THE UNIVERSITY ATLAS

Twenty-second Edition

GEORGE PHILIP

LONDON · MELBOURNE · MILWAUKEE

Edited by
Harold Fullard, M.Sc., Consultant Cartographer,
H.C. Darby, C.B.E., Litt.D., F.B.A., Emeritus Professor of Geography, University of Cambridge and
B.M. Willett, B.A., Cartographic Editor,
D. Gaylard, Assistant Cartographic Editor

Maps prepared by George Philip Cartographic Services Ltd under the direction of A.G. Poynter, M.A., Director of Cartography.

First Edition February 1937
Twenty-second Edition Autumn 1983
Reprinted 1984

British Library Cataloguing in Publication Data
The University atlas. – 22nd ed
1. Atlases, British
I. Fullard, Harold II. Darby, H.C.
912 G1021

ISBN 0 540 05432 1

Printed in Great Britain by George Philip Printers Ltd., London

Preface

During the course of over forty-five years since its original publication the University Atlas has been through twenty-one editions, each of which has in its turn been revised and improved.

For the eighth edition in 1958, the atlas was completely redesigned because it was considered that only an entirely new version would meet the needs of the post-war years. In that edition we made two significant changes: a substantial increase in the scale of the sectional maps, and a re-arrangement of the atlas into an easily portable size, convenient for frequent use and able to stand on a bookshelf.

For the twelfth edition in 1967, the style of colouring of the maps was completely changed to provide lighter and clearer layer colours. This in turn made possible the inclusion of hill-shading to complement the layer colouring and bring out clearly relief features without impairing the detail of names, settlements and communications.

For the nineteenth edition in 1978 the content of the atlas was completely re-examined, and the lay-out of a large number of maps was redesigned – in particular those covering Asia, Australasia and Latin America. This enabled larger scales to be provided for (a) China, south-east Asia, Japan, the Tashkent area and the southern Urals; (b) south-east Australia and New Guinea; and (c) Mexico, the West Indies and eastern Brazil. Other new maps covered the Indian Ocean, the North Sea, the French departments, the Benelux countries, Switzerland, Alaska and California. The design of yet other maps was altered to secure a more effective presentation, e.g., the world maps of climate.

As in previous editions, international boundaries have been drawn to show the *de facto* situation where there are rival claims to territory.

Spellings of names are in the forms given in the latest official lists, and generally agree with the rules of the Permanent Committee on Geographical Names and the United States Board on Geographic Names. A list of recent place-name changes and a table showing the transcription of Chinese place-names from the Wade-Giles system into Pinyin appear at the end of the index, which contains over 50,000 entries.

We gratefully acknowledge the help of many official organisations and individuals.

H. FULLARD
H.C. DARBY

Contents

iii Preface
iv-vii Contents
viii Population of Countries

The following information appears after the index section

Recent Placename Changes
Chinese Placenames
Meaning of Geographical Terms

World

1 **General Reference**

2-3 **The World**
Geology 1:95M
Volcanoes 1:280M
Earthquakes 1:280M

4-5 **The World** 1:100M
Climatic Regions

6 **The World** 1:190M
Seasonal Temperature and Ocean Currents
Annual Range of Temperature

7 **The World** 1:190M
Seasonal Pressure and Prevailing Winds
Annual Precipitation

8-9 **The World** 1:73.2M
Density of Population

10-11 **The World** 1:80M
Political

12-13 **Polar Regions** 1:35M

14-15 **The Atlantic Ocean** 1:45M

Europe & The British Isles

16 **Europe** 1:20M
Physical

17 **Europe** 1:40M
Climate

18 **Europe** 1:35M
Structure
Annual Precipitation

19 **The North Sea** 1:6M
Oil and Gas

20 **Europe** 1:20M
Density of Population

21 **Europe** 1:20M
Political

22 **The British Isles** 1:4M
Geology

23 **The British Isles** 1:4M
Physical

24 **The British Isles** 1:4M
Climate
Annual Precipitation, Pressure and Wind

25 **The British Isles** 1:8.5M
Climate
January and July temperature
Duration of Bright Sunshine

26	**The British Isles** Administrative *Prior to the reorganisation of local government in the U.K. 1974-75*	1:4M
27	**The British Isles** Administrative	1:4M
28-89	**South and South-east England**	1:1M
30	**South-west England**	1:1M
31	**Wales**	1:1M
32-33	**Northern England**	1:1M
34-35	**Southern Scotland**	1:1M
36-37	**Northern Scotland**	1:1M
38-39	**Ireland**	1:1.25M
40	**The British Isles** Density of Population	1:4M

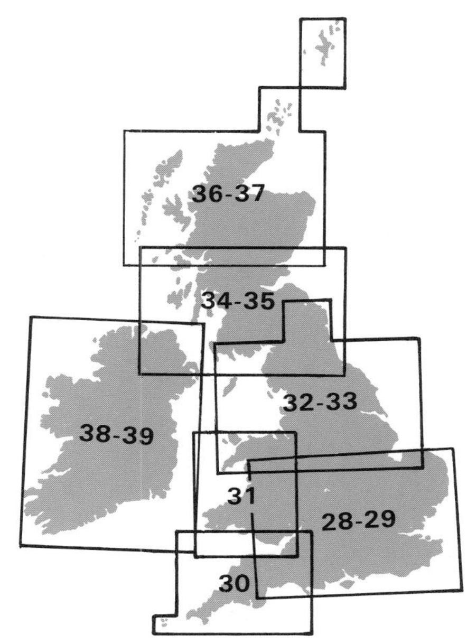

36-37
34-35
32-33
38-39
31
28-29
30

Europe

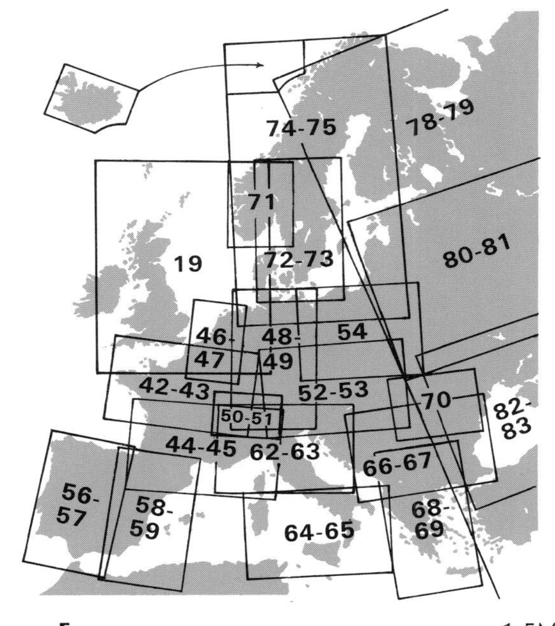

74-75
78-79
71
19
72-73
80-81
46-47
48-49
54
42-43
52-53
50-51
70
82-83
44-45
62-63
66-67
56-57
58-59
68-69
64-65

41	**France** Administrative	1:5M
42-43	**Northern France**	1:2.5M
44-45	**Southern France**	1:2.5M
46-47	**The Netherlands, Belgium and Luxembourg**	1:1.25M
48-49	**Germany and Switzerland**	1:2.5M
50-51	**Switzerland**	1:1M
52-53	**Austria, Czechoslovakia and Hungary**	1:2.5M
54	**Poland**	1:3M
55	**Spain and Portugal**	1:5M
56-57	**Western Spain and Portugal**	1:2.5M
58-59	**Eastern Spain**	1:2.5M
60-61	**The Mediterranean Lands**	1:10M
62-63	**Northern Italy and Western Yugoslavia**	1:2.5M
64-65	**Southern Italy**	1:2.5M
66-67	**Eastern Yugoslavia and Bulgaria**	1:2.5M
68-69	**Greece and Albania**	1:2.5M
70	**Romania**	1:2.5M
71	**Southern Norway**	1:2.5M
72-73	**Denmark and Southern Sweden**	1:2.5M
74-75	**Scandinavia and the Baltic Lands** **Iceland**	1:5M 1:5M
76-77	**U.S.S.R.**	1:20M
78-79	**U.S.S.R. in Europe**	1:10M
80-81	**European Russia — Central**	1:5M
82-83	**European Russia — South**	1:5M

Asia

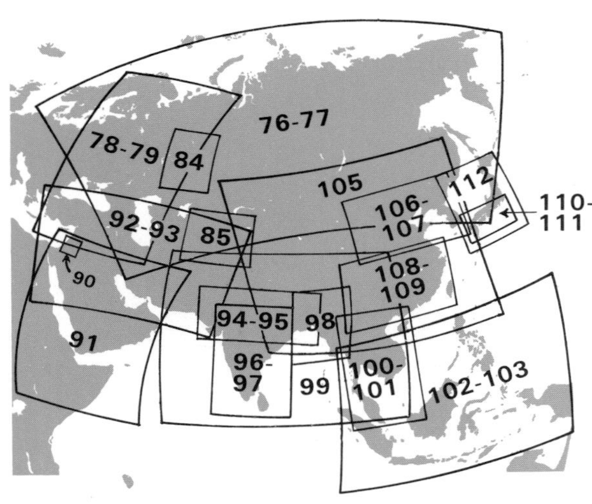
76-77
78-79
84
105
106-107
112
110-111
92-93
85
90
108-109
94-95
98
91
96-97
99
100-101
102-103

84	**The Southern Urals**	1:5M
85	**The Tashkent Region**	1:5M
86	**Asia** Physical	1:50M
87	**Asia** Political	1:50M
88	**Asia** Climate	1:100M
89	**Asia** Annual Rainfall The Evolution of the Monsoons	1:80M
90	**Israel and West Jordan**	1:1M
91	**Arabia and the Horn of Africa**	1:15M
92-93	**The Near and Middle East**	1:10M
94-95	**The Indo-Gangetic Plain** **Jammu and Kashmir**	1:6M
96-97	**Southern India and Sri Lanka**	1:6M
98	**Bangladesh, North-eastern India and Burma**	1:6M
99	**South Asia**	1:20M
100-101	**Mainland South-east Asia**	1:6M
102-103	**Indonesia** **Java and Madura**	1:12.5M 1:7.5M
104	**Southern and Eastern Asia** Density of Population	1:30M
105	**China**	1:20M
106-107	**Northern China and Korea**	1:6M
108-109	**Southern China**	1:6M
110-111	**Southern Japan**	1:2.5M
112	**Japan**	1:7.5M

Africa

113	**Africa** Political Density of Population	 1:40M 1:80M
114	**Africa** Physical Annual Rainfall	1:40M 1:80M
115	**Africa** Climate	1:80M
116-117	**Northern Africa**	1:15M
118-119	**North-west Africa**	1:8M
120-121	**West Africa**	1:8M
122-123	**The Nile Valley** **The Nile Delta**	1:8M 1:4M
124-125	**Central and South Africa**	1:15M
126-127	**East Africa**	1:8M
128-129	**Southern Africa**	1:8M

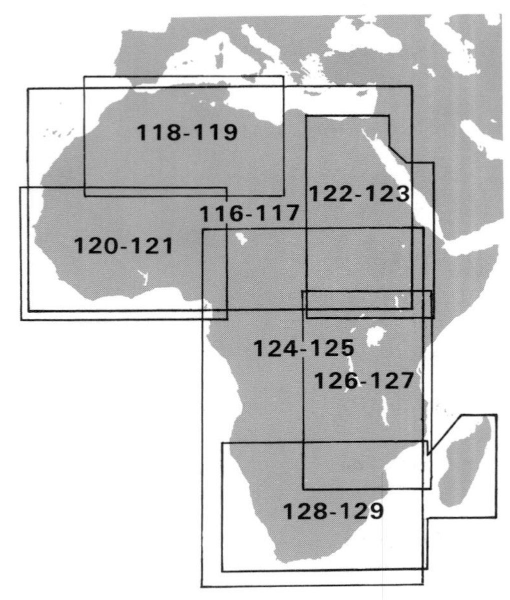
118-119
122-123
116-117
120-121
124-125
126-127
128-129

Australasia

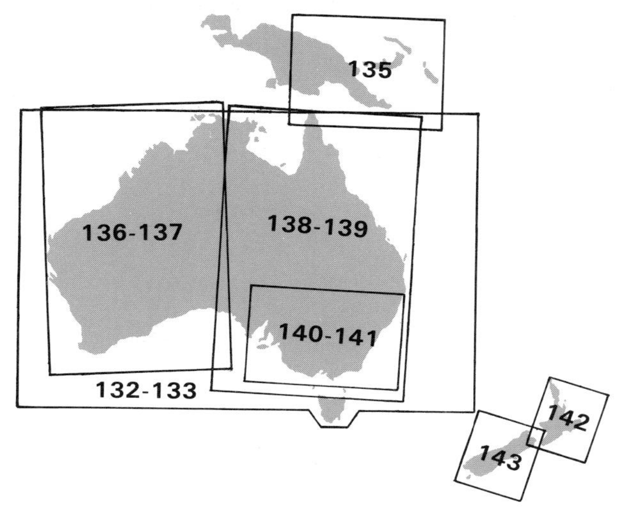
135
136-137
138-139
140-141
132-133
142
143

Page	Map	Scale
130-131	**The Pacific Ocean**	1:54M
132-133	**Australia**	1:12M
134	**Australia** Climate	1:60M
135	**Papua New Guinea**	1:6.5M
136-137	**Western Australia**	1:8M
138-139	**Eastern Australia**	1:8M
140-141	**South-east Australia**	1:4M
142	**New Zealand — North Island** Climate	1:3.5M 1:25M
143	**New Zealand — South Island** Population Annual Rainfall	1:3.5M 1:15M 1:25M

The Americas

Page	Map	Scale
144-145	**North America** Physical Annual Rainfall United States: Administrative	1:30M 1:70M 1:40M
146	**North America** Climate	1:70M
147	**Alaska** **Hawaiian Islands** **Puerto Rico and Virgin Islands** **Aleutian Islands**	1:12M 1:5M 1:5M 1:5M
148-149	**Canada**	1:15M
150-151	**Eastern Canada**	1:7M
152-153	**Western Canada**	1:7M
154-155	**The United States**	1:12M
156-157	**Eastern United States** Density of Population	1:6M 1:50M
158-159	**Middle United States**	1:6M
160-161	**Western United States** U.S.A.: Soils	1:6M 1:50M
162	**North-eastern United States**	1:3M
163	**Southern California**	1:3M
164-165	**Mexico**	1:8M
166-167	**Central America and the Antilles**	1:8M
168	**South America** Physical	1:30M
169	**South America** Climate	1:80M
170-171	**Eastern Brazil**	1:8M
172-173	**Central South America**	1:8M
174-175	**South America — North** Political	1:16M 1:80M
176	**South America — South**	1:16M

Index

Principal Countries of the World

Country	Area in thousands of square km	Population in thousands	Density of population per sq. km.	Capital Population in thousands
Afghanistan	647	15 540	24	Kabul (588)
Albania	29	2 734	94	Tiranë (192)
Algeria	2 382	18 594	8	Algiers (1 503)
Angola	1 247	7 078	6	Luanda (475)
Argentina	2 767	26 863	10	Buenos Aires (8 436)
Australia	7 687	14 727	2	Canberra (227)
Austria	84	7 507	89	Vienna (1 587)
Bangladesh	144	88 656	616	Dacca (1 730)
Belgium	31	9 859	318	Brussels (1 042)
Belize	23	145	6	Belmopan (4)
Benin	113	3 567	32	Porto-Novo (104)
Bhutan	47	1 298	28	Thimphu (60)
Bolivia	1 099	5 600	5	Sucre (63)
				La Paz (655)
Botswana	600	819	1	Gaborone (37)
Brazil	8 512	119 099	14	Brasilia (763)
Brunei	6	213	37	Bandar Seri
				Begawan (37)
Bulgaria	111	8 862	80	Sofia (1 032)
Burma	677	35 289	52	Rangoon (2 276)
Burundi	28	4 512	161	Bujumbura (157)
Cambodia	181	8 872	49	Phnom Penh (2 000)
Cameroon	475	8 503	18	Yaoundé (314)
Canada	9 976	23 343	2	Ottawa (718)
Central African Rep.	623	2 370	4	Bangui (187)
Chad	1 284	4 524	4	Ndjamena (179)
Chile	757	11 104	15	Santiago (3 692)
China	9 597	982 550	102	Peking (7 570)
Colombia	1 139	27 520	24	Bogota (2 855)
Congo	342	1 537	5	Brazzaville (290)
Costa Rica	51	2 245	44	San José (563)
Cuba	115	9 833	86	Havana (1 861)
Cyprus	9	629	68	Nicosia (147)
Czechoslovakia	128	15 312	120	Prague (1 176)
Denmark	43	5 124	119	Copenhagen (1 251)
Djibouti	22	119	5	Djibouti (62)
Dominican Republic	49	5 431	111	Santo Domingo (1 103)
Ecuador	284	8 354	29	Quito (743)
Egypt	1 001	41 995	42	Cairo (5 084)
El Salvador	21	4 813	229	San Salvador (366)
Equatorial Guinea	28	363	13	Rey Malabo (37)
Ethiopia	1 222	31 065	25	Addis Abeba (1 210)
Fiji	18	631	35	Suva (118)
Finland	337	4 788	14	Helsinki (893)
France	547	53 788	98	Paris (9 863)
French Guiana	91	64	1	Cayenne (25)
Gabon	268	551	2	Libréville (186)
Gambia	11	601	55	Banjul (48)
Germany, East	108	16 737	155	East Berlin (1 111)
Germany, West	249	61 658	248	Bonn (285)
Ghana	239	11 450	48	Accra (738)
Greece	132	9 599	73	Athens (2 101)
Greenland	2 176	50	0.02	Godthåb (9)
Guatemala	109	7 262	67	Guatemala (793)
Guinea	246	5 014	20	Conakry (526)
Guinea-Bissau	36	777	22	Bissau (109)
Guyana	215	884	4	Georgetown (187)
Haiti	28	5 009	179	Port-au-Prince (791)
Honduras	112	3 691	33	Tegucigalpa (274)
Hong Kong	1	5 068	4 827	Victoria (849)
Hungary	93	10 711	115	Budapest (2 060)
Iceland	103	228	2	Reykjavik (83)
India	3 288	683 810	208	Delhi (3 647)
Indonesia	2 027	7 383	73	Jakarta (4 576)
Iran	1 648	37 447	23	Tehran (4 496)
Iraq	435	13 084	28	Baghdad (2 969)
Irish Republic	70	3 440	49	Dublin (525)
Israel	21	3 871	184	Jerusalem (376)
Italy	301	57 140	190	Rome (2 898)
Ivory Coast	322	7 973	25	Abidjan (850)
Jamaica	11	2 192	199	Kingston (573)
Japan	372	117 057	315	Tokyo (8 349)
Jordan	98	2 779	28	Amman (712)
Kenya	583	16 402	28	Nairobi (835)
Korea, North	121	17 914	148	Pyongyang (1 500)
Korea, South	98	37 449	382	Seoul (6 879)
Kuwait	18	1 356	75	Kuwait (775)
Laos	237	3 721	16	Vientiane (177)
Lebanon	10	3 161	316	Beirut (702)
Lesotho	30	1 339	45	Maseru (29)
Liberia	111	1 873	17	Monrovia (172)
Libya	1 760	2 977	2	Tripoli (551)
Luxembourg	3	364	140	Luxembourg (78)
Madagascar	587	8 742	15	Antananarivo (400)
Malawi	118	5 968	51	Lilongwe (103)
Malaysia	330	13 436	41	Kuala Lumpur (452)
Mali	1 240	6 906	6	Bamako (404)
Malta	0.3	369	1 153	Valletta (14)
Mauritania	1 031	1 634	2	Nouakchott (135)
Mauritius	2	959	480	Port Louis (141)
Mexico	1 973	71 911	36	Mexico (13 994)
Mongolia	1 565	1 595	1	Ulan Bator (400)
Morocco	447	20 242	45	Rabat (596)
Mozambique	783	12 130	15	Maputo (384)
Namibia	824	852	1	Windhoek (61)
Nepal	141	14 010	99	Katmandu (210)
Netherlands	41	14 220	347	Amsterdam (965)
New Zealand	269	3 176	12	Wellington (321)
Nicaragua	130	2 703	21	Managua (500)
Niger	1 267	5 305	4	Niamey (130)
Nigeria	924	77 082	83	Lagos (1 477)
Norway	324	4 092	13	Oslo (645)
Oman	212	891	4	Muscat (25)
Pakistan	804	82 441	103	Islamabad (77)
Panama	76	1 837	24	Panama (546)
Papua New Guinea	462	3 082	7	Port Moresby (113)
Paraguay	407	3 067	8	Asunción (565)
Peru	1 285	17 780	14	Lima (3 303)
Philippines	300	48 400	161	Manila (1 438)
Poland	313	35 815	114	Warsaw (1 543)
Portugal	92	9 933	108	Lisbon (1 612)
Puerto Rico	9	3 188	358	San Juan (515)
Romania	238	22 201	93	Bucharest (1 934)
Rwanda	26	5 046	194	Kigali (90)
Saudi Arabia	2 150	8 367	4	Riyadh (667)
Senegal	196	5 661	29	Dakar (799)
Sierra Leone	72	3 474	48	Freetown (214)
Singapore	0.6	2 391	4 122	Singapore (2 308)
Somali Republic	638	3 645	6	Mogadishu (400)
South Africa	1 221	29 285	24	Pretoria (562)
				Cape Town (1 097)
Spain	505	37 430	74	Madrid (3 520)
Sri Lanka	66	14 738	223	Colombo (1 412)
Sudan	2 506	18 681	8	Khartoum (334)
Surinam	163	352	2	Paramaribo (151)
Swaziland	17	547	32	Mbabane (24)
Sweden	450	8 320	18	Stockholm (1 380)
Switzerland	41	6 329	154	Berne (282)
Syria	185	8 979	49	Damascus (1 142)
Taiwan	36	17 479	486	Taipei (3 050)
Tanzania	945	17 982	19	Dar-es-Salaam (757)
Thailand	514	46 455	90	Bangkok (4 702)
Togo	56	2 699	48	Lomé (135)
Trinidad and Tobago	5	1 156	227	Port of Spain (63)
Tunisia	164	6 363	39	Tunis (944)
Turkey	781	45 218	58	Ankara (2 204)
Uganda	236	13 225	56	Kampala (331)
United Arab Emirates	84	1 040	12	Abu Dhabi (236)
U.S.S.R.	22 402	265 542	12	Moscow (8 011)
United Kingdom	245	55 945	228	London (6 696)
United States	9 363	229 805	25	Washington (3 045)
Upper Volta	274	6 908	25	Ouagadougou (169)
Uruguay	178	2 899	16	Montevideo (1 230)
Venezuela	912	13 913	15	Caracas (2 576)
Vietnam	330	52 742	160	Hanoi (2 571)
Western Samoa	3	156	55	Apia (32)
Yemen, North	195	5 926	30	Sana (448)
Yemen, South	288	1 969	7	Aden (285)
Yugoslavia	256	22 471	88	Belgrade (775)
Zaïre	2 345	28 291	12	Kinshasa (2 008)
Zambia	753	5 680	8	Lusaka (538)
Zimbabwe	391	7 360	19	Harare (633)

SETTLEMENTS

Settlement symbols in order of size

LONDON   Stuttgart   Sevilla   Bergen   Bath   Biarritz   Srikolayatji

Settlement symbols and type styles vary according to the scale of each map and indicate the importance of towns on the map rather than specific population figures

∴ Sites of Archæological or Historical importance

BOUNDARIES

International Boundaries

International Boundaries (Undemarcated or Undefined)

Internal Boundaries

International boundaries show the *de facto* situation where there are rival claims to territory

National and Provincial Parks

COMMUNICATIONS

Motorways

Motorways under construction

Principal Roads

Other Roads

Road Tunnels

Principal Railways

Other Railways

Railways under construction

Railway Tunnels

Passes

Principal Canals

Principal Oil Pipelines

3386 Principal Shipping Routes (Distances in Nautical Miles)

Tracks and Seasonal Roads

Airports

PHYSICAL FEATURES

Perennial Streams

Seasonal Streams

▲ 8848 Spot Height in metres

Seasonal Lakes, Salt Flats

Swamps, Marshes

▼ 8050 Sea Depths. in metres

Permanent Ice

Wells in Desert

1134 Height of Lake Surface Above Sea Level, in metres

Height of Land Above Sea Level in metres: 6000, 4000, 3000, 2000, 1500, 1000, 400, 200, 0

Land Below Sea Level

Depth of Sea in metres: 0, 200, 2000, 4000, 5000, 6000, 8000

Some of the maps have different contours to highlight and clarify the principal relief features

Abbreviations of measures used   mm Millimetres   m Metres   km Kilometres   °C Degrees Celsius   mb Millibars

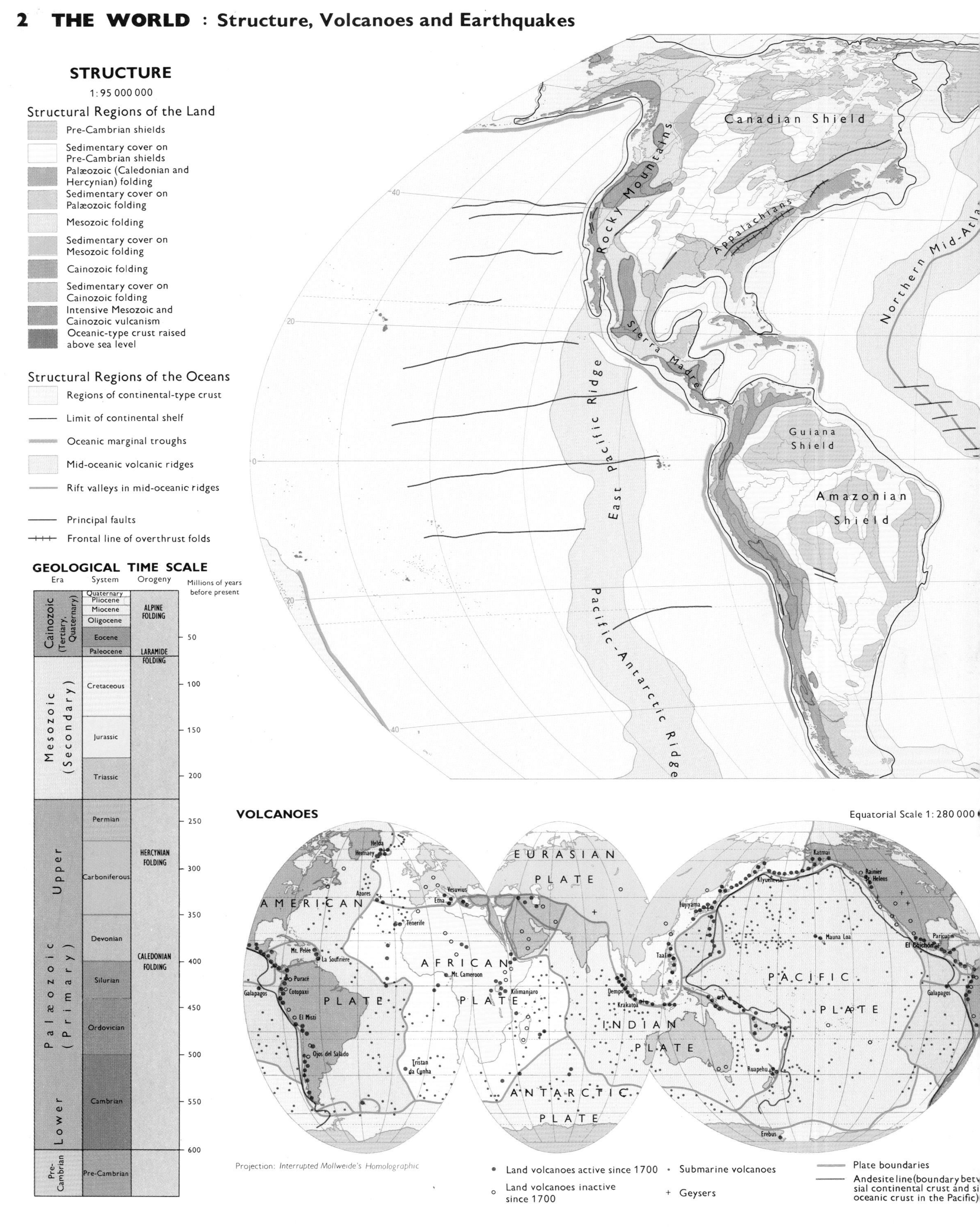
STRUCTURE
1:95 000 000
Structural Regions of the Land
Pre-Cambrian shields
Sedimentary cover on Pre-Cambrian shields
Palæozoic (Caledonian and Hercynian) folding
Sedimentary cover on Palæozoic folding
Mesozoic folding
Sedimentary cover on Mesozoic folding
Cainozoic folding
Sedimentary cover on Cainozoic folding
Intensive Mesozoic and Cainozoic vulcanism
Oceanic-type crust raised above sea level
Structural Regions of the Oceans
Regions of continental-type crust
Limit of continental shelf
Oceanic marginal troughs
Mid-oceanic volcanic ridges
Rift valleys in mid-oceanic ridges
Principal faults
Frontal line of overthrust folds
GEOLOGICAL TIME SCALE
Era
System
Orogeny
Millions of years before present
Cainozoic (Tertiary, Quaternary)
Quaternary
Pliocene
Miocene
Oligocene
Eocene
Paleocene
ALPINE FOLDING
LARAMIDE FOLDING
Mesozoic (Secondary)
Cretaceous
Jurassic
Triassic
Palæozoic (Primary)
Upper
Lower
Permian
Carboniferous
Devonian
Silurian
Ordovician
Cambrian
HERCYNIAN FOLDING
CALEDONIAN FOLDING
Pre-Cambrian
Pre-Cambrian
50
100
150
200
250
300
350
400
450
500
550
600
Canadian Shield
Rocky Mountains
Appalachians
Northern Mid-Atla
Sierra Madre
East Pacific Ridge
Guiana Shield
Amazonian Shield
Pacific-Antarctic Ridge
40
20
0
20
40
VOLCANOES
Equatorial Scale 1:280 000
EURASIAN PLATE
AMERICAN PLATE
AFRICAN PLATE
INDIAN PLATE
PACIFIC PLATE
ANTARCTIC PLATE
Hekla
Heimaey
Azores
Vesuvius
Etna
Tenerife
Mt. Pelée
La Soufrière
Puracé
Cotopaxi
Galapagos
El Misti
Ojos del Salado
Tristan da Cunha
Mt. Cameroon
Kilimanjaro
Dempo
Krakatoa
Taal
Fujiyama
Klyuchevsk
Katmai
Rainier
Helens
Mauna Loa
Paricutin
El Chichón
Ruapehu
Erebus
Projection: Interrupted Mollweide's Homolographic
Land volcanoes active since 1700
Land volcanoes inactive since 1700
Submarine volcanoes
Geysers
Plate boundaries
Andesite line (boundary betw sial continental crust and si oceanic crust in the Pacific)

1: 95 000 000

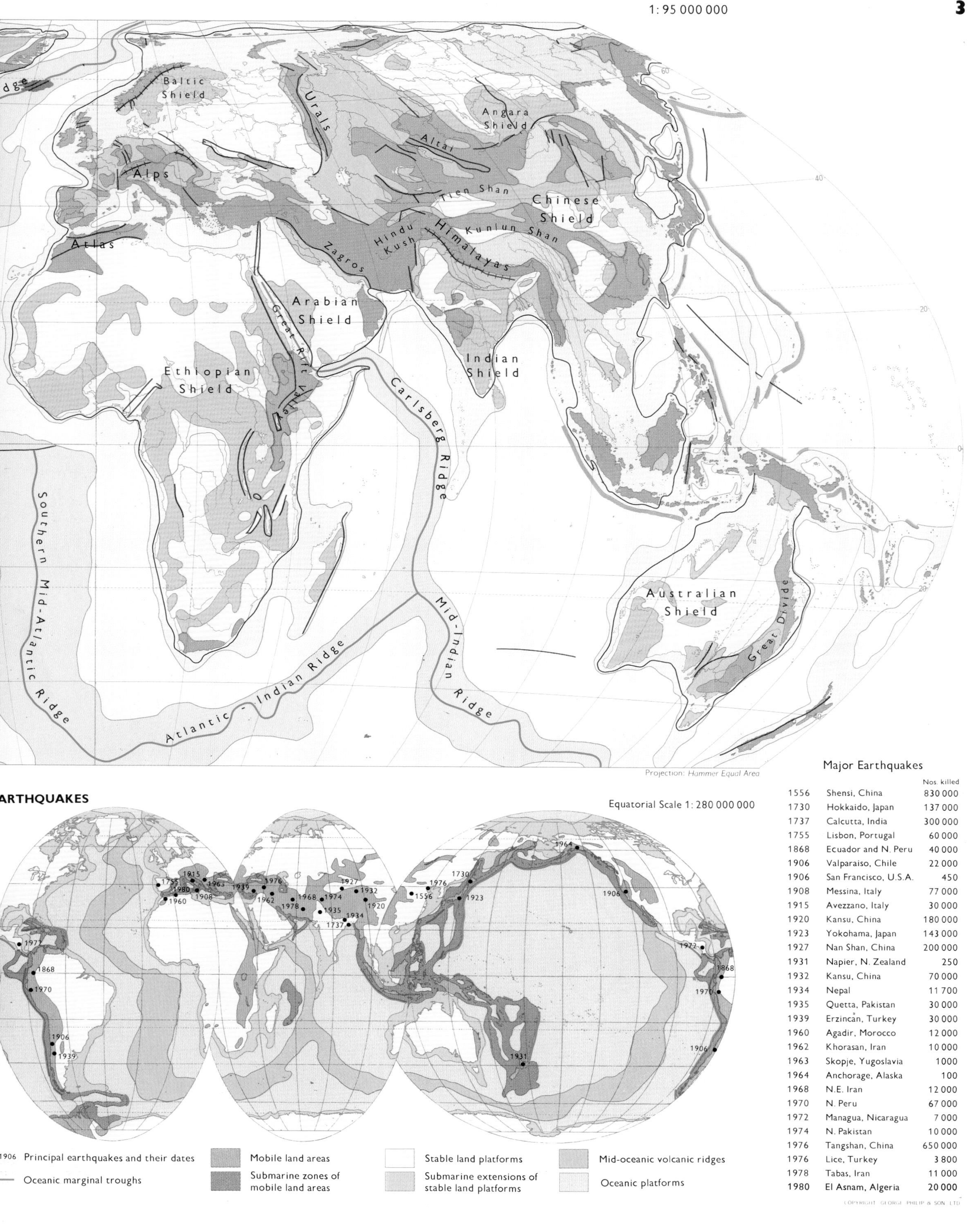
Baltic Shield
Urals
Angara Shield
Altai
Alps
Tien Shan
Chinese Shield
Atlas
Hindu Kush
Himalayas
Kunlun Shan
Zagros
Arabian Shield
Great Rift Valley
Indian Shield
Ethiopian Shield
Carlsberg Ridge
Southern Mid-Atlantic Ridge
Mid-Indian Ridge
Atlantic - Indian Ridge
Australian Shield
Great Divide
Projection: Hammer Equal Area

ARTHQUAKES

Equatorial Scale 1: 280 000 000

1906 Principal earthquakes and their dates

Oceanic marginal troughs

Mobile land areas

Submarine zones of mobile land areas

Stable land platforms

Submarine extensions of stable land platforms

Mid-oceanic volcanic ridges

Oceanic platforms

Major Earthquakes

		Nos. killed
1556	Shensi, China	830 000
1730	Hokkaido, Japan	137 000
1737	Calcutta, India	300 000
1755	Lisbon, Portugal	60 000
1868	Ecuador and N. Peru	40 000
1906	Valparaiso, Chile	22 000
1906	San Francisco, U.S.A.	450
1908	Messina, Italy	77 000
1915	Avezzano, Italy	30 000
1920	Kansu, China	180 000
1923	Yokohama, Japan	143 000
1927	Nan Shan, China	200 000
1931	Napier, N. Zealand	250
1932	Kansu, China	70 000
1934	Nepal	11 700
1935	Quetta, Pakistan	30 000
1939	Erzincan, Turkey	30 000
1960	Agadir, Morocco	12 000
1962	Khorasan, Iran	10 000
1963	Skopje, Yugoslavia	1000
1964	Anchorage, Alaska	100
1968	N.E. Iran	12 000
1970	N. Peru	67 000
1972	Managua, Nicaragua	7 000
1974	N. Pakistan	10 000
1976	Tangshan, China	650 000
1976	Lice, Turkey	3 800
1978	Tabas, Iran	11 000
1980	El Asnam, Algeria	20 000

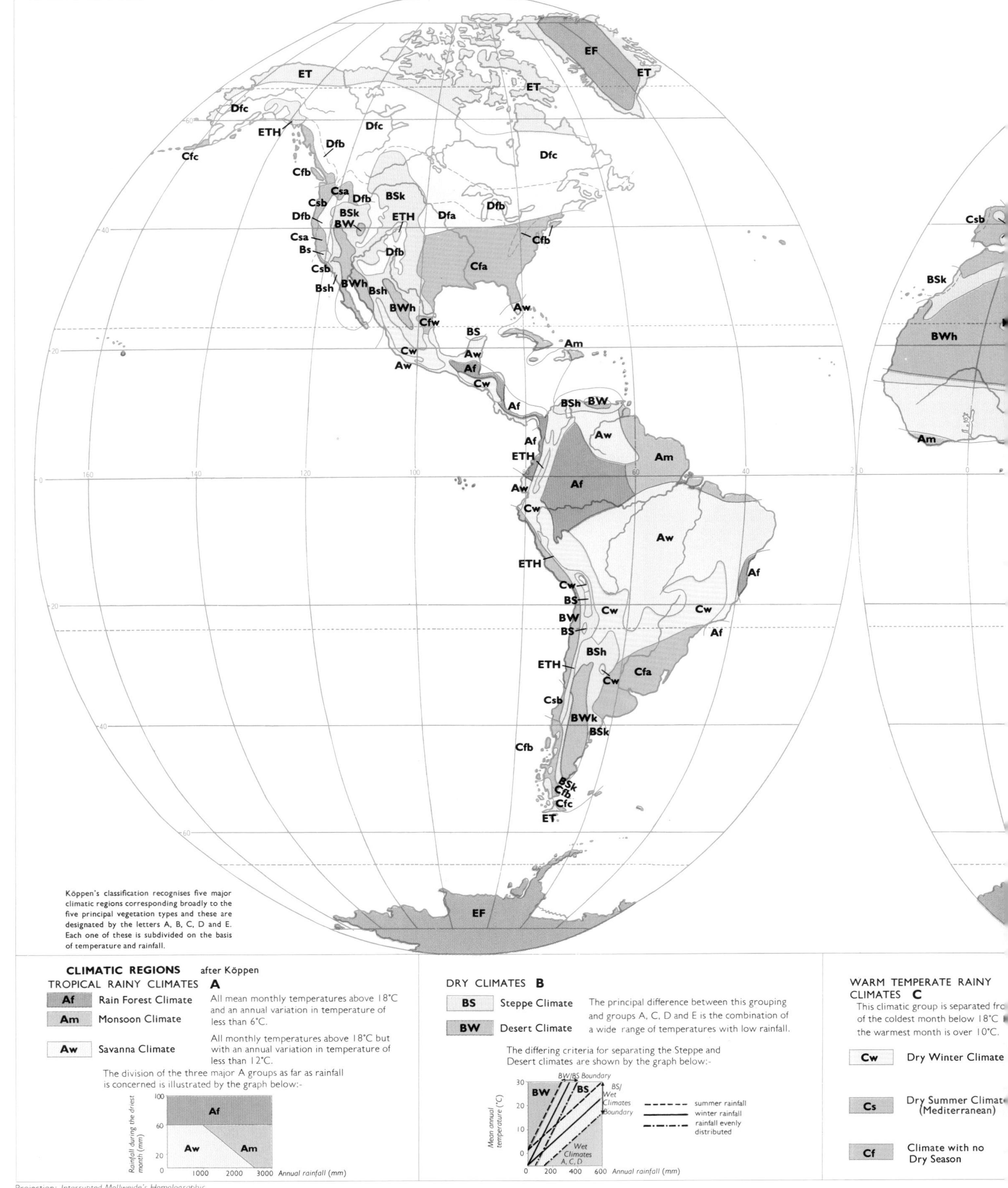
EF
ET
ET
ET
Dfc
ETH
Dfc
Dfb
Cfc
Dfc
Cfb
Csa
Dfb
BSk
Csb
BSk
Dfb
Dfb
ETH
Dfa
BW
Csa
Bs
Cfb
Dfb
Csb
Cfa
Bsh
BWh
Bsh
BWh
Aw
Cfw
BS
Am
Cw
Aw
Aw
Af
Cw
Af
BSh
BW
Af
Aw
ETH
Am
Af
Aw
Cw
Aw
ETH
Af
Cw
BS
Cw
Cw
BW
BS
Af
BSh
ETH
Cw
Cfa
Csb
BWk
BSk
Cfb
BSk
Cfb
Cfc
ET
EF
Csb
BSk
BWh
Am
Köppen's classification recognises five major climatic regions corresponding broadly to the five principal vegetation types and these are designated by the letters A, B, C, D and E. Each one of these is subdivided on the basis of temperature and rainfall.

CLIMATIC REGIONS after Köppen

TROPICAL RAINY CLIMATES **A**

Af	Rain Forest Climate	All mean monthly temperatures above 18°C and an annual variation in temperature of less than 6°C.
Am	Monsoon Climate	
Aw	Savanna Climate	All monthly temperatures above 18°C but with an annual variation in temperature of less than 12°C.

The division of the three major A groups as far as rainfall is concerned is illustrated by the graph below:-

Rainfall during the driest month (mm)
100
60
20
0
Af
Aw
Am
1000
2000
3000
Annual rainfall (mm)

DRY CLIMATES **B**

BS	Steppe Climate	The principal difference between this grouping and groups A, C, D and E is the combination of a wide range of temperatures with low rainfall.
BW	Desert Climate	

The differing criteria for separating the Steppe and Desert climates are shown by the graph below:-

BW/BS Boundary
BW
BS
BS/ Wet Climates Boundary
Wet Climates A, C, D
Mean annual temperature (°C)
30
20
10
0
0
200
400
600
Annual rainfall (mm)
summer rainfall
winter rainfall
rainfall evenly distributed

WARM TEMPERATE RAINY CLIMATES **C**

This climatic group is separated fro of the coldest month below 18°C the warmest month is over 10°C.

Cw	Dry Winter Climate
Cs	Dry Summer Climate (Mediterranean)
Cf	Climate with no Dry Season

Projection: *Interrupted Mollweide's Homolographic*

ET
Cfc
ETH
Cfc
Dfc
ET
Dfd
Dfc
ET
Dfc
Dfb
Dfb
Dwc
ETH
Cfb
Dfb
Cfa
Cfa
Cfa
BSk
Dwb
Dfb
BWk
Cfb
Cfa
BSk
Dwa
Cfb
Csa
Cfb
Dfb
Dfb
ETH
BWk
Csb
BSk
Cfa
BSk
Dfb
ETH
Dfc
Cwa
BSh
Dfb
BWh
BWh
BSh
Cwa
Cfa
BWh
BWh
BSh
BSh
Cwa
Aw
Am
Am
BSh
Cw
Aw
Am
Am
Cwb
Af
BS
BSh
Cwb
Cf
Af
Af
Cf
Cwb
Aw
Aw
Aw
Af
Cf
Aw
Cwa
Aw
Af
BWh
Aw
BSh
BSh
Cw
Cw
Aw
Cwb
BSh
BWh
BWk
Cfa
Csa
BSh
BSk
Cfa
Csb
BSk
Cfb
Csb
BWk
Csa
Csb
Cfb
Cfb
Cfb
Cfb
EF
EF

COLD TEMPERATE RAINY CLIMATES **D**

Dw	Dry Winter Climate	The mean temperature of the coldest month is below −3°C but the mean temperature of the warmest month is still over 10°C.
Df	Dry Summer Climate	

POLAR CLIMATES **E**

ET	Tundra Climate	The mean temperature of the warmest month is below 10°C giving permanently frozen subsoil.
EF	Polar Climate	The mean temperature of the warmest month is below 0°C giving permanent ice and snow.

oup A by having the mean temperature
ove −3°C. The mean temperature of

e wettest month of summer has at least
times as much rain as the driest
nter month.

e wettest month of winter has at least
ree times as much rain as the driest
onth of summer. The driest summer
onth itself has less than 30mm rainfall.

en rainfall throughout the year.

The classification is in some cases subdivided by the addition of the following letters after the major types:-

Used with groups C and D	**a**	Hot summer—mean temperature of the hottest month above 22°C and with more than four months of over 10°C.
	b	Warm summer—mean temperature of the hottest month below 22°C but still with more than four months of over 10°C.
	c	Cool short summer—mean temperature of the hottest month below 22°C but with less than four months of over 10°C.
Used with group D	**d**	Cool short summer and cold winter—mean temperature of the hottest month below 22°C, and of the coldest month below −38°C.
Used with group B	**h**	Hot dry climate—mean annual temperature above 18°C.
	k	Cool dry climate—mean annual temperature below 18°C.
Used with group E	**H**	Polar climate due to elevation being over 1500m

THE WORLD : Temperature and Ocean Currents

1:190 000 000

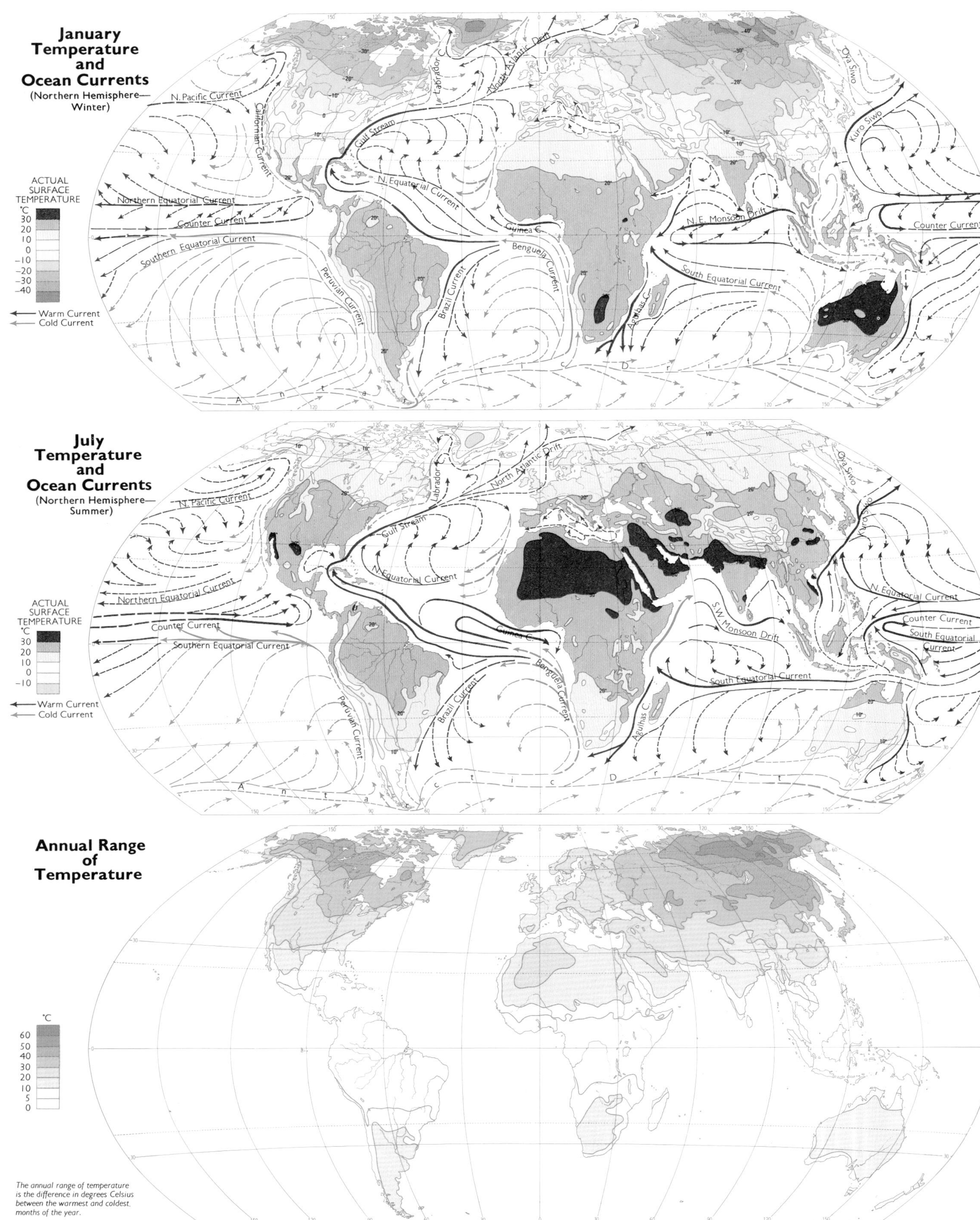

January Temperature and Ocean Currents
(Northern Hemisphere—Winter)
ACTUAL SURFACE TEMPERATURE
°C
30
20
10
0
−10
−20
−30
−40
Warm Current
Cold Current
N. Pacific Current
Californian Current
Labrador C.
North Atlantic Drift
Oya Siwo
Kuro Siwo
Gulf Stream
N. Equatorial Current
Northern Equatorial Current
Counter Current
Southern Equatorial Current
Guinea C.
Benguela Current
N. E. Monsoon Drift
Counter Current
South Equatorial Current
Peruvian Current
Brazil Current
Agulhas C.
Antarctic Drift
July Temperature and Ocean Currents
(Northern Hemisphere—Summer)
ACTUAL SURFACE TEMPERATURE
°C
30
20
10
0
−10
Warm Current
Cold Current
N. Pacific Current
Labrador C.
North Atlantic Drift
Oya Siwo
Kuro Siwo
Gulf Stream
N. Equatorial Current
Northern Equatorial Current
Counter Current
Southern Equatorial Current
Guinea C.
Benguela Current
S.W. Monsoon Drift
N. Equatorial Current
Counter Current
South Equatorial Current
South Equatorial Current
Peruvian Current
Brazil Current
Agulhas C.
Antarctic Drift
Annual Range of Temperature
°C
60
50
40
30
20
10
5
0

The annual range of temperature is the difference in degrees Celsius between the warmest and coldest months of the year.

Projection: *Hammer Equal Area*

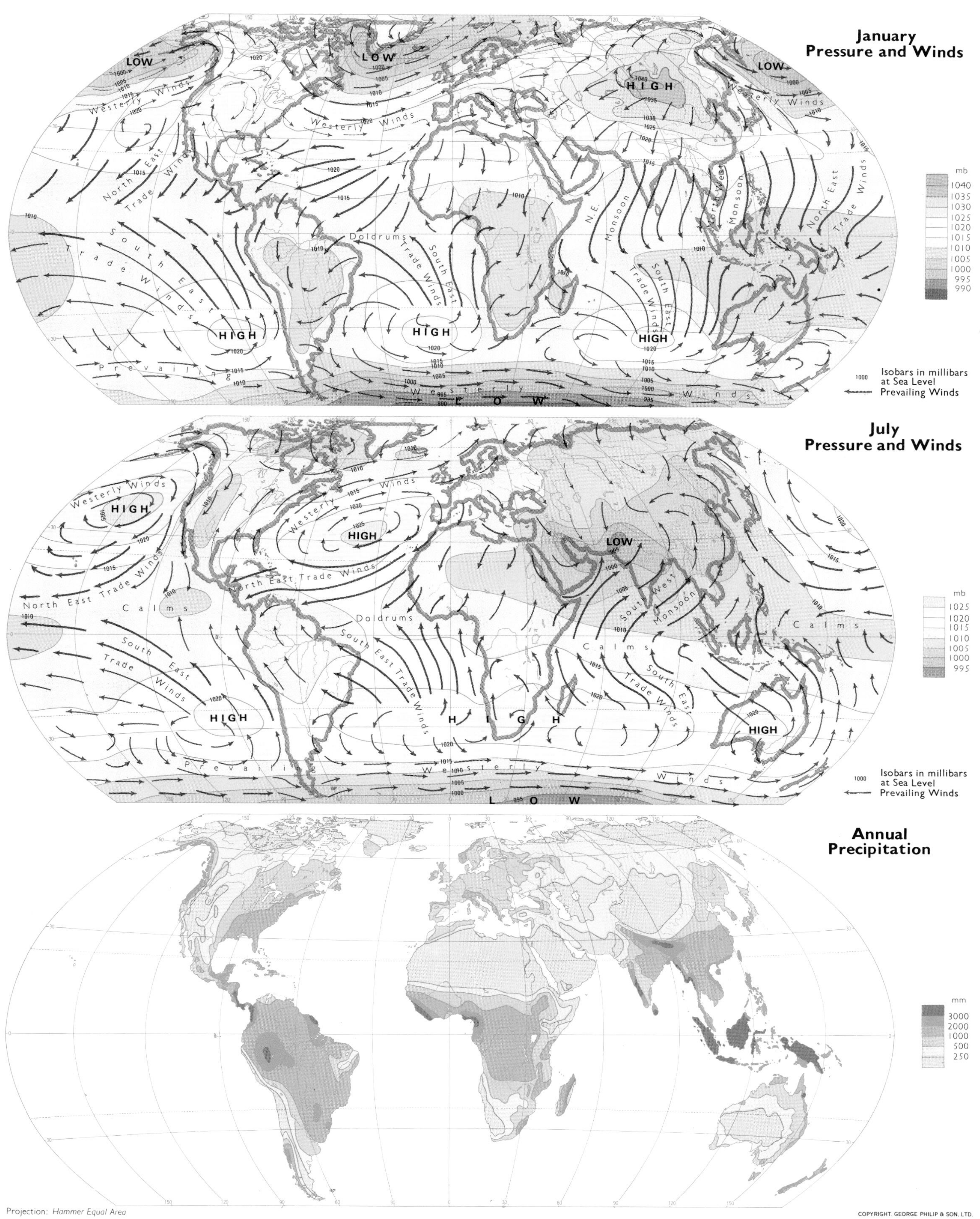
January
Pressure and Winds
LOW
HIGH
Westerly Winds
North East Trade Winds
South East Trade Winds
N.E. Monsoon
North West Monsoon
Doldrums
Prevailing Westerly Winds
mb
1040
1035
1030
1025
1020
1015
1010
1005
1000
995
990
1000 Isobars in millibars at Sea Level
Prevailing Winds
July
Pressure and Winds
Calms
South West Monsoon
mb
1025
1020
1015
1010
1005
1000
995
Annual
Precipitation
mm
3000
2000
1000
500
250

Projection: *Hammer Equal Area*

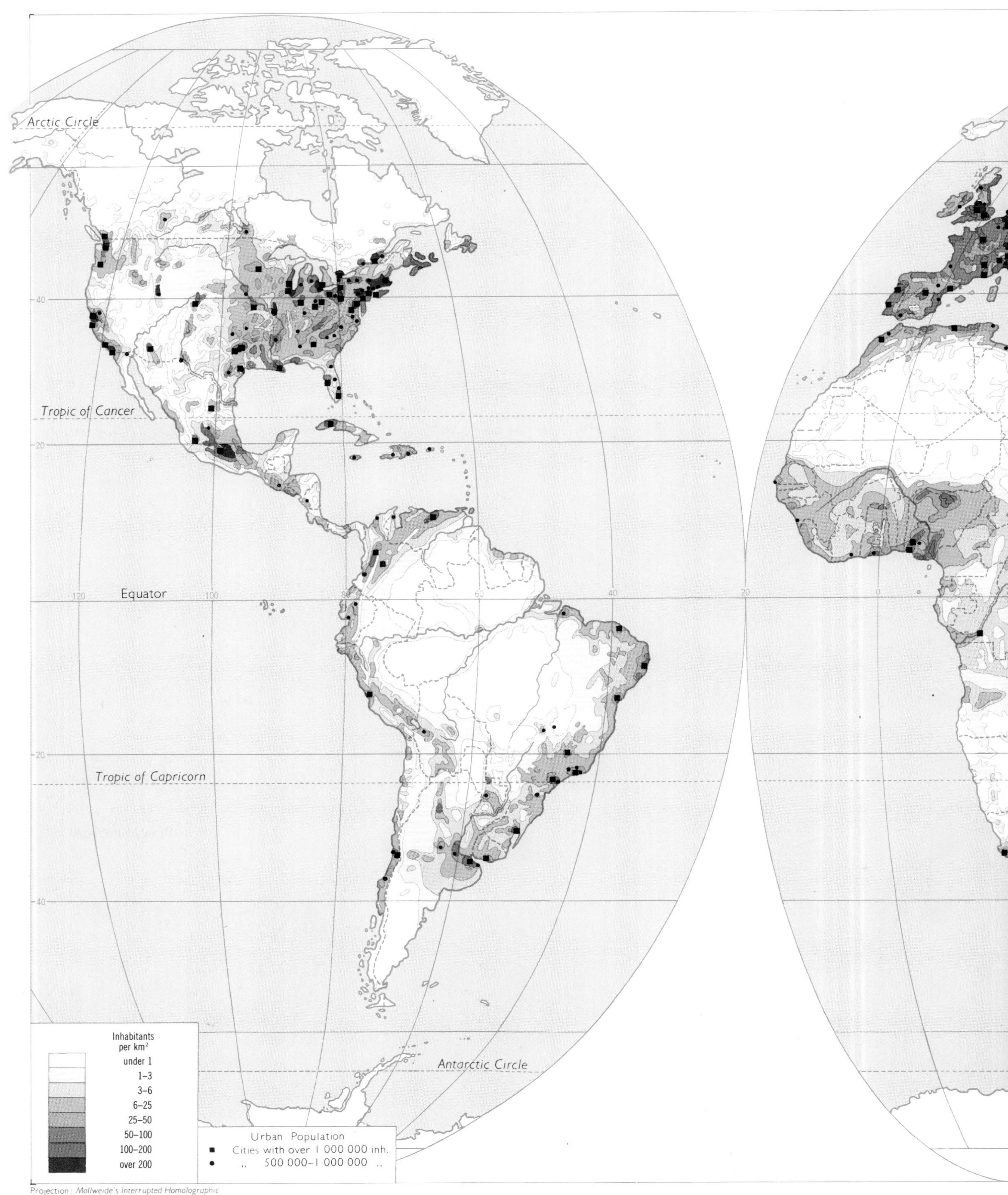
Arctic Circle
Tropic of Cancer
Equator
Tropic of Capricorn
Antarctic Circle
40
20
20
40
120
100
80
60
40
20
0
20
Inhabitants per km²
under 1
1–3
3–6
6–25
25–50
50–100
100–200
over 200
Urban Population
Cities with over 1 000 000 inh.
,, 500 000–1 000 000 ,,

Projection: *Mollweide's interrupted Homolographic*

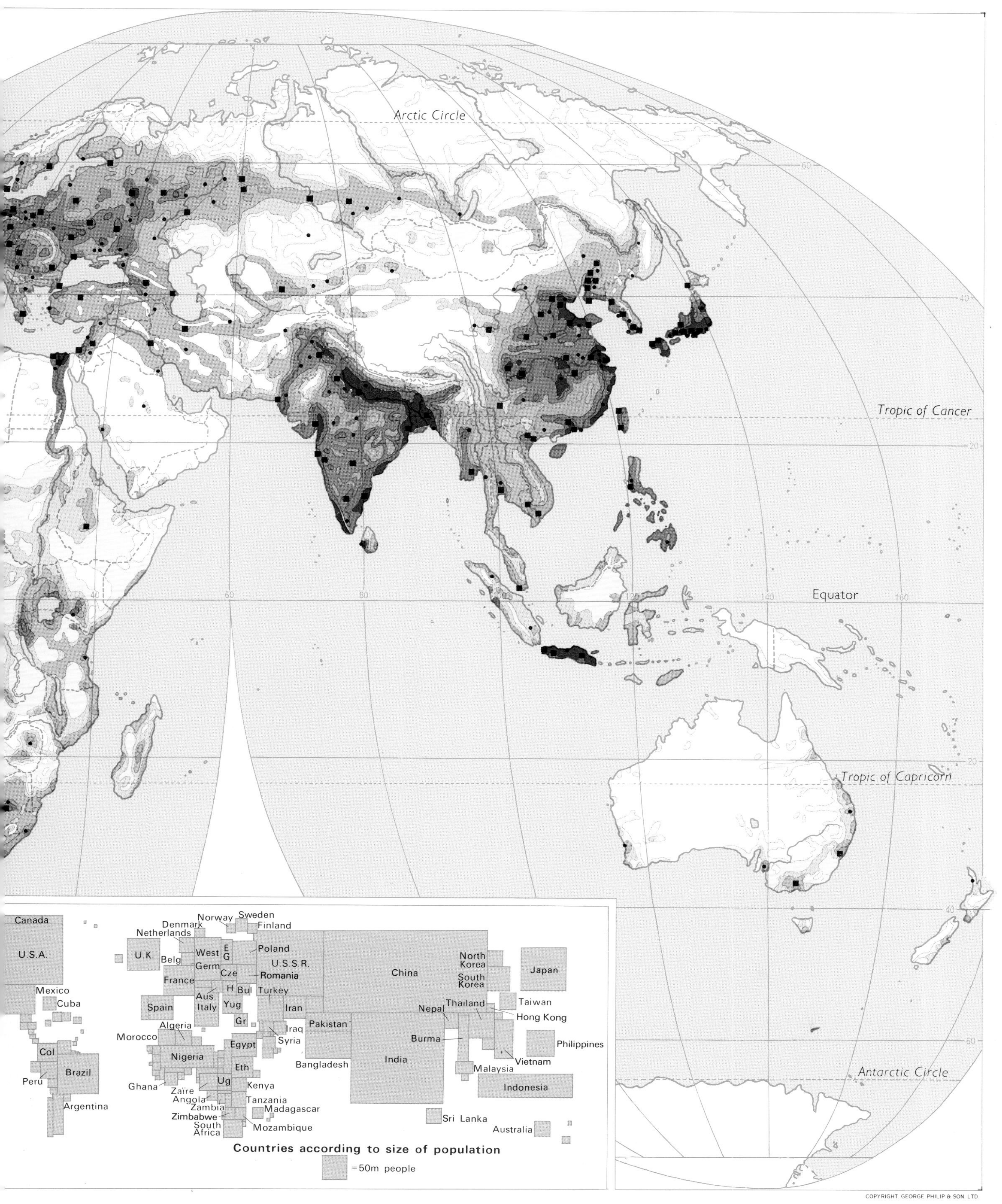
Arctic Circle
Tropic of Cancer
Equator
Tropic of Capricorn
Antarctic Circle
Canada
U.S.A.
Mexico
Cuba
Col
Peru
Brazil
Argentina
Norway
Sweden
Denmark
Netherlands
Finland
U.K.
Belg
West Germ
E G
Poland
U.S.S.R.
Romania
France
Cze
H
Bul
Aus
Italy
Yug
Turkey
Spain
Gr
Iran
Algeria
Iraq
Syria
Morocco
Egypt
Nigeria
Eth
Ghana
Ug
Kenya
Zaïre
Angola
Zambia
Tanzania
Madagascar
Zimbabwe
South Africa
Mozambique
Pakistan
Bangladesh
India
Nepal
China
North Korea
South Korea
Japan
Thailand
Taiwan
Hong Kong
Burma
Philippines
Vietnam
Malaysia
Indonesia
Sri Lanka
Australia
Countries according to size of population
=50m people

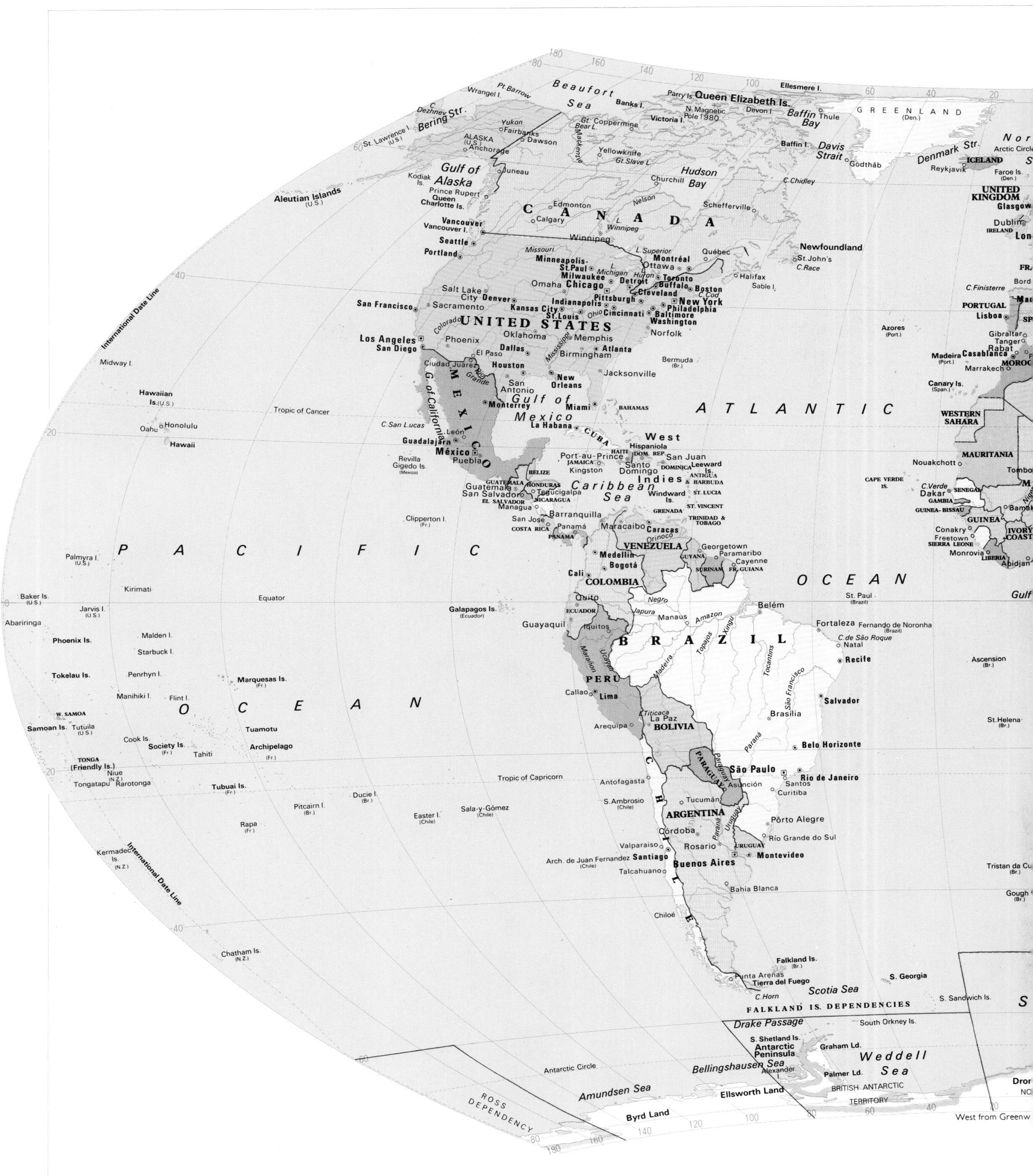
Beaufort Sea
Pt. Barrow
Wrangel I.
C. Dezhnev
Bering Str.
St. Lawrence I. (U.S.)
Yukon
Fairbanks
ALASKA (U.S.)
Anchorage
Dawson
Gulf of Alaska
Juneau
Kodiak Is.
Prince Rupert
Queen Charlotte Is.
Aleutian Islands (U.S.)
Banks I.
Parry Is.
Queen Elizabeth Is.
Ellesmere I.
Devon I.
N. Magnetic Pole 1980
Victoria I.
Gt. Bear L.
Coppermine
Mackenzie
Yellowknife
Gt. Slave L.
Baffin Bay
Thule
Baffin I.
Davis Strait
Godthåb
GREENLAND (Den.)
Denmark Str.
ICELAND
Reykjavik
Arctic Circle
Faroe Is. (Den.)
UNITED KINGDOM
Glasgow
Dublin
IRELAND
Hudson Bay
Churchill
C. Chidley
Nelson
Schefferville
CANADA
Edmonton
Calgary
L. Winnipeg
Winnipeg
Vancouver
Vancouver I.
Seattle
Portland
Missouri
L. Superior
Montréal
Québec
Newfoundland
St. John's
C. Race
Minneapolis-St. Paul
Milwaukee
L. Michigan
L. Huron
Ottawa
Toronto
Detroit
Buffalo
Boston
C. Cod
Halifax
Sable I.
Omaha
Chicago
Cleveland
Pittsburgh
New York
Philadelphia
Salt Lake City
Denver
Indianapolis
Kansas City
St. Louis
Ohio
Cincinnati
Baltimore
Washington
Norfolk
San Francisco
Sacramento
Colorado
UNITED STATES
Oklahoma
Memphis
Los Angeles
San Diego
Phoenix
Dallas
Atlanta
Birmingham
El Paso
Ciudad Juarez
Rio Grande
Houston
Mississippi
New Orleans
Jacksonville
San Antonio
Bermuda (Br.)
Gulf of Mexico
Monterrey
Miami
BAHAMAS
La Habana
CUBA
MEXICO
G. of California
C. San Lucas
León
Guadalajara
México
Puebla
Revilla Gigedo Is. (Mexico)
West Indies
Hispaniola
HAITI
DOM. REP.
Port-au-Prince
San Juan
JAMAICA
Kingston
Santo Domingo
DOMINICA
Leeward Is.
ANTIGUA & BARBUDA
BELIZE
GUATEMALA
HONDURAS
Guatemala
Tegucigalpa
San Salvador
EL SALVADOR
NICARAGUA
Managua
Caribbean Sea
Windward Is.
ST. LUCIA
GRENADA
ST. VINCENT
TRINIDAD & TOBAGO
Barranquilla
San José
COSTA RICA
Panamá
PANAMA
Maracaibo
Caracas
Orinoco
VENEZUELA
Georgetown
GUYANA
Paramaribo
SURINAM
Cayenne
FR. GUIANA
Medellín
Bogotá
Cali
COLOMBIA
Clipperton I. (Fr.)
ATLANTIC OCEAN
PACIFIC OCEAN
Quito
ECUADOR
Galapagos Is. (Ecuador)
Guayaquil
Iquitos
Negro
Japura
Manaus
Amazon
Belém
Xingu
Tapajos
BRAZIL
Fortaleza
Fernando de Noronha (Brazil)
C. de São Roque
Natal
Recife
Madeira
Tocantins
São Francisco
Marañón
Ucayali
PERU
Callao
Lima
Salvador
Brasília
L. Titicaca
La Paz
BOLIVIA
Arequipa
Belo Horizonte
Paraná
PARAGUAY
Paraguay
São Paulo
Rio de Janeiro
Santos
Asunción
Curitiba
Antofagasta
S. Ambrosio (Chile)
Tucumán
ARGENTINA
CHILE
Uruguay
Pôrto Alegre
Córdoba
Rio Grande do Sul
Valparaiso
Rosario
URUGUAY
Montevideo
Arch. de Juan Fernandez (Chile)
Santiago
Buenos Aires
Talcahuano
Bahía Blanca
Chiloé
Falkland Is. (Br.)
Punta Arenas
Tierra del Fuego
C. Horn
Scotia Sea
S. Georgia
S. Sandwich Is.
FALKLAND IS. DEPENDENCIES
Drake Passage
South Orkney Is.
S. Shetland Is.
Antarctic Peninsula
Graham Ld.
Weddell Sea
Bellingshausen Sea
Alexander I.
Palmer Ld.
BRITISH ANTARCTIC TERRITORY
Antarctic Circle
Amundsen Sea
Ellsworth Land
Byrd Land
ROSS DEPENDENCY
International Date Line
Midway I.
Hawaiian Is. (U.S.)
Oahu
Honolulu
Hawaii
Tropic of Cancer
Palmyra I. (U.S.)
Kirimati
Baker Is. (U.S.)
Jarvis I. (U.S.)
Equator
Abariringa
Phoenix Is.
Malden I.
Starbuck I.
Tokelau Is.
Penrhyn I.
Marquesas Is. (Fr.)
Manihiki I.
Flint I.
W. SAMOA
Samoan Is.
Tutuila (U.S.)
Tuamotu Archipelago (Fr.)
Cook Is.
Society Is. (Fr.)
Tahiti
TONGA (Friendly Is.)
Niue (N.Z.)
Tongatapu
Rarotonga
Tubuai Is. (Fr.)
Tropic of Capricorn
Ducie I. (Br.)
Pitcairn I. (Br.)
Easter I. (Chile)
Sala-y-Gômez (Chile)
Rapa (Fr.)
Kermadec Is. (N.Z.)
Chatham Is. (N.Z.)
Azores (Port.)
C. Finisterre
PORTUGAL
Lisboa
Gibraltar
Tangier
Rabat
Madeira (Port.)
Casablanca
Marrakech
Canary Is. (Span.)
WESTERN SAHARA
MAURITANIA
Nouakchott
CAPE VERDE IS.
C. Verde
Dakar
SENEGAL
GAMBIA
GUINEA-BISSAU
GUINEA
Conakry
Freetown
SIERRA LEONE
Monrovia
LIBERIA
Abidjan
St. Paul (Brazil)
Ascension (Br.)
St. Helena (Br.)
Tristan da Cunha (Br.)
Gough I. (Br.)
West from Greenwich

Projection: *Hammer Equal Area*

ARCTIC OCEAN
Laptev Sea
East Siberian Sea
Barents Sea
Kara Sea
UNION OF SOVIET SOCIALIST REPUBLICS
RUSSIAN SOVIET FEDERATIVE SOCIALIST REPUBLIC
Bering Sea
Sea of Okhotsk
MONGOLIA
CHINA
TIBET
JAPAN
Sea of Japan
East China Sea
South China Sea
PACIFIC OCEAN
Tropic of Cancer
TRUST TERRITORY OF THE PACIFIC ISLANDS (U.S.)
Northern Marianas (U.S.)
Caroline Is.
Marshall Is.
KIRIBATI
TUVALU
Equator
PHILIPPINES
MALAYSIA
INDONESIA
PAPUA NEW GUINEA
SOLOMON IS.
Arafura Sea
Timor Sea
AUSTRALIA
WESTERN AUSTRALIA
NORTHERN TERRITORY
QUEENSLAND
SOUTH AUSTRALIA
NEW SOUTH WALES
VICTORIA
TASMANIA
Great Australian Bight
Tasman Sea
NEW ZEALAND
New Caledonia (Fr.)
VANUATU
FIJI
INDIAN OCEAN
Arabian Sea
Bay of Bengal
INDIA
PAKISTAN
AFGHANISTAN
IRAN (PERSIA)
IRAQ
SAUDI ARABIA
OMAN
SOUTH YEMEN
Persian Gulf
Red Sea
Gulf of Aden
Caspian Sea
Black Sea
Mediterranean Sea
TURKEY
EGYPT
LIBYA
SUDAN
CHAD
NIGER
NIGERIA
ETHIOPIA
SOMALI REP.
KENYA
TANZANIA
ZAÏRE (CONGO)
ANGOLA
ZAMBIA
ZIMBABWE
MOZAMBIQUE
NAMIBIA
BOTSWANA
SOUTH AFRICA
MADAGASCAR
Mozambique Chan.
BURMA
THAILAND
Tropic of Capricorn
SOUTHERN OCEAN
Antarctic Circle
Enderby Land
Wilkes Land
AUSTRALIAN DEPENDENCY
Ross Sea
S. Magnetic Pole 1980

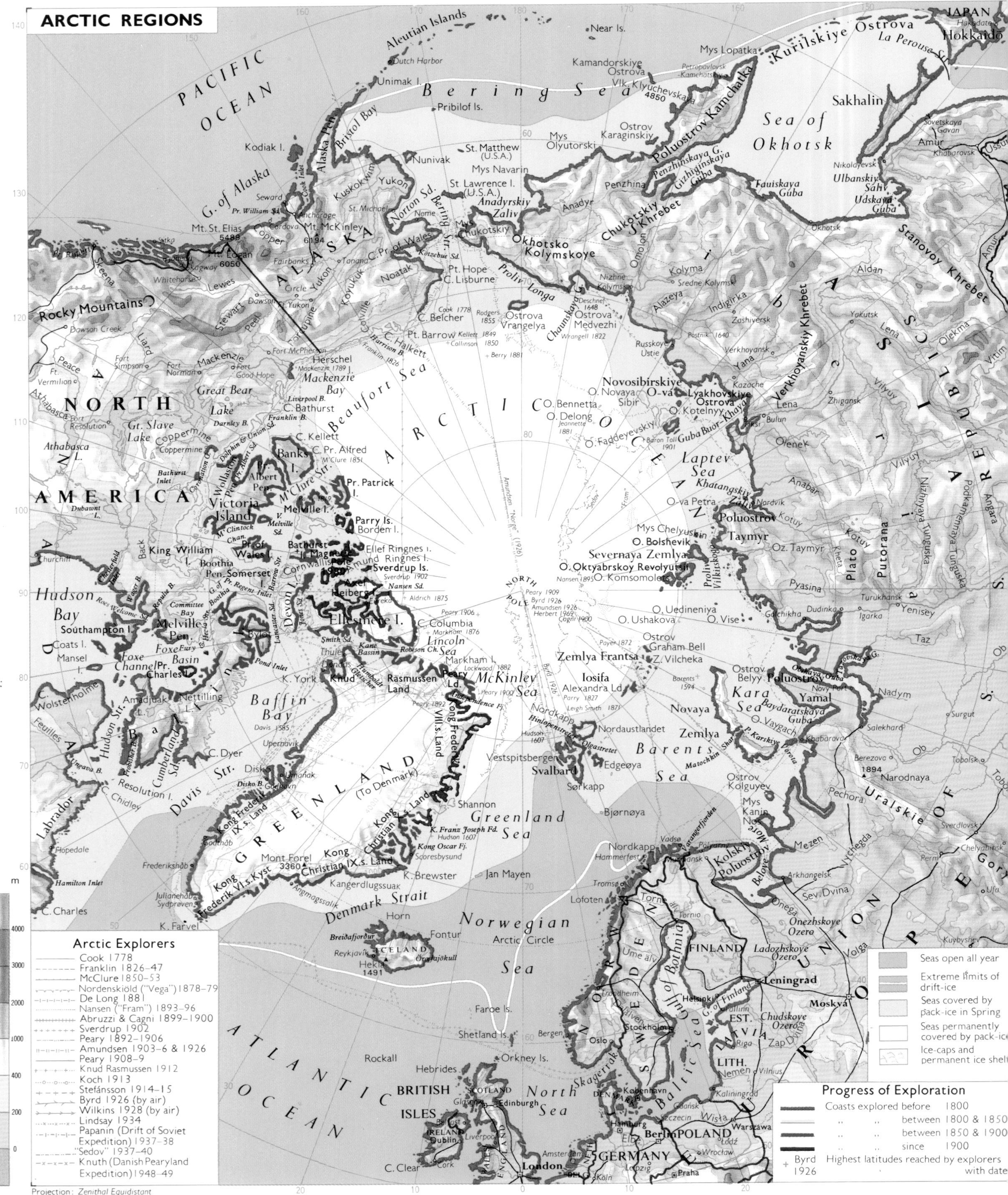

ARCTIC REGIONS
Arctic Explorers
Cook 1778
Franklin 1826–47
McClure 1850–53
Nordenskiöld ("Vega") 1878–79
De Long 1881
Nansen ("Fram") 1893–96
Abruzzi & Cagni 1899–1900
Sverdrup 1902
Peary 1892–1906
Amundsen 1903–6 & 1926
Peary 1908–9
Knud Rasmussen 1912
Koch 1913
Stefánsson 1914–15
Byrd 1926 (by air)
Wilkins 1928 (by air)
Lindsay 1934
Papanin (Drift of Soviet Expedition) 1937–38
"Sedov" 1937–40
Knuth (Danish Pearyland Expedition) 1948–49
Seas open all year
Extreme limits of drift-ice
Seas covered by pack-ice in Spring
Seas permanently covered by pack-ice
Ice-caps and permanent ice shelf
Progress of Exploration
Coasts explored before 1800
" " between 1800 & 1850
" " between 1850 & 1900
" " since 1900
Byrd 1926 Highest latitudes reached by explorers with date
m
4000
3000
2000
1000
400
200
0
Projection: Zenithal Equidistant
PACIFIC OCEAN
Bering Sea
Sea of Okhotsk
ARCTIC OCEAN
Beaufort Sea
Laptev Sea
Kara Sea
Barents Sea
Greenland Sea
Norwegian Sea
ATLANTIC OCEAN
North Sea
Baffin Bay
Davis Str.
Denmark Strait
Hudson Bay
Lincoln Sea
McKinley Sea
NORTH AMERICA
ALASKA
GREENLAND (To Denmark)
ICELAND
BRITISH ISLES
NORWAY
SWEDEN
FINLAND
EURO OPEAN
UNION OF SOVIET S.
GERMANY
POLAND
Rocky Mountains
Aleutian Islands
Victoria Island
Ellesmere I.
Baffin I.
Novaya Zemlya
Severnaya Zemlya
Zemlya Frantsa Iosifa
Svalbard
Vestspitsbergen
Novosibirskiye O-va
Sakhalin
NORTH POLE
Arctic Circle
Mt. McKinley 6194
Mt. St. Elias 5488
Mt. Logan 6050
Mont Forel 3360
Hekla 1491
Leningrad
Moskva
London
Berlin

1:35 000 000

400 0 400 800 1200 km

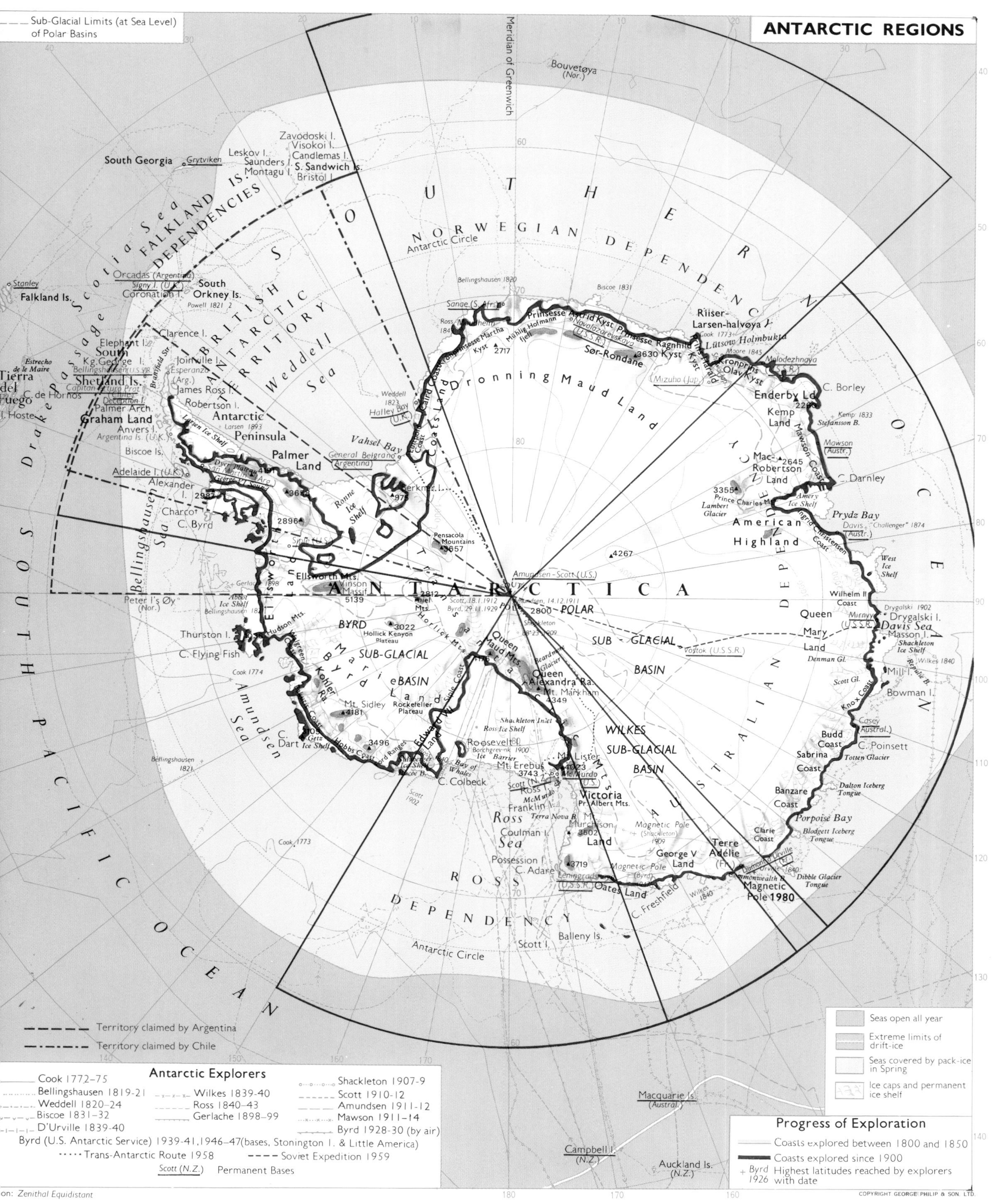
ANTARCTIC REGIONS
Sub-Glacial Limits (at Sea Level) of Polar Basins
Meridian of Greenwich
Bouvetøya (Nor.)
Zavodoski I.
Visokoi I.
Leskov I.
Candlemas I.
Saunders I.
Montagu I.
S. Sandwich Is.
Bristol I.
South Georgia
Grytviken
FALKLAND IS. DEPENDENCIES
Scotia Sea
Orcadas (Argentina)
Signy I. (U.K.)
Coronation I.
South Orkney Is.
Powell 1821
Stanley
Falkland Is.
Drake Passage
Elephant I.
Clarence I.
South Shetland Is.
Kg. George I.
Estrecho de le Maire
Tierra del Fuego
C. de Hornos
I. Hoste
Joinville I.
Esperanza (Arg.)
James Ross I.
Robertson I.
Palmer Arch.
Deception I.
Graham Land
Anvers I.
Antarctic Peninsula
Larsen 1893
Larsen Ice Shelf
Biscoe Is.
Palmer Land
Adelaide I. (U.K.)
Alexander I.
Charcot I.
C. Byrd
Bellingshausen Sea
BRITISH ANTARCTIC TERRITORY
Weddell Sea
Weddell 1823
Halley Bay (U.K.)
Vahsel Bay
General Belgrano (Argentina)
Ronne Ice Shelf
Berkner I.
Pensacola Mountains
Peter I's Øy (Nor.)
Abbot Ice Shelf
Thurston I.
C. Flying Fish
Cook 1774
Amundsen Sea
Ellsworth Land
Ellsworth Mts.
Vinson Massif 5139
BYRD SUB-GLACIAL BASIN
Hollick Kenyon Plateau
Marie Byrd Land
Mt. Sidley 4181
Rockefeller Plateau
Hudson Mts.
Kohler Ra.
C. Dart
Getz Ice Shelf
Bellingshausen 1821
Edward VII Land
Horlick Mts.
Thiel Mts.
Queen Maud Mts.
Queen Alexandra Ra.
Mt. Markham 4349
Beardmore Glacier
Shackleton Inlet
Ross Ice Shelf
Roosevelt I.
Bay of Whales
C. Colbeck
Mt. Erebus 3743
Scott (N.Z.)
McMurdo (U.S.)
Ross I.
Franklin I.
Ross Sea
Coulman I.
Possession I.
C. Adare
Terra Nova B.
Victoria Land
Pr. Albert Mts.
Mt. Murchison 3602
Cook 1773
Scott 1902
ROSS DEPENDENCY
Balleny Is.
Scott I.
Antarctic Circle
Oates Land
C. Freshfield
Leningradskaya (U.S.S.R.)
Magnetic Pole (Byrd)
George V Land
Terre Adélie (Fr.)
Dumont d'Urville (Fr.)
Commonwealth B.
Magnetic Pole 1980
Dibble Glacier Tongue
ANTARCTICA
SOUTH POLE
Amundsen-Scott (U.S.)
Amundsen, 14.12.1911
Scott, 18.1.1912
Byrd, 29.11.1929
2800 POLAR SUB-GLACIAL BASIN
Vostok (U.S.S.R.)
WILKES SUB-GLACIAL BASIN
AUSTRALIAN DEPENDENCY
NORWEGIAN DEPENDENCY
Antarctic Circle
Bellingshausen 1820
Biscoe 1831
Sanae (S. Afr.)
Prinsesse Martha Kyst
Prinsesse Astrid Kyst
Prinsesse Ragnhild Kyst
Novolazarevskaya (U.S.S.R.)
Mühlig Hofmann fjell
Sør-Rondane
Dronning Maud Land
Mizuho (Jap.)
Riiser-Larsen-halvøya
Lützow Holmbukta
Kronprins Olav Kyst
Molodezhnaya (U.S.S.R.)
Enderby Ld.
C. Borley
Kemp Land
Kemp 1833
Stefansson B.
Mawson (Austr.)
Mawson Coast
Mac-Robertson Land
C. Darnley
Prince Charles Mts.
Lambert Glacier
Amery Ice Shelf
Prydz Bay
Davis (Austr.)
"Challenger" 1874
Ingrid Christensen Coast
American Highland
West Ice Shelf
Wilhelm II Coast
Drygalski 1902
Drygalski I.
Mirnyy (U.S.S.R.)
Davis Sea
Masson I.
Shackleton Ice Shelf
Wilkes 1840
Queen Mary Land
Denman Gl.
Mill I.
Bowman I.
Scott Gl.
Knox Coast
Casey (Austral.)
Budd Coast
C. Poinsett
Totten Glacier
Sabrina Coast
Banzare Coast
Dalton Iceberg Tongue
Porpoise Bay
Blodgett Iceberg Tongue
Clarie Coast
SOUTHERN OCEAN
SOUTH PACIFIC OCEAN
Macquarie Is. (Austral.)
Campbell I. (N.Z.)
Auckland Is. (N.Z.)
Territory claimed by Argentina
Territory claimed by Chile
Antarctic Explorers
Cook 1772-75
Bellingshausen 1819-21
Weddell 1820-24
Biscoe 1831-32
D'Urville 1839-40
Wilkes 1839-40
Ross 1840-43
Gerlache 1898-99
Shackleton 1907-9
Scott 1910-12
Amundsen 1911-12
Mawson 1911-14
Byrd 1928-30 (by air)
Byrd (U.S. Antarctic Service) 1939-41, 1946-47 (bases, Stonington I. & Little America)
Trans-Antarctic Route 1958
Soviet Expedition 1959
Scott (N.Z.) Permanent Bases
Seas open all year
Extreme limits of drift-ice
Seas covered by pack-ice in Spring
Ice caps and permanent ice shelf
Progress of Exploration
Coasts explored between 1800 and 1850
Coasts explored since 1900
Byrd 1926 Highest latitudes reached by explorers with date

Projection: Zenithal Equidistant

ARCTIC OCEAN
Greenland Sea
Norwegian Sea
Barents Sea
Kara Sea
Svalbard
Zemlya Frantsa Iosifa
Novaya Zemlya
Severnaya Zemlya
GREENLAND
ICELAND
Denmark Strait
Davis Strait
Baffin Bay
Baffin Island
Ellesmere Island
Queen Elizabeth Islands
Beaufort Sea
Hudson Bay
Labrador
Newfoundland
Labrador Basin
C A N A D A
UNITED STATES
Gulf of Mexico
Florida
CUBA
West Indies
Caribbean Sea
Sargasso Sea
Bermuda
Azores
Madeira
Islas Canarias
Canary Basin
Cape Verde Basin
NORTH ATLANTIC OCEAN
North American Basin
Northern Mid-Atlantic Ridge
NORTH EQUATORIAL CURRENT
NORTH ATLANTIC DRIFT
Tropic of Cancer
Bay of Biscay
North Sea
Mediterranean Sea
UNITED KINGDOM
IRELAND
FRANCE
SPAIN
PORTUGAL
MOROCCO
ALGERIA
TUNISIA
LIBYA
WESTERN SAHARA
MAURITANIA
NIGER
NIGERIA
SWEDEN
FINLAND
U.S.S.R.
POLAND
ROMANIA
GREECE
VENEZUELA
COLOMBIA
Sahara
GUINEA CURRENT

BRAZIL
BOLIVIA
ARGENTINA
PERU
CHILE
PARAGUAY
URUGUAY
Mato Grosso
Brasília
São Paulo
Rio de Janeiro
Belo Horizonte
Salvador
Recife
Fortaleza
Pôrto Alegre
Montevideo
Buenos Aires
Rosario
Córdoba
Santiago
Valparaíso
Asunción
La Paz
Lima
Callao
Manaus
Tierra del Fuego
Drake Passage
Falkland Is. (Islas Malvinas)
FALKLAND IS. DEPENDENCIES
South Georgia
South Orkney Is.
South Shetland Is.
South Sandwich Is.
Scotia Sea
Weddell Sea
BRITISH ANTARCTIC TERRITORY
Antarctic Peninsula
Graham Land
Palmer Land
Ellsworth Land
Byrd Land
Ross Sea
Coats Land
Dronning Maud Land
Enderby Land
SOUTH ATLANTIC OCEAN
SOUTHERN OCEAN
PACIFIC OCEAN
South East Pacific Basin
Chile Rise
PERUVIAN COLD CURRENT
BENGUELA COLD CURRENT
EQUATORIAL CURRENT
WEST WIND DRIFT
CAPE HORN COLD CURRENT
Brazil Basin
Angola Basin
Cape Basin
Agulhas Basin
Argentine Basin
Atlantic Indian Ridge
Southern Mid-Atlantic Ridge
Walvis Ridge
Cape Town
Ascension
St. Helena
Tristan da Cunha
Gough I.
Bouvetøya
Antarctic Circle
Tropic of Capricorn
Equatorial Limit of Icebergs
Direction of Currents
Principal Shipping Routes (Distances in Nautical Miles)
Projection: Mollweide
COPYRIGHT GEORGE PHILIP & SON, LTD

1:20 000 000

200 0 200 400 600 800 km

Projection: Bonne. West from Greenwich 0 East from Greenwich

m 4000 2000 1000 400 200 0 200 2000 4000 m

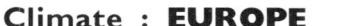

1: 40 000 000

400 0 400 800 1200 1600 km

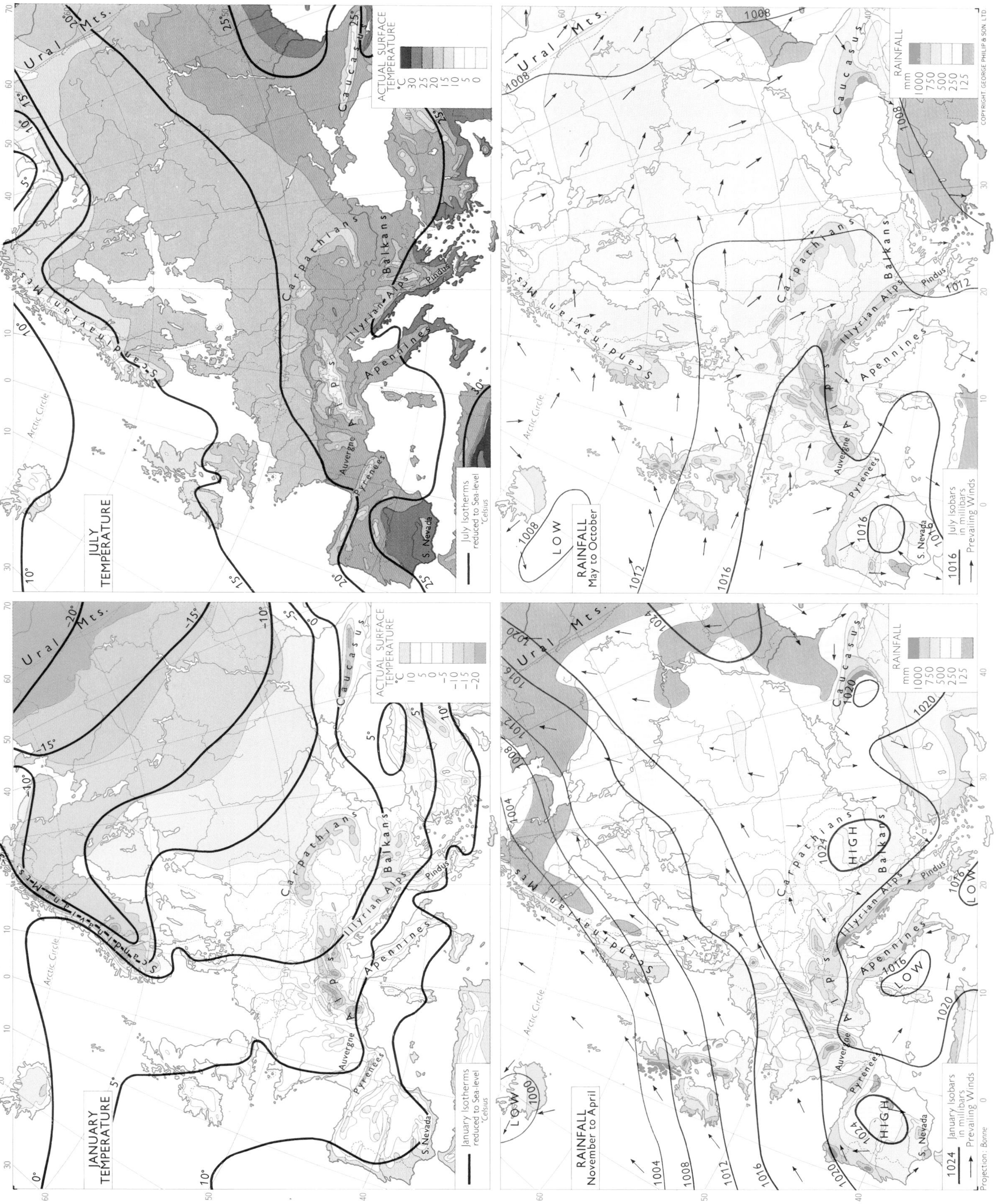

JULY TEMPERATURE

ACTUAL SURFACE TEMPERATURE
°C
30
25
20
15
10
5
0

July Isotherms reduced to Sea-level °Celsius

RAINFALL May to October

RAINFALL
mm
1000
750
500
250
125

1016 July Isobars in millibars

Prevailing Winds

JANUARY TEMPERATURE

ACTUAL SURFACE TEMPERATURE
°C
10
5
0
–5
–10
–15
–20

January Isotherms reduced to Sea-level °Celsius

RAINFALL November to April

RAINFALL
mm
1000
750
500
250
125

1024 January Isobars in millibars

Prevailing Winds

Projection: Bonne

1:35 000 000

400 0 400 800 1200 km

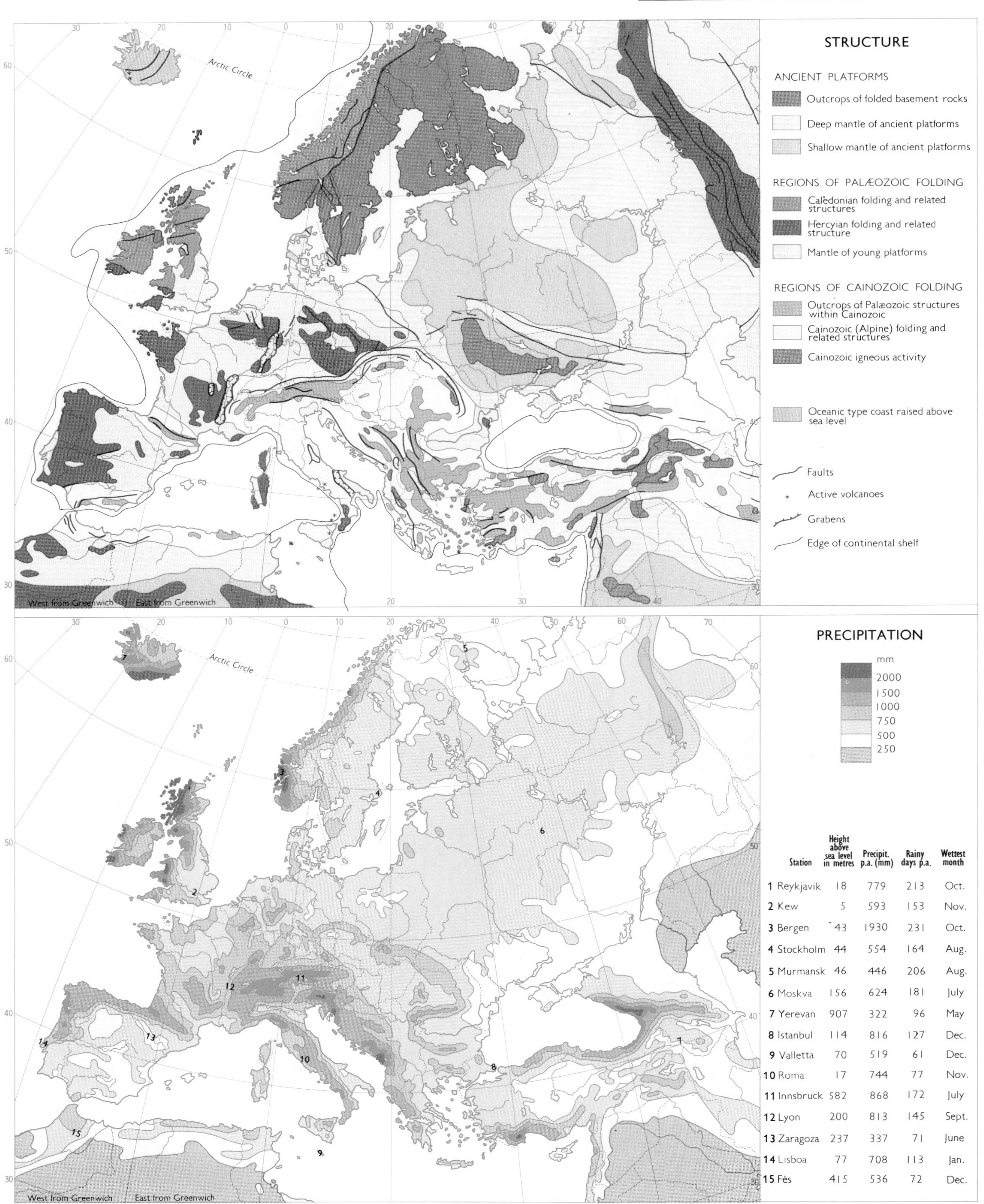
STRUCTURE
ANCIENT PLATFORMS
Outcrops of folded basement rocks
Deep mantle of ancient platforms
Shallow mantle of ancient platforms
REGIONS OF PALÆOZOIC FOLDING
Calèdonian folding and related structures
Hercyian folding and related structure
Mantle of young platforms
REGIONS OF CAINOZOIC FOLDING
Outcrops of Palæozoic structures within Cainozoic
Cainozoic (Alpine) folding and related structures
Cainozoic igneous activity
Oceanic type coast raised above sea level
Faults
Active volcanoes
Grabens
Edge of continental shelf
Arctic Circle
West from Greenwich
East from Greenwich
PRECIPITATION
mm
2000
1500
1000
750
500
250
Projection: Bonne

Station	Height above sea level in metres	Precipit. p.a. (mm)	Rainy days p.a.	Wettest month
1 Reykjavik	18	779	213	Oct.
2 Kew	5	593	153	Nov.
3 Bergen	43	1930	231	Oct.
4 Stockholm	44	554	164	Aug.
5 Murmansk	46	446	206	Aug.
6 Moskva	156	624	181	July
7 Yerevan	907	322	96	May
8 Istanbul	114	816	127	Dec.
9 Valletta	70	519	61	Dec.
10 Roma	17	744	77	Nov.
11 Innsbruck	582	868	172	July
12 Lyon	200	813	145	Sept.
13 Zaragoza	237	337	71	June
14 Lisboa	77	708	113	Jan.
15 Fès	415	536	72	Dec.

1:6 000 000

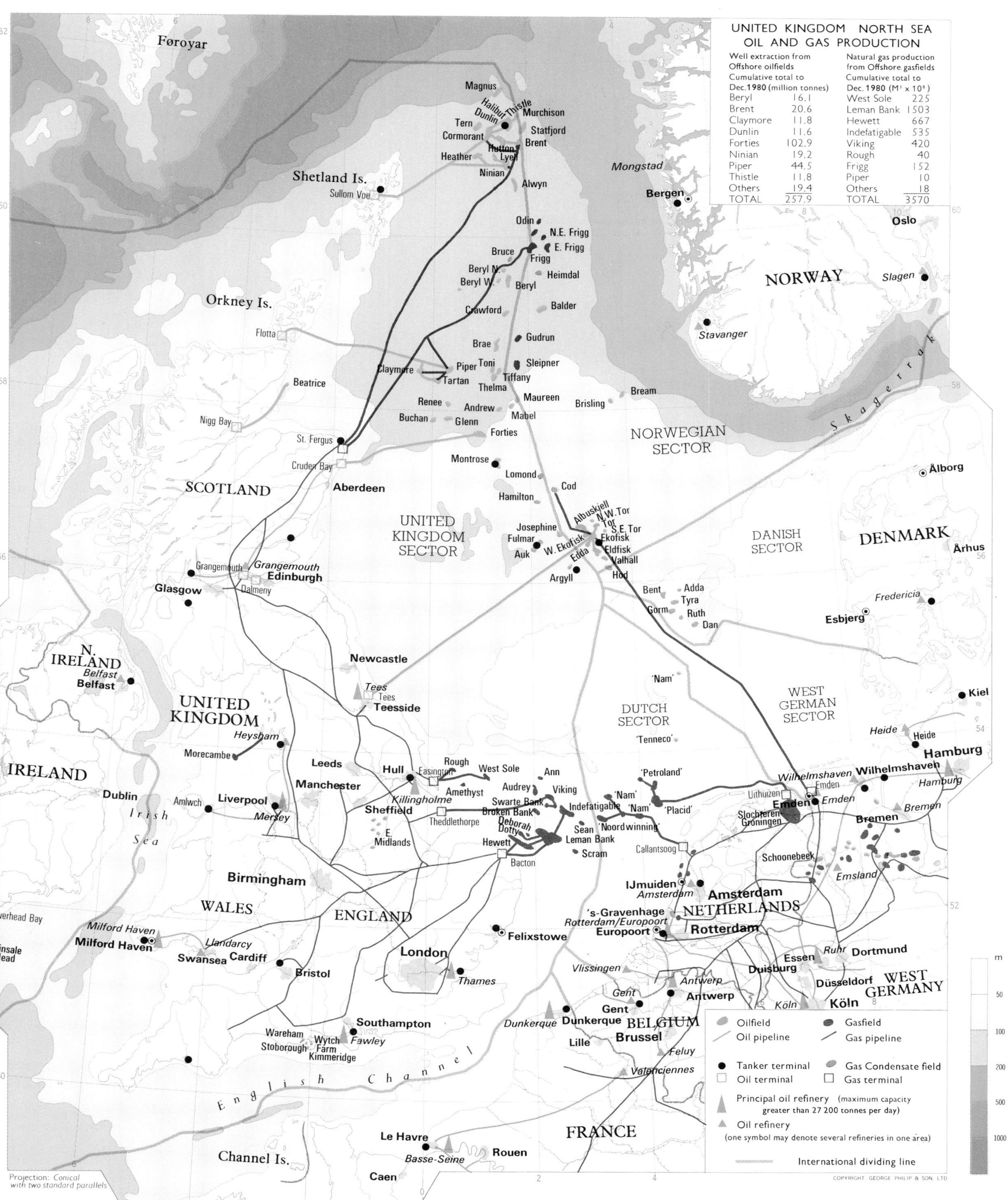

UNITED KINGDOM NORTH SEA OIL AND GAS PRODUCTION

Well extraction from Offshore oilfields Cumulative total to Dec.1980 (million tonnes)		Natural gas production from Offshore gasfields Cumulative total to Dec.1980 (M³ x 10⁸)	
Beryl	16.1	West Sole	225
Brent	20.6	Leman Bank	1503
Claymore	11.8	Hewett	667
Dunlin	11.6	Indefatigable	535
Forties	102.9	Viking	420
Ninian	19.2	Rough	40
Piper	44.5	Frigg	152
Thistle	11.8	Piper	10
Others	19.4	Others	18
TOTAL	257.9	TOTAL	3570

Føroyar
Magnus
Halibut
Thistle
Dunlin
Murchison
Tern
Cormorant
Statfjord
Brent
Hutton
Lyell
Heather
Ninian
Alwyn
Shetland Is.
Sullom Voe
Mongstad
Bergen
Oslo
Odin
N.E. Frigg
E. Frigg
Frigg
Bruce
Beryl N.
Beryl W.
Beryl
Heimdal
Crawford
Balder
NORWAY
Slagen
Orkney Is.
Flotta
Stavanger
Brae
Gudrun
Piper
Toni
Sleipner
Claymore
Tartan
Tiffany
Thelma
Beatrice
Skagerrak
Bream
Renee
Andrew
Maureen
Brisling
Buchan
Glenn
Mabel
Nigg Bay
Forties
St. Fergus
NORWEGIAN SECTOR
Cruden Bay
Montrose
Aberdeen
SCOTLAND
Lomond
Cod
Ålborg
Hamilton
UNITED KINGDOM SECTOR
Albuskjell
N.W. Tor
Tor
S.E. Tor
Ekofisk
Josephine
Fulmar
W. Ekofisk
Edda
Eldfisk
Valhall
Auk
Hod
Argyll
DANISH SECTOR
DENMARK
Århus
Grangemouth
Edinburgh
Dalmeny
Glasgow
Bent
Adda
Tyra
Gorm
Ruth
Dan
Fredericia
Esbjerg
N. IRELAND
Belfast
Newcastle
'Nam'
Kiel
Tees
Teesside
UNITED KINGDOM
DUTCH SECTOR
WEST GERMAN SECTOR
Heysham
Heide
'Tenneco'
Morecambe
Hamburg
IRELAND
Leeds
Rough
Easington
West Sole
Ann
'Petroland'
Wilhelmshaven
Hull
Manchester
Killingholme
Amethyst
Audrey
Viking
Emden
Uithuizen
Dublin
Amlwch
Liverpool
Mersey
Irish Sea
Sheffield
Theddlethorpe
Swarte Bank
Broken Bank
Indefatigable
'Nam'
'Placid'
Slochteren
Groningen
Bremen
E. Midlands
Deborah
Dotty
Hewett
Sean
Leman Bank
Scram
'Noordwinning'
Callantsoog
Bacton
Schoonebeek
Emsland
Birmingham
IJmuiden
Amsterdam
NETHERLANDS
WALES
ENGLAND
's-Gravenhage
Rotterdam/Europoort
Europoort
Rotterdam
Milford Haven
Llandarcy
Felixstowe
Ruhr
Dortmund
Kinsale Head
Swansea
Cardiff
London
Essen
Duisburg
Bristol
Thames
Vlissingen
Antwerp
Düsseldorf
WEST GERMANY
Gent
Köln
Southampton
Dunkerque
BELGIUM
Wareham
Wytch Farm
Fawley
Stoborough
Kimmeridge
Lille
Brussel
Feluy
Valenciennes
English Channel
Le Havre
Basse-Seine
Rouen
FRANCE
Channel Is.
Caen
Oilfield
Gasfield
Oil pipeline
Gas pipeline
Tanker terminal
Gas Condensate field
Oil terminal
Gas terminal
Principal oil refinery (maximum capacity greater than 27 200 tonnes per day)
Oil refinery
(one symbol may denote several refineries in one area)
International dividing line
Projection: Conical with two standard parallels

EUROPE : Density of Population

1: 20 000 000

200 0 200 400 600 800 km

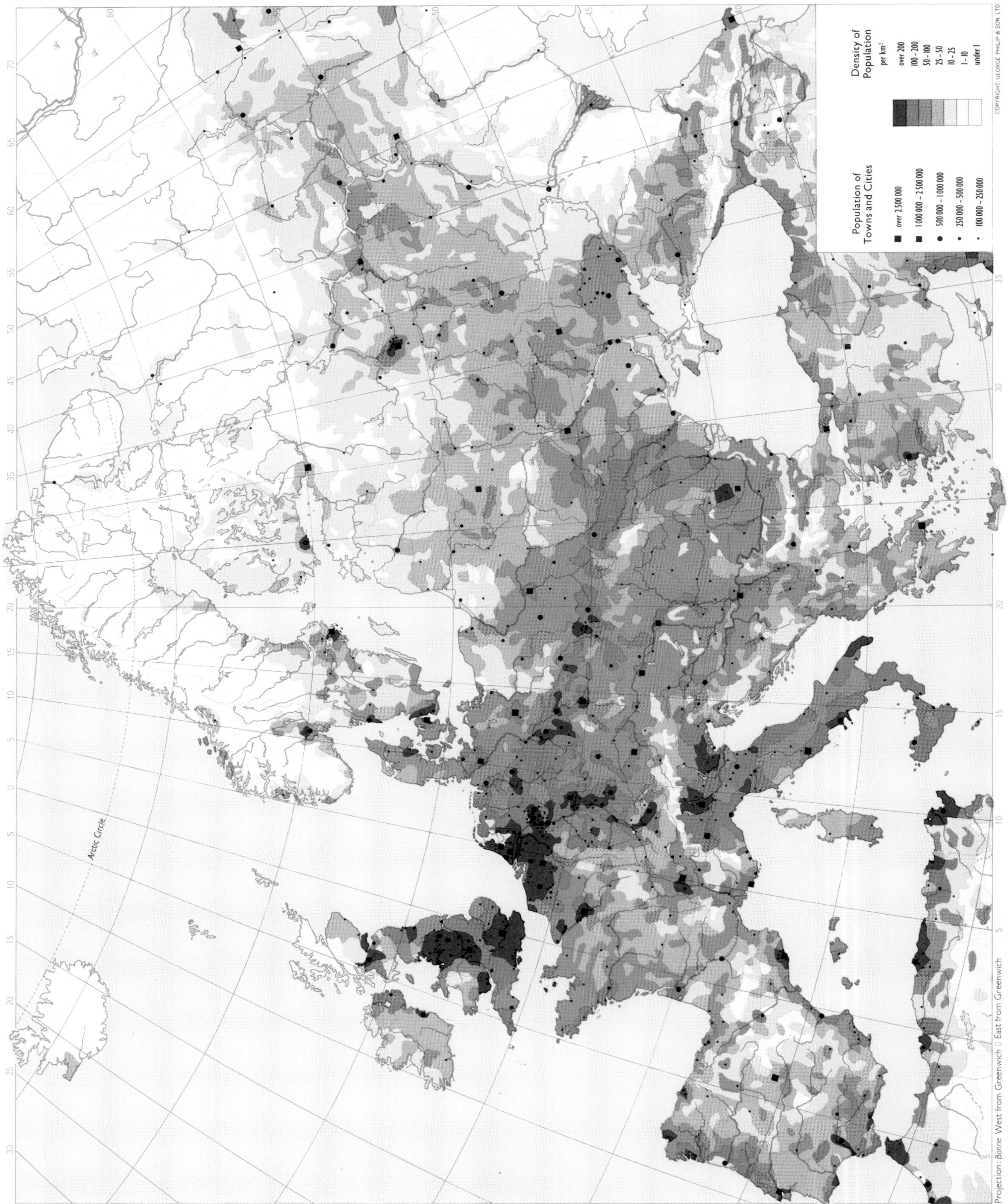
Density of Population
per km²
over 200
100 - 200
50 - 100
25 - 50
10 - 25
1 - 10
under 1
Population of Towns and Cities
over 2 500 000
1 000 000 - 2 500 000
500 000 - 1 000 000
250 000 - 500 000
100 000 - 250 000
Arctic Circle
Projection: Bonne West from Greenwich 0 East from Greenwich

1:20 000 000

200 0 200 400 600 800 km

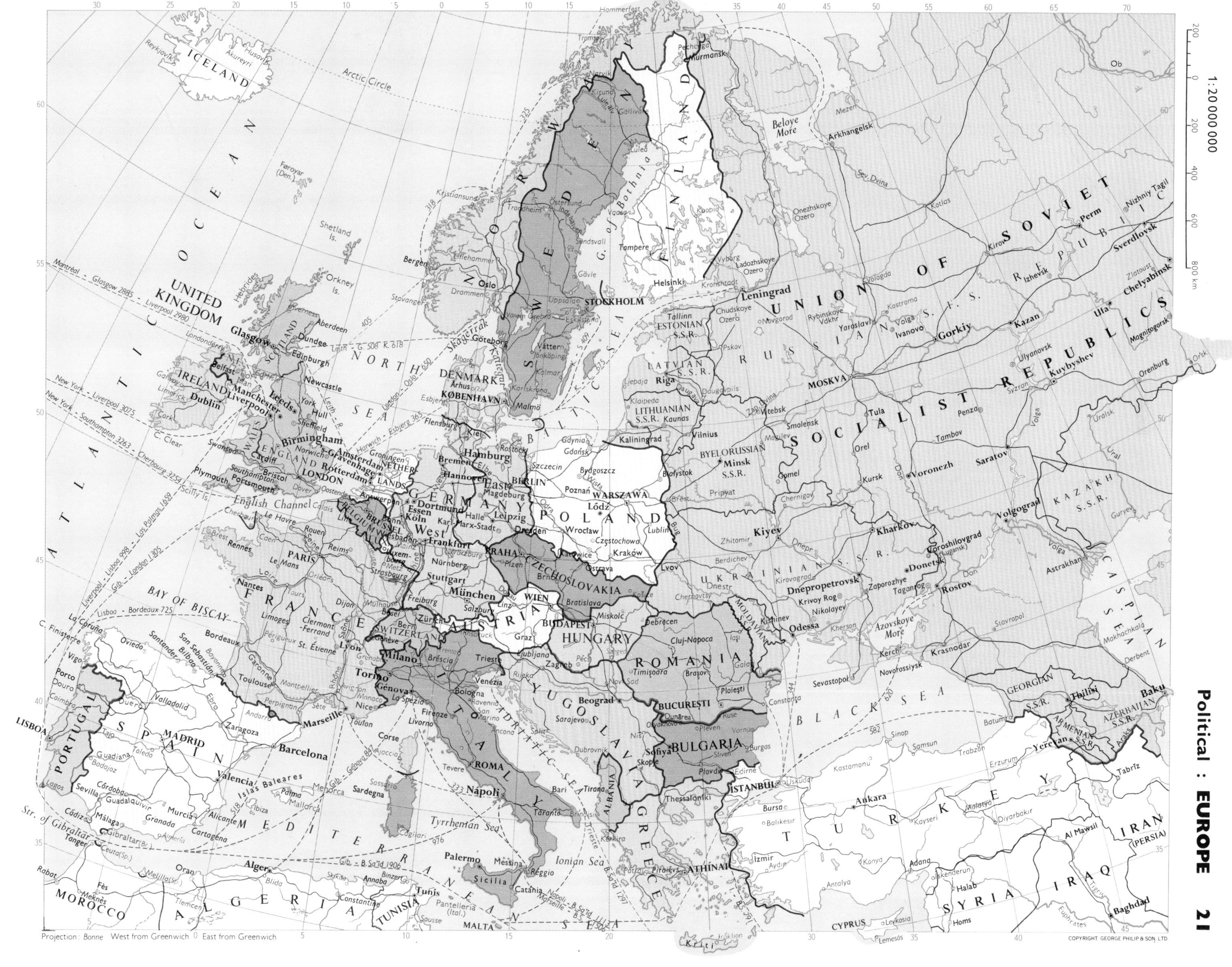
UNION OF SOVIET SOCIALIST REPUBLICS
R.S.F.S.R.
UKRAINIAN S.S.R.
BYELORUSSIAN S.S.R.
ESTONIAN S.S.R.
LATVIAN S.S.R.
LITHUANIAN S.S.R.
MOLDAVIAN S.S.R.
GEORGIAN S.S.R.
ARMENIAN S.S.R.
AZERBAIJAN S.S.R.
KAZAKH S.S.R.
FINLAND
SWEDEN
NORWAY
DENMARK
POLAND
CZECHOSLOVAKIA
HUNGARY
ROMANIA
BULGARIA
YUGOSLAVIA
ALBANIA
GREECE
TURKEY
SYRIA
IRAQ
IRAN (PERSIA)
CYPRUS
AUSTRIA
SWITZERLAND
ITALY
FRANCE
BELGIUM
GERMANY
East
West
UNITED KINGDOM
IRELAND
ICELAND
SPAIN
PORTUGAL
MOROCCO
ALGERIA
TUNISIA
MALTA
ATLANTIC OCEAN
NORTH SEA
BALTIC SEA
BLACK SEA
CASPIAN SEA
MEDITERRANEAN SEA
BAY OF BISCAY
English Channel
Tyrrhenian Sea
Ionian Sea
Arctic Circle
MOSKVA
Leningrad
Kiyev
Minsk
Riga
Vilnius
Tallinn
Helsinki
STOCKHOLM
Oslo
KØBENHAVN
BERLIN
WARSZAWA
PRAHA
WIEN
BUDAPEST
BUCUREŞTI
Sofiya
Beograd
Tirana
ATHINAI
ISTANBUL
Ankara
LONDON
PARIS
BRUSSEL
Amsterdam
Bern
ROMA
MADRID
LISBOA
Dublin
Tunis
Alger
Projection: Bonne West from Greenwich 0 East from Greenwich
COPYRIGHT GEORGE PHILIP & SON, LTD.

BRITISH ISLES : Solid Geology

1: 4 000 000

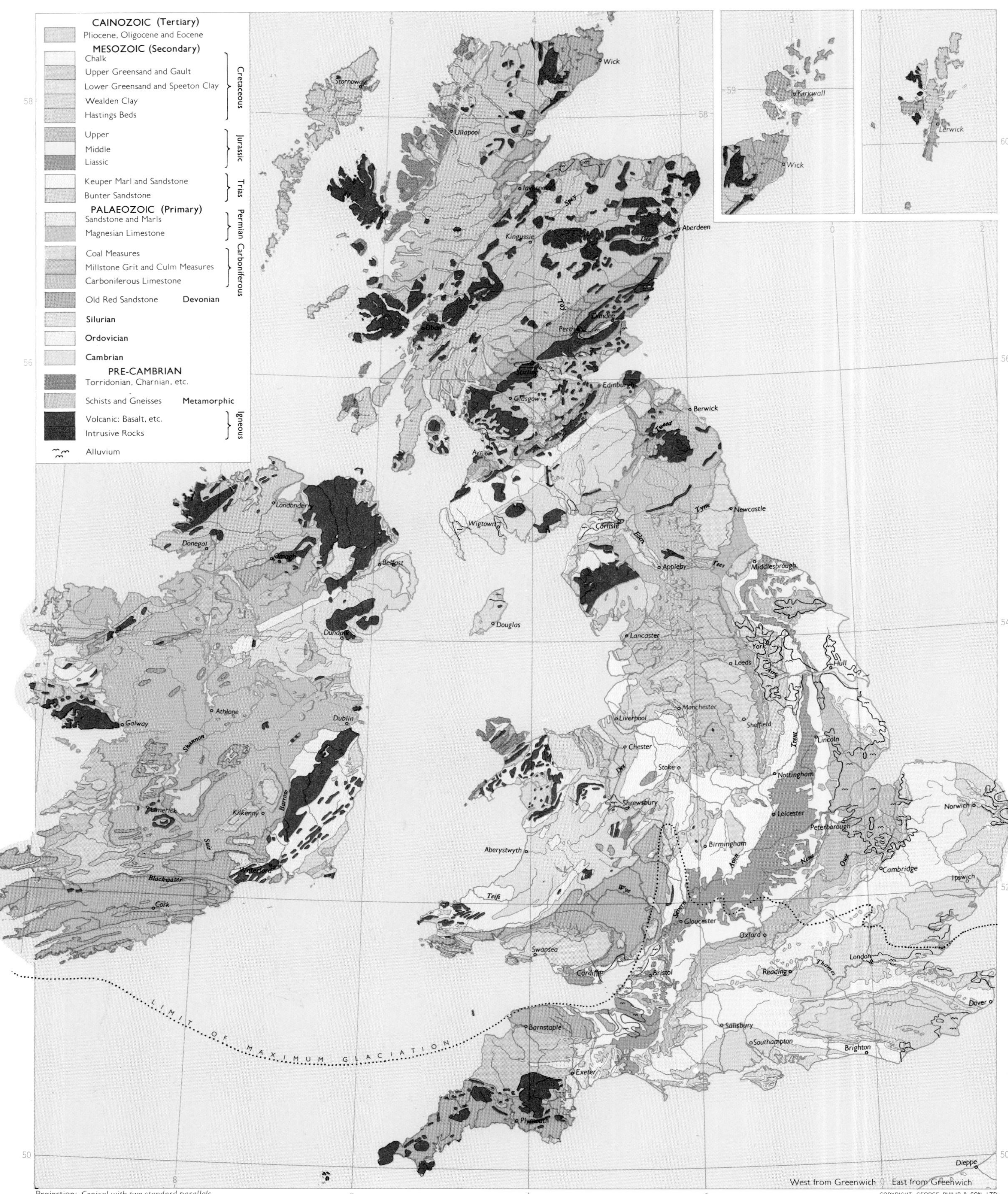
50 0 50 100 150 km
CAINOZOIC (Tertiary)
Pliocene, Oligocene and Eocene
MESOZOIC (Secondary)
Chalk
Upper Greensand and Gault
Lower Greensand and Speeton Clay
Wealden Clay
Hastings Beds
Cretaceous
Upper
Middle
Liassic
Jurassic
Keuper Marl and Sandstone
Bunter Sandstone
Trias
PALAEOZOIC (Primary)
Sandstone and Marls
Magnesian Limestone
Permian
Coal Measures
Millstone Grit and Culm Measures
Carboniferous Limestone
Carboniferous
Old Red Sandstone
Devonian
Silurian
Ordovician
Cambrian
PRE-CAMBRIAN
Torridonian, Charnian, etc.
Schists and Gneisses
Metamorphic
Volcanic: Basalt, etc.
Intrusive Rocks
Igneous
Alluvium
Stornoway
Wick
Ullapool
Kirkwall
Lerwick
Spey
Kingussie
Aberdeen
Dee
Tay
Dundee
Perth
Oban
Stirling
Glasgow
Edinburgh
Berwick
Tweed
Ayr
Londonderry
Wigtown
Carlisle
Eden
Tyne
Newcastle
Donegal
Omagh
Belfast
Appleby
Tees
Middlesbrough
Douglas
Dundalk
Lancaster
York
Leeds
Aire
Hull
Athlone
Galway
Dublin
Manchester
Liverpool
Sheffield
Trent
Lincoln
Shannon
Chester
Stoke
Dee
Nottingham
Limerick
Kilkenny
Barrow
Shrewsbury
Leicester
Norwich
Peterborough
Suir
Aberystwyth
Birmingham
Avon
Nene
Ouse
Cambridge
Ipswich
Blackwater
Waterford
Cork
Teifi
Wye
Severn
Gloucester
Oxford
Swansea
Cardiff
Bristol
Reading
Thames
London
Dover
LIMIT OF MAXIMUM GLACIATION
Barnstaple
Salisbury
Southampton
Brighton
Exeter
Plymouth
Dieppe
West from Greenwich
East from Greenwich
Projection: Conical with two standard parallels

1: 4 000 000

50 0 50 100 150 km

ATLANTIC
OCEAN
NORTH
SEA
IRISH SEA
CELTIC
SEA
ENGLISH CHANNEL
Strait of Dover
Dogger
Bank
Devil's
Hole
238
Shetland Is.
Unst
Yell
Fetlar
Out Skerries
Whalsay
St. Magnus B.
Mainland
Bressay
Foula
Sumburgh Hd.
Fair Isle
Orkney
Is.
Westray
Rousay
Mull Head
N. Ronaldsay
Start Point
Sanday
Stronsay
Mainland
Hoy Sound
Hoy
Pentland Firth
S. Ronaldsay
Dunnet Hd.
John o' Groats
Duncansby Hd.
Wick
Thurso
Morven
Pentland Firth
Stroma
C. Wrath
L. Eriboll
Butt of Lewis
Flannan Is.
Lewis
Harris
799
St. Kilda
Outer Hebrides
North Uist
Benbecula
South Uist
Barra
Barra Hd.
Little Minch
North Minch
Eddrachillis B.
Ben Hope
927
B. More Assynt
998
L. Shin
Helmsdale
Morven
706
Dornoch Firth
Tarbat Ness
Moray Firth
Cromarty Firth
L. Broom
L. Ewe
L. Gairloch
L. Torridon
L. Maree
B. Dearg
1081
B. Wyvis
1045
North West Highlands
Skye
1009
Cuillin Hills
Canna
Rhum
Eigg
Muck
Sound of Sleat
L. Carron
Carn Eige
1182
Glen Affric
L. Ness
Inverness
Findhorn
Spey
Strath Spey
Cairn Gorm
1245
Ben Macdui
1311
Glen Gorry
Glen Mor
L. Morar
L. Shiel
Spean
2347
Ben Nevis
Pt. of Ardnamurchan
Coll
Tiree
Mull
Staffa
Iona
Ben More
966
Oban
L. Linnhe
Grampian Mountains
Lochnagar
1154
Kinnairds Hd.
Ythan
Deveron
Don
Dee
Aberdeen
Girdle Ness
North Esk
South Esk
Tummel
Pass of Killiecrankie
Schiehallion
1081
B. Lawers
1214
L. Tay
Tay
Strathmore
Sidlaw Hills
Dundee
Firth of Tay
Earn
Perth
Fife Ness
Firth of Lorn
L. Awe
L. Katrine
The Trossachs
Ochil Hills
L. Leven
B. Lomond
974
L. Lomond
Forth
Firth of Forth
Bass Rock
Lennox Hills
Colonsay
Jura
Sound of Jura
L. Fyne
Islay
Gigha
Bute
Kintyre
Goat Fell
874
Arran
Firth of Clyde
Glasgow
Clyde
Edinburgh
Pentland Hills
Moorfoot Hills
Lammermuir Hills
St. Abb's Hd.
Berwick
Tweed
Irvine
Ayr
Southern Uplands
Broad Law
830
Ettrick
Teviot
Cheviot Hills
The Cheviot
816
Coquet
Doon
Merrick
843
Nith
Annan
Esk
L. Ryan
Galloway
Luce B.
Mull of Galloway
Wigtown B.
Solway Firth
N. Tyne
S. Tyne
Tyne
Newcastle
Sunderland
Carlisle
Eden
Cross Fell
893
Wear
Pennines
Tees
Middlesbrough
Cleveland
Robin Hood's Bay
North York Moors
454
Swale
Ure
Vale of York
Vale of Pickering
Flamborough Hd.
Bridlington B.
Derwent
Cumbrian Mts.
Lake District
Scafell Pikes
978
Windermere
Wensleydale
Whernside
737
Lune
Pt. of Ayre
I. of Man
Snaefell
620
Calf of Man
St. Bees Hd.
Barrow-in-Furness
I. of Walney
Morecambe Bay
Forest of Bowland
Ribble
Fylde
Nidd
Wharfe
York
Yorkshire Wolds
Holderness
Leeds
Calder
Aire
Hull
Humber
Spurn Hd.
Liverpool Bay
Lancashire Plain
Manchester
Mersey
Liverpool
Wirral
Gt. Ormes Head
636
Sheffield
Don
Sherwood Forest
Lincoln Heath
Lincoln
Lincolnshire Wolds
Witham
Cheshire Plain
Chester
Dee
Holy I.
Anglesey
Caernarfon Bay
Menai Strait
Snowdon
1085
Clwyd
Conwy
L. Bala
Berwyn
Cambrian Mountains
Stoke
Trent
Dove
Derwent
The Wash
The Fens
Bure
Wensum
Norfolk Broads
Norwich
Yare
Waveney
Breckland
Cadair Idris
892
L. Vyrnwy
Mawddach
Tremadoc Bay
Bardsey I.
Braich-y-Pwll
Shrewsbury
The Wrekin
407
The Long Mynd
Wenlock Edge
Cannock Chase
Charnwood Forest
Vale of Belvoir
Welland
Rockingham Forest
Nene
Ouse
Birmingham
Clee Hills
Teme
Severn
Plynlimon
752
Ystwyth
Cardigan Bay
Radnor Forest
Wye
Lugg
Malvern Hills
Avon
Vale of Evesham
Northampton Uplands
Cam
Cambridge
Deben
Orwell
Stour
Ipswich
The Naze
The Sandlings
Teifi
Mynydd Eppynt
Mynydd Prescelly
Tywi
Black Mts.
Brecon Beacons
886
Forest of Dean
Gloucester
330
Cotswolds
Windrush
Cherwell
Oxford
Thame
Chiltern Hills
Chelmer
Blackwater
Foulness
St. David's Hd.
St. Brides B.
Milford Haven
Carmarthen B.
Gower
Swansea
Neath
Swansea B.
Taff
Worms Hd.
Cardiff
Vale of Glamorgan
Usk
Bristol Channel
Severn
Bristol
Avon
Vale of White Horse
Marlborough Downs
Berkshire Downs
Kennet
Reading
Thames
London
Lea
Colne
Wey
North Foreland
Lundy
Barnstaple B.
Hartland Pt.
Exmoor
Dunkery Beacon
520
Brendon Hills
Quantock Hills
Parrett
Vale of Taunton
Mendip Hills
Walbury Hill
297
Salisbury Plain
Test
Hampshire Downs
North Downs
Medway
Vale of Kent
Leith Hill
294
The Weald
Forest Ridges
Romney Marsh
Rother
Dover
Dungeness
Taw
Torridge
Tamar
High Willhays
621
Dartmoor
Blackdown Hills
Exe
Exeter
Otter
Cranborne Chase
Stour
North Dorset Downs
South Dorset Downs
Frome
I. of Purbeck
New Forest
Southampton
South Downs
Arun
Ouse
Selsey Bill
Beachy Hd.
The Solent
The Needles
I. of Wight
St. Catherine's Pt.
Portland Bill
Lyme Bay
Brown Willy
419
Bodmin Moor
Camel
Fowey
Plymouth
Dart
Tor B.
Start Pt.
Bolt Hd.
Whitesand Bay
St. Ives B.
Land's End
Mount's B.
Falmouth B.
Lizard Point
Isles of Scilly
St. Mary's
172
Malin Hd.
Lough Swilly
Sheep Haven
Giant's Causeway
Rathlin I.
Fair Hd
Mull of Kintyre
North Channel
Bloody Foreland
Aran I.
Errigal
752
L. Foyle
Foyle
Londonderry
Derryveagh Mts.
Finn
Sperrin Mts.
Sawel
683
Bann
Trostan
554
Mts. of Antrim
Gweebarra B.
Bluestack
676
Rossan Pt.
Derg
Mourne
L. Neagh
Belfast
Belfast L.
272
Ards
Lagan
Donegal Bay
Erne
L. Erne
Blackwater
Killala Bay
Sligo Bay
Broad Haven
Erris Hd.
Mullet Pen.
Ox Mts.
Upper L. Erne
Bann
Mourne Mts.
Strangford L.
Dundrum B.
Sl. Donard
852
Sl. Gullion
Carlingford L.
Dundalk B.
Clogher Hd.
Blacksod B.
Achill Hd.
Achill I.
Nephin
806
L. Conn
Moy
Arrow
L. Allen
Clare I.
Clew B.
Inishbofin
Mweelrea
819
L. Sheelin
Blackwater
L. Mask
L. Corrib
Connemara
Slyne Hd.
Bertraghboy B.
Kilkieran B.
Galway Bay
Aran Is.
Central Plain
Inny
L. Ree
Suck
Boyne
Brosna
Shannon
Bog of Allen
Liffey
Dublin
Dublin B.
Ireland's Eye
Lambay I.
Sl. Bloom Mts.
529
Sl. Elva
345
Slieve Aughty
Mal Bay
L. Derg
Slieve Bernagh
Wicklow Mts.
Lugnaquilla
926
Wicklow Hd.
Keeper Hill
694
Nore
Barrow
Slaney
Mt. Leinster
796
Loop Hd.
Shannon
Limerick
Golden Vale
Feale
Maigue
Tralee B.
Galty Mts.
920
Suir
Comeragh Mts.
Knockmealdown Mts.
Cahore Pt.
Wexford Harbour
Greenore Pt.
Carnsore Pt.
St. George's Channel
Brandon
953
Dingle B.
Lakes of Killarney
Macgillycuddy's Reeks
1041
Mts. of Kerry
Boggeragh Mts.
Nagles Mts.
Blackwater
Lee
Cork
Mine Hd.
Hook Hd.
Waterford Harbour
Dungarvan Harbour
Youghal Harbour
Kenmare
Caha Mts.
Shehy Mts.
Bandon
Cork Harbour
Old Head of Kinsale
Bantry Bay
Mizen Hd.
Fastnet
C. Clear
Clear I.
Galley Hd.
Strumble Hd.
m
1000
400
200
100
0
50
100
200
m
Projection: Conical with two standard parallels
West from Greenwich 0 East from Greenwich

BRITISH ISLES : Annual Precipitation

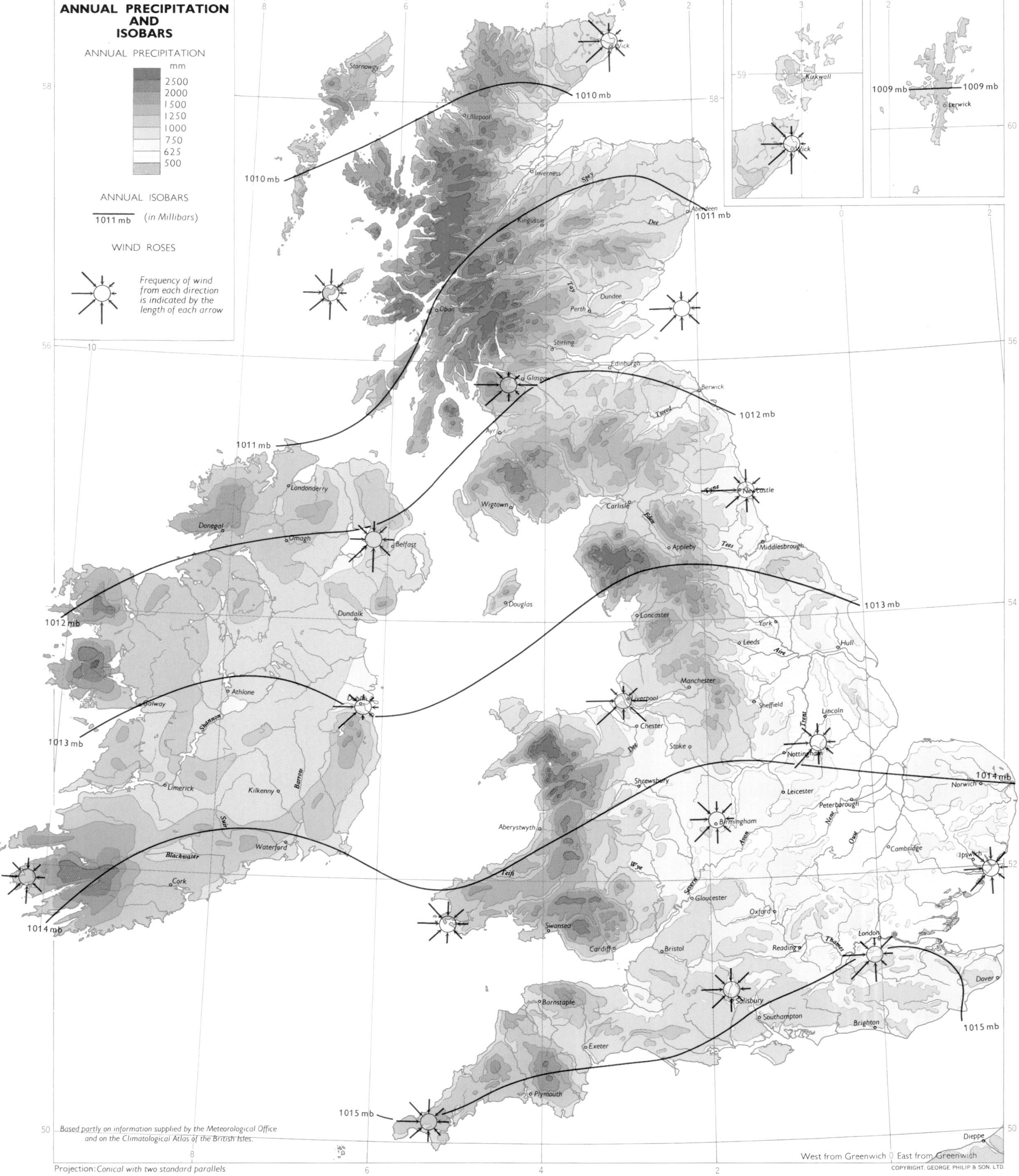
1:4 000 000
50 0 50 100 150 km
ANNUAL PRECIPITATION AND ISOBARS
ANNUAL PRECIPITATION
mm
2500
2000
1500
1250
1000
750
625
500
ANNUAL ISOBARS
1011 mb (in Millibars)
WIND ROSES
Frequency of wind from each direction is indicated by the length of each arrow
1010 mb
1011 mb
1012 mb
1013 mb
1014 mb
1015 mb
1009 mb
Stornoway
Wick
Ullapool
Inverness
Kingussie
Aberdeen
Oban
Perth
Dundee
Stirling
Edinburgh
Glasgow
Berwick
Ayr
Kirkwall
Lerwick
Londonderry
Donegal
Omagh
Belfast
Wigtown
Carlisle
Newcastle
Appleby
Middlesbrough
Douglas
Dundalk
Lancaster
York
Leeds
Hull
Manchester
Sheffield
Athlone
Galway
Dublin
Liverpool
Chester
Lincoln
Stoke
Nottingham
Limerick
Kilkenny
Shrewsbury
Leicester
Norwich
Peterborough
Aberystwyth
Birmingham
Waterford
Cork
Cambridge
Ipswich
Gloucester
Oxford
Swansea
Cardiff
Bristol
Reading
London
Dover
Barnstaple
Salisbury
Southampton
Brighton
Exeter
Plymouth
Dieppe
Spey
Dee
Tay
Tweed
Tyne
Eden
Tees
Aire
Trent
Shannon
Barrow
Suir
Blackwater
Teifi
Wye
Severn
Avon
Nene
Ouse
Thames
Based partly on information supplied by the Meteorological Office and on the Climatological Atlas of the British Isles.
West from Greenwich 0 East from Greenwich
Projection: Conical with two standard parallels

1:8 500 000

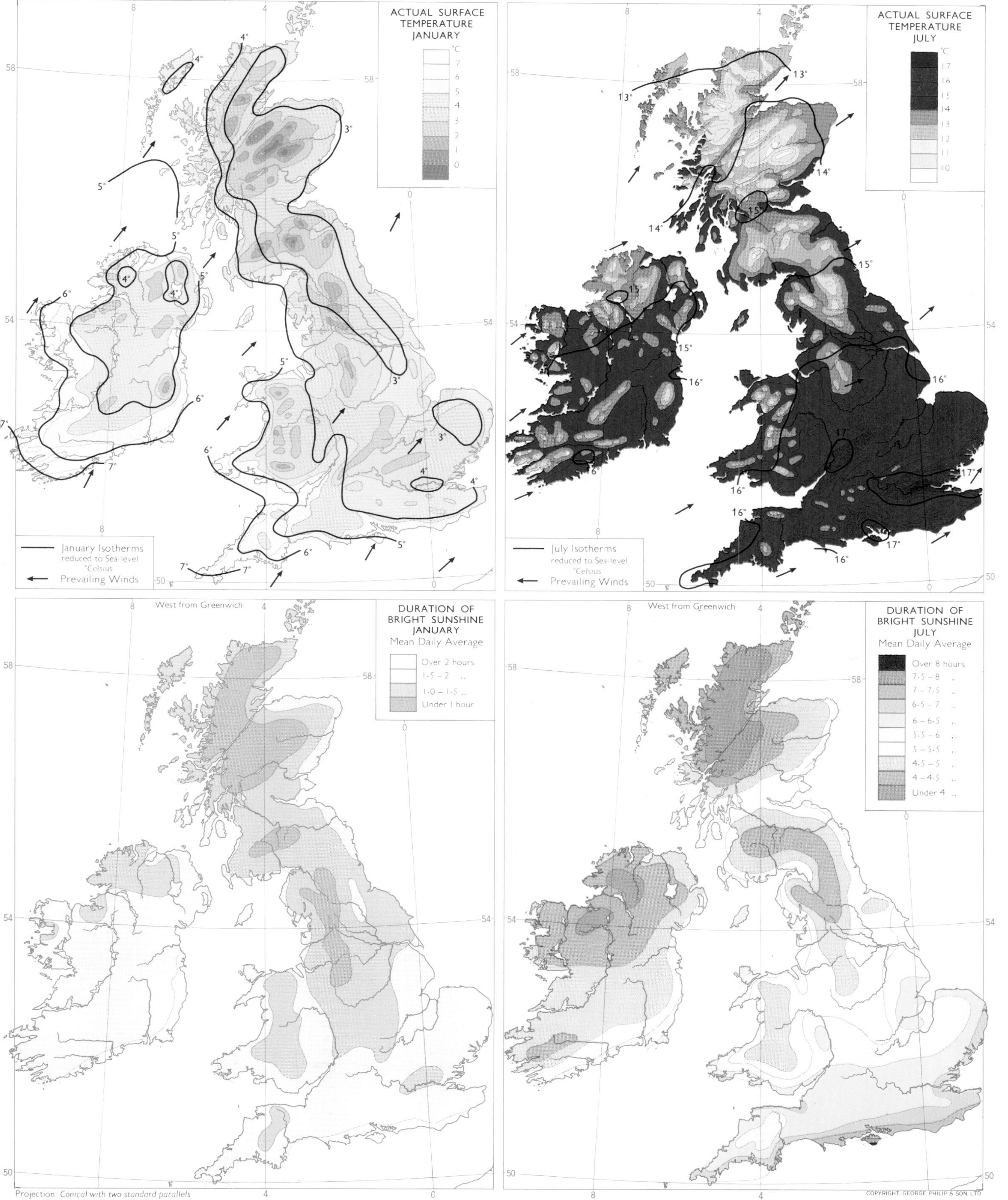

50 0 50 100 150 200 250 300 km
ACTUAL SURFACE TEMPERATURE JANUARY
°C
7
6
5
4
3
2
1
0
January Isotherms reduced to Sea-level °Celsius
Prevailing Winds
ACTUAL SURFACE TEMPERATURE JULY
°C
17
16
15
14
13
12
11
10
July Isotherms reduced to Sea-level °Celsius
Prevailing Winds
West from Greenwich
DURATION OF BRIGHT SUNSHINE JANUARY
Mean Daily Average
Over 2 hours
1·5 – 2 ..
1·0 – 1·5 ..
Under 1 hour
DURATION OF BRIGHT SUNSHINE JULY
Mean Daily Average
Over 8 hours
7·5 – 8 ..
7 – 7·5 ..
6·5 – 7 ..
6 – 6·5 ..
5·5 – 6 ..
5 – 5·5 ..
4·5 – 5 ..
4 – 4·5 ..
Under 4 ..

Projection: *Conical with two standard parallels*

BRITISH ISLES : Old Counties

1:4 000 000

50 0 50 100 150 km
Orkney Is.
Westray
N. Ronaldsay
Sanday
ORKNEY
Mainland
Stronsay
Hoy
Kirkwall
South Ronaldsay
Thurso
Wick
CAITHNESS
Shetland Is.
Unst
Yell
Mainland
ZETLAND
Foula
Lerwick
Fair I.
Pentland Firth
Thurso
Wick
CAITHNESS
SUTHERLAND
Lairg
Golspie
Stornoway
Lewis
Harris
North Uist
Benbecula
South Uist
Barra
Outer Hebrides
North Minch
Ullapool
ROSS AND CROMARTY
Invergordon
Moray Firth
Lossiemouth
Elgin
Dingwall
Nairn
NAIRN
Inverness
MORAY
BANFF
Banff
Fraserburgh
Peterhead
ABERDEEN
Aberdeen
Portree
Skye
Kyle of Lochalsh
Kingussie
Ballater
Balmoral
KINCARDINE
Stonehaven
Rhum
Eigg
Mallaig
INVERNESS
SCOTLAND
Fort William
Blair Atholl
ANGUS
Forfar
Montrose
Arbroath
Coll
Tiree
Inner Hebrides
Ballachulish
PERTH
Crieff
Perth
Dundee
Cupar
St. Andrews
FIFE
Staffa
Iona
Mull
Oban
ARGYLL
Firth of Lorn
Colonsay
Jura
Lochgilphead
Stirling
Kinross
Kirkcaldy
Leven
Firth of Forth
CL.-Clackmannan
KIN.-Kinross
W. Loth-West Lothian
STIRLING
Falkirk
Dunfermline
Helensburgh
Greenock
Rothesay
Dumbarton
Paisley
Glasgow
Edinburgh
Leith
E. LOTHIAN
Haddington
Dunbar
MIDLOTHIAN
RENFREW
Hamilton
Motherwell
Islay
Kintyre
BUTE
Arran
Kilmarnock
Saltcoats
Irvine
Prestwick
Ayr
LANARK
PEEBLES
Peebles
Galashiels
Duns
BERWICK
Berwick-on-Tweed
SELKIRK
Jedburgh
Hawick
Moffat
ROXBURGH
Campbeltown
Firth of Clyde
AYR
Sanquhar
DUMFRIES
Dumfries
KIRKCUDBRIGHT
WIGTOWN
Wigtown
Stranraer
Kirkcudbright
Solway Firth
Mull of Galloway
Malin Hd.
Tory I.
Portrush
Coleraine
North Channel
Aran I.
Letterkenny
DONEGAL
Londonderry
LONDONDERRY
Lifford
ANTRIM
Ballymena
Larne
Antrim
Bangor
Donegal
NORTHERN IRELAND
TYRONE
ULSTER
L. Neagh
Belfast
Omagh
Lisburn
DOWN
Downpatrick
Donegal Bay
Killala Bay
Erris Hd.
Bundoran
Sligo
FERMANAGH
Enniskillen
LEITRIM
Armagh
ARMAGH
Monaghan
Newry
MONAGHAN
Dundrum
Ballina
SLIGO
Clones
CAVAN
Cavan
Dundalk
Greenore
LOUTH
Achill I.
MAYO
Castlebar
Westport
Clare I.
CONNACHT
ROSCOMMON
Roscommon
Carrick-on-Shannon
LONGFORD
Longford
Ceanannus Mor
An Uaimh
Drogheda
MEATH
Connemara
Corrib
GALWAY
Galway
Galway Bay
Athlone
WESTMEATH
Mullingar
Balbriggan
IRELAND
Athenry
Tullamore
OFFALY
Dublin
DUBLIN
(Baile Atha Cliath)
Dun Laoghaire
Bray
Birr
Port Laoise
LAOIS
KILDARE
Naas
LEINSTER
WICKLOW
Wicklow
CLARE
Ennis
Nenagh
Carlow
Athy
Arklow
Kilrush
Loop Hd.
Shannon
Limerick
Thurles
TIPPERARY
Kilkenny
KILKENNY
CARLOW
Listowel
LIMERICK
Rath Luirc
Tipperary
Clonmel
Carrick-on-Suir
Enniscorthy
WEXFORD
New Ross
Wexford
Tralee
MUNSTER
KERRY
Killarney
Mallow
Fermoy
WATERFORD
Waterford
Rosslare
Carnsore Pt.
Dungarvan
Youghal
Cahirciveen
CORK
Cork
Blarney
Cobh
Cork Harbour
Bandon
Kinsale
Bantry
Castletown Bere
C. Clear
ATLANTIC OCEAN
IRISH SEA
St. George's Channel
NORTH SEA
ENGLISH CHANNEL
NORTHUMBERLAND
Alnwick
Newcastle
Tynemouth
South Shields
Gateshead
Sunderland
Durham
DURHAM
Hartlepool
Stockton
TEESSIDE
Middlesbrough
Whitby
Carlisle
CUMBERLAND
Whitehaven
St. Bee's Hd.
Appleby
Kendal
WESTMORLAND
Darlington
NORTH RIDING
Northallerton
Scarborough
Windermere
ISLE OF MAN
Douglas
Barrow
Flamborough Hd.
ENGLAND
YORKSHIRE
Ripon
York
EAST RIDING
Beverley
Hull
Lancaster
Morecambe Bay
Keighley
WEST RIDING
Leeds
LANCASHIRE
Blackpool
Preston
Burnley
Blackburn
Halifax
Bradford
Huddersfield
Wakefield
Bolton
Oldham
Barnsley
Scunthorpe
Spurn Hd.
Grimsby
Liverpool Bay
St. Helens
Salford
Manchester
Doncaster
Rotherham
Sheffield
LINDSEY
Llandudno
Birkenhead
Liverpool
Stockport
Holyhead
ANGLESEY
Llangefni
Caernarvon
Rhyl
Flint
Chester
FLINT
Macclesfield
DERBY
Chesterfield
Mansfield
Lincoln
LINCOLN
Denbigh
DENBIGH
CHESHIRE
Crewe
Matlock
NOTTS
Nottingham
Caernarvon Bay
CAERNARVON
Wrexham
Stoke-on-Trent
Derby
KESTEVEN
Boston
The Wash
Grantham
HOLLAND
STAFFORD
Stafford
Burton upon Trent
Kings Lynn
NORFOLK
Norwich
Gt. Yarmouth
Lowestoft
MERIONETH
Dolgellau
Shrewsbury
Wolverhampton
LEICESTER
Oakham
RUTLAND
Peterborough
HUNTS & PETERBOROUGH
Huntingdon
CAMBS
MONTGOMERY
Welshpool
SHROPSHIRE
Walsall
Birmingham
Leicester
Coventry
Cardigan Bay
Aberystwyth
Kidderminster
Rugby
Corby
SUFFOLK
Bury St. Edmunds
EAST
WEST
RADNOR
Presteigne
WORCESTER
Worcester
WARWICK
Leamington
Warwick
NORTHAMPTON
Wellingborough
Cambridge
Ipswich
Llandrindod Wells
HEREFORD
Hereford
Stratford-on-Avon
Northampton
Bedford
ISLE OF ELY
Fishguard
CARDIGAN
Cardigan
WALES
BRECKNOCK
BEDFORD
Buckingham
Colchester
Harwich
The Naze
St. David's Hd.
PEMBROKE
CARMARTHEN
Carmarthen
Brecon
Cheltenham
Gloucester
GLOUCESTER
OXFORD
BUCKS
Luton
HERTFORD
Hertford
ESSEX
Chelmsford
Merthyr Tydfil
Monmouth
MONMOUTH
Oxford
Aylesbury
St. Albans
Watford
Milford Haven
Pembroke
Haverfordwest
Llanelli
Swansea
GLAMORGAN
Rhondda
Newport
Port Talbot
Southend
Cardiff
Bristol
Swindon
BERKS
Slough
Windsor
Reading
LONDON
Kingston
Chatham
Gillingham
Maidstone
Margate
Canterbury
Bristol Channel
Weston-super-Mare
Bath
Trowbridge
WILTS
Aldershot
SURREY
Reigate
KENT
Lundy
Ilfracombe
Wells
Guildford
Ashford
Dover
Folkestone
Hartland Point
Barnstaple
SOMERSET
Salisbury
Winchester
HANTS
SUSSEX
Taunton
Yeovil
Southampton
Chichester
WEST
EAST
Lewes
Hastings
Eastbourne
Bude
DEVON
DORSET
Axminster
Dorchester
Poole
Bournemouth
Portsmouth
Worthing
Brighton
Newhaven
Exeter
Newport
Isle of Wight
Weymouth
CORNWALL
St. Austell
Devonport
Plymouth
Torquay
Truro
Camborne
Penzance
Falmouth
Start Pt.
Land's End
Lizard
Isles of Scilly
Dieppe

Projection: *Conical with two standard parallels*

West from Greenwich 0 East from Greenwich

1:4 000 000

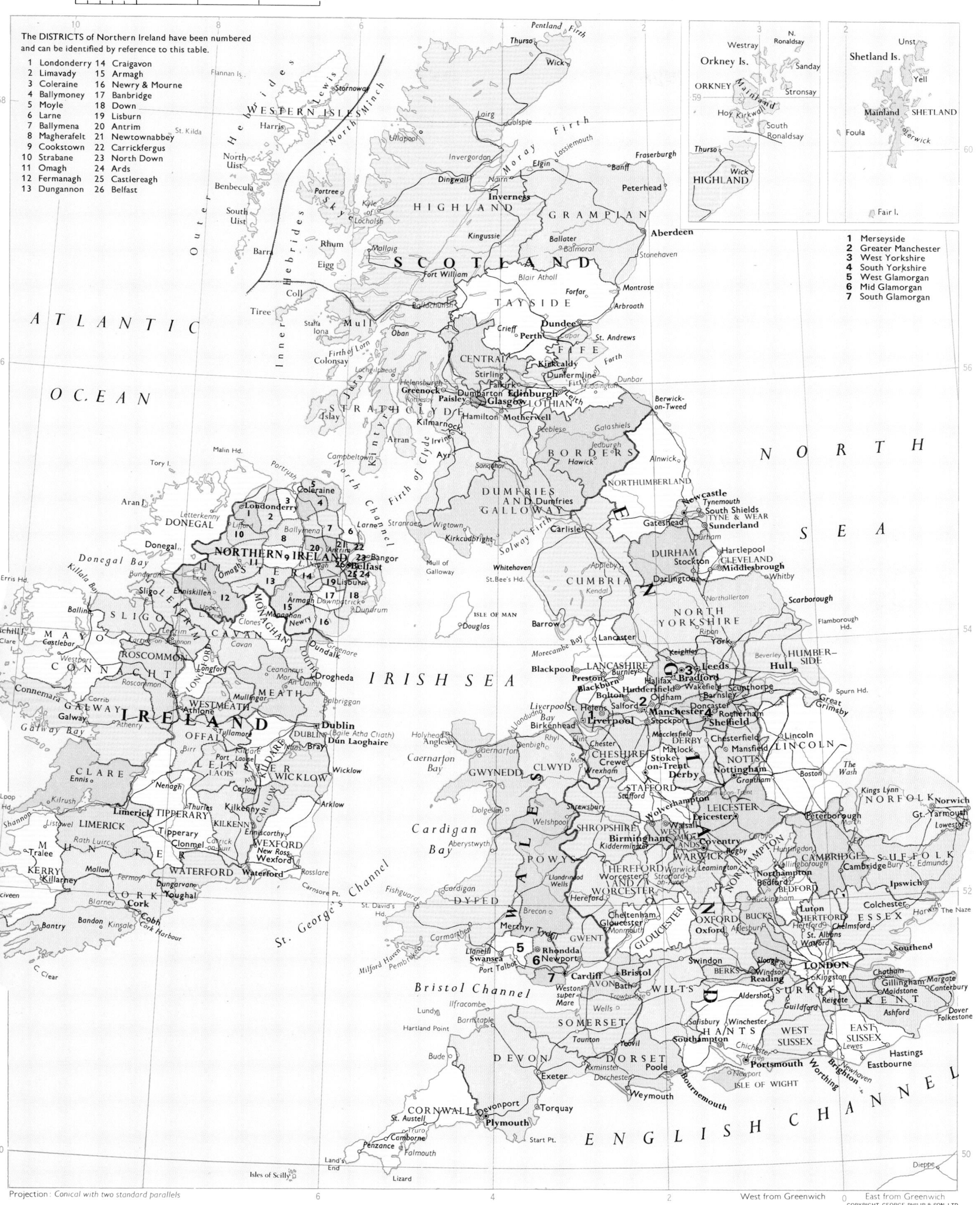
50 0 50 100 150 km
The DISTRICTS of Northern Ireland have been numbered and can be identified by reference to this table.
1 Londonderry
2 Limavady
3 Coleraine
4 Ballymoney
5 Moyle
6 Larne
7 Ballymena
8 Magherafelt
9 Cookstown
10 Strabane
11 Omagh
12 Fermanagh
13 Dungannon
14 Craigavon
15 Armagh
16 Newry & Mourne
17 Banbridge
18 Down
19 Lisburn
20 Antrim
21 Newtownabbey
22 Carrickfergus
23 North Down
24 Ards
25 Castlereagh
26 Belfast
1 Merseyside
2 Greater Manchester
3 West Yorkshire
4 South Yorkshire
5 West Glamorgan
6 Mid Glamorgan
7 South Glamorgan
Orkney Is.
ORKNEY
Shetland Is.
SHETLAND
ATLANTIC OCEAN
NORTH SEA
IRISH SEA
ENGLISH CHANNEL
Bristol Channel
Cardigan Bay
St. George's Channel
North Channel
SCOTLAND
HIGHLAND
GRAMPIAN
TAYSIDE
FIFE
CENTRAL
LOTHIAN
STRATHCLYDE
BORDERS
DUMFRIES AND GALLOWAY
WESTERN ISLES
NORTHERN IRELAND
IRELAND
DONEGAL
SLIGO
LEITRIM
MAYO
ROSCOMMON
CAVAN
MONAGHAN
LOUTH
MEATH
WESTMEATH
LONGFORD
OFFALY
GALWAY
DUBLIN
KILDARE
LAOIS
WICKLOW
CARLOW
CLARE
LIMERICK
TIPPERARY
KILKENNY
WEXFORD
WATERFORD
KERRY
CORK
ENGLAND
WALES
NORTHUMBERLAND
TYNE & WEAR
DURHAM
CLEVELAND
CUMBRIA
NORTH YORKSHIRE
HUMBERSIDE
LANCASHIRE
CHESHIRE
DERBY
NOTTS
LINCOLN
STAFFORD
LEICESTER
SHROPSHIRE
WEST MIDLANDS
WARWICK
NORTHAMPTON
CAMBRIDGE
NORFOLK
SUFFOLK
HEREFORD AND WORCESTER
GLOUCESTER
OXFORD
BUCKS
BEDFORD
HERTFORD
ESSEX
GWYNEDD
CLWYD
POWYS
DYFED
GWENT
AVON
WILTS
BERKS
SURREY
KENT
SOMERSET
DORSET
HANTS
WEST SUSSEX
EAST SUSSEX
DEVON
CORNWALL
ISLE OF MAN
ISLE OF WIGHT
LONDON
Edinburgh
Glasgow
Aberdeen
Dundee
Inverness
Belfast
Dublin
Newcastle
Leeds
Bradford
Liverpool
Manchester
Sheffield
Birmingham
Bristol
Cardiff
Plymouth
Southampton
Portsmouth
Norwich
Projection: Conical with two standard parallels
West from Greenwich
East from Greenwich
COPYRIGHT, GEORGE PHILIP & SON, LTD.

GWYNEDD
Oswestry
Whittington
Wem
Eccleshall
Stafford
Trent
Weston
Abbots Bromley
Tutbury
Burton upon Trent
Long Eaton
Aran Fawddwy 905
L. Vyrnwy
Llanfyllin
Llanymynech
Myddle
Shawbury
Hinstock
STAFFORDSHIRE
Gnosall
Penkridge
Rugeley
Cannock Chase
Ashby de la Zouch
Swadlincote
Coalville
Shepshed
Dolgellau
Cader Idris 892
Tal-y-llyn
Welshpool
Severn
Shrewsbury
Bicton
Crudgington
High Ercall
Wellington
Telford
Newport
Oakengates
Hednesford
Cannock 243
Lichfield
Ibstock
Machynlleth
Corris
Long Mt.
Minsterley
Stiper stones
The Long Mynd
Wrekin 407
Dawley
Coalbrookdale
Ironbridge
Madeley
Brownhills
Walsall
Tamworth
Market Bosworth
Wednesfield
Willenhall
WOLVERHAMPTON
Darlaston
Wednesbury
Bilston
Coseley
Tipton
Dudley
Oldbury
Sutton Coldfield
Atherstone
Nuneaton
Hinckley
Tregynon
Berriew
Carno
Caersws
Newtown
Much Wenlock
Wenlock Edge
Broseley
Worfield
Bridgnorth
Brierley Hill
Stourbridge
Smethwick
Warley
BIRMINGHAM
Bedworth
Plynlimon (Pumlumon) 752
Kerry
Bishop's Castle
Clun Forest
SHROPSHIRE
Clee Hills
Ditton Priors 541
Halesowen
WEST MIDLANDS
Solihull
Meriden
COVENTRY
Rugby
Severn
Llanidloes
Clun
Clunbury
Craven Arms
Bromfield
Ludlow
Highley
Wyre Forest
Kidderminster
Bewdley
Stourport-on-Severn
Hartlebury
Hampton in Arden
Knowle
Kenilworth
Rheidol
Llangurig
St. Harmon
Llanbister
Teme
Knighton
Leintwardine
Cleobury Mortimer
Bromsgrove
Redditch
Warwick
Royal Leamington Spa
Ystwyth
Rhayader
Elan
POWYS
660 Radnor Forest
Presteigne
Wigmore
Brimfield
Mortimers Cross
Tenbury
Stanford on Teme
Ombersley
Droitwich
Henley-in-Arden
Studley
Llandrindod Wells
New Radnor
Kingsland
Eardisland
Pembridge
Leominster
Martley
WARWICKSHIRE
Stratford-upon-Avon
Tregaron
Newbridge on Wye
Drygarn Fawr 645
Hundred House
Bromyard
Worcester
HEREFORD AND WORCESTER
Kington
Weobley
Bodenham
Alcester
Builth Wells
Painscastle
Newchurch
Eardisley
Clifford
Credenhill
Marden
Pershore
Evesham
Kineton
Banbury
DYFED
Mynydd Eppynt
Hay-on-Wye
Dorstone
Great Malvern
Malvern Wells
Kempsey
Severn Stoke
Bredon Hill 293
Chipping Campden
Edge Hill 226
Llandovery
Brecon
Talgarth
Peterchurch
Hereford
Ledbury
Upton upon-Severn
Tewkesbury
Shipston-on-Stour
Deddington
Black Mountains 811
Longtown
Madley
Fownhope
Much Marcle
Dymock
Moreton-in-Marsh
Mynydd du (Black Mt.)
Fforest Fawr
886 Brecon Beacons
Crickhowell
Ross-on-Wye
Newent
Gloucester
Cheltenham
Charlton Kings
Cleeve Cloud 330
Stow-on-the-Wold
Chipping Norton
Abergavenny
Monmouth
Symond's Yat
Cinderford
Churchdown
Brockworth
Bourton-on-the-Water
Witney
Oxford
Merthyr Tydfil
Brynmawr
Tredegar
Ebbw Vale
Blaenavon
Abertillery
Abersychan
Newnham
Forest of Dean
Blakeney
Lydney
GLOUCESTERSHIRE
Stroud
Cirencester
Windrush
Pontardawe
Aberdare
Mountain Ash
Rhondda
Bargoed
New Tredegar
Pontypool
GWENT
Cwmbran
Raglan
Tintern
Chepstow
Minchinhampton
Thames
Abingdon
Neath
Swansea
Port Talbot
Maesteg
MID GLAMORGAN
Pontypridd
Treharris
Tonyrefail
Caerphilly
Newport
Bedwas
Risca
Hengoed
Berkeley
Dursley
Tetbury
Faringdon
Didcot
Margam
Swansea Bay
Pyle
Llantrisant
Almondsbury
Severn
Malmesbury
Stratton St. Margaret
Swindon
Vale of White Horse
Wantage
Porthcawl
Bridgend
SOUTH GLAMORGAN
CARDIFF
Rumney
Filton
AVON
Mangotsfield
Wroughton
Marlborough Downs
Berkshire Downs
Cowbridge
Llantwit Major
Penarth
Barry
Clevedon
BRISTOL
Kingswood
Chippenham
Calne
Marlborough
Newbury
Nash Pt.
St. Donats
Bristol Channel
Weston-super-Mare
Keynsham
Bath
Corsham
Melksham
Devizes
Vale of Pewsey
Bradford on Avon
Trowbridge
WILTSHIRE
Collingbourne Kingston
Basingstoke
Bridgwater Bay
Foreland Pt.
Porlock B.
Lynton
Porlock
Minehead
Burnham-on-Sea
Mendip Hills
Midsomer Norton
Radstock
Frome
Westbury
Warminster
Salisbury Plain
Andover
Exmoor 520
Dunster
Watchet
Highbridge
Wookey Hole
Wells
Shepton Mallet
Cheddar
Glastonbury
Street
Polden Hills
Brendon Hills
Quantock Hills 384
Bridgwater
SOMERSET
Dulverton
Wiveliscombe
Taunton
Sparkford
Wincanton
Salisbury
Winchester
HAMPSHIRE
South Molton
Milverton
Norton Fitzwarren
Yeo
Shaftesbury
Romsey
Eastleigh
Bampton
Wellington
Blackdown Hills 315
Yeovil
Sherborne
Cranborne Chase
Totton
SOUTHAMPTON
Tiverton
Cullompton
Crewkerne
Blackmoor Vale
New Forest
Hythe
DEVON
Crediton
Silverton
Honiton
Axminster
N. Dorset Downs 275
DORSET
Blandford Forum
Ringwood
Exeter
Ottery St. Mary
Bridport
Wimborne Minster
Ferndown
Christchurch
Lymington
Portsmouth
Teign
Topsham
Exmouth
Budleigh Salterton
Sidmouth
Lyme Regis
Lyme B.
Dorchester
S. Dorset Downs
Wareham
Poole
Bournemouth
Poole Har.
Swanage
Durlston Head
St. Alban's Hd.
Chesil Beach
Weymouth
I. of Portland
Portland Bill
The Needles
ISLE OF WIGHT
Newport
Cowes
Ryde
Ventnor
St. Catherine's Pt.
The Solent
Projection: Conical with two standard parallels
m
800
600
400
200
100
0
50
m

1:1 000 000
10 0 10 20 30 40 km
The Wash
LINCOLNSHIRE
NORFOLK
Norfolk Broads
Breckland
CAMBRIDGESHIRE
SUFFOLK
BEDFORDSHIRE
HERTFORDSHIRE
ESSEX
LONDON
SURREY
KENT
WEST SUSSEX
EAST SUSSEX
The Fens
East Anglian Heights
Chiltern Hills
North Downs
South Downs
The Weald
Romney Marsh
I. of Thanet
I. of Sheppey
R. Thames
Strait of Dover
FRANCE
Calais
Boulogne
C. Gris-Nez
Hunstanton
King's Lynn
Wisbech
Spalding
Stamford
Peterborough
March
Ely
Huntingdon
St. Ives
St. Neots
Cambridge
Newmarket
Bury St. Edmunds
Thetford
East Dereham
Fakenham
Cromer
Sheringham
Norwich
Great Yarmouth
Lowestoft
Beccles
Ipswich
Woodbridge
Felixstowe
Harwich
Colchester
Clacton-on-Sea
Frinton-on-Sea
Walton-on-the-Naze
Sudbury
Haverhill
Stowmarket
Aldeburgh
Southwold
Kettering
Corby
Wellingborough
Northampton
Bedford
Milton Keynes
Bletchley
Luton
Dunstable
Hitchin
Letchworth
Stevenage
Welwyn Garden City
Hertford
Harlow
Bishop's Stortford
Saffron Walden
Braintree
Chelmsford
Maldon
Witham
Basildon
Southend-on-Sea
Shoeburyness
Aylesbury
Hemel Hempstead
St. Albans
Watford
High Wycombe
Slough
Windsor
Maidenhead
Reading
Bracknell
Woking
Guildford
Farnborough
Aldershot
Reigate
Redhill
Crawley
Horsham
Haywards Heath
East Grinstead
Tunbridge Wells
Tonbridge
Sevenoaks
Maidstone
Rochester
Chatham
Gillingham
Gravesend
Dartford
Sheerness
Sittingbourne
Faversham
Whitstable
Herne Bay
Margate
Broadstairs
Ramsgate
Canterbury
Deal
Dover
Folkestone
Hythe
Ashford
Rye
Hastings
Bexhill
Eastbourne
Lewes
Newhaven
Seaford
Brighton
Hove
Worthing
Littlehampton
Bognor Regis
Chichester
Selsey Bill
Beachy Hd.
Dungeness
West from Greenwich
East from Greenwich
52
51

Based upon the Ordnance Survey Map with the permission of the Controller of Her Majesty's Stationery Office. Crown Copyright Reserved.

Motorways
Motorways under construction

1:1 000 000

10 0 10 20 30 40 km

SCILLY ISLES

on same scale

Based upon the Ordnance Survey Map with the permission of the Controller of Her Majesty's Stationery Office. Crown Copyright Reserved.

m 600 400 200 100 0

0 50 m

Projection: Conical with two standard parallels

West from Greenwich

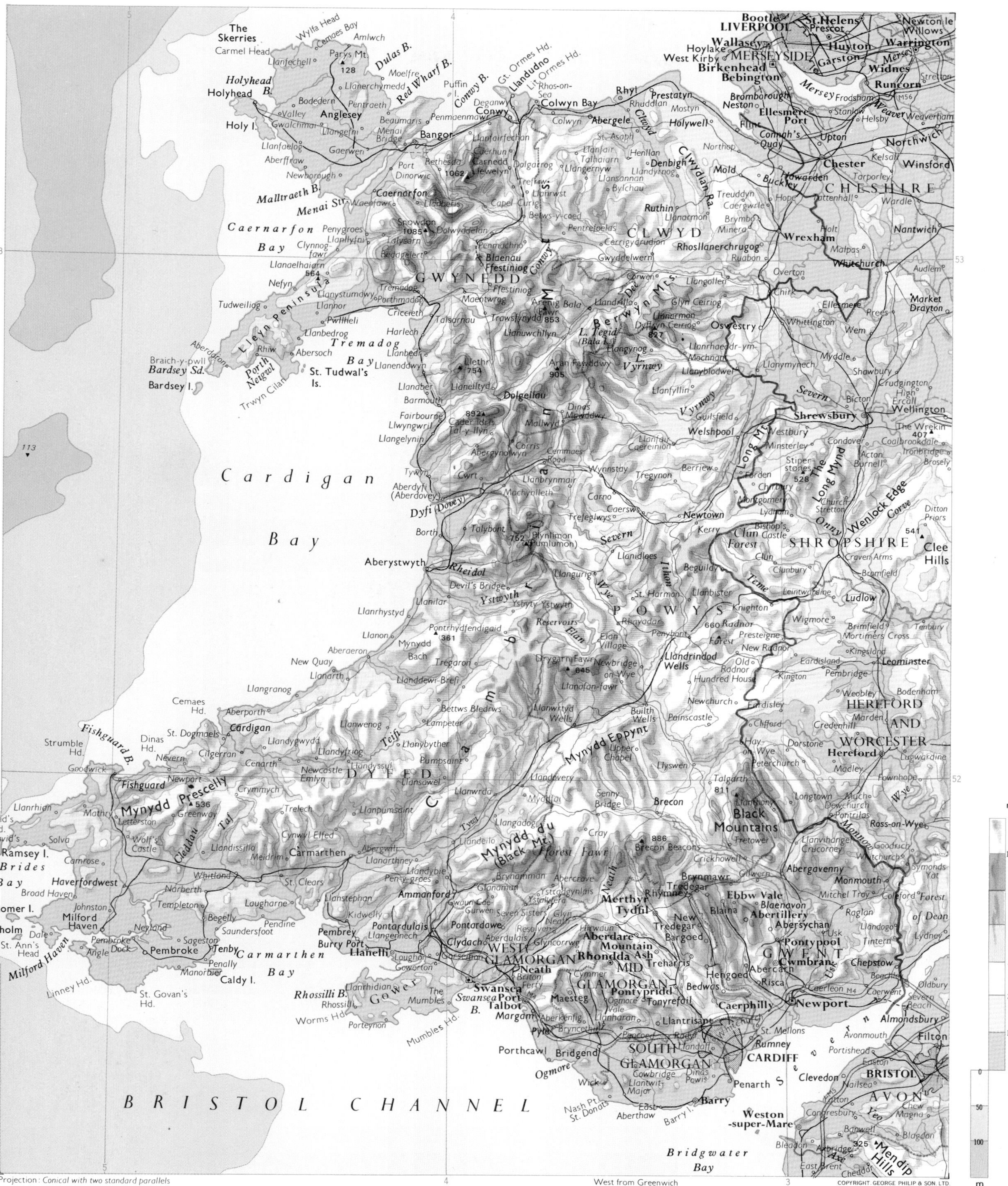
1:1 000 000
10 0 10 20 30 40 km
Cardigan Bay
BRISTOL CHANNEL
Carmarthen Bay
Tremadog Bay
Caernarfon Bay
GWYNEDD
CLWYD
POWYS
DYFED
WEST GLAMORGAN
MID GLAMORGAN
SOUTH GLAMORGAN
GWENT
SHROPSHIRE
CHESHIRE
HEREFORD AND WORCESTER
AVON
MERSEYSIDE
Anglesey
LIVERPOOL
Chester
Wrexham
Shrewsbury
Aberystwyth
Swansea
CARDIFF
Newport
BRISTOL
Hereford
Snowdon 1085
Cader Idris 892
Black Mountains
Mynydd Prescelly
Projection: Conical with two standard parallels
Motorways
Motorways under construction
West from Greenwich

DUMFRIES AND GALLOWAY
Galloway
Dumfries
Maxwelltown
Corsock
Collin
Dalton
Ecclefechan
Canonbie
Annan
Eaglesfield
Gretna
Gretna Green
Crocketford
Haugh of Urr
New Abbey
Bankend
Ruthwell
Cummertrees
Newton Stewart
Minnigaff
New Luce
L. Ken
Laurieston
Creetown
Gatehouse of Fleet
Castle Douglas
Dalbeattie
Criffell
569
Kirkbean
Ringford
Kirkcowan
Glenluce
Wigtown
Caulkerbush
Southerness
Auchencairn
Sandhead
Kirkinner
Kirkcudbright
Whauphill
Luce Bay
Port William
Sorbie
The Machars
Garlieston
Wigtown Bay
Dundrennan
Kirkcudbright B.
Port Logan
Drummore
Whithorn
Isle of Whithorn
Burrow Hd.
Mull of Galloway
Solway Firth
Roadhead
Longtown
Smithfield
Gilsland
Irthing
Rockcliffe
Brampton
Bowness-on-Solway
P. Carlisle
Stanwix
Carlisle
Hayton
Cumwhinton
Kirkbride
Newton Arlosh
Silloth
Abbey Town
Wampool
Wigton
Red Dial
Thursby
Beckfoot
Allonby
Aspatria
Crosby
Mealsgate
Caldew
Maryport
Fothergill
Flimby
Seaton
Ellen
Dearham
Bothel
High Pike
658
Caldbeck
Skelton
Greystoke
Workington
Cockermouth
Bassenthwaite L.
Great Clifton
Harrington
Distington
Parton
Thornthwaite
Skiddaw
931
Greta
Keswick
Penrith
Threlkeld
Pooley Bridge
Whitehaven
Lowes Water
Crummock Water
Derwent Water
Rowrah
Frizington
Cleator Moor
Buttermere
Thirlmere
950
Helvellyn
Ullswater
Hackthorpe
Patterdale
Shap
St. Bees Head
St. Bees
Ennerdale Water
Lake District
Borrowdale
Egremont
Beckermet
Calder Bridge
Calder Hall
Seascale
Wast Water
Scafell Pikes
978
Kirkstone Pass
Grasmere
Grasmere L.
Rydal
Ambleside
Haweswater
High Borrow Bridge
Gosforth
Boot
Irt
Esk
Hawkshead
Coniston
Coniston Water
Windermere
Staveley
Ravenglass
Broughton-in-Furness
Bowness-on-Windermere
Torver
Kendal
Bootle
600
Black Combe
Gawthwaite
Newby Bridge
Whicham
Millom
Grizebeck
Greenodd
Lindale
Ulverston
Cartmel
Haverigg
Duddon R.
Leven
Cark
Grange-over-Sands
Arnside
Dalton-in-Furness
Aldingham
Vickerstown
Barrow-in-Furness
Morecambe B.
Carnforth
Bolton-le-Sands
I. of Walney
Rampside
Morecambe
Hilpsford Pt.
Heysham
Lancaster
Ward's Stone
560
Caton
Galgate
Lune
Cockerham
Knott End
Pilling
Preesall
Fleetwood
Rossall Pt.
Garstang
Bleasdale Moors
Thornton Cleveleys
Wyre
Poulton-le-Fylde
Blackpool
Woodplumpton
Longridge
LANCASHIRE
Preston
Fulwood
Kirkham
Penwortham
Walton le Dale
St. Annes
Lytham
R. Ribble
Longton
Tarleton
Leyland
Euxton
Southport
Birkdale
Ainsdale
Rufford
Chorley
Standish
Horwich
Formby
Formby Pt.
Ormskirk
Skelmersdale
Wigan
Westhoughton
MERSEYSIDE
Maghull
Crosby
Litherland
Kirkby
St. Helens
Ashton-in-Makerfield
Atherton
Hindley
Leigh
Bootle
LIVERPOOL
Prescot
New Brighton
Wallasey
Hoylake
West Kirby
Birkenhead
Bebington
Port Sunlight
Bromborough
Neston
Huyton
Garston
Speke
Widnes
Mersey
Newton-le-Willows
Urmston
Irlam
Warrington
Lymm
Runcorn
Frodsham
Helsby
Ellesmere Port
Stanlow
Weaver
Weaverham
Northwich
Flint
Connah's Quay
Upton
Chester
CHESHIRE
Kelsall
Tarporley
Winsford
Middlewich
Hawarden
Buckley
Mold
Hope
Wrexham
Holt
Malpas
Whitchurch
Overton
Chirk
Ellesmere
Prees
Oswestry
Whittington
SHROPSHIRE
Market Drayton
Audlem
Madeley
Nantwich
Crewe
Wardle
Sandbach
Alsager
Kidsgrove
Newcastle-under-Lyme
Keele
Trentham
STOKE ON TRENT
Longton
Stone
STAFFORDSHIRE
Uttoxeter
Cheadle
Leek
Biddulph
Congleton
Holmes Chapel
Knutsford
Wilmslow
Alderley Edge
Macclesfield
Bollington
Buglawton
552
Altrincham
Hale
Sale
Stretford
Salford
MANCHESTER
Stockport
Cheadle
Gatley
Denton
Hyde
Marple
Ashton under Lyne
Stalybridge
Dukinfield
Swinton
Eccles
Prestwich
Radcliffe
Middleton
Oldham
Royton
Heywood
Rochdale
Littleborough
Bury
Farnworth
Tyldesley
Bolton
Ramsbottom
GREATER MANCHESTER
Darwen
Rawtenstall
Bacup
Haslingden
Todmorden
Blackburn
Accrington
Oswaldtwistle
Great Harwood
Rishton
Padiham
Burnley
Nelson
Colne
Brierfield
Whalley
Clitheroe
Pendle Hill
558
Barrowford
Barnoldswick
Gisburn
Earby
Keighley
Skipton
Aire
Bolton-by-Bowland
Slaidburn
Forest of Bowland
Hodder
Ribble
Gargrave
Hellifield
Long Preston
Threshfield
Settle
Giggleswick
Malham Tarn
Kettlewell
Grassington
Wharfe
Horton in Ribblesdale
Pen-y-Ghent
693
Ingleton
Ingleborough
723
Greta
High Bentham
Burton
Kirkby Lonsdale
Milnthorpe
Crooklands
Whernside
737
Dent
Garsdale Head
Sedbergh
Hawes
Wensleydale
Langstrothdale Chase
Askrigg
Great Shunner Fell
713
Swale
Keld
Rogan's Seat
671
Reeth
Tebay
Grayrigg
Orton
Ravenstonedale
Kirkby Stephen
Stainmore Forest
Bowes
Brough
Crosby Ravensworth
Hoff
Appleby
Kirkby Thore
Temple Sowerby
Mickle Fell
790
Middleton in Teesdale
Mickleton
Cotherstone
Teesdale
Tees
Cross Fell
893
Melmerby
Kirkoswald
Lazonby
Eden
High Hesket
Croglin
Alston
Allenheads
Weardale
Wearhead
St. Johns Chapel
Stanhope
Wolsingham
Edmondbyers
Castleside
Collier Law
516
Derwent
Cold Fell
622
Lambley
Haltwhistle
Greenhead
HADRIAN'S WALL
Haydon Bridge
Hexham
Corbridge
Catton
Allendale Town
Allen
S. Tyne
Slaley
Chollerton
Stamfordham
Humshaugh
Wark
Colwell
NORTHUMBERLAND
Pennines
CUMBRIA
IRISH SEA
Pt. of Ayre
Jurby Hd.
Andreas
Bride
Ramsey B.
Ramsey
Sulby
Ballaugh
Maughold
Maughold Hd.
Kirk Michael
Snaefell
620
Laxey
Peel
Glen Helen
Clay Hd.
St. John's
Onchan
ISLE OF MAN
Patrick
Glenmaye
S. Barrule
483
Foxdale
Douglas
Douglas Hd.
Bradda Hd.
Port Erin
Colby
Ballasalla
Castletown
Port St. Mary
Langness
Calf of Man
The Skerries
Carmel Head
Wylfa Head
Cemaes Bay
Amlwch
Llanfechell
Parys Mt.
128
Dulas B.
Moelfre
Llanerchymedd
Red Wharf B.
Holyhead B.
Holyhead
Holy I.
Valley
Bodedern
Pentraeth
Anglesey
Llangefni
Beaumaris
Puffin I.
Conwy B.
Gt. Ormes Hd.
Llandudno
Lt. Ormes Hd.
Rhos-on-Sea
Deganwy
Conwy
Colwyn Bay
Rhyl
Prestatyn
Rhuddlan
Mostyn
Holywell
Abergele
Clwyd
St. Asaph
Menai Bridge
Bangor
Penmaenmawr
Llanfairfechan
Llanfaelog
Aberffraw
Gaerwen
Newborough
Malltraeth B.
Port Dinorwic
Bethesda
Carnedd Llewelyn
1062
Llanfair Talhaiarn
Henllan
Denbigh
Llangernyw
Llansannan
Bylchau
Clwydian Ra.
Caernarfon
Menai Str.
Llanberis
Capel Curig
Trefriw
Llanrwst
Betws-y-Coed
Ruthin
Llanarmon
Treuddyn
Caergwrle
Brymbo
Minera
Caernarfon Bay
Penygroes
Llanllyfni
Clynnog-fawr
Snowdon
1085
Dolwyddelan
Talysarn
GWYNEDD
Pentrefoelas
CLWYD
Cerrigydrudion
Beddgelert
Penmachno
Blaenau Ffestiniog
Conwy
Gwyddelwern
Rhosllanerchrugog
Ruabon
Llangollen
Corwen
Dee
Llanaelhaiarn
564
Nefyn
Llanystumdwy
Porthmadog
Tremadog
Ffestiniog
Maentwrog
853
Llandrillo
Glyn Ceiriog
Berwyn Mts.
827
Llanarmon Dyffryn Ceiriog
Tudweiliog
Lleyn Peninsula
Llannor
Pwllheli
Criccieth
Harlech
Talsarnau
Trawsfynydd
Arenig Fawr
Bala
Bala L.
L. Tegid
55
54
53
4
3
2
m
1000
800
600
400
200
100
0
50

Projection: Conical with two standard parallels

Motorways

Motorways under construction

1:1 000 000

10 0 10 20 30 40 km
NORTH SEA
TYNE AND WEAR
CLEVELAND
NORTH YORKSHIRE
HUMBERSIDE
WEST YORKSHIRE
SOUTH YORKSHIRE
DERBYSHIRE
NOTTINGHAMSHIRE
LINCOLNSHIRE
NORFOLK
Continuation Northwards on same scale
BORDERS
NORTHUMBERLAND
Cheviot Hills
The Cheviot 816
HADRIAN'S WALL
Berwick-upon-Tweed
Tweedmouth
Scremerston
Holy I.
Budle Bay
Farne Is.
Bamburgh
Seahouses
N. Sunderland
Beadnell
Embleton
Longhoughton
Lesbury
Alnmouth
Alnwick
Warkworth
Amble
Coquet I.
Hauxley
Broomhill
Druridge B.
Widdrington
Ellington
Ashington
Newbiggin-by-the-Sea
Bedlington
Blyth
Morpeth
Cramlington
Seaton Delaval
Hartley
Whitley B.
Tynemouth
South Shields
Jarrow
Wallsend
Newcastle-upon-Tyne
Gateshead
Sunderland
Washington
Houghton-le-Spring
Chester-le-Street
Hetton-le-Hole
Easington
Durham
Stanley
Consett
Leadgate
Hexham
Prudhoe
Corbridge
Haltwhistle
Haydon Bridge
Greenhead
Gilsland
Allendale Town
Allenheads
Alston
Cold Fell 622
Kielder
Kielder Res.
Peel Fell 602
Sighty Crag 519
Bellingham
Otterburn
Rochester
Elishaw
Simonside 441
Rothbury
Longframlington
Alwinton
Coquet
Glanton
Wooler
Chatton
Belford
Lowick
Norham
Coldstream
Kelso
Jedburgh
Roxburgh
Morebattle
Yetholm
Ancrum
St. Boswells
Earlston
Gordon
Greenlaw
Westruther
Duns
Preston
Chirnside
Swinton
Leitholm
Whitley Bay
Tynemouth
Hartlepool
Peterlee
Seaham
Easington Colliery
Horden
Redcar
Marske by the Sea
Saltburn by the Sea
Teesside
Middlesbrough
Stockton-on-Tees
Billingham
Eston
Guisborough
Skelton
Loftus
Staithes
Kettle Ness
Whitby
Robin Hood's Bay
North York Moors
Cleveland Hills
Hambleton Hills
Fylingdales Moor
Scarborough
Scalby Ness
Pickering
Vale of Pickering
Kirkbymoorside
Helmsley
Thirsk
Northallerton
Filey
Filey Bay
Flamborough Head
Bridlington
Bridlington Bay
Driffield
Malton
York
Ripon
Harrogate
Knaresborough
Wetherby
Tadcaster
Selby
Leeds
Otley
Pudsey
Morley
Dewsbury
Wakefield
Castleford
Pontefract
Goole
Howden
Beverley
Hornsea
Withernsea
Holderness
KINGSTON-UPON-HULL
Haltemprice
Cottingham
Hessle
Humber
Barton upon Humber
Scunthorpe
Brigg
Immingham
Great Grimsby
Cleethorpes
Spurn Hd.
Mouth of the Humber
Donna Nook
Louth
Mablethorpe
Sutton-on-Sea
Skegness
Ingoldmells Pt.
Gibraltar Pt.
The Wash
Boston
Spilsby
Horncastle
Market Rasen
Gainsborough
Lincoln
Sleaford
Grantham
Newark on-Trent
Isle of Axholme
Doncaster
Thorne
Barnsley
Rotherham
SHEFFIELD
Worksop
East Retford
Chesterfield
Mansfield
Sutton in Ashfield
Matlock
Alfreton
Ripley
Hucknall
NOTTINGHAM
Ilkeston
Heanor
Belper
Ashbourne
DERBY
Long Eaton
West Bridgford
Beeston
Stapleford
Carlton
Hunstanton
Heacham
Burnham Market
Wells-next-the-Sea
Blakeney
Cley
Weybourne
Holt
Fakenham
West from Greenwich
East from Greenwich
Based upon the Ordnance Survey Map with the permission of the Controller of Her Majesty's Stationery Office. Crown Copyright Reserved.
COPYRIGHT, GEORGE PHILIP & SON. LTD.

Pt. of Ardnamurchan
Ardnamurchan
Sunart
L. Leven
Blackwater Res.
Coll
Tobermory
L. Sunart
Rannoch Moor
Glen Coe
Morvern
L. Frisa
Tiree
Hynish B.
Treshnish Isles
L. Tuath
Gometra
Ulva
Staffa
L. na Keal
Mull
Ben More 966
Passage of Tiree
Sd. of Mull
Loch Linnhe
Lismore
Kerrera
Oban
L. Spelve
L. Scridain
Ross of Mull
Iona
L. Buie
Firth of Lorn
Seil
Luing
Garvellachs
Scarba
G. of Corryvreckan
Torran Rocks
Dubh Artach
Loch Etive
B. Cruachan 1124
Loch Awe
L. Avich
L. Tulla
Glen Orchy
Ben Lui 1130
Ben More 1174
L. Voil
L. Katrine
The Trossachs
Loch Lomond
Colonsay
Oronsay
Passage of Oronsay
ATLANTIC
OCEAN
L. Tarbert
Jura
Paps of Jura 784
Sound of Jura
Sound of Islay
Islay
Port Askaig
Bridgend
Bowmore
Port Charlotte
L. Indaal
Portnahaven
Laggan B.
Port Ellen
Ardbeg
The Oa
Mull of Oa
Ardmore Pt.
Gigha I.
Crinan Cdn.
Lochgilphead
Knapdale
W. L. Tarbert
Tarbert
Loch Fyne
Argyll
Kyles of Bute
Rothesay
Bute
Dunoon
Greenock
Gourock
Helensburgh
Dumbarton
Alexandria
Glasgow
Paisley
Renfrew
Johnstone
Barrhead
Largs
Cumbrae Is.
Sd. of Bute
West Kilbride
Arran
Goat Fell 874
Brodick
Lamlash
Holy I.
Kilbrannan Sound
Firth of Clyde
Kintyre
Campbeltown
Machrihanish
Southend
Mull of Kintyre
Sanda I.
Pladda
Stevenston
Ardrossan
Saltcoats
Irvine
Kilmarnock
Kilwinning
Troon
Prestwick
Ayr
Heads of Ayr
Maybole
Girvan
Ailsa Craig 334
Carrick
Inishtrahull
Malin Pen.
Glengad Hd.
Inishowen Pen.
Moville
Lough Foyle
Rathlin
Giants Causeway
Benbane Hd.
Ballycastle B.
Ballycastle
Fair Hd.
Portrush
Portstewart
Coleraine
Ballymoney
Limavady
Londonderry
NORTH CHANNEL
Mountains of Antrim
Trostan 554
Red B.
Garron Pt.
Carnlough
Glenarm
Larne
Larne Lough
Ballymena
NORTHERN IRELAND
ULSTER
LONDONDERRY
ANTRIM
TYRONE
Sperrin Mts.
Sawel 683
L. Beg
Antrim
Lough Neagh
Ballyclare
Whitehead
Carrickfergus
Belfast Lough
Bangor
Copeland I.
Donaghadee
Newtownards
Holywood
BELFAST
Newtownabbey
Omagh
Dungannon
Corsewall Pt.
Kirkcolm
Stranraer
L. Ryan
The Rhins
Portpatrick
Luce Bay
Port Logan
Drummore
Mull of Galloway
Newton Stewart
Glenluce
Wigtown
Whithorn
Port William
Burrow Hd.
Galloway
Rhinns of Kells
Projection: Conical with two standard parallels
West from Greenwich

1:1 000 000

10 0 10 20 30 40 km

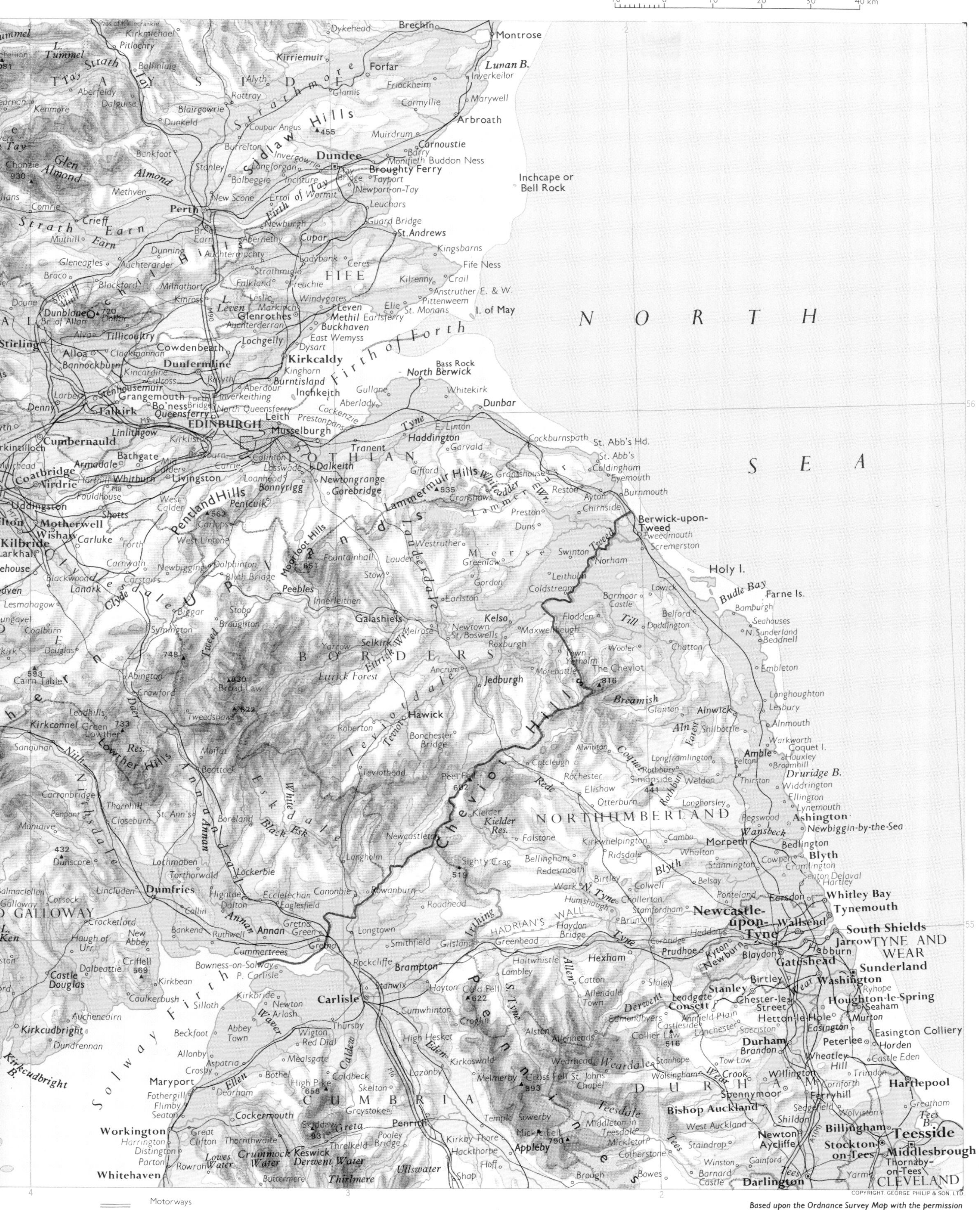

Pass of Killiecrankie
Kirkmichael
Pitlochry
L. Tummel
Dykehead
Brechin
Montrose
Kirriemuir
Lunan B.
Forfar
Inverkeilor
Strath Tay
Ballinluig
Alyth
Glamis
Friockheim
Aberfeldy
Dalguise
Rattray
Strathmore
Carmyllie
Marywell
Kenmore
Blairgowrie
Sidlaw Hills
455
Dunkeld
Coupar Angus
Muirdrum
Arbroath
Carnoustie
Barry
Burrelton
Dundee
Monifieth
Buddon Ness
Glen Almond
Bankfoot
Invergowrie
Broughty Ferry
Chonzie
930
Stanley
Longforgan
Tayport
Inchcape or Bell Rock
Almond
Balbeggie
Inchture
Newport-on-Tay
Methven
New Scone
Errol
Firth of Tay
Wormit
Leuchars
Comrie
Perth
Guard Bridge
Crieff
Newburgh
St. Andrews
Strath Earn
Abernethy
Cupar
Muthill
Bridge of Earn
Dunning
Auchtermuchty
Kingsbarns
Ladybank
Ceres
Gleneagles
Auchterarder
FIFE
Fife Ness
Strathmiglo
Braco
Blackford
Falkland
Freuchie
Kilrenny
Crail
Milnathort
Anstruther E. & W.
Leslie
Markinch
Pittenweem
Doune
Kinross
L. Leven
Windygates
Leven
Elie
St. Monans
I. of May
Dunblane
720
Dollar
Glenrothes
Methil
Earlsferry
NORTH
Br. of Allan
Auchterderran
Buckhaven
Alva
Tillicoultry
East Wemyss
Stirling
Cowdenbeath
Lochgelly
Dysart
Firth of Forth
Alloa
Clackmannan
Bannockburn
Dunfermline
Kirkcaldy
Bass Rock
Kincardine
Kinghorn
North Berwick
Culross
Rosyth
Aberdour
Burntisland
Larbert
Stenhousemuir
Inverkeithing
Inchkeith
Gullane
Whitekirk
Grangemouth
Forth Bridges
Aberlady
Dunbar
Denny
Falkirk
Bo'ness
North Queensferry
Queensferry
Cockenzie
Prestonpans
Linlithgow
Leith
Tyne
E. Linton
EDINBURGH
Musselburgh
Haddington
Cumbernauld
Kirkliston
Cockburnspath
St. Abb's Hd.
St. Abb's
Bathgate
Tranent
Garvald
LOTHIAN
Coldingham
Armadale
Calder
Currie
Dalkeith
Coatbridge
Whitburn
Loanhead
Gifford
Lammermuir Hills
Eyemouth
Airdrie
Livingston
Lasswade
Newtongrange
Grantshouse
Bonnyrigg
Gorebridge
535
Burnmouth
Fauldhouse
Cranshaws
Whiteadder Wr.
Reston
Uddingston
Pentland Hills
West Calder
Penicuik
Ayton
Chirnside
562
Motherwell
Shotts
Preston
Duns
Berwick-upon-Tweed
Tweedmouth
Wishaw
Carlops
Lammermuir
Scremerston
Kilbride
Carluke
West Linton
Forth
Westruther
Swinton
Moorfoot Hills
Lauder
Merse
Norham
Carnwath
Newbigging
Dolphinton
651
Fountainhall
Greenlaw
Holy I.
Stow
Gordon
Lauderdale
Leitholm
Blackwood
Blyth Bridge
Lowick
Bude Bay
Farne Is.
Lanark
Peebles
Coldstream
Barmoor Castle
Lesmahagow
Innerleithen
Earlston
Bamburgh
Clydesdale
Biggar
Stobo
Galashiels
Kelso
Flodden
Belford
Seahouses
Coalburn
Broughton
Melrose
Newtown St. Boswells
Maxwellheugh
Till
Doddington
N. Sunderland
Beadnell
Douglas
Symington
Selkirk
Yarrow
Roxburgh
Chatton
748
Tweed
BORDERS
Wooler
Town Yetholm
Ettrick Wr.
Morebattle
The Cheviot
Embleton
593
Abington
830
Ettrick Forest
Ancrum
Jedburgh
816
Cairn Table
Broad Law
Breamish
Longhoughton
Crawford
Glanton
Alnwick
Lesbury
Leadhills
822
Teviotdale
Hawick
Green Lowther
733
Tweedsmuir
Kirkconnel
Robertson
Aln
Shilbottle
Alnmouth
Bonchester Bridge
Cheviot Hills
Sanquhar
Lowther Hills
Res.
Moffat
Alwinton
Forest
Warkworth
Coquet I.
Amble
Hauxley
Coquet
Longframlington
Broomhill
Felton
Catcleugh
Rothbury
Druridge B.
Beattock
Teviothead
Rochester
Simonside
Thirston
Widdrington
Carronbridge
Peel Fell
602
441
Weldon
Elishaw
Ellington
Esk
Whiteadder
Rede
Otterburn
Longhorsley
Lynemouth
Thornhill
Penpont
Closeburn
Kielder
Kielder Res.
NORTHUMBERLAND
Pegswood
Ashington
Annan
St. Ann's
Boreland
Black Esk
Newcastleton
Falstone
Kirkwhelpington
Cambo
Wansbeck
Newbiggin-by-the-Sea
Moniaive
432
Dunscore
Nithsdale
Lochmaben
Langholm
Bellingham
Ridsdale
Morpeth
Whalton
Bedlington
Blyth
Sighty Crag
Stannington
Cowpen
Cramlington
Torthorwald
Lockerbie
519
Redesmouth
Birtley
Blyth
Belsay
Seaton Delaval
Hartley
Corsock
Lincluden
Dumfries
Hightae
Ecclefechan
Canonbie
Rowanburn
Wark
N. Tyne
Colwell
Ponteland
Earsdon
Whitley Bay
Dalton
Eaglesfield
Roadhead
Humshaugh
Chollerton
Tynemouth
GALLOWAY
Collin
Irthing
Stamfordham
Newcastle-upon-Tyne
Wallsend
Crocketford
Gretna Green
HADRIAN'S WALL
Brunton
South Shields
New Abbey
Bankend
Ruthwell
Annan
Longtown
Haydon Bridge
Heddon
Jarrow
TYNE AND WEAR
Haugh of Urr
Gretna
Smithfield
Gilsland
Greenhead
Corbridge
Prudhoe
Ryton
Newburn
Hebburn
Cummertrees
Tyne
Blaydon
Criffell
Bowness-on-Solway
Rockcliffe
Brampton
Haltwhistle
Hexham
Gateshead
Sunderland
Castle Douglas
Dalbeattie
569
P. Carlisle
Lambley
Catton
Staley
Birtley
Washington
Kirkbean
Hayton
Cold Fell
622
Allendale Town
Leadgate
Stanley
Ryhope
Caulkerbush
Kirkbride
Derwent
Consett
Chester-le-Street
Houghton-le-Spring
Silloth
Newton Arlosh
Carlisle
Wear
Seaham
Auchencairn
Cumwhinton
Edmundbyers
Annfield Plain
Hetton-le-Hole
Murton
Solway Firth
Waver
Thursby
Croglin
Castleside
Lanchester
Kirkcudbright
Abbey Town
Wigton
High Hesket
Alston
Allenheads
Collier Law
Sacriston
Easington
Easington Colliery
Dundrennan
Beckfoot
Red Dial
Caldew
Kirkoswald
516
Durham
Peterlee
Allonby
Aspatria
Eden
Weardale
Stanhope
Brandon
Horden
Kirkcudbright B.
Mealsgate
Wearhead
Tow Law
Wheatley Hill
Castle Eden
Crosby
Ellen
Bothel
Coldbeck
Lazonby
Melmerby
Cross Fell
St. John's Chapel
Wolsingham
Crook
Willington
Trimdon
Maryport
High Pike
658
893
DURHAM
Hartlepool
Dearham
Skelton
Cornforth
Ferryhill
Fothergill
Flimby
CUMBRIA
Pennines
Spennymoor
Seaton
Greystoke
Teesdale
Bishop Auckland
Sedgefield
Greatham
Cockermouth
Penrith
Temple Sowerby
Middleton in Teesdale
Shildon
Wolviston
Tees B.
Skiddaw
Greta
Pooley Bridge
Kirkby Thore
West Auckland
Billingham
Teesside
Workington
931
Mickle Fell
Newton Aycliffe
Great Clifton
Threlkeld
Hackthorpe
Appleby
790
Mickleton
Staindrop
Stockton-on-Tees
Middlesbrough
Harrington
Thornthwaite
Distington
Keswick
Cotherstone
Parton
Lowes Water
Crummock Water
Derwent Water
Hoff
Winston
Gainford
Thornaby-on-Tees
Rowrah
Ullswater
Shap
Brough
Bowes
Barnard Castle
Tees
Yarm
CLEVELAND
Whitehaven
Buttermere
Thirlmere
Darlington
SEA
M9
M8
M90

Motorways
Motorways under construction

Based upon the Ordnance Survey Map with the permission of the Controller of Her Majesty's Stationery Office. Crown Copyright Reserved.

SHETLAND ISLANDS
on same scale
Herma Ness
Haroldswick
Baltasound
Unst
Balta
Bluemull Sd.
Cullivoe
Uyeasound
Mu Ness
Ramna Stacks
Whale Firth
Point of Fethaland
Fetlar
North Roe
Mid Yell
Yell
The Snap
The Faither
Ronas Hill
450
Colgrave Sd.
Yell Sound
Burravoe
Esha Ness
Hillswick
Sullom Voe
Lunna Ness
St. Magnus Bay
SHETLAND
Skaw
Taing
Out Skerries
Brae
Muckle Roe
Papa Stour
Whalsay
Sd. of Papa
The Haa
Sandness
S Nesting Bay
Walls
Mainland
Vaila
Gruting Voe
Score Hd.
Lerwick
I. of Noss
Scalloway
Bressay
Bard Hd.
West Burra
Clift Sound
Bressay Sd.
Kettla Ness
293
Helli Ness
Hoswick
Mousa
St. Ninian's I.
Scousburgh
Boddam
Fitful Hd
B. of Quendale
Sumburgh Hd.
C. Wrath
Butt of Lewis
Port of Ness
South Dell
Ness
Cellar Hd.
Borve
Barvas
North Tolsta
Tolsta Hd.
Shawbost
Carloway
Broad Bay
Back
Tiumpan Hd.
Great Bernera
Gallan Hd.
291
Newmarket
Portaguiran
Stornoway
Melbost
Eye Peninsula
Bayble
Uig
Callanish
L. Roag
Chicken Hd.
Lewis
Aird Brenish
575
Gisla
Lochs
Crossbost
Loch Langavat
Balallan
L. Erisort
Cromore
Park
Kintaravay
Gravir
Kebock Hd.
Scarp
Husinish
Husinish Pt.
N.Harris
Ardvourlie Castle
571
Beinn Mhor
L. Shell
799
W. L. Tarbert
Ardhasig
Sd. of Shiant
Shiant Is.
Taransay
L. Seaforth
Tarbert
Harris
WESTERN
Sd. of Taransay
Toe Hd.
Scalpay
E. L. Tarbert
Scarastavore
S.Harris
Leverburgh
Sound of Harris
Pabbay
Sd. of Pabbay
Berneray
Rodel
Renish Pt.
Haskeir Is.
Griminish Pt.
ISLES
Rubha Hunish
Sollas
Lochmaddy
North Uist
L. Maddy
Paible
Clachan
Sound of Monach
Carinish
L. Eport
347
Eaval
Monach Is.
Baleshare
Grimsay
Ronay
Gramisdale
Benbecula
Ardivachar Pt.
L. Bee
Wiay
Bagh nam Faoileann
Howmore
South Uist
605
Hecla
Rubha Ardvule
620
B. Mhor
L. Eynort
Daliburgh
Lochboisdale
L. Boisdale
Sound of Barra
Sd. of Eriskay
Eriskay
Greian Hd.
Barra
384
Castlebay
Bruernish Pt.
Vatersay
Sandray
Pabbay
Mingulay
Berneray
Barra Head
241
Outer Hebrides
Little Minch
North Minch
The Minch
Inner Hebrides
Kilmaluag
Vaternish Pt.
Uig
Loch Snizort
Waternish
Dunvegan Head
Trotternish
The Storr
719
Stein
Sound of Raasay
Rona
Inner Sound
Milovaig
Lephin
Dunvegan
Roskhill
Portree
488
Skye
Raasay
Bracadale
L. Bracadale
Coillore
L. Harport
Fernilea
Carbost
Drynoch
Narrows
Scalpay
Minginish
Sligachan
Cuillin Hills
Glenbrittle
Bla Bheinn
928
1009
Broadford
Rubh' an Dunain
Soay Sd.
Soay
L. Scavaig
Elgol
L. Eishort
Eilean Iarmain
Teangue
Cuillin Sound
Canna
Armadale
Ardavasar
Sound of Sleat
Sanday
Sd. of Canna
Kinloch
Pt. of Sleat
Rhum
810
Sound of Rhum
Eigg
394
Sd. of Eigg
Muck
Kinlochbervie
L. Inchard
L. Laxford
Handa I.
Scourie
Eddrachillis Bay
Pt. of Stoer
Drumbeg
Quinag
Stoer
Assynt
Lochinver
Enard Bay
Rhu Coigach
Summer Isles
L. Lurgainn
L. Broom
Ullapool
Coigach
Gruinard B.
Greenstone Pt.
Mellon Charles
Aultbea
An Teallach
1062
L. na Sealga
L. Ewe
Melvaig
Poolewe
Fionn Loch
Braemore
Longa I.
L. Gairloch
Gairloch
Henderson
Kerrysdale
Talladale
981
Slioch
L. Maree
L. Fannich
Kinlochewe
Achnasheen
L. Torridon
1053
Torridon
Fasag
Shieldaig
Achnashellach
Applecross Forest
Applecross
Coulags
Carron
Monar Forest
L. Monar
1062
L. Kishorn
Lochcarron
Toscaig
Crowlin Is.
Stromemore
Plockton
Stromeferry
L. Carron
Kyle of Lochalsh
Auchtertyre
Dornie
Mullardoch
Carn Eige
1182
Kyleakin
L. Alsh
Glenelg
Invershiel
A' Chralaig
1120
The Saddle
1010
Glen Shiel
L. Hourn
L. Quoich
Ladhar B.
1019
Knoydart
Inverie
Tomdoun
Glen Garry
L. Nevis
Mallaig
1040
Sgurr na Ciche
Morar
Tarbet
Loch Morar
L. Arkaig
983
Culvain
Arisaig
Lochailort
Glenfinnan
Caledonian Canal
Kinlocheil
Corpach
Sd. of Arisaig
882
Moidart
Kinlochmoidart
L. Eil
Shona I.
L. Moidart
Loch Shiel
Fort William
1347
Ben Nevis
Ardgour
888
Sunart
Corran
North Ballachulish
Ardnamurchan
Salen
Pt. of Ardnamurchan
Kilchoan
Mingary
527
Strontian
Sorisdale
Coll
Clabhach
L. Sunart
South Ballachulish
1148
Tobermory
Arinagour
Caliach Pt.
Calgary
Dervaig
Drimnin
Morvern
Kingairloch
L. Frisa
Loch Linnhe
Portnacroish
Coles
Sd. of Mull
Lochaline
Tiree
Scarinish
Passage of Tiree
Treshnish Isles
L. Tuath
Salen
Lismore I.
Loch Etive
Hynish B.
Hynish
1000
800
600
400
200
100
0
50
100
m
Projection: Conical with two standard parallels

1:1 000 000

10 0 10 20 30 40 km

ORKNEY ISLANDS
on same scale
Papa Westray
Westray
N. Ronaldsay
N. Ronaldsay Firth
The North Sound
Westray Firth
Eday
Sanday
Sanday Sound
Papa Stronsay
Stronsay
Eynhallow Sd.
Rousay
Egilsay
Wyre
Gairsay
Shapinsay
L. of Harray
L. of Stenness
Kirkwall
Mainland
Deer Sd.
Copinsay
Graemsay
Hoy
Ward Hill
Scapa Flow
Flotta
Burray
S. Walls
Swona
South Ronaldsay
Pentland Firth
Stroma
Pentland Skerries
Duncansby Hd.
Auskerry
Dunnet Hd.
Thurso
Wick
Sinclair's B.
Noss Head
Kyle of Tongue
Loch Hope
Ben Hope
Loch Loyal
Strath Naver
Strath Halladale
Strathmore
L. Naver
B. Klibreck
L. nan Clar
Strath of Kildonan
Morven
Helmsdale
Ord of Caithness
B. Dhorain
Loch Shin
Brora
L. Brora
Golspie
L. Fleet
Dornoch Firth
Tarbat Ness
Easter Ross
B. Wyvis
Cromarty Firth
Moray Firth
Black Isle
Dingwall
Inverness
Beauly F.
Caledonian Canal
Nairn
Burghead B
Lossiemouth
Elgin
Forres
Spey B.
Buckie
Banff
Fraserburgh
Kinnairds Hd.
Peterhead
Buchan Ness
Buchan
Keith
Strathbogie
Formartine
Ellon
Deveron
Ythan
Hills of Cromdale
Carn Glas-choire
Grantown-on-Spey
L. Duntelchaig
Loch Ness
Strath Glass
Glen Moriston
Monadhliath Mts.
Strath Dearn
Strathspey
Cairn Gorm
Cairngorm Mts.
B. Avon
B. Macdhui
Braeriach
Braemar
Balmoral Forest
Lochnagar
Mt. Keen
The Buck
Ladder Hills
Grampian
Inverurie
Don
Aberdeen
Girdle Ness
Mar
Dee
Stonehaven
Glen Esk
North Esk
Braes of Angus
South Esk
Howe of the Mearns
Laurencekirk
Brechin
Montrose
NORTH SEA
Lunan B.
Arbroath
Forfar
Kirriemuir
Strathmore
Sidlaw Hills
Dundee
Carnoustie
Buddon Ness
Broughty Ferry
Grampian Mountains
Forest of Atholl
Glen Garry
Beinn a' Ghlo
Glas Maol
Glen Shee
Blair Atholl
Pitlochry
Loch Rannoch
L. Tummel
Schiehallion
Tay
Strath Tay
Aberfeldy
Dunkeld
Blairgowrie
Glen Lyon
B. Lawers
Loch Tay
Breadalbane
Rannoch Moor
L. Laidon
L. Tulla
L. Ericht
B. Alder
L. Laggan
Creag Meagaidh
Dalwhinnie
Kingussie
Newtonmore
Aviemore
Spean
Blackwater Res.
SCOTLAND
Highland
Tayside
West from Greenwich

DISTRICTS IN NORTHERN IRELAND

1 Londonderry
2 Limavady
3 Coleraine
4 Ballymoney
5 Moyle
6 Larne
7 Ballymena
8 Magherafelt
9 Cookstown
10 Strabane
11 Omagh
12 Fermanagh
13 Dungannon
14 Craigavon
15 Armagh
16 Newry and Mourne
17 Banbridge
18 Down
19 Lisburn
20 Antrim
21 Newtownabbey
22 Carrickfergus
23 North Down
24 Ards
25 Castlereagh
26 Belfast

1:1 250 000

10 0 10 20 30 40 50 km

ATLANTIC
OCEAN
LEINSTER
MUNSTER
OFFALY
LAOIS
KILDARE
WICKLOW
CARLOW
WEXFORD
KILKENNY
WATERFORD
TIPPERARY
LIMERICK
CLARE
KERRY
CORK
Galway Bay
Aran Is. (Galway)
Inishmore
North Sound
South Sound
Liscannor Bay
Mal Bay
Mouth of the Shannon
Tralee B.
Brandon B.
Dingle Bay
Smerwick Har.
Gt. Blasket I.
St. Finian's Bay
Valentia I.
Kenmare R.
Bantry Bay
Dunmanus B.
Roaringwater B.
Clear I.
Fastnet Rock
Glandore Har.
Rosscarbery Bay
Clonakilty Bay
Courtmacsherry Bay
Kinsale Harbour
Old Head of Kinsale
Cork Harbour
Youghal Bay
Dungarvan Harbour
Tramore Bay
Waterford Harbour
Bannow Bay
Wexford Harbour
Tacumshin L.
Lady's I. Lake
Saltee Is.
Carnsore Pt.
Tuskar Rock
Arklow
Wicklow
Greystones
Bray
Dun Laoghaire (Dunleary)
Limerick
Ennis
Galway
Tralee
Killarney
Kenmare
Bantry
Skibbereen
Macroom
Mallow
Fermoy
Cork
Kinsale
Bandon
Clonmel
Waterford
New Ross
Wexford
Enniscorthy
Kilkenny
Carlow
Thurles
Nenagh
Tipperary
Cashel
Roscrea
Tullamore
Kildare
Athy
Macgillycuddy's Reeks
Slieve Mish
Galty Mts.
Knockmealdown Mts.
Comeragh Mts.
Silvermine Mts.
Slieve Bloom
Nagles Mts.
Boggeragh Mts.
Shehy Mts.
Caha Mts.
Ballyhoura Hills
Mullaghareirk Mts.
Slieve Aughty
Arra Mts.
Blackstairs Mt.
Shannon
Barrow
Nore
Suir
Blackwater
Lee
Grand Canal
Projection: Conical with two standard parallels
West from Greenwich
Motorways
COPYRIGHT GEORGE PHILIP & SON, LTD

1:4 000 000

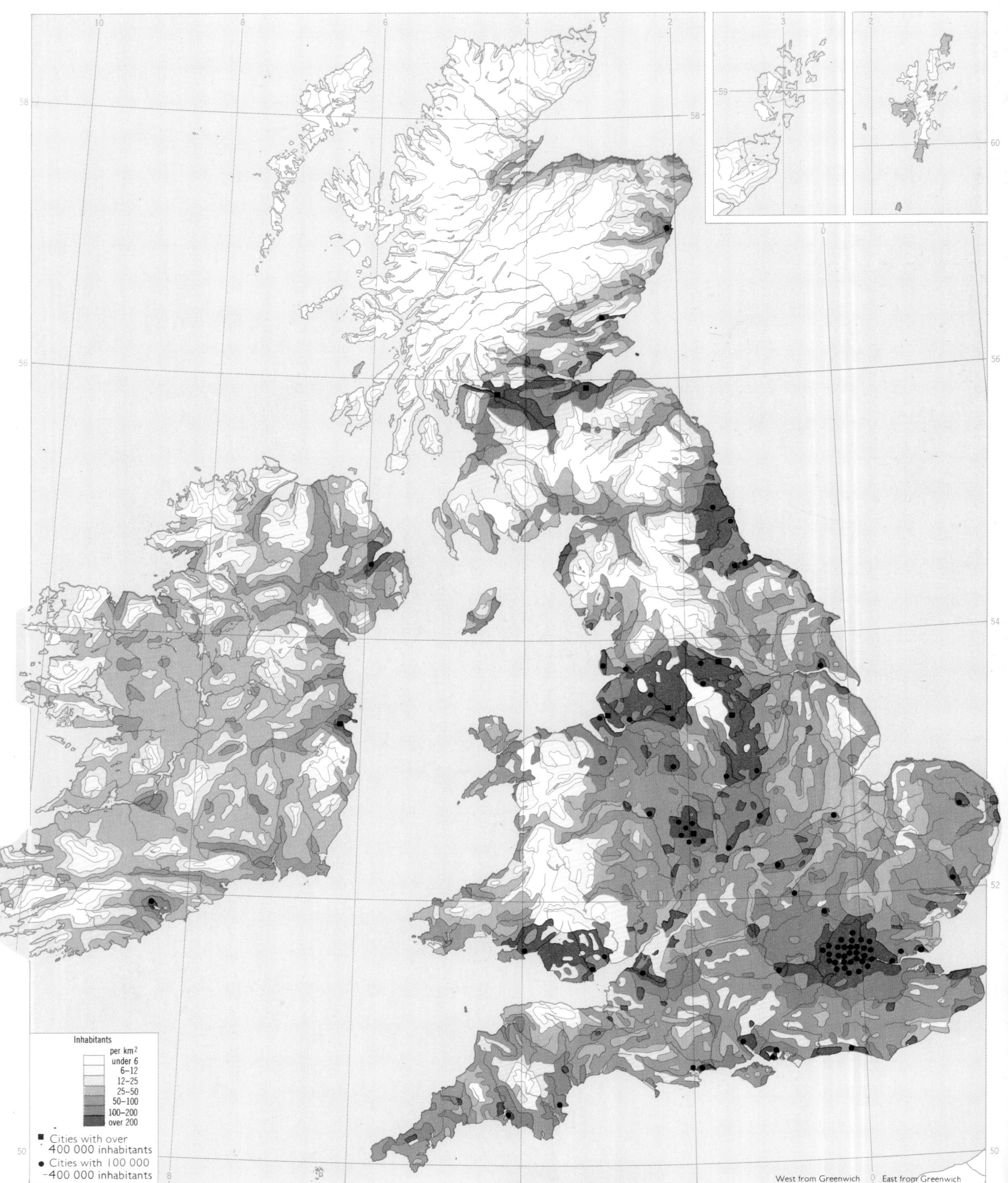
50 0 50 100 150 km
Inhabitants per km2
under 6
6–12
12–25
25–50
50–100
100–200
over 200
Cities with over 400 000 inhabitants
Cities with 100 000 -400 000 inhabitants
West from Greenwich
East from Greenwich

Projection: *Conical with two standard parallels*

1:5 000 000

50 0 50 100 150 200 km

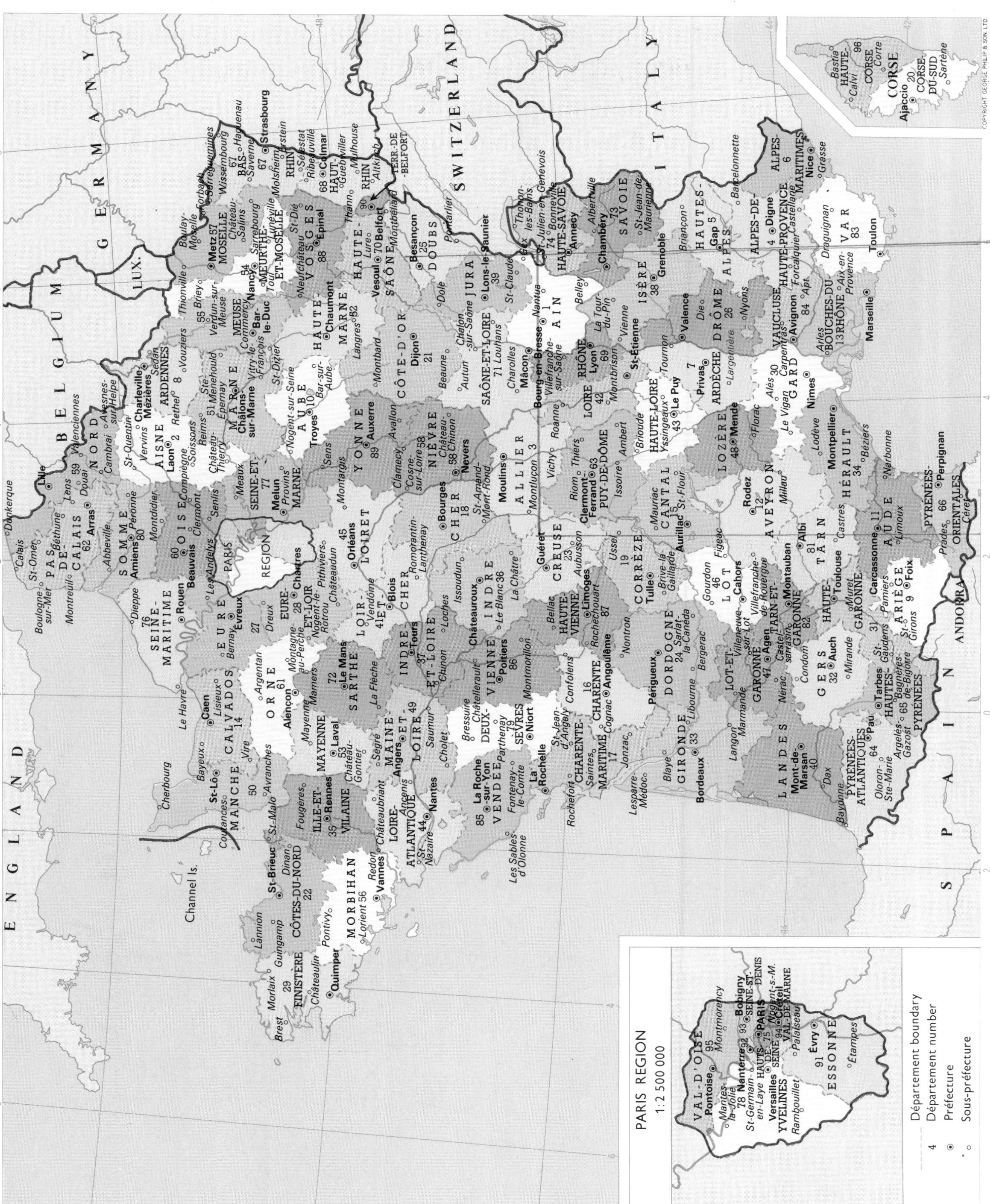
ENGLAND
BELGIUM
GERMANY
LUX.
SWITZERLAND
ITALY
SPAIN
ANDORRA
Channel Is.
CORSE
HAUTE-CORSE 2B
CORSE-DU-SUD 2A
Bastia
Ajaccio
PARIS REGION
1:2 500 000
VAL-D'OISE 95
YVELINES 78
HAUTS-DE-SEINE 92
SEINE-ST-DENIS 93
PARIS 75
VAL-DE-MARNE 94
ESSONNE 91
Département boundary
4 Département number
Préfecture
Sous-préfecture
COPYRIGHT GEORGE PHILIP & SON, LTD

E N G L A N D
English Channel
Exeter
Plymouth
Dartmoor
Torquay
Paignton
Falmouth
Penzance
Land's End
Lizard Pt.
Lyme Bay
Weymouth
Portland Bill
Southampton
Eastleigh
Portsmouth
Bournemouth
Poole
Brighton
Worthing
Eastbourne
Hastings
South Downs
Isle of Wight
CHANNEL ISLANDS
Alderney
Guernsey
St. Peter Port
Sark
Herm
Jersey
St. Helier
Cherbourg
Baie de la Seine
Le Havre
Rouen
Dieppe
Caen
Golfe de St-Malo
St-Malo
St-Brieuc
Brest
Quimper
Lorient
Vannes
Rennes
Nantes
St. Nazaire
Angers
Le Mans
Laval
Tours
Poitiers
La Rochelle
Niort
Rochefort
Angoulême
Cognac
Saintes
Royan
Alençon
Cholet
La Roche-sur-Yon
Ile d'Ouessant
Mer d'Iroise
Belle-Ile
Ile de Groix
Baie de Bourgneuf
Ile de Noirmoutier
Ile d'Yeu
Pertuis Breton
Ile de Ré
Pertuis d'Antioche
Ile d'Oléron
Les-Sables-d'Olonne
Monts d'Arrée
Montagne Noire
Collines de Normandie
Collines du Perche
CALVADOS
ANJOU
ANGOUMOIS
AUNIS
CHARENTE-MARITIME
DEUX-SÈVRES
VIENNE
Plaines et Seuil du Poitou
m
4000
3000
2000
1500
1000
400
200
0
200
2000
m
DÉPARTEMENTS IN THE PARIS AREA
1 Ville de Paris
2 Seine-St-Denis
3 Val-de-Marne
4 Hauts-de-Seine
Projection: Conical with two standard parallels
West from Greenwich
East from Greenwich

1:2 500 000

10 0 10 20 30 40 50 60 70 80 90 100 km

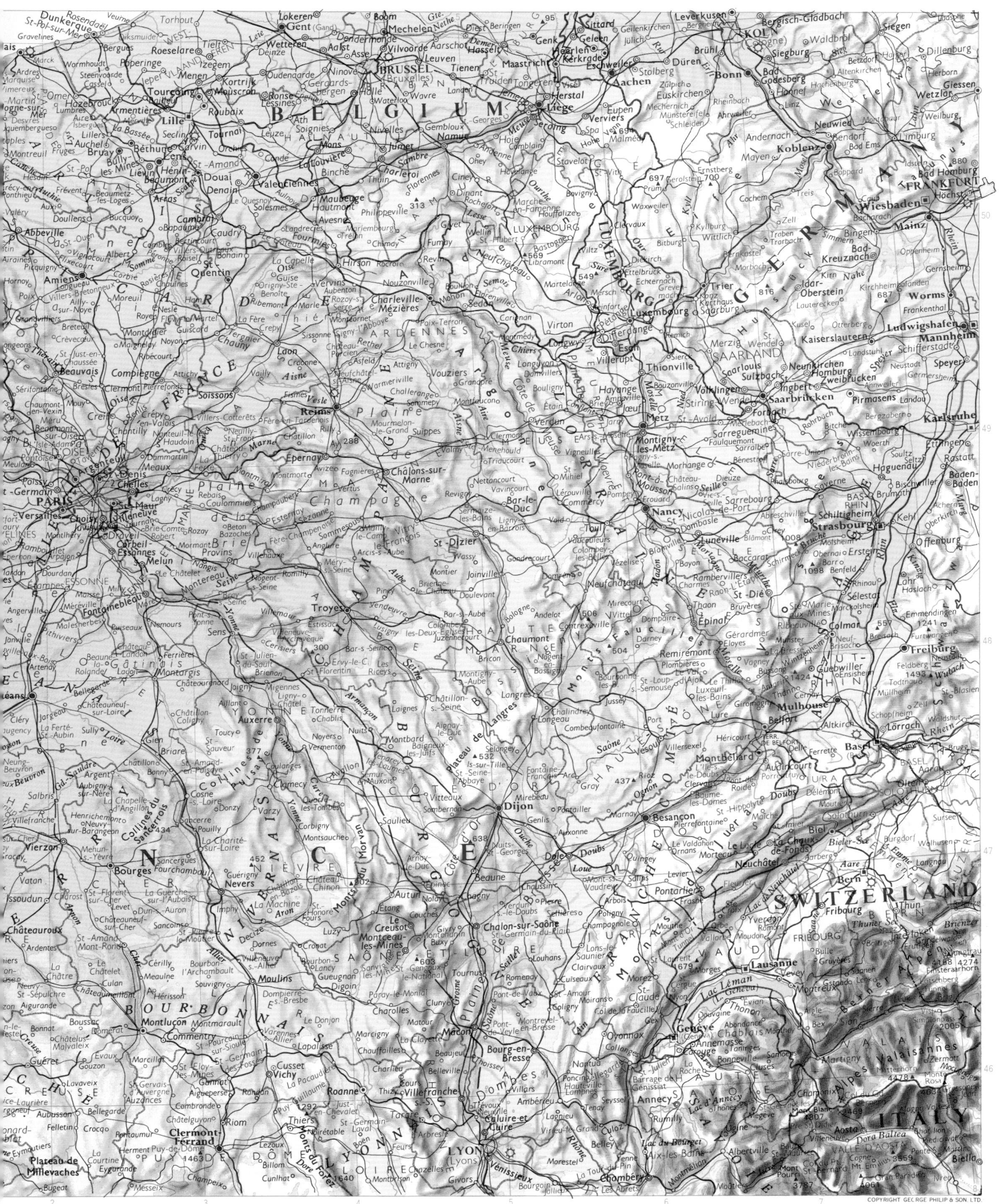
BELGIUM
GERMANY
LUXEMBOURG
SWITZERLAND
ITALY
FRANCE
SAARLAND
ARDENNES
Champagne
BOURGOGNE
BOURBONNAIS
LORRAINE
ALSACE
JURA
VAUD
VALAIS
Alpes Valaisannes
FRANCHE-COMTÉ
PARIS
BRUSSEL
Lille
Liège
Aachen
Köln
Bonn
Koblenz
Wiesbaden
Mainz
FRANKFURT
Mannheim
Ludwigshafen
Worms
Karlsruhe
Saarbrücken
Trier
Luxembourg
Metz
Nancy
Strasbourg
Reims
Troyes
Dijon
Besançon
Mulhouse
Basel
Freiburg
Bern
Lausanne
Genève
Lyon
Clermont-Ferrand
Bourges
Nevers
Moulins
Orléans
Amiens
Dunkerque
Gent
Maastricht
Lac Léman
Plateau de Langres
Monts du Forez
Plateau de Millevaches
Montbéliard
Belfort
Épinal
Colmar
Chalon-sur-Saône
Mâcon
Annecy
Chambéry
Roanne
Vichy
Montluçon
Châteauroux
Vierzon
Auxerre
Chaumont
Charleville-Mézières
Sedan
Verdun
Thionville
Namur
Charleroi
Mons
Valenciennes
Cambrai
St-Quentin
Laon
Soissons
Beauvais
Compiègne
Melun
Fontainebleau
Versailles
Sens
Neuchâtel
Fribourg
Aosta
Biella

ATLANTIC
OCEAN
Golfe de
Gascogne
Ile de Noirmoutier
Ile d'Yeu
Ile de Ré
Ile d'Oléron
Pertuis Breton
Pertuis d'Antioche
Cholet
Thouars
Bressuire
Châtellerault
Poitiers
Loches
Châteauroux
Bourges
Nevers
Moulins
Montluçon
Vichy
Clermont-Ferrand
Riom
Thiers
Limoges
La Roche-sur-Yon
Les Sables-d'Olonne
Luçon
Niort
La Rochelle
Rochefort
Saintes
Cognac
Angoulême
Royan
Périgueux
Bergerac
Libourne
Bordeaux
Bègles
Arcachon
Marmande
Agen
Cahors
Montauban
Toulouse
Albi
Rodez
Millau
Aurillac
Tulle
Brive-la-Gaillarde
Castres
Carcassonne
Narbonne
Béziers
Perpignan
Tarbes
Pau
Lourdes
Bayonne
Biarritz
Dax
Mont-de-Marsan
Auch
Foix
Pamiers
Andorra
Pamplona
Tudela
Huesca
Zaragoza
Lérida
Gerona
Figueras
Manresa
Vendée
Deux-Sèvres
Vienne
Indre
Creuse
Haute-Vienne
Corrèze
Charente
Charente-Maritime
Dordogne
Gironde
Landes
Lot-et-Garonne
Lot
Aveyron
Tarn
Tarn-et-Garonne
Haute-Garonne
Gers
Hautes-Pyrénées
Pyrénées-Atlantiques
Ariège
Aude
Pyrénées-Orientales
Cantal
Puy-de-Dôme
Allier
Cher
AUNIS
SAINTONGE
ANGOUMOIS
LIMOUSIN
PÉRIGORD
GASCOGNE
BÉARN
NAVARRE
ROUSSILLON
BOURBONNAIS
AUVERGNE
NAVARRA
ARAGON
CATALUÑA
SPAIN
Plateau de Millevaches
Causse Méjean
Mts de Lacaune
Sierra de la Peña
Sierra de Guara
Sierra del Cadí
Pic d'Aneto
Puy de Dôme
Puy de Sancy
Golfe

Projection: *Conical with two standard parallels* West from Greenwich East from Greenwich

1:2 500 000

10 0 10 20 30 40 50 60 70 80 90 100 km

SWITZERLAND
ITALY
FRANCE
CORSICA
LIGURIAN SEA
MEDITERRANEAN SEA
Golfo di Génova
Golfe du Lion
PROVENCE
DAUPHINÉ
SAVOIE
HAUTE-SAVOIE
ALPES-DE-HAUTE-PROVENCE
ALPES-MARITIMES
HAUTES-ALPES
VAUCLUSE
BOUCHES-DU-RHÔNE
VAR
DRÔME
ISÈRE
AIN
JURA
VALAIS
VAUD
PIEMONTE
LOMBARDIA
LIGURIA
GRAUBÜNDEN
HAUTE-CORSE
CORSE-DU-SUD
ILES D'HYÈRES
LYON
MARSEILLE
TORINO
MILANO
GENOVA
Genève
Lausanne
Bern
Luzern
Grenoble
Chambéry
Annecy
Avignon
Nice
Toulon
Aix-en-Provence
Cannes
Monaco
San Remo
Savona
La Spezia
Livorno
Bastia
Ajaccio
Bonifacio
Valence
St-Étienne
Mâcon
Dijon
Novara
Pavia
Bergamo
Brescia
Cuneo
Asti
Alessandria
Piacenza
Parma
Cremona
Mont Blanc 4807
Matterhorn 4478
Lac Léman
Lago Maggiore
Lac du Bourget
Mont Cinto 2710
Elba
Capraia
Gorgona
Pianosa
Côte d'Azur
COPYRIGHT. GEORGE PHILIP & SON. LTD.

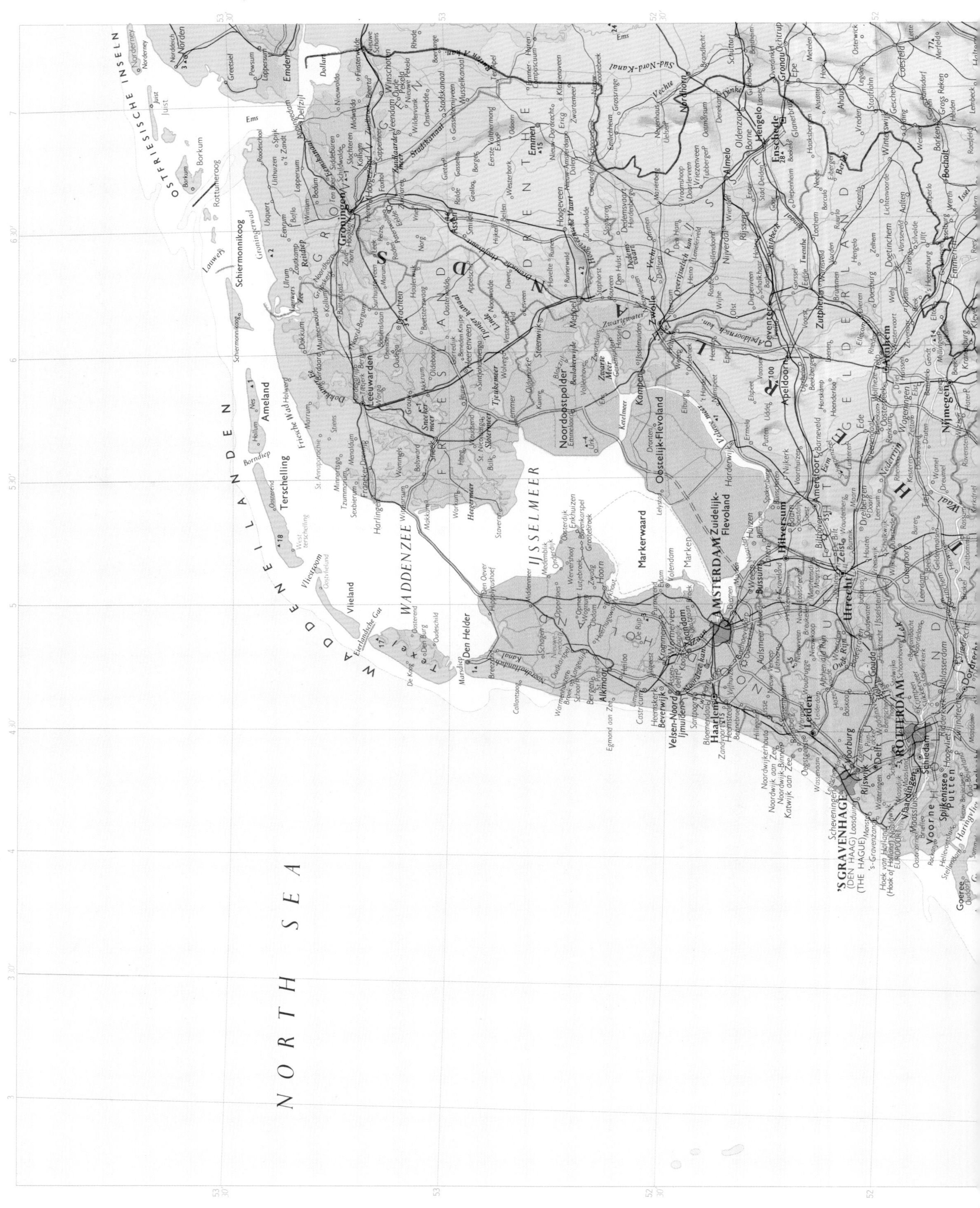
NORTH SEA
WADDENEILANDEN
OSTFRIESISCHE INSELN
WADDENZEE
IJSSELMEER
Markerwaard
Texel
Vlieland
Terschelling
Ameland
Schiermonnikoog
Borkum
Den Helder
Alkmaar
Haarlem
AMSTERDAM
Leiden
'S GRAVENHAGE (DEN HAAG) (THE HAGUE)
ROTTERDAM
Utrecht
Hilversum
Amersfoort
Apeldoorn
Arnhem
Nijmegen
Deventer
Zwolle
Kampen
Hengelo
Enschede
Almelo
Emmen
Assen
Groningen
Leeuwarden
Harlingen
Sneek
Drachten
Heerenveen
Hoogeveen
Meppel
Noordoostpolder
Oostelijk-Flevoland
Zuidelijk-Flevoland
Emden

BELGIUM
GERMANY
FRANCE
LUXEMBOURG
BRUSSEL (BRUXELLES)
Antwerpen
(Gand) Gent
Brugge
Oostende
Lille
Roubaix
Tourcoing
Kortrijk (Courtrai)
Liège
Namur
Charleroi
Mons
Maastricht
Aachen
KÖLN (COLOGNE)
DÜSSELDORF
ESSEN
DORTMUND
Bochum
Duisburg
Bonn
Luxembourg
Trier
Eindhoven
Breda
Tilburg
Valenciennes
Cambrai
St-Quentin
Charleville-Mézières
Projection: Conical with two standard parallels
East from Greenwich
1:1 250 000
10 5 0 10 20 30 40 50 km
m 600 400 200 100 50 10 0
0 10 50 m

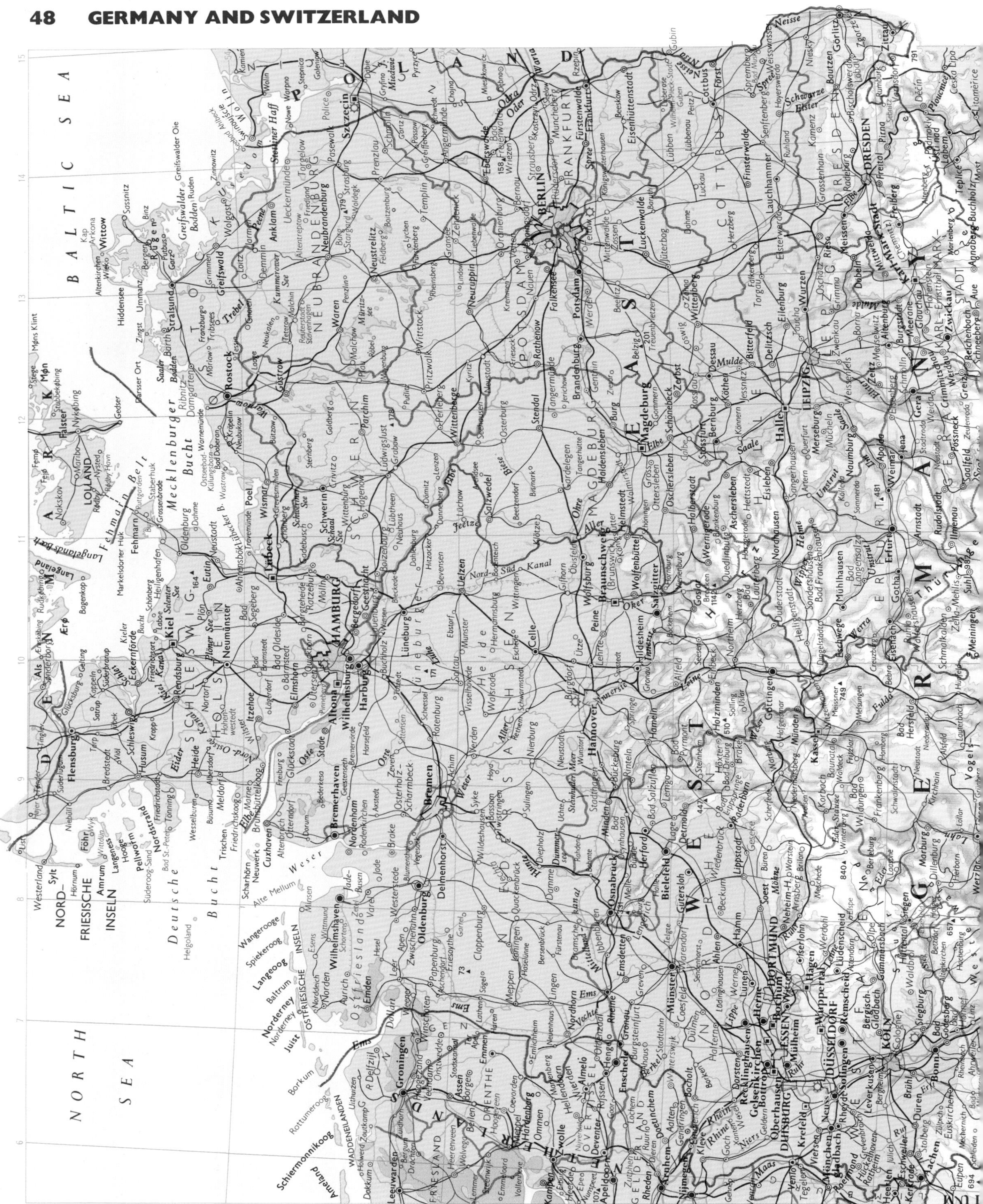
NORTH SEA
BALTIC SEA
Deutsche Bucht
Mecklenburger Bucht
HAMBURG
BERLIN
DRESDEN
LEIPZIG
HANNOVER
Bremen
DORTMUND
ESSEN
DÜSSELDORF
KÖLN
DUISBURG
Magdeburg
Rostock
Szczecin
Kiel
Lübeck
Halle
Braunschweig
Kassel
Münster
Osnabrück
Bielefeld
Groningen
NORDFRIESISCHE INSELN
OSTFRIESISCHE INSELN
WADDENEILANDEN
Lüneburger Heide
Mittelland Kanal

1:2 500 000

10 0 10 20 30 40 50 60 70 80 90 100 km

Conical with two standard parallels

East from Greenwich

m 4000 3000 2000 1500 1000 400 200 0

FRANCE
HAUTE-SAÔNE
DOUBS
JURA
HAUT-RHIN
BELFORT
Sundgau
Porte de Bourgogne
Franches Montagnes
Jura
Schweizer Mittelland
BERN
FRIBOURG
VAUD
NEUCHÂTEL
SOLOTHURN
BASEL-LANDSCHAFT
VALAIS
HAUTE-SAVOIE
SAVOIE
GENÈVE
VALLE D'AOSTA
Berner Oberland
Berner Alpen
Freiburger Alpen
Alpes Pennines
Chablais
Faucigny
Genevois
Pays de Gex
Gruyère
Ober-Aargau
Valle d'Aosta
Alpi Graie
Lac Léman (L. Geneva)
Lac de Neuchâtel
Bielersee
Thunersee
Brienzersee
Lac d'Annecy
Lac du Bourget
Schwarzwald
Vosges
Montagnes du Lomont 839
MULHOUSE
BASEL (BASLE)
BERN (BERNE)
LAUSANNE
GENÈVE (GENEVA)
BESANÇON
Belfort
Montbéliard
Vesoul
Lure
Luxeuil-les-Bains
Pontarlier
Champagnole
St-Claude
Oyonnax
Bellegarde-s.-V.
Annecy
Rumilly
Aix-les-Bains
Belley
Albertville
Ugine
Annemasse
Thonon-les-Bains
Evian-les-Bains
Montreux
Vevey
Morges
Nyon
Yverdon
Neuchâtel
La Chaux-de-Fonds
Le Locle
Biel (Bienne)
Solothurn
Grenchen
Fribourg (Freiburg)
Thun
Spiez
Olten
Aarau
Liestal
Delémont
Porrentruy
Lörrach
Chamonix-Mont-Blanc
Martigny
Sion
Sierre
Aosta
Matterhorn (Mte Cervino) 4478
Monte Rosa
Dufourspitze 4634
Mont Blanc 4807
Projection: Conical with two standard parallels

1:1 000 000

10 0 10 20 30 40 km

W. GERMANY
WÜRTTEMBERG
BAYERN
AUSTRIA
TIROL
VORARLBERG
LIECHTENSTEIN
ITALY
LOMBARDIA
TRENTINO
PIEMONTE
ZÜRICH
SCHAFFHAUSEN
THURGAU
ST. GALLEN
APPENZELL
SCHWYZ
ZUG
GLARUS
GRAUBÜNDEN
TICINO
NIDWALDEN
Bodensee (L. Constance)
Lago Maggiore
Lago di Lugano
Lago di Como
Lago d'Iseo
Lago d'Idro
Lago di Garda
Lago di Varese
Lago d'Orta
Zürichsee
Walensee
Zugersee
Vierwaldstättersee
Allgäuer Alpen
Allgäu
Lechtaler Alpen
Ötztaler Alpen
Bregenzer Wald
Rätikon
Montafon
Silvretta Gruppe
Prätigau
Unterengadin
Oberengadin
Glarner Alpen
Urner Alpen
Lepontine Alpen
Oberland
Adula-Gruppe
Alpi Retiche
Alpi Orobie
Valtellina
Val Camonica
Val Seriana
Brianza
National-Park
Toggenburg
Churfirsten
Singen
Radolfzell
Konstanz
Überlingen
Friedrichshafen
Ravensburg
Weingarten
Lindau
Bregenz
Kempten
Füssen
Schongau
Marktoberdorf
Immenstadt
Sonthofen
Oberstdorf
Dornbirn
Feldkirch
Bludenz
Landeck
Imst
Vaduz
Chur
Davos
St. Moritz
Schaffhausen
Winterthur
Frauenfeld
St. Gallen
Rorschach
Arbon
Wil
Wetzikon
Uster
Zug
Luzern
Schwyz
Altdorf
Glarus
Bellinzona
Locarno
Lugano
Chiavenna
Sondrio
Tirano
Morbegno
Como
Lecco
Varese
Bergamo
Gallarate
Verbania
Domodóssola
Riva del Garda
Chiasso
Mendrisio
Saronno
Cantu
Seregno
Clusone
Lóvere
Bormio
Ortles 3899
Mte. Adamello 3554
P. Bernina 4049
P. Kesch 3418
Schesaplana 2964
Tödi 3620
Sántis 2501
Mythen 1899
East from Greenwich

8 30′ 9 9 30′ 10 10 30′

47 30′ 47 46 30′ 46

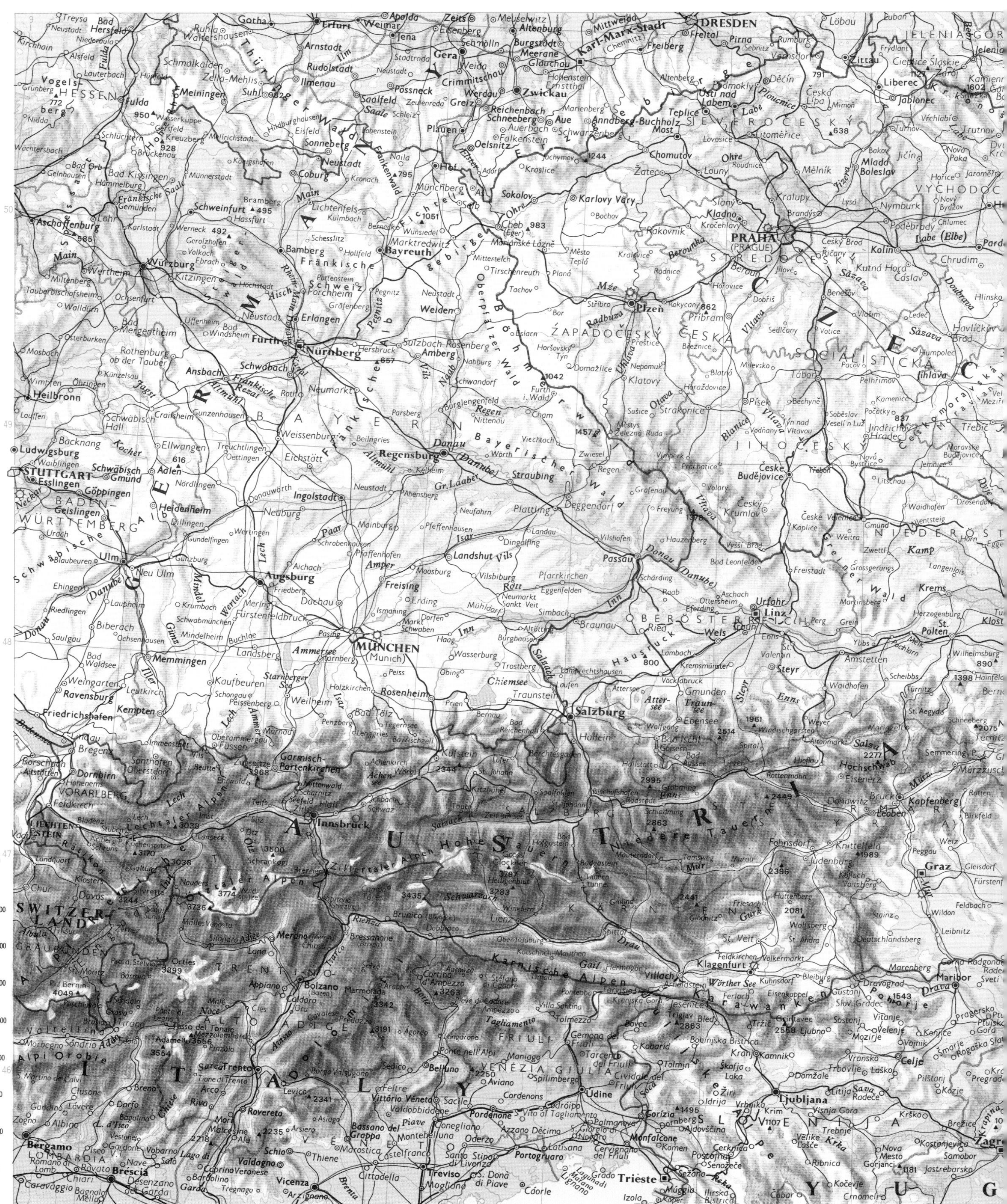
DRESDEN
Karl-Marx-Stadt
Erfurt
Weimar
Jena
Gera
Zwickau
Plauen
Chemnitz
Hof
Bayreuth
Bamberg
Würzburg
Nürnberg
Fürth
Erlangen
Regensburg
Ingolstadt
Augsburg
MÜNCHEN
(Munich)
Ulm
STUTTGART
Heilbronn
Ludwigsburg
Aschaffenburg
Fulda
Coburg
Schweinfurt
Landshut
Passau
Straubing
Memmingen
Kempten
Rosenheim
Salzburg
Linz
Wels
Steyr
Innsbruck
Graz
Klagenfurt
Villach
Leoben
Kapfenberg
St. Pölten
Krems
PRAHA
(PRAGUE)
Plzeň
Karlovy Vary
Cheb
Chomutov
Most
Teplice
Ústí nad Labem
Děčín
Liberec
Jablonec
Kladno
Kolín
Jihlava
Tábor
Písek
České Budějovice
Český Krumlov
Ljubljana
Maribor
Celje
Kranj
Trieste
Gorizia
Udine
Bolzano
Merano
Trento
Belluno
Treviso
Vicenza
Bergamo
Brescia
Rovereto
SWITZERLAND
LIECHTENSTEIN
VORARLBERG
BADEN-WÜRTTEMBERG
HESSEN
BAYERN
AUSTRIA
ITALY
ZÁPADOČESKÝ
SEVEROČESKÝ
STŘEDOČESKÝ
JIHOČESKÝ
ČESKÁ SOCIALISTICKÁ
VENEZIA GIULIA
FRIULI
Donau (Danube)
Inn
Vltava
Labe (Elbe)
Drau
Drava
Bodensee
Chiemsee
Hohe Tauern
Niedere Tauern
Zillertaler Alpen
Karnische Alpen
Karawanken
Böhmer Wald
Bayerischer Wald
Thüringer Wald
Fränkische Alb
Schwäbische Alb
Grossglockner
3797
3774
3436
2963
Projection: Conical with two standard parallels

1:2 500 000

10 0 10 20 30 40 50 60 70 80 90 100 km

POLAND
CZECHOSLOVAKIA
SLOVENSKÁ SOCIALISTICKÁ REPUBLIKA
HUNGARY
ROMANIA
YUGOSLAVIA
U.S.S.R.
Wrocław (Breslau)
Opole
Częstochowa
Radomsko
Kielce
Gory Świętokrzyskie
Ostrowiec-Świetokrzyski
Zamość
Katowice
Kraków
Tarnów
Rzeszów
Przemyśl
Jarosław
Nowy Sącz
Bielsko-Biała
Ostrava
Olomouc
Brno
Žilina
Trenčín
Nitra
Trnava
Bratislava
Košice
Prešov
Banská Bystrica
Vysoké Tatry
Nízke Tatry
Slovenské Rudohorie
Wien (Vienna)
Floridsdorf
Győr
Komárno
Esztergom
Budapest
Miskolc
Eger
Debrecen
Nyíregyháza
Szolnok
Kecskemét
Szeged
Székesfehérvár
Veszprém
Balaton
Pécs
Kaposvár
Szombathely
Nagykanizsa
Subotica
Kikinda
Timişoara
Arad
Oradea
Satu Mare
Uzhgorod
Mukachevo
Duna (Donau)
Tisza
Maros
Osijek
Sombor
Dunaújváros
Sopron
Neusiedler See

17 East from Greenwich 18 19 20 21

1:3 000 000

20 0 20 40 60 80 100 km

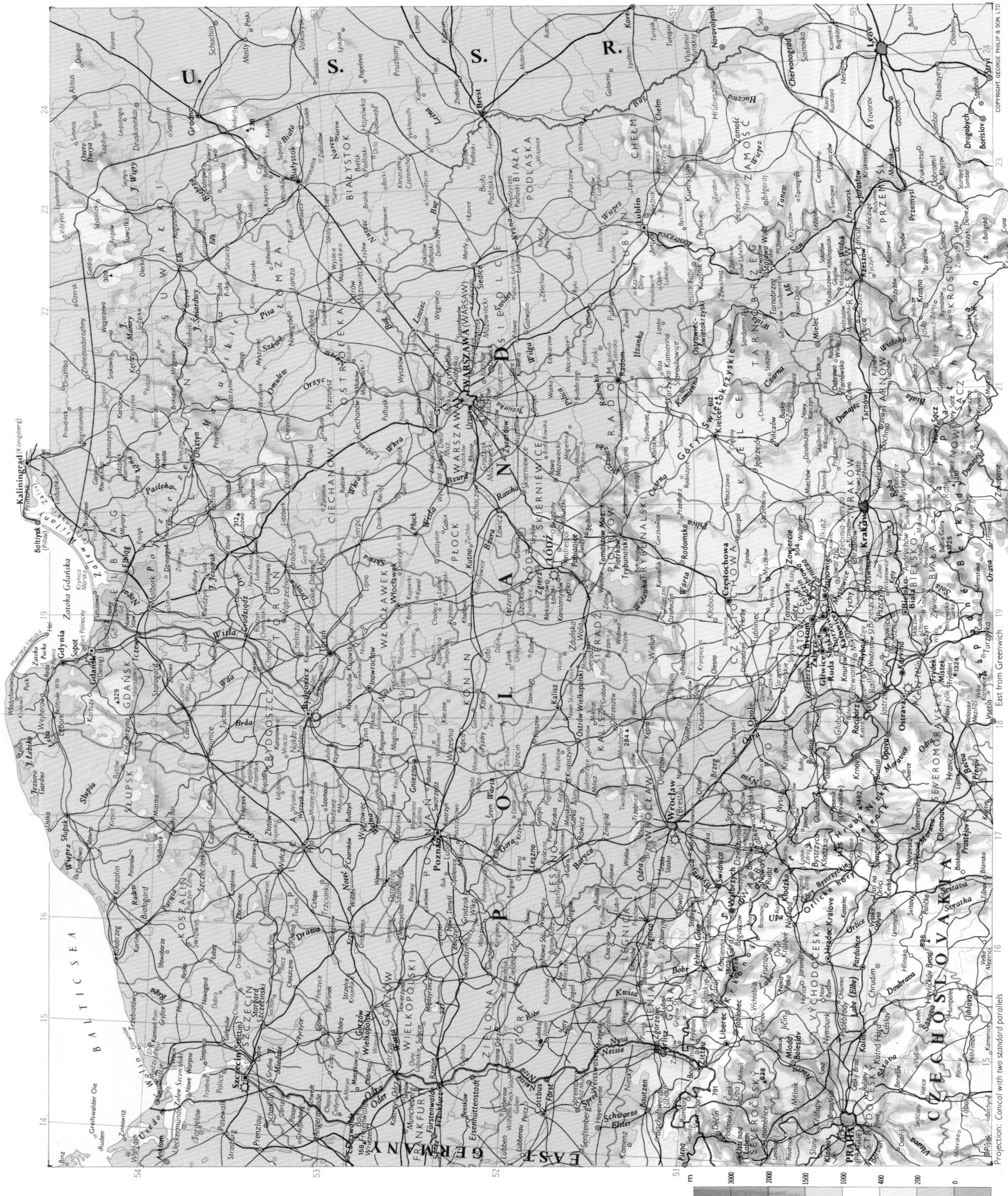
U. S. S. R.
POLAND
BALTIC SEA
EAST GERMANY
CZECHOSLOVAKIA
WARSZAWA (WARSAW)
Kaliningrad (Königsberg)
Zatoka Gdańska
East from Greenwich
Projection: Conical with two standard parallels
COPYRIGHT, GEORGE PHILIP & SON, LTD.
m
3000
2000
1500
1000
400
200
0

1:5 000 000

50 0 50 100 150 200 km

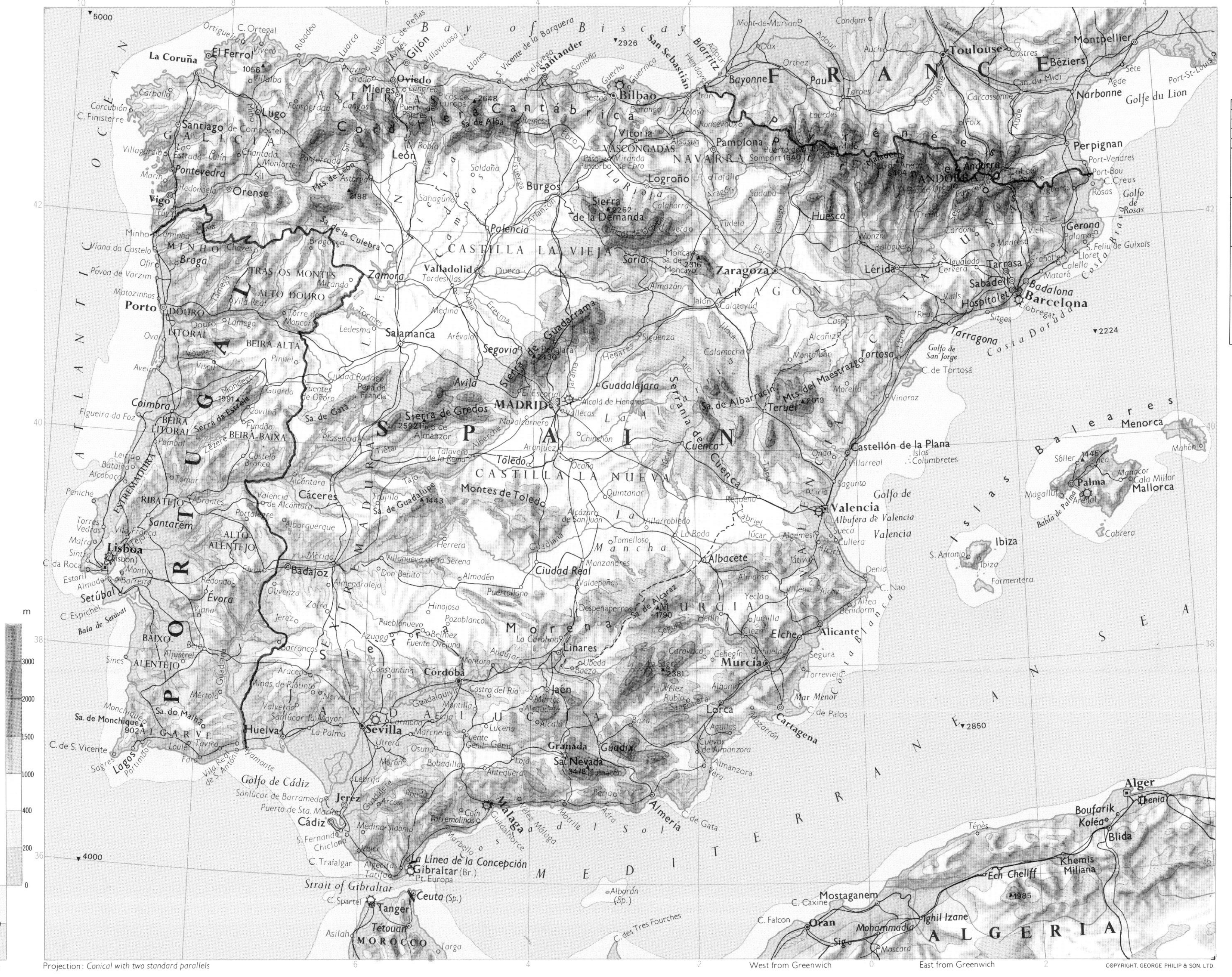
FRANCE
SPAIN
PORTUGAL
ALGERIA
MOROCCO
Bay of Biscay
Golfe du Lion
Islas Baleares
ATLANTIC OCEAN
MEDITERRANEAN SEA
Strait of Gibraltar
Golfo de Cádiz
Golfo de Valencia
MADRID
Lisboa
Barcelona
Valencia
Sevilla
Málaga
Zaragoza
Bilbao
Porto
Granada
Murcia
Córdoba
Alicante
Cartagena
Valladolid
Salamanca
Toledo
Cádiz
Gibraltar (Br.)
Tanger
Ceuta (Sp.)
Alger
Oran
Mallorca
Menorca
Ibiza
Palma
Sa. Nevada
Sierra Morena
Sierra de Guadarrama
Sierra de Gredos
Montes de Toledo
Serranía de Cuenca
Cordillera Cantábrica
Pyrénées
ANDORRA
CASTILLA LA VIEJA
CASTILLA LA NUEVA
ARAGÓN
CATALUÑA
GALICIA
ASTURIAS
EXTREMADURA
ANDALUCÍA
La Mancha
MINHO
TRÁS OS MONTES
ALTO DOURO
BEIRA ALTA
BEIRA BAIXA
BEIRA LITORAL
DOURO LITORAL
ESTREMADURA
RIBATEJO
ALTO ALENTEJO
BAIXO ALENTEJO
ALGARVE
West from Greenwich
East from Greenwich
Projection: Conical with two standard parallels
COPYRIGHT, GEORGE PHILIP & SON, LTD.
m 3000 2000 1500 1000 400 200 0
0 200 m

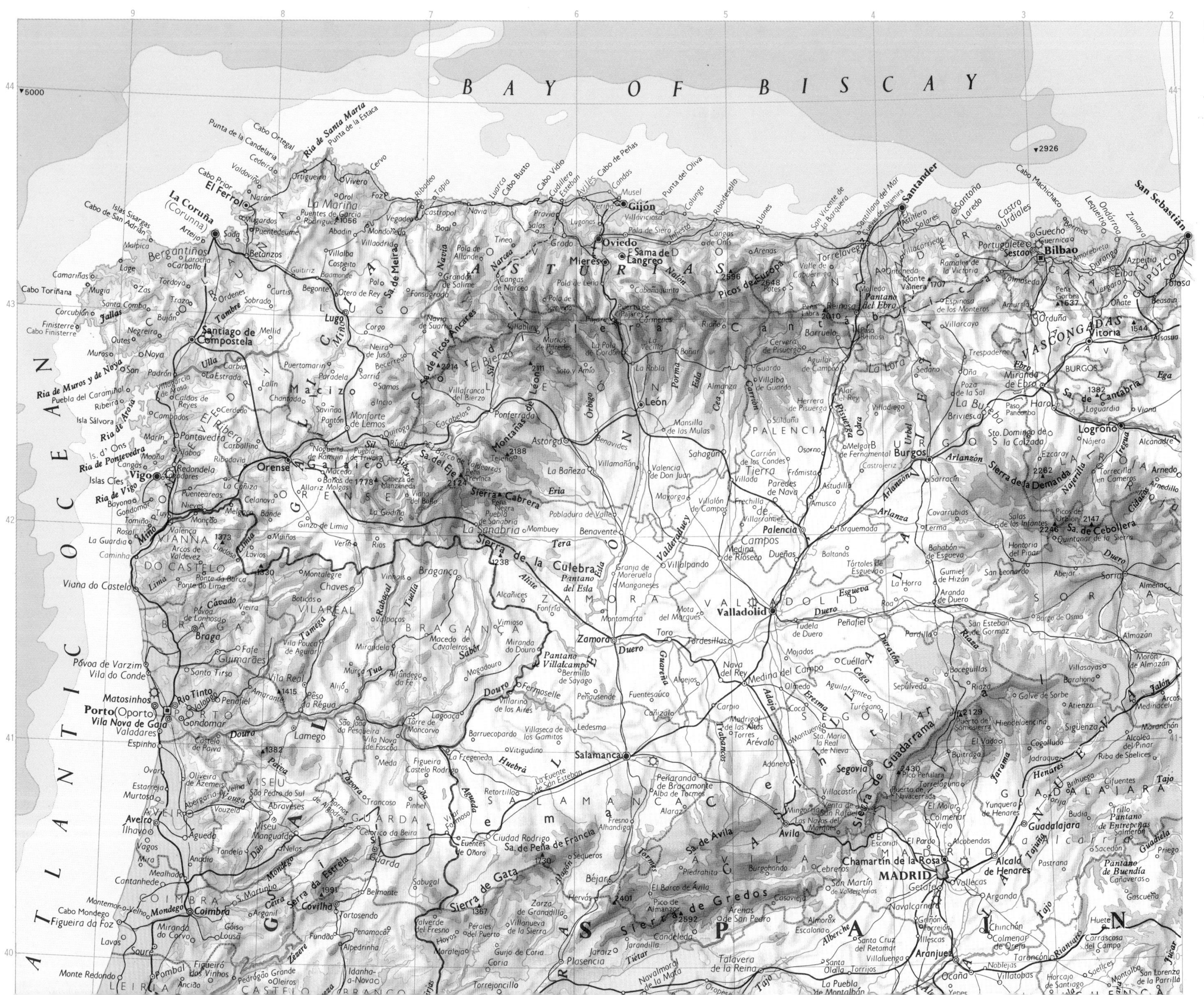
BAY OF BISCAY
ATLANTIC OCEAN
SPAIN
San Sebastián
Bilbao
Santander
Gijón
Oviedo
León
Burgos
Logroño
Vitoria
Palencia
Valladolid
Zamora
Salamanca
Segovia
Avila
MADRID
Guadalajara
Alcalá de Henares
Aranjuez
Lugo
Orense
La Coruña (Corunna)
El Ferrol
Santiago de Compostela
Pontevedra
Vigo
Porto (Oporto)
Vila Nova de Gaia
Matosinhos
Aveiro
Coimbra
Braga
Bragança
Viseu
Guarda
Covilhã
Plasencia
Béjar
Sierra de Gredos
Sierra de Gata
Sierra de Guadarrama
Duero
Douro
Ebro
Pisuerga
Tormes
Esla
Miño
Cabo Ortegal
Cabo Finisterre
Cabo Mondego
Ría de Arosa
Ría de Vigo
Islas Cíes
Picos de Europa
Sierra de la Demanda
Montañas de León
Sierra Cabrera
Sierra de la Culebra

MEDITERRANEAN SEA
Golfo de Cádiz
Strait of Gibraltar
MOROCCO
Golfo de Almería
Costa del Sol
Baía de Setúbal
LISBOA (LISBON)
Setúbal
Évora
Badajoz
Mérida
Cáceres
Córdoba
Sevilla (Seville)
Huelva
Cádiz
Jerez de la Frontera
Málaga
Granada
Almería
Jaén
Gibraltar (Br.)
Algeciras
Ceuta (Sp.)
Tétouan
Tanger (Tangier)
Larache
Melilla (Sp.)
Alborán (Sp.)
Faro
Sierra Nevada
Sierra Morena
Sierra de Segura
Montes de Toledo
Ciudad Real
Puertollano
Linares
Úbeda
Antequera
Algarve
Cabo de São Vicente
Projection: Conical with two standard parallels
West from Greenwich
COPYRIGHT. GEORGE PHILIP & SON. LTD.

1:2 500 000

10 0 10 20 30 40 50 60 70 80 90 100 km

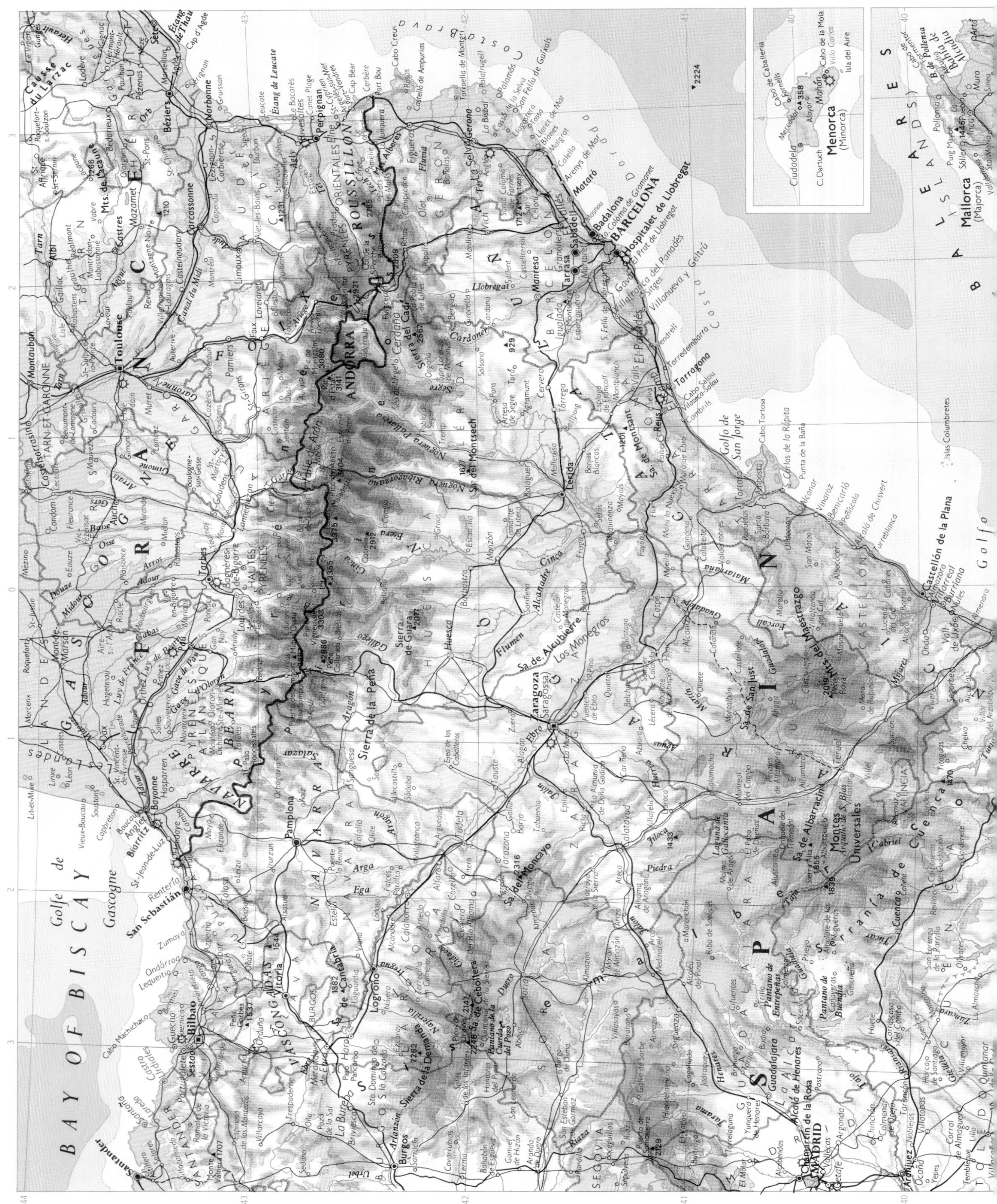
BAY OF BISCAY
Golfe de Gascogne
Menorca
(Minorca)
Mallorca
(Majorca)
BARCELONA
ANDORRA
Toulouse
Perpignan
Zaragoza
Pamplona
Bilbao
San Sebastián
Burgos
Logroño
Huesca
Lérida
Tarragona
Castellón de la Plana
MADRID

1:2 500 000

10 0 10 20 30 40 50 60 70 80 90 100 km

M E D I T E R R A N E A N S E A
A L G E R I A
M O R O C C O
ALGER (Algiers)
Blida
Boufarik
Koléa
Médéa
Khemis Miliana
Miliana
Ech Cheliff
Ténès
C. Kramis
Mostaganem
Arzew
C. Caxine
C. Falcon
Mascara
Mohammadia
Sig
ORAN
Ighil Izane
Sidi-Bel-Abbès
Aïn Témouchent
Beni Saf
Nedroma
Tiaret
Melilla (Sp.)
C. Tres Forcas
Nador
Berkane
Alborán (Sp.)
Ibiza (Iviza)
Formentera
Cabrera
Valencia
Albufera de Valencia
Sueca
Cullera
Gandía
Alcira
Játiva
Alcoy
Alicante
Elche
Torrevieja
Mar Menor
Cabo de Palos
Cartagena
Murcia
Orihuela
Lorca
Águilas
Golfo de Mazarrón
Cabo de Gata
Golfo de Almería
Almería
Sierra de Gádor
Sa. de los Filabres
Sierra Nevada
Guadix
Granada
Linares
Úbeda
Baeza
Albacete
Hellín
Yecla
Jumilla
Villena
Valdepeñas
Manzanares
Daimiel
Tomelloso
Sierra Morena
Sierra de Alcaraz
Sierra de Segura
Cabo Sacratif
Motril
Adra
2850
3478
3392
West from Greenwich
East from Greenwich

Projection: Conical with two standard parallels

m 3000 2000 1500 1000 400 200 0

0 200 2000 m

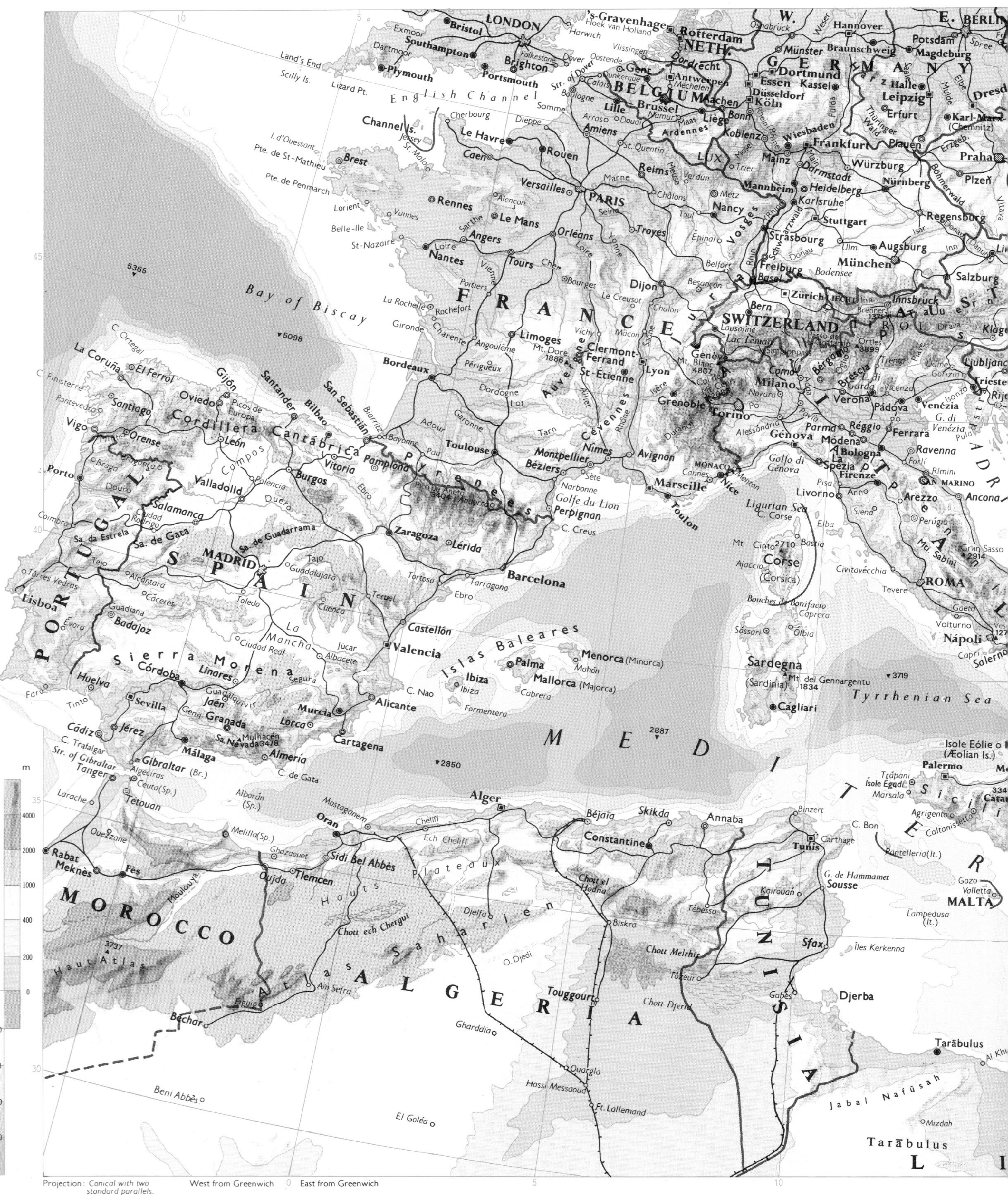
LONDON
Bristol
Southampton
Brighton
Portsmouth
Plymouth
Exmoor
Dartmoor
Land's End
Scilly Is.
Lizard Pt.
English Channel
Channel Is.
Jersey
Folkestone
Dover
Harwich
Str. of Dover
's-Gravenhage
Hoek van Holland
Rotterdam
Vlissingen
Dordrecht
NETH.
Oostende
Dunkerque
Calais
Boulogne
Gent
Antwerpen
Mechelen
BELGIUM
Brussel
Namur
Lille
Arras
Douai
Somme
Maas
Ardennes
Liège
Aachen
LUX.
Trier
Osnabrück
Weser
Hannover
Münster
Braunschweig
Magdeburg
Potsdam
BERLIN
Spree
W.
E.
GERMANY
Essen
Dortmund
Kassel
Düsseldorf
Köln
Halle
Leipzig
Dresden
Bonn
Koblenz
Wiesbaden
Erfurt
Karl-Marx-Stadt (Chemnitz)
Thüringer Wald
Frankfurt
Plauen
Erzgeb.
Praha
Mainz
Darmstadt
Würzburg
Mannheim
Heidelberg
Nürnberg
Plzeň
Karlsruhe
Stuttgart
Regensburg
Ulm
Augsburg
Donau
München
Strasbourg
Freiburg
Basel
Bodensee
Zürich
Salzburg
Innsbruck
Inn
Brenner
Cherbourg
Dieppe
Le Havre
Rouen
Amiens
St. Quentin
I. d'Ouessant
Pte. de St-Mathieu
Pte. de Penmarch
Brest
St. Malo
Caen
Reims
Meuse
Verdun
Marne
Versailles
PARIS
Seine
Châlons
Metz
Nancy
Vosges
Lorient
Rennes
Alençon
Le Mans
Vannes
Belle-Ile
Sarthe
Angers
St-Nazaire
Loire
Nantes
Orléans
Troyes
Tours
Cher
Yonne
Toul
Épinal
Belfort
Rhin
Bay of Biscay
5365
5098
Poitiers
Vienne
Bourges
FRANCE
Dijon
Besançon
Jura
Le Creusot
La Rochelle
Rochefort
Chalon
Bern
SWITZERLAND
Lausanne
Lac Léman
Genève
Simplon Pass
Mt. Blanc 4807
Gironde
Charente
Limoges
Vichy
Mâcon
Saône
Angoulême
Mt. Dore 1886
Clermont-Ferrand
St-Étienne
Lyon
Périgueux
Dordogne
Lot
Auvergne
Allier
Isère
Grenoble
Col du Mt. Cenis
Torino
Po
Bordeaux
Garonne
Cévennes
Rhône
Durance
Alessandria
Adour
Tarn
Nîmes
Bayonne
Biarritz
Pau
Toulouse
Montpellier
Avignon
Béziers
Sète
Narbonne
Golfe du Lion
Perpignan
C. Creus
Marseille
Cannes
MONACO
Menton
Nice
Toulon
Pyrenees
Pico de Aneto 3404
Andorra
C. Ortegal
La Coruña
El Ferrol
C. Finisterre
Pontevedra
Santiago
Vigo
Oviedo
Gijón
Picos de Europa
Santander
Bilbao
San Sebastián
Cordillera Cantábrica
León
Orense
Miño
Campos
Vitoria
Pamplona
Burgos
Ebro
Porto
Braga
Douro
Valladolid
Palencia
Duero
Salamanca
Ciudad Rodrigo
Coimbra
Sa. da Estrela
Sa. de Gata
Sa. de Guadarrama
Zaragoza
Lérida
MADRID
Tajo
Guadalajara
SPAIN
PORTUGAL
Tejo
Tôrres Vedras
Alcántara
Lisboa
Cáceres
Toledo
Cuenca
Teruel
Tortosa
Tarragona
Barcelona
Guadiana
Évora
Badajoz
La Mancha
Ciudad Real
Júcar
Albacete
Castellón
Valencia
Sierra Morena
Linares
Córdoba
Segura
Huelva
Faro
Tinto
Sevilla
Guadalquivir
Jaén
Genil
Granada
Murcia
Lorca
Alicante
C. Nao
Cádiz
Jérez
Mulhacén
Sa. Nevada 3478
Cartagena
C. Trafalgar
Str. of Gibraltar
Algeciras
Gibraltar (Br.)
Málaga
Almería
C. de Gata
Tanger
Ceuta (Sp.)
Tétouan
Larache
Alborán (Sp.)
Islas Baleares
Ibiza
Formentera
Palma
Mallorca (Majorca)
Cabrera
Menorca (Minorca)
Mahón
2850
2887
MEDITERRANEAN
Como
Milano
Bergamo
Brescia
Adda
Trento
Udine
Gorizia
Isonzo
Trieste
Rijeka
Ljubljana
Klagenfurt
Drava
L. di Garda
Vicenza
Verona
Novara
Pavia
Pádova
Venézia
G. di Venézia
Pula
Parma
Réggio
Módena
Ferrara
Génova
Golfo di Génova
Ravenna
Forlì
Bologna
La Spezia
Pisa
Firenze
Arno
Livorno
Rimini
SAN MARINO
Arezzo
Ancona
Siena
Perúgia
Ligurian Sea
C. Corse
Elba
Bastia
Mt Cinto 2710
Corse (Corsica)
Ajaccio
Gran Sasso 2914
Mt. Sabini
Civitavécchia
Tevere
ROMA
Bouches de Bonifacio
Caprera
Sássari
Ólbia
Gaeta
Volturno
Nápoli
Capri
Salerno
Sardegna (Sardinia)
Mt. del Gennargentu 1834
3719
Tyrrhenian Sea
Cágliari
Isole Eólie (Æolian Is.)
Palermo
Trápani
Ísole Egadi
Marsala
Sicilia
Agrigento
Caltanissetta
Alger
Mostaganem
Oran
Chellif
Ech Cheliff
Béjaïa
Skikda
Annaba
Binzert
Constantine
Tunis
Carthage
C. Bon
Pantelleria (It.)
Melilla (Sp.)
Ghazaouet
Sidi Bel Abbès
Tlemcen
Ouezzane
Rabat
Meknès
Fès
Oujda
Moulouya
MOROCCO
Plateaux
Hauts
Chott el Hodna
Djelfa
Saharien
Chott ech Chergui
G. de Hammamet
Sousse
Kairouan
Tébessa
Gozo
Valletta
MALTA
Lampedusa (It.)
Biskra
Chott Melrhir
Sfax
Îles Kerkenna
3737
Haut Atlas
Atlas
ALGERIA
O. Djedi
Aïn Sefra
Touggourt
Tozeur
Gabès
Djerba
Figuig
Béchar
Chott Djerid
TUNISIA
Ghardaïa
Ouargla
Hassi Messaoud
Ft. Lallemand
Beni Abbès
El Goléa
Tarābulus
Jabal Nafūsah
Mizdah
Al Khums
35
40
45
30
10
5
0
m
4000
2000
1000
400
200
0
200
1000
2000
3000
m

Projection: Conical with two standard parallels.

West from Greenwich 0 East from Greenwich

1:10 000 000

100 0 100 200 300 400 km

POLAND
Poznań
Płock
Warszawa
Wisła (Vistula)
Łódź
Pinsk
Brest
Polesye
Chernigov
Desna
Konotop
Sumy
Belgorod
Nezhin
Kharkov
Volgograd
Radom
Lublin
Kielce
Wrocław
Legnica
Lutsk
Rovno
Styr
Goryn
Pripyat
Bug
Kiyev
Dnepr
Pereyaslav-Khmelnitskiy
Zhitomir
Belaya Tserkov
Poltava
Kremenchug
(Dnieper)
Slavyansk
Artemovsk
Donets
Voroshilovgrad (Lugansk)
Kamensk-Shakhtinskiy
Tsimlyanskoye Vdkhr.
Chorzów
Kraków
Tarnów
Przemyśl
Lvov
Berdichev
Vinnitsa
Cherkassy
Pavlograd
Gorlovka
Makeyevka
Shakhty
Don
Novocherkassk
Ostrava
Jablunkov
Těšín
CZECHOSLOVAKIA
Tatry
2655
Slavkov
Kamenets-Podol'skiy
Uman
Kirovograd
Dneprodzerzhinsk
Dnepropetrovsk
Donetsk
Rostov
Manych
Mogilev-Podolskiy
Krivoy Rog
Zaporozhye
Taganrog
Azov
Oz. Manych Gudilo
Kolomyya
Prut
Balta
Pervomaysk
Zhdanov (Mariupol)
Yeisk
Váh
Hron
Košice
Banská Štiavnica
Chernovtsy
Beltsy
MOLDAVIAN S.S.R.
Voznesensk
Nikolayev
Melitopol
Berdyansk
Tikhoretsk
Stavropol
Bratislava
Miskolc
Tokaj
Tisza
Botoşani
Pietrosul 2305
Iaşi
Kishinev
Tiraspol
Bendery
Kherson
Perekop
Sea of Azov
Kerch
Krasnodar
Armavir
Budapest
HUNGARY
Debrecen
Pietrosul 2102
Siret
Odessa
Belgorod-Dnestrovskiy
Karkinitskiy Zaliv
Krymskaya (Crimea)
Feodosiya
Kuban
Maykop
Raab
Kecskemét
Oradea
Körös
Cluj-Napoca
ROMANIA
Balaton
Hódmezővásárhely
Szeged
Arad
Mureş
Braşov (Oraşul Stalin)
Galaţi
Ismail
M. Tarkhankut
Yevpatoriya
Simferopol
1545
Novorossiysk
Tuapse
Pécs
Sibiu
Negoiu 2535
Brăila
Sulina
Sevastopol
Balaklava
Yalta
Zagreb
Drava
Subotica
Sombor
Timişoara
Carpaţii Meridionali
Sukhumi
Novi Sad
Petrovaradin
Porţile de Fier
Ploieşti
Dobruja
Poti
Brod
Sava
Beograd
Turnu-Severin
Piteşti
Constanţa
BLACK SEA
Banja Luka
Bucureşti
Silistra
Batumi
Smederevo
Orşova
Craiova
Tolbukhin
2211
BOSNA
Kragujevac
Dunărea (Danube)
Ruse
Ince Burnu
Sinop
Trabzon
Rize
Sarajevo
Bosna
Drina
SRBIJA
Vidin
Morava
Niš
Pleven
Iskur
Stara Planina
Târnovo
Shipchenski Pr.
Sliven
Varna
Inebolu
Samsun
Giresun
Tirebolu
Kuzey Anadolu Dağlari
Sebin Karahisar
Dalmacija
Mostar
Novi Pazar
Durmitor 2522
Sofiya
BULGARIA
Burgas
Zonguldak
Kastamonu
2565
Amasya
Tokat
Erzincan
Lastovo
Dubrovnik (Ragusa)
CRNA GORA
Kotor
Cetinje
Musala 2925
Maritsa
Plovdiv
Edirne
İstanbul
Karadeniz Boğazi (Bosporus)
Ereğli
Çankiri
Çorum
Sivas
Shkodër
Skopje
2764
Šar Pl.
Vardar
Rhodopi Planina
Üsküdar
İzmit
Bolu
Kizil Irmak
Yozgat
Fırat
Gargano
Barletta
Bari
Tirana
Durrës
Elbasan
ALBANIA
Strumica
Sérrai
Kaválla
Tekirdağ
Marmara Denizi
İznik Gölü
Beypazari
Ankara
TURKEY
Keban
Bitola
Alexandroúpolis
Enez
Bursa
Bilecik
Sakarya
Gürün
Malatya
Brindisi
Thessaloníki
Gelibolu (Gallipoli)
Bandirma
Eskişehir
Sivrihisar
Kirşehir
Kayseri
Táranto
Vlorë
Aliákmon
Óros Olimbos 2917
Áthos 2033
Gökçeada
Çanakkale Boğazi
Çanakkale
Troy
Balikesir
Kütahya
Tuz Gölü
Erciyas Daği 3770
Golfo di Táranto
Str. of Otranto
Límnos
Afyon Karahisar
Bolvadin
Aksaray
Niğde
Maraş
Gaziantep
C. Sta. Maria di Leuca
Kérkira
Nótia Píndhos
Lárisa
Vólos
Voríai Sporádhes
Aegean Sea
Lésvos
Ayvalik
Eğridir Gölü
Beyşehir Gölü
Konya
Seyhan
Osmaniye
La Sila 1929
GREECE
Évvoia
Khíos
Manisa
Turgutlu
İzmir
Alaşehir
Büyük Menderes
Eğridir
Isparta
Karaman
Toros Dağlari
Tarsus
Adana
İskenderun
Halab
Ionian Sea
Levkás
Návpaktos
Thívai
Sámos
Aydin
Denizli
Burdur
Mersin
İskenderun Körfezi
Kefallinía
Korinthiakós Kólpos
Athínai
Piraiévs
Ikaría
Muğla
Antalya
Silifke
Antakya
SYRIA
Réggio
Pátrai
Kórinthos
Kikládhes
Náxos
Dhodhekánisos
Elmali
3086
Antalya Körfezi
Al Ladhiqiyah
Ḥamā'
C. Spartivento
Zákinthos
Olympia
Návplion
Sífros
Pelopónnisos
Spárti
Íos
Ródhos
Baniyas
Str. di Messina
Kalamata
Pílos
Mílos
Thíra
Ródhos
4486
Megiste (Kastellórizo)
Levkosia (Nicosia)
Morfou
Ammókhostos (Famagusta)
Larnax
Homs
Tarabulus
5121
Ákra Taínaron
Kíthira
Kárpathos
CYPRUS
Troodhos 1951
Lemesós
LEBANON
3083
Dimashq (Damascus)
Andikíthira
Khaniá
Ídhi Oros 2456
Iráklion
Kríti
Bayrût (Beirut)
Şayda
Zahle
Jabal ash Sheikh 2814
Jabal ad Durūz
4135
MEDITERRANEAN SEA
Akko
Haifa
Bosra
ISRAEL
Jordan
Tel Aviv-Yafo
Jerusalem
'Ammān
JORDAN
Gaza
Bahr el Miyet
Karak
3174
Cyrene
Derna
Al Marj (Barce)
Khalij Bómba
Rashid
Bahra el Burullus
Dumyât
Bûr Saîd
El 'Arîsh
Petra
Ma'ān
Banghāzī
Tobruq
Khalîg el Salûm
El Iskandarîya
El Maḥalla el Kubra
Tanta
Suez Canal
El Qantara
Ismâ 'iliya
Buheirat Murrat-el-Kubra
Gebel el Tîh
Elat
Al 'Aqabah
Khalīj Surt
Salûm
Matrûḥ
El 'Alamein
EL QÂHIRA
El Suweis
Barqa
EGYPT
Khalîg es Suweis
Es Sînâ'
2637
Khalīj al 'Aqaba
LIBYA
El Faiyûm
Nile
Beni Suêf

- - - - - - Division between Greeks and Turks in Cyprus; Turks to the north.

SWITZERLAND
FRANCE
LIGURIAN SEA
Golfo di Génova
CORSE
(CORSICA)
ILES D'HYERES
Côte d'Azur
MILANO
(Milan)
TORINO
(Turin)
GENOVA
(Genoa)
MARSEILLE
(Marseilles)
Lyon
(Lyons)
Genève
(GENEVA)
Lausanne
Bern
(BERNE)
Luzern
Zürich-see
Neuchâtel
Fribourg
Grenoble
Avignon
Aix-en-Provence
Toulon
Nice
MONACO
Cannes
Ajaccio
Bastia
Livorno
(Leghorn)
Pisa
Lucca
La Spezia
Parma
Piacenza
Cremona
Brescia
Bergamo
Como
Novara
Pavia
Alessandria
Asti
Cúneo
Savona
San Remo
Imperia
Elba
Capraia
Montecristo
Lac Léman
(L. de Genève)
Lago Maggiore
L. di Como
L. di Lugano
Lac d'Annecy
Lac du Bourget
VALAIS
TICINO
GRAUBÜNDEN
PIEMONTE
LOMBARDIA
SAVOIE
HAUTE-SAVOIE
VAUCLUSE
BOUCHES-DU-RHÔNE
ALPES-DE-HAUTE-PROVENCE
ALPES-MARITIMES
HAUTE-CORSE
CORSE-DU-SUD
LIECHTENSTEIN
VORARLBERG
Arcipelago Toscano
Rhône
Durance
Po
Isère
2650
4000
3000
2000
1500
1000
400
200
0
200
2000
m

Projection: Conical with two standard parallels

East from Greenwich

1:2 500 000

10 0 10 20 30 40 50 60 70 80 90 100 km

Innsbruck
Hohe Tauern
Niedere Tauern
Graz
Klagenfurt
Villach
Wörther See
Karnische Alpen
Karawanken
Bolzano
Dolomiti
Marmolada
3342
Belluno
FRIULI
VENEZIA GIULIA
Udine
Pordenone
Vittorio Veneto
Treviso
Bassano
Vicenza
Pádova
Mestre
Venézia (Venice)
Golfo di Venézia
Chióggia
Rovigo
Ferrara
Foci del Po
Porto Tolle
Valli di Comácchio
Ravenna
Faenza
Forlì
Imola
Lugo
Cesena
Rímini
SAN MARINO
Pésaro
Fano
Senigállia
Ancona
Ósimo
Macerata
Civitanova
Fermo
MARCHE
Urbino
Gubbio
Perúgia
Assisi
L. Trasimeno
Foligno
Spoleto
UMBRIA
Terni
Rieti
L'Aquila
ABRUZZI
Gran Sasso d'Italia
Pescara
Chieti
Ortona
Vasto
Térmoli
Viterbo
L. di Bolsena
L. di Vico
L. di Bracciano
Civitavécchia
ROMA (ROME)
Tívoli
Avezzano
Sulmona
MOLISE
Tremiti
Pianosa
Palagruža
Vieste
Monte Sant'Ángelo
S. Marco
L. di Lésina
L. di Varano
A D R I A T I C S E A
Trieste
G. di Trieste
Gorízia
Monfalcone
Koper
Piran
Poreč
Rovinj
Pula
Brionski (Brijuni)
Rt. Kamenjak
Kvarner
Kvarnerić
Cres
Krk
Rab
Lošinj
Pag
Rijeka (Fiume)
Ljubljana
Kranj
Bled
Triglav
2863
Celje
Maribor
Ptuj
Murska Sobota
Zagreb
Karlovac
Sisak
Velika Kapela
Mala Kapela
Velebit Planina
Gospić
Zadar
Dugi Otok
Kornat
Šibenik
Split
Trogir
Brač
Hvar
Vis
Korčula
Lastovo
Mljet
Pelješac
Dinara Planina
Bihać
Banja Luka
BOSNA
HERCEGOVINA
Bjelovar
Varaždin
Koprivnica
Nagykanizsa
Zalaegerszeg
Keszthely
Balaton
Bakony Hegység
Szombathely
HUNGARY
Drava
Sava
Kupa
Una
Y U G O S L A V I A
A U S T R I A
I T A L Y

FOR CONTINUATION SEE PAGE 66

Iles Sanguinaires
G. d'Ajaccio
C. di Muro
CORSE
G. de Valinco
Propriano
Sartène
Porto-Vecchio
CORSICA
CORSE-DU-SUD
Iles Cerbicales
Solenzara
Favone
Zonza
Levie
Bonifacio
I. de Cavallo
Bouches de Bonifacio
Santa Teresa Gallura
Maddalena
La Maddalena
Caprera
Punta dello Scorno
Asinara
Golfo dell' Asinara
Costa Smeralda
Coghinas
Aggius
Calangianus
Tempio Pausania
Golfo Aranci
G. di Ólbia
Tavolara
Porto Torres
Sorso
Sennori
Ósilo
Sássari
C. dell'Argentiera
M. Limbara
Ólbia
L. di Coghinas
Oschiri
Ozieri
Tanaunella
Posada
Ittiri
Alghero
Pattada
Budduso
Siniscola
Villanova Monteleone
1259
Bonorva
Bitti
C. Comino
Orune
Bosa
Nùoro
Temo
Oliena
Dorgali
Macomer
Golfo di Orosei
SARDEGNA
Ghilarza
L. del Tirso
Fonni
C. Mannu
Sorgono
Monti del Gennargentu
1834
Baunei
C. di Monte Santu
Cabras
Oristano
Arbatax
Laconi
Lanusei
Golfo di Oristano
M. Arci
812
Arborea
Terralba
Jerzu
Nurri
S. Gavino Monreale
Sanluri
Mandas
Flumendosa
SARDINIA
Gúspini
Arbus
C. Pécora
Gonnosfanadiga
Senorbì
1236
Villacidro
S. Vito
Villaputzu
Fluminimaggiore
M. Linas
Serramanna
Muravera
Iglesias
Cixerri
Dolianova
Assemini
Sestu
Pta. Serpeddì
1069
Portoscuso
Gonnesa
Siliqua
Sinnai
C. Ferrato
Carloforte
Carbonia
Selargius
Quartu Sant'Elena
San Pietro
1116
Santadi
Cagliari
Golfo di Cágliari
Sant'Antioco
Serpentara
C. Carbonara
Sant' Antíoco
Porto Botte
Pula
Teulada
G. di Pálmas
C. Spartivento
Vatican City
ROMA
(Rome)
Tivoli
Subiaco
Fregene
Palestrina
Valmontone
Lido di Ostia (Lido di Roma)
Tevere (Tiber)
Frosinone
Velletri
Alatri
Véroli
Sora
Prática di Mare
Albano Laziale
Aprília
Cori
Ferentino
Cisterna di Latina
Frosinone
Ceccano
Latina
Sezze
Priverno
Anzio
Nettuno
Sonnino
Fondi
Pontínia
1533
Sabáudia
Terracina
Fórmia
Monte Circeo
541
Gaeta
Golfo di Gaeta
Zannone
Palmarola
Ponza
Ísole Ponziane
283
Ventotene
TYRRHENIAN
SEA
3719
3589
Ustica
C. San Vito
PALERMO
Bagheria
Trápani
Érice
1110
Levanzo
Maréttimo
Ísole Ègadi
Favignana
Alcamo
Calatafimi
Salemi
Stagnone
Marsala
Corleone
1613
Castelvetrano
Partanna
Mazara del Vallo
Menfi
Sciacca
Belice
Campobello di Mazara
Ribera
Platani
Cattólica Eraclea
Siculiana
Porto Empédocle
Agrigento
Favara
Sicilian Channel
Iles de la Galite
C. Serrat
C. Blanc
Cani
Bizerte (Binzert)
Menzel-Bourguiba
Plane
Zembra
Mateur
Golfe de Tunis
C. Bon
El Kala
Tabarka
ALGERIA
Tébourba
TUNIS
Halq el Oued
Kelibia
Menzel-Temime
Bou Salem
Béja
Medjerda
Soliman
TUNISIA
Téboursouk
Nabeul
Zaghouan
Hammamet
Pantelleria
Pantelleria (It.)
836
1319
MEDITE
Projection: Conical with two standard parallels
East from Greenwich
m
3000
2000
1500
1000
400
200
37
0
200
2000
4000
m

1:2 500 000

10 0 10 20 30 40 50 60 70 80 90 100 km

A D R I A T I C
S E A
I O N I A N
S E A
R A N E A N S E A
Strait of Otranto
G. di Manfredónia
Golfo di Táranto
G. di Salerno
G. di Policastro
Golfo di Sant'Eufémia
Golfo di Squillace
G. di Gióia
Golfo di Catánia
Isole Eólie o Lípari (Æolian Is.)
Strómboli
Salina
Lípari
Vulcano
Filicudi
Alicudi
Panarea
BASILICATA
CALABRIA
Monti Nebrodi
Etna
3340
Monte Sant'Ángelo
Foggia
Barletta
Trani
Bisceglie
Molfetta
Bari
Monopoli
Brindisi
Lecce
Otranto
C. d'Otranto
Gallipoli
C. Santa Maria di Leuca
Táranto
Matera
Potenza
Salerno
Benevento
Avellino
Campobasso
Cerignola
Manfredónia
Altamura
Gravina
Grottáglie
Mandúria
Nardò
Galatina
Cosenza
Crotone
Catanzaro
Vibo Valéntia
Réggio
Messina
Str. di Messina
Milazzo
Taormina
Catánia
Acireale
Augusta
Siracusa
Noto
Ragusa
Módica
Vittória
Cómiso
Caltagirone
Piazza Armerina
Enna
Pachino
C. Passero
C. Spartivento
C. delle Colonne
C. Rizzuto
Capo Vaticano
Pta. dell'Alice
Sinni
Bradano
Basento
Agri
Crati
Neto
Sele
Ófanto
Kérkira (Corfu)
Kérkira
Durrësi (Durazzo)
Tirana
Vlora
Berati
Fieri
Shkumbini
Drini
Laguna e Nartës
Karaburuni
Otthonoi
Erikoúsa
Samothráki
Gastoúri
Levkímmi
3065
4116

HUNGARY
YUGOSLAVIA
ALBANIA
ADRIATIC SEA
CRNA GORA (MONTENEGRO)
BOSNA
HERCEGOVINA
SRBIJA
MAKEDONIJA
DALMACIJA
Autonomna Pokrajina Vojvodina
Socijalisticka Autonomna Pokrajina Kosovo
TOLNA
SOMOGY
BARANYA
CSONGRÁD
BIHOR
ARAD
TIMIŞ
CARAŞ SEVERIN
Nagykanizsa
Kaposvár
Szekszárd
Pécs
Mohács
Baja
Kiskunhalas
Kiskunmajsa
Hódmezővásárhely
Szeged
Makó
Orosháza
Gyula
Arad
Timişoara
Lugoj
Hunedoara
Caransebeş
Reşiţa
Subotica
Sombor
Novi Sad
Zrenjanin
Kikinda
Vršac
Pančevo
Beograd (Belgrade)
Zemun
Smederevo
Požarevac
Kragujevac
Čačak
Kruševac
Niš
Leskovac
Priština
Prizren
Skopje
Kumanovo
Tetovo
Prilep
Bitola
Ohrid
Ohridsko Jezero (L. Ohrid)
Prespansko Jezero (L. Prespa)
Titograd
Nikšić
Kotor
Dubrovnik
Mostar
Sarajevo
Zenica
Tuzla
Banja Luka
Osijek
Vukovar
Vinkovci
Slavonski Brod
Tirana
Durrësi (Durazzo)
Shkodra
Skadarsko Jezero
Elbasani
Vidin
Drava
Sava
Dunav (Danube)
Tisa
Morava
Drina
Bosna
Neretva
Vardar
Dinara
Prokletije
Korab
Šar Planina
Kopaonik
Fruška Gora
Durmitor 2522
Korčula
Hvar
Lastovo
Mljet
Projection: Conical with two standard parallels
East from Greenwich
19
20
22
46
45
44
43
42
41
m
3000
2000
1500
1000
400
200
0
200
2000
m

1:2 500 000

10 0 10 20 30 40 50 60 70 80 90 100 km

U. S. S. R.
UKRAINIAN S.S.R.
BULGARIA
TURKEY
BLACK SEA
VALAHIA (WALACHIA)
DOBROGEA
MUREŞ
HARGHITA
BACĂU
VASLUI
COVASNA
VRANCEA
SIBIU
BRAŞOV
IZMAIL
BRĂILA
BUZĂU
PRAHOVA
DÎMBOVIŢA
VÎLCEA
ARGEŞ
IALOMIŢA
CĂLĂRAŞI
GIURGIU
TELEORMAN
OLT
DOLJ
TULCEA
CONSTANŢA
KIRKLARELI
ISTANBUL
TEKIRDAĞ
Munţii Făgăraş
Munţii Ciuc
Munţii Vrancei
Stara Planina (Balkan)
Sredna Gora
Rodopi
Sredni Rodopi
Iztochni Rodopi
Istranca Dağları
Karadeniz Boğazı (Bosporus)
Dunărea (Danube)
Dunay (Danube)
Lacul Razelm
Burgaski Zaliv
BUCUREŞTI (Bucharest)
Ploieşti
Piteşti
Craiova
Braşov
Sibiu
Bacău
Galaţi
Brăila
Buzău
Tulcea
Constanţa
Ruse (Ruschuk)
Giurgiu
Sofiya (Sofia)
Plovdiv
Stara Zagora
Burgas
Varna
Pleven
Tolbukhin (Dobrich Bazargic)
Edirne (Adrianople)
İSTANBUL
Üsküdar

BULGARIA
YUGOSLAVIA
ALBANIA
Sofiya
Plovdiv
Stara Zagora
Pleven
Vratsa
Lovech
Sliven
Yambol
Khaskovo
Pernik
Edirne
Çanakkale
Saros Körfezi
Samothráki
Límnos
Thásos
Kavála
Thessaloníki (Salonica)
Thermaïkós Kólpos
Lárisa
Vólos
Skopje
Kumanovo
Prilep
Bitola
Ohrid
Priština
Niš
Leskovac
Prizren
Titograd (Podgorica)
Shkodra
Tirana (Tiranë)
Durrësi (Durazzo)
Vlora (Valona)
Korça
Berati
Kérkira (Corfu)
Ioánnina

SEA OF CRETE
(Sea of Candia)
IONIAN SEA
AEGEAN SEA
KIKLÁDHES
(CYCLADES)
ARKHIPÉLAGOS
ATTIKI KAI
PELOPÓNNISOS KAI DHITIKÍ IPROTIKÍ ÉLLAS
DHODEKÁNISOS
(DODECANESE)
TURKEY
MUĞLA
AYDIN
ATHÍNAI
(ATHENS)
Piraiévs
(Piræus)
Kallithéa
Kórinthos
(Corinth)
Corinth Canal
Pátrai
Lamía
Khalkís
(Chalcis)
Iráklion
(Candia)
Khaniá
(Canea)
Réthimnon
Kíthira
(Cerigo)
Náxos
Páros
Míkonos
Tínos
Ándros
Síros
Mílos
Thíra
Íos
Amorgós
Astipálaia
Ikaría
Khíos
(Chios)
Psará
Skíros
Skópelos
Kefallinía
(Cephalonia)
Zákinthos
(Zante)
Itháki
(Ithaca)
Levkás
(Santa Maura)
Sámos
Kos
Ródhos
(Rhodes)
Kárpathos
Kásos
Saronikós Kólpos
Argolikós Kólpos
Lakonikós Kólpos
Messiniakós Kólpos
Kiparissiakós Kólpos
Korinthiakós Kólpos
Pátraikós Kólpos
Kólpos Kisámou
Kólpos Khanion
Kólpos Mesaras
Kólpos Merabellou
Stenón Kárpathos
Stenón Kasos
Kerme Körfezi
Mandalya Körfezi
Kuşada Körfezi
Taïyetos Óros
Párnon Óros
Ókhi Óros
Ídhi Óros
5015
Continuation Eastwards on same scale
East from Greenwich
Projection: Conical with two standard parallels
COPYRIGHT GEORGE PHILIP & SON LTD.
1:2 500 000
10 0 10 20 30 40 50 60 70 80 90 100 km
m
3000
2000
1500
1000
400
200
0
200
2000

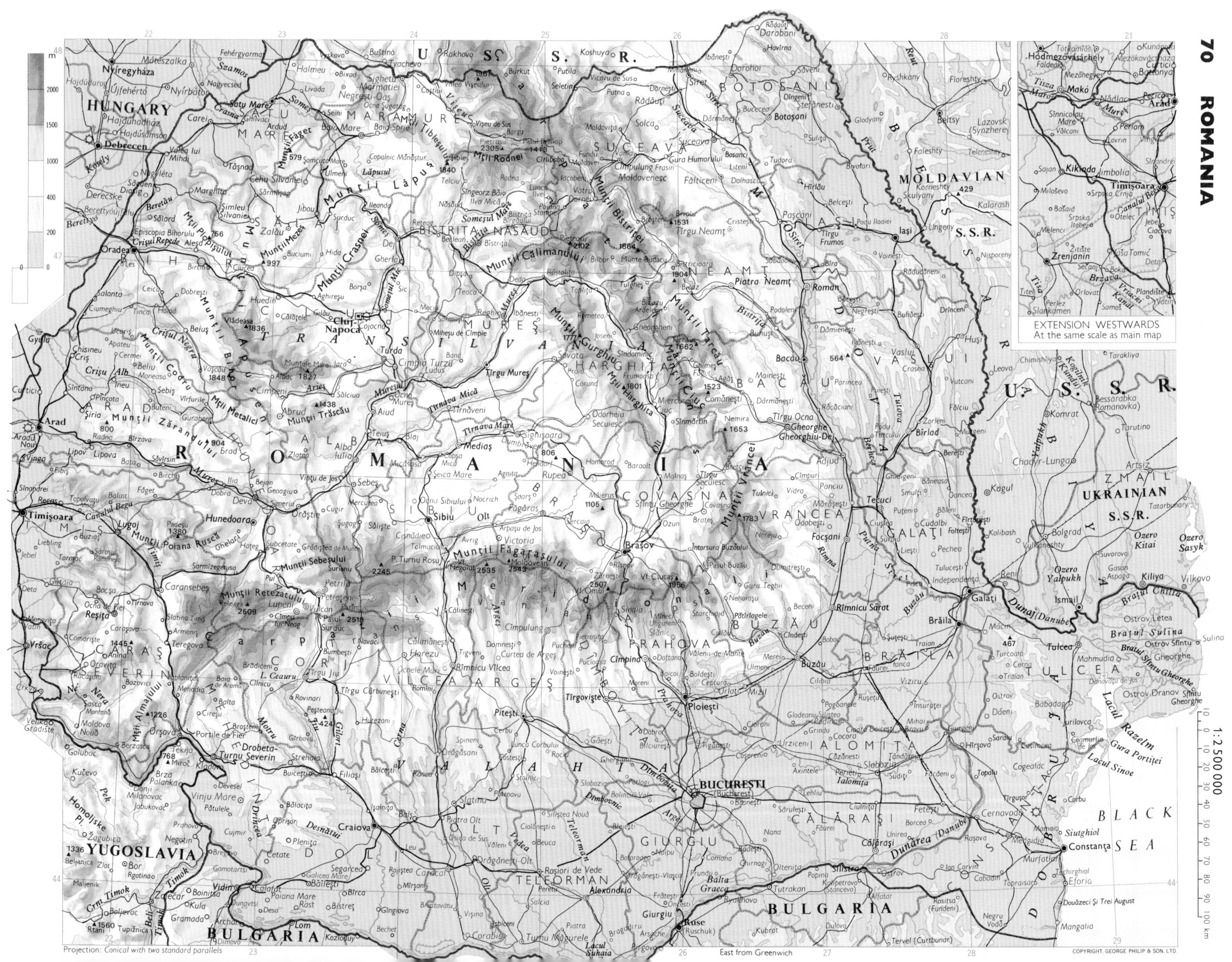
1:2 500 000
10 0 10 20 30 40 50 60 70 80 90 100 km
EXTENSION WESTWARDS
At the same scale as main map
COPYRIGHT, GEORGE PHILIP & SON, LTD.
Projection: Conical with two standard parallels
East from Greenwich
m
2000
1500
1000
400
200
0
ROMANIA
BUCUREŞTI
HUNGARY
YUGOSLAVIA
BULGARIA
MOLDAVIAN S.S.R.
UKRAINIAN S.S.R.
U. S. S. R.
BLACK SEA
Iaşi
Cluj-Napoca
Timişoara
Constanţa
Galaţi
Brăila
Braşov
Ploieşti
Craiova
Oradea
Arad
Sibiu
Bacău
Debrecen
Munţii Făgăraşului
Munţii Călimanului
Munţii Retezatului
Dunărea
Prut
Siret
Olt
Mureş

1:2 500 000

10 0 10 20 30 40 50 60 70 80 90 100 km

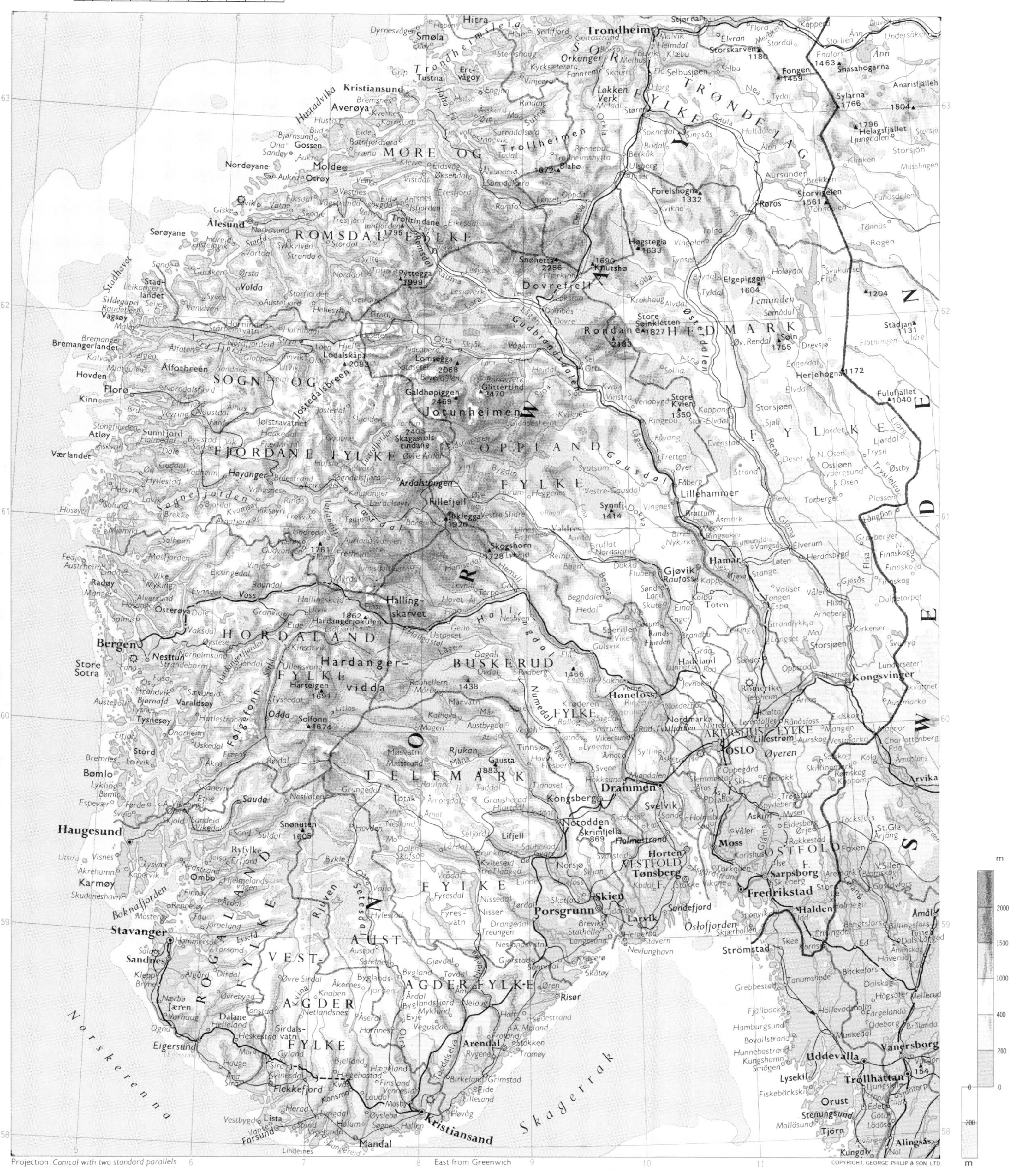

SØR TRØNDELAG
MØRE OG ROMSDAL FYLKE
SOGN OG FJORDANE FYLKE
HEDMARK FYLKE
OPPLAND FYLKE
HORDALAND FYLKE
BUSKERUD FYLKE
TELEMARK FYLKE
AKERSHUS FYLKE
ØSTFOLD
VESTFOLD
ROGALAND FYLKE
AUST-AGDER FYLKE
VEST-AGDER FYLKE
SWEDEN
Trondheim
Kristiansund
Molde
Ålesund
Bergen
Stavanger
Haugesund
Kristiansand
Mandal
Arendal
Skien
Porsgrunn
Larvik
Tønsberg
Horten
Drammen
Kongsberg
OSLO
Lillestrøm
Hamar
Lillehammer
Gjøvik
Røros
Moss
Fredrikstad
Sarpsborg
Halden
Kongsvinger
Elverum
Trondheimsleia
Trollheimen
Dovrefjell
Snøhetta 2286
Rondane
Jotunheimen
Galdhøpiggen 2469
Glittertind 2470
Jostedalsbreen
Hardangervidda
Hardangerjøkulen
Hallingskarvet
Sognefjorden
Gudbrandsdalen
Østerdalen
Femunden
Mjøsa
Øyeren
Oslofjorden
Skagerrak
Norskerenna
Stadlandet
Karmøy
Strömstad
Uddevalla
Trollhättan
Vänersborg
Arvika

Projection: Conical with two standard parallels

East from Greenwich

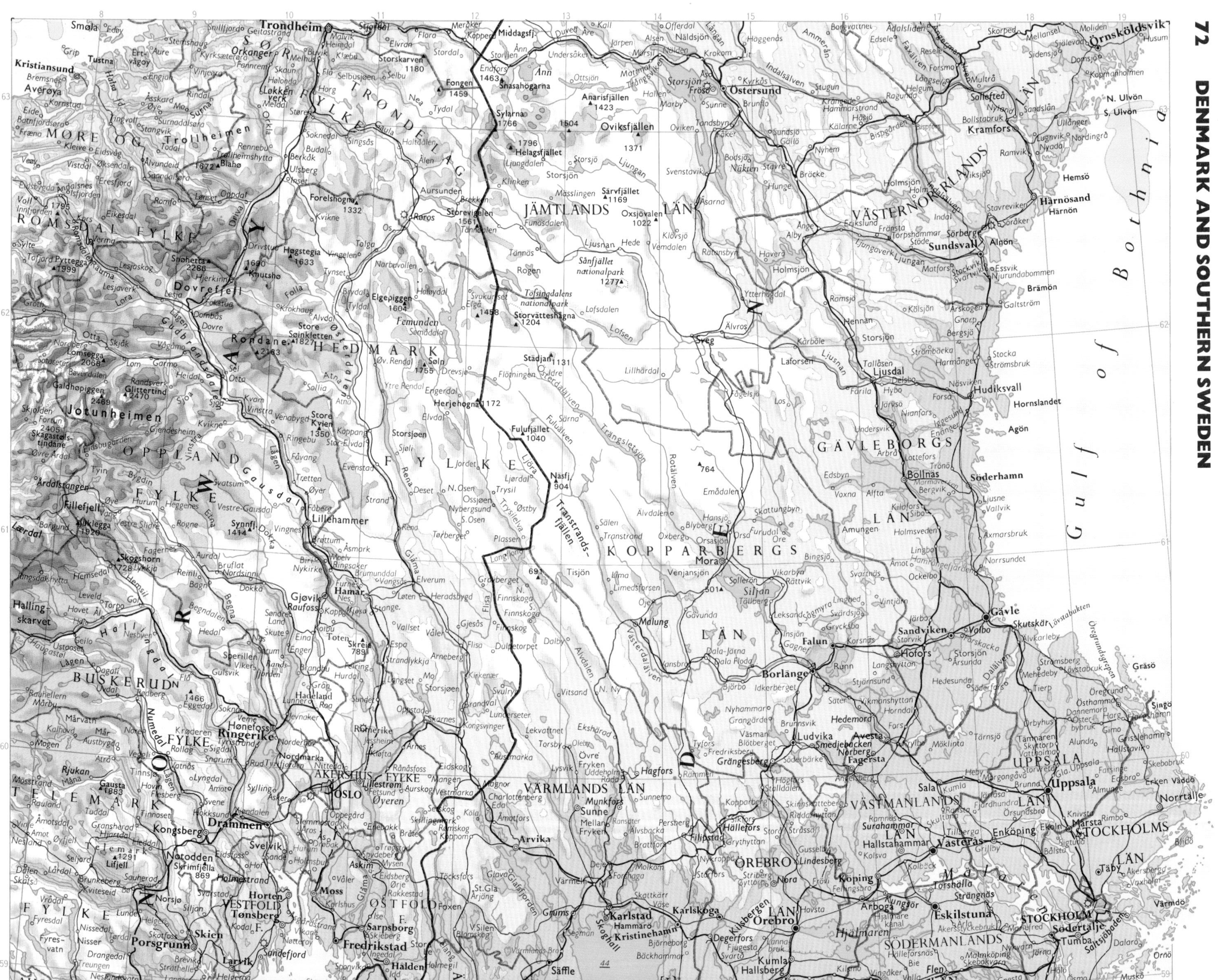

Gulf of Bothnia
VÄSTERNORRLANDS LÄN
JÄMTLANDS LÄN
GÄVLEBORGS LÄN
KOPPARBERGS LÄN
UPPSALA LÄN
STOCKHOLMS LÄN
VÄSTMANLANDS LÄN
SÖDERMANLANDS
ÖREBRO LÄN
VÄRMLANDS LÄN
SØR TRØNDELAG FYLKE
MØRE OG ROMSDAL FYLKE
HEDMARK FYLKE
OPPLAND FYLKE
BUSKERUD FYLKE
AKERSHUS FYLKE
ØSTFOLD
VESTFOLD
TELEMARK FYLKE
Örnsköldsvik
Härnösand
Kramfors
Sundsvall
Hudiksvall
Söderhamn
Bollnäs
Gävle
Sandviken
Falun
Borlänge
Mora
Östersund
Uppsala
Stockholm
Västerås
Eskilstuna
Örebro
Karlstad
Arvika
Trondheim
Kristiansund
Røros
Lillehammer
Hamar
Oslo
Drammen
Moss
Sarpsborg
Fredrikstad
Halden
Tønsberg
Skien
Porsgrunn
Kongsberg
Jotunheimen
Dovrefjell
Rondane

1:2 500 000

10 0 10 20 30 40 50 60 70 80 90 100 km

BALTIC SEA
Kattegat
Skagerrak
Norskerenna
Jammerbugt
GERMANY
POLAND
DENMARK
JYLLAND
SJÆLLAND
FYN
LOLLAND
FALSTER
KALMAR LÄN
JÖNKÖPINGS LÄN
KRONOBERGS LÄN
BLEKINGE LÄN
MALMÖHUS
KRISTIANSTADS
HALLANDS
SKARABORGS LÄN
ÖSTERGÖTLANDS
Bornholm
Gotland
Öland
Anholt
Læsø
Samsø
Møn
Fehmarn
Rügen
Göteborg
Malmö
København
Helsingborg
Helsingør
Ålborg
Århus
Odense
Esbjerg
Kiel
Flensburg
Jönköping
Linköping
Norrköping
Nyköping
Kalmar
Karlskrona
Visby
Trelleborg
Rønne
Słupsk
Lębork
Kristianstad
Halmstad
Växjö
Ystad
Lund
Roskilde
Randers
Viborg
Vejle
Kolding
Fredericia
Horsens
Herning
Holstebro
Skive
Frederikshavn
Hjørring
Skagen
Grenen
Nyborg
Svendborg
Nakskov
Næstved
Slagelse
Holbæk
Hillerød
Kalundborg
Rendsburg
Schleswig
Husum
Trollhättan
Uddevalla
Borås
Alingsås
Varberg
Falkenberg
Ängelholm
Landskrona
Eslöv
Hässleholm
Nybro
Västervik
Oskarshamn
Motala
Mjölby
Eksjö
Nässjö
Vetlanda
Ljungby
Värnamo
Mariestad
Skövde
Lidköping
Falköping
Vänersborg
Kungälv
Mölndal
Arendal
Tvedestrand
Store Bælt
Lille Bælt
Femer Bælt
Fehmarn Belt
Langelands Bælt
Kalmarsund
Limfjorden
Ålborg Bugt
Kieler Bucht
Hanöbukten
Bornholmsgattet
Fakse Bugt
Holmsland Klit
East from Greenwich
Projection: Conical with two standard parallels

m 2000 1500 1000 400 200 0 0 200 m

ICELAND
on the same scale as general map
West from Greenwich
Arctic Circle
Reykjavík
Keflavík
Akranes
Hafnarfjörður
Akureyri
Húsavík
Sauðárkrókur
Siglufjörður
Ísafjörður
Seyðisfjörður
Faxaflói
Breiðafjörður
Húnaflói
Vatnajökull
Langjökull
Hofsjökull
Mýrdalsjökull
Vestmannaeyjar
NORWEGIAN SEA
Lofoten
Vesterålen
Vestfjorden
Moskenstraumen
Narvik
Tromsø
Hammerfest
Nordkapp
Vadsø
Lopphavet
Kiruna
Gällivare
Luleå
Boden
Piteå
Skellefteå
Umeå
Örnsköldsvik
Härnösand
Kramfors
Sollefteå
Östersund
Trondheim
Steinkjer
Levanger
Namsos
Mosjøen
Mo
Bodø
Kristiansund
Molde
Ålesund
Oulu
Kemi
Tornio
Haparanda
Rovaniemi
Kokkola
Jakobstad
Vaasa
Kajaani
Iisalmi
Kuopio
Jyväskylä
NORRBOTTEN
VÄSTERBOTTEN
N.-TRONDELAG
SØR-TRONDELAG
Arctic Circle

1:5 000 000

50 0 50 100 150 200 km

Projection: Conical with two standard parallels
East from Greenwich
COPYRIGHT GEORGE PHILIP & SON, LTD.
B A L T I C   S E A
G U L F   O F   F I N L A N D
D E N M A R K
S W E D E N
N O R W A Y
P O L A N D
W E S T   G E R M A N Y
E A S T
E S T O N I A N   S.S.R.
L A T V I A
L I T H U A N I A N   S.S.R.
R.   S.   F.   S.   R.
U.   S.   S.   R.
Svealand
Götaland
Skagerrak
Kattegat
The Sound
Store Bælt
Lille Bælt
Rīgas Jūras Līcis (Gulf of Riga)
Zatoka Gdańska
Ålands hav
STOCKHOLM
OSLO
HELSINKI (Helsingfors)
KØBENHAVN (Copenhagen)
Tallinn
Riga
Göteborg
Malmö
Gdańsk
Gdynia
Szczecin (Stettin)
Hamburg
Bremen
Kiel
Lübeck
Rostock
Bergen
Stavanger
Kristiansand
Turku (Åbo)
Tampere
Uppsala
Norrköping
Linköping
Örebro
Västerås
Kalmar
Karlskrona
Visby
Gotland
Öland
Bornholm
Rønne
Hiiumaa (Dagö)
Saaremaa (Ösel)
Åland (Ahvenanmaa)
Mariehamn (Maarianhamina)
Vänern
Vättern
Sjælland
Fyn
Lolland
Falster
Århus
Ålborg
Odense
Esbjerg
Kaliningrad
Klaipėda
Liepaja
Ventspils
Jelgava
Kaunas
Vilnius
Grodno
Białystok
Bydgoszcz
Toruń
Elbląg
Groningen
Oldenburg
Wilhelmshaven
m
2000
1500
1000
400
200
0
200

R.S.F.S.R.
1. Daghestan A.S.S.R.
2. Kabardino-Balkar A.S.S.R.
3. Mari A.S.S.R.
4. Mordovian A.S.S.R.
5. North Ossetian A.S.S.R.
6. Tatar A.S.S.R.
7. Udmurt A.S.S.R.
8. Chuvash A.S.S.R.
9. Checheno-Ingush A.S.S.R.
AZERBAIJAN
10. Nakhichevan A.S.S.R.
GEORGIA
11. Abkhaz A.S.S.R.
12. Adzhar A.S.S.R.
m
4000
2000
1000
400
200
0
200
m
Projection: Conical Orthomorphic with two standard parallels
East from Greenwich

1:20 000 000
200 0 200 400 600 800 km
Mys Dezhneva (East C.)
St. Lawrence I. (U.S.A.)
Chukotskoye More
Ostrov Vrangelya
East Siberian Sea
Laptev Sea
OCEAN
Novosibirskiye Ostrova
Ostrova Delong
Ostrov Kotelnyy
Lyakhovskiye Ostrova
Proliv Dmitriya Lapteva
Ostrov Komsomolets
Ostrov Oktyabrskoy Revolyutsii
Ostrov Bolshevik
Severnaya Zemlya
Proliv Vilkitskogo
Poluostrov Taymyr
Gory Byrranga
Mys Arkticheskiy
Nordvik
Tiksi
Khatanga
Verkhoyansk
Verkhoyanskiy Khrebet
Khrebet Cherskogo
Srednekolymsk
Chukotskiy Khrebet
Koryakskiy Khrebet
Anadyrskiy Zaliv
Bering Sea
Poluostrov Kamchatka
Petropavlovsk-Kamchatskiy
Penzhinskaya Guba
Zaliv Shelikhova
Magadan
Okhotsk
Sea of Okhotsk
Arctic Circle
YAKUT A.S.S.R.
Yakutsk
Vilyuysk
Olekminsk
Aldan
Lena
SOCIALIST REPUBLIC
Stanovoy Khrebet
Dzhugdzhur
Sakhalin
Okha
Nikolayevsk-na-Amure
Komsomolsk
Khabarovsk
Sovetskaya Gavan
Yuzhno-Sakhalinsk
Khrebet Sikhote Alin
Vladivostok
Nakhodka
Kurilskiye Ostrova
Hokkaido
Sapporo
Hakodate
Sea of Japan
Honshū
Nii-gata
Kanazawa
To-yama
Krasnoyarsk
Bratsk
Kirensk
Nizhneudinsk
Angarsk
Irkutsk
Ulan Ude
Chita
Blagoveshchensk
Birobidzhan
Ozero Baykal
BURYAT A.S.S.R.
Yablonovyy Khrebet
Ulaanbaatar (Ulan Bator)
MONGOLIA
Hangayn Nuruu
Hentiyn Nuruu
Edrengiyn Nuruu
Tung Pei (Manchuria)
Haerhpin
Ch'angch'un
Shenyang (Mukden)
Fushun
Anshan
Lüta
Pei'p'ing
Changchiak'ou (Kalgan)
Paot'ou
Inner Mongolia
REPUBLIC
NORTH KOREA
P'yongyang
Sŏul
SOUTH KOREA
Pusan
Chongjin
Boundaries of U.S.S.R.
Boundaries of S.S.R.
Boundaries of A.S.S.R.
COPYRIGHT. GEORGE PHILIP & SON, LTD.

P-ov. Rybachiy
Murmansk
Kolguyev
M. Kanin Nos
P-ov. Kanin
Cheshskaya Guba
Ostrov Morzhovets
Malozemelskaya Tundra
Bolshezemelskaya Tundra
Timanskiy Kryazh
Arctic Circle
Vorkuta
Kolskiy Poluostrov
Kandalakshskiy Zaliv
Beloye More (White Sea)
Dvinskaya Guba
Onezhskaya Guba
Arkhangelsk (Archangel)
Lappland
Gulf of Bothnia
SWEDEN
NORWAY
FINLAND
KARELIAN A.S.S.R.
Ladozhskoye Ozero
Onezhskoye Ozero
Petrozavodsk
Helsinki
Stockholm
Tallinn
G. of Finland
LENINGRAD
ESTONIAN S.S.R.
LATVIAN S.S.R.
Riga
Rigas Juras Licis
LITHUANIAN S.S.R.
Kaunas
Vilnius
Kaliningrad (Königsberg)
BYELORUSSIAN S.S.R.
Minsk
(WHITE RUSSIA)
Polesye (Pripet-Marshes)
WARSZAWA (Warsaw)
POLAND
MOSKVA (Moscow)
Novgorod
Pskov
Smolensk
Vitebsk
Mogilev
Gomel
Bryansk
Tula
Kalinin
Yaroslavl
Rybinsk
Vologda
Kostroma
Ivanovo
Vladimir
Ryazan
GORKIY (Gorki)
Kazan
Cheboksary
Ulyanovsk
Penza
KUYBYSHEV
Syktyvkar
Kotlas
Kirov
Perm
Izhevsk
Ufa
SVERDLOVSK
Nizhniy Tagil
Zlatoust
Magnitogorsk
Orenburg
Severnyye Uvaly
Valdayskaya Vozvyshennost
RUSSIAN SOVIET FEDERATIVE SOCIALIST REPUBLIC
KOMI A.S.S.R.
UDMURT A.S.S.R.
MARI A.S.S.R.
CHUVASH
TATAR A.S.S.R.
MORDOVIAN A.S.S.R.
BASHKIR A.S.S.R.
Ural

1:10 000 000

100 0 100 200 300 400 km

1 Kabardino-Balkar A.S.S.R.
2 North Ossetian A.S.S.R.
3 Nakhichevan A.S.S.R. (Azer.)
4 Checheno-Ingush A.S.S.R.

Projection: Conical with two standard parallels

-------- Division between Greeks and Turks in Cyprus; Turks to the North.

East from Greenwich

m 4000 2000 1000 400 200 0

0 200 1000 2000 4000 m

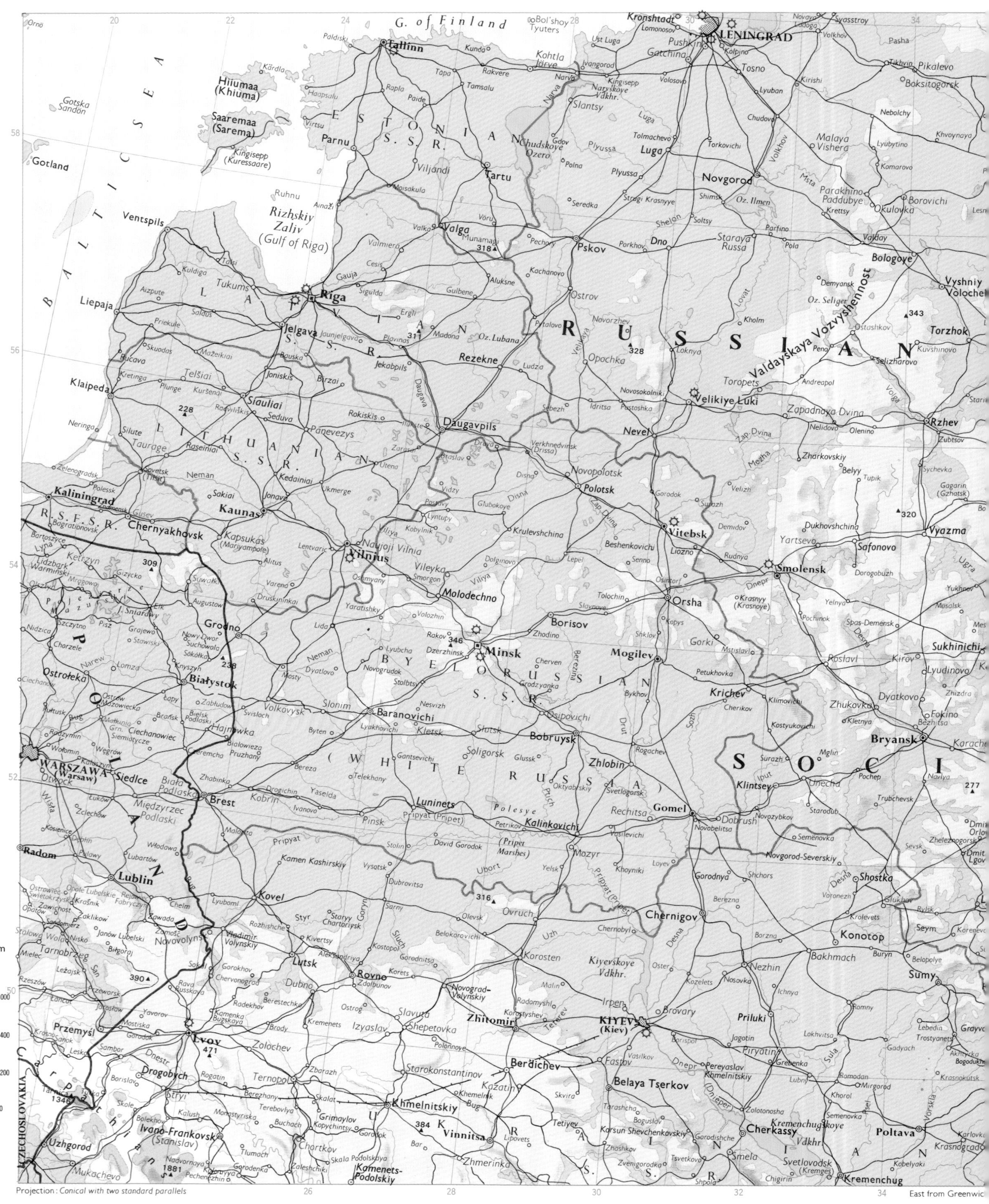

Projection: Conical with two standard parallels

East from Greenwich

1:5 000 000

50 0 50 100 150 200 km

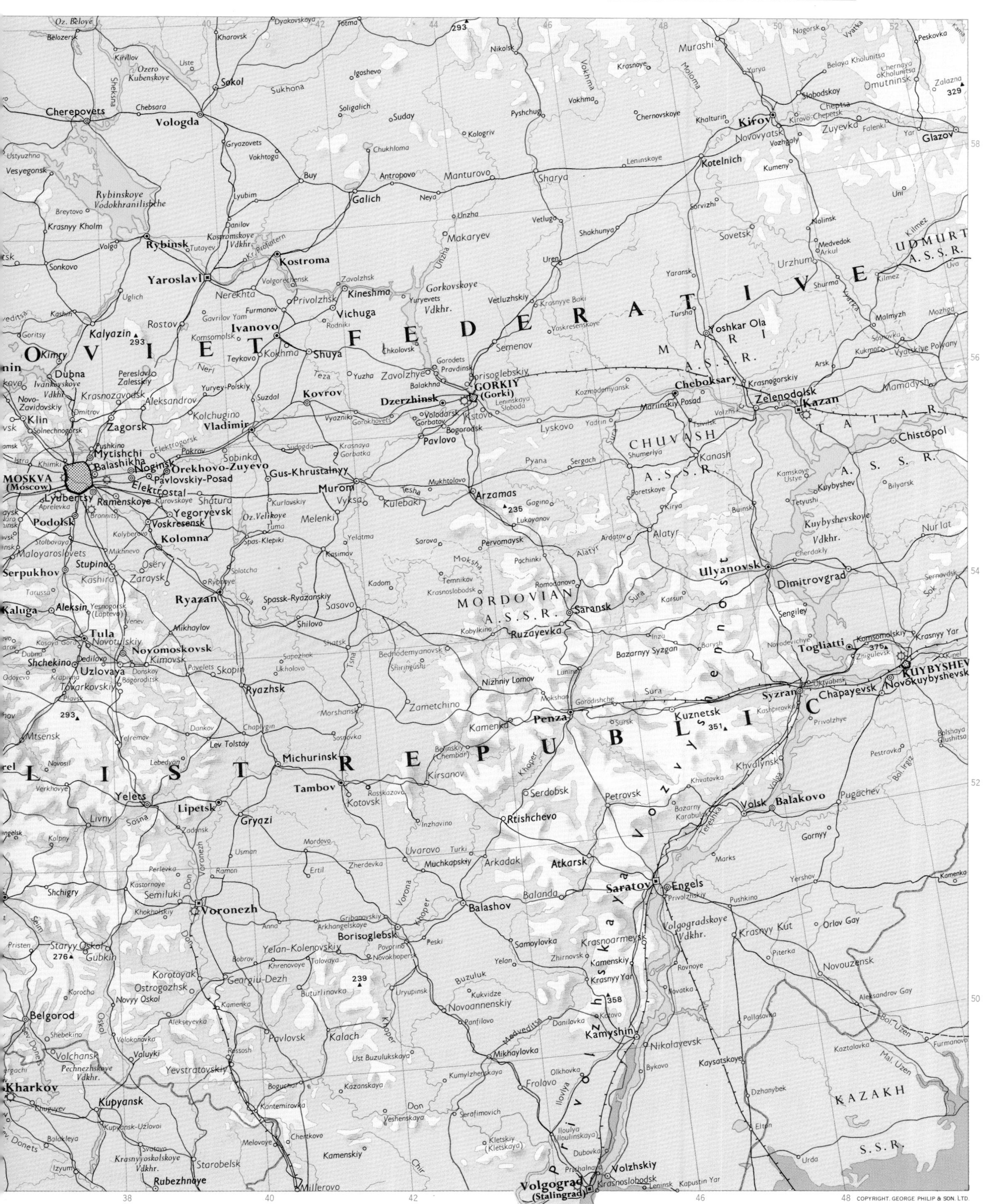

SOVIET FEDERATIVE SOCIALIST REPUBLIC
MARI A.S.S.R.
CHUVASH A.S.S.R.
TATAR A.S.S.R.
MORDOVIAN A.S.S.R.
UDMURT A.S.S.R.
KAZAKH S.S.R.
Privolzhskaya Vozvyshennost
MOSKVA (Moscow)
Cherepovets
Vologda
Sokol
Kharovsk
Belozersk
Kirillov
Ozero Kubenskoye
Sheksna
Sukhona
Totma
Dyakovskaya
Nikolsk
Igoshevo
Soligalich
Suday
Kologriv
Chukhloma
Gryazovets
Vokhtoga
Buy
Antropovo
Manturovo
Sharya
Galich
Neya
Rybinskoye Vodokhranilishche
Vesyegonsk
Ustyuzhna
Breytovo
Krasnyy Kholm
Rybinsk
Tutayev
Kostromskoye Vdkhr.
Danilov
Lyubim
Kostroma
Yaroslavl
Sonkovo
Uglich
Kashin
Kalyazin
293
Nerekhta
Volgorechensk
Zavolzhsk
Kineshma
Gorkovskoye Vdkhr.
Privolzhsk
Vichuga
Rodniki
Furmanov
Gavrilov Yam
Rostov
Ivanovo
Komsomolsk
Teykovo
Kokhma
Shuya
Kimry
Dubna
Pereslavl Zalesskiy
Yuryev-Polskiy
Aleksandrov
Kolchugino
Vladimir
Suzdal
Kovrov
Dzerzhinsk
GORKIY (Gorki)
Balakhna
Gorodets
Pravdinsk
Zavolzhye
Borisoglebskiy
Semenov
Chkolovsk
Vetluzhskiy
Krasnyye Baki
Voskresenskoye
Uren
Vetluga
Shakhunya
Unzha
Makaryev
Pyshchug
Vokhma
Krasnoye
Murashi
Moloma
Chernovskoye
Khalturin
Kirov
Novovyatsk
Kirovo-Chepetsk
Slobodskoy
Yurya
Nagorsk
Vyatka
Belaya Kholunitsa
Omutninsk
Zalazna 329
Peskovka
Kama
Zuyevka
Glazov
Falenki
Kotelnich
Leninskoye
Kumeny
Uni
Sovetsk
Nolinsk
Medvedok
Arkul
Urzhum
Kilmez
Uva
Yaransk
Shurma
Sorvizhi
Tursha
Yoshkar Ola
Malmyzh
Mozhga
Kukmor
Vyatskiye Polyany
Arsk
Mamadysh
Cheboksary
Kozmodemyansk
Marinskiy Posad
Krasnogorskiy
Zelenodolsk
Kazan
Volzhsk
Tsivilsk
Kanash
Shumerlya
Chistopol
Kamskoye Ustye
Kuybyshev
Bilyarsk
Tetyushi
Kuybyshevskoye Vdkhr.
Nurlat
Buinsk
Poretskoye
Kirya
Alatyr
Ardatov
Ulyanovsk
Dimitrovgrad
Cherdakly
Sengiley
Togliatti
Komsomolskiy
Zhigulevsk 375
Krasnyy Yar
KUYBYSHEV
Novokuybyshevsk
Chapayevsk
Syzran
Kuznetsk 351
Privolzhye
Khvalynsk
Balakovo
Volsk
Pugachev
Khvatovka
Bazarnyy Karabulak
Marks
Saratov
Engels
Privolzhskiy
Volgogradskoye Vdkhr.
Krasnyy Kut
Orlov Gay
Piterka
Novouzensk
Aleksandrov Gay
Pallasovka
Kaztalovka
Bolshoy Uzen
Malyy Uzen
Dzhanybek
Elton
Urda
Kapustin Yar
Leninsk
Volzhskiy
Krasnoslobodsk
Volgograd (Stalingrad)
Kamyshin
Nikolayevsk
Bykovo
Kaysatskoye
Krasnoarmeysk
Kamenskiy
Krasnyy Yar
358
Kotovo
Olkhovka
Frolovo
Ilovlya
Kletskiy (Kletskaya)
Dubovka
Mikhaylovka
Medveditsa
Danilovka
Serafimovich
Veshenskaya
Kamenskiy
Chir
Don
Millerovo
Kazanskaya
Kumylzhenskaya
Novoannenskiy
Panfilovo
Uryupinsk
Buzuluk
Kukvidze
Yelan
Samoylovka
Balashov
Balanda
Atkarsk
Arkadak
Rtishchevo
Serdobsk
Petrovsk
Penza
Kamenka
Belinskiy (Chembar)
Kirsanov
Khoper
Tambov
Rasskazovo
Kotovsk
Inzhavino
Uvarovo
Muchkapskiy
Zherdevka
Borisoglebsk
Povorino
Peski
Gribanovskiy
Arkhangelskoye
Anna
Bobrov
Talovaya
Buturlinovka
239
Kalach
Pavlovsk
Ust Buzulukskaya
Bogushar
Kantemirovka
Chertkovo
Melovoye
Starobelsk
Rubezhnoye
Kupyansk
Kharkov
Chuguyev
Balakleya
Izyum
Svatovo
Krasnyy Oskol
Valuyki
Volchansk
Pechenezhskoye Vdkhr.
Belgorod
Shebekino
Korocha
Novyy Oskol
Alekseyevka
Ostrogozhsk
Korotoyak
Georgiu-Dezh
Starvy Oskol 276
Gubkin
Voronezh
Semiluki
Kastornoye
Shchigry
Livny
Yelets
Lipetsk
Gryazi
Usman
Ertil
Mordovo
Michurinsk
Lev Tolstoy
Chaplygin
Dankov
Lebedyan
Ryazhsk
Skopin
Morshansk
Sosnovka
Zametchino
Nizhniy Lomov
Mokshan
Lunino
Sura
Ruzayevka
Saransk
Kovylkino
Insar
Krasnoslobodsk
Temnikov
Kadom
Sasovo
Shilovo
Spassk-Ryazanskiy
Ryazan
Rybnoye
Zaraysk
Kashira
Stupino
Serpukhov
Kolomna
Voskresensk
Yegoryevsk
Shatura
Kurlovskiy
Gus-Khrustalnyy
Murom
Vyksa
Kulebaki
Melenki
Arzamas 235
Lukoyanov
Pervomaysk
Sarova
Moksha
Pochinki
Romodanovo
Lyskovo
Pyana
Sergach
Vorsma
Pavlovo
Bogorodsk
Kstovo
Volodarsk
Gorbatov
Vyazniki
Gorokhovets
Sudogda
Pokrov
Sobinka
Orekhovo-Zuyevo
Noginsk
Pavlovskiy-Posad
Elektrostal
Balashikha
Mytishchi
Zagorsk
Pushkino
Lyubertsy
Ramenskoye
Bronnitsy
Podolsk
Klin
Solnechnogorsk
Dmitrov
Novo-Zavidovskiy
Konakovo
Ivankovskoye Vdkhr.
Maloyaroslavets
Kaluga
Aleksin
Tula
Novotulskiy
Shchekino
Novomoskovsk
Kimovsk
Uzlovaya
Bogoroditsk
Donskoy
Tovarkovskiy
Plavsk
Yefremov
Mtsensk
Novosil
Verkhovye
Efremov
Kaluga
Kashira
Oka
Tesha
Yeldtma
Sosna
Oskol
Voronezh
Don
Sura
Volga
Vorona
Tsna
Ural
Samara
Bol. Irgiz
Chernaya Kholunitsa
Cheptsa
Yadrin
Kirya
Inza
Barysh
Bazarnyy Syzgan
Gorodishche
Sursk
Karsun
Zhirnovsk
Rovnoye
Novyy Uzen
Tereshka
Gornyy
Yershov
Pushkino
Pestravka
Bolshaya Glushitsa
Furmanovo
Kamenka
Sernovodsk
Sok
38
40
42
44
46
48
50
52
50
52
54
56
58

Lvov
Rovno
Dubno
Zhitomir
Korosten
Kiyevskoye Vdkhr.
KIYEV (Kiev)
Nezhin
Bakhmach
Sumy
Belopolye
Starvy Oskol
Belgorod
Kharkov
Priluki
Romny
Poltava
Berdichev
Fastov
Belaya Tserkov
Khmelnitskiy
Ternopol
Ivano-Frankovsk (Stanislav)
Vinnitsa
Zhmerinka
Kremenchugskoye Vdkhr.
Cherkassy
Smela
Kremenchug
Kamenets-Podolskiy
Chernovtsy
Uman
Talnoye
Kirovograd
Dneprodzerzhinsk
Dneprodzerzhinskoye Vdkhr.
Dnepropetrovsk
Pavlograd
Slavyansk
Kramatorsk
Artemovsk
Konstantinovka
Gorlovka
Krasnoarmeisk
Makeyevka
Donetsk (Stalino)
Zaporozhye
Krivoy Rog
Nikopol
Pervomaysk
Beltsy
Kishinev
Tiraspol
Bendery
Odessa
Nikolayev
Kherson
Novaya Kakhovka
Kakhovskoye Vdkhr.
Melitopol
Zhdanov
Berdyansk
Izmail
Galati
Braila
Ploiesti
BUCURESTI (Bucharest)
Constanța
Brașov
Bacău
Iasi
ROMANIA
Ruse (Rusčuk)
Tolbukhin
Varna
Burgas
BULGARIA
Karkinitskiy Zaliv
Dzhankoi
Krymskiy P.-ov. (Crimea)
Yevpatoriya
Simferopol
Sevastopol
Yalta
Feodosiya
Kerch
Novorossiysk
AZOVSKOYE MORE (Sea of Azov)
BLACK SEA
Karadeniz Boğazi (Bosporus)
İstanbul
Üsküdar
MARMARA DENIZI (Sea of Marmara)
Edirne
Kirklareli
İzmit
Adapazari
Zonguldak
Kastamonu
Sinop
Samsun
Amasya
Tokat
Çorum
Bursa
Ankara
TURKEY

Projection: Conical with two standard parallels

Yelan-Kolenovskiy
Povorino
Peski
Samoylovka
Krasnoarmeysk
Zhirnovsk
Kamenskiy
Krasnyy Kut
Orlov Gay
Oz. Chalkar
Chalkar
Dzhambeyty
Bobrov
Khrenovoye
Talovaya
Novokhopersk
Yelan
Georgiu-Dezh
Ostrogozhsk
Buturlinovka
239
Uryupinsk
Buzuluk
Kukvidze
Novoannenskiy
Panfilovo
Krasnyy Yar
358
Vozvyshennost
Rovnoye
Piterka
Novouzensk
Kushum
Chapayevo
Kamenka
Kalach
Pavlovsk
Medveditsa
Danilovka
Kotovo
Novatka
Volgogradskoye
Vdkhr.
Pallasovka
Aleksandrov Gay
Mergenevskiy
Karsha
Bol. Uzen
Ural
Rossosh
Khoper
Ust Buzulukskaya
Mikhaylovka
Kamyshin
Nikolayevsk
Kaztalovka
Mal. Uzen
Furmanovo
Antonovo
Bazartobe
Bogurhar
Kumylzhenskaya
Olkhovka
Bykovo
Kaysatskoye
Kazanskaya
Frolovo
Ilovlya
Kantemirovka
Don
Veshenskaya
Serafimovich
Dzhanybek
Kalmykovo
Melovoye
Chertkovo
Kletskiy (Kletskaya)
Ilovlya (Iloulinskaya)
Privolzhskaya
Elton
Inderborskiy
K A Z A K H
S. S. R.
Starobelsk
Kamenskiy
Chir
Dubovka
Sovetskaya
Prichalnaya
Volzhskiy
Urda
donetsk
Millerovo
Volgograd (Stalingrad)
Leninsk
Kapustin Yar
Shungay
Kalach na Donu
Krasnoslobodsk
Zelenyy
Voroshilovgrad (Lugansk)
Glubokiy
Surovikino
Krasnoarmeysk
Vladimirovka
Topoli
Kamensk-Shakhtinskiy
Chernyshkovskiy
Volga
Verkhniy Baskunchak
Morozovsk
Lenin
Akhtubinsk (Petropavlovskiy)
Makhambet (Yamankhalinka)
Krasnodon
Sverdlovsk
Tsimlyanskoye Vdkhr.
Krasnyy Luch
Belaya Kalitva
Rovenki
Gukovo
Krasnodonetskaya
Sinegorski
Novobogatinskoye
Novoshakhtinsk
Artemovski
Tsimlyansk
Kotelnikovo
Gurvev
Shakhty
Ust-Donetskiy
Konstantinovski
Obilnoye
Kopanovka
Kamenolomni
Volgodonsk
Dubovskoye
Yenotayevka
-28
Tuzlov
Novocherkassk
Zavetnoye
Rostov
Bolshaya Martynovka
Zimovniki
Azov
Bataysk
K A L M Y K
Veselovskoye Vdkhr.
Manych
Kuberle
Krasnyy Yar
Ganyushkino
Mechetinskaya
Zernograd
A. S. S. R.
Astrakhan
Yeya
Proletarskaya
Remontnoye
Kushchevskaya
Yegorlykskaya
Ergeni Vozvyshennost
Kamyzyak
Gigant
Oz. Manych-Gudilo
Krasnoye
Salsk
Elista (Stepnoi)
-28
Peschanokopskoye
Yegorlyk
Leninsk
Priyutnoye
Kirovski
Pavlovskaya
Belaya Glina
Divnoye
Liman
Kultay
Kanevskaya
Krasnogvardeyskoye
Prikaspiyskaya Nizmennost
Kalaus
C A S P I A N S E A
Ipatovo
Tikhoretsk
Kaspiyskiy
Timashevsk
Novoaleksandrovskaya
Kropotkin
Svetlograd (Petrovskoye)
Arzgir
O. Kulaly
Mangyshlakskiy Zaliv
Korenovsk
Izobil'nyy
Blagodarnoye
Beloye Ozero
Kuma
M. Tyub Karagan
Fort Shevchenko
P-ov. Mangyshlak
Ust-Labinsk
Krasnodar
Armavir
Stavropol
Prikumsk
Staryy Biryuzyak
Kuban
Kurgan (Kurgannaya)
831
Nevinnomyssk
Vladimirovka
Tyuleniy
Zelenokumsk (Vorontsovo-Aleksandrovskoye)
Bryanskoye
Maykop
Labinsk
Urup
Kursavka
Apsheronsk
Laba
Mineralnyye Vody
O. Chechen
Neftegorsk
Cherkessk
Aleksandriyskaya
Shevchenko
Georgievsk
Lopatin
Dakhovskaya
Yessentuki
Pyatigorsk
Kizlyar
Kislovodsk
Prokhladnyy
Mozdok
CHECHENO-
Terek
Karachayevsk
Krasnaya Polyana
Nalchik
Mayskiy
Nartkala
Malgobek
INGUSH
Gudermes
Sulak
Sochi
Teberda
Kizil Yurt
Matsesta
KABARDINO-BALKAR A.S.S.R.
Elkhotovo
Groznyy
A.S.S.R.
Makhachkala
Adler
Tyrnyauz
Beslan
N. OSSETIAN A.S.S.R.
Khasavyurt
Gagra
Elbrus 5633
Ordzhonikidze
Kumtorkala
ABKHAZ A.S.S.R.
Kodori
5203
Kaspiysk
Gudauta
Novyy Afon
Buynaksk
Sukhumi
Inguri
Tkvarcheli
Sadon
Kazbek 5047
Tebulos 4492
Izberbash
Novokayakent
Ochamchire
Gali
Dzhvari
Tsageri
Rioni
Oni
Akusha
Khunzakh
Zugdidi
G E O R G I A
Tlyarata
Dagestanskiye Ogni
800
Anaklia
Kutaisi
Tkibuli
Sachkhere
Chiatura
Tskhinvali (Staliniri)
Dusheti
Kuli
Derbent
Mikha-Tskhakaya
Zestafoni
Khashuri
Gori
Telavi
Kvareli
Lagodekhi
Kasumkent
Poti
Samtredia
Mikhaylovka
Kobuleti
S. S. R.
Kaspi
Mtskheta
Gurdzhaani
Samur
Khachmas
Makharadze
Tbilisi
Signakhi
Zakataly
Akhty
Kuba
Batumi
Khulo
Borzhomi
Citeli Ckaro
Alazan
ADZHAR A.S.S.R.
Akhaltsikhe
Khrami
Marneuli
Rustavi
Mirzaani
Divichi
Vale
Shaumyani
Iori
Sheki (Nukha)
Bazar Dyuzi 4466
Siazan
Hopa
Akhalkalaki
Mingechaurskoye Vdkhr.
Baba dag 3629
Borçka
Akstafa
Kura
Kutkashen
Pazar
Artvin
Ardahan
Çildir
Alaverdi
Mashtaga
Görele
Akçaabat
Ardanuç
Kisir 3192
Tauz
Shamkhor
Mingechaur
Agdash
Geokchay
Shemakha
Sumgait
O. Artem
Tirebolu
Trabzon
Rize
Kaçkar 3937
Leninakan
Kirovakan
Kirovabad
Chanlar
Yevlakh
Lyaki
Surakhany
Zyrya
Sürmene
Dilizhan
Dashkesan
AZERBAIJAN
BAKU
Aragats 4090
Sevan
Kyurdamir
Oltu
Çakırgöl 3063
Artik
Chorentsavan
Ozero Sevan
Mir-Bashir
Barda
S.S.R.
Kazi Magomed
Kamo
Gümüşane
Kars
Şelim
Narman
Sarıkamış
ARMENIAN S.S.R.
Terter
Alyata
Digor
Agdzhabedi
Sabirabad
Ali-Bayramly
Bayburt
Tortum
Kagizman
Echmiadzin
Yerevan
Martuni
Agdam
Imishly
Karachala
Aras
M. Byandovan
Harşit
Çoruh
Ispir
D A Eg L A R I
50 48 46 44 42 40
Kavkaz
(Caucasus)
Bolshoy Kavkaz

East from Greenwich 40 42 44 46 48 50

1:5 000 000

50 0 50 100 150 200 km

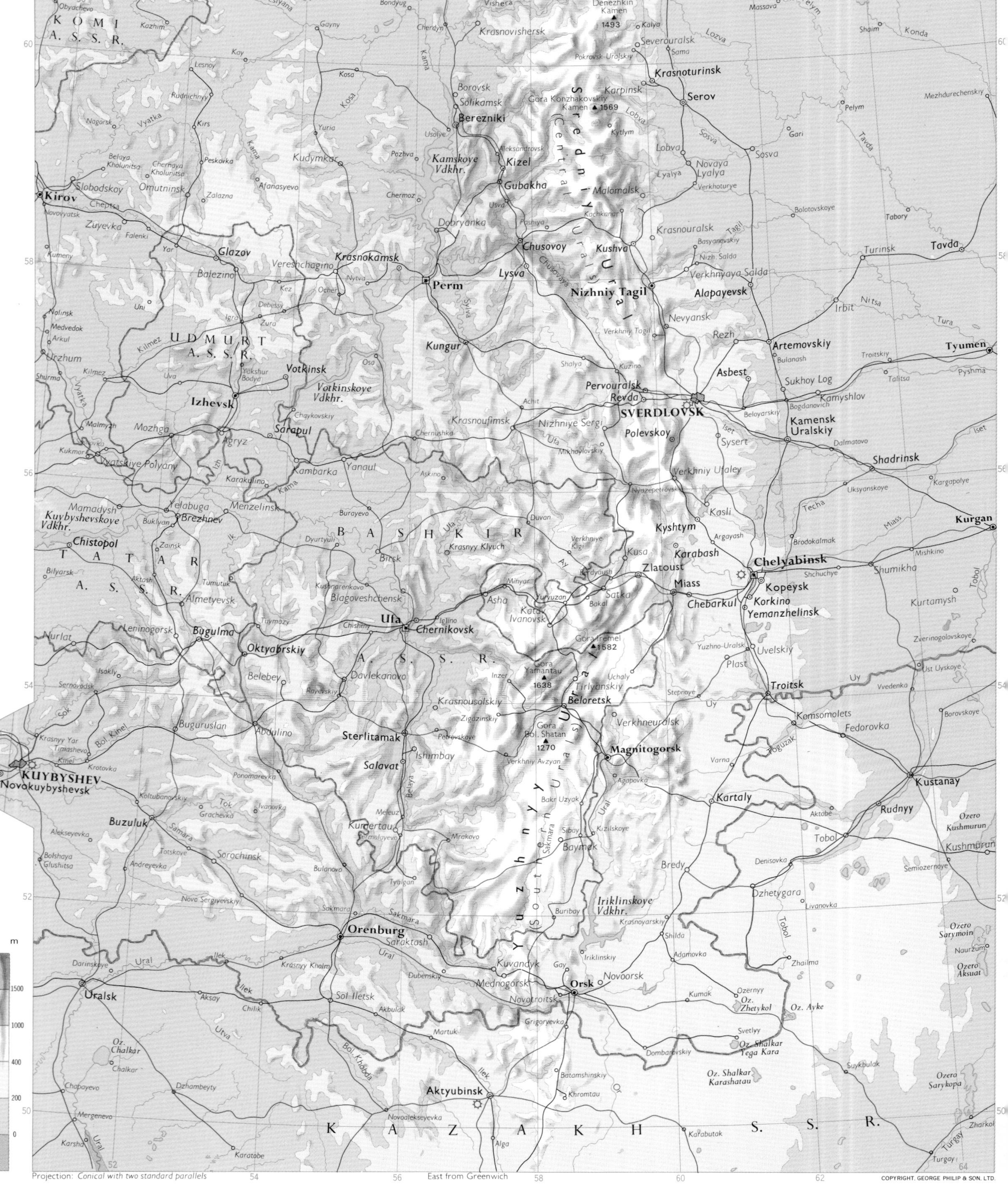

KOMI A.S.S.R.
UDMURT A.S.S.R.
TATAR A.S.S.R.
BASHKIR A.S.S.R.
KAZAKH S.S.R.
Sredniy Ural (Central Urals)
Yuzhnyy Ural (Southern Urals)
Gora Denezhkin Kamen 1493
Gora Konzhakovskiy Kamen 1569
Gora Iremel 1582
Gora Yamantau 1638
Gora Bol. Shatan 1270
Kirov
Slobodskoy
Omutninsk
Glazov
Balezino
Izhevsk
Votkinsk
Sarapul
Mozhga
Agryz
Vyatskiye Polyany
Yelabuga
Brezhnev
Menzelinsk
Chistopol
Kuybyshevskoye Vdkhr.
Almetyevsk
Leninogorsk
Bugulma
Oktyabrskiy
Nurlat
Buguruslan
Abdulino
KUYBYSHEV
Novokuybyshevsk
Buzuluk
Sorochinsk
Orenburg
Uralsk
Sol Iletsk
Aktyubinsk
Perm
Krasnokamsk
Vereshchagino
Kudymkar
Berezniki
Solikamsk
Kamskoye Vdkhr.
Kizel
Gubakha
Chusovoy
Lysva
Dobryanka
Kungur
Krasnovishersk
Krasnoturinsk
Karpinsk
Serov
Severouralsk
Kushva
Nizhniy Tagil
Alapayevsk
Verkhnyaya Salda
Nevyansk
Rezh
Artemovskiy
Asbest
Pervouralsk
Revda
SVERDLOVSK
Polevskoy
Kamensk Uralskiy
Shadrinsk
Kurgan
Tyumen
Turinsk
Tavda
Irbit
Kamyshlov
Sukhoy Log
Krasnoufimsk
Nizhniye Sergi
Votkinskoye Vdkhr.
Kambarka
Yanaul
Birsk
Blagoveshchensk
Ufa
Chernikovsk
Belebey
Davlekanovo
Sterlitamak
Ishimbay
Salavat
Kumertau
Meleuz
Asha
Katav Ivanovsk
Satka
Zlatoust
Miass
Chebarkul
Kyshtym
Karabash
Kasli
Verkhniy Ufaley
Chelyabinsk
Kopeysk
Korkino
Yemanzhelinsk
Troitsk
Plast
Uvelskiy
Beloretsk
Magnitogorsk
Verkhneuralsk
Kartaly
Kustanay
Rudnyy
Baymak
Sibay
Orsk
Novotroitsk
Mednogorsk
Kuvandyk
Novoorsk
Iriklinskoye Vdkhr.
Dzhetygara
Kushmurun
Komsomolets
Fedorovka
Ural
Tobol
Uy
Kama
Belaya
Sakmara
Ilek

Projection: Conical with two standard parallels

East from Greenwich

1:5 000 000

50 0 50 100 150 200 km

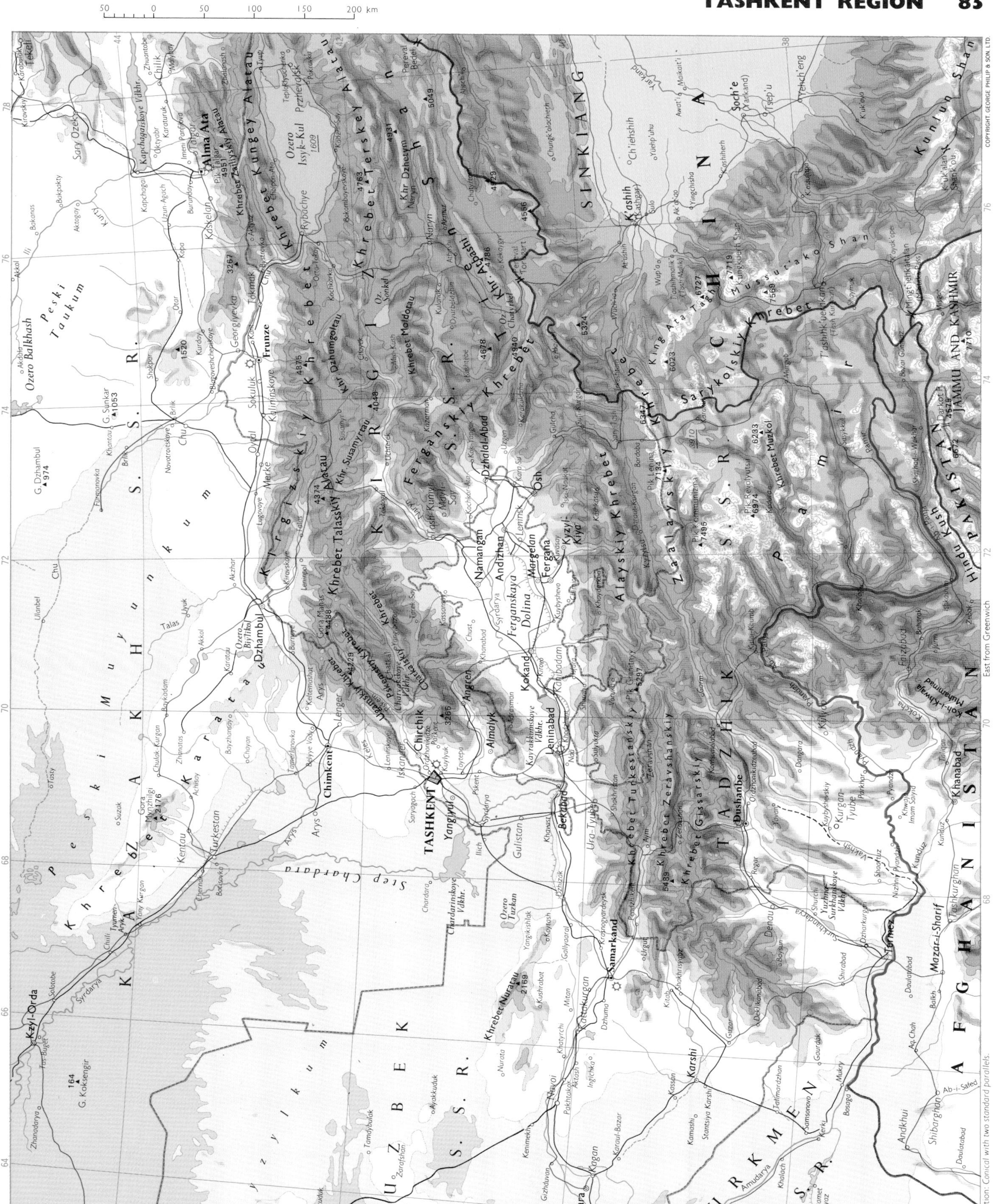

TASHKENT
Alma Ata
Frunze
Dzhambul
Chimkent
Turkestan
Kzyl-Orda
Samarkand
Bukhara
Karshi
Dushanbe
Leninabad
Kokand
Fergana
Andizhan
Namangan
Osh
Chirchik
Angren
Almalyk
Yangiyul
Termez
Mazar-i-Sharif
Kashi (Kashgar)
Soch'e (Yarkand)
Rybach'ye
Tokmak
Chardzhou
Ozero Issyk-Kul
Ozero Balkhash
Peski Taukum
Peski Muyunkum
Kyzylkum
Step Chardara
Chardarinskoye Vdkhr.
Kayrakkumskoye Vdkhr.
Ferganskaya Dolina
Khrebet Karatau
Khrebet Talasskiy Alatau
Khrebet Kungey Alatau
Zailiyskiy Alatau
Khrebet Terskey Alatau
Alayskiy Khrebet
Zaalayskiy Khrebet
Khrebet Turkestanskiy
Khrebet Zeravshanskiy
Khrebet Gissarskiy
Khrebet Nuratau
Sarykolskiy Khrebet
Kunlun Shan
Hindu Kush
Pamir
Tien Shan
Pik Lenina 7134
Pik Kommunizma 7495
K I R G I Z S. S. R.
K A Z A K H S. S. R.
U Z B E K S. S. R.
T A D Z H I K S. S. R.
T U R K M E N S. S. R.
A F G H A N I S T A N
C H I N A
S I N K I A N G
JAMMU AND KASHMIR
PAKISTAN
m 6000 4000 3000 2000 1500 1000 400 200 0
East from Greenwich
Projection: Conical with two standard parallels.

1:50 000 000

500 0 500 1000 1500 2000 km

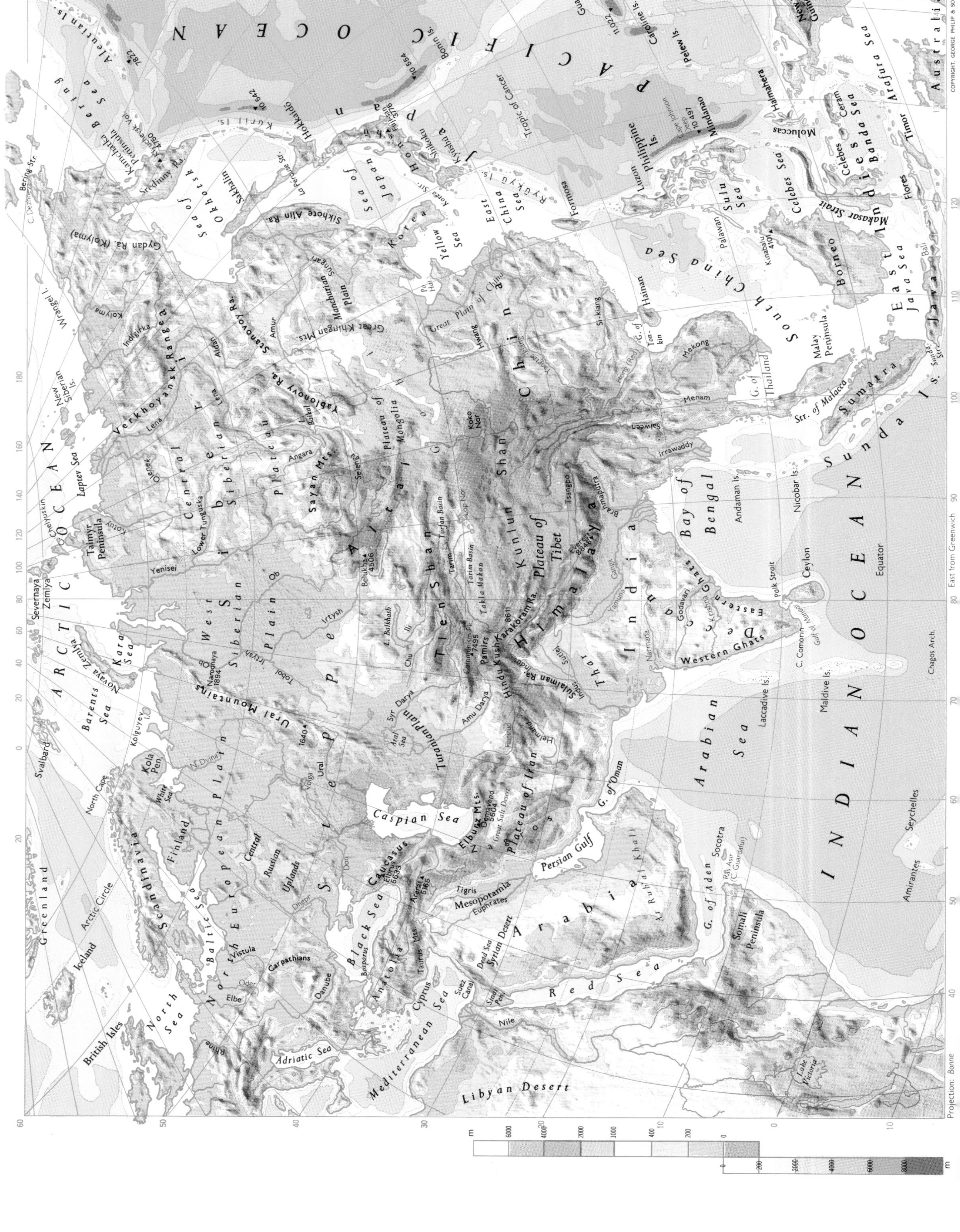

Projection: Bonne

East from Greenwich

1:50 000 000

0 500 1000 1500 2000 km

East from Greenwich

Projection: Bonne

1:100 000 000

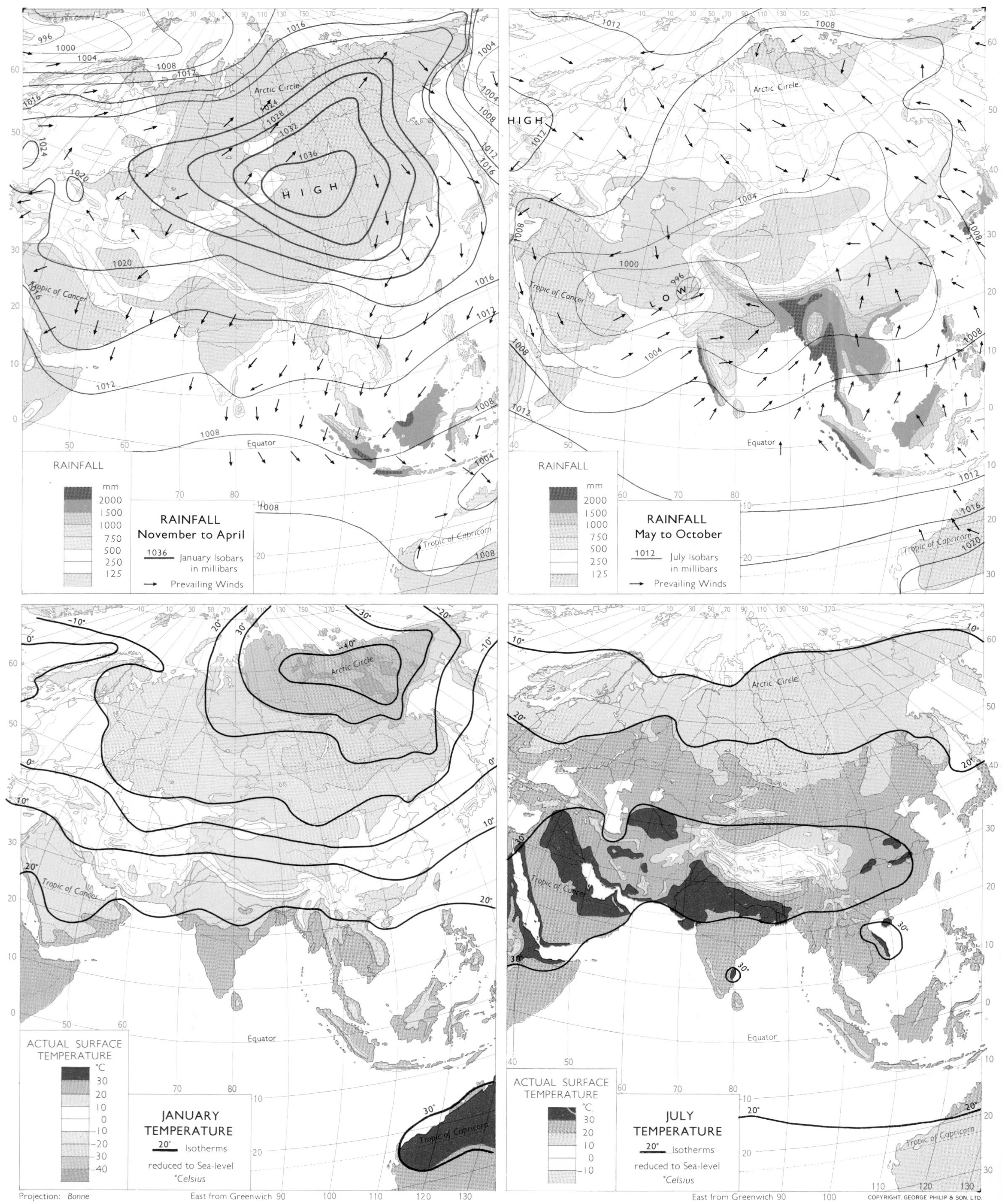
RAINFALL November to April
1036 January Isobars in millibars
Prevailing Winds
RAINFALL mm
2000
1500
1000
750
500
250
125
HIGH
Arctic Circle
Tropic of Cancer
Equator
Tropic of Capricorn
RAINFALL May to October
1012 July Isobars in millibars
LOW
JANUARY TEMPERATURE
20° Isotherms reduced to Sea-level °Celsius
ACTUAL SURFACE TEMPERATURE °C
30
20
10
0
-10
-20
-30
-40
JULY TEMPERATURE
Projection: Bonne
East from Greenwich

INDIA: MONSOONS

THEIR EVOLUTION IS SHOWN BY MONTHLY CLIMATE MAPS

RAINFALL
mm per month
mm
25
50
100
200
400

— ISOTHERMS
Temperature in degrees Celsius

— ISOBARS
(Pressure in millibars)

← WINDS

Ural Mts.
Caucasus
Elburz
Tropic of Cancer
Altai
Tien Shan
Pamirs
Hindu Kush
Kunlun
Himalaya
Deccan
Yablonovyy Mts.
Stanovoy Mts.
Khingan Mts.
Arctic Circle
Equator

mm
3000
2000
1000
500
250

1:80 000 000

East from Greenwich

JANUARY
FEBRUARY
MARCH
APRIL
MAY
JUNE
JULY
AUGUST
SEPTEMBER
OCTOBER
NOVEMBER
DECEMBER

Projection: *Lambert's Equivalent Azimuthal*

ISRAEL AND WEST JORDAN

1:1 000 000

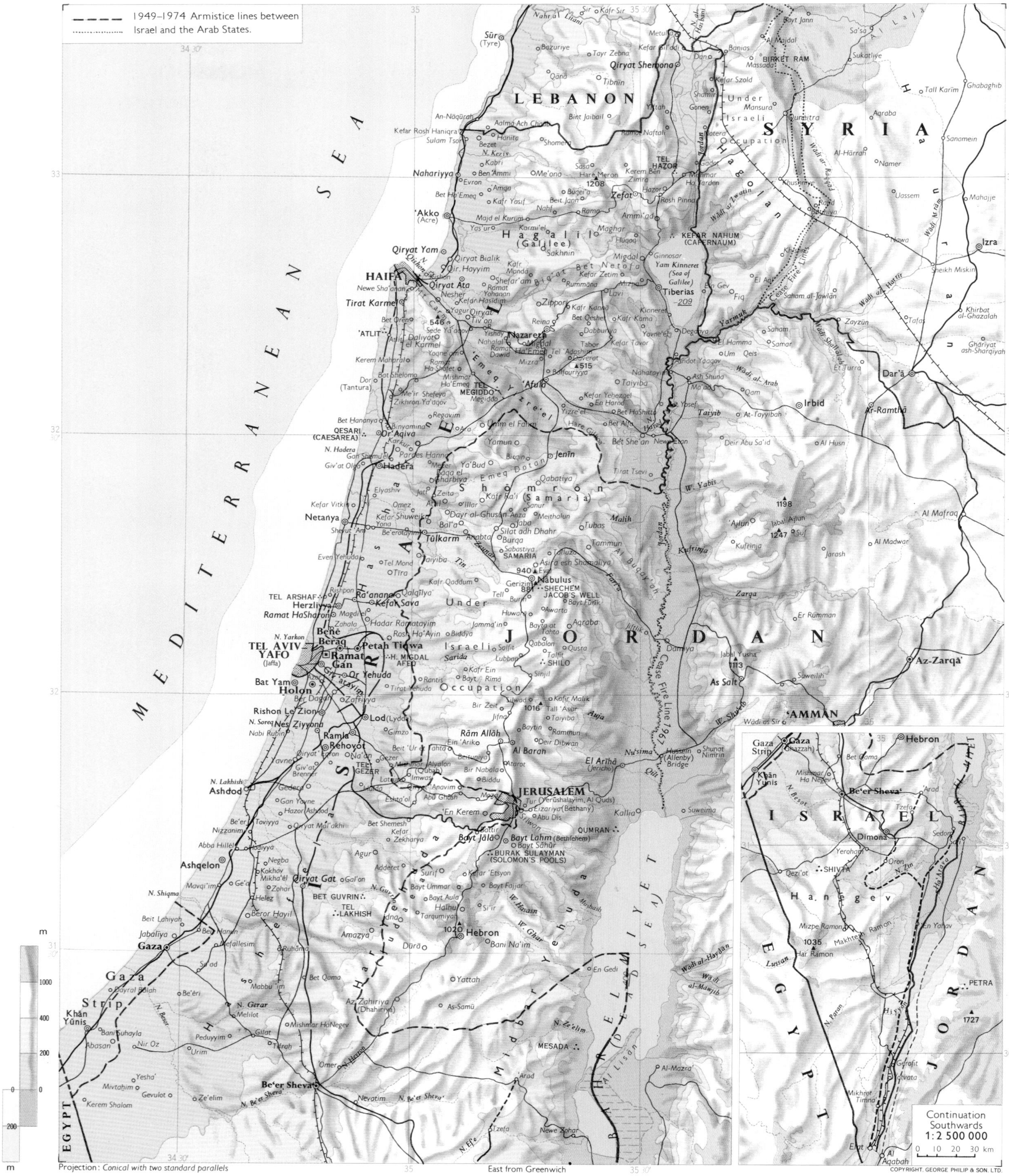

10 0 10 20 30 40 km

1949–1974 Armistice lines between Israel and the Arab States.
MEDITERRANEAN SEA
LEBANON
SYRIA
JORDAN
ISRAEL
Under Israeli Occupation
HAIFA
TEL AVIV-YAFO
JERUSALEM
Nazareth
Nablus
Tiberias
Yam Kinneret (Sea of Galilee)
Be'er Sheva
Hebron
Gaza
Gaza Strip
Ashdod
Ashqelon
Netanya
Hadera
'Akko (Acre)
Nahariyya
Zefat
Qiryat Shemona
Irbid
'AMMAN
As Salt
Az-Zarqa'
Dar'ā
El Arīhā (Jericho)
Bayt Lahm (Bethlehem)
Ram Allāh
Tulkarm
Jenin
Hagalil (Galilee)
Shomron (Samaria)
Hanegev
Ceasefire Line 1967
Yarmuk
Jordan
Bahrat Lut (Dead Sea)
EGYPT
Continuation Southwards
1:2 500 000
0 10 20 30 km
Elat
Al 'Aqabah
Dimona
Mizpe Ramon
PETRA
1000
400
200
0
200
m

Projection: Conical with two standard parallels

East from Greenwich

1:15 000 000

100 0 100 200 300 400 500 600 km

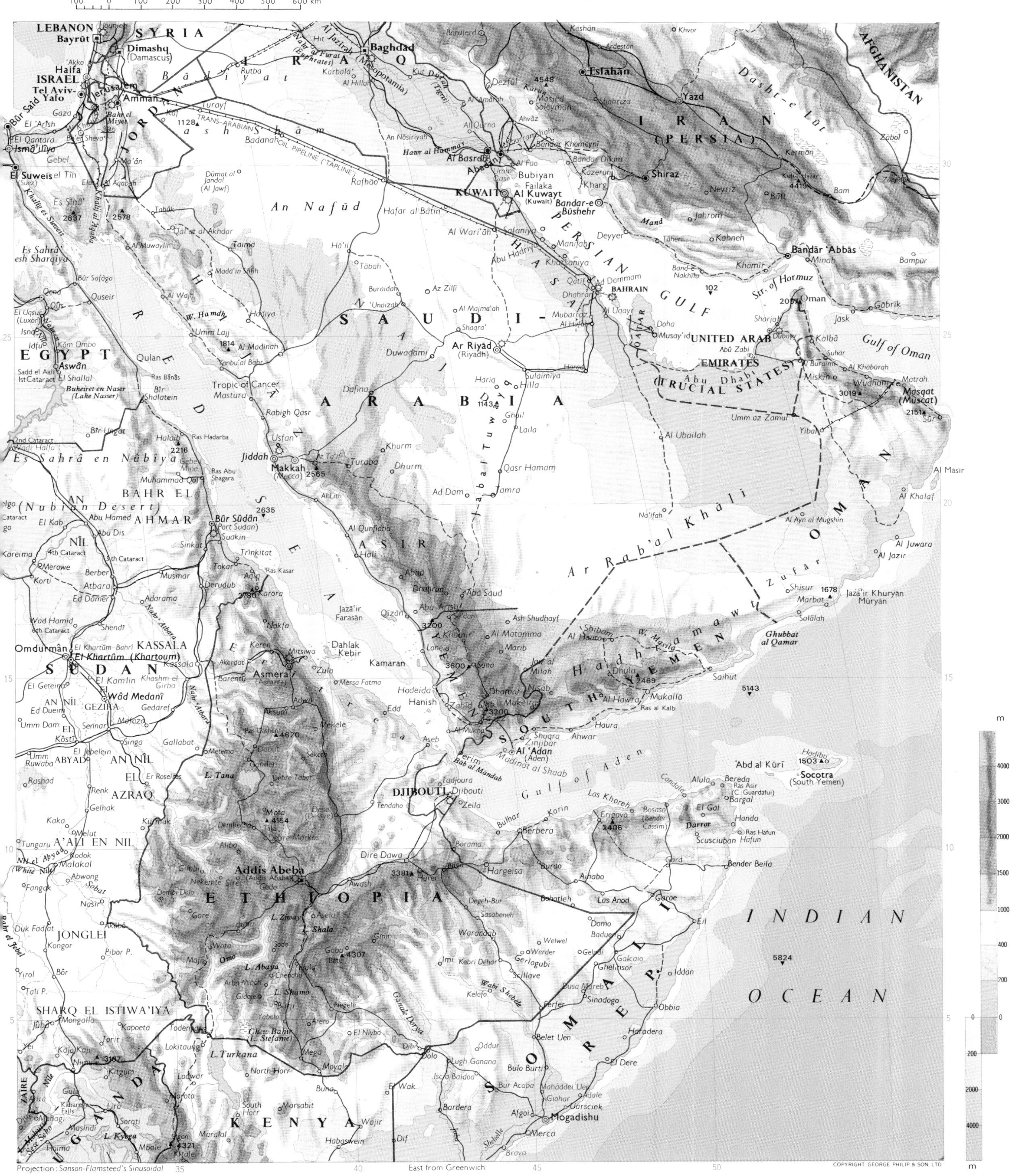
LEBANON
Bayrût
SYRIA
Dimashq (Damascus)
ISRAEL
Haifa
Tel Aviv-Yafo
Jerusalem
Ammān
JORDAN
IRAQ
Baghdād
Esfahān
Yazd
IRAN (PERSIA)
AFGHANISTAN
Dasht-e Lūt
Shiraz
Kermān
Al Basrah
KUWAIT
Al Kuwayt
Bandar-e Būshehr
An Nafūd
PERSIAN GULF
BAHRAIN
QATAR
Bandar 'Abbās
Str. of Hormuz
Gulf of Oman
UNITED ARAB EMIRATES (TRUCIAL STATES)
Abu Dhabi
Masqat (Muscat)
SAUDI ARABIA
Ar Riyād (Riyadh)
Tropic of Cancer
Jiddah
Makkah (Mecca)
EGYPT
Aswân
Buheiret en Naser (Lake Nasser)
Es Sahrâ en Nûbîya
RED SEA
BAHR EL AHMAR
Bûr Sûdân (Port Sudan)
Ar Rab' al Khali
OMAN
Zufar
Hadhramawt
SOUTH YEMEN
YEMEN
Sana
Al 'Adan (Aden)
Bab al Mandab
Gulf of Aden
Socotra (South Yemen)
SUDAN
Omdurmân
El Khartûm (Khartoum)
KASSALA
Asmera
Eritrea
DJIBOUTI
ETHIOPIA
Addis Abeba
L. Tana
SOMALI REP.
Mogadishu
INDIAN OCEAN
KENYA
UGANDA
L. Turkana
JONGLEI
SHARQ EL ISTIWA'IYA
A'ALI EN NIL
Projection: Sanson-Flamsteed's Sinusoidal
East from Greenwich
COPYRIGHT GEORGE PHILIP & SON LTD

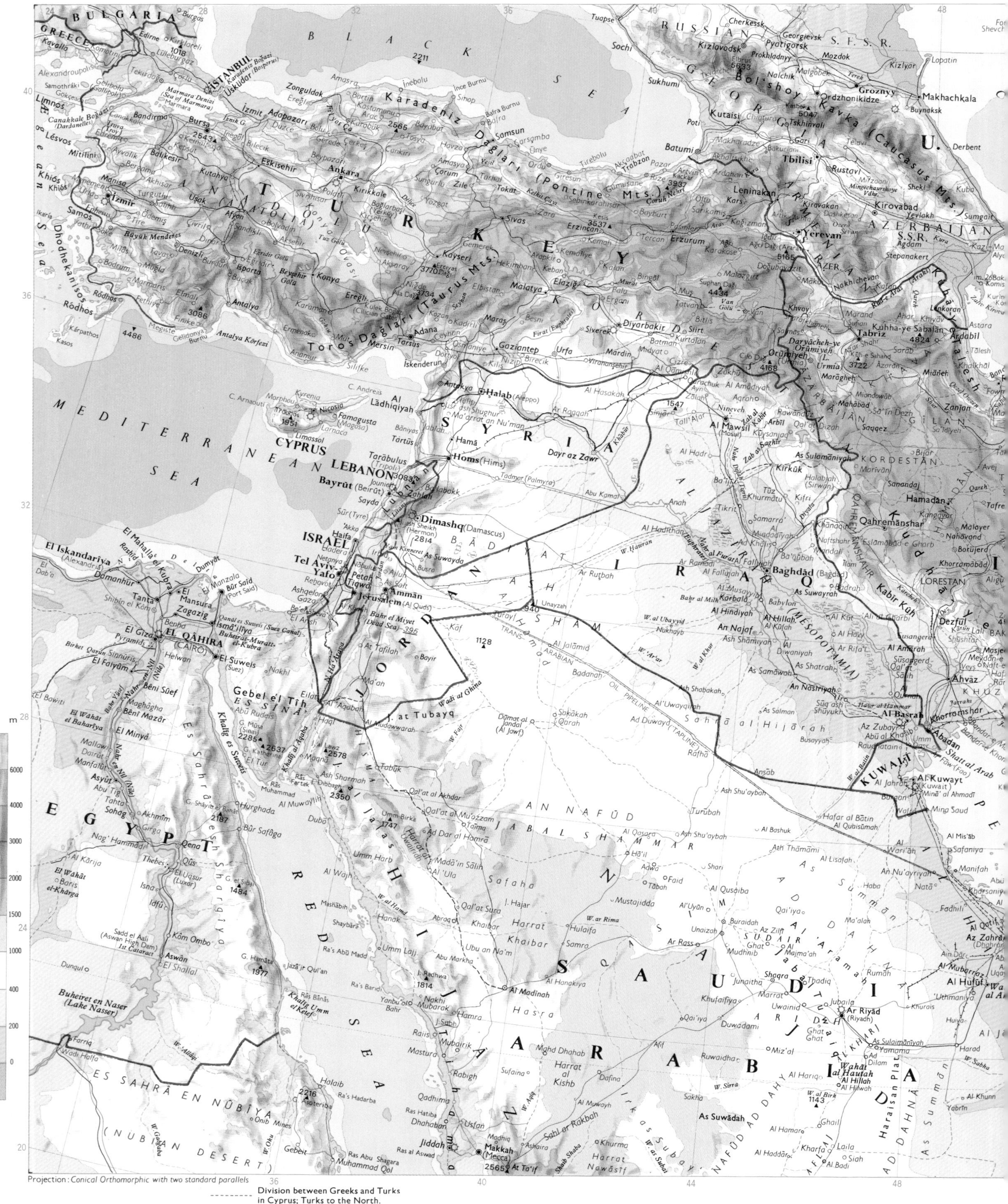
BULGARIA
GREECE
BLACK SEA
RUSSIAN S.F.S.R.
GEORGIA
ARMENIA
AZERBAIJAN S.S.R.
TURKEY
ANADOLU (ANATOLIA)
Karadeniz Dağlari (Pontine Mts.)
Toros Dağlari (Taurus Mts.)
Bol'shoy Kavkaz (Caucasus Mts.)
MEDITERRANEAN SEA
CYPRUS
LEBANON
SYRIA
ISRAEL
JORDAN
IRAQ
AL JAZIRAH
(MESOPOTAMIA)
KUWAIT
EGYPT
SAUDI ARABIA
RED SEA
AN NAFŪD
JABAL SHAMMAR
BĀDIYAT ASH SHĀM
ES SAHRĀ EN NŪBĪYA
(NUBIAN DESERT)
İSTANBUL
Ankara
İzmir
Bursa
Konya
Adana
Kayseri
Sivas
Erzurum
Trabzon
Samsun
Antalya
Mersin
Gaziantep
Diyarbakır
Tbilisi
Yerevan
Baku
Batumi
Sochi
Groznyy
Makhachkala
Nicosia
Famagusta
Halab (Aleppo)
Homs (Hims)
Hamā
Dimashq (Damascus)
Bayrūt (Beirūt)
Tarābulus (Tripoli)
Haifa
Tel Aviv-Yafo
Jerusalem (Al Quds)
'Ammān
Dayr az Zawr
Al Mawsil (Mosul)
Kirkūk
Baghdād
Al Basrah
Al Kuwayt (Kuwait)
Tabrīz
Hamadān
El Iskandarîya (Alexandria)
EL QÂHIRA (CAIRO)
El Suweis (Suez)
Asyût
Aswân
Buheiret en Naser (Lake Nasser)
Wadi Halfa
Jiddah
Makkah (Mecca)
Al Madīnah
Ar Riyāḍ (Riyadh)
Al Hufūf

Projection: Conical Orthomorphic with two standard parallels

Division between Greeks and Turks in Cyprus; Turks to the North.

AFGHANISTAN
PAKISTAN
N.W. FRONTIER PROVINCE
BALUCHISTAN
PUNJAB
SIND
RAJASTHAN
HARYANA
HIMACHAL PRADESH
JAMMU AND KASHMIR
MADHYA PRADESH
GUJARAT
ARABIAN SEA
Gulf of Kutch
Rann of Kutch
Little Rann
Mouths of the Indus
THAR DESERT (Great Indian Desert)
THAL DESERT
Salt Range
Toba Kakar
Sulaiman Range
Kirthar Range
Pab Hills
Gir Hills
Vindhya
Satpura
Tropic of Cancer
Kabul
Ghazni
Kandahar
Quetta
Peshawar
Kohat
Bannu
Islamabad
Rawalpindi
Srinagar
Jammu
Sialkot
Gujranwala
Lahore
Amritsar
Faisalabad
Sargodha
Jhang
Multan
Dera Ismail Khan
Dera Ghazi Khan
Bahawalpur
Sukkur
Jacobabad
Shikarpur
Larkana
Nawabshah
Hyderabad
KARACHI
Ludhiana
Jullundur
Patiala
Chandigarh
Simla
Ambala
DELHI
Rohtak
Hissar
Bikaner
Jodhpur
Ajmer
Jaipur
Alwar
Kota
Udaipur
Ujjain
Indore
Bhopal
AHMADABAD
Vadodara
Bhavnagar
Rajkot
Jamnagar
Porbandar
Bhuj
Junagadh
Mandvi
Veraval
Projection: Conical with two standard parallels
m
6000
4000
3000
2000
1500
1000
400
200
0
200
2000
m

1:6 000 000

50 0 50 100 150 200 250 km

JAMMU AND KASHMIR
On same scale as Main Map
U.S.S.R.
GILGIT AGENCY
N.W. FRONTIER PROVINCE
PUNJAB
JAMMU AND KASHMIR
HIMACHAL PRADESH
Karakoram Range
Kunlun Shan
Deosai Mountains
Zaskar Mountains
SODA PLAINS
Gilgit
Srinagar
Rawalpindi
Islamabad
Abbottabad
Jammu
Sialkot
Wazirabad
Gujrat
Jhelum
Leh
Kargil
Skardu
Nanga Parbat 8126
Rakaposhi
Masherbrum 7821
CHINESE REPUBLIC
Kangtissu Shan
Aling Kangri
Chenmo Shan
TIBET
NEPAL
Mt. Everest 8848
Makalu 8481
Kanchenjunga 8598
Annapurna 8078
Dhaulagiri 8172
Manaslu 8156
Katmandu
Lalitpur
Bhaktapur
SIKKIM
Gangtok
Darjeeling
BHUTAN
Punakha
ASSAM
Garo Hills
BANGLADESH
Dacca
Narayanganj
Rajshahi
Khulna
Barisal
Jessore
Mymensingh
UTTAR PRADESH
BIHAR
MADHYA PRADESH
Siwalik Range
Mahabharat Range
Kanpur
Lucknow
Allahabad
Varanasi
Gorakhpur
Bareilly
Moradabad
Rampur
Shahjahanpur
Faizabad
Jaunpur
Patna
Gaya
Muzaffarpur
Darbhanga
Bhagalpur
Monghyr
Ranchi
Jamshedpur
Dhanbad
Asansol
Durgapur
Burdwan
Kharagpur
Calcutta
Howrah
Jabalpur
Bilaspur
Raigarh
Sambalpur
Raurkela
Balasore
Rajmahal Hills
Kaimur Hills
Panna Hills
Maikala Range
Chota Nagpur
Sundarbans
Mouths of the Ganga
The Sandheads
Ganga
Brahmaputra
East from Greenwich
COPYRIGHT. GEORGE PHILIP & SON. LTD.

NEPAL
UTTAR PRADESH
RAJASTHAN
MADHYA PRADESH
MAHARASHTRA
ORISSA
KANPUR
Lucknow
Allahabad
Varanasi
Patna
Jabalpur
Nagpur
Bhopal
Indore
Jaipur
Agra
Gwalior
AHMADABAD
BOMBAY
Pune
HYDERABAD
Secunderabad
Vishakhapatnam
Gulf of Cambay
Chilka Lake

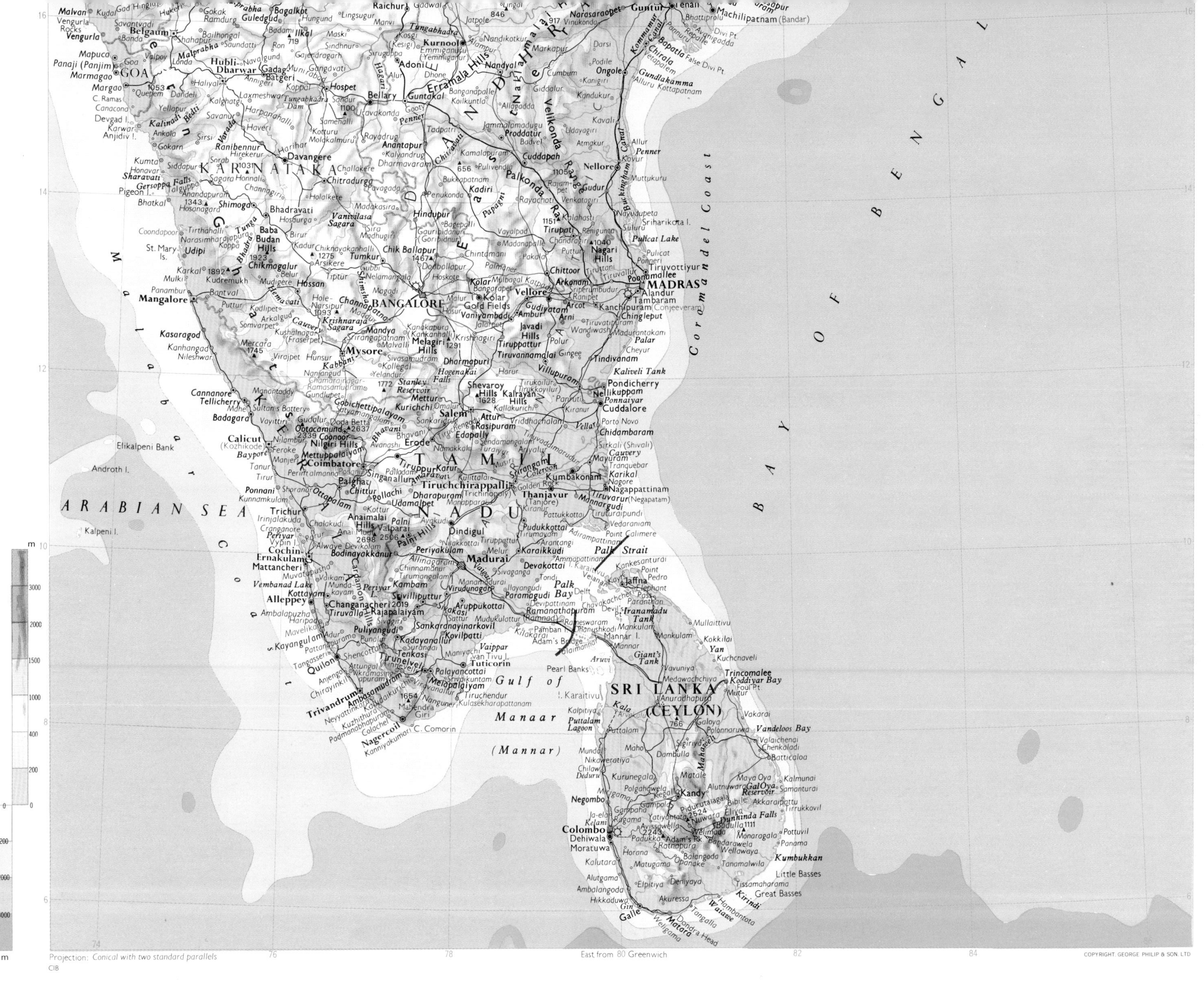

1:6 000 000
50 0 50 100 150 200 250 km
BAY OF BENGAL
ARABIAN SEA
Malabar Coast
Coromandel Coast
SRI LANKA (CEYLON)
TAMIL NADU
KARNATAKA
Gulf of Manaar
(Mannar)
Palk Strait
Palk Bay
Adam's Bridge
MADRAS
BANGALORE
Mysore
Coimbatore
Madurai
Tiruchchirappalli
Thanjavur (Tanjore)
Salem
Vellore
Pondicherry
Cuddalore
Nellore
Kurnool
Guntur
Ongole
Bellary
Hospet
Hubli-Dharwar
Belgaum
GOA
Panaji (Panjim)
Marmagao
Margao
Mangalore
Udipi
Shimoga
Davangere
Chitradurga
Tumkur
Hassan
Calicut (Kozhikode)
Cannanore
Tellicherry
Trichur
Cochin
Ernakulam
Alleppey
Quilon
Trivandrum
Nagercoil
C. Comorin
Tuticorin
Palayancottai
Tirunelveli
Dindigul
Cardamom Hills
Nilgiri Hills
Javadi Hills
Erramala Hills
Velikonda Range
Palkonda Range
Jaffna
Trincomalee
Anuradhapura
Kandy
Colombo
Dehiwala
Moratuwa
Negombo
Galle
Matara
Dondra Head
Batticaloa
Kumbukkan
Little Basses
Great Basses
Hambantota
Kirindi
Mannar I.
Puttalam Lagoon
Point Calimere
Pearl Banks
Vembanad Lake
Pulicat Lake
Elikalpeni Bank
Androth I.
Kalpeni I.
St. Mary Is.
Anjidiv I.
Vengurla Rocks
Vengurla
Malvan
Machilipatnam (Bandar)
Chirala
Bapatla
Nagapattinam
Karikal
Kumbakonam
Chingleput
Kanchipuram (Conjeeveram)
Arkonam
Tambaram
Tirupati
Chittoor
Cuddapah
Nandyal
Adoni
Anantapur
Hindupur
Kolar Gold Fields
Erode
Tiruppur
Pollachi
Palghat
Karur
Pudukkottai
Ramanathapuram
Rameswaram
Sivakasi
Virudunagar
Kovilpatti
East from 80 Greenwich
Projection: Conical with two standard parallels
CIB
m 3000 2000 1500 1000 400 200 0
0 200 2000 4000 m

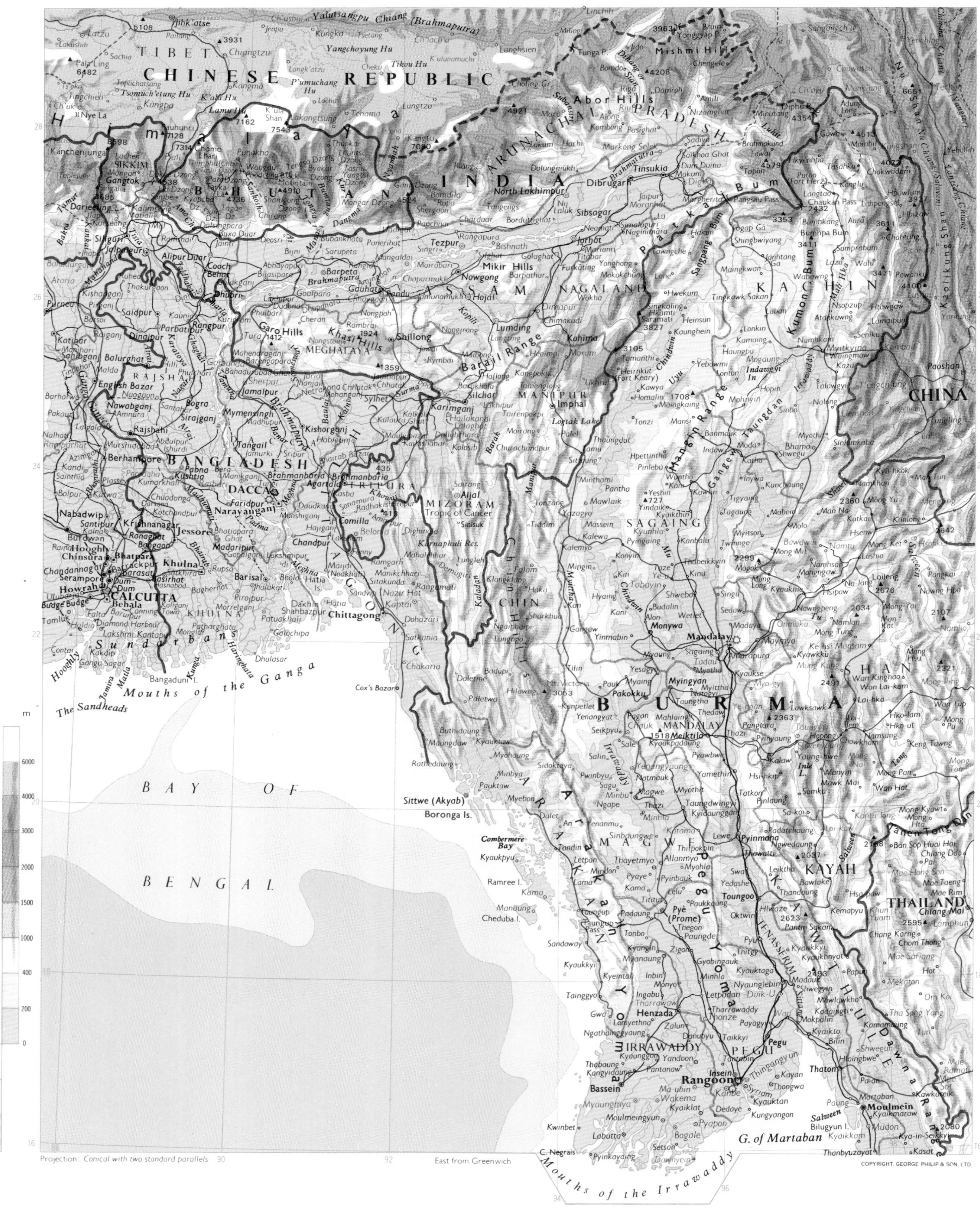
1: 6 000 000
50 0 50 100 150 200 250 km
CHINESE REPUBLIC
TIBET
INDIA
BHUTAN
SIKKIM
ASSAM
ARUNACHAL PRADESH
NAGALAND
MANIPUR
MEGHALAYA
TRIPURA
MIZORAM
BANGLADESH
BURMA
CHINA
THAILAND
KACHIN
SAGAING
CHIN
MANDALAY
SHAN
MAGWE
KAYAH
PEGU
IRRAWADDY
KAWTHULE
ARAKAN
RAJSHAHI
KHULNA
CHITTAGONG
BAY OF BENGAL
Mouths of the Ganga
Mouths of the Irrawaddy
The Sandheads
G. of Martaban
Yalutsangpu Chiang (Brahmaputra)
Mishmi Hills
Abor Hills
Garo Hills
Khasi Hills
Mikir Hills
Barail Range
Patkai Bum
Kumon Bum
Sundarbans
Tropic of Cancer
Karnaphuli Res.
Arakan Yoma
Pegu Yoma
CALCUTTA
DACCA
Rangoon
Mandalay
Chittagong
Shillong
Imphal
Sittwe (Akyab)
Boronga Is.
Combermere Bay
Ramree I.
Cheduba I.
C. Negrais
Moulmein
Bassein
Henzada
Pegu
Toungoo
Monywa
Myingyan
Pakokku
Meiktila
Dibrugarh
Tinsukia
Jorhat
Tezpur
Gauhati
Nowgong
Silchar
Sylhet
Comilla
Khulna
Jessore
Rajshahi
Darjeeling
Gangtok
Cox's Bazar
Projection: Conical with two standard parallels
East from Greenwich
m
6000
4000
3000
2000
1500
1000
400
200
0
200
2000
m

1:20 000 000

200 0 200 400 600 800 km

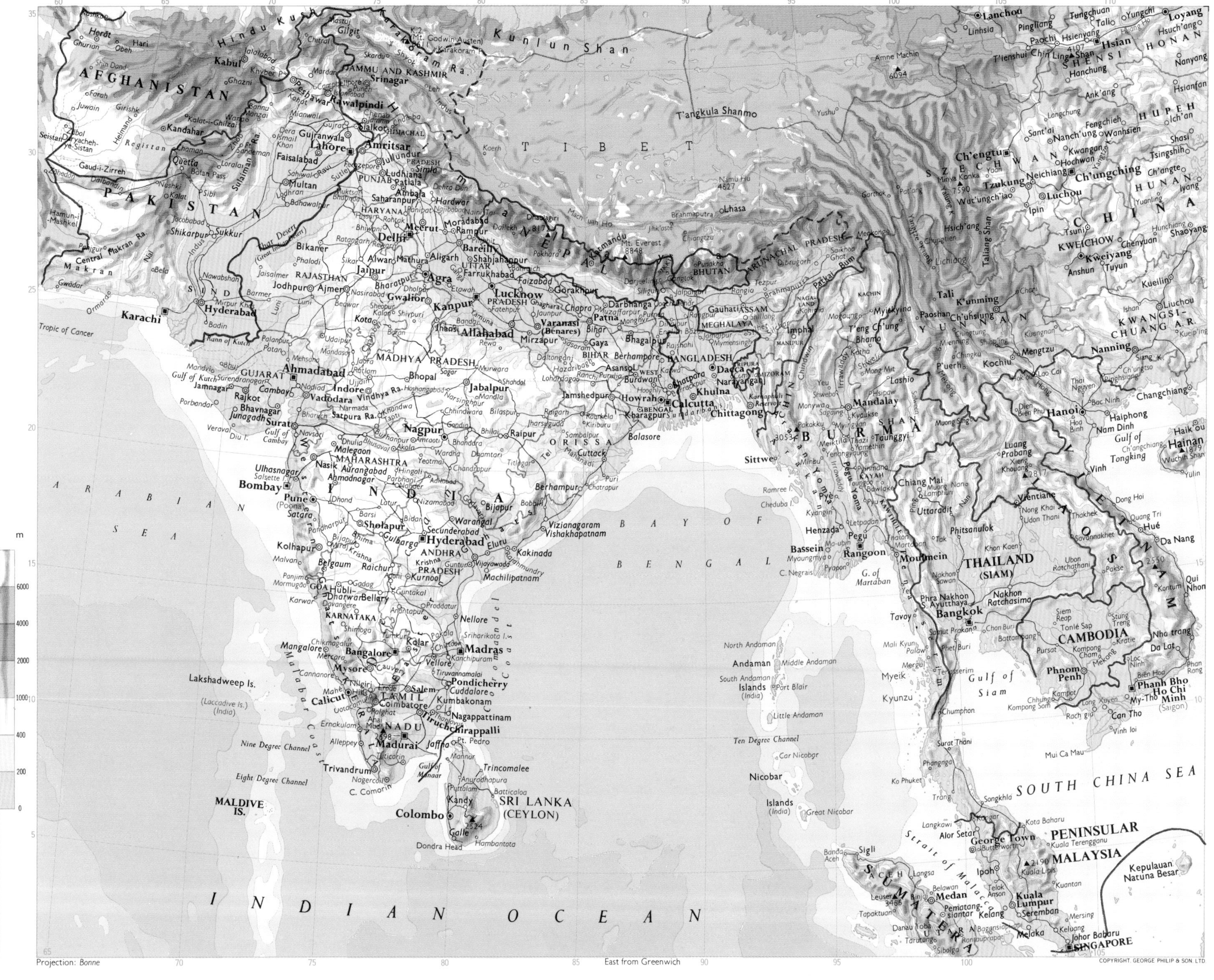
AFGHANISTAN
PAKISTAN
INDIA
TIBET
NEPAL
BHUTAN
BANGLADESH
BURMA
THAILAND (SIAM)
CAMBODIA
LAOS
VIETNAM
CHINA
PENINSULAR MALAYSIA
SUMATERA
SRI LANKA (CEYLON)
MALDIVE IS.
ARABIAN SEA
BAY OF BENGAL
INDIAN OCEAN
SOUTH CHINA SEA
Gulf of Siam
Strait of Malacca
Tropic of Cancer
Kunlun Shan
Hindu Kush
Mt. Everest 8848
Karachi
Bombay
Delhi
Calcutta
Madras
Colombo
Rangoon
Bangkok
Hanoi
Kabul
Lhasa
SINGAPORE
Projection: Bonne
East from Greenwich
COPYRIGHT GEORGE PHILIP & SON LTD.

J. GLEN

Gulf of Tonkin
Hainan
Hai'k'ou
Nanning
HANOI
Haiphong
Da Nang
Hue
Vinh
Vientiane
Luang Prabang
Mekong
THAILAND (SIAM)
BANGKOK
Thon Buri
CAMBODIA
Tonle Sap
Battambang
Moulmein
Rangoon
Gulf of Martaban
Mandalay
Pegu
Chiang Mai
Nakhon Ratchasima (Khorat)
Ubon Ratchathani
Pakse
Qui Nhon
Central Highlands

1:6 000 000

50 0 50 100 150 200 250 km

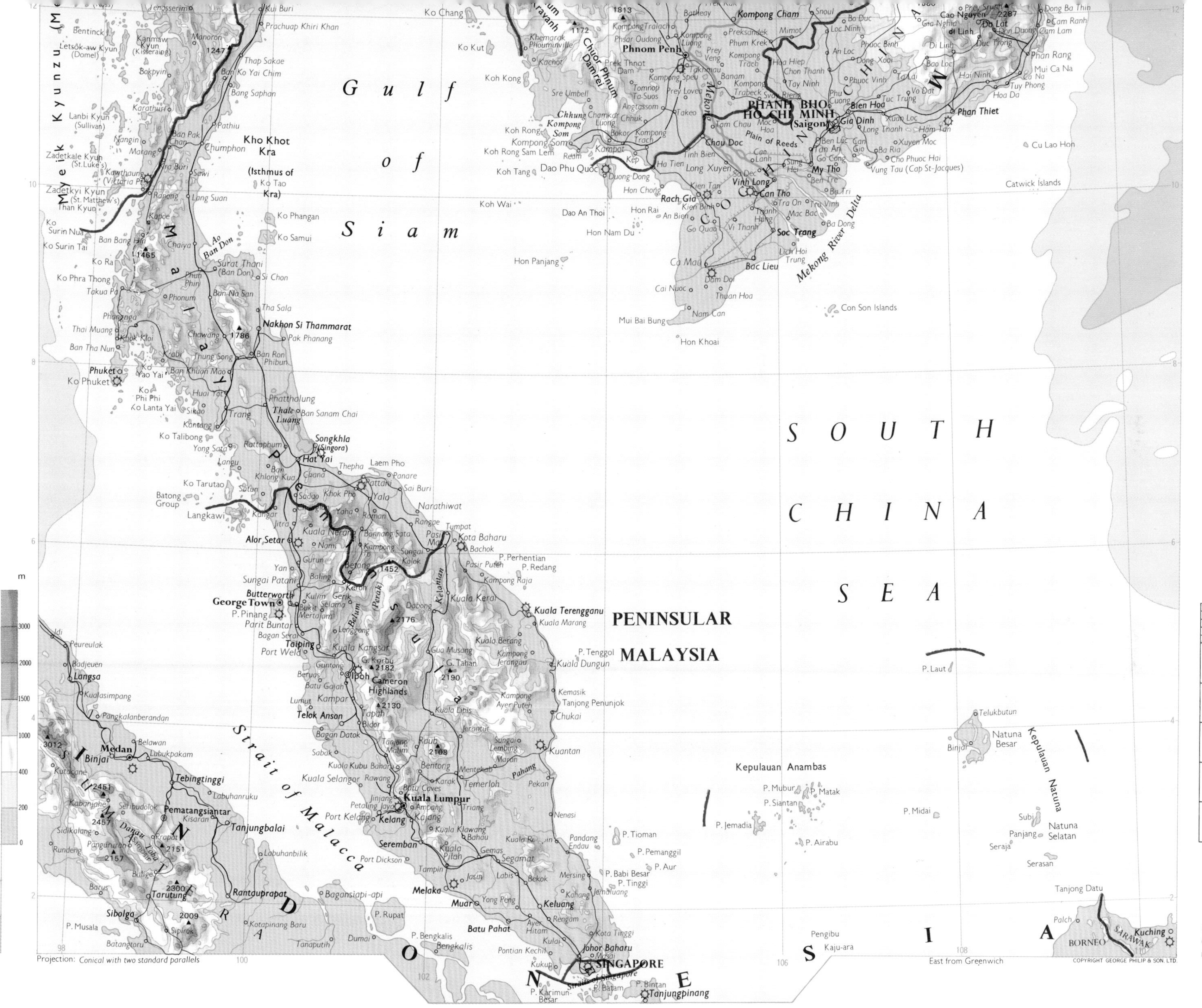
Gulf of Siam
SOUTH CHINA SEA
PENINSULAR MALAYSIA
Strait of Malacca
INDONESIA
SINGAPORE
Kuala Lumpur
Phnom Penh
PHANH BHO HO CHI MINH (Saigon)
Mekong River Delta
Plain of Reeds
Kepulauan Natuna
Kepulauan Anambas
George Town
Medan
Kuching
BORNEO
SARAWAK
Projection: Conical with two standard parallels
East from Greenwich
COPYRIGHT GEORGE PHILIP & SON. LTD.

Rangoon
Moulmein
G. of Martaban
Tak
Uttaradit
Nong Khai
Udon Thani
Thakhek
Dong Hoi
Hue
Da Nang (Tourane)
Hsisha
Chuntao
THAILAND (SIAM)
Phitsanulok
Savannakhet
LAOS
Ubon Ratchathani
Nakhon Ratchasima (Khorat)
Phnom Dangrek
Phra Nakhon Si Ayutthaya
Bangkok
VIET-NAM
Tavoy
Mergui
Battambang
Siem Reap
CAMBODIA
Tonle Sap
Nha Trang
Mui Varella
Chanthaburi
Gulf of Siam
Phnom Penh
Kompong Cham
Kratie
Phan Rang
PHANH BHO HO CHI MINH (Saigon)
Vung Tau
Kampot
Phu Quoc
Can Tho
Ca Mau
Con Son
ANDAMAN SEA
Chumphon
Kho Khot Kra
Ranong
Ko Samui
Surat Thani
Nakhon Si Thammarat
Phuket
Songkhla (Singora)
Pattani
Kota Baharu
SOUTH CHINA SEA
Palawan
Islands (Philippines)
Spratly I.
Amboyna I.
Kota Belud
Kota Kinabalu (Jesselton)
SABAH
Strait of Malacca
George Town
Alor Setar
Langkawi
Kuala Terengganu
MALAYSIA
PENINSULAR MALAYSIA
Ipoh
Kuala Lumpur
Port Kelang
Melaka
Kuantan
Johor Baharu
SINGAPORE
Bandar Seri Begawan
BRUNEI
Miri
Sabang
Banda Aceh (Kutaraja)
ACEH
Medan
Belawan
Simeulue
Sibolga
Nias
Kepulauan Natuna Besar
Kepulauan Anambas
Kuching
SARAWAK
Sibu
Bintulu
Singkawang
Pontianak
BORNEO
KALIMANTAN
Padang
Bukittinggi
Pakanbaru
RIAU
Kepulauan Riau
Kepulauan Lingga
Singkep
Siberut
JAMBI
Jambi
Palembang
Bangka
Pangkalpinang
Belitung (Billiton)
Tanjungpandan
INDONESIA
Banjarmasin
Balikpapan
Bengkulu
Tanjungkarang
LAMPUNG
Greater Sunda Islands
JAVA SEA
Madura
JAKARTA
Bogor
Bandung
Cirebon
Semarang
Surabaya
Yogyakarta
Surakarta
Malang
BALI
Lombok
JAWA (JAVA)
INDIAN OCEAN
Java Trench
Kepulauan Mentawai
Enggano
6073
6650
NUSA TENGGARA
Projection: Mercator
East from Greenwich
100
105
110
115
15
10
5
0
m
4000
3000
2000
1500
1000
400
200
0
200
2000
4000
6000
8000

1:12 500 000
100 0 100 200 300 400 500 km
JAVA AND MADURA
1:7 500 000
50 0 50 100 150 200 250 300 km
Jakarta
Serang
Tangerang
Bekasi
Bogor
Sukabumi
Bandung
Cirebon
Purwakarta
Subang
Garut
Tegal
Pemalang
Pekalongan
Batang
Semarang
Kudus
Japara
Demak
Rembang
Tuban
Salatiga
Surakarta
Magelang
Yogyakarta
Klaten
Madiun
Ponorogo
Kediri
Blitar
Malang
Surabaya
Sidoarjo
Pasuruan
Probolinggo
Kraksaan
Bondowoso
Situbondo
Jember
Bali
Madura
Nusa Kambangan
Nusa Barung
Bawean
Kepulauan Karimunjawa
Cilacap
Ngawi
Nganjuk
Kendal
Tulungagung
Trenggalek
Purwokerto
Banyumas
Kebumen
Purworejo
Wates
Bantul
Pacitan
Wonosari
Slamet 3428
Semeru 3676
Raung 3332
Lawu 3265
Merbabu 3142
3078
3019
2563
TENGAH
TIMUR
Selat Madura
Selat Sunda
Teluk Pelabuhan Ratu
P. Rakatau (Krakatau)
Tg. Gede
Tg. Indramayu
Indramayu
Merak
Banten
Anyer-Lor
Labuhan
Pelabuhanratu
Rangkasbitung
Babuyan Chan.
C. Engaño
Claveria
Aparri
Laoag
Vigan
Tuguegarao
Ilagan
Bontoc
Baguio
Solano
Bayombong
San Fernando
Lingayen Gulf
Dagupan
Tarlac
Cabanatuan
San Jose
Angeles
Olongapo
Bataan
Manila
Manila Bay
Quezon City
Cavite
Batangas
Lucena
Polillo Islands
Lamon Bay
Cape San Ildefonso
Cape Encanto
Casiguran
Palanan Pt.
Palanan
Sierra Madre
LUZON
Lubang Is.
Cape Calavite
Mindoro
Mindoro Str.
Marinduque
Burias
Sibuyan
Tablas
Sibuyan Sea
Masbate
Samar
Catanduanes
Lagonoy Gulf
Legaspi
Sorsogon
Naga
Daet
Virac
Yog Point
San Bernardino Strait
Catarman
Calbayog
Wright
Taft
Borongan
Visayan Sea
Panay
Iloilo
Roxas
Ormoc
Tacloban
Leyte
Guiuan
Calicoan
Cebu
Bacolod
Negros
Dumaguete
Bohol
Tagbilaran
Dinagat
Siargao
Surigao
Butuan
Cagayan de Oro
Iligan
Dipolog
Mindanao
Pagadian
Cotabato
Davao
Digos
Davao G.
Moro G.
Zamboanga
Basilan Str.
Basilan
Isabela
Jolo
Sulu Arch.
Tawitawi
Sibutu Passage
Samales Group
Tapul Group
Sarangani Bay
Sarangani Is.
C. S. Agustin
Mindanao Trench
(Philippine Trench)
10 497
9540
Busuanga
Calamian Group
Culion
Cuyo Is.
Taytay
Dumaran
Puerto Princesa
5576
SULU SEA
PACIFIC
OCEAN
Yap Islands
Ulithi Atoll
8597
Ngulu Atoll
8527
Sorol Atoll
Babelthuap
Koror
Angaur
8138
Caroline Islands
(U.S. Trust Territory of the Pacific Islands)
Sonsorol Islands
Pulo Anna
Merir
5798
Tobi
Helen Atoll
Kepulauan Mapia
Kepulauan Asia
Equator
CELEBES SEA
Kepulauan Talaud
Kepulauan Nenusa
Karakelong
Salebabu
Kaburuang
Pulau Sangihe
Tahuna
Siau
Kepulauan Sangihe
Tahulandang
Biaro
Bangka
Manado
2022
Kema
Kotamobagu
Gorontalo
UTARA
Teluk Tomini
Kepulauan Togian
Toli-toli
Tg. Mangkalihat
Makasar
Donggala
Palu
Poso
Tokala 2630
3311
TENGAH
SULAWESI (CELEBES)
SELATAN
Palopo
Rantemario 3455
Kolonodale
Teluk Tolo
Mekongga 2799
TENGGARA
Kendari
Wowoni
Pare-pare
Watampone
Ujung Pandang
Lompobatang 2871
Teluk Bone
Muna
Butung
Baubau
Kabaena
Salayar
Kepulauan Banggai
Peleng
Taliabu
Mangole
Kepulauan Sula
Sanana
MOLUCCA SEA
Morotai
Halmahera
Tobelo
Galela
Ternate
Tidore
Makian
Teluk Buli
Teluk Weda
Weda
Kep. Bacan
Bacan
Labuha
Obi
Kepulauan Obi
Tg. Libobo
Waigeo
Salawati
Batanta
Misool
Selat Dampier
Sorong
Jazirah Doberai (Vogelkop)
Manokwari
Kwoka 3000
Kepulauan Schouten
Biak
Supiori
Numfoor
Yapen
Selat Yapen
Serui
Teluk Cendrawasih
IRIAN JAYA
Pegunungan Van Rees
Pegunungan Maoke
Pengunungan Sudirman
Pegunungan Jayawijaya
Puncak Jaya 5029
4750
4702
Jayapura (Hollandia)
Sarmi
PAPUA NEW GUINEA
Wamena
Tanahmerah
Teluk Flamingo
Pulau Yos Sudarso
Merauke
Tg. Vals
Okaba
Fakfak
Kaimana
Teluk Berau
Tg. Fatagar
Teluk Kamrau
Kepulauan Watubela
Kepulauan Gorong
Seram
(Ceram)
Bula
Wahai
Ambon
Buru
Namlea
Namrole
SERAM SEA
BANDA SEA
Kepulauan Banda
7440
5888
Kepulauan Kai
Tual
Kai Besar
Kai Ketil
Kepulauan Aru
Wokam
Kobroor
Trangan
Dobo
Tg. Ngabordamlu
Kepulauan Tanimbar
Yamdena
Saumlaki
Selaru
Selu
Larat
Wetar
Kepulauan Kisar
Romang
Leti
Kepulauan Leti
Sermata
Babar
Damar
Teun
Nila
Serua
Barat Daya
MALUKU
Banda
Flores
Ende
Maumere
Ruteng
Bima
Sumbawa
Sumba
Waingapu
Sawu Sea
Alor
Pantar
Lomblen
Adonara
Kalabahi
Selat Ombai
Timor
Dili
Viqueque
Tata Mailau 2920
Kefamenanu
Kupang
Roti
Semau
Sawu
Raijua
Dana
NUSA TENGGARA TIMUR
ARAFURA SEA
Kepulauan Tukangbesi
Wangiwangi
Batuata (Watuata I.)
Kepulauan Bone Rate
Kalaotoa
2382
5123
COPYRIGHT, GEORGE PHILIP & SON, LTD.

1: 30 000 000

200 0 200 400 600 800 1000 km

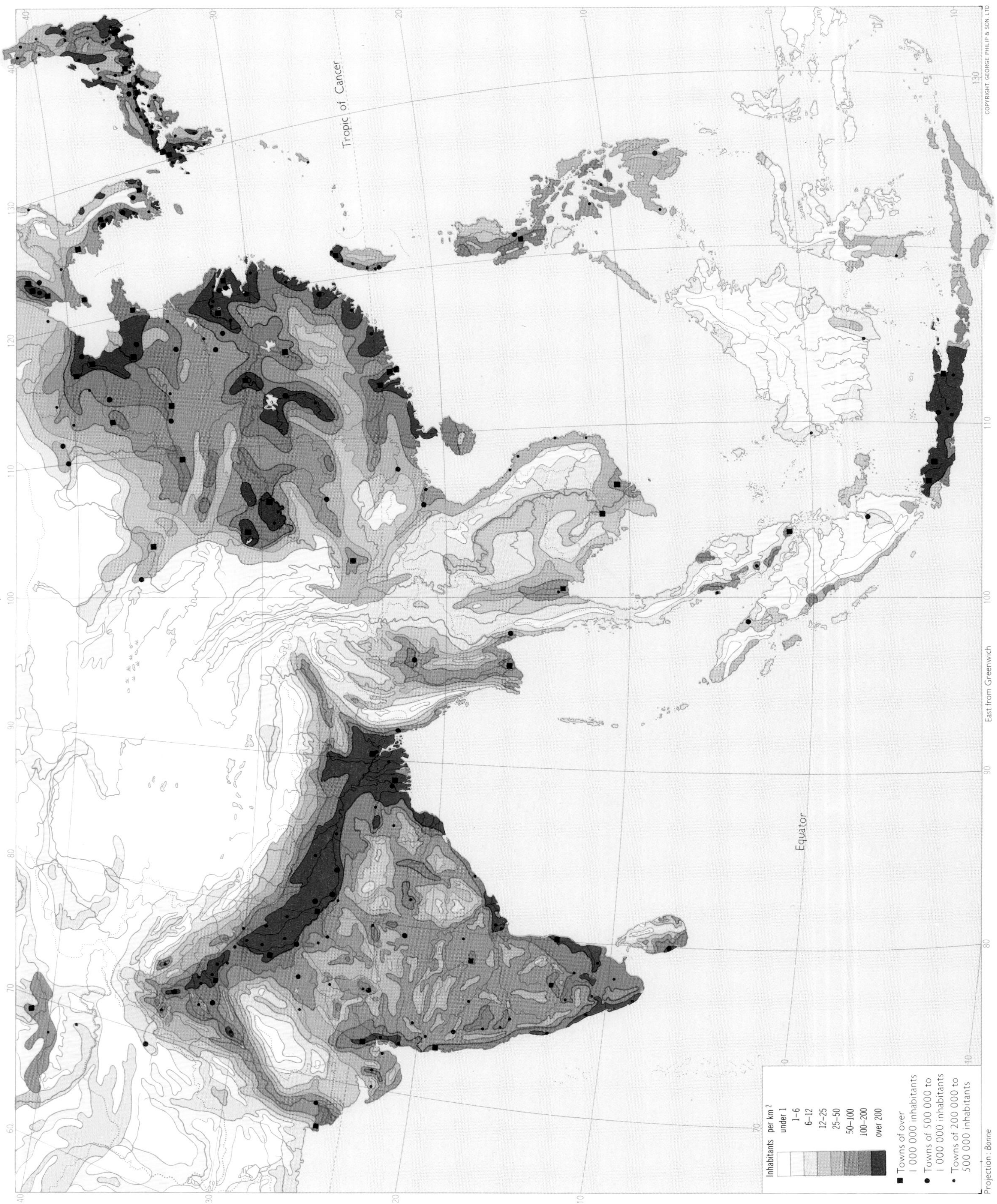
Tropic of Cancer
Equator
East from Greenwich
Inhabitants per km²
under 1
1–6
6–12
12–25
25–50
50–100
100–200
over 200
Towns of over 1 000 000 inhabitants
Towns of 500 000 to 1 000 000 inhabitants
Towns of 200 000 to 500 000 inhabitants
Projection: Bonne

1:20 000 000

200 0 200 400 600 800 km

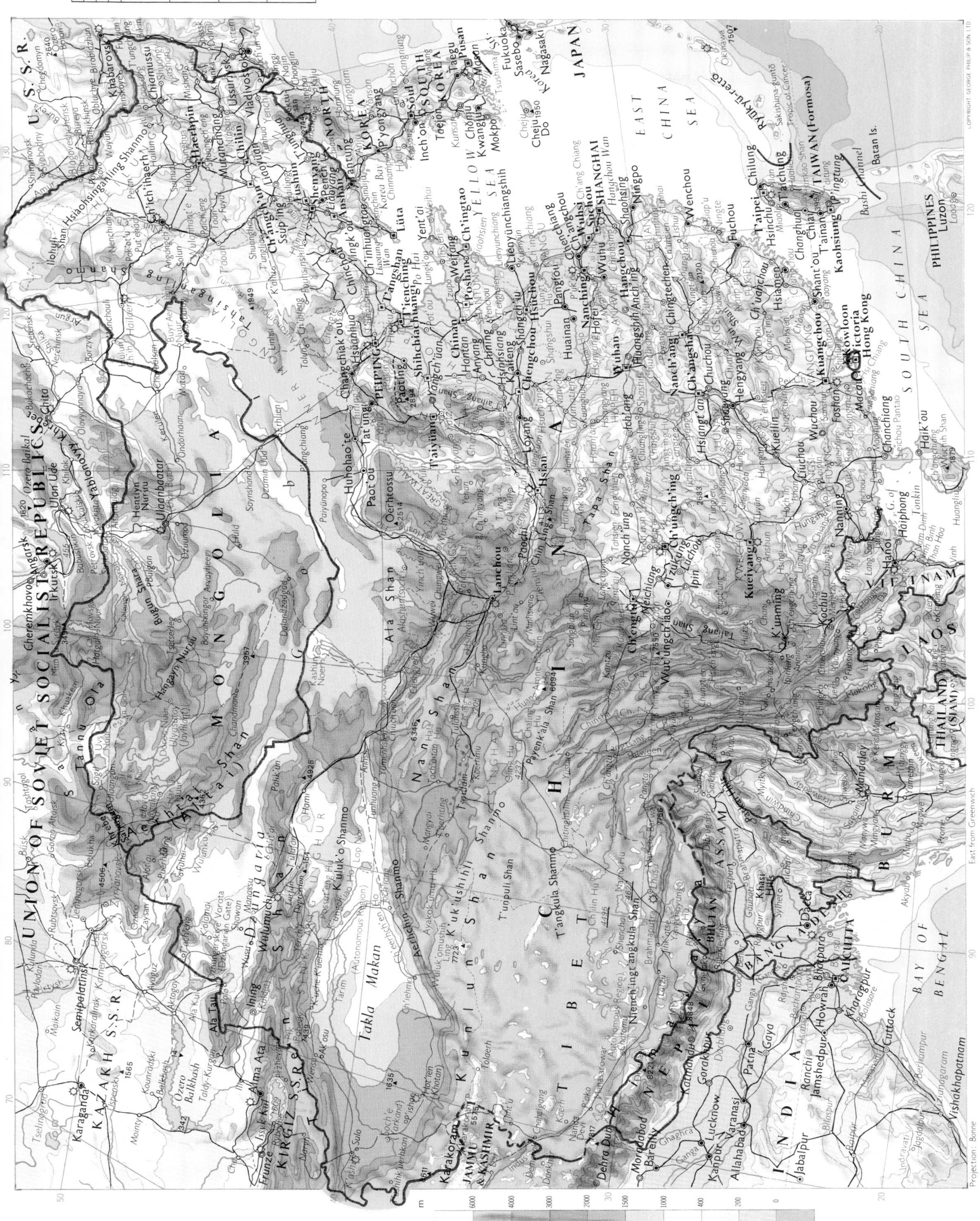
UNION OF SOVIET SOCIALIST REPUBLICS
U. S. S. R.
MONGOLIA
TIBET
CHINA
JAPAN
NORTH KOREA
SOUTH KOREA
EAST CHINA SEA
YELLOW SEA
SOUTH CHINA SEA
BAY OF BENGAL
INDIA
NEPAL
BHUTAN
ASSAM
BURMA
LAOS
THAILAND (SIAM)
PHILIPPINES
TAIWAN (Formosa)
PEIPING
SHANGHAI
HONG KONG
CALCUTTA
Projection: Bonne
East from Greenwich
COPYRIGHT GEORGE PHILIP & SON LTD

MONGOLIA
ÖVÖR HANGAY
DUNDGOVĬ
DORNOGOVĬ
SÜHBAATAR
ÖMNÖGOVĬ
Gobi
CHINA
NINGSIA-HUI A.R.
Oerhtossu (Ordos)
Ala Shan
Lang Shan
Tach'ing Shan
THE GREAT WALL
Huang Ho (Yellow River)
Paiyü Shan
Ch'in Ling Shan
Funiu Shan
T'aihang Shan
Chungt'iao Shan
Wei Ho
Lo Ho
Fen Ho
PEIP'ING (Peking)
T'AIYÜAN (Yangch'ü)
HSIAN (Sian)
Lanchou
Paot'ou
Huhohaot'e
Tat'ung
Changchiak'ou (Kalgan)
Shihchiachuangi
Chengchou (Chengchow)
K'aifeng
Loyang
Yinch'uan
Hanchung (Nancheng)
Nanyang
Paoting
Projection: Conical with two standard parallels

HAERHPIN (Harbin)
H E I L U N G K I A N G
U.S.S.R.
Ozero Khanka
Vladivostok
Ussuriysk (Voroshilov)
Razdolnoye
Artem
Mutanchiang
Ningan
Ch'angch'un
Chilin (Kirin)
Shuangliao
Ssup'ing
Liaoyüan
Fushun
SHENYANG (Mukden)
Pench'i
Liaoyang
Anshan
Chinchou
Yingk'ou
Tantung
Sinŭiju
L I A O N I N G
K I R I N
Pei (Manchuria)
Ch'angpai Shan
Paektu-san
2744
Liaotung Wan
Liaotung Pantao
Korea Bay
LÜTA (Dairen)
Lüshun (Port Arthur)
Po Hai (Gulf of Chihli)
T'angshan
TIENCHING (Tientsin)
T'angku
Taku
Ch'inhuangtao (Chinwangtao)
Shanhaikuan
NORTH KOREA
P'yŏngyang
Wŏnsan
Hŭngnam
Hamhŭng
Chongjin
Tongjosŏn Man
Kaesŏng
Cease Fire Line
SOUL (Seoul)
Inch'ŏn
Yŏngdŭngpo
Ŭijŏngbu
Ch'unch'ŏn
Kangnŭng
Wŏnju
Suwŏn
SOUTH KOREA
Taejŏn
Taegu
Pusan
Kwangju
Mokpo
Yŏsu
Masan
Ulsan
Pohang
Kunsan
Chŏnju
Ullŭng Do
Cheju Do
Cheju
Sogipo
1950
SEA OF JAPAN
Korea Strait
Tsushima
Tsushima-kaikyō
Iki
JAPAN
Sasebo
Nagasaki
Karatsu
Nakadōri-jima
Fukue-jima
Shantung Pantao
Laichou Wan
Yent'ai (Chefoo)
Weihai
Weifang
Tzupo
CH'INGTAO (Tsingtao)
Chiaochou Wan
Lienyünchiangshih (Hsinhailien)
Haichou Wan
K I A N G S U
YELLOW SEA
East from Greenwich

KANSU
SHENSI
SZECHWAN
KWEICHOW
YUNNAN
KWANGSI CHUANG AUTONOMOUS REGION
KACHIN
BURMA
SHAN STATE
LAOS
THAILAND
VIETNAM
Gulf of Tonkin
CH'ENGTU
CH'UNGCH'ING
(Chungking)
K'unming
Kueiyang
Nanning
Hanoi
Haiphong
Hanchung
(Nancheng)
Nanch'ung
Wanhsien
Tzukung
Neichiang
Luchou
Ipin
Tsuni
Anshun
Kochiu
Liuchou
Ha Dong
Nam Dinh
Luang Prabang
Phong Saly
Nam Tha
Weichou Tao
Leichou Pantao
(Luichow Peninsula)
Fai Tsi Long Archipelago
Ningching Shan
Sülung Shan
Tahsüeh Shan
Chiunglai Shan
Kaolikung Shan
Wuliang Shan
Ailao Shan
Taliang Shan
Tapa Shan
Nu Shan
Yünling Shan
Salween
Mekong
Minya Konka
7600
5500
4038
3054
3143
3233
3670
2683
2320
4000
3000
2000
1500
1000
400
200
0
m

Projection: Conical with two standard parallels

1:6 000 000

50 0 50 100 150 200 250 km

HONAN
KIANGSU
ANHWEI
HUPEH
CHEKIANG
KIANGSI
HUNAN
FUKIEN
KWANGTUNG
KWANGSI CHUANG
TAIWAN
(FORMOSA)
HONG KONG (U.K.)
Kowloon
VICTORIA
KUANGCHOU (Canton)
Macau (Macao) (Port.)
SHANGHAI
NANCHING (Nanking)
Hangchou
Suchou (Soochow)
Wuhsi
Ch'angchou
Chenchiang
Nant'ung
Ningpo
Shaohsing
Wenchou
Fuchou (Foochow)
Hsiamen (Amoy)
Chinmen Tao (Quemoy)
Ch'uanchou
Changchou
Shant'ou (Swatow)
Ch'aoan
Shaokuan
Foshan
Chiangmen
Ch'angsha
Hsiangt'an
Chuchou
Hengyang
Shaoyang
Yüehyang
Nanch'ang
Chiuchiang
Kanchou
Chingtechen
Shangjao
Linch'uan
WUHAN
Hank'ou
Hanyang
Wuch'ang
Huangshih
Shashih
Ich'ang
Hsiangfan
Nanyang
Hsinyang (Sinyang)
Hofei
Anch'ing
Wuhu
Pangfou
Huainan
Yangchou
T'AIPEI
Chilung
Hsinchu
T'aichung
Changhua
Chiai
T'ainan
Kaohsiung
P'ingtung
Hualien
Chanchiang (Tsamkong)
Wuchou
Chungyang Shanmo
Wui Shan
Tapieh Shan
Nanling
Formosa Strait
Luzon Strait
SOUTH CHINA SEA
Tropic of Cancer
Ch'ang Chiang (Yangtze)
Poyang Hu
Tungt'ing Hu
Chou Shan
Hsinkao Shan
3997
3931
1816
1725
1629
2120
2164
1703
1834
112
114
116
118
120
122
20
22
24
26
28
30
32

S E A O F J A P A N
SOUTH KOREA
Oki-Shotō
Dōgo
Daimanji-San 608
Saigō
H O N S
CHŪGOKU - DISTRICT
Shimane-Hantō
Matsue
Jizō-Zaki
Sakaiminato
Yonago
Hirata
Shinji-Ko
Hi-no-Misaki
Taisha
Izumo
Yasugi
Daitō
Kisuki
Iwami
Tottori
Kurayoshi
TOTTORI
Toyooka
Ōda
Gōtsu
Hamada
SHIMANE
Chūgoku-Sanchi
Tsuyama
Niimi
Ochiai
OKAYAMA
Tōjō
Shōbara
Miyoshi
Takahashi
Okayama
Himeji
Tatsuno
Aioi
Akō
Bizen
Saidaiji
Takasago
Kakogawa
Masuda
HIROSHIMA
Kake
Ōta-Gawa
Yakage
Sōja
Kurashiki
Fuchū
Ibara
Fukuyama
Kasaoka
Tamano
Mi-Shima
Ōmi-Shima
Hagi
Tsuno-Shima
Aono-Yama
Kanmuri-Yama 1339
HIROSHIMA
Saijō
Mihara
Onomichi
Harima-Nada
Awaji-Shima
Shōdo-Shima
Tonoshō
Takamatsu
Sakaide
Marugame
Zentsūji
KAGAWA
Naruto
Tokushima
Hibiki-Nada
Nagato
YAMAGUCHI
Yamaguchi
Mine
Toyoura
Tokuji
Hōfu
Ōtake
Iwakuni
Kure
Takehara
In'no-shima
Hiroshima-Wan
Genkai-Nada
Shimonoseki
Onoda
Ube
Tokuyama
Kudamatsu
Hikari
Yanai
Aki-Nada
Hiuchi-Nada
Kan'onji
Imabari
Kawanoe
Niihama
Iyo-mishima
Saijō
Komatsujima
Anan
TOKUSHIMA
KITAKYŪSHŪ
Suō-Nada
Nakama
Nōgata
Yukuhashi
Ō-Shima
Iki
Katsumoto
Gō-no-ura
Iki-Kaikyō
Higasi-Suidō
Kara-Saki
Tsushima
Izuhara
Kō-Saki
Naga-Shima
Iwai-Jima
Hime-Jima
Oshima
Yashiro-Jima
Matsuyama
Heigun-To
Iyo
Shikoku-Sanchi
KOCHI
EHIME
FUKUOKA
Iizuka
Takawa
Nakatsu
Buzen
Kunisaki
Bungotakada
Usa
Fukuma
Ō-Shima
Yobuko
Karatsu
Ikitsuki-Shima
Hirado
Hirado-Shima
Matsuura
Imari
SAGA
Tsukushi-Sanchi
Amagi
Tosu
Hita
Kurume
Saga
Takeo
Sasebo
Kashima
Yanagawa
Kitsuki
Beppu-Wan
Beppu
Ōita
Hōgo-Kaikyō
Yufu-Dake 1584
Iyo-Nada
Sada-Misaki-Hantō
Ōzu
Yawatahama
Uwajima
Kōchi
Tosa-yamada
Nankoku
Aki
Susaki
Tosa-Wan
Muroto
Muroto-Misaki
SHIKOKU
SHIKOKU - DISTRICT
Nakamura
Sukumo
Tosa-shimizu
Ashizuri-Zaki
Oki-no-Shima
Tsurumi-Saki
Bungo-Suidō
Saganoseki
Usuki
Tsukumi
Saiki
ŌITA
Kujū-San 1787
Taketa
Aso
Ōmuta
Arao
Omura-Wan
Ōmura
NAGASAKI
Nagasaki
Isahaya
Unzen-Dake 1360
Shimabara
Kumamoto
KUMAMOTO
Uto
Tamana
Kikuchi
Takachiho
Nobeoka
Nomo-Zaki
Tachibana-Wan
Amakusa-Nada
Amakusa-Shotō
Hondo
Shimo-Jima
Kami-Jima
Yatsushiro
Yatsushiro-Kai
Kyūshū-Sanchi
MIYAZAKI
Hyūga
Hitoyoshi
Ushibuka
Minamata
Izumi
Akune
Ōkuchi
Saito
KYŪSHŪ
KYŪSHŪ - DISTRICT
Kobayashi
Kirishima-Yama
Miyazaki
Miyakonojō
Sendai
Koshiki-Rettō
Kami-koshiki-Jima
Shimo-koshiki-Jima
Kushikino
Kagoshima
Kokubu
Nichinan
Taniyama
Kaseda
Noma-Saki
Makurazaki
Bō-no-Misaki
Kagoshima-Wan
Tarumizu
Kanoya
Kushima
Shibushi-Wan
Ibusuki
Kaimon-Dake 924
Ōsumi-Hantō
Sata-Misaki
Projection: Lambert's Conformal Conic

1:2 500 000

10 0 10 20 30 40 50 60 70 80 90 100 km

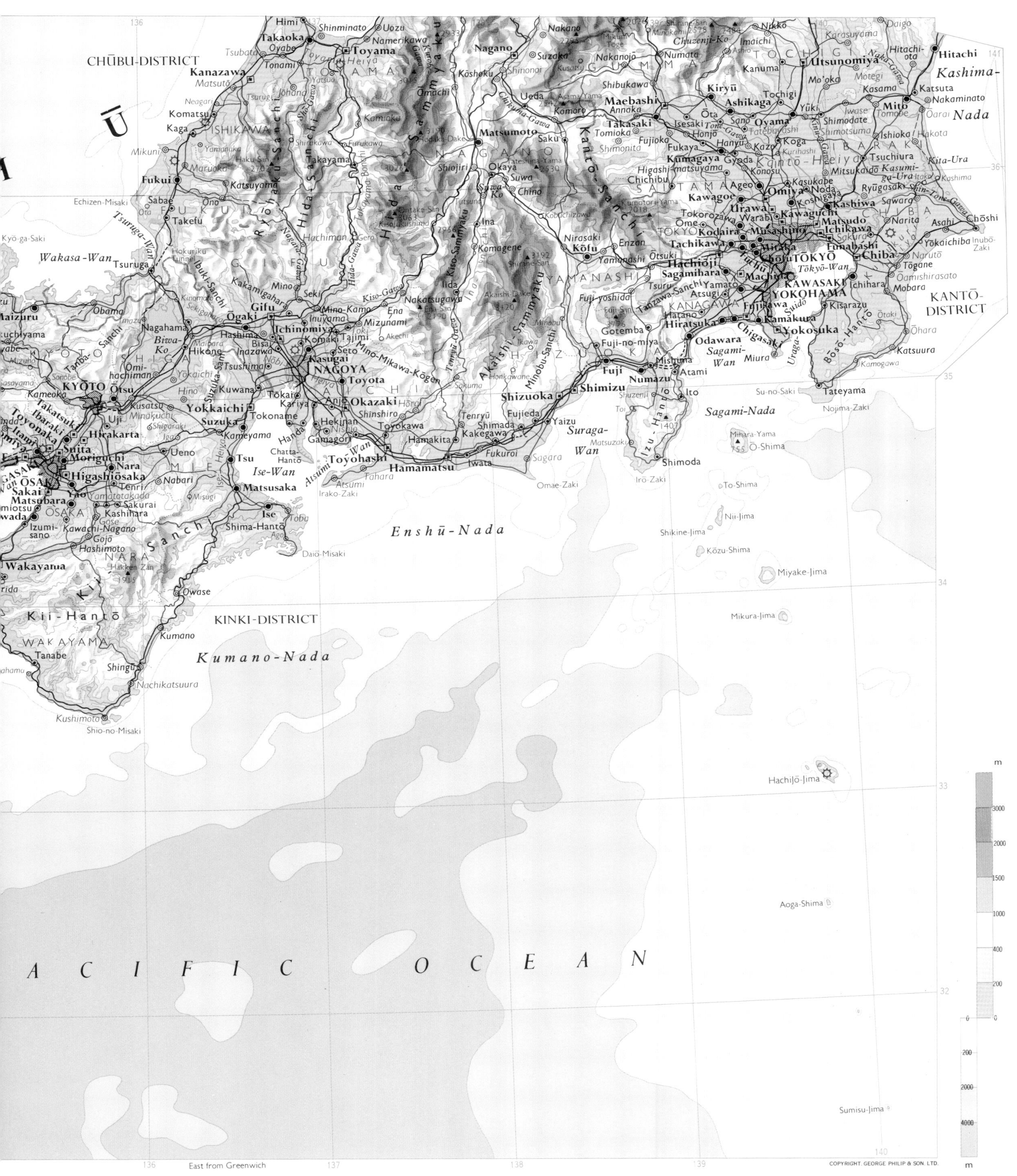
CHŪBU-DISTRICT
KINKI-DISTRICT
KANTŌ-DISTRICT
Himi
Takaoka
Shinminato
Uozu
Namerikawa
Toyama
Kanazawa
Komatsu
Kaga
Mikuni
Fukui
Katsuyama
Sabae
Takefu
Echizen-Misaki
Tsuruga-Wan
Tsuruga
Kyō-ga-Saki
Wakasa-Wan
Maizuru
Obama
Nagahama
Biwa-Ko
Hikone
Omi-hachiman
KYOTO
Otsu
Kameoka
Takatsuki
Ibaraki
Toyonaka
Itami
Suita
Moriguchi
Hirakarta
Uji
Higashiōsaka
Nara
Yao
Sakai
Matsubara
Izumi-sano
Kashihara
Sakurai
Tenri
Kawachi-Nagano
Gojō
Hashimoto
Wakayama
Kii-Hantō
WAKAYAMA
Tanabe
Shingū
Kumano
Nachikatsuura
Kushimoto
Shio-no-Misaki
Kumano-Nada
Owase
Ise
Shima-Hantō
Daiō-Misaki
Matsusaka
Tsu
Ise-Wan
Ueno
Nabari
Kameyama
Suzuka
Yokkaichi
Kuwana
Tsushima
NAGOYA
Kasugai
Ichinomiya
Gifu
Ōgaki
Hashima
Seki
Mino
Inuyama
Tajimi
Mizunami
Seto
Toyota
Okazaki
Anjō
Kariya
Tōkai
Tokoname
Handa
Chatta-Hantō
Hekinan
Nishio
Gamagōri
Toyohashi
Toyokawa
Shinshiro
Atsumi-Wan
Irako-Zaki
Hamamatsu
Iwata
Hamakita
Fukuroi
Kakegawa
Shimada
Fujieda
Yaizu
Shizuoka
Shimizu
Fuji
Numazu
Mishima
Atami
Ito
Izu-Hantō
Shimoda
Irō-Zaki
Omae-Zaki
Suraga-Wan
Enshū-Nada
Takayama
Matsumoto
Nagano
Ueda
Komoro
Saku
Suwa
Okaya
Chino
Shiojiri
Ina
Komagene
Iida
Nakatsugawa
Ena
Kōfu
Nirasaki
Ōtsuki
Fuji-yoshida
Gotemba
Fuji-no-miya
Odawara
Hiratsuka
Chigasaki
Fujisawa
Kamakura
Yokosuka
Miura
Sagami-Wan
Sagami-Nada
YOKOHAMA
KAWASAKI
TŌKYŌ
Tōkyō-Wan
Hachiōji
Sagamihara
Machida
Atsugi
Yamato
Tachikawa
Kodaira
Musashino
Mitaka
Chōfu
Fuchū
Tokorozawa
Ōme
Kawagoe
Urawa
Ōmiya
Kawaguchi
Ageo
Kumagaya
Fukaya
Gyoda
Kōnosu
Chichibu
Takasaki
Maebashi
Isesaki
Honjō
Kiryū
Ashikaga
Ōta
Tochigi
Oyama
Koga
Utsunomiya
Kanuma
Nikkō
Numata
Shibukawa
Mito
Hitachi
Katsuta
Nakaminato
Kashima-Nada
Tsuchiura
Ishioka
Shimodate
Yūki
Ryūgasaki
Noda
Kashiwa
Matsudo
Ichikawa
Funabashi
Chiba
Narita
Sakura
Chōshi
Asahi
Yōkaichiba
Tōgane
Mobara
Ichihara
Kisarazu
Tateyama
Bōsō-Hantō
Katsuura
Uraga-Suido
Nojima-Zaki
Ō-Shima
To-Shima
Nii-Jima
Shikine-Jima
Kōzu-Shima
Miyake-Jima
Mikura-Jima
Hachijō-Jima
Aoga-Shima
Sumisu-Jima
PACIFIC OCEAN
East from Greenwich
COPYRIGHT GEORGE PHILIP & SON LTD.

1:7 500 000

1:40 000 000

400 0 400 800 1200 1600 km

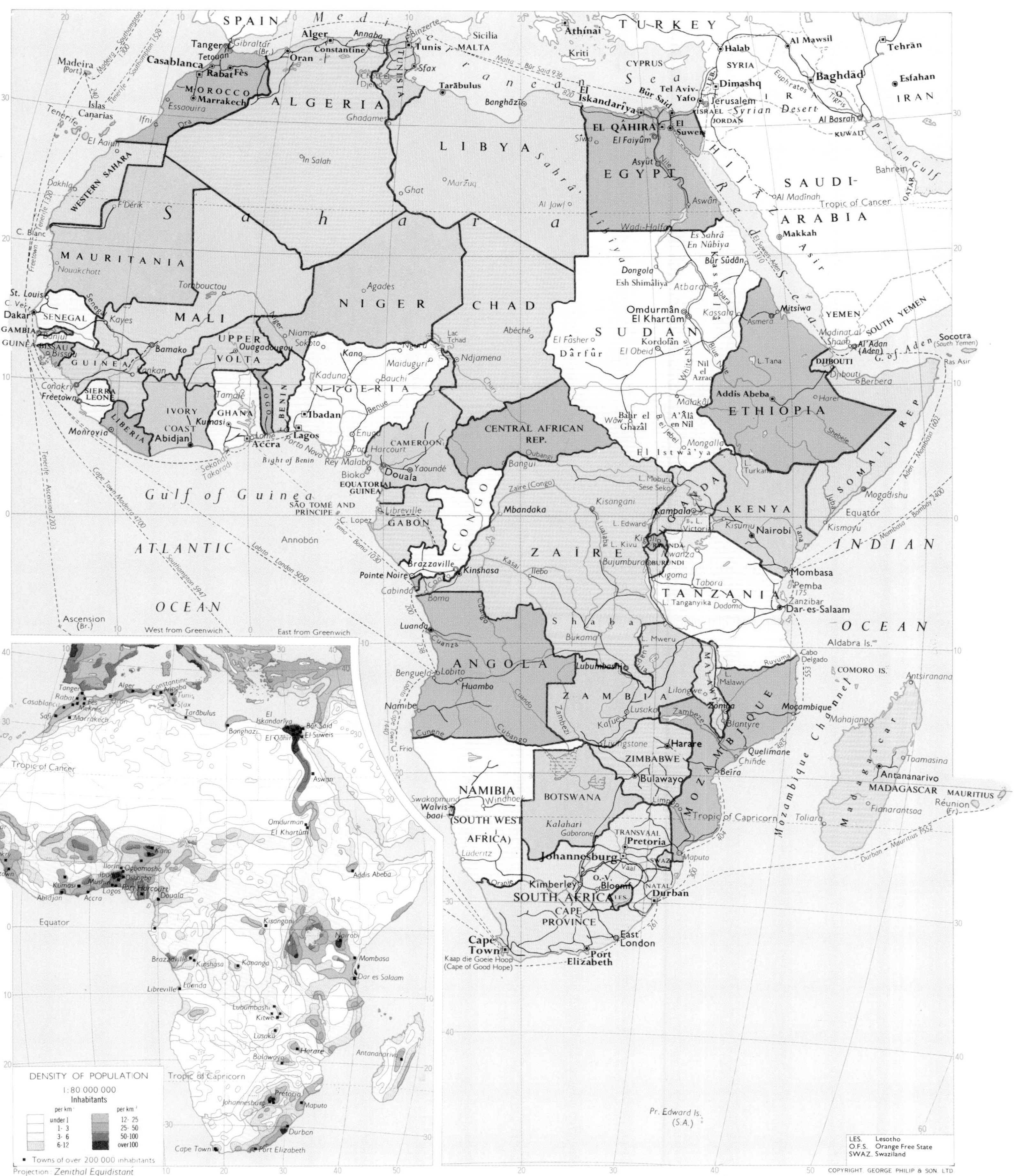
DENSITY OF POPULATION
1:80 000 000
Inhabitants
per km²
under 1
1- 3
3- 6
6-12
12- 25
25- 50
50-100
over 100
■ Towns of over 200 000 inhabitants
LES. Lesotho
O.F.S. Orange Free State
SWAZ. Swaziland
ALGERIA
LIBYA
EGYPT
SUDAN
CHAD
NIGER
MALI
MAURITANIA
NIGERIA
ETHIOPIA
KENYA
TANZANIA
ZAÏRE
ANGOLA
ZAMBIA
ZIMBABWE
BOTSWANA
SOUTH AFRICA
MADAGASCAR
ATLANTIC OCEAN
INDIAN OCEAN

Projection: Zenithal Equidistant

1: 40 000 000

400 0 400 800 1200 1600 km

ANNUAL RAINFALL
1: 80 000 000

mm
3000
2000
1000
500
250

Projection : *Lambert's Equivalent Azimuthal*

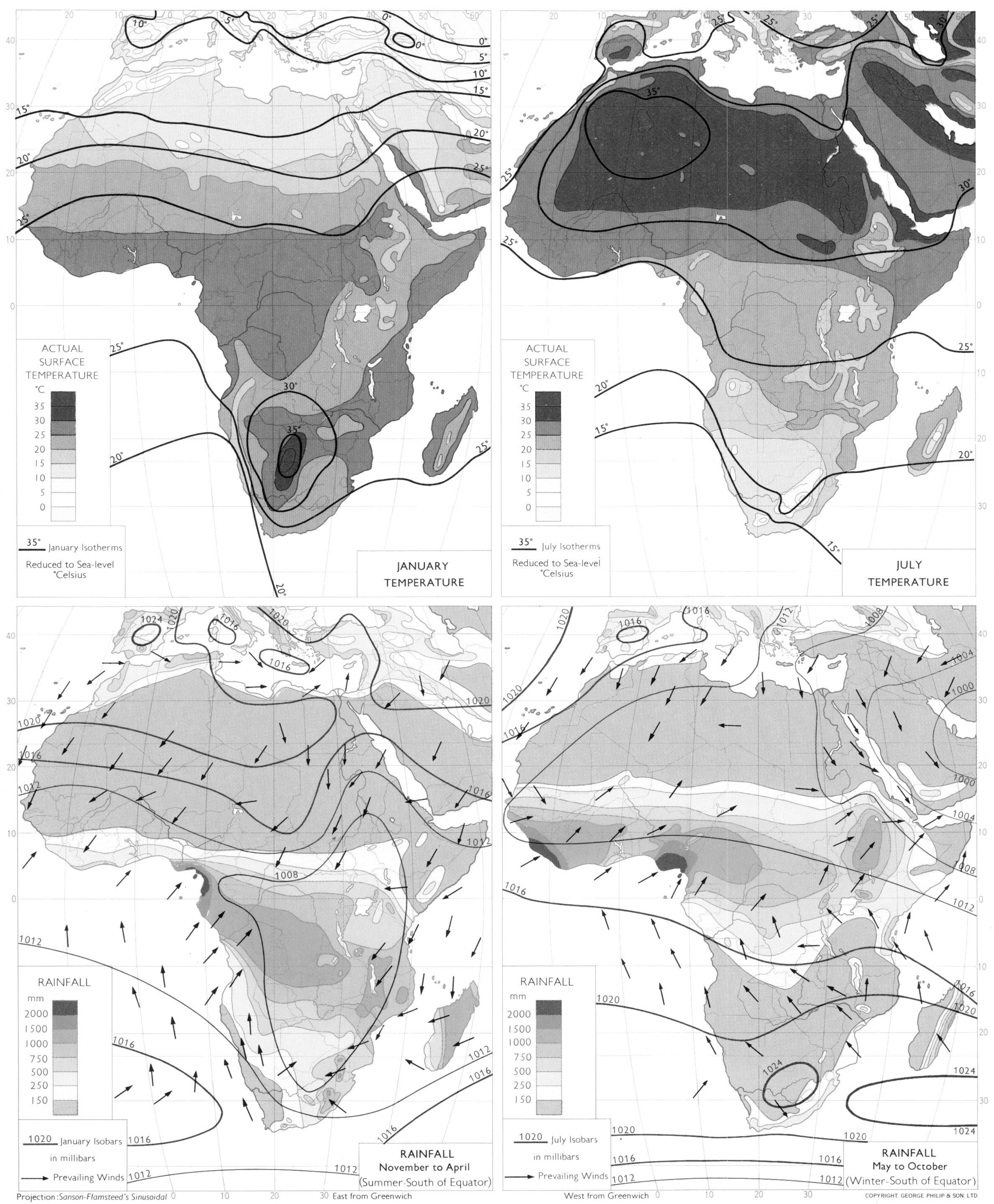
ACTUAL SURFACE TEMPERATURE
°C
35
30
25
20
15
10
5
0
35° January Isotherms
Reduced to Sea-level °Celsius
JANUARY TEMPERATURE
35° July Isotherms
Reduced to Sea-level °Celsius
JULY TEMPERATURE
RAINFALL
mm
2000
1500
1000
750
500
250
150
1020 January Isobars in millibars
Prevailing Winds
RAINFALL
November to April
(Summer-South of Equator)
1020 July Isobars in millibars
Prevailing Winds
RAINFALL
May to October
(Winter-South of Equator)
Projection: Sanson-Flamsteed's Sinusoidal
East from Greenwich
West from Greenwich

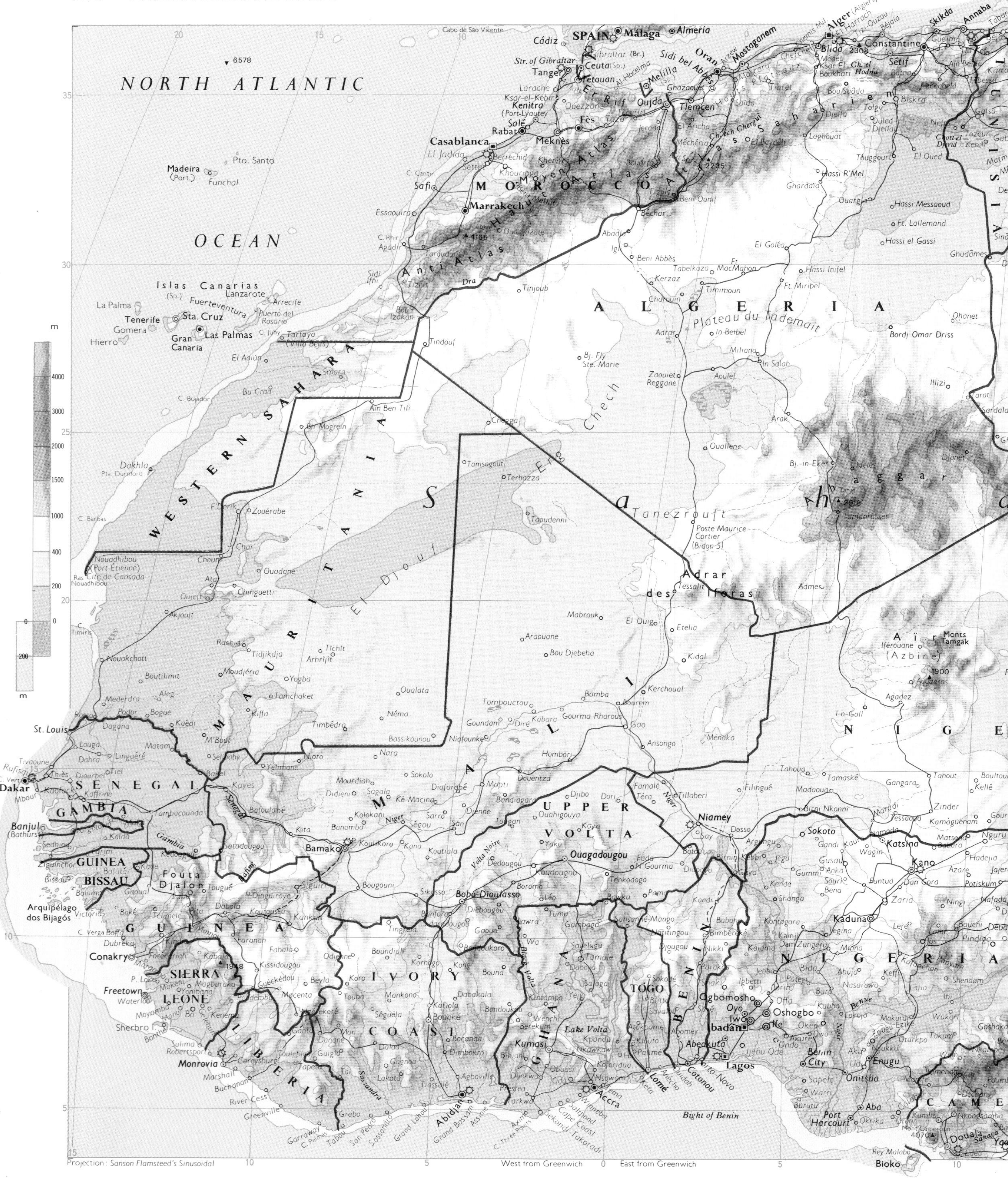
NORTH ATLANTIC
OCEAN
Madeira (Port.)
Pto. Santo
Funchal
Islas Canarias (Sp.)
Lanzarote
Fuerteventura
Arrecife
Puerto del Rosario
La Palma
Tenerife
Sta. Cruz
Gomera
Hierro
Gran Canaria
Las Palmas
C. Juby
Tarfaya (Villa Bens)
El Aaiún
Smara
Bu Craa
C. Bojador
WESTERN SAHARA
Dakhla
Pta. Durnford
C. Barbas
Nouadhibou (Port Etienne)
Ras Nouadhibou
Cite de Cansada
SPAIN
Málaga
Almería
Cádiz
Str. of Gibraltar
Gibraltar (Br.)
Tanger
Ceuta (Sp.)
Tetouan
Melilla (Sp.)
Al-Hoceima
Larache
Ksar-el-Kebir
Kenitra (Port-Lyautey)
Salé
Rabat
Casablanca
El Jadida
Berrechid
Settat
Khouribga
Meknès
Fès
Taza
Oujda
Ouezzane
Er Rif
Safi
C. Cantin
Essaouira
Marrakech
C. Rhir
Agadir
Taroudant
Ouarzazate
Tiznit
Sidi Ifni
Bou Izakan
Anti Atlas
Haut Atlas
Moyen Atlas
4165
MOROCCO
Dra
Tindouf
Tinjoub
Cabo de São Vicente
Oran
Mostaganem
Sidi bel Abbès
Tlemcen
Ghazaouet
Alger (Algiers)
Blida
Médéa
Ksar El Boukhari
Chech Chergui
Ch. el Hodna
Constantine
Skikda
Annaba
Sétif
Batna
Biskra
Bou Saâda
Djelfa
Laghouat
Touggourt
El Oued
Ouled Djellal
Saïda
Mascara
Tiaret
Chott el Djerid
Hassi R'Mel
Ghardaïa
Ouargla
Hassi Messaoud
Ft. Lallemand
Hassi el Gassi
El Goléa
Béchar
Beni Ounif
Abadla
Beni Abbès
Tabelkaza
Ft. MacMahon
Kerzaz
Timimoun
Hassi Inifel
Ft. Miribel
Charouin
ALGERIA
Plateau du Tademait
Adrar
In Belbel
Bordj Omar Driss
Ohanet
Zaouiet Reggane
Bj. Fly Ste. Marie
Aoulef
In Salah
Arak
Illizi
Ouallene
Bj.-in-Eker
Ahaggar
Tahat
2918
Tamanrasset
Djanet
Chech
Tanezrouft
Poste Maurice Cortier (Bidon 5)
Erg
Taoudenni
Tamsagout
Terhazza
Chegga
Aïn Ben Tili
Bir Mogrein
F'Derik
Zouérate
MAURITANIA
Choum
Char
Atar
Ouadane
Chinguetti
Ouiet
Akjoujt
C. Timiris
El Djouf
Nouakchott
Boutilimit
Rachid
Tidjikdja
Tichit
Arhrijit
Moudjéria
Yogba
Aleg
Mederdra
Tamchaket
Kiffa
Oualata
Néma
Timbédra
Bassikounou
Rosso
Podor
Bogué
Kaédi
M'Bout
Sélibaby
St. Louis
Dagana
Louga
Matam
Dahra
Linguéré
SENEGAL
Tivaouane
Thiès
Rufisque
C. Vert
Dakar
Mbour
Diourbel
Kaolack
Kaffrine
Bakel
Kayes
GAMBIA
Banjul (Bathurst)
Georgetown
Tambacounda
Kolda
Sedhiou
Ziguinchor
Gambia
GUINEA BISSAU
Bissau
Bafatá
Bolama
Arquipélago dos Bijagós
Fouta Djalon
Labé
Boké
Tougué
Dabola
Mamou
Kouroussa
Kankan
Kindia
Faranah
C. Verga
Dubréka
Conakry
Forécariah
Kabala
1948
GUINEA
SIERRA LEONE
Freetown
Waterloo
Moyamba
Kenema
Makeni
Sherbro I.
Bonthe
Sulima
LIBERIA
Robertsport
Monrovia
Careysburg
Marshall
Buchanan
River Cess
Greenville
Garraway
C. Palmas
Harper
Kissidougou
Guéckédou
Macenta
Beyla
Nzérékoré
Ganta
Tapeta
Odienné
Touba
Man
Danané
Guiglo
Séguéla
Mankono
Korhogo
Katiola
Bouaké
Boundiali
Kong
Bouna
Dabakala
Bondoukou
Daloa
Gagnoa
Lakota
Dimbokro
Bocanda
Tiassalé
Agboville
Abidjan
Grand Bassam
Assinie
Grand Lahou
Sassandra
San Pedro
Tabou
Grabo
Sassandra
IVORY COAST
Mali
MALI
Tombouctou
Kabara
Dire
Goundam
Niafounké
Gourma-Rharous
Bourem
Gao
Ansongo
Ménaka
Hombori
Kidal
Tessalit
Adrar des Iforas
Aguelhok
El Ouig
Etelia
Mabrouk
Araouane
Bou Djebeha
Kerchoual
Bamba
Nioro
Nara
Yélimané
Sokolo
Mourdiah
Diafarabé
Mopti
Djenné
Douentza
Bandiagara
Ké-Macina
Ségou
San
Kita
Bamako
Koulikoro
Kolokani
Banamba
Bafoulabé
Satadougou
Sikasso
Bougouni
Koutiala
Niger
Bafing
Senegal
UPPER VOLTA
Ouagadougou
Ouahigouya
Djibo
Dori
Kaya
Yako
Koudougou
Tenkodogo
Fada N'Gourma
Diapaga
Bobo-Dioulasso
Diébougou
Gaoua
Banfora
Volta Noire
Léo
Po
Bawku
Tumu
Lawra
Wa
Black Volta
Gambaga
Tamale
Salaga
Yeji
Kintampo
Wenchi
Berekum
Sunyani
Lake Volta
Kumasi
Obuasi
Dunkwa
Kpandu
Nkawkaw
Koforidua
Accra
Tema
Winneba
Saltpond
Cape Coast
Sekondi-Takoradi
Axim
C. Three Points
Tarkwa
Prestea
GHANA
TOGO
Sansanné-Mango
Sokodé
Atakpamé
Palimé
Lomé
Aného
BENIN
Natitingou
Djougou
Kandi
Parakou
Nikki
Savalou
Abomey
Ouidah
Cotonou
Porto-Novo
Bight of Benin
Niamey
Tillabéri
Famalé
Téra
Say
Dosso
Filingué
Tahoua
Madaoua
Birni Nkonni
Maradi
Zinder
Tessaoua
Gouré
Agadez
In-Gall
Aïr
Monts Tamgak
(Azbine)
Iférouane
1900
Tanout
NIGER
Sokoto
Gusau
Katsina
Kano
Zaria
Kaduna
Jos
Bauchi
Ilorin
Ogbomosho
Oyo
Oshogbo
Iwo
Ife
Ibadan
Abeokuta
Lagos
Ijebu Ode
Ondo
Akure
Benin City
Sapele
Warri
Onitsha
Enugu
Port Harcourt
Aba
Calabar
NIGERIA
Kaduna
Benue
Lokoja
Makurdi
CAMEROON
Bioko
Rey Malabo
Douala
Mont Cameroun
4070
Kumba
Sanaga
Projection: Sanson Flamsteed's Sinusoidal
West from Greenwich
East from Greenwich
m
4000
3000
2000
1500
1000
400
200
0
200
m

1:15 000 000

100 0 100 200 300 400 500 600 km

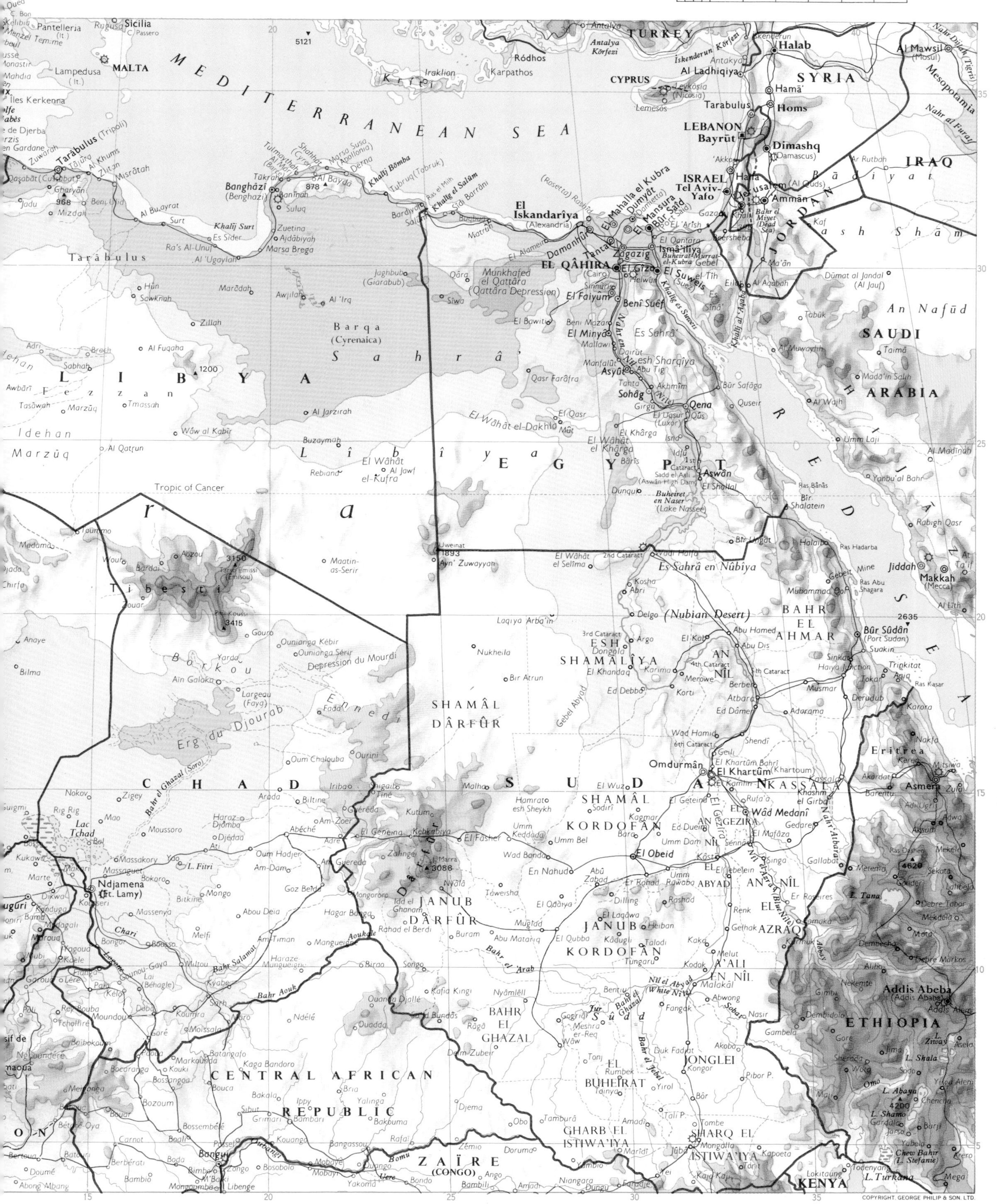
MEDITERRANEAN SEA
Sicilia
MALTA
Pantelleria
Lampedusa (It.)
Îles Kerkenna
Ródhos
Iraklion
Karpathos
Kriti
CYPRUS
Levkosia (Nicosia)
Lemesós
TURKEY
Antalya
Antalya Körfezi
İskenderun Körfezi
İskenderun
Antakya
Halab
Al Ladhiqiya
SYRIA
Hamā'
Homs
Tarabulus
LEBANON
Bayrūt
Dimashq (Damascus)
ISRAEL
Tel Aviv-Yafo
Jerusalem
'Ammān
JORDAN
IRAQ
Al Mawsil (Mosul)
Mesopotamia
Nahr Dijlah (Tigris)
Nahr al Furat
Ar Rutbah
Bādiyat ash Shām
Dūmat al Jandal (Al Jauf)
An Nafūd
SAUDI ARABIA
Taimā
Tabūk
Madā'in Salih
Al Wajh
Umm Lajj
Al Madīnah
Yanbu'al Bahr
Rabigh
Jiddah
Makkah (Mecca)
At Ta'if
Al Lith
HIJAZ
Tarabulus (Tripoli)
Misrātah
Banghāzī (Benghazi)
Al Bayda
Darna
Tubruq (Tobruk)
Khalīj Bōmba
Khalīj Surt
Surt
Es Sider
Zuetina
Ajdābiyah
Marsa Brega
Gharyān
Mizdah
Beni Ulid
Al Buayrat
Tarābulus
Jaghbub (Giarabub)
Hūn
Sawknah
Zillah
Marādah
Awjilah
Al 'Irq
Barqa (Cyrenaica)
Sahrâ Lîbîya
LIBYA
Fezzan
Sabhah
Awbārī
Tasāwah
Marzūq
Tmassah
Al Fuqaha
Al Jarzirah
Wāw al Kabīr
Al Qatrun
Idehan Marzūq
Buzaymah
Rebiana
El Wāhāt el-Kufra
Al Jawf
Tropic of Cancer
Sīwa
Qāra
Munkhafed el Qattâra (Qattâra Depression)
El Iskandarîya (Alexandria)
El Mahalla el Kubra
Dumyât (Damietta)
El Mansura
Bûr Sa'îd (Port Said)
Damanhûr
Tanta
Zagazig
Ismâ'iliya
EL QÂHIRA (Cairo)
El Gîza
Helwân
El Suweis (Suez)
El Faiyûm
Beni Suef
El Minya
Mallawi
Asyût
Sohâg
Qena
Qus
El Uqsur (Luxor)
Isna
Idfu
Aswân
Sadd el Aali (Aswan High Dam)
Buheiret en Naser (Lake Nasser)
El Wâhât el-Dakhla
El Wâhât el Khârga
El Khârga
Qasr Farâfra
El Bawiti
Es Sahrâ' esh Sharqîya
EGYPT
Bûr Safâga
Quseir
Ras Banas
Uweinat 1893
Ayn' Zuwayyah
Maatin-as-Serir
Wadi Halfa
2nd Cataract
Es Sahrâ en Nûbiya (Nubian Desert)
Delgo
Argo
3rd Cataract
4th Cataract
5th Cataract
6th Cataract
ESH SHAMALIYA
Dongola
Karima
Merowe
Abu Hamed
Berber
Atbara
Ed Damer
Shendi
Bûr Sûdân (Port Sudan)
Suakin
Tokar
BAHR EL AHMAR
RED SEA
Halaib
Omdurmân
El Khartûm
El Khartûm Bahrî
Kassala
Wad Medanî
El Obeid
Er Roseires
Malakâl
Juba
NUBA
Sennâr
Kosti
Mitsiwa
Asmera
Eritrea
Akordat
Gonder
L. Tana
Dese
Debre Markos
Addis Abeba
Nazret
ETHIOPIA
L. Shala
L. Abaya
L. Shamo
Chew Bahir (L. Stefanie)
L. Turkana
KENYA
Mega
Dembidolo
Gore
Jima
Gambela
Fangak
Bentiu
Kodok
Aweil
Wau
Tonj
Rumbek
Bor
Pibor P.
Kapoeta
Yei
Torit
SHAMÂL DÂRFÛR
JANUB DÂRFÛR
SHAMÂL KORDOFÂN
JANUB KORDOFÂN
A'ALI EN NÎL
BAHR EL GHAZAL
EL BUHEIRAT
JONGLEI
GHARB EL ISTIWA'IYA
SHARQ EL ISTIWA'IYA
EL GEZIRA
AN NÎL
AN NÎL EL AZRAQ
Nîl el Abyad (White Nile)
Nîl el Azraq (Blue Nile)
Bahr el Jebel
Bahr el 'Arab
Nahr Atbara
El Fasher
El Geneina
Nyala
Jebel Marra
3088
Umm Keddada
En Nahud
Umm Ruwaba
Dilling
Kadugli
Talodi
Rashad
Tibesti
3415
3150
Bardaï
Aozou
Zouar
Borkou
Faya (Largeau)
Fada
Ennedi
Erg du Djourab
Ounianga Kebir
Ounianga Sérir
Depression du Mourdi
Bilma
Tummo
CHAD
Lac Tchad
Bol
Mao
Moussoro
Ati
Oum Hadjer
Abéché
Adré
Am-Dam
Mongo
Ndjamena (Ft. Lamy)
Massenya
Massakory
Bahr el Ghazal
Bahr Salamat
Chari
Am Timan
Biltine
Iriba
Bokoro
Kélo
Moundou
Sarh
Doba
Koumra
Goz Beida
CENTRAL AFRICAN REPUBLIC
Bangui
Bambari
Bossangoa
Bouar
Berbérati
Bria
Ndélé
Birao
Kaga Bandoro
Sibut
Mobaye
Bangassou
Zémio
Obo
Djema
Rafai
ZAÏRE (CONGO)
Uele
Bomu
Ubangi
Bondo
Aketi
Bumba
Libenge
15
20
25
30
35
40
10
5
COPYRIGHT. GEORGE PHILIP & SON. LTD.

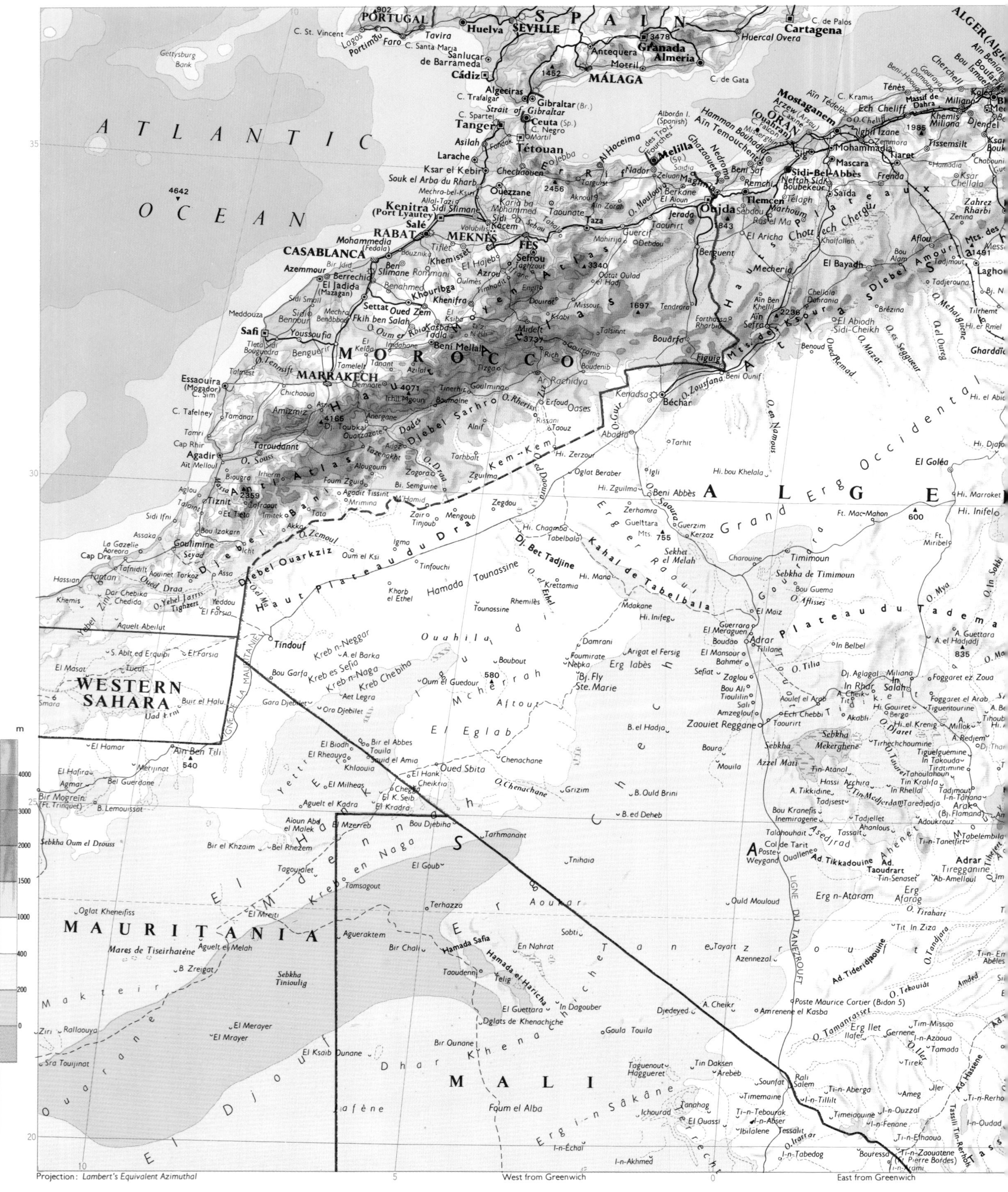

Projection: Lambert's Equivalent Azimuthal

1:8 000 000

50 0 50 100 150 200 250 300 km

MEDITERRANEAN SEA
SICILY
Marsala
Agrigento
Caltanissetta
CATANIA
Siracusa
Ragusa
Etna 3340
C. Spartivento
C. Passero
Pantelleria (Italian)
Linosa I. (Italian)
Lampione I. (Italian)
Lampedusa (Italian)
Gozo
Valletta
MALTA
Bizerte (Binzert)
C. Bon
Halq el Oued
Kelibia
TUNIS
Nabeul
Hammamet
G. de Hammamet
Kalaa-Kebira
Sousse
Monastir
Moknine
Mahdia
Kairouan
Sfax
Iles Kerkenna
G. de Gabès
Gabès
Djerba I.
Zarzis
Bahiret el Bibane
Medenine
Tatahouine
TUNISIA
Chott Djerid
Gafsa
Nefta
Tozeur
Béja
Jendouba
El Kef
Thala
Tébessa
Annaba
Skikda
Jijel
Bejaia
CONSTANTINE
Guelma
Sétif
El Eulma
Bordj bou Arreridj
Batna
Biskra
Khenchela
Bou Saâda
M'sila
Tolga
Chott Melrhir
Ouled Djellal
El Meghaier
El Oued
Touggourt
Ouargla
Guerrara
Hassi Messaoud
Ft. Lallemand
Grand Erg Oriental
Ghudamis
Plateau du Tinrhert
Al Hammādah al Ḥamrā'
Tarābulus (Tripoli)
Tājūrā'
Leptis Magna (Labdah)
Zuwārah
Jabal Nafūsah
Gharyān
Nālūt
Misurata
Zlīṭan
Tarhūnah
Banī Walīd
AL KHUMS
AL JABAL AL GHARB
Khalij Surt (Gulf of Sidra)
Surt
Sabkhat Tāwurghā'
Bu Nujaym
MISRĀTAH
Banghāzī (Benghazi)
Ajdābiyah
Marsa Brega
Jabal as Sawdā'
Hūn
Waddān
Al Jufrah
Zillah
SABHAH
Al Harūj al Aswad
Sabhah (Sebha)
Awbārī
Marzūq
Idehan Marzūq
Idehan
Tmassah
Al Qaṭrūn
Ghat
Djanet
Tassili n' Ajjer
Tamanrasset
Ahaggar
In Amenas
Bordj Omar Driss
Tropic of Cancer
Sarīr Tibasti
Ténéré
Tibesti
Tarso Emissi 3150
Emi Koussi 3415
Pic Toussidé 3265
Bardaï
Zouar
Massif de Kemet
Plateau du Djado
Djado
Chirfa
Bilma
Ségueddine
Toummo
Madama
I A
L I B Y A
A W B Ā R Ī
R
A
BANGHĀZĪ
N I G E R
C H A D
Massif de Terazit

Projection: Lambert's Equivalent Azimuthal

Gambia and Senegal have agreed to the amalgamation of their economies and armies. This new confederation is known as Senegambia.

1:8 000 000

50 0 50 100 150 200 250 300 km

ALGERIA
Adrar des Iforhas
Aïr (Azbine)
NIGER
Ténéré
Talak
Tahoua
NIGERIA
BENIN
GHANA
TOGO
CAMEROON
CHAD
EQUATORIAL GUINEA
Slave Coast
Bight of Benin
Niger Delta
Bight of Bonny
GULF OF GUINEA
Lac Tchad
N.E. NIGERIA
on same scale as general map
SOKOTO
KANO
KADUNA
BAUCHI
BORNO
NIGER
OYO
PLATEAU
GONGOLA
BENUE
ANAMBRA
BENDEL
CROSS RIVER
Niamey
LAGOS
IBADAN
ACCRA
Lomé
Cotonou
Porto-Novo
Kano
Kaduna
Zaria
Maiduguri
Port-Harcourt
Enugu
Abuja
Douala
Yaoundé
Agadez (Agadès)
Zinder
Maradi
Sokoto
Ilorin
Ogbomosho
Oshogbo
Abeokuta
Benin City
Onitsha
Aba
Calabar
Jos
Bauchi
Yola
Makurdi
Tamale
Kumasi
Monts Bagzane 1900
Massif de Terazit
Mts. Atsoum
Mts. Gan Goriama
Vogel Pk 2042
Shebshi Mts.
Rey Malabo
BIOKO
Pico Santa Isabel 2850
Mt. Cameroun 4070
East from Greenwich
COPYRIGHT GEORGE PHILIP & SON, LTD

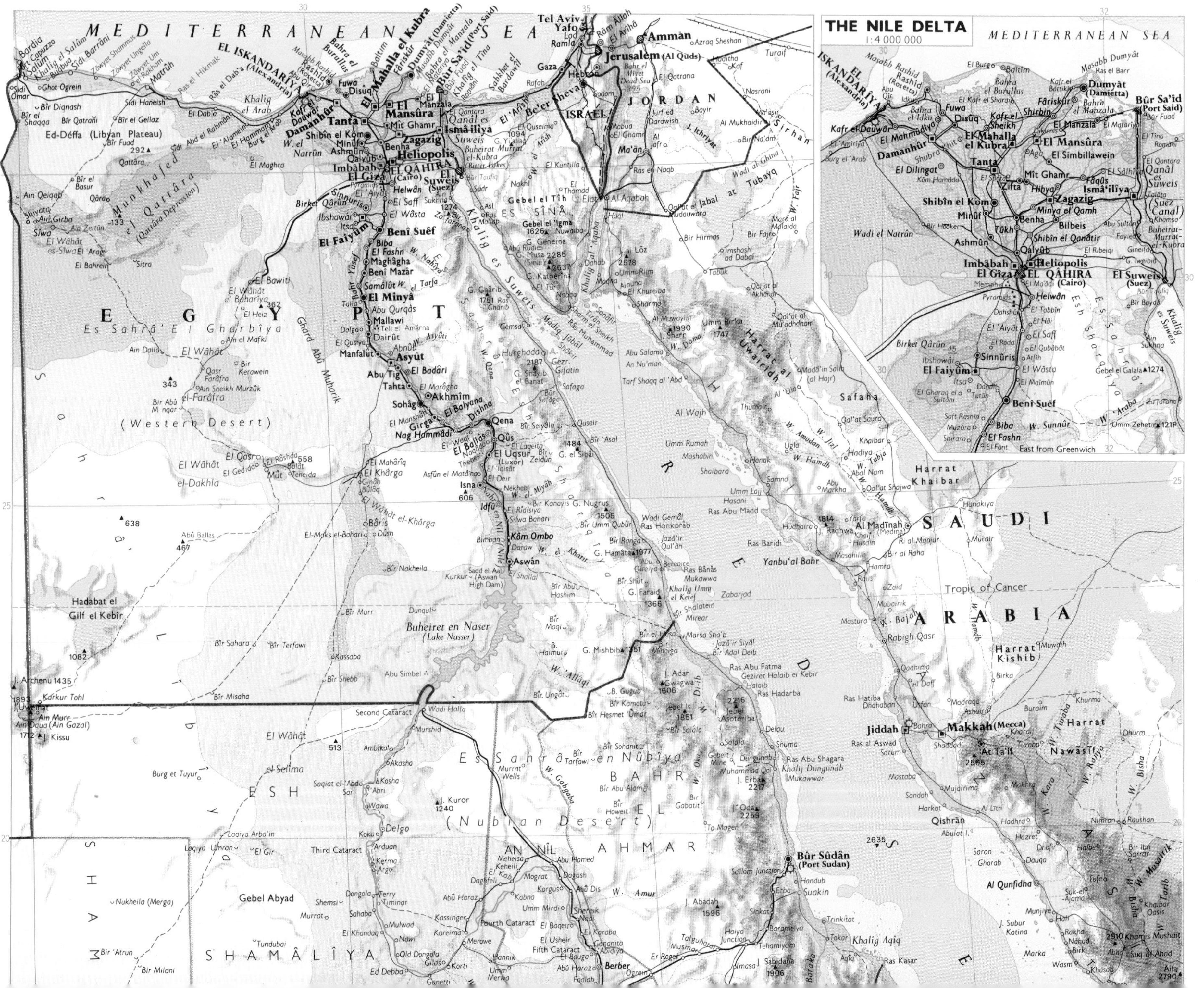
MEDITERRANEAN SEA
EL ISKANDARÎYA (Alexandria)
EL QÂHIRA (Cairo)
Bûr Sa'îd (Port Said)
Suweis (Suez)
Jerusalem (Al Quds)
Ammân
JORDAN
ISRAEL
EGYPT
Es Sahrâ' El Gharbîya
(Western Desert)
Khalig es Suweis
Buheiret en Naser (Lake Nasser)
Aswân
Tropic of Cancer
SAUDI ARABIA
Makkah (Mecca)
Jiddah
Al Madînah (Medina)
Bûr Sûdân (Port Sudan)
Es Sahrâ en Nûbîya (Nubian Desert)
BAHR EL AHMAR
SHAMÂLÎYA
THE NILE DELTA
1:4 000 000
MEDITERRANEAN SEA
East from Greenwich

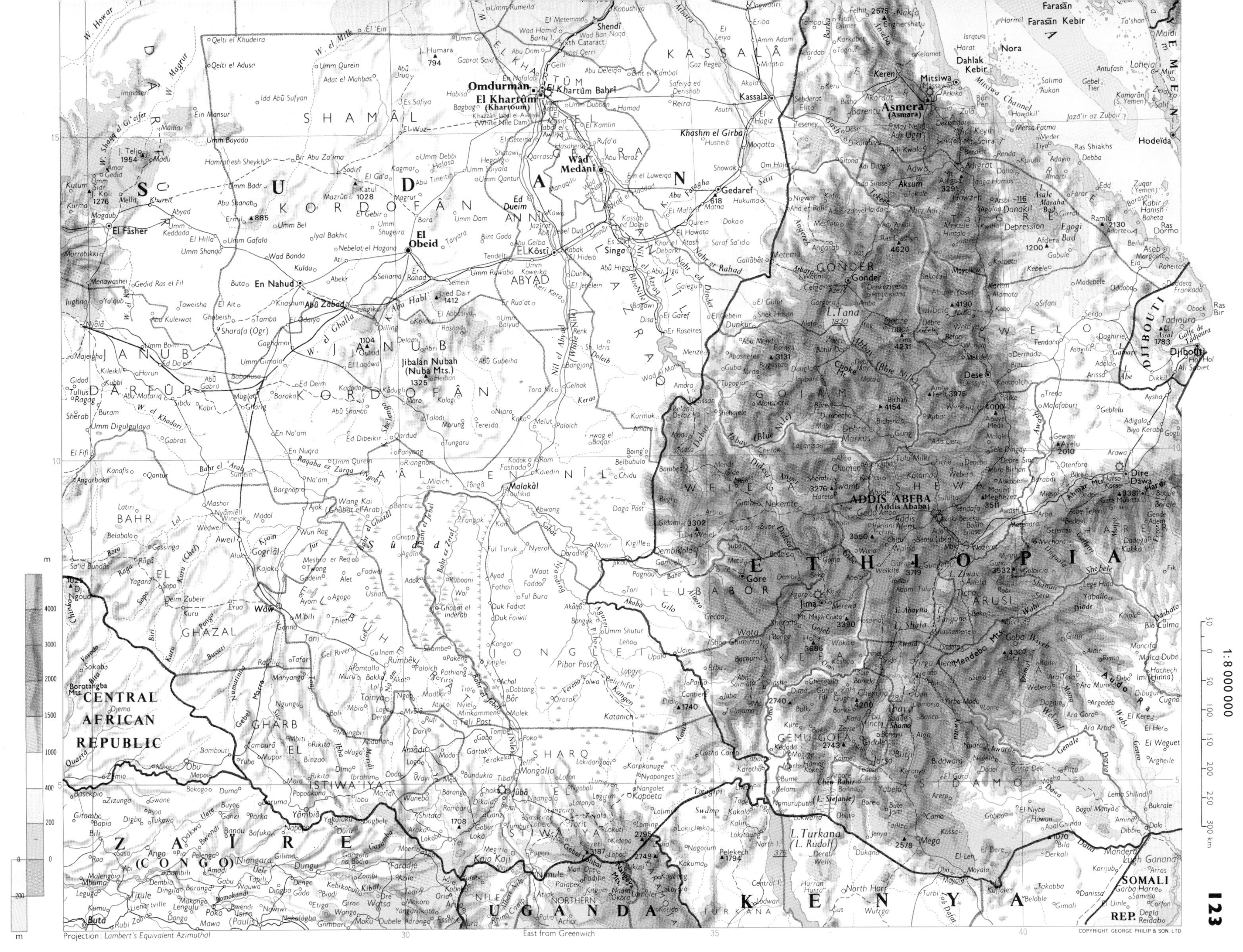
1:8 000 000
50 0 50 100 150 200 250 300 km
SUDAN
ETHIOPIA
ADDIS ABEBA (Addis Ababa)
DJIBOUTI
YEMEN
KENYA
UGANDA
SOMALI REP.
CENTRAL AFRICAN REPUBLIC
ZAIRE (CONGO)
Omdurman
El Khartûm (Khartoum)
El Khartûm Bahri
Wad Medani
El Obeid
En Nahud
El Fâsher
Kassala
Gedaref
Malakâl
Wâw
Jûba
Asmera (Asmara)
Mitsiwa
Gonder
Dese
Jima
Gore
Dire Dawa
Harer
Djibouti
Hodeida
L. Tana
L. Turkana (L. Rudolf)
Danakil Depression
Jibalan Nubah (Nuba Mts.)
Farasan Kebir
Dahlak Kebir
m
4000
3000
2000
1500
1000
400
200
0
200
Projection: Lambert's Equivalent Azimuthal
East from Greenwich
COPYRIGHT GEORGE PHILIP & SON, LTD

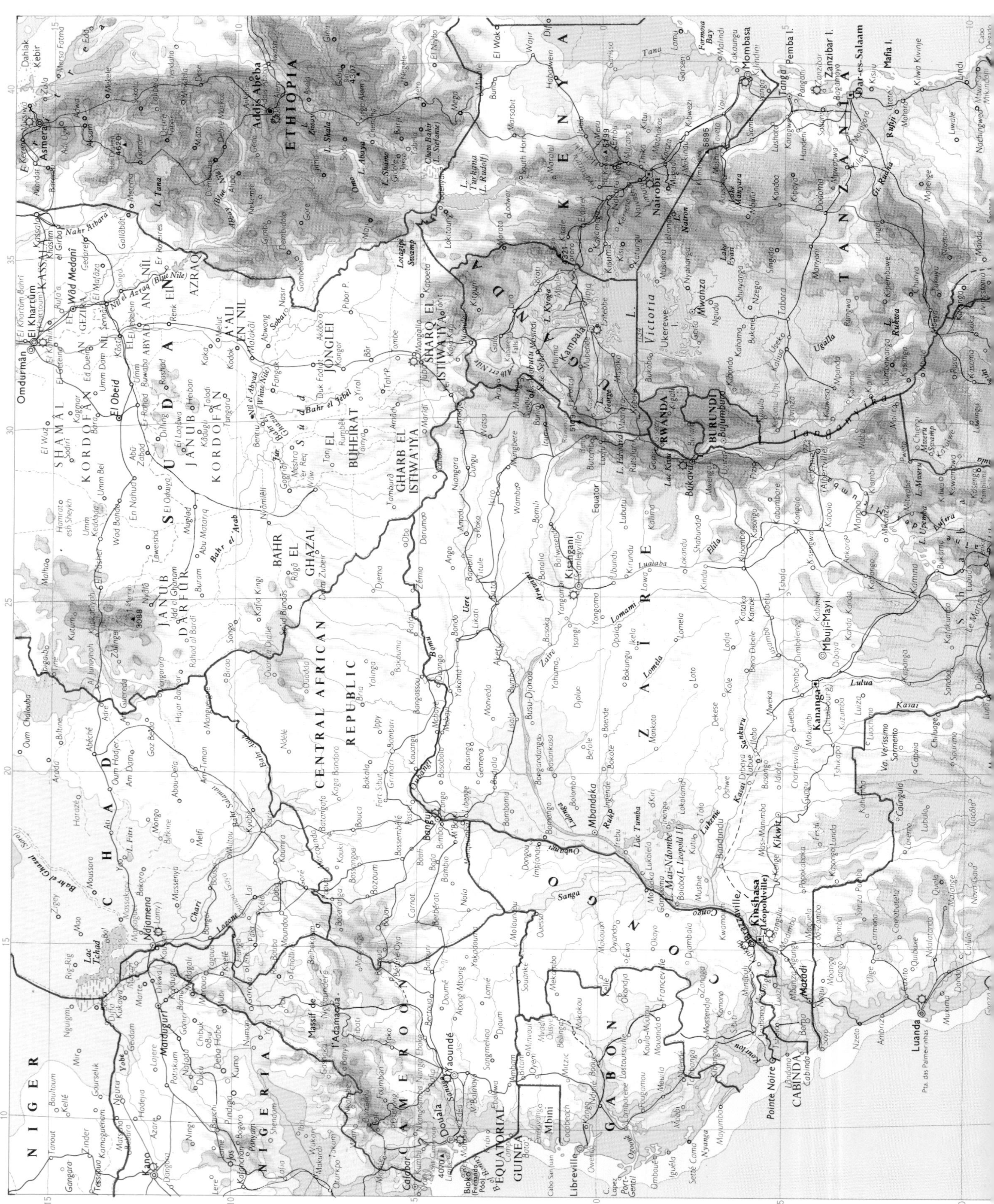
ETHIOPIA
Addis Abeba
Asmera
Nairobi
Mombasa
Dar-es-Salaam
Zanzibar I.
Pemba I.
Mafia I.
Kampala
Kigali
RWANDA
BURUNDI
Bujumbura
Victoria
Lake Tanganyika
El Khartûm
Omdurman
CENTRAL AFRICAN REPUBLIC
Bangui
Kisangani
Kinshasa
Brazzaville
Luanda
CABINDA
Pointe Noire
Libreville
GABON
EQUATORIAL GUINEA
Mbini
Douala
Yaoundé
Ndjamena
Lac Tchad
Kano
NIGER
NIGERIA
Maiduguri
Massif de l'Adamaoua
Mbuji-Mayi
Kananga
Mbandaka

1:15 000 000

100 0 100 200 300 400 500 600 km

MADAGASCAR
On same scale as General Map
COPYRIGHT GEORGE PHILIP & SON, LTD
INDIAN OCEAN
ATLANTIC OCEAN
Mozambique Channel
ZIMBABWE
BOTSWANA
NAMIBIA
(SOUTH WEST AFRICA)
SOUTH AFRICA
LESOTHO
SWAZILAND
TRANSVAAL
NATAL
ORANJE-VRYSTAAT (O.F.S.)
CAPE PROVINCE
Kalahari
Harare (Salisbury)
Bulawayo
Lusaka
Beira
Maputo (Lourenço Marques)
Pretoria
Johannesburg
Durban
Pietermaritzburg
Bloemfontein
Kimberley
East London
Port Elizabeth
Cape Town (Kaapstad)
Windhoek
Gaborone
Antananarivo (Tananarive)
Toliara
Tropic of Capricorn
East from Greenwich

m 6000 4000 3000 2000 1500 1000 400 200 0

0 200 m

Projection: Sanson Flamsteed's Sinusoidal

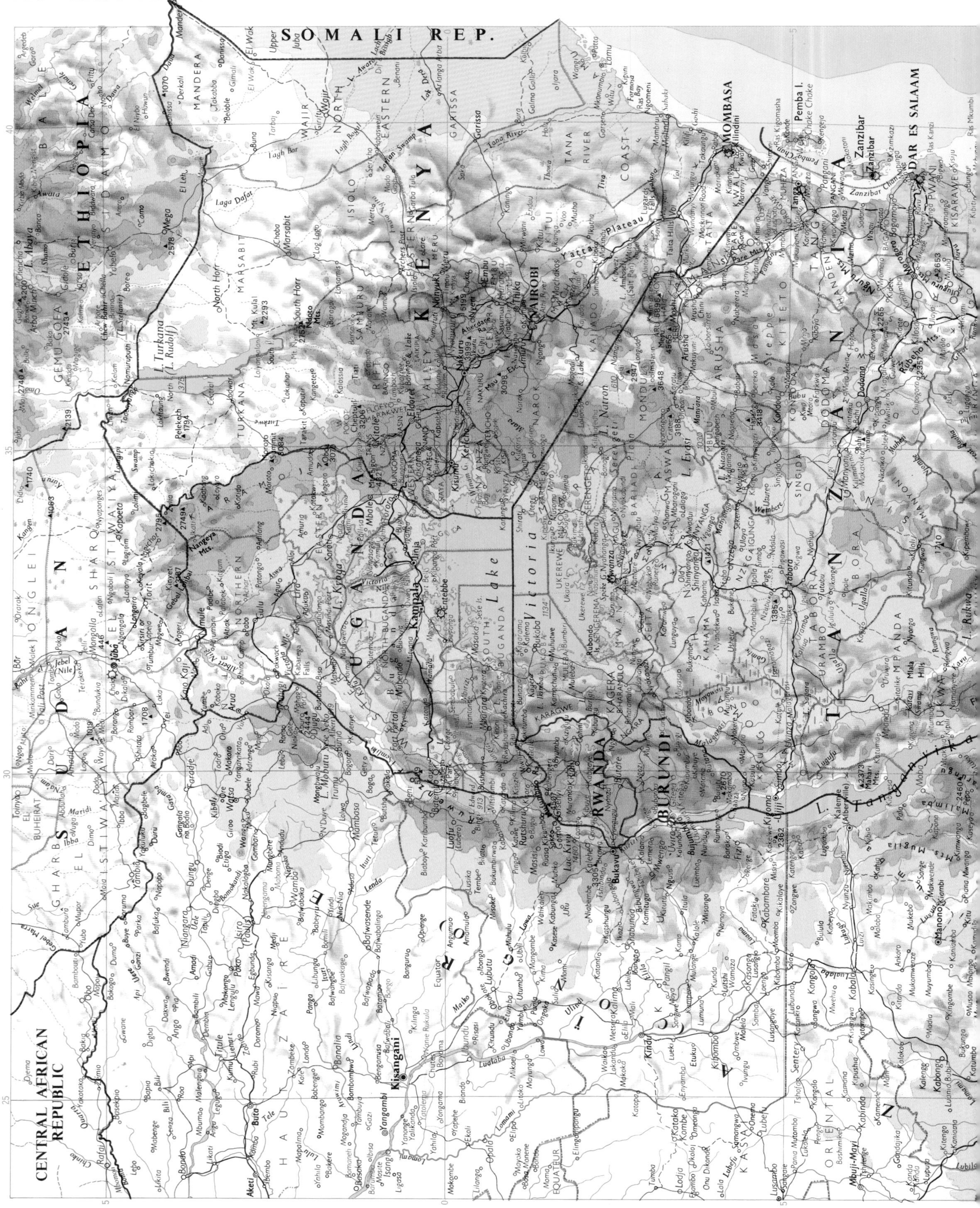

SOMALI REP.

ETHIOPIA

KENYA

UGANDA

SUDAN

TANZANIA

RWANDA

BURUNDI

ZAIRE

CENTRAL AFRICAN REPUBLIC

Lake Victoria

L. Tanganyika

L. Turkana (L. Rudolf)

NAIROBI

MOMBASA

DAR ES SALAAM

Zanzibar

Pemba I.

Kampala

Kisangani

1:8 000 000

50 0 50 100 150 200 250 300 km

INDIAN OCEAN
MOZAMBIQUE
ZIMBABWE
ZAMBIA
MALAWI
BOTSWANA
ANGOLA
TRANSVAAL
Lusaka
HARARE (Salisbury)
Bulawayo
Blantyre
Beira
Livingstone
Lubumbashi (Elisabethville)
Ndola
Kitwe
Mufulira
Luanshya
Chingola
Likasi
Kolwezi
Lilongwe
Kariba Lake
Mtwara-Mikindani
Lindi
Moçambique
Angoche
Quelimane
Chinde
I. do Bazaruto
I. Benguérua
Serowe
Gweru
Kadoma
Kwekwe
Masvingo
Mutare
Tete
Zambezi
Limpopo
Projection: Lambert's Equivalent Azimuthal
East from Greenwich
COPYRIGHT, GEORGE PHILIP & SON, LTD.

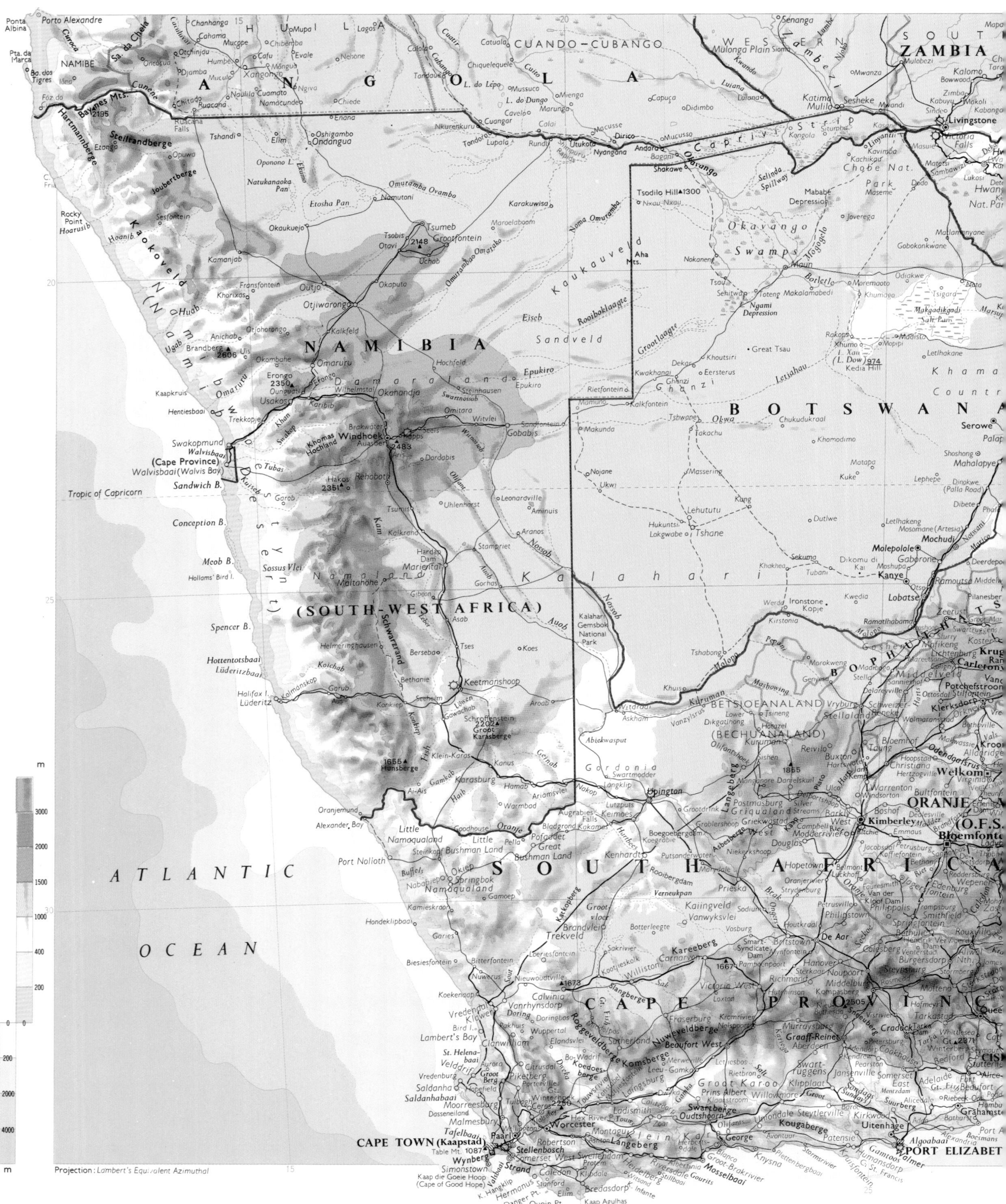
ANGOLA
CUANDO-CUBANGO
ZAMBIA
NAMIBIA
(SOUTH-WEST AFRICA)
BOTSWANA
SOUTH AFRICA
CAPE PROVINCE
ATLANTIC
OCEAN
Tropic of Capricorn
Porto Alexandre
Ponta Albina
NAMIBE
Baynes Mts.
2195
Cunene
Ruacana Falls
Ondangua
Etosha Pan
Tsumeb
Grootfontein
Otavi
2148
Outjo
Otjiwarongo
Kaokoveld
Namib Desert
Brandberg
2606
Omaruru
Erongo
2350
Usakos
Karibib
Okahandja
Hentiesbaai
Swakopmund
Walvisbaai
(Cape Province)
Walvisbaai (Walvis Bay)
Sandwich B.
Windhoek
2483
Khomas Hochland
Gobabis
Rehoboth
Hakos
2351
Conception B.
Meob B.
Sossus Vlei
Maltahöhe
Mariental
Hardap Dam
Spencer B.
Hottentotsbaai
Lüderitzbaai
Lüderitz
Halifax I.
Keetmanshoop
Schwarzrand
Bethanie
Karasberge
2202
Hunsberge
1655
Karasburg
Oranjemund
Alexander Bay
Kalahari
Kalahari Gemsbok National Park
Nossob
Auob
Caprivi Strip
Okavango Swamps
Maun
Ngami Depression
Tsodilo Hill 1300
Aha Mts.
Kaukauveld
Sandveld
Ghanzi
Makgadikgadi Salt Pans
Livingstone
Victoria Falls
Chobe Nat. Park
Mababe Depression
Serowe
Mahalapye
Molepolole
Gaborone
Mochudi
Kanye
Lobatse
Tshabong
BETSJOEANALAND
(BECHUANALAND)
Kuruman
Vryburg
Kimberley
Bloemfontein
ORANJE
(O.F.S.)
Welkom
Klerksdorp
Potchefstroom
Upington
Gordonia
Little Namaqualand
Bushman Land
Port Nolloth
Springbok
Namaqualand
Kenhardt
Prieska
Griqualand West
Hondeklipbaai
Kamieskroon
Garies
Bitterfontein
Vanrhynsdorp
Calvinia
Trekveld
Carnarvon
Victoria West
De Aar
Colesberg
Middelburg
Graaff-Reinet
Cradock
Beaufort West
Nuweveldberge
Groot Karoo
Klein Karoo
Lambert's Bay
Clanwilliam
St. Helena-baai
Saldanha
Saldanhabaai
Malmesbury
Paarl
Worcester
Stellenbosch
CAPE TOWN (Kaapstad)
Table Mt. 1087
Tafelbaai
Wynberg
Simonstown
Kaap die Goeie Hoop
(Cape of Good Hope)
Hermanus
Bredasdorp
Kaap Agulhas
Mosselbaai
George
Knysna
Oudtshoorn
Uitenhage
PORT ELIZABETH
Algoabaai
Grahamstown
m
3000
2000
1500
1000
400
200
0
200
2000
4000
m
Projection: Lambert's Equivalent Azimuthal

1:8 000 000

50 0 50 100 150 200 250 300 km

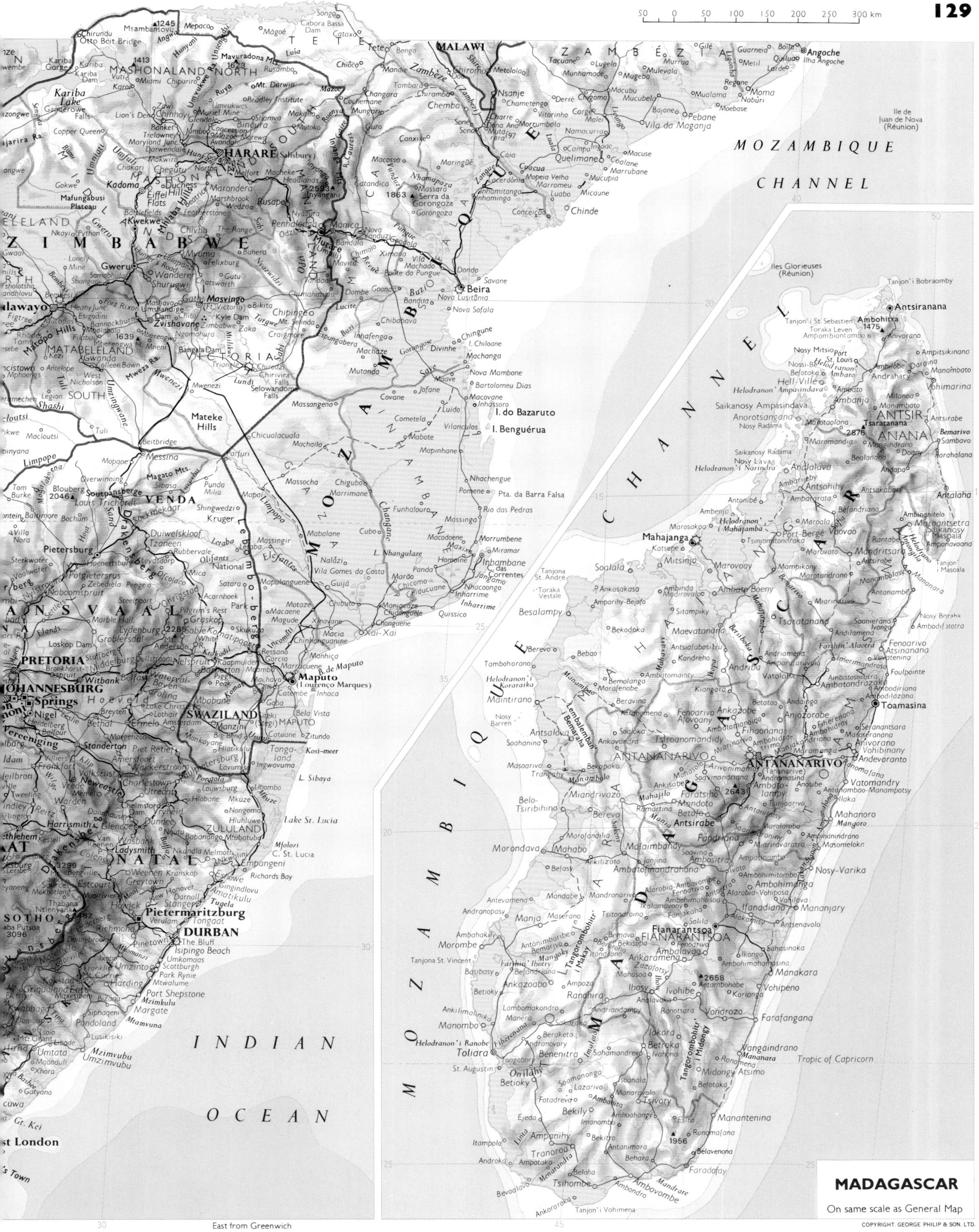

MOZAMBIQUE CHANNEL

INDIAN OCEAN

MADAGASCAR

On same scale as General Map

East from Greenwich

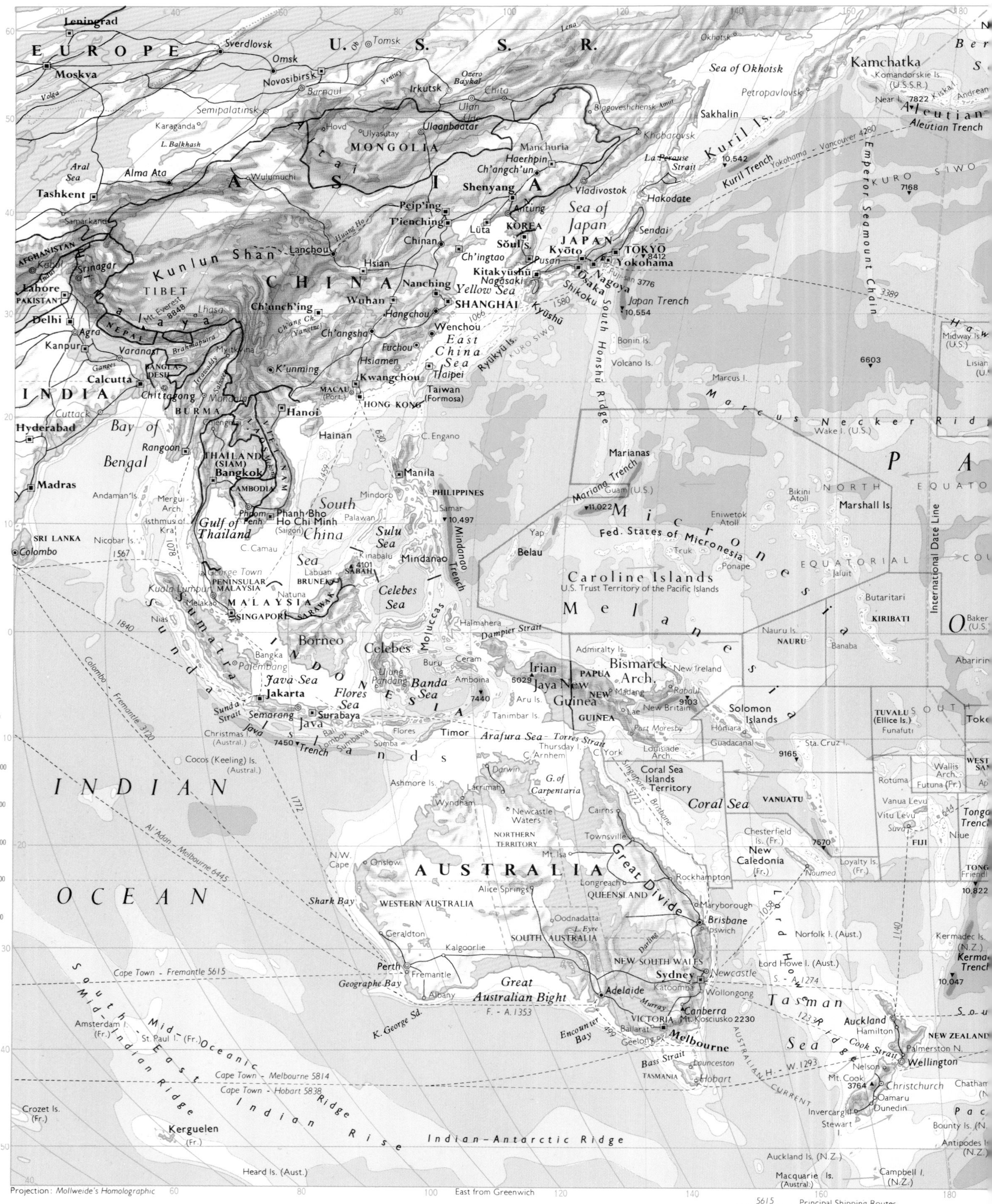
EUROPE
U. S. S. R.
Leningrad
Moskva
Sverdlovsk
Omsk
Novosibirsk
Tomsk
Barnaul
Irkutsk
Ozero Baykal
Chita
Ulan Ude
Semipalatinsk
Karaganda
L. Balkhash
Aral Sea
Alma Ata
Tashkent
Samarkand
Wulumuchi
Hovd
Ulyasutay
Ulaanbaatar
MONGOLIA
Altai
ASIA
Manchuria
Haerhpin
Ch'angch'un
Shenyang
Vladivostok
Blagoveshchensk
Amur
Khabarovsk
Sakhalin
Sea of Okhotsk
Okhotsk
Lena
Kamchatka
Petropavlovsk
Komandorskie Is. (U.S.S.R.)
Near I.
7822
Kiska I.
Aleutian
Aleutian Trench
Bering Sea
Kuril Is.
La Pérouse Strait
10,542
Kuril Trench
Yokohama - Vancouver 4280
Emperor Seamount Chain
KURO SIWO
7168
Hakodate
Sea of Japan
Sendai
JAPAN
TŌKYŌ
Yokohama
8412
Kyōto
Nagoya
Ōsaka
Shikoku
Kyūshū
Nagasaki
Kitakyūshū
Fuji-san 3776
Japan Trench
10,554
KOREA
Sŏul
Pusan
Antung
Lüta
Pei'ping
T'ienching
Chinan
Ch'ingtao
Yellow Sea
Hsian
Lanchou
Huang Ho
Kunlun Shan
TIBET
CHINA
Nanching
SHANGHAI
Wuhan
Hangchou
Ch'unch'ing
Chang Chiang (Yangtze)
Ch'angsha
Wenchou
East China Sea
Fuchou
Hsiamen
Taipei
Taiwan (Formosa)
Ryūkyū Is.
K'unming
Kwangchou
MACAU (Port.)
HONG KONG
Hanoi
Hainan
Lhasa
Mt. Everest 8848
Himalaya
NEPAL
Brahmaputra
AFGHANISTAN
Kabul
Srinagar
Lahore
PAKISTAN
Delhi
Agra
Kanpur
Ganges
Varanasi
BANGLADESH
Calcutta
Chittagong
Mandalay
BURMA
Irrawaddy
Salween
Mekong
INDIA
Cuttack
Hyderabad
Bay of Bengal
Rangoon
Madras
THAILAND (SIAM)
Bangkok
LAOS
VIETNAM
CAMBODIA
Phnom Penh
Phanh Bho Ho Chi Minh (Saigon)
Gulf of Thailand
Andaman Is.
Mergui Arch.
Isthmus of Kra
SRI LANKA
Colombo
Nicobar Is.
South China Sea
C. Camau
Palawan
Mindoro
Manila
PHILIPPINES
Samar
10,497
Mindanao
Mindanao Trench
Sulu Sea
Kinabalu 4101
SABAH
Labuan
BRUNEI
George Town
PENINSULAR MALAYSIA
Kuala Lumpur
Melaka
MALAYSIA
SINGAPORE
SARAWAK
Natuna
Celebes Sea
Nias
Sumatra
Sunda Is.
Borneo
INDONESIA
Celebes
Moluccas
Halmahera
Dampier Strait
Bangka
Palembang
Java Sea
Jakarta
Sunda Strait
Semarang
Surabaya
Java
Bali
Lombok
Sumbawa
Flores
Sumba
Timor
Flores Sea
Banda Sea
Ujung Pandang
Buru
Ceram
Amboina
7440
Aru Is.
Tanimbar Is.
Irian Jaya
5029
New Guinea
PAPUA NEW GUINEA
Bismarck Arch.
Admiralty Is.
New Ireland
Madang
Rabaul
New Britain
9103
Lae
Port Moresby
Java Trench
7450
Christmas I. (Austral.)
Cocos (Keeling) Is. (Austral.)
Arafura Sea
Torres Strait
Thursday I.
C. York
Darwin
C. Arnhem
G. of Carpentaria
Ashmore Is.
Wyndham
Larrimah
Newcastle Waters
NORTHERN TERRITORY
Cairns
Louisiade Arch.
Coral Sea Islands Territory
Coral Sea
Townsville
Mt. Isa
Great Divide
Rockhampton
Longreach
QUEENSLAND
N.W. Cape
Onslow
AUSTRALIA
Alice Springs
WESTERN AUSTRALIA
Shark Bay
Oodnadatta
L. Eyre
SOUTH AUSTRALIA
Maryborough
Brisbane
Ipswich
Darling
Geraldton
Kalgoorlie
Perth
Fremantle
Geographe Bay
Albany
Great Australian Bight
F. - A. 1353
K. George Sd.
NEW SOUTH WALES
Sydney
Newcastle
Katoomba
Wollongong
Adelaide
Murray
Canberra
Mt. Kosciusko 2230
VICTORIA
Ballarat
Geelong
Melbourne
Encounter Bay
Bass Strait
Launceston
TASMANIA
Hobart
AUSTRALIAN CURRENT
Tasman Sea
Lord Howe Rise
Lord Howe I. (Aust.)
Norfolk I. (Aust.)
S. - A. 1274
Auckland
Hamilton
NEW ZEALAND
Palmerston N.
Cook Strait
Wellington
Nelson
Mt. Cook 3764
Christchurch
Oamaru
Dunedin
Invercargill
Stewart I.
Chatham
Bounty Is. (N.Z.)
Antipodes Is. (N.Z.)
Auckland Is. (N.Z.)
Macquarie Is. (Austral.)
Campbell I. (N.Z.)
Kermadec Is. (N.Z.)
Kermadec Trench
10,047
Tonga Trench
10,822
Fiji
Suva
Vanua Levu
Viti Levu
Niue
Loyalty Is. (Fr.)
Nouméa
New Caledonia (Fr.)
Chesterfield Is. (Fr.)
7570
VANUATU
Rotuma
Wallis Arch.
Futuna (Fr.)
Sta. Cruz I.
9165
Solomon Islands
Honiara
Guadacanal
TUVALU (Ellice Is.)
Funafuti
Nauru I.
NAURU
Banaba
KIRIBATI
Butaritari
Abariringa
Baker I. (U.S.)
Jaluit
Marshall Is.
Eniwetok Atoll
Bikini Atoll
NORTH EQUATORIAL
EQUATORIAL
International Date Line
Caroline Islands
U.S. Trust Territory of the Pacific Islands
Ponape
Truk
Fed. States of Micronesia
Micronesia
Melanesia
Belau
Yap
Guam (U.S.)
Mariana Trench
11,022
Marianas
Wake I. (U.S.)
Marcus Necker Ridge
Marcus I.
6603
Midway Is. (U.S.)
Volcano Is.
Bonin Is.
South Honshū Ridge
1580
1066
630
1459
1078
1567
1840
Colombo - Fremantle 3120
1772
Al 'Adan - Melbourne 6445
Cape Town - Fremantle 5615
Cape Town - Melbourne 5814
Cape Town - Hobart 5838
Singapore - Brisbane 3772
1058
1140
1233
644
3389
H. - W. 1293
INDIAN OCEAN
Amsterdam I. (Fr.)
St. Paul I. (Fr.)
Mid-Oceanic Ridge
South-East Indian Ridge
Mid-Indian Ridge
Indian Rise
Indian-Antarctic Ridge
Crozet Is. (Fr.)
Kerguelen (Fr.)
Heard Is. (Aust.)
PACIFIC
m
6000
4000
2000
1000
200
0
200
2000
4000
6000
8000

Projection: *Mollweide's Homolographic*   East from Greenwich

5615 Principal Shipping Routes *(Distances in Nautical Miles)*

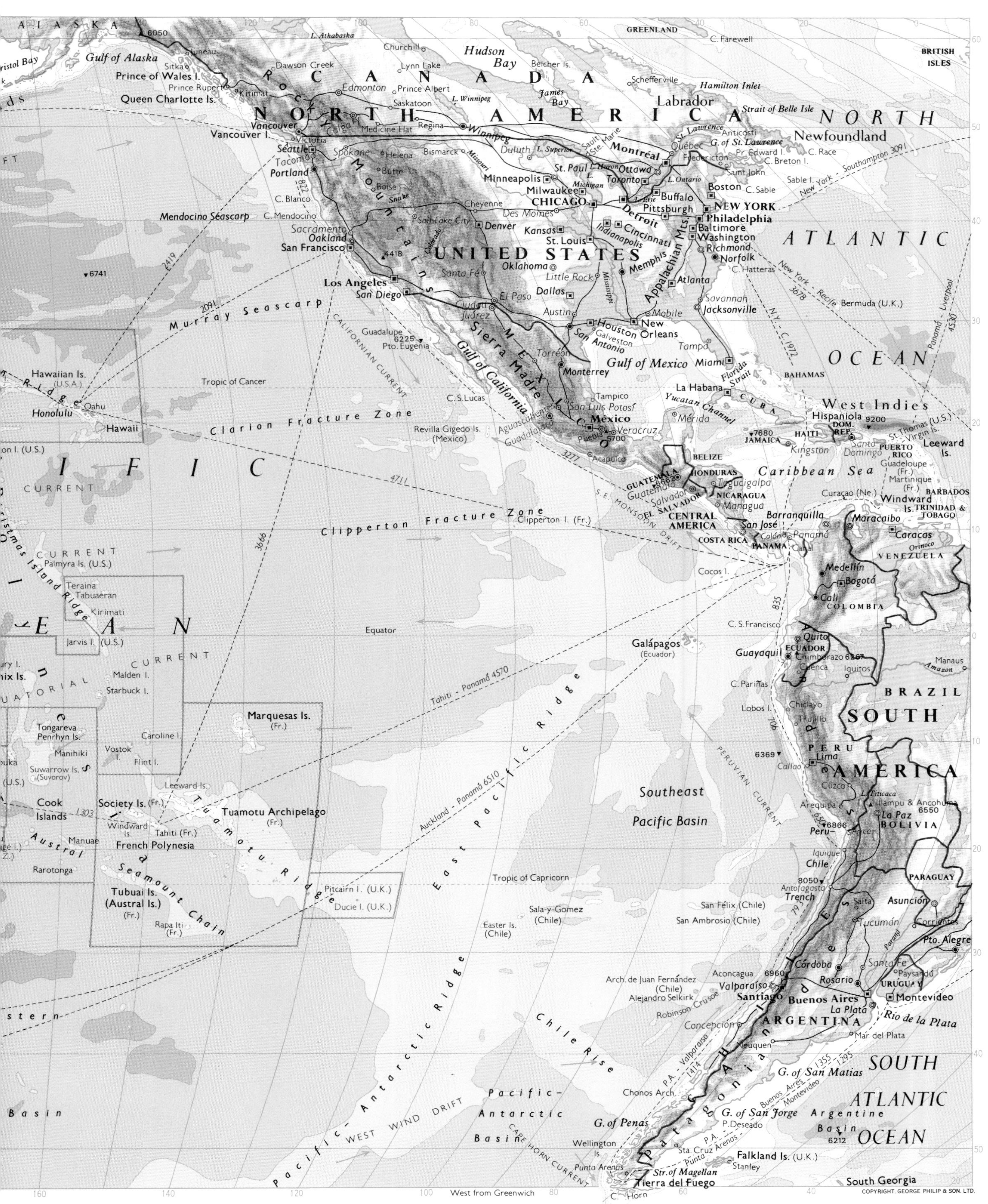
ALASKA
6050
Gulf of Alaska
Sitka
Juneau
Prince of Wales I.
Prince Rupert
Kitimat
Queen Charlotte Is.
L. Athabaska
Dawson Creek
Edmonton
Prince Albert
Saskatoon
Churchill
Lynn Lake
Hudson Bay
Belcher Is.
James Bay
L. Winnipeg
CANADA
NORTH AMERICA
Schefferville
Labrador
Hamilton Inlet
Strait of Belle Isle
NORTH
GREENLAND
C. Farewell
BRITISH ISLES
Vancouver
Vancouver I.
Victoria
Calgary
Medicine Hat
Regina
Winnipeg
Rocky Mountains
Seattle
Tacoma
Spokane
Helena
Bismarck
Missouri
Duluth
L. Superior
Sault Ste. Marie
Montréal
Québec
St. Lawrence
Anticosti
G. of St. Lawrence
Newfoundland
Pr. Edward I.
Fredericton
C. Race
C. Breton I.
Portland
Butte
Boise
Snake
St. Paul
L. Huron
Ottawa
Minneapolis
Michigan
Toronto
L. Ontario
Saint John
Sable I.
Boston
C. Sable
New York - Southampton 3091
822
C. Blanco
Milwaukee
CHICAGO
L. Erie
Buffalo
Detroit
NEW YORK
Pittsburgh
Philadelphia
Cheyenne
Des Moines
Mendocino Seascarp
C. Mendocino
Salt Lake City
Denver
Kansas
Cincinnati
Indianapolis
Baltimore
Washington
Richmond
Norfolk
Sacramento
Oakland
San Francisco
Colorado
4418
UNITED STATES
St. Louis
Memphis
Appalachian Mts.
ATLANTIC
C. Hatteras
2419
6741
Oklahoma
Santa Fé
Little Rock
Mississippi
Atlanta
New York - Recife 3678
Los Angeles
San Diego
El Paso
Dallas
Savannah
Jacksonville
Bermuda (U.K.)
Panamá - Liverpool 4530
2091
Murray Seascarp
Ciudad Juárez
Austin
Mobile
New Orleans
Guadalupe
6225
Pto. Eugenia
Houston
Galveston
San Antonio
Tampa
N.Y. - C. 1972
CALIFORNIAN CURRENT
Sierra Madre
Gulf of California
MEXICO
Torreón
Gulf of Mexico
Miami
OCEAN
Hawaiian Is. (U.S.A.)
Tropic of Cancer
Monterrey
Florida Strait
BAHAMAS
Oahu
Honolulu
Hawaii
C.S.Lucas
La Habana
CUBA
Tampico
Yucatan Channel
West Indies
San Luis Potosí
Mérida
Hispaniola
9200
Clarion Fracture Zone
Revilla Gigedo Is. (Mexico)
Aguascalientes
Guadalajara
México
Puebla
5700
Veracruz
7680
JAMAICA
HAITI
DOM. REP.
St. Thomas (U.S.)
Virgin Is.
Kingston
Santo Domingo
PUERTO RICO
Leeward Is.
3277
Acapulco
BELIZE
Guadeloupe (Fr.)
Martinique (Fr.)
I F I C
CURRENT
4711
GUATEMALA
6662
Guatemala
HONDURAS
Tegucigalpa
Caribbean Sea
BARBADOS
Curaçao (Ne.)
Windward Is.
TRINIDAD & TOBAGO
EL SALVADOR
Salvador
NICARAGUA
Managua
S.E. MONSOON DRIFT
Barranquilla
Maracaibo
Clipperton Fracture Zone
Clipperton I. (Fr.)
CENTRAL AMERICA
San José
COSTA RICA
Colón
Panamá
PANAMA
Canal
Caracas
Orinoco
VENEZUELA
CURRENT
Palmyra Is. (U.S.)
3666
Cocos I.
Medellín
Bogotá
Teraina
Tabuaeran
Kirimati
Christmas Island Ridge
835
Cali
COLOMBIA
E A N
Jarvis I. (U.S.)
Equator
C. S.Francisco
Quito
ECUADOR
Galápagos (Ecuador)
Guayaquil
Chimborazo 6267
Cuenca
Iquitos
Manaus
Amazon
CURRENT
EQUATORIAL
Malden I.
Starbuck I.
Tahiti - Panamá 4570
C. Pariñas
BRAZIL
Lobos I.
Chiclayo
Trujillo
SOUTH
Tongareva
Penrhyn Is.
Marquesas Is. (Fr.)
Caroline I.
Manihiki
Vostok I.
Flint I.
East Pacific Ridge
706
PERU
6369
Lima
Callao
Suwarrow Is. (Suvorov)
Leeward Is.
Auckland - Panamá 6510
PERUVIAN CURRENT
AMERICA
Southeast Pacific Basin
Cuzco
L. Titicaca
Illampu & Ancohuma 6550
La Paz
BOLIVIA
Cook Islands
1303
Society Is. (Fr.)
Tuamotu Archipelago (Fr.)
Arequipa
6866
Peru-
Arica
Windward Is.
Tahiti (Fr.)
Tuamotu Ridge
Manuae
French Polynesia
Austral Seamount Chain
Iquique
Chile
Rarotonga
8050
Antofagasta
Trench
PARAGUAY
Tropic of Capricorn
Pitcairn I. (U.K.)
Ducie I. (U.K.)
Tubuai Is. (Austral Is.) (Fr.)
Rapa Iti (Fr.)
Sala-y-Gomez (Chile)
Easter Is. (Chile)
San Félix (Chile)
San Ambrosio (Chile)
Salta
Asunción
Tucumán
Corrientes
Paraná
Pto. Alegre
Andes
Córdoba
Santa Fe
Paysandú
Aconcagua
6960
Arch. de Juan Fernández (Chile)
Alejandro Selkirk
Robinson Crusoe
Valparaíso
Santiago
Rosario
Buenos Aires
La Plata
URUGUAY
Montevideo
Río de la Plata
Pacific-Antarctic Ridge
Chile Rise
Concepción
ARGENTINA
Mar del Plata
Neuquén
P.A. - Valparaíso 1414
1355
1295
G. of San Matias
SOUTH ATLANTIC
Chonos Arch.
Buenos Aires - Montevideo
Pacific-Antarctic Basin
Patagonia
G. of San Jorge
Argentine Basin
P. Deseado
6212
OCEAN
Basin
WEST WIND DRIFT
G. of Penas
CAPE HORN CURRENT
Wellington Is.
Sta. Cruz
P.A. - Punta Arenas
Falkland Is. (U.K.)
Stanley
Punta Arenas
Str. of Magellan
Tierra del Fuego
South Georgia
C. Horn
160
140
120
100
West from Greenwich
80
60
40
20
COPYRIGHT, GEORGE PHILIP & SON, LTD.

Java Trench
TIMOR SEA
INDIAN OCEAN
WESTERN AUSTRALIA
NORTHERN TERRITORY
SOUTH AUSTRALIA
Kimberley
Canning Basin
Great Sandy Desert
Gibson Desert
Great Victoria Desert
Nullarbor Plain
Great Australian Bight
Tanami Desert
Darwin
Perth
Fremantle
Geraldton
Carnarvon
Broome
Port Hedland
Kalgoorlie
Albany
Esperance
Wyndham
Katherine
Ayers Rock
Mt. Olga
Macdonnell Ras.
Musgrave Ranges
Hamersley Ra.
King George Sound
Projection: Bonne
East from Greenwich

1:14 000 000
100 0 100 200 300 400 500 600 km
CORAL SEA
CORAL SEA ISLANDS TERRITORY
PACIFIC OCEAN
TASMAN SEA
QUEENSLAND
NEW SOUTH WALES
VICTORIA
TASMANIA
Gulf of Carpentaria
Cape York Peninsula
Great Barrier Reef
Great Dividing Range
Louisiade Archipelago
Misima I.
Rossel I.
Tagula I.
San Cristobal
Rennell
Thursday I.
Banks I.
Prince of Wales I.
C. York
Newcastle B.
Endeavour Str.
P. Musgrave
Shelburne B.
C. Grenville
Temple B.
Duifken Pt.
Albatross B.
Weipa
Wenlock
C. Weymouth
C. Direction
Archer
C. Keer-Weer
Holroyd
Coen
Princess Charlotte B.
Bathurst B.
C. Melville
Osprey Rf.
Coleman
Normanby
C. Flattery
C. Bedford
Cooktown
Laura
Mitchell
C. Tribulation
Trinity Bay
Mossman
Mareeba
Chillagoe
C. Grafton
Cairns
Atherton
Bartle Frere 1612
Innisfail
Gilbert
Normanton
Burketown
Croydon
Ravenshoe
Einasleigh
Forsayth
Gregory Ra.
Newcastle Ra.
Hinchinbrook I.
Ingham
Palm Is.
Halifax B.
Townsville
C. Cleveland
C. Bowling Green
Home Hill
Bowen
Whitsunday I.
Cumberland Is.
Proserpine
Collinsville
Repulse B.
Mackay
Palmerston
Sarina
Broad Sd.
Swain Rfs.
C. Townshend
Townshend I.
Saumarez Rf.
Lihou Rfs & Cays
Wessel Is.
English Co. Is.
C. Wilberforce
Melville B.
Gove
C. Arnhem
P. Bradshaw
Caledon B.
C. Grey
Blue Mud B.
Alyangula
Groote Eylandt
C. Beatrice
Limmen Bight
Maria I.
Sir Edward Pellew Group
Vanderlin I.
Borroloola
McArthur
Mornington I.
C. van Diemen
Wellesley Is.
Bentinck I.
Barkly Tableland
Dobbyn
Camooweal
Austral Downs
Leichhardt
Kajabbi
Norman
Flinders
Mount Isa
Mary Kathleen
Cloncurry
Julia Cr.
Richmond
Pentland
Charters Towers
Hughenden
Duchess
Dajarra
Urandangi
Selwyn Range
Selwyn
Georgina
Winton
Muttaburra
Boulia
Diamantina
Hay
Belyando
Denham Ra.
Netherdale
Isaac
Peak Ra.
Connors Ra.
Blair Athol
Clermont
Aramac
Longreach
Ilfracombe
Barcaldine
Alpha
Capricorn
Emerald
Nogoa
Mackenzie
Drummond Ra.
Thomson
Bedourie
Eyre Cr.
L. Machattie
Simpson Desert
Jundah
Barcoo
Blackall
Warrego Ra.
Springsure
Mt. Morgan
Rockhampton
Yeppoon
Keppel B.
C. Capricorn
Curtis I.
P. Curtis
Gladstone
Biloela
Bustard Head
Dawson
Expedition Ra.
Windorah
Yaraka
Birdsville
Grey Range
Adavale
Augathella
1312
Theodore
Monto
Childers
Bundaberg
Burnett
Hervey Bay
Sandy C.
Fraser I.
Pialba
Maryborough
Gayndah
Taroom
Wandoan
Murgon
Wondai
Kingaroy
Gympie
Nambour
Bribie I.
Moreton B.
Moreton I.
Brisbane
Ipswich
Southport
N. Stradbroke I.
Toowoomba
Dalby
Condamine
Miles
Roma
Mitchell
Injune
Charleville
Quilpie
Bulloo
Cooper Creek
Wyandra
Balonne
Cunnamulla
St. George
Moonie
Thargomindah
Goondiwindi
Dirranbandi
Mungindi
Macintyre
Warwick
Stanthorpe
Mt. Barney
Sutherland Pt.
C. Byron
Lismore
Ballina
Casino
Clarence
Grafton
Tenterfield
Inverell
Glen Innes
Armidale
Round Mountain
Coffs Harbour
Macleay
Kempsey
Port Macquarie
New England Range
Gwydir
Moree
Warialda
Narrabri
Barwon
Walgett
Liverpool Plains
Liverpool Ra.
Gunnedah
Tamworth
Barrington Tops
Taree
Muswellbrook
Singleton
Maitland
Newcastle
Sugarloaf Pt.
P. Stephens
Hawkesbury R.
SYDNEY
Port Jackson
Wollongong
Shellharbour
Nowra
Jervis B.
Goulburn
Canberra
Queanbeyan
Batemans B.
Bega
Twofold B.
Disaster B.
Mallacoota Inlet
C. Howe
C. Everard
Snowy
Kosciusko 2230
Australian Alps
Bombala
Cooma
Hume
Albury
Wagga Wagga
Tumut
Yass
Young
Cowra
Cootamundra
Junee
Narrandera
Leeton
Griffith
Hay
Murrumbidgee
Riverina
Deniliquin
Lachlan
Hillston
Forbes
Parkes
Condobolin
L. Cargelligo
Orange
Bathurst
Lithgow
Katoomba
Mudgee
Wellington
Dubbo
Gilgandra
Castlereagh
Macquarie
Narromine
Bogan
Nyngan
Cobar
Bourke
Coonamble
Darling
Paroo
Warrego
Tibooburra
L. Callabonna
L. Frome
Paroo Chan.
Broken Hill
Wilcannia
Menindee
Main Barrier Ra.
Ivanhoe
Wentworth
Mildura
Balranald
Murray
Renmark
Loxton
Pinnaroo
Ouyen
Swan Hill
Kerang
Echuca
Shepparton
Benalla
Mt. Bogong 1986
Wangaratta
Bendigo
Castlemaine
Maryborough
Ararat
Stawell
Horsham
Wimmera
Bordertown
Naracoorte
Kingston S.E.
Penola
Mt. Gambier
Millicent
Hamilton
Ballarat
MELBOURNE
Geelong
Colac
Warrnambool
Port Fairy
Portland
Discovery B.
C. Bridgewater
C. Northumberland
C. Otway
Port Phillip B.
Phillip I.
Wonthaggi
Yallourn
Moe
Traralgon
Sale
Bairnsdale
Orbost
Gippsland
Ninety Mile Beach
Corner Inlet
Wilsons Promontory
Bass Strait
King I.
Hunter I.
C. Grim
Cape Barren I.
C. Portland
Flinders I.
Furneaux Group
Clarke I.
Devonport
Burnie
Ulverstone
Beaconsfield
Launceston
Scottsdale
Ben Lomond
St. Marys
Sandy C.
Zeehan
Mt. Ossa 1617
Great L.
Queenstown
Strahan
Macquarie Harb.
Freycinet Penin.
New Norfolk
Hobart
Huonville
Low Rocky Pt.
P. Davey
Tasman Penin.
P. Arthur
Storm B.
Bruny I.
S.E. Cape
L. Eyre (North)
L. Eyre (South)
L. Blanche
L. Gregory
Strzelecki Cr.
Warburton
Macumba
Hanson Ra.
Denison Ra.
L. Yamma Yamma
Marree
Leigh Creek
Copley
Woomera
L. Torrens
Pimba
Flinders Ranges
St. Mary's Pk. 1089
Hawker
Quorn
L. Macfarlane
Mt. Brown 965
Port Augusta
Whyalla
Iron Knob
Port Pirie
Peterborough
Jamestown
Burra
Wallaroo
Kadina
Spencer Gulf
Yorke Penin.
G. St. Vincent
Port Lincoln
Gawler
Adelaide
Murray Bridge
Mt. Lofty Ra.
Alexandrina
The Coorong
Encounter B.
Victor Harbor
Kangaroo I.
Backstairs Pass.
Investigator Str.
Tropic of Capricorn
Bird I.
Cato I.
Avon Is.
Chesterfield Is.
Bellona Rfs.
Lord Howe I.
140 145 150 155 160
10 15 20 25 30 35

1:60 000 000

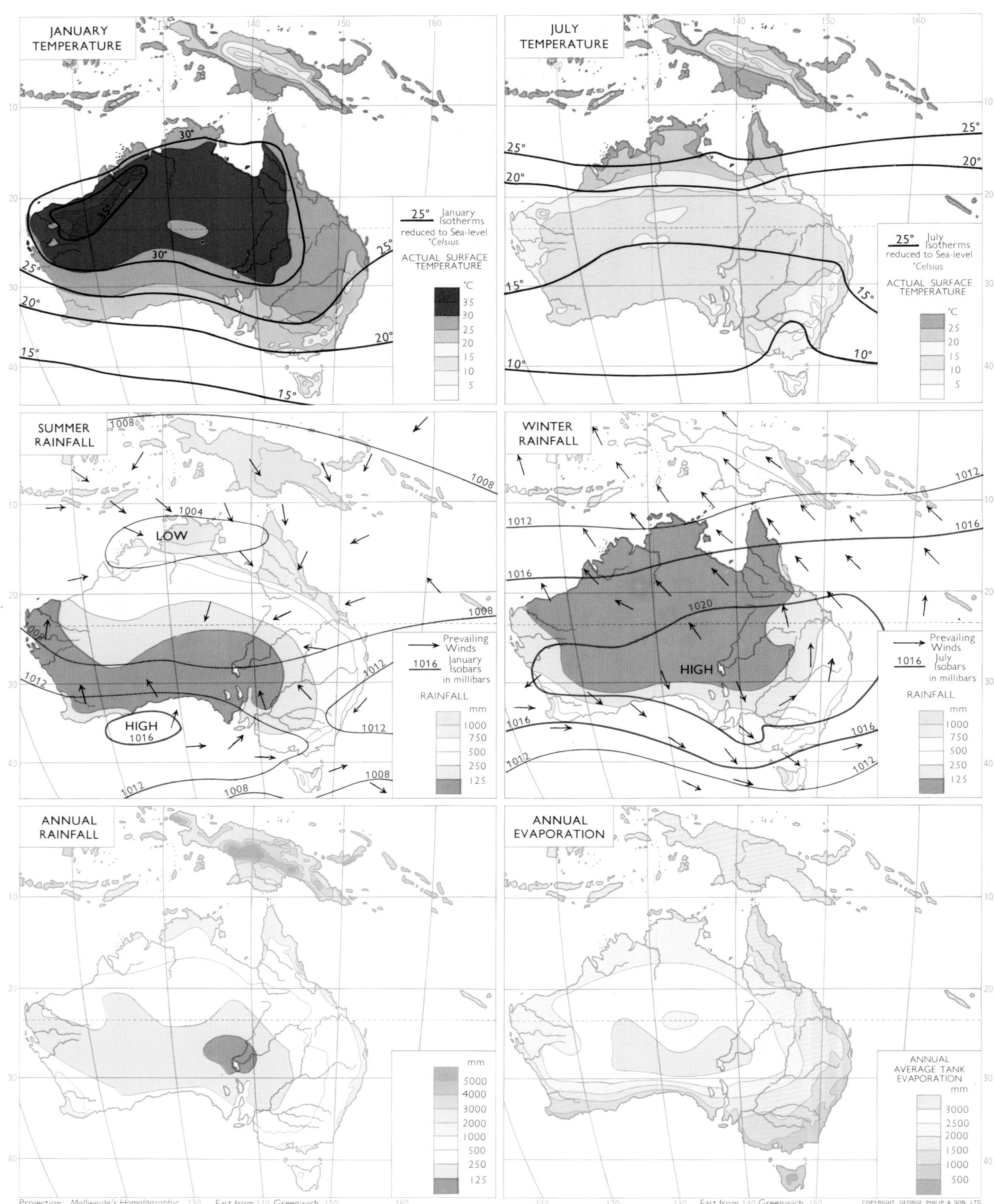
JANUARY TEMPERATURE
25° January Isotherms reduced to Sea-level °Celsius
ACTUAL SURFACE TEMPERATURE
°C 35 30 25 20 15 10 5
JULY TEMPERATURE
25° July Isotherms reduced to Sea-level °Celsius
ACTUAL SURFACE TEMPERATURE
°C 25 20 15 10 5
SUMMER RAINFALL
LOW
HIGH 1016
Prevailing Winds
1016 January Isobars in millibars
RAINFALL mm 1000 750 500 250 125
WINTER RAINFALL
HIGH
Prevailing Winds
1016 July Isobars in millibars
RAINFALL mm 1000 750 500 250 125
ANNUAL RAINFALL
mm 5000 4000 3000 2000 1000 500 250 125
ANNUAL EVAPORATION
ANNUAL AVERAGE TANK EVAPORATION mm 3000 2500 2000 1500 1000 500
Projection: Mollweide's Homolographic
East from Greenwich

1:6 500 000

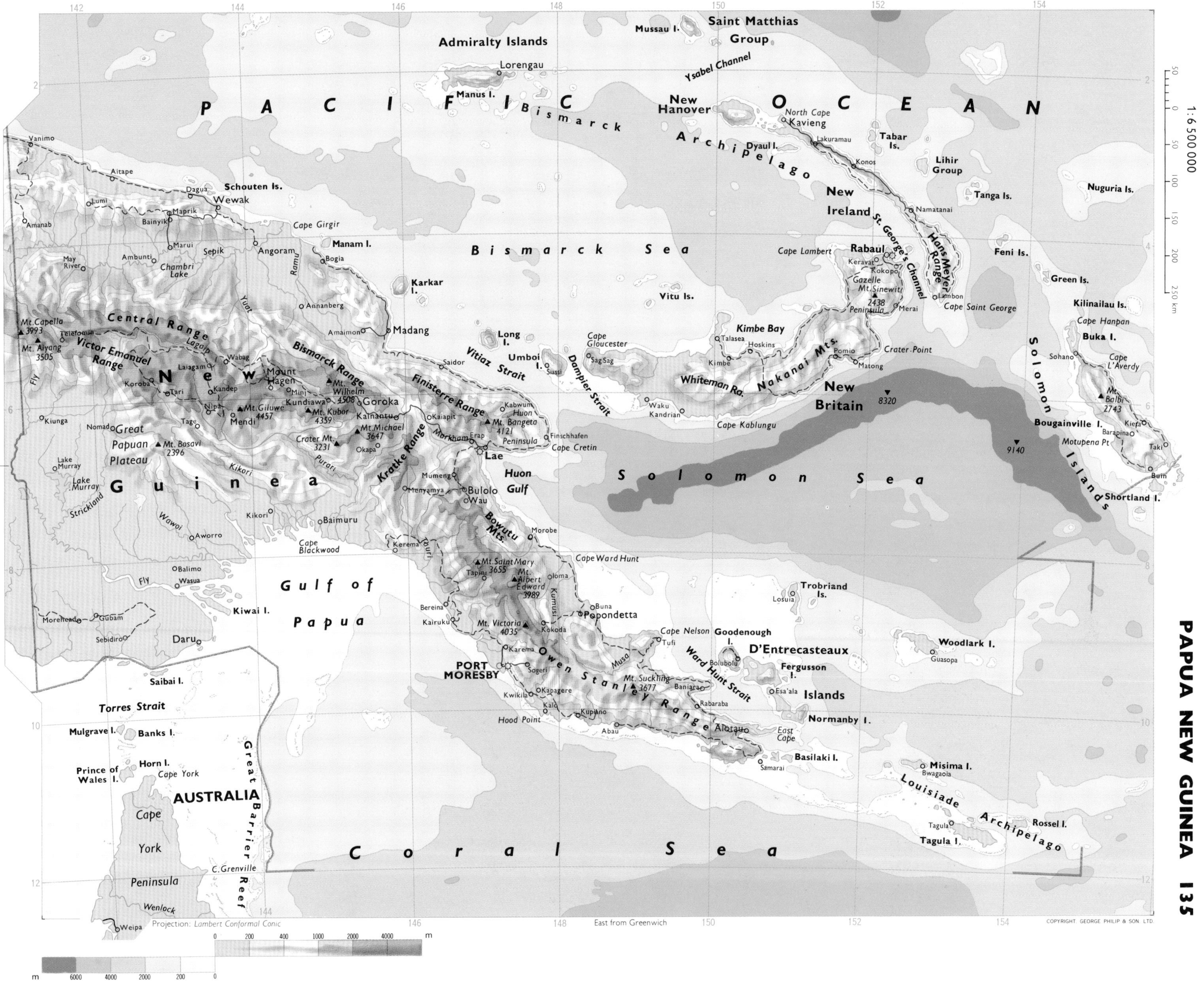
50 0 50 100 150 200 250 km
P A C I F I C O C E A N
Bismarck Archipelago
Bismarck Sea
Solomon Sea
Coral Sea
Gulf of Papua
New Guinea
Solomon Islands
Louisiade Archipelago
D'Entrecasteaux Islands
Admiralty Islands
Manus I.
Lorengau
Saint Matthias Group
Mussau I.
Ysabel Channel
New Hanover
North Cape
Kavieng
Dyaul I.
New Ireland
Tabar Is.
Lihir Group
Tanga Is.
Feni Is.
Green Is.
Nuguria Is.
Kilinailau Is.
Cape Hanpan
Buka I.
Cape L'Averdy
Mt. Balbi 2743
Bougainville I.
Motupena Pt
Shortland I.
Hans Meyer Range
St. George's Channel
Cape Saint George
Rabaul
Cape Lambert
Mt. Sinewit 2438
Kimbe Bay
Cape Gloucester
Whiteman Ra.
Nakanai Mts.
New Britain
Crater Point
Cape Kablungu
8320
9140
Vitu Is.
Long I.
Umboi I.
Vitiaz Strait
Dampier Strait
Karkar I.
Manam I.
Schouten Is.
Wewak
Cape Girgir
Vanimo
Aitape
Sepik
Ramu
Angoram
Chambri Lake
Madang
Central Range
Victor Emanuel Range
Mt. Capella 3993
Mt. Aiyang 3505
Bismarck Range
Mt. Wilhelm 4508
Mount Hagen
Goroka
Mt. Giluwe 4457
Mt. Kubor 4359
Mendi
Mt. Michael 3647
Crater Mt. 3231
Finisterre Range
Kratke Range
Huon Peninsula
Mt. Bangeta 4121
Finschhafen
Cape Cretin
Lae
Huon Gulf
Bulolo
Wau
Bowutu Mts.
Great Papuan Plateau
Mt. Bosavi 2396
Lake Murray
Strickland
Fly
Kikori
Purari
Baimuru
Cape Blackwood
Kiunga
Balimo
Kiwai I.
Daru
Morehead
Mt. Saint Mary 3655
Mt. Albert Edward 3989
Mt. Victoria 4035
Kokoda
Popondetta
Cape Ward Hunt
Cape Nelson
PORT MORESBY
Owen Stanley Range
Mt. Suckling 3677
Hood Point
Ward Hunt Strait
Goodenough I.
Fergusson I.
Normanby I.
Trobriand Is.
Woodlark I.
Alotau
East Cape
Samarai
Basilaki I.
Misima I.
Tagula I.
Rossel I.
Saibai I.
Torres Strait
Mulgrave I.
Banks I.
Prince of Wales I.
Horn I.
Cape York
AUSTRALIA
Great Barrier Reef
C. Grenville
Cape York Peninsula
Wenlock
Weipa
Projection: Lambert Conformal Conic
East from Greenwich
COPYRIGHT GEORGE PHILIP & SON LTD.

TIMOR SEA
INDONESIA
INDIAN OCEAN
NORTHERN TERRITORY
Tanami Desert
Great Sandy Desert
Gibson Desert
Timor
Roti
Sawa
Sumba
Sumbawa
Melville I.
Bathurst I.
Darwin
Port Darwin
Katherine
Cobourg Pen.
Van Diemen Gulf
Dundas Str.
Clarence Str.
Joseph Bonaparte Gulf
Cambridge Gulf
Bonaparte Archipelago
Wyndham
Cockburn Ra.
Carr Boyd Ra.
Durack Range
King Leopold Ranges
Mt. Ord 1007
Mt. Hann 776
Halls Creek
Fitzroy Crossing
Derby
King Sound
Buccaneer Archipelago
Broome
Roebuck B.
Lagrange B.
Eighty Mile Beach
Wallal Downs
Port Hedland
Dampier Archipelago
Dampier
Roebourne
Onslow
Exmouth Gulf
North West C.
Exmouth
Learmonth
Hamersley Range
Chichester Ra.
Mt. Bruce 1236
Tom Price
Ophthalmia Ra.
Mt. Newman 1053
Marble Bar
Nullagine
Rowley Shoals
Scott Reef
Lake Mackay
Lake Disappointment
Macdonnell Ranges
Mt. Liebig 1524
Mt. Zeil 1510
Mt. Singleton 808
Tropic of Capricorn
Gregory Lake
L. Macdonald
Ashburton
Fitzroy

1:8 000 000

50 0 50 100 150 200 250 300 km

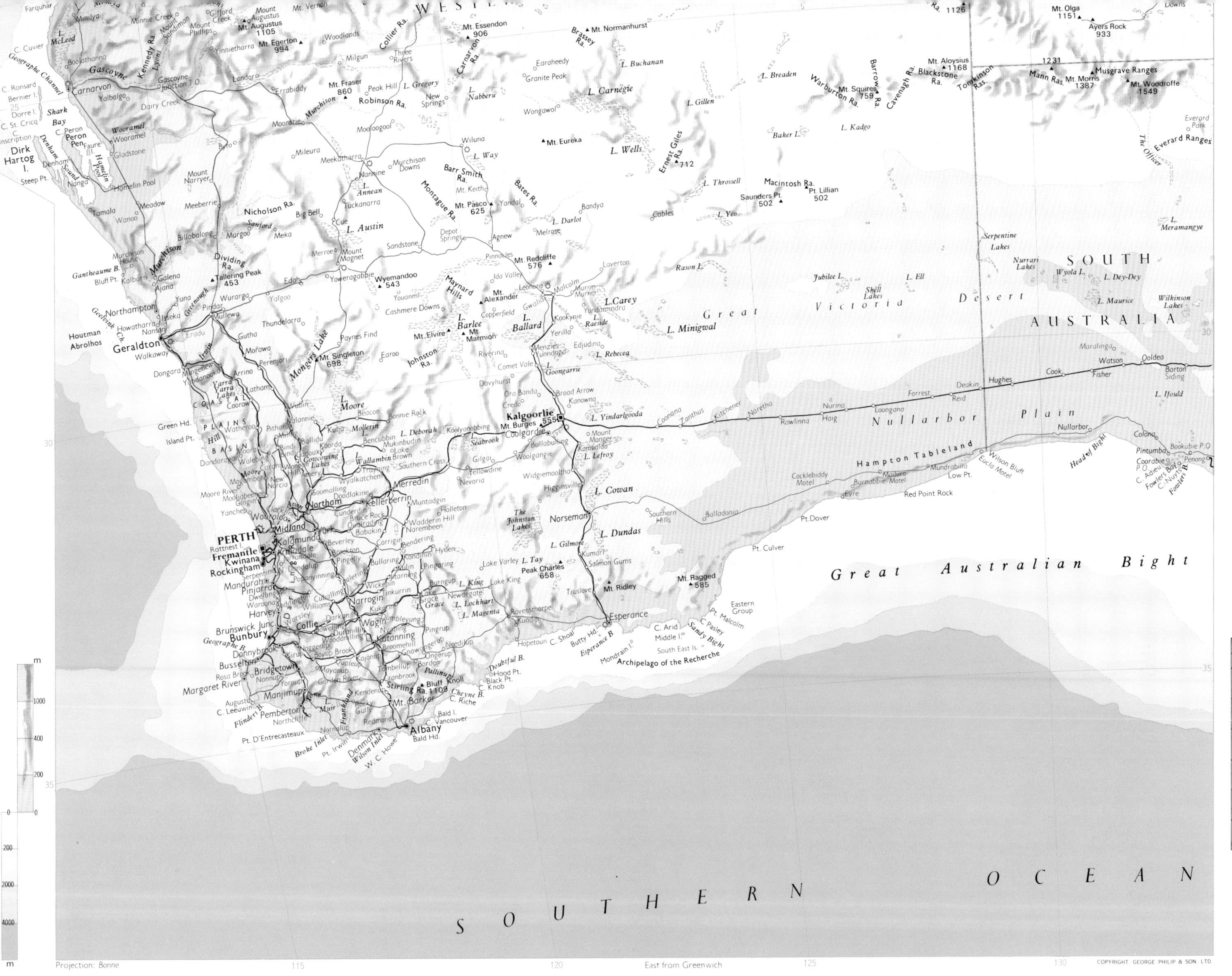

SOUTH AUSTRALIA
WESTERN
Great Victoria Desert
Nullarbor Plain
Hampton Tableland
Great Australian Bight
SOUTHERN OCEAN
PERTH
Fremantle
Kwinana
Rockingham
Midland
Northam
Geraldton
Carnarvon
Kalgoorlie
Coolgardie
Norseman
Esperance
Albany
Bunbury
Busselton
Mandurah
Pinjarra
Collie
Narrogin
Merredin
Northampton
Shark Bay
Dirk Hartog I.
Houtman Abrolhos
Archipelago of the Recherche
Eucla Motel
Ooldea
Cook
Forrest
Rawlinna
L. Carnegie
L. Wells
L. Barlee
L. Moore
L. Austin
Ayers Rock 933
Mt. Olga 1151
Musgrave Ranges
Everard Ranges
Warburton Ra.
Projection: Bonne
East from Greenwich
COPYRIGHT GEORGE PHILIP & SON LTD

Gulf of Carpentaria
CORAL SEA
Great Barrier Reef
Bass Strait
TASMANIA
NORTHERN TERRITORY
GREAT QUEENSLAND
Great Dividing Range
Arnhem Land
Simpson Desert
Barkly Tableland
Cape York Peninsula
Townsville
Cairns
Mount Isa
Rockhampton
Mackay
Gladstone
Hobart
Launceston
Alice Springs
Wellesley Is.
Groote Eylandt
Sir Edward Pellew Group
Hinchinbrook I.
Cumberland Islands
Northumberland Islands
Furneaux Group
Flinders Island
King Island

1:8 000 000

50 0 50 100 150 200 250 300 km

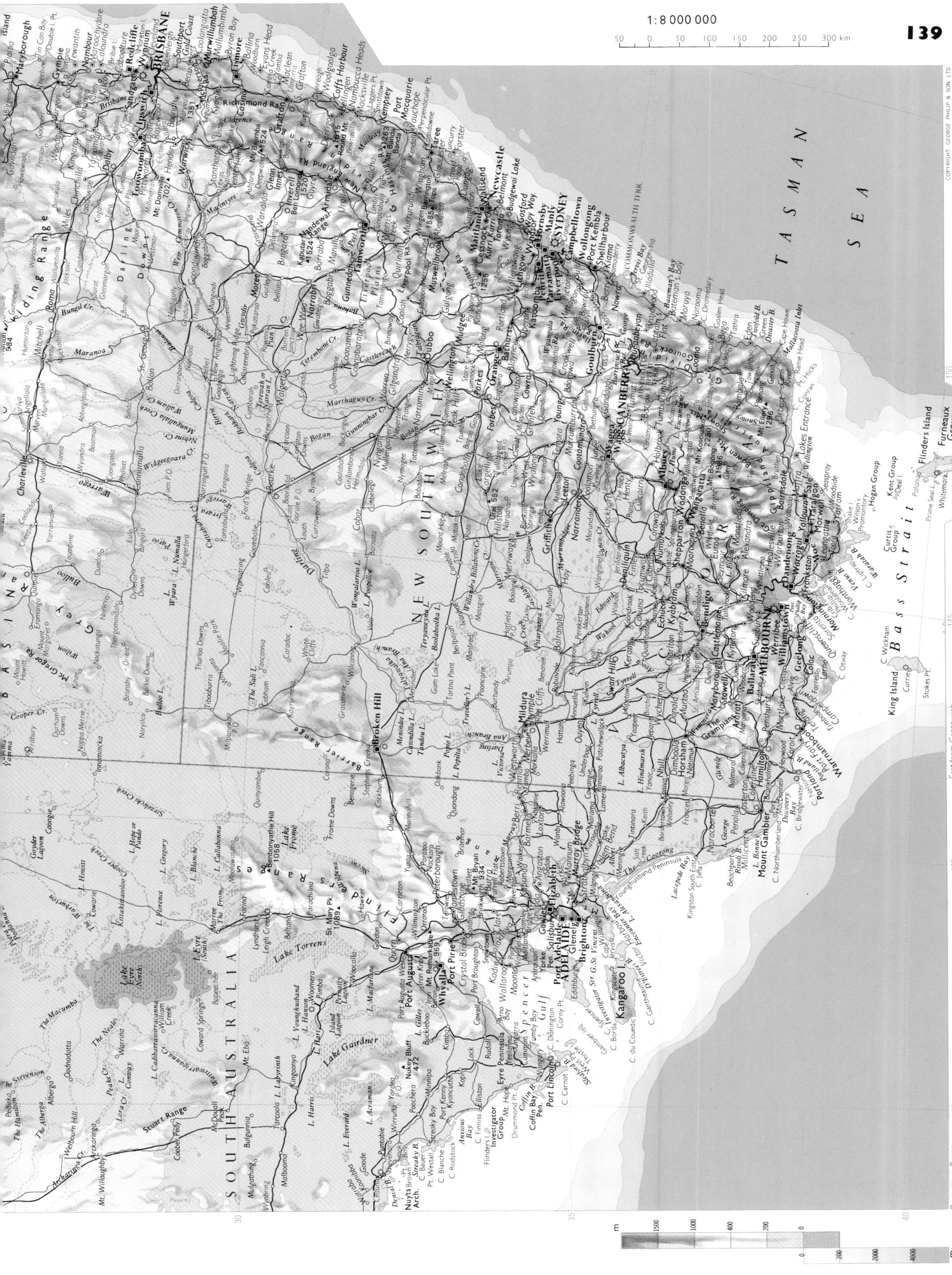

TASMAN SEA

NEW SOUTH WALES

SOUTH AUSTRALIA

Bass Strait

m 1500 1000 400 200 0

0 200 2000 4000 m

East from Greenwich

Projection: Bonne

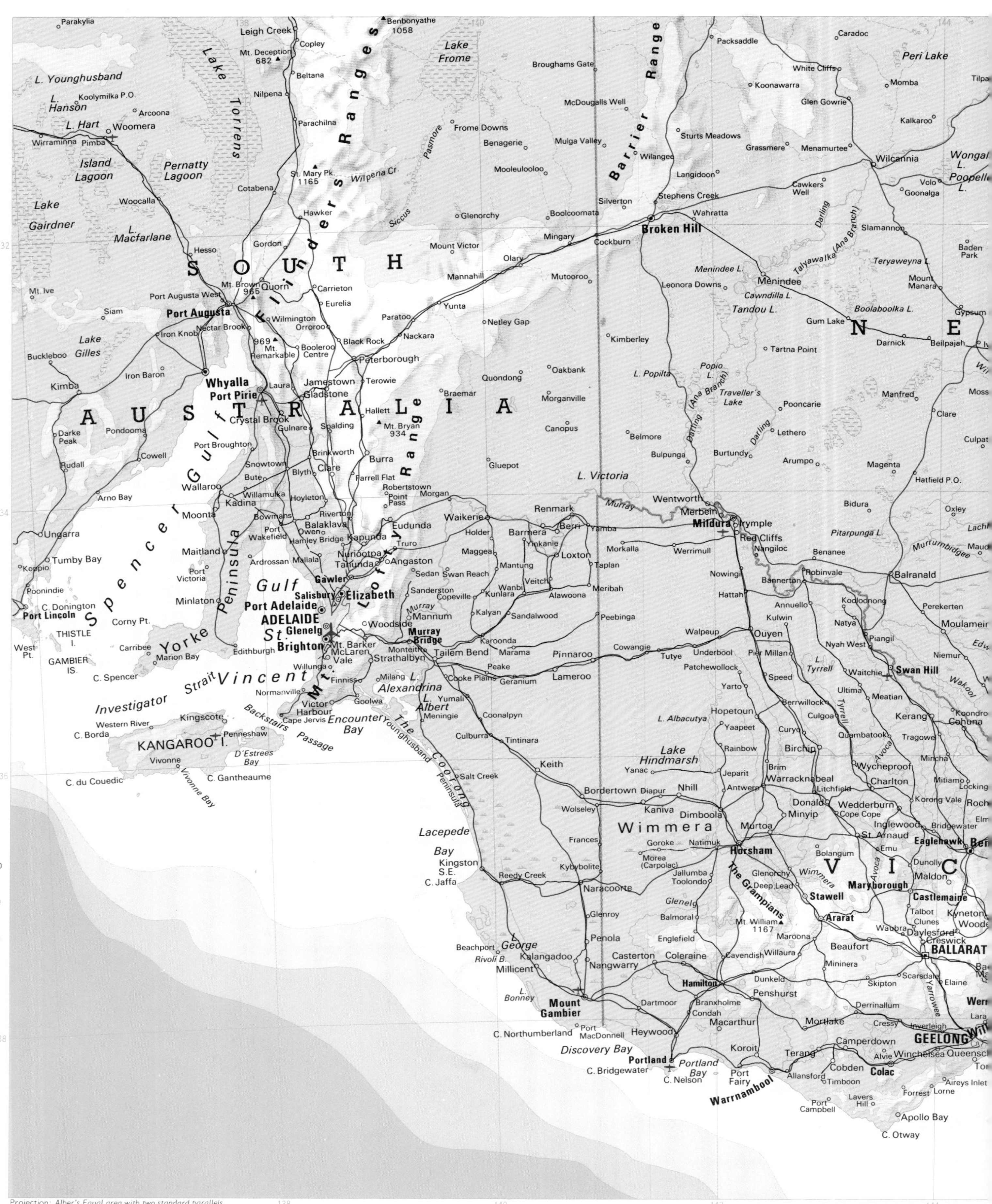

SOUTH AUSTRALIA
NEW SOUTH WALES
VIC
Parakylia
Leigh Creek
Copley
Benbonyathe
1058
Mt. Deception
682
Beltana
Nilpena
Parachilna
Lake Torrens
Flinders Ranges
Lake Frome
L. Younghusband
L. Hanson
Koolymilka P.O.
Arcoona
L. Hart
Woomera
Wirraminna
Pimba
Island Lagoon
Pernatty Lagoon
Lake Gairdner
Woocalla
L. Macfarlane
Hesso
Cotabena
St. Mary Pk.
1165
Wilpena Cr.
Hawker
Gordon
Quorn
Mt. Brown
965
Carrieton
Eurelia
Port Augusta West
Port Augusta
Mt. Ive
Siam
Wilmington
Orroroo
Nectar Brook
Iron Knob
Lake Gilles
Buckleboo
Black Rock
Booleroo Centre
Mt. Remarkable
969
Peterborough
Iron Baron
Kimba
Whyalla
Port Pirie
Laura
Jamestown
Terowie
Gladstone
Crystal Brook
Hallett
Mt. Bryan
934
Gulnare
Spalding
Darke Peak
Pondooma
Port Broughton
Cowell
Brinkworth
Burra
Rudall
Spencer Gulf
Snowtown
Clare
Blyth
Bute
Farrell Flat
Wallaroo
Robertstown
Point Pass
Morgan
Arno Bay
Kadina
Willamulka
Hoyleton
Moonta
Bowmans
Riverton
Ungarra
Port Wakefield
Balaklava
Owen
Hamley Bridge
Kapunda
Eudunda
Tumby Bay
Maitland
Yorke Peninsula
Nuriootpa
Tanunda
Truro
Angaston
Koppio
Port Victoria
Ardrossan
Mallala
Gawler
Sedan
Swan Reach
Poonindie
Gulf
Salisbury
Elizabeth
Minlaton
Port Adelaide
ADELAIDE
Mt. Lofty Ranges
Sanderston
Copeville
C. Donington
Port Lincoln
Corny Pt.
Glenelg
St. Vincent
Brighton
Woodside
Murray Bridge
Mannum
Kalyan
Sandalwood
THISTLE I.
West Pt.
GAMBIER IS.
Carribee
Marion Bay
Edithburgh
Mt. Barker
McLaren Vale
Strathalbyn
Willunga
Tailem Bend
C. Spencer
Investigator Strait
Finniss
Milang
L. Alexandrina
Normanville
Victor Harbour
Goolwa
Cape Jervis
Encounter Bay
Backstairs Passage
Western River
Kingscote
C. Borda
Penneshaw
KANGAROO I.
Vivonne
D'Estrees Bay
C. du Couedic
C. Gantheaume
Vivonne Bay
L. Albert
Meningie
Yumali
The Coorong
Younghusband Peninsula
Salt Creek
Lacepede Bay
Kingston S.E.
C. Jaffa
Beachport
Rivoli B.
L. George
Millicent
Kalangadoo
L. Bonney
Mount Gambier
C. Northumberland
Port MacDonnell
Discovery Bay
C. Bridgewater
Portland
Portland Bay
C. Nelson
Heywood
Port Fairy
Warrnambool
Barrier Range
Broughams Gate
McDougalls Well
Pasmore
Frome Downs
Benagerie
Mulga Valley
Mooleulooloo
Siccus
Glenorchy
Boolcoomata
Silverton
Mount Victor
Mingary
Cockburn
Broken Hill
Olary
Mannahill
Mutooroo
Yunta
Paratoo
Nackara
Netley Gap
Kimberley
Oakbank
Quondong
Braemar
Morganville
Canopus
Gluepot
L. Victoria
Waikerie
Holder
Barmera
Renmark
Berri
Yamba
Loxton
Maggea
Mantung
Morkalla
Taplan
Wanbi
Kunlara
Alawoona
Meribah
Peebinga
Karoonda
Marama
Pinnaroo
Peake
Lameroo
Cooke Plains
Geranium
Coonalpyn
Culburra
Tintinara
Keith
Bordertown
Wolseley
Frances
Naracoorte
Glenroy
Penola
Reedy Creek
Kybybolite
Nangwarry
Casterton
Coleraine
Packsaddle
Koonawarra
Sturts Meadows
Wilangee
Langidoon
Stephens Creek
Wahratta
Menindee L.
Menindee
Leonora Downs
Cawndilla L.
Tandou L.
Kinchega
L. Popilta
Popio L.
Traveller's Lake
Pooncarie
Darling
Lethero
Belmore
Bulpunga
Burtundy
Arumpo
Wentworth
Merbein
Mildura
Irymple
Red Cliffs
Nangiloc
Werrimull
Nowingi
Hattah
Kulwin
Ouyen
Walpeup
Underbool
Cowangie
Tutye
Patchewollock
Speed
Yarto
L. Albacutya
Hopetoun
Yaapeet
Rainbow
Lake Hindmarsh
Yanac
Jeparit
Diapur
Nhill
Kaniva
Dimboola
Wimmera
Goroke
Natimuk
Horsham
Morea (Carpolac)
Jallumba
Toolondo
The Grampians
Mt. William
1167
Balmoral
Englefield
Cavendish
Hamilton
Dartmoor
Branxholme
Condah
Macarthur
Koroit
Caradoc
Peri Lake
White Cliffs
Momba
Glen Gowrie
Kalkaroo
Menamurtee
Grassmere
Wilcannia
Cawkers Well
Volo
Goonalga
Slamannon
Talyawalka (Ana Branch)
Teryaweyna L.
Mount Manara
Boolaboolka L.
Gum Lake
Darnick
Tartna Point
Manfred
Clare
Magenta
Hatfield P.O.
Bidura
Oxley
Pitarpunga L.
Benanee
Balranald
Murrumbidgee
Robinvale
Bannerton
Annuello
Kooloonong
Natya
Perekerten
Nyah West
Piangil
Moulamein
Swan Hill
Waitchie
L. Tyrrell
Ultima
Meatian
Berriwillock
Culgoa
Kerang
Cohuna
Koondrook
Quambatook
Tragowel
Birchip
Warracknabeal
Wycheproof
Charlton
Brim
Litchfield
Donald
Minyip
Murtoa
Wedderburn
Cope Cope
St. Arnaud
Inglewood
Bridgewater
Eaglehawk
Emu
Bolangum
Dunolly
Maldon
Glenorchy
Deep Lead
Stawell
Maryborough
Castlemaine
Ararat
Talbot
Clunes
Kyneton
Waubra
Daylesford
Creswick
Maroona
Willaura
Beaufort
BALLARAT
Mininera
Dunkeld
Penshurst
Scarsdale
Skipton
Elaine
Derrinallum
Mortlake
Cressy
Inverleigh
GEELONG
Terang
Camperdown
Alvie
Winchelsea
Cobden
Colac
Allansford
Timboon
Port Campbell
Lavers Hill
Forrest
Lorne
Aireys Inlet
Apollo Bay
C. Otway
m
2000
1500
1000
400
200
0
200
2000
4000
m

Projection: *Alber's Equal area with two standard parallels*

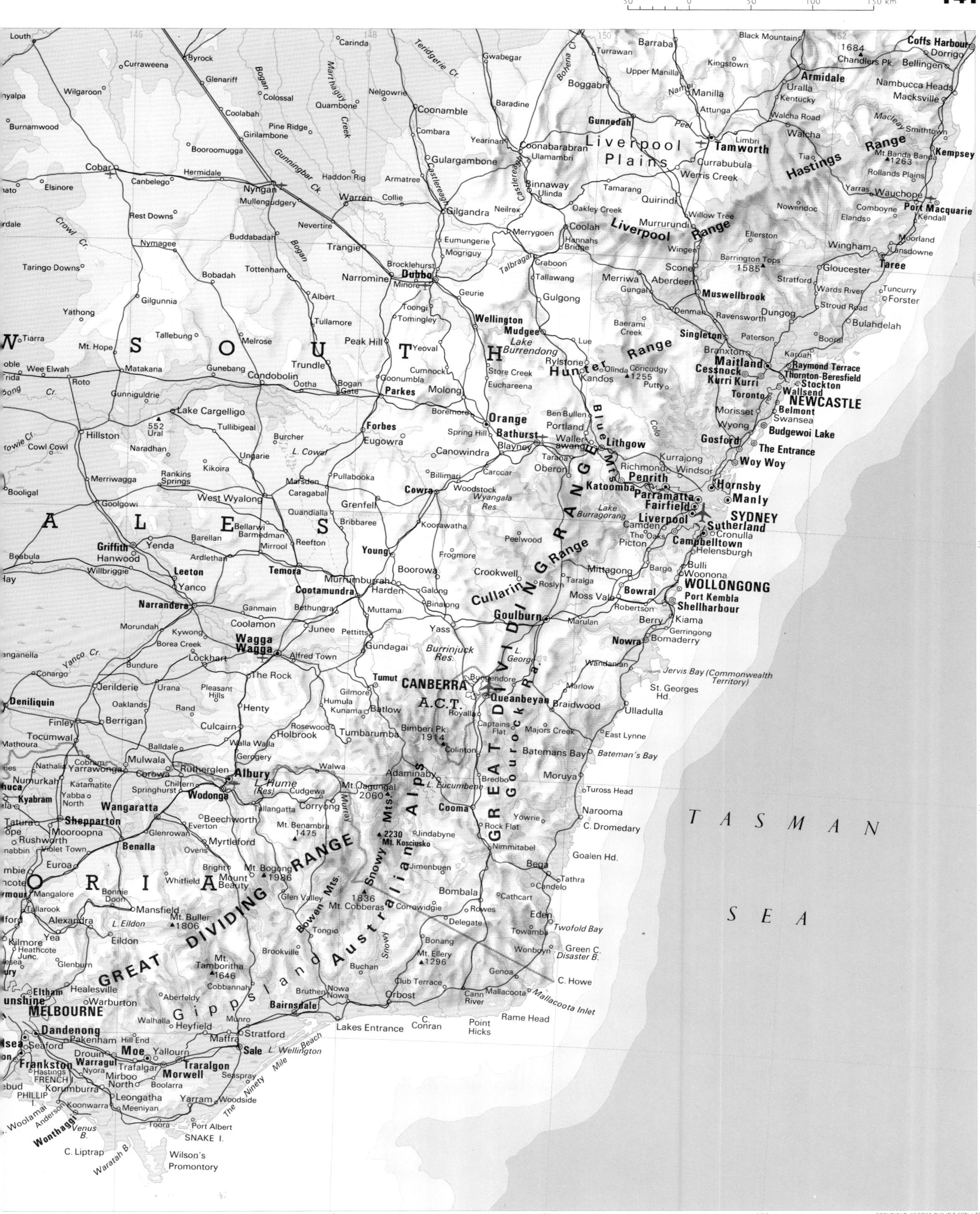
Coffs Harbour
Dorrigo
Bellingen
Armidale
Uralla
Kentucky
Nambucca Heads
Macksville
Walcha
Walcha Road
Tamworth
Kempsey
Hastings
Range
Wauchope
Port Macquarie
Liverpool Plains
Liverpool Range
Gunnedah
Boggabri
Barraba
Manilla
Quirindi
Murrurundi
Werris Creek
Coonabarabran
Coonamble
Gilgandra
Dubbo
Narromine
Trangie
Nyngan
Cobar
Warren
Wellington
Mudgee
Gulgong
Scone
Aberdeen
Muswellbrook
Singleton
Taree
Gloucester
Forster
Tuncurry
Dungog
Maitland
Cessnock
Kurri Kurri
Raymond Terrace
NEWCASTLE
Gosford
The Entrance
Woy Woy
Hornsby
Manly
SYDNEY
Parramatta
Fairfield
Liverpool
Penrith
Katoomba
Lithgow
Bathurst
Orange
Parkes
Forbes
Cowra
Condobolin
Lake Cargelligo
Hillston
West Wyalong
Young
Temora
Cootamundra
Griffith
Leeton
Narrandera
Wagga Wagga
Junee
Goulburn
Bowral
Mittagong
Campbelltown
WOLLONGONG
Port Kembla
Shellharbour
Kiama
Nowra
Jervis Bay (Commonwealth Territory)
Ulladulla
CANBERRA
A.C.T.
Queanbeyan
Yass
Tumut
Gundagai
Batemans Bay
Moruya
Narooma
Cooma
Bega
Eden
Twofold Bay
C. Howe
Mallacoota Inlet
Albury
Wodonga
Wangaratta
Shepparton
Benalla
Deniliquin
Mt. Kosciusko
Snowy Mts.
Australian Alps
Bowen Mts.
GREAT DIVIDING RANGE
Gippsland
Bairnsdale
Lakes Entrance
Sale
Traralgon
Morwell
Moe
Warragul
Dandenong
MELBOURNE
Frankston
Wonthaggi
Wilson's Promontory
The Ninety Mile Beach
Blue Mts.
Hunter Range
Cullarin Range
Gourock Ra.
N E W S O U T H W A L E S
V I C T O R I A
T A S M A N S E A

NEW ZEALAND – NORTH ISLAND

1:3 500 000

20 0 20 40 60 80 100 km

TASMAN SEA

JANUARY TEMPERATURE
1:25 000 000

ACTUAL SURFACE TEMPERATURE

°C
20
15
10
5
0

20° Isotherms reduced to Sea-level
°Celsius

JULY TEMPERATURE
1:25 000 000

SUMMER AND WINTER RAINFALL

mm
1000
750
500
250

1012 Isobars in millibars

Prevailing Winds

SUMMER RAINFALL
November to April
1:25 000 000

WINTER RAINFALL
May to October
1:25 000 000

m
3000
2000
1000
400
200
0
200
2000
m

Projection: Conical with two standard parallels

East from Greenwich

1:3 500 000

20 0 20 40 60 80 100 km

POPULATION
1:15 000 000
Inhabitants per km²
under 1
1–3
3–6
6–12
12–25
25–50
50–100
over 100

○ Towns of 50–100 000 inhabitants
■ Towns of over 100 000 inhabitants

ANNUAL RAINFALL
1:15 000 000
mm
3000
2000
1250
750
500

Projection: Conical with two standard parallels

East from Greenwich

ARCTIC OCEAN
ATLANTIC
PACIFIC
Greenland
Iceland
Greenland Sea
Denmark Strait
Davis Strait
Baffin Bay
Baffin Island
Ellesmere I.
Axel Heiberg
Sverdrup Land
Queen Elizabeth Islands
Devon I.
Prince of Wales I.
Victoria I.
Banks I.
Beaufort Sea
Hudson Bay
James Bay
Hudson Strait
Ungava Peninsula
Labrador
Laurentian Plateau
Newfoundland
Gulf of St Lawrence
Nova Scotia
Bay of Fundy
Southampton I.
Foxe Basin
Melville Pen.
Boothia Pen.
Gulf of Boothia
Great Bear L.
Great Slave L.
Lake Winnipeg
L. Superior
L. Michigan
L. Huron
L. Erie
L. Ontario
Mackenzie Mts.
Rocky Mountains
Coast Mountains
Selkirk Mts.
Cascade Range
Sierra Nevada
Coast Range
Great Basin
Wasatch Mountains
Colorado Plateau
Great Plains
Llano Estacado
Appalachian Mts.
Allegheny Mts.
Blue Ridge
Cumberland Plateau
Ozark Plateau
Brooks Range
Alaska Range
Alaska Pen.
Gulf of Alaska
Alexander Archipelago
Queen Charlotte Islands
Vancouver I.
Aleutian Islands
Bering Sea
Bering Strait
Mendocino Seascarp
Murray Seascarp
New York
Philadelphia
Washington
Montreal
Ottawa
Toronto
Detroit
Chicago
St. Louis
Minneapolis
Kansas City
Winnipeg
Regina
Edmonton
Calgary
Denver
Seattle
Portland
San Francisco
Los Angeles

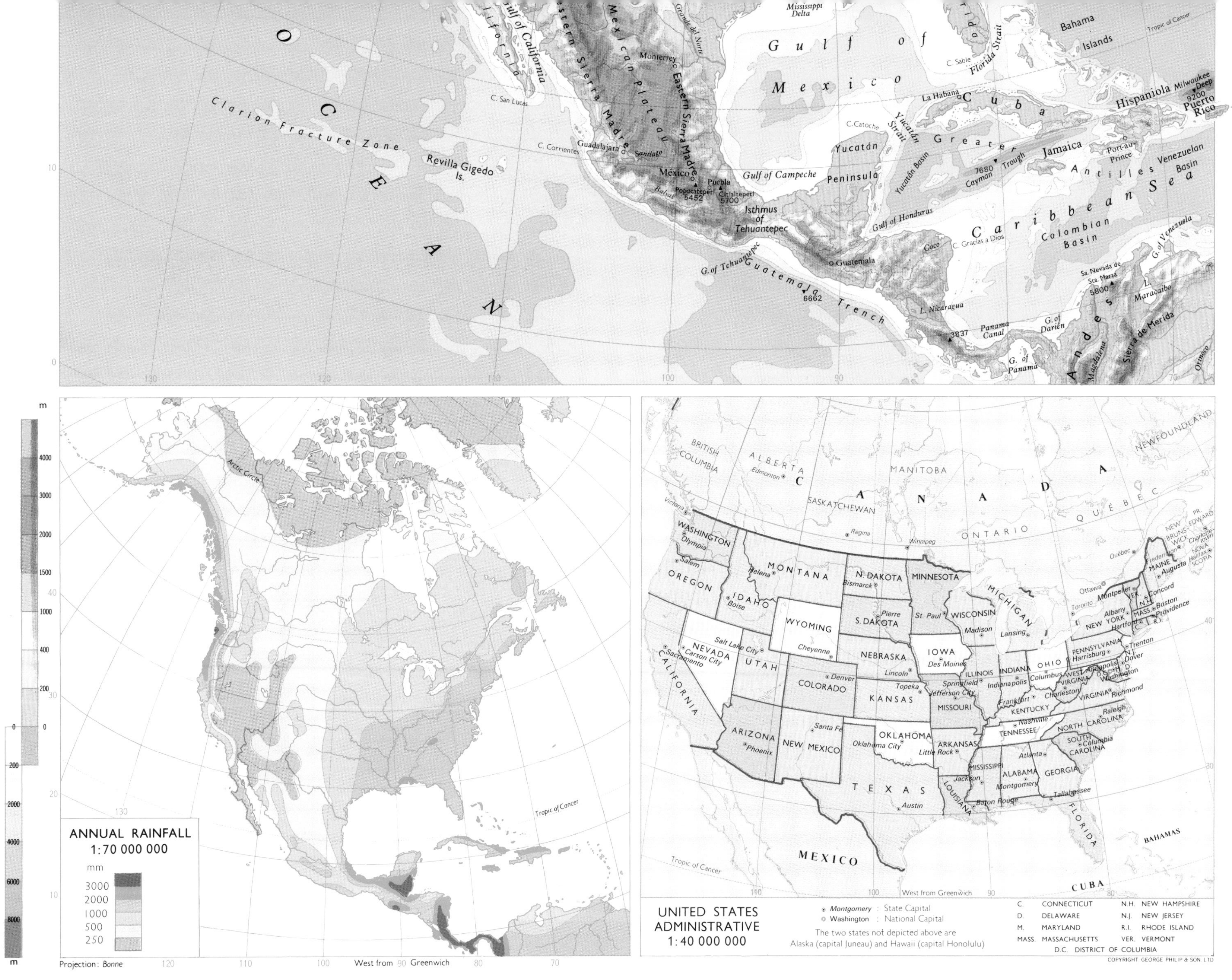
Gulf of Mexico
Mississippi Delta
Bahama Islands
Tropic of Cancer
Florida Strait
C. Sable
La Habana
Cuba
Hispaniola
Milwaukee Deep 9200
Puerto Rico
Port-au-Prince
Jamaica
Greater Antilles
Caribbean Sea
Venezuelan Basin
Colombian Basin
Cayman Trough 7680
Yucatán Basin
Yucatán Strait
C. Catoche
Yucatán Peninsula
Gulf of Campeche
Gulf of Honduras
C. Gracias a Dios
Coco
L. Nicaragua
3837
Panama Canal
G. of Panamá
G. of Darién
Sa. Nevada de Sta. Marta 5800
L. Maracaibo
G. of Venezuela
Sierra de Mérida
Magdalena
Andes
Orinoco
Guatemala
Isthmus of Tehuantepec
G. of Tehuantepec
Guatemala Trench
6662
México
Puebla
Popocatepetl 5452
Citlaltepetl 5700
Balsas
Guadalajara
Santiago
Monterrey
Grande del Norte
Eastern Sierra Madre
Mexican Plateau
Western Sierra Madre
Gulf of California
California
C. San Lucas
C. Corrientes
Revilla Gigedo Is.
Clarion Fracture Zone
OCEAN
ANNUAL RAINFALL
1:70 000 000
mm
3000
2000
1000
500
250
Arctic Circle
Tropic of Cancer
Projection: Bonne
West from 90 Greenwich
m
4000
3000
2000
1500
1000
400
200
0
200
2000
4000
6000
8000
m
CANADA
BRITISH COLUMBIA
ALBERTA
Edmonton
SASKATCHEWAN
Regina
MANITOBA
Winnipeg
ONTARIO
QUÉBEC
NEWFOUNDLAND
Victoria
WASHINGTON
Olympia
OREGON
Salem
IDAHO
Boise
MONTANA
Helena
N. DAKOTA
Bismarck
MINNESOTA
St. Paul
S. DAKOTA
Pierre
WYOMING
Cheyenne
NEVADA
Carson City
CALIFORNIA
Sacramento
UTAH
Salt Lake City
COLORADO
Denver
NEBRASKA
Lincoln
IOWA
Des Moines
WISCONSIN
Madison
MICHIGAN
Lansing
KANSAS
Topeka
MISSOURI
Jefferson City
ILLINOIS
Springfield
INDIANA
Indianapolis
OHIO
Columbus
ARIZONA
Phoenix
NEW MEXICO
Santa Fe
OKLAHOMA
Oklahoma City
ARKANSAS
Little Rock
TEXAS
Austin
LOUISIANA
Baton Rouge
MISSISSIPPI
Jackson
ALABAMA
Montgomery
GEORGIA
Atlanta
FLORIDA
Tallahassee
TENNESSEE
Nashville
KENTUCKY
Frankfort
WEST VIRGINIA
Charleston
VIRGINIA
Richmond
NORTH CAROLINA
Raleigh
SOUTH CAROLINA
Columbia
PENNSYLVANIA
Harrisburg
NEW YORK
Albany
Trenton
Dover
Annapolis
Washington
Hartford
Providence
Boston
Concord
Montpelier
MAINE
Augusta
Ottawa
Toronto
Québec
Fredericton
NEW BRUNSWICK
P.E. ISLAND
Charlottetown
NOVA SCOTIA
Halifax
MEXICO
CUBA
BAHAMAS
Tropic of Cancer
West from Greenwich
UNITED STATES
ADMINISTRATIVE
1:40 000 000
⊛ Montgomery : State Capital
⊙ Washington : National Capital
The two states not depicted above are
Alaska (capital Juneau) and Hawaii (capital Honolulu)
C. CONNECTICUT
D. DELAWARE
M. MARYLAND
MASS. MASSACHUSETTS
N.H. NEW HAMPSHIRE
N.J. NEW JERSEY
R.I. RHODE ISLAND
VER. VERMONT
D.C. DISTRICT OF COLUMBIA
COPYRIGHT GEORGE PHILIP & SON LTD

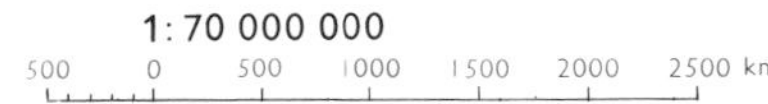
1: 70 000 000
500 0 500 1000 1500 2000 2500 km

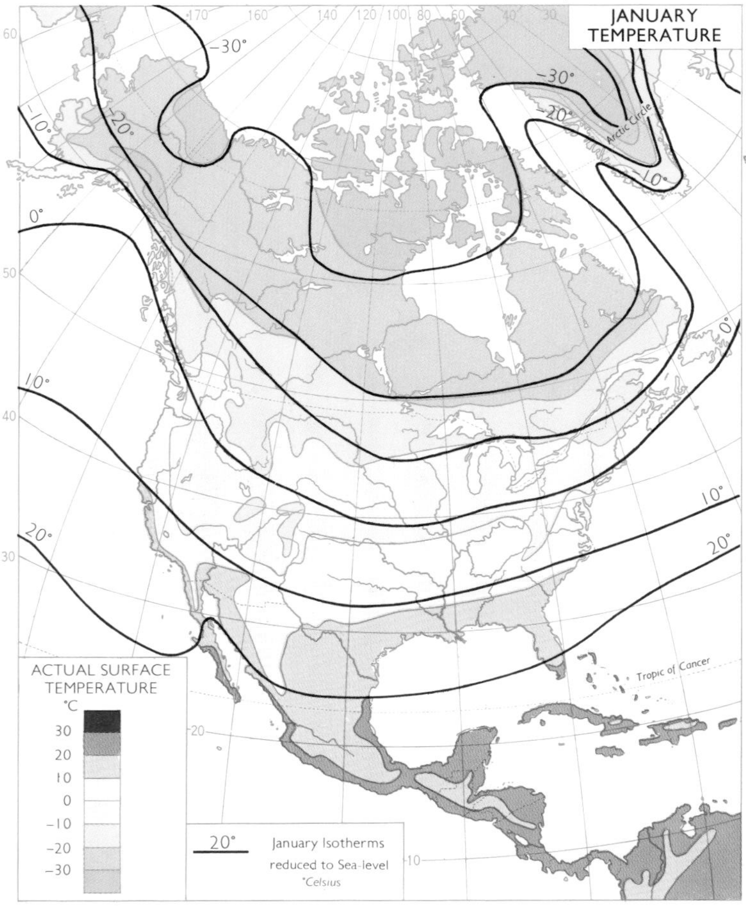

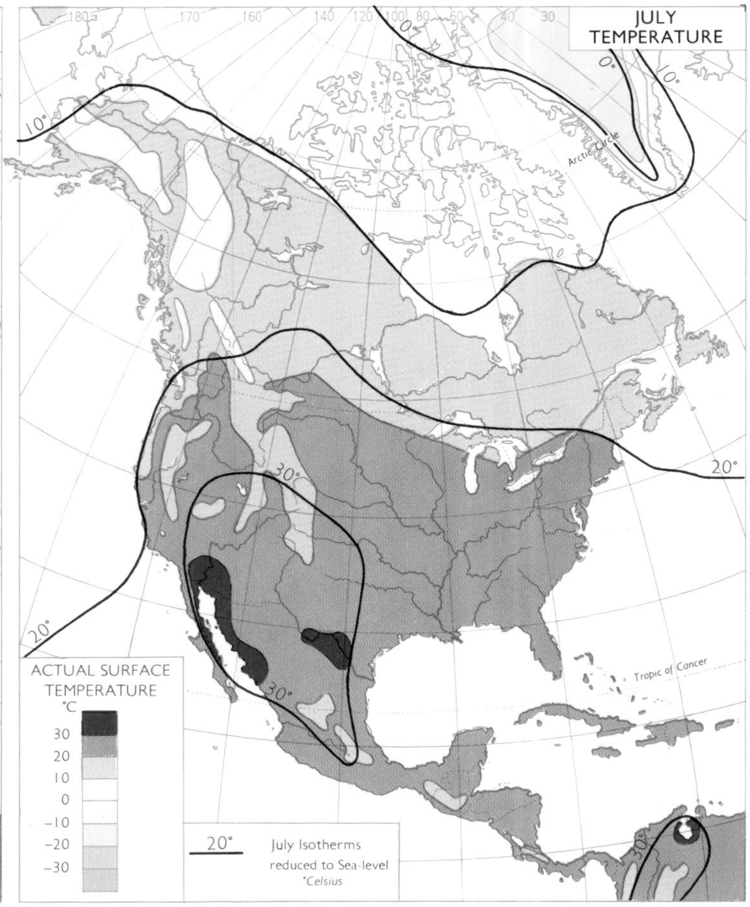

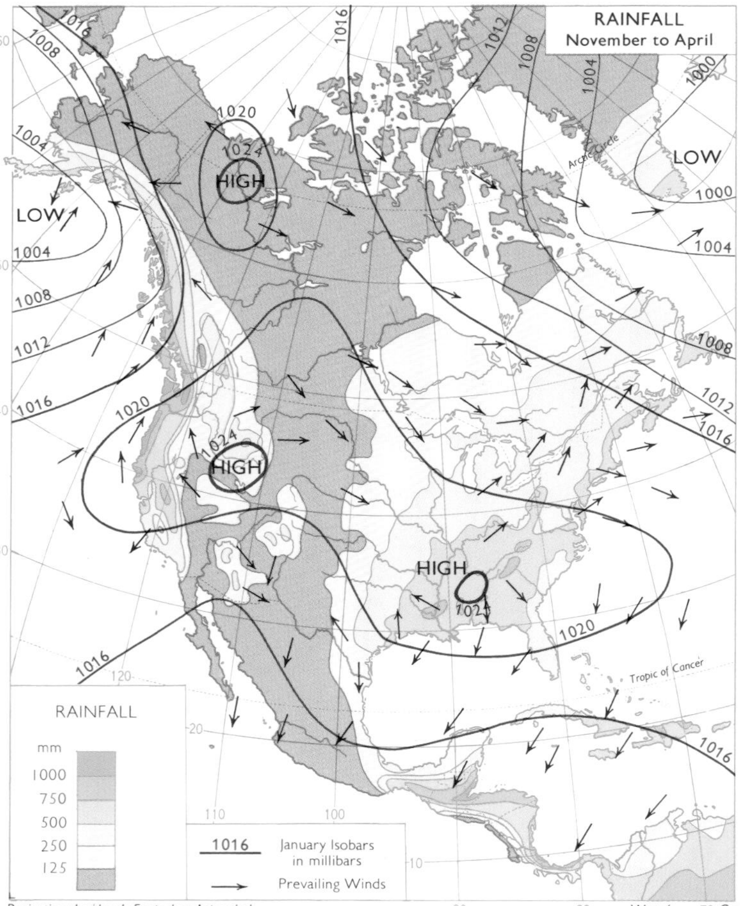

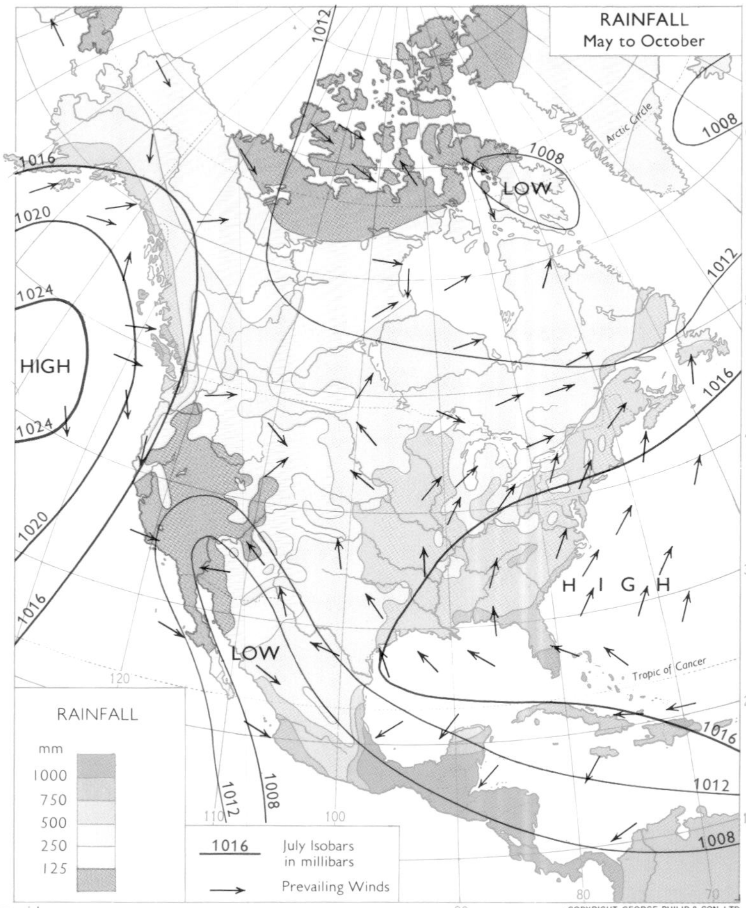

JANUARY TEMPERATURE

ACTUAL SURFACE TEMPERATURE
°C
30
20
10
0
−10
−20
−30

20° January Isotherms reduced to Sea-level °Celsius

JULY TEMPERATURE

ACTUAL SURFACE TEMPERATURE
°C
30
20
10
0
−10
−20
−30

20° July Isotherms reduced to Sea-level °Celsius

RAINFALL November to April

RAINFALL
mm
1000
750
500
250
125

1016 January Isobars in millibars

→ Prevailing Winds

RAINFALL May to October

RAINFALL
mm
1000
750
500
250
125

1016 July Isobars in millibars

→ Prevailing Winds

Projection: *Lambert's Equivalent Azimuthal*

West from Greenwich

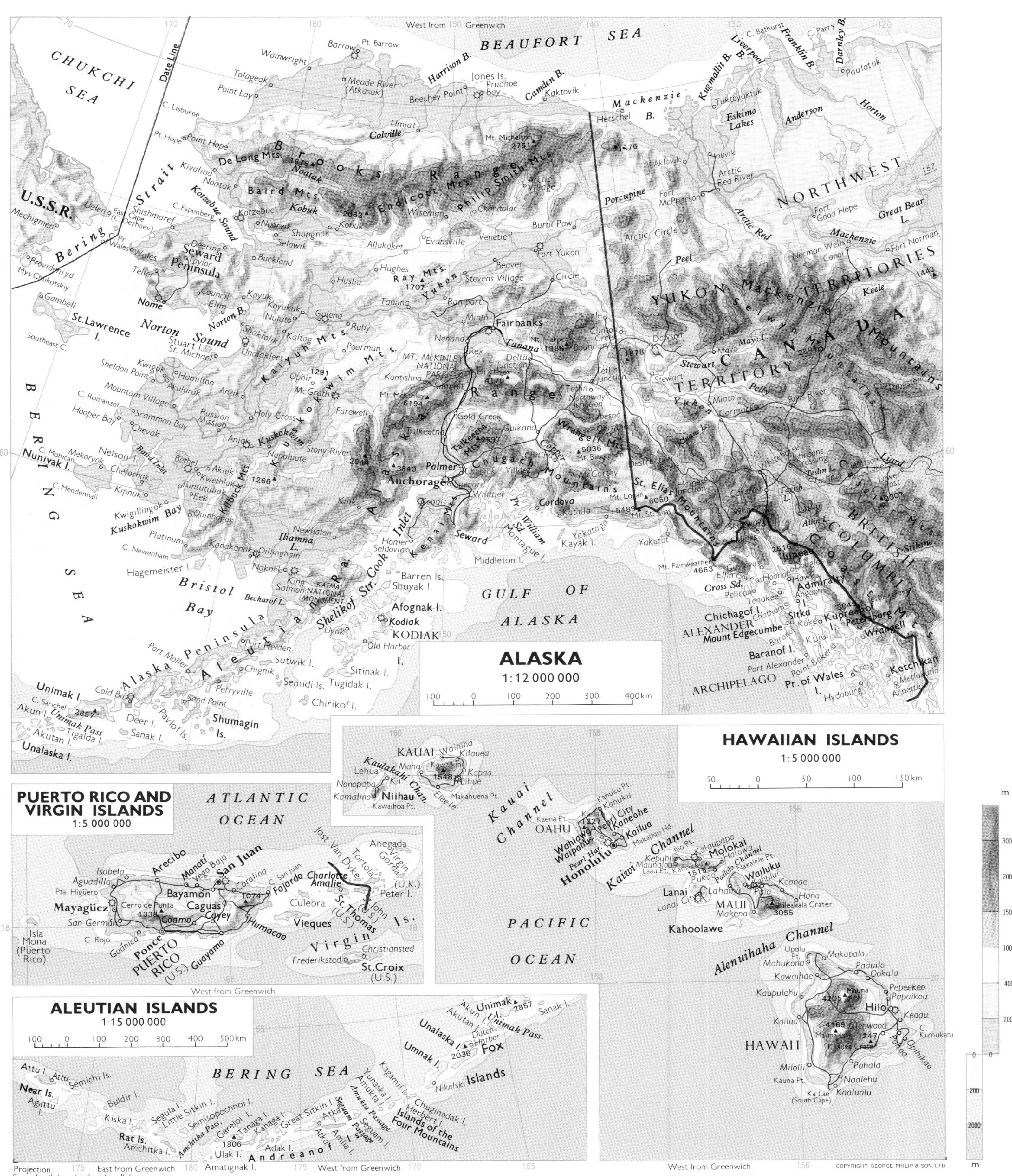
ALASKA
1:12 000 000
100 0 100 200 300 400 km
HAWAIIAN ISLANDS
1:5 000 000
50 0 50 100 150 km
PUERTO RICO AND VIRGIN ISLANDS
1:5 000 000
ALEUTIAN ISLANDS
1:15 000 000
100 0 100 200 300 400 500 km
West from Greenwich
East from Greenwich
Projection: Conical with two standard parallels
COPYRIGHT, GEORGE PHILIP & SON, LTD.
CHUKCHI SEA
BEAUFORT SEA
BERING SEA
GULF OF ALASKA
Bristol Bay
Norton Sound
Kotzebue Sound
Bering Strait
Date Line
U.S.S.R.
Brooks Range
De Long Mts.
Baird Mts.
Endicott Mts.
Philip Smith Mts.
Alaska Range
Kuskokwim Mts.
Chugach Mountains
Wrangell Mts.
St. Elias Mountains
Coast Mts.
Mackenzie Mountains
Selwyn Mountains
YUKON TERRITORY
NORTHWEST TERRITORIES
CANADA
BRITISH COLUMBIA
Alaska Peninsula
Seward Peninsula
Aleutian Ra.
Kenai Mts.
Cook Inlet
Shelikof Str.
Barrow
Pt. Barrow
Wainwright
Prudhoe Bay
Kotzebue
Nome
Fairbanks
Anchorage
Palmer
Seward
Valdez
Cordova
Juneau
Sitka
Ketchikan
Skagway
Whitehorse
Dawson
Kodiak
KODIAK I.
St. Lawrence I.
Nunivak I.
Unimak I.
Unalaska I.
Shumagin Is.
ALEXANDER ARCHIPELAGO
Chichagof I.
Baranof I.
Admiralty I.
Pr. of Wales I.
Mt. McKinley 6194
Mt. Logan 6050
Mt. Fairweather 4663
MT. McKINLEY NATIONAL PARK
KATMAI NATIONAL MONUMENT
KAUAI
Niihau
OAHU
Honolulu
Molokai
Lanai
MAUI
Kahoolawe
HAWAII
Hilo
Mauna Kea 4205
Mauna Loa 4169
Haleakala Crater 3055
Kauai Channel
Kaiwi Channel
Alenuihaha Channel
PACIFIC OCEAN
ATLANTIC OCEAN
San Juan
Arecibo
Mayagüez
Ponce
PUERTO RICO (U.S.)
Isla Mona (Puerto Rico)
Culebra
Vieques
Virgin Is.
Charlotte Amalie
St. Thomas (U.S.)
St. Croix (U.S.)
Anegada
Virgin Gorda
Tortola
Christiansted
Frederiksted
Attu I.
Near Is.
Rat Is.
Andreanof Is.
Islands of the Four Mountains
Fox Islands
Umnak I.
Unalaska I.
Unimak I.
Amchitka I.
Adak I.
Atka I.
Kiska I.

PACIFIC OCEAN
ALASKA
YUKON TERRITORY
NORTHWEST TERRITORIES
BRITISH COLUMBIA
ALBERTA
SASKATCHEWAN
MANITOBA
WASHINGTON
OREGON
IDAHO
MONTANA
WYOMING
NORTH DAKOTA
SOUTH DAKOTA
NEBRASKA
MINNESOTA
NEVADA
UTAH
CALIFORNIA
UNITED STATES
INUVIK
CENTRAL ARCTIC
Anchorage
Fairbanks
Whitehorse
Juneau
Vancouver
Victoria
Seattle
Portland
Edmonton
Calgary
Regina
Saskatoon
Winnipeg
Yellowknife
Great Slave L.
Great Bear Lake
Lake Athabasca
Lake Winnipeg
Amundsen Gulf
Victoria Island
Banks Island
Coronation Gulf
Queen Maud Gulf
Viscount Melville Sound
Queen Charlotte Is.
Vancouver I.
Rocky Mountains
Mackenzie Mountains
Coast Mountains
Cassiar Mountains
Columbia Mountains
Salt Lake City
San Francisco
Minneapolis
Omaha
Projection: Bonne
m
3000
2000
1500
1000
400
200
0
200
2000
m

1:15 000 000

100 0 100 200 300 400 500 600 km

GREENLAND
ATLANTIC OCEAN
Baffin Bay
Davis Strait
Hudson Strait
Ungava Bay
Hudson Bay
James Bay
Foxe Basin
Foxe Channel
BAFFIN I.
Gulf of St. Lawrence
NEWFOUNDLAND
LABRADOR
COAST OF LABRADOR
QUEBEC
ONTARIO
NEW BRUNSWICK
NOVA SCOTIA
PR. EDWARD I.
MAINE
NEW HAMPSHIRE
VERMONT
MASS.
NEW YORK
PENNSYLVANIA
NEW JERSEY
OHIO
INDIANA
MONTREAL
Québec
Ottawa
TORONTO
Boston
NEW YORK
Buffalo
DETROIT
Cleveland
Halifax
St. John's
Lake Superior
L. Huron
L. Michigan
Lake Erie
Ontario
Cumberland Peninsula
Cumberland Sd.
Frobisher Bay
Resolution I.
Southampton I.
Ungava Peninsula
Belle Isle
Str. of Belle Isle
Cabot Str.
I. d'Anticosti
Sable I. (Nova Scotia)
ST. PIERRE et MIQUELON (Fr.)
West from Greenwich
COPYRIGHT, GEORGE PHILIP & SON, LTD.

N. W. TERRITORIES

HUDSON BAY

JAMES BAY

MANITOBA

ONTARIO

LAKE SUPERIOR

LAKE HURON

LAKE MICHIGAN

LAKE ERIE

LAKE ONTARIO

WISCONSIN

MICHIGAN

ILLINOIS

NEW YORK

m

1500

1000

400

200

0

0

200

2000

4000

m

Lambert's Equivalent Azimuthal

INDIANA OHIO PENNSYLVANIA

1:7 000 000

50 0 50 100 150 200 250 300 km

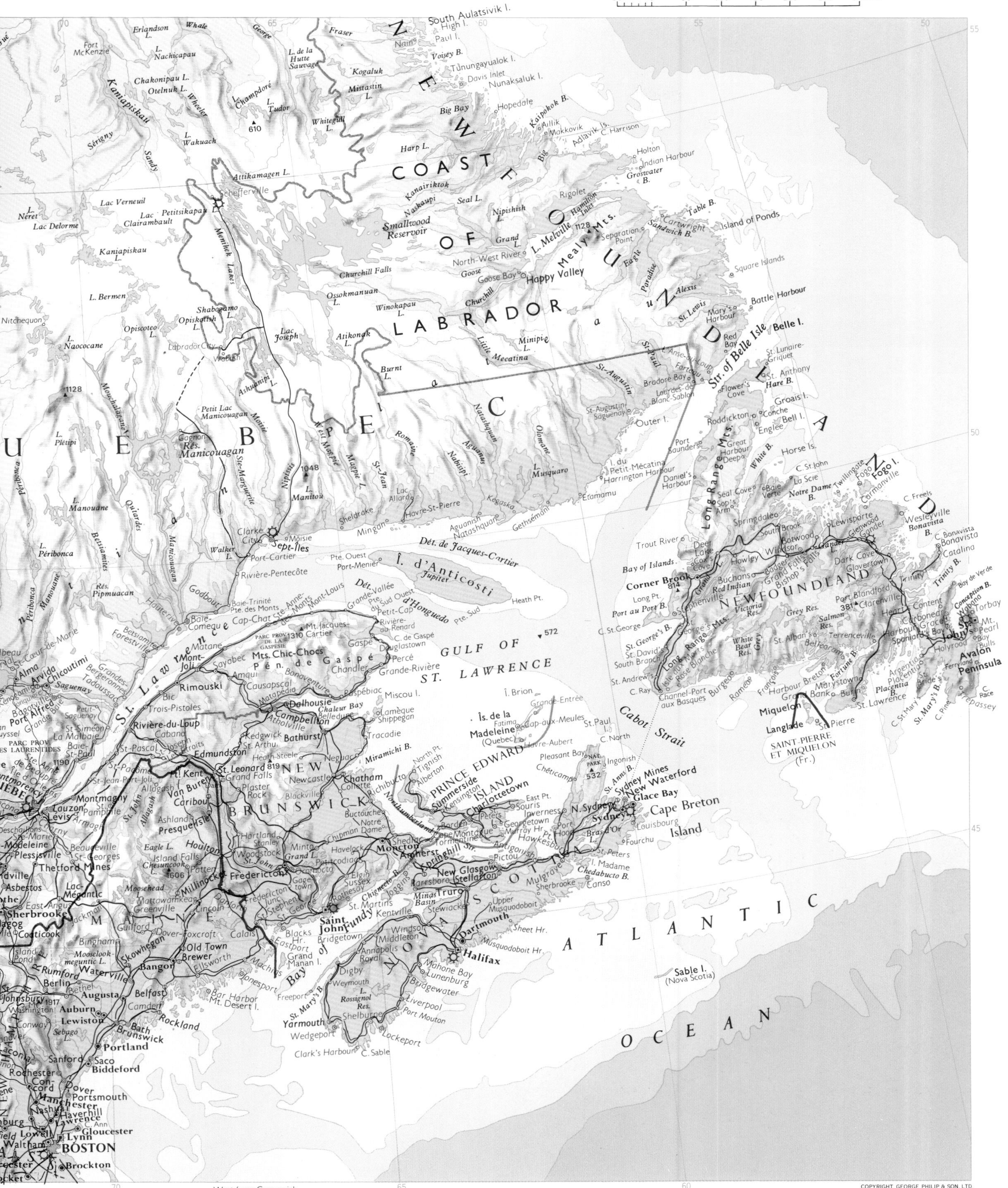
NEWFOUNDLAND
COAST OF LABRADOR
QUEBEC
South Aulatsivik I.
High I.
Paul I.
Nain
Voisey B.
Tunungayualok I.
Davis Inlet
Nunaksaluk I.
Hopedale
Kaipokok B.
Makkovik
Adlavik Is.
C. Harrison
Holton
Indian Harbour
Groswater B.
Rigolet
Hamilton Inlet
Table B.
Cartwright
Sandwich B.
Island of Ponds
Separation Point
Square Islands
Battle Harbour
Alexis
Paradise
Eagle
Mealy Mts.
1128
L. Melville
Happy Valley
Goose Bay
North-West River
Grand L.
Nipishish L.
Seal L.
Naskaupi
Kanairiktok
Harp L.
Big Bay
Mistastin L.
Kogaluk
Fraser
Whitegull L.
L. de la Hutte Sauvage
Erlandson L.
Whale
George
Fort McKenzie
L. Nachicapau
Chakonipau L.
Otelnuk L.
Champdoré
L. Tudor
610
Kaniapiskau
Wheeler
Sérigny
Sandy
L. Wakuach
Attikamagen L.
Schefferville
L. Petitsikapau
Lac Verneuil
Lac Clairambault
L. Néret
Lac Delorme
Kaniapiskau L.
Menihek Lakes
Smallwood Reservoir
Churchill Falls
Ossokmanuan L.
Winokapau L.
Churchill
Goose
L. Bermen
Nitchequon
Shabogamo L.
Opiskotish L.
Opiscoteo L.
Lac Joseph
Labrador City
Wabush
Atikonak L.
Ashuanipi L.
L. Naococane
1128
Burnt L.
Minipi L.
Little Mecatina
St. Lewis
Mary's Harbour
Red Bay
Belle I.
Str. of Belle Isle
Anse-au-Loup
Forteau
Brador Bay
Lourdes-de-Blanc-Sablon
St. Paul
St.-Augustin
St.-Augustin-Saguenay
Outer I.
Port Saunders
Harrington Harbour
I. du Petit-Mécatina
Daniel's Harbour
Etamamu
St. Lunaire-Griquet
St. Anthony
Hare B.
Flower's Cove
Groais I.
Roddickton
Conche
Bell I.
Englee
Great Harbour Deep
Horse Is.
C. St. John
White B.
La Scie
Long Range Mts.
Seal Cove
Baie Verte
Sop's Arm
Notre Dame B.
Twillingate
Fogo
Fogo I.
Carmanville
C. Freels
Wesleyville
Bonavista B.
C. Bonavista
Bonavista
Catalina
Trinity B.
Trinity
Springdale
South Brook
Botwood
Lewisporte
Glenwood
Gander
Gander L.
Windsor
Grand Falls
Bishop's Falls
Dark Cove
Glovertown
Howley
Deer Lake
Trout River
Bay of Islands
Corner Brook
814
Buchans
Red Indian L.
Victoria Res.
NEWFOUNDLAND
Port Blandford
Clarenville
381
Long Pt.
Port au Port B.
Stephenville
C. St. George
St. George's B.
St. David's
South Branch
Grey Res.
Salmon Res.
White Bear Res.
St. Alban's
Terrenceville
Belleoram
Conception B.
Bay de Verde
Torbay
St. John's
Mt. Pearl
Bay Bulls
Holyrood
Heart's Content
Carbonear
Harbour Grace
Spaniard's Bay
Avalon Peninsula
Argentia
Placentia
Placentia B.
St. Mary's B.
Ferryland
C. Race
Trepassey
C. Pine
C. St. Mary
St. Lawrence
Burin
Marystown
Fortune B.
Grand Bank
Harbour Breton
Burgeo
Ramea
Channel-Port aux Basques
C. Ray
St. Andrew's
Miquelon
Langlade
St. Pierre
SAINT-PIERRE ET MIQUELON (Fr.)
Cabot Strait
C. North
Ingonish
532
Chéticamp
Pleasant Bay
St. Paul I.
Sydney Mines
New Waterford
N. Sydney
Glace Bay
Sydney
Cape Breton Island
Louisbourg
Bras d'Or L.
Fourchu
Inverness
Port Hood
St. Peters
I. Madame
Chedabucto B.
Canso
Mulgrave
Antigonish
Sherbrooke
Pictou
New Glasgow
Stellarton
Truro
Upper Musquodoboit
Sheet Hr.
Musquodoboit Hr.
Dartmouth
Halifax
Sable I. (Nova Scotia)
Mahone Bay
Lunenburg
Bridgewater
Liverpool
Port Mouton
Lockeport
C. Sable
Clark's Harbour
Shelburne
Wedgeport
Yarmouth
Rossignol L.
Annapolis Royal
Digby
Weymouth
Middleton
Windsor
Kentville
Minas Basin
Stewiacke
NOVA SCOTIA
Springhill
Amherst
Parrsboro
Bay of Fundy
St. Martins
Saint John
Sussex
Moncton
Shediac
Sackville
PRINCE EDWARD ISLAND
Summerside
Kensington
Charlottetown
Souris
East Pt.
Georgetown
North Pt.
Tignish
Alberton
Borden
Northumberland Str.
Î. Brion
Îs. de la Madeleine (Quebec)
Cap-aux-Meules
Grande-Entrée
Havre-Aubert
GULF OF ST. LAWRENCE
572
Miscou I.
Lamèque
Shippegan
Tracadie
Miramichi B.
Chatham
Newcastle
Richibucto
Buctouche
Chipman
Havelock
Minto
Grand L.
Fredericton
Oromocto
Gagetown
Woodstock
Hartland
Stanley
NEW BRUNSWICK
Bathurst
Campbellton
Dalhousie
Chaleur Bay
Edmundston
St. Leonard
Grand Falls
Plaster Rock
Heath Steele
819
Kedgwick
Atholville
Perth
Blackville
St. Stephen
St. George
Fredericton Junc.
Calais
Eastport
Grand Manan I.
Blacks Hr.
Machias
Jonesport
Bar Harbor
Mt. Desert I.
Ellsworth
Bangor
Brewer
Old Town
Belfast
Camden
Rockland
Augusta
Waterville
Skowhegan
Dover-Foxcroft
Guilford
Bingham
Moosehead L.
Greenville
Millinocket
Houlton
Presque Isle
Caribou
Van Buren
Ft. Kent
Allagash
St. John
Ashland
Eagle L.
Island Falls
Chesuncook L.
1606
Mattawamkeag
Lincoln
Danforth
Mooselookmeguntic L.
Rumford
Berlin
Bethel
St. Johnsbury
1917
Mt. Washington
Conway
Sebago L.
Auburn
Lewiston
Bath
Brunswick
Portland
Saco
Biddeford
Sanford
Rochester
Concord
Dover
Portsmouth
Manchester
Nashua
Haverhill
Lawrence
Lowell
C. Ann
Gloucester
Lynn
Waltham
BOSTON
Brockton
Jackman
Coaticook
Sherbrooke
East Angus
Lac-Mégantic
Asbestos
Thetford Mines
Plessisville
St. Georges
Beauceville
Montmagny
Lauzon
Lévis
Armagh
QUEBEC
Montmorency
St. Pamphile
St. Pascal
Rivière-du-Loup
Cabano
Trois-Pistoles
Bic
Rimouski
Mont-Joli
Matane
Sayabec
Amqui
Causapscal
Matapédia
Mts. Chic-Chocs
Pén. de Gaspé
Mt. Jacques-Cartier
1310
PARC PROV. DE LA GASPÉSIE
Bonaventure
Chandler
Paspébiac
Gaspé
Douglastown
Percé
Grande-Rivière
C. de Gaspé
Rivière-au-Renard
Ste.-Anne-des-Monts
Cap-Chat
Mont-Louis
Grande-Vallée
Petit-Cap
Pte. Sud Ouest
Dét. d'Honguedo
Pte.-Sud
Heath Pt.
Î. d'Anticosti
Jupiter
Port-Menier
Pte. Ouest
Dét. de Jacques-Cartier
Baie-Comeau
Baie-Trinité
Pte. des Monts
Godbout
Hauterive
Betsiamites
Forestville
Grandes-Bergeronnes
Tadoussac
Saguenay
Chicoutimi
Arvida
Alma
Port Alfred
Bagotville
La Malbaie
St. Siméon
Baie-St.-Paul
PARC PROV. DES LAURENTIDES
1190
St. Lawrence
Rivière-Pentecôte
Port-Cartier
Sept-Îles
Clarke City
Moisie
Walker L.
Sheldrake
Mingan
Havre-St.-Pierre
Aguanish
Natashquan
Kegaska
Gethsémani
L. Musquaro
Olomane
Natashquan
Aguanus
Nabisipi
Romaine
St.-Jean
Magpie L.
West Magpie
Lac Allard
1048
L. Manitou
Nipissis
Moisie
Ste.-Marguerite
Manicouagan
Rés. Manicouagan
Gagnon
Petit Lac Manicouagan
Outardes
Betsiamites
Rés. Pipmuacan
L. Manouane
L. Péribonca
L. Plétipi
Péribonca
Manouane
St.-Cœur-de-Marie
Mouchalagane

West from Greenwich

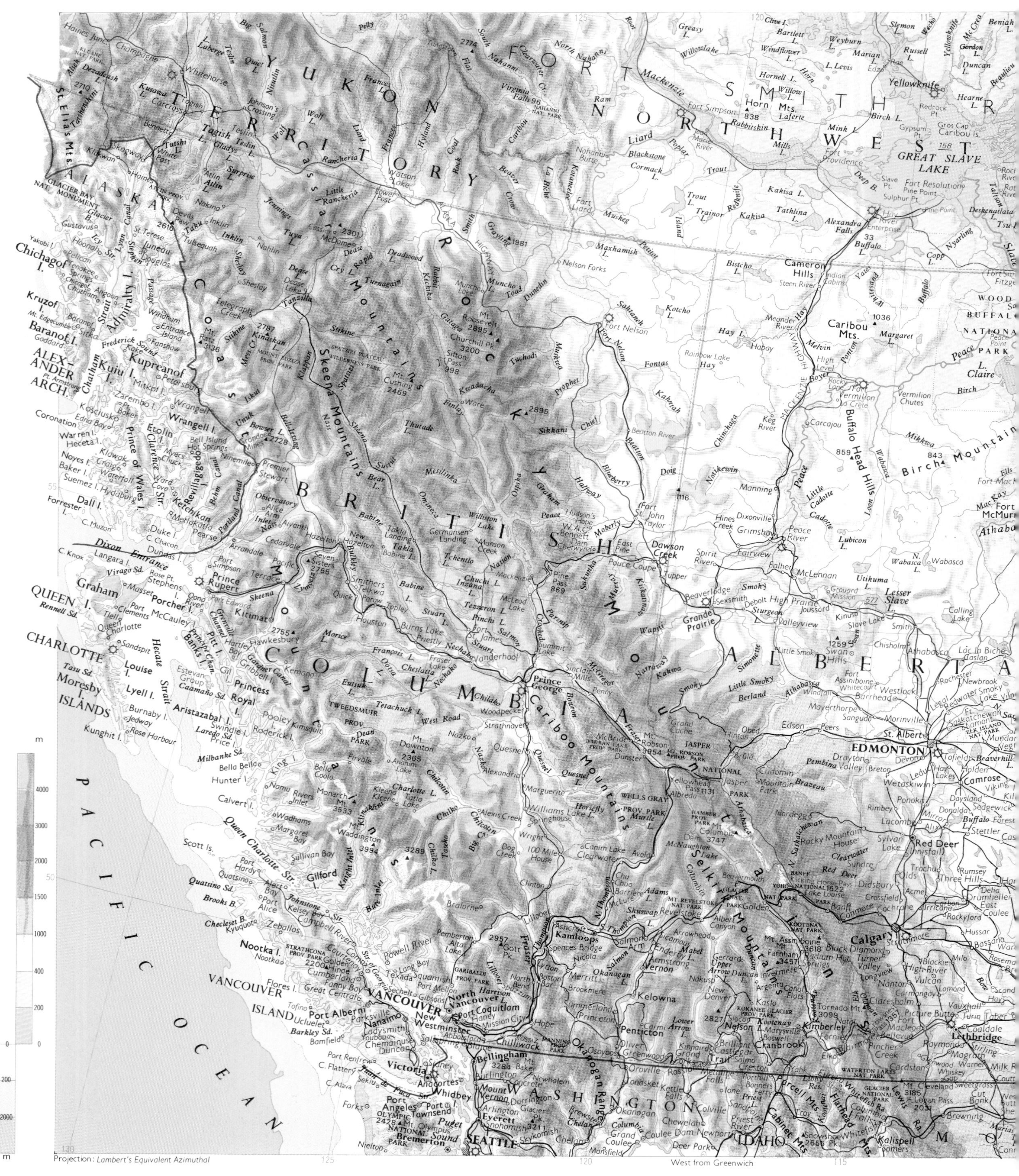
YUKON TERRITORY
NORTHWEST TERRITORIES
BRITISH COLUMBIA
ALBERTA
ALASKA
WASHINGTON
IDAHO
PACIFIC OCEAN
QUEEN CHARLOTTE ISLANDS
VANCOUVER ISLAND
Whitehorse
Yellowknife
Fort Simpson
Fort Nelson
Fort St. John
Dawson Creek
Grande Prairie
Peace River
Prince Rupert
Prince George
Kamloops
Kelowna
Penticton
Vernon
Nelson
Cranbrook
Lethbridge
Calgary
Red Deer
EDMONTON
St. Albert
VANCOUVER
North Vancouver
New Westminster
Victoria
Nanaimo
Port Alberni
Bellingham
Everett
SEATTLE
Bremerton
Port Angeles
Juneau
Skeena Mountains
Cassiar Mountains
Coast Mountains
Cariboo Mountains
Selkirk Mountains
Rocky Mountains
Caribou Mts.
Birch Mountains
Buffalo Head Hills
GREAT SLAVE LAKE
Lesser Slave L.
Williston Lake
Peace
Fraser
Mackenzie
Liard
Athabasca
Mt. Robson 3954
Mt. Waddington 3994
Mt. Assiniboine 3618
JASPER NATIONAL PARK
BANFF NAT. PARK
WOOD BUFFALO NATIONAL PARK
Dixon Entrance
Hecate Strait
Queen Charlotte Str.
Juan de Fuca Str.
Graham I.
Moresby I.
Chichagof I.
Baranof I.
Admiralty I.
Prince of Wales I.
Revillagigedo I.
Projection: Lambert's Equivalent Azimuthal
West from Greenwich
m
4000
3000
2000
1500
1000
400
200
0
200
2000
m

1:7 000 000

50 0 50 100 150 200 250 300 km

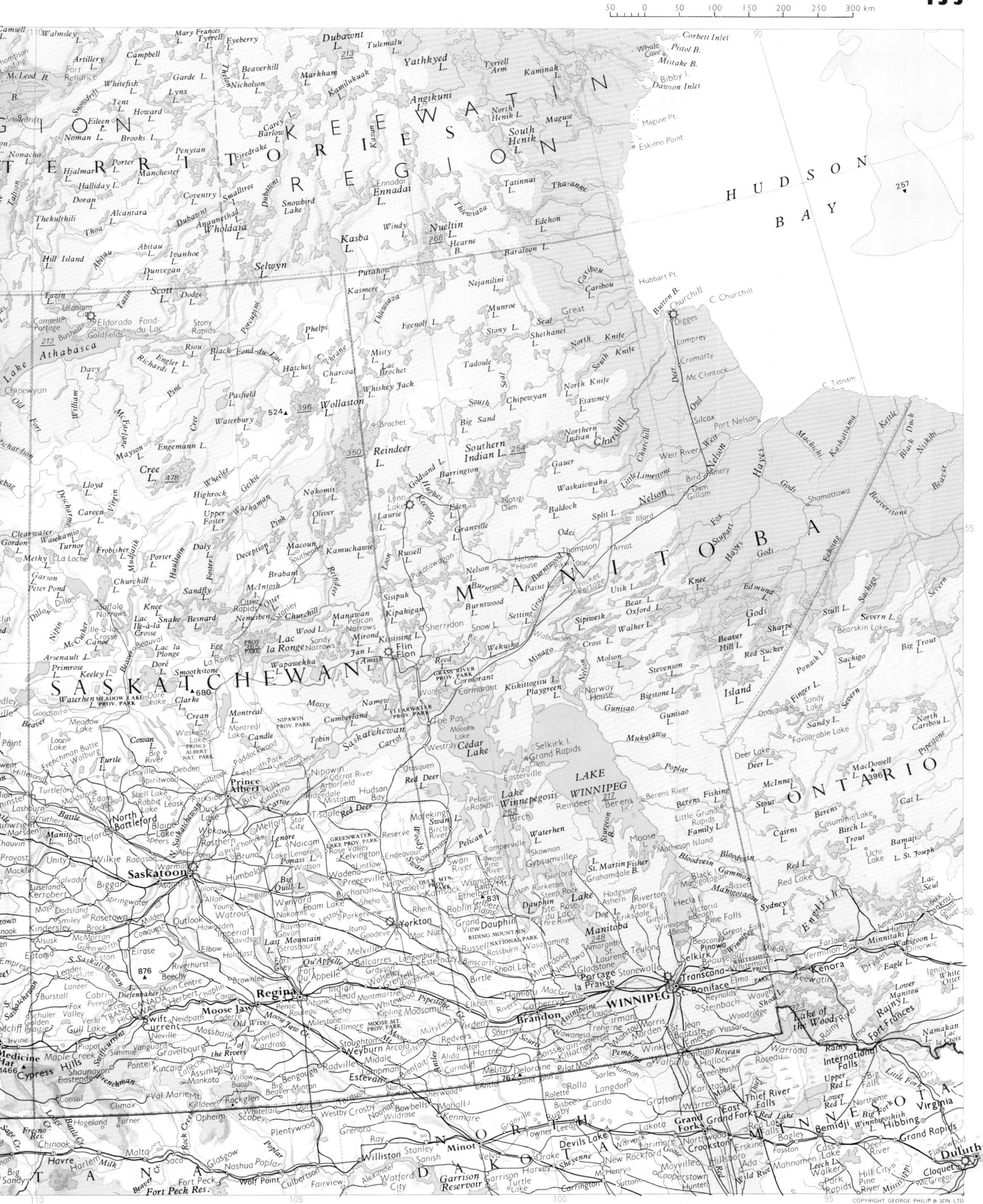
KEEWATIN REGION
TERRITORIES
HUDSON BAY
MANITOBA
SASKATCHEWAN
ONTARIO
NORTH DAKOTA
MINNESOTA
LAKE WINNIPEG
Lake Winnipegosis
Lake Manitoba
Lake Athabasca
Wollaston L.
Reindeer L.
Southern Indian L.
Cedar Lake
Lake of the Woods
Churchill
C. Churchill
Flin Flon
The Pas
Prince Albert
North Battleford
Saskatoon
Regina
Moose Jaw
Swift Current
Medicine Hat
Yorkton
Brandon
WINNIPEG
St. Boniface
Transcona
Portage la Prairie
Dauphin
Kenora
Fort Frances
International Falls
Grand Forks
Minot
Duluth
Thompson
Lynn Lake
Estevan
Weyburn
Nelson
Hayes
Dubawnt L.
Yathkyed L.
Nueltin L.
Kasba L.
Eskimo Point
Dawson Inlet
Corbett Inlet
Lake Athabasca
Cree L.
Lac la Ronge
Cypress Hills
Garrison Reservoir
Fort Peck Res.
Red Lake
Island L.
Gods L.
Big Trout L.
Lac Seul
Rainy River
Hubbart Pt.
C. Tatnam
Port Nelson
RIDING MOUNTAIN NATIONAL PARK
PRINCE ALBERT NAT. PARK
TRANS CANADA HIGHWAY
60
55
50
110
105
100
95
90

CANADA
ALBERTA
SASKATCHEWAN
BRITISH COLUMBIA
Vancouver
Victoria
Calgary
Saskatoon
Regina
Lethbridge
Medicine Hat
Moose Jaw
PACIFIC OCEAN
WASHINGTON
Seattle
Tacoma
Spokane
OREGON
Portland
Eugene
IDAHO
Boise
MONTANA
Great Falls
Billings
Helena
Butte
Missoula
WYOMING
Casper
Cheyenne
NORTH DAKOTA
SOUTH DAKOTA
NEBRASKA
CALIFORNIA
Sacramento
San Francisco
Oakland
San Jose
Fresno
Bakersfield
LOS ANGELES
Long Beach
San Bernardino
San Diego
NEVADA
Reno
Las Vegas
UTAH
Salt Lake City
Ogden
Great Salt Lake
COLORADO
Denver
Colorado Springs
Pueblo
ARIZONA
Phoenix
Tucson
NEW MEXICO
Albuquerque
Santa Fe
El Paso
TEXAS
Lubbock
Amarillo
Midland
Odessa
San Angelo
KANSAS
OKLAHOMA
ROCKY MOUNTAINS
Yellowstone National Park
Grand Canyon
MEXICO
Tijuana
Mexicali
Ciudad Juárez
Hermosillo
Chihuahua
Monterrey
Torreón
Nuevo Laredo
Laredo
SONORA
CHIHUAHUA
COAHUILA
DURANGO
BAJA CALIFORNIA NORTE
BAJA CALIFORNIA SUR
Golfo de California
Projection: Albers' Equal Area with two standard parallels
West from Greenwich
130
110
105
100
45
40
35
30
m
4000
3000
2000
1500
1000
400
200
0
200
2000

1:12 000 000

100 0 100 200 300 400 500 km

C A N A D A
O N T A R I O
Q U E B E C
Lake Winnipeg
Lake Nipigon
Thunder Bay
Lake Superior
Duluth
Sault Ste. Marie
Sudbury
L. Nipissing
Georgian Bay
Lake Huron
Lake Michigan
Lake Erie
Lake Ontario
TORONTO
Hamilton
Kingston
Ottawa
MONTREAL
Québec
L. Champlain
NEW BRUNSWICK
MAINE
VERMONT
NEW HAMPSHIRE
MASS.
CONN.
R.I.
NEW YORK
Boston
Providence
Hartford
New Haven
Albany
Syracuse
Rochester
Buffalo
Niagara Falls
PENNSYLVANIA
PHILADELPHIA
Pittsburgh
Harrisburg
Scranton
Allentown
NEW JERSEY
Newark
Trenton
Atlantic City
Wilmington
Baltimore
Washington D.C.
MARYLAND
DEL.
Delaware Bay
Chesapeake Bay
VIRGINIA
Richmond
Norfolk
Newport News
Portsmouth
WEST VIRGINIA
Charleston
Huntington
Wheeling
OHIO
Cleveland
Akron
Youngstown
Toledo
Columbus
Dayton
Cincinnati
DETROIT
MICHIGAN
Lansing
Grand Rapids
Flint
Saginaw
INDIANA
Indianapolis
Ft. Wayne
South Bend
Gary
Evansville
ILLINOIS
CHICAGO
Rockford
Peoria
Springfield
WISCONSIN
Milwaukee
Madison
Green Bay
MINNESOTA
Minneapolis
St. Paul
IOWA
Des Moines
Cedar Rapids
Davenport
Waterloo
MISSOURI
St. Louis
Kansas City
St. Joseph
Springfield
KENTUCKY
Louisville
Lexington
TENNESSEE
Nashville
Memphis
Knoxville
Chattanooga
NORTH CAROLINA
Charlotte
Greensboro
Winston Salem
Raleigh
Durham
Asheville
SOUTH CAROLINA
Columbia
Charleston
GEORGIA
Atlanta
Augusta
Macon
Savannah
Columbus
ALABAMA
Birmingham
Montgomery
Mobile
MISSISSIPPI
Jackson
LOUISIANA
Baton Rouge
New Orleans
Shreveport
ARKANSAS
Little Rock
OKLAHOMA
Tulsa
Dallas
Houston
Galveston
Beaumont
FLORIDA
Jacksonville
Tallahassee
Orlando
Tampa
St. Petersburg
Miami
West Palm Beach
Key West
Florida Keys
Everglades
Delta of the Mississippi
G U L F O F M E X I C O
A T L A N T I C O C E A N
BAHAMAS
Grand Bahama I.
Gt. Abaco
Andros I.
Eleuthera I.
Cat I.
Long I.
Exuma Sound
N.W. Providence Chan.
N.E. Providence Channel
Appalachian Mts.
Adirondack Mts.
Blue Ridge
Cumberland Plateau
Ozark Plateau
Boston Mts.
Ouachita Mts.
Mississippi
Ohio
Missouri
Tennessee
Arkansas
Red River
St. Lawrence
Long I.
Martha's Vineyard
C. Cod
C. Hatteras
C. Fear
C. Canaveral
C. Sable
Albemarle Sd.
Pamlico Sd.
45
40
35
30
25
95
90
85
80
75
70
65
COPYRIGHT GEORGE PHILIP & SON LTD

QUEBEC
ONTARIO
NEW YORK
PENNSYLVANIA
OHIO
INDIANA
MICHIGAN
WISCONSIN
KENTUCKY
WEST VIRGINIA
VIRGINIA
MARYLAND
DELAWARE
NEW JERSEY
VERMONT
NEW HAMPSHIRE
MASSACHUSETTS
LAKE SUPERIOR
LAKE HURON
LAKE MICHIGAN
LAKE ONTARIO
LAKE ERIE
Georgian Bay
MONTREAL
Ottawa
TORONTO
BUFFALO
DETROIT
CLEVELAND
PITTSBURGH
PHILADELPHIA
BALTIMORE
WASHINGTON D.C.
NEW YORK
BOSTON
CHICAGO
MILWAUKEE
INDIANAPOLIS
CINCINNATI
Columbus
Louisville
Richmond

1:6 000 000

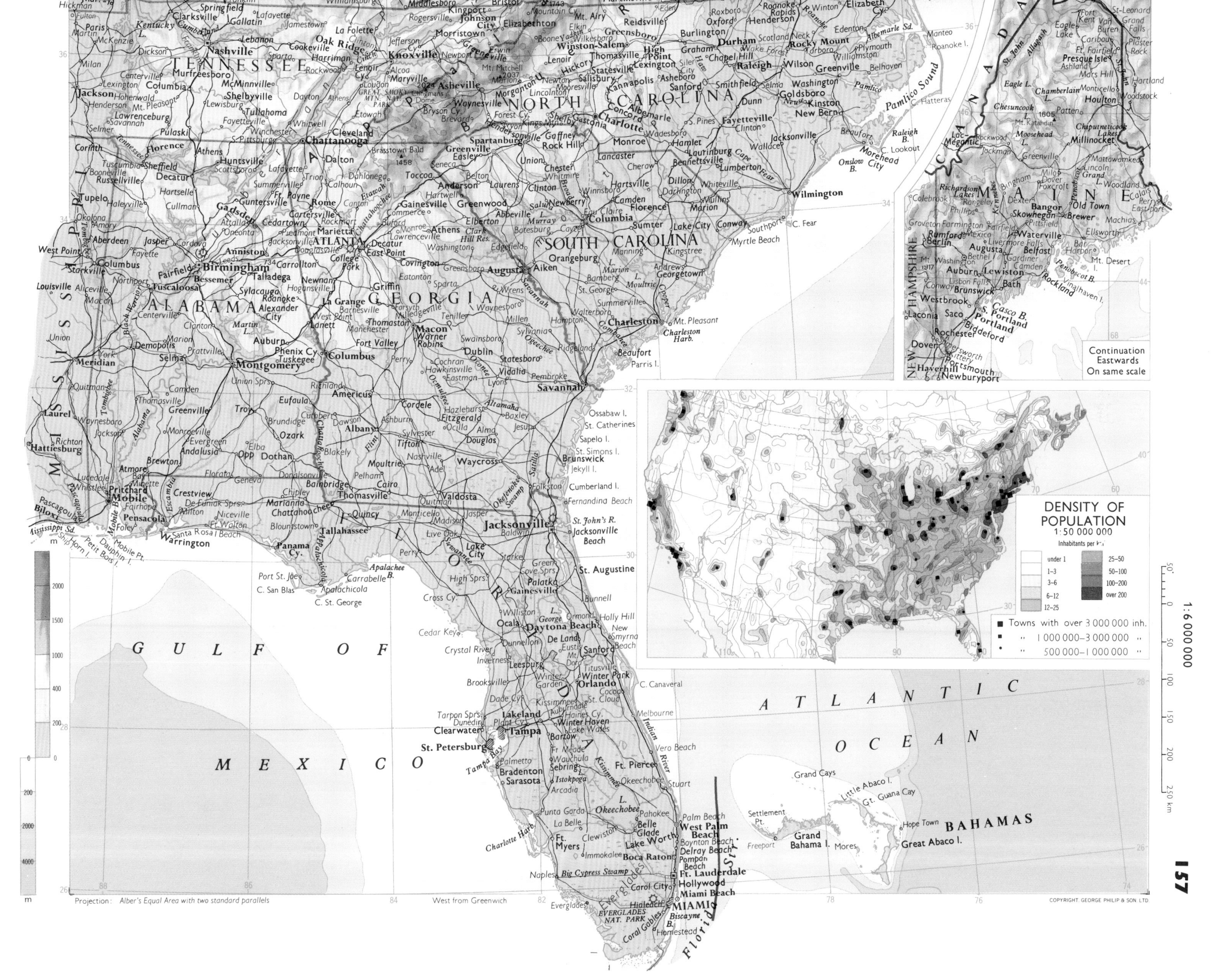
50 0 50 100 150 200 250 km
TENNESSEE
NORTH CAROLINA
SOUTH CAROLINA
GEORGIA
ALABAMA
MISSISSIPPI
FLORIDA
MAINE
NEW HAMPSHIRE
CANADA
GULF OF MEXICO
ATLANTIC OCEAN
BAHAMAS
Nashville
Knoxville
Chattanooga
Asheville
Charlotte
Raleigh
Durham
Wilmington
Columbia
Charleston
Savannah
Augusta
Atlanta
Macon
Columbus
Montgomery
Birmingham
Mobile
Pensacola
Tallahassee
Jacksonville
Orlando
Tampa
St. Petersburg
Miami
Bangor
Portland
Continuation Eastwards On same scale
DENSITY OF POPULATION
1:50 000 000
under 1
1–3
3–6
6–12
12–25
25–50
50–100
100–200
over 200
Towns with over 3 000 000 inh.
1 000 000–3 000 000
500 000–1 000 000
Projection: Alber's Equal Area with two standard parallels
West from Greenwich
COPYRIGHT GEORGE PHILIP & SON LTD.

CANADA
LAKE SUPERIOR
LAKE MICHIGAN
MICHIGAN
WISCONSIN
MINNESOTA
NORTH DAKOTA
SOUTH DAKOTA
IOWA
NEBRASKA
ILLINOIS
MISSOURI
KANSAS
COLORADO
WYOMING
MONTANA
MILWAUKEE
CHICAGO
MINNEAPOLIS
St. Paul
ST. LOUIS
DENVER
Omaha
Des Moines
Duluth
Bismarck
Pierre
Lincoln
Topeka
Cheyenne
Laramie Mountains

1:6 000 000

50 0 50 100 150 200 250 km

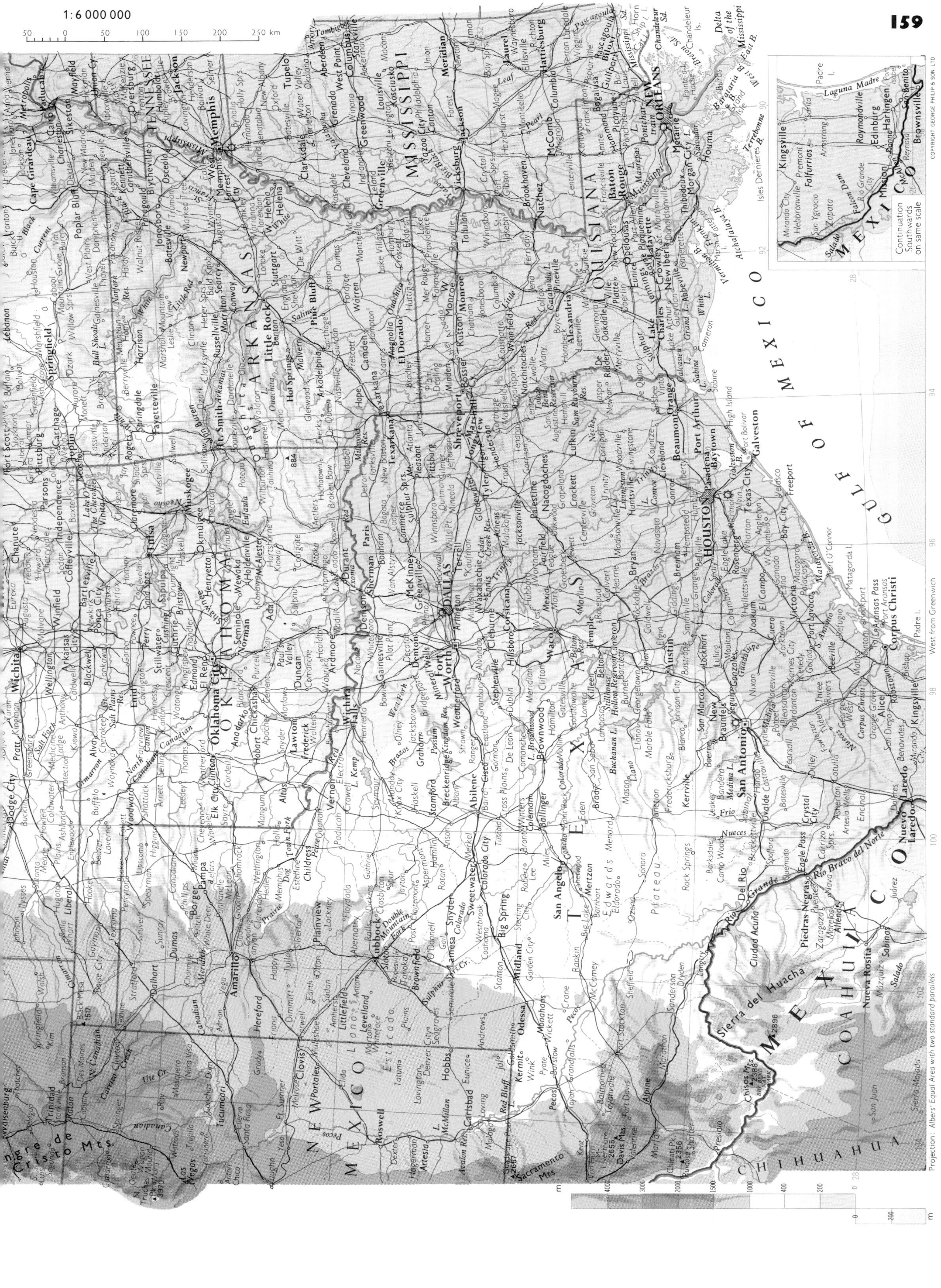

OKLAHOMA
ARKANSAS
TENNESSEE
MISSISSIPPI
LOUISIANA
TEXAS
NEW MEXICO
MEXICO
COAHUILA
CHIHUAHUA
GULF OF MEXICO
Sangre de Cristo Mts.
Llano Estacado
Edwards Plateau
Sierra del Huacha
Continuation Southwards on same scale
West from Greenwich

Projection: Albers' Equal Area with two standard parallels

1:6 000 000

50 0 50 100 150 200

BRITISH COLUMBIA
ALBERTA
SASKATCHEWAN
CANADA
WASHINGTON
OREGON
IDAHO
MONTANA
WYOMING
NEVADA
Bighorn Mountains
Lewis Range
Bitterroot Range
Lemhi Range
Salmon River Mountains
Clearwater Mountains
Cabinet Mountains
Blue Mountains
Wallowa Mts.
Olympic Mts.
Wind River Range
Uinta Mountains
Medicine Bow Range
Shoshone Mountains
Independence Mts.
Diamond Mts.
Ruby Mts.
Great Salt Lake
Salt Lake City
SEATTLE
PORTLAND
VANCOUVER
Victoria
Tacoma
Spokane
Boise
Helena
Missoula
Billings
Great Falls
Butte
Idaho Falls
Pocatello
Ogden
Provo
Reno
Sacramento
Eugene
Salem
Yakima
Casper
Rock Springs
Juan de Fuca Strait

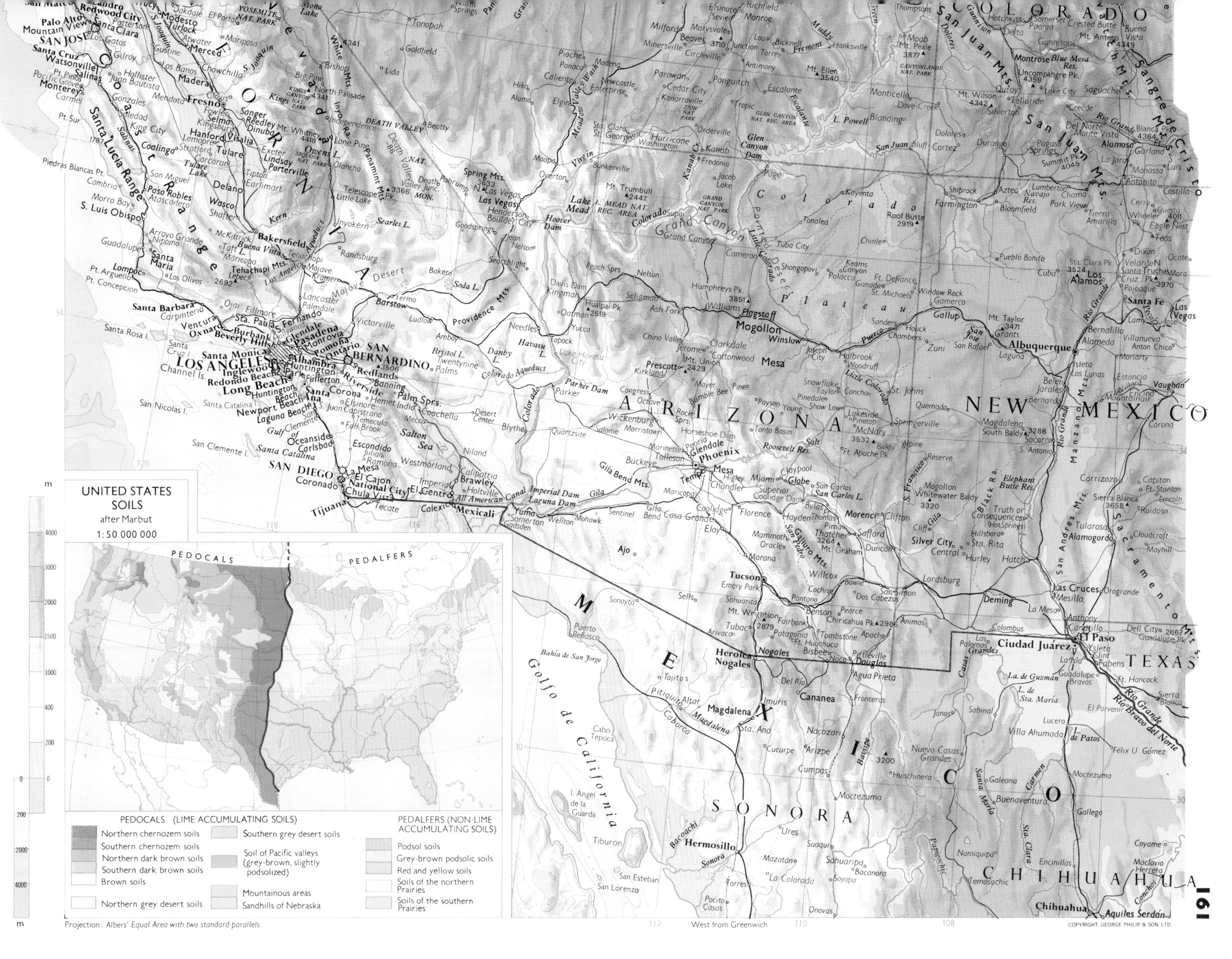
UNITED STATES
SOILS
after Marbut
1:50 000 000
PEDOCALS
PEDALFERS
PEDOCALS (LIME ACCUMULATING SOILS)
Northern chernozem soils
Southern chernozem soils
Northern dark brown soils
Southern dark brown soils
Brown soils
Northern grey desert soils
Southern grey desert soils
Soil of Pacific valleys (grey-brown, slightly podsolized)
Mountainous areas
Sandhills of Nebraska
PEDALFERS (NON-LIME ACCUMULATING SOILS)
Podsol soils
Grey-brown podsolic soils
Red and yellow soils
Soils of the northern Prairies
Soils of the southern Prairies
CALIFORNIA
NEVADA
ARIZONA
NEW MEXICO
COLORADO
TEXAS
MEXICO
SONORA
CHIHUAHUA
Golfo de California
Colorado Plateau
LOS ANGELES
SAN DIEGO
SAN BERNARDINO
Phoenix
Tucson
Albuquerque
Santa Fe
El Paso
Ciudad Juárez
Hermosillo
Chihuahua
Las Vegas
Fresno
Bakersfield
Projection: Albers' Equal Area with two standard parallels
West from Greenwich
COPYRIGHT. GEORGE PHILIP & SON. LTD.

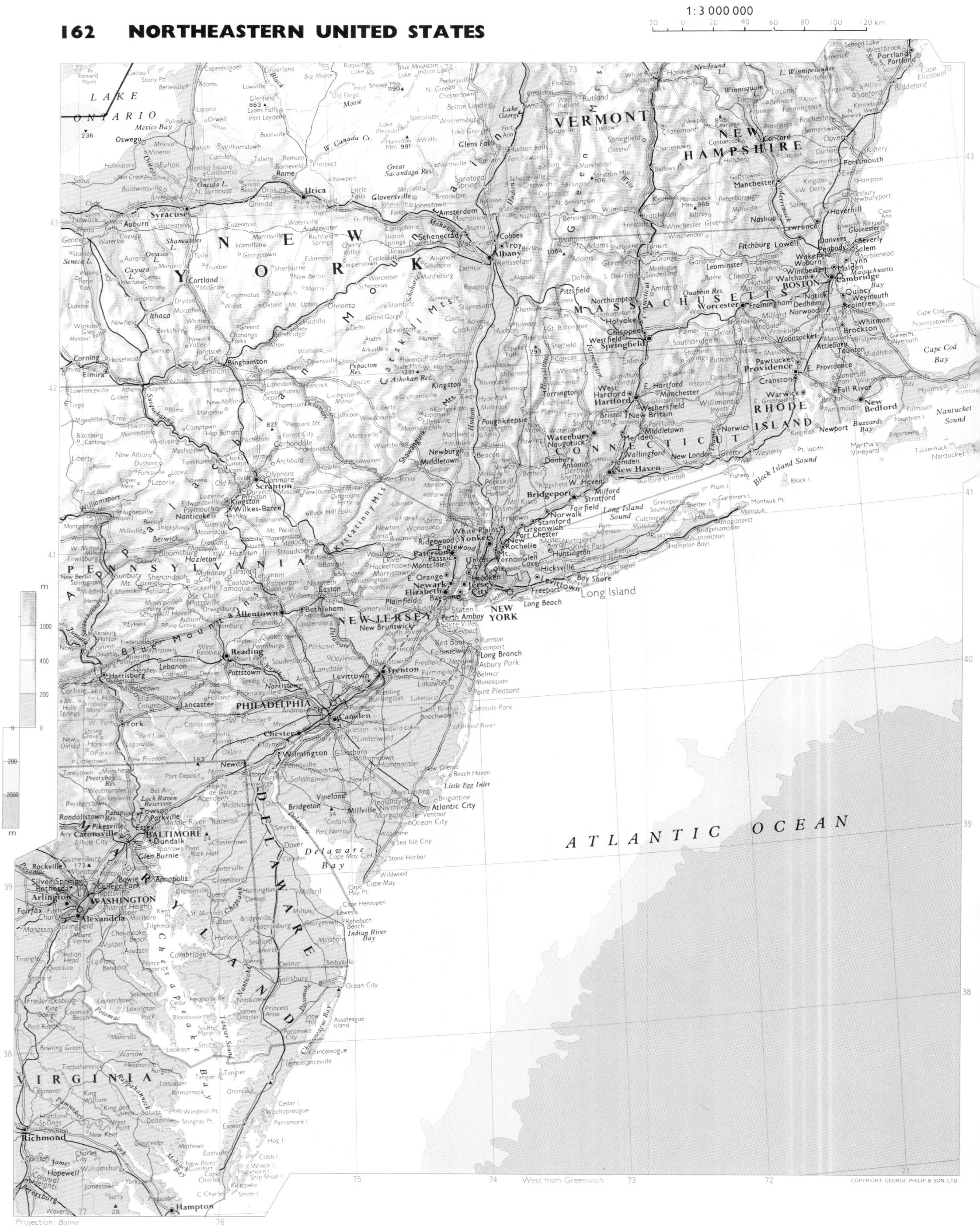

1:3 000 000

20 0 20 40 60 80 100 120 km

ATLANTIC OCEAN

Projection: Bonne

West from Greenwich

1:3 000 000

20 0 20 40 60 80 100 120 140 km

m

4000

3000

2000

1500

1000

400

200

0

200

2000

m

Projection: Bonne

West from Greenwich

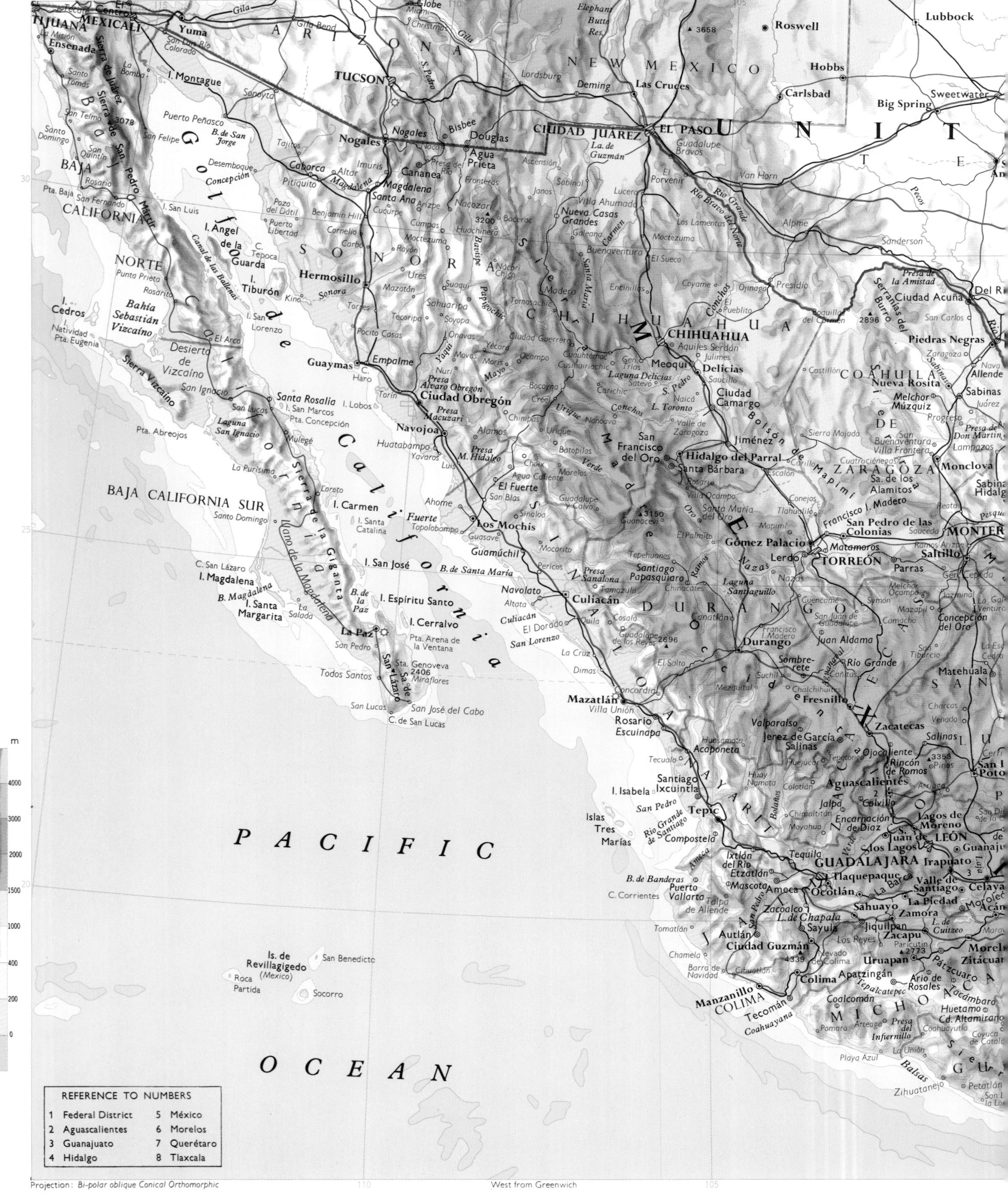
PACIFIC OCEAN
Golfo de California
BAJA CALIFORNIA NORTE
BAJA CALIFORNIA SUR
SONORA
CHIHUAHUA
COAHUILA
DURANGO
ZACATECAS
NAYARIT
JALISCO
COLIMA
MICHOACÁN
ARIZONA
NEW MEXICO
TIJUANA
MEXICALI
Ensenada
TUCSON
Nogales
CIUDAD JUÁREZ
EL PASO
Hermosillo
Guaymas
Ciudad Obregón
Navojoa
Los Mochis
CHIHUAHUA
Delicias
Hidalgo del Parral
TORREÓN
Gómez Palacio
Saltillo
Culiacán
Mazatlán
Durango
Zacatecas
Aguascalientes
Tepic
GUADALAJARA
Colima
Manzanillo
La Paz
Santa Rosalía
Is. de Revillagigedo (Mexico)
REFERENCE TO NUMBERS
1 Federal District
2 Aguascalientes
3 Guanajuato
4 Hidalgo
5 México
6 Morelos
7 Querétaro
8 Tlaxcala
Projection: Bi-polar oblique Conical Orthomorphic
West from Greenwich

GULF OF MEXICO
Golfo de Campeche
UNITED STATES
TEXAS
LOUISIANA
MISSISSIPPI
ALABAMA
GEORGIA
FLORIDA
ARKANSAS
Wichita Falls
Denison
Sherman
Paris
Texarkana
Camden
El Dorado
Greenville
Tuscaloosa
Opelika
Columbus
McRae
Denton
DALLAS
FORT WORTH
Ranger
Cleburne
Marshall
Longview
Tyler
Monroe
Tallulah
Vicksburg
Jackson
Meridian
Selma
Montgomery
Phenix City
Americus
Cordele
Albany
Tifton
Waycross
Troy
Dothan
Valdosta
Tallahassee
Corsicana
Palestine
Hillsboro
Waco
Brownwood
Toledo Bend Res.
Nacogdoches
Shreveport
Natchez
Laurel
Hattiesburg
Flomaton
Jim Woodruff Res.
Lufkin
Sam Rayburn Res.
Alexandria
McComb
Bogalusa
MOBILE
Pensacola
Panama City
Apalachee Bay
Lake City
Temple
Huntsville
Bryan
Baton Rouge
Hammond
Biloxi
Gulfport
Mobile Bay
C. San Blas
Suwannee
Austin
Navasota
Lake Charles
Lafayette
Beaumont
NEW ORLEANS
Breton Sound
HOUSTON
Port Arthur
Atchafalaya Bay
Terrebonne B.
Mississippi Delta
Rosenberg
Galveston
Clearwater
SAN ANTONIO
Victoria
Dilley
Nueces
Alice
Corpus Christi
Laredo
Kingsville
Nuevo Laredo
Zapata
Camargo
Mc Allen
Laguna Madre
Harlingen
Brownsville
Reynosa
Matamoros
Valle Hermoso
Montemorelos
Santa Teresa
Méndez
San Fernando
Linares
Villagrán
Santander-Jiménez
La Pesca
Soto la Marina
Ciudad Victoria
Sierra de Tamaulipas
TAMAULIPAS
Aldama
Pta. Jerez
Ciudad Mante
Ciudad Madero
Tampico
Altamira
Pánuco
Ciudad Valles
Laguna de Tamiahua
Tantoyuca
C. Rojo
Tamazunchale
Tuxpan
Poza Rica
Papantla
Nautla
Huauchinango
Pachuca
Tulancingo
Teziutlán
Jalapa
Zempoala
MÉXICO
Tlaxcala
Apizaco
PUEBLA
Coatepec
Veracruz
Amecameca
Orizaba
Córdoba
Alvarado
Tlacotalpan
San Andrés Tuxtla
Coatzacoalcos
Cuernavaca
Tehuacán
Cosamaloapan
Iguala
Acatlán
Acayucan
Minatitlán
Cárdenas
Villahermosa
TABASCO
Frontera
Paraíso
Comalcalco
Chilapa
Chilpancingo
Tlaxiaco
Oaxaca
OAXACA
Istmo de Tehuantepec
Matías Romero
Juchitán
Ixtepec
Tehuantepec
Salina Cruz
Golfo de Tehuantepec
Acapulco
Ometepec
Miahuatlán
Pochutla
Puerto Escondido
Puerto Ángel
Pta. Maldonado
Arriaga
Tonalá
Tuxtla Gutiérrez
San Cristóbal de las Casas
Comitán
CHIAPAS
Huixtla
Tapachula
Coatepeque
C. Tecún Umán
Retalhuleu
Isla Desterrada
Isla Pérez
Canal de Yucatán
C. Catoche
Rio Lagartos
El Cuyo
Pta. Yalkubul
Progreso
Dzilam de Bravo
Motul
Temax
Tizimín
Izamal
Espita
Mérida
Dzibilchaltún
YUCATÁN
Valladolid
Chichén Itzá
Maxcanú
Sotuta
Mayapán
Ticul
Calkiní
Uxmal
Tekax
Peto
Tenabo
Campeche
Hopelchén
Bolonchenticul
Edzná
Felipe Carrillo Puerto
QUINTANA ROO
Champotón
Chenkán
José Carpizo
Ciudad del Carmen
Laguna de Términos
Palizada
CAMPECHE
Concepción
Matamoros
Bacalar
Chetumal
B. de Chetumal
Corozal
Orange Walk
Pto. Juárez
El Díaz
Puerto Morelos
Isla Cozumel
Cozumel
Vigía Chico
B. de la Ascensión
B. del Espíritu Santo
Banco Chinchorro
Ambergris Cay
Turneffe Is.
Belize City
Belmopan
BELIZE
Dangriga
Tikal
Uaxactún
Flores
La Libertad
L. Petén Itzá
Benque Viejo
Golfo de Honduras
Monkey River
Punta Gorda
San Luis
Livingston
Puerto Barrios
Puerto Cortés
Tela
La Ceiba
Islas de la Bahía
Roatán
Puerto Castilla
Trujillo
GUATEMALA
L. de Izabal
Cobán
Huehuetenango
Totonicapán
Sololá
Quezaltenango
Antigua
Mazatenango
San Marcos
Zacapa
Chiquimula
Jalapa
Amatitlán
San Pedro Sula
El Progreso
HONDURAS
Santa Rosa de Copán
Comayagua
Yoro
Juticalpa
Tegucigalpa
Patuca
CUBA
Guane
La Fé
La Esperanza
C. San Antonio
C. Corrientes
COPYRIGHT, GEORGE PHILIP & SON, LTD

GULF OF MEXICO
Isla Desterrada
Isla Pérez
Canal de Yucatán
Straits of Florida
Florida Keys
Florida Bay
Dry Tortugas
Key West
MIAMI
Hialeah
Fort Lauderdale
Boca Raton
West Palm Beach
Fort Myers
Naples
C. Romano
Everglades
The Everglades
C. Sable
Florida City
L. Okeechobee
Little Abaco I.
Grand Bahama I.
Great Abaco I.
Northwest Providence Channel
Northeast Providence Channel
Bimini Is.
Berry Is.
Eleuthera I.
Nassau
New Providence I.
Andros Island
Great Bahama Bank
Great Guana Cay
Great Exuma
Santaren Channel
Cay Sal Bank
Canal Nicolás
Canal Viejo de Bahama
(Havana) LA HABANA
MARIANAO
Guanabacoa
Matanzas
San Antonio de los Baños
Guanajay
Bahía Honda
La Esperanza
Pinar del Río
San Luis
Los Palacios
Güines
Batabanó
Jagüey Grande
Cárdenas
Colón
Jovellanos
Sagua la Grande
Santa Clara
Caibarién
Placetas
Cienfuegos
Trinidad
Sancti-Spíritus
Morón
Ciego de Avila
Florida
Camagüey
Nuevitas
Victoria de las Tunas
Manzanillo
Bayamo
Sierra Maestra
Golfo de Guacanayabo
CUBA
Isla de la Juventud
Nueva Gerona
Archipiélago de los Canarreos
C. San Antonio
C. Corrientes
GREATER ANTILLES
Cayman Islands (Br.)
Cayman Brac
Little Cayman
Georgetown
Grand Cayman
Montego Bay
Falmouth
St. Ann's Bay
Lucea
Savanna la Mar
Black River
Mandeville
May Pen
Spanish Town
Pedro Cays (Jamaica)
Swan Islands (U.S.A. & Honduras)
Bajo Nuevo (Colombia)
CARIBBEAN
Progreso
Mérida
Motul
Izamal
Tizimín
Valladolid
Ticul
Peto
Campeche
Champotón
Ciudad del Carmen
Laguna de Términos
YUCATÁN
QUINTANA ROO
CAMPECHE
Isla Cozumel
C. Catoche
Banco Chinchorro
Chetumal
Ambergris Cay
Turneffe Is.
Belize City
Belmopan
BELIZE
Swan Islands
Golfo de Honduras
Islas de la Bahía
Roatán
Puerto Barrios
Puerto Cortés
Tela
La Ceiba
San Pedro Sula
El Progreso
Trujillo
C. Camarón
Laguna Caratasca
C. Gracias á Dios
Mosquitia
Cayos Miskitos (Nicaragua)
HONDURAS
Tegucigalpa
Comayagua
Choluteca
GUATEMALA
Cobán
Huehuetenango
Quetzaltenango
Antigua
Escuintla
Mazatenango
Jalapa
Chiquimula
Zacapa
L. de Izabal
Livingston
Flores
L. Petén Itzá
SAN SALVADOR
EL SALVADOR
Santa Ana
Usulután
San Miguel
Golfo de Fonseca
NICARAGUA
Chinandega
León
MANAGUA
Masaya
Granada
Diriamba
Boaco
Juigalpa
Matagalpa
Estelí
Puerto Cabezas
Bluefields
Lago de Nicaragua
San Juan del Norte
Islas del Maíz (Nicaragua, U.S.A.)
I. de Providencia (Colombia)
I. de San Andrés (Colombia)
Cayos Roncador (U.S.A. & Colombia)
Golfo de Papagayo
COSTA RICA
San José
Cartago
Alajuela
Puntarenas
Limón
Pen. de Nicoya
Pen. de Osa
Golfo Dulce
Puerto Armuelles
David
Golfo de Chiriquí
Laguna de Chiriquí
Colón
PANAMÁ
Golfo de Panamá
Arch. de las Perlas
Pen. de Azuero
Archipiélago de las Mulatas
Golfo del Darién
Serranía del Darién
Is. de San Bernardo
CARTAGENA

Projection: Bi-polar oblique Conical Orthomorphic

1:8 000 000

50 0 50 100 150 200 250 300 km

ATLANTIC OCEAN
Tropic of Cancer
Turks Islands (Br.)
Caicos Islands (Br.)
Turks I. Passage
Caicos Passage
Crooked I. Passage
San Salvador (Watling I., Guanahani)
Cat I.
Conception I.
Rum Cay
Long I.
Clarence Town
Atwood or Samana Cay
Crooked I.
Plana Cays
Mayaguana I.
Albert Town
Snug Corner
Acklins I.
Mira por vos Cay
Hogsty Reef
Little Inagua I.
Great Inagua I.
Lake Rose
Matthew Town
Baracoa
Guantánamo
Paso de los Vientos (Windward Passage)
Pta. de Maisi
I. de la Tortue
Port-de-Paix
Cap-Haïtien
Fort-Liberté
Monte Cristi
La Isabela
Puerto Plata
C. Frances Viejo
San Francisco de Macoris
Santiago de los Cabelleros
Vega
Cord. Central
3175
Golfe de la Gonâve
Gonaïves
Hinche
St.-Marc
HAITI
DOMINICAN REP.
Jérémie
I. de la Gonâve
PORT-AU-PRINCE
San Juan
Massif de la Hotte
2280
Enriquillo
Les Cayes
Jacmel
Barahona
Aquin
Pointe-à-Gravois
Pedernales
Azua de Compostela
Bani
San Cristóbal
SANTO DOMINGO
San Pedro de Macoris
Hato Mayor
Higüey
La Romana
C. Engano
I. Saona
Sabana de La Mar
Samana
HISPANIOLA
I. Beata
C. Beata
ANTILLES
Canal de la Mona
Isla Mona (U.S.A.)
Mayagüez
Aguadilla
Arecibo
Bayamón
SAN JUAN
Fajardo
Ponce
Caguas
Guayama
1338
PUERTO RICO (U.S.A.)
Charlotte Amalie
Virgin Is. (U.S.A.)
Virgin Is. (Br.)
Anegada
Anegada Passage
Virgin Gorda
Tortola
Road Town
Frederiksted
Christiansted
St. Croix
Sombrero (Anguilla)
Anguilla (Br.)
St.-Martin (Guad.)
St.-Barthélemy (Fr.)
St. Maarten (Neth.)
Saba (Neth.)
St. Eustatius (Neth.)
Basseterre
ST. KITTS-NEVIS
Nevis
Barbuda
ANTIGUA & BARBUDA
St. Johns
Antigua
Redonda
Montserrat (Br.)
Guadeloupe Passage
LEEWARD ISLANDS
LESSER ANTILLES
Moule
Désirade
Ste-Rose
GUADELOUPE (Fr.)
Pointe-a-Pitre
Basse-Terre
Marie-Galante (Fr.)
Grand-Bourg
I. des Saintes (Guad.)
Dominica Passage
Portsmouth
DOMINICA
Roseau
I. de Aves (Bird I.) (Venezuela)
Martinique Passage
Mt. Pelée 1397
Ste. Marie
François
Rivière-Pilot
Fort-de-France
MARTINIQUE
St. Lucia Channel (Fr.)
Castries
ST. LUCIA
Soufrière
St. Vincent Passage
Soufrière 1234
ST. VINCENT
Kingstown
Bridgetown
BARBADOS
Speightstown
The Grenadines
Hillsborough
WINDWARD ISLANDS
St. George's
GRENADA
CARIBBEAN SEA
Neth. Antilles
Aruba (Neth.)
Curaçao (Neth.)
Bonaire (Neth.)
Willemstad
Pta. Gallinas
C. San Román
Pen. de la Guajira
Pen. de Paraguaná
Pta. Espada
Punto Fijo
Punta Cardón
Puerto Cumarebo
Golfo de Venezuela
Riohacha
C. San Juan de Guía
Uribia
GUAJIRA
Santa Marta
Ciénaga
Barranquilla
Soledad
Sabanalarga
Fundación
Valledupar
Calamar
Plato
Agustín Codazzi
MAGDALENA
CÉSAR
Zambrano
Corozal
Magangué
Mompós
El Banco
Sahagún
Caucasia
Ayapel
BOLÍVAR
Simití
San Rafael
MARACAIBO
La Concepción
Altagracia
Mene de Mauroa
Santa Rita
Cabimas
Villa del Rosario
Cuidad Ojeda
Mene Grande
Machiques
Lago de Maracaibo
ZULIA
La Ceiba
Catatumbo
Encontrados
San Carlos del Zulia
NORTE DE SANTANDER
Cúcuta
Ocaña
TÁCHIRA
Coro
FALCÓN
Tocuyo
Puerto Cabello
Maracay
Maiquetía
La Guaira
CARACAS
DISTRITO FEDERAL
San Felipe
YARACUY
Carora
LARA
BARQUISIMETO
Yaritagua
Valencia
Los Teques
Villa de Cura
S. Juan de los Morros
Altagracia de Orituco
El Tocuyo
San Carlos
COJEDES
TRUJILLO
Trujillo
Valera
Acarigua
PORTUGUESA
Guanare
Barinas
MÉRIDA
Mérida
Cord. de Mérida
BARINAS
Ciudad Bolivia
Libertad
Santa Bárbara
Achaguas
San Fernando de Apure
Apure
El Baúl
Calabozo
GUÁRICO
El Sombrero
Valle de la Pascua
Santa María de Ipire
Orinoco
VENEZUELA
I. La Tortuga
C. Codera
Higuerote
Río Chico
Puerto La Cruz
Barcelona
Cumaná
Carúpano
Río Caribe
I. Margarita
La Asunción
Porlamar
NUEVA ESPARTA
SUCRE
Cariaco
Caripito
Maturín
MONAGAS
Caicara
Anaco
Cantaura
El Tigre
ANZOÁTEGUI
Pariaguán
Soledad
Ciudad Bolívar
Ciudad Guayana
Tucupita
DELTA AMACURO
Sierra Imataca
Upata
El Callao
Tumeremo
Guasipati
Emb de Guri
I. Blanquilla (Ven.)
I. Los Hermanos (Ven.)
I. Orchila (Ven.)
Is. de Aves (Ven.)
Is. Los Roques (Ven.)
Is. Los Testigos (Ven.)
Tobago
Scarborough
Pen. de Paria
Dragon's Mouth
Port of Spain
Arima
Galera Pt.
Trinidad
Güiria
Golfo de Paria
San Fernando
Río Claro
TRINIDAD & TOBAGO
Serpent's Mouth
West from Greenwich
COPYRIGHT. GEORGE PHILIP & SON. LTD.

1:30 000 000

ATLANTIC OCEAN
PACIFIC OCEAN
SOUTH ATLANTIC OCEAN
Caracas
Trinidad
Bogotá
Medellín
Cali
Quito
Guayaquil
Lima
La Paz
Manaus
Belém
Fortaleza
Recife
Salvador
Brasília
Belo Horizonte
Rio de Janeiro
São Paulo
Asunción
Pôrto Alegre
Montevideo
Buenos Aires
La Plata
Rosario
Córdoba
Tucumán
Santiago
Valparaíso
Georgetown
Barranquilla
Maracaibo
Equator
Tropic of Capricorn
Guiana Highlands
Brazilian Highlands
Llanos
Selvas
Andes
Gran Chaco
Pampas
Patagonia
Plateau of Mato Grosso
Plateau of Borborema
Bolivian Plateau
Atacama Desert
Amazon
Orinoco
Paraná
Paraguay
Uruguay
Madeira
Negro
São Francisco
Tocantins
Araguaia
Xingu
Tapajós
Purus
Juruá
Falkland Islands
West Falkland
East Falkland
Tierra del Fuego
Magellan's Strait
C. Horn
Chiloé I.
Chonos Archipelago
Argentine Basin
Peru Chile Trench
Chile Rise
Aconcagua 6960
Ojos del Salado 6863
Huascarán 6768
Chimborazo 6267
Cotopaxi 5897
Ancohuma & Illampu 6550
Roraima 2810
Pico da Bandeira 2890
Projection: Lambert's Equivalent Azimuthal
West from Greenwich

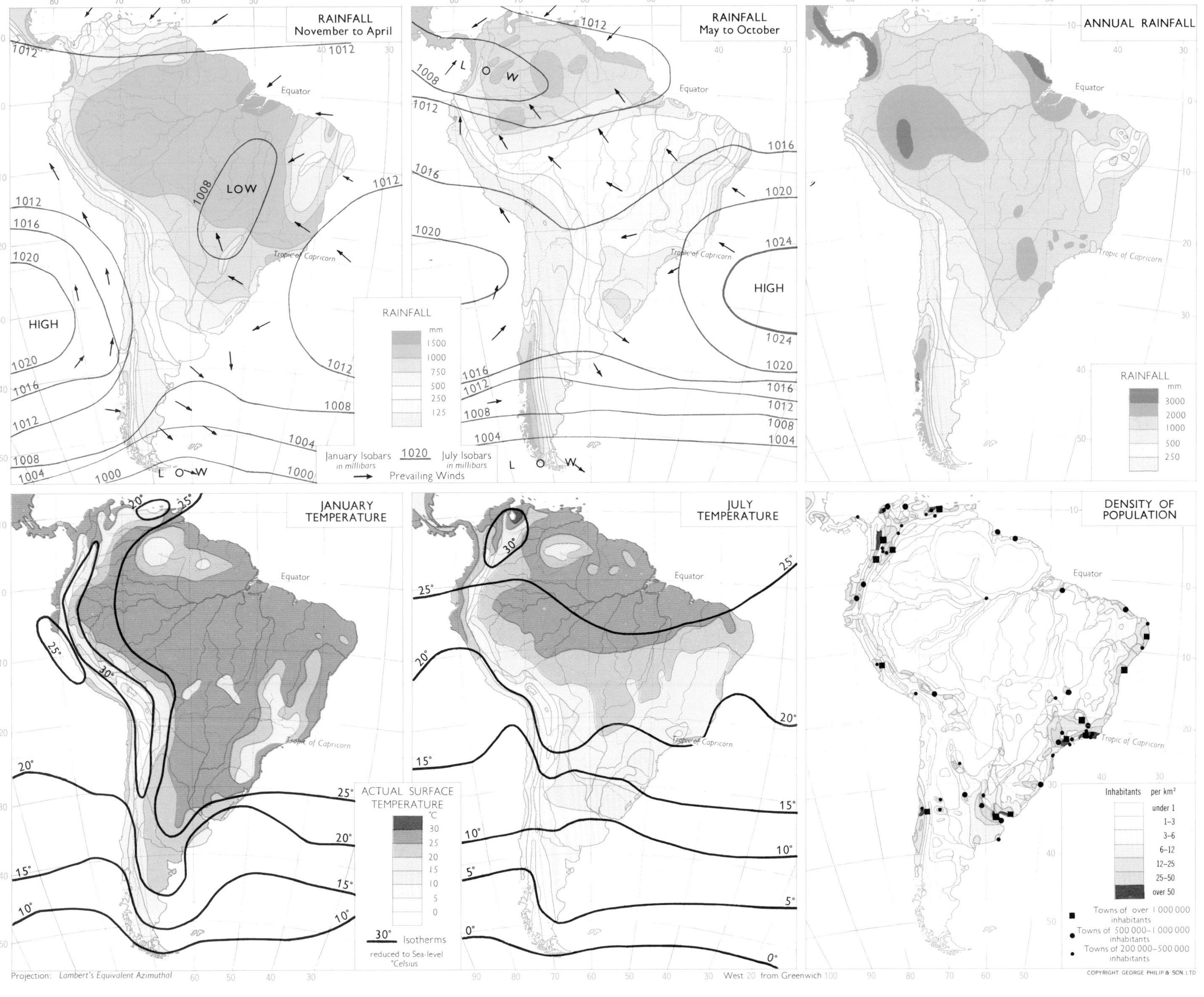
RAINFALL November to April
RAINFALL May to October
ANNUAL RAINFALL
LOW
HIGH
Equator
Tropic of Capricorn
RAINFALL mm
1500
1000
750
500
250
125
January Isobars in millibars
1020
July Isobars in millibars
Prevailing Winds
RAINFALL mm
3000
2000
1000
500
250
JANUARY TEMPERATURE
JULY TEMPERATURE
DENSITY OF POPULATION
ACTUAL SURFACE TEMPERATURE °C
30
25
20
15
10
5
0
30° Isotherms reduced to Sea-level °Celsius
Inhabitants per km²
under 1
1–3
3–6
6–12
12–25
25–50
over 50
Towns of over 1 000 000 inhabitants
Towns of 500 000–1 000 000 inhabitants
Towns of 200 000–500 000 inhabitants
Projection: Lambert's Equivalent Azimuthal
West 20 from Greenwich
COPYRIGHT GEORGE PHILIP & SON LTD

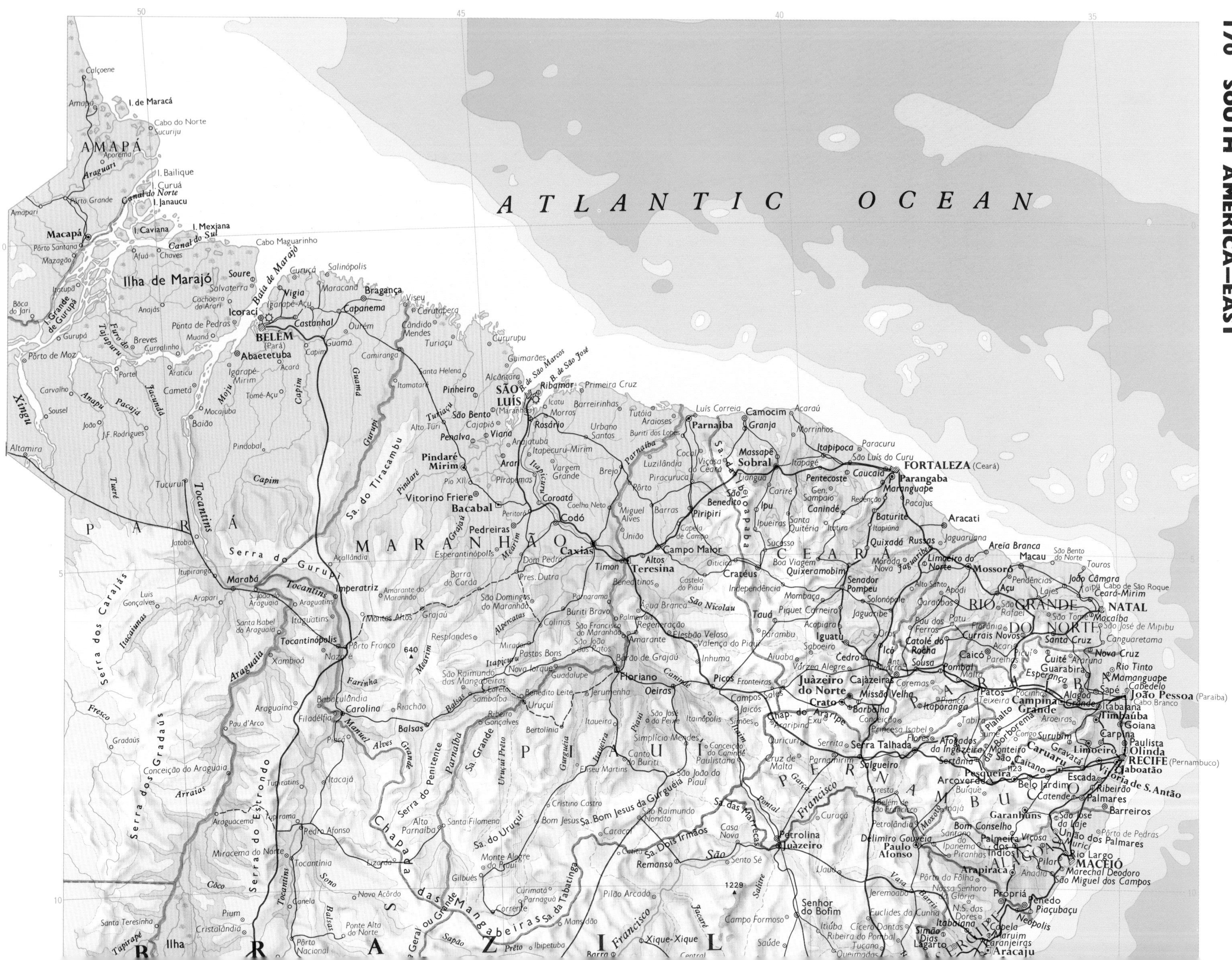
ATLANTIC OCEAN
AMAPÁ
Macapá
Ilha de Marajó
BELÉM (Pará)
PARÁ
MARANHÃO
SÃO LUÍS
PIAUÍ
Teresina
CEARÁ
FORTALEZA (Ceará)
RIO GRANDE DO NORTE
NATAL
PARAÍBA
João Pessoa (Paraíba)
PERNAMBUCO
RECIFE (Pernambuco)
ALAGOAS
MACEIÓ
Aracaju
BRAZIL
Tocantins
Serra do Gurupi
Chapada das Mangabeiras
Serra dos Gradaús
Serra dos Carajás

ATLANTIC OCEAN
ESPÍRITO SANTO
RIO DE JANEIRO
SÃO PAULO
PARANÁ
MINAS GERAIS
GOIÁS
BAHIA
SALVADOR (Bahia)
BELO HORIZONTE
BRASÍLIA
DISTRITO FEDERAL
GOIÂNIA
Anápolis
Uberlândia
Uberaba
Ribeirão Prêto
CAMPINAS
SANTOS
SANTO ANDRÉ
NITERÓI
CAMPOS
Vitória
Vila Velha
Juiz de Fora
Montes Claros
Teófilo Otoni
Gov. Valadares
Vitória da Conquista
Feira de Santana
Ilhéus
Itabuna
Jequié
CURITIBA
Paranaguá
Ponta Grossa
Londrina
Maringá
Presidente Prudente
Bauru
Marília
Sorocaba
Piracicaba
Jundiaí
Taubaté
Volta Redonda
Petrópolis
Nova Iguaçu
Cabo Frio
Cabo de São Tomé
Tropic of Capricorn
West from Greenwich
Projection: Lambert's Equivalent Azimuthal

1:8 000 000

50 0 50 100 150 200 250 300 km

2000 1500 1000 400 200 0

0 200 2000 4000 m

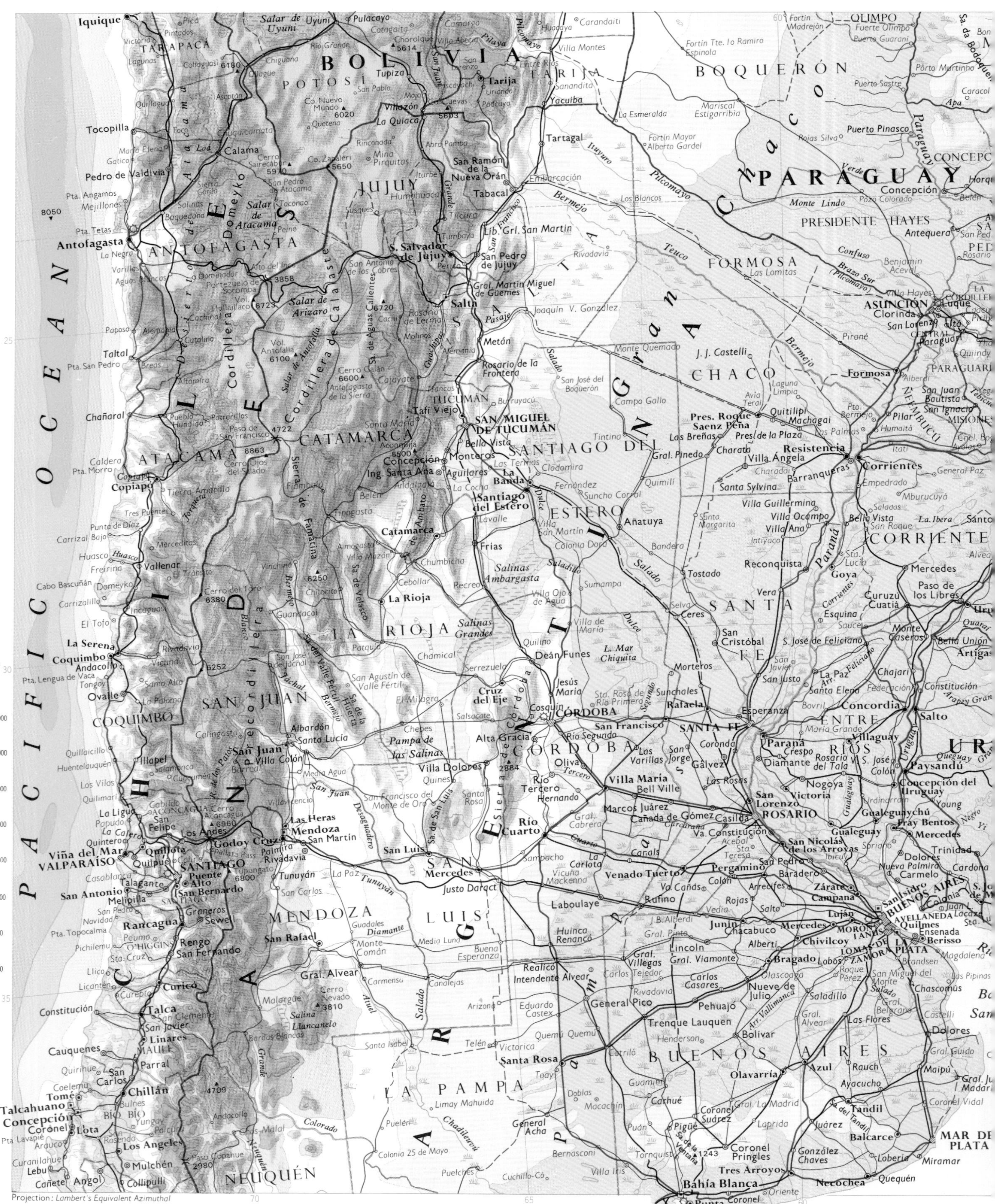

PACIFIC OCEAN
BOLIVIA
PARAGUAY
CHILE
ARGENTINA
Gran Chaco
Desierto de Atacama
Cordillera de los Andes
Iquique
Tocopilla
Antofagasta
Taltal
Chañaral
Copiapó
Vallenar
La Serena
Coquimbo
Ovalle
Viña del Mar
VALPARAÍSO
SANTIAGO
San Antonio
Rancagua
Curicó
Talca
Linares
Chillán
Talcahuano
Concepción
Los Angeles
Salta
S. Salvador de Jujuy
SAN MIGUEL DE TUCUMÁN
Catamarca
La Rioja
Santiago del Estero
CÓRDOBA
Mendoza
San Juan
San Luis
San Rafael
Río Cuarto
Santa Rosa
Bahía Blanca
ROSARIO
SANTA FE
Paraná
Corrientes
Resistencia
Formosa
ASUNCIÓN
BUENOS AIRES
LA PLATA
MAR DEL PLATA
Tandil
Concordia
Paysandú
Salto
TUCUMÁN
CATAMARCA
LA RIOJA
SAN JUAN
MENDOZA
SAN LUIS
LA PAMPA
CÓRDOBA
SANTA FE
ENTRE RÍOS
CORRIENTES
CHACO
FORMOSA
SANTIAGO DEL ESTERO
JUJUY
SALTA
BOQUERÓN
PRESIDENTE HAYES
ATACAMA
ANTOFAGASTA
TARAPACÁ
COQUIMBO
POTOSÍ
TARIJA
NEUQUÉN
Projection: Lambert's Equivalent Azimuthal

1:8 000 000

50 0 50 100 150 200 250 300 km

BELO HORIZONTE
N. Lima
Itabirito
Congonhas
Cons. Lafaiete
Ouro Prêto
Ponte Nova
Vitória
Vila Velha
Guarapari
Castelo
Cachoeiro de Itapemirim
Oliveira
Campo Belo
São João del Rei
Ubá
Muriaé
Carangola
Alegre
Itaperuna
Guarus
CAMPOS
Cabo de São Tomé
Barbacena
Lavras
Cataguases
Leopoldina
Santos Dumont
Juiz de Fora
Três Rios
Além Paraíba
RIO DE JANEIRO
Nova Friburgo
Macaé
Petrópolis
DUQUE DE CAXIAS
SÃO GONÇALO
NITERÓI
RIO DE JANEIRO
Cabo Frio
La. de Araruama
Tropic of Capricorn
Volta Redonda
Barra do Pirai
Barra Mansa
Nova Iguaçu
Angra dos Reis
Ilha Grande
Baía da Ilha Grande
Pta. de Juatinga
Três Corações
Varginha
Alfenas
Guaxupé
Poços de Caldas
Pouso Alegre
Itajubá
Ouro Fino
Cruzeiro
Guaratinguetá
Taubaté
S. J. dos Campos
Jacareí
Mogi das Cruzes
SÃO PAULO
SANTO ANDRÉ
SANTOS
Guarujá
São Vicente
Ilha de São Sebastião
Pta. do Boi
Itanhaém
Jundiaí
CAMPINAS
Americana
Mogi-Mirim
Bragança Paulista
Sorocaba
Itu
Piracicaba
Limeira
Rio Claro
São Carlos
Araraquara
Araras
Pinhal
São João da Boa Vista
Mococa
Ribeirão Prêto
Jaboticabal
Bebedouro
Passos
Batatais
São Seb. do Paraíso
Franca
Olímpia
S. José do Rio Prêto
Mirassol
Catanduva
Taquaritinga
Novo Horizonte
Penápolis
Lins
SÃO PAULO
Bauru
Jaú
Garça
Marília
Tupã
Adamantina
Birigui
Araçatuba
Andradina
Três Lagoas
Mirandópolis
Presidente Prudente
Rancharia
Assis
Ourinhos
Avaré
Botucatu
Tatuí
Itapetininga
Itapeva
Itararé
Jaguariaíva
Paranapiacaba
Iguape
Ilha Comprida
Ilha do Cardoso
Registro
Londrina
Arapongas
Apucarana
Maringá
Paranavaí
Cornélio Procópio
Jacarèzinho
Cianorte
Cruzeiro do Oeste
Campo Mourão
Guaíra
PARANÁ
B R A Z I L
Cascavel
Guarapuava
Ponta Grossa
Castro
Palmeira
CURITIBA
1889
Antonina
Paranaguá
Guaratuba
Lapa
Irati
União da Vitória
Pto. União
Rio Negro
Mafra
São Francisco do Sul
Joinvile
Itajaí
Blumenau
Brusque
Caçador
Joaçaba
Chapecó
SANTA CATARINA
Campos Novos
Rio do Sul
Lajes
Ilha de Santa Catarina
Florianópolis
1808
Laguna
Tubarão
Cabo Santa Marta Grande
Criciúma
Araranguá
Foz do Iguaçu
Itaipu Dam
Iguaçu Falls
Oviedo
Hernandarias
ALTO PARANÁ
Eldorado
MISIONES
Posadas
Encarnación
Oberá
Erechim
Passo Fundo
Caràzinho
Santo Ângelo
Cruz Alta
São Luis Gonzaga
Santa Rosa
São Borja
Vacaria
Bento Gonçalves
Caxias do Sul
RIO GRANDE DO SUL
Santiago
Santa Maria
Santa Cruz do Sul
Montenegro
Nôvo Hamburgo
Taquara
São Leopoldo
PÔRTO ALEGRE
Osorio
Alegrete
Cachoeira do Sul
Rio Pardo
São Gabriel
Santana do Livramento
Rivera
Dom Pedrito
Bagé
Camaquã
Lagoa dos Patos
Mostardas
Pelotas
Rio Grande
Tacuarembó
URUGUAY
Melo
Jaguarão
Lagoa Mirim
Lagoa Mangueira
Santa Vitória do Palmar
Treinta y Tres
Minas
Rocha
San Carlos
Maldonado
MONTEVIDEO
Plata
ATLANTIC OCEAN
5304
Tropic of Capricorn
25
30
35
55
50
45
40
West from Greenwich

PACIFIC OCEAN
COLOMBIA
VENEZUELA
ECUADOR
PERU
BOLIVIA
AMAZONAS
ACRE
RORAIMA
RONDÔNIA
Bogotá
Caracas
Quito
Lima
La Paz
Manaus
Medellín
Guayaquil
Maracaibo
Port of Spain
TRINIDAD & TOBAGO
Equator
Milne Edwards Trench
Peru-Chile Trench
Projection: Sanson-Flamsteed's Sinusoidal

1:16 000 000

200 100 0 200 400 600 km
ATLANTIC OCEAN
Equator
POLITICAL
1:80 000 000
VENEZUELA
COLOMBIA
ECUADOR
PERU
BOLIVIA
BRAZIL
PARAGUAY
ARGENTINA
URUGUAY
CHILE
PACIFIC OCEAN
Falkland Is.
Tierra del Fuego
FR. GUIANA
AMAPÁ
PARÁ
MARANHÃO
PIAUÍ
CEARÁ
RIO GRANDE DO NORTE
PARAÍBA
PERNAMBUCO
ALAGOAS
SERGIPE
BAHIA
GOIÁS
MINAS GERAIS
ESPIRITO SANTO
MATO GROSSO
DIST. FED.
Planalto do Mato Grosso
Paramaribo
Cayenne
Macapá
Belém (Pará)
São Luís (Maranhão)
Fortaleza (Ceará)
Natal
João Pessoa (Paraíba)
RECIFE (Pernambuco)
Maceió
Aracaju
Salvador (Bahia)
Teresina
Ilhéus
Brasília
Goiânia
Belo Horizonte
Vitória
Campo Grande
Juiz de Fora
Petrópolis
Niterói
RIO DE JANEIRO
Campinas
Ilha de Marajó
Fernando de Noronha (Braz.)
Trindade (Braz.)
Rocas
6059
1678
1850
1340
2787
2890
55
50
45
40
35
30

1:16 000 000

200 100 0 200 400 600 km
MATO GROSSO DO SUL
PARAGUAY
Chaco Boreal
Chaco Central
Asunción
Concepción
Tropic of Capricorn
Antofagasta
Tocopilla
Calama
Desierto de Atacama
Salta
San Salvador de Jujuy
Tarija
San Miguel de Tucumán
Santiago del Estero
Catamarca
La Rioja
Copiapó
Peru–Chile Trench
Richards Deep
Richard's Deep
La Serena
Coquimbo
Ovalle
San Juan
Córdoba
Mendoza
Valparaiso
Viña del Mar
SANTIAGO
Rancagua
Talca
Talcahuano
Concepción
Chillán
Temuco
Valdivia
Osorno
Puerto Montt
Ancud
I. de Chiloé
Archipiélago de los Chonos
Pen. de Taitao
G. de Penas
I. Wellington
Canal Concepción
Estrecho Nelson
Arch. Reina Adelaida
Estrecho de Magallanes (Magellan's Str.)
I. Santa Inés
Punta Arenas
Tierra del Fuego
Canal Beagle
I. Hoste
Cabo de Hornos (C. Horn)
Islas Diego Ramirez
I. de los Estados (Staten I.)
Río Gallegos
Santa Cruz
Bahía Grande
San Julián
Pto. Deseado
Comodoro Rivadavia
Golfo San Jorge
Trelew
Rawson
Golfo Nuevo
Península Valdés
Golfo San Matías
Viedma
Carmen de Patagones
Bahía Blanca
Neuquén
San Carlos de Bariloche
Mar del Plata
Tandil
Necochea
Tres Arroyos
Río de la Plata
La Plata
BUENOS AIRES
MONTEVIDEO
Maldonado
URUGUAY
Rosario
Santa Fe
Paraná
Resistencia
Corrientes
Posadas
Encarnación
RIO GRANDE DO SUL
Pôrto Alegre
Lagoa dos Patos
Pelotas
Rio Grande
Lagoa Mirim
SANTA CATARINA
Florianópolis
PARANÁ
Curitiba
Paranaguá
SÃO PAULO
Santos
RIO DE JANEIRO
Campinas
Londrina
Maringá
Ribeirão Prêto
ARGENTINA
CHILE
BRAZIL
SOUTH ATLANTIC OCEAN
FALKLAND ISLANDS (ISLAS MALVINAS) (Br.)
West Falkland
East Falkland
Stanley
Falkland Sound
South Georgia (Br.)
5830
6800
3600
4058
3700
2469
705
700

INDEX

The number printed in bold type against each index entry indicates the map page where the feature will be found. The geographical coordinates which follow the name are sometimes only approximate but are close enough for the place name to be located.
An open square □ signifies that the name refers to an administrative subdivision of a country while a solid square ■ follows the name of a country. (□) follows the old county names of the U.K.
The alphabetical order of names composed of two or more words is governed primarily by the first word and then by the second. This rule applies even if the second word is a description or its abbreviation, R.,L.,I. for example. Names composed of a proper name (Gibraltar) and a description (Strait of) are positioned alphabetically by the proper name. If the same place name occurs twice or more times in the index and all are in the same country, each is followed by the name of the administrative subdivision in which it is located. The names are placed in the alphabetical order of the subdivisions. If the same place name occurs twice or more in the index and the places are in different countries they will be followed by their country names, the latter governing the alphabetical order. In a mixture of these situations the primary order is fixed by the alphabetical sequence of the countries and the secondary order by that of the country subdivisions.

A. C. T. – Australian Capital Territory
A. R. – Autonomous Region
A. S. S. R. – Autonomous Soviet Socialist Republic
Afghan. – Afghanistan
Afr. – Africa
Ala. – Alabama
Alas. – Alaska
Alg. – Algeria
Alta. – Alberta
Amer. – America
And. P. – Andhra Pradesh
Ang. – Angola
Arch. – Archipelago
Arg. – Argentina
Ariz. – Arizona
Ark. – Arkansas
Atl. Oc. – Atlantic Ocean
Austral. – Australia
B. – Baie, Bahía, Bay, Bucht, Bugt
B.A. – Buenos Aires
B.C. – British Columbia
Bangla. – Bangladesh
Barr. – Barrage
Bay. – Bayern
Belg. – Belgium
Berks. – Berkshire
Bol. – Bolshoi
Bots. – Botswana
Br. – British
Bri. – Bridge
Bt. – Bight
Bucks. – Buckinghamshire
Bulg. – Bulgaria
C. – Cabo, Cap, Cape
C. Prov. – Cape Province
Calif. – California
Camb. – Cambodia
Cambs. – Cambridgeshire
Can. – Canada
Cat. – Cataract, Cataracta
Cent. – Central
Chan. – Channel
Co. – Country
Colomb. – Colombia
Colo. – Colorado
Conn. – Connecticut
Cord. – Cordillera
Cr.. – Creek
Cumb. – Cumbria
Czech. – Czechoslovakia
D.C. – District of Columbia
Del. – Delaware
Dep. – Dependency
Derby. – Derbyshire
Des. – Desert
Dist. – District
Dj. – Djebel
Dumf. & Gall. – Dumfries and Galloway
E. – East
Eng. – England
Fed. – Federal, Federation
Fla. – Florida
For. – Forest
Fr. – France, French
Fs. – Falls
Ft. – Fort
G. – Golf, Golfo, Gulf, Guba
Ga. – Georgia
Germ. – Germany
Glam. – Glamorgan
Glos. – Gloucestershire
Gr. – Grande, Great, Greater, Group
H.K. – Hong Kong
H.P. – Himachal Pradesh
Hants. – Hampshire
Harb. – Harbor, Harbour
Hd. – Head
Here. & Worcs. – Hereford and Worcester
Herts. – Hertfordshire
Holl. – Holland
Hung. – Hungary
I.o.M. – Isle of Man
I. of W. – Isle of Wight
I.(s). – Île, Ilha, Insel, Isla, Island
Id. – Idaho
Ill. – Illinois
Ind. – Indiana
Ind. Oc. – Indian Ocean
J. – Jabal, Jabel, Jazira
Junc. – Junction
K. – Kap, Kapp
K. – Kuala
Kal. – Kalmyk A.S.S.R.
Kans. – Kansas
Kpl. – Kapell
Ky. – Kentucky
L. – Lac, Lacul, Lago, Lagoa, Lake, Limni, Loch, Lough
La. – Lousiana
Lancs. – Lancashire
Leb. – Lebanon
Leics. – Leicestershire
Lim. – Limerick
Lincs. – Lincolnshire
Lit. – Little
Lr. – Lower
Lt. Ho. – Light House
Mad. P. – Madhya Pradesh
Madag. – Madagascar
Malay. – Malaysia
Man. – Manitoba
Manch. – Manchester
Maran. – Maranhão
Mass. – Massachusetts
Md. – Maryland
Me. – Maine
Mend. – Mendoza
Mer. – Méridionale
Mich. – Michigan
Mid. – Middle
Minn. – Minnesota
Miss. – Mississippi
Mo. – Missouri
Mong. – Mongolia
Mont. – Montana
Moroc. – Morocco
Mozam. – Mozambique
Mt.(e). – Mont, Monte, Monti, Montaña, Mountain
Mys. – Mysore
N. – North, Northern, Nouveau
N.B. – New Brunswick
N.C. – North Carolina
N.D. – North Dakota
N.H. – New Hampshire
N.I. – North Island
N.J. – New Jersey
N. Mex. – New Mexico
N.S. – Nova Scotia
N.S.W. – New South Wales
N.T. – Northern Territory
N.W.T. – North West Territory
N.Y. – New York
N.Z. – New Zealand
Nat. – National
Nat Park. – National Park
Nebr. – Nebraska
Neth. – Netherlands
Nev. – Nevada
Newf. – Newfoundland
Nic. – Nicaragua
Northants. – Northamptonshire
Northumb. – Northumberland
Notts. – Nottinghamshire
O. – Oued, ouadi
O.F.S. – Orange Free State
Okla. – Oklahoma
Ont. – Ontario
Or. – Orientale
Oreg. – Oregon
Os. – Ostrov
Oxon. – Oxfordshire
Oz. – Ozero
P. – Pass, Passo, Pasul, Pulau
P.E.I. – Prince Edward Island
P.N.G. – Papua New Guinea
P.O. – Post Office
P. Rico. – Puerto Rico
Pa. – Pennsylvania
Pac. Oc. – Pacific Ocean
Pak. – Pakistan
Pass. – Passage
Pen. – Peninsula, Peninsule
Phil. – Philippines
Pk. – Park, Peak
Plat. – Plateau
P-ov. – Poluostrov
Port. – Portugal, Portuguese
Prom. – Promontory
Prov. – Province, Provincial
Pt. – Point
Pta. – Ponta, Punta
Pte. – Pointe
Qué. – Québec
Queens. – Queensland
R. – Rio, River
R.I. – Rhode Island
R.S.F.S.R. – Russian Soviet Federal Socialist Republic
Ra.(s). – Range(s)
Raj. – Rajasthan
Reg. – Region
Rep. – Republic
Res. – Reserve, Reservoir
Rhld. – Pfz. – Rheinland – Pfalz
S. – San, South
S. Afr. – South Africa
S. Austral. – South Australia
S.D: – South Dakota
S.-Holst. – Schleswig-Holstein
S.I. – South Island
S. Leone – Sierra Leone
S.S.R. – Soviet Socialist Republic
S.-U. – Sinkiang-Uighur
Sa. – Serra, Sierra
Sard. – Sardinia
Sask. – Saskatchewan
Scot. – Scotland
Sd. – Sound
Sept. – Septentrionale
Sib. – Siberia
Som. – Somerset
Span. – Spanish
Sprs. – Springs
St. – Saint
Sta. – Santa, Station
Staffs. – Staffordshire
Ste. – Sainte
Sto. – Santo
Str. – Strait, Stretto
Switz. – Switzerland
T.O. – Telegraph Office
Tas. – Tasmania
Tenn. – Tennessee
Terr. – Territory
Tex. – Texas
Tg. – Tanjung
Thai. – Thailand
Tipp. – Tipperary
Trans. – Transvaal
U.K. – United Kingdom
U.S.A. – United States of America
U.S.S.R. – Union of Soviet Socialist Republics
Ukr. – Ukraine
Ut.P. – Uttar Pradesh
Utd. – United
Va. – Virginia
Vdkhr. – Vodokhranilishche
Venez. – Venezuela
Vic. – Victoria
Viet. – Vietnam
Vol. – Volcano
Vt. – Vermont
W. – Wadi, West
W.A. – Western Australia
W. Isles – Western Isles
Wash. – Washington
Wilts. – Wiltshire
Wis. – Wisconsin
Wlkp. – Wielkopolski
Wyo. – Wyoming
Yorks. – Yorkshire
Yug. – Yugoslavia
Zimb. – Zimbabwe

Please refer to the table at the end of the index for recent placename changes in Angola, Iran, Madagascar, Mozambique, Vietnam and Zimbabwe. There is also a table giving the Pin Yin equivalents of the modified Wade-Giles nameforms for the principal Chinese placenames which appear in this Atlas.

A

Aabenraa-Sønderborg Amt □ **73** 55 0N 9 30 E
Aachen **48** 50 47N 6 4 E
Aadorf **15** 47 30N 8 55 E
Aaiun **116** 27 9N 13 12W
Aal **73** 55 39N 8 18 E
Aâlâ en Nîl □ **123** 8 50N 29 55 E
Aalen **49** 48 49N 10 6 E
Aalma ech Chaab **90** 33 7N 35 9 E
Aalsmeer **46** 52 17N 4 43 E
Aalsö **73** 56 23N 10 52 E
Aalst, Belg. **47** 50 56N 4 2 E
Aalst, Neth. **152** 50 57N 4 20 E
Aalten **46** 51 56N 6 35 E
Aalter **47** 51 5N 3 28 E
Aarau **50** 47 23N 8 4 E
Aarburg **50** 47 2N 7 16 E
Aardenburg **47** 51 16N 3 28 E
Aare, R. **50** 47 33N 8 14 E
Aareavaara **74** 67 27N 23 29 E
Aargau □ **50** 47 26N 8 10 E
Aarhus Amt □ **73** 56 15N 10 15 E
Aarle **47** 51 30N 5 38 E
Aarschot **47** 50 59N 4 49 E
Aarsele **47** 51 0N 3 26 E
Aartrijke **47** 51 7N 3 6 E
Aarwangen **50** 47 15N 7 46 E
Aasleagh **38** 53 37N 9 40W
Aastrup **73** 55 34N 8 49 E
Aba, Congo **126** 3 58N 30 17 E
Aba, Nigeria **121** 5 10N 7 19 E
Âbâ, Jazîrat **123** 13 30N 32 31 E
Abadan **92** 30 22N 48 20 E
Abade, Ethiopia **123** 9 22N 38 3 E
Abade, Iran **93** 31 8N 52 40 E
Abadin **56** 43 21N 7 29W
Abadla **118** 31 2N 2 45W
Abaeté **171** 19 9 S 45 27W
Abaeté, R. **171** 18 2 S 45 12W
Abaetetuba **170** 1 40 S 48 50W
Abai **173** 25 58 S 55 54W
Abak **121** 4 58N 7 50 E
Abakaliki **121** 6 22N 8 2 E
Abakan **77** 53 40N 91 10 E
Abal Nam **122** 25 20N 38 37 E
Abalemma **121** 16 12N 7 50 E
Aballetuba **170** 1 40 S 51 15W
Abanilla **59** 38 12N 1 3W
Abano Terme **63** 45 22N 11 46 E
Abarán **59** 38 12N 1 23W
Abarqu **93** 31 10N 53 20 E
Abasan **90** 31 19N 34 21 E
Abasberes **123** 11 33N 35 23 E
Abashiri **112** 44 0N 144 15 E
Abashiri-Wan **112** 44 0N 144 30 E
Abau **135** 10 11 S 148 46 E
Abaújszántó **53** 48 16N 21 12 E
Abaya L. **123** 6 30N 37 50 E
Abbadia San Salvatore **63** 42 53N 11 40 E
Abbay, R., (Nîl el Azraq) **123** 10 17N 35 22 E
Abbaye, Pt. **156** 46 58N 88 4W
Abbetorp **73** 56 57N 16 8 E
Abbeville, France **43** 50 6N 1 49 E
Abbeville, La., U.S.A. **159** 30 0N 92 7W
Abbeville, S.C., U.S.A. **157** 34 12N 82 21W
Abbey **39** 53 7N 8 25W
Abbey Town **32** 54 50N 3 18W
Abbeydorney **39** 52 21N 9 40W
Abbeyfeale **39** 52 23N 9 20W
Abbeyleix **39** 52 55N 7 20W
Abbeyside **39** 52 5N 7 36W
Abbiategrasso **62** 45 23N 8 55 E
Abbieglassie **139** 27 15 S 147 28 E
Abbotabad **94** 34 10N 73 15 E
Abbots Bromley **28** 52 50N 1 52W
Abbots Langley **29** 51 43N 0 25W
Abbotsbury **28** 50 40N 2 36W
Abbotsford, Can. **152** 49 0N 122 10W
Abbotsford, U.S.A. **158** 44 55N 90 20W
Abcoude **46** 52 17N 4 59 E
'Abd al Kuri **91** 12 5N 52 20 E
Abdulino **84** 53 42N 53 40 E
Abe, L. **123** 11 8N 41 47 E
Abéché **117** 13 50N 20 35 E
Abejar **58** 41 48N 2 47W
Abekr **123** 12 45N 28 50 E
Abêlessa **118** 22 58N 4 47 E
Abelti **123** 8 10N 37 30 E
Abengourou **120** 6 42N 3 27W
Åbenrå **73** 55 3N 9 25 E
Abeokuta **121** 7 3N 3 19 E
Aber **126** 2 12N 32 25 E
Aber-soch **31** 52 50N 4 31W
Aberaeron **31** 52 15N 4 16W
Aberayron = Aberaeron **31** 52 15N 4 16W
Abercarn **31** 51 39N 3 9W
Aberchirder **37** 57 34N 2 40W
Abercorn **139** 25 12 S 151 5 E
Abercorn = Mbala **127** 8 46 S 31 17 E
Abercrave **31** 51 48N 3 42W
Aberdare **31** 51 43N 3 27W
Aberdare Ra. **126** 0 15 S 36 50 E
Aberdaron **31** 52 48N 4 41W
Aberdeen, Austral. **141** 32 9 S 150 56 E
Aberdeen, Can. **153** 52 20N 106 8W
Aberdeen, S. Afr. **128** 32 28 S 24 2 E
Aberdeen, U.K. **37** 57 9N 2 6W
Aberdeen, Md., U.S.A. **162** 39 30N 76 14W
Aberdeen, S.D., U.S.A. **158** 45 30N 98 30W
Aberdeen, Wash., U.S.A. **160** 47 0N 123 50W
Aberdeen (□) **26** 57 18N 2 30W
Aberdour **35** 56 2N 3 18W
Aberdovey **31** 52 33N 4 3W
Aberdulais **31** 51 41N 3 46W
Aberfeldy, Austral. **141** 37 42 S 146 22 E
Aberfeldy, U.K. **37** 56 37N 3 50W
Aberffraw **31** 53 11N 4 28W
Aberfoyle **34** 56 10N 4 23W
Abergaria-a-Velha **56** 40 41N 8 32W
Abergavenny **31** 51 49N 3 1W
Abergele **31** 53 17N 3 35W
Abergwili **31** 51 52N 4 18W
Abergynolwyn **31** 52 39N 3 58W
Aberkenfig **31** 51 33N 3 36W
Aberlady **35** 56 0N 2 51W
Abernathy **159** 33 49N 101 49W
Abernethy **35** 56 19N 3 18W
Aberporth **31** 52 8N 4 32W
Abersychan **31** 51 44N 3 3W
Abertillery **31** 51 44N 3 9W
Aberystwyth **31** 52 25N 4 6W
Abha **122** 18 0N 42 34 E
Abhayapuri **98** 26 24N 90 38 E
Abidiya **122** 18 18N 34 3 E
Abidjan **120** 5 26N 3 58W
Abilene, Kans., U.S.A. **158** 39 0N 97 16W
Abilene, Texas, U.S.A. **159** 32 22N 99 40W
Abingdon, U.K. **28** 51 40N 1 17W
Abingdon, Ill., U.S.A. **158** 40 53N 90 23W
Abingdon, Va., U.S.A. **157** 36 46N 81 56W
Abington **35** 55 30N 3 42W
Abington Reef **138** 18 0 S 149 35 E
Abitan L. **153** 60 27N 107 15W
Abitan, R. **153** 59 53N 109 3W
Abitibi L. **150** 48 40N 79 40W
Abiy Adi **123** 13 39N 39 3 E
Abkhaz A.S.S.R. □ **83** 43 0N 41 0 E
Abkit **77** 64 10N 157 10 E
Abnûb **122** 27 18N 31 4 E
Åbo = Turku **75** 60 27N 22 14 E
Abo, Massif d' **119** 21 41N 16 8 E
Abocho **121** 7 35N 6 56 E
Abohar **94** 30 10N 74 10 E
Aboisso **120** 5 30N 3 5W
Abomey **121** 7 10N 2 5 E
Abondance **45** 46 18N 6 42 E
Abong Mbang **124** 4 0N 13 8 E
Abonnema **121** 4 41N 6 49 E
Abony **53** 47 12N 20 3 E
Aboso **120** 5 23N 1 57W
Abou Deïa **117** 11 20N 19 20 E
Aboyne **37** 57 4N 2 48W
Abqaiq **92** 26 0N 49 45 E
Abra Pampa **172** 22 43 S 65 42W
Abrantes **57** 39 24N 8 7W
Abraveses **56** 40 41N 7 55 E
Abreojos, Pta. **164** 26 50N 113 40W
Abreschviller **43** 48 39N 7 6 E
Abrets, Les **45** 45 32N 5 35 E
Abri, Esh Shimâliya, Sudan **123** 20 50N 30 27 E
Abri, Kordofân, Sudan **123** 11 40N 30 21 E
Abrolhos, Arquipélago dos **171** 18 0 S 38 30W
Abrolhos, banka **171** 18 0 S 38 0W
Abrud **70** 46 19N 23 5 E
Abruzzi □ **63** 42 15N 14 0 E
Absaroka Ra. **160** 44 40N 110 0W
Abū al Khasib **92** 30 25N 48 0 E
Abū 'Ali **92** 27 20N 49 27 E
Abu Arish **91** 16 53N 42 48 E
Abû Ballas **122** 24 26N 27 36 E
Abu Deleiq **123** 15 57N 33 48 E
Abū Dhabī **93** 24 28N 54 36 E
Abû Dis **90** 31 47N 35 16 E
Abu Dis **122** 19 12N 33 38 E
Abu Dom **123** 16 18N 32 25 E
Abû Gabra **123** 11 2N 26 50 E
Abû Ghôsh **90** 31 48N 35 6 E
Abû Gubeiha **123** 11 30N 31 15 E
Abu Habl, W. **123** 12 37N 31 0 E
Abu Hamed **122** 19 32N 33 13 E
Abû Haraz, Esh Shimâliya, Sudan **122** 19 8N 32 18 E
Abû Haraz, Nîl el Azraq, Sudan **123** 14 35N 34 30 E
Abû Higar **123** 12 50N 33 59 E
Abu Kamal **92** 34 30N 41 0 E
Abu Markha **92** 25 4N 38 22 E
Abu Qîr **122** 31 18N 30 0 E
Abu Qireiya **122** 24 5N 35 28 E
Abu Qurqâs **122** 28 1N 30 44 E
Abu Salama **122** 27 10N 35 51 E
Abû Simbel **122** 22 18N 31 40 E
Abu Tig **122** 27 4N 31 15 E
Abu Tiga **123** 12 47N 34 12 E
Abû Zabad **123** 12 25N 29 10 E
Abu Zenîma **122** 29 0N 33 15 E
Abuja **121** 9 16N 7 2 E
Abunã **174** 9 40 S 65 20W
Abunã, R. **174** 9 41 S 65 20W
Aburatsu **110** 31 34N 131 24 E
Aburo, Mt. **126** 2 4N 30 53 E
Abut Hd. **143** 43 7 S 170 15 E
Abwong **123** 9 2N 32 14 E
Åby **73** 58 40N 16 10 E
Aby, Lagune **120** 5 15N 3 14W
Acacías **174** 3 59N 73 46W
Acajutla **166** 13 36N 89 50W
Açallândia **170** 5 0 S 47 50W
Acámbaro **164** 20 0N 100 40W
Acaponeta **164** 22 30N 105 20W
Acapulco de Juárez **165** 16 51N 99 56W
Acarai, Serra **175** 1 50N 57 50W
Acaraú **170** 2 53 S 40 7W
Acari **170** 6 31 S 36 38W
Acarigua **174** 9 33N 69 12W
Acatlan **165** 18 10N 98 3W
Acayucán **165** 17 59N 94 58W
Accéglio **62** 44 28N 6 59 E
Accomac **156** 37 43N 75 40W
Accra **121** 5 35N 0 6W
Accrington **32** 53 46N 2 22W
Acebal **172** 33 20 S 60 50W
Aceh □ **102** 4 0N 97 30 E
Acerenza **65** 40 50N 15 58 E
Acerra **65** 40 57N 14 22 E
Aceuchal **57** 38 39N 6 30W
Achaguas **174** 7 46N 68 14W
Achak Gomba **99** 33 30N 96 25 E
Achalpur **96** 21 22N 77 32 E
Achavanich **37** 58 22N 3 25W
Achel **47** 51 15N 5 29 E
A'ch'eng **107** 45 33N 127 0 E
Achenkirch **52** 47 32N 11 45 E
Achensee **52** 47 26N 11 45 E
Acher **94** 23 10N 72 32 E
Achern **49** 48 37N 8 5 E
Acheron, R. **143** 42 16 S 173 4 E
Achill **38** 53 56N 9 55W
Achill Hd. **38** 53 59N 10 15W
Achill I. **38** 53 58N 10 5W
Achill Sd. **38** 53 53N 9 55W
Achillbeg I. **38** 53 51N 9 58W
Achim **48** 53 1N 9 2 E
Achimota **121** 5 35N 0 15W
Achinsk **77** 56 20N 90 20 E
Achisay **85** 43 35N 68 53 E
Achit **84** 56 48N 57 54 E
Achnasheen **36** 57 35N 5 5W
Achnashellach **36** 57 28N 5 20W
Achol **123** 6 35N 31 32 E
A'Chralaig, Mt. **36** 57 11N 5 10W
Acireale **65** 37 37N 15 9 E
Ackerman **159** 33 20N 89 8W
Acklin's I. **167** 22 30N 74 0W
Acland, Mt. **133** 24 50 S 148 20 E
Aclare **38** 54 4N 8 54W
Acle **29** 52 38N 1 32 E
Acme **152** 51 33N 113 30W
Aconcagua **172** 32 50 S 70 0W
Aconcagua □ **172** 32 15 S 70 30W
Aconcagua, Cerro **172** 32 39 S 70 0W
Aconquija, Mt. **172** 27 0 S 66 0W
Acopiara **170** 6 6 S 39 27W
Açores, Is. dos **14** 38 44N 29 0W
Acquapendente **63** 42 45N 11 50 E
Acquasanta **63** 42 46N 13 24 E
Acquaviva delle Fonti **65** 40 53N 16 50 E
Acqui **62** 44 40N 8 28 E
Acre = 'Akko **90** 32 35N 35 4 E
Acre □ **174** 9 1 S 71 0W
Acre, R. **174** 10 45 S 68 25W
Acri **65** 39 29N 16 23 E
Acs **53** 47 42N 18 0 E
Acton Burnell **28** 52 37N 2 41W
Açu **170** 5 34 S 36 54W
Ad Dam **91** 20 33N 44 45 E
Ad Dammam **92** 26 20N 50 5 E
Ad Dar al Hamra **92** 27 20N 37 45 E
Ad Dawhah **93** 25 15N 51 35 E
Ad Dilam **92** 23 55N 47 10 E
Ada, Ethiopia **123** 8 48N 38 51 E
Ada, Ghana **121** 5 44N 0 40 E
Ada, Minn., U.S.A. **158** 47 20N 96 30W
Ada, Okla., U.S.A. **159** 34 50N 96 45W
Ada, Yugo. **66** 45 49N 20 9 E
Adair C. **12** 71 50N 71 0W
Adaja, R. **56** 41 15N 4 50W
Adale **91** 2 58N 46 27 E
Ådalslinden **72** 63 27N 16 55 E
Adam **93** 22 15N 57 28 E
Adamantina **171** 21 42 S 51 4W
Adamaoua, Massif de l' **121** 7 20N 12 20 E
Adamawa Highlands = Adamaoua **121** 7 20N 12 20 E
Adamello, Mt. **62** 46 10N 10 34 E
Adami Tulu **123** 7 53N 38 41 E
Adaminaby **141** 36 0 S 148 45 E
Adamovka **84** 51 32N 59 56 E
Adams, Mass., U.S.A. **162** 42 38N 73 8W
Adams, N.Y., U.S.A. **162** 43 50N 76 3W
Adams, Wis., U.S.A. **158** 43 59N 89 50W
Adam's Bridge **97** 9 15N 79 40 E
Adams L. **152** 51 10N 119 40W
Adams Mt. **160** 46 10N 121 28W
Adam's Peak **97** 6 55N 80 45 E
Adamuz **57** 38 2N 4 32W
Adana **92** 37 0N 35 16 E
Adanero **56** 40 56N 4 36W
Adapazari **92** 40 48N 30 25 E
Adarama **123** 17 10N 34 52 E
Adare **39** 52 34N 8 48W
Adare, C. **13** 71 0 S 171 0 E
Adavale **139** 25 52 S 144 32 E
Adayio **123** 14 29N 40 50 E
Adda, R. **62** 45 25N 9 30 E
Addis Ababa = Addis Abeba **123** 9 2N 38 42 E
Addis Abeba **123** 9 2N 38 42 E
Addis Alem **123** 9 0N 38 17 E
Addlestone **29** 51 22N 0 30W
Addo **29** 33 32 S 25 44 E
Addu Atoll **87** 0 30 S 73 0 E
Adebour **121** 13 17N 11 50 E
Adel **157** 31 10N 83 28W
Adelaide, Austral. **140** 34 52 S 138 30 E
Adelaide, Bahamas **166** 25 0N 77 31W
Adelaide I. **13** 67 15 S 68 30W
Adelaide Pen. **148** 68 15N 97 30W
Adelaide River **136** 13 15 S 131 7 E
Adelanto **163** 34 35N 117 22W
Adelboden **50** 46 29N 7 33 E
Adele, I. **136** 15 32 S 123 9 E
Adélie, Terre **13** 67 0 S 140 0 E
Ademuz **58** 40 5N 1 13W
Aden **91** 12 50N 45 0 E
Aden, G. of **91** 13 0N 50 0 E
Adendorp **128** 33 25 S 24 30 E
Adhoi **94** 23 26N 70 32 E
Adi **103** 4 15 S 133 30 E
Adi Daro **123** 14 20N 38 14 E
Adi Keyih **123** 14 51N 39 22 E
Adi Kwala **123** 14 38N 38 48 E
Adi Ugri **123** 14 58N 38 48 E
Adieu, C. **137** 32 0 S 132 10 E
Adieu Pt. **136** 15 14 S 124 35 E
Adigala **123** 10 24N 42 15 E
Adige, R. **63** 45 9N 11 25 E
Adigrat **123** 14 20N 39 26 E
Adilabad **96** 19 33N 78 35 E
Adin **160** 41 10N 121 0W
Adin Khel **93** 32 45N 68 5 E
Adinkerke **47** 51 5N 2 36 E
Adirampattinam **97** 10 28N 79 20 E
Adirondack Mts. **156** 44 0N 74 15W
Adis Dera **123** 10 12N 38 46 E
Adjohon **121** 6 41N 2 32 E
Adjud **70** 46 7N 27 10 E
Adjumani **126** 3 20N 31 50 E
Adlavik Is. **151** 55 2N 58 45W
Adler **83** 43 28N 39 52 E
Adliswil **51** 47 19N 8 32 E
Admer **119** 20 21N 5 27 E
Admer, Erg d' **119** 24 0N 9 5 E
Admiralty B. **13** 62 0 S 59 0W
Admiralty G. **136** 14 20 S 125 55 E
Admiralty I. **147** 57 40N 134 35W
Admiralty Inlet **160** 48 0N 122 40W
Admiralty Is. **135** 2 0 S 147 0 E
Admiralty Ra. **13** 72 0 S 164 0 E
Ado **121** 6 36N 2 56 E
Ado Ekiti **121** 7 38N 5 12 E
Adok **123** 8 10N 30 20 E
Adola **123** 11 14N 41 44 E
Adonara **103** 8 15 S 123 5 E
Adoni **97** 15 33N 77 18W
Adony **53** 47 6N 18 52 E
Adour, R. **44** 43 32N 1 32W
Adra, India **95** 23 30N 86 42 E
Adra, Spain **59** 36 43N 3 3W
Adraj **91** 20 1N 51 0 E
Adrano **65** 37 40N 14 49 E
Adrar **118** 27 51N 0 11W
Adrar des Iforhas **121** 19 40N 1 40 E
Adrasman **85** 40 38N 69 58 E
Adré **117** 13 40N 22 20 E
Adri **119** 27 32N 13 2 E
Adria **63** 45 4N 12 3 E
Adrian, Mich., U.S.A. **156** 41 55N 84 0W
Adrian, Tex., U.S.A. **159** 35 19N 102 37W
Adriatic Sea **60** 43 0N 16 0 E
Adrigole **39** 51 44N 9 42W
Adua **103** 1 45 S 129 50 E
Aduku **126** 2 03N 32 45 E
Adula **51** 46 30N 9 3 E
Adung Long **98** 28 7N 97 42 E
Adur **97** 9 8N 76 40 E
Adwa, Ethiopia **123** 14 15N 38 52 E
Adwa, Si Arab. **92** 27 15N 42 35 E
Adwick le Street **33** 53 35N 1 12W
Adzhar A.S.S.R. □ **83** 42 0N 42 0 E
Adzopé **120** 6 7N 3 49W
Æbelø I. **73** 55 39N 10 10 E
Æbeltoft **73** 56 12N 10 41 E
Æbeltoft Vig. B. **73** 56 9N 10 35 E
Ægean Is. **61** 38 0N 25 0 E
Ægean Sea **61** 37 0N 25 0 E
Aenemuiden **47** 51 30N 3 40 E
Ænes **71** 60 5N 6 8 E
Æolian Is. = Eólie, I. **65** 38 40N 15 7 E
Aerhchin Shanmo **105** 38 0N 88 0 E
Aerhshan **105** 47 93N 119 59 E
Aerht'ai Shan **105** 48 0N 90 0 E
Æro **73** 54 53N 10 20 E
Ærø **73** 54 52N 10 25 E
Ærøskøbing **73** 54 53N 10 24 E
Aesch **50** 47 28N 7 36 E
Aëtós **69** 37 15N 21 50 E
Afafi, Massif d' **119** 22 11N 14 48 E
Afanasyevo **84** 58 52N 53 15 E
Afándou **69** 36 18N 28 12 E
Afarag, Erg **118** 23 50N 2 47 E
Afdera, Mt. **123** 13 16N 41 5 E
Affreville = Khemis Miliania **118** 36 11N 2 14 E
Affric, L. **36** 57 15N 5 5W
Affric, R. **37** 57 15N 4 50W
Afghanistan ■ **93** 33 0N 65 0 E
Afgoi **91** 2 7N 44 59 E
Afif **92** 23 53N 42 56 E
Afikpo **121** 5 53N 7 54 E
Aflisses, O. **118** 28 30N 0 50 E
Aflou **118** 34 7N 2 3 E
Afodo **123** 10 18N 34 49 E
Afogados da Ingàzeira **170** 7 45 S 37 39W
Afognak I. **147** 58 10N 152 50W

Afragola **65** 40 54N 14 15 E
Africa **114** 10 0N 20 0 E
Afton **162** 42 14N 75 31W
Aftout **118** 26 50N 3 45W
Afuá **170** 0 15 S 50 10W
Afula **90** 32 37N 35 17 E
Afyon Karahisar **92** 38 20N 30 15 E
Agadès **121** 16 58N 7 59 E
Agadir **118** 30 28N 9 35W
Agadir Tissint **118** 29 57N 7 16W
Agano, R. **112** 37 50N 139 30 E
Agapa **77** 71 27N 89 15 E
Agapovka **84** 53 18N 59 8 E
Agar **94** 23 40N 76 2 E
Agaro **123** 7 50N 36 38 E
Agartala **98** 23 50N 91 23 E
Agassiz **152** 49 14N 121 46W
Agat **123** 15 38N 38 16 E
Agattu I. **147** 52 25N 172 30 E
Agbelouvé **121** 6 35N 1 14 E
Agboville **120** 5 55N 4 15W
Agdam **83** 40 0N 46 58 E
Agdash **83** 40 44N 47 22 E
Agde **44** 43 19N 3 28 E
Agde, C. d' **44** 43 16N 3 28 E
Agdz **118** 30 47N 6 30W
Agen **44** 44 12N 0 38 E
Ageo **111** 35 58N 139 36 E
Ager Tay **119** 20 0N 17 41 E
Agersø **73** 55 13N 11 12 E
Agger **73** 56 47N 8 13 E
Aggersborg **73** 57 0N 9 16 E
Aggius **64** 40 56N 9 4 E
Aghalee **38** 54 32N 6 17W
Aghavannagh **39** 52 55N 6 25W
Aghern **39** 52 5N 8 10W
Aghil Mts. **93** 36 0N 77 0 E
Aghil Pass **93** 36 15N 76 35 E
Aginskoye **77** 51 6N 114 32 E
Agira **65** 37 40N 14 30 E
Aglou **118** 29 50N 9 50W
Agly, R. **44** 42 46N 3 3 E
Agna Branca **170** 7 57 S 47 19W
Agnes **137** 28 0 S 120 30 E
Agnew **137** 28 1 S 120 30 E
Agnews Hill **38** 54 51N 5 55W
Agnibilékrou **120** 7 10N 3 11W
Agnita **70** 45 59N 24 40 E
Agnone **65** 41 49N 14 20 E
Ago **111** 33 36N 135 29 E
Agofie **121** 8 27N 0 15 E
Agogna, R. **62** 45 8N 8 42 E
Agogo, Ghana **121** 6 50N 1 1W
Agogo, Sudan **123** 7 50N 28 45 E
Agon **42** 49 2N 1 34W
Agön **72** 61 33N 17 25 E
Agon I. **72** 61 34N 17 23 E
Agordo **63** 46 18N 12 2 E
Agout, R. **44** 43 47N 1 41 E
Agra **94** 27 17N 77 58 E
Agrado **174** 2 15N 75 46W
Agramunt **58** 41 48N 1 6 E
Agreda **58** 41 51N 1 55W
Agri **73** 56 14N 10 32 E
Ağri Daği **92** 39 50N 44 15 E
Agri, R. **65** 40 17N 16 15 E
Agrigento **64** 37 19N 13 33 E
Agrinion **69** 38 37N 21 27 E
Agrøpoli **65** 40 23N 14 59 E
Agryz **84** 56 33N 53 2 E
Agua Caliente, Mexico **164** 26 30N 108 20W
Agua Caliente, U.S.A. **163** 32 29N 116 59W
Agua Caliente Springs **163** 32 56N 116 19W
Agua Clara **175** 20 25 S 52 45W
Agua Prieta **164** 31 20N 109 32W
Aguadas **174** 5 40N 75 38W
Aguadilla **147** 18 27N 67 10W
Aguadulce **166** 8 15N 80 32W
Aguanaval, R. **164** 23 45N 103 10W
Aguanga **163** 33 27N 116 51W
Aguanus, R. **151** 50 13N 62 5W
Aguapei, R. **171** 21 0 S 51 0W
Aguapey, R. **172** 29 7 S 56 36W
Aguaray Guazú, R. **172** 24 47 S 57 19W
Aguarico, R. **174** 0 0 77 30W
Aguas Blancas **172** 24 15 S 69 55W
Aguas Calientes, Sierra de **172** 25 26 S 67 27W
Águas Formosas **171** 17 5 S 40 57W
Aguas, R. **58** 41 20N 0 30W
Aguascalientes **164** 22 0N 102 12W
Aguascalientes □ **164** 22 0N 102 20W
Agudo **57** 38 59N 4 52W
Agueda **56** 40 34N 8 27W
Agueda, R. **56** 40 45N 6 37W
Aguelt el Kadra **118** 25 3N 7 6W
Agueni N'Ikko **118** 32 29N 5 47W
Aguié **121** 13 31N 7 46 E
Aguilafuente **56** 41 13N 4 7W
Aguilar **57** 37 31N 4 40W
Aguilar de Campóo **56** 42 47N 4 15W
Aguilares **172** 27 26 S 65 35W
Aguilas **59** 37 23N 1 35W
Aguja, C. de la **174** 11 18N 74 12W
Aguja, Pta. **174** 6 0 S 81 0W
Agulaa **123** 13 40N 39 40 E
Agulhas, Kaap **128** 34 52 S 20 0 E
Agung **102** 8 20 S 115 28 E
Agur, Israel **90** 31 42N 34 55 E
Agur, Uganda **126** 2 28N 32 55 E
Agůš **70** 46 28N 26 15 E
Agusan, R. **103** 9 20N 125 50 E
Agvali **83** 42 36N 46 8 E
Aha Mts. **128** 19 45 S 21 0 E
Ahaggar **119** 23 0N 6 30 E
Ahamansu **121** 7 38N 0 35 E
Ahar **92** 38 35N 47 0 E
Ahascragh **38** 53 24N 8 20W
Ahaura **143** 42 20 S 171 32 E
Ahaura, R. **143** 42 21 S 171 34 E
Ahaus **48** 52 4N 7 1 E
Ahelledjem **119** 26 37N 6 58 E
Ahimanawa Ra. **130** 39 5 S 176 30 E
Ahipara B. **142** 35 5 S 173 5 E
Ahiri **96** 19 30N 80 0 E
Ahlen **48** 51 45N 7 52 E
Ahmad Wal **94** 29 18N 65 58 E
Ahmadabad (Ahmedabad) **94** 23 0N 72 40 E
Ahmadnagar (Ahmednagar) **96** 19 7N 74 46 E
Ahmadpur **94** 29 12N 71 10 E
Ahmar Mts. **123** 9 20N 41 15 E
Ahoada **121** 5 8N 6 36 E
Ahoghill **38** 54 52N 6 23W
Ahome **164** 25 55N 109 11W
Ahr, R. **48** 50 25N 6 52 E
Ahrensbök **48** 54 0N 10 34 E
Ahrweiler **48** 50 31N 7 3 E
Ahsā, Wahatāal **92** 25 50N 49 0 E
Ahuachapán **166** 13 54N 89 52W
Ahuriri, R. **143** 44 31 S 170 12 E
Åhus **73** 55 56N 14 18 E
Ahvāz **92** 31 20N 48 40 E
Ahvenanmaa **75** 60 15N 20 0 E
Ahzar **121** 15 30N 3 20 E
Aibaq **93** 36 15N 68 5 E
Aichach **49** 48 28N 11 9 E
Aichi-ken □ **111** 35 0N 137 15 E
Aidone **65** 37 26N 14 26 E
Aiello Cálabro **65** 39 6N 16 12 E
Aigle **50** 46 18N 6 58 E
Aignay-le-Duc **43** 47 40N 4 43 E
Aigre **44** 45 54N 0 1 E
Aigua **173** 34 13 S 54 46W
Aigueperse **44** 46 3N 3 13 E
Aigues-Mortes **45** 43 35N 4 12 E
Aiguilles **45** 44 47N 6 51 E
Aiguillon **44** 44 18N 0 21 E
Aiguillon, L' **44** 46 20N 1 16W
Aigurande **44** 46 27N 1 49 E
Aihui **105** 50 16N 127 28 E
Aija **174** 9 50 S 77 45W
Aijal **98** 23 40N 92 44 E
Aiken **157** 33 34N 81 50W
Ailao Shan **108** 24 0N 101 30 E
Aillant-sur-Tholon **43** 47 52N 3 20 E
Aillik **151** 55 11N 59 18W
Ailly-sur-Noye **43** 49 45N 2 20 E
Ailsa Craig, I. **34** 55 15N 5 7W
Aim **77** 59 0N 133 55 E
Aimere **103** 8 45 S 121 3 E
Aimogasta **172** 28 33 S 66 50W
Aimorés **171** 19 30 S 41 4W
Aimorés, Serra dos **171** 17 50 S 40 30W
Ain □ **45** 46 5N 5 20 E
Ain Banaiyah **93** 23 0N 51 0 E
Aïn-Beïda **119** 35 50N 7 35 E
Ain ben Khellil **118** 33 15N 0 49W
Ain Ben Tili **118** 25 59N 9 27W
Aïn Benian **118** 36 48N 2 55 E
'Ain Dalla **122** 27 20N 27 23 E
Ain Dar **92** 25 55N 49 10 E
Ain el Mafki **122** 27 30N 28 15 E
Ain Girba **122** 29 20N 25 14 E
Aïn M'lila **119** 36 2N 6 35 E
Ain Qeiqab **122** 29 42N 24 55 E
Ain, R. **45** 45 52N 5 11 E
Aïn Rich **118** 34 38N 24 55 E
Aïn-Sefra **118** 32 47N 0 37W
Ain Sheikh Murzûk **122** 26 47N 27 45 E
Ain Sukhna **122** 29 32N 32 20 E
Aïn Tédelès **118** 36 0N 0 21 E
Aïn-Témouchent **118** 35 16N 1 8W
Aïn Touta **119** 35 26N 5 54 E
Aïn Zeitûn **122** 29 10N 25 48 E
Aïn Zorah **118** 34 37N 3 32W
Ainabo **91** 9 0N 46 25 E
Ainazi **80** 57 50N 24 24 E
Aine Galakka **117** 18 10N 18 30 E
Ainos Óros **69** 38 10N 20 35 E
Ainsdale **32** 53 37N 3 2W
Ainsworth **158** 42 33N 99 52W
Aioi **110** 34 48N 134 28 E
Aion **77** 69 50N 169 0 E
Aipe **174** 3 13N 75 15W
Aïr **121** 18 30N 8 0 E
Airaines **43** 49 58N 1 55 E
Aird Brenish, C. **36** 58 8N 7 8W
Aird, The, dist. **37** 57 26N 4 30W
Airdrie **35** 55 53N 3 57W
Aire **43** 50 37N 2 22 E
Aire, Isla del **58** 39 48N 4 16 E
Aire, R. **43** 49 18N 5 0 E
Aire-sur-l'Adour **44** 43 42N 0 15W
Aireys Inlet **140** 38 29 S 144 5 E
Airolo **51** 46 32N 8 37 E
Airvault **42** 46 50N 0 8W
Aisgill **32** 54 23N 2 21W
Aishihik **147** 61 40N 137 46W
Aisne □ **43** 49 42N 3 40 E
Aisne, R. **43** 49 26N 2 50 E
Aït Melloul **118** 30 25N 9 29W
Aitana, Sierra de **59** 38 35N 0 24W
Aitape **135** 3 11 S 142 22 E
Aith **37** 59 8N 2 38W
Aitkin **158** 46 32N 93 43W
Aitolia Kai Akarnania □ **69** 38 45N 21 18 E
Aitolikón **69** 38 26N 21 21 E
Aitoska Planina **67** 42 45N 27 30 E
Aiuaba **170** 6 38 S 40 7W
Aiud **70** 46 19N 23 44 E
Aix-en-Provence **45** 43 32N 5 27 E
Aix-la-Chapelle = Aachen **48** 50 47N 6 4 E
Aix-les-Bains **45** 45 41N 5 53 E
Aix-les-Thermes **44** 42 43N 1 51 E
Aix-sur-Vienne **44** 45 48N 1 8 E
Aiyang, Mt. **135** 5 10 S 141 20 E
Aiyangpienmen **107** 40 55N 124 30 E
Aiyansh **152** 55 17N 129 2W
Aiyina **69** 37 45N 23 26 E
Aiyínion **68** 40 28N 22 28 E
Aiyion **69** 38 15N 22 5 E
Aizenay **42** 46 44N 1 38W
Aizpute **80** 56 43N 21 40 E
Aizuwakamatsu **112** 37 30N 139 56 E
Ajaccio **45** 41 55N 8 40 E
Ajaccio, G. d' **45** 41 52N 8 40 E
Ajalpán **165** 18 22N 97 15W
Ajana **137** 27 56 S 114 35 E
Ajanta Ra. **96** 20 28N 75 50 E
Ajax, Mt. **143** 42 35 S 172 5 E
Ajdabiyah **119** 30 54N 20 4 E
Ajdīr, Raïs **119** 33 4N 11 44 E
Ajdovščina **63** 45 54N 13 54 E
Ajibar **123** 10 35N 38 36 E
'Ajlun **90** 32 18N 35 47 E
Ajman **93** 25 25N 55 30 E
Ajmer **94** 26 28N 74 37 E
Ajo **161** 32 18N 112 54W
Ajoie **50** 47 22N 7 0 E
Ajok **123** 9 15N 28 28 E
Ajua **120** 4 50N 1 55W
Ak Dağ **92** 36 30N 30 0 E
Akaba **121** 8 10N 1 2 E
Akabli **118** 26 49N 1 31 E
Akaishi-Dake **111** 35 27N 138 9 E
Akaishi-Sammyaku **111** 35 25N 138 10 E
Akaki Beseka **123** 8 55N 38 45 E
Akala **123** 15 39N 36 13 E
Akaroa **143** 43 49 S 172 59 E
Akaroa Harb. **131** 43 54 S 172 59 E
Akasha **122** 21 10N 30 32 E
Akashi **110** 34 45N 135 0 E
Akbou **119** 36 31N 4 31 E
Akbulak **84** 51 1N 55 37 E
Akdala **85** 45 2N 74 35 E
Akechi **111** 35 18N 137 23 E
Akegbe **121** 6 17N 7 28 E
Akelamo **103** 1 35N 129 40 E
Akershus Fylke □ **71** 60 10N 11 15 E
Akeru, R. **96** 17 25N 80 0 E
Aketi **124** 2 38N 23 47 E
Akhaïa □ **69** 38 5N 21 45 E
Akhalkalaki **83** 41 27N 43 25 E
Akhaltsikhe **83** 41 40N 43 0 E
Akharnaí **69** 38 5N 23 44 E
Akhelóös, R. **69** 38 5N 21 25 E
Akhendriá **69** 34 58N 25 16 E
Akhéron, R. **68** 39 31N 20 29 E
Akhisar **92** 38 56N 27 48 E
Akhladhókambos **69** 37 31N 22 35 E
Akhmîm **122** 26 31N 31 47 E
Akhnur **95** 32 52N 74 45 E
Akhtopol **67** 42 6N 27 56 E
Akhtubinsk (Petropavlovskiy) **83** 48 27N 46 7 E
Akhty **83** 41 30N 47 45 E
Akhtyrka **80** 50 25N 35 0 E
Aki **110** 33 30N 133 54 E
Aki-Nada **110** 34 5N 132 40 E
Akiak **147** 60 50N 161 12W
Akimiski I. **150** 52 50N 81 30W
Akimovka **82** 46 44N 35 0 E
Akincilar **69** 37 57N 27 25 E
Akinum **138** 6 15 S 149 30 E
Åkirkeby **73** 55 4N 14 55 E
Akita **112** 39 45N 140 0 E
Akita-ken □ **112** 39 40N 140 30 E
Akjoujt **120** 19 45N 14 15W
Akka **118** 29 28N 8 9W
'Akko **90** 32 35N 35 4 E
Akkol, Kazakh, U.S.S.R. **85** 45 0N 75 39 E
Akkol, Kazakh, U.S.S.R. **85** 43 36N 70 45 E
Akköy **69** 37 30N 27 18 E
Akkrum **46** 53 3N 5 50 E
Aklampa **121** 8 15N 2 10 E
Aklavik, Can. **147** 68 12N 135 0W
Aklavik, N.W.T., Can. **147** 68 12N 135 0W
Akmuz **85** 41 15N 76 10 E
Aknoul **118** 34 40N 3 55W
Akō **110** 34 45N 134 24 E
Ako **121** 10 19N 10 48 E
Akobo, R. **123** 7 10N 34 25 E
Akola **96** 20 42N 77 2 E
Akonolinga **121** 3 50N 12 18 E
Akordat **123** 15 30N 37 40 E
Akosombo Dam **121** 6 20N 0 5 E
Ak'osu **105** 41 15N 80 14 E
Akot, India **96** 21 10N 77 10 E
Akot, Sudan **123** 6 31N 30 9 E
Akpatok I. **149** 60 25N 68 8W
Akranes **74** 64 19N 22 6W
Åkrehamn **71** 59 15N 5 10 E
Akreïjit **120** 18 19N 9 11W
Akrítas Venétiko, Ákra **69** 36 43N 21 54 E
Akron, Colo., U.S.A. **158** 40 13N 103 15W
Akron, Ohio, U.S.A. **156** 41 7N 81 31W
Akrotiri, Ákra **68** 40 26N 25 27W
Aksai Chih, L. **95** 35 15N 79 55 E
Aksaray **92** 38 25N 34 2 E
Aksarka **76** 66 31N 67 50 E
Aksehir **92** 38 18N 31 30 E
Aksenovo Zilovskoye **77** 53 20N 117 40 E
Aksuat, Ozero **84** 51 32N 64 34 E
Aksum **123** 14 5N 38 40 E
Aktash, R.S.F.S.R., U.S.S.R. **84** 52 2N 52 7 E
Aktash, Uzbek S.S.R., U.S.S.R. **85** 39 55N 65 55 E
Aktobe **84** 52 55N 62 22 E
Aktogay **85** 44 25N 76 44 E
Aktyubinsk **79** 50 17N 57 10 E
Aktyuz **85** 42 54N 76 7 E
Aku **121** 6 40N 7 18 E
Akulurak **147** 62 40N 164 35W
Akun I. **147** 54 15N 165 30W
Akune **110** 32 1N 130 12 E
Akure **121** 7 15N 5 5 E
Akureyri **74** 65 40N 18 6W
Akusha **83** 42 18N 47 30 E
Akutan I. **147** 53 30N 166 0W
Akzhar **85** 43 8N 71 37 E
Al Abyār **119** 32 9N 20 29 E
Al Amadiyah **92** 37 5N 43 30 E
Al Amārah **92** 31 55N 47 15 E
Al Aqabah **92** 29 37N 35 0 E
Al Ashkhara **93** 21 50N 59 30 E
Al Ayn al Mugshin **91** 19 35N 54 40 E
Al 'Azīzīyah **119** 32 30N 13 1 E
Al Badi **92** 22 0N 46 35 E
Al Barah **90** 31 55N 35 12 E
Al Barkāt **119** 24 56N 10 14 E
Al Basrah **92** 30 30N 47 50 E
Al Baydā **117** 32 30N 21 40 E
Al Bu'ayrāt **119** 31 24N 15 44 E
Al Buqay'ah **90** 32 15N 35 30 E
Al Dīwaniyah **92** 32 0N 45 0 E
Al Fallujah **92** 33 20N 43 55 E
Al Fāw **92** 30 0N 48 30 E
Al Hadithan **92** 34 0N 41 13 E
Al Hamad **92** 31 30N 39 30 E
Al Hamar **92** 22 23N 46 6 E
Al Hariq **92** 23 29N 46 27 E
Al Hasakah **92** 36 35N 40 45 E
Al Hauta **91** 16 5N 48 20 E
Al Havy **92** 32 5N 46 5 E
Al Hillah, Iraq **92** 32 30N 44 25 E
Al Hillah, Si Arab. **92** 23 35N 46 50 E
Al Hilwah **92** 23 24N 46 48 E
Al Hindiya **92** 32 30N 44 10 E
Al Hoceïma **118** 35 8N 3 58W
Al Hufrah, Awbārī, Libya **119** 25 32N 14 1 E
Al Hufrah, Misrātah, Libya **119** 29 5N 18 3 E
Al Hufuf **92** 25 25N 49 45 E
Al Husayyāt **119** 30 24N 20 37 E
Al Husn **90** 32 29N 35 52 E
Al Irq **117** 29 5N 21 35 E
Al Ittihad = Madinat al Shaab **91** 12 50N 45 0 E
Al Jahrah **92** 29 25N 47 40 E
Al Jalāmid **92** 31 20N 39 45 E
Al Jarzirah **117** 26 10N 21 20 E
Al Jawf **117** 24 10N 23 24 E
Al Jazir **91** 18 30N 56 31 E
Al Jubail **92** 27 0N 49 50 E
Al Juwara **91** 19 0N 57 13 E
Al Khābūrah **93** 23 57N 57 5 E
Al Khalih **90** 31 32N 35 6 E
Al Khums (Homs) **119** 32 40N 14 17 E
Al Kut **92** 32 30N 46 0 E
Al Kuwayt **92** 29 20N 48 0 E
Al Ladhiqiyah **92** 35 30N 35 45 E
Al Lith **122** 20 9N 40 15 E
Al Madīnah **92** 24 35N 39 52 E
Al-Mafraq **90** 32 17N 36 14 E
Al Majma'ah **92** 25 57N 45 22 E
Al Manamah **93** 26 10N 50 30 E
Al Marj **117** 32 25N 20 30 E
Al Masīrah **91** 20 25N 58 50 E
Al Mawsil **92** 36 15N 43 5 E
Al Miqdadīyah **92** 34 0N 45 0 E
Al Mubarraz **92** 25 30N 49 40 E
Al Muharraq **93** 26 15N 50 40 E
Al Mukha **91** 13 18N 43 15 E
Al Musayyib **92** 32 40N 44 25 E
Al Muwaylih **92** 27 40N 35 30 E
Al Qaddāhīyah **119** 31 15N 15 9 E
Al Qamishli **92** 37 10N 41 10 E
Al Qaryah ash Sharqīyah **119** 30 28N 13 40 E
Al Qaşabāt **119** 32 39N 14 1 E
Al Qatif **92** 26 35N 50 0 E
Al Qatrun **119** 24 56N 15 3 E
Al Quaisūmah **92** 28 10N 46 20 E
Al Quds **90** 31 47N 35 10 E
Al Qunfidha **122** 19 3N 41 4 E
Al Quraiyat **93** 23 17N 58 53 E
Al Qurnah **92** 31 1N 47 25 E
Al 'Ula **92** 26 35N 38 0 E
Al Uqaylah **119** 30 12N 19 10 E
Al Uqayr **92** 25 40N 50 15 E
Al' Uwayqilah **92** 30 30N 42 10 E
Al 'Uyūn **92** 26 30N 43 50 E
Al Wajh **122** 26 10N 36 30 E
Al Wakrah **93** 25 10N 51 40 E

Al Warīah 92 27 50N 47 30 E
Al Wātīyah 119 32 28N 11 57 E
Ala, Italy 62 45 46N 11 0 E
Ala, Sweden 72 61 13N 17 9 E
Ala Shan 105 40 0N 104 0 E
Alabama □ 157 31 0N 87 0W
Alabama, R. 157 31 30N 87 35W
Alaçati 69 38 16N 26 23 E
Alaejos 56 41 18N 5 13W
Alagna Valsésia 62 45 51N 7 56 E
Alagôa Grande 170 7 3 S 35 35W
Alagôas □ 170 9 0 S 36 0W
Alagoinhas 171 12 0 S 38 20W
Alagón 58 41 46N 1 12W
Alagón, R. 56 39 50N 6 50W
Alajuela 166 10 2N 84 8W
Alakamisy 129 21 19 S 47 14 E
Alakurtti 78 67 0N 30 30 E
Alam Ajaib 122 25 55N 27 14 E
Alameda, Spain 57 37 12N 4 39W
Alameda, Calif., U.S.A. 163 37 46N 122 15W
Alameda, N. Mex., U.S.A. 161 35 10N 106 43W
Alameda, S.D., U.S.A. 160 43 2N 112 30W
Alamitos, Sierra de los 164 26 30N 102 20W
Alamo 161 37 21N 115 10W
Alamogordo 161 32 59N 106 0W
Alamos 164 27 0N 109 0W
Alamosa 161 37 30N 106 0W
Åland 75 60 15N 20 0 E
Aland 96 17 36N 76 35 E
Alandroal 57 38 41N 7 24W
Ålands hav 75 60 10N 19 30 E
Alange, Presa de 57 38 45N 6 18W
Alangouassou 120 7 30N 4 34W
Alanis 57 38 3N 5 43W
Alanya 92 36 38N 32 0 E
Alaotra, L. 129 17 30 S 48 30 E
Alapayevsk 84 57 52N 61 42 E
Alar del Rey 56 42 38N 4 20W
Alaraz 56 40 45N 5 17W
Alaşehir 79 38 23N 28 30 E
Alashantsoch'i 106 38 59N 105 45 E
Alaska □ 147 65 0N 150 0W
Alaska, G. of 147 58 0N 145 0W
Alaska Highway 152 60 0N 130 0W
Alaska Pen. 147 56 0N 160 0W
Alaska Range 147 62 50N 151 0W
Alássio 62 44 1N 8 10 E
Alatri 64 41 44N 13 21 E
Alatyr 81 54 45N 46 35 E
Alatyr, R. 81 54 45N 45 30 E
Alausí 174 2 0 S 78 50W
Álava □ 58 42 48N 2 28W
Alava, C. 160 48 10N 124 40W
Alaverdi 83 41 2N 44 37 E
Alawoona 140 34 45 S 140 30 E
Alaykel 85 40 15N 74 25 E
Alayor 58 39 57N 4 8 E
Alayskiy Khrebet 85 39 45N 72 0 E
Alazan, R. 83 41 25N 46 35 E
Alba 62 44 41N 8 1 E
Alba □ 70 46 10N 23 30 E
Alba de Tormes 56 40 50N 5 30W
Alba-Iulia 70 46 8N 23 39 E
Albac 70 46 28N 23 1 E
Albacete 59 39 0N 1 50W
Albacete □ 59 38 50N 2 0W
Albacutya, L. 140 35 45 S 141 58 E
Ålbæk 73 57 36N 10 25 E
Ålbæk Bugt 73 57 35N 10 40 E
Albaida 59 38 51N 0 31W
Albalate de las Nogueras 58 40 22N 2 18W
Albalate del Arzobispo 58 41 6N 0 31W
Albania ■ 68 41 0N 20 0 E
Albano Laziale 64 41 44N 12 40 E
Albany, Austral. 137 35 1 S 117 58 E
Albany, Ga., U.S.A. 157 31 40N 84 10W
Albany, Minn., U.S.A. 158 45 37N 94 38W
Albany, N.Y., U.S.A. 162 42 29N 73 47W
Albany, Oreg., U.S.A. 160 44 41N 123 0W
Albany, Tex., U.S.A. 159 32 45N 99 20W
Albany, R. 150 52 17N 81 31W
Albardón 172 31 20 S 68 30W
Albarracín 58 40 25N 1 26W
Albarracín, Sierra de 58 40 30N 1 30W
Albatross B. 138 12 45 S 141 30 E
Albatross Pt. 142 38 7 S 174 44 E
Albegna, R. 63 42 40N 11 28 E
Albemarle 157 35 27N 80 15W
Albemarle Sd. 157 36 0N 76 30W
Albenga 62 44 3N 8 12 E
Alberche, R. 56 40 10N 4 30W
Alberdi 172 26 14 S 58 20W
Alberes, Mts. 58 42 28N 2 56W
Alberga 139 27 12 S 135 28 E
Alberga, R. 136 26 50 S 133 40 E
Alberique 59 39 7N 0 31W
Alberni 152 49 20N 124 50W
Albersdorf 48 54 8N 9 19 E
Albert, Austral. 141 32 22 S 147 30 E
Albert, Can. 151 45 51N 64 38W
Albert, France 43 50 0N 2 38 E
Albert Canyon 152 51 8N 117 41W
Albert Edward, Mt. 135 8 20 S 147 24 E
Albert Edward Ra. 136 18 17 S 127 57 E
Albert L., Austral. 140 35 30 S 139 10 E
Albert L., U.S.A. 160 42 40N 120 8W
Albert Lea 158 43 32N 93 20W
Albert, L. = Mobutu Sese Seko, L. 126 1 30N 31 0 E
Albert Nile, R. 126 3 16N 31 38 E
Albert Town 167 22 37N 74 33 E
Alberta □ 152 54 40N 115 0W
Alberti 172 35 1 S 60 16W
Albertinia 128 34 11 S 21 34 E
Albertirsa 53 47 14N 19 37 E
Albertkanaal 47 51 14N 4 26 E
Alberton 151 46 50N 64 0W
Albertville 45 45 40N 6 22 E
Albertville = Kalemie 126 5 55 S 29 9 E
Albi 44 43 56N 2 9 E
Albia 158 41 0N 92 50W
Albina 175 5 37N 54 15W
Albina, Pta. 128 15 52 S 11 44 E
Albino 62 45 47N 9 48 E
Albion, Idaho, U.S.A. 160 42 21N 113 37W
Albion, Mich., U.S.A. 156 42 15N 84 45W
Albion, Nebr., U.S.A. 158 41 47N 98 0W
Alblasserdam 46 51 52N 4 40 E
Albocácer 58 40 21N 0 1 E
Alböke 73 56 57N 16 47 E
Alborán, I. 57 35 57N 3 0W
Alborea 59 39 17N 1 24W
Ålborg 73 57 2N 9 54 E
Ålborg Bugt 73 56 50N 10 35 E
Alborz, Reshteh-Ye Kūkhā-Ye 93 36 0N 52 0 E
Albox 59 37 23N 2 8W
Albreda 152 52 35N 119 10W
Albrighton 28 52 38N 2 17W
Albuera, La 57 38 45N 6 49W
Albufeira 57 37 5N 8 15W
Albula, R. 51 46 38N 9 30 E
Albuñol 59 36 48N 3 11W
Albuquerque 161 35 5N 106 47W
Albuquerque, Cayos de 166 12 10N 81 50W
Alburno, Mte. 65 40 32N 15 20 E
Alburquerque 57 39 15N 6 59W
Albury 141 36 3 S 146 56 E
Albuskjell, oilfield 19 56 40N 3 0 E
Alby 72 62 30N 15 28 E
Alcácer do Sal 57 38 22N 8 33W
Alcalá de Chisvert 58 40 19N 0 13 E
Alcalá de Guadaira 57 37 20N 5 50W
Alcalá de Henares 58 40 28N 3 22W
Alcalá de los Gazules 57 36 29N 5 43W
Alcalá la Real 57 37 27N 3 57W
Alcamo 64 37 59N 12 55 E
Alcanadre 58 42 24N 2 7W
Alcanadre, R. 58 41 43N 0 12W
Alcanar 58 40 33N 0 28 E
Alcanede 57 39 25N 8 49W
Alcanena 57 39 27N 8 40W
Alcañices 57 41 41N 6 21W
Alcañiz 58 41 2N 0 8W
Alcântara 170 2 20 S 44 30W
Alcántara 57 39 41N 6 57W
Alcantara L. 153 60 57N 108 9W
Alcantarilla 59 37 59N 1 12W
Alcaracejos 57 38 24N 4 58W
Alcaraz 59 38 40N 2 29W
Alcaraz, Sierra de 59 38 40N 2 20W
AlcáRovas 57 38 23N 8 9W
Alcarria, La 58 40 31N 2 45W
Alcaudete 57 37 35N 4 5W
Alcázar de San Juan 59 39 24N 3 12W
Alcester 28 52 13N 1 52W
Alcira 59 39 9N 0 30W
Alcoa 157 35 50N 84 0W
Alcobaça, Brazil 171 17 30 S 39 13W
Alcobaça, Port. 57 39 32N 9 0W
Alcobendas 58 40 32N 3 38W
Alcolea del Pinar 58 41 2N 2 28W
Alcora 58 40 5N 0 14W
Alcoutim 57 37 25N 7 28W
Alcova 160 42 37N 106 52W
Alcoy 59 38 43N 0 30W
Alcubierre, Sierra de 58 41 45N 0 22W
Alcublas 58 39 48N 0 43W
Alcudia 58 39 51N 3 9 E
Alcudia, Bahía de 58 39 45N 3 14 E
Alcudia, Sierra de la 57 38 34N 4 30W
Aldabra Is. 11 9 22 S 46 28 E
Aldama 165 22 25N 98 4W
Aldan 77 58 40N 125 30 E
Aldan, R. 77 62 30N 135 10 E
Aldborough 33 54 6N 1 21W
Aldbourne 28 51 28N 1 38W
Aldbrough 33 53 50N 0 7W
Aldeburgh 29 52 9N 1 35 E
Aldeia Nova 57 37 55N 7 24W
Alden I. 71 61 19N 4 45 E
Alder 160 45 27N 112 3W
Alder Pk. 163 35 53N 12 22W
Alderbury 28 51 4N 1 45W
Alderley Edge 32 53 18N 2 15W
Aldermaston 28 51 23N 1 9W
Alderney, I. 42 49 42N 2 12W
Aldershot 29 51 15N 0 43W
Aldersyde 152 50 40N 113 53W
Aldingham 32 54 8N 3 3W
Aledo 158 41 10N 90 50W
Alefa 123 11 55N 36 55 E
Aleg 120 17 3N 13 55W
Alegre 173 20 50 S 41 30W
Alegrete 173 29 40 S 56 0W
Aleisk 76 52 40N 83 0 E
Alejandro Selkirk, I. 131 33 50 S 80 15W
Aleksandriya, U.S.S.R. 79 50 45N 26 22 E
Aleksandriya, U.S.S.R. 82 48 42N 33 3 E
Aleksandriyskaya 83 43 59N 47 0 E
Aleksandrov 81 56 23N 38 44 E
Aleksandrov Gay. 81 50 15N 48 35 E
Aleksandrovac 66 44 28N 21 13 E
Aleksandrovka 82 48 55N 32 20 E
Aleksandrovo 67 43 14N 24 51 E
Aleksandrovsk 84 59 9N 57 33 E
Aleksandrovsk-Sakhaliniskiy 77 50 50N 142 20 E
Aleksandrovskiy Zavod 77 50 40N 117 50 E
Aleksandrovskoye 76 60 35N 77 50 E
Aleksandrów Kujawski 54 52 53N 18 43 E
Aleksandrów Łódzki 54 51 49N 19 17 E
Alekseyevka, R.S.F.S.R., U.S.S.R. 81 50 43N 38 40 E
Alekseyevka, R.S.F.S.R., U.S.S.R. 84 52 35N 51 17 E
Aleksin 81 54 31N 37 9 E
Aleksinac 66 43 31N 21 42 E
Além Paraíba 173 21 52 S 42 41W
Alemania, Argent. 172 25 40 S 65 30W
Alemania, Chile 172 25 10 S 69 55W
Ålen 71 62 51N 11 17 E
Alençon 42 48 27N 0 4 E
Alentejo, Alto- 55 39 0N 7 40W
Alentejo, Baixo- 55 38 0N 8 30W
Alenuihaha Chan. 147 20 25N 156 0W
Aleppo 92 36 10N 37 15 E
Aléria 45 42 5N 9 26 E
Alert B. 152 50 30N 127 35W
Alès 45 44 9N 4 5 E
Aleşd 70 47 3N 22 22 E
Alessándria 62 44 54N 8 37 E
Ålestrup 73 56 42N 9 29 E
Ålesund 71 62 28N 6 12 E
Alet 123 8 14N 29 2 E
Alet-les-Bains 44 43 0N 2 14 E
Aletschgletscher 50 46 28N 8 2 E
Aletschhorn 50 46 28N 8 0 E
Aleutian Is. 147 52 0N 175 0W
Aleutian Ra. 147 55 0N 155 0W
Alexander 158 47 51N 103 40W
Alexander Arch. 147 57 0N 135 0W
Alexander B. 128 28 36 S 16 33 E
Alexander City 157 32 58N 85 57W
Alexander I. 13 69 0 S 70 0W
Alexander, Mt. 137 28 58 S 120 16 E
Alexandra, Austral. 141 37 8 S 145 40 E
Alexandra, N.Z. 143 45 14 S 169 25 E
Alexandra Falls 152 60 29N 116 18W
Alexandria, Austral. 138 19 5 S 136 40 E
Alexandria, Brazil 171 6 25 S 38 1W
Alexandria, B.C., Can. 152 52 35N 122 27W
Alexandria, Ont., Can. 150 45 19N 74 38W
Alexandria, Rumania 70 43 57N 25 24 E
Alexandria, S. Afr. 128 33 38 S 26 28 E
Alexandria, U.K. 34 55 59N 4 40W
Alexandria, Ind., U.S.A. 156 40 18N 85 40W
Alexandria, La., U.S.A. 159 31 20N 92 30W
Alexandria, Minn., U.S.A. 158 45 50N 95 20W
Alexandria, S.D., U.S.A. 158 43 40N 97 45W
Alexandria, Va., U.S.A. 162 38 47N 77 1W
Alexandria = El Iskandarîya 122 31 0N 30 0 E
Alexandria Bay 156 44 20N 75 52W
Alexandrina, L. 140 35 25 S 139 10 E
Alexandroúpolis 68 40 50N 25 54 E
Alexis Creek 152 52 0N 123 20W
Alexis, R. 151 52 33N 56 8W
Alfambra 58 40 33N 1 5W
Alfândega da Fé 56 41 20N 6 59W
Alfaro 58 42 10N 1 50W
Alfatar 67 43 59N 27 13 E
Alfeld 48 52 0N 9 49 E
Alfenas 173 21 40 S 44 0W
Alfiós, R. 69 37 36N 21 54 E
Alfonsine 63 44 30N 12 1 E
Alford, Grampian, U.K. 37 57 13N 2 42W
Alford, Lincs., U.K. 33 53 16N 0 10 E
Alfred 162 43 28N 70 40W
Alfred Town 141 35 8 S 147 30 E
Alfredton 142 40 41 S 175 54 E
Alfreton 33 53 6N 1 22W
Alfriston 29 50 48N 0 10 E
Alfta 72 61 21N 16 4 E
Alftanes 74 64 29N 22 10W
Alga 84 49 53N 57 20 E
Algaba, La 57 37 27N 6 1W
Algar 57 36 40N 5 39W
Ålgård 71 58 46N 5 53 E
Ålgård 71 58 46N 5 53 E
Algarinejo 57 37 19N 4 9W
Algarve 57 37 15N 8 10W
Algeciras 57 36 9N 5 28W
Algemesí 59 39 11N 0 27W
Alger 118 36 42N 3 8 E
Algeria ■ 118 35 10N 3 11 E
Alghero 64 40 34N 8 20 E
Algiers = Alger 118 36 42N 3 8 E
Algoabaai 128 33 50 S 25 45 E
Algodonales 57 36 54N 5 24W
Algodor, R. 56 39 51N 3 48W
Algoma, Mich., U.S.A. 156 44 35N 87 27W
Algoma, Oreg., U.S.A. 160 42 25N 121 54W
Algonquin Prov. Pk. 150 45 50N 78 30W
Alhama de Almeria 59 36 57N 2 34W
Alhama de Aragón 58 41 18N 1 54W
Alhama de Granada 57 37 0N 3 59W
Alhama de Murcia 59 37 51N 1 25W
Alhambra, Spain 59 38 54N 3 4W
Alhambra, U.S.A. 163 34 8N 118 10W
Alhaurín el Grande 57 36 39N 4 41W
Alhucemas = Al-Hoceïma 118 35 8N 3 58W
Ali al Gharbi 92 32 30N 46 45 E
Ali Bayramly 83 39 43N 48 52 E
Ali Khel 94 33 56N 69 35 E
Ali Sabieh 123 11 10N 42 44 E
Ália 64 37 47N 13 42 E
Aliabad 93 28 10N 57 35 E
Aliaga 58 40 40N 0 42W
Aliakmon, R. 68 40 10N 22 0 E
Alibag 96 18 38N 72 56 E
Alibo 123 9 52N 37 5 E
Alibunar 66 45 5N 20 57 E
Alicante 59 38 23N 0 30W
Alicante □ 59 38 30N 0 37W
Alice, S. Afr. 128 32 48 S 26 55 E
Alice, U.S.A. 159 27 47N 98 1W
Alice Arm 152 55 29N 129 31W
Alice Downs 136 17 45 S 127 56 E
Alice, Punta dell' 65 39 23N 17 10 E
Alice, R., Queens., Austral. 138 15 35 S 142 20 E
Alice, R., Queens., Austral. 138 24 2 S 144 50 E
Alice Springs 138 23 40 S 135 50 E
Alicedale 128 33 15 S 26 4 E
Aliceville 157 33 9N 88 10W
Alick Cr. 138 20 35 S 142 10 E
Alicudi, I. 65 38 33N 14 20 E
Alida 153 49 25N 101 55W
Aligarh, India 93 27 55N 78 10 E
Aligarh, Raj., India 94 25 55N 76 15 E
Aligarh, Ut. P., India 94 27 55N 78 10 E
Aligudarz 92 33 25N 49 45 E
Alijó 56 41 16N 7 27W
Alimena 65 37 42N 14 4 E
Alimnia 69 36 16N 27 43 E
Aling Kangri 99 31 45N 84 45 E
Alingaabro 73 56 56N 10 32 E
Alingsås 73 57 56N 12 31 E
Alipore 95 22 32N 88 24 E
Alipur 94 29 25N 70 55 E
Alipur Duar 98 26 30N 89 35 E
Aliquippa 156 40 38N 80 18W
Aliste, R. 56 41 48N 6 14W
Alivérion 69 38 24N 24 2 E
Aliwal North 128 30 45 S 26 45 E
Alix 152 52 24N 113 11W
Aljezur 57 37 18N 8 49W
Aljustrel 57 37 55N 8 10W
Alkamari 121 13 27N 11 10 E
Alken 47 50 53N 5 18 E
Alkhalaf 91 20 30N 58 13 E
Alkmaar 46 52 37N 4 45 E
All American Canal 161 32 45N 115 0W
Allada 121 6 41N 2 9 E
Allah Dad 94 25 38N 67 34 E
Allahabad 95 25 25N 81 58 E
Allakaket 147 66 30N 152 45W
Allakh Yun 77 60 50N 137 5 E
Allal Razi 118 34 30N 6 39W
Allan 153 51 53N 106 4W
Allanche 44 45 14N 2 57 E
Allanmyo 98 19 16N 95 17 E
Allanridge 128 27 45 S 26 40 E
Allansford 140 38 26 S 142 39 E
Allanton 143 45 55 S 170 15 E
Allanwater 150 50 14N 90 10W
Allaqi, Wadi 122 22 15N 34 55 E
Allard Lake 151 50 40N 63 10W
Allariz 56 42 11N 7 50W
Allassac 44 45 15N 1 29 E
Alle 47 49 51N 4 58 E
Allegan 156 42 32N 85 52W
Allegheny Mts. 156 38 0N 80 0W
Allegheny, R. 156 41 14N 79 50W
Allègre 44 45 12N 3 41 E
Allen, Bog of 39 53 15N 7 0W
Allen, L. 38 54 30N 8 5W
Allen R. 35 54 53N 2 13W
Allenby (Hussein) Bridge 90 31 53N 35 33 E
Allendale 35 54 55N 2 15W
Allende 164 28 20N 100 50W
Allenheads 35 54 49N 2 12W
Allentown 162 40 36N 75 30W
Allentsteig 52 48 41N 15 20 E
Allenwood 39 53 16N 6 53W
Alleppey 97 9 30N 76 28 E
Alleröd 73 55 54N 12 19 E
Alleur 47 50 39N 5 31 E
Allevard 45 45 24N 6 5 E
Alliance, Nebr., U.S.A. 158 42 10N 102 50W
Alliance, Ohio, U.S.A. 156 40 53N 81 7W
Allier □ 44 46 25N 3 0 E
Allier, R. 43 46 57N 3 4 E
Alligator Cr., Queens., Austral. 138 21 20 S 149 12 E
Alligator Cr., Queens., Austral. 138 19 23 S 146 58 E
Allihies 39 51 39N 10 4W
Allingåbrl 73 56 28N 10 20 E
Allingåbro 73 56 28N 10 20 E
Allinge 73 55 17N 14 50 E
Alliston 150 44 9N 79 52W
Alloa 35 56 7N 3 49W
Allonby 32 54 45N 3 27W
Allos 45 44 15N 6 38 E
Alma, Can. 151 48 35N 71 40W
Alma, Kans., U.S.A. 158 39 1N 96 22W
Alma, Mich., U.S.A. 156 43 25N 84 40W
Alma, Nebr., U.S.A. 158 40 10N 99 25W
Alma, Wis., U.S.A. 158 44 19N 91 54W
Alma Ata 85 43 15N 76 57 E
Almada 57 38 40N 9 9W
Almaden 138 17 22 S 144 40 E

Almadén **57** 38 49N 4 52W
Almagro **57** 38 50N 3 45W
Almalyk **85** 40 50N 69 35 E
Almanor, L. **160** 40 15N 121 11W
Almansa **59** 38 51N 1 5W
Almanza **56** 42 39N 5 3W
Almanzor, Pico de **56** 40 15N 5 18W
Almanzora, R. **59** 37 22N 2 21W
Almarcha, La **58** 39 41N 2 24W
Almas **171** 11 33 S 47 9W
Almaş, Mţii **70** 44 49N 22 12 E
Almazán **58** 41 30N 2 30W
Almazora **58** 39 57N 0 3W
Almeirim, Brazil **175** 1 30 S 52 0W
Almeirim, Port. **57** 39 12N 8 37W
Almelo **46** 52 22N 6 42 E
Almenar **58** 41 43N 2 12W
Almenara, Brazil **171** 16 11 S 40 42W
Almenara, Spain **58** 39 46N 0 14W
Almenara, Sierra de **59** 37 34N 1 32W
Almendralejo **57** 38 41N 6 26W
Almería **59** 36 52N 2 32W
Almería □ **59** 37 20N 2 20W
Almería, G. de **59** 36 41N 2 28W
Almetyevsk **84** 54 53N 52 20 E
Almhult **73** 56 32N 14 10 E
Almirante **166** 9 10N 82 30W
Almiropótamos **69** 38 16N 24 11 E
Almirós **69** 39 11N 22 45 E
Almodôvar **57** 37 31N 8 2W
Almodóvar del Campo **57** 38 43N 4 10W
Almogia **57** 36 50N 4 32W
Almonaster la Real **57** 37 52N 6 48W
Almond R. **35** 56 27N 3 27W
Almondsbury **28** 51 33N 2 34W
Almonte, R. **57** 39 41N 6 12W
Almora **95** 29 38N 79 4 E
Almoradi **59** 38 7N 0 46W
Almorox **56** 40 14N 4 24W
Almoustarat **121** 17 35N 0 8 E
Älmult **73** 56 33N 14 8 E
Almuñécar **57** 36 43N 3 41W
Almunia, La de Doña Godina **58** 41 29N 1 23W
Almvik **73** 57 49N 16 30 E
Aln, R. **35** 55 24N 1 35W
Alness **37** 57 41N 4 15W
Alness R. **37** 57 45N 4 20W
Alnif **118** 31 10N 5 8W
Alnmouth **35** 55 24N 1 37W
Alnön I. **72** 62 26N 17 33 E
Alnwick **35** 55 25N 1 42W
Aloi **126** 2 16N 33 10 E
Alon **98** 22 12N 95 5 E
Alonsa **153** 50 50N 99 0W
Alor, I. **103** 8 15 S 124 30 E
Alor Setar **101** 6 7N 100 22 E
Alora **57** 36 49N 4 46W
Alosno **57** 37 33N 7 7W
Alot'ai **105** 47 52N 88 7 E
Alotau **135** 10 16 S 150 30 E
Alougoum **118** 30 17N 6 56W
Aloysius Mt. **137** 26 0 S 128 38 E
Alpaugh **163** 35 53N 119 29W
Alpedrinha **56** 40 6N 7 27W
Alpena **156** 45 6N 83 24W
Alpercatas, R. **170** 6 2 S 44 19W
Alpes-de-Haute-Provence □ **45** 44 8N 6 10 E
Alpes-Maritimes □ **45** 43 55N 7 10 E
Alpes Valaisannes **50** 46 4N 7 30 E
Alpha **138** 23 39 S 146 37 E
Alphen **47** 51 29N 4 58 E
Alphen aan den Rijn **46** 52 7N 4 40 E
Alphington **30** 50 41N 3 32W
Alpi Apuan **62** 44 7N 10 14 E
Alpi Craie **43** 45 40N 7 0 E
Alpi Lepontine **51** 46 22N 8 27 E
Alpi Orobie **62** 46 7N 10 0 E
Alpi Retiche **51** 46 45N 10 0 E
Alpiarça **57** 39 15N 8 35W
Alpine, Ariz., U.S.A. **161** 33 57N 109 4W
Alpine, Calif., U.S.A. **163** 32 50N 116 46W
Alpine, Tex., U.S.A. **159** 30 35N 103 35W
Alpnach **51** 46 57N 8 17 E
Alrewas **28** 52 43N 1 44W
Alrø **73** 55 52N 10 5 E
Alroy Downs **138** 19 20 S 136 5 E
Als **73** 56 46N 10 18 E
Alsace **43** 48 15N 7 25 E
Alsager **32** 53 7N 2 20W
Alsask **153** 51 21N 109 59W
Alsásua **58** 42 54N 2 10W
Alseda **73** 57 27N 15 20 E
Alsen **72** 63 23N 13 56 E
Alsfeld **48** 50 44N 9 19 E
Alsh, L. **36** 57 15N 5 39W
Alsónémedi **53** 47 34N 19 15 E
Alsten **74** 65 58N 12 40 E
Alston **32** 54 48N 2 26W
Alta **74** 69 57N 23 10 E
Alta Gracia **172** 31 40 S 64 30W
Alta Lake **152** 50 10N 123 0W
Alta, Sierra **58** 40 31N 1 30W
Alta Sierra **163** 35 42N 118 33W
Altaelva **74** 69 46N 23 45 E
Altafjorden **74** 70 5N 23 5 E
Altagracia **174** 10 45N 71 30W
Altai = Aerht'ai Shan **105** 48 0N 90 0 E
Altamaha, R. **157** 31 50N 82 0W
Altamira, Brazil **175** 3 0 S 52 10W
Altamira, Chile **172** 25 47 S 69 51W
Altamira, Colomb. **174** 2 3N 75 47W
Altamira, Mexico **165** 22 24N 97 55W
Altamira, Cuevas de **56** 43 20N 4 5W
Altamont **162** 42 43N 74 3W
Altamura **65** 40 50N 16 33 E
Altanbulag **54** 50 19N 106 30 E
Altar **164** 30 40N 111 50W
Altarnun **30** 50 35N 4 30W
Altata **164** 24 30N 108 0W
Altavista **156** 37 9N 79 22W
Altdorf **51** 46 52N 8 36 E
Altea **59** 38 38N 0 2W
Altenberg **48** 50 46N 13 47 E
Altenbruch **48** 53 48N 8 44 E
Altenburg **48** 50 59N 12 28 E
Altenkirchen **48** 50 41N 7 38 E
Altenmarkt **52** 47 43N 14 39 E
Alter do Chão **57** 39 12N 7 40W
Altkirch **43** 47 37N 7 15 E
Altnaharra **37** 58 17N 4 27W
Alto Adige = Trentino-Alto Adige **62** 46 5N 11 0 E
Alto Araguaia **175** 17 15 S 53 20W
Alto Chindio **127** 16 19 S 35 25 E
Alto Cuchumatanes **164** 15 30N 91 10W
Alto del Inca **172** 24 10 S 68 10W
Alto Ligonha **127** 15 30 S 38 11 E
Alto Molocue **127** 15 50 S 37 35 E
Alto Paraná □ **173** 25 0 S 54 50W
Alto Parnaíba **170** 9 6 S 45 57W
Alto Santo **170** 5 31 S 38 15W
Alto Turi **170** 2 54 S 45 38W
Alto Uruguay, R. **173** 27 0 S 53 30W
Alton, U.K. **29** 51 8N 0 59W
Alton, Ill., U.S.A. **158** 38 55N 90 5W
Alton, N.H., U.S.A. **162** 43 27N 71 13W
Alton Downs **139** 26 7 S 138 57 E
Altona **48** 53 32N 9 56 E
Altoona **156** 40 32N 78 24W
Altopáscio **62** 43 50N 10 40 E
Altos **170** 5 3 S 42 28W
Altrincham **32** 53 25N 2 21W
Altstätten **51** 47 22N 9 33 E
Alturas **160** 41 36N 120 37W
Altus **159** 34 30N 99 25W
Alucra **83** 40 22N 38 47 E
Aluksône **80** 57 24N 27 3 E
Alula **91** 11 50N 50 45 E
Alupka **82** 44 23N 34 2 E
Alushta **82** 44 40N 34 25 E
Alusi **103** 7 35 S 131 40 E
Alustante **58** 40 36N 1 40W
Alva, U.K. **35** 56 9N 3 49W
Alva, U.S.A. **159** 36 50N 98 50W
Alvaiázere **56** 39 49N 8 23W
Alvangen **73** 58 0N 12 7 E
Älvängen **73** 57 58N 12 8 E
Alvarado, Mexico **165** 18 40N 95 50W
Alvarado, U.S.A. **159** 32 25N 97 15W
Alvaro Obregón, Presa **164** 27 55N 109 52W
Alvastra **73** 58 20N 14 44 E
Alvdal **71** 62 6N 10 37 E
Alvear **172** 29 5 S 56 30W
Alvechurch **28** 52 22N 1 58W
Alverca **57** 38 56N 9 1W
Alveringen **47** 51 1N 2 43 E
Alvesta **73** 56 54N 14 35 E
Älvho **72** 61 30N 14 45 E
Alvie, Austral. **140** 38 14 S 143 30 E
Alvie, U.K. **37** 57 10N 3 50W
Alvin **159** 29 23N 95 12W
Alvito **57** 38 15N 8 0W
Älvkarleby **75** 60 32N 17 40 E
Alvra, Pic d' **51** 46 35N 9 50 E
Älvros **72** 62 3N 14 38 E
Älvsborgs län □ **73** 58 30N 12 30 E
Älvsby **74** 65 42N 20 52 E
Älvsbyn **74** 65 40N 20 0 E
Alvsered **73** 57 14N 12 51 E
Alwar **94** 27 38N 76 34 E
Alwaye **97** 10 8N 76 24 E
Alwinton **35** 55 20N 2 7W
Alwyn, oilfield **19** 60 30N 1 45 E
Alyangula **133** 13 55 S 136 30 E
Alyaskitovyy **77** 64 45N 141 30 E
Alyata **83** 39 58N 49 25 E
Alyth **37** 56 38N 3 15W
Alzada **158** 45 3N 104 22W
Alzano Lombardo **62** 45 44N 9 43 E
Alzette, R. **47** 49 45N 6 6 E
Alzey **49** 49 48N 8 4 E
Am-Dam **117** 12 40N 20 35 E
Am Djeress **117** 16 15N 22 50 E
Am Guereda **117** 12 53N 21 14 E
Am Timan **117** 11 0N 20 10 E
Am-Zoer **124** 14 13N 21 23 E
Amadeus, L. **137** 24 54 S 131 0 E
Amadi, Congo **126** 3 40N 26 40 E
Amadi, Sudan **123** 5 29N 30 25 E
Amadi, Zaïre **126** 3 40N 26 40 E
Amadia **92** 37 6N 43 30 E
Amadjuak **149** 64 0N 72 39W
Amadjuak L. **149** 65 0N 71 8W
Amadora **57** 38 45N 9 13W
Amaga **174** 6 3N 75 42W
Amagansett **162** 40 58N 72 8W
Amagasaki **111** 34 42N 135 20 E
Amager **73** 55 37N 12 35 E
Amagi **110** 33 25N 130 39 E
Amagunze **121** 6 20N 7 40 E
Amaimon **135** 5 12 S 145 30 E
Amakusa-Nada **110** 32 35N 130 5 E
Amakusa-Shotō **110** 32 15N 130 10 E
Amål **72** 59 2N 12 40 E
Åmål **72** 59 3N 12 42 E
Amalapuram **96** 16 35N 81 55 E
Amalfi, Colomb. **174** 6 55N 75 4W
Amalfi, Italy **65** 40 39N 14 34 E
Amaliás **69** 37 47N 21 22 E
Amalner **96** 21 5N 75 5 E
Amambaí **173** 23 5 S 55 13W
Amambaí, R. **173** 23 22 S 53 56W
Amambay □ **173** 23 0 S 56 0W
Amambay, Cordillera de **173** 20 30 S 56 0W
Amami-O-Shima **112** 28 0N 129 0 E
Amanab **135** 3 40 S 141 14 E
Amandola **63** 42 59N 13 21 E
Amanfrom **121** 7 20N 0 25 E
Amangeldy **76** 50 10N 65 10 E
Amantea **65** 39 8N 16 3 E
Amapá **170** 2 5N 50 50W
Amapá □ **170** 1 40N 52 0W
Amar Gedid **123** 14 27N 25 13 E
Amara, Iraq **92** 31 57N 47 12 E
Amara, Sudan **123** 10 25N 34 10 E
Amarante, Brazil **170** 6 14 S 42 50W
Amarante, Port. **56** 41 16N 8 5W
Amarante do Maranhão **170** 5 36 S 46 45W
Amaranth **153** 50 36N 98 43W
Amarapura **98** 21 54N 96 3 E
Amaravati, R. **97** 10 50N 77 42 E
Amaravati = Amraoti **96** 20 55N 77 45 E
Amareleja **57** 38 12N 7 13W
Amargosa **171** 13 2 S 39 36W
Amargosa, R. **163** 36 14N 116 51W
Amargosa Ra., mts **163** 36 25N 116 40W
Amarillo **159** 35 14N 101 46W
Amaro Leite **171** 13 58 S 49 9W
Amaro, Mt. **63** 42 5N 14 6 E
Amarpur, India **99** 23 30N 91 45 E
Amarpur, Bihar, India **95** 25 5N 87 0 E
Amarpur, Tripura, India **99** 23 30N 91 45 E
Amasra **92** 41 45N 32 30 E
Amassama **121** 5 1N 6 2 E
Amasya **92** 40 40N 35 50 E
Amatignak I. **147** 51 19N 179 10W
Amatikulu **129** 29 3 S 31 33 E
Amatitlán **166** 14 29N 90 38W
Amatrice **63** 42 38N 13 16 E
Amay **47** 50 33N 5 19 E
Amazon, R. **175** 2 0 S 53 30W
Amazonas □, Brazil **174** 4 20 S 64 0W
Amazonas □, Colomb. **174** 1 0 S 72 0W
Amazonas □, Venez. **174** 3 30N 66 0W
Amazonas, R. **175** 2 0 S 53 30W
Ambad **96** 19 38N 75 50 E
Ambahakily **129** 21 36 S 43 41 E
Ambala **94** 30 23N 76 56 E
Ambalangoda **97** 6 15N 80 5 E
Ambalapuzha **97** 9 25N 76 25 E
Ambalavao **129** 21 50 S 46 56 E
Ambalindum **138** 23 23 S 134 40 E
Ambam **124** 2 20N 11 15 E
Ambanifilao **129** 12 48 S 49 47 E
Ambanja **129** 13 40 S 48 27 E
Ambararata **129** 13 41 S 48 27 E
Ambarchik **77** 69 40N 162 20 E
Ambarijeby **129** 14 56 S 47 41 E
Ambarnath **96** 19 12N 73 22 E
Ambaro, B. d' **129** 13 23 S 48 38 E
Ambasamudram **97** 8 43N 77 25 E
Ambato **174** 1 5 S 78 42W
Ambato-Boéni **129** 16 28 S 46 43 E
Ambato, Sierra de **172** 28 25N 66 10W
Ambatolampy **129** 19 20 S 47 35 E
Ambatondrazaka **129** 17 55 S 48 28 E
Ambatosoratra **129** 17 37 S 48 31 E
Ambenja **129** 15 17 S 46 58 E
Ambeno **103** 9 20 S 124 30 E
Amberg **49** 49 25N 11 52 E
Ambergris Cay **165** 18 0N 88 0W
Ambérieu-en-Bugey **45** 45 57N 5 20 E
Amberley **143** 43 9 S 172 44 E
Ambert **44** 45 33N 3 44 E
Ambevongo **129** 15 25 S 42 26 E
Ambia **129** 16 11 S 45 33 E
Ambidédi **120** 14 35N 11 47W
Ambikapur **95** 23 15N 83 15 E
Ambikol **122** 21 20N 30 50 E
Ambilobé **125** 13 10 S 49 3 E
Ambinanindrano **129** 20 5 S 48 23 E
Ambjörnarp **73** 57 25N 13 17 E
Amble **35** 55 20N 1 36W
Ambler **162** 40 9N 75 13W
Ambleside **32** 54 26N 2 58W
Amblève **47** 50 21N 6 10 E
Amblève, R. **47** 50 25N 5 45 E
Ambo, Begemdir & Simen, Ethiopia **123** 12 20N 37 30 E
Ambo, Shewa, Ethiopia **123** 9 0N 37 48 E
Ambo, Peru **174** 10 5 S 76 10W
Ambodifototra **129** 16 59 S 49 52 E
Ambodilazana **129** 18 6 S 49 10 E
Ambohimahasoa **129** 21 7 S 47 13 E
Ambohimanga du Sud **129** 20 52 S 47 36 E
Ambon **103** 3 35 S 128 20 E
Ambongao, Cones d' **129** 17 0 S 45 0 E
Amboseli L. **126** 2 40 S 37 10 E
Ambositra **129** 20 31 S 47 25 E
Amboy **163** 34 33N 115 51W
Ambre, C. d' **129** 12 40 S 49 10 E
Ambre, Mt. d' **125** 12 30 S 49 10 E
Ambriz **124** 7 48 S 13 8 E
Ambrizete **124** 7 10 S 12 52 E
Ambunti **135** 4 13 S 142 52 E
Ambut **97** 12 48N 78 43 E
Amby **139** 26 30 S 148 11 E
Amchitka I. **147** 51 30N 179 0W
Amchitka P. **147** 51 30N 179 0W
Amderma **76** 69 45N 61 30 E
Ameca **164** 20 30N 104 0W
Ameca, R. **164** 20 40N 105 15W
Amecameca **165** 19 10N 98 57W
Ameland **46** 53 27N 5 45 E
Amélia **63** 42 34N 12 25 E
Amèlie-les-Bains-Palalda **44** 42 29N 2 41 E
Amen **77** 68 45N 180 0 E
Amendolaro **65** 39 58N 16 34 E
Amenia **162** 41 51N 73 33W
America **47** 51 27N 5 59 E
American Falls **160** 42 46N 112 56W
American Falls Res. **160** 43 0N 112 50W
American Highland **13** 73 0 S 75 0 E
Americana **173** 22 45 S 47 20W
Americus **157** 32 0N 84 10W
Amersfoort, Neth. **46** 52 9N 5 23 E
Amersfoort, S. Afr. **129** 26 59 S 29 53 E
Amersham **29** 51 40N 0 38W
Amery, Austral. **137** 31 9 S 117 5 E
Amery, Can. **153** 56 34N 94 3W
Ames **158** 42 0N 93 40W
Amesbury, U.K. **28** 51 10N 1 46W
Amesbury, U.S.A. **162** 42 50N 70 52W
Amesdale **153** 50 2N 92 55W
Ameson **150** 49 50N 84 35W
Amethyst, gasfield **19** 53 38N 0 40 E
Amfiklia **69** 38 38N 22 35 E
Amfilokhía **69** 38 52N 21 9 E
Amfipolis **68** 40 48N 23 52 E
Ámfissa **69** 38 32N 22 22 E
Amga, R. **77** 61 0N 132 0 E
Amgu **77** 45 45N 137 15 E
Amherst, Burma **99** 16 2N 97 20 E
Amherst, Can. **151** 45 48N 64 8W
Amherst, Mass., U.S.A. **162** 42 21N 72 30W
Amherst, Tex., U.S.A. **159** 34 0N 102 24W
Amherst, Mt. **136** 18 11 S 126 59 E
Amherstburg **150** 42 6N 83 6W
Amiata Mte. **63** 42 54N 11 40 E
Amiens **43** 49 54N 2 16 E
Amigdhalokefáli **69** 35 23N 23 30 E
Amili **98** 28 25N 95 52 E
Amindaion **68** 40 42N 21 42 E
Amirante Is. **11** 6 0 S 53 0 E
Amisk L. **153** 54 35N 102 15W
Amistati, Presa **164** 29 24N 101 0W
Amite **159** 30 47N 90 31W
Åmli **71** 58 45N 8 32 E
Amlia I. **147** 52 5N 173 30W
Amlwch **31** 53 24N 4 21W
Amm Adam **123** 16 20N 36 1 E
'Ammān **90** 32 0N 35 52 E
Ammanford **31** 51 48N 4 0W
Ammerån **72** 63 9N 16 13 E
Ammerån **72** 63 9N 16 13 E
Ammersee **49** 48 0N 11 7 E
Ammerzoden **46** 51 49N 5 13 E
Ammi'ad **90** 32 55N 35 32 E
Amnat Charoen **100** 15 51N 104 38 E
Amne Machin **105** 34 30N 100 0 E
Amnéville **43** 49 16N 6 9 E
Amo Chiang, R. **108** 22 56N 101 47 E
Amorebieta **58** 43 13N 2 44W
Amorgós **69** 36 50N 25 57 E
Amory **57** 33 59N 88 30W
Amos **150** 48 35N 78 5W
Åmot **71** 59 54N 9 54 E
Åmot **71** 59 34N 8 0 E
Åmotsdal **71** 59 37N 8 26 E
Amour, Djebel **118** 33 42N 1 37 E
Amoy = Hsiamen **109** 24 25N 118 4 E
Amozoc **165** 19 2N 98 3W
Ampang **101** 3 8N 101 45 E
Ampanihy **129** 24 40 S 44 45 E
Amparihy Est. **129** 23 57 S 47 20 E
Ampasindava, B. d' **129** 13 40 S 48 15 E
Ampasindava, Presqu'île d' **129** 13 42 S 47 55W
Amper **121** 9 25N 9 40 E
Ampère **119** 35 44N 5 27 E
Ampleforth **33** 54 13N 1 8W
Ampombiantambo **129** 12 42 S 48 57 E
Amposta **58** 40 43N 0 34 E
Ampotaka **129** 25 3 S 44 41 E
Ampoza **129** 22 20 S 44 44 E
Ampthill **29** 52 3N 0 30W
Amqa **90** 32 59N 35 10 E
Amqui **151** 48 28N 67 27W
Amraoti **96** 20 55N 77 45 E
Amreli **94** 21 35N 71 17 E
Amrenene el Kasba **118** 22 10N 0 30 E
Amriswil **51** 47 33N 9 18 E
Amritsar **94** 31 35N 74 57 E
Amroha **95** 28 53N 78 30 E
Amrum **48** 54 37N 8 21 E
Amsel **119** 22 47N 5 29 E
Amsterdam, Neth. **46** 52 23N 4 54 E
Amsterdam, U.S.A. **162** 42 58N 74 10W
Amsterdam, I. **11** 37 30 S 77 30 E
Amstetten **52** 48 7N 14 51 E
Amu Darya, R. **76** 37 50N 65 0 E
Amuay **174** 11 50N 70 10W
Amukta I. **147** 52 29N 171 20W
Amund Ringnes I. **12** 78 20N 96 25W
Amundsen Gulf **148** 71 0N 124 0W
Amundsen Sea **13** 72 10 S 115 0W
Amungen **72** 61 10N 15 40 E

Amuntai 102 2 28S 115 25E
Amur, R. 77 53 30N 122 30E
Amurang 103 1 5N 124 40E
Amuri Pass 143 42 31S 172 11E
Amurrio 58 43 3N 3 0W
Amurzet 77 47 50N 131 5E
Amusco 56 42 10N 4 28W
Amvrakikós Kólpos 69 39 0N 20 55E
Amvrosiyvka 83 47 43N 38 30E
Amzeglouf 118 26 50N 0 1E
An 98 22 29N 96 54E
An Bien 101 9 45N 105 0E
An Geata Mór, (Binghamstown) 38 54 13N 10 0W
An Hoa 100 15 30N 108 20E
An Loc 101 11 40N 106 50E
An Nafud 92 28 15N 41 0E
An Najaf 92 32 3N 44 15E
An-Nâqûrah 90 33 7N 35 8E
An Nasiriyah 92 31 0N 46 15E
An Nawfaliyah 119 30 54N 17 58E
An Nhon (Binh Dinh) 100 13 55N 109 7E
An Nîl □ 123 17 30N 33 0E
An Nîl el Abyad □ 123 14 0N 32 15E
An Nu'ayriyah 92 27 30N 48 30E
An Teallach, Mt. 36 57 49N 5 18W
An Thoi, Dao 101 9 58N 104 0E
An Tuc 100 13 57N 108 39E
An Uaimh 38 53 39N 6 40W
Ana-Sira 71 58 17N 6 25E
Anabta 90 32 19N 35 7E
Anabuki 110 34 2N 134 11E
Anaco 174 9 27N 64 28W
Anaconda 160 46 7N 113 0W
Anacortes 160 48 30N 122 40W
Anadarko 159 35 4N 98 15W
Anadia, Brazil 170 9 42S 36 18W
Anadia, Port. 56 40 26N 8 27W
Anadolu 92 38 0N 29 0E
Anadyr 77 64 35N 177 20E
Anadyr, R. 77 66 50N 171 0E
Anadyrskiy Zaliv 77 64 0N 180 0E
Anáfi 69 36 22N 25 48E
Anafópoulo 69 36 17N 25 50E
Anagni 64 41 44N 13 8E
Anah 92 34 25N 42 0E
Anaheim 163 33 50N 118 0W
Anahim Lake 152 52 28N 125 18W
Anáhuac 164 27 14N 100 9W
Anai Mudi, Mt. 97 10 12N 77 20E
Anaimalai Hills 97 10 20N 76 40E
Anajás 170 0 59S 49 57W
Anajatuba 170 3 16S 44 37W
Anakapalle 96 17 42N 83 06E
Anakie 138 23 32S 147 45E
Anaklia 83 42 22N 41 35E
Analalava 129 14 35S 48 0E
Analapasy 129 25 11S 46 40E
Anam 121 6 19N 6 41E
Anambar, R. 94 30 10N 68 50E
Anambas, Kepulauan 102 3 20N 106 30E
Anamoose 158 47 55N 100 7W
Anamosa 158 42 7N 91 17W
Anamur 92 36 8N 32 58E
Anan 110 33 54N 134 40E
Anand 94 22 32N 72 59E
Anandpur 96 21 16N 86 13E
Anánes 69 36 33N 24 9E
Anantapur 97 14 39N 77 42E
Anantnag 95 33 45N 75 10E
Ananyev 82 47 44N 29 57E
Anapa 82 44 55N 37 25E
Anápolis 171 16 15S 48 50W
Anar 93 30 55N 55 13E
Anarak 93 33 25N 53 40E
Anatolia = Anadolu 92 38 0N 29 0E
Anatone 160 46 9N 117 4W
Añatuya 172 28 20S 62 50W
Anaunethad L. 153 60 55N 104 25W
Anaye 117 19 15N 12 50E
Anbyŏn 107 39 1N 127 35E
Ancaster 33 52 59N 0 32W
Ancenis 42 47 21N 1 10W
Anch'i 109 25 3N 118 13E
Anch'ing 109 30 37N 117 0E
Anch'iu 107 36 25N 119 10E
Ancholme, R. 33 53 42N 0 32W
Anchorage 147 61 10N 149 50W
Ancião 56 39 56N 8 27W
Ancohuma, Nevada 174 16 0S 68 50W
Ancon 164 8 57N 79 33W
Ancón 174 11 50S 77 10W
Ancona 63 43 37N 13 30E
Ancrum 35 55 31N 2 35W
Ancud 176 42 0S 73 50W
Ancud, G. de 176 42 0S 73 0W
Andacollo, Argent. 172 37 10S 70 42W
Andacollo, Chile 172 30 15S 71 10W
Andado 138 25 25S 135 15E
Andalgalá 172 27 40S 66 30W
Åndalsnes 71 62 35N 7 43E
Andalucía 57 37 35N 5 0W
Andalusia 157 31 51N 86 30W
Andalusia = Andalucía 57 37 35N 5 0W
Andaman Is. 101 12 30N 92 30E
Andaman Sea 101 13 0N 96 0E
Andaman Str. 101 12 15N 92 20E
Andara 128 18 2S 21 9E
Andarai 171 12 48S 41 20W
Andeer 51 46 36N 9 26E
Andelfingen 51 47 36N 8 41E
Andelot 43 46 51N 5 56E
Andelys, Les 42 49 15N 1 25E
Andenne 47 50 30N 5 5E
Andéranboukane 121 15 26N 3 2E
Anderlecht 47 50 50N 4 19E
Anderlues 47 50 25N 4 16E
Andermatt 51 46 38N 8 35E
Andernach 48 50 24N 7 25E
Andernos 44 44 44N 1 6W
Anderslöv 73 55 26N 13 19E
Anderson, Austral. 141 38 32S 145 27E
Anderson, Calif., U.S.A. 160 40 30N 122 19W
Anderson, Ind., U.S.A. 156 40 5N 85 40W
Anderson, Mo., U.S.A. 159 36 43N 94 29W
Anderson, S.C., U.S.A. 157 34 32N 82 40W
Anderson, Mt. 129 25 5S 30 42E
Anderson, R. 147 69 42N 129 0W
Anderstorp 73 57 19N 13 39E
Andes 162 42 12N 74 47W
Andes, mts. 174 20 0S 68 0W
Andfjorden 74 69 10N 16 20E
Andhra, L. 96 18 30N 73 32E
Andhra Pradesh □ 97 15 0N 80 0E
Andikíthira 69 35 52N 23 15E
Andímilos 69 36 47N 24 12E
Andíparos 69 37 0N 25 3E
Andípaxoi 69 39 9N 20 13E
Andípsara 69 38 30N 25 29E
Andizhan 76 41 10N 72 0E
Andkhui 93 36 52N 65 8E
Andoharano 129 22 58S 43 45E
Andol 96 17 51N 78 4E
Andong 107 36 40N 128 43E
Andorra ■ 58 42 30N 1 30E
Andorra La Vella 58 42 31N 1 32E
Andover, U.K. 28 51 13N 1 29W
Andover, U.S.A. 162 40 59N 74 44W
Andradina 171 20 54S 51 23W
Andrahary, Mt. 129 13 37S 49 17E
Andraitx 58 39 35N 2 25E
Andramasina 129 19 11S 47 35E
Andrano-Velona 129 18 10S 46 52E
Andranopasy 129 21 17S 43 44E
Andreanof Is. 147 51 0N 178 0W
Andreapol 80 56 40N 32 17E
Andreas 32 54 23N 4 25W
Andrespol 54 51 45N 19 34E
Andrew, oilfield 19 58 4N 1 24E
Andrews, S.C., U.S.A. 157 33 29N 79 30W
Andrews, Tex., U.S.A. 159 32 18N 102 33W
Andreyevka 84 52 19N 51 55E
Ándria 65 41 13N 16 17E
Andrian 65 46 30N 11 13E
Andriba 129 17 30S 46 58E
Andrijevica 66 42 45N 19 48E
Andrítsaina 69 37 29N 21 52E
Androka 129 24 58S 44 2E
Ándros 69 37 50N 24 50E
Andros I. 166 24 30N 78 0W
Andros Town 166 24 43N 77 47W
Andrychów 54 49 51N 19 18E
Andújar 57 38 3N 4 5W
Aneby 73 57 48N 14 49E
Anécho 121 6 12N 1 34E
Anegada I. 147 18 45N 64 20W
Anergane 118 31 4N 7 14W
Aneto, Pico de 58 42 37N 0 40E
Anfeg 119 22 29N 5 58E
Anfu 109 27 23N 114 37E
Ang Thong 100 14 35N 100 31E
Anga 77 60 35N 132 0E
Angamos, Punta 172 23 1S 70 32W
Anganch'i 98 47 9N 123 48E
Angara, R. 77 58 30N 97 0E
Angarsk 77 52 30N 104 0E
Angas Downs 137 24 49S 132 14E
Angas Ra. 137 23 0S 127 50E
Angaston 140 34 30S 139 8E
Ånge 72 62 31N 15 35E
Ångebo 72 61 58N 16 22E
Angel de la Guarda, I. 164 29 30N 113 30W
Ängelholm 73 56 15N 12 58E
Angellala 139 26 24S 146 54E
Angels Camp 163 38 8N 120 30W
Ängelsberg 72 59 58N 16 0E
Angenong 99 31 57N 94 10E
Anger, R. 123 9 30N 36 35E
Angereb 123 13 11N 37 7E
Angereb, R. 123 14 0N 36 0E
Ångermanälven 72 62 40N 18 0E
Angermünde 48 53 1N 14 0E
Angers 42 47 30N 0 35W
Angerville 43 48 19N 2 0E
Ångesån 74 66 50N 22 15E
Anghiari 63 43 32N 12 3E
Angical 171 12 0S 44 42W
Angical do Piauí 171 6 5S 42 44W
Angikuni L. 153 62 0N 100 0W
Angkor 100 13 22N 103 50E
Angle 31 51 40N 5 3W
Anglem Mt. 143 46 45S 167 53E
Anglés 58 41 57N 2 38E
Anglesey (□) 26 53 17N 4 20W
Anglesey, I. 31 53 17N 4 20W
Anglet 44 43 29N 1 31W
Angleton 159 29 12N 95 23W
Angleur 47 50 36N 5 35E
Anglure 43 48 35N 3 50E
Angmagssalik 12 65 40N 37 20W
Angmering 29 50 48N 0 28W
Ango 126 4 10N 26 5E
Angoche 127 16 8S 40 0E
Angoche, I. 127 16 20S 39 50E
Angol 172 37 56S 72 45W
Angola 156 41 40N 85 0W
Angola ■ 125 12 0S 18 0E
Angoon 147 57 40N 134 40W
Angoram 135 4 4S 144 4E
Angoulême 44 45 39N 0 10E
Angoumois 44 45 30N 0 25E
Angra dos Reis 173 23 0S 44 10W
Angra-Juntas 128 27 39S 15 31E
Angran 76 80 59N 69 3E
Angren 85 41 1N 70 12E
Angtassom 101 11 1N 104 41E
Angu 126 3 25N 24 28E
Anguilla ■ 167 18 14N 63 5W
Angurugu 138 14 0S 136 25E
Angus (□) 26 56 45N 2 55W
Angus, Braes of 37 56 51N 3 0W
Anhanduí, R. 173 21 46S 52 9W
Anhée 47 50 18N 4 53E
Anholt 73 56 42N 11 33E
Anhsi 105 40 30N 96 0E
Anhsiang 109 29 24N 112 9E
Anhua, Hunan, China 109 28 22N 111 10E
Anhua, Kwangsi-Chuang, China 108 25 10N 108 21E
Anhwei □ 109 33 15N 116 50E
Ani, Kiangsi, China 109 28 50N 115 32E
Ani, Shansi, China 106 35 3N 111 2E
Aniak 147 61 58N 159 50W
Anicuns 171 16 28S 49 58W
Ánidhros 69 36 38N 25 43E
Anié 121 7 42N 1 8E
Animas 161 31 58N 108 58W
Ånimskog 73 58 53N 12 35E
Anin 101 15 36N 97 50E
Anivorano 129 18 44S 48 58E
Anjangaon 96 21 10N 77 20E
Anjar 94 23 6N 70 10E
Anjen 109 26 42N 113 19E
Anjiabé 129 12 7S 49 20E
Anjidiv I. 97 14 40N 74 10E
Anjō 111 34 57N 137 5E
Anjou 42 47 20N 0 15W
Anjozorobe 129 18 22S 47 52E
Anju 107 39 36N 125 40E
Anka 121 12 13N 5 58E
Ank'ang 108 32 38N 109 5E
Ankara 92 40 0N 32 54E
Ankaramena 129 21 57S 46 39E
Ankazoabo 129 22 18S 44 31E
Ankazobé 129 18 20S 47 10E
Ankazotokana 129 21 20S 48 9E
Ankisabé 129 19 17S 46 29E
Anklesvar 96 21 38N 73 3E
Ankober 123 9 35N 39 40E
Ankoro 126 6 45S 26 55E
Ankuang 107 45 19N 123 40E
Ankuo 106 38 25N 115 19E
Anlu 109 31 12N 113 38E
Anlung 108 25 6N 106 31E
Anmyŏn Do 107 36 25N 126 25E
Ånn 72 63 19N 12 34E
Ann Arbor 156 42 17N 83 45W
Ann C., Antarct. 13 66 30S 50 30E
Ann C., U.S.A. 162 42 39N 70 37W
Ann, gasfield 19 53 40N 2 5E
Ånn L. 72 63 15N 12 35E
Anna, U.S.A. 159 37 28N 89 10W
Anna, U.S.S.R. 81 51 38N 40 23E
Anna Branch, R. 139 34 2S 141 50E
Anna Plains 136 19 17S 121 37E
Annaba 119 36 50N 7 46E
Annaberg-Buchholz 48 50 34N 12 58E
Annagassan 38 53 53N 6 20W
Annagh Hd. 38 54 15N 10 5W
Annaka 111 36 19N 138 54E
Annalee, R. 38 54 3N 7 15W
Annalong 38 54 7N 5 55W
Annam = Trung-Phan 101 16 30N 107 30E
Annamitique, Chaîne 100 17 0N 106 0E
Annan 35 55 0N 3 17W
Annan, R. 35 54 58N 3 18W
Annanberg 135 4 52S 144 42E
Annandale 35 55 10N 3 25W
Annapolis 162 39 0N 76 30W
Annapolis Royal 151 44 44N 65 32W
Annapurna 95 28 34N 83 50E
Annascaul 39 52 10N 10 3W
Anne, oilfield 19 55 24N 5 7E
Annean, L. 137 26 54S 118 14E
Anneberg 73 57 32N 12 6E
Annecy 45 45 55N 6 8E
Annecy, L. d' 45 45 52N 6 10E
Annemasse 45 46 12N 6 16E
Annestown 39 52 8N 7 18W
Annette 147 55 2N 131 35W
Annfield Plain 33 54 52N 1 45W
Annie Peak 137 33 53S 119 59E
Anning 108 24 58N 102 30E
Anningle 136 21 50S 133 7E
Anniston 157 33 45N 85 50W
Annobón 114 1 35S 3 35E
Annonay 45 45 15N 4 40E
Annonciation, L' 150 46 25N 74 55W
Annot 45 43 58N 6 38E
Annotto Bay 166 18 17N 77 3W
Annuello 140 34 53S 142 55E
Annville 162 40 18N 76 32W
Áno Arkhánai 69 35 16N 25 11E
Áno Porróia 68 41 17N 23 2E
Áno Viánnos 69 35 2N 25 21E
Anoka 158 45 10N 93 26W
Anorotsangana 129 13 56S 47 55E
Anp'ing, Hopei, China 106 38 13N 115 31E
Anp'ing, Liaoning, China 107 41 10N 123 30E
Ans 47 50 39N 5 32E
Ansai 106 36 54N 109 10E
Ansbach 49 49 17N 10 34E
Anse au Loup, L' 151 51 32N 56 50W
Anse, L' 150 46 47N 88 28W
Anseba, R. 123 16 15N 37 45E
Anserma 174 5 13N 75 48W
Anseroeul 47 50 43N 3 32E
Anshan 107 41 3N 122 58E
Anshun 105 26 2N 105 57E
Ansley 158 41 19N 99 24W
Ansó 58 42 51N 0 48W
Anson 159 32 46N 99 54W
Anson B. 136 13 20S 130 6E
Ansongo 121 15 25N 0 35E
Ansonia 162 41 21N 73 6W
Ansonville 150 48 46N 80 43W
Anstey 28 52 41N 1 14W
Anstey Hill 109 34 51S 138 44E
Anstruther 35 56 14N 2 40W
Ansudu 103 2 11S 139 22E
Antabamba 174 14 40S 73 0W
Antakya 92 36 14N 36 10E
Antalaha 129 14 57S 50 20E
Antalya 92 36 52N 30 45E
Antalya Körfezi 92 36 15N 31 30E
Antananrivo 125 18 55S 47 35E
Antanimbaribé 129 21 30S 44 48E
Antarctic Pen. 13 67 0S 60 0W
Antarctica 125 90 0S 0 0
Antela, Laguna 56 42 7N 7 40W
Antelope 127 21 2S 28 31E
Anten 73 58 5N 12 22E
Antenor Navarro 170 6 44S 38 27W
Antequera, Parag. 172 24 8S 57 7W
Antequera, Spain 57 37 5N 4 33W
Antero Mt. 161 38 45N 106 43W
Anthemoús 68 40 31N 23 15E
Anthony, Kans., U.S.A. 159 37 8N 98 2W
Anthony, N. Mex., U.S.A. 161 32 1N 106 37W
Anthony Lagoon 138 18 0S 135 30E
Anti Atlas, Mts. 118 30 30N 6 30W
Antibes 45 43 34N 7 6E
Antibes, C. d' 45 43 31N 7 7E
Anticosti, Î. de 151 49 30N 63 0W
Antifer, C. d' 42 49 41N 0 10E
Antigo 158 45 8N 89 5W
Antigonish 151 45 38N 61 58W
Antigua 166 14 34N 90 41W
Antigua Bahama, Canal de la 166 22 10N 77 30W
Antigua, I. 167 17 0N 61 50W
Antilla 166 20 40N 75 50W
Antimony 161 38 7N 112 0W
Antioch 163 38 7N 121 45W
Antioquia 174 6 40N 75 55W
Antioquia □ 174 7 0N 75 30W
Antipodes Is. 130 49 45S 178 40E
Antler 158 48 58N 101 18W
Antler, R. 153 49 8N 101 0W
Antlers 159 34 15N 95 35W
Antofagasta 172 23 50S 70 30W
Antofagasta □ 172 24 0S 69 0W
Antofagasta de la Sierra 172 26 5S 67 20W
Antofallá 172 25 30S 68 5W
Antofalla, Salar de 172 25 40S 67 45W
Antoing 47 50 34N 3 27E
Anton 159 33 49N 102 5W
Anton Chico 161 35 12N 105 5W
Antongil, B. d' 129 15 30S 49 50E
Antonibe 129 15 7S 47 24E
Antonibe, Presqu'île d' 129 15 30S 49 50E
Antonina 173 25 26S 48 42W
Antonito 161 37 4N 106 1W
Antonovo 83 49 25N 51 42E
Antony 30 50 22N 4 13W
Antrain 42 48 28N 1 30W
Antrim 38 54 43N 6 13W
Antrim □ 38 54 42N 6 20W
Antrim Co. 38 54 58N 6 20W
Antrim, Mts. of 38 54 57N 6 8W
Antrim Plateau 136 18 8S 128 20E
Antrodoco 63 42 25N 13 4E
Antropovo 81 58 26N 42 51E
Antsalova 129 18 40S 44 37E
Antse 106 36 15N 112 15E
Antsirabé 129 19 55S 47 2E
Antsohihy 129 14 50S 47 50E
Ant'u 107 43 6N 128 54E
Antung 107 40 10N 124 18E
Antungwei 107 35 10N 119 20E
Antwerp 140 36 17S 142 4E
Antwerp = Antwerpen 47 51 13N 4 25E
Antwerpen 47 51 13N 4 25E
Antwerpen □ 47 51 15N 4 40E
Antz'u 106 39 31N 116 41E
Anupgarh 94 29 10N 73 10E
Anuradhapura 97 8 22N 80 28E
Anvaing 47 50 41N 3 34E
Anvers = Antwerp(en) 47 51 13N 4 25E
Anvers I. 13 64 30S 63 40W
Anvik 147 62 37N 160 20W
Anxious B. 139 33 24S 134 45E
Anyama 120 5 30N 4 3W
Anyang 106 36 7N 114 26E
Anyer-Lor 103 6 5S 105 56E
Anyüan 109 25 9N 115 21E
Anza, Jordan 90 32 22N 35 12E
Anza, U.S.A. 163 33 35N 116 39W

Anza Borrego Desert State Park 163 33 0N 116 26W
Anzhero-Sudzhensk 76 56 10N 83 40 E
Anzio 64 41 28N 12 37 E
Aoga-Shima 111 32 28N 139 46 E
Aoiz 58 42 46N 1 22W
Aomori 112 40 45N 140 45 E
Aomori-ken □ 112 40 45N 140 40 E
Aonla 95 28 16N 79 11 E
Aono-Yama 110 34 28N 131 48 E
Aorangi Mts. 142 41 49 S 175 22 E
Aoreora 118 28 51N 10 53W
Aosta 62 45 43N 7 20 E
Aoudéras 121 17 45N 8 20 E
Aouinet Torkoz 118 28 31N 9 46W
Aoukar □ 118 23 50N 2 45W
Aouker 120 23 48N 4 0W
Aoulef el Arab 118 26 55N 1 2 E
Aoullouz 118 30 44N 8 1W
Apa 108 32 55N 101 40 E
Apa, R. 172 22 6 S 58 2W
Apache, Ariz., U.S.A. 161 31 46N 109 6W
Apache, Okla., U.S.A. 159 34 53N 98 22W
Apahanuerhch'i 106 43 58N 116 2 E
Apalachee B. 157 30 0N 84 0W
Apalachicola 157 29 40N 85 0W
Apalachicola, R. 157 30 0N 85 0W
Apapa 121 6 25N 3 25 E
Apaporis, R. 174 0 30 S 70 30W
Aparecida do Taboado 171 20 5 S 51 5W
Aparri 103 18 22N 121 38 E
Aparurén 174 5 6N 62 8W
Apateu 70 46 36N 21 47 E
Apatin 66 45 40N 19 0 E
Apatzingán 164 19 0N 102 20W
Apeldoorn 46 52 13N 5 57 E
Apeldoornsch Kanal 46 52 29N 6 5 E
Apen 48 53 12N 7 47 E
Apenam 102 8 35 S 116 13 E
Apennines 16 44 20N 10 20 E
Apía 174 5 5N 75 58W
Apiacás, Serra dos 174 9 50 S 57 0W
Apiaí 174 24 31 S 48 50W
Apinajé 171 11 31 S 48 18W
Apiti 142 39 58 S 175 54 E
Apizaco 165 19 26N 98 9W
Aplahoué 121 6 56N 1 41 E
Aplao 174 16 0 S 72 40W
Apo, Mt. 103 6 53N 125 14 E
Apodi 170 5 39 S 37 48W
Apolda 48 51 1N 11 30 E
Apollo Bay 140 38 45 S 143 40 E
Apollonia, Greece 69 36 58N 24 43 E
Apollonia, Libya 117 32 52N 21 59 E
Apolo 174 14 30 S 68 30W
Aporé, R. 171 19 27 S 50 57W
Aporema 170 1 14N 50 49W
Apostle Is. 158 46 50N 90 30W
Apóstoles 173 28 0 S 56 0W
Apostolovo 82 47 39N 33 39 E
Apoteri 174 4 2N 58 32W
Appalachian Mts. 156 38 0N 80 0W
Appelscha 46 52 57N 6 21 E
Appenninі 65 41 0N 15 0 E
Appeninno Ligure 62 44 30N 9 0 E
Appenzell 51 47 20N 9 25 E
Appenzell-Ausser Rhoden □ 51 47 23N 9 23 E
Appenzell-Inner Rhoden □ 51 47 20N 9 25 E
Appiano 63 46 27N 11 17 E
Appingedam 46 53 19N 6 51 E
Apple Valley 163 34 30N 117 11W
Appleby 32 54 35N 2 29W
Applecross 36 57 26N 5 50W
Applecross For. 36 57 27N 5 40W
Appledore, Devon, U.K. 30 51 3N 4 12W
Appledore, Kent, U.K. 29 51 2N 0 47 E
Appleton 156 44 17N 88 25W
Approuague 170 4 20N 52 0W
Apreivka 81 55 33N 37 4 E
Apricena 65 41 47N 15 25 E
Aprigliano 65 39 17N 16 19 E
Aprília 64 41 38N 12 38 E
Apsheronsk 83 44 28N 39 42 E
Apsley Str. 136 11 35 S 130 28 E
Apt 45 43 53N 5 24 E
Apucarana 173 23 55 S 51 33W
Apulia = Puglia 65 41 0N 16 30 E
Apure □ 174 7 10N 68 50W
Apure, R. 174 8 0N 69 20W
Apurimac, R. 174 12 10 S 73 30W
Apurito, R. 174 7 50N 67 0W
Apuseni, Munţii 70 46 30N 22 45 E
Aq Chah 93 37 0N 66 5 E
'Aqaba 122 29 31N 35 0 E
'Aqaba, Khalīj al 92 28 15N 33 20 E
Aqiq 122 18 14N 38 12 E
Aqiq, Khalîg 122 18 20N 38 10 E
'Aqraba 90 32 9N 35 20 E
'Aqrah 92 36 46N 43 45 E
Aquanish 151 50 14N 62 2W
Aquasco 162 38 35N 76 43W
Aquidaba 171 10 17 S 37 2W
Aquidauana 175 20 30 S 55 50W
Aquila, L' 63 42 21N 13 24 E
Aquiles Serdán 164 28 37N 105 54W
Aquin 167 18 16N 73 24W
Ar Ramadi 92 33 25N 43 20 E
Ar-Ramthā 90 32 34N 36 0 E
Ar Rass 92 25 50N 43 40 E
Ar Rifai 92 31 50N 46 10 E
Ar Riyād 92 24 41N 46 42 E
Ar Rub 'al Khālī 91 21 0N 51 0 E
Ar Rutbah 92 33 0N 40 15 E
Arab, Khalîg el 122 30 55N 29 0 E
Arab, Shott al 92 30 0N 48 31 E
Araba 121 13 7N 5 0 E
Arabatskaya Strelka 82 45 40N 35 0 E
Arabba 63 46 30N 11 51 E
Arabelo 174 4 55N 64 13W
Arabia 86 25 0N 45 0 E
Arabian Desert 122 28 0N 32 20 E
Arabian Sea 86 16 0N 65 0 E
Aracajú 170 10 55 S 37 4W
Aracataca 174 10 38N 74 9W
Aracati 170 4 30 S 37 44W
Araçatuba 173 21 10 S 50 30W
Aracena 57 37 53N 6 38W
Aracruz 171 19 49 S 40 16W
Araçuai 171 16 52 S 42 4W
Araçuai, R. 171 16 46 S 42 2W
Arad 66 46 10N 21 20 E
Arada 117 15 0N 20 20 E
Aradu Nou 66 46 8N 21 20 E
Arafura Sea 103 10 0 S 135 0 E
Aragats 83 40 30N 44 15 E
Aragón 58 41 25N 1 0W
Aragón, R. 58 42 35N 0 50W
Aragona 64 37 24N 13 36 E
Aragua □ 174 10 0N 67 10W
Aragua de Barcelona 174 9 28N 64 49W
Araguacema 170 8 50 S 49 20W
Araguaçu 171 12 49 S 49 51W
Araguaia, R. 170 7 0 S 49 15W
Araguaina 170 7 12 S 48 12W
Araguari 171 18 38 S 48 11W
Araguari, R. 170 1 0N 51 40W
Araguatins 170 5 38 S 48 7W
Araioses 170 2 53 S 41 55W
Arak 118 25 20N 3 45 E
Arāk 92 34 0N 49 40 E
Arakan □ 98 19 0N 94 15 E
Arakan Coast 99 19 0N 94 0 E
Arakan Yoma 98 20 0N 94 30 E
Arákhova 69 38 28N 22 35 E
Araks, R. = Aras, Rud-e 92 39 10N 47 10 E
Aral Sea = Aralskoye More 76 44 30N 60 0 E
Aralsk 76 46 50N 61 20 E
Aralskoye More 76 44 30N 60 0 E
Aramac 138 22 58 S 145 14 E
Arambagh 95 22 53N 87 48 E
Aramū, Mţii de 70 47 10N 22 30 E
Aran Fawddwy, Mt. 31 52 48N 3 40W
Aran, I. 38 55 0N 8 30W
Aran Is. 39 53 5N 9 42W
Aranci 64 41 5N 3 40W
Aranci, Golfo 64 41 0N 9 35 E
Aranda de Duero 58 41 39N 3 42W
Arandelovac 66 44 18N 20 37 E
Aranga 142 35 44 S 173 40 E
Aranjuez 56 40 1N 3 40W
Aranos 125 24 9 S 19 7 E
Aransas Pass 159 28 0N 97 9W
Aranyaprathet 101 13 41N 102 30 E
Aranzazu 174 5 16N 75 30W
Arao 110 32 59N 130 25 E
Araouane 120 18 55N 3 30W
Arapahoe 158 40 22N 99 53W
Arapari 170 5 34 S 49 15W
Arapawa I. 131 41 13 S 174 20 E
Arapey Grande, R. 172 30 55 S 57 49W
Arapiraca 170 9 45 S 36 39W
Arapkir 92 39 5N 38 30 E
Arapongas 173 23 29 S 51 28W
Arapuni 130 38 3 S 175 37 E
Araranguá 173 29 0 S 49 30W
Araraquara 171 21 50 S 48 0W
Araras 173 5 15 S 60 35W
Ararás, Serra dos 173 25 0 S 53 10W
Ararat, Austral. 140 37 16 S 143 0 E
Ararat, Turkey 92 39 50N 44 15 E
Ararat, Mt. = Ağri Daği 92 39 50N 44 15 E
Arari 170 3 28 S 44 47W
Araria 95 26 9N 87 33 E
Araripe 171 7 12 S 40 8W
Araripe, Chapada do 170 7 20 S 40 0W
Araripina 170 7 33 S 40 34W
Araro 123 4 41N 38 50 E
Araruama, Lagoa de 173 22 53 S 42 12W
Araruna 170 6 52 S 35 44W
Aras 71 59 42N 10 31 E
Aras, Rud-e 92 39 10N 47 10 E
Araticu 170 1 58 S 49 51W
Arauca 174 7 0N 70 40W
Arauca □ 174 6 40N 71 0W
Arauca, R. 174 7 30N 69 0W
Arauco 172 37 16 S 73 25W
Arauco □ 172 37 40 S 73 25W
Araújos 171 19 56 S 45 14W
Arauquita 174 7 2N 71 25W
Araure 174 9 34N 69 13W
Arawa 123 9 57N 41 58 E
Arawhata 143 43 59 S 168 38 E
Arawhata, R. 143 44 0 S 168 40 E
Araxá 171 19 35 S 46 55W
Araya, Pen. de 174 10 40N 64 0W
Arba 123 9 0N 40 20 E
Arba Jahan 126 2 5N 39 2 E
Arba, L' 118 36 40N 3 9 E
Arba Minch 123 6 0N 37 30 E
Arbah, Wadi al 90 30 30N 35 5 E
Arbatax 64 39 57N 9 42 E
Arbedo 51 46 12N 9 3 E
Arbeláez 174 4 17N 74 26W
Arbīl 92 36 15N 44 5 E
Arboga 72 59 24N 15 52 E
Arbois 43 46 55N 5 46 E
Arbon 51 47 31N 9 26 E
Arbore 123 5 3N 36 50 E
Arborea 64 39 46N 8 34 E
Arborfield 153 53 6N 103 39W
Arborg 153 50 54N 97 13W
Arbrå 72 61 28N 16 22 E
Arbresle, L' 45 45 50N 4 26 E
Arbroath 37 56 34N 2 35W
Arbuckle 160 39 3N 122 2W
Arbus 64 39 30N 8 33 E
Arbuzinka 82 47 52N 31 25 E
Arc 43 47 28N 5 34 E
Arcachon 44 44 40N 1 10W
Arcachon, Bassin d' 44 44 42N 1 10W
Arcadia, Fla., U.S.A. 157 27 20N 81 50W
Arcadia, La., U.S.A. 159 32 34N 92 53W
Arcadia, Nebr., U.S.A. 158 41 29N 99 4W
Arcadia, Wis., U.S.A. 158 44 13N 91 29W
Arcata 160 40 55N 124 4W
Arcévia 63 43 29N 12 58 E
Archangel = Arkhangelsk 78 64 40N 41 0 E
Archar 66 43 50N 22 54 E
Archbald 162 41 30N 75 31W
Archena 59 38 9N 1 16W
Archer B. 138 13 20 S 141 30 E
Archer, R. 138 13 25 S 142 50 E
Archers Post 126 0 35N 37 35 E
Archidona 57 37 6N 4 22W
Archiestown 37 57 28N 3 20W
Arci, Monte 64 39 47N 8 44 E
Arcidosso 63 42 51N 11 30 E
Arcila = Asilah 118 35 29N 6 0W
Arcis-sur-Aube 43 48 32N 4 10 E
Arckaringa 139 27 56 S 134 45 E
Arckaringa Cr. 139 28 10 S 135 22 E
Arco, Italy 62 45 55N 10 54 E
Arco, U.S.A. 160 43 45N 113 16W
Arcola 153 49 40N 102 30W
Arcoona 140 31 2 S 137 1 E
Arcos, Brazil 171 20 17 S 45 32W
Arcos, Spain 58 41 12N 2 16W
Arcos de los Frontera 57 36 45N 5 49W
Arcot 97 12 53N 79 20 E
Arcoverde 170 8 25 S 37 4W
Arctic Ocean 12 78 0N 160 0W
Arctic Red, R. 147 66 0N 132 0W
Arctic Red River 147 67 15N 134 0W
Arctic Village 147 68 5N 145 45W
Arda, R., Bulg. 67 41 40N 25 40 E
Arda, R., Italy 62 44 53N 9 52 E
Ardabil 92 38 15N 48 18 E
Ardagh 39 52 30N 9 5W
Ardakan 93 30 20N 52 5 E
Årdal 71 59 9N 6 13 E
Ardales 57 36 53N 4 51W
Årdalstangen 71 61 14N 7 43 E
Ardara 38 54 47N 8 25W
Ardatov 81 54 51N 46 15 E
Ardavasar 36 57 3N 5 54 E
Ardbeg 34 55 38N 6 6W
Ardcath 38 53 36N 6 21W
Ardcharnich 36 57 52N 5 5W
Ardchyle 34 56 26N 4 24W
Ardèche □ 45 44 42N 4 16 E
Ardee 38 53 51N 6 32W
Arden Stby. 73 56 46N 9 52 E
Ardennes 47 49 30N 5 10 E
Ardennes □ 43 49 35N 4 40 E
Ardentes 43 46 45N 1 50 E
Ardentinny 34 56 3N 4 56 E
Arderin, Mt. 39 53 3N 7 40W
Ardestan 93 33 20N 52 25 E
Ardfert 39 52 20N 9 49W
Ardfinnan 39 52 20N 7 53W
Ardglass 38 54 16N 5 38W
Ardgour 36 56 45N 5 25W
Ardgroom 39 51 44N 9 53W
Ardhas, R. 68 41 36N 26 25 E
Ardhasig 36 57 55N 6 51W
Ardhéa 68 40 58N 22 3 E
Ardila, R. 57 38 10N 7 20W
Ardingly 29 51 3N 0 3W
Ardino 67 41 34N 25 9 E
Ardivachar Pt. 36 57 23N 7 25W
Ardkearagh 39 51 48N 10 11W
Ardkeen 38 54 27N 5 31W
Ardlethan 141 34 22 S 146 53 E
Ardlui 34 56 19N 4 43W
Ardmore, Austral. 138 21 39 S 139 11 E
Ardmore, Okla., U.S.A. 159 34 10N 97 5W
Ardmore, Pa., U.S.A. 162 39 58N 75 18W
Ardmore, S.D., U.S.A. 158 43 0N 103 40W
Ardmore Hd. 39 51 58N 7 43W
Ardmore Pt. 34 55 40N 6 0W
Ardnacrusha 39 52 43N 8 38W
Ardnamurchan, Pen. 36 56 43N 6 0W
Ardnamurchan Pt. 36 56 44N 6 14W
Ardnaree 38 54 6N 9 8W
Ardnave Pt. 34 55 54N 6 20W
Ardooie 47 50 59N 3 13 E
Ardore Marina 65 38 11N 16 10 E
Ardrahan 39 53 10N 8 48W
Ardres 43 50 50N 2 0 E
Ardrishaig 34 56 0N 5 27W
Ardrossan, Austral. 140 34 26 S 137 53 E
Ardrossan, U.K. 34 55 39N 4 50W
Ards □ 38 54 35N 5 30W
Ards Pen. 38 54 30N 5 25W
Ardud 70 47 37N 22 52 E
Ardunac 83 41 8N 42 5 E
Ardvoulie Castle 36 58 0N 6 45W
Ardwell 37 57 20N 3 5W
Åre 72 63 22N 13 15 E
Arecibo 147 18 29N 66 42W
Areia Branca 170 5 0 S 37 0W
Aremark 71 59 15N 11 42 E
Arena de la Ventana, Punta 164 24 4N 109 52W
Arenales, Cerro 176 47 5 S 73 40W
Arenas 56 43 17N 4 50W
Arenas de San Pedro 56 40 12N 5 5W
Arenas, Pta. 174 10 20N 62 39W
Arendal 71 58 28N 8 46 E
Arendonk 47 51 19N 5 5 E
Arendsee 48 52 52N 11 27 E
Arenig Fach, Mt. 31 52 55N 3 45 E
Arenig Fawr, Mt. 31 52 56N 3 45W
Arenys de Mar 58 41 35N 2 33 E
Arenzano 62 44 24N 8 40 E
Areópolis 69 36 40N 22 22 E
Arequipa 174 16 20 S 71 30W
Arero 123 4 41N 38 50 E
Arês 171 6 11 S 35 9W
Arès 44 44 47N 1 8W
Arévalo 56 41 3N 4 43W
Arezzo 63 43 28N 11 50 E
Arga, R. 58 42 30N 1 50W
Argalastí 68 39 13N 23 13 E
Argamasilla de Alba 59 39 8N 3 5W
Arganda 58 40 19N 3 26W
Arganil 56 40 13N 8 3W
Argayash 84 55 29N 60 52 E
Argelès-Gazost 44 43 0N 0 6W
Argelès-sur-Mer 44 42 34N 3 1 E
Argent-sur-Sauldre 43 47 33N 2 25 E
Argenta, Can. 152 50 20N 116 55W
Argenta, Italy 63 44 37N 11 50 E
Argentan 42 48 45N 0 1W
Argentário, Mte. 63 42 23N 11 11 E
Argentat 44 45 6N 1 56 E
Argentera 62 44 23N 6 58 E
Argenteuil 43 48 57N 2 14 E
Argentia 151 47 18N 53 58W
Argentiera, C. dell' 64 40 44N 8 8 E
Argentière, Aiguilles d' 50 45 58N 7 2 E
Argentina 174 0 34N 74 17W
Argentina ■ 176 35 0 S 66 0W
Argentino, L. 176 50 10 S 73 0W
Argenton-sur-Creuse 44 46 36N 1 30 E
Argentré 42 48 5N 0 40W
Argeş □ 70 45 0N 24 45 E
Argeş, R. 70 44 30N 25 50 E
Arghandab, R. 94 32 15N 66 23 E
Argo 122 19 28N 30 30 E
Argo, I. 122 19 28N 30 30 E
Argolikós Kólpos 69 37 20N 22 52 E
Argolis □ 69 37 38N 22 50 E
Argonne 43 49 0N 5 20 E
Árgos 69 37 40N 22 43 E
Árgos Orestikón 68 40 27N 21 26 E
Argostólion 69 38 12N 20 33 E
Arguedas 58 42 11N 1 36W
Arguello, Pt. 163 34 34N 120 40W
Argun, R. 77 53 20N 121 28 E
Argungu 121 12 40N 4 31 E
Argus Pk. 163 35 52N 117 26W
Argyle 158 48 23N 96 49W
Argyle Downs 136 16 17 S 128 47 E
Argyle, L. 136 16 20 S 128 40 E
Argyll (□) 26 56 18N 5 15W
Argyll, Dist. 34 56 14N 5 10W
Argyll, oilfield 19 56 8N 3 5 E
Argyrádhes 68 39 27N 19 58 E
Århus 73 56 8N 10 11 E
Aria 142 38 33 S 175 0 E
Ariamsvlei 128 28 9 S 19 51 E
Ariana 119 36 52N 10 12 E
Ariano Irpino 65 41 10N 15 4 E
Ariano nel Polèsine 63 44 56N 12 5 E
Aribinda 121 14 17N 0 52W
Arica, Chile 174 18 32 S 70 20W
Arica, Colomb. 174 2 0 S 71 50W
Arica, Peru 174 1 30 S 75 30W
Arid, C. 137 34 1 S 123 10 E
Arida 111 33 29N 135 44 E
Ariège □ 44 42 56N 1 30 E
Ariège, R. 44 42 56N 1 25 E
Arieş, R. 70 46 24N 23 20 E
Arilje 66 43 44N 20 7 E
Arima 167 10 38N 61 17W
Arinagour 34 56 38N 6 31W
Arinos, R. 174 11 15 S 57 0W
Ario de Rosales 164 19 12N 101 42W
Aripuanã 174 9 25 S 60 30W
Aripuanã, R. 174 7 30 S 60 25W
Ariquemes 174 9 55 S 63 6W
Arisaig 36 56 55N 5 50W
Arisaig, Sd. of 36 56 50N 5 50W
Arîsh, W. el 122 30 25N 34 52 E
Arismendi 174 8 29N 68 22W
Arissa 123 11 10N 41 35 E
Aristazabal, I. 152 52 40N 129 10W
Arita 110 33 11N 129 54 E
Arivaca 161 31 37N 111 25W
Arivonimamo 129 19 1 S 47 11 E
Ariyalur 97 11 8N 79 8 E
Ariza 58 41 19N 2 3W
Arizaro, Salar de 172 24 40 S 67 50W
Arizona 172 35 45 S 65 25W
Arizona □ 161 34 20N 111 30W
Arizpe 164 30 20N 110 11W

Arjang 72 59 24N 12 9 E
Årjäng 72 59 24N 12 8 E
Arjeplog 74 66 3N 18 2 E
Arjona, Colomb. 174 10 14N 75 22W
Arjona, Spain 57 37 56N 4 4W
Arjuno 103 7 49S 112 19 E
Arka 77 60 15N 142 0 E
Arkadak 81 51 58N 43 19 E
Arkadelphia 159 34 5N 93 0W
Arkadhia □ 69 37 30N 22 20 E
Arkaig, L. 36 56 58N 5 10W
Arkansas □ 159 35 0N 92 30W
Arkansas City 159 37 4N 97 3W
Arkansas, R. 159 35 20N 93 30W
Árkathos, R. 68 39 20N 21 4 E
Arkhángelos 69 36 13N 28 7 E
Arkhangelsk 78 64 40N 41 0 E
Arkhangelskoye 81 51 32N 40 58 E
Arkiko 123 15 33N 39 30 E
Arkle R. 32 54 25N 2 0W
Arklow 39 52 48N 6 10W
Arklow Hd. 39 52 46N 6 10W
Árkoi 69 37 24N 26 44 E
Arkona, Kap 48 54 41N 13 26 E
Arkonam 97 13 7N 79 43 E
Arkösund 73 58 29N 16 56 E
Arkoúdhi 69 38 33N 20 43 E
Arkticheskiy, Mys 77 81 10N 95 0 E
Arkul 84 57 17N 50 3 E
Arkville 162 42 9N 74 37W
Arlanc 44 45 25N 3 42 E
Arlanza, R. 56 42 6N 4 0W
Arlanzón, R. 56 42 12N 4 0W
Arlberg Pass 49 49 9N 10 12 E
Arlee 160 47 10N 114 4W
Arles 45 43 41N 4 40 E
Arlesheim 50 47 30N 7 37 E
Arless 39 52 53N 7 1W
Arlington, S. Afr. 129 28 1S 27 53 E
Arlington, Oreg., U.S.A. 160 45 48N 120 6W
Arlington, S.D., U.S.A. 158 44 25N 97 4W
Arlington, Va., U.S.A. 162 38 52N 77 5W
Arlington, Vt., U.S.A. 162 43 5N 73 9W
Arlington, Wash., U.S.A. 160 48 11N 122 4W
Arlon 47 49 42N 5 49 E
Arlöv 73 55 38N 13 5 E
Arly 121 11 35N 1 28 E
Armadale, Austral. 137 32 12S 116 0 E
Armadale, Lothian, U.K. 35 55 54N 3 42W
Armadale, Skye, U.K. 36 57 24N 5 54W
Armagh, Can. 137 46 41N 70 32W
Armagh, U.K. 38 54 22N 6 40W
Armagh □ 38 54 18N 6 37W
Armagh Co. 38 54 16N 6 35W
Armagnac 44 43 44N 0 10 E
Armançon, R. 43 47 51N 4 7 E
Armavir 83 45 2N 41 7 E
Armenia 174 4 35N 75 45W
Armenian S.S.R. □ 83 40 0N 41 0 E
Armeniş 70 45 13N 22 17 E
Armentières 43 50 40N 2 50 E
Armero 174 4 58N 74 54W
Armidale 141 30 30S 151 40 E
Armour 158 43 20N 98 25W
Armoy 38 55 8N 6 20W
Arms 150 49 34N 86 3W
Armstead 160 45 0N 112 56W
Armstrong, B.C., Can. 152 50 25N 119 10W
Armstrong, Ont., Can. 150 50 18N 89 4W
Armstrong, U.S.A. 159 26 59N 90 48W
Armstrong Cr. 136 16 35S 131 40 E
Armur 96 18 48N 78 16 E
Arnaia 68 40 30N 23 40 E
Arnarfjörður 74 65 48N 23 40W
Arnay-le-Duc 43 47 10N 4 27 E
Arnedillo 58 42 13N 2 14W
Arnedo 58 42 12N 2 5W
Árnes 74 66 1N 21 31W
Årnes 71 60 7N 11 28 E
Arnett 159 36 9N 99 44W
Arney 38 54 17N 7 41W
Arnhem 46 51 58N 5 55 E
Arnhem B. 138 12 20S 136 10 E
Arnhem, C. 138 12 20S 137 0 E
Arnhem Ld. 138 13 10S 135 0 E
Arni 97 12 43N 79 19 E
Arnissa 68 40 47N 21 49 E
Arno Bay 140 33 54S 136 34 E
Arno, R. 62 43 44N 10 20 E
Arnold, N.Z. 143 42 29S 171 25 E
Arnold, U.K. 33 53 0N 1 8W
Arnold, Calif., U.S.A. 163 38 15N 120 20W
Arnold, Nebr., U.S.A. 158 41 29N 100 10W
Arnoldstein 52 46 33N 13 43 E
Arnot 153 55 46N 96 41W
Arnøy 74 70 9N 20 40 E
Arnprior 150 45 26N 76 21W
Arnsberg 48 51 25N 8 10 E
Arnside 32 54 12N 2 49W
Arnstadt 48 50 50N 10 56 E
Aroa 174 10 26N 68 54W
Aroab 125 26 41S 19 39 E
Aroánia Óri 69 37 56N 22 12 E
Aroche 57 37 56N 6 57W
Aroeiras 170 7 31S 35 41W
Arolla 50 46 2N 7 29 E
Arolsen 48 51 23N 9 1 E
Arona 62 45 45N 8 32 E
Arosa 51 46 47N 9 41 E
Arosa, Ría de 56 42 28N 8 57W
Arpajon, Cantal, France 44 44 54N 2 28 E
Arpajon, Seine et Oise, France 43 48 37N 2 12 E
Arpino 64 41 40N 13 35 E
Arra Mts. 39 52 50N 8 22W
Arrabury 139 26 45S 141 0 E
Arrah 95 25 35N 84 32 E
Arraias 171 12 56S 46 57W
Arraias, R. 170 7 30S 49 20W
Arraiolos 57 38 44N 7 59W
Arran, I. 34 55 34N 5 12W
Arrandale 152 54 57N 130 0W
Arras 43 50 17N 2 46 E
Arreau 44 42 54N 0 22 E
Arrecife 116 28 59N 13 40W
Arrecifes 172 34 06S 60 9W
Arrée, Mts. d' 42 48 26N 3 55W
Arriaga, Chiapas, Mexico 165 16 15N 93 52W
Arriaga, San Luís de Potosi, Mexico 164 21 55N 101 23W
Arrild 73 55 8N 8 58 E
Arrililah P.O. 138 23 43S 143 54 E
Arrino 137 29 30S 115 40 E
Arrochar 34 56 12N 4 45W
Arrojado, R. 171 13 24S 44 20W
Arromanches-les-Bains 42 49 20N 0 38W
Arronches 57 39 8N 7 16W
Arrou 42 48 6N 1 8 E
Arrow L. 38 54 3N 8 20W
Arrow Rock Res. 160 43 45N 115 50W
Arrowhead 152 50 40N 117 55W
Arrowhead, L. 163 34 16N 117 10W
Arrowsmith, Mt. 143 30 7N 141 38 E
Arrowtown 143 44 57S 168 50 E
Arroyo de la Luz 57 39 30N 6 38W
Arroyo Grande 163 35 9N 120 32W
Års 73 56 48N 9 30 E
Ars 44 46 13N 1 30W
Ars-sur-Moselle 43 49 5N 6 4 E
Arsenault L. 153 53 6N 108 32W
Arsiero 63 45 49N 11 22 E
Arsikere 97 13 15N 76 15 E
Arsk 81 56 10N 49 50 E
Årskogen 72 62 8N 17 20 E
Árta 69 39 8N 21 2 E
Artá 58 39 40N 3 20 E
Árta □ 68 39 15N 26 0 E
Arteaga 164 18 50N 102 20W
Arteijo 56 43 19N 8 29W
Artem,Os. 83 40 28N 50 20 E
Artémou 120 15 38N 12 16W
Artemovsk 82 48 35N 37 55 E
Artemovski 83 54 45N 93 35 E
Artemovskiy 84 57 21N 61 54 E
Artenay 43 48 5N 1 50 E
Artern 48 51 22N 11 18 E
Artesa de Segre 58 41 54N 1 3 E
Artesia 159 32 55N 104 25W
Artesia Wells 159 28 17N 99 18W
Artesian 158 44 2N 97 54W
Arth 51 47 4N 8 31 E
Arthez-de-Béarn 44 43 29N 0 38W
Arthington 120 6 35N 10 45W
Arthur Cr. 138 22 30S 136 25 E
Arthur Pt. 138 22 7S 150 3 E
Arthur, R. 138 41 2S 144 40 E
Arthur's Pass 143 42 54S 171 35 E
Arthur's Town 167 24 38N 75 42W
Arthurstown 39 52 15N 6 58W
Artigas 172 30 20S 56 30W
Artigavan 38 54 51N 7 24W
Artik 83 40 38N 44 50 E
Artillery L. 153 63 9N 107 52W
Artois 43 50 20N 2 30 E
Artotína 69 38 42N 22 2 E
Artvin 92 41 14N 41 44 E
Aru, Kepulauan 103 6 0S 134 30 E
Arua 126 3 1N 30 58 E
Aruanã 171 15 0S 51 10W
Aruba I. 167 12 30N 70 0W
Arudy 44 43 7N 0 28W
Arumpo 140 33 48S 142 55 E
Arun, R. 95 27 30N 87 15 E
Arun R. 29 50 48N 0 33W
Arunachal Pradesh □ 98 28 0N 95 0 E
Arundel 29 50 52N 0 32W
Aruppukottai 97 9 31N 78 8 E
Arusha 126 3 20S 36 40 E
Arusha □ 126 4 0S 36 30 E
Arusha Chini 126 3 32S 37 20 E
Arusi □ 123 7 45N 39 00 E
Aruvi 97 8 48N 79 53 E
Aruwimi, R. 126 1 30N 25 0 E
Arva 38 53 57N 7 35W
Arvada 160 44 43N 106 6W
Arvaklu 97 8 20N 79 58 E
Arvayheer 105 46 15N 102 48 E
Arve, R. 45 46 11N 6 8 E
Arvi 96 20 59N 78 16 E
Arvida 151 48 25N 71 14W
Arvidsjaur 74 65 35N 19 10 E
Arvika 72 59 40N 12 36 E
Arvin 163 35 12N 118 50W
Arys 85 42 26N 68 48 E
Arys, R. 85 42 45N 68 15 E
Arzachena 64 41 5N 9 27 E
Arzamas 81 55 27N 43 55 E
Arzew 118 35 50N 0 23W
Arzgir 83 45 18N 44 23 E
Arzignano 63 45 30N 11 20 E
As 47 51 1N 5 35 E
Aš 52 50 13N 12 12 E
As Salt 90 32 2N 35 43 E
As Samawah 92 31 15N 45 15 E
As-Samū 90 31 24N 35 4 E
As Sulaimānīyah 92 35 35N 45 29 E
As Sulṭon 119 31 4N 17 8 E
As Suwaih 93 22 10N 59 33 E
As Suwayda 92 32 40N 36 30 E
As Suwayrah 92 32 55N 45 0 E
Asab 128 25 30S 18 0 E
Asaba 121 6 12N 6 38 E
Asadabad 92 34 50N 48 10 E
Asafo 120 6 20N 2 40W
Asahi 111 35 43N 140 39 E
Asahi-Gawa, R. 110 34 36N 133 58 E
Asahikawa 112 43 45N 142 30 E
Asale, L. 123 14 0N 40 20 E
Asama-Yama 111 36 24N 138 31 E
Asamankese 121 5 50N 0 40W
Asankrangwa 120 5 45N 2 30W
Asansol 95 23 40N 87 1 E
Åsarna 72 62 40N 14 20 E
Åsarna 72 62 39N 14 22 E
Asbe Teferi 123 9 4N 40 49 E
Asbesberge 128 29 0S 23 0 E
Asbest 84 57 0N 61 30 E
Asbestos 151 45 47N 71 58W
Asbury Park 162 40 15N 74 1W
Ascensión 164 31 6N 107 59W
Ascensión, B. de la 165 19 50N 87 20W
Ascension, I. 15 8 0S 14 15W
Aschach 49 48 23N 14 0 E
Aschaffenburg 49 49 58N 9 8 E
Aschendorf 48 53 2N 7 22 E
Aschersleben 48 51 45N 11 28 E
Asciano 63 43 14N 11 32 E
Áscoli Piceno 63 42 51N 13 34 E
Áscoli Satriano 65 41 11N 15 32 E
Ascona 51 46 9N 8 46 E
Ascope 174 7 46S 79 8W
Ascot 29 51 24N 0 41W
Ascotán 172 21 45S 68 17W
Aseb 123 13 0N 42 40 E
Åseda 73 57 10N 15 20 E
Åseda 73 57 10N 15 20 E
Asedjrad 118 24 51N 1 29 E
Asela 123 8 0N 39 0 E
Asenovgrad 67 42 1N 24 51 E
Åseral 71 58 37N 7 25 E
Åseral 71 58 38N 7 26 E
Asfeld 43 49 27N 4 5 E
Asfordby 29 52 45N 0 57W
Asfûn el Matâ'na 122 25 26N 32 30 E
Åsgårdstrand 71 59 22N 10 27 E
Ash 29 51 17N 1 16 E
Ash Fork 161 35 14N 112 32W
Ash Grove 159 37 21N 93 36W
Ash Shām,Bādiyat 92 31 30N 40 0 E
Ash Shāmīyah 92 31 55N 44 35 E
Ash Shatrah 92 31 30N 46 10 E
Ash Shuna 90 32 32N 35 34 E
Asha 84 55 0N 57 16 E
Ashaira 122 21 40N 40 40 E
Ashanti 121 7 30N 2 0W
Ashau 100 16 6N 107 22 E
Ashbourne, Ireland 38 53 31N 6 24W
Ashbourne, U.K. 33 53 2N 1 44W
Ashburn 157 31 42N 83 40W
Ashburton, N.Z. 143 43 53S 171 48 E
Ashburton, U.K. 30 50 31N 3 45W
Ashburton Downs 136 23 25S 117 4 E
Ashburton, R., Austral. 136 21 40S 114 56 E
Ashburton, R., N.Z. 131 44 2S 171 50 E
Ashby-de-la-Zouch 28 52 45N 1 29W
Ashchurch 28 52 0N 2 7W
Ashcroft 152 50 40N 121 20W
Ashdod 90 31 49N 34 35 E
Ashdot Ya'aqov 90 32 39N 35 35 E
Ashdown Forest 29 51 4N 0 2 E
Asheboro 157 35 43N 79 46W
Asherton 159 28 25N 99 43W
Asheville 157 35 39N 82 30W
Asheweig, R. 150 54 17N 87 12W
Ashford, Austral. 139 29 15S 151 3 E
Ashford, Derby., U.K. 33 53 13N 1 43W
Ashford, Kent, U.K. 29 51 8N 0 53 E
Ashford, U.S.A. 160 46 45N 122 2W
Ashikaga 111 36 28N 139 29 E
Ashington 35 55 12N 1 35W
Ashio 111 36 38N 139 27 E
Ashizuri-Zaki 110 32 35N 132 50 E
Ashkarkot 94 33 3N 67 58 E
Ashkhabad 76 38 0N 57 50 E
Ashland, Kans., U.S.A. 159 37 13N 99 43W
Ashland, Ky., U.S.A. 156 38 25N 82 40W
Ashland, Me., U.S.A. 151 46 34N 68 26W
Ashland, Mont., U.S.A. 160 45 41N 106 12W
Ashland, Nebr., U.S.A. 158 41 5N 96 27W
Ashland, Ohio, U.S.A. 156 40 52N 82 20W
Ashland, Oreg., U.S.A. 160 42 10N 122 38W
Ashland, Pa., U.S.A. 162 40 45N 76 22W
Ashland, Va., U.S.A. 156 37 46N 77 30W
Ashland, Wis., U.S.A. 158 46 40N 90 52W
Ashley, N.D., U.S.A. 158 46 3N 99 23W
Ashley, Pa., U.S.A. 162 41 14N 75 53W
Ashmont 152 54 7N 111 29W
Ashmore Is. 136 12 14S 123 50 E
Ashmore Reef 136 12 14S 123 5 E
Ashmûn 122 30 18N 30 55 E
Ashokan Res. 162 41 56N 74 13W
Ashquelon 90 31 42N 34 55 E
Ashtabula 156 41 52N 80 50W
Ashti 96 18 50N 75 15 E
Ashton, S. Afr. 128 33 50S 20 5 E
Ashton, U.S.A. 160 44 6N 111 30W
Ashton-in-Makerfield 32 53 29N 2 39W
Ashton-u.-Lyne 32 53 30N 2 8 E
Ashuanipi, L. 151 52 45N 66 15W
Ashurst 142 40 16S 175 45 E
Ashurstwood 29 51 6N 0 2 E
Ashwater 30 50 43N 4 18W
Ashwick 28 51 13N 2 31W
Asia 86 45 0N 75 0 E
Asia, Kepulauan 103 1 0N 131 13 E
Asiago 63 45 52N 11 30 E
Asifabad 96 19 30N 79 24 E
Asilah 118 35 29N 6 0W
Asinara 64 41 5N 8 15 E
Asinara, G. dell' 64 41 0N 8 30 E
Asinara I. 64 41 5N 8 15 E
Asino 76 57 0N 86 0 E
Asir 91 18 40N 42 30 E
Asir, Ras 91 11 55N 51 10 E
Aska 96 19 37N 84 42 E
Askeaton 39 52 37N 8 58W
Asker 71 59 50N 10 26 E
Askersund 73 58 53N 14 55 E
Askim 71 59 35N 11 10 E
Askino 84 56 5N 56 34 E
Askja 74 65 3N 16 48W
Åskloster 73 57 13N 12 11 E
Askrigg 32 54 19N 2 6W
Asl 122 29 33N 32 44 E
Aslackby 33 52 53N 0 23W
Asmar 93 35 10N 71 27 E
Asmera (Asmara) 123 15 19N 38 55 E
Asnæs 73 55 40N 11 0 E
Åsnen 73 56 35N 15 45 E
Åsnes 71 60 37N 11 59 E
Asni 118 31 17N 7 58W
Aso 110 33 0N 130 42 E
Aso-Zan 110 32 53N 131 6 E
Asoa 126 4 35N 25 48 E
Asola 62 45 12N 10 25 E
Asotin 60 46 14N 117 2W
Aspatria 32 54 45N 3 20W
Aspe 59 38 20N 0 40W
Aspen 161 39 12N 106 56W
Aspermont 159 33 11N 100 15W
Aspiring, Mt. 143 44 23S 168 46 E
Aspres 45 44 32N 5 44 E
Aspur 94 23 58N 74 7 E
Asquith 153 52 8N 107 13W
Assa 118 28 35N 9 6W
Assaba, Massif de l' 120 16 10N 11 45W
Assam □ 98 25 45N 92 30 E
Assamakka 121 19 21N 5 38 E
Assateague I. 162 38 5N 75 6W
Asse 47 50 54N 4 6 E
Assebroek 47 51 11N 3 17 E
Assekrem 119 23 16N 5 49 E
Assémini 64 39 18N 9 0 E
Assen 46 53 0N 6 35 E
Assendelft 46 52 29N 4 45 E
Assenede 47 51 14N 3 46 E
Assens, Odense, Denmark 73 56 41N 10 3 E
Assens, Randers, Denmark 73 55 16N 9 55 E
Assesse 47 50 22N 5 2 E
Assiniboia 153 49 40N 105 59W
Assiniboine, R. 153 49 53N 97 8W
Assinica L. 150 50 30N 75 20W
Assinie 120 5 9N 3 17W
Assis 173 22 40S 50 20W
Assisi 63 43 4N 12 36 E
Ássos 69 38 22N 20 33 E
Assynt 36 58 25N 5 10W
Assynt, L. 36 58 25N 5 15W
Astakidha 69 35 53N 26 50 E
Astalfort 44 44 4N 0 40 E
Astara 79 38 30N 48 50 E
Astee 39 52 33N 9 36W
Asten 47 51 24N 5 45 E
Asti 62 44 54N 8 11 E
Astillero 56 43 24N 3 49W
Astipálaia 69 36 32N 26 22 E
Aston, C. 149 70 10N 67 40W
Aston Clinton 29 51 48N 0 44W
Astorga 56 42 29N 6 8W
Astoria 160 46 16N 123 50W
Åstorp 73 56 6N 12 55 E
Astrakhan 83 46 25N 48 5 E
Astudillo 56 42 12N 4 22W
Asturias 56 43 15N 6 0W
Astwood Bank 28 52 15N 1 55W
Asunción 172 25 21S 57 30W
Asunción, La 174 11 2N 63 53W
Åsunden 73 57 47N 13 18 E
Asutri 123 15 25N 35 45 E
Aswa, R. 126 2 30N 33 5 E
Aswad,Rasal 122 21 20N 39 0 E
Aswân 122 24 4N 32 57 E
Aswân High Dam = Sadd el Aali 122 24 5N 32 54 E
Asyût 122 27 11N 31 4 E
Asyûti, Wadi 122 27 18N 31 20 E
Aszód 53 47 39N 19 28 E
At Tafilah 92 30 45N 35 30 E
At Ta'if 122 21 5N 40 27 E
Atacama 172 25 40S 67 40W
Atacama □ 172 27 30S 70 0W
Atacama, Desierto de 176 24 0S 69 20W
Atacama, Salar de 172 24 0S 68 20W
Ataco 174 3 35N 75 23W
Atakor 119 23 27N 5 31 E
Atakpamé 121 7 31N 1 13 E
Atalaia 114 9 25S 36 0W

Atalándi **69** 38 39N 22 58E
Atalaya **174** 10 45S 73 50W
Ataléia **171** 18 3S 41 6W
Atami **111** 35 0N 139 55E
Atankawng **98** 25 50N 97 47E
Atar **116** 20 30N 13 5W
Atara **77** 63 10N 129 10E
Ataram, Erg d' **118** 23 57N 2 0E
Atarfe **57** 37 13N 3 40W
Atascadero **163** 35 32N 120 44W
Atasu **76** 48 30N 71 0E
Atauro **103** 8 10S 125 30E
Atbara **122** 17 42N 33 59E
Atbara, R. **122** 17 40N 33 56E
Atbashi **85** 41 10N 75 48E
Atbashi, Khrebet **85** 40 50N 75 30E
Atchafalaya B. **159** 29 30N 91 20W
Atchison **158** 39 40N 95 0W
Atebubu **121** 7 47N 1 0W
Ateca **58** 41 20N 1 49W
Aterno, R. **63** 42 18N 13 45E
Atesine, Alpi **62** 46 55N 11 30E
Atessa **63** 42 5N 14 27E
Ath **47** 50 38N 3 47E
Ath Thamami **92** 27 45N 35 30E
Athabasca **152** 54 45N 113 20W
Athabasca, L. **153** 59 15N 109 15W
Athabasca, R. **153** 58 40N 110 50W
Athboy **38** 53 37N 6 55W
Athea **39** 52 27N 9 18W
Athenry **39** 53 18N 8 45W
Athens, Ala., U.S.A. **157** 34 49N 86 58W
Athens, Ga., U.S.A. **157** 33 56N 83 24W
Athens, N.Y., U.S.A. **162** 42 15N 73 48W
Athens, Ohio, U.S.A. **156** 39 52N 82 6W
Athens, Pa., U.S.A. **162** 41 57N 76 36W
Athens, Tex., U.S.A. **159** 32 11N 95 48W
Athens = Athínai **69** 37 58N 23 46E
Atherstone **28** 52 35N 1 32W
Atherton, Austral. **138** 17 17S 145 30E
Atherton, U.K. **32** 53 32N 2 30W
Athiéme **121** 6 37N 1 40E
Athínai **69** 37 58N 23 46E
Athleague **38** 53 34N 8 17W
Athlone **38** 53 26N 7 57W
Athni **96** 16 44N 75 6E
Athol **143** 45 30S 168 35E
Atholl, Forest of **37** 56 51N 3 50W
Atholville **151** 47 59N 66 43W
Áthos, Mt. **68** 40 9N 24 22E
Athus **47** 49 34N 5 50E
Athy **39** 53 0N 7 0W
Ati **123** 13 5N 29 2E
Atiak **126** 3 12N 32 2E
Atiamuri **142** 38 24S 176 5E
Atico **174** 16 14S 73 40W
Atienza **58** 41 12N 2 52W
Atikokan **150** 48 45N 91 37W
Atikonak L. **151** 52 40N 64 32W
Atka, U.S.A. **147** 52 5N 174 40W
Atka, U.S.S.R. **77** 60 50N 151 48E
Atkarsk **81** 51 55N 45 2E
Atkasuk (Meade River) **147** 70 30N 157 20W
Atkinson **158** 42 35N 98 59W
Atlanta, Ga., U.S.A. **157** 33 50N 84 24W
Atlanta, Tex., U.S.A. **159** 33 7N 94 8W
Atlantic **158** 41 25N 95 0W
Atlantic City **162** 39 25N 74 25W
Atlantic Ocean **14** 0 0 20 0W
Atlántico □ **174** 10 45N 75 0W
Atlas, Great, Mts. **114** 33 0N 5 0W
Atlin **147** 59 31N 133 41W
Atlin Lake **147** 59 26N 133 45W
'Atlit **90** 32 42N 34 56E
Atløy **71** 61 21N 4 58E
Atmakur **97** 14 37N 79 40E
Atmore **157** 31 2N 87 30W
Atnarko **152** 52 25N 126 0W
Atō **110** 34 25N 131 40E
Atoka **159** 34 22N 96 10W
Átokos **69** 38 28N 20 49E
Atolia **163** 35 19N 117 37W
Atotonilco el Alto **164** 20 20N 98 40W
Atouguia **57** 39 20N 9 20W
Atoyac, R. **165** 16 30N 97 31W
Atrafors **73** 57 02N 12 40E
Atrak, R. **93** 37 50N 57 0E
Ätran **73** 57 7N 12 57E
Atrato, R. **174** 6 40N 77 0W
Atrauli **94** 28 2N 78 20E
Atri **63** 42 35N 14 0E
Atsbi **122** 13 52N 39 50E
Atsumi **111** 34 35N 137 4E
Atsumi-Wan **111** 34 44N 137 13E
Atsuta **112** 43 24N 141 26E
Attalla **157** 34 2N 86 5W
Attawapiskat **150** 52 56N 82 24W
Attawapiskat, L. **150** 52 18N 87 54W
Attawapiskat, R. **150** 52 57N 82 18W
Attendorn **48** 51 8N 7 54E
Attersee **52** 47 55N 13 31E
Attert **47** 49 45N 5 47E
Attica **156** 40 20N 87 15W
Attichy **43** 49 25N 3 3E
Attigny **43** 49 28N 4 35E
Attikamagen L. **151** 55 0N 66 30W
Attikí Kai Arkhipélagos □ **69** 38 10N 23 40E
Attil **90** 32 23N 35 4E
Attleboro **162** 41 56N 71 18W
Attleborough **29** 52 32N 1 1E
Attock **94** 33 52N 72 20E
Attopeu **100** 14 48N 106 50E
Attu **147** 52 55N 173 10W
Attunga **141** 30 55S 150 50E
Attur **97** 11 35N 78 30E
Attymon **39** 53 20N 8 37W
Atuel, R. **172** 36 17S 66 50W
Atvidaberg **73** 58 12N 16 0E
Atwater **163** 37 21N 120 37W
Atwood **158** 39 52N 101 3W
Au Sable Pt. **150** 46 0N 86 0W
Au Sable, R. **156** 44 25N 83 20W
Aubagne **45** 43 17N 5 37E
Aubange **47** 49 34N 5 48E
Aubarede Pt. **103** 17 15N 122 20E
Aube □ **43** 48 15N 4 0E
Aubel **47** 50 42N 5 51E
Aubenas **45** 44 37N 4 24E
Aubenton **43** 49 50N 4 12E
Auberry **163** 37 7N 119 29W
Aubigny-sur-Nère **43** 47 30N 2 24E
Aubin **44** 44 33N 2 15E
Aubrac, Mts. d' **44** 44 38N 2 58E
Auburn, Ala., U.S.A. **157** 32 37N 85 30W
Auburn, Calif., U.S.A. **160** 38 50N 121 4W
Auburn, Ind., U.S.A. **156** 41 20N 85 0W
Auburn, Nebr., U.S.A. **158** 40 25N 95 50W
Auburn, N.Y., U.S.A. **162** 42 57N 76 39W
Auburn, Penn., U.S.A. **162** 40 36N 76 6W
Auburn Range **139** 25 15S 150 30E
Auburndale **157** 28 5N 81 45W
Aubusson **44** 45 57N 2 11E
Auch **44** 43 39N 0 36E
Auchel **43** 50 30N 2 29E
Auchenblae **37** 56 54N 2 26W
Auchencairn **35** 54 51N 3 52W
Auchi **121** 7 6N 6 13E
Auchinleck **34** 55 28N 4 18W
Auchness **37** 58 0N 4 36W
Auchterarder **35** 56 18N 3 43W
Auchterderran **35** 56 8N 3 16W
Auchtermuchty **35** 56 18N 3 15W
Auchtertyre **36** 57 17N 5 35W
Auckland **142** 36 52S 174 46E
Auckland □ **142** 38 35S 177 0E
Auckland Is. **142** 51 0S 166 0E
Aude □ **44** 43 8N 2 28E
Aude, R. **44** 44 13N 3 15E
Auden **150** 50 14N 87 53W
Auderghem **47** 50 49N 4 26E
Auderville **42** 49 43N 1 57W
Audierne **42** 48 1N 4 34W
Audincourt **43** 47 30N 6 50E
Audlem **32** 52 59N 2 31W
Audo Ra. **123** 6 20N 41 50E
Audrey, gasfield **19** 53 35N 2 0E
Audubon **158** 41 43N 94 56W
Aue **48** 50 34N 12 43E
Auerbach **48** 50 30N 12 25E
Auffay **42** 49 43N 1 07E
Augathella **139** 25 48S 146 35E
Augher **38** 54 25N 7 10W
Aughnacloy **38** 54 25N 6 58W
Aughrim, Clare, Ireland **39** 53 0N 8 57W
Aughrim, Galway, Ireland **39** 53 18N 8 19W
Aughrim, Wicklow, Ireland **39** 52 52N 6 20W
Aughrus More **38** 53 34N 10 10W
Augrabies Falls **128** 28 35S 20 20E
Augsburg **49** 48 22N 10 54E
Augusta, Italy **65** 37 14N 15 12E
Augusta, Ark., U.S.A. **159** 35 17N 91 25W
Augusta, Ga., U.S.A. **157** 33 29N 81 59W
Augusta, Kans., U.S.A. **159** 37 40N 97 0W
Augusta, Me., U.S.A. **151** 44 20N 69 46E
Augusta, Mont., U.S.A. **160** 47 30N 112 29W
Augusta, Wis., U.S.A. **158** 44 41N 91 8W
Augustenborg **73** 54 57N 9 53E
Augustine **159** 31 30N 94 37W
Augusto Cardosa **127** 12 40S 34 50E
Augustów **54** 53 51N 23 00E
Augustus Downs **138** 18 35S 139 55E
Augustus I. **136** 15 20S 124 30E
Augustus, Mt. **137** 24 20S 116 50E
Auk, oilfield **19** 56 25N 2 15E
Aukan **123** 15 29N 40 50E
Aukum **163** 38 34N 120 43W
Auld, L. **136** 22 32S 123 44E
Auldearn **37** 57 34N 3 50W
Aulla **62** 44 12N 9 57E
Aulnay **44** 46 2N 0 22W
Aulne, R. **42** 48 17N 4 16W
Ault **158** 40 40N 104 42W
Ault-Onival **42** 50 5N 1 29E
Aultbea **36** 57 50N 5 36W
Aulus-les-Bains **44** 42 49N 1 19E
Aumale **43** 49 46N 1 46E
Aumont-Aubrac **44** 44 43N 3 17E
Auna **121** 10 9N 4 42E
Aundh **96** 17 33N 74 23E
Aunis **44** 46 0N 0 50W
Auponhia **103** 1 58S 125 27E
Aups **45** 43 37N 6 15E
Aur, P. **101** 2 35N 104 10E
Aura **98** 26 59N 97 57E
Aurahorten, Mt. **71** 59 15N 6 53E
Auraiya **95** 26 28N 79 33E
Aurangabad, Bihar, India **95** 24 45N 84 18E
Aurangabad, Maharashtra, India **96** 19 50N 75 23E
Auray **42** 47 40N 3 0W
Aurès **119** 35 8N 6 30E
Aurich **48** 53 28N 7 30E
Aurilândia **171** 16 44S 50 28W
Aurillac **44** 44 55N 2 26E
Aurlandsvangen **71** 60 55N 7 12E
Auronza **63** 46 33N 12 27E
Aurora, Brazil **171** 6 57S 38 58W
Aurora, S. Afr. **128** 32 40S 18 29E
Aurora, Colo., U.S.A. **158** 39 44N 104 55W
Aurora, Ill., U.S.A. **156** 41 42N 88 12W
Aurora, Mo., U.S.A. **159** 36 58N 93 42W
Aurora, Nebr., U.S.A. **158** 40 55N 98 0W
Aurora, N.Y., U.S.A. **162** 42 45N 76 42W
Aurskog **71** 59 55N 11 26E
Aurukun Mission **138** 13 20S 141 45E
Aus **128** 26 35S 16 12E
Auskerry I. **37** 59 2N 2 35W
Aust-Agder fylke □ **75** 58 55N 7 40E
Austad **71** 58 58N 7 37E
Austerlitz = Slavikov **53** 49 10N 16 52E
Austevoll **71** 60 5N 5 13E
Austin, Austral. **137** 27 40S 117 50E
Austin, Minn., U.S.A. **158** 43 37N 92 59W
Austin, Nev., U.S.A. **160** 39 30N 117 1W
Austin, Tex., U.S.A. **159** 30 20N 97 45W
Austin, L. **137** 27 40S 118 0E
Austral Downs **138** 20 30S 137 45E
Austral Is. = Tubuai, Îles **143** 25 0S 150 0E
Australia ■ **133** 23 0S 135 0E
Australian Alps **141** 36 30S 148 8E
Australian Cap. Terr. **139** 35 15S 149 8E
Australian Dependency **13** 73 0S 90 0E
Austria ■ **52** 47 0N 14 0E
Austvågøy **74** 68 20N 14 40E
Autelbas **47** 49 39N 5 52E
Auterive **44** 43 21N 1 29E
Authie, R. **43** 50 22N 1 38E
Autlan **164** 19 40N 104 30W
Autun **43** 46 58N 4 17E
Auvelais **47** 50 27N 4 38E
Auvergne, Austral. **136** 15 39S 130 1E
Auvergne, France **44** 45 20N 3 0E
Auxerre **43** 47 48N 3 32E
Auxi-le-Château **43** 50 15N 2 8E
Auxonne **43** 47 10N 5 20E
Auzances **44** 46 2N 2 30E
Avaldsnes **71** 59 21N 5 20E
Avallon **43** 47 30N 3 53E
Avalon **163** 33 21N 118 20W
Avalon Pen. **151** 47 30N 53 20W
Avalon Res. **159** 32 30N 104 30W
Avanigadda **97** 16 0N 80 56E
Avaré **173** 23 4S 48 58W
Ávas **68** 40 57N 25 56E
Avawata Mts. **163** 35 30N 116 20W
Avebury **28** 51 25N 1 52W
Aveh **92** 35 40N 49 15E
Aveiro, Brazil **175** 3 10S 55 5W
Aveiro, Port. **56** 40 37N 8 38W
Aveiro □ **56** 40 40N 8 35W
Avelgem **47** 50 47N 3 27E
Avellaneda **172** 34 50S 58 10W
Avellino **65** 40 54N 14 46E
Avenal **163** 36 0N 120 8W
Avenchen **50** 46 53N 7 2E
Averøya **71** 63 0N 7 35E
Aversa **65** 40 58N 14 11E
Avery **160** 47 22N 115 56W
Aves, Islas de **174** 12 0N 67 40W
Avesnes-sur-Helpe **43** 50 8N 3 55E
Avesta **72** 60 9N 16 10E
Aveton Gifford **30** 50 17N 3 51W
Aveyron □ **44** 44 22N 2 45E
Avezzano **63** 42 2N 13 24E
Avgó **69** 35 33N 25 37E
Aviá Terai **172** 26 45S 60 50W
Aviano **63** 46 3N 12 35E
Avich, L. **34** 56 17N 5 25W
Aviemore **37** 57 11N 3 50W
Avigliana **62** 45 7N 7 13E
Avigliano **65** 40 44N 15 41E
Avignon **45** 43 57N 4 50E
Ávila **56** 40 39N 4 43W
Ávila □ **56** 40 30N 5 0W
Avila Beach **163** 35 11N 120 44W
Ávila, Sierra de **56** 40 40N 5 0W
Avilés **56** 43 35N 5 57W
Avionárion **69** 38 31N 24 8E
Avisio, R. **63** 46 14N 11 18E
Aviz **57** 39 4N 7 53W
Avize **43** 48 59N 4 0E
Avoca, Austral. **139** 37 5S 143 26E
Avoca, Ireland **39** 52 52N 6 13W
Avoca, R., Austral. **140** 35 40S 143 43E
Avoca, R., Ireland **39** 52 48N 6 10W
Avoch **37** 57 34N 4 10W
Avola, Can. **152** 51 45N 119 19W
Avola, Italy **65** 36 56N 15 7E
Avon **158** 43 0N 98 3W
Avon □ **28** 51 30N 2 40W
Avon Downs **133** 19 58S 137 25E
Avon Is. **133** 19 37S 158 17E
Avon, R., Austral. **137** 31 40S 116 7E
Avon, R., Avon, U.K. **28** 51 30N 2 43W
Avon, R., Grampian, U.K. **37** 57 25N 3 25W
Avon, R., Hants., U.K. **28** 50 44N 1 45W
Avon, R., Warwick, U.K. **28** 52 0N 2 9W
Avondale, N.Z. **142** 36 54S 174 42E
Avondale, Rhod. **127** 17 43S 30 58E
Avonlea **153** 50 0N 105 0W
Avonmouth **28** 51 30N 2 42W
Avranches **42** 48 40N 1 20W
Avrig **70** 45 43N 24 21E
Avrillé **44** 46 28N 1 28W
Avtovac **66** 43 9N 18 35E
Avu Meru □ **126** 3 20S 36 50E
Awag el Baqar **123** 10 10N 33 10E
Awaji **111** 34 32N 135 1E
Awaji-Shima **110** 34 30N 134 50E
Awali **93** 26 0N 50 30E
Awantipur **95** 33 55N 75 3E
Awanui **142** 35 4S 173 17E
Awarja, R. **96** 18 0N 76 15E
Awarta **90** 32 10N 35 17E
Awarua Pt. **143** 44 15S 168 5E
Awasa, L. **123** 7 0N 38 30E
Awash **123** 9 1N 40 10E
Awash, R. **123** 11 30N 42 0E
Awaso **120** 6 15N 2 22W
Awatere, R. **143** 41 37S 174 10E
Awbarī **119** 26 46N 12 57E
Awe, L. **34** 56 15N 5 15W
Aweil **123** 8 42N 27 20E
Awgu **121** 6 4N 7 24E
Awjilah **117** 29 8N 21 7E
Aworro **135** 7 43S 143 11E
Ax-les-Thermes **44** 42 44N 1 50E
Axarfjörður **74** 66 15N 16 45W
Axbridge **28** 51 17N 2 50W
Axe Edge **32** 53 14N 2 2W
Axe R. **28** 51 17N 2 52W
Axel **47** 51 16N 3 55E
Axel Heiberg I. **12** 80 0N 90 0W
Axelfors **73** 57 26N 13 7E
Axholme, Isle of **33** 53 30N 1 10E
Axim **120** 4 51N 2 15W
Axintele **70** 44 37N 26 47E
Axiós, R. **68** 40 57N 22 35E
Axmarsbruk **72** 61 3N 17 10E
Axminster **30** 50 47N 3 1W
Axmouth **30** 50 43N 3 2W
Axstedt **48** 53 26N 8 43E
Axvall **73** 58 23N 13 34E
Ay **43** 49 3N 4 0E
Ay, R. **84** 56 8N 57 40E
Ayabaca **174** 4 40S 79 53W
Ayabe **111** 35 20N 135 20E
Ayacucho, Argent. **172** 37 5S 58 20W
Ayacucho, Peru **174** 13 0S 74 0W
Ayaguz **76** 48 10N 80 0E
Ayakkuduk **85** 41 12N 65 12E
Ayakok'umu Hu **105** 37 30N 89 20E
Ayakudi **97** 10 57N 77 6E
Ayamonte **57** 37 12N 7 24W
Ayan **77** 56 30N 138 16E
Ayancık **82** 41 57N 34 18E
Ayapel **174** 8 19N 75 9W
Ayapel, Sa. de **174** 7 45N 75 30W
Ayaş **82** 40 10N 32 14E
Ayaviri **174** 14 50S 70 35W
Aydın □ **92** 37 40N 27 40E
Aye **47** 50 14N 5 18E
Ayenngré **121** 8 40N 1 1E
Ayer Hitam **101** 1 55N 103 11E
Ayeritam **101** 5 24N 100 15E
Ayers Rock **136** 25 23S 131 5E
Ayiá **68** 39 43N 22 45E
Áyia Anna **69** 38 52N 23 24E
Ayía Marína, Kásos, Greece **69** 35 27N 26 53E
Ayía Marína, Leros, Greece **69** 37 11N 26 48E
Ayía Paraskeví **68** 39 14N 26 16E
Ayía Rouméli **69** 35 14N 23 58E
Ayiássos **69** 39 5N 26 23E
Áyios Andréas **69** 37 21N 22 45E
Áyios Evstrátios **68** 39 34N 24 58E
Áyios Ioánnis, Ákra **69** 35 20N 25 40E
Áyios Kírikos **69** 37 34N 26 17E
Áyios Matthaíos **68** 39 30N 19 47E
Áyios Míron **69** 35 15N 25 1E
Áyios Nikólaos **69** 35 11N 25 41E
Áyios Pétros **69** 38 38N 20 33E
Áyios Yeóryios **69** 37 28N 23 57E
Ayíkathonísi **69** 37 28N 27 0E
Ayke, Ozero **84** 51 57N 61 36E
Aylesbury **29** 51 48N 0 49W
Aylesford **29** 51 18N 0 29E
Aylmer L. **148** 64 0N 108 30W
Aylsham **29** 52 48N 1 16E
Ayn Zālah **92** 36 45N 42 35E
'Ayn Zaqqūt **119** 29 0N 19 30E
Ayna **59** 38 34N 2 3W
Aynho **28** 51 59N 1 15W
Ayni **85** 39 23N 68 32E
Ayolas **172** 27 10S 56 59W
Ayom **123** 7 49N 28 23E
Ayon, Ostrov **77** 69 50N 169 0E
Ayora **59** 39 3N 1 3W
Ayr, Austral. **138** 19 35S 147 25E
Ayr, U.K. **34** 55 28N 4 37W
Ayr (□) **26** 55 25N 4 25W
Ayr, Heads of **34** 55 25N 4 43W
Ayr, R. **34** 55 29N 4 40W
Ayre, Pt. of **37** 58 55N 2 43W
Ayre, Pt. of I.o.M. **32** 54 27N 4 21W
Aysgarth **32** 54 18N 2 0W
Aysha **123** 10 50N 42 23E
Ayton **138** 15 45S 145 25E
Ayton, Borders, U.K. **35** 55 51N 2 6W
Ayton, N. Yorks., U.K. **33** 54 15N 0 29W
Aytos **67** 42 47N 27 16E
Aytoska Planina **67** 42 45N 27 30E
Ayu, Kepulauan **103** 0 35N 131 5E
Ayutla, Guat. **166** 14 40N 92 10W

Ayutla, Mexico 165 16 58N 99 17W
Ayutthaya = Phra Nakhon Si A. 101 14 25N 100 30E
Ayvalık 92 39 20N 26 46E
Aywaille 47 50 28N 5 40E
Az Zahiriya 90 31 25N 34 58E
Az Zahran 92 26 10N 50 7E
Az-Zarqā 90 32 5N 36 4E
Az Zāwiyah 119 32 52N 12 56E
Az-Zilfī 92 26 12N 44 52E
Az Zintān 119 31 59N 12 9E
Az Zubayr 92 30 20N 47 50E
Azambuja 57 39 4N 8 51W
Azamgarh 95 26 35N 83 13E
Azaouak, Vallée de l' 121 15 50N 3 20E
Azärbāijān □ 92 37 0N 44 30E
Azare 121 11 55N 10 10E
Azay-le-Rideau 42 47 16N 0 30E
Azazga 119 36 48N 4 22E
Azbine = Aïr 121 18 0N 8 0E
Azeffoun 119 36 51N 4 26E
Azemmour 118 33 14N 9 20W
Azerbaijan S.S.R. □ 83 40 20N 48 0E
Azezo 123 12 28N 37 15E
Azilal,Beni Mallal 118 32 0N 6 30W
Azimganj 95 24 14N 84 16E
Aznalcóllar 57 37 32N 6 17W
Azogues 174 2 35S 78 0W
Azor 90 32 2N 34 48E
Azores, Is. 14 38 44N 29 0W
Azov 83 47 3N 39 25E
Azov Sea = Azovskoye More 82 46 0N 36 30E
Azovskoye More 82 46 0N 36 30E
Azovy 76 64 55N 64 35E
Azpeitia 58 43 12N 2 19W
Azrou 118 33 28N 5 19W
Aztec 161 36 54N 108 0W
Azúa de Compostela 167 18 25N 70 44W
Azuaga 57 38 16N 5 39W
Azuara 58 41 15N 0 53W
Azuara, R. 58 41 12N 0 55W
Azúcar, Presa del 165 26 0N 99 5W
Azuer, R. 57 38 50N 3 15W
Azuero, Pen. de 166 7 30N 80 30W
Azul 172 36 42S 59 43W
Azusa 163 34 8N 117 52W
Azzaba 119 36 48N 7 6E
Azzano Décimo 63 45 53N 12 46E

B

B. Curri 68 42 22N 20 5E
Ba Don 100 17 45N 106 26E
Ba Dong 101 9 40N 106 33E
Ba Ngoi = Cam Lam 101 11 50N 109 10E
Ba, R. 56 13 5N 109 0E
Ba Tri 101 10 2N 106 36E
Baa 103 10 50S 123 0E
Baamonde 56 43 7N 7 44W
Baar 51 47 12N 8 32E
Baarle Nassau 47 51 27N 4 56E
Baarlo 47 51 20N 6 6E
Baarn 46 52 12N 5 17E
Bāb el Māndeb 91 12 35N 43 25E
Baba Burnu 68 39 29N 26 2E
Baba dag 83 41 0N 48 55E
Baba, Mt. 67 42 44N 23 59E
Babaçulândia 170 7 13S 47 46W
Babadag 70 44 53N 28 44E
Babaeski 67 41 26N 27 6E
Babahoyo 174 1 40S 79 30W
Babakin 137 32 7S 118 1E
Babana 121 10 31N 3 46E
Babar, Alg. 119 35 10N 7 6E
Babar, Pak. 94 31 7N 69 32E
Babar, I. 103 8 0S 129 30E
Babarkach 94 29 45N 68 0E
Babayevo 81 59 24N 35 55E
Babb 160 48 56N 113 27W
Babbitt 163 38 32N 118 39W
Babenhausen 49 49 57N 8 56E
Babi Besar, P. 101 2 25N 103 59E
Babia Gora 54 49 38N 19 38E
Babile 123 9 16N 42 11E
Babinda 138 17 20S 145 56E
Babine 152 55 20N 126 35W
Babine L. 152 54 48N 126 0W
Babine, R. 152 55 45N 127 44W
Babo 103 2 30S 133 30E
Babócsa 53 46 2N 17 21E
Babol 93 36 40N 52 50E
Babol Sar 93 36 45N 52 45E
Baboma 126 2 30N 28 10E
Baborówo Kietrz 53 50 7N 18 1E
Baboua 124 5 49N 14 58E
Babuna, mts. 66 41 30N 21 40E
Babura 121 12 51N 8 59E
Babusar Pass 95 35 12N 73 59E
Babushkin 81 55 45N 37 40E
Babušnica 66 43 7N 22 27E
Babylon, Iraq 92 32 40N 44 30E
Babylon, U.S.A. 162 40 42N 73 20W
Bač 66 45 29N 19 17E
Bac Can 100 22 08N 105 49E
Bac Giang 100 21 16N 106 11E
Bac Kan 101 22 5N 105 50E
Bac Lieu = Vinh Loi 101 9 17N 105 43E
Bac Ninh 100 21 13N 106 4E
Bac Phan 100 22 0N 105 0E
Bac Quang 100 22 30N 104 48E
Bacabal 170 4 15N 44 45W
Bacalar 165 18 12N 87 53W
Bacan,Pulau 103 0 50S 127 30E
Bacarès, Le 44 42 47N 3 3E
Bacarra 103 18 15N 120 37E
Baccarat 43 48 28N 6 42E
Bacchus Marsh 140 37 43S 144 27E
Bacerac 164 30 18N 108 50W
Bach Long Vi,Dao 100 20 10N 107 40E
Bachaquero 174 9 56N 71 8W
Bacharach 49 50 3N 7 46E
Bachclina 76 57 45N 67 20E
Bachok 101 6 4N 102 25E
Bachuma 123 6 31N 36 1E
Bačina 66 43 42N 21 23E
Back 36 58 17N 6 20W
Back, R. 148 65 10N 104 0W
Bačka Palanka 66 45 17N 19 27E
Bačka Topola 66 45 49N 19 39E
Bäckefors 73 58 48N 12 9E
Bački Petrovac 66 45 29N 19 32E
Backnang 49 48 57N 9 26E
Backstairs Passage 133 35 40S 138 5E
Bacolod 103 10 40N 122 57E
Bacqueville 42 49 47N 1 0E
Bacs-Kiskun □ 53 46 43N 19 30E
Bácsalmás 53 46 8N 19 17E
Bacton 29 52 50N 1 29E
Bacuit 103 11 20N 119 20E
Bacup 32 53 42N 2 12W
Bacŭu 70 46 35N 26 55E
Bacŭu □ 70 46 30N 26 45E
Bad Aussee 52 47 43N 13 45E
Bad Axe 150 43 48N 82 59W
Bad Bergzabem 49 49 6N 8 0E
Bad Bramstedt 48 53 56N 9 53E
Bad Doberan 48 54 6N 11 55E
Bad Driburg 48 51 44N 9 0E
Bad Ems 49 50 22N 7 44E
Bad Frankenhausen 48 51 21N 11 3E
Bad Freienwalde 52 52 46N 14 2E
Bad Godesberg 48 50 41N 7 4E
Bad Hersfeld 48 50 52N 9 42E
Bad Hofgastein 52 47 17N 13 6E
Bad Homburg 49 50 17N 8 33E
Bad Honnef 48 50 39N 7 13E
Bad Ischl 52 47 44N 13 38E
Bad Kissingen 49 50 11N 10 5E
Bad Kreuznach 49 49 47N 7 47E
Bad Lands 158 43 40N 102 10W
Bad Lauterberg 48 51 38N 10 29E
Bad Leonfelden 52 48 31N 14 18E
Bad Lippspringe 48 51 47N 8 46E
Bad Mergentheim 49 49 29N 9 47E
Bad Münstereifel 48 50 33N 6 46E
Bad Nauheim 49 50 24N 8 45E
Bad Oeynhausen 48 52 16N 8 45E
Bad Oldesloe 48 53 56N 10 17E
Bad Orb 49 50 16N 9 21E
Bad Pyrmont 48 51 59N 9 5E
Bad, R. 158 44 10N 100 50W
Bad Ragaz 51 47 0N 9 30E
Bad St. Peter 48 54 23N 8 32E
Bad Salzuflen 48 52 8N 8 44E
Bad Segeberg 48 53 58N 10 16E
Bad Tölz 49 47 43N 11 34E
Bad Waldsee 49 47 56N 9 46E
Bad Wildungen 48 51 7N 9 10E
Bad Wimpfen 49 49 12N 9 10E
Bad Windsheim 49 49 29N 10 25E
Badagara 97 11 35N 75 40E
Badagri 121 6 25N 2 55E
Badajoz 57 38 50N 6 59W
Badajoz □ 57 38 40N 6 30W
Badakhshan □ 93 36 30N 71 0E
Badalona 58 41 26N 2 15E
Badalzai 94 29 50N 65 35E
Badampahar 96 22 10N 86 10E
Badanah 92 30 58N 41 30E
Badas 102 4 33N 114 25E
Badas, Kepulauan 102 0 45N 107 5E
Baddo, R. 93 28 15N 65 0E
Bade 103 7 10S 139 35E
Baden, Austria 53 48 1N 16 13E
Baden, Switz. 51 47 28N 8 18E
Baden-Baden 49 48 45N 8 15E
Baden Park 140 32 8S 144 12E
Baden-Württemberg □ 49 48 40N 9 0E
Badenoch 37 58 16N 4 5W
Badenscoth 37 57 27N 2 30W
Badeso 123 9 58N 40 52E
Badgastein 52 47 7N 13 9E
Badger, Can. 151 49 0N 56 4W
Badger, U.S.A. 163 36 38N 119 1W
Badghis □ 93 35 0N 63 0E
Badgom 95 34 1N 74 45E
Badhoevedorp 46 52 20N 4 47E
Badia Polesine 63 45 6N 11 30E
Badin 94 24 38N 68 54E
Badnera 96 20 48N 77 44E
Badogo 120 11 2N 8 13W
Badrinath 95 30 45N 79 30E
Baduen 91 7 15N 47 40E
Badulla 97 7 1N 81 7E
Badupi 98 21 36N 93 27E
Bække 73 55 35N 9 6E
Baena 57 37 37N 4 20W
Baerami Creek 141 32 27S 150 27E
Baetas 174 6 5S 62 15W
Baexem 47 51 13N 5 53E
Baeza, Ecuador 174 0 25S 77 45W
Baeza, Spain 59 37 57N 3 25W
Bafa 93 31 40N 55 25E
Bafa Gölü 69 37 30N 27 29E
Bafatá 120 12 8N 15 20W
Baffin Bay 12 72 0N 64 0W
Baffin I. 149 68 0N 75 0W
Bafia 121 4 40N 11 10E
Bafilo 121 9 22N 1 22E
Bafing, R. 120 11 40N 10 45W
Baflo 46 53 22N 6 31E
Bafoulabé 120 13 50N 10 55W
Bafq 93 31 40N 55 20E
Bafra 82 41 34N 35 54E
Baft 93 29 15N 56 38E
Bafut 121 6 6N 10 2E
Bafwakwandji 126 1 12N 26 52E
Bafwasende 126 1 3N 27 5E
Bagalkot 96 16 10N 75 40E
Bagamoyo 126 6 28S 38 55E
Bagamoyo □ 126 6 20S 38 30E
Bagan Datok 101 3 59N 100 47E
Bagan Serai 101 5 1N 100 32E
Bagan Siapiapi 102 2 12N 100 50E
Baganga 103 7 34N 126 33E
Bagasra 94 21 59N 71 77E
Bagawi 123 12 20N 34 18E
Bagdad 163 34 35N 115 53W
Bagdarin 77 54 26N 113 36E
Bagé 173 31 20S 54 15W
Bagenalstown = Muine Bheag 39 52 42N 6 57W
Baggs 160 41 8N 107 46W
Baggy Pt. 30 51 11N 4 12W
Bagh 95 33 59N 73 45E
Bagh nam Faoileann, B. 36 57 22N 7 13W
Baghdād 92 33 20N 44 30E
Bagherhat 98 22 40N 89 47E
Bagheria 64 38 5N 13 30E
Baghin 93 30 12N 56 45E
Baghlan 93 36 12N 69 0E
Baghlan □ 93 36 0N 68 30E
Baginbun Hd. 39 52 10N 6 50W
Bagley 158 47 30N 95 22W
Bagnacavallo 63 44 25N 11 58E
Bagnara Cálabra 65 38 16N 15 49E
Bagnères-de-Bigorre 44 43 5N 0 9E
Bagnères-de-Luchon 44 42 47N 0 38E
Bagni di Lucca 62 44 1N 10 37E
Bagno di Romagna 63 43 50N 11 59E
Bagnoles-de-l'Orne 42 48 32N 0 25W
Bagnolo Mella 62 45 27N 10 14E
Bagnols-les-Bains 44 44 30N 3 40E
Bagnols-sur-Cèze 45 44 10N 4 36E
Bagnorégio 63 42 38N 12 7E
Bagolino 62 45 49N 10 28E
Bagotville 151 48 22N 70 54W
Bagrdan 66 44 5N 21 11E
Bagshot 29 51 22N 0 41W
Baguio 103 16 26N 120 34E
Bahabón de Esgueva 58 41 52N 3 43W
Bahadurabad 98 25 11N 89 44E
Bahadurgarh 94 28 40N 76 57E
Bahama, Canal Viejo de 166 22 10N 77 30W
Bahama Is. 167 24 40N 74 0W
Bahamas ■ 167 24 0N 74 0W
Baharîya, El Wâhât el 122 28 0N 28 50E
Bahau 101 2 48N 102 26E
Bahawalnagar 94 30 0N 73 15E
Bahawalpur 94 29 37N 71 40E
Bahawalpur □ 94 29 5N 71 3E
Baheri 95 28 45N 79 34E
Baheta 123 13 27N 42 10E
Bahi 126 5 58S 35 21E
Bahi Swamp 126 6 10S 35 0E
Bahia = Salvador 171 13 0S 38 30W
Bahia □ 171 12 0N 42 0W
Bahía Blanca 172 38 35S 62 13W
Bahía de Caráquez 174 0 40S 80 27W
Bahía Honda 166 22 54N 83 10W
Bahía, Islas de la 166 16 45N 86 15W
Bahia Laura 176 48 10S 66 30W
Bahia Negra 174 20 5S 58 5W
Bahir Dar Giyorgis 123 11 33N 37 25E
Bahmer 118 27 32N 0 10W
Bahönye 53 46 25N 17 28E
Bahr Aouk 124 9 20N 20 40E
Bahr Dar 123 11 37N 37 10E
Bahr el Abiad 123 9 30N 31 40E
Bahr el Ahmer □ 122 20 0N 35 0E
Bahr el Arab 123 9 50N 27 10E
Bahr el Azraq 123 10 30N 35 0E
Bahr el Ghazâl □ 123 7 0N 28 0E
Bahr el Ghazâl, R. 123 9 0N 30 0E
Bahr el Jebel 123 7 30N 30 30E
Bahr Salamat 124 10 0N 19 0E
Bahr Yûsef 122 28 25N 30 35E
Bahra 92 21 25N 39 32E
Bahra el Burullus 122 31 28N 30 48E
Bahra el Manzala 122 31 28N 32 01E
Bahraich 95 27 38N 81 50E
Bahrain ■ 93 26 0N 50 35E
Bahramabad 93 30 28N 56 2E
Bahu Kalat 93 25 50N 61 20E
Bai 120 13 35N 3 28W
Bai Bung, Mui 101 8 38N 104 44E
Bai Duc 100 18 3N 105 49E
Bai Thuong 100 19 54N 105 23E
Baia-Mare 70 47 40N 23 17E
Baia-Sprie 70 47 41N 23 43E
Baião 170 2 40S 49 40W
Baïbokoum 117 7 40N 14 45E
Baidoa 91 3 8N 43 30E
Baie Comeau 151 49 12N 68 10W
Baie de l'Abri 151 50 3N 67 0W
Baie Johan Beetz 151 50 18N 62 50W
Baie St. Paul 151 47 28N 70 32W
Baie Trinité 151 49 25N 67 20W
Baie Verte 151 49 55N 56 12W
Baignes 44 45 28N 0 25W
Baigneux-les-Juifs 43 47 31N 4 39E
Ba'ījī 92 35 0N 43 30E
Baikal, L. 77 53 0N 108 0E
Bailadila, Mt. 96 18 43N 81 15E
Baildon 33 53 52N 1 46W
Baile Atha Cliath = Dublin 39 53 20N 6 18W
Bailei 123 6 44N 40 18E
Bailén 57 38 8N 3 48W
Baileux 47 50 2N 4 23E
Bailhongal 97 15 55N 74 53E
Bailique, Ilha 170 1 2N 49 58W
Bailleul 43 50 44N 2 41E
Baillieborough 38 53 55N 7 0W
Baimuru 135 7 35S 144 51E
Bain-de-Bretagne 42 47 50N 1 40W
Bainbridge, U.K. 32 54 18N 2 7W
Bainbridge, Ga., U.S.A. 157 30 53N 84 34W
Bainbridge, N.Y., U.S.A. 162 42 17N 75 29W
Baing 103 10 14S 120 34E
Bainville 158 48 8N 104 10W
Bainyik 135 3 40S 143 4E
Baird 159 32 25N 99 25W
Baird Inlet 147 64 49N 164 18W
Baird Mts. 147 67 10N 160 15W
Bairnsdale 141 37 48S 147 36E
Baissa 121 7 14N 10 38E
Baitadi 95 29 35N 80 25E
Baixa Grande 171 11 57S 40 11W
Baiyuda 122 17 35N 32 07E
Baja 53 46 12N 18 59E
Baja California 164 32 10N 115 12W
Baja, Pta. 164 29 50N 116 0W
Bajah, Wadi 122 23 14N 39 20E
Bajana 94 23 7N 71 49E
Bajimba 139 29 22S 152 0E
Bajimba, Mt. 139 29 17S 152 6E
Bajina Bašta 66 43 58N 19 35E
Bajitpur 95 24 13N 91 0E
Bajmok 66 45 57N 19 24E
Bajo Boquete 167 8 49N 82 27W
Bajoga 121 10 57N 11 20E
Bajool 138 23 40S 150 35E
Bak 53 46 43N 16 51E
Bakal 84 54 56N 58 48E
Bakala 117 6 15N 20 20E
Bakanas 85 44 50N 76 15E
Bakar 63 45 18N 14 32E
Bakel, Neth. 47 51 30N 5 45E
Bakel, Senegal 120 14 56N 12 20W
Baker, Calif., U.S.A. 163 35 16N 116 8W
Baker, Mont., U.S.A. 158 46 22N 104 12W
Baker, Nev., U.S.A. 160 38 59N 114 7W
Baker, Oreg., U.S.A. 160 44 50N 117 55W
Baker Is. 130 0 10N 176 35E
Baker, L., Austral. 137 26 54S 126 5E
Baker, L., Can. 148 64 0N 96 0W
Baker Lake 148 64 20N 96 3W
Baker Mt. 160 48 50N 121 49W
Baker's Dozen Is. 150 56 45N 78 45W
Bakersfield 163 35 25N 119 0W
Bakewell 33 53 13N 1 40W
Bakhchisaray 82 44 40N 33 45E
Bakhmach 80 51 10N 32 45E
Bakhtiari □ 92 32 0N 49 0E
Bakia 123 5 18N 25 45E
Bakinskikh Komissarov 92 39 20N 49 15E
Bakırköy 67 40 59N 28 53E
Bakkafjörðr 74 66 2N 14 48W
Bakkagerði 74 65 31N 13 49W
Bakke 71 58 25N 6 39E
Bakony Forest = Bakony Hegység 53 47 10N 17 30E
Bakony Hegység 53 47 10N 17 30E
Bakony, R. 53 47 35N 17 54E
Bakori 121 11 34N 7 25E
Bakouma 117 5 40N 22 56E
Bakov 52 50 27N 14 55E
Bakpakty 85 44 35N 76 40E
Bakr Uzyak 84 52 59N 58 38E
Baku 83 40 25N 49 45E
Bakwanga = Mbuji Mayi 124 6 9S 23 40E
Bal'a 90 32 20N 35 6E
Bala, L. = Tegid, L. 31 52 53N 3 38W
Balabac I. 102 8 0N 117 0E
Balabac, Selat 102 7 53N 117 5E
Balabagh 94 34 25N 70 12E
Balabakk 92 34 0N 36 10E
Balabalangan, Kepulauan 102 2 20S 117 30E
Balaghat 96 21 49N 80 12E
Balaghat Ra. 96 18 50N 76 30E
Balaguer 58 41 50N 0 50E
Balakhna 81 56 35N 43 32E
Balaklava, Austral. 140 34 7S 138 22E
Balaklava, U.S.S.R. 82 44 30N 33 30E
Balakleya 82 49 28N 36 55E
Balakovo 81 52 4N 47 55E
Balallan 36 58 5N 6 35W
Balancán 165 17 48N 91 32W
Balanda 81 51 30N 44 40E
Balangir 96 20 43N 83 35E
Balapur 96 21 22N 76 45E
Balashikha 81 55 49N 37 59E
Balashov 81 51 30N 43 10E
Balasinor 94 22 57N 73 23E
Balasore 96 21 35N 87 3E

Balassagyarmat 53 48 4N 19 15 E
Balât 122 25 36N 29 19 E
Balaton 53 46 50N 17 40 E
Balatonfüred 53 46 58N 17 54 E
Balatonszentgyörgy 53 46 41N 17 19 E
Balazote 59 38 54N 2 09W
Balbeggie 35 56 26N 3 19W
Balbi, Mt. 135 5 55 S 154 58 E
Balblair 37 57 39N 4 11W
Balboa 166 9 0N 79 30W
Balbriggan 38 53 35N 6 10W
Balcarce 172 38 0 S 58 10W
Balcarres 153 50 50N 103 35W
Balchik 67 43 28N 28 11 E
Balclutha 143 46 15 S 169 45 E
Bald Hd. 137 35 6 S 118 1 E
Bald Hill, W. Australia, Austral. 137 31 36 S 116 13 E
Bald Hill, W. Australia, Austral. 137 24 55 S 119 57 E
Bald I. 137 34 57 S 118 27 E
Bald Knob 159 35 20N 91 35W
Baldegger-See 51 47 12N 8 17 E
Balder, oilfield 19 59 10N 2 20 E
Balderton 33 53 3N 0 46W
Baldock 29 51 59N 0 11W
Baldock L. 153 56 33N 97 57W
Baldoyle 38 53 24N 6 10W
Baldwin, Fla., U.S.A. 156 30 15N 82 10W
Baldwin, Mich., U.S.A. 156 43 54N 85 53W
Baldwinsville 162 43 10N 76 19W
Bale 63 45 4N 13 46 E
Baleares □ 58 39 30N 3 0 E
Baleares, Islas 58 39 30N 3 0 E
Balearic Is. = Baleares, Islas 58 39 30N 3 0 E
Baleia,Ponta da 171 17 40 S 39 7W
Balen 47 51 10N 5 10 E
Baler 103 15 46N 121 34 E
Balerna 51 45 52N 9 0 E
Baleshare I. 36 57 30N 7 21W
Balezino 84 58 2N 53 6 E
Balfate 166 15 48N 86 25W
Balfe's Creek 138 20 12 S 145 55 E
Balfour, S. Afr. 129 26 38 S 28 35 E
Balfour, U.K. 37 59 2N 2 54W
Balfour Downs 137 22 45 S 120 50 E
Balfouriyya 90 32 38N 35 18 E
Balfron 34 56 4N 4 20W
Bali 121 5 54N 10 0 E
Bali □ 102 8 20 S 115 0 E
Bali, I. 102 8 20 S 115 0 E
Bali, Selat 103 8 30 S 114 35 E
Baligród 54 49 20N 22 17 E
Balikesir 92 39 35N 27 58 E
Balikpapan 102 1 10 S 116 55 E
Balimbing 103 5 10N 120 3 E
Balimo 135 8 6 S 142 57 E
Baling 101 5 41N 100 55 E
Balintore 37 57 45N 3 55W
Balipara 99 26 50N 92 45 E
Balit 95 36 15N 74 40 E
Baliza 175 16 0 S 52 20W
Balk 46 52 54N 5 35 E
Balkan Mts. = Stara Planina 67 43 15N 23 0 E
Balkan Pen. 16 42 0N 22 0 E
Balkh = Wazirabad 93 36 44N 66 47 E
Balkh □ 93 36 30N 67 0 E
Balkhash 76 46 50N 74 50 E
Balkhash, Ozero 76 40 0N 74 50 E
Balla, Ireland 38 53 48N 9 7W
Balla, Pak. 99 24 10N 91 35 E
Ballachulish 36 56 40N 5 10W
Balladonia 137 32 27 S 123 51 E
Ballagan Pt. 38 54 0N 6 6W
Ballaghaderreen 38 53 55N 8 35W
Ballantrae 34 55 6N 5 0W
Ballara 140 32 19 S 140 45 E
Ballarat 139 37 33 S 143 50 E
Ballard, L. 137 29 20 S 120 10 E
Ballarpur 96 19 50N 79 23 E
Ballater 37 57 2N 3 2W
Ballaugh 32 54 20N 4 32W
Balldale 141 36 20N 146 33 E
Ballenas, Canal de las 164 29 10N 113 45W
Balleni 70 45 48N 27 51 E
Balleny Is. 13 66 30 S 163 0 E
Ballia 95 25 46N 84 12 E
Ballickmoyler 39 52 54N 7 2W
Ballidu 137 30 35 S 116 45 E
Ballina, Austral. 139 28 50 S 153 31 E
Ballina, Mayo, Ireland 38 54 7N 9 10W
Ballina, Tipp., Ireland 39 52 49N 8 27W
Ballinagar 39 53 15N 7 21W
Ballinagh = Bellananagh 38 53 55N 7 25W
Ballinalack 38 53 38N 7 28W
Ballinalea 39 53 0N 6 8W
Ballinalee 38 53 46N 7 40W
Ballinamallard 38 54 30N 7 36W
Ballinameen 38 53 54N 8 19W
Ballinamore 38 54 3N 7 48W
Ballinamore Bridge 38 53 30N 8 24W
Ballinascarty 39 51 40N 8 52W
Ballinasloe 39 53 20N 8 12W
Ballincollig 39 51 52N 8 35W
Ballindaggin 39 52 33N 6 43W
Ballinderry 38 53 2N 8 13W
Ballinderry R. 38 54 40N 6 32W
Ballindine 38 53 40N 8 57W
Ballineen 39 51 43N 8 57W
Balling 73 56 38N 8 51 E
Ballingarry, Lim., Ireland 39 53 1N 8 3W
Ballingarry, Tipp., Ireland 39 52 29N 8 50W
Ballingarry, Tipp., Ireland 39 52 35N 7 32W
Ballingeary 39 51 51N 9 13W
Ballinger 159 31 45N 99 58W
Ballinhassig 39 51 48N 8 33W
Ballinlough 38 53 45N 8 39W
Ballinluig 37 56 40N 3 40W
Ballinrobe 38 53 36N 9 13W
Ballinskelligs 39 51 50N 10 17W
Ballinskelligs B. 39 51 46N 10 11W
Ballintober 38 53 43N 8 25W
Ballintoy 38 55 13N 6 20W
Ballintra 38 54 35N 8 9W
Ballinunty 39 52 36N 7 40W
Ballinure 39 52 34N 7 46W
Ballivian 172 22 41 S 62 10W
Ballivor 38 53 32N 6 50W
Ballo Pt. 79 8 55N 13 18W
Balloch 34 56 0N 4 35W
Ballon 39 48 10N 0 16 E
Ballston Spa 162 43 0N 73 51W
Ballybay 38 54 8N 6 52W
Ballybofey 38 54 48N 7 47W
Ballyboghil 38 53 32N 6 16W
Ballybogy 38 55 8N 6 33W
Ballybunion 39 52 30N 9 40W
Ballycanew 39 52 37N 6 18W
Ballycarney 39 52 35N 6 44W
Ballycastle 38 55 12N 6 15W
Ballycastle B. 38 55 12N 6 15W
Ballyclare, Ireland 38 53 40N 8 0W
Ballyclare, U.K. 38 54 46N 6 0W
Ballyclerahan 39 52 25N 7 48W
Ballycolla 39 52 53N 7 27W
Ballyconneely 38 53 27N 10 5W
Ballyconneely B. 38 53 23N 10 8W
Ballyconnell 38 54 7N 7 35W
Ballycotton 39 51 50N 8 0W
Ballycroy 38 54 2N 9 49W
Ballydavid 39 53 12N 8 28W
Ballydavid Hd. 39 52 15N 10 20W
Ballydehob 39 51 34N 9 28W
Ballydonegan 39 51 37N 10 12W
Ballydonegan B. 39 51 38N 10 6W
Ballyduff, Kerry, Ireland 39 52 27N 9 40W
Ballyduff, Waterford, Ireland 39 52 9N 8 2W
Ballyforan 38 53 29N 8 18W
Ballygar 38 53 33N 8 20W
Ballygarrett 39 52 34N 6 15W
Ballygawley 38 54 27N 7 2W
Ballyglass 38 53 45N 9 9W
Ballygorman 38 55 23N 7 20W
Ballyhahill 39 52 33N 9 13W
Ballyhaise 38 54 3N 7 20W
Ballyhalbert 38 54 30N 5 28W
Ballyhaunis 38 53 47N 8 47W
Ballyheige I. 39 52 22N 9 51W
Ballyhoura Hills 39 52 18N 8 33W
Ballyjamesduff 38 53 52N 7 11W
Ballylanders 39 52 25N 8 21W
Ballylaneen 39 52 10N 7 25W
Ballylongford 39 52 34N 9 30W
Ballylooby 39 52 20N 7 59W
Ballylynan 39 52 57N 7 02W
Ballymacoda 39 51 53N 7 56W
Ballymagorry 38 54 52N 7 26W
Ballymahon 39 53 35N 7 45W
Ballymena 38 54 53N 6 18W
Ballymena □ 38 54 53N 6 18W
Ballymoe 38 53 41N 8 28W
Ballymoney 38 55 5N 6 30W
Ballymoney □ 38 55 5N 6 23W
Ballymore 39 53 30N 7 40W
Ballymore Eustace 39 53 8N 6 38W
Ballymote 38 54 5N 8 30W
Ballymurphy 39 52 33N 6 52W
Ballymurray 38 53 36N 8 8W
Ballynabola 39 52 21N 6 50W
Ballynacally 39 52 42N 9 7W
Ballynacargy 38 53 35N 7 32W
Ballynacorra 39 51 53N 8 10W
Ballynagore 38 53 24N 7 29W
Ballynahinch 38 54 24N 5 55W
Ballynahown 38 53 21N 7 52W
Ballynameen 38 54 58N 6 41W
Ballynamona 39 52 5N 8 39W
Ballynure 38 54 47N 5 59W
Ballyquintin, Pt. 38 54 20N 5 30W
Ballyragget 39 52 47N 7 20W
Ballyroan 39 52 57N 7 20W
Ballyronan 38 54 43N 6 32W
Ballyroney 38 54 17N 6 8W
Ballysadare 38 54 12N 8 30W
Ballyshannon 38 54 30N 8 10W
Ballyvaughan 39 53 7N 9 10W
Ballyvourney 39 51 57N 9 10W
Ballyvoy 38 55 11N 6 11W
Ballywalter 38 54 33N 5 30W
Ballywilliam 39 52 27N 6 52W
Balmaceda 176 46 0 S 71 50W
Balmaclellan 35 55 6N 4 5W
Balmazújváros 53 47 37N 21 21 E
Balmedie 37 57 14N 2 4W
Balmhorn 50 46 26N 7 42 E
Balmoral 140 37 15 S 141 48 E
Balmoral For. 37 57 0N 3 15W
Balmorhea 159 31 2N 103 41W
Balnapaling 37 57 42N 4 2W
Balonne, R. 139 28 47 S 147 56 E
Balovale 125 13 30 S 23 15 E
Balquhidder 34 56 22N 4 22W
Balrampur 95 27 30N 82 20 E
Balranald 140 34 38 S 143 33 E
Balş 70 44 22N 24 5 E
Balsas 165 18 0N 99 40W
Balsas, R., Goias, Brazil 170 9 0 S 48 0W
Balsas, R., Maranhão, Brazil 170 7 15 S 44 35W
Balsas, R., Mexico 164 18 30N 101 20W
Bålsta 72 59 35N 17 30 E
Balsthal 50 47 19N 7 41 E
Balta, Rumania 70 44 54N 22 38 E
Balta, U.S.A. 158 48 12N 100 7W
Balta, U.S.S.R. 82 48 2N 29 45 E
Balta, I. 36 60 44N 0 49W
Baltanás 56 41 56N 4 15W
Baltasound 36 60 47N 0 53W
Baltic Sea 75 56 0N 20 0 E
Baltiisk 75 54 38N 19 55 E
Baltim 122 31 35N 31 10 E
Baltimore, Ireland 39 51 29N 9 22W
Baltimore, U.S.A. 162 39 18N 76 37W
Baltinglass 39 52 57N 6 42W
Baltrum 48 53 43N 7 25 E
Baluchistan □ 93 27 30N 65 0 E
Balurghat 95 25 15N 88 44 E
Balvicar 34 56 17N 5 38W
Balygychan 77 63 56N 154 12 E
Bam 93 29 7N 58 14 E
Bam La 99 29 25N 98 35 E
Bama 121 11 33N 13 33 E
Bamako 120 12 34N 7 55W
Bamba 121 17 5N 1 0W
Bambari 117 5 40N 20 35 E
Bambaroo 107 18 50 S 146 11 E
Bamberg, Ger. 49 49 54N 10 53 E
Bamberg, U.S.A. 157 33 19N 81 1W
Bambesi 123 9 45N 34 40 E
Bambey 120 14 42N 16 28W
Bambili 126 3 40N 26 0 E
Bamboo 138 14 34 S 143 20 E
Bambouti 126 5 25N 27 12 E
Bambuí 171 20 1 S 45 58W
Bamburgh 35 55 36N 1 42W
Bamenda 121 5 57N 10 11 E
Bamfield 152 48 45N 125 10W
Bamford 33 53 21N 1 41W
Bamian □ 93 35 0N 67 0 E
Bamkin 121 6 3N 11 27 E
Bampton, Devon, U.K. 30 50 59N 3 29W
Bampton, Oxon., U.K. 28 51 44N 1 33W
Bampur 93 27 15N 60 21 E
Bampur, R. 93 27 20N 59 30 E
Ban Aranyaprathet 100 13 41N 102 30 E
Ban Ban 100 19 31N 103 15 E
Ban Bang Hin 101 9 32N 98 35 E
Ban Bua Chum 101 15 11N 101 12 E
Ban Bua Yai 100 15 33N 102 26 E
Ban Chiang Klang 100 19 15N 100 55 E
Ban Chik 100 17 15N 102 22 E
Ban Choho 100 15 2N 102 9 E
Ban Dan Lan Hoi 100 17 0N 99 35 E
Ban Don 100 12 53N 107 48 E
Ban Don = Surat Thani 101 9 8N 99 20 E
Ban Don, Go 101 9 20N 99 25 E
Ban Dong 100 19 14N 100 3 E
Ban Hong 100 18 18N 98 50 E
Ban Houei Sai 101 20 22N 100 32 E
Ban Kaeng 100 17 29N 100 7 E
Ban Kantang 101 7 25N 99 31 E
Ban Keun 100 18 22N 102 35 E
Ban Khai 100 12 46N 101 18 E
Ban Khe Bo 101 19 10N 104 39 E
Ban Kheun 100 20 13N 101 7 E
Ban Khlong Kua 101 6 57N 100 8 E
Ban Khuan Mao 101 7 50N 99 37 E
Ban Khun Yuam 100 18 49N 97 57 E
Ban Ko Yai Chim 101 11 17N 99 26 E
Ban Kok 100 16 40N 103 40 E
Ban Laem 100 13 13N 99 59 E
Ban Lao Ngam 100 15 28N 106 10 E
Ban Le Kathe 100 15 49N 98 53 E
Ban Mae Chedi 100 19 11N 99 31 E
Ban Mae Laeng 100 20 1N 99 17 E
Ban Mae Sariang 100 18 0N 97 56 E
Ban Me Thuot 100 12 40N 108 3 E
Ban Mi 100 15 3N 100 32 E
Ban Muong Mo 100 19 4N 103 58 E
Ban Na Mo 100 17 7N 105 40 E
Ban Na San 101 8 33N 99 52 E
Ban Na Tong 100 20 56N 101 47 E
Ban Nam Bac 100 20 38N 102 20 E
Ban Nam Ma 100 22 2N 101 37 E
Ban Ngang 100 15 59N 106 11 E
Ban Nong Bok 100 17 5N 104 48 E
Ban Nong Boua 100 15 40N 106 33 E
Ban Nong Pling 100 15 40N 100 10 E
Ban Pak Chan 101 10 32N 98 51 E
Ban Phai 100 16 4N 102 44 E
Ban Pong 100 13 50N 99 55 E
Ban Ron Phibun 101 8 9N 99 51 E
Ban Sanam Chai 101 7 33N 100 25 E
Ban Sangkha 100 14 37N 103 52 E
Ban Tak 100 17 2N 99 4 E
Ban Tako 100 14 5N 102 40 E
Ban Takua Pa 101 8 55N 98 25 E
Ban Tha Dua 100 17 59N 98 39 E
Ban Tha Li 100 17 37N 101 25 E
Ban Tha Nun 101 8 12N 98 18 E
Ban Thahine 100 14 12N 105 33 E
Ban Thateng 101 15 25N 106 27 E
Ban Xien Kok 100 20 54N 100 39 E
Ban Yen Nhan 100 20 57N 106 2 E
Baña, La, Punta de 58 40 33N 0 40 E
Banadar Daryay Oman □ 93 25 30N 56 0 E
Banadia 174 6 54N 71 49W
Banagher 39 53 12N 8 0W
Banalia 126 1 32N 25 5 E
Banam 101 11 20N 105 17 E
Banamba 120 13 29N 7 22W
Banana 138 24 28 S 150 8 E
Bananal, I. do 171 11 30 S 50 30W
Banaras = Varanasi 95 25 22N 83 8 E
Banas, R., Gujarat, India 94 24 25N 72 30 E
Banas, R., Madhya Pradesh, India 95 24 15N 81 30 E
Bânâs, Ras. 122 23 57N 35 50 E
Banat □ 66 45 45N 21 15 E
Banbridge 38 54 21N 6 17W
Banbridge □ 38 54 21N 6 16W
Banbury 28 52 4N 1 21W
Banchory 37 57 3N 2 30W
Bancroft 150 45 3N 77 51W
Bancroft = Chililabombwe 127 12 18 S 27 43 E
Band 67 46 30N 24 25 E
Band-i-Turkistan, Ra. 93 35 2N 64 0 E
Banda 95 25 30N 80 26 E
Banda Aceh 102 5 35N 95 20 E
Banda Banda, Mt. 141 31 10 S 152 28 E
Banda Elat 103 5 40 S 133 5 E
Banda, Kepulauan 103 4 37 S 129 50 E
Banda, La 172 27 45 S 64 10W
Banda, Punta 164 31 47N 116 50W
Banda Sea 103 6 0 S 130 0 E
Bandama, R. 120 6 32N 5 30W
Bandanwara 94 26 9N 74 38 E
Bandar = Masulipatnam 97 16 12N 81 12 E
Bandar 'Abbās 93 27 15N 56 15 E
Bandar-e Būshehr 93 28 55N 50 55 E
Bandar-e Chārak 93 26 45N 54 20 E
Bandar-e Deylam 92 30 5N 50 10 E
Bandar-e Lengeh 93 26 35N 54 58 E
Bandar-e Ma'shur 92 30 35N 49 10 E
Bandar-e-Nakhīlu 93 26 58N 53 30 E
Bandar-e-Pahlavi 92 37 30N 49 30 E
Bandar-e Rīg 93 29 30N 50 45 E
Bandar-e Shah 93 37 0N 54 10 E
Bandar-e-Shahpur 92 30 30N 49 5 E
Bandar Maharani = Muar 101 2 3N 102 34 E
Bandar Penggaram = Batu Pahat 101 1 50N 102 56 E
Bandar Seri Begawan 102 4 52N 115 0 E
Bandawe 127 11 58 S 34 5 E
Bande, Belg. 47 50 10N 5 25 E
Bande, Spain 56 42 3N 7 58W
Bandeira, Pico da 173 20 26 S 41 47W
Bandeirante 171 13 41 S 50 48W
Bandera, Argent. 172 28 55 S 62 20W
Bandera, U.S.A. 159 29 45N 99 3W
Banderas, Bahía de 164 20 40N 105 30W
Bandi-San 112 37 36N 140 4 E
Bandia, R. 96 19 30N 80 25 E
Bandiagara 120 14 12N 3 29W
Bandirma 92 40 20N 28 0 E
Bandon 39 51 44N 8 45W
Bandon, R. 39 51 40N 8 11W
Bandula 127 19 0 S 33 7 E
Bandundu 124 3 15 S 17 22 E
Bandung 103 6 36 S 107 48 E
Bandya 137 27 40 S 122 5 E
Bañeres 59 38 44N 0 38W
Banes 167 21 0N 75 42W
Bañeza, La 56 42 17N 5 54W
Banff, Can. 152 51 10N 115 34W
Banff, U.K. 37 57 40N 2 32W
Banff Nat. Park 152 51 30N 116 15W
Banfora 120 10 40N 4 40W
Bang Fai, R. 100 16 57N 104 45 E
Bang Hieng, R. 100 16 24N 105 40 E
Bang Krathum 100 16 34N 100 18 E
Bang Lamung 100 13 3N 100 56 E
Bang Mun Nak 100 16 2N 100 23 E
Bang Pa In 100 14 14N 100 35 E
Bang Rakam 100 16 45N 100 7 E
Bang Saphan 101 11 14N 99 28 E
Bangala Dam 127 21 7 S 31 25 E
Bangalore 97 12 59N 77 40 E
Bangangte 121 5 8N 10 32 E
Bangaon 95 23 0N 88 47 E
Bangassou 124 4 55N 23 55 E
Bangeta, Mt. 135 6 21 S 147 3 E
Banggai 103 1 40 S 123 30 E
Banggi, P. 102 7 50N 117 0 E
Banghāzī 119 32 11N 20 3 E
Bangil 103 7 36 S 112 50 E
Bangjang 123 11 23N 32 41 E
Bangka, Pulau, Celebes, Indon. 103 1 50N 125 5 E
Bangka, Pulau, Sumatera, Indon. 102 2 0 S 105 50 E
Bangka, Selat 102 3 30 S 105 30 E
Bangkalan 103 7 2 S 112 46 E
Bangkinang 102 0 18N 101 5 E
Bangko 102 2 5 S 102 9 E
Bangkok 100 13 45N 100 31 E
Bangladesh ■ 98 24 0N 90 0 E
Bangolo 120 7 1N 7 29W
Bangor, Me., U.S.A. 151 44 48N 68 42W

Place	Page	Lat.	Long.
Bangor, Pa., U.S.A.	162	40 51N	75 13W
Bangor, N.I., U.K.	38	54 40N	5 40W
Bangor, Wales, U.K.	31	53 13N	4 9W
Bangued	103	17 40N	120 37 E
Bangui	124	4 23N	18 35 E
Banguru	126	0 30N	27 10 E
Bangweulu, L.	127	11 0 S	30 0 E
Bangweulu Swamp	127	11 20 S	30 15 E
Banham	29	52 27N	1 3 E
Bani	167	18 16N	70 22W
Bani Bangou	121	15 3N	2 42 E
Bani, Djebel	118	29 16N	8 0W
Bani Na'im	90	31 31N	35 10 E
Bani, R.	120	12 40N	6 30W
Bani Suhayla	90	31 21N	34 19 E
Bania	120	9 4N	3 6W
Baniara	135	9 44 S	149 54 E
Banihal Pass	95	33 30N	75 12 E
Banīnah	119	32 0N	20 12 E
Baniyas	92	35 10N	36 0 E
Banja Luka	66	44 49N	17 26 E
Banjak, Kepulauan	102	2 10N	97 10 E
Banjar	103	7 24 S	108 30 E
Banjarmasin	102	3 20 S	114 35 E
Banjarnegara	103	7 24 S	109 42 E
Banjul	120	13 28N	16 40W
Banka Banka	138	18 50 S	134 0 E
Bankend	35	55 2N	3 31W
Bankeryd	73	57 53N	14 6 E
Banket	127	17 27 S	30 19 E
Bankfoot	35	56 30N	3 31W
Bankhead	37	57 11N	2 10W
Bankilaré	121	14 35N	0 44 E
Bankipore	95	25 35N	85 10 E
Banks I., B.C., Can.	152	53 20N	130 0W
Banks I., N. W. Terr., Can.	12	73 15N	121 30W
Banks I., P.N.G.	135	10 10 S	142 15 E
Banks Peninsula	143	43 45 S	173 15 E
Banks Str.	138	40 40 S	148 10 E
Bankura	95	23 11N	87 18 E
Bankya	66	42 43N	23 8 E
Bann R., Down, U.K.	38	54 30N	6 31W
Bann R., Londonderry, U.K.	38	55 10N	6 34W
Bannalec	42	47 57N	3 42W
Bannang Sata	101	6 16N	101 16 E
Bannerton	140	34 42 S	142 47 E
Banning, Can.	150	48 44N	91 56W
Banning, U.S.A.	163	33 58N	116 58W
Banningville = Bandundu	124	3 15 S	17 22 E
Bannockburn, Zimb.	127	20 17 S	29 48 E
Bannockburn, U.K.	35	56 5N	3 55W
Bannow	39	52 12N	6 50W
Bannow B.	39	52 13N	6 48W
Bannu	93	33 0N	70 18 E
Bañolas	58	42 16N	2 44 E
Banon	45	44 2N	5 38 E
Baños de la Encina	57	38 10N	3 46W
Baños de Molgas	56	42 15N	7 40W
Bánovce	53	48 44N	18 16 E
Banská Bystrica	53	48 46N	19 14 E
Banská Stiavnica	53	48 25N	18 55 E
Bansko	67	41 52N	23 28 E
Banswara	94	23 32N	74 24 E
Bantama	121	7 48N	0 42W
Bante	121	8 25N	1 53 E
Banteer	39	52 8N	8 53W
Banten	103	6 5 S	106 8 E
Bantry	39	51 40N	9 28W
Bantry, B.	39	51 35N	9 50W
Bantul	103	7 55 S	110 19 E
Bantva	94	21 29N	70 12 E
Bantval	97	12 55N	75 0 E
Banu	93	35 35N	69 5 E
Banwell	28	51 19N	2 51W
Banya	67	42 33N	24 50 E
Banyo	121	6 52N	11 45 E
Banyuls	44	42 29N	3 8 E
Banyumas	103	7 32 S	109 18 E
Banyuwangi	103	8 13 S	114 21 E
Banzare Coast	13	66 30 S	125 0 E
Banzyville = Mobayi	124	4 15N	21 8 E
Bao Ha	100	22 11N	104 21 E
Bao Lac	100	22 57N	105 40 E
Bao Loc	101	11 32N	107 48 E
Bap	94	27 23N	72 18 E
Bapatla	97	15 55N	80 30 E
Bapaume	43	50 7N	2 50 E
Bâqa el Gharbiya	90	32 25N	35 2 E
Baqūbah	92	33 45N	44 50 E
Baquedano	172	23 20 S	69 52W
Bar, U.S.S.R.	82	49 4N	27 40 E
Bar, Yugo.	66	42 8N	19 8 E
Bar Harbor	151	44 15N	68 20W
Bar-le-Duc	43	48 47N	5 10 E
Bar-sur-Aube	43	48 14N	4 40 E
Bar-sur-Seine	43	48 7N	4 20 E
Barabai	102	2 32 S	115 34 E
Barabinsk	76	55 20N	78 20 E
Baraboo	158	43 28N	89 46W
Baracoa	167	20 20N	74 30W
Baradero	172	33 52 S	59 29W
Baradine	141	30 56 S	149 4 E
Baraga	158	46 49N	88 29W
Barahona, Dom. Rep.	167	18 13N	71 7W
Barahona, Spain	58	41 17N	2 39W
Barail Range	99	25 15N	93 20 E
Barakhola	99	25 0N	92 45 E
Barakot	95	21 33N	84 59 E
Barakula	139	26 30 S	150 33 E
Baralaba	138	24 13 S	149 50 E
Baralzon L.	153	60 0N	98 3W
Baramati	96	18 11N	74 33 E
Baramba	96	20 25N	85 23 E
Barameiya	122	18 32N	36 38 E
Baramula	95	34 15N	74 20 E
Baran	94	25 9N	76 40 E
Baranoa	174	10 48N	74 55W
Baranof I.	147	57 0N	135 10W
Baranovichi	80	53 10N	26 0 E
Baranów Sandomierski	54	50 29N	21 30 E
Baranya □	53	46 0N	18 15 E
Barão de Cocais	171	19 56 S	43 28W
Barão de Grajaú	170	6 45 S	43 1W
Barão de Melgaço	174	11 50 S	60 45W
Baraolt	70	46 5N	25 34 E
Barapasi	103	2 15 S	137 5 E
Barapina	135	6 21 S	155 25 E
Barasat	95	22 46N	88 31 E
Barasoli	123	13 38N	42 0W
Barat Daya,Kepuluan	103	7 30 S	128 0 E
Barataria B.	159	29 15N	89 45W
Baraut	94	29 13N	77 7 E
Baraya	174	3 10N	75 4W
Barbacena	173	21 15 S	43 56W
Barbacoas, Colomb.	174	1 45N	78 0W
Barbacoas, Venez.	174	9 29N	66 58W
Barbados ■	167	13 0N	59 30W
Barbalha	170	7 19 S	39 17W
Barban	63	45 0N	14 4 E
Barbastro	58	42 2N	0 5 E
Barbate	57	36 13N	5 56W
Barberton, S. Afr.	129	25 42 S	31 2 E
Barberton, U.S.A.	156	41 0N	81 40W
Barbigha	95	25 21N	85 47 E
Barbourville	157	36 57N	83 52W
Barbuda I.	167	17 30N	61 40W
Barca d'Alva	56	41 0N	7 0W
Barca, La	164	20 20N	102 40W
Barcaldine	138	23 33 S	145 13 E
Barcarrota	57	38 31N	6 51W
Barce = Al Marj	117	32 25N	20 40 E
Barcellona Pozzo di Gotto	65	38 8N	15 15 E
Barcelona, Spain	58	41 21N	2 10 E
Barcelona, Venez.	174	10 10N	64 40W
Barcelona □	58	41 30N	2 0 E
Barcelonette	45	44 23N	6 40 E
Barcelos	174	1 0 S	63 0W
Barcin	54	52 52N	17 55 E
Barcoo, R.	138	28 29 S	137 46 E
Barcs	53	45 58N	17 28 E
Barczewo	54	53 50N	20 42 E
Bard, Hd.	36	60 6N	1 5W
Barda	83	40 25N	47 10 E
Bardai	119	21 25N	17 0 E
Bardas Blancas	172	35 49 S	69 45W
Bardejov	53	49 18N	21 15 E
Bardera	91	2 20N	42 27 E
Bardi	62	44 38N	9 43 E
Bardiyah	117	31 45N	25 0 E
Bardney	33	53 13N	0 19W
Bardo	54	50 31N	16 42 E
Bardoc	137	30 18 S	121 12 E
Bardoli	96	21 12N	73 5 E
Bardsey, I.	31	52 46N	4 47W
Bardsey Sound	31	52 47N	4 46W
Bardstown	156	37 50N	85 29W
Bareilly	95	28 22N	79 27 E
Barellan	141	34 16 S	146 24 E
Barengapara	98	25 14N	90 14 E
Barentin	42	49 33N	0 58 E
Barenton	42	48 38N	0 50W
Barents Sea	12	73 0N	39 0 E
Barentu	123	15 2N	37 35 E
Barfleur	42	49 40N	1 17W
Barford	28	52 15N	1 35W
Barga	62	44 5N	10 30 E
Bargal	91	11 25N	51 0 E
Bargara	138	24 50 S	152 25 E
Barge	62	44 43N	7 19 E
Barge, La	160	41 12N	110 4W
Bargnop	123	9 32N	28 25 E
Bargo	141	34 18 S	150 35 E
Bargoed	31	51 42N	3 22W
Bargteheide	48	53 42N	10 13 E
Barguzin	77	53 37N	109 37 E
Barh	95	25 29N	85 46 E
Barhaj	95	26 18N	83 44 E
Barham	29	51 12N	1 10 E
Barhi	95	24 15N	85 25 E
Bari, India	94	26 39N	77 39 E
Bari, Italy	65	41 6N	16 52 E
Bari Doab	94	30 20N	73 0 E
Baria = Phuoc Le	101	10 39N	107 19 E
Bariadi □	126	2 45 S	34 40 E
Barika	118	35 23N	5 22 E
Barinas	174	8 36N	70 15W
Barinas □	174	8 10N	69 50W
Baring C.	148	70 0N	117 30W
Baringo	126	0 47N	36 16 E
Baringo □	126	0 55N	36 0 E
Baringo, L.	126	0 47N	36 16 E
Barinitas	174	8 45N	70 25W
Baripada	96	21 57N	86 45 E
Bariri	171	22 4 S	48 44W
Bârîs	122	24 42N	30 31 E
Barisal	98	22 30N	90 20 E
Barisan, Bukit	102	3 30 S	102 15 E
Barito, R.	102	2 50 S	114 50 E
Barjac	45	44 20N	4 22 E
Barjols	45	43 34N	6 2 E
Barjūji, W.	119	25 26N	12 12 E
Bark L.	150	46 58N	82 25W
Barka	122	17 30N	37 34 E
Barkah	93	23 40N	58 0 E
Barker, Mt.	139	35 4 S	138 55 E
Barking	29	51 31N	0 10 E
Barkley Sound	152	48 50N	125 10W
Barkly Downs	138	20 30 S	138 30 E
Barkly East	129	30 58 S	27 33 E
Barkly Tableland	138	19 50 S	138 40 E
Barkly West	128	28 5 S	24 31 E
Barkol, Wadi	122	17 40N	32 0 E
Barksdale	159	29 47N	100 2W
Barlborough	33	53 17N	1 17W
Barlby	33	53 48N	1 3W
Barlee, L.	137	29 15 S	119 30 E
Barlee, Mt.	137	24 35 S	128 10 E
Barlee Ra.	137	23 30 S	116 0 E
Barlett	163	36 29N	118 2W
Barletta	65	41 20N	16 17 E
Barlinek	54	53 0N	15 15 E
Barlingbo	73	57 35N	18 27 E
Barlow L.	153	62 00N	103 0W
Barmby Moor	33	53 55N	0 47W
Barmedman	141	34 9 S	147 21 E
Barmer	94	25 45N	71 20 E
Barmera	140	34 15 S	140 28 E
Barmoor	35	55 38N	2 0W
Barmouth	31	52 44N	4 3W
Barmstedt	48	53 47N	9 46 E
Barna	39	53 14N	9 10W
Barnaderg	38	53 29N	8 43W
Barnagar	94	23 7N	75 19 E
Barnard Castle	32	54 33N	1 55W
Barnato	141	31 38 S	145 0 E
Barnaul	76	53 20N	83 40 E
Barnby Moor	33	53 21N	1 0W
Barne Inlet	13	80 15 S	160 0 E
Barnes	141	36 2 S	144 47 E
Barnesville	157	33 6N	84 9W
Barnet	29	51 37N	0 15W
Barnetby le Wold	33	53 34N	0 24W
Barneveld, Neth.	96	52 7N	5 36 E
Barneveld, U.S.A.	162	43 16N	75 14W
Barneville	42	49 23N	1 46W
Barney, Mt.	133	28 17 S	152 44 E
Barngo	138	25 3 S	147 20 E
Barnhart	159	31 10N	101 8W
Barnoldswick	32	53 55N	2 11W
Barnsley	33	53 33N	1 29W
Barnstaple	30	51 5N	4 3W
Barnstaple B.	30	51 5N	4 25W
Barnsville	158	46 43N	96 28W
Baro	121	8 35N	6 18 E
Baro, R.	123	8 25N	33 40 E
Baroda	94	25 29N	76 35 E
Baroda = Vadodara, India	93	22 20N	73 10 E
Baroda = Vadodara, Gujarat, India	94	22 20N	73 10 E
Baron Ra.	136	23 30 S	127 45 E
Barpali	96	21 11N	83 35 E
Barpathar	98	26 17N	93 53 E
Barpeta	95	26 20N	91 10 E
Barqa	117	27 0N	20 0 E
Barqin	119	27 33N	13 34 E
Barques, Pte. aux	156	44 5N	82 55W
Barquinha	57	39 28N	8 25W
Barquísimeto	174	9 58N	69 13W
Barr, France	43	48 25N	7 28 E
Barr, U.K.	34	55 13N	4 44W
Barr Smith Ra.	137	27 10 S	120 15 E
Barra, Brazil	170	11 5 S	43 10W
Barra, Gambia	120	13 21N	16 36W
Barra da Estiva	171	13 38 S	41 19W
Barra de Navidad	164	19 12N	104 41W
Barra do Corda	170	5 30 S	45 10W
Barra do Mendes	171	11 43 S	42 4W
Barra do Piraí	173	22 30 S	43 50W
Barra Falsa, Pta. da	129	22 58 S	35 37 E
Barra Hd.	36	56 47N	7 40W
Barra, I.	36	57 0N	7 30W
Barra Mansa	173	22 35 S	44 12W
Barra, Sd. of	36	57 4N	7 25W
Barraba	141	30 21 S	150 35 E
Barrackpur	95	22 44N	88 30 E
Barrafranca	65	37 22N	14 10 E
Barranca, Lima, Peru	174	10 45 S	77 50W
Barranca, Loreto, Peru	174	4 50 S	76 50W
Barrancabermeja	174	7 0N	73 50W
Barrancas, Colomb.	174	10 57N	72 50W
Barrancas, Venez.	174	8 55N	62 5W
Barrancos	57	38 10N	6 58W
Barranqueras	172	27 30 S	59 0W
Barranquilla, Atlántico, Colomb.	174	11 0N	74 50W
Barranquilla, Vaupés, Colomb.	174	1 39N	72 19W
Barras, Brazil	170	4 15 S	42 18W
Barras, Colomb.	174	1 45 S	73 13W
Barraute	150	48 26N	77 38W
Barre, U.S.A.	156	44 15N	72 30W
Barre, U.S.A.	162	42 26N	72 6W
Barreal	172	31 33 S	69 28W
Barreiras	171	12 8 S	45 0W
Barreirinhas	170	2 30 S	42 50W
Barreiro	57	38 40N	9 6W
Barreiros	170	8 49 S	35 12W
Barrême	45	43 57N	6 23 E
Barren I.	101	12 17N	95 50 E
Barren Is., Madag.	129	18 25 S	43 40 E
Barren Is., U.S.A.	147	58 45N	152 0W
Barren Junc.	139	30 5 S	149 0 E
Barretos	171	20 30 S	48 35W
Barrhead, Can.	152	54 10N	114 24W
Barrhead, U.K.	34	55 48N	4 23W
Barrhill	34	55 7N	4 46W
Barrie	150	44 24N	79 40W
Barrier, C.	142	36 25 S	175 32 E
Barrier Ra., Austral.	140	31 0 S	141 30 E
Barrier Ra., N.Z.	143	44 5 S	169 42 E
Barrier Rf., Gt.	138	19 0 S	149 0 E
Barrière	152	51 12N	120 7W
Barrington, Austral.	133	31 58 S	151 55 E
Barrington, Ill., U.S.A.	156	42 8N	88 5W
Barrington, R.I., U.S.A.	162	41 43N	71 20W
Barrington L.	153	56 55N	100 15W
Barrington Tops.	141	32 6 S	151 28 E
Barringun	139	29 1 S	145 41 E
Barrow	147	71 16N	156 50W
Barrow Creek T.O.	138	21 30 S	133 55 E
Barrow I.	136	20 45 S	115 20 E
Barrow-in-Furness	32	54 8N	3 15W
Barrow Pt.	138	14 20 S	144 40 E
Barrow, Pt.	147	71 22N	156 30W
Barrow, R.	39	52 10N	6 57W
Barrow Ra.	137	26 0 S	127 40 E
Barrow Strait	12	74 20N	95 0W
Barrow upon Humber	33	53 41N	0 22W
Barrowford	32	53 51N	2 14W
Barruecopardo	56	41 4N	6 40W
Barruelo	56	42 54N	4 17W
Barry, S. Glam., U.K.	31	51 23N	3 19W
Barry, Tayside, U.K.	35	56 29N	2 45W
Barry I.	31	51 23N	3 17W
Barry's Bay	150	45 29N	77 41W
Barry's Pt.	39	51 36N	8 40W
Barsalogho	121	13 25N	1 3W
Barsat	95	36 10N	72 45 E
Barsi	96	18 10N	75 50 E
Barsø	73	55 7N	9 33 E
Barsoi	99	25 48N	87 57 E
Barstow, Calif., U.S.A.	163	34 58N	117 2W
Barstow, Tex., U.S.A.	170	31 30N	103 25W
Barthélemy, Col	100	19 26N	104 6 E
Bartica	174	6 25N	58 40W
Bartle Frere, Mt.	138	17 27 S	145 50 E
Bartlesville	159	36 50N	95 58W
Bartlett	159	30 46N	97 30W
Bartlett, L.	152	63 5N	118 20W
Bartolomeu Dias	127	21 10 S	35 8 E
Barton	33	54 28N	1 38W
Barton Siding	137	30 31 S	132 39 E
Barton-upon-Humber	33	53 41N	0 27W
Bartoszyce	54	54 15N	20 55 E
Bartow	157	27 53N	81 49W
Barú, I. de	174	10 15N	75 35W
Baruth	48	52 3N	13 31 E
Barvas	36	58 21N	6 31W
Barvaux	47	50 21N	5 29 E
Barvenkovo	82	48 57N	37 0 E
Barwani	94	22 2N	74 57 E
Barwell	28	52 35N	1 22W
Barysh	81	49 2N	25 18 E
Bas-Rhin □	43	48 40N	7 30 E
Bašaid	66	45 38N	20 25 E
Basa'idu	93	26 35N	55 20 E
Basal	94	33 33N	72 13 E
Basalt	163	38 0N	118 15W
Basankusa	124	1 5N	19 50 E
Basawa	94	34 15N	70 50 E
Bascharage	47	49 34N	5 55 E
Bascuñán, Cabo	172	28 52 S	71 35W
Basècles	47	50 32N	3 39 E
Basel (Basle)	50	47 35N	7 35 E
Basel Landschaft □	50	47 26N	7 45 E
Basel-Stadt □	50	47 35N	7 35 E
Basento, R.	65	40 35N	16 10 E
Bashi Channel	105	21 15N	122 0 E
Bashkir A.S.S.R. □	84	54 0N	57 0 E
Basilaki, I.	135	10 35 S	151 0 E
Basilan, Selat	103	6 50N	122 0 E
Basilanl, I.	103	6 35N	122 0 E
Basildon	29	51 34N	0 29 E
Basilicata □	65	40 30N	16 0 E
Basim	96	20 3N	77 0 E
Basin	160	44 22N	108 2W
Basing	28	51 16N	1 3W
Basingstoke	28	51 15N	1 5W
Basirhat	98	22 40N	88 54 E
Baskatong Res.	150	46 46N	75 50W
Baskerville C.	136	17 10 S	122 15 E
Basle = Basel	50	47 35N	7 35 E
Basmat	96	19 15N	77 12 E
Basoda	94	23 52N	77 54 E
Basodino	51	46 25N	8 28 E
Basoka	126	1 16N	23 40 E
Basongo	124	4 15 S	20 20 E
Basque Provinces = Vascongadas	58	42 50N	2 45W
Basra = Al Basrah	92	30 30N	47 50 E
Bass Rock	35	56 5N	2 40W
Bass Strait	138	39 15 S	146 30 E
Bassano, del Grappa	63	45 45N	11 45 E
Bassari	121	9 19N	0 57 E
Bassas da India	125	22 0 S	39 0 E
Basse	120	13 13N	14 15W
Basse-Terre, I.	167	16 0N	61 40W
Bassecourt	50	47 20N	7 15 E
Bassée, La	43	50 31N	2 49 E
Bassein, Burma	98	16 30N	94 30 E
Bassein, India	96	19 26N	72 48 E
Bassein Myit	99	16 45N	94 30 E
Bassenthwaite, L.	32	54 40N	3 14W
Basseterre	167	17 17N	62 43W
Bassett, Nebr., U.S.A.	158	42 37N	99 30W
Bassett, Va., U.S.A.	157	36 48N	79 59W
Bassevelde	47	51 15N	3 41 E

Bassi 94 30 44N 76 21 E
Bassigny 43 48 0N 5 10 E
Bassikounou 120 15 55N 6 1W
Bassilly 47 50 40N 3 56 E
Bassum 48 52 50N 8 42 E
Båstad 73 56 25N 12 51 E
Båstad 73 56 25N 12 51 E
Bastak 93 27 15N 54 25 E
Bastar 96 19 25N 81 40 E
Basti 95 26 52N 82 55 E
Bastia 45 42 40N 9 30 E
Bastia Umbra 63 43 4N 12 34 E
Bastide, La 44 44 35N 3 55 E
Bastogne 47 50 1N 5 43 E
Baston 29 52 43N 0 19W
Bastrop 159 30 5N 97 22W
Basuto 128 19 50 S 26 25 E
Basutoland = Lesotho 129 29 0 S 28 0 E
Basyanovskiy 84 58 19N 60 44 E
Bat Yam 90 32 2N 34 44 E
Bata, Eq. Guin. 124 1 57N 9 50 E
Bata, Rumania 70 46 1N 22 4 E
Bataan 103 14 40N 120 25 E
Bataan Pen. 103 14 38N 120 30 E
Batabanó 166 22 40N 82 20W
Batabanó, G. de 167 22 30N 82 30W
Batac 103 18 3N 120 34 E
Batagoy 77 67 38N 134 38 E
Batak 67 41 57N 24 12 E
Batalha 57 39 40N 8 50W
Batama 126 0 58N 26 33 E
Batamay 77 63 30N 129 15 E
Batamshinskiy 84 50 36N 58 16 E
Batang 103 6 55 S 109 40 E
Batangafo 117 7 25N 18 20 E
Batangas 103 13 35N 121 10 E
Batanta, I. 103 0 55N 130 40 E
Bataszék 66 46 10N 18 44 E
Batatais 173 20 54 S 47 37W
Batavia 156 43 0N 78 10W
Bataysk 83 47 3N 39 45 E
Batchelor 136 13 4 S 131 1 E
Bateman's B. 141 35 40 S 150 12 E
Batemans Bay 141 35 44 S 150 11 E
Bates Ra. 137 27 25 S 121 0 E
Batesburg 157 33 54N 81 32W
Batesville, Ark., U.S.A. 159 35 48N 91 40W
Batesville, Miss., U.S.A. 159 34 17N 89 58W
Batesville, Tex., U.S.A. 159 28 59N 99 38W
Batetski 80 58 47N 30 16 E
Bath, U.K. 28 51 22N 2 22W
Bath, Maine, U.S.A. 151 43 50N 69 49W
Bath, N.Y., U.S.A. 156 42 20N 77 17W
Batheay 101 11 59N 104 57 E
Bathford 28 51 23N 2 18W
Bathgate 35 55 54N 3 38W
Bâthie, La 46 45 37N 6 28 E
Bathmen 46 52 15N 6 29 E
Bathurst, Austral. 141 33 25 S 149 31 E
Bathurst, Can. 151 47 37N 65 43W
Bathurst B. 138 14 16 S 144 25 E
Bathurst C. 147 70 30N 128 30W
Bathurst, C. 147 70 34N 128 0W
Bathurst, Gambia = Banjul 120 13 28N 16 40W
Bathurst Harb. 138 43 15 S 146 10 E
Bathurst I., Austral. 136 11 30 S 130 10 E
Bathurst I., Can. 12 76 30N 130 10W
Bathurst Inlet 148 66 50N 108 1W
Batie 120 9 53N 2 53W
Batley 33 53 43N 1 38W
Batlow 141 35 31 S 148 9 E
Batman 92 37 55N 41 5 E
Batna 119 35 34N 6 15 E
Batoka 127 16 45 S 27 15 E
Baton Rouge 159 30 30N 91 5W
Batong, Ko 101 6 32N 99 12 E
Batopilas 164 27 45N 107 45W
Batouri 124 4 30N 14 25 E
Battambang 100 13 7N 103 12 E
Batticaloa 97 7 43N 81 45 E
Battice 47 50 39N 5 50 E
Battipáglia 65 40 38N 15 0 E
Battir 90 31 44N 35 8 E
Battle, Can. 153 52 58N 110 52W
Battle, U.K. 29 50 55N 0 30 E
Battle Camp 138 15 20 S 144 40 E
Battle Creek 156 42 20N 85 36W
Battle Harbour 151 52 16N 55 35W
Battle Lake 158 46 20N 95 43W
Battle Mountain 160 40 45N 117 0W
Battle, R. 153 52 43N 108 15W
Battlefields 127 18 37 S 29 47 E
Battleford 153 52 45N 108 15W
Battonya 53 46 16N 21 3 E
Batu Caves 101 3 15N 101 40 E
Batu Gajah 101 4 28N 101 3 E
Batu, Kepulauan 102 0 30 S 98 25 E
Batu, Mt. 123 6 55N 39 45 E
Batu Pahat 101 1 50N 102 56 E
Batuata, P. 103 6 30 S 122 20 E
Batulaki 103 5 40N 125 30 E
Batumi 83 41 30N 41 30 E
Baturadja 102 4 11 S 104 15 E
Baturité 170 4 28 S 38 45W
Baturité, Serra de 170 4 25 S 39 0W
Baubau 103 5 25 S 123 50 E
Bauchi 121 10 22N 9 48 E
Bauchi □ 121 10 0N 10 0 E
Baud 42 47 52N 3 1W
Baudette 158 48 46N 94 35W
Baudouinville = Moba 126 7 0 S 29 48 E
Baudour 47 50 29N 3 50 E
Bauer, C. 139 32 44 S 134 4 E
Baugé 42 47 31N 0 8W
Bauhinia Downs 138 24 35 S 149 18 E
Baule, La 42 47 18N 2 23W
Bauma 51 47 3N 8 53 E
Baume les Dames 43 47 22N 6 22 E
Baunei 64 40 2N 9 41 E
Bauru 173 22 10 S 49 0W
Baús 175 18 22 S 52 47W
Bauska 80 56 25N 25 15 E
Bautzen 48 51 11N 14 25 E
Baux, Les 45 43 45N 4 51 E
BavaniSte 66 44 49N 20 53 E
Bavaria = Bayern 49 49 7N 11 30 E
Båven 72 59 35N 17 30 E
Bavispe, R. 164 29 30N 109 11W
Bawdsey 29 52 1N 1 27 E
Bawdwin 98 23 5N 97 50 E
Bawean 102 5 46 S 112 35 E
Bawku 121 11 3N 0 19W
Bawlake 98 19 11N 97 21 E
Bawnboy 38 54 8N 7 40W
Bawtry 33 53 25N 1 1W
Baxley 157 31 43N 82 23W
Baxter Springs 159 37 3N 94 45W
Bay Bulls 151 47 19N 52 50W
Bay City, Mich., U.S.A. 156 43 35N 83 51W
Bay City, Oreg., U.S.A. 160 45 45N 123 58W
Bay City, Tex., U.S.A. 159 28 59N 95 55W
Bay de Verde 151 48 5N 52 54W
Bay, Laguna de 103 14 20N 121 11 E
Bay of Islands 142 35 15 S 174 6 E
Bay St. Louis 159 30 18N 89 22W
Bay Shore 162 40 44N 73 15W
Bay Springs 159 31 58N 89 18W
Bay View 142 39 25 S 176 50 E
Baya 127 11 53 S 27 25 E
Bayamo 166 20 20N 76 40W
Bayamón 147 18 24N 66 10W
Bayan Kara Shan 99 34 0N 98 0 E
Bayan-Ovoo 106 47 47N 112 5 E
Bayana 94 26 55N 77 18 E
Bayanaul 76 50 45N 75 45 E
Bayandalay 106 43 30N 103 29 E
Bayanga 124 2 53N 16 19 E
Bayanhongor 105 46 8N 100 43 E
Bayard 158 41 48N 103 17W
Baybay 103 10 40N 124 55 E
Bayble 36 58 12N 6 13W
Bayburt 92 40 15N 40 20 E
Bayerischer Wald 49 49 0N 13 0 E
Bayern □ 49 49 7N 11 30 E
Bayeux 42 49 17N 0 42W
Bayfield 158 46 50N 90 48W
Bayir 92 30 45N 36 55 E
Baykadam 85 43 48N 69 58 E
Baykal, Oz. 77 53 0N 108 0 E
Baykit 77 61 50N 95 50 E
Baykonur 76 47 48N 65 50 E
Baymak 84 52 36N 58 19 E
Baynes Mts. 128 17 15 S 13 0 E
Bayombong 103 16 30N 121 10 E
Bayon 43 48 30N 6 20 E
Bayona 56 42 6N 8 52W
Bayonne, France 44 43 30N 1 28W
Bayonne, U.S.A. 162 40 41N 74 7W
Bayovar 174 5 50 S 81 0W
Baypore, R. 97 11 10N 75 47 E
Bayram-Ali 76 37 37N 62 10 E
Bayreuth 49 49 56N 11 35 E
Bayrischzell 49 47 39N 12 1 E
Bayrūt 92 33 53N 35 31 E
Baysun 85 38 12N 67 12 E
Bayt Aula 90 31 37N 35 2 E
Bayt Fajjar 90 31 38N 35 9 E
Bayt Fūrīk 90 32 11N 35 20 E
Bayt Jala 90 31 43N 35 11 E
Bayt Lahm 90 31 43N 35 12 E
Bayt Rīma 90 32 2N 35 6 E
Bayt Sāhūr 90 31 42N 35 13 E
Bayt Ummar 90 31 38N 35 7 E
Bayta at Tahtā 90 32 9N 35 18 E
Baytin 90 31 56N 35 14 E
Baytown 159 29 42N 94 57W
Bayzhansay 85 43 14N 69 54 E
Bayzo 121 13 52N 4 35 E
Baza 59 37 30N 2 47W
Bazar Dyuzi 83 41 12N 48 10 E
Bazarny Karabulak 81 52 30N 46 20 E
Bazarnyy Syzgan 81 53 45N 46 40 E
Bazartobe 83 49 26N 51 45 E
Bazaruto, I. do 129 21 40 S 35 28 E
Bazas 44 44 27N 0 13W
Bazuriye 90 33 15N 35 16 E
Beabula 141 34 26 S 145 9 E
Beach 158 46 57N 104 0W
Beach Haven 162 39 34N 74 14W
Beachley 28 51 37N 2 39W
Beachport 140 37 29 S 140 0 E
Beachwood 162 39 55N 74 8W
Beachy Head 29 50 44N 0 16 E
Beacon, Austral. 137 30 26 S 117 52 E
Beacon, U.S.A. 162 41 32N 73 58W
Beaconia 153 50 25N 96 31W
Beaconsfield, Austral. 133 41 11 S 146 48 E
Beaconsfield, U.K. 29 51 36N 0 39W
Beadnell 35 55 33N 1 38W
Beagle Bay 136 16 32 S 122 54 E
Beagle, Canal 176 55 0 S 68 30W
Bealanana 129 14 33N 48 44 E
Bealey 143 43 2 S 171 36 E
Beaminster 28 50 48N 2 44W
Bear I. 39 51 38N 9 50W
Bear I. Nor. 12 74 30N 19 0 E
Bear L., B.C., Can. 152 56 10N 126 52W
Bear L., Man., Can. 153 55 8N 96 0W
Bear L., U.S.A. 160 42 0N 111 20W
Bearcreek 160 45 11N 109 6W
Beardmore 150 49 36N 87 57W
Beardmore Glacier 13 84 30 S 170 0 E
Beardstown 158 40 0N 90 25W
Bearn 44 43 28N 0 36W
Bearpaw Mt. 160 48 15N 109 55W
Bearsden 34 55 55N 4 21W
Bearskin Lake 150 53 58N 91 2W
Bearsted 29 51 15N 0 35 E
Beas de Segura 59 38 15N 2 53W
Beasain 58 43 3N 2 11W
Beata, C. 167 17 40N 71 30W
Beata, I. 167 17 34N 71 31W
Beatrice, Zimb. 127 18 15 S 30 55 E
Beatrice, U.S.A. 158 40 20N 96 40W
Beatrice, C. 138 14 20 S 136 55 E
Beatrice, oilfield 19 58 7N 3 6W
Beattock 35 55 19N 3 27W
Beatton, R. 152 56 15N 120 45W
Beatton River 152 57 26N 121 20W
Beatty 163 36 58N 116 46W
Beaucaire 45 43 48N 4 39 E
Beauce, Plaines de 43 48 10N 2 0 E
Beauceville 151 46 13N 70 46W
Beaudesert 139 27 59 S 153 0 E
Beaufort, Austral. 140 37 25 S 143 25 E
Beaufort, Malay. 102 5 30N 115 40 E
Beaufort, N.C., U.S.A. 157 34 45N 76 40W
Beaufort, S.C., U.S.A. 157 32 25N 80 40W
Beaufort Sea 12 72 0N 140 0W
Beaufort-West 128 32 18 S 22 36 E
Beaugency 43 47 47N 1 38 E
Beauharnois 150 45 20N 73 52W
Beaujeu 45 46 10N 4 35 E
Beaujolais 45 46 0N 4 25 E
Beaulieu, Loiret, France 44 47 31N 2 49 E
Beaulieu, Vendée, France 45 46 41N 1 37W
Beaulieu, U.K. 28 50 49N 1 27W
Beaulieu, R. 152 62 3N 113 11W
Beauly 37 57 29N 4 27W
Beauly Firth 37 57 30N 4 20W
Beauly, R. 37 57 26N 4 28W
Beaumaris 31 53 16N 4 7W
Beaumetz-les-Loges 43 50 15N 2 40 E
Beaumont, Belg. 47 50 15N 4 14 E
Beaumont, France 44 44 45N 0 46 E
Beaumont, N.Z. 143 45 50 S 169 33 E
Beaumont, Calif., U.S.A. 163 33 56N 116 58W
Beaumont, Tex., U.S.A. 159 30 5N 94 8W
Beaumont-le-Roger 42 49 4N 0 47 E
Beaumont-sur-Oise 43 49 9N 2 17 E
Beaune 43 47 2N 4 50 E
Beaune-la-Rolande 43 48 4N 2 25 E
Beauraing 47 50 7N 4 57 E
Beausejour 153 50 5N 96 35 E
Beausset, Le 45 43 10N 5 46 E
Beauvais 43 49 25N 2 8 E
Beauval 153 55 9N 107 37W
Beauvoir, Deux Sèvres, France 44 46 12N 0 30W
Beauvoir, Vendée, France 42 46 55N 2 1W
Beaver, Alaska, U.S.A. 147 66 20N 147 30W
Beaver, Okla., U.S.A. 159 36 52N 100 31W
Beaver, Utah, U.S.A. 161 38 20N 112 45W
Beaver City 158 40 13N 99 50W
Beaver Dam 158 43 28N 88 50W
Beaver Falls 156 40 44N 80 20W
Beaver Hill L. 153 54 16N 94 59W
Beaver I. 150 45 40N 85 31W
Beaver, R. 152 59 52N 124 20W
Beaver, R 150 55 55N 87 48W
Beaver, R. 153 55 26N 107 45W
Beaverhill L., Man., Can. 153 54 5N 94 50W
Beaverhill L., N.W.T., Can. 153 63 2N 111 22W
Beaverhill L., Alb., 152 53 27N 112 32W
Beaverlodge 152 55 11N 119 29W
Beavermouth 152 51 32N 117 23W
Beaverstone, R. 150 54 59N 89 25W
Beawar 94 26 3N 74 18 E
Bebedouro 173 21 0 S 48 25W
Bebington 32 53 23N 3 1W
Beboa 129 17 22 S 44 33 E
Bebra 48 50 59N 9 48 E
Beccles 29 52 27N 1 33 E
Bečej 66 45 36N 20 3 E
Beceni 70 45 23N 26 48 E
Becerreá 56 42 51N 7 10W
Béchar 118 31 38N 2 18 E
Becharof L. 147 58 0N 156 30W
Bechuanaland = Botswana 125 23 0 S 24 0 E
Bechyně 52 49 17N 14 29 E
Beckermet 32 54 26N 3 31W
Beckfoot 32 54 50N 3 25W
Beckingham 33 53 24N 0 49W
Beckley 156 37 50N 81 8W
Bécon 42 47 30N 0 50W
Bečva, R. 53 49 31N 17 40 E
Bedale 33 54 18N 1 35W
Bédar 59 37 11N 1 59W
Bédarieux 44 43 37N 3 10 E
Bédarrides 45 44 2N 4 54 E
Beddone, Mt. 138 25 50 S 134 20 E
Bedele 123 8 31N 35 44 E
Bedel,Pereval 85 41 26N 78 26 E
Bederkesa 48 53 37N 8 50 E
Bedford, Can. 150 45 7N 72 59W
Bedford, S. Afr. 128 32 40 S 26 10 E
Bedford, U.K. 29 52 8N 0 29W
Bedford, Ind., U.S.A. 156 38 50N 86 30W
Bedford, Iowa, U.S.A. 158 40 40N 94 41W
Bedford, Ohio, U.S.A. 156 41 23N 81 32W
Bedford, Va., U.S.A. 156 37 25N 79 30W
Bedford □ 29 52 4N 0 28W
Bedford, C. 138 15 14 S 145 21 E
Bedford Downs 136 17 19 S 127 20 E
Bedford Level 29 52 25N 0 5 E
Bedków 54 51 36N 19 44 E
Bedlington 35 55 8N 1 35W
Bednesti 152 53 50N 123 10W
Bednja, R. 63 46 12N 16 25 E
Bednodemyanovsk 81 53 55N 43 15 E
Bedourie 138 24 30 S 139 30 E
Bedretto 51 46 31N 8 31 E
Bedum 47 53 18N 6 36 E
Bedwas 31 51 36N 3 10W
Bedworth 28 52 28N 1 29W
Bedzin 54 50 19N 19 7 E
Bee L. 36 57 22N 7 21W
Beebyn 137 27 0 S 117 48 E
Beech Grove 156 39 40N 86 2W
Beechey Point 147 70 27N 149 18W
Beechworth 141 36 22 S 146 43 E
Beechy 153 50 53N 107 24W
Beeford 33 53 58N 0 18W
Beek, Gelderland, Neth. 46 51 55N 6 11 E
Beek, Limburg, Neth. 47 50 57N 5 48 E
Beek, Noord Brabant, Neth. 47 51 32N 5 38 E
Beekbergen 46 52 10N 5 58 E
Beelitz 48 52 14N 12 58 E
Beemem 47 51 9N 3 21 E
Beenleigh 139 27 43 S 153 10 E
Beer 30 50 41N 3 5W
Be'er Sheva' 90 31 15N 34 48 E
Be'er Sheva', N. 90 31 12N 34 40 E
Be'er Toviyyao 90 31 44N 34 42 E
Be'eri 90 31 25N 34 30 E
Be'erotayim 90 32 19N 34 59 E
Beersheba = Be'er Sheva' 90 31 15N 34 48 E
Beerta 46 53 11N 7 6 E
Beerze, R. 46 51 39N 5 20 E
Beesd 46 51 53N 5 11 E
Beesel 47 51 16N 6 2 E
Beeskow 48 52 9N 14 14 E
Beeston 33 52 55N 1 11W
Beetaloo 138 17 15 S 133 50 E
Beetsterzwaag 46 53 4N 6 5 E
Beetzendorf 48 52 42N 11 6 E
Beeville 159 28 27N 97 44W
Befale 124 0 25N 20 45 E
Befandriana 125 21 55 S 44 0 E
Befotaka, Diégo-Suarez, Madag. 129 14 30 S 48 0 E
Befotaka, Fianarantsoa, Madag. 129 23 49 S 47 0 E
Beg, L. 38 54 48N 6 28W
Bega 141 36 41 S 149 51 E
Bega, Canalul 66 45 37N 20 46 E
Begelly 31 51 45N 4 44W
• Begemdir & Simen □ 123 13 55N 37 30 E
Begna 71 60 41N 9 42 E
Begonte 56 43 10N 7 40W
Begu-Sarai 95 25 24N 86 9 E
Beguildy 31 52 25N 3 11W
Béhagle = Lai 117 9 25N 16 30 E
Behara 125 24 55 S 46 20 E
Behbehan 92 30 30N 50 15 E
Behror 94 27 51N 76 20 E
Behshahr 93 36 45N 53 35 E
Beida (Al Bayda) 117 32 30N 21 40 E
Beighton 33 53 21N 1 21W
Beilen 46 52 52N 6 27 E
Beilngries 49 49 1N 11 27 E
Beilpajah 140 32 54 S 143 52 E
Beilul 123 13 2N 42 20 E
Beinn a' Ghlo, Mt. 37 56 51N 3 42W
Beinn Mhor, Mt. 36 57 59N 6 39W
Beira 127 19 50 S 34 52 E
Beira-Alta 55 40 35N 7 35W
Beira-Baixa 55 40 2N 7 30W
Beira-Litoral 55 40 5N 8 30W
Beirut = Bayrūt 92 33 53N 35 31 E
Beit Bridge 127 14 58 S 30 15 E
Beit Hanum 90 31 32N 34 32 E
Beit Lahiya 90 31 32N 34 30 E
Beit 'Ur et Tahta 90 31 54N 35 5 E
Beit Yosef 90 32 34N 35 33 E
Beitbridge 127 22 12 S 30 0 E
Beith 34 55 45N 4 38W
Beituniya 90 31 54N 35 10 E
Beiuş 70 46 40N 22 21 E
Beja 57 38 2N 7 53W
Béja 119 36 43N 9 12 E
Beja □ 57 37 55N 7 55W
Béjaïa 119 36 42N 5 2 E
Béjar 56 40 23N 5 46W
Bejestan 93 34 30N 58 5 E
Bekabad 85 40 13N 69 14 E
Bekasi 103 6 20 S 107 0 E
Békés 53 46 47N 21 9 E
Békés □ 53 46 45N 21 0 E
Békéscsaba 53 46 40N 21 10 E
Bekily 129 24 13 S 45 19 E
Bekkevoort 47 50 57N 4 58 E
Bekkjarvik 71 60 1N 5 13 E

*Renamed Gonder

Bekoji 123 7 40N 38 20 E
Bekok 101 2 20N 103 7 E
Bekopaka 129 19 9 S 44 45 E
Bekwai 121 6 30N 1 34W
Bel Air 162 39 32N 76 21W
Bela, India 95 25 50N 82 0 E
Bela, Pak. 94 26 12N 66 20 E
Bela Crkva 66 44 55N 21 27 E
Bela Palanka 66 43 13N 22 17 E
Bela Vista, Brazil 173 22 12 S 56 20W
Bela Vista, Mozam. 129 26 10 S 32 44 E
Bélâbre 44 46 34N 1 8 E
Belaia, Mt. 123 11 25N 36 8 E
Belalcázar 57 38 35N 5 10W
Belanovica 66 44 15N 20 23 E
Belavenona 129 24 50 S 47 4 E
Belawan 102 3 33N 98 32 E
Belaya Glina 83 46 5N 40 48 E
Belaya Kalitva 83 48 13N 40 50 E
Belaya Kholunitsa 84 58 41N 50 13 E
Belaya, R. 84 55 54N 53 33 E
Belaya Tserkov 80 49 45N 30 10 E
Belbroughton 28 52 23N 2 5W
Belceşti 70 47 19N 27 7 E
Belchatów 54 51 21N 19 22 E
Belcher, C. 12 75 0N 160 0W
Belcher Is. 150 56 15N 78 45W
Belchite 58 41 18N 0 43W
Belclare 38 53 29N 8 55W
Belcoo 38 54 18N 7 52W
Belderg 38 54 18N 9 33W
Beldringe 73 55 28N 10 21 E
Belebey 84 54 7N 54 7 E
Belém de São Francisco 170 8 46 S 38 58W
Belém (Pará) 170 1 20 S 48 30W
Belén, Argent. 172 27 40 S 67 5W
Belén, Colomb. 174 1 26N 75 56W
Belén, Parag. 172 23 30 S 57 6W
Belen 161 34 40N 106 50W
Belene 67 43 39N 25 10 E
Bélesta 44 42 55N 1 56 E
Belet Uen 91 4 30N 45 5 E
Belev 81 53 50N 36 5 E
Belfast, N.Z. 143 43 27 S 172 39 E
Belfast, S. Afr. 129 25 42 S 30 2 E
Belfast, U.K. 38 54 35N 5 56W
Belfast, U.S.A. 151 44 30N 69 0W
Belfast □ 38 54 35N 5 56W
Belfast, L. 38 54 40N 5 50W
Belfeld 47 51 18N 6 6 E
Belfeoram 151 47 32N 55 30W
Belfield 158 46 54N 103 11W
Belford 35 55 36N 1 50W
Belfort 43 47 38N 6 50 E
Belfort □ 43 47 38N 6 52 E
Belfry 160 45 10N 109 2W
Belgaum 97 15 55N 74 35 E
Belgioioso 62 45 9N 9 21 E
Belgium ■ 47 51 30N 5 0 E
Belgooly 138 51 44N 8 30W
Belgorod 82 50 35N 36 35 E
Belgorod Dnestrovskiy 82 46 11N 30 23 E
Belgrade 160 45 50N 111 10W
Belgrade = Beograd 66 44 50N 20 37 E
Belgrove 143 41 27 S 172 59 E
Belhaven 157 35 34N 76 35W
Beli 121 7 52N 10 58 E
Beli Drim, R. 66 42 25N 20 34 E
Beli Manastir 66 45 45N 18 36 E
Beli Timok, R. 66 43 39N 22 14 E
Belice, R. 64 37 44N 12 58 E
Belinga 124 1 10N 13 2 E
Belingwe 127 20 29 S 29 57 E
Belingwe, N., mt. 127 20 37 S 29 55 E
Belinsky (Chembar) 81 53 0N 43 25 E
Belinţ 66 45 48N 21 54 E
Belinyu 102 1 35 S 105 50 E
Beliton, Is. 102 3 10 S 107 50 E
Belitung, I. 102 3 10 S 107 50 E
Beliu 70 46 30N 22 0 E
Belize ■ 165 17 0N 88 30W
Belize City 165 17 25N 88 0W
Beljanica 66 44 08N 21 43 E
Bell 151 53 50N 53 10 E
Bell Bay 138 41 6 S 146 53 E
Bell I. 151 50 46N 55 35W
Bell Irving, R. 152 56 12N 129 5W
Bell Peninsula 149 63 50N 82 0W
Bell, R. 150 49 48N 77 38W
Bell Rock = Inchcape Rock 35 56 26N 2 24W
Bell Ville 172 32 40 S 62 40W
Bella Bella 152 52 10N 128 10W
Bella Coola 152 52 25N 126 40W
Bella Unión 172 30 15 S 57 40W
Bella Vista, Corrientes, Argent. 172 28 33 S 59 0W
Bella Vista, Tucuman, Argent. 172 27 10 S 65 25W
Bella Yella 120 7 24N 10 9W
Bellacorick 38 54 8N 9 35W
Bellaghy 38 54 50N 6 31W
Bellágio 62 45 59N 9 15 E
Bellaire 156 40 1N 80 46W
Bellananagh 38 53 55N 7 25W
Bellarena 38 55 7N 6 57W
Bellarwi 141 34 6 S 147 13 E
Bellary 97 15 10N 76 56 E
Bellata 139 29 53 S 149 46 E
Bellavary 38 53 54N 9 9W
Belle Fourche 158 44 43N 103 52W
Belle Fourche, R. 158 44 25N 105 0W
Belle Glade 157 26 43N 80 38W
Belle Ile 42 47 20N 3 10W
Belle Isle 151 51 57N 55 25W
Belle-Isle-en-Terre 42 48 33N 3 23W
Belle Isle, Str. of 151 51 30N 56 30W
Belle, La 157 26 45N 81 22W
Belle Plaine, Iowa, U.S.A. 158 41 51N 92 18W
Belle Plaine, Minn., U.S.A. 158 44 35N 93 48W
Belledonne 45 45 11N 6 0 E
Belledune 151 47 55N 65 50W
Belleek 38 54 30N 8 6W
Bellefontaine 156 40 20N 83 45W
Bellefonte 156 40 56N 77 45W
Bellegarde, Ain, France 45 46 4N 5 49 E
Bellegarde, Creuse, France 43 45 59N 2 19 E
Bellegarde, Loiret, France 43 48 0N 2 26 E
Belleoram 151 47 31N 55 25W
Belleville, Can. 150 44 10N 77 23W
Belleville, Rhône, France 45 46 7N 4 45 E
Belleville, Vendée, France 42 46 48N 1 28W
Belleville, Ill., U.S.A. 158 38 30N 90 0W
Belleville, Kans., U.S.A. 158 39 51N 97 38W
Belleville, N.Y., U.S.A. 162 43 46N 76 10W
Bellevue, Can. 152 49 35N 114 22W
Bellevue, U.S.A. 160 43 25N 144 23W
Belley 45 45 46N 5 41 E
Bellin (Payne Bay) 149 60 0N 70 0W
Bellingen 141 30 25 S 152 50 E
Bellingham, U.K. 35 55 09N 2 16W
Bellingham, U.S.A. 160 48 45N 122 27W
Bellingshausen Sea 13 66 0 S 80 0W
Bellinzona 51 46 11N 9 1 E
Bello 174 6 20N 75 33W
Bellona Reefs 133 21 26 S 159 0 E
Bellows Falls 162 43 10N 72 30W
Bellpat 94 29 0N 68 5 E
Bellpuig 58 41 37N 1 1 E
Belluno 63 46 8N 12 6 E
Bellville 159 29 58N 96 18W
Belmar 162 40 10N 74 2W
Bélmez 57 38 17N 5 17W
Belmont, Austral. 141 33 4 S 151 42 E
Belmont, U.S.A. 162 43 27N 71 29W
Belmonte, Brazil 171 16 0 S 39 0W
Belmonte, Port. 56 40 21N 7 20W
Belmonte, Spain 58 39 34N 2 43W
Belmopan 165 17 18N 88 30W
Belmore 140 33 34 S 141 13 E
Belmullet 38 54 13N 9 58W
Belo Horizonte 171 19 55 S 43 56W
Belo Jardim 170 8 20 S 36 26W
Belo-sur-Mer 129 20 42 S 44 33 E
Belo-sur-Tsiribihana 129 19 40 S 43 30 E
Belogorsk, R.S.F.S.R., U.S.S.R. 77 51 0N 128 20 E
Belogorsk, Ukraine, U.S.S.R. 82 45 3N 34 35 E
Belogradchik 66 43 37N 22 40 E
Belogradets 67 43 22N 27 18 E
Beloha 129 25 10 S 45 3 E
Beloit, Kans., U.S.A. 158 39 32N 98 9W
Beloit, Wis., U.S.A. 158 42 35N 89 0W
Belokholunitskiy 81 58 55N 50 43 E
Belomorsk 78 64 35N 34 30 E
Belonia 98 23 15N 91 30 E
Belopolye 80 51 14N 34 20 E
Beloretsk 84 53 58N 58 24 E
Belovo 76 54 30N 86 0 E
Beloyarskiy 84 56 45N 61 24 E
Beloye More 78 66 30N 38 0 E
Beloye, Oz. 78 60 10N 37 35 E
Beloye Ozero 83 45 15N 46 50 E
Belozersk 81 60 0N 37 30 E
Belpasso 65 37 37N 15 0 E
Belper 33 53 2N 1 29W
Belsay 35 55 6N 1 53W
Belsele 47 51 9N 4 6 E
Belsito 64 37 50N 13 47 E
Beltana 140 30 48 S 138 25 E
Belterra 175 2 45 S 55 0W
Beltinci 63 46 37N 16 20 E
Belton, Humberside, U.K. 33 53 33N 0 49W
Belton, Norfolk, U.K. 29 52 35N 1 39 E
Belton, S.C., U.S.A. 157 34 31N 82 39W
Belton, Tex., U.S.A. 159 31 4N 97 30W
Beltra, Mayo, Ireland 38 53 57N 9 24W
Beltra, Sligo, Ireland 38 54 12N 8 36W
Beltra L. 38 53 56N 9 28W
Beltsy 82 47 48N 28 0 E
Belturbet 38 54 6N 7 28W
Belukha 76 49 50N 86 50 E
Beluran 102 5 48N 117 35 E
Beluša 53 49 5N 18 27 E
Belušió 66 43 50N 21 10 E
Belvedere Marittimo 65 39 37N 15 52 E
Belvès 44 44 46N 1 0 E
Belvidere, Ill., U.S.A. 158 42 15N 88 55W
Belvidere, N.J., U.S.A. 162 40 48N 75 5W
Belville 38 54 40N 9 22W
Belvis de la Jara 57 39 45N 4 57W
Belyando, R. 138 21 38 S 146 50 E
Belyj Jar 76 58 26N 84 39 E
Belyy 80 55 48N 32 51 E
Belyy, Ostrov 76 73 30N 71 0 E
Belyye Vody 85 42 25N 69 50 E
Belz 80 50 23N 24 1 E
Belzig 48 52 8N 12 36 E
Belzoni 159 33 12N 90 30W
Bemaraha, Plat. du 129 18 40 S 44 45 E
Bemarivo, Majunga, Madag. 129 17 6 S 44 31 E
Bemarivo, Tuléar, Madag. 129 21 45 S 44 45 E
Bemarivo, R. 129 21 45 S 44 45 E
Bemavo 129 21 33 S 45 25 E
Bembéréke 121 10 11N 2 43 E
Bembesi 127 20 0 S 28 58 E
Bembesi, R. 127 20 0 S 28 58 E
Bembézar, R. 57 38 0N 5 20W
Bembridge 28 50 41N 1 4W
Bemidji 158 47 30N 94 50W
Bemmel 46 51 54N 5 54 E
Ben Alder 37 55 59N 4 30W
Ben Avon 37 57 6N 3 28W
Ben Bheigeir, Mt. 34 55 43N 6 6W
Ben Bullen 141 33 12 S 150 2 E
Ben Chonzie 35 56 27N 4 0W
Ben Cruachan, Mt. 34 56 26N 5 8W
Ben Dearg 37 57 47N 4 58W
Ben Dearg, mt. 37 56 54N 3 49W
Ben Dhorain 37 58 7N 3 50W
Ben Dorian 34 56 30N 4 42W
Ben Gardane 119 33 11N 11 11 E
Ben Hee 37 58 16N 4 43W
Ben Hope, mt. 37 58 24N 4 36W
Ben Klibreck 37 58 14N 4 25W
Ben Lawers, mt. 37 56 33N 4 13W
Ben Lomond, mt. 139 30 1 S 151 43 E
Ben Lomond mt. 138 41 38 S 147 42 E
Ben Lomond, mt. 34 56 12N 4 39W
Ben Loyal 37 58 25N 4 25W
Ben Luc 101 10 39N 106 29 E
Ben Lui, mt. 34 56 24N 4 50W
Ben Macdhui 37 57 4N 3 40W
Ben Mhor 36 57 16N 7 21W
Ben More, Mull, U.K. 34 56 26N 6 2W
Ben More, Perth, U.K. 34 56 23N 4 31W
Ben More Assynt 37 58 7N 4 51W
Ben Nevis, mt., N.Z. 143 45 15 S 169 0 E
Ben Nevis, mt., U.K. 36 56 48N 5 0W
Ben Ohau Ra. 143 44 1 S 170 4 E
Ben Quang 100 17 3N 106 55 E
Ben Stack 36 58 20N 4 58W
Ben Tharsiunn 37 57 47N 4 20W
Ben Venue 34 56 13N 4 28W
Ben Vorlich 34 56 22N 4 15W
Ben Wyvis, mt. 37 57 40N 4 35W
Bena 121 11 20N 5 50 E
Bena Dibele 124 4 4 S 22 50 E
Benagalbón 57 36 45N 4 15W
Benagerie 140 31 25 S 140 22 E
Benahmed 118 33 4N 7 9W
Benalla 141 36 30 S 146 0 E
Benambra, Mt. 141 36 31 S 147 34 E
Benamejí 57 37 16N 4 33W
Benanee 140 34 31 S 142 52 E
Benares = Varanasi 95 25 22N 83 8 E
Benavente, Port. 57 38 59N 8 49W
Benavente, Spain 56 42 2N 5 43W
Benavides, Spain 56 42 30N 5 54W
Benavides, U.S.A. 159 27 35N 98 28W
Benbane Hd. 38 55 15N 6 30W
Benbaun, Mt. 38 53 30N 9 50W
Benbecula, I. 36 57 26N 7 21W
Benbonyathe, Mt. 140 30 25 S 139 11 E
Benburb 38 54 25N 6 42W
Bencubbin 137 30 48 S 117 52 E
Bend 160 44 2N 121 15W
Bendel □ 121 6 0N 6 0 E
Bender Beila 91 9 30N 50 48 E
Bender Cassim 91 11 12N 49 18 E
Bendering 137 32 23 S 118 18 E
Bendery 82 46 50N 29 50 E
Bendigo 140 36 40 S 144 15 E
Beneden Knijpe 46 52 58N 5 59 E
Benedick 162 38 31N 76 41W
Beneditinos 170 5 27 S 42 22W
Benedito Leite 170 7 13 S 44 34W
Benei Beraq 129 32 5N 34 50 E
Bènéna 120 13 9N 4 17W
Beneraird, Mt. 34 55 4N 4 57W
Benešov 52 49 46N 14 41 E
Bénestroff 43 48 54N 6 45 E
Benet 44 46 22N 0 35W
Benevento 65 41 7N 14 45 E
Benfeld 43 48 22N 7 34 E
Beng Lovea 100 12 36N 105 34 E
Benga 127 16 11 S 33 40 E
Bengal, Bay of 99 15 0N 90 0 E
Bengawan Solo 103 7 5 S 112 25 E
Benghazi = Banghāzī 119 32 11N 20 3 E
Bengkalis 102 1 30N 102 10 E
Bengkulu 102 3 50 S 102 12 E
Bengkulu □ 102 3 48 S 102 16 E
Bengough 153 49 25N 105 10W
Benguela 125 12 37 S 13 25 E
Benguerir 118 32 16N 7 56W
Benguérua, Î. 129 21 58 S 35 28 E
Benha 122 30 26N 31 8 E
Beni 126 0 30N 29 27 E
Beni Abbès 118 30 5N 2 5W
Beni Haoua 118 36 30N 1 30 E
Benî Mazâr 122 28 32N 30 44 E
Beni Mellal 118 32 21N 6 21W
Beni Ounif 118 32 0N 1 10W
Beni, R. 174 10 30 S 66 0W
Beni Saf 118 35 17N 1 15W
Benî Suêf 122 29 5N 31 6 E
Beniah L. 152 63 23N 112 17W
Benicarló 58 40 23N 0 23 E
Benicia 163 38 3N 122 9W
Benidorm 59 38 33N 0 9W
Benidorm,Islote de 59 38 31N 0 9W
Benin ■ 121 10 0N 2 0 E
Benin, Bight of 121 5 0N 3 0 E
Benin City 121 6 20N 5 31 E
Benington 33 52 59N 0 5 E
Benisa 59 38 43N 0 03 E
Benjamin Aceval 172 24 58 S 57 34W
Benjamin Constant 174 4 40 S 70 15W
Benjamin Hill 164 30 10N 111 10W
Benkelman 158 40 7N 101 32W
Benlidi 138 24 35 S 144 50 E
Benmore Pk. 143 44 25 S 170 8 E
Bennane Hd. 34 55 9N 5 2W
Bennebroek 46 52 19N 4 36 E
Bennekom 46 52 0N 5 41 E
Bennett 147 59 56N 134 53W
Bennettsbridge 39 52 36N 7 12W
Bennettsville 157 34 38N 79 39W
Bennington 162 42 52N 73 12W
Benoa 102 8 50 S 115 20 E
Bénodet 42 47 53N 4 7W
Benoni 129 26 11 S 28 18 E
Benoud 118 32 20N 0 16 E
Benque Viejo 165 17 5N 89 8W
Bensheim 49 49 40N 8 38 E
Benson, U.K. 28 51 37N 1 6W
Benson, U.S.A. 161 31 59N 110 19W
Bent 93 26 20N 59 25 E
Benteng 103 6 10 S 120 30 E
Bentinck I. 138 17 3 S 139 35 E
Bentiu 123 9 10N 29 55 E
Bentley, Hants., U.K. 29 51 12N 0 52W
Bentley, S. Yorks, U.K. 33 53 33N 1 9W
Bento Gonçalves 173 29 10 S 51 31W
Benton, Ark., U.S.A. 159 34 30N 92 35W
Benton, Calif., U.S.A. 163 37 48N 118 32W
Benton, Ill., U.S.A. 158 38 0N 88 55W
Benton, Pa., U.S.A. 162 41 12N 76 23W
Benton Harbor 156 42 10N 86 28W
Bentong 101 3 31N 101 55 E
Bentu Liben 123 8 32N 38 21 E
Benue □ 121 7 30N 7 30 E
Benue Plateau □ 121 8 0N 8 30 E
Benue, R. 121 7 50N 6 30 E
Benwee Hd. 38 54 20N 9 50W
Beo 103 4 25N 126 50 E
Beograd 66 44 50N 20 37 E
Beowawe 160 40 45N 117 0W
Beppu 110 33 15N 131 30 E
Beppu-Wan 110 33 18N 131 34 E
Ber Dagan 90 32 1N 34 49 E
Bera 98 24 5N 89 37 E
Beragh 38 54 34N 7 10W
Berakit 123 14 38N 39 29 E
Berati 68 40 43N 19 59 E
Berber 122 18 0N 34 0 E
Berbéra 117 10 33N 16 35 E
Berbera 91 10 30N 45 2 E
Berbérati 124 4 15N 15 40 E
Berberia, Cabo 59 38 39N 1 24 E
Berbice, R. 174 5 20N 58 10W
Berceto 62 44 30N 10 0 E
Berchtesgaden 49 47 37N 13 1 E
Berck-sur-Mer 43 50 25N 1 36 E
Berdichev 82 49 57N 28 30 E
Berdsk 76 54 47N 83 2 E
Berdyansk 82 46 45N 36 50 E
Berdyaush 84 55 9N 59 9 E
Bere Alston 30 50 29N 4 11W
Bere Regis 28 50 45N 2 13W
Berea 156 37 35N 84 18W
Berebere 103 2 25N 128 45 E
Bereda 91 11 45N 51 0 E
Bereina 135 8 39 S 146 30 E
Berekum 120 7 29N 2 34W
Berenice 122 24 2N 35 25 E
Berens I. 153 52 18N 97 18W
Berens, R. 153 51 21N 97 0W
Berens River 153 52 25N 97 0W
Berestechko 80 50 22N 25 5 E
Bereşti 70 46 6N 27 50 E
Berettyo, R. 53 47 32N 21 47 E
BerettyóIjfalu 53 47 13N 21 33 E
Beretău, R. 70 47 30N 22 7 E
Berevo 129 19 44 S 44 58 E
Berevo-sur-Ranobe 129 17 14 S 44 17 E
Bereza 80 52 31N 24 51 E
Berezhany 80 49 26N 24 58 E
Berezina, R. 80 54 10N 28 10 E
Berezna 80 51 35N 30 46 E
Berezniki 84 59 24N 56 46 E
Berezovka 82 47 25N 30 55 E
Berezovo 76 64 0N 65 0 E
Berg 71 59 10N 11 18 E
Berga, Spain 58 42 6N 1 48 E
Berga, Kalmar, Sweden 73 57 14N 16 3 E
Berga, Kronoberg, Sweden 73 56 55N 14 0 E
Bergama 92 39 8N 27 15 E
Bergambacht 46 51 56N 4 48 E
Bérgamo 62 45 42N 9 40 E
Bergantiños 56 43 20N 8 40W
Bergedorf 48 53 28N 10 12 E
Bergeijk 47 51 19N 5 21 E
Bergen, Ger. 48 54 24N 13 26 E
Bergen, Norway 71 60 23N 5 20 E
Bergen-Binnen 46 52 40N 4 43 E
Bergen-op-Zoom 47 51 30N 4 18 E
Bergerac 44 44 51N 0 30 E
Bergheim 48 50 57N 6 38 E
Berghem 46 51 46N 5 33 E

Bergisch-Gladbach **48** 50 59N 7 9 E
Bergkvara **73** 56 23N 16 5 E
Bergschenhoek **46** 51 59N 4 30 E
Bergsjö **72** 61 59N 17 3 E
Berguent **118** 34 1N 2 0W
Bergues **43** 50 58N 2 24 E
Bergum **46** 53 13N 5 59 E
Bergvik **72** 61 16N 16 50 E
Berhala, Selat **102** 1 0 S 104 15 E
Berhampore **95** 24 2N 88 27 E
Berhampur **96** 19 15N 84 54 E
Berheci, R. **70** 46 7N 27 19 E
Berhungra **139** 34 46 S 147 52 E
Bering Sea **130** 58 0N 167 0 E
Bering Str. **147** 66 0N 170 0W
Beringarra **137** 26 0 S 116 55 E
Beringen, Belg. **47** 51 3N 5 14 E
Beringen, Switz. **51** 47 38N 8 34 E
Beringovskiy **77** 63 3N 179 19 E
Berislav **82** 46 50N 33 30 E
Berisso **172** 34 40 S 58 0W
Berja **59** 36 50N 2 56W
Berkane **118** 34 52N 2 20W
Berkel, R. **46** 52 8N 6 12 E
Berkeley **163** 37 52N 122 20W
Berkeley Springs **156** 39 38N 78 12W
Berkhamsted **29** 51 45N 0 33W
Berkhout **46** 52 38N 4 59 E
Berkner I. **13** 79 30 S 50 0W
Berkovitsa **67** 43 16N 23 8 E
Berkshire **162** 42 19N 76 11W
Berkshire □ **28** 51 30N 1 20W
Berkshire Downs **28** 51 30N 1 30W
Berkyk **71** 62 50N 9 59 E
Berlaar **47** 51 7N 4 39 E
Berland, R. **152** 54 0N 116 50W
Berlanga **57** 38 17N 5 50W
Berlave **47** 51 2N 4 0 E
Berleburg **48** 51 3N 8 22 E
Berlenga, I. **75** 39 25N 9 30W
Berlick **47** 51 22N 6 9 E
Berlin, Ger. **48** 52 32N 13 24 E
Berlin, Md., U.S.A. **162** 38 19N 75 12W
Berlin, N.H., U.S.A. **156** 44 29N 71 10W
Berlin, N.Y., U.S.A. **162** 42 42N 73 23W
Berlin, E. □ **48** 52 30N 13 30 E
Berlin, W. □ **48** 52 30N 13 20 E
Bermeja, Sierra **57** 36 45N 5 11W
Bermejo, R., Formosa, Argent. **172** 26 30 S 58 50W
Bermejo, R., San Juan, Argent. **172** 30 0 S 68 0W
Bermeo **58** 43 25N 2 47W
Bermillo de Sayago **56** 41 22N 6 8W
Bermuda, I. **10** 32 45N 65 0W
Bern (Berne) **50** 46 57N 7 28 E
Bern (Berne) □ **50** 46 45N 7 40 E
Bernalda **65** 40 24N 16 44 E
Bernalillo **161** 35 17N 106 37W
Bernam, R. **101** 3 45N 101 5 E
Bernardo de Irigoyen **173** 26 15 S 53 40W
Bernardsville **162** 40 43N 74 34W
Bernasconi **172** 37 55 S 63 44W
Bernau **49** 47 53N 12 20 E
Bernay **42** 49 5N 0 35 E
Berndorf **52** 47 59N 16 1 E
Berne = Bern **50** 46 57N 7 28 E
Berner Alpen **50** 46 27N 7 35 E
Berneray, I. **36** 56 47N 7 38W
Bernese Oberland = Oberland • **50** 46 27N 7 35 E
Bernier I. **137** 24 50 S 113 12 E
Bernina Pass **51** 46 22N 9 54 E
Bernina, Piz **51** 46 20N 9 54 E
Bernissart **47** 50 28N 3 39 E
Beroroha **125** 21 40 S 45 10 E
Bérouboúey **121** 10 34N 2 46 E
Beroun **52** 49 57N 14 5 E
Berounka, R. **52** 50 0N 13 47 E
Berovo **66** 41 42N 22 51 E
Berrahal **119** 36 54N 7 33 E
Berre **45** 43 28N 5 11 E
Berre, Étang de **45** 43 27N 5 5 E
Berrechid **118** 33 18N 7 36W
Berri **140** 34 14 S 140 35 E
Berriedale **37** 58 12N 3 30W
Berriew **31** 52 36N 3 12W
Berrigan **141** 35 38 S 145 49 E
Berrouaghia **118** 36 10N 2 53 E
Berrwillock **140** 35 36 S 142 59 E
Berry, Austral. **141** 34 46 S 150 43 E
Berry, France **43** 47 0N 2 0 E
Berry Hd. **30** 50 24N 3 29W
Berry Is. **166** 25 40N 77 50W
Berryville **159** 36 23N 93 35W
Bersenbrück **48** 52 33N 7 56 E
Berst Ness **37** 59 16N 3 0W
Berthaund **158** 40 21N 105 5W
Berthier Is. **136** 14 29 S 124 59 E
Berthold **158** 48 19N 101 45W
Bertincourt **43** 50 5N 2 58 E
Bertoua **124** 4 30N 13 45 E
Bertraghboy, B. **38** 53 22N 9 54W
Bertrand **158** 40 35N 99 38W
Bertrange **47** 49 37N 6 3 E
Bertrix **47** 49 51N 5 15 E
Beruas **101** 4 30N 100 47 E
Berufjörður **74** 64 48N 14 29W
Berur Hayil **90** 31 34N 34 38 E
Berwick **162** 41 4N 76 17W
Berwick (□) **26** 55 46N 2 30W
Berwick-upon-Tweed **35** 55 47N 2 0W
Berwyn Mts. **31** 52 54N 3 26W
Beryl N., oilfield **19** 59 37N 1 30 E
Beryl, oilfield **19** 59 28N 1 30 E
Beryl W., oilfield **19** 59 32N 1 20 E
Berzasca **66** 44 39N 21 58 E
Berzence **53** 46 12N 17 11 E
Besal **95** 35 4N 73 56 E
Besalampy **129** 16 43 S 44 29 E
Besançon **43** 47 9N 6 0 E
Besar **102** 2 40 S 116 0 E
Beserah **101** 3 50N 103 21 E
Beshenkovichi **80** 55 2N 29 29 E
Beška **66** 45 8N 20 6 E
Beskids, Mts. **53** 49 35N 18 40 E
Beslan **83** 43 22N 44 28 E
Besna Kobila **66** 42 31N 22 10 E
Besnard L. **153** 55 25N 106 0W
Beşparmak Daği **69** 37 32N 27 30 E
Bessarabiya **70** 46 20N 29 0 E
Bessarabka **82** 46 21N 28 51 E
Bessbrook **38** 54 12N 6 25W
Bessèges **45** 44 18N 4 8 E
Bessemer **158** 46 27N 90 0W
Bessin **42** 49 21N 1 0W
Bessines-sur-Gartempe **42** 46 6N 1 22 E
Best **47** 51 31N 5 23 E
Bet Alfa **90** 32 31N 35 25 E
Bet Guvrin **90** 31 37N 34 54 E
Bet Hashitta **90** 32 31N 35 27 E
Bet Ha'tmeq **90** 32 58N 35 8 E
Bet Qeshet **90** 32 41N 35 21 E
Bet She'an **90** 32 30N 35 30 E
Bet Tadjine, Djebel **118** 29 0N 3 30W
Bet Yosef **90** 32 34N 35 33 E
Betafo **129** 19 50 S 46 51 E
Betanzos **56** 43 15N 8 12W
Bétaré-Oya **124** 5 40N 14 5 E
Betekom **47** 50 59N 4 47 E
Bétera **58** 39 35N 0 28W
Bethal **129** 26 27 S 29 28 E
Bethanien **125** 26 31 S 17 8 E
Bethany, S. Afr. **128** 29 34 S 25 59 E
Bethany, U.S.A. **158** 40 18N 94 0W
Bethany = Eizarilya **90** 31 47N 35 15 E
Bethel, U.S.A. **147** 60 50N 161 50W
Bethel, Conn., U.S.A. **162** 41 22N 73 25W
Bethesda, U.K. **31** 53 11N 4 3W
Bethesda, U.S.A. **162** 38 59N 77 6W
Bethlehem, S. Afr. **129** 28 14 S 28 18 E
Bethlehem, U.S.A. **162** 40 39N 75 24W
Bethlehem = Bayt Lahm **90** 31 43N 35 12 E
Bethulie **128** 30 30 S 25 59 E
Béthune **43** 50 30N 2 38 E
Béthune, R. **42** 49 56N 1 5 E
Bethungra **141** 34 45 S 147 51 E
Betijoque **174** 9 23N 70 44W
Betim **171** 19 58 S 44 13W
Betioky **129** 23 48 S 44 20 E
Beton Bazoches **43** 48 42N 3 15 E
Betong **101** 5 45N 101 5 E
Betoota **138** 25 40 S 140 42 E
Betroka **129** 23 16 S 46 0 E
Betsiamites **151** 48 56N 68 40W
Betsiamites, R. **151** 48 56N 68 40W
Betsiboka, R. **129** 17 0 S 47 0 E
Betsjoeanaland **128** 26 30 S 22 30 E
Bettembourg **47** 49 31N 6 6 E
Betterton **162** 39 52N 76 4W
Betteshanger **29** 51 14N 1 20 E
Bettiah **95** 26 48N 84 33 E
Bettles **147** 66 54N 150 50W
Bèttola **62** 44 46N 9 35 E
Bettws Bledrws **31** 52 9N 4 2W
Bettyhill **37** 58 31N 4 12W
Betul **96** 21 48N 77 59 E
Betung **102** 2 0 S 103 10 E
Betws-y-Coed **31** 53 4N 3 49W
Beuca **70** 44 14N 24 56 E
Beuil **45** 44 6N 7 0 E
Beulah, Can. **153** 50 16N 101 02W
Beulah, U.S.A. **158** 47 18N 101 47W
Beuvronne, La **46** 48 59N 2 41 E
Bevensen **48** 53 5N 10 34 E
Beveren **47** 51 12N 4 16 E
Beverley, Austral. **137** 32 9 S 116 56 E
Beverley, U.K. **33** 53 52N 0 26W
Beverlo **47** 51 7N 5 13 E
Beverly, Can. **152** 53 36N 113 21W
Beverly, Mass., U.S.A. **162** 42 32N 70 50W
Beverly, Wash., U.S.A. **160** 46 55N 119 59W
Beverly Hills **163** 34 4N 118 29W
Beverwijk **46** 52 28N 4 38 E
Bewdley **28** 52 23N 2 19W
Bex **50** 46 15N 7 0 E
Bexhill **29** 50 51N 0 29 E
Bexley **29** 51 26N 0 10 E
Beyin **120** 5 1N 2 41W
Beykoz **67** 41 8N 29 7 E
Beyla **120** 8 30N 8 38W
Beynat **44** 45 8N 1 44 E
Beyneu **76** 45 10N 55 3 E
Beypazarı **92** 40 10N 31 48 E
Beyşehir Gölü **92** 37 40N 31 45 E
Bezdan **66** 45 28N 18 57 E
Bezerros **171** 8 14 S 35 45W
Bezet **90** 33 4N 35 8 E
Bezhitsa **80** 53 19N 34 17 E
Béziers **44** 43 20N 3 12 E
Bezwada = Vijayawada **97** 16 31N 80 39 E
Bhachau **93** 23 20N 70 16 E
Bhadarwah **95** 32 58N 75 46 E
Bhadra, R. **97** 13 0N 76 0 E
Bhadrakh **96** 21 10N 86 30 E
Bhadravati **97** 13 49N 76 15 E
Bhagalpur **95** 25 10N 87 0 E
Bhairab **98** 22 51N 89 34 E
Bhairab Bazar **98** 24 4N 90 58 E
Bhaisa **96** 19 10N 77 58 E
Bhakkar **94** 31 40N 71 5 E
Bhakra Dam **95** 31 30N 76 45 E
Bhamo **98** 24 15N 97 15 E
Bhamragarh **96** 19 30N 80 40 E
Bhandara **96** 21 5N 79 42 E
Bhanrer Ra. **94** 23 40N 79 45 E
Bharat = India **93** 24 0N 78 0 E
Bharatpur **94** 27 15N 77 30 E
Bharuch **96** 21 47N 73 0 E
Bhatghar L. **96** 18 10N 73 48 E
Bhatiapara Ghat **98** 23 13N 89 42 E
Bhatkal **97** 13 58N 74 35 E
Bhatpara **95** 22 50N 88 25 E
Bhattiprolu **97** 16 7N 80 45 E
Bhaun **94** 32 55N 72 40 E
Bhaunagar = Bhavnagar **94** 21 45N 72 10 E
Bhavani **97** 11 27N 77 43 E
Bhavani, R. **97** 11 30N 77 15 E
Bhavnagar **94** 21 45N 72 10 E
Bhawanipatna **96** 19 55N 83 30 E
Bhera **94** 32 29N 72 57 E
Bhilsa = Vidisha **94** 23 28N 77 53 E
Bhilwara **94** 25 25N 74 38 E
Bhima, R. **96** 17 20N 76 30 E
Bhimber **95** 32 59N 74 3 E
Bhimvaram **96** 16 30N 81 30 E
Bhind **95** 26 30N 78 46 E
Bhir **96** 19 4N 75 58 E
Bhiwandi **96** 19 15N 73 0 E
Bhiwani **94** 28 50N 76 9 E
Bhola **98** 22 45N 90 35 E
Bhongir **96** 17 30N 78 56 E
Bhopal **94** 23 20N 77 53 E
Bhor **96** 18 12N 73 53 E
Bhubaneswar **96** 20 15N 85 50 E
Bhuj **94** 23 15N 69 49 E
Bhumibol Dam **100** 17 15N 98 58 E
Bhusaval **96** 21 15N 69 49 E
Bhutan ■ **98** 27 25N 89 50 E
Biafra, B. of = Bonny, Bight of **121** 3 30N 9 20 E
Biak **103** 1 0 S 136 0 E
Biała **54** 50 24N 17 40 E
Biała Piska **54** 53 37N 22 5 E
Biała Podlaska **54** 52 4N 23 6 E
Biała Podlaska □ **54** 52 0N 23 0 E
Biała, R. **54** 49 46N 20 53 E
Białogard **54** 54 2N 15 58 E
Biały Bór **54** 53 53N 16 51 E
Białystok **54** 53 10N 23 10 E
Białystok □ **54** 53 9N 23 10 E
Biancavilla **65** 37 39N 14 50 E
Biano Plateau = Manika Plateau **127** 9 55 S 26 24 E
Biaro **103** 2 5N 125 26 E
Biarritz **44** 43 29N 1 33W
Biasca **51** 46 22N 8 58 E
Biba **122** 28 55N 31 0 E
Bibaī **112** 43 19N 141 52 E
Bibby I. **153** 61 55N 93 0W
Biberach **49** 48 5N 9 49 E
Biberist **50** 47 11N 7 34 E
Bibey, R. **56** 42 24N 7 13W
Bibiani **120** 6 30N 2 8W
Bibile **97** 7 10N 81 25 E
Biboohra **138** 16 56 S 145 25 E
Bibungwa **126** 2 40 S 28 15 E
Bibury **28** 51 46N 1 50W
Bic **151** 48 20N 68 41W
Bicaj **68** 42 0N 20 25 E
Bicaz **70** 46 53N 26 5 E
Biccari **65** 41 23N 15 12 E
Bicester **28** 51 53N 1 9W
Biche, La, R. **152** 59 57N 123 50W
Bichena **123** 10 28N 38 10 E
Bickerton I. **138** 13 45 S 136 10 E
Bicknell, Ind., U.S.A. **156** 38 50N 87 20W
Bicknell, Utah, U.S.A. **161** 38 16N 111 35W
Bicsad **70** 47 56N 23 28 E
Bicton **28** 52 43N 2 47W
Bida **121** 9 3N 5 58 E
Bidar **96** 17 55N 77 35 E
Biddeford **151** 43 30N 70 28W
Biddenden **29** 51 7N 0 40 E
Biddu **90** 31 50N 35 8 E
Biddulph **32** 53 8N 2 11W
Biddwara **123** 5 11N 38 34 E
Biddya **90** 32 7N 35 4 E
Bideford **30** 51 1N 4 13W
Bideford Bay **30** 51 5N 4 20W
Bidford on Avon **28** 52 9N 1 53W
Bidor **101** 4 6N 101 15 E
Bidura **140** 34 10 S 143 21 E
Bié **125** 12 22 S 16 55 E
Bié Plateau **125** 12 0 S 16 0 E
Bieber **160** 41 4N 121 6W
Biel (Bienne) **50** 47 8N 7 14 E
Bielawa **54** 50 43N 16 37 E
Bielé Karpaty **53** 49 5N 18 0 E
Bielefeld **48** 52 2N 8 31 E
Bielersee **50** 47 6N 7 5 E
Biella **62** 45 33N 8 3 E
Bielsk Podlaski **54** 52 47N 23 12 E
Bielsko-Biała **54** 49 50N 19 8 E
Bielsko-Biała □ **54** 49 45N 19 15 E
Bien Hoa **101** 10 57N 106 49 E
Bienfait **153** 49 10N 102 50W
Bienne = Biel **50** 47 8N 7 14 E
Bienvenida **57** 38 18N 6 12W
Bienville, L. **150** 55 5N 72 40W
Biescas **58** 42 37N 0 20W
Biesiesfontein **128** 30 57 S 17 58 E
Bietigheim **49** 48 57N 9 8 E
Bievre **47** 49 57N 5 1 E
Biferno, R. **65** 41 40N 14 38 E
Big B. **151** 55 43N 60 35W
Big Bear City **163** 34 16N 116 51W
Big Bear L. **163** 34 15N 116 56W
Big Beaver **153** 49 10N 105 10W
Big Beaver House **150** 52 59N 89 50W
Big Bell **137** 27 21 S 117 40 E
Big Belt Mts. **160** 46 50N 111 30W
Big Bend **129** 26 50 S 32 2 E
Big Bend Nat. Park **159** 29 15N 103 15W
Big Black, R. **159** 32 35N 90 30W
Big Blue, R. **158** 40 20N 96 40W
Big Cr. **152** 51 42N 122 41W
Big Creek **163** 37 11N 119 14W
Big Cypress Swamp **157** 26 12N 81 10W
Big Delta **147** 64 15N 145 0W
Big Falls **158** 48 11N 93 48W
Big Horn **160** 46 11N 107 25W
Big Horn Mts. = Bighorn Mts. **160** 44 30N 107 30W
Big Horn R. **160** 45 30N 108 10W
Big Lake **159** 31 12N 101 25W
Big Moose **162** 43 49N 74 58W
Big Muddy, R. **158** 48 25N 104 45W
Big Pine **163** 37 12N 118 17W
Big Piney **160** 42 32N 110 3W
Big Quill L. **153** 51 55N 105 22W
Big, R. **151** 54 50N 58 55W
Big Rapids **156** 43 42N 85 27W
Big River **153** 53 50N 107 0W
Big Sable Pt. **156** 44 5N 86 30W
Big Salmon **147** 61 50N 136 0W
Big Sand L. **153** 57 45N 99 45W
Big Sandy **160** 48 12N 110 9W
Big Sandy Cr. **158** 38 52N 103 11W
Big Sioux, R. **158** 44 20N 96 53W
Big Smoky Valley **163** 38 30N 117 15W
Big Snowy Mt. **160** 46 50N 109 15W
Big Spring **159** 32 10N 101 25W
Big Springs **158** 41 4N 102 3W
Big Stone City **158** 45 20N 96 30W
Big Stone Gap **157** 36 52N 82 45W
Big Stone L. **158** 44 25N 96 35W
Big Sur **163** 36 15N 121 48W
Big Trout L. **150** 53 40N 90 0W
Biganos **44** 44 39N 0 59W
Bigbury **30** 50 17N 3 52W
Bigbury B. **30** 50 18N 3 58W
Bigerymunal, Mt. **137** 27 25 S 120 40 E
Bigfork **160** 48 3N 114 2W
Biggar **153** 52 4N 108 0W
Bigge I. **136** 14 35 S 125 10 E
Biggenden **139** 25 31 S 152 4 E
Biggleswade **29** 52 6N 0 16W
Bighorn Mts. **160** 44 30N 107 30W
Bignona **120** 12 52N 16 23W
Bigorre **44** 43 5N 0 2 E
Bigstone L. **153** 53 42N 95 44W
Bigtimber **160** 45 53N 110 0W
Bigwa **126** 7 10 S 39 10 E
Bihaó **63** 44 49N 15 57 E
Bihar **95** 25 5N 85 40 E
Bihar □ **95** 25 0N 86 0 E
Biharamulo **126** 2 25 S 31 25 E
Biharamulo □ **126** 2 30 S 31 20 E
Biharkeresztes **53** 47 8N 21 44 E
Bihé Plateau **125** 12 0 S 16 0 E
Bihor □ **70** 47 0N 22 10 E
Bihor, Munţii **70** 46 29N 22 47 E
Bijagós, Arquipélago dos **120** 11 15N 16 10W
Bijaipur **94** 26 2N 77 36 E
Bijapur, Mad. P., India **96** 18 50N 80 50 E
Bijapur, Mysore, India **96** 16 50N 75 55 E
Bijar **92** 35 52N 47 35 E
Bijeljina **66** 44 46N 19 17 E
Bijni **98** 26 30N 90 40 E
Bijnor **94** 29 27N 78 11 E
Bikaner **94** 28 2N 73 18 E
Bikapur **95** 26 30N 82 7 E
Bikin **77** 46 50N 134 20 E
Bikini, atoll **130** 12 0N 167 30 E
Bikoro **124** 0 48 S 18 15 E
Bikoué **121** 5 55 S 11 50 E
Bilād Banī Bū 'Ali **93** 22 0N 59 20 E
Bilara **94** 26 14N 73 53 E
Bilaspara **98** 26 13N 90 14 E
Bilaspur, India **99** 22 2N 82 15 E
Bilaspur, Mad. P., India **95** 22 2N 82 15 E
Bilaspur, Punjab, India **94** 31 19N 76 50 E
Bilauk Taungdan **100** 13 0N 99 0 E
Bilbao **58** 43 16N 2 56W
Bilbor **70** 47 18N 25 30 E
Bildudalur **74** 65 41N 23 36W
Bilecik **92** 40 5N 30 5 E
Bileóa **66** 42 53N 18 27 E
Bilibino **77** 68 3N 166 20 E
Bilibiza **127** 12 30 S 40 20 E
Bilin **98** 17 14N 97 15 E
Bilir **77** 65 40N 131 20 E
Bilishti **68** 40 37N 20 59 E
Bill **158** 43 18N 105 18W
Billa **121** 8 55N 12 15 E
Billabalong **137** 27 25 S 115 49 E
Billericay **29** 51 38N 0 25 E
Billesdon **29** 52 38N 0 56W

Billiluna 136 19 37 S 127 41 E
Billimari 71 33 41 S 148 37 E
Billingham 33 54 36N 1 18W
Billinghay 33 53 5N 0 17W
Billings 160 45 43N 108 29W
Billingsfors 72 58 59N 12 15 E
Billingshurst 29 51 2N 0 28W
Billom 44 45 43N 3 20 E
Bilma 117 18 50N 13 30 E
Bilo Gora 66 45 53N 17 15 E
Biloela 138 24 24 S 150 31 E
Biloxi 159 30 30N 89 0W
Bilpa Morea Claypan 138 25 0 S 140 0 E
Bilston 28 52 34N 2 5W
Bilthoven 46 52 8N 5 12 E
Biltine 117 14 40N 20 50 E
Bilugyun 98 16 24N 97 32 E
Bilyana 138 18 5 S 145 50 E
Bilyarsk 84 54 58N 50 22 E
Bilzen 47 50 52N 5 31 E
Bima 103 8 22 S 118 49 E
Bimban 122 24 24N 32 54 E
Bimberi Peak, mt. 141 35 44 S 148 51 E
Bimbila 121 8 54N 0 5 E
Bimbo 124 4 15N 18 33 E
Bina-Etawah 94 24 13N 78 14 E
Binačka Morava, R. 66 42 30N 19 35 E
Binalbagan 103 10 12N 122 50 E
Binalong 141 34 40 S 148 39 E
Binatang 102 2 10N 111 40 E
Binbrook 33 53 26N 0 9W
Binche 47 50 26N 4 10 E
Binda 139 27 52 S 147 21 E
Bindi Bindi 137 30 37 S 116 22 E
Bindle 139 27 40 S 148 45 E
Bindura 127 17 18 S 31 18 E
Bingara, N.S.W., Austral. 139 29 52 S 150 36 E
Bingara, Queens., Austral. 139 28 10 S 144 37 E
Bingen 49 49 57N 7 53 E
Bingerville 120 5 18N 3 49W
Bingham, U.K. 33 52 57N 0 55W
Bingham, U.S.A. 151 45 5N 69 50W
Bingham Canyon 160 40 31N 112 10W
Binghamton 38 42 9N 75 54W
Bingley 32 53 51N 1 50W
Bingöl 92 39 20N 41 0 E
Binh Dinh = An Nhon 100 13 55N 109 7 E
Binh Khe 100 13 57N 108 51 E
Binh Son 100 15 20N 108 40 E
Binjai 102 3 50N 98 30 E
Binnaway 141 31 28 S 149 24 E
Binongko 103 5 55 S 123 55 E
Binscarth 153 50 37N 101 17W
Bint 93 26 22N 59 25 E
Bint Jaibail 90 33 8N 35 25 E
Bintan 102 1 0N 104 0 E
Bintulu 102 3 10N 113 0 E
Binyamina 90 32 32N 34 56 E
Binza 123 5 25N 28 40 E
Binzert = Bizerte 119 37 15N 9 50 E
Bio-Bío □ 172 37 35 S 72 0W
Bio Culma 123 7 20N 42 15 E
Biograd 63 43 56N 15 29 E
Biokovo 66 43 23N 17 0 E
Biougra 118 30 15N 9 14W
Biq'at Bet Netofa 90 32 49N 35 22 E
Bir 93 19 0N 75 54 E
Bîr Abû Hashim 122 23 42N 34 6 E
Bîr Abû M'nqar 122 26 33N 27 33 E
Bir Adal Deib 122 22 35N 36 10 E
Bir al Malfa 119 31 58N 15 18 E
Bir 'Asal 122 25 55N 34 20 E
Bir Autrun 117 18 15N 26 40 E
Bir Dhu'fân 119 31 59N 14 32 E
Bîr Diqnash 122 31 3N 25 23 E
Bir el Abbes 118 26 7N 6 9W
Bir-el-Ater 119 34 46N 8 3 E
Bîr el Basur 122 29 51N 25 49 E
Bîr el Gellaz 122 30 50N 26 40 E
Bîr el Shaqqa 122 30 54N 25 1 E
Bir Fuad 122 30 35N 26 28 E
Bir Haimur 122 22 45N 33 40 E
Bîr Kanayis 122 24 59N 33 15 E
Bîr Kerawein 122 27 10N 28 25 E
Bir Lemouissat 118 25 0N 10 32W
Bîr Maql 122 23 7N 33 40 E
Bîr Misaha 122 22 13N 27 59 E
Bir Mogreïn, (Fort Trinquet) 116 25 10N 11 25W
Bîr Murr 122 23 28N 30 10 E
Bîr Nabala 90 31 52N 35 12 E
Bîr Nakheila 122 24 1N 30 50 E
Bîr Qâtrani 122 30 55N 26 10 E
Bîr Ranga 122 24 25N 35 15 E
Bir Ras 123 12 0N 44 0 E
Bîr Sahara 122 22 54N 28 40 E
Bîr Seiyâla 122 25 10N 34 50 E
Bir Sguine 118 30 1N 5 39W
Bîr Shalatein 122 23 5N 35 25 E
Bîr Shebb 122 22 25N 29 40 E
Bîr Shût 122 23 50N 35 15 E
Bîr Terfawi 122 22 57N 28 55 E
Bîr Umm Qubûr 122 24 35N 34 2 E
Bîr Ungât 122 22 8N 33 48 E
Bîr Za'farâna 122 29 10N 32 40 E
Bîr Zāmus 119 24 16N 15 6 E
Bîr Zeidûn 122 25 45N 34 40 E
Bir Zeit 90 31 59N 35 11 E
Bira 103 2 3 S 132 2 E
Bîra 70 47 2N 27 3 E
Biramfero 120 11 40N 9 10W
Birao 117 10 20N 22 40 E
Birawa 126 2 20 S 28 48 E
Bîrca 70 43 59N 23 36 E
Birch 29 51 50N 0 54 E
Birch Hills 153 52 59N 105 25W
Birch I. 153 52 26N 99 54W
Birch L., N.W.T., Can. 152 62 4N 116 33W
Birch L., Ont., Can. 150 51 23N 92 18W
Birch L., U.S.A. 150 47 48N 91 43W
Birch Mts. 152 57 30N 113 10W
Birch River 153 52 24N 101 6W
Birchington 29 51 22N 1 18 E
Birchip 140 35 56 S 142 55 E
Birchiş 70 45 58N 22 0 E
Birchwood 143 45 55 S 167 53 E
Bird 153 56 30N 94 13W
Bird City 158 39 48N 101 33W
Bird I., Austral. 133 22 10 S 155 28 E
Bird I., S. Afr. 128 32 3 S 18 17 E
Birdaard 46 53 18N 5 53 E
Birdhip 139 35 52 S 142 50 E
Birdlip 28 51 50N 2 7W
Birdsville 138 25 51 S 139 20 E
Birdum 136 15 39 S 133 13 E
Birecik 92 37 0N 38 0 E
Bireuen 102 5 14N 96 39 E
Birhan 123 10 45N 37 55 E
Birifo 120 13 30N 14 0 E
Birigui 173 21 18 S 50 16W
Birimgan 138 22 41 S 147 25 E
Birjand 93 32 57N 59 10 E
Birk 122 18 8N 41 30 E
Birka 122 22 11N 40 38 E
Birkdale 32 53 38N 3 2W
Birkenhead, N.Z. 142 36 49 S 174 46 E
Birkenhead, U.K. 32 53 24N 3 1W
Birket Qârûn 122 29 30N 30 40 E
Birkfeld 52 47 21N 15 45 E
Birkhadem 118 36 43N 3 3 E
Bîrlad 70 46 15N 27 38 E
Birmingham, U.K. 28 52 30N 1 55W
Birmingham, U.S.A. 157 33 31N 86 50W
Birmitrapur 96 22 30N 84 10 E
Birni Ngaouré 121 13 5N 2 51 E
Birni Nkonni 121 13 55N 5 15 E
Birnin Gwari 121 11 0N 6 45 E
Birnin Kebbi 121 12 32N 4 12 E
Birnin Kudu 121 11 30N 9 29 E
Birobidzhan 77 48 50N 132 50 E
Birqin 90 32 23N 35 15 E
Birr 39 53 7N 7 55W
Birrie, R. 139 29 43 S 146 37 E
Birs, R. 50 47 24N 7 32 E
Birsilpur 94 28 11N 72 58 E
Birsk 84 55 25N 55 30 E
Birtin 70 46 59N 22 31 E
Birtle 153 50 30N 101 5W
Birtley, Northumberland, U.K. 35 55 5N 2 12W
Birtley, Tyne & Wear, U.K. 35 54 53N 1 34W
Birur 93 13 30N 75 55 E
Biryuchiy, Ostrov 82 46 10N 35 0 E
Birzai 80 56 11N 24 45 E
Bîrzava 70 46 7N 21 59 E
Bisa 103 1 10 S 127 40 E
Bisáccia 65 41 0N 15 20 E
Bisacquino 64 37 42N 13 13 E
Bisai 111 35 16N 136 44 E
Bisalpur 95 28 14N 79 48 E
Bisbal, La 58 41 58N 3 2 E
Bisbee 161 31 30N 110 0W
Biscay, B. of 14 45 0N 2 0W
Biscayne B. 157 25 40N 80 12W
Biscéglie 65 41 14N 16 30 E
Bischofshofen 52 47 26N 13 14 E
Bischofswerda 48 51 8N 14 11 E
Bischofszell 51 47 29N 9 15 E
Bischwiller 43 48 41N 7 50 E
Biscoe I. 13 66 0 S 67 0W
Biscostasing 150 47 18N 82 9W
Biscucuy 174 9 22N 69 59W
Biševo, I. 63 42 57N 16 3 E
Bisha 123 15 30N 37 31 E
Bisha, Wadi 122 20 30N 43 0 E
Bishop, Calif., U.S.A. 163 37 20N 118 26W
Bishop, Tex., U.S.A. 159 27 35N 97 49W
Bishop Auckland 33 54 40N 1 40W
Bishop's Castle 28 52 29N 3 0W
Bishop's Cleeve 28 51 56N 2 3W
Bishop's Falls 151 49 2N 55 30W
Bishop's Frome 28 52 8N 2 29W
Bishops Lydeard 28 51 4N 3 12W
Bishop's Nympton 30 50 58N 3 44W
Bishop's Stortford 29 51 52N 0 11 E
Bishop's Waltham 28 50 57N 1 13W
Bishopsteignton 30 50 32N 3 32W
Bishopstoke 28 50 58N 1 19W
Bisignano 65 39 30N 16 17 E
Bisina, L. 126 1 38N 33 56 E
Biskra 119 34 50N 5 44 E
Biskupiec 54 53 53N 20 58 E
Bislig 103 8 15N 126 27 E
Bismarck 158 46 49N 100 49W
Bismarck Arch. 135 2 30 S 150 0 E
Bismarck Ra. 135 5 35 S 145 0 E
Bismarck Sea 135 4 10 S 146 50 E
Bismark 48 52 39N 11 31 E
Biso 126 1 44N 31 26 E
Bison 158 45 34N 102 28W
Bispfors 74 63 1N 16 39 E
Bispgarden 72 63 2N 16 40 E
Bissagos = Bijagós 120 11 15N 16 10W
Bissau 120 11 45N 15 45W
Bissett 153 51 2N 95 41W
Bissikrima 120 10 50N 10 58W
Bistcho L. 152 59 45N 118 50W
Bistreţu 70 43 54N 23 23 E
Bistrica = Ilirska Bistrica 63 45 34N 14 14 E
Bistriţa 70 47 9N 24 35 E
Bistriţa Năsăud □ 70 47 15N 24 30 E
Bistriţa, R. 70 47 10N 24 30 E
Bistriţei, Munţii 70 47 15N 25 40 E
Biswan 95 27 29N 81 2 E
Bisztynek 54 54 8N 20 53 E
Bitam 124 2 5N 11 25 E
Bitche 43 48 58N 7 25 E
Bitkine 124 11 59N 18 13 E
Bitlis 92 38 20N 42 3 E
Bitola (Bitolj) 66 41 5N 21 21 E
Bitonto 65 41 7N 16 40 E
Bitter Creek 160 41 39N 108 36W
Bitter L., Gt. 122 30 15N 32 40 E
Bitter L. = Buheirat-Murrat el Kubra 122 30 15N 32 40 E
Bitterfeld 48 51 36N 12 20 E
Bitterfontein 128 31 0 S 18 32 E
Bitteroot, R. 160 46 30N 114 20W
Bitterroot Range 160 46 0N 114 20W
Bitterwater 163 36 23N 121 0W
Bitti 64 40 29N 9 20 E
Bitton 28 51 25N 2 27W
Bittou 121 11 17N 0 18W
Bitumount 152 57 26N 112 40W
Biu 121 10 40N 12 3 E
Bivolari 70 47 31N 27 27 E
Bivolu 70 47 16N 25 58 E
Biwa-Ko 111 35 15N 135 45 E
Biwabik 158 47 33N 92 19W
Biylikol, Ozero 85 43 5N 70 45 E
Biysk 76 52 40N 85 0 E
Bizana 129 30 50 S 29 52 E
Bizen 110 34 43N 134 8 E
Bizerte (Binzert) 119 37 15N 9 50 E
Bjandovan, Mys 83 39 45N 49 28 E
Bjargtangar 74 65 30N 24 30W
Bjärka-Säby 73 58 16N 15 44 E
Bjarnanes 74 64 20N 15 6W
Bjelasica 66 42 50N 19 40 E
Bjelo Polje 66 43 1N 19 45 E
Bjelovar 66 45 56N 16 49 E
Bjerringbro 73 56 23N 9 39 E
Björbo 72 60 27N 14 44 E
Björkhamre 72 61 24N 16 25 E
Björkhult 73 57 50N 15 40 E
Björneborg 72 59 14N 14 16 E
Bjuv 73 56 5N 12 55 E
Bla Bheinn 36 57 14N 6 7W
Blaby 28 52 34N 1 10W
Blace 66 43 18N 21 17 E
Blachownia 54 50 49N 18 56 E
Black Combe, mt. 32 54 16N 3 20W
Black Diamond 152 50 45N 114 14W
Black Esk R. 35 55 14N 3 13W
Black Forest = Schwarzwald 49 48 0N 8 0 E
Black Hd., Ireland 39 53 9N 9 18W
Black Hd., Antrim, U.K. 38 54 56N 5 42W
Black Hd., Cornwall, U.K. 30 50 1N 5 6W
Black Hills 158 44 0N 103 50W
Black I. 153 51 12N 96 30W
Black Island Sd. 162 41 10N 71 45W
Black Isle, Reg. 37 57 35N 4 15W
Black L., Can. 153 59 12N 105 15W
Black L., U.S.A. 156 45 28N 84 15W
Black Mesa, Mt. 159 36 57N 102 55W
Black Mt. = Mynydd Du 31 51 45N 3 45W
Black Mountain 141 30 18 S 151 39 E
Black Mts. 31 51 52N 3 5W
Black Pt. 137 34 30 S 119 25 E
Black R. 38 53 54N 7 42W
Black, R., Ark., U.S.A. 159 36 15N 90 45W
Black, R., N.Y., U.S.A. 162 43 59N 76 40W
Black, R., Wis., U.S.A. 158 44 18N 90 52W
Black, R., Vietnam = Da, R. 100 21 15N 105 20 E
Black Range, Mts. 161 33 30N 107 55W
Black River 166 18 0N 77 50W
Black Rock 140 32 50 S 138 44 E
Black Sea 21 43 30N 35 0 E
Black Volta, R. 120 9 0N 2 40W
Black Warrior, R. 157 33 0N 87 45W
Blackall 138 24 25 S 145 45 E
Blackball 143 42 22 S 171 26 E
Blackbull 138 17 55 S 141 45 E
Blackburn 32 53 44N 2 30W
Blackburn, Mt. 147 61 5N 142 3W
Blackbutt 139 26 51 S 152 6 E
Blackdown Hills 28 50 57N 3 15W
Blackduck 158 47 43N 94 32W
Blackfoot 160 43 13N 112 12W
Blackfoot, R. 160 47 0N 113 35W
Blackford 35 56 15N 3 48W
Blackie 152 50 36N 113 37W
Blackmoor Gate 30 51 9N 3 55W
Blackmoor Vale 28 50 54N 2 28W
Blackpool 32 53 48N 3 3W
Blackridge 138 22 35 S 147 35 E
Blackrock 39 53 18N 6 11W
Blacks Harbour 151 45 3N 66 49W
Blacksburg 156 37 17N 80 23W
Blacksod B. 38 54 6N 10 0W
Blacksod Pt. 38 54 7N 10 5W
Blackstairs Mt. 39 52 33N 6 50W
Blackstone 156 37 6N 78 0W
Blackstone, R. 152 61 5N 122 55W
Blackstone Ra. 137 26 00 S 129 00 E
Blackville 151 46 44N 65 50W
Blackwater, Austral. 138 23 35 S 148 53 E
Blackwater, Can. 152 53 20N 123 0W
Blackwater, Ireland 39 52 26N 6 20W
Blackwater Cr. 139 25 56 S 144 30 E
Blackwater, R., Limerick, Ireland 39 51 55N 7 50W
Blackwater, R., Meath, Ireland 38 53 40N 6 40W
Blackwater, R., Essex, U.K. 29 51 44N 0 53 E
Blackwater, R., Ulster, U.K. 38 54 31N 6 35W
Blackwater Res. 37 56 42N 4 45W
Blackwell 159 36 55N 97 20W
Blackwells Corner 163 35 37N 119 47W
Blackwood 35 55 40N 3 56W
Blackwood, C. 135 7 49 S 144 31 E
Bladel 47 51 22N 5 13 E
Bladinge 73 56 52N 14 29 E
Blädinge 73 56 52N 14 29 E
Blaenau Ffestiniog 31 53 0N 3 57W
Blaenavon 31 51 46N 3 5W
Blagaj 66 43 16N 17 55 E
Blagdon 28 51 19N 2 42W
Blagnac 44 43 38N 1 24 E
Blagodarnoye 83 45 7N 43 37 E
Blagoevgrad (Gorna Dzhumayo) 66 42 2N 23 5 E
Blagoveshchensk, Amur, U.S.S.R. 77 50 20N 127 30 E
Blagoveshchensk, Urals, U.S.S.R. 84 55 1N 55 59 E
Blagoveshchenskoye 85 43 18N 74 12 E
Blaina 31 51 46N 3 10W
Blaine 160 48 59N 122 43W
Blaine Lake 153 52 51N 106 52W
Blainville 43 48 33N 6 23 E
Blair 158 41 38N 96 10W
Blair Athol 138 22 42 S 147 31 E
Blair Atholl 37 56 46N 3 50W
Blairgowrie 37 56 36N 3 20W
Blairmore 152 49 40N 114 25W
Blaj 70 46 10N 23 57 E
Blake Pt. 158 48 12N 88 27W
Blakely 157 31 22N 85 0W
Blakeney, Glos., U.K. 28 51 45N 2 29W
Blakeney, Norfolk, U.K. 29 52 57N 1 1 E
Blâmont 43 48 35N 6 50 E
Blanc, C., Maurit. 116 20 50N 17 0W
Blanc, C., Tunisia 119 37 15N 9 56 E
Blanc, Le 44 46 37N 1 3 E
Blanc, Mont 45 45 48N 6 50 E
Blanc Sablon 151 51 24N 57 8W
Blanca, Bahía 176 39 10 S 61 30W
Blanca Peak 161 37 35N 105 29W
Blanchard 159 35 8N 97 40W
Blanche, C. 139 33 1 S 134 9 E
Blanche L., S. Austral., Austral. 139 29 15 S 139 40 E
Blanche L., W. Austral., Austral. 136 22 25 S 123 17 E
Blanco, S. Afr. 128 33 55 S 22 23 E
Blanco, U.S.A. 159 30 7N 98 30W
Blanco, C., C. Rica 166 9 34N 85 8W
Blanco, C., Peru 174 4 10 S 81 10W
Blanco, C., Spain 59 39 21N 2 51 E
Blanco, C., U.S.A. 160 42 50N 124 40W
Blanco, R. 172 31 54 S 69 42W
Blanda 74 65 20N 19 40W
Blandford Forum 28 50 52N 2 10W
Blanding 161 37 35N 109 30W
Blanes 58 41 40N 2 48 E
Blangy 43 49 14N 0 17 E
Blanice, R. 52 49 10N 14 5 E
Blankenberge 47 51 20N 3 9 E
Blankenburg 48 51 46N 10 56 E
Blanquefort 44 44 55N 0 38W
Blanquilla, La 174 11 51N 64 37W
Blanquillo 173 32 53 S 55 37W
Blansko 53 49 22N 16 40 E
Blantyre 127 15 45 S 35 0 E
Blaricum 46 52 16N 5 14 E
Blarney 39 51 57N 8 35W
Błaski 54 51 38N 18 30 E
Blatná 52 49 25N 13 52 E
Blatnitsa 67 43 41N 28 32 E
Blatten 50 46 16N 8 0 E
Blåvands Huk 75 55 33N 8 4 E
Blaydon 35 54 56N 1 47W
Blaye 44 45 8N 0 40W
Blaye-les-Mines 44 44 1N 2 8 E
Blayney 141 33 32 S 149 14 E
Blaze, Pt. 136 12 56 S 130 11 E
Błazowa 54 49 53N 22 7 E
Bleadon 28 51 18N 2 57W
Blean 29 51 18N 1 3 E
Bleasdale Moors 32 53 57N 2 40W
Bleckede 48 53 18N 10 43 E
Bled 63 46 27N 14 7 E
Blednaya, Gora 76 65 50N 65 30 E
Bléharis 47 50 31N 3 25 E
Bleiburg 52 46 35N 14 49 E
Blejeşti 70 44 19N 25 27 E
Blekinge län □ 73 56 20N 15 20 E
Blenheim 143 41 38 S 174 5 E

Place	Page	Lat.	Long.
Bléone, R.	**45**	44 5N	6 0E
Bletchingdon	**28**	51 51N	1 16W
Bletchley	**29**	51 59N	0 44W
Bleymard, Le	**44**	44 30N	3 42E
Blidet Amor	**119**	32 59N	5 58E
Blidö	**72**	59 37N	18 53E
Blidsberg	**73**	57 56N	13 30E
Bligh Sound	**143**	44 47S	167 32E
Blind River	**150**	46 10N	82 58W
Blinishti	**68**	41 52N	19 58E
Blinnenhorn	**51**	46 26N	8 19E
Blisworth	**29**	52 11N	0 56W
Blitar	**103**	8 5S	112 11E
Blitta	**121**	8 23N	1 6E
Block I.	**162**	41 11N	71 35W
Blockley	**28**	52 1N	1 45W
Bloemendaal	**46**	52 24N	4 39E
Bloemfontein	**128**	29 6S	26 14E
Bloemhof	**128**	27 38S	25 32E
Blofield	**29**	52 38N	1 25E
Blois	**42**	47 35N	1 20E
Blokziji	**46**	52 43N	5 58E
Blomskog	**72**	59 16N	12 2E
Blonduös	**74**	65 40N	20 12W
Bloodsworth Is.	**162**	38 9N	76 3W
Bloodvein, R.	**153**	51 47N	96 43W
Bloody Foreland	**38**	55 10N	8 18W
Bloomer	**158**	45 8N	91 30W
Bloomfield, Iowa, U.S.A.	**158**	40 44N	92 26W
Bloomfield, N. Mexico, U.S.A.	**161**	36 46N	107 59W
Bloomfield, Nebr., U.S.A.	**158**	42 38N	97 15W
Bloomfield R.	**138**	15 56S	145 22E
Bloomingdale	**162**	41 33N	74 26W
Bloomington, Ill., U.S.A.	**158**	40 49N	89 0W
Bloomington, Ind., U.S.A.	**156**	39 10N	86 30W
Bloomsburg	**162**	41 0N	76 30W
Blora	**103**	6 57S	111 25E
Blossburg	**162**	41 40N	77 4W
Blouberg	**129**	23 8S	29 0E
Blountstown	**157**	30 28N	85 5W
Bloxham	**28**	52 1N	1 22W
Bludenz	**52**	47 10N	9 50E
Blue I.	**156**	41 40N	87 40W
Blue Lake	**160**	40 53N	124 0W
Blue Mesa Res.	**161**	38 30N	107 15W
Blue Mountain Lake	**162**	43 52N	74 30W
Blue Mountain Peak	**167**	18 0N	76 40W
Blue Mts., Austral.	**133**	33 40S	150 0E
Blue Mts., Jamaica	**167**	18 0N	76 40W
Blue Mts., Ore., U.S.A.	**160**	45 15N	119 0W
Blue Mts., Pa., U.S.A.	**156**	40 30N	76 0W
Blue Mud B.	**138**	13 30S	136 0E
Blue Nile = Nîl el Azraq	**123**	12 30N	34 30E
Blue Nile □ = An Nîl el Azraq □	**123**	12 30N	34 30E
Blue Nile, R. = Nîl el Azraq	**123**	10 30N	35 0E
Blue Ridge, Mts.	**157**	36 30N	80 15W
Blue Stack Mts.	**38**	54 46N	8 5W
Blueberry, R.	**152**	56 45N	120 49W
Bluefield	**156**	37 18N	81 14W
Bluefields	**166**	12 0N	83 50W
Bluemull Sd.	**36**	60 45N	1 0W
Blueskin B.	**143**	45 44S	170 38E
Bluff, Austral.	**138**	23 35S	149 4E
Bluff, N.Z.	**143**	46 37S	168 20E
Bluff, U.S.A.	**147**	64 50N	147 15W
Bluff Downs	**138**	19 37S	145 30E
Bluff Harbour	**143**	46 36S	168 21E
Bluff Knoll, Mt.	**137**	34 24S	118 15E
Bluff Pt.	**137**	27 50S	114 5E
Bluffton	**156**	40 43N	85 9W
Blumenau	**173**	27 0S	49 0W
Blumenthal	**48**	53 5N	12 20E
Blümisalphorn	**50**	46 30N	7 47E
Blundeston	**29**	52 33N	1 42E
Blunt	**158**	44 32N	100 0W
Bly	**160**	42 23N	121 0W
Blyberg	**72**	61 9N	14 11E
Blyth, Austral.	**140**	33 49S	138 28E
Blyth, Northumberland, U.K.	**35**	55 8N	1 32W
Blyth, Notts., U.K.	**33**	53 22N	1 2W
Blyth Bridge	**35**	55 41N	3 22W
Blyth, R.	**35**	55 8N	1 30W
Blythburgh	**29**	52 19N	1 36E
Blythe	**161**	33 40N	114 33W
Blyton	**33**	53 25N	0 42W
Bo, Norway	**71**	59 25N	9 3E
Bo, S. Leone	**120**	7 55N	11 50W
Bo Duc	**101**	11 58N	106 50E
Bō-no-Misaki	**110**	31 15N	130 13E
Boa I.	**38**	54 30N	7 50W
Boa Nova	**171**	14 22S	40 10W
Boa Viagem	**170**	5 7S	39 44W
Boa Vista	**174**	2 48N	60 30W
Boaco	**166**	12 29N	85 35W
Boal	**56**	43 25N	6 49W
Boat of Garten	**37**	57 15N	3 45W
Boatman	**139**	27 16S	146 55E
Bobadah	**141**	32 19S	146 41E
Bobbili	**96**	18 35N	83 30E
Bóbbio	**62**	44 47N	9 22E
Bobcaygeon	**150**	44 33N	78 33W
Böblingen	**57**	48 41N	9 1E
Bobo-Dioulasso	**120**	11 8N	4 13W
Boboc	**67**	45 13N	26 59E
Bobolice	**54**	53 58N	16 37E
Boboshevo	**66**	42 9N	23 0E
Bobov Dol	**66**	42 20N	23 0E
Bóbr, R.	**54**	51 50N	15 15E
Bobrinets	**82**	48 4N	32 5E
Bobrov	**81**	51 5N	40 2E
Bobruysk	**80**	53 10N	29 15E
Bobures	**174**	9 15N	71 11W
Boca de Uracoa	**174**	9 8N	62 20W
Bôca do Acre	**174**	8 50S	67 27W
Bocage	**41**	49 0N	1 0W
Bocaiúva	**171**	17 7S	43 49W
Bocanda	**120**	7 5N	4 31W
Bocaranga	**117**	7 0N	15 35E
Bocas del Dragon	**174**	11 0N	61 50W
Bocas del Toro	**166**	9 15N	82 20W
Bocdam	**36**	59 55N	1 16W
Boceguillas	**58**	41 20N	3 39W
Bochnia	**54**	49 58N	20 27E
Bocholt, Belg.	**47**	51 10N	5 35E
Bocholt, Ger.	**48**	51 50N	6 35E
Bochov	**52**	50 9N	13 3E
Bochum	**48**	51 28N	7 12E
Bockenem	**48**	52 1N	10 8E
Bocoyna	**164**	27 52N	107 35W
Bocq, R.	**47**	50 20N	4 55E
Boçsa Montanû	**66**	45 21N	21 47E
Boda	**124**	4 19N	17 26E
Böda	**73**	57 15N	17 3E
Boda	**74**	57 15N	17 0E
Bodaybo	**77**	57 50N	114 0E
Boddam	**37**	57 28N	1 46W
Boddington	**137**	32 50S	116 30E
Bodedern	**31**	53 17N	4 29W
Bodegraven	**46**	52 5N	4 46E
Boden	**74**	65 50N	21 42E
Bodenham	**28**	52 9N	2 41W
Bodensee	**51**	47 35N	9 25E
Bodenteich	**48**	52 49N	10 41E
Boderg, L.	**38**	53 52N	8 0W
Bodhan	**96**	18 40N	77 55E
Bodiam	**29**	51 1N	0 33E
Bodinayakkanur	**97**	10 2N	77 10E
Bodinga	**121**	12 58N	5 10E
Bodinnick	**30**	50 20N	4 37W
Bodio	**51**	46 23N	8 55E
Bodmin	**30**	50 28N	4 44W
Bodmin Moor	**30**	50 33N	4 36W
Bodø	**74**	67 17N	14 24E
Bodrog, R.	**53**	48 15N	21 35E
Bodrum	**92**	37 5N	27 30E
Bódva, R.	**53**	48 19N	20 45E
Bodyke	**39**	52 53N	8 38W
Boechout	**47**	51 10N	4 30E
Boegoebergdam	**128**	29 7S	22 9E
Boekelo	**46**	52 12N	6 49E
Boelenslaan	**46**	53 10N	6 10E
Boën	**45**	45 44N	4 0E
Boende	**124**	0 24S	21 12E
Boerne	**159**	29 48N	98 41W
Boertange	**46**	53 1N	7 12E
Boezinge	**47**	50 54N	2 52E
Boffa	**120**	10 16N	14 3W
Bofin L.	**38**	53 51N	7 55W
Bofors	**72**	59 19N	14 34E
Bogale	**98**	21 16N	92 24E
Bogalusa	**159**	30 50N	89 55W
Bogan Gate	**141**	33 7S	147 49E
Bogan, R.	**141**	32 45S	148 8E
Bogantungan	**138**	23 41S	147 17E
Bogata	**159**	33 26N	95 10W
Bogatió	**66**	44 51N	19 30E
Bogdan, Mt.	**67**	42 37N	24 20E
Bogdanovitch	**84**	56 47N	62 1E
Bogenfels	**125**	27 25S	15 25E
Bogense	**73**	55 34N	10 5E
Boggabilla	**139**	28 36S	150 24E
Boggabri	**141**	30 45S	150 0E
Boggeragh Mts.	**39**	52 2N	8 55W
Boghari = Ksar el Boukhari	**118**	35 51N	2 52E
Bogia	**135**	4 9S	145 0E
Bognor Regis	**29**	50 47N	0 40W
Bogø	**73**	54 55N	12 2E
Bogo	**103**	11 3N	124 0E
Bogodukhov	**80**	50 9N	35 33E
Bogong, Mt.	**141**	36 47S	147 17E
Bogor	**103**	6 36S	106 48E
Bogoro	**121**	9 37N	9 29E
Bogoroditsk	**81**	53 47N	38 8E
Bogorodsk	**81**	56 4N	43 30E
Bogorodskoye	**77**	52 22N	140 30E
Bogoso	**120**	5 38N	2 3W
Bogotá	**174**	4 34N	74 0W
Bogotol	**76**	56 15N	89 50E
Bogra	**98**	24 51N	89 22E
Boguchany	**77**	58 40N	97 30E
Boguchar	**83**	49 55N	40 32E
Bogué	**120**	16 45N	14 10W
Boguslav	**82**	49 47N	30 53E
Boguszów Lubawka	**54**	50 43N	15 56E
Bohain	**43**	49 59N	3 28E
Bohemia	**52**	50 0N	14 0E
Bohemia Downs	**136**	18 53S	126 14E
Bohemian Forest = Böhmerwald	**49**	49 30N	12 40E
Bohena Cr.	**139**	30 17S	149 42E
Boheraphuca	**39**	53 1N	7 45W
Bohinjska Bistrica	**63**	46 17N	14 1E
Böhmerwald	**49**	49 30N	12 40E
Bohmte	**48**	52 24N	8 20E
Bohola	**38**	53 54N	9 4W
Boholl, I.	**103**	9 50N	124 10E
Bohotleh	**91**	8 20N	46 25E
Boi	**121**	9 35N	9 27E
Boi, Pta. de	**173**	23 55S	45 15W
Boiano	**65**	41 28N	14 29E
Boiestown	**151**	46 27N	66 26W
Boigu I.	**138**	9 15S	143 30E
Boileau, C.	**136**	17 40S	122 7E
Boipeba, I. de	**171**	13 39S	38 55W
Bois, Les	**50**	47 11N	6 50E
Bois, R.	**171**	18 35S	50 2W
Boischot	**47**	51 3N	4 47E
Boisdale L.	**36**	57 9N	7 19W
Boise	**160**	43 43N	116 9W
Boise City	**159**	36 45N	102 30W
Boissevain	**153**	49 15N	100 0W
Boite, R.	**63**	46 24N	12 13E
Boitzenburg	**48**	55 16N	13 36E
Boizenburg	**48**	53 22N	10 42E
Bojador C.	**116**	26 0N	14 30W
Bojanow	**54**	51 43N	16 42E
Bøjden	**73**	55 6N	10 7E
Bojnurd	**93**	37 30N	57 20E
Bojonegoro	**103**	7 11S	111 54E
Boju	**121**	7 22N	7 55E
Boka	**66**	45 22N	20 52E
Boka Kotorska	**66**	42 23N	18 32E
Bokala	**120**	8 31N	4 33W
Boké	**120**	10 56N	14 17W
Bokhara, R.	**139**	29 55S	146 42E
Bokkos	**121**	9 17N	9 1E
Boknafjorden	**71**	59 14N	5 40E
Bokombayevskoye	**85**	47 7N	77 0E
Bokoro	**117**	12 25N	17 14E
Bokote	**124**	0 12S	21 8E
Bokpyin	**101**	11 18N	98 42E
Boksitogorsk	**80**	59 32N	33 56E
Bokungu	**124**	0 35S	22 50E
Bol, Chad	**124**	13 30N	15 0E
Bol, Yugo.	**63**	43 18N	16 38E
Bolama	**120**	11 30N	15 30W
Bolan Pass	**93**	29 50N	67 20E
Bolangum	**140**	36 42S	142 54E
Bolaños, R.	**164**	22 0N	104 10W
Bolbec	**42**	49 30N	0 30E
Bolchereche	**76**	56 4N	74 45E
Boldeşti	**70**	45 3N	26 2E
Bole	**123**	6 36N	37 20E
Bolekhov	**80**	49 0N	24 0E
Bolesławiec	**54**	51 17N	15 37E
Bolgary	**78**	55 3N	48 50E
Bolgatanga	**121**	10 44N	0 53W
Bolgrad	**82**	45 40N	28 32E
Boli	**123**	6 2N	28 48E
Bolinao C.	**103**	16 30N	119 55E
Bolívar, Argent.	**172**	36 15S	60 53W
Bolívar, Antioquía, Colomb.	**174**	5 50N	76 1W
Bolívar, Cauca, Colomb.	**174**	2 0N	77 0W
Bolivar, Mo., U.S.A.	**159**	37 38N	93 22W
Bolivar, Tenn., U.S.A.	**159**	35 14N	89 0W
Bolivar □	**174**	9 0N	74 40W
Bolivia ■	**174**	17 6S	64 0W
Boljevac	**66**	43 51N	21 58E
Bolkhov	**81**	53 25N	36 0E
Bollène	**45**	44 18N	4 45E
Bollington	**32**	53 18N	2 8W
Bollnäs	**72**	61 21N	16 24E
Bollon	**139**	28 2S	147 29E
Bollstabruk	**72**	63 1N	17 40E
Bollullos	**57**	37 19N	6 32W
Bolmen	**73**	56 55N	13 40E
Bolney	**29**	50 59N	0 11W
Bolo Silase	**123**	8 51N	39 27E
Bolobo	**124**	2 6S	16 20E
Bologna	**63**	44 30N	11 20E
Bologne	**43**	48 10N	5 8E
Bologoye	**80**	57 55N	34 0E
Bolomba	**124**	0 35N	19 0E
Bolonchenticul	**165**	20 0N	89 49W
Bolong	**103**	6 6N	122 16E
Bolotovskoye	**84**	58 31N	62 28E
Boloven, Cao Nguyen	**100**	15 10N	106 30E
Bolpur	**95**	23 40N	87 45E
Bolsena	**63**	42 40N	11 58E
Bolsena, L. di	**63**	42 35N	11 55E
Bolshaya Glushitsa	**81**	52 24N	50 29E
Bolshaya Khobda, R.	**84**	50 50N	54 53E
Bolshaya Kinel, R.	**84**	53 14N	50 30E
Bolshaya Lepetrikha	**82**	47 11N	33 57E
Bolshaya Martynovka	**83**	47 12N	41 46E
Bolshaya Shatan, Gora	**84**	53 37N	58 3E
Bolshevik, Ostrov	**77**	78 30N	102 0E
Bolshezemelskaya Tundra	**78**	67 0N	56 0E
Bolshoi Kavkas	**83**	42 50N	44 0E
Bolshoi Tuters, O.	**80**	59 44N	26 57E
Bolshoy Atlym	**76**	62 25N	66 50E
Bolshoy Tokmak	**82**	47 16N	35 42E
Bol'soj T'uters, O.	**80**	59 44N	26 57E
Bolsover	**33**	53 14N	1 18W
Bolsward	**46**	53 3N	5 32E
Bolt Head	**30**	50 13N	3 48W
Bolt Tail	**30**	50 13N	3 55W
Boltaña	**58**	42 28N	0 4E
Boltigen	**50**	46 38N	7 24E
Bolton	**32**	53 35N	2 26W
Bolton Abbey	**32**	53 59N	1 53W
Bolton by Bowland	**32**	53 56N	2 21W
Bolton Landing	**162**	43 32N	73 35W
Bolton le Sands	**32**	54 7N	2 49W
Bolton-on-Dearne	**33**	53 31N	1 19W
Bolu	**92**	40 45N	31 35E
Bolubolu	**135**	9 21S	150 20E
Bolus Hd.	**39**	51 48N	10 20W
Bolvadin	**92**	38 45N	31 57E
Bolzano (Bozen)	**63**	46 30N	11 20E
Bom Conselho	**170**	9 42S	37 26W
Bom Despacho	**171**	19 43S	45 15W
Bom Jardim	**171**	7 47S	35 35W
Bom Jesus	**170**	9 4S	44 22W
Bom Jesus da Gurguéia, Serra	**170**	9 0S	43 0W
Bom Jesus da Lapa	**171**	13 15S	43 25W
Boma	**124**	5 50S	13 4E
Bomaderry	**141**	34 52S	150 37E
Bômba, Khalīj	**117**	32 20N	23 15E
Bomba, La	**164**	31 53N	115 2W
Bombala	**141**	36 56S	149 15E
Bombarral	**57**	39 15N	9 9W
Bombay	**96**	18 55N	72 50E
Bomboma	**124**	2 25N	18 55E
Bombombwa	**126**	2 18N	19 3E
Bomi Hills	**120**	7 1N	10 38E
Bomili	**126**	1 45N	27 5E
Bomokandi, R.	**126**	3 10N	28 15E
Bomongo	**124**	1 27N	18 21E
Bomu, R.	**124**	4 40N	23 30E
Bon C.	**119**	37 1N	11 2E
Bon Sar Pa	**100**	12 24N	107 35E
Bonaduz	**15**	46 49N	9 25E
Bonaire, I.	**167**	12 10N	68 15W
Bonang	**141**	37 11S	148 41E
Bonanza	**166**	13 54N	84 35W
Bonaparte Archipelago	**136**	14 0S	124 30E
Boñar	**56**	42 52N	5 19W
Bonarbridge	**37**	57 53N	4 20W
Bonäset	**72**	63 16N	18 45E
Bonaventure	**151**	48 5N	65 32W
Bonavista	**151**	48 40N	53 5W
Bonavista, C.	**151**	48 42N	53 5W
Bonchester Bri.	**35**	55 23N	2 36W
Bonchurch	**28**	50 36N	1 11W
Bondeno	**63**	44 53N	11 22E
Bondo	**124**	3 55N	23 53E
Bondoukoro	**120**	9 51N	4 25W
Bondoukou	**120**	8 2N	2 47W
Bondowoso	**120**	7 56S	113 49E
Bondyug	**84**	60 29N	55 56E
Bone Rate, I.	**103**	7 25S	121 5E
Bone Rate, Kepulauan	**103**	6 30S	121 10E
Bone, Teluk	**103**	4 10S	120 50E
Bonefro	**65**	41 42N	14 55E
Bo'ness	**35**	56 0N	3 38W
Bong Son = Hoai Nhon	**100**	14 26N	109 1E
Bongandanga	**124**	1 24N	21 3E
Bonge	**123**	6 5N	37 16E
Bongor	**117**	10 35N	15 20E
Bongouanou	**120**	6 42N	4 15W
Bonham	**159**	33 30N	96 10W
Bonherden	**47**	51 1N	4 32E
Bonifacio	**45**	41 24N	9 10E
Bonifacio, Bouches de	**64**	41 12N	9 15E
Bonin Is.	**130**	27 0N	142 0E
Bonito de Santa Fé	**171**	7 19S	38 31W
Bonn	**48**	50 43N	7 6E
Bonnat	**44**	46 20N	1 53E
Bonne B.	**151**	40 31N	58 0W
Bonne Espérance, I.	**151**	51 24N	57 40W
Bonne Terre	**159**	37 55N	90 38W
Bonners Ferry	**160**	48 38N	116 21W
Bonnert	**47**	49 43N	5 49E
Bonnétable	**42**	48 11N	0 25E
Bonneuil Matours	**42**	46 41N	0 34E
Bonneville	**45**	46 5N	6 24E
Bonney, L.	**140**	37 50S	140 20E
Bonnie Doon	**141**	37 2S	145 53E
Bonnie Rock	**137**	30 29S	118 22E
Bonny, France	**43**	47 34N	2 50E
Bonny, Nigeria	**121**	4 25N	7 13E
Bonny, Bight of	**121**	3 30N	9 20E
Bonny, R.	**121**	4 20N	7 14E
Bonnyrigg	**35**	55 52N	3 8W
Bonnyville	**153**	54 20N	110 45W
Bonoi	**103**	1 45S	137 41E
Bonorva	**64**	40 25N	8 47E
Bonsall	**163**	33 16N	117 14W
Bontang	**102**	0 10N	117 30E
Bonthain	**103**	5 34S	119 56E
Bonthe	**120**	7 30N	12 33W
Bonyeri	**120**	5 1N	2 46W
Bonyhád	**53**	46 18N	18 32E
Bonython Ra.	**136**	23 40S	128 45E
Boogardie	**137**	28 2S	117 45E
Bookabie P.O.	**137**	31 50S	132 41E
Booker	**159**	36 29N	100 30W
Boolaboolka, L.	**140**	32 38S	143 10E
Boolarra	**141**	38 20S	146 20E
Boolathanna	**137**	21 40S	113 41E
Boolcoomata	**140**	31 57S	140 33E
Booleroo Centre	**140**	32 53S	138 21E
Booligal	**141**	33 58S	144 53E
Booloo Downs	**137**	23 52S	119 33E
Boom	**47**	51 6N	4 20E
Boonah	**139**	27 58S	152 41E
Boondall	**108**	27 20S	153 4E
Boone, Iowa, U.S.A.	**158**	42 5N	93 53W
Boone, N.C., U.S.A.	**157**	36 14N	81 43W
Booneville, Ark., U.S.A.	**159**	35 10N	93 54W
Booneville, Miss., U.S.A.	**157**	34 39N	88 34W
Boongoondoo	**138**	22 55S	145 55E
Boonville, Ind., U.S.A.	**156**	38 3N	87 13W
Boonville, Mo., U.S.A.	**158**	38 57N	92 45W
Boonville, N.Y., U.S.A.	**162**	43 31N	75 20W
Booral	**141**	32 30S	151 56E

Boorindal 139 30 22 S 146 11 E
Booroomugga 141 31 17 S 146 27 E
Boorowa 141 34 28 S 148 44 E
Boot 32 54 24N 3 18W
Boothia, Gulf of 149 71 0N 91 0W
Boothia Pen. 148 71 0N 94 0W
Bootle, Cumb., U.K. 32 54 17N 3 24W
Bootle, Merseysude, U.K. 32 53 28N 3 1W
Booué 124 0 5 S 11 55 E
Bopeechee 139 29 36 S 137 22 E
Bophuthatswana □ 126 26 0 S 26 0 E
Bopo 79 7 33N 7 50 E
Boppard 49 50 13N 7 36 E
Boquete 166 8 46N 82 27W
Boquillas 164 29 17N 102 53W
Bor 52 49 41N 12 45 E
Bôr 123 6 10N 31 40 E
Bor, Sweden 73 57 9N 14 10 E
Bor, Yugo. 66 44 8N 22 7 E
Borah, Mt. 160 44 19N 113 46W
Borang 123 4 50N 30 59 E
Borås 73 57 43N 12 56 E
Borås 73 57 43N 12 56 E
Borazjan 93 29 22N 51 10 E
Borba, Brazil 174 4 12 S 59 34W
Borba, Port. 57 38 50N 7 26W
Borborema, Planalto da 170 7 0 S 37 0W
Borçka 83 41 25N 41 41 E
Borculo 46 52 7N 6 31 E
Borda, C. 140 35 45 S 136 34 E
Bordeaux 44 44 50N 0 36W
Borden, Austral. 137 34 3 S 118 12 E
Borden, Can. 151 46 18N 63 47W
Borden I. 12 78 30N 111 30W
Borders □ 35 55 45N 2 50W
Bordertown 140 36 19 S 140 45 E
Borðeyri 74 65 12N 21 6W
Bordighera 62 43 47N 7 40 E
Bordj bou Arridj 119 36 4N 4 45 E
Bordj Djeneiene 119 31 47N 10 3 E
Bordj el Hobra 119 32 9N 4 51 E
Bordj Fly Ste. Marie 118 27 19N 2 32W
Bordj-in-Eker 119 24 9N 5 3 E
Bordj Ménaiel 119 36 46N 3 43 E
Bordj Nili 118 33 28N 3 2 E
Bordj Zelfana 119 32 27N 4 15 E
Bordoba 85 39 31N 73 16 E
Bordon Camp 29 51 6N 0 52W
Borea Creek 141 35 5 S 146 35 E
Borehamwood 29 51 40N 0 15W
Borek Wlkp. 54 51 54N 17 11 E
Boreland 35 55 12N 3 16W
Boremore 141 33 15 S 149 0 E
Borensberg 73 58 34N 15 17 E
Borgarnes 74 64 32N 21 55W
Borgefjellet 74 65 20N 13 45 E
Borger, Neth. 46 52 54N 6 33 E
Borger, U.S.A. 159 35 40N 101 20W
Borgerhout 47 51 12N 4 28 E
Borghamn 73 58 23N 14 41 E
Borgholm 73 56 52N 16 39 E
Bórgia 65 38 50N 16 30 E
Borgie R. 37 58 28N 4 20W
Borgo San Dalmazzo 62 44 19N 7 29 E
Borgo San Lorenzo 63 43 57N 11 21 E
Borgo Val di Taro 62 44 29N 9 47 E
Borgomanero 62 45 41N 8 28 E
Borgonovo Val Tidone 62 45 1N 9 28 E
Borgorose 63 42 12N 13 14 E
Borgosésia 62 45 43N 8 17 E
Borgvattnet 72 63 26N 15 48 E
Borhaug 71 58 6N 6 33 E
Borikhane 100 18 33N 103 43 E
Borisoglebsk 81 51 27N 42 5 E
Borisoglebskiy 81 56 28N 43 59 E
Borisov 80 54 17N 28 28 E
Borisovka 85 43 15N 68 10 E
Borisovo-Sudskoye 81 59 58N 35 57 E
Borispol 80 50 21N 30 59 E
Borja, Peru 174 4 20 S 77 40W
Borja, Spain 58 41 48N 1 34W
Borjas Blancas 58 41 31N 0 52 E
Borkou 117 18 15N 18 50 E
Borlänge 72 60 29N 15 26 E
Borley, C. 13 66 15 S 52 30 E
Bormida, R. 62 44 35N 8 10 E
Bórmio 62 46 28N 10 22 E
Born 47 51 2N 5 49 E
Borna 48 51 8N 12 31 E
Borndiep, Str. 46 53 27N 5 35 E
Borne 46 52 18N 6 46 E
Bornem 47 51 6N 4 14 E
Borneo, I. 102 1 0N 115 0 E
Bornholm, I. 73 55 10N 15 0 E
Bornholmsgattet 73 55 15N 14 20 E
Borno □ 121 12 30N 12 30 E
Bornos 57 36 48N 5 42W
Bornu Yassa 121 12 14N 12 25 E
Borodino 80 55 31N 35 40 E
Borogontsy 77 62 42N 131 8 E
Boromo 120 11 45N 2 58W
Boron 163 35 0N 117 39W
Boronga Is. 98 19 58N 93 6 E
Borongan 103 11 37N 125 26 E
Bororen 138 24 13 S 151 33 E
Borotangba Mts. 123 6 30N 25 0 E
Boroughbridge 33 54 6N 1 23W
Borovan 67 43 27N 23 45 E
Borovichi 80 58 25N 33 55 E
Borovsk, Moscow, U.S.S.R. 81 55 12N 36 24 E
Borovsk, Urals, U.S.S.R. 84 59 43N 56 40 E
Borovskoye 84 53 48N 64 12 E
Borradaile, Mt. 136 12 5 S 132 51 E
Borrby 73 55 27N 14 10 E
Borrego Springs 163 33 15N 116 23W
Borriol 58 40 4N 0 4W
Borris 39 32 36N 6 57W
Borris-in-Ossory 39 52 57N 7 40W
Borrisokane 39 53 0N 8 8W
Borrisoleigh 39 52 48N 7 58W
Borroloola 138 16 4 S 136 17 E
Borrowdale 32 54 31N 3 10W
Borsa 70 47 41N 24 50 E
Borsod-Abaúj-Zemplén □ 53 48 20N 21 0 E
Borssele 47 51 26N 3 45 E
Bort-les-Orgues 44 45 24N 2 29 E
Borth 31 52 29N 4 3W
Borujerd 92 33 55N 48 50 E
Borve 36 58 25N 6 28W
Borzhomi 83 41 48N 43 28 E
Borzna 80 51 18N 32 26 E
Borzya 77 50 24N 116 31 E
Bos. Dubica 63 45 10N 16 50 E
Bos. Gradiška 66 45 10N 17 15 E
Bos. Grahovo 63 44 12N 16 26 E
Bos. Kostajnica 63 45 11N 16 33 E
Bos. Krupa 63 44 53N 16 10 E
Bos. Novi 63 45 2N 16 22 E
Bos. Petrovac 63 44 35N 16 21 E
Bos. Samac 66 45 3N 18 29 E
Bosa 64 40 17N 8 32 E
Bosaga 85 37 33N 65 41 E
Bosanska Brod 66 45 10N 18 0 E
Bosanski Novi 63 45 2N 16 22 E
Bosavi, Mt. 135 6 30 S 142 49 E
Bosbury 28 52 5N 2 27W
Boscastle 30 50 42N 4 42W
Boscotrecase 65 40 46N 14 28 E
Bosham 29 50 50N 0 51W
Boshoek 128 25 30 S 27 9 E
Boshof 128 28 31 S 25 13 E
Boshrūyeh 93 33 50N 57 30 E
Bosilegrad 66 42 30N 22 27 E
Boskoop 46 52 4N 4 40 E
Boskovice 53 49 29N 16 40 E
Bosna i Hercegovina □ 66 44 0N 18 0 E
Bosna, R. 66 44 50N 18 10 E
Bosnia = Bosna 66 44 0N 18 0 E
Bosnik 103 1 5 S 136 10 E
Bōsō-Hantō 111 35 20N 140 20 E
Bosobolo 124 4 15N 19 50 E
Bosporus = Karadeniz Boğazı 92 41 10N 29 10 E
Bossangoa 117 6 35N 17 30 E
Bossekop 74 69 57N 23 15 E
Bossembélé 117 5 25N 17 40 E
Bossier City 159 32 28N 93 38W
Bosso 121 13 43N 13 19 E
Bossut C. 136 18 42 S 121 35 E
Boston, U.K. 33 52 59N 0 2W
Boston, U.S.A. 162 42 20N 71 0W
Boston Bar 152 49 52N 121 22W
Bosut, R. 66 45 5N 19 2 E
Boswell, Can. 152 49 28N 116 45W
Boswell, U.S.A. 159 34 1N 95 30W
Botad 94 22 15N 71 40 E
Botany Bay 139 34 0 S 151 14 E
Botene 100 17 35N 101 12 E
Botevgrad 67 42 55N 23 47 E
Bothaville 128 27 23 S 26 34 E
Bothel 32 54 43N 3 16W
Bothnia, G. of 74 63 0N 21 0 E
Bothwell 138 42 20 S 147 1 E
Boticas 56 41 41N 7 40W
Botlетle R. 128 20 10 S 24 10 E
Botoroaga 70 44 8N 25 32 E
Botoşani 70 47 42N 26 41 E
Botoşani □ 70 47 50N 26 50 E
Botro 120 7 51N 5 19W
Botswana ■ 125 22 0 S 24 0 E
Bottesford 33 52 57N 0 48W
Bottineau 158 48 49N 100 25W
Bottrop 48 51 34N 6 59 E
Botucatu 173 22 55 S 48 30W
Botwood 151 49 6N 55 23W
Bou Alam 118 33 50N 1 26 E
Bou Ali 118 27 11N 0 4W
Bou Djébéha 120 18 25N 2 45W
Bou Garfa 118 27 4N 7 59W
Bou Guema 118 28 49N 0 19 E
Bou Iblane, Djebel 118 33 50N 4 0W
Bou Ismail 118 36 38N 2 42 E
Bou Izakarn 118 29 12N 6 46W
Bou Kahil, Djebel 118 34 22N 9 23 E
Bou Saâda 119 35 11N 4 9 E
Bou Salem 119 36 45N 9 2 E
Bouaké 120 7 40N 5 2W
Bouar 124 6 0N 15 40 E
Bouârfa 118 32 32N 1 58 E
Bouca 117 6 45N 18 25 E
Boucau 44 43 32N 1 29W
Boucaut B. 138 12 0 S 134 25 E
Bouches-du-Rhône □ 45 43 37N 5 2 E
Bouda 118 27 50N 0 27W
Boudenib 118 31 59N 3 31W
Boudry 50 46 57N 6 50 E
Boufarik 118 36 34N 2 58 E
Bougainville C. 136 13 57 S 126 4 E
Bougainville I. 135 6 0 S 155 0 E
Bougainville Reef 138 15 30 S 147 5 E
Bougaroun, C. 119 37 6N 6 30 E
Bougie = Béjaïa 119 36 42N 5 2 E
Bougouni 120 11 30N 7 20W
Bouillon 47 49 44N 5 3 E
Bouïra 119 36 20N 3 59 E
Boujad 118 32 46N 6 24W
Bouladuff 39 52 42N 7 55W
Boulder, Austral. 132 30 46 S 121 30 E
Boulder, Colo., U.S.A. 158 40 3N 105 10W
Boulder, Mont., U.S.A. 160 46 14N 112 4W
Boulder City 161 36 0N 114 50W
Boulder Creek 163 37 7N 122 7W
Boulder Dam = Hoover Dam 161 36 0N 114 45W
Bouleau, Lac au 150 47 40N 77 35W
Boulhaut 118 33 30N 7 1W
Boulia 138 22 52 S 139 51 E
Bouligny 43 49 17N 5 45 E
Boulogne, R. 42 46 50N 1 25W
Boulogne-sur-Gesse 44 43 18N 0 38 E
Boulogne-sur-Mer 43 50 42N 1 36 E
Boulsa 121 12 39N 0 34W
Boultoum 121 14 45N 10 25 E
Boumalne 118 31 25N 6 0W
Boun Neua 100 21 38N 101 54 E
Boun Tai 100 21 23N 101 58 E
Bouna 120 9 10N 3 0W
Boundary 147 64 11N 141 2W
Boundary Pk. 163 37 51N 118 21W
Boundiali 120 9 30N 6 20W
Bountiful 160 40 57N 111 58W
Bounty I. 130 46 0 S 180 0 E
Bour Khaya 77 71 50N 133 10 E
Bourbon-l'Archambault 44 46 36N 3 4 E
Bourbon-Lancy 44 46 37N 3 45 E
Bourbonnais 44 46 28N 3 0 E
Bourbonne 43 47 59N 5 45 E
Bourem 121 17 0N 0 24W
Bourg 44 45 3N 0 34W
Bourg-Argental 45 45 18N 4 32 E
Bourg-de-Péage 45 45 2N 5 3 E
Bourg-en-Bresse 45 46 13N 5 12 E
Bourg-St.-Andéol 45 44 23N 4 39 E
Bourg-St.-Maurice 45 45 35N 6 46 E
Bourg-St.-Pierre 50 45 57N 7 12 E
Bourganeuf 44 45 57N 1 45 E
Bourges 43 47 9N 2 25 E
Bourget, L. du 45 45 44N 5 52 E
Bourgneuf 42 47 2N 1 58W
Bourgneuf, B. de 42 47 3N 2 10W
Bourgneuf, Le 42 48 10N 0 59W
Bourgogne 43 47 0N 4 30 E
Bourgoin-Jallieu 45 45 36N 5 17 E
Bourke 139 30 8 S 145 55 E
Bourlamaque 150 48 5N 77 56W
Bourne 29 52 46N 0 22W
Bournemouth 28 50 43N 1 53W
Bourriot-Bergonce 44 44 7N 0 14W
Bourton-on-the-Water 28 51 53N 1 45W
Bouscat, Le 44 44 53N 0 32W
Boussac 44 46 22N 2 13 E
Boussens 44 43 12N 0 58 E
Bousso 117 10 34N 16 52 E
Boussu 47 50 26N 3 48 E
Bouthillier, Le 151 47 47N 64 55W
Boutilimit 120 17 45N 14 40W
Bouvet I. 15 55 0 S 3 30 E
Bouznika 118 33 46N 7 6W
Bouzonville 43 49 17N 6 32 E
Bova Marina 65 37 59N 15 56 E
Bovalino Marina 65 38 9N 16 10 E
Bovec 63 46 20N 13 33 E
Bovenkarspel 46 52 41N 5 14 E
Bóves 62 44 19N 7 29 E
Boves 62 44 19N 7 33 E
Bovey Tracey 30 50 36N 3 40W
Bovigny 47 50 12N 5 55 E
Bovill 160 46 58N 116 27W
Bovino 65 41 15N 15 20 E
Bow Island 152 49 50N 111 23W
Bow, R. 152 51 10N 115 0W
Bowbells 158 48 47N 102 19W
Bowdle 158 45 30N 100 2W
Bowelling 137 33 25 S 116 30 E
Bowen 138 20 0 S 148 16 E
Bowen Mts. 141 37 0 S 148 0 E
Bowen, R. 138 20 24 S 147 20 E
Bowes 32 54 31N 1 59W
Bowie, U.S.A. 162 39 0N 76 47W
Bowie, Ariz., U.S.A. 161 32 15N 109 30W
Bowie, Tex., U.S.A. 159 33 33N 97 50W
Bowland, Forest of 32 54 0N 2 30W
Bowling Green, Ky., U.S.A. 156 37 0N 86 25W
Bowling Green, Ohio, U.S.A. 156 41 22N 83 40W
Bowling Green, Va., U.S.A. 162 38 3N 77 21W
Bowling Green, C. 138 19 19 S 147 25 E
Bowman 158 46 12N 103 21W
Bowman, I. 13 65 0 S 104 0 E
Bowmans 140 34 10 S 138 17 E
Bowmanville 150 43 55N 78 41W
Bowmore 34 55 45N 6 18W
Bowness, Can. 152 50 55N 114 25W
Bowness, Solway, U.K. 32 54 57N 3 13W
Bowness, Windermere, U.K. 32 54 22N 2 56W
Bowral 141 34 26 S 150 27 E
Bowraville 139 30 37 S 152 52 E
Bowron, R. 152 54 3N 121 50W
Bowser L. 152 56 30N 129 30W
Bowsman 153 52 14N 101 12W
Bowutu Mts. 135 7 45 S 147 10 E
Bowwood 127 17 5 S 26 20 E
Box 28 51 24N 2 16W
Box Hill 29 51 16N 0 16W
Boxelder Creek 160 47 20N 108 30W
Boxholm 73 58 12N 15 3 E
Boxley 29 51 17N 0 34 E
Boxmeer 47 51 38N 5 56 E
Boxtel 47 51 36N 5 9 E
Boyabat 82 41 28N 34 42 E
Boyacá □ 174 5 30N 72 30W
Boyanup 137 33 30 S 115 40 E
Boyce 159 31 25N 92 39W
Boyd L. 150 61 30N 103 20W
Boyer, R. 152 58 27N 115 57W
Boyle 38 53 58N 8 19W
Boyne City 156 45 13N 85 1W
Boyne, R. 38 53 40N 6 34W
Boynton Beach 157 26 31N 80 3W
Boyoma, Chutes 124 0 12N 25 25 E
Boyup Brook 137 33 50 S 116 23 E
Bozburun 69 36 43N 28 8 E
Bozcaada 68 39 49N 26 3 E
Bozeat 29 52 14N 0 41W
Bozeman 160 45 40N 111 0W
Bozepole Wlk. 54 54 33N 17 56 E
Bozevac 66 44 32N 21 24 E
Bozouls 44 44 28N 2 43 E
Bozoum 117 6 25N 16 35 E
Bozovici 70 44 56N 22 1 E
Bra 62 44 41N 7 50 E
Brabant □ 47 50 46N 4 30 E
Brabant L. 153 54 18N 108 5W
Brabrand 73 56 9N 10 7 E
BraC 63 43 20N 16 40 E
Bracadale 36 57 22N 6 24W
Bracadale, L. 36 57 20N 6 30W
Bracciano 63 42 6N 12 10 E
Bracciano, L. di 63 42 8N 12 11 E
Bracebridge 150 45 2N 79 19W
Bracebridge Heath 33 53 13N 0 32W
Brach 119 27 31N 14 20 E
Bracieux 43 47 30N 1 30 E
Bräcke 72 62 45N 15 26 E
Brackettville 159 29 21N 100 20W
Brackley 28 52 3N 1 9W
Bracknell 29 51 24N 0 45W
Braco 35 56 16N 3 55W
Brad 70 46 10N 22 50 E
Brádano, R. 65 40 41N 16 20 E
Bradda Hd. 32 54 6N 4 46W
Bradenton 157 27 25N 82 35W
Bradford, U.K. 33 53 47N 1 45W
Bradford, Pa., U.S.A. 156 41 58N 78 41W
Bradford, Vt., U.S.A. 162 43 59N 72 9W
Bradford-on-Avon 28 51 20N 2 15W
Brading 28 50 41N 1 9W
Bradley, Ark., U.S.A. 159 33 7N 93 39W
Bradley, Calif., U.S.A. 163 35 52N 120 48W
Bradley, S.D., U.S.A. 158 45 10N 97 40W
Bradley Institute 127 17 7 S 31 25 E
Bradore Bay 151 51 27N 57 18W
Bradshaw 136 15 21 S 130 16 E
Bradwell-on-Sea 29 51 44N 0 55 E
Bradworthy 30 50 54N 4 22W
Brady 159 31 8N 99 25W
Brae 36 60 23N 1 20W
Brae, oilfield 19 58 45N 1 18 E
Brædstrup 73 55 58N 9 37 E
Braemar, Queens., Austral. 139 25 35 S 152 20 E
Braemar, S. Austral., Austral. 140 33 12 S 139 35 E
Braemar, U.K. 37 57 2N 3 20W
Braemar, dist. 37 57 2N 3 20W
Braemore, Grampian, U.K. 37 58 16N 3 33W
Braemore, Highland, U.K. 36 57 45N 5 2W
Braeriach Mt. 37 57 4N 3 44W
Braga 56 41 35N 8 25W
Braga □ 56 41 30N 8 30W
Bragado 172 35 2 S 60 27W
Bragança, Brazil 170 1 0 S 47 2W
Bragança, Port. 56 41 48N 6 50W
Bragança □ 56 41 30N 6 45W
Bragança Paulista 173 22 55 S 46 32W
Brahmanbaria 98 23 50N 91 15 E
Brahmani, R. 96 21 0N 85 15 E
Brahmaputra, R. 98 26 30N 93 30 E
Brahmaur 93 32 28N 76 32 E
Braich-y-Pwll 31 52 47N 4 46W
Braidwood 141 35 27 S 149 49 E
Brailsford 33 52 58N 1 35W
Braine-l'Alleud 47 50 42N 4 23 E
Braine-le-Comte 47 50 37N 4 8 E
Brainerd 158 46 20N 94 10W
Braintree, U.K. 29 51 53N 0 34 E
Braintree, U.S.A. 162 42 11N 71 0W
Braithwaite Pt. 138 12 5 S 133 50 E
Brak, R. 128 29 50 S 23 10 E
Brake 48 53 19N 8 30 E
Brakel 46 51 49N 5 5 E
Brakne-Hoby 73 56 12N 15 8 E
Bräkne-Hoby 73 56 14N 15 6 E
Brakpan 129 26 13 S 28 20 E
Brakwater 128 22 28 S 17 3 E
Brålanda 73 58 34N 12 21 E
Brålanda 73 58 34N 12 21 E
Brańla 70 45 19N 27 59 E
Brańla □ 70 45 5N 27 30 E
Bralorne 152 50 50N 123 15W
Bramford 29 52 5N 1 6 E
Bramminge 73 55 28N 8 42 E

Name	Page	Lat.	Long.
Bramon	**72**	62 14N	17 40E
Brampton, Can.	**150**	43 45N	79 45W
Brampton, Cambs., U.K.	**29**	52 19N	0 13W
Brampton, Cumb., U.K.	**32**	54 56N	2 43W
Bramsche	**48**	52 25N	7 58E
Bramshott	**29**	51 5N	0 47W
Bramwell	**138**	12 8S	142 37E
Brancaster	**29**	52 58N	0 40E
Branco, Cabo	**170**	7 9S	34 47W
Branco, R.	**174**	0 0	61 15W
Brande	**73**	55 57N	9 8E
Brandenburg	**48**	52 24N	12 33E
Brander, Pass of	**34**	56 25N	5 10W
Branderburgh	**37**	57 43N	3 17W
Brandfort	**128**	28 40S	26 30E
Brandon, Can.	**153**	49 50N	99 57W
Brandon, Durham, U.K.	**33**	54 46N	1 37W
Brandon, Suffolk, U.K.	**29**	52 27N	0 37E
Brandon, U.S.A.	**156**	43 48N	73 4W
Brandon, U.S.A.	**162**	44 2N	73 5W
Brandon B.	**39**	52 17N	10 8W
Brandon, Mt.	**39**	52 15N	10 15W
Brandon Pt.	**39**	52 18N	10 10W
Brandsen	**172**	35 10S	58 15W
Brandval	**71**	60 19N	12 1E
Brandvlei	**128**	30 25S	20 30E
Brandýs	**52**	50 10N	14 40E
Branford	**162**	41 15N	72 48W
Braniewo	**54**	54 25N	19 50E
Brännarp	**73**	56 46N	12 38E
Bransby	**139**	28 10S	142 0E
Bransfield Str.	**13**	63 0S	59 0W
Branson, Colo., U.S.A.	**159**	37 4N	103 53W
Branson, Mo., U.S.A.	**159**	36 40N	93 18W
Branston	**33**	53 13N	0 28W
Brantford	**150**	43 15N	80 15W
Brantôme	**44**	45 22N	0 39E
Branxholme	**140**	37 52S	141 49E
Branxton	**141**	32 38S	151 21E
Branzi	**62**	46 0N	9 46E
Bras d'or, L.	**151**	45 50N	60 50W
Brasiléia	**174**	11 0S	68 45W
Brasília	**171**	15 47S	47 55E
Braslav	**80**	55 38N	27 0E
Braslovče	**63**	46 21N	15 3E
Brașov	**70**	45 38N	25 35E
Brașov □	**70**	45 45N	25 15E
Brass	**121**	4 35N	6 14E
Brass, R.	**121**	4 15N	6 13E
Brasschaat	**47**	51 19N	4 27E
Brassey, Barisan	**102**	5 0N	117 15E
Brassey Ra.	**137**	25 8S	122 15E
Brasstown Bald, Mt.	**157**	34 54N	83 45W
Brassus, Le	**50**	46 35N	6 13E
Brasted	**29**	51 16N	0 8E
Bratislava	**53**	48 10N	17 7E
Bratsk	**77**	56 10N	101 30E
Bratteborg	**73**	57 37N	14 4E
Brattleboro	**162**	42 53N	72 37W
Brattvær	**71**	63 25N	7 48E
Brațul Chilia, R.	**70**	45 25N	29 20E
Brațul Sfintu Gheorghe, R.	**70**	45 0N	29 20E
Brațul Sulina, R.	**70**	45 10N	29 20E
Bratunac	**66**	44 13N	19 21E
Braunau	**52**	48 15N	13 3E
Braunschweig	**48**	52 17N	10 28E
Braunton	**30**	51 6N	4 9W
Brava	**91**	1 20N	44 8E
Bråvikeh	**72**	58 38N	16 32E
Bravo del Norte, R.	**164**	30 30N	105 0W
Brawley	**163**	32 58N	115 30W
Bray, France	**43**	49 15N	1 40E
Bray, Ireland	**39**	53 12N	6 6W
Bray, U.K.	**29**	51 30N	0 42W
Bray Hd.	**39**	51 52N	10 26W
Bray, Mt.	**138**	14 0N	134 30E
Bray-sur-Seine	**43**	48 25N	3 14E
Brazeau, R.	**152**	52 55N	115 14W
Brazil	**156**	39 30N	87 8W
Brazil ■	**174**	5 0N	20 0W
Brazilian Highlands	**170**	18 0S	46 30W
Brazo Sur, R.	**172**	25 30S	58 0W
Brazos, R.	**159**	30 30N	96 20W
Brazzaville	**124**	4 9S	15 12E
Brčko	**66**	44 54N	18 46E
Breadalbane, Austral.	**138**	23 50S	139 35E
Breadalbane, U.K.	**34**	56 30N	4 15W
Breaden, L.	**137**	25 51S	125 28E
Breage	**30**	50 6N	5 17W
Breaksea Sd.	**143**	45 35S	166 35E
Bream Bay	**142**	35 56S	174 28E
Bream Head	**142**	35 51S	174 36E
Bream Tail	**142**	36 3S	174 36E
Breamish, R.	**35**	55 30N	1 55W
Breas	**172**	25 29S	70 24W
Brebes	**103**	6 52S	109 3E
Brechin	**37**	56 44N	2 40W
Brecht	**47**	51 21N	4 38E
Breckenridge, Colo., U.S.A.	**160**	39 30N	106 2W
Breckenridge, Minn., U.S.A.	**158**	46 20N	96 36W
Breckenridge, Tex., U.S.A.	**159**	32 48N	98 55W
Breckland	**23**	52 30N	0 40E
Brecknock (□)	**26**	51 58N	3 25W
Břeclav	**53**	48 46N	16 53E
Brecon	**31**	51 57N	3 23W
Brecon Beacons	**31**	51 53N	3 27W
Breda	**47**	51 35N	4 45E
Bredaryd	**73**	57 10N	13 45E
Bredasdorp	**128**	34 33S	20 2E
Bredbo	**141**	35 58S	149 10E
Brede	**29**	50 56N	0 37E
Bredene	**47**	51 14N	2 59E
Bredon Hill	**28**	52 3N	2 2W
Bredy	**84**	52 26N	60 21E
Bree	**47**	51 8N	5 35E
Breezand	**46**	52 53N	4 49E
Bregalnica, R.	**66**	41 50N	22 20E
Bregenz	**52**	47 30N	9 45E
Bregning	**73**	56 8N	8 30E
Bréhal	**42**	48 53N	1 30W
Bréhat, I. de	**42**	48 51N	3 0W
Breiðafjörður	**74**	65 15N	23 15W
Breil	**45**	43 56N	7 31E
Breisach	**49**	48 2N	7 37E
Brejinho de Nazaré	**170**	11 1S	48 34W
Brejo	**170**	3 41S	42 47W
Brekke	**71**	61 1N	5 26E
Bremangerlandet	**71**	61 51N	5 0E
Bremangerpollen	**71**	61 51N	5 0E
Bremen	**48**	53 4N	8 47E
Bremen □	**48**	53 6N	8 46E
Bremer I.	**138**	12 5S	136 45E
Bremerhaven	**48**	53 34N	8 35E
Bremerton	**160**	47 30N	122 38W
Bremervörde	**48**	53 28N	9 10E
Bremgarten	**51**	47 21N	8 21E
Bremnes	**71**	59 47N	5 8E
Bremsnes	**71**	63 6N	7 40E
Brendon Hills	**28**	51 6N	3 25W
Brenes	**57**	37 32N	5 54W
Brenham	**159**	30 5N	96 27W
Brenner Pass	**52**	47 0N	11 30E
Breno	**62**	45 57N	10 20E
Brent, Can.	**150**	46 2N	78 29W
Brent, U.K.	**29**	51 33N	0 18W
Brent, oil and gasfield	**19**	61 0N	1 45E
Brenta, R.	**63**	45 11N	12 18E
Brentwood, U.K.	**29**	51 37N	0 19W
Brentwood, U.S.A.	**163**	37 55N	121 42W
Bréscia	**62**	45 33N	10 13E
Breskens	**47**	51 23N	3 33E
Breslau = Wrocław.	**54**	51 5N	17 5E
Bresle, R.	**43**	50 4N	1 21E
Bresles	**43**	49 25N	2 13E
Bressanone	**63**	46 43N	11 40E
Bressay	**36**	60 10N	1 6W
Bressay I.	**36**	60 10N	1 5W
Bressay Sd.	**36**	60 8N	1 10W
Bresse, La	**43**	48 0N	6 53E
Bresse, Plaine de	**43**	46 20N	5 10E
Bressuire	**42**	46 51N	0 30W
Brest, France	**42**	48 24N	4 31W
Brest, U.S.S.R.	**80**	52 10N	23 40E
Bretagne	**42**	48 0N	3 0W
Bretçu	**70**	46 7N	26 18E
Breteuil	**43**	49 38N	2 18E
Breton	**152**	53 7N	114 28W
Breton Sd.	**159**	29 40N	89 12W
Brett, C.	**142**	35 10S	174 20E
Bretten	**49**	49 2N	8 43E
Bretuil	**42**	48 50N	0 53E
Breukelen	**46**	52 10N	5 0E
Brevard	**157**	35 19N	82 42W
Breves	**170**	1 40S	50 29W
Brevik	**71**	59 4N	9 42E
Brewarrina	**139**	30 0S	146 51E
Brewer	**151**	44 43N	68 50W
Brewer, Mt.	**163**	36 44N	118 28W
Brewerton	**162**	43 14N	76 9W
Brewood	**28**	52 41N	2 10W
Brewster, N.Y., U.S.A.	**162**	41 23N	73 37W
Brewster, Wash., U.S.A.	**160**	48 10N	119 51W
Brewster, Kap	**12**	70 7N	22 0W
Brewton	**157**	31 9N	87 2W
Breyten	**129**	26 16S	30 0E
Breytovo	**81**	58 18N	37 50E
Brézina	**118**	33 4N	1 14E
Březnice	**52**	49 32N	13 57E
Breznik	**66**	42 44N	22 50E
Brezno	**53**	48 50N	19 40E
Bria	**117**	6 30N	21 58E
Briançon	**45**	44 54N	6 39E
Briare	**43**	47 38N	2 45E
Bribbaree	**141**	34 10S	147 51E
Bribie I.	**139**	27 0S	152 58E
Brickaville	**129**	18 49S	49 4E
Bricon	**43**	48 5N	5 0E
Bricquebec	**42**	49 29N	1 39W
Bride	**32**	54 24N	4 23W
Bridestowe	**30**	50 41N	4 7W
Bridge	**29**	51 14N	1 8E
Bridge of Allan	**35**	56 9N	3 57W
Bridge of Don	**37**	57 10N	2 8W
Bridge of Earn	**35**	56 20N	3 25W
Bridge of Orchy	**34**	56 29N	4 48W
Bridge of Weir	**34**	55 51N	4 35W
Bridge, R.	**152**	50 50N	122 40W
Bridgehampton	**162**	40 56N	72 18W
Bridgend, Islay, U.K.	**34**	55 46N	6 15W
Bridgend, Mid Glam., U.K.	**31**	51 30N	3 35W
Bridgeport, Calif., U.S.A.	**163**	38 14N	119 15W
Bridgeport, Conn., U.S.A.	**162**	41 12N	73 12W
Bridgeport, Nebr., U.S.A.	**158**	41 42N	103 10W
Bridgeport, Tex., U.S.A.	**159**	33 15N	97 45W
Bridger	**160**	45 20N	108 58W
Bridgeton	**162**	39 29N	75 10W
Bridgetown, Austral.	**137**	33 58S	116 7E
Bridgetown, Barbados	**167**	13 0N	59 30W
Bridgetown, Can.	**151**	44 55N	65 18W
Bridgetown, Ireland	**39**	52 13N	6 33W
Bridgeville	**162**	38 45N	75 36W
Bridgewater, Austral.	**140**	36 36S	143 59E
Bridgewater, Can.	**151**	44 25N	64 31W
Bridgewater, Mass., U.S.A.	**162**	41 59N	70 56W
Bridgewater, N.Y., U.S.A.	**162**	42 58N	75 15W
Bridgewater, S.D., U.S.A.	**158**	43 34N	97 29W
Bridgewater, C.	**140**	38 23S	141 23E
Bridgnorth	**28**	52 33N	2 25W
Bridgwater	**28**	51 7N	3 0W
Bridgwater B.	**28**	51 15N	3 15W
Bridlington	**33**	54 6N	0 11W
Bridlington B.	**33**	54 4N	0 10W
Bridport, Austral.	**138**	40 59S	147 23E
Bridport, U.K.	**28**	50 43N	2 45W
Brie-Comte-Robert	**43**	48 40N	2 35E
Brie, Plaine de	**43**	48 35N	3 10E
Briec	**42**	48 6N	4 0W
Brielle	**46**	51 54N	4 10E
Brienne-le-Château	**43**	48 24N	4 30E
Brienon	**43**	48 0N	3 35E
Brienz	**50**	46 46N	8 2E
Brienzersee	**50**	46 44N	7 53E
Brierfield	**32**	53 49N	2 15W
Brierley Hill	**28**	52 29N	2 7W
Briey	**43**	49 14N	5 57E
Brig	**50**	46 18N	7 59E
Brigantine	**162**	39 24N	74 22W
Brigg	**33**	53 33N	0 30W
Briggsdale	**158**	40 40N	104 20W
Brigham City	**160**	41 30N	112 1W
Brighouse	**33**	53 42N	1 47W
Brighstone	**29**	50 38N	1 36W
Bright	**141**	36 42S	146 56E
Brightlingsea	**29**	51 49N	1 1E
Brighton, Austral.	**140**	35 5S	138 30E
Brighton, Can.	**150**	44 2N	77 44W
Brighton, U.K.	**29**	50 50N	0 9W
Brighton, U.S.A.	**158**	39 59N	104 50W
Brightstone	**28**	50 38N	1 23W
Brightwater	**143**	41 22S	173 9E
Brignogan-Plage	**42**	48 40N	4 20W
Brignoles	**45**	43 25N	6 5E
Brigstock	**29**	52 27N	0 38W
Brihuega	**58**	40 45N	2 52W
Brikama	**120**	13 15N	16 45W
Brill	**28**	51 49N	1 3W
Brilliant	**152**	49 19N	117 38W
Brilon	**48**	51 23N	8 32E
Brim	**140**	36 3S	142 27E
Brimfield	**28**	52 18N	2 42W
Brindisi	**65**	40 39N	17 55E
Brinkley	**159**	34 55N	91 15W
Brinklow	**28**	52 25N	1 22W
Brinkworth, Austral.	**140**	33 42S	138 26E
Brinkworth, U.K.	**28**	51 33N	1 59W
Brinyan	**37**	59 8N	3 0W
Brion I.	**151**	47 46N	61 26W
Brionne	**42**	49 11N	0 43E
Brionski, I.	**63**	44 55N	13 45E
Brioude	**44**	45 18N	3 23E
Briouze	**42**	48 42N	0 23W
Brisbane	**139**	27 25S	153 2E
Brisbane, R.	**139**	27 24S	153 9E
Brisignella	**63**	44 14N	11 46E
Bristol, U.K.	**28**	51 26N	2 35W
Bristol, Conn., U.S.A.	**162**	41 44N	72 57W
Bristol, Pa., U.S.A.	**162**	40 6N	74 52W
Bristol, R.I., U.S.A.	**162**	41 40N	71 15W
Bristol, S.D., U.S.A.	**158**	45 25N	97 43W
Bristol B.	**147**	58 0N	160 0W
Bristol Channel	**30**	51 18N	4 30W
Bristol I.	**13**	58 45S	28 0W
Bristol L.	**161**	34 23N	116 0W
Briston	**29**	52 52N	1 4E
Bristow	**159**	35 5N	96 28W
British Antarctic Territory	**13**	66 0S	45 0W
British Columbia □	**152**	55 0N	125 15W
British Guiana = Guyana	**174**	5 0N	59 0W
British Honduras = Belize	**165**	17 0N	88 30W
British Isles	**16**	55 0N	4 0W
Briton Ferry	**31**	51 37N	3 50W
Brits	**129**	25 37S	27 48E
Britstown	**128**	30 37S	23 30E
Britt	**150**	45 46N	80 34W
Brittany = Bretagne	**42**	48 0N	3 0W
Brittas	**39**	53 14N	6 29W
Brittatorp	**73**	57 3N	14 58E
Britton	**158**	45 50N	97 47W
Brive-la-Gaillarde	**44**	45 10N	1 32E
Briviesca	**58**	42 32N	3 19W
Brixham	**30**	50 24N	3 31W
Brixton	**138**	23 32S	144 57E
Brixworth	**29**	52 20N	0 54W
Brize Norton	**28**	51 46N	1 35W
Brlik, U.S.S.R.	**76**	44 0N	74 5E
Brlik, Kazakh S.S.R., U.S.S.R.	**85**	44 5N	73 31E
Brlik, Kazakh S.S.R., U.S.S.R.	**85**	43 40N	73 49E
Brno	**53**	49 10N	16 35E
Bro	**72**	59 13N	13 2E
Broach = Bharuch	**96**	21 47N	73 0E
Broad Arrow	**137**	30 23S	121 15E
Broad B.	**36**	58 14N	6 16W
Broad Chalke	**28**	51 2N	1 54W
Broad Clyst	**30**	50 46N	3 27W
Broad Haven, Ireland	**38**	54 20N	9 55W
Broad Haven, U.K.	**31**	51 46N	5 6W
Broad Law, Mt.	**35**	55 30N	3 22W
Broad, R.	**157**	34 30N	81 26W
Broad Sd., Austral.	**138**	22 0S	149 45E
Broad Sd., U.K.	**30**	49 56N	6 19W
Broadalbin	**162**	43 3N	74 12W
Broadford, Austral.	**141**	37 14S	145 4E
Broadford, Clare, Ireland	**39**	52 48N	8 38W
Broadford, Limerick, Ireland	**39**	52 21N	8 59W
Broadford, U.K.	**36**	57 14N	5 55W
Broadhembury	**30**	50 49N	3 16W
Broadhurst Ra.	**136**	22 30S	122 30E
Broads, The	**29**	52 45N	1 30E
Broadsound Ra.	**133**	22 50S	149 30E
Broadstairs	**29**	51 21N	1 28E
Broadus	**158**	45 28N	105 27W
Broadview	**153**	50 22N	102 35W
Broadway, Ireland	**39**	52 13N	6 23W
Broadway, U.K.	**28**	52 2N	1 51W
Broadwindsor	**28**	50 49N	2 49W
Broager	**73**	54 53N	9 40E
Broaryd	**73**	57 7N	13 15E
Brochet, Man., Can.	**153**	57 53N	101 40W
Brochet, Manitoba, Can.	**153**	57 55N	101 40W
Brochet, Québec, Can.	**150**	47 12N	72 42W
Brochet, L.	**153**	58 36N	101 35W
Brock	**153**	51 26N	108 43W
Brocken	**48**	51 48N	10 40E
Brockenhurst	**28**	50 49N	1 34W
Brocklehurst	**141**	32 9S	148 38E
Brockman Mt.	**137**	22 25S	117 15E
Brockville	**150**	44 35N	75 41W
Brockway	**158**	47 18N	105 46W
Brockworth	**28**	51 51N	2 9W
Brod	**66**	41 35N	21 17E
Brodarevo	**66**	43 14N	19 44E
Brodeur Pen.	**149**	72 30N	88 10W
Brodick	**34**	55 34N	5 9W
Brodnica	**54**	53 15N	19 25E
Brodokalmak	**84**	55 35N	62 6E
Brody	**80**	50 5N	25 10E
Broechem	**47**	51 11N	4 38E
Broek	**46**	52 26N	5 0E
Broek op Langedijk	**46**	52 41N	4 49E
Brogan	**160**	44 14N	117 32W
Broglie	**42**	49 0N	0 30E
Brok	**54**	52 43N	21 52E
Broke Inlet	**137**	34 55S	116 25E
Broken Bank, gasfield	**19**	53 20N	2 4E
Broken Bow, Nebr., U.S.A.	**158**	41 25N	99 35W
Broken Bow, Okla., U.S.A.	**159**	34 2N	94 43W
Broken Hill	**140**	31 58S	141 29E
Broken Hill = Kabwe	**127**	14 27S	28 28E
Brokind	**73**	58 13N	15 42E
Bromborough	**32**	53 20N	3 0W
Bromham	**28**	51 23N	2 3W
Bromhead	**153**	49 18N	103 40W
Bromley	**29**	51 20N	0 5E
Bromölla	**73**	56 5N	14 28E
Brompton	**33**	54 22N	1 25W
Bromsgrove	**28**	52 20N	2 3W
Bromyard	**28**	52 12N	2 30W
Brønderslev	**73**	57 16N	9 57E
Brong Ahafo	**120**	7 50N	2 0E
Bronkhorstspruit	**129**	25 46S	28 45E
Bronnitsy	**81**	55 27N	38 10E
Bronte, Italy	**65**	37 48N	14 49E
Bronte, U.S.A.	**159**	31 54N	100 18W
Bronte Park	**138**	42 8S	146 30E
Brookeborough	**38**	54 19N	7 23W
Brookfield	**158**	39 50N	93 4W
Brookhaven	**159**	31 40N	90 25W
Brookings, Oreg., U.S.A.	**160**	42 4N	124 10W
Brookings, S.D., U.S.A.	**158**	44 20N	96 45W
Brooklands	**138**	18 5S	144 0E
Brookmere	**152**	49 52N	120 53W
Brooks	**152**	50 35N	111 55W
Brooks B.	**152**	50 15N	127 55W
Brooks L.	**153**	61 55N	106 35W
Brooks Ra.	**147**	68 40N	147 0W
Brooksville	**157**	28 32N	82 21W
Brookton	**137**	32 22S	116 57E
Brookville	**156**	39 25N	85 0W
Brooloo	**139**	26 30S	152 43E
Broom, L.	**36**	57 55N	5 15W
Broome	**136**	18 0S	122 15E
Broomehill	**137**	31 51S	117 39E
Broomfield	**28**	51 46N	0 28E
Broomhill	**35**	55 19N	1 36W
Broons	**42**	48 20N	2 16W
Brora	**37**	58 0N	3 50W
Brora L.	**37**	58 3N	3 58W
Brora, R.	**37**	58 4N	3 52W
Brosarp	**73**	55 44N	14 8E
Brösarp	**73**	55 43N	14 6E
Broseley	**28**	52 36N	2 30W
Brosna, R.	**39**	53 8N	8 0W
Broșteni	**70**	47 14N	25 43E
Brotas de Macaúbas	**171**	12 0S	42 38W
Brothers	**160**	43 56N	120 39W
Brothertoft	**33**	53 0N	0 5W
Brotton	**33**	54 34N	0 55W
Brøttum	**71**	61 2N	10 34E

Brough, Cumbria, U.K. 32 54 32N 2 19W
Brough, Humberside, U.K. 33 53 44N 0 35W
Brough Hd. 37 59 8N 3 20W
Broughams Gate 140 30 51 S 140 59 E
Broughshane 38 54 54N 6 12W
Broughton, Austral. 138 20 10 S 146 20 E
Broughton, Borders, U.K. 35 55 37N 3 25W
Broughton, Humberside, U.K. 33 53 33N 0 36W
Broughton, Northampton, U.K. 29 52 22N 0 45W
Broughton, Yorkshire, U.K. 33 54 26N 1 8W
Broughton-in-Furness 32 54 17N 3 12W
Broughty Ferry 35 56 29N 2 50W
Broumov 53 50 35N 16 20 E
Brouwershaven 46 51 45N 3 55 E
Brouwershavensche Gat 46 51 46N 3 50 E
Brovary 80 50 34N 30 48 E
Brovst 73 57 6N 9 31 E
Browerville 158 46 3N 94 50W
Brown, Mt. 140 32 30 S 138 0 E
Brown, Pt. 139 32 32 S 133 50 E
Brown Willy, Mt. 30 50 35N 4 34W
Brownfield 159 33 10N 102 15W
Browngrove 38 53 33N 8 49W
Brownhills 28 52 38N 1 57W
Browning 160 48 35N 113 10W
Brownlee 153 50 43N 106 1W
Browns Bay 142 36 40 S 174 40 E
Brownstown Hd. 39 52 8N 7 8W
Brownsville, Oreg., U.S.A. 160 44 29N 123 0W
Brownsville, Tenn., U.S.A. 159 35 35N 89 15W
Brownsville, Tex., U.S.A. 159 25 56N 97 25W
Brownwood 159 31 45N 99 0W
Brownwood, L. 159 31 51N 98 35W
Browse I. 136 14 7 S 123 33 E
Broxburn 35 55 56N 3 23W
Broye, R. 50 46 52N 6 58 E
Brozas 57 39 37N 6 47W
Bruas 101 4 31N 100 46 E
Bruay-en-Artois 43 50 29N 2 33 E
Bruce Bay 143 43 35 S 169 42 E
Bruce, gasfield 19 59 45N 1 32 E
Bruce Mines 150 46 20N 83 45W
Bruce, Mt. 136 22 37 S 118 8 E
Bruce Rock 137 31 52 S 118 8 E
Bruchsal 49 49 9N 8 39 E
Bruck a.d. Leitha 53 48 1N 16 47 E
Bruck a.d. Mur 52 47 24N 15 16 E
Brückenau 49 50 17N 9 48 E
Brŭdiceni 70 45 3N 23 4 E
Brue, R. 28 51 10N 2 59W
Bruernish Pt. 36 57 0N 7 22W
Bruff 39 52 29N 8 35W
Brugelette 47 50 35N 3 52 E
Bruges = Brugge 47 51 13N 3 13 E
Brugg 50 47 29N 8 11 E
Brugge 47 51 13N 3 13 E
Brühl 48 50 49N 6 51 E
Bruinisse 47 51 40N 4 5 E
Brûlé 152 53 15N 117 58W
Brûlon 42 47 58N 0 15W
Brûly 47 49 58N 4 32 E
Brumado 171 14 14 S 41 40W
Brumado, R. 171 14 13 S 41 40W
Brumath 43 48 43N 7 40 E
Brummen 46 52 5N 6 10 E
Brumunddal 71 60 53N 10 56 E
Brunchilly 138 18 50 S 134 30 E
Brundidge 157 31 43N 85 45W
Bruneau 160 42 57N 115 55W
Bruneau, R. 160 42 45N 115 50W
Brunei = Bandar Seri Begawan 102 4 52N 115 0 E
Brunei ■ 102 4 50N 115 0 E
Brunette Downs 138 18 40 S 135 55 E
Brunflo 72 63 5N 14 50 E
Brunico 63 46 50N 11 55 E
Brünig, Col de 50 46 46N 8 8 E
Brunkeberg 71 59 26N 8 28 E
Brunna 72 59 52N 17 25 E
Brunnen 51 46 59N 8 37 E
Brunner 143 42 27 S 171 20 E
Brunner, L. 143 42 27 S 171 20 E
Brunnsvik 72 60 12N 15 8 E
Bruno 153 52 20N 105 30W
Brunsberg 72 59 38N 12 52 E
Brunsbüttelkoog 48 53 52N 9 13 E
Brunssum 47 50 57N 5 59 E
Brunswick, Ga., U.S.A. 157 31 10N 81 30W
Brunswick, Md., U.S.A. 156 39 20N 77 38W
Brunswick, Me., U.S.A. 151 43 53N 69 50W
Brunswick, Mo., U.S.A. 158 39 26N 93 10W
Brunswick = Braunschweig 48 52 17N 10 28 E
Brunswick B. 136 15 15 S 124 50 E
Brunswick Junction 137 33 15 S 115 50 E
Brunswick, Pen. de 176 53 30 S 71 30W
Bruntál 53 50 0N 17 27 E
Brunton 35 55 2N 2 6W
Bruny I. 138 43 20 S 147 15 E
Bruree 39 52 25N 8 40W
Brus Laguna 166 15 47N 84 35W
Brusartsi 66 43 40N 23 5 E
Brush 158 40 17N 103 33W
Brusio 51 46 14N 10 8 E
Brusque 173 27 5 S 49 0W
Brussel 47 50 51N 4 21 E
Brussels = Bruxelles 47 50 51N 4 21 E
Brustem 47 50 48N 5 14 E
Bruthen 141 37 42 S 147 50 E
Bruton 28 51 6N 2 28W
Bruvik 71 60 29N 5 40 E
Bruxelles 47 50 51N 4 21 E
Bruyères 43 48 10N 6 40 E
Brwinow 54 52 9N 20 40 E
Bryagovo 67 41 58N 25 8 E
Bryan, Ohio, U.S.A. 156 41 30N 84 30W
Bryan, Texas, U.S.A. 159 30 40N 96 27W
Bryan, Mt. 140 33 30 S 139 0 E
Bryansk 80 53 13N 34 25 E
Bryanskoye 83 44 9N 47 10 E
Bryant 58 44 39N 97 26W
Bryggja 71 61 56N 5 27 E
Bryher I. 30 49 57N 6 21W
Brymbo 31 53 4N 3 5W
Brynamman 31 51 49N 3 52W
Bryncethin 31 51 33N 3 34W
Bryne 71 58 44N 5 38 E
Brynmawr 31 51 48N 3 11W
Bryrup 73 56 2N 9 30 E
Bryson City 157 35 28N 83 25W
Bryte 163 38 35N 121 33W
Brza Palanka 66 44 28N 22 37 E
Brzava, R. 66 45 21N 20 45 E
Brzeg 54 50 52N 17 30 E
Brzeg Dln 54 51 16N 16 41 E
Brzesko 54 49 59N 20 34 E
Brześć Kujawski 54 52 36N 18 55 E
Brzeszcze 54 49 59N 19 10 E
Brzeziny 54 51 49N 19 42 E
Brzozów 54 49 41N 22 3 E
Bu Athiah 119 30 1N 15 30 E
Bu Craa 116 26 45N 17 2 E
Buapinang 103 4 40 S 121 30 E
Buayan 103 5 3N 125 28 E
Buba 120 11 40N 14 59W
Bubanza 126 3 6 S 29 23 E
Bucaramanga 174 7 0N 73 0W
Buccaneer Arch. 136 16 7 S 123 20 E
Bucchiánico 63 42 20N 14 10 E
Bucecea 70 47 47N 26 28 E
Bŭceşti 70 46 50N 27 11 E
Buchach 80 49 5N 25 25 E
Buchan, Austral. 141 37 30 S 148 12 E
Buchan, U.K. 37 57 32N 2 8W
Buchan Ness 37 57 29N 1 48W
Buchan, oilfield 19 57 55N 0 0
Buchanan, Can. 153 51 40N 102 45W
Buchanan, Liberia 120 5 57N 10 2W
Buchanan Cr. 138 17 10 S 138 6 E
Buchanan, L., Queens., Austral. 138 21 35 S 145 52 E
Buchanan, L., W. Australia, Austral. 137 25 33 S 123 2 E
Buchanan, L., U.S.A. 159 30 50N 98 25W
Buchans 151 49 50N 56 52W
Bucharest = Bucureşti 70 44 27N 26 10 E
Buchholz 48 53 19N 9 51 E
Buchloe 49 48 3N 10 45 E
Buchlyvie 34 56 7N 4 20W
Buchon, Pt. 163 35 15N 120 54W
Buchs 51 47 10N 9 28 E
Buck Hill Falls 162 41 11N 75 16W
Buck, The, mt. 37 57 19N 3 0W
Buckden 29 52 17N 0 16W
Bückeburg 48 52 16N 9 2 E
Buckeye 161 33 28N 112 40W
Buckfastleigh 30 50 28N 3 47W
Buckhannon 156 39 2N 80 10W
Buckhaven 35 56 10N 3 2W
Buckie 37 57 40N 2 58W
Buckingham, Can. 150 45 37N 75 24W
Buckingham, U.K. 29 52 0N 0 59W
Buckingham □ 29 51 50N 0 55W
Buckingham B. 138 12 10 S 135 40 E
Buckingham Can. 97 14 0N 80 5 E
Buckinguy 139 31 3 S 147 30 E
Buckland 147 66 0N 161 5W
Buckland Brewer 30 50 56N 4 14W
Buckle Hd. 136 14 26 S 127 52 E
Buckleboo 140 32 54 S 136 12 E
Buckley, U.K. 31 53 10N 3 5W
Buckley, U.S.A. 160 47 10N 122 2W
Bucklin 159 37 37N 99 40W
Bucksburn 37 57 10N 2 10W
Bucquoy 43 50 9N 2 43 E
Buctouche 151 46 30N 64 45W
Bucureşti 70 44 27N 26 10 E
Bucyrus 156 40 48N 83 0W
Budacul, Munte 41 47 5N 25 40 E
Budafok 53 47 26N 19 2 E
Budalin 98 22 20N 95 10 E
Budapest 53 47 29N 19 5 E
Budaun 95 28 5N 79 10 E
Budd Coast 13 67 0 S 112 0 E
Buddabadah 141 31 56 S 147 14 E
Buddon Ness 35 56 29N 2 42W
Buddusò 64 40 35N 9 18 E
Bude 30 50 49N 4 33W
Bude Bay 30 50 50N 4 40W
Budel 47 51 17N 5 34 E
Budeşti 70 44 13N 26 30 E
Budge Budge 95 22 30N 88 25 E
Budgewoi Lake 141 33 13 S 151 34 E
Budia 58 40 38N 2 46W
Búdir 74 64 49N 23 23W
Budjala 124 2 50N 19 40 E
Budle B. 35 55 37N 1 45W
Budleigh Salterton 30 50 37N 3 19W
Búdrio 63 44 31N [illegible] 31 E
Budva 66 42 17N 18 50 E
Budzyn 54 52 54N 16 59 E
Buea 121 4 10N 9 9 E
Buellton 163 34 37N 120 12W
Buena 162 39 31N 74 56W
Buena Vista, Colo., U.S.A. 161 38 56N 106 6W
Buena Vista, Va., U.S.A. 156 37 47N 79 23W
Buena Vista L. 163 35 15N 119 21W
Buenaventura 164 29 50N 107 30W
Buenaventura, B. de 174 3 48N 77 17W
Buendía, Pantano de 58 40 25N 2 43W
Buenópolis 171 17 54 S 44 11W
Buenos Aires, Argent. 172 34 30 S 58 20W
Buenos Aires, Colomb. 174 1 36N 73 18W
Buenos Aires, C. Rica 166 9 10N 83 20W
Buenos Aires □ 172 36 30 S 60 0W
Buenos Aires, Lago 176 46 35 S 72 30W
Buesaco 174 1 23N 77 9W
Buffalo, Can. 153 50 49N 110 42W
Buffalo, Mo., U.S.A. 159 37 40N 93 5W
Buffalo, Okla., U.S.A. 159 36 55N 99 42W
Buffalo, S.D., U.S.A. 159 45 39N 103 31W
Buffalo, Wyo., U.S.A. 160 44 25N 106 50W
Buffalo Center 147 64 2N 145 50W
Buffalo Head Hills 152 57 25N 115 55W
Buffalo L. 152 52 27N 112 54W
Buffalo Narrows 153 55 51N 108 29W
Buffalo, R. 152 57 50N 117 1W
Buffels, R. 129 29 36 S 17 15 E
Buford 157 34 5N 84 0W
Bug, R., Poland 54 51 20N 23 40 E
Bug, R., U.S.S.R. 82 48 0N 31 0 E
Buga 174 4 0N 77 0W
Buganda □ 126 0 0N 31 30 E
Buganga 126 0 25N 32 0 E
Bugeat 44 45 36N 1 55 E
Buggenhout 47 51 1N 4 12 E
Buggs I. L. 157 36 20N 78 30W
Buglawton 32 53 12N 2 11W
Bugle 30 50 23N 4 46W
Bugojno 66 44 2N 17 25 E
Bugsuk, I. 102 8 15N 117 15 E
Bugue, Le 44 44 55N 0 56 E
Bugulma 84 54 33N 52 48 E
Buguma 121 4 42N 6 55 E
Bugun Shara 105 49 0N 104 0 E
Buguruslan 84 53 39N 52 26 E
Buheirat-Murrat-el-Kubra 122 30 15N 32 40 E
Buhl, Idaho, U.S.A. 160 42 35N 114 54W
Buhl, Minn., U.S.A. 158 47 30N 92 46W
Buhŭeşti 70 46 47N 27 32 E
Buhuşi 70 46 41N 26 45 E
Buick 159 37 8N 91 2W
Bŭicoi 70 45 3N 25 52 E
Buie L. 34 56 20N 5 55W
Bŭileşti 70 44 01N 23 20 E
Builth Wells 31 52 10N 3 26W
Buina Qara 93 36 20N 67 0 E
Buinsk 81 55 0N 48 18 E
Buíque 170 8 37 S 37 9W
Buis-les-Baronnies 45 44 17N 5 16 E
Buit, L. 151 50 59N 63 13W
Buitenpost 46 53 15N 6 9 E
Buitrago 56 41 0N 3 38W
Bujalance 57 37 54N 4 23W
Buján 56 42 59N 8 36W
Bujaraloz 58 41 29N 0 10W
Buje 63 45 24N 13 39 E
Buji 135 9 8 S 142 11 E
Bujnurd 93 37 35N 57 15 E
Bujumbura (Usumbura) 126 3 16 S 29 18 E
Bük 53 47 22N 16 45 E
Buk 54 52 21N 16 17 E
Buka I. 135 5 10 S 154 35 E
Bukachacha 77 52 55N 116 50 E
Bukama 127 9 10 S 25 50 E
Bukandula 126 0 13N 31 50 E
Bukavu 126 2 20 S 28 52 E
Bukene 126 4 15 S 32 48 E
Bukhara 85 39 48N 64 25 E
Bukima 126 1 50 S 33 25 E
Bukit Mertajam 101 5 22N 100 28 E
Bukittinggi 102 0 20 S 100 20 E
Bukkapatnam 97 14 14N 77 46 E
Buklyan 84 55 42N 52 10 E
Bukoba 126 1 20 S 31 49 E
Bukoba □ 126 1 30 S 32 0 E
Bukowno 54 50 17N 19 35 E
Bukrale 123 4 32N 42 0 E
Bukuru 121 9 42N 8 48 E
Bukuya 126 0 40N 31 52 E
Bula 120 12 7N 15 43W
Bülach 51 47 31N 8 32 E
Bulahdelah 141 32 23 S 152 13 E
Bulan 103 12 40N 123 52 E
Bulanash 84 57 16N 62 0 E
Bulandshahr 94 28 28N 77 58 E
Bulanovo 84 52 27N 55 10 E
Bulantai 99 36 33N 92 18 E
Bûlâq 122 25 10N 30 38 E
Bulawayo 127 20 7 S 28 32 E
Buldana 96 20 30N 76 18 E
Buldir I. 147 52 20N 175 55 E
Bulford 28 51 11N 1 45W
Bulgan 105 48 45N 103 34 E
Bulgaria ■ 67 42 35N 25 30 E
Bulgroo 138 25 47 S 143 58 E
Bulgunnia 139 30 10 S 134 53 E
Bulhar 91 10 25N 44 30 E
Buli, Teluk 103 1 5N 128 25 E
Buliluyan, C. 102 8 20N 117 15 E
Bulki 123 6 11N 36 31 E
Bulkington 163 52 29N 1 25W
Bulkley, R. 152 55 15N 127 40W
Bulkur 77 71 50N 126 30 E
Bull Shoals L. 159 36 40N 93 5W
Bullabulling 137 31 1 S 120 32 E
Bullange 47 50 24N 6 15 E
Bullaque, R. 57 39 20N 4 13W
Bullara 136 22 40 S 114 3 E
Bullaring 137 32 30 S 117 45 E
Bullas 59 38 2N 1 40W
Bulle 50 46 37N 7 3 E
Buller Gorge 143 41 40 S 172 10 E
Buller, Mt. 141 37 10 S 146 28 E
Buller, R. 143 41 44 S 171 36 E
Bullfinch 137 30 58 S 119 3 E
Bulli 141 34 15 S 150 57 E
Bullock Cr. 138 17 51 S 143 45 E
Bulloo Downs, Queens., Austral. 139 28 31 S 142 57 E
Bulloo Downs, W.A., Austral. 137 24 0 S 119 32 E
Bulloo L. 139 28 43 S 142 25 E
Bulloo, R. 139 28 43 S 142 30 E
Bulls 142 40 10 S 175 24 E
Bully-les-Mines 43 50 27N 2 44 E
Bulnes 172 36 42 S 72 19W
Bulo Burti 91 3 50N 45 33 E
Bulolo 135 7 10 S 146 40 E
Bulpunga 140 33 47 S 141 45 E
Bulqiza 68 40 30N 20 21 E
Bulsar 96 20 40N 72 58 E
Bultfontein 128 28 18 S 26 10 E
Bulu Karakelong 103 4 35N 126 50 E
Buluan 103 9 0N 125 30 E
Bŭlŭciţa 70 44 23N 23 8 E
Bulukumba 103 5 33 S 120 11 E
Bulun 77 70 37N 127 30 E
Bulwell 33 53 1N 1 12W
Bumba 124 2 13N 22 30 E
Bumbiri I. 126 1 40 S 31 55 E
Bumble Bee 161 34 8N 112 18W
Bumbum 121 14 10N 8 10 E
Bumhkang 98 26 51N 97 40 E
Bumhpa Bum 98 26 51N 97 14 E
Bumi, R. 127 17 30 S 28 30 E
Bumtang, R. 98 26 56N 90 53 E
Buna, Kenya 124 2 58N 39 30 E
Buna, P.N.G. 135 8 42 S 148 27 E
Bunaiyin 92 23 10N 51 8 E
Bunaw 39 51 47N 9 50W
Bunazi 126 1 3 S 31 23 E
Bunbeg 38 55 4N 8 18W
Bunbury 132 33 20 S 115 35 E
Bunclody 39 52 40N 6 40W
Buncrana 38 55 8N 7 28W
Bundaberg 139 24 54 S 152 22 E
Bünde 48 52 11N 8 33 E
Bundey, R. 138 21 46 S 135 37 E
Bundi 94 25 30N 75 35 E
Bundooma 138 24 54 S 134 16 E
Bundoran 38 54 24N 8 17W
Bundukia 123 5 14N 30 55 E
Bundure 141 35 10 S 146 1 E
Bŭneasa 70 45 56N 27 55 E
Bunessan 34 56 18N 6 15W
Bung Kan 100 18 23N 103 37 E
Bungay 29 52 27N 1 26 E
Bungendore 141 35 14 S 149 30 E
Bungil Cr. 138 27 5 S 149 5 E
Bungō-Suidō 110 33 0N 132 15 E
Bungoma 126 0 34N 34 34 E
Bungotakada 110 33 35N 131 25 E
Bungu 126 7 35 S 39 0 E
Bunguran N. Is. 102 4 45N 108 0 E
Bunia 126 1 35N 30 20 E
Bunji 95 35 45N 74 40 E
Bunju 102 3 35N 117 50 E
Bunker Hill 163 39 15N 117 8W
Bunkerville 161 36 47N 114 6W
Bunkie 159 31 1N 92 12W
Bunmahon 39 52 8N 7 22W
Bunnanaddan 38 54 3N 8 35W
Bunnell 157 29 28N 81 12W
Bunnik 46 52 4N 5 12 E
Bunnyconnellan 38 54 7N 9 1W
Bunnythorpe 142 40 16 S 175 39 E
Buñol 59 39 25N 0 47W
Bunsbeek 47 50 50N 4 56 E
Bunschoten 46 52 14N 5 22 E
Buntingford 29 51 57N 0 1W
Buntok 102 1 40 S 114 58 E
Bununu 121 9 51N 9 32 E
Bununu Doss 121 10 6N 9 25 E
Bunwell 29 52 30N 1 9 E
Bunyoro □ = Western □ 126 1 45N 31 30 E
Bunza 121 12 8N 4 0 E
Búoareyri 74 65 2N 14 13W
Buol 103 1 15N 121 32 E
Buon Brieng 100 13 9N 108 12 E
Buong Long 100 13 44N 106 59 E
Buorkhaya, Mys 77 71 50N 133 10 E
Buqbuq 122 31 29N 25 29 E
Buqei'a 90 32 58N 35 20 E
Bur Acaba 91 3 12N 44 20 E
Bûr Fuad 122 31 15N 32 20 E
Bûr Safâga 122 26 43N 33 57 E
Bûr Sa'îd 122 31 16N 32 18 E
Bûr Sûdân 122 19 32N 37 9 E
Bûr Taufiq 122 29 54N 32 32 E
Bura 126 1 4 S 39 58 E

Buraidah 92 26 20N 44 8E
Buraimī, Al Wāhāt al 93 24 15N 55 43E
Burak Sulayman 90 31 42N 35 7E
Burama 91 9 55N 43 7E
Burao 91 9 32N 45 32E
Buras 159 29 20N 89 33W
Burayevo 84 55 50N 55 24E
Burbage, Derby, U.K. 32 53 15N 1 55W
Burbage, Leics., U.K. 28 52 31N 1 20W
Burbage, Wilts., U.K. 28 51 21N 1 40W
Burbank 163 34 9N 118 23W
Burcher 141 33 30S 147 16E
Burdekin, R. 138 19 38S 147 25E
Burdett 152 49 50N 111 32W
Burdur 92 37 45N 30 22E
Burdwan 95 23 16N 87 54E
Bure 123 10 40N 37 4E
Bure, R. 29 52 38N 1 45E
Bureba, La 58 42 36N 3 24W
Buren 46 51 55N 5 20E
Burfell 74 64 5N 20 56W
Burford 28 51 48N 1 38W
Burg, Magdeburg, Ger. 48 52 16N 11 50E
Burg, Schleswig-Holstein, Ger. 48 54 25N 11 10E
Burg el Arab 122 30 54N 29 32E
Burg et Tuyur 122 20 55N 27 56E
Burgan 92 29 0N 47 57E
Burgas 67 42 33N 27 29E
Burgaski Zaliv 67 42 30N 27 39E
Burgdorf, Ger. 48 52 27N 10 0E
Burgdorf, Switz. 50 47 3N 7 37E
Burgenland □ 53 47 20N 16 20E
Burgeo 151 47 37N 57 38W
Burgersdorp 128 31 0S 26 20E
Burges, Mt. 137 30 50S 121 5E
Burgess 162 37 53N 76 21W
Burgess Hill 29 50 57N 0 7W
Burgh-le-Marsh 33 53 10N 0 15E
Burghclere 28 51 19N 1 20W
Burghead 37 57 42N 3 30W
Burghead B. 37 57 40N 3 33W
Búrgio 64 37 35N 13 18E
Bürglen 51 46 53N 8 40E
Burglengenfeld 49 49 11N 12 2E
Burgo de Osma 58 41 35N 3 4W
Burgohondo 56 40 26N 4 47W
Burgos 58 42 21N 3 41W
Burgos □ 58 42 21N 3 42W
Burgstädt 48 50 55N 12 49E
Burgsteinfurt 48 52 9N 7 23E
Burgsvik 73 57 3N 18 19E
Burguillos del Cerro 57 38 23N 6 35W
Burgundy = Bourgogne 43 47 0N 4 30E
Burhanpur 96 21 18N 76 20E
Burhou Rocks 42 49 45N 2 15W
Buri Pen. 123 15 25N 39 55E
Burias, I. 103 12 55N 123 5E
Buribay 84 51 57N 58 10E
Burica, Punta 166 8 3N 82 51W
Burigi, L. 126 2 2S 31 22E
Burin, Can. 151 47 1N 55 14W
Burin, Jordan 90 32 11N 35 15E
Buriram 100 15 0N 103 0E
Buriti Alegre 171 18 9S 49 3W
Buriti Bravo 170 5 50S 43 50W
Buriti dos Lopes 170 3 10S 41 52W
Burji 123 5 29N 37 51E
Burkburnett 159 34 7N 98 35W
Burke 160 47 31N 115 56W
Burke, R. 138 23 12S 139 33E
Burketown 138 17 45S 139 33E
Burk's Falls 150 45 37N 79 24W
Burley, Hants, U.K. 28 50 49N 1 41W
Burley, N. Yorks., U.K. 33 53 55N 1 46W
Burley, U.S.A. 160 42 37N 113 55W
Burlingame 163 37 35N 122 21W
Burlington, Colo., U.S.A. 158 39 21N 102 18W
Burlington, Iowa, U.S.A. 158 40 50N 91 5W
Burlington, Kans., U.S.A. 158 38 15N 95 47W
Burlington, N.C., U.S.A. 157 36 7N 79 27W
Burlington, N.J., U.S.A. 162 40 5N 74 50W
Burlington, Wash., U.S.A. 160 48 29N 122 19W
Burlington, Wis., U.S.A. 156 42 41N 88 18W
Burlyu-Tyube 76 46 30N 79 10E
Burma ■ 98 21 0N 96 30E
Burnabbie 137 32 7S 126 21E
Burnaby I. 152 52 25N 131 19W
Burnamwood 141 31 7S 144 53E
Burnet 159 30 45N 98 11W
Burnett, R. 133 24 45S 152 23E
Burney 160 40 56N 121 41W
Burnfoot 38 55 4N 7 15W
Burngup 137 33 2S 118 42E
Burnham, Essex, U.K. 29 51 37N 0 50E
Burnham, Somerset, U.K. 28 51 14N 3 0W
Burnham Market 29 52 57N 0 43E
Burnie 138 41 4S 145 56E
Burnley 32 53 47N 2 15W
Burnmouth 35 55 50N 2 4W
Burnoye 85 42 36N 70 47E
Burns, Oreg., U.S.A. 160 43 40N 119 4W
Burns, Wyo., U.S.A. 158 41 13N 104 18W
Burns Lake 152 54 20N 125 45W
Burnside, L. 137 25 25S 123 0E
Burnt Paw 147 67 2N 142 43W
Burntisland 35 56 4N 3 14W
Burntwood L. 153 55 22N 100 26W
Burntwood, R. 153 56 8N 96 34W
Burqa 90 32 18N 35 11E
Burra 140 33 40S 138 55E
Burragorang, L. 141 33 52S 150 37E
Burramurra 138 20 25N 137 15E
Burravoe 36 60 30N 1 3W
Burray I. 37 58 50N 2 54W
Burreli 68 41 36N 20 1E
Burrelton 35 56 30N 3 16W
Burren 39 53 9N 9 5W
Burren Junction 139 30 7S 148 59E
Burrendong Dam 139 32 39S 149 6E
Burrendong Res. 141 32 45S 149 10E
Burriana 58 39 50N 0 4W
Burrinjuck Res. 141 35 0S 148 36E
Burro, Serranías del 164 29 0N 102 0W
Burrow Hd. 34 54 40N 4 23W
Burrundie 136 13 32S 131 42E
Burruyacú 172 26 30S 64 40W
Burry Port 31 51 41N 4 17W
Bursa 92 40 15N 29 5E
Burseryd 73 57 12N 13 17E
Burstall 153 50 39N 109 54W
Burstwick 33 53 43N 0 6W
Burton 32 54 10N 2 43W
Burton Agnes 33 54 4N 0 18W
Burton Bradstock 28 50 41N 2 43W
Burton Fleming 33 54 8N 0 20W
Burton L. 150 54 45N 78 20W
Burton Latimer 29 52 23N 0 41W
Burton upon Stather 33 53 39N 0 41W
Burton-upon-Trent 28 52 48N 1 39W
Burtonport 38 54 59N 8 26W
Burtundy 140 33 45S 142 15E
Burtville 137 28 42S 122 33E
Buru, I. 103 3 30S 126 30E
Burufu 120 10 25N 2 50W
Burujird 92 33 58N 48 41E
Burullus, Bahra el 122 31 25N 31 0E
Burunday 85 43 20N 76 51E
Burundi ■ 126 3 15S 30 0E
Burung 102 0 21N 108 25E
Bururi 126 3 57S 29 37E
Burutu 121 5 20N 5 29E
Burwash 29 50 59N 0 24E
Burwash Landing 147 61 21N 139 0W
Burwell, U.K. 29 52 17N 0 20E
Burwell, U.S.A. 158 41 49N 99 8W
Bury 32 53 36N 2 19W
Bury St. Edmunds 29 52 15N 0 42E
Buryat A.S.S.R. □ 77 53 0N 110 0E
Burzenin 54 51 28N 18 47E
Busalla 62 44 34N 8 58E
Busango Swamp 127 14 15S 25 45E
Busayyah 92 30 0N 46 10E
Busby 152 53 55N 114 0W
Bushati 68 41 58N 19 34E
Bushell 153 59 31N 108 45W
Bushenyi 126 0 35S 30 10E
Bushey 29 51 38N 0 20W
Bushman Land 128 29 30S 19 30E
Bushmills 38 55 14N 6 32W
Bushnell, Ill., U.S.A. 158 40 32N 90 30W
Bushnell, Nebr., U.S.A. 158 41 18N 103 50W
Busia □ 126 0 25N 34 6E
Busie 120 10 29N 2 22W
Businga 124 3 16N 20 59E
Buskerud fylke □ 75 60 13N 9 0E
Busko Zdrój 54 50 28N 20 42E
Busovača 66 44 6N 17 53E
Busra 92 32 30N 36 25E
Bussa 121 10 11N 4 32E
Bussang 43 47 50N 6 50E
Busselton 137 33 42S 115 15E
Bussigny 50 46 33N 6 33E
Bussum 46 52 16N 5 10E
Bustard Hd. 133 24 0S 151 48E
Busto Arsizio 62 45 40N 8 50E
Busto, C. 56 43 34N 6 28W
Busu-Djanoa 124 1 50N 21 5E
Busuangal, I. 103 12 10N 120 0E
Büsum 48 54 7N 8 50E
Buta 126 2 50N 24 53E
Butare 126 2 31S 29 52E
Bute 140 33 51S 138 2E
Bute (□) 26 55 40N 5 10W
Bute, I. 34 55 48N 5 2W
Bute Inlet 152 50 40N 124 53W
Bute, Kyles of 34 55 55N 5 10W
Bute, Sd. of 34 55 43N 5 8W
Butemba 126 1 9N 31 37E
Butembo 126 0 9N 29 18E
Butera 65 37 10N 14 10E
Bütgenbach 47 50 26N 6 12E
Buthidaung 98 20 52N 92 32E
Butiaba 126 1 50N 31 20E
Butler 158 38 17N 94 18W
Bütschwil 51 47 23N 9 5E
Butte, Mont., U.S.A. 160 46 0N 112 31W
Butte, Nebr., U.S.A. 158 42 56N 98 54W
Butterfield, Mt. 137 24 45S 128 7E
Buttermere 32 54 32N 3 17W
Butterworth 101 5 24N 100 23E
Buttevant 39 52 14N 8 40E
Buttfield, Mt. 137 24 45S 128 9E
Button B. 153 58 45N 94 23W
Buttonwillow 163 35 24N 119 28W
Butty Hd. 137 33 54S 121 39E
Butuan 103 8 57N 125 33E
Butuku-Luba 121 3 29N 8 33E
Butung, I. 103 5 0S 122 45E
Buturlinovka 81 50 50N 40 35E
Butzbach 48 50 24N 8 40E
Buxar 95 25 34N 83 58E
Buxton, S. Afr. 128 27 38S 24 42E
Buxton, U.K. 32 53 16N 1 54W
Buxy 43 46 44N 4 40E
Buyaga 77 59 50N 127 0E
Buynaksk 83 42 36N 47 42E
Buyr Nuur 105 47 50N 117 42E
Büyük çekmece 67 41 2N 28 35E
Büyük Kemikli Burun 68 40 20N 26 15E
Büyük Menderes, R. 79 37 45N 27 40E
Buzançais 42 46 54N 1 25E
Buzau, Pasul 70 45 35N 26 12E
Buzaymah 117 24 35N 22 0E
Buzen 110 33 35N 131 5E
Buzet 63 45 24N 13 58E
Buzi, R. 127 19 52S 34 30E
Buziaş 66 45 38N 21 36E
Buzuluk 84 52 48N 52 12E
Buzuluk, R. 81 50 50N 52 12E
Buzũu 70 45 10N 26 50E
Buzũu □ 70 45 20N 26 30E
Buzũu, R. 70 45 10N 27 20E
Buzzards Bay 162 41 45N 70 38W
Bwagaoia 135 10 40S 152 52E
Bwana Mkubwe 127 13 8S 28 38E
Byala, Ruse, Bulg. 67 43 28N 25 44E
Byala, Varna, Bulg. 67 42 53N 27 55E
Byala Slatina 67 43 26N 23 55E
Byandovan, Mys 83 39 45N 49 28E
Bychawa 54 51 1N 22 36E
Byczyha 54 51 7N 18 12E
Bydgoszcz 54 53 10N 18 0E
Bydgoszcz □ 54 53 16N 17 33E
Byelorussian S.S.R. □ 80 53 30N 27 0E
Byers 158 39 46N 104 13W
Byfield 28 52 10N 1 15W
Bygland 71 58 50N 7 48E
Byglandsfjord 71 58 40N 7 50E
Byglandsfjorden 71 58 44N 7 50E
Byhalia 159 34 53N 89 41W
Bykhov 80 53 31N 30 14E
Bykle 71 59 20N 7 22E
Bykovo 83 49 50N 45 25E
Bylas 161 33 11N 110 9W
Bylchau 31 53 9N 3 32W
Bylderup 73 54 57N 9 6E
Bylot I. 149 73 13N 78 34W
Byrd Land = Marie Byrd Land 13 79 30S 125 0W
Byrd Sub-Glacial Basin 13 82 0S 120 0W
Byro 137 26 5S 116 11E
Byrock 141 30 40S 146 27E
Byron B. 151 54 42N 57 40W
Byron, C. 133 28 38S 153 40W
Byrranga, Gory 77 75 0N 100 0E
Byrum 73 57 16N 11 0E
Byske 74 64 57N 21 11E
Byske, R. 74 65 20N 20 0E
Bystrovka 85 42 47N 75 42E
Bystrzyca Kłodzka 54 50 19N 16 39E
Byten 80 52 50N 25 27E
Bytom 54 50 25N 19 0E
Bytom Ordz. 54 51 44N 15 48E
Bytów 54 54 10N 17 30E
Byumba 126 1 35S 30 4E
Byvalla 72 61 22N 16 27E
Bzéma 117 24 50N 22 20E
Bzenec 53 48 58N 17 18E

C

Ca Mau = Quan Long 101 9 7N 105 8E
Ca Mau, Mui = Bai Bung 101 8 35N 104 42E
Ca Na 101 11 20N 108 54E
Ca, R. 100 18 45N 105 45E
Caacupé 172 25 23N 57 5W
Caamano Sd. 152 52 55N 129 25W
Caatingas 170 7 0S 52 30W
Caazapá 172 26 8S 56 19W
Caazapá □ 173 26 10S 56 0W
Caballería, Cabo de 58 40 5N 4 5E
Cabañaquinta 56 43 10N 5 38W
Cabanatuan 103 15 30N 121 5E
Cabanes 58 40 9N 0 2E
Cabano 151 47 40N 68 56E
Cabazon 163 33 55N 116 47W
Cabbage Tree Hd. 108 27 20S 153 5E
Cabedelo 170 7 0S 34 50W
Cabeza del Buey 57 38 44N 5 13W
Cabildo 172 32 30S 71 5W
Cabimas 174 10 30N 71 25W
Cabinda 124 5 40S 12 11E
Cabinda □ 124 5 0S 12 30E
Cabinet Mts. 160 48 0N 115 30W
Cables 137 27 55S 123 25E
Cableskill 162 42 39N 74 30W
Cabo Blanco 176 47 56S 65 47W
Cabo Delgado □ 127 10 35S 40 35E
Cabo Frio 173 22 51S 42 3W
Cabo Pantoja 174 1 0S 75 10W
Cabonga Reservoir 150 47 20N 76 40W
Cabool 159 37 10N 92 8W
Caboolture 139 27 5S 152 58E
Cabora Bassa Dam 127 15 20S 32 50E
Caborca (Heroica) 164 30 40N 112 10W
Cabot Strait 151 47 15N 59 40W
Cabra 57 37 30N 4 28W
Cabra del Santo Cristo 59 37 42N 3 16W
Cabrach 37 57 20N 3 0W
Cabras 64 39 57N 8 30E
Cabrera, I. 59 39 6N 2 59E
Cabrera, Sierra 56 42 12N 6 40W
Cabri 153 50 35N 108 25W
Cabriel, R. 59 39 20N 1 20W
Cabruta 174 7 50N 66 10W
Caburan 103 6 3N 125 45E
Cabuyaro 174 4 18N 72 49W
Çacabelos 56 42 36N 6 44W
Čačak 66 43 54N 20 20E
Cáceres, Brazil 174 16 5S 57 40W
Cáceres, Colomb. 174 7 35N 75 20W
Cáceres, Spain 57 39 26N 6 23W
Cáceres □ 57 39 45N 6 0W
Cache B. 150 46 26N 80 1W
Cache Bay 150 46 22N 80 0W
Cachepo 57 37 20N 7 49W
Cacheu 120 12 14N 16 8W
Cachi 172 25 5S 66 10W
Cachimbo, Serra do 175 9 30S 55 0W
Cáchira 174 7 21N 73 17W
Cachoeira 171 12 30S 39 0W
Cachoeira Alta 171 18 48S 50 58W
Cachoeira de Itapemirim 173 20 51S 41 7W
Cachoeira do Sul 173 30 3S 52 53W
Cachoeiro do Arari 170 1 1S 48 58W
Cachopo 57 37 20N 7 49W
Cacolo 124 10 9S 19 21E
Caconda 125 13 48S 15 8E
Caçu 171 18 37S 51 4W
Caculé 171 14 30S 42 13W
Cadamstown 39 53 7N 7 39W
Cadarga 139 26 8S 150 58E
Cadaux 137 30 48S 117 15E
Čadca 53 49 26N 18 45E
Caddo 159 34 8N 96 18W
Cadenazzo 51 46 9N 8 57E
Cader Idris 31 52 43N 3 56W
Cadereyta Jiménez 165 25 40N 100 0W
Cadí, Sierra del 58 42 17N 1 42E
Cadibarrawirracanna, L. 139 28 52S 135 27E
Cadillac, Can. 150 48 14N 78 23W
Cadillac, France 44 44 38N 0 20W
Cadillac, U.S.A. 156 44 16N 85 25W
Cadiz 103 11 30N 123 15E
Cádiz 57 36 30N 6 20W
Cádiz □ 57 36 36N 5 45W
Cádiz, G. de 57 36 40N 7 0W
Cadomin 152 53 2N 117 20W
Cadotte, R. 152 56 43N 117 10W
Cadours 44 43 44N 1 2E
Cadoux 137 30 46S 117 7E
Caen 42 49 10N 0 22W
Caenby Corner 33 53 23N 0 32W
Caergwrle 29 53 6N 3 3W
Caerhun 31 53 14N 3 50W
Caerleon 31 51 37N 2 57W
Caernarfon 31 53 8N 4 17W
Caernarfon B. 31 53 4N 4 40W
Caernarvon = Caernarfon 31 53 8N 4 17W
Caernarvon (□) 26 53 8N 4 17W
Caerphilly 31 51 34N 3 13W
Caersws 31 52 32N 3 27W
Caerwent 31 51 37N 2 47W
Cæsarea = Qesari 90 32 30N 34 53E
Caeté 171 20 0S 43 40W
Caetité 171 13 50S 42 50W
Cafayate 172 26 2S 66 0W
Cafu 128 16 30S 15 8E
Cagayan de Oro 103 8 30N 124 40E
Cagayan, R. 103 18 25N 121 42E
Cagli 63 43 32N 12 38E
Cágliari 64 39 15N 9 6E
Cágliari, G. di 64 39 8N 9 10E
Cagnano Varano 65 41 49N 15 47E
Cagnes-sur-Mer 45 43 40N 7 9E
Caguas 147 18 14N 66 4W
Caha Mts. 39 51 45N 9 40W
Caher I. 38 53 44N 10 1W
Caherconlish 39 52 36N 8 30W
Cahermore 39 51 35N 10 2W
Cahir 39 52 23N 7 56W
Cahirciveen 39 51 57N 10 13W
Cahore Pt. 39 52 34N 6 11W
Cahors 44 44 27N 1 27E
Cahuapanas 174 5 15S 77 0W
Cai Ban, Dao 100 21 10N 107 27E
Cai Nuoc 101 8 56N 105 1E
Caianda 127 11 29S 23 31E
Caibarién 166 22 30N 79 30W
Caicara 174 7 38N 66 10W
Caicó 170 6 20S 37 0W
Caicos Is. 167 21 40N 71 40W
Caicos Passage 167 22 45N 72 45W
Caihaique 176 45 30S 71 45W
Caird Coast 13 75 0S 25 0W
Cairn Gorm 37 57 7N 3 40W
Cairn Table 35 55 30N 4 0W
Cairngorm Mts. 37 57 6N 3 42W
Cairnryan 34 54 59N 5 0W
Cairns 138 16 57S 145 45E
Cairo, Ga., U.S.A. 157 30 52N 84 12W
Cairo, Illinois, U.S.A. 159 37 0N 89 10W
Cairo, N.Y., U.S.A. 162 42 18N 74 0W
Cairo = El Qâhira 122 30 1N 31 14E
Cairo Montenotte 62 44 23N 8 16E
Caister-on-Sea 29 52 38N 1 43E
Caistor 33 53 29N 0 20W
Caithness (□) 26 58 25N 3 25W
Caithness, Ord of, C. 37 58 35N 3 37W

Caiundo 125 15 50S 17 52E
Caiza 174 20 2S 65 40W
Cajamarca 174 7 5S 78 28W
Cajapió 170 2 58S 44 48W
Cajarc 44 44 29N 1 50E
Cajàzeiros 170 7 0S 38 30W
Çajetina 66 43 47N 19 42E
Čajniče 66 43 34N 19 5E
Çakirgöl 83 40 33N 39 40E
Cala 57 37 59N 6 21W
Cala Cadolar 59 38 38N 1 35E
Cala, R. 57 37 50N 6 8W
Calabar 121 4 57N 8 20E
Calabozo 174 9 0N 67 20W
Calábria □ 65 39 24N 16 30E
Calaburras, Pta. de 57 36 30N 4 38W
Calaceite 58 41 1N 0 11E
Calafat 70 43 58N 22 59E
Calafate 176 50 25S 72 25W
Calahorra 58 42 18N 1 59W
Calais, France 43 50 57N 1 56E
Calais, U.S.A. 151 45 5N 67 20W
Calais, Pas de 160 50 57N 1 20E
Calalaste, Sierra de 172 25 0S 67 0W
Calama, Brazil 174 8 0S 62 50W
Calama, Chile 172 22 30S 68 55W
Calamar, Bolívar, Colomb. 174 10 15N 74 55W
Calamar, Vaupés, Colomb. 174 1 58N 72 32W
Calamian Group 103 11 50N 119 55E
Calamocha 58 40 50N 1 17W
Calanaque 174 0 5S 64 0W
Calañas 57 37 40N 6 53W
Calanda 58 40 56N 0 15W
Calang 102 4 30N 95 43E
Calangiánus 64 40 56N 9 12E
Calapan 103 13 25N 121 7E
Calasparra 59 38 14N 1 41W
Calatafimi 64 37 56N 12 50E
Calatayud 58 41 20N 1 40W
Calauag 103 13 55N 122 15E
Calavà, C. 65 38 11N 14 55E
Calavite, Cape 103 13 26N 120 10E
Calbe 48 51 57N 11 47E
Calca 174 13 10S 72 0W
Calci 62 43 44N 10 31E
Calcidica = Khalkidhiki □ 170 40 25N 23 40E
Calcutta 95 22 36N 88 24E
Caldaro 63 46 23N 11 15E
Caldas □ 174 5 15N 75 30W
Caldas da Rainha 57 39 24N 9 8W
Caldas de Reyes 56 42 36N 8 39W
Caldas Novas 171 17 45S 48 38W
Caldbeck 32 54 45N 3 3W
Calder Bridge 32 54 27N 3 31W
Calder Hall 32 54 26N 3 31W
Calder, R. 33 53 44N 1 21W
Caldera 172 27 5S 70 55W
Caldew R. 32 54 54N 2 59W
Caldiran 92 39 7N 44 0E
Caldwell, Idaho, U.S.A. 160 43 45N 116 42W
Caldwell, Kans., U.S.A. 159 37 5N 97 37W
Caldwell, Texas, U.S.A. 159 30 30N 96 42W
Caldy I. 31 51 38N 4 42W
Caledon, S. Afr. 128 34 14S 19 26E
Caledon, U.K. 38 54 22N 6 50W
Caledon B. 138 12 45S 137 0E
Caledon, R. 128 30 0S 26 46E
Caledonian Can. 37 56 50N 5 6W
Calella 58 41 37N 2 40E
Calemba 128 16 0S 15 38E
Calera, La 172 32 50S 71 10W
Calexico 161 32 40N 115 33W
Calf of Man 32 54 4N 4 48W
Calgary, Can. 152 51 0N 114 10W
Calgary, U.K. 34 56 34N 6 17W
Calhoun 157 34 30N 84 55W
Cali 174 3 25N 76 35W
Caliach Pt. 34 56 37N 6 20W
Calicoan, I. 103 10 59N 125 50E
Calicut 93 11 15N 75 43E
Calicut, (Kozhikode) 97 11 15N 75 43E
Caliente 161 37 43N 114 34W
California 158 38 37N 92 30W
California □ 160 37 25N 120 0W
California, Baja 164 32 10N 115 12W
California, Baja, T.N. □ 164 30 0N 115 0W
California, Baja, T.S. □ 164 25 50N 111 50W
California City 163 35 7N 117 57W
California, Golfo de 164 27 0N 111 0W
California Hot Springs 163 35 51N 118 41W
California, Lr. = California, Baja 164 25 50N 111 50W
Calilegua 172 23 45S 64 42W
Călimăneşti 70 45 14N 24 20E
Calingasta 172 31 15S 69 30W
Calipatria 161 33 8N 115 30W
Calistoga 160 38 36N 122 32W
Calitri 65 40 54N 15 25E
Calkini 165 20 21N 90 3W
Callabonna, L. 139 29 40S 140 5E
Callac 42 48 25N 3 27W
Callafo 91 6 48N 43 47E
Callan 39 52 33N 7 25W
Callanish 36 58 12N 6 43W
Callantsoog 46 52 50N 4 42E
Callao 174 12 0S 77 0W
Callaway 158 41 20N 99 56W
Calles 165 23 2N 98 42W
Callicoon 162 41 46N 75 3W
Callide 138 24 18S 150 28E
Calling Lake 152 55 15N 113 12W
Callington 30 56 30N 4 19W
Calliope 138 24 0S 151 16E
Callosa de Ensarriá. 59 38 40N 0 8W
Callosa de Segura 59 38 1N 0 53W
Callow 38 53 58N 9 2W
Calne 28 51 26N 2 0W
Calola 128 16 25S 17 48E
Calore, R. 65 41 8N 14 45E
Caloundra 139 26 45S 153 10E
Calpe 59 38 39N 0 3E
Calshot 28 50 49N 1 18W
Calstock, Can. 150 49 47N 84 9W
Calstock, U.K. 30 50 30N 4 13W
Caltabellotta 64 37 36N 13 11E
Caltagirone 65 37 13N 14 30E
Caltanissetta 65 37 30N 14 3E
Caluire-et-Cuire 45 45 49N 4 51E
Calulo 124 10 1S 14 56E
Calumbo 124 9 0S 13 20E
Caluso 62 45 18N 7 52E
Calvados □ 42 49 5N 0 15W
Calvert 159 30 59N 96 50W
Calvert Hills 138 17 15S 137 20E
Calvert I. 152 51 30N 128 0W
Calvert, R. 138 16 17S 137 44E
Calvert Ra. 136 24 0S 122 30E
Calvillo 164 21 51N 102 43W
Calvinia 128 31 28S 19 45E
Calwa 163 36 42N 119 46W
Calzada Almuradiel 59 38 32N 3 28W
Calzada de Calatrava 57 38 42N 3 46W
Cam Lam 101 11 54N 109 10E
Cam Pha 100 21 1N 107 18E
Cam, R. 29 52 21N 0 16E
Cam Ranh 101 11 54N 109 12E
Cam Xuyen 100 18 15N 106 0E
Camabatela 124 8 20S 15 26E
Camacã 171 15 24S 39 30W
Camaçari 171 12 41S 38 18W
Camacho 164 24 25N 102 18W
Camaguán 174 8 6N 67 36W
Camagüey 166 21 20N 78 0W
Camaiore 62 43 57N 10 18E
Camamu 171 13 57S 39 7W
Camaná 174 16 30S 72 50W
Camaquã, R. 173 30 50S 52 50W
Camaret 42 48 16N 4 37W
Camargo 174 20 38S 65 15E
Camargue 45 43 34N 4 34E
Camarillo 163 34 13N 119 2W
Camariñas 56 43 8N 9 12W
Camarón, C. 166 16 0N 85 0W
Camarones, Argent. 176 44 50S 65 40W
Camarones, Chile 174 19 0S 69 58W
Camas 160 45 35N 122 24W
Camas Valley 160 43 0N 123 46W
Cambados 56 42 31N 8 49W
Cambará 173 23 2S 50 5W
Cambay 94 22 23N 72 33E
Cambay, G. of 94 20 45N 72 30E
Camberley 29 51 20N 0 44W
Cambil 59 37 40N 3 33W
Cambo 35 55 9N 1 57W
Cambo-les-Bains 44 43 22N 1 23W
Cambodia ■ 100 12 15N 105 0E
Camborne 30 50 13N 5 18W
Cambrai 43 50 11N 3 14E
Cambria 163 35 44N 121 6W
Cambrian Mts. 31 52 25N 3 52W
Cambridge, Can. 150 43 23N 80 15W
Cambridge, Jamaica 166 18 18N 77 54W
Cambridge, N.Z. 142 37 54S 175 29E
Cambridge, U.K. 29 52 13N 0 8E
Cambridge, Idaho, U.S.A. 160 44 36N 116 52W
Cambridge, Mass., U.S.A. 162 42 20N 71 8W
Cambridge, Md., U.S.A. 162 38 33N 76 2W
Cambridge, Minn., U.S.A. 158 45 34N 93 15W
Cambridge, Nebr., U.S.A. 158 40 20N 100 12W
Cambridge, N.Y., U.S.A. 162 43 2N 73 22W
Cambridge, Ohio, U.S.A. 156 40 1N 81 22W
Cambridge Bay 148 69 10N 105 0W
Cambridge Gulf 136 14 45S 128 0E
Cambridgeshire □ 29 52 12N 0 7E
Cambrils 58 41 8N 1 3E
Cambuci 173 21 35S 41 55W
Camden, Austral. 141 34 1S 150 43E
Camden, U.K. 29 51 33N 0 10W
Camden, Ala., U.S.A. 157 31 59N 87 15W
Camden, Ark., U.S.A. 159 33 30N 92 50W
Camden, Del., U.S.A. 162 39 7N 75 33W
Camden, Me., U.S.A. 151 44 14N 69 6W
Camden, N.J., U.S.A. 162 39 57N 75 1W
Camden, N.Y., U.S.A. 162 43 20N 75 45W
Camden, S.C., U.S.A. 157 34 17N 80 34W
Camden, B. 147 71 0N 145 0W
Camden Sound 136 15 27S 124 25E
Camel R. 30 50 28N 4 49W
Camelford 30 50 37N 4 41W
Camembert 42 48 53N 0 10E
Cámeri 62 45 30N 8 40E
Camerino 63 43 10N 13 4E
Cameron, Ariz., U.S.A. 161 35 55N 111 31W
Cameron, La., U.S.A. 159 29 50N 93 18W
Cameron, Mo., U.S.A. 158 39 42N 94 14W
Cameron, Tex., U.S.A. 159 30 53N 97 0W
Cameron Falls 150 49 8N 88 19W
Cameron Highlands 101 4 27N 101 22E
Cameron Hills 152 59 48N 118 0W
Cameron Mts. 143 46 1S 167 0E
Cameroon ■ 124 3 30N 12 30E
Camerota 65 40 2N 15 21E
Cameroun, Mt. 121 4 45N 8 55E
Cameroun, R. 121 4 0N 9 35E
Camerton 28 51 18N 2 27W
Cametá 170 2 0S 49 30W
Caminha 56 41 50N 8 50W
Camino 163 38 47N 120 40W
Camira Creek 139 29 15S 152 58E
Camiranga 170 1 48S 46 17W
Cammachmore 37 57 2N 2 9W
Camocim 170 2 55S 40 50W
Camogli 62 44 21N 9 9E
Camolin 39 52 37N 6 26W
Camooweal 138 19 56S 138 7E
Camopi, R. 175 3 12N 52 17W
Camp Crook 158 45 36N 103 59W
Camp Hill 162 40 15N 76 56W
Camp Nelson 163 36 8N 118 39W
Camp Wood 159 29 47N 100 0W
Campagna 65 40 40N 15 5E
Campana 172 34 10S 58 55W
Campana, I. 176 48 20S 75 10W
Campanario 57 38 52N 5 36W
Campania □ 65 40 50N 14 45E
Campbell 163 37 17N 121 57W
Campbell, C. 143 41 47S 174 18E
Campbell I. 142 52 30S 169 0E
Campbell L. 153 63 14N 106 55W
Campbell River 152 50 5N 125 20W
Campbell Town 138 41 52S 147 30E
Campbellpur 94 33 46N 72 20E
Campbellsville 156 37 23N 85 12W
Campbellton, Alta., Can. 152 53 32N 113 15W
Campbellton, N.B., Can. 151 47 57N 66 43W
Campbelltown, Austral. 141 34 4S 150 49E
Campbelltown, U.K. 37 57 34N 4 2W
Campbeltown 34 55 25N 5 36W
Campeche 165 19 50N 90 32W
Campeche □ 165 19 50N 90 32W
Campeche, Golfo de 165 19 30N 93 0W
Camperdown 140 38 14S 143 9E
Camperville 153 51 59N 100 9W
Campi Salentina 65 40 22N 18 2E
Campidano 64 39 30N 8 40E
Campillo de Altobuey 58 39 36N 1 49W
Campillo de Llerena 57 38 30N 5 50W
Campillos 57 37 4N 4 51W
Campina Grande 170 7 20S 35 47W
Campiña, La 57 37 45N 4 45W
Campina Verde 171 19 31S 49 28W
Campinas 173 22 50S 47 0W
Campine 47 51 8N 5 20E
Campinho 170 14 30S 39 10W
Campli 63 42 44N 13 40E
Campo 124 2 15N 9 58E
Campo Beló 171 21 0S 45 30W
Campo de Criptana 59 39 25N 3 7W
Campo de Gibraltar 57 36 15N 5 25W
Campo Flórido 171 19 47S 48 35W
Campo Formoso 170 10 30S 40 20W
Campo Grande 175 20 25S 54 40W
Campo Maior, Brazil 170 4 50S 42 12W
Campo Maior, Port. 57 38 59N 7 7W
Campo Mourão 171 24 3S 52 22W
Campo Tencia 51 46 26N 8 43E
Campo Túres 63 46 53N 11 55E
Campoalegre 174 2 41N 75 20W
Campobasso 65 41 34N 14 40E
Campobello di Licata 64 37 16N 13 55E
Campobello di Mazara 64 37 38N 12 45E
Campofelice 64 37 54N 13 53E
Camporeale 64 37 53N 13 3E
Campos 173 21 50S 41 20W
Campos Altos 171 19 41S 46 10W
Campos Belos 171 13 10S 46 45W
Campos del Puerto 59 39 26N 3 1E
Campos Novos 173 27 21S 51 20W
Campos Sales 170 7 4S 40 23W
Camprodón 58 42 19N 2 23E
Campsie Fells 23 56 2N 4 20W
Camptown 162 41 44N 76 14W
Campuya, R. 174 1 10S 74 0W
Camrose, Can. 152 53 0N 112 50W
Camrose, U.K. 31 51 50N 5 2W
Camsall L. 153 72 32N 106 47W
Camsell Portage 153 59 37N 109 15W
Camurra 139 29 21S 149 52E
Can Gio 101 10 25N 106 58E
Can Tho 101 10 2N 105 46E
Canada ■ 148 60 0N 100 0W
Cañada de Gómez 73 32 55S 61 30W
Canadian 159 35 56N 100 25W
Canadian, R. 159 36 0N 98 45W
Canairiktok, R. 151 54 30N 62 30W
Canajoharie 162 42 54N 74 35W
Çanakkale 68 40 8N 26 30E
Çanakkale Boğazi 68 40 0N 26 0E
Canal de l'Est 43 48 45N 5 35E
Canal Flats 152 50 10N 115 48W
Canal latéral à la Garonne 44 44 25N 0 15E
Canalejas 172 35 15S 66 34W
Canals 172 33 35S 62 40W
Canáls 59 38 58N 0 35W
Canandaigua 156 42 55N 77 18W
Cananea 164 31 0N 110 20W
Canarias, Islas 116 29 30N 17 0W
Canarreos, Arch. de los 166 21 35N 81 40W
Canary Is. = Canarias, Islas 116 29 30N 17 0W
Canastra, Serra da 171 20 0S 46 20W
Canatlán 164 24 31N 104 47W
Canaveral, C. 157 28 28N 80 31W
Cañaveras 58 40 27N 2 14W
Canavieiras 171 15 39S 39 0W
Canbelego 141 31 32S 146 18E
Canberra 141 35 15S 149 8E
Canby, Calif., U.S.A. 160 41 26N 120 58W
Canby, Minn., U.S.A. 158 44 44N 96 15W
Canby, Oregon, U.S.A. 160 45 24N 122 45W
Cancale 42 48 40N 1 50W
Candala 91 11 30N 49 58E
Candas 56 43 35N 5 45W
Candé 42 47 34N 1 0W
Candea = Iráklion 69 35 20N 25 12E
Candela 65 41 8N 15 31E
Candelaria 173 27 29S 55 44W
Candelaria, Pta. de la 56 43 45N 8 0W
Candeleda 56 40 10N 5 14W
Candelo 141 36 47S 149 43E
Candia = Iráklion 69 35 20N 25 12E
Cândido de Abreu 171 24 35S 51 20W
Cândido Mendes 170 1 27S 45 43W
Candle L. 153 53 50N 105 18W
Cando 158 48 30N 99 14W
Canea = Khaniá 69 35 30N 24 4E
Canela 170 10 15S 48 25W
Canelli 62 44 44N 8 18E
Canelones 172 34 32S 56 10W
Canet-Plage 44 42 41N 3 2E
Cañete, Chile 172 37 50S 73 30W
Cañete, Cuba 167 20 36N 74 43W
Cañete, Peru 174 13 0S 76 30W
Cañete, Spain 58 40 3N 1 54W
Cañete de las Torres 57 37 53N 4 19W
Canfranc 58 42 42N 0 31W
Cangamba 125 13 40S 19 54E
Cangas 56 42 16N 8 47W
Cangas de Narcea 56 43 10N 6 32W
Cangas de Onís 56 43 21N 5 8W
Canguaretama 170 6 20S 35 5W
Canguçu 173 31 22S 52 43W
Canhotinho 171 8 53S 36 12W
Cani, Is. 119 36 21N 10 5E
Canicado 125 24 2S 33 2E
Canicattì 64 37 21N 13 50E
Canicattini 65 37 1N 15 3E
Canim, L. 152 51 45N 120 50W
Canim Lake 152 51 17N 120 54W
Canindé 170 4 22S 39 19W
Canindé, R. 170 6 15S 42 52W
Canipaan 102 8 33N 117 15E
Canisbay 37 58 38N 3 6W
Canisp Mt. 36 58 8N 5 5W
Cañitas 164 23 36N 102 43W
Cañiza, La 56 42 13N 8 16W
Cañizal 56 41 20N 5 22W
Canjáyar 59 37 1N 2 44W
Çankırı 92 40 40N 33 30E
Cankuzo 126 3 10S 30 31E
Canlaon, Mt. 103 9 27N 118 25E
Canmore 152 51 7N 115 18W
Cann River 141 37 35S 149 7E
Canna I. 36 57 3N 6 33W
Canna, Sd. of 36 57 1N 6 30W
Cannanore 97 11 53N 75 27E
Cannes 45 43 32N 7 0E
Cannich 37 57 20N 4 48W
Canning Basin 136 19 50S 124 0E
Canning Town 95 22 23N 88 40E
Cannington 28 51 8N 3 4W
Cannock 28 52 42N 2 2W
Cannock Chase, hills 23 52 43N 2 0W
Cannon Ball, R. 158 46 20N 101 20W
Cannondale, Mt. 138 25 13S 148 57E
Caño Colorado 174 2 18N 68 22W
Canoe L. 153 55 10N 108 15W
Canol 147 65 15N 126 50W
Canon City 158 39 30N 105 20W
Canonbie 35 55 4N 2 58W
Canopus 140 33 29S 140 42E
Canora 153 51 40N 102 30W
Canosa di Púglia 65 41 13N 16 4E
Canourgue, Le 44 44 26N 3 13E
Canowindra 141 33 35S 148 38E
Canso 151 45 20N 61 0W
Cantabria, Sierra de 58 42 40N 2 30W
Cantabrian Mts. = Cantábrica 56 43 0N 5 10W
Cantábrica, Cordillera 56 43 0N 5 10W
Cantal □ 44 45 4N 2 45E
Cantanhede 56 40 20N 8 36W
Cantaura 174 9 19N 64 21W
Cantavieja 58 40 31N 0 25W
Çantavir 66 45 55N 19 46E
Canterbury, Austral. 138 25 23S 141 53E
Canterbury, U.K. 29 51 17N 1 5E
Canterbury □ 143 43 45S 171 19E
Canterbury Bight 143 44 16S 171 55E
Canterbury Plains 143 43 55S 171 22E
Cantil 163 35 18N 117 58W
Cantillana 57 37 36N 5 50W
Canto do Buriti 170 8 7S 42 58W
Canton, Ga., U.S.A. 157 34 13N 84 29W
Canton, Ill., U.S.A. 158 40 32N 90 0W
Canton, Mass., U.S.A. 162 42 9N 71 9W
Canton, Miss., U.S.A. 159 32 40N 90 1W
Canton, Mo., U.S.A. 158 40 10N 91 33W
Canton, Ohio, U.S.A. 156 40 47N 81 22W
Canton, Okla., U.S.A. 159 36 5N 98 36W

Canton, Pa., U.S.A. 162 41 39N 76 51W
Canton, S.D., U.S.A. 158 43 20N 96 35W
Canton = Kuangchou 109 23 10N 113 10 E
•Canton I. 130 2 30 S 172 0W
Canton L. 159 36 12N 98 40W
Cantù 62 45 44N 9 8 E
Canudos 174 7 13 S 58 5W
Canulloit 161 31 58N 106 36W
Canutama 174 6 30 S 64 20W
Canvey 29 51 32N 0 35 E
Canyon, Can. 147 47 25N 84 36W
Canyon, Texas, U.S.A. 159 35 0N 101 57W
Canyon, Wyo., U.S.A. 160 44 43N 110 36W
Canyonlands Nat. Park 161 38 25N 109 30W
Canyonville 160 42 55N 123 14W
Canzo 62 45 54N 9 18 E
Cao Bang 100 22 40N 106 15 E
Cao Lanh 101 10 27N 105 38 E
Caoles 34 56 32N 6 43W
Caolisport, Loch 34 55 54N 5 40W
Cáorle 63 45 36N 12 51 E
Cap-aux-Meules 151 47 23N 61 52W
Cap Chat 151 49 6N 66 40W
Cap-de-la-Madeleine 150 46 22N 72 31W
Cap Haïtien 167 19 40N 72 20W
Cap St.-Jacques = Vung Tau 101 10 21N 107 4 E
Capa Stilo 65 38 25N 16 25 E
Capáccio 65 40 26N 15 4 E
Capaia 124 8 27 S 20 13 E
Capanaparo, R. 174 7 0N 67 30W
Capanema 170 1 12 S 47 11W
Caparo, R. 174 7 30N 70 30W
Capatárida 174 11 11N 70 37W
Capbreton 44 43 39N 1 26W
Capdenac 44 44 34N 2 5 E
Cape Barren I. 138 40 25 S 148 15 E
Cape Breton Highlands Nat. Park 151 46 50N 60 40W
Cape Breton I. 151 46 0N 60 30W
Cape Charles 162 37 15N 75 59W
Cape Coast 121 5 5N 1 15W
Cape Cod B. 162 41 50N 70 18W
Cape Dorset 149 64 14N 76 32W
Cape Dyer 149 66 40N 61 22W
Cape Fear, R. 157 34 30N 78 25W
Cape Girardeau 159 37 20N 89 30W
Cape Jervis 140 35 40 S 138 5 E
Cape May 162 39 1N 74 53W
Cape May C.H. 162 39 5N 74 50W
Cape May Pt. 162 38 56N 74 56W
Cape Montague 151 46 5N 62 25W
Cape Palmas 120 4 25N 7 49W
Cape Preston 136 20 51 S 116 12 E
Cape Province □ 128 32 0 S 23 0 E
Cape, R. 138 20 37 S 147 1 E
Cape Tormentine 151 46 8N 63 47W
Cape Town (Kaapstad) 128 33 55 S 18 22 E
Cape Verde Is. 14 17 10N 25 20W
Cape York Peninsula 138 33 34 S 115 33 E
Capel 29 51 8N 0 18W
Capel Curig 31 53 6N 3 55W
Capela 170 10 30 S 37 0W
Capela de Campo 170 4 40 S 41 55W
Capelinha 171 17 42 S 42 31W
Capella 138 23 2 S 148 1 E
Capella, G. 138 4 45 S 140 50 E
Capella, Mt. 135 5 4 S 141 8 E
Capelle, La 43 49 59N 3 50 E
Capendu 44 43 11N 2 31 E
Capernaum = Kefar Nahum 90 32 54N 35 32 E
Capestang 44 43 20N 3 2 E
Capim 170 1 41 S 47 47W
Capim, R. 170 3 0 S 48 0W
Capinópolis 171 18 41 S 49 35W
Capitan 161 33 40N 105 41W
Capitola 163 36 59N 121 57W
Capivara, Serra da 171 14 35 S 45 0W
Capizzi 65 37 50N 14 26 E
Čapljina 66 43 35N 17 43 E
Capoche, R. 127 15 0 S 32 45 E
Cappamore 39 52 38N 8 20W
Cappoquin 39 52 9N 7 46W
Capraia, I. 62 43 2N 9 50 E
Caprarola 63 42 21N 12 11 E
Capreol 150 46 43N 80 56W
Caprera, I. 64 41 12N 9 28 E
Capri, I. 65 40 34N 14 15 E
Capricorn, C. 133 23 30 S 151 13 E
Capricorn Group 138 23 30 S 151 55 E
Capricorn Ra. 136 23 20 S 117 0 E
Caprino Veronese 62 45 37N 10 47 E
Caprivi Strip 128 18 0 S 23 0 E
Captainganj 95 26 55N 83 45 E
Captain's Flat 141 35 35 S 149 27 E
Captieux 44 44 18N 0 16W
Cápua 65 41 7N 14 15 E
Capulin 159 36 48N 103 59W
Caquetá □ 174 1 0N 74 0W
Caquetá, R. 174 1 0N 76 20W
Cáqueza 174 4 25N 73 57W
Carabobo 174 10 10N 68 5W
Caracal 70 44 8N 24 22 E
Caracaraí 174 1 50N 61 8W
Caracas 174 10 30N 66 55W
Caracol, Piauí, Brazil 170 9 15 S 43 45W
Caracol, Rondonia, Brazil 174 9 15 S 64 20W
Caradoc 140 30 35 S 143 5 E
Caragabal 141 33 49 S 147 45 E
Caragh L. 39 52 3N 9 50W
Caráglio 62 44 25N 7 25 E
Caraí 171 17 12 S 41 42W
Carajás, Serra dos 170 6 0 S 51 30W
Caramanta 174 5 33N 75 38W
Carangola 173 20 50 S 42 5W
Carani 137 30 57 S 116 28 E
Caransebeş 70 45 28N 22 18 E
Carapelle, R. 65 41 20N 15 35 E
Caraş Severin □ 66 45 10N 22 10 E
Caraşova 66 45 11N 21 51 E
Caratasca, Laguna 166 15 30N 83 40W
Caratec 42 48 40N 3 55W
Caratinga 171 19 50 S 42 10W
Caratunk 151 45 13N 69 55W
Caraúbas 170 7 43 S 36 31W
Caravaca 59 38 8N 1 52W
Caravággio 62 45 30N 9 39 E
Caravelas 171 17 45 S 39 15W
Caraveli 174 15 45 S 73 25W
Caràzinho 173 28 0 S 53 0W
Carballino 56 42 26N 8 5W
Carballo 56 43 13N 8 41W
Carberry 153 49 50N 99 25W
Carbia 56 42 48N 8 14W
Carbó 164 29 42N 110 58W
Carbon 152 51 30N 113 9W
Carbonara, C. 64 39 8N 9 30 E
Carbondale, Colo, U.S.A. 160 39 30N 107 10W
Carbondale, Ill., U.S.A. 159 37 45N 89 10W
Carbondale, Pa., U.S.A. 162 41 37N 75 30W
Carbonear 151 47 42N 53 13W
Carboneras 59 37 0N 1 53W
Carboneras de Guadazaón 58 39 54N 1 50W
Carbonia 64 39 10N 8 30 E
Carbost 36 57 19N 6 21W
Carbury 38 53 22N 6 58W
Carcabuey 57 37 27N 4 17W
Carcagente 59 39 8N 0 28W
Carcajou 152 57 47N 117 6W
Carcasse, C. 167 18 30N 74 28W
Carcassonne 44 43 13N 2 20 E
Carche 59 38 26N 1 9W
Carcoar 141 33 36 S 149 8 E
Carcross 147 60 13N 134 45W
Cardabia 136 23 2 S 113 55 E
Cardamom Hills 97 9 30N 77 15 E
Cárdenas, Cuba 166 23 0N 81 30W
Cárdenas, San Luis Potosí, Mexico 166 22 0N 99 41W
Cárdenas, Tabasco, Mexico 165 17 59N 93 21W
Cardenete 58 39 46N 1 41W
Cardiff 31 51 28N 3 11W
Cardiff-by-the-Sea 163 33 1N 117 17W
Cardigan 31 52 6N 4 41W
Cardigan (□) 26 52 6N 4 41W
Cardigan B. 31 52 30N 4 30W
Cardington 29 52 7N 0 23W
Cardón 174 11 37N 70 14W
Cardona, Spain 58 41 56N 1 40 E
Cardona, Uruguay 172 33 53 S 57 18W
Cardoner, R. 58 42 0N 1 33 E
Cardross 153 49 50N 105 40W
Cardston 152 49 15N 113 20W
Cardwell 138 18 14 S 146 2 E
Careen L. 153 57 0N 108 11W
Carei 70 47 40N 22 29 E
Carentan 42 49 19N 1 15W
Carey, Idaho, U.S.A. 160 43 19N 113 58W
Carey, Ohio, U.S.A. 156 40 58N 83 22W
Carey, L. 137 29 0 S 122 15 E
Carey L. 153 62 12N 102 55W
Careysburg 120 6 34N 10 30W
Cargados Garajos, Is. 11 17 0 S 59 0 E
Cargelligo, L. 139 33 17 S 146 24 E
Cargèse 45 42 7N 8 35 E
Carhaix-Plouguer 42 48 18N 3 36W
Carhué 172 37 10 S 62 50W
Cariacica 171 20 16 S 40 25W
Cariaco 174 10 29N 63 33W
Caribaná, Pta. 174 8 37N 76 52W
Caribbean Sea 167 15 0N 75 0W
Cariboo Mts. 152 53 0N 121 0W
Caribou, Can. 153 53 15N 121 55W
Caribou, U.S.A. 151 46 55N 68 0W
Caribou I. 150 47 22N 85 49W
Caribou Is. 152 61 55N 113 15W
Caribou L., Man., Can. 153 59 21N 96 10W
Caribou L., Ont., Can. 150 50 25N 89 5W
Caribou Mts. 152 59 12N 115 40W
Caribou, R., Man., Can. 153 59 20N 94 44W
Caribou, R., N.W.T., Can. 152 61 27N 125 45W
Carichic 164 27 56N 107 3W
Carignan 43 49 38N 5 10 E
Carignano 62 44 55N 7 40 E
Carillo 164 26 50N 103 55W
Carinda 141 30 28 S 147 41 E
Cariñena 58 41 20N 1 13W
Carinhanha 171 14 15 S 44 0W
Carinhanha, R. 171 14 20 S 43 47W
Carini 64 38 9N 13 10 E
Carinish 36 57 31N 7 20W
Carinola 64 41 11N 13 58 E
Carinthia □ = Kärnten 52 46 52N 13 30 E
Caripito 174 10 8N 63 6W
Caririacu 171 7 2 S 39 17W
Carisbrooke 28 50 42N 1 19W
Caritianas 174 9 20 S 63 0W
Cark 32 54 11N 2 59W
Carlentini 65 37 15N 15 2 E
Carleton Place 150 45 8N 76 9W
Carleton Rode 29 52 30N 1 6 E
Carletonville 128 26 23 S 27 22 E
Carlin 160 40 50N 116 5W
Carlingford 38 54 3N 6 10W
Carlingford, L. 38 54 0N 6 5W
Carlinville 158 39 20N 89 55W
Carlisle, U.K. 32 54 54N 2 55W
Carlisle, U.S.A. 162 40 12N 77 10W
Carlitte, Pic 44 42 35N 1 43 E
Carloforte 64 39 10N 8 18 E
Carlops 35 55 47N 3 20W
Carlos Casares 172 35 53 S 61 20W
Carlos Chagas 171 17 43 S 40 45W
Carlos Tejedor 172 35 25 S 62 25W
Carlota, La 172 33 30 S 63 20W
Carlow 39 52 50N 6 58W
Carlow □ 39 52 43N 6 50W
Carloway 36 58 17N 6 48W
Carlsbad, Calif., U.S.A. 163 33 11N 117 25W
Carlsbad, N. Mex., U.S.A. 159 32 20N 104 7W
Carlton 33 52 58N 1 6W
Carlton Colville 29 52 27N 1 41 E
Carlton Miniott 33 54 13N 1 22W
Carluke 35 55 44N 3 50W
Carlyle, Can. 153 49 40N 102 20W
Carlyle, U.S.A. 158 38 38N 89 23W
Carmacks 147 62 5N 136 16W
Carmagnola 62 44 50N 7 42 E
Carman 153 49 30N 98 0W
Carmangay 152 50 10N 113 10W
Carmanville 151 49 23N 54 19W
Carmarthen 31 51 52N 4 20W
Carmarthen (□) 26 53 40N 4 18W
Carmarthen B. 31 51 40N 4 30W
Carmaux 44 44 3N 2 10 E
Carmel, Calif., U.S.A. 163 36 38N 121 55W
Carmel, N.Y., U.S.A. 162 41 25N 73 38W
Carmel Hd. 31 53 24N 4 34W
Carmel Mt. 90 32 45N 35 3 E
Carmel Valley 163 36 29N 121 43W
Carmelo 172 34 0 S 58 10W
Carmen, Colomb. 174 9 43N 75 8W
Carmen, Parag. 173 27 13 S 56 12W
Carmen de Patagones 176 40 50 S 63 0W
Carmen, I. 164 26 0N 111 20W
Carmen, R. 164 30 42N 106 29W
Cármenes 56 42 58N 5 34W
Carmensa 172 35 15 S 67 40W
Carmi 156 38 6N 88 10W
Carmichael 163 38 38N 121 19W
Carmila 138 21 55 S 149 24 E
Carmo do Paranaiba 171 18 59 S 46 21W
Carmona 57 37 28N 5 42W
Carmyllie 37 56 36N 2 41W
Carn Ban 37 57 6N 4 15W
Carn Eige 36 57 17N 5 9W
Carn Glas Chorie 37 57 20N 3 50W
Carn Mor 37 57 14N 3 13W
Carn na Saobhaidh 37 57 12N 4 20W
Carna 39 53 20N 9 50W
Carnarvon, Queens., Austral. 138 24 48 S 147 45 E
Carnarvon, W. Austral., Austral. 137 24 51 S 113 42 E
Carnarvon, S. Afr. 128 30 56 S 22 8 E
Carnarvon Ra., Queensland, Austral. 138 25 15 S 148 30 E
Carnarvon Ra., W.A., Austral. 137 25 0 S 120 45 E
Carnaxide 57 38 43N 9 14W
Carncastle 38 54 55N 5 52W
Carndonagh 38 55 15N 7 16W
Carnduff 153 49 10N 101 50W
Carnedd Llewelyn, Mt. 31 53 9N 3 58W
Carnegie, L. 137 26 5 S 122 30 E
Carnew 39 52 43N 6 30W
Carney 38 54 20N 8 30W
Carnforth 32 54 8N 2 47W
Carnic Alps = Karnische Alpen 63 46 34N 12 50 E
Carnlough 38 55 0N 6 0W
Carno 31 52 34N 3 31W
Carnon 44 43 32N 3 59 E
Carnot 124 4 59N 15 56 E
Carnot B. 136 17 20 S 121 30 E
Carnoustie 35 56 30N 2 41W
Carnsore Pt. 39 52 10N 6 20W
Carnwath 35 55 42N 3 38W
Caro 156 43 29N 83 27W
Carolina, Brazil 170 7 10 S 47 30W
Carolina, S. Afr. 129 26 5 S 30 6 E
Carolina, La 57 38 17N 3 38W
Caroline I. 131 9 15 S 150 3W
Caroline Is. 130 8 0N 150 0 E
Caroline Pk. 143 45 57 S 167 15 E
Carolside 152 51 20N 111 40W
Caron 153 50 30N 105 50W
Caroni, R. 174 6 0N 62 40W
Carora 174 10 11N 70 5W
Carovigno 65 40 42N 17 40 E
Carpathians, Mts. 53 49 40N 19 30 E
Carpaţii Meridionali 70 45 30N 25 0 E
Carpenédolo 62 45 22N 10 25 E
Carpentaria Downs 138 18 44 S 144 20 E
Carpentaria, G. of 133 14 0 S 139 0 E
Carpentras 45 44 3N 5 2 E
Carpi 62 44 47N 10 52 E
Carpina 170 7 51 S 35 15W
Carpino 65 41 50N 15 51 E
Carpinteria 163 34 25N 119 31W
Carpio 56 41 13N 5 7W
Carpolac = Morea 140 36 45 S 141 18 E
Carr Boyd Ra. 136 16 15 S 128 35 E
Carra L. 38 53 41N 9 12W
Carrabelle 157 29 52N 84 40W
Carracastle 38 53 57N 8 42W
Carradale 34 55 35N 5 30W
Carraipia 174 11 16N 72 22W
Carrara 62 44 5N 10 7 E
Carrascosa del Campo 58 40 2N 2 45W
Carrauntohill, Mt. 39 52 0N 9 49W
Carraweena 139 29 10 S 140 0 E
Carrbridge 37 57 17N 3 50W
Carriacou, I. 167 12 30N 61 28W
Carribee 140 35 7 S 136 57 E
Carrick 38 54 40N 8 39W
Carrick, dist. 34 55 12N 4 38W
Carrick-on-Shannon 38 53 57N 8 7W
Carrick-on-Suir 39 52 22N 7 30W
Carrick Ra. 143 45 15 S 169 8 E
Carrickart 38 55 10N 7 47W
Carrickbeg 39 52 20N 7 25W
Carrickboy 38 53 36N 7 40W
Carrickfergus 36 54 43N 5 50W
Carrickfergus □ 38 54 43N 5 49W
Carrickmacross 38 54 0N 6 43W
Carrieton 140 32 25 S 138 31 E
Carrigaholt 39 52 37N 9 42W
Carrigahorig 39 53 4N 8 10W
Carrigaline 39 51 49N 8 22W
Carrigallen 38 53 59N 7 40W
Carrigan Hd. 38 54 38N 8 40W
Carrignavar 39 52 0N 8 29W
Carrigtwohill 39 51 55N 8 15W
Carrington 158 47 30N 99 7W
Carrión de los Condes 56 42 20N 4 37W
Carrión, R. 56 42 42N 4 47W
Carrizal 174 12 1N 72 11W
Carrizal Bajo 172 28 5 S 71 20W
Carrizalillo 172 29 0 S 71 30W
Carrizo Cr. 159 36 30N 103 40W
Carrizo Springs 159 28 28N 99 50W
Carrizozo 161 33 40N 105 57W
Carroll 158 42 2N 94 55W
Carrollton, Ga., U.S.A. 157 33 36N 85 5W
Carrollton, Ill., U.S.A. 158 39 20N 90 25W
Carrollton, Ky., U.S.A. 156 38 40N 85 10W
Carrollton, Mo., U.S.A. 158 39 19N 93 24W
Carron L. 36 57 22N 5 35W
Carron R., U.K. 36 57 30N 5 30W
Carron R., U.K. 37 57 51N 4 21W
Carrot, R. 153 53 50N 101 17W
Carrot River 153 53 17N 103 35W
Carrouges 42 48 34N 0 10W
Carrowkeel 38 55 7N 7 12W
Carrowmore L. 38 54 12N 9 48W
Carruthers 153 52 52N 109 16W
Carryduff 38 54 32N 5 52W
Çarşamba 92 41 15N 36 45 E
Carsoli 63 42 7N 13 3 E
Carson 158 46 27N 101 29W
Carson City 160 39 12N 119 46W
Carson Sink 160 39 50N 118 40W
Carsonville 156 43 25N 82 39W
Carsphairn 34 55 13N 4 15W
Carstairs 35 55 42N 3 41W
Cartagena, Colomb. 174 10 25N 75 33W
Cartagena, Spain 59 37 38N 0 59W
Cartago, Colomb. 174 4 45N 75 55W
Cartago, C. Rica 166 9 50N 84 0W
Cartaret 42 49 23N 1 47W
Cartaxo 57 39 10N 8 47W
Cartaya 57 37 16N 7 9W
Cartersville 157 34 11N 84 48W
Carterton 142 41 2 S 175 31 E
Carthage, Ark., U.S.A. 159 34 4N 92 32W
Carthage, Ill., U.S.A. 158 40 25N 91 10W
Carthage, Mo., U.S.A. 159 37 10N 94 20W
Carthage, N.Y., U.S.A. 156 43 59N 75 37W
Carthage, S.D., U.S.A. 158 44 14N 97 38W
Carthage, Texas, U.S.A. 159 32 8N 94 20W
Cartier I. 136 12 31 S 123 29 E
Cartmel 32 54 13N 2 57W
Cartwright 151 53 41N 56 58W
Caruaru 170 8 15 S 35 55W
Carúpano 174 10 45N 63 15W
Carutapera 170 1 13 S 46 1W
Caruthersville 159 36 10N 89 40W
Carvarzere 63 45 8N 12 7 E
Carvin 43 50 30N 2 57 E
Carvoeiro 174 1 30 S 61 59W
Carvoeiro, Cabo 57 39 21N 9 24W
Casa Agapito 174 2 3N 73 58W
Casa Branca, Brazil 171 21 46 S 47 4W
Casa Branca, Port. 57 38 29N 8 12W
Casa Grande 161 32 53N 111 51W
Casa Nova 170 9 10 S 41 5W
Casablanca, Chile 172 33 20 S 71 25W
Casablanca, Moroc. 118 33 36N 7 36W
Casacalenda 65 41 45N 14 50 E
Casalbordino 63 42 10N 14 34 E
Casale Monferrato 62 45 8N 8 28 E
Casalmaggiore 62 44 59N 10 25 E
Casalpusterlengo 62 45 10N 9 40 E
Casamance, R. 120 12 54N 15 0W
Casamássima 65 40 58N 16 55 E
Casanare, R. 174 6 30N 71 20W
Casarano 65 40 0N 18 10 E
Casares 57 36 27N 5 16W
Casas Grandes 164 30 22N 108 0W
Casas IbáPez 59 39 17N 1 30W
Casasimarro 59 39 22N 2 3W
Casatejada 56 39 54N 5 40W
Casavieja 56 40 17N 4 46W
Cascade, Idaho, U.S.A. 160 44 30N 116 2W

*Renamed Abariringa

Cascade, Mont., U.S.A. 160 47 16N 111 46W
Cascade Locks 160 45 44N 121 54W
Cascade Pt. 143 44 1S 168 20E
Cascade Ra. 160 45 0N 121 30W
Cascais 57 38 41N 9 25W
Cascina 62 43 40N 10 32E
Caselle Torinese 62 45 12N 7 39E
Caserta 65 41 5N 14 20E
Cashel 39 52 31N 7 53W
Cashla B. 39 53 12N 9 37W
Cashmere 160 47 31N 120 30W
Cashmere Downs 137 28 57S 119 35E
Casigua 174 11 2N 71 1W
Casiguran 103 16 15N 122 15E
Casilda 172 33 10S 61 10W
Casimcea 70 44 45N 28 23E
Casino 139 28 52S 153 3E
Casiquiare, R. 174 2 45N 66 20W
Caslan 152 54 38N 112 31W
Casma 174 9 30S 78 20W
Casmalia 163 34 50N 120 32W
Casola Valsenio 63 44 12N 11 40E
Cásoli 63 42 7N 14 18E
Caspe 58 41 14N 0 1W
Casper 160 42 52N 106 27W
Caspian Sea 79 43 0N 50 0E
Casquets 42 49 46N 2 15W
Cass City 156 43 34N 83 15W
Cass Lake 158 47 23N 94 38W
Cassá de la Selva 58 41 53N 2 52E
Cassano Iónio 65 39 47N 16 20E
Cassel 43 50 48N 2 30E
Casselton 158 47 0N 97 15W
Cássia 171 20 36S 46 56W
Cassiar 152 59 16N 129 40W
Cassiar Mts. 152 59 30N 130 30W
Cassils 152 50 29N 112 15W
Cassinga 125 15 5S 16 23E
Cassino 64 41 30N 13 50E
Cassiporé, C. 170 3 50N 51 5W
Cassis 45 43 14N 5 32E
Cassville 159 36 45N 93 59W
Cástagneto Carducci 62 43 9N 10 36E
Castaic 163 34 30N 118 38W
Castanhal 170 1 18S 47 55W
Castanheiro 174 0 17S 65 38W
Casteau 47 50 32N 4 2E
Castéggio 62 45 1N 9 8E
Castejón de Monegros 58 41 37N 0 15W
Castel di Sangro 65 41 41N 14 5E
Castel San Giovanni 62 45 4N 9 25E
Castel San Pietro 63 44 23N 11 30E
Castelbuono 65 37 56N 14 4E
Casteldelfino 62 44 35N 7 4E
Castelfiorentino 62 43 36N 10 58E
Castelfranco Emília 62 44 37N 11 2E
Castelfranco Veneto 63 45 40N 11 56E
Casteljaloux 44 44 19N 0 6E
Castellabate 65 40 18N 14 55E
Castellammare del Golfo 64 38 2N 12 53E
Castellammare di Stábia 65 40 47N 14 29E
Castellammare, G. di 64 38 5N 12 55E
Castellamonte 62 45 23N 7 42E
Castellana Grotte 65 40 53N 17 10E
Castellane 45 43 50N 6 31E
Castellaneta 65 40 40N 16 57E
Castellar de Santisteban 59 38 16N 3 8W
Castelleone 62 45 19N 9 47E
Castelli 172 36 7S 57 47W
Castelló de Ampurias 58 42 15N 3 4E
Castellón □ 58 40 15N 0 5W
Castellón de la Plana 58 39 58N 0 3W
Castellote 58 40 48N 0 15W
Castelltersol 58 41 45N 2 8E
Castelmáuro 65 41 50N 14 40E
Castelnau-de-Médoc 44 45 2N 0 48W
Castelnaudary 44 43 20N 1 58E
Castelnovo ne' Monti 62 44 27N 10 26E
Castelnuovo di Val di Cécina 62 43 12N 10 54E
Castelo 173 20 53S 41 42E
Castelo Branco 56 39 50N 7 31W
Castelo Branco □ 56 39 52N 7 45W
Castelo de Paiva 56 41 2N 8 16W
Castelo de Vide 57 39 25N 7 27W
Castelo do Piaúi 170 5 20S 41 33W
Castelsarrasin 44 44 2N 1 7E
Casteltérmini 64 37 32N 13 38E
Castelvetrano 64 37 40N 12 46E
Casterton 140 37 30S 141 30E
Castets 44 43 52N 1 6W
Castiglione del Lago 63 43 7N 12 3E
Castiglione della Pescáia 62 42 46N 10 53E
Castiglione della Stiviere 62 45 23N 10 30E
Castiglione Fiorentino 63 43 20N 11 55E
Castilblanco 57 39 17N 5 5W
Castilla La Nueva 57 39 45N 3 20W
Castilla La Vieja 56 41 55N 4 0W
Castilla, Playa de 57 37 0N 6 33W
Castille = Castilla 56 40 0N 3 30W
Castilletes 174 11 51N 71 19W
Castillón 164 28 20N 103 38W
Castillon-en-Couserans 44 42 56N 1 1E
Castillon-la-Bataille 44 44 51N 0 2W
Castillonès 44 44 39N 0 37E
Castillos 173 34 12S 53 52W
Castle Acre 29 52 42N 0 42W
Castle Cary 28 51 5N 2 32W
Castle Dale 160 39 11N 111 1W
Castle Donington 28 52 50N 1 20W
Castle Douglas 35 54 57N 3 57W
Castle Eden 54 54 45N 1 20W
Castle Point 142 40 54N 176 15E
Castle Rock, Colo., U.S.A. 158 39 26N 104 50W
Castle Rock, Wash., U.S.A. 160 46 20N 122 58W
Castlebar 38 53 52N 9 17W
Castlebay 36 56 57N 7 30W
Castlebellingham 38 53 53N 6 22W
Castleblakeney 38 53 26N 8 28W
Castleblayney 38 54 7N 6 44W
Castlebridge 39 52 23N 6 28W
Castlecliff 142 39 57S 174 59E
Castlecomer 39 52 49N 7 13W
Castleconnell 39 52 44N 8 30W
Castledawson 38 54 47N 6 35W
Castlederg 38 54 43N 7 35W
Castledermot 39 52 55N 6 50W
Castlefinn 38 54 47N 7 35W
Castleford 33 53 43N 1 21W
Castlegar 152 49 20N 117 40W
Castlegate 160 39 45N 110 57W
Castlegregory 39 52 16N 10 0W
Castlehill 38 51 1N 9 49W
Castleisland 39 52 14N 9 28W
Castlemaine, Austral. 140 37 2S 144 12E
Castlemaine, Ireland 39 52 10N 9 42W
Castlemaine Harb. 39 52 8N 9 50W
Castlemartyr 39 51 54N 8 3W
Castlepollard 38 53 40N 7 20W
Castlereagh 38 53 47N 8 30W
Castlereagh □ 38 54 33N 5 33W
Castlereagh B. 138 12 10S 135 10E
Castlereagh, R. 141 30 12S 147 32E
Castleside 32 54 50N 1 52W
Castleton, Derby., U.K. 33 53 20N 1 47W
Castleton, N. Yorks., U.K. 33 54 27N 0 57W
Castleton, U.S.A. 162 43 37N 73 11W
Castletown, Geoghegan, Ireland 38 53 27N 7 30W
Castletown, Laois, Ireland 38 52 58N 7 31W
Castletown, Meath, Ireland 39 53 47N 6 41W
Castletown, I. of Man 32 54 4N 4 40W
Castletown, U.K. 37 58 35N 3 22W
Castletown Bearhaven 39 51 40N 9 54W
Castletownroche 39 52 10N 8 28W
Castletownshend 39 51 31N 9 11W
Castlevale 138 24 30S 146 48E
Castlewellan 38 54 16N 5 57W
Castor 152 52 15N 111 50W
Castorland 162 43 53N 75 31W
Castres 44 43 37N 2 13E
Castricum 46 52 33N 4 40E
Castries 167 14 0N 60 50W
Castril 59 37 48N 2 46W
Castro, Brazil 173 24 45S 50 0W
Castro, Chile 176 42 30S 73 50W
Castro Alves 171 12 46S 39 26W
Castro del Río 57 37 41N 4 29W
Castro Marim 57 37 13N 7 26W
Castro Urdiales 58 43 23N 3 19W
Castro Verde 57 37 41N 8 4W
Castrojeriz 56 42 17N 4 9W
Castropol 56 43 32N 7 0W
Castroreale 65 38 5N 15 15E
Castrovillari 65 39 49N 16 11E
Castroville, Calif., U.S.A. 163 36 46N 121 45W
Castroville, Tex, U.S.A. 159 29 20N 98 53W
Castuera 57 38 43N 5 37W
Casummit L. 150 51 29N 92 22W
Cat Ba 100 20 50N 107 0E
Cat I., Bahamas 167 24 30N 75 30W
Cat I., U.S.A. 159 30 15N 89 7W
Çat L. 150 51 40N 91 50W
Çata 53 47 58N 18 38E
Catacamas 166 14 54N 85 56W
Catacaos 174 5 20S 80 45W
Cataguases 173 21 23S 42 39W
Catahoula L. 159 31 30N 92 5W
Catalão 171 18 10S 47 57W
Çatalca 92 41 9N 28 28E
Catalina 151 48 31N 53 4W
Catalonia = Cataluña 58 41 40N 1 15E
Cataluña 58 41 40N 1 15E
Catamarca 172 28 30S 65 50W
Catamarca □ 172 28 30S 65 50W
Catanduanas, Is. 103 13 50N 124 20E
Catanduva 173 21 5S 48 58W
Catánia 65 37 31N 15 4E
Catánia, G. di 65 37 25N 15 8E
Catanzaro 65 38 54N 16 38E
Catarman 103 12 28N 124 1E
Catastrophe C. 136 34 59S 136 0E
Catcleugh 35 55 19N 2 22W
Cateau, Le 43 50 6N 3 30E
Cateel 103 7 47N 126 24E
Catende 170 8 40S 35 43W
Caterham 29 51 16N 0 4W
Cathcart, Austral. 141 36 2S 149 24E
Cathcart, S. Afr. 128 32 18S 27 10E
Catine 41 46 30N 0 15W
Catio 120 11 17N 15 15W
Catismiña 174 4 5N 63 52W
Catita 170 9 31S 43 1W
Catlettsburg 156 38 23N 82 38W
Cato I. 133 23 15S 155 32E
Catoche, C. 165 21 40N 87 0W
Catolé 171 7 19S 36 1W
Catolé do Rocha 170 6 21S 37 45W
Caton 32 54 5N 2 41W
Catonsville 162 39 16N 76 44W
Catral 59 38 10N 0 47W
Catria, Mt. 63 43 28N 12 42E
Catrimani 174 0 27N 61 41W
Catrine 34 55 30N 4 20W
Catsfield 29 50 53N 0 28E
Catskill 162 42 14N 73 52W
Catskill Mts. 162 42 15N 74 15W
Catt, Mt. 138 13 49S 134 23E
Catterick 33 54 23N 1 38W
Cattólica 63 43 58N 12 43E
Cattólica Eraclea 64 37 27N 13 24E
Catton 35 54 56N 2 16W
Catu 171 12 21S 38 23W
Catuala 128 16 25S 19 2E
Catur 127 13 45S 35 30E
Catwick Is. 101 10 0N 109 0E
Cauca □ 174 2 30N 76 50W
Cauca, R. 174 7 25N 75 30W
Caucasia 174 8 0N 75 12W
Caucasus Mts. = Bolshoi Kavkas 83 42 50N 44 0E
Caucaia 170 3 40S 38 35W
Caudebec-en-Caux 42 49 30N 0 42E
Caudete 59 38 42N 1 2W
Caudry 43 50 7N 3 22E
Caulkerbush 35 54 54N 3 40W
Caulnes 42 48 18N 2 10W
Caulónia 65 38 23N 16 25E
Caungula 124 8 15S 18 50E
Cáuquenes 172 36 0S 72 30W
Caura, R. 174 6 20N 64 30W
Cauresi, R. 127 17 40S 33 10E
Causapscal 151 48 19N 67 12W
Causeway 39 52 25N 9 45W
Caussade 44 44 10N 1 33E
Cauterets 44 42 52N 0 8W
Cauvery, R. 93 12 0N 77 45E
Caux 42 49 38N 0 35E
Cava dei Tirreni 65 40 42N 14 42E
Cávado, R. 56 41 37N 8 15W
Cavaillon 45 43 50N 5 2E
Cavalaire-sur-Mer 45 43 10N 6 33E
Cavalcante 171 13 48S 47 30W
Cavalerie, La 44 44 0N 3 10E
Cavalese 63 46 17N 11 29E
Cavalier 158 48 50N 97 39W
Cavalli Is. 142 35 0S 173 58E
Cavallo, I. 45 41 22N 9 16E
Cavally, R. 120 5 0N 7 40W
Cavan 38 54 0N 7 22W
Cavan □ 38 53 58N 7 10W
Cavanagh Ra. 137 26 10S 122 50E
Cavárzere 63 45 8N 12 6E
Cave City 156 37 13N 85 57W
Cavenagh Range 137 26 12S 127 55E
Cavendish 140 37 31S 142 2E
Cavers 150 48 55N 87 41W
Caviana, Ilha 170 0 15N 50 0W
Cavite 103 14 20N 120 55E
Cavour 62 44 47N 7 22E
Cavtat 66 42 35N 18 13E
Cawdor 37 57 31N 3 56W
Cawkers Well 140 31 41S 142 57E
Cawndilla, L. 140 32 30S 142 15E
Cawnpore = Kanpur 95 26 35N 80 20E
Cawood 33 53 50N 1 7W
Cawston 29 52 47N 1 10E
Caxias 174 5 0S 43 27W
Caxias do Sul 173 29 10S 51 10W
Caxine, C. 118 35 56N 0 27W
Caxito 124 8 30S 13 30E
Cay Sal Bank 166 23 45N 80 0W
Cayambe 174 0 3N 78 22W
Cayce 157 33 59N 81 2W
Cayenne 175 5 0N 52 18W
Cayes, Les 167 18 15N 73 46W
Cayeux-sur-Mer. 43 50 10N 1 30E
Cayey 147 18 7N 66 10W
Caylus 44 44 15N 1 47E
Cayman Brac, I. 166 19 43N 79 49W
Cayman Is. 166 19 40N 79 50W
Cayo 165 17 10N 89 0W
Cayo Romano, I. 167 22 0N 73 30W
Cayuga 162 42 28N 76 30W
Cayuga L. 162 42 45N 76 45W
Cazalla de la Sierra 57 37 56N 5 45W
Cazaux et de Sanguinet, Étang de 44 44 29N 1 10W
Cazenovia 162 42 56N 75 51W
Cazères 44 43 13N 1 5E
Çazin 63 44 57N 15 57E
Čazma 63 45 45N 16 39E
Cazombo 125 12 0S 22 48E
Cazorla, Spain 59 37 55N 3 2W
Cazorla, Venez. 174 8 1N 67 0W
Cazorla, Sierra de 59 38 5N 2 55W
Cea, R. 56 42 40N 5 5W
Ceamurlia de Jos 67 44 43N 28 47E
Ceanannus Mor 38 53 42N 6 53W
Ceará = Fortaleza 170 3 35S 38 35W
Ceará □ 170 5 0S 40 0W
Ceará Mirim 170 5 38S 35 25W
Ceauru, L. 70 44 58N 23 11E
Cebaco, I. 166 7 33N 81 9W
Cebollar 172 29 10S 66 35W
Cebollera, Sierra de 58 42 0N 2 30W
Cebreros 56 40 27N 4 28W
Cebú 103 10 18N 123 54E
Cebú, I. 103 10 15N 123 40E
Ceccano 64 41 34N 13 18E
Cece 53 46 46N 18 39E
Cechi 120 6 15N 4 25W
Cecil Plains 139 27 30S 151 11E
Cecilton 162 39 24N 75 52W
Cécina 62 43 19N 10 33E
Cécina, R. 62 43 19N 10 40E
Ceclavin 56 39 50N 6 45W
Cedar City 161 37 41N 113 3W
Cedar Creek Res. 159 32 15N 96 0W
Cedar Falls 158 42 39N 92 29W
Cedar I. 162 37 35N 75 32W
Cedar Key 157 29 9N 83 5W
Cedar L. 153 53 20N 100 10W
Cedar Pt. 162 38 18N 76 25W
Cedar, R. 158 41 50N 91 20W
Cedar Rapids 158 42 0N 91 38W
Cedarburg 156 43 18N 87 55W
Cedartown 157 34 1N 85 15W
Cedarvale 152 55 1N 128 22W
Cedarville 160 41 37N 120 13W
Cedeira 56 43 39N 8 2W
Cedral 164 23 50N 100 42W
Cedrino, R. 64 40 8N 9 25E
Cedro 170 6 34S 39 3W
Cedros, I. de 164 28 10N 115 20W
Ceduna 139 32 7S 133 46E
Cedynia 54 52 53N 14 12E
Ceepeecee 152 49 52N 126 42W
Cefalù 65 38 3N 14 1E
Cega, R. 56 41 17N 4 10W
Cegléd 53 47 11N 19 47E
Céglie Messápico 65 40 39N 17 31E
Cehegín 59 38 6N 1 48W
Cehu-Silvaniei 70 47 24N 23 9E
Ceiba, La 166 15 40N 86 50W
Ceica 70 46 53N 22 10E
Ceira, R. 56 40 15N 7 55W
Cekhira 119 34 20N 10 5E
Celano 63 42 6N 13 30E
Celanova 56 42 9N 7 58W
Celaya 164 20 31N 100 37W
Celbridge 39 53 20N 6 33W
Celebes I. = Sulawesi 103 2 0S 120 0E
Celebes Sea 103 3 0N 123 0E
Celga 123 12 38N 37 3E
Çelina 156 40 32N 84 31W
Čelić 66 44 43N 18 47E
Celje 63 46 16N 15 18E
Cellar Hd. 36 58 25N 6 10W
Celldömölk 53 47 16N 17 10E
Celle 48 52 37N 10 4E
Celles 47 50 42N 3 28E
Celorica da Beira 56 40 38N 7 24W
Cemaes Bay 31 53 24N 4 27W
Cemaes Hd. 31 52 7N 4 44W
Çement 159 34 56N 98 8W
Čemerno 66 43 26N 20 26E
Cemmaes Road 31 52 39N 3 41W
Cenarth 31 52 3N 4 32W
Cenis, Col du Mt. 45 45 15N 6 55E
Ceno, R. 62 44 40N 9 52E
Cenon 44 44 50N 0 33W
Centallo 62 44 30N 7 35E
Centenário do Sul 171 22 48S 51 57W
Center, N.D., U.S.A. 158 47 9N 101 17W
Center, Texas, U.S.A. 159 31 50N 94 10W
Centerfield 160 39 9N 111 56W
Centerville, Ala., U.S.A. 157 32 55N 87 7W
Centerville, Calif., U.S.A. 163 36 44N 119 30W
Centerville, Iowa, U.S.A. 158 40 45N 92 57W
Centerville, Miss., U.S.A. 159 31 10N 91 3W
Centerville, S.D., U.S.A. 158 43 10N 96 58W
Centerville, Tenn., U.S.A. 157 35 46N 87 29W
Centerville, Tex., U.S.A. 159 31 15N 95 56W
Cento 63 44 43N 11 16E
Central 170 11 8S 42 8W
Central □, Kenya 126 0 30S 33 30E
Central □, Malawi 126 13 30S 33 30E
Central □, U.K. 34 56 0N 4 30W
Central □, Zambia 127 14 25S 28 50E
Central African Republic ■ 124 7 0N 20 0E
Central Auckland □ 142 37 30S 175 30E
Central City, Ky., U.S.A. 156 37 20N 87 7W
Central City, Nebr., U.S.A. 158 41 8N 98 0W
Central, Cordillera, C. Rica 166 10 10N 84 5W
Central, Cordillera, Dom. Rep. 167 19 15N 71 0W
Central I., L. Turkana 126 3 30N 36 0E
Central Islip 162 40 49N 73 13W
Central Makran Range 93 26 30N 64 15E
Central Patricia 150 51 30N 90 9W
Central Ra. 135 5 0S 143 0E
Central Russian Uplands 16 54 0N 36 0E
Central Siberian Plateau 77 65 0N 105 0E
Central Square 162 43 17N 76 9W
Centralia, Ill., U.S.A. 158 38 32N 89 5W
Centralia, Mo., U.S.A. 158 39 12N 92 6W
Centralia, Wash., U.S.A. 160 46 46N 122 59W
Centúripe 65 37 37N 14 41E
Cephalonia = Kefallinía 69 38 28N 20 30E
Cepin 66 45 32N 18 34E

Ceprano **64** 41 33N 13 30 E
Ceptura **70** 45 1N 26 21 E
Ceram I. = Seram I. **103** 3 10 S 129 0 E
Ceram Sea **103** 2 30 S 128 30 E
Cerbère **44** 42 26N 3 10 E
Cerbicales, Îles **45** 41 33N 9 22 E
Cerbu **70** 44 46N 24 46 E
Cercal **57** 37 48N 8 40W
Cercemaggiore **65** 41 27N 14 43 E
Cerdaña **58** 42 22N 1 35 E
Cerdedo **56** 42 33N 8 23W
Cerea **63** 45 12N 11 13 E
Ceres, Argent. **172** 29 55 S 61 55W
Ceres, Brazil **171** 15 17 S 49 35W
Ceres, Italy **62** 45 19N 7 22 E
Ceres, S. Afr. **128** 33 21 S 19 18 E
Ceres, U.K. **35** 56 18N 2 57W
Ceres, U.S.A. **163** 37 35N 120 57W
Céret **44** 42 30N 2 42 E
Ceretè **174** 8 53N 75 48W
Cerfontaine **47** 50 11N 4 26 E
Cerignola **65** 41 17N 15 53 E
Cerigo = Kíthira **69** 36 9N 23 0 E
Cérilly **44** 46 37N 2 50 E
Cerisiers **43** 48 8N 3 30 E
Cerizay **42** 46 50N 0 40W
Çerkeş **92** 40 40N 32 58 E
Cerknica **63** 45 48N 14 21 E
Çermerno **66** 43 35N 20 25 E
Cerna **70** 44 4N 28 17 E
Cerna, R. **70** 44 45N 24 0 E
Cernavodă **70** 44 22N 28 3 E
Cernay **43** 47 44N 7 10 E
Cerne Abbas **28** 50 49N 2 29W
Cernik **66** 45 17N 17 22 E
Cerralvo, I. **164** 24 20N 109 45 E
Cerreto Sannita **65** 41 17N 14 34 E
Cerrig-y-druidion **31** 53 2N 3 34W
Cerritos **164** 22 20N 100 20W
Cerro **161** 36 47N 105 36W
Cêrro Corá **171** 6 3 S 36 21W
Cerro de Punta, Mt. **147** 18 10N 67 0W
Certaldo **62** 43 32N 11 2 E
Cervaro, R. **65** 41 21N 15 30 E
Cervera **58** 41 40N 1 16 E
Cervera de Pisuerga **56** 42 51N 4 30W
Cervera del Rio Alhama **58** 42 2N 1 58W
Cérvia **63** 44 15N 12 20 E
Cervignano del Friuli **63** 45 49N 13 20 E
Cervinara **65** 41 2N 14 36 E
Cervo **56** 43 40N 7 24W
Cervoine **45** 42 20N 9 29 E
Cesanâtico **63** 44 12N 12 22 E
César □ **174** 9 0N 73 30W
Cesaro **65** 37 50N 14 38 E
Cesena **63** 44 9N 12 14 E
Cesenático **63** 44 12N 12 22 E
Cēsis **80** 57 17N 25 28 E
Česká Třebová **53** 49 54N 16 27 E
České Budějovice **52** 48 55N 14 25 E
České Velenice **52** 48 45N 15 1 E
Českézemě **52** 50 0N 14 0 E
Ceskomoravská Vrchovina **52** 49 20N 15 45 E
Český Brod **52** 50 4N 14 52 E
Český Krumlov **52** 48 43N 14 21 E
Český Těšin **53** 49 45N 18 39 E
Çeşme **69** 38 20N 26 23 E
Cess, R. **120** 5 25N 9 35W
Cessnock **141** 32 50 S 151 21 E
Cestos, R. **120** 5 30N 9 30W
Cetate **70** 44 7N 23 2 E
Cetina, R. **63** 43 50N 16 30 E
Cetinje **66** 42 23N 18 59 E
Cetraro **65** 39 30N 15 56 E
Ceuta **118** 35 52N 5 18W
Ceva **62** 44 23N 8 0 E
Cévennes, mts. **44** 44 10N 3 50 E
Ceylon = Sri Lanka ■ **97** 7 30N 80 50 E
Cha-am **100** 12 48N 99 58 E
Cha Pa **100** 22 21N 103 50 E
Chaam **47** 51 30N 4 52 E
Chabeuil **45** 44 54N 5 1 E
Chabjuwardoo B. **137** 23 0 S 113 30 E
Chablais **45** 46 20N 6 36 E
Chablis **43** 47 47N 3 48 E
Chabounia **118** 35 30N 2 38 E
Chacabuco **172** 34 40 S 60 27W
Chacewater **30** 50 15N 5 8W
Chachapoyas **174** 6 15 S 77 50W
Chachoengsao **100** 13 42N 101 5 E
Chachran **93** 28 55N 70 30 E
Chachro **94** 25 5N 70 15 E
Chaco □ **172** 25 0 S 61 0W
Chaco Austral **176** 27 30 S 61 40W
Chaco Boreal **172** 22 30 S 60 10W
Chaco Central **176** 24 0 S 61 0W
Chad ■ **117** 12 30N 17 15 E
Chadan **77** 51 17N 91 35 E
Chadileuvú, R. **172** 37 0 S 65 55W
Chadiza **127** 14 10 S 33 34 E
Chadron **158** 42 50N 103 0W
Chadyr-Lunga **82** 46 3N 28 51 E
Chae Hom **100** 18 43N 99 35 E
Chaem, R. **100** 18 11N 98 38 E
Chaeryŏng **107** 38 24N 125 36 E
Chafurray **174** 3 10N 73 14W
Chagai **93** 29 30N 63 0 E
Chagai Hills **93** 29 30N 63 0 E
Chagda **77** 58 45N 130 30 E
Chagford **30** 50 40N 3 50W
Chagny **43** 46 57N 4 45 E
Chagoda **80** 59 10N 35 25 E
Chagos Arch. **86** 6 0 S 72 0 E
Chāh Bahār **93** 25 20N 60 40 E
Ch'ahaerhyuichungch'i **106** 41 18N 112 48 E
Ch'ahanch'elo **106** 41 41N 114 15 E
Chahar Buriak **93** 30 15N 62 0 E
Chāhr-e Babak **93** 30 10N 55 20 E
Chahsikiang **105** 32 32N 79 41 E
Chahtung **98** 26 41N 98 10 E
Chai-nat **100** 15 11N 100 8 E
Chaibasa **99** 22 42N 85 49 E
Chaillé-les-Marais **44** 46 25N 1 2W
Chaise Dieu, La **44** 45 20N 3 40 E
Chaiya **101** 9 23N 99 14 E
Chaiyaphum **100** 15 48N 102 2 E
Chaize-le-Vicomté, La **42** 46 40N 1 18W
Chaj Doab **94** 32 0N 73 0 E
Chajari **172** 30 42N 58 0W
Chakaria **98** 21 45N 92 5 E
Chake Chake **126** 5 15 S 39 45 E
Chakhansur **93** 31 10N 62 0 E
Chaklashi **94** 22 40N 72 52 E
Chakonipau, L. **151** 56 18N 68 30W
Chakradharpur **95** 22 45N 85 40 E
Chakwadam **98** 27 29N 98 31 E
Chakwal **94** 32 50N 72 45 E
Chala **174** 15 48 S 74 20W
Chalais **44** 45 16N 0 3 E
Chalakudi **97** 10 18N 76 20 E
Chalcatongo **165** 17 4N 97 34W
Chalchihuites **164** 23 29N 103 53W
Chalcis = Khalkís **69** 38 27N 23 42 E
Chale **28** 50 35N 1 19W
Chaleur B. **151** 47 55N 65 30W
Chalfant **163** 37 32N 118 21W
Chalfont St. Peter **29** 51 36N 0 33W
Chalhuanca **174** 14 15 S 73 5W
Ch'aling **109** 26 47N 113 45 E
Chaling Hu **105** 34 55N 98 0 E
Chalisgaon **96** 20 30N 75 10 E
Chalkar **83** 50 35N 51 52 E
Chalkar Oz. **83** 50 33N 51 45 E
Chalky Inlet **143** 46 3 S 166 31 E
Challans **42** 46 50N 1 52W
Challapata **174** 19 0 S 66 50W
Challerange **43** 49 18N 4 46 E
Challis **160** 44 32N 114 25W
Chalna **95** 22 36N 89 35 E
Chalon-sur-Saône **43** 46 48N 4 50 E
Chalonnes **42** 47 20N 0 45W
Châlons-sur-Marne **43** 48 58N 4 20 E
Châlus **44** 45 39N 0 58 E
Cham, Ger. **49** 49 12N 12 40 E
Cham, Switz. **51** 47 11N 8 28 E
Cham, Cu Lao **100** 15 57N 108 30 E
Chama, R. **127** 36 57N 106 37W
Chaman **93** 30 58N 66 25 E
Chamarajanagar-Ramasamudram **97** 11 52N 76 52 E
Chamartín de la Rosa **58** 40 28N 3 40W
Chamba, India **94** 32 35N 76 10 E
Chamba, Tanz. **125** 11 37 S 37 0 E
Chambal, R. **94** 26 0N 76 55 E
Chamberlain, Austral. **136** 15 58 S 127 54 E
Chamberlain, U.S.A. **158** 43 50N 99 21W
Chambers **161** 35 13N 109 30W
Chambersburg **156** 39 53N 77 41W
Chambéry **45** 45 34N 5 55 E
Chambeshi **127** 12 39 S 28 1 E
Chambeshi, R. **124** 10 20 S 31 58 E
Chambois **42** 48 48N 0 6 E
Chambon-Feugerolles, Le **45** 45 24N 4 18 E
Chãmbon, Le **45** 45 35N 4 26 E
Chambord **151** 48 25N 72 6W
Chamboulive **44** 45 26N 1 42 E
Chambri L. **135** 4 15 S 143 10 E
Chamela **164** 19 32N 105 5W
Chamical **172** 30 22 S 66 27W
Chamkar Luong **101** 11 0N 103 45 E
Chamonix **45** 45 55N 6 51 E
Champa **95** 22 2N 82 43 E
Champagne, Can. **152** 60 49N 136 30W
Champagne, France **43** 49 0N 4 40 E
Champagnole **43** 46 45N 5 55 E
Champaign **156** 40 8N 88 14W
Champassak **100** 14 53N 105 52 E
Champaubert **43** 48 50N 3 45 E
Champdeniers **44** 46 29N 0 25W
Champeix **44** 45 37N 3 8 E
Champerico **166** 14 18N 91 55W
Champier **50** 45 27N 5 17 E
Champion B. **137** 28 44 S 114 36 E
Champlain **151** 46 27N 72 24W
Champotón **165** 19 20N 90 50W
Chamusca **57** 39 21N 8 29W
Chana **101** 6 55N 100 44 E
Chañaral **172** 26 15 S 70 50W
Chanasma **94** 23 44N 72 5 E
Chanca, R. **57** 37 49N 7 15W
Chanchiang **109** 21 15N 110 20 E
Chancy **50** 46 8N 6 0 E
Chanda **96** 19 57N 79 25 E
Chandalar **147** 67 30N 148 35W
Chandausi **95** 28 27N 78 49 E
Chandeleur Is. **59** 29 45N 88 53W
Chandeleur Sd. **159** 29 58N 88 40W
Chandernagore **95** 22 52N 88 24 E
Chandigarh **94** 30 30N 76 58 E
Chandler, Can. **151** 48 18N 64 46W
Chandler, Ariz., U.S.A. **161** 33 20N 111 56W
Chandler, Okla., U.S.A. **159** 35 43N 97 20W
Chandler's Ford **28** 50 59N 1 23W
Chandlers Peak **141** 30 24 S 152 10 E
Chandmani **105** 45 20N 97 59 E
Chandpur, Bangla. **98** 22 8N 90 55 E
Chandpur, India **94** 29 8N 78 19 E
Chang **94** 26 59N 68 30 E
Ch'ang Chiang, R. **109** 31 40N 121 50 E
Chang, Ko **101** 12 0N 102 23 E
Changa **95** 33 53N 77 35 E
Changanacheri **97** 9 25N 76 31 E
Changane, R. **125** 23 30 S 33 50 E
Ch'anganpao **108** 26 9N 109 42 E
Changchiak'ou **106** 40 50N 114 53 E
Ch'angchiang **100** 19 19N 108 43 E
Ch'angchih **106** 36 11N 113 6 E
Ch'angchou **109** 31 47N 119 58 E
Changchou **109** 24 31N 117 40 E
Ch'angch'un **107** 43 58N 125 19 E
Ch'angch'unling **107** 45 22N 125 28 E
Changdori **107** 38 30N 127 40 E
Ch'angfeng **109** 32 27N 117 9 E
Changhsing **109** 31 0N 119 56 E
Ch'anghua **109** 30 10N 119 15 E
Changhua **109** 24 2N 120 30 E
Changhŭng **107** 34 41N 126 52 E
Changhŭngni **107** 40 24N 128 19 E
Ch'angi **107** 36 51N 119 23 E
Changjin **107** 40 23N 127 15 E
Changjin-chŏsuji **107** 40 30N 127 15 E
Changkuangts'ai Ling **107** 45 50N 128 50 E
Changli **107** 39 40N 119 19 E
Ch'angling **107** 44 16N 123 57 E
Ch'anglo, Fukien, China **109** 25 58N 119 31 E
Ch'anglo, Fukien, China **109** 26 40N 117 20 E
Ch'anglo, Kwangtung, China **109** 24 4N 115 37 E
Changlun **101** 6 25N 100 26 E
Changming **108** 31 44N 104 44 E
Ch'angning, Hunan, China **109** 26 25N 112 15 E
Ch'angning, Szechwan, China **108** 28 38N 104 57 E
Ch'angning, Yunnan, China **108** 24 50N 99 36 E
Ch'angpai **107** 41 26N 128 0 E
Ch'angpai Shan **107** 42 25N 129 0 E
Changpei **106** 41 7N 114 51 E
Ch'angp'ing **106** 40 12N 116 12 E
Changp'ing **109** 25 18N 117 24 E
Changpu **109** 24 2N 117 31 E
Ch'angsha **109** 28 15N 113 0 E
Ch'angshan **109** 28 57N 118 31 E
Ch'angshou **108** 29 50N 107 2 E
Ch'angshu **109** 31 33N 120 45 E
Ch'angshun **108** 25 59N 106 25 E
Ch'angt'ai **109** 24 34N 117 50 E
Ch'angte **109** 29 5N 111 42 E
Ch'angt'ing **109** 25 52N 116 20 E
Ch'angt'u **107** 42 47N 124 0 E
Ch'angtu **108** 31 10N 97 14 E
Ch'angt'u Shan **109** 30 15N 122 20 E
Ch'angwu **106** 35 9N 107 42 E
Changwu **107** 42 24N 122 30 E
Ch'angyang **109** 30 28N 111 9 E
Ch'angyatien **106** 40 40N 108 46 E
Changyeh **105** 38 56N 100 37 E
Changyŏn **107** 38 15N 125 6 E
Ch'angyüan **106** 35 17N 114 50 E
Chanhanga **128** 16 0 S 14 8 E
Chanhua **107** 37 42N 118 8 E
Chani **108** 25 36N 103 49 E
Channapatna **97** 12 40N 77 15 E
Channel Is. **42** 49 30N 2 40W
Channel Islands **163** 33 30N 119 0W
Channing, Mich., U.S.A. **156** 46 9N 88 1W
Channing, Tex., U.S.A. **159** 35 45N 102 20W
Chantada **56** 42 36N 7 46W
Chanthaburi **100** 12 38N 102 12 E
Chantilly **43** 49 12N 2 29 E
Chantonnay **42** 46 40N 1 3W
Chantrey Inlet **148** 67 48N 96 20W
Chanute **159** 37 45N 85 25W
Chanyü **107** 44 39N 122 45 E
Chanza, R. **57** 37 49N 7 15W
Ch'ao Hu **109** 31 40N 117 30 E
Chao Phraya Lowlands **100** 15 30N 100 0 E
Chao Phraya, R. **100** 13 32N 100 36 E
Ch'aoan **109** 23 41N 116 33 E
Chaoan **109** 23 47N 117 5 E
Chaoch'eng, Shansi, China **106** 36 26N 111 43 E
Chaoch'eng, Shantung, China **106** 36 3N 115 35 E
Chaochiao **108** 28 1N 102 49 E
Chaoch'ing **109** 23 7N 112 24 E
Chaohsien **106** 37 45N 114 46 E
Ch'aohsien **109** 31 41N 117 49 E
Chaop'ing **109** 24 1N 110 59 E
Chaot'ung **108** 27 19N 103 42 E
Ch'aoyang, Kwangtung, China **109** 23 10N 116 30 E
Ch'aoyang, Liaoning, China **107** 41 46N 120 16 E
Chaoyüan, Heilungkiang, China **107** 45 30N 125 8 E
Chaoyüan, Shantung, China **107** 37 22N 120 24 E
Chap Kuduk **76** 48 45N 55 5 E
Chapala **127** 15 50 S 37 35 E
Chapala, Lago de **164** 20 10N 103 20W
Chaparmukh **98** 26 12N 92 31 E
Chapayevo **83** 50 25N 51 10 E
Chapayevsk **81** 53 0N 49 40 E
Chapecó **173** 27 14 S 52 41W
Chapel-en-le-Frith **32** 53 19N 1 54W
Chapel Hill **157** 35 53N 79 3W
Chapelle-d'Angillon, La **43** 47 21N 2 25 E
Chapelle Glain, La **42** 47 38N 1 11W
Chapeyevo **84** 50 12N 51 10 E
Chapleau **150** 47 50N 83 24W
Chaplin **153** 50 28N 106 40W
Chaplino **82** 48 8N 36 15 E
Chaplygin **81** 53 15N 39 55 E
Chapra **95** 25 48N 84 50 E
Char **116** 21 40N 12 45W
Chara **77** 56 54N 118 12 E
Charadai **172** 27 35 S 60 0W
Charagua **174** 19 45 S 63 10W
Charak **93** 26 46N 54 18 E
Charalá **174** 6 17N 73 10W
Charaña **174** 17 30 S 69 35W
Charapita **174** 0 37 S 74 21W
Charata **172** 27 13 S 61 14W
Charcas **164** 23 10N 101 20W
Charcoal L. **153** 58 49N 102 22W
Charcot I. **13** 70 0 S 75 0W
Chard, Can. **153** 55 55N 111 10W
Chard, U.K. **28** 50 52N 2 59W
Chardara **76** 41 16N 67 59 E
Chardara, Step **85** 42 20N 68 0 E
Charduar **98** 26 51N 92 46 E
Chardzhou **85** 39 6N 63 34 E
Charente-Maritime □ **44** 45 50N 0 35W
Charente □ **44** 45 50N 0 16W
Charente, R. **44** 45 41N 0 30W
Charentsavan **83** 40 35N 44 41 E
Chârib, G. **122** 28 6N 32 54 E
Charikar **93** 35 0N 69 10 E
Charing **29** 51 12N 0 49 E
Charité, La **43** 47 10N 3 0 E
Chariton R. **158** 39 19N 92 58W
Charkhari **95** 25 24N 79 45 E
Charkhi Dadri **94** 28 37N 76 17 E
Charlbury **28** 51 52N 1 29W
Charlemont **38** 54 26N 6 40W
Charleroi **47** 50 24N 4 27 E
Charles, C. **162** 37 10N 75 52W
Charles City, Iowa, U.S.A. **158** 43 2N 92 41W
Charles City, Va., U.S.A. **162** 37 20N 77 4W
Charles L. **153** 59 50N 110 33W
Charles, Pk. **137** 32 53 S 121 8 E
Charles Town **156** 39 20N 77 50W
Charleston, Miss., U.S.A. **159** 34 2N 90 3W
Charleston, Mo., U.S.A. **159** 36 52N 89 20W
Charleston, S.C., U.S.A. **157** 32 47N 79 56W
Charleston, W. Va., U.S.A. **157** 38 24N 81 36W
Charlestown, Ireland **38** 53 58N 8 48W
Charlestown, S. Afr. **129** 27 26 S 29 53 E
Charlestown, Ind., U.S.A. **156** 38 29N 85 40W
Charlestown, N.H., U.S.A. **162** 43 14N 72 24W
Charlestown of Aberlour **37** 57 27N 3 13W
Charlesville **124** 5 27 S 20 59 E
Charleville **139** 26 24 S 146 15 E
Charleville-Mézières **43** 49 44N 4 40 E
Charleville = Rath Luirc **39** 52 21N 8 40W
Charlevoix **156** 45 19N 85 14W
Charlieu **45** 46 10N 4 10 E
Charlotte, Mich., U.S.A. **156** 42 36N 84 48W
Charlotte, N.C., U.S.A. **157** 35 16N 80 46W
Charlotte Amalie **147** 18 22N 64 56W
Charlotte Harb. **157** 26 45N 82 10W
Charlotte Waters **136** 25 56N 134 54 E
Charlottenberg **72** 59 54N 12 17 E
Charlottesville **156** 38 1N 78 30W
Charlottetown **151** 46 14N 63 8W
Charlton, Austral. **140** 36 16 S 143 24 E
Charlton, U.S.A. **158** 40 59N 93 20W
Charlton I. **150** 52 0N 79 20W
Charlton Kings **28** 51 52N 2 3W
Charlwood **29** 51 8N 0 12W
Charmes **43** 48 22N 6 17 E
Charminster **28** 50 43N 2 28W
Charmouth **28** 50 45N 2 54W
Charnwood Forest **23** 52 43N 1 18W
Charny **151** 46 43N 71 15W
Charolles **45** 46 27N 4 16 E
Charost **43** 47 0N 2 7 E
Charouïne **118** 29 0N 0 15W
Charre **127** 17 19 S 35 10 E
Charroux **44** 46 9N 0 25 E
Charsadda **94** 34 7N 71 45 E
Charters Towers **138** 20 5 S 146 13 E
Chartham **29** 51 14N 1 1 E
Chartre, La **42** 47 42N 0 34 E
Chartres **42** 48 29N 1 30 E
Chascomús **172** 35 30 S 58 0W
Chasefu **127** 11 55 S 32 58 E
Chaslands Mistake **143** 46 38 S 169 22 E
Chasseneuil-sur-Bonnieure **44** 45 52N 0 29 E
Chata **94** 27 42N 77 30 E
Châtaigneraie, La **42** 46 38N 0 45W
Chatal Balkan = Udvoy Balkan **67** 42 50N 26 50 E
Château-Chinon **43** 47 4N 3 56 E
Château d'Oex **50** 46 28N 7 8 E

Château-du-Loir 42 47 40N 0 25 E
Château Gontier 42 47 50N 0 42W
Château-la-Vallière 42 47 30N 0 20 E
Château-Landon 43 48 8N 2 40 E
Château, Le 44 45 52N 1 12W
Château Porcien 43 49 31N 4 13 E
Château Renault 42 47 36N 0 56 E
Château-Salins 43 48 50N 6 30 E
Château-Thierry 43 49 3N 3 20 E
Châteaubourg 43 48 7N 1 25W
Châteaubriant 42 47 43N 1 23W
Châteaudun 42 48 3N 1 20 E
Châteaugiron 42 48 3N 1 30W
Châteaulin 42 48 11N 4 8W
Châteaumeillant 44 46 35N 2 12 E
Châteauneuf 42 48 35N 1 15 E
Châteauneuf-du-Faou 42 48 11N 3 50W
Châteauneuf-sur-Charente 44 45 36N 0 3W
Châteauneuf-sur-Cher 43 46 52N 2 18 E
Châteauneuf-sur-Loire 43 47 52N 2 13 E
Châteaurenard 45 43 53N 4 51 E
Châteauroux 43 46 50N 1 40 E
Châtel-Guyon 44 45 55N 3 4 E
Châtel St. Denis 50 46 32N 6 54 E
Châtelaillon-Plage 44 46 5N 1 5W
Châtelard, Le 50 46 4N 6 57 E
Châtelaudren 42 48 33N 2 59W
Chatelet 47 50 24N 4 32 E
Châtelet, Le, Cher, France 44 46 40N 2 20 E
Châtelet, Le, Seine et Marne, France 43 48 30N 2 47 E
Châtellerault 42 46 50N 0 30 E
Châtelus-Malvaleix 44 46 18N 2 1 E
Chatham, N.B., Can. 151 47 2N 65 28W
Chatham, Ont., Can. 150 42 24N 82 11W
Chatham, U.K. 29 51 22N 0 32 E
Chatham, Alaska, U.S.A. 147 57 30N 135 0W
Chatham, La., U.S.A. 159 32 22N 92 26W
Chatham, N.Y., U.S.A. 162 42 21N 73 32W
Chatham Is. 130 44 0 S 176 40W
Chatham Str. 152 57 0N 134 40W
Châtillon, Loiret, France 43 47 36N 2 44 E
Châtillon, Marne, France 43 49 5N 3 43 E
Chatillon 62 45 45N 7 40 E
Châtillon-Coligny 43 47 50N 2 51 E
Châtillon-en-Bazois 43 47 3N 3 39 E
Châtillon-en-Diois 45 44 41N 5 29 E
Châtillon-sur-Seine 43 47 50N 4 33 E
Châtillon-sur-Sèvre 42 46 56N 0 45W
Chatkal, R. 85 41 38N 70 1 E
Chatkalskiy Khrebet 85 41 30N 70 45 E
Chatmohar 95 24 15N 89 26 E
Chatra 95 24 12N 84 56 E
Chatrapur 96 19 22N 85 2 E
Châtre, La 44 46 35N 1 59 E
Chatsworth 127 19 32 S 30 46 E
Chatta-Hantō 111 34 45N 136 55 E
Chattahoochee 157 30 43N 84 51W
Chattanooga 157 35 2N 85 17W
Chatteris 29 52 27N 0 3 E
Chatton 35 55 34N 1 55W
Chaturat 100 15 34N 101 51 E
Chatyrkel, Ozero 85 40 40N 75 18 E
Chatyrtash 85 40 55N 76 25 E
Chau Phu 101 10 42N 105 7 E
Chaudes-Aigues 44 44 51N 3 1 E
Chauffailes 44 46 13N 4 20 E
Chauk 98 20 53N 94 49 E
Chaukan La 99 27 0N 97 15 E
Chaukan Pass 98 27 8N 97 10 E
Chaulnes 43 49 48N 2 47 E
Chaumont 43 48 7N 5 8 E
Chaumont-en-Vexin 43 49 16N 1 53 E
Chaumont-sur-Loire 42 47 29N 1 11 E
Chaunay 44 46 13N 0 9 E
Chauny 43 49 37N 3 12 E
Chausey, Îs. 42 48 52N 1 49W
Chaussin 43 46 59N 5 22 E
Chauvin 153 52 45N 110 10W
Chaux de Fonds, La 50 47 7N 6 50 E
Chaves, Brazil 170 0 15 S 49 55W
Chaves, Port. 56 41 45N 7 32W
Chavuma 125 13 10 S 22 55 E
Chawang 101 8 25N 99 30 E
Ch'aya 108 30 35N 98 3 E
Chayan 85 43 5N 69 25 E
Chayek 85 41 55N 74 30 E
Chaykovskiy 84 56 47N 54 9 E
Chazelles-sur-Lyon 45 45 39N 4 22 E
Cheadle, Gr. Manchester, U.K. 32 53 23N 2 14W
Cheadle, Staffs., U.K. 32 52 59N 1 59W
Cheadle Hulme 32 53 22N 2 12W
Cheb (Eger) 52 50 9N 12 20 E
Chebarkul 84 55 0N 60 25 E
Cheboksary 81 56 8N 47 30 E
Cheboygan 156 45 38N 84 29W
Chebsara 81 59 10N 38 45 E
Chech, Erg 118 25 0N 2 15W
Chechaouen 118 35 9N 5 15W
Chechen 83 43 59N 47 40 E
Chech'eng 106 34 4N 115 13 E
Checheno-Ingush, A.S.S.R. □ 83 43 30N 45 29 E
Chechon 107 37 8N 128 12 E
Checiny 54 50 46N 20 37 E
Checleset B. 152 50 5N 127 35W
Checotah 159 35 31N 95 30W
Chedabucto B. 151 45 25N 61 8W
Cheddar 28 51 16N 2 47W
Cheddleton 32 53 5N 2 2W
Cheduba I. 98 18 45N 93 40 E
Cheepie 139 26 43 S 144 59 E
Ch'eerhch'en Ho, R. 105 39 30N 88 15 E
Chef-Boutonne 44 46 7N 0 4W
Chefoo = Yent'ai 107 37 30N 121 12 E
Chefornak 147 60 10N 164 15W
Chegdomyn 77 51 7N 132 52 E
Chegga 118 25 15N 5 40W
Chehalis 160 46 44N 122 59W
Cheju 107 33 28N 126 30 E
Cheju Do 107 33 29N 126 34 E
Chejung 109 27 13N 119 52 E
Chekalin 81 54 10N 36 10 E
Chekao 109 31 46N 117 45 E
Chekiang □ 109 29 30N 120 0 E
Chela, Sa. da 128 16 20 S 13 20 E
Chelan, Can. 153 52 38N 103 22 E
Chelan, U.S.A. 160 47 49N 120 0W
Chelan, L. 152 48 5N 120 30W
Cheleken 76 39 26N 53 7 E
Chelforó 176 39 0 S 66 40W
Chéliff, O. 118 36 0N 0 8 E
Chelkar 76 47 40N 59 32 E
Chelkar Tengiz, Solonchak 76 48 0N 62 30 E
Chellala Dahrania 118 33 2N 0 1 E
Chelles 43 48 52N 2 33 E
Chełm 54 51 8N 23 30 E
Chełm □ 54 51 15N 23 30 E
Chelmarsh 28 52 29N 2 25W
Chełmek 54 50 6N 19 16 E
Chelmer, R. 29 51 45N 0 42 E
Chełmno 54 53 20N 18 30 E
Chelmsford 29 51 44N 0 29 E
Chełmża 54 53 10N 18 39 E
Chelsea, Austral. 141 38 5 S 145 8 E
Chelsea, Okla., U.S.A. 159 36 35N 95 25W
Chelsea, Vermont, U.S.A. 162 43 59N 72 27W
Cheltenham 28 51 55N 2 5W
Chelva 58 39 45N 1 0W
Chelyabinsk 84 55 10N 61 24 E
Chelyuskin, C. 86 77 30N 103 0 E
Chemainus 152 48 55N 123 48W
Chemikovsk 78 56 31N 58 11 E
Chemillé 42 47 14N 0 45W
Chemnitz = Karl-Marx-Stadt 48 50 50N 12 55 E
Chemor 101 4 44N 101 6 E
Chemult 160 43 14N 121 54W
Chen, Gora 77 65 10N 141 20 E
Chenab, R. 94 30 40N 73 30 E
Chenachane, O. 118 25 30N 3 30W
Chenan 106 33 16N 109 1 E
Chenango Forks 162 42 15N 75 51W
Chencha 123 6 15N 37 32 E
Ch'ench'i 109 28 1N 110 13 E
Ch'enchiachiang 107 34 25N 119 50 E
Chenchiang 109 32 12N 119 27 E
Chenchieh 108 23 15N 107 9 E
Chênée 47 50 37N 5 37 E
Cheney 160 47 38N 117 34W
Chenfeng 108 25 25N 105 51 E
Chengan 108 28 30N 107 30 E
Ch'engch'eng 106 35 6N 109 52 E
Ch'engchiang 108 24 40N 102 55 E
Chengchou 106 34 38N 113 43 E
Chengchow = Chengchou 106 34 38N 113 43 E
Chengelee 98 28 47N 96 16 E
Chengho 109 27 25N 118 46 E
Ch'enghsi Hu 109 32 22N 116 12 E
Ch'enghsien, Chekiang, China 109 29 30N 120 48 E
Ch'enghsien, Kansu, China 106 33 42N 105 36 E
Ch'engk'ou 108 31 58N 108 48 E
Ch'engku 106 33 9N 107 22 E
Ch'engkung 108 24 53N 102 45 E
Ch'engmai 100 19 44N 109 59 E
Ch'engpu 109 26 12N 110 5 E
Ch'engte 107 41 0N 117 58 E
Chengting 106 38 8N 114 37 E
Ch'engtu 108 30 45N 104 0 E
Ch'engtung Hu 109 32 17N 116 23 E
Ch'engtzut'uan 107 39 30N 122 30 E
Ch'engwu 106 35 0N 115 56 E
Ch'engyang 107 36 20N 120 16 E
Chengyang 109 32 36N 114 23 E
Chengyangkuan 109 32 29N 116 37 E
Chenhai 109 29 57N 121 42 E
Ch'enhsien 109 25 48N 113 2 E
Chenhsiung 108 27 27N 104 50 E
Chenhsü 109 27 20N 120 16 E
Chenkán 165 19 8N 90 58W
Chenk'ang 108 24 4N 99 18 E
Chenlai 107 45 52N 123 12 E
Chenning 108 25 57N 105 51 E
Chenp'ing 106 33 2N 112 14 E
Ch'enp'ing 108 31 52N 109 31 E
Chenyüan, Kansu, China 106 35 59N 107 2 E
Chenyüan, Kweichow, China 108 27 0N 108 20 E
Cheo Reo = Hau Bon 101 13 25N 108 28 E
Cheom Ksan 100 14 13N 104 56 E
Chepelare 67 41 44N 24 40 E
Chepén 174 7 10 S 79 15W
Chepes 172 31 20 S 66 35W
Chepo 166 9 10N 79 6W
Chepstow 31 51 38N 2 40W
Cheptsa, R. 81 58 36N 50 4 E
Cheptulil, Mt. 126 1 25N 35 35 E
Chequamegon B. 158 46 40N 90 30W
Chequeche 127 14 13 S 38 30 E
Cher □ 43 47 10N 2 30 E
Chér, R. 43 47 10N 2 10 E
Cheran 98 25 45N 90 44 E
Cherasco 62 44 39N 7 50 E
Cheratte 47 50 40N 5 41 E
Cheraw 157 34 42N 79 54W
Cherbourg 42 49 39N 1 40W
Cherchell 118 36 35N 2 12 E
Cherdakly 81 54 25N 48 50 E
Cherdyn 84 60 24N 56 29 E
Cheremkhovo 77 53 32N 102 40 E
Cherepanovo 76 54 15N 83 30 E
Cherepovets 81 59 5N 37 55 E
Chergui, Chott Ech 118 34 10N 0 25 E
Cheri 121 13 26N 11 21 E
Cherikov 80 53 32N 31 20 E
Cheriton 28 51 3N 1 9W
Cheriton Fitzpaine 30 50 51N 3 38W
Cherkessk 83 44 25N 42 10 E
Cherlak 76 54 15N 74 55 E
Chermoz 84 58 46N 56 10 E
Chernak 85 43 24N 68 2 E
Chernaya Kholunitsa 84 58 51N 51 52 E
Cherni, Mt. 67 42 35N 23 18 E
Chernigov 80 51 28N 31 20 E
Chernikovsk 84 54 48N 56 8 E
Chernobyl 80 51 13N 30 15 E
Chernogorsk 77 54 5N 91 10 E
Chernomorskoye 82 45 31N 32 46 E
Chernovskoye 81 58 48N 47 20 E
Chernovtsy 82 48 0N 26 0 E
Chernoye 77 70 30N 89 10 E
Chernushka 84 56 29N 56 3 E
Chernyakhovsk 80 54 29N 21 48 E
Chernyshevskiy 77 62 40N 112 30 E
Chernyshkovskiy 83 48 30N 42 28 E
Cherokee, Iowa, U.S.A. 158 42 40N 95 30W
Cherokee, Okla., U.S.A. 159 36 45N 98 25W
Cherokees, L. of the 159 36 50N 95 12W
Cherquenco 176 38 35 S 72 0W
Cherrapunji 99 25 17N 91 47 E
Cherry Creek 160 39 50N 114 58W
Cherry Valley, U.S.A. 162 42 48N 74 45W
Cherry Valley, U.S.A. 163 33 59N 116 57W
Cherryvale 159 37 20N 95 33W
Cherskiy 77 68 45N 161 18 E
Cherskogo Khrebet 77 65 0N 143 0 E
Chertkovo 83 49 25N 40 19 E
Chertsey 29 51 23N 0 30W
Cherven 80 53 45N 28 13 E
Cherven-Bryag 67 43 17N 24 7 E
Cherwell, R. 28 51 46N 1 18W
Chesapeake Bay 162 38 0N 76 12W
Chesapeake Beach 162 38 41N 76 32W
Chesha B. = Cheshskaya G. 78 67 20N 47 0 E
Chesham 29 51 42N 0 36W
Cheshire □ 32 53 14N 2 30W
Cheshunt 29 51 42N 0 1W
Chesil Beach 23 50 37N 2 33W
Cheslatta L. 152 53 49N 125 20W
Chesne, Le 43 49 30N 4 45 E
Cheste 59 39 30N 0 41W
Chester, U.K. 32 53 12N 2 53W
Chester, Calif., U.S.A. 160 40 22N 121 22W
Chester, Ill., U.S.A. 158 37 58N 89 50W
Chester, Mont., U.S.A. 160 48 31N 111 0W
Chester, Pa., U.S.A. 162 39 54N 75 20W
Chester, S.C., U.S.A. 157 34 44N 81 13W
Chester, Va., U.S.A. 162 37 21N 77 27W
Chester, Vt., U.S.A. 162 43 16N 72 36W
Chester-le-Street 33 54 53N 1 34W
Chesterfield, Can. 148 63 0N 91 0W
Chesterfield, U.K. 33 53 14N 1 26W
Chesterfield, U.S.A. 162 37 23N 77 31W
Chesterfield I. 129 16 20 S 43 58 E
Chesterfield, Îles 133 19 52 S 158 15 E
Chesterfield Inlet 148 63 30N 90 45W
Chesterton Range 138 25 30 S 147 27 E
Chestertown 162 39 13N 76 4W
Chesuncook L. 151 46 0N 69 10W
Chetaibi 119 37 1N 7 20 E
Cheticamp 151 46 37N 60 59W
Chetumal 165 18 30N 88 20W
Chetumal, Bahía de 165 18 40N 88 10W
Chetwynd 152 55 45N 121 45W
Chevanceaux 44 45 18N 0 14W
Cheviot Hills 35 55 20N 2 30W
Cheviot Ra. 138 25 20 S 143 45 E
Cheviot, The 35 55 29N 2 8W
Chew Bahir 123 4 40N 30 50 E
Chew Magna 28 51 21N 2 37W
Chewelah 160 48 17N 117 43W
Cheyenne, Okla., U.S.A. 159 35 40N 99 40W
Cheyenne, Wyo., U.S.A. 158 41 9N 104 49W
Cheyenne, R. 158 44 50N 101 0W
Cheyenne Wells 158 38 51N 102 23W
Cheylard, Le 45 44 55N 4 25 E
Cheyne B. 137 34 35 S 118 50 E
Chhabra 94 24 40N 76 54 E
Chhang 102 12 15N 104 14 E
Chhatak 95 25 5N 91 37 E
Chhatarpur 95 24 55N 79 43 E
Chhep 100 13 45N 105 24 E
Chhindwara 95 22 2N 78 59 E
Chhlong 101 12 15N 105 58 E
Chhuk 101 10 46N 104 8 E
Chi, R. 100 15 11N 104 43 E
Chiaho 109 25 33N 112 15 E
Chiahsiang 106 35 25N 116 21 E
Chiahsien, Hensi, China 106 38 6N 110 28 E
Chiahsien, Honan, China 106 33 58N 113 13 E
Chiahsing 109 30 45N 120 43 E
Chiai 109 23 29N 120 25 E
Chiali 109 23 10N 120 11 E
Chialing Chiang, R. 108 30 2N 106 19 E
Chiamussu 105 46 50N 130 21 E
Chian, Kiangsi, China 109 27 8N 115 0 E
Chian, Kirin, China 107 41 6N 126 10 E
Chiang Dao 100 19 22N 98 58 E
Chiang Kham 100 19 32N 100 18 E
Chiang Khan 100 17 52N 101 36 E
Chiang Khong 100 20 17N 100 24 E
Chiang Mai 100 18 47N 98 59 E
Chiang Saen 100 20 16N 100 5 E
Chiangch'eng 108 22 36N 101 50 E
Chiangchiat'un 107 40 54N 120 36 E
Chiangching 108 29 13N 106 15 E
Chiangchun 109 23 5N 120 5 E
Chianghua 109 25 2N 111 45 E
Chiangk'ou 108 27 42N 108 50 E
Chiangling 109 30 21N 112 5 E
Chiangmen 109 22 37N 113 3 E
Chiangpei 108 29 47N 106 29 E
Chiangp'ing 108 21 36N 108 8 E
Chiangshan 109 28 45N 118 37 E
Chiangta 108 31 28N 99 12 E
Chiangti 108 27 1N 103 37 E
Chiangyin 109 31 50N 120 18 E
Chiangyü 108 31 47N 104 45 E
Chiangyung 109 25 16N 111 20 E
Chianie 125 15 35 S 13 40 E
Ch'iaochia 108 26 57N 103 3 E
Chiaochou Wan 107 36 10N 120 15 E
Chiaoho, Hopei, China 106 38 1N 116 17 E
Chiaoho, Kirin, China 107 43 42N 127 19 E
Chiaohsien 107 36 20N 120 0 E
Chiaoling 109 24 40N 117 10 E
Chiaotso 106 35 17N 113 18 E
Chiapa de Corzo 165 16 42N 93 0W
Chiapa, R. 165 16 42N 93 0W
Chiapas □ 165 17 0N 92 45W
Chiaramonte Gulfi 65 37 1N 14 41 E
Chiaravalle 63 38 41N 16 24 E
Chiaravalle Centrale 65 38 41N 16 25 E
Chiari 62 45 31N 9 55 E
Chiashan 109 32 37N 118 8 E
Chiasso 51 45 50N 9 0 E
Chiating 109 31 21N 121 15 E
Chiautla 165 18 18N 98 34W
Chiávari 62 44 20N 9 20 E
Chiavenna 62 46 18N 9 23 E
Chiawang 107 34 30N 117 22 E
Chiayü 109 29 59N 113 54 E
Chiba 111 35 30N 140 7 E
Chiba-ken □ 111 35 30N 140 20 E
Chibabava 129 20 25 S 33 35 E
Chibemba 125 15 48 S 14 8 E
Chibougamau 150 49 56N 74 24W
Chibougamau L. 150 49 50N 74 20W
Chibougamau, R. 150 49 50N 75 40W
Chibuk 121 10 52N 12 50 E
Chibuto 129 24 40 S 33 33 E
Chic-Chocs, Mts. 151 48 55N 66 0W
Chic-Chocs, Parc Prov. des 151 48 55N 66 20W
Chicacole = Srikakulam 97 18 14N 84 4 E
Chicago 156 41 53N 87 40W
Chicago Heights 156 41 29N 87 37W
Chicago North 156 42 20N 87 50W
Chichagof I. 152 58 0N 136 0W
Chichaoua 118 31 32N 8 44W
Chichén Itzá 165 20 40N 88 32W
Chichester 29 50 50N 0 47W
Chichester Ra. 136 21 35 S 117 45 E
Chich'i 109 30 4N 118 34 E
Ch'ichiang 108 29 0N 106 40 E
Chichibu 111 35 5N 139 10 E
Ch'ich'ihaerh 105 47 22N 123 57 E
Chichiriviche 174 10 56N 68 16W
Ch'ich'un 109 30 14N 115 25 E
Chickasha 159 35 0N 98 0W
Chicken Hd. 31 58 10N 6 15W
Chiclana de la Frontera 57 36 26N 6 9W
Chiclayo 174 6 42 S 79 50W
Chico 160 39 45N 121 54W
Chico, R., Chubut, Argent. 160 44 0 S 67 0W
Chico, R., Santa Cruz, Argent. 176 49 30 S 69 30W
Chicoa 125 15 35 S 32 20 E
Chicomo 129 24 31 S 34 6 E
Chicontepec 165 20 58N 98 10W
Chicopee 162 42 6N 72 37W
Chicoutimi 151 48 28N 71 5W
Chidambaram 97 11 20N 79 45 E
Chiddingfold 29 51 6N 0 37W
Chidenguele 129 24 55 S 34 2 E
Chidley C. 149 60 23N 64 26W
Chiehhsiu 106 37 0N 111 55 E
Ch'iehmo 105 38 8N 85 32 E
Chiehshou 106 33 20N 115 24 E
Chiehyang 109 23 37N 116 19 E
Chiem Hoa 100 22 12N 105 17 E
Chiemsee 49 47 53N 12 27 E
Chiench'ang 107 41 16N 124 28 E
Chiench'angying 107 40 8N 118 50 E
Ch'iench'engchen 108 27 12N 109 50 E

Place	Page	Lat.	Long.
Ch'ienchiang, Hupeh, China	**109**	30 25N	112 51 E
Ch'ienchiang, Kwangsi-Chuang, China	**108**	23 40N	108 58 E
Ch'ienchiang, Szechwan, China	**108**	29 31N	108 46 E
Chiench'uan	**108**	26 28N	99 52 E
Chiengi	**124**	8 45 S	29 10 E
Chienho	**108**	26 39N	108 35 E
Ch'ienhsi	**108**	27 3N	106 0 E
Ch'ienhsien	**106**	34 30N	108 10 E
Chienko	**108**	32 0N	105 23 E
Chienli	**109**	29 49N	112 53 E
Chienou	**109**	27 5N	118 20 E
Ch'ienshan, Anhwei, China	**109**	30 41N	116 35 E
Ch'ienshan, Kiangsi, China	**109**	28 18N	117 40 E
Chienshih	**108**	30 40N	109 43 E
Chienshui	**108**	23 37N	102 49 E
Chiente	**109**	29 29N	119 16 E
Chienti, R.	**63**	43 15N	13 30 E
Chienwei	**108**	29 13N	103 56 E
Chienyang	**109**	27 21N	118 5 E
Ch'ienyang, Hunan, China	**109**	27 18N	110 10 E
Ch'ienyang, Kansu, China	**106**	34 35N	107 2 E
Chienyang	**108**	30 24N	104 33 E
Chierhkalang	**107**	43 6N	122 54 E
Chieri	**62**	45 0N	7 50 E
Chiese, R.	**62**	45 45N	10 35 E
Chieti	**63**	42 22N	14 10 E
Chièvres	**47**	50 35N	3 48 E
Chigasaki	**111**	35 19N	139 24 E
Chignecto B.	**151**	45 48N	64 40W
Chignik	**147**	56 15N	158 27W
Chigorodó	**174**	7 41N	76 42W
Chiguana	**172**	21 0 S	67 50W
Chihari	**107**	38 40N	126 30 E
Ch'ihch'i	**109**	21 59N	112 58 E
Chihchiang, Hunan, China	**108**	27 27N	109 41 E
Chihchiang, Hupei, China	**109**	30 19N	111 30 E
Chihchin	**108**	26 42N	105 45 E
Ch'ihfeng	**107**	42 18N	118 57 E
Chihkou	**107**	35 55N	119 13 E
Chihli, G. of = Po Hai	**107**	38 40N	119 0 E
Ch'ihshui	**108**	29 29N	105 38 E
Ch'ihshui Ho, R.	**108**	28 53N	105 48 E
Chihsi	**107**	45 20N	130 55 E
Ch'ihsien	**106**	34 33N	114 47 E
Chihsien, Honan, China	**106**	35 25N	114 5 E
Chihsien, Hopei, China	**106**	37 34N	115 34 E
Chihsien, Shansi, China	**106**	36 8N	110 39 E
Chihtan	**106**	36 56N	108 47 E
Chihte	**109**	30 9N	117 0 E
Chihuahua	**164**	28 40N	106 3W
Chihuahua □	**164**	28 40N	106 3W
Chihuatlán	**164**	19 14N	104 35W
Chiili	**85**	44 20N	66 15 E
Chik Ballapur	**97**	13 25N	77 45 E
Chikawawa	**127**	16 2 S	34 50 E
Chikhli	**96**	20 20N	76 18 E
Chikmagalur	**97**	13 15N	75 45 E
Chikodi	**96**	16 26N	74 38 E
Chikonde	**127**	12 16 S	31 38 E
Ch'ik'ou	**107**	38 37N	117 35 E
Chikugo	**110**	33 14N	130 28 E
Chikuma-Gawa, R.	**111**	36 59N	138 35 E
Chilac	**165**	18 20N	97 24W
Chilako, R.	**152**	53 53N	122 57W
Chilam Chavki	**95**	35 5N	75 5 E
Chilanga	**127**	15 33 S	28 16 E
Chilant'ai	**106**	39 45N	105 45 E
Chilapa	**165**	17 40N	99 20W
Chilas	**95**	35 25N	74 5 E
Chilaw	**93**	7 30N	79 50 E
Chilcotin, R.	**152**	51 44N	122 23W
Childers	**139**	25 15 S	152 17 E
Childress	**159**	34 30N	100 50W
Chile ■	**176**	35 0 S	71 15W
Chilecito	**172**	29 0 S	67 40W
Chilete	**174**	7 10 S	78 50W
Chilham	**29**	51 15N	0 59 E
Chilik, Kazakh S.S.R., U.S.S.R.	**84**	51 7N	53 55 E
Chilik, Kirgiz S.S.R., U.S.S.R.	**85**	43 33N	78 17 E
Chililabombwe (Bancroft)	**125**	12 18 S	27 43 E
Chilin	**105**	43 53N	126 38 E
Ch'ilin Hu	**105**	31 50N	89 0 E
Chilka L.	**96**	19 40N	85 25 E
Chilko, L.	**152**	52 60N	124 10W
Chilko, R.	**152**	52 6N	124 9W
Chillagoe	**138**	17 14 S	144 33 E
Chillán	**172**	36 40 S	72 10W
Chillicothe, Ill., U.S.A.	**158**	40 55N	89 32W
Chillicothe, Mo., U.S.A.	**158**	39 45N	93 30W
Chillicothe, Ohio, U.S.A.	**156**	39 53N	82 58W
Chilliwack	**152**	49 10N	122 0W
Chilo	**94**	27 12N	73 32 E
Chiloane, I.	**129**	20 40 S	34 55 E
Chiloé, I. de	**176**	42 50 S	73 45W
Chilpancingo	**165**	17 30N	99 40W
Chiltern	**141**	36 10 S	146 36 E
Chiltern Hills	**29**	51 44N	0 42W
Chilton	**156**	44 1N	88 12W
Chiluage	**124**	9 15 S	21 42 E
Chilubula	**127**	10 14 S	30 51 E
Chilumba	**127**	10 28 S	34 12 E
Chilung	**109**	25 3N	121 45 E
Chilwa, L. (Shirwa)	**127**	15 15 S	35 40 E
Chimacum	**160**	48 1N	122 53W
Chimaltitán	**164**	21 46N	103 50W
Chimán	**166**	8 45N	78 40W
Chimay	**47**	50 3N	4 20 E
Chimbay	**76**	42 57N	59 47 E
Chimborazo	**174**	1 20 S	78 55W
Chimbote	**174**	9 0 S	78 35W
Ch'imen	**109**	29 56N	117 47 E
Chimion	**85**	40 15N	71 32 E
Chimishliya	**70**	46 34N	28 44 E
Chimkent	**85**	42 18N	69 36 E
Chimo	**107**	36 23N	120 27 E
Chimpembe	**127**	9 31 S	29 33 E
Chin □	**98**	22 0N	93 0 E
Chin Chiang, R.	**109**	28 23N	115 48 E
Chin Hills	**98**	22 30N	93 30 E
Chin Ho, R.	**106**	35 2N	113 25 E
Chin Ling Shan	**106**	34 0N	107 0 E
Ch'in Shui, R.	**109**	26 13N	115 15 E
China	**164**	25 40N	99 20W
China ■	**105**	30 0N	110 0 E
China Lake	**163**	35 44N	117 37W
Chinacates	**164**	25 0N	105 14W
Chinacota	**174**	7 37N	72 36W
Ch'inan	**106**	34 50N	105 35 E
Chinan	**106**	36 32N	117 0 E
Chinandega	**166**	12 30N	87 0W
Chinati Pk.	**159**	30 0N	104 25W
Chincha Alta	**174**	13 20 S	76 0W
Chinch'eng	**106**	35 30N	112 50 E
Chinchi	**106**	37 57N	106 6 E
Chinch'i	**109**	27 54N	116 44 E
Chinchiang, Fukien, China	**109**	24 54N	118 35 E
Chinchiang, Kiangsi, China	**109**	29 44N	115 59 E
Chinchiang, Yunnan, China	**108**	26 14N	100 34 E
Chinchilla	**139**	26 45 S	150 38 E
Chinchilla de Monte Aragón	**59**	38 53N	1 40W
Chinchón	**58**	40 9N	3 26W
Chinchorro, Banco	**165**	18 35N	87 20W
Ch'inchou	**108**	21 58N	108 35 E
Chinchou	**107**	41 8N	121 6 E
Chinch'uan	**108**	31 30N	101 55 E
Chincoteague	**162**	37 58N	75 21W
Chincoteague B.	**162**	38 5N	75 8W
Chinde	**127**	18 45 S	36 30 E
Chindo	**107**	34 28N	126 15 E
Chindwin, R.	**98**	21 26N	95 15 E
Chineni	**95**	33 2N	75 15 E
Ch'ing Chiang, R.	**109**	29 51N	112 22 E
Ch'ing Hai	**105**	37 0N	100 20 E
Ching Ho, R.	**106**	34 29N	109 5 E
Ching Shan	**109**	31 40N	111 30 E
Chinga	**127**	15 13 S	38 35 E
Chingan	**109**	28 52N	115 22 E
Ch'ingchen	**108**	26 32N	106 30 E
Ch'ingch'eng	**107**	37 11N	117 42 E
Chingchiang	**109**	32 2N	120 16 E
Ch'ingchiang, Kiangsi, China	**109**	28 5N	115 30 E
Ch'ingchiang, Kiangsu, China	**107**	33 33N	119 4 E
Ch'ingchien	**106**	37 12N	110 6 E
Chingch'uan	**106**	35 15N	107 22 E
Ch'ingfeng	**106**	35 54N	115 7 E
Chinghai	**106**	38 56N	116 55 E
Ch'inghomen	**107**	41 45N	121 25 E
Chinghsi	**108**	23 8N	106 25 E
Ch'inghsien	**106**	38 35N	116 48 E
Chinghsien	**109**	30 42N	118 23 E
Ch'inghsü	**106**	37 40N	112 20 E
Chinghung	**108**	22 0N	100 49 E
Chingi Chiang, R.	**108**	29 32N	103 44 E
Chingku	**108**	23 28N	100 42 E
Chingleput	**97**	12 42N	79 58 E
Ch'ingliu	**109**	26 12N	116 48 E
Chinglo	**106**	38 24N	111 54 E
Ch'inglung	**108**	25 48N	105 14 E
Chingmen	**109**	30 58N	112 6 E
Chingning, Chekiang, China	**109**	27 58N	119 38 E
Chingning, Kansu, China	**106**	35 30N	105 45 E
Chingola	**127**	12 31 S	27 53 E
Chingole	**127**	13 4 S	34 17 E
Chingpien	**106**	37 24N	108 36 E
Chingpo Hu	**107**	43 50N	128 50 E
Ch'ingp'u	**109**	31 9N	121 6 E
Chingshan	**109**	31 2N	113 3 E
Chingshih	**109**	29 40N	111 50 E
Ch'ingshui	**106**	34 44N	106 2 E
Chingsing	**106**	38 5N	114 8 E
Chingt'ai	**106**	37 10N	104 8 E
Ch'ingtao	**107**	36 5N	120 25 E
Chingte	**109**	30 19N	118 31 E
Chingtechen	**109**	29 19N	117 15 E
Ch'ingt'ien	**109**	28 9N	120 17 E
Chingtung	**108**	24 22N	100 50 E
Chingtzukuan	**106**	33 13N	111 2 E
Chinguar	**125**	12 18 S	16 45 E
Chinguetti	**116**	20 25N	12 15W
Chingune	**129**	20 33 S	35 0 E
Ch'ingyang	**105**	36 5N	107 40 E
Chingyang	**106**	34 32N	108 52 E
Ch'ingyang, Anhwei, China	**109**	30 38N	117 50 E
Ch'ingyang, Ningsia Hui, China	**106**	36 5N	107 40 E
Chingyü	**107**	42 22N	126 45 E
Chingyüan	**106**	36 35N	104 40 E
Ch'ingyüan, Chekiang, China	**109**	27 37N	119 3 E
Ch'ingyüan, Kwangtung, China	**109**	23 42N	112 58 E
Ch'ingyüan, Liaoning, China	**107**	42 6N	124 55 E
Ch'ingyün	**107**	37 53N	117 23 E
Chinhae	**107**	35 9N	128 40 E
Chinhanguanine	**129**	25 21 S	32 30 E
Chinhsi	**107**	40 49N	120 55 E
Chinhsiang	**106**	35 5N	116 18 E
Chinhsien, Hopei, China	**106**	38 2N	115 2 E
Chinhsien, Kiangsi, China	**109**	28 22N	116 14 E
Chinhsien, Liaoning, China	**107**	39 6N	121 3 E
Chinhua	**109**	29 9N	119 41 E
Ch'inhuangtao	**107**	39 57N	119 40 E
Chining, Inner Mongolia, China	**106**	41 2N	113 8 E
Chining, Shantung, China	**106**	35 19N	116 36 E
Chiniot	**94**	31 45N	73 0 E
Chinipas	**164**	27 22N	108 32W
Chinju	**107**	35 12N	128 2 E
Chink'ou	**109**	30 20N	114 7 E
Chinle	**161**	36 14N	109 38W
Chinmen	**109**	24 27N	118 21 E
Chinmen Tao, I.	**109**	24 25N	118 25 E
Chinnamanur	**97**	9 50N	77 16 E
Chinnampo	**107**	38 52N	125 28 E
Chinning	**108**	24 40N	102 35 E
Chinnur	**96**	18 57N	79 43 E
Chino, Japan	**111**	35 59N	138 9 E
Chino, U.S.A.	**163**	34 1N	117 41W
Chino Valley	**161**	34 54N	112 28W
Chinon	**42**	47 10N	0 15 E
Chinook, Can.	**153**	51 28N	110 59W
Chinook, U.S.A.	**160**	48 35N	109 19W
Chinp'ing, Kweichow, China	**108**	26 40N	109 7 E
Chinp'ing, Yunnan, China	**108**	22 46N	103 15 E
Chinsali	**124**	10 30 S	32 2 E
Chinsha	**108**	27 29N	106 15 E
Chinsha Chiang, R. = Yangtze Chiang, R.	**108**	27 30N	99 30 E
Chinshan	**109**	30 3N	121 13 E
Ch'inshui	**106**	35 41N	112 11 E
Chintamani	**97**	13 26N	78 3 E
Chint'an	**109**	31 45N	119 35 E
Chint'ang	**108**	30 51N	104 27 E
Chinwangtao = Ch'inhuangtao	**107**	39 57N	119 40 E
Ch'inyang	**106**	35 5N	112 55 E
Ch'inyüan	**106**	36 31N	112 15 E
Chióggia	**63**	45 13N	12 15 E
Chíos = Khíos	**69**	38 27N	26 9 E
Chip Lake	**152**	53 35N	115 35W
Chipai L.	**150**	52 56N	87 53W
Chipata (Ft . Jameson)	**127**	13 38 S	32 28 E
Chipewyan L.	**153**	58 0N	98 27W
Chipinga	**127**	20 13 S	32 36 E
Chipiona	**57**	36 44N	6 26W
Chipley	**157**	30 45N	85 32W
Chiplun	**96**	17 31N	73 34 E
Chipman	**151**	46 6N	65 53W
Chipoka	**127**	13 57 S	34 28 E
Chiporovtsi	**66**	43 24N	22 52 E
Chippenham	**28**	51 27N	2 7W
Chippewa Falls	**158**	44 55N	91 22W
Chippewa, R.	**158**	44 45N	91 55W
Chipping Campden	**28**	52 4N	1 48W
Chipping Norton	**28**	51 56N	1 32W
Chipping Ongar	**29**	51 43N	0 15 E
Chipping Sodbury	**28**	51 31N	2 23W
Chiquian	**174**	10 10 S	77 0W
Chiquimula	**166**	14 51N	89 37W
Chiquinquirá	**174**	5 37N	73 50W
Chir, R.	**83**	48 45N	42 10 E
Chirala	**97**	15 50N	80 20 E
Chiramba	**127**	16 55 S	34 39 E
Chiran	**110**	31 22N	130 27 E
Chiras	**93**	35 14N	65 40 E
Chirawa	**94**	28 14N	75 42 E
Chirayinkil	**97**	8 41N	76 49 E
Chirbury	**28**	52 35N	3 6W
Chirchik	**85**	41 29N	69 35 E
Chirfa	**117**	20 55N	12 14 E
Chiricahua Pk.	**161**	31 53N	109 14W
Chirikof I.	**147**	55 50N	155 40W
Chiriquí, Golfo de	**166**	8 0N	82 10W
Chiriquí, Lago de	**166**	9 10N	82 0W
Chiriquí, Vol.	**166**	8 55N	82 35W
Chirivira Falls	**127**	21 10 S	32 12 E
Chirk	**31**	52 57N	3 4W
Chirmiri	**99**	23 15N	82 20 E
Chirnogi	**70**	44 7N	26 32 E
Chirnside	**35**	55 47N	2 11W
Chiromo	**125**	16 30 S	35 7 E
Chirpan	**67**	42 10N	25 19 E
Chirripó Grande, cerro	**166**	9 29N	83 29W
Chisamba	**127**	14 55 S	28 20 E
Chisapani Garhi	**99**	27 30N	84 2 E
Ch'ishan	**106**	34 28N	107 35 E
Chishan	**106**	35 36N	110 59 E
Ch'ishan	**109**	22 44N	120 31 E
Chishmy	**84**	54 35N	55 23 E
Chisholm	**152**	54 55N	114 10W
Chishou	**108**	28 12N	109 43 E
Chishui	**109**	27 14N	115 10 E
Chisimba Falls	**127**	10 12 S	30 56 E
Chisineu Criş	**66**	46 32N	21 37 E
Chisledon	**28**	51 30N	1 44W
Chisone, R.	**62**	45 0N	7 5 E
Chisos Mts.	**159**	29 20N	103 15W
Chistian Mandi	**94**	29 50N	72 55 E
Chistopol	**81**	55 25N	50 38 E
Chita, Colomb.	**174**	6 11N	72 28W
Chita, U.S.S.R.	**77**	52 0N	113 25 E
Chitado	**125**	17 10 S	14 8 E
Ch'it'ai	**105**	44 1N	89 28 E
Chitapur	**96**	17 10N	76 50 E
Chitembo	**125**	13 30 S	16 50 E
Chitina	**147**	61 30N	144 30W
Chitinghsilin	**105**	32 51N	92 28 E
Chitipa	**127**	9 41 S	33 19 E
Chitokoloki	**125**	13 43 S	23 4 E
Chitorgarh	**94**	24 52N	74 43 E
Chitrakot	**96**	19 20N	81 40 E
Chitral	**93**	35 50N	71 56 E
Chitravati, R.	**97**	14 30N	78 0 E
Chitré	**167**	7 59N	80 27W
Chitse	**106**	36 54N	114 52 E
Chittagong	**98**	22 19N	91 55 E
Chittagong □	**98**	24 5N	91 25 E
Chittoor	**97**	13 15N	79 5 E
Chittur	**97**	10 40N	76 45 E
Chitu	**123**	8 38N	37 58 E
Ch'itung, Hunan, China	**109**	26 47N	112 7 E
Ch'itung, Kiangsu, China	**109**	31 49N	121 40 E
Chiuant'u	**107**	42 33N	128 19 E
Chiuchaohua	**108**	32 20N	105 45 E
Chiuch'engch'i	**108**	27 10N	108 42 E
Chiuchiang, Kiangsi, China	**109**	29 43N	115 55 E
Chiuchiang, Kwangtung, China	**109**	22 50N	112 50 E
Chiuch'üan	**105**	39 46N	98 34 E
Chiuhsiangch'eng	**109**	33 13N	114 50 E
Chiukuanch'eng	**106**	35 50N	115 22 E
Chiuling Shan	**109**	28 50N	114 20 E
Chiuliuch'eng	**108**	24 32N	109 15 E
Chiulung	**108**	28 59N	101 32 E
Ch'iungchou Haihsia	**100**	20 10N	110 15 E
Ch'iunghai	**100**	19 15N	110 26 E
Chiunglai	**108**	30 25N	103 30 E
Chiunglai Shan	**108**	31 20N	102 50 E
Ch'iungshan	**100**	19 51N	110 26 E
Chiuningkang	**109**	26 48N	114 6 E
Ch'iupei	**108**	24 3N	104 12 E
Chiushench'iu	**106**	33 10N	115 8 E
Chiushengch'i	**108**	27 31N	109 12 E
Chiusi	**63**	43 1N	11 58 E
Chiut'ai	**107**	44 10N	125 49 E
Chiutaosha	**106**	35 39N	103 45 E
Chiuwuch'ing	**106**	39 23N	116 53 E
Chiva	**59**	39 27N	0 41W
Chivasso	**62**	45 10N	7 52 E
Chivilcoy	**172**	35 0 S	60 0W
Chiwanda	**127**	11 23 S	34 55 E
Chiwefwe	**127**	13 37 S	29 31 E
Chiyang	**107**	37 0N	117 13 E
Ch'iyang	**109**	20 35N	111 52 E
Chiyüan	**106**	35 5N	112 39 E
Chiyün	**109**	28 35N	120 2 E
Chizera	**127**	13 10 S	25 0 E
Chkalov = Orenburg	**78**	52 0N	55 5 E
Chkolovsk	**81**	56 50N	43 10 E
Chlumec	**52**	50 9N	15 29 E
Chmielnik	**54**	50 37N	20 43 E
Cho Bo	**100**	20 46N	105 10 E
Cho Do	**107**	38 30N	124 40 E
Cho Phuoc	**101**	10 26N	107 18 E
Choba	**126**	2 30N	38 5 E
Chobe National Park	**128**	21 30 S	25 0 E
Chobe, R.	**128**	18 10 S	24 10 E
Chobol	**121**	11 53N	13 1 E
Chochiwŏn	**107**	36 37N	127 18 E
Chocianów	**54**	51 35N	15 33 E
Chociwel	**54**	53 29N	15 21 E
Chocó □	**174**	6 0N	77 0W
Chocontá	**174**	5 9N	73 41W
Chodaków	**54**	52 16N	20 18 E
Chodavaram	**96**	17 40N	82 50 E
Chodecz	**54**	52 56N	19 2 E
Chodziez	**54**	52 58N	17 0 E
Choele Choel	**176**	39 11 S	65 40W
Chōfu	**111**	35 39N	139 33 E
Chohsien	**106**	39 30N	116 0 E
Choiseul I.	**130**	7 0 S	156 40 E
Choisy-le-Roi	**43**	48 45N	2 24 E
Choix	**164**	26 40N	108 10W
Chojna	**54**	52 58N	14 25 E
Chojnice	**54**	53 42N	17 40 E
Chojnów	**54**	51 25N	15 58 E
Choke Mts.	**123**	11 18N	37 15 E
Chokurdakh	**77**	70 38N	147 55 E
Cholame	**163**	35 44N	120 18W
Cholet	**42**	47 4N	0 52W
Chollerton	**35**	55 4N	2 7W
Cholpon-Ata	**85**	42 40N	77 6 E
Cholsey	**28**	51 34N	1 10W
Cholu	**106**	40 19N	115 5 E
Choluteca	**166**	13 20N	87 14W
Choluteca, R.	**166**	13 5N	87 20W
Chom Bung	**100**	13 37N	99 36 E
Chom Thong	**100**	18 25N	98 41 E
Choma	**127**	16 48 S	26 59 E
Chomen Swamp	**123**	9 20N	37 10 E

Chomu 94 27 15N 75 40 E
Chomutov 52 50 28N 13 23 E
Chon Buri 100 13 22N 100 59 E
Chon Thanh 101 11 24N 106 36 E
Chŏnan 107 36 48N 127 9 E
Chonburi 101 13 21N 101 1 E
Chone 174 0 40 S 80 0W
Chong Kai 100 13 57N 103 35 E
Chong Mek 100 15 10N 105 27 E
Chŏngdo 107 35 38N 128 42 E
Chŏngha 107 36 12N 129 21 E
Chŏngjin 107 41 47N 129 50 E
Chŏngju 107 39 40N 125 5 E
Chŏngułp 107 35 35N 126 50 E
Chŏnju 107 35 50N 127 4 E
Chonos, Arch. de los 176 45 0 S 75 0W
Chopda 96 21 20N 75 15 E
Chopim, R. 173 25 35 S 53 5W
Choptank, R. 162 38 41N 76 0W
Chorbat La 95 34 42N 76 37 E
Chorley 32 53 39N 2 39W
Chormet el Melah 119 30 11N 16 29 E
Chorolque, Cerro 172 20 59 S 66 5W
Choroszcz 54 53 10N 22 59 E
Chortkov 80 49 2N 25 46 E
Chorul Tso 95 32 30N 82 30 E
Chŏrwŏn 107 38 15N 127 10 E
Chorzele 54 53 15N 21 2 E
Chorzów 54 50 18N 19 0 E
Chos-Malal 172 37 15 S 70 5W
Chosan 107 40 50N 125 47 E
Choshi 111 35 45N 140 45 E
Choszczno 54 53 7N 15 25 E
Choteau 160 47 50N 112 10W
Chotila 94 22 30N 71 15 E
Chotzu 106 40 52N 112 33 E
Chou Shan 109 30 2N 122 6 E
Chouchih 106 34 8N 108 14 E
Chouch'ü 106 33 46N 104 18 E
Chouning 109 27 15N 119 13 E
Chouts'un 107 36 48N 117 52 E
Ch'ouyang 108 23 14N 104 35 E
Chowchilla 163 37 11N 120 12W
Chowkham 98 20 52N 97 28 E
Choybalsan 105 48 4N 114 30 E
Christchurch, N.Z. 143 43 33 S 172 47 E
Christchurch, U.K. 28 50 44N 1 47W
Christiana, S. Afr. 128 27 52 S 25 8 E
Christiana, U.S.A. 162 39 40N 75 40W
Christiansfeld 73 55 21N 9 29 E
Christiansö, I. 73 55 19N 15 12 E
Christiansted 147 17 45N 64 42W
Christie B. 153 62 32N 111 10W
Christina, R. 153 56 40N 111 3W
Christmas Cr. 136 18 53 S 125 55 E
Christmas Creek 136 18 29 S 125 23 E
Christmas I., Ind. Oc. 142 10 0 S 105 40 E
Christmas I., Pac. Oc. 131 1 58N 157 27W
Christopher L. 137 24 49 S 127 42 E
Chrudim 52 49 58N 15 43 E
Chrzanów 54 50 10N 19 21 E
Chtimba 127 10 35 S 34 13 E
Chu 85 43 36N 73 42 E
Ch'u Chiang, R. 108 30 2N 106 19 E
Chu Chua 152 51 22N 120 10W
Chu Lai 100 15 28N 108 45 E
Chu, R., U.S.S.R. 85 45 0N 67 44 E
Chu, R., Viet. 100 19 53N 105 45 E
Chuadanga 98 23 38N 88 51 E
Ch'üanchou, Fukien, China 109 24 56N 118 35 E
Ch'üanchou, Kwangsi-Chuang, China 109 25 59N 111 4 E
Chuangho 107 39 42N 123 0 E
Chüannan 109 24 50N 114 40 E
Chūbu □ 112 36 45N 137 30 E
Chubut, R. 176 43 0 S 70 0W
Chuch'eng 107 36 0N 119 16 E
Chuch'i 108 32 19N 109 52 E
Chuchi, Chekiang, China 109 29 43N 120 14 E
Chuchi, Honan, China 106 34 27N 115 39 E
Chuchi L. 152 55 12N 124 30W
Ch'uching 108 25 34N 103 45 E
Chuchou 109 27 50N 113 10 E
Chudleigh 30 50 35N 3 36W
Chudovo 80 59 10N 31 30 E
Chudskoye, Oz. 80 58 13N 27 30 E
Ch'üehshan 109 32 48N 114 1 E
Chugach Mts. 147 62 0N 146 0W
Chugiak 147 61 7N 149 10W
Chuginadak I. 147 52 50N 169 45W
Chūgoku □ 110 35 0N 133 0 E
Chūgoku-Sanchi 110 35 0N 133 0 E
Chuguyev 82 49 55N 36 45 E
Chugwater 158 41 48N 104 47W
Chuhai 109 22 17N 113 34 E
Chühsien 107 35 35N 118 49 E
Ch'uhsien, China 109 28 57N 118 58 E
Ch'uhsien, China 109 32 18N 118 18 E
Chuhsien 105 28 57N 118 58 E
Ch'ühsien 108 30 51N 107 1 E
Ch'uhsiung 108 25 2N 101 32 E
Chüjung 109 31 56N 119 10 E
Chukai 101 4 13N 103 25 E
Chukhloma 81 58 45N 42 40 E
Chūko 111 36 44N 139 27 E
Chukotskiy Khrebet 77 68 0N 175 0 E
Chukotskiy, Mys 77 66 10N 169 3 E
Chukotskoye More 77 68 0N 175 0W
Chula Vista 163 32 39N 117 8W
Chulak-Kurgan 85 43 46N 69 9 E
Chülu 106 37 13N 115 1 E
Chulucanas 174 5 0 S 80 0W
Chum Phae 100 16 32N 102 6 E
Chum Saeng 100 15 55N 100 15 E
Chumar 95 32 40N 78 35 E
Chumatien 109 33 0N 114 4 E
Chumbicha 172 29 0 S 66 10W
Chumerna 67 42 45N 25 55 E
Chumikan 77 54 40N 135 10 E
Chumphon 101 10 35N 99 14 E
Chumuare 127 14 31 S 31 50 E
Chumunjin 107 37 55N 127 44 E
Chunchŏn 107 37 58N 127 44 E
Chunga 127 15 0 S 26 2 E
Ch'ungan 109 27 45N 118 0 E
Ch'ungch'ing, Szechwan, China 108 29 30N 106 30 E
Ch'ungch'ing, Szechwan, China 108 30 27N 103 43 E
Chungch'üantzu 106 39 22N 102 42 E
Chunggang ŭp 107 41 48N 126 48 E
Chunghsiang 109 31 10N 112 35 E
Chunghsien 108 30 17N 108 4 E
Chunghwa 107 38 52N 125 47 E
Ch'ungi 109 25 42N 114 19 E
Ch'ungjen 109 27 44N 116 2 E
Chungju 107 36 58N 127 58 E
Chungkang 107 43 42N 127 37 E
Chungking = Ch'ungch'ing 108 29 30N 106 30 E
Ch'ungli 106 40 5N 115 12 E
Chungli 109 24 57N 121 13 E
Ch'ungming 109 31 27N 121 24 E
Ch'ungming Tao, I. 109 31 35N 121 40 E
Chungmu 107 34 50N 128 20 E
Chungning 106 35 22N 105 40 E
Chungshan, Kwangsi-Chuang, China 109 24 30N 111 17 E
Chungshan, Kwangtung, China 109 22 31N 113 20 E
Ch'ungshuiho 106 39 54N 111 34 E
Ch'ungte 109 30 32N 120 26 E
Chungt'iaoshan 106 35 0N 111 30 E
Chungtien 108 27 51N 99 42 E
Ch'ungtso 108 22 20N 107 20 E
Chungtu 108 24 41N 109 42 E
Chungwei 106 37 35N 105 10 E
Chungyang 106 37 24N 111 10 E
Chungyang Shanmo 109 23 10N 121 0 E
Chungyüan 100 19 9N 110 28 E
Chünhsien 109 32 40N 111 15 E
Chunian 94 31 10N 74 0 E
Chunya 127 8 30 S 33 27 E
Chunya □ 126 7 48 S 33 0 E
Ch'unyang 107 43 42N 129 26 E
Chuquibamba 174 15 47N 72 44W
Chuquicamata 172 22 15 S 69 0W
Chuquisaca □ 172 23 30 S 63 30W
Chur 51 46 52N 9 32 E
Churachandpur 98 24 20N 93 40 E
Church Hill 38 55 0N 7 53W
Church House 152 50 20N 125 10W
Church Stretton 28 52 32N 2 49W
Churchdown 28 51 53N 2 9W
Churchill 153 58 47N 94 11W
Churchill, C. 153 58 46N 93 12W
Churchill Falls 151 53 36N 64 19W
Churchill L. 153 55 55N 108 20W
Churchill Pk. 152 58 10N 125 10W
Churchill, R., Man., Can. 153 58 47N 94 12W
Churchill, R., Newf., Can. 151 53 19N 60 10W
Churchill, R., Sask., Can. 153 58 47N 94 12W
Churchtown 39 52 12N 6 20W
Churfisten 51 47 8N 9 17 E
Churston Ferrers 30 50 23N 3 32W
Churu 94 28 20N 75 0 E
Churuguaro 174 10 49N 69 32W
Churwalden 51 46 47N 9 33 E
Chusan 109 32 13N 110 24 E
Chushul 95 33 40N 78 40 E
Chusovaya, R. 84 58 18N 56 22 E
Chusovoy 84 58 15N 57 40 E
Chust 85 41 0N 71 13 E
Ch'ützu 106 36 24N 107 27 E
Chuuronjang 107 41 35N 129 40 E
Chuvash A.S.S.R. □ 81 55 30N 48 0 E
Chuwassu 108 28 48N 97 27 E
Ch'üwu 106 35 35N 111 23 E
Ch'üyang 106 38 37N 114 41 E
Chüyeh 106 35 23N 116 6 E
Ciacova 66 45 35N 21 10 E
Cicero 156 41 48N 87 48W
Cicero Dantas 170 10 36 S 38 23W
Cidacos, R. 58 42 15N 2 10W
Cide 82 41 40N 32 50 E
Ciechanów 54 52 52N 20 38 E
Ciechanów □ 54 53 0N 20 30 E
Ciechocinek 54 52 53N 18 45 E
Ciego de Avila 166 21 50N 78 50W
Ciénaga 174 11 1N 74 15W
Ciénaga de Oro 174 8 53N 75 37W
Cienfuegos 166 22 10N 80 30W
Cieplice Śląskie Zdrój 54 50 50N 15 40 E
Cierp 44 42 55N 0 40 E
Cies, Islas 56 42 12N 8 55W
Cieszyn 54 49 45N 18 35 E
Cieza 59 38 17N 1 23W
Cifuentes 58 40 47N 2 37W
Ciha Pa. 101 22 20N 103 47 E
Cijara, Pantano de 57 39 18N 4 52W
Cijulang 103 7 42 S 108 27 E
Cikampek 103 6 23 S 107 28 E
Cilacap 103 7 43 S 109 0 E
Cıldır 83 41 10N 43 20 E
Cilgerran 31 52 4N 4 39W
Cilician Gates P. 92 37 20N 34 52 E
Cilician Taurus 92 36 40N 34 0 E
Cîlnicu 70 44 54N 23 4 E
Cimarron, Kans., U.S.A. 159 37 50N 100 20W
Cimarron, N. Mex., U.S.A. 159 36 30N 104 52W
Cimarron, R. 159 37 10N 102 10W
Cîmpia Turzii 70 46 34N 23 53 E
Cîmpina 70 45 10N 25 45 E
Cîmpulung, Argeş, Rumania 70 45 17N 25 3 E
Cîmpulung, Suceava, Rumania 70 47 32N 25 30 E
Cîmpuri 67 46 0N 26 50 E
Cinca, R. 58 42 20N 0 9 E
Cincer 66 43 55N 17 5 E
Cinch, R. 157 36 0N 84 15W
Cincinnati 156 39 10N 84 26W
Cincinnatus 162 42 33N 75 54W
Cinderford 28 51 49N 2 30W
Cîndeşti 70 45 15N 26 42 E
Ciney 47 50 18N 5 5 E
Cinigiano 63 42 53N 11 23 E
Cinogli 63 43 23N 13 10 E
Cinto, Mt. 45 42 24N 8 54 E
Cioranii 70 44 45N 26 25 E
Çiotat, La 45 43 12N 5 36 E
Čiovo 63 43 30N 16 17 E
Cipó 171 11 6 S 38 31W
Circle, Alaska, U.S.A. 147 65 50N 144 10W
Circle, Montana, U.S.A. 158 47 26N 105 35W
Circleville, Ohio, U.S.A. 156 39 35N 82 57W
Circleville, Utah, U.S.A. 161 38 12N 112 24W
Cirebon 103 6 45 S 108 32 E
Cirencester 28 51 43N 1 59W
Cireşu 70 44 47N 22 31 E
Cirey-sur-Vezouze 43 48 35N 6 57 E
Ciriè 62 45 14N 7 35 E
Cirò 65 39 23N 17 3 E
Cisco 159 32 25N 99 0W
Cislău 70 45 14N 26 33 E
Cisna 54 49 12N 22 20 E
Cisneros 174 6 33N 75 4W
Cisnădie 70 45 42N 24 9 E
Cisterna di Latina 64 41 35N 12 50 E
Cisternino 65 40 45N 17 26 E
Cité de Cansado 116 20 51N 17 0W
Citega (Kitega) 126 3 30 S 29 58 E
Citeli-Ckaro 83 41 33N 46 0 E
Citlaltépetl, mt. 165 19 0N 97 20W
Citrusdal 128 32 35 S 19 0 E
Città della Pieve 63 42 57N 12 0 E
Città di Castello 63 43 27N 12 14 E
Città Sant' Angelo 63 42 32N 14 5 E
Cittadella 63 45 39N 11 48 E
Cittaducale 63 42 24N 12 58 E
Cittanova 65 38 22N 16 0 E
Ciucaş, mt. 70 45 31N 25 56 E
Ciudad Acuña 164 29 20N 101 10W
Ciudad Altamirano 164 18 20N 100 40W
Ciudad Bolívar 174 8 5N 63 30W
Ciudad Camargo 164 27 41N 105 10W
Ciudad de Valles 165 22 0N 98 30W
Ciudad del Carmen 165 18 20N 97 50W
Ciudad Delicias = Delicias 164 28 10N 105 30W
Ciudad Guerrero 164 28 33N 107 28W
Ciudad Guzmán 164 19 40N 103 30W
Ciudad Juárez 164 31 40N 106 28W
Ciudad Madero 165 22 19N 97 50W
Ciudad Mante 165 22 50N 99 0W
Ciudad Obregón 164 27 28N 109 59W
Ciudad Piar 174 7 27N 63 19W
Ciudad Real 57 38 59N 3 55W
Ciudad Real □ 57 38 50N 4 0W
Ciudad Rodrigo 56 40 35N 6 32W
Ciudad Trujillo = Sto. Domingo 167 18 30N 70 0W
Ciudad Victoria 165 23 41N 99 9W
Ciudadela 58 40 0N 3 50 E
Ciulniţa 70 44 26N 27 22 E
Civa, B. 82 41 20N 36 40 E
Cividale del Friuli 63 46 6N 13 25 E
Civita Castellana 63 42 18N 12 24 E
Civitanova Marche 63 43 18N 13 41 E
Civitavécchia 63 42 6N 11 46 E
Civitella del Tronto 63 42 48N 13 40 E
Civray 44 46 10N 0 17 E
Çivril 92 38 20N 29 55 E
Cixerri, R. 64 39 45N 8 40 E
Cizre 92 37 19N 42 10 E
Clabach 34 56 38N 6 36W
Clabby 38 54 24N 7 22W
Clach Leathad 34 56 36N 7 52W
Clachan, N. Uist., U.K. 36 57 33N 7 20W
Clachan, Strathclyde, U.K. 34 55 45N 5 35W
Clackline 137 31 40 S 116 32 E
Clackmannan 35 56 10N 3 50W
Clackmannan (□) 26 56 10N 3 47W
Clacton-on-Sea 29 51 47N 1 10 E
Cladich 34 56 21N 5 5W
Claire, L. 152 58 35N 112 5W
Clairemont 159 33 9N 100 44W
Clairvaux-les-Laes 45 46 35N 5 45 E
Clamecy 43 47 28N 3 30 E
Clane 39 53 18N 6 40W
Clanfield 29 50 56N 1 0W
Clanton 157 32 48N 86 36W
Clanwilliam 128 32 11 S 18 52 E
Clar, L. nan 37 58 17N 4 8W
Clara 39 53 20N 7 38W
Clara, R. 138 19 8 S 142 30 E
Claraville 163 35 24N 118 20W
Clare, N.S.W., Austral. 140 33 24 S 143 54 E
Clare, S. Austral., Austral. 140 33 50 S 138 37 E
Clare, N. Ireland, U.K. 38 54 25N 6 19W
Clare, Suffolk, U.K. 29 52 5N 0 36 E
Clare, U.S.A. 156 43 47N 84 45W
Clare □ 39 52 20N 7 38W
Clare I. 38 53 48N 10 0W
Clare, R. 38 53 20N 9 0W
Clarecastle 39 52 50N 8 58W
Clareen 39 53 4N 7 49W
Claregalaway 39 53 20N 8 57W
Claremont 162 43 23N 72 20W
Claremont Pt. 138 14 1 S 143 41 E
Claremore 159 36 20N 95 20W
Claremorris 38 53 45N 9 0W
Clarence I. 13 61 30 S 53 50W
Clarence, I. 176 54 0 S 72 0W
Clarence, R., Austral. 139 29 25 S 153 22 E
Clarence, R., N.Z. 143 42 10 S 173 56 E
Clarence Str., Austral. 136 12 0 S 131 0 E
Clarence Str., U.S.A. 152 55 40N 132 10W
Clarence Town 167 23 6N 74 59W
Clarendon, Ark., U.S.A. 159 34 41N 91 20W
Clarendon, Tex., U.S.A. 159 34 58N 100 54W
Clarenville 151 48 10N 54 1W
Claresholm 152 50 0N 113 45W
Clarie Coast 13 67 0 S 135 0 E
Clarinbridge 39 53 13N 8 55W
Clarinda 158 40 45N 95 0W
Clarion 158 42 41N 93 46W
Clark 158 44 55N 97 45W
Clark Fork 160 48 9N 116 9W
Clark Fork, R. 160 48 0N 115 40W
Clark Hill Res. 157 33 45N 82 20W
Clarkdale 161 34 53N 112 3W
Clarke City 151 50 12N 66 38W
Clarke, I. 138 40 32 S 148 10 E
Clarke L. 153 54 24N 106 54W
Clarke Ra. 138 20 45 S 148 20 E
Clarks Fork, R. 160 45 0N 109 30W
Clark's Harbour 151 43 25N 65 38W
Clarks Station 163 38 8N 116 42W
Clarks Summit 162 41 31N 75 44W
Clarksburg 156 39 18N 80 21W
Clarksdale 159 34 12N 90 33W
Clarkston 160 46 28N 117 2W
Clarksville, Ark., U.S.A. 159 35 29N 93 27W
Clarksville, Tenn., U.S.A. 157 36 32N 87 20W
Clarksville, Tex., U.S.A. 159 33 37N 94 59W
Claro, R. 171 19 8 S 50 40W
Clashmore 37 57 53N 4 8W
Clatskanie 160 46 9N 123 12W
Clatteringshaws L. 34 55 3N 4 17W
Claude 159 35 8N 101 22W
Claudio 171 20 26 S 44 46W
Claudy 38 54 55N 7 10W
Claunie L. 36 57 8N 5 6W
Claveria 103 18 37N 121 15 E
Claverley 28 52 32N 2 19W
Clay 163 38 17N 121 10W
Clay Center 158 39 27N 97 9W
Clay Cross 33 53 11N 1 26W
Clay Hd. 32 54 13N 4 23W
Claydon 29 52 6N 1 7 E
Clayette, La 45 46 17N 4 19 E
Claymont 162 39 48N 75 28W
Claymore, oilfield 19 58 30N 0 15W
Claypool 161 33 27N 110 55W
Clayton, Idaho, U.S.A. 160 44 12N 114 31W
Clayton, N. Mex., U.S.A. 159 36 30N 103 10W
Cle Elum 160 47 15N 120 57W
Cleady 39 51 53N 9 32W
Clear C. 39 51 26N 9 30W
Clear I. 39 51 26N 9 30W
Clear Lake, Calif., U.S.A. 160 39 5N 122 47W
Clear Lake, S.D., U.S.A. 158 44 48N 96 41W
Clear Lake, Wash., U.S.A. 160 48 27N 122 15W
Clear Lake Res. 160 41 55N 121 10W
Clearfield, Pa., U.S.A. 156 41 0N 78 27W
Clearfield, Utah, U.S.A. 160 41 10N 112 0W
Clearmont 160 44 43N 106 29W
Clearwater, Can. 152 51 38N 120 2W
Clearwater, U.S.A. 157 27 58N 82 45W
Clearwater Cr. 152 61 36N 125 30W
Clearwater L. 150 56 10N 75 0W
Clearwater, Mts. 160 46 20N 115 30W
Clearwater Prov. Park 153 54 0N 101 0W
Clearwater, R., Alta., Can. 152 52 22N 114 57W
Clearwater, R., Alta., Can. 153 56 44N 111 23W
Clearwater, R., B.C., Can. 152 51 38N 120 3W
Cleat 37 58 45N 2 56W
Cleator Moor 32 54 30N 3 32W
Cleburne 159 32 18N 97 25W
Cleddau R. 31 51 46N 4 44W
Clee Hills 23 52 26N 2 35W

Cleethorpes 33 53 33N 0 2W
Cleeve Cloud 28 51 56N 2 0W
Cleggan 38 53 33N 10 7W
Clelles 45 44 50N 5 38E
Clemency 47 49 35N 5 53E
Clent 28 52 25N 2 6W
Cleobury Mortimer 28 52 23N 2 28W
Clerke Reef 136 17 22S 119 20E
Clerks Rocks 13 56 0S 36 30W
Clermont 133 22 49S 147 39E
Clermont-en-Argonne 43 49 5N 5 4E
Clermont-Ferrand 44 45 46N 3 4E
Clermont-l'Hérault 44 43 38N 3 26E
Clerval 43 47 25N 6 30E
Cléry-Saint-André 43 47 50N 1 46E
Cles 62 46 21N 11 4E
Clevedon 28 51 26N 2 52W
Cleveland, Austral. 139 27 30S 153 15E
Cleveland, Miss., U.S.A. 159 33 43N 90 43W
Cleveland, Ohio, U.S.A. 156 41 28N 81 43W
Cleveland, Okla., U.S.A. 159 36 21N 96 33W
Cleveland, Tenn., U.S.A. 157 35 9N 84 52W
Cleveland, Tex., U.S.A. 159 30 18N 95 0W
Cleveland □ 33 54 35N 1 8E
Cleveland, C. 138 19 11S 147 1E
Cleveland Hills 33 54 25N 1 11W
Clevelândia 173 26 24S 52 23W
Clevvaux 47 50 4N 6 2E
Clew Bay 38 53 54N 9 50W
Clewiston 157 26 44N 80 50W
Cley 29 52 57N 1 3E
Clifden, Ireland 38 53 30N 10 2W
Clifden, N.Z. 143 46 1S 167 42E
Clifden B. 38 53 29N 10 5W
Cliff 161 33 0N 108 44W
Cliffe 29 51 27N 0 31E
Cliffony 38 54 25N 8 28W
Clifford 28 52 6N 3 6W
Clift Sound 36 60 4N 1 17W
Clifton, Austral. 139 27 59S 151 53E
Clifton, Ariz., U.S.A. 161 33 8N 109 23W
Clifton, Tex., U.S.A. 159 31 46N 97 35W
Clifton Forge 156 37 49N 79 51W
Climax 153 49 10N 108 20W
Clingmans Dome 157 35 35N 83 30W
Clint 161 31 37N 106 11W
Clinton, B.C., Can. 152 51 6N 121 35W
Clinton, Ont., Can. 150 43 37N 81 32W
Clinton, N.Z. 143 46 12S 169 23E
Clinton, Ark., U.S.A. 159 35 37N 92 30W
Clinton, Conn., U.S.A. 162 41 17N 72 32W
Clinton, Ill., U.S.A. 158 40 8N 89 0W
Clinton, Ind., U.S.A. 156 39 40N 87 22W
Clinton, Iowa, U.S.A. 158 41 50N 90 12W
Clinton, Mass., U.S.A. 162 42 26N 71 40W
Clinton, Mo., U.S.A. 158 38 20N 93 46W
Clinton, N.C., U.S.A. 157 35 5N 78 15W
Clinton, Okla., U.S.A. 159 35 30N 99 0W
Clinton, S.C., U.S.A. 157 34 30N 81 54W
Clinton, Tenn., U.S.A. 157 36 6N 84 10W
Clinton C. 138 22 30S 150 45E
Clinton Colden L. 148 64 58N 107 27W
Clintonville 158 44 35N 88 46W
Clipperton, I. 143 10 18N 109 13W
Clipston 29 52 26N 0 58W
Clisson 42 47 5N 1 16W
Clitheroe 32 53 52N 2 23W
Clive 142 39 36S 176 58E
Clive L. 152 63 13N 118 54W
Cloates, Pt. 136 22 43S 113 40E
Clocolan 129 28 55S 27 34E
Clodomira 172 27 35S 64 14W
Clogh 39 52 51N 7 11W
Cloghan, Donegal, Ireland 38 54 50N 7 56W
Cloghan, Offaly, Ireland 39 53 13N 7 53W
Cloghan, W'meath, Ireland 38 53 33N 7 15W
Clogheen 39 52 17N 8 0W
Clogher 38 54 25N 7 10W
Clogher Hd. 38 53 48N 6 15W
Cloghjordan 39 52 57N 8 2W
Cloghran 38 53 26N 6 14W
Clonakilty 39 51 37N 8 53W
Clonakilty B. 39 51 33N 8 50W
Clonbur 38 53 32N 9 21W
Cloncurry, Austral. 138 20 40S 140 28E
Cloncurry, Ireland 38 53 26N 6 47W
Cloncurry, R. 138 18 37S 140 40E
Clondalkin 39 53 20N 6 25W
Clonee 38 53 25N 6 28W
Cloneen 39 52 28N 7 36W
Clones 38 54 10N 7 13W
Clonkeen 39 51 59N 9 20W
Clonmany 38 55 16N 7 24W
Clonmel 39 52 22N 7 42W
Clonmore 39 52 49N 6 35W
Clonroche 39 52 27N 6 42W
Clontarf 38 53 22N 6 10W
Cloonakool 38 54 6N 8 47W
Cloone 38 53 57N 7 47W
Cloonfad 38 53 41N 8 45W
Cloppenburg 48 52 50N 8 3E
Cloquet 158 46 40N 92 30W
Clorinda 172 25 16S 57 45W
Closeburn 35 55 13N 3 45W
Cloud Peak 160 44 30N 107 10W
Cloudcroft 161 33 0N 105 48W
Cloudy B. 143 41 25S 174 10E
Clough, Ballymena, U.K. 38 54 58N 6 16W
Clough, Down, U.K. 38 54 18N 5 50W
Cloughton 33 54 20N 0 27W
Clova 37 56 50N 3 4W
Clovelly 30 51 0N 4 25W
Cloverdale 160 38 49N 123 0W
Clovis, Calif., U.S.A. 163 36 54N 119 45W
Clovis, N. Mex., U.S.A. 159 34 20N 103 10W
Clowne 33 53 18N 1 16W
Cloyne 39 51 52N 8 7W
Club Terrace 141 37 35S 148 58E
Cluj-Napoca 70 46 47N 23 38E
Cluj □ 70 46 45N 23 30E
Clun 28 52 26N 3 2W
Clun Forest 28 52 27N 3 7W
Clunbury 28 52 25N 2 55W
Clunes, Austral. 140 37 20S 143 45E
Clunes, U.K. 36 56 57N 4 58W
Cluny 45 46 26N 4 38E
Cluses 45 46 5N 6 35E
Clusone 62 45 54N 9 58E
Clutha, R. 143 46 20S 169 49E
Clwyd □ 31 53 5N 3 20W
Clwyd, R. 31 53 12N 3 30W
Clwydian Ra. 31 53 10N 3 15W
Clydach 31 51 42N 3 54W
Clyde, Austral. 139 28 48S 143 40E
Clyde, Can. 149 70 30N 68 30W
Clyde, N.Z. 143 45 12S 169 20E
Clyde, Firth of 34 55 20N 5 0W
Clyde, R. 34 55 46N 4 58W
Clydebank 34 55 54N 4 25W
Clydesdale 35 55 42N 3 50W
Clynnog-fawr 31 53 2N 4 22W
Côa, R. 56 40 45N 7 0W
Coachella 163 33 44N 116 13W
Coachella Canal 163 32 43N 114 57W
Coachford 39 51 54N 8 48W
Coachman's Cove 151 50 6N 56 20W
Coagh 38 54 39N 6 37W
Coahoma 159 32 17N 101 20W
Coahuayana, R. 164 18 41N 103 45W
Coahuayutla 164 18 19N 101 42W
Coahuila □ 164 27 0N 112 30W
Coal Creek Flat 143 45 27S 169 19E
Coal I. 143 46 8S 166 40E
Coal, R. 152 59 39N 126 57W
Coalane 127 17 48S 37 2E
Coalbrookdale 28 52 38N 2 30W
Coalburn 35 55 35N 3 55W
Coalcomán 164 18 40N 103 10W
Coaldale, Can. 152 49 45N 112 35W
Coaldale, U.S.A. 163 38 2N 117 55W
Coaldale, Pa., U.S.A. 162 40 50N 75 54W
Coalgate 159 34 35N 96 13W
Coalinga 163 36 10N 120 21W
Coalisland 38 54 33N 6 42W
Coalspur 152 53 15N 117 0W
Coalville, U.K. 28 52 43N 1 21W
Coalville, U.S.A. 160 40 58N 111 24W
Coamo 147 18 5N 66 22W
Coaraci 171 14 38S 39 32W
Coari 174 4 8S 63 7W
Coast □ 126 2 40S 39 45E
Coast Mts. 152 52 0N 126 0W
Coast Range 163 40 0N 124 0W
Coastal Plains Basin 137 30 10S 115 30E
Coatbridge 35 55 52N 4 2W
Coatepec 165 19 27N 96 58W
Coatepeque 166 14 46N 91 55W
Coatesville 162 39 59N 75 30W
Coaticook 151 45 10N 71 46W
Coats I. 149 62 30N 83 0W
Coats Land 13 77 0S 25 0W
Coatzacoalcos 165 18 7N 94 35W
Cobadin 70 44 5N 28 13E
Cobalt 150 47 25N 79 42W
Cobán 166 15 30N 90 21W
Cobar 141 31 27S 145 48E
Cobb I. 162 37 17N 75 42W
Cobbannah 141 37 37S 147 12E
Cobberas, Mt. 141 36 53S 148 12E
Cobden 140 38 20S 143 3E
Cóbh 39 51 50N 8 18W
Cobija 174 11 0S 68 50W
Cobourg 150 43 58N 78 10W
Cobourg Pen. 136 11 20S 132 15E
Cobram 141 35 54S 145 40E
Cobre 160 41 6N 114 25W
Cóbué 125 12 0S 34 58E
Coburg 49 50 15N 10 58E
Coca 56 41 13N 4 32W
Coca, R. 174 0 25S 77 5W
Cocal 170 3 28S 41 34W
Cocanada = Kakinada 96 16 55N 82 20E
Cocentaina 59 38 45N 0 27W
Cocha, La 172 27 50S 65 40W
Cochabamba 174 17 15S 66 20W
Coche, I. 174 10 47N 63 56W
Cochem 49 50 8N 7 7E
Cochemane 127 17 0S 32 54E
Cochilha Grande de Albardão 173 28 30S 51 30W
Cochin 97 9 55N 76 22E
Cochin China 101 10 30N 106 0E
Cochin China = Nam-Phan 101 10 30N 106 0E
Cochise 161 32 6N 109 58W
Cochran 157 32 25N 83 23W
Cochrane, Alta., Can. 152 51 11N 114 30W
Cochrane, Ont., Can. 150 49 0N 81 0W
Cochrane, L. 176 47 10S 72 0W
Cochrane, R. 153 57 53N 101 34W
Cockatoo I. 136 16 6S 123 37E
Cockburn 140 32 5S 141 0E
Cockburn, Canal 176 54 30S 72 0W
Cockburn, C. 136 11 20S 132 52E
Cockburn I. 150 45 55N 83 22W
Cockburn Ra. 136 15 46S 128 0E
Cockburnspath 35 55 56N 2 23W
Cockenzie 35 55 58N 2 59W
Cockerham 32 53 58N 2 49W
Cockermouth 32 54 40N 3 22W
Cockeysville 162 39 29N 76 39W
Cockfield 29 52 8N 0 47E
Cocklebiddy 137 32 0S 126 3E
Coco Chan. 101 13 50N 93 25E
Coco Is. 101 14 0N 93 12E
Coco, Pta. 174 2 58N 77 43W
Coco, R. (Wanks) 166 14 10N 85 0W
Cocoa 157 28 22N 80 40W
Cocobeach 124 0 59N 9 34E
Cocoli, R. 120 12 0N 14 0W
Cocora 70 44 45N 27 3E
Côcos 171 14 10S 44 33W
Cocos (Keeling) Is. 11 12 12S 96 54E
Côcos, R. 171 12 44S 44 48W
Cod, C. 162 42 8N 70 10W
Cod, gasfield 19 57 8N 2 35E
Codajás 174 3 40S 62 0W
Coddenham 29 52 8N 1 8E
Codera, C. 174 10 35N 66 4W
Coderre 153 50 11N 106 31W
Codigoro 63 44 50N 12 5E
Codó 170 4 30S 43 55W
Codogno 62 45 10N 9 42E
Codróipo 63 45 57N 13 0E
Codru, Munţii 70 46 30N 22 15E
Cods Hd. 39 51 40N 10 7W
Cody 160 44 35N 109 0W
Coe Hill 150 44 52N 77 50W
Coelemu 172 36 30S 72 48W
Coelho Neto 170 4 15S 43 0W
Coen 138 13 52S 143 12E
Coesfeld 48 51 56N 7 10E
Coeur d'Alene 160 47 45N 116 51W
Coevorden 46 52 40N 6 44E
Coffeyville 159 37 0N 95 40W
Coffin B. Pen. 136 34 20S 135 10E
Coffs Harbour 141 30 16S 153 5E
Cofre de Perote, Cerro 165 19 30N 97 10W
Cofrentes 59 39 13N 1 5W
Cogealac 70 44 36N 28 36E
Coggeshall 29 51 53N 0 41E
Coghinas, R. 64 40 55N 8 48E
Cognac 44 45 41N 0 20W
Cogne 62 45 37N 7 21E
Cogolludo 58 40 59N 3 10W
Cohagen 160 47 2N 106 45W
Cohoes 162 42 47N 73 42W
Cohuna 140 35 45S 144 15E
Coiba I. 166 7 30N 81 40W
Coig, R. 176 51 0S 70 20W
Coigach, dist. 36 58 0N 5 10W
Coillore 36 57 21N 6 23W
Coimbatore 97 11 2N 76 59E
Coimbra 56 40 15N 8 27W
Coimbra □ 56 40 12N 8 25W
Coin 57 36 40N 4 48W
Cojedes □ 174 9 20N 68 20W
Cojimies 174 0 20N 80 0W
Cojocna 70 46 45N 23 50E
Cojutepequé 166 13 41N 88 54W
Coka 66 45 57N 20 12E
Cokeville 160 42 4N 111 0W
Col di Tenda 62 44 7N 7 36E
Colaba Pt. 96 18 54N 72 47E
Colac 140 38 21S 143 35E
Colachel 97 8 10N 77 15E
Colares 57 38 48N 9 30W
Colatina 171 19 32S 40 37W
Colbinabbin 141 36 38S 144 48E
Colby, U.K. 32 54 6N 4 42W
Colby, U.S.A. 158 39 27N 101 2W
Colchagua □ 172 34 30S 71 0W
Colchester 29 51 54N 0 55E
Cold Fell 32 54 54N 2 40W
Coldingham 35 55 53N 2 10W
Coldstream 35 55 39N 2 14W
Coldwater 159 37 18N 99 24W
Coldwell 150 48 45N 86 30W
Colebrook 138 42 31S 147 12E
Colebrooke 30 50 45N 3 44W
Coleford 28 51 46N 2 38W
Coleman, Can. 152 49 40N 114 30W
Coleman, U.S.A. 159 31 52N 99 30W
Coleman, R. 138 15 6S 141 38E
Colenso 129 28 44S 29 50E
Coleraine, Austral. 140 37 36S 141 40E
Coleraine, U.K. 38 55 8N 6 40E
Coleraine □ 38 55 8N 6 40E
Coleridge, L. 143 43 17S 171 30E
Coleroon, R. 97 11 0N 79 0E
Colesberg 128 30 45S 25 5E
Coleshill 28 52 30N 1 42W
Coleville 163 38 44N 119 30W
Colfax, La., U.S.A. 159 31 35N 92 39W
Colfax, Wash., U.S.A. 160 46 57N 117 28W
Colgrave Sd. 36 60 35N 1 0W
Colhué Huapi, L. 176 45 30S 69 0W
Cólico 62 46 8N 9 22E
Coligny 128 46 24N 5 21E
Colima 164 19 10N 103 40W
Colima □ 164 19 10N 103 40W
Colima, Nevado de 164 19 30N 103 40W
Colina 172 33 13S 70 45W
Colina do Norte 120 12 28N 15 0W
Colinas, Goiás, Brazil 171 14 15S 48 2W
Colinas, Maranhão, Brazil 170 6 0S 44 10W
Colinton, Austral. 141 35 50S 149 10E
Colinton, U.K. 35 55 54N 3 17W
Coll, I. 34 56 40N 6 35W
Collaguasi 172 21 5S 68 45W
Collarada, Peña 58 42 43N 0 29W
Collarenebri 139 29 33S 148 36E
Collbran 161 39 16N 107 58W
Colle Salvetti 62 43 34N 10 27E
Colle Sannita 65 41 22N 14 48E
Colléchio 62 44 23N 10 10E
Colleen Bawn 127 21 0S 29 12E
College Park, Ga., U.S.A. 157 33 42N 84 27W
College Park, Md., U.S.A. 162 39 0N 76 55W
Collette 151 46 40N 65 30W
Collie, N.S.W., Austral. 141 31 41S 148 18E
Collie, W. Austral., Austral. 137 33 22S 116 8E
Collier B. 136 16 10S 124 15E
Collier Law Pk. 32 54 47N 1 59W
Collier Ra. 137 24 45S 119 10E
Collin 35 55 4N 3 30W
Colline Metallifere 62 43 10N 11 0E
Collingbourne 28 51 16N 1 39W
Collingswood 162 39 55N 75 4W
Collingwood, Austral. 138 22 20S 142 31E
Collingwood, Can. 150 44 29N 80 13W
Collingwood, N.Z. 143 40 25S 172 40E
Collingwood B. 138 9 30S 149 30E
Collins 150 50 17N 89 27W
Collinsville 138 20 30S 147 56E
Collipulli 172 37 55S 72 30W
Collison Ra. 136 14 49S 127 25E
Collo 119 36 58N 6 37E
Collon 38 53 46N 6 29W
Collonges 45 46 9N 5 52E
Collooney 38 54 11N 8 28W
Colmar 43 48 5N 7 20E
Colmars 45 44 11N 6 39E
Colmenar 57 36 54N 4 20W
Colmenar de Oreja 58 40 6N 3 25W
Colmenar Viejo 56 40 39N 3 47W
Colmor 159 36 18N 104 36W
Colne 32 53 51N 2 11W
Colne, R., Essex, U.K. 29 51 55N 0 50E
Colne, R., Herts., U.K. 29 51 36N 0 30W
Colnett, Cabo 164 31 0N 116 20W
Colo, R. 141 33 25S 150 52E
Cologna Véneta 63 45 19N 11 21E
Colomb-Béchar = Béchar 118 31 38N 2 18E
Colombey-les-Belles 43 48 32N 5 54E
Colombey-les-deux Églises 43 48 20N 4 50E
Colômbia 171 20 10S 48 40W
Colombia 174 3 24N 79 49W
Colombia ■ 174 3 45N 73 0W
Colombier 50 46 58N 6 53E
Colombo 97 6 56N 79 58E
Colombus, Kans., U.S.A. 159 37 15N 94 30W
Colombus, Nebr., U.S.A. 158 41 30N 97 25W
Colombus, N.Mex., U.S.A. 161 31 54N 107 43W
Colome 158 43 20N 99 44W
Colón, Argent. 172 32 12S 58 30W
Colón, Cuba 166 22 42N 80 54W
Colón, Panama 166 9 20N 80 0W
Colonel Hill 167 22 50N 74 21W
Colonella 63 42 52N 13 50E
Colonia del Sacramento 173 34 25S 57 50W
Colonia Dora 172 28 34S 62 59W
Colonia Las Heras 176 46 30S 69 0W
Colonia Sarmiento 176 45 30S 68 15W
Colonial Hts. 162 37 15N 77 25W
Colonne, C. delle 65 39 2N 17 11E
Colonsay 153 51 59N 105 52W
Colonsay, I. 34 56 4N 6 12W
Colorado □ 154 37 40N 106 0W
Colorado Aqueduct 161 34 17N 114 10W
Colorado City 159 32 25N 100 50W
Colorado Desert 154 34 20N 116 0W
Colorado Plateau 161 36 40N 110 30W
Colorado, R., Argent. 172 37 30S 69 0W
Colorado, R., Ariz., U.S.A. 161 33 30N 114 30W
Colorado, R., Calif., U.S.A. 161 34 0N 114 33W
Colorado, R., Tex., U.S.A. 159 29 40N 96 30W
Colorado Springs 158 38 55N 104 50W
Colorno 62 44 55N 10 21E
Colossal 141 30 52S 147 3E
Colotepec 165 15 47N 97 3W
Colotlán 164 22 6N 103 16W
Colpy 37 57 23N 2 35W
Colsterworth 29 52 48N 0 37W
Coltishall 29 52 44N 1 21E
Colton, Calif., U.S.A. 163 34 4N 117 20W
Colton, Wash., U.S.A. 160 46 41N 117 6W
Columbia, La., U.S.A. 159 32 7N 92 5W
Columbia, Miss., U.S.A. 159 31 16N 89 50W
Columbia, Mo., U.S.A. 158 38 58N 92 20W
Columbia, Pa., U.S.A. 162 40 2N 76 30W
Columbia, S.C., U.S.A. 157 34 0N 81 0W

Columbia, Tenn., U.S.A. 157 35 40N 87 0W
Columbia, C. 12 83 0N 70 0W
Columbia City 156 41 8N 85 30W
Columbia, District of □ 156 38 55N 77 0W
Columbia Falls 160 48 25N 114 16W
Columbia Heights 158 45 5N 93 10W
Columbia, Mt. 152 52 8N 117 20W
Columbia Basin 160 47 30N 118 30W
Columbia, R. 160 45 49N 120 0W
Columbretes, Is. 58 39 50N 0 50E
Columbus, Ga., U.S.A. 157 32 30N 84 58W
Columbus, Ind., U.S.A. 156 39 14N 85 55W
Columbus, Miss., U.S.A. 157 33 30N 88 26W
Columbus, Mont., U.S.A. 160 45 45N 109 14W
Columbus, N.D., U.S.A. 158 48 52N 102 48W
Columbus, Ohio, U.S.A. 156 39 57N 83 1W
Columbus, Tex., U.S.A. 159 29 42N 96 33W
Columbus, Wis., U.S.A. 158 43 20N 89 2W
Colunda 125 12 7S 23 36E
Colunga 56 43 29N 5 16W
Colusa 160 39 15N 122 1W
Colville 160 48 33N 117 54W
Colville, C. 142 36 29S 175 21E
Colville, R. 147 69 15N 152 0W
Colwell 35 55 4N 2 4W
Colwich 28 52 48N 1 58W
Colwyn 31 53 17N 3 43W
Colwyn Bay 31 53 17N 3 44W
Colyton 30 50 44N 3 4W
Comácchio 63 44 41N 12 10E
Comalcalco 165 18 16N 93 13W
Comallo 176 41 0S 70 5W
Comana 70 44 10N 26 10E
Comanche, Okla., U.S.A. 159 34 27N 97 58W
Comanche, Tex., U.S.A. 159 31 55N 98 35W
Comăneşti 70 46 25N 26 26E
Comayagua 166 14 25N 87 37W
Combahee, R. 157 32 45N 80 50W
Combara 141 31 10S 148 22E
Combe Martin 30 51 12N 4 2W
Combeaufontaine 43 47 38N 5 54E
Comber 38 54 33N 5 45W
Combermere Bay 98 19 37N 93 34E
Comblain 47 50 29N 5 35E
Combles 43 50 0N 2 50E
Combourg 42 48 25N 1 46W
Comboyne 141 31 34S 152 34E
Combronde 44 45 58N 3 5E
Comeragh Mts. 39 52 17N 7 35W
Comercinho 171 16 19S 41 47W
Comet 138 23 36S 148 38E
Comet Vale 137 29 55S 121 4E
Comilla 98 23 28N 91 10E
Comines 47 50 46N 3 0E
Comino, C. 64 40 28N 9 47E
Cómiso 65 36 57N 14 35E
Comitán 165 16 18N 92 9W
Commentry 44 46 20N 2 46E
Commerce, Ga., U.S.A. 157 34 10N 83 25W
Commerce, Tex., U.S.A. 159 33 15N 95 50W
Commercy 43 48 40N 5 34E
Committee B. 149 68 30N 86 30W
Commonwealth B. 13 67 0S 144 0E
Commoron Cr., R. 139 28 22S 150 8E
Communism Pk. = Kommunizma, Pk. 93 38 40N 72 20E
Como 62 45 48N 9 5E
Como, L. di 62 46 5N 9 17E
Comodoro Rivadavia 176 45 50S 67 40W
Comores, Arch. des 11 10 0S 50 0E
Comores, Is. 11 12 10S 44 15E
Comorin, C. 97 8 3N 77 40E
Comorişte 70 45 10N 21 35E
Comoro Is. 11 12 10S 44 15E
Comox 152 49 42N 124 55W
Compiègne 43 49 24N 2 50E
Compíglia Maríttima 62 43 4N 10 37E
Comporta 57 38 22N 8 46W
Compostela 164 21 15N 104 53W
Comprida, I. 173 24 50S 47 42W
Compton, U.K. 28 51 2N 1 19W
Compton, U.S.A. 163 33 54N 118 13W
Compton Downs 139 30 28S 146 30E
Comrie 35 56 22N 4 0W
Con Cuong 100 19 2N 104 54E
Côn Dao 101 8 45N 106 45E
Con Son, Is. 101 8 41N 106 37E
Conakry 120 9 29N 13 49W
Conara Junction 138 41 50S 147 26E
Conargo 141 35 16S 145 10E
Conatlán 164 24 30N 104 42W
Concarneau 42 47 52N 3 56W
Conceição, Brazil 170 7 33S 38 31W
Conceição, Mozam. 127 18 47S 36 7E
Conceição da Barra 171 18 35S 39 45W
Conceição do Araguaia 170 8 0S 49 2W
Conceição do Canindé 170 7 54S 41 34W
Conceição do Mato Dentro 171 19 1S 43 25W
Concepción 165 18 15N 90 5W
Concepción, Argent. 172 27 20S 65 35W
Concepción, Boliv. 174 15 50S 61 40W
Concepción, Chile 172 36 50S 73 0W
Concepción, Colomb. 174 0 5N 75 37W
Concepción, Parag. 172 23 30S 57 20W
Concepción, Venez. 174 10 48N 71 46W
Concepción □ 172 37 0S 72 30W
Concepcion, C. 154 34 30N 120 34W
Concepción del Oro 164 24 40N 101 30W
Concepción del Uruguay 172 32 35S 58 20W
Concepción, L. 174 17 20S 61 10W
Concepción, La = Ri-Aba 121 3 28N 84 0E
Concepción, Punta 164 26 55N 111 50W
Concepción, R. 164 30 32N 113 2W
Conception B. 128 23 55S 14 22E
Conception I. 167 23 52N 75 9W
Conception, Pt. 163 34 27N 120 28W
Concession 127 17 27S 30 56E
Conchas Dam 159 35 25N 104 10W
Conche 151 50 48N 55 58W
Conches-en-Ouche 50 48 58N 0 58E
Concho 161 34 32N 109 43W
Concho, R. 159 31 30N 100 8W
Conchos, R., Chihnahua, Mexico 164 29 20N 105 0W
Conchos, R., Tamaulipas, Mexico 165 25 0N 97 32W
Concon 172 32 56S 71 33W
Concord, Calif., U.S.A. 163 37 59N 122 2W
Concord, N.C., U.S.A. 157 35 28N 80 35W
Concord, N.H., U.S.A. 162 43 12N 71 30W
Concórdia, Argent. 172 31 20S 58 2W
Concórdia, Brazil 174 4 36S 66 36W
Concordia, Colomb. 174 2 39N 72 47W
Concordia, Mexico 164 23 18N 106 2W
Concordia, U.S.A. 158 39 35N 97 40W
Concordia, La 165 16 8N 92 38W
Concots 44 44 26N 1 40E
Concrete 160 48 35N 121 49W
Condah 140 37 57S 141 44E
Condamine, R. 133 27 7S 149 48E
Condat 44 45 21N 2 46E
Conde 171 11 49S 37 37W
Condé 43 50 26N 3 34E
Conde 158 45 13N 98 5W
Condé-sur-Noireau 42 48 51N 0 33W
Condeúba 171 15 0S 42 0W
Condobolin 141 33 4S 147 6E
Condom 44 43 57N 0 22E
Condon 160 45 15N 120 8W
Condove 62 45 8N 7 19E
Condover 28 52 39N 2 46W
Conegliano 63 45 53N 12 18E
Conejera, I. 59 39 11N 2 58E
Conejos 164 26 14N 103 53W
Conflans-en-Jarnisy 43 49 10N 5 52E
Confolens 44 46 2N 0 40E
Confuso, R. 172 24 10S 59 0W
Congleton 32 53 10N 2 12W
Congo 170 7 48S 36 40W
Congo ■ 124 1 0S 16 0E
Congo Basin 114 0 10S 24 30E
Congo, Democratic Rep. of = Zaïre ■ 124 3 0S 22 0E
Congo (Kinshasa) ■ = Zaïre ■ 124 1 0S 16 0E
Congo, R. = Zaïre, R. 124 1 30N 28 0E
Congonhas 173 20 30S 43 52W
Congresbury 28 51 20N 2 49W
Congress 161 34 11N 112 56W
Congucu 113 31 25S 52 30W
Conil 57 36 17N 6 10W
Coningsby 33 53 7N 0 9W
Conisbrough 33 53 29N 1 12W
Coniston, Can. 150 46 29N 80 51W
Coniston, U.K. 32 54 22N 3 6W
Coniston Water 32 54 20N 3 5W
Conjeeveram = Kancheepuram 97 12 52N 79 45E
Conjuboy 138 18 35S 144 45E
Conklin 153 55 38N 111 5W
Conlea 139 30 7S 144 35E
Conn, L. 38 54 3N 9 15W
Conna 39 52 5N 8 8W
Connacht 38 53 23N 8 40W
Connah's Quay 31 53 13N 3 6W
Conneaut 156 41 55N 80 32W
Connecticut □ 162 41 40N 72 40W
Connecticut, R. 162 41 17N 72 21W
Connel 34 56 27N 5 24W
Connel Park 34 55 22N 4 15W
Connell 160 46 45N 118 58W
Connemara 38 53 29N 9 45W
Conner, La 160 48 22N 122 27W
Connersville 156 39 40N 85 10W
Connonagh 39 51 35N 9 8W
Connor, Mt. 136 14 34S 126 4E
Connors Ra. 138 21 40S 149 10E
Conoble 141 32 55S 144 42E
Cononaco, R. 174 1 20S 76 30W
Conquest 153 51 32N 107 14W
Conquet, Le 42 48 21N 4 46W
Conrad 160 48 11N 112 0W
Conran, C. 141 37 49S 148 44E
Conroe 159 30 15N 95 28W
Conselheiro Lafaiete 173 20 40S 43 48W
Conselheiro Pena 171 19 10S 41 30W
Consett 32 54 52N 1 50W
Conshohocken 162 40 5N 75 18W
Consort 153 52 1N 110 46W
Constance = Konstanz 49 47 39N 9 10E
Constance, L. = Bodensee 51 47 35N 9 25E
Constanţa 70 44 14N 28 38E
Constanţa □ 70 44 15N 28 15E
Constantia 162 43 15N 76 1W
Constantina 57 37 51N 5 40W
Constantine 119 36 25N 6 42E
Constitución, Chile 172 35 20S 72 30W
Constitución, Uruguay 172 31 0S 58 10W
Consuegra 57 39 28N 3 43W
Consul 153 49 20N 109 30W
Contact 160 41 50N 114 56W
Contai 95 21 54N 87 55E
Contamana 174 7 10S 74 55W
Contarina 63 45 2N 12 13E
Contas, R. 171 13 5S 41 53W
Contes 45 43 49N 7 19E
Conthey 50 46 14N 7 28E
Contin 37 57 34N 4 35W
Contoocook 162 43 13N 71 45W
Contra Costa 129 25 9S 33 30E
Contres 43 47 24N 1 26E
Contrexéville 43 48 6N 5 53E
Convención 174 8 28N 73 21W
Conversano 65 40 57N 17 8E
Convoy 38 54 52N 7 40W
Conway, Ark., U.S.A. 159 35 5N 92 30W
Conway, N.H., U.S.A. 162 43 58N 71 8W
Conway, S.C., U.S.A. 157 33 49N 79 2W
Conway = Conwy 31 53 17N 3 50W
Conway, L. 139 28 17S 135 35E
Conwy 31 53 17N 3 50W
Conwy Bay 31 53 17N 3 57W
Conwy, R. 31 53 18N 3 50W
Coober Pedy 136 29 1S 134 43E
Coobina 137 23 22S 120 10E
Cooch Behar 98 26 22N 89 29E
Cook, Austral. 137 30 37S 130 25E
Cook, U.S.A. 158 47 49N 92 39W
Cook, Bahia 176 55 10S 70 0W
Cook Inlet 147 59 0N 151 0W
Cook Is. 131 20 0S 160 0W
Cook, Mount 143 43 36S 170 9E
Cook Strait 143 41 15S 174 29E
Cooke Plains 140 35 23S 139 34E
Cookeville 157 36 12N 85 30W
Cookham 29 51 33N 0 42W
Cookhouse 128 32 44S 25 47E
Cookstown 38 54 40N 6 43W
Cookstown □ 38 54 40N 6 43W
Cooktown 138 15 30S 145 16E
Coolabah 141 31 1S 146 43E
Cooladdi 139 26 37S 145 23E
Coolah 141 31 48S 149 41E
Coolamon 141 34 46S 147 8E
Coolaney 38 54 10N 8 36W
Coolangatta 139 28 11S 153 29E
Coole 38 53 42N 7 23W
Coolgardie 137 30 55S 121 8E
Coolgreany 39 52 46N 6 14W
Coolibah 136 15 33S 130 56E
Coolidge 161 33 1N 111 35W
Coolidge Dam 161 33 10N 110 30W
Coolmore 38 54 33N 8 12W
Cooma 141 36 12S 149 8E
Coomacarrea Mts. 39 51 59N 10 0W
Coonabarabran 141 31 14S 149 18E
Coonalpyn 140 35 43S 139 52E
Coonamble 141 30 56S 148 27E
Coonana 137 31 0S 123 0E
Coondapoor 97 13 42N 74 40E
Coongie 139 27 9S 140 8E
Coongoola 139 27 43S 145 47E
Cooninie, L. 139 26 4S 139 59E
Coonoor 97 11 10N 76 45E
Cooper 159 33 20N 95 40W
Cooper Cr. 139 28 29S 137 46E
Cooper, R. 157 33 0N 79 55W
Coopersburg 162 40 31N 75 23W
Cooperstown, N.D., U.S.A. 158 47 30N 98 14W
Cooperstown, New York, U.S.A. 162 42 42N 74 57W
Coorabie P.O. 137 31 54S 132 18E
Coorabulka 138 23 41S 140 20E
Coorong, The 133 35 50S 139 20E
Coorow 137 29 53S 116 2E
Cooroy 139 26 22S 152 54E
Coos Bay 160 43 26N 124 7W
Cootamundra 141 34 36S 148 1E
Cootehill 38 54 5N 7 5W
Cooyar 139 26 59S 151 51E
Cooyeana 138 24 29S 138 45E
Copahué, Paso 172 37 49S 71 8W
Copainalá 165 17 8N 93 11W
Copake Falls 162 42 7N 73 31W
Copán 166 14 50N 89 9W
Cope 158 39 44N 102 50W
Cope, Cabo 59 37 26N 1 28W
Cope Cope 140 36 27S 143 5E
Copeland I. 38 54 38N 5 33W
Copenhagen 162 43 54N 75 41W
Copenhagen = København 73 55 41N 12 34E
Copertino 65 40 17N 18 2W
Copeville 140 34 47S 139 51E
Copiapó 172 27 15S 70 20E
Copiapó, R. 172 27 19S 70 56W
Copinsay I. 37 58 54N 2 40W
Coplay 162 40 44N 75 29W
Copley 140 30 24S 138 26E
Copp L. 152 60 14N 114 40W
Copparo 63 44 52N 11 49E
Copper Center 147 62 10N 145 25W
Copper Cliff 150 46 28N 81 4W
Copper Harbor 156 47 31N 87 55W
Copper Mountain 152 49 20N 120 30W
Copper Queen 127 17 29S 29 18E
Copper R. 147 61 30N 144 30W
Copperbelt □ 127 13 15N 27 30E
Copperfield 137 29 1S 120 26E
Coppermine 148 67 50N 115 5W
Coppermine, R. 148 67 49N 115 4W
Copperopolis 163 37 58N 120 38W
Cöppingen 49 48 42N 9 40E
Copythorne 28 50 56N 1 34W
Coquet, I. 35 55 21N 1 30W
Coquet, R. 35 55 18N 1 45W
Coquilhatville = Mbandaka 124 0 1N 18 18E
Coquille 160 43 15N 124 6W
Coquimbo 172 30 0S 71 20W
Coquimbo □ 172 31 0S 71 0W
Cora, oilfield 19 55 45N 4 45E
Corabia 70 43 48N 24 30E
Coraçáo de Jesus 171 11 39S 39 56W
Coracora 174 15 5S 73 45W
Coradi, Is. 65 40 27N 71 10E
Coral Harbour 149 64 8N 83 10W
Coral Rapids 150 50 20N 81 40W
Coral Sea 142 15 0S 150 0E
Coral Sea Islands Terr. 133 20 0S 155 0E
Corato 65 41 12N 16 22E
Corbeil-Essonnes 43 48 36N 2 26E
Corbie 43 49 54N 2 30E
Corbières, mts. 44 42 55N 2 35E
Corbigny 43 47 16N 3 40E
Corbin 156 37 0N 84 3W
Corbion 47 49 48N 5 0E
Corbones, R. 57 37 25N 5 35W
Corbridge 35 54 58N 2 0W
Corby, Lincs., U.K. 29 52 49N 0 31W
Corby, Northants., U.K. 29 52 29N 0 41W
Corcoles, R. 59 39 12N 2 40W
Corcoran 163 36 6N 119 35W
Corcubión 56 42 56N 9 12W
Cord. de Caravaya 174 14 0S 70 30W
Cordele 157 31 55N 83 49W
Cordell 159 35 18N 99 0W
Cordenons 63 45 59N 12 42E
Cordes 44 44 5N 1 57E
Cordillera Oriental 174 5 0N 74 0W
Cordisburgo 171 19 7S 44 21W
Córdoba 172 31 20S 64 10W
Cordoba 164 26 20N 103 20W
Córdoba, Mexico 165 18 50N 97 0W
Córdoba, Spain 57 37 50N 4 50W
Córdoba □, Argent. 172 31 22S 64 15W
Córdoba □, Colomb. 174 8 20N 75 40W
Córdoba □, Spain 57 38 5N 5 0W
Córdoba, Sierra de 172 31 10S 64 25W
Cordon 103 16 42N 121 32E
Cordova, Ala., U.S.A. 157 33 45N 87 12W
Cordova, Alaska, U.S.A. 147 60 36N 145 45W
Corella 58 42 7N 1 48W
Corella, R. 138 19 34S 140 47E
Coremas 170 7 1S 37 58W
Corfe Castle 28 50 58N 2 3W
Corfe Mullen 28 50 45N 2 0W
Corfield 138 21 40S 143 21E
Corfu = Kerkira 68 39 38N 19 50E
Corgo 56 42 56N 7 25W
Cori 64 41 39N 12 53E
Coria 56 40 0N 6 33W
Coricudgy, Mt. 141 32 51S 150 24E
Corigliano Cálabro 65 39 36N 16 31E
Coringa Is. 138 16 58S 149 58E
Corinna 138 41 35S 145 10E
Corinth, Miss., U.S.A. 157 34 54N 88 30W
Corinth, N.Y., U.S.A. 162 43 15N 73 50W
Corinth = Korinthos 69 37 56N 22 55E
Corinth Canal 69 37 48N 23 0E
Corinth, G. of = Korinthiakós 69 38 16N 22 30E
Corinto, Brazil 171 18 20S 44 30W
Corinto, Nic. 166 12 30N 87 10W
Corj □ 70 45 5N 23 25E
Cork 39 51 54N 8 30W
Cork □ 39 51 50N 8 50W
Cork Harbour 39 51 46N 8 16W
Corlay 42 48 20N 3 5W
Corleone 64 37 48N 13 16E
Corleto Perticara 65 40 23N 16 2E
Çorlu 67 41 11N 27 49E
Cormack L. 152 60 56N 121 37W
Cormóns 63 45 58N 13 29E
Cormorant 153 54 14N 100 35W
Cormorant L. 153 54 15N 100 50W
Cormorant, oilfield 19 61 0N 1 10E
Corn Hill, Mt. 38 53 48N 7 43W
Corn Is. 167 12 0N 83 0W
Cornelio 164 29 55N 111 8W
Cornélio Procópio 173 23 7S 50 40W
Cornell 158 45 10N 91 8W
Corner Brook 151 48 57N 57 58W
Corner Inlet 133 38 45S 146 20E
Cornforth 33 54 42N 1 28W
Corniglio 62 44 29N 10 5E
Corning, Ark., U.S.A. 159 36 27N 90 34W
Corning, Calif., U.S.A. 160 39 56N 122 9W
Corning, Iowa, U.S.A. 158 40 57N 94 40W
Corning, N.Y., U.S.A. 162 42 10N 77 3W
Cornwall, Austral. 138 41 33S 148 7E
Cornwall, Can. 150 45 2N 74 44W
Cornwall, U.S.A. 162 40 17N 76 25W
Cornwall □ 30 50 26N 4 40W
Cornwall, C. 30 50 8N 5 42W
Cornwallis I. 12 75 8N 95 0W
Corny Pt. 140 34 55S 137 0E
Coro 174 11 25N 69 41W
Coroaci 171 18 35S 42 17W

Coroatá 170 4 20S 44 0W
Corocoro 174 17 15S 69 19W
Corofin 39 53 27N 8 50W
Coroico 174 16 0S 67 50W
Coromandel, Brazil 171 18 28S 47 13W
Coromandel, N.Z. 142 36 45S 175 31E
Coromandel Coast 97 12 30N 81 0E
Coromandel Pen. 142 37 0S 175 45E
Coromandel Ra. 142 37 0S 175 40E
Coromorant, L. 153 54 20N 100 50W
Corona, Austral. 139 31 16S 141 24E
Corona, Calif., U.S.A. 163 33 49N 117 36W
Corona, N. Mex., U.S.A. 161 34 15N 105 32W
Coronada B. 166 9 0N 83 40W
Coronado 163 32 45N 117 9W
Coronado, Bahía de 166 9 0N 83 40W
Coronation 152 52 5N 111 27W
Coronation Gulf 148 68 25N 112 0W
Coronation I., Antarct. 13 60 45S 46 0W
Coronation I., U.S.A. 152 55 52N 134 20W
Coronation Is. 136 14 57S 124 55E
Coronda 172 31 58S 60 56W
Coronel 172 37 0S 73 10W
Coronel Bogado 172 27 11S 56 18W
Coronel Dorrego 172 38 40S 61 10W
Coronel Fabriciano 171 19 31S 42 38W
Coronel Murta 171 16 37S 42 11W
Coronel Oviedo 172 25 24S 56 30W
Coronel Pringles 172 38 0S 61 30W
Coronel Suárez 172 37 30S 62 0W
Coronel Vidal 172 37 28S 57 45W
Coronie 170 5 55N 56 25W
Corovoda 68 40 31N 20 14E
Corowa 141 35 58S 146 21E
Corozal, Belize 165 18 30N 88 30W
Corozal, Colomb. 174 9 19N 75 18W
Corpach 36 56 50N 5 9W
Corps 45 44 50N 5 56E
Corpus 173 27 10S 55 30W
Corpus Christi 159 27 50N 97 28W
Corpus Christi L. 159 28 5N 97 54W
Corque 174 18 10S 67 50W
Corral de Almaguer 58 39 45N 3 10W
Corran 36 56 44N 5 14W
Corrandibby Ra. 137 26 0S 115 20E
Corraun Pen. 38 53 58N 10 15W
Corrégio 62 44 46N 10 47E
Corrente 170 10 27S 45 10W
Corrente, R. 170 13 8S 43 28W
Correntes, C. das 129 24 6S 35 34E
Correntina 171 13 20S 44 39W
Corrèze □ 44 45 20N 1 45E
Corrib, L. 38 53 25N 9 10W
Corrie 34 55 39N 5 10W
Corrientes 172 27 30S 58 45W
Corrientes □ 172 28 0S 57 0W
Corrientes, C., Colomb. 174 5 30N 77 34W
Corrientes, C., Cuba 166 21 43N 84 30W
Corrientes, C., Mexico 164 20 25N 105 42W
Corrientes, R., Argent. 172 30 21S 59 33W
Corrientes, R., Colomb. 174 3 15S 75 58W
Corrigan 159 31 0N 94 48W
Corrigin 137 32 20S 117 53E
Corringham 33 53 25N 0 42W
Corris 31 52 41N 3 49W
Corrowidgie 141 36 56S 148 50E
Corry 156 41 55N 79 39W
Corryong 141 36 12S 147 53E
Corryvrecken, G. of 34 56 10N 5 44W
Corse, C. 45 43 1N 9 25E
Corse-du-Sud □ 45 41 45N 9 0E
Corse, Î 45 42 0N 9 0E
Corsewall Pt. 34 55 0N 5 10W
Corsham 28 51 25N 2 11W
Corsica = Corse 45 42 0N 9 0E
Corsicana 159 32 5N 96 30W
Corsley 28 51 12N 2 14W
Corsock 35 55 54N 3 56W
Corté 45 42 19N 9 11E
Corte do Pinto 57 37 42N 7 29W
Cortegana 57 37 52N 6 49W
Cortez 161 37 24N 108 35W
Cortina d'Ampezzo 63 46 32N 12 9E
Cortland 162 42 35N 76 11W
Corton 29 52 31N 1 46E
Cortona 63 43 16N 12 0E
Coruche 57 38 57N 8 30W
Çorum 92 40 30N 35 5E
Corumbá, Goias, Brazil 171 16 0S 48 50W
Corumbá, Mato Grosso, Brazil 174 19 0S 57 30W
Corumbá R. 171 17 25S 48 30W
Corumbaíba 171 18 9S 48 34W
Coruña □ 56 43 0N 8 37E
Coruña, La 56 43 20N 8 25W
Coruña, La □ 56 43 10N 8 30W
Corund 70 46 30N 25 13E
Corunna = La Coruña 56 43 20N 8 25W
Coruripe 171 10 5S 36 10W
Corvallis 160 44 36N 123 15W
Corve, R. 28 52 22N 2 43W
Corvette, L. de la 150 53 25N 73 55W
Corwen 31 52 59N 3 23W
Corydon 158 40 42N 93 22W
Cosalá 164 24 28N 106 40W
Cosamaloapán 165 18 23N 95 50W
Coseley 28 52 33N 2 6W
Cosenza 65 39 17N 16 14E
Coşereni 70 44 38N 26 35E
Cosham 28 50 51N 1 3W
Coshocton 156 40 17N 81 51W
Cosne-s.-Loire 43 47 24N 2 54E
Coso Junction 163 36 3N 117 57W
Coso Pk. 163 36 13N 117 44W
Cospeito 56 43 12N 7 34W
Cosquín 172 31 15S 64 30W
Cossato 62 45 34N 8 10E
Cossé-le-Vivien 42 47 57N 0 54W
Costa Azul 50 43 25N 6 50E
Costa Blanca 59 38 25N 0 10W
Costa Brava 58 41 30N 3 0E
Costa del Sol 57 36 30N 4 30W
Costa Dorada 58 40 45N 1 15E
Costa Mesa 163 33 39N 117 55W
Costa Rica 164 31 20N 112 40W
Costa Rica ■ 166 10 0N 84 0W
Costa Smeralda 64 41 5N 9 35E
Costelloe 39 53 20N 9 33W
Costessey 29 52 40N 1 11E
Costigliole d'Asti 62 44 48N 8 11E
Costilla 161 37 0N 105 30W
Coştiui 70 47 53N 24 2E
Cosumnes, R. 163 38 14N 121 25W
Coswig 48 51 52N 12 31E
Cotabato 103 7 14N 124 15E
Cotabena 140 31 42S 138 11E
Cotagaita 172 20 45S 65 30W
Côte d'Azur 45 43 25N 6 50E
Côte d'Or 43 47 10N 4 50E
Côte d'Or □ 43 47 30N 4 50E
Côte, La 50 46 25N 6 15E
Côte-St. André, La 45 45 24N 5 15E
Coteau des Prairies 158 44 30N 97 0W
Coteau du Missouri, Plat. du 154 47 0N 101 0W
Cotegipe 171 12 2S 44 15W
Cotentin 42 49 30N 1 30W
Côtes de Meuse 43 49 15N 5 22E
Côtes-du-Nord □ 42 48 25N 2 40W
Cotherstone 32 54 34N 1 59W
Cotiella 58 42 31N 0 19E
Cotina, R. 66 43 36N 19 9E
Cotonou 121 6 20N 2 25E
Cotopaxi, Vol. 174 0 30S 78 30W
Cotronei 65 39 9N 16 27E
Cotswold Hills 28 51 42N 2 10W
Cottage Grove 160 43 48N 123 2W
Cottbus 48 51 44N 14 20E
Cottbus □ 48 51 43N 13 30E
Cottenham 29 52 18N 0 8E
Cottingham 36 53 47N 0 23W
Cottonwood, Can. 152 53 5N 121 50W
Cottonwood, U.S.A. 161 34 48N 112 1W
Coubre, Pte. de la 44 45 42N 1 15W
Couches 43 46 53N 4 30E
Couço 57 38 59N 8 17W
Coudersport 156 41 45N 78 1W
Couedic, C. du 140 36 5S 136 40E
Couëron 42 47 13N 1 44W
Coueson, R. 42 48 20N 1 15W
Couhé-Vérac 44 46 18N 0 12E
Couillet 47 50 23N 4 28E
Coulags 36 57 26N 5 24W
Coulanges, Deux Sèvres, France 44 46 58N 0 35W
Coulanges, Yonne, France 43 47 30N 3 30E
Coulee City 160 47 44N 119 12W
Coulman I. 13 73 35S 170 0E
Coulommiers 43 48 50N 3 3E
Coulonge, R. 150 45 52N 76 46W
Coulport 34 56 3N 4 53W
Coulterville 163 37 42N 120 12W
Council 147 64 55N 163 45W
Council Bluffs 158 41 20N 95 50W
Council Grove 158 38 41N 96 30W
Coupar Angus 35 56 33N 3 17W
Courantyne, R. 174 5 0N 57 45W
Courçon 44 46 15N 0 50W
Cours 45 46 7N 4 19E
Courseulles 42 49 20N 0 29W
Court-St.-Etienne 47 50 38N 4 34E
Courtenay 152 49 45N 125 0W
Courtine, La 44 45 43N 2 16E
Courtland 163 38 20N 121 34W
Courtmacsherry 39 51 38N 8 43W
Courtmacsherry B. 39 51 37N 8 37W
Courtown 39 52 39N 6 14W
Courtrai = Kortrijk 47 50 50N 3 17E
Courville 42 48 28N 1 15E
Coutances 42 49 3N 1 28W
Couterne 42 48 30N 0 25W
Coutras 44 45 3N 0 8W
Coutts 152 49 0N 111 57W
Couvet 50 46 57N 6 38E
Couvin 47 50 3N 4 29E
Covarrubias 58 42 4N 3 31W
Covasna 70 45 50N 26 10E
Covasna □ 70 45 50N 26 0E
Cove Bay 37 57 5N 2 5W
Coventry 28 52 25N 1 31W
Coventry L. 153 61 15N 106 15W
Cover R. 32 54 14N 1 45W
Coverack 30 50 2N 5 6W
Covilhã 56 40 17N 7 31W
Covina 163 34 5N 117 52W
Covington, Ga., U.S.A. 157 33 36N 83 50W
Covington, Ky., U.S.A. 156 39 5N 84 30W
Covington, Okla., U.S.A. 159 36 21N 97 36W
Covington, Tenn., U.S.A. 159 35 34N 89 39W
Cowal Creek Settlement 138 10 54S 142 20E
Cowal, dist. 34 56 5N 5 8W
Cowal, L. 141 33 40S 147 25E
Cowan 153 52 5N 100 45W
Cowan, L. 137 31 45S 121 45E
Cowan L. 153 54 0N 107 15W
Cowangie 140 35 12S 141 26E
Coward Springs 139 29 24S 136 48E
Cowarie 139 27 45S 138 15E
Cowarna 137 30 55S 122 40E
Cowbridge 31 51 28N 3 28W
Cowcowing Lakes 137 30 55S 117 20E
Cowdenbeath 35 56 7N 3 20W
Cowell 140 33 39S 136 56E
Cowes 28 50 45N 1 18W
Cowfold 29 50 58N 0 16W
Cowl Cowl 141 33 36S 145 18E
Cowley 28 51 43N 1 12W
Cowpen 35 55 8N 1 34W
Cowra 141 33 49S 148 42E
Coxim 175 18 30S 54 55W
Cox's Bazar 98 21 26N 91 59E
Cox's Cove 151 49 7N 58 5W
Coyame 164 29 28N 105 6W
Coylton 34 55 26N 4 31W
Coyuca de Benítez 165 17 1N 100 8W
Coyuca de Catalán 164 18 58N 100 41W
Cozad 158 40 55N 99 57W
Cozie, Alpi 62 44 50N 6 59E
Cozumel 165 20 31N 86 55W
Cozumel, Isla de 165 20 30N 86 40W
Craanford 39 52 40N 6 23W
Craboon 141 32 3S 149 30E
Cracow 139 25 17S 150 17E
Cradock 128 32 8S 25 36E
Craggie 37 57 25N 4 6W
Craig, Alaska, U.S.A. 147 55 30N 133 5W
Craig, Colo., U.S.A. 160 40 32N 107 44W
Craigavon = Portadown 38 54 27N 6 26W
Craigavon = Lurgan 38 54 28N 6 20W
Craigellachie 37 57 29N 3 9W
Craighouse 34 55 50N 5 58W
Craigmore 127 20 28S 32 30E
Craignish, L. 34 56 11N 5 32W
Craigtown 37 58 30N 3 53W
Crail 35 56 16N 2 38W
Crailsheim 49 49 7N 10 5E
Craiova 70 44 21N 23 48E
Cramlington 35 55 5N 1 36W
Crampel 117 7 8N 19 81E
Cramsie 138 23 20S 144 15E
Cranberry Portage 153 54 35N 101 23W
Cranborne 28 50 55N 1 55W
Cranborne Chase 29 50 56N 2 6W
Cranbrook, Tas., Austral. 138 42 0S 148 5E
Cranbrook, W. Austral., Austral. 137 34 18S 117 33E
Cranbrook, Can. 152 49 30N 115 46W
Cranbrook, U.K. 29 51 6N 0 33E
Crandon 158 45 32N 88 52W
Crane, Oregon, U.S.A. 160 43 21N 118 39W
Crane, Texas, U.S.A. 159 31 26N 102 27W
Cranfield Pt. 38 54 1N 6 3W
Cranleigh 29 51 8N 0 29W
Cranshaws 35 55 51N 2 30W
Cranston 162 41 47N 71 27W
Cranwell 33 53 4N 0 29W
Craon 42 47 50N 0 58W
Craonne 43 49 27N 3 46E
Crasna 70 46 32N 27 51E
Crasna, R. 70 47 44N 27 35E
Crater Lake 160 42 55N 122 3W
Crater Mt. 135 6 37S 145 7E
Crater Pt. 135 5 25S 152 9E
Crateús 170 5 10S 40 50W
Crathie 37 57 3N 3 12W
Crati, R. 65 39 41N 16 30E
Crato, Brazil 171 7 10S 39 25W
Crato, Port. 57 39 16N 7 39W
Crau 45 43 32N 4 40E
Craughwell 39 53 15N 8 44W
Craven Arms 28 52 27N 2 49W
Crawford, U.K. 35 55 28N 3 40W
Crawford, U.S.A. 158 42 40N 103 25W
Crawford, oilfield 19 59 7N 1 30E
Crawfordsville 156 40 2N 86 51W
Crawley 29 51 7N 0 10W
Cray 31 51 55N 3 38W
Crazy Mts. 160 46 14N 110 30W
Creag Meagaidh, mt. 37 56 57N 4 38W
Crean L. 153 54 5N 106 9W
Crèche, La 44 46 23N 0 19W
Crécy-en-Brie 43 48 50N 2 53E
Crécy-en-Ponthieu 43 50 15N 1 53E
Crécy-sur-Serre 43 49 40N 3 32E
Credenhill 28 52 6N 2 49W
Crediton 30 50 47N 3 39W
Credo 137 30 28S 120 45E
Cree L. 153 57 30N 106 30W
Cree, R., Can. 153 58 57N 105 47W
Cree, R., U.K. 34 54 51N 4 24W
Creede 161 37 56N 106 59W
Creegh 39 52 45N 9 25W
Creel 164 27 45N 107 38W
Creeside 34 55 4N 4 41W
Creeslough 38 55 8N 7 55W
Creetown 34 54 54N 4 23W
Creeves 39 52 33N 9 3W
Creggan 38 54 39N 7 0W
Cregganbaun 38 53 42N 9 48W
Creighton 158 42 30N 97 52W
Creil 43 49 15N 2 34E
Crema 62 45 21N 9 40E
Cremona 62 45 8N 10 2E
Crepaja 66 45 1N 20 38E
Crêpy 43 49 37N 3 32E
Crêpy-en-Valois 43 49 14N 2 54E
Cres 63 44 58N 14 25E
Cresbard 158 45 13N 98 57W
Crescent, Okla., U.S.A. 159 35 38N 97 36W
Crescent, Oreg., U.S.A. 160 43 30N 121 37W
Crescent City 160 41 45N 124 12W
Crescentino 62 45 11N 8 7E
Crespino 63 44 59N 11 51E
Crespo 172 32 2S 60 19W
Cressman 150 47 40N 72 55W
Cressy 140 38 2S 143 40E
Crest 45 44 44N 5 2E
Crested Butte 161 38 57N 107 0W
Crestline 163 34 14N 117 18W
Creston, Can. 152 49 10N 116 31W
Creston, Calif., U.S.A. 163 35 32N 120 33W
Creston, Iowa, U.S.A. 158 41 0N 94 20W
Creston, Wash., U.S.A. 160 47 47N 118 36W
Creston, Wyo., U.S.A. 160 41 46N 107 50W
Crestone 161 35 2N 106 0W
Crestview, Calif., U.S.A. 163 37 46N 118 58W
Crestview, Fla., U.S.A. 157 30 45N 86 35W
Creswick 140 37 25S 143 51E
Crete 158 40 38N 96 58W
Crete = Kriti 69 35 15N 25 0E
Crete, La, Can. 152 58 10N 116 29W
Crete, La, Alta., Can. 152 58 11N 116 24W
Crete, Sea of 69 26 0N 25 0E
Cretin, C. 135 6 40S 147 53E
Creus, C. 58 42 20N 3 19E
Creuse □ 44 46 0N 2 0E
Creuse, R. 44 47 0N 0 34E
Creusot, Le 43 46 50N 4 24E
Creuzburg 48 51 3N 10 15E
Crevalcore 63 44 41N 11 10E
Crèvecœur-le-Grand 43 49 37N 2 5E
Crevillente 59 38 12N 0 48W
Crewe 32 53 6N 2 28W
Crewkerne 28 50 53N 2 48W
Crianlarich 34 56 24N 4 37W
Crib Point 139 38 22S 145 13E
Criccieth 31 52 55N 4 15W
Criciúma 173 28 40S 49 23W
Crick 28 52 22N 1 9W
Crickhowell 31 51 52N 3 8W
Cricklade 28 51 38N 1 50W
Crieff 35 56 22N 3 50W
Criffell Mt. 35 54 56N 3 38W
Crikvenica 63 45 11N 14 40E
Crillon, Mt. 152 58 39N 137 14W
Crimea = Krymskaya 82 45 0N 34 0E
Crimmitschau 48 50 48N 12 23E
Crimond 37 57 35N 1 53W
Crinan Canal 34 56 4N 5 30W
Crinkill 39 53 5N 7 55E
Cristalândia 170 10 36S 49 11W
Cristeşti 70 47 15N 26 33E
Cristino Castro 170 8 49S 44 13W
Crişul Alb, R. 66 46 25N 21 40E
Crişul Negru, R. 70 46 38N 22 26E
Crişul Repede, R. 70 47 20N 22 25E
Crivitz 48 53 35N 11 39E
Crixás 171 14 27S 49 58W
Crna Gora □ 66 42 40N 19 20E
Crna Trava 66 42 49N 22 19E
Crni Drim, R. 66 41 17N 20 40E
Crni Timok, R. 66 43 53N 22 0E
Črnoljeva Planina 66 42 20N 21 0E
Črnomeij 63 45 33N 15 10E
Croagh Patrick, mt. 38 53 46N 9 40W
Croatia = Hrvatska 63 45 20N 16 0E
Crocker, Barisan 102 5 0N 116 30E
Crocketford 35 55 3N 3 49W
Crockets Town 38 54 8N 9 7W
Crockett 159 31 20N 95 30W
Crocodile Is. 138 11 43S 135 8E
Crocodile, R. 129 25 30S 31 15E
Crocq 44 45 52N 2 21E
Croghan 38 53 55N 8 13W
Croglin 32 54 50N 2 37W
Crohy Hd. 38 54 55N 8 28W
Croisic, Le 42 47 18N 2 30W
Croisic, Pte. du. 42 47 19N 2 31W
Croix, La, L. 150 48 20N 92 15W
Croker, C. 136 10 58S 132 35E
Croker, I. 136 11 12S 132 32E
Crolly 38 55 2N 8 16W
Cromalt Hills 36 58 0N 5 2W
Cromarty, Can. 153 58 3N 94 9W
Cromarty, U.K. 37 57 40N 4 2W
Cromarty Firth 37 57 40N 4 15W
Cromdale, Hills of 37 57 20N 3 28W
Cromer 29 52 56N 1 18E
Cromore 36 58 6N 6 23W
Cromwell, N.Z. 143 45 3S 169 14E
Cromwell, U.S.A. 162 41 36N 72 39W
Cronat 43 46 43N 3 40E
Crondall 29 51 13N 0 51W
Cronulla 141 34 3S 151 8E
Crook 33 54 43N 1 45W
Crooked I. 167 22 50N 74 10W
Crooked Island Passage 167 23 0N 74 30W
Crooked, R., Can. 152 54 10N 122 35W
Crooked, R., U.S.A. 160 44 30N 121 0W
Crooklands 32 54 16N 2 43W
Crookston, Minn., U.S.A. 158 47 50N 96 40W
Crookston, Nebr., U.S.A. 158 42 56N 100 45W
Crookstown 39 51 50N 8 50W
Crooksville 156 39 45N 82 8W

Crookwell 141 34 28S 149 24E
Croom 39 52 32N 8 43W
Crosby, Cumb., U.K. 32 54 45N 3 25W
Crosby, Merseyside, U.K. 32 53 30N 3 2W
Crosby, Minn., U.S.A. 158 46 28N 93 57W
Crosby, N.D., U.S.A. 153 48 55N 103 18W
Crosby Ravensworth 32 54 34N 2 35W
Crosbyton 159 33 37N 101 12W
Cross City 157 29 35N 83 5W
Cross Fell 32 54 44N 2 29W
Cross L. 153 54 45N 97 30W
Cross Plains 159 32 8N 99 7W
Cross, R. 121 4 46N 8 20E
Cross River □ 121 6 0N 8 0E
Cross Sound 147 58 20N 136 30W
Crossakiel 38 53 43N 7 2W
Crossbost 36 58 8N 6 27W
Crossdoney 38 53 57N 7 27W
Crosse, La, Kans., U.S.A. 158 38 33N 99 20W
Crosse, La, Wis., U.S.A. 158 43 48N 91 13W
Crossett 159 33 10N 91 57W
Crossfarnoge Pt. 39 52 10N 6 37W
Crossfield 152 51 25N 114 0W
Crossgar 38 54 22N 5 46W
Crosshaven 39 51 48N 8 19W
Crosshill 34 55 19N 4 39W
Crossley, Mt. 143 42 50S 172 5E
Crossmaglen 38 54 5N 6 37W
Crossmolina 38 54 6N 9 21W
Croton-on-Hudson 162 41 12N 73 55W
Crotone 65 39 5N 17 6E
Crouch, R. 29 51 37N 0 53E
Crow Agency 160 45 40N 107 30W
Crow Hd. 39 51 34N 10 9W
Crow, R. 152 59 41N 124 20W
Crow Sound 30 49 56N 6 16W
Crowborough 29 51 3N 0 9E
Crowell 159 33 59N 99 45W
Crowl Creek 141 32 0S 145 30E
Crowland 29 52 41N 0 10W
Crowle 33 53 36N 0 49W
Crowley 159 30 15N 92 20W
Crowley, L. 163 37 53N 118 42W
Crowlin Is. 36 57 20N 5 50W
Crown Point 156 41 24N 87 23W
Crows Landing 163 37 23N 121 6W
Crows Nest 139 27 16S 152 4E
Crowsnest Pass 152 49 40N 114 40W
Croyde 30 51 7N 4 13W
Croydon, Austral. 138 18 13S 142 14E
Croydon, U.K. 29 51 18N 0 5W
Crozet, Île 11 46 27S 52 0E
Crozon 42 48 15N 4 30W
Cruces, Pta. 174 6 39N 77 32W
Cruden Bay 37 57 25N 1 50W
Crudgington 28 52 46N 2 33W
Crumlin 38 54 38N 6 12W
Crummer Peaks 138 6 40S 144 0E
Crummock Water L. 32 54 33N 3 18W
Crusheen 39 52 57N 8 52W
Cruz, C. 166 19 50N 77 50W
Cruz das Almas 171 12 40S 39 6W
Cruz de Malta 170 8 15S 40 20W
Cruz del Eje 172 30 45S 64 50W
Cruz, La, Colomb. 174 1 35N 76 58W
Cruz, La, C. Rica 166 11 4N 85 39W
Cruz, La, Mexico 164 23 55N 106 54W
Cruzeiro 173 22 50S 45 0W
Cruzeiro do Oeste 173 23 46S 53 4W
Cruzeiro do Sul 174 7 35S 72 35W
Cry L. 152 58 45N 128 5W
Cryfow Sl. 54 51 2N 15 24E
Crymmych 31 51 59N 4 40W
Crystal Brook 140 33 21S 138 12E
Crystal City, Mo., U.S.A. 158 38 15N 90 23W
Crystal City, Tex., U.S.A. 159 28 40N 99 50W
Crystal Falls 156 46 9N 88 11W
Crystal River 157 28 54N 82 35W
Crystal Springs 159 31 59N 90 25W
Čáslav 52 49 54N 15 22E
Csongrád 53 46 43N 20 12E
Csongrád □ 53 46 32N 20 15E
Csorna 53 47 38N 17 18E
Csurgo 53 46 16N 17 9E
Ctesiphon 92 33 9N 44 35E
Cu Lao Hon 101 10 54N 108 18E
Cua Rao 100 19 16N 104 27E
Cuácua, R. 127 18 0S 36 0E
Cuamato 128 17 2S 15 7E
Cuamba = Nova Preixo 127 14 45S 36 22E
Cuando 128 16 25S 22 2E
Cuando Cubango □ 128 16 25S 20 0E
Cuando, R. 125 14 0S 19 30E
Cuangar 128 17 28S 14 40E
Cuango 124 6 15S 16 35E
Cuarto, R. 172 33 25S 63 2W
Cuatrociénegas de Carranza 164 26 59N 102 5W
Cuauhtémoc 164 28 25N 106 52W
Cuba, Port. 57 38 10N 7 54W
Cuba, U.S.A. 161 36 0N 107 0W
Cuba ■ 166 22 0N 79 0W
Cuballing 137 32 50S 117 10E
Cubango, R. 128 16 15S 17 45E
Cuchi 125 14 37S 17 10E
Cuchumatanes, Sierra de los 166 15 35N 91 25W
Cuckfield 29 51 0N 0 8W
Cucurpe 164 30 20N 110 43W
Cucurrupí 174 4 23N 76 56W
Cúcuta 174 7 54N 72 31W
Cudahy 156 42 54N 87 50W
Cudalbi 70 45 46N 27 41E
Cuddalore 97 11 46N 79 45E
Cuddapah 97 14 30N 78 47E
Cuddapan, L. 138 25 45S 141 26E
Cudgewa 141 36 10S 147 42E
Cudillero 56 43 33N 6 9W
Cudworth 33 53 35N 1 25W
Cue 137 27 25S 117 54E
Cuéllar 56 41 23N 4 21W
Cuenca, Ecuador 174 2 50S 79 9W
Cuenca, Spain 58 40 5N 2 10W
Cuenca □ 58 40 0N 2 0W
Cuenca, Serranía de 58 39 55N 1 50W
Cuencamé 164 24 53N 103 41W
Cuerda del Pozo, Pantano de la 58 41 51N 2 44W
Cuernavaca 165 18 50N 99 20W
Cuero 159 29 5N 97 17W
Cuers 45 43 14N 6 5E
Cuervo 159 35 5N 104 25W
Cuesmes 47 50 26N 3 56E
Cuevas de Altamira 56 43 20N 4 5W
Cuevas del Almanzora 59 37 18N 1 58W
Cuevo 174 20 25N 63 30W
Cugir 70 43 48N 23 25E
Cugno 123 6 14N 42 31E
Cuhimbre 174 0 10S 75 23W
Cuiabá 175 15 30S 56 0W
Cuiabá, R. 175 16 50S 56 30W
Cuidad Bolivar 174 8 21N 70 34W
Cuilcagh, Mt. 38 54 12N 7 50W
Cuilco 166 15 24N 91 58W
Cuillin Hills 36 57 14N 6 15W
Cuillin Sd. 36 57 4N 6 20W
Cuima 125 13 0S 15 45E
Cuiseaux 45 46 30N 5 22E
Cuité 170 6 29S 36 9W
Cuito, R. 128 16 50S 19 30E
Cuitzeo, L. 164 19 55N 101 5W
Cujmir 70 44 13N 22 57E
Culan 44 46 34N 2 20E
Cŭlaraşi 43 44 14N 27 23E
Culbertson 158 48 9N 104 30W
Culburra 140 35 50S 139 58E
Culcairn 141 35 45S 147 3E
Culdaff 38 55 17N 7 10W
Culebra, I. 147 18 19N 65 17W
Culebra, Sierra de la 56 41 55N 6 20W
Culemborg 46 51 58N 5 14E
Culgoa 140 35 44S 143 6E
Culgoa, R. 139 29 56S 146 20E
Culiacán 164 24 50N 107 40W
Culiacán, R. 164 24 30N 107 42W
Cŭlimani, Munţii 70 47 12N 25 0E
Cŭlineşti 70 45 21N 24 18E
Culion, I. 103 11 54N 120 1E
Cúllar de Baza 59 37 35N 2 34W
Cullarin Range 141 34 30S 149 30E
Cullaville 38 54 4N 6 40W
Cullen, Austral. 136 13 58S 131 54E
Cullen, U.K. 37 57 45N 2 50W
Cullen Pt. 138 11 57S 141 54E
Cullera 59 39 9N 0 17W
Cullin L. 38 53 58N 9 12W
Cullivoe 36 60 43N 1 0W
Cullman 157 34 13N 86 50W
Culloden Moor 37 57 29N 4 7W
Cullompton 30 50 52N 3 23W
Cullyhanna 38 54 8N 6 35W
Culm, R. 30 50 46N 3 31W
Culoz 45 45 47N 5 46E
Culpataro 140 33 40S 144 22E
Culpeper 156 38 29N 77 59W
Culrain 37 57 55N 4 25W
Culross 35 56 4N 3 38W
Cults 37 57 8N 2 10W
Culuene, R. 175 12 15S 53 10W
Culvain Mt. 36 56 55N 5 19W
Culver, Pt. 137 32 54S 124 43E
Culverden 143 42 47S 172 49E
Cumali 69 36 42N 27 28E
Cumaná 174 10 30N 64 5W
Cumari 171 18 16S 48 11W
Cumberland, Can. 152 49 40N 125 0W
Cumberland, Md., U.S.A. 156 39 40N 78 43W
Cumberland, Wis., U.S.A. 158 45 32N 92 3W
Cumberland (□) 26 54 44N 2 55W
Cumberland I. 157 30 52N 81 30W
Cumberland Is. 138 20 35S 149 10E
Cumberland L. 153 54 3N 102 18W
Cumberland Pen. 149 67 0N 64 0W
Cumberland Plat. 157 36 0N 84 30W
Cumberland, R. 157 36 15N 87 0W
Cumberland Sd. 149 65 30N 66 0W
Cumborah 139 29 40S 147 45E
Cumbrae Is. 34 55 46N 4 54W
Cumbres Mayores 57 38 4N 6 39W
Cumbria □ 32 54 35N 2 55W
Cumbrian Mts. 32 54 30N 3 0W
Cumbum 97 15 40N 79 10E
Cuminestown 37 57 32N 2 17W
Cummerower See 48 53 47N 12 52E
Cummertrees 35 55 0N 3 20W
Cummings Mtn. 163 35 2N 118 34W
Cummins 139 34 16S 135 43E
Cumnock, Austral. 141 32 59S 148 46E
Cumnock, U.K. 34 55 27N 4 18W
Cumnor 28 51 44N 1 20W
Cumpas 164 30 0N 109 48W
Cumuruxatiba 171 17 6S 39 13W
Cumwhinton 32 54 51N 2 49W
Cuñaré 174 0 49N 72 32W
Cuncumén 172 31 53S 70 38W
Cunderdin 137 31 37S 117 12E
Cundinamarca □ 174 5 0N 74 0W
Cunene, R. 128 17 0S 15 0E
Cúneo 62 44 23N 7 31E
Cunillera, I. 59 38 59N 1 13E
Cunlhat 44 45 38N 3 32E
Cunnamulla 139 28 2S 145 38E
Cunninghame, Reg. 34 55 38N 4 35W
Cuorgnè 62 45 23N 7 39E
Cupar, Can. 153 50 57N 104 10W
Cupar, U.K. 35 56 20N 3 0W
Cupica 174 6 50N 77 30W
Cupica, Golfo de 174 6 25N 77 30W
Ćuprija 66 43 57N 21 26E
Curaçá 170 8 59S 39 54W
Curaçao, I. 167 12 10N 69 0W
Curanilahue 172 37 29S 73 28W
Curaray, R. 174 1 30S 75 30W
Curatabaca 174 6 19N 62 51W
Curbarado 174 7 3N 76 54W
Curbur 137 26 28S 115 55E
Cure, La 50 46 28N 6 4E
Curepto 172 35 8S 72 1W
Curiapo 174 8 33N 61 5W
Curicó 172 34 55S 71 20W
Curicó □ 172 34 50S 71 15W
Curimatá 170 10 2S 44 17W
Curiplaya 174 0 16N 74 52W
Curitiba 173 25 20S 49 10W
Curlew Mts. 38 54 0N 8 20W
Curoca Norte 128 16 15S 12 58E
Currabubula 141 31 16S 150 44E
Curracunya 139 28 29S 144 9E
Curraglass 39 52 5N 8 4W
Currais Novos 170 6 13S 36 30W
Curralinho 170 1 35S 49 30W
Curran, L. = Terewah, L. 139 29 50S 147 24E
Currane L. 39 51 50N 10 8W
Currant 160 38 51N 115 32W
Curranyalpa 141 30 53S 144 39E
Curraweena 141 30 47S 145 54E
Currawilla 138 25 10S 141 20E
Current, R. 159 37 15N 91 10W
Currie, Austral. 138 39 56S 143 53E
Currie, U.K. 35 55 53N 3 17W
Currie, U.S.A. 160 40 16N 114 45W
Currie, Mt. 129 30 29S 29 21E
Currituck Sd. 157 36 20N 75 50W
Curry Rivel 28 51 2N 2 52W
Curryglass 39 51 40N 9 50W
Curtea-de-Argeş 70 45 12N 24 42E
Curtis, Spain 56 43 7N 8 4W
Curtis, U.S.A. 158 40 41N 100 32W
Curtis, I. 138 23 35S 151 10E
Curtis, Pt. 138 23 53S 151 21E
Curuá, I. 170 0 48N 50 10W
Curuapanema, R. 175 7 0S 54 30W
Curuçá 170 0 35S 47 50W
Curuguaty 173 24 19S 55 49W
Curupira, Serra 174 1 25N 64 30W
Cururupu 170 1 50S 44 50W
Curuzú Cuatiá 172 29 50S 58 5W
Curvelo 171 18 45S 44 27W
Curyo 140 35 50S 142 47E
Cushendall 38 55 5N 6 3W
Cushendun 38 55 8N 6 3W
Cushina 39 53 11N 7 10W
Cushing, Mt. 152 57 35N 126 57W
Cusihuiriáchic 164 28 10N 106 50W
Cussabat 119 32 39N 14 1E
Cusset 44 46 8N 3 28E
Custer 158 43 45N 103 38W
Cut Bank 160 48 40N 112 15W
Cutchogue 162 41 1N 72 30W
Cuthbert 157 31 47N 84 47W
Cutler 163 36 31N 119 17W
Cutra L. 39 53 2N 8 48W
Cutro 65 39 1N 16 58E
Cuttaburra, R. 139 29 43S 144 22E
Cuttack 96 20 25N 85 57E
Cuvier, C. 137 23 14S 113 22E
Cuvier I. 142 36 27S 175 50E
Cuxhaven 48 53 51N 8 41E
Cuyabeno 174 0 16S 75 53W
Cuyahoga Falls 156 41 8N 81 30W
Cuyo 103 10 50N 121 5E
Cuyuni, R. 175 7 0N 59 30W
Cuzco 174 13 32S 72 0W
Cuzco, Mt. 174 20 0S 66 50W
Cŭzŭneşti 70 44 36N 27 3E
Čvrsnica, Mt. 66 43 36N 17 35E
Cwmbran 31 51 39N 3 0W
Cwrt 31 52 35N 3 55W
Cyangugu 126 2 29S 28 54E
Cybinka 54 52 12N 14 46E
Cyclades = Kikladhes 69 37 20N 24 30E
Cygnet 138 43 8S 147 1E
Cymmer 31 51 37N 3 38W
Cynthiana 156 38 23N 84 10W
Cynwyl Elfed 31 51 55N 4 22W
Cypress Hills 153 49 40N 109 30W
Cyprus ■ 92 35 0N 33 0E
Cyrenaica □ 117 27 0N 20 0E
Cyrene 117 32 39N 21 18E
Czaplinek 54 53 34N 16 14E
Czar 153 52 27N 110 50W
Czarne 54 53 42N 16 58E
Czarnków 54 52 55N 16 38E
Czechoslovakia ■ 53 49 0N 17 0E
Czechowice-Dziedzice 54 49 54N 18 59E
Czeladz 54 50 16N 19 2E
Czempin 54 52 9N 16 33E
Czersk 54 53 46N 17 58E
Czerwiensk 54 52 1N 15 13E
Czerwionka 54 50 7N 18 37E
Częstochowa 54 50 49N 19 7E
Częstochowa □ 54 50 45N 19 0E
Czlopa 54 53 6N 16 6E
Człuchów 54 53 41N 17 22E

D

Da Lat 101 11 56N 108 25E
Da Nang 100 16 4N 108 13E
Da, R. 100 21 15N 105 20E
Daarlerveen 46 52 26N 6 34E
Dab'a, Ras el 122 31 3N 28 31E
Dabai 121 11 25N 5 15E
Dabajuro 174 11 2N 70 40W
Dabakala 120 8 15N 4 20W
Dabatou 120 11 50N 9 20W
Dabburiya 90 32 42N 35 22E
Daberas 128 25 27S 18 30E
Dabhoi 94 22 10N 73 20E
Dabie 54 53 27N 14 45E
Dabola 120 10 50N 11 5W
Dabong 101 5 23N 103 1E
Dabou 120 5 20N 4 23W
Daboya 121 9 30N 1 20W
Dabra Berhan 123 9 42N 39 15E
Dabra Sina 123 9 51N 39 45E
Dabra Tabor 123 11 50N 37 58E
Dabra Zabit 123 11 48N 38 30E
Dabrowa Górnicza 54 50 15N 19 10E
Dabrowa Tarnówska 54 50 10N 20 59E
Dabrówno 54 53 27N 20 2E
Dabus, R. 123 10 12N 35 0E
Dacca 98 23 43N 90 26E
Dacca □ 98 24 0N 90 25E
Dachau 49 48 16N 11 27E
Dadanawa 174 3 0N 59 30W
Daday 82 41 28N 33 35E
Daddato 123 12 24N 42 45E
Dade City 157 28 20N 82 12W
Dadiya 121 9 35N 11 24E
Dadra and Nagar Haveli □ 96 20 5N 73 0E
Dadri = Charkhi Dadri 94 28 37N 76 17E
Dadu 94 26 45N 67 45E
Daer R. 35 55 23N 3 39W
Daet 103 14 2N 122 55E
Dagaio 123 6 8N 40 40E
Dagana 120 16 30N 15 20W
Dagash 122 19 19N 33 25E
Dagestan, A.S.S.R. □ 83 42 30N 47 0E
Daggett 163 34 43N 116 52W
Daggs Sd. 143 45 23S 166 45E
Daghfeli 122 19 18N 32 40E
Daghirie 123 11 40N 41 50E
Dagö = Hiiumaa 80 58 50N 22 45E
Dagoreti 126 1 18S 36 4E
Dagua 135 3 27S 143 20E
Dagupan 103 16 3N 120 20E
Dahab 122 28 30N 34 31E
Dahlak Kebir 123 15 50N 40 10E
Dahlenburg 48 53 11N 10 43E
Dahlonega 157 34 35N 83 59W
Dahme 48 51 51N 13 25E
Daho 121 10 28N 11 18E
Dahomey ■ = Benin ■ 121 8 0N 2 0E
Dahra 120 15 22N 15 30W
Dahra, Massif de 118 36 7N 1 21E
Dai Hao 100 18 1N 106 25E
Dai-Sen 110 35 22N 133 32E
Daigo 111 36 46N 140 21E
Dailly 34 55 16N 4 44W
Daimanji-San 110 36 14N 133 20E
Daimiel 59 39 5N 3 35W
Daintree 138 16 20S 145 20E
Daiō-Misaki 111 34 15N 136 45E
Dairen = Lüta 107 38 55N 121 40E
Dairût 122 27 34N 30 43E
Dairymple 34 55 24N 4 36W
Daisetsu-Zan 112 43 30N 142 57E
Daitari 96 21 10N 85 46E
Daitō 110 35 19N 132 58E
Dajarra 138 21 42S 139 30E
Dak Dam 100 12 20N 107 21E
Dak Nhe 100 15 28N 107 48E
Dak Pek 100 15 4N 107 44E
Dak Song 101 12 19N 107 35E
Dak Sui 100 14 55N 107 43E
Dakala 121 14 27N 2 27E
Dakar 120 14 34N 17 29W
Dakhla 116 23 50N 15 53W
Dakhla, El Wâhât el- 122 25 30N 28 50E
Dakhovskaya 83 44 13N 40 13E
Dakingari 121 11 37N 4 1E
Dakor 94 22 45N 73 11E
Dakoro 121 14 31N 6 46E
Dakota City 158 42 27N 96 28W
Dakota, North 158 47 30N 100 0W
Đakovica 66 42 22N 20 26E
Dakovo 66 45 19N 18 24E
Dakra 120 15 22N 15 30W
Dalaba 120 10 42N 12 15W
Dalälven, L. 72 61 27N 17 15E
Dalandzadgad 106 43 27N 104 30E

Dalarö **75** 59 8N 18 24 E
Dalat **101** 12 3N 108 32 E
Dalbandin **93** 29 0N 4 23 E
Dalbeattie **35** 54 55N 3 50W
Dalbosjön, L. **73** 58 40N 12 45 E
Dalby, Austral. **139** 27 10 S 151 17 E
Dalby, Sweden **73** 55 42N 13 22 E
Dale, Sogn og Fjordane, Norway **71** 61 27N 7 28 E
Dale, Sogn og Fjordane, Norway **71** 61 22N 5 23 E
Dale, U.K. **31** 51 42N 5 11W
Dalen, Neth. **46** 52 42N 6 46 E
Dalen, Norway **71** 59 26N 8 0 E
Dalet **98** 19 59N 93 51 E
Daletme **98** 21 36N 92 46 E
Dalfsen **46** 52 31N 6 16 E
Dalga **122** 27 39N 30 41 E
Dalgaranger, Mt. **137** 27 50 S 117 5 E
Dalhalvaig **37** 58 28N 3 53W
Dalhart **159** 36 0N 102 30W
Dalhousie, Can. **151** 48 0N 66 26W
Dalhousie, India **94** 32 38N 76 0 E
Daliburgh **36** 57 10N 7 23W
Dalj **174** 45 28N 18 58 E
Dalkeith **35** 55 54N 3 5W
Dalkey **39** 53 16N 6 7W
Dall I. **152** 54 59N 133 25W
Dallarnil **139** 25 19 S 152 2 E
Dallas, U.K. **37** 57 33N 3 32W
Dallas, Oregon, U.S.A. **160** 45 0N 123 15W
Dallas, Texas, U.S.A. **159** 32 50N 96 50W
Dallol **123** 14 14N 40 17 E
Dalmacija **66** 43 20N 17 0 E
Dalmally **34** 56 25N 5 0W
Dalmatia = Dalmacija **66** 43 20N 17 0 E
Dalmatovo **84** 56 16N 62 56 E
Dalmellington **34** 55 20N 4 25W
Dalneretchensk **77** 45 50N 133 40 E
Daloa **120** 7 0N 6 30W
Dalry **34** 55 44N 4 42W
Dalrymple, Mt. **133** 21 1 S 148 39 E
Dalsjöfors **73** 57 46N 18 5 E
Dalskog **73** 58 44N 12 18 E
Dalton, Can. **150** 48 11N 84 1W
Dalton, Cumbria, U.K. **33** 54 9N 3 11W
Dalton, Dumfries, U.K. **35** 55 3N 3 22W
Dalton, N. Yorks., U.K. **33** 54 28N 1 32W
Dalton, Ga., U.S.A. **103** 34 45N 85 0W
Dalton, Mass., U.S.A. **162** 42 28N 73 11W
Dalton, Nebr., U.S.A. **158** 41 27N 103 0W
Dalton Post **152** 66 42N 137 0W
Daltonganj **95** 24 0N 84 4 E
Dalvik **74** 65 58N 18 32W
Dalwhinnie **37** 56 56N 4 14W
Daly City **163** 37 42N 122 28W
Daly L. **153** 56 32N 105 39W
Daly, R. **136** 13 21 S 130 18 E
Daly Waters **138** 16 15 S 133 24 E
Dalystown **38** 53 26N 7 23W
Dam **170** 4 45N 55 0W
Dam Doi **101** 8 59N 105 12 E
Dam Gillan **153** 56 20N 94 40W
Dam Ha **100** 21 21N 107 36 E
Dama, Wadi **122** 27 12N 35 50 E
Daman **96** 20 25N 72 57 E
Daman □ **96** 20 25N 72 58 E
Damanhûr **122** 31 0N 30 30 E
Damar, I. **103** 7 15 S 128 30 E
Damaraland **128** 21 0 S 17 0 E
Damascus = Dimashq **92** 33 30N 36 18 E
Damaturu **121** 11 45N 11 55 E
Damāvand **93** 36 0N 52 0 E
Damāvand, Qolleh-ye **93** 35 45N 52 10 E
Damba, Angola **124** 6 44 S 15 29 E
Damba, Ethiopia **123** 15 10N 38 47 E
Dâmbovnic, R. **70** 44 28N 25 18 E
Dame Marie **167** 18 36N 74 26W
Damerham **28** 50 57N 1 52W
Dames Quarter **162** 38 11N 75 54W
Damghan **93** 36 10N 54 17 E
Damietta = Dumyât **122** 31 24N 31 48 E
Damin **93** 27 30N 60 40 E
Damiya **90** 32 6N 35 34 E
Damman **92** 26 25N 50 2 E
Dammarie **43** 48 20N 1 30 E
Dammartin **43** 49 3N 2 41 E
Dammastock **51** 46 38N 8 24 E
Damme **48** 52 32N 8 12 E
Damodar, R. **95** 23 17N 87 35 E
Damoh **95** 23 50N 79 28 E
Dampier **136** 20 41 S 116 42 E
Dampier Arch. **136** 20 38 S 116 32 E
Dampier Downs **136** 18 24 S 123 5 E
Dampier, Selat **103** 0 40 S 131 0 E
Dampier Str. **135** 5 50 S 148 0 E
Damrei, Chuor Phnum **101** 12 30N 103 0 E
Damville **42** 48 51N 1 5 E
Damvillers **43** 49 20N 5 21 E
Dan Chadi **121** 12 47N 5 17 E
Dan Dume **121** 11 28N 7 8 E
Dan Gora **121** 11 30N 8 7 E
Dan Gulbi **121** 11 40N 6 15 E
Dan, oilfield **19** 55 30N 5 10 E
Dan Sadau **121** 11 25N 6 20 E
Dana **103** 11 0 S 122 52 E
Dana, Lac **150** 50 53N 77 20W
Dana, Mt **163** 37 54N 119 12W
Danakil Depression **123** 12 45N 41 0 E
Danao **103** 10 31N 124 1 E
Danbury **162** 41 23N 73 29W
Danby L. **161** 34 17N 115 0W
Dand **94** 31 28N 65 32 E
Dandaragan **137** 30 40 S 115 40 E
Dandeldhura **95** 29 20N 80 35 E
Dandeli **93** 15 5N 74 30 E
Dandenong **141** 38 0 S 145 15 E
Dandkandi **98** 23 32N 90 43 E
Danforth **151** 45 39N 67 57W
Dang Raek **101** 14 40N 104 0 E
Dangara **85** 38 6N 69 22 E
• Danger Is. **131** 10 53 S 165 49W
Danger Pt. **128** 34 40 S 19 17 E
Dangla **123** 11 18N 36 56 E
Dangora **121** 11 30N 8 7 E
Dangrek, Phnom **100** 14 15N 105 0 E
Daniel **160** 42 56N 110 2W
Daniel's Harbour **151** 50 13N 57 35W
Danielskull **128** 28 11 S 23 33 E
Danielson **162** 41 50N 71 52W
Danilov **81** 58 16N 40 13 E
Danilovgrad **66** 42 38N 19 9 E
Danilovka **81** 50 25N 44 12 E
Danissa **126** 3 15N 40 58 E
Danja **121** 11 29N 7 30 E
Dankalwa **121** 11 52N 12 12 E
Dankama **121** 13 20N 7 44 E
Dankhar Gompa **93** 32 10N 78 10 E
Dankov **81** 53 20N 39 5 E
Danli **166** 14 4N 86 35W
Dannemora **75** 60 12N 17 51 E
Dannenberg **48** 53 7N 11 4 E
Dannevirke **142** 40 12 S 176 8 E
Dannhauser **129** 28 0 S 30 3 E
Dansalan **103** 8 2N 124 30 E
Dansville **156** 42 32N 77 41W
Dantan **95** 21 57N 87 20 E
Danube, R. **53** 45 0N 28 20W
Danubyo **98** 17 15N 95 35 E
Danvers **162** 42 34N 70 55 E
Danville, Ill., U.S.A. **156** 40 10N 87 40W
Danville, Ky., U.S.A. **156** 37 40N 84 45W
Danville, Pa., U.S.A. **162** 40 58N 76 37W
Danville, Va., U.S.A. **157** 36 40N 79 20W
Danzig = Gdansk **54** 54 22N 18 40 E
Dão **103** 10 30N 122 6 E
Dão, R. **56** 40 28N 8 0W
Daosa **94** 26 52N 76 20 E
Daoud = Aïn Beida **119** 35 50N 7 29 E
Daoulas **42** 48 22N 4 17W
Dapango **121** 10 55N 0 16 E
Dar al Hamra, Ad **92** 27 22N 37 43 E
Dar es Salaam **126** 6 50 S 39 12 E
Dar'á **90** 32 36N 36 7 E
Darab **93** 28 50N 54 30 E
Darabani **70** 48 10N 26 39 E
Daraj **119** 30 10N 10 28 E
Daraut Kurgan **85** 39 33N 72 11 E
Daravica **66** 42 32N 20 8 E
Daraw **121** 24 22N 32 51 E
Darazo **121** 11 1N 10 24W
Darband **94** 34 30N 72 50 E
Darbhanga **95** 26 15N 86 8 E
Darby **160** 46 2N 114 7W
D'Arcy **152** 50 35N 122 30W
Darda **66** 45 40N 18 41 E
Dardanelle **163** 38 2N 119 50W
Dardanelles = Canakkale Boğlazi **92** 40 0N 26 20 E
Dardenelle **159** 35 12N 93 9W
Darent, R. **29** 51 22N 0 12 E
Darfield **143** 43 29 S 172 7 E
Darfo **62** 45 43N 10 11 E
Dargai **94** 34 25N 71 45 E
Dargan Ata **76** 40 40N 62 20 E
Dargaville **142** 35 57 S 173 52 E
Darharala **120** 8 23N 4 20W
Dari **123** 5 48N 30 26 E
Darién, G. del **174** 9 0N 77 0W
Darién, Serranía del **174** 8 30N 77 30W
Dariganga **106** 45 5N 113 45 E
Darinskoye **84** 51 20N 51 44 E
Darjeeling **95** 27 3N 88 18 E
Dark Cove **151** 48 47N 54 13W
Darkan **137** 33 20 S 116 43 E
Darke Peak **140** 33 27 S 136 12 E
Darkot Pass **95** 36 45N 73 26 E
Darlaston **28** 52 35N 2 1W
Darling Downs **139** 28 30 S 152 0 E
Darling, R. **140** 34 4 S 141 54 E
Darling Ra. **137** 32 30 S 116 0 E
Darlington, U.K. **33** 54 33N 1 33W
Darlington, S.C., U.S.A. **157** 34 18N 79 50W
Darlington, Wis., U.S.A. **158** 42 43N 90 7W
Darlot, L. **137** 27 48 S 121 35 E
Darłowo **54** 54 25N 16 25 E
Darmstadt **49** 49 51N 8 40 E
Darnall **129** 29 23 S 31 18 E
Darnétal **42** 49 25N 1 10 E
Darney **43** 48 5N 6 0 E
Darnick **140** 32 48 S 143 38 E
Darnley B. **147** 69 30N 123 30W
Darnley, C. **13** 68 0 S 69 0 E
Daroca **58** 41 9N 1 25W
Darr **138** 23 13 S 144 7 E
Darr, R. **138** 23 39 S 143 50 E
Darragh **39** 52 47N 9 7W
Darran Mts. **143** 44 37 S 167 59 E
Darrington **160** 48 14N 121 37W
Darror, R. **91** 10 30N 50 0 E
Darsana **98** 23 35N 88 48 E
Darsi **97** 15 46N 79 44 E
Darsser Ort **48** 44 27N 12 30 E
Dart, R., N.Z. **143** 44 20 S 168 20 E
Dart, R., U.K. **30** 50 24N 3 36W
Renamed Pukapuka
Dartford **29** 51 26N 0 15 E
Dartington **30** 50 26N 3 42W
Dartmoor, Austral. **140** 37 56N 141 19 E
Dartmoor, U.K. **30** 50 36N 4 0W
Dartmouth, Austral. **138** 23 31 S 144 44 E
Dartmouth, Can. **151** 44 40N 63 30W
Dartmouth, U.K. **30** 50 21N 3 35W
Dartmouth, L. **139** 26 4 S 145 18 E
Darton **33** 53 36N 1 32W
Dartuch, C. **58** 39 55N 3 49 E
Daru, P.N.G. **135** 9 3 S 143 13 E
Daru, S. Leone **120** 8 0N 10 52W
Darvel **34** 55 37N 4 20W
Darvel Bay **103** 4 50N 118 20 E
Darwen **32** 53 42N 2 29W
Darwha **96** 20 15N 77 45 E
Darwin, Austral. **136** 12 25 S 130 51 E
Darwin, U.S.A. **163** 36 15N 117 35W
Darwin, Mt. **127** 16 45 S 31 33 E
Darwin River **136** 12 50 S 130 58 E
Daryacheh-ye-Sistan **93** 31 0N 61 0 E
Daryapur **96** 20 55N 77 20 E
Dase **123** 14 53N 37 15 E
Dashato, R. **123** 7 25N 42 40 E
Dashkesan **83** 40 40N 46 0 E
Dasht-e Kavīr **93** 34 30N 55 0 E
Dasht-e Lut **93** 31 30N 58 0 E
Dasht-i-Khash **93** 32 0N 62 0 E
Dasht-i-Margo **93** 30 40N 62 30 E
Dasht-i-Nawar **94** 33 52N 68 0 E
Dasht, R. **93** 25 40N 62 20 E
Daska **94** 32 20N 74 20 E
Dassa-Zoume **121** 7 46N 2 14 E
Dasseneiland **128** 33 37 S 18 3 E
Datça **69** 36 46N 27 40 E
Datia **95** 25 39N 78 27 E
Dattapur **96** 20 45N 78 15 E
Daugava **80** 57 0N 24 0 E
Daugavpils **80** 55 53N 26 32 E
Daulat Yar **93** 34 30N 65 45 E
Daulatabad **96** 19 57N 75 15 E
Daun **49** 50 5N 6 53 E
Dauphin, Can. **153** 51 9N 100 5W
Dauphin, U.S.A. **162** 40 22N 76 56W
Dauphin I. **157** 30 16N 88 10W
Dauphin L. **153** 51 20N 99 45W
Dauphiné **45** 45 15N 5 25 E
Dauqa **122** 19 30N 41 0 E
Daura, Kano, Nigeria **121** 13 2N 8 21 E
Daura, N.-E., Nigeria **121** 11 31N 11 24 E
Davadi **120** 14 10N 16 3W
Davangere **97** 14 25N 75 50 E
Davao **103** 7 0N 125 40 E
Davao, G. of **103** 6 30N 125 48 E
Davar Panab **93** 27 25N 62 15 E
Dave **74** 52 55N 1 50W
Davenport, Calif., U.S.A. **163** 37 1N 122 12W
Davenport, Iowa, U.S.A. **158** 41 30N 90 40W
Davenport, Wash., U.S.A. **160** 47 40N 118 5W
Davenport Downs **138** 24 8 S 141 7 E
Davenport Ra. **138** 20 28 S 134 0 E
Daventry **28** 52 16N 1 10W
David **166** 8 30N 82 30W
David City **158** 41 18N 97 10W
David Gorodok **80** 52 4N 27 8 E
Davidson **153** 51 16N 105 59W
Davik **71** 61 53N 5 33 E
Davis **163** 38 33N 121 45W
Davis Dam **161** 35 11N 114 35W
Davis Inlet **151** 55 50N 60 45W
Davis Mts. **159** 30 42N 104 15W
Davis Str. **149** 65 0N 58 0W
Davlekanovo **84** 54 13N 55 3 E
Davos **51** 46 48N 9 49 E
Davy L. **153** 58 53N 108 18W
Davyhurst **137** 30 2 S 120 40 E
Dawa, R. **123** 5 0N 39 5 E
Dawaki, Jos, Nigeria **121** 9 25N 9 33 E
Dawaki, Kano, Nigeria **121** 12 5N 8 23 E
Dawayima **90** 31 33N 34 55 E
Dawes Ra. **138** 24 40 S 150 40 E
Dawley **28** 52 40N 2 29W
Dawlish **30** 50 34N 3 28W
Dawna Range **98** 16 30N 98 30 E
Dawnyein **98** 15 54N 95 36 E
Dawros Hd. **38** 54 48N 8 32W
Dawson, Can. **147** 64 10N 139 30W
Dawson, Ga., U.S.A. **157** 31 45N 84 28W
Dawson, N.D., U.S.A. **158** 46 56N 99 45W
Dawson Creek **152** 55 45N 120 15W
Dawson, I. **176** 53 50 S 70 50W
Dawson Inlet **153** 61 50N 93 25W
Dawson, R. **133** 23 25 S 150 10 E
Dawson Range **138** 24 30 S 149 48 E
Dawson's **127** 17 0 S 30 57 E
Daylesford **140** 37 21 S 144 9 E
Dayr al-Ghusūn **90** 32 21N 35 4 E
Dayr az Zawr **92** 35 20N 40 5 E
Daysland **152** 52 50N 112 20W
Dayton, Ohio, U.S.A. **156** 39 45N 84 10W
Dayton, Tenn., U.S.A. **157** 35 30N 85 1W
Dayton, Wash., U.S.A. **160** 46 20N 118 0W
Daytona Beach **157** 29 14N 81 0W
Dayville **160** 44 33N 119 37W
De Aar **128** 30 39 S 24 0 E
De Bilt **46** 52 6N 5 11 E
De Funiak Springs **157** 30 42N 86 10W
De Grey **136** 20 12 S 119 12 E
De Grey, R. **136** 20 0 S 119 13 E
De Kalb **158** 41 55N 88 45W
De Koog **46** 53 6N 4 46 E
De Land **157** 29 1N 81 19W
De Leon **159** 32 9N 98 35W
De Long Mts. **147** 68 10N 163 0W
De Long, Ostrova **77** 76 40N 149 20 E
De Panne **47** 51 6N 2 34 E
De Pere **156** 44 28N 88 1W
De Queen **159** 34 3N 94 24W
De Quincy **159** 30 30N 93 27W
De Ridder **159** 30 48N 93 15W
De Rijp **46** 52 33N 4 51 E
De Smet **158** 44 25N 97 35W
De Tour Village **156** 45 49N 83 56W
De Witt **159** 34 19N 91 20W
Dead Sea = Miyet, Bahr el **92** 31 30N 35 30 E
Deadwood **58** 44 25N 103 43W
Deadwood L. **152** 59 10N 128 30W
Deaf Adder Cr. **136** 13 0 S 132 47 E
Deakin **137** 30 46 S 129 58 E
Deal **29** 51 13N 1 25 E
Dealesville **128** 28 41 S 25 44 E
Dean, Forest of **28** 51 50N 2 35W
Deán Funes **172** 30 20 S 64 20W
Dearborn **150** 42 18N 83 15W
Dearham **32** 54 43N 3 28W
Dease L. **152** 58 40N 130 5W
Dease Lake **152** 58 25N 130 6W
Dease, R. **152** 59 56N 128 32W
Death Valley **163** 36 27N 116 52W
Death Valley Junc. **163** 36 21N 116 30W
Death Valley Nat. Monument **163** 36 30N 117 0W
Deauville **42** 49 23N 0 2 E
Deba Habe **121** 10 14N 11 20 E
Debaltsevo **82** 48 22N 38 26 E
Debar **66** 41 21N 20 37 E
Debba **123** 14 20N 41 18 E
Debden **153** 53 30N 106 50W
Debdou **118** 33 59N 3 0W
Debeeti **128** 23 45 S 26 32 E
Deben, R. **29** 52 4N 1 19 E
Debenham **29** 52 14N 1 10 E
Debessy **84** 57 39N 53 49 E
Dębica **54** 50 2N 21 25 E
Deblin **54** 51 34N 21 50 E
Debo, L. **120** 15 14N 3 57W
Debolt **152** 55 12N 118 1W
Deborah, gasfield **19** 53 4N 1 50 E
Deborah, L. **137** 30 45 S 119 0 E
Debrc **66** 44 38N 19 53 E
Debre Birhan **123** 9 41N 39 31 E
Debre Markos **123** 10 20N 37 40 E
Debre May **123** 11 20N 37 25 E
Debre Sina **123** 9 51N 39 50 E
Debre Tabor **123** 11 50N 38 26 E
Debrecen **53** 47 33N 21 42 E
Dečani **66** 42 30N 20 10 E
Decatur, Ala., U.S.A. **157** 34 35N 87 0W
Decatur, Ga., U.S.A. **157** 33 47N 84 17W
Decatur, Ill., U.S.A. **158** 39 50N 89 0W
Decatur, Ind., U.S.A. **156** 40 52N 85 28W
Decatur, Texas, U.S.A. **159** 33 15N 97 35W
Decazeville **44** 44 34N 2 15 E
Deccan **97** 14 0N 77 0 E
Deception I. **13** 63 0 S 60 15W
Deception L. **153** 56 33N 104 13W
Deception, Mt. **140** 30 42 S 138 16 E
Decize **43** 46 50N 3 28 E
Decollatura **65** 39 2N 16 21 E
Decorah **158** 43 20N 91 50W
Deda **70** 46 56N 24 50 E
Dedaye **98** 16 24N 95 53 E
Deddington **28** 51 58N 1 19W
Dedemsvaavt **46** 52 36N 6 28 E
Dedham **162** 42 14N 71 10W
Dedilovo **81** 53 59N 37 50 E
Dédougou **120** 12 30N 3 35W
Deduru Oya **97** 7 32N 81 45 E
Dedza **127** 14 20 S 34 20 E
Dee, R., Eng.-Wales, U.K. **31** 53 15N 3 7W
Dee, R., Scot., U.K. **37** 57 4N 2 7W
Deel R. **38** 53 35N 7 9W
Deelish **39** 51 41N 9 18W
Deep B. **152** 61 15N 116 35W
Deep Lead **140** 37 0 S 142 43 E
Deep Well **138** 24 20 S 134 0 E
Deepdale **136** 26 22 S 114 20 E
Deeping Fen **29** 52 45N 0 15W
Deeping, St. Nicholas **29** 52 44N 0 11W
Deepwater **139** 29 25 S 151 51 E
Deer I. **147** 54 55N 162 20W
Deer Lake, Newf., Can. **151** 49 11N 57 27W
Deer Lake, Ontario, Can. **153** 52 36N 94 20W
Deer Lodge **160** 46 25N 112 40W
Deer Park **160** 47 55N 117 21W
Deer, R. **153** 58 23N 94 13W
Deer River **158** 47 21N 93 44W
Deer Sound **37** 58 58N 2 50W
Deeral **138** 17 14 S 145 55 E
Deerdepoort **128** 24 37 S 26 27 E
Deering **147** 66 5N 162 50W
Deerlijk **47** 50 51N 3 22 E
Deerness **37** 58 57N 2 44W
Deesa **94** 24 18N 72 10 E
Deferiet **162** 44 2N 75 41W
Defiance **156** 41 20N 84 20W
Deganwy **31** 53 18N 3 49W
Deganya **90** 32 43N 35 34 E
Degebe, R. **57** 38 21N 7 37W
Degeh-Bur **91** 8 11N 43 31 E

Degema 121 4 50N 6 48 E
Degerfors 74 64 16N 19 46 E
Degersfor 73 59 20N 14 28 E
Degersheim 51 47 23N 9 12 E
Degersiö 72 63 13N 18 3 E
Deggendorf 49 48 49N 12 59 E
Degloor 96 18 34N 77 33 E
Deh Bīd 93 30 39N 53 11 E
Deh Kheyr 93 28 45N 54 40 E
Deh Titan 93 33 45N 63 50 E
Dehibat 119 32 0N 10 47 E
Dehiwala 97 6 50N 79 51 E
Dehkhvareqan 92 37 50N 45 55 E
Dehra Dun 94 30 20N 78 4 E
Dehri 95 24 50N 84 15 E
Deinze 47 50 59N 3 32 E
Deir Abu Sa'id 90 32 30N 38 42 E
Deir Dibwan 90 31 55N 35 15 E
Dej 70 47 10N 23 52 E
Deje 72 59 35N 13 29 E
Dekar 128 18 30 S 23 10 E
Dekemhare 123 15 6N 39 0 E
Dekese 124 3 24 S 21 24 E
Dekhkanabad 85 38 21N 66 30 E
Del Mar 163 32 58N 117 16W
Del Norte 161 37 47N 106 27W
Del Rey, Rio 121 4 30N 8 48 E
Del Rio, Mexico 164 29 22N 100 54W
Del Rio, U.S.A. 159 29 15N 100 50W
Delabole 30 50 37N 4 45W
Delagoa B. 129 25 50 S 32 45 E
Delagua 159 32 35N 104 40W
Delai 122 17 21N 36 6 E
Delambre I. 136 20 27 S 117 4 E
Delano 163 35 48N 119 13W
Delareyville 128 26 41 S 25 26 E
Delavan 158 42 40N 88 39W
Delaware 156 40 20N 83 0W
Delaware □ 162 39 0N 75 40W
Delaware B. 162 38 50N 75 0W
Delaware City 162 39 34N 75 36W
Delaware, R. 162 39 20N 75 25W
Delčevo 66 41 58N 22 46 E
Delchirach 37 57 23N 3 20W
Delegate 141 37 4 S 148 56 E
Delémont 50 47 22N 7 20 E
Delft 46 52 1N 4 22 E
Delft I. 97 9 30N 79 40 E
Delfzijl 46 53 20N 6 55 E
Delgado, C. 127 10 45 S 40 40 E
Delgerhet 106 45 50N 110 30 E
Delgo 122 20 6N 30 40 E
Delhi, India 94 28 38N 77 17 E
Delhi, U.S.A. 162 42 17N 74 56W
Deli Jovan 66 44 13N 22 9 E
Delia 152 51 38N 112 23W
Delice, R. 92 39 45N 34 15 E
Delicias 164 28 10N 105 30W
Delicias, Laguna 164 28 7N 105 40W
Delimiro Gouveia 170 9 23 S 37 59W
Delitzsch 48 51 32N 12 22 E
Dell City 161 31 58N 105 19W
Dell Rapids 158 43 53N 96 44W
Delle 43 47 30N 7 2 E
Dellys 119 36 50N 3 57 E
Delmar, Del., U.S.A. 162 38 27N 75 34W
Delmar, N.Y., U.S.A. 162 42 5N 73 50W
Delmenhorst 48 53 3N 8 37 E
Delmiro 170 9 24 S 38 6W
Delnice 63 45 23N 14 50 E
Deloraine, Austral. 138 41 30 S 146 40 E
Deloraine, Can. 153 49 15N 100 29W
Delorme, L. 151 54 31N 69 52W
Delovo 66 44 55N 20 52 E
Delphi 156 40 37N 86 40W
Delphos 156 40 51N 84 17W
Delportshoop 128 28 22 S 24 20 E
Delray Beach 157 26 27N 80 4W
Delsbo 72 61 48N 16 32 E
Delta, Colo., U.S.A. 161 38 44N 108 5W
Delta, Utah, U.S.A. 160 39 21N 112 29W
Delta Amacuro □ 174 8 30N 61 30W
Deltaville 162 37 33N 76 20W
Delungra 139 29 39 S 150 51 E
Delvin 38 53 37N 7 8W
Delvina 68 39 59N 20 4 E
Delvinákion 68 39 57N 20 32 E
Demak 103 6 50 S 110 40 E
Demanda, Sierra de la 58 42 15N 3 0W
Demba 124 5 28 S 22 15 E
Dembecha 123 10 32N 37 30 E
Dembi 123 8 5N 36 25 E
Dembia 126 3 33N 25 48 E
Dembidolo 123 8 34N 34 50 E
Demchok 93 32 40N 79 29 E
Demer, R. 47 51 0N 5 8 E
Demerais, L. 150 47 35N 77 0W
Demerara, R. 174 7 0N 58 0W
Demidov 80 55 10N 31 30 E
Deming 161 32 10N 107 50W
Demini, R. 174 0 46N 62 56W
Demmin 48 53 54N 13 2 E
Demmit 152 55 20N 119 50W
Demnate 118 31 44N 6 59W
Demonte 62 44 18N 7 18 E
Demopolis 157 32 30N 87 48W
Dempo, Mt. 102 4 10 S 103 15 E
Demyansk 80 57 30N 32 27 E
Den Bemmel 46 51 43N 4 26 E
Den Burg 46 53 3N 4 47 E
Den Chai 100 17 59N 100 4 E
Den Dungen 47 51 41N 5 22 E
Den Haag = 's Gravenhage 46 52 7N 4 17 E
Den Ham 46 52 28N 6 30 E
Den Helder 46 52 57N 4 45 E
Den Hulst 46 52 36N 6 16 E
Den Oever 46 52 56N 5 2 E
Denain 43 50 20N 3 22 E
Denair 163 37 32N 120 48W
Denau 85 38 16N 67 54 E
Denbigh 31 53 12N 3 26W
Denbigh (□) 26 53 8N 3 30W
Denby Dale 33 53 35N 1 40W
Denchin 99 31 35N 95 15 E
Dendang 102 3 7 S 107 56 E
Dender, R. 47 51 2N 4 6 E
Denderhoutem 47 50 53N 4 2 E
Denderleeuw 47 50 54N 4 5 E
Dendermonde 47 51 2N 4 5 E
Deneba 123 9 47N 39 10 E
Denekamp 46 52 22N 7 1 E
Denezhkin Kamen, Gora 84 60 25N 59 32 E
Denge 121 12 52N 5 21 E
Dengi 121 9 25N 9 55 E
Denham 137 25 56 S 113 31 E
Denham Ra. 138 21 55 S 147 46 E
Denham Sd. 137 25 45 S 113 15 E
Denholm 153 52 40N 108 0W
Denia 59 38 49N 0 8 E
Denial B. 139 32 14 S 133 32 E
Deniliquin 141 35 30 S 144 58 E
Denison, Iowa, U.S.A. 158 42 0N 95 18W
Denison, Texas, U.S.A. 159 33 50N 96 40W
Denison Plains 136 18 35 S 128 0 E
Denison Range 136 28 30 S 136 5 E
Denisovka 84 52 28N 61 46 E
Denizli 92 37 42N 29 2 E
Denkez Iyesus 123 12 27N 37 43 E
Denman 141 32 24 S 150 42 E
Denmark 137 34 59 S 117 18 E
Denmark ■ 73 55 30N 9 0 E
Denmark Str. 14 66 0N 30 0W
Dennis Hd. 37 59 23N 2 26W
Denniston 143 41 45 S 171 49 E
Denny 35 56 1N 3 55W
Denpasar 102 8 45 S 115 5 E
Dent 32 54 17N 2 28W
Denton, E. Sussex, U.K. 29 50 48N 0 5 E
Denton, Gr. Manchester, U.K. 32 53 26N 2 10W
Denton, Lincs., U.K. 33 52 52N 0 42W
Denton, Md., U.S.A. 162 38 53N 75 50W
Denton, Mont., U.S.A. 160 47 25N 109 56W
Denton, Texas, U.S.A. 159 33 12N 97 10W
D'Entrecasteaux, C. 137 34 50 S 115 59 E
D'Entrecasteaux Is. 135 9 0 S 151 0 E
D'Entrecasteaux Pt. 137 34 50 S 115 57 E
Dents du Midi 50 46 10N 6 56 E
Denu 121 6 4N 1 8 E
Denver, Colo., U.S.A. 158 39 45N 105 0W
Denver, Pa., U.S.A. 162 40 14N 76 8W
Denver City 159 32 58N 102 48W
Deoband 94 29 42N 77 43 E
Deobhog 96 19 53N 82 44 E
Deogarh 96 21 32N 84 45 E
Deoghar 95 24 30N 86 59 E
Deolali 96 19 50N 73 50 E
Deoli 94 25 50N 75 50 E
Deoria 95 26 31N 83 48 E
Deosai, Mts. 95 35 40N 75 0 E
Deposit 162 42 5N 75 23W
Depot Spring 137 27 55 S 120 3 E
Depuch I. 136 20 35 S 117 44 E
Deputatskiy 77 69 18N 139 54 E
Dera Ghazi Khan 94 30 5N 70 43 E
Dera Ismail Khan 94 31 50N 70 50 E
Dera Ismail Khan □ 94 32 30N 70 0 E
Derati Wells 126 3 52N 36 37 E
Derbent 74 42 5N 48 15 E
Derby, Austral. 136 17 18 S 123 38 E
Derby, U.K. 33 52 55N 1 28W
Derby, U.S.A. 162 41 20N 73 5W
Derby □ 33 52 55N 1 28W
Derecske 53 47 20N 21 33 E
Derg, L. 39 53 0N 8 20W
Derg, R. 38 54 42N 7 26W
Dergachi 81 50 3N 36 3 E
Dergaon 99 26 45N 94 0 E
Dermantsi 67 43 8N 24 17 E
Derna 117 32 40N 22 35 E
Dernieres Isles 159 29 0N 90 45W
Derriana, L. 39 51 54N 10 1W
Derrinallum 140 37 57 S 143 15 E
Derry R. 39 52 43N 6 35W
Derrybrien 39 53 4N 8 38W
Derrygonnelly 38 54 25N 7 50W
Derrygrogan 39 53 19N 7 23W
Derrykeighan 38 55 8N 6 30W
Derrylin 38 54 12N 7 34W
Derry = Londonderry 38 55 0N 7 19W
Derrynasaggart Mts. 39 51 58N 9 15W
Derryrush 38 53 23N 9 40W
Derryveagh Mts. 38 55 0N 8 40W
Derudub 122 17 31N 36 7 E
Dervaig 34 56 35N 6 13W
Derval 42 47 40N 1 41W
Dervéni 69 38 8N 22 25 E
Derwent 153 53 41N 110 58W
Derwent, R., Derby, U.K. 33 52 53N 1 17W
Derwent, R., N. Yorks., U.K. 33 53 45N 0 57W
Derwent, R., Tyne & Wear, U.K. 35 54 58N 1 40W
Derwentwater, L. 32 53 34N 3 9W
Des Moines, Iowa, U.S.A. 158 41 35N 93 37W
Des Moines, N. Mex., U.S.A. 159 36 50N 103 51W
Des Moines, R. 158 40 23N 91 25W
Desaguadero, R., Argent. 172 33 28 S 67 15W
Desaguadero, R., Boliv. 174 17 30 S 68 0W
Desborough 29 52 27N 0 50W
Deschaillons 151 46 32N 72 7W
Descharme, R. 153 56 51N 109 13W
Deschutes, R. 160 45 30N 121 0W
Dese 123 11 5N 39 40 E
Deseado, R. 176 40 0 S 69 0W
Desemboque 164 30 30N 112 27W
Desenzano del Gardo 62 45 28N 10 32 E
Desert Center 161 33 45N 115 27W
Desert Hot Springs 163 33 58N 116 30W
Desertmartin 38 54 47N 6 40W
Desford 28 52 38N 1 19W
Désirade, I. 167 16 18N 61 3W
Deskenatlata L. 152 60 55N 112 3W
Desna, R. 80 52 0N 33 15 E
Desnǔtui, R. 70 44 15N 23 27 E
Desolación, I. 176 53 0 S 74 0W
Despeñaperros, Paso 59 38 24N 3 30W
Despotovac 66 44 6N 21 30 E
Dessa 121 14 44N 1 6 E
Dessau 48 51 49N 12 15 E
Dessel 47 51 15N 5 7 E
Dessye = Dese 123 11 5N 39 40 E
D'Estress B. 140 35 55 S 137 45 E
Desuri 94 25 18N 73 35 E
Desvrès 43 50 40N 1 48 E
Det Udom 100 14 54N 105 5 E
Detinjá, R. 66 43 51N 19 45 E
Detmold 48 51 55N 8 50 E
Detour Pt. 156 45 37N 86 35W
Detroit, Mich., U.S.A. 150 42 13N 83 22W
Detroit, Tex., U.S.A. 159 33 40N 95 10W
Detroit Lakes 158 46 50N 95 50W
Dett 127 18 32 S 26 57 E
Dettifoss 74 65 49N 16 24W
Děčin 52 50 47N 14 12 E
Deurne, Belg. 47 51 12N 4 24 E
Deurne, Neth. 47 51 27N 5 49 E
Deutsche Bucht 48 54 10N 7 51 E
Deutschlandsberg 52 46 49N 15 14 E
Deux-Acren, Les 47 50 44N 3 51 E
Deux-Sèvres □ 42 46 35N 0 20W
Deva 70 45 53N 22 55 E
Devakottai 97 9 55N 78 45 E
Devaprayag 95 30 13N 78 35 E
Dévaványa 53 47 2N 20 59 E
Deveci Daği 82 40 10N 36 0 E
Devecser 53 47 6N 17 26 E
Deventer 46 52 15N 6 10 E
Deveron, R. 37 57 40N 2 31W
Devesel 70 44 28N 22 41 E
Devgad, I. 97 14 48N 74 5 E
Devil R., Pk. 143 40 56 S 172 37 E
Devils Bridge 31 52 23N 3 50W
Devils Den 163 35 46N 119 58W
Devils Lake 158 48 5N 98 50W
Devils Paw, mt. 152 58 47N 134 0W
Devils Pt. 97 9 26N 80 6 E
Devilsbit Mt. 39 52 50N 7 58W
Devin 67 41 44N 24 24 E
Devizes 28 51 21N 2 0W
Devnya 67 43 13N 27 33 E
Devolli, R. 68 40 57N 20 15 E
Devon 152 53 24N 113 44W
Devon I. 12 75 47N 88 0W
Devonport, Austral. 138 41 10 S 146 22 E
Devonport, N.Z. 142 36 49 S 174 49 E
Devonport, U.K. 30 50 23N 4 11W
Devonshire □ 30 50 50N 3 40W
Dewas 94 22 59N 76 3 E
Dewetsdorp 128 29 33 S 26 39 E
Dewgad Baria 94 22 40N 73 55 E
Dewsbury 33 53 42N 1 38W
Dexter, Mo., U.S.A. 159 36 50N 90 0W
Dexter, N. Mex., U.S.A. 159 33 15N 104 25W
Dey-Dey, L. 137 29 12 S 131 4 E
Deyhuk 93 33 15N 104 25W
Deyyer 93 27 55N 51 55 E
Dezadeash L. 152 60 28N 136 58W
Dezfūl 92 32 20N 48 30 E
Dezh Shahpur 92 35 30N 46 25 E
Dezhneva, Mys 77 66 10N 169 3 E
Dhaba 92 27 25N 35 40 E
Dháfni 69 37 48N 22 1 E
Dhahaban 122 21 58N 39 3 E
Dhahiriya = Qz Zahiriya 90 31 25N 34 58 E
Dhahran 92 26 9N 50 10 E
Dhama Dzong 99 28 15N 91 15 E
Dhamási 68 39 43N 22 11 E
Dhampur 95 29 19N 78 33 E
Dhamtari 96 20 42N 81 35 E
Dhanbad 95 23 50N 86 30 E
Dhangarhi 99 28 55N 80 40 E
Dhankuta 95 26 55N 87 20 E
Dhanora 96 20 20N 80 22 E
Dhar 94 22 35N 75 26 E
Dharampur, Mad. P., India 94 22 13N 75 18 E
Dharampur, Maharashtra, India 96 20 32N 73 17 E
Dharapuram 97 10 45N 77 34 E
Dharmapuri 97 12 10N 78 10 E
Dharmavaram 97 14 29N 77 44 E
Dharmsala, (Dharamsala) 94 32 16N 73 23 E
Dhaulagiri Mt. 95 28 45N 83 45 E
Dhebar, L. 94 24 10N 74 0 E
Dhenkanal 96 20 45N 85 35 E
Dhenoúsa 69 37 8N 25 48 E
Dhesfina 69 38 25N 22 31 E
Dheskáti 68 39 55N 21 49 E
Dhespotikó 69 36 57N 24 58 E
Dhidhimótikhon 68 41 22N 26 29 E
Dhikti, Mt. 69 35 8N 25 29 E
Dhilianáta 69 38 15N 20 34 E
Dhílos 69 37 23N 25 15 E
Dhimitsána 69 37 36N 22 3 E
Dhirfis, Mt. 69 38 40N 23 54 E
Dhodhekánisos 69 36 35N 27 0 E
Dhofar 91 17 0N 54 10 E
Dhokós 69 37 20N 23 20 E
Dholiana 68 39 54N 20 32 E
Dholka 94 22 44N 72 29 E
Dholpur 94 26 45N 77 59 E
Dhomokós 69 39 10N 22 18 E
Dhond 96 18 26N 74 40 E
Dhoraji 94 21 45N 70 37 E
Dhoxáthon 68 41 9N 24 16 E
Dhragonisi 69 37 27N 25 29 E
Dhrangadhra 94 22 59N 71 31 E
Dhriopós 69 37 35N 24 35 E
Dhrol 94 22 40N 70 25 E
Dhubaibah 93 23 25N 54 35 E
Dhubri 98 26 2N 90 2 E
Dhulasar 98 21 52N 90 14 E
Dhulia 96 20 58N 74 50 E
Dhupdhara 98 25 58N 91 4 E
Dhurm 122 20 18N 42 53 E
Di Linh 101 11 35N 108 4 E
Di Linh, Cao Nguyen 101 11 30N 108 0 E
Día, I. 69 35 26N 25 13 E
Diable, Mt. 163 37 53N 121 56W
Diablerets, Les 50 46 22N 7 10 E
Diablo Range 163 37 0N 121 5W
Diafarabé 120 14 17N 4 57W
Diala 120 13 59N 10 0W
Dialakoro 120 12 18N 7 54W
Diallassagou 120 13 47N 3 41W
Diamante 172 32 5 S 60 40W
Diamante, R. 172 34 31 S 66 56W
Diamantina 171 18 5 S 43 40W
Diamantina, R. 138 22 25 S 142 20 E
Diamantino 175 14 30 S 56 30W
Diamond Harbour 95 22 11N 88 14 E
Diamond Is. 138 17 25 S 151 5 E
Diamond Mts. 160 40 0N 115 58W
Diamond Springs 163 38 42N 120 49W
Diamondville 160 41 51N 110 30W
Diano Marina 62 43 55N 8 3 E
Dianópolis 171 11 38 S 46 50W
Dianra 120 8 45N 6 14W
Diaole, Î. du. 170 5 15N 52 45W
Diapaga 121 12 5N 1 46 E
Diapangou 121 12 5N 0 10 E
Diapur 140 36 19 S 141 29 E
Diariguila 120 10 35N 10 2W
Dibai (Dubai) 93 25 15N 55 20 E
Dibaya 124 6 20 S 22 0 E
Dibaya Lubue 124 4 12 S 19 54 E
Dibba 93 25 45N 56 16 E
Dibbi 123 4 10N 41 52 E
Dibden 28 50 53N 1 24W
Dibega 92 35 50N 43 46 E
Dibër 68 41 38N 20 15 E
Dibete 128 23 45 S 26 32 E
Dibi 123 4 10N 41 52 E
Dibrugarh 98 27 29N 94 55 E
Dibulla 174 11 17N 73 19W
Dickinson 158 46 50N 102 40W
Dickson 157 36 5N 87 22W
Dickson City 162 41 29N 75 40W
Dicomano 63 43 53 S 11 30 E
Didam 46 51 57N 6 8 E
Didcot 28 51 36N 1 14W
Didesa, W. 123 9 40N 35 50 E
Didiéni 120 14 5N 7 50W
Didsbury 152 51 35N 114 10W
Didwana 94 27 17N 74 25 E
Die 45 44 47N 5 22 E
Diébougou 120 11 0N 3 15W
Diefenbaker L. 153 51 0N 106 55W
Diego Garcia, I. 11 9 50 S 75 0 E
Diégo Suarez 129 12 25 S 49 20 E
Diekirch 47 49 52N 6 10 E
Diélette 42 49 33N 1 52W
Diéma 120 14 32N 9 3W
Diemen 46 52 21N 4 58 E
Dieméring 120 12 29N 16 47W
Dien Ban 100 15 53N 108 16 E
Diên Biên Phu 100 21 20N 103 0 E
Dien Khanh 101 12 15N 109 6 E
Diepenheim 46 52 12N 6 33 E
Diepenveen 46 52 18N 6 9 E
Diepholz 48 52 37N 8 22 E
Diepoldsau 51 47 23N 9 40 E
Dieppe 42 49 54N 1 4 E
Dieren 46 52 3N 6 6 E
Dierks 159 34 9N 94 0W
Diessen 47 51 29N 5 10 E
Diessenhofen 51 47 42N 8 46 E
Diest 47 50 58N 5 4 E
Dietikon 51 47 24N 8 24 E
Dieulefit 45 44 54N 5 4 E
Dieuze 43 48 30N 6 40 E

Name	Page	Lat.	Long.
Diever	**46**	52 51N	6 19 E
Diffa	**121**	13 34N	12 33 E
Differdange	**47**	49 31N	5 54 E
Dig	**94**	27 28N	77 20 E
Digba	**126**	4 25N	25 42 E
Digboi	**98**	27 23N	95 38 E
Digby	**151**	44 41N	65 50W
Digges	**153**	58 40N	94 0W
Digges Is.	**149**	62 40N	77 50W
Digges Lamprey	**153**	58 33N	94 8W
Dighinala	**98**	23 15N	92 5 E
Dighton	**158**	38 30N	100 26W
Digne	**45**	44 5N	6 12 E
Digoin	**44**	46 29N	3 58 E
Digos	**103**	6 45N	125 20 E
Digranes	**74**	66 4N	14 44 E
Digras	**96**	20 6N	77 45 E
Dihang, R.	**99**	27 30N	96 30 E
Dijlah	**92**	37 0N	42 30 E
Dijle, R.	**47**	50 58N	4 41 E
Dijon	**43**	47 20N	5 0 E
Dikala	**123**	4 45N	31 28 E
Dikhal	**123**	11 8N	42 20 E
Dikomu di Kai, Mt.	**128**	24 51 S	24 36 E
Diksmuide	**47**	51 2N	2 52 E
Dikson	**76**	73 40N	80 5 E
Dikumbiya	**123**	14 45N	37 30 E
Dikwa	**121**	12 4N	13 30 E
Dila	**123**	6 14N	38 22 E
Dilam	**92**	23 55N	47 10 E
Dilbeek	**47**	50 51N	4 17 E
Dili	**103**	8 39 S	125 34 E
Dilizhan	**83**	41 46N	44 57 E
Dillenburg	**48**	50 44N	8 17 E
Dilley	**159**	28 40N	99 12W
Dilling	**123**	12 3N	29 35 E
Dillingen	**49**	49 22N	6 42 E
Dillingham	**147**	59 5N	158 30W
Dillon, Can.	**153**	55 56N	108 56W
Dillon, Mont., U.S.A.	**160**	45 9N	112 36W
Dillon, S.C., U.S.A.	**157**	34 26N	79 20W
Dillon, R.	**153**	55 56N	108 56W
Dillsburg	**162**	40 7N	77 2W
Dilolo	**14**	10 28 S	22 18 E
Dilsen	**47**	51 2N	5 44 E
Dilston	**138**	41 22 S	147 10 E
Dima	**123**	6 19N	36 15 E
Dimapur	**98**	25 54N	93 45 E
Dimas	**164**	23 43N	106 47W
Dimashq	**92**	33 30N	36 18 E
Dimbelenge	**124**	4 30N	23 0 E
Dimbokro	**120**	6 45N	4 30W
Dimboola	**140**	36 28 S	142 0 E
Dîmboviţa □	**70**	45 0N	25 30 E
Dîmbovita, R.	**70**	44 40N	26 0 E
Dimbulah	**138**	17 2 S	145 4 E
Dimitriya Lapteva, Proliv	**77**	73 0N	140 0 E
Dimitrovgrad, Bulg.	**67**	42 5N	25 35 E
Dimitrovgrad, U.S.S.R.	**81**	54 25N	49 33 E
Dimitrovgrad, Yugo.	**66**	43 0N	22 48 E
Dimmitt	**159**	34 36N	102 16W
Dimo	**123**	5 19N	29 10 E
Dimona	**90**	31 2N	35 1 E
Dimovo	**66**	43 43N	22 50 E
Dinagat I.	**103**	10 10N	125 40 E
Dinajpur	**98**	25 33N	88 43 E
Dinan	**42**	48 28N	2 2W
Dinant	**47**	50 16N	4 55 E
Dinapore	**95**	25 38N	85 5 E
Dinar	**92**	38 5N	30 15 E
Dinard	**42**	48 38N	2 6W
Dinaric Alps	**16**	44 0N	17 30 E
Dinas Hd.	**31**	52 2N	4 56W
Dinas Mawddwy	**31**	52 44N	3 41W
Dinas Powis	**31**	51 25N	3 14W
Dinder, Nahr ed	**123**	12 32N	35 0 E
Dindi, R.	**96**	16 24N	78 15 E
Dindigul	**97**	10 25N	78 0 E
Dingelstädt	**48**	51 19N	10 19 E
Dingila	**126**	3 25N	26 25 E
Dingle	**39**	52 9N	10 17W
Dingle B.	**39**	52 3N	10 20W
Dingle Harbour	**39**	52 7N	10 12W
Dingmans Ferry	**162**	41 13N	74 55W
Dingo	**138**	23 38 S	149 19 E
Dingolfing	**49**	48 38N	12 30 E
Dinguiraye	**120**	11 30N	10 35W
Dingwall	**37**	57 36N	4 26W
Dingyadi	**121**	13 0N	0 53 E
Dinh Lap	**100**	21 33N	107 6 E
Dinh, Mui	**101**	11 22N	109 1 E
Dinhata	**98**	26 8N	89 27 E
Dinkel	**46**	52 30N	6 58 E
Dinokwe (Palla Road)	**128**	23 29 S	26 37 E
Dinosaur National Monument	**160**	40 30N	108 45W
Dinslaken	**47**	51 34N	6 41 E
Dintel, R.	**47**	51 39N	4 22 E
Dinuba	**163**	36 37N	119 22W
Dinxperlo	**46**	51 52N	6 30 E
Dio	**73**	56 37N	14 15 E
Diosgyör	**53**	48 7N	20 43 E
Diosig	**70**	47 18N	22 2 E
Dioundiou	**121**	12 37N	3 33 E
Diourbel	**120**	14 39N	16 12W
Diphu Pass	**98**	28 9N	97 20 E
Diplo	**94**	24 25N	69 35 E
Dipolog	**103**	8 36N	123 20 E
Dipşa	**70**	46 58N	24 27 E
Dipton	**143**	45 54 S	168 22 E
Dir	**93**	35 08N	71 59 E
Diré	**120**	15 20N	3 25W

Name	Page	Lat.	Long.
Dire Dawa	**123**	9 35N	41 45 E
Direction, C.	**138**	12 51 S	143 32 E
Diriamba	**166**	11 51N	86 19W
Dirico	**125**	17 50 S	20 42 E
Dirk Hartog I.	**137**	25 50 S	113 5 E
Dirranbandi	**139**	28 33 S	148 17 E
Disa	**123**	12 5N	34 15 E
Disappointment, C.	**160**	46 20N	124 0W
Disappointment L.	**136**	23 20 S	122 40 E
Disaster B.	**141**	37 15 S	150 0 E
Discovery	**148**	63 0N	115 0W
Discovery B.	**140**	38 10 S	140 40 E
Disentis	**51**	46 42N	8 50 E
Dishna	**122**	26 9N	32 32 E
Disina	**121**	11 35N	9 50 E
Disko	**12**	69 45N	53 30W
Disko Bugt	**12**	69 10N	52 0W
Disna	**80**	55 32N	28 11 E
Disna, R.	**80**	55 20N	27 30 E
Dison	**47**	50 37N	5 51 E
Diss	**29**	52 23N	1 6 E
Disteghil Sar	**95**	36 20N	75 5 E
Distington	**32**	54 35N	3 33W
District Heights	**162**	38 51N	76 53W
District of Columbia □	**162**	38 55N	77 0W
Distrito Federal □, Brazil	**171**	15 45 S	47 45W
Distrito Federal □, Venez.	**174**	10 30N	66 55W
Disûq	**122**	31 8N	30 35 E
Ditchingham	**29**	52 28N	1 26 E
Ditchling & Beacon	**29**	50 59N	0 7W
Ditinn	**120**	10 53N	12 11W
Dittisham	**30**	50 22N	3 36W
Ditton Priors	**28**	52 30N	2 33W
Diu, I.	**94**	20 45N	70 58 E
Diver	**150**	46 44N	79 30W
Dives	**42**	49 18N	0 8W
Dives, R.	**42**	49 18N	0 7W
Divi Pt.	**97**	15 59N	81 9 E
Divichi	**83**	41 15N	48 57 E
Divide	**160**	45 48N	112 47W
Dividing Ra.	**137**	27 45 S	116 0 E
Divinopólis	**171**	20 10 S	44 54W
Divisões, Serra dos	**171**	17 0 S	51 0W
Divnoye	**83**	45 55N	43 27 E
Divo	**120**	5 48N	5 15W
Diwal Kol	**94**	34 23N	67 52 E
Dixie	**160**	45 37N	115 27W
Dixon, Calif., U.S.A.	**163**	38 27N	121 49W
Dixon, Ill., U.S.A.	**158**	41 50N	89 30W
Dixon, Mont., U.S.A.	**160**	47 19N	114 25W
Dixon, N. Mex., U.S.A.	**161**	36 15N	105 57W
Dixon Entrance	**153**	54 30N	132 0W
Dixonville	**152**	56 32N	117 40W
Diyarbakir	**92**	37 55N	40 18 E
Dizzard Pt.	**30**	50 46N	4 38W
Djabotaoure	**121**	8 35N	0 58 E
Djado	**119**	21 4N	12 14 E
Djado, Plateau du	**119**	21 29N	12 21 E
Djakarta = Jakarta	**103**	6 9 S	106 49 E
Djakovo	**66**	45 19N	18 24 E
Djamâa	**119**	33 32N	5 59 E
Djamba	**128**	16 45 S	13 58 E
Djambala	**124**	2 20 S	14 30 E
Djanet	**119**	24 35N	9 32 E
Djang	**121**	5 30N	10 5 E
Djaul I.	**135**	2 58 S	150 57 E
Djawa = Jawa	**103**	7 0 S	110 0 E
Djebiniana	**119**	35 1N	11 0 E
Djelfa	**118**	34 40N	3 15 E
Djema	**126**	6 9N	25 15 E
Djeneïene	**119**	31 45N	10 9 E
Djenné	**120**	14 0N	4 30W
Djenoun, Garet el	**119**	25 4N	5 31 E
Djerba	**119**	33 52N	10 51 E
Djerba, Île de	**119**	33 56N	11 0 E
Djerid, Chott	**119**	33 42N	8 30 E
Djibo	**121**	14 15N	1 35W
Djibouti	**123**	11 30N	43 5 E
Djibouti ■	**123**	11 30N	42 15 E
Djidjelli	**119**	36 52N	5 50 E
Djirlange	**101**	11 44N	108 15 E
Djofra	**119**	28 59N	15 47 E
Djolu	**124**	0 45N	22 5 E
Djorf el Youdi	**118**	32 14N	9 8W
Djougou	**121**	9 40N	1 45 E
Djoum	**124**	2 41N	12 35 E
Djourab, Erg du	**117**	16 40N	18 50 E
Djugu	**126**	1 55N	30 35 E
Djúpivogur	**74**	64 39N	14 17W
Djursholm	**72**	59 25N	18 6 E
Djursland	**73**	56 27N	10 45 E
Dmitriev-Lgovskiy	**80**	52 10N	35 0 E
Dmitriya Lapteva, Proliv	**77**	73 0N	140 0 E
Dmitrov	**81**	56 25N	37 32 E
Dmitrovsk Orlovskiy	**80**	52 29N	35 10 E
Dneiper, R. = Dnepr	**82**	52 29N	35 10 E
Dnepr, R.	**82**	50 0N	31 0 E
Dneprodzerzhinsk	**82**	48 32N	34 30 E
Dneprodzerzhinskoye Vdkhr.	**77**	49 0N	34 0 E
Dnepropetrovsk	**82**	48 30N	35 0 E
Dneprorudnoye	**82**	47 21N	34 58 E
Dnestr, R.	**82**	48 30N	26 30 E
Dnestrovski = Belgorod	**82**	50 35N	36 35 E
Dniester = Dnestr	**82**	48 30N	26 30 E
Dno	**80**	57 50N	29 58 E
Doan Hung	**100**	21 38N	105 10 E
Doba	**117**	8 40N	16 50 E
Dobané	**126**	6 20N	24 39 E
Dobbiaco	**63**	46 44N	12 13 E

Name	Page	Lat.	Long.
Dobbyn	**138**	19 44 S	139 59 E
Dobczyce	**54**	49 52N	20 25 E
Döbeln	**48**	51 7N	13 10 E
Doberai, Jazirah	**103**	1 25 S	133 0 E
Dobiegniew	**54**	52 59N	15 45 E
Doblas	**172**	37 5 S	64 0W
Dobo	**103**	5 45 S	134 15 E
Doboj	**66**	44 46N	18 6 E
Dobra, Poland	**54**	53 34N	15 20 E
Dobra, Dîmboviţa, Rumania	**67**	44 52N	25 40 E
Dobra, Hunedoara, Rumania	**70**	45 54N	22 36 E
Dobre Miasto	**54**	53 58N	20 26 E
Dobrinishta	**67**	41 49N	23 34 E
Dobriš	**52**	49 46N	14 10 E
Dobrodzien	**54**	50 45N	18 25 E
Dobrogea	**70**	44 30N	28 15 E
Dobruja = Dobrogea	**70**	44 30N	28 15 E
Dobrush	**80**	52 28N	30 35 E
Dobryanka	**84**	58 27N	56 25 E
Dobrzyn n. Wisła	**54**	52 39N	19 22 E
Dobtong	**123**	6 25N	31 40 E
Doc, Mui	**100**	17 58N	106 30 E
Doce, R.	**171**	19 37 S	39 49W
Docking	**29**	52 55N	0 39 E
Doda	**95**	33 10N	75 34 E
Döda Fallet	**72**	63 4N	16 35 E
Doddington	**29**	52 29N	0 3 E
Dodecanese = Dhodhekánisos	**69**	36 35N	27 0 E
Dodewaard	**46**	51 55N	5 39 E
Dodge Center	**158**	44 1N	92 57W
Dodge City	**159**	37 42N	100 0W
Dodge L.	**153**	59 50N	105 36W
Dodgeville	**158**	42 55N	90 8W
Dodman Pt.	**30**	50 13N	4 49W
Dodo	**123**	5 10N	29 57 E
Dodola	**123**	6 59N	39 11 E
Dodoma	**126**	6 8 S	35 45 E
Dodoma □	**126**	6 0 S	36 0 E
Dodsland	**153**	51 50N	108 45W
Dodson	**160**	48 23N	108 4W
Doesburg	**46**	52 1N	6 9 E
Doetinchem	**46**	51 59N	6 18 E
Doftana	**70**	45 17N	25 45 E
Dog Creek	**152**	51 35N	122 14W
Dog L., Man., Can.	**152**	51 2N	98 31W
Dog L., Ont., Can.	**150**	48 12N	89 16W
Dog, R.	**152**	57 50N	94 40W
Doganbey	**69**	37 40N	27 10 E
Dogi	**93**	32 20N	62 50 E
Dogliani	**62**	44 35N	7 55 E
Dōgo	**110**	36 15N	133 16 E
Dōgo-San	**110**	35 2N	133 13 E
Dògondoutchi	**121**	13 38N	4 2 E
Dogoraoua	**121**	14 0N	5 31 E
Dogran	**94**	31 48N	73 35 E
Dohad	**94**	22 50N	74 15 E
Dohazari	**99**	22 10N	92 5 E
Doheny	**150**	47 4N	72 35W
Doherty	**150**	46 58N	79 44W
Doi, I.	**103**	2 21N	127 49 E
Doi Luang	**101**	18 20N	101 30 E
Doi Saket	**100**	18 52N	99 9 E
Doig, R., Alta., Can.	**152**	56 57N	120 0W
Doig, R., B.C., Can.	**152**	56 25N	120 40W
Dois Irmãos, Serra	**171**	8 30 S	41 5W
Dokka	**71**	60 49N	10 7 E
Dokka, R.	**71**	61 7N	10 0 E
Dokkum	**46**	53 20N	5 59 E
Dokkumer Ee, R.	**46**	53 18N	5 52 E
Dokri Mohenjodaro	**94**	27 25N	68 7 E
Dol	**42**	48 34N	1 47W
Dolak, Pulau = Kolepom, P.	**103**	8 0 S	138 30 E
Doland	**158**	44 55N	98 5W
Dolbeau	**151**	48 53N	72 18W
Dôle	**43**	47 7N	5 31 E
Doleib, W.	**123**	10 30N	33 15 E
Dolgarrog	**31**	53 11N	3 50W
Dolgellau	**31**	52 44N	3 53W
Dolgelly = Dolgellau	**31**	52 44N	3 53W
Dolginovo	**80**	54 39N	27 29 E
Dolianovo	**64**	39 23N	9 11 E
Dolinskaya	**82**	48 16N	32 36 E
Dolisie	**124**	4 0 S	13 10 E
Dolj □	**70**	44 10N	23 30 E
Dolla	**39**	52 47N	8 12W
Dollar	**35**	56 9N	3 41W
Dollart	**46**	53 20N	7 10 E
Dolna Banya	**67**	42 18N	23 44 E
Dolni Dubnik	**67**	43 24N	24 26 E
Dolo	**63**	45 25N	12 4 E
Dolo Bay	**123**	4 11N	42 3 E
Dolomites = Dolomiti	**63**	46 30N	11 40 E
Dolomiti	**63**	46 30N	11 40 E
Dolores, Argent.	**172**	36 20 S	57 40W
Dolores, Mexico	**164**	28 53N	108 27W
Dolores, Uruguay	**172**	33 34 S	58 15W
Dolores, Colo., U.S.A.	**161**	37 30N	108 30W
Dolores, Tex., U.S.A.	**159**	27 40N	99 38W
Dolores, R.	**159**	38 30N	108 55W
Đolovo	**66**	44 55N	20 52 E
Dolphin and Union Str.	**148**	69 5N	114 45W
Dolphin C.	**176**	51 10 S	50 0W
Dolphinton	**35**	55 42N	3 28W
Dolsk	**54**	51 59N	17 3 E
Dolton	**30**	50 53N	4 2W
Dolwyddelan	**31**	53 3N	3 53W
Dom	**50**	46 6N	7 50 E
Dom Joaquim	**171**	18 57 S	43 16W
Dom Pedrito	**173**	31 0 S	54 40W

Name	Page	Lat.	Long.
Dom Pedro	**170**	4 29 S	44 27W
Doma	**121**	8 25N	8 18 E
Domasi	**127**	15 22 S	35 10 E
Domat Ems	**51**	46 50N	9 27 E
Domazlice	**52**	49 28N	13 0 E
Dombarovskiy	**84**	50 46N	59 32 E
Dombås	**71**	62 6N	9 4 E
Dombasle	**43**	49 8N	5 10 E
Dombe Grande	**125**	12 56 S	13 8 E
Dombes	**45**	46 3N	5 0 E
Dombóvár	**53**	46 21N	18 9 E
Dombrád	**53**	48 13N	21 54 E
Domburg	**47**	51 34N	3 30 E
Domel, I = Letsok-aw-kyun	**101**	11 30N	98 25 E
Domérat	**44**	46 21N	2 32 E
Domett	**143**	42 53 S	173 12 E
Domeyko	**172**	29 0 S	71 30W
Domeyko, Cordillera	**172**	24 30 S	69 0W
Domfront	**42**	48 37N	0 40W
Dominador	**172**	24 21 S	69 20W
Dominica I.	**167**	15 20N	61 20W
Dominica Passage	**167**	15 10N	61 20W
Dominican Rep. ■	**167**	19 0N	70 30W
Dömitz	**48**	53 9N	11 13 E
Domme	**44**	44 48N	1 12 E
Dommel, R.	**47**	51 30N	5 20 E
Dommerby	**73**	56 33N	9 5 E
Domo	**91**	7 50N	47 10 E
Domodossóla	**62**	46 6N	8 19 E
Dompaire	**43**	48 14N	6 14 E
Dompierre	**44**	46 31N	3 41 E
Dompin	**120**	5 10N	2 5W
Domrémy	**43**	48 26N	5 40 E
Domsjö	**72**	63 16N	18 41 E
Domville, Mt.	**139**	28 1 S	151 15 E
Domvraina	**69**	38 15N	22 59 E
Domzale	**63**	46 9N	3 6 E
Don Benito	**57**	38 53N	5 51W
Don, C.	**136**	11 18 S	131 46 E
Don Duong	**101**	11 51N	108 35 E
Don Martin, Presa de	**164**	27 30N	100 50W
Don Pedro Res.	**163**	37 43N	120 24W
Don, R., India	**97**	16 40N	75 55W
Don, R., Eng., U.K.	**33**	53 41N	0 51W
Don, R., Scot., U.K.	**37**	57 14N	2 5W
Don, R., U.S.S.R.	**83**	49 35N	41 40 E
Dona Ana	**127**	17 25 S	35 17 E
Donabate	**38**	53 30N	6 9W
Donadea	**38**	53 20N	6 45W
Donaghadee	**38**	54 38N	5 32W
Donaghmore, Ireland	**39**	52 54N	7 37W
Donaghmore, U.K.	**38**	54 33N	6 50W
Donald	**140**	36 23 S	143 0 E
Donalda	**152**	52 35N	112 34W
Donaldsonville	**159**	30 2N	91 50W
Donalsonville	**157**	31 3N	84 52W
Donard	**39**	53 1N	6 37W
Donau-Kanal	**49**	49 1N	11 27 E
Donau, R.	**53**	47 55N	17 20 E
Donaueschingen	**49**	47 57N	8 30 E
Donawitz	**52**	47 22N	15 4 E
Doncaster	**33**	53 31N	1 9W
Dondo, Angola	**74**	9 45 S	14 25 E
Dondo, Mozam.	**127**	19 33 S	34 46 E
Dondo, Teluk	**103**	0 29N	120 45 E
Dondra Head	**97**	5 55N	80 40 E
Donegal	**38**	54 39N	8 8W
Donegal □	**38**	54 53N	8 0W
Donegal B.	**38**	54 30N	8 35W
Donegal Har.	**38**	54 35N	8 15W
Donegal Pt.	**39**	52 44N	9 38W
Doneraile	**39**	52 13N	8 37W
Donets, R.	**81**	48 50N	38 45 E
Donetsk	**82**	48 0N	37 45 E
Dong	**121**	9 20N	12 15 E
Dong Ba Thin	**101**	12 8N	109 13 E
Dong Dang	**100**	21 4N	106 57 E
Dong Giam	**100**	19 15N	105 31 E
Dong Ha	**100**	16 49N	107 8 E
Dong Hene	**100**	16 16N	105 18 E
Dong Hoi	**100**	17 29N	106 36 E
Dong Khe	**100**	22 26N	106 27 E
Dong Van	**100**	23 16N	105 22 E
Dong Xoai	**101**	11 32N	106 55 E
Donga	**121**	7 45N	10 2 E
Dongara	**137**	29 14 S	114 57 E
Dongargarh	**96**	21 10N	80 40 E
Dongen	**47**	51 38N	4 56 E
Donges	**42**	47 18N	2 4W
Donggala	**103**	0 30 S	119 40 E
Dongola	**122**	19 9N	30 22 E
Dongou	**124**	2 0N	18 5 E
Donhead	**28**	51 1N	2 8W
Donington	**33**	52 54N	0 12W
Donington, C.	**140**	34 45 S	136 0 E
Doniphan	**159**	36 40N	90 50W
Donja Stubica	**63**	45 59N	16 0 E
Donji Dušnik	**66**	43 12N	22 5 E
Donji Miholjac	**66**	45 45N	18 10 E
Donji Milanovac	**66**	44 28N	22 6 E
Donji Vakuf	**66**	44 8N	17 24 E
Donjon, Le	**44**	46 22N	3 48 E
Dønna	**74**	66 6N	12 30 E
Donna	**74**	66 6N	12 30 E
Donna	**159**	26 12N	98 2W
Donna Nook, Pt.	**33**	53 29N	0 9 E
Donnaconna	**151**	46 41N	71 41W
Donnelly's Crossing	**142**	35 42 S	173 38 E
Donnybrook	**137**	33 34 S	115 48 E
Donor's Hills	**138**	18 42 S	140 33 E
Donoughmore	**39**	52 0N	8 42W
Donskoy	**81**	53 55N	38 15W

Donya Lendava **63** 46 35N 16 25 E
Donzère **45** 44 28N 4 43 E
Donzy **43** 47 20N 3 6 E
Dooagh **38** 53 59N 10 7W
Doochary **38** 54 54N 8 10W
Doodlakine **137** 31 34 S 117 51 E
Dooega Hd. **38** 53 54N 10 3W
Doon L. **34** 55 15N 4 22W
Doon, R. **34** 55 26N 4 41W
Doonbeg **39** 52 44N 9 31W
Doonbeg R. **39** 52 42N 9 20W
Doorn **46** 52 2N 5 20 E
Dor (Tantura) **90** 32 37N 34 55 E
Dora Báltea, R. **62** 45 42N 7 25 E
Dora, L. **136** 22 0 S 123 0 E
Dora Riparia, R. **62** 45 7N 7 24 E
Dorada, La **174** 5 30N 74 40W
Dorading **123** 8 30N 33 5 E
Doran L. **153** 61 13N 108 6W
Dorat, Le **44** 46 14N 1 5 E
Dörby **73** 56 20N 16 12 E
Dorchester, Dorset, U.K. **28** 50 42N 2 28W
Dorchester, Oxon., U.K. **28** 51 38N 1 10W
Dorchester, C. **149** 65 27N 77 27W
Dordogne □ **44** 45 5N 0 40 E
Dordogne, R. **44** 45 2N 0 36W
Dordrecht, Neth. **46** 51 48N 4 39 E
Dordrecht, S. Afr. **128** 31 20 S 27 3 E
Doré L. **153** 54 46N 107 17W
Doré Lake **153** 54 38N 107 54W
Dore, Mt. **44** 45 32N 2 50 E
Dore, R. **44** 45 59N 3 28 E
Dores **37** 57 22N 4 20W
Dores do Indaiá **171** 19 27 S 45 36W
Dorfen **49** 48 16N 12 10 E
Dorgali **64** 40 18N 9 35 E
Dori **121** 14 3N 0 2W
Doring, R. **128** 32 30 S 19 30 E
Dorion **150** 45 23N 74 3W
Dorking **29** 51 14N 0 20W
Dormaa-Ahenkro **120** 7 15N 2 52W
Dormo, Ras **123** 13 14N 42 35 E
Dornach **50** 47 29N 7 37 E
Dornberg **63** 45 45N 13 50 E
Dornbirn **52** 47 25N 9 45 E
Dornes **43** 46 48N 3 18 E
Dornie **36** 57 17N 5 30W
Dornoch **37** 57 52N 4 0W
Dornoch, Firth of **37** 57 52N 4 0W
Dornogovi □ **106** 44 0N 110 0 E
Doro **121** 16 9N 0 51W
Dorog **53** 47 42N 18 45 E
Dorogobuzh **80** 54 50N 33 10 E
Dorohoi **70** 47 56N 26 30 E
Döröö Nuur **105** 47 40N 93 30 E
Dorre I. **137** 25 13 S 113 12 E
Dorrigo **141** 30 20 S 152 44 E
Dorris **160** 41 59N 121 58W
Dorset □ **28** 50 48N 2 25W
Dorsten **48** 51 40N 6 55 E
Dorstone **28** 52 4N 3 0W
Dortmund **48** 51 32N 7 28 E
Dörtyol **92** 36 52N 36 12 E
Dorum **48** 53 40N 8 33 E
Doruma **126** 4 42N 27 33 E
Dorya, W. **123** 5 15N 41 30 E
Dos Bahías, C. **176** 44 58 S 65 32W
Dos Cabezas **161** 32 1N 109 37W
Dos Hermanas **57** 37 16N 5 55W
Dos Palos **163** 36 59N 120 37W
Dosara **121** 12 20N 6 5 E
Doshi **93** 35 35N 68 50 E
Dosso **121** 13 0N 3 13 E
Döstrup **73** 56 41N 9 42 E
Dot **152** 50 12N 121 25W
Dothan **157** 31 10N 85 25W
Dottignies **47** 50 44N 3 19 E
Dotty, gasfield **19** 53 3N 1 48 E
Douai **43** 50 21N 3 4 E
Douala **121** 4 0N 9 45 E
Douarnenez **42** 48 6N 4 21W
Double Island Pt. **139** 25 56 S 153 11 E
Doubrava, R. **52** 49 40N 15 30 E
Doubs □ **43** 47 10N 6 20 E
Doubs, R. **43** 46 53N 5 1 E
Doubtful B. **137** 34 15 S 119 28 E
Doubtful Sd. **143** 45 20 S 166 49 E
Doubtless B. **142** 34 55 S 173 26 E
Doucet **150** 48 15N 76 35W
Doudeville **42** 49 43N 0 47 E
Doué **42** 47 11N 0 20W
Douentza **120** 14 58N 2 48W
Douglas, S. Afr. **128** 29 4 S 23 46 E
Douglas, U.K. **32** 54 9N 4 29W
Douglas, U.K. **35** 55 33N 3 50W
Douglas, Alaska, U.S.A. **147** 58 23N 134 32W
Douglas, Ariz., U.S.A. **161** 31 21N 109 30W
Douglas, Ga., U.S.A. **157** 31 32N 82 52W
Douglas, Wyo., U.S.A. **158** 42 45N 105 20W
Douglas Hd. **32** 54 9N 4 28W
Douglastown **151** 48 46N 64 24W
Douglasville **157** 33 46N 84 43W
Douirat **118** 33 2N 4 11W
Doukáton, Ákra **69** 38 34N 20 30 E
Doulevant **43** 48 22N 4 53 E
Doullens **43** 50 10N 2 20 E
Doulus Hd. **39** 51 57N 10 19W
Doumé **124** 4 15N 13 25 E
Douna **120** 12 40N 6 0W
Dounby **37** 59 4N 3 13W
Doune **35** 56 12N 4 3W
Dounreay **37** 58 40N 3 28W
Dour **47** 50 24N 3 46 E
Dourada, Serra **171** 13 10 S 48 45W
Dourados **173** 22 9 S 54 50W
Dourados, R. **173** 21 58 S 54 18W
Dourdan **43** 48 30N 2 0 E
Douro Litoral □ **55** 41 10N 8 20W
Douro, R. **56** 41 1N 8 16W
Douŭzeci Si Trei August **70** 43 50N 28 40 E
Douvaine **45** 46 19N 6 16 E
Douz **119** 33 25N 9 0 E
Dove **32** 52 51N 1 36W
Dove Brook **151** 53 40N 57 40W
Dove Creek **161** 37 53N 108 59W
Dove Dale **33** 53 10N 1 47W
Dove, R. **33** 54 20N 0 55W
Dover, Austral. **138** 43 18 S 147 2 E
Dover, U.K. **29** 51 7N 1 19 E
Dover, Del., U.S.A. **162** 39 10N 75 31W
Dover, N.H., U.S.A. **162** 43 5N 70 51W
Dover, N.J., U.S.A. **162** 40 53N 74 34W
Dover, Ohio, U.S.A. **156** 40 32N 81 30W
Dover-Foxcroft **151** 45 14N 69 14W
Dover Plains **162** 41 43N 73 35W
Dover, Pt. **137** 32 32 S 125 32 E
Dover, Str. of **16** 51 0N 1 30 E
Doveridge **32** 52 54N 1 49 E
Dovey, R. **31** 52 32N 4 0W
Dovre **71** 62 0N 9 15 E
Dovrefjell **71** 62 15N 9 33 E
Dowa **127** 13 38 S 33 58 E
Dowagiac **156** 42 0N 86 8W
Dowlatabad **93** 28 20N 50 40 E
Down □ **38** 54 20N 5 50W
Down, Co. **38** 54 20N 6 0W
Downey **160** 42 29N 112 3W
Downham **29** 52 26N 0 15 E
Downham Market **29** 52 36N 0 22 E
Downhill **38** 55 10N 6 48W
Downieville **160** 39 34N 120 50W
Downpatrick **38** 54 20N 5 43W
Downpatrick Hd. **38** 54 20N 9 21W
Downs Division **139** 27 10 S 150 44 E
Downs, The **38** 53 30N 7 15W
Downsville **162** 42 5N 74 60W
Downton **28** 51 0N 1 44W
Dowra **38** 54 11N 8 2W
Doylestown **162** 40 21N 75 10W
Doyung **99** 33 40N 99 25 E
Dra, Cap **118** 28 58N 11 0W
Draa, O. **118** 30 29N 6 1W
Drachten **46** 53 7N 6 5 E
Drăgăneşti **70** 44 9N 24 32 E
Drăgăneşti-Viaşca **70** 44 5N 25 33 E
Dragaš **66** 42 5N 20 35 E
Drăgăsani **70** 44 39N 24 17 E
Dragina **66** 44 30N 19 25 E
Dragocvet **66** 44 0N 21 15 E
Dragonera, I. **58** 39 35N 2 19 E
Dragon's Mouth **174** 11 0N 61 50W
Dragovistica, (Berivol) **66** 42 22N 22 39 E
Draguignan **45** 43 30N 6 27 E
Drain **160** 43 45N 123 17W
Drake, Austral. **139** 28 55 S 152 25 E
Drake, U.S.A. **158** 47 56N 100 31W
Drake Passage **13** 58 0 S 68 0W
Drakensberg **129** 31 0 S 25 0 E
Dráma **68** 41 9N 24 10 E
Dráma □ **68** 41 10N 24 0 E
Drammen **71** 59 42N 10 12 E
Drangajökull **74** 66 9N 22 15W
Drangan **39** 52 32N 7 36W
Drangedal **71** 59 6N 9 3 E
Dranov, Ostrov **70** 44 55N 29 30 E
Draperstown **38** 54 48N 6 47 E
Dras **95** 34 25N 75 48 E
Drau, R. **52** 47 46N 13 33 E
Drava, R. **66** 45 50N 18 0W
Draveil **43** 48 41N 2 25 E
Dravograd **63** 46 36N 15 5 E
Drawa, R. **54** 53 6N 15 56 E
Drawno **54** 53 13N 15 46 E
Drawsko Pom **54** 53 35N 15 50 E
Drayton Valley **152** 53 25N 114 58W
Dreghorn **34** 55 36N 4 30W
Dreibergen **46** 52 3N 5 17 E
Drejö **73** 54 58N 10 25 E
Dren **66** 43 8N 20 44 E
Drenagh **38** 55 3N 6 55W
Drenthe □ **54** 52 52N 6 40 E
Drentsche Hoofdvaart **46** 52 39N 6 4 E
Dresden **48** 51 2N 13 45 E
Dresden □ **48** 51 12N 14 0 E
Dreumel **47** 51 51N 5 26 E
Dreux **42** 48 44N 1 23 E
Drezdenko **54** 52 50N 15 49 E
Driel **46** 51 57N 5 49 E
Driffield **33** 54 0N 0 25W
Driftwood **150** 49 8N 81 23 E
Drigana **119** 20 51N 12 17 E
Driggs **160** 43 50N 111 8W
Drimnin **36** 56 36N 6 0W
Drimoleague **39** 51 40N 9 15W
Drin-i-zi, R. **68** 41 37N 20 28 E
Drina, R. **66** 44 30N 19 10 E
Drincea, R. **70** 44 20N 22 55 E
Drînceni **70** 46 49N 28 10 E
Drini, R. **68** 42 20N 20 0 E
Drinjača, R. **66** 44 20N 19 0 E
Driva **71** 62 33N 9 38 E
Driva, R. **71** 62 34N 9 33 E
Drivstua **71** 62 26N 9 37 E
Drniš **63** 43 51N 16 10 E
Drøbak **71** 59 39N 10 39 E
Dröbak **75** 59 39N 10 48 E
Drobbakk **71** 59 39N 10 39 E
Drobin **54** 52 42N 19 58 E
Drogheda **38** 53 45N 6 20W
Drogichin **80** 52 15N 25 8 E
Drogobych **80** 49 20N 23 30 E
Droichead Nua **39** 53 11N 6 50W
Droitwich **28** 52 16N 2 10W
Dromahair **38** 54 13N 8 18W
Dromara **38** 54 21N 6 1W
Dromard **38** 54 14N 8 40W
Drôme □ **45** 44 38N 5 15 E
Drôme, R. **45** 44 46N 4 46 E
Dromedary, C. **141** 36 17 S 150 10 E
Dromiskin **38** 53 56N 6 25W
Dromod **38** 53 52N 7 55W
Dromore, Down, U.K. **38** 54 24N 6 10W
Dromore, Tyrone, U.K. **38** 54 31N 7 28W
Dromore West **38** 54 15N 8 50W
Dronero **62** 44 29N 7 22 E
Dronfield, Austral. **138** 21 12 S 140 3 E
Dronfield, U.K. **33** 53 18N 1 29W
Dronninglund **73** 57 10N 10 19 E
Dronrijp **46** 53 11N 5 39 E
Drosendorf **52** 48 52N 15 37 E
Drouin **141** 38 10 S 145 53 E
Drouzhba **67** 43 22N 28 0 E
Drum **38** 54 6N 7 9W
Drumbeg, N. Ire., U.K. **38** 54 33N 6 0W
Drumbeg, Scot., U.K. **36** 58 15N 5 12W
Drumcard **38** 54 14N 7 42W
Drumcliffe **38** 54 20N 8 30W
Drumcondra **38** 53 50N 6 40W
Drumheller **152** 51 25N 112 40W
Drumjohn **34** 55 14N 4 15W
Drumkeerin **38** 54 10N 8 8W
Drumlish **38** 53 50N 7 47W
Drummond **160** 46 46N 113 4W
Drummond I. **150** 46 0N 83 40W
Drummond Pt. **139** 34 9 S 135 16 E
Drummond Ra. **138** 23 45 S 147 10 E
Drummondville **150** 45 55N 72 25W
Drummore **34** 54 41N 4 53W
Drumquin **38** 54 38N 7 30W
Drumright **159** 35 59N 96 38W
Drumshanbo **38** 54 2N 8 4W
Drumsna **38** 53 57N 8 0W
Drunen **47** 51 41N 5 8 E
Druridge B. **35** 55 16N 1 32W
Druskinankaj **80** 54 3N 23 58 E
Drut, R. **80** 52 32N 30 0 E
Druten **46** 51 53N 5 36 E
Druya **80** 55 45N 27 15 E
Druzhina **77** 68 14N 145 18 E
Drvar **63** 44 21N 16 2 E
Drvenik **63** 43 27N 16 3 E
Dry Tortugas **166** 24 38N 82 55W
Dryanovo **67** 42 59N 25 28 E
Dryden, Can. **153** 49 50N 92 50W
Dryden, N.Y., U.S.A. **162** 42 30N 76 18W
Dryden, Tex., U.S.A. **159** 30 3N 102 3W
Drygalski I. **13** 66 0 S 92 0 E
Drygarn Fawr **31** 52 13N 3 39W
Drymen **70** 56 4N 4 28W
Drynoch **36** 57 17N 6 18W
Drysdale I. **138** 11 41 S 136 0 E
Drysdale, R. **136** 13 59 S 126 51 E
Dschang **121** 5 32N 10 3 E
Du **121** 10 26N 1 34W
Du Bois **156** 41 8N 78 46W
Du Quoin **158** 38 0N 89 10W
Duanesburg **162** 42 45N 74 11W
Duaringa **138** 23 42 S 149 42 E
Duba **92** 27 10N 35 40 E
Dubai = Dubayy **93** 25 18N 55 20 E
Dubawnt, L. **153** 63 4N 101 42W
Dubawnt, R. **153** 64 33N 100 6W
Dubayy **93** 25 18N 55 20 E
Dubbeldam **46** 51 47N 4 43 E
Dubbo **141** 32 11 S 148 35 E
Dubele **126** 2 56N 29 35 E
Dübendorf **51** 47 24N 8 37 E
Dubenskiy **84** 51 27N 56 38 E
Dubh Artach **34** 56 8N 6 40W
Dubica **63** 45 17N 16 48 E
Dublin, Ireland **38** 53 20N 6 18W
Dublin, Ga., U.S.A. **157** 32 30N 83 0W
Dublin, Tex., U.S.A. **159** 32 0N 98 20W
Dublin □ **38** 53 24N 6 20W
Dublin, B. **39** 53 24N 6 20W
Dubna **81** 54 8N 36 52 E
Dubno **80** 50 25N 25 45 E
Dubois **160** 44 7N 112 9W
Dubossary **82** 47 15N 29 10 E
Dubossasy Vdkhr. **82** 47 30N 29 0 E
Dubovka **83** 49 5N 44 50 E
Dubovskoye **83** 47 28N 42 40 E
Dubrajpur **95** 23 48N 87 25 E
Dubrékah **120** 9 46N 13 31W
Dubrovitsa **80** 51 31N 26 35 E
Dubrovnik **66** 42 39N 18 6 E
Dubrovskoye **77** 58 55N 111 0 E
Dubuque **158** 42 30N 90 41W
Duchesne **160** 40 14N 110 22W
Duchess **138** 21 20 S 139 50 E
Ducie I. **131** 24 47 S 124 40W
Duck Cr., N.S.W., Austral. **139** 31 4 S 147 6 E
Duck Cr., W. Australia, Austral. **136** 22 37 S 116 53 E
Duck Lake **153** 52 50N 106 16W
Duck, Mt. **153** 51 27N 100 35W
Duck Mt. Prov. Parks **153** 51 45N 101 0W
Duckwall Mtn. **163** 37 58N 120 7W
Duddington **29** 52 36N 0 32W
Duddon R. **32** 54 12N 3 15W
Düdelange **47** 49 29N 6 5 E
Duderstadt **48** 51 30N 10 15 E
Dudhi **99** 24 15N 83 10 E
Dudhnai **98** 25 59N 90 47 E
Düdingen **50** 46 52N 7 12 E
Dudinka **77** 69 30N 86 0 E
Dudley **28** 52 30N 2 5W
Dudna, R. **96** 19 36N 76 20 E
Dueñas **56** 41 52N 4 33W
Dŭeni **70** 44 51N 28 10 E
Dueodde **73** 54 59N 15 4 E
Dueré **171** 11 20 S 49 17W
Duero, R. **56** 41 37N 4 25W
Duff Is. **142** 9 0 S 167 0 E
Duffel **47** 51 6N 4 30 E
Duffield **33** 52 59N 1 30W
Dufftown **37** 57 26N 3 9W
Dufourspitz **50** 45 56N 7 52 E
Dugi, I. **63** 44 0N 15 0 E
Dugo Selo **63** 45 51N 16 18 E
Duhak **93** 33 20N 57 30 E
Duifken Pt. **138** 12 33 S 141 38 E
Duisburg **48** 51 27N 6 42 E
Duitama **174** 5 50N 73 2W
Duiveland **47** 51 38N 4 0 E
Duiwelskloof **129** 23 42 S 30 10 E
Dukana **126** 3 59N 37 20 E
Dukati **68** 40 16N 19 32 E
Duke I. **152** 54 50N 131 20W
Dukhan **93** 25 25N 50 50 E
Dukhovshchina **80** 55 15N 32 27 E
Duki **93** 30 14N 68 25 E
Dukla **54** 49 30N 21 35 E
Duku, North-Eastern, Nigeria **121** 10 43N 10 43 E
Duku, North-Western, Nigeria **121** 11 11N 4 55 E
Dulas B. **31** 53 22N 4 16W
Dulawan **103** 7 5N 124 20 E
Dulce, Golfo **166** 8 40N 83 20W
Dulce, R. **172** 29 30 S 63 0W
Duleek **38** 53 40N 6 24W
Dŭlgopol **67** 43 3N 27 22 E
Dullewala **94** 31 50N 71 25 E
Dülmen **48** 51 49N 7 18 E
Dulnain Bridge **37** 57 19N 3 40W
Dulovo **67** 43 48N 27 9 E
Dululu **138** 23 48 S 150 15 E
Duluth **158** 46 48N 92 10W
Dulverton **28** 51 2N 3 33W
Dum Dum **95** 22 39N 88 26 E
Dum Duma **99** 27 40N 95 40 E
Dumaguete **103** 9 17N 123 15 E
Dumai **102** 1 35N 101 20 E
Dumaran I. **103** 10 33N 119 50 E
Dumaring **103** 1 46N 118 10 E
Dumas, Ark., U.S.A. **159** 33 52N 91 30W
Dumas, Okla., U.S.A. **159** 35 50N 101 58W
Dümat al Jandal **92** 29 55N 39 40 E
Dumba I. **71** 61 43N 4 50 E
Dumbarton **34** 55 58N 4 35W
Dumbleyung **137** 33 17 S 117 42 E
Dumbrŭveni **70** 46 14N 24 34 E
Dumfries **35** 55 4N 3 37W
Dumfries & Galloway □ **35** 54 30N 4 0W
Dumfries (□) **26** 55 0N 3 30W
Dŭmienesti **70** 46 44N 27 1 E
Dumka **95** 24 0N 87 22 E
Dumoine L. **150** 46 55N 77 55W
Dumoine, R. **150** 46 13N 77 51W
Dumraon **95** 25 33N 84 8 E
Dumyât **122** 31 24N 31 48 E
Dumyât, Masabb **122** 31 28N 32 0 E
Dun Laoghaire, (Dunleary) **39** 53 17N 6 9W
Dun-le-Palestel **44** 46 18N 1 39 E
Dun-sur-Auron **43** 46 53N 2 33 E
Duna, R. **53** 45 51N 18 48 E
Dunaff Hd. **38** 55 18N 7 30W
Dunaföldvár **53** 46 50N 18 57 E
Dunai, R. **53** 47 50N 18 52 E
Dunaj, R. **67** 45 17N 29 32 E
Dunajec, R. **54** 50 12N 20 52 E
Dunajska Streda **53** 48 0N 17 37 E
Dunamanagh **38** 54 53N 7 20W
Dunans **34** 56 4N 5 9W
Dunany Pt. **38** 53 51N 6 15W
Dunapatai **53** 46 39N 19 4 E
Dunaszekcsö **53** 46 22N 18 45 E
Dunaújváros **53** 47 0N 18 57 E
Dunav, R. **66** 45 0N 20 21 E
Dunavtsi **66** 43 57N 22 53 E
Dunback **143** 45 23 S 170 36 E
Dunbar, Austral. **138** 16 0 S 142 22 E
Dunbar, U.K. **35** 56 0N 2 32W
Dunbarton (□) **26** 56 4N 4 42W
Dunbeath **37** 58 15N 3 25W
Dunblane **35** 56 10N 3 58W
Dunboyne **38** 53 25N 6 30W
Duncan, Can. **152** 48 45N 123 40W
Duncan, Ariz., U.S.A. **161** 32 46N 109 6W
Duncan, Okla., U.S.A. **159** 34 25N 98 0W
Duncan L. **152** 62 51N 113 58W
Duncan, L., Brit. Col., Can. **150** 50 20N 117 0W
Duncan, L., Qué., Can. **152** 53 29N 77 58W
Duncan Pass. **101** 11 0N 92 30 E
Duncan Town **166** 22 15N 75 45W

Duncansby 37 58 37N 3 3W
Duncansby Head 37 58 39N 3 0W
Dunchurch 28 52 21N 1 19W
Duncormick 39 53 14N 6 40W
Dundalk, Ireland 38 53 55N 6 45W
Dundalk, U.S.A. 162 39 15N 76 31W
Dundalk, B. 38 53 55N 6 15W
Dundas 150 43 17N 79 59W
Dundas I. 152 54 30N 130 50W
Dundas, L. 137 32 35S 121 50E
Dundas Str. 136 11 15S 131 35E
Dundee, S. Afr. 129 28 11S 30 15E
Dundee, U.K. 35 56 29N 3 0W
Dundee, U.S.A. 162 42 32N 76 59W
Dundgovi □ 106 45 10N 106 0E
Dundo 124 7 23S 20 48E
Dundonald 38 54 37N 5 50W
Dundoo 139 27 40S 144 37E
Dundrennan 35 54 49N 3 56W
Dundrum, Ireland . 39 53 17N 6 15W
Dundrum, U.K. 38 54 17N 5 50W
Dundwara 95 27 48N 79 9E
Dunedin, N.Z. 143 45 50S 170 33E
Dunedin, U.S.A. 157 28 1N 82 45W
Dunedin, R. 152 59 30N 124 5W
Dunfanaghy 38 55 10N 7 59W
Dunfermline 35 56 5N 3 28W
Dungannon 38 54 30N 6 47W
Dungannon □ 38 54 30N 6 55W
Dungarpur 94 23 52N 73 45E
Dungarvan 39 52 6N 7 40W
Dungarvan Harb. 39 52 5N 7 35W
Dungas 121 13 4N 9 20E
Dungavel 35 55 37N 4 7W
Dungbura La 99 34 41N 93 18E
Dungeness 29 50 54N 0 59E
Dungiven 38 54 55N 6 56W
Dunglow 38 54 57N 8 20W
Dungo, L. do 128 17 15S 19 0E
Dungog 141 32 22S 151 40E
Dungourney 39 51 58N 8 5W
Dungu 124 2 32N 28 22E
Dungunâb 122 21 10N 37 9E
Dungunâb, Khalîg 122 21 5N 37 12E
Dunhinda Falls 97 7 5N 81 6E
Dunières 45 45 13N 4 20E
Dunk I. 138 17 59S 146 14E
Dunkeld, Austral. 140 37 40S 142 22E
Dunkeld, U.K. 37 56 34N 3 36W
Dunkerque 43 51 2N 2 20E
Dunkery Beacon 28 51 15N 3 37W
Dunkineely 38 54 38N 8 22W
Dunkirk 156 42 30N 79 18W
Dunkirk = Dunkerque 43 51 2N 2 20E
Dunkuj 123 11 15N 33 0E
Dunkur 123 11 58N 35 58E
Dunkwa, Central, Ghana 120 6 0N 1 47W
Dunkwa, Central, Ghana 121 5 30N 1 0W
Dunlap 158 41 50N 95 30W
Dunlavin 39 53 3N 6 40W
Dunleary = Dun Laoghaire 39 53 17N 6 8W
Dunleer 38 53 50N 6 23W
Dunlin, oilfield 19 61 12N 1 40E
Dunloe, Gap of 39 52 2N 9 40W
Dunlop 34 55 43N 4 32W
Dunloy 38 55 1N 6 25W
Dunmanus B. 39 51 31N 9 50W
Dunmanway 39 51 43N 9 8W
Dunmara 138 16 42S 133 25E
Dunmod 105 47 45N 106 58E
Dunmore, Ireland 38 53 37N 8 44W
Dunmore, U.S.A. 162 41 27N 75 38W
Dunmore East 39 52 9N 7 0W
Dunmore Town 166 25 30N 76 39W
Dunmurry 38 54 33N 6 0W
Dunn 157 35 18N 78 36W
Dunnellon 157 29 4N 82 28W
Dunnet 37 58 37N 3 20W
Dunnet B. 37 58 37N 3 23W
Dunnet Hd. 37 58 38N 3 22W
Dunning, U.K. 35 56 18N 3 37W
Dunning, U.S.A. 158 41 52N 100 4W
Dunolly 140 36 51S 143 44E
Dunoon 34 55 57N 4 56W
Dunqul 122 23 40N 31 10E
Duns 35 55 47N 2 20W
Dunscore 35 55 8N 3 48W
Dunseith 158 48 49N 100 2W
Dunsford 30 50 41N 3 40W
Dunshaughlin 38 53 31N 6 32W
Dunsmuir 160 41 0N 122 10W
Dunstable 29 51 53N 0 31W
Dunstan Mts. 143 44 53S 169 35E
Dunster, Can. 152 53 8N 119 50W
Dunster, U.K. 28 51 11N 3 28W
Dunston 28 52 46N 2 7W
Duntelchaig, L. 37 57 20N 4 18W
Dunton Green 29 51 17N 0 11E
Duntroon 143 44 51S 170 40E
Dunûrea, R. 70 45 0N 29 40E
Dunvegan 36 57 26N 6 35W
Dunvegan Hd. 36 57 30N 6 42W
Dunvegan L. 153 60 8N 107 10W
Duong Dong 101 10 13N 103 58E
Dupree 158 45 4N 101 35W
Dupuyer 160 48 11N 112 31W
Duque de Caxias 173 22 45S 43 19W
Dura 90 31 31N 35 1E
Durack 136 15 33S 127 52E
Durack Ra. 136 16 50S 127 40E
Durance, R. 45 43 55N 4 45E
Durand 156 42 54N 83 58W
Durango, Mexico 164 24 3N 104 39W
Durango, Spain 58 43 13N 2 40W
Durango, U.S.A. 161 37 10N 107 50W
Durango □ 164 25 0N 105 0W
Duranillin 137 33 30S 116 45E
Durant 159 34 0N 96 25W
Duratón, R. 56 41 27N 4 0W
Durazno 172 33 25S 56 38W
Durazzo = Durrësi 68 41 19N 19 28E
Durban, France 44 43 0N 2 49W
Durban, S. Afr. 129 29 49S 31 1E
Dúrcal 57 37 0N 3 34W
Đurdevac 66 46 2N 17 3E
Düren 48 50 48N 6 30E
Durg 96 21 15N 81 22E
Durgapur 95 23 30N 87 9E
Durham, Can. 150 44 10N 80 49W
Durham, U.K. 33 54 47N 1 34W
Durham, N.C., U.S.A. 157 36 0N 78 55W
Durham, N.H., U.S.A. 162 43 8N 70 56W
Durham □ 32 54 42N 1 45W
Durham Downs 139 26 6S 149 3E
Durlstone Hd. 28 50 35N 1 58W
Durmitor Mt. 66 43 18N 19 0E
Dŭrmŭneşti 70 46 21N 26 33E
Durness 37 58 34N 4 45W
Durness, Kyle of 37 58 35N 4 55W
Durrandella 138 24 3S 146 35E
Durrësi 68 41 19N 19 28E
Durrie 138 25 40S 140 15E
Durrington 28 51 12N 1 47W
Durrow 39 53 20N 7 31W
Durrus 39 51 37N 9 32W
Dursey Hd. 39 51 34N 10 41W
Dursey I. 39 51 36N 10 12W
Dursley 28 51 41N 2 21W
Durtal 42 47 40N 0 18W
Duru 126 4 20N 28 50E
Durup 73 56 45N 8 57E
D'Urville Island 143 40 50S 173 55E
Duryea 162 41 20N 75 45W
Dusa Mareb 91 5 40N 46 33E
Dûsh 122 24 35N 30 41E
Dushak 76 37 20N 60 10E
Dushanbe 85 38 33N 68 48E
Dusheti 83 42 0N 44 55E
Dushore 162 41 31N 76 24W
Dusky Sd. 143 45 47S 166 30E
Dussejour, C. 136 14 45S 128 13E
Düsseldorf 48 51 15N 6 46E
Dussen 46 51 44N 4 59E
Duszniki Zdrój 54 51 26N 16 22E
Dutch Harbour 147 53 54N 166 35W
Dutlhe 128 23 58S 23 46E
Dutsan Wai 121 10 50N 8 10E
Dutton, R. 138 20 44S 143 10E
Duvan 84 55 42N 57 54E
Duved 72 63 24N 12 55E
Duvno 66 43 42N 17 13E
Duwadami 92 24 35N 44 15E
Duzdab = Zāhedān 93 29 30N 60 50E
Dve Mogili 67 43 47N 25 55E
Dvina, Sev. 78 56 30N 24 0E
Dvina, Zap. 80 61 40N 45 30E
Dvinsk = Daugavpils 80 55 33N 26 32E
Dvinskaya Guba 78 65 0N 39 0E
Dvor 63 45 4N 16 22E
Dvorce 53 49 50N 17 34E
Dvur Králové 52 50 27N 15 50E
Dwarka 94 22 18N 69 8E
Dwellingup 137 32 43S 116 4E
Dwight 156 41 5N 88 25W
Dyakovskoya 81 60 5N 41 12E
Dyatkovo 80 53 48N 34 27E
Dyaul, I. 138 3 0S 150 55E
Dyce 37 57 12N 2 11W
Dyer 163 37 40N 118 5W
Dyer, C. 149 67 0N 61 0W
Dyerbeldzhin 85 41 13N 74 54E
Dyersburg 159 36 2N 89 20W
Dyfed □ 31 52 0N 4 30W
Dyje, R. 53 48 50N 16 45E
Dyke Acland Bay 138 8 45S 148 45E
Dykehead 37 56 43N 3 0W
Dyle, R. 47 50 58N 4 41E
Dymchurch 29 51 2N 1 0E
Dymock 28 51 58N 2 27W
Dynevor Downs 139 28 10S 144 20E
Dynów 54 49 50N 22 11E
Dypvag 71 79 40N 9 8E
Dyrnes 71 63 25N 7 52E
Dysart, Can. 153 50 57N 104 2W
Dysart, U.K. 35 56 8N 3 8W
Dysjön 72 62 38N 15 31E
Dyulgeri 67 42 18N 27 23E
Dyurtyuli 84 55 9N 54 4E
Dzambeyty 83 50 15N 52 30E
Dzaudzhikau = Ordzhonikidze 83 43 0N 44 35E
Dzerzhinsk 80 53 40N 27 7E
Dzhailma 76 51 30N 61 50E
Dzhalal-Abad 84 40 56N 73 0E
Dzhalinda 77 53 40N 124 0E
Dzhambeyty 84 50 16N 52 35E
Dzhambul 85 42 54N 71 22E
Dzhambul, Gora 85 44 54N 73 0E
Dzhankoi 82 45 40N 34 30E
Dzhanybek 83 49 25N 46 50E
Dzhardzhan 77 68 10N 123 5E
Dzharkurgan 85 37 31N 67 25E
Dzhelinde 77 70 0N 114 20E
Dzherzhinsk 80 53 48N 27 19E
Dzhetygara 84 52 11N 61 12E
Dzhetym, Khrebet 85 41 30N 77 0E
Dzhezkazgan 76 47 10N 67 40E
Dzhizak 85 40 6N 67 50E
Dzhugdzur, Khrebet 77 57 30N 138 0E
Dzhuma 85 39 42N 66 40E
Dzhumgoltau, Khrebet 85 42 15N 74 30E
Dzhungarskiye Vorota 76 45 0N 82 0E
Dzhvari 83 42 42N 42 4E
Działdowo 54 53 15N 20 15E
Działoszyce 54 50 22N 20 20E
Działoszyn 54 51 6N 18 50E
Dzibilchaltún 165 21 5N 89 36W
Dzierzgon 54 53 58N 19 20E
Dzierzoniow 54 50 45N 16 39E
Dzilam de Bravo 165 21 24N 88 53W
Dzioua 119 33 14N 5 14E
Dziwnów 54 54 2N 14 45E
Dzungaria 105 44 10N 88 0E
Dzungarian Gates = Dzhungarskiye V. 105 45 0N 82 0E

E

Eabamet, L. 150 51 30N 87 46W
Eads 158 38 30N 102 46W
Eagle, Alaska, U.S.A. 147 64 44N 141 29W
Eagle, Colo., U.S.A. 160 39 45N 106 55W
Eagle Butt 158 45 1N 101 12W
Eagle Grove 158 42 37N 93 53W
Eagle L., Calif., U.S.A. 160 40 35N 120 50W
Eagle L., Me., U.S.A. 151 46 23N 69 22W
Eagle Lake 159 29 35N 96 21W
Eagle Nest 161 36 33N 105 13W
Eagle Pass 159 28 45N 100 35W
Eagle Pk. 163 38 10N 119 25W
Eagle Pt. 136 16 11S 124 23E
Eagle, R. 151 53 36N 57 26W
Eagle River 158 45 55N 89 17W
Eaglehawk 140 36 43S 144 16E
Eagles Mere 162 41 25N 76 33W
Eaglesfield 35 55 3N 3 12W
Eagleshan 34 55 44N 4 18W
Eakring 33 53 9N 0 59W
Ealing 29 51 30N 0 19W
Earaheedy 137 25 34S 121 29E
Earby 32 53 55N 2 8W
Eardisland 28 52 14N 2 50W
Eardisley 28 52 8N 3 0W
Earith 29 52 21N 0 1E
Earl Grey 153 50 57N 104 43W
Earl Shilton 28 52 35N 1 20W
Earl Soham 29 52 14N 1 15E
Earle 159 35 18N 90 26W
Earlimart 163 35 53N 119 16W
Earls Barton 29 52 16N 0 44W
Earl's Colne 29 51 56N 0 43E
Earlsferry 35 56 11N 2 50W
Earlston 35 55 39N 2 40W
Earn, L. 34 56 23N 4 14W
Earn, R. 35 56 20N 3 19W
Earnslaw, Mt. 143 44 32S 168 27E
Earoo 137 29 34S 118 22E
Earsdon 35 55 4N 1 30W
Earth 159 34 18N 102 30W
Easebourne 29 51 0N 0 42W
Easington, Durham, U.K. 33 54 50N 1 24W
Easington, Yorks., U.K. 33 54 40N 0 7W
Easington Colliery 33 54 49N 1 19W
Easingwold 33 54 8N 1 11W
Easky 38 54 17N 8 58W
Easley 157 34 52N 82 35W
East Aberthaw 31 51 23N 3 23W
East Anglian Hts. 29 52 10N 0 17E
East Angus 151 45 30N 71 40W
East, B. 159 29 2N 89 16W
East Barming 29 51 15N 0 29E
East Bathurst 151 47 35N 65 40W
East Bengal 99 24 0N 90 0E
East Bergholt 29 51 58N 1 2E
East Beskids, mts. 53 49 30N 18 45E
East Brent 28 51 14N 2 55W
East C., N.Z. 142 37 42S 178 35E
East C., P.N.G. 135 10 13S 150 53E
East Chicago 156 41 40N 87 30W
East China Sea 105 30 5N 126 0E
East Coulee 152 51 23N 112 27W
East Cowes 28 50 45N 1 17W
East Dereham 29 52 40N 0 57E
East Falkland 176 51 30S 58 30W
East Fen 33 53 4N 0 5E
East Florenceville 151 46 26N 67 36W
East Grand Forks 158 47 55N 97 5W
East Greenwich 162 41 40N 71 27W
East Grinstead 29 51 8N 0 1W
East Harling 29 52 26N 0 55E
East Hartford 162 41 46N 72 39W
East Helena 160 46 37N 111 58W
East Ilsley 28 51 33N 1 15W
East Indies 102 0 0 120 0E
East Jordan 156 45 10N 85 7W
East Kilbride 35 55 46N 4 10W
East Kirkby 33 53 5N 1 15W
East Lansing 156 42 44N 84 37W
East Linton 35 56 0N 2 40W
East Liverpool 156 40 39N 80 35W
East London 129 33 0S 27 55E
East Looe 30 50 22N 4 28W
East Los Angeles 163 34 1N 118 9W
East Lynne 141 35 35S 150 16E
East Main (Eastmain) 151 52 20N 78 30W
East Markham 33 53 15N 0 53W
East Midlands, oilfield 19 53 20N 0 45W
East Moor 33 53 15N 1 30W
East, Mt. 137 29 0S 122 30E
East Orange 162 40 46N 74 13W
East P. 151 46 27N 61 58W
East Pakistan = Bangladesh 99 24 0N 90 0E
East Pine 152 55 48N 120 5W
East Point 157 33 40N 84 28W
East Providence 162 41 49N 71 23W
East Retford 33 53 19N 0 55W
East St. Louis 158 38 36N 90 10W
East Schelde, R. 47 51 38N 3 40E
E. Siberian Sea 77 73 0N 160 0E
East Stroudsburg 162 41 0N 75 1[illegible]W
East Sussex □ 29 50 55N 0 20E
East Tawas 156 44 17N 83 31W
East Toorale 139 30 27S 145 28E
East Walker, R. 163 38 52N 119 10W
East Wemyss 35 56 8N 3 5W
East Woodhay 28 51 21N 1 26W
Eastbourne, N.Z. 142 41 19S 174 55E
Eastbourne, U.K. 29 50 46N 0 18E
Eastchurch 29 51 23N 0 53E
Eastend 153 49 32N 108 50W
Easter Islands 143 27 0S 109 0W
Easter Ross, dist. 37 57 50N 4 35W
Easter Skeld 36 60 12N 1 27W
Eastern □ 126 0 0S 38 30E
Eastern Cr. 138 20 40S 141 35E
Eastern Ghats 97 15 0N 80 0E
Eastern Group, Is. 137 33 30S 124 30E
Eastern Province □ 120 8 15N 11 0W
Easterville 153 53 8N 99 49W
Easthampton 162 42 16N 72 40W
Eastland 159 32 26N 98 45W
Eastleigh 28 50 58N 1 21W
Eastmain (East Main) 150 52 20N 78 30W
Eastmain, R. 150 52 27N 72 26W
Eastman 157 32 13N 83 41W
Eastnor 28 52 2N 2 22W
Easton, Dorset, U.K. 28 50 32N 2 27W
Easton, Northants., U.K. 29 52 37N 0 31W
Easton, Somerset, U.K. 28 51 28N 2 42W
Easton, Md., U.S.A. 162 38 47N 76 7W
Easton, Pa., U.S.A. 162 40 41N 75 15W
Easton, Wash., U.S.A. 160 47 14N 121 8W
Eastport, Maine, U.S.A. 151 44 57N 67 0W
Eastport, N.Y., U.S.A. 162 40 50N 72 44W
Eastry 29 51 15N 1 19E
Eastview 150 45 27N 75 40W
Eastville 162 37 21N 75 57W
Eastwood 33 53 2N 1 17W
Eaton, U.K. 29 52 52N 0 46W
Eaton, U.S.A. 158 40 35N 104 42W
Eaton, L. 136 22 55S 130 57E
Eaton Socon 29 52 13N 0 18W
Eatonia 153 51 13N 109 25W
Eatonton 157 33 22N 83 24W
Eatontown 162 40 18N 74 7W
Eau Claire, S.C., U.S.A. 157 34 5N 81 2W
Eau Claire, Wis., U.S.A. 158 44 46N 91 30W
Eauze 44 43 53N 0 7E
Eaval, Mt. 36 57 31N 7 12W
Ebagoola 138 14 15S 143 12E
Eban 121 9 40N 4 50E
Ebberston 33 54 14N 0 35W
Ebbw Vale 31 51 47N 3 12W
Ebeggui 119 26 2N 6 0E
Ebeltoft 75 56 12N 10 41E
Ebensee 52 47 48N 13 46E
Eberbach 49 49 27N 8 59E
Eberswalde 48 52 49N 13 50E
Ebikon 51 47 5N 8 21E
Ebingen 49 48 13N 9 1E
Ebino 110 32 2N 130 48E
Ebnat-Kappel 51 47 16N 9 7E
Eboli 65 40 39N 15 2E
Ebolowa 121 2 55N 11 10E
Ebony 128 22 6S 15 15E
Ébrié, Lagune 120 5 12N 4 40W
Ebro, Pantano del 56 43 0N 3 58W
Ebro, R. 58 41 49N 1 5W
Ebstorf 48 53 2N 10 23E
Ecaussines-d' Enghien 47 50 35N 4 11E
Ecclefechan 35 55 3N 3 18W
Eccleshall 28 52 52N 2 14W
Eceabat 68 40 11N 26 21E
Éceuillé 42 47 10N 1 19E
Ech Chebbi 118 26 41N 0 29E
Echallens 50 46 38N 6 38E
Echaneni 77 27 33S 32 6E
Echelles, Les 45 45 27N 5 45E
Echizen-Misaki 111 35 59N 135 57E
Echmiadzin 83 40 12N 44 19E
Echo Bay, N.W.T., Can. 148 66 10N 117 40W
Echo Bay, Ont., Can. 150 46 29N 84 4W
Echoing, R. 153 55 51N 92 5W
Echt, Neth. 47 51 7N 5 52E
Echt, U.K. 37 57 8N 2 26W
Echternach 47 49 49N 6 3E
Echuca 141 36 3S 144 46E
Ecija 57 37 30N 5 10W
Eck L. 34 56 5N 5 0W
Eckernförde 48 54 26N 9 50E
Eckington 33 53 19N 1 21W
Eclipse Is. 136 13 54S 126 19E
Écommoy 42 47 50N 0 17E
Ecoporanga 171 18 23S 40 50W

Écos 43 49 9N 1 35 E
Écouché 42 48 42N 0 10W
Ecuador ■ 174 2 0S 78 0W
Ed 73 58 55N 11 55 E
Ed Dabbura 122 17 40N 34 15 E
Ed Damer 122 17 27N 34 0 E
Ed Debba 122 18 0N 30 51 E
Ed-Déffa 122 30 40N 26 30 E
Ed Deim 123 10 10N 28 20 E
Ed Dueim 123 14 0N 32 10 E
Ed Dzong 99 32 11N 90 12 E
Edah 137 28 16S 117 10 E
Edam, Can. 153 53 11N 108 46W
Edam, Neth. 46 52 31N 5 3 E
Edapally 97 11 19N 78 3 E
Eday, I. 37 59 11N 2 47W
Eday Sd. 37 59 12N 2 45W
Edd 123 14 0N 41 30 E
Edda, oilfield 19 56 25N 3 15 E
Edderton 37 57 50N 4 10W
Eddrachillis B. 36 58 16N 5 10W
Eddystone 30 50 11N 4 16W
Eddystone Pt. 138 40 59S 148 20 E
Ede, Neth. 46 52 4N 5 40 E
Ede, Nigeria 121 7 45N 4 29 E
Ede, Sweden 72 62 10N 16 50 E
Edea 121 3 51N 10 9 E
Edegem 47 51 10N 4 27 E
Edehon L. 153 60 25N 97 15W
Edekel, Adrar 119 23 56N 6 47 E
Eden, Austral. 141 37 3S 149 55 E
Eden, U.K. 38 54 44N 5 47W
Eden, Tex., U.S.A. 159 31 16N 99 50W
Eden, Wyo., U.S.A. 160 42 2N 109 27W
Eden L. 153 56 38N 100 15W
Eden, R. 32 54 57N 3 2W
Edenbridge 29 51 12N 0 4 E
Edenburg 128 29 43S 25 58 E
Edendale 143 46 19S 168 48 E
Edenderry 39 53 21N 7 3W
Edenton 157 36 5N 76 36W
Edenville 129 27 37S 27 34 E
Ederny 38 54 32N 7 40W
Edgar 158 40 25N 98 0W
Edgartown 162 41 22N 70 28W
Edge Hill 28 52 7N 1 28W
Edge I. 12 77 45N 22 30 E
Edgecumbe 142 37 59S 176 47 E
Edgefield 157 33 43N 81 59W
Edgeley 158 46 27N 98 41W
Edgemont 158 43 15N 103 53W
Edgeøya 12 77 45N 22 30 E
Edgeworthstown = Mostrim 38 53 42N 7 36W
Edhessa 68 40 48N 22 5 E
Edievale 143 45 49S 169 22 E
Edina, Liberia 120 6 0N 10 19W
Edina, U.S.A. 158 40 6N 92 10W
Edinburg 159 26 22N 98 10W
Edinburgh 35 55 57N 3 12W
Edington 28 51 17N 2 6W
Edirne 67 41 40N 26 45 E
Edison 163 35 21N 118 52W
Edithburgh 140 35 5S 137 43 E
Edjeleh 119 28 25N 9 40 E
Edjudina 137 29 48S 122 23 E
Edmeston 162 42 42N 75 15W
Edmond 159 35 37N 97 30W
Edmondbyers 32 54 50N 1 59W
Edmonds 160 47 47N 122 22W
Edmonton, Austral. 138 17 2S 145 46 E
Edmonton, Can. 152 53 30N 113 30W
Edmund L. 153 54 45N 93 17W
Edmundston 151 47 23N 68 20W
Edna 159 29 0N 96 40W
Edna Bay 152 55 55N 133 40W
Edolo 62 46 10N 10 21 E
Edouard, L. 126 0 25S 29 40 E
Edremit 92 39 40N 27 0 E
Edsbyn 72 61 23N 15 49 E
Edsel Ford Ra. 13 77 0S 143 0W
Edsele 72 63 25N 16 32 E
Edson 152 53 40N 116 28W
Eduardo Castex 172 35 50S 64 25W
Edward I. 150 48 22N 88 37W
Edward, L. (Idi Amin Dada, L.) 126 0 25S 29 40 E
Edward, R. 140 35 0S 143 30 E
Edward VII Pen. 13 80 0S 160 0W
Edwards 163 34 55N 117 51W
Edwards Plat. 159 30 30N 101 5W
Edwardsville 162 41 15N 75 56W
Edzell 37 56 49N 2 40W
Edzo 152 62 49N 116 4W
Eefde 46 52 10N 6 13 E
Eek 147 60 10N 162 0W
Eekloo 47 51 11N 3 33 E
Eelde 46 53 8N 6 34 E
Eem, R. 46 52 16N 5 20 E
Eems Kanaal 46 53 18N 6 46 E
Eems, R. 46 53 26N 6 57 E
Eenrum 46 53 22N 6 28 E
Eernegem 47 51 8N 3 2 E
Eerste Valthermond 46 52 53N 6 58 E
Eersterivier 128 34 0S 18 45 E
Efate, I. (Vate) 46 17 40S 168 25 E
Eferding 52 48 18N 14 1 E
Eferi 119 24 30N 9 28 E
Effingham 156 39 8N 88 30W
Effiums 121 6 35N 8 0 E
Effretikon 51 47 25N 8 42 E
Efiduasi 121 6 45N 1 25W
Eforie Sud 70 44 1N 28 37 E
Ega, R. 58 42 32N 1 58W
Egadi, Isole 64 37 55N 12 10 E
Eganville 150 45 32N 77 5W
Egeland 158 48 42N 99 6W
Egenolf L. 153 59 3N 100 0W
Eger 53 47 53N 20 27 E
Eger, R. 53 47 43N 20 32 E
Egersund = Eigersund 75 58 26N 6 1 E
Egerton, Mt. 137 24 42S 117 44 E
Egg L. 153 55 5N 105 30W
Eggenburg 52 48 38N 15 50 E
Eggiwil 50 46 52N 7 47 E
Egham 29 51 25N 0 33W
Egilsay I. 37 59 10N 2 56W
Eginbah 136 20 53S 119 47 E
Egletons 44 45 24N 2 3 E
Eglisau 51 47 35N 8 31 E
Egmond-aan-Zee 46 52 37N 4 38 E
Egmont, C. 142 39 16S 173 45 E
Egmont, Mt. 142 39 17S 174 5 E
Egogi Bad 123 13 10N 41 30 E
Egremont 32 54 28N 3 33W
Eğridir Gölü 92 37 53N 30 50 E
Egton 33 54 27N 0 45W
Egtved 73 55 38N 9 18 E
Egua 174 5 5N 68 0W
Eguas, R. 171 13 26S 44 14W
Egume 121 7 30N 7 14 E
Eguzon 44 46 27N 1 33 E
Egvekinot 77 66 19N 179 50W
Egyek 53 47 39N 20 52 E
Egypt ■ 122 28 0N 31 0 E
Eha Amufu 121 6 30N 7 40 E
Ehime-ken □ 110 33 30N 132 40 E
Ehingen 49 48 16N 9 43 E
Ehrwald 52 47 24N 10 56 E
Eibar 58 43 11N 2 28W
Eibergen 46 52 6N 6 39 E
Eichstätt 49 48 53N 11 12 E
Eidanger 71 59 7N 9 43 E
Eide 71 60 31N 6 44 E
Eider, R. 48 54 15N 8 50 E
Eidsberg 71 59 32N 11 16 E
Eidsfoss 71 59 36N 10 2 E
Eidsvold 139 25 25S 151 12 E
Eidsvoll 75 60 19N 11 14 E
Eifel 49 50 10N 6 45 E
Eiffel Flats 127 18 20S 30 0 E
Eigersund 71 58 26N 6 1 E
Eigg, I. 36 56 54N 6 10W
Eigg, Sd. of 36 56 52N 6 15W
Eighty Mile Beach 136 19 30S 120 40 E
Eil 91 8 0N 49 50 E
Eil, L. 36 56 50N 5 15W
Eilat 90 29 30N 34 56 E
Eildon 141 37 14S 145 55 E
Eildon, L. 139 37 10S 146 0 E
Eileen L. 153 62 16N 107 37W
Eilenburg 48 51 28N 12 38 E
Ein 'Arik 90 31 54N 35 8 E
Ein el Luweiqa 123 14 5N 33 50 E
Einasleigh 138 18 32S 144 5 E
Einasleigh, R. 138 17 30S 142 17 E
Einbeck 48 51 48N 9 50 E
Eindhoven 47 51 26N 5 30 E
Einsiedeln 51 47 7N 8 46 E
Eiríksjökull 74 64 46N 20 24W
Eirlandsche Gat 46 53 12N 4 54 E
Eirunepé 174 6 35S 70 0W
Eisden 47 50 59N 5 42 E
Eisenach 48 50 58N 10 18 E
Eisenberg 48 50 59N 11 50 E
Eisenerz 52 47 32N 15 54 E
Eisenhüttenstadt 48 52 9N 14 41 E
Eisenkappel 52 46 29N 14 36 E
Eisenstadt 53 47 51N 16 31 E
Eiserfeld 47 50 50N 8 0 E
Eisfeld 49 50 25N 10 54 E
Eishort, L. 36 57 9N 6 0W
Eisleben 48 51 31N 11 31 E
Eizariya (Bethany) 90 31 47N 35 15 E
Ejby 73 55 25N 9 56 E
Eje, Sierra del 56 42 24N 6 54W
Ejea de los Caballeros 58 42 7N 1 9W
Ejido 174 8 33N 71 14W
Ejura 121 7 25N 1 25 E
Ejutla 165 16 34N 96 44W
Ekalaka 158 45 55N 104 30 E
Ekawasaki 110 33 13N 132 46 E
Ekeryd 73 57 37N 14 6 E
Eket 121 4 38N 7 56W
Eketahuna 142 40 38S 175 43 E
Ekhinos 68 41 16N 25 1W
Ekibastuz 76 51 40N 75 22 E
Ekimchan 77 53 0N 133 0W
Ekofisk, oilfield 19 56 35N 3 30 E
Ekofisk, W., oilfield 19 56 35N 3 5 E
Ekoli 126 0 23S 24 13 E
Ekoln, I. 72 59 45N 17 40 E
Eksjö 73 57 40N 14 58W
Ekwan Pt. 150 53 16N 82 7W
Ekwan, R. 150 53 12N 82 15W
El Abiodh 118 32 53N 0 31 E
El Aïoun 118 34 33N 2 30W
El 'Aiyat 122 29 36N 31 15 E
El Alamein 122 30 48N 28 58 E
El Aqaba 90 29 31N 35 0 E
El Arahal 57 37 15N 5 33W
El Araq 122 28 40N 26 20 E
El Arba 118 36 28N 3 12 E
El Arba du Rharb 118 34 50N 5 59W
El Aricha 118 34 13N 1 16W
El Arīhā 90 31 52N 35 27 E
El Arish 138 17 49S 146 1 E
El 'Arîsh 122 31 8N 33 50 E
El Arnaud 119 36 7N 5 49 E
El Arrouch 119 36 37N 6 53 E
• El Asnam 118 36 10N 1 20 E
El Astillero 56 43 24N 3 49W
El Badâri 122 27 4N 31 25 E
El Bahrein 122 28 30N 26 25 E
El Ballâs 122 26 2N 32 43 E
El Balyana 122 26 10N 32 3 E
El Baqeir 122 18 40N 33 40 E
El Barco de Ávila 56 40 21N 5 31W
El Barco de Valdeorras 56 42 23N 7 0W
El Bauga 122 18 18N 33 52 E
El Baúl 174 8 57N 68 17W
El Bawiti 122 28 25N 28 45 E
El Bayadh 118 33 40N 1 1 E
El Bierzo 56 42 45N 6 30W
El Biodh 118 26 0N 6 32W
El Bluff 166 11 59N 83 40W
El Bonillo 59 38 57N 2 35W
El Cajon 163 32 49N 117 0W
El Callao 174 7 25N 61 50W
El Camp 58 41 5N 1 10 E
El Campo 159 29 10N 96 20W
El Carmen 174 1 16N 66 52W
El Castillo 57 37 41N 6 19W
El Centro 161 32 50N 115 40W
El Cerro, Boliv. 174 17 30S 61 40W
El Cerro, Spain 57 37 45N 6 57W
El Cocuy 174 6 25N 72 27W
El Coronil 57 37 5N 5 38W
El Cuy 176 39 55S 68 25W
El Cuyo 165 21 30N 87 40W
El Dab'a 122 31 0N 28 27 E
El Dátil 164 30 7N 112 15W
El Deir 122 25 25N 32 20 E
El Dere 91 3 50N 47 8 E
El Diaz 165 21 1N 87 17W
El Difícul 174 9 51N 74 14W
El Díos 164 20 40N 87 20W
El Diviso 174 1 22N 78 14W
El Djouf 120 20 0N 11 30 E
El Dorado, Colomb. 174 1 11N 71 52W
El Dorado, Ark., U.S.A. 159 33 10N 92 40W
El Dorado, Kans., U.S.A. 159 37 55N 96 56W
El Dorado, Venez. 174 6 55N 61 30W
El Dorado Springs 159 37 54N 93 59W
El Eglab 118 26 20N 4 30W
El Escorial 56 40 35N 4 7W
El Faiyûm 122 29 19N 30 50 E
El Fâsher 123 13 33N 25 26 E
El Fashn 122 28 50N 30 54 E
El Ferrol 56 43 29N 3 14W
El Fifi 123 10 4N 25 0 E
El Fuerte 164 26 30N 108 40W
El Gal 91 10 58N 50 20 E
El Gebir 123 13 40N 29 40 E
El Gedida 122 25 40N 28 30 E
El Geneina 117 13 27N 22 45 E
El Geteina 123 14 50N 32 27 E
El Gezira 123 14 0N 33 0 E
El Gezira □ 123 15 0N 33 0 E
El Gîza 122 30 0N 31 10 E
El Goléa 118 30 30N 2 50 E
El Guettar 119 34 5N 4 38 E
El Hadjire 119 32 36N 5 30 E
El Hagiz 123 15 15N 35 50 E
El Hajeb 118 33 41N 5 23W
El Hammâm 122 30 52N 29 25 E
El Hank, Alg. 118 25 38N 5 29W
El Hank, Maurit. 118 24 37N 7 0W
El Haql 122 29 15N 34 59 E
El Hawata 123 13 25N 34 42 E
El Heiz 122 27 50N 28 40 E
El 'Idisât 122 25 30N 32 35 E
El Iskandarîya 122 31 0N 30 0 E
El Istwâ'ya □ 123 5 0N 30 0 E
El Jadida 118 33 16N 9 31W
El Jorf Lasfar, C. 118 33 5N 8 54W
El Kab 122 19 27N 32 46 E
El Kala 119 36 50N 8 30 E
El Kamlin 123 15 3N 33 11 E
El Kantara, Alg. 119 35 14N 5 45 E
El Kantara, Tunisia 119 33 45N 10 58 E
El Karaba 122 18 32N 33 41 E
El Kef 119 36 12N 8 47 E
El Kelâa des Srarhna 118 32 4N 7 27W
El Khandaq 122 18 30N 30 30 E
El Khârga 122 25 30N 30 33 E
El Khartûm 123 15 31N 32 35 E
El Khartûm Bahrî 123 15 40N 32 31 E
El-Khroubs 119 36 10N 6 55 E
El Khureiba 122 28 3N 35 10 E
El Kseur 119 36 46N 4 49 E
El Ksiba 118 32 45N 6 1W
El Kuntilla 122 30 1N 34 45 E
El Ladhiqiya 92 35 20N 35 30 E
El Laqeita 122 25 50N 33 15 E
El Leiya 123 16 15N 35 28 E
El Mafâza 123 13 38N 34 30 E
El Mahalla el Kubra 122 31 0N 31 0 E
El Mahârîq 122 25 35N 30 35 E
El Maiz 118 28 19N 0 9W
El-Maks el-Bahari 122 24 30N 30 40 E
El Manshâh 122 26 26N 31 50 E
El Mansour 118 27 47N 0 14W
El Mansûra 122 31 0N 31 19 E
El Mantico 174 7 27N 62 32W
El Manzala 122 31 10N 31 50 E
El Marâgha 122 26 35N 31 10 E
El Masid 123 15 15N 33 0 E
El Matariya 122 31 15N 32 0 E
El Meghaier 119 33 55N 5 58 E
El Melfa 119 31 58N 15 18 E
El Meraguen 118 28 0N 0 7W
El Metemma 123 16 50N 33 10 E
El Miamo 174 7 39N 61 46W
El Milagro 172 30 59S 65 59W
El Milheas 118 25 27N 6 57W
El Milia 119 36 51N 6 13 E
El Minyâ 122 28 7N 30 33 E
El Molar 58 40 42N 3 45W
El Monte 163 34 4N 118 2W
El Mreyye 120 18 0N 6 0W
El Obeid 123 13 8N 30 10 E
El Oro = Sta. María del Oro 164 25 50N 105 20W
El Oro de Hidalgo 165 19 48N 100 8W
El Oued 119 33 20N 6 58 E
El Ouig 120 19 31N 0 27 E
El Palmar 174 7 58N 61 53W
El Palmito, Presa 164 25 40N 105 3W
El Panadés 58 41 10N 1 30 E
El Pao 174 9 38N 68 8W
El Pardo 56 40 31N 3 47W
El Paso 161 31 50N 106 30W
El Paso Robles 163 35 38N 120 41W
El Pedernoso 59 39 29N 2 45W
El Pedroso 57 37 51N 5 45W
El Pilar 174 10 32N 63 9W
El Pobo de Dueñas 58 40 46N 1 39W
El Portal 163 37 44N 119 49W
El Porvenir, Mexico 164 31 15N 105 51W
El Porvenir, Venez. 174 4 42N 71 19W
El Prat de Llobregat 58 41 18N 2 3 E
El Progreso 166 15 26N 87 51W
El Provencío 59 39 23N 2 35W
El Pueblito 164 29 3N 105 4W
El Qahîra 122 30 1N 31 14 E
El Qantara 122 30 51N 32 20 E
El Qasr 122 25 44N 28 42 E
El Qubba 123 11 10N 27 5 E
El Quseima 122 30 40N 34 15 E
El Qusîya 122 27 29N 30 44 E
El Râshda 122 25 36N 28 57 E
El Reno 159 35 30N 98 0W
El Rheauya 118 25 52N 6 30W
El Ribero 56 42 30N 8 30W
El Rîdisiya 122 24 56N 32 51 E
El Rio 163 34 14N 119 10W
El Ronquillo 57 37 44N 6 10W
El Rubio 57 37 22N 5 0W
El Saff 122 29 34N 31 16 E
El Salado 174 8 56N 73 55W
El Salto 164 23 47N 105 22W
El Salvador ■ 166 13 50N 89 0W
El Sancejo 57 37 4N 5 6W
El Sauce 166 13 0N 86 40W
El Shallal 122 24 0N 32 53 E
El Suweis 122 29 58N 32 31 E
El Temblador 174 8 59N 62 44W
El Thamad 122 29 40N 34 28 E
El Tigre 174 8 55N 64 15W
El Tocuyo 174 9 47N 69 48W
El Tofo 172 29 22S 71 18W
El Tránsito 172 28 52S 70 17W
El Tûr 122 28 14N 33 36 E
El Turbio 176 51 30S 72 40W
El Uqsur 122 25 41N 32 38 E
El Vado 58 41 2N 3 18W
El Vallés 58 41 35N 2 20 E
El Vigía 174 8 38N 71 39W
El Wak 124 2 49N 40 56 E
El Waqf 122 25 37N 32 15 E
El Wâsta 122 29 19N 31 12 E
El Weguet 123 5 28N 42 17 E
Ela 123 12 50N 42 20 E
Elafónisos 69 36 29N 22 56 E
Elaine 140 37 44S 144 2 E
Elamanchili = Yellamanchilli 96 17 26N 82 50 E
Elan R. 31 52 17N 3 40W
Elan Village 31 52 18N 3 34W
Elands 141 31 37S 152 20 E
Elandsvlei 128 32 19S 19 31 E
Élassa 69 35 18N 26 21 E
Elassón 68 39 53N 22 12 E
Elat 103 5 40S 133 5 E
Elateia 69 38 37N 22 46 E
Eläzığ 92 38 37N 39 22 E
Elba 157 31 27N 86 4W
Elba, I. 62 42 48N 10 15 E
Elbasani 68 41 9N 20 9 E
Elbasani-Berati 68 40 58N 20 0 E
Elbe, R. 48 53 15N 10 7 E
Elbert, Mt. 161 39 12N 106 36W
Elberta 156 44 35N 86 14W
Elberton 157 34 7N 82 51W
Elbeuf 42 49 17N 1 2 E
Elbląg □ 54 54 15N 19 30 E
Elblag (Elbing) 54 54 10N 19 25 E
Elbow 153 51 7N 106 35W
Elbrus, Mt. 83 43 30N 42 30 E
Elburg 46 52 26N 5 50 E
Elburz Mts. = Alborz 93 36 0N 52 0 E
Elche 59 38 15N 0 42W
Elche de la Sierra 59 38 27N 2 3W
Elcho I. 138 11 55S 135 45 E
Elda 59 38 29N 0 47W
Eldfisk, oilfield 19 56 25N 3 30 E
Eldon, Iowa, U.S.A. 97 40 50N 92 12W
Eldon, Mo., U.S.A. 158 38 20N 92 38W
Eldora 158 42 20N 93 5W
Eldorado, Argent. 173 26 28S 54 43W

*Renamed Ech Cheliff

Eldorado, Ont., Can. 97 44 40N 77 32W
Eldorado, Sask., Can. 153 59 35N 108 30W
Eldorado, Mexico 164 24 0N 107 30W
Eldorado, Ill., U.S.A. 156 37 50N 88 25W
Eldorado, Tex., U.S.A. 159 30 52N 100 35W
Eldoret 126 0 30N 35 25 E
Electra 159 34 0N 99 0W
Eleele 147 21 54N 159 35W
Elefantes, R. 129 24 0S 32 30 E
Elektrogorsk 81 55 56N 38 50 E
Elektrostal 81 55 41N 38 32 E
Elele 121 5 5N 6 50 E
Elena 67 42 55N 25 53 E
Elephant Butte Res. 161 33 45N 107 30W
Elephant I. 13 61 0S 55 0W
Elephant Pass 97 9 35N 80 25 E
Elesbão Veloso 170 6 13S 42 8W
Eleshnitsa 67 41 52N 23 36 E
Eleuthera I. 166 25 0N 76 20W
Elevsis 69 38 4N 23 26 E
Elevtheroúpolis 68 40 52N 24 20 E
Elfin Cove 147 58 11N 136 20W
Elgåhogna, Mt. 72 62 7N 12 7 E
Elgepiggen 71 62 10N 11 21 E
Elgeyo-Marakwet □ 126 0 45N 35 30 E
Elgg 51 47 29N 8 52 E
Elgin, Can. 151 45 48N 65 10W
Elgin, U.K. 37 57 39N 3 20W
Elgin, Ill., U.S.A. 156 42 0N 88 20W
Elgin, N.D., U.S.A. 158 46 24N 101 46W
Elgin, Nebr., U.S.A. 158 41 58N 98 3W
Elgin, Nev., U.S.A. 161 37 27N 114 36W
Elgin, Oreg., U.S.A. 160 45 37N 118 0W
Elgin, Texas, U.S.A. 159 30 21N 97 22W
Elgol 36 57 9N 6 6W
Elgon, Mt. 126 1 10N 34 30 E
Elham 29 51 9N 1 7 E
Eliase 103 8 10S 130 55 E
Elida 159 33 56N 103 41W
Elie 153 49 48N 97 52W
Elie de Beaumont, Mt. 143 43 30S 170 20 E
Elikón, Mt. 69 38 18N 22 45 E
Elim 147 64 35N 162 20W
Elin Pelin 126 42 40N 23 38 E
Elisabethville = Lubumbashi 127 11 32S 27 38 E
Eliseu Martins 170 8 13S 43 42W
Elishaw 35 55 16N 2 14W
Elista 83 46 16N 44 14 E
Elit 123 15 10N 37 0 E
Elizabeth, Austral. 140 34 42S 138 41 E
Elizabeth, U.S.A. 162 40 37N 74 12W
Elizabeth City 157 36 18N 76 16W
Elizabetha 126 1 3N 23 37 E
Elizabethton 157 36 20N 82 13W
Elizabethtown, Ky., U.S.A. 156 37 40N 85 54W
Elizabethtown, Pa., U.S.A. 162 40 8N 76 36W
Elizondo 58 43 12N 1 30W
Elk City 159 35 25N 99 25W
Elk Grove 163 38 25N 121 22W
Elk Island Nat. Park 152 53 47N 112 59W
Elk Lake 150 47 40N 80 25W
Elk Point 153 53 54N 110 55W
Elk River, Idaho, U.S.A. 160 46 50N 116 8W
Elk River, Minn., U.S.A. 158 45 17N 93 34W
Elkedra 138 21 9S 135 26 E
Elkedra, R. 138 21 8S 136 22 E
Elkhart, Ind., U.S.A. 156 41 42N 85 55W
Elkhart, Kans., U.S.A. 159 37 3N 101 54W
Elkhorn 153 49 59N 101 14W
Elkhorn, R. 158 42 0N 98 15W
Elkhotovo 83 43 19N 44 15 E
Elkhovo 67 42 10N 26 40 E
Elkin 157 36 17N 80 50W
Elkins 156 38 53N 79 53W
Elko, Can. 152 49 20N 115 10W
Elko, U.S.A. 160 40 40N 115 50W
Elkton 162 39 36N 75 50W
Ell, L. 137 29 13S 127 46 E
Elland 33 53 41N 1 49W
Ellecom 46 52 2N 6 6 E
Ellef Ringnes I. 12 78 30N 102 2W
Ellen, Mt. 161 38 4N 110 56W
Ellen R. 32 54 44N 3 24W
Ellendale, Austral. 136 17 56S 124 48 E
Ellendale, U.S.A. 158 46 3N 98 30W
Ellensburg 160 47 0N 120 30W
Ellenville 162 41 42N 74 23W
Eller Beck Bri. 33 54 23N 0 40W
Ellerston 141 31 49S 151 20 E
Ellery, Mt. 141 37 28S 148 40 E
Ellesmere 32 52 55N 2 53W
Ellesmere I. 12 79 30N 80 0W
Ellesmere, L. 131 43 46S 172 27 E
Ellesmere Port 32 53 17N 2 55W
Ellesworth Land 13 74 0S 85 0W
Ellezelles 47 50 44N 3 42 E
Ellice Is. 130 8 0S 176 0 E
Ellicott City 162 39 16N 76 48W
Ellington 35 55 14N 1 34W
Ellinwood 158 38 27N 98 37W
Elliot, Austral. 138 17 33S 133 32 E
Elliot, S. Afr. 129 31 22S 27 48 E
Elliot Lake 150 46 35N 82 35W
Ellis 158 39 0N 99 39W
Ellisville 157 31 38N 89 12W
Ellon 37 57 21N 2 5W
Ellore = Eluru 96 16 48N 81 8 E
Ells, R. 152 57 18N 111 40W
Ellsworth 158 38 47N 98 15W
Ellsworth Land 13 76 0S 89 0W
Ellwangen 49 48 57N 10 9 E
Ellwood City 156 40 52N 80 19W
Elm 51 46 54N 9 10 E
Elma, Can. 153 49 52N 95 55W
Elma, U.S.A. 160 47 0N 123 30 E
Elmer 162 39 36N 75 10W
Elmhurst 156 41 52N 87 58W
Elmina 121 5 5N 1 21W
Elmira, Can. 151 46 30N 61 59W
Elmira, U.S.A. 162 42 8N 76 49W
Elmira Heights 162 42 8N 76 50W
Elmore, Austral. 140 36 30S 144 37 E
Elmore, U.S.A. 163 33 7N 115 49W
Elmshorn 48 53 44N 9 40 E
Elmswell 29 52 14N 0 53 E
Elorza 174 7 3N 69 31W
Eloy 161 32 46N 111 46W
Éloyes 43 48 6N 6 36 E
Elphin, Ireland 38 53 50N 8 11W
Elphin, U.K. 36 58 4N 5 3W
Elphinstone 138 21 30S 148 17 E
Elrose 153 51 12N 108 0W
Elsas 150 48 32N 82 55W
Elsinore, Austral. 141 31 35S 145 11 E
Elsinore, Cal., U.S.A. 163 33 40N 117 15W
Elsinore, Utah, U.S.A. 161 38 40N 112 2W
Elsinore = Helsingor 73 56 2N 12 35 E
Elspe 48 51 10N 8 1 E
Elspeet 46 52 17N 5 48 E
Elst 46 51 55N 5 51 E
Elsterwerda 48 51 27N 13 32 E
Elstree 29 51 38N 0 16W
Elten 46 51 52N 6 9 E
Eltham, Austral. 141 37 43S 145 12 E
Eltham, N.Z. 142 39 26S 174 19 E
Elton 83 49 5N 46 52 E
Eluru 96 16 48N 81 8 E
Elvas 57 38 50N 7 17W
Elven 42 47 44N 2 36W
Elverum 71 60 53N 11 34 E
Elvire, Mt. 137 21 52S 116 50 E
Elvire, R. 136 17 51S 128 11 E
Elvo, R. 62 45 32N 8 14 E
Elvran 71 63 24N 11 3 E
Elwood, Ind., U.S.A. 156 40 20N 85 50W
Elwood, Nebr., U.S.A. 158 40 38N 99 51W
Ely, U.K. 29 52 24N 0 16 E
Ely, Minn., U.S.A. 158 47 54N 91 52W
Ely, Nev., U.S.A. 160 39 10N 114 50W
Elyashiv 90 32 23N 34 55 E
Elyria 156 41 22N 82 8W
Emådalen 72 61 20N 14 44 E
Emaiygi, R. 80 58 30N 26 30 E
Emba 76 48 50N 58 8 E
Embarcación 172 23 10S 64 0W
Embarras Portage 153 58 27N 111 28W
Embleton 35 55 30N 1 38W
Embo 37 57 55N 4 0W
Embóna 69 36 13N 27 51 E
Embrach 51 47 30N 8 36 E
Embrun 45 44 34N 6 30 E
Embu 126 0 32S 37 38 E
Embu □ 126 0 30S 37 35 E
Emden 48 53 22N 7 12 E
Emeq Hula 90 33 5N 35 8 E
'Emeq Yizre'el 90 32 35N 35 12 E
Emerald 138 23 32S 148 10 E
Emerson 153 49 0N 97 10W
Emery 161 38 59N 111 17W
Emery Park 161 32 10N 110 59W
Emi Koussi, Mt. 117 20 0N 18 55 E
Emilia-Romagna □ 62 44 33N 10 40 E
Emilius, Mt. 62 45 41N 7 23 E
Eminabad 94 32 2N 74 8 E
Emine 67 42 40N 27 56 E
Emlichheim 48 52 37N 6 51 E
Emly 39 52 28N 8 20W
Emmaboda 73 56 37N 15 32 E
Emmaus 162 40 32N 75 30W
Emme, R. 50 47 0N 7 42 E
Emmeloord 46 52 44N 5 46 E
Emmen, Neth. 47 52 48N 6 57 E
Emmen, Switz. 51 47 4N 8 17 E
Emmendingen 49 48 7N 7 51 E
Emmental 50 47 0N 7 35 E
Emmer-Compascum 46 52 49N 7 2 E
Emmerich 48 51 50N 6 12 E
Emmet 138 24 45S 144 30 E
Emmetsburg 158 43 3N 94 40W
Emmett 160 43 51N 116 33W
Emöd 53 47 57N 20 47 E
Emona 67 42 43N 27 53 E
Empalme 164 28 1N 110 49W
Empangeni 129 28 50S 31 52 E
Empedrado 172 28 0S 58 46W
Empoli 62 43 43N 10 57 E
Emporia, Kans., U.S.A. 158 38 25N 96 16W
Emporia, Va., U.S.A. 157 36 41N 77 32W
Emporium 156 41 30N 78 17W
Empress 153 50 57N 110 0W
Emptinne 47 50 19N 5 8 E
Ems, R. 48 52 37N 7 16 E
Emsdetten 48 52 11N 7 31 E
Emsworth 29 50 51N 0 56 E
Emu 140 36 44S 143 26 E
Emu Park 138 23 13S 150 50 E
Emu Ra. 136 23 0S 122 0 E
Emyvale 38 54 20N 6 57W
En Gedi 90 31 28N 35 25 E
En Harod 90 32 33N 35 22 E
'En Kerem 90 31 47N 35 6 E
En Nahud 123 12 45N 28 25 E
en Namous, O. 118 31 15N 0 10W
Ena 111 35 25N 137 25 E
Ena-San 111 35 26N 137 36 E
Enafors 72 63 17N 12 20 E
Enambú 174 1 1N 70 17W
Enana 128 17 30S 16 23 E
Enånger 72 61 30N 17 9 E
Enard B. 36 58 5N 5 20W
Enbetsu 112 44 44N 141 47 E
Encantadas, Serra 173 30 40S 53 0W
Encanto, Cape 103 20 20N 121 40 E
Encarnación 173 27 15S 56 0W
Encarnación de Diaz 164 21 30N 102 20W
Ench'eng 106 37 9N 116 16 E
Enchi 120 5 53N 2 48W
Encinal 159 28 3N 99 25W
Encinillas 164 33 3N 117 17W
Encinitas 163 33 3N 117 17W
Encino 161 34 46N 106 16W
Encounter B. 140 35 45S 138 45 E
Encruzilhada 171 15 31S 40 54W
Endau 101 2 40N 103 38 E
Endau, R. 101 2 30N 103 30 E
Ende 103 8 45S 121 30 E
Endeavour 153 52 10N 102 39W
Endeavour Str. 138 10 45S 142 0 E
Endelave 73 55 46N 10 18 E
Enderbury I. 131 3 8S 171 5W
Enderby, Can. 152 50 35N 119 10W
Enderby, U.K. 28 52 35N 1 15W
Enderby I. 136 20 35S 116 30 E
Enderby Land 13 66 0S 53 0 E
Enderlin 158 46 45N 97 41W
Endicott, N.Y., U.S.A. 162 42 6N 76 2W
Endicott, Wash., U.S.A. 160 47 0N 117 45W
Endicott Mts. 147 68 0N 152 30W
Endröd 53 46 55N 20 47 E
Endyalgout I. 136 11 40S 132 35 E
Enebakk 71 59 46N 11 9 E
Enez 68 40 45N 26 5 E
Enfida 119 36 6N 10 28 E
Enfield, U.K. 29 51 39N 0 4W
Enfield, U.S.A. 162 43 34N 71 57W
Engadin 51 46 45N 10 10 E
Engadine, Lower = Engiadina Bassa 51 46 51N 10 18 E
Engadine, Upper = Engiadin 'Ota 51 46 38N 10 0 E
Engano, C. 167 18 30N 68 20W
Engaño, C. 103 18 35N 122 23 E
Engeddi 90 31 28N 35 25 E
Engelberg 51 46 48N 8 26 E
Engels 81 51 28N 46 6 E
Engemann L. 153 55 55N 106 55W
Enger 71 60 35N 10 20 E
Enggano, I. 102 5 20S 102 40 E
Enghien 47 50 37N 4 2 E
Engiadin 'Ota 51 46 38N 10 0 E
Engiadina Bassa 51 46 51N 10 18 E
Engkilili 102 1 3N 111 42 E
England 159 34 30N 91 58W
England □ 27 53 0N 2 0W
Englee 151 50 45N 56 5W
Englefield 140 37 21S 141 48 E
Englehart 150 47 49N 79 52W
Engler L. 153 59 8N 106 52W
Englewood, Colo., U.S.A. 158 39 40N 105 0W
Englewood, Kans., U.S.A. 159 37 7N 99 59W
Englewood, N.J., U.S.A. 162 40 54N 73 59W
English Bazar 95 24 58N 88 21 E
English Channel 42 50 0N 2 0W
English Company Is. 133 12 0S 137 0 E
English, R. 153 50 30N 93 50W
English River 150 49 20N 91 0W
Enid 159 36 26N 97 52W
Enipévs, R. 68 39 22N 22 17 E
Eniwetok 131 11 30N 152 16 E
Enjil 118 33 12N 4 32W
Enkeldoorn 127 19 2S 30 52 E
Enkhuizen 46 52 42N 5 17 E
Enköping 72 59 37N 17 4 E
Enlo 108 24 0N 107 7 E
Enna 65 37 34N 14 15 E
Ennadai 153 61 8N 100 53W
Ennadai L. 153 61 0N 101 0W
Ennedi 117 17 15N 22 0 E
Ennell L. 38 53 29N 7 25W
Ennerdale Water 32 54 32N 3 24W
Enngonia 139 29 21S 145 50 E
Enningdal 71 58 59N 11 33 E
Ennis, Ireland 39 52 51N 8 59W
Ennis, Mont., U.S.A. 160 45 27N 111 48W
Ennis, Texas, U.S.A. 159 32 15N 96 40W
Enniscorthy 39 52 30N 6 35W
Enniskean 39 51 44N 8 56W
Enniskerry 39 53 12N 6 10W
Enniskillen 38 54 20N 7 40W
Ennistimon 39 52 56N 9 18W
Enns 52 48 12N 14 28 E
Enns, R. 52 48 8N 14 27 E
Enoggera Range 108 27 26S 152 56 E
Enoggera Res. 109 27 27S 152 55 E
Enontekiö 74 68 23N 23 37 E
Enp'ing 109 22 11N 112 18 E
Enriquillo, L. 167 18 20N 72 5W
Ens 46 52 38N 5 50 E
Enschede 46 52 13N 6 53 E
Ensenada, Argent. 172 34 55S 57 55W
Ensenada, Mexico 164 31 50N 116 50W
Enshih 108 30 18N 109 27 E
Enshū-Nada 111 34 27N 137 38 E
Ensisheim 43 47 50N 7 20 E
Enstone 28 51 55N 1 25W
Entebbe 126 0 4N 32 28 E
Enter 46 52 17N 6 35 E
Enterprise, Can. 152 60 47N 115 45W
Enterprise, Oreg., U.S.A. 160 45 30N 117 11W
Enterprise, Utah, U.S.A. 161 37 37N 113 36W
Entlebuch 50 46 59N 8 4 E
Entrance 152 53 25N 117 50W
Entre Rios, Boliv. 172 21 30S 64 25W
Entre Rios, Mozam. 127 14 57S 37 20 E
Entre Rios □ 172 30 30S 58 30W
Entre Rios, Bahia 171 11 56S 38 5W
Entrecasteaux, Pt. d' 137 34 50S 115 56 E
Entrepeñas, Pantano de 58 40 34N 2 42W
Entwistle 152 53 30N 115 0W
Enugu 121 6 30N 7 30 E
Enugu Ezike 121 7 0N 7 29 E
Enumclaw 160 47 12N 122 0W
Envermeu 42 49 53N 1 15 E
Envigado 174 6 10N 75 35W
Enza, R. 62 44 33N 10 22 E
Enzan 111 35 42N 138 44 E
Eólie o Lípari, Is. 65 38 30N 14 50 E
Epa 138 8 28S 146 52 E
Epanomí 68 40 25N 22 59 E
Epe, Neth. 47 52 21N 5 59 E
Epe, Nigeria 121 6 36N 3 59 E
Épernay 43 49 3N 3 56 E
Épernon 43 48 35N 1 40 E
Ephesus 92 38 0N 27 30 E
Ephraim 160 39 30N 111 37W
Ephrata, Pa., U.S.A. 162 40 11N 76 11W
Ephrata, Wash., U.S.A. 160 47 28N 119 32W
Epila 58 41 36N 1 17W
Épinac-les-Mines 43 46 59N 4 31 E
Épinal 43 48 19N 6 27 E
Episcopia Bihorului 70 47 12N 21 55 E
Epitálion 69 37 37N 21 30 E
Eport L. 36 57 33N 7 10W
Epping 29 51 42N 0 8 E
Epping Forest 29 51 40N 0 5 E
Epsom 29 51 19N 0 16W
Epukiro 125 21 30S 19 0 E
Epworth 33 53 30N 0 50W
Equatorial Guinea ■ 124 2 0S 78 0W
Équeurdreville-Hainneville 42 49 40N 1 40W
Er Rahad 123 12 45N 30 32 E
Er Rif 118 35 1N 4 1W
Er Roseires 123 11 55N 34 30 E
Er Rumman 90 32 9N 35 48 E
Eradu 137 28 40S 115 2 E
Erandol 96 20 56N 75 20 E
Erap 135 6 37S 146 51 E
Erāwadī Myit, R. = Irrawaddy, R. 98 19 30N 95 15 E
Erba, Italy 62 45 49N 9 12 E
Erba, Sudan 122 19 5N 36 40 E
Ercha 77 69 45N 147 20 E
Erciyas Daği 92 38 30N 35 30 E
Erdene 106 44 30N 111 10 E
Erding 49 48 18N 11 55 E
Erebus, Mt. 13 77 35S 167 0 E
Erechim 173 27 35S 52 15W
Ereğli 92 41 15N 31 30 E
Erei, Monti 65 37 20N 14 20 E
Erembodegem 47 50 56N 4 4 E
Eresma, R. 56 41 13N 4 30W
Eressós 69 39 11N 25 57 E
Erewadi Myitwanya 99 15 30N 95 0 E
Erfenis Dam 128 28 30S 26 50 E
Erfjord 71 59 20N 6 14 E
Erfoud 118 31 30N 4 15W
Erfurt 48 50 58N 11 2 E
Erfurt □ 48 51 10N 10 30 E
Ergani 92 38 26N 39 49 E
Erğene, R. 67 41 20N 27 0 E
Ergeni Vozyshennost 83 47 0N 44 0 E
Erhlien 106 43 42N 112 2 E
Erhlin 109 23 54N 120 22 E
Erhtao Chiang, R. 107 42 35N 128 10 E
Erhyüan 108 26 7N 99 57 E
Eria, R. 56 42 10N 6 8W
Eriba 123 16 40N 36 10 E
Eriboll, L. 37 58 28N 4 41W
Érica 46 52 43N 6 56 E
Érice 64 38 4N 12 34 E
Ericht, L. 37 56 50N 4 25W
Erie 156 42 10N 80 7W
Erigavo 91 10 35N 47 35 E
Erikoúsa 68 39 55N 19 14 E
Eriksdale 153 50 52N 98 7W
Erikslund 72 62 31N 15 54 E
Erímanthos 69 37 57N 21 50 E
Erimo-misaki 112 41 50N 143 15 E
Eriskay I. 36 57 4N 7 18W
Eriskay, Sd. of 36 57 5N 7 20W
Erisort L. 36 58 5N 6 30W
Eriswil 50 47 5N 7 46 E
Erith 152 53 25N 116 46W
Erithraí 69 38 13N 23 20 E
Eritrea □ 123 14 0N 41 0 E
Erjas, R. 56 39 45N 6 52W
Erker, L. 72 59 51N 18 29 E
Erlangen 49 49 35N 11 0 E
Erldunda 138 25 14S 133 12 E
Ermelo, Neth. 46 52 35N 5 35 E
Ermelo, S. Afr. 129 26 31S 29 59 E

Ermenak 92 36 44N 33 0E
Ermióni 69 37 23N 23 15E
Ermoúpolis = Siros 69 37 28N 24 57E
Ernakulam 97 9 59N 76 19E
Erne, Lough 38 54 26N 7 46W
Erne, R. 38 54 30N 8 16W
Ernée 42 48 18N 0 56W
Ernest Giles Ra. 137 27 0S 123 45E
Erode 97 11 24N 77 45E
Eromanga 139 26 40S 143 11E
Erongo 128 21 39S 15 58E
Erongoberg 128 21 45S 15 32E
Erp 47 51 36N 5 37E
Erquelinnes 47 50 19N 4 8E
Erquy 42 48 38N 2 29W
Erquy, Cap d' 42 48 39N 2 29W
Err, Piz d' 51 46 34N 9 43E
Errabiddy 137 25 25S 117 5E
Erramala Hills 97 15 30N 78 15E
Errer, R. 123 42 35N 8 40E
Errigal, Mt. 38 55 2N 8 8W
Errill 39 52 52N 7 40W
Erris Hd. 38 54 19N 10 0W
Errochty, L. 37 56 45N 4 10W
Errogie 37 57 16N 4 23W
Errol 35 56 24N 3 13W
Erseka 68 40 22N 20 40E
Erskine 158 47 37N 96 0W
Erstein 43 48 25N 7 38E
Erstfeld 51 46 50N 8 38E
Ertil 81 51 55N 40 50E
Ertvågøy 71 63 12N 8 25E
Ertvelde 47 51 11N 3 45E
Erundu 128 20 39S 16 26E
Eruwa 121 7 33N 3 26E
Ervalla 72 59 28N 15 16E
Ervy-le-Châtel 43 48 2N 3 55E
Erwin 157 36 10N 82 28W
Erzgebirge 48 50 25N 13 0E
Erzin 77 50 15N 95 10E
Erzincan 92 39 46N 39 30E
Erzurum 92 39 57N 41 15E
Es Sahrâ' Esh Sharqîya 122 26 0N 33 30E
Es Sider 119 30 50N 18 21E
Es Sînâ' 122 29 0N 34 0E
Es Souk 121 18 48N 1 2E
Es Sûkî 123 13 20N 34 58E
Esa'ala 135 9 45S 150 49E
Esambo 126 3 48S 23 30E
Esan-misaki 112 41 40N 141 10E
Esbjerg 73 55 29N 8 29E
Escada 170 8 22S 35 14W
Escalante 161 37 47N 111 37W
Escalante, R. 161 37 45N 111 0W
Escalón 164 26 40N 104 20W
Escalona 56 40 9N 4 29W
Escambia, R. 157 30 45N 87 15W
Escanaba 156 45 44N 87 5W
Escant, R. 47 51 2N 3 45E
Esch-sur-Alzette 47 49 32N 6 0E
Eschallens 50 46 39N 6 38E
Eschede 48 52 44N 10 13E
Escholzmatt 50 46 55N 7 56E
Eschwege 48 51 10N 10 3E
Eschweiler 48 50 49N 6 14E
Escondida, La 164 24 6N 99 55W
Escondido 163 33 9N 117 4W
Escrick 33 53 53N 1 3W
Escuinapa 164 22 50N 105 50W
Escuintla 166 14 20N 90 48W
Escuminac 151 48 0N 67 0W
Escutillas = Ceba 174 6 33N 70 24W
Eséka 121 3 41N 10 44E
Esens 48 53 40N 7 35E
Esera, R. 58 42 24N 0 22E
Esfahan □ 93 33 0N 53 0E
Esgueva, R. 56 41 46N 4 14W
Esh Sham = Dimashq 92 33 30N 36 18E
Esh Shamâlîya □ 122 19 0N 31 0E
Esha Ness 36 60 30N 1 36W
Eshowe 129 28 50S 31 30E
Eshta' ol 90 31 47N 35 0E
Esiama 120 4 48N 2 25W
Esino, R. 63 43 28N 13 8E
Esk R. 32 54 23N 3 21W
Esk, R., Dumfries, U.K. 35 54 58N 3 4W
Esk, R., N. Yorks., U.K. 33 54 27N 0 36W
Eskdale 35 55 12N 3 4W
Eskifjördur 74 65 3N 13 55W
Eskilstuna 72 59 22N 16 32E
Eskimo Ls. 147 69 15N 132 17W
Eskimo Pt. 153 61 10N 94 3W
Eskişehir 92 39 50N 30 35E
Esla, R. 56 41 45N 5 50W
Eslöv 73 55 50N 13 20E
Esmeralda, La 172 22 16S 62 33W
Esmeraldas 174 1 0N 79 40W
Esneux 47 50 32N 5 33E
Espa 71 60 35N 11 15E
Espada, Pta. 174 12 5N 71 7W
Espalion 44 44 32N 2 47E
Espalmador, I. 59 38 48N 1 26E
Espanola 150 46 15N 81 46W
Espardell, I. del 59 38 47N 1 25E
Esparraguera 58 41 33N 1 52E
Esparta 166 9 59N 84 40W
Espejo 57 37 40N 4 34W
Espenberg, C. 147 66 35N 163 40W
Esperança 170 7 1S 35 51W
Esperance 137 33 45S 121 55E
Esperance B. 137 33 48S 121 55E
Esperantinópolis 170 4 53S 44 53W
Esperanza 172 31 29S 61 3W
Esperanza, La, Argent. 172 24 9S 64 52W
Esperanza, La, Boliv. 174 14 20S 62 0W
Esperanza, La, Cuba 166 22 46N 83 44W
Esperanza, La, Hond. 166 14 15N 88 10W
Espéraza 44 42 56N 2 14E
Espevær Lt. Ho. 71 59 35N 5 7E
Espichel, C. 57 38 22N 9 16W
Espiel 57 38 11N 5 1W
Espigão, Serra do 173 26 35S 50 30W
Espinal 174 4 9N 74 53W
Espinazo, Sierra del = Espinhaço, Serra do 171 17 30S 43 30W
Espinhaço, Serra do 171 17 30S 43 30W
Espinho 56 41 1N 8 38W
Espinilho, Serra do 173 28 30S 55 0W
Espino 174 8 34N 66 1W
Espinosa de los Monteros 56 43 5N 3 34W
Espírito Santo □ 171 20 0S 40 45W
Espíritu Santo, B. del 165 19 15N 79 40W
Espíritu Santo, I. 164 24 30N 110 23W
Espita 165 21 1N 88 19W
Esplanada 171 11 47S 37 57W
Espluga de Francolí 58 41 24N 1 7E
Espuña, Sierra de 59 37 51N 1 35W
Espungabera 129 20 29S 32 45E
Esquel 176 42 40S 71 20W
Esquimalt 148 48 30N 123 23W
Esquina 172 30 0S 59 30W
Essaouira (Mogador) 118 31 32N 9 42W
Essarts, Les 42 46 47N 1 12W
Essebie 126 2 58N 30 40E
Essen, Belg. 47 51 28N 4 28E
Essen, Ger. 48 51 28N 6 59E
Essendon, Mt. 137 25 0S 120 30E
Essequibo, R. 174 5 45N 58 50W
Essex 162 39 18N 76 29W
Essex □ 29 51 48N 0 30E
Esslingen 49 48 43N 9 19E
Essonne □ 43 48 30N 2 20E
Essvik 72 62 18N 17 24E
Estadilla 58 42 4N 0 16E
Estados, I. de los 176 54 40S 64 30W
Estagel 44 42 47N 2 40E
Estância 170 11 16S 37 26W
Estancia 161 34 50N 106 1W
Estarreja 56 40 45N 8 35W
Estats, P. d' 44 42 40N 1 40E
Estavayer le Lac 50 46 51N 6 51E
Estcourt 129 28 58S 29 53E
Este 63 45 12N 11 40E
Esteban 56 43 33N 6 5W
Estelí 166 13 9N 86 22W
Estella 58 42 40N 2 0W
Estelline, S.D., U.S.A. 158 44 39N 96 52W
Estelline, Texas, U.S.A. 159 34 35N 100 27W
Estena, R. 57 39 23N 4 44W
Estepa 57 37 17N 4 52W
Estepona 57 36 24N 5 7W
Esterhazy 153 50 37N 102 5W
Esternay 43 48 44N 3 33E
Esterri de Aneu 58 42 38N 1 5E
Estevan 153 49 10N 102 59W
Estevan Group 152 53 3N 129 38W
Estherville 158 43 25N 94 50W
Estissac 43 48 16N 3 48E
Eston, Can. 153 51 8N 108 40W
Eston, U.K. 33 54 33N 1 6W
Estonian S.S.R. □ 80 48 30N 25 30E
Estoril 57 38 42N 9 23W
Estrada, La 56 42 43N 8 27W
Estrêla, Serra da 56 40 10N 7 45W
Estrella 59 38 25N 3 35W
Estremadura 57 39 0N 9 0W
Estremoz 57 38 51N 7 39W
Estrondo, Serra do 170 7 20S 48 0W
Esztergom 53 47 47N 18 44E
Et Tieta 118 29 37N 9 15W
Et Turra 90 32 39N 35 39E
Étables-sur-Mer 42 48 38N 2 51W
Etah 95 27 35N 78 40E
Étain 43 49 13N 5 38E
Étalle 47 49 40N 5 36E
Etamamu 151 50 18N 59 59W
Étampes 43 48 26N 2 10E
Étang 43 46 52N 4 10E
Etanga 128 17 55S 13 00E
Étaples 43 50 30N 1 39E
Etawah 95 26 48N 79 6E
Etawah, R. 157 34 20N 84 15W
Etawney L. 153 57 50N 96 50W
Etchingham 29 51 0N 0 27E
Eteh 121 7 2N 7 28E
Etelia 121 19 10N 0 55E
Éthe 47 49 35N 5 35E
Ethel Creek 136 22 55S 120 11E
Ethel, Oued el 118 28 31N 3 37W
Ethelbert 153 51 32N 100 25W
Ethiopia ■ 91 8 0N 40 0E
Ethiopian Highlands 114 10 0N 37 0E
Etive, L. 34 56 30N 5 12W
Etna, Mt. 65 37 45N 15 0E
Etne 71 59 40N 5 56E
Etoile 127 11 33S 27 30E
Etolin I. 152 56 5N 132 20W
Eton 29 51 29N 0 37W
Etoshapan 128 18 40S 16 30E
Etowah 157 35 20N 84 30W
Étrépagny 42 49 18N 1 36E
Étretat 42 49 42N 0 12E
Etroits, Les 151 47 24N 68 54W
Etropole 68 43 50N 24 0E
Ettelbrüch 47 49 50N 6 5E
Ettelbruck 47 49 51N 6 5E
Etten 47 51 34N 4 38E
Ettington 28 52 8N 1 38W
Ettlingen 49 48 58N 8 25E
Ettrick Forest 35 55 30N 3 0W
Ettrick Water 35 55 31N 2 55W
Etuku 126 3 42S 25 45E
Etzatlán 164 20 48N 104 5W
Etzna 165 19 35N 90 15W
Eu 42 50 3N 1 26E
Euboea = Évvoia 69 38 40N 23 40E
Euchareena 141 32 57S 149 6E
Eucla Basin 137 31 19S 126 9E
Euclid 156 41 32N 81 31W
Euclides da Cunha 170 10 31S 39 1W
Eucumbene, L. 141 36 2S 148 40E
Eudora 159 33 5N 91 17W
Eudunda 140 34 12S 139 7E
Eufaula, Ala., U.S.A. 157 31 55N 85 11W
Eufaula, Okla., U.S.A. 159 35 20N 95 33W
Eufaula, L. 159 35 15N 95 28W
Eugene 160 44 0N 123 8W
Eugenia, Punta 164 27 50N 115 5W
Eugowra 141 33 22S 148 24E
Eulo 139 28 10S 145 3E
Eumungerie 141 31 56N 148 36E
Eunice, La., U.S.A. 159 30 35N 92 28W
Eunice, N. Mex., U.S.A. 159 32 30N 103 10W
Eupen 47 50 37N 6 3E
Euphrates = Furat, Nahr al 92 33 30N 43 0E
Eure □ 42 49 6N 1 0E
Eure-et-Loir □ 42 48 22N 1 30E
Eureka, Can. 12 80 0N 85 56W
Eureka, Calif., U.S.A. 160 40 50N 124 0W
Eureka, Kans., U.S.A. 157 37 50N 96 20W
Eureka, Mont., U.S.A. 160 48 53N 115 6W
Eureka, Nev., U.S.A. 160 39 32N 116 2W
Eureka, S.D., U.S.A. 158 45 49N 99 38W
Eureka, Utah, U.S.A. 160 40 0N 112 0W
Eureka, Mt. 137 26 35S 121 35E
Eurelia 140 32 33S 138 35E
Euroa 141 36 44S 145 35E
Europa, Île 125 22 20S 40 22E
Europa, Picos de 56 43 10N 5 0W
Europa Pt. 55 36 2N 6 32W
Europa Pt. = Europa, Pta. de 57 36 3N 5 21W
Europa, Pta. de 57 36 3N 5 21W
Europe 16 20 0N 20 0E
Europoort 46 51 57N 4 10E
Euskirchen 48 50 40N 6 45E
Eustis 157 28 54N 81 36W
Eutin 48 54 7N 10 38E
Eutsuk L. 152 53 20N 126 45W
Euxton 32 53 41N 2 42W
Eva Downs 138 18 1S 134 52E
Eval, Mt. 90 32 15N 35 15E
Evanger 71 60 39N 6 7E
Evans 158 40 25N 104 43W
Evans Head 139 29 7S 153 27E
Evans L. 150 50 50N 77 0W
Evans P. 158 41 0N 105 35W
Evanston, Ill., U.S.A. 156 42 0N 87 40W
Evanston, Wy., U.S.A. 160 41 10N 111 0W
Evansville, Ind., U.S.A. 156 38 0N 87 35W
Evansville, Wis., U.S.A. 158 42 47N 89 18W
Evanton 37 57 40N 4 20W
Evato 129 20 37S 47 10E
Évaux-les-Bains 44 46 12N 2 29E
Eveleth 158 47 35N 92 40W
Even Yahuda 90 32 16N 34 53E
Evensk 77 61 57N 159 14E
Evenstad 71 61 25N 11 7E
Everard, C. 141 37 49S 149 17E
Everard, L. 139 31 30S 135 0E
Everard Ras. 137 27 5S 132 28E
Evercreech 28 51 8N 2 30W
Everdale 141 31 52S 144 46E
Evere 47 50 52N 4 25E
Everest, Mt. 95 28 5N 86 58E
Everett 160 48 0N 122 10W
Evergem 47 51 7N 3 43E
Everglades 157 26 0N 80 30W
Evergreen 157 31 28N 86 55W
Everöd 73 55 53N 14 5E
Everson 160 48 57N 122 22W
Everton 141 36 25S 146 33E
Evesham 28 52 6N 1 57W
Evian-les-Bains 45 46 24N 6 35E
Evinayong 124 1 50N 10 35E
Évinos, R. 69 38 27N 21 40E
Évisa 45 42 15N 8 48E
Évora 57 38 33N 7 57W
Évora □ 57 38 33N 7 50W
Évreux 42 49 0N 1 8E
Évritania □ 69 39 5N 21 30E
Évron 42 48 23N 1 58W
Évros □ 68 41 10N 26 0E
Évrótas, R. 69 36 50N 22 40E
Évvoia 69 38 30N 24 0E
Évvoia □ 69 38 40N 23 40E
Ewe, L. 36 57 49N 5 38W
Ewell 29 51 20N 0 15W
Ewhurst 29 51 9N 0 25W
Ewing 158 42 18N 98 22W
Ewo 124 0 48S 14 45E
Exaltación 174 13 10S 65 20W
Excelsior 139 33 6S 149 59W
Excelsior Springs 158 39 20N 94 10W
Excideuil 44 45 20N 1 4E
Exe, R. 30 50 38N 3 27W
Exeter, U.K. 30 50 43N 3 31W
Exeter, Calif., U.S.A. 163 36 17N 119 9W
Exeter, Nebr., U.S.A. 158 40 43N 97 30W
Exeter, N.H., U.S.A. 162 43 0N 70 58W
Exford 28 51 8N 3 39W
Exloo 46 52 53N 6 52E
Exmes 42 48 45N 0 10E
Exminster 30 50 40N 3 29W
Exmoor 30 51 10N 3 59W
Exmore 162 37 32N 75 50W
Exmouth, Austral. 136 22 6S 114 0E
Exmouth, U.K. 30 50 37N 3 26W
Exmouth G. 136 22 15S 114 15E
Expedition Range 138 24 30S 149 12E
Exton 29 52 42N 0 38W
Extremadura 57 39 30N 6 5W
Exu 171 7 31S 39 43W
Exuma Sound 166 24 30N 76 20W
Eyam 33 53 17N 1 40W
Eyasi, L. 126 3 30S 35 0E
Eyawaddi Myii 98 15 50N 95 6E
Eye, Camb., U.K. 29 52 36N 0 11W
Eye, Norfolk, U.K. 29 52 19N 1 9E
Eye Pen. 36 58 13N 6 10W
Eyeberry L. 153 63 8N 104 43W
Eyemouth 35 55 53N 2 5W
Eygurande 44 45 40N 2 26E
Eyhatten 47 50 43N 6 1E
Eyisen 82 41 0N 36 50E
Eyjafjorður 74 66 15N 18 30W
Eymet 44 44 40N 0 25E
Eymoutiers 44 45 40N 1 45E
Eynhallow Sd. 37 59 8N 3 7W
Eynort, L. 36 57 13N 7 18W
Eynsham 28 51 47N 1 21W
Eyrarbakki 74 63 52N 21 9W
Eyre 137 32 15S 126 18E
Eyre Cr. 138 26 40S 139 0E
Eyre, L. 133 29 30S 137 26E
Eyre L., (North) 139 28 30S 137 20E
Eyre L., (South) 139 29 18S 137 25E
Eyre Mts. 143 45 25S 168 25E
Eyre Pen. 139 33 30S 137 17E
Eyrecourt 39 53 12N 8 8W
Ez Zeidab 122 17 25N 33 55E
Ez Zergoun, W. 118 32 45N 2 25E
Ezcaray 58 42 19N 3 0W
Ezine 68 39 48N 26 12E

F

Fabens 161 31 30N 106 8W
Fåborg 73 55 6N 10 15E
Fabriano 63 43 20N 12 52E
Fabrizia 43 38 29N 16 19E
Făcăeni 70 44 32N 27 53E
Facatativá 174 4 49N 74 22W
Facture 44 44 39N 0 58W
Fada 117 17 13N 21 34E
Fada-n-Gourma 121 12 10N 0 30E
Fadd 53 46 28N 18 49E
Faddeyevski, Ostrov 77 76 0N 150 0E
Fadhili 92 26 55N 49 10E
Fadlab 122 17 42N 34 2E
Faenza 63 44 17N 11 53E
Fafa 121 15 22N 0 48E
Fafe 56 41 27N 8 11W
Fagam 121 11 1N 10 1E
Fågelsjö 72 61 50N 14 35E
Fagerhult 73 57 8N 15 40E
Fagernes 75 60 59N 9 14E
Fagersta 72 60 1N 15 46E
Fåglavik 73 58 6N 13 6E
Fagnano Castello 65 39 31N 16 4E
Fagnano, L. 176 54 30S 68 0W
Fagnières 43 48 58N 4 20E
Fahral 93 29 0N 59 0E
Fahūd 93 22 18N 56 28E
Faid 92 27 1N 42 52E
Faido 51 46 29N 8 48E
Fair, C. 138 12 24S 143 16E
Fair Hd. 38 55 14N 6 10W
Fair Isle 23 59 30N 1 40W
Fair Oaks 163 38 39N 121 16W
Fairbank 161 31 44N 110 12W
Fairbanks 147 64 59N 147 40W
Fairbourne 31 52 42N 4 3W
Fairbury 158 40 5N 97 5W
Fairfax, Okla., U.S.A. 159 36 37N 96 45W
Fairfax, Va., U.S.A. 162 38 51N 77 18W
Fairfield, Austral. 141 33 53S 150 57E
Fairfield, Ala., U.S.A. 157 33 30N 87 0W
Fairfield, Calif., U.S.A. 163 38 14N 122 1W
Fairfield, Conn., U.S.A. 162 41 8N 73 16W
Fairfield, Idaho, U.S.A. 160 43 27N 114 52W
Fairfield, Ill., U.S.A. 156 38 20N 88 20W
Fairfield, Iowa, U.S.A. 158 41 0N 91 58W
Fairfield, Mont., U.S.A. 160 47 40N 112 0W
Fairfield, Texas, U.S.A. 159 31 40N 96 0W
Fairford, Can. 153 51 37N 98 38W
Fairford, U.K. 28 51 42N 1 48W
Fairhope 157 30 35N 87 50W
Fairlie, N.Z. 143 44 5S 170 49E
Fairlie, U.K. 34 55 44N 4 52W
Fairlight 29 50 53N 0 40E
Fairmead 163 37 5N 120 10W
Fairmont, Minn., U.S.A. 158 43 37N 94 30W
Fairmont, W. Va., U.S.A. 156 39 29N 80 10W
Fairmont Hot Springs 152 50 20N 115 56W
Fairmount 163 34 45N 118 26W

Fairplay 161 39 9N 107 0W
Fairport 156 43 8N 77 29W
Fairview, Austral. 138 15 31S 144 17E
Fairview, Can. 152 56 5N 118 25W
Fairview, N. Dak., U.S.A. 158 47 49N 104 7W
Fairview, Okla., U.S.A. 159 36 19N 98 30W
Fairview, Utah, U.S.A. 160 39 50N 111 0W
Fairweather, Mt. 147 58 55N 137 45W
Faith 158 45 2N 102 4W
Faither, The, C. 36 60 34N 1 30W
Faizabad, Afghan. 93 37 7N 70 33E
Faizabad, India 95 26 45N 82 10E
Faizpur 96 21 14N 75 49E
Fajardo 147 18 20N 65 39W
Fakenham 29 52 50N 0 51E
Fakfak 103 3 0S 132 15E
Fakiya 170 42 10N 27 4E
Fakobli 120 7 23N 7 23W
Fakse 73 55 15N 12 8E
Fakse B. 73 55 11N 12 15E
Fakse Ladeplads 73 55 16N 12 9E
Fak'u 107 42 31N 123 26E
Falaise 42 48 54N 0 12W
Falaise, Mui 100 19 6N 105 45E
Falakrón Óros 68 41 15N 23 58E
Falam 98 23 0N 93 45E
Falcarragh 38 55 8N 8 8W
Falces 58 42 24N 1 48W
Falcón □ 174 11 0N 69 50W
Falcon, C. 118 35 50N 0 50W
Falcón Dam 159 26 50N 99 20W
Falconara Marittima 63 43 37N 13 23E
Faldingworth 33 53 21N 0 22W
Faléa 120 12 16N 11 17W
Falelatai 84 13 55S 171 59W
Falenki 84 58 22N 51 35E
Faleshty 82 47 32N 27 44E
Falfurrias 159 27 8N 98 8W
Falher 152 55 44N 117 15W
Falkenberg, Ger. 48 51 34N 13 13E
Falkenberg, Sweden 73 56 54N 12 30E
Falkensee 48 52 35N 13 6E
Falkenstein 48 50 27N 12 24E
Falkirk 35 56 0N 3 47W
Falkland 35 56 15N 3 13W
Falkland Is. 176 51 30S 59 0W
Falkland Is. Dep. 13 57 0S 40 0W
Falkland Sd. 176 52 0S 60 0W
Falkonéra 69 36 50N 23 52E
Falköping 73 58 12N 13 33E
Fall Brook 161 33 25N 117 12W
Fall River 162 41 45N 71 5W
Fall River Mills 160 41 1N 121 30W
Fallbrook 163 33 23N 117 15W
Fallmore 38 54 6N 10 5W
Fallon, Mont., U.S.A. 158 46 52N 105 8W
Fallon, Nev., U.S.A. 160 39 31N 118 51W
Falls Church 162 38 53N 77 11W
Falls City, Nebr., U.S.A. 158 40 0N 95 40W
Falls City, Oreg., U.S.A. 160 44 54N 123 29W
Falmey 121 12 36N 2 51E
Falmouth, Jamaica 166 18 30N 77 40W
Falmouth, U.K. 30 50 9N 5 5W
Falmouth, Ky., U.S.A. 156 38 40N 84 20W
Falmouth, Mass., U.S.A. 162 41 34N 70 38W
Falmouth B. 30 50 7N 5 3E
False B. 128 34 15S 18 40E
False Divi Pt. 97 15 35N 80 50E
Falset 58 41 7N 0 50E
Falso, C. 166 15 12N 83 21W
Falster 73 54 45N 11 55E
Falsterbo 73 55 23N 12 50E
Falsterbokanalen 73 55 25N 12 56E
Falstone 35 55 10N 2 26W
Faluja 90 31 48N 31 37E
Falun 72 60 37N 15 37E
Famagusta 92 35 8N 33 55E
Famaka 123 11 24N 34 52E
Famatina, Sierra, de 172 29 5S 68 0W
Family L. 153 51 54N 95 27W
Famoso 163 35 37N 119 12W
Fampotabe 129 15 56S 50 8E
Fan i Madh, R. 68 41 56N 20 16E
Fana, Mali 120 13 0N 6 56W
Fana, Norway 71 60 16N 5 20E
Fanad Hd. 38 55 17N 7 40W
Fanambana 129 13 34S 50 0E
Fanárion 68 39 24N 21 47E
Fanch'ang 109 31 2N 118 13E
Fanchiat'un 107 43 42N 125 5E
Fanchih 106 39 14N 113 19E
Fandriana 129 20 14S 47 21E
Fang 100 19 55N 99 13E
Fangch'eng, Honan, China 106 33 16N 112 59E
Fangch'eng, Kwangsi-Chuang, China 108 21 46N 108 21E
Fanghsien 109 32 0N 111 0E
Fangliao 109 22 22N 130 35E
Fangshan 106 38 0N 111 16E
Fangtzu 107 36 39N 119 15E
Fannich, L. 36 57 40N 5 0W
•Fanning I. 131 3 51N 159 22W
Fanny Bay 152 49 27N 124 48W
Fanø 73 55 25N 8 25E
Fano 63 43 50N 13 0E
Fanø, I. 73 55 25N 8 25E
Fanshaw 152 57 11N 133 30W
Fao (Al Fāw) 92 30 0N 48 30E
Faqirwali 94 29 27N 73 0E

*Renamed Tubuaeran

Fara in Sabina 63 42 13N 12 44E
Farab 85 39 9N 63 36E
Faraday Seamount Group 14 50 0N 27 0W
Faradje 126 3 50N 29 45E
Farafangana 129 22 49S 47 50E
Farâfra, El Wâhât el- 122 27 15N 28 20E
Farah 93 32 20N 62 7E
Farah □ 93 32 25N 62 10E
Farahalana 129 14 26S 50 10E
Faraid, Gebel 122 23 33N 35 19E
Faraid Hd. 37 58 35N 4 48W
Faramana 120 11 56N 4 45W
Faranah 120 10 3N 10 45W
Farasān, Jazā'ir 91 16 45N 41 55E
Farasan Kebir 91 16 40N 42 0E
Faratsiho 129 19 24S 46 57E
Fardes, R. 59 37 25N 3 10W
Fareham 28 50 52N 1 11W
Farewell 147 62 30N 154 0W
Farewell, C. 143 40 29S 172 43E
Farewell C. = Farvel, K. 12 59 48N 43 55W
Farewell Spit 143 40 35S 173 0E
Farfán 174 0 16N 76 41W
Fargo 158 47 0N 97 0W
Faria, R. 90 32 12N 35 27E
Faribault 158 44 15N 93 19W
Faridkot 94 30 44N 74 45E
Faridpur, Bangla. 98 23 15N 90 0E
Faridpur, India 95 18 14N 79 34E
Farila 72 61 48N 15 50E
Färila 72 61 48N 15 50E
Farim 120 12 27N 15 17W
Farimān 93 35 40N 60 0E
Farina 139 30 3S 138 15E
Faringdon 28 51 39N 1 34W
Faringe 72 59 55N 18 7E
Farinha, R. 170 6 15S 47 30W
Färjestaden 73 56 38N 16 25E
Farmakonisi 69 37 17N 27 8E
Farmerville 159 32 48N 92 23W
Farmingdale 162 40 12N 74 10W
Farmington, Calif., U.S.A. 163 37 56N 121 0W
Farmington, N. Mex., U.S.A. 161 36 45N 108 28W
Farmington, N.H., U.S.A. 162 43 25N 71 3W
Farmington, Utah, U.S.A. 160 41 0N 111 58W
Farmington, R. 162 41 51N 72 38W
Farmville 156 37 19N 78 22W
Farnborough 29 51 17N 0 46W
Farne Is. 35 55 38N 1 37W
Farnham 29 51 13N 0 49W
Farnham, Mt. 152 45 20N 72 55W
Farnworth 32 53 33N 2 24W
Faro, Brazil 175 2 0S 56 45W
Faro, Port. 57 37 2N 7 55W
Fårö 75 58 0N 19 10E
Faro □ 57 37 12N 8 10W
Faroe Is. 16 62 0N 7 0W
Farquhar, C. 137 23 38S 113 36E
Farquhar, Mt. 136 22 18S 116 53E
Farr 37 57 21N 4 13W
Farranfore 39 52 10N 9 32W
Farrars, Cr. 138 25 35S 140 43E
Farrashband 93 28 57N 52 5E
Farrell 156 41 13N 80 29W
Farrell Flat 140 33 48S 138 48E
Farrukhabad 95 27 30N 79 32E
Fars □ 93 29 30N 55 0E
Fársala 68 39 17N 22 23E
Farsø 73 56 46N 9 19E
Farsö 73 56 48N 9 20E
Farstrup 73 56 59N 9 28E
Farsund 71 58 5N 6 55E
Fartura, Serra da 173 26 21S 52 52W
Faru 121 12 48N 6 12E
Farum 73 55 49N 12 21E
Farvel, Kap 12 59 48N 43 55W
Farwell 159 34 25N 103 0W
Faryab 93 28 7N 57 14E
Fasa 93 29 0N 53 32E
Fasag 36 57 33N 5 32W
Fasano 65 40 50N 17 20E
Fashoda 123 9 50N 32 2E
Faskari 79 11 42N 6 58E
Faslane 34 56 3N 4 49W
Fastnet Rock 39 51 22N 9 37W
Fastov 80 50 7N 29 57E
Fatehgarh 95 27 25N 79 35E
Fatehpur, Raj., India 94 28 0N 75 4E
Fatehpur, Ut. P., India 95 27 8N 81 7E
Fatick 120 14 19N 16 27W
Fatima 151 47 24N 61 53W
Fátima 57 39 37N 8 39W
Fatoya 120 11 37N 9 10W
Faucilles, Monts 43 48 5N 5 50E
Fauldhouse 35 55 50N 3 44W
Faulkton 158 45 4N 99 8W
Faulquemont 43 49 3N 6 36E
Fauquembergues 43 50 36N 2 5E
Faure I. 137 25 52S 113 50E
Fauresmith 128 29 44S 25 17E
Fauske 74 67 17N 15 25E
Fauvillers 47 49 51N 5 40E
Faux-Cap 129 25 33S 45 32E
Favara 64 37 19N 13 39E
Faversham 29 51 18N 0 54E
Favignana 64 37 56N 12 18E
Favone 45 41 47N 9 26E

Favourable Lake 150 52 50N 93 39W
Fawley 28 50 49N 1 20W
Fawn, R. 150 52 22N 88 20W
Fawnskin 163 34 16N 116 56W
Faxaflói 74 64 29N 23 0W
Faxälven 72 63 13N 17 13E
Faya = Largeau 117 17 58N 19 6E
Fayence 45 43 38N 6 42E
Fayette, Ala., U.S.A. 157 33 40N 87 50W
Fayette, La., U.S.A. 156 40 22N 86 52W
Fayette, Mo., U.S.A. 158 39 10N 92 40W
Fayetteville, Ark., U.S.A. 159 36 0N 94 5W
Fayetteville, N.C., U.S.A. 157 35 0N 78 58W
Fayetteville, Tenn., U.S.A. 157 35 0N 86 30W
Fayón 58 41 15N 0 20E
Fazeley 28 52 36N 1 42W
Fazenda Nova 171 16 11S 50 48W
Fazilka 94 30 27N 74 2E
Fazilpur 94 29 18N 70 29E
F'Derik 116 22 40N 12 45W
Fé, La 166 22 2N 84 15W
Feakle 39 52 56N 8 41W
Feale, R. 39 52 26N 9 28W
Fear, C. 157 33 45N 78 0W
Fearn 37 57 47N 4 0W
Fearnan 37 56 34N 4 6W
Feather, R. 160 39 30N 121 20W
Featherston 142 41 6S 175 20E
Featherstone 127 18 42S 30 55E
Fécamp 42 49 45N 0 22E
Fedala = Mohammeda 118 33 44N 7 21W
Fedamore 39 52 33N 8 36W
Federación 172 31 0S 57 55W
Federalsburg 162 38 42N 75 47W
Fedjadj, Chott el 119 33 52N 9 14E
Fedje 71 60 47N 4 43E
Fedorovka 84 53 38N 62 42E
Feeagh L. 38 53 56N 9 35W
Feeny 38 54 54N 7 0W
Fehérgyarmat 53 48 0N 22 30E
Fehmarn 48 54 26N 11 10E
Fehmarn Bælt 73 54 35N 11 20E
Feihsiang 106 36 32N 114 47E
Feihsien 107 35 12N 118 0E
Feilding 142 40 13S 175 35E
•Feira 65 15 35S 30 16E
Feira de Santana 171 12 15S 38 57W
Fejér □ 53 47 9N 18 30E
Fejø 73 54 55N 11 30E
Felanitx 59 39 27N 3 7E
Feldbach 52 46 57N 15 52E
Feldberg 48 53 20N 13 26E
Feldberg, mt. 49 47 51N 7 58E
Feldis 51 46 48N 9 26E
Feldkirch 52 47 15N 9 37E
Feldkirchen 52 46 44N 14 6E
Felhit 123 16 40N 38 1E
Felipe Carrillo Puerto 165 19 38N 88 3W
Felixlândia 171 18 47S 44 55W
Felixstowe 29 51 58N 1 22W
Felletin 44 45 53N 2 11E
Felpham 29 50 47N 0 38W
Felton, U.K. 35 55 18N 1 42W
Felton, U.S.A. 163 37 3N 122 4W
Feltre 63 46 1N 11 55E
Feltwell 29 52 29N 0 32E
Femø 73 54 58N 11 53E
Femunden 71 62 10N 11 53E
Fen Ho, R. 106 35 36N 110 42E
Fench'ing 108 24 35N 99 54E
Fénérive 129 17 22S 49 25E
Fenerwa 123 13 5N 39 3E
Fengári 68 40 25N 25 32E
Fengchen 106 40 30N 113 0E
Fengch'eng, Kiangsi, China 109 28 10N 115 43E
Fengch'eng, Liaoning, China 107 40 30N 124 2E
Fengchieh 108 31 3N 109 28E
Fengch'iu 106 35 2N 114 24E
Fenghsiang 106 34 26N 107 18E
Fenghsien, Kiangsu, China 106 34 42N 116 34E
Fenghsien, Shanghai, China 109 30 55N 121 27E
Fenghsien, Shensi, China 106 33 56N 106 41E
Fenghsin 109 28 42N 115 23E
Fenghua 109 29 40N 121 24E
Fenghuang 108 27 58N 109 19E
Fenghuangtsui 106 33 30N 109 27E
Fengi 108 25 35N 100 18E
Fengjun 107 39 51N 118 8E
Fengk'ai 109 23 26N 111 30E
Fengkang 108 27 58N 107 47E
Fengloho 109 31 29N 112 29E
Fengning 106 41 12N 116 32E
Fengshan, Hopei, China 107 41 13N 117 6E
Fengshan, Kwangsi-Chuang, China 108 24 32N 107 3E
Fengt'ai, Anhwei, China 109 32 44N 116 43E
Fengt'ai, Peip'ing, China 106 39 51N 116 17E
Fengteng 106 36 25N 114 14E
Fengtu 108 29 58N 107 59E
Fengyuang 109 32 52N 117 32E
Fenhsi 106 36 38N 111 31E
Feni 109 27 48N 114 41E
Feni Is. 135 4 0S 153 40E
Fenit 39 52 17N 9 51W

*Renamed Luangwa

Fennagh 39 52 42N 6 50W
Fennimore 158 42 58N 90 41W
Fenny 98 22 55N 91 32E
Fenny Bentley 33 53 4N 1 43W
Fenny Compton 28 52 9N 1 20W
Fenny Stratford 29 51 59N 0 42W
Feno, C. de 45 41 58N 8 33E
Fenoarivo 129 18 26S 46 34E
Fens, The 29 52 45N 0 2E
Fenton, Can. 153 53 0N 105 35W
Fenton, U.S.A. 156 42 47N 83 44W
Fenwick 34 55 38N 4 25W
Fenyang 106 37 19N 111 46E
Feodosiya 82 45 2N 35 28E
Fer, C. de 119 37 3N 7 10E
Ferbane 39 53 17N 7 50W
Ferdows 93 33 58N 58 2E
Fère-Champenoise 43 48 45N 4 0E
Fère-en-Tardenois 43 49 10N 3 30E
Fère, La 43 49 40N 3 20E
Ferentino 64 41 42N 13 14E
Ferfer 91 5 18N 45 20E
Fergana 85 40 23N 71 46E
Ferganskaya Dolina 85 40 50N 71 30E
Ferganskiy Khrebet 85 41 0N 73 50E
Fergus 150 43 43N 80 24W
Fergus Falls 158 46 25N 96 0W
Fergus, R. 39 52 45N 9 0W
Ferguson 150 47 50N 73 30W
Fergusson I. 135 9 30S 150 45E
Fériana 119 34 59N 8 33E
Feričanci 66 45 32N 18 0E
Ferkane 119 34 37N 7 26E
Ferkéssédougou 120 9 35N 5 6W
Ferlach 52 46 32N 14 18E
Ferland 150 50 19N 88 27W
Ferlo, Vallée du 120 15 15N 14 15W
Fermanagh (□) 38 54 21N 7 40W
Fermo 63 43 10N 13 42E
Fermoselle 56 41 19N 6 27W
Fermoy 39 52 4N 8 18W
Fernagh 38 54 2N 7 51W
Fernan Nuñ,z 57 37 40N 4 44W
Fernández 172 27 55S 63 50W
Fernandina 157 30 40N 81 30W
Fernando de Noronha, I. 170 4 0S 33 10W
Fernando do Noronho □ 170 4 0S 33 10W
Fernando Póo = Bioko 113 3 30N 8 40E
Fernandópolis 171 20 16S 50 14W
Ferndale, Calif., U.S.A. 160 40 37N 124 12W
Ferndale, Wash., U.S.A. 160 48 51N 122 41W
Ferness 37 57 28N 3 44W
Fernhurst 29 51 3N 0 43W
Fernie 152 49 30N 115 5W
Fernilea 36 57 18N 6 24W
Fernlees 138 23 51S 148 7E
Fernley 160 39 42N 119 20W
Feroke 97 11 9N 75 46E
Ferozepore 94 30 55N 74 40E
Férrai 68 40 53N 26 10E
Ferrandina 65 40 30N 16 28E
Ferrara 63 44 50N 11 36E
Ferrato, C. 64 39 18N 9 39E
Ferreira do Alentejo 57 38 4N 8 6W
Ferreñafe 174 6 35S 79 50W
Ferret, C. 44 44 38N 1 15W
Ferrette 43 47 30N 7 20E
Ferriday 159 31 35N 91 33W
Ferrières 43 48 5N 2 48E
Ferriete 62 44 40N 9 30E
Ferrol 56 43 29N 8 15W
Ferron 160 39 3N 111 3W
Ferros 171 19 14S 43 2W
Ferryhill 33 54 42N 1 32W
Ferryland 151 47 2N 52 53W
Ferté Bernard, La 42 48 10N 0 40E
Ferté, La 43 48 57N 3 6E
Ferté-Mace, La 42 48 35N 0 21W
Ferté-St. Aubin, La 43 47 42N 1 57E
Ferté-Vidame, La 42 48 37N 0 53E
Fertile 158 47 37N 96 18W
Fertília 64 40 37N 8 13E
Fertöszentmiklós 53 47 35N 16 53E
Fès 118 34 0N 5 0W
Feschaux 47 50 9N 4 54E
Feshi 124 6 0S 18 10E
Fessenden 158 47 42N 99 44W
Fet 71 59 57N 11 12E
Feteşti 70 44 22N 27 51E
Fethaland, Pt. 36 60 39N 1 20W
Fethard 39 52 29N 7 42W
Fethiye 92 36 36N 29 10E
Fetlar, I. 36 60 36N 0 52W
Fettercairn 37 56 50N 2 33W
Feuerthalen 51 47 32N 8 38E
Feurs 45 45 45N 4 13E
Fezzan 117 27 0N 15 0E
Ffestiniog 31 52 58N 3 56W
Fforest Fawr, mt. 31 51 52N 3 35W
Fiambalá 172 27 45S 67 37W
Fianarantsoa 125 21 20S 46 45E
Fianarantsoa □ 129 19 30S 47 0E
Fianga 117 9 55N 15 20E
Fibiş 66 45 57N 21 26E
Fichot, I. 151 51 12N 55 40W
Fichtelgebirge 49 50 10N 12 0E
Ficksburg 129 28 51S 27 53E
Fiddown 39 52 20N 7 20W
Fidenza 62 44 51N 10 3E
Field 150 46 31N 80 1W

Field I. 136 12 5S 132 23E
Field, R. 138 23 48S 138 0E
Fields Finds 137 29 0S 117 10E
Fierenana 129 18 29S 48 24E
Fiéri 68 40 43N 19 33E
Fiesch 50 46 25N 8 12E
Fife □ 35 56 13N 3 2W
Fife Ness 35 56 17N 2 35W
Fifth Cataract 123 18 15N 33 50E
Figeac 44 44 37N 2 2E
Figline Valdarno 63 43 37N 11 28E
Figtree 127 20 22S 28 20E
Figueira da Foz 56 40 7N 8 54W
Figueiró dos Vinhos 56 39 55N 8 16W
Figueras 58 42 18N 2 58E
Figuig 118 32 5N 1 11W
Fihaonana 129 18 36S 47 12E
Fiherenana, R. 129 22 50S 44 0E
Fiji ■ 142 17 20S 179 0E
Fiji Is. 130 17 20S 179 0E
Fik 90 32 46N 35 41E
Fika 121 11 15N 11 13E
Filabres, Sierra de los 59 37 13N 2 20W
Filadélfia, Brazil 170 7 21S 47 30W
Filadélfia, Italy 65 38 47N 16 17E
Filadelfia 172 22 25S 60 0W
Fil'akovo 53 48 17N 19 50E
Filby 29 52 40N 1 39E
Filchner Ice Shelf 13 78 0S 60 0W
Filer 160 42 30N 114 35W
Filey 33 54 13N 0 18W
Filey B. 33 54 12N 0 15W
Filiaşi 70 44 32N 23 31E
Filiátes 68 39 38N 20 16E
Filiatrá 69 37 9N 21 35E
Filicudi, I. 65 38 35N 14 33E
Filiouri, R. 68 41 15N 25 40E
Filipstad 72 59 43N 14 9E
Filisur 51 46 41N 9 40E
Fillmore, Can. 153 49 50N 103 25W
Fillmore, U.S.A. 163 34 23N 118 58W
Filottrano 63 43 28N 13 20E
Filton 28 51 29N 2 34E
Filyos 82 41 34N 32 4E
Filyos çayi 92 41 35N 32 10E
Finale Ligure 62 44 10N 8 21E
Finale nell' Emília 63 44 50N 11 18E
Fiñana 59 37 10N 2 50W
Fincham 29 52 38N 0 30E
Findhorn 37 57 39N 3 36W
Findhorn, R. 37 57 38N 3 38W
Findlay 156 41 0N 83 41W
Findon 29 50 53N 0 24W
Finea 38 53 46N 7 23W
Finedon 29 52 20N 0 40W
Finger L. 153 53 9N 93 30W
Fingest 29 51 35N 0 52W
Finglas 38 53 22N 6 18W
Fingõe 127 15 12S 31 50E
Finike 92 36 21N 30 10E
Finistère □ 42 48 20N 4 0W
Finisterre 56 42 54N 9 16W
Finisterre, C. 56 42 50N 9 19W
Finisterre Ra. 135 6 0S 146 30E
Finke 138 25 34S 134 35E
Finke, R. 138 24 54S 134 16E
Finland ■ 78 70 0N 27 0E
Finland, G. of 78 60 0N 26 0E
Finlay, R. 152 55 50N 125 10W
Finley, Austral. 141 35 38S 145 35E
Finley, U.S.A. 158 47 35N 97 50W
Finn, R. 38 54 50N 7 55W
Finnart 34 56 7N 4 48W
Finnigan, Mt. 138 15 49S 145 17E
Finniss 140 35 24S 138 48E
Finniss, C. 139 33 38S 134 51E
Finnmark fylke □ 74 69 30N 25 0E
Finschhafen 135 6 33S 147 50E
Finse 71 60 36N 7 30E
Finspång 73 58 45N 15 43E
Finsta 72 59 45N 18 34E
Finsteraarhorn 50 46 31N 8 10E
Finsterwalde 48 51 37N 13 42E
Finsterwolde 46 53 12N 7 6E
Finstown 37 59 0N 3 8W
Fintona 38 54 30N 7 20W
Fintown 38 54 52N 8 8W
Finucanel I. 132 20 19S 118 30E
Finvoy 38 55 0N 6 29W
Fionn L. 36 57 46N 5 30W
Fionnphort 34 56 19N 6 23W
Fiora, R. 63 42 25N 11 35E
Fiordland National Park 143 45 0S 167 50E
Fiorenzuola d'Arda 62 44 56N 9 54E
Fiq 90 32 46N 35 41E
Fire River 150 48 47N 83 36W
Firebag, R. 153 57 45N 111 21W
Firebaugh 163 36 52N 120 27W
Firedrake L. 153 61 25N 104 30W
Firenze 63 43 47N 11 15E
Firkessédougou 120 9 35N 5 6W
Firmi 44 44 32N 2 19E
Firminy 45 45 23N 4 18E
Firoz Kohi 93 34 45N 63 0E
Firozabad 95 27 10N 78 25E
First Cataract 122 24 1N 32 51E
Firūzābād 93 28 52N 52 35E
Firuzkuh 93 35 50N 52 40E
Firvale 152 52 27N 126 13W
Fish, R. 128 27 40S 17 30E
Fisher 137 30 30S 131 0E
Fisher B. 153 51 35N 97 13W
Fishguard 31 51 59N 4 59W
Fishguard B. 31 52 2N 4 58W
Fishing L. 153 52 10N 95 24W
Fishkill 162 41 32N 73 53W
Fishtoft 33 52 27N 0 2E
Fishtown 120 4 24N 7 45E
Fiskivötn 74 64 50N 20 45W
Fiskum 71 59 42N 9 46E
Fismes 43 49 20N 3 40E
Fister 71 59 10N 6 5E
Fitchburg 162 42 35N 71 47W
Fitero 58 42 4N 1 52W
Fitful Hd. 36 59 54N 1 20W
Fitjar 71 59 55N 5 17E
Fitri, L. 124 12 50N 17 28E
Fitz Roy 176 47 10S 67 0W
Fitzgerald, Can. 152 59 51N 111 36W
Fitzgerald, U.S.A. 157 31 45N 83 10W
Fitzmaurice, R. 136 14 50S 129 50E
Fitzpatrick 150 47 29N 72 46W
Fitzroy Crossing 136 18 9S 125 38E
Fitzroy, R., Queens., Austral. 138 23 32S 150 52E
Fitzroy, R., W. Australia, Austral. 136 17 25S 124 0E
Fiume = Rijeka 63 45 20N 14 21E
Fiumefreddo Brúzio 65 39 14N 16 4E
Five Alley 39 53 9N 7 51W
Five Points 163 36 26N 120 6W
Fivemiletown 38 54 23N 7 20W
Fizi 126 4 17S 28 55E
Fjæra 71 59 52N 6 22E
Fjaere 71 58 23N 8 36E
Fjellerup 73 56 29N 10 34E
Fjerritslev 73 57 5N 9 15E
Fkih ben Salah 118 32 45N 6 45W
Fla 71 60 25N 9 26E
Flå 71 63 13N 10 18E
Flagler 158 39 20N 103 4W
Flagstaff 161 35 10N 111 40W
Flagstone 152 49 4N 115 10W
Flaherty, I. 150 56 15N 79 15W
Flåm 75 60 52N 7 14E
Flambeau, R. 158 45 40N 90 50W
Flamborough 33 54 7N 0 7W
Flamborough Hd. 33 54 8N 0 4W
Flaming Gorge Dam 160 40 50N 109 25W
Flaming Gorge L. 160 41 15N 109 30W
Flamingo, Teluk 103 5 30S 138 0E
Flanders = Flandres 47 51 10N 3 15E
Flandre Occidental □ 47 51 0N 3 0E
Flandre Orientale □ 47 51 0N 4 0E
Flandreau 158 44 5N 96 38W
Flandres, Plaines des 47 51 10N 3 15E
Flannan Is. 23 58 9N 7 52W
Flaren L. 73 57 2N 14 5E
Flåsjön 74 64 5N 15 50E
Flat, R. 152 61 51N 128 0W
Flat River 159 37 50N 90 30W
Flatey, Barðastrandarsýsla, Iceland 74 66 10N 17 52W
Flatey, Suður-þingeyjarsýsla, Iceland 74 65 22N 22 56W
Flathead L. 160 47 50N 114 0W
Flattery, C., Austral. 138 14 58S 145 21E
Flattery, C., U.S.A. 160 48 21N 124 43W
Flavy-le-Martel 43 49 43N 3 12E
Flawil 51 47 26N 9 11E
Flaxton 158 48 52N 102 24W
Flèche, La 42 47 42N 0 5W
Fleeming, C. 136 11 15S 131 21E
Fleet 29 51 16N 0 50W
Fleetwood, U.K. 32 53 55N 3 1W
Fleetwood, U.S.A. 162 40 27N 75 49W
Flekkefjord 71 58 18N 6 39E
Flémalle 47 50 36N 5 28E
Flensborg Fjord 73 54 50N 9 40E
Flensburg 48 54 46N 9 28E
Flers 42 48 47N 0 33W
Flesberg 71 59 51N 9 22E
Fletton 29 52 34N 0 13W
Fleurance 44 43 52N 0 40E
Fleurier 50 46 54N 6 35E
Fleurus 47 50 29N 4 32E
Flickerbäcken 72 61 47N 12 34E
Flims 51 46 50N 9 17E
Flin Flon 153 54 46N 101 53W
Flinders B. 137 34 19S 115 9E
Flinders Group, Is. 138 14 11S 144 15E
Flinders I. 138 40 0S 148 0E
Flinders, R. 138 17 36S 140 36E
Flinders Ranges 140 31 30S 138 30E
Flinders Reefs 138 17 37S 148 31E
Flint 156 43 5N 83 19W
Flint (□) 26 53 15N 3 12W
Flint, I. 131 11 26S 151 48W
Flint, R. 157 31 20N 84 10W
Flinton 139 27 55S 149 32E
Fliseryd 73 57 6N 16 15E
Flitwick 29 51 59N 0 30W
Flix 58 41 14N 0 32E
Flixecourt 43 50 0N 2 5E
Flobecq 47 50 44N 3 45E
Floda 72 60 30N 14 53E
Flodden 35 55 37N 2 8W
Floodwood 158 46 55N 92 55W
Flora, N. Tröndelag, Norway 71 63 27N 11 22E
Flora, Sogn & Fjordane, Norway 71 61 35N 5 1E
Flora, U.S.A. 156 38 40N 88 30W
Florac 44 44 20N 3 37E
Florala 157 31 0N 86 20W
Florânia 170 6 8S 36 49W
Floreffe 47 50 26N 4 46E
Florence, Ala., U.S.A. 157 34 50N 87 50W
Florence, Ariz., U.S.A. 161 33 0N 111 25W
Florence, Colo., U.S.A. 158 38 26N 105 0W
Florence, Oreg., U.S.A. 160 44 0N 124 3W
Florence, S.C., U.S.A. 157 34 5N 79 50W
Florence = Firenze 63 43 47N 11 15E
Florence, L. 139 28 53S 138 9E
Florennes 47 50 15N 4 35E
Florensac 44 43 23N 3 28E
Florenville 47 49 40N 5 19E
Flores, Azores 16 39 13N 31 13W
Flores, Brazil 170 7 51S 37 59W
Flores, Guat. 166 16 50N 89 40W
Flores I. 152 49 20N 126 10W
Flores, I. 103 8 35S 121 0E
Flores Sea 102 6 30S 124 0E
Floresta 170 9 46S 37 26W
Floresville 159 29 10N 98 10W
Floriano 170 6 50S 43 0W
Florianópolis 173 27 30S 48 30W
Florida, Cuba 166 21 32N 78 14W
Florida, Uruguay 173 34 7S 56 10W
Florida □ 157 28 30N 82 0W
Florida B. 167 25 0N 81 20W
Florida Keys 167 25 0N 80 40W
Florida, Strait of 167 25 0N 80 0W
Florídia 65 37 6N 15 9E
Flórina 68 40 48N 21 26E
Flórina □ 68 40 45N 21 20E
Florningen 72 61 50N 12 16E
Florø 71 61 35N 5 1E
Flosta 71 58 32N 8 56E
Flower's Cove 151 51 14N 56 46W
Floydada 159 33 58N 101 18W
Flüela Pass 51 46 45N 9 57E
Fluk 103 1 42S 127 38E
Flumen, R. 58 41 50N 0 25W
Flumendosa, R. 64 39 30N 9 25E
Fluminimaggiore 64 39 25N 8 30E
Flums 51 47 6N 9 21E
Flushing = Vlissingen 47 51 26N 3 34E
Fluviá, R. 58 42 12N 3 7E
Fly, R. 135 8 25S 143 0E
Foam Lake 153 51 40N 103 32W
Foča 66 43 31N 18 47E
Focşani 70 45 41N 27 15E
Fofo Fofo 138 8 9S 147 6E
Foggaret el Arab 118 27 3N 2 59E
Foggaret ez Zoua 118 27 20N 3 0E
Fóggia 65 41 28N 15 31E
Foggo 121 11 21N 9 57E
Foglia, R. 63 43 50N 12 32E
Fogo 151 49 43N 54 17W
Fogo I. 151 49 40N 54 5W
Fohnsdorf 52 47 12N 14 40E
Föhr 48 54 40N 8 30E
Foia, Cerro da 57 37 19N 8 10W
Foix 44 42 58N 1 38E
Fojnica 66 43 59N 17 51E
Fokang 109 23 52N 113 31E
Fokino 80 53 30N 34 10E
Fokís □ 69 38 30N 22 15E
Fokstua 71 62 8N 9 16E
Folda, Nord-Trøndelag, Norway 74 64 41N 10 50E
Folda, Nordland, Norway 74 67 38N 14 50E
Földeák 53 46 19N 20 30E
Folette, La 157 36 23N 84 9W
Foley 128 30 25N 87 40W
Foleyet 150 48 15N 82 25W
Folgefonni 71 60 23N 6 34E
Foligno 63 42 58N 12 40E
Folkestone 29 51 5N 1 11E
Folkston 157 30 55N 82 0W
Follett 159 36 30N 100 12W
Follónica 62 42 55N 10 45E
Folsom 160 38 41N 121 7W
Fond-du-Lac 153 59 19N 107 12W
Fond du lac 158 43 46N 88 26W
Fond-du-Lac, R. 153 59 17N 106 0W
Fondak 118 35 34N 5 35W
Fondi 64 41 21N 13 25E
Fonfría 56 41 37N 6 9W
Fongen 71 63 11N 11 38E
Fonni 64 40 5N 9 16E
Fonsagrada 56 43 8N 7 4W
Fonseca, G. de 166 13 10N 87 40W
Fontaine-Française 43 47 32N 5 21E
Fontainebleau 43 48 24N 2 40E
Fontas, R. 152 58 14N 121 48W
Fonte Boa 174 2 25S 66 0W
Fontem 121 5 32N 9 52E
Fontenay-le-Comte 44 46 28N 0 48W
Fontenelle 151 48 54N 64 33W
Fontur 74 66 23N 14 32W
Fonyód 53 46 44N 17 33E
Foochow = Fuchou 109 26 5N 119 18E
Foping 106 33 22N 108 19E
Foppiano 62 46 21N 8 24E
Föra 73 57 1N 16 51E
Forbach 43 49 10N 6 52E
Forbes 141 33 22S 148 0E
Forbesganj 95 26 17N 87 18E
Forcados 121 5 26N 5 26E
Forcados, R. 121 5 25N 5 20E
Forcall, R. 58 40 40N 0 12W
Forcalquier 45 43 58N 5 47E
Forchheim 49 49 42N 11 4E
Forclaz, Col de la 50 46 3N 7 1E
Ford City 163 35 9N 119 27W
Førde 71 61 27N 5 53E
Fordingbridge 28 50 56N 1 48W
Fordongianus 44 40 0N 8 50E
Fords Bridge 139 29 41S 145 29E
Fordyce 159 33 50N 92 20W
Forécariah 120 9 20N 13 10W
Forel 12 66 52N 36 55W
Foremost 152 49 26N 111 25W
Forenza 65 40 50N 15 50E
Forest, Belg. 47 50 49N 4 20E
Forest, U.S.A. 159 32 21N 89 27W
Forest City, Ark., U.S.A. 159 35 0N 90 50W
Forest City, Iowa, U.S.A. 158 43 12N 93 39W
Forest City, N.C., U.S.A. 157 35 23N 81 50W
Forest Grove 160 45 31N 123 4W
Forest Lawn 152 51 4N 114 0W
Forest Row 29 51 6N 0 3E
Forestburg 152 52 35N 112 1W
Forestier Pen. 138 43 0S 148 0E
Forestville, Can. 151 48 48N 69 20W
Forestville, U.S.A. 156 44 41N 87 29W
Forez, Mts. du 44 45 40N 3 50E
Forfar 37 56 40N 2 53W
Forges-les-Eaux 43 49 37N 1 30E
Forget 150 49 40N 102 50W
Forked River 162 39 50N 74 12W
Forks 160 47 56N 124 23W
Forksville 162 41 29N 76 35W
Forlì 63 44 14N 12 2E
Forman 158 46 9N 97 43W
Formazza 62 46 23N 8 26E
Formby Pt. 32 53 33N 3 7W
Formentera, I. 59 38 40N 1 30E
Formentor, C. de 58 39 58N 3 13E
Fórmia 64 41 15N 13 34E
Formiga 171 20 27S 45 25W
Formigine 62 44 37N 10 51E
Formiguères 44 42 37N 2 5E
Formosa, Argent. 172 26 15S 58 10W
Formosa, Brazil 171 15 32S 47 20W
Formosa = Taiwan ■ 109 24 0N 121 0E
Formosa □ 172 26 5S 58 10W
Formosa Bay 126 2 40S 40 20E
Formosa Strait 109 24 40N 120 0E
Formoso, R. 171 10 34S 49 56W
Fornaes, C. 73 56 27N 10 58E
Fornells 58 40 4N 4 4E
Fornos de Algodres 56 40 38N 7 32W
Fornovo di Taro 62 44 42N 10 7E
Forres 37 57 37N 3 38W
Forrest, Vic., Austral. 140 38 22S 143 40E
Forrest, W. Australia, Austral. 137 30 51S 128 6E
Forrest Lakes 137 29 12S 128 46E
Forrest, Mt. 137 24 48S 127 45E
Forrières 47 50 8N 5 17E
Fors, Jämtland, Sweden 72 63 0N 16 40E
Fors, Kopparberg, Sweden 72 60 14N 16 20E
Forsa 72 61 44N 16 55E
Forsand 71 58 54N 6 5E
Forsayth 138 18 33S 143 34E
Forsbacka 72 60 39N 16 54E
Forse 72 63 8N 17 1E
Forserum 73 57 42N 14 30E
Forshaga 72 59 33N 13 29E
Forshem 73 58 38N 13 30E
Forsmo 72 63 16N 17 11E
Forst 48 51 43N 14 37E
Forster 141 32 12S 152 31E
Forsyth, Ga., U.S.A. 157 33 4N 83 55W
Forsyth, Mont., U.S.A. 160 46 14N 106 37W
Forsyth I. 143 40 58S 174 5E
Fort Albany 150 52 15N 81 35W
Fort Ann 162 43 25N 73 30W
Fort Apache 161 33 50N 110 0W
Fort Archambault = Sarh 117 9 5N 18 23E
Fort Assiniboine 152 54 20N 114 45W
Fort Augustus 37 57 9N 4 40W
Fort Babine 152 55 22N 126 37W
Fort Beaufort 128 32 46S 26 40E
Fort Benton 160 47 50N 110 40W
Fort Bragg 160 39 28N 123 50W
Fort Bretonnet = Bousso 117 10 34N 16 52E
Fort Bridger 160 41 22N 110 20W
Fort Charlet = Djanet 119 24 35N 9 32E
Fort Chimo 149 58 6N 68 25W
Fort Chipewyan 153 58 42N 111 8W
Fort Collins 158 40 30N 105 4W
Fort Coulonge 150 45 50N 76 45W
Fort Crampel = Kaga Bandoro 117 7 8N 19 18E
Fort-Dauphin 129 25 2S 47 0E
Fort Davis 159 30 38N 103 53W
Fort-de-France 167 14 36N 61 2W
Fort de Polignac = Illizi 119 26 31N 8 32E
Fort de Possel = Possel 124 5 5N 19 10E
Fort Defiance 161 35 47N 109 4W
Fort Dodge 158 42 29N 94 10W
Fort Flatters = Bordj Omar Driss 119 27 10N 6 40E
Fort Foureau = Kousseri 117 12 0N 14 55E
Fort Frances 153 48 35N 93 25W
Fort Franklin 148 65 30N 123 45W
Fort Garland 161 37 28N 105 30W

Fort George **151** 53 50N 79 0W
Fort George, R. **150** 53 50N 77 0W
Fort Good-Hope **147** 66 14N 128 40W
Fort Gouraud = F'Dérik **116** 22 40N 12 45W
Fort Grahame **152** 56 30N 124 35W
Fort Hancock **161** 31 19N 105 56W
Fort Hauchuca **161** 31 32N 110 30W
Fort Hertz (Putao) **99** 27 28N 97 30E
Fort Hope **150** 51 30N 88 10W
Fort Irwin **163** 35 16N 116 34W
Fort Jameson = Chipata **127** 13 38S 32 38E
Fort Johnston **127** 14 25S 35 16E
Fort Kent **151** 47 12N 68 30W
Fort Klamath **160** 42 45N 122 0W
Fort Lallemand **119** 31 13N 6 17E
Fort-Lamy = Ndjamena **117** 12 4N 15 8E
Fort Lapperrine = Tamanrasset **119** 22 56N 5 30E
Fort Laramie **158** 42 15N 104 30W
Fort Lauderdale **157** 26 10N 80 5W
Fort Liard **152** 60 20N 123 30W
Fort Liberté **167** 19 42N 71 51W
Fort Lupton **158** 40 8N 104 48W
Fort Mackay **152** 57 12N 111 41W
Fort McKenzie **151** 57 20N 69 0W
Fort Macleod **152** 49 45N 113 30W
Fort MacMahon **118** 29 51N 1 45E
Fort McMurray **152** 56 44N 111 23W
Fort McPherson **147** 67 30N 134 55W
Fort Madison **158** 40 39N 91 20W
Fort Meade **157** 27 45N 81 45W
Fort Miribel **118** 29 31N 2 55E
Fort Morgan **158** 40 10N 103 50W
Fort Myers **157** 26 30N 82 0W
Fort Nelson **152** 58 50N 122 38W
Fort Nelson, R. **152** 59 32N 124 0W
Fort Norman **147** 64 57N 125 30W
Fort Pacot (Chirfa) **119** 20 55N 12 14E
Fort Payne **157** 34 25N 85 44W
Fort Peck **160** 47 1N 105 30W
Fort Peck Dam **160** 48 0N 106 20W
Fort Peck Res. **160** 47 40N 107 0W
Fort Pierce **158** 27 29N 80 19W
Fort Pierre **158** 44 25N 100 25W
Fort Pierre Bordes **118** 20 0N 2 55E
Fort Portal **126** 0 40N 30 20E
Fort Providence **152** 61 21N 117 40W
Fort Qu'Appelle **153** 50 45N 103 50W
Fort Randall **147** 55 10N 162 48W
Fort Reliance **153** 63 0N 109 20W
Fort Resolution **152** 61 10N 113 40W
Fort Rixon **127** 20 2S 29 17E
Fort Roseberry = Mansa **127** 11 10S 28 50E
Fort Rupert (Rupert House) **150** 51 30N 78 40W
Fort Saint **119** 30 13N 9 31E
Fort St. James **152** 54 30N 124 10W
Fort St. John **152** 56 15N 120 50W
Fort Sandeman **94** 31 20N 69 25E
Fort Saskatchewan **152** 53 40N 113 15W
Fort Scott **159** 38 0N 94 40W
Fort Selkirk **147** 62 43N 137 22W
Fort Severn **150** 56 0N 87 40W
Fort Shevchenko **83** 44 30N 50 10E
Fort Sibut = Sibut **117** 5 52N 19 10E
Fort Simpson **152** 61 45N 121 23W
Fort Smith, Can. **152** 60 0N 111 51W
Fort Smith, U.S.A. **159** 35 25N 94 25W
Fort Stanton **161** 33 33N 105 36W
Fort Stockton **159** 30 48N 103 2W
Fort Sumner **159** 34 24N 104 8W
Fort Thomas **161** 33 2N 109 59W
Fort Trinquet = Bir Mogrein **116** 25 10N 11 25W
Fort Valley **157** 32 33N 83 52W
Fort Vermilion **152** 58 24N 116 0W
Fort Victoria **127** 20 8S 30 55E
Ft. Walton Beach **157** 30 25N 86 40W
Fort Wayne **156** 41 5N 85 10W
Fort William **36** 56 48N 5 8W
Fort William = Thunder Bay **150** 48 20N 89 10W
Fort Worth **159** 32 45N 97 25W
Fort Yates **158** 46 8N 100 38W
Fort Yukon **147** 66 35N 145 12W
Fortaleza **170** 3 35S 38 35W
Forte Coimbra **174** 19 55S 57 48W
Forte Rocadas **125** 16 38S 15 22E
Forteau **151** 51 28N 57 1W
Fortescue **136** 21 4S 116 4E
Fortescue, R. **136** 21 20S 116 5E
Forth, Firth of **35** 56 5N 2 55W
Forthassa Rharbia **118** 32 52N 1 11W
Forties, oilfield **19** 57 40N 1 0E
Fortín Corrales **174** 22 21S 60 35W
Fortín Guachalla **174** 22 22S 62 23W
Fortín Rojas Silva **172** 22 40S 59 3W
Fortín Siracuas **174** 21 3S 61 46W
Fortín Teniente Montania **172** 22 1S 59 45W
Fortore, R. **63** 41 40N 15 0E
Fortrose **143** 46 38S 168 45E
Fortuna, Spain **59** 38 11N 1 7W
Fortuna, Cal., U.S.A. **160** 48 38N 124 8W
Fortuna, N.D., U.S.A. **158** 48 55N 103 48W
Fortune Bay **151** 47 30N 55 22W
Forty Mile **147** 64 20N 140 30W
Forūr **93** 26 20N 54 30E
Fos **62** 43 20N 4 57E
Fos do Jordão **174** 9 30S 72 14W
Fos-sur-Mer **45** 43 26N 4 56E
Foshan **109** 23 4N 113 5E
Fossacesia **63** 42 15N 14 30E
Fossano **62** 44 39N 7 40E
Fosses-la-Ville **47** 50 24N 4 41E
Fossil **160** 45 0N 120 9W
Fossilbrook **138** 17 47S 144 29E
Fossombrone **63** 43 41N 12 49E
Fosston **158** 47 33N 95 39W
Foster, R. **153** 55 47N 105 49W
Fosters Ra. **138** 21 35S 133 48E
Fostoria **156** 41 8N 83 25W
Fou Chiang, R. **108** 30 3N 106 21E
Fouch'eng **106** 37 52N 116 8E
Fougamou **124** 1 38S 11 39E
Fougéres **42** 48 21N 1 14W
Fouhsinshih **107** 42 13N 121 51E
Foul Pt. **97** 8 35N 81 25E
Foula, I. **23** 60 10N 2 5W
Fouling **108** 29 40N 107 20E
Foulpointe **129** 17 41S 49 31E
Foum el Alba **118** 20 45N 3 0W
Foum el Kreneg **118** 29 0N 0 58W
Foum Tatahouine **119** 32 57N 10 29E
Foum Zguid **118** 30 2N 6 59W
Foumban **121** 5 45N 10 50E
Foundiougne **120** 14 5N 16 32W
Founing **107** 33 47N 119 48E
Fountain, Colo., U.S.A. **158** 38 42N 104 40W
Fountain, Utah, U.S.A. **160** 39 41N 111 50W
Fountain Springs **163** 35 54N 118 51W
Foup'ing **106** 38 55N 114 13E
Four Mts., Is. of the **147** 52 0N 170 30W
Fourchambault **43** 47 0N 3 3E
Fourchu **151** 45 43N 60 17W
Fourcroy, C. **136** 11 45S 130 2E
Fourmies **43** 50 1N 4 2E
Fournás **69** 39 3N 21 52E
Foúrnoi **69** 37 36N 26 32E
Fours **43** 46 50N 3 42E
Foushan **106** 35 58N 111 51E
Fouta Djalon **120** 11 20N 12 10W
Foux, Cap-à- **167** 19 43N 73 27W
Fouyang **109** 32 55N 115 52E
Foveaux Str. **143** 46 42S 168 10E
Fowler, Calif., U.S.A. **163** 36 41N 119 41W
Fowler, Colo., U.S.A. **158** 38 10N 104 0W
Fowler, Kans., U.S.A. **159** 37 28N 100 7W
Fowlers B. **137** 31 59S 132 34E
Fowlers Bay **137** 32 0S 132 29E
Fowlerton **159** 28 26N 98 50W
Fox Is. **147** 52 30N 166 0W
Fox, R. **153** 56 3N 93 18W
Fox Valley **153** 50 30N 109 25W
Foxboro **162** 42 4N 71 16W
Foxe Basin **149** 68 30N 77 0W
Foxe Channel **149** 66 0N 80 0W
Foxe Pen. **149** 65 0N 76 0W
Foxen, L. **72** 59 25N 11 55E
Foxhol **46** 53 10N 6 43E
Foxpark **160** 41 4N 106 6W
Foxton **142** 40 29S 175 18E
Foyle, Lough **38** 55 6N 7 8W
Foynes **38** 52 30N 9 5W
Foz **56** 43 33N 7 20W
Foz do Cunene **128** 17 15S 11 55E
Foz do Gregório **174** 6 47S 71 0W
Foz do Iguaçu **173** 25 30S 54 30W
Frackville **162** 40 46N 76 15W
Fraga **58** 41 32N 0 21E
Fraire **47** 50 16N 4 31E
Frameries **47** 50 24N 3 54E
Framlingham **29** 52 14N 1 20E
Franca **171** 20 25S 47 30W
Francavilla al Mare **63** 42 25N 14 16E
Francavilla Fontana **65** 40 32N 17 35E
France ■ **41** 47 0N 3 0E
Frances **140** 36 41S 140 55E
Frances Creek **136** 13 25S 132 3E
Frances L. **152** 61 23N 129 30W
Frances, R. **152** 60 16N 129 10W
Francés Viejo, C. **167** 19 40N 70 0W
Franceville **124** 1 40S 13 32E
Franche Comté □ **43** 46 30N 5 50E
Franches Montagnes **50** 47 10N 7 0E
Francis-Garnier **118** 36 30N 1 30E
Francis Harbour **151** 52 34N 55 44W
Francisco I. Madero, Coahuila, Mexico **164** 25 48N 103 18W
Francisco I. Madero, Durango, Mexico **164** 24 32N 104 22W
Francisco Sá **171** 16 28S 43 30W
Francistown **125** 21 7S 27 33E
Francofonte **65** 37 13N 14 50E
François **151** 47 35N 56 45W
Francois L. **152** 54 0N 125 30W
François, Le **167** 14 38N 60 57W
Francorchamps **47** 50 27N 5 57E
Franeker **46** 53 12N 5 33E
Frankado **123** 12 30N 43 12E
Frankenberg **48** 51 3N 8 47E
Frankenthal **49** 49 32N 8 21E
Frankford = Kilcormac **39** 53 10N 7 43W
Frankfort, Ind., U.S.A. **156** 40 20N 86 33W
Frankfort, Kans., U.S.A. **158** 39 42N 96 26W
Frankfort, Ky., U.S.A. **156** 38 12N 84 52W
Frankfort, Mich., U.S.A. **156** 44 38N 86 14W
Frankfort, N.Y., U.S.A. **162** 43 2N 75 4W
Frankfurt □ **48** 52 30N 14 0E
Frankfurt am Main **49** 50 7N 8 40E
Frankfurt an der Oder **48** 52 50N 14 31E
Fränkische Alb **49** 49 20N 11 30E
Fränkische Saale **49** 50 7N 9 49E
Fränkische Saale, R. **49** 50 7N 9 49E
Fränkische Schweiz **49** 49 45N 11 10E
Frankland, R. **137** 35 0S 116 48E
Franklin, Ky., U.S.A. **157** 36 40N 86 30W
Franklin, La., U.S.A. **159** 29 45N 91 30W
Franklin, Mass., U.S.A. **162** 42 4N 71 23W
Franklin, Nebr., U.S.A. **158** 40 9N 98 55W
Franklin, N.H., U.S.A. **162** 43 28N 71 39W
Franklin, N.J., U.S.A. **162** 41 9N 74 38W
Franklin, Pa., U.S.A. **156** 41 22N 79 45W
Franklin, Tenn., U.S.A. **157** 35 54N 86 53W
Franklin, Va., U.S.A. **157** 36 40N 76 58W
Franklin, W. Va., U.S.A. **156** 38 38N 79 21W
*Franklin □ **149** 71 0N 99 0W
Franklin B. **147** 69 45N 126 0W
Franklin D. Roosevelt L. **160** 48 30N 118 16W
Franklin I. **13** 76 10S 168 30E
Franklin, L. **160** 40 20N 115 26W
Franklin Mts., Can. **148** 66 0N 125 0W
Franklin Mts., N.Z. **143** 44 55S 167 45E
Franklin Str. **148** 72 0N 96 0W
Franklinton **159** 30 53N 90 10W
Franklyn Mt. **143** 42 4S 172 42E
Franks Peak **160** 43 50N 109 5W
Frankston **141** 38 8S 145 8E
Frankton Junc. **142** 37 47S 175 16E
Fränsta **72** 62 30N 16 11E
Frant **29** 51 5N 0 17E
Frantsa Josifa, Zemlya **76** 76 0N 62 0E
Franz **150** 48 25N 84 30W
Franz Josef Fd. **12** 73 20N 22 0E
Franz Josef Land = Frantsa Josifa **76** 76 0N 62 0E
Franzburg **48** 54 9N 12 52E
Frascati **64** 41 48N 12 41E
Fraser I. **139** 25 15S 153 10E
Fraser L. **152** 54 0N 124 50W
Fraser, Mt. **137** 25 35S 118 20E
Fraser, R., B.C., Can. **152** 49 7N 123 11W
Fraser, R., Newf., Can. **151** 56 39N 63 10W
Fraserburg **128** 31 55S 21 30E
Fraserburgh **37** 57 41N 2 0W
Fraserdale **150** 49 55N 81 37W
Frasertown **142** 38 58S 177 28E
Frashëri **68** 40 23N 20 26E
Frasne **43** 46 50N 6 10E
Frater **150** 47 20N 84 25W
Frauenfeld **51** 47 34N 8 54E
Fray Bentos **172** 33 10S 58 15W
Frazier Downs P.O. **136** 18 48S 121 42E
Frechilla **56** 42 8N 4 50W
Fredericia **73** 55 34N 9 45E
Frederick, Md., U.S.A. **162** 39 25N 77 23W
Frederick, Okla., U.S.A. **159** 34 22N 99 0W
Frederick, S.D., U.S.A. **158** 45 55N 98 29W
Frederick Reef **133** 20 58S 154 23E
Frederick Sd. **153** 57 10N 134 0W
Fredericksburg, Tex., U.S.A. **159** 30 17N 98 55W
Fredericksburg, Va., U.S.A. **162** 38 16N 77 29W
Frederickstown **159** 37 35N 90 15W
Fredericton **151** 45 57N 66 40W
Fredericton Junc. **151** 45 41N 66 40W
Frederiksberg **72** 60 12N 14 25E
Frederiksborg Amt □ **73** 55 50N 12 10E
Frederikshåb **12** 62 0N 49 30W
Frederikshavn **73** 57 28N 10 31E
Frederikssund **73** 55 50N 12 3E
Frederiksted **147** 17 43N 64 53W
Fredonia, Ariz., U.S.A. **161** 36 59N 112 36W
Fredonia, Kans., U.S.A. **159** 37 34N 95 50W
Fredonia, N.Y., U.S.A. **156** 42 26N 79 20W
Fredrikstad **71** 59 13N 10 57E
Freehold **162** 40 15N 74 18W
Freel Pk. **163** 38 52N 119 53W
Freeland **162** 41 3N 75 48W
Freeling, Mt. **136** 22 35S 133 06E
Freels, C. **151** 49 15N 53 30W
Freeman, Calif., U.S.A. **163** 35 35N 117 53W
Freeman, S.D., U.S.A. **158** 43 25N 97 20W
Freeport, Bahamas **167** 25 45N 88 30E
Freeport, Can. **151** 44 15N 66 20W
Freeport, Ill., U.S.A. **158** 42 18N 89 40W
Freeport, N.Y., U.S.A. **162** 40 39N 73 35W
Freeport, Tex., U.S.A. **159** 28 55N 95 22W
Freetown **120** 8 30N 13 10W
Freevater Forest **37** 57 51N 4 45W
Fregenal de la Sierra **57** 38 10N 6 39W
Fregene **64** 41 50N 12 12E
Fregeneda, La **56** 40 58N 6 54W
Fréhel C. **42** 48 40N 2 20W
Freiberg **48** 50 55N 13 20E
Freibourg = Fribourg **50** 46 49N 7 9E
Freiburg, Baden, Ger. **49** 48 0N 7 52E
Freiburg, Sachsen, Ger. **48** 53 49N 9 17E
Freiburger Alpen **50** 46 37N 7 10E
Freire **176** 39 0S 72 50W
Freirina **172** 28 30S 70 27W
Freising **49** 48 24N 11 47E
Freistadt **52** 48 30N 14 30E
Freital **48** 51 0N 13 40E
Fréjus **45** 43 25N 6 44E
Fremantle **137** 32 1S 115 47E
Fremont, Calif., U.S.A. **163** 37 32N 122 57W
Fremont, Mich., U.S.A. **156** 43 29N 85 59W
Fremont, Nebr., U.S.A. **158** 41 30N 96 30W
Fremont, Ohio, U.S.A. **156** 41 20N 83 5W
Fremont, L. **160** 43 0N 109 50W
**Now part of Central Arctic and Baffin*
Fremont, R. **161** 38 15N 110 20W
French Camp **163** 37 53N 121 16W
French Cr. **156** 41 30N 80 2W
French Guiana ■ **175** 4 0N 53 0W
French I. **141** 38 20S 145 22E
French Terr. of Afars & Issas □ = Djibouti **123** 11 30N 42 15E
Frenchglen **160** 42 56N 119 0W
Frenchman Butte **153** 53 36N 109 36W
Frenchman Creek, R. **158** 40 34N 101 35W
Frenchman, R. **160** 49 25N 108 20W
Frenchpark **38** 53 53N 8 25W
Frenda **118** 35 2N 1 1E
Fresco, R. **175** 7 15S 51 30W
Freshfield, C. **13** 68 25S 151 10E
Freshford **39** 52 45N 7 25W
Freshwater **28** 50 42N 1 31W
Fresnillo **164** 23 10N 103 0W
Fresno **163** 36 47N 119 50W
Fresno Alhandiga **56** 40 42N 5 37W
Fresno Res. **160** 48 47N 110 0W
Freswick **37** 58 35N 3 5W
Freuchie **35** 56 14N 3 8W
Freudenstadt **49** 48 27N 8 25E
Freux **47** 49 59N 5 27E
Frévent **43** 50 15N 2 17E
Frew, R. **138** 20 0S 135 38E
Frewena **138** 19 50S 135 50E
Freycinet, C. **137** 34 9S 115 0E
Freycinet Pen. **138** 42 10S 148 25E
Fria **120** 10 27N 13 32W
Fria, La **174** 8 13N 72 15W
Friant **163** 36 59N 119 43W
Frías **172** 28 40S 65 5W
Fribourg **50** 46 49N 7 9E
Fribourg □ **50** 45 40N 7 0E
Frick **50** 47 31N 8 1E
Fridafors **73** 56 25N 14 39E
Fridaythorpe **33** 54 2N 0 40W
Friedberg, Bayern, Ger. **49** 48 21N 10 59E
Friedberg, Hessen, Ger. **10** 50 19N 8 45E
Friedland **49** 53 40N 13 33E
Friedrichshafen **49** 47 39N 9 29E
Friedrichskoog **48** 54 1N 8 52E
Friedrichsort **48** 54 24N 10 11E
Friedrichstadt **48** 54 23N 9 6E
Friendly (Tonga) Is. **130** 19 50S 174 30W
Friesach **52** 46 57N 14 24E
Friesack **48** 52 43N 12 35E
Friesche Wad **46** 53 22N 5 44E
Friesland □ **46** 53 5N 5 50E
Friesoythe **48** 53 1N 7 51E
Frigate, L. **150** 53 15N 74 45W
Frigg E., gasfield **19** 59 50N 2 20E
Frigg, gasfield **19** 59 50N 2 15E
Frigg N.E., gasfield **19** 60 0N 2 17E
Frillesås **73** 57 20N 12 12E
Frimley **29** 51 18N 0 43W
Frinnaryd **73** 57 55N 14 50E
Frinton-on-Sea **29** 51 50N 1 16E
Frio, C. **128** 18 0S 12 0E
Frio, R. **159** 29 40N 99 40W
Friockheim **37** 56 39N 2 40W
Friona **159** 34 40N 102 42W
Frisa, Loch **34** 56 34N 6 5W
Frisian Is. **48** 53 30N 6 0E
Fristad **73** 57 50N 13 0E
Fritch **159** 35 40N 101 35W
Fritsla **73** 57 33N 12 47E
Fritzlar **48** 51 8N 9 19E
Friuli-Venezia-Giulia □ **63** 46 0N 13 0E
Frizington **32** 54 33N 3 30W
Frobisher B. **149** 63 0N 67 0W
Frobisher L. **153** 56 20N 108 15W
Frobisher Sd. **149** 62 30N 66 0W
Frodsham **32** 53 17N 2 45W
Frogmore **141** 34 15S 148 52E
Frohavet **74** 64 5N 9 35E
Froid **158** 48 20N 104 29W
Froid-Chapelle **47** 50 9N 4 19E
Frolovo **83** 49 45N 43 30E
Fromberg **160** 45 19N 108 58W
Frombork **54** 54 21N 19 41E
Frome **28** 51 16N 2 17W
Frome Downs **140** 31 13S 139 46E
Frome, L. **140** 30 45S 139 45E
Frome, R. **28** 50 44N 2 5W
Fromentine **42** 46 53N 2 9W
Frómista **56** 42 16N 4 25W
Front Range **160** 40 0N 105 10W
Front Royal **156** 38 55N 78 10W
Fronteira **57** 39 3N 7 39W
Fronteiras **170** 7 5S 40 37W
Frontera **165** 18 30N 92 40W
Frontignan **44** 43 27N 3 45E
Frosinone **64** 41 38N 13 20E
Frosolone **65** 41 34N 14 27E
Frostburg **156** 39 43N 78 57W
Frostisen **74** 68 14N 17 10E
Frouard **43** 48 47N 6 8E
Frövi **72** 59 28N 15 24E
Frower Pt. **39** 51 40N 8 30W
Froya **71** 63 43N 8 40E
Frøya **71** 63 43N 8 40E
Fröya I. **74** 63 45N 8 45E
Fruges **43** 50 30N 2 8E
Frumoasa **70** 46 28N 25 48E
Frunze **85** 42 54N 74 36E
Fruška Gora **66** 45 7N 19 30E
Frutal **171** 20 0S 49 0W
Frutigen **50** 46 35N 7 38E
Frýdek-Místek **53** 49 40N 18 20E

Name	Page	Lat.	Long.
Frýdlant, Severočeský, Czech.	**52**	50 56N	15 9E
Frýdlant, Severomoravsky, Czech.	**53**	49 35N	18 20E
Fryvaldov = Jesenik	**53**	50 0N	17 8E
Fthiótis □	**69**	38 50N	22 25E
Fu	**72**	60 57N	14 44E
Fuan	**109**	27 9N	119 38E
Fucécchio	**62**	43 44N	10 51E
Fuch'ing	**109**	25 43N	119 22E
Fuchou, Fukien, China	**109**	26 5N	119 18E
Fuchou, Liaoning, China	**107**	39 45N	121 45E
Fuchū	**110**	34 34N	133 14E
Fūchū	**111**	35 40N	139 29E
Fuch'üan	**108**	26 42N	107 33E
Fuch'uan	**109**	24 50N	111 16E
Fucino, L.	**44**	42 0N	13 30E
Fuencaliente	**57**	38 25N	4 18W
Fuengirola	**57**	36 32N	4 41W
Fuente-Alamo	**59**	38 44N	1 24W
Fuente de Cantos	**57**	38 15N	6 18W
Fuente de San Esteban, La	**56**	40 49N	6 15W
Fuente del Maestre	**57**	38 31N	6 28W
Fuente el Fresno	**57**	39 14N	3 46W
Fuente Ovejuna	**57**	38 15N	5 25W
Fuentes de Andalucía	**57**	37 28N	5 20W
Fuentes de Ebro	**58**	41 31N	0 38W
Fuentes de León	**57**	38 5N	6 32W
Fuentes de Oñoro	**56**	40 33N	6 52W
Fuentesaúco	**56**	41 15N	5 30W
Fuerte Olimpo	**172**	21 0S	58 0W
Fuerte, R.	**164**	26 0N	109 0W
Fuerteventura, I.	**116**	28 30N	14 0W
Fuertey	**38**	53 37N	8 16W
Fufeng	**106**	34 20N	107 51E
Fŭget	**70**	45 52N	22 10E
Fŭget, Munţii	**70**	45 50N	22 9E
Fugløysund	**74**	70 15N	20 20E
Fŭgŭraş	**70**	45 48N	24 58E
Fŭgŭraş, Munţii	**70**	45 40N	24 40E
Fuhai	**105**	47 6N	87 23E
Fuhsien, Liaoning, China	**107**	39 38N	122 0E
Fuhsien, Shensi, China	**106**	36 2N	109 20E
Fuhsingchen	**108**	22 47N	101 5E
Fujaira	**93**	25 7N	56 18E
Fuji	**111**	35 9N	138 39E
Fuji-no-miya	**111**	35 20N	138 40E
Fuji-San	**111**	35 22N	138 44E
Fuji-yoshida	**111**	35 50N	138 46E
Fujieda	**111**	34 52N	138 16E
Fujioka	**111**	36 15N	139 5E
Fujisawa	**111**	35 22N	139 29E
Fukien □	**109**	26 0N	117 30E
Fukou	**106**	34 3N	114 27E
Fuku	**106**	39 2N	111 3E
Fukuchiyama	**111**	35 25N	135 9E
Fukui	**111**	36 0N	136 10E
Fukui-ken □	**111**	36 0N	136 12E
Fukuma	**110**	33 46N	130 28E
Fukung	**108**	26 58N	98 54E
Fukuoka	**110**	33 30N	130 30E
Fukuoka-ken □	**110**	33 30N	131 0E
Fukuroi	**111**	34 45N	137 55E
Fukushima	**112**	37 30N	140 15E
Fukushima-ken □	**112**	37 30N	140 15E
Fukuyama	**110**	34 35N	133 20E
Fŭlciu	**70**	46 17N	28 7E
Fulda	**48**	50 32N	9 41E
Fullerton, Calif., U.S.A.	**163**	33 52N	117 58W
Fullerton, Nebr., U.S.A.	**158**	41 25N	98 0W
Fulmar, oilfield	**19**	56 30N	2 8E
Fülöpszállás	**53**	46 49N	19 16E
Fŭlticeni	**70**	47 21N	26 20W
Fulton, Mo., U.S.A.	**158**	38 50N	91 55W
Fulton, N.Y., U.S.A.	**162**	43 20N	76 22W
Fuluälven	**72**	61 18N	13 4E
Fulufjället	**72**	61 32N	12 41E
Fulungch'üan	**107**	44 24N	124 37E
Fülüpszállás	**53**	46 49N	19 16E
Fumay	**43**	50 0N	4 40E
Fumbusi	**121**	10 25N	1 20W
Fumel	**44**	44 30N	0 58E
Fumin	**108**	25 14N	102 29E
Funabashi	**111**	35 45N	140 0E
Funafuti, I.	**130**	8 30S	179 0E
Funchal	**116**	32 45N	16 55W
Fundación	**174**	10 31N	74 11W
Fundão, Brazil	**171**	19 55S	40 24W
Fundão, Port.	**56**	40 8N	7 30W
Fundu	**127**	14 58S	30 14E
Fundy, B. of	**151**	45 0N	56 0W
Funes	**174**	1 0N	77 28W
Funing, Hopei, China	**107**	39 54N	119 12E
Funing, Yunnan, China	**108**	23 37N	105 36E
Funiu Shan	**106**	33 40N	112 30E
Funsi	**120**	10 21N	1 54W
Funtua	**121**	11 30N	7 18E
Fupien	**108**	31 18N	102 27E
Fup'ing	**106**	34 47N	109 7E
Fur	**73**	56 50N	9 0E
Furat, Nahr al	**92**	33 30N	43 0E
Furbero	**165**	20 22N	97 31W
Furka Pass	**51**	46 34N	8 35E
Furmanov	**81**	57 25N	41 3E
Furmanovka	**85**	44 17N	72 57E
Furmanovo	**83**	49 42N	49 25E
Furnas, Reprêsa de	**173**	20 50S	45 0W
Furneaux Group	**138**	40 10S	147 50E
Furness, Pen.	**32**	54 12N	3 10W
Fürstenau	**48**	52 32N	7 40E
Fürstenfeld	**52**	47 3N	16 3E
Fürstenfeldbruck	**49**	48 10N	11 15E
Fürstenwalde	**48**	52 20N	14 3E
Fürth	**49**	49 29N	11 0E
Fürth i. Wald	**49**	49 19N	12 51E
Furtwangen	**49**	48 3N	8 14E
Furudal	**72**	61 10N	15 11E
Furukawa	**111**	36 14N	137 11E
Furusund	**72**	59 40N	18 55E
Fury and Hecla Str.	**149**	69 56N	84 0W
Fusa	**71**	60 12N	5 37E
Fusagasugá	**174**	4 21N	74 22W
Fuscaldo	**65**	39 25N	16 1E
Fushan	**107**	37 30N	121 5E
Fushë Arrëzi	**68**	42 4N	20 2E
Fushun, Liaoning, China	**107**	41 50N	123 55E
Fushun, Szechwan, China	**108**	29 13N	105 0E
Fush'un Chiang, R.	**109**	30 5N	120 5E
Fusio	**51**	46 27N	8 40E
Füssen	**49**	47 35N	10 43E
Fusui	**108**	22 35N	107 58E
Fusung	**107**	42 15N	127 20E
Futago-Yama	**110**	33 35N	131 36E
Futing	**109**	27 15N	120 10E
Futuk	**121**	9 45N	10 56E
Futuna I.	**130**	14 25S	178 20E
Fŭurei	**70**	45 6N	27 19E
Fuwa	**122**	31 12N	30 33E
Fuyang	**109**	30 5N	119 56E
Fuyang Ho, R.	**106**	38 14N	116 5E
Fuyü	**107**	45 10N	124 50E
Fuyüan	**105**	47 40N	132 30E
Füzesgyarmat	**53**	47 21N	21 14E
Fwaka	**125**	12 5S	29 25E
Fylde	**32**	53 50N	2 58W
Fylingdales Moor	**33**	54 22N	0 32W
Fyn	**73**	55 20N	10 30E
Fyne, L.	**34**	56 0N	5 20W
Fyns Amt □	**73**	55 15N	10 30E
Fynshav	**73**	54 59N	9 59E
Fyresvatn	**71**	59 6N	8 10E
Fyvie	**37**	57 26N	2 24W

G

Name	Page	Lat.	Long.
Gaanda	**121**	10 10N	12 27E
Gaba	**123**	6 20N	35 7E
Gaba Tula	**82**	0 20N	38 35E
Gabah, C.	**91**	8 0N	50 0E
Gabarin	**121**	11 8N	10 27E
Gabbs	**163**	38 52N	117 55W
Gabela	**124**	11 0S	14 37E
Gaberones = Gaborone	**128**	24 37S	25 57E
Gabès	**119**	33 53N	10 2E
Gabès, Golfe de	**119**	34 0N	10 30E
Gabgaba, W.	**122**	22 10N	33 5E
Gabin	**54**	52 23N	19 41E
Gabon ■	**124**	0 10S	10 0E
Gaborone	**128**	24 37S	25 57E
Gabrovo	**67**	42 52N	25 27E
Gacé	**42**	48 49N	0 20E
Gach Saran	**93**	30 15N	50 45E
Gacko	**66**	43 10N	18 33E
Gada	**121**	13 38N	5 36E
Gadag	**97**	15 30N	75 45E
Gadamai	**123**	17 11N	36 10E
Gadap	**94**	25 5N	67 28E
Gadarwara	**95**	22 50N	78 50E
Gäddede	**74**	64 30N	14 15E
Gadebusch	**48**	53 41N	11 6E
Gadein	**123**	8 10N	28 45E
Gadhada	**94**	22 0N	71 35E
Gadmen	**51**	46 45N	8 16E
Gádor, Sierra de	**59**	36 57N	2 45W
Gadsden, Ala., U.S.A.	**157**	34 1N	86 0W
Gadsden, Ariz., U.S.A.	**161**	32 35N	114 47W
Gadwal	**96**	16 10N	77 50E
Gaerwen	**31**	53 13N	4 17W
Gaeta	**64**	41 12N	13 35E
Gaeta, G. di	**64**	41 0N	13 25E
Gaffney	**157**	35 10N	81 31W
Gafsa	**119**	34 24N	8 51E
Gagarin (Gzhatsk)	**80**	55 30N	35 0E
Gagetown	**151**	45 46N	66 29W
Gagino	**81**	55 15N	45 10E
Gagliano del Capo	**65**	39 50N	18 23E
Gagnef	**72**	60 36N	15 5E
Gagnoa	**120**	6 4N	5 55W
Gagnon	**151**	51 50N	68 5W
Gagnon, L.	**153**	62 3N	110 27W
Gagra	**83**	43 20N	40 10E
Gah	**44**	43 12N	0 27W
Gahini	**126**	1 50S	30 30E
Gahmar	**95**	25 27N	83 55E
Gaibandha	**98**	25 20N	89 36E
Gaïdhouronisi	**69**	34 53N	25 41E
Gail	**159**	32 48N	101 25W
Gail, R.	**52**	46 37N	13 15E
Gaillac	**44**	43 54N	1 54E
Gaillon	**42**	49 10N	1 20E
Gaima	**135**	8 9S	142 59E
Gainesville, Fla., U.S.A.	**157**	29 38N	82 20W
Gainesville, Ga., U.S.A.	**157**	34 17N	83 47W
Gainesville, Mo., U.S.A.	**159**	36 35N	92 26W
Gainesville, Tex., U.S.A.	**159**	33 40N	97 10W
Gainford	**33**	54 34N	1 44W
Gainsborough	**33**	53 23N	0 46W
Gairdner L.	**140**	31 30S	136 0E
Gairloch	**36**	57 42N	5 40W
Gairloch L.	**36**	57 43N	5 45W
Gairlochy	**36**	56 55N	5 0W
Gairsay, I.	**37**	59 4N	2 59W
Gais	**51**	47 22N	9 27E
Gaithersburg	**162**	39 9N	77 12W
Gaj	**66**	45 28N	17 3E
Gajale	**121**	11 25N	8 10E
Gajiram	**121**	12 29N	13 9E
Gakuch	**95**	36 7N	73 45E
Gal Oya Res.	**97**	8 5N	80 55E
Galachipa	**98**	22 8N	90 26E
Galadi	**121**	13 5N	6 20E
Galán, Cerro	**172**	25 55S	66 52W
Galana, R.	**126**	3 0S	39 10E
Galangue	**125**	13 48S	16 3E
Galanta	**53**	48 11N	17 45E
Galápagos, Is.	**131**	0 0	89 0W
Galas, R.	**101**	4 55N	101 57E
Galashiels	**35**	55 37N	2 50W
Galatás	**69**	37 30N	23 26E
Galatea	**142**	38 24S	176 45E
Galaţi	**70**	45 27N	28 2E
Galaţi □	**70**	45 45N	27 30E
Galatina	**65**	40 10N	18 10E
Galátone	**65**	40 8N	18 3E
Galax	**157**	36 42N	80 57W
Galaxídhion	**69**	38 22N	22 23E
Galbally	**39**	52 24N	8 17W
Galbraith	**138**	16 25S	141 30E
Galdhøpiggen	**71**	61 38N	8 18E
Galeana	**164**	24 50N	100 4W
Galela	**103**	1 50N	127 55E
Galena, Austral.	**137**	27 48S	114 42E
Galena, U.S.A.	**147**	64 42N	157 0W
Galeota Point	**167**	10 8N	61 0W
Galera	**59**	37 45N	2 33W
Galera, Pta. de la	**174**	10 48N	75 16W
Galesburg	**158**	40 57N	90 23W
Galey R.	**39**	52 30N	9 23W
Galgate	**32**	53 59N	2 47W
Galheirão, R.	**171**	12 23S	45 5W
Galheiros	**171**	13 18S	46 25W
Galicea Mare	**70**	44 4N	23 19E
Galich, R.S.F.S.R., U.S.S.R.	**81**	58 23N	42 18E
Galich, Uk., U.S.S.R.	**80**	49 10N	24 40E
Galiche	**67**	43 34N	23 50E
Galicia	**56**	42 43N	8 0W
Galijp	**46**	53 10N	5 58E
Galilee = Hagalil	**90**	32 53N	35 18E
Galilee, L.	**138**	22 20S	145 50E
Galite, Is. de la	**119**	37 30N	8 59E
Galivro Mts.	**161**	32 40N	110 30W
Gallan Hd.	**36**	58 14N	7 0W
Gallarate	**62**	45 40N	8 48E
Gallatin	**157**	36 24N	86 27W
Galle	**97**	6 5N	80 10E
Gallego	**164**	29 49N	106 22W
Gállego, R.	**58**	42 23N	0 30W
Gallegos, R.	**176**	51 50S	71 0W
Galley Hd.	**39**	51 32N	8 56W
Galliate	**62**	45 27N	8 44E
Gallinas, Pta.	**174**	12 28N	71 40W
Gallipoli	**65**	40 8N	18 0E
Gallipoli = Gelibolu	**68**	40 28N	26 43E
Gallipolis	**156**	38 50N	82 10W
Gällivare	**74**	67 9N	20 40E
Gällö	**72**	62 56N	15 15E
Gallo, C. di	**64**	38 13N	13 19E
Gallocanta, Laguna de	**58**	40 58N	1 30W
Galloway	**34**	55 0N	4 25W
Galloway, Mull of	**34**	54 38N	4 50W
Gallup	**161**	35 30N	108 54W
Gallur	**58**	41 52N	1 19W
Gallyaaral	**85**	40 2N	67 35E
Galmi	**121**	13 58N	5 41E
Gal'on	**90**	31 38N	34 51E
Galong	**141**	34 37S	148 34E
Galoya	**93**	8 10N	80 55E
Galston	**34**	55 36N	4 22W
Galt, Can.	**150**	43 21N	80 19W
Galt, U.S.A.	**163**	38 15N	121 18W
Galtström	**72**	62 10N	17 30E
Galtür	**52**	46 58N	10 11E
Galty Mts.	**39**	52 22N	8 10W
Galtymore, Mt.	**39**	52 22N	8 12W
Galva	**158**	41 10N	90 0W
Galve de Sorbe	**58**	41 13N	3 10W
Galveston	**159**	29 15N	94 48W
Galveston B.	**159**	29 30N	94 50W
Gálvez, Argent.	**172**	32 0S	61 20W
Gálvez, Spain	**57**	39 42N	4 16W
Galway	**39**	53 16N	9 4W
Galway □	**38**	53 16N	9 3W
Galway B.	**39**	53 10N	9 20W
Gam, R.	**100**	21 55N	105 12E
Gamagōri	**111**	34 50N	137 14E
Gamare, L.	**123**	11 32N	41 40E
Gamarra	**174**	8 20N	73 45W
Gamawa	**121**	12 10N	10 31E
Gambaga	**121**	10 30N	0 28W
Gambat	**94**	27 17N	68 26E
Gambela	**123**	8 14N	34 38E
Gambell	**147**	63 55N	171 50W
Gambia ■	**120**	13 25N	16 0W
Gambia, R.	**120**	13 20N	15 45W
Gambier, C.	**136**	11 56S	130 57E
Gambier Is.	**140**	35 3S	136 30E
Gamboli	**94**	29 53N	68 24E
Gamboma	**124**	1 55S	15 52E
Gamboola	**138**	16 29S	143 43E
Gameleira	**170**	7 50S	50 0W
Gamerco	**161**	35 33N	108 56W
Gamleby	**73**	57 54N	16 20W
Gamlingay	**29**	52 9N	0 11W
Gammelgarn	**171**	57 24N	18 49E
Gammon, R.	**153**	51 24N	95 44W
Gamōda-Saki	**110**	33 50N	134 45E
Gan (Addu Atoll)	**87**	0 10S	71 10E
Gan Shemu'el	**90**	32 28N	34 56E
Gan Yavne	**90**	31 48N	34 42E
Ganado, Ariz., U.S.A.	**161**	35 46N	109 41W
Ganado, Tex., U.S.A.	**159**	29 4N	96 31W
Gananoque	**150**	44 20N	76 10W
Ganaveh	**93**	29 35N	50 35E
Gand	**47**	51 2N	3 37E
Gandak, R.	**95**	27 0N	84 8E
Gandava	**94**	28 32N	67 32E
Gander	**151**	48 18N	54 29W
Gander L.	**151**	48 58N	54 35W
Ganderowe Falls	**127**	17 20S	29 10E
Gandesa	**58**	41 3N	0 26E
Gand = Gent	**47**	51 2N	3 37E
Gandhi Sagar	**94**	24 40N	75 40E
Gandi	**121**	12 55N	5 49E
Gandía	**59**	38 58N	0 9W
Gandino	**62**	45 50N	9 52E
Gandole	**121**	8 28N	11 35E
Gandu	**171**	13 45S	39 30W
Ganedidalem = Gani	**103**	0 48S	128 14E
Ganetti	**122**	18 0N	31 10E
Ganga, Mouths of the	**95**	21 30N	90 0E
Ganga, R.	**95**	25 0N	88 0E
Ganganagar	**94**	29 56N	73 56E
Gangapur	**94**	26 32N	76 37E
Gangara	**121**	14 35N	8 40E
Gangavati	**97**	15 30N	76 36E
Gangaw	**98**	22 5N	94 15E
Ganges	**44**	43 56N	3 42E
Ganges = Ganga, R.	**95**	25 0N	88 0E
Gangoh	**94**	29 46N	77 18E
Gangtok	**98**	27 20N	88 37E
Ganj	**95**	27 45N	78 47E
Ganmain	**141**	34 47S	147 1E
Gannat	**44**	46 7N	3 11E
Gannett Pk.	**160**	43 15N	109 47W
Gannvalley	**158**	44 3N	98 57W
Ganserdorf	**53**	48 20N	16 43E
Ganta (Gompa)	**120**	7 15N	8 59W
Gantheaume B.	**137**	27 40S	114 10E
Gantheaume, C.	**140**	36 4S	137 25E
Gantsevichi	**80**	52 42N	26 30E
Ganyushkino	**83**	46 35N	49 20E
Ganzi	**123**	4 30N	31 15E
Gao □	**121**	18 0N	1 0E
Gao Bang	**101**	22 37N	106 18E
Gaoua	**120**	10 20N	3 8W
Gaoual	**120**	11 45N	13 25W
Gaouz	**118**	31 52N	4 20W
Gap	**45**	44 33N	6 5E
Gar Dzong	**93**	32 20N	79 55E
Gara, L.	**38**	53 57N	8 26W
Garachiné	**166**	8 0N	78 12W
Garanhuns	**170**	8 50S	36 30W
Garawe	**120**	4 35N	8 0W
Garba Tula	**126**	0 30N	38 32E
Garber	**159**	36 30N	97 36W
Garberville	**160**	40 11N	123 50W
Garboldisham	**29**	52 24N	0 57E
Garça	**171**	22 14S	49 37W
Garças, R.	**170**	8 43S	39 41W
Gard □	**45**	44 2N	4 10E
Garda, L. di	**62**	45 40N	10 40E
Gardanne	**45**	43 27N	5 27E
Garde L.	**153**	62 50N	106 13W
Gardelegen	**48**	52 32N	11 21E
Garden City, Kans., U.S.A.	**159**	38 0N	100 45W
Garden City, Tex., U.S.A.	**159**	31 52N	101 28W
Garden Grove	**163**	33 47N	117 55W
Gardenstown	**37**	57 40N	2 20W
Gardez	**94**	33 31N	68 59E
Gardhiki	**69**	38 50N	21 55E
Gardian	**117**	15 45N	19 40E
Gardiner, Can.	**150**	49 19N	81 2W
Gardiner, Mont., U.S.A.	**160**	45 3N	110 53W
Gardiner, New Mexico, U.S.A.	**159**	36 55N	104 29W
Gardiners I.	**162**	41 4N	72 5W
Gardner	**162**	42 35N	72 0W
Gardner Canal	**152**	53 27N	128 8W
Gardnerville	**160**	38 59N	119 47W
Gardo	**91**	9 18N	49 20E
Gare, L.	**34**	56 1N	4 50W
Garelochhead	**34**	56 7N	4 50W
Gareloi I.	**147**	51 49N	178 50W
Garešnica	**66**	45 36N	16 56E
Garéssio	**62**	44 12N	8 1E
Garey	**163**	34 53N	120 19W
Garfield, Utah, U.S.A.	**160**	40 45N	112 15W
Garfield, Wash., U.S.A.	**160**	47 3N	117 8W
Garforth	**33**	53 48N	1 22W
Gargaliánoi	**69**	37 4N	21 38E
Gargano, Mte.	**65**	41 43N	15 43E
Gargans, Mt.	**44**	45 37N	1 39E
Gargantua, C.	**150**	47 35N	85 0W
Gargoune	**121**	15 56N	0 13E
Gargrave	**32**	53 58N	2 7W
Garhshankar	**94**	31 13N	76 11E
Gari	**84**	59 26N	62 21E
Garibaldi	**152**	49 56N	123 15W
Garibaldi Prov. Park	**152**	49 50N	122 40W

Garies 125 30 32S 17 59E
Garigliano, R. 64 41 13N 13 44E
Garissa 126 0 25S 39 40E
Garissa □ 126 0 20S 40 0E
Garkida 121 10 27N 12 36E
Garko 121 11 45N 8 53E
Garland 160 41 47N 112 10W
Garlasco 62 45 11N 8 55E
Garlieston 34 54 47N 4 22W
Garm 85 39 0N 70 20E
Garmab 94 32 50N 65 30E
Garmisch-Partenkirchen 49 47 30N 11 5E
Garmo 126 61 51N 8 48E
Garmouth 37 57 40N 3 8W
Garmsar 93 35 20N 52 25E
Garner 158 43 4N 93 37W
Garnett 158 38 18N 95 12W
Garo Hills 95 25 30N 90 30E
Garoe 91 8 35N 48 40E
Garoke 139 36 45S 141 30E
Garona, R. 58 42 55N 0 45E
Garonne, R. 44 45 2N 0 36W
Garoua (Garwa) 121 9 19N 13 21E
Garraway 120 4 35N 8 0W
Garrel 48 52 58N 7 59E
Garrigues 44 43 40N 3 30E
Garrison, Ireland 38 54 25N 8 5W
Garrison, Mont., U.S.A. 160 46 37N 112 56W
Garrison, N.D., U.S.A. 158 31 50N 94 28W
Garrison, Tex., U.S.A. 159 47 39N 101 27W
Garrison Res. 158 47 30N 102 0W
Garron Pt. 38 55 3N 6 0W
Garrovillas 57 39 40N 6 33W
Garrucha 59 37 11N 1 49W
Garry L., Can. 148 65 58N 100 18W
Garry L., U.K. 37 57 5N 4 52W
Garry, R. 37 56 47N 3 47W
Garsdale Head 32 54 19N 2 19W
Garsen 124 2 20S 40 5E
Garson L., Alta., Can. 153 56 19N 110 2W
Garson L., Sask., Can. 153 56 20N 110 1W
Garstang 32 53 53N 2 47W
Garston 32 53 21N 2 55W
Gartempe, R. 44 46 47N 0 49E
Gartok 93 31 59N 80 30E
Gartz 48 54 17N 13 21E
Garu, Ghana 121 10 55N 0 20W
Garu, Nigeria 121 13 35N 5 25E
Garub 128 26 37S 16 0E
Garupá 170 1 25S 51 35W
Garut 103 7 14S 107 53E
Garvagh 38 55 0N 6 41W
Garvaghey 38 54 29N 7 8W
Garvald 35 55 55N 2 39W
Garváo 57 37 42N 8 21W
Garvellachs, Is. 34 56 14N 5 48W
Garvie Mts. 143 45 30S 168 50E
Garwa 95 24 11N 83 47E
Garwolin 54 51 55N 21 38E
Gary 156 41 35N 87 20W
Garzón 174 2 10N 75 40W
Gasan Kuli 76 37 40N 54 20E
Gascogne 44 43 45N 0 20E
Gascogne, G. de 58 44 0N 2 0W
Gascony = Gascogne 44 43 45N 0 20E
Gascoyne Junc. Teleg. Off. 137 25 2S 115 17E
Gascoyne, R. 137 24 52S 113 37E
Gascueña 58 40 18N 2 31W
Gash, W. 123 15 0N 37 15E
Gashaka 121 7 20N 11 29E
Gasherbrum 95 35 40N 76 40E
Gashua 121 12 54N 11 0E
Gasmata 138 6 15S 150 30E
Gaspé 151 48 52N 64 30W
Gaspé, C. 151 48 48N 64 7W
Gaspé Pass. 151 49 10N 64 0W
Gaspé Pen. 151 48 45N 65 40W
Gaspésie, Parc Prov. de la 151 48 55N 65 50W
Gaspesian Prov. Park 151 49 0N 66 45W
Gassaway 156 38 42N 80 43W
Gasselte 46 52 58N 6 48E
Gasselternijveen 46 52 59N 6 51E
Gássino Torinese 62 45 8N 7 50E
Gassol 121 8 34N 10 25E
Gastonia 157 35 17N 81 10W
Gastoúni 69 37 51N 21 15E
Gastoúri 68 39 34N 19 54E
Gastre 176 42 10S 69 15W
Gata, C. de 59 36 41N 2 13W
Gata, Sierra de 56 40 20N 6 20W
Gataga, R. 152 58 35N 126 59W
Gatchina 80 59 35N 30 0E
Gatehouse of Fleet 34 54 53N 4 10W
Gateshead 35 54 57N 1 37W
Gatesville 159 31 29N 97 45W
Gaths 127 26 2S 30 32E
Gatico 172 22 40S 70 20W
Gatinais 43 48 5N 2 40E
Gâtine, Hauteurs de 44 46 35N 0 45W
Gatineau, Parc de la 150 45 20N 76 0W
Gatineau, R. 150 45 27N 75 42W
Gatley 32 53 25N 2 15W
Gatooma 125 18 20S 29 52E
Gattinara 62 45 37N 8 22E
Gatun, L. 166 9 7N 79 56W
Gaucín 57 36 31N 5 19W
Gaud-i-Zirreh 93 29 45N 62 0E
Gauer L. 153 57 0N 97 50W
Gauhati 98 26 10N 91 45E
Gauja, R. 80 57 10N 24 45E
Gaula, R. 71 62 57N 11 0E
Gaurain-Ramecroix 47 50 36N 3 30E
Gaurdak 85 37 50N 66 4E
Gaussberg, Mt. 13 66 45S 89 0E
Gausta 71 59 50N 8 37E
Gausta, Mt. 75 59 48N 8 40E
Gavá 58 41 18N 2 0E
Gavarnie 44 42 44N 0 3W
Gavater 93 25 10N 61 23E
Gavdhopoúla 69 34 56N 24 0E
Gávdhos 69 34 50N 24 5E
Gavere 47 50 55N 3 40E
Gavião 57 39 28N 7 50W
Gaviota 163 34 29N 120 13W
Gavle 72 60 41N 17 13E
Gävle 72 60 40N 17 9E
Gävleborgs Lan □ 72 61 20N 16 15E
Gavorrano 62 42 55N 10 55E
Gavray 42 49 55N 1 20W
Gavrilov Yam 81 57 10N 39 37E
Gávrion 69 37 54N 24 44E
Gawachab 128 27 4S 17 55E
Gawai 98 27 56N 97 40E
Gawilgarh Hills 96 21 15N 76 45E
Gawler 140 34 30S 138 42E
Gawler Ranges 136 32 30S 135 45E
Gawthwaite 32 54 16N 3 6W
Gay 84 51 27N 58 27E
Gaya, India 95 24 47N 85 4E
Gaya, Niger 121 11 58N 3 28E
Gaya, Nigeria 121 11 57N 9 0E
Gaylord 156 45 1N 84 35W
Gayndah 139 25 35S 151 39E
Gayny 84 60 18N 54 19E
Gaysin 82 48 57N 28 25E
Gayton 29 52 45N 0 35E
Gayvoron 82 48 22N 29 45E
Gaywood 29 52 46N 0 26E
Gaza 90 31 30N 34 28E
Gaza □ 129 23 10S 32 45E
Gaza Strip 90 31 29N 34 25E
Gazaoua 121 13 32N 7 55E
Gazelle Pen. 135 4 40S 152 0E
Gazi 126 1 3N 24 30E
Gaziantep 92 37 6N 37 23E
Gbanga 120 7 19N 9 13W
Gbekebo 121 6 26N 4 48E
Gboko 121 7 17N 9 4E
Gbongan 121 7 28N 4 20E
Gcuwa 129 32 20S 28 11E
Gdansk 54 54 22N 18 40E
Gdansk □ 54 54 10N 18 30E
Gdanska, Zatoka 54 54 30N 19 20E
Gdov 80 58 40N 27 55E
Gdynia 54 54 35N 18 33E
Geashill 39 53 14N 7 20W
Gebe, I. 103 0 5N 129 25E
Gebeit Mine 122 21 3N 36 29E
Gecoa 123 7 30N 35 18E
Gedaref 123 14 2N 35 28E
Gedera 90 31 49N 34 46E
Gedinne 47 49 59N 4 56E
Gedney 29 52 47N 0 5W
Gedo 123 9 2N 37 25E
Gèdre 44 42 47N 0 2E
Gedser 73 54 35N 11 55E
Gedser Odde, C. 73 54 30N 12 5E
Geel 47 51 10N 4 59E
Geelong 140 38 10S 144 22E
Geelvink Chan. 137 28 30S 114 0E
Geer, R. 47 50 51N 5 42E
Geestenseth 48 53 31N 8 51E
Geesthacht 48 53 25N 10 20E
Geffen 46 51 44N 5 28E
Geh 126 26 10N 60 0E
Geia 90 31 38N 34 37E
Geidam 121 12 57N 11 57E
Geikie, R. 153 57 45N 103 52W
Geilenkirchen 48 50 58N 6 8E
Geili 123 16 1N 32 37E
Geilo 71 60 32N 8 14E
Geinica 53 48 51N 20 55E
Geisingen 49 47 55N 8 37E
Geita 126 2 48S 32 12E
Geita □ 126 2 50S 32 10E
Gel, R. 123 7 5N 29 10E
Gel River 123 7 5N 29 10E
Gela, Golfo di 65 37 0N 14 8E
Geladi 91 6 59N 46 30E
Gelderland □ 46 52 5N 6 10E
Geldermalsen 46 51 53N 5 17E
Geldern 48 51 32N 6 18E
Geldrop 47 51 25N 5 32E
Geleen 47 50 57N 5 49E
Gelehun 120 8 20N 11 40W
Gelendzhik 82 44 33N 38 17E
Gelibolu 68 40 28N 26 43E
Gelnhausen 49 50 12N 9 12E
Gelsenkirchen 48 51 30N 7 5E
Gelting 48 54 43N 9 53E
Gemas 101 2 37N 102 36E
Gembloux 47 50 34N 4 43E
Gembu 121 8 58N 12 31E
Gemena 124 3 20N 19 40E
Gemerek 92 39 15N 36 10E
Gemert 47 51 33N 5 41E
Gemiston 128 26 15S 28 10E
Gemlik 92 40 28N 29 13E
Gemmi 50 46 25N 7 37E
Gemona del Friuli 63 46 16N 13 7E
Gemsa 122 27 39N 33 35E
Gemu-Gofa □ 123 5 40N 36 40E
Gemünden 49 50 3N 9 43E
Genale 123 6 0N 39 30E
Genappe 47 50 37N 4 27E
Gençay 44 46 23N 0 23E
Gendringen 46 51 52N 6 21E
Gendt 46 51 53N 5 59E
Geneina, Gebel 122 29 2N 33 55E
Genemuiden 46 52 38N 6 2E
General Acha 172 37 20S 64 38W
General Alvear, B. A., Argent. 172 36 0S 60 0W
General Alvear, Mend., Argent. 172 35 0S 67 40W
General Artigas 172 26 52S 56 16W
General Belgrano 172 36 0S 58 30W
General Cabrera 172 32 53S 63 58W
General Cepeda 164 25 23N 101 27W
General Guido 172 36 40S 57 50W
General Juan Madariaga 172 37 0S 57 0W
General La Madrid 172 37 30S 61 10W
General MacArthur 103 11 18N 125 28E
General Martin Mignuel de Güemes 172 24 50S 65 0W
General Paz 172 27 45S 57 36W
General Paz, L. 176 44 0S 72 0W
General Pico 172 35 45S 63 50W
General Pinedo 172 27 15S 61 30W
General Pinto 172 34 45S 61 50W
General Roca 176 30 0S 67 40W
General Sampaio 170 4 2S 39 29W
General Santos 103 6 12N 125 14E
General Toshevo 67 43 42N 28 6E
General Treviño 165 26 14N 99 29W
General Trías 164 28 21N 106 22W
General Viamonte 172 35 1S 61 3W
General Villegas 172 35 0S 63 0W
Generoso, Mte. 51 45 56N 9 2E
Genesee 160 46 31N 116 59W
Genesee, R. 156 41 35N 78 0W
Geneseo, Ill., U.S.A. 158 41 25N 90 10W
Geneseo, Kans., U.S.A. 158 38 32N 98 8W
Geneva, Ala., U.S.A. 157 31 2N 85 52W
Geneva, Nebr., U.S.A. 158 40 35N 97 35W
Geneva, N.Y., U.S.A. 162 42 53N 77 0W
Geneva, Ohio, U.S.A. 156 41 49N 80 58W
Geneva = Genève 50 46 12N 6 9E
Geneva, L. 156 42 38N 88 30W
Geneva, L. = Léman, Lac 50 46 26N 6 30E
Genève 50 46 12N 6 9E
Genève □ 50 46 10N 6 10E
Gengenbach 49 48 25N 8 0E
Genichesk 82 46 12N 34 50E
Genil, R. 57 37 12N 3 50W
Génissiat, Barrage de 45 46 1N 5 48E
Genk 47 50 58N 5 32E
Genkai-Nada 110 34 0N 130 0E
Genlis 43 47 15N 5 12E
Gennargentu, Mt. del 64 40 0N 9 10E
Gennep 47 51 41N 5 59E
Gennes 42 47 20N 0 17W
Genoa, Austral. 141 37 29S 149 35E
Genoa, Nebr., U.S.A. 158 41 31N 97 44W
Genoa, N.Y., U.S.A. 162 42 40N 76 32W
Genoa = Génova 62 44 24N 8 57E
Génova 62 44 24N 8 56E
Génova, Golfo di 62 44 0N 9 0E
Gent 47 51 2N 3 37E
Gentbrugge 47 51 3N 3 47E
Genteng 103 7 25S 106 23E
Genthin 48 52 24N 12 10E
Gentio do Ouro 170 11 25S 42 30W
Geographe B. 137 33 30S 113 20E
Geographe Chan. 137 24 30S 113 0E
Geokchay 83 40 42N 47 43E
George, Can. 151 46 12N 62 32W
George, S. Afr. 128 33 58S 22 29E
George, L., New South Wales, Austral. 141 35 10S 149 25E
George, L., S. Austral., Austral. 140 37 25S 140 0E
George, L., W. A., Austral. 137 22 45S 123 40E
George, L., Uganda 126 0 5N 30 10E
George, L., Fla., U.S.A. 157 29 15N 81 35W
George, L., N.Y., U.S.A. 162 43 30N 73 30W
George, Mt. 137 25 17S 119 0E
George, R. 151 58 49N 66 10W
George River = Port Nouveau 149 58 30N 65 50W
George Sound 143 44 52S 167 25E
George Town, Austral. 138 41 5S 146 49E
George Town, Bahamas 166 23 33N 75 47W
George Town, Malay. 101 5 25N 100 19E
George V Coast 13 67 0S 148 0E
George West 159 28 18N 98 5W
Georgetown, Austral. 133 18 17S 143 33E
Georgetown, Ont., Can. 150 43 40N 80 0W
Georgetown, P.E.I., Can. 151 46 13N 62 24W
Georgetown, Cay. Is. 166 19 20N 81 24W
Georgetown, Gambia 120 13 30N 14 47W
Georgetown, Guyana 174 6 50N 58 12W
Georgetown, Colo., U.S.A. 160 39 46N 105 49W
Georgetown, Del., U.S.A. 162 38 42N 75 23W
Georgetown, N.Y., U.S.A. 162 42 46N 75 44W
Georgetown, Ohio, U.S.A. 156 38 50N 83 50W
Georgetown, S.C., U.S.A. 157 33 22N 79 15W
Georgetown, Tex., U.S.A. 159 30 45N 98 10W
Georgi Dimitrov 67 42 15N 23 54E
Georgia □ 156 32 0N 82 0W
Georgia, Str. of 152 49 25N 124 0W
Georgian B. 150 45 15N 81 0W
Georgian S.S.R. □ 83 41 0N 45 0E
Georgievsk 83 44 12N 43 28E
Georgina Downs 138 21 10S 137 40E
Georgina, R. 138 23 30S 139 47E
Georgiu-Dezh 81 51 3N 39 20E
Georgiyevka 85 43 3N 74 43E
Gera 48 50 53N 12 5E
Gera □ 48 50 45N 11 30E
Geraardsbergen 47 50 45N 3 53E
Geral de Goias, Serra 171 12 0S 46 0W
Geral do Paranã Serra 171 15 0S 47 0W
Geral, Serra, Bahia, Brazil 171 14 0S 41 0W
Geral, Serra, Goiás, Brazil 170 11 15S 46 30W
Geral, Serra, Santa Catarina, Brazil 173 26 25S 50 0W
Geraldine, N.Z. 143 44 5S 171 15E
Geraldine, U.S.A. 160 47 45N 110 18W
Geraldton, Austral. 137 28 48S 114 32E
Geraldton, Can. 150 49 44N 86 59W
Geranium 140 35 23S 140 11E
Gerardmer 43 48 3N 6 50E
Gerdine, Mt. 147 61 32N 152 30W
Gerede 82 40 45N 32 10E
Gérgal 59 37 7N 2 31W
Geriban 91 7 10N 48 55E
Gerik 101 5 25N 100 8E
Gering 158 41 51N 103 40W
Gerizim 90 32 13N 35 15E
Gerlach 160 40 43N 119 27W
Gerlachovka, Mt. 53 49 11N 20 7E
Gerlafingen 50 47 10N 7 34E
Gerlev 73 56 36N 10 9E
Gerlogubi 91 6 53N 45 3E
German Planina 66 42 33N 22 0E
Germansen Landing 152 55 43N 124 40W
Germany, East ■ 48 52 0N 12 0E
Germany, West ■ 48 52 0N 9 0E
Germersheim 49 49 13N 8 0E
Germiston 125 26 11S 28 10E
Gernsheim 49 49 44N 8 29E
Gero 111 35 48N 137 14E
Gerogery 141 35 50S 147 1E
Gerolstein 49 50 12N 6 24E
Gerona 58 41 58N 2 46E
Gerona □ 58 42 11N 2 30E
Gérouville 47 49 37N 5 26E
Gerrans B. 30 50 12N 4 57W
Gerrard 152 50 30N 117 17W
Gerrards Cross 29 51 35N 0 32W
Gerrild 73 56 30N 10 50E
Gerringong 141 34 46S 150 47E
Gers □ 44 43 35N 0 38E
Gersau 51 47 0N 8 32E
Gersoppa Falls 97 14 12N 74 46E
Gerufa 128 19 8S 26 0E
Gerze 92 41 45N 35 10E
Geseke 48 51 38N 8 29E
Geser 103 3 50N 130 35E
Gesso, R. 62 44 21N 7 20E
Gesves 47 50 24N 5 4E
Getafe 56 40 18N 3 44W
Gethsémani 151 50 13N 60 40W
Gettysburg, Pa., U.S.A. 156 39 47N 77 18W
Gettysburg, S.D., U.S.A. 158 45 3N 99 56W
Getz Ice Shelf 13 75 0S 130 0W
Geul, R. 47 50 53N 5 43E
Geurie 141 32 22S 148 50E
Gevaudan 44 44 40N 3 40E
Gevgelija 66 41 9N 22 30E
Gévora, R. 57 38 53N 6 57W
Gex 45 46 21N 6 3E
Geyikli 68 39 50N 26 12E
Geyser 160 47 17N 110 30W
Geysir 74 64 19N 20 18W
Geyve 82 40 32N 30 18E
Ghaghara, R. 95 26 0N 84 20E
Ghail 92 21 40N 46 20E
Ghalla, Wadi el 123 12 0N 28 58E
Ghana ■ 121 6 0N 1 0W
Ghandhi Dam 93 24 30N 75 35E
Ghansor 95 22 39N 80 1E
Ghanzi 128 21 50S 21 45E
Ghanzi □ 128 21 50S 21 45E
Gharbîya, Es Sahrâ el 122 27 40N 26 30E
Ghard Abû Muharik 122 26 50N 30 0E
Ghardaïa 118 32 31N 3 37E
Gharyān 119 32 10N 13 0E
Ghāt 119 24 59N 10 19E
Ghat Ghat 92 26 0N 45 5E
Ghatal 95 22 40N 87 46E
Ghatampur 95 26 8N 80 13E
Ghatprabha, R. 96 16 15N 75 20E
Ghazal, Bahr el 117 15 0N 17 0E
Ghazaouet 118 35 8N 1 50W
Ghaziabad 94 28 42N 77 35E
Ghazipur 95 25 38N 83 35E
Ghazni 94 33 30N 68 17E
Ghazni □ 93 33 0N 68 0E
Ghedi 62 45 24N 10 16E
Ghelari 70 45 42N 22 45E
Ghelinsor 91 6 35N 46 55E
Ghent = Gand 47 51 4N 3 43E

Gheorghe Gheorghiu-Dej 70 46 17N 26 47 E
Gheorgheni 70 46 43N 25 41 E
Ghergani 70 44 37N 25 37 E
Gherla 70 47 0N 23 57 E
Ghilarza 64 40 8N 8 50 E
Ghisonaccia 45 42 1N 9 26 E
Ghizao 94 33 30N 65 59 E
Ghizar, R. 95 36 10N 73 4 E
Ghod, R. 96 18 40N 74 15 E
Ghorat □ 93 34 0N 64 20 E
Ghost River, Can. 150 50 10N 91 27W
Ghost River, Ont., Can. 150 51 25N 83 20W
Ghot Ogrein 122 31 10N 25 20 E
Ghotaru 94 27 20N 70 1 E
Ghotki 94 28 5N 69 30 E
Ghudāmis 119 30 11N 9 29 E
Ghugri 95 22 39N 80 41 E
Ghugus 96 20 0N 79 0 E
Ghulam Mohammad Barrage 94 25 30N 67 0 E
Ghuriān 93 34 17N 61 25 E
Gia Dinh 101 10 49N 106 42 E
Gia Lai = Pleiku 101 14 3N 108 0 E
Gia Nghia 101 12 0N 107 42 E
Gia Ngoc 100 14 50N 108 58 E
Gia Vuc 100 14 42N 108 34 E
Giamda Dzong 99 30 3N 93 2 E
Giannutri, I. 62 42 16N 11 5 E
Giant Forest 163 36 36N 118 43W
Giant Mts. = Krkonose 52 50 50N 16 10 E
Giant's Causeway 38 55 15N 6 30W
Giarabub = Jaghbub 117 29 42N 24 38 E
Giarre 65 37 44N 15 10 E
Giaveno 62 45 3N 7 20 E
Gibara 166 21 0N 76 20W
Gibbon 158 40 49N 98 45W
Gibe, R. 123 6 25N 36 10 E
Gibellina 64 37 48N 13 0 E
Gibeon 128 25 7 S 17 45 E
Gibraléon 57 37 23N 6 58W
Gibraltar 57 36 7N 5 22W
Gibraltar Pt. 33 53 6N 0 20 E
Gibraltar, Str. of 57 35 55N 5 40W
Gibson Des. 136 24 0 S 126 0 E
Gibsons 152 49 24N 123 32W
Gida. G. 12 72 30N 77 0 E
Giddalur 97 15 20N 78 57 E
Gidde 123 5 40N 37 25 E
Giddings 159 30 11N 96 58W
Gide 123 9 52N 35 5 E
Gien 43 47 40N 2 36 E
Giessen 48 50 34N 8 40 E
Gieten 46 53 0N 6 46 E
Gif-sur-Yvette 46 48 42N 2 8 E
Gifatin, Geziret 122 27 10N 33 50 E
Gifford 35 55 54N 2 45W
Gifford Creek 137 24 3 S 116 16 E
Gifhorn 48 52 29N 10 32 E
Gifu 111 35 30N 136 45 E
Gifu-ken □ 111 36 0N 137 0 E
Gigant 83 46 28N 41 30 E
Giganta, Sa. de la 164 25 30N 111 30W
Gigen 67 43 40N 24 28 E
Giggleswick 32 54 5N 2 19W
Gigha, I. 39 55 42N 5 45W
Giglio, I. 62 42 20N 10 52 E
Gignac 44 43 39N 3 32 E
Gigüela, R. 58 39 47N 3 0W
Gijón 56 43 32N 5 42W
Gil I. 152 53 12N 129 15W
Gila Bend 161 33 0N 112 46W
Gila Bend Mts. 161 33 15N 113 0W
Gila, R. 161 33 5N 108 40W
Gilau 138 5 38 S 149 3 E
Gilbedi 121 13 40N 5 45 E
•Gilbert Is. 130 1 0 S 176 0 E
Gilbert Plains 153 51 9N 100 28W
Gilbert, R. 138 16 35 S 141 15 E
Gilbert River 138 18 9 S 142 52 E
Gilberton 138 19 16 S 143 35 E
Gilbués 170 9 50 S 45 21W
Gilford 38 54 23N 6 20W
Gilford I. 152 50 40N 126 30W
Gilgai 137 31 15 S 119 56 E
Gilgandra 141 31 43 S 148 39 E
Gilgil 126 0 30 S 36 20 E
Gilgit 95 35 50N 74 15 E
Gilgit, R. 95 35 50N 74 25 E
Gilgunnia 141 32 26 S 146 2 E
Gilgulgul 139 26 26 S 150 0 E
Gilima 126 3 53N 28 15 E
Giljeva Planina 66 43 9N 20 0 E
Gill L. 38 54 15N 8 25W
Gillam 153 56 20N 94 40W
Gilleleje 73 56 8N 12 19 E
Gillen, L. 137 26 11 S 124 38 E
Gilles, L. 140 32 50 S 136 45 E
Gillespie Pt. 143 43 24 S 169 49 E
Gillett 162 41 57N 76 48W
Gillette 158 44 20N 105 38W
Gilliat 138 20 40 S 141 28 E
Gillingham, Dorset, U.K. 28 51 2N 2 15W
Gillingham, Kent, U.K. 29 51 23N 0 34 E
Gilmer 159 32 44N 94 55W
Gilmore 141 35 14 S 148 12 E
Gilmore, L. 137 32 29 S 121 37 E
Gilmour 150 44 48N 77 37W
Gilo 123 7 35N 34 30 E
Gilo, R. 161 33 5N 108 40W
Gilort, R. 70 44 38N 23 32 E
Gilroy 163 37 1N 121 37W
Gilsland 32 55 0N 2 34W
Gilău 70 46 45N 23 23W
Giluwe, Mt. 135 6 8 S 143 52 E
Gilwern 31 51 49N 3 5W
Gilze 47 51 32N 4 57 E
Gimåfors 72 62 40N 16 25 E
Gimbi 123 9 3N 35 42 E
Gimigliano 65 38 53N 16 32 E
Gimli 153 50 40N 97 10W
Gimmi 123 9 0N 37 20 E
Gimo 72 60 11N 18 12 E
Gimont 44 43 38N 0 52 E
Gimzo 90 31 56N 34 56 E
Gin Ganga 97 6 5N 80 7 E
Gin Gin 139 25 0 S 151 44 E
Ginâh 122 25 21N 30 30 E
Gindie 138 23 44 S 148 8 E
Gineta, La 59 39 8N 2 1W
Gingin 137 31 22 S 115 54 E
Gîngiova 70 43 54N 23 50 E
Ginir 123 7 12N 40 40 E
Ginosa 65 40 35N 16 45 E
Ginowan 112 26 15N 127 47 E
Ginzo de Limia 56 42 3N 7 47W
Giohar 91 2 20N 45 15 E
Gióia del Colle 65 40 49N 16 55 E
Gióia, G. di 65 38 30N 15 50 E
Gióia Táuro 65 38 26N 15 53 E
Gioiosa Iónica 65 38 20N 16 19 E
Gióna, Óros 69 38 38N 22 14 E
Giong, Teluk 103 4 50N 118 20 E
Giovi, P. dei 45 44 30N 8 55 E
Giovinazzo 65 41 10N 16 40 E
Gippsland 133 37 45 S 147 15 E
Gir Hills 94 21 0N 71 0 E
Girab 94 26 2N 70 38 E
Giralla 136 22 31 S 114 15 E
Giraltovce 53 49 7N 21 32 E
Girard 159 37 30N 94 50W
Girardot 174 4 18N 74 48W
Girdle Ness 37 57 9N 2 2W
Giresun 92 40 45N 38 30 E
Girga 122 26 17N 31 55 E
Girgir, C. 135 3 50 S 144 35 E
Giridih 95 24 10N 86 21 E
Girifalco 65 38 49N 16 25 E
Girilambone 141 31 16 S 146 57 E
Girishk 93 31 47N 64 24 E
Giro 121 11 7N 4 42 E
Giromagny 43 47 44N 6 50 E
Gironde □ 44 44 45N 0 30W
Gironde, R. 44 45 27N 0 53W
Gironella 58 42 2N 1 53 E
Giru 138 19 30 S 147 5 E
Girvan 34 55 15N 4 50W
Girvan R. 34 55 18N 4 51W
Gisborne 142 38 39 S 178 5 E
Gisburn 32 53 56N 2 16W
Gisenyi 126 1 41 S 29 30 E
Giske 71 62 30N 6 3 E
Gisla 36 58 7N 6 53W
Gislaved 73 57 19N 13 32 E
Gisors 43 49 15N 1 40 E
Gissarskiy, Khrebet 85 39 0N 69 0 E
Gistel 47 51 9N 2 59 E
Giswil 50 46 50N 8 11 E
Gitega (Kitega) 126 3 26 S 29 56 E
Gits 47 51 0N 3 6 E
Giubiasco 51 46 11N 9 1 E
Giugliano in Campania 65 40 55N 14 12 E
Giulianova 63 42 45N 13 58 E
Giurgeni 70 44 45N 27 38 E
Giurgiu 70 43 52N 25 57 E
Giv'at Brenner 90 31 52N 34 47 E
Give 73 55 51N 9 13 E
Givet 43 50 8N 4 49 E
Givors 45 45 35N 4 45 E
Givry, Belg. 47 50 23N 4 2 E
Givry, France 43 46 41N 4 46 E
Giza (El Giza) 122 30 1N 31 11 E
Gizhduvan 85 40 6N 64 41 E
Gizhiga 77 62 0N 150 27 E
Gizhiginskaya, Guba 77 61 0N 158 0 E
Gizycko 54 54 2N 21 48 E
Gizzeria 65 38 57N 16 10 E
Gjegjan 68 41 58N 20 3 E
Gjerpen 71 59 15N 9 33 E
Gjerstad 71 58 54N 9 0 E
Gjiri-i-Vlorës 68 40 29N 19 27 E
Gjirokastër 68 40 7N 20 16 E
Gjoa Haven 148 68 20N 96 0W
Gjovdal 71 58 52N 8 19 E
Gjøvik 71 60 47N 10 43 E
Glace Bay 151 46 11N 59 58W
Glacier B. 152 58 30N 136 10W
Glacier Nat. Park 152 51 15N 117 30W
Glacier National Park 160 48 35N 113 40W
Glacier Peak Mt. 160 48 7N 121 7W
Gladewater 159 32 30N 94 58W
Gladstone, Queens., Austral. 74 23 52 S 151 16 E
Gladstone, S.A., Austral. 140 33 15 S 138 22 E
Gladstone, W. Australia, Austral. 137 25 57 S 114 17 E
Gladstone, Can. 153 50 13N 98 57W
Gladstone, U.S.A. 156 45 52N 87 1W
Gladwin 156 43 59N 84 29W
Gladys L. 152 59 50N 133 0W
Glafsfjorden 72 59 30N 12 45 E
Głagów Małapolski 53 50 10N 21 56 E
Glåma 74 65 48N 23 0W
Glåma, R. 71 60 30N 12 8 E
Glamis 37 56 37N 3 0W
Glamorgan (□) 26 51 37N 3 35W
Glamorgan, Vale of 23 50 45N 3 15W
Glan, Phil. 103 5 45N 125 20 E
Glan, Sweden 73 58 37N 16 0 E
Glanaman 31 51 48N 3 56W
Glanaruddery Mts. 39 52 20N 9 27W
Glandore 39 51 33N 9 7W
Glandore Harb. 39 51 33N 9 8W
Glanerbrug 46 52 13N 6 58 E
Glanton 35 55 25N 1 54W
Glanworth 39 52 10N 8 25W
Glarner Alpen 51 46 50N 9 0 E
Glärnisch 51 47 0N 9 0 E
Glarus 51 47 3N 9 4 E
Glarus □ 51 47 0N 9 5 E
Glas Maol 37 56 52N 3 20W
Glasco, Kans., U.S.A. 158 39 25N 97 50W
Glasco, N.Y., U.S.A. 162 42 3N 73 57W
Glasgow, U.K. 34 55 52N 4 14W
Glasgow, Ky., U.S.A. 156 37 2N 85 55W
Glasgow, Mont., U.S.A. 160 48 12N 106 35W
Glasnevin 38 53 22N 6 18W
Glassboro 162 39 42N 75 7W
Glasslough 38 54 20N 6 53W
Glastonbury, U.K. 28 51 9N 2 42W
Glastonbury, U.S.A. 162 41 42N 72 27W
Glatt, R. 51 47 28N 8 32 E
Glattfelden 51 47 33N 8 30 E
Glauchau 48 50 50N 12 33 E
Glazov 81 58 9N 52 40 E
Glbovo 67 42 1N 24 43 E
Gleichen 152 50 50N 113 0W
Gleisdorf 52 47 6N 15 44 E
Glemsford 29 52 6N 0 41 E
Glen Affric 36 57 15N 5 0W
Glen Afton 142 37 46 S 175 4 E
Glen Almond 35 56 28N 3 50W
Glen B. 38 54 43N 8 45W
Glen Burnie 162 39 10N 76 37W
Glen Canyon Dam 161 37 0N 111 25W
Glen Canyon Nat. Recreation Area 161 37 30N 111 0W
Glen Coe 23 56 40N 5 0W
Glen Cove 162 40 51N 73 37W
Glen Esk 37 56 53N 2 50W
Glen Etive 34 56 37N 5 0W
Glen Florrie 136 22 55 S 115 59 E
Glen Garry, Inv., U.K. 36 57 3N 5 7W
Glen Garry, Per., U.K. 37 56 47N 4 5W
Glen Gowrie 140 31 4 S 143 10 E
Glen Helen 32 54 14N 4 35W
Glen Innes 139 29 40 S 151 39 E
Glen Lyon, U.K. 37 56 35N 4 20W
Glen Lyon, U.S.A. 162 41 10N 76 7W
Glen Massey 142 37 38 S 175 2 E
Glen Mor 37 57 12N 4 37 E
Glen Moriston 36 57 10N 4 58W
Glen Orchy 34 56 27N 4 52W
Glen Orrin 37 57 30N 4 45W
Glen Oykel 37 58 5N 4 50W
Glen, R. 29 52 50N 0 7W
Glen Shee 37 56 45N 3 25W
Glen Shiel 36 57 8N 5 20W
Glen Spean 37 56 53N 4 40W
Glen Trool Lodge 34 55 5N 4 30W
Glen Ullin 158 46 48N 101 46W
Glen Valley 141 36 54 S 147 28 E
Glenade 38 54 22N 8 17W
Glenamoy 38 54 14N 9 40W
Glénans, Îs. de 42 47 42N 4 0W
Glenariff 141 30 50 S 146 33 E
Glenarm 38 54 58N 5 58W
Glenart Castle 39 52 48N 6 12W
Glenavy, N.Z. 143 44 54 S 171 7 E
Glenavy, U.K. 38 54 36N 6 12W
Glenbarr 34 55 34N 5 40W
Glenbeigh 39 52 3N 9 57W
Glenbrittle 36 57 13N 6 18W
Glenbrook 142 33 46 S 150 37 E
Glenburn 141 37 37 S 145 26 E
Glencoe, S. Afr. 129 28 11 S 30 11 E
Glencoe, U.S.A. 158 44 45N 94 10W
Glencolumbkille 38 54 43N 8 41W
Glendale, Can. 150 46 45N 84 2W
Glendale, Zimb. 127 17 22 S 31 5 E
Glendale, Ariz., U.S.A. 161 33 40N 112 8W
Glendale, Calif., U.S.A. 163 34 7N 118 18W
Glendale, Oreg., U.S.A. 160 42 44N 123 29W
Glendive 158 47 7N 104 40W
Glendo 158 42 30N 105 0W
Glendora 163 34 8N 117 52W
Gleneagles 35 56 16N 3 44W
Glenealy 39 52 59N 6 10W
Gleneely 38 52 14N 7 8W
Glenelg, Austral. 140 34 58 S 138 31 E
Glenelg, U.K. 36 57 13N 5 37W
Glenelg, R. 140 38 4 S 140 59 E
Glenfarne 38 54 17N 8 0W
Glenfield 162 43 43N 75 24W
Glenfinnan 36 56 52N 5 28W
Glengad Hd. 38 55 19N 7 11W
Glengariff 39 51 45N 9 33W
Glengormley 38 54 41N 5 57W
Glengyle 138 24 48 S 139 37 E
Glenham 143 46 26 S 168 52 E
Glenhope 143 41 40 S 172 39 E
Glenisland 38 53 54N 9 24W
Glenkens, The 34 55 10N 4 15W
Glenluce 34 54 53N 4 50W
Glenmary, Mt. 143 44 0 S 169 55 E
Glenmaye 32 54 11N 4 42W
Glenmora 159 31 1N 92 34W
Glenmorgan 139 27 14 S 149 42 E
Glenn, oilfield 19 57 55N 0 15 E
Glennagevlagh 38 53 36N 9 41W
Glennamaddy 38 53 37N 8 33W
Glenn's Ferry 160 43 0N 115 15W
Glenoe 38 54 47N 5 50W
Glenorchy, S. Austral., Austral. 140 31 55 S 139 46 E
Glenorchy, Tas., Austral. 138 42 49 S 147 18 E
Glenorchy, Vic., Austral. 140 36 55 S 142 41 E
Glenore 138 17 50 S 141 12 E
Glenormiston 138 22 55 S 138 50 E
Glenreagh 139 30 2 S 153 1 E
Glenrock 160 42 53N 105 55W
Glenrothes 35 56 12N 3 11W
Glenrowan 141 36 29 S 146 13 E
Glenroy, S. Australia, Austral. 140 37 13 S 140 48 E
Glenroy, W. Australia, Austral. 136 17 16 S 126 14 E
Glenroy, S. Afr. 132 26 23 S 28 17 E
Glens Falls 162 43 19N 73 39W
Glentane 38 53 25N 8 30W
Glenties 38 54 48N 8 18W
Glenville 156 38 56N 80 50W
Glenwood, Alta., Can. 152 49 21N 113 31W
Glenwood, Newf., Can. 151 49 0N 54 47W
Glenwood, Ark., U.S.A. 159 34 20N 93 30W
Glenwood, Hawaii, U.S.A. 147 19 29N 155 10W
Glenwood, Iowa, U.S.A. 158 41 7N 95 41W
Glenwood, Minn., U.S.A. 158 45 38N 95 21W
Glenwood Sprs. 160 39 39N 107 15W
Gletsch 51 46 34N 8 22 E
Glettinganes 51 65 30N 13 37W
Glin 39 52 34N 9 17W
Glina 63 45 20N 16 6 E
Glinojeck 54 52 49N 20 21 E
Glinsk 39 53 23N 9 49W
Glittertind 71 61 40N 8 32 E
Gliwice (Gleiwitz) 54 50 22N 18 41 E
Globe 161 33 25N 110 53W
Glodeanu-Siliştea 70 44 50N 26 48 E
Glödnitz 52 46 53N 14 7 E
Glodyany 70 47 45N 27 31 E
Gloggnitz 52 47 41N 15 56 E
Głogów 54 51 37N 16 5 E
Głogowek 54 50 21N 17 53 E
Gloria, La 174 8 37N 73 48W
Glorieuses, Îs. 129 11 30 S 47 20 E
Glossop 32 53 27N 1 56W
Gloucester, Austral. 141 32 0 S 151 59 E
Gloucester, U.K. 28 51 52N 2 15W
Gloucester, U.S.A. 162 42 38N 70 39W
Gloucester, Va., U.S.A. 162 37 25N 76 32W
Gloucester, C. 135 5 26 S 148 21 E
Gloucester City 162 39 54N 75 8W
Gloucester, I. 138 20 0 S 148 30 E
Gloucestershire □ 28 51 44N 2 10W
Gloversville 162 43 5N 74 18W
Glovertown 151 48 40N 54 03W
Głubczyce 54 50 13N 17 52 E
Glubokiy 83 48 35N 40 25 E
Glubokoye 80 55 10N 27 45 E
Głucholazy 54 50 19N 17 24 E
Glücksburg 48 54 48N 9 34 E
Glückstadt 48 53 46N 9 28 E
Gluepot 140 33 45 S 140 0 E
Glukhov 80 51 40N 33 50 E
Glussk 80 52 53N 28 41 E
Głowno 54 51 59N 19 42 E
Glyn-ceiriog 31 52 56N 3 12W
Glyn Neath 31 51 45N 3 37W
Glyncorrwg 31 51 40N 3 39W
Glyngøre 73 56 46N 8 52 E
Glynn 39 52 29N 6 55W
Gmünd, Kärnten, Austria 52 46 54N 13 31 E
Gmünd, Niederösterreich, Austria 52 48 45N 15 0 E
Gmunden 52 47 55N 13 48 E
Gnarp 72 62 3N 17 16 E
Gnesta 72 59 3N 17 17 E
Gniew 54 53 50N 18 50 E
Gniewkowo 54 52 54N 18 25 E
Gniezno 54 52 30N 17 35 E
Gnoien 48 53 58N 12 41 E
Gnopp 123 8 47N 29 50 E
Gnosall 28 52 48N 2 15W
Gnosjö 73 57 22N 13 43 E
Gnowangerup 137 33 58 S 117 59 E
Go Cong 101 10 22N 106 40 E
Gō-no-ura 110 33 44N 129 40 E
Goa 97 15 33N 73 59 E
Goa □ 97 15 33N 73 59 E
Goageb 128 26 49 S 17 15 E
Goalen Hd. 141 36 33 S 150 4 E
Goalpara 98 26 10N 90 40 E
Goalundo 95 23 50N 89 47 E
Goaso 120 6 48N 2 30W
Goat Fell 34 55 37N 5 11W
Goba, Ethiopia 123 7 1N 39 59 E
Goba, Mozam. 125 26 15 S 32 13 E
Gobabis 128 22 16 S 19 0 E
Gobi, desert 105 44 0N 111 0 E
Gobichettipalayam 97 11 31N 77 21 E
Gobō 111 33 53N 135 10 E
Gobo 123 5 40N 30 10 E

• Renamed Kiribati

Goch 48 51 40N 6 9E
Gochas 125 24 59S 19 25E
Godalming 29 51 12N 0 37W
Godavari Point 96 17 0N 82 20E
Godavari, R. 96 19 5N 79 0E
Godbout 151 49 20N 67 38W
Godda 95 24 50N 87 20E
Goddua 119 26 26N 14 19E
Godech 66 43 1N 23 4E
Godegård 73 58 43N 15 8E
Goderich 150 43 45N 81 41W
Goderville 42 49 38N 0 22E
Godhavn 12 69 15N 53 38W
Godhra 94 22 49N 73 40E
Godmanchester 29 52 19N 0 11W
Gödöllö 53 47 38N 19 25E
Godoy Cruz 172 32 56S 68 52W
Godrevy Pt. 30 50 15N 5 24W
Gods L. 153 54 40N 94 15W
Gods, R. 153 56 22N 92 51W
Godshill 28 50 38N 1 13W
Godstone 29 51 15N 0 3W
Godthåb 12 64 10N 51 46W
Godwin Austen (K2) 93 36 0N 77 0E
Goeie Hoop, Kaap die 128 34 24S 18 30E
Goeland, L. 150 49 50N 76 48W
Goeree 46 51 50N 4 0E
Goes 47 51 30N 3 55E
Goffstown 162 43 1N 71 36W
Gogama 150 47 35N 81 43W
Gogango 138 23 40S 150 2E
Gogebic, L. 158 46 30N 89 34W
Gogha 94 21 32N 72 9E
Gogolin 54 50 30N 18 0E
Gogra, R. = Ghaghara 99 26 0N 84 20E
Gogriâl 123 8 30N 28 0E
Goiana 170 7 33S 34 59W
Goiandira 171 11 46S 46 40W
Goianésia 171 15 18S 49 7W
Goiânia 171 16 35S 49 20W
Goiás 171 15 55S 50 10W
Goiás □ 170 12 10S 48 0W
Goiatuba 171 18 1S 49 23W
Goil L. 34 56 8N 4 52W
Goirle 47 51 31N 5 4E
Góis 56 40 10N 8 6W
Goisern 52 47 38N 13 38E
Gojam □ 123 10 55N 36 30E
Gojeb, W. 123 7 12N 36 40E
Gojō 111 34 21N 135 42E
Gojra 94 31 10N 72 40E
Gokak 97 16 11N 74 52E
Gokarannath 95 27 57N 80 39E
Gokarn 97 14 33N 74 17E
Gökçeada 68 40 10N 26 0E
Gokteik 99 22 26N 97 0E
Gokurt 94 29 47N 67 26E
Gøl 73 57 4N 9 42E
Gola 95 28 3N 80 32E
Gola I. 38 55 4N 8 20W
Golaghat 98 26 30N 94 0E
Golakganj 95 26 8N 89 52E
Golaya Pristen 82 46 29N 32 23E
Golchikha 12 71 45N 84 0E
Golconda 160 40 58N 117 32W
Gold Beach 160 42 25N 124 25W
Gold Coast, Austral. 139 28 0S 153 25E
Gold Coast, W. Afr. 121 4 0N 1 40W
Gold Creek 147 62 45N 149 45W
Gold Hill 160 42 28N 123 2W
Gold Point 163 37 21N 117 21W
Gold River 152 49 40N 126 10E
Goldach 51 47 28N 9 28E
Goldau 51 47 3N 8 33E
Goldberg 48 53 34N 12 6E
Golden, Can. 152 51 20N 117 0W
Golden, Ireland 39 52 30N 8 0W
Golden, U.S.A. 158 39 42N 105 30W
Golden Bay 143 40 40S 172 50E
Golden Gate 160 37 54N 122 30W
Golden Hinde, mt. 152 49 40N 125 44W
Golden Prairie 153 50 13N 109 37W
Golden Rock 97 10 45N 78 48E
Golden Vale 39 52 33N 8 17W
Goldendale 160 45 53N 120 48W
Goldfield 163 37 45N 117 13W
Goldfields 153 59 28N 108 29W
Goldpines 153 50 45N 93 05W
Goldsand L. 153 57 2N 101 8W
Goldsboro 157 35 24N 77 59W
Goldsmith 159 32 0N 102 40W
Goldsworthy 136 20 21S 119 30E
Goldsworthy, Mt. 136 20 23S 119 31E
Goldthwaite 159 31 25N 98 32W
Goleen 39 51 30N 9 43W
Golegã 57 39 24N 8 29W
Goleniów 54 53 35N 14 50E
Goleta 163 34 27N 119 50W
Golfito 166 8 41N 83 5W
Golfo degli Aranci 65 41 0N 9 38E
Goliad 159 28 40N 97 22W
Golija 66 43 22N 20 15E
Golija, Mts. 66 43 5N 18 45E
Golina 54 52 15N 18 4E
Golo, R. 45 42 31N 9 32E
Golovanesvsk 82 48 25N 30 30E
Gölpazari 82 40 17N 30 17E
Golra 94 33 37N 72 56E
Golspie 37 57 58N 3 58W
Golub Dobrzyn 54 53 7N 19 2E
Golubac 66 44 38N 21 38E
Golyama Kamchiya, R. 67 43 2N 27 18E
Goma, Ethiopia 123 8 29N 36 53E
Goma, Rwanda 126 2 11S 29 18E
Goma, Zaïre 126 1 37S 29 10E
Gomare 128 19 25S 22 8E
Gomati, R. 95 26 30N 81 50E
Gombari 126 2 45N 29 3E
Gombe 121 10 19N 11 2E
Gombe, R. 126 4 30S 32 50E
Gombi 121 10 12N 12 45E
Gomel 80 52 28N 31 0E
Gomera, I. 116 28 10N 17 5W
Gometra I. 34 56 30N 6 18W
Gómez Palacio 164 25 40N 104 40W
Gommern 48 52 54N 11 47E
Gomogomo 103 6 25S 134 53E
Gomoh 99 23 52N 86 10E
Gomotartsi 66 44 6N 22 57E
Goms 50 46 30N 8 15E
Gonābād 93 34 15N 58 45E
Gonaïves 167 19 20N 72 50W
Gonâve, G. de la 167 19 29N 72 42W
Gonâve, I. de la 167 18 45N 73 0W
Gönc 53 48 28N 21 14E
Gonda 95 27 9N 81 58E
Gondab-e Kāvūs 93 37 20N 55 25E
Gondal 94 21 58N 70 52E
Gonder 123 12 23N 37 30E
Gondia 96 21 30N 80 10E
Gondola 127 19 4S 33 37E
Gondomar, Port. 56 41 10N 8 35W
Gondomar, Spain 56 42 7N 8 45W
Gondrecourt-le-Château 43 48 26N 5 30E
Gongola □ 121 8 0N 12 0E
Gongola, R. 121 10 30N 10 22E
Goniadz 54 53 30N 22 44E
Goniri 121 11 30N 12 15E
Gonnesa 64 39 17N 8 27E
Gonno-Altaysk 76 51 50N 86 5E
Gonnos 68 39 52N 22 29E
Gonnosfanadiga 64 39 30N 8 39E
Gonzales, Calif., U.S.A. 163 36 35N 121 30W
Gonzales, Tex., U.S.A. 159 29 30N 97 30W
González Chaves 172 38 02S 60 05W
Good Hope, C. of = Goeie Hoop 128 34 24S 18 30E
Goode 139 31 58S 133 45E
Goodenough I. 135 9 20S 150 15E
Gooderham 150 44 54N 78 21W
Goodeve 153 51 4N 103 10W
Gooding 160 43 0N 114 50W
Goodland 158 39 22N 101 44W
Goodnight 159 35 4N 101 13W
Goodooga 139 29 1S 147 28E
Goodrich 28 51 52N 2 38W
Goodsoil 153 54 24N 109 13W
Goodsprings 161 35 51N 115 30W
Goodwick 31 52 0N 5 0W
Goodwin, Mt. 136 14 13S 129 32E
Goodwood 29 50 53N 0 44W
Goole 33 53 42N 0 52W
Goolgowi 141 33 58S 145 41E
Goolwa 140 35 30S 138 47E
Goomalling 137 31 15S 116 42E
Goombalie 139 29 59S 145 26E
Goonalga 140 31 45S 143 37E
Goonda 127 19 48S 33 57E
Goondiwindi 139 28 30S 150 21E
Goongarrie 137 30 2S 121 8E
Goonumbla 141 32 59S 148 11E
Goonyella 138 21 47S 147 58E
Goor 46 52 13N 6 33E
Gooray 139 28 25S 150 2E
Goose Bay 151 53 15N 60 20W
Goose L. 160 42 0N 120 30W
Goose R. 151 53 20N 60 35W
Goothinga 138 17 36S 140 50E
Gooty 97 15 7N 77 41E
Gop 93 22 5N 69 50E
Gopalganj, Bangla. 98 23 1N 89 50E
Gopalganj, India 95 26 28N 84 30E
Goppenstein 50 46 23N 7 46E
Göppingen 49 48 42N 9 40E
Gor 59 37 23N 2 58W
Góra 54 51 40N 16 31E
Gorakhpur 95 26 47N 83 32E
Gorbatov 81 56 12N 43 2E
Gorbea, Peña 58 43 1N 2 50W
Gorda 163 35 53N 121 26W
Gorda, Punta 166 14 10N 83 10W
Gordon, Austral. 140 32 7S 138 20E
Gordon, U.K. 35 55 41N 2 32W
Gordon, U.S.A. 158 42 49N 102 6W
Gordon B. 136 11 35S 130 10E
Gordon Downs 136 18 48S 128 40E
Gordon L., Alta., Can. 153 56 30N 110 25W
Gordon L., N.W.T., Can. 152 63 5N 113 11W
Gordon, R. 138 42 27S 145 30E
Gordon River 137 34 10S 117 15E
Gordonia 128 28 13S 21 10E
Gordonvale 138 17 5S 145 50E
Gore 139 28 17S 151 30E
Goré 117 7 59N 16 49E
Gore, Ethiopia 123 8 12N 35 32E
Gore, N.Z. 143 46 5S 168 58E
Gore B. 150 45 57N 82 28W
Gorebridge 35 55 51N 3 2W
Goresbridge 39 52 38N 7 0W
Gorey 39 52 41N 6 18W
Gorgan 93 36 55N 54 30E
Gorge, The 138 18 27S 145 30E
Gorgona, I. 174 3 0N 78 10W
Gorgona I. 62 43 27N 9 52E
Gorgora 123 12 15N 37 17E
Gori 83 42 0N 44 7E
Gorinchem 46 51 50N 4 59E
Goring, Oxon, U.K. 28 51 31N 1 8W
Goring, Sussex, U.K. 29 50 49N 0 26W
Gorinhatã 171 19 15S 49 45W
Goritsy 81 57 4N 36 43E
Gorizia 63 45 56N 13 37E
Gorka 54 51 39N 16 58E
Gorki = Gorkiy 81 56 20N 44 0E
Gorkiy 81 57 20N 44 0E
Gorkovskoye Vdkhr. 81 57 2N 43 4E
Gorleston 29 52 35N 1 44E
Gorlev 73 55 30N 11 15E
Gorlice 54 49 35N 21 11E
Görlitz 54 51 10N 14 59E
Gorlovka 81 48 25N 37 58E
Gorman, Calif., U.S.A. 163 34 47N 118 51W
Gorman, Tex., U.S.A. 159 32 15N 98 43W
Gorna Oryakhovitsa 67 43 7N 25 40E
Gorna Radgona 63 46 40N 16 2E
Gornja Tuzla 66 44 35N 18 46E
Gornji Grad 63 46 20N 14 52E
Gornji Milanovac 66 44 00N 20 29E
Gornji Vafuk 66 43 57N 17 34E
Gorno Ablanovo 67 43 37N 25 43E
Gorno Filinskoye 76 60 5N 70 0E
Gornyy 81 51 50N 48 30E
Gorodenka 82 48 41N 25 29E
Gorodets 81 56 38N 43 28E
Gorodische 81 53 13N 45 40E
Gorodnitsa 80 50 46N 27 26E
Gorodnya 80 51 55N 31 33E
Gorodok, Byelorussia, U.S.S.R. 80 55 30N 30 3E
Gorodok, Ukraine, U.S.S.R. 80 49 46N 23 32E
Goroka 135 6 7S 145 25E
Goroke 140 36 43S 141 29E
Gorokhov 80 50 15N 24 45E
Gorokhovets 81 56 13N 42 39E
Gorom Gorom 121 14 26N 0 14W
Goromonzi 127 17 52S 31 22E
Gorong, Kepulauan 103 4 5S 131 15E
Gorongosa, Sa. da 127 18 27S 32 2E
Gorongose, R. 129 20 40S 34 30E
Gorontalo 103 0 35N 123 13E
Goronyo 121 13 29N 5 39E
Gorredijk 46 53 0N 6 3E
Gorron 42 48 25N 0 50W
Gorseinon 31 51 40N 4 2W
Gorssel 46 52 12N 6 12E
Gort 39 53 4N 8 50W
Gortin 38 54 43N 7 13W
Gorumahisani 96 22 20N 86 24E
Gorumna I. 39 53 15N 9 44W
Gorzkowice 54 51 13N 19 36E
Gorzno 54 53 12N 19 38E
Gorzów Slaski 54 51 3N 18 22E
Gorzów Wielkopolski 54 52 43N 15 15E
Gorzów Wielkopolski □ 54 52 45N 15 30E
Gosainthan, Mt. 99 28 20N 85 45E
Gosberton 33 52 52N 0 10W
Göschenen 51 46 40N 8 36E
Göse 111 34 27N 135 44E
Gosford 141 33 23N 151 18E
Gosforth 32 54 24N 3 27W
Goshen, S. Afr. 128 25 50S 25 0E
Goshen, Calif., U.S.A. 163 36 21N 119 25W
Goshen, Ind., U.S.A. 156 41 36N 85 46W
Goshen, N.Y., U.S.A. 162 41 23N 74 21W
Goslar 48 51 55N 10 23E
Gospič 63 44 35N 15 23E
Gosport 28 50 48N 1 8W
Gossa, I. 71 62 52N 6 50E
Gossau 51 47 25N 9 15E
Gosse, R. 138 19 32S 134 37E
Gostivar 66 41 48N 20 57E
Gostyn 54 51 50N 17 3E
Gostynin 54 52 26N 19 29E
Göta 73 58 6N 12 10E
Göta älv 73 57 42N 11 54E
Göta Kanal 73 58 35N 14 15E
Götaland, reg. 73 58 0N 14 0E
Göteborg 73 57 43N 11 59E
Göteborg & Bohus □ 75 58 20N 11 50E
Gotemba 111 35 18N 138 56E
Götene 73 58 32N 13 30E
Gotha 48 50 56N 10 42E
Gothenburg 158 40 58N 100 8W
Gothenburg = Göteborg 73 57 43N 11 59E
Gotse Delchev (Nevrokop) 67 41 43N 23 46E
Gotska Sandön 75 58 24N 19 15E
Götsu 110 35 0N 132 14E
Göttingen 48 51 31N 9 55E
Gottwaldov (Zlin) 53 49 14N 17 40E
Gouda 46 52 1N 4 42E
Goudhurst 29 51 7N 0 28E
Goudiry 120 14 15N 12 45E
Gough I. 15 40 10S 9 45W
Gouin Res. 150 48 35N 74 40W
Gouitafla 120 7 30N 5 53W
Goula Touila 118 21 50N 1 57E
Goulburn 141 34 44S 149 44E
Goulburn Is. 138 11 40S 133 20E
Gould, mt. 137 25 46S 117 18E
Goulia 120 10 1N 7 11W
Goulimine 118 28 50N 10 0W
Goulmima 118 31 41N 4 57W
Gouménissa 68 40 56N 22 37E
Goumeur 119 20 40N 18 30E
Goundam 135 16 25N 3 45W
Gounou-Gaya 124 9 38N 15 31E
Goúra 69 37 56N 22 20E
Gourara 118 29 0N 0 30E
Gouraya 118 36 31N 1 56E
Gourdon, France 44 44 44N 1 23E
Gourdon, U.K. 37 56 50N 2 15W
Gouré 121 14 0N 10 10E
Gourits, R. 128 34 15S 21 45E
Gourma Rharous 121 16 55N 2 5W
Gournay-en-Bray 43 49 29N 1 44E
Gouro 117 19 30N 19 30E
Gourock 34 55 58N 4 49W
Gourock Ra. 141 36 0S 149 25E
Gourselik 121 13 31N 10 52E
Goursi 120 12 42N 2 37W
Gouvêa 171 18 27S 43 44W
Gouzon 44 46 12N 2 14E
Govan 153 51 20N 105 0W
Gove 133 12 25S 136 55E
Goverla 82 49 9N 24 30E
Governador Valadares 171 18 15S 41 57W
Governor's Harbour 166 25 10N 76 14W
Gowan 138 25 0S 145 0E
Gowanda 156 42 29N 78 58W
Gower, The 31 51 35N 4 10W
Gowerton 31 51 38N 4 2W
Gowna, L. 38 53 52N 7 35W
Gowran 39 52 38N 7 5W
Goya 172 29 10S 59 10W
Goyder's Lagoon 139 27 3S 139 58E
Goyllarisquizga 174 10 19S 76 31W
Goz Beïda 117 12 20N 21 30E
Goz Regeb 123 16 3N 35 33E
Gozdnica 54 51 28N 15 4E
Gozo (Ghaudex) 60 36 0N 14 13E
Graaff-Reinet 128 32 13S 24 32E
Graasten 73 54 57N 9 34E
Grabow 48 53 17N 11 31E
Grabów 54 51 31N 18 7E
Grabs 51 47 11N 9 27E
Gračac 63 44 18N 15 57E
Gračanica 66 44 43N 18 18E
Graçay 43 47 10N 1 50E
Grace 160 42 38N 111 46W
Grace, L., (North) 137 33 10S 118 20E
Grace, L., (South) 137 33 15S 118 25E
Graceville 158 45 36N 96 23W
Gracevka 84 52 55N 52 52E
Gracias a Dios, C. 166 15 0N 83 20W
Gradačac 66 44 52N 18 26E
Gradaús 170 7 43S 51 11W
Gradaús, Serra dos 170 8 0S 50 45W
Gradeska Planina 66 41 30N 22 15E
Gradets 67 42 46N 26 30E
Gradignan 66 44 47N 0 36W
Gradnitsa 67 42 57N 24 58E
Grado, Italy 63 45 40N 13 20E
Grado, Spain 56 43 23N 6 4W
Gradule 139 28 32S 149 15E
Grady 159 34 52N 103 15W
Graeca, Lacul 70 44 5N 26 10E
Graemsay I. 37 58 56N 3 17W
Graénalon, L. 74 64 10N 17 20W
Grafham Water 29 52 18N 0 17W
Grafton, Austral. 139 29 38S 152 58E
Grafton, U.S.A. 158 48 30N 97 25W
Grafton, C. 133 16 51S 146 0E
Gragnano 65 40 42N 14 30E
Graham, Can. 150 49 20N 90 30W
Graham, N.C., U.S.A. 157 36 5N 79 22W
Graham, Tex., U.S.A. 159 33 7N 98 38W
Graham Bell, Os. 76 80 5N 70 0E
Graham I. 152 53 40N 132 30W
Graham Land 13 65 0S 64 0W
Graham Mt. 161 32 46N 109 58W
Graham, R. 152 56 31N 122 17W
Grahamdale 153 51 23N 98 30W
Grahamstown 128 33 19S 26 31E
Grahamsville 162 41 51N 74 33W
Grahovo 66 42 40N 18 4E
Graïba 119 34 30N 10 13E
Graide 47 49 58N 5 4E
Graigue 39 52 51N 6 56W
Graiguenamanagh 39 52 32N 6 58W
Grain Coast 120 4 20N 10 0W
Grainthorpe 33 53 27N 0 5E
Graivoron 80 50 29N 35 39E
Grajaú 170 5 50S 46 30W
Grajaú, R. 170 3 41S 44 48W
Grajewo 54 53 39N 22 30E
Gramada 66 43 49N 22 39E
Gramat 44 44 48N 1 43E
Gramisdale 36 57 29N 7 18W
Grammichele 65 37 12N 14 37E
Grampian □ 37 57 0N 3 0W
Grampians, Mts. 140 37 0S 142 20E
Gran Canaria 116 27 55N 15 35W
Gran Chaco 156 25 0S 61 0W
Gran Paradiso 62 49 33N 7 17E
Gran Sabana, La 174 5 30N 61 30W
Gran Sasso d'Italia, Mt. 44 42 25N 13 30E
Granada, Nic. 166 11 58N 86 0W
Granada, Spain 59 37 10N 3 35W
Granada, U.S.A. 158 38 5N 102 13W
Granada □ 57 37 5N 4 30W
Granard 38 53 47N 7 30W
Granbo 72 61 16N 16 33E
Granbury 159 32 28N 97 48W
Granby 150 45 25N 72 45W
Grand Bahama I. 166 26 40N 78 30W
Grand Bank 151 47 6N 55 48W
Grand Bassa 120 6 0N 10 2W

Grand Bassam 120 5 10N 3 49W
Grand Béréby 120 4 38N 6 55W
Grand-Bourg 167 15 53N 61 19W
Grand Canal 39 53 15N 8 10W
Grand Canyon National Park 161 36 15N 112 20W
Grand Cayman 166 19 20N 81 20W
Grand Cess 120 4 40N 8 12W
Grand 'Combe, La 45 44 13N 4 2E
Grand Coulee 160 47 48N 119 1W
Grand Coulee Dam 160 48 0N 118 50W
Grand Erg Occidental 118 30 20N 1 0E
Grand Erg Oriental 119 30 0N 6 30E
Grand Falls 151 47 2N 67 46W
Grand Forks, Can. 152 49 0N 118 30W
Grand Forks, U.S.A. 158 48 0N 97 3W
Grand-Fougeray 42 47 43N 1 44W
Grand Fougeray, Le 42 47 44N 1 43W
Grand Haven 156 43 3N 86 13W
Grand I. 150 46 30N 86 40W
Grand Island 158 40 59N 98 25W
Grand Isle 159 29 15N 89 58W
Grand Junction 161 39 0N 108 30W
Grand L., N.B., Can. 151 45 57N 66 7W
Grand L., Newf., Can. 151 48 45N 57 45W
Grand L., Newf., Can. 151 53 40N 60 30W
Grand L., Newf., Can. 151 49 0N 57 30W
Grand L., U.S.A. 159 29 55N 92 45W
Grand Lac 150 47 35N 77 35W
Grand Lahou 120 5 10N 5 0W
Grand Lake 160 40 20N 105 54W
Grand-Leez 47 50 35N 4 45E
Grand Lieu, Lac de 42 47 6N 1 40W
Grand Manan I. 151 44 45N 66 52W
Grand Marais, Can. 158 47 45N 90 25W
Grand Marais, U.S.A. 156 46 39N 85 59W
Grand Mère 150 46 36N 72 40W
Grand Motte, La 45 48 35N 1 4E
Grand Popo 121 6 15N 1 44E
Grand Portage 150 47 58N 89 41W
Grand Pressigny, Le 42 46 55N 0 48E
Grand, R., Mo., U.S.A. 160 39 23N 93 27W
Grand, R., S.D., U.S.A. 160 45 45N 101 30W
Grand Rapids, Can. 153 53 12N 99 19W
Grand Rapids, Mich., U.S.A. 156 42 57N 85 40W
Grand Rapids, Minn., U.S.A. 158 47 19N 93 29W
Grand St.-Bernard, Col. du 50 45 53N 7 11E
Grand Teton 160 43 45N 110 57W
Grand Valley 160 39 30N 108 2W
Grand View 153 51 11N 100 51W
Grandas de Salime 56 43 13N 6 53W
Grande 170 11 30S 44 30W
Grande, B. 176 50 30S 68 20W
Grande Baie 151 48 19N 70 52W
Grande Cache 152 53 53N 119 8W
Grande, Coxilha 173 28 18S 51 30W
Grande de Santiago, R. 164 21 20N 105 50W
Grande Dixence, Barr. de la 50 46 5N 7 23E
Grande-Entrée 151 47 30N 61 40W
Grande, I. 171 23 9S 44 14W
Grande, La 160 45 15N 118 0W
Grande Prairie 152 55 15N 118 50W
Grande, R., Jujuy, Argent. 172 23 9S 65 52W
Grande, R., Mendoza, Argent. 172 36 52S 69 45W
Grande R. 174 18 35S 63 0W
Grande, R., Brazil 171 20 0S 50 0W
Grande, R., Spain 59 39 6N 0 48W
Grande, R., U.S.A. 159 29 20N 100 40W
Grande Rivière 151 48 26N 64 30W
Grande, Serra, Goiás, Brazil 170 11 15S 46 30W
Grande, Serra, Maranhao, Brazil 170 4 30S 41 20W
Grande, Serra, Piauí, Brazil 170 8 0S 45 0W
Grande Vallée 151 49 14N 65 8W
Grandes Bergeronnes 151 48 16N 69 35W
Grandfalls 159 31 21N 102 51W
Grandglise 47 50 30N 3 42E
Grandoe Mines 152 56 29N 129 54W
Grândola 57 38 12N 8 35W
Grandpré 43 49 20N 4 50E
Grandson 50 46 49N 6 39E
Grandview, Can. 153 51 10N 100 42W
Grandview, U.S.A. 160 46 13N 119 58W
Grandvilliers 43 49 40N 1 57E
Graneros 172 34 5S 70 45W
Graney L. 39 53 0N 8 40W
Grange 38 54 24N 8 32W
Grange, La, Austral. 136 18 45S 121 43E
Grange, La, U.S.A. 163 37 42N 120 27W
Grange, La, Ga., U.S.A. 157 33 4N 85 0W
Grange, La, Ky., U.S.A. 156 38 20N 85 20W
Grange, La, Tex., U.S.A. 159 29 54N 96 52W
Grange-over-Sands 32 54 12N 2 55W
Grangemouth 35 56 1N 3 43W
Granger 160 46 25N 120 5W
Grangesberg 72 60 6N 15 1E
Grängesberg 72 60 6N 15 1E
Grangetown 33 54 36N 1 7W
Grangeville 160 45 57N 116 4W
Granite City 158 38 45N 90 3W
Granite Falls 158 44 45N 95 35W
Granite Mtn. 163 33 5N 116 28W
Granite Peak 137 25 40S 121 20E
Granite Pk., mt. 160 45 8N 109 52W
Granitnyy, Pik 85 39 32N 70 20E
Granity 143 41 39S 171 51E
Granja 170 3 17S 40 50W
Granja de Moreruela 56 41 48N 5 44W
Granja de Torrehermosa 57 38 19N 5 35W
Gränna 73 58 1N 14 28E
Granollers 58 41 39N 2 18E
Gransee 48 53 0N 13 10E
Grant, Can. 150 50 6N 86 18W
Grant, U.S.A. 158 40 53N 101 42W
Grant City 158 40 30N 94 25W
Grant, I. 136 11 10S 132 52E
Grant, Mt. 163 38 34N 118 48W
Grant Range Mts. 161 38 30N 115 30W
Grantham 33 52 55N 0 39W
Grantown-on-Spey 37 57 19N 3 36W
Grants 161 35 14N 107 57W
Grant's Pass 160 42 30N 123 22W
Grantsburg 158 45 46N 92 44W
Grantshouse 35 55 53N 2 17W
Grantsville 160 40 35N 112 32W
Granville, France 42 48 50N 1 35W
Granville, U.K. 38 54 30N 6 47W
Granville, N.D., U.S.A. 158 48 18N 100 48W
Granville, N.Y., U.S.A. 162 43 24N 73 16W
Granville L. 153 56 18N 100 30W
Grao de Gandía 59 39 0N 0 27W
Grapeland 159 31 30N 95 25W
Gras, L. de 148 64 30N 110 30W
Graskop 129 24 56S 30 49E
Gräsmark 72 59 58N 12 44E
Grasmere, Austral. 139 35 1S 117 45E
Grasmere, U.K. 32 54 28N 3 2W
Gräsö 72 60 21N 18 28E
Graso 72 60 28N 18 35E
Grasonville 162 38 57N 76 13W
Grass, R. 153 56 3N 96 33W
Grass Range 160 47 0N 109 0W
Grass River Prov. Park 153 54 40N 100 50W
Grass Valley, Calif., U.S.A. 160 39 18N 121 0W
Grass Valley, Oreg., U.S.A. 160 45 28N 120 48W
Grassano 65 40 38N 16 17E
Grasse 45 43 38N 6 56E
Grassington 32 54 5N 2 0W
Grassmere 140 31 24S 142 38E
Grate's Cove 151 48 8N 53 0W
Graubünden (Grisons) □ 51 46 45N 9 30E
Graulhet 44 43 45N 1 58E
Graus 58 42 11N 0 20E
Gravatá 170 6 59S 35 29W
Grave 46 51 46N 5 44E
Grave, Pte. de 44 45 34N 1 4W
's-Graveland 46 52 15N 5 7E
Gravelbourg 153 49 50N 106 35W
Gravelines 43 51 0N 2 10E
's-Gravendeel 46 51 47N 4 37E
's-Gravenhage 46 52 7N 4 17E
's-Gravenpolder 47 51 28N 3 54E
's-Gravensance 46 52 0N 4 9E
Graversfors 73 58 42N 16 8E
Gravesend, Austral. 139 29 35S 150 20E
Gravesend, U.K. 29 51 25N 0 22E
Gravina di Púglia 65 40 48N 16 25E
Gravir 36 58 2N 6 25W
Gravois, Pointe-à 167 16 15N 73 45W
Gravone, R. 45 42 3N 8 54E
Grävsnäs 73 58 5N 12 29E
Gray 43 47 27N 5 35E
Grayling 156 44 40N 84 42W
Grayling, R. 152 59 21N 125 0W
Grayrigg 32 54 22N 2 40W
Grays Harbor 160 46 55N 124 8W
Grays L. 160 43 8N 111 30W
Grays Thurrock 29 51 28N 0 23E
Grayson 153 50 45N 102 40W
Grayvoron 80 50 29N 35 39E
Graz 52 47 4N 15 27E
Grazalema 57 36 46N 5 23W
Grdelica 66 42 55N 22 3E
Greasy L. 152 62 55N 122 12W
Great Abaco I. 166 26 15N 77 10W
Great Australia Basin 133 26 0S 140 0E
Great Australian Bight 137 33 30S 130 0E
Great Ayton 33 54 29N 1 8W
Great Baddow 29 51 43N 0 31E
Great Bahama Bank 166 23 15N 78 0W
Great Barrier I. 142 36 11S 175 25E
Great Barrier Reef 138 19 0S 149 0E
Great Barrington 162 42 11N 73 22W
Great Basin 154 40 0N 116 30W
Great Bear L. 148 65 0N 120 0W
Great Bear, R. 148 65 0N 124 0W
Great Belt 73 55 20N 11 0E
Great Bena 162 41 57N 75 45W
Great Bend 158 38 25N 98 55W
Great Bentley 29 51 51N 1 5E
Great Bernera, I. 137 58 15N 6 50W
Great Bitter Lake 122 30 15N 32 40E
Great Blasket, I. 39 52 5N 10 30W
Great Britain 16 54 0N 2 15W
Great Bushman Land 128 29 20S 19 20E
Great Central 152 49 20N 125 10W
Great Chesterford 29 52 4N 0 11E
Great Clifton 32 54 39N 3 29W
Great Coco I. 101 14 10N 93 25E
Great Divide 141 23 0S 146 0E
Great Dunmow 29 51 52N 0 22E
Great Exuma I. 166 23 30N 75 50W
Great Falls, Can. 153 50 27N 96 1W
Great Falls, U.S.A. 160 47 27N 111 12W
Great Fish R., S. Afr. 128 33 28S 27 5E
Great Fish R., S. Afr. 128 31 30S 20 16E
Great Gonerby 33 52 56N 0 40W
Great Guana Cay 166 24 0N 76 20W
Great Hanish 123 13 40N 43 0E
Great Harbour Deep 151 50 35N 56 25W
Great Harwood 32 52 41N 2 49W
Great I., Can. 153 58 53N 96 35W
Great I., Ireland 39 51 52N 8 15W
Great Inagua I. 167 21 0N 73 20W
Gt. Indian Desert = Thar Desert 94 28 0N 72 0E
Great Jarvis 151 47 39N 57 12W
Great Karoo = Groot Karoo 128 32 30S 23 0E
Great Lake 138 41 50S 146 30E
Great Lakes 153 44 0N 82 0W
Great Malvern 28 52 7N 2 19W
Great Massingham 29 52 47N 0 41E
Great Missenden 29 51 42N 0 42W
Gt. Namaqualand = Groot Namakwaland 128 26 0S 18 0E
Great Orme's Head 31 53 20N 3 52W
Great Ouse, R. 29 52 20N 0 8E
Great Palm I. 138 18 45S 146 40E
Great Papuan Plateau 135 6 30S 142 25E
Great Plains 50 45 0N 100 0W
Great Ruaha, R. 126 7 30S 35 0E
Great Salt Lake 160 41 0N 112 30W
Great Salt Lake Desert 160 40 20N 113 50W
Great Salt Plains Res. 159 36 40N 98 15W
Great Sandy Desert 136 21 0S 124 0E
Great Sandy I. = Fraser I. 139 25 15S 153 0E
Great Scarcies, R. 120 9 30N 12 40W
Great Shefford 28 51 29N 1 27W
Great Shelford 29 52 9N 0 9E
Great Shunner Fell 32 54 22N 2 16W
Great Sitkin I. 147 52 0N 176 10W
Great Slave L. 152 61 23N 115 38W
Great Stour, R. 29 51 21N 1 15E
Gt. Sugar Loaf, mt. 39 53 10N 6 10W
Great Torrington 30 50 57N 4 9W
Gt. Victoria Des. 137 29 30S 126 30E
Great Wall 106 38 30N 109 30E
Gt. Waltham 29 51 47N 0 29E
Great Whale, R. 150 55 20N 75 30W
Great Whernside, mt. 32 54 9N 1 59W
Great Winterhoek, mt. 128 33 07S 19 10E
Great Wyrley 28 52 40N 2 1W
Great Yarmouth 29 52 40N 1 45E
Great Yeldham 29 52 1N 0 33E
Greater Antilles 167 17 40N 74 0W
Greater Manchester □ 32 53 30N 2 15W
Greatham 33 54 38N 1 14W
Grebbestad 73 58 42N 11 15E
Grebenka 80 50 9N 32 22E
Greco, Mt. 64 41 48N 14 0E
Gredos, Sierra de 56 40 20N 5 0W
Greece ■ 68 40 0N 23 0E
Greeley, Colo., U.S.A. 158 40 30N 104 40W
Greeley, Nebr., U.S.A. 158 41 36N 98 32W
Green B. 156 45 0N 87 30W
Green Bay 156 44 30N 88 0W
Green C. 141 37 13S 150 1E
Green Cove Springs 157 29 59N 81 40W
Green Hammerton 33 54 2N 1 17W
Green Hd. 137 30 5S 114 56E
Green Is. 135 4 35S 154 10E
Green Island 143 45 55S 170 26E
Green Lowther, Mt. 35 55 22N 3 44W
Green R., Ky., U.S.A. 156 37 54N 87 30W
Green R., Utah, U.S.A. 161 39 0N 110 6W
Green R., Wyo., U.S.A. 161 43 2N 110 2W
Green R., Wyo., U.S.A. 160 41 44N 109 28W
Greenbush 158 48 46N 96 10W
Greencastle, U.K. 38 54 2N 6 5W
Greencastle, U.S.A. 156 39 40N 86 48W
Greene 162 42 20N 75 45W
Greenfield, Calif., U.S.A. 163 35 15N 119 0W
Greenfield, Calif., U.S.A. 163 36 19N 121 15W
Greenfield, Ind., U.S.A. 156 39 47N 85 51W
Greenfield, Iowa, U.S.A. 158 41 18N 94 28W
Greenfield, Mass., U.S.A. 162 42 38N 72 38W
Greenfield, Miss., U.S.A. 159 37 28N 93 50W
Greenhead 35 54 58N 2 31W
Greening 150 48 10N 74 55W
Greenisland 38 54 42N 5 50W
Greenland 12 66 0N 45 0W
Greenland Sea 12 73 0N 10 0W
Greenlaw 35 55 42N 2 28W
Greenock 34 55 57N 4 46W
Greenodd 32 54 14N 3 3W
Greenore 38 54 2N 6 8W
Greenore Pt. 39 52 15N 6 20W
Greenough, R. 137 28 54S 115 36E
Greenport 162 41 5N 72 23W
Greensboro, Ga., U.S.A. 157 33 34N 83 12W
Greensboro, Md., U.S.A. 162 38 59N 75 48W
Greensboro, N.C., U.S.A. 157 36 7N 79 46W
Greensburg, Ind., U.S.A. 156 39 20N 85 30W
Greensburg, Kans., U.S.A. 159 37 38N 99 20W
Greensburg, Pa., U.S.A. 156 40 18N 79 31W
Greenstone Pt. 36 57 55N 5 38W
Greenville, Liberia 120 5 7N 9 6W
Greenville, Ala., U.S.A. 157 31 50N 86 37W
Greenville, Calif., U.S.A. 160 40 8N 121 0W
Greenville, Ill., U.S.A. 158 38 53N 89 22W
Greenville, Me., U.S.A. 151 45 30N 69 32W
Greenville, Mich., U.S.A. 156 43 12N 85 14W
Greenville, Miss., U.S.A. 159 33 25N 91 0W
Greenville, N.C., U.S.A. 157 35 37N 77 26W
Greenville, N.H., U.S.A. 162 42 46N 71 49W
Greenville, N.Y., U.S.A. 162 42 25N 74 1W
Greenville, Ohio, U.S.A. 156 40 5N 84 38W
Greenville, Pa., U.S.A. 156 41 23N 80 22W
Greenville, S.C., U.S.A. 157 34 54N 82 24W
Greenville, Tenn., U.S.A. 157 36 13N 82 51W
Greenville, Tex., U.S.A. 159 33 5N 96 5W
Greenwater Lake Prov. Park 153 52 32N 103 30W
Greenway 31 51 56N 4 49W
Greenwich, U.K. 29 51 28N 0 0
Greenwich, Conn., U.S.A. 162 41 1N 73 38W
Greenwich, N.Y., U.S.A. 162 43 2N 73 36W
Greenwood, Can. 152 49 10N 118 40W
Greenwood, Miss., U.S.A. 159 33 30N 90 4W
Greenwood, S.C., U.S.A. 157 34 13N 82 13W
Greenwood, Mt. 136 13 48S 130 4E
Gregory 158 43 14N 99 20W
Gregory Downs 138 18 35S 138 45E
Gregory, L. 139 28 55S 139 0E
Gregory L. 136 20 5S 127 0E
Gregory, L. 137 25 38S 119 58E
Gregory Lake 136 20 10S 127 30E
Gregory, R. 138 17 53S 139 17E
Gregory Ra., Queens., Austral. 138 19 30S 143 40E
Gregory Ra., W. Austral., Austral. 136 21 20S 121 12E
Greian Hd. 36 57 1N 7 30W
Greiffenberg 48 53 6N 13 57E
Greifswald 48 54 6N 13 23E
Greifswalder Bodden 48 54 12N 13 35E
Greifswalder Oie 48 54 15N 13 55E
Grein 52 48 14N 14 51E
Greiner Wald 52 48 30N 15 0E
Greiz 48 50 39N 12 12E
Gremikha 78 67 50N 39 40E
Grenå 73 56 25N 10 53E
Grenada 159 33 45N 89 50W
Grenada I. ■ 167 12 10N 61 40W
Grenade 44 43 47N 1 17E
Grenadines 167 12 40N 61 20W
Grenchen 50 47 12N 7 24E
Grenen 73 57 44N 10 40E
Grenfell, Austral. 141 33 52S 148 8E
Grenfell, Can. 153 50 30N 102 56W
Grenoble 45 45 12N 5 42E
Grenora 158 48 38N 103 54W
Grenville, C. 138 12 0S 143 13E
Grenville Chan. 152 53 40N 129 46W
Gréoux-les-Bains 45 43 55N 5 52E
Gresham 160 45 30N 122 31W
Gresik 103 9 13S 112 38E
Gressoney St. Jean 62 45 49N 7 47E
Greta 32 54 9N 2 36W
Greta R. 32 54 36N 3 5W
Gretna, U.K. 35 54 59N 3 4W
Gretna, U.S.A. 159 30 0N 90 2W
Gretna Green 35 55 0N 3 3W
Gretton 29 52 33N 0 40W
Grevelingen Krammer 46 51 44N 4 0E
Greven 48 52 7N 7 36E
Grevená 68 40 4N 21 25E
Grevená □ 68 40 2N 21 25E
Grevenbroich 48 51 6N 6 32E
Grevenmacher 47 49 41N 6 26E
Grevesmühlen 48 53 51N 11 10E
Grevie 73 56 22N 12 46E
Grevinge 73 55 48N 11 34E
Grey, C. 138 13 0S 136 35E
Grey, R. 143 42 27S 171 12E
Grey Range 133 27 0S 143 30E
Grey Res. 151 48 20N 56 30W
Greyabbey 38 54 32N 5 35W
Greybull 160 44 30N 108 3W
Greystone 32 54 39N 2 52W
Greystones 39 53 9N 6 4W
Greytown, N.Z. 142 41 5S 175 29E
Greytown, S. Afr. 129 29 1S 30 36E
Gribanovskiy 81 51 28N 41 50E
Gribbell I. 152 53 23N 129 0W
Gribbin Head 30 50 18N 4 41W
Gridley 160 39 27N 121 47W
Griekwastad 128 28 49S 23 15E
Griffin 157 33 17N 84 14W
Griffith 141 34 18S 146 2E
Griffith Mine 153 50 47N 93 25W
Grigoryevka 84 50 48N 58 18E
Grijalva, R. 164 16 20N 92 20W
Grijpskerk 46 53 16N 6 18E
Grillby 72 59 38N 17 15E

Grim, C. **133** 40 45S 144 45E
Grimaïlov **80** 49 20N 26 5E
Grimari **117** 5 43N 20 0E
Grimbergen **47** 50 56N 4 22E
Grimeton **73** 57 6N 12 25E
Griminish Pt. **36** 57 40N 7 30W
Grimma **48** 51 14N 12 44E
Grimmen **48** 54 6N 13 2E
Grimsay I. **36** 57 29N 7 12W
Grimsby **33** 53 35N 0 5W
Grimsel Pass **51** 46 34N 8 23E
Grímsey **74** 66 33N 18 0W
Grimshaw **152** 56 10N 117 40W
Grimstad **71** 58 22N 8 35E
Grindelwald **50** 46 38N 8 2E
Grindsted **73** 55 46N 8 55E
Grindstone Island **151** 47 25N 62 0W
Grindu **70** 44 44N 26 50E
Grinduşul, Mt. **70** 46 40N 26 7E
Griñón **56** 40 13N 3 51W
Grinnell **158** 41 45N 92 43W
Grip **71** 63 16N 7 37E
Griqualand East **129** 30 30S 29 0E
Griqualand West **128** 28 40S 23 30E
Griquet **151** 51 30N 55 35W
Grisolles **44** 43 49N 1 19E
Grisons □ **49** 46 40N 9 30E
Grisslehamm **72** 60 5N 18 49E
Grita, La **174** 8 8N 71 59W
Gritley **37** 58 56N 2 45W
Grivegnée **47** 50 37N 5 36E
Griz Nez **43** 50 50N 1 35E
Grizebeck **32** 54 16N 3 10W
Grmeč Planina **63** 44 43N 16 16E
Groais I. **151** 50 55N 55 35W
Groblersdal **129** 25 15S 29 25E
Grobming **52** 47 27N 13 54E
Grocka **66** 44 40N 20 42E
Grodek **80** 52 46N 23 38E
Grodkow **54** 50 43N 17 40E
Grodno **80** 53 42N 23 52E
Grodzisk Mazowiecki **54** 52 7N 20 37E
Grodzisk Wlkp. **54** 52 15N 16 22E
Grodzyanka **80** 53 31N 28 42E
Groenlo **46** 52 2N 6 37E
Groesbeck **159** 31 32N 96 34W
Groesbeek **46** 51 47N 5 58E
Groix **42** 47 38N 3 29W
Groix, I. de **42** 47 38N 3 28W
Grójec **54** 51 50N 20 58E
Grolloo **46** 52 56N 6 41E
Gronau **48** 52 13N 7 2E
Grong **74** 64 25N 12 8E
Groningen **46** 53 15N 6 35E
Groningen □ **46** 53 16N 6 40E
Groninger Wad **46** 53 27N 6 30E
Grönskåra **73** 57 5N 15 43E
Gronsveld **47** 50 49N 5 44E
Groom **159** 35 12N 100 59W
Groomsport **38** 54 41N 5 37W
Groot Berg, R. **128** 32 50S 18 20E
Groot-Brakrivier **128** 34 2S 22 18E
Groot Karoo **128** 32 35S 23 0E
Groot Namakwaland = Namaland **128** 26 0S 18 0E
Groot, R. **128** 33 10S 23 35E
Groote Eylandt **138** 14 0S 136 50E
Grootebroek **46** 52 41N 5 13E
Grootfontein **128** 19 31S 18 6E
Grootlaagte, R. **128** 21 10S 21 20E
Gros C. **152** 61 59N 113 32W
Grosa, Punta **59** 39 6N 1 36E
Grósio **62** 46 18N 10 17E
Grosne, R. **45** 46 30N 4 40E
Gross Glockner **52** 47 5N 12 40E
Gross Ottersleben **48** 52 5N 11 33E
Grossa, Pta. **170** 1 20N 50 0W
Grossenbrode **48** 54 21N 11 4E
Grossenhain **48** 51 17N 13 32E
Grosseto **62** 42 45N 11 7E
Grossgerungs **52** 48 34N 14 57E
Grosswater B. **151** 54 20N 57 40W
Grote Gette, R. **47** 50 51N 5 6E
Grote Nete, R. **47** 51 8N 4 34E
Groton, U.S.A. **162** 41 22N 72 12W
Groton, U.S.A. **162** 42 36N 76 22W
Grottaglie **65** 40 32N 17 25E
Grottaminarda **65** 41 5N 15 4E
Grouard Mission **152** 55 33N 116 9W
Grouin, Pointe du **42** 48 43N 1 51W
Groundhog, R. **150** 48 45N 82 20W
Grouse Creek **160** 41 51N 113 57W
Grouw **46** 53 5N 5 51E
Groveland **163** 37 50N 120 14W
Grovelsjön **72** 62 6N 12 16E
Grover City **163** 35 7N 120 37W
Groveton **159** 31 5N 95 4W
Groznjan **63** 45 22N 13 43E
Groznyy **83** 43 20N 45 45E
Grubbenvorst **47** 51 25N 6 9E
Grubišno Polje **66** 45 44N 17 12E
Grudusk **54** 53 3N 20 38E
Grudziadz **54** 53 30N 18 47E
Gruinard B. **36** 57 56N 5 35W
Gruissan **44** 43 8N 3 7E
Grumo Appula **65** 41 2N 16 43E
Grums **72** 59 22N 13 5E
Grünau **125** 27 45S 18 26E
Grünberg **48** 50 37N 8 55E
Grundy Center **158** 42 22N 92 45W
Grungedal **71** 59 44N 7 43E
Gruting Voe **36** 60 12N 1 32W
Gruver **159** 36 19N 101 20W
Gruyères **50** 46 35N 7 4E
Gruza **66** 43 54N 20 46E
Gryazi **81** 52 30N 39 58E
Gryazovets **81** 58 50N 40 20E
Grybów **54** 49 36N 20 55E
Grycksbo **72** 60 40N 15 29E
Gryfice **54** 53 55N 15 13E
Gryfino **54** 53 16N 14 29E
Grytgöl **73** 58 49N 15 33E
Grythyttan **72** 59 41N 14 32E
Grytviken **13** 53 50S 37 10W
Gstaad **50** 46 28N 7 18E
Gua **99** 22 18N 85 20E
Gua Musang **101** 4 53N 101 58E
Guacanayabo, Golfo de **166** 20 40N 77 20W
Guacara **174** 10 14N 67 53W
Guachípas **172** 25 40S 65 30W
Guachiría, R. **174** 5 30N 71 30W
Guadajoz, R. **57** 37 50N 4 51W
Guadalajara, Mexico **164** 20 40N 103 20W
Guadalajara, Spain **58** 40 37N 3 12W
Guadalajara □ **58** 40 47N 3 0W
Guadalcanal **57** 38 5N 5 52W
Guadalcanal, I. **130** 9 32S 160 12E
Guadalén, R. **59** 38 30N 3 7W
Guadales **172** 34 30S 67 55W
Guadalete, R. **57** 36 45N 5 47W
Guadalhorce, R. **57** 36 50N 4 42W
Guadalimar, R. **59** 38 10N 2 53W
Guadalmena, R. **59** 38 31N 2 50W
Guadalmez, R. **57** 38 33N 4 42W
Guadalope, R. **58** 41 0N 0 13W
Guadalquivir, R. **57** 38 0N 4 0W
Guadalupe, Brazil **170** 6 44S 43 47W
Guadalupe, Spain **57** 39 27N 5 17W
Guadalupe, U.S.A. **163** 34 59N 120 33W
Guadalupe Bravos **164** 31 20N 106 10W
Guadalupe de los Reyes **164** 25 23N 104 15W
Guadalupe I. **131** 29 0N 118 50W
Guadalupe Pk. **161** 31 50N 105 30W
Guadalupe, R. **159** 29 25N 97 30W
Guadalupe, Sierra de **55** 39 28N 5 30W
Guadalupe y Calvo **164** 26 6N 106 58W
Guadarrama, Sierra de **56** 41 0N 4 0W
Guadeloupe, I. **167** 16 20N 61 40W
Guadeloupe Passage **167** 16 50N 68 15W
Guadiamar, R. **57** 37 9N 6 20W
Guadiana Menor, R. **59** 37 45N 3 7W
Guadiana, R. **57** 37 45N 7 35W
Guadiaro, R. **57** 36 39N 5 17W
Guadiato, R. **57** 37 55N 4 53W
Guadiela, R. **58** 40 30N 2 23W
Guadix **59** 37 18N 3 11W
Guafo, Boca del **176** 43 35S 74 0W
Guaina **174** 5 9N 63 36W
Guainía □ **174** 2 30N 69 00W
Guaira **173** 24 5S 54 10W
Guaira, La **174** 10 36N 66 56W
Guaitecas, Islas **176** 44 0S 74 30W
Guajará-Mirim **174** 10 50S 65 20W
Guajira, La □ **174** 11 30N 72 30W
Guajira, Pen. de la **167** 12 0N 72 0W
Gualan **166** 15 8N 89 22W
Gualdo Tadino **63** 43 14N 12 46E
Gualeguay **172** 33 10S 59 20W
Gualeguaychú **172** 33 3S 58 31W
Guam I. **130** 13 27N 144 45E
Guamá **170** 1 37S 47 29W
Guama **174** 10 16N 68 49W
Guamá, R. **170** 1 29S 48 30W
Guamareyes **174** 0 30S 73 0W
Guaminí **172** 37 1S 62 28W
Guampí, Sierra de **174** 6 0N 65 35W
Guamuchil **164** 25 25N 108 3W
Guanabacoa **166** 23 8N 82 18W
Guanabara □ **173** 23 0S 43 25W
Guanacaste **166** 10 40N 85 30W
Guanacaste, Cordillera del **166** 10 40N 85 4W
Guanacevío **164** 25 40N 106 0W
Guanajay **166** 22 56N 82 42W
Guanajuato **164** 21 0N 101 20W
Guanajuato □ **164** 20 40N 101 20W
Guanambi **171** 14 13S 42 47W
Guanare **174** 8 42N 69 12W
Guanare, R. **174** 8 50N 68 50W
Guandacol **172** 29 30S 68 40W
Guane **166** 22 10N 84 0W
Guanhães **171** 18 47S 42 57W
Guanica **147** 17 58N 66 55W
Guanipa, R. **174** 9 20N 63 30W
Guanta **174** 10 14N 64 36W
Guantánamo **167** 20 10N 75 20W
Guapí **174** 2 36N 77 54W
Guápiles **166** 10 10N 83 46W
Guaporé **173** 12 0S 64 0W
Guaporé, R. **174** 13 0S 63 0W
Guaqui **174** 16 41S 68 54W
Guara, Sierra de **58** 42 19N 0 15W
Guarabira **170** 6 51S 35 29W
Guarapari **173** 20 40S 40 30W
Guarapuava **171** 25 20S 51 30W
Guaratinguetá **173** 22 49S 45 9W
Guaratuba **173** 25 53S 48 38W
Guard Bridge **35** 56 21N 2 52W
Guarda **56** 40 32N 7 20W
Guarda □ **56** 40 40N 7 20W
Guardafui, C. = Asir, Ras **91** 11 55N 51 10E
Guardamar del Segura **59** 38 5N 0 39W
Guardavalle **65** 38 31N 16 30E
Guardia, La **56** 41 56N 8 52W
Guardiagrele **63** 42 11N 14 11E
Guardo **56** 42 47N 4 50W
Guareña **57** 38 51N 6 6W
Guareña, R. **56** 41 25N 5 25W
Guaria □ **172** 25 45S 56 30W
Guárico □ **174** 8 40N 66 35W
Guarujá **173** 24 2S 46 25W
Guarus **173** 21 30S 41 20W
Guasave **164** 25 34N 108 27W
Guasdualito **174** 7 15N 70 44W
Guasipati **174** 7 28N 61 54W
Guasopa **135** 9 12S 152 56E
Guastalla **62** 44 55N 10 40E
Guatemala **166** 14 40N 90 30W
Guatemala ■ **166** 15 40N 90 30W
Guatire **174** 10 28N 66 32W
Guaviare, R. **174** 3 30N 71 0W
Guaxupé **173** 21 10S 47 5W
Guayabal **174** 4 43N 71 37W
Guayama **147** 17 59N 66 7W
Guayaquil **174** 2 15S 79 52W
Guayaquil, Golfo de **174** 3 10S 81 0W
Guaymallen **172** 32 50S 68 45W
Guaymas **164** 27 50N 111 0W
Guba, Ethiopia **123** 4 52N 39 18E
Guba, Zaïre **127** 10 38S 26 27E
Gubakha **84** 58 52N 57 36E
Gubam **135** 8 39S 141 53E
Gúbbio **63** 43 20N 12 34E
Gubio **121** 12 30N 12 42E
Gubkin **81** 51 17N 37 32E
Guča **66** 43 46N 20 15E
Guchil **101** 5 35N 102 10E
Gudalur **97** 11 30N 76 29E
Gudata **83** 43 7N 40 32E
Gudbransdal **75** 61 33N 10 0E
Guddu Barrage **93** 28 30N 69 50E
Gudenå **73** 56 27N 9 40E
Gudermes **83** 43 24N 46 20E
Gudhjem **73** 55 12N 14 58E
Gudiña, La **56** 42 4N 7 8W
Gudivada **96** 16 30N 81 15E
Gudiyatam **97** 12 57N 78 55E
Gudmundra **72** 62 56N 17 47E
Gudrun, gasfield **19** 58 50N 1 48E
Gudur **97** 14 12N 79 55E
Guebwiller **43** 47 55N 7 12E
Guecho **58** 43 21N 2 59W
Guéckédou **120** 8 40N 10 5W
Guelma **119** 36 25N 7 29E
Guelph **150** 43 35N 80 20W
Guelt es Stel **118** 35 12N 3 1E
Guelttara **118** 29 23N 2 10W
Guemar **119** 33 30N 6 57E
Guéméné-Penfao **42** 47 38N 1 50W
Guéméné-sur-Scorff **42** 48 4N 3 13W
Güemes **172** 24 50S 65 0W
Guéné **121** 11 44N 3 16E
Guer **42** 47 54N 2 8W
Guérande **42** 47 20N 2 26W
Guerche, La **42** 47 57N 1 16W
Guerche-sur-l'Aubois, La **43** 46 58N 2 56E
Guercif **118** 34 14N 3 21W
Guéréda **124** 14 31N 22 5E
Guéret **44** 46 11N 1 51E
Guérigny **43** 47 6N 3 10E
Guernica **58** 43 19N 2 40W
Guernsey **158** 42 19N 104 45W
Guernsey I. **42** 49 30N 2 35W
Guerrara, Oasis, Alg. **119** 32 51N 4 35E
Guerrara, Saoura, Alg. **118** 28 5N 0 8W
Guerrero □ **165** 17 30N 100 0W
Guerzim **118** 29 45N 1 47W
Güeş ti **74** 44 48N 25 19E
Guestling Green **29** 50 53N 0 40E
Gueugnon **45** 45 36N 4 3E
Gueydan **159** 30 3N 92 30W
Guezendi = Ghesendor **119** 21 14N 18 14E
Guglia, P. dal **51** 46 28N 9 45E
Guglionesi **63** 51 55N 14 54E
Guhra **93** 27 36N 56 8E
Guia Lopes da Laguna **173** 21 26S 56 7W
Guiana Highlands **174** 5 0N 60 0W
Guibes **128** 26 41S 16 49E
Guider **121** 9 55N 13 59E
Guidimouni **121** 13 42N 9 31E
Guiglo **120** 6 45N 7 30W
Guija **125** 34 35S 33 15E
Guijo de Coria **56** 40 6N 6 28W
Guildford **29** 51 14N 0 34W
Guilford, Conn., U.S.A. **162** 41 15N 72 40W
Guilford, Me., U.S.A. **151** 45 12N 69 25W
Guillaumes **45** 44 5N 6 52E
Guillestre **45** 44 39N 6 40E
Guilsfield **31** 52 42N 3 9W
Guilvinec **42** 47 48N 4 17W
Guimarães, Braz. **170** 2 9S 44 35W
Guimarães, Port. **56** 41 28N 8 24W
Guimaras I. **103** 10 35N 122 37E
Guinea ■ **120** 10 20N 10 0W
Guinea Bissau ■ **120** 12 0N 15 0W
Guinea, Gulf of **121** 3 0N 2 30E
Guinea, Port. = Guinea Bissau **120** 12 0N 15 0W
Güines **166** 22 50N 82 0W
Guingamp **42** 48 34N 3 10W
Guipavas **42** 48 26N 4 29W
Guipúzcoa □ **58** 43 12N 2 15W
Guir, O. **118** 39 29N 2 58W
Guirgo **121** 11 54N 1 21W
Güiria **174** 10 32N 62 18W
Guisborough **33** 54 32N 1 2W
Guiscard **43** 49 40N 3 0E
Guise **43** 49 52N 3 35E
Guitiriz **56** 43 11N 7 50W
Guivan **103** 11 5N 125 55E
Gujan-Mestras **44** 44 38N 1 4W
Gujar Khan **84** 33 15N 73 21E
Gujarat □ **94** 23 20N 71 0E
Gujranwala **94** 32 10N 74 12E
Gujrat **94** 32 40N 74 2E
Gukhothae **101** 17 2N 99 50E
Gukovo **83** 48 1N 39 58E
Gulak **121** 10 50N 13 30E
Gulargambone **141** 31 20S 148 30E
Gulbahar **93** 35 5N 69 10E
Gulbargā **96** 17 20N 76 50E
Gulbene **80** 57 8N 26 52E
Gulcha **85** 40 19N 73 26E
Guldborg Sd. **73** 54 39N 11 50E
Guledgud **97** 16 3N 75 48E
Gulf Basin **136** 15 20S 129 0E
Gulfport **159** 30 28N 89 3W
Gulgong **141** 32 20S 149 30E
Gulistan, Pak. **94** 30 36N 66 35E
Gulistan, U.S.S.R. **85** 40 29N 68 46E
Gulkana **147** 62 15N 145 48W
Gull Lake **153** 50 10N 108 29W
Gullane **35** 56 2N 2 50W
Gullegem **47** 50 51N 3 13E
Gullringen **73** 57 48N 15 44E
Güllük **69** 37 12N 27 36E
Gulma **121** 12 40N 4 23E
Gulmarg **95** 34 3N 74 25E
Gulnam **123** 6 55N 29 30E
Gulnare **140** 33 27S 138 27E
Gulpaigan **92** 33 26N 50 20E
Gulpen **47** 50 49N 5 53E
Gülpinar **68** 39 32N 26 10E
Gulshad **76** 46 45N 74 25E
Gulsvik **71** 60 24N 9 38E
Gulu **126** 2 48N 32 17E
Gulwe **126** 6 30S 36 25E
Gulyaypole **82** 47 45N 36 21E
Gum Lake **140** 32 42S 143 9E
Gumal, R. **94** 32 5N 70 5E
Gumbaz **94** 30 2N 69 0E
Gumel **121** 12 39N 9 22E
Gumiel de Hizán **58** 41 46N 3 41W
Gumlu **138** 19 53S 147 41E
Gumma-ken □ **111** 36 30N 138 20E
Gummersbach **48** 51 2N 7 32E
Gummi **121** 12 4N 5 9E
Gümüsane **92** 40 30N 39 30E
Gümüşhaciköy **82** 40 50N 35 18E
Gumzai **103** 5 28S 134 42E
Guna **94** 24 40N 77 19E
Guna Mt. **123** 11 50N 37 40E
Gundagai **141** 35 3S 148 6E
Gundih **103** 7 10S 110 56E
Gundlakamma, R. **97** 15 30N 80 15E
Gunebang **141** 33 5S 146 38E
Gungal **141** 32 17S 150 32E
Gungi **123** 10 20N 38 3E
Gungu **124** 5 43S 19 20E
Gunisao L. **153** 53 33N 96 15W
Gunisao, R. **153** 53 56N 97 53W
Gunnedah **141** 30 59S 150 15E
Gunniguldrie **141** 33 12S 146 8E
Gunningbar Cr. **141** 31 14S 147 6E
Gunnison, Colo., U.S.A. **161** 38 32N 106 56W
Gunnison, Utah, U.S.A. **160** 39 11N 111 48W
Gunnison, R. **161** 38 50N 108 30W
Gunnworth **153** 51 20N 108 9W
Guntakal **97** 15 11N 77 27E
Guntersville **157** 34 18N 86 16W
Guntong **101** 4 36N 101 3E
Guntur **96** 16 23N 80 30E
Gunungapi **103** 6 45S 126 30E
Gunungsitoli **102** 1 15N 97 30E
Gunungsugih **102** 4 58S 105 7E
Gunupur **96** 19 5N 83 50E
Gunworth **153** 51 20N 108 10W
Gunza **124** 10 50S 13 50E
Gunzenhausen **49** 49 6N 10 45E
Gupis **95** 36 15N 73 20E
Gura **94** 25 12N 71 39E
Gura Humorului **70** 47 35N 25 53E
Gura Teghii **70** 45 30N 26 25E
Gurage, mt. **123** 8 20N 38 20E
Gurchan **92** 34 55N 49 25E
Gurdaspur **94** 32 5N 75 25E
Gurdon **159** 33 55N 93 10W
Gurdzhaani **83** 41 43N 45 52E
Gurgan **93** 36 51N 54 25E
Gurgaon **94** 28 33N 77 10E
Gurghiu, Munţii **70** 46 41N 25 15E
Gurguéia, R. **170** 6 50S 43 24W
Guria **62** 44 30N 9 0E
Gurk, R. **52** 46 48N 14 20E
Gurkha **95** 28 5N 84 40E
Gurla Mandhata **95** 30 30N 81 10E
Gurley **139** 29 45S 149 48E
Gurnard's Head **30** 50 12N 5 37W
Gurnet Pt. **162** 42 1N 70 34W
Gurrumbah **138** 17 30S 144 55E
Gurun **101** 5 49N 100 27E
Gürün **92** 38 41N 37 22E
Gurupá **175** 1 25S 51 45W
Gurupá, I. Grande de **175** 1 0S 51 45W
Gurupi **171** 11 43S 49 4W
Gurupi, R. **170** 3 20S 47 20W
Gurupi, Serra do **170** 5 0S 47 30W
Guryev **83** 47 5N 52 0E
Gus **126** 3 2N 36 57E

Gus-Khrsutalnyy **81** 55 42N 40 35 E
Gusau **121** 12 18N 6 31 E
Gusev **80** 54 35N 22 20 E
Gushiago **121** 9 55N 0 15W
Gusinje **66** 42 35N 19 50 E
Gúspini **64** 39 32N 8 38 E
Gusselby **72** 59 38N 15 14 E
Güssing **53** 47 3N 16 20 E
Gustanj **63** 46 36N 14 49 E
Gustavus **147** 58 25N 135 58W
Gustine **163** 37 21N 121 0W
Güstrow **48** 53 47N 12 12 E
Gusum **73** 58 16N 16 30 E
Gŭtaia **70** 45 26N 21 30 E
Gütersloh **48** 51 54N 8 25 E
Gutha **137** 28 58 S 115 55 E
Guthalungra **138** 19 52 S 147 50 E
Guthrie **159** 35 55N 97 30W
Guttannen **51** 46 38N 8 18 E
Guttenberg **158** 42 46N 91 10W
Guyana ■ **174** 5 0N 59 0W
Guyenne **44** 44 30N 0 40 E
Guyman **159** 36 45N 101 30W
Guyra **139** 30 15 S 151 40 E
Guzar **85** 38 36N 66 15 E
Guzmán, Laguna de **164** 31 25N 107 25W
Gwa **98** 17 30N 94 40 E
Gwaai **127** 19 15 S 27 45 E
Gwabegar **141** 30 31 S 149 0 E
Gwadabawa **121** 13 20N 5 15 E
Gwādar **93** 25 10N 62 18 E
Gwagwada **121** 10 15N 7 15 E
Gwalchmai **31** 53 16N 4 23W
Gwalia **137** 28 54 S 121 20 E
Gwalior **94** 26 12N 78 10 E
Gwanara **121** 18 55N 3 10 E
Gwanda **127** 20 55 S 29 0 E
Gwandu **121** 12 30N 4 41 E
Gwane **126** 4 45N 25 48 E
Gwaram **121** 11 15N 9 51 E
Gwarzo **121** 12 20N 8 55 E
Gwasero **121** 9 30N 8 30 E
Gwaun-Cae-Gurwen **31** 51 46N 3 51W
Gweebarra B. **38** 54 52N 8 21W
Gweedore **38** 55 4N 8 15W
Gweek **30** 50 6N 5 12W
Gwelo **125** 19 28 S 29 45 E
Gwennap **30** 50 12N 5 9W
Gwent □ **31** 51 45N 2 55W
Gweta **128** 20 12 S 25 17 E
Gwi **121** 9 0N 7 10 E
Gwinn **156** 46 15N 87 29W
Gwio Kura **121** 12 40N 11 2 E
Gwolu **120** 10 58N 1 59W
Gwoza **121** 11 12N 13 40 E
Gwyddelwern **31** 53 2N 3 23W
Gwydir, R. **139** 29 27 S 149 48 E
Gwynedd □ **31** 53 0N 4 0W
Gya La **95** 28 45N 84 45 E
Gyangtse **99** 28 50N 89 33 E
Gydanskiy P-ov. **76** 70 0N 78 0 E
Gyland **71** 58 24N 6 45 E
Gympie **139** 26 11 S 152 38 E
Gyobingauk **98** 18 13N 95 39 E
Gyoda **111** 36 10N 139 30 E
Gyoma **53** 46 56N 20 58 E
Gyöngyös **53** 47 48N 20 15 E
Györ **53** 47 41N 17 40 E
Györ-Sopron □ **53** 47 40N 17 20 E
Gypsum Palace **140** 32 37 S 144 9 E
Gypsum Pt. **152** 61 53N 114 35W
Gypsumville **153** 51 45N 98 40W
Gyttorp **72** 59 31N 14 58 E
Gyula **53** 46 38N 21 17 E
Gzhatsk = Gagarin **80** 55 30N 35 0 E

H

Ha Coi **100** 21 26N 107 46 E
Ha Dong **100** 20 58N 105 46 E
Ha Giang **100** 22 50N 104 59 E
Ha Nam = Phu-Ly **100** 20 35N 105 50 E
Ha Tien **101** 10 23N 104 29 E
Ha Tinh **100** 18 20N 105 54 E
Ha Trung **100** 20 0N 105 50 E
Haa, The **36** 60 20N 1 0 E
Haacht **47** 50 59N 4 37 E
Haag **49** 48 11N 12 12 E
Haaksbergen **46** 52 9N 6 45 E
Haaltert **47** 50 55N 4 1 E
Haamstede **47** 51 42N 3 45 E
Haapamäki **74** 62 18N 24 28 E
Haapsalu **80** 58 56N 23 30 E
Haarby **73** 55 13N 10 8 E
Haarlem **46** 52 23N 4 39 E
Haast **143** 43 51 S 169 1 E
Haast P. **143** 44 6 S 169 21 E
Haast, R. **143** 43 50 S 169 2 E
Haastrecht **46** 52 0N 4 47 E
Hab Nadi Chauki **94** 25 0N 66 50 E
Hab, R. **93** 25 15N 67 8 E
Haba **92** 27 10N 47 0 E
Habana, La **166** 23 8N 82 22W
Habaswein **126** 1 2N 39 30 E
Habay **152** 58 50N 118 44W
Habay-la-Neuve **47** 49 44N 5 38 E
Habiganj **98** 24 24N 91 30 E
Hablingbo **73** 57 12N 18 16 E
Habo **73** 57 55N 14 6 E
Haccourt **47** 50 44N 5 40 E
Hachenburg **48** 50 40N 7 49 E
Hachijō-Jima **111** 33 5N 139 45 E
Hachinohe **112** 40 30N 141 29 E
Hachiōji **111** 35 30N 139 30 E
Hachŏn **107** 40 29N 129 2 E
Hachy **47** 49 42N 5 41 E
Hacketstown **39** 52 52N 6 35W
Hackett **152** 52 9N 112 28W
Hackettstown **162** 40 51N 74 50W
Hackney **29** 51 33N 0 2W
Hackthorpe **32** 54 37N 2 42W
Hadali **94** 32 16N 72 11 E
Hadarba, Ras **122** 22 4N 36 51 E
Hadd, Ras al **93** 22 35N 59 50 E
Haddenham **29** 51 46N 0 56W
Haddington **35** 55 57N 2 48W
Haddon Rig **141** 31 27 S 147 52 E
Hadeija **121** 12 30N 10 5 E
Hadeija, R. **121** 12 20N 9 30W
Haden **139** 27 13 S 151 54 E
Hadera **90** 32 27N 34 55 E
Haderslev **73** 55 15N 9 30 E
Hadhra **122** 20 10N 41 5 E
Hadhramaut = Hadramawt **91** 15 30N 49 30 E
Hadibu **91** 12 35N 54 2 E
Hadjeb el Aïoun **119** 35 21N 9 32 E
Hadleigh **29** 52 3N 0 58 E
Hadley **28** 52 42N 2 28W
Hadlow **29** 51 12N 0 20 E
Hadong **107** 35 5N 127 44 E
Hadramawt **91** 15 30N 49 30 E
Hadrians Wall **35** 55 0N 2 30W
Hadsten **73** 56 19N 10 3 E
Hadsund **73** 56 44N 10 8 E
Haeju **107** 38 3N 125 45 E
Haenam **107** 34 34N 126 15 E
Haerhpin **107** 45 45N 126 45 E
Hafar al Batin **92** 28 25N 46 50 E
Hafizabad **94** 32 5N 73 40 E
Haflong **98** 25 10N 93 5 E
Hafnarfjörður **74** 64 4N 21 57W
Haft-Gel **92** 31 30N 49 32 E
Hafun **91** 10 25N 51 16 E
Hafun, Ras **91** 10 29N 51 20 E
Hagalil **90** 32 53N 35 18 E
Hagar Banga **117** 10 40N 22 45 E
Hagari, R. **97** 14 0N 76 45 E
Hagemeister I. **147** 58 42N 161 0W
Hagen **48** 51 21N 7 29 E
Hagenow **48** 53 25N 11 10 E
Hagerman **159** 33 5N 104 22W
Hagerstown **156** 39 39N 77 46W
Hagetmau **44** 43 39N 0 37W
Hagfors **72** 60 3N 13 45 E
Häggenås **72** 63 24N 14 55 E
Hagi, Iceland **74** 65 28N 23 25W
Hagi, Japan **110** 34 30N 131 30 E
Hagion Evstratios **68** 39 30N 25 0 E
Hagion Óros **68** 40 37N 24 6 E
Hags Hd. **39** 52 57N 9 30W
Hague, C. de la **42** 49 44N 1 56W
Hague, The = s'-Gravenhage **47** 52 7N 4 17 E
Haguenau **43** 48 49N 7 47 E
Hai □ **126** 3 10 S 37 10 E
Hai Duong **100** 20 56N 106 19 E
Haian, Kiangsu, China **109** 32 37N 120 33 E
Haian, Kwangtung, China **109** 20 18N 110 11 E
Haich'eng, Fukien, China **109** 24 24N 117 51 E
Haich'eng, Liaoning, China **107** 40 52N 122 45 E
Haichou **107** 34 34N 119 6 E
Haichou Wan **107** 35 0N 119 30 E
Haidar Khel **94** 33 58N 68 38 E
Haifa **90** 32 46N 35 0 E
Haifeng **109** 22 59N 115 21 E
Haig **137** 30 55 S 126 10 E
Haiger **48** 50 44N 8 12 E
Haik'ang **109** 20 56N 110 4 E
Haik'ou **100** 20 5N 110 20 E
Hā'il **92** 27 28N 42 2 E
Hailaerh **105** 49 12N 119 42 E
Hailakandi **98** 24 42N 92 34 E
Hailey **160** 43 30N 114 15W
Haileybury **150** 47 30N 79 38W
Hailin **107** 44 32N 129 24 E
Hailing Tao **109** 21 37N 111 65 E
Hailsham **29** 50 52N 0 17 E
Hailun **105** 47 27N 126 56 E
Hailung **107** 42 30N 125 40 E
Hailuoto **74** 65 3N 24 45 E
Haimen, Chekiang, China **109** 28 39N 121 25 E
Haimen, Kwangtung, China **109** 23 15N 116 35 E
Hainan **100** 19 0N 110 0 E
Hainan Str. = Ch'iungcho Haihsia **100** 20 10N 110 15 E
Hainaut □ **47** 50 30N 4 0 E
Hainburg **53** 48 9N 16 56 E
Haines, Alaska, U.S.A. **147** 59 20N 135 36W
Haines, Oreg., U.S.A. **160** 44 51N 117 59W
Haines City **157** 28 6N 81 35W
Haines Junction **147** 60 45N 137 30W
Hainfeld **52** 48 3N 15 48 E
Haining **109** 30 23N 120 30 E
Hainton **33** 53 21N 0 13W
Haiphong **100** 20 47N 106 35 E
Hait'an Tao **109** 25 35N 119 45 E
Haiti ■ **167** 19 0N 72 30W
Haiya Junc. **122** 18 20N 36 40 E
Haiyang **107** 36 45N 121 15 E
Haiyen **109** 30 28N 120 57 E
Haiyüan, Kwangsi-Chuang, China **108** 22 6N 107 25 E
Haiyüan, Ningsia Hui, China **106** 36 32N 105 40 E
Haja **103** 3 19 S 129 37 E
Hajdú-Bihar □ **53** 47 30N 21 30 E
Hajdúböszörmény **53** 47 40N 21 30 E
Hajdúdurog **53** 47 48N 21 30 E
Hajdúhadház **53** 47 40N 21 40 E
Hajdúnánás **53** 47 50N 21 26 E
Hajdúsámson **53** 47 37N 21 42 E
Hajdúszobaszló **53** 47 27N 21 22 E
Haji Langar **93** 35 50N 79 20 E
Hajiganj **98** 23 15N 90 50 E
Hajipur **95** 25 45N 85 20 E
Hajr **93** 24 0N 56 34 E
Haka **98** 22 39N 93 37 E
Hakansson, Mts. **127** 8 40 S 25 45 E
Hakantorp **73** 58 18N 12 55 E
Håkantorp **73** 58 18N 12 55 E
Hakataramea **143** 44 30 S 170 30 E
Hakataramea, R. **143** 44 35 S 170 40 E
Hakken-Zan **111** 34 10N 135 54 E
Hakodate **112** 41 45N 140 44 E
Hakota **111** 36 5N 140 30 E
Haku-San **111** 36 9N 136 46 E
Hakun **98** 26 46N 95 42 E
Hala **93** 25 43N 68 20 E
Hala Hu **105** 38 15N 97 40 E
Halab = Aleppo **92** 36 10N 37 15 E
Halabjah **92** 35 10N 45 58 E
Halaib **122** 22 5N 36 30 E
Halanzy **47** 49 33N 5 44 E
Halawa **147** 21 9N 156 47W
Halbe **122** 19 40N 42 15 E
Halberstadt **48** 51 53N 11 2 E
Halberton **30** 50 55N 3 24W
Halcombe **142** 40 8 S 175 30 E
Halcyon, Mt. **103** 13 0N 121 30 E
Halden **72** 59 7N 11 23 E
Haldensleben **48** 52 17N 11 30 E
Haldia **99** 22 5N 88 3 E
Haldwani **95** 29 25N 79 30 E
Hale **32** 53 24N 2 21W
Hale, R. **138** 24 56 S 135 53 E
Haleakala Crater **147** 20 43N 156 12W
Halen **47** 50 57N 5 6 E
Halesowen **28** 52 27N 2 2W
Halesworth **29** 52 21N 1 30 E
Haleyville **157** 34 15N 87 40W
Half Assini **120** 5 1N 2 50W
Halfmoon B. **143** 46 50 S 168 5 E
Halfway **160** 44 56N 117 8W
Halfway, R. **152** 56 12N 121 32W
Halhul **90** 31 35N 35 7 E
Hali **122** 18 40N 41 15 E
Haliburton **150** 45 3N 78 30W
Halibut, oilfield **19** 61 20N 1 36 E
Halifax, Austral. **138** 18 32 S 146 22 E
Halifax, Can. **151** 44 38N 63 35W
Halifax, U.K. **32** 53 43N 1 51W
Halifax, U.S.A. **162** 40 25N 76 55W
Halifax B. **138** 18 50 S 147 0 E
Halifax I. **128** 26 38 S 15 4 E
Halil, R. **93** 27 40N 58 30 E
Halkirk **37** 58 30N 3 30W
Hall **52** 47 17N 11 30 E
Hall Land **12** 81 20N 60 0W
Hall Pt. **136** 15 40 S 124 23 E
Hallabro **73** 56 22N 15 5 E
Halland **73** 56 55N 12 50 E
Hallands län □ **73** 56 50N 12 50 E
Hallands Väderö **73** 56 27N 12 34 E
Hallandsås **73** 56 22N 13 0 E
Halle, Belg. **47** 50 44N 4 13W
Halle, Nordrhein-Westfalen, Ger. **48** 52 4N 8 20 E
Halle, Sachsen-Anhalt, Ger. **48** 51 29N 12 0 E
Halle □ **48** 51 28N 11 58 E
Hällefors **72** 59 47N 14 31 E
Hallein **52** 47 40N 13 5 E
Hällekis **73** 58 38N 13 27 E
Hallett **140** 33 25 S 138 55 E
Hallettsville **159** 29 28N 96 57W
Hallevadsholm **73** 58 37N 11 33 E
Hällevadsholm **73** 58 35N 11 33 E
Halley Bay **13** 75 31 S 26 36W
Hallia, R. **96** 16 55N 79 10 E
Halliday **158** 47 20N 102 25W
Halliday L. **153** 61 21N 108 56W
Hallim **107** 33 24N 126 15 E
Hallingdal, R. **71** 60 34N 9 12 E
Hallingskeid **71** 60 40N 7 17 E
Hällnäs **74** 64 19N 19 36 E
Hallock **153** 48 47N 97 57W
Hallow **28** 52 14N 2 15W
Hall's Creek **136** 18 16 S 127 46 E
Hallsberg **72** 59 5N 15 7 E
Hallstahammar **72** 59 38N 16 15 E
Hallstatt **52** 47 33N 13 38 E
Hallstavik **72** 60 5N 18 37 E
Hallstead **162** 41 56N 75 45W
Hallwiler See **50** 47 16N 8 12 E
Hallworthy **30** 50 38N 4 34W
Halmahera, I. **103** 0 40N 128 0 E
Halmeu **70** 47 57N 23 2 E
Halmstad **73** 56 41N 12 52 E
Halq el Oued **119** 36 53N 10 10 E
Hals **73** 56 59N 10 18 E
Halsa **71** 63 3N 8 14 E
Halsafjorden **71** 63 5N 8 10 E
Hälsingborg = Helsingborg **73** 56 3N 12 42 E
Halstad **158** 47 21N 96 41W
Halstead **29** 51 59N 0 39 E
Haltdalen **71** 62 56N 11 8 E
Haltern **48** 51 44N 7 10 E
Haltwhistle **35** 54 58N 2 27W
Ham **128** 49 44N 3 3 E
Ham Tan **101** 10 40N 107 45 E
Ham Yen **100** 22 4N 105 3 E
Hamā **92** 35 5N 36 40 E
Hamab **128** 28 7 S 19 16 E
Hamad **123** 15 20N 33 32 E
Hamada **110** 34 50N 132 10 E
Hamadān **92** 34 52N 48 32 E
Hamadān □ **92** 35 0N 49 0 E
Hamadh **122** 24 55N 39 3 E
Hamadia **118** 35 28N 1 57 E
Hamakita **111** 34 45N 137 47 E
Hamale **120** 10 56N 2 45W
Hamamatsu **111** 34 45N 137 45 E
Hamar **71** 60 48N 11 7 E
Hamar Koke **123** 51 5N 36 45 E
Hamarøy **74** 68 5N 15 38 E
Hamâta, Gebel **122** 24 17N 35 0 E
Hambantota **93** 6 10N 81 10 E
Hamber Prov. Park **152** 52 20N 118 0W
Hambledon **28** 50 56N 1 6W
Hambleton Hills **33** 54 17N 1 12W
Hamburg, Ger. **48** 53 32N 9 59 E
Hamburg, Ark., U.S.A. **159** 33 15N 91 47W
Hamburg, Iowa, U.S.A. **158** 40 37N 95 38W
Hamburg, Pa., U.S.A. **162** 40 33N 76 0W
Hamburg □ **48** 53 30N 10 0 E
Hamden **162** 41 21N 72 56W
Hame **75** 61 30N 24 0 E
Hämeen Lääni **75** 61 24N 24 10 E
Hämeenlinna **75** 61 0N 24 28 E
Hamelin Pool **137** 26 22 S 114 20 E
Hamelin Pool Bay **137** 26 10 S 114 5 E
Hameln **48** 52 7N 9 24 E
Hamersley **136** 22 20 S 117 37 E
Hamersley Ra. **136** 22 0 S 117 45 E
Hamhung **107** 40 0N 127 30 E
Hami **105** 42 47N 93 32 E
Hamilton, Austral. **140** 37 45 S 142 2 E
Hamilton, Can. **150** 43 20N 79 50W
Hamilton, N.Z. **142** 37 47 S 175 19 E
Hamilton, U.K. **35** 55 47N 4 2W
Hamilton, Alas., U.S.A. **147** 62 55N 164 0W
Hamilton, Mont., U.S.A. **160** 46 20N 114 6W
Hamilton, N.Y., U.S.A. **162** 42 49N 75 31W
Hamilton, Ohio, U.S.A. **156** 39 20N 84 35W
Hamilton, Tex., U.S.A. **159** 31 40N 98 5W
Hamilton Downs **106** 21 25 S 142 23 E
Hamilton, gasfield **19** 56 54N 2 13 E
Hamilton Hotel **138** 22 45 S 140 40 E
Hamilton Inlet **151** 54 0N 57 30W
Hamilton Mt. **162** 43 25N 74 22W
Hamilton, R., Queens., Austral. **138** 23 30 S 139 47 E
Hamilton, R., S. Austral., Austral. **136** 26 40 S 134 20 E
Hamiota **153** 50 11N 100 38W
Hamlet **157** 34 56N 79 40W
Hamley Bridge **140** 34 17 S 138 35 E
Hamlin **159** 32 58N 100 8W
Hamm **48** 51 40N 7 58 E
Hammam bou Hadjar **118** 35 23N 0 58W
Hammamet **119** 36 24N 10 38 E
Hammamet, G. de **119** 36 10N 10 48 E
Hammarö, I. **72** 59 20N 13 30 E
Hammarstrand **72** 63 7N 16 20 E
Hamme **47** 51 6N 4 8 E
Hamme-Mille **47** 50 47N 4 43 E
Hammel **73** 56 16N 9 52 E
Hammelburg **49** 50 7N 9 54 E
Hammenton **156** 39 40N 74 47W
Hammeren **73** 55 18N 14 47 E
Hammerfest **74** 70 39N 23 41 E
Hammersmith **29** 51 30N 0 15W
Hammond, Ind., U.S.A. **156** 41 40N 87 30W
Hammond, La., U.S.A. **159** 30 32N 90 30W
Hammonton **162** 39 38N 74 48W
Hamnavoe **36** 60 25N 1 5W
Hamneda **73** 56 41N 13 51 E
Hamoir **47** 50 25N 5 32 E
Hamont **47** 51 15N 5 32 E
Hampden **143** 45 18 S 170 50 E
Hampshire □ **28** 51 3N 1 20W
Hampshire Downs **28** 51 10N 1 10W
Hampton, Ark., U.S.A. **159** 33 35N 92 29W
Hampton, Iowa, U.S.A. **158** 42 42N 93 12W
Hampton, N.H., U.S.A. **162** 42 56N 70 48W
Hampton, S.C., U.S.A. **157** 32 52N 81 2W
Hampton, Va., U.S.A. **162** 37 4N 76 18W
Hampton Bays **162** 40 53N 72 31W
Hampton Harbour **136** 20 30 S 116 30 E
Hampton in Arden **28** 52 26N 1 42W
Hampton Tableland **137** 32 0N 127 0 E
Hamra **92** 24 2N 38 55 E
Hamrange **72** 60 59N 17 5 E
Hamrat esh Sheykh **123** 14 45N 27 55 E
Hamre **71** 60 33N 5 20 E
Hamun Helmand **93** 31 15N 61 15 E
Hamun-i-Lora, Pak. **93** 29 38N 64 58 E
Hamun-i-Lora, Pak. **93** 29 38N 64 58 E
Hamun-i-Mashkel **93** 28 30N 63 0 E
Hamyang **107** 35 32N 127 42 E
Han Chiang, R., Hupeh, China **109** 30 35N 114 15 E

Han Chiang, R., Kwangtung, China 109 23 30N 116 48 E
Hana 147 20 45N 155 59W
Hanak 122 25 32N 37 0 E
Hanamaki 112 39 23N 141 7 E
Hanang □ 126 4 10 S 35 40 E
Hanang, mt. 126 4 30 S 35 25 E
Hanau 49 50 8N 8 56 E
Hanbogd 106 43 11N 107 10 E
Hanch'eng 106 35 30N 110 30 E
Hanchiang 109 25 29N 119 5 E
Hanch'uan 109 30 39N 113 46 E
Hanchuang 107 34 36N 117 22 E
Hanchung 106 33 10N 107 2 E
Hancock, Mich., U.S.A. 158 47 10N 88 35W
Hancock, Minn., U.S.A. 158 45 26N 95 46W
Hancock, Pa., U.S.A. 162 41 57N 75 19W
Handa, Japan 111 34 53N 137 0 E
Handa, Somalia 91 10 37N 51 2 E
Handa I. 36 58 23N 5 10W
Handen 72 59 12N 18 12 E
Handeni 124 5 25 S 38 2 E
Handeni □ 126 5 30 S 38 0 E
Handlová 155 48 45N 18 35 E
Handub 122 19 15N 37 25 E
Handwara 95 34 21N 74 20 E
Handzame 47 51 2N 3 0 E
Hanegev 90 30 50N 35 0 E
Haney 152 49 12N 122 40W
Hanford 163 36 25N 119 39W
Hang Chat 100 18 20N 99 21 E
Hang Dong 100 18 41N 98 55 E
Hangang, R. 107 37 50N 126 30 E
Hangayn Nuruu 105 47 30N 100 0 E
Hangchinch'i 106 39 54N 108 56 E
Hangchinhouch'i 106 41 55N 107 15 E
Hangchou 109 30 15N 120 8 E
Hangchou Wan 109 30 30N 121 30 E
Hanger 73 57 6N 13 58 E
Hangklip, K. 128 34 26 S 18 48 E
Hangö (Hanko) 75 59 59N 22 57 E
Hanhongor 106 43 55N 104 28 E
Hanish J. 91 13 45N 42 46 E
Hanita 90 33 5N 35 10 E
Hankinson 158 46 9N 96 58W
Hanko = Hangö 75 59 59N 22 57 E
Hank'ou 109 30 40N 114 18 E
Hankow = Hank'ou 109 30 40N 114 18 E
Hanksville 161 38 19N 110 45W
Hanku 107 39 16N 117 50 E
Hanle 95 32 42N 79 4 E
Hanmer 143 42 32 S 172 50 E
Hann, Mt. 136 16 0 S 126 0 E
Hann, R. 136 17 26 S 126 17 E
Hanna 152 51 40N 111 54W
Hannaford 158 47 23N 98 18W
Hannah 158 48 58N 98 42W
Hannah B. 150 51 40N 80 0W
Hannahs Bridge 141 31 55 S 149 41 E
Hannibal, Mo., U.S.A. 158 39 42N 91 22W
Hannibal, N.Y., U.S.A. 162 43 19N 76 35W
Hannik 122 18 12N 32 20 E
Hanningfield Water 29 51 40N 0 30 E
Hannover 48 52 23N 9 43 E
Hannut 47 50 40N 5 4 E
Hanö 73 56 0N 14 50 E
Hanö, I. 73 56 2N 14 50 E
Hanöbukten 73 55 35N 14 30 E
Hanoi 100 21 5N 105 55 E
Hanover, S. Afr. 128 31 4 S 24 29 E
Hanover, N.H., U.S.A. 162 43 43N 72 17W
Hanover, Pa., U.S.A. 162 39 46N 76 59W
Hanover, Va., U.S.A. 162 37 46N 77 22W
Hanover = Hannover 48 52 23N 9 43 E
Hanover, I. 176 51 0 S 74 50W
Hanpan, C. 135 5 0 S 154 35 E
Hans Meyer Ra. 135 4 20 S 152 55 E
Hansholm 73 57 8N 8 38 E
Hanshou 109 28 55N 111 58 E
Hansi 94 29 10N 75 57 E
Hansjö 72 61 10N 14 40 E
Hanson, L. 140 31 0 S 136 15 E
Hanson Range 136 27 0 S 136 30 E
Hansted 73 57 8N 8 36 E
Hantan 105 36 42N 114 30 E
Hante 47 50 19N 4 11 E
Hanton 106 36 42N 114 30 E
Hanwood 141 34 26 S 146 3 E
Hanyang 109 30 35N 114 0 E
Hanyin 108 32 53N 108 37 E
Hanyü 111 36 10N 139 32 E
Hanyüan 108 29 21N 102 43 E
Haoch'ing 108 26 34N 100 12 E
Haokang 105 47 25N 132 8 E
Haopi 106 35 57N 114 13 E
Haparanda 74 65 52N 24 8 E
Hapert 47 51 22N 5 15 E
Happy 159 34 47N 101 50W
Happy Camp 160 41 52N 123 30W
Happy Valley 151 53 15N 60 20W
Hapsu 107 41 13N 128 51 E
Hapur 94 28 45N 77 45 E
Haql 92 29 10N 35 0 E
Har 103 5 16 S 133 14 E
Har-Ayrag 106 45 47N 109 16 E
Har Tuv 90 31 46N 35 0 E
Har Us Nuur 105 48 0N 92 10 E
Har Yehuda 90 31 35N 34 57 E
Harad 92 24 15N 49 0 E
Haradera 91 4 33N 47 38 E
Haradh 92 24 15N 49 0 E
Haramsøya 71 62 39N 6 12 E
Haran 92 36 48N 39 0 E
Harat 123 16 5N 39 26 E
Haraze 117 14 20N 19 12 E
Haraze-Mangueigne 117 7 22N 17 3 E
Harbin = Haerhpin 107 45 45N 126 45 E
Harboør 73 56 38N 8 10 E
Harbor Beach 156 43 50N 82 38W
Harbor Springs 156 45 28N 85 0W
Harbour Breton 151 47 29N 55 50W
Harbour Deep 151 50 25N 56 30W
Harbour Grace 151 47 40N 53 22W
Harburg 48 53 27N 9 58 E
Hårby 73 55 13N 10 7 E
Harcourt 138 24 17 S 149 55 E
Harda 94 22 27N 77 5 E
Hardangerfjorden. 71 60 15N 6 0 E
Hardangerjøkulen 71 60 30N 7 0 E
Hardangervidda 71 60 20N 7 20 E
Hardap Dam 128 24 32 S 17 50 E
Hardegarijp 46 53 13N 5 57 E
Harden 141 34 32 S 148 24 E
Hardenberg 46 52 34N 6 37 E
Harderwijk 46 52 21N 5 38 E
Hardey, R. 136 22 45 S 116 8 E
Hardin 160 45 50N 107 35W
Harding 129 30 22 S 29 55 E
Harding Ra. 136 16 17 S 124 55 E
Hardisty 152 52 40N 111 18W
Hardman 160 45 12N 119 49W
Hardoi 95 27 26N 80 15 E
Hardwar 94 29 58N 78 16 E
Hardy 159 36 20N 91 30W
Hardy, Pen. 176 55 30 S 68 20W
Hare B. 151 51 15N 55 45W
Hare Gilboa 90 32 31N 35 25 E
Hare Meron 90 32 59N 35 24 E
Harelbeke 47 50 52N 3 20 E
Haren, Ger. 48 52 47N 7 18 E
Haren, Neth. 46 53 11N 6 36 E
Harer 123 9 20N 42 8 E
Harer □ 123 7 12N 42 0 E
Hareto 123 9 23N 37 6 E
Harfleur 42 49 30N 0 10 E
Hargeisa 91 9 30N 44 2 E
Hargshamn 72 60 12N 18 30 E
Hari, R., Afghan. 93 34 20N 64 30 E
Hari, R., Indon. 102 1 10 S 101 50 E
Haricha, Hamada el 118 22 40N 3 15W
Harihar 97 14 32N 75 44 E
Harim, J. al 60 26 0N 56 10 E
Harima-Nada 110 34 30N 134 35 E
Haringey 29 51 35N 0 7W
Haringhata, R. 98 22 0N 89 58 E
Haringvliet 46 51 48N 4 10 E
Haripad 97 9 14N 76 28 E
Harirúd 93 35 0N 61 0 E
Harkat 122 20 25N 39 40 E
Harlan, Iowa, U.S.A. 158 41 37N 95 20W
Harlan, Tenn., U.S.A. 157 36 58N 83 20W
Harlech 31 52 52N 4 7W
Harlem 160 48 29N 108 39W
Harleston 29 52 25N 1 18 E
Harlingen, Neth. 46 53 11N 5 25 E
Harlingen, U.S.A. 159 26 30N 97 50W
Harlow 29 51 47N 0 9 E
Harlowton 160 46 30N 109 54W
Harmånger 72 61 55N 17 20 E
Harmil 123 16 30N 40 10 E
Harney Basin 160 43 30N 119 0W
Harney L. 160 43 0N 119 0W
Harney Pk. 158 43 52N 103 33W
Härnön 72 62 36N 18 0 E
Harnösand 72 62 38N 18 5 E
Haro 58 42 35N 2 55W
Haro, C. 164 27 50N 110 55W
Haroldswick 36 60 48N 0 50W
Håroy 73 55 13N 10 8 E
Harp L. 151 55 5N 61 50W
Harpe, La 158 40 30N 91 0W
Harpenden 29 51 48N 0 20W
Harpenhalli 97 14 47N 76 2 E
Harper 120 4 25N 7 43 E
Harper Mt. 147 64 15N 143 57W
Harplinge 73 56 45N 12 45 E
Harport L. 36 57 20N 6 20W
Harput 92 38 48N 39 15 E
Harrand 94 29 28N 70 3 E
Harrat al Kishb 92 22 30N 40 15 E
Harrat al Umuirid 92 26 50N 38 0 E
Harrat Khaibar 122 25 45N 40 0 E
Harrat Nawāsīf 122 21 30N 42 0 E
Harray, L. of 37 59 0N 3 15W
Harricana, R. 150 50 30N 79 10W
Harrietsham 29 51 15N 0 41 E
Harriman 157 36 0N 84 35W
Harrington, U.K. 32 54 37N 3 55W
Harrington, U.S.A. 162 38 56N 75 35W
Harrington Harbour 151 50 31N 59 30W
Harris 36 57 50N 6 55W
Harris L. 136 31 10 S 135 10 E
Harris Mts. 143 44 49 S 168 49 E
Harris, Sd. of 36 57 44N 7 6W
Harrisburg, Ill., U.S.A. 159 37 42N 88 30W
Harrisburg, Nebr., U.S.A. 158 41 36N 103 46W
Harrisburg, Oreg., U.S.A. 160 44 25N 123 10W
Harrisburg, Pa., U.S.A. 162 40 18N 76 52W
Harrismith 129 28 15 S 29 8 E
Harrison, Ark., U.S.A. 159 36 10N 93 4W
Harrison, Idaho, U.S.A. 160 47 30N 116 51W
Harrison, Nebr., U.S.A. 158 42 42N 103 52W
Harrison B. 147 70 25N 151 0W
Harrison, C. 151 55 0N 58 0W
Harrison L. 152 49 33N 121 50W
Harrisonburg 156 38 28N 78 52W
Harrisonville 158 38 45N 93 45W
Harriston 150 43 57N 80 53W
Harrisville 150 44 40N 83 19W
Harrogate 33 53 59N 1 32W
Harrow 29 51 35N 0 15W
Harry, L. 139 29 23 S 138 19 E
Harsefeld 48 53 26N 9 31 E
Harskamp 46 52 8N 5 46 E
Harstad 74 68 48N 16 30 E
Hart 156 43 42N 86 21W
Hart, L. 140 31 10 S 136 25 E
Hartbees, R. 128 29 8 S 20 48 E
Hartberg 52 47 17N 15 58 E
Harteigen, Mt. 71 60 11N 7 5 E
Hartest 29 52 7N 0 41 E
Hartford, Conn., U.S.A. 162 41 47N 72 41W
Hartford, Ky., U.S.A. 156 37 26N 86 50W
Hartford, S.D., U.S.A. 158 43 40N 96 58W
Hartford, Wis., U.S.A. 158 43 18N 88 25W
Hartford City 156 40 22N 85 20W
Harthill 35 55 52N 3 45W
Hartland, Can. 151 46 20N 67 32W
Hartland, U.K. 30 50 59N 4 29W
Hartland Pt. 30 51 2N 4 32W
Hartlebury 28 52 20N 2 13W
Hartlepool 33 54 42N 1 11W
Hartley, Zimb. 127 18 10 S 30 7 E
Hartley, U.K. 35 55 5N 1 27W
Hartley Bay 152 53 25N 129 15W
Hartmannberge 128 17 0 S 13 0 E
Hartney 153 49 30N 100 35W
Hartpury 28 51 55N 2 18W
Hartselle 157 34 25N 86 55W
Hartshorne 159 34 51N 95 30W
Hartsville 157 34 23N 80 2W
Hartwell 157 34 21N 82 52W
Harunabad 94 29 35N 73 2 E
Harur 97 12 3N 78 29 E
Harvard, Mt. 161 39 0N 106 5W
Harvey, Austral. 137 33 5 S 115 54 E
Harvey, Ill., U.S.A. 156 41 40N 87 50W
Harvey, N.D., U.S.A. 158 47 50N 99 58W
Harwell 28 51 40N 1 17W
Harwich 29 51 56N 1 18 E
Harwood 33 53 54N 1 30W
Haryana □ 94 29 0N 76 10 E
Harz 48 51 40N 10 40 E
Harzé 47 50 27N 5 40 E
Harzgerode 48 51 38N 11 8 E
Hasa 92 26 0N 49 0 E
Hasaheisa 123 14 25N 33 20 E
Hasani 122 25 0N 37 8 E
Hasanpur 94 28 51N 78 9 E
Haselünne 48 52 40N 7 30 E
Hasharon 90 32 12N 34 49 E
Hashefela 90 31 30N 34 43 E
Hashima 111 35 20N 136 40 E
Hashimoto 111 34 19N 135 37 E
Hasjö 72 63 2N 16 20 E
Håsjö 72 63 1N 16 5 E
Haskell, Kans., U.S.A. 159 35 51N 95 40W
Haskell, Tex., U.S.A. 159 33 10N 99 45W
Haskier Is. 36 57 42N 7 40W
Haslach 49 48 16N 8 7 E
Hasle 73 55 11N 14 44 E
Haslemere 29 51 5N 0 41W
Haslev 73 55 18N 11 57 E
Haslingden 32 53 43N 2 20W
Hasparren 44 43 24N 1 18W
Hassan 92 13 0N 76 5 E
Hasselt, Belg. 47 50 56N 5 21 E
Hasselt, Neth. 46 52 36N 6 6 E
Hassene, Ad. 118 21 0N 4 0 E
Hassfurt 49 50 2N 10 30 E
Hassi Berrekrem 119 33 45N 5 16 E
Hassi Daoula 119 33 4N 5 38 E
Hassi el Biod 119 28 30N 6 0 E
Hassi el Heïda 74 29 34N 0 14W
Hassi Inifel 118 29 50N 3 41 E
Hassi Marroket 119 30 10N 3 0 E
Hassi Messaoud 119 31 43N 6 8 E
Hassi Taguenza 172 29 8N 0 23W
Hassi Zerzour 118 30 51N 3 56W
Hässleby 73 57 37N 15 30 E
Hässleholmen 73 56 9N 13 45 E
Hastière-Lavaux 47 50 13N 4 49 E
Hastigrow 37 58 32N 3 15W
Hastings, Austral. 141 38 18 S 145 12 E
Hastings, N.Z. 142 39 39 S 176 52 E
Hastings, U.K. 29 50 51N 0 36 E
Hastings, Mich., U.S.A. 156 42 40N 82 20W
Hastings, Minn., U.S.A. 158 44 41N 92 51W
Hastings, Nebr., U.S.A. 158 40 34N 98 22W
Hastings Ra. 141 31 15 S 152 14 E
Hästveda 73 56 17N 13 55 E
Hat Nhao 101 14 46N 106 32 E
Hat Yai 101 7 1N 100 27 E
Hatanbulag 106 43 8N 109 14 E
Hatano 111 35 22N 139 14 E
Hatch 161 32 45N 107 8W
Hatches Creek 138 20 56 S 135 12 E
Hatchet L. 153 58 36N 103 40W
Haţeg 70 45 36N 22 55 E
Haţeg, Mţii 70 45 25N 23 0 E
Hatert 46 51 49N 5 50 E
Hatfield 29 51 46N 0 11W
Hatfield Broad Oak 29 51 48N 0 16 E
Hatfield Post Office 140 33 54N 143 49 E
Hatgal 105 50 26N 100 9 E
Hatherleigh 30 50 49N 4 4W
Hathersage 33 53 20N 1 39W
Hathras 94 27 36N 78 6 E
Hatia 99 22 30N 91 5 E
Hato de Corozal 174 6 11N 71 45W
Hato Mayor 167 18 46N 69 15W
Hattah 140 34 48N 142 17 E
Hattem 46 52 28N 6 4 E
Hatteras, C. 157 35 10N 75 30W
Hattiesburg 159 31 20N 89 20W
Hatton, Can. 153 50 2N 109 50W
Hatton, U.K. 37 57 24N 1 57W
Hatvan 53 47 40N 19 45 E
Hau Bon (Cheo Reo) 100 13 25N 108 28 E
Hau Duc 100 15 20N 108 13 E
Hauchinango 164 20 12N 97 45W
Haug 71 60 23N 10 26 E
Haugastøl 71 60 30N 7 50 E
Haugesund 71 59 23N 5 13 E
Haugh of Urr 35 55 0N 3 51W
Haughangaroa Ra. 142 38 42 S 175 40 E
Haughley 29 52 13N 0 59 E
Haukelisæter 71 59 51N 7 9 E
Haulerwijk 46 53 4N 6 20 E
Haultain, R. 153 55 51N 106 46W
Haungpa 98 25 29N 96 7 E
Haura 91 13 50N 47 35 E
Hauraki Gulf 142 36 35 S 175 5 E
Hausruck 52 48 6N 13 30 E
Haut Atlas 118 32 0N 7 0W
Haut-Rhin □ 43 48 0N 7 15 E
Haut Zaïre □ 126 2 20N 26 0 E
Hauta Oasis 92 23 40N 47 0 E
Hautah, Wahāt al 92 23 40N 47 0 E
Haute-Corse □ 45 42 30N 9 30 E
Haute-Garonne □ 44 43 28N 1 30 E
Haute-Loire □ 44 45 5N 3 50 E
Haute-Marne □ 43 48 10N 5 20 E
Haute-Saône □ 43 47 45N 6 10 E
Haute-Savoie □ 45 46 0N 6 20 E
Haute-Vienne □ 44 45 50N 1 10 E
Hauterive 151 49 10N 68 16W
Hautes-Alpes □ 45 44 42N 6 20 E
Hautes Fagnes 47 50 34N 6 6 E
Hautes-Pyrénées □ 44 43 0N 0 10 E
Hauteville-Lompnes 45 45 59N 5 35 E
Hautmont 43 50 15N 3 55 E
Hautrage 47 50 29N 3 46 E
Hauts-de-Seine □ 43 48 52N 2 15 E
Hauts Plateaux 118 34 14N 1 0 E
Hauxley 35 55 21N 1 35W
Havana 158 40 19N 90 3W
Havana = La Habana 166 23 8N 82 22W
Havant 29 50 51N 0 59W
Havasu, L. 161 34 18N 114 8W
Havdhem 73 57 10N 18 20 E
Havelange 47 50 23N 5 15 E
Havelian 94 34 2N 73 10 E
Havelock, N.B., Can. 151 46 2N 65 24W
Havelock, Ont., Can. 150 44 26N 77 53W
Havelock, N.Z. 143 41 17 S 173 48 E
Havelock I. 101 11 55N 93 2 E
Havelte 46 52 46N 6 14 E
Haverfordwest 31 51 48N 4 59W
Haverhill, U.K. 29 52 6N 0 27 E
Haverhill, U.S.A. 162 42 50N 71 2W
Haveri 97 14 53N 75 24 E
Haverigg 32 54 12N 3 16W
Havering 29 51 33N 0 20 E
Haverstraw 162 41 12N 73 58W
Håverud 73 58 50N 12 28 E
Havîrna 70 48 4N 26 43 E
Havlíčkuv Brod 52 49 36N 15 33 E
Havnby 73 55 5N 8 34 E
Havre 160 48 40N 109 34W
Havre-Aubert 151 47 12N 62 0W
Havre de Grace 162 39 33N 76 6W
Havre, Le 42 49 30N 0 5 E
Havre St. Pierre 151 50 18N 63 33W
Havza 92 41 0N 35 35 E
Haw, R. 157 37 43N 80 52W
Hawaii □ 147 20 30N 157 0W
Hawaii I. 147 20 0N 155 0W
Hawaiian Is. 147 20 30N 156 0W
Hawarden, Can. 153 51 25N 106 36W
Hawarden, U.K. 31 53 11N 3 2W
Hawarden, U.S.A. 158 43 2N 96 28W
Hawea Flat 143 44 40 S 169 19 E
Hawea Lake 143 44 28 S 169 19 E
Hawera 142 39 35 S 174 19 E
Hawes 32 54 18N 2 12W
Hawes Water, L. 32 54 32N 2 48W
Hawick 35 55 25N 2 48W
Hawk Junction 150 48 30N 84 38W
Hawkchurch 30 50 47N 2 56W
Hawkdun Ra. 143 44 53 S 170 5 E
Hawke B. 142 39 25N 177 20 E
Hawker 28 31 59 S 138 22 E
Hawke's Bay □ 142 39 45 S 176 35 E
Hawke's Harbour 151 53 2N 55 50W
Hawkesbury 150 45 35N 74 40W
Hawkesbury I. 152 53 37N 129 3W
Hawkesbury Pt. 138 11 55 S 134 5 E
Hawkesbury River 133 33 50 S 151 44W
Hawkesbury Upton 28 51 34N 2 19W
Hawkhurst 29 51 2N 0 31 E
Hawkinsville 157 32 17N 83 30W
Hawkshead 32 54 23N 3 0W
Hawkwood 139 25 45 S 150 50 E
Hawley, Minn., U.S.A. 158 46 58N 96 20W
Hawley, Pa., U.S.A. 162 41 28N 75 11W
Haworth 32 53 50N 1 57W
Hawsker 33 54 27N 0 34W
Hawthorne 163 38 31N 118 37W
Hawzen 123 13 58N 39 28 E

Haxby **33** 54 1N 1 4W
Haxtun **158** 40 40N 102 39W
Hay, Austral. **141** 34 30S 144 51E
Hay, U.K. **31** 52 4N 3 9W
Hay, C. **136** 14 5S 129 29E
Hay L. **152** 58 50N 118 50W
Hay Lakes **152** 53 12N 113 2W
Hay, R., Austral. **138** 24 10S 137 20E
Hay, R., Can. **152** 60 0N 116 56W
Hay River **152** 60 51N 115 44W
Hay Springs **158** 42 40N 102 38W
Hayange **43** 49 20N 6 2E
Hayato **110** 31 40N 130 43E
Hayburn Wyke **33** 54 22N 0 28W
Haycock **147** 65 10N 161 20W
Hayden, Ariz., U.S.A. **161** 33 2N 110 54W
Hayden, Wyo., U.S.A. **160** 40 30N 107 22W
Haydenville **162** 42 22N 72 42W
Haydon **138** 18 0S 141 30E
Haydon Bridge **35** 54 58N 2 15W
Haye Descartes, La **42** 46 58N 0 42E
Haye-du-Puits, La **42** 49 17N 1 33W
Hayes **158** 44 22N 101 1W
Hayes Pen. **12** 75 30N 65 0W
Hayes, R. **153** 57 3N 92 12W
Hayle **30** 50 12N 5 25W
Haymana **92** 39 30N 32 35E
Haynesville **159** 33 0N 93 7W
Hays, Can. **152** 50 6N 111 48W
Hays, U.S.A. **158** 38 55N 99 25W
Hayton **32** 54 55N 2 45W
Hayward, Calif., U.S.A. **163** 37 40N 122 5W
Hayward, Wis., U.S.A. **158** 46 2N 91 30W
Hayward's Heath **29** 51 0N 0 5W
Hazard **156** 37 18N 83 10W
Hazaribagh **95** 23 58N 85 26E
Hazaribagh Road **95** 24 12N 85 57E
Hazebrouck **43** 50 42N 2 31E
Hazelton, Can. **152** 55 20N 127 42W
Hazelton, U.S.A. **158** 46 30N 100 15W
Hazen **160** 39 37N 119 2W
Hazerswoude **46** 52 5N 4 36E
Hazlehurst **157** 31 50N 82 35W
Hazleton **156** 40 58N 76 0W
Hazlett, L. **136** 21 30S 128 48E
Hazrat Imam **93** 37 15N 68 50E
Heacham **29** 52 55N 0 30E
Head of Bight **137** 31 30S 131 25E
Headcorn **29** 51 10N 0 39E
Headford **38** 53 28N 9 6W
Headington **28** 51 46N 1 13W
Headlands **127** 18 15S 32 2E
Healdsburg **160** 38 33N 122 51W
Healdton **159** 34 16N 97 31W
Healesville **141** 37 35S 145 30E
Heanor **33** 53 1N 1 20W
Heard I. **11** 53 0S 74 0E
Hearne **159** 30 54N 96 35W
Hearne B. **153** 60 10N 99 10W
Hearne L. **152** 62 20N 113 10W
Hearst **150** 49 40N 83 41W
Heart, R. **158** 46 40N 101 30W
Heart's Content **151** 47 54N 53 27W
Heath Mts. **143** 45 39S 167 9E
Heath Pt. **151** 49 8N 61 40W
Heath Steele **151** 47 17N 66 5W
Heathcote **141** 36 56S 144 45E
Heather, oilfield **19** 60 55N 0 50E
Heathfield **29** 50 58N 0 18E
Heathsville **162** 37 55N 76 28W
Heavener **159** 34 54N 94 36W
Hebbronville **159** 27 20N 98 40W
Hebburn **35** 54 59N 1 30W
Hebden Bridge **32** 53 45N 2 0W
Hebel **139** 28 58S 147 47E
Heber Springs **159** 35 29N 91 39W
Hebgen, L. **160** 44 50N 111 15W
Hebrides, U.K. **36** 57 30N 7 0W
Hebrides, Inner Is., U.K. **36** 57 20N 6 40W
Hebrides, Outer Is., U.K. **36** 57 50N 7 25W
Hebron, Can. **149** 58 12N 62 38W
Hebron, N.D., U.S.A. **158** 46 56N 102 2W
Hebron, Nebr., U.S.A. **158** 40 15N 97 33W
Hebron (Al Khalil) **90** 31 32N 35 6E
Heby **72** 59 56N 16 53E
Hecate Str. **152** 53 10N 130 30W
Hechingen **49** 48 20N 8 58E
Hechtel **47** 51 8N 5 22E
Heckington **33** 52 59N 0 17W
Hecla **158** 45 56N 98 8W
Hecla I. **153** 51 10N 96 43W
Hecla Mt. **36** 57 18N 7 15W
Heddal **71** 59 36N 9 20E
Heddon **35** 55 0N 1 47W
Hédé **42** 48 18N 1 49W
Hede **72** 62 23N 13 30E
Hedemora **72** 60 18N 15 58E
Hedgehope **143** 46 12S 168 34E
Hedley **159** 34 53N 100 39W
Hedmark □ **75** 61 17N 11 40E
Hedmark fylke □ **71** 61 17N 11 40E
Hednesford **28** 52 43N 2 0W
Hedon **33** 53 44N 0 11W
Hedrum **71** 59 7N 10 5E
Heeg **46** 52 58N 5 37E
Heegermeer **46** 52 56N 5 32E
Heemskerk **46** 52 31N 4 40E
Heemstede **46** 52 22N 4 37E
Heer **47** 50 50N 5 43E
Heerde **46** 52 24N 6 2E
's Heerenburg **46** 51 53N 6 16E
's Heerenloo **46** 52 19N 5 36E
Heerenveen **46** 52 57N 5 55E
Heerhugowaard **46** 52 40N 4 51E
Heerlen **47** 50 55N 6 0E
Heerlerheide **47** 50 54N 5 58E
Heers **47** 50 45N 5 18E
Heesch **46** 51 44N 5 32E
Heestert **47** 50 47N 3 25E
Heeze **47** 51 23N 5 35E
Hegyalja, Mts. **53** 48 25N 21 25E
Heich'engchen **106** 36 16N 106 19E
Heide **48** 54 10N 9 7E
Heide, oilfield **19** 54 5N 9 5E
Heidelberg, Ger. **49** 49 23N 8 41E
Heidelberg, C. Prov., S. Afr. **128** 34 6S 20 59E
Heidelberg, Trans., S. Afr. **129** 26 30S 28 23E
Heidenheim **49** 48 40N 10 10E
Heigun-To **110** 33 47N 132 14E
Heikant **47** 51 15N 4 1E
Heilam **37** 58 31N 4 40W
Heilbron **129** 27 16S 27 59E
Heilbronn **49** 49 8N 9 13E
Heiligenblut **52** 47 2N 12 51E
Heiligenhafen **48** 54 21N 10 58E
Heiligenstadt **48** 51 22N 10 9E
Heilungkiang □ **46** 48 0N 128 0E
Heim **71** 63 26N 9 5E
Heimdal, gasfield **19** 59 35N 2 15E
Heino **46** 52 26N 6 14E
Heinola **75** 61 13N 26 24E
Heinsburg **153** 53 50N 110 30W
Heinsch **47** 49 42N 5 44E
Heinsun **98** 25 52N 95 35E
Heinze Is. **101** 14 25N 97 45E
Heirnkut **98** 25 14N 94 44E
Heishan **107** 41 40N 122 3E
Heishui, Liaoning, China **107** 42 6N 119 22E
Heishui, Szechwan, China **108** 32 15N 103 0E
Heist **47** 51 20N 3 15E
Heist-op-den-Berg **47** 51 5N 4 44E
Heistad **71** 59 35N 9 40E
Hejaz = Hijāz **92** 26 0N 37 30E
Hekelegem **47** 50 55N 4 7E
Hekimhan **92** 38 50N 38 0E
Hekinan **111** 34 52N 137 0E
Hekla **74** 63 56N 19 35W
Hel **54** 54 38N 18 50E
Helagsfjället **72** 62 54N 12 25E
Helchteren **47** 51 4N 5 22E
Helden **47** 51 19N 6 0E
Helechosa **57** 39 22N 4 53W
Helena, Ark., U.S.A. **159** 34 30N 90 35W
Helena, Mont., U.S.A. **160** 46 40N 112 0W
Helendale **163** 34 45N 117 19W
Helensburgh, Austral. **141** 34 11S 151 1E
Helensburgh, U.K. **34** 56 0N 4 44W
Helensville **142** 36 41S 174 29E
Helets **90** 31 36N 34 39E
Helgasjön **73** 57 0N 14 50E
Helgeland **74** 66 20N 13 30E
Helgeroa **71** 59 0N 9 45E
Helgoland, I. **48** 54 10N 7 51E
Helgum **72** 63 25N 16 50E
Heligoland = Helgoland **48** 54 10N 7 51E
Heliopolis **122** 30 6N 31 17E
Hell-Ville **129** 13 25S 48 16E
Hellebæk **73** 56 4N 12 32E
Helleland **71** 58 33N 6 7E
Hellendoorn **46** 52 24N 6 27E
Hellertown **162** 40 35N 75 21W
Hellevoetsluis **46** 51 50N 4 8E
Helli Ness **36** 60 3N 1 10W
Hellick Kenyon Plateau **13** 82 0S 110 0W
Hellifield **32** 54 0N 2 13W
Hellín **59** 38 31N 1 40W
Hellum **73** 57 16N 10 10E
Helmand □ **93** 31 20N 64 0E
Helmand, R. **94** 34 0N 67 0E
Helmond **47** 51 29N 5 41E
Helmsdale **37** 58 7N 3 40W
Helmsley **33** 54 15N 1 2W
Helmstedt **48** 52 16N 11 0E
Helnæs **73** 55 9N 10 0E
Helper **160** 39 44N 110 56W
Helperby **33** 54 8N 1 20W
Helsby **32** 53 16N 2 47W
Helsingborg **73** 56 3N 12 42E
Helsinge **73** 56 2N 12 12E
Helsingfors = Helsinki **75** 60 15N 25 3E
Helsingør **73** 56 2N 12 35E
Helsinki (Helsingfors) **75** 60 15N 25 3E
Helston **30** 50 7N 5 17W
Helvick Hd. **39** 52 3N 7 33W
Helvoirt **47** 51 38N 5 14E
Helwân **122** 29 50N 31 20E
Hem **71** 59 26N 10 0E
Hemavati, R. **97** 12 50N 67 0E
Hemel Hempstead **29** 51 45N 0 28W
Hemet **163** 33 45N 116 59W
Hemingford **158** 42 21N 103 4W
Hemphill **159** 31 21N 93 49W
Hempstead **159** 30 5N 96 5W
Hempton **29** 52 50N 0 49E
Hemse **73** 57 15N 18 22E
Hemsö, I. **72** 62 43N 18 5E
Hemsön **72** 62 42N 18 5E
Hemsworth **33** 53 37N 1 21W
Hemyock **30** 50 55N 1 13W
Hen & Chicken Is. **142** 35 58S 174 45E
Henares, R. **58** 40 55N 3 0W
Hendaye **44** 43 23N 1 47W
Henderson, Argent. **172** 36 18S 61 43W
Henderson, U.K. **36** 57 42N 5 47W
Henderson, Ky., U.S.A. **156** 37 50N 87 38W
Henderson, Nev., U.S.A. **161** 36 2N 115 0W
Henderson, Pa., U.S.A. **157** 35 25N 88 40W
Henderson, Tex., U.S.A. **159** 32 5N 94 49W
Hendersonville **157** 35 21N 82 28W
Hendon **139** 28 5S 151 50E
Hendorf **70** 46 4N 24 5E
Henfield **29** 50 56N 0 17W
Hengch'eng **106** 38 26N 106 26E
Hengelo, Gelderland, Neth. **46** 52 3N 6 19E
Hengelo, Overijssel, Neth. **46** 52 16N 6 48E
Hengfeng **109** 28 25N 117 35E
Henghsien **108** 22 36N 109 16E
Hengoed **31** 51 39N 3 14W
Hengshan, Hunan, China **109** 27 15N 112 51E
Hengshan, Shansi, China **106** 37 56N 108 53E
Hengshui **106** 37 43N 115 42E
Hengtaohotze **107** 44 55N 129 3E
Hengyang **109** 26 51N 112 30E
Hengyanghsien **109** 26 58N 112 21E
Hénin-Beaumont **43** 50 25N 2 58E
Henley **29** 51 32N 0 53W
Henley-in-Arden **28** 52 18N 1 47W
Henllan **31** 53 13N 3 29W
Henlopen, C. **162** 38 48N 75 5W
Henlow **29** 51 2N 0 18W
Hennan, L. **72** 62 3N 15 55E
Henne **73** 55 44N 8 11E
Hennebont **42** 47 49N 3 19W
Hennenman **128** 27 59S 27 1E
Hennessy **159** 36 8N 97 53W
Hennigsdorf **48** 52 38N 13 13E
Henribourg **153** 53 25N 105 38W
Henrichemont **43** 47 20N 2 21E
Henrietta **159** 33 50N 98 15W
Henrietta Maria C. **150** 55 9N 82 20W
Henry **158** 41 5N 89 20W
Henryetta **159** 35 2N 96 0W
Henstridge **28** 50 59N 2 24W
Hentiyn Nuruu **105** 48 30N 108 30E
Henty **141** 35 30N 147 0E
Henzada **98** 17 38N 95 35E
Heppner **160** 45 27N 119 34W
Herad **71** 58 8N 6 47E
Héraðsflói **74** 65 42N 14 12W
Héradsvötn **74** 65 25N 19 5W
Herald Cays **138** 16 58S 149 9E
Herāt **93** 34 20N 62 7E
Herāt □ **93** 35 0N 62 0E
Hérault □ **44** 43 34N 3 15E
Hérault, R. **44** 43 20N 3 32E
Herbert **153** 50 30N 107 10W
Herbert Downs **138** 23 7S 139 9E
Herbert I. **147** 52 49N 170 10W
Herbert, R. **138** 18 31S 146 17E
Herberton **138** 17 28S 145 25E
Herbertstown **39** 52 32N 8 29W
Herbiers, Les **42** 46 52N 1 0W
Herbignac **42** 47 27N 2 18W
Herborn **48** 50 40N 8 19E
Herby **54** 50 45N 18 50E
Hercegnovi **66** 42 30N 18 33E
Herðubreið **74** 65 11N 16 21W
Herdla **71** 60 34N 4 56E
Hereford, U.K. **28** 52 4N 2 42W
Hereford, U.S.A. **159** 34 50N 102 28W
Hereford and Worcester □ **28** 52 10N 2 30W
Herefordshire □ **26** 52 15N 2 50W
Herefoss **71** 58 32N 8 32E
Herekino **142** 35 18S 173 11E
Herent **47** 50 54N 4 40E
Herentals **47** 51 12N 4 51E
Herenthout **47** 51 8N 4 45E
Herfølge **73** 55 26N 12 9E
Herford **48** 52 7N 8 40E
Héricourt **43** 47 32N 6 55E
Herington **158** 38 43N 97 0W
Herisau **51** 47 22N 9 17E
Hérisson **44** 46 32N 2 42E
Herjehogna **75** 61 43N 12 7E
Herk, R. **47** 50 56N 5 12E
Herkenbosch **47** 51 9N 6 4E
Herkimer **162** 43 0N 74 59W
Herm I. **42** 49 30N 2 28W
Herma Ness **36** 60 50N 0 54W
Hermagor **52** 46 38N 13 23E
Herman **158** 45 51N 96 8W
Hermandez **163** 36 24N 120 46W
Hermann **158** 38 40N 91 25W
Hermannsburg **48** 52 49N 10 6E
Hermannsburg Mission **136** 23 57S 132 45E
Hermanus **128** 34 27S 19 12E
Herment **44** 45 45N 2 24E
Hermidale **141** 31 30S 146 42E
Hermiston **160** 45 50N 119 16W
Hermitage **143** 43 44S 170 5E
Hermitage B. **151** 47 33N 56 10W
Hermite, Is. **176** 55 50S 68 0W
Hermon, Mt. = Sheikh, J. ash **92** 33 20N 36 0E
Hermosillo **164** 29 10N 111 0W
Hernad, R. **53** 48 20N 21 15E
Hernandarias **173** 25 20S 54 40W
Hernando, Argent. **172** 32 28S 63 40W
Hernando, U.S.A. **159** 34 50N 89 59W
Herndon **162** 40 43N 76 51W
Herne, Belg. **47** 50 44N 4 2E
Herne, Ger. **48** 51 33N 7 12E
Herne Bay **29** 51 22N 1 8E
Herne Hill **137** 31 45S 116 5E
Herning **73** 56 8N 8 58E
Heroica Nogales **164** 31 14N 110 56W
Heron Bay **150** 48 40N 85 25W
Heröy **71** 62 18N 5 45E
Herreid **158** 45 53N 100 5W
's Herrenbroek **46** 52 32N 6 1E
Herrera **57** 39 12N 4 50W
Herrera de Alcántar **57** 39 39N 7 25W
Herrera de Pisuerga **56** 42 35N 4 20W
Herrera del Duque **57** 39 10N 5 3W
Herrero, Punta **165** 19 17N 87 27W
Herrick **138** 41 5S 147 55E
Herrin **159** 37 50N 89 0W
Herrljunga **73** 58 5N 13 1E
Hersbruck **49** 49 30N 11 25E
Herschel I. **147** 69 35N 139 5W
Herseaux **47** 50 43N 3 15E
Herselt **47** 51 3N 4 53E
Herserange **47** 49 30N 5 48E
Hershey **162** 40 17N 76 39W
Herstal **47** 50 40N 5 38E
Herstmonceux **29** 50 53N 0 21E
Hersvik **71** 61 10N 4 53E
Hertford **29** 51 47N 0 4W
Hertford □ **29** 51 51N 0 5W
's Hertogenbosch **47** 51 42N 5 18E
Hertzogville **128** 28 9S 25 30E
Hervás **56** 40 16N 5 52W
Herve **47** 50 38N 5 48E
Hervey B. **133** 25 0S 152 52E
• Hervey Is. **131** 19 30S 159 0W
Hervey Junction **150** 46 50N 72 29W
Herwijnen **46** 51 50N 5 7E
Herzberg, Cottbus, Ger. **48** 51 40N 13 13E
Herzberg, Niedersachsen, Ger. **48** 51 38N 10 20E
Herzele **47** 50 53N 3 53E
Herzliyya **90***32 10N 34 50E
Herzogenbuchsee **50** 47 11N 7 42E
Herzogenburg **52** 48 17N 15 41E
Hesdin **43** 50 21N 2 0E
Hesel **48** 53 18N 7 36E
Heskestad **71** 58 28N 6 22E
Hesperange **47** 49 35N 6 10E
Hesperia **163** 34 25N 117 18W
Hesse = Hessen **48** 50 57N 9 20E
Hessen □ **48** 50 57N 9 20E
Hessle **33** 53 44N 0 28E
Hetch Hetchy Aqueduct **163** 37 36N 121 25W
Heteren **46** 51 58N 5 46E
Hethersett **29** 52 35N 1 10E
Hettinger **158** 46 8N 102 38W
Hetton-le-Hole **35** 54 49N 1 26W
Hettstedt **48** 51 39N 11 30E
Heugem **47** 50 49N 5 42E
Heule **47** 50 51N 3 15E
Heusden, Belg. **47** 51 2N 5 17E
Heusden, Neth. **46** 51 44N 5 8E
Hève, C. de la **42** 49 30N 0 5E
Heverlee **47** 50 52N 4 42E
Heves □ **53** 47 50N 20 0E
Hevron, N. **90** 31 28N 34 52E
Hewett, C. **149** 70 16N 67 45W
Hewett, gasfield **19** 53 5N 1 50E
Hex River **128** 33 30S 19 35E
Hexham **35** 54 58N 2 7W
Heybridge **29** 51 44N 0 42E
Heyfield **141** 37 59S 146 47E
Heysham **32** 54 5N 2 53W
Heytesbury **28** 51 11N 2 7W
Heythuysen **47** 51 15N 5 55E
Heywood, Austral. **140** 38 8S 141 37E
Heywood, U.K. **32** 53 36N 2 13W
Hi-no-Misaki **110** 35 26N 132 38E
Hi Vista **163** 34 44N 117 46W
Hiamen **109** 31 52N 121 15E
Hiawatha, Kans., U.S.A. **158** 39 55N 95 33W
Hiawatha, Utah, U.S.A. **160** 39 37N 111 1W
Hibbing **158** 47 30N 93 0W
Hibbs B. **138** 42 35S 145 15E
Hibbs, Pt. **138** 42 38S 145 15E
Hibernia Reef **136** 12 0S 123 23E
Hibiki-Nada **110** 34 0N 130 0E
Hickman **159** 36 35N 89 8W
Hickory **157** 35 46N 81 17W
Hicks Bay **142** 37 34S 178 21E
Hicksville **162** 40 46N 73 30W
Hida-Gawa **70** 47 10N 23 9E
Hida-Gawa, R. **111** 35 26N 137 3E
Hida-Sammyaku **111** 36 30N 137 40E
Hida-Sanchi **111** 36 10N 137 0E
Hidaka **110** 35 30N 134 44E
Hidalgo □ **164** 20 30N 99 10W
Hidalgo del Parral **164** 26 58N 105 40W
Hidalgo, Presa M. **164** 26 30N 108 35W
Hiddensee **48** 54 30N 13 6E
Hidrolândia **171** 17 0S 49 15W
Hieflau **52** 47 36N 14 46E
Hiendelaencina **58** 41 5N 3 0W
Hierro I. **116** 27 57N 17 56E
Higashi-matsuyama **111** 36 2N 139 25E
Higashiōsaka **111** 34 40N 135 37E

*Renamed Manuae

Higasi-Suidō 110 34 0N 129 30 E
Higgins 159 36 9N 100 1W
Higginsville 137 31 42 S 121 38 E
Higgs I. L. 157 36 20N 78 30W
High Atlas = Haut Atlas 118 32 30N 5 0W
High Bentham 32 54 8N 2 31W
High Borrow Bri. 32 54 26N 2 43W
High Bridge 162 40 40N 74 54W
High Ercall 28 52 46N 2 37W
High Hesket 32 54 47N 2 49W
High I. 151 56 40N 61 10W
High Island 159 29 32N 94 22W
High Level 152 58 31N 117 8W
High Pike, mt. 32 54 43N 3 4W
High Point 157 35 57N 79 58W
High Prairie 152 55 30N 116 30W
High River 152 50 30N 113 50W
High Springs 157 29 50N 82 40W
High Tatra 53 49 30N 20 00 E
High Veld = Hoëveld 129 26 30 S 30 0 E
High Willhays, hill 30 50 41N 3 59W
High Wycombe 29 51 37N 0 45W
Higham Ferrers 29 52 18N 0 36W
Highbank 138 47 34 S 171 45 E
Highbridge 28 51 13N 2 59W
Highbury 138 16 25 S 143 9 E
Highclere 28 51 20N 1 22W
Highland □ 36 57 30N 5 0W
Highland Pk. 156 42 10N 87 50W
Highland Springs 162 37 33N 77 20W
Highley 28 52 25N 2 23W
Highmore 158 44 35N 99 26W
Highrock L. 153 57 5N 105 32W
Hightae 35 55 5N 3 27W
Hightstown 162 40 16N 74 31W
Highworth 28 51 38N 1 42W
Higley 161 33 27N 111 46W
Higüay 167 18 37N 68 42W
Higüero, Pta. 147 18 22N 67 16W
Hiiumaa 80 58 50N 22 45 E
Hijar 58 41 10N 0 27W
Hijāz 91 26 0N 37 30 E
Hiji 110 33 22N 131 32 E
Hijken 46 52 54N 6 30 E
Hikari 110 33 58N 131 58 E
Hiketa 110 34 13N 134 24 E
Hiko 161 37 30N 115 13W
Hikone 111 35 15N 136 10 E
Hikurangi, East Court 142 37 55 S 178 4 E
Hikurangi, Mt. 142 37 55 S 178 4 E
Hilawng 98 21 23N 93 48 E
Hildburghhausen 49 50 24N 10 43 E
Hildesheim 48 52 9N 9 55 E
Hilgay 29 52 34N 0 23 E
Hill 150 45 40N 74 45W
Hill City, Idaho, U.S.A. 160 43 20N 115 2W
Hill City, Kans., U.S.A. 158 39 25N 99 51W
Hill City, Minn., U.S.A. 158 46 57N 93 35W
Hill City, S.D., U.S.A. 158 43 58N 103 35W
Hill End 141 38 1 S 146 9 E
Hill Island L. 153 60 30N 109 50W
Hill, R. 137 30 23 S 115 3 E
Hilla, Iraq 92 32 30N 44 27 E
Hilla, Si Arab. 92 23 35N 46 50 E
Hillared 73 57 37N 13 10 E
Hillegom 46 52 18N 4 35 E
Hillerød 73 55 56N 12 19 E
Hillerstorp 73 57 20N 13 52 E
Hilli 98 25 17N 89 1 E
Hillingdon 29 51 33N 0 29W
Hillman 156 45 5N 83 52W
Hillmond 153 53 26N 109 41W
Hillsboro, Kans., U.S.A. 158 38 28N 97 10W
Hillsboro, N. Mex., U.S.A. 161 33 0N 107 35W
Hillsboro, N. Mex., U.S.A. 161 33 0N 107 35W
Hillsboro, N.D., U.S.A. 158 47 23N 97 9W
Hillsboro, N.H., U.S.A. 156 43 8N 71 56W
Hillsboro, Oreg., U.S.A. 160 45 31N 123 0W
Hillsboro, Tex., U.S.A. 159 32 0N 97 10W
Hillsborough, U.K. 38 54 28N 6 6W
Hillsborough, W. Indies 167 12 28N 61 28W
Hillsdale, Mich., U.S.A. 156 41 55N 84 40W
Hillsdale, N.Y., U.S.A. 162 42 11N 73 30W
Hillside 136 21 45 S 119 23 E
Hillsport 150 49 27N 85 34W
Hillston 141 33 30 S 145 31 E
Hillswick 36 60 29N 1 28W
Hilltown 38 54 12N 6 8W
Hilo 147 19 44N 155 5W
Hilonghilong, mt. 103 9 10N 125 45 E
Hilpsford Pt. 32 54 4N 3 12W
Hilvarenbeek 47 51 29N 5 8 E
Hilversum 46 52 14N 5 10 E
Himachal Pradesh □ 94 31 30N 77 0 E
Himalaya 99 29 0N 84 0 E
Himara 68 40 8N 19 43 E
Himatnagar 93 23 37N 72 57 E
Hime-Jima 110 33 43N 131 40 E
Himeji 110 34 50N 134 40 E
Himi 111 36 50N 137 0 E
Himmerland 73 56 45N 9 30 E
Hims = Homs 92 34 40N 36 45 E
Hinako, Kepulauan 102 0 50N 97 20 E
Hinche 167 19 9N 72 1W
Hinchinbrook I. 138 18 20 S 146 15 E
Hinckley, U.K. 28 52 33N 1 21W
Hinckley, U.S.A. 160 39 18N 112 41W
Hindås 73 57 42N 12 27 E
Hindaun 94 26 44N 77 5 E
Hinde Rapids (Hells Gate) 126 5 25 S 27 3 E
Hinderwell 33 54 32N 0 45W
Hindhead 29 51 6N 0 42W
Hindley 32 53 32N 2 35W
Hindmarsh L. 140 36 5 S 141 55 E
Hindol 95 20 40N 85 10 E
Hinds 143 43 59 S 171 36 E
Hindsholm 73 55 30N 10 40 E
Hindu Bagh 94 30 56N 67 57 E
Hindu Kush 93 36 0N 71 0 E
Hindubagh 93 30 56N 67 57 E
Hindupur 97 13 49N 77 32 E
Hines Creek 152 56 20N 118 40W
Hinganghat 96 20 30N 78 59 E
Hingeon 47 50 32N 4 59 E
Hingham, U.K. 29 52 35N 0 59 E
Hingham, U.S.A. 160 48 40N 110 29W
Hingol, R. 93 25 30N 65 30 E
Hingoli 96 19 41N 77 15 E
Hinkley Pt. 28 50 59N 3 32W
Hinlopenstretet 12 79 35N 18 40 E
Hinna 121 10 25N 11 28 E
Hinnøy 74 68 40N 16 28 E
Hino 111 35 0N 136 15 E
Hinojosa 55 38 30N 5 17W
Hinojosa del Duque 57 38 30N 5 17W
Hinokage 110 32 39N 131 24 E
Hinsdale 160 48 26N 107 2W
Hinstock 28 52 50N 2 28W
Hinterrhein, R. 51 46 40N 9 25 E
Hinton, Can. 152 53 26N 117 34W
Hinton, U.S.A. 156 37 40N 80 51W
Hinwil 51 47 18N 8 51 E
Hippolytushoef 46 52 54N 4 58 E
Hirado 110 33 22N 129 33 E
Hirado-Shima 110 33 20N 129 30 E
Hirakarta 111 34 48N 135 40 E
Hirakud 96 21 32N 83 51 E
Hirakud Dam 96 21 32N 83 45 E
Hirara 112 24 48N 125 17 E
Hirata 110 35 24N 132 49 E
Hiratsuka 111 35 19N 139 21 E
Hirhafok 119 23 49N 5 45 E
Hirlǎu 70 47 23N 27 0 E
Hiromi 110 33 13N 132 36 E
Hirosaki 112 40 34N 140 28 E
Hiroshima 110 34 30N 132 30 E
Hiroshima-ken □ 112 34 50N 133 0 E
Hiroshima-Wan 110 34 5N 132 20 E
Hirsoholmene 73 57 30N 10 36 E
Hirson 43 49 55N 4 4 E
Hîrşova 70 44 40N 27 59 E
Hirtshals 73 57 36N 9 57 E
Hirwaun 31 51 43N 3 30W
Hisoy 71 58 26N 8 44 E
Hispaniola, I. 165 19 0N 71 0W
Hissar 94 29 12N 75 45 E
Histon 29 52 15N 0 6 E
Hita 110 33 20N 130 58 E
Hitachi 111 36 36N 140 39 E
Hitachiota 111 36 30N 140 30 E
Hitchin 29 51 57N 0 16W
Hitoyoshi 110 32 13N 130 45 E
Hitra 71 63 30N 8 45 E
Hitzacker 48 53 9N 11 1 E
Hiuchi-Nada 110 34 5N 133 20 E
Hjalmar L. 153 61 33N 109 25W
Hjälmare Kanal 72 59 20N 15 59 E
Hjälmaren 72 59 18N 15 40 E
Hjartdal 71 59 37N 8 41 E
Hjärtsäter 73 58 35N 12 3 E
Hjerkinn 71 62 13N 9 33 E
Hjerpsted 73 55 2N 8 39 E
Hjo 73 58 22N 4 17 E
Hjørring 73 57 29N 9 59 E
Hjorted 73 57 37N 16 19 E
Hjortkvarn 73 58 54N 15 26 E
Hko-ut 98 21 40N 97 46 E
Hkyenhpa 98 27 43N 97 25 E
Hlaingbwe 98 17 8N 97 50 E
Hlinsko 52 49 45N 15 54 E
Hlohovec 53 48 26N 17 49 E
Hlwaze 98 18 54N 96 37 E
Ho 121 6 37N 0 27 E
Ho Chi Minh, Phanh Bho 101 10 58N 106 40 E
Ho Thuong 100 19 32N 105 48 E
Hoa Binh 100 20 50N 105 20 E
Hoa Da (Phan Ri) 100 11 16N 108 40 E
Hoa Hiep 101 11 34N 105 51 E
Hoadley 152 52 45N 114 30W
Hoai Nhon (Bon Son) 100 14 28N 109 1 E
Hoare B. 149 65 17N 62 55W
Hobart, Austral. 138 42 50 S 147 21 E
Hobart, U.S.A. 159 35 0N 99 5W
Hobbs 159 32 40N 103 3W
Hobjærg 73 56 19N 9 32 E
Hobo 174 2 35N 75 30W
Hoboken, Belg. 47 51 11N 4 21 E
Hoboken, U.S.A. 162 40 45N 74 4W
Hobro 73 56 39N 9 46 E
Hobscheid 47 49 42N 5 57 E
Hoburg C. 73 56 54N 18 8 E
Hoburgen 73 56 55N 18 7 E
Hochang 108 27 8N 104 45 E
Hochatown 159 34 11N 94 39W
Hochdorf 51 47 10N 8 17 E
Hochiang 108 28 48N 105 48 E
Hochien 106 38 26N 116 5 E
Hoch'ih 108 24 43N 108 2 E
Hoching 106 35 37N 110 43 E
Hoch'iu 109 32 21N 116 13 E
Höchst 49 50 6N 8 33 E
Hoch'ü 106 39 26N 111 8 E
Hoch'uan 108 30 2N 106 18 E
Hockenheim 49 49 18N 8 33 E
Hod, oilfield 19 56 10N 3 25 E
Hodaka-Dake 111 36 17N 137 39 E
Hodde 73 55 42N 8 39 E
Hodder R. 32 53 57N 2 27W
Hoddesdon 29 51 45N 0 1W
Hodeïda 91 14 50N 43 0 E
Hodge, R. 33 54 14N 0 55W
Hodgson 153 51 13N 97 36W
Hódmezóvásárhely 53 46 28N 20 22 E
Hodna, Chott el 119 35 30N 5 0 E
Hodonin 53 48 50N 17 0 E
Hodsager 73 56 19N 8 51 E
Hoeamdong 107 42 30N 130 16 E
Hoëdic, I. 42 47 21N 2 52W
Hoegaarden 47 50 47N 4 53 E
Hoek van Holland 46 52 0N 4 7 E
Hoeksche Waard 46 51 46N 4 25 E
Hoenderloo 46 52 7N 5 52 E
Hoengsŏng 107 37 29N 127 59 E
Hoensbroek 47 50 55N 5 55 E
Hoeryong 107 42 30N 129 58 E
Hoeselt 47 50 51N 5 29 E
Hoëveld 129 26 30 S 30 0 E
Hoeven 47 51 35N 4 35 E
Hoeyang 107 38 43N 127 36 E
Hof, Ger. 49 50 18N 11 55 E
Hof, Iceland 74 64 33N 14 40W
Höfðakaupstaður 74 65 50N 20 19W
Hofei 109 31 52N 117 15 E
Hoff 32 54 34N 2 31W
Hofgeismar 48 51 29N 9 23 E
Hofors 72 60 35N 16 15 E
Hofsjökull 74 64 49N 18 48W
Hofsós 74 65 53N 19 26W
Hōfu 110 34 3N 131 34 E
Hofuf 92 25 20N 49 40 E
Hög-Gia, Mt. 71 62 23N 10 7 E
Hog I. 162 37 26N 75 42W
Hogan Group 139 39 13 S 147 1 E
Höganäs 73 56 13N 12 34 E
Hogansville 157 33 14N 84 50W
Hogarth, Mt. 138 21 50 S 137 0 E
Hogeland 160 48 51N 108 40W
Högen 72 61 47N 14 11 E
Hogenaki Falls 97 12 6N 77 50 E
Högfors, Örebro, Sweden 72 59 58N 15 3 E
Högfors, Västmanlands, Sweden 72 60 2N 16 3 E
Hoggar = Ahaggar 119 23 0N 6 30 E
Hōgo-Kaikyo 110 33 20N 131 58 E
Hog's Back, hill 29 51 13N 0 40W
Hogs Hd. 39 51 46N 10 13W
Högsäter 73 58 38N 12 5 E
Högsby 73 57 10N 16 1 E
Högsjo 72 59 4N 15 44 E
Hogsthorpe 33 53 13N 0 19 E
Hogsty Reef 167 21 41N 73 48W
Hohe Rhön 49 50 24N 9 58 E
Hohe Tauern 52 47 11N 12 40 E
Hohenau 53 48 36N 16 55 E
Hohenems 52 47 22N 9 42 E
Hohenstein Ernstthal 48 50 48N 12 43 E
Hohenwald 157 35 35N 87 30W
Hohenwestedt 48 54 6N 9 40 E
Hohoe 121 7 8N 0 32 E
Hohsi 108 24 9N 102 38 E
Hohsien, Anhwei, China 109 31 43N 118 22 E
Hohsien, Kwangsi-Chuang, China 109 24 25N 111 31 E
Hohsüeh 109 30 2N 112 25 E
Hôi An 100 15 30N 108 19 E
Hoi Xuan 100 20 25N 105 9 E
Hoisington 158 38 33N 98 50W
Højer 73 54 58N 8 42 E
Hōjō 110 33 58N 132 46 E
Hok 73 57 31N 14 16 E
Hokensås 73 58 0N 14 5 E
Hökensås 73 58 0N 14 5 E
Hökerum 73 57 51N 13 16 E
Hokianga Harbour 142 35 31 S 173 22 E
Hokitika 143 42 42 S 171 0 E
Hokkaidō 112 43 30N 143 0 E
Hokkaidō □ 112 43 30N 143 0 E
Hokksund 71 59 44N 9 59 E
Hok'ou, Kansu, China 106 36 9N 103 29 E
Hok'ou, Kwantang, China 109 23 13N 112 45 E
Hok'ou, Yunnan, China 108 22 39N 103 57 E
Hokow 101 22 39N 103 57 E
Hol-Hol. 123 11 20N 42 50 E
Holan Shan 106 38 50N 105 50 E
Holbæk 73 55 43N 11 43 E
Holbeach 29 52 48N 0 1 E
Holbeach Marsh 29 52 52N 0 5 E
Holborn Hd. 37 58 37N 3 30W
Holbrook, Austral. 141 35 42 S 147 18 E
Holbrook, U.S.A. 161 35 0N 110 0W
Holden 152 53 13N 112 11W
Holden Fillmore 160 39 0N 112 26W
Holdenville 159 35 5N 96 25W
Holder 140 34 21 S 140 0 E
Holderness 33 53 45N 0 5W
Holdfast 153 50 58N 105 25W
Holdrege 153 40 25N 99 30W
Hole 71 60 6N 10 12 E
Hole-Narsipur 97 12 48N 76 16 E
Holešov 53 49 20N 17 35 E
Holguín 166 20 50N 76 20W
Holinkoerh 106 40 23N 111 53 E
Holič 53 48 49N 17 10 E
Holkham 29 52 57N 0 48 E
Holla, Mt. 123 7 5N 36 35 E
Hollabrunn 52 48 34N 16 5 E
Hollams Bird I. 128 24 40 S 14 30 E
Holland 156 42 47N 86 7W
Holland Fen 33 53 0N 0 8W
Holland-on-Sea 29 51 48N 1 12 E
Hollandia = Jajapura 103 2 28 S 140 38 E
Hollands Bird I. 128 24 40 S 14 30 E
Hollandsch Diep 47 51 41N 4 30 E
Hollandsch IJssel, R. 46 51 55N 4 34 E
Hollandstoun 37 59 22N 2 25W
Höllen 71 58 6N 7 49 E
Holleton 137 31 55 S 119 0 E
Hollidaysburg 156 40 26N 78 25W
Hollis 159 34 45N 99 55W
Hollister 161 36 51N 121 24W
Hollum 46 53 26N 5 38 E
Holly 158 38 7N 102 7W
Holly Hill 157 29 15N 81 3W
Holly Springs 159 34 45N 89 25W
Hollymount 38 53 40N 9 7W
Hollywood, Ireland 39 53 6N 6 35W
Hollywood, Calif., U.S.A. 154 34 7N 118 25W
Hollywood, Fla., U.S.A. 157 26 0N 80 9W
Holm 72 62 40N 16 40 E
Holman Island 148 71 0N 118 0W
Hólmavík 74 65 42N 21 40W
Holme, Humberside,, U.K. 33 53 50N 0 48W
Holme, N. Yorks., U.K. 32 53 34N 1 50W
Holmedal 71 59 46N 5 50 E
Holmedal, Fjordane 71 61 22N 5 11 E
Holmegil 72 59 10N 11 44 E
Holmes Chapel 32 53 13N 2 21W
Holmes Reefs 138 16 27 S 148 0 E
Holmestrand 71 59 31N 10 14 E
Holmfirth 33 53 34N 1 48W
Holmsbu 71 59 32N 10 27 E
Holmsjön 72 62 26N 15 20 E
Holmsland Klit 73 56 0N 8 5 E
Holmsund 74 63 41N 20 20 E
Holmwood 29 51 12N 0 19W
Hölö 72 59 3N 17 36 E
Holo Ho, R. 107 44 54N 122 22 E
Holod 70 46 49N 22 8 E
Holon 90 32 2N 34 47 E
Holroyd, R. 138 14 10 S 141 36 E
Holsen 71 61 25N 6 8 E
Holstebro 73 56 22N 8 37 E
Holsworthy 30 50 48N 4 21W
Holt, Iceland 74 63 33N 19 48W
Holt, Clwyd, U.K. 31 53 4N 2 52W
Holt, Norfolk, U.K. 29 52 55N 1 4 E
Holte 73 55 50N 12 29 E
Holten 46 52 17N 6 26 E
Holton Harbour 151 54 31N 57 12W
Holton le Clay 33 53 29N 0 3W
Holtville 161 32 50N 115 27W
Holum 71 58 6N 7 32 E
Holwerd 46 53 22N 5 54 E
Holy Cross 147 62 10N 159 52W
Holy I., England, U.K. 35 55 42N 1 48W
Holy I., Scotland, U.K. 34 55 31N 5 4W
Holy I., Wales, U.K. 31 53 17N 4 37W
Holyhead 31 53 18N 4 38W
Holyhead B. 31 53 20N 4 35W
Holyoke, Mass., U.S.A. 162 42 14N 72 37W
Holyoke, Nebr., U.S.A. 158 40 39N 102 18W
Holyrood 151 47 27N 53 8W
Holywell 31 53 16N 3 14W
Holywood 38 54 38N 5 50W
Holzminden 48 51 49N 9 31 E
Homa Bay 126 0 36 S 34 22 E
Homa Bay □ 126 0 50 S 34 30 E
Homalin 98 24 55N 95 0 E
Homberg 48 51 2N 9 20 E
Hombori 121 15 20N 1 38W
Homburg 49 49 19N 7 21 E
Home B. 149 68 40N 67 10W
Home Hill 138 19 43 S 147 25 E
Homedale 160 43 42N 116 59W
Homer, Alaska, U.S.A. 147 59 40N 151 35W
Homer, La., U.S.A. 159 32 50N 93 4W
Homestead, Austral. 138 20 20 S 145 40 E
Homestead, U.S.A. 157 25 29N 80 27W
Hominy 159 36 26N 96 24W
Homnabad 96 17 45N 77 5 E
Homoine 129 23 55 S 35 8 E
Homorod 70 46 5N 25 15 E
Homs = Al Khums 119 32 40N 14 17 E
Homs (Hims) 92 34 40N 36 45 E
Hon Chong 101 10 16N 104 38 E
Hon Me 100 19 23N 105 56 E
Honan □ 106 34 10N 113 10 E
Honbetsu 112 43 7N 143 37 E
Honda 174 5 12N 74 45W
Hondeklipbaai 125 30 19 S 17 17 E
Hondo, Japan 110 32 27N 130 12 E
Hondo, U.S.A. 159 29 22N 99 6W
Hondo, R. 165 18 25N 88 21W
Honduras ■ 166 14 40N 86 30W
Honduras, Golfo de 166 16 50N 87 0W
Hönefoss 71 60 10N 10 12 E
Honey L. 160 40 13N 120 14W
Honfleur 42 49 25N 0 13 E
Höng 73 55 30N 11 14 E
Hong Gai 100 20 57N 107 5 E
Hong Kong ■ 109 22 11N 114 14 E

Hong, R. **100** 20 17N 106 34 E
Hongchŏn **107** 37 44N 127 53 E
Hongha, R. **101** 22 0N 104 0 E
Hongor **106** 45 56N 112 50 E
Hongsa **100** 19 43N 101 20 E
Hongsŏng **107** 36 37N 126 38 E
Honguedo, Détroit d' **151** 49 15N 64 0W
Hongwon **107** 40 0N 127 56 E
Honiara **142** 9 30 S 160 0 E
Honington **33** 52 58N 0 35W
Honiton **30** 50 48N 3 11W
Honjo, Akita, Japan **112** 39 23N 140 3 E
Honjo, Gumma, Japan **111** 36 14N 139 11 E
Honkawane **111** 35 5N 138 5 E
Honkorâb, Ras **122** 24 35N 35 10 E
Honolulu **147** 21 19N 157 52W
Honshū **112** 36 0N 138 0 E
Hontoria del Pinar **58** 41 50N 3 10W
Hoo **29** 51 25N 0 33 E
Hood Mt. **160** 45 15N 122 0W
Hood, Pt. **137** 34 23 S 119 34 E
Hood Pt. **135** 10 4 S 147 45 E
Hood River **160** 45 45N 121 37W
Hoodsport **160** 47 24N 123 7W
Hooge **48** 54 31N 8 36 E
Hoogerheide **47** 51 26N 4 20 E
Hoogeveen **46** 52 44N 6 30 E
Hoogeveensche Vaart **46** 52 42N 6 12 E
Hoogezand **46** 53 11N 6 45 E
Hooghly-Chinsura **95** 22 53N 88 27 E
Hooghly, R. **95** 21 59N 88 10 E
Hoogkerk **46** 53 13N 6 30 E
Hooglede **47** 50 59N 3 5 E
Hoogstraten **47** 51 24N 4 46 E
Hoogvliet **46** 51 52N 4 21 E
Hook **29** 51 17N 0 55W
Hook Hd. **39** 52 8N 6 57W
Hook I. **138** 20 4 S 149 0 E
Hook of Holland = Hoek v. Holland **47** 52 0N 4 7 E
Hooker **159** 36 55N 101 10W
Hooker Cr. **136** 18 23 S 130 50 E
Hoonah **147** 58 15N 135 30W
Hooper Bay **147** 61 30N 166 10W
Hoopersville **162** 38 16N 76 11W
Hoopeston **156** 40 30N 87 40W
Hoopstad **128** 27 50 S 25 55 E
Höör **73** 55 55N 13 33 E
Hoorn **46** 52 38N 5 4 E
Hoover Dam **161** 36 0N 114 45W
Hop Bottom **162** 41 41N 75 47W
Hopà **83** 41 28N 41 30 E
Hope, Can. **152** 49 25N 121 25 E
Hope, U.K. **31** 53 7N 3 2W
Hope, Ark., U.S.A. **159** 33 40N 93 30W
Hope, N.D., U.S.A. **158** 47 21N 97 42W
Hope Bay **13** 65 0 S 55 0W
Hope, L. **139** 28 24 S 139 18 E
Hope L. **37** 58 24N 4 38W
Hope Pt. **147** 68 20N 166 50W
Hope Town **157** 26 30N 76 30W
Hopedale, Can. **151** 55 28N 60 13W
Hopedale, U.S.A. **162** 42 8N 71 33W
Hopefield **128** 33 3 S 18 22 E
Hopei □ **107** 39 25N 116 45 E
Hopelchén **165** 19 46N 89 50W
Hopeman **37** 57 42N 3 26W
Hopen **71** 63 27N 8 2 E
Hopetoun **137** 33 57 S 120 7 E
Hopetown, Austral. **140** 35 42 S 142 22 E
Hopetown, S. Afr. **128** 29 34 S 24 3 E
Hopewell **162** 37 18N 77 17W
Hopien-Ts'un **108** 27 40N 101 55 E
Hopin **98** 21 14N 96 53 E
Hop'ing **109** 24 26N 114 56 E
Hopkins **158** 40 31N 94 45W
Hopkins, L. **136** 24 15 S 128 35 E
Hopkinsville **157** 36 52N 87 26W
Hopland **160** 39 0N 123 7W
Hopo **108** 31 24N 99 0 E
Hoptrup **73** 55 11N 9 28 E
Hop'u **108** 21 41N 109 10 E
Hoquiam **160** 46 50N 123 55W
Hōrai **111** 34 58N 137 32 E
Horazdovice **52** 49 19N 13 42 E
Hörby **73** 55 50N 13 44 E
Horcajo de Santiago **58** 39 50N 3 1W
Hordaland fylke □ **71** 60 25N 6 15 E
Horden **33** 54 45N 1 17W
Hordern Hills **136** 20 40 S 130 20 E
Hordio **91** 10 36N 51 8 E
Horezu **70** 45 6N 24 0 E
Horgen **51** 47 15N 8 35 E
Horgoš **66** 46 10N 20 0 E
Horice **52** 50 21N 15 39 E
Horley **29** 51 10N 0 10W
Horlick Mts. **13** 84 0 S 102 0W
Hormoz **93** 27 35N 55 0 E
Hormuz, I. **93** 27 8N 56 28 E
Hormuz Str. **93** 26 30N 56 30 E
Horn, Austria **52** 48 39N 15 40 E
Horn, Isafjarðarsýsla, Iceland **74** 66 28N 22 28W
Horn, Suður-Múlasýsla, Iceland **74** 65 10N 13 31W
Horn, Neth. **47** 51 12N 5 57 E
Horn, Cape = Hornos, C. de **176** 55 50 S 67 30W
Horn Head **38** 55 13N 8 0W
Horn I., Austral. **138** 10 37 S 142 17 E
Horn I., P.N.G. **135** 10 35 S 142 20 E
Horn, I. **157** 30 17N 88 40W
Horn Mts. **152** 62 15N 119 15W
Horn, R. **152** 61 30N 118 1W
Hornachuelos **57** 37 50N 5 14W
Hornavan **74** 66 15N 17 30 E
Hornbæk, Frederiksborg, Denmark **73** 56 5N 12 26 E
Hornbæk, Viborg, Denmark **73** 56 28N 9 58 E
Hornbeck **159** 31 22N 93 20W
Hornbrook **160** 41 58N 122 37W
Hornburg **48** 52 2N 10 36 E
Hornby **143** 43 33 S 172 33 E
Horncastle **33** 53 13N 0 8W
Horndal **72** 60 18N 16 23 E
Horndean **29** 50 56N 1 5W
Hornell **156** 42 23N 77 41W
Hornell L. **152** 62 20N 119 25W
Hornepayne **150** 49 14N 84 48W
Hornindal **71** 61 58N 6 30 E
Horningsham **28** 51 11N 2 16W
Hornitos **163** 37 30N 120 14W
Hornnes **71** 58 34N 7 45 E
Hornos, Cabo de **176** 55 50 S 67 30 E
Hornoy **43** 49 50N 1 54 E
Hornsberg, Jamtland, Sweden **72** 63 14N 14 40 E
Hornsberg, Kronobergs, Sweden **72** 56 37N 13 47 E
Hornsby **141** 33 42 S 151 2 E
Hornsea **33** 53 55N 0 10W
Hornslandet Pen. **72** 61 35N 17 37 E
Hornslet **73** 56 18N 10 19 E
Hornu **47** 50 26N 3 50 E
Hörnum **73** 54 44N 8 18 E
Horovice **52** 49 48N 13 53 E
Horqueta **172** 23 15 S 56 55W
Horra, La **56** 41 44N 3 53W
Horred **73** 57 22N 12 28 E
Horse Cr. **158** 41 33N 104 45W
Horse Is. **151** 50 15N 55 50W
Horsefly L. **152** 52 25N 121 0W
Horseheads **162** 42 10N 76 49W
Horseleap **38** 53 25N 7 34W
Horsens **73** 55 52N 9 51 E
Horsens Fjord **73** 55 50N 10 0 E
Horseshoe **137** 25 27 S 118 31 E
Horseshoe Dam **161** 33 45N 111 35W
Horsforth **33** 53 50N 1 39W
Horsham, Austral. **140** 36 44 S 142 13 E
Horsham, U.K. **29** 51 4N 0 20W
Horsham St. Faith **29** 52 41N 1 15 E
Horsovsky Tyn **52** 49 31N 12 58 E
Horst **47** 51 27N 6 3 E
Horsted Keynes **29** 51 2N 0 1W
Horten **71** 59 25N 10 32 E
Hortobágy, R. **53** 47 30N 21 6 E
Horton **158** 39 42N 95 30W
Horton-in-Ribblesdale **32** 54 9N 2 19W
Horton, R. **147** 69 56N 126 52W
Hörvik **73** 56 2N 14 45 E
Horw **51** 47 1N 8 19 E
Horwich **32** 53 37N 2 33W
Horwood, L. **150** 48 10N 82 20W
Hosaina **123** 7 30N 37 47 E
Hosdurga **97** 13 40N 76 17 E
Hose, Pegunungan **102** 2 5N 114 6 E
Hoshan **109** 31 24N 116 20 E
Hoshangabad **94** 22 45N 77 45 E
Hoshiarpur **94** 31 30N 75 58 E
Hoshui **106** 36 0N 107 59 E
Hoshun **106** 37 19N 113 34 E
Hosingen **47** 50 1N 6 6 E
Hoskins **135** 5 29 S 150 27 E
Hosmer **158** 45 36N 99 29W
Hososhima **110** 32 26N 131 40 E
Hospental **51** 46 37N 8 34 E
Hospet **97** 15 15N 76 20 E
Hospital **39** 52 30N 8 28W
Hospitalet de Llobregat **58** 41 21N 2 6 E
Hospitalet, L' **44** 42 36N 1 47 E
Hoste, I. **176** 55 0 S 69 0W
Hostens **44** 44 30N 0 40W
Hoswick **36** 60 0N 1 15W
Hot **100** 18 8N 98 29 E
Hot Creek Ra. **160** 39 0N 116 0W
Hot Springs, Ark, U.S.A. **159** 34 30N 93 0W
Hot Springs, S.D., U.S.A. **158** 43 25N 103 30W
Hotagen, L. **74** 63 50N 14 30 E
Hotazel **128** 27 17 S 23 00 E
Hotchkiss **161** 38 55N 107 47W
Hotham, C. **136** 12 2 S 131 18 E
Hot'ien **105** 37 7N 79 55 E
Hoting **74** 64 8N 16 15 E
Hotolishti **68** 41 10N 20 25 E
Hotse **106** 35 14N 115 27 E
Hotte, Massif de la **167** 18 30N 73 45W
Hottentotsbaai **128** 26 8 S 14 59 E
Hotton **47** 50 16N 5 26 E
Houat, I. **42** 47 24N 2 58W
Houck **161** 35 15N 109 15W
Houdan **43** 48 48N 1 35 E
Houdeng-Goegnies **47** 50 29N 4 10 E
Houei Sai **100** 20 18N 100 26 E
Houffalize **47** 50 8N 5 48 E
Houghton **158** 47 9N 88 39W
Houghton L. **156** 44 20N 84 40W
Houghton-le-Spring **35** 54 51N 1 28W
Houghton Regis **29** 51 54N 0 32W
Houhora **142** 34 49 S 173 9 E
Houille, R. **47** 50 8N 4 50 E
Houlton **151** 46 5N 68 0W
Houma **159** 29 35N 90 50W
Houmt Souk = Djerba **119** 33 53N 10 37 E
Houndé **120** 11 34N 3 31W
Hounslow **29** 51 29N 0 20W
Hourn L. **36** 57 7N 5 35W
Hourtin **44** 45 11N 1 4W
Housatonic, R. **162** 41 10N 73 7W
Houston, Can. **152** 54 25N 126 30W
Houston, Mo., U.S.A. **159** 37 20N 92 0W
Houston, Tex., U.S.A. **159** 29 50N 95 20W
Houten **46** 52 2N 5 10 E
Houthalen **47** 51 2N 5 23 E
Houthem **47** 50 48N 2 57 E
Houthulst **47** 50 59N 2 57 E
Houtman Abrolhos **137** 28 43 S 113 48 E
Houyet **47** 50 11N 5 1 E
Hova **73** 58 53N 14 14 E
Høvag **71** 58 10N 8 15 E
Hövåg **71** 58 10N 8 16 E
Hovd **105** 48 1N 91 39 E
Hovden **71** 59 33N 7 22 E
Hove **29** 50 50N 0 10W
Hoveton **29** 52 45N 1 23 E
Hovingham **33** 54 10N 0 59W
Hovmantorp **73** 56 47N 15 7 E
Hövsgöl **106** 43 37N 109 39 E
Hovsta **72** 59 22N 15 15 E
Howakil **123** 15 10N 40 16 E
Howar, W., (Shau) **123** 17 0N 25 30 E
Howard, Austral. **139** 25 16 S 152 32 E
Howard, Kans., U.S.A. **159** 37 30N 96 16W
Howard, S.D., U.S.A. **158** 44 2N 97 30W
Howard I. **138** 12 10 S 135 24 E
Howard L. **153** 62 15N 105 57W
Howatharra **137** 28 29 S 114 33 E
Howden **33** 53 45N 0 52W
Howe **160** 43 48N 113 0W
Howe, C. **141** 37 30 S 150 0 E
Howell **156** 42 38N 84 0W
Howick, N.Z. **142** 36 54 S 174 48 E
Howick, S. Afr. **129** 29 28 S 30 14 E
Howick Group **138** 14 20 S 145 30 E
Howitt, L. **139** 27 40 S 138 40 E
Howley **151** 49 12N 57 2W
Howmore **36** 57 18N 7 23W
Howrah **95** 22 37N 88 27 E
Howth **38** 53 23N 6 3W
Howth Hd. **38** 53 21N 6 0W
Hoxne **29** 52 22N 1 11 E
Höxter **48** 51 45N 9 26 E
Hoy I. **37** 58 50N 3 15W
Hoy Sd. **37** 58 57N 3 20W
Hoya **48** 52 47N 9 10 E
Høyanger **71** 61 25N 6 50 E
Höydalsmo **71** 59 30N 8 15 E
Hoyerswerda **48** 51 26N 14 14 E
Hoylake **32** 53 24N 3 11W
Höyland **71** 58 50N 5 43 E
Hoyleton **140** 34 2 S 138 34 E
Hoyos **56** 40 9N 6 45W
Hoyüan **109** 23 50N 114 40 E
Hpawlum **98** 27 12N 98 12 E
Hpettintha **98** 24 14N 95 23 E
Hpizow **98** 26 57N 98 24 E
Hpungan Pass **99** 27 30N 96 55 E
Hrádec Králové **52** 50 15N 15 50 E
Hrádek **53** 48 46N 16 16 E
Hranice **53** 49 34N 17 45 E
Hron, R. **53** 48 0N 18 4 E
Hrubieszów **54** 50 49N 23 51 E
Hrubý Nízký Jeseník **53** 50 7N 17 10 E
Hrvatska **63** 45 20N 16 0 E
Hsenwi **98** 23 22N 97 55 E
Hsi Chiang, R. **109** 22 20N 113 20 E
Hsiach'engtzu, Heilungkiang, China **107** 44 41N 130 27 E
Hsiach'engtzu, Schechwan, China **108** 29 24N 101 46 E
Hsiachiang **109** 27 33N 115 10 E
Hsiaching **106** 36 57N 115 59 E
Hsiach'uan Shan **109** 21 40N 112 37 E
Hsiahsien **106** 35 12N 111 11 E
Hsiai **106** 34 17N 116 11 E
Hsiakuan **108** 25 39N 100 9 E
Hsiamen **109** 24 30N 118 7 E
Hsian **106** 34 17N 109 0 E
Hsiang Chiang, R. **109** 29 30N 113 10 E
Hsiangch'eng, Honan, China **106** 33 50N 113 29 E
Hsiangch'eng, Honan, China **106** 33 13N 114 50 E
Hsiangch'eng, Szechwan, China **108** 29 0N 99 46 E
Hsiangchou **108** 23 58N 109 41 E
Hsiangfan **109** 32 7N 112 9 E
Hsianghsiang **109** 27 46N 112 30 E
Hsiangning **106** 36 1N 110 47 E
Hsiangshan **109** 29 18N 121 37 E
Hsiangshuik'ou **107** 34 12N 119 34 E
Hsiangt'an **109** 27 55N 112 52 E
Hsiangtu **108** 23 14N 106 57 E
Hsiangyang **109** 32 2N 112 6 E
Hsiangyin **109** 28 40N 112 53 E
Hsiangyüan **106** 36 32N 113 2 E
Hsiangyün **108** 25 29N 100 35 E
Hsiaochin **108** 31 1N 102 23 E
Hsiaofeng **109** 30 36N 119 33 E
Hsiaohsien **106** 34 2N 116 56 E
Hsiaohsinganling Shanmo **105** 48 45N 127 0 E
Hsiaoi **106** 37 7N 111 46 E
Hsiaokan **109** 30 57N 113 53 E
Hsiaoshan **109** 30 10N 120 15 E
Hsiaot'ai Shan **107** 36 18N 116 38 E
Hsiap'u **109** 26 58N 119 57 E
Hsiawa **107** 42 38N 120 31 E
Hsich'ang **108** 27 50N 102 18 E
Hsichieht'o **108** 30 24N 108 13 E
Hsich'uan **109** 33 0N 111 24 E
Hsich'ung **108** 31 0N 105 48 E
Hsiehch'eng **107** 34 48N 117 15 E
Hsiehmaho **109** 31 38N 111 12 E
Hsienchü **109** 28 51N 120 44 E
Hsienfeng **108** 29 40N 109 7 E
Hsienhsien **106** 38 2N 116 12 E
Hsienning **109** 29 51N 114 15 E
Hsienshui Ho, R. **108** 30 5N 101 5 E
Hsienyang **106** 34 22N 108 48 E
Hsienyu **109** 25 24N 118 40 E
Hsifei Ho, R. **109** 32 38N 116 39 E
Hsifeng, Kweichow, China **108** 27 5N 106 42 E
Hsifeng, Liaoning, China **107** 42 44N 124 42 E
Hsifengchen **106** 35 40N 107 42 E
Hsifengk'ou **107** 40 24N 118 19 E
Hsiho **106** 34 2N 105 12 E
Hsihsia, Honan, China **106** 33 30N 111 30 E
Hsihsia, Shantung, China **107** 37 25N 120 48 E
Hsihsiang **108** 33 1N 107 40 E
Hsihsien, Honan, China **109** 32 24N 114 52 E
Hsihsien, Shensi, China **106** 36 41N 110 56 E
Hsihua **106** 33 47N 114 31 E
Hsilamunlun Ho, R. **107** 43 24N 123 42 E
Hsiliao Ho, R. **107** 43 24N 123 42 E
Hsilin **108** 24 30N 105 3 E
Hsin Chiang, R. **109** 28 50N 116 40 E
Hsin Ho, R. **107** 43 33N 123 31 E
Hsinchan **107** 43 52N 127 20 E
Hsinch'ang **109** 29 30N 120 54 E
Hsincheng **106** 34 25N 113 46 E
Hsinch'eng, Hopei, China **106** 39 15N 115 59 E
Hsinch'eng, Kwangsi-Chuang, China **108** 24 4N 108 40 E
Hsinchiang **106** 35 40N 111 15 E
Hsinchien **108** 23 58N 102 47 E
Hsinchin **107** 39 25N 121 59 E
Hsinching **108** 30 25N 103 49 E
Hsinchi'u **107** 41 53N 119 40 E
Hsinchou **109** 30 52N 114 48 E
Hsinchu **109** 24 48N 120 58 E
Hsinfeng, Kiangsi, China **109** 25 27N 114 58 E
Hsinfeng, Kiangsi, China **109** 26 7N 116 11 E
Hsinfeng, Kwangtung, China **109** 24 4N 114 12 E
Hsingan **109** 25 39N 110 39 E
Hsingch'eng **107** 40 40N 120 48 E
Hsingho **106** 40 52N 113 58 E
Hsinghsien **106** 38 31N 111 4 E
Hsinghua **107** 32 55N 119 52 E
Hsinghua Wan **109** 25 20N 119 20 E
Hsingi **108** 25 5N 104 55 E
Hsinging **109** 26 25N 110 44 E
Hsingjen **108** 25 25N 105 13 E
Hsingjenp'ao **106** 37 0N 105 0 E
Hsingkuo **109** 26 26N 115 16 E
Hsinglung **107** 40 29N 117 32 E
Hsingning **109** 24 8N 115 43 E
Hsingp'ing **106** 34 18N 108 26 E
Hsingshan **109** 31 10N 110 51 E
Hsingt'ai **106** 37 5N 114 38 E
Hsingyeh **108** 22 45N 109 52 E
Hsinhailien = Lienyünchiangshih **107** 34 37N 119 13 E
Hsinhsiang **106** 35 15N 113 54 E
Hsinhsien, Shansi, China **106** 38 24N 112 47 E
Hsinhsien, Shantung, China **106** 36 15N 115 40 E
Hsinhsing **109** 22 45N 112 11 E
Hsinhua **109** 27 43N 111 18 E
Hsinhui **109** 22 32N 113 0 E
Hsini **109** 22 12N 110 53 E
Hsining **105** 36 37N 101 46 E
Hsink'ai Ho, R. **107** 41 10N 122 5 E
Hsinkan **109** 27 45N 115 21 E
Hsinkao Shan **109** 23 25N 120 52 E
Hsinlit'un **107** 42 2N 122 19 E
Hsinlo **106** 38 15N 114 40 E
Hsinmin **107** 42 0N 122 52 E
Hsinpaoan **106** 40 27N 115 23 E
Hsinpin **107** 41 43N 125 2 E
Hsinp'ing **108** 24 6N 101 58 E
Hsinshao **109** 27 20N 111 26 E
Hsint'ai **107** 35 54N 117 44 E
Hsint'ien **109** 25 56N 112 13 E
Hsints'ai **109** 32 44N 114 59 E
Hsinyang **109** 32 10N 114 6 E
Hsinyeh **109** 37 31N 112 21 E
Hsinyü **109** 27 48N 114 56 E
Hsipaw **98** 22 37N 97 18 E
Hsip'ing, Honan, China **106** 33 34N 110 45 E
Hsip'ing, Honan, China **106** 33 23N 114 2 E
Hsishni **109** 30 27N 115 13 E
Hsitalahai **106** 40 38N 109 38 E
Hsiu Shui, R. **109** 29 13N 116 0 E
Hsiujen **109** 24 26N 110 14 E
Hsiunghsien **106** 38 50N 116 11 E
Hsiungyüeh **107** 40 12N 122 12 E
Hsiuning **109** 29 51N 118 15 E
Hsiushan **108** 28 27N 108 59 E
Hsiushui **109** 29 2N 114 34 E

Hsiuwen 108 26 52N 106 35 E
Hsiuyen 107 40 19N 123 15 E
Hsiyang 106 37 27N 113 46 E
Hsüanch'eng 109 30 54N 118 41 E
Hsüanen 108 29 59N 109 24 E
Hsüanhan 108 31 25N 107 38 E
Hsüanhua 106 40 38N 115 5 E
Hsüanwei 108 26 13N 104 5 E
Hsüch'ang 106 34 1N 113 53 E
Hsüchou 107 34 15N 117 10 E
Hsüehfeng Shan 109 27 0N 110 30 E
Hsüehweng Shan 109 24 24N 121 12 E
Hsun Chiang, R. 109 23 30N 111 30 E
Hsünhsien 106 35 40N 114 32 E
Hsüni 106 35 6N 108 20 E
Hsüntien 108 25 33N 103 15 E
Hsünwu 109 24 57N 115 28 E
Hsünyang 108 32 48N 109 27 E
Hsüp'u 109 27 56N 110 36 E
Hsüshui 106 39 1N 115 39 E
Hsüwen 109 20 20N 110 9 E
Hsüyung 108 28 6N 105 21 E
Htawgaw 98 25 57N 98 23 E
Hua Hin 100 12 34N 99 58 E
Huaan 109 25 1N 117 33 E
Huachacalla 164 18 45 S 68 17W
Huachinera 164 30 9N 108 55W
Huachipato 172 36 45 S 73 09W
Huacho 174 11 10 S 77 35W
Huachón 174 10 35 S 76 0W
Huachou 109 21 38N 110 35 E
Huacrachuco 174 8 35 S 76 50W
Huahsien, Honan, China 106 35 33N 114 34 E
Huahsien, Shensi, China 106 34 31N 109 46 E
Huai Yot 101 7 45N 99 37 E
Huaiachen 106 40 33N 114 30 E
Huaian, Hopei, China 106 40 33N 114 30 E
Huaian, Kiangsu, China 107 33 31N 119 8 E
Huaichi 109 24 0N 112 8 E
Huaihua 109 27 34N 109 56 E
Huaijen 106 39 50N 113 7 E
Huaijou 106 40 20N 116 37 E
Huainan 109 32 39N 117 2 E
Huaining 109 30 21N 116 42 E
Huaite 107 43 30N 124 50 E
Huaitechen 107 43 52N 124 45 E
Huaiyang 106 33 50N 115 2 E
Huaiyüan, Anhwei, China 109 32 58N 117 13 E
Huaiyüan, Kwangsi-Chuang, China 108 24 36N 108 27 E
Huajuapan 165 17 50N 98 0W
Huajung 109 29 34N 112 34 E
Hualien 109 24 0N 121 30 E
Huallaga, R. 174 5 30 S 76 10W
Hualpai Pk. 161 35 8N 113 58W
Huan Chiang, R. 106 36 4N 107 40 E
Huancabamba 174 5 10 S 79 15W
Huancané 174 15 10 S 69 50W
Huancapi 174 13 25 S 74 0W
Huancavelica 174 12 50 S 75 5W
Huancayo 174 12 5 S 75 0W
Huanchiang 108 24 50N 108 15 E
Huang Ho, R. 107 36 50N 118 20 E
Huangchiakopa 106 40 20N 109 18 E
Huangch'uan 109 32 8N 115 4 E
Huanghsien, Hunen, China 108 27 22N 109 10 E
Huanghsien, Shantung, China 107 37 38N 120 30 E
Huangkang 109 30 27N 114 50 E
Huanglienp'u 108 25 32N 99 44 E
Huangling 106 35 36N 109 17 E
Huangliu 105 18 20N 108 50 E
Huanglung 106 35 37N 109 58 E
Huanglungt'an 109 32 38N 110 33 E
Huangmei 109 30 4N 115 56 E
Huangshih 109 30 10N 115 2 E
Huangt'uan 107 36 55N 121 41 E
Huangyang 109 26 37N 111 42 E
Huangyen 109 28 37N 121 12 E
Huanhsien 106 36 32N 107 10 E
Huaning 108 24 12N 102 55 E
Huanjen 107 41 16N 125 21 E
Huanp'ing 108 26 54N 107 55 E
Huant'ai 107 36 57N 118 5 E
Huánuco 174 9 55 S 76 15W
Huap'ing 108 26 37N 101 13 E
Huap'itientzu 107 43 30N 130 2 E
Huaraz 174 9 30 S 77 32W
Huarmey 174 10 5 S 78 5W
Huasamota 164 22 30N 104 30W
Huascarán 174 9 0 S 77 30W
Huasco 172 28 24 S 71 15W
Huasco, R. 172 28 27 S 71 13W
Huasna 163 35 6N 120 24W
Huatabampo 164 26 50N 109 50W
Huate 106 41 57N 114 4 E
Huatien 107 42 58N 126 50 E
Huauchinango 165 20 11N 98 3W
Huautla 164 18 20N 96 50W
Huautla de Jiménez 165 18 8N 96 51W
Huay Namota 164 21 56N 104 30W
Huayin 106 34 36N 110 2 E
Huayllay 174 11 03 S 76 21W
Huayüan 108 28 30N 109 25 E
Hubbard 159 31 50N 96 50W
Hubbart Pt. 153 59 21N 94 41W
Hubli-Dharwar 97 15 22N 75 15 E
Huchang 107 41 25N 127 2 E
Huchuetenango 164 15 25N 91 30W
Hückelhoven-Ratheim 48 51 6N 6 3 E
Hucknall 33 53 3N 1 12W
Huddersfield 33 53 38N 1 49W
Hudi 122 17 43N 34 28 E
Hudiksvall 72 61 43N 17 10 E
Hudson, Can. 153 50 6N 92 09W
Hudson, Mich., U.S.A. 156 41 50N 84 20W
Hudson, N.H., U.S.A. 162 42 46N 71 26W
Hudson, N.Y., U.S.A. 162 42 15N 73 46W
Hudson, Wis., U.S.A. 158 44 57N 92 45W
Hudson, Wyo., U.S.A. 160 42 54N 108 37W
Hudson B. 153 59 0N 91 0W
Hudson Bay, Can. 149 60 0N 86 0W
Hudson Bay, Sask., Can. 153 52 51N 102 23W
Hudson Falls 162 43 18N 73 34W
Hudson, R. 162 40 42N 74 2W
Hudson Str. 148 62 0N 70 0W
Hudson's Hope 152 56 0N 121 54W
Hué 100 16 30N 107 35 E
Huebra, R. 56 40 54N 6 28W
Huedin 70 46 52N 23 2 E
Huehuetenango 166 15 20N 91 28W
Huejúcar 164 22 21N 103 13W
Huelgoat 42 48 22N 3 46W
Huelma 59 37 39N 3 28W
Huelva 57 37 18N 6 57W
Huelva □ 57 37 40N 7 0W
Huelva, R. 57 37 46N 6 15W
Huentelauquén 172 31 38 S 71 33W
Huércal Overa 59 37 23N 1 57W
Huerta, Sa. de la 172 31 10 S 67 30W
Huertas, C. de las 59 38 21N 0 24W
Huerva, R. 58 41 13N 1 15W
Huesca 58 42 8N 0 25W
Huesca □ 58 42 20N 0 1 E
Huéscar 59 37 44N 2 35W
Huétamo 164 18 36N 100 54W
Huete 58 40 10N 2 43W
Hugh, R. 138 25 1 S 134 10 E
Hugh Town 30 49 55N 6 19W
Hughenden 138 20 52 S 144 10 E
Hughes, Austral. 137 30 42 S 129 31 E
Hughes, U.S.A. 147 66 0N 154 20W
Hughesville 162 41 14N 76 44W
Hugo, Colo., U.S.A. 158 39 12N 103 27W
Hugo, Okla., U.S.A. 159 34 0N 95 30W
Hugoton 159 37 18N 101 22W
Huhehot = Huhohaot'e 106 40 50N 110 39 E
Huhohaot'e 106 40 50N 110 39 E
Huhsien 106 34 8N 108 34 E
Huian 109 25 4N 118 47 E
Huianp'u 106 37 30N 106 40 E
Huiarau Ra. 142 38 45 S 176 55 E
Huich'ang 109 25 32N 115 45 E
Huichapán 165 20 24N 99 40W
Huichou 109 23 5N 114 24 E
Huifa Ho, R. 107 43 6N 126 53 E
Huihsien, Honan, China 106 35 32N 113 54 E
Huihsien, Kansu, China 106 33 46N 106 6 E
Huila 128 15 30 S 15 0 E
Huila □ 174 2 30N 75 45W
Huila, Nevado del 174 3 0N 76 0W
Huilai 109 23 4N 116 18 E
Huili 108 26 39N 102 11 E
Huimin 107 37 29N 117 29 E
Huinan 107 42 40N 126 5 E
Huinca Renancó 172 34 51 S 64 22W
Huining 106 35 41N 105 8 E
Huinung 106 39 0N 106 45 E
Huiroa 142 39 15 S 174 30 E
Huise 47 50 54N 3 36 E
Huishui 108 26 8N 106 35 E
Huissen 46 51 57N 5 57 E
Huiting 106 34 6N 116 4 E
Huitse 108 26 22N 103 15 E
Huit'ung 108 26 56N 109 36 E
Huixtla 165 15 9N 92 28W
Huiya 92 24 40N 49 15 E
Huizen 46 52 18N 5 14 E
Hukawng Valley 99 26 30N 96 30 E
Hukou 109 29 45N 116 13 E
Hukuma 123 14 55N 36 2 E
Hukuntsi 128 23 58 S 21 45 E
Hula 123 6 33N 38 30 E
Hulaifa 92 25 58N 41 0 E
Hulan 105 46 0N 126 44 E
Huld 106 45 5N 105 30 E
Hülda 90 31 50N 34 51 E
Hull, Can. 150 45 20N 75 40W
Hull, U.K. 33 53 45N 0 20W
Hullavington 28 51 31N 2 9W
Hulme End 32 53 8N 1 51W
Hulst 47 51 17N 4 2 E
Hultsfred 73 57 30N 15 52 E
Hulun Ch'ih 105 49 1N 117 32 E
Humacao 147 18 9N 65 50W
Humahuaca 172 23 10 S 65 25W
Humaitá 174 7 35 S 62 40W
Humaita 172 27 2 S 58 31W
Humansdorp 128 34 2 S 24 46 E
Humber, Mouth of 33 53 32N 0 8 E
Humber, R. 33 53 40N 0 10W
Humberside □ 33 53 50N 0 30W
Humbert River 136 16 30 S 130 45 E
Humble 159 29 59N 95 10W
Humboldt, Can. 153 52 15N 105 9W
Humboldt, Iowa, U.S.A. 158 42 42N 94 15W
Humboldt, Tenn., U.S.A. 157 35 50N 88 55W
Humboldt Gletscher 12 79 30N 62 0W
Humboldt, R. 160 40 55N 116 0W
Humbolt Mts. 143 44 30 S 168 15 E
Hume 163 36 48N 118 54W
Hume, L. 141 36 0 S 147 0 E
Humenné 53 48 55N 21 50 E
Humphreys, Mt. 163 37 17N 118 40W
Humphreys Pk. 161 35 24N 111 38W
Humpolec 52 49 31N 15 20 E
Humshaugh 35 55 3N 2 8W
Humula 141 35 30 S 147 46 E
Hün 119 29 2N 16 0 E
Hun Chiang, R. 107 40 52N 125 42 E
Huna Floi 74 65 50N 20 50W
Hunan □ 109 27 30N 111 30 E
Hunch'un 107 42 52N 130 21 E
Hundested 73 55 58N 11 52 E
Hundred House 31 52 11N 3 17W
Hundred Mile House 152 51 38N 121 18W
Hundshögen, mt. 72 62 57N 13 46 E
Hunedoara 70 45 40N 22 50 E
Hunedoara □ 70 45 45N 22 54 E
Hünfeld 48 50 40N 9 47 E
Hung Chiang, R. 108 27 7N 109 57 E
Hung Ho, R. 109 32 24N 115 32 E
Hung Liu Ho, R. 106 38 3N 109 10 E
Hung Yen 100 20 39N 106 4 E
Hungan 109 31 18N 114 33 E
Hungary ■ 53 47 20N 19 20 E
Hungary, Plain of 16 47 0N 20 0 E
Hungchiang 109 27 6N 110 0 E
Hungerford, Austral. 139 28 58 S 144 24 E
Hungerford, U.K. 28 51 25N 1 30W
Hunghai Wan 109 22 45N 115 15 E
Hunghu 109 29 49N 113 30 E
Hüngnam 107 39 55N 127 45 E
Hungshui Ho, R. 108 23 24N 110 12 E
Hungtech'eng 106 36 48N 107 6 E
Hungt'ou Hsü 109 22 4N 121 25 E
Hungt'se Hu 107 33 15N 118 45 E
Hungtung 106 36 15N 111 37 E
Hungya 108 29 56N 103 25 E
Hungyüan 108 32 46N 102 42 E
Huni Valley 120 5 33N 1 56W
Hunmanby 33 54 12N 0 19W
Hunsberge 128 27 58 S 17 5 E
Hunsrück, mts. 49 50 0N 7 30 E
Hunstanton 29 52 57N 0 30 E
Hunsur 97 12 16N 76 16 E
Hunte, R. 48 52 47N 8 28 E
Hunter, N.Z. 143 44 36 S 171 2 E
Hunter, N.D., U.S.A. 158 47 12N 97 17W
Hunter, N.Y., U.S.A. 162 42 13N 74 13W
Hunter Hills, The 143 44 26 S 170 46 E
Hunter, I. 138 40 30 S 144 54 E
Hunter I. 152 51 55N 128 0W
Hunter Mts. 143 45 43 S 167 25 E
Hunter, R. 143 44 21 S 169 27 E
Hunter Ra. 141 32 45 S 150 15 E
Hunters Road 127 19 9 S 29 49 E
Hunterston 34 55 43N 4 55W
Hunterton 139 26 12 S 148 30 E
Hunterville 142 39 56 S 175 35 E
Huntingburg 156 38 20N 86 58W
Huntingdon, Can. 150 45 10N 74 10W
Huntingdon, U.K. 29 52 20N 0 11W
Huntingdon, N.Y., U.S.A. 162 40 52N 73 25W
Huntingdon, Pa., U.S.A. 156 40 28N 78 1W
Huntingdon & Peterborough (□) 26 52 23N 0 10W
Huntingdon I. 151 53 48N 56 45W
Huntington, U.K. 33 54 0N 1 4W
Huntington, Id., U.S.A. 160 44 22N 117 21W
Huntington, Ind., U.S.A. 156 40 52N 85 30W
Huntington, Ut., U.S.A. 160 39 24N 111 1W
Huntington, W. Va., U.S.A. 156 38 20N 82 30W
Huntington Beach 163 33 40N 118 0W
Huntington Park 161 34 58N 118 15W
Huntly, N.Z. 142 37 34 S 175 11 E
Huntly, U.K. 37 57 27N 2 48W
Huntsville, Can. 150 45 20N 79 14W
Huntsville, Ala., U.S.A. 157 34 45N 86 35W
Huntsville, Tex., U.S.A. 159 30 50N 95 35W
Hunyani Dams. 127 18 0 S 31 10 E
Hunyani, R. 127 18 0 S 31 10 E
Hunyüan 106 39 44N 113 42 E
Hunza, R. 95 36 24N 75 50 E
Huohsien 106 36 38N 111 43 E
Huon, G. 135 7 0 S 147 30 E
Huon Pen. 135 6 20 S 147 30 E
Huong Hoa 100 16 37N 106 45 E
Huong Khe 100 18 13N 105 41 E
Huonville 138 43 0 S 147 5 E
Huoshaop'u 107 43 23N 130 26 E
Hupei □ 109 31 5N 113 5 E
Hurbanovo 53 47 51N 18 11 E
Hurezani 70 44 49N 23 40 E
Hurghada 122 27 15N 33 50 E
Hŭrghita □ 70 46 30N 25 30 E
Hŭrghita Mţii 70 46 25N 25 35 E
Hurley, N. Mex., U.S.A. 161 32 45N 108 7W
Hurley, Wis., U.S.A. 158 46 26N 90 10W
Hurlford 34 55 35N 4 29W
Hurliness 37 58 47N 3 15W
Hurlock 162 38 38N 75 52W
Huron, Calif., U.S.A. 163 36 12N 120 6W
Huron, S.D., U.S.A. 158 44 30N 98 20W
Hurricane 161 37 10N 113 12W
Hursley 28 51 1N 1 23W
Hurso 123 9 35N 41 33 E
Hurstbourne Tarrant 28 51 17N 1 27W
Hurstpierpoint 29 50 56N 0 11W
Hurum, Buskerud, Norway 71 59 36N 10 23 E
Hurum, Oppland, Norway 71 61 9N 8 46 E
Hurunui, R. 143 42 54 S 173 18 E
Hurup 73 56 46N 8 25 E
Husaby 73 58 35N 13 25 E
Húsavík 74 66 3N 17 21W
Husband's Bosworth 28 52 27N 1 3W
Husi 70 46 41N 28 7 E
Husinish Pt. 36 57 59N 7 6W
Huskvarna 73 57 47N 14 15 E
Huslia 147 65 40N 156 30W
Husøy 71 61 3N 4 44 E
Hussar 152 51 3N 112 41W
Hussein (Allenby) Br. 90 31 53N 35 33 E
Hustopéce 53 48 57N 16 43 E
Husum, Ger. 48 54 27N 9 3 E
Husum, Sweden 72 63 21N 19 12 E
Hutchinson, Kans., U.S.A. 159 38 3N 97 59W
Hutchinson, Minn, U.S.A. 158 44 50N 94 22W
Huttenberg 52 46 56N 14 33 E
Hüttental 47 50 53N 8 1 E
Huttig 159 33 5N 92 10W
Hutton, Mt. 139 25 51 S 148 20 E
Hutton, oilfield 19 61 0N 1 30 E
Hutton Ra. 137 24 45 S 124 30 E
Huttwil 50 47 7N 7 50 E
Huwarā 90 32 9N 35 15 E
Huwun 123 4 23N 40 6 E
Huy 47 50 31N 5 15 E
Huyton 32 53 25N 2 52W
Hvaler 71 59 4N 11 1 E
Hvammsfjörður 74 65 4N 22 5W
Hvammur 74 65 13N 21 49W
Hvar 63 43 10N 16 45 E
Hvar, I. 63 43 11N 16 28 E
Hvarski Kanal 63 43 15N 16 35 E
Hvítá, Arnessýsla, Iceland 74 64 0N 20 58W
Hvítá, Mýrasýsla, Iceland 74 64 40N 21 5W
Hvítárvatn 74 63 37N 19 50W
Hvitsten 71 59 35N 10 42 E
Hwachon-chŏsuji 107 38 5N 127 50 E
Hwang Ho = Huang Ho, R. 107 36 50N 118 20 E
Hwekum 98 26 7N 95 22 E
Hyannis, Mass., U.S.A. 162 41 39N 70 17W
Hyannis, Nebr., U.S.A. 158 41 60N 101 45W
Hyargas Nuur 105 49 12N 93 34 E
Hyattsville 162 38 59N 76 55W
Hybo 72 61 49N 16 15 E
Hydaburg 147 55 15N 132 45W
Hyde, N.Z. 143 45 18 S 170 16 E
Hyde, U.K. 32 53 26N 2 6W
Hyde Park 162 41 47N 73 56W
Hyden 137 32 24 S 118 46 E
Hyderabad, India 96 17 10N 78 29 E
Hyderabad, Pak. 94 25 23N 68 36 E
Hyderabad □ 94 25 3N 68 24 E
Hyères 45 43 8N 6 9 E
Hyères, Is. d' 45 43 0N 6 28 E
Hyesan 107 41 20N 128 10 E
Hyland Post 139 57 40N 128 10W
Hyland, R. 152 59 52N 128 12W
Hylestad 71 59 6N 7 29 E
Hyllested 71 56 17N 10 46 E
Hyltebruk 73 56 59N 13 15 E
Hymia 95 33 40N 78 2 E
Hyndman Pk. 160 44 4N 114 0W
Hynish 34 56 27N 6 54W
Hynish B. 34 56 29N 6 40W
Hyōgo-ken □ 110 35 15N 135 0 E
Hyrum 160 41 35N 111 56W
Hysham 160 46 21N 107 11W
Hythe 29 51 4N 1 5 E
Hyūga 110 32 25N 131 35 E
Hyvinkä 75 60 38N 24 50 E

I

I Ho, R. 107 34 10N 118 4 E
I-n-Azaoua 119 20 45N 7 31 E
I-n-Échaïe 118 20 10N 2 5W
I-n-Gall 121 6 51N 7 1 E
I-n-Tabedog 118 19 54N 1 3 E
Iabès, Erg 118 27 30N 2 2W
Iaco, R. 174 10 25 S 70 30W
Iaçu 171 12 45 S 40 13W
Iakora 129 23 6 S 46 40 E
Ialomiţa □ 70 44 30N 27 30 E
Ianca 70 45 6N 27 29 E
Iar Connacht 39 53 20N 9 20W
Iara 70 46 31N 23 35 E
Iaşi □ 70 47 20N 27 0 E
Iaşi (Jassy) 70 47 10N 27 40 E
Iauaretê 174 0 30N 69 5W
Iaucdjovac, (Port Harrison) 149 58 25N 78 15W
Iba 103 15 22N 120 0 E
Ibadan 121 7 22N 3 58 E
Ibagué 174 4 27N 73 14W
Ibaiti 171 23 50 S 50 10W
Iballja 68 42 12N 20 0 E
Ibar, R. 66 43 15N 20 40 E
Ibara 110 34 36N 133 28 E

Ibaraki-ken □ 111 36 10N 140 10 E
Ibararaki 111 34 49N 135 34 E
Ibarra 174 0 21N 78 7W
Ibba 123 4 49N 29 2 E
Ibba, Bahr el 123 5 30N 28 55 E
Ibbenbüren 48 52 16N 7 41 E
Ibembo 126 2 35N 23 35 E
Ibera, Laguna 172 28 30 S 57 9W
Iberian Peninsula 16 40 0N 5 0W
Iberville 150 45 19N 73 17W
Iberville, Lac d' 150 55 55N 73 15W
Ibi 121 8 15N 9 50 E
Ibiá 171 19 30 S 46 30W
Ibicaraí 171 14 51 S 39 36W
Ibicuí 171 14 51 S 39 59W
Ibicuy 172 33 55 S 59 10W
Ibioapaba, Serra da 170 20 14 S 40 25W
Ibipetuba 171 11 0 S 44 32W
Ibiracu 171 19 50 S 40 30W
Ibitiara 171 12 39 S 42 13W
Ibiza 59 38 54N 1 26 E
Ibiza, I. 59 39 0N 1 30 E
Iblei, Monti 65 37 15N 14 45 E
Ibo 127 12 22 S 40 32 E
Ibonma 103 3 22 S 133 31 E
Ibotirama 171 12 13 S 43 12W
Ibriktepe 68 41 2N 26 33 E
Ibshawâi 122 29 21N 30 40 E
Ibstock 28 52 42N 1 23W
Ibu 103 1 35N 127 25 E
Ibuki-Sanchi 111 35 25N 136 34 E
Ibûneşti 70 46 45N 24 50 E
Iburg 48 52 10N 8 3 E
Ibusuki 110 31 12N 130 32 E
Ibwe Munyama 127 16 5 S 28 31 E
Ica 174 14 0 S 75 30W
Ica, R. 174 2 55 S 69 0W
Icabarú 174 4 20N 61 45W
Içana 174 1 21N 69 0W
Icatu 170 2 46 S 44 4W
Iceland, I. ■ 74 65 0N 19 0W
Icha 77 55 30N 156 0 E
Ichang 109 25 25N 112 55 E
Ich'ang 109 30 40N 111 20 E
Ichchapuram 96 19 10N 84 40 E
Icheng 109 32 16N 119 12 E
Ich'eng, Hupeh, China 109 31 43N 112 12 E
Ich'eng, Shansi, China 106 35 42N 111 40 E
Ichihara 111 35 28N 140 5 E
Ichikawa 111 35 44N 139 55 E
Ichilo, R. 174 16 30 S 64 45W
Ichinomiya, Gifu, Japan 111 35 18N 136 48 E
Ichinomiya, Kumamoto, Japan 110 32 58N 131 5 E
Ichinoseki 112 38 55N 141 8 E
Ichŏn 107 37 17N 127 27 E
Icht 118 29 6N 8 54W
Ichtegem 47 51 5N 3 1 E
Ich'uan 106 36 4N 110 6 E
Ich'un 105 47 42N 128 54 E
Ichün 106 35 23N 109 7 E
Ich'un, Heilungkiang, China 105 47 42N 128 54 E
Ich'un, Kiangsi, China 109 27 47N 114 22 E
Icó 170 6 24 S 38 51W
Icoraci 170 1 18 S 48 28W
Icy C. 12 70 25N 162 0W
Icy Str. 153 58 20N 135 30W
Ida Grove 158 42 20N 95 25W
Ida Valley 137 28 42 S 120 29 E
Idabel 159 33 53N 94 50W
Idaga Hamus 123 14 13N 39 35 E
Idah 121 6 10N 6 40 E
Idaho □ 160 44 10N 114 0W
Idaho City 160 43 50N 115 52W
Idaho Falls 160 43 30N 112 10W
Idaho Springs 160 39 49N 105 30W
Idanha-a-Nova 56 39 50N 7 15W
Idanre 121 7 8N 5 5 E
Idar-Oberstein 49 49 43N 7 19 E
Idd el Ghanam 117 11 30N 24 25 E
Iddan 91 6 10N 49 5 E
Idehan 119 27 10N 11 30 E
Idehan Marzūq 119 24 50N 13 51 E
Idelès 119 23 58N 5 53 E
Idfû 122 25 0N 32 49 E
Idhi Oros 69 35 15N 24 45 E
Idhra 69 37 20N 23 28 E
Idi 102 4 55N 97 45 E
Idi Amin Dada, L. 93 0 25 S 29 40 E
Idiofa 124 4 55 S 19 42 E
Idkerberget 72 60 22N 15 15 E
Idle 33 53 50N 1 45W
Idle, R. 33 53 27N 0 49W
Idmiston 28 51 8N 1 43W
Idna 90 31 34N 34 58 E
Idria 163 36 25N 120 41W
Idrija 63 46 0N 14 5 E
Idritsa 80 56 25N 28 57 E
Idstein 49 50 13N 8 17 E
Idsworth 29 50 50N 0 56W
Idutywa 125 32 8 S 28 18 E
Ieper 47 50 51N 2 53 E
Ierápetra 69 35 0N 25 44 E
Ierissós 68 40 22N 23 52 E
Ierissóu Kólpos 68 40 27N 23 57 E
Ierzu 64 39 48N 9 32 E
Ieshima-Shotō 110 34 40N 134 32 E
Iesi 63 43 32N 13 12 E
Ifach, Punta 59 38 38N 0 5 E
Ifanadiana 129 21 29 S 47 39 E
Ife 121 7 30N 4 31 E
Iférouâne 121 19 5N 8 35 E
Ifni 118 29 25N 10 10W
Ifon 121 6 58N 5 40 E
Iga 111 34 45N 136 10 E
Iganga 126 0 30N 33 28 E
Igarapava 171 20 3 S 47 47W
Igarapé Açu 170 1 4 S 47 33W
Igarapé-Mirim 170 1 59 S 48 58W
Igarka 77 67 30N 87 20 E
Igatimi 173 24 5 S 55 30W
Igatpuri 96 19 40N 73 35 E
Igbetti 121 8 44N 4 8 E
Igbo-Ora 121 7 10N 3 15 E
Igboho 121 8 40N 3 50 E
Iggesund 72 61 39N 17 10 E
Igherm 118 30 7N 8 18W
Ighil Izane 118 35 44N 0 31 E
Iglene 118 22 57N 4 58 E
Iglésias 64 39 19N 8 27 E
Igli 118 30 25N 2 12W
Iglino 84 54 50N 56 26 E
Igloolik Island 149 69 20N 81 30W
Igma 118 29 9N 6 11W
Igma, Gebel el 122 28 55N 34 0 E
Ignace 150 49 30N 91 40W
Igoshevo 81 59 25N 42 35 E
Igoumenítsa 68 39 32N 20 18 E
Igra 84 57 33N 53 7 E
Iguaçu, Cat. del 173 25 41N 54 26W
Iguaçu, R. 173 25 30 S 53 10W
Iguala 165 18 20N 99 40W
Igualada 58 41 37N 1 37 E
Iguape 171 24 43 S 47 33W
Iguape, R. 173 24 40 S 48 0W
Iguassu = Iguaçu 173 25 41N 54 26W
Iguatu 170 6 20 S 39 18W
Iguéla 124 2 0 S 9 16 E
Igumale 121 6 47N 7 55 E
Igunga □ 126 4 20 S 33 45 E
Ihiala 121 5 40N 6 55 E
Ihosy 129 22 24 S 46 8 E
Ihotry, L. 129 21 56 S 43 41 E
Ihsien, Anwhei, China 109 29 53N 117 57E
Ihsien, Hopeh, China 106 39 21N 115 29E
Ihsien, Liaoning, China 107 41 34N 121 15E
Ihsien, Shantung, China 107 37 11N 119 55E
Ihuang 109 27 32N 115 57 E
Ii 74 65 15N 25 30 E
Iida 111 35 35N 138 0 E
Iiey 138 18 53 S 141 12 E
Iijoki 74 65 20N 26 15 E
Iisalmi 74 63 32N 27 10 E
Iizuka 110 33 38N 130 42 E
Ijebu-Igbo 121 6 56N 4 1 E
Ijebu-Ode 121 6 47N 3 52 E
IJmuiden 46 52 28N 4 35 E
IJssel, R. 46 52 35N 5 50 E
IJsselmeer 46 52 45N 5 20 E
IJsselmuiden 46 52 34N 5 57 E
IJsselstein 46 52 1N 5 2 E
Ijui, R. 173 27 58 S 55 20W
Ijūin 110 31 37N 130 24 E
IJzendijke 47 51 19N 3 37 E
IJzer, R. 47 51 9N 2 44 E
Ik, R. 84 55 55N 52 36 E
Ikamatua 41 42 15 S 171 41 E
Ikare 121 7 18N 5 40 E
Ikaría, I. 69 37 35N 26 10 E
Ikast 73 56 8N 9 10 E
Ikawa 111 35 13N 138 15 E
Ikeda 111 34 1N 133 48 E
Ikeja 121 6 28N 3 45 E
Ikela 124 1 0 S 23 35 E
Ikerre 121 7 25N 5 19 E
Ikhtiman 67 42 27N 23 48 E
Iki 110 33 45N 129 42 E
Iki-Kaikyō 110 33 40N 129 45 E
Ikimba L. 126 1 30 S 31 20 E
Ikire 121 7 10N 4 15 E
Ikirun 121 7 54N 4 40 E
Ikitsuki-Shima 110 33 23N 129 26 E
Ikole 121 7 40N 5 37 E
Ikom 121 6 0N 8 42 E
Ikopa, R. 129 17 45 S 46 40 E
Ikot Ekpene 121 5 12N 7 40 E
Ikungu 126 1 33 S 33 42 E
Ikuno 110 35 10N 134 48 E
Ila 121 8 0N 4 51 E
Ilam 95 26 58N 87 58 E
Ilan, China 105 46 14N 129 33 E
Ilan, Taiwan 109 24 45N 121 44 E
Ilanskiy 77 56 14N 96 3 E
Ilanz 51 46 46N 9 12 E
Ilaomita, R. 47 44 47N 27 0 E
Ilaro Agege 121 6 53N 3 3 E
Ilayangudi 97 9 34N 78 37 E
Ilbilbie 138 21 45 S 149 20 E
Ilchester 28 51 0N 2 41W
Ile-à-la Crosse 153 55 27N 107 53W
Ile-à-la-Crosse, Lac 153 55 40N 107 45W
Île Bouchard, L' 42 47 7N 0 26 E
Île de France □ 43 49 0N 2 20 E
Ilebo 124 4 17 S 20 47 E
Ileje □ 127 9 30 S 33 25 E
Ilek 84 51 32N 53 21 E
Ilek, R. 84 51 30N 53 22 E
Ilen R. 39 51 38N 9 19W
Ilero 121 8 0N 3 20 E
Ilesha, West-Central, Nigeria 121 7 37N 4 40 E
Ilesha, Western, Nigeria 121 8 57N 3 28E
Ilford 153 56 4N 95 35W
Ilfov □ 70 44 20N 26 0 E
Ilfracombe, Austral. 138 23 30 S 144 30 E
Ilfracombe, U.K. 30 51 13N 4 8W
Ilha Grande, Baia da 171 23 9S 44 30W
Ílhavo 56 40 33N 8 43W
Ilheus 171 14 49 S 39 2W
Ili 85 45 53N 77 10 E
Ilia 70 45 57N 22 40 E
Ilia □ 69 37 45N 21 35 E
Iliamna L. 147 59 35N 155 30W
Iliang, Yunnan, China 108 24 54N 103 9E
Iliang, Yunnan, China 108 27 35N 104 1E
Ilich 85 40 50N 68 27 E
Ilico 172 34 50 S 72 20W
Iliff 158 40 50N 103 3W
Ilíki 69 38 24N 23 15 E
Ilio Pt. 147 21 13N 157 16W
Iliodhrómia 68 39 12N 23 50 E
Ilion 162 43 0N 75 3W
Ilirska Bistrica 63 45 34N 14 14 E
Iliysk 76 44 10N 77 10 E
Ilkal 97 15 57N 76 8 E
Ilkeston 33 52 59N 1 19W
Ilkley 21 53 56N 1 49W
Illana B. 103 7 35N 123 45 E
Illapel 172 32 0 S 71 10W
'Illar 90 32 23N 35 7 E
Ille 44 42 40N 2 37 E
Ille-et-Vilaine □ 42 48 10N 1 30W
Iller, R. 49 47 53N 10 10 E
Illescás 56 40 8N 3 51W
Illig 91 7 47N 49 45 E
Illimani, Mte. 174 16 30 S 67 50W
Illinois □ 155 40 15N 89 30W
Illinois, R. 155 40 10N 90 20W
Illizi 119 26 31N 8 32 E
Illora 57 37 17N 3 53W
Ilmen, Oz. 80 58 15N 31 10 E
Ilmenau 48 50 41N 10 55 E
Ilminster 28 50 55N 2 56W
Ilo 174 17 40 S 71 20W
Ilobu 121 7 45N 4 25 E
Ilohuli Shan 105 51 20N 124 20 E
Iloilo 103 10 45N 122 33 E
Ilok 66 45 15N 19 20 E
Ilora 121 7 45N 3 50 E
Ilorin 121 8 30N 4 35 E
Ilovatka 81 50 30N 46 50 E
Ilovlya 83 49 15N 44 2 E
Ilovlya, R. 83 49 38N 44 20 E
Iłowa 54 51 30N 15 10 E
Ilubabor □ 123 7 25N 35 0 E
Ilukste 80 55 55N 26 20 E
Ilung 108 31 34N 106 24 E
Ilva Mică 70 47 17N 24 40 E
Ilwaki 103 7 55 S 126 30 E
Ilyichevsk 82 46 10N 30 35 E
Imabari 110 34 4N 133 0 E
Imadahane 118 32 8N 7 0W
Imaichi 111 36 6N 139 16 E
Imaloto, R. 129 23 10 S 45 15 E
Iman = Dalneretchensk 77 45 50N 133 40 E
Imari 110 33 15N 129 52 E
Imasa 122 18 0N 36 12 E
Imathía □ 68 40 30N 22 15 E
Imbâbah 122 30 5N 31 12 E
Imbler 160 45 31N 118 0W
Imbros = Imroz 68 40 10N 26 0 E
Imen 108 24 40N 102 9 E
Imeni Panfilova 85 43 23N 77 7 E
Imeni Poliny Osipenko 77 55 25N 136 29 E
Imeri, Serra 174 0 50N 65 25W
Imerimandroso 129 17 26 S 48 35 E
Imi (Hinna) 123 6 35N 42 30 E
Imi n'Tanoute 118 31 13N 8 51 E
Imienp'o 107 45 0N 128 16 E
Imishly 83 39 49N 48 4 E
Imiteg 118 29 43N 8 10W
Imlay 160 40 45N 118 9W
Immingham 33 53 37N 0 12W
Immokalee 157 26 25N 81 20W
Imo □ 121 5 15N 7 20 E
Imola 63 44 20N 11 42 E
Imotski 66 43 27N 17 21 E
Imperatriz 170 5 30 S 47 29W
Impéria 62 43 52N 8 0 E
Imperial, Can. 153 51 21N 105 28W
Imperial, Calif., U.S.A. 161 32 52N 115 34W
Imperial, Nebr., U.S.A. 158 40 38N 101 39W
Imperial Beach 163 32 35N 117 8W
Imperial Dam 161 32 50N 114 30W
Imperial Valley 163 32 55N 115 30W
Imperieuse Reef 136 17 36 S 118 50 E
Impfondo 124 1 40N 18 0 E
Imphal 98 24 48N 93 56 E
Imphy 43 46 56N 3 15 E
Imroz = Gökçeada 68 40 10N 26 0 E
Imst 52 47 15N 10 44 E
Imuruan B. 103 10 40N 119 10 E
In Belbel 118 27 55N 1 12 E
In Delimane 121 15 52N 1 31 E
In-Gall 121 16 51N 7 1 E
In Rhar 118 27 10N 1 59 E
In Salah 118 27 10N 2 32 E
In Tallak 121 16 19N 3 15 E
Ina 111 35 50N 138 0 E
Ina-Bonchi 111 35 45N 137 58 E
Inagh 39 52 53N 9 11W
Inajá 170 8 54 S 37 49W
Inangahua Junc. 143 41 52 S 171 59 E
Inanwatan 103 2 10 S 132 5 E
Iñapari 174 11 0 S 69 40W
Inari 74 68 54N 27 5 E
Inari, L. 74 69 0N 28 0 E
Inazawa 111 35 15N 136 47 E
Inca 58 39 43N 2 54 E
Incaguasi 172 29 12 S 71 5W
Ince 32 53 32N 2 38W
İnce Burnu 92 42 2N 35 0 E
Inch 39 52 42N 8 8W
Inch Br. 39 52 49N 9 6W
Inchard, Loch 36 58 28N 5 2W
Inchcape Rock 35 56 26N 2 24W
Inchigeelagh 39 51 50N 9 8W
Inchini 123 8 55N 37 37 E
Inchkeith, I. 35 56 2N 3 8W
Inchnadamph 36 58 9N 5 0W
Inch'ŏn 107 37 27N 126 40 E
Inchture 35 56 26N 3 8W
Incio 56 42 39N 7 21W
Incomáti, R. 129 25 15 S 32 35 E
Incudine, Mte. l' 45 41 50N 9 12 E
Inda Silase 123 14 10N 38 15 E
Indaal L. 34 55 44N 6 20W
Indalsälven 72 62 36N 17 30 E
Indaw 98 24 15N 96 5 E
Indbir 123 8 7N 37 52 E
Indefatigable, gasfield 19 53 20N 2 40 E
Independence, Calif., U.S.A. 163 36 51N 118 7W
Independence, Iowa, U.S.A. 158 42 27N 91 52W
Independence, Kans., U.S.A. 159 37 10N 95 50W
Independence, Mo., U.S.A. 158 39 3N 94 25W
Independence, Oreg., U.S.A. 160 44 53N 123 6W
Independence Fjord 12 82 10N 29 0W
Independence Mts. 160 41 30N 116 2W
Independência 170 5 23 S 40 19W
Independencia, La 165 16 31N 91 47W
Independenta 70 45 25N 27 42 E
Inderborskly 83 48 30N 51 42 E
India ■ 87 20 0N 80 0 E
Indian Cabins 152 59 52N 117 2W
Indian Harbour 151 54 27N 57 13W
Indian Head 153 50 30N 103 35W
Indian House L. 151 56 30N 64 30W
Indian Lake 162 43 47N 74 16W
Indian Ocean 11 5 0 S 75 0 E
Indian River B. 162 38 36N 75 4W
Indiana 156 40 38N 79 9W
Indiana □ 156 40 0N 86 0W
Indianapolis 156 39 42N 86 10W
Indianola, Iowa, U.S.A. 158 41 20N 93 38W
Indianola, Miss., U.S.A. 159 33 27N 90 40W
Indianópolis 171 19 2 S 47 55 E
Indiapora 171 19 57 S 50 17W
Indiaroba 171 11 32 S 37 31W
Indiga 78 67 50N 48 50 E
Indigirka, R. 77 69 0N 147 0 E
Indija 66 45 6N 20 7 E
Indio 163 33 46N 116 15W
Indonesia ■ 102 5 0 S 115 0 E
Indore 94 22 42N 75 53 E
Indramaju 103 6 21 S 108 20 E
Indramaju, Tg. 103 6 20 S 108 20 E
Indravati, R. 96 19 0N 81 15 E
Indre □ 43 47 12N 1 39 E
Indre-et-Loire □ 42 47 12N 0 40 E
Indre, R. 42 47 2N 1 8 E
Indre Söndeled 71 58 46N 9 5 E
Indus, Mouth of the 94 24 00N 68 00 E
Indus, R. 94 28 40N 70 10 E
İnebolu 92 41 55N 33 40E
Infante, Kaap 128 34 27 S 20 51 E
Infantes 59 38 43N 3 1W
Infiernillo, Presa del 164 18 9N 102 0W
Infiesto 56 43 21N 5 21W
Ingá 171 7 17 S 35 36W
Ingatestone 29 51 40N 0 23W
Ingelmunster 47 50 56N 3 16 E
Ingende 124 0 12 S 18 57 E
Ingenio Santa Ana 172 27 25 S 65 40W
Ingesvang 73 56 10N 9 20 E
Ingham 138 18 43 S 146 10 E
Ingichka 85 39 47N 65 58 E
Ingleborough, mt. 32 54 11N 2 23W
Inglefield Land 143 78 30N 70 0W
Ingleton 32 54 9N 2 29W
Inglewood, Queensland, Austral. 139 28 25 S 151 8 E
Inglewood, Vic., Austral. 140 36 29 S 143 53 E
Inglewood, N.Z. 142 39 9 S 174 14 E
Inglewood, U.S.A. 163 33 58N 118 21W
Ingoldmells, Pt. 33 53 11N 0 21 E
Ingólfshöfði 74 63 48N 16 39W
Ingolstadt 49 48 45N 11 26 E
Ingomar 160 46 43N 107 37W
Ingonish 151 46 42N 60 18W
Ingore 120 12 24N 15 48W
Ingul, R. 82 47 30N 32 15 E
Ingulec 82 47 42N 33 4 E
Ingulets, R. 82 47 20N 33 20 E
Inguri, R. 83 42 58N 42 17 E
Inhaca, I. 129 26 1 S 32 57 E
Inhafenga 129 20 36 S 33 47 E
Inhambane 125 23 54 S 35 30 E

Inhambane □ **129** 22 30 S 34 20 E
Inhambupe **171** 11 47 S 38 21W
Inhaminga **127** 18 26 S 35 0 E
Inharrime **129** 24 30 S 35 0 E
Inharrime, R. **129** 24 30 S 35 0 E
Inhassoro **127** 21 50 S 35 15 E
Inhuma **170** 6 40 S 41 42W
Inhumas **171** 16 22 S 49 30W
Iniesta **59** 39 27N 1 45W
Ining, Kwangsi-Chuang, China **109** 25 8N 109 57 E
Ining, Sinkiang-Uigur, China **105** 43 54N 81 21 E
Inírida, R. **174** 3 0N 68 40W
Inishark **38** 53 36N 10 17W
Inishark I. **38** 53 38N 10 17W
Inishbofin I., Donegal, Ireland **38** 55 10N 8 10W
Inishbofin I., Galway, Ireland **38** 53 35N 10 12W
Inisheer **39** 53 3N 9 32W
Inishfree B. **38** 55 4N 8 20W
Inishkea Is. **38** 54 8N 10 10W
Inishmaan I. **39** 53 5N 9 35W
Inishmore, I. **39** 53 8N 9 45W
Inishmurray I. **38** 54 26N 8 40W
Inishowen Hd. **38** 55 14N 6 56W
Inishowen, Pen. **38** 55 14N 7 15W
Inishrush **38** 54 52N 6 32W
Inishtooskert I. **39** 52 10N 10 35W
Inishturk I. **38** 53 42N 10 8W
Inishvickillane **39** 52 3N 10 37W
Inistioge **39** 52 30N 7 5W
Injune **139** 25 46 S 148 32 E
Inkberrow **28** 52 13N 1 59W
Inklin **152** 58 56N 133 5W
Inklin, R. **152** 58 50N 133 10W
Inkom **160** 42 51N 112 7W
Inkpen Beacon **28** 51 22N 1 28W
Inle Aing **98** 20 30N 96 58 E
Inn, R. **49** 48 35N 13 28 E
Innamincka **139** 27 44 S 140 46 E
Innellan **34** 55 54N 4 58W
Inner Mongolia □ **106** 44 50N 117 40 E
Inner Sound **36** 57 30N 5 55W
Innerleithen **35** 55 37N 3 4W
Innertkirchen **50** 46 43N 8 14 E
Innetalling I. **150** 56 0N 79 0W
Innfield **38** 53 25N 6 50W
Inniscrone **38** 54 13N 69 0W
Innisfail, Austral. **138** 17 33 S 146 5 E
Innisfail, Can. **152** 52 0N 113 57W
Innishannon **39** 51 45N 8 40W
Inniskeen **38** 54 0N 6 35W
In'no-shima **110** 34 19N 133 10 E
Innsbruck **52** 47 16N 11 23 E
Ino **110** 33 33N 133 26 E
Inocência **171** 19 47 S 51 48W
Inongo **124** 1 35 S 18 30 E
Inosu **174** 12 22N 71 38W
Inoucdjouac (Port Harrison) **149** 58 27N 78 6W
Inowrocław **54** 52 50N 18 20 E
Inpundong **107** 41 25N 126 34 E
Inquisivi **174** 16 50 S 66 45W
Ins **50** 47 1N 7 7 E
Insch **37** 57 20N 2 39W
Inscription, C. **137** 25 29 S 112 59 E
Insein **98** 17 15N 96 0 E
Însurăţei **70** 44 50N 27 40 E
Intendente Alvear **172** 35 12 S 63 32W
Interior **158** 43 46N 101 59W
Interlaken, Switz. **50** 46 41N 7 50 E
Interlaken, U.S.A. **162** 42 37N 76 43W
International Falls **158** 48 36N 93 25W
Interview I. **101** 12 55N 92 42 E
Inthanon, Mt. **101** 18 35N 98 29 E
Intiyaco **172** 28 50 S 60 0W
Intragna **51** 46 11N 8 42 E
Inubō-Zaki **111** 35 42N 140 52 E
Inútil, B. **176** 53 30 S 70 15W
Inuvik **147** 68 16N 133 40W
Inuyama **111** 35 23N 136 56 E
Inver B. **38** 54 35N 8 28W
Inverallochy **37** 57 40N 1 56W
Inveran, Ireland **39** 53 14N 9 28W
Inveran, U.K. **37** 57 58N 4 26W
Inveraray **34** 56 13N 5 5W
Inverbervie **37** 56 50N 2 17W
Invercargill **143** 46 24 S 168 24 E
Inverell **139** 29 45 S 151 8 E
Invergarry **37** 57 5N 4 48W
Invergordon **37** 57 41N 4 10W
Invergowrie **35** 56 29N 3 5W
Inverie **36** 57 2N 5 40W
Inverkeilor **37** 56 38N 2 33W
Inverkeithing **35** 56 2N 3 24W
Inverleigh **140** 38 6 S 144 3 E
Invermere **152** 50 30N 116 2W
Invermoriston **37** 57 13N 4 38W
Inverness, Can. **151** 46 15N 61 19W
Inverness, U.K. **37** 57 29N 4 12W
Inverness, U.S.A. **157** 28 50N 82 20W
Inverness (□) **26** 57 6N 4 40W
Invershiel **36** 57 13N 5 25W
Inverurie **37** 57 15N 2 21W
Inverway **136** 17 50 S 129 38 E
Investigator Group **136** 34 45 S 134 20 E
Investigator Str. **140** 35 30 S 137 0 E
Inyanga **127** 18 12 S 32 40 E
Inyangahi, mt. **127** 18 20 S 32 20 E
Inyantue **127** 18 30 S 26 40 E
Inyazura **127** 18 40 S 31 40 E
Inyo Range **161** 37 0N 118 0W
Inyokern **163** 35 37N 117 54W
Inywa **98** 22 4N 94 44 E
Inza **81** 53 55N 46 25 E
Inzell **49** 47 48N 12 15 E
Inzer **84** 54 14N 57 34 E
Inzhavino **81** 52 22N 42 23 E
Ioánnina (Janinà) □ **68** 39 39N 20 57 E
Iōhen **110** 32 58N 132 32 E
Iola **159** 38 0N 95 20W
Ioma **135** 8 19 S 147 52 E
Ion Corvin **70** 44 7N 27 50 E
Iona I. **34** 56 20N 6 25W
Ionava **80** 55 8N 24 12 E
Ione, Calif., U.S.A. **163** 38 20N 121 0W
Ione, Wash., U.S.A. **160** 48 44N 117 29W
Ionia **156** 42 59N 85 7W
Ionian Is. = Ionioi Nisoi **69** 38 40N 20 0 E
Ionian Sea **61** 37 30N 17 30 E
Iónioi Nísoi **69** 38 40N 20 8 E
Ioniškis **80** 56 13N 23 35 E
Iori, R. **83** 41 12N 46 10 E
Íos, I. **69** 36 41N 25 20 E
Iowa □ **158** 42 18N 93 30W
Iowa City **158** 41 40N 91 35W
Iowa Falls **158** 42 30N 93 15W
Ipala **126** 4 30 S 33 5 E
Ipameri **171** 17 44 S 48 9W
Ipanema **75** 9 48 S 41 45W
Ipáti **69** 38 52N 22 14 E
Ipatovo **83** 45 45N 42 50 E
Ipel, R. **53** 48 10N 19 35 E
Ipiales **174** 0 50N 77 37W
Ipiaú **171** 14 8 S 39 44W
Ipin **108** 28 48N 104 33 E
Ipinlang **108** 25 5N 101 58 E
Ipirá **171** 12 10 S 39 44W
Ípiros □ **68** 39 30N 20 30 E
Ipixuna **174** 7 0 S 71 40W
Ipoh **101** 4 35N 101 5 E
Iporá **171** 16 28 S 51 7W
Ippy **117** 6 5N 21 7 E
Ipsárion Óros **68** 40 40N 24 40 E
Ipswich, Austral. **139** 27 35 S 152 46 E
Ipswich, U.K. **29** 52 4N 1 9 E
Ipswich, N.H., U.S.A. **162** 42 40N 70 50W
Ipswich, S.D., U.S.A. **158** 45 28N 99 20W
Ipu **170** 4 23 S 40 44W
Ipueiras **170** 4 33 S 40 43W
Ipupiara **171** 11 49 S 42 37W
Iput, R. **80** 53 0N 32 10 E
Iquique **174** 20 19 S 70 5W
Iquitos **174** 3 45 S 73 10W
Iracoubo **175** 5 30N 53 10W
Iráklia, I. **69** 36 50N 25 28 E
Iráklion **69** 35 20N 25 12 E
Iráklion □ **69** 35 10N 25 10 E
Irako-Zaki **111** 34 35N 137 1 E
Irala **173** 25 55 S 54 35W
Iramba □ **126** 4 30 S 34 30 E
Iran ■ **93** 33 0N 53 0 E
Iran, Pegunungan **102** 2 20N 114 50 E
Iran, Plateau of **43** 33 00N 55 0 E
Iranamadu Tank **97** 9 23N 80 29 E
Iranshahr **93** 27 75N 60 40 E
Irapa **174** 10 34N 62 35W
Irapuato **164** 20 40N 101 40W
Iraq ■ **92** 33 0N 44 0 E
Irarrar, W. **118** 20 10N 1 30 E
Irati **173** 25 25 S 50 38W
Irbid **90** 32 35N 35 48 E
Irbit **84** 57 41N 63 3 E
Irchester **29** 52 17N 0 40W
Irebu **124** 0 40 S 17 55 E
Irecê **170** 11 18 S 41 52W
Iregua, R. **58** 42 22N 2 24 E
Ireland ■ **38** 53 0N 8 0W
Ireland's Eye **38** 53 25N 6 4W
Irele **121** 7 40N 5 40 E
Iremel, Gora **84** 54 33N 58 50 E
Iret **77** 60 10N 154 5 E
Irgiz, Bol. **81** 52 10N 49 10 E
Irharharene **119** 27 37N 7 30 E
Irharrhar, O. **119** 27 30N 6 0 E
Irhyangdong **107** 41 15N 129 30 E
Iri **107** 35 59N 127 0 E
Irian Jaya □ **103** 4 0 S 137 0 E
Iriba **124** 15 7N 22 15 E
Irié **120** 8 15N 9 10W
Iriklinskiy **84** 51 39N 58 38 E
Iringa **126** 7 48 S 35 43 E
Iringa □, Tanz. **126** 7 48 S 35 43 E
Iringa □, Tanz. **127** 9 0 S 35 0 E
Irinjalakuda **97** 10 21N 76 14 E
Iriomote-Jima **112** 24 19N 123 48 E
Iriona **166** 15 57N 85 11W
Irish Sea **32** 54 0N 5 0W
Irish Town **93** 40 55 S 145 9 E
Irkeshtam **85** 39 41N 73 55 E
Irkutsk **77** 52 10N 104 20 E
Irlam **32** 53 26N 2 27W
Irma **153** 52 55N 111 14W
Irmak **92** 39 58N 33 25 E
Irō-Zaki **111** 34 36N 138 51 E
Iroise **42** 48 15N 4 45W
Iron Baron **140** 33 3 S 137 11 E
Iron Gate = Porţile de Fier **70** 44 42N 22 30 E
Iron Knob **140** 32 46 S 137 8 E
Iron, L. **38** 53 37N 7 34W
Iron Mountain **156** 45 49N 88 4W
Iron River **158** 46 6N 88 40W
Ironbridge **28** 52 38N 2 29W
Ironhurst **138** 18 5 S 143 28 E
Ironstone Kopje, Mt. **128** 25 17 S 24 5 E
Ironton, Mo., U.S.A. **159** 37 40N 90 40W
Ironton, Ohio, U.S.A. **156** 38 35N 82 40W
Ironwood **158** 46 30N 90 10W
Iroquois Falls **150** 48 46N 80 41W
Irpen **80** 50 30N 30 8 E
Irrara Cr. **139** 29 35 S 145 31 E
Irrawaddy **98** 17 0N 95 0 E
Irrawaddy □ **98** 17 0N 95 0 E
Irrawaddy, R. **98** 15 50N 95 6 E
Irsina **65** 40 45N 16 15 E
Irt R. **32** 54 24N 3 25W
Irthing R. **35** 54 25N 2 48W
Irthlingborough **29** 52 20N 0 37W
Irtysh, R. **76** 53 36N 75 30 E
Irumu **126** 1 32N 29 53 E
Irún **58** 43 20N 1 52W
Irurzun **58** 42 55N 1 50W
Irvine, Can. **153** 49 57N 110 16W
Irvine, U.K. **34** 55 37N 4 40W
Irvine, U.S.A. **156** 37 42N 83 58W
Irvinestown **38** 54 28N 7 38W
Irwin, Pt. **137** 35 5 S 116 55 E
Irwin, R. **137** 29 15 S 114 54 E
Irymple **140** 34 14 S 142 8 E
Is-sur-Tille **43** 47 30N 5 10 E
Isa **121** 13 14N 6 24 E
Isaac, R. **138** 22 55 S 149 20 E
Isabel **158** 45 27N 101 22W
Isabela, Dom. Rep. **167** 19 58N 71 2W
Isabela, Pto Rico **147** 18 30N 67 01W
Isabela, Cord. **166** 13 30N 85 25W
Isabela, I. **164** 21 51N 105 55W
Isabella Ra. **136** 21 0 S 121 4 E
Ísafjarðardjúp **74** 66 10N 23 0W
Ísafjörður **74** 66 5N 23 9W
Isagarh **94** 24 48N 77 51 E
Isahaya **110** 32 52N 130 2 E
Isaka **126** 3 56 S 32 59 E
Isakly **84** 54 8N 51 32 E
Isangi **124** 0 52N 24 10 E
Isar, R. **49** 48 40N 12 30 E
Isarco, R. **63** 46 40N 11 35 E
Ísari **69** 37 22N 22 0 E
Isbergues **43** 50 36N 2 24 E
Isbiceni **70** 43 45N 24 40 E
Íschia, I. **64** 40 45N 13 51 E
Iscuandé **174** 2 28N 77 59W
Isdell, R. **136** 16 27 S 124 51 E
Ise **111** 34 25N 136 45 E
Ise-Heiya **111** 34 40N 136 30 E
Ise-Wan **111** 34 43N 136 43 E
Isefjord **73** 55 53N 11 50 E
Iseltwald **50** 46 43N 7 58 E
Isenthal **51** 46 55N 8 34 E
Iseo **62** 45 40N 10 3 E
Iseo, L. di **62** 45 45N 10 3 E
Iseramagazi **126** 4 37 S 32 10 E
Isère □ **45** 45 15N 5 40 E
Isère, R. **44** 45 15N 5 30 E
Iserlohn **48** 51 22N 7 40 E
Isérnia **65** 41 35N 14 12 E
Isesaki **111** 36 19N 139 12 E
Iset, R. **84** 56 36N 66 24 E
Iseyin **121** 8 0N 3 36 E
Isfara **85** 40 7N 70 38 E
Ishan **108** 24 30N 108 41 E
Ishara **121** 6 40N 3 40 E
Ishigaki **112** 24 20N 124 10 E
Ishikari-Wan **112** 43 20N 141 20 E
Ishikawa **112** 26 25N 127 48 E
Ishikawa-ken □ **111** 36 30N 136 30 E
Ishim **76** 56 10N 69 18 E
Ishim, R. **76** 57 45N 71 10 E
Ishimbay **84** 53 28N 56 2 E
Ishinomaki **112** 38 32N 141 20 E
Ishioka **111** 36 11N 140 16 E
Ishizuchi-Yama **110** 33 45N 133 6 E
Ishkashim **85** 36 44N 71 37 E
Ishkuman **95** 36 30N 73 50 E
Ishmi **68** 41 33N 19 34 E
Ishpeming **156** 46 30N 87 40W
Ishua **121** 7 15N 5 50 E
Ishui **107** 35 50N 118 32 E
Ishurdi **98** 24 9N 89 3 E
Isigny-sur-Mer **42** 49 19N 1 6W
Işik **82** 40 40N 32 35 E
Isil Kul **76** 54 55N 71 16 E
Isili **44** 39 45N 9 6 E
Isiolo **126** 0 24N 37 33 E
Isipingo **129** 30 00 S 30 57 E
Isipingo Beach **129** 30 00 S 30 57 E
Isiro **126** 2 53N 27 58 E
Iskander **85** 41 36N 69 41 E
İskenderun **92** 36 32N 36 10 E
Iskilip **82** 40 50N 34 20 E
Iskut, R. **152** 56 45N 131 49W
Iskyr, R. **67** 43 35N 24 20 E
Isla Cristina **57** 37 13N 7 17W
Isla, La **174** 6 51N 76 56W
Isla, R. **37** 56 32N 3 20W
Islamabad **94** 33 40N 73 0 E
Islamkot **94** 24 42N 70 13 E
Islampur **96** 17 2N 72 9 E
Island Falls, Can. **150** 49 35N 81 20W
Island Falls, U.S.A. **151** 46 0N 68 25W
Island L. **153** 53 47N 94 25W
Island Lagoon **140** 31 30 S 136 40 E
Island Pt. **137** 30 20 S 115 1 E
Island Pond **156** 44 50N 71 50W
Island, R. **152** 60 25N 121 12W
Islands, B. of, Can. **151** 49 11N 58 15W
Islands, B. of, N.Z. **142** 35 20 S 174 20 E
Islay, I. **34** 55 46N 6 10W
Islay Sound **34** 55 45N 6 5W
Isle-Adam, L' **43** 49 6N 2 14 E
Isle aux Morts **151** 47 35N 59 0W
Isle-Jourdain, L', Gers, France **44** 43 36N 1 5 E
Isle-Jourdain, L', Vienne, France **42** 46 13N 0 31 E
Isle, L', Tarn, France **44** 43 52N 1 49 E
Isle, L', Vaucluse, France **45** 43 55N 5 3 E
Isle of Whithorn **34** 54 42N 4 22W
Isle of Wight □ **28** 50 40N 1 20W
Isle Ornsay **36** 57 9N 5 50W
Isle Royale **158** 48 0N 88 50W
Isle-sur-la-Sorgue, L' **45** 43 55N 5 2 E
Isle-sur-le-Doubs, L' **43** 47 26N 6 34 E
Isle Vista **163** 34 27N 119 52W
Isleham **29** 52 21N 0 24 E
Islet, L' **151** 47 4N 70 23W
Isleta **161** 34 58N 106 46W
Isleton **163** 38 10N 121 37W
Islip **28** 51 49N 1 12W
Ismail **82** 45 22N 28 46 E
Ismâ'ilîya **122** 30 37N 32 18 E
Ismay **158** 46 33N 104 44W
Isna **122** 25 17N 32 30 E
Isogstalo **95** 34 15N 78 46 E
Ísola del Liri **64** 41 39N 13 32 E
Ísola della Scala **62** 45 16N 11 0 E
Ísola di Capo Rizzuto **65** 38 56N 17 5 E
Isparta **92** 37 47N 30 30 E
Isperikh **67** 43 43N 26 50 E
Íspica **65** 36 47N 14 53 E
Israel ■ **90** 32 0N 34 50 E
Isseka **137** 28 22 S 114 35 E
Issia **120** 6 33N 6 33W
Issoire **44** 45 32N 3 15 E
Issoudun **43** 46 57N 2 0 E
Issyk-Kul, Ozero **85** 42 25N 77 15 E
İstanbul **92** 41 0N 29 0 E
Istmina **174** 5 10N 76 39W
Istok **66** 42 45N 20 24 E
Istokpoga, L. **157** 27 22N 81 14W
Istra, U.S.S.R. **81** 55 55N 36 50 E
Istra, Yugo. **63** 45 10N 14 0 E
Istranca Dağlari **67** 41 48N 27 30 E
Istres **45** 43 31N 4 59 E
Istria = Istra **63** 45 10N 14 0 E
Itá **172** 25 29N 57 21W
Itabaiana, Paraíba, Brazil **170** 7 18 S 35 19W
Itabaiana, Sergipe, Brazil **170** 10 41 S 37 26W
Itabaianinha **170** 11 16 S 37 47W
Itaberaba **171** 12 32 S 40 18W
Itaberaí **171** 16 2 S 49 48W
Itabira **171** 19 37 S 43 13W
Itabirito **173** 20 15 S 43 48W
Itabuna **171** 14 48 S 39 16W
Itacaiunas, R. **170** 5 21 S 49 8W
Itacajá **170** 8 19 S 47 46W
Itaete **171** 13 0 S 41 5W
Itaguaçu **171** 19 48 S 40 51W
Itaguari, R. **171** 14 11 S 44 40W
Itaguatins **170** 5 47 S 47 29W
Itaim, R. **170** 7 2 S 42 2W
Itainópolis **170** 7 24 S 41 31W
Itaituba **175** 4 10 S 55 50W
Itajaí **173** 27 0 S 48 45W
Itajubá **173** 22 24 S 45 30W
Itajuípe **171** 14 41 S 39 22W
Itaka **127** 8 50 S 32 49 E
Itako **111** 35 56N 140 33 E
Italy ■ **60** 42 0N 13 0 E
Itamataré **170** 2 16 S 46 24W
Itambacuri **171** 18 1 S 41 42W
Itambé **171** 15 15 S 40 37W
Itambe, mt. **170** 18 30 S 43 15W
Itampolo **129** 24 41 S 43 57 E
Itanhaém **121** 24 9 S 46 47W
Itanhém **171** 17 9 S 40 20W
Itano **110** 34 1N 134 28 E
Itapaci **171** 14 57 S 49 34W
Itapagé **170** 3 41 S 39 34W
Itaparica, I. de **171** 12 54 S 38 42W
Itapebi **171** 15 56 S 39 32W
Itapecerica **171** 20 28 S 45 7W
Itapecuru-Mirim **170** 3 24 S 44 20W
Itapecuru, R. **170** 3 20 S 44 15W
Itaperuna **171** 21 10 S 42 0W
Itapetinga **171** 15 15 S 40 15W
Itapetininga **173** 23 36 S 48 7W
Itapeva **173** 23 59 S 48 59W
Itapicuru **170** 10 50 S 38 40W
Itapicuru, R. **170** 5 40 S 44 30W
Itapipoca **170** 3 30 S 39 35W
Itapiúna **170** 4 33 S 38 57W
Itaporanga **171** 7 18 S 38 10W
Itapuá □ **173** 26 40 S 55 40W
Itapuranga **171** 15 35 S 49 59W
Itaquari **173** 20 12 S 40 25W
Itaquatiana **174** 2 58 S 58 30W
Itaquí **172** 29 0 S 56 30W
Itararé **173** 24 6 S 49 23W
Itarsi **94** 22 36N 77 51 E
Itarumã **171** 18 42 S 51 25W
Itatí **172** 27 16 S 58 15W
Itatira **170** 4 30 S 39 37W
Itatuba **174** 5 40 S 63 20W
Itaueira **170** 7 36 S 43 2W

Itaueira, R. 170 6 41 S 42 55 W
Itaúna 171 20 4 S 44 34 W
Itchen, R. 28 50 57 N 1 20 W
Itéa 69 38 25 N 22 25 E
Ithaca 162 42 25 N 76 30 W
Ithaca = Itháki 69 38 25 N 20 43 E
Itháki, I. 69 38 25 N 20 40 E
Ithon R. 31 52 16 N 3 23 W
It'iaoshan 106 37 10 N 104 2 E
Itinga 171 16 36 S 41 47 W
Itiruçu 171 13 31 S 40 9 W
Itiúba 171 10 43 S 39 51 W
Ito 111 34 58 N 139 5 E
Itonamas, R. 174 13 0 S 64 25 W
Itsa 122 29 15 N 30 40 E
Itsukaichi 110 34 22 N 132 8 E
Itsuki 110 32 24 N 130 50 E
Itteville 46 48 31 N 2 21 E
Ittiri 64 40 38 N 8 32 E
Itu, Brazil 173 23 10 S 47 15 W
Itu, Hupeh, China 109 30 24 N 111 26 E
Itu, Shantung, China 107 36 41 N 118 28 E
Itu, Nigeria 121 5 10 N 7 58 E
Ituaçu 171 13 50 S 41 18 W
Ituango 174 7 4 N 75 45 W
Ituiutaba 171 19 0 S 49 25 W
Itumbiara 171 18 20 S 49 10 W
Ituna 153 51 10 N 103 30 W
It'ung 107 43 20 N 125 17 E
Itunge Port 127 9 40 S 33 55 E
Itupiranga 170 5 9 S 49 20 W
Iturama 171 19 44 S 50 11 W
Iturbe 172 23 0 S 65 25 W
Ituri, R. 126 1 45 N 26 45 E
Iturup, Ostrov 77 45 0 N 148 0 E
Ituverava 171 20 20 S 47 47 W
Ituyuro, R. 172 22 40 S 63 50 W
Itzehoe 48 53 56 N 9 31 E
Ivalo 74 68 38 N 27 35 E
Ivalojoki 74 68 30 N 27 0 E
Ivanaj 68 42 17 N 19 25 E
Ivanhoe, N.S.W., Austral. 140 32 56 S 144 20 E
Ivanhoe, N.T., Austral. 136 15 41 S 128 41 E
Ivanhoe, U.S.A. 163 36 23 N 119 13 W
Ivanhoe L. 153 60 25 N 106 30 W
Ivanió Grad 63 45 41 N 16 25 E
Ivanjica 66 43 35 N 20 12 E
Ivanjscie 63 46 12 N 16 13 E
Ivankovskoye Vdkhr. 81 56 48 N 36 55 E
Ivano-Frankovsk, (Stanislav) 80 49 0 N 24 40 E
Ivanovka 84 52 34 N 53 23 E
Ivanovo, Byelorussia, U.S.S.R. 80 52 7 N 25 29 E
Ivanovo, R.S.F.S.R., U.S.S.R. 81 57 5 N 41 0 E
Ivato 129 20 37 S 47 10 E
Ivaylovgrad 67 41 32 N 26 8 E
Ivinghoe 29 51 50 N 0 38 W
Ivinheima, R. 173 21 48 S 54 15 W
Iviza = Ibiza 59 39 0 N 1 30 E
Ivohibe 129 22 31 S 46 57 E
Ivolândia 171 16 34 S 50 51 W
Ivory Coast ■ 120 7 30 N 5 0 W
Ivösjön 73 56 8 N 14 25 E
Ivrea 62 45 30 N 7 52 E
Ivugivik, (N.D. d'Ivugivic) 149 62 24 N 77 55 W
Ivybridge 30 50 24 N 3 56 W
Iwahig 102 8 35 N 117 32 E
Iwai-Jima 110 33 47 N 131 58 E
Iwaki 112 37 3 N 140 55 E
Iwakuni 110 34 15 N 132 8 E
Iwami 110 35 32 N 134 15 E
Iwamisawa 112 43 12 N 141 46 E
Iwanai 112 42 58 N 140 30 E
Iwanuma 112 38 7 N 140 58 E
Iwase 110 36 21 N 140 6 E
Iwata 111 34 49 N 137 59 E
Iwate-ken □ 112 39 30 N 141 30 E
Iwate-San 112 39 51 N 141 0 E
Iwo 121 7 39 N 4 9 E
Iwonicz-Zdroj 54 49 37 N 21 47 E
Ixiamas 174 13 50 S 68 5 W
Ixopo 129 30 11 S 30 5 E
Ixtepec 165 16 40 N 95 10 W
Ixtlán de Juárez 165 17 23 N 96 28 W
Ixtlán del Rio 164 21 5 N 104 28 W
Ixworth 29 52 18 N 0 50 E
Iyang, Honan, China 106 34 9 N 112 25 E
Iyang, Hunan, China 109 28 36 N 112 20 E
Iyang, Kiangsi, China 109 28 23 N 117 25 E
Iyo 110 33 45 N 132 45 E
Iyo-mishima 110 33 58 N 133 30 E
Iyo-Nada 110 33 40 N 132 20 E
Izabal, L. 166 15 30 N 89 10 W
Izamal 165 20 56 N 89 1 W
Izberbash 83 42 35 N 47 45 E
Izbica Kujawski 54 52 25 N 18 30 E
Izegem 47 50 55 N 3 12 E
Izgrev 67 43 36 N 26 58 E
Izh, R. 84 55 58 N 52 38 E
Izhevsk 84 56 51 N 53 14 E
Izmail 82 45 22 N 28 46 E
İzmir (Smyrna) 79 38 25 N 27 8 E
İzmit 92 40 45 N 29 50 E
Izola 63 45 32 N 13 39 E
Izu-Hantō 111 34 45 N 139 0 E
Izuhara 110 34 12 N 129 17 E
Izumi 110 32 5 N 130 22 E
Izumiotsu 111 34 30 N 135 24 E
Izumisano 111 34 40 N 135 43 E
Izumo 110 35 20 N 132 55 E
Izyaslav 80 50 5 N 25 50 E
Izyum 82 49 12 N 37 28 E

J

Jaba 123 6 20 N 35 7 E
Jaba' 90 32 20 N 35 13 E
Jabaliya 90 31 32 N 34 27 E
Jabalón, R. 59 38 45 N 3 35 W
Jabalpur 95 23 9 N 79 58 E
Jablah 92 35 20 N 36 0 E
Jablanac 63 44 42 N 14 56 E
Jablonec 52 50 43 N 15 10 E
Jablonica 53 48 37 N 17 26 E
Jabłonowo 54 53 23 N 19 10 E
Jaboatão 170 8 7 S 35 1 W
Jaboticabal 173 21 15 S 48 17 W
Jabukovac 66 44 22 N 22 21 E
Jaburu 174 5 30 S 64 0 W
Jaca 58 42 35 N 0 33 W
Jacala 165 21 1 N 99 11 W
Jacaré, R. 170 10 3 S 42 13 W
Jacareí 173 23 20 S 46 0 W
Jacarèzinho 173 23 5 S 50 0 W
Jáchal 172 30 5 S 69 0 W
Jáchymov 52 50 22 N 12 55 E
Jacinto 171 16 10 S 40 17 W
Jack Lane B. 151 55 45 N 60 35 W
Jackfish 150 48 45 N 87 0 W
Jackman 151 45 35 N 70 17 W
Jacksboro 159 33 14 N 98 15 W
Jackson, Austral. 139 26 39 S 149 39 E
Jackson, Ala., U.S.A. 157 31 32 N 87 53 W
Jackson, Calif., U.S.A. 159 37 25 N 89 42 W
Jackson, Ill., U.S.A. 163 38 25 N 120 47 W
Jackson, Ky., U.S.A. 156 37 35 N 83 22 W
Jackson, Mich., U.S.A. 156 42 18 N 84 25 W
Jackson, Minn., U.S.A. 158 43 35 N 95 30 W
Jackson, Miss., U.S.A. 159 32 20 N 90 10 W
Jackson, Ohio, U.S.A. 156 39 0 N 82 40 W
Jackson, Tenn., U.S.A. 157 35 40 N 88 50 W
Jackson, Wyo., U.S.A. 160 43 30 N 110 49 W
Jackson Bay, Can. 152 50 32 N 125 57 W
Jackson Bay, N.Z. 143 43 58 S 168 42 E
Jackson, C. 143 40 59 S 174 20 E
Jackson, L. 160 43 55 N 110 40 W
Jacksons 143 42 46 S 171 32 E
Jacksonville, Ala., U.S.A. 157 33 49 N 85 45 W
Jacksonville, Calif., U.S.A. 163 37 52 N 120 24 W
Jacksonville, Fla., U.S.A. 157 30 15 N 81 38 W
Jacksonville, Ill., U.S.A. 158 39 42 N 90 15 W
Jacksonville, N.C., U.S.A. 157 34 50 N 77 29 W
Jacksonville, Oreg., U.S.A. 160 42 13 N 122 56 W
Jacksonville, Tex., U.S.A. 159 31 58 N 95 12 W
Jacksonville Beach 157 30 19 N 81 26 W
Jacmel 167 18 20 N 72 40 W
Jacob Lake 161 36 45 N 112 12 W
Jacobabad 94 28 20 N 68 29 E
Jacobeni 70 47 25 N 25 20 E
Jacobina 170 11 11 S 40 30 W
Jacob's Well 90 32 13 N 35 13 E
Jacques Cartier, Mt. 151 48 57 N 66 0 W
Jacques Cartier Pass 151 49 50 N 62 30 W
Jacqueville 120 5 12 N 4 25 W
Jacuí, R. 173 30 2 S 51 15 W
Jacuipe, R. 171 12 30 S 39 5 W
Jacundá, R. 170 1 57 S 50 26 W
Jade 48 53 22 N 8 14 E
Jadebusen, B. 48 53 30 N 8 15 E
Jadoigne 47 50 43 N 4 52 E
Jadotville = Likasi 127 10 55 S 26 48 E
Jadovnik 66 43 20 N 19 45 E
Jadraque 58 40 55 N 2 55 W
Jādū 119 32 0 N 12 0 E
Jaén, Peru 174 5 25 S 78 40 W
Jaén, Spain 57 37 44 N 3 43 W
Jaén □ 57 37 50 N 3 30 W
Jafène 118 20 35 N 5 30 W
Jaffa = Tel Aviv-Yafo 90 32 4 N 34 48 E
Jaffa, C. 140 36 58 S 139 40 E
Jaffna 97 9 45 N 80 2 E
Jaffrey 162 42 50 N 72 4 W
Jagadhri 94 30 10 N 77 20 E
Jagadishpur 95 25 30 N 84 21 E
Jagdalpur 96 19 3 N 82 6 E
Jagersfontein 128 29 44 S 25 27 E
Jaghbub 117 29 42 N 24 38 E
Jagraon 93 30 50 N 75 25 E
Jagst, R. 49 49 13 N 10 0 E
Jagtial 96 18 50 N 79 0 E
Jaguaquara 171 13 32 S 39 58 W
Jaguariaíva 173 24 10 S 49 50 W
Jaguaribe 170 5 53 S 38 37 W
Jaguaribe, R. 170 6 0 S 38 35 W
Jaguaruana 170 4 50 S 37 47 W
Jagüey 166 22 35 N 81 7 W
Jagungal, Mt. 141 36 8 S 148 22 E
Jahangirabad 94 28 19 N 78 4 E
Jahrom 92 28 30 N 53 31 E
Jaicós 170 7 21 S 41 8 W
Jainti 98 26 45 N 89 40 E
Jaintiapur 98 25 8 N 92 7 E
Jaipur 94 27 0 N 76 10 E
Jajarm 93 37 5 N 56 20 E
Jajce 66 44 19 N 17 17 E
Jajere 121 11 58 N 11 25 E
Jajpur 96 20 53 N 86 22 E
Jakarta 103 6 9 S 106 49 E
Jakobstad (Pietarsaari) 74 63 40 N 22 43 E
Jakupica 66 41 45 N 21 22 E
Jal 159 32 8 N 103 8 W
Jala 93 27 30 N 62 40 E
Jalalabad, Afghan. 94 34 30 N 70 29 E
Jalalabad, India 95 26 41 N 79 42 E
Jalalpur Jattan 94 32 38 N 74 19 E
Jalama 163 34 29 N 120 29 W
Jalapa, Guat. 166 14 45 N 89 59 W
Jalapa, Mexico 165 19 30 N 96 50 W
Jalas, Jabal al 92 27 30 N 36 30 E
Jalaun 95 26 8 N 79 25 E
Jales 171 20 16 S 50 33 W
Jaleswar 95 26 38 N 85 48 E
Jalgaon, Maharashtra, India 96 21 2 N 76 31 E
Jalgaon, Maharashtra, India 96 21 0 N 75 42 E
Jalhay 47 50 33 N 5 58 E
Jalingo 121 8 55 N 11 25 E
Jalisco □ 164 20 0 N 104 0 W
Jalkot 95 35 20 N 73 24 E
Jallas, R. 56 42 57 N 9 0 W
Jallumba 140 36 55 N 141 57 E
Jalna 96 19 48 N 75 57 E
Jalón, R. 58 41 20 N 1 40 W
Jalpa 164 21 38 N 102 58 W
Jalpaiguri 98 26 32 N 88 46 E
Jalq 93 27 35 N 62 33 E
Jaluit I. 130 6 0 N 169 30 E
Jamaari 121 11 44 N 9 53 E
Jamaica, I. ■ 166 18 10 N 77 30 W
Jamalpur, Bangla. 98 24 52 N 90 2 E
Jamalpur, India 95 25 18 N 86 28 E
Jamalpurganj 95 23 2 N 88 1 E
Jamanxim, R. 175 6 30 S 55 50 W
Jambe 103 1 15 S 132 10 E
Jambes 47 50 27 N 4 52 E
Jambi 102 1 38 S 103 30 E
Jambusar 94 22 3 N 72 51 E
Jamdena, I. = Yamdena 103 7 45 S 131 20 E
James B. 150 53 30 N 80 0 W
James, R., Dak., U.S.A. 158 44 50 N 98 0 W
James, R., Va., U.S.A. 162 37 0 N 76 27 W
James Ranges 136 24 10 S 132 0 E
James Ross I. 13 63 58 S 50 94 W
Jamestown, Austral. 140 33 10 S 138 32 E
Jamestown, S. Afr. 128 31 6 S 26 45 E
Jamestown, Ky., U.S.A. 156 37 0 N 85 5 W
Jamestown, N.D., U.S.A. 158 47 0 N 98 30 W
Jamestown, N.Y., U.S.A. 156 42 5 N 79 18 W
Jamestown, Tenn., U.S.A. 157 36 25 N 85 0 W
Jamestown, Va., U.S.A. 162 37 12 N 76 46 W
Jamiltepec 165 16 17 N 97 49 W
Jamkhandi 97 16 30 N 75 15 E
Jamma'in 90 32 8 N 35 12 E
Jammalamadugu 97 14 51 N 78 25 E
Jammerbugt 73 57 15 N 9 20 E
Jammu 94 32 43 N 74 54 E
Jammu & Kashmir □ 95 34 25 N 77 0 E
Jamnagar 94 22 30 N 70 0 E
Jamner 96 20 45 N 75 45 E
Jamoigne 47 49 41 N 5 24 E
Jampur 94 29 39 N 70 32 E
Jamrud 94 34 2 N 71 24 E
Jamshedpur 95 22 44 N 86 20 E
Jamtara 95 23 59 N 86 41 E
Jämtlands län □ 72 62 40 N 13 50 E
Jamuna, R. 98 23 51 N 89 45 E
Jamurki 98 24 9 N 90 2 E
Jan Kemp 128 27 55 S 24 51 E
Jan L. 153 54 56 N 102 55 W
Jan Mayen Is. 12 71 0 N 11 0 W
Janaúba 171 15 48 S 43 19 W
Janaucu, I. 170 0 30 N 50 10 W
Jand 94 33 30 N 72 0 E
Janda, Laguna de la 57 36 15 N 5 45 W
Jandaia 171 17 6 S 50 7 W
Jandaq 92 34 3 N 54 22 E
Jandola 94 32 20 N 70 9 E
Jandowae 139 26 45 S 151 7 E
Jandrain-Jandrenouilles 47 50 40 N 4 58 E
Jándula, R. 57 38 25 N 3 55 W
Jane Pk. 142 45 15 S 168 20 E
Janesville 158 42 39 N 89 1 W
Janga 121 10 5 N 1 0 W
Jangaon 96 17 44 N 79 5 E
Janhtang Ga 98 26 32 N 96 38 E
Jani Khel 93 32 45 N 68 25 E
Janja 66 44 40 N 19 17 E
Janjevo 66 42 35 N 21 19 E
Janjina 66 42 58 N 17 25 E
Janos 164 30 45 N 108 10 W
Jánoshalma 53 46 18 N 19 21 E
Jánosháza 53 47 8 N 17 12 E
Jánossomorja 53 47 47 N 17 11 E
Janów 54 50 43 N 22 30 E
Janów Lubelski 54 50 48 N 22 23 E
Janów Podlaski 54 52 11 N 23 11 E
Janowiec Wlkp. 54 52 45 N 17 30 E
Januária 171 15 25 S 44 25 W
Janub Dârfûr □ 123 11 0 N 25 0 E
Janub Kordofân □ 123 12 0 N 30 0 E
Janville 43 48 10 N 1 50 E
Janzé 42 47 55 N 1 28 W
Jaop'ing 109 23 43 N 117 0 E
Jaora 94 23 40 N 75 10 E
Jaoyang 106 38 14 N 115 44 E
Japan ■ 112 36 0 N 136 0 E
Japan, Sea of 112 40 0 N 135 0 E
Japan Trench 142 28 0 N 145 0 E
Japara 103 6 30 S 110 40 E
Japen, I. = Yapen 103 1 50 S 136 0 E
Japero 103 4 59 S 137 11 E
Japurá 174 1 48 S 66 30 W
Japurá, R. 174 3 8 S 64 46 W
Jaque 174 7 27 N 78 15 W
Jaques Cartier, Détroit de 151 50 0 N 63 30 W
Jara, La 161 37 16 N 106 0 W
Jaraguá 171 15 45 S 49 20 W
Jaraicejo 57 39 40 N 5 49 W
Jaraiz 56 40 4 N 5 45 W
Jarales 161 34 44 N 106 51 W
Jarama, R. 58 40 50 N 3 20 W
Jarandilla 56 40 8 N 5 39 W
Jaranwala 94 31 15 N 73 20 E
Jarash 90 32 17 N 35 54 E
Järbo 72 60 42 N 16 38 E
Jarbridge 160 41 56 N 115 27 W
Jardim 172 21 28 S 56 9 W
Jardín, R. 59 38 50 N 2 10 W
Jardines de la Reina, Is. 166 20 50 N 78 50 W
Jargalant = Hovd 105 48 1 N 91 38 E
Jargeau 43 47 50 N 2 7 E
Jarmen 48 53 56 N 13 20 E
Järna, Kopp., Sweden 72 60 33 N 14 26 E
Järna, Stockholm, Sweden 72 59 7 N 17 35 E
Jarnac 44 45 40 N 0 11 W
Jarny 43 49 9 N 5 53 E
Jarocin 54 51 59 N 17 29 E
Jaroměř 52 50 22 N 15 52 E
Jarosław 54 50 2 N 22 42 E
Järpås 73 58 23 N 12 57 E
Järpås 73 58 23 N 12 57 E
Järpen 72 63 21 N 13 26 E
Jarrahdale 137 32 24 S 116 5 E
Jarres, Plaine des 100 19 27 N 103 10 E
Jarrow 35 54 58 N 1 28 W
Jarso 123 5 15 N 37 30 E
Järved 72 63 16 N 18 43 E
Jarvis I. 131 0 15 S 159 55 W
Jarvornik 53 50 23 N 17 2 E
Jarwa 95 27 45 N 82 30 E
Jaša Tomió 66 45 26 N 20 50 E
Jasien 54 51 46 N 15 0 E
Jasin 101 2 20 N 102 26 E
Jāsk 93 25 38 N 57 45 E
Jasło 54 49 45 N 21 30 E
Jasper, Can. 152 52 55 N 118 5 W
Jasper, Ala., U.S.A. 157 33 48 N 87 16 W
Jasper, Ark., U.S.A. 97 36 0 N 93 10 W
Jasper, Fla., U.S.A. 157 30 31 N 82 58 W
Jasper, La., U.S.A. 159 30 59 N 93 58 W
Jasper, S.D., U.S.A. 158 43 52 N 96 22 W
Jasper Nat. Park 152 52 50 N 118 8 W
Jasper Place 152 53 33 N 113 25 W
Jastrebarsko 63 45 41 N 15 39 E
Jastrowie 54 53 26 N 16 49 E
Jastrzebie Zdroj 54 49 57 N 18 35 E
Jászapáti 53 47 32 N 20 10 E
Jászárokszállás 53 47 39 N 20 1 E
Jászberény 53 47 30 N 19 55 E
Jászkiser 53 47 27 N 20 20 E
Jászladány 53 47 23 N 20 18 E
Jatai 171 17 50 S 51 45 W
Jati 94 24 27 N 68 19 E
Jatibarang 103 6 28 S 108 18 E
Jatinegara 103 6 13 S 106 52 E
Játiva 59 39 0 N 0 32 W
Jatobal 170 4 35 S 49 33 W
Jatt 90 32 24 N 35 2 E
Jaú 173 22 10 S 48 30 W
Jau al Milah 91 15 15 N 45 40 E
Jauche 47 50 41 N 4 57 E
Jauja 174 11 45 S 75 30 W
Jaunelgava 80 56 35 N 25 0 E
Jaunpur 95 25 46 N 82 44 E
Java = Jawa 103 7 0 S 110 0 E
Java Sea 102 4 35 S 107 15 E
Javadi Hills 97 12 40 N 78 40 E
Jávea 59 38 48 N 0 10 E
Javhlant = Ulyasutay 105 47 45 N 96 49 E
Javla 96 17 18 N 75 9 E
Javron 42 48 25 N 0 25 W
Jawa 103 7 0 S 110 0 E
Jawor 54 51 4 N 16 11 E
Jaworzno 54 50 13 N 19 22 E
Jay 159 33 17 N 94 46 W
Jayawijaya, Pengunungan 103 7 0 S 139 0 E
Jaydot 153 49 15 N 110 15 W
Jaynagar 99 26 43 N 86 9 E
Jayton 159 33 17 N 100 35 W
Jazminal 164 24 56 N 101 25 W
Jean 161 35 47 N 115 20 W
Jean Marie River 152 61 32 N 120 38 W
Jean Rabel 167 19 50 N 73 30 W
Jeanerette 159 29 52 N 91 38 W
Jebba, Moroc. 118 35 11 N 4 43 W
Jebba, Nigeria 121 9 9 N 4 48 E
Jebel 66 40 35 N 21 15 E
Jebel Aulia 123 15 10 N 32 31 E
Jebel Qerri 123 16 16 N 32 50 E
Jedburgh 35 55 28 N 2 33 W
Jedlicze 54 49 43 N 21 40 E
Jedlnia-Letnisko 54 51 25 N 21 19 E
Jedrzejów 54 50 35 N 20 15 E

Jedway 152 52 17N 131 14W
Jeetze, R. 48 52 58N 11 6E
Jefferson, Iowa, U.S.A. 158 42 3N 94 25W
Jefferson, Tex., U.S.A. 159 32 45N 94 23W
Jefferson, Wis., U.S.A. 158 43 0N 88 49W
Jefferson City 157 36 8N 83 30W
Jefferson, Mt., Calif., U.S.A. 163 38 51N 117 0W
Jefferson, Mt., Oreg., U.S.A. 160 44 45N 121 50W
Jeffersonville 156 38 20N 85 42W
Jega 121 12 15N 4 23E
Jekabpils 80 56 29N 25 57E
Jelenia Góra 54 50 50N 15 45E
Jelenia Góra □ 54 51 0N 15 30E
Jelgava 80 56 41N 22 49E
Jelica 66 43 50N 20 17E
Jelli 123 5 25N 31 45E
Jellicoe 150 49 40N 87 30W
Jelšava 53 48 37N 20 15E
Jemaja 103 3 5N 105 45E
Jemaluang 101 2 16N 103 52E
Jemappes 47 50 27N 3 54E
Jember 103 8 11S 113 41E
Jembongan, I. 102 6 45N 117 20E
Jemmapes = Azzaba 119 36 48N 7 6E
Jemnice 52 49 1N 15 34E
Jena, Ger. 48 50 56N 11 33E
Jena, U.S.A. 159 31 41N 92 7W
Jench'iu 106 38 43N 116 5E
Jendouba 119 36 29N 8 47E
Jenhochieh 108 26 29N 101 45E
Jenhsien 106 37 8N 114 37E
Jenhua 109 25 5N 113 45E
Jenhuai 108 27 53N 106 17E
Jenin 90 32 28N 35 18E
Jenkins 156 37 13N 82 41W
Jennings 159 30 10N 92 45W
Jennings, R. 152 59 38N 132 5W
Jenny 73 57 47N 16 35E
Jeparit 140 36 8S 142 1E
Jequié 171 13 51S 40 5W
Jequitai, R. 171 17 4S 44 50W
Jequitinhonha 171 16 30S 41 0W
Jequitinhonha, R. 171 15 51S 38 53W
Jerada 118 34 40N 2 10W
Jerantut 101 3 56N 102 22E
Jérémie 167 18 40N 74 10W
Jeremoabo 170 10 4S 38 21W
Jerez de García Salinas 164 22 39N 103 0W
Jerez de la Frontera 57 36 41N 6 7W
Jerez de los Caballeros 57 38 20N 6 45W
Jerez, Punta 165 22 58N 97 40W
Jericho 138 23 38S 146 6E
Jericho = El Arīhā 90 31 52N 35 27E
Jerichow 48 52 30N 12 2E
Jerilderie 141 35 20S 145 41E
Jermyn 162 41 31N 75 31W
Jerome 161 34 50N 112 0W
Jersey City 162 40 41N 74 8W
Jersey, I. 42 49 13N 2 7W
Jersey Shore 156 41 17N 77 18W
Jerseyville 158 39 5N 90 20W
Jerumenha 171 7 5S 43 30W
Jerusalem 90 31 47N 35 10E
Jervaulx 33 54 19N 1 41W
Jervis B. 141 35 8S 150 46E
Jervis, C. 139 35 38S 138 6E
Jesenice 63 46 28N 14 3E
Jesenik 53 50 0N 17 8E
Jeseník (Frývaldov) 53 50 15N 17 11E
Jesenske 53 48 20N 20 10E
Jesselton = Kota Kinabalu 102 6 0N 116 12E
Jessnitz 48 51 42N 12 19E
Jessore 98 23 10N 89 10E
Jesup 157 31 30N 82 0W
Jesús Carranza 165 17 28N 95 1W
Jesús María 172 30 59S 64 5W
Jetmore 159 38 10N 99 57W
Jetpur 94 21 45N 70 10E
Jette 47 50 53N 4 20E
Jevnaker 71 60 15N 10 26E
Jewett 159 31 20N 96 8W
Jewett City 162 41 36N 72 0W
Jeypore 96 18 50N 82 38E
Jeziorany 54 53 58N 20 46E
J.F. Rodrigues 170 2 55S 50 20W
Jhajjar 94 28 37N 76 14E
Jhal Jhao 93 26 20N 65 35E
Jhalakati 98 22 39N 90 12E
Jhalawar 94 24 35N 76 10E
Jhang Maghiana 94 31 15N 72 15E
Jhansi 95 25 30N 78 36E
Jharia 95 23 45N 86 18E
Jharsaguda 99 21 50N 84 5E
Jharsuguda 96 21 50N 84 5E
Jhelum 94 33 0N 73 45E
Jhelum, R. 95 31 50N 72 10E
Jhunjhunu 94 28 10N 75 20E
Jiangshan 95 28 45N 118 37E
Jibão, Serra do 171 14 48S 45 0W
Jibiya 121 13 5N 7 12E
Jibou 70 47 15N 23 17E
Jicín 52 50 25N 15 20E
Jicarón, I. 166 7 10N 81 50W
Jiddah 92 21 29N 39 16E
Jido 99 29 2N 94 58E
Jifna 90 31 58N 35 13E
Jiggalong 136 23 24S 120 47E
Jihk'atse 107 29 15N 88 53E
Jihlava 52 49 28N 15 35E
Jihočeský □ 52 49 8N 14 35E
Jihomoravský □ 53 49 5N 16 30E
Jiht'u 105 33 27N 79 42E
Jijiga 91 9 20N 42 50E
Jijona 59 38 34N 0 30W
Jikamshi 121 12 12N 7 45E
Jiloca, R. 58 41 0N 1 20W
Jílové 52 49 52N 14 29E
Jim Jim Cr. 136 12 50S 132 32E
Jima 123 7 40N 36 55E
Jimbolia 66 45 47N 20 57E
Jimena de la Frontera 57 36 27N 5 24W
Jimenbuen 141 36 42S 148 53E
Jiménez 164 27 10N 105 0W
Jind 94 29 19N 76 16E
Jindabyne 141 36 25S 148 35E
Jindrichuv Hradeç 52 49 10N 15 2E
Jinja 126 0 25N 33 12E
Jinjang 101 3 13N 101 39E
Jinjini 120 7 20N 3 42W
Jinnah Barrage 93 32 58N 71 33E
Jinotega 166 13 6N 85 59W
Jinotepe 166 11 50N 86 10W
Jiparaná (Machado), R. 174 8 45S 62 20W
Jipijapa 174 1 0S 80 40W
Jiquilpán 164 19 57N 102 42W
Jisresh Shughur 92 35 49N 36 18E
Jitarning 137 32 48S 117 57E
Jitra 101 6 16N 100 25E
Jiu, R. 70 44 50N 23 20E
Jiuchin 109 25 53N 116 0E
Jiuli 108 24 6N 97 54E
Jizera, R. 52 50 21N 14 48E
Jizl Wadi 122 26 30N 38 0E
Jizō-zaki 110 35 34N 133 20E
Joaçaba 173 27 5S 51 31W
Joaíma 171 16 39S 41 2W
João 170 2 46S 50 59W
João Amaro 171 12 46S 40 22W
João Câmara 170 5 32S 35 48W
João de Almeida 125 15 10S 13 50E
João Pessoa 170 7 10S 34 52W
João Pinheiro 171 17 45S 46 10W
Joaquim Távora 171 23 30S 49 58W
Joaquín V. González 172 25 10S 64 0W
Jobourg, Nez de 42 49 41N 1 57W
Joch'iang 105 39 2N 88 0E
Jódar 59 37 50N 3 21W
Jodhpur 94 26 23N 73 2E
Joe Batt's Arm 151 49 44N 54 10W
Joensuu 78 62 37N 29 49E
Joeuf 43 49 12N 6 1E
Jofane 125 21 15S 34 18E
Joggins 151 45 42N 64 27W
Jogjakarta = Yogyakarta 103 7 49S 110 22E
Jōhana 111 36 37N 136 57E
Johannesburg, S. Afr. 129 26 10S 28 8E
Johannesburg, U.S.A. 163 35 22N 117 38W
Johannisnäs 72 62 45N 16 15E
Johansfors, Halland, Sweden 73 56 50N 12 58E
Johansfors, Kronoberg, Sweden 73 56 42N 15 32E
John Days, R. 160 45 0N 120 0W
John o' Groats 37 58 39N 3 3W
Johnshaven 37 56 48N 2 20W
Johnson 159 37 35N 101 48W
Johnson City, N.Y., U.S.A. 162 42 7N 75 57W
Johnson City, Tenn., U.S.A. 157 36 18N 82 21W
Johnson City, Tex., U.S.A. 159 30 15N 98 24W
Johnson Cy. 156 42 9N 67 0W
Johnson Ra. 137 29 40S 119 15E
Johnsondale 163 35 58N 118 32W
Johnsons Crossing 152 60 29N 133 18W
Johnsonville 142 41 13S 174 48E
Johnston 31 51 45N 5 5W
Johnston Falls = Mambilima Falls 127 10 31S 28 45E
Johnston I. 131 17 10N 169 8E
Johnston Lakes 137 32 20S 120 45E
Johnston Ra. 137 29 40S 119 20E
Johnstone 34 55 50N 4 31W
Johnstone Str. 152 50 28N 126 0W
Johnstown, Ireland 39 52 46N 7 34W
Johnstown, N.Y., U.S.A. 162 43 1N 74 20W
Johnstown, Pa., U.S.A. 156 40 19N 78 53W
Johnstown Bridge 38 53 23N 6 53W
Johor □ 101 2 5N 103 20E
Johor Baharu 101 1 28N 103 46E
Johor, S. 101 1 45N 103 47E
Joigny 43 48 0N 3 20E
Joinvile 173 26 15S 48 55E
Joinville 43 48 27N 5 10E
Joinville I. 13 63 15S 55 30W
Jojutla 165 18 37N 99 11W
Jokkmokk 74 66 35N 19 50E
Jökulsá á Brú 74 65 40N 14 16W
Jökulsá Fjöllum 74 65 30N 16 15W
Jökulsa R. 74 65 30N 16 15W
Jolan 163 35 58N 121 9W
Joliet 156 41 30N 88 0W
Joliette 150 46 3N 73 24W
Jolo I. 103 6 0N 121 0E
Jome, I. 103 1 16S 127 30E
Jönåker 73 58 44N 16 40E
Jönaker 73 58 44N 16 43E
Jones C. 150 54 33N 79 35W
Jones Sound 12 76 0N 89 0W
Jonesboro, Ark., U.S.A. 159 35 50N 90 45W
Jonesboro, Ill., U.S.A. 159 37 26N 89 18W
Jonesboro, La., U.S.A. 159 32 15N 92 41W
Jonesport 151 44 32N 67 38W
Jönköping 73 57 45N 14 10E
Jönköpings län □ 75 57 30N 14 30E
Jonquière 151 48 27N 71 14W
Jonsberg 73 58 30N 16 48E
Jonsered 73 57 45N 12 10E
Jonzac 44 45 27N 0 28W
Joplin 159 37 0N 94 25W
Jordan, Phil. 103 10 41N 122 38E
Jordan, Mont., U.S.A. 160 47 25N 106 58W
Jordan, N.Y., U.S.A. 162 43 4N 76 29W
Jordan ■ 92 31 0N 36 0E
Jordan, R. 90 32 10N 35 32E
Jordan Valley 160 43 0N 117 2W
Jordânia 171 15 45S 40 11W
Jordanów 54 49 41N 19 49E
Jorhat 98 26 45N 94 20E
Jörn 74 65 4N 20 1E
Jørpeland 71 59 3N 6 1E
Jorquera, R. 172 28 3S 69 58W
Jos 121 9 53N 8 51E
Jošanička Banja 66 43 24N 20 47E
José Batlle y OrdóPez 173 33 20S 55 10W
Josefow 54 52 10N 21 11E
Joseni 70 47 42N 25 29E
Joseph 160 45 27N 117 13W
Joseph Bonaparte G. 136 14 35S 128 50E
Joseph City 161 35 0N 110 16W
Joseph, Lac 151 52 45N 65 18W
Josephine, oilfield 19 58 35N 2 45E
Joshua Tree 163 34 8N 116 19W
Joshua Tree Nat. Mon. 163 33 56N 116 5W
Josselin 42 47 57N 2 33W
Jostedal 71 61 35N 7 15E
Jostedalsbre, Mt. 71 61 45N 7 0E
Jotunheimen 71 61 35N 8 25E
Jounieh 92 33 59N 35 30E
Jourdanton 159 28 54N 98 32W
Journe 46 52 58N 5 48E
Joussard 152 55 22N 115 57W
Joux, Lac de 50 46 39N 6 18E
Jouzjan □ 93 36 10N 66 0E
Jovellanos 166 22 40N 81 10W
Jowai 98 25 26N 92 12E
Joyce's Country, dist. 38 53 32N 9 30W
Joyeuse 45 44 29N 4 16E
Jozini Dam 129 27 27S 32 7E
Ju Shui, R. 109 28 36N 116 4E
Juan Aldama 164 24 20N 103 23W
Juan Bautista 161 36 55N 121 33W
Juan Bautista Alberdi 172 34 26S 61 48W
Juan de Fuca Str. 160 48 15N 124 0W
Juan de Nova, I. 129 17 3S 42 45E
Juan Fernández, Arch. de 131 33 50S 80 0W
Juan José Castelli 172 25 57S 60 37W
Juan L. Lacaze 172 34 26S 57 25W
Juárez, Argent. 172 37 40S 59 43W
Juárez, Mexico 164 27 37N 100 44W
Juárez, Sierra de 164 32 0N 116 0W
Juatinga, Ponta de 171 23 17S 44 30W
Juàzeiro 170 9 30S 40 30W
Juàzeiro do Norte 170 7 10S 39 18W
Jûbâ 123 4 57N 31 35E
Juba, R. 91 1 30N 42 35E
Jubaila 92 24 55N 46 25E
Jûbâl 122 27 30N 34 0E
Jubbulpore = Jabalpur 95 23 9N 79 58E
Jübek 48 54 31N 9 24E
Jubga 83 44 19N 38 48E
Jubilee L. 137 29 0S 126 50E
Juby, C. 116 28 0N 12 59W
Júcar, R. 58 40 8N 2 13W
Júcaro 166 21 37N 78 51W
Juch'eng 109 25 32N 113 39E
Juchitán 165 16 27N 95 5W
Judaea = Yehuda 90 31 35N 34 57E
Judenburg 52 47 12N 14 38E
Judith Gap 160 46 48N 109 46W
Judith Pt. 162 41 20N 71 30W
Judith, R. 160 47 30N 109 30W
Juian 109 27 45N 120 38E
Juich'ang 109 29 40N 115 39E
Juigalpa 166 12 6N 85 26W
Juillac 44 45 20N 1 19E
Juist, I. 48 53 40N 7 0E
Juiz de Fora 171 21 43S 43 19W
Jujuy 172 24 10S 65 25W
Jujuy □ 172 23 20S 65 40W
Jukao 109 32 24N 120 35E
Julesberg 158 41 0N 102 20W
Juli 174 16 10S 69 25W
Julia Cr. 138 20 0S 141 11E
Julia Creek 138 20 39S 141 44E
Juliaca 174 15 25S 70 10W
Julian 163 33 4N 116 38W
Julian Alps = Julijske Alpe 63 46 15N 14 1E
Julianakanaal 47 51 6N 5 52E
Julianehåb 12 60 43N 46 0W
Julianstown 38 53 40N 6 16W
Jülich 48 50 55N 6 20E
Julier P. 51 46 28N 9 32E
Julijske Alpe 63 46 15N 14 1E
Julimes 164 28 25N 105 27W
Jullundur 94 31 20N 75 40E
Jumbo 127 17 30S 30 58E
Jumento, Cayos 167 23 0N 75 40E
Jumet 47 50 27N 4 25E
Jumilla 59 38 28N 1 19W
Jumla 95 29 15N 82 13E
Jumna, R. = Yamuna 94 27 0N 78 30E
Junagadh 94 21 30N 70 30E
Junan 109 32 58N 114 31E
Junction, Tex., U.S.A. 159 30 29N 99 48W
Junction, Utah, U.S.A. 161 38 10N 112 15W
Junction B. 138 11 52S 133 55E
Junction City, Kans., U.S.A. 158 39 4N 96 55W
Junction City, Oreg., U.S.A. 160 44 20N 123 12W
Jundah 138 24 46S 143 2E
Jundiaí 173 23 10S 47 0W
Juneau 147 58 26N 134 30W
Junee 141 34 53S 147 35E
Jung Chiang, R. 108 23 25N 110 0E
Jungan 108 25 14N 109 23E
Jungch'ang 108 29 27N 105 33E
Jungch'eng 107 37 9N 122 23E
Jungchiang 108 25 56N 108 31E
Jungching 108 29 49N 102 55E
Jungfrau 50 46 32N 7 58E
Jungho 106 35 21N 110 32E
Junghsien, Kwangsi-Chuang, China 109 22 52N 110 33E
Junghsien, Szechwan, China 108 29 29N 104 22E
Junglinster 47 49 43N 6 15E
Jungshahi 94 24 52N 67 44E
Jungshui 108 24 14N 109 23E
Juniata, R. 162 40 30N 77 40W
Junín 172 34 33S 60 57W
Junín de los Andes 176 39 45S 71 0W
Junnar 96 19 12N 73 58E
Junquera, La 58 42 25N 2 53E
Junta, La 159 38 0N 103 30W
Juntura 160 43 44N 119 4W
Juparanã, Lagoa 171 19 35S 40 18W
Jupiter, R. 151 49 29N 63 37W
Juquiá 171 24 19S 47 38W
Jur, Nahr el 123 8 45N 29 0E
Jura 43 46 35N 6 5E
Jura □ 43 46 47N 5 45E
Jura, I. 34 56 0N 5 50W
Jura, Paps of, mts. 34 55 55N 6 0W
Jura, Sd. of 34 55 57N 5 45W
Jura Suisse 50 47 10N 7 0E
Jurado 174 7 7N 77 46W
Jurby Hd. 32 54 23N 4 31W
Jurien B. 132 30 17S 115 0E
Jurilovca 70 44 46N 28 52W
Jurm 93 36 50N 70 45E
Juruá, R. 174 2 30S 66 0W
Juruena, R. 174 7 20S 58 3W
Juruti 175 2 9S 56 4W
Jushan 107 36 54N 121 30E
Jussey 43 47 50N 5 55E
Justo Daract 172 33 52S 65 12W
Jüterbog 48 51 59N 13 6E
Juticalpa 166 14 40N 85 50W
Jutland 16 56 0N 8 0E
Jutphaas 46 52 2N 5 6E
Jutung 109 32 19N 121 14E
Juvigny-sous-Andaine 42 48 32N 0 30W
Juvisy 43 48 43N 2 23E
Juwain 93 31 45N 61 30E
Juyüan 109 24 46N 113 16E
Juzennecourt 43 48 10N 5 0E
Jye-kundo 99 33 0N 96 50E
Jylhama 74 64 34N 26 40E
Jylland 73 56 15N 9 20E
Jylland (Jutland) 73 56 25N 9 30E
Jyväskylä 74 62 14N 25 44E

K

K. Sedili Besar 101 1 55N 104 5E
K2, Mt. 95 36 0N 77 0E
Ka Lae (South C.) 147 18 55N 155 41W
Kaaia, Mt. 147 21 31N 158 9W
Kaap die Goeie Hoop 128 34 24S 18 30E
Kaap Plato 128 28 30S 24 0E
Kaapkruis 128 21 43S 14 0E
Kaapstad = Cape Town 125 33 56S 18 27E
Kaatsheuvel 47 51 39N 5 2E
Kabaena, I. 103 5 15S 122 0E
Kabala 120 9 38N 11 37W
Kabale 126 1 15S 30 0E
Kabalo 126 6 0S 27 0E
Kabambare 126 4 41S 27 39E
Kabango 127 8 35S 28 30E
Kabanjahe 102 8 2N 98 27E
Kabara 120 16 40N 2 50W
Kabardinka 82 44 40N 37 57E
Kabardino-Balkar, A.S.S.R. □ 83 43 30N 43 30E
Kabarega Falls 126 2 15N 31 38E
Kabasalan 103 7 47N 122 44E
Kabba 121 7 57N 6 3E
Kabe 110 34 31N 132 31E
Kabi 121 13 30N 12 35E
Kabin Buri 100 13 57N 101 43E
Kabinakagami L. 150 48 54N 84 25W
Kabinda 126 6 23S 24 28E
Kablungu, C. 135 6 20S 150 1E
Kabna 122 19 6N 32 40E
Kabompo 127 13 30S 24 14E
Kabompo, R. 127 13 50S 24 10E
Kabondo 127 8 58S 25 40E
Kabongo 126 7 22S 25 33E
Kabou 121 9 28N 0 55E
Kaboudia, Rass 119 35 13N 11 10E

Kabra 138 23 25 S 150 25 E
Kabūd Gonbad 93 37 5 N 59 45 E
Kabuiri 121 11 30 N 13 30 E
Kabul 94 34 28 N 69 18 E
Kabul □ 93 34 0 N 68 30 E
Kabul, R. 94 34 30 N 69 13 E
Kabunga 126 1 38 S 28 3 E
Kaburuang 103 3 50 N 126 30 E
Kabushiya 123 16 54 N 33 41 E
Kabwe 127 14 30 S 28 29 E
Kabwum 135 6 11 S 147 15 E
Kačanik 66 42 13 N 21 12 E
Kachanovo 80 57 25 N 27 38 E
Kachebera 127 13 56 S 32 50 E
Kachin □ 98 26 0 N 97 0 E
Kachira, Lake 126 0 40 S 31 0 E
Kachiry 76 53 10 N 75 50 E
Kachisi 123 9 40 N 37 57 E
Kachkanar 84 58 42 N 59 33 E
Kachot 101 11 30 N 103 3 E
Kaçkar 83 40 45 N 41 30 E
Kadaingti 98 17 37 N 97 32 E
Kadan Kyun, I. 101 12 30 N 98 20 E
Kadanai, R. 94 32 0 N 66 10 E
Kadarkút 53 46 13 N 17 39 E
Kadayanallur 97 9 3 N 77 22 E
Kaddi 121 13 40 N 5 40 E
Kade 121 6 7 N 0 56 W
Kadgo, L. 137 25 30 S 125 30 E
Kadi 94 23 18 N 72 23 E
Kadina 140 34 0 S 137 43 E
Kadiri 97 14 12 N 78 13 E
* Kadiyevka 83 48 35 N 38 30 E
Kadoka 158 43 50 N 101 31 W
Kadom 81 54 37 N 42 24 E
Kaduna 121 10 30 N 7 21 E
Kaduna □ 121 11 0 N 7 30 E
Kaduna, R. 121 10 5 N 8 10 E
Kadyoha 120 8 58 N 5 53 W
Kadzhi-Say 85 42 8 N 77 10 E
Kaedi 120 16 9 N 13 28 W
Kaelé 121 10 15 N 14 15 E
Kaena Pt. 147 21 35 N 158 17 W
Kaeng Khoï 100 14 35 N 101 0 E
Kaeo 142 35 6 S 173 49 E
Kaerh, China 105 31 45 N 80 22 E
Kaerh, Sudan 123 5 35 N 31 20 E
Kaesŏng 107 37 58 N 126 35 E
Kaf 92 31 25 N 37 20 E
Kafakumba 124 9 38 S 23 46 E
Kafan 79 39 18 N 46 15 E
Kafanchan 121 9 40 N 8 20 E
Kafareti 121 10 25 N 11 12 E
Kaffrine 120 14 8 N 15 36 W
Kafia Kingi 117 9 20 N 24 25 E
Kafinda 127 12 32 S 30 20 E
Kafirévs, Ákra 69 38 9 N 24 8 E
Kafiristan 93 35 0 N 70 30 E
Kafr Ana 70 32 2 N 34 48 E
Kafr 'Ein 90 32 3 N 35 7 E
Kafr el Dauwâr 122 31 8 N 30 8 E
Kafr Kama 90 32 44 N 35 26 E
Kafr Kannā 90 32 45 N 35 20 E
Kafr Malik 90 32 0 N 35 18 E
Kafr Mandā 90 32 49 N 35 15 E
Kafr Quaddum 90 32 14 N 35 7 E
Kafr Ra'i 90 32 23 N 35 9 E
Kafr Sir 90 33 19 N 35 23 E
Kafr Yasif 90 32 58 N 35 10 E
Kafue 127 15 46 S 28 9 E
Kafue Flats 127 15 32 S 27 0 E
Kafue Gorge 127 16 0 S 28 0 E
Kafue Hook 127 14 58 S 26 0 E
Kafue Nat. Park 65 15 30 S 25 40 E
Kafue, R. 125 15 30 S 26 0 E
Kafulwe 127 9 0 S 29 1 E
Kaga, Afghan. 94 34 14 N 70 10 E
Kaga, Japan 111 36 16 N 136 15 E
Kagamil I. 147 53 0 N 169 40 W
Kagan 85 39 43 N 64 33 E
Kagawa-ken □ 110 34 15 N 134 0 E
Kagera R. 126 1 15 S 31 20 E
Kagoshima 110 31 36 N 130 40 E
Kagoshima-ken □ 110 30 0 N 130 0 E
Kagoshima-Wan 110 31 0 N 130 40 E
Kagul 82 45 50 N 28 15 E
Kahajan, R. 102 2 10 S 114 0 E
Kahama 126 4 8 S 32 30 E
Kahama □ 126 3 40 S 32 0 E
Kahang 101 2 12 N 103 32 E
Kahe 126 3 30 S 37 25 E
Kahemba 124 7 18 S 18 55 E
Kaherekoua Mts. 143 45 45 S 167 15 E
Kahniah, R. 152 58 15 N 120 55 W
Kahnuj 93 27 55 N 57 40 E
Kahoka 158 40 25 N 91 42 W
Kahoolawe, I. 147 20 33 N 156 35 W
Kahuku & Pt. 147 21 41 N 157 57 W
Kahulai 147 20 54 N 156 28 W
Kahurangi, Pt. 143 40 50 S 172 10 E
Kahuta 94 33 35 N 73 24 E
Kai Kai 128 19 52 S 21 15 E
Kai, Kepulauan 103 5 55 S 132 45 W
Kaiama 121 9 36 N 4 1 E
Kaiapit 135 6 18 S 146 18 E
Kaiapoi 143 42 24 S 172 40 E
Kaibara 111 35 8 N 135 5 E
K'aichien 109 23 45 N 111 47 E
K'aifeng 106 34 50 N 114 27 E
Kaihsien 107 40 25 N 122 25 E
K'aihsien 108 31 12 N 108 25 E
K'aihua 109 29 9 N 118 24 E
Kaiingveld 128 30 0 S 22 0 E
Kaikohe 142 35 25 S 173 49 E
Kaikoura 143 42 25 S 173 43 E
Kaikoura Pen. 143 42 25 S 173 43 E
Kaikoura Ra. 143 41 59 S 173 41 E
Kailahun 120 8 18 N 10 39 W
Kailashahar 98 25 19 N 92 0 E
Kaili 108 26 32 N 107 57 E
K'ailu 107 43 35 N 121 12 E
Kailua 147 19 39 N 156 0 W
Kaimana 103 3 30 S 133 45 E
Kaimanawa Mts. 142 39 15 S 175 56 E
Kaimata 143 42 34 S 171 28 E
Kaimganj 95 27 33 N 79 24 E
Kaimon-Dake 110 31 11 N 130 32 E
Kaimur Hill 95 24 30 N 82 0 E
Kainan 110 34 9 N 135 12 E
Kainantu 135 6 18 S 145 52 E
Kaingaroa Forest 142 38 30 S 176 30 E
Kainji Res. 121 10 1 N 4 40 E
Kaipara Harb. 142 36 25 S 174 14 E
K'aip'ing 109 22 31 N 112 32 E
Kaipokok B. 151 54 54 N 59 47 W
Kairana 94 29 33 N 77 15 E
Kairiru, I. 138 3 20 S 143 20 E
Kaironi 103 0 47 S 133 40 E
Kairouan 119 35 45 N 10 5 E
Kairuku 135 8 51 S 146 35 E
Kaiserslautern 49 49 30 N 7 43 E
Kaitaia 142 35 8 S 173 17 E
Kaitangata 143 46 17 S 169 51 E
Kaithal 94 29 48 N 76 26 E
Kaitu, R. 94 33 20 N 70 20 E
Kaiwi Channel 147 21 13 N 157 30 W
K'aiyang 108 27 4 N 106 55 E
K'aiyüan, Liaoning, China 107 42 33 N 124 4 E
K'aiyüan, Yunnan, China 108 23 47 N 103 10 E
Kaiyuh Mts. 147 63 40 N 159 0 W
Kajaani 74 64 17 N 27 46 E
Kajabbi 138 20 0 S 140 1 E
Kajan, R. 102 2 40 N 116 40 E
Kajang 101 2 59 N 101 48 E
Kajeli 103 3 20 S 127 10 E
Kajiado 126 1 53 S 36 48 E
Kajiki 110 31 44 N 130 40 E
Kajo Kaji 123 3 58 N 31 40 E
Kajoa, I. 103 0 1 N 127 28 E
Kajuagung 102 32 8 S 104 46 E
Kakabeka Falls 150 48 24 N 89 37 W
Kakamas 125 28 45 S 20 33 E
Kakamega 126 0 20 N 34 46 E
Kakamega □ 126 0 20 N 34 46 E
Kakamigahara 111 35 28 N 136 48 E
Kakanj 66 44 9 N 18 7 E
Kakanui Mts. 143 45 10 S 170 30 E
Kakapotahi 143 43 0 S 170 45 E
Kake, Japan 110 34 36 N 132 19 E
Kake, U.S.A. 147 57 0 N 134 0 W
Kakegawa 111 34 45 N 138 1 E
Kakhib 83 42 28 N 46 34 E
Kakhovskoye Vdkhr. 82 47 5 N 34 16 E
Kakia 125 24 48 S 23 22 E
Kakinada = Cocanada 99 16 50 N 82 11 E
Kakinada (Cocanada) 96 16 50 N 82 11 E
Kakisa L. 152 60 56 N 117 43 W
Kakisa, R. 152 61 3 N 117 10 W
Kakogawa 110 34 46 N 134 51 E
Kaktovik 147 70 8 N 143 50 W
Kakwa, R. 152 54 37 N 118 28 W
Kala 121 12 2 N 14 40 E
Kala Oya. 97 8 15 N 80 0 E
Kala Shank'ou 95 35 42 N 78 20 E
Kalaa-Kebira 119 35 59 N 10 32 E
Kalabagh 94 33 0 N 71 28 E
Kalabáka 68 39 42 N 21 39 E
Kalabo 125 14 58 S 22 33 E
Kalach 81 50 22 N 41 0 E
Kaladan, R. 99 21 30 N 92 45 E
Kalahari, Des. 128 24 0 S 22 0 E
Kalahari Gemsbok Nat. Pk. 128 26 0 S 20 30 E
Kalahasti 97 13 45 N 79 44 E
Kalai-Khumb 85 38 28 N 70 46 E
Kalaja e Turrës 68 41 10 N 19 28 E
Kalakamati 129 20 40 S 27 25 E
Kalakan 77 55 15 N 116 45 E
K'alak'unlun Shank'ou 95 35 33 N 77 46 E
Kalam 95 35 34 N 72 30 E
Kalama, U.S.A. 160 46 0 N 122 55 W
Kalama, Zaïre 126 2 52 S 28 35 E
Kalamariá 68 40 33 N 22 55 E
Kalamata 69 37 3 N 22 10 E
Kalamazoo 156 42 20 N 85 35 W
Kalamazoo, R. 156 42 40 N 86 12 W
Kalamb 96 18 3 N 74 48 E
Kalambo Falls 127 8 37 S 31 35 E
Kálamos, I. 69 38 37 N 20 55 E
Kalamoti 69 38 15 N 26 4 E
Kalamunda 137 32 0 S 116 0 E
Kalangadoo 140 37 34 S 140 41 E
Kalannie 137 30 22 S 117 5 E
Kalao, I. 103 7 21 S 121 0 E
Kalaotoa, I. 103 7 20 S 121 50 E
Kälarne 72 62 59 N 16 8 E
Kalárovo 53 47 54 N 18 0 E
Kalasin 100 16 26 N 103 30 E
Kalat 93 29 8 N 66 31 E
Kalat □ 93 27 0 N 64 30 E
Kalat-i-Ghilzai 93 32 15 N 66 58 E
Kálathos (Calato) 69 36 9 N 28 8 E
Kalaupapa 147 21 12 N 156 59 W
Kalaus, R. 83 45 40 N 43 30 E
Kalávrita 69 38 3 N 22 8 E
Kalaw 98 20 37 N 96 35 E
Kalba 120 9 30 N 2 42 W
Kalbarri 137 27 40 S 114 10 E
Kaldhovd 71 60 5 N 8 20 E
Kalecik 82 40 4 N 33 26 E
Kalegauk Kyun 99 15 33 N 97 35 E
Kalehe 126 2 6 S 28 50 E
Kalema 126 1 12 S 31 55 E
Kalemie 124 5 55 S 29 9 E
Kalemyo 98 23 11 N 94 4 E
Kalety 54 50 35 N 18 52 E
Kalewa 98 22 41 N 95 32 E
Kálfafellsstaður 74 64 11 N 15 53 W
Kalgan = Changchiak'ou 106 40 50 N 114 53 E
Kalgoorlie 137 30 40 S 121 22 E
Kaliakra, Nos 67 43 21 N 28 30 E
Kalianda 102 5 50 S 105 45 E
Kalibo 103 11 43 N 122 22 E
Kaliganj Town 98 23 25 N 89 8 E
Kalima 126 2 33 S 26 32 E
Kalimantan Barat □ 102 0 0 110 30 E
Kalimantan Selatan □ 102 4 10 S 115 30 E
Kalimantan Tengah □ 102 2 0 S 113 30 E
Kalimantan Timor □ 102 1 30 N 116 30 E
Kálimnos, I. 69 37 0 N 27 0 E
Kalimpong 95 27 4 N 88 35 E
Kalinadi, R. 97 14 50 N 74 20 E
Kalinin 81 56 55 N 35 55 E
Kaliningrad 80 54 42 N 20 32 E
Kalinino 83 45 12 N 38 59 E
Kalininskoye 85 42 50 N 73 49 E
Kalinkovichi 80 52 12 N 29 20 E
Kalinovik 66 43 31 N 18 29 E
Kalipetrovo (Starčevo) 67 44 5 N 27 14 E
Kaliro 126 0 56 N 33 30 E
Kalirrákhi 68 40 40 N 24 35 E
Kalispell 160 48 10 N 114 22 W
Kalisz 54 51 45 N 18 8 E
Kalisz □ 54 51 30 N 18 0 E
Kalisz Pom 54 53 17 N 15 55 E
Kaliua 126 5 5 S 31 48 E
Kaliveli Tank 97 12 5 N 79 50 E
Kalix R. 74 67 0 N 22 0 E
Kalka 94 30 56 N 76 57 E
Kalkaroo 140 31 12 S 143 54 E
Kalkaska 150 44 44 N 85 11 W
Kalkfeld 128 20 57 S 16 14 E
Kalkfontein 128 22 4 S 20 57 E
Kalkfontein Dam 128 29 30 S 24 15 E
Kalkrand 128 24 1 S 17 35 E
Kall L. 72 63 35 N 13 10 E
Kallakurichi 97 11 44 N 79 1 E
Kållandsö 73 58 40 N 13 5 E
Källby 73 58 30 N 13 8 E
Kallia 86 31 46 N 35 30 E
Kallidaikurichi 97 8 38 N 77 31 E
Kallinge 73 56 15 N 15 18 E
Kallithéa 69 37 55 N 23 41 E
Kallmeti 68 41 51 N 19 41 E
Kallonís, Kólpos 69 39 10 N 26 10 E
Kallsjön 74 63 38 N 13 0 E
Kalltorp 73 58 23 N 13 20 E
Kalmalo 121 13 40 N 5 20 E
Kalmar 73 56 40 N 16 20 E
Kalmar län □ 73 57 25 N 16 15 E
Kalmar sund 73 56 40 N 16 25 E
Kalmthout 47 51 23 N 4 29 E
Kalmyk A.S.S.R. □ 83 46 5 N 46 1 E
Kalmykovo 83 49 0 N 51 35 E
Kalna 95 23 13 N 88 25 E
Kalo 135 10 1 S 147 48 E
Kalocsa 53 46 32 N 19 0 E
Kalofer 67 42 37 N 24 59 E
Kalol, Gujarat, India 94 23 15 N 72 33 E
Kalol, Gujarat, India 94 22 37 N 73 31 E
Kalola 127 10 0 S 28 0 E
Kalolímnos 69 37 4 N 27 8 E
Kalomo 127 17 0 S 26 30 E
Kalonerón 69 37 20 N 21 38 E
Kalpi 95 26 8 N 79 47 E
Kalrayan Hills 97 11 45 N 78 40 E
Kalsubai, Mt. 96 17 35 N 73 45 E
Kaltbrunn 51 47 13 N 9 2 E
Kaltungo 121 9 48 N 11 19 E
Kalu 94 25 5 N 67 39 E
Kaluga 81 54 35 N 36 10 E
Kalulushi 127 12 50 S 28 3 E
Kalundborg 73 55 41 N 11 5 E
Kalush 80 42 9 N 24 12 E
Kałuszyn 54 52 13 N 21 52 E
Kalutara 97 6 35 N 80 0 E
Kalwaria 54 49 53 N 19 41 E
Kalya 84 60 15 N 59 59 E
Kalyan, Austral. 140 34 55 S 139 49 E
Kalyan, India 96 20 30 N 74 3 E
Kalyani 174 17 53 N 76 59 E
Kalyazin 81 57 15 N 37 45 E
Kam Keut 101 18 20 N 104 48 E
Kama, Burma 98 22 10 N 95 10 E
Kama, Zaïre 126 3 30 S 27 5 E
Kama, R. 84 60 0 N 53 0 E
Kamachumu 126 1 37 S 31 37 E
Kamae 110 32 48 N 131 56 E
Kamaguenam 121 13 36 N 10 30 E
Kamaing 98 24 26 N 94 55 E
Kamaishi 112 39 20 N 142 0 E
Kamakura 111 35 19 N 139 33 E
Kamalia 94 30 44 N 72 42 E
Kamalino 147 21 50 N 160 14 W
Kamamaung 98 17 21 N 97 40 E
Kamango 126 0 40 N 29 52 E
Kamapanda 127 12 5 S 24 0 E
Kamaran 91 15 28 N 42 35 E
Kamashi 85 38 51 N 65 23 E
Kamativi 127 18 15 S 0 27 E
Kamba 121 11 50 N 3 45 E
Kambalda 137 31 10 S 121 37 E
Kambam 97 9 45 N 77 16 E
Kambar 94 27 37 N 68 1 E
Kambarka 84 56 15 N 54 11 E
Kambia 120 9 3 N 12 53 W
Kambolé 127 8 47 S 30 48 E
Kambove 127 10 51 S 26 33 E
Kamchatka, P-ov. 77 57 0 N 160 0 E
Kamde 138 8 0 S 140 58 E
Kamen 76 53 50 N 81 30 E
Kamen Kashirskiy 80 51 39 N 24 56 E
Kamenica 66 44 25 N 19 40 E
Kamenice 52 49 18 N 15 2 E
Kamenjak, Rt. 63 44 47 N 13 55 E
Kamenka, R.S.F.S.R., U.S.S.R. 78 65 58 N 44 0 E
Kamenka, R.S.F.S.R., U.S.S.R. 81 50 47 N 39 20 E
Kamenka Bugskaya 80 50 8 N 24 16 E
Kamenka Dneprovskaya 82 47 29 N 34 14 E
Kamensk 76 56 25 N 62 45 E
Kamensk Shakhtinskiy 83 48 23 N 40 20 E
Kamensk-Uralskiy 84 56 25 N 62 2 E
Kamenskiy 81 50 48 N 45 25 E
Kamenskoye 77 62 45 N 165 30 E
Kamenyak 67 43 24 N 26 57 E
Kamenz 48 51 17 N 14 7 E
Kameoka 111 35 0 N 135 35 E
Kames 34 55 53 N 5 15 W
Kameyama 111 34 51 N 126 27 E
Kami 68 42 17 N 20 18 E
Kami-Jima 110 32 27 N 130 20 E
Kami-koshiki-Jima 110 31 50 N 129 52 E
Kamiah 160 46 12 N 116 2 W
Kamien Krajenskie 54 53 32 N 17 32 E
Kamien Pomorski 54 53 57 N 14 43 E
Kamiensk 54 51 12 N 19 29 E
Kamiita 110 34 6 N 134 22 E
Kamilonision 69 35 50 N 26 15 E
Kamilukuak, L. 153 62 22 N 101 40 W
Kamina 127 8 45 S 25 0 E
Kaminak L. 153 62 10 N 95 0 W
Kamioka 111 36 25 N 137 15 E
Kamituga Mungombe 126 3 2 S 28 10 E
Kamiyaku 112 30 25 N 130 30 E
Kamloops 152 50 40 N 120 20 W
Kamo 143 35 42 S 174 20 E
Kamogawa 111 35 5 N 140 5 E
Kamoke 94 32 4 N 74 4 E
Kamono 124 3 10 S 13 20 E
Kamp, R. 52 48 35 N 15 26 E
Kampala 126 0 20 N 32 30 E
Kampar 101 4 18 N 101 9 E
Kampar, R. 102 0 30 N 102 0 E
Kampen 46 52 33 N 5 53 E
Kamperland 47 51 34 N 3 43 E
Kamphaeng Phet 100 16 28 N 99 30 E
Kampolombo, L. 127 11 30 S 29 35 E
Kampong Ayer Puteh 101 4 15 N 103 10 E
Kampong Jerangau 101 4 50 N 103 10 E
Kampong Raja 101 5 45 N 102 35 E
Kampong Sedili Besar 101 1 56 N 104 8 E
Kampong To 101 6 3 N 101 13 E
Kampot 101 10 36 N 104 10 E
Kamptee 94 21 9 N 79 19 E
Kampti 120 10 7 N 3 25 W
Kampuchea ■ = Cambodia 100 12 15 N 105 0 E
Kamrau, Teluk 103 3 30 S 133 45 E
Kamsack 153 51 34 N 101 54 W
Kamskove Ustye 81 55 10 N 49 20 E
Kamskoye Vdkhr. 78 58 0 N 56 0 E
Kamuchawie L. 153 56 18 N 101 59 W
Kamui-Misaki 112 45 3 N 142 30 E
Kamyshin 81 50 10 N 45 30 E
Kamyshlov 84 56 50 N 62 43 E
Kamyzyak 83 46 4 N 48 10 E
Kan 98 20 53 N 93 49 E
Kan Chiang, R. 109 29 45 N 116 10 E
Kanaaupscow 150 54 2 N 76 30 W
Kanab 161 37 3 N 112 29 W
Kanab Creek 161 37 0 N 112 40 W
Kanaga I. 147 51 45 N 177 22 W
Kanagawa-ken □ 111 35 20 N 139 20 E
Kanairiktok, R. 151 55 2 N 60 18 W
Kanakanak 147 59 0 N 158 58 W
Kanakapura 97 12 33 N 77 28 E
Kanália 68 39 30 N 22 53 E
Kananga 124 5 55 S 22 18 E
Kanarraville 161 37 34 N 113 12 W
Kanash 81 55 48 N 47 32 E
Kanawha, R. 156 39 40 N 82 0 W
Kanayis, Ras el 122 31 30 N 28 5 E
Kanazawa 111 36 30 N 136 38 E
Kanbalu 98 17 55 N 85 24 E
Kanchanaburi 100 14 8 N 99 31 E
Kanchenjunga, Mt. 95 27 50 N 88 10 E
Kanchipuram (Conjeeveram) 97 12 52 N 79 45 E
Kanchou 109 25 51 N 114 59 E
Kanch'üan 106 36 19 N 109 19 E
Kanda Kanda 124 6 52 S 23 48 E
Kandagach 79 49 20 N 57 15 E
Kandahar 94 31 32 N 65 30 E
Kandahar □ 94 31 0 N 65 0 E
Kandalaksha 78 67 9 N 32 30 E
Kandalakshkiyzaliv 78 66 0 N 35 0 E

* *Renamed Stakhanov*

Name	Page	Lat.	Long.
Kandalu	93	29 55N	63 20 E
Kandangan	102	2 50 S	115 20 E
Kandanos	69	35 19N	23 44 E
Kandé	121	9 57N	1 53 E
Kandep	135	5 54 S	143 32 E
Kander, R.	50	46 33N	7 38 E
Kandersteg	50	46 30N	7 40 E
Kandewu	127	14 1 S	26 16 E
Kandhíla	69	37 46N	22 22 E
Kandhkot	94	28 16N	69 8 E
Kandhla	94	29 18N	77 19 E
Kandi, Benin	121	11 7N	2 55 E
Kandi, India	95	23 58N	88 5 E
Kandinduna	127	13 58 S	24 19 E
Kandira	92	41 5N	30 10 E
Kandla	94	23 0N	70 10 E
Kandos	141	32 45 S	149 58 E
Kandrach	93	25 30N	65 30 E
Kandrian	135	6 14 S	149 37 E
Kandukur	95	15 12N	79 57 E
Kandy	97	7 18N	80 43 E
Kane	156	41 39N	78 53W
Kane Bassin	12	79 30N	68 0W
Kanel	120	13 18N	14 35W
Kaneohe	147	21 25N	157 48W
Kanevskaya	83	46 3N	39 3 E
Kanfanar	63	45 7N	13 50 E
Kang	93	30 55N	61 55 E
Kangaba	120	11 56N	8 25W
Kangar	101	6 27N	100 12 E
Kangaroo I.	140	35 45 S	137 0 E
Kangaroo Mts.	138	23 25 S	142 0 E
Kangavar	92	34 40N	48 0 E
Kangean, Kepulauan	102	6 55 S	115 23 E
Kangerdlugsuaé	12	68 10N	32 20W
Kanggye	107	41 0N	126 35 E
Kanggyŏng	107	36 10N	126 0 E
Kanghwa	107	37 45N	126 30 E
K'angkang	108	32 46N	101 3 E
Kangnŭng	107	37 45N	128 54 E
Kango	124	0 11N	10 5 E
K'angp'ing	107	43 45N	123 20 E
Kangpokpi	98	25 8N	93 58 E
K'angting	108	30 2N	102 0 E
Kangtissu Shan	95	31 0N	82 0 E
Kangto, Mt.	99	27 50N	92 35 E
Kangyao	107	44 15N	126 40 E
Kangyidaung	98	16 56N	94 54 E
Kanhangad	97	12 21N	74 58 E
Kanheri	96	19 13N	72 50 E
Kani, China	99	29 25N	95 25 E
Kani, Ivory C.	120	8 29N	6 36W
Kaniama	126	7 30 S	24 12 E
Kaniapiskau L.	151	54 10N	69 55W
Kaniapiskau, R.	151	57 40N	69 30 E
Kanibadam	85	40 17N	70 25 E
Kanin Nos, Mys	78	68 45N	43 20 E
Kanin, P-ov.	78	68 0N	45 0 E
Kanina	68	40 23N	19 30 E
Kaniva	140	36 22 S	141 18 E
Kanjiza	66	46 3N	20 4 E
Kanjut Sar	95	36 15N	75 25 E
Kankakee	156	41 6N	87 50W
Kankakee, R.	156	41 13N	87 0W
Kankan	120	10 30N	9 15W
Kanker	96	20 10N	81 40 E
Kankouchen	107	40 30N	119 27 E
Kanku	106	34 45N	105 12 E
Kankunskiy	77	57 37N	126 8 E
Kanmuri-Yama	110	34 30N	132 4 E
Kannabe	110	34 32N	133 23 E
Kannapolis	157	35 32N	80 37W
Kannauj	95	27 3N	79 26 E
Kannod	93	22 45N	76 40 E
Kano	121	12 2N	8 30 E
Kano □	121	12 30N	9 0 E
Kan'onji	110	34 7N	133 39 E
Kanoroba	120	9 7N	6 8W
Kanowit	102	2 14N	112 20 E
Kanowna	137	30 32 S	121 31 E
Kanoya	110	31 25N	130 50 E
Kanózuga	54	49 58N	22 25 E
Kanpetlet	98	21 10N	93 59 E
Kanpur	95	26 35N	80 20 E
Kansas □	158	38 40N	98 0W
Kansas City, Kans., U.S.A.	158	39 0N	94 40W
Kansas City, Mo., U.S.A.	158	39 3N	94 30W
Kansas, R.	158	39 15N	96 20W
Kansenia	127	10 20 S	26 0 E
Kansk	77	56 20N	95 37 E
Kansŏng	107	38 24N	128 30 E
Kansu □	105	35 30N	104 30 E
Kant	85	42 53N	74 51 E
Kant'angtzu	106	37 28N	104 33 E
Kantché	121	13 31N	8 30 E
Kantemirovka	83	49 43N	39 55 E
Kantharalak	100	14 39N	104 39 E
Kantishna	147	63 31N	151 5W
Kantō □	111	36 0N	140 0 E
Kantō-Heiya	111	36 0N	139 30 E
Kantō-Sanchi	111	35 50N	138 50 E
Kantu-long	98	19 57N	97 36 E
Kanturk	39	52 10N	8 55W
Kantzu	108	31 37N	100 0 E
Kanuma	111	36 44N	139 42 E
Kanus	128	27 50 S	18 39 E
Kanye	128	25 0 S	25 28 E
Kanyu	128	20 7 S	24 37 E
Kanyü	107	34 53N	119 9 E
Kanzene	127	10 30 S	25 12 E
Kanzi, Ras	126	7 1 S	39 33 E
Kaoan	109	28 25N	115 22 E
Kaochou	109	21 55N	110 52 E
Kaohofu	109	30 43N	116 49 E
Kaohsien	108	28 21N	104 31 E
Kaohsiung	109	22 35N	120 16 E
Kaok'eng	109	27 39N	114 4 E
Kaoko Otavi	125	18 12 S	13 45 E
Kaokoveld	128	19 0 S	13 0 E
Kaolack	120	14 5N	16 8W
Kaolan Shan	109	21 55N	113 15 E
Kaolikung Shan	108	26 0N	98 55 E
Kaomi	107	36 25N	119 45 E
Kaopao Hu	109	32 50N	119 15 E
Kaop'ing	106	35 48N	112 55 E
K'aoshant'un	107	44 25N	124 27 E
Kaot'ang	106	36 51N	116 13 E
Kaoyang	106	38 42N	115 47 E
Kaoyu	109	32 46N	119 32 E
Kaoyüan	107	37 7N	118 0 E
Kapaa	147	22 5N	159 19W
Kapadvanj	94	23 5N	73 0 E
Kapagere	135	9 46 S	147 42 E
Kapanga	124	8 30 S	22 40 E
Kapanovka	83	47 28N	46 50 E
Kapata	127	14 16 S	26 15 E
Kapellen	47	51 19N	4 25 E
Kapello, Ákra	69	36 9N	23 3 E
Kapema	127	10 45 S	28 22 E
Kapfenberg	52	47 26N	15 18 E
Kapiri Mposhi	127	13 59 S	28 43 E
Kapiskau	150	52 50N	82 1W
Kapiskau, R.	150	52 47N	81 55W
Kapit	102	2 0N	113 5 E
Kapiti I.	142	40 50 S	174 56 E
Kaplice	52	48 42N	14 30 E
Kapoe	101	9 34N	98 32 E
Kapoeta	123	4 50N	33 35 E
Kápolnásnyék	53	47 16N	18 41 E
Kaponga	143	39 29 S	174 9 E
Kapos, R.	53	46 30N	18 20 E
Kaposvár	53	46 25N	17 47 E
Kappeln	48	54 37N	9 56 E
Kapps	128	22 32 S	17 18 E
Kaprije	63	43 42N	15 43 E
Kaprijke	47	51 13N	3 38 E
Kapsan	107	41 4N	128 19 E
Kapsukas	80	54 33N	23 19 E
Kapuas Hulu, Pegunungan	102	1 30N	113 30 E
Kapuas, R.	102	0 20N	111 40 E
Kapuka	127	10 30 S	32 55 E
Kapulo	127	8 18 S	29 15 E
Kapunda	140	34 20 S	138 56 E
Kapurthala	94	31 23N	75 25 E
Kapuskasing	150	49 25N	82 30W
Kapuskasing, R.	150	49 49N	82 0W
Kapustin Yar	83	48 37N	45 40 E
Kaputar, Mt.	139	30 15 S	150 10 E
Kaputir	126	2 5N	35 28 E
Kapuvár	53	47 36N	17 1 E
Kara, Turkey	69	38 29N	26 19 E
Kara, U.S.S.R.	76	69 10N	65 25 E
Kara Bogaz Gol, Zaliv	76	41 0N	53 30 E
Kara Burun	69	38 41N	26 28 E
Kara, I.	69	36 58N	27 30 E
Kara Kalpak A.S.S.R. □	76	43 0N	60 0 E
Kara Kum	76	39 30N	60 0 E
Kara-Saki	110	34 41N	129 30 E
Kara Sea	76	75 0N	70 0 E
Kara Su	85	40 44N	72 53 E
Kara, Wadi	122	20 40N	42 0 E
Karabash	84	55 29N	60 14 E
Karabekaul	85	38 30N	64 8 E
Karabük	82	41 10N	32 30 E
Karabulak	85	44 54N	78 30 E
Karaburuni	68	40 25N	19 20 E
Karabutak	84	49 59N	60 14 E
Karachala	83	39 45N	48 53 E
Karachayevsk	83	43 50N	42 0 E
Karachev	80	53 10N	35 5 E
Karachi	94	24 53N	67 0 E
Karachi □	94	25 30N	67 0 E
Karad	96	17 15N	74 10 E
Karadeniz Boğazı	92	41 10N	29 5 E
Karadeniz Dağlari	92	41 30N	35 0 E
Karaga	121	9 58N	0 28W
Karagajly	76	49 26N	76 0 E
Karaganda	76	49 50N	73 0 E
Karaginskiy, Ostrov	77	58 45N	164 0 E
Karagwe □	126	2 0 S	31 0 E
Karaikal	97	10 59N	79 50 E
Karaikkudi	97	10 0N	78 45 E
Karaitivu I.	97	9 45N	79 52 E
Karaj	93	35 4N	51 0 E
Karak, Jordan	90	31 14N	35 40 E
Karak, Malay.	101	3 25N	102 2 E
Karakas	76	48 20N	83 30 E
Karakitang	103	3 14N	125 28 E
Karakobis	128	22 3 S	20 37 E
Karakoram	95	35 20N	76 0 E
Karakoram P. = K'alak'unlun Shank'ou	95	35 33N	77 46 E
Karakoram Pass	93	35 20N	78 0 E
Karakul, Tadzhik, S.S.R., U.S.S.R.	85	39 2N	73 33 E
Karakul, Uzbek S.S.R., U.S.S.R.	85	39 22N	63 50 E
Karakuldzha	85	40 39N	73 26 E
Karakulino	84	56 1N	53 43 E
Karalon	77	57 5N	115 50 E
Karaman	92	37 14N	33 13 E
Karambu	102	3 53 S	116 6 E
Karamea	143	41 14 S	172 6 E
Karamea Bight	143	41 22 S	171 40 E
Karamea, R.	143	41 13 S	172 26 E
Karamet Niyaz	85	37 45N	64 34 E
Karamoja □	126	3 0N	34 15 E
Karamsad	94	22 35N	72 50 E
Karanganjar	103	7 38 S	109 37 E
Karanja	96	20 29N	77 31 E
Karapoit	142	37 53 S	175 32 E
Karaşar	82	40 21N	31 55 E
Karasburg	128	28 0 S	18 44 E
Karasino	76	66 50N	86 50 E
Karasjok	74	69 27N	25 30 E
Karasuk	76	53 44N	78 2 E
Karasuk □	126	2 12N	35 15 E
Karasuyama	111	36 39N	140 9 E
Karatau	85	43 10N	70 28 E
Karatau, Khrebet	85	43 30N	69 30 E
Karativu, I.	97	8 22N	79 52 E
Karatiya	90	31 39N	34 43 E
Karatobe	84	49 44N	53 30 E
Karatoya, R.	98	24 7N	89 36 E
Karaturuk	85	43 35N	78 0 E
Karaul-Bazar	85	39 30N	64 48 E
Karauli	94	26 30N	77 4 E
Karavasta	68	40 53N	19 28 E
Karawa	124	3 18N	20 17 E
Karawanken	52	46 30N	14 40 E
Karazhal	76	48 2N	70 49 E
Karbala	92	32 47N	44 3 E
Kårböle	72	61 59N	15 22 E
Karcag	53	47 19N	21 1 E
Karcha, R.	95	34 15N	75 57 E
Kärda	73	57 10N	13 49 E
Kardeljevo	66	43 2N	17 27 E
Kardhámila	69	38 35N	26 5 E
Kardhítsa	68	39 23N	21 54 E
Kardhítsa □	68	39 15N	21 50 E
Kärdla	80	58 50N	22 40 E
Kareeberge	128	30 50 S	22 0 E
Kareima	122	18 30N	31 49 E
Karelian A.S.S.R. □	78	65 30N	32 30 E
Karema, P.N.G.	135	9 12 S	147 18 E
Karema, Tanz.	126	6 49 S	30 24 E
Karen	101	12 49N	92 53 E
Karganrud	92	37 55N	49 0 E
Kargapolye	84	55 57N	64 24 E
Kargasok	76	59 3N	80 53 E
Kargat	76	55 10N	80 15 E
Kargı	82	41 11N	34 30 E
Kargil	95	34 32N	76 12 E
Kargowa	54	52 5N	15 51 E
Karguéri	121	13 36N	10 30 E
Kariai	69	40 14N	24 19 E
Kariba	127	16 28 S	28 36 E
Kariba Dam	125	16 30 S	28 35 E
Kariba Gorge	127	16 30 S	28 35 E
Kariba Lake	127	16 40 S	28 25 E
Karibib	128	21 0 S	15 56 E
Karikal	97	10 59N	79 50 E
Karikkale	92	39 55N	33 30 E
Karimata, Kepulauan	102	1 40 S	109 0 E
Karimata, Selat	102	2 0 S	108 20 E
Karimnagar	96	18 26N	79 10 E
Karimundjawa, Kepulauan	102	5 50 S	110 30 E
Karin	91	10 50N	45 52 E
Káristos	69	38 1N	24 29 E
Karitane	51	45 38 S	170 39 E
Kariya	111	34 58N	137 1 E
Karkal	97	13 15N	74 56 E
Karkar I.	135	4 40 S	146 0 E
Karkinitskiy Zaliv	82	45 36N	32 35 E
Karkur	90	32 29N	34 57 E
Karkur Tohl	122	22 5N	25 5 E
Karl Libknekht	80	51 40N	35 45 E
Karl-Marx-Stadt	48	50 50N	12 55 E
Karl-Marx-Stadt □	48	50 45N	13 0 E
Karla, L = Voiviis, Limni	68	39 35N	22 45 E
Karlino	54	54 3N	15 53 E
Karlobag	63	44 32N	15 5 E
Karlovac	63	45 31N	15 36 E
Karlovka	82	49 29N	35 8 E
Karlovy Vary	52	50 13N	12 51 E
Karlsborg	73	58 33N	14 33 E
Karlshamn	73	56 10N	14 51 E
Karlskoga	72	59 22N	14 33 E
Karlskrona	73	56 10N	15 35 E
Karlsruhe	49	49 3N	8 23 E
Karlstad, Sweden	72	59 23N	13 30 E
Karlstad, U.S.A.	158	48 38N	96 30W
Karmøy	71	59 15N	5 15 E
Karnal	94	29 42N	77 2 E
Karnali, R.	95	29 0N	82 0 E
Karnaphuli Res.	98	22 40N	92 20 E
Karnataka □	97	13 15N	77 0 E
Karnes City	159	28 53N	97 53W
Karni	120	10 45N	2 40W
Karnische Alpen	52	46 36N	13 0 E
Karnobat	67	42 40N	27 0 E
Kärnten □	52	46 52N	13 30 E
Karo	120	12 16N	2 22W
Karoi	127	16 48 S	29 45 E
Karonga	127	9 57 S	33 55 E
Karoonda	140	35 1 S	139 59 E
Karos, Is.	69	36 54N	25 40 E
Karousâdhes	68	39 47N	19 45 E
Karpalund	73	56 4N	14 5 E
Kárpathos, I.	69	35 37N	27 10 E
Kárpathos, Stenón	69	36 0N	27 30 E
Karpinsk	84	59 45N	60 1 E
Karpogory	78	63 59N	44 27 E
Karrebaek	73	55 12N	11 39 E
Kars	92	40 40N	43 5 E
Karsakpay	76	47 55N	66 40 E
Karsha	83	49 45N	51 35 E
Karshi	85	38 53N	65 48 E
Karsun	81	54 14N	46 57 E
Kartál Óros	68	41 15N	25 13 E
Kartaly	84	53 3N	60 40 E
Kartapur	94	31 27N	75 32 E
Kartuzy	54	54 22N	18 10 E
Karuah	141	32 37 S	151 56 E
Karufa	103	3 50 S	133 20 E
Karumba	138	17 31 S	140 50 E
Karumo	126	2 25 S	32 50 E
Karumwa	126	3 12 S	32 38 E
Karungu	126	0 50 S	34 10 E
Karunjie	136	16 18 S	127 12 E
Karup	73	56 19N	9 10 E
Karur	97	10 59N	78 2 E
Karviná	53	49 53N	18 25 E
Karwar	93	14 55N	74 13 E
Karwi	95	25 12N	80 57 E
Kas Kong	101	11 27N	102 12 E
Kasache	127	13 25 S	34 20 E
Kasai	110	34 55N	134 52 E
Kasai Occidental □	127	6 30 S	22 30 E
Kasai Oriental □	126	5 0 S	24 30 E
Kasai, R.	124	8 20 S	22 0 E
Kasaji	127	10 25 S	23 27 E
Kasama, Japan	111	36 23N	140 16 E
Kasama, Zambia	127	10 16 S	31 9 E
Kasandong	107	41 18N	126 55 E
Kasane	128	17 34 S	24 50 E
Kasanga	127	8 30 S	31 10 E
Kasangulu	124	4 15 S	15 15 E
Kasaoka	110	34 30N	133 30 E
Kasaragod	97	12 30N	74 58 E
Kasat	98	15 56N	98 13 E
Kasba	98	25 51N	87 37 E
Kasba L.	153	60 20N	102 10W
Kasba Tadla	118	32 36N	6 17W
Kaschmar	93	35 16N	58 26 E
Kaseberga	73	55 24N	14 8 E
Kaseda	110	31 25N	130 19 E
Kasempa	127	13 30 S	25 44 E
Kasenga	127	10 20 S	28 45 E
Kasese	126	0 13N	30 3 E
Kasewa	127	14 28 S	28 53 E
Kasganj	95	27 48N	78 42 E
Kashabowie	150	48 40N	90 26W
Kashan	93	34 5N	51 30 E
Kashgar = K'oshin	105	39 29N	75 58 E
Kashihara	111	34 35N	135 37 E
Kashima, Ibaraki, Japan	111	35 58N	140 38 E
Kashima, Saga, Japan	110	33 7N	130 6 E
Kashima-Nada	111	36 0N	140 45 E
Kashimbo	127	11 12 S	26 19 E
Kashin	81	57 20N	37 36 E
Kashipur, Orissa, India	96	19 16N	83 3 E
Kashipur, Ut. P., India	95	29 15N	79 0 E
Kashira	81	54 45N	38 10 E
Kashiwa	111	35 52N	139 59 E
Kashiwazaki	112	37 22N	138 33 E
Kashkasu	85	39 54N	72 44 E
Kashmir □	95	32 44N	74 54 E
Kashmor	94	28 28N	69 32 E
Kashpirovka	81	53 0N	48 30 E
Kashum Tso	99	34 45N	86 0 E
Kashun Noerh	105	42 25N	101 0 E
Kasimov	81	54 55N	41 20 E
Kasing	126	6 15 S	26 58 E
Kaskaskia, R.	158	37 58N	89 57W
Kaskattama, R.	153	57 3N	90 4W
Kaskelan	85	43 20N	76 35 E
Kaskinen (Kaskö)	74	62 22N	21 15 E
Kaskö (Kaskinen)	74	62 22N	21 15 E
Kasli	84	55 53N	60 46 E
Kaslo	152	49 55N	117 0W
Kasmere L.	153	59 34N	101 10W
Kasonawedjo	127	1 50 S	137 41 E
Kasongo	126	4 30 S	26 33 E
Kasongo Lunda	124	6 35 S	17 0 E
Kásos, I.	69	35 20N	26 55 E
Kásos, Stenón	69	35 30N	26 30 E
Kaspi	83	41 54N	44 17 E
Kaspiysk	83	42 52N	47 40 E
Kaspiyskiy	83	45 22N	47 23 E
Kassab ed Doleib	123	13 30N	33 35 E
Kassaba	122	22 40N	29 55 E
Kassala	123	15 23N	36 26 E
Kassala □	123	15 20N	36 26 E
Kassan	85	39 2N	65 35 E
Kassandra	68	40 0N	23 30 E
Kassansay	85	41 15N	71 31 E
Kassel	48	51 19N	9 32 E
Kassinger	122	18 46N	31 51 E
Kassiopi	80	39 48N	19 55 E
Kassue	103	6 58 S	139 21 E
Kastamonu	92	41 25N	33 43 E
Kastav	63	45 22N	14 20 E
Kastélli	69	35 29N	23 38 E
Kastéllion	69	35 12N	25 20 E
Kastellorizon = Megiste	61	36 8N	29 34 E
Kastellou, Ákra	69	35 30N	27 15 E
Kasterlee	47	51 15N	4 59 E
Kastlösa	73	56 26N	16 25 E
Kastó, I.	69	38 35N	20 55 E
Kastóri	69	37 10N	22 17 E
Kastoría	68	40 30N	21 19 E
Kastoría □	68	40 30N	21 15 E
Kastorías	68	40 30N	21 20 E
Kastornoye	81	51 55N	38 2 E
Kástron	68	39 53N	25 8 E

Name	Page	Lat.	Long.
Kastrosikiá	69	39 6N	20 36 E
Kasugai	111	35 12N	136 59 E
Kasukabe	111	35 58N	139 49 E
Kasulu	126	4 37S	30 5 E
Kasulu □	126	4 37S	30 5 E
Kasumi	110	35 38N	134 38 E
Kasumiga-Ura	111	36 0N	140 25 E
Kasumkent	83	41 47N	48 15 E
Kasungu	127	13 0S	33 29 E
Kasur	94	31 5N	74 25 E
Kata	77	58 46N	102 40 E
Kataba	127	16 10S	25 10 E
Katako Kombe	126	3 25S	24 20 E
Katákolon	69	37 38N	21 19 E
Katale	126	4 52S	31 7 E
Katalla	147	60 10N	144 35W
Katama	123	9 35N	38 36 E
Katamatite	141	36 6S	145 41 E
Katanda	126	0 55S	29 21 E
Katanga = Shaba	126	8 0S	25 0 E
Katanghan □	93	36 0N	69 0 E
Katangi	96	21 56N	79 50 E
Katangli	77	51 42N	143 14 E
Katanich	123	6 0N	33 40 E
Katanning	132	33 40S	117 33 E
Katastári	69	37 50N	20 45 E
Katav Ivanovsk	84	54 45N	58 12 E
Katavi Swamps	126	6 50S	31 10 E
Kateríni	68	40 18N	22 37 E
Katesbridge	38	54 18N	6 8W
Katha	99	24 10N	96 30 E
Katherina, Gebel	122	28 30N	33 57 E
Katherine	136	14 27S	132 20 E
Kathiawar, dist.	93	22 20N	71 0 E
Kathua	95	32 23N	75 30 E
Kati	120	12 41N	8 4W
Katiet	102	2 21S	99 44 E
Katihar	95	25 34N	87 36 E
Katima Mulilo	125	17 28S	24 13 E
Katima Mulilo Rapids	128	17 28S	24 13 E
Katimbira	127	12 40S	34 0 E
Katiola	120	8 10N	5 10W
Katkopberg	128	30 0S	20 0 E
Katlanovo	66	41 52N	21 40 E
Katmai Nat. Monument	147	58 30N	155 0W
Katmai, vol.	147	58 20N	154 59W
Katmandu	95	27 45N	85 12 E
Kato Akhaïa	69	38 8N	21 33 E
Kato Stazros	68	40 39N	23 43 E
Katol	96	21 17N	78 38 E
Katompi	124	6 2S	26 23 E
Katonga, R.	126	0 15N	31 50 E
Katoomba	141	33 41S	150 19 E
Katowice	54	50 17N	19 5 E
Katowice □	53	50 15N	19 0 E
Katrine L.	34	56 15N	4 30W
Katrineholm	72	59 9N	16 12 E
Katsepe	129	15 45S	46 15 E
Katsina	121	7 10N	9 20 E
Katsina Ala, R.	121	6 52N	9 40 E
Katsumoto	110	33 51N	129 42 E
Katsuta	111	36 25N	140 31 E
Katsuura	111	35 15N	140 20 E
Katsuyama	111	36 3N	136 30 E
Kattakurgan	85	39 55N	66 15 E
Kattawaz	93	32 48N	68 23 E
Kattawaz-Urgun □	93	32 10N	62 20 E
Kattegat	73	57 0N	11 20 E
Katumba	126	7 40S	25 17 E
Katungu	126	2 55S	40 3 E
Katwa	95	23 30N	89 25 E
Katwijk-aan-Zee	46	52 12N	4 24 E
Katy	54	51 2N	16 45 E
Kau Tao	101	10 6N	99 48 E
Kauai Chan.	147	21 45N	158 50W
Kauai, I.	147	19 30N	155 30W
Kaufakha	90	31 29N	34 40 E
Kaufbeuren	49	47 42N	10 37 E
Kaufman	159	32 35N	96 20W
Kaukauna	156	44 20N	88 13W
Kaukauveld	128	20 0S	20 15 E
Kaukonen	74	67 31N	24 53 E
Kaulille	47	51 11N	5 31 E
Kauliranta	74	66 27N	23 41 E
Kaunas	80	54 54N	23 54 E
Kaunghein	98	25 41N	95 26 E
Kaupulehu	147	19 43N	155 53W
Kaura Namoda	121	12 37N	6 33 E
Kautokeino	74	69 0N	23 4 E
Kavacha	77	60 16N	169 51 E
Kavadarci	66	41 26N	22 3 E
Kavaja	68	41 11N	19 33 E
Kavali	97	14 55N	80 1 E
Kaválla	68	40 57N	24 28 E
Kaválla □	68	41 05N	24 30 E
Kaválla Kólpos	68	40 50N	24 25 E
Kavanayén	174	5 38N	61 48W
Kavarna	67	43 26N	28 22 E
Kavieng	135	2 36S	150 51 E
Kavkaz, Bolshoi	83	42 50N	44 0 E
Kavousi	69	35 7N	25 51 E
Kaw = Caux	175	4 30N	52 15W
Kawa	123	13 42N	32 34 E
Kawachi-Nagano	111	34 28N	135 31 E
Kawagoe	111	35 55N	139 29 E
Kawaguchi	111	35 52N	138 45 E
Kawaihae	147	20 3N	155 50W
Kawaihoa Pt.	147	21 47N	160 12W
Kawaikini, Mt.	147	22 0N	159 30W
Kawakawa	142	35 23S	174 6 E
Kawama	127	9 30S	28 30 E
Kawambwa	127	9 48S	29 3 E
Kawanoe	110	34 1N	133 34 E
Kawarau	143	45 3S	169 0 E
Kawardha	95	22 0N	81 17 E
Kawasaki	111	35 35N	138 42 E
Kawau I.	142	36 25S	174 52 E
Kawene	150	48 45N	91 15W
Kawerau	142	38 7S	176 42 E
Kawhia Harbour	142	38 5S	174 51 E
Kawick Peak	163	37 58N	116 57W
Kawkareik	98	16 33N	98 14 E
Kawlin	98	23 47N	95 41 E
Kawnro	99	22 48N	99 8 E
Kawthaung	101	10 5N	98 36 E
Kawthoolei □ = Kawthuk	98	18 0N	97 30 E
Kawthuk □	98	18 0N	97 30 E
Kawya	98	16 40N	97 50 E
Kay	84	59 57N	52 59 E
Kaya	121	13 25N	1 10W
Kayah □	98	19 15N	97 15 E
Kayaho	107	43 5N	129 46 E
Kayak I.	147	60 0N	144 30W
Kayan	98	16 54N	96 34 E
Kayangulam	97	9 10N	76 33 E
Kaycee	160	43 45N	106 46W
Kayenta	161	36 46N	110 15W
Kayes	120	14 25N	11 30W
Kayima	120	8 54N	11 15W
Kayl	47	49 29N	6 2 E
Kayomba	127	13 11S	24 2 E
Kayoro	121	11 0N	1 28W
Kayrakkumskoye Vdkhr.	85	40 20N	70 0 E
Kayrunnera	139	30 40S	142 30 E
Kaysatskoye	83	49 47N	46 49 E
Kayseri	92	38 45N	35 30 E
Kaysville	160	41 2N	111 58W
Kazachinskoye	77	56 16N	107 36 E
Kazachye	77	70 52N	135 58 E
Kazakh S.S.R. □	85	50 0N	58 0 E
Kazakhstan	84	51 11N	53 0 E
Kazan	81	55 48N	49 3 E
Kazan, R.	153	64 2N	95 30W
Kazanluk	67	42 38N	25 35 E
Kazanskaya	83	49 50N	40 30 E
Kazarman	85	41 24N	73 59 E
Kazatin	82	49 45N	28 50 E
Kazerun	93	29 38N	51 40 E
Kazhim	80	60 21N	51 33 E
Kazi Magomed	83	40 3N	49 0 E
Kazimierza Wielki	54	50 15N	20 30 E
Kazincbarcika	53	48 17N	20 36 E
Kazo	111	36 7N	139 36 E
Kaztalovka	83	49 47N	48 43 E
Kazu	98	25 27N	97 46 E
Kazumba	124	6 25S	22 5 E
Kazvin	92	36 15N	50 0 E
Kazym, R.	76	63 40N	68 30 E
Kcynia	54	53 0N	17 30 E
Ké	120	13 58N	5 18W
Ke-hsi Mansam	98	21 56N	97 50 E
Ke-Macina	120	14 5N	5 20W
Kéa	69	37 35N	24 22 E
Kea	30	50 13N	5 4W
Kéa, I.	69	37 30N	24 22 E
Keaau	147	19 37N	155 3W
Keady	38	54 15N	6 42W
Keal, Loch na	34	56 30N	6 5W
Kealkill	39	51 45N	9 20W
Keams Canyon	161	35 53N	110 9W
Keanae	147	20 52N	156 9W
Kearney	158	40 45N	99 3W
Kearsage, Mt.	162	43 25N	71 51W
Keban	92	38 50N	38 50 E
Kebele	123	12 52N	40 40 E
Kebi	120	9 18N	6 37W
Kebili	119	33 47N	9 0 E
Kebkabiya	117	13 50N	24 0 E
Kebnekaise, mt.	74	67 54N	18 33 E
Kebock Hd.	36	58 1N	6 20W
Kebri Dehar	91	6 45N	44 17 E
Kebumen	103	7 42S	109 40 E
Kecel	53	46 31N	19 16 E
Kechika, R.	152	59 41N	127 12W
Kecskemét	53	46 57N	19 35 E
Kedada	123	5 30N	35 58 E
Kedah □	101	5 50N	100 40 E
Kedainiai	80	55 15N	23 57 E
Kedgwick	151	47 40N	67 20W
Kedia Hill	128	21 28S	24 37 E
Kediri	103	7 51S	112 1 E
Kédougou	120	12 35N	12 10W
Kedzierzyn	54	50 20N	18 12 E
Keefers	152	50 0N	121 40W
Keel	38	53 59N	10 2W
Keelby	33	53 34N	0 15W
Keele	32	53 0N	2 17W
Keele, R.	147	64 15N	127 0W
Keeler	163	36 29N	117 52W
Keeley L.	153	54 54N	108 8W
Keeling Is. = Cocos Is.	142	12 12S	96 54 E
Keelung = Chilung	109	25 3N	121 45 E
Keen, Mt.	37	56 58N	2 54W
Keenagh	38	53 36N	7 50W
Keene, Calif., U.S.A.	163	35 13N	118 33W
Keene, N.H., U.S.A.	162	42 57N	72 17W
Keeper, Mt.	39	52 46N	8 17W
Keer-Weer, C.	138	14 0S	141 32 E
Keerbergen	47	51 1N	4 38 E
Keeten Mastgat	47	51 36N	4 0 E
Keetmanshoop	128	26 35S	18 8 E
Keewatin	158	47 23N	93 0W
Keewatin □	153	63 20N	94 40W
Keewatin, R.	153	56 29N	100 46W
Kefa □	123	6 55N	36 30 E
Kefallinía, I.	69	38 28N	20 30 E
Kefamenanu	103	9 28S	124 38 E
Kefar Ata	90	32 48N	35 7 E
Kefar Etsyon	90	31 39N	35 7 E
Kefar Hasidim	90	32 47N	35 5 E
Kefar Hittim B.	90	32 48N	35 27 E
Kefar Nahum	90	32 54N	35 22 E
Kefar Sava	90	32 11N	34 54 E
Kefar Szold	90	33 11N	35 34 E
Kefar Vitkin	90	32 22N	34 53 E
Kefar Yehezqel	90	32 34N	35 22 E
Kefar Yona	90	32 20N	34 54 E
Kefar Zekharya	90	31 43N	34 57 E
Keffi	121	8 55N	7 43 E
Keflavík	74	64 2N	22 35W
Keg River	152	57 54N	117 7W
Kegalla	97	7 15N	80 21 E
Kegashka	151	50 14N	61 18W
Kegworth	28	52 50N	1 17W
Kehl	49	48 34N	7 50 E
Keighley	32	53 52N	1 54W
Keimaneigh, P. of	39	51 49N	9 17W
Keimoes	128	28 41S	21 0 E
Keiss	37	58 33N	3 6W
Keïta	121	14 46N	5 56 E
Keith, Austral.	140	36 0S	140 20 E
Keith, U.K.	37	57 33N	2 58W
Keith Arm	148	65 20N	122 15W
Kekaygyr	85	40 42N	75 32 E
Kekri	94	26 0N	75 10 E
Kël	77	69 30N	124 10 E
Kelamet	123	16 0N	38 20 E
Kelang	101	3 2N	101 26 E
Kelani Ganga, R.	97	6 58N	79 50 E
Kelantan □	101	5 10N	102 0 E
Kelantan, R.	101	6 13N	102 14 E
Kělcyra	68	40 22N	20 12 E
Keld	32	54 24N	2 11W
Keles, R.	85	41 1N	68 37 E
Kelheim	49	48 58N	11 57 E
Kelibia	119	36 50N	11 3 E
Kellas	37	57 33N	3 23W
Kellé, Congo	124	0 8S	14 38 E
Kellé, Niger	121	14 18N	10 10 E
Keller	160	48 2N	118 44W
Kellerberrin	137	31 36S	117 38 E
Kellett C.	12	72 0N	126 0W
Kellogg	160	47 30N	116 5W
Kelloselkä	74	66 56N	28 53 E
Kells, Ireland	39	52 33N	7 18W
Kells, U.K.	38	54 48N	6 13W
Kells = Ceanannas Mor	38	53 42N	6 53W
Kells, Rhinns of	34	55 9N	4 22W
Kelmentsy	80	48 30N	26 50 E
Kélo	124	9 10N	15 45 E
Kelowna	152	49 50N	119 25W
Kelsale	29	52 15N	1 30 E
Kelsall	32	53 14N	2 44W
Kelsey Bay	152	50 25N	126 0W
Kelso, N.Z.	143	45 54S	169 15 E
Kelso, U.K.	35	55 36N	2 27W
Kelso, U.S.A.	160	46 10N	122 57W
Keltemashat	85	42 25N	70 8 E
Keluang	101	2 3N	103 18 E
Kelvedon	29	51 50N	0 43 E
Kelvington	153	52 10N	103 30W
Kem	78	65 0N	34 38 E
Kem-Kem	118	30 40N	4 30W
Kem, R.	78	64 45N	32 20 E
Kema	103	1 22N	125 8 E
Kemah	92	39 32N	39 5 E
Kemano	152	53 35N	128 0W
Kemapyu	98	18 49N	97 19 E
Kemasik	101	4 25N	103 25 E
Kembolcha	123	11 29N	39 42 E
Kemenets-Podolskiy	82	48 40N	26 30 E
Kemerovo	76	55 20N	85 50 E
Kemi	74	65 44N	24 34 E
Kemi älv = Kemijoki	74	65 47N	24 32 E
Kemijärvi	74	66 43N	27 22 E
Kemijoki	74	65 47N	24 32 E
Kemmel	47	50 47N	2 50 E
Kemmerer	160	41 52N	110 30W
Kemnay	37	57 14N	2 28W
Kemp Coast	13	69 0S	55 0 E
Kemp L.	159	33 45N	99 15W
Kempsey, Austral.	141	31 1S	152 50 E
Kempsey, U.K.	28	52 8N	2 11W
Kempston	29	52 7N	0 30W
Kempt, L.	150	47 25N	74 22W
Kempten	49	47 42N	10 18 E
Kemptville	150	45 0N	75 38W
Ken L.	35	55 0N	4 8W
Kenadsa	118	31 48N	2 26W
Kenai	147	60 35N	151 20W
Kenai Mts.	147	60 0N	150 0W
Kendal, Indon.	103	6 56S	110 14 E
Kendal, U.K.	32	54 19N	2 44W
Kendall	141	31 35S	152 44 E
Kendall, R.	138	14 4S	141 35 E
Kendallville	156	41 25N	85 15W
Kendari	103	3 50S	122 30 E
Kendawangan	102	2 32S	110 17 E
Kende	121	11 30N	4 12 E
Kendenup	137	34 30S	117 38 E
Kendrapara	96	20 35N	86 30 E
Kendrick	160	46 43N	116 41W
Kendrikí Kai Dhitikí Makedhonia □	68	40 30N	22 0 E
Kene Thao	100	17 44N	101 25 E
Kenema	120	7 50N	11 14W
Keng Kok	100	16 26N	105 12 E
Keng Tawng	98	20 45N	98 18 E
Keng Tung, Burma	99	21 0N	99 30 E
Keng Tung, Burma	99	21 0N	99 30 E
Kenge	124	4 50S	16 55 E
Kengeja	126	5 26S	39 45 E
Kengma	108	23 34N	99 24 E
Kenhardt	128	29 19S	21 12 E
Kenilworth	28	52 22N	1 35W
Kenimekh	85	40 16N	65 7 E
Kéninkoumou	120	15 17N	12 18W
Kénitra (Port Lyautey)	118	34 15N	6 40W
Kenmare, Ireland	39	51 52N	9 35W
Kenmare, U.S.A.	158	48 40N	102 4W
Kenmare, R.	39	51 40N	10 0W
Kenmore	37	56 35N	4 0W
Kenn Reef	133	21 12S	155 46 E
Kennebec	158	43 56N	99 54W
Kennedy	127	18 52S	27 10 E
Kennedy, C. = Canaveral, C.	157	28 28N	80 31W
Kennedy, Mt.	148	60 19N	139 0W
Kennedy Ra.	137	24 45S	115 10 E
Kennedy Taungdeik	99	23 35N	94 4 E
Kennet, R.	28	51 24N	1 7W
Kenneth Ra.	137	23 50S	117 8 E
Kennett	159	36 7N	90 0W
Kennett Square	162	39 51N	75 43W
Kennewick	160	46 11N	119 2W
Kenninghall	29	52 26N	1 0 E
Kénogami	151	48 25N	71 15W
Kenogami, R.	150	51 6N	84 28W
Kenora	153	49 50N	94 35W
Kenosha	156	42 33N	87 48W
Kensington, Can.	151	46 28N	63 34W
Kensington, U.S.A.	158	39 48N	99 2W
Kensington Downs	138	22 31S	144 19 E
Kent, Ohio, U.S.A.	156	41 8N	81 20W
Kent, Oreg., U.S.A.	160	45 11N	120 45W
Kent, Tex., U.S.A.	159	31 5N	104 12W
Kent □	29	51 12N	0 40 E
Kent Gr.	138	39 30S	147 20 E
Kent Pen.	148	68 30N	107 0W
Kent Pt.	162	38 50N	76 22W
Kent, Vale of	23	51 12N	0 30 E
Kentau	85	43 32N	68 36 E
Kentdale	137	34 54S	117 3 E
Kentisbeare	30	50 51N	3 18W
Kentland	156	40 45N	87 25W
Kenton, U.K.	30	50 37N	3 28W
Kenton, U.S.A.	156	40 40N	83 35W
Kentucky	141	30 45S	151 28 E
Kentucky □	156	37 20N	85 0W
Kentucky Dam	156	37 2N	88 15W
Kentucky L.	157	36 0N	88 0W
Kentucky, R.	156	38 41N	85 11W
Kentville	151	45 6N	64 29W
Kentwood	159	31 0N	90 30W
Kenya ■	126	2 20N	38 0 E
Kenya, Mt.	126	0 10S	37 18 E
Keo Nena, Deo	100	18 23N	105 10 E
Keokuk	158	40 25N	91 24W
Kep, Camb.	101	10 29N	104 19 E
Kep, Viet.	100	21 24N	106 16 E
Kep-i-Gjuhëzës	68	40 28N	19 15 E
Kep-i-Palit	68	41 25N	19 21 E
Kep-i-Rodonit	68	41 32N	19 30 E
Kepi	103	6 32S	139 19 E
Kepice	54	54 16N	16 51 E
Kepler Mts.	143	45 25S	167 20 E
Kepno	54	51 18N	17 58 E
Keppel B.	133	23 21S	150 55 E
Kepsut	92	39 40N	28 15 E
Kepuhi	147	22 13N	159 21W
Kepulauan, R.	103	5 30S	139 0 E
Kepulauan Sunda, Ketjil Barat □	102	8 50S	117 30 E
Kepulauan Sunda, Ketjil Timor □	103	9 30S	122 0 E
Kerala □	97	11 0N	76 15 E
Kerama-Shotō	112	26 12N	127 22 E
Keran	95	34 35N	73 59 E
Kerang	140	35 40S	143 55 E
Keratéa	69	37 48N	23 58 E
Keraudren, C., Tas., Austral.	136	40 22S	144 47 E
Keraudren, C., W. Austral., Austral.	138	19 58S	119 45 E
Keravat	135	4 17S	152 2 E
Keray	93	26 15N	57 30 E
Kerch	82	45 20N	36 20 E
Kerchinskiy Proliv	82	45 10N	36 30 E
Kerchoual	121	17 20N	0 20 E
Kerem Maharal	90	32 39N	34 59 E
Kerema	135	7 58S	145 50 E
Keren	123	15 45N	38 28 E
Kerewan	120	13 35N	16 10W
Kerguelen I.	11	48 15S	69 10 E
Kerhonkson	162	41 46N	74 11W
Keri	69	37 40N	20 49 E
Keri Kera	123	12 21N	32 37 E
Kericho	126	0 22S	35 15 E
Kericho □	126	0 30S	35 15 E
Kerikeri	143	35 12S	173 59 E
Kerinci	102	2 5S	101 0 E
Kerkdriel	46	51 47N	5 20 E
Kerkenna, Iles	119	34 48N	11 1 E
Kerki	85	37 50N	65 12 E
Kérkira	68	39 38N	19 50 E
Kerkrade	47	50 53N	6 4 E
Kerma	122	19 33N	30 32 E
Kermadec Is.	130	31 8S	175 16W
Kermān	93	30 15N	57 1 E
Kerman	163	36 43N	120 4W

Kermãn □ 93 30 0N 57 0 E
Kermanshah 92 34 23N 47 0 E
Kermanshah □ 92 34 0N 46 30 E
Kerme Körfezi 69 36 55N 27 50 E
Kermen 67 42 30N 26 16 E
Kermit 159 31 56N 103 3W
Kern, R. 163 35 16N 119 18W
Kerns 51 46 54N 8 17 E
Kernville 163 35 45N 118 26W
Keroh 101 5 43N 101 1 E
Kerr, Pt. 142 34 25 S 173 5 E
Kerrera I. 34 56 24N 5 32W
Kerrobert 157 52 0N 109 11W
Kerrville 159 30 1N 99 8W
Kerry 31 52 28N 3 16W
Kerry □ 39 52 7N 9 35W
Kerry Hd. 39 52 26N 9 56W
Kerrysdale 36 57 41N 5 39W
Kersa 123 9 28N 41 48 E
Kerstinbo 72 60 16N 16 58 E
Kerteminde 73 55 28N 10 39 E
Kertosono 103 7 38 S 112 9 E
Keru 123 15 40N 37 5 E
Kerulen, R. 105 48 48N 117 0 E
Kerzaz 118 29 29N 1 25W
Kerzers 50 46 59N 7 12 E
Kesagami L. 150 50 23N 80 15W
Kesagami, R. 150 51 4N 79 45W
Kesan 68 41 49N 26 38 E
Kesch, Piz 51 46 38N 9 53 E
Kesh 38 54 31N 7 43W
Keski Suomen □ 74 62 45N 25 15 E
Kessel, Belg. 47 51 8N 4 38 E
Kessel, Neth. 47 51 17N 6 3 E
Kessel-Lo 47 50 53N 4 43 E
Kessingland 29 52 25N 1 41 E
Kestell 129 28 17 S 28 42 E
Kestenga 78 66 0N 31 50 E
Kesteren 46 51 56N 5 34 E
Keswick 32 54 35N 3 9W
Keszthely 53 46 50N 17 15 E
Keta 121 5 49N 1 0 E
Ketapang 102 1 55 S 110 0 E
Ketchikan 147 55 25N 131 40W
Ketchum 160 43 50N 114 27W
Kete Krachi 121 7 55N 0 1W
Ketef, Khalig Umm el 122 23 40N 35 35 E
Ketelmeer 46 32 36N 5 46 E
Keti Bandar 94 24 8N 67 27 E
Ketri 94 28 1N 75 50 E
Kętrzyn 54 54 7N 21 22 E
Kettering 29 52 24N 0 44W
Kettla, Ness 36 60 3N 1 20W
Kettle Falls 160 48 41N 118 2W
Kettle Ness 33 54 32N 0 41W
Kettle, R. 153 56 23N 94 34W
Kettleman City 163 36 1N 119 58W
Kettlewell 32 54 8N 2 2W
Kety 54 49 51N 19 16 E
Kevin 160 48 45N 111 58W
Kewanee 158 41 18N 90 0W
Kewaunee 156 44 27N 87 30W
Keweenaw B. 156 46 56N 88 23W
Keweenaw Pen. 156 47 30N 88 0W
Keweenaw Pt. 156 47 26N 87 40W
Kexby 33 53 21N 0 41W
Key Harbour 150 45 50N 80 45W
Key, L. 38 54 0N 8 15W
Key West 166 24 40N 82 0W
Keyingham 33 53 42N 0 7W
Keyling Inlet 136 14 50 S 129 40 E
Keymer 29 50 55N 0 5W
Keynsham 28 51 25N 2 30W
Keynshamburg 127 19 15 S 29 40 E
Keyport 162 40 26N 74 12W
Keyser 156 39 26N 79 0W
Keystone, S.D., U.S.A. 158 43 54N 103 27W
Keystone, W. Va., U.S.A. 156 37 30N 81 30W
Keyworth 28 52 52N 1 8W
Kez 84 57 55N 53 46 E
Kezhma 77 59 15N 100 57 E
Kezmarok 53 49 10N 20 28 E
Khabarovo 76 69 30N 60 30 E
Khabarovsk 77 48 20N 135 0 E
Khachmas 83 41 31N 48 42 E
Khachraud 94 23 25N 75 20 E
Khadari, W. el 123 10 35N 26 16 E
Khadro 94 26 11N 68 50 E
Khadyzhensk 83 44 26N 39 32 E
Khadzhilyangar 95 35 45N 79 20 E
Khagaria 95 25 18N 86 32 E
Khaibar 92 25 38N 39 28 E
Khaibor 122 25 49N 39 16 E
Khaipur, Bahawalpur, Pak. 94 29 34N 72 17 E
Khaipur, Hyderabad, Pak. 94 27 32N 68 49 E
Khair 94 27 57N 77 46 E
Khairabad 95 27 33N 80 47 E
Khairagarh 95 21 27N 81 2 E
Khairpur 93 27 32N 68 49 E
Khairpur □ 94 23 30N 69 8 E
Khakhea 125 24 48 S 23 22 E
Khalach 85 38 4N 64 52 E
Khalfallah 118 34 33N 0 16 E
Khalij-e-Fars □ 93 28 20N 51 45 E
Khalilabad 95 26 48N 83 5 E
Khálki 68 39 36N 22 30 E
Khálki, I. 69 36 15N 27 35 E
Khalkidhikí □ 68 40 25N 23 20 E
Khalkís 69 38 27N 23 42 E
Khalmer-Sede = Tazovskiy 76 67 30N 78 30 E
Khalmer Yu 76 67 58N 65 1 E
Khalturin 81 58 40N 48 50 E
Kham Kent 100 18 15N 104 43 E
Khamaria 96 23 10N 80 52 E
Khama's Country 128 21 45 S 26 30 E
Khamba Dzong 99 28 25N 88 30W
Khambhalia 94 22 14N 69 41 E
Khamgaon 96 20 42N 76 37 E
Khammam 96 17 11N 80 6 E
Khãn Yũnis 90 31 21N 34 18 E
Khan Yunus 90 31 21N 34 18 E
Khanabad, Afghan. 93 36 45N 69 5 E
Khanabad, U.S.S.R. 85 40 59N 70 38 E
Khãnaqin 92 34 23N 45 25 E
Khandrá 69 35 3N 26 8 E
Khandwa 96 21 49N 76 22 E
Khandyga 77 62 30N 134 50 E
Khanewal 94 30 20N 71 55 E
Khanga Sidi Nadji 119 34 50N 6 50 E
Khanh Duong 100 12 44N 108 44 E
• Khanh Hung 101 9 36N 105 58 E
Khaniá 69 35 30N 24 4 E
Khaniá □ 69 35 0N 24 0 E
Khanion Kólpos 69 35 33N 23 55 E
Khanka, Oz. 76 45 0N 132 30 E
Khanna 94 30 42N 76 16 E
Khanpur 94 28 42N 70 35 E
Khantau 85 44 13N 73 48 E
Khanty-Mansiysk 76 61 0N 69 0 E
Khapalu 95 35 10N 76 20 E
Kharagpur 95 22 20N 87 25 E
Kharaij 122 21 25N 41 0 E
Kharan Kalat 93 28 34N 65 21 E
Kharanaq 93 32 20N 54 45 E
Kharda 96 18 40N 75 40 E
Khardung La 95 34 20N 77 43 E
Kharfa 92 22 0N 46 35 E
Kharg, Jazireh 92 29 15N 50 28 E
Khârga, El Wâhât el 122 25 0N 30 0 E
Khargon, India 93 21 45N 75 35 E
Khargon, India 96 21 45N 75 40 E
Kharit, Wadi el 122 24 5N 34 10 E
Kharkov 82 49 58N 36 20 E
Kharmanli 67 41 55N 25 55 E
Kharovsk 81 59 56N 40 13 E
Kharsaniya 92 27 10N 49 10 E
Khartoum = El Khartûm 123 15 31N 32 35 E
Khartoum □ 123 16 0N 33 0 E
Khasab 93 26 14N 56 15 E
Khasavyurt 83 43 30N 46 40 E
Khasebake 128 20 42 S 24 29 E
Khash 93 28 15N 61 5 E
Khashm el Girba 123 14 59N 35 58 E
Khasi Hills 98 25 30N 91 30 E
Khaskovo 67 41 56N 25 30 E
Khatanga 77 72 0N 102 20 E
Khatanga, Zaliv 12 66 0N 112 0 E
Khatauli 94 29 17N 77 43 E
Khatyrchi 85 40 2N 65 58 E
Khatyrka 77 62 3N 175 15 E
Khavar □ 92 37 20N 46 0 E
Khavast 85 40 10N 68 49 E
Khawa 122 29 45N 40 25 E
Khaydarken 85 39 57N 71 20 E
Khazzãn Jabal el Awliyâ 123 15 24N 32 20 E
Khe Bo 100 19 8N 104 41 E
Khe Long 100 21 29N 104 46 E
Khed, Maharashtra, India 96 18 51N 73 56 E
Khed, Maharashtra, India 96 17 43N 73 27 E
Khed Brahma 93 24 7N 73 5 E
Khekra 94 28 52N 77 20 E
Khemarak Phouminville 101 11 37N 102 59 E
Khemis Miliana 118 36 11N 2 14 E
Khemisset 118 33 50N 6 1W
Khemmarat 100 16 10N 105 15 E
Khenchela 119 35 28N 7 11 E
Khenifra 118 32 58N 5 46W
Khenmarak Phouminville 102 11 40N 102 58 E
Kherrata 119 36 27N 5 13 E
Kherson 82 46 35N 32 35 E
Khersónisos Akrotíri 69 35 30N 24 10 E
Khetinsiring 99 32 54N 92 50 E
Khiliomódhion 69 37 48N 22 51 E
Khilok 77 51 30N 110 45 E
Khimki 81 55 50N 37 20 E
Khingan, mts. 86 47 0N 119 30 E
Khíos 69 38 27N 26 9 E
Khisar-Momina Banya 67 42 30N 24 44 E
Khiuma = Hiiumaa 80 58 50N 22 45 E
Khiva 76 41 30N 60 18 E
Khiyav 92 38 30N 47 45 E
Khlaouia 118 25 50N 6 32W
Khlong Khlung 100 16 12N 99 43 E
Khlong, R. 101 15 30N 98 50 E
Khmelnitsky 82 49 23N 27 0 E
Khmer Republic ■ = Cambodia 100 12 15N 105 0 E
Khoai, Hon 101 8 26N 104 50 E
Khodzhent 85 40 14N 69 37 E
Khoi 92 38 40N 45 0 E
Khojak P. 93 30 55N 66 30 E
Khok Kloi 101 8 17N 98 19 E
Khok Pho 101 6 43N 101 6 E
Khokholskiy 81 51 35N 38 50 E
Kholm 80 57 10N 31 15 E
*Renamed Soc Trang
Kholmsk 77 35 5N 139 48 E
Khomas Hochland 128 22 40 S 16 0 E
Khomayn 92 33 40N 50 7 E
Khomo 128 21 7 S 24 35 E
Khon Kaen 100 16 30N 102 47 E
Khong, Camb. 101 13 55N 105 56 E
Khong, Laos 100 14 7N 105 51 E
Khong, R., Laos 101 15 0N 106 50 E
Khong, R., Thai. 101 17 45N 104 20 E
Khong Sedone 100 15 34N 105 49 E
Khonh Hung (Soc Trang) 101 9 37N 105 50 E
Khonu 77 66 30N 143 25 E
Khoper, R. 81 52 0N 43 20 E
Khor el 'Atash 123 13 20N 34 15 E
Khóra 69 37 3N 21 42 E
Khóra Sfákion 69 35 15N 24 9 E
Khorasan □ 93 34 0N 58 0 E
Khorat = Nakhon Ratchasima 100 14 59N 102 12 E
Khorat, Cao Nguyen 100 15 30N 102 50 E
Khorat Plat. 101 15 30N 102 50 E
Khorb el Ethel 118 28 44N 6 11W
Khorog 85 37 30N 71 36 E
Khorol 82 49 48N 33 15 E
Khorramabad 92 33 30N 48 25 E
Khorramshahr 92 30 29N 48 15 E
Khota Kota 127 12 55 S 34 15 E
Khotan = Hot'ien 105 37 7N 79 55 E
Khotin 82 48 31N 26 27 E
Khouribga 118 32 58N 6 50W
Khowai 98 24 5N 91 40 E
Khoyniki 80 51 54N 29 55 E
Khrami, R. 83 41 30N 44 30 E
Khrenovoye 81 51 4N 40 6 E
Khristianá, I. 69 36 14N 25 13 E
Khromtau 84 50 17N 58 27 E
Khtapodhiá, I. 69 37 24N 25 34 E
Khu Khan 100 14 42N 104 12 E
Khufaifiya 92 24 50N 44 35 E
Khugiani 94 31 28N 66 14 E
Khulna 98 22 45N 89 34 E
Khulna □ 98 22 45N 89 35 E
Khulo 83 41 33N 42 19 E
Khunzakh 83 42 35N 46 42 E
Khur 93 32 55N 58 18 E
Khurai 94 24 3N 78 23 E
Khurais 92 24 55N 48 5 E
Khurja 94 28 15N 77 58 E
Khurma 92 21 58N 42 3 E
Khũryãn Mũryãn, Jazã 'ir 91 17 30N 55 58 E
Khush 93 32 55N 62 10 E
Khushab 94 32 20N 72 20 E
Khuzdar 94 27 52N 66 30 E
Khuzestan □ 92 31 0N 50 0 E
Khvalynsk 81 52 30N 48 2 E
Khvatovka 81 52 24N 46 32 E
Khvor 93 33 45N 55 0 E
Khvormuj 93 28 40N 51 30 E
Khvoy 92 38 35N 45 0 E
Khvoynaya 80 58 49N 34 28 E
Khwaja Muhammad 93 36 0N 70 0 E
Khyber Pass 94 34 10N 71 8 E
Kiabukwa 127 8 40 S 24 48 E
Kiadho, R. 96 19 50N 76 55 E
Kiama 141 34 40 S 150 50 E
Kiamba 126 6 0N 124 40 E
Kiambi 126 7 15 S 28 0 E
Kiambu 126 1 8 S 36 50 E
Kiangsi □ 109 27 20N 115 40 E
Kiangsu □ 109 33 0N 119 50 E
Kiania 129 20 18 S 47 8 E
Kiaohsien = Chiaohsien 107 36 20N 120 0 E
Kibæk 73 56 2N 8 51 E
Kibanga Port 126 0 10 S 32 58 E
Kibangou 124 3 18 S 12 22 E
Kibara 126 2 8 S 33 30 E
Kibara, Mts. 126 8 25 S 27 10 E
Kibombo 126 3 57 S 25 53 E
Kibondo 126 3 35 S 30 45 E
Kibondo □ 126 4 0 S 30 55 E
Kibumbu 126 3 32 S 29 45 E
Kibungu 126 2 10 S 30 32 E
Kibuye, Burundi 126 3 39 S 29 59 E
Kibuye, Rwanda 126 2 3 S 29 21 E
Kibwesa 126 6 30 S 29 58 E
Kibwezi 124 2 27 S 37 57 E
Kibworth Beauchamp 29 52 33N 0 59W
Kičevo 66 41 34N 20 59 E
Kichiga 77 59 50N 163 5 E
Kicking Horse Pass 152 51 27N 116 25W
Kidal 121 17 50N 1 22 E
Kidderminster 28 52 24N 2 13W
Kidete 126 6 25 S 37 17 E
Kidira 120 14 28N 12 13W
Kidlington 28 51 49N 1 18W
Kidnappers, C. 142 39 38 S 177 5 E
Kidsgrove 32 53 6N 2 15W
Kidston 138 18 52 S 144 8 E
Kidstones 32 54 15N 2 2W
Kidugalle 126 6 49 S 38 15 E
Kidwelly 31 51 44N 4 20W
Kiel 48 54 16N 10 8 E
Kiel Canal = Nord-Ostee-Kanal 48 54 15N 9 40 E
Kielce 54 50 58N 20 42 E
Kielce □ 54 51 0N 20 40 E
Kielder 35 55 14N 2 35W
Kieldrecht 47 51 17N 4 11 E
Kieler Bucht 48 54 30N 10 30 E
Kien Binh 101 9 55N 105 19 E
Kien Hung 101 9 43N 105 17 E
Kien Tan 101 10 7N 105 17 E
Kienchwan 99 26 30N 99 45 E
Kienge 127 10 30 S 27 30 E
Kiessé 121 13 29N 4 1 E
Kieta 135 6 12 S 155 36 E
Kiev = Kiyev 80 50 30N 30 28 E
Kiffa 120 16 50N 11 15W
Kifisiá 69 38 4N 23 49 E
Kifissós, R. 69 38 30N 23 0 E
Kifri 92 34 45N 45 0 E
Kigali 126 1 5 S 30 4 E
Kigarama 126 1 1 S 31 50 E
Kigoma □ 126 5 0 S 30 0 E
Kigoma-Ujiji 126 5 30 S 30 0 E
Kigomasha, Ras 126 4 58 S 38 58 E
Kihee 139 27 23 S 142 37 E
Kihikihi 142 38 2 S 175 22 E
Kii-Hantō 111 34 0N 135 45 E
Kii-Sanchi 111 34 20N 136 0 E
Kijik 147 60 20N 154 20W
Kikai-Jima 112 28 19N 129 58 E
Kikinda 66 45 50N 20 30 E
Kikládhes □ 69 37 0N 25 0 E
Kikládhes, Is. 69 37 20N 24 30 E
Kikoira 141 33 59 S 146 40 E
Kikori 135 7 13 S 144 15 E
Kikori, R. 135 7 5 S 144 0 E
Kikuchi 110 32 59N 130 47 E
Kikwit 124 5 5 S 18 45 E
Kil 72 59 30N 13 20 E
Kilafors 72 61 14N 16 36 E
Kilakarai 97 9 12N 78 47 E
Kilauea 147 22 13N 159 25W
Kilauea Crater 147 19 24N 155 17W
Kilbaha 39 52 35N 9 51W
Kilbeggan 38 53 22N 7 30W
Kilbeheny 39 52 18N 8 13W
Kilbennan 38 53 33N 8 54W
Kilbirnie 34 55 46N 4 42W
Kilbrannan Sd. 34 55 40N 5 23W
Kilbride 39 52 56N 6 5W
Kilbrien 39 52 12N 7 40W
Kilbrittain 39 51 40N 8 42W
Kilbuck Mts. 147 60 30N 160 0W
Kilchberg 51 47 18N 8 33 E
Kilchoan 36 56 42N 6 8W
Kilcock 38 53 24N 6 40W
Kilcoe 39 51 33N 9 26W
Kilcogan 39 53 13N 8 52W
Kilconnell 39 53 20N 8 25W
Kilcoo 38 54 14N 6 1W
Kilcormac 39 53 11N 7 44W
Kilcoy 139 26 59 S 152 30 E
Kilcreggan 34 55 59N 4 50W
Kilcrohane 39 51 35N 9 44W
Kilcullen 39 53 8N 6 45W
Kilcurry 38 54 3N 6 26W
Kildare 39 53 10N 6 50W
Kildare □ 39 53 10N 6 50W
Kildavin 39 52 41N 6 42W
Kildemo 39 52 37N 8 50W
Kildonan 37 58 10N 3 50W
Kildorrery 39 52 15N 8 25W
Kilembe 126 0 15N 30 3 E
Kilfenora 39 53 0N 9 13W
Kilfinan 34 55 57N 5 19W
Kilfinnane 39 52 21N 8 30W
Kilgarvan 39 51 54N 9 28W
Kilgore 159 32 22N 94 40W
Kilham 33 54 4N 0 22W
Kilian Qurghan 93 36 52N 78 3 E
Kilifi 126 3 40 S 39 48 E
Kilifi □ 126 3 30 S 39 40 E
Kilimanjaro □ 126 4 0 S 38 0 E
Kilimanjaro, Mt. 126 3 7 S 37 20 E
Kilinailau, Is. 135 4 45 S 155 20 E
Kilindini 126 4 4 S 39 40 E
Kilis 92 36 50N 37 10 E
Kiliya 82 45 28N 29 16 E
Kilju 107 40 57N 129 25 E
Kilkea 39 52 57N 6 55W
Kilkee 39 52 41N 9 40W
Kilkeel 38 54 4N 6 0W
Kilkelly 38 53 53N 8 50W
Kilkenny 39 52 40N 7 17W
Kilkenny □ 39 52 35N 7 15W
Kilkerrin 38 52 32N 8 36W
Kilkhampton 30 50 53N 4 30W
Kilkieran 39 53 20N 9 45W
Kilkieran B. 38 53 18N 9 45W
Kilkis 68 40 58N 22 57 E
Kilkis □ 68 41 5N 22 50 E
Kilkishen 39 52 49N 8 45W
Kilknock 38 53 42N 8 53W
Kill 39 52 11N 7 20W
Killadoon 38 53 44N 9 53W
Killadysert 39 52 40N 9 7W
Killala 38 54 13N 9 12W
Killala B. 38 54 20N 9 12W
Killaloe 39 52 48N 8 28W
Killam 152 52 47N 111 51W
Killane 39 53 20N 7 6W
Killard, Pt. 38 54 18N 5 31W
Killare 38 53 28N 7 34W
Killarney, Man., Can. 150 49 10N 99 40W
Killarney, Ont., Can. 153 45 55N 81 30W
Killarney, Ireland 39 52 2N 9 30W
Killarney, L's. of 39 52 0N 9 30W
Killary Harb. 38 53 38N 9 52W
Killashandra 38 54 1N 7 32W
Killashee 38 53 40N 7 52W
Killavally 38 53 22N 7 23W
Killavullen 39 52 8N 8 32W

Killchianaig 34 56 2N 5 48W
Killdeer, Can. 153 49 6N 106 22W
Killdeer, U.S.A. 158 47 26N 102 48W
Killeagh 39 51 56N 8 0W
Killean 34 55 38N 5 40W
Killeen 159 31 7N 97 45W
Killeenleigh 39 51 58N 8 49W
Killeigh 39 53 14N 7 27W
Killenaule 39 52 35N 7 40W
Killianspick 39 52 21N 7 18W
Killiecrankie P. 37 56 44N 3 46W
Killimor 39 53 10N 8 17W
Killin 34 56 28N 4 20W
Killiney 39 53 15N 6 8W
Killingdal 71 62 47N 11 26 E
Killinghall 33 54 1N 1 33W
Killini 69 37 55N 21 8 E
Killini, Mts. 69 37 54N 22 25 E
Killinick 39 52 15N 6 29W
Killorglin 39 52 6N 9 48W
Killough 38 54 16N 5 40W
Killtullagh 39 53 17N 8 37W
Killucan 38 53 30N 7 10W
Killurin 39 52 23N 6 35W
Killybegs 38 54 38N 8 26W
Killyleagh 38 54 24N 5 40W
Kilmacolm 34 55 54N 4 39W
Kilmacthomas 39 52 13N 7 27W
Kilmaganny 39 52 26N 7 20W
Kilmaine 38 53 33N 9 10W
Kilmaley 39 52 50N 9 11W
Kilmallock 39 52 22N 8 35W
Kilmaluag 36 57 40N 6 18W
Kilmanagh 39 52 38N 7 28W
Kilmarnock, U.K. 34 55 36N 4 30W
Kilmarnock, U.S.A. 162 37 43N 76 23W
Kilmartin 34 56 8N 5 29W
Kilmaurs 34 55 37N 4 33W
Kilmeaden 39 52 15N 7 15W
Kilmeedy 39 52 25N 8 55W
Kilmelford 34 56 16N 5 30W
Kilmez 84 56 58N 50 55 E
Kilmez, R. 84 56 58N 50 28 E
Kilmichael 39 51 49N 9 4W
Kilmichael Pt. 39 52 44N 6 8W
Kilmihill 39 52 44N 9 18W
Kilmore, Austral. 141 37 25 S 144 53 E
Kilmore, Ireland 39 52 12N 6 35W
Kilmore Quay 39 52 10N 6 36W
Kilmuir 37 57 44N 4 7W
Kilmurry 39 52 47N 9 30W
Kilmurvy 39 53 9N 9 46W
Kilnaleck 38 53 52N 7 21W
Kilninver 34 56 20N 5 30W
Kilombero □ 127 8 0 S 37 0 E
Kilondo 127 9 45 S 34 20 E
Kilosa 126 6 48 S 37 0 E
Kilosa □ 126 6 48 S 37 0 E
Kilpatrick 39 51 46N 8 42W
Kilrea 38 54 58N 6 34W
Kilrenny 35 56 15N 2 40W
Kilronan 39 53 8N 9 40W
Kilrush 39 52 39N 9 30W
Kilsby 28 52 20N 1 11W
Kilsheelan 39 52 23N 7 37W
Kilsmo 72 59 6N 15 35 E
Kilsyth 35 55 58N 4 3W
Kiltamagh 38 53 52N 9 0W
Kiltealy 39 52 34N 6 45W
Kiltegan 39 52 53N 6 35W
Kiltoom 38 53 30N 8 0W
Kilwa □ 127 9 0 S 39 0 E
Kilwa Kisiwani 127 8 58 S 39 32 E
Kilwa Kivinje 127 8 45 S 39 25 E
Kilwa Masoko 127 8 55 S 39 30 E
Kilwinning 34 55 40N 4 41W
Kilworth 39 52 10N 8 15W
Kilworth, mts. 39 52 10N 8 15W
Kim 159 37 18N 103 20W
Kimamba 126 6 45 S 37 10 E
Kimba 140 33 8 S 136 23 E
Kimball, Nebr., U.S.A. 158 41 17N 103 20W
Kimball, S.D., U.S.A. 158 43 47N 98 57W
Kimbe 135 5 33 S 150 11 E
Kimbe B. 135 5 15 S 150 30 E
Kimberley, N.S.W., Austral. 140 32 50 S 141 4 E
Kimberley, W. Australia, Austral. 136 16 20 S 127 0 E
Kimberley, Can. 152 49 40N 115 59W
Kimberley, S. Afr. 128 28 43 S 24 46 E
Kimberley, dist. 132 16 20 S 127 0 E
Kimberley Downs 136 17 24 S 124 22 E
Kimberly 160 42 33N 114 25W
Kimbolton 29 52 17N 0 23W
Kimchŏn 107 36 11N 128 4 E
Kimi 69 38 38N 24 6 E
Kimje 107 35 48N 126 45 E
Kimmeridge, oilfield 19 50 36N 2 6W
Kimolos 69 36 48N 24 37 E
Kimolos, I. 69 36 48N 24 35 E
Kimovsk 81 54 0N 38 29 E
Kimparana 120 12 48N 5 0W
Kimry 81 56 55N 37 15 E
Kimsquit 152 52 45N 126 57W
Kimstad 73 58 35N 15 58 E
Kinabalu, mt. 102 6 0N 116 0 E
Kinaros, I. 69 36 59N 26 15 E
Kinaskan L. 152 57 38N 130 8W
Kinawley 38 54 14N 7 40W
Kinbrace 37 58 16N 3 56W
Kincaid 153 49 40N 107 0W
Kincardine, Can. 150 44 10N 81 40W
Kincardine, Fife, U.K. 35 56 4N 3 43W
Kincardine, Highland, U.K. 37 57 52N 4 20W
Kincardine (□) 26 56 56N 2 28W
Kincraig 37 57 8N 3 57W
Kindersley 153 51 30N 109 10W
Kindia 120 10 0N 12 52W
Kindu 126 2 55 S 25 50 E
Kinel 84 53 15N 50 40 E
Kineshma 81 57 30N 42 5 E
Kinesi 126 1 25 S 33 50 E
Kineton 28 52 10N 1 30W
King and Queen 162 37 42N 76 50W
King City 163 36 11N 121 8W
King Cr. 138 24 35 S 139 30 E
King Edward, R. 136 14 14 S 126 35 E
King Frederick VI Land 12 63 0N 43 0W
King Frederick VIII Land 12 77 30N 25 0W
King George 162 38 15N 77 10W
King George B. 176 51 30 S 60 30W
King George I. 13 60 0 S 60 0W
King George Is. 149 53 40N 80 30W
King George Sd. 132 35 5 S 118 0 E
King I., Austral. 138 39 50 S 144 0 E
King I., Can. 152 52 10N 127 40W
King I. = Kadah Kyun 101 12 30N 98 20 E
King, L. 137 33 10 S 119 35 E
King Leopold Ranges 136 17 20 S 124 20 E
King, Mt. 138 25 10 S 147 30 E
King Sd. 136 16 50 S 123 20 E
King William I. 148 69 10N 97 25W
King William, L. 50 42 14 S 146 15 E
King William's Town 128 32 51 S 27 22 E
Kingairloch, dist. 36 56 37N 5 30W
Kingaroy 139 26 32 S 151 51 E
Kingarrow 38 54 55N 8 5W
Kingarth 34 55 45N 5 2W
Kingfisher 159 35 50N 97 55W
Kinghorn 35 56 4N 3 10W
Kingisepp 80 59 25N 28 40 E
Kingisepp (Kuressaare) 80 58 15N 22 15 E
Kingman, Ariz., U.S.A. 161 35 12N 114 2W
Kingman, Kans., U.S.A. 159 37 41N 96 9W
Kings B. 12 78 0N 15 0 E
Kings Canyon National Park 163 37 0N 118 35W
King's Lynn 29 52 45N 0 25 E
Kings Mountain 157 35 13N 81 20W
Kings Park 162 40 53N 73 16W
King's Peak 160 40 46N 110 27W
King's, R. 39 52 32N 7 12W
Kings, R. 163 36 10N 119 50W
King's Sutton 28 52 1N 1 16W
King's Worthy 28 51 6N 1 18W
Kingsbarns 35 56 18N 2 40W
Kingsbridge 30 50 17N 3 46W
Kingsburg 163 36 35N 119 36W
Kingsbury 28 52 33N 1 41W
Kingscote 140 35 33 S 137 31 E
Kingscourt 38 53 55N 6 48W
Kingskerswell 30 50 30N 3 34W
Kingsland 28 52 15N 2 49W
Kingsley 158 42 37N 95 58W
Kingsley Dam 158 41 20N 101 40W
Kingsport 157 36 33N 82 36W
Kingsteignton 30 50 32N 3 35W
Kingston, Can. 150 44 14N 76 30W
Kingston, Jamaica 166 18 0N 76 50W
Kingston, N.Z. 143 45 20 S 168 43 E
Kingston, U.K. 28 51 23N 1 40W
Kingston, N.Y., U.S.A. 162 41 55N 74 0W
Kingston, Pa., U.S.A. 162 41 19N 75 58W
Kingston, R.I., U.S.A. 162 41 29N 71 30W
Kingston South East 140 36 51 S 139 55 E
Kingston-upon-Thames 29 51 23N 0 20W
Kingstown, Austral. 141 30 29 S 151 6 E
Kingstown, St. Vinc. 167 13 10N 61 10W
Kingstree 157 33 40N 79 48W
Kingsville, Can. 150 42 2N 82 45W
Kingsville, U.S.A. 159 27 30N 97 53W
Kingswear 30 50 21N 3 33W
Kingswood 28 51 26N 2 31W
Kington 28 52 12N 3 2W
Kingtung 99 24 30N 100 50 E
Kingussie 37 47 5N 4 2W
Kinistino 153 52 57N 105 2W
Kinkala 124 4 18 S 14 49 E
Kinki □ 111 35 0N 135 30 E
Kinleith 142 38 20 S 175 56 E
Kinloch, N.Z. 143 44 51 S 168 20 E
Kinloch, L. More, U.K. 37 58 17N 4 50W
Kinloch, Rhum, U.K. 36 57 0N 6 18W
Kinloch Rannoch 37 56 41N 4 12W
Kinlochbervie 36 58 28N 5 5W
Kinlochewe 36 57 37N 5 20W
Kinlochiel 36 56 52N 5 20W
Kinlochleven 36 56 42N 4 59W
Kinlochmoidart 36 56 47N 5 43W
Kinloss 37 57 38N 3 37W
Kinlough 38 54 27N 8 16W
Kinn 71 61 34N 4 45 E
Kinna 73 57 32N 12 42 E
Kinnaird 152 49 17N 117 39W
Kinnaird's Hd. 37 57 40N 2 0W
Kinnared 73 57 2N 13 7 E
Kinnegad 38 53 28N 7 8W
Kinneret 90 32 44N 35 34 E
Kinneret, Yam 90 32 45N 35 35 E
Kinneviken, B. 73 58 38N 18 20 E
Kinnitty 39 53 6N 7 44W
Kino 164 28 45N 111 59W
Kinoje, R. 150 52 8N 81 25W
Kinomoto 111 35 30N 136 13 E
Kinoni, C. Afr. 123 5 40N 26 10 E
Kinoni, Uganda 126 0 41 S 30 28 E
Kinping 101 22 56N 103 15 E
Kinrooi 47 51 9N 5 45 E
Kinross 35 56 13N 3 25W
Kinross (□) 26 56 13N 3 25W
Kinsale 39 51 42N 8 31W
Kinsale Harbour 39 51 40N 8 30W
Kinsale Head, gasfield 19 51 20N 8 0W
Kinsale Old Hd. 39 51 37N 8 32W
Kinsarvik 71 60 22N 6 43 E
Kinshasa 124 4 20 S 15 15 E
Kinsley 159 37 57N 99 30W
Kinston 157 35 18N 77 35W
Kintampo 121 8 5N 1 41W
Kintap 102 3 51 S 115 13 E
Kintaravay 36 58 4N 6 42W
Kintore 37 57 14N 2 20W
Kintore Ra. 137 23 15 S 128 47 E
Kintyre, Mull of 34 55 17N 5 4W
Kintyre, pen. 34 55 30N 5 35W
Kinu 98 22 46N 95 37 E
Kinu-Gawa, R. 111 35 36N 139 57 E
Kinushseo, R. 150 55 15N 83 45W
Kinuso 152 55 25N 115 25W
Kinvara 39 53 8N 8 57W
Kinyangiri 126 4 35 S 34 37 E
Kióni 69 38 27N 20 41 E
Kiosk 150 46 6N 78 53W
Kiowa, Kans., U.S.A. 159 37 3N 98 30W
Kiowa, Okla., U.S.A. 159 34 45N 95 50W
Kipahigan L. 153 55 20N 101 55W
Kipanga 126 6 15 S 35 20 E
Kiparissia 69 37 15N 21 40 E
Kiparissiakós Kólpos 69 37 25N 21 25 E
Kipawa Res. Prov. Park 150 47 0N 78 30W
Kipembawe 124 7 38 S 33 27 E
Kipengere Ra. 127 9 12 S 34 15 E
Kipili 126 7 28 S 30 32 E
Kipini 126 2 30 S 40 32 E
Kipling 153 50 6N 102 38W
Kipnuk 147 59 55N 164 7W
Kippen 34 56 8N 4 12W
Kippure, Mt. 39 53 11N 6 23W
Kipushi 127 11 48 S 27 12 E
Kir 124 1 29 S 19 25 E
Kirandul 96 18 33N 81 10 E
Kiratpur 94 29 32N 78 12 E
Kirchberg 50 47 5N 7 35 E
Kirchhain 48 50 49N 8 54 E
Kirchheim 49 48 38N 9 20 E
Kirchheim Bolanden 49 49 40N 8 0 E
Kirchschlag 53 47 30N 16 19 E
Kircubbin 38 54 30N 5 33W
Kirensk 77 57 50N 107 55 E
Kirgiz S.S.R. □ 85 42 0N 75 0 E
Kirgiziya Steppe 79 50 0N 55 0 E
Kiri 124 1 29 S 19 25 E
Kiriburu 96 22 0N 85 0 E
Kirikkale 92 39 51N 33 32 E
Kirikopuni 142 35 50 S 174 1 E
Kirillov 81 59 51N 38 14 E
Kirin □ 107 43 50N 125 45 E
Kirindi, R. 97 6 15N 81 20 E
Kirishi 80 51 28N 31 59 E
Kirishima-Yama 110 31 58N 130 55 E
Kiriwina Is. = Trobriand Is. 138 8 40 S 151 0 E
Kirk Michael 32 54 17N 4 35W
Kirkbean 35 54 56N 3 35W
Kirkbride 32 54 54N 3 13W
Kirkburton 33 53 36N 1 42W
Kirkby 32 53 29N 2 54W
Kirkby-in-Ashfield 33 53 6N 1 15W
Kirkby Lonsdale 32 54 13N 2 36W
Kirkby Malzeard 33 54 10N 1 38W
Kirkby Moorside 33 54 16N 0 56W
Kirkby Steven 32 54 27N 2 23W
Kirkby Thore 32 54 38N 2 34W
Kirkcaldy 35 56 7N 3 10W
Kirkcolm 34 54 59N 5 4W
Kirkconnel 35 55 23N 4 0W
Kirkcowan 34 54 53N 4 38W
Kirkcudbright 35 54 50N 4 3W
Kirkcudbright (□) 26 55 4N 4 0W
Kirkcudbright B. 35 54 46N 4 0W
Kirkeby 73 55 7N 8 33 E
Kirkee 96 18 34N 73 56 E
Kirkenær 71 60 27N 12 3 E
Kirkenes 74 69 40N 30 5 E
Kirkham 32 53 47N 2 53W
Kirkinner 34 54 59N 4 28W
Kirkintilloch 35 55 57N 4 10W
Kirkjubæjarklaustur 74 63 47N 18 4W
Kirkland, Ariz., U.S.A. 161 34 29N 112 46W
Kirkland, Wash., U.S.A. 160 47 40N 122 10W
Kirkland Lake 150 48 9N 80 2W
Kırklareli 67 41 44N 27 15 E
Kirkliston 35 55 55N 3 27W
Kirkliston Ra. 143 44 25 S 170 34 E
Kirkmichael 37 56 43N 3 31W
Kirkoswald 32 54 46N 2 41W
Kirkoswold 34 55 19N 4 48W
Kirkstone P. 32 54 29N 2 55W
Kirksville 158 40 8N 92 35W
Kirkuk 92 35 30N 44 21 E
Kirkwall 37 58 59N 2 59W
Kirkwhelpington 35 55 9N 2 0W
Kirkwood 128 33 22 S 25 15 E
Kirlampudi 96 17 12N 82 12 E
Kirn 49 49 46N 7 29 E
Kirov, R.S.F.S.R., U.S.S.R. 81 54 3N 34 12 E
Kirov, R.S.F.S.R., U.S.S.R. 84 58 35N 49 40 E
Kirovabad 83 40 45N 46 10 E
Kirovakan 83 41 0N 44 0 E
Kirovo 85 40 26N 70 36 E
Kirovo-Chepetsk 81 58 28N 50 0 E
Kirovograd 82 48 35N 32 20 E
Kirovsk, R.S.F.S.R., U.S.S.R. 78 67 48N 33 50 E
Kirovsk, Ukraine, U.S.S.R. 83 48 35N 38 30 E
Kirovski 83 45 51N 48 11 E
Kirovskiy 85 44 52N 78 12 E
Kirovskoye 85 42 39N 71 35 E
Kirriemuir, Can. 153 51 56N 110 20W
Kirriemuir, U.K. 37 56 41N 3 0W
Kirs 84 59 21N 52 14 E
Kirsanov 81 52 35N 42 40 E
Kirşehir 92 39 14N 34 5 E
Kirstonia 128 25 30 S 23 45 E
Kirtachi 121 12 52N 2 30 E
Kirthar Range 93 27 0N 67 0 E
Kirtling 29 52 11N 0 27 E
Kirtlington 28 51 54N 1 9W
Kirton 39 52 56N 0 3W
Kirton-in-Lindsey 33 53 29N 0 35W
Kiruna 74 67 52N 20 15 E
Kirundu 124 0 50 S 25 35 E
Kirup 137 33 40 S 115 50 E
Kiryū 111 36 24N 139 20 E
Kiryu 81 55 5N 46 45 E
Kirzhach 81 56 12N 38 50 E
Kisa 73 58 0N 15 39 E
Kisaga 126 4 30 S 34 23 E
Kisalaya 166 14 40N 84 3W
Kisámou, Kólpos 69 35 30N 23 38 E
Kisanga 126 2 30N 26 35 E
Kisangani 126 0 35N 25 15 E
Kisar, I. 103 8 5 S 127 10 E
Kisaran 102 2 47N 99 29 E
Kisarawe 126 6 53 S 39 0 E
Kisarawe □ 126 7 3 S 39 0 E
Kisarazu 111 35 23N 139 55 E
Kisbér 53 47 30N 18 0 E
Kiselevsk 76 54 5N 86 6 E
Kishanganga, R. 95 34 50N 74 15 E
Kishanganj 95 26 3N 88 14 E
Kishangarh 94 27 50N 70 30 E
Kishi 121 9 1N 3 45 E
Kishinev 82 47 0N 28 50 E
Kishinoi 82 47 1N 28 50 E
Kishiwada 111 34 28N 135 22 E
Kishkeam 39 52 15N 9 12 E
Kishon 90 32 33N 35 12 E
Kishorganj 98 24 26N 90 40 E
Kishorn L. 36 57 22N 5 40W
Kishtwar 95 33 20N 75 48 E
Kisii 126 0 40 S 34 45 E
Kisii □ 126 0 40 S 34 45 E
Kisiju 124 7 23 S 39 19 E
Kısır, Dağ 83 41 0N 43 5 E
Kisizi 126 1 0 S 29 58 E
Kiska I. 147 52 0N 177 30 E
Kiskatinaw, R. 152 56 8N 120 10W
Kiskittogisu L. 153 54 13N 98 20W
Kiskomárom = Zalakomár 53 46 33N 17 10 E
Kiskőrös 53 46 37N 19 20 E
Kiskundorozsma 53 46 16N 20 5 E
Kiskunfelégyháza 53 46 42N 19 53 E
Kiskunhalas 53 46 28N 19 37 E
Kiskunmajsa 53 46 30N 19 48 E
Kislovodsk 83 43 50N 42 45 E
Kismayu 113 0 20 S 42 30 E
Kiso-Gawa, R. 111 35 2N 136 45 E
Kiso-Sammyaku 111 35 30N 137 45 E
Kisofukushima 111 35 52N 137 43 E
Kisoro 126 1 17 S 29 48 E
Kispest 53 47 27N 19 9 E
Kissidougou 120 9 5N 10 0W
Kissimmee 157 28 18N 81 22W
Kissimmee, R. 157 27 20N 81 0W
Kississing L. 153 55 34N 100 47W
Kistanje 63 43 58N 15 55 E
Kisterenye 53 48 3N 19 50 E
Kisújszállás 53 47 12N 20 50 E
Kisuki 110 35 17N 132 54 E
Kisumu 126 0 3 S 34 45 E
Kisvárda 53 48 14N 22 4 E
Kiswani 126 4 5 S 37 57 E
Kiswere 127 9 27 S 39 30 E
Kit Carson 158 38 48N 102 45W
Kita 120 13 5N 9 25W
Kita-Ura 111 36 0N 140 34 E
Kitab 85 39 7N 66 52 E
Kitakami, R. 112 38 25N 141 19 E
Kitakyūshū 110 33 50N 130 50 E
Kitale 126 1 0N 35 12 E
Kitami 112 43 48N 143 54 E
Kitangiri, L. 126 4 5 S 34 20 E
Kitano-Kaikyō 110 34 17N 134 58 E
Kitaya 127 10 38 S 40 8 E
Kitchener, Austral. 137 30 55 S 124 8 E
Kitchener, Can. 150 43 27N 80 29W
Kitchigami, R. 150 50 35N 78 5W
Kitega = Citega 126 3 30 S 29 58 E
Kiteto □ 126 5 0 S 37 0 E
Kitgum Matidi 126 3 17N 32 52 E
Kíthira 69 36 9N 23 0 E
Kíthira, I. 69 36 8N 23 0 E
Kíthnos 69 37 26N 24 27 E

Kíthnos, I. **69** 37 25N 24 25 E
Kitimat **152** 54 3N 128 38W
Kitinen, R. **74** 67 34N 26 40 E
Kitiyab **123** 17 13N 33 35 E
Kitros **68** 40 22N 22 34 E
Kitsuki **110** 33 35N 131 37 E
Kittakittaooloo, L. **139** 28 3 S 138 14 E
Kittanning **156** 40 49N 79 30W
Kittatinny Mts. **162** 41 0N 75 0W
Kittery **162** 43 7N 70 42W
Kitui **126** 1 17 S 38 0 E
Kitui □ **126** 1 30 S 38 25 E
Kitwe **127** 12 54 S 28 7 E
Kitzbühel **52** 47 27N 12 24 E
Kitzingen **49** 49 44N 10 9 E
Kivalina **147** 67 45N 164 40W
Kivalo **74** 66 18N 26 0 E
Kivarli **94** 24 33N 72 46 E
Kivotós **68** 40 13N 21 26 E
Kivu □ **126** 3 10 S 27 0 E
Kivu, L. **126** 1 48 S 29 0 E
Kiwai I. **135** 8 35 S 143 30 E
Kiyev **80** 50 30N 30 28 E
Kiyevskoye Vdkhr. **80** 51 0N 30 0 E
Kizel **84** 59 3N 57 40 E
Kiziguru **126** 1 46 S 30 23 E
Kizil Jilga **95** 35 26N 79 50 E
Kizil Kiya **76** 40 20N 72 35 E
Kızılcahaman **82** 40 30N 32 30 E
Kızılırmak **83** 39 15N 36 0 E
Kizilskoye **84** 52 44N 58 54 E
Kizimkazi **126** 6 28 S 39 30 E
Kizlyar **83** 43 51N 46 40 E
Kizyl-Arvat **76** 38 58N 56 15 E
Kjellerup **73** 56 17N 9 25 E
Klabat, Teluk **102** 1 30 S 105 40 E
Kladanj **66** 44 14N 18 42 E
Kladnica **66** 43 23N 20 2 E
Kladno **52** 50 10N 14 7 E
Kladovo **66** 44 36N 22 33 E
Klaeng **100** 12 47N 101 39 E
Klagenfurt **52** 46 38N 14 20 E
Klagerup **73** 55 36N 13 17 E
Klagshamn **73** 55 32N 12 53 E
Klagstorp **73** 55 22N 13 23 E
Klaipeda **80** 55 43N 21 10 E
Klakring **73** 55 42N 9 59 E
Klamath Falls **160** 42 20N 121 50W
Klamath Mts. **160** 41 20N 123 0W
Klamath, R. **160** 41 40N 123 30W
Klang = Kelang **101** 3 1N 101 33 E
Klangklang **98** 22 41N 93 26 E
Klanjec **63** 46 3N 15 45 E
Klappan, R. **152** 58 0N 129 43W
Klarälven **72** 60 32N 13 15 E
Klaten **103** 7 43 S 110 36 E
Klatovy **52** 49 23N 13 18 E
Klawak **152** 55 35N 133 0W
Klawer **128** 31 44 S 18 36 E
Klazienaveen **46** 52 44N 7 0 E
Kłecko **54** 52 38N 17 25 E
Kleczew **54** 52 22N 18 9 E
Kleena Kleene **152** 52 0N 124 50W
Klein **160** 46 26N 108 31W
Klein-Karas **128** 27 33 S 18 7 E
Klein Karoo **128** 33 45 S 21 30 E
Kleine Gette, R. **47** 50 51N 5 6 E
Kleine Nete, R. **47** 51 12N 4 46 E
KlekovaCa, mt. **63** 44 25N 16 32 E
Klemtu **152** 52 35N 128 55W
Klenovec, Czech. **53** 48 36N 19 54 E
Klenovec, Yugo. **66** 31 32N 20 49 E
Klepp **71** 59 48N 5 36 E
Klerksdorp **128** 26 51 S 26 38 E
Kletnya **80** 53 30N 33 2 E
Kletsk **80** 53 5N 26 45 E
Kletskiy **83** 49 20N 43 0 E
Kleve **48** 51 46N 6 10 E
Klickitat **160** 45 50N 12 10W
Klimovichi **80** 53 36N 32 0 E
Klin **81** 56 28N 36 48 E
Klinaklini, R. **152** 51 21N 125 40W
Klinte **73** 53 35N 10 12 E
Klintehamn **73** 57 22N 18 12 E
Klintsey **80** 52 50N 32 10 E
Klipplaat **128** 33 0 S 24 22 E
Klisura **67** 42 40N 24 28 E
Klitmøller **73** 57 3N 8 30 E
Kljajićevo **66** 45 45N 19 17 E
Ključ **63** 44 32N 16 48 E
Kłobuck **54** 50 55N 19 5 E
Kłodzko **54** 50 28N 16 38 E
Kloetinge **47** 51 30N 3 56 E
Klondike **147** 64 0N 139 26W
Kloosterzande **47** 51 22N 4 1 E
Klosi **68** 41 28N 20 10 E
Klosterneuburg **53** 48 18N 16 19 E
Klosters **51** 46 52N 9 52 E
Kloten, Sweden **72** 59 54N 15 19 E
Kloten, Switz. **51** 47 27N 8 35 E
Klötze **48** 52 38N 11 9 E
Klouto **121** 6 57N 0 44 E
Klovborg **73** 55 56N 9 30 E
Klövsjöfj, mt. **72** 62 36N 13 57 E
Kluane, L. **147** 61 15N 138 40W
Kluang = Keluang **101** 1 59N 103 20 E
Kluczbork **54** 50 58N 18 12 E
Klundert **47** 51 40N 4 32 E
Klyuchevskaya, Guba **83** 55 50N 160 30 E
Kmelnitski **80** 49 23N 27 0 E
Knapdale, dist. **34** 55 55N 5 30W
Knaresborough **33** 54 1N 1 29W
Knebworth **29** 51 52N 0 11W
Knee L., Man., Can. **153** 55 3N 94 45W
Knee L., Sask., Can. **153** 55 51N 107 0W
Knesselare **47** 51 9N 3 26 E
Knezha **67** 43 30N 23 56 E
Knic **66** 43 53N 20 45 E
Knight Inlet **152** 50 45N 125 40W
Knighton **31** 52 21N 3 2W
Knights Ferry **163** 37 50N 120 40W
Knight's Landing **160** 38 50N 121 43W
Knin **63** 44 1N 16 17 E
Knittelfeld **52** 47 13N 14 51 E
Knjazevac **66** 43 35N 22 18 E
Knob, C. **137** 34 32 S 119 16 E
Knock **38** 53 48N 8 55W
Knockananna **39** 52 52N 6 34W
Knockhoy Mt. **39** 51 49N 9 27W
Knocklayd Mt. **38** 55 10N 6 15W
Knocklofty **39** 52 20N 7 49W
Knockmahon **39** 52 8N 7 21W
Knockmealdown Mts. **39** 52 16N 8 0W
Knocknaskagh Mt. **39** 52 7N 8 25W
Knokke **47** 51 20N 3 17 E
Knott End **32** 53 55N 3 0W
Knottingley **33** 53 42N 1 15W
Knowle **28** 52 23N 1 43W
Knox **156** 41 18N 86 36W
Knox, C. **152** 54 11N 133 5W
Knox City **159** 33 26N 99 38W
Knox Coast **13** 66 30 S 108 0 E
Knoxville, Iowa, U.S.A. **158** 41 20N 93 5W
Knoxville, Pa., U.S.A. **157** 41 57N 77 26W
Knoxville, Tenn., U.S.A. **157** 35 58N 83 57W
Knoydart, dist. **36** 57 3N 5 33W
Knurów **54** 50 13N 18 38 E
Knutsford **32** 53 18N 2 22W
Knutshø **71** 62 18N 9 41 E
Knysna **128** 34 2 S 23 2 E
Knyszyn **54** 53 20N 22 56 E
Ko Chang **101** 12 0N 102 20 E
Ko Ho, R. **109** 32 58N 117 13 E
Ko Kha **100** 18 11N 99 24 E
Ko Kut **101** 11 40N 102 32 E
Ko Phangan **101** 9 45N 100 10 E
Ko Phra Thong **101** 9 6N 98 15 E
Kō-Saki **110** 34 5N 129 13 E
Ko Samui **101** 9 30N 100 0 E
Koartac (Notre Dame de Koartac) **149** 61 5N 69 36 E
Koba, Aru, Indon. **103** 6 37 S 134 37 E
Koba, Bangka, Indon. **102** 2 26 S 106 14 E
Kobarid **63** 46 15N 13 30 E
Kobayashi **110** 31 56N 130 59 E
Kōbe **111** 34 45N 135 10 E
Kobelyaki **82** 49 11N 34 9 E
København **73** 55 41N 12 34 E
Koblenz, Ger. **49** 50 21N 7 36 E
Koblenz, Switz. **50** 47 37N 8 14 E
Kobo **123** 12 2N 39 56 E
Kobrin **80** 52 15N 24 22 E
Kobroor, Kepulauan **103** 6 10 S 134 30 E
Kobuchizawa **111** 35 52N 138 19 E
Kobuk **147** 66 55N 157 0W
Kobuk, R. **147** 66 55N 157 0W
Kobuleti **83** 41 55N 41 45 E
Kobylin **54** 51 43N 17 12 E
Kobyłka **54** 52 21N 21 10 E
Kobylkino **81** 54 8N 43 46 E
Kobylnik **80** 54 58N 26 39 E
Kočani **66** 41 55N 22 25 E
Koçarli **69** 37 45N 27 43 E
Koceljevo **66** 44 28N 19 50 E
Kočevje **63** 45 39N 14 50 E
Kochang **107** 35 41N 127 55 E
Kochas **95** 25 15N 83 56 E
Kōchi **110** 33 30N 133 35 E
Kōchi-Heiya **110** 33 28N 133 30 E
Kōchi-ken □ **110** 33 40N 133 30 E
Kochiu **108** 23 25N 103 7 E
Kochkor-Ata **85** 41 1N 72 29 E
Kochkorka **85** 42 13N 75 46 E
Kodaikanai **97** 10 13N 77 32 E
Kodaira **111** 35 44N 139 29 E
Koddiyar Bay **97** 8 33N 81 15 E
Kodiak **147** 57 30N 152 45W
Kodiak I. **147** 57 30N 152 45W
Kodiang **101** 6 21N 100 18 E
Kodinar **94** 20 46N 70 46 E
Kodori, R. **83** 43 0N 41 40 E
Koekelare **47** 51 5N 2 59 E
K'oerch'inyuich-'iench'i **107** 46 5N 122 5 E
Koerhmu **105** 36 22N 94 55 E
Koersel **47** 51 3N 5 17 E
Koes **125** 26 0 S 19 15 E
Köflach **13** 47 4N 15 4 E
Koforidua **121** 6 3N 0 17W
Kōfu **111** 35 40N 138 30 E
Koga **111** 36 11N 139 43 E
Kogaluk, R. **151** 56 12N 61 44W
Kogan **139** 27 2 S 150 40 E
Kogin Baba **121** 7 55N 11 35 E
Kogizman **92** 40 5N 43 10 E
Kogon **121** 11 20N 14 32W
Kogota **112** 38 33N 141 3 E
Koh-i-Bab, mts. **93** 34 30N 67 0 E
Koh-i-Khurd **94** 33 30N 65 59 E
Koh-i-Mazar **94** 32 30N 66 25 E
Kohat **94** 33 40N 71 29 E
Kohima **98** 25 35N 94 10 E
Kohler Ra. **13** 77 0N 110 0W
Kohtla-Järve **80** 59 20N 27 20 E
Kohukohu **142** 36 31 S 173 38 E
Koindong **107** 40 28N 126 18 E
Kojabuti **103** 2 36 S 140 37 E
Kojetin **53** 49 21N 17 20 E
Kojima **110** 34 20N 133 38 E
Kōjo **110** 34 33N 133 55 E
Kojō **107** 38 58N 127 58 E
Kojonup **137** 33 48 S 117 10 E
Kok Yangak **85** 41 2N 73 12 E
Koka **122** 20 5N 30 35 E
Kokand **85** 40 30N 70 57 E
Kokanee Glacier Prov. Park **152** 49 47N 117 10W
Kokas **103** 2 42 S 132 26 E
Kokava **53** 48 35N 19 50 E
Kokchetav **76** 53 20N 69 10 E
Kokemäenjoki **75** 61 32N 21 44 E
Kokemäenjoki = Kumo älv **75** 61 32N 21 44 E
Kokhma **81** 56 55N 41 18 E
Kokkola (Gamlakarleby) **74** 63 50N 23 8 E
Koko, Mid-Western, Nigeria **121** 6 5N 5 28 E
Koko, North-Western, Nigeria **121** 11 28N 4 29 E
Koko Kyunzu **101** 14 10N 93 25 E
Koko-Nor = Ch'ing Hai **105** 37 0N 100 20 E
Koko Shili **99** 35 20N 91 0 E
Kokoda **135** 8 54 S 147 47 E
Kokolopozo **120** 5 8N 6 5W
Kokomo **156** 40 30N 86 6W
Kokopo **135** 4 22 S 152 19 E
Kokoro **121** 14 12N 0 55 E
Kokoura **77** 71 35N 144 50 E
Koksan **107** 38 46N 126 40 E
Koksengir, Gora **85** 44 21N 65 6 E
Koksoak, R. **149** 54 5N 64 10W
Kokstad **125** 30 32 S 29 29 E
Kokubu **110** 31 44N 130 46 E
Kola **78** 68 45N 33 8 E
Kola, I. **103** 5 35 S 134 30 E
Kola Pen. = Kolskiy P-ov. **78** 67 30N 38 0 E
Kolagede **103** 7 54 S 110 26 E
Kolahoi **95** 34 12N 75 22 E
Kolahun **120** 8 15N 10 4W
Kolaka **103** 4 3 S 121 46 E
K'olamai **105** 45 30N 84 55 E
K'olan **106** 38 43N 111 32 E
Kolar **97** 13 12N 78 15 E
Kolar Gold Fields **97** 12 58N 78 16 E
Kolari **74** 67 20N 23 48 E
Kolarovgrad **67** 43 27N 26 42 E
Kolarovo **53** 47 56N 18 0 E
Kolašin **66** 42 50N 19 31 E
Kolayat **93** 27 50N 72 50 E
Kolby **73** 55 49N 10 33 E
Kolby Kås **73** 55 48N 10 32 E
Kolchugino **81** 56 17N 39 22 E
Kolda **120** 12 55N 14 50W
Koldewey I. **12** 77 0N 18 0W
Kolding **73** 55 30N 9 29 E
Kole **124** 3 16 S 22 42 E
Koléa **118** 36 38N 2 46 E
*Kolepom, Pulau **103** 8 0 S 138 30 E
Kölfors **72** 62 9N 16 30 E
Kolguyev, Ostrov **78** 69 20N 48 30 E
Kolham **46** 53 11N 6 44 E
Kolhapur **96** 16 43N 74 15 E
Kolia **120** 9 46N 6 28W
Kolin **52** 50 2N 15 9 E
Kolind **73** 56 21N 10 34 E
Kölleda **48** 51 11N 11 14 E
Kollegal **97** 12 9N 77 9 E
Kolleru L. **96** 16 40N 81 10 E
Kollum **46** 53 17N 6 10 E
Kolmanskop **128** 26 45 S 15 14 E
Köln **48** 50 56N 6 58 E
Koło **54** 52 14N 18 40 E
Kołobrzeg **54** 54 10N 15 35 E
Kologriv **81** 58 48N 44 25 E
Kolokani **120** 13 35N 7 45W
Kolomna **81** 55 8N 38 45 E
Kolomyya **82** 48 31N 25 2 E
Kolondiéba **120** 11 5N 6 54W
Kolonodale **103** 2 3 S 121 25 E
Kolosib **98** 24 15N 92 45 E
Kolpashevo **76** 58 20N 83 5 E
Kolpino **80** 59 44N 30 39 E
Kolpny **81** 52 12N 37 10 E
Kolskiy Poluostrov **78** 67 30N 38 0 E
Kolskiy Zaliv **78** 69 23N 34 0 E
Koltubanovskiy **84** 52 57N 52 2 E
Kolubara, R. **66** 44 35N 20 15 E
Kolumna **54** 51 36N 19 14 E
Koluszki **54** 51 45N 19 46 E
Kolwezi **124** 10 40 S 25 25 E
Kolyberovo **81** 55 15N 38 40 E
Kolyma, R. **77** 64 40N 153 0 E
Kolymskoye, Okhotsko **77** 63 0N 157 0 E
Kôm Ombo **122** 24 25N 32 52 E
Komagene **111** 35 44N 137 58 E
Komaki **111** 35 17N 136 55 E
Komandorskiye Ostrava **77** 55 0N 167 0 E
Komárno **53** 47 49N 18 5 E
Komárom **53** 47 43N 18 7 E
Komárom □ **53** 47 35N 18 20 E
Komarovo **80** 58 38N 33 40 E
Komatsu **111** 36 25 S 136 30 E
Komatsukima **110** 34 0N 134 35 E
Kombissiri **121** 12 4N 1 20W
Kombori **120** 13 26N 3 56W

*Renamed Yos Sudarso, Pulau

Kombóti **69** 39 6N 21 5 E
Komen **63** 45 49N 13 45 E
Komenda **121** 5 4N 1 28W
Komi, A.S.S.R. □ **84** 64 0N 55 0 E
Komiza **63** 43 3N 16 11 E
Komló **53** 46 15N 18 16 E
Kommamur Canal **97** 16 0N 80 25 E
Kommunarsk **83** 48 30N 38 45 E
Kommunizma, Pik **85** 39 0N 72 2 E
Komnes **71** 59 30N 9 55 E
Komodo **103** 8 37 S 119 20 E
Komoé **120** 5 12N 3 44W
Komono **124** 3 15 S 13 20 E
Komoran, Pulau **103** 8 18 S 138 45 E
Komoro **111** 36 19N 138 26 E
Komorze **54** 62 8N 17 38 E
Komotiri **68** 41 9N 25 26 E
Kompong Bang **101** 12 24N 104 40 E
Kompong Cham **101** 11 54N 105 30 E
Kompong Chhnang **101** 12 20N 104 35 E
Kompong Chikreng **100** 13 5N 104 18 E
Kompong Kleang **101** 13 6N 104 8 E
Kompong Luong **101** 11 49N 104 48 E
Kompong Pranak **101** 13 35N 104 55 E
Kompong Som **101** 10 38N 103 30 E
Kompong Som, Chhung **101** 10 50N 103 32 E
Kompong Speu **101** 11 26N 104 32 E
Kompong Sralao **100** 14 5N 105 46 E
Kompong Thom **100** 12 35N 104 51 E
Kompong Trabeck, Camb. **100** 13 6N 105 14 E
Kompong Trabeck, Camb. **101** 11 9N 105 28 E
Kompong Trach, Camb. **101** 11 25N 105 48 E
Kompong Trach, Camb. **118** 10 34N 104 28 E
Kompong Tralach **101** 11 54N 104 47 E
Komrat **82** 46 18N 28 40 E
Komsberge **128** 32 40 S 20 45 E
Komsomolabad **85** 38 50N 69 55 E
Komsomolets **84** 53 45N 62 2 E
Komsomolets, Ostrov **77** 80 30N 95 0 E
Komsomolsk, R.S.F.S.R., U.S.S.R. **77** 50 30N 137 0 E
Komsomolsk, Turkmen S.S.R., U.S.S.R. **85** 39 2N 63 36 E
Komsomolskiy **81** 53 30N 49 40 E
Kona, Niger **121** 13 33N 8 3 E
Kona, Nigeria **121** 8 58N 11 15 E
Konakovo **81** 56 52N 36 45 E
Konam Dzong **99** 29 5N 93 0 E
Konawa **159** 34 59N 96 46W
Kondagaon **96** 19 35N 81 35 E
Konde **126** 4 57 S 39 45 E
Kondiá **68** 39 52N 25 10 E
Kondinin **137** 32 34 S 118 8 E
Kondoa **126** 4 55 S 35 50 E
Kondoa □ **126** 5 0 S 36 0 E
Kondratyevo **77** 57 30N 98 30 E
Konduga **121** 11 35N 13 26 E
Kong **120** 8 54N 4 36W
Kong Christian IX.s Land **12** 68 0N 36 0W
Kong Christian X.s Land **12** 74 0N 29 0W
Kong Frederik VIII.s Land **12** 78 30N 26 0W
Kong Frederik VI.s Kyst **12** 63 0N 43 0W
Kong, Koh **101** 11 20N 103 0 E
Kong Oscar Fjord **12** 72 20N 24 0W
Kong, R. **100** 13 32N 105 58 E
Konga **73** 56 30N 15 6 E
Kongeå **73** 55 24N 8 39 E
Kongju **107** 36 30N 127 0 E
Konglu **98** 27 13N 97 57 E
Kongolo **126** 5 22 S 27 0 E
Kongoussi **121** 13 19N 1 32W
Kongsberg **71** 59 39N 9 39 E
Kongsvinger **71** 60 12N 12 2 E
Kongsvoll **71** 62 20N 9 36 E
Kongwa **126** 6 11 S 36 26 E
Koni **127** 10 40 S 27 11 E
Koni, Mts. **127** 10 36 S 27 10 E
Koniecpol **54** 50 46N 19 40 E
Königsberg = Kaliningrad **80** 54 42N 20 32 E
Königslutter **48** 52 14N 10 50 E
Königswusterhausen **48** 52 19N 13 38 E
Konin **54** 52 12N 18 15 E
Konin □ **54** 52 15N 18 30 E
Konispol **68** 39 42N 20 10 E
Kónitsa **68** 40 5N 20 48 E
Köniz **50** 46 56N 7 25 E
Konjic **66** 43 42N 17 58 E
Konjice **63** 46 20N 15 28 E
Konkouré, R. **120** 10 30N 13 40W
Könnern **48** 51 40N 11 45 E
Konnur **96** 16 14N 74 49 E
Kono **120** 8 30N 11 5W
Konoğlu **82** 40 35N 31 50 E
Konolfingen **50** 46 54N 7 38 E
Konongo **121** 6 40N 1 15W
Konos **135** 3 10 S 151 44 E
Konosha **78** 61 0N 40 5 E
Kōnosu **111** 36 3N 139 31 E
Konotop **80** 51 12N 33 7 E
Konskaya, R. **82** 47 30N 35 0 E
Konskie **54** 51 15N 20 23 E
Konsmo **71** 58 16N 7 23 E
Konstantinovka **82** 48 32N 37 39 E
Konstantinovski, R.S.F.S.R., U.S.S.R. **81** 57 45N 39 35 E

CIB

Konstantinovski, R.S.F.S.R., U.S.S.R. **83** 47 33N 41 10 E
Konstantynów Łódzki **54** 51 45N 19 20 E
Konstanz **49** 47 39N 9 10 E
Kontagora **121** 10 23N 5 27 E
Kontich **47** 51 8N 4 26 E
Kontum **100** 14 24N 108 0 E
Kontum, Plat. du **100** 14 30N 108 0 E
Konya **92** 37 52N 32 35 E
Konyin **98** 22 58N 94 42 E
Konz Karthaus **49** 49 41N 6 36 E
Konza **124** 1 45 S 37 0 E
Konzhakovskiy Kamen, Gora **84** 59 38N 59 8 E
Koog **12** 52 27N 4 49 E
Kookynie **137** 29 17 S 121 22 E
Koolan I. **136** 16 0 S 123 45 E
Kooline **136** 22 57 S 116 20 E
Kooloonong **140** 34 48 S 143 10 E
Koolyanobbing **137** 30 48 S 119 36 E
Koolymilka P.O. **140** 30 58 S 136 32 E
Koondrook **140** 35 33 S 144 8 E
Koorawatha **141** 34 2 S 148 33 E
Koorda **137** 30 48 S 117 35 E
Kooskia **160** 46 9N 115 59W
Koostatak **153** 51 26N 97 26W
Kootenai, R. **160** 48 30N 115 30W
Kootenay L. **153** 49 45N 117 0W
Kootenay Nat. Park **152** 51 0N 116 0W
Kootingal **173** 31 1 S 151 3 E
Kopa **85** 43 31N 75 50 E
Kopaonik Planina **66** 43 10N 21 0 E
Kopargaon **96** 19 51N 74 28 E
Kópavogur **74** 64 6N 21 55W
Koper **63** 45 31N 13 44 E
Kopervik **71** 59 17N 5 17 E
Kopeysk **84** 55 7N 61 37 E
Kopi **139** 33 24 S 135 40 E
Köping **72** 59 31N 16 3 E
Kopiste **63** 42 48N 16 42 E
Kopliku **68** 42 15N 19 25 E
Köpmanholmen **72** 63 10N 18 35 E
Köpmannebro **73** 58 45N 12 30 E
Koppal **97** 15 23N 76 5 E
Koppang **71** 61 34N 11 3 E
Kopparberg **75** 59 52N 15 0 E
Kopparbergs län □ **147** 61 20N 14 15 E
Koppeh Dāgh **93** 38 0N 58 0 E
Kopperå **71** 63 24N 11 50 E
Kopperå **71** 63 24N 11 52 E
Koppio **140** 34 26 S 135 51 E
Koppom **72** 59 43N 12 10 E
Koprivlen **67** 41 36N 23 53 E
Koprivnica **63** 46 12N 16 45 E
Koprivshtitsa **67** 42 40N 24 19 E
Kopychintsy **80** 49 7N 25 58 E
Korab, mt. **66** 41 44N 20 40 E
Korakiána **68** 39 42N 19 45 E
Koraput **96** 18 50N 82 40 E
Korba **95** 22 20N 82 45 E
Korbach **48** 51 17N 8 50 E
Korbu, G. **101** 4 41N 101 18 E
Korça **68** 40 37N 20 50 E
Korça □ **68** 40 40N 20 50 E
Korčula **63** 42 57N 17 8 E
Korčula, I. **63** 42 57N 17 0 E
Korčulanski Kanal **63** 43 3N 16 40 E
Kordestān □ **92** 36 0N 47 0 E
Korea **107** 40 0N 127 0 E
Korea Bay **107** 39 0N 124 0 E
Korea, South ■ **107** 36 0N 128 0 E
Korea Strait **107** 34 0N 129 30 E
Koregaon **96** 17 40N 74 10 E
Korenevo **80** 51 27N 34 55 E
Korenovsk **83** 45 12N 39 22 E
Korets **80** 50 40N 27 5 E
Korgus **122** 19 16N 33 48 E
Korhogo **120** 9 29N 5 28W
Koribundu **120** 7 41N 11 46W
Koridina **139** 29 42 S 143 25 E
Korim **103** 0 58 S 136 10 E
Korinthia □ **69** 37 50N 22 35 E
Korinthiakós Kólpos **69** 38 16N 22 30 E
Kórinthos **69** 37 56N 22 55 E
Korioumé **120** 16 35N 3 0W
Kōriyama **112** 37 24N 140 23 E
Korkino **84** 54 54N 61 23 E
Körmend **53** 47 5N 16 35 E
Kornat, I. **63** 43 50N 15 20 E
Korneshty **82** 47 21N 28 1 E
Korneuburg **53** 48 20N 16 20 E
Korning **73** 56 30N 9 44 E
Kornsjø **71** 58 57N 11 39 E
Kornstad **71** 62 59N 7 27 E
Koro, Ivory C. **120** 8 32N 7 30W
Koro, Mali **120** 14 1N 2 58W
Koroba **135** 5 44 S 142 47 E
Korocha **81** 50 55N 37 30 E
Korogwe **124** 5 5 S 38 25 E
Korogwe □ **126** 5 0 S 38 20 E
Koroit **140** 38 18 S 142 24 E
Korong Vale **140** 36 22 S 143 45 E
Koróni **69** 36 48N 21 57 E
Korónia, Limni **68** 40 47N 23 37 E
Koronis **69** 37 12N 25 35 E
Koronowo **54** 53 19N 17 55 E
Koror **103** 7 20N 134 28 E
Körös, R. **53** 46 45N 20 20 E
Köröstarcsa **53** 46 53N 21 3 E
Korosten **80** 50 57N 28 25 E
Korotoyak **81** 51 1N 39 2 E
Korraraika, B. de **129** 17 45 S 43 57 E
Korsakov **77** 46 30N 142 42 E
Korshavn **71** 58 2N 7 0 E
Korshunovo **77** 58 37N 110 10 E
Korsör **73** 55 20N 11 9 E
Korsze **54** 54 11N 21 9 E
Kortemark **47** 51 2N 3 3 E
Kortessem **47** 50 52N 5 23 E
Korti **122** 18 0N 31 40 E
Kortrijk **47** 50 50N 3 17 E
Korumburra **141** 38 26 S 145 50 E
Korwai **94** 24 7N 78 5 E
Koryakskiy Khrebet **77** 61 0N 171 0 E
Koryŏng **107** 35 44N 128 15 E
Kos **69** 36 52N 27 19 E
Kos, I. **69** 36 50N 27 15 E
Kosa, Ethiopia **123** 7 50N 36 50 E
Kosa, U.S.S.R. **84** 59 56N 55 0 E
Kosa, R. **84** 60 11N 55 10 E
Kosaya Gora **81** 54 10N 37 30 E
Koschagy **79** 46 40N 54 0 E
Kosciusko **159** 33 3N 89 34W
Kosciusko, I. **152** 56 0N 133 40W
Kosciusko, Mt. **141** 36 27 S 148 16 E
Kösély, R. **53** 47 25N 21 30 E
Kosgi **96** 16 58N 77 43 E
Kosha **122** 20 50N 30 30 E
Koshigaya **111** 35 54N 139 48 E
K'oshih **105** 39 29N 75 58 E
K'oshihk'ot'engch'i **107** 43 17N 117 24 E
Koshiki-Rettō **110** 31 45N 129 49 E
Kōshoku **111** 36 38N 138 6 E
Koshtëbë **85** 41 5N 74 15 E
Kosi **94** 27 48N 77 29 E
Kosi-meer **129** 27 0 S 32 50 E
Košice **53** 48 42N 21 15 E
Kosjerič **66** 44 0N 19 55 E
Koslan **78** 63 28N 48 52 E
Kosŏng **107** 38 40N 128 22 E
Kosovska-Mitrovica **66** 42 54N 20 52 E
Kosścian **54** 52 5N 16 40 E
Kosścierzyna **54** 54 8N 17 59 E
Kosso **120** 5 3N 5 47W
Kostajnica **63** 45 17N 16 30 E
Kostanjevica **63** 45 51N 15 27 E
Kostelec **53** 50 14N 16 35 E
Kostenets **67** 42 15N 23 52 E
Koster **128** 25 52 S 26 54 E
Kôstî **123** 13 8N 32 43 E
Kostolac **66** 44 43N 21 15 E
Kostroma **81** 57 50N 41 58 E
Kostromskoye Vdkhr. **81** 57 52N 40 49 E
Kostrzyn **54** 52 24N 17 14 E
Kostyukovichi **80** 53 10N 32 4 E
Koszalin **54** 54 12N 16 8 E
Koszalin □ **54** 54 10N 16 10 E
Kőszeg **53** 47 23N 16 33 E
Kot Adu **94** 30 30N 71 0 E
Kot Moman **94** 32 13N 73 0 E
Kota **94** 25 14N 75 49 E
Kota Baharu **101** 6 7N 102 14 E
Kota Kinabalu **102** 6 0N 116 12 E
Kota-Kota = Khota Kota **127** 12 55 S 34 15 E
Kota Tinggi **101** 1 44N 103 53 E
Kotaagung **102** 5 38 S 104 29 E
Kotabaru **102** 3 20 S 116 20 E
Kotabumi **102** 4 49 S 104 46 E
Kotamobagu **103** 0 57N 124 31 E
Kotaneelee, R. **152** 60 11N 123 42W
Kotawaringin **102** 2 28 S 111 27 E
Kotchandpur **98** 23 24N 89 1 E
Kotcho L. **152** 59 7N 121 12W
Kotel **67** 42 52N 26 26 E
Kotelnich **81** 58 20N 48 10 E
Kotelnikovo **83** 47 45N 43 15 E
Kotelnyy, Ostrov **77** 75 10N 139 0 E
Kothagudam **96** 17 30N 80 40 E
Kothapet **96** 19 21N 79 28 E
Köthen **48** 51 44N 11 59 E
Kothi **95** 24 45N 80 40 E
Kotiro **94** 26 17N 67 13 E
Kotka **75** 60 28N 26 58 E
Kotlas **78** 61 15N 47 0 E
Kotlenska Planina **67** 42 56N 26 30 E
Kotli **94** 33 30N 73 55 E
Kotmul **95** 35 32N 75 10 E
Kotohira **110** 34 11N 133 49 E
Kotonkoro **121** 11 3N 5 58 E
Kotor **66** 42 25N 18 47 E
Kotor Varoš **66** 44 38N 17 22 E
Kotoriba **63** 46 23N 16 48 E
Kotovo **81** 50 22N 44 45 E
Kotovsk **82** 47 55N 29 35 E
Kotputli **94** 27 43N 76 12 E
Kotri **94** 25 22N 68 22 E
Kotri, R. **96** 19 45N 80 35 E
Kótronas **69** 36 38N 22 29 E
Kötschach-Mauthen **52** 46 41N 13 1 E
Kottayam **97** 9 35N 76 33 E
Kottur **97** 10 34N 76 56 E
Kotturu **93** 14 45N 76 10 E
Kotuy, R. **77** 70 30N 103 0 E
Kotzebue **147** 66 50N 162 40W
Kotzebue Sd. **147** 66 30N 164 0W
Kouango **124** 5 0N 20 10 E
Koudekerke **47** 51 29N 3 33 E
Koudougou **120** 12 10N 2 20W
Koufonísi, I. **69** 34 56N 26 8 E
Koufonisia, I. **69** 36 57N 25 35 E
Kougaberge **128** 33 48 S 24 20 E
Kouibli **120** 7 15N 7 14W
Kouilou, R. **124** 4 10 S 12 5 E
Kouki **124** 7 22N 17 3 E
Koula Moutou **124** 1 15 S 12 25 E
Koulen **100** 13 50N 104 40 E
Koulikoro **120** 12 40N 7 50W
Koumala **138** 21 38 S 149 15 E
Koumankoun **120** 11 58N 6 6W
Koumbia, Guin. **120** 11 54N 13 40W
Koumbia, Upp. Vol. **120** 11 10N 3 50W
Koumboum **120** 10 25N 13 0W
Koumpenntoum **120** 13 59N 14 34W
Koumra **117** 8 50N 17 35 E
Koumradskiy **76** 47 20N 75 0 E
Koundara **120** 12 29N 13 18W
Kountze **159** 30 20N 94 22W
Koupangtzu **107** 41 22N 121 46 E
Koupéla **121** 12 11N 0 21 E
Kourizo, Passe de **119** 22 28N 15 27 E
Kouroussa **120** 10 45N 9 45W
Koussané **120** 14 53N 11 14W
Kousseri **117** 12 0N 14 55 E
Koutiala **120** 12 25N 5 35W
Kouto **120** 9 53N 6 25W
Kouvé **121** 6 25N 0 59 E
KovaCica **66** 45 5N 20 38 E
Kovel **80** 51 10N 24 20 E
Kovilpatti **97** 9 10N 77 50 E
Kovin **66** 44 44N 20 59 E
Kovrov **81** 56 25N 41 25 E
Kovur, Andhra Pradesh, India **96** 17 3N 81 39 E
Kovur, Andhra Pradesh, India **97** 14 30N 80 1 E
Kowal **54** 52 32N 19 7 E
Kowalewo Pomorskie **54** 53 10N 18 52 E
Kowkash **150** 50 20N 87 20W
Kowloon **109** 22 20N 114 15 E
Kowŏn **107** 39 26N 127 14 E
Kōyama **110** 31 20N 130 56 E
Koyan, Pegunungan **102** 3 15N 114 30 E
Koyang **106** 33 31N 116 11 E
Koytash **85** 40 11N 67 19 E
Koyuk **147** 64 55N 161 20W
Koyukuk, R. **147** 65 45N 156 30W
Koyulhisar **82** 40 20N 37 52 E
Koza **112** 26 19N 127 46 E
Kozan **92** 37 35N 35 50 E
Kozàni **68** 40 19N 21 47 E
Kozàni □ **68** 40 18N 21 45 E
Kozara, Mts. **63** 45 0N 17 0 E
Kozarac **63** 44 58N 16 48 E
Kozelsk **80** 54 2N 35 38 E
Kozhikode = Calicut **97** 11 15N 75 43 E
Kozhva **78** 65 10N 57 0 E
Koziegłowy **54** 50 37N 19 8 E
Kozje **63** 46 5N 15 35 E
Kozle **54** 50 20N 18 8 E
Kozlodui **67** 43 45N 23 42 E
Kozlovets **67** 43 30N 25 20 E
Kozmin **54** 51 48N 17 27 E
Kōzu-Shima **111** 34 13N 139 10 E
Kozuchów **54** 51 45N 15 31 E
Kpabia **121** 9 10N 0 20W
Kpandae **121** 8 30N 0 2W
Kpandu **121** 7 2N 0 18 E
Kpessi **121** 8 4N 1 16 E
Kra Buri **101** 10 22N 98 46 E
Kra, Isthmus of = Kra, Kho Khot **101** 10 15N 99 30 E
Kra, Kho Khot **101** 10 15N 99 30 E
Krabbendijke **47** 51 26N 4 7 E
Krabi **101** 8 4N 98 55 E
Kragan **103** 6 43 S 111 38 E
Kragerø **71** 58 52N 9 25 E
Kragujevac **66** 44 2N 20 56 E
Krajenka **54** 53 18N 16 59 E
Krakatau = Rakata, Pulau **102** 6 10 S 105 20 E
Krakor **100** 12 32N 104 12 E
Kraków **54** 50 4N 19 57 E
Kraków □ **53** 50 0N 20 0 E
Kraksaan **103** 7 43 S 113 23 E
Kraksmala **73** 57 2N 15 20 E
Kråkstad **71** 59 40N 10 50 E
Kråkstad **71** 59 39N 10 55 E
Kralanh **100** 13 35N 103 25 E
Králiky **53** 50 6N 16 45 E
Kraljevo **66** 43 44N 20 41 E
Kralovice **52** 49 59N 13 29 E
Královsky Chlmec **53** 48 27N 22 0 E
Kralupy **52** 50 13N 14 20 E
Kramatorsk **82** 48 50N 37 30 E
Kramer **161** 35 0N 117 38W
Kramfors **72** 62 55N 17 48 E
Kramis, C. **118** 36 26N 0 45 E
Krångede **72** 63 9N 16 10 E
Krångede **72** 63 9N 16 6 E
Kraniá **68** 39 53N 21 18 E
Kranidhion **69** 37 20N 23 10 E
Kranj **63** 46 16N 14 22 E
Kranjska Gora **63** 46 29N 13 48 E
Kranzberg **128** 21 59 S 15 37 E
Krapina **63** 46 10N 15 52 E
Krapina, R. **63** 46 0N 15 55 E
Krapivna **81** 53 58N 37 10 E
Krapkowice **54** 50 29N 17 56 E
Kras Polyana **83** 43 40N 40 25 E
Krashyy Klyuch **84** 55 23N 56 39 E
Kraskino **77** 42 44N 130 48 E
Krăslava **80** 55 52N 27 12 E
Kraslice **52** 50 19N 12 31 E
Krasnaya Gorbatka **81** 55 52N 41 45 E
Krasnik Fabryezny **54** 50 58N 22 11 E
Krasnoarmeisk **82** 48 18N 37 11 E
Krasnoarmeysk, R.S.F.S.R., U.S.S.R. **81** 50 32N 45 50 E
Krasnoarmeysk, R.S.F.S.R., U.S.S.R. **83** 48 30N 44 25 E
Krasnodar **83** 45 5N 38 50 E
Krasnodonetskaya **83** 48 5N 40 50 E
Krasnog Dardeiskoye **82** 45 32N 34 16 E
Krasnogorskiy **81** 56 10N 48 28 E
Krasnograd **82** 49 27N 35 27 E
Krasnogvardeysk **85** 39 46N 67 16 E
Krasnogvardeyskoye **83** 45 52N 41 33 E
Krasnoïarsk **77** 56 8N 93 0 E
Krasnokamsk **84** 58 4N 55 48 E
Krasnokutsk **80** 50 10N 34 50 E
Krasnoperekopsk **82** 46 0N 33 54 E
Krasnoselkupsk **76** 65 20N 82 10 E
Krasnoslobodsk **83** 48 42N 44 33 E
Krasnoturinsk **84** 59 46N 60 12 E
Krasnoufimsk **84** 56 57N 57 46 E
Krasnouralsk **84** 58 21N 60 3 E
Krasnousolskiy **84** 53 54N 56 27 E
Krasnovishersk **84** 60 23N 57 3 E
Krasnovodsk **79** 40 0N 52 52 E
Krasnoyarsk **77** 56 8N 93 0 E
Krasnoyarskiy **84** 51 58N 59 55 E
Krasnoye, Kal., U.S.S.R. **83** 46 16N 45 0 E
Krasnoye, R.S.F.S.R., U.S.S.R. **81** 59 15N 47 40 E
Krasnoye, Ukr., U.S.S.R. **80** 49 56N 24 42 E
Krasnozavodsk **81** 56 38N 38 16 E
Krasny Liman **82** 48 58N 37 50 E
Krasny Sulin **83** 47 52N 40 8 E
Krasnystaw **54** 50 57N 23 5 E
Krasnyy **80** 49 56N 24 42 E
Krasnyy Kholm, R.S.F.S.R., U.S.S.R. **81** 58 10N 37 10 E
Krasnyy Kholm, R.S.F.S.R., U.S.S.R. **84** 51 35N 54 9 E
Krasnyy Kut **81** 50 50N 47 0 E
Krasnyy Luch **83** 48 13N 39 0 E
Krasnyy Yar, Kal., U.S.S.R. **83** 46 43N 48 23 E
Krasnyy Yar, R.S.F.S.R., U.S.S.R. **81** 50 42N 44 45 E
Krasnyy Yar, R.S.F.S.R., U.S.S.R. **81** 53 30N 50 22 E
Krasnyyoskolskoye, Vdkhr. **82** 49 30N 37 30 E
Kraśnik **54** 50 55N 22 5 E
Kraszna, R. **53** 48 0N 22 20 E
Kratie **100** 12 32N 106 10 E
Kratke Ra. **135** 6 45 S 146 0 E
Kratovo **66** 42 6N 22 10 E
Kravanh, Chuor Phnum **101** 12 0N 103 32 E
Krawang **103** 6 19N 107 18 E
Krefeld **48** 51 20N 6 22 E
Kremaston, Limni **69** 38 52N 21 30 E
Kremenchug **82** 49 5N 33 25 E
Kremenchugskoye Vdkhr. **82** 49 20N 32 30 E
Kremenets **82** 50 8N 25 43 E
Kremenica **66** 40 55N 21 25 E
Kremennaya **82** 49 1N 38 10 E
Kremikovtsi **67** 42 46N 23 28 E
Kremmen **48** 52 45N 13 1 E
Kremmling **160** 40 10N 106 30W
Kremnica **53** 48 45N 18 50 E
Krems **52** 48 25N 15 36 E
Kremsmünster **52** 48 3N 14 8 E
Kretinga **80** 55 53N 21 15 E
Krettamia **118** 28 47N 3 27W
Krettsy **80** 58 15N 32 30 E
Kreuzlingen **51** 47 38N 9 10 E
Kribi **121** 2 57N 9 56 E
Krichem **67** 46 16N 24 28 E
Krichev **80** 53 45N 31 50 E
Kriens **51** 47 2N 8 17 E
Krim, mt. **63** 45 53N 14 30 E
Krimpen **46** 51 55N 4 34 E
Krionéri **69** 38 20N 21 35 E
Krishna, R. **96** 16 30N 77 0 E
Krishnagiri **97** 12 32N 78 16 E
Krishnanagar **95** 23 24N 88 33 E
Krishnaraja Sagara **97** 12 20N 76 30 E
Kristianopel **73** 56 12N 16 0 E
Kristiansand **71** 58 9N 8 1 E
Kristianstad **73** 56 2N 14 9 E
Kristianstad □ **75** 56 15N 14 0 E
Kristiansund **71** 63 7N 7 45 E
Kristiinankaupunki **74** 62 16N 21 21 E
Kristinehamn **72** 59 18N 14 13 E
Kristinestad **74** 62 16N 21 21 E
Kriti, I. **69** 35 15N 25 0 E
Kritsá **69** 35 10N 25 41 E
Kriva Palanka **66** 42 11N 22 19 E
Kriva, R. **66** 42 12N 22 18 E
Krivaja, R. **66** 44 15N 18 22 E
Krivelj **66** 44 8N 22 5 E
Krivoy Rog **82** 47 51N 33 20 E
Krizevci **63** 46 3N 16 32 E
Krk **63** 45 5N 14 36 E
Krk, I. **63** 45 8N 14 40 E
Krka, R. **63** 45 50N 15 30 E
Krkonoše **52** 50 50N 16 10 E
Krnov **53** 50 5N 17 40 E
Krobia **54** 51 47N 16 59 E
Kročehlavy **52** 50 8N 14 9 E
Kroeng Krai **101** 14 55N 98 30 E
Krokawo **54** 54 47N 18 9 E
Krokeai **69** 36 53N 22 32 E
Kroken, Norway **71** 58 57N 9 8 E
Kroken, Sweden **71** 59 2N 11 23 E
Krokom **72** 63 20N 14 30 E

Krolevets 80 51 35N 33 20 E
Kroměríz 53 49 18N 17 21 E
Krommenie 46 52 30N 4 46 E
Krompachy 53 48 54N 20 52 E
Kromy 80 52 40N 35 48 E
Kronobergs län □ 73 56 45N 14 30 E
Kronprins Harald Kyst 13 70 0 S 35 1 E
Kronprins Olav Kyst 13 69 0 S 42 0 E
Kronprinsesse Märtha Kyst 13 73 30 S 10 0W
Kronshtadt 80 60 5N 29 35 E
Kroonstad 125 27 43 S 27 19 E
Kröpelin 48 54 4N 11 48 E
Kropotkin 77 45 25N 40 35 E
Kropp 48 54 24N 9 32 E
Krósniewice 54 52 15N 19 11 E
Krosno 54 49 35N 21 56 E
Krosno □ 54 49 30N 22 0 E
Krosno Odrz 54 52 3N 15 7 E
Krościenko 54 49 29N 20 25 E
Krotoszyn 54 51 42N 17 23 E
Krotovka 84 53 18N 51 10 E
Krraba 68 41 13N 20 0 E
Krško 63 45 57N 15 30 E
Krstača, mt. 66 42 57N 20 8 E
Kruger Nat. Pk. 129 24 0 S 31 40 E
Krugersdorp 129 26 5 S 27 46 E
Kruidfontein 128 32 48 S 21 59 E
Kruiningen 47 51 27N 4 2 E
Kruis, Kaap 128 21 55 S 13 57 E
Kruishoutem 47 50 54N 3 32 E
Kruisland 47 51 34N 4 25 E
Kruja 68 41 32N 19 46 E
Krulevshchina 80 55 5N 27 45 E
Kruma 68 42 37N 20 28 E
Krumovgrad 67 41 29N 25 38 E
Krung Thep = Bangkok 100 13 45N 100 35 E
Krupanj 66 44 25N 19 22 E
Krupina 53 48 22N 19 5 E
Krupinica, R. 53 48 15N 19 5 E
Kruševac 66 43 35N 21 28 E
Krušovo 66 41 23N 21 19 E
Kruszwica 54 52 40N 18 20 E
Kruzof I. 152 57 10N 135 40W
Krylbo 72 60 7N 16 15 E
Krymsk Abinsk 82 44 50N 38 0 E
Krymskaya 82 45 0N 34 0 E
Krynica 54 49 25N 20 57 E
Krynica Morska 54 54 23N 19 28 E
Krynki 54 53 17N 23 43 E
Kryulyany 70 47 12N 29 9 E
Krzepice 54 50 58N 18 50 E
Krzeszowice 54 50 8N 19 37 E
Krzywin 54 51 58N 16 50 E
Krzyz 54 52 52N 16 0 E
Ksabi, Alg. 118 29 8N 0 58W
Ksabi, Moroc. 118 32 51N 4 13W
Ksar Chellala 118 35 13N 2 19 E
Ksar el Boukhari 118 35 51N 2 52 E
Ksar el Kebir 118 35 0N 6 0W
*Ksar es Souk 118 31 58N 4 20W
Ksar Rhilane 119 33 0N 9 39 E
Ksiba 118 32 46N 6 0W
Ksour, Mts. des 118 32 45N 0 30W
Kstovo 81 56 12N 44 13 E
Kuachou 109 32 14N 119 24 E
Kuala 102 2 46N 105 47 E
Kuala Berang 101 5 5N 103 1 E
Kuala Dungun 101 4 45N 103 25 E
Kuala Kangsar 101 4 46N 100 56 E
Kuala Kerai 101 5 30N 102 12 E
Kuala Klawang 101 2 56N 102 5 E
Kuala Kubu Baharu 101 3 34N 101 39 E
Kuala Lipis 101 4 10N 102 3 E
Kuala Lumpur 101 3 9N 101 41 E
Kuala Marang 101 5 12N 103 13 E
Kuala Nerang 101 6 16N 100 37 E
Kuala Pilah 101 2 45N 102 15 E
Kuala Rompin 101 2 49N 103 29 E
Kuala Selangor 101 3 20N 101 15 E
Kuala Terengganu 101 5 20N 103 8 E
Kuala Trengganu 101 5 20N 103 8 E
Kualakahi Chan 147 22 2N 159 53W
Kualakapuas 102 2 55 S 114 20 E
Kualakurun 102 1 10 S 113 50 E
Kualapembuang, Indon. 102 3 14 S 112 38 E
Kualapembuang, Indon. 102 2 52 S 111 45 E
Kuanaan 107 34 8N 119 24 E
Kuanch'eng 107 40 39N 118 32 E
Kuandang 103 0 56N 123 1 E
Kuangan 108 30 30N 106 35 E
Kuangch'ang 109 26 50N 116 15 E
Kuangchou 109 23 12N 113 12 E
Kuangfeng 109 28 26N 118 12 E
Kuanghan 108 30 56N 104 15 E
Kuanghua 109 32 22N 111 43 E
Kuangjao 107 37 5N 118 25 E
Kuangling 106 39 47N 114 10 E
Kuangnan 108 24 3N 105 3 E
Kuangning 109 23 40N 112 23 E
Kuangshi 109 29 55N 115 25 E
Kuangshun 108 26 5N 106 16 E
Kuangte 109 30 54N 119 26 E
Kuangtse 109 27 30N 117 24 E
Kuangwuch'eng 106 37 49N 108 51 E
Kuangyüan 108 32 22N 105 50 E
Kuanhsien 108 31 0N 103 40 E
Kuanling 108 25 55N 105 35 E
Kuanp'ing 109 31 39N 110 16 E
Kuantan 101 3 49N 103 20 E
Kuant'ao 106 36 31N 115 16 E
Kuantaok'ou 106 34 18N 111 1 E
K'uantien 107 40 47N 124 43 E
Kuanyang 109 25 29N 111 9 E
Kuanyün 107 34 17N 119 15 E
Kuaram 123 12 25N 39 30 E
Kuba 83 41 21N 48 32 E
Kubak 93 27 10N 63 10 E
Kuban, R. 82 45 5N 38 0 E
Kubenskoye, Oz. 81 59 40N 39 25 E
Kuberle 83 47 0N 42 20 E
Kubokawa 110 33 12N 133 8 E
Kubor 135 6 10 S 144 44 E
Kubrat 67 43 49N 26 31 E
Kučevo 66 44 30N 21 40 E
Kucha Gompa 95 34 25N 76 56 E
Kuchaman 94 27 13N 74 47 E
Kuch'ang 108 24 58N 102 45 E
Kuchang 109 28 37N 109 56 E
K'uche K'uerhlo 105 41 43N 82 54 E
Kuchenspitze 49 47 3N 10 14 E
Kuchiang 109 27 11N 114 47 E
Kuching 102 1 33N 110 25 E
Kuchinoerabu-Jima 112 30 28N 130 11 E
Kuchinotsu 110 32 36N 130 11 E
Kuçove = Qytet Stalin 68 40 47N 19 57 E
Kud, R. 94 26 30N 66 12 E
Kuda 93 23 10N 71 15 E
Kudalier, R. 96 18 20N 78 40 E
Kudamatsu 110 34 0N 131 52 E
Kudara 85 38 25N 72 39 E
Kudat 102 6 55N 116 55 E
Kudremukh, Mt. 97 13 15N 75 20 E
Kuduarra Well 136 20 38 S 126 20 E
Kudus 103 6 48 S 110 51 E
Kudymkar 84 59 1N 54 39 E
Kuei Chiang, R. 109 23 33N 111 18 E
Kueich'i 109 28 17N 117 11 E
Kueich'ih 109 30 42N 117 30 E
Kueichu 108 26 25N 106 40 E
Kueihsien 108 23 6N 109 36 E
Kueilin 109 25 20N 110 18 E
Kueip'ing 108 23 24N 110 5 E
Kueiting 108 26 30N 107 17 E
Kueitung 109 26 12N 114 0 E
Kueiyang, Hunan, China 109 25 44N 112 43 E
Kueiyang, Kweichow, China 108 26 35N 106 43 E
K'uerhlo 105 41 44N 86 9 E
Kufra, El Wâhât el 117 24 17N 23 15 E
Kufrinja 90 32 20N 35 41 E
Kufstein 52 47 35N 12 11 E
Kugmallit B. 147 29 0N 134 0W
Kugong, I. 150 56 18N 79 50W
Kūh-e-Alijuq 93 31 30N 51 41 E
Kūh-e-Dinar 93 30 10N 51 0 E
Kūh-e-Hazaran 93 29 35N 57 20 E
Kūh-e-Jebel Barez 93 29 0N 58 0 E
Kūh-e-Sorkh 93 35 30N 58 45 E
Kūh-e-Taftan 93 28 40N 61 0 E
Kūhak 93 27 12N 63 10 E
Kūhha-ye-Bashakerd 93 26 45N 59 0 E
Kūhha-ye Sabalān 93 38 15N 47 45 E
Kuhnsdorf 52 46 37N 14 38 E
Kuhpayeh 93 32 44N 52 20 E
Kui Buri 101 12 3N 99 52 E
Kuinre 46 52 47N 5 51 E
Kuiseb, R. 125 23 40 S 15 30 E
Kuiu I. 147 56 40N 134 15W
Kujangdong 107 39 57N 126 1 E
Kuji 112 40 11N 141 46 E
Kujū-San 110 33 5N 131 15 E
Kujukuri-Heiya 111 35 45N 140 30 E
Kukavica, mt. 66 42 48N 21 57 E
Kukawa 121 12 58N 13 27 E
Kukerin 137 33 13 S 118 0 E
Kukësi 68 42 5N 20 20 E
Kukësi □ 68 42 25N 20 15 E
Kukko 123 8 26N 41 35 E
Kukmor 84 56 11N 50 54 E
Kukup 101 1 20N 103 27 E
K'uk'ushihli Shanmo 105 35 20N 91 0 E
Kukvidze 81 50 40N 43 15 E
Kula, Bulg. 66 43 52N 22 36 E
Kula, Yugo. 66 45 37N 19 32 E
Kulai 101 1 44N 103 35 E
Kulal, Mt. 126 2 42N 36 57 E
Kulaly, O. 83 45 0N 50 0 E
Kulanak 85 41 22N 75 30 E
Kulasekharapattanam 97 8 20N 78 0 E
Kuldiga 80 56 58N 21 59 E
Kuldja = Ining 105 43 54N 81 21 E
Kuldu 123 12 50N 28 30 E
Kulebaki 81 55 22N 42 25 E
Kulen Vakuf 63 44 35N 16 2 E
Kulgam 95 33 36N 75 2 E
Kuli 83 42 2N 46 12 E
Kulim 101 5 22N 100 34 E
Kulin 137 32 40 S 118 2 E
Kulja 137 30 28 S 117 18 E
Küllük 69 37 12N 27 36 E
Kulm 158 46 22N 98 58W
K'uloch'akonnoerh 106 43 25N 114 50 E
Kulsary 76 46 59N 54 1 E
Kultay 83 45 5N 51 40 E
Kulti 95 23 43N 86 50 E
Kulu 93 37 12N 115 2 E
Kulumadau 138 9 15 S 152 50 E
K'ulunch'i 107 42 44N 121 44 E
Kulunda 76 52 45N 79 15 E
Kulungar 94 34 0N 69 2 E
Kulwin 140 35 0 S 142 42 E
Kulyab 85 37 55N 69 50 E
Kum Tekei 76 43 10N 79 30 E
Kuma 110 33 39N 132 54 E
Kuma, R. 83 44 55N 45 57 E
Kumaganum 121 13 8N 10 38 E
Kumagaya 111 36 9N 139 22 E
Kumak 84 51 10N 60 8 E
Kumamoto 110 32 45N 130 45 E
Kumamoto-ken □ 110 32 30N 130 40 E
Kumano 111 33 54N 136 5 E
Kumano-Nada 111 33 47N 136 20 E
Kumanovo 66 42 9N 21 42 E
Kumara 143 42 37 S 171 12 E
Kumarkhali 98 23 51N 89 15 E
Kumarl 137 32 47 S 121 33 E
Kumasi 120 6 41N 1 38W
Kumba 121 4 36N 9 24 E
Kumbakonam 97 10 58N 79 25 E
Kumbarilla 139 27 15 S 150 55 E
Kumbo 121 6 15N 10 36 E
Kumbukkan Oya 97 6 35N 81 40 E
Kümchŏn 107 38 10N 126 29 E
Kumdok 95 33 32N 78 10 E
Kumeny 81 58 10N 49 47 E
Kümhwa 107 38 17N 127 28 E
Kumi 126 1 30N 33 58 E
Kumkale 68 40 30N 26 13 E
Kumla 72 59 8N 15 10 E
Kumo 121 10 1N 11 12 E
Kumon Bum 98 26 30N 97 15 E
Kumotori-Yama 111 35 51N 138 57 E
Kumta 97 14 29N 74 32 E
Kumtorkala 83 43 2N 46 50 E
Kumukahi, C. 147 19 31N 154 49W
Kumusi, R. 135 8 16 S 148 13 E
Kumylzhenskaya 83 49 51N 42 38 E
Kunágota 53 46 26N 21 3 E
Kunama 141 35 35 S 148 4 E
Kunar 93 34 30N 71 3 E
Kunashir, Ostrov 77 44 0N 146 0 E
Kunch 95 26 0N 79 10 E
Kunda 80 59 30N 26 34 E
Kundiawa 135 6 2 S 145 1 E
Kundip 137 33 42 S 120 10 E
Kundla 94 21 21N 71 25 E
Kunduz 93 36 50N 68 50 E
Kunduz □ 93 36 50N 68 50 E
Kunene, R. 128 17 15 S 13 40 E
Kungala 139 29 58 S 153 7 E
Kungälv 73 57 53N 11 59 E
Kungan 109 30 4N 112 12 E
Kungch'eng 109 24 50N 110 49 E
K'ungch'iao Ho 105 41 48N 86 47 E
Küngdong 107 39 9N 126 5 E
Kungey Alatau, Khrebet 85 42 50N 77 0 E
Kunghit I. 152 52 6N 131 3W
Kungho 105 36 28N 100 45 E
Kungka 108 28 44N 100 22 E
Kungkuan 108 21 51N 109 33 E
Kungrad 76 43 6N 58 54 E
Kungsbacka 73 57 30N 12 5 E
Kungshan 108 27 41N 97 37 E
Kungt'an 108 28 49N 108 38 E
Kungur 84 57 25N 56 57 E
Kungurri 138 21 3 S 148 46 E
Kungyangon 98 16 27N 96 1 E
Kungyingtzu 107 43 38N 121 0 E
Kunhar, R. 95 35 0N 73 40 E
Kunhegyes 53 47 22N 20 36 E
Kunimi-Dake 110 32 33N 131 1 E
Kuningan 103 6 59 S 108 29 E
Kunisaki 110 33 33N 131 45 E
Kunlara 140 34 54 S 139 55 E
Kunlong 98 23 20N 98 50 E
Kunlun Shan 105 36 0N 86 30 E
Kunmadaras 53 47 28N 20 45 E
K'unming 108 25 5N 102 40 E
Kunnamkulam 97 10 38N 76 7 E
Kunrade 47 50 53N 5 57 E
Kunsan 107 35 59N 126 45 E
K'unshan 109 31 22N 121 0 E
Kunszentmárton 53 46 50N 20 20 E
Kununurra 136 15 40 S 128 39 E
Kunwarara 138 22 55 S 150 9 E
Kuohsien 106 38 57N 112 46 E
Kuopio 74 62 53N 27 35 E
Kuopion Lääni □ 74 63 25N 27 10 E
Kupa, R. 63 45 30N 16 10 E
Kupang 103 10 19 S 123 39 E
Kupeik'ou 107 40 42N 117 9 E
Kupiano 135 10 4 S 148 14 E
Kupreanof I. 147 56 50N 133 30W
Kupres 66 44 1N 17 15 E
Kupyansk 82 49 45N 37 35 E
Kupyansk-Uzlovoi 82 49 52N 37 34 E
Kur, R. 98 26 50N 91 0 E
Kura, R. 83 40 20N 47 30 E
Kurahashi-Jima 110 34 8N 132 31 E
Kuranda 138 16 48 S 145 35 E
Kurandvad 96 16 45N 74 39 E
Kurashiki 110 34 40N 133 50 E
Kurayoshi 110 35 26N 133 50 E
Kurday 85 43 21N 74 59 E
Kurdistan, reg. 92 37 30N 42 0 E
Kurduvadi 96 18 8N 75 29 E
Kure 110 34 14N 132 32 E
Kuressaare = Kingisepp 80 58 15N 22 15 E
Kurgaldzhino 76 50 35N 70 20 E
Kurgan, R.S.F.S.R., U.S.S.R. 77 64 5N 172 50W
Kurgan, R.S.F.S.R., U.S.S.R. 84 55 26N 65 18 E
Kurgan-Tyube 85 37 50N 68 47 E
Kuria Muria I = Khy ryān Muryān J. 91 17 30N 55 58 E
Kurichchi 97 11 36N 77 35 E
Kuridala 138 21 16 S 140 29 E
Kurigram 98 25 49N 89 39 E
Kurihashi 111 36 8N 139 42 E
Kuril Trench 142 44 0N 153 0 E
Kurilskiye Ostrova 77 45 0N 150 0 E
Kuring Kuru 128 17 42 S 18 32 E
Kuringen 47 50 56N 5 18 E
Kurino 110 31 57N 130 43 E
KüRKkkuyu 68 39 35N 26 27 E
Kurkur 122 23 50N 32 0 E
Kurkûrah 119 31 30N 20 1 E
Kurla 96 19 5N 72 52 E
Kurlovski 81 55 25N 40 40 E
Kurma 123 13 55N 24 40 E
Kurmuk 123 10 33N 34 21 E
Kurnalpi 137 30 29 S 122 16 E
Kurnool 97 15 45N 78 0 E
Kurobe-Gawe, R. 111 36 55N 137 25 E
Kurogi 110 33 12N 130 40 E
Kurovskoye 81 55 35N 38 55 E
Kurow 143 44 4 S 170 29 E
Kurrajong, N.S.W., Austral. 141 33 33 S 150 42 E
Kurrajong, W.A., Austral. 137 28 39 S 120 59 E
Kurram, R. 94 33 30N 70 15 E
Kurri Kurri 141 32 50 S 151 28 E
Kuršenai 80 56 1N 23 3 E
Kurseong 95 26 56N 88 18 E
Kursk 81 51 42N 36 11 E
Kuršumlija 66 43 9N 21 19 E
Kuršumlijska Banja 66 43 3N 21 11 E
Kurtalon 92 37 55N 41 40 E
Kurtamysh 84 54 55N 64 27 E
Kurty, R. 85 44 16N 76 42 E
Kuru (Chel), Bahr el 123 8 10N 26 50 E
Kuruman 128 27 28 S 23 28 E
Kurume 110 33 15N 130 30 E
Kurunegala 97 7 30N 80 18 E
Kurya 77 61 15N 108 10 E
Kusa 84 55 20N 59 29 E
Kuşadası 69 37 52N 27 15 E
Kuşadası Körfezı 69 37 56N 27 0 E
Kusatsu, Gumma, Japan 111 36 37N 138 36 E
Kusatsu, Shiga, Japan 111 34 58N 136 5 E
Kusawa L. 152 60 20N 136 13W
Kusel 49 49 31N 7 25 E
Kushchevskaya 83 46 33N 39 35 E
Kushikino 110 31 44N 130 16 E
Kushima 110 31 29N 131 14 E
Kushimoto 111 33 28N 135 47 E
Kushin 109 32 12N 115 48 E
Kushiro 112 43 0N 144 25 E
Kushiro, R. 112 42 59N 144 23 E
Kushk 93 34 55N 62 30 E
Kushka 76 35 20N 62 18 E
Kushmurun 84 52 27N 64 36 E
Kushmurun, Ozero 84 52 40N 64 48 E
Kushnarenkovo 84 55 6N 55 22 E
Kushol 95 33 40N 76 36 E
Kushrabat 85 40 18N 66 32 E
Kushtia 98 23 55N 89 5 E
Kushum, R. 83 50 40N 50 20 E
Kushva 84 58 18N 59 45 E
Kuskokwim Bay 147 59 50N 162 56W
Kuskokwim Mts. 147 63 0N 156 0W
Kuskokwim, R. 147 61 48N 157 0W
Küsnacht 51 47 19N 8 15 E
Kussa 123 4 9N 38 58 E
Küssnacht 51 47 5N 8 26 E
Kustanay 84 53 10N 63 35 E
Kusu 110 33 16N 131 9 E
Kusung 108 28 25N 105 12 E
Kut, Ko 101 11 40N 102 35 E
Kutá Horq 52 49 57N 15 16 E
Kutahya 92 39 30N 30 2 E
Kutaisi 83 42 19N 42 40 E
Kutaradja = Banda Aceh 102 5 35N 95 20 E
Kutatjane 102 3 45N 97 50 E
Kutch, G. of 94 22 50N 69 15 E
Kutch, Rann of 94 24 0N 70 0 E
Kut'ien 109 26 36N 118 48 E
Kutina 63 45 29N 16 48 E
Kutiyana 94 21 36N 70 2 E
Kutjevo 66 45 23N 17 55 E
Kutkai 98 23 27N 97 56 E
Kutkashen 83 40 58N 47 47 E
Kutná Hora 52 49 57N 15 16 E
Kutno 54 52 15N 19 23 E
Kuttabul 138 21 5 S 148 48 E
Kutu 124 2 40 S 18 11 E
Kutum 123 14 20N 24 10 E
Kúty 53 48 40N 17 3 E
Kuŭptong 107 40 45N 126 1 E
Kuurne 47 50 51N 3 18 E
Kuvandyk 84 51 28N 57 21 E
Kuvasay 85 40 18N 71 59 E
Kuvshinovo 80 57 2N 34 11 E
Kuwait = Al Kuwayt 92 29 30N 47 30 E
Kuwait ■ 92 29 30N 47 30 E
Kuwana 111 35 0N 136 43 E
Kuyang 106 41 8N 110 1 E
Kuybyshev 81 55 27N 78 19 E
Kuybyshevo, Ukraine S.S.R., U.S.S.R. 82 47 25N 36 40 E
Kuybyshevo, Uzbek S.S.R., U.S.S.R. 85 40 20N 71 15 E
Kuybyshevskiy 85 37 52N 68 44 E
Kuybyshevskoye Vdkhr. 81 55 2N 49 30 E

*Renamed Ar Rachidya.

Kuyeh Ho, R. 106 38 30N 110 44 E
Kuylyuk 85 41 14N 69 17 E
Kuyto, Oz. 78 64 40N 31 0 E
Kuyüan, Hopeh, China 106 41 34N 115 38 E
Kuyüan, Ningsia Hui, China 106 36 1N 106 17 E
Kuzhithura 97 8 18N 77 11 E
Kuzino 84 57 1N 59 27 E
Kuzmin 66 45 2N 19 25 E
Kuznetsk 81 53 12N 46 40 E
Kuzomen 78 66 22N 36 50 E
Kvænangen 74 69 55N 21 15 E
Kvam 71 61 40N 9 42 E
Kvamsøy 71 61 7N 6 28 E
Kvarken 74 63 30N 21 0 E
Kvarner 63 44 50N 14 10 E
Kvarnerič 63 44 43N 14 37 E
Kvarnsveden 72 60 32N 15 25 E
Kvarntorp 72 59 8N 15 17 E
Kvås 71 58 16N 7 14 E
Kvernes 71 63 1N 7 44 E
Kvillsfors 73 57 24N 15 29 E
Kvina, R. 71 58 43N 6 52 E
Kvinesdal 71 58 18N 6 59 E
Kviteseid 71 59 24N 8 29 E
Kwabhaca 129 30 51 S 29 0 E
Kwadacha, R. 152 57 28N 125 38W
Kwakhanai 128 21 39 S 21 16 E
Kwakoegron 175 5 25N 55 25W
Kwale, Kenya 126 4 15 S 39 31 E
Kwale, Nigeria 121 6 18N 5 28 E
Kwale □ 126 4 15 S 39 10 E
Kwamouth 124 3 9 S 16 20 E
Kwando, R. 128 16 48 S 22 45 E
Kwangdaeri 107 40 31N 127 32 E
Kwangju 107 35 9N 126 54 E
Kwangsi-Chuang A.R. □ 109 24 0N 109 0 E
Kwangtung □ 109 23 45N 114 0 E
Kwara □ 121 8 0N 5 0 E
Kwaraga 128 20 26 S 24 32 E
Kwataboahegan, R. 150 51 9N 80 50W
Kwatisore 103 3 7 S 139 59 E
Kweichow □ 108 27 20N 107 0 E
Kweiyang = Kueiyang 108 26 35N 106 43 E
Kwethluk 147 60 45N 161 34W
Kwidzyn 54 54 45N 18 58 E
Kwigillingok 147 59 50N 163 10W
Kwiguk 147 63 45N 164 35W
Kwikila 135 9 49 S 147 38 E
Kwimba □ 126 3 0 S 33 0 E
Kwinana 137 32 15 S 115 47 E
Kwitaba 126 3 56 S 29 39 E
Kya-in-Seikkyi 98 16 2N 98 8 E
Kyabe 117 9 30N 19 0 E
Kyabra Cr. 139 25 36 S 142 55 E
Kyabram 139 36 19 S 145 4 E
Kyaiklat 98 16 46N 96 52 E
Kyaikmaraw 98 16 23N 97 44 E
Kyaikthin 98 23 32N 95 40 E
Kyaikto 100 17 20N 97 3 E
Kyakhta 77 50 30N 106 25 E
Kyangin 98 18 20N 95 20 E
Kyaring Tso 99 31 5N 88 25 E
Kyaukhnyat 98 18 15N 97 31 E
Kyaukpadaung 99 20 52N 95 8 E
Kyaukpyu 99 19 28N 93 30 E
Kyaukse 98 21 36N 96 10 E
Kyauktaw 98 21 16N 96 44 E
Kyawkku 98 21 48N 96 56 E
Kyburz 163 38 47N 120 18W
Kybybolite 140 36 53 S 140 55 E
Kyegegwa 126 0 30N 31 0 E
Kyeintali 98 18 0N 94 29 E
Kyela □ 127 9 45 S 34 0 E
Kyenjojo 126 0 40N 30 37 E
Kyidaunggan 98 19 53N 96 12 E
Kyle Dam 127 20 15 S 31 0 E
Kyle, dist. 34 55 32N 4 25W
Kyle of Lochalsh 36 57 17N 5 43W
Kyleakin 36 57 16N 5 44W
Kyneton 140 37 10 S 144 29 E
Kynuna 138 21 37 S 141 55 E
Kyō-ga-Saki 111 35 45N 135 15 E
Kyoga, L. 126 1 35N 33 0 E
Kyogle 139 28 40 S 153 0 E
Kyongju 107 35 51N 129 14 E
Kyongpyaw 99 17 12N 95 10 E
Kyŏngsŏng 107 41 35N 129 36 E
Kyōto 111 35 0N 135 45 E
Kyōto-fu □ 111 35 15N 135 30 E
Kyrinia 92 35 20N 33 20 E
Kyritz 48 52 57N 12 25 E
Kyrkebyn 72 59 18N 13 3 E
Kyrping 71 59 45N 6 5 E
Kyshtym 84 55 42N 60 34 E
Kystatyam 77 67 20N 123 10 E
Kytalktakh 77 65 30N 123 40 E
Kytlym 84 59 30N 59 12 E
Kyu-hkok 98 24 4N 98 4 E
Kyulyunken 77 64 10N 137 5 E
Kyunhla 98 23 25N 95 15 E
Kyuquot 152 50 3N 127 25W
Kyuquot Sd. 83 50 0N 127 25W
Kyurdamir 83 40 25N 48 3 E
Kyūshū 110 33 0N 131 0 E
Kyūshū □ 110 33 0N 131 0 E
Kyūshū-Sanchi 110 32 45N 131 40 E
Kyustendil 66 42 25N 22 41 E
Kyusyur 77 70 39N 127 15 E
Kywong 141 34 58 S 146 44 E
Kyzyl 77 51 50N 94 30 E
Kyzyl-Kiya 85 40 16N 72 8 E
Kyzyl Orda 85 44 56N 65 30 E
Kyzyl Rabat 76 37 45N 74 55 E
Kyzylkum 84 42 30N 65 0 E
Kyzylsu, R. 85 39 11N 72 2 E
Kzyl-orda 85 44 48N 65 28 E

L

Laa 53 48 43N 16 23 E
Laage 48 53 55N 12 21 E
Laasphe 48 50 56N 8 23 E
Laau Pt. 147 21 57N 159 40W
Laba, R. 83 45 0N 40 30 E
Laban, Burma 98 25 52N 96 40 E
Laban, Ireland 39 53 8N 8 50W
Labasheeda 39 52 37N 9 15W
Labastide 44 43 28N 2 39 E
Labastide-Murat 44 44 39N 1 33 E
Labbézenga 121 15 2N 0 48 E
Labdah = Leptis Magna 119 32 40N 14 12 E
Labé 120 11 24N 12 16W
Labe, R. 52 50 3N 15 20 E
Laberec, R. 53 21 57N 49 7 E
Laberge, L. 152 61 11N 135 12W
Labin 63 45 5N 14 8 E
Labinsk 83 44 40N 40 48W
Labis 101 2 22N 103 2 E
Labiszyn 54 52 57N 17 54 E
Laboa 103 8 6 S 122 50 E
Laboe 48 54 25N 10 13 E
Labouheyre 44 44 13N 0 55W
Laboulaye 172 34 10 S 63 30W
Labrador City 151 52 57N 66 55W
Labrador, Coast of ■ 149 53 20N 61 0W
Labranzagrande 174 5 33N 72 34W
Lábrea 174 7 15 S 64 51W
Labrède 44 44 41N 0 32W
Labuan, I. 102 5 15N 115 38W
Labuha 103 0 30 S 127 30 E
Labuhan 103 6 26 S 105 50 E
Labuhanbajo 103 8 28 S 120 1 E
Labuissière 47 50 19N 4 11 E
Labuk, Telok 102 6 10N 117 50 E
Labutta 98 16 9N 94 46 E
Labytnangi 78 66 29N 66 40 E
Lac Allard 151 50 33N 63 24W
Lac Bouchette 151 48 16N 72 11W
Lac du Flambeau 158 46 1N 89 51W
Lac Édouard 151 47 40N 72 16W
Lac la Biche 152 54 45N 111 58W
Lac-Mégantic 151 45 35N 70 53W
Lac Seul 153 50 28N 92 0W
Lac Thien 100 12 25N 108 11 E
Lacanau, Étang de 44 44 58N 1 7W
Lacanau Médoc 44 44 59N 1 5W
Lacantum, R. 165 16 36N 90 40W
Lacara, R. 57 39 7N 6 25W
Lacaune 44 43 43N 2 40 E
Lacaune, Mts. de 44 43 43N 2 50 E
Laccadive Is. = Lakshadweep Is. 86 10 0N 72 30 E
Laceby 33 53 32N 0 10W
Lacepede B. 140 36 40 S 139 40 E
Lacepede Is. 136 16 55 S 122 0 E
Lacerdónia 127 18 3 S 35 35 E
Lachen, Sikkim 98 47 12N 8 51 E
Lachen, Switz. 51 47 12N 8 51 E
Lachi 94 33 25N 71 20 E
Lachine 150 45 30N 73 40W
Lachlan 139 42 50 S 147 3 E
Lachlan, R. 140 34 22 S 143 55 E
Lachmangarh 94 27 50N 75 4 E
Lachute 150 45 39N 74 21 E
Lackagh Hills 38 54 14N 8 0W
Lackawanna 156 42 49N 78 50W
Lackawaxen 162 41 29N 74 59W
Lacock 28 51 24N 2 8W
Lacombe 152 52 30N 113 44W
Lacona 162 43 37N 76 5W
Láconi 64 39 54N 9 4 E
Laconia 162 43 32N 71 30W
Lacq 44 43 25N 0 35W
Lacrosse 160 46 51N 117 58W
Ladainha 171 17 39 S 41 44W
Ladakh Ra. 95 34 0N 78 0 E
Ladder Hills 37 57 14N 3 13W
Ladhar Bheinn 36 57 5N 5 37W
Ladhon, R. 69 37 40N 21 50 E
Lâdik 82 40 57N 35 58 E
Ladismith 128 33 28 S 21 15 E
Lâdiz 93 28 55N 61 15 E
Ladnun 94 27 38N 74 25 E
Ladock 30 50 19N 4 58W
Ladoga, L. = Ladozhskoye Oz. 78 61 15N 30 30 E
Ladon 43 48 0N 2 30 E
Ladozhskoye Ozero 76 61 15N 30 30 E
Ladrone Is. = Mariana Is. 130 17 0N 145 0 E
Lady Babbie 127 18 30 S 29 20 E
Lady Beatrix L. 150 5 20N 76 50W
Lady Edith Lagoon 136 20 36 S 126 47 E
Lady Grey 128 30 43 S 27 13 E
Ladybank 35 56 16N 3 8W
Ladybrand 128 29 9 S 27 29 E
Lady's I. Lake 39 52 12N 6 23W
Ladysmith, Can. 152 49 0N 123 49W
Ladysmith, S. Afr. 129 28 32 S 29 46 E
Ladysmith, U.S.A. 158 45 27N 91 4W
Lae 135 6 40 S 147 2 E
Laem Ngop 101 12 10N 102 26 E
Laem Pho 101 6 55N 101 19 E
Læsø 73 57 15N 10 53 E
Læsø Rende 73 57 20N 10 45 E
Lafayette, Colo., U.S.A. 158 40 0N 105 2W
Lafayette, Ga., U.S.A. 157 34 44N 85 15W
Lafayette, La., U.S.A. 159 30 18N 92 0W
Lafayette, Tenn., U.S.A. 157 36 35N 86 0W
Laferté 150 48 37N 78 48W
Laferte, R. 152 61 53N 117 44W
Laffan's Bridge 39 52 36N 7 45W
Lafia 121 8 30N 8 34 E
Lafiagi 121 8 52N 5 20 E
Lafleche 153 49 45N 106 40W
Lafon 123 5 5N 32 29 E
Laforest 150 47 4N 81 12W
Laforsen 72 61 56N 15 3 E
Lagaip, R. 135 5 4 S 141 52 E
Lagan 73 56 32N 12 58 E
Lagan, R. 38 54 35N 5 55W
Lagarfljót 74 65 40N 14 18W
Lagarto 170 10 54 S 37 41W
Lagarto, Serra do 173 23 0 S 57 15W
Lage, Ger. 48 52 0N 8 47 E
Lage, Spain 56 43 13N 9 0W
Lage-Mierde 47 51 25N 5 9 E
Lågen 71 61 29N 10 2 E
Lågen, R. 75 61 30N 10 20 E
Lägerdorf 48 53 53N 9 35 E
Lagg 34 56 57N 5 50W
Laggan, Grampian, U.K. 37 57 24N 3 6W
Laggan, Highland, U.K. 37 57 3N 4 48W
Laggan B. 34 55 40N 6 20W
Laggan L. 37 56 57N 4 30W
Laggers Pt. 139 30 52 S 153 4 E
Laghman □ 93 34 20N 70 0 E
Laghouat 118 33 50N 2 59 E
Laghy 38 54 37N 8 7W
Lagnieu 45 45 55N 5 20 E
Lagny 43 48 52N 2 40 E
Lago 65 39 9N 16 8 E
Lagôa 57 37 8N 8 27W
Lagoaça 56 41 11N 6 44W
Lagodekhi 83 41 50N 46 22 E
Lagónegro 65 40 8N 15 45 E
Lagonoy Gulf 103 13 50N 123 50 E
Lagos, Nigeria 121 6 25N 3 27 E
Lagos, Port. 57 37 5N 8 41W
Lagos de Moreno 164 21 21N 101 55W
Lagrange 136 14 13 S 125 46 E
Lagrange B. 136 18 38 S 121 42 E
Laguardia 58 42 33N 2 35W
Laguépie 44 44 8N 1 57 E
Laguna, Brazil 173 28 30 S 48 50W
Laguna, U.S.A. 161 35 3N 107 28W
Laguna Beach 163 33 31N 117 52W
Laguna Dam 161 32 55N 114 30W
Laguna de la Janda 57 36 15N 5 45W
Laguna Limpia 172 26 32 S 59 45W
Laguna Madre 165 27 0N 97 20W
Laguna Veneta 63 45 23N 12 25 E
Lagunas, Chile 172 21 0 S 69 45W
Lagunas, Peru 174 5 10 S 75 35W
Lagunillas 174 10 8N 71 16W
Lahad Datu 103 5 0N 118 30 E
Lahaina 147 20 52N 156 41W
Lahan Sai 100 14 25N 102 52 E
Lahanam 100 16 16N 105 16 E
Lahardaun 38 54 2N 9 20W
Laharpur 95 27 43N 80 56 E
Lahat 102 3 45 S 103 30 E
Lahe 98 19 18N 93 36 E
Lahewa 102 1 22N 97 12 E
Lahijan 93 37 10N 50 6 E
Lahn, R. 48 50 52N 8 35 E
Laholm 73 56 30N 13 2 E
Laholmsbukten 73 56 30N 12 45 E
Lahontan Res. 160 39 28N 118 58W
Lahore 94 31 32N 74 22 E
Lahore □ 94 31 55N 74 5 E
Lahpongsel 98 27 7N 98 25 E
Lahr 49 48 20N 7 52 E
Lahti 75 60 58N 25 40 E
Lai (Béhagle) 117 9 25N 16 30 E
Lai Chau 100 22 5N 103 3 E
Lai-hka 98 21 16N 97 40 E
Laiagam 135 5 33 S 143 30 E
Laian 109 32 27N 118 25 E
Laichou Wan 107 37 30N 119 30 E
Laidley 139 27 39 S 152 20 E
Laidon L. 37 56 40N 4 40W
Laifeng 108 29 31N 109 18 E
Laigle 42 48 46N 0 38 E
Laignes 43 47 50N 4 20 E
Laihsi 107 36 51N 120 30 E
Laikipia □ 126 0 30N 36 30 E
Laila 92 22 10N 46 40 E
Laillahue, Mt. 174 17 0 S 69 30W
Laingsburg 128 33 9 S 20 52 E
Laipin 108 23 42N 109 16 E
Lairg 37 58 1N 4 24W
Lais 102 3 35 S 102 0 E
Laishui 106 39 23N 115 42 E
Laiwu 107 36 12N 117 38 E
Laiyang 107 36 58N 120 41 E
Laiyüan 106 39 19N 114 41 E
Laja, R. 164 20 55N 100 46W
Lajes, Rio Grande d. N., Brazil 170 5 41 S 36 14W
Lajes, Sta. Catarina, Brazil 173 27 48 S 50 20W
Lajinha 171 20 9 S 41 37W
Lajkovac 66 44 27N 20 14 E
Lajosmizse 53 47 3N 19 32 E
Lak Sao 100 18 11N 104 59 E
Laka Chih 95 30 40N 81 10 E
Lakaband 94 31 2N 69 15 E
Lakar 103 8 15 S 128 17 E
Lake Alpine 163 38 29N 120 0W
Lake Andes 158 43 10N 98 32W
Lake Anse 156 46 42N 88 25W
Lake Arthur 159 30 8N 92 40W
Lake Brown 137 30 56 S 118 20 E
Lake Cargelligo 141 33 15 S 146 22 E
Lake Charles 159 31 10N 93 10W
Lake City, Colo, U.S.A. 161 38 3N 107 27W
Lake City, Fla., U.S.A. 157 30 10N 82 40W
Lake City, Iowa, U.S.A. 158 42 12N 94 42W
Lake City, Mich., U.S.A. 156 44 20N 85 10W
Lake City, Minn., U.S.A. 158 44 28N 92 21W
Lake City, S.C., U.S.A. 157 33 51N 79 44W
Lake Coleridge 143 43 17 S 171 30 E
Lake District 23 54 30N 3 10W
Lake George 162 43 25N 73 43W
Lake Grace 137 33 7 S 118 28 E
Lake Harbour 149 62 30N 69 50W
Lake Havasu City 161 34 25N 114 29W
Lake Hughes 163 34 41N 118 26W
Lake Isabella 163 35 38N 118 28W
Lake King 137 33 5 S 119 45 E
Lake Lenore 153 52 24N 104 59W
Lake Louise 152 51 30N 116 10W
Lake Mason 137 27 30 S 119 30 E
Lake Mead Nat. Rec. Area 161 36 0N 114 30W
Lake Mills 158 43 23N 93 33W
Lake Murray 135 6 48 S 141 29 E
Lake Nash 138 20 57 S 138 0 E
Lake of the Woods 155 49 0N 95 0W
Lake Pleasant 162 43 28N 74 25W
Lake Providence 159 32 49N 91 12W
Lake River 150 54 22N 82 31W
Lake Superior Prov. Park 150 47 45N 84 45W
Lake Tekapo 143 43 55 S 170 30 E
Lake Traverse 150 45 56N 78 4W
Lake Varley 137 32 48 S 119 30 E
Lake Village 159 33 20N 91 19W
Lake Wales 157 27 55N 81 32W
Lake Worth 157 26 36N 80 3W
Lakefield 150 44 25N 78 16W
Lakehurst 162 40 1N 74 19W
Lakeland 157 28 0N 82 0W
Lakenheath 29 52 25N 0 30 E
Lakes Entrance 141 37 50 S 148 0 E
Lakeside, Ariz., U.S.A. 161 34 12N 109 59W
Lakeside, Calif., U.S.A. 163 32 52N 116 55W
Lakeside, Nebr., U.S.A. 158 42 5N 102 24W
Lakeview, N.Y., U.S.A. 156 42 43N 78 57W
Lakeview, Oreg., U.S.A. 160 42 15N 120 22W
Lakewood, Calif., U.S.A. 163 33 51N 118 8W
Lakewood, N.J., U.S.A. 162 40 5N 74 13W
Lakhaniá 69 35 58N 27 54 E
Lákhi 69 35 24N 23 27 E
Lakhimpur 95 27 14N 94 7 E
Lakhipur, Assam, India 98 24 48N 93 0 E
Lakhipur, Assam, India 98 26 2N 90 18 E
Lakhonpheng 100 15 54N 105 34 E
Lakhpat 94 23 48N 68 47 E
Laki 74 64 4N 18 14W
Lakin 159 37 58N 101 18W
Lakitusaki, R. 150 54 21N 82 25W
Lakki 93 32 38N 70 50 E
Lakonía □ 69 36 55N 22 30 E
Lakonikós Kólpos 69 36 40N 22 40 E
Lakor, I. 103 8 15 S 128 17 E
Lakota, Ivory C. 120 5 50N 5 30W
Lakota, U.S.A. 158 48 0N 98 22W
Laksefjorden 74 70 45N 26 50 E
Lakselv 74 70 2N 24 56 E
Lakselvbukt 74 69 26N 19 40 E
Lakshadweep Is. 86 10 0N 72 30 E
Laksham 98 23 14N 91 8 E
Lakshmi Kantapur 95 22 5N 88 20 E
Lakshmipur 98 22 38N 88 16 E
Lakuramau 135 2 54 S 151 15 E
Lala Ghat 99 24 30N 92 40 E
Lala Musa 94 32 40N 73 57 E
Lalago 126 3 28 S 33 58 E
Lalapanzi 127 19 20 S 30 15 E
Lalganj 95 25 52N 85 13 E
Lalibala 123 12 8N 39 10 E
Lalin 107 45 14N 126 52 E
Lalín 56 42 40N 8 5W
Lalin Ho, R. 107 45 28N 125 43 E
Lalinde 44 44 50N 0 44 E
Lalitapur 99 26 36N 85 32 E
Lalitpur 95 24 42N 78 28 E
Lam 100 21 21N 106 31 E
Lam Pao Res. 100 16 50N 103 15 E
Lama Kara 121 9 30N 1 15 E
Lamaing 99 15 25N 97 53 E
Lamaipum 98 25 40N 97 57 E
Lamar, Colo., U.S.A. 158 38 9N 102 35W
Lamar, Mo., U.S.A. 159 37 30N 94 20W
Lamas 174 6 28 S 76 31W
Lamastre 45 44 59N 4 35 E
Lamaya 108 29 50N 99 56 E
Lamb Hd. 37 59 5N 2 32W
Lambach 52 48 6N 13 51 E
Lamballe 42 48 29N 2 31W
Lambaréné 124 0 20 S 10 12 E
Lambay I. 38 53 30N 6 0W

Lambayeque □ 174 6 45 S 80 0W
Lamberhurst 29 51 5N 0 21 E
Lambert 158 47 44N 104 39W
Lambert, C. 135 4 11 S 151 31 E
Lambert Land 12 79 12N 20 30W
Lambesc 45 43 39N 5 16 E
Lambeth 29 51 27N 0 7W
Lambi Kyun, (Sullivan I.) 101 10 50N 98 20 E
Lámbia 69 37 52N 21 53 E
Lambley 35 54 56N 2 30W
Lambon 135 4 45 S 152 48 E
Lambourn 28 51 31N 1 31W
Lambro, R. 62 45 18N 9 20 E
Lambs Hd. 39 51 44N 10 10W
Lame 121 10 27N 9 12 E
Lame Deer 160 45 45N 106 40W
Lamego 56 41 5N 7 52W
Lameque 151 47 45N 64 38W
Lameroo 140 35 19 S 140 33 E
Lamesa 159 32 45N 101 57W
Lamhult 73 57 12N 14 36 E
Lamia 69 38 55N 22 41 E
• Lamitan 103 6 40N 122 10 E
Lammermuir 35 55 50N 2 25W
Lammermuir Hills 35 55 50N 2 40W
Lamoille 160 40 47N 115 31W
Lamon Bay 103 14 30N 122 20 E
Lamont, Can. 152 53 46N 112 50W
Lamont, U.S.A. 163 35 15N 118 55W
Lampa 174 15 10 S 70 30W
Lampang 100 18 18N 99 31 E
Lampasas 159 31 5N 98 10W
Lampaul 42 48 28N 5 7W
Lampazos de Naranjo 164 27 2N 100 32W
Lampedusa, I. 60 35 36N 12 40 E
Lampeter 31 52 6N 4 6W
Lampione, I. 119 35 33N 12 20 E
Lampman 153 49 25N 102 50W
Lamprechtshausen 52 48 0N 12 58 E
Lampung 102 1 48 S 115 0 E
Lamu, Burma 98 19 14N 94 10 E
Lamu, Kenya 126 2 10 S 40 55 E
Lamy 161 35 30N 105 58W
Lan Tsan Kiang (Mekong) 87 18 0N 104 15 E
Lanai City 147 20 50N 156 56W
Lanai I. 147 20 50N 156 55W
Lanak La 95 34 27N 79 32 E
Lanaken 47 50 53N 5 39 E
Lanak'o Shank'ou = Lanak La 95 34 27N 79 32 E
Lanao, L. 103 7 52N 124 15 E
Lanark 35 55 40N 3 48W
Lanark (□) 26 55 37N 3 50W
Lancashire □ 32 53 40N 2 30W
Lancaster, Can. 151 45 17N 66 10W
Lancaster, U.K. 32 54 3N 2 48W
Lancaster, Calif., U.S.A. 163 34 47N 118 8W
Lancaster, Ky., U.S.A. 156 37 40N 84 40W
Lancaster, Pa., U.S.A. 162 40 4N 76 19W
Lancaster, S.C., U.S.A. 157 34 45N 80 47W
Lancaster, Va., U.S.A. 162 37 46N 76 28W
Lancaster, Wis., U.S.A. 158 42 48N 90 43W
Lancaster Sd. 12 74 13N 84 0W
Lancer 153 50 48N 108 53W
Lanchester 33 54 50N 1 44W
Lanch'i 109 29 11N 119 30 E
Lanchou 106 36 5N 103 55 E
Lanciano 63 42 15N 14 22 E
Lancing 29 50 49N 0 19W
Łancut 54 50 10N 22 20 E
Lancy 50 46 12N 6 8 E
Lândana 124 5 11 S 12 5 E
Landau 49 49 12N 8 7 E
Landeck 52 47 9N 10 34 E
Landen 47 50 45N 5 3 E
Lander, Austral. 136 20 25 S 132 0 E
Lander, U.S.A. 160 42 50N 108 49W
Landerneau 42 48 28N 4 17W
Landeryd 73 57 7N 13 15 E
Landes □ 44 43 57N 0 48W
Landes, Les 44 44 20N 1 0W
Landete 58 39 56N 1 25W
Landi Kotal 94 34 7N 71 6 E
Landivisiau 42 48 31N 4 6W
Landkey 30 51 2N 4 0W
Landor 137 25 10 S 117 0 E
Landquart 51 46 58N 9 32 E
Landquart, R. 51 46 50N 9 47 E
Landrecies 43 50 7N 3 40 E
Land's End, Can. 12 76 10N 123 0W
Land's End, U.K. 30 50 4N 5 43W
Landsberg 49 48 3N 10 52 E
Landsborough Cr. 138 22 28 S 144 35 E
Landsbro 73 57 24N 14 56 E
Landschaft 50 47 28N 7 40 E
Landshut 48 48 31N 12 10 E
Landskrona 73 56 53N 12 50 E
Landvetter 73 57 41N 12 17 E
Lane 73 58 25N 12 3 E
Laneffe 47 50 17N 4 35 E
Lanesboro 162 41 57N 75 34W
Lanesborough 38 53 40N 8 0W
Lanett 157 33 0N 85 15W
Lang Bay 152 49 17N 124 21W
Lang Qua 100 22 16N 104 27 E
Lang Shan 106 41 0N 106 20 E
Lang Suan 101 9 57N 99 4 E
Langaa 73 56 23N 9 51 E
Lángadhás 68 40 46N 23 2 E
Langádhia 69 37 43N 22 1 E
Långan 72 63 19N 14 44 E

*Renamed Isabela

Langara I. 152 54 14N 133 1W
Langavat L. 36 58 4N 6 48W
Langchen Khambah (Sutlej) 95 31 25N 80 0 E
Langch'i 109 31 10N 119 10 E
Langchung 108 31 31N 105 58 E
Langdon 158 48 47N 98 24W
Langdorp 47 50 59N 4 52 E
Langeac 44 45 7N 3 29 E
Langeb, R. 122 17 28N 36 50 E
Langeberge, C. Prov., S. Afr. 128 28 15 S 22 33 E
Langeberge, C. Prov., S. Afr. 128 33 55 S 21 20 E
Langeland 73 54 56N 10 48 E
Langelands Bælt 73 54 55N 10 56 E
Langemark 47 50 55N 2 55 E
Langen 49 53 36N 8 36 E
Langenburg 153 50 51N 101 43W
Langeness 48 54 34N 8 35 E
Langenlois 52 48 29N 15 40 E
Langensalza 48 51 6N 10 40 E
Langenthal 50 47 13N 7 47 E
Langeoog 48 53 44N 7 33 E
Langeskov 73 55 22N 10 35 E
Langesund 71 59 0N 9 45 E
Langhem 73 57 36N 13 14 E
Länghem 73 57 36N 13 14 E
Langhirano 62 44 39N 10 16 E
Langholm 35 55 9N 2 59W
Langidoon 140 31 36 S 142 2 E
Langjökull 74 64 39N 20 12W
Langkawi I. 101 6 20N 99 45 E
Langkawi, P. 101 6 25N 99 45 E
Langkon 102 6 30N 116 40 E
Langk'ouhsü 109 26 8N 115 10 E
Langlade, Can. 150 48 14N 76 10W
Langlade, St. P. & M. 151 46 50N 56 20W
Langlo 139 26 26 S 146 5 E
Langlois 160 42 54N 124 26W
Langnau 50 46 56N 7 47 E
Langness 32 54 3N 4 37W
Langogne 44 44 43N 3 50 E
Langon 44 44 33N 0 16W
Langøya 74 68 45N 15 10 E
Langport 28 51 2N 2 51W
Langres 43 47 52N 5 20 E
Langres, Plateau de 43 47 45N 5 20 E
Langsa 102 4 30N 97 57 E
Långsele 72 63 12N 17 4 E
Långshyttan 72 60 27N 16 2 E
Langson 100 21 52N 106 42 E
Langstrothdale Chase 32 54 14N 2 13W
Langtai 108 26 6N 105 20 E
Langtao 98 27 15N 97 34 E
Langting 98 25 31N 93 7 E
Langtoft 29 52 42N 0 19W
Langtree 30 50 55N 4 11W
Langtry 159 29 50N 101 33W
Langu 101 6 53N 99 47 E
Languedoc □ 44 43 58N 3 22 E
Langwies 51 46 50N 9 44 E
Lanhsien 106 38 17N 111 38 E
Lanigan 153 51 51N 105 2W
Lank'ao 106 34 50N 114 49 E
Lanna 72 59 16N 14 56 E
Lannemezan 44 43 8N 0 23 E
Lannercost 138 18 35 S 146 0 E
Lannilis 42 48 35N 4 32W
Lannion 42 48 46N 3 29W
Lanouaille 44 45 24N 1 9 E
Lanp'ing 108 26 25N 99 24 E
Lansdale 162 40 14N 75 18W
Lansdowne 141 31 48 S 152 30 E
Lansdowne House 150 52 14N 87 53W
Lansford 162 40 48N 75 55W
Lanshan 109 25 18N 112 6 E
Lansing 156 42 47N 84 32W
Lanslebourg-Mont-Cenis 45 45 17N 6 52 E
Lanta Yai, Ko 101 7 35N 99 3 E
Lant'ien 106 34 3N 109 20 E
Lants'ang 108 22 40N 99 58 E
Lants'ang Chiang, R. 108 30 0N 98 0 E
Lantsien 99 32 4N 96 6 E
Lants'un 107 36 24N 120 10 E
Lantuna 103 8 19 S 124 8 E
Lanus 172 34 44 S 58 27W
Lanusei 64 39 53N 9 31 E
Lanzarote, I. 116 29 0N 13 40W
Lanzo Torinese 62 45 16N 7 29 E
Lao Bao 100 16 35N 106 30 E
Lao Cai 100 22 30N 103 57 E
Lao, R. 65 39 45N 15 45 E
Laoag 103 18 7N 120 34 E
Laoang 103 12 32N 125 8 E
Laoha Ho, R. 107 43 24N 120 39 E
Laois □ 39 53 0N 7 20W
Laon 43 49 33N 3 35 E
Laona 156 45 32N 88 41W
Laos ■ 100 17 45N 105 0 E
Lapa 173 25 46 S 49 44W
Lapalisse 44 46 15N 3 44 E
Laparan Cap, I. 103 6 0N 120 0 E
Lapeer 156 43 3N 83 20W
Lapford 30 50 52N 3 49W
Lapi □ 74 67 0N 27 0 E
Lapland = Lappland 74 68 7N 24 0 E
Laporte 162 41 27N 76 30W
Lapovo 66 44 10N 21 2 E
Lappland 74 68 7N 24 0 E
Laprida 172 37 34 S 60 45W
Laptev Sea 77 76 0N 125 0 E
Lapush 160 47 56N 124 33W
Lăpuşu, R. 70 47 25N 23 40 E
Lar 93 27 40N 54 14 E
Lara 140 38 2 S 144 26 E
Lara □ 174 10 10N 69 50W
Larabanga 120 9 16N 1 56W
Laracha 56 43 15N 8 35W
Larache 118 35 10N 6 5W
Laragh 39 53 0N 6 20W
Laragne-Montéglin 45 44 18N 5 49 E
Laramie 158 41 15N 105 29W
Laramie Mts. 158 42 0N 105 30W
Laranjeiras 170 10 48 S 37 10W
Laranjeiras do Sul 173 25 23 S 52 23W
Larantuka 103 8 5 S 122 55 E
Larap 103 14 18N 122 39 E
Larat, I. 103 7 0 S 132 0 E
Larbert 35 56 2N 3 50W
Lärbro 73 57 47N 18 50 E
Larch, R. 149 57 30N 71 0W
Lårdal 71 59 20N 8 25 E
Lårdal 71 59 25N 8 10 E
Larde 127 16 28 S 39 43 E
Larder Lake 150 48 5N 79 40W
Lárdhos, Ákra 69 36 4N 28 10 E
Laredo, Spain 58 43 26N 3 28W
Laredo, U.S.A. 159 27 34N 99 29W
Laredo Sd. 152 52 30N 128 53W
Laren 46 52 16N 5 14 E
Largeau (Faya) 117 17 58N 19 6 E
Largentière 45 44 34N 4 18 E
Largs 34 55 48N 4 51W
Lari 62 43 34N 10 35 E
Lariang 103 1 35 S 119 25 E
Larimore 158 47 55N 97 35W
Larino 65 41 48N 14 54 E
Lárisa 68 39 38N 22 28 E
Lárisa □ 68 39 39N 22 24 E
Larkana 94 27 32N 68 2 E
Larkollen 71 59 20N 10 41 E
Larnaca 92 35 0N 33 35 E
Lárnax 92 35 0N 33 35 E
Larne 38 54 52N 5 50W
Larne L. 38 54 52N 5 50W
Larned 158 38 15N 99 10W
Laroch 36 56 40N 5 9W
Larochette 47 49 47N 6 13 E
Laroquebrou 44 44 58N 2 12 E
Larrey, Pt. 136 19 55 S 119 7 E
Larrimah 136 15 35 S 133 12 E
Larsen Ice Shelf 13 67 0 S 62 0W
Larteh 121 5 50N 0 5W
Laru 126 2 54N 24 25 E
Larvik 71 59 4N 10 0 E
Laryak 76 61 15N 80 0 E
Larzac, Causse du 44 44 0N 3 17 E
Las Animas 159 38 8N 103 18W
Las Anod 91 8 26N 47 19 E
Las Blancos 59 37 38N 0 49W
Las Bonitas 174 7 50N 65 40W
Las Brenãs 172 27 5 S 61 7W
Las Cabezas de San Juan 57 37 0N 5 58W
Las Cruces 161 32 25N 106 50W
Las Flores 172 36 0 S 59 0W
Las Heras, Mendoza, Argent. 173 32 51 S 68 49W
Las Heras, Santa Cruz, Argent. 176 46 30 S 69 0W
Las Huertas, Cabo de 59 38 22N 0 24W
Las Khoreh 91 11 4N 48 20 E
Las Lajas 176 38 30 S 70 25W
Las Lajitas 174 6 55N 65 39W
Las Lomitas 172 24 35 S 60 50W
Las Marismas 57 37 5N 6 20W
Las Mercedes 174 9 7N 66 24W
Las Navas de la Concepción 57 37 56N 5 30W
Las Navas de Tolosa 57 38 18N 3 38W
Las Palmas, Argent. 172 27 8 S 58 45W
Las Palmas, Canary Is. 116 28 10N 15 28W
Las Palmas □ 116 28 10N 15 28W
Las Piedras 173 34 35 S 56 20W
Las Plumas 176 43 40 S 67 15W
Las Rosas 172 32 30 S 61 40W
Las Tablas 166 7 49N 80 14W
Las Termas 172 27 29 S 64 52W
Las Tres Marías, Is. 164 20 12N 106 30W
Las Varillas 172 32 0 S 62 50W
Las Vegas, Nev., U.S.A. 161 36 10N 115 5W
Las Vegas, N.M., U.S.A. 161 35 35N 105 10W
Lascano 173 33 35 S 54 18W
Lascaux 44 45 5N 1 10 E
Lashburn 153 53 10N 109 40W
Lashio 98 22 56N 97 45 E
Lashkar 94 26 10N 78 10 E
Łasin 54 53 30N 19 2 E
Lasithi □ 69 35 5N 25 50 E
Lask 54 51 34N 19 8 E
Laskill 33 54 19N 1 6W
Laško 63 46 10N 15 16 E
Lassance 171 17 54 S 44 34W
Lassay 42 48 27N 0 30W
Lassen, Pk. 160 40 20N 121 0W
Lasswade 35 55 53N 3 8W
Last Mountain L. 153 51 5N 105 14W
Lastoursville 124 0 55 S 12 38 E
Lastovo 63 42 46N 16 55 E
Lastovo, I. 63 42 46N 16 55 E
Lastovski Kanal 63 42 50N 17 0 E
Lat Yao 100 15 45N 99 48 E
Latacunga 174 0 50 S 78 35W
Latakia = Al Ladhiqiya 92 35 30N 35 45 E
Latchford 150 47 20N 79 50W
Laterza 65 40 38N 16 47 E
Latham 137 29 44 S 116 20 E
Lathen 48 52 51N 7 21 E
Latheron 37 58 17N 3 20W
Lathrop Wells 163 36 39N 116 24W
Latiano 65 40 33N 17 43 E
Latina 64 41 26N 12 53 E
Latisana 63 45 47N 13 1 E
Latium = Lazio 63 42 0N 12 30 E
Laton 163 36 26N 119 41W
Latorica, R. 53 48 31N 22 0 E
Latouche 147 60 0N 148 0W
Latouche Treville, C. 136 18 27 S 121 49 E
Latrobe 138 38 8 S 146 44 E
Latrobe, Mt. 139 39 0 S 146 23 E
Latrónico 65 40 5N 16 0 E
Latrun 90 31 50N 34 58 E
Latur 96 18 25N 76 40 E
Latvia, S.S.R. □ 80 56 50N 24 0 E
Latzu 105 29 10N 87 45 E
Lauchhammer 48 51 35N 13 40 E
Laudal 71 58 15N 7 30 E
Lauder 35 55 43N 2 45W
Lauderdale 35 55 43N 2 44W
Lauenburg 48 53 23N 10 33 E
Läufelfingen 50 47 24N 7 52 E
Laufen 50 47 25N 7 30 E
Laugarbakki 74 65 20N 20 55W
Laugharne 31 51 45N 4 28W
Laujar 59 37 0N 2 54W
Launceston, Austral. 138 41 24 S 147 8 E
Launceston, U.K. 30 50 38N 4 21W
Laune, R. 39 52 5N 9 40W
Launglon Bok 101 13 50N 97 54 E
Laupheim 49 48 13N 9 53 E
Laura, Queens., Austral. 133 15 32 S 144 32 E
Laura, S.A., Austral. 140 33 10 S 138 18 E
Lauragh 39 51 46N 9 46W
Laureana di Borrello 65 38 28N 16 5 E
Laurel, Del., U.S.A. 162 38 33N 75 34W
Laurel, Md., U.S.A. 162 39 6N 76 51W
Laurel, Miss., U.S.A. 159 31 50N 89 0W
Laurel, Mont., U.S.A. 160 45 46N 108 49W
Laurencekirk 37 56 50N 2 30W
Laurencetown 39 53 14N 8 11W
Laurens 157 34 32N 82 2W
Laurentian Plat. 151 52 0N 70 0W
Laurentides, Parc Prov. des 151 47 45N 71 15W
Lauria 65 40 3N 15 50 E
Laurie I. 13 60 0 S 46 0W
Laurie L. 153 56 35N 101 57W
Laurieston 35 54 57N 4 2W
Laurinburg 157 34 50N 79 25W
Laurium 156 47 14N 88 26W
Lausanne 50 46 32N 6 38 E
Laut Kecil, Kepulauan 102 4 45 S 115 40 E
Laut, Kepulauan 102 4 45N 108 0 E
Lauterbach 48 50 39N 9 23 E
Lauterbrunnen 50 46 36N 7 55 E
Lauterecken 49 49 39N 7 35 E
Lauwe 47 50 47N 3 12 E
Lauwers 46 53 32N 6 23 E
Lauwers Zee 46 53 21N 6 13 E
Lauzon 151 46 48N 71 10W
Lava Hot Springs 160 42 38N 112 1W
Lavadores 56 42 14N 8 41W
Lavagna 62 44 18N 9 22 E
Laval 42 48 4N 0 48W
Lavalle 172 28 15 S 65 15W
Lavandou, Le 45 43 8N 6 22 E
Lávara 68 41 19N 26 22 E
Lavardac 44 44 12N 0 20 E
Lavaur 44 43 42N 1 49 E
Lavaux 50 46 30N 6 45 E
Lavaveix 44 46 5N 2 8 E
Lavelanet 44 42 57N 1 51 E
Lavello 65 41 4N 15 47 E
Lavendon 29 52 11N 0 39W
Lavenham 29 52 7N 0 48 E
Laverendrye Prov. Park 150 46 15N 17 15W
Laverne 159 36 43N 99 58W
Lavers Hill 140 38 40 S 143 25 E
Laverton 137 28 44 S 122 29 E
Lavi 90 32 47N 35 25 E
Lavik 71 61 6N 5 25 E
Lávkos 69 39 9N 23 14 E
Lavos 56 40 6N 8 49W
Lavras 173 21 20 S 45 0W
Lavre 57 38 46N 8 22W
Lavrentiya 77 65 35N 171 0W
Lávrion 69 37 40N 24 4 E
Lavumisa 129 27 20 S 31 55 E
Lawas 102 4 55N 115 40 E
Lawele 103 5 16 S 123 3 E
Lawers 35 56 31N 4 9W
Lawksawk 98 21 15N 96 52 E
Lawn Hill 138 18 36 S 138 33 E
Lawng Pit 99 26 45N 98 35 E
Lawra 120 10 39N 2 51W
Lawrence, Austral. 173 29 30 S 153 8 E
Lawrence, Kans., U.S.A. 158 39 0N 95 10W
Lawrence, Mass., U.S.A. 162 42 40N 71 9W
Lawrenceburg, Ind., U.S.A. 156 39 5N 84 50W
Lawrenceburg, Tenn., U.S.A. 157 35 12N 87 19W
Lawrenceville, Ga., U.S.A. 157 33 55N 83 59W

Lawrenceville, Pa., U.S.A. 162 42 0N 77 8W
Laws 163 37 24N 118 20W
Lawton 159 34 33N 98 25W
Lawu Mt. 103 7 40S 111 13E
Laxa 72 59 0N 14 37E
Laxey 32 54 15N 4 23W
Laxfield 29 52 18N 1 23E
Laxford, L. 36 58 25N 5 10W
Laxmeshwar 97 15 9N 75 28E
Laysan I. 143 25 30N 167 0W
Laytonville 160 39 44N 123 29W
Laytown 38 53 40N 6 15W
Laza 98 26 30N 97 38E
Lazarevac 66 44 23N 20 17E
Lazio □ 63 42 10N 12 30E
Lazonby 32 54 45N 2 42W
Łazy 54 50 27N 19 24E
Łbzenica 54 53 18N 17 15E
Lea 33 53 22N 0 45W
Lea, R. 29 51 40N 0 3W
Leach 101 12 21N 103 46E
Lead 158 44 20N 103 40W
Leadenham 33 53 5N 0 33W
Leader 153 50 50N 109 30W
Leadhills 35 55 25N 3 47W
Leadville 161 39 17N 106 23W
Leaf, R., Can. 149 58 47N 70 4W
Leaf, R., U.S.A. 159 31 45N 89 20W
Leakey 159 29 45N 99 45W
Leaksville 157 36 30N 79 49W
Lealui 125 15 10S 23 2E
Leamington, Can. 150 42 3N 82 36W
Leamington, N.Z. 130 37 55S 175 29E
Leamington, U.K. 28 52 18N 1 32W
Leamington, U.S.A. 160 39 37N 112 17W
Leandro Norte Alem 173 27 34S 55 15W
Leane L. 39 52 2N 9 32W
Leaoto, Mt. 70 45 20N 25 20E
Leap 39 51 34N 9 11W
Learmonth 136 22 40S 114 10E
Leask 153 53 5N 106 45W
Leatherhead 29 51 18N 0 20W
Leavenworth, Mo., U.S.A. 158 39 25N 95 0W
Leavenworth, Wash., U.S.A. 160 47 44N 120 37W
Łeba 54 54 45N 17 32E
Lebak 103 6 32N 124 5E
Lebane 66 42 56N 21 44E
Lebanon, Ind., U.S.A. 156 40 3N 86 55W
Lebanon, Kans., U.S.A. 158 39 50N 98 35W
Lebanon, Ky., U.S.A. 156 37 35N 85 15W
Lebanon, Mo., U.S.A. 159 37 40N 92 40W
Lebanon, Oreg., U.S.A. 160 44 31N 122 57W
Lebanon, Pa., U.S.A. 162 40 20N 76 28W
Lebanon, Tenn., U.S.A. 157 36 15N 86 20W
Lebanon ■ 92 34 0N 36 0E
Lebbeke 47 51 0N 4 8E
Lebec 163 34 36N 118 59W
Lebedin 80 50 35N 34 30E
Lebedyan 81 53 0N 39 10E
Lebomboberge 129 24 30S 32 0E
Łebork 54 54 33N 17 46E
Lebrija 57 36 53N 6 5W
Lebu 172 37 40S 73 47W
Lecce 65 40 20N 18 10E
Lecco 62 45 50N 9 27E
Lecco, L. di. 62 45 51N 9 22E
Lécera 58 41 13N 0 43W
Lech 52 47 13N 10 9E
Lech, R. 49 48 45N 10 45E
Lechlade 28 51 42N 1 40W
Lechtaler Alpen 52 47 15N 10 30E
Lectoure 44 43 56N 0 38E
Łeczyca 54 52 5N 19 45E
Ledbury 28 52 3N 2 25W
Lede 47 50 58N 3 59E
Ledeberg 47 51 2N 3 45E
Ledec 52 49 41N 15 18E
Ledesma 56 41 6N 5 59W
Leduc 152 53 20N 113 30W
Ledyczek 54 53 33N 16 59E
Lee, U.K. 28 50 47N 1 11W
Lee, U.S.A. 160 40 35N 115 36W
Lee Vining 163 37 58N 119 7W
Leech L. 158 47 9N 94 23W
Leedey 159 35 53N 99 24W
Leeds, U.K. 33 53 48N 1 34W
Leeds, U.S.A. 157 33 32N 86 30W
Leek, Neth. 46 53 10N 6 24E
Leek, U.K. 32 53 7N 2 2W
Leende 47 51 21N 5 33E
Leer 48 53 13N 7 29E
Leerdam 46 51 54N 5 6E
Leersum 46 52 0N 5 26E
Leesburg 157 28 47N 81 52W
Leeston 143 43 45N 172 19E
Leesville 159 31 12N 93 15W
Leeton 141 34 23S 146 23E
Leeuwarden 46 53 15N 5 48E
Leeuwin, C. 137 34 20S 115 9E
Leeward Is. 167 16 30N 63 30W
Lefors 159 35 30N 100 50W
Lefroy, L. 137 31 21S 121 40E
Legal 152 53 55N 113 45W
Legendre I. 136 20 22S 116 55E
Leghorn = Livorno 62 43 32N 10 18E
Legion 127 21 25S 28 30E
Legionowo 54 52 25N 20 50E
Léglise 47 49 48N 5 32E
Legnago 63 45 10N 11 19E
Legnano 62 45 35N 8 55E
Legnica 54 51 12N 16 10E
Legnica □ 54 51 30N 16 0E
Legoniel 38 54 38N 6 0W
Legrad 63 46 17N 16 51E
Legume 139 28 20S 152 12E
Leh 95 34 15N 77 35E
Lehi 160 40 20N 112 0W
Lehighton 162 40 50N 75 44W
Lehinch 39 52 56N 9 21E
Lehliu 70 44 29N 26 20E
Lehrte 48 52 22N 9 58E
Lehua, I. 147 22 1N 160 6W
Lehututu 128 23 54S 21 55E
Lei Shui, R. 109 26 56N 112 39E
Leiah 94 30 58N 70 58E
Leibnitz 52 46 47N 15 34E
Leicester 28 52 39N 1 9W
Leicester □ 28 52 40N 1 10W
Leichhardt, R. 133 17 50S 139 49E
Leichhardt Ra. 138 20 46S 147 40E
Leichou Chiang, R. 109 20 52N 110 10E
Leichou Pantao 108 20 40N 110 10E
Leiden 46 52 9N 4 30E
Leiderdorp 46 52 9N 4 32E
Leidschendam 46 52 5N 4 24E
Leie, R. 47 51 2N 3 45E
Leigh, Gr. Manch., U.K. 32 53 29N 2 31W
Leigh, Here. & Worcs., U.K. 28 52 10N 2 21W
Leigh Creek 140 30 28S 138 24E
Leighlinbridge 39 52 45N 7 2W
Leighton Buzzard 29 51 55N 0 39W
Leignon 47 50 16N 5 7E
Leiktho 98 19 13N 96 35E
Leinster, Mt. 39 52 38N 6 47W
Leinster, prov. 39 53 0N 7 10W
Leintwardine 28 52 22N 2 51W
Leipo 108 28 15N 103 34E
Leipzig 48 51 20N 12 23E
Leipzig □ 48 51 20N 12 30E
Leiria 57 39 46N 8 53W
Leiria □ 57 39 46N 8 53W
Leisler, Mt. 136 23 23S 129 30E
Leiston 29 52 13N 1 35E
Leith 35 55 59N 3 10W
Leith Hill 29 51 10N 0 23W
Leitha, R. 53 47 57N 17 5E
Leitholm 35 55 42N 2 16W
Leitrim 38 54 0N 8 5W
Leitrim □ 38 54 8N 8 0W
Leiyang 109 26 24N 112 51E
Leiza 58 43 5N 1 55W
Lek, R. 46 51 54N 4 38E
Lekáni 68 41 10N 24 35E
Leke 47 51 6N 2 54E
Lekhainá 69 37 57N 21 16E
Lekkerkerk 46 51 54N 4 41E
Leknice 61 51 34N 14 45E
Leksula 103 3 46S 126 31E
Leland 159 33 25N 90 52W
Leland Lakes 153 60 0N 110 59W
Lelant 30 50 11N 5 26W
Leleque 176 42 15S 71 0W
Lelu 98 19 4N 95 30E
Lelystad 46 52 30N 5 25E
Lema 121 12 58N 4 13E
Lemagrut, mt. 123 3 9S 35 22E
Leman Bank, gasfield 19 53 5N 2 20E
Léman, Lac 50 46 26N 6 30E
Lemelerveld 46 52 26N 6 20E
Lemera 126 3 0S 28 55E
Lemery 103 13 58N 120 56E
Lemesós 92 34 42N 33 1E
Lemgo 48 52 2N 8 52E
Lemhi Ra. 160 44 30N 113 30W
Lemmer 46 52 51N 5 43E
Lemmon 158 45 59N 102 10W
Lemon Grove 163 32 45N 117 2W
Lemoore 163 36 23N 119 46W
Lempdes 44 45 22N 3 17E
Lemvig 73 56 33N 8 20E
Lemyethna 98 21 10N 95 52E
Lena, R. 77 64 30N 127 0E
Lenadoon Pt. 38 54 19N 9 3W
Lencloître 42 46 50N 0 20E
Lençóis 171 12 35S 41 43W
Lendalfoot 34 55 12N 4 55W
Lendelede 47 50 53N 3 16E
Lendinara 63 45 4N 11 37E
Lene L. 38 53 40N 7 12W
Lengau de Vaca, Punta 172 30 14S 71 38W
Lenger 85 42 12N 69 54E
Lengerich 48 52 12N 7 50E
Lenggong 101 5 6N 100 58E
Lengyeltóti 53 46 40N 17 40E
Lenham 29 51 14N 0 44E
Lenhovda 73 57 0N 15 16E
Lenia 123 4 10N 37 25E
Lenin 83 48 20N 40 56E
Lenina, Pik 85 39 20N 72 55E
Leninabad 85 40 17N 69 37E
Leninakan 83 41 0N 42 50E
Leningrad 80 59 55N 30 20E
Leninogorsk, Kazakh S.S.R., U.S.S.R. 76 50 20N 83 30E
Leninogorsk, R.S.F.S.R., U.S.S.R. 84 54 36N 52 30E
Leninpol 85 42 29N 71 55E
Leninsk, R.S.F.S.R., U.S.S.R. 83 48 40N 45 15E
Leninsk, Uzbek S.S.R., U.S.S.R. 85 40 38N 72 15E
Leninsk-Kuznetskiy 76 55 10N 86 10E
Leninskaya 81 56 7N 44 29E
Leninskoye, R.S.F.S.R., U.S.S.R. 77 47 56N 132 38E
Leninskoye, R.S.F.S.R., U.S.S.R. 81 58 23N 47 3E
Leninskoye, Uzbek S.S.R., U.S.S.R. 85 41 45N 69 23E
Lenk 50 46 27N 7 28E
Lenkoran 79 39 45N 48 50E
Lenmalu 103 1 58S 130 0E
Lennard, R. 136 17 22S 124 20E
Lennox Hills 34 56 3N 4 12W
Lennoxtown 34 55 58N 4 14W
Leno 62 45 24N 10 14E
Lenoir 157 35 55N 81 36W
Lenoir City 157 35 40N 84 20W
Lenora 158 39 39N 100 1W
Lenore L. 153 52 30N 104 59W
Lenox 162 42 20N 73 18W
Lens, Belg. 47 50 33N 3 54E
Lens, France 43 50 26N 2 50E
Lens St. Remy 47 50 39N 5 7E
Lensk (Mukhtuya) 77 60 48N 114 55E
Lenskoye 82 45 3N 34 1E
Lent 46 51 52N 5 52E
Lentini 65 37 18N 15 0E
Lenwood 163 34 53N 117 7W
Lenzburg 50 47 23N 8 11E
Lenzen 48 53 6N 11 26E
Lenzerheide 51 46 44N 9 34E
Léo 120 11 3N 2 2W
Leoben 52 47 22N 15 5E
Leola 158 45 47N 98 58W
Leominster, U.K. 28 52 15N 2 43W
Leominster, U.S.A. 162 42 32N 71 45W
Léon 44 43 53N 1 18W
León, Mexico 164 21 7N 101 30W
León, Nic. 166 12 20N 86 51W
León, Spain 56 42 38N 5 34W
Leon 158 40 40N 93 40W
León □ 56 42 40N 5 55W
León, Montañas de 56 42 30N 6 18W
Leonardtown 162 38 19N 76 39W
Leonel, Mte. 65 46 15N 8 5E
Leonforte 65 37 39N 14 22E
Leongatha 141 38 30S 145 58E
Leonidhion 69 37 9N 22 52E
Leonora 137 28 49S 121 19E
Leonora Downs 140 32 29S 142 5E
Léopold II, Lac = Mai-Ndombe 124 2 0S 18 0E
Leopoldina 173 21 28S 42 40W
Leopoldo Bulhões 171 16 37S 48 46W
Leopoldsburg 47 51 7N 5 13E
Léopoldville = Kinshasa 124 4 20S 15 15E
Leoti 158 38 31N 101 19W
Leoville 153 53 39N 107 33W
Lépa, L. do 128 17 0S 19 0E
Lepe 57 37 15N 7 12W
Lepel 80 54 50N 28 40E
Lephin 36 57 26N 6 43W
Lepikha 77 64 45N 125 55E
Lépo, L. do 128 17 0S 19 0E
Lepontine Alps 62 46 22N 8 27E
Lepsény 53 47 0N 18 15E
Leptis Magna 119 32 40N 14 12E
Lequeitio 58 43 20N 2 32W
Lerbäck 72 58 56N 15 2E
Lercara Friddi 64 37 42N 13 36E
Lerdo 164 25 32N 103 32W
Léré 124 9 39N 14 13E
Lere 121 9 43N 9 18E
Leribe 129 28 51S 28 3E
Lérici 62 44 4N 9 48E
Lérida 58 41 37N 0 39E
Lérida □ 58 42 6N 1 0E
Lérins, Is. de 45 43 31N 7 3E
Lerma 56 42 0N 3 47W
Léros, I. 69 37 10N 26 50E
Lérouville 43 48 50N 5 30E
Lerrig 39 52 22N 9 47W
Lerwick 36 60 10N 1 10W
Les 70 46 58N 21 50E
Lesbos, I. = Lésvos 69 39 0N 26 20E
Lesbury 35 55 25N 1 37W
Lésina, L. di 63 41 53N 15 25E
Lesja 71 62 7N 8 51E
Lesjaverk 71 62 12N 8 34E
Lesko 54 49 30N 22 23E
Leskov, I. 13 56 0S 28 0W
Leskovac 68 43 0N 21 58E
Leskovec 68 40 10N 20 34E
Leslie, U.K. 35 56 12N 3 12W
Leslie, U.S.A. 159 35 50N 92 35W
Lesmahagow 35 55 38N 3 55W
Lesna 54 51 0N 15 15E
Lesneven 42 48 35N 4 20W
Lesnič a 66 44 39N 19 20E
Lesnoy 84 59 47N 52 9E
Lesnoye 80 58 15N 35 31E
Lesotho ■ 129 29 40S 28 0E
Lesozavodsk 77 45 30N 133 20E
Lesparre-Médoc 44 45 18N 0 57W
Lessay 42 49 14N 1 30W
Lesse, R. 47 50 15N 4 54E
Lesser Antilles 167 12 30N 61 0W
Lesser Slave L. 152 55 30N 115 25W
Lessines 47 50 42N 3 50E
Lestock 153 51 19N 103 59W
Lesuer I. 136 13 50S 127 17E
Lesuma 128 17 58S 25 12E
Lésvos, I. 69 39 0N 26 20E
Leswalt 34 54 56N 5 6W
Leszno 54 51 50N 16 30E
Leszno □ 54 51 45N 16 30E
Letchworth 29 51 58N 0 13W
Letea, Ostrov 70 45 18N 29 20E
Lethbridge 152 49 45N 112 45W
Lethero 140 33 33S 142 30E
Lethlhakeng 128 24 0S 24 59E
Leti 103 8 10S 127 40E
Leti, Kepulauan 103 8 10S 128 0E
Letiahau, R. 128 21 40S 23 30E
Leticia 174 4 0S 70 0W
Letpadan 98 17 45N 96 0E
Letpan 98 19 28N 93 52E
Letsôk-aw-Kyun (Domel I.) 101 11 30N 98 25E
Letterbreen 38 54 18N 7 43W
Letterfrack 38 53 33N 9 58W
Letterkenny 38 54 57N 7 42W
Lettermacaward 38 54 51N 8 18W
Lettermore I. 39 53 18N 9 40W
Lettermullan 39 53 15N 9 44W
Letterston 31 51 56N 5 0W
Lettoch 37 57 22N 3 30W
Leu 70 44 10N 24 0E
Leucadia 163 33 4N 117 18W
Leucate 44 42 56N 3 3E
Leucate, Étang de 44 42 50N 3 0E
Leuchars 35 56 23N 2 53W
Leuk 50 46 19N 7 37E
Leukerbad 50 46 24N 7 36E
Leupegem 47 50 50N 3 36E
Leuser, G. 102 4 0N 96 51E
Leutkirch 49 47 49N 10 1E
Leuven (Louvain) 47 50 52N 4 42E
Leuze, Hainaut, Belg. 47 50 36N 3 37E
Leuze, Namur, Belg. 47 50 33N 4 54E
Lev Tolstoy 81 53 13N 39 29E
Levádhia 69 38 27N 22 54E
Levan 160 39 37N 111 32W
Levanger 74 63 45N 11 19E
Levani 68 40 40N 19 28E
Lévanto 62 44 10N 9 37E
Levanzo, I. 64 38 0N 12 19E
Levelland 159 33 38N 102 17W
Leven, Fife, U.K. 35 56 12N 3 0W
Leven, Humb., U.K. 33 53 54N 0 18W
Leven, Banc du 129 12 30S 47 45E
Leven, L. 35 56 12N 3 22W
Leven R. 33 54 27N 1 15W
Levens 45 43 50N 7 12E
Leveque C. 136 16 20S 123 0E
Leverano 65 40 16N 18 0E
Leverburgh 36 57 46N 7 0W
Leverkusen 48 51 2N 6 59E
Levet 43 46 56N 2 22E
Levice 53 48 13N 18 35E
Levick, Mt. 13 75 0S 164 0E
Levico 63 46 0N 11 18E
Levie 45 41 40N 9 7E
Levier 43 46 58N 6 8E
Levin 142 40 37S 175 18E
Levis 151 46 48N 71 9W
Levis, L. 152 62 37N 117 58W
Levítha, I. 69 37 0N 26 28E
Levittown, N.Y., U.S.A. 162 40 41N 73 31W
Levittown, Pa., U.S.A. 162 40 10N 74 51W
Levka 67 41 52N 26 15E
Lévka, Mt. 69 35 18N 24 3E
Levkás 69 38 48N 20 43E
Levkás, I. 69 38 40N 20 43E
Levkimmi 68 39 25N 20 3E
Levkôsia = Nicosia 92 35 10N 33 25E
Levoča 53 48 59N 20 35E
Levroux 43 47 0N 1 38E
Levski 67 43 21N 25 10E
Levskigrad 67 42 38N 24 47E
Lewe 98 19 38N 96 7E
Lewellen 158 41 22N 102 5W
Lewes, U.K. 29 50 53N 0 2E
Lewes, U.S.A. 156 38 45N 75 8W
Lewes, L. 148 60 30N 134 20W
Lewin Brzeski 54 50 45N 17 37E
Lewis, Butt of 36 58 30N 6 12W
Lewis, I. 36 58 10N 6 40W
Lewis, R. 160 48 0N 113 15W
Lewis Ra. 136 20 3S 128 50E
Lewisburg, Pa., U.S.A. 162 40 57N 76 57W
Lewisburg, Tenn., U.S.A. 157 35 29N 86 46W
Lewisham 29 51 27N 0 1W
Lewisporte 151 49 15N 55 3W
Lewiston, U.K. 37 57 19N 4 30W
Lewiston, Idaho, U.S.A. 160 45 58N 117 0W
Lewiston, Utah, U.S.A. 160 42 0N 111 56W
Lewistown, Mont., U.S.A. 160 47 0N 109 25W
Lewistown, Pa., U.S.A. 156 40 37N 77 33W
Lexington, Ill., U.S.A. 158 40 37N 88 47W
Lexington, Ky., U.S.A. 156 38 6N 84 30W
Lexington, Md., U.S.A. 162 38 16N 76 27W
Lexington, Miss., U.S.A. 159 33 8N 90 2W
Lexington, Mo., U.S.A. 158 39 7N 93 55W
Lexington, N.C., U.S.A. 157 35 50N 80 13W
Lexington, Nebr., U.S.A. 158 40 48N 99 45W
Lexington, N.Y., U.S.A. 162 42 15N 74 22W
Lexington, Oreg., U.S.A. 160 45 29N 119 46W

Place	Page	Lat.	Long.
Lexington, Tenn., U.S.A.	**157**	35 38N	88 25W
Leyburn	**33**	54 19N	1 50W
Leyland	**32**	53 41N	2 42W
Leysdown on Sea	**29**	51 23N	0 57 E
Leysin	**50**	46 21N	7 0 E
Leyte, I.	**103**	11 0N	125 0 E
Lezay	**44**	46 17N	0 0 E
Lèze, R.	**44**	43 28N	1 25 E
Lezha	**68**	41 47N	19 42 E
Lézignan-Corbières	**44**	43 13N	2 43 E
Lezoux	**44**	45 49N	3 21 E
Lgov	**80**	51 42N	35 10 E
Lhanbryde	**37**	57 38N	3 12W
Lhariguo	**99**	30 29N	93 4 E
Lhasa	**105**	29 39N	91 6 E
Lhokseumawe	**102**	5 20N	97 10 E
Lhuntsi Dzong	**98**	27 39N	91 10 E
Li, Finland	**74**	65 20N	25 20 E
Li, Thai.	**100**	17 48N	98 57 E
Li Shui, R.	**109**	29 24N	112 1 E
Liádhoi, I.	**69**	36 50N	26 11 E
Liang Liang	**103**	5 58N	121 30 E
Liang Shan	**108**	23 42N	99 48 E
Lianga	**103**	8 38N	126 6 E
Liangch'eng, Inner Mongolia, China	**106**	40 26N	112 14 E
Liangch'eng, Shantung, China	**107**	35 35N	119 32 E
Lianghok'ou	**108**	29 10N	108 44 E
Lianghsiang	**106**	39 44N	116 8 E
Liangp'ing	**108**	30 41N	107 49 E
Liangpran, Gunong	**102**	1 0N	114 23 E
Liangtang	**106**	33 56N	106 12 E
Liao Ho, R.	**107**	40 39N	122 12 E
Liaoch'eng	**106**	36 26N	115 58 E
Liaochung	**107**	41 30N	122 42 E
Liaoning □	**107**	41 15N	122 0 E
Liaotung Pantao	**107**	40 0N	122 22 E
Liaotung Wan	**107**	40 30N	121 30 E
Liaoyang	**107**	41 17N	123 11 E
Liaoyüan	**107**	42 55N	125 10 E
Liapádhes	**68**	39 42N	19 40 E
Liard, R.	**152**	61 51N	121 18W
Liari	**94**	25 37N	66 30 E
Libau = Liepaja	**80**	56 30N	21 0 E
Libby	**160**	48 20N	115 10W
Libenge	**124**	3 40N	18 55 E
Liberal, Kans., U.S.A.	**159**	37 4N	101 0W
Liberal, Mo., U.S.A.	**159**	37 35N	94 30W
Liberec	**52**	50 47N	15 7 E
Liberia	**166**	10 40N	85 30W
Liberia ■	**120**	6 30N	9 30W
Libertad	**174**	8 20N	69 37W
Libertad, La	**166**	16 47N	90 7W
Liberty, Mo., U.S.A.	**158**	39 15N	94 24W
Liberty, N.Y., U.S.A.	**162**	41 48N	74 45W
Liberty, Pa., U.S.A.	**162**	41 34N	77 6W
Liberty, Tex., U.S.A.	**159**	30 5N	94 50W
Libiaz	**53**	50 7N	19 21 E
Libin	**47**	49 59N	5 15 E
Lîbîya, Sahrâ'	**114**	27 35N	25 0 E
Libohava	**68**	40 3N	20 10 E
Libourne	**44**	44 55N	0 14W
Libramont	**47**	49 55N	5 23 E
Librazhdi	**68**	41 12N	20 22 E
Libreville	**124**	0 25N	9 26 E
Libya ■	**117**	28 30N	17 30 E
Libyan Plateau = Ed-Déffa	**122**	30 40N	26 30 E
Licantén	**172**	34 55 S	72 0W
Licata	**64**	37 6N	13 55 E
Lich'eng	**106**	36 59N	113 31 E
Lichfield	**28**	52 40N	1 50W
Lichiang	**108**	26 54N	100 12 E
Lichin	**107**	37 32N	118 20 E
Lichtaart	**47**	51 13N	4 55 E
Lichtenburg	**128**	26 8 S	26 8 E
Lichtenfels	**49**	50 7N	11 4 E
Lichtenvoorde	**46**	51 59N	6 34 E
Lichtervelde	**47**	51 2N	3 9 E
Lich'uan, Hupeh, China	**109**	30 18N	108 51 E
Lich'uan, Kiangsi, China	**109**	27 14N	116 51 E
Licosa, Punta	**65**	40 15N	14 53 E
Lida, U.S.A.	**163**	37 30N	117 30W
Lida, U.S.S.R.	**80**	53 53N	25 15 E
Lidhult	**73**	56 50N	13 27 E
Lidingö	**73**	59 22N	18 8 E
Lidköping	**73**	58 31N	13 14 E
Lido, Italy	**63**	45 25N	12 23 E
Lido, Niger	**121**	12 54N	3 44 E
Lido di Ostia	**64**	41 44N	12 14 E
Lidzbark	**54**	53 15N	19 49 E
Lidzbark Warminski	**54**	54 7N	20 34 E
Liebenwalde	**48**	52 51N	13 23 E
Lieberose	**48**	51 59N	14 18 E
Liebling	**66**	45 36N	21 20 E
Liechtenstein ■	**49**	47 8N	9 35 E
Liederkerke	**47**	50 52N	4 5 E
Liège	**47**	50 38N	5 35 E
Liège □	**47**	50 32N	5 35 E
Liegnitz = Legnica	**54**	51 12N	16 10 E
Liempde	**47**	51 35N	5 23 E
Lienart	**126**	3 3N	25 31 E
Lienartville	**126**	3 3N	25 31 E
Liench'eng	**109**	25 47N	116 48 E
Lienchiang, Fukien, China	**109**	26 11N	119 32 E
Lienchiang, Kwangtung, China	**109**	21 36N	110 16 E
Lienhsien	**109**	24 50N	112 23 E
Lienp'ing	**109**	24 22N	114 30 E
Lienshan, Kwangtung, China	**109**	24 37N	112 2 E
Lienshan, Yunnan, China	**108**	24 48N	97 54 E
Lienshankuan	**107**	40 58N	123 46 E
Lienshui	**107**	33 46N	119 18 E
Lienyüan	**109**	27 41N	111 40 E
Lienyünchiang	**107**	34 47N	119 30 E
Lienyünchiangshih	**107**	34 37N	119 13 E
Lienz	**52**	46 50N	12 46 E
Liepāja	**80**	56 30N	21 0 E
Lier	**47**	51 7N	4 34 E
Lierneux	**47**	50 17N	5 47 E
Lieshout	**47**	51 31N	5 36 E
Lieşta	**70**	45 38N	27 34 E
Liestal	**50**	47 29N	7 44 E
Lieşti	**70**	45 38N	27 34 E
Liévin	**43**	50 24N	2 47 E
Lièvre, R.	**150**	45 31N	75 26W
Liezen	**52**	47 34N	14 15 E
Liffey, R.	**39**	53 21N	6 20W
Lifford	**38**	54 50N	7 30W
Liffré	**42**	48 12N	1 30W
Lifjell	**71**	59 27N	8 45 E
Lightning Ridge	**139**	29 22 S	148 0 E
Lignano	**63**	45 42N	13 8 E
Ligny-en-Barrois	**43**	48 36N	5 20 E
Ligny-le-Châtel	**43**	47 54N	3 45 E
Ligoúrion	**69**	37 37N	23 2 E
Ligua, La	**172**	32 30 S	71 16W
Liguria □	**62**	44 30N	9 0 E
Ligurian Sea	**62**	43 20N	9 0 E
Lihir Group	**135**	3 0 S	152 35 E
Lihou Reefs and Cays	**138**	17 25 S	151 40 E
Lihsien, Hopeh, China	**106**	38 29N	115 34 E
Lihsien, Hunan, China	**109**	29 38N	111 45 E
Lihsien, Kansu, China	**106**	34 11N	105 2 E
Lihsien, Szechwan, China	**108**	31 28N	103 17 E
Lihue	**147**	21 59N	159 24W
Lihwa	**99**	30 4N	100 18 E
Likasi	**127**	10 55 s	26 48 E
Likati	**124**	3 20N	24 0 E
Likhoslavl	**80**	57 12N	35 30 E
Likhovski	**83**	48 10N	40 10 E
Likoma I.	**127**	12 3 s	34 45 E
Likumburu	**127**	9 43 s	35 8 E
Liling	**109**	27 40N	113 30 E
Lill	**47**	51 15N	4 50 E
Lille	**43**	50 38N	3 3 E
Lille Bælt	**73**	55 30N	9 45 E
Lillebonne	**42**	49 30N	0 32 E
Lillehammer	**71**	61 8N	10 30 E
Lillers	**43**	50 35N	2 28 E
Lillesand	**71**	58 15N	8 23 E
Lillestrøm	**71**	59 58N	11 5 E
Lillian Point, Mt.	**137**	27 40 s	126 6 E
Lillo	**58**	39 45N	3 20W
Lillooet, R.	**152**	49 15N	121 57W
Lilongwe	**127**	14 0 s	33 48 E
Liloy	**103**	8 4N	122 39 E
Lilun	**108**	28 3N	100 27 E
Lim, R.	**66**	43 0N	19 40 E
Lima, Indon.	**103**	3 37 s	128 4 E
Lima, Peru	**174**	12 0 s	77 0W
Lima, Sweden	**72**	60 55N	13 20 E
Lima, Mont., U.S.A.	**160**	44 41N	112 38W
Lima, Ohio, U.S.A.	**156**	40 42N	84 5W
Lima, R.	**56**	41 50N	8 18W
Limanowa	**54**	49 42N	20 22 E
Limassol	**92**	34 42N	33 1 E
Limavady	**38**	55 3N	6 58W
Limavady □	**38**	55 0N	6 55W
Limay Mahuida	**172**	37 10 s	66 45W
Limay, R.	**176**	39 40 s	69 45W
Limbang	**102**	4 42N	115 6 E
Limbara, Monti	**64**	40 50N	9 10 E
Limbdi	**94**	22 34N	71 51 E
Limbourg	**47**	50 37N	5 56 E
Limbourg □	**47**	51 2N	5 25 E
Limbri	**141**	31 3 s	151 5 E
Limbunya	**136**	17 14 s	129 50 E
Limburg	**49**	50 22N	8 4 E
Limburg □	**47**	51 20N	5 55 E
Limedsforsen	**72**	60 52N	13 25 E
Limeira	**173**	22 35 s	47 28W
Limenária	**68**	40 38N	24 32 E
Limerick	**39**	52 40N	8 38W
Limerick □	**39**	52 30N	8 50W
Limerick Junction	**39**	52 30N	8 12W
Limestone, R.	**153**	56 31N	94 7W
Limfjorden	**73**	56 55N	9 0 E
Limia, R.	**56**	41 55N	8 8W
Limmared	**73**	57 34N	13 20 E
Limmat, R.	**51**	47 26N	8 20 E
Limmen	**46**	52 34N	4 42 E
Limmen Bight	**138**	14 40 s	135 35 E
Limmen Bight R.	**138**	15 7 s	135 44 E
Limni	**69**	38 43N	23 18 E
Limnos, I.	**68**	39 50N	25 5 E
Limoeiro	**170**	7 52 s	25 27W
Limoeiro do Norte	**170**	5 5 s	38 0W
Limoges	**44**	45 50N	1 15 E
Limón	**167**	10 0N	83 2W
Limon	**158**	39 18N	103 38W
Limone	**62**	44 12N	7 32 E
Limousin	**44**	46 0N	1 0 E
Limousin, Plateau de	**44**	46 0N	1 0 E
Limoux	**44**	43 4N	2 12 E
Limpopo, R.	**129**	23 15 s	32 5 E
Limpsfield	**29**	51 15N	0 1 E
Limu Ling, mts.	**100**	19 0N	109 20 E
Limuru	**126**	1 2 s	36 35 E
Lin	**68**	41 4N	20 38 E
Linan	**109**	30 13N	119 40 E
Linares	**172**	35 50 s	71 40W
Linàres	**174**	1 23N	77 31W
Linares, Mexico	**165**	24 50N	99 40W
Linares, Spain	**59**	38 10N	3 40W
Linares □	**172**	36 0 s	71 0W
Linas Mte.	**64**	39 25N	8 38 E
Linchenchen	**106**	36 28N	110 0 E
Linch'eng	**106**	37 26N	114 34 E
Linch'i	**106**	35 46N	113 53 E
Linchiang	**107**	41 50N	126 55 E
Linchin	**106**	35 6N	110 33 E
Linch'ing	**106**	36 56N	115 45 E
Linch'ü	**107**	36 30N	118 32 E
Linch'uan	**109**	28 0N	116 20 E
Lincluden	**35**	55 5N	3 40W
Lincoln, Argent.	**172**	34 55N	61 30W
Lincoln, N.Z.	**143**	43 38 s	172 30 E
Lincoln, U.K.	**33**	53 14N	0 32W
Lincoln, Ill., U.S.A.	**158**	40 10N	89 20W
Lincoln, Kans., U.S.A.	**158**	39 6N	98 9W
Lincoln, Maine, U.S.A.	**151**	45 27N	68 29W
Lincoln, N. Mex., U.S.A.	**161**	33 30N	105 26W
Lincoln, Nebr., U.S.A.	**158**	40 50N	96 42W
Lincoln, N.H., U.S.A.	**162**	44 3N	71 40W
Lincoln □	**33**	53 14N	0 32W
Lincoln Sea	**12**	84 0N	55 0W
Lincoln Wolds	**33**	53 20N	0 5W
Lincolnton	**157**	35 30N	81 15W
Lind, Austral.	**138**	18 58 s	144 30 E
Lind, U.S.A.	**160**	47 0N	118 33W
Lindale	**32**	54 14N	2 54W
Lindås	**71**	60 44N	5 10 E
Lindås, Norway	**71**	60 44N	5 9 E
Lindås, Sweden	**73**	56 38N	15 35 E
Lindau	**49**	47 33N	9 41 E
Linde	**46**	52 50N	6 57 E
Linden, Guyana	**174**	6 0N	58 10W
Linden, Calif., U.S.A.	**163**	38 1N	121 5W
Linden, Tex., U.S.A.	**159**	33 0N	94 20W
Lindenheuvel	**47**	50 59N	5 48 E
Lindenwold	**162**	39 49N	72 59W
Linderöd	**73**	55 56N	13 47 E
Linderödsåsen	**73**	55 53N	13 53 E
Lindesberg	**72**	59 36N	15 15 E
Lindesnes	**71**	57 58N	7 3 E
Lindfield	**29**	51 2N	0 5W
Lindi	**127**	9 58 s	39 38 E
Lindi □	**127**	9 40 s	38 30 E
Lindi, R.	**126**	1 25N	25 50 E
Lindoso	**56**	41 52N	8 11W
Lindow	**48**	52 58N	12 58 E
Lindsay, Can.	**150**	44 22N	78 43W
Lindsay, Calif., U.S.A.	**163**	36 14N	119 6W
Lindsay, Okla., U.S.A.	**159**	34 51N	97 37W
Lindsborg	**158**	38 35N	97 40W
Línea de la Concepción, La	**55**	36 15N	5 23W
Línea de la Concepción, La	**57**	36 15N	5 23W
Linfen	**106**	36 5N	111 32 E
Lingakok	**99**	29 55N	87 38 E
Lingayer	**103**	16 1N	120 14 E
Lingayer G.	**103**	16 10N	120 15 E
Lingch'iu	**106**	39 28N	114 10 E
Lingch'uan, Kwangsi Chuang, China	**109**	25 25N	110 20 E
Lingch'uan, Shansi, China	**106**	35 46N	113 26 E
Lingen	**48**	52 32N	7 21 E
Lingfield	**29**	51 11N	0 1W
Lingga, Kepulauan	**102**	0 10 s	104 30 E
Linghed	**72**	60 48N	15 55 E
Linghsien, Hunan, China	**109**	26 26N	113 45 E
Linghsien, Shantung, China	**106**	37 21N	116 34 E
Lingle	**158**	42 10N	104 18W
Lingling	**109**	26 13N	111 37 E
Lingpi	**107**	33 33N	117 33 E
Lingshan	**108**	22 26N	109 17 E
Lingshih	**106**	36 51N	111 47 E
Lingshou	**106**	38 18N	114 22 E
Lingshui	**100**	18 27N	110 0 E
Lingt'ai	**106**	35 4N	107 37 E
Linguéré	**120**	15 25N	15 5W
Lingwu	**106**	38 5N	106 20 E
Lingyün	**108**	24 24N	106 31 E
Linh Cam	**100**	18 31N	105 31 E
Linhai	**109**	28 51N	121 7 E
Linhares	**171**	19 25 s	40 4W
Linho	**106**	40 50N	107 30 E
Linhsi	**107**	43 37N	118 8 E
Linhsia	**105**	35 36N	103 5 E
Linhsiang	**109**	29 29N	113 30 E
Linhsien	**106**	37 57N	110 57 E
Lini	**107**	35 5N	118 20 E
Linju	**106**	34 14N	112 45 E
Link	**68**	41 4N	20 38 E
Linkao	**100**	19 56N	109 42 E
Linkinhorne	**30**	50 31N	4 22W
Linköping	**73**	58 28N	15 36 E
Link'ou	**107**	45 18N	130 15 E
Linli	**109**	29 27N	111 39 E
Linlithgow	**35**	55 58N	3 38W
Linn, Mt.	**160**	40 0N	123 0W
Linney Head	**31**	51 37N	5 4W
Linnhe, L.	**34**	56 36N	5 25W
Linosa	**119**	35 51N	12 50 E
Lins	**173**	21 40 s	49 44W
Linshui	**108**	30 18N	106 55 E
Linslade	**29**	51 55N	0 40W
Lint'ao	**106**	35 20N	104 0 E
Linth, R.	**49**	46 54N	9 0 E
Linthal	**51**	46 54N	9 0 E
Lintlaw	**153**	52 4N	103 14W
Linton, Can.	**151**	47 15N	72 16W
Linton, U.K.	**29**	52 6N	0 19 E
Linton, Ind., U.S.A.	**156**	39 0N	87 10W
Linton, N. Dak., U.S.A.	**158**	46 21N	100 12W
Lints'ang	**108**	23 45N	100 0 E
Lint'ung	**106**	34 24N	109 13 E
Linville	**139**	26 50 s	152 11 E
Linwu	**109**	25 17N	112 33 E
Linxe	**44**	43 56N	1 13W
Linyanti, R.	**128**	18 10 s	24 10 E
Linyüan	**107**	41 18N	119 15 E
Linz, Austria	**52**	48 18N	14 18 E
Linz, Ger.	**48**	50 33N	7 18 E
Lion-d'Angers, Le	**42**	47 37N	0 43W
Lion, G. du	**44**	43 0N	4 0 E
Lioni	**65**	40 52N	15 10 E
Lion's Den	**127**	17 15 s	30 5 E
Lion's Head	**150**	44 58N	81 15W
Liozno	**80**	55 0N	30 50 E
Lipali	**127**	15 50 s	35 50 E
Lípari	**65**	38 26N	14 58 E
Lípari, Is.	**65**	38 40N	15 0 E
Lipetsk	**81**	52 45N	39 35 E
Lipiany	**54**	53 2N	14 58 E
Lip'ing	**108**	26 16N	109 8 E
Lipkany	**82**	48 14N	26 25 E
Lipljan	**66**	42 31N	21 7 E
Lipnik	**53**	49 32N	17 36 E
Lipno	**54**	52 49N	19 15 E
Lipo	**108**	25 25N	107 53 E
Lipova	**66**	46 8N	21 42 E
Lipovets	**82**	49 12N	29 1 E
Lippstadt	**48**	51 40N	8 19 E
Lipsco	**54**	51 10N	21 36 E
Lipscomb	**159**	36 16N	100 28W
Lipsko	**54**	51 9N	21 40 E
Lipsói, I.	**69**	37 19N	26 50 E
Liptovsky Svaty Milkula	**53**	49 6N	19 35 E
Liptrap C.	**141**	38 50 s	145 55 E
Lip'u	**109**	24 30N	110 23 E
Lira	**126**	2 17N	32 57 E
Liri, R.	**64**	41 25N	13 45 E
Liria	**58**	39 37N	0 35W
Lisala	**124**	2 12N	21 38 E
Lisbellaw	**38**	54 20N	7 32W
Lisboa	**57**	38 42N	9 10W
Lisboa □	**57**	39 0N	9 12W
Lisbon	**158**	46 30N	97 46W
Lisbon = Lisboa	**57**	38 42N	9 10W
Lisburn	**38**	54 30N	6 9W
Lisburne, C.	**147**	68 50N	166 0W
Liscannor	**39**	52 57N	9 24W
Liscannor, B.	**39**	52 57N	9 24W
Liscarroll	**39**	52 15N	8 44W
Liscia, R.	**64**	41 5N	9 17 E
Liscomb	**151**	45 2N	62 0W
Lisdoonvarna	**39**	53 2N	9 18W
Lishe Ho, R.	**108**	24 18N	101 32 E
Lishih	**106**	37 30N	111 7 E
Lishu	**107**	43 20N	124 37 E
Lishuchen	**107**	45 5N	130 40 E
Lishui, Chekiang, China	**109**	28 27N	119 54 E
Lishui, Kiangsu, China	**109**	31 38N	119 2 E
Lisianski I.	**130**	25 30N	174 0W
Lisieux	**42**	49 10N	0 12 E
Lisischansk	**83**	48 55N	38 30 E
Liskeard	**30**	50 27N	4 29W
Lismore, N.S.W., Austral.	**139**	28 44 s	153 21 E
Lismore, Vic., Austral.	**133**	37 58 s	143 21 E
Lismore, Ireland	**39**	52 8N	7 58W
Lismore I.	**34**	56 30N	5 30W
Lisnacree	**38**	54 4N	6 5W
Lisnaskea	**38**	54 15N	7 27W
Liss	**29**	51 3N	0 53W
Lissatinning Bri.	**39**	51 55N	10 1W
Lisse	**46**	52 16N	4 33 E
Lisselton	**39**	52 30N	9 34W
Lissycasey	**39**	52 44N	9 12W
List	**48**	55 1N	8 26 E
Lista, Norway	**71**	58 7N	6 39 E
Lista, Sweden	**75**	59 19N	16 16 E
Lister, Mt.	**13**	78 0 s	162 0 E
Liston	**139**	28 39 s	152 6 E
Listowel, Can.	**150**	43 44N	80 58W
Listowel, Ireland	**39**	52 27N	9 30W
Listowel Dns.	**139**	25 10 s	145 12 E
Lit-et-Mixe	**44**	44 2N	1 15W
Lit'ang, Kwangsi-Chuang, China	**108**	23 11N	109 5 E
Lit'ang, Szechwan, China	**108**	30 4N	100 18 E
Litang	**103**	5 27N	118 31 E
Lit'ang Ho, R.	**108**	28 5N	101 28 E
Litcham	**29**	52 43N	0 49 E
Litchfield, Austral.	**140**	36 18 s	142 52 E
Litchfield, Conn., U.S.A.	**162**	41 44N	73 12W
Litchfield, Ill., U.S.A.	**158**	39 10N	89 40W
Litchfield, Minn., U.S.A.	**158**	45 5N	95 0W
Liteni	**70**	47 32N	26 32 E
Litherland	**32**	53 29N	3 0W
Lithgow	**141**	33 25 s	150 8 E
Lithínon, Ákra	**69**	34 55N	24 44 E
Lithuania S.S.R. □	**80**	55 30N	24 0 E
Litija	**63**	46 3N	14 50 E

Lititz 162 40 9N 76 18W
Litókhoron 68 40 8N 22 34 E
Litoměrice 52 50 33N 14 10 E
Litomysi 53 49 52N 16 20 E
Litschau 52 48 58N 15 4 E
Little Abaco I. 157 26 50N 77 30W
Little Aden 91 12 41N 45 6 E
Little America 13 79 0N 160 0W
Little Andaman I. 101 10 40N 92 15 E
Little Barrier I. 142 36 12 S 175 8 E
Little Belt 72 55 8N 9 55 E
Little Belt Mts. 160 46 50N 111 0W
Little Blue, R. 158 40 18N 97 45W
Little Bushman Land 128 29 10 S 18 10 E
Little Cadotte, R. 152 56 41N 117 6W
Little Cayman, I. 166 19 41N 80 3W
Little Churchill, R. 153 57 30N 95 22W
Little Coco I. 101 14 0N 93 15 E
Little Colorado, R. 161 36 0N 111 31W
Little Current 150 45 55N 82 0W
Little Current, R. 150 50 57N 84 36W
Little Egg Inlet 162 39 30N 74 20W
Little Falls, Minn., U.S.A. 158 45 58N 94 19W
Little Falls, N.Y., U.S.A. 162 43 3N 74 50W
Lit. Grand Rapids 153 52 0N 95 29W
Lit. Humbaldt, R. 160 41 20N 117 27W
Lit. Inagua I. 167 21 40N 73 50W
Little Lake 163 35 58N 117 58W
Little Longlac 150 49 42N 86 58W
Little Marais 158 47 24N 91 8W
Little Mecatiná I. 151 50 30N 59 25W
Little Minch 36 57 35N 6 45W
Lit. Miquelon I. 151 46 45N 56 25W
Lit. Missouri R. 158 46 40N 103 50W
Little Namaqualand 128 29 0 S 17 9 E
Little Ormes Hd. 31 53 19N 3 47W
Little Ouse, R. 29 52 25N 0 50 E
Little Para, R. 109 34 47 S 138 25 E
Little Rann of Kutch 94 23 25N 71 25 E
Little Red, R. 159 35 40N 92 15W
Little River 143 43 45 S 172 49 E
Little Rock 159 34 41N 92 10W
Little Ruaha, R. 126 7 50 S 35 30 E
Little Sable Pt. 156 43 40N 86 32W
Little Scarcies, R. 125 9 30N 12 25W
Little Sioux, R. 147 42 20N 95 55W
Little Smoky 152 54 44N 117 11W
Little Smoky River 152 55 40N 117 38W
Little Snake, R. 160 40 45N 108 15W
Little Wabash, R. 156 38 40N 88 20W
Little Walsingham 29 52 53N 0 51 E
Little Whale, R. 150 55 50N 75 0W
Littleborough 32 53 38N 2 8W
Littlefield 159 33 57N 102 17W
Littlefork 158 48 24N 93 35W
Littlehampton, Austral. 109 35 3 S 138 52 E
Littlehampton, U.K. 29 50 48N 0 32W
Littlemill 37 57 31N 3 49W
Littleport 29 52 27N 0 18 E
Littlestone-on-Sea 29 50 59N 0 59 E
Littlestown 162 39 45N 77 3W
Littleton Common 162 42 32N 71 28W
Litu 108 28 24N 101 16 E
Liuan 109 31 45N 116 30 E
Liuch'eng 108 24 39N 109 14 E
Liuchou 108 24 15N 109 22 E
Liuchuang 107 33 9N 120 18 E
Liuheng Tao 109 29 43N 122 8 E
Liuho, Kiangsu, China 109 32 20N 118 51 E
Liuho, Kirin, China 107 42 16N 125 42 E
Liukou 107 40 57N 118 18 E
Liuli 127 11 3 S 34 38 E
Liupa 106 33 40N 107 0 E
Liuwa Plain 125 14 20 S 22 30 E
Liuyang 109 28 9N 113 38 E
Livada 70 47 52N 23 5 E
Livadherón 68 40 2N 21 57 E
Livanovka 84 52 6N 61 59 E
Livarot 42 49 0N 0 9 E
Live Oak 157 30 17N 83 0W
Liveringa 136 18 3 S 124 10 E
Livermore 163 37 41N 121 47W
Livermore, Mt. 159 30 45N 104 8W
Liverpool, Austral. 141 33 54 S 150 58 E
Liverpool, Can. 151 44 5N 64 41W
Liverpool, U.K. 32 53 25N 3 0W
Liverpool, U.S.A. 162 43 6N 76 13W
Liverpool Bay, Can. 147 70 0N 128 0W
Liverpool Bay, U.K. 23 53 30N 3 20W
Liverpool Plains 141 31 15 S 150 15 E
Liverpool Ra. 141 31 50 S 150 30 E
Livingston, Guat. 166 15 50N 88 50W
Livingston, U.K. 45 55 52N 3 33W
Livingston, Calif., U.S.A. 163 37 23N 120 43W
Livingston, Mont., U.S.A. 160 45 40N 110 40W
Livingstone 159 30 44N 94 54W
Livingstone Falls 126 5 25 S 13 35 E
Livingstone I. 13 63 0 S 60 15W
Livingstone (Maramba) 127 17 46 S 25 52 E
Livingstone Memorial 127 12 20 S 30 18 E
Livingstone Mts., N.Z. 143 45 15 S 168 9 E
Livingstone Mts., Tanz. 127 9 40 S 34 20 E
Livingstonia 127 10 38 S 34 5 E
Livno 66 43 50N 17 0 E
Livny 81 52 30N 37 30 E
Livorno 62 43 32N 10 18 E
Livramento 173 30 55 S 55 30W
Livramento do Brumado 171 13 39 S 41 50W
Livron-sur-Drôme 45 44 46N 4 51 E
Liwale 127 9 48 S 37 58 E
Liwale □ 127 9 0 S 38 0 E
Liwale Chini 127 9 40 S 38 0 E
Lixnaw 39 52 24N 9 37W
Lixoúrion 69 38 14N 20 24 E
Liyang 109 31 22N 119 30 E
Lizard 30 49 58N 5 10W
Lizard I. 138 14 42 S 145 30 E
Lizard Pt. 30 49 57N 5 11W
Lizarda 170 9 36 S 46 41W
Lizzano 65 40 23N 17 25 E
Ljig 66 44 13N 20 18 E
Ljubija 63 44 55N 16 35 E
Ljubinje 66 42 58N 18 5 E
Ljubljana 63 46 4N 14 33 E
Ljubno 63 46 25N 14 46 E
Ljubovija 66 44 11N 19 22 E
Ljubuški 66 43 12N 17 34 E
Ljung 73 58 1N 13 3 E
Ljungan 72 62 18N 17 23 E
Ljungan, R. 74 62 30N 14 30 E
Ljungaverk 72 62 30N 16 5 E
Ljungby 73 56 49N 13 55 E
Ljusdal 72 61 46N 16 3 E
Ljusnan 72 61 12N 17 8 E
Ljusnan, R. 75 62 0N 15 20 E
Ljusne 72 61 13N 17 7 E
Ljutomer 63 46 31N 16 11 E
Lki 67 41 28N 23 43 E
Llagostera 58 41 50N 2 54 E
Llanaber 31 52 45N 4 5W
Llanaelhaiarn 31 52 59N 4 24W
Llanafan-fawr 31 52 12N 3 29W
Llanarmon Dyffryn Ceiriog 31 52 53N 3 15W
Llanarth 31 52 12N 4 19W
Llanarthney 31 51 51N 4 9W
Llanbedr 31 52 40N 4 7W
Llanbedrog 31 52 52N 4 29W
Llanberis 31 53 7N 4 7W
Llanbister 31 52 22N 3 19W
Llanbrynmair 31 52 36N 3 19W
Llancanelo, Salina 172 35 40 S 69 8W
Llandaff 31 51 29N 3 13W
Llanddewi-Brefi 31 52 11N 3 57W
Llandilo 31 51 45N 4 0W
Llandogo 31 51 44N 2 40W
Llandovery 31 51 59N 3 49W
Llandrillo 31 52 56N 3 27W
Llandrindod Wells 31 52 15N 3 23W
Llandudno 31 53 19N 3 51W
Llandybie 31 51 49N 4 0W
Llandyfriog 31 52 2N 4 26W
Llandygwydd 31 52 3N 4 33W
Llandyrnog 31 53 10N 3 19W
Llandyssul 31 52 3N 4 20W
Llanelli 31 51 41N 4 11W
Llanelltyd 31 52 45N 3 54W
Llanenddwyn 31 52 48N 4 7W
Llanerchymedd 31 53 20N 4 22W
Llanes 56 43 25N 4 50W
Llanfaelog 31 53 13N 4 29W
Llanfair Caereinion 31 52 39N 3 20W
Llanfair Talhaiarn 31 53 13N 3 37W
Llanfairfechan 31 53 15N 3 58W
Llanfechell 31 52 23N 4 25W
Llanfyllin 31 52 47N 3 17W
Llangadog 31 51 56N 3 53W
Llangefni 31 53 15N 4 20W
Llangelynin 31 52 39N 4 7W
Llangennech 31 51 41N 4 10W
Llangerniew 31 53 12N 3 41W
Llangollen 31 52 58N 3 10W
Llangranog 31 52 11N 4 29W
Llangurig 31 52 25N 3 36W
Llangynog 31 52 50N 3 24W
Llanharan 31 51 32N 3 28W
Llanidloes 31 52 28N 3 31W
Llanilar 31 52 22N 4 2W
Llanllyfni 31 53 2N 4 18W
Llannor 31 52 55N 4 25W
Llano Estacado 154 34 0N 103 0W
Llano R. 159 30 50N 99 0W
Llanon 31 52 17N 4 9W
Llanos 174 3 25N 71 35W
Llanpumpsaint 31 51 56N 4 19W
Llanrhaedr-ym-Mochnant 31 52 50N 3 18W
Llanrhidian 31 51 36N 4 11W
Llanrhystyd 31 52 19N 4 9W
Llanrwst 31 53 8N 3 49W
Llansannan 31 53 10N 3 35W
Llansawel 31 52 0N 4 1W
Llanstephan 31 51 46N 4 24W
Llanthony 31 51 57N 3 2W
Llantrisant 31 51 33N 3 22W
Llanuwchllyn 31 52 52N 3 41W
Llanvihangel Crucorney 31 51 53N 2 58W
Llanwenog 31 52 6N 4 11W
Llanwrda 31 51 58N 3 52W
Llanwrtyd Wells 31 52 6N 3 39W
Llanybldwel 28 52 47N 3 8W
Llanybyther 31 52 4N 4 10W
Llanymynech 28 52 48N 3 6W
Llanystymdwy 31 52 56N 4 17W
Llera 165 23 19N 99 1W
Llerena 57 38 17N 6 0W
Llethr Mt. 31 52 47N 3 58W
Lleyn Peninsula 31 52 55N 4 35W
Llico 172 34 46 S 72 5W
Llobregat, R. 58 41 19N 2 9 E
Lloret de Mar 58 41 41N 2 53 E
Lloyd B. 138 12 45 S 143 27 E
Lloyd Barrage 95 27 46N 68 50 E
Lloyd L. 153 57 22N 108 57W
Lloydminster 153 53 20N 110 0W
Lluchmayor 59 39 29N 2 53 E
Llullaillaco, volcán 172 24 30 S 68 30W
Llwyngwril 31 52 41N 4 6W
Llyswen 31 52 2N 3 18W
Lo 47 50 59N 2 45 E
Lo Ho, Honan, China 106 34 48N 113 4 E
Lo Ho, Shensi, China 106 34 41N 110 6 E
Lo, R. 100 21 18N 105 25 E
Loa 161 38 18N 111 46W
Loa, R. 172 21 30 S 70 0W
Loan 109 27 24N 115 49 E
Loanhead 35 55 53N 3 10W
Loano 62 44 8N 8 14 E
Loans 34 55 33N 4 39W
Lobatse 125 25 12 S 25 40 E
Löbau 48 51 5N 14 42 E
Lobaye, R. 128 4 30N 17 0 E
Lobbes 47 50 21N 4 16 E
Lobenstein 48 50 25N 11 39 E
Lobería 172 38 10 S 58 40W
Łobez 54 53 38N 15 39 E
Lobito 125 12 18 S 13 35 E
Lobón, Canal de 57 38 50N 6 55W
Lobos 172 35 2 S 59 0W
Lobos, I. 164 21 27N 97 13W
Lobos, Is. 168 6 35 S 80 45W
Lobstick L. 151 54 0N 65 12W
Lobva 84 59 10N 60 30 E
Lobva, R. 84 59 8N 60 48 E
Loc Binh 100 21 46N 106 54 E
Loc Ninh 101 11 50N 106 34 E
Locarno 51 46 10N 8 47 E
Loch Raven Res. 162 39 26N 76 33W
Lochaber 36 56 55N 5 0W
Lochailort 36 56 53N 5 40W
Lochaline 36 56 32N 5 47W
Loch'ang 109 25 10N 113 20 E
Lochans 34 54 52N 5 1W
Lochboisdale 36 57 10N 7 20W
Lochbuie 34 56 21N 5 52W
Lochcarron 36 57 25N 5 30W
Lochdonhead 34 56 27N 5 40W
Loche L., La 153 56 40N 109 30W
Loche, La 153 56 29N 109 26W
Lochearnhead 34 56 24N 4 19W
Lochem 46 52 9N 6 26 E
Loch'eng 108 24 47N 108 54 E
Loches 42 47 7N 1 0 E
Lochgelly 35 56 7N 3 18W
Lochgilphead 34 56 2N 5 37W
Lochgoilhead 34 56 10N 4 54W
Lochiang 108 31 21N 104 28 E
Lochih 108 30 18N 105 0 E
Loch'ing 109 28 8N 120 57 E
Loch'ing Wan 109 28 4N 121 5 E
Lochinver 36 58 9N 5 15W
Lochlaggan Hotel 37 56 59N 4 25W
Lochmaben 35 55 8N 3 27W
Lochmaddy 36 57 36N 7 10W
Lochnagar, Queens., Austral. 138 24 34 S 144 52 E
Lochnagar, Queens., Austral. 138 23 33 S 145 38 E
Lochnagar, Mt. 37 56 57N 3 14W
Łochow 54 52 33N 21 42 E
Lochranza 34 55 42N 5 18W
Lochs Park, Reg. 36 58 7N 6 33W
Loch'uan 106 35 48N 109 35 E
Lochwinnoch 34 55 47N 4 39W
Lochy, L. 37 56 58N 4 55W
Lochy, R. 36 56 52N 5 3W
Lock 139 33 34 S 135 46 E
Lock Haven 156 41 7N 77 31W
Lockeford 163 38 10N 121 9W
Lockeport 151 43 47N 65 4W
Lockerbie 35 55 7N 3 21W
Lockhart, Austral. 141 35 14 S 146 40 E
Lockhart, U.S.A. 159 29 55N 97 40W
Lockhart, L. 137 33 15 S 119 3 E
Lockington 140 36 16 S 144 34 E
Lockport 156 43 12N 78 42W
Locle, Le 50 47 3N 6 44 E
Locminé 42 47 54N 2 51W
Locri 65 38 14N 16 14 E
Locronan 42 48 7N 4 15W
Loctudy 42 47 50N 4 12W
Lod 90 31 57N 34 54 E
Lodalskåpa 71 61 47N 7 13 E
Loddon 29 52 32N 1 29 E
Lodève 44 43 44N 3 19 E
Lodge Grass 160 45 21N 107 27W
Lodgepole 158 41 12N 102 40W
Lodgepole Cr. 158 41 20N 104 30W
Lodhran 94 29 32N 71 30 E
Lodi, Italy 62 45 19N 9 30 E
Lodi, U.S.A. 163 38 12N 121 16W
Lodja 124 3 30 S 23 23 E
Lodji 103 1 38 S 127 28 E
Lodosa 58 42 25N 2 4W
Lodose 73 58 5N 12 10 E
Lödöse 73 58 2N 12 9 E
Lodwar 126 3 10N 35 40 E
Łodz 54 51 45N 19 27 E
Łodz □ 54 51 45N 19 27 E
Loengo 126 4 48 S 26 30 E
Lofer 52 47 35N 12 41 E
Lofoten 74 68 10N 13 0 E
Lofoten Is. 74 68 30N 15 0 E
Lofsen 72 62 7N 13 57 E
Loftahammar 73 57 54N 16 41 E
Loftsdalen 72 62 10N 13 20 E
Loftus 33 54 33N 0 52W
Lofty Ra. 136 24 15 S 119 30 E
Loga 121 13 37N 3 14 E
Logan, Kans., U.S.A. 158 39 23N 99 35W
Logan, Ohio, U.S.A. 156 39 25N 82 22 E
Logan, Utah, U.S.A. 160 41 45N 111 50W
Logan, Mt. 147 60 41N 140 22W
Logan Pass 152 48 41N 113 44W
Logansport 156 31 58N 93 58W
Loganville 162 39 51N 76 42W
Logo 123 5 20N 30 18 E
Logo Dergo 123 6 10N 29 18 E
Logroño 58 42 28N 2 32W
•Logroño □ 58 42 28N 2 27W
Logrosán 57 39 20N 5 32W
Løgstør 73 56 58N 9 14 E
Lohardaga 95 23 27N 84 45 E
Loheia 91 15 45N 42 40 E
Lohja 75 60 12N 24 5 E
Loho 106 33 33N 114 5 E
Lohr 49 50 0N 9 35 E
Loikaw 98 19 40N 97 17 E
Loimaa 75 60 50N 23 5 E
Loir-et-Cher □ 43 47 40N 1 20 E
Loire □ 45 45 40N 4 5 E
Loire-Atlantique □ 42 47 25N 1 40W
Loire, R. 42 47 16N 2 10W
Loiret □ 43 47 58N 2 10 E
Loitz 48 53 58N 13 8 E
Loja, Ecuador 174 3 59 S 79 16W
Loja, Spain 57 37 10N 4 10W
Lojung 108 24 27N 109 36 E
Loka 123 4 13N 31 0 E
Lokandu 124 2 30 S 25 45 E
Løken 71 59 48N 11 29 E
Lokerane 128 24 54 S 24 42 E
Lokeren 47 51 6N 3 59 E
Lokhvitsa 80 50 25N 33 18 E
Lokichokio 126 4 19N 34 13 E
Lokitaung 124 4 12N 35 48 E
Lokka 74 67 49N 27 45 E
Løkken, Denmark 73 57 22N 9 41 E
Løkken, Norway 71 63 8N 9 45 E
Loknya 80 56 49N 30 4 E
Lokobo 123 4 20N 30 30 E
Lokoja 121 7 47N 6 45 E
Lokolama 124 2 35 S 19 50 E
Loktung 100 18 41N 109 5 E
Lokuti 123 4 21N 33 15 E
Lokwei 100 19 12N 110 30 E
Lol 123 5 28N 29 36 E
Lol, R. 123 9 0N 28 10 E
Lola 120 7 52N 8 29W
Lolibai, Gebel 123 3 50N 33 50 E
Lolimi 123 4 35N 34 0 E
Loliondo 124 2 2 S 35 39 E
Lolland 73 54 45N 11 30 E
Lollar 48 50 39N 8 43 E
Lolo 160 46 50N 114 8W
Lolodorf 121 3 16N 10 49 E
Lolungchung 126 30 43N 96 7 E
Lom 67 43 48N 23 20 E
Lom Kao 100 16 53N 101 14 E
Lom, R. 66 43 45N 23 7 E
Lom Sak 100 16 47N 101 15 E
Loma 160 47 59N 110 29W
Loma Linda 163 34 3N 117 16W
Lomami, R. 126 1 0 S 24 40 E
Lomas de Zamóra 172 34 45 S 58 25W
Lombadria 136 16 31 S 122 54 E
Lombard 160 46 7N 111 28W
Lombardia □ 62 45 35N 9 45 E
Lombardy = Lombardia 62 45 35N 9 45 E
Lombez 44 43 29N 0 55 E
Lomblen, I. 103 8 30 S 123 32 E
Lombok, I. 102 8 35 S 116 20 E
Lomé 121 6 9N 1 20 E
Lomela 124 2 5 S 23 52 E
Lomela, R. 124 1 30 S 22 50 E
Lomello 62 45 11N 8 46 E
Lometa 159 31 15N 98 25W
Lomie 124 3 13N 13 38 E
Loming 123 4 27N 33 40W
Lomma 73 55 43N 13 6 E
Lomme, R. 47 50 8N 5 10 E
Lommel 47 51 14N 5 19 E
Lomond 152 50 24N 112 36W
Lomond, gasfield 19 57 18N 1 12 E
Lomond, L. 34 56 8N 4 38W
Lomond, mt. 139 30 0 S 151 45 E
Lomphat 101 13 30N 106 59 E
Lompobatang, mt. 103 5 24 S 119 56 E
Lompoc 163 34 41N 120 32W
Lomsegga 71 61 49N 8 21 E
Łomza 54 53 10N 22 2 E
Łomza □ 54 53 0N 22 30 E
Lonan 106 34 6N 110 10 E
Lonavla 96 18 46N 73 29 E
Loncoche 176 39 20 S 72 50W
Londa 97 15 30N 74 30 E
Londe, La 45 43 8N 6 14 E
Londerzeel 47 51 0N 4 19 E
Londiani 126 0 10 S 35 33 E
Londinières 42 49 50N 1 25 E
London, Can. 150 43 0N 81 15W
London, U.K. 29 51 30N 0 5W
London, Ky., U.S.A. 156 37 11N 84 5W
London, Ohio, U.S.A. 156 39 54N 83 28W
London □ 29 51 30N 0 5W
Londonderry 38 55 0N 7 20W

*Renamed La Rioja

Londonderry, C. 136 13 45 S 126 55 E
Londonderry, Co. 38 55 0 N 7 20 W
Londonderry, I. 176 55 0 S 71 0 W
Londrina 173 23 0 S 51 10 W
Lone Pine 163 36 35 N 118 2 W
Long Beach, Calif., U.S.A. 163 33 46 N 118 12 W
Long Beach, N.Y., U.S.A. 162 40 35 N 73 40 W
Long Beach, Wash., U.S.A. 160 46 20 N 124 1 W
Long Bennington 33 52 59 N 0 45 W
Long Branch 162 40 19 N 74 0 W
Long Clawson 29 52 51 N 0 56 W
Long Crendon 29 51 47 N 1 0 W
Long Eaton 33 52 54 N 1 16 W
Long Gully 109 35 1 S 138 40 E
Long I., Austral. 138 22 8 S 149 53 E
Long I., Bahamas 167 23 20 N 75 10 W
Long I., Can. 150 44 23 N 66 19 W
Long I., Ireland 39 51 30 N 9 35 W
Long I., P.N.G. 135 5 20 S 147 5 E
Long I., U.S.A. 162 40 50 N 73 20 W
Long I. Sd. 162 41 10 N 73 0 W
Long Itchington 28 52 16 N 1 24 W
Long L. 150 49 30 N 86 50 W
Long, L. 34 56 4 N 4 50 W
Long L. 162 43 57 N 74 25 W
Long Melford 29 52 5 N 0 44 E
Long Mt. 31 52 38 N 3 7 W
Long Mynd 23 52 35 N 2 50 W
Long Pine 158 43 33 N 99 50 W
Long Pocket 138 18 30 S 146 0 E
Long Pt., Can. 151 48 47 N 58 46 W
Long Pt., N.Z. 143 46 34 S 169 36 E
Long Preston 32 54 0 N 2 16 W
Long Ra. 151 49 30 N 57 30 W
Long Range Mts 151 48 0 N 58 30 W
Long Reef 136 13 55 S 125 45 E
Long Str. 12 70 0 N 175 0 E
Long Sutton 29 52 47 N 0 9 E
Long Thanh 101 10 47 N 106 57 E
Long Xuyen 101 10 19 N 105 28 E
Longá 69 36 53 N 21 55 E
Longa I. 36 57 45 N 5 50 W
Longarone 63 46 15 N 12 18 E
Longburn 142 40 23 S 175 35 E
Longdam 99 28 12 N 98 16 E
Longeau 43 47 47 N 5 20 E
Longford, Austral. 138 41 32 S 147 3 E
Longford, Ireland 38 53 43 N 7 50 W
Longford, U.K. 28 51 53 N 2 14 W
Longford □ 38 53 42 N 7 45 W
Longforgan 35 56 28 N 3 8 W
Longframlington 35 55 18 N 1 47 W
Longhawan 102 2 15 N 114 55 E
Longhorsley 35 55 15 N 1 46 W
Longhoughton 35 55 26 N 1 38 W
Longido 126 2 43 S 36 35 E
Longiram 102 0 5 S 115 45 E
Longkin 98 25 39 N 96 22 E
Longlac 150 49 45 N 86 25 W
Longlier 47 49 52 N 5 27 E
Longling 99 24 42 N 98 58 E
Longmont 158 40 10 N 105 4 W
Longnawan 102 21 50 N 114 55 E
Longobucco 65 39 27 N 16 37 E
Longone, R. 117 10 0 N 15 40 E
Longreach 138 23 28 S 144 14 E
Longridge 32 53 50 N 2 37 W
Long's Peak 160 40 20 N 105 50 W
Longside 37 57 30 N 1 57 W
Longton, Austral. 138 21 0 S 145 55 E
Longton, Lancs., U.K. 32 53 43 N 2 48 W
Longton, Stafford, U.K. 32 53 00 N 2 8 W
Longtown 32 55 1 N 2 59 W
Longué 42 47 22 N 0 8 W
Longueau 42 49 52 N 2 22 E
Longuyon 43 49 27 N 5 35 E
Longview, Can. 152 50 32 N 114 10 W
Longview, Tex., U.S.A. 159 32 30 N 94 45 W
Longview, Wash., U.S.A. 160 46 9 N 122 58 W
Longvilly 47 50 2 N 5 50 E
Longwy 43 49 30 N 5 45 E
Lonigo 63 45 23 N 11 22 E
Loning 106 34 28 N 111 42 E
Löningen 48 54 43 N 7 44 E
Lonja, R. 63 45 30 N 16 40 E
Lonkor Tso 95 32 40 N 83 15 E
Lonoke 159 34 48 N 91 57 W
Lonouaille 44 46 30 N 1 35 E
Lons-le-Saunier 43 46 40 N 5 31 E
Lønsdal 74 66 46 N 15 26 E
Lønstrup 73 57 29 N 9 47 E
Looc 103 12 20 N 112 5 E
Lookout, C., Can. 150 55 18 N 83 56 W
Lookout, C., U.S.A. 157 34 30 N 76 30 W
Lookout, Pt. 162 38 2 N 76 21 W
Loolmalasin, mt. 126 3 0 S 35 53 E
Loomis 153 49 15 N 108 45 W
Loon L. 153 44 50 N 77 15 W
Loon Lake 153 54 2 N 109 10 W
Loon-op-Zand 47 51 38 N 5 5 E
Loon, R., Alta., Can. 152 57 8 N 115 3 W
Loon, R., Man., Can. 153 55 53 N 101 59 W
Loongana 137 30 52 S 127 5 E
Loop Hd. 39 52 34 N 9 55 W
Loosduinen 46 52 3 N 4 14 E
Lop Buri 100 14 48 N 100 37 E
Lop Nor 105 40 20 N 90 10 E
Lopare 66 44 39 N 18 46 E
Lopatin 83 43 50 N 47 35 E
Lopatina, G. 77 50 0 N 143 30 E
Lopaye 123 6 37 N 33 40 E
Lopera 57 37 56 N 4 14 W
Lopez 162 41 27 N 76 20 W
Lopez C. 124 0 47 S 8 40 E
Lop'ing, Kiangsi, China 109 28 57 N 117 5 E
Lop'ing, Yunnan, China 108 24 56 N 104 20 E
Lopodi 123 5 5 N 33 15 E
Loppem 47 51 9 N 3 12 E
Loppersum 46 53 20 N 6 44 E
Lopphavet 74 70 27 N 21 15 E
Lora Cr. 139 28 10 S 135 22 E
Lora del Río 57 37 39 N 5 33 W
Lora, La 56 42 45 N 4 0 W
Lora, R. 93 32 0 N 67 15 E
Lorain 156 41 20 N 82 5 W
Loralai 94 30 29 N 68 30 E
Lorca 59 37 41 N 1 42 W
Lord Howe I. 130 31 33 S 159 6 E
Lordsburg 161 32 15 N 108 45 W
Lorengau 135 2 1 S 147 15 E
Loreto, Brazil 170 7 5 S 45 30 W
Loreto, Italy 63 43 26 N 13 36 E
Loreto, Mexico 164 26 1 N 111 21 W
Loreto Aprutina 63 42 24 N 13 59 E
Lorgues 45 43 28 N 6 22 E
Lorica 174 9 14 N 75 49 W
Lorient 42 47 45 N 3 23 W
Lorne, Austral. 140 38 33 S 143 59 E
Lorne, U.K. 34 56 26 N 5 10 W
Lorne, Firth of 34 56 20 N 5 40 W
Lörrach 49 47 36 N 7 38 E
Lorraine 43 49 0 N 6 0 E
Lorrainville 150 47 21 N 79 23 W
Los Alamos, Calif., U.S.A. 163 34 44 N 120 17 W
Los Alamos, N. Mex., U.S.A. 161 35 57 N 106 17 W
Los Altos 163 37 23 N 122 7 W
Los Andes 172 32 50 S 70 40 W
Los Ángeles 172 37 28 S 72 23 W
Los Angeles 163 34 0 N 118 10 W
Los Angeles Aqueduct 163 35 25 N 118 0 W
Los Banos 163 37 8 N 120 56 W
Los Barrios 57 36 11 N 5 30 W
Los Blancos, Argent. 172 23 45 S 62 30 W
Los Blancos, Spain 59 37 38 N 0 49 W
Los Gatos 163 37 15 N 121 59 W
Los, Îles de 120 9 30 N 13 50 W
Los Lamentos 164 30 36 N 105 50 W
Los Lunas 161 34 55 N 106 47 W
Los Mochis 164 25 45 N 109 5 W
Los Monegros 58 41 29 N 0 3 W
Los Muertos, Punta de 59 36 57 N 1 54 W
Los Olivos 163 34 40 N 120 7 W
Los Palacios 166 22 35 N 83 15 W
Los Palacios y Villafranca 57 37 10 N 5 55 W
Los Reyes 164 19 21 N 99 7 W
Los Roques, Is. 167 11 50 N 66 45 W
Los Santos de Maimona 57 38 37 N 6 22 W
Los Testigos, Is. 174 11 23 N 63 6 W
Los Vilos 172 32 0 S 71 30 W
Los Yébenes 57 39 36 N 3 55 W
Loshan, Honan, China 109 32 12 N 114 32 E
Loshan, Szechwan, China 108 29 34 N 103 44 E
Loshkalakh 77 62 45 N 147 20 E
Lošinj, I. 63 44 55 N 14 45 E
Losser 46 52 16 N 7 1 E
Lossiemouth 37 57 43 N 3 17 W
Lostwithiel 30 50 24 N 4 41 W
Losuia 135 8 30 S 151 4 E
Lot □ 44 44 39 N 1 40 E
Lot-et-Garonne □ 44 44 22 N 0 30 E
Lot, R. 44 44 18 N 0 20 E
Lota, Austral. 108 27 28 S 153 11 E
Lota, Chile 172 37 5 S 73 10 W
Løten 71 60 51 N 11 21 E
Lothian, (□) 26 55 55 N 3 35 W
Lothiers 43 46 42 N 1 33 E
Lotien 108 25 29 N 106 39 E
Lot'ien 109 30 47 N 115 20 E
Lot'ing 107 39 26 N 118 56 E
Loting 109 22 46 N 111 34 E
Lötschberg 49 46 25 N 7 53 E
Lotschbergtunnel 50 46 26 N 7 43 E
Lottefors 72 61 25 N 16 24 E
Lotung, China 100 18 44 N 109 9 E
Lotung, Taiwan 109 24 41 N 121 46 E
Lotz'u 108 25 19 N 102 18 E
Lotzukou 107 43 44 N 130 20 E
Lotzwil 50 47 12 N 7 48 E
Loudéac 42 48 11 N 2 47 W
Loudon 157 35 41 N 84 22 W
Loudun 42 47 0 N 0 5 E
Loué 42 47 59 N 0 9 W
Loue, R. 42 47 4 N 6 10 E
Louga 120 15 45 N 16 5 W
Loughborough 28 52 46 N 1 11 W
Loughbrickland 38 54 19 N 6 19 W
Loughmore 39 52 45 N 7 50 W
Loughor 31 51 39 N 4 5 W
Loughrea 39 53 11 N 8 33 W
Loughros More, B. 38 54 48 N 8 30 W
Louhans 45 46 38 N 5 12 E
Louis Gentil 118 32 16 N 8 31 W
Louis Trichardt 125 23 0 S 29 55 E
Louis XIV, Pte. 150 54 37 N 79 45 W
Louisa 156 38 5 N 82 40 W
Louisbourg 151 45 55 N 60 0 W
Louisbourg Nat. Historic Park 151 45 58 N 60 20 W
Louisburgh 38 53 46 N 9 49 W
Louise I. 152 52 55 N 131 40 W
Louiseville 150 46 20 N 73 0 W
Louisiade Arch. 135 11 10 S 153 0 E
Louisiana 158 39 25 N 91 0 W
Louisiana □ 159 30 50 N 92 0 W
Louisville, Ky., U.S.A. 156 38 15 N 85 45 W
Louisville, Miss., U.S.A. 159 33 7 N 89 3 W
Loulay 44 46 3 N 0 30 W
Loulé 57 37 9 N 8 0 W
Lount L. 153 50 10 N 94 20 W
Louny 52 50 20 N 13 48 E
Loup City 158 41 19 N 98 57 W
Loupe, La 42 48 29 N 1 1 E
Lourdes 44 43 6 N 0 3 W
Lourdes-de-Blanc-Sablon 151 51 24 N 57 12 W
Lourenço-Marques, B. de 129 25 50 S 32 45 E
Lourenço-Marques = Maputo 129 25 58 S 32 32 E
Loures 57 38 50 N 9 9 W
Lourinhã 57 39 14 N 9 17 W
Louroux Béconnais, Le 42 47 30 N 0 55 W
Lousã 56 40 7 N 8 14 W
Louth, Austral. 141 30 30 S 145 8 E
Louth, Ireland 38 53 47 N 6 33 W
Louth, U.K. 33 53 23 N 0 0 W
Louth □ 38 53 55 N 6 30 W
Louti 109 27 45 N 111 58 E
Loutrá Aidhipsoú 69 38 54 N 23 2 E
Loutráki 69 38 0 N 22 57 E
Louveigné 47 50 32 N 5 42 E
Louvière, La 47 50 27 N 4 10 E
Louviers 42 49 12 N 1 10 E
Lovat, R. 80 56 30 N 31 20 E
Love 153 53 29 N 104 10 W
Loveland 158 40 27 N 105 4 W
Lovell 160 44 51 N 108 20 W
Lovelock 160 40 17 N 118 25 W
Lóvere 62 45 50 N 10 4 E
Loviisa = Lovisa 75 60 31 N 26 20 E
Loving 159 32 17 N 104 4 W
Lovington 159 33 0 N 103 20 W
Lovios 56 41 55 N 8 4 W
Lovisa (Loviisa) 75 60 28 N 26 12 E
Lovosice 52 50 30 N 14 2 E
Lovran 63 45 18 N 14 15 E
Lovrin 66 45 58 N 20 48 E
Lövstabukten 72 60 35 N 17 45 E
Low Pt. 137 32 25 S 127 25 E
Low Rocky Pt. 133 42 59 S 145 29 E
Lowa 124 1 25 S 25 47 E
Lowa, R. 126 1 15 S 27 40 E
Lowell 162 42 38 N 71 19 W
Lower Arrow L. 152 49 40 N 118 5 W
Lower Austria = Niederösterreich 52 48 25 N 15 40 E
Lower Beeding 29 51 2 N 0 15 W
Lower Hermitage 109 34 49 S 138 46 E
Lower Hutt 142 41 10 S 174 55 E
Lower L. 160 41 17 N 120 3 W
Lower Lake 160 38 56 N 122 36 W
Lower Neguac 151 47 20 N 65 10 W
Lower Post 152 59 58 N 128 30 W
Lower Sackville 151 44 45 N 63 43 W
Lower Saxony = Niedersachsen 48 52 45 N 9 0 E
Lower Seal, L. 150 56 30 N 74 23 W
Lower Woolgar 138 19 47 S 143 27 E
Lowes Water L. 32 54 35 N 3 23 W
Lowestoft 29 52 29 N 1 44 E
Lowick 35 55 38 N 1 57 W
Łowicz 54 52 6 N 19 55 E
Lowther Hills 35 55 20 N 3 40 W
Lowville 162 43 48 N 75 30 W
Loxton 140 34 28 S 140 31 E
Loyal L. 37 58 24 N 4 20 W
Loyalty Is. 130 21 0 S 167 30 E
Loyang 106 34 41 N 112 28 E
Loyauté, Îles 130 21 0 S 167 30 E
Loyeh 108 24 48 N 106 34 E
Loyev 80 57 7 N 30 40 E
Loyoro 126 3 22 N 34 14 E
Loyüan 109 26 30 N 119 33 E
Loz 63 45 43 N 14 14 E
Lozère □ 44 44 35 N 3 30 E
Loznica 66 44 32 N 19 14 E
Lozovaya 82 49 0 N 36 27 E
Lozva, R. 84 59 36 N 62 20 E
Lu 98 45 0 N 8 29 E
Lü-Tao 109 22 47 N 121 20 E
Luabo 147 18 30 S 36 10 E
Luacano 124 11 15 S 21 37 E
Lualaba, R. 126 5 45 S 26 50 E
Luampa 127 15 4 S 24 20 E
Luan 103 6 10 N 124 25 E
Luan Chau 100 21 38 N 103 24 E
Luan Ho, R. 107 39 25 N 119 15 E
Luanch'eng 106 37 53 N 114 39 E
Luanda 124 8 58 S 13 9 E
Luang Doi 100 18 30 N 101 0 E
Luang Prabang 100 19 45 N 102 10 E
Luang Thale 101 7 30 N 100 15 E
Luangwa, R. 125 14 25 S 30 25 E
Luangwa Val. 127 13 30 S 31 30 E
Luanho 107 40 56 N 117 42 E
Luanhsien 107 39 45 N 118 44 E
Luanping 107 40 56 N 117 42 E
Luanshya 127 13 3 S 28 28 E
Luapula □ 127 11 0 S 29 0 E
Luapula, R. 127 12 0 S 28 50 E
Luarca 56 43 32 N 6 32 W
Luashi 127 10 50 S 23 36 E
Lubalo 124 9 10 S 19 15 E
Luban 54 51 5 N 15 15 E
Lubana, Osero 80 56 45 N 27 0 E
Lubang Is. 103 13 50 N 120 12 E
Lubartów 54 51 28 N 22 42 E
Lubawa 54 53 30 N 19 48 E
Lubban 90 32 9 N 35 14 E
Lubbeek 47 50 54 N 4 50 E
Lübben 48 51 56 N 13 54 E
Lübbenau 48 51 49 N 13 59 E
Lubbock 159 33 40 N 102 0 W
Lubcroy 37 57 58 N 4 47 W
Lübeck 48 53 52 N 10 41 E
Lübecker Bucht 48 54 3 N 11 0 E
Lubefu 126 4 47 S 24 27 E
Lubefu, R. 126 4 47 S 24 27 E
Lubero = Luofu 126 0 1 S 29 15 E
Lubicon L. 152 56 23 N 115 56 W
Lubien Kujawski 54 52 23 N 19 9 E
Lubin 54 51 24 N 16 11 E
Lublin 54 51 12 N 22 38 E
Lublin □ 54 51 5 N 22 30 E
Lubliniec 54 50 43 N 18 45 E
Lubny 80 50 3 N 32 58 E
Lubok Antu 102 1 3 N 111 50 E
Lubon 54 52 21 N 16 51 E
Lubongola 126 2 35 S 27 50 E
Lubotin 53 49 17 N 20 53 E
Lubraniec 54 52 33 N 18 50 E
Lubsko 54 51 45 N 14 57 E
Lübtheen 48 53 18 N 11 4 E
Lubuagan 103 17 21 N 121 10 E
Lubudi 124 6 50 S 21 20 E
Lubudi, R. 127 9 30 S 25 0 E
Lubuhanbilik 102 2 33 N 100 14 E
Lubuk Linggau 102 3 15 S 102 55 E
Lubuk Sikaping 102 0 10 N 100 15 E
Lubumbashi 127 11 32 S 27 28 E
Lubunda 126 5 12 S 26 41 E
Lubungu 127 14 35 S 26 24 E
Lubutu 126 0 45 S 26 30 E
Luc An Chau 100 22 6 N 104 43 E
Luc-en-Diois 45 44 36 N 5 28 E
Luc, Le 45 43 23 N 6 21 E
Lucan 38 53 21 N 6 27 W
Lucania, Mt. 147 60 48 N 141 25 W
Lucca 62 43 50 N 10 30 E
Luccens 50 46 43 N 6 51 E
Luce Bay 138 54 45 N 4 48 W
Lucea 166 18 25 N 78 10 W
Lucedale 157 30 55 N 88 34 W
Lucena, Phil. 103 13 56 N 121 37 E
Lucena, Spain 57 37 27 N 4 31 W
Lucena del Cid 58 40 9 N 0 17 W
Lučenec 53 48 18 N 19 42 E
Lucera 65 41 30 N 15 20 E
Lucerne = Luzern 51 47 3 N 8 18 E
Lucerne Valley 163 34 27 N 116 57 W
Lucero 164 30 49 N 106 30 W
Luchai 108 24 33 N 109 48 E
Luchena, R. 59 37 50 N 2 0 W
Luch'eng 106 36 18 N 113 15 E
Lucheringo, R. 127 12 0 S 36 5 E
Luch'i 109 28 17 N 110 10 E
Luchiang, China 109 31 14 N 117 17 E
Luchiang, Taiwan 109 24 1 N 120 22 E
Luchou 108 28 53 N 105 22 E
Lüchow 48 52 58 N 11 8 E
Luch'uan 109 22 20 N 110 14 E
Lucindale 93 36 59 S 140 23 E
Lucira 125 14 0 S 12 35 E
Luckau 48 51 50 N 13 43 E
Luckenwalde 48 52 5 N 13 11 E
Lucknow 95 26 50 N 81 0 E
Lucomagno, Paso del 51 46 34 N 8 49 E
Luçon 44 46 28 N 1 10 W
Luda Kamchiya, R. 67 42 50 N 27 0 E
Ludbreg 63 46 15 N 16 38 E
Lüdenscheid 48 51 13 N 7 37 E
Lüderitz 128 26 41 S 15 8 E
Ludewa □ 127 10 0 S 34 50 E
Ludgershall 28 51 15 N 1 38 W
Ludgvan 30 50 9 N 5 30 W
Ludhiana 94 30 57 N 75 56 E
Lüdinghausen 48 51 46 N 7 28 E
Ludington 156 43 58 N 86 27 W
Ludlow, U.K. 28 52 23 N 2 42 W
Ludlow, Calif., U.S.A. 163 34 43 N 116 10 W
Ludlow, Vt., U.S.A. 162 43 25 N 72 40 W
Luduş 70 46 29 N 24 5 E
Ludvika 72 60 8 N 15 14 E
Ludwigsburg 49 48 53 N 9 11 E
Ludwigshafen 49 49 27 N 8 27 E
Ludwigslust 48 53 19 N 11 28 E
Ludza 80 56 32 N 27 43 E
Lue 141 32 38 S 149 50 E
Luebo 124 5 21 S 21 17 E
Lüehyang 106 33 20 N 106 3 E
Lueki 126 3 20 S 25 48 E
Luena, Zaïre 127 9 28 S 25 43 E
Luena, Zambia 127 10 40 S 30 25 E
Luepa 174 5 43 N 61 31 W
Lufeng, Kwangtung, China 109 23 2 N 115 37 E
Lufeng, Yunnan, China 108 25 10 N 102 5 E
Lufira R. 124 9 30 S 27 0 E
Lufkin 159 31 25 N 94 40 W
Lufupa 127 10 32 S 24 50 E
Luga 80 58 40 N 29 55 E
Luga, R. 80 59 5 N 28 30 E
Lugano 51 46 0 N 8 57 E
Lugano, L. di 51 46 0 N 9 0 E

Lugansk = Voroshilovgrad 83 48 35N 39 29 E
Lugard's Falls 126 3 6S 38 41 E
Lugela 127 16 25S 36 43 E
Lugenda, R. 127 12 35S 36 50 E
Lugh Ganana 91 3 48N 42 40 E
Lugnaquilla, Mt. 39 52 48N 6 28W
Lugnvik 72 62 56N 17 55 E
Lugo, Italy 63 44 25N 11 53 E
Lugo, Spain 56 43 2N 7 35W
Lugo □ 56 43 0N 7 30W
Lugoj 66 45 42N 21 57 E
Lugones 56 43 26N 5 50W
Lugovoy 76 43 0N 72 20 E
Lugovoye 85 42 55N 72 43 E
Lugwardine 28 52 4N 2 38W
Luhe, R. 48 53 7N 10 0 E
Luhsi, Yunan, China 108 24 31N 103 46 E
Luhsi, Yunnan, China 108 24 27N 98 36 E
Luhuo 108 31 24N 100 41 E
Lui 106 33 52N 115 28 E
Luiana 125 17 25S 22 30W
Luichart L. 37 57 36N 4 43W
Luichow Pen. = Leichou Pantao 108 20 40N 110 5 E
Luing I. 34 56 15N 5 40W
Luino 62 46 0N 8 42 E
Luís 164 26 36N 109 11W
Luís Correia 170 3 0S 41 35W
Luís Gomes 171 6 25S 38 23W
Luís Gonçalves 170 5 37S 50 25W
Luisa 124 7 40S 22 30 E
Luiza 124 7 40S 22 30 E
Luizi 126 6 0S 27 25 E
Luján 172 34 45S 59 5W
Lukanga Swamp 127 14 30S 27 40 E
Lukenie, R. 124 3 0S 18 50 E
Lukhisaral 95 27 11N 86 5 E
Lukolela 124 1 10S 17 12 E
Lukosi 127 18 30S 26 30 E
Lukovit 67 43 13N 24 11 E
Lukoyanov 81 55 2N 44 20 E
Lukuhu 108 27 46N 100 50 E
Lukulu 125 14 35S 23 25 E
Lula 126 0 30N 25 10 E
Lule, R. 74 65 35N 22 10 E
Luleå 74 65 35N 22 10 E
Lüleburgaz 67 41 23N 27 28 E
Luliang 108 25 3N 103 39 E
Luling 159 29 45N 97 40W
Lulonga, R. 124 1 0N 19 0 E
Lulua, R. 124 6 30S 22 50 E
Luluabourg = Kananga 124 5 55S 22 18 E
Lulung 107 39 55N 118 57 E
Lumai 125 13 20S 21 25 E
Lumajang 103 8 8S 113 16 E
Lumbala, Angola 125 12 36S 22 30 E
Lumbala, Angola 125 14 18S 21 18 E
Lumberton, Miss., U.S.A. 159 31 4N 89 28W
Lumberton, N. Mex., U.S.A. 161 36 58N 106 57W
Lumberton, N.C., U.S.A. 157 34 37N 78 59W
Lumbres 43 50 40N 2 5 E
Lumbwa 126 0 12S 35 28 E
Lumby 152 50 10N 118 50W
Lumding 98 25 46N 93 10 E
Lumege 125 11 45S 20 50 E
Lumeyen 123 4 55N 33 28 E
Lumi 135 3 30S 142 2 E
Lummen 47 50 59N 5 12 E
Lumphanan 37 57 8N 2 41W
Lumsden, N.Z. 143 45 44S 168 27 E
Lumsden, U.K. 37 57 16N 2 51W
Lumut 101 4 13N 100 37 E
Lumut, Tg. 102 3 50S 105 58 E
Lunan 108 24 47N 103 16 E
Lunan B. 37 56 40N 2 25W
Lunavada 94 23 8N 73 37 E
Lunca 70 47 22N 25 1 E
Lund, Norway 74 68 42N 18 9 E
Lund, Sweden 73 55 41N 13 12 E
Lund, U.S.A. 160 38 53N 115 0W
Lunda 124 9 40S 20 12 E
Lundazi 125 12 20S 33 7 E
Lunde 71 59 17N 9 5 E
Lunderskov 73 55 29N 9 19 E
Lundi, R. 127 21 15S 31 25 E
Lundu 102 1 40N 109 50 E
Lundy, I. 30 51 10N 4 41W
Lune, R. 32 54 0N 2 51W
Lüneburg 48 53 15N 10 23 E
Lüneburg Heath = Lüneburger Heide 48 53 0N 10 0 E
Lüneburger Heide 48 53 0N 10 0 E
Lunel 45 43 39N 4 9 E
Lünen 48 51 36N 7 31 E
Lunenburg 151 44 22N 64 18W
Lunéville 43 48 36N 6 30 E
Lung Chiang, R. 108 24 30N 109 15 E
Lunga, R. 127 13 0S 26 33 E
Lungan 108 23 11N 107 41 E
Lungch'ang 108 29 20N 105 19 E
Lungch'ih 108 29 25N 103 24 E
Lungchou 108 22 24N 106 50 E
Lungch'üan 109 28 5N 119 7 E
Lungch'uan, Kwangtung, China 109 24 6N 115 15 E
Lungch'uan, Yunnan, China 108 24 16N 97 58 E
Lungern 50 46 48N 8 10 E
Lungholt 74 63 35N 18 10 E
Lunghsi 106 35 3N 104 38 E
Lunghsien 106 34 47N 107 0 E
Lunghua 107 41 18N 117 42 E
Lunghui 109 27 18N 110 52 E
Lungi Airport 120 8 40N 16 47 E
Lungk'ou 107 37 42N 120 21 E
Lungkuan 106 40 45N 115 43 E
Lungkukang 108 32 18N 99 7 E
Lungleh 98 22 55N 92 45 E
Lungli 108 26 27N 106 58 E
Lunglin 108 24 43N 105 26 E
Lungling 108 24 38N 98 35 E
Lungmen 109 23 44N 114 15 E
Lungming 108 23 4N 107 14 E
Lungnan 109 24 54N 114 47 E
Lungngo 98 21 57N 93 36 E
Lungshan 108 29 27N 109 23 E
Lungsheng 109 25 48N 110 0 E
Lungte 106 35 38N 106 6 E
Lungyen 109 25 9N 117 0 E
Lungyu 109 29 2N 119 10 E
Luni 94 26 0N 73 6 E
Luni, R. 94 25 40N 72 20 E
Luninets 80 52 15N 27 0 E
Luning 163 38 30N 118 10W
Lunino 81 53 35N 45 6 E
Lunna Ness 36 60 27N 1 4W
Lunner 71 60 19N 10 35 E
Lunsemfwa Falls 127 14 30S 29 6 E
Lunsemfwa, R. 127 14 50S 30 10 E
Lunteren 46 52 5N 5 38 E
Luofu 126 0 1S 29 15 E
Luozi 124 4 54S 14 0 E
Lupeni 70 45 21N 23 13 E
Łupków 53 49 15N 22 4 E
Lupundu 127 14 18S 26 45 E
Luque, Parag. 172 25 19S 57 25W
Luque, Spain 57 37 35N 4 16W
Luray 156 38 39N 78 26W
Lure 43 47 40N 6 30 E
Luremo 124 8 30S 17 50 E
Lurgainn L. 36 58 1N 5 15W
Lurgan 38 54 28N 6 20W
Luristan 92 33 20N 47 0 E
Lusaka 127 15 28S 28 16 E
Lusambo 126 4 58S 23 28 E
Luseland 153 52 5N 109 24W
Lushan, Honan, China 106 33 45N 113 10 E
Lushan, Kweichow, China 108 26 33N 107 58 E
Lushan, Szechwan, China 108 30 10N 102 59 E
Lushih 106 34 4N 110 2 E
Lushnja 68 40 55N 19 41 E
Lushoto 126 4 47S 38 20 E
Lushoto □ 126 4 45S 38 20 E
Lushui 108 25 51N 98 55 E
Lüshun 107 38 48N 121 16 E
Lusignan 44 46 26N 0 8 E
Lusigny-sur-Barse 43 48 16N 4 15 E
Lusk, Ireland 38 53 32N 6 10W
Lusk, U.S.A. 158 42 47N 104 27W
Luss 34 56 6N 4 40W
Lussac-les-Châteaux 44 46 24N 0 43 E
Lussanvira 171 20 42S 51 7W
Lüta 107 38 55N 121 40 E
Luti 108 7 14S 157 0 E
Luting 108 29 56N 102 12 E
Luton 29 51 53N 0 24W
Lutong 102 4 30N 114 0 E
Lutry 50 46 31N 6 42 E
Lutsk 80 50 50N 25 15 E
Lutterworth 28 52 28N 1 12W
Luverne 158 43 35N 96 12W
Luvua 127 8 48S 25 17 E
Luwegu, R. 127 9 30S 36 20 E
Luwingu, Mt. 124 10 15S 30 2 E
Luwuk 103 10 0S 122 40 E
Luxembourg 47 49 37N 6 9 E
Luxembourg □ 47 49 58N 5 30 E
Luxembourg ■ 47 50 0N 6 0 E
Luxeuil-les-Bains 43 47 49N 6 24 E
Luxor = El Uqsur 122 25 41N 32 38 E
Luy de Béarn, R. 44 43 39N 0 48W
Luy de France, R. 44 43 39N 0 48W
Luy, R. 44 43 39N 1 9W
Luyksgestel 47 51 17N 5 20 E
Luz, Brazil 171 19 48S 45 40W
Luz, France 44 42 53N 0 1 E
Luzern 51 47 3N 8 18 E
Luzern □ 50 47 2N 7 55 E
Luzerne 162 41 17N 75 54W
Luziânia 171 16 20S 48 0W
Luzilândia 170 3 28S 42 22W
Luzon, I. 103 16 0N 121 0 E
Luzy 43 46 47N 3 58 E
Luzzi 65 39 28N 16 17 E
Lvov 80 49 40N 24 0 E
Lwówek 54 52 28N 16 10 E
Lwówek Śląski 54 51 7N 15 38 E
Lyakhovichi 80 53 2N 26 32 E
Lyakhovskiye, Ostrova 77 73 40N 141 0 E
Lyaki 83 40 34N 47 22 E
Lyall Mt. 142 45 16S 167 32 E
*Lyallpur 94 31 30N 73 5 E
Lyalya, R. 84 59 9N 61 29 E
Lyaskovets 67 43 6N 25 44 E
Lybster 37 58 18N 3 16W
Lychen 48 53 13N 13 20 E
Lyckeby 73 56 12N 15 37 E
Lycksele 74 64 38N 18 40 E
Lydd 29 50 57N 0 56 E
Lydda = Lod 90 31 57N 34 54 E
*Renamed Faisalabad
Lydenburg 129 25 10S 30 29 E
Lydford 30 50 38N 4 7W
Lydham 28 52 31N 2 59W
Lyell 143 41 48S 172 4 E
Lyell I. 152 52 40N 131 35W
Lyell, oilfield 19 60 55N 1 12 E
Lyell Range 143 41 38S 172 20 E
Lygnern 73 57 30N 12 15 E
Lykens 162 40 34N 76 42W
Lykling 71 59 42N 5 12 E
Lyman 160 41 24N 110 15W
Lyme Bay 23 50 36N 2 55W
Lyme Regis 30 50 44N 2 57W
Lyminge 29 51 7N 1 6 E
Lymington 28 50 46N 1 32W
Lymm 32 53 23N 2 30W
Lympne 29 51 4N 1 2 E
Lynchburg 156 37 23N 79 10W
Lynd, R. 138 16 28S 143 18 E
Lynd Ra. 139 25 30S 149 20 E
Lynden 160 48 56N 122 32W
Lyndhurst, N.S.W., Austral. 138 33 41S 149 2 E
Lyndhurst, Queens., Austral. 138 19 12S 144 20 E
Lyndhurst, S. Australia, Austral. 139 30 15S 138 18 E
Lyndhurst, U.K. 28 50 53N 1 33W
Lyndon, R. 137 23 29S 114 6 E
Lyneham 28 51 30N 1 57W
Lyngdal, Agder, Norway 71 58 8N 7 7 E
Lyngdal, Buskerud, Norway 71 59 54N 9 32 E
Lynher Reef 136 15 27S 121 55 E
Lynmouth 30 51 14N 3 50W
Lynn 162 42 28N 70 57W
Lynn Canal 152 58 50N 135 20W
Lynn L. 153 56 30N 101 40W
Lynn Lake 153 56 51N 101 3W
Lynton 30 51 14N 3 50W
Lyntupy 80 55 4N 26 23 E
Lynx L. 153 62 25N 106 15W
Lyø 73 55 3N 10 9 E
Lyon 45 45 46N 4 50 E
Lyonnais 45 45 45N 4 15 E
Lyons, Colo., U.S.A. 158 40 17N 105 15W
Lyons, Ga., U.S.A. 157 32 10N 82 15W
Lyons, Kans., U.S.A. 158 38 24N 98 13W
Lyons, N.Y., U.S.A. 162 43 3N 77 0W
Lyons = Lyon 45 45 46N 4 50 E
Lyons Falls 162 43 37N 75 22W
Lyons, R. 137 25 2S 115 9 E
Lyrestad 73 58 48N 14 4 E
Lysá 52 50 11N 14 51 E
Lysekil 73 58 17N 11 26 E
Lyskovo 81 56 0N 45 3 E
Lyss 50 47 4N 7 19 E
Lysva 84 58 07N 57 49 E
Lysvik 72 60 1N 13 9 E
Lytchett Minster 28 50 44N 2 3W
Lytham St. Anne's 32 53 45N 2 58W
Lythe 33 54 30N 0 40W
Lytle 159 29 14N 98 46W
Lyttelton 143 43 35S 172 44 E
Lytton 152 50 13N 121 31W
Lyuban 80 59 16N 31 18 E
Lyubim 81 58 20N 40 50 E
Lyubimets 67 41 50N 26 5 E
Lyubomi 81 51 10N 24 2 E
Lyubotin 82 50 0N 36 4 E
Lyubytino 80 58 50N 33 16 E
Lyudinovo 80 53 52N 34 28 E

M

Ma, R. 100 19 47N 105 56 E
Ma'ad 90 32 37N 35 36 E
Maam Cross 38 53 28N 9 32W
Maamba 128 17 17S 26 28 E
Ma'an 92 30 12N 35 44 E
Maanshan 109 31 40N 118 30 E
Maarheeze 47 51 19N 5 36 E
Maarianhamina 75 60 5N 19 55 E
Maarn 47 52 3N 5 22 E
Maarssen 46 52 9N 5 2 E
Maartensdijk 46 52 9N 5 10 E
Maas 38 54 49N 8 21W
Maas, R. 47 51 48N 4 55 E
Maasbracht 47 51 9N 5 54 E
Maasbree 47 51 22N 6 3 E
Maasdam 46 51 48N 4 34 E
Maasdijk 46 51 58N 4 13 E
Maaseik 47 51 6N 5 45 E
Maasin 102 10 5N 124 55 E
Maasland 46 51 57N 4 16 E
Maasniel 47 51 12N 6 1 E
Maassluis 47 51 56N 4 16 E
Maastricht 47 50 50N 5 40 E
Maatin-es-Sarra 117 21 45N 22 0 E
Maave 129 21 4S 34 47 E
Mabein 98 23 29N 96 37 E
Mabel L. 152 50 35N 118 43W
Mabel, oilfield 19 58 6N 1 36 E
Mabenge 126 4 15N 24 12 E
Mablethorpe 33 53 21N 0 14 E
Mabrouk 121 19 29N 1 15W
Mabton 127 46 13N 120 1W
Mac Bac 101 9 46N 106 7 E
Mc Grath 147 62 58N 155 40W
Macachin 172 37 10S 63 43W
Macadam Ra. 136 14 40S 129 50 E
Macaé 173 22 20S 41 55W
Macaguane 174 6 35N 71 43W
Macaíba 170 5 15S 35 21W
Macajuba 171 12 9S 40 22W
McAlester 159 34 57N 95 40W
Macamic 150 48 45N 79 0W
Macão 57 39 35N 7 59W
Macao = Macau ■ 109 22 16N 113 35 E
Macapá 175 0 5N 51 10W
Macarani 171 15 33S 40 24W
Macarena, Serranía de la 174 2 45N 73 55W
Macarthur 140 38 5S 142 0 E
McArthur, R. 136 16 45S 136 0 E
McArthur River 138 16 27S 137 7 E
Macau 170 5 0S 36 40W
Macau ■ 109 22 16N 113 35 E
Macaúbas 171 13 2S 42 42W
McBride 152 53 20N 120 10W
McCamey 159 31 8N 102 15W
McCammon 160 42 41N 112 11W
McCarthy 147 61 25N 143 0W
McCauley I. 152 53 40N 130 15W
Macclesfield 32 53 16N 2 9W
McClintock 153 57 50N 94 10W
McClintock Chan. 148 72 0N 102 0W
McClintock Ra., Mts. 136 18 44S 127 38 E
McCloud 160 41 14N 122 5W
McCluer Gulf 103 2 20S 133 0 E
McCluer I. 136 11 5S 133 0 E
McClure, L. 163 37 35N 120 16W
McClusky 158 47 30N 100 31W
McComb 159 31 20N 90 30W
McConnell Creek 152 56 53N 126 30W
McCook 158 40 15N 100 35W
McCulloch 152 49 45N 119 15W
McCusker, R. 153 55 32N 108 39W
McDame 152 59 44N 128 59W
McDermitt 160 42 0N 117 45W
McDonald I. 11 54 0S 73 0 E
Macdonald L. 137 23 30S 129 0 E
Macdonald Ra. 136 15 35S 124 50 E
Macdonnell Ranges 136 23 40S 133 0 E
McDouall Peak 139 29 51S 134 55 E
Macdougall L. 148 66 00N 98 27W
McDougalls Well 140 31 8S 141 15 E
MacDowell L. 150 52 15N 92 45W
Macduff 37 57 40N 2 30W
Mace 150 48 55N 80 0W
Maceda 56 42 16N 7 39W
Macedo da Cavaleiros 124 11 25S 16 45 E
Macedo de Cavaleiros 56 41 31N 6 57W
Macedonia = Makedonija 66 41 53N 21 40 E
Macedonia = Makhedonia 68 40 39N 22 0 E
Maceió 170 9 40S 35 41W
Maceira 57 39 41N 8 55W
Macenta 120 8 35N 9 20W
Macerata 63 43 19N 13 28 E
McFarland 163 35 41N 119 14W
Macfarlane, L. 140 32 0S 136 40 E
McFarlane, R. 153 59 12N 107 58W
McGehee 159 33 40N 91 25W
McGill 160 39 27N 114 50W
Macgillycuddy's Reeks, mts. 39 52 2N 9 45W
McGraw 162 42 35N 76 4W
MacGregor 153 49 57N 98 48W
McGregor, Iowa, U.S.A. 158 42 58N 91 15W
McGregor, Minn., U.S.A. 158 46 37N 93 17W
McGregor, R. 152 55 10N 122 0W
McGregor Ra. 139 27 0S 142 45 E
Mach 93 29 50N 67 20 E
Machacalis 171 17 5S 40 45W
Machachi 174 0 30S 78 15W
Machado, R. = Jiparana 174 8 45S 62 20W
Machagai 172 26 56S 60 2W
Machakos 126 1 30S 37 15 E
Machakos □ 126 1 30S 37 15 E
Machala 174 3 10S 79 50W
Machanga 129 20 59S 35 0 E
Machar Marshes 123 9 28N 33 21 E
Machattie, L. 138 24 50S 139 48 E
Machava 129 25 54S 32 28 E
Machece 127 19 15S 35 32 E
Machecoul 42 47 0N 1 49W
Machelen 47 50 55N 4 26 E
Mach'eng 109 31 11N 115 2 E
Mcherrah 118 27 0N 4 30W
Machevna 77 61 20N 172 20 E
Machezo, mt. 57 39 21N 4 20W
Machiang 108 26 30N 107 35 E
Mach'iaoho 107 44 41N 130 32 E
Machias 151 44 40N 67 34W
Machichaco, Cabo 58 43 28N 2 47W
Machichi, R. 153 57 3N 92 6W
Machida 111 35 28N 139 23 E
Machilipatnam 99 16 12N 81 12 E
Machilipatnam = Masulipatnam 96 16 12N 131 15 E
Machine, La 43 46 54N 3 27 E
Mchinja 127 9 44S 39 45 E
Mchinji 127 13 47S 32 58 E
Machiques 174 10 4N 72 34W
Machrihanish 34 55 25N 5 42W
Machupicchu 174 13 8S 72 30W
Machynlleth 31 52 36N 3 51W
•Macias Nguema Biyoga 113 3 30N 8 40 E
McIlwraith Ra. 138 13 50S 143 20 E
•Renamed Bioko

Macina **120** 14 40N 4 50W
Macina, Canal de **120** 13 50N 5 40W
McIntosh **158** 45 57N 101 20W
McIntosh L. **153** 55 11N 104 41W
MacIntosh Range, Mts. **137** 24 45 S 121 33 E
Macintyre, R. **139** 28 37 S 149 40 E
Macizo Galaico **56** 42 30N 7 30W
Mackay, Austral. **138** 21 8 S 149 11 E
Mackay, U.S.A. **160** 43 58N 113 37W
Mackay, L. **136** 22 30 S 129 0 E
Mackay, R. **152** 57 10N 111 38W
McKay Ra. **137** 23 0 S 122 30 E
McKeesport **156** 40 21N 79 50W
Mackenzie **152** 55 20N 123 05W
McKenzie **157** 36 10N 88 31W
Mackenzie Bay **147** 69 0N 137 30W
Mackenzie City = Linden **174** 6 0N 58 10W
Mackenzie Highway **152** 58 0N 117 15W
Mackenzie Mts. **147** 64 0N 128 0W
Mackenzie Plains **143** 44 10 S 170 25W
Mackenzie, R., Austral. **138** 23 38 S 149 46 E
Mackenzie, R., Can. **148** 69 10N 134 20W
McKenzie, R. **160** 44 2N 122 30W
*Mackenzie, Terr. **149** 61 30N 144 30W
McKerrow L. **143** 44 25 S 168 5 E
Mackinaw City **156** 45 47N 84 44W
McKinlay **138** 21 16 S 141 18 E
McKinlay, R. **138** 20 50 S 141 28 E
McKinley, Mt. **147** 63 10N 151 0W
McKinley Sea **12** 84 0N 10 0W
McKinney **159** 33 10N 96 40W
Mackinnon Road **126** 3 40 S 39 1 E
Mackintosh Ra. **137** 27 39 S 125 32 E
McKittrick **163** 35 18N 119 39W
Mackmyra **72** 60 40N 17 3 E
Macksville **141** 30 40 S 152 56 E
McLaren Vale **140** 35 13 S 138 31 E
McLaughlin **158** 45 50N 100 50W
Maclean **139** 29 26 S 153 16 E
McLean **159** 35 15N 100 35W
McLeansboro **158** 38 5N 88 30W
Maclear **129** 31 2 S 28 23 E
Macleay, R. **141** 30 56 S 153 0 E
McLennan **152** 55 42N 116 50W
MacLeod, B. **152** 62 53N 110 0W
McLeod L. **137** 24 9 S 113 47 E
McLeod, L. **137** 24 50 S 114 0 E
MacLeod Lake **152** 54 58N 123 0W
McIlwraith Ra., Mts. **138** 13 43 S 143 23 E
McLoughlin, Mt. **160** 42 30N 122 30W
McLure **152** 51 2N 120 13W
McMillan L. **159** 32 40N 104 20W
McMinnville, Oreg., U.S.A. **160** 45 16N 123 11W
McMinnville, Tenn., U.S.A. **157** 35 43N 85 45W
McMorran **153** 51 19N 108 42W
McMurdo Sd. **13** 77 0 S 170 0 E
McMurray = Fort McMurray **152** 56 45N 111 27W
McNary **161** 34 4N 109 53W
McNaughton L. **152** 52 0N 118 10W
Macnean L. **38** 54 19N 7 52W
MacNutt **153** 51 5N 101 36W
Macodoene **129** 23 32 S 35 5 E
Macomb **158** 40 25N 90 40W
Macomer **64** 40 16N 8 48 E
Mâcon **45** 46 19N 4 50 E
Macon, Ga., U.S.A. **157** 32 50N 83 37W
Macon, Miss., U.S.A. **157** 33 7N 88 31W
Macon, Mo., U.S.A. **158** 39 40N 92 26W
Macondo **125** 12 37 S 23 46 E
Macosquink **38** 55 5N 6 43W
Macossa **127** 17 55 S 33 56 E
Macoun L. **153** 56 32N 103 50W
Macovane **129** 21 30 S 35 0 E
McPherson **158** 38 25N 97 40W
McPherson Pk. **163** 34 53N 119 53W
Macpherson Ra. **139** 28 15 S 153 15 E
Macquarie Harbour **138** 42 15 S 145 15 E
Macquarie Is. **130** 50 0 S 160 0 E
Macquarie, R. **139** 30 50 S 147 30 E
McRae, Mt. **136** 22 17 S 117 35 E
MacRobertson Coast **13** 68 30 S 63 0 E
Macroom **39** 51 54N 8 57W
McSwyne's B. **38** 54 37N 8 25W
Macu **174** 0 25N 69 15W
Macugnaga **62** 45 57N 7 58 E
Macuirima **127** 19 14 S 35 5 E
Macuiza **127** 8 7 S 34 29 E
Macujer **174** 0 24N 73 0W
Macumba, R. **133** 27 11 S 136 0 E
Macuse **127** 17 45 S 37 17 E
Macuspana **165** 17 46N 92 36W
Macusse **128** 17 48 S 20 23 E
Mácuzari, Presa **164** 27 10N 109 10W
Macuze **127** 17 45 S 37 17 E
Madā 'in Sālih **122** 26 51N 37 58 E
Madagali **121** 10 56N 13 33 E
Madagascar ■ **129** 20 0 S 47 0 E
Madagascar, I. **129** 20 0 S 47 0 E
Madam **120** 7 58N 3 32W
Madama **119** 22 0N 14 0 E
Madame I. **151** 45 30N 60 58W
Madanapalle **97** 13 33N 78 34 E
Madang **135** 5 12 S 145 49 E
Madaoua **121** 14 5N 6 27 E
Madara **121** 11 45N 10 35 E
Madaripur **98** 23 2N 90 15 E
Madauk **98** 17 56N 96 52 E
Madawaska **150** 45 30N 77 55W
Madawaska, R. **150** 45 27N 76 21W

*Now part of Fort Smith □

Madaya **98** 22 20N 96 10 E
Madbar **123** 6 17N 30 45 E
Maddalena, I. **64** 41 15N 9 23 E
Maddalena, La **64** 41 13N 9 25 E
Maddaloni **65** 41 4N 14 23 E
Maddy, L. **36** 57 36N 7 8W
Made **47** 51 41N 4 49 E
Madebele **123** 12 30N 41 10 E
Madeira, Is. **116** 32 50N 17 0W
Madeira, R. **174** 5 30 S 61 20W
Madeleine, Is. de la **151** 47 30N 61 40W
Madeley **28** 52 38N 2 28W
Madely **32** 52 59N 2 20W
Madenda **127** 13 42 S 35 1W
Madera **163** 37 0N 120 1W
Madha **96** 18 0N 75 55 E
Madhubani **95** 26 21N 86 7 E
Madhumati, R. **98** 22 53N 89 52 E
Madhupur **126** 24 18N 86 37 E
Madhya Pradesh □ **94** 21 50N 81 0 E
Madi Opei **126** 3 47N 33 5 E
Madill **159** 34 5N 96 49W
Madimba, Mozam. **127** 4 58 S 15 6 E
Madimba, Zaïre **124** 5 0 S 15 0 E
Madinat al Shaab **91** 12 50N 45 0 E
Madingou **124** 4 10 S 13 33 E
Madirovalo **129** 16 26 S 46 32 E
Madison, Fla., U.S.A. **157** 30 29N 83 26W
Madison, Ind., U.S.A. **156** 38 42N 85 20W
Madison, Nebr., U.S.A. **158** 41 53N 97 25W
Madison, S.D., U.S.A. **158** 44 0N 97 8W
Madison, Wis., U.S.A. **158** 43 5N 89 25W
Madison City **158** 43 5N 93 10W
Madison Junc. **160** 44 42N 110 56W
Madison, R. **160** 45 0N 111 48W
Madisonville **156** 37 42N 87 30W
Madista **128** 21 15 S 25 6 E
Madiun **103** 7 38 S 111 32 E
Madol **123** 9 3N 27 45 E
Madona **80** 56 53N 26 5 E
Madonie, Le, Mts. **64** 37 50N 13 50 E
Madoonga **174** 26 56 S 117 35 E
Madras, India **97** 13 8N 80 19 E
Madras, U.S.A. **160** 44 40N 121 10W
Madras = Tamil Nadu □ **97** 11 0N 77 0 E
Madre de Dios, I. **176** 50 20N 75 10W
Madre de Dios, R. **174** 11 30 S 67 30W
Madre del Sur, Sierra **165** 17 30N 100 0W
Madre, Laguna **165** 25 0N 97 30W
Madre Occidental, Sierra **164** 27 0N 107 0W
Madre Oriental, Sierra **164** 25 0N 100 0W
Madre, Sierra, Mexico **165** 16 0N 93 0W
Madre, Sierra, Phil. **103** 17 0N 122 0 E
Madri **94** 24 16N 73 32 E
Madrid **56** 40 25N 3 45W
Madrid □ **56** 40 30N 3 45W
Madridejos **57** 39 28N 3 33W
Madrigal de las Altas Torres **56** 41 5N 5 0W
Madrona, Sierra **57** 38 27N 4 16W
Madroñera **57** 39 26N 5 42W
Madu **123** 14 37N 26 4 E
Madura Motel **137** 31 55 S 127 0 E
Madura, Selat **103** 7 30 S 113 20 E
Madurai **97** 9 55N 78 10 E
Madurantakam **97** 12 30N 79 50 E
Madurta **109** 35 1 S 138 44 E
Maduru Oya **97** 7 40N 81 7 E
Madzhalis **83** 42 9N 47 47 E
Mae Chan **100** 20 9N 99 52 E
Mae Hong Son **100** 19 16N 98 8 E
Mae Khlong, R. **100** 13 24N 100 0 E
Mae Phrik **100** 17 27N 99 7 E
Mae Ramat **100** 16 58N 98 31 E
Mae Rim **100** 18 54N 98 57 E
Mae Sot **100** 16 43N 98 34 E
Mae Suai **100** 19 39N 99 33 E
Mae Tha **100** 18 28N 99 8 E
Maebaru **110** 33 33N 130 12 E
Maebashi **111** 36 24N 139 4 E
Maella **58** 41 8N 0 7 E
Maentwrog **31** 52 57N 4 0W
Maerhk'ang **108** 31 51N 102 28 E
Mâeruş **70** 45 53N 25 31 E
Maesteg **31** 51 36N 3 40W
Maestra, Sierra **166** 20 15N 77 0W
Maestrazgo, Mts. del **58** 40 30N 0 25W
Maevatanana **125** 16 56N 46 49 E
Ma'fan **119** 25 56N 14 56 E
Mafeking, Can. **153** 52 40N 101 10W
*Mafeking, S. Afr. **128** 25 50 S 25 38 E
Maféré **120** 5 30N 3 2W
Mafeteng **128** 29 51 S 27 15 E
Maffe **47** 50 21N 5 19 E
Maffra **141** 37 53 S 146 58 E
Mafia □ **126** 7 50 S 39 45 E
Mafia I. **126** 7 45 S 39 50 E
Mafou **109** 31 34N 115 15 E
Mafra, Brazil **173** 26 10N 50 0W
Mafra, Port. **57** 38 55N 9 20W
Mafungabusi Plateau **127** 18 30 S 29 8 E
Magadan **77** 59 30N 151 0 E
Magadi **126** 1 54 S 36 19 E
Magadi, L. **126** 1 54 S 36 19 E
Magaliesburg **129** 26 1 S 27 32 E
Magallanes, Estrecho de **176** 52 30 S 75 0W
Magangué **174** 9 14N 74 45W
Magaria **121** 13 4N 9 5W
Magburaka **120** 8 47N 12 0W
Magdal **90** 32 51N 35 30 E

*Renamed Mafikeng

Magdalen Is. = Madeleine, Is. de la **151** 47 30N 61 40W
Magdalena, Argent. **172** 35 5 S 57 30W
Magdalena, Boliv. **174** 13 13 S 63 57W
Magdalena, Mexico **164** 30 50N 112 0W
Magdalena, U.S.A. **161** 34 10N 107 20W
Magdalena □ **174** 10 0N 74 0W
Magdalena, B. **164** 24 30N 112 10W
Magdalena, I. **164** 24 40N 112 15W
Magdalena, Llano de la **164** 25 0N 111 30W
Magdalena, mt. **102** 4 25N 117 55 E
Magdalena, R., Colomb. **174** 8 30N 74 0W
Magdalena, R., Mexico **164** 30 50N 112 0W
Magdeburg **48** 52 8N 11 36 E
Magdeburg □ **48** 52 20N 11 40 E
Magdelaine Cays **138** 16 33 S 150 18 E
Magdiel **90** 32 10N 34 54 E
Magdub **123** 13 42N 25 5 E
Magee **159** 31 53N 89 45W
Magee, I. **38** 54 48N 5 44W
Magelang **103** 7 29 S 110 13 E
Magellan's Str. **176** 52 30 S 75 0W
Magellan's Str. = Magallanes, Est. de **176** 52 30 S 75 0W
Magenta, Austral. **140** 33 51 S 143 34 E
Magenta, Italy **62** 45 28N 8 53 E
Magenta, L. **137** 33 30 S 119 10 E
Maggea **140** 34 28 S 140 2 E
Maggia **51** 46 15N 8 42 E
Maggia, R. **51** 46 18N 8 36 E
Maggiorasca, Mt. **62** 44 33N 9 29 E
Maggiore, L. **62** 46 0N 8 35 E
Maghama **120** 15 32N 12 57W
Maghar **90** 32 54N 35 24 E
Maghera **38** 54 51N 6 40W
Magherafelt **38** 54 44N 6 37W
Maghnia **118** 34 50N 1 43W
Maghull **32** 53 31N 2 56W
Magilligan **38** 55 10N 6 53W
Magilligan Pt. **38** 55 10N 6 58W
Magione **63** 43 10N 12 12 E
Maglaj **66** 44 33N 18 7 E
Magliano in Toscana **63** 42 36N 11 18 E
Máglie **65** 40 8N 18 17 E
Magnac-Laval **44** 46 13N 1 11 E
Magnetic Pole, 1976, (South) **13** 68 48 S 139 30 E
Magnetic Pole, 1976(North) **12** 76 12N 100 12W
Magnisia □ **69** 39 24N 22 46 E
Magnitogorsk **84** 53 27N 59 4 E
Magnolia, Ark., U.S.A. **159** 33 18N 93 12W
Magnolia, Miss., U.S.A. **159** 31 8N 90 28W
Magnor **71** 59 56N 12 15 E
Magnus, oilfield **19** 61 40N 1 20 E
Magny-en-Vexin **43** 49 9N 1 47 E
Màgoé **127** 15 45 S 31 42 E
Magog **151** 45 18N 72 9W
Magoro **126** 1 45N 34 12 E
Magosta = Famagusta **92** 35 8N 33 55 E
Magoye **127** 16 1 S 27 30 E
Magpie L. **151** 51 0N 64 40W
Magrath **152** 49 25N 112 50W
Magro, R. **59** 39 20N 0 45W
Magruder Mt. **163** 37 25N 117 33W
Magrur, W. **123** 16 5N 26 30 E
Magu □ **126** 2 45 S 33 15 E
Maguarinho, C. **170** 0 15 S 48 30W
Maguire's Bri. **38** 54 18N 7 28W
Maguse L. **153** 61 40N 95 10W
Maguse Pt. **153** 61 20N 93 50W
Maguse River **153** 61 20N 94 25W
Magwe **98** 20 10N 95 0 E
Maha Sarakham **100** 16 12N 103 16 E
Mahābād **92** 36 50N 45 45 E
Mahabaleshwar **96** 17 58N 73 50 E
Mahabarat Lekh **95** 28 30N 82 0 E
Mahabo **129** 20 23 S 44 40 E
Mahad **96** 18 6N 73 29 E
Mahadeo Hills **94** 22 20N 78 30 E
Mahadeopur **96** 18 48N 80 0 E
Mahagi **126** 2 20N 31 0 E
Mahajamba, B. de la **129** 15 24 S 47 5 E
Mahajamba, R. **129** 17 0 S 47 30 E
Mahajan **94** 28 48N 73 56 E
Mahajilo, R. **129** 19 30 S 46 0 E
Mahakam, R. **102** 1 0N 114 40 E
Mahalapye **128** 23 1 S 26 51 E
Mahalla el Kubra **122** 31 10N 31 0 E
Mahallāt **93** 33 55N 50 30 E
Mahanadi R. **96** 20 33N 85 0 E
Mahanagh **38** 53 31N 8 42W
Mahanoro **129** 19 54 S 48 48 E
Mahanoy City **162** 40 48N 76 10W
Maharashtra □ **96** 19 30N 75 30 E
Maharès **119** 34 32N 10 29 E
Mahari Mts. **126** 6 20 S 30 0 E
Mahasolo **129** 19 7 S 46 22 E
Mahaweli Ganga **97** 8 0N 81 10 E
Mahaxay **100** 17 22N 105 48 E
Mahboobabad **96** 17 42N 80 2 E
Mahbubnagar **96** 16 45N 77 59 E
Mahd Dhahab **92** 25 55N 45 30 E
Mahdia **119** 35 28N 11 0 E
Mahé **97** 11 42N 75 34 E
Mahe **95** 33 10N 78 32 E
Mahendra Giri, mt. **97** 8 20N 77 30 E
Mahendraganj **98** 25 20N 89 45 E
Mahenge **127** 8 45 S 36 35 E
Maheno **143** 45 10 S 170 50 E
Mahia Pen. **142** 39 9 S 177 55 E
Mahirija **118** 34 0N 3 16W
Mahlaing **98** 21 6N 95 39 E
Mahmiya **123** 17 5N 33 50 E
Mahmud Kot **94** 30 16N 71 0 E
Mahmudia **70** 45 5N 29 5 E
Mahnomen **158** 47 22N 95 57W
Mahoba **95** 25 15N 79 55 E
Mahón **58** 39 50N 4 18 E
Mahone Bay **151** 44 30N 64 20W
Mahopac **162** 41 22N 73 45W
Mahsū **108** 30 31N 100 19 E
Mahukona **147** 20 11N 155 52W
Mahuta **121** 11 32N 4 58 E
Mai-Ndombe, L. **124** 2 0 S 18 0 E
Mai-Sai **100** 20 20N 99 55 E
Maibara **111** 35 19N 136 17 E
Maîche **43** 47 16N 6 48 E
Maicuru, R. **175** 1 0 S 54 30W
Máida **65** 38 51N 16 21 E
Maidan Khula **94** 33 36N 69 50 E
Maiden Bradley **28** 51 9N 2 18W
Maiden Newton **28** 50 46N 2 35W
Maidenhead **29** 51 31N 0 42W
Maidi **123** 16 20N 42 45 E
Maidstone, Can. **153** 53 5N 109 20W
Maidstone, U.K. **29** 51 16N 0 31 E
Maiduguri **121** 12 0N 13 20 E
Maignelay **43** 49 32N 2 30 E
Maigualida, Sierra **174** 5 30N 65 10W
Maijdi **98** 22 48N 91 10 E
Maikala Ra. **96** 22 0N 81 0 E
Mailly-le-Camp **43** 48 41N 4 12 E
Mailsi **94** 29 48N 72 15 E
Maimana **93** 35 53N 64 38 E
Main Barrier Ra. **133** 31 10 S 141 20 E
Main Centre **153** 50 35N 107 21W
Main Coast Ra. **138** 16 22 S 145 10 E
Main, R., Ger. **49** 50 13N 11 0 E
Main, R., U.K. **38** 54 49N 6 20W
Mainburg **49** 48 37N 11 49 E
Maindargi **96** 17 33N 74 21 E
Maine **42** 48 0N 0 0 E
Maine □ **151** 45 20N 69 0W
Maine-et-Loire □ **42** 47 31N 0 30W
Maine, R. **39** 52 10N 9 40W
Maïne-Soroa **121** 13 13N 12 2 E
Maingkwan **98** 26 15N 96 45 E
Mainit, L. **103** 9 31N 125 30 E
Mainkaing **98** 24 48N 95 16 E
Mainland, I., Orkneys, U.K. **37** 59 0N 3 10W
Mainland, I., Shetlands, U.K. **36** 60 15N 1 22W
Mainpuri **95** 27 18N 79 4 E
Maintenon **43** 48 35N 1 35 E
Maintirano **129** 18 3 S 44 1 E
Mainvault **47** 50 39N 3 43 E
Mainz **49** 50 0N 8 17 E
Maipú **172** 37 0 S 58 0W
Maipures **174** 5 11N 67 49W
Maiquetía **174** 10 36N 66 57W
Maira, R. **62** 44 29N 7 15 E
Mairabari **98** 26 30N 92 30 E
Mairipotaba **171** 17 18 S 49 28W
Maisi **167** 20 17N 74 9W
Maisi, C. **167** 20 10N 74 10W
Maisse **43** 48 24N 2 21 E
Maissin **47** 49 58N 5 10 E
Maitland, N.S.W., Austral. **141** 32 44 S 151 36 E
Maitland, S. Australia, Austral. **140** 34 23 S 137 40 E
Maitland, L. **137** 27 11 S 121 3 E
Maiyema **121** 12 5N 4 25 E
Maíz, Islas del **166** 12 15N 83 4W
Maizuru **111** 35 25N 135 22 E
Majagual **174** 8 33N 74 38W
Majalengka **103** 6 55 S 108 14 E
Majd el Kurum **90** 32 56N 35 15 E
Majene **103** 3 27 S 118 57 E
Majevica Planina **66** 44 45N 18 50 E
Maji **123** 6 20N 35 30 E
Major **153** 51 52N 109 37W
Majorca, I. = Mallorca, I. **58** 39 30N 3 0 E
Majors Creek **141** 35 33 S 149 45 E
Majunga **125** 15 40 S 46 25 E
Majunga □ **129** 17 0 S 47 0 E
Maka **120** 13 40N 14 10W
Makak **121** 3 36N 11 0 E
Makale **103** 3 6 S 119 51 E
Makamba **126** 4 8 S 29 49 E
Makamik **150** 48 45N 79 0W
Makapuu Hd. **147** 21 19N 157 39W
Makarewa **143** 46 20 S 168 21 E
Makari **124** 12 35N 14 28 E
Makarikari = Makgadikgadi **128** 20 40 S 25 45 E
Makarovo **77** 57 40N 107 45 E
Makarska **66** 43 20N 17 2 E
Makaryev **81** 57 52N 43 50 E
Makasar = Ujung Pandang **103** 5 10 S 119 20 E
Makasar, Selat **103** 1 0 S 118 20 E
Makat **76** 47 39N 53 19 E
Makedhonía □ **68** 40 39N 22 0 E
Makedonija □ **66** 41 53N 21 40 E
Makena **147** 20 39N 156 27W
Makeni **120** 8 55N 12 5W
Maker **30** 50 20N 4 10W
Makeyevka **82** 48 0N 38 0 E
Makgadikgadi **128** 20 40 S 25 45 E
Makgadikgadi Salt Pans **128** 20 40 S 25 45 E
Makgobistad **128** 25 45 S 25 12 E

Makhachkala 83 43 0N 47 15 E
Makharadze 83 41 55N 42 2 E
Makian, I. 103 0 12N 127 20 E
†Makin, I. 130 3 30N 174 0 E
Makindu 124 2 7 S 37 40 E
Makinsk 76 52 37N 70 26 E
Makkah 122 21 30N 39 54 E
Makkovik 151 55 0N 59 10W
Makkum 46 53 3N 5 25 E
Maklakovo 77 58 16N 92 29 E
Makó 53 46 14N 20 33 E
Makokou 124 0 40N 12 50 E
Makongo 126 3 15N 26 17 E
Makoro 126 3 10N 29 59 E
Makoua 124 0 5 S 15 50 E
Maków Podhal 54 49 43N 19 45 E
Makrá, I. 69 36 15N 25 54 E
Makrai 93 22 2N 77 0 E
Makran 93 26 13N 61 30 E
Makran Coast Range 93 25 40N 4 0 E
Makrana 94 27 2N 74 46 E
Mákri 68 40 52N 25 40 E
Maksimkin Yar 76 58 58N 86 50 E
Maktar 119 35 48N 9 12 E
Mākū 92 39 15N 44 31 E
Makuan 108 23 2N 104 24 E
Makum 98 27 30N 95 23 E
Makumbe 128 20 15 S 24 26 E
Makumbi 124 5 50 S 20 43 E
Makunda 128 22 30 S 20 7 E
Makurazaki 110 31 15N 130 20 E
Makurdi 120 7 43N 8 28 E
Makwassie 128 27 17 S 26 0 E
Mal 98 26 51N 86 45 E
Mal B. 39 52 50N 9 30W
Mal-i-Gjalicës së Lumës 68 42 2N 20 25 E
Mal i Gribës 68 40 17N 9 45 E
Mal i Nemërçkës 68 40 15N 20 15 E
Mal i Tomorit 68 40 42N 20 11 E
Mala Kapela 63 44 45N 15 30 E
Mala, Pta. 166 7 28N 80 2W
Malabang 103 7 36N 124 3 E
Malabar Coast 97 11 0N 75 0 E
Malacca = Melaka 101 2 15N 102 15 E
Malacca, Str. of 101 3 0N 101 0 E
Malacky 53 48 27N 17 0 E
Malad City 160 41 10N 112 20 E
Maladetta, Mt. 59 42 40N 0 30 E
Malafaburi 123 10 37N 40 30 E
Málaga, Colomb. 174 6 42N 72 44W
Málaga, Spain 57 36 43N 4 23W
Malaga 159 32 12N 104 2W
Málaga □ 57 36 38N 4 58W
Malagarasi 126 5 5 S 30 50 E
Malagarasi, R. 126 3 50 S 30 30 E
Malagasy Rep. ■ = Madagascar ■ 129 20 0 S 47 0 E
Malagón 57 39 11N 3 52W
Malagón, R. 57 37 40N 7 20W
Malahide 38 53 26N 6 10W
Malaimbandy 129 20 20 S 45 36 E
Malakâl 123 9 33N 31 50 E
Malakand 94 34 40N 71 55 E
Malakoff 159 32 10N 95 55W
Malakwa 152 50 55N 118 50W
Malamyzh 77 50 0N 136 50 E
Malang 103 7 59 S 112 35 E
Malanje 124 9 30 S 16 17 E
Mälaren 72 59 30N 17 10 E
Malargüe 172 35 40 S 69 30W
Malartic 150 48 9N 78 9W
Malatya 92 38 25N 38 20 E
Malawi ■ 127 13 0 S 34 0 E
Malawi, L. (Lago Niassa) 127 12 30 S 34 30 E
Malay Pen. 101 7 25N 100 0 E
*Malaya □ 101 4 0N 102 0 E
Malaya Belözerka 82 47 12N 34 56 E
Malaya Vishera 80 58 55N 32 25 E
Malaybalay 103 8 5N 125 15 E
Malayer 92 34 19N 48 51 E
Malaysia ■ 102 5 0N 110 0 E
*Malaysia, Western □ 101 5 0N 102 0 E
Malazgirt 92 39 10N 42 33 E
Malbaie, La 151 47 40N 70 10W
Malbon 138 21 5 S 140 17 E
Malbooma 139 30 41 S 134 11 E
Malbork 54 54 3N 19 10 E
Malca Dube 123 6 40N 41 52 E
Malchin 48 53 43N 12 44 E
Malchow 48 53 29N 12 25 E
Malcolm 137 28 51 S 121 25 E
Malcolm, Pt., S. Australia, Austral. 109 34 52 S 138 29 E
Malcolm, Pt., W. Australia, Austral. 137 33 48 S 123 45 E
Malczyce 54 51 14N 16 29 E
Maldegem 47 51 14N 3 26 E
Malden, Mass., U.S.A. 162 42 26N 71 5W
Malden, Mo., U.S.A. 159 36 35N 90 0W
Malden I. 143 4 3 S 155 1W
Maldive Is. ■ 86 2 0N 73 0W
Maldon, Austral. 140 37 0 S 144 6 E
Maldon, U.K. 29 51 43N 0 41 E
Maldonado 173 35 0 S 55 0W
Maldonado, Punta 165 16 19N 98 35W
Malé 62 46 20N 10 55 E
Malé Karpaty 53 48 30N 17 20 E
Malea, Ákra 69 36 28N 23 7 E
Malegaon 96 20 30N 74 30 E
Malei 127 17 12 S 36 58 E
Malela 126 4 22 S 26 8 E
Malenge 127 12 40 S 26 42 E
Målerås 73 56 54N 15 34 E
Malerkotla 94 30 32N 75 58 E
Máles 69 36 6N 25 35 E
Malesherbes 43 48 15N 2 24 E
Maleske Planina 66 41 38N 23 7 E
Malestroit 42 47 49N 2 25W
Malfa 65 38 35N 14 50 E
Malgobek 83 43 30N 44 52 E
Malgomaj L. 74 64 40N 16 30 E
Malgrat 58 41 39N 2 46 E
Malham Tarn 32 54 6N 2 11W
Malhão, Sa. do 55 37 25N 8 0W
Malheur L. 160 43 19N 118 42W
Malheur, R. 160 43 55N 117 55W
Mali 120 12 10N 12 20W
Mali ■ 121 15 0N 10 0W
Mali H Ka R. 98 25 42N 97 30 E
Mali Kanal 66 45 36N 19 24 E
Mali Kyun, I. 101 13 0N 98 20 E
Mali, R. 99 26 20N 97 40 E
Malibu 163 34 2N 118 41W
Malih, Nahr al 90 32 20N 35 29 E
Malik 103 0 39 S 123 16 E
Malili 103 2 42 S 121 23 E
Malimba, Mts. 126 7 30 S 29 30 E
Malin, Ireland 38 55 18N 7 16W
Malin, U.S.S.R. 80 50 46N 29 15 E
Malin Hd. 38 55 18N 7 16W
Malin Pen. 38 55 20N 7 17W
Malinau 102 3 35N 116 30 E
Malindi 126 3 12 S 40 5 E
Maling, Mt. 103 1 0N 121 0 E
Malingping 103 6 45 S 106 2 E
Malinyi 127 8 56 S 36 0 E
Maliqi 68 40 45N 20 48 E
Malita 103 6 19N 125 39 E
Malkapur, Maharashtra, India 96 16 57N 74 0W
Malkapur, Maharashtra, India 96 20 53N 76 17 E
Małkinia Grn. 54 52 42N 21 58 E
Malko Turnovo 67 41 59N 27 31 E
Mallacoota 141 37 40 S 149 40 E
Mallacoota Inlet 141 37 40 S 149 40 E
Mallaha 90 33 6N 35 35 E
Mallaig 36 57 0N 5 50W
Mallala 140 34 26 S 138 30 E
Mallawan 95 27 4N 80 12 E
Mallawi 122 27 44N 30 44 E
Mallemort 45 43 44N 5 11 E
Málles Venosta 62 46 42N 10 32 E
Mállia 69 35 17N 25 27 E
Mallina P.O. 136 20 53 S 118 2 E
Mallorca, I. 58 39 30N 3 0 E
Mallow 39 52 8N 8 40W
Malltraeth B. 31 53 7N 4 30W
Mallwyd 31 52 43N 3 41W
Malmbäck 73 57 34N 14 28 E
Malmberget 74 67 11N 20 40 E
Malmèdy 47 50 25N 6 2 E
Malmesbury, S. Afr. 128 33 28 S 18 41 E
Malmesbury, U.K. 28 51 35N 2 5W
Malmö 75 55 36N 12 59 E
Malmöhus län □ 73 55 45N 13 30 E
Malmslätt 73 58 27N 15 33 E
Malmyzh 84 56 31N 50 41 E
Malmyzh Mozhga 81 56 35N 50 30 E
Malnaş 70 46 2N 25 49 E
Malo Konare 67 42 12N 24 24 E
Maloarkhangelsk 81 52 28N 36 30 E
Maloja 51 46 25N 9 35 E
Maloja Pass 51 46 23N 9 42 E
Malolos 103 14 50N 121 2 E
Malomalsk 84 58 45N 59 53 E
Malombe L. 127 14 40 S 35 15 E
Malomir 67 42 16N 26 30 E
Malone 156 44 50N 74 19W
Malorad 67 43 28N 23 41 E
Malorita 80 51 41N 24 3 E
Maloyaroslovets 81 55 2N 36 20 E
Malozemelskaya Tundra 78 67 0N 50 0 E
Malpartida 57 39 26N 6 30W
Malpas 32 53 3N 2 47W
Malpelo I. 174 4 3N 80 35W
Malpica 56 43 19N 8 50W
Malprabha, R. 97 15 40N 74 50 E
Malta, Brazil 170 6 54 S 37 31W
Malta, Idaho, U.S.A. 160 42 15N 113 50W
Malta, Mont., U.S.A. 160 48 20N 107 55W
Malta ■ 64 35 50N 14 0 E
Maltahöhe 125 24 55 S 17 0 E
Maltby 33 53 25N 1 12W
Malters 50 47 3N 8 11 E
Malton 33 54 9N 0 48W
Maluku □ 103 3 0 S 128 0 E
Maluku, Kepulauan 103 3 0 S 128 0 E
Malumfashi 121 11 48N 7 39 E
Malung, China 108 25 18N 103 20 E
Malung, Sweden 72 60 42N 13 44 E
Malvalli 97 12 28N 77 8 E
Malvan 97 16 2N 73 30 E
Malvern, U.K. 28 52 7N 2 19W
Malvern, U.S.A. 159 34 22N 92 50W
Malvern Hills 28 52 0N 2 19W
Malvern Wells 28 52 4N 2 19W
Malvérnia 129 22 6 S 31 42 E
Malvik 71 63 25N 10 40 E
Malvinas Is. = Falkland Is. 174 51 30 S 59 0W
Malya 126 3 5 S 33 38 E
Malybay 85 43 30N 78 25 E
Mama 77 58 18N 112 54 E
Mamadysh 81 55 44N 51 23 E
Mamaia 70 44 18N 28 37 E
Mamaku 142 38 5 S 176 8 E
Mamanguape 170 6 50 S 35 4W
Mamasa 103 2 55 S 119 20 E
Mambasa 126 1 22N 29 3 E
Mamberamo, R. 103 2 0 S 137 50 E
Mambilima Falls 127 10 31 S 28 45 E
Mambirima 127 11 25 S 27 33 E
Mambo 126 4 52 S 38 22 E
Mambrui 126 3 5 S 40 5 E
Mameigwess L. 150 52 35N 87 50W
Mamer 47 49 38N 6 2 E
Mamers 42 48 21N 0 22 E
Mamfe 121 5 50N 9 15 E
Mammamattawa 150 50 25N 84 23W
Mámmola 65 38 23N 16 13 E
Mammoth 161 32 46N 110 43W
Mamoré, R. 175 9 55 S 65 20W
Mamou 120 10 15N 12 0W
Mampatá 120 11 54N 14 53W
Mampawah 102 0 30N 109 5 E
Mampong 121 7 6N 1 26W
Mamuju 103 2 50 S 118 50 E
Man 120 7 30N 7 40W
Man, I. of 32 54 15N 4 30W
Man Na 98 23 27N 97 19 E
Man O' War Peak 151 56 58N 61 40W
Man, R. 96 17 20N 75 0 E
Man Tun 98 23 2N 98 38 E
Mana, Fr. Gui. 175 5 45N 53 55W
Mana, U.S.A. 147 22 3N 159 45W
Mana, R. 123 6 20N 40 41 E
Måna, R. 71 59 55N 8 50 E
Manaar, Gulf of 97 8 30N 79 0 E
Manacacías, R. 174 4 23N 72 4W
Manacapuru 174 3 10 S 60 50W
Manacles, The 30 50 3N 5 5W
Manacor 58 39 32N 3 12 E
Manage 47 50 31N 4 15 E
Managua 166 12 0N 86 20W
Managua, L. 166 12 20N 86 30W
Manaia 142 39 33 S 174 8 E
Manakana 129 13 45 S 50 4 E
Manakara 129 22 8 S 48 1 E
Manakau Mt. 143 42 15 S 173 42 E
Manam I. 135 4 5 S 145 0 E
Manamâh, Al 93 26 11N 50 35 E
Manambao, R. 129 17 35 S 44 45 E
Manambato 129 13 43 S 49 7 E
Manambolo, R. 129 19 20 S 45 0 E
Manambolosy 129 16 2 S 49 40 E
Mananara 129 16 10 S 49 30 E
Mananara, R. 129 23 25 S 48 10 E
Mananjary 129 21 13 S 48 20 E
Manantenina 129 24 17 S 47 19 E
Manaos = Manaus 174 3 0 S 60 0W
Manapouri 143 45 34 S 167 39 E
Manapouri, L. 143 45 32 S 167 32 E
Manar, R. 96 18 50N 77 20 E
Manas, Gora 85 42 22N 71 2 E
Manas, R. 99 26 12N 90 40 E
Manasarowar, L. 105 30 45N 81 20 E
Manasarowar L. 105 30 45N 81 20 E
Manasir 93 24 30N 51 10 E
Manaslu, Mt. 95 28 33N 84 33 E
Manasquan 162 40 7N 74 3W
Manassa 161 37 12N 105 58W
Manassas 162 38 45N 77 28W
Manassu 105 44 18N 86 13 E
Manati 147 18 26N 66 29W
Manaung Kyun 98 18 45N 93 40 E
Manaus 174 3 0 S 60 0W
Manawan L. 153 55 24N 103 14W
Manawatu, R. 142 40 28 S 175 12 E
Manay 103 7 17N 126 33 E
Manby 33 53 22N 0 6 E
Mancelona 156 44 54N 85 5W
Mancha, La 59 39 10N 2 54W
Mancha Real 57 37 48N 3 39W
Manchaster, L. 108 27 29 S 152 46 E
Manche □ 42 49 10N 1 20W
Manchester, U.K. 32 53 30N 2 15W
Manchester, Conn., U.S.A. 162 41 47N 72 30W
Manchester, Ga., U.S.A. 157 32 53N 84 32W
Manchester, Iowa, U.S.A. 158 42 28N 91 27W
Manchester, Ky., U.S.A. 156 38 40N 83 45W
Manchester, N.H., U.S.A. 162 42 58N 71 29W
Manchester, Pa., U.S.A. 162 40 4N 76 43W
Manchester, Vt., U.S.A. 162 43 10N 73 5W
Manchester L. 153 61 28N 107 29W
Manchouli 105 49 46N 117 24 E
Manchuria = Tung Pei 107 44 0N 126 0 E
Manciano 63 42 35N 11 30 E
Mancifa 123 6 53N 41 50 E
Mand, R. 93 28 20N 52 30 E
Manda, Chunya, Tanz. 127 6 51 S 32 29 E
Manda, Jombe, Tanz. 127 10 30 S 34 40 E
Mandabé 125 21 0 S 44 55 E
Mandaguari 173 23 32 S 51 42W
Mandah 106 44 27N 108 20 E
Mandal 71 58 2N 7 25 E
Mandalay 99 22 0N 96 10 E
Mandalay = Mandale 98 22 0N 96 10 E
Mandale 99 22 0N 96 10 E
Mandalgovi 106 45 45N 106 20 E
Mandali 92 33 52N 45 28 E
Mandalya Körfezi 69 37 15N 27 20 E
Mandan 158 46 50N 101 0W
Mandapeta 96 16 47N 81 56 E
Mandar, Teluk 103 3 35 S 119 4 E
Mandas 64 39 40N 9 8 E
Mandasaur 93 24 3N 75 8 E
Mandasor (Mandsaur) 94 24 3N 75 8 E
Mandawai (Katingan), R. 102 1 30 S 113 0 E
Mandelieu-la-Napoule 45 43 34N 6 57 E
Mandera 126 3 55N 41 42 E
Mandera □ 126 3 30N 41 0 E
Manderfeld 47 50 20N 6 20 E
Mandi, India 94 31 39N 76 58 E
Mandi, Zambia 127 14 30 S 23 45 E
Mandimba 125 14 20 S 35 40 E
Mandioli 103 0 40 S 127 20 E
Mandla 95 22 39N 80 30 E
Mandø 73 55 18N 8 33 E
Mandoto 129 19 34 S 46 17 E
Mandoúdhion 69 38 48N 23 29 E
Mandra 94 33 23N 73 12 E
Mandráki 69 36 36N 27 11 E
Mandrase, R. 129 25 10 S 46 30 E
Mandritsara 129 15 50 S 48 49 E
Mandsaur (Mandasor) 94 24 3N 75 8 E
Mandurah 137 32 36 S 115 48 E
Mandúria 65 40 25N 17 38 E
Mandvi 96 22 51N 69 22 E
Mandya 97 12 30N 77 0 E
Mandzai 94 30 55N 67 6 E
Mané 121 12 59N 1 21W
Manea 29 52 29N 0 10 E
Maner, R. 97 18 30N 79 40 E
Maneroo 138 23 22 S 143 53 E
Maneroo Cr. 138 23 21 S 143 53 E
Manfalût 122 27 20N 30 52 E
Manfred 140 33 19 S 143 45 E
Manfredónia 65 41 40N 15 55 E
Manfredónia, G. di 65 41 30N 16 10 E
Manga, Brazil 171 14 46 S 43 56W
Manga, Upp. Vol. 121 11 40N 1 4W
Mangabeiras, Chapada das 170 10 0 S 46 30W
Mangahan 142 40 26 S 175 48 E
Mangalagiri 96 16 26N 80 36 E
Mangaldai 98 26 26N 92 2 E
Mangalia 70 43 50N 28 35 E
Mangalore, Austral. 141 36 56 S 145 10 E
Mangalore, India 97 12 55N 74 47 E
Manganeses 56 41 45N 5 43W
Mangaon 96 18 15N 73 20 E
Manger 71 60 38N 5 3W
Mangerton Mt. 39 51 59N 9 30W
Manggar 102 2 50 S 108 10 E
Manggawitu 103 4 8 S 133 32 E
Mangin Range 98 24 15N 95 45 E
Mangla Dam 95 33 32N 73 50 E
Manglaur 94 29 44N 77 49 E
Mangoche 125 14 25 S 35 16 E
Mangoky, R. 129 21 55 S 44 40 E
Mangole I. 103 1 50 S 125 55 E
Mangombe 126 1 20 S 26 48 E
Mangonui 142 35 1 S 173 32 E
Mangotsfield 28 51 29N 2 29W
Mangualde 56 40 38N 7 48W
Mangueigne 117 10 40N 21 5 E
Mangueira, Lagoa da 173 33 0 S 52 50W
Manguéni, Hamada 119 22 47N 12 56 E
Mangum 159 34 50N 99 30W
Mangyai 105 37 50N 91 38 E
Mangyshlak P-ov. 83 43 40N 52 30 E
Manhattan, Kans., U.S.A. 158 39 10N 96 40W
Manhattan, Nev., U.S.A. 163 38 31N 117 3W
Manhiça 129 25 23 S 32 49 E
Manhuaçu 171 20 15 S 42 2W
Manhui 106 41 1N 107 14 E
Manhumirim 171 20 22 S 41 57W
Mani 99 34 52N 87 11 E
Maní 174 4 49N 72 17W
Mania, R. 129 19 55 S 46 10 E
Maniago 63 46 11N 12 40 E
Manica 127 18 58 S 32 59 E
Manica e Sofala □ 129 19 10 S 33 45 E
Manicaland □ 127 19 0 S 32 30 E
Manicoré 174 6 0 S 61 10W
Manicouagan L. 151 51 25N 68 15W
Manicouagan, R. 151 49 30N 68 30W
Manifah 92 27 30N 49 0 E
Manifold 138 22 41 S 150 40 E
Manigotagan 153 51 6N 96 8W
Manigotagan L. 153 50 52N 95 37W
Manihiki I. 131 10 24 S 161 1W
Manika, Plat. de 127 10 0 S 25 5 E
Manikganj 98 23 52N 90 0 E
Manila, Phil. 103 14 40N 121 3 E
Manila, U.S.A. 160 41 0N 109 44W
Manila B. 103 14 0N 120 0 E
Manilla 141 30 45 S 150 43 E
Manimpé 120 14 11N 5 28W
Maningory 129 17 9 S 49 30 E
Manipur □ 98 24 30N 94 0 E
Manipur, R. 98 23 45N 93 40 E
Manisa 92 38 38N 27 30 E
Manistee 156 44 15N 86 20W
Manistee, R. 156 44 15N 86 21W
Manistique 156 45 59N 86 18W
Manito L. 153 52 43N 109 43W
Manitoba □ 153 55 30N 97 0W
Manitoba, L. 153 51 0N 98 45W
Manitou 153 49 15N 98 32W
Manitou I. 150 47 22N 87 30W

Renamed Peninsular Malaysia
†Renamed Butaritari

Manitou Is. 156 45 8N 86 0W
Manitou L., Ont., Can. 153 49 15N 93 0W
Manitou L., Qué., Can. 151 50 55N 65 17W
Manitoulin I. 150 45 40N 82 30W
Manitowaning 150 45 46N 81 49W
Manitowoc 156 44 8N 87 40W
Manizales 174 5 5N 75 32W
Manja 129 21 26S 44 20E
Manjacaze 125 24 45S 34 0E
Manjakandriana 129 18 55S 47 47E
Manjeri 97 11 7N 76 11E
Manjhand 94 25 50N 68 10E
Manjil 92 36 46N 49 30E
Manjimup 137 34 15S 116 6E
Manjra, R. 96 18 20N 77 20E
Mankaiana 129 26 38S 31 6E
Mankato, Kans., U.S.A. 158 39 49N 98 11W
Mankato, Minn., U.S.A. 158 44 8N 93 59W
Mankono 120 8 10N 6 10W
Mankota 153 49 25N 107 5W
Manlay 106 44 9N 106 50E
Manlleu 58 42 2N 2 17E
Manly, N.S.W., Austral. 141 33 48S 151 17E
Manly, Queens., Austral. 108 27 27S 153 11E
Manmad 96 20 18N 74 28E
Mann Ranges, Mts. 137 26 6S 130 5E
Manna 102 4 25S 102 55E
Mannahill 140 32 25S 140 0E
Mannar 97 9 1N 79 54E
Mannar, G. of 97 8 30N 79 0E
Mannar I. 97 9 5N 79 45E
Mannargudi 97 10 45N 79 32E
Männedorf 51 47 15N 8 43E
Mannheim 49 49 28N 8 29E
Manning, Can. 152 56 53N 117 39W
Manning, U.S.A. 157 33 40N 80 9W
Manning Prov. Park 152 49 5N 120 45W
Mannington 156 39 35N 80 25W
Manningtree 29 51 56N 1 3E
Mannu, C. 64 40 2N 8 24E
Mannu, R. 64 39 35N 8 56E
Mannum 140 34 57S 139 12E
Mano 120 8 3N 12 12W
Manokwari 103 0 54S 134 0E
Manolás 69 38 4N 21 21E
Manombo 129 22 57S 43 28E
Manono 124 7 15S 27 25E
Manorbier 31 51 38N 4 48W
Manorhamilton 38 54 19N 8 11W
Manosque 45 43 49N 5 47E
Manouane L. 151 50 45N 70 45W
Manpojin 107 41 6N 126 24E
Manresa 58 41 48N 1 50E
Mans, Le 42 48 0N 0 10E
Mansa, Gujarat, India 94 23 27N 72 45E
Mansa, Punjab, India 94 30 0N 75 27E
Mansa, Zambia 127 11 13S 28 55E
Mansel I. 149 62 0N 79 50W
Mansenra 94 34 20N 73 11E
Mansfield, Austral. 141 37 4S 146 6E
Mansfield, U.K. 33 53 8N 1 12W
Mansfield, La., U.S.A. 159 32 2N 93 40W
Mansfield, Mass., U.S.A. 162 42 2N 71 12W
Mansfield, Ohio, U.S.A. 156 40 45N 82 30W
Mansfield, Pa., U.S.A. 162 41 48N 77 4W
Mansfield, Wash., U.S.A. 160 47 51N 119 44W
Mansfield Woodhouse 33 53 11N 1 11W
Mansi 98 24 40N 95 44E
Mansidão 170 10 43S 44 2W
Mansilla de las Mulas 56 42 30N 5 25W
Mansle 44 45 52N 0 9E
Manso, R. 171 14 0S 52 0W
Mansôa 120 12 0N 15 20W
Manson Cr. 152 55 37N 124 25W
Mansoura, Djebel 119 36 1N 4 31E
Manta 174 1 0S 80 40W
Mantalingajan, Mt. 102 8 55N 117 45E
Mantare 126 2 42S 33 13E
Manteca 163 37 50N 121 12W
Mantecal 174 7 34N 69 17W
Mantekomu Hu 99 34 40N 89 0E
Mantena 171 18 47S 40 59W
Manteo 157 35 55N 75 41W
Mantes-la-Jolie 43 49 0N 1 41E
Manthani 96 18 40N 79 35E
Manthelan 42 47 9N 0 47E
Manti 160 39 23N 111 32W
Mantiqueira, Serra da 173 22 0S 44 0W
Manton, U.K. 29 52 37N 0 41W
Manton, U.S.A. 156 44 23N 85 25W
Mantorp 73 58 21N 15 20E
Mântova 62 45 10N 10 47E
Mänttä 74 62 0N 24 40E
Mantua = Mántova 62 45 10N 10 47E
Mantung 140 34 35S 140 3E
Manturova 81 58 10N 44 30E
Manu 174 12 10S 71 0W
Manucan 103 8 14N 123 3E
Manuel Alves Grande, R. 170 7 27S 47 35W
Manuel Alves, R. 171 11 19S 48 28W
Manui I. 103 3 35S 123 5E
Manukau 142 37 1S 174 55E
Manukau Harbour 142 37 3S 174 45E
Manunui 142 38 54S 175 21E
Manus I. 135 2 0S 147 0E
Manvi 97 15 57N 76 59E
Manville, R.I., U.S.A. 162 41 58N 71 28W
Manville, Wyo., U.S.A. 158 42 48N 104 36W
Manwath 96 19 19N 76 32E
Many 159 31 36N 93 28W
Manyane 128 23 21S 21 42E
Manyara L. 126 3 40S 35 50E
Manych-Gudilo, Oz. 83 46 24N 42 38E
Manych, R. 83 47 0N 41 15E
Manyonga, R. 126 4 5S 34 0E
Manyoni 126 5 45S 34 55E
Manyoni □ 126 6 30S 34 30E
Manzai 94 32 20N 70 15E
Manzala, Bahra el 122 31 10N 31 56E
Manzanares 59 39 0N 3 22W
Manzaneda, Cabeza de 56 42 12N 7 15W
Manzanillo, Cuba 166 20 20N 77 10W
Manzanillo, Mexico 164 19 0N 104 20W
Manzanillo, Pta. 166 9 30N 79 40W
Manzano Mts. 161 34 30N 106 45W
Manzini 129 26 30S 31 25E
Mao 117 14 4N 15 19E
Maohsing 107 45 31N 124 32E
Maoke, Pengunungan 102 3 40S 137 30E
Maolin 107 43 55N 123 25E
Maoming 109 21 39N 110 54E
Maopi T'ou 109 21 56N 120 43E
Maoping 109 30 51N 110 54E
Maowen 108 31 41N 103 52E
Mapastepec 165 15 26N 92 54W
Mapia, Kepulauan 103 0 50N 134 20E
Mapien 108 28 48N 103 39E
Mapimí 164 25 50N 103 31W
Mapimí, Bolsón de 164 27 30N 103 15W
Map'ing 109 31 36N 113 33E
Mapinga 126 6 40S 39 12E
Mapinhane 129 22 20S 35 0E
Maple Creek 153 49 55N 109 29W
Mapleton 160 44 4N 123 58W
Maplewood 158 38 33N 90 18W
Mappinga 109 34 58S 138 52E
Maprik 135 3 44S 143 3E
Mapuca 97 15 36N 73 46E
Mapuera, R. 174 0 30S 58 25W
Maputo 129 25 58S 32 32E
Maqnā 92 28 25N 34 50E
Maquela do Zombo 124 6 0S 15 15E
Maquinchao 176 41 15S 68 50W
Maquoketa 158 42 4N 90 40W
Mar Chiquita, L. 172 30 40S 62 50W
Mar del Plata 172 38 0S 57 30W
Mar Menor, L. 59 37 40N 0 45W
Mar, Reg. 37 57 11N 2 53W
Mar, Serra do 173 25 30S 49 0W
Mara, Bangla. 98 28 11N 94 7E
Mara, Tanz. 126 1 30S 34 32E
Mara □, Tanz. 126 1 45S 34 20E
Mara □, Tanz. 126 1 30S 34 32E
Maraã 174 1 43S 65 25W
Marabá 170 5 20S 49 5W
Maracá, I. de 170 2 10N 50 30W
Maracaibo 174 10 40N 71 37W
Maracaibo, Lago de 174 9 40N 71 30W
Maracaju 173 21 38S 55 9W
Maracanã 170 0 46S 47 27W
Maracás 171 13 26S 40 27W
Maracay 174 10 15N 67 36W
Marādah 119 29 4N 19 4E
Maradi 121 13 35N 8 10E
Maradun 121 12 35N 6 18E
Marāgheh 92 37 30N 46 12E
Maragogipe 171 12 46S 38 55W
Marajó, B. de 170 1 0S 48 30W
Marajó, Ilha de 170 1 0S 49 30W
Maralal 124 1 0N 36 38E
Maralinga 137 29 45S 131 15E
Marama 140 35 10S 140 10E
Marampa 120 8 45N 10 28W
Maramureș □ 70 47 45N 24 0E
Maran 101 3 35N 102 45E
Marana 161 32 30N 111 9W
Maranboy 136 14 40S 132 40E
Maranchón 58 41 6N 2 15W
Marand 92 38 30N 45 45E
Marandellas 127 18 5S 31 42E
Maranguape 170 3 55S 38 50W
Maranhão = São Luis 170 2 31S 44 16W
Maranhão □ 170 5 0S 46 0W
Marañón, R. 174 4 50S 75 35W
Marano, L. di 63 45 42N 13 13E
Maranoa R. 139 27 50S 148 37E
Maraş 92 37 37N 36 53E
Marașești 70 45 52N 27 5E
Maratea 65 39 59N 15 43E
Marateca 57 38 34N 8 40W
Marathókambos 69 37 43N 26 42E
Marathon, Austral. 138 20 51S 143 32E
Marathon, Can. 150 48 44N 86 23W
Marathón 69 38 11N 23 58E
Marathon, N.Y., U.S.A. 162 42 25N 76 3W
Marathon, Tex., U.S.A. 159 30 15N 103 15W
Maratua, I. 103 2 10N 118 35E
Maraú 171 14 6S 39 0W
Marazion 30 50 8N 5 29W
Marbat 91 17 0N 54 45E
Marbella 57 36 30N 4 57W
Marble Bar 136 21 9S 119 44E
Marble Falls 159 30 30N 98 15W
Marblehead 162 42 29N 70 51W
Marburg 48 50 49N 8 44E
Marby 72 63 7N 14 18E
Marcal, R. 53 47 21N 17 15E
Marcali 53 46 35N 17 25E
Marcaria 62 45 7N 10 34E
March 29 52 33N 0 5E
Marchand = Rommani 118 33 20N 6 40W
Marché 44 46 0N 1 20E
Marche □ 63 43 22N 13 10E
Marche-en-Famenne 47 50 14N 5 19E
Marchena 57 37 18N 5 23W
Marches = Marche 63 43 22N 13 10E
Marciana Marina 62 42 44N 10 12E
Marcianise 65 41 3N 14 16E
Marcigny 45 46 17N 4 2E
Marcillac-Vallon 44 44 29N 2 27E
Marcillat 44 46 12N 2 38E
Marcinelle 47 50 24N 4 26E
Marck 43 50 57N 1 57E
Marckolsheim 43 48 10N 7 30E
Marcos Juárez 172 32 42S 62 5W
Marcus I. 130 24 0N 153 45E
Mardan 94 34 20N 72 0E
Marden 28 52 7N 2 42W
Mardie 136 21 12S 115 59E
Mardin 92 37 20N 40 36E
Marechal Deodoro 170 9 43S 35 54W
Maree L. 36 57 40N 5 30W
Mareeba 138 16 59S 145 28E
Mareham le Fen 33 53 7N 0 3W
Marek 103 4 41S 120 24E
Marek = Stanke Dimitrov 66 42 27N 23 9E
Maremma 62 42 45N 11 15E
Maréna 120 14 0N 7 30W
Marenberg 63 46 38N 15 13E
Marengo 158 41 42N 92 5W
Marennes 126 45 49N 1 5W
Marenyi 126 4 22S 39 8E
Marerano 129 21 23S 44 52E
Marèttimo, I. 64 37 58N 12 5E
Mareuil-sur-Lay 44 46 32N 1 14W
Marfa 159 30 15N 104 0W
Marfleet 33 53 45N 0 15W
Margable 123 12 54N 42 38E
Margam 31 51 33N 3 45W
Marganets 82 47 40N 34 40E
Margao 97 14 12N 73 58E
Margaree Harbour 151 46 26N 61 8W
Margaret Bay 152 51 20N 127 20W
Margaret L. 152 58 56N 115 25W
Margaret, R. 136 12 57S 131 16E
Margaret River 137 33 57S 115 7E
Margarita, Isla de 174 11 0N 64 0W
Margarition 68 39 22N 20 26E
Margate, S. Afr. 129 30 50S 30 20E
Margate, U.K. 29 51 23N 1 24E
Margate City 162 39 20N 74 31W
Margelan 85 40 27N 71 42E
Margeride, Mts. de la 44 44 43N 3 38E
Margherita 98 27 16N 95 40E
Margherita di Savola 65 41 25N 16 5E
Marghita 70 47 22N 22 22E
Margonin 54 52 58N 17 5E
Margreten 47 50 49N 5 49E
Marguerite 152 52 30N 122 25W
Marhoum 118 34 27N 0 11W
Mari, A.S.S.R. □ 81 56 30N 48 0E
María Elena 172 22 18S 69 40W
María Grande 172 31 45S 59 55W
Maria, I. 138 14 52S 135 45E
Maria I. 138 42 35S 148 0E
Maria van Diemen, C. 142 34 29S 172 40E
Mariager 73 56 40N 10 0E
Mariager Fjord 73 56 42N 10 19E
Mariakani 126 3 50S 39 27E
Marian L. 152 63 0N 116 15W
Mariana 171 20 23S 43 25W
Mariana Is. 130 17 0N 145 0E
Mariana Trench 130 13 0N 145 0W
Marianao 166 23 8N 82 24W
Mariani 98 26 39N 94 19E
Marianna, Ark., U.S.A. 159 34 48N 90 48W
Marianna, Fla., U.S.A. 157 30 45N 85 15W
Mariannelund 73 57 37N 15 35E
Mariánské Lázně 52 49 57N 12 41E
Marias, R. 160 48 26N 111 40W
Mariato, Punta 166 7 12N 80 52W
Mariazell 52 47 47N 15 19E
Marib 91 15 25N 45 20E
Maribo 73 54 48N 11 30E
Maribor 63 46 36N 15 40E
Marico, R. 128 24 25S 26 30E
Maricopa, Ariz., U.S.A. 161 33 5N 112 2W
Maricopa, Calif., U.S.A. 163 35 7N 119 27W
Marîdî 123 4 55N 29 25E
Marîdî, W. 123 5 25N 29 21E
Marie Galante, I. 167 15 56N 61 16W
Mariecourt 149 61 30N 72 0W
Mariefred 72 59 15N 17 12E
Mariehamn (Maarianhamina) 75 60 5N 19 57E
Marienberg, Ger. 48 50 40N 13 10E
Marienberg, Neth. 47 52 30N 6 35E
Marienberg, P.N.G. 138 3 54S 144 10E
Marienbourg 47 50 6N 4 31E
Mariental 128 24 36S 18 0E
Mariestad 73 58 43N 13 50E
Marietta, Ga., U.S.A. 157 34 0N 84 30W
Marietta, Ohio, U.S.A. 156 39 27N 81 27W
Marignane 45 43 25N 5 13E
Mariinsk 76 56 10N 87 20E
Mariinskiy Posad 81 56 10N 47 45E
Marilia 173 22 0S 50 0W
Marillana 136 22 37S 119 24E
Marín 56 42 23N 8 42W
Marina 163 36 41N 121 48W
Marina di Cirò 65 39 22N 17 8E
Mariña, La 56 43 30N 7 40W
Marina Plains 138 14 37S 143 57E
Marinduque, I. 103 13 25N 122 0E
Marine City 156 42 45N 82 29W
Marinel, Le 127 10 25S 25 17E
Marineo 64 37 57N 13 23E
Marinette, Ariz., U.S.A. 161 33 41N 112 16W
Marinette, Wis., U.S.A. 156 45 4N 87 40W
Maringá 173 23 35S 51 50W
Marinha Grande 57 39 45N 8 56W
Marino 109 35 3S 138 31E
Marino Rocks 109 35 3S 138 31E
Marion, Austral. 109 34 59S 138 33E
Marion, Ala., U.S.A. 157 32 33N 87 20W
Marion, Ill., U.S.A. 159 37 45N 88 55W
Marion, Ind., U.S.A. 156 40 35N 85 40W
Marion, Iowa, U.S.A. 158 42 2N 91 36W
Marion, Kans., U.S.A. 158 38 25N 97 2W
Marion, Mich., U.S.A. 156 44 7N 85 8W
Marion, N.C., U.S.A. 157 35 42N 82 0W
Marion, Ohio, U.S.A. 156 40 38N 83 8W
Marion, S.C., U.S.A. 157 34 11N 79 22W
Marion, Va., U.S.A. 157 36 51N 81 29W
Marion Bay 140 35 12S 136 59E
Marion, L. 157 33 30N 80 15W
Marion Reef 138 19 10S 152 17E
Maripa 174 7 26N 65 9W
Mariposa 163 37 31N 119 59W
Mariscal Estigarribia 172 22 3S 60 40W
Maritime Alps = Alpes Maritimes 62 44 10N 7 10E
Maritsa 67 42 1N 25 50E
Maritsá 69 36 22N 28 10E
Maritsa, R. 67 42 15N 24 0E
Mariyampole = Kapsukas 80 54 33N 23 19E
Marjan 93 32 5N 68 20E
Mark 34 55 2N 5 1W
Marka 122 18 14N 41 19E
Markapur 97 15 44N 79 19E
Markaryd 73 56 28N 13 35E
Marke 47 50 48N 3 14E
Marked Tree 159 35 35N 90 24W
Markelo 46 52 14N 6 30E
Markelsdorfer Huk 48 54 33N 11 0E
Marken 46 52 26N 5 12E
Markerwaard 46 52 33N 5 15E
Market Bosworth 28 52 37N 1 24W
Market Deeping 29 52 40N 0 20W
Market Drayton 32 52 55N 2 30W
Market Harborough 29 52 29N 0 55W
Market Lavington 28 51 17N 1 59W
Market Rasen 33 53 24N 0 20W
Market Weighton 33 53 52N 0 40W
Markethill 38 54 18N 6 31W
Markfield 28 52 42N 1 18W
Markham I. 12 84 0N 0 45W
Markham L. 153 62 30N 102 35W
Markham Mts. 13 83 0S 164 0E
Markham, R. 135 6 41S 147 2E
Marki 54 52 20N 21 2E
Markinch 35 56 12N 3 9W
Markleeville 163 38 42N 119 47W
Markoupoulon 69 37 53N 23 57E
Markovac 66 44 14N 21 7E
Markovo 77 64 40N 169 40E
Markoye 121 14 39N 0 2E
Marks 81 51 45N 46 50E
Marks Tey 29 51 53N 0 48E
Marksville 159 31 10N 92 2W
Markt Schwaben 49 48 14N 11 49E
Marktredwitz 49 50 1N 12 2E
Marlboro, Can. 152 53 30N 116 50W
Marlboro, U.S.A. 162 42 19N 71 33W
Marlboro, N.Y., U.S.A. 162 41 36N 73 58W
Marlborough, Austral. 138 22 46S 149 52E
Marlborough, U.K. 28 51 26N 1 44W
Marlborough □ 143 41 45S 173 33E
Marlborough Downs 28 51 25N 1 55W
Marle 43 49 43N 3 47E
Marlin 159 31 25N 96 50W
Marlow, Austral. 141 35 17S 149 55E
Marlow, Ger. 48 54 8N 12 34E
Marlow, U.K. 29 51 34N 0 47W
Marlow, U.S.A. 159 34 40N 97 58W
Marly-le-Grand 50 46 47N 7 10E
Marmagao 97 15 25N 73 56E
Marmande 44 44 30N 0 10E
Marmara denizi 92 40 45N 28 15E
Marmara, I. 82 40 35N 27 38E
Marmara, Sea of = Marmara denizi 92 40 45N 28 15E
Marmaris 92 36 50N 28 14E
Marmarth 158 46 21N 103 52W
Marmion L. 150 48 55N 91 30W
Marmion Mt. 137 29 16S 119 50E
Marmolada, Mte. 63 46 25N 11 55E
Marmolejo 57 38 3N 4 13W
Marmora 150 44 28N 77 41W
Marnay 43 47 20N 5 48E
Marne 48 53 57N 9 1E
Marne □ 43 49 0N 4 10E
Marne, R. 43 48 53N 4 25E
Marnhull 28 50 58N 2 20W
Maro 124 8 30N 19 0E
Maroa 174 2 43N 67 33W
Maroala 129 15 23S 47 59E
Maroantsetra 129 15 26S 49 44E
Marocco ■ 129 32 0N 5 50W
Maromandia 129 14 13S 48 5E
Maroni, R. 175 4 0N 52 0W
Marónia 68 40 53N 25 24E
Maroochydore 139 26 29S 153 5E
Maroona 140 37 27S 142 54E
Maros, R. 53 46 25N 20 20E
Marosakoa 129 15 26S 46 38E

Marostica 63 45 44N 11 40 E
Maroua 121 10 40N 14 20 E
Marovoay 129 16 6 S 46 39 E
Marple 32 53 23N 2 5W
Marquard 128 28 40 S 27 28 E
Marqueira 57 38 41N 9 9W
Marquesas Is. = Marquises 131 9 30 S 140 0W
Marquette 156 46 30N 87 21W
Marquise 43 50 50N 1 40 E
Marquises, Is. 131 9 30 S 140 0W
Marra 139 31 12 S 144 10 E
Marra, Gebet 123 7 20N 27 35 E
Marradi 63 44 5N 11 37 E
Marrakech 118 31 40N 8 0W
Marrat 92 25 0N 45 35 E
Marrawah 138 40 55 S 144 42 E
Marrecas, Serra das 170 9 0 S 41 0W
Marree 139 29 39 S 138 1 E
Marrimane 129 22 58 S 33 34 E
Marromeu 125 18 40 S 36 25 E
Marroqui, Punta 56 36 0N 5 37W
Marrowie Creek 141 33 23 S 145 40 E
Marrubane 127 18 0 S 37 0 E
Marrum 46 53 19N 5 48 E
Marrupa 127 13 8 S 37 30 E
Mars, Le 158 43 0N 96 0W
Marsa Susa (Apollonia) 117 32 52N 21 59 E
Marsabit 126 2 18N 38 0 E
Marsabit □ 126 2 45N 37 45 E
Marsala 64 37 48N 12 25 E
Marsciano 63 42 54N 12 20 E
Marsden 141 33 47N 147 32 E
Marsdiep 46 52 58N 4 46 E
Marseillan 44 43 23N 3 31 E
Marseille 45 43 18N 5 23 E
Marseilles = Marseille 45 43 18N 5 23 E
Marsh I. 159 29 35N 91 50W
Marshall, Liberia 120 6 8N 10 22W
Marshall, Ark., U.S.A. 159 35 58N 92 40W
Marshall, Mich., U.S.A. 156 42 17N 84 59W
Marshall, Minn., U.S.A. 158 44 25N 95 45W
Marshall, Mo., U.S.A. 158 39 8N 93 15W
Marshall, Tex., U.S.A. 159 32 29N 94 20W
Marshall Is. 130 9 0N 171 0 E
Marshall, R. 138 22 59 S 136 59 E
Marshalltown 158 42 0N 93 0W
Marshfield, U.K. 28 51 27N 2 18W
Marshfield, Mo., U.S.A. 159 37 20N 92 58W
Marshfield, Wis., U.S.A. 158 44 42N 90 10W
Mársico Nuovo 65 40 26N 15 43 E
Marske by the sea 33 54 35N 1 0W
Märsta 72 59 37N 17 52 E
Marstal 73 54 51N 10 30 E
Marston Moor 33 53 58N 1 17W
Marstrand 73 57 53N 11 35 E
Mart 159 31 34N 96 51W
Marta, R. 63 42 18N 11 47 E
Martaban 98 16 30N 97 35 E
Martaban, G. of 98 15 40N 96 30 E
Martano 65 40 14N 18 18 E
Martapura 102 3 22 S 114 56 E
Marte 121 12 23N 13 46 E
Martebo 73 57 45N 18 30 E
Martelange 47 49 49N 5 43 E
Martés, Sierra 59 39 20N 1 0W
Marthaguy Creek 141 30 50 S 147 45 E
Martham 29 52 42N 1 38 E
Martha's Vineyard 162 41 25N 70 35W
Martigné Ferchaud 42 47 50N 1 20W
Martigny 50 46 6N 7 3 E
Martigues 45 43 24N 5 4 E
Martil 118 35 36N 5 15W
Martin, Czech. 53 49 6N 18 48 E
Martin, S.D., U.S.A. 158 43 11N 101 45W
Martin, Tenn., U.S.A. 159 36 23N 88 51W
Martin, L. 157 32 45N 85 50W
Martin, R. 58 41 2N 0 43W
Martina 51 46 53N 10 28 E
Martina Franca 65 40 42N 17 20 E
Martinborough 142 41 14 S 175 29 E
Martinez 163 38 1N 122 8W
Martinho Campos 171 19 20 S 45 13W
Martinique, I. 167 14 40N 61 0W
Martinique Passage 167 15 15N 61 0W
Martinon 69 38 25N 23 15 E
Martinópolis 173 22 11 S 51 12W
Martins 171 6 5 S 37 55W
Martinsberg 52 48 22N 15 9 E
Martinsburg 156 39 30N 77 57W
Martinsville, Ind., U.S.A. 156 39 29N 86 23W
Martinsville, Va., U.S.A. 157 36 41N 79 52W
Martley 28 52 14N 2 22W
Martock 28 50 58N 2 47W
Marton 142 40 4 S 175 23 E
Martorell 58 41 28N 1 56 E
Martos 57 37 44N 3 58W
Martre, La, L. 148 63 8N 117 16W
Martre, La, R. 148 63 0N 118 0W
Martuk 84 50 46N 56 31 E
Martuni 83 40 9N 45 10 E
Maru 121 12 22N 6 22 E
Marudi 102 4 10N 114 25 E
Maruf 93 31 30N 67 0 E
Marugame 110 34 15N 133 55 E
Maruggio 65 40 20N 17 33 E
Marui 135 4 4 S 143 2 E
Maruim 170 10 45 S 37 5W
Marulan 141 34 43 S 150 3 E
Marum 46 53 9N 6 16 E
Marunga 128 17 20 S 20 2 E
Marungu, Mts. 126 7 30 S 30 0 E
Maruoka 111 36 9N 136 16 E
Marvejols 44 44 33N 3 19 E
Marvine Mt. 161 38 44N 111 40W
Marwar 94 25 43N 73 45 E
Mary 76 37 40N 61 50 E
Mary Frances L. 153 63 19N 106 13W
Mary Kathleen 138 20 35 S 139 48 E
Maryborough, Queens., Austral. 139 25 31 S 152 37 E
Maryborough, Vic., Austral. 140 37 0 S 143 44 E
Maryets 81 56 17N 49 47 E
Maryfield 153 49 50N 101 35W
Marykirk 37 56 47N 2 30W
Maryland □ 156 39 10N 76 40W
Maryland Jc. 127 12 45 S 30 31 E
Maryport 32 54 43N 3 30W
Mary's Harbour 151 52 18N 55 51W
Marystown 151 47 10N 55 10W
Marysvale 161 38 25N 112 17W
Marysville, Can. 152 49 35N 116 0W
Marysville, Calif., U.S.A. 160 39 14N 121 40W
Marysville, Kans., U.S.A. 158 39 50N 96 38W
Marysville, Ohio, U.S.A. 156 40 15N 83 20W
Marytavy 30 50 34N 4 6W
Maryvale 139 28 4 S 152 12 E
Maryville 157 35 50N 84 0W
Marywell 37 56 35N 2 31W
Marzo, Punta 174 6 50N 77 42W
Marzuq 119 25 53N 14 10 E
Masada = Mesada 90 31 20N 35 19 E
Masafa 127 13 50 S 27 30 E
Masai 101 1 29N 103 55 E
Masai Steppe 126 4 30 S 36 30 E
Masaka 126 0 21 S 31 45 E
Masakali 121 13 2N 12 32 E
Masalima, Kepulauan 102 5 10 S 116 50 E
Masamba 103 2 30 S 120 15 E
Masan 107 35 11N 128 32 E
Masanasa 59 39 25N 0 25W
Masandam, Ras 93 26 30N 56 30 E
Masasi 127 10 45 S 38 52 E
Masasi □ 127 10 45 S 38 50 E
Masaya 166 12 0N 86 7W
Masba 121 10 35N 13 1 E
Mascara 118 35 26N 0 6 E
Mascota 164 20 30N 104 50W
Masela 103 8 9 S 129 51 E
Maseme 147 18 46 S 25 3 E
Maseru 128 29 18 S 27 30 E
Mashaba 127 20 2 S 30 29 E
Mashabih 92 25 35N 36 30 E
Masham 33 54 15N 1 40W
Mashan 108 23 44N 108 14 E
Masherbrum, mt. 95 35 38N 76 18 E
Mashhad 93 36 20N 59 35 E
Mashi 121 13 0N 7 54 E
Mashiki 110 32 51N 130 53 E
Mashki Chah 93 29 5N 62 30 E
Mashkode 150 47 2N 84 7W
Mashonaland, North, □ 127 16 30 S 30 0 E
Mashonaland, South, □ 127 18 0 S 31 30 E
Mashtagi 83 40 35N 50 0 E
Masi 74 69 26N 23 50 E
Masi-Manimba 124 4 40 S 18 5 E
Masindi 126 1 40N 31 43 E
Masindi Port 126 1 43N 32 2 E
Masirah 91 20 25N 58 50 E
Masisea 174 8 35 S 74 15W
Masisi 126 1 23 S 28 49 E
Masjed Solyman 92 31 55N 49 25 E
Mask, L. 38 53 36N 9 24W
Maski 97 15 56N 76 46 E
Maslen Nos 67 42 18N 27 48 E
Maslinica 63 43 24N 16 13 E
Masnou 58 41 28N 2 20 E
Masoala, C. 129 15 59 S 50 13 E
Masoarivo 129 19 3 S 44 19 E
Masohi 103 3 2 S 128 15 E
Masomeloka 129 20 17 S 48 37 E
Mason, Nev., U.S.A. 163 38 56N 119 8W
Mason, S.D., U.S.A. 158 45 12N 103 27W
Mason, Tex., U.S.A. 159 30 45N 99 15W
Mason B. 143 46 55 S 167 45 E
Mason City 160 48 0N 119 0W
Masqat 93 23 37N 58 36 E
Massa 62 44 2N 10 7 E
Massa Maríttima 62 43 3N 10 52 E
Massa, O. 118 30 0N 9 30W
Massachusetts □ 162 42 25N 72 0W
Massachusetts B. 162 42 30N 70 0W
Massada 90 33 12N 35 45 E
Massafra 65 40 35N 17 8 E
Massaguet 124 12 28N 15 26 E
Massakory 117 13 0N 15 49 E
Massangena 129 21 34 S 33 0 E
Massapê 170 3 31 S 40 19W
Massarosa 62 43 53N 10 17 E
Massat 44 42 53N 1 21 E
Massava 84 60 40N 62 6 E
Massawa = Mitsiwa 123 15 35N 39 25 E
Massena 156 44 52N 74 55W
Massenya 117 11 30N 16 25 E
Masset 152 54 0N 132 0W
Massiac 44 45 15N 3 11 E
Massif Central 44 45 30N 2 21 E
Massillon 156 40 47N 81 30W
Massinga 125 23 15 S 35 22 E
Massingir 129 23 46 S 32 4 E
Mässlingen 98 62 42N 12 48 E
Massman 138 16 25 S 145 25 E
Masson I. 13 66 10 S 93 20 E
Mastaba 122 20 52N 39 30 E
Mastanli = Momchilgrad 21 41 33N 25 23 E
Masterton 142 40 56 S 175 39 E
Mástikho, Ákra 68 38 10N 26 2 E
Mastuj 95 36 20N 72 36 E
Mastung 93 29 50N 66 42 E
Mastura 122 23 7N 38 52 E
Masuda 110 34 40N 131 51 E
Masulipatam 96 16 12N 81 12 E
Maswa □ 126 1 20 S 34 0 E
Mat, R. 68 41 40N 20 0 E
Mata de São João 171 12 31 S 38 17W
Matabeleland North □ 127 20 0 S 28 0 E
Matabeleland South □ 127 19 0 S 29 0 E
Mataboor 103 1 41 S 138 3 E
Matachel, R. 57 38 32N 6 0W
Matachewan 150 47 56N 80 39W
Matad 105 47 12N 115 29 E
Matadi 124 5 52 S 13 31 E
Matador 153 50 49N 107 56W
Matagalpa 166 13 10N 85 40W
Matagami 150 49 45N 77 34W
Matagami, L. 150 49 50N 77 40W
Matagorda 159 28 43N 96 0W
Matagorda, B. 159 28 30N 96 15W
Matagorda I. 159 28 10N 96 40W
Matak, P. 101 3 18N 106 16 E
Matakana 141 32 59 S 145 54 E
Matale 97 7 30N 80 44 E
Matam 120 15 34N 13 17W
Matamata 142 37 48 S 175 47 E
Matameye 121 13 26N 8 28 E
Matamoros, Campeche, Mexico 165 25 53N 97 30W
Matamoros, Coahuila, Mexico 164 25 45N 103 1W
Matamoros, Puebla, Mexico 165 18 2N 98 17W
Matamoros, Tamaulipas, Mexico 165 25 50N 97 30W
Matana, D. 103 2 30 S 121 25 E
Matandu, R. 127 8 35 S 39 40 E
Matane 151 48 50N 67 33W
Mat'ang, Szechwan, China 108 31 54N 102 55 E
Mat'ang, Yunnan, China 108 23 30N 104 4 E
Matankari 121 13 46N 4 1 E
Matanuska 148 61 38N 149 0W
Matanzá 174 7 22N 73 2W
Matanzas 166 23 0N 81 40W
Matapá, Ákra 69 36 22N 22 27 E
Matapedia 151 48 0N 66 59W
Matara 97 5 58N 80 30 E
Mataram 102 8 41 S 116 10 E
Matarani 174 16 50 S 72 10W
Mataranka 136 14 55 S 133 4 E
Mataró 58 41 32N 2 29 E
Matarraña, R. 58 40 55N 0 8 E
Mataruška Banja 66 43 40N 20 45 E
Matata 142 37 54 S 176 48 E
Matatiele 129 30 20 S 28 49 E
Mataura 143 46 11 S 168 51 E
Mataura, R. 143 45 49 S 168 44 E
Matehuala 164 23 40N 100 50W
Mateira 171 18 54 S 50 30W
Mateke Hills 127 21 48 S 31 0 E
Matélica 63 43 15N 13 0 E
Matera 65 40 40N 16 37 E
Mátészalka 53 47 58N 22 20 E
Matetsi 127 18 12 S 26 0 E
Mateur 119 37 0N 9 48 E
Mateyev Kurgan 83 47 35N 38 47 E
Matfors 72 62 21N 17 2 E
Matha 44 45 52N 0 20W
Matheson I. 153 51 45N 96 56W
Mathews 162 37 26N 76 19W
Mathias Pass 143 43 7 S 171 6 E
Mathis 159 28 4N 97 48W
Mathoura 141 35 50 S 144 55 E
Mathry 31 51 56N 5 6W
Mathura 94 27 30N 77 48 E
Mati 103 6 55N 126 15 E
Mati, R. 68 41 40N 20 0 E
Matias Romero 165 16 53N 95 2W
Matibane 127 14 49 S 40 45 E
Matien 109 32 55N 116 26 E
Matlock 33 53 8N 1 32W
Matmata 119 33 30N 9 59 E
Matna 123 13 49N 35 10 E
Mato Grosso □ 175 14 0 S 55 0W
Mato Grosso, Planalto do 174 15 0 S 54 0W
Mato Verde 171 15 23 S 42 52W
Matochkin Shar 76 73 10N 56 40 E
Matong 135 5 36 S 151 50 E
Matopo Hills 127 20 36 S 28 20 E
Matopos 127 20 20 S 28 29 E
Matour 45 46 19N 4 29 E
Matozinhos 56 41 11N 8 42W
Matrah 93 23 37N 58 30 E
Matrûh 122 31 19N 27 9 E
Matsang Tsangpo (Brahmaputra), R. 99 29 25N 88 0 E
Matsena 121 13 5N 10 5 E
Matsesta 83 43 34N 39 44 E
Matsu Tao 109 26 9N 119 56 E
Matsubara 111 34 33N 135 34 E
Matsudo 111 35 47N 139 54 E
Matsue 110 35 25N 133 10 E
Matsumae 112 41 26N 140 7 E
Matsumoto 111 36 15N 138 0 E
Matsusaka 111 34 34N 136 32 E
Matsutō 111 36 31N 136 34 E
Matsuura 110 33 20N 129 49 E
Matsuyama 110 33 45N 132 45 E
Mattagami, R. 150 50 43N 81 29W
Mattancheri 97 9 50N 76 15 E
Mattawa 150 46 20N 78 45W
Mattawamkeag 151 45 30N 68 30W
Matterhorn, mt. 50 45 58N 7 39 E
Mattersburg 53 47 44N 16 24 E
Matthew Town 167 20 57N 73 40W
Matthew's Ridge 174 7 37N 60 10W
Mattice 150 49 40N 83 20W
Mattituck 162 40 58N 72 32W
Mattmar 72 63 18N 13 54 E
Mattoon 156 39 30N 88 20W
Matua 102 2 58 S 110 52 E
Matuba 129 24 28 S 32 49 E
Matucana 174 11 55 S 76 15W
Matun 94 33 22N 69 58 E
Maturín 174 9 45N 63 11W
Matutina 171 19 13 S 45 58W
Matzuzaki 111 34 43N 138 50 E
Mau-é-ele 129 24 18 S 34 2 E
Mau Escarpment 126 0 40 S 36 0 E
Mau Ranipur 95 25 16N 79 8 E
Mauagami, R. 150 49 30N 82 0W
Maubeuge 43 50 17N 3 57 E
Maubourguet 44 43 29N 0 1 E
Mauchline 34 55 31N 4 23W
Maud 37 57 30N 2 8W
Maud, Pt. 137 23 6 S 113 45 E
Maude 140 34 29 S 144 18 E
Maudheim 13 71 5 S 11 0W
Maudin Sun 99 16 0N 94 30 E
Maués 174 3 20 S 57 45W
Mauganj 99 24 50N 81 55 E
Maughold 32 54 18N 4 17W
Maughold Hd. 32 54 18N 4 17W
Maui I. 147 20 45N 156 20 E
Maulamyaing 99 16 30N 97 40 E
Maule □ 172 36 5 S 72 30W
Mauleon 44 43 14N 0 54W
Maulvibazar 98 24 29N 91 42 E
Maum 38 53 31N 9 35W
Maumee 156 41 35N 83 40W
Maumee, R. 156 41 42N 83 28W
Maumere 103 8 38 S 122 13 E
Maumturk Mts. 38 53 32N 9 42W
Maun 128 20 0 S 23 26 E
Mauna Kea, Mt. 147 19 50N 155 28W
Mauna Loa, Mt. 147 19 50N 155 28W
Maunath Bhanjan 95 25 56N 83 33 E
Maungaturoto 142 36 6 S 174 23 E
Maungdow 98 21 14N 94 5 E
Maungmagan Is. 99 14 0 S 97 48 E
Maungmagan Kyunzu 101 14 0N 97 48 E
Maupin 160 45 12N 121 9W
Maure-de-Bretagne 42 47 53N 2 0W
Maureen, oilfield 19 58 5N 1 45 E
Maurepas L. 159 30 18N 90 35W
Maures, mts. 45 43 15N 6 15 E
Mauriac 44 45 13N 2 19 E
Maurice L. 137 29 30 S 131 0 E
Mauriceville 142 40 45 S 175 35 E
Maurienne 45 45 15N 6 20 E
Mauritania ■ 116 20 50N 10 0W
Mauritius ■ 11 20 0 S 57 0 E
Mauron 42 48 9N 2 18W
Maurs 44 44 43N 2 12 E
Maurthe, R. 43 48 47N 6 9 E
Mauston 158 43 48N 90 5W
Mauterndorf 52 47 9N 13 40 E
Mauvezin 44 43 44N 0 53 E
Mauzé-sur le Mignon 44 46 12N 0 41W
Mavelikara 97 9 14N 76 32 E
Mavinga 125 15 50 S 20 10 E
Mavli 94 24 45N 73 55 E
Mavqi'im 90 31 38N 34 32 E
Mavrova 68 40 26N 19 32 E
Mavuradonha Mts. 127 16 30 S 31 30 E
Mawa 126 2 45N 26 33 E
Mawana 94 29 6N 77 58 E
Mawand 94 29 33N 68 38 E
Mawer 153 50 46N 106 22W
Mawgan 30 50 4N 5 10W
Mawkmai 98 20 14N 97 50 E
Mawlaik 98 23 40N 94 26 E
Mawlawkho 98 17 50N 97 38 E
Mawson Base 13 67 30 S 65 0 E
Max 158 47 50N 101 20W
Maxcanú 165 20 40N 90 10W
Maxhamish L. 152 59 50N 123 17W
Maxixe 129 23 54 S 35 17 E
Maxwellheugh 35 55 35N 2 23W
Maxwelltown 142 39 51 S 174 49 E
Maxwelton, Queens., Austral. 138 15 45 S 142 30 E
Maxwelton, Queens., Austral. 138 20 43 S 142 41 E
May Downs 138 22 38 S 148 55 E
May, I. of 35 56 11N 2 32W
May Nefalis 123 15 0N 38 12 E
May Pen 166 17 58N 77 15W
May River 135 4 19 S 141 58 E
Maya 58 43 12N 1 29W
Maya Gudo, Mt. 123 7 30N 37 8 E
Maya Mts. 165 16 30N 89 0W
Maya, R. 77 58 20N 135 0 E

Place	Page	Lat.	Long.
Mayaguana Island	**167**	21 30N	72 44W
Mayagüez	**147**	18 12N	67 9W
Mayahi	**121**	13 58N	7 40E
Mayals	**58**	41 22N	0 30E
Mayang	**108**	27 53N	109 48E
Mayanup	**137**	33 58S	116 25E
Mayapán	**165**	20 38N	89 27W
Mayarf	**167**	20 40N	75 39W
Mayarí	**167**	20 40N	75 41W
Mayavaram = Mayuram	**97**	11 3N	79 42E
Maybell	**160**	40 30N	108 4W
Maybole	**34**	55 21N	4 41W
Maychew	**123**	12 50N	39 42E
Maydena	**138**	42 45S	146 39E
Maydos	**68**	40 13N	26 20E
Mayen	**49**	50 18N	7 10E
Mayenne	**42**	48 20N	0 38W
Mayenne □	**42**	48 10N	0 40W
Mayer	**161**	34 28N	112 17W
Mayerthorpe	**152**	53 57N	115 8W
Mayfield, Derby., U.K.	**33**	53 1N	1 47W
Mayfield, E. Sussex, U.K.	**29**	51 1N	0 17E
Mayfield, Ky., U.S.A.	**157**	36 45N	88 40W
Mayfield, N.Y., U.S.A.	**162**	43 6N	74 16W
Mayhill	**161**	32 58N	105 30W
Maykop	**83**	44 35N	40 25E
Mayli-Say	**85**	41 17N	72 24E
Maymyo	**100**	22 2N	96 28E
Maynard	**162**	42 30N	71 33W
Maynard Hills	**137**	28 35S	119 50E
Mayne, Le, L.	**151**	57 5N	68 30W
Mayne, R.	**138**	23 40S	142 10E
Maynooth, Can.	**150**	45 14N	77 56W
Maynooth, Ireland	**38**	53 22N	6 38W
Mayo	**147**	63 38N	135 57W
Mayo □	**139**	53 47N	9 7W
Mayo Bridge	**38**	54 11N	6 13W
Mayo L.	**147**	63 45N	135 0W
Mayo, R.	**164**	26 45N	109 47W
Mayon, Mt.	**103**	13 15N	123 42E
Mayor I.	**142**	37 16S	176 17E
Mayorga	**56**	42 10N	5 16W
Mays Landing	**162**	39 27N	74 44W
Mayskiy	**83**	43 47N	43 59E
Mayson L.	**153**	57 55N	107 10W
Maysville	**156**	38 43N	84 16W
Mayu, I.	**103**	1 30N	126 30E
Mayuram	**97**	11 3N	79 42E
Mayville	**158**	47 30N	97 23W
Mayya	**77**	61 44N	130 18E
Mazabuka	**127**	15 52S	27 44E
Mazagán = El Jadida	**118**	33 11N	8 17W
Mazagão	**175**	0 20S	51 50W
Mazama	**152**	49 43N	120 8W
Mazamet	**44**	43 30N	2 20E
Mazán	**174**	3 15S	73 0W
Mazapil	**164**	24 38N	101 34W
Mazar-i-Sharif	**93**	36 41N	67 0E
Mazar, O.	**118**	32 0N	1 38E
Mazara del Vallo	**64**	37 40N	12 34E
Mazarredo	**176**	47 10S	66 50W
Mazarrón	**59**	37 38N	1 19W
Mazarrón, Golfo de	**59**	37 27N	1 19W
Mazaruni, R.	**174**	6 15N	60 0W
Mazatán	**164**	29 0N	110 8W
Mazatenango	**166**	14 35N	91 30W
Mazatlán	**164**	23 10N	106 30W
Māzhān	**93**	32 30N	59 0E
Mazheikyai	**80**	56 20N	22 20E
Mazinān	**93**	36 25N	56 48E
Mazoe	**127**	17 28S	30 58E
Mazoe R.	**125**	16 45S	32 30E
Mazoi	**127**	16 42S	33 7E
Mazrûb	**123**	14 0N	29 20E
Mazurian Lakes = Mazurski, Pojezierze	**54**	53 50N	21 0E
Mazurski, Pojezierze	**54**	53 50N	21 0E
Mazzarino	**65**	37 19N	14 12E
Mbaba	**120**	14 59N	16 44W
Mbabane	**129**	26 18S	31 6E
Mbagne	**120**	16 6N	14 47W
M'bahiakro	**120**	7 33N	4 19W
M'Baiki	**124**	3 53N	18 1E
Mbala	**127**	8 46S	31 17E
Mbale	**126**	1 8N	34 12E
Mbalmayo	**121**	3 33N	11 33E
Mbamba Bay	**127**	11 13S	34 49E
Mbandaka	**124**	0 1S	18 18E
Mbanga	**121**	4 30N	9 33E
Mbanza Congo	**124**	6 18S	14 16E
Mbanza Ngungu	**124**	5 12S	14 53E
Mbarara	**126**	0 35S	30 25E
Mbatto	**120**	6 28N	4 22W
Mbenkuru, R.	**127**	9 25S	39 50E
Mberubu	**121**	6 10N	7 38E
Mbesuma	**127**	10 0S	32 2E
Mbeya	**127**	8 54S	33 29E
Mbeya □	**126**	8 15S	33 30E
Mbia	**123**	6 15N	29 18E
Mbimbi	**127**	13 25S	23 2E
Mbinga	**127**	10 50S	35 0E
Mbinga □	**127**	10 50S	35 0E
Mbini □	**124**	1 30N	10 0E
Mbiti	**123**	5 42N	28 3E
Mboki	**123**	5 19N	25 58E
Mboro	**120**	15 9N	16 54W
Mboune	**120**	14 42N	13 34W
Mbour	**120**	14 22N	16 54W
Mbout	**120**	16 1N	12 38W
Mbozi □	**127**	9 0S	32 50E
Mbuji-Mayi	**126**	6 9S	23 40E
Mbulu	**124**	3 45S	35 30E
Mbulu □	**126**	3 52S	35 33E
Mbumbi	**128**	18 26S	19 59E
Mburucuyá	**172**	28 1S	58 14W
M'chounech	**119**	34 57N	6 1E
M'Clure Str., Can.	**10**	75 0N	118 0W
M'Clure Str., Can.	**12**	74 0N	120 0W
Mdennah	**118**	24 37N	6 0W
Mead L.	**161**	36 1N	114 44W
Meade, Can.	**150**	49 26N	83 51W
Meade, U.S.A.	**159**	37 18N	100 25W
Meadow	**137**	26 35S	114 40E
Meadow Lake	**153**	54 10N	108 26W
Meadow Lake Prov. Park	**153**	54 27N	109 0W
Meadville	**156**	41 39N	80 9W
Meaford	**150**	44 36N	80 35W
Mealfuarvonie, Mt.	**37**	57 15N	4 34W
Mealhada	**56**	40 22N	8 27W
Mealsgate	**32**	54 46N	3 14W
Mealy Mts.	**151**	53 10N	60 0W
Meander, R. = Menderes, Büyük	**92**	37 45N	27 40E
Meander River	**152**	59 2N	117 42W
Meare's, C.	**160**	45 37N	124 0W
Mearim, R.	**170**	3 4S	44 35W
Mearns, Howe of the	**37**	56 52N	2 26W
Measham	**28**	52 43N	1 30W
Meath □	**38**	53 32N	6 40W
Meath Park	**153**	53 27N	105 22W
Meatian	**140**	35 34S	143 21E
Meaulne	**44**	46 36N	2 28E
Meaux	**43**	48 58N	2 50E
Mecanhelas	**127**	15 12S	35 54E
Mecca	**163**	33 37N	116 3W
Mecca = Makkah	**122**	21 30N	39 54E
Mechanicsburg	**162**	40 12N	77 0W
Mechanicville	**162**	42 54N	73 41W
Mechara	**123**	8 36N	40 20E
Mechelen, Anvers, Belg.	**47**	51 2N	4 29E
Mechelen, Limbourg, Belg.	**47**	50 58N	5 41E
Méchéria	**118**	33 35N	0 18W
Mechernich	**48**	50 35N	6 39E
Mechetinskaya	**83**	46 45N	40 32E
Mecidiye	**68**	40 38N	26 32E
Mecitözü	**82**	40 32N	35 25E
Mecklenburg B.	**48**	54 20N	11 40E
Meconta	**127**	14 59S	39 50E
Meda	**56**	40 57N	7 18W
Meda P.O.	**136**	17 22S	123 59E
Meda, R.	**136**	17 20S	124 30E
Medaguine	**118**	33 41N	3 26E
Medak	**96**	18 1N	78 15E
Medan	**102**	3 40N	98 38E
Medanosa, Pta.	**176**	48 0S	66 0W
Medawachchiya	**97**	8 30N	80 30E
Meddouza, cap	**118**	32 33N	9 9W
Médéa	**118**	36 12N	2 50E
Mededa	**66**	43 44N	19 15E
Medeiros Neto	**171**	17 20S	40 14W
Medel, Pic	**51**	46 37N	8 55E
Medellín	**174**	6 15N	75 35W
Medemblik	**46**	52 46N	5 8E
Meder	**123**	14 42N	40 44E
Mederdra	**120**	17 0N	15 38W
Medford, Oreg., U.S.A.	**160**	42 20N	122 52W
Medford, Wis., U.S.A.	**158**	45 9N	90 21W
Medford Lakes	**162**	39 52N	74 48W
Medgidia	**70**	44 15N	28 19E
Medi	**123**	5 4N	30 42E
Media	**162**	39 55N	75 23W
Media Agua	**172**	31 58S	68 25W
Media Luna	**172**	34 45S	66 44W
Mediaş	**70**	46 9N	24 22E
Medical Lake	**160**	47 41N	117 42W
Medicina	**63**	44 29N	11 38E
Medicine Bow	**160**	41 56N	106 11W
Medicine Hat	**153**	50 0N	110 45W
Medicine Lake	**158**	48 30N	104 30W
Medicine Lodge	**159**	37 20N	98 37W
Medina, Brazil	**171**	16 15S	41 29W
Medina, Colomb.	**174**	4 30N	73 21W
Medina, N.D., U.S.A.	**158**	46 57N	99 20W
Medina, N.Y., U.S.A.	**156**	43 15N	78 27W
Medina, Ohio, U.S.A.	**156**	41 9N	81 50W
Medina = Al Madīnah	**92**	24 35N	39 52E
Medina de Ríoseco	**56**	41 53N	5 3W
Medina del Campo	**56**	41 18N	4 55W
Medina L.	**159**	29 35N	98 58W
Medina, R.	**159**	29 10N	98 20W
Medina-Sidonia	**57**	36 28N	5 57W
Medinaceli	**58**	41 12N	2 30W
Mediterranean Sea	**60**	35 0N	15 0E
Medjerda, O.	**119**	36 35N	8 30E
Medkovets	**67**	43 37N	23 10E
Medley	**153**	54 25N	110 16W
Mednogorsk	**84**	51 24N	57 37E
Médoc	**44**	45 10N	0 56W
Medstead, Can.	**153**	53 19N	108 5W
Medstead, U.K.	**28**	51 7N	1 4W
Medulin	**63**	44 49N	13 55E
Medveda	**66**	42 50N	21 32E
Medveditsa, R.	**81**	50 30N	44 0E
Medvedok	**81**	57 20N	50 1E
Medvezhi, Ostrava	**77**	71 0N	161 0E
Medvezhyegorsk	**78**	63 0N	34 25E
Medway, R.	**29**	51 12N	0 23E
Medyn	**81**	54 59N	35 56E
Medzev	**53**	48 43N	20 55E
Medzilaborce	**53**	49 17N	21 52E
Meeandh	**108**	27 26S	153 6E
Meeberrie	**137**	26 57S	116 0E
Meekatharra	**137**	26 32S	118 29E
Meeker	**160**	40 1N	107 58W
Meelpaeg L.	**151**	48 18N	56 35W
Meeniyan	**141**	38 35S	146 0E
Meer	**47**	51 27N	4 45E
Meerane	**48**	50 51N	12 30E
Meerbeke	**47**	50 50N	4 3E
Meerle	**47**	51 29N	4 48E
Meerssen	**47**	50 53N	5 50E
Meerut	**94**	29 1N	77 50E
Meeteetsa	**160**	44 10N	108 56W
Meeuwen	**47**	51 6N	5 31E
Mega	**123**	3 57N	38 30E
Megálo Khorío	**69**	36 27N	27 24E
Megálo Petalí, I.	**69**	38 0N	24 15E
Megalópolis	**69**	37 25N	22 7E
Meganisi, I.	**69**	38 39N	20 48E
Mégantic	**151**	45 36N	70 56W
Mégara	**69**	37 58N	23 22E
Megarine	**119**	33 14N	6 2E
Megdhova, R.	**69**	39 10N	21 45E
Megen	**46**	51 49N	5 34E
Mégève	**45**	45 51N	6 37E
Meghalaya □	**98**	25 50N	91 0E
Meghalayap	**99**	25 40N	89 55E
Meghezez, Mt.	**123**	9 18N	39 26E
Meghna, R.	**98**	23 45N	90 40E
Megiddo	**90**	32 36N	35 11E
Mégiscane, L.	**150**	48 35N	75 55W
Megiste	**61**	36 8N	29 34E
Mehadia	**70**	44 56N	22 23E
Mehaigne, R.	**47**	50 32N	5 13E
Mehaïguene, O.	**118**	32 20N	2 45E
Meharry, Mt.	**132**	22 59S	118 35E
Mehedinti □	**70**	44 40N	22 45E
Meheisa	**122**	19 38N	32 57E
Mehndawal	**95**	26 58N	83 5E
Mehsana	**94**	23 39N	72 26E
Mehun-sur-Yèvre	**43**	47 10N	2 13E
Mei Chiang, R.	**109**	24 24N	116 35E
Meia Ponte, R.	**171**	18 32S	49 36W
Meichuan	**109**	30 9N	115 33E
Meidrim	**31**	51 51N	4 3W
Meiganga	**124**	6 20N	14 10E
Meigh	**38**	54 8N	6 22W
Meihsien, Kwangtung, China	**109**	24 18N	116 7E
Meihsien, Shensi, China	**106**	34 16N	107 42E
Meijel	**47**	51 21N	5 53E
Meiktila	**98**	21 0N	96 0E
Meilen	**51**	47 16N	8 39E
Meiningen	**48**	50 32N	10 25E
Meio, R.	**171**	13 36S	49 7W
Meira, Sierra de	**56**	43 15N	7 15W
Meiringen	**50**	46 43N	8 12E
Meishan	**108**	30 3N	103 51E
Meissen	**48**	51 10N	13 29E
Meit'an	**108**	27 48N	107 28E
Meithalun	**90**	32 21N	35 16E
Méjean	**44**	44 15N	3 30E
Mejillones	**172**	23 10S	70 30W
Meka	**137**	27 25S	116 48E
Mekambo	**124**	1 2N	14 5E
Mekdela	**123**	11 24N	39 10E
Mekhtar	**93**	30 30N	69 15E
Meklong = Samut Songkhram	**101**	13 24N	100 1E
Meknès	**118**	33 57N	5 33W
Meko	**121**	7 27N	2 52E
Mekong, R.	**101**	18 0N	104 15E
Mekongga	**103**	3 50S	121 30E
Mekoryok	**147**	60 20N	166 20W
Melagiri Hills	**97**	12 20N	77 30E
Melah, Sebkhet el	**118**	29 20N	1 30W
Melaka	**101**	2 15N	102 15E
Melaka □	**101**	2 20N	102 15E
Melalap	**102**	5 10N	116 5E
Mélambes	**69**	35 8N	24 40E
Melanesia	**130**	4 0S	155 0E
Melapalaiyam	**97**	8 39N	77 44E
Melbost	**36**	58 12N	6 20W
Melbourn	**29**	52 5N	0 1E
Melbourne, Austral.	**141**	37 50S	145 0E
Melbourne, U.K.	**28**	52 50N	1 25W
Melbourne, U.S.A.	**157**	28 13N	80 14W
Melcésine	**62**	45 46N	10 48E
Melchor Múzquiz	**164**	27 50N	101 40W
Melchor Ocampo (San Pedro Ocampo)	**164**	24 52N	101 40W
Méldola	**63**	44 7N	12 3E
Meldorf	**48**	54 5N	9 5E
Mêle-sur-Sarthe, Le	**42**	48 31N	0 22E
Melegnano	**62**	45 21N	9 20E
Melekess = Dimitrovgrad	**81**	54 25N	49 33E
Melenci	**66**	45 32N	20 20E
Melenki	**81**	55 20N	41 37E
Meleuz	**84**	52 58N	55 55E
Melfi, Chad	**117**	11 0N	17 59E
Melfi, Italy	**65**	41 0N	15 40E
Melfort, Can.	**153**	52 50N	104 37W
Melfort, Zimb.	**127**	18 0S	31 25E
Melfort, Loch	**34**	56 13N	5 33W
Melgaço	**56**	42 7N	8 15W
Melgar de Fernamental	**56**	42 27N	4 17W
Melhus	**71**	63 17N	10 18E
Melick	**47**	51 10N	6 1E
Melide	**51**	45 57N	8 57E
Meligalá	**69**	37 15N	21 59E
Melilla	**118**	35 21N	2 57W
Melilot	**42**	31 22N	34 37E
Melipilla	**172**	33 42S	71 15W
Mélissa Óros	**69**	37 32N	26 4E
Melita	**153**	49 15N	101 5W
Mélito di Porto Salvo	**65**	37 55N	15 47E
Melitopol	**82**	46 50N	35 22E
Melk	**52**	48 13N	15 20E
Melksham	**28**	51 22N	2 9W
Mellan-Fryken	**72**	59 45N	13 10E
Mellansel	**74**	63 25N	18 17E
Melle, Belg.	**47**	51 0N	3 49E
Melle, France	**44**	46 14N	0 10W
Melle, Ger.	**48**	52 12N	8 20E
Mellégue, O.	**119**	36 32N	8 51E
Mellen	**158**	46 19N	90 36W
Mellerud	**73**	58 41N	12 28E
Mellette	**158**	45 11N	98 29W
Mellid	**56**	42 55N	8 1W
Mellish Reef	**133**	17 25S	155 50E
Mellit	**123**	14 15N	25 40E
Mellon Charles	**36**	57 52N	5 37W
Melmerby	**32**	54 44N	2 35W
Melnik	**67**	40 58N	23 25E
Mělník	**52**	50 22N	14 23E
Melo	**173**	32 20S	54 10W
Melolo	**103**	9 53S	120 40E
Melones Res.	**163**	37 57N	120 31W
Melouprey	**100**	13 48N	105 16E
Melovoye	**83**	49 25N	40 5E
Melrhir, Chott	**119**	34 25N	6 24E
Melrose, N.S.W., Austral.	**141**	32 42S	146 57E
Melrose, W. Australia, Austral.	**137**	27 50S	121 15E
Melrose, U.K.	**35**	55 35N	2 44W
Melrose, U.S.A.	**159**	34 27N	103 33W
Mels	**51**	47 3N	9 25E
Melsele	**47**	51 13N	4 17E
Melsonby	**33**	54 28N	1 41W
Melstone	**160**	46 45N	108 0W
Melsungen	**48**	51 8N	9 34E
Melton	**29**	52 51N	1 1E
Melton Constable	**29**	52 52N	1 1E
Melton Mowbray	**29**	52 46N	0 52W
Melun	**43**	48 32N	2 39E
Melunga	**128**	17 15S	16 22E
Melur	**97**	10 2N	78 23E
Melut	**123**	10 30N	32 20E
Melvaig	**36**	57 48N	5 49W
Melvich	**37**	58 33N	3 55W
Melville	**153**	50 55N	102 50W
Melville B.	**138**	12 0S	136 45E
Melville, C.	**138**	14 11S	144 30E
Melville I., Austral.	**136**	11 30S	131 0E
Melville I., Can.	**12**	75 30N	111 0W
Melville, L., Newf., Can.	**151**	53 45N	59 40W
Melville, L., Newf., Can.	**151**	59 30N	53 40W
Melville Pen.	**149**	68 0N	84 0W
Melvin L.	**38**	54 26N	8 10W
Melvin, R.	**152**	59 11N	117 31W
Mélykút	**53**	46 11N	19 25E
Memaliaj	**68**	40 25N	19 58E
Memba	**127**	14 11S	40 30E
Memboro	**103**	9 30S	119 30E
Membrilla	**59**	38 59N	3 21W
Memel	**129**	27 38S	29 36E
Memel = Klaipeda	**80**	55 43N	21 10E
Memmingen	**49**	47 59N	10 12E
Memphis, Tenn., U.S.A.	**159**	35 7N	90 0W
Memphis, Tex., U.S.A.	**159**	34 45N	100 30W
Mena	**159**	34 40N	94 15W
Menai Bridge	**31**	53 14N	4 11W
Menai Strait	**31**	53 7N	4 20W
Ménaka	**121**	15 59N	2 18E
Menaldum	**46**	53 13N	5 40E
Menamurtee	**140**	31 25S	143 11E
Menarandra, R.	**129**	25 0S	44 50E
Menard	**159**	30 57N	99 58W
Menasha	**156**	44 13N	88 27W
Menate	**102**	0 12S	112 47E
Mendawai, R.	**102**	1 30S	113 0E
Mende	**44**	44 31N	3 30E
Mendebo Mts.	**123**	7 0N	39 22E
Mendenhall, C.	**147**	59 44N	166 10W
Menderes, R.	**92**	37 25N	28 45E
Mendez	**165**	25 7N	98 34W
Mendhar	**95**	33 35N	74 10E
Mendi, Ethiopia	**123**	9 47N	35 4E
Mendi, P.N.G.	**135**	6 11S	143 47E
Mendip Hills	**28**	51 17N	2 40W
Mendlesham	**29**	52 15N	1 4E
Mendocino	**160**	39 26N	123 50W
Mendong Gompa	**95**	31 16N	85 11E
Mendota, Calif., U.S.A.	**163**	36 46N	120 24W
Mendota, Ill., U.S.A.	**158**	41 35N	89 5W
Mendoza	**172**	32 50S	68 52W
Mendoza □	**172**	33 0S	69 0W
Mendrisio	**51**	45 52N	8 59E
Mene Grande	**174**	9 49N	70 56W
Menemen	**92**	38 18N	27 10E
Menen	**47**	50 47N	3 7E
Menfi	**64**	37 36N	12 57E
Meng-pan	**99**	23 5N	100 19E
Meng-so	**101**	22 33N	99 31E
Meng-wang	**99**	22 17N	100 32E
Meng Wang	**101**	22 18N	100 31E
Mengch'eng	**106**	33 17N	116 34E
Mengeš	**63**	46 24N	14 35E
Menggala	**102**	4 20S	105 15E
Menghai	**108**	21 58N	100 28E
Menghsien	**106**	34 54N	112 47E
Mengibar	**57**	37 58N	3 48W
Mengla	**108**	21 28N	101 29E
Menglien	**108**	22 21N	99 36E

Mengoub 118 29 49N 5 26W
Mengpolo 108 24 24N 99 14 E
Mengshan 109 24 12N 110 31 E
Mengting 108 23 33N 98 5 E
Mengtz = Mengtzu 108 23 25N 103 20 E
Mengtzu 108 23 25N 103 20 E
Mengyin 107 35 40N 117 55 E
Menihek L. 151 54 0N 67 0W
Menin 47 50 47N 3 7 E
Menindee 140 32 20N 142 25 E
Menindee, L. 140 32 20N 142 25 E
Meningie 140 35 43 S 139 20 E
Menkúng 99 28 38N 98 24 E
Menlo Park 163 37 27N 122 12W
Menominee 156 45 9N 87 39W
Menominee, R. 156 45 30N 87 50W
Menomonie 158 44 50N 91 54W
Menor, Mar 59 37 43N 0 48W
Menorca, I. 58 40 0N 4 0 E
Mentawai, Kepulauan 102 2 0 S 99 0 E
Mentekab 101 3 29N 102 21 E
Menton 45 43 50N 7 29 E
Menyamya 135 7 10 S 145 59 E
Menzel-Bourguiba 119 39 9N 9 49 E
Menzel Chaker 119 35 0N 10 26 E
Menzelinsk 84 55 53N 53 1 E
Menzies 137 29 40 S 120 58 E
Me'ona (Tarshiha) 90 33 1N 35 15 E
Meoqui 164 28 17N 105 29W
Mepaco 127 15 57 S 30 48 E
Meppel 47 52 42N 6 12 E
Meppen 48 52 41N 7 20 E
Mequinenza 58 41 22N 0 17 E
Mer Rouge 159 32 47N 91 48W
Merabéllou, Kólpos 69 35 10N 25 50 E
Merai 135 4 52 S 152 19 E
Merak 103 5 55 S 106 1 E
Meramangye, L. 137 28 25 S 132 13 E
Merano (Meran) 63 46 40N 11 10 E
Merate 62 45 42N 9 23 E
Merauke 103 8 29 S 140 24 E
Merbabu, Mt. 103 7 30 S 110 40 E
Merbein 140 34 10 S 142 2 E
Merca 91 1 48N 44 50 E
Mercadal 58 39 59N 4 5 E
Mercara 97 12 30N 75 45 E
Mercato Saraceno 63 43 57N 12 11 E
Merced 163 37 18N 120 30W
Merced Pk. 163 37 36N 119 24W
Merced, R. 163 37 21N 120 58W
Mercedes, Buenos Aires, Argent. 172 34 40 S 59 30W
Mercedes, Corrientes, Argent. 172 29 10 S 58 5W
Mercedes, San Luis, Argent. 172 33 5 S 65 21W
Mercedes, Uruguay 172 33 12 S 58 0W
Merceditas 172 28 20 S 70 35W
Mercer 142 37 16 S 175 5 E
Merchtem 47 50 58N 4 14 E
Mercy C. 149 65 0N 62 30W
Merdrignac 42 48 11N 2 27W
Mere, Belg. 47 50 55N 3 58 E
Mere, U.K. 28 51 5N 2 16W
Meredith C. 176 52 15 S 60 40W
Meredith, L. 159 35 30N 101 35W
Merei 70 45 7N 26 43 E
Merelbeke 47 51 0N 3 45 E
Méréville 43 48 20N 2 5 E
Merewa 123 7 40N 36 54 E
Mergenevo 84 49 56N 51 18 E
Mergenevskiy 83 49 59N 51 15 E
Mergui 101 12 30N 98 35 E
Mergui Arch. = Myeik Kyunzu 101 11 30N 97 30 E
Meribah 140 34 43 S 140 51 E
Mérida, Mexico 165 20 50N 89 40W
Mérida, Spain 57 38 55N 6 25W
Mérida, Venez. 174 8 36N 71 8W
Mérida □ 174 8 30N 71 10W
Mérida, Cord. de 174 9 0N 71 0W
Meriden, U.K. 28 52 27N 1 36W
Meriden, U.S.A. 162 41 33N 72 47W
Meridian, Idaho, U.S.A. 160 43 41N 116 25W
Meridian, Miss., U.S.A. 157 32 20N 88 42W
Meridian, Tex., U.S.A. 159 31 55N 97 37W
Mering 49 48 15N 11 0 E
Merioneth (□) 26 52 49N 3 55W
Merirumã 175 1 15N 54 50W
Merke 85 42 52N 73 11 E
Merkel 159 32 30N 100 0W
Merkem 47 50 57N 2 51 E
Merksem 47 51 16N 4 25 E
Merksplas 47 51 22N 4 52 E
Merlebach 43 49 5N 6 52 E
Merlerault, Le 42 48 41N 0 16 E
Mermaid Mt. 108 27 29 S 152 49 E
Mermaid Reef 136 17 6 S 119 36 E
Mern 73 55 3N 12 3 E
Merowe 122 18 29N 31 46 E
Merredin 137 31 28 S 118 18 E
Merrick, Mt. 34 55 8N 4 30W
Merrill, Oregon, U.S.A. 160 42 2N 121 37W
Merrill, Wis., U.S.A. 158 45 11N 89 41W
Merrimack, R. 162 42 49N 70 49W
Merritt 152 50 10N 120 45W
Merriwa 141 32 6 S 150 22 E
Merriwagga 141 33 47 S 145 43 E
Merroe 137 27 53 S 117 50 E
Merry I. 150 55 29N 77 31W
Merrygoen 141 31 51 S 149 12 E
Merryville 159 30 47N 93 31W
Mersa Fatma 123 14 57N 40 17 E
Mersch 47 49 44N 6 7 E
Merse, dist. 35 55 40N 2 30W
Mersea I. 29 51 48N 0 55 E
Merseburg 48 51 20N 12 0 E
Mersey, R. 32 53 20N 2 56W
Merseyside □ 32 53 25N 2 55W
Mersin 92 36 51N 34 36 E
Mersing 101 2 25N 103 50 E
Merta 94 26 39N 74 4 E
Mertert 47 49 43N 6 29 E
Merthyr Tydfil 31 51 45N 3 23W
Mértola 57 37 40N 7 40 E
Merton 29 51 25N 0 13W
Mertzig 47 49 51N 6 1 E
Mertzon 159 31 17N 100 48W
Méru 43 49 13N 2 8 E
Meru 126 0 3N 37 40 E
Meru □ 126 0 3N 37 46 E
Meru, mt. 126 3 15 S 36 46 E
Merville 43 50 38N 2 38 E
Méry-sur-Seine 43 48 31N 3 54 E
Merzifon 82 40 53N 35 32 E
Merzig 49 49 26N 6 37 E
Merzouga, Erg Tin 119 24 0N 11 4 E
Mesa 161 33 20N 111 56W
Mesa, La, Colomb. 174 4 38N 74 28W
Mesa, La, Calif., U.S.A. 163 32 48N 117 5W
Mesa, La, N. Mex., U.S.A. 161 32 6N 106 48W
Mesach Mellet 119 24 30N 11 30 E
Mesada 90 31 20N 35 19 E
Mesagne 65 40 34N 17 48 E
Mesaras, Kólpos 69 35 6N 24 47 E
Meschede 48 51 20N 8 17 E
Mesfinto 123 13 30N 37 22 E
Mesgouez, L. 150 51 20N 75 0W
Meshchovsk 80 54 22N 35 17 E
Meshed = Mashhad 93 36 20N 59 35 E
Meshoppen 162 41 36N 76 3W
Mesick 156 44 24N 85 42W
Mesilinka, R. 152 56 6N 124 30W
Mesilla 161 32 20N 107 0W
Meslay-du-Maine 42 47 58N 0 33W
Mesocco 51 46 23N 9 12 E
Mesolóngion 69 38 27N 21 28 E
Mesopotamia, reg. 92 33 30N 44 0 E
Mesoraca 65 39 5N 16 47 E
Mésou Volímais 69 37 53N 27 35 E
Mess Cr. 152 57 55N 131 14W
Messac 42 47 49N 1 50W
Messad 118 34 8N 3 30 E
Méssaména 121 3 48N 12 49 E
Messancy 47 49 36N 5 49 E
Messeix 44 45 37N 2 33 E
Messina, Italy 65 38 10N 15 32 E
Messina, S. Afr. 129 22 20 S 30 12 E
Messina, Str. di 65 38 5N 15 35 E
Messini 69 37 4N 22 1 E
Messinia □ 69 37 10N 22 0 E
Messiniakós, Kólpos 69 36 45N 22 5 E
Mestà, Akra 69 38 16N 25 53 E
Mesta, R. 67 41 30N 24 0 E
Mestanza 57 38 35N 4 4W
Město Teplá 52 49 59N 12 52 E
Mestre 63 45 30N 12 13 E
Mestre, Espigão 171 12 30 S 46 10W
Městys Zelezná Ruda 52 49 8N 13 15 E
Meta □ 174 3 30N 73 0W
Meta, R. 174 6 20N 68 5W
Metagama 150 47 0N 81 55W
Metaline Falls 160 48 52N 117 22W
Metán 172 25 30 S 65 0W
Metauro, R. 63 43 45N 12 59 E
Metchosin 152 48 15N 123 37W
Metehara 123 8 58N 39 57 E
Metema 123 12 56N 36 13 E
Metengobalame 127 14 49 S 34 30 E
Méthana 69 37 35N 23 23 E
Metheringham 33 53 9N 0 22W
Methlick 37 57 26N 2 13W
Methóni 69 36 49N 21 42 E
Methuen, Mt. 136 15 54 S 124 44 E
Methven, N.Z. 143 43 38 S 171 40 E
Methven, U.K. 35 56 25N 3 35W
Methwin, Mt. 137 25 3 S 120 45 E
Methwold 29 52 30N 0 33 E
Methy L. 153 56 28N 109 30W
Metil 125 16 24 S 39 0 E
Metkovets 67 43 37N 23 10 E
Metkovió 66 43 6N 17 39 E
Metlakatla 147 55 10N 131 33W
Metlaoui 119 34 24N 8 24 E
Metlika 63 45 40N 15 20 E
Metowra 139 25 3 S 146 15 E
Metropolis 159 37 10N 88 47W
Métsovon 68 39 48N 21 12 E
Mettet 47 50 19N 4 41 E
Mettuppalaiyam 97 11 18N 76 59 E
Mettur 97 11 48N 77 47 E
Mettur Dam 95 11 45N 77 45 E
Metulla 90 33 17N 35 34 E
Metz 43 49 8N 6 10 E
Meulaboh 102 4 11N 96 3 E
Meulan 43 49 0N 1 52 E
Meung-sur-Loire 43 47 50N 1 40 E
Meureudu 102 5 19N 96 10 E
Meurthe-et-Moselle □ 43 48 52N 6 0 E
Meuse □ 43 49 8N 5 25 E
Meuse, R. 47 50 45N 5 41 E
Meuselwitz 48 51 3N 12 18 E
Mevagissey 30 50 16N 4 48W
Mevagissey Bay 30 50 15N 4 40W
Mexborough 33 53 29N 1 18W
Mexia 159 31 38N 96 32W
Mexiana, I. 170 0 0 49 30W
Mexicali 164 32 40N 115 30W
México 165 19 20N 99 10W
Mexico, Me., U.S.A. 156 44 35N 70 30W
Mexico, Mo., U.S.A. 158 39 10N 91 55W
Mexico, N.Y., U.S.A. 162 43 28N 76 18W
Mexico ■ 164 20 0N 100 0W
México □ 164 19 20N 99 10W
Mexico, G. of 165 25 0N 90 0W
Mey 37 58 38N 3 14W
Meyenburg 48 53 19N 12 15 E
Meymac 44 45 32N 2 10 E
Meyrargues 45 43 38N 5 32 E
Meyrueis 44 44 12N 3 27 E
Meyssac 44 45 3N 1 40 E
Mezdra 67 43 12N 23 35 E
Mèze 44 43 27N 3 36 E
Mezen 78 65 50N 44 20 E
Mezha, R. 80 55 50N 31 45 E
Mezhdurechenskiy 84 59 36N 65 56 E
Mezidon 42 49 5N 0 1W
Mézières 43 49 45N 4 42 E
Mézilhac 45 44 49N 4 21 E
Mézin 44 44 4N 0 16 E
Mezöberény 53 46 49N 21 3 E
Mezöfalva 53 46 55N 18 49 E
Mezöhegyes 53 46 19N 20 49 E
Mezokövácsháza 53 46 25N 20 57 E
Mezökövesd 53 47 49N 20 35 E
Mézos 44 44 5N 1 10W
Mezötúr 53 47 0N 20 41 E
Mezquital 164 23 29N 104 23W
Mezzolombardo 62 46 13N 11 5 E
Mgeta 127 8 22 S 38 6 E
Mglin 80 53 2N 32 50 E
Mhlaba Hills 127 18 30 S 30 30 E
Mhow 94 22 33N 75 50 E
Mi-Shima 110 34 46N 131 9 E
Miahuatlán 165 16 21N 96 36W
Miajadas 57 39 9N 5 54W
Mialar 94 26 15N 70 20 E
Miallo 138 16 28 S 145 22 E
Miami, Ariz., U.S.A. 161 33 25N 111 0W
Miami, Fla., U.S.A. 157 25 52N 80 15W
Miami, Tex., U.S.A. 159 35 44N 100 38W
Miami Beach 157 25 49N 80 6W
Miami, R. 156 39 20N 84 40W
Miamisburg 156 39 40N 84 11W
Miandowāb 92 37 0N 46 5 E
Miandrivazo 125 19 50 S 45 56 E
Miāneh 92 37 30N 47 40 E
Mianwali 94 32 38N 71 28 E
Miaoli 109 24 34N 120 48 E
Miarinarivo 129 18 57 S 46 55 E
Miass 84 54 59N 60 6 E
Miass, R. 84 56 6N 64 30 E
Miasteczko Kraj 54 53 7N 17 1 E
Miastko 54 54 0N 16 58 E
Mica Dam 152 52 5N 118 32W
Mica Res. 152 51 55N 118 00W
Michael, Mt. 135 6 27 S 145 22 E
Michalovce 29 48 44N 21 54 E
Micheldever 28 51 7N 1 17W
Michelson, Mt. 147 69 20N 144 20W
Michelstadt 49 49 40N 9 0 E
Michigan □ 155 44 40N 85 40W
Michigan City 156 41 42N 86 56W
Michigan, L. 156 44 0N 87 0W
Michih 106 37 49N 110 7 E
Michikamau L. 151 54 0N 64 0W
Michipicoten 150 47 55N 84 55W
Michipicoten I. 150 47 40N 85 50W
Michoacan □ 164 19 0N 102 0W
Michurin 67 42 9N 27 51 E
Michurinsk 81 52 58N 40 27 E
Mickle Fell 32 54 38N 2 16W
Mickleover 33 52 55N 1 32W
Mickleton, Oxon., U.K. 28 52 5N 1 48W
Mickleton, Yorks., U.K. 32 54 36N 2 3W
Miclere 138 22 34 S 147 32 E
Micronesia 130 17 0N 160 0 E
Micŭsasa 70 46 7N 24 7 E
Mid Calder 35 55 53N 3 23W
Mid Glamorgan □ 31 51 40N 3 25W
Mid Yell 36 60 36N 1 5W
Midai, P. 101 3 0N 107 47 E
Midale 153 49 25N 103 20W
Midas 160 41 14N 116 56W
Middagsfjället 72 63 27N 12 19 E
Middelbeers 47 51 28N 5 15 E
Middelburg, Neth. 47 51 30N 3 36 E
Middelburg, C. Prov., S. Afr. 128 31 30 S 25 0 E
Middelburg, Trans., S. Afr. 129 25 49N 29 28 E
Middelfart 73 55 30N 9 43 E
Middelharnis 46 51 46N 4 10 E
Middelkerke 47 51 11N 2 49 E
Middelrode 47 51 41N 5 26 E
Middelveld 128 29 45 S 22 30 E
Middle Alkali L. 160 41 30N 120 3W
Middle Andaman I. 101 12 30N 92 30 E
Middle Brook 151 48 40N 54 20W
Middle I. 137 28 55 S 113 55 E
Middle River 162 39 19N 76 25W
Middle Zoy 28 51 5N 2 54W
Middleboro 162 41 49N 70 55W
Middleburg, N.Y., U.S.A. 162 42 36N 74 19W
Middleburg, Pa., U.S.A. 162 40 47N 77 3W
Middlebury 162 44 0N 73 9W
Middleham 33 54 17N 1 49W
Middlemarch 143 45 30 S 170 9 E
Middlemarsh 28 50 51N 2 29W
Middleport 156 39 0N 82 5W
Middlesbrough 33 54 35N 1 14W
Middlesex, Belize 165 17 2N 88 31W
Middlesex, U.S.A. 162 40 36N 74 30W
Middleton, Can. 151 44 57N 65 4W
Middleton, Gr. Manchester, U.K. 32 53 33N 2 12W
Middleton, Norfolk, U.K. 29 52 43N 0 29 E
Middleton Cheney 28 52 4N 1 17W
Middleton Cr. 138 22 35 S 141 51 E
Middleton I. 147 59 30N 146 28W
Middleton-in-Teesdale 32 54 38N 2 5W
Middleton in the Wolds 33 53 56N 0 35W
Middleton P.O. 138 22 22 S 141 32 E
Middletown, U.K. 38 54 18N 6 50W
Middletown, Conn., U.S.A. 162 41 37N 72 40W
Middletown, Del., U.S.A. 162 39 30N 84 21W
Middletown, N.Y., U.S.A. 162 41 28N 74 28W
Middletown, Pa., U.S.A. 162 40 12N 76 44W
Middlewich 32 53 12N 2 28W
Midelt 118 32 46N 4 44W
Midhurst, N.Z. 142 39 17 S 174 18 E
Midhurst, U.K. 29 50 59N 0 44W
Midi, Canal du 44 43 45N 1 21 E
Midi d'Ossau 58 42 50N 0 25W
Midland, Austral. 137 31 54 S 115 59 E
Midland, Can. 150 44 45N 79 50W
Midland, Mich., U.S.A. 156 43 37N 84 17W
Midland, Tex., U.S.A. 159 32 0N 102 3W
Midland Junc. 137 31 50 S 115 58 E
Midlands □ 127 19 40 S 29 0 E
Midleton 39 51 52N 8 12W
Midlothian, Austral. 138 17 10 S 141 12 E
Midlothian, U.S.A. 159 32 30N 97 0W
Midlothian (□) 26 55 45N 3 15W
Midnapore 95 22 25N 87 21 E
Midongy du Sud 129 23 35 S 47 1 E
Midongy, Massif de 129 23 30 S 47 0 E
Midskog 73 58 56N 14 5 E
Midsomer Norton 28 51 17N 2 29W
Midvale 160 40 39N 111 58W
Midway Is. 130 28 13N 177 22W
Midwest 160 43 27N 106 11W
Midwolda 46 53 12N 6 52 E
Midzur 66 43 24N 22 40 E
Mie-ken □ 111 34 30N 136 10 E
Miechów 54 50 21N 20 5 E
Miedzyborz 54 51 39N 17 24 E
Miedzychód 54 52 35N 15 53 E
Miedzylesie 54 50 41N 16 40 E
Miedzyrzec Podlaski 54 51 58N 22 45 E
Miedzyrzecz 54 52 26N 15 35 E
Miedzyzdroje 54 53 56N 14 26 E
Miejska Górka 54 51 39N 16 58 E
Miélan 44 43 27N 0 19 E
Mielelek 138 6 1 S 148 58 E
Mianch'ih 106 34 48N 111 40 E
Mienchu 108 31 22N 104 7 E
Mienga 128 17 12 S 19 48 E
Mienhsien 106 33 11N 106 36 E
Mienning 108 28 30N 102 10 E
Mienyang, Hupei, China 109 30 10N 113 20 E
Mienyang, Szechwan, China 108 31 28N 104 46 E
Miercurea Ciuc 70 46 21N 25 48 E
Mieres 56 43 18N 5 48W
Mierlo 47 51 27N 5 37 E
Mieso 123 9 15N 40 43 E
Mieszkowice 54 52 47N 14 30 E
Migdal 90 32 51N 35 30 E
Migdal Afeq 90 32 5N 34 58 E
Migennes 43 47 58N 3 31 E
Migliarino 63 44 54N 11 56 E
Miguel Alemán, Presa 165 18 15N 96 40W
Miguel Alves 170 4 11 S 42 55W
Miguel Calmon 170 11 26 S 40 36W
Mihara 110 34 24N 133 5 E
Mihara-Yama 111 34 43N 139 23 E
Mihsien 106 34 31N 113 22 E
Mii 108 26 50N 102 3 E
Mijares, R. 58 40 15N 0 50W
Mijas 57 36 36N 4 40W
Mijdrecht 46 52 13N 4 53 E
Mijilu 121 10 22N 13 19 E
Mikese 126 6 48 S 37 55 E
Mikha Tskhakaya 83 42 15N 42 7 E
Mikhailovgrad 67 43 27N 23 16 E
Mikhailovka 82 47 16N 35 27 E
Mikhaylov 81 54 20N 39 0 E
Mikhaylovka, Azerbaijan, U.S.S.R. 83 41 31N 48 52 E
Mikhaylovka, R.S.F.S.R., U.S.S.R. 81 50 3N 43 5 E
Mikhaylovski 84 56 27N 59 7 E
Mikhnevo 81 55 4N 37 59 E
Miki, Hyōgō, Japan 110 34 48N 134 59 E
Miki, Kagawa, Japan 110 34 12N 134 7 E
Mikinai 69 37 43N 22 46 E
Mikindani 127 10 15 S 40 2 E
Mikkeli 75 61 43N 27 25 E
Mikkeli □ 74 62 0N 28 0 E
Mikkelin Lääni □ 74 61 56N 28 0 E
Mikkwa, R. 152 58 25N 114 46W
Mikniya 123 17 0N 33 45 E
Mikołajki 54 53 49N 21 37 E

Mikołów 53 50 10N 18 50 E
Mikonos, I. 69 37 30N 25 25 E
Mikrón Dhérion 68 41 19N 26 6 E
Mikulov 53 48 48N 16 39 E
Mikumi 126 7 26 S 37 9 E
Mikun 78 62 20N 50 0 E
Mikuni 111 36 13N 136 9 E
Mikuni-Tōge 111 36 50N 138 40 E
Mikura-Jima 111 33 52N 139 36 E
Mila 119 36 27N 6 16 E
Milaca 158 45 45N 93 40W
Milagro 174 2 0 S 79 30W
Milan, Mo., U.S.A. 158 40 10N 93 5W
Milan, Tenn., U.S.A. 157 35 55N 88 45W
Milan = Milano 62 45 28N 9 10 E
Milang, S. Australia, Austral. 139 32 2 S 139 10 E
Milang, S. Australia, Austral. 140 35 24 S 138 58 E
Milange 127 16 3 S 35 45 E
Milano 62 45 28N 9 10 E
Milâs 92 37 20N 27 50 E
Milazzo 65 38 13N 15 13 E
Milbank 158 45 17N 96 38W
Milborne Port 28 50 58N 2 28W
Milden 153 51 29N 107 32W
Mildenhall 29 52 20N 0 30 E
Mildura 140 34 13 S 142 9 E
Miléai 68 39 20N 23 9 E
Miles, Austral. 139 26 40 S 150 23 E
Miles, U.S.A. 159 31 39N 100 11W
Miles City 158 46 30N 105 50W
Milestone 153 49 59N 104 31W
Mileto 65 38 37N 16 3 E
Miletto, Mte. 65 41 26N 14 23 E
Mileurà 137 26 22 S 117 20 E
Milevsko 52 49 27N 14 21 E
Milford, Ireland 39 52 20N 8 52W
Milford, Conn., U.S.A. 162 41 13N 73 4W
Milford, Del., U.S.A. 162 38 52N 75 27W
Milford, Mass., U.S.A. 162 42 8N 71 30W
Milford, N.H., U.S.A. 162 42 50N 71 39W
Milford, Pa., U.S.A. 162 41 20N 74 47W
Milford, Utah, U.S.A. 161 38 20N 113 0W
Milford Haven 31 51 43N 5 2W
Milford Haven, B. 31 51 40N 5 10W
Milford on Sea 28 50 44N 1 36W
Milford Sd. 143 44 34 S 167 47 E
Milgun 137 25 6 S 118 18 E
Milh, Ras el 117 32 0N 24 55 E
Miliana, Aïn Salah, Alg. 118 27 20N 2 32 E
Miliana, Médéa, Alg. 118 36 12N 2 15 E
Milicz 54 51 31N 17 19 E
Miling 137 30 30 S 116 17 E
Militello in Val di Catánia 65 37 16N 14 46 E
Milk, R. 160 48 40N 107 15W
Milk River 152 49 10N 112 5W
Mill 47 51 41N 5 48 E
Mill City 160 44 45N 122 28W
Mill, I. 13 66 0 S 101 30 E
Mill Valley 163 37 54N 122 32W
Millau 44 44 8N 3 4 E
Millbrook, U.K. 30 50 19N 4 12W
Millbrook, U.S.A. 162 41 47N 73 42W
Millbrook Res. 109 34 50 S 138 49 E
Mille Lacs, L. 158 46 10N 93 30W
Mille Lacs, L. des 150 48 45N 90 35W
Milledgeville 157 33 7N 83 15W
Millen 157 32 50N 81 57W
Miller 158 44 35N 98 59W
Millerovo 83 48 57N 40 28 E
Miller's Flat 143 45 39 S 169 23 E
Millersburg 162 40 32N 76 58W
Millerton, N.Z. 143 41 39 S 171 54 E
Millerton, U.S.A. 162 41 57N 73 32W
Millerton, L. 163 37 0N 119 42W
Milleur Pt. 34 55 2N 5 5W
Millevaches, Plat. de 44 45 45N 2 0 E
Millicent 140 37 34 S 140 21 E
Millingen 46 51 52N 6 2 E
Millinocket 151 45 45N 68 45W
Millisle 38 54 38N 5 33W
Millmerran 139 27 53 S 151 16 E
Millom 32 54 13N 3 16W
Millport 34 55 45N 4 55W
Mills L. 152 61 30N 118 20W
Millsboro 162 38 36N 75 17W
Millstreet 39 52 4N 9 5W
Milltown, Galway, Ireland 38 53 37N 8 54W
Milltown, Kerry, Ireland 39 52 9N 9 42W
Milltown, U.K. 37 57 33N 4 48W
Milltown Malbay 39 52 51N 9 25W
Millville, N.J., U.S.A. 162 39 22N 75 0W
Millville, Pa., U.S.A. 162 41 7N 76 32W
Millwood Res. 159 33 45N 94 0W
Milly 43 48 24N 2 20 E
Milly Milly 137 26 4 S 116 43 E
Milna 63 43 20N 16 28 E
Milnathort 35 56 14N 3 25W
Milne Inlet 149 72 30N 80 0W
Milne, R. 138 21 10 S 137 33 E
Milngavie 34 55 57N 4 20W
Milnor 158 46 19N 97 29W
Milnthorpe 32 54 14N 2 47W
Milo, Can. 152 50 34N 112 53W
Milo, China 108 24 28N 103 23 E
Milolii 147 22 8N 159 42W
Mílos 69 36 44N 24 25 E
Mílos, I. 69 36 44N 24 25 E
Milo evo 66 45 42N 20 20 E
Miłoslaw 54 52 12N 17 32 E
Milovaig 36 57 27N 6 45W
Milparinka P.O. 139 29 46 S 141 57 E
Miltenberg 49 49 41N 9 13 E
Milton, N.Z. 143 46 7 S 169 59 E
Milton, Dumf. & Gall., U.K. 34 55 18N 4 50W
Milton, Hants., U.K. 28 50 45N 1 40W
Milton, Northants, U.K. 29 52 12N 0 55W
Milton, Calif., U.S.A. 163 38 3N 120 51W
Milton, Del., U.S.A. 162 38 47N 75 19W
Milton, Fla., U.S.A. 157 30 38N 87 0W
Milton, Pa., U.S.A. 162 41 0N 76 53W
Milton Abbot 30 50 35N 4 16W
Milton-Freewater 160 45 57N 118 24W
Milton Keynes 29 52 3N 0 42W
Milverton 28 51 2N 3 15W
Milwaukee 156 43 9N 87 58W
Milwaukie 160 45 27N 122 39W
Mim 120 6 57N 2 33W
Mimizan 44 44 12N 1 13W
Mimon 52 50 38N 14 43 E
Mimoso 171 15 10 S 48 5W
Min Chiang, R., China 105 28 48N 104 33 E
Min Chiang, R., Fukien, China 109 26 5N 119 37 E
Min Chiang, R., Szechwan, China 108 28 48N 104 33 E
Min-Kush 85 41 4N 74 28 E
Mina 161 38 21N 118 9W
Mina Pirquitas 172 22 40 S 66 40W
Mina Saud 92 28 45N 48 20 E
Minā'al Ahmadī 92 29 5N 48 10 E
Mīnāb 93 27 10N 57 1 E
Minago, R. 153 54 33N 98 13W
Minakami 111 36 49N 138 59 E
Minaki 153 50 0N 94 40W
Minakuchi 111 34 58N 136 10 E
Minamata 110 32 10N 130 30 E
Minamitane 112 30 25N 130 54 E
Minas Basin 151 45 20N 64 12W
Minas de Rio Tinto 57 37 42N 6 22W
Minas de San Quintín 57 38 49N 4 23W
Minas Gerais □ 171 18 50 S 46 0W
Minas Novas 171 17 15 S 42 36W
Minas, Sierra de las 166 15 9N 89 31W
Minatitlán 165 17 58N 94 35W
Minbu 98 20 10N 95 0 E
Minbya 98 20 22N 93 16 E
Mincha 140 36 1 S 144 6 E
Minch'in 106 38 42N 103 11 E
Minch'ing 109 26 13N 118 51 E
Minchinhampton 28 51 42N 2 10W
Mincio, R. 62 45 8N 10 55 E
Mindanao, I. 103 8 0N 125 0 E
•Mindanao Sea 103 9 0N 124 0 E
Mindanao Trench 103 8 0N 128 0 E
Mindelheim 49 48 4N 10 30 E
Minden, Ger. 48 52 18N 8 54 E
Minden, U.S.A. 159 32 40N 93 20W
Mindiptana 103 5 45 S 140 22 E
Mindon 98 19 21N 94 44 E
Mindoro, I. 103 13 0N 121 0 E
Mindoro Strait 103 12 30N 120 30 E
Mindouli 124 4 12 S 14 28 E
Mine 110 34 12N 131 7 E
Mine Hd. 39 52 0N 7 37W
Minehead 28 51 12N 3 29W
Mineola, N.Y., U.S.A. 162 40 45N 73 38W
Mineola, Tex., U.S.A. 159 32 40N 95 30W
Minera 31 53 3N 3 7W
Mineral King 163 36 27N 118 36W
Mineral Wells 159 32 50N 98 5W
Mineralnyye Vody 83 44 18N 43 15 E
Minersville, Pa., U.S.A. 162 40 40N 76 17W
Minersville, Utah, U.S.A. 161 38 14N 112 58W
Minervino Murge 65 41 6N 16 4 E
Minette 157 30 54N 87 43W
Minetto 162 43 24N 76 28W
Mingan 151 50 20N 64 0W
Mingary, Austral. 140 32 8 S 140 45 E
Mingary, U.K. 36 56 42N 6 5W
Mingch'i 109 26 24N 117 12 E
Mingchiang 109 32 28N 114 8 E
Mingechaur 83 40 52N 47 0 E
Mingechaurskoye Vdkhr. 83 40 56N 47 20 E
Mingela 138 19 52 S 146 38 E
Mingenew 137 29 12 S 115 21 E
Mingera Cr. 138 20 38 S 138 10 E
Mingin 98 22 50N 94 30 E
Minginish, Dist. 36 57 14N 6 15W
Minglanilla 58 39 34N 1 38W
Mingulay I. 36 56 50N 7 40W
Minho □ 55 41 25N 8 20W
Minho, R. 55 41 58N 8 40W
Minhou 109 26 0N 119 18 E
Minhow = Fuchou 109 26 5N 119 18 E
Minhsien 106 34 26N 104 2 E
Minidoka 160 42 47N 113 34W
Minigwal L. 137 29 31 S 123 14 E
Minilya 137 23 55 S 114 0 E
Minilya, R. 137 23 45 S 114 0 E
Mininera 140 37 37 S 142 58 E
Minióevo 66 43 42N 22 18 E
Minipi, L. 151 52 25N 60 45W
Minj 135 5 54 S 144 30 E
Mink L. 152 61 54N 117 40W
Minlaton 140 34 45 S 137 35 E
Minna 121 9 37N 6 30 E
*Renamed Bohol Sea
Minneapolis, Kans., U.S.A. 158 39 11N 97 40W
Minneapolis, Minn., U.S.A. 158 44 58N 93 20W
Minnesota □ 158 46 40N 94 0W
Minnesund 71 60 23N 11 14 E
Minnie Creek 137 24 3 S 115 42 E
Minnigaff 34 54 58N 4 30W
Minnitaki L. 150 49 47N 91 5W
Mino 111 35 32N 136 55 E
Mino-Kamo 111 35 23N 137 2 E
Mino-Mikawa-Kōgen 111 35 10N 137 30 E
Miño, R. 56 41 58N 8 40W
Minobu 111 35 22N 138 26 E
Minobu-Sanchi 111 35 14N 138 20 E
Minorca = Menorca 58 40 0N 4 0 E
Minore 141 32 14 S 148 27 E
Minot 158 48 10N 101 15W
Minquiers, Les 42 48 58N 2 8W
Minsen 48 53 43N 7 58 E
Minsk 80 53 52N 27 30 E
Minsk Mazowiecki 54 52 10N 21 33 E
Minster 29 51 20N 1 20 E
Minster-on-Sea 29 51 25N 0 50 E
Minsterley 28 52 38N 2 56W
Mintaka Pass 93 37 0N 74 58 E
Minthami 98 23 55N 94 16 E
Mintlaw 37 57 32N 1 59W
Minto 147 64 55N 149 20W
Minto L. 150 48 0N 84 45W
Minton 153 49 10N 104 35W
Minturn 160 39 45N 106 25W
Minturno 64 41 15N 13 43 E
Minûf 122 30 26N 30 52 E
Minusinsk 77 53 50N 91 20 E
Minutang 98 28 15N 96 30 E
Minvoul 124 2 9N 12 8 E
Minya Konka 108 29 34N 101 53 E
Minyar 84 55 4N 57 33 E
Minyip 140 36 29 S 142 36 E
Mionica 66 44 14N 20 6 E
Mios Num, I. 103 1 30 S 135 10 E
Miquelon 151 47 3N 56 20W
Miquelon, St. Pierre et, □ 151 47 8N 56 24W
Mir-Bashir 83 40 11N 46 58 E
Mira, Italy 63 45 26N 12 9 E
Mira, Port. 56 40 26N 8 44W
Mira, R. 57 37 30N 8 30W
Mirabella Eclano 65 41 3N 14 59 E
Miracema do Norte 170 9 33 S 48 24W
Mirador 170 6 22 S 44 22W
Miraflores 164 23 21N 109 45W
Miraj 96 16 50N 74 45 E
Miram 138 21 15 S 148 55 E
Miram Shah 94 33 0N 70 0 E
Miramar, Argent. 172 38 15 S 57 50W
Miramar, Mozam. 129 23 50 S 35 35 E
Miramas 45 43 33N 4 59 E
Mirambeau 44 45 23N 0 35W
Miramichi B. 151 47 15N 65 0W
Miramont-de-Guyenne 44 44 37N 0 21 E
Miranda 175 20 10 S 56 15W
Miranda de Ebro 58 42 41N 2 57W
Miranda do Corvo 56 40 6N 8 20W
Miranda do Douro 56 41 30N 6 16W
Mirando City 159 27 28N 98 59W
Mirandola 62 44 53N 11 2 E
Mirandópolis 173 21 9 S 51 6W
Mirango 127 13 32 S 34 58 E
Mirano 63 45 29N 12 6 E
Miraporvos, I. 167 22 9N 74 30W
Mirassol 173 20 46 S 49 28W
Mirboo North 141 38 24 S 146 10 E
Mirear, I. 122 23 15N 35 41 E
Mirebeau, Côte d'Or, France 43 47 25N 5 20 E
Mirebeau, Vienne, France 42 46 49N 0 10 E
Mirecourt 43 48 20N 6 10 E
Mirgorod 80 49 58N 33 50 E
Miri 102 4 18N 114 0 E
Miriam Vale 138 24 20 S 151 33 E
Mirim, Lagoa 173 32 45 S 52 50W
Mirimire 174 11 10N 68 43W
Mirny 13 66 0 S 95 0 E
Mirnyy 77 62 33N 113 53 E
Mirond L. 153 55 6N 102 47W
Mirosławiec 54 53 20N 16 5 E
Mirpur 95 33 15N 73 50 E
Mirpur Bibiwari 94 28 33N 67 44 E
Mirpur Khas 94 25 30N 69 0 E
Mirpur Sakro 94 24 33N 67 41 E
Mirrool 141 34 19 S 147 10 E
Mirror 152 52 30N 113 7W
Mîrsani 70 44 1N 23 59 E
Mirsk 54 50 58N 15 23 E
Miryang 107 35 31N 128 44 E
Mirzaani 83 41 24N 46 5 E
Mirzapur 95 25 10N 82 45 E
Misantla 165 19 56N 96 50W
Miscou I. 151 47 57N 64 31W
Misery, Mt. 108 34 52 S 138 48 E
Mish'ab, Ra'as al 92 28 15N 48 43 E
Mishan 105 45 31N 132 2 E
Mishawaka 156 41 40N 86 8W
Mishbih, Gebel 122 22 48N 34 38 E
Mishima 111 35 10N 138 52 E
Mishkino 84 55 20N 63 55 E
Mishmar Aiyalon 90 31 52N 34 57 E
Mishmar Ha' Emeq 90 32 37N 35 7 E
Mishmar Ha Negev 90 31 22N 34 48 E
Mishmar Ha Yarden 90 33 0N 35 56 E
Mishmi Hills 98 29 0N 96 0 E
Misilmeri 64 38 2N 13 25 E
Misima I. 135 10 40 S 152 45 E
Misión, La 164 32 5N 116 50W
Misiones □, Argent. 173 27 0 S 55 0W
Misiones □, Parag. 172 27 0 S 56 0W
Miskin 93 23 44N 56 52 E
Miskitos, Cayos 166 14 26N 82 50W
Miskolc 53 48 7N 20 50 E
Misoke 126 0 42 S 28 2 E
Misoöl, I. 103 2 0 S 130 0 E
Misrātah 119 32 18N 15 3 E
Missanabie 150 48 20N 84 6W
Missão Velha 170 7 15 S 39 10W
Misserghin 118 35 44N 0 49W
Missinaibi L. 150 48 23N 83 40W
Missinaibi, R. 150 50 30N 82 40W
Mission, S.D., U.S.A. 158 43 21N 100 36W
Mission, Tex., U.S.A. 159 26 15N 98 30W
Mission City 152 49 10N 122 15W
Missisa L. 150 52 20N 85 7W
Mississagi 150 46 15N 83 9W
Mississippi, R. 159 35 30N 90 0W
Mississippi Sd. 159 30 25N 89 0W
Missoula 160 47 0N 114 0W
Missouri □ 158 38 25N 92 30W
Missouri, Little, R. 160 46 0N 111 35W
Missouri, R. 158 40 20N 95 40W
Mistake B. 153 62 8N 93 0W
Mistassini L. 150 51 0N 73 40W
Mistassini, R. 151 48 42N 72 20W
Mistastin L. 151 55 57N 63 20W
Mistatim 153 52 52N 103 22W
Mistelbach 53 48 34N 16 34 E
Misterbianco 65 37 32N 15 0 E
Misterton, Notts., U.K. 33 53 27N 0 49W
Misterton, Som., U.K. 28 50 51N 2 46W
Mistretta 65 37 56N 14 20 E
Misty L. 153 58 53N 101 40W
Misugi 111 34 31N 136 16 E
Misumi 110 32 37N 130 27 E
Mît Ghamr 122 30 42N 31 12 E
Mitaka 111 35 40N 139 33 E
Mitan 85 40 0N 66 35 E
Mitatib 123 15 59N 36 12 E
Mitchel Troy 31 51 46N 2 45W
Mitcheldean 28 51 51N 2 29W
Mitchell, Austral. 139 26 29 S 147 58 E
Mitchell, Ind., U.S.A. 156 38 42N 86 25W
Mitchell, Nebr., U.S.A. 158 41 58N 103 45W
Mitchell, Oreg., U.S.A. 160 44 31N 120 8W
Mitchell, S.D., U.S.A. 158 43 40N 98 0W
Mitchell, Mt. 157 35 40N 82 20W
Mitchell, R. 138 15 12 S 141 35 E
Mitchelstown 39 52 16N 8 18W
Mitchelton 108 27 25 S 152 59 E
Mitha Tiwana 94 32 13N 72 6 E
Mithimna 68 39 20N 26 12 E
Mitiamo 140 36 12 S 144 15 E
Mitilini 69 39 6N 26 35 E
Mitilini = Lesvos 68 39 0N 26 20 E
Mitilinoi 69 37 42N 26 56 E
Mitla 165 16 55N 96 24W
Mito 111 36 20N 140 30 E
Mitsinjo 129 16 1 S 45 52 E
Mitsiwa 123 15 35N 39 25 E
Mitsiwa Channel 123 15 30N 40 0 E
Mitsukaidō 111 36 1N 139 59 E
Mittagong 141 34 28 S 150 29 E
Mittelland 50 46 50N 7 23 E
Mittelland Kanal 48 52 23N 7 45 E
Mittenwalde 48 52 16N 13 33 E
Mittweida 48 50 59N 13 0 E
Mitu 108 25 21N 100 32 E
Mitú 174 1 8N 70 3W
Mituas 174 3 52N 68 49W
Mitumba 126 7 8 S 31 2 E
Mitumba, Chaîne des 126 10 0 S 26 20 E
Mitwaba 127 8 2N 27 17 E
Mityana 126 0 23N 32 2 E
Mitzick 124 0 45N 11 40 E
Miura 111 35 12N 139 40 E
Mius, R. 83 47 30N 39 0 E
Mixteco, R. 165 18 11N 98 30W
Miyagi-Ken □ 112 38 15N 140 45 E
Miyâh, W. el 122 25 10N 33 30 E
Miyake-Jima 111 34 0N 139 30 E
Miyako 112 39 40N 141 75 E
Miyako-Jima 112 24 45N 125 20 E
Miyakonojō 110 31 32N 131 5 E
Miyanojō 110 31 54N 130 27 E
Miyanoura-Dake 112 30 20N 130 26 E
Miyata 110 33 49N 130 42 E
Miyazaki 110 31 56N 131 30 E
Miyazaki-ken □ 110 32 0N 131 30 E
Miyazu 110 35 35N 135 10 E
Miyet, Bahr el 92 31 30N 35 30 E
Miyoshi 110 34 48N 132 51 E
Miyün 106 40 22N 116 49 E
Mizamis = Ozamiz 103 8 15N 123 50 E
Mizdah 119 31 30N 13 0 E
Mizen Hd., Cork, Ireland 39 51 27N 9 50W
Mizen Hd., Wick., Ireland 39 52 52N 6 4W
Mizil 70 44 59N 26 29 E
Mizoram □ 98 23 0N 92 40 E
Mizuho 111 35 6N 135 17 E
Mizunami 111 35 22N 137 15 E
Mjöbäck 73 57 28N 12 53 E
Mjölby 73 58 20N 15 10 E
Mjømna 71 60 55N 4 55 E

Mjörn 73 57 55N 12 25 E
Mjøsa 71 60 40N 11 0 E
Mkata 126 5 45 S 38 20 E
Mkokotoni 126 5 55 S 39 15 E
Mkomazi 126 4 40 S 38 7 E
Mkulwe 127 8 37 S 32 20 E
Mkumbi, Ras 126 7 38 S 39 55 E
Mkushi 127 14 25 S 29 15 E
Mkushi River 127 13 40 S 29 30 E
Mkuze, R. 129 27 45 S 32 30 E
Mkwaya 126 6 17 S 35 40 E
Mladá Boleslav 52 50 27N 14 53 E
Mladenovac 66 44 28N 20 44 E
Mlala Hills 126 6 50 S 31 40 E
Mlange 127 16 2 S 35 33 E
Mlava, R. 66 44 35N 21 18 E
Mława 54 53 9N 20 25 E
Mlinište 63 44 15N 16 50 E
Mljet, I. 66 42 43N 17 30 E
Młynary 54 54 12N 19 46 E
Mme 121 6 18N 10 14 E
Mo, Hordaland, Norway 71 60 49N 5 48 E
Mo, Telemark, Norway 71 59 28N 7 50 E
Mo, Sweden 72 61 19N 16 47 E
Mo i Rana 74 66 15N 14 7 E
Moa, I. 103 8 0 S 128 0 E
Moa, R. 120 7 0N 11 40W
Moab 161 38 40N 109 35W
Moabi 124 2 24 S 10 59 E
Moalie Park 139 29 42 S 143 3 E
Moaña 56 42 18N 8 43W
Moanda 124 1 28 S 13 21 E
Moapo 161 36 45N 114 37W
Moate 39 53 25N 7 43W
Moba 126 7 0 S 29 48 E
Mobara 111 35 25N 140 18 E
Mobaye 124 4 25N 21 5 E
Mobayi 124 4 15N 21 8 E
Moberley 158 39 25N 92 25W
Moberly, R. 152 56 12N 120 55W
Mobert 150 48 41N 85 40W
Mobile 157 30 41N 88 3W
Mobile B. 157 30 30N 88 0W
Mobile, Pt. 157 30 15N 88 0W
Mobjack B. 162 37 16N 76 22W
Möborg 73 56 24N 8 21 E
Mobridge 158 45 40N 100 28W
Mobutu Sese Seko, L. 126 1 30N 31 0 E
Moc Chav 100 20 50N 104 38 E
Moc Hoa 101 10 46N 105 56 E
Mocabe Kasari 127 9 58 S 26 12 E
Mocajuba 170 2 35 S 49 30W
Moçambique 127 15 3 S 40 42 E
Moçambique □ 127 14 45 S 38 30 E
Mocanaqua 162 41 9N 76 8W
Mochiang 108 23 25N 101 44 E
Mochiara Grove 128 20 43 S 21 50 E
Mochudi 128 24 27 S 26 7 E
Mocimboa da Praia 127 11 25 S 40 20 E
Mociu 70 46 46N 24 3 E
Möckeln 73 56 40N 14 15 E
Mockhorn I. 162 37 10N 75 52W
Moclips 160 47 14N 124 10W
Moçâmedes □ 128 16 35 S 12 30 E
Mocoa 174 1 15N 76 45W
Mococa 173 21 28 S 47 0W
Mocorito 164 25 20N 108 0W
Moctezuma 164 30 12N 106 26W
Moctezuma, R. 165 21 59N 98 34W
Mocuba 125 16 54 S 37 25 E
Moda 98 24 22N 96 29 E
Modane 45 45 12N 6 40 E
Modasa 94 23 30N 73 21 E
Modave 47 50 27N 5 18 E
Modbury, Austral. 109 34 50 S 138 41 E
Modbury, U.K. 30 50 21N 3 53W
Modder, R. 128 28 50 S 24 50 E
Modderrivier 128 29 2 S 24 38 E
Módena 62 44 39N 10 55 E
Modena 161 37 55N 113 56W
Modesto 163 37 43N 121 0W
Módica 65 36 52N 14 45 E
Modigliana 63 44 9N 11 48 E
Modjokerto 103 7 29 S 112 25 E
Modlin 54 52 24N 20 41 E
Mödling 53 48 5N 16 17 E
Modo 123 5 31N 30 33 E
Modra 53 48 19N 17 20 E
Modreeny 39 52 57N 8 6W
Modriča 66 44 57N 18 17 E
Moe 141 38 12 S 146 19 E
Moebase 127 17 3 S 38 41 E
Moei, R. 101 17 25N 98 10 E
Moëlan-s-Mer 42 47 49N 3 38W
Moelfre 31 53 21N 4 15W
Moengo 175 5 45N 54 20W
Moergestel 47 51 33N 5 11 E
Moësa, R. 51 46 12N 9 10 E
Moffat 35 55 20N 3 27W
Moga 94 30 48N 75 8 E
Mogadiscio = Mogadishu 91 2 2N 45 25 E
Mogadishu 91 2 2N 45 25 E
Mogador = Essaouira 118 31 32N 9 42W
Mogadouro 56 41 22N 6 47W
Mogami-gawa, R. 112 38 45N 140 0 E
Mogaung 98 25 20N 97 0 E
Møgeltønder 73 54 57N 8 48 E
Mogente 59 38 52N 0 45W
Moggil 108 27 34 S 152 52 E
Mogho 123 4 54N 40 16 E
Mogi das Cruzes 173 23 45 S 46 20W
Mogi-Guaçu, R. 173 20 53 S 48 10W
Mogi-Mirim 173 22 20 S 47 0W
Mogielnica 54 51 42N 20 41 E
Mogilev 80 53 55N 30 18 E
Mogilev Podolskiy 82 48 20N 27 40 E
Mogilno 54 52 39N 17 55 E
Mogincual 125 15 35 S 40 25 E
Mogliano Veneto 63 45 33N 12 15 E
Mogocha 77 53 40N 119 50 E
Mogoi 103 1 55 S 133 10 E
Mogok 98 23 0N 96 40 E
Mogollon 161 33 25N 108 55W
Mogollon Mesa 161 43 40N 111 0W
Mogriguy 141 32 3 S 148 40 E
Moguer 57 37 15N 6 52W
Mogumber 137 31 2 S 116 3 E
Mohács 53 45 58N 18 41 E
Mohaka, R. 142 39 7 S 177 12 E
Mohall 158 48 46N 101 30W
Mohammadābād 93 37 30N 59 5 E
Mohammedia 118 33 44N 7 21W
Mohave Desert 161 35 0N 117 30W
Mohawk 161 32 45N 113 50W
Mohawk, R. 162 42 47N 73 42W
Moheda 73 57 1N 14 35 E
Mohembo 125 18 15 S 21 43 E
Moher, Cliffs of 39 52 58N 9 30W
Mohican, C. 147 60 10N 167 30W
Mohill 38 53 57N 7 52W
Möhne, R. 48 51 29N 8 10 E
Mohnyin 98 24 47N 96 22 E
Moholm 73 58 37N 14 5 E
Mohon 43 49 45N 4 44 E
Mohoro 126 8 6 S 39 8 E
Moia 123 5 3N 28 2 E
Moidart, L. 36 56 47N 5 40W
Moinabad 96 17 44N 77 16 E
Moineşti 70 46 28N 26 21 E
Mointy 76 47 40N 73 45 E
Moira 38 54 28N 6 16W
Moirais 69 35 4N 24 56 E
Moirans 45 45 20N 5 33 E
Moirans-en-Montagne 45 46 26N 5 43 E
Moisäkula 80 58 3N 24 38 E
Moisie 151 50 7N 66 1W
Moisie, R. 151 50 6N 66 5W
Moissac 44 44 7N 1 5 E
Moita 57 38 38N 8 58W
Mojácar 59 37 6N 1 55W
Mojados 56 41 26N 4 40W
Mojave 163 35 8N 118 8W
Mojave Desert 163 35 0N 116 30W
Mojo, Boliv. 172 21 48 S 65 33W
Mojo, Ethiopia 123 8 35N 39 5 E
Mojo, I. 102 8 10 S 117 40 E
Moju, R. 170 1 40 S 48 25W
Mokai 142 38 32 S 175 56 E
Mokambo 127 12 25 S 28 20 E
Mokameh 95 25 24N 85 55 E
Mokau, R. 142 38 35 S 174 55 E
Mokelumne Hill 163 38 18N 120 43W
Mokelumne, R. 163 38 23N 121 25W
Mokhós 69 35 16N 25 27 E
Mokhotlong 129 29 22 S 29 2 E
Mokihinui 143 41 33 S 171 58 E
Moknine 119 35 35N 10 58 E
Mokokchung 99 26 15N 94 30 E
Mokpalin 98 17 26N 96 53 E
Mokpo 107 34 50N 126 30 E
Mokra Gora 66 42 50N 20 30 E
Mokronog 63 45 57N 15 9 E
Moksha, R. 81 54 45N 43 40 E
Mokshan 81 52 25N 44 35 E
Mokta Spera 120 16 38N 9 6W
Moktama Kwe 99 15 40N 96 30 E
Mol 47 51 11N 5 5 E
Mola, C. de la 58 39 53N 4 20 E
Mola di Bari 65 41 3N 17 5 E
Moland 71 59 11N 8 6 E
Moláoi 69 36 49N 22 56 E
Molat, I. 63 44 15N 14 50 E
Molchanovo 76 57 40N 83 50 E
Mold 31 53 10N 3 10W
Moldava nad Bodvou 53 48 38N 21 0 E
Moldavia = Moldova 70 46 30N 27 0 E
Moldavian S.S.R.□ 82 47 0N 28 0 E
Molde 71 62 45N 7 9 E
Moldotau, Khrebet 85 41 35N 75 0 E
Moldova 70 46 30N 27 0 E
Moldova Nouă 70 44 45N 21 41 E
Moldoveanu, mt. 67 45 36N 24 45 E
Mole Creek 138 41 32 S 146 24 E
Mole, R. 29 51 13N 0 15W
Molepolole 125 24 28 S 25 28 E
Moléson 50 46 33N 7 1 E
Molesworth 143 42 5 S 173 16 E
Molfetta 65 41 12N 16 35 E
Molina de Aragón 58 40 46N 1 52W
Moline 158 41 30N 90 30W
Molinella 63 44 38N 11 40 E
Molinos 172 25 28 S 66 15W
Moliro 126 8 12 S 30 30 E
Molise □ 63 41 45N 14 30 E
Moliterno 65 40 14N 15 50 E
Mollahat 98 22 56N 89 48 E
Mölle 73 56 17N 12 31 E
Molledo 56 43 8N 4 6W
Mollendo 174 17 0 S 72 0W
Mollerin, L. 137 30 30 S 117 35 E
Mollerusa 58 41 37N 0 54 E
Mollina 57 37 8N 4 38W
Mölln 48 53 37N 10 41 E
Mollösund 73 58 4N 11 30 E
Mölltorp 73 58 30N 14 26 E
Mölndal 73 57 40N 12 3 E
Mölnlycke 73 57 40N 12 8 E
Molo 98 23 22N 96 53 E
Molochansk 82 47 15N 35 23 E
Molochaya, R. 82 47 0N 35 30 E
Molodechno 80 54 20N 26 50 E
Molokai, I. 147 21 8N 157 0W
Moloma, R. 81 59 0N 48 15 E
Molong 141 33 5 S 148 54 E
Molopo, R. 125 25 40 S 24 30 E
Mólos 69 38 47N 22 37 E
Molotov, Mys 77 81 10N 95 0 E
Moloundou 124 2 8N 15 15 E
Molsheim 43 48 33N 7 29 E
Molson L. 153 54 22N 95 32W
Molteno 128 31 22 S 26 22 E
Molu, I. 103 6 45 S 131 40 E
Molucca Sea 103 4 0 S 124 0 E
Moluccas = Maluku, Is. 103 1 0 S 127 0 E
Molusi 128 20 21 S 24 29 E
Moma, Mozam. 127 16 47 S 39 4 E
Moma, Zaïre 126 1 35 S 23 52 E
Momanga 128 18 7 S 21 41 E
Momba 140 30 58 S 143 30 E
Mombaça 170 15 43 S 48 43W
Mombasa 126 4 2 S 39 43 E
Mombetsu, Hokkaido, Japan 112 42 27N 142 4 E
Mombetsu, Hokkaido, Japan 112 44 21N 143 22 E
Mombuey 56 42 3N 6 20W
Momchilgrad 67 41 33N 25 23 E
Momi 126 1 42 S 27 0 E
Momignies 47 50 2N 4 10 E
Mompós 174 9 14N 74 26W
Møn 73 54 57N 12 15 E
Mon, R. 99 20 25N 94 30 E
Mona, Canal de la 167 18 30N 67 45W
Mona, I. 167 18 5N 67 54W
Mona Passage 167 18 0N 67 40W
Mona, Punta, C. Rica 166 9 37N 82 36W
Mona, Punta, Spain 57 36 43N 3 45W
Monach Is. 36 57 32N 7 40W
Monach, Sd. of 36 57 34N 7 26W
Monaco ■ 44 43 46N 7 23 E
Monadhliath Mts. 37 57 10N 4 4W
Monadnock Mt. 162 42 52N 72 7W
Monagas □ 174 9 20N 63 0W
Monaghan 38 54 15N 6 58W
Monaghan □ 38 54 10N 7 0W
Monahans 159 31 35N 102 50W
Monapo 127 14 50 S 40 12 E
Monar For. 36 57 27N 5 10W
Monar L. 36 57 26N 5 8W
Monarch Mt. 152 51 55N 125 57W
Monasterevan 39 53 10N 7 5W
Monastier-sur-Gazeille, Le 44 44 57N 3 59 E
Monastir 119 35 50N 10 49 E
Monastyriska 80 49 8N 25 14 E
Monavullagh Mts. 39 52 14N 7 35W
Moncada 58 39 30N 0 24W
Moncalieri 62 45 0N 7 40 E
Moncalvo 62 45 3N 8 15 E
Moncarapacho 57 37 5N 7 46W
Moncayo, Sierra del 58 41 48N 1 50W
Mönchengladbach 48 51 12N 6 23 E
Monchique 57 37 19N 8 38W
Monchique, Sa. de, 55 37 18N 8 39W
Monclova 164 26 50N 101 30W
Monção 56 42 4N 8 27W
Moncontant 42 46 43N 0 36W
Moncontour 42 48 22N 2 38W
Moncton 151 46 7N 64 51W
Mondego, Cabo 56 40 11N 8 54W
Mondego, R. 56 40 28N 8 0W
Mondeodo 103 3 21 S 122 9 E
Mondolfo 63 43 45N 13 8 E
Mondoñedo 56 43 25N 7 23W
Mondoví 62 44 23N 7 56 E
Mondovi 158 44 37N 91 40W
Mondragon 45 44 13N 4 44 E
Mondragone 64 41 8N 13 52 E
Mondrain I. 137 34 9 S 122 14 E
Monduli □ 126 3 0 S 36 0 E
Monemvasía 69 36 41N 23 3 E
Monessen 156 40 9N 79 50W
Monesterio 57 38 6N 6 15W
Monestier-de-Clermont 45 44 55N 5 38 E
Monet 150 48 10N 75 40W
Monêtier-les-Bains, Le 45 44 58N 6 30 E
Monett 159 36 55N 93 56W
Moneygall 39 52 54N 7 59W
Moneymore 38 54 42N 6 40W
Monfalcone 63 45 49N 13 32 E
Monflanquin 44 44 32N 0 47 E
Monforte 57 39 6N 7 25W
Monforte de Lemos 56 42 31N 7 33W
Mong Cai 101 21 27N 107 54 E
Möng Hsu 99 21 54N 98 30 E
Mong Hta 98 19 50N 98 35 E
Mong Ket 98 23 8N 98 22 E
Möng Kung 98 21 35N 97 35 E
Mong Kyawt 98 19 56N 98 45 E
Mong Lang 101 20 29N 97 52 E
Möng Nai 98 20 32N 97 55 E
Möng Pai 98 19 40N 97 15 E
Mong Pawk 99 22 4N 99 16 E
Mong Ping 98 21 22N 99 2 E
Mong Pu 98 20 55N 98 44 E
Mong Ton 98 20 25N 98 45 E
Mong Tung 98 22 2N 97 41 E
Mong Wa 99 21 26N 100 27 E
Mong Yai 98 22 28N 98 3 E
Mongalla 123 5 8N 31 55 E
Monger, L. 137 29 25 S 117 5 E
Monghyr 95 25 23N 86 30 E
Mongla 98 22 8N 89 35 E
Mongngaw 98 22 47N 96 59 E
Mongo 117 12 14N 18 43 E
Mongolia ■ 105 47 0N 103 0 E
Mongonu 121 12 40N 13 32 E
Mongororo 124 12 22N 22 26 E
Mongoumba 124 3 33N 18 40 E
Mongpang 101 23 5N 100 25 E
Mongu 125 15 16 S 23 12 E
Mongua 128 16 43 S 15 20 E
Moniaive 35 55 11N 3 55W
Monifieth 35 56 30N 2 48W
Monistral-St.-Loire 45 45 17N 4 11 E
Monitor, Pk. 163 38 52N 116 35W
Monitor, Ra. 163 38 30N 116 45W
Monivea 38 53 22N 8 42W
Monk 153 47 7N 69 59W
Monkey Bay 127 14 7 S 35 1 E
Monkey River 165 16 22N 88 29W
Monki 54 53 23N 22 48 E
Monkira 138 24 46 S 140 30 E
Monkoto 124 1 38 S 20 35 E
Monmouth, U.K. 31 51 48N 2 43W
Monmouth, U.S.A. 158 40 50N 90 40W
Monmouth (□) 26 51 34N 3 5W
Monnow R. 28 51 54N 2 48W
Mono, L. 163 38 0N 119 9W
Mono, Punta del 166 12 0N 83 30W
Monolith 163 35 7N 118 22W
Monópoli 65 40 57N 17 18 E
Monor 53 47 21N 19 27 E
Monóvar 59 38 28N 0 53W
Monowai 143 45 53 S 167 25 E
Monowai, L. 143 45 53 S 167 25 E
Monreal del Campo 58 40 47N 1 20W
Monreale 64 38 6N 13 16 E
Monroe, La., U.S.A. 159 32 32N 92 4W
Monroe, Mich., U.S.A. 156 41 55N 83 26W
Monroe, N.C., U.S.A. 157 35 2N 80 37W
Monroe, Utah, U.S.A. 161 38 45N 111 39W
Monroe, Wis., U.S.A. 158 42 38N 89 40W
Monroe City 158 39 40N 91 40W
Monroeton 162 41 43N 76 29W
Monroeville 157 31 33N 87 15W
Monrovia, Liberia 120 6 18N 10 47W
Monrovia, U.S.A. 161 34 7N 118 1W
Mons 47 50 27N 3 58 E
Møns Klint 73 54 57N 12 33 E
Monsaraz 57 38 28N 7 22W
Monse 103 4 0 S 123 10 E
Monségur 44 44 38N 0 4 E
Monsélice 63 43 13N 11 45 E
Monster 46 52 1N 4 10 E
Mont-aux-Sources 129 28 44 S 28 52 E
Mont-de-Marsin 44 43 54N 0 31W
Mont d'Or, Tunnel 43 46 45N 6 18 E
Mont-Dore, Le 44 45 35N 2 50 E
Mont Joli 151 48 37N 68 10W
Mont Laurier 150 46 35N 75 30W
Mont Luis 151 42 31N 2 6 E
Mont St. Michel 42 48 40N 1 30W
Mont-sur-Marchienne 47 50 23N 4 24 E
Mont Tremblant Prov. Park 150 46 30N 74 30W
Montabaur 48 50 26N 7 49 E
Montacute 109 34 53 S 138 45 E
Montagnac 44 43 29N 3 28 E
Montagnana 63 45 13N 11 29 E
Montagu 128 33 45 S 20 8 E
Montagu, I. 164 58 30 S 26 15W
Montague, Can. 151 46 10N 62 39W
Montague, Calif., U.S.A. 160 41 47N 122 30W
Montague, Mass., U.S.A. 162 42 31N 72 33W
Montague, I. 164 31 40N 144 46W
Montague I. 147 60 0N 147 0W
Montague Ra. 137 29 15 S 119 30 E
Montague Sd. 136 14 28 S 125 20 E
Montaigu 42 46 59N 1 18W
Montalbán 58 40 50N 0 45W
Montalbano di Elicona 65 38 1N 15 0 E
Montalbano Iónico 65 40 17N 16 33 E
Montalbo 58 39 53N 2 42W
Montalcino 63 43 4N 11 30 E
Montalegre 56 41 49N 7 47W
Montalto di Castro 63 42 20N 11 36 E
Montalto Uffugo 65 39 25N 16 9 E
Montalvo 163 34 15N 119 12W
Montamarta 56 41 39N 5 49W
Montaña 174 6 0 S 73 0W
Montana 50 46 19N 7 29 E
Montana □ 154 47 0N 110 0W
Montánchez 57 39 15N 6 8W
Montañita 174 1 30N 75 28W
Montargis 43 48 0N 2 43 E
Montauban 44 44 0N 1 21 E
Montauk 162 41 3N 71 57W
Montauk Pt. 162 41 4N 71 52W
Montbard 43 47 38N 4 20 E
Montbéliard 43 47 31N 6 48 E
Montblanch 58 41 23N 1 4 E
Montbrison 45 45 36N 4 3 E
Montcalm, Pic de 44 42 40N 1 25 E
Montceau-les-Mines 43 46 40N 4 23 E
Montchanin 62 46 47N 4 30 E
Montclair 162 40 53N 74 49W
Montcornet 43 49 40N 4 0 E

Montcuq 44 44 21N 1 13 E
Montdidier 43 49 38N 2 35 E
Monte Albán 165 17 2N 96 45W
Monte Alegre 175 2 0S 54 0W
Monte Alegre de Goiás 171 13 14S 47 10W
Monte Alegre de Minas 171 18 52S 48 52W
Monte Azul 171 15 9S 42 53W
Monte Bello Is. 136 20 30S 115 45 E
Monte Carlo 45 43 46N 7 23 E
Monte Carmelo 171 18 43S 47 29W
Monte Caseros 172 30 10S 57 50W
Monte Comán 172 34 40S 68 0W
Monte Cristi 167 19 52N 71 39W
Monte Libano 16 8 5N 75 29W
Monte Lindo, R. 172 25 30S 58 40W
Monte Quemado 172 25 53S 62 41W
Monte Redondo 56 39 53N 8 50W
Monte San Savino 43 43 20N 11 42 E
Monte Sant' Angelo 65 41 42N 15 59 E
Monte Santo, C. di 64 40 5N 9 42 E
Monte Visto 161 37 40N 106 8W
Monteagudo 173 27 14S 54 8W
Montealegre 59 38 48N 1 17W
Montebello 150 45 40N 74 55W
Montebelluna 63 45 47N 12 3 E
Montebourg 42 49 30N 1 20W
Montecastrilli 63 42 40N 12 30 E
Montecatini Terme 62 43 55N 10 48 E
Montecito 163 34 26N 119 40W
Montecristi 174 1 0S 80 40W
Montecristo, I. 62 42 20N 10 20 E
Montefalco 63 42 53N 12 38 E
Montefiascone 63 42 31N 12 2 E
Montefrío 57 37 20N 3 39W
Montegnée 47 50 38N 5 31 E
Montego B. 166 18 30N 78 0W
Montegranaro 63 43 13N 13 38 E
Monteiro 170 7 22S 37 38W
Monteith 140 35 11S 139 23 E
Montejicar 59 37 33N 3 30W
Montejinnie 136 16 40S 131 45 E
Montekomu Hu 99 34 40N 89 0 E
Montelíbano 174 8 5N 75 29W
Montélimar 45 44 33N 4 45 E
Montella 65 40 50N 15 0 E
Montellano 57 36 59N 5 36W
Montello 158 43 49N 89 21W
Montelupo Fiorentino 62 43 44N 11 2 E
Montemór-o-Novo 57 38 40N 8 12W
Montemór-o-Velho 56 40 11N 8 40W
Montemorelos 165 25 11N 99 42W
Montendre 44 45 16N 0 26W
Montenegro 173 29 39S 51 29W
Montenegro □ 66 42 40N 19 20 E
Montenero di Bisaccia 63 42 0N 14 47 E
Montepuez 127 13 8S 38 59 E
Montepuez, R. 127 12 40S 40 15 E
Montepulciano 63 43 5N 11 46 E
Montereale 63 42 31N 13 13 E
Montereau 43 48 22N 2 57 E
Monterey 163 36 35N 121 57W
Monterey, B. 163 36 50N 121 55W
Montería 174 8 46N 75 53W
Monteros 172 27 11S 65 30W
Monterotondo 63 42 3N 12 36 E
Monterrey 164 25 40N 100 30W
Montes Altos 170 5 50S 47 4W
Montes Claros 171 16 30S 43 50W
Montes de Toledo 57 39 35N 4 30W
Montesano 160 47 0N 123 39W
Montesárchio 65 41 5N 14 37 E
Montescaglioso 65 40 34N 16 40 E
Montesilvano 63 42 30N 14 8 E
Montevarchi 63 43 30N 11 32 E
Monteverde 124 8 45S 16 45 E
Montevideo 173 34 50S 56 11W
Montezuma 158 41 32N 92 35W
Montfaucon, Haute-Loire, France 45 45 11N 4 20 E
Montfaucon, Meuse, France 43 49 16N 5 8 E
Montfort 47 51 7N 5 58 E
Montfort-l'Amaury 43 48 47N 1 49 E
Montfort-sur-Meu 42 48 8N 1 58W
Montgenèvre 45 44 56N 6 42 E
Montgomery, U.K. 31 52 34N 3 9W
Montgomery, Ala., U.S.A. 157 32 20N 86 20W
Montgomery, Pa., U.S.A. 162 41 10N 76 53W
Montgomery, W. Va., U.S.A. 156 38 9N 81 21W
Montgomery = Sahiwal 94 30 45N 73 8 E
Montgomery (□) 26 52 34N 3 9W
Montgomery Pass 163 37 58N 118 20W
Montguyon 44 45 12N 0 12W
Monthey 50 46 15N 6 56 E
Monticelli d'Ongina 62 45 3N 9 56 E
Monticello, Ark., U.S.A. 159 33 40N 91 48W
Monticello, Fla., U.S.A. 157 30 35N 83 50W
Monticello, Ind., U.S.A. 156 40 40N 86 45W
Monticello, Iowa, U.S.A. 158 42 18N 91 18W
Monticello, Ky., U.S.A. 157 36 52N 84 50W
Monticello, Minn., U.S.A. 158 45 17N 93 52W
Monticello, Miss., U.S.A. 159 31 35N 90 8W
Monticello, N.Y., U.S.A. 162 41 37N 74 42W
Monticello, Utah, U.S.A. 161 37 55N 109 27W
Montichiari 62 45 28N 10 29 E
Montieri 43 48 30N 4 45 E
Montignac 44 45 4N 1 10 E
Montignies-sur-Sambre 47 50 24N 4 29 E
Montigny-les-Metz 43 49 7N 6 10 E
Montigny-sur-Aube 43 47 57N 4 45 E
Montijo 57 38 52N 6 39W
Montijo, Presa de 57 38 55N 6 26W
Montilla 57 37 36N 4 40W
Montivideo 158 44 55N 95 40W
Montlhéry 43 48 39N 2 15 E
Montluçon 44 46 22N 2 36 E
Montmagny 151 46 58N 70 34W
Montmarault 53 46 11N 2 54 E
Montmartre 153 50 14N 103 27W
Montmédy 43 49 30N 5 20 E
Montmélian 45 45 30N 6 4 E
Montmirail 43 48 51N 3 30 E
Montmoreau-St.-Cybard 44 45 23N 0 8 E
Montmorency 151 46 53N 71 11W
Montmorillon 44 46 26N 0 50 E
Montmort 43 48 55N 3 49 E
Monto 138 24 52S 151 12 E
Montório al Vomano 63 42 35N 13 38 E
Montoro 57 38 1N 4 27W
Montour Falls 162 42 20N 76 51W
Montpelier, Idaho, U.S.A. 160 42 15N 111 29W
Montpelier, Ohio, U.S.A. 156 41 34N 84 40W
Montpelier, Vt., U.S.A. 156 44 15N 72 38W
Montpellier 44 43 37N 3 52 E
Montpezat-de-Quercy 44 44 15N 1 30 E
Montpon-Ménestrol 44 45 2N 0 11 E
Montréal, Can. 150 45 31N 73 34W
Montréal, France 44 43 13N 2 8 E
Montréal L. 153 54 20N 105 45W
Montreal Lake 153 54 3N 105 46W
Montredon-Labessonnié 44 43 45N 2 18 E
Montréjeau 44 43 6N 0 35 E
Montrésor 42 47 10N 1 10 E
Montreuil 43 50 27N 1 45 E
Montreuil-Bellay 42 47 8N 0 9W
Montreux 50 46 26N 6 55 E
Montrevault 42 47 17N 1 2W
Montrevel-en-Bresse 45 46 21N 5 8 E
Montrichard 42 47 20N 1 10 E
Montrose, U.K. 37 56 43N 2 28W
Montrose, Col., U.S.A. 161 38 30N 107 52W
Montrose, Pa., U.S.A. 162 41 50N 75 55W
Montrose, oilfield 19 57 20N 1 35 E
Montross 162 38 6N 76 50W
Monts, Pte des 151 49 27N 67 12W
Montsalvy 44 44 41N 2 30 E
Montsant, Sierra de 58 41 17N 0 1 E
Montsauche 43 47 13N 4 0 E
Montsech, Sierra del 58 42 0N 0 45 E
Montseny 58 42 29N 1 2 E
Montserrat, I. 167 16 40N 62 10W
Montserrat, mt. 58 41 36N 1 49 E
Montuenga 56 41 3N 4 38W
Montuiri 58 39 34N 2 59 E
Monveda 124 2 52N 21 30 E
Monymusk 37 57 13N 2 32W
Monyo 98 17 59N 95 30 E
Mônywa 98 22 7N 95 11 E
Monza 62 45 35N 9 15 E
Monze 127 16 17S 27 29 E
Monze, C. 94 24 47N 66 37 E
Monzón 58 41 52N 0 10 E
Mook 46 51 46N 5 54 E
Mo'oka 111 36 26N 140 1 E
Moolawatana 139 29 55S 139 45 E
Mooleulooloo 140 31 36S 140 32 E
Mooliabeenee 137 31 20S 116 2 E
Mooloogool 137 26 2S 119 5 E
Moomin, Cr. 139 29 44S 149 20 E
Moonah, R. 138 22 3S 138 33 E
Moonbeam 150 49 20N 82 10W
Mooncoin 39 52 18N 7 17W
Moonie 139 27 46S 150 20 E
Moonie, R. 139 27 45S 150 0 E
Moonta 140 34 6S 137 32 E
Moora 137 30 37S 115 58 E
Mooraberree 138 25 13S 140 54 E
Moorarie 137 25 56S 117 35 E
Moorcroft 158 44 17N 104 58W
Moore, L. 137 29 50S 117 35 E
Moore, R. 137 31 22S 115 30 E
Moore Reefs 138 16 0S 149 5 E
Moore River Native Settlement 137 31 1S 115 56 E
Moorebank 47 33 56S 150 56 E
Moorefield 156 39 5N 78 59W
Mooresville 157 35 36N 80 45W
Moorfoot Hills 35 55 44N 3 8W
Moorhead 158 47 0N 97 0W
Moorland 141 31 46S 152 38 E
Mooroopna 141 36 25S 145 22 E
Moorpark 163 34 17N 118 53W
Moorreesburg 128 33 6S 18 38 E
Moorslede 47 50 54N 3 4 E
Moosburg 49 48 28N 11 57 E
Moose Factory 150 51 20N 80 40W
Moose I. 153 51 42N 97 10W
Moose Jaw 153 50 24N 105 30W
Moose Jaw R. 153 50 34N 105 18W
Moose Lake, Can. 153 53 43N 100 20W
Moose Lake, U.S.A. 158 46 27N 92 48W
Moose Mountain Cr. 153 49 13N 102 12W
Moose Mtn. Prov. Park 153 49 48N 102 25W
Moose, R. 150 51 20N 80 25W
Moose River 150 50 48N 81 17W
Moosehead L. 151 45 40N 69 40W
Moosomin 153 50 9N 101 40W
Moosonee 150 51 17N 80 39W
Moosup 162 41 44N 71 52W
Mopeia 125 17 30S 35 40 E
Mopipi 128 21 6S 24 55 E
Mopoi 123 5 6N 26 54 E
Moppin 139 29 12S 146 45 E
Mopti 120 14 30N 4 0W
Moqatta 123 14 38N 35 50 E
Moquegua 174 17 15S 70 46W
Mór 53 47 25N 18 12 E
Móra 57 38 55N 8 10W
Mora, Sweden 72 61 2N 14 38 E
Mora, Minn., U.S.A. 158 45 52N 93 19W
Mora, N. Mex., U.S.A. 161 35 58N 105 21W
Mora de Ebro 58 41 6N 0 38 E
Mora de Rubielos 58 40 15N 0 45W
Mora la Nueva 58 41 7N 0 39 E
Morača, R. 66 42 40N 19 20 E
Morada Nova 170 5 7S 38 23W
Morada Nova de Minas 171 18 37S 45 22W
Moradabad 94 28 50N 78 50 E
Morafenobe 129 17 50S 44 53 E
Morag 54 53 55N 19 56 E
Moral de Calatrava 59 38 51N 3 33W
Moraleja 56 40 6N 6 43W
Morales 174 2 45N 76 38W
Moramanga 129 18 56S 48 12 E
Moran, Kans., U.S.A. 159 37 53N 94 35W
Moran, Wyo., U.S.A. 160 43 53N 110 37W
Morano Cálabro 65 39 51N 16 8 E
Morant Cays 166 17 22N 76 0W
Morant Pt. 166 17 55N 76 12W
Morar 36 56 58N 5 49W
Morar L. 36 56 57N 5 40W
Moratalla 59 38 14N 1 49W
Moratuwa 97 6 45N 79 55 E
Morava, R. 53 49 50N 16 50 E
Moravatío 164 19 51N 100 25W
Moravia, Iowa, U.S.A. 158 40 50N 92 50W
Moravia, N.Y., U.S.A. 162 42 43N 76 25W
Moravian Hts. = Ceskemoravská V. 52 49 30N 15 40 E
Moravica, R. 66 43 40N 20 8 E
Moravice, R. 53 49 50N 17 43 E
Moravița 66 45 17N 21 14 E
Moravska Trebová 53 49 45N 16 40 E
Moravské Budějovice 52 49 4N 15 49 E
Morawa 137 29 13S 116 0 E
Morawhanna 174 8 30N 59 40W
Moray (□) 26 57 32N 3 25W
Moray Firth 37 57 50N 3 30W
Morbach 49 49 48N 7 7 E
Morbegno 62 46 8N 9 34 E
Morbihan □ 42 47 55N 2 50W
Morcenx 44 44 0N 0 55W
Mordelles 42 48 5N 1 52W
Morden 153 49 15N 98 10W
Mordovian S.S.R.□ 81 54 20N 44 30 E
Mordovo 81 52 13N 40 50 E
More L. 37 58 18N 4 52W
Møre og Romsdal □ 71 63 0N 9 0 E
Morea 140 36 45S 141 18 E
Moreau, R. 158 45 15N 102 45W
Morebattle 35 55 30N 2 20W
Morecambe 32 54 5N 2 52W
Morecambe B. 32 54 7N 3 0W
Morecambe, gasfield 19 53 57N 3 40W
Moree 139 29 28S 149 54 E
Morehead, P.N.G. 135 8 41S 141 41 E
Morehead, U.S.A. 156 38 12N 83 22W
Morehead City 157 34 46N 76 44W
Moreira 174 0 34S 63 26W
Morelia 164 19 40N 101 11W
Morella, Austral. 138 23 0S 143 47 E
Morella, Spain 58 40 35N 0 2 E
Morelos 164 26 42N 107 40W
Morelos □ 165 18 40N 99 10W
Morena, Sierra 57 38 20N 4 0W
Morenci 161 33 7N 109 20W
Moreni 70 44 59N 25 36 E
Moreno 171 8 7S 35 6W
Mores, I. 157 26 15N 77 35W
Moresby I. 152 52 30N 131 40W
Morestel 45 45 40N 5 28 E
Moret 43 48 22N 2 48 E
Moreton B. 133 27 10S 153 10 E
Moreton, I. 139 27 10S 153 25 E
Moreton-in-Marsh 28 51 59N 1 42W
Moreton Telegraph Office 138 12 22S 142 30 E
Moretonhampstead 30 50 39N 3 45W
Moreuil 43 49 46N 2 30 E
Morez 45 46 31N 6 2 E
Morgan, Austral. 140 34 0S 139 35 E
Morgan, U.S.A. 160 41 3N 111 44W
Morgan City 159 29 40N 91 15W
Morgan Hill 163 37 8N 121 39W
Morganfield 156 37 40N 87 55W
Morganton 157 35 46N 81 48W
Morgantown 156 39 39N 79 58W
Morganville, Queens., Austral. 139 25 10S 152 0 E
Morganville, S. Australia, Austral. 140 33 10S 140 32 E
Morgat 42 48 15N 4 32 E
Morgenzon 129 26 45S 29 36 E
Morges 50 46 31N 6 29 E
Morhange 43 48 55N 6 38 E
Mori 62 45 51N 10 59 E
Morialmée 47 50 17N 4 30 E
Morialta Falls Reserve 109 34 54S 138 43 E
Moriarty 161 35 3N 106 2W
Morice L. 152 53 50N 127 40W
Morichal 174 2 10N 70 34W
Morichal Largo, R. 174 8 55N 63 0W
Moriguchi 111 34 44N 135 34 E
Moriki 121 12 52N 6 30 E
Morinville 152 53 49N 113 41W
Morioka 112 39 45N 141 8 E
Moris 164 28 8N 108 32W
Morisset 141 33 6S 151 30 E
Morkalla 140 34 23S 141 10 E
Morlaàs 44 43 21N 0 18W
Morlaix 42 48 36N 3 52W
Morlanwelz 47 50 28N 4 15 E
Morley 33 53 45N 1 36W
Mormanno 65 39 53N 15 59 E
Mormant 43 48 37N 2 52 E
Morney 139 25 22S 141 23 E
Morningside 108 27 28S 153 4 E
Mornington, Victoria, Austral. 141 38 15S 145 5 E
Mornington, W. Australia, Austral. 136 17 31S 126 6 E
Mornington, Ireland 38 53 42N 6 17W
Mornington I. 138 16 30S 139 30 E
Mornington, I. 176 49 50S 75 30W
Mórnos, R. 69 38 30N 22 0 E
Moro 123 10 50N 30 9 E
Moro G. 103 6 30N 123 0 E
Morobe 135 7 49S 147 38 E
Morocco ■ 118 32 0N 5 50W
Morococha 174 11 40S 76 5W
Morogoro 126 6 50S 37 40 E
Morogoro □ 126 8 0S 37 0 E
Morokweng 125 26 12S 23 45 E
Moroleón 164 20 8N 101 32W
Morombé 129 21 45S 43 22 E
Moron 172 34 39S 58 37W
Morón 166 22 0N 78 30W
Morón de Almazán 58 41 29N 2 27W
Morón de la Frontera 57 37 6N 5 28W
Morondava 129 20 17S 44 17 E
Morondo 120 8 57N 6 47W
Morongo Valley 163 34 3N 116 37W
Moronou 120 6 16N 4 59W
Morotai, I. 103 2 10N 128 30 E
Moroto 124 2 28N 34 42 E
Moroto Summit, Mt. 126 2 30N 34 43 E
Morozov (Bratan), mt. 67 42 30N 25 10 E
Morozovsk 83 48 25N 41 50 E
Morpeth 35 55 11N 1 41W
Morrelganj 98 22 28N 89 51 E
Morrilton 159 35 10N 92 45W
Morrinhos, Ceara, Brazil 170 3 14S 40 7W
Morrinhos, Minas Gerais, Brazil 171 17 45S 49 10W
Morrinsville 142 37 40S 175 32 E
Morris, Can. 153 49 25N 97 22W
Morris, Ill., U.S.A. 156 41 20N 88 20W
Morris, Minn., U.S.A. 158 45 33N 95 56W
Morris, N.Y., U.S.A. 162 42 33N 75 15W
Morris, Mt. 137 26 9S 131 4 E
Morrisburg 150 44 55N 75 7W
Morrison 158 41 47N 90 0W
Morristown, Ariz., U.S.A. 161 33 54N 112 45W
Morristown, N.J., U.S.A. 162 40 48N 74 30W
Morristown, S.D., U.S.A. 158 45 57N 101 44W
Morristown, Tenn., U.S.A. 157 36 18N 83 20W
Morrisville, N.Y., U.S.A. 162 42 54N 75 39W
Morrisville, Pa., U.S.A. 162 40 13N 74 47W
Morro Agudo 171 20 44S 48 4W
Morro Bay 163 35 27N 120 54W
Morro do Chapéu 171 11 33S 41 9W
Morro, Pta. 172 27 6S 71 0W
Morros 170 2 52S 44 3W
Morrosquillo, Golfo de 167 9 35N 75 40W
Morrum 73 56 12N 14 45 E
Morrumbene 125 23 31S 35 16 E
Mors 73 56 50N 8 45 E
Morshank 81 53 28N 41 50 E
Mörsil 72 63 19N 13 40 E
Mortagne, Charente Maritime, France 44 45 28N 0 49W
Mortagne, Orne, France 42 48 30N 0 32 E
Mortagne, Vendée, France 42 46 59N 0 57W
Mortagne-au-Perche 42 48 31N 0 33 E
Mortagne, R. 43 48 30N 6 30 E
Mortain 42 48 40N 0 57W
Mortara 62 45 15N 8 43 E
Morte Bay 30 51 10N 4 13W
Morte Pt. 30 51 13N 4 14W
Morteau 43 47 3N 6 35 E
Mortehoe 30 51 21N 4 12W
Morteros 172 30 50S 62 0W
Mortes, R. das 171 11 45S 50 44W
Mortimer's Cross 28 52 17N 2 50W
Mortlake 140 38 5S 142 50 E
Morton, Tex., U.S.A. 159 33 39N 102 49W
Morton, Wash., U.S.A. 160 46 33N 122 17W
Morton Fen 29 52 45N 0 23W
Mortsel 47 51 11N 4 27 E
Morundah 141 34 57S 146 19 E
Moruya 141 35 58N 150 3 E
Morvan, Mts. du 43 47 5N 4 0 E

Name	Page	Lat.	Long.
Morven, Austral.	**139**	26 22 S	147 5 E
Morven, N.Z.	**143**	44 50 S	171 6 E
Morven, dist.	**34**	56 38N	5 44W
Morven, mt., Grampian, U.K.	**37**	57 8N	3 1W
Morven, mt., Highland, U.K.	**37**	58 15N	3 40W
Morvern	**36**	56 38N	5 44W
Morwell	**141**	38 10 S	146 22 E
Moryn	**54**	52 51N	14 22 E
Mosalsk	**80**	54 30N	34 55 E
Mosbach	**49**	49 21N	9 9 E
Mosciano Sant' Ángelo	**63**	42 42N	13 52 E
Moscos Is.	**101**	14 0N	97 30 E
Moscow, Idaho, U.S.A.	**160**	46 45N	116 59W
Moscow, Pa., U.S.A.	**162**	41 20N	75 31W
Moscow = Moskva	**81**	55 45N	37 35 E
Mosel, R.	**49**	50 22N	7 36 E
Moselle □	**43**	48 59N	6 33 E
Moselle, R.	**47**	50 22N	7 36 E
Moses Lake	**160**	47 16N	119 17W
Mosgiel	**143**	45 53 S	170 21 E
Moshi	**126**	3 22 S	37 18 E
Moshi □	**126**	3 22 S	37 18 E
Moshupa	**128**	24 46 S	25 29 E
Mósina	**54**	52 15N	16 50 E
Mosjøen	**74**	65 51N	13 12 E
Moskenesøya	**74**	67 58N	13 0 E
Moskenstraumen	**74**	67 47N	13 0 E
Moskva	**81**	55 45N	37 35 E
Moskva, R.	**81**	55 5N	38 51 E
Moslavačka Gora	**63**	45 40N	16 37 E
Mošćenice	**63**	45 17N	14 16 E
Mosomane (Artesia)	**128**	24 2 S	26 19 E
Mosonmagyaróvár	**53**	47 52N	17 18 E
Mo orin	**66**	45 19N	20 4 E
Mospino	**82**	47 52N	38 0 E
Mosquera	**174**	2 35N	78 30W
Mosquero	**159**	35 48N	103 57W
Mosqueruela	**58**	40 21N	0 27W
Mosquitia	**166**	15 20N	84 10W
Mosquitos, Golfo de los	**166**	9 15N	81 10W
Moss	**71**	59 27N	10 40 E
Moss Vale	**141**	34 32 S	150 25 E
Mossaka	**124**	1 15 S	16 45 E
Mossâmedes, Angola	**125**	15 7 S	12 11 E
Mossâmedes, Brazil	**171**	16 7 S	50 11W
Mossbank	**153**	49 56N	105 56W
Mossburn	**143**	45 41 S	168 15 E
Mosselbaai	**128**	34 11 S	22 8 E
Mossendjo	**124**	2 55 S	12 42 E
Mosses, Col des	**49**	46 25N	7 7 E
Mossgiel	**140**	33 15 S	144 30 E
Mossley	**32**	53 31N	2 1W
Mossman	**138**	16 28 S	145 23 E
Mossoró	**170**	5 10 S	37 15W
Mossuril	**127**	14 58 S	40 42 E
Mossy, R.	**153**	54 5N	102 58W
Most	**52**	50 31N	13 38 E
Mostar	**66**	43 22N	17 50 E
Mostardas	**173**	31 2 S	50 51W
Mostefa, Rass	**119**	36 55N	11 3 E
Mosterøy	**71**	59 5N	5 37 E
Mostiska	**80**	49 48N	23 4 E
Mostrim	**38**	53 42N	7 38W
Mosty	**80**	53 27N	24 38 E
Mostyn	**31**	53 18N	3 14W
Mosul = Al Mawsil	**92**	36 20N	43 5 E
Mosulpo	**107**	33 20N	126 17 E
Mosvatn, L.	**71**	59 52N	8 5 E
Mota del Cuervo	**58**	39 30N	2 52W
Mota del Marqués	**56**	41 38N	5 11W
Motagua, R.	**166**	15 44N	88 14W
Motala	**73**	58 32N	15 1 E
Motcombe	**28**	51 1N	2 12W
Motegi	**111**	36 32N	140 11 E
Mothe-Achard, La	**42**	46 37N	1 40W
Motherwell	**35**	55 48N	4 0W
Motihari	**95**	26 37N	85 1 E
Motilla del Palancar	**58**	39 34N	1 55W
Motnik	**63**	46 14N	14 54 E
Motocurunya	**174**	4 24N	64 5W
Motovun	**63**	45 20N	13 50 E
Motozintea de Mendoza	**165**	15 21N	92 14W
Motril	**59**	36 44N	3 37W
Motrul, R.	**70**	44 44N	22 59 E
Mott	**158**	46 25N	102 14W
Motte-Chalançon, La	**45**	44 30N	5 21 E
Motte, La	**45**	44 20N	6 3 E
Mottisfont	**28**	51 22N	1 32W
Mottola	**65**	40 38N	17 0 E
Motueka	**143**	41 7 S	173 1 E
Motul	**165**	21 0N	89 20W
Motupena Pt.	**135**	6 30 S	155 10 E
Mouchalagane, R.	**151**	50 56N	68 41W
Moúdhros	**68**	39 50N	25 18 E
Moudjeria	**120**	17 50N	12 15W
Moudon	**50**	46 40N	6 49 E
Mouila	**124**	1 50 S	11 0 E
Moulamein	**140**	35 3 S	144 1 E
Moule, Le	**167**	16 20N	61 22W
Moulins	**44**	46 35N	3 19 E
Moulmein	**98**	16 30N	97 40 E
Moulmeingyun	**98**	16 23N	95 16 E
Moulouya, O.	**118**	35 8N	2 22W
Moulton, U.K.	**29**	52 17N	0 51W
Moulton, U.S.A.	**159**	29 35N	97 8W
Moultrie	**157**	31 11N	83 47W
Moultrie, L.	**157**	33 25N	80 10W
Mound City, Mo., U.S.A.	**158**	40 2N	95 25W
Mound City, S.D., U.S.A.	**158**	45 46N	100 3W
Moúnda, Ákra	**69**	38 5N	20 45 E
Moundou	**117**	8 40N	16 10 E
Moundsville	**156**	39 53N	80 43W
Moung	**100**	12 46N	103 27 E
Mount Airy	**162**	36 31N	80 37W
Mount Amherst	**136**	18 24 S	126 58 E
Mount Angel	**160**	45 4N	122 46W
Mount Augustus	**137**	24 20 S	116 56 E
Mount Barker, S.A., Austral.	**140**	35 5 S	138 52 E
Mount Barker, W.A., Austral.	**137**	34 38 S	117 40 E
Mount Barker Junc.	**109**	35 1 S	138 52 E
Mount Beauty	**141**	36 47 S	147 10 E
Mount Bellew Bridge	**38**	53 28N	8 30W
Mount Buckley	**138**	20 6 S	148 0 E
Mount Carmel, Ill., U.S.A.	**156**	38 20N	87 48W
Mount Carmel, Pa., U.S.A.	**162**	40 46N	76 25W
Mount Clemens	**150**	42 35N	82 50W
Mount Coolon	**138**	21 25 S	147 25 E
Mount Cootatha Park	**108**	27 29 S	152 57 E
Mount Crosby	**108**	27 32 S	152 48 E
Mount Darwin	**125**	16 47 S	31 38 E
Mount Desert I.	**151**	44 25N	68 25W
Mount Dora	**157**	28 49N	81 32W
Mount Douglas	**138**	21 35 S	146 50 E
Mount Edgecumbe	**147**	57 8N	135 22W
Mount Elizabeth	**136**	16 0 S	125 50 E
Mount Enid	**136**	21 42 S	116 26 E
Mount Forest	**150**	43 59N	80 43W
Mount Fox	**138**	18 45 S	145 45 E
Mount Gambier	**140**	37 50 S	140 46 E
Mount Garnet	**138**	17 37 S	145 6 E
Mount Goldsworthy	**132**	20 25 S	119 39 E
Mount Gravatt	**108**	27 32 S	153 5 E
Mount Hagen	**135**	5 52 S	144 16 E
Mount Hope, N.S.W., Austral.	**141**	32 51 S	145 51 E
Mount Hope, S.A., Austral.	**139**	34 7 S	135 23 E
Mount Hope, U.S.A.	**156**	37 52N	81 9W
Mount Horeb	**158**	43 0N	89 42W
Mount Howitt	**139**	26 31 S	142 16 E
Mount Isa	**138**	20 42 S	139 26 E
Mount Ive	**140**	32 25 S	136 5 E
Mount Keith	**137**	27 15 S	120 30 E
Mount Kisco	**162**	41 12N	73 44W
Mount Laguna	**163**	32 52N	116 25W
Mount Larcom	**138**	23 48 S	150 59 E
Mount Lavinia	**93**	6 50N	79 50 E
Mount Lofty Ra.	**133**	34 35 S	139 5 E
Mount McKinley Nat. Pk.	**147**	64 0N	150 0W
Mount Magnet	**137**	28 2 S	117 47 E
Mount Manara	**140**	32 29 S	143 58 E
Mount Margaret	**139**	26 54 S	143 21 E
Mount Maunganui	**142**	37 40 S	176 14 E
Mount Monger	**137**	31 0 S	122 0 E
Mount Morgan	**138**	23 40 S	150 25 E
Mount Morris	**156**	42 43N	77 50W
Mount Mulligan	**138**	16 45 S	144 47 E
Mount Narryer	**137**	26 30 S	115 55 E
Mount Newman	**136**	23 18 S	119 45 E
Mount Nicholas	**137**	22 54 S	120 27 E
Mount Oxide	**138**	19 30 S	139 29 E
Mount Pearl	**151**	47 31N	52 47W
Mount Penn	**162**	40 20N	75 54W
Mount Perry	**139**	25 13 S	151 42 E
Mount Phillips	**137**	24 25 S	116 15 E
Mount Pleasant, Iowa, U.S.A.	**158**	41 0N	91 35W
Mount Pleasant, Mich., U.S.A.	**156**	43 35N	84 47W
Mount Pleasant, S.C., U.S.A.	**157**	32 45N	79 48W
Mount Pleasant, Tenn., U.S.A.	**157**	35 31N	87 11W
Mount Pleasant, Tex., U.S.A.	**159**	33 5N	95 0W
Mount Pleasant, Ut., U.S.A.	**160**	39 40N	111 29W
Mount Pocono	**162**	41 8N	75 21W
Mount Rainier Nat. Park.	**160**	46 50N	121 43W
Mount Revelstoke Nat. Park	**152**	51 5N	118 30W
Mount Robson	**152**	52 56N	119 15W
Mount Robson Prov. Park	**152**	53 0N	119 0W
Mount Samson	**108**	27 18 S	152 51 E
Mount Sandiman	**137**	24 25 S	115 30 E
Mount Shasta	**160**	41 20N	122 18W
Mount Somers	**143**	43 45 S	171 27 E
Mount Sterling, Ill., U.S.A.	**158**	40 0N	90 40W
Mount Sterling, Ky., U.S.A.	**158**	38 0N	84 0W
Mount Surprise	**138**	18 10 S	144 17 E
Mount Talbot	**38**	53 31N	8 18W
Mount Tom Price	**137**	22 50 S	117 40 E
Mount Upton	**162**	42 26N	75 23W
Mount Vernon, Austral.	**137**	24 15 S	118 15 E
Mount Vernon, D.C., U.S.A.	**162**	38 47N	77 10W
Mount Vernon, Ill., U.S.A.	**162**	38 17N	88 57W
Mount Vernon, Ind., U.S.A.	**158**	38 17N	88 57W
Mount Vernon, N.Y., U.S.A.	**156**	40 57N	73 49W
Mount Vernon, Ohio, U.S.A.	**156**	40 20N	82 30W
Mount Vernon, Wash., U.S.A.	**160**	48 27N	122 18W
Mount Victor	**140**	32 11 S	139 44 E
Mount Whaleback	**132**	23 18 S	119 44 E
Mount Willoughby	**139**	27 58 S	134 8 E
Mountain Ash	**31**	51 42N	3 22W
Mountain Center	**163**	33 42N	116 44W
Mountain City, Nev., U.S.A.	**160**	41 54N	116 0W
Mountain City, Tenn., U.S.A.	**157**	36 30N	81 50W
Mountain Dale	**162**	41 41N	74 32W
Mountain Grove	**159**	37 5N	92 20W
Mountain Home, Ark., U.S.A.	**159**	36 20N	92 25W
Mountain Home, Idaho, U.S.A.	**160**	43 11N	115 45W
Mountain Iron	**158**	47 30N	92 87W
Mountain Park.	**152**	52 50N	117 15W
Mountain View, Ark., U.S.A.	**159**	35 52N	92 10W
Mountain View, Calif., U.S.A.	**161**	37 26N	122 5W
Mountain Village	**147**	62 10N	163 50W
Mountainair	**161**	34 35N	106 15W
Mountcharles	**38**	54 37N	8 12W
Mountfield	**38**	54 34N	7 10W
Mountmellick	**39**	53 7N	7 20W
Mountnorris	**38**	54 15N	6 29W
Mountnorris B.	**136**	11 25 S	132 45 E
Mountrath	**39**	53 0N	7 30W
Mounts Bay	**30**	50 3N	5 27W
Mountsorrel	**28**	52 43N	1 9W
Mountvernon	**152**	48 25N	122 20W
Mouping	**107**	37 24N	121 35 E
Moura, Austral.	**138**	24 35 S	149 58 E
Moura, Brazil	**174**	1 25 S	61 45W
Moura, Port.	**57**	38 7N	7 30W
Mourão	**57**	38 22N	7 22W
Mourdi, Depression du	**117**	18 10N	23 0 E
Mourdiah	**120**	14 35N	7 25W
Moure, La	**158**	46 27N	98 17W
Mourenx	**44**	43 23N	0 36W
Mouri	**121**	5 6N	1 14W
Mourilyan	**138**	17 35 S	146 3 E
Mourmelon-le-Grand	**43**	49 8N	4 22 E
Mourne Mts.	**38**	54 10N	6 0W
Mourne, R.	**38**	54 45N	7 39W
Mouroubra	**137**	29 42 S	117 52 E
Mourzouq	**119**	25 53N	14 10W
Mousa I.	**36**	60 0N	1 10W
Mouscron	**47**	50 45N	3 12 E
Moussoro	**117**	13 50N	16 35 E
Mouthe	**43**	46 44N	6 12 E
Moutier	**50**	47 16N	7 21 E
Moutiers	**45**	45 29N	6 31 E
Mouting	**108**	25 22N	101 32 E
Moutong	**103**	0 28N	121 13 E
Mouy	**43**	49 18N	2 20 E
Mouzáki	**68**	39 25N	21 37 E
Movas	**164**	28 10N	109 25W
Moville	**38**	55 11N	7 3W
Moxhe	**47**	50 38N	5 5 E
Moxotó, R.	**170**	9 19 S	38 14W
Moy, Inverness, U.K.	**37**	57 22N	4 3W
Moy, Ulster, U.K.	**38**	54 27N	6 40W
Moy, R.	**38**	54 5N	8 50W
Moyagee	**137**	27 48 S	117 48 E
Moyahua	**164**	21 16N	103 10W
Moyale, Ethiopia	**123**	3 34N	39 4 E
Moyale, Kenya	**126**	3 30N	39 0 E
Moyamba	**120**	8 15N	12 30W
Moyasta	**39**	52 40N	9 31W
Moycullen	**39**	53 20N	9 10W
Moyie	**152**	49 17N	115 50W
Moyle □	**38**	55 10N	6 15W
Moylett	**38**	53 57N	7 7W
Moynalty	**38**	53 48N	6 52W
Moyne	**39**	52 45N	7 43W
Moyobamba	**174**	6 0 S	77 0W
Moyvalley	**38**	53 26N	6 55W
Moza	**90**	31 48N	35 8 E
Mozambique = Moçambique	**125**	15 3 S	40 42 E
Mozambique ■	**129**	19 0 S	35 0 E
Mozambique Chan.	**129**	20 0 S	39 0 E
Mozdok	**83**	43 45N	44 48 E
Mozhaisk	**81**	55 30N	36 2 E
Mozhga	**84**	56 26N	52 15 E
Mozirje	**63**	46 22N	14 58 E
Mozua	**126**	3 57N	24 2 E
Mozyr	**80**	52 0N	29 15 E
Mpanda	**126**	6 23 S	31 40 E
Mpanda □	**126**	6 23 S	31 40 E
Mpésoba	**120**	12 31N	5 39W
Mpika	**127**	11 51 S	31 25 E
Mpraeso	**121**	6 50N	0 50W
Mpulungu	**127**	8 51 S	31 5 E
Mpwapwa	**124**	6 30 S	36 30 E
Mpwapwa □	**126**	6 30 S	36 20 E
Mragowo	**54**	53 57N	21 18 E
Mrakovo	**84**	52 43N	56 38 E
Mramor	**66**	43 20N	21 45 E
Mrhaïer	**119**	33 55N	5 58 E
Mrimina	**118**	29 50N	7 9W
Mrkonjić Grad	**66**	44 26N	17 4 E
Mrkopalj	**63**	45 21N	14 52 E
Mrocza	**54**	53 16N	17 35 E
Msab, Oued en	**119**	32 35N	5 20 E
Msaken	**119**	35 49N	10 33 E
M'Salu, R.	**127**	12 25 S	39 15 E
Msambansovu, mt.	**127**	15 50 S	30 3 E
M'sila	**119**	35 46N	4 30 E
Msoro	**125**	13 35 S	31 50 E
Msta, R.	**80**	58 30N	33 30 E
Mstislavl	**80**	54 0N	31 50 E
Mszana Dolna	**54**	49 41N	20 5 E
Mszczonów	**54**	51 58N	20 33 E
Mtama	**127**	10 17 S	39 21 E
Mtilikwe, R.	**127**	21 0 S	31 12 E
Mtsensk	**81**	53 25N	36 30 E
Mtskheta	**83**	41 52N	44 45 E
Mtwara	**124**	10 20 S	40 20 E
Mtwara □	**126**	1 0 S	39 0 E
Mtwara-Mikindani	**127**	10 20 S	40 20 E
Mu Gia, Deo	**100**	17 40N	105 47 E
Mu Ness	**36**	60 41N	0 50W
Mu, R.	**98**	21 56N	95 38 E
Muaná	**170**	1 25 S	49 15W
Muanda	**124**	6 0 S	12 20 E
Muang Chiang Rai	**100**	19 52N	99 50 E
Muang Kalasin	**101**	16 26N	103 30 E
Muang Lampang	**101**	18 16N	99 32 E
Muang Lamphun	**100**	18 40N	98 53 E
Muang Nan	**101**	18 52N	100 42 E
Muang Phetchabun	**101**	16 23N	101 12 E
Muang Phichit	**101**	16 29N	100 21 E
Muang Ubon	**101**	15 15N	104 50 E
Muang Yasothon	**101**	15 50N	104 10 E
Muar	**101**	2 3N	102 34 E
Muar, R.	**101**	2 15N	102 48 E
Muarabungo	**102**	1 40 S	101 10 E
Muaradjuloi	**102**	0 12 S	114 3 E
Muaraenim	**102**	3 40 S	103 50 E
Muarakaman	**102**	0 2 S	116 45 E
Muaratebo	**102**	1 30 S	102 26 E
Muaratembesi	**102**	1 42 S	103 2 E
Muaratewe	**102**	0 50 S	115 0 E
Mubairik	**92**	23 22N	39 8 E
Mubarakpur	**95**	26 12N	83 24 E
Mubende	**126**	0 33N	31 22 E
Mubi	**121**	10 18N	13 16 E
Mubur, P.	**101**	3 20N	106 12 E
Mucajaí, Serra do	**174**	2 23N	61 10W
Much Dewchurch	**28**	51 58N	2 45W
Much Marcle	**28**	51 59N	2 27W
Much Wenlock	**28**	52 36N	2 34W
Muchalls	**37**	57 2N	2 10W
Mücheln	**48**	51 18N	11 49 E
Muchinga Mts.	**127**	11 30 S	31 30 E
Muchkapskiy	**81**	51 52N	42 28 E
Mŭcin	**70**	45 16N	28 8 E
Muck, I.	**36**	56 50N	6 15W
Muckadilla	**139**	26 35 S	148 23 E
Muckle Roe I.	**36**	60 22N	1 22W
Muckross Hd.	**38**	54 37N	8 35W
Mucubela	**129**	16 53 S	37 49 E
Mucugê	**171**	13 5 S	37 49 E
Mucuri	**171**	18 0 S	40 0W
Mucurici	**171**	18 6 S	40 31W
Mud I.	**108**	27 20 S	153 14 E
Mud L.	**160**	40 15N	120 15W
Mudanya	**82**	40 25N	28 50 E
Muddy, R.	**161**	38 30N	110 55W
Mudgee	**141**	32 32 S	149 31 E
Mudhnib	**92**	25 50N	44 18 E
Mudjatik, R.	**153**	56 1N	107 36W
Mudon	**98**	16 15N	97 44 E
Muecate	**127**	14 55 S	39 34 E
Muêda	**127**	11 36 S	39 28 E
Muela, La	**58**	41 36N	1 7W
Mueller Ra., Mts.	**136**	18 18 S	126 46 E
Muerto, Mar	**165**	16 10N	94 10W
Muff	**38**	55 4N	7 16W
Mufindi □	**127**	8 30 S	35 20 E
Mufou Shan	**109**	29 15N	114 20 E
Mufulira	**127**	12 32 S	28 15 E
Mufumbiro Range	**126**	1 25 S	29 30 E
Mugardos	**56**	43 27N	8 15W
Muge	**57**	39 3N	8 40W
Muge, R.	**57**	39 15N	8 18W
Múggia	**63**	45 36N	13 47 E
Mugi	**110**	33 40N	134 25 E
Mugia	**56**	43 3N	9 17W
Mugila, Mts.	**126**	7 0 S	28 50 E
Muğla	**92**	37 15N	28 28 E
Múglizh	**67**	42 37N	25 32 E
Mugu	**95**	29 45N	82 30 E
Muhammad Qol	**122**	20 53N	37 9 E
Muhammad Râs	**122**	27 50N	34 0 E
Muhammadabad	**95**	26 4N	83 25 E
Muharraqa = Sa'ad	**90**	31 28N	34 33 E
Muhesi, R.	**126**	6 40 S	35 5 E
Muheza □	**126**	5 0 S	39 0 E
Mühldorf	**49**	48 14N	12 23 E
Mühlhausen	**48**	51 12N	10 29 E
Mühlig-Hofmann-fjella	**13**	72 30 S	5 0 E
Muhutwe	**126**	1 35 S	31 45 E
Mui Bai Bung	**101**	8 35N	104 42 E
Mui Ron	**101**	18 7N	106 27 E
Muiden	**46**	52 20N	5 4 E
Muine Bheag	**39**	52 42N	6 59W
Muiños	**56**	41 58N	7 59W
Muir, L.	**137**	34 30 S	116 40 E
Muir of Ord	**37**	57 30N	4 35W
Muirdrum	**35**	56 31N	2 40W
Muirkirk	**35**	55 31N	4 6W
Muja	**123**	12 2N	39 30 E
Mukachevo	**80**	48 27N	22 45 E
Mukah	**102**	2 55N	112 5 E
Mukalla	**91**	14 33N	49 2 E
Mukawwa, Geziret	**122**	23 55N	35 53 E
Mukdahan	**100**	16 32N	104 43 E
Mukden = Shenyang	**107**	41 48N	123 27 E

Mukeiras **91** 13 59N 45 52 E
Mukhtolovo **81** 55 29N 43 15 E
Mukinbudin **137** 30 55 S 118 5 E
Mukombwe **127** 15 48 S 26 32 E
Mukomuko **102** 2 20 S 101 10 E
Mukomwenze **126** 6 49 S 27 15 E
Mukry **85** 37 54N 65 12 E
Muktsar **94** 30 30N 74 30 E
Muktsar Bhatinda **94** 30 15N 74 57 E
Mukur **94** 32 50N 67 50 E
Mukutawa, R. **153** 53 10N 97 24W
Mukwela **127** 17 0 S 26 40 E
Mula **59** 38 3N 1 33W
Mula, R. **96** 19 16N 74 20 E
Mulanay **103** 13 30N 122 30 E
Mulange **126** 3 40 S 27 10 E
Mulatas, Arch. de las **166** 6 51N 78 31W
Mulchén **172** 37 45 S 72 20W
Mulde, R. **48** 50 55N 12 42 E
Mule Creek **158** 43 19N 104 8W
Muleba **126** 1 50 S 31 37 E
Muleba □ **126** 2 0 S 31 30 E
Mulegé **164** 26 53N 112 1W
Mulegns **51** 46 32N 9 38 E
Mulengchen **107** 44 32N 130 14 E
Muleshoe **159** 34 17N 102 42W
Mulga Valley **140** 31 8 S 141 3 E
Mulgathing **139** 30 15 S 134 0 E
Mulgrave **151** 45 38N 61 31W
Mulgrave I. **135** 10 5 S 142 10 E
Mulhacén **59** 37 4N 3 20W
Mülheim **48** 51 26N 6 53W
Mulhouse **43** 47 40N 7 20 E
Muli, China **99** 28 21N 100 40 E
Muli, China **108** 27 50N 101 15 E
Mull Head **37** 59 23N 2 53W
Mull I. **34** 56 27N 6 0W
Mull, Ross of, dist. **34** 56 20N 6 15W
Mull, Sound of **34** 56 30N 5 50W
Mullagh **39** 53 13N 8 25W
Mullaghareirk Mts. **39** 52 20N 9 10W
Mullaittvu **97** 9 15N 80 55 E
Mullardoch L. **36** 57 30N 5 0W
Mullen **158** 42 5N 101 0W
Mullengudgery **141** 31 43 S 147 29 E
Mullens **156** 37 34N 81 22W
Muller, Pegunungan **102** 0 30N 113 30 E
Muller Ra. **138** 5 30 S 143 0 E
Mullet Pen. **38** 54 10N 10 2W
Mullewa **137** 28 29 S 115 30 E
Mullheim **49** 47 48N 7 37 E
Mulligan, R. **138** 26 40 S 139 0 E
Mullin **159** 31 33N 98 38W
Mullinahone **39** 52 30N 7 31W
Mullinavat **39** 52 23N 7 10W
Mullingar **38** 53 31N 7 20W
Mullins **157** 34 12N 79 15W
Mullion **30** 50 1N 5 15W
Mullsjö **73** 57 56N 13 55 E
Mullumbimby **139** 28 30 S 153 30 E
Mulobezi **127** 16 45 S 25 7 E
Mulrany **38** 53 54N 9 47W
Mulroy B. **38** 55 15N 7 45W
Mulshi L. **96** 18 30N 73 20 E
Multai **96** 21 39N 78 15 E
Multan **94** 30 15N 71 30 E
Multan □ **94** 30 29N 72 29 E
Multrå **72** 63 10N 17 24 E
Mulumbe, Mts. **127** 8 40 S 27 30 E
Mulungushi Dam **127** 14 48 S 28 48 E
Mulvane **159** 37 30N 97 15W
Mulwad **122** 18 45N 30 39 E
Mulwala **141** 35 59 S 146 0 E
Mumbles **31** 51 34N 4 0W
Mumbles Hd. **31** 51 33N 4 0W
Mumbwa **125** 15 0 S 27 0 E
Mumeng **135** 7 1 S 146 37 E
Mumra **83** 45 45N 47 41 E
Mun **101** 15 17N 103 0 E
Mun, R. **100** 15 19N 105 30 E
Muna, I. **103** 5 0 S 122 30 E
Muna Sotuta **165** 20 29N 89 43W
Munawwar **95** 32 47N 74 27 E
Münchberg **49** 50 11N 11 48 E
Müncheberg **48** 52 30N 14 9 E
München **49** 48 8N 11 33 E
Munchen-Gladbach = Mönchengladbach **48** 51 12N 6 23 E
Muncho Lake **152** 59 0N 125 50W
Munchŏn **107** 39 14N 127 19 E
Münchwilen **51** 47 38N 8 59 E
Muncie **156** 40 10N 85 20W
Mundakayam **97** 9 30N 76 32 E
Mundala, Puncak **103** 4 30 S 141 0 E
Mundare **152** 53 35N 112 20W
Munday **159** 33 26N 99 39W
Münden **48** 51 25N 9 42 E
Mundesley **29** 52 53N 1 24 E
Mundiwindi **136** 23 47 S 120 9 E
Mundo Novo **171** 11 50 S 40 29W
Mundo, R. **59** 38 30N 2 15W
Mundra **94** 22 54N 69 26 E
Mundrabilla **137** 31 52 S 127 51 E
Munera **59** 39 2N 2 29W
Muneru, R. **96** 16 45N 80 3 E
Mungallala **139** 26 25 S 147 34 E
Mungallala Cr. **139** 28 53 S 147 5 E
Mungana **138** 17 8 S 144 27 E
Mungaoli **94** 24 24N 78 7 E
Mungari **127** 17 12 S 33 42 E
Mungbere **124** 2 36N 28 28 E
Mungindi **139** 28 58 S 149 1 E
Munhango **125** 12 10 S 18 38 E
Munhango R. **125** 11 30 S 19 30 E
Munich = München **49** 48 8N 11 35 E
Munising **156** 46 25N 86 39W
Munjiye **122** 18 47N 41 20W
Munka-Ljungby **73** 56 16N 12 58 E
Munkedal **73** 58 28N 11 40 E
Munkfors **72** 59 50N 13 30 E
Muñoz Gamero, Pen. **176** 52 30 S 73 5 E
Munro **141** 37 56 S 147 11 E
Munroe L. **153** 59 13N 98 35W
Munsan **107** 37 51N 126 48 E
Munshiganj **98** 23 33N 90 32 E
Münsingen **50** 46 52N 7 32 E
Munster **43** 48 2N 7 8 E
Münster, Niedersachsen, Ger. **48** 52 59N 10 5 E
Münster, Nordrhein-Westfalen, Ger. **48** 51 58N 7 37 E
Münster, Switz. **51** 46 30N 8 17 E
Munster □ **39** 52 20N 8 40W
Muntadgin **137** 31 45 S 118 33 E
Muntele Mare **70** 46 30N 23 12 E
Muntok **102** 2 5 S 105 10 E
Muon Pak Beng **101** 19 51N 101 4 E
Muong Beng **100** 20 23N 101 46 E
Muong Boum **100** 22 24N 102 49 E
Muong Er **100** 20 49N 104 1 E
Muong Hai **100** 21 3N 101 49 E
Muong Hiem **100** 20 5N 103 22 E
Muong Houn **100** 20 8N 101 23 E
Muong Hung **100** 20 56N 103 53 E
Muong Kau **100** 15 6N 105 47 E
Muong Khao **100** 19 47N 103 29 E
Muong Khoua **100** 21 5N 102 31 E
Muong La **101** 20 52N 102 5 E
Muong Liep **100** 18 29N 101 40 E
Muong May **100** 14 49N 106 56 E
Muong Ngeun **100** 20 36N 101 3 E
Muong Ngoi **100** 20 43N 102 41 E
Muong Nhie **100** 22 12N 102 28 E
Muong Nong **100** 16 22N 106 30 E
Muong Ou Tay **100** 22 7N 101 48 E
Muong Oua **100** 18 18N 101 20 E
Muong Pak Bang **100** 19 54N 101 8 E
Muong Penn **100** 20 13N 103 52 E
Muong Phalane **100** 16 39N 105 34 E
Muong Phieng **100** 19 6N 101 32 E
Muong Phine **100** 16 32N 106 2 E
Muong Sai **100** 20 42N 101 59 E
Muong Saiapoun **100** 18 24N 101 31 E
Muong Sen **100** 19 24N 104 8 E
Muong Sing **100** 21 11N 101 9 E
Muong Son **100** 20 27N 103 19 E
Muong Soui **100** 19 33N 102 52 E
Muong Va **100** 21 53N 102 19 E
Muong Xia **100** 20 19N 104 50 E
Muonio **74** 67 57N 23 40 E
Muonio älv **74** 67 48N 23 25 E
Muotathal **51** 46 58N 8 46 E
Muotohora **142** 38 18 S 177 40 E
Mupa **125** 16 5 S 15 50 E
Muqaddam, Wadi **123** 17 0N 32 0 E
Mur-de-Bretagne **42** 48 12N 3 0W
Mur, R. **52** 47 7N 13 55 E
Mura, R. **63** 46 37N 16 9 E
Murallón, Cuerro **176** 49 55 S 73 30W
Muralto **51** 46 11N 8 49 E
Muranda **126** 1 52 S 29 20 E
Murang'a **126** 0 45 S 37 9 E
Murashi **81** 59 30N 49 0 E
Murat **44** 45 7N 2 53 E
Murau **52** 47 6N 14 10 E
Muravera **64** 39 25N 9 35 E
Murça **56** 41 24N 7 28W
Murchison **143** 41 49 S 172 21 E
Murchison Downs **137** 26 45 S 118 55 E
Murchison Falls = Kabarega Falls **126** 2 15N 31 38 E
Murchison House **137** 27 39 S 114 14 E
Murchison Mts. **143** 45 13 S 167 23 E
Murchison, oilfield* **19** 61 25N 1 40 E
Murchison, R. **137** 26 45 S 116 15 E
Murchison Ra. **138** 20 0 S 134 10 E
Murchison Rapids **127** 15 55 S 34 35 E
Murcia **59** 38 2N 1 10W
Murcia □ **59** 37 50N 1 30W
Murdo **158** 43 56N 100 43W
Murdoch Pt. **138** 14 37 S 144 55 E
Murdock Hill **109** 34 59 S 138 55 E
Mure, La **45** 44 55N 5 48 E
Mureş □ **70** 46 45N 24 40 E
Mureşul, R. **70** 46 15N 20 13 E
Muret **44** 43 30N 1 20 E
Murfatlar **70** 44 10N 28 26 E
Murfreesboro **157** 35 50N 86 21W
Murg **51** 47 8N 9 13 E
Murgab **85** 38 10N 73 59 E
Murgeni **70** 46 12N 28 1 E
Murgenthal **50** 47 16N 7 50 E
Murgon **139** 26 15 S 151 54 E
Murgoo **137** 27 24 S 116 28 E
Muri **51** 47 17N 8 21 E
Muriaé **173** 21 8 S 42 23W
Murias de Paredes **56** 42 52N 6 19W
Murici **170** 9 19 S 35 56W
Muriel Mine **127** 17 14 S 30 40 E
Muritiba **171** 12 55 S 39 15W
Murits see **48** 53 25N 12 40 E
Murjo Mt. **103** 6 36 S 110 53 E
Murka **126** 3 27 S 38 0 E
Murmansk **78** 68 57N 33 10 E
Murmerwoude **46** 53 18N 6 0 E
Murnau **49** 47 40N 11 11 E
Muro, France **45** 42 34N 8 54 E
Muro, Spain **58** 39 45N 3 3 E
Muro, C. di **45** 41 44N 8 37 E
Muro Lucano **65** 40 45N 15 30 E
Murom **81** 55 35N 42 3 E
Muroran **112** 42 25N 141 0 E
Muros **56** 42 45N 9 5W
Muros y de Noya, Ria de **56** 42 45N 9 0W
Muroto **110** 33 18N 134 9 E
Muroto-Misaki **110** 33 15N 134 10 E
Murowana Gosślina **54** 52 35N 17 0 E
Murphy **160** 43 11N 116 33W
Murphys **163** 38 8N 120 28W
Murphysboro **159** 37 50N 89 20W
Murrat **122** 18 51N 29 33 E
Murray, Ky., U.S.A. **157** 36 40N 88 20W
Murray, Utah, U.S.A. **160** 40 41N 111 58W
Murray Bridge **140** 35 6 S 139 14 E
Murray Downs **138** 21 4 S 134 40 E
Murray Harb. **151** 46 0N 62 28W
Murray, L., P.N.G. **135** 7 0 S 141 35 E
Murray, L., U.S.A. **157** 34 8N 81 30W
Murray, R., S. Australia, Austral. **140** 35 20 S 139 22 E
Murray, R., W. Australia, Austral. **133** 32 33 S 115 45 E
Murray, R., Can. **152** 56 11N 120 45W
Murraysburg **128** 31 58 S 23 47 E
Murree **94** 33 56N 73 28 E
Murrieta **163** 33 33N 117 13W
Murrin Murrin **137** 28 50 S 121 45 E
Murrough **39** 53 7N 9 18W
Murrumbidgee, R. **140** 34 40 S 143 0 E
Murrumburrah **141** 34 32 S 148 22 E
Murrurundi **141** 31 42 S 150 51 E
Murshid **122** 21 40N 31 10 E
Murshidabad **95** 24 11N 88 19 E
Murska Sobota **63** 46 39N 16 12 E
Murtazapur **96** 20 40N 77 25 E
Murten **50** 46 56N 6 7 E
Murten-see **50** 46 56N 7 4 E
Murtle L. **152** 52 8N 119 38W
Murtoa **140** 36 35 S 142 28 E
Murton **33** 54 51N 1 22W
Murtosa **56** 40 44N 8 40W
Muru **123** 6 36N 29 16 E
Murungu **126** 4 12 S 31 10 E
Murupara **142** 38 28 S 176 42 E
Murwara **95** 23 46N 80 28 E
Murwillumbah **139** 28 18 S 153 27 E
Mürz, R. **52** 47 30N 15 25 E
Mürzzuschlag **52** 47 36N 15 41 E
Muş **92** 38 45N 41 30 E
Musa, Gebel (Sinai) **122** 28 32N 33 59 E
Musa Khel **94** 30 29N 69 52 E
Musa Qala (Musa Kala) **93** 32 20N 64 50 E
Musa, R. **135** 9 3 S 148 55 E
Musaffargarh **93** 30 10N 71 10 E
Musairik, Wadi **122** 19 30N 43 10 E
Musala, I. **102** 1 41N 98 28 E
Musalla, mt. **67** 42 13N 23 37 E
Musan **107** 42 12N 129 12 E
Musangu **127** 10 28 S 23 55 E
Musasa **126** 3 25 S 31 30 E
Musashino **111** 35 42N 139 34 E
Muscat = Masqat **93** 23 37N 58 36 E
Muscat & Oman = Oman **91** 23 0N 58 0 E
Muscatine **158** 41 25N 91 5W
Musel **56** 43 34N 5 42W
Musetula **127** 14 28 S 24 1 E
Musgrave Ras. **137** 26 0 S 132 0 E
Mushie **124** 2 56 S 17 4 E
Mushin **121** 6 32N 3 21 E
Musi, R., India **96** 17 10N 79 25 E
Musi, R., Indon. **102** 2 55 S 103 40 E
Muskeg, R. **152** 60 20N 123 20W
Muskegon **156** 43 15N 86 17W
Muskegon Hts. **156** 43 12N 86 17W
Muskegon, R. **156** 43 25N 86 0W
Muskogee **159** 35 50N 95 25W
Muskwa, R. **152** 58 47N 122 48W
Musmar **122** 18 6N 35 40 E
Musofu **127** 13 30 S 29 0 E
Musoma **126** 1 30 S 33 48 E
Musoma □ **126** 1 50 S 34 30 E
Musquaro, L. **151** 50 38N 61 5W
Musquodoboit Harbour **151** 44 50N 63 9W
Mussau I. **135** 1 30 S 149 40 E
Musselburgh **35** 55 57N 3 3W
Musselkanaal **46** 52 57N 7 0 E
Musselshell, R. **160** 46 30N 108 15W
Mussidan **44** 45 2N 0 22 E
Mussomeli **64** 37 35N 13 43 E
Musson **47** 49 33N 5 42 E
Mussooree **94** 30 27N 78 6 E
Mussuco **128** 17 2 S 19 3 E
Mustafa Kemalpaşa **92** 40 3N 28 25 E
Mustajidda **92** 26 30N 41 50 E
Mustang **95** 29 10N 83 55 E
Mustapha, C. **119** 36 55N 11 3 E
Musters, L. **176** 45 20 S 69 25W
Musudan **107** 40 50N 129 43 E
Muswellbrook **141** 32 16 S 150 56 E
Muszyna **53** 49 22N 20 55 E
Mût **122** 25 28N 28 58 E
Mut **92** 36 40N 33 28 E
Mutan Chiang, R. **107** 46 18N 129 31 E
Mutanchiang **107** 44 40N 129 35 E
Mutanda, Mozam. **129** 21 0 S 33 34 E
Mutanda, Zambia **127** 12 15 S 26 13 E
Muthill **35** 56 20N 3 50W
Mutis **174** 1 4N 77 25W
Mutooroo **140** 32 26 S 140 55 E
Mutshatsha **127** 10 35 S 24 20 E
Mutsu-Wan **112** 41 5N 140 55 E
Muttaburra **138** 22 38 S 144 29 E
Muttama **141** 34 46 S 148 8 E
Mutton Bay **151** 50 50N 59 2W
Mutton I. **39** 52 50N 9 31W
Mutuáli **127** 14 55 S 37 0 E
Mutung **108** 29 35N 106 51 E
Mutunópolis **171** 13 40 S 49 15W
Muvatupusha **97** 9 53N 76 35 E
Muxima **124** 9 25 S 13 52 E
Muy, Le **45** 43 28N 6 34 E
Muy Muy **166** 12 39N 85 36W
Muya **77** 56 27N 115 39 E
Muyaga **126** 3 14 S 30 33 E
Muyunkum, Peski **85** 44 12N 71 0 E
Muzaffarabad **95** 34 25N 73 30 E
Muzaffargarh **94** 30 5N 71 14 E
Muzaffarnagar **94** 29 26N 77 40 E
Muzaffarpur **95** 26 7N 85 32 E
Muzhi **76** 65 25N 64 40 E
Muzillac **42** 47 35N 2 30W
Muzkol, Khrebet **85** 38 22N 73 20 E
Muzo **174** 5 32N 74 6W
Muzon C. **152** 54 40N 132 40W
Mvôlô **123** 6 10N 29 53 E
Mwadui **126** 3 35 S 33 40 E
Mwandi Mission **127** 17 30 S 24 51 E
Mwango **126** 6 48 S 24 12 E
Mwanza, Katanga, Congo **126** 7 55 S 26 43 E
Mwanza, Kwango, Congo **127** 5 29 S 17 43 E
Mwanza, Malawi **126** 16 58 S 24 28 E
Mwanza, Tanz. **126** 2 30 S 32 58 E
Mwanza □ **126** 2 0 S 33 0 E
Mwaya **126** 9 32 S 33 55 E
Mweelrea, Mt. **38** 53 37N 9 48W
Mweka **124** 4 50 S 21 40 E
Mwenga **126** 3 1 S 28 21 E
Mwepo **127** 11 50 S 26 10 E
Mweru, L. **127** 9 0 S 29 0 E
Mweza Range **127** 21 0 S 30 0 E
Mwimbi **127** 8 38 S 31 39 E
Mwinilunga **127** 11 43 S 24 25 E
Mwinilunga, Mt. **127** 11 43 S 24 25 E
My Tho **101** 10 29N 106 23 E
Mya, O. **119** 30 46N 4 44 E
Myadh **124** 1 16N 13 10 E
Myanaung **98** 18 25N 95 10 E
Myaungmya **98** 16 30N 95 0 E
Mybster **37** 58 27N 3 24W
Myddfai **31** 51 59N 3 47W
Myddle **28** 52 49N 2 47W
Myerstown **162** 40 22N 76 18W
Myingyan **98** 21 30N 95 30 E
Myitkyina **98** 25 30N 97 26 E
Myittha, R. **98** 16 15N 94 34 E
Myjava **53** 48 41N 17 37 E
Mylor **109** 35 3 S 138 46 E
Mymensingh **98** 24 45N 90 24 E
Myndmere **158** 46 23N 97 7W
Mynydd Bach, Hills **31** 52 16N 4 6W
Mynydd Eppynt, Mts. **31** 52 4N 3 30W
Mynydd Prescelly, mt. **31** 51 57N 4 48W
Mynzhilgi, Gora **85** 43 48N 68 51 E
Myogi **101** 21 24N 96 28 E
Myrdal **71** 60 43N 7 10 E
Mýrdalsjökull **74** 63 40N 19 6W
Myrrhee **136** 36 46 S 146 17 E
Myrtle Beach **157** 33 43N 78 50W
Myrtle Creek **160** 43 0N 123 19W
Myrtle Point **160** 43 0N 124 4W
Myrtleford **141** 36 34 S 146 44 E
Myrtletown **108** 27 23 S 153 8 E
Mysen **71** 59 33N 11 20 E
Myslenice **54** 49 51N 19 57 E
Myslibórz **54** 52 55N 14 50 E
Mysłowice **54** 50 15N 19 12 E
Mysore **97** 12 17N 76 41 E
Mysore □ = Karnataka **142** 13 15N 77 0 E
Mystic **162** 41 21N 71 58W
Mystishchi **81** 55 50N 37 50 E
Myszkow **54** 50 45N 19 22 E
Mythen **51** 47 2N 8 42 E
Myton **160** 40 10N 110 2W
Mývatn **74** 65 36N 17 0W
Mze, R. **52** 49 47N 12 50 E
Mzimba **127** 11 48 S 33 33 E
Mzuzu **127** 11 30 S 33 55 E

N

N' Dioum **120** 16 31N 14 39W
Na-lang **98** 22 42N 97 33 E
Na Noi **100** 18 19N 100 43 E
Na Phao **100** 17 35N 105 44 E
Na Sam **100** 22 3N 106 37 E
Na San **100** 21 12N 104 2 E
Naaldwijk **46** 51 59N 4 13 E
Naalehu **147** 19 4N 155 35W
Na'am **123** 9 42N 28 27 E
Na'an **90** 31 53N 34 52 E
Naantali **75** 60 29N 22 2 E
Naarden **46** 52 18N 5 9 E
Naas **39** 53 12N 6 40W
Nababeep **128** 29 36 S 17 46 E
Nabadwip **95** 23 34N 88 20 E
Nabari **111** 34 37N 136 5 E

Nabas 103 11 47N 122 6 E
Nabberu, L. 137 25 30 S 120 30 E
• Naberezhnyye Chelny 84 55 42N 52 19 E
Nabesna 147 62 33N 143 10W
Nabeul 119 36 30N 10 51 E
Nabha 94 30 26N 76 14 E
Nabi Rubin 90 31 56N 34 44 E
Nabire 103 3 15 S 136 27 E
Nabisar 94 25 8N 69 40 E
Nabispi, R. 151 50 14N 62 13W
Nabiswera 126 1 27N 32 15 E
Nablus = Nābulus 90 32 14N 35 15 E
Naboomspruit 129 24 32 S 28 40 E
Nābulus 90 32 14N 35 15 E
Nabúri 127 16 53 S 38 59 E
Nacala-Velha 127 14 32 S 40 34 E
Nacaome 166 13 31N 87 30W
Nacaroa 127 14 22 S 39 56 E
Naches 160 46 48N 120 49W
Nachikatsuura 111 33 33N 135 58 E
Nachingwea 127 10 49 S 38 49 E
Nachingwea □ 127 10 30 S 38 30 E
Nachna 94 27 34N 71 41 E
Náchod 53 50 25N 16 8 E
Nacimento Res. 163 35 46N 120 53W
Nacka 72 59 17N 18 12 E
Nackara 140 32 48 S 139 12 E
Naco, Mexico 164 31 20N 109 56W
Naco, U.S.A. 161 31 24N 109 58W
Nacogdoches 159 31 33N 95 30W
Nácori Chico 164 29 39N 109 1W
Nacozari 164 30 30N 109 50W
Nadi 122 18 40N 33 41 E
Nadiad 94 22 41N 72 56 E
Nador 118 35 14N 2 58W
Nadushan 93 32 2N 53 35 E
Nadvornaya 80 48 40N 24 35 E
Nadym 76 63 35N 72 42 E
Nadym, R. 76 65 30N 73 0 E
Nærbø 71 58 40N 5 39 E
Næstved 73 55 13N 11 44 E
Nafada 121 11 8N 11 20 E
Näfels 51 47 6N 9 4 E
Nafferton 33 54 1N 0 24W
Naft Shāh 92 34 0N 45 30 E
Nafūd ad Dahy 92 22 0N 45 0 E
Nafūsah, Jabal 119 32 12N 12 30 E
Nag Hammâdi 122 26 2N 32 18 E
Naga 103 13 38N 123 15 E
Naga Hills 99 26 0N 94 30 E
Naga, Kreb en 118 24 12N 6 0W
Naga-Shima, Kagoshima, Japan 110 32 10N 130 9 E
Naga-Shima, Yamaguchi, Japan 110 33 55N 132 5 E
Nagagami, R. 150 49 40N 84 40W
Nagahama, Ehime, Japan 111 33 36N 132 29 E
Nagahama, Shiga, Japan 111 35 23N 136 16 E
Nagai Parkar 94 24 28N 70 46 E
Nagaland □ 98 26 0N 94 30 E
Nagambie 141 36 47 S 145 10 E
Nagano 111 36 40N 138 10 E
Nagano-ken □ 111 36 15N 138 0 E
Nagaoka 112 37 27N 138 50 E
Nagappattinam 97 10 46N 79 51 E
Nagar Parkar 93 24 30N 70 35 E
Nagara-Gawa, R. 111 35 1N 136 43 E
Nagari Hills 97 15 30N 79 45 E
Nagarjuna Sagar 96 16 35N 79 17 E
Nagasaki 110 32 47N 129 50 E
Nagasaki-ken □ 110 32 50N 129 40 E
Nagato 110 34 19N 131 5 E
Nagaur 94 27 15N 73 45 E
Nagbhir 96 20 34N 79 42 E
Nagchu Dzong 99 31 22N 91 54 E
Nagercoil 97 8 12N 77 33 E
Nagina 95 29 30N 78 30 E
Nagineh 93 34 20N 57 15 E
Nagold 49 48 38N 8 40 E
Nagoorin 138 24 17 S 151 15 E
Nagorsk 81 59 18N 50 48 E
Nagorum 126 4 1N 34 33 E
Nagoya 111 35 10N 136 50 E
Nagpur 96 21 8N 79 10 E
Nagrong 99 32 46N 84 16 E
Nagua 167 19 23N 69 50W
Nagyatád 53 46 14N 17 22 E
Nagyecsed 53 47 53N 22 24 E
Nagykanizsa 53 46 28N 17 0 E
Nagykörös 53 46 55N 19 48 E
Nagyléta 53 47 23N 21 55 E
Naha 112 26 13N 127 42 E
Nahalal 90 32 41N 35 12 E
Nahanni Butte 152 61 2N 123 20W
Nahanni Nat. Pk. 152 61 15N 125 0W
Naharayim 90 32 28N 35 33 E
Nahariyya 90 33 1N 35 5 E
Nahāvand 92 34 10N 48 30 E
Nahe, R. 49 49 48N 7 33 E
Nahf 90 32 56N 35 18 E
Nahîya, Wadi 122 27 37N 32 0 E
Nahlin 152 58 55N 131 38W
Nahud 122 18 12N 41 40 E
Naiapu 70 44 12N 25 47 E
Naicá 164 27 53N 105 31W
Naicam 153 52 30N 104 30W
Na'ifah 91 19 59N 50 46 E
Naila 49 50 19N 11 43 E
Nailsea 28 51 25N 2 44W
Nailsworth 28 51 41N 2 12W
Nain 151 56 34N 61 40W
*Renamed Brezhnev
Na'in 93 32 54N 53 0 E
Naini Tal 95 29 23N 79 30 E
Nainpur 93 22 30N 80 10 E
Naintré 42 46 46N 0 29 E
Naira, I. 103 4 28 S 130 0 E
Nairn 37 57 35N 3 54W
Nairn (□) 26 57 28N 3 52W
Nairn R. 37 57 32N 3 58W
Nairobi 126 1 17 S 36 48 E
Naivasha 126 0 40 S 36 30 E
Naivasha □ 126 0 40 S 36 30 E
Naivasha L. 126 0 48 S 36 20 E
Najac 44 44 14N 1 58 E
Najafābād 93 32 40N 51 15 E
Najd 92 26 30N 42 0 E
Nájera 58 42 26N 2 48W
Najerilla, R. 58 42 15N 2 45W
Najibabad 94 29 40N 78 20 E
Najin 107 42 12N 130 15 E
Naju 107 35 3N 126 43 E
Naka-Gawa, R. 111 36 20N 140 36 E
Naka-no-Shima 112 29 51N 129 46 E
Nakalagba 126 2 50N 27 58 E
Nakama 110 33 56N 130 43 E
Nakaminato 111 36 21N 140 36 E
Nakamura 110 33 0N 133 0 E
Nakanai Mts. 135 5 40 S 151 0 E
Nakano 111 36 45N 138 22 E
Nakanojō 111 36 35N 138 51 E
Nakatane 112 30 31N 130 57 E
Nakatsu 110 33 40N 131 15 E
Nakatsugawa 111 35 29N 137 30 E
Nakelele Pt. 147 21 2N 156 35W
Nakfa 123 16 40N 38 25 E
Nakhichevan, A.S.S.R. □ 79 39 14N 45 30 E
Nakhl 122 29 55N 33 43 E
Nakhl Mubarak 92 24 10N 38 10 E
Nakhodka 77 43 10N 132 45 E
Nakhon Nayok 100 14 12N 101 13 E
Nakhon Pathom 100 13 49N 100 3 E
Nakhon Phanom 100 17 23N 104 43 E
Nakhon Ratchasima (Khorat) 100 14 59N 102 12 E
Nakhon Sawan 100 15 35N 100 10 E
Nakhon Si Thammarat 100 8 29N 100 0 E
Nakhon Thai 100 17 17N 100 50 E
Nakina, B.C., Can. 152 59 12N 132 52W
Nakina, Ont., Can. 150 50 10N 86 40W
Nakło n. Noteoja 54 53 9N 17 38 E
Naknek 147 58 45N 157 0W
Nakodar 94 31 8N 75 31 E
Nakomis 127 39 19N 89 19W
Nakskov 73 54 50N 11 8 E
Näkten 72 62 48N 14 38 E
Naktong, R. 107 35 7N 128 57 E
Nakur 94 30 2N 77 32 E
Nakuru 126 0 15 S 35 5 E
Nakuru □ 126 0 15 S 35 5 E
Nakuru, L. 126 0 23 S 36 5 E
Nakusp 152 50 20N 117 45W
Nal, R. 94 27 0N 65 50 E
Nalchik 83 43 30N 43 33 E
Nälden 72 63 21N 14 14 E
Näldsjön 72 63 25N 14 15 E
Nalerigu 121 10 35N 0 25W
Nalgonda 96 17 6N 79 15 E
Nalhati 95 24 17N 87 52 E
Nalinnes 47 50 19N 4 27 E
Nallamalai Hills 97 15 30N 78 50 E
Nalón, R. 56 43 35N 6 10W
Nālūt 119 31 54N 11 0 E
Nam Can 101 8 46N 104 59 E
Nam Dinh 100 20 25N 106 5 E
Nam Du, Hon 101 9 41N 104 21 E
'Nam', gasfields 19 53 17N 3 36 E
Nam Ngum 100 18 35N 102 34 E
'Nam', oilfield 19 54 50N 4 40 E
Nam-Phan 101 10 30N 106 0 E
Nam Phong 100 16 42N 102 52 E
Nam Tha 100 20 58N 101 30 E
Nam Tok 100 14 14N 99 4 E
Nam Tso = Namu Hu 105 30 45N 90 30 E
Namacurra 125 17 30 S 36 50 E
Namakkal 97 11 13N 78 13 E
Namaland, Africa 128 26 0 S 18 0 E
Namaland, S. Afr. 128 30 0 S 18 0 E
Namangan 85 41 0N 71 40 E
Namapa 127 13 43 S 39 50 E
Namasagali 126 1 2N 33 0 E
Namatanai 135 3 40 S 152 29 E
Nambala 120 14 1N 5 58W
Namber 103 1 2 S 134 57 E
Nambour 139 26 32 S 152 58 E
Nambucca Heads 141 30 37 S 153 0 E
Namcha Barwa 105 29 40N 95 10 E
Namche Bazar 95 27 51N 86 47 E
Namchonjŏm 107 38 15N 126 26 E
Namêche 47 50 28N 5 0 E
Namecund 127 14 54 S 37 37 E
Nameh 102 2 34N 116 21 E
Nameponda 127 15 50 S 39 50 E
Namerikawa 111 36 46N 137 20 E
Námestovo 53 49 24N 19 25 E
Nametil 127 15 40 S 39 15 E
Náměšt nad Oslavou 53 49 12N 16 10 E
Namew L. 153 54 14N 101 56W
Namhsan 98 22 48N 97 42 E
Nami 101 6 2N 100 46 E
Namib Desert = Namib Woestyn 128 22 30 S 15 0 E
Namib-Woestyn 128 22 30 S 15 0 E
Namibia □ 128 22 0 S 18 9 E
Namiquipa 164 29 15N 107 25W
Namja Pass 95 30 0N 82 25 E
Namkhan 98 23 50N 97 41 E
Namlea 103 3 10 S 127 5 E
Namoi, R. 141 30 12 S 149 30 E
Namous, O. 118 30 44N 0 18W
Nampa 160 43 40N 116 40W
Nampula 127 15 6 S 39 7 E
Namrole 103 3 46 S 126 46 E
Namsen 74 64 27N 11 42 E
Namsen, R. 74 64 40N 12 45 E
Namsos 74 64 28N 11 0 E
Namtu 98 23 5N 97 28 E
Namtumbo 127 10 30 S 36 4 E
Namu 152 51 52N 127 41W
Namu Hu 105 30 45N 90 30 E
Namur 47 50 27N 4 52 E
Namur □ 47 50 17N 5 0 E
Namutoni 128 18 49 S 16 55 E
Namwala 127 15 44 S 26 30 E
Namwŏn 107 35 23N 127 23 E
Namysłow 54 51 6N 17 42 E
Nan 100 18 48N 100 46 E
Nan Ling 109 25 0N 112 30 E
Nan, R. 100 15 42N 100 9 E
Nan Shan 105 38 30N 99 0 E
Nana 70 44 17N 26 34 E
Nānā, W. 119 30 0N 15 24 E
Nanaimo 152 49 10N 124 0W
Nanam 107 41 44N 129 40 E
Nan'an 109 24 58N 118 23 E
Nanango 139 26 40 S 152 0 E
Nanao 109 23 26N 117 1 E
Nanch'ang 109 28 40N 115 50 E
Nanchang, Fukien, China 109 24 26N 117 18 E
Nanchang, Hupei, China 109 31 47N 111 42 E
Nanch'eng 109 27 33N 116 35 E
Nancheng = Hanchung 106 33 10N 107 2 E
Nanchiang 108 32 21N 106 50 E
Nanchiao 108 22 2N 100 15 E
Nanchien 106 25 5N 100 30 E
Nanching 109 32 3N 118 47 E
Nanchishan Liehtao 108 27 28N 121 4 E
Nanch'uan 108 29 7N 107 16 E
Nanch'ung 108 30 50N 106 4 E
Nancy 43 48 42N 6 12 E
Nanda Devi, Mt. 95 30 30N 80 30 E
Nandan 110 34 10N 134 42 E
Nander 96 19 10N 77 20 E
Nandewar Ra. 139 30 15 S 150 35 E
Nandi □ 126 0 15N 35 0 E
Nandikotkur 97 15 52N 78 18 E
Nandura 96 20 52N 76 25 E
Nandurbar 96 21 20N 74 15 E
Nandyal 97 15 30N 78 30 E
Nanfeng 109 27 10N 116 24 E
Nanga 137 26 7 S 113 45 E
Nanga Eboko 121 4 41N 12 22 E
Nanga Parbat, mt. 95 35 10N 74 35 E
Nangade 127 11 5 S 39 36 E
Nangapinoh 102 0 20 S 111 14 E
Nangarhar □ 93 34 20N 70 0 E
Nangatajap 102 1 32 S 110 34 E
Nangeya Mts. 126 3 30N 33 30 E
Nangis 43 48 33N 3 0 E
Nangodi 121 10 58N 0 42W
Nangola 120 12 41N 6 35W
Nangwarry 140 37 33 S 140 48 E
Nanhsien 109 29 22N 112 25 E
Nanhsiung 109 25 10N 114 18 E
Nanhua 108 25 15N 101 20 E
Nanhui 109 31 3N 121 46 E
Nani Hu 109 31 10N 118 55 E
Nanjangud 97 12 6N 76 43 E
Nanjeko 127 5 31 S 23 30 E
Nanjirinji 127 9 41 S 39 5 E
Nankana Sahib 94 31 27N 73 38 E
Nank'ang 109 25 38N 114 45 E
Nanking = Nanching 109 32 5N 118 45 E
Nankoku 110 33 29N 133 38 E
Nankung 106 37 22N 115 20 E
Nanling 109 30 56N 118 19 E
Nannine 137 26 51 S 118 18 E
Nanning 108 22 48N 108 20 E
Nannup 137 33 59 S 115 48 E
Nanpa 108 32 13N 104 51 E
Nanp'an Chiang, R. 108 25 0N 106 11 E
Nanpara 95 27 52N 81 33 E
Nanp'i 106 38 4N 116 34 E
Nanp'ing, Fukien, China 109 26 38N 118 10 E
Nanp'ing, Hupeh, China 109 29 55N 112 2 E
Nanpu 108 31 19N 106 2 E
Nanripe 127 13 52 S 38 52 E
Nansei-Shotō 112 26 0N 128 0 E
Nansen Sd. 12 81 0N 91 0W
Nansio 126 2 3 S 33 4 E
Nanson 137 28 35 S 114 45 E
Nant 44 44 1N 3 18 E
Nantes 42 47 12N 1 33W
Nanteuil-le-Haudouin 43 49 9N 2 48 E
Nantiat 44 46 1N 1 11 E
Nanticoke 162 41 12N 76 1W
Nanticoke, R. 162 38 16N 75 56W
Nanton, Can. 152 50 21N 113 46W
Nanton, China 108 24 59N 107 32 E
Nantua 45 46 10N 5 35 E
Nantucket 162 41 17N 70 6W
Nantucket I. 155 41 16N 70 3W
Nantucket Sd. 162 41 30N 70 15W
Nant'ung 109 32 0N 120 55 E
Nantwich 32 53 5N 2 31W
Nanuque 171 17 50 S 40 21W
Nanutarra 136 22 32 S 115 30 E
Nanyang 106 33 0N 112 32 E
Nan'yō 110 34 3N 131 49 E
Nanyüan 106 39 48N 116 24 E
Nanyuki 126 0 2N 37 4 E
Nao, C. de la 59 38 44N 0 14 E
Nao Chou Tao 109 20 55N 110 35 E
Nao, La, Cabo de 59 38 44N 0 14 E
Naococane L. 151 52 50N 70 45W
Naogaon 98 24 52N 88 52 E
Napa 163 38 18N 122 17W
Napa, R. 163 38 10N 122 19W
Napamute 147 61 30N 158 45W
Napanee 150 44 15N 77 0W
Napanoch 162 41 44N 74 2W
Nape 100 18 18N 105 6 E
Nape Pass = Keo Neua, Deo 100 18 23N 105 10 E
Napf 50 47 1N 7 56 E
Napiéolédougou 120 9 18N 5 35W
Napier 142 39 30 S 176 56 E
Napier Broome B. 136 14 2 S 126 37 E
Napier Downs 136 17 11 S 124 36 E
Napier Pen. 138 12 4 S 135 43 E
Naples 157 26 10N 81 45W
Naples = Nápoli 65 40 50N 14 5 E
Nap'o 108 23 44N 106 49 E
Napo □ 174 0 30 S 77 0W
Napo, R. 174 3 5 S 73 0W
Napoleon, N. Dak., U.S.A. 158 46 32N 99 49W
Napoleon, Ohio, U.S.A. 156 41 24N 84 7W
Nápoli 65 40 50N 14 5 E
Nápoli, G. di 65 40 40N 14 10 E
Napopo 126 4 15N 28 0 E
Napoule, La 45 43 31N 6 56 E
Nappa 32 53 58N 2 14W
Nappa Merrie 139 27 36 S 141 7 E
Naqâda 122 25 53N 32 42 E
Nara, Japan 111 34 40N 135 49 E
Nara, Mali 120 15 25N 7 20W
Nara, Canal 94 26 0N 69 20 E
Nara-ken □ 111 34 30N 136 0 E
Nara Visa 159 35 39N 103 10W
Naracoorte 140 36 58 S 140 45 E
Naradhan 141 33 34 S 146 17 E
Narasapur 96 16 26N 81 50 E
Narasaropet 96 16 14N 80 4 E
Narathiwat 101 6 40N 101 55 E
Narayanganj 98 23 31N 90 33 E
Narayanpet 96 16 45N 77 30 E
Narberth 31 51 48N 4 45W
Narbonne 44 43 11N 3 0 E
Narborough 28 52 34N 1 12W
Narcea, R. 56 43 15N 6 30W
Nardò 65 40 10N 18 0 E
Nare Head 30 50 12N 4 55W
Narembeen 137 32 7 S 118 17 E
Naretha 137 31 0 S 124 45 E
Nari, R. 94 29 10N 67 50 E
Narin 93 36 5N 69 0 E
Narinda, B. de 129 14 55 S 47 30 E
Narino □ 174 1 30N 78 0W
Narita 111 35 47N 140 19 E
Narmada, R. 94 22 40N 77 30 E
Narnaul 94 28 5N 76 11 E
Narni 63 42 30N 12 30 E
Naro, Ghana 120 10 22N 2 27W
Naro, Italy 64 37 18N 13 48 E
Naro Fominsk 81 55 23N 36 32 E
Narodnaya, G. 78 65 5N 60 0 E
Narok 126 1 20 S 33 30 E
Narok □ 126 1 20 S 33 30 E
Narón 56 43 32N 8 9W
Narooma 141 36 14 S 150 4 E
Narowal 94 32 6N 74 52 E
Narrabri 139 30 19 S 149 46 E
Narran, R. 139 28 37 S 148 12 E
Narrandera 141 34 42 S 146 31 E
Narraway, R. 152 55 44N 119 55W
Narrogin 137 32 58 S 117 14 E
Narromine 141 32 12 S 148 12 E
Narrows, str. 36 57 20N 6 5W
Narsampet 96 17 57N 79 58 E
Narsinghpur 95 22 54N 79 14 E
Naruto 110 34 11N 134 37 E
Narutō 111 35 36N 140 25 E
Naruto-Kaikyō 110 34 14N 134 39 E
Narva 80 59 10N 28 5 E
Narva, R. 80 59 10N 27 50 E
Narvik 74 68 28N 17 26 E
Narvskoye Vdkhr. 80 59 10N 28 5 E
Narwana 94 29 39N 76 6 E
Naryan-Mar 78 68 0N 53 0 E
Naryilco 139 28 37 S 141 53 E
Narym 76 59 0N 81 58 E
Narymskoye 76 49 10N 84 15 E
Naryn 85 41 26N 75 58 E
Naryn, R. 85 40 52N 71 36 E
Nasa 74 66 29N 15 23 E
Nasa, mt. 74 66 32N 15 23 E
Nasarawa 121 8 32N 7 41 E
Naseby, N.Z. 143 45 1 S 170 10 E
Naseby, U.K. 29 52 24N 0 59W
Naser, Buheirat en 122 23 0N 32 30 E
Nash Pt. 31 51 24N 3 34W
Nashua, Iowa, U.S.A. 158 42 55N 92 34W
Nashua, Mont., U.S.A. 160 48 10N 106 25W
Nashua, N.H., U.S.A. 162 42 50N 71 25W
Nashville, Ark., U.S.A. 159 33 56N 93 50W

Nashville, Ga., U.S.A. **157** 31 13N 83 15W
Nashville, Tenn., U.S.A. **157** 36 12N 86 46W
Našice **66** 45 32N 18 4 E
Nasielsk **54** 52 35N 20 50 E
Nasik **96** 20 2N 73 50 E
Nasirabad, Bangla. **95** 24 42N 90 30 E
Nasirabad, India **94** 26 15N 74 45 E
Nasirabad, Pak. **96** 28 25N 68 25 E
Naskaupi, R. **151** 53 47N 60 51W
Naso **65** 38 8N 14 46 E
Nass, R. **152** 55 0N 129 40W
Nassau, Bahamas **166** 25 0N 77 30W
Nassau, U.S.A. **162** 42 30N 73 34W
Nassau, Bahía **176** 55 20S 68 0W
Nasser City = Kôm Ombo **122** 24 25N 32 52 E
Nasser, L. = Naser, Buheiret en **122** 23 0N 32 30 E
Nassian **120** 7 58N 2 57W
Nässjö **73** 57 38N 14 45 E
Nastopoka Is. **150** 57 0N 77 0W
Näsum **73** 56 10N 14 29 E
Näsviken **72** 61 46N 16 52 E
Nata, Bots. **128** 20 7S 26 4 E
Nata, China **100** 19 37N 109 17 E
Nata, Si Arab. **92** 27 15N 48 35 E
Nata, Tanz. **125** 2 0S 34 25 E
Natagaima **174** 3 37N 75 6W
Natal, Brazil **170** 5 47S 35 13W
Natal, Can. **152** 49 43N 114 51W
Natal, Indon. **102** 0 35N 99 0 E
Natal □ **129** 28 30S 30 30 E
Natalinci **66** 44 15N 20 49 E
Natanz **93** 33 30N 51 55 E
Natashquan **151** 50 14N 61 46W
Natashquan Pt. **151** 50 8N 61 40W
Natashquan, R. **151** 50 7N 61 50W
Natchez **159** 31 35N 91 25W
Natchitoches **159** 31 47N 93 4W
Naters **50** 46 19N 8 0 E
Nathalia **141** 36 1S 145 7 E
Nathdwara **94** 24 55N 73 50 E
Natick **162** 42 16N 71 19W
Natih **93** 22 25N 56 30 E
Natimuk **140** 36 42S 142 0 E
Nation, R. **152** 55 30N 123 32W
National City **163** 32 45N 117 7W
National Mills **153** 52 52N 101 40W
Natitingou **121** 10 20N 1 26 E
Natividad, I. de **164** 27 50N 115 10W
Natkyizin **101** 14 57N 97 59 E
Natogyi **98** 21 25N 95 39 E
Natoma **158** 39 14N 99 0W
Natron L. **126** 2 20S 36 0 E
Natrûn, W. el. **122** 30 25N 30 0 E
Natuna Besar, Kepulauan **101** 4 0N 108 15 E
Natuna Selatan, Kepulauan **101** 2 45N 109 0 E
Naturaliste, C. **132** 33 32S 115 0 E
Naturaliste C. **138** 40 50S 148 15 E
Naturaliste Channel **137** 25 20S 113 0 E
Natya **140** 34 57S 143 13 E
Nau **85** 40 9N 69 22 E
Nau-Nau **128** 18 57S 21 4 E
Nau Qala **94** 34 5N 68 5 E
Naubinway **150** 46 7N 85 27W
Naucelle **44** 44 13N 2 20 E
Nauders **52** 46 54N 10 30 E
Nauen **48** 52 36N 12 52 E
Naujoji Vilnia **80** 54 48N 25 27 E
Naumburg **48** 51 10N 11 48 E
Nauru I. **130** 0 25N 166 0 E
Naurzum **84** 51 32N 64 34 E
Naushahra **93** 34 0N 72 0 E
Nauta **174** 4 20S 73 35W
Nautanwa **99** 27 20N 83 25 E
Nautla **165** 20 20N 96 50W
Nava **164** 28 25N 100 46W
Nava del Rey **56** 41 22N 5 6W
Navacerrada, Puerto de **56** 40 47N 4 0W
Navahermosa **57** 39 41N 4 28W
Navalcarnero **56** 40 17N 4 5W
Navalmoral de la Mata **56** 39 52N 5 16W
Navalvillar de Pela **57** 39 9N 5 24W
Navan = An Uaimh **38** 53 39N 6 40W
Navarino, I. **176** 55 0S 67 30W
Navarra □ **58** 42 40N 1 40W
Navarre **44** 43 15N 1 20 E
Navarreux **44** 43 20N 0 47W
Navasota **159** 30 20N 96 5W
Navassa I. **167** 18 30N 75 0W
Nave **62** 45 35N 10 17 E
Navenby **33** 53 7N 0 32W
Naver L. **37** 58 18N 4 20W
Naver, R. **37** 58 34N 4 15W
Navia **56** 43 24N 6 42W
Navia de Suarna **56** 42 58N 6 59W
Navia, R. **56** 43 15N 6 50W
Navidad **172** 33 57S 71 50W
Navlya **80** 52 53N 34 15 E
Navoi **85** 40 9N 65 22 E
Navojoa **164** 27 0N 109 30W
Navolato **164** 24 47N 107 42W
Navolok **78** 62 33N 39 57 E
Návpaktos **69** 38 23N 21 42 E
Návplion **69** 37 33N 22 50 E
Navrongo **121** 10 57N 0 58W
Navsari **96** 20 57N 72 59 E
Nawa Kot **94** 28 21N 71 24 E
Nawabganj **98** 24 35N 81 14 E
Nawabganj, Bara Banki **95** 26 56N 81 14 E
Nawabganj, Bareilly **95** 28 32N 79 40 E
Nawabshah **94** 26 15N 68 25 E
Nawada **95** 24 50N 85 25 E
Nawakot **95** 28 0N 85 10 E
Nawalgarh **96** 27 50N 75 15 E
Nawansnahr **95** 32 33N 74 48 E
Nawapara **95** 20 52N 82 33 E
Nawi **122** 18 32N 30 50 E
Nawng Hpa **98** 21 52N 97 52 E
Náxos **69** 37 8N 25 25 E
Náxos, I. **69** 37 5N 25 30 E
Nay **44** 43 10N 0 18W
Nay Band **93** 27 20N 52 40 E
Naya **174** 3 13N 77 22W
Naya, R. **174** 3 13N 77 22W
Nayakhan **77** 62 10N 159 0 E
Nayarit □ **164** 22 0N 105 0W
Nayé **120** 14 28N 12 12W
Nayung **108** 26 50N 105 17 E
Nazaré, Bahia, Brazil **171** 13 0S 39 0W
Nazaré, Goiás, Brazil **170** 6 23S 47 40W
Nazaré, Port. **57** 39 36N 9 4W
Nazaré Antônio de Jesus **171** 13 2S 39 0W
Nazaré da Mata **171** 7 44S 35 14W
Nazareth, Israel **90** 32 42N 35 17 E
Nazareth, U.S.A. **162** 40 44N 75 19W
Nazas **164** 25 10N 104 0W
Nazas, R. **164** 25 20N 104 4W
Naze **112** 28 22N 129 27 E
Naze, The **29** 51 43N 1 19 E
Nazeret **123** 8 45N 39 15 E
Nazir Hat **98** 22 35N 91 55 E
Nazko **152** 53 1N 123 37W
Nazko, R. **152** 53 7N 123 34W
Nchacoongo **129** 24 20S 35 9 E
Nchanga **127** 12 30S 27 49 E
Ncheu **127** 14 50S 34 37 E
Ndala **126** 4 45S 33 23 E
Ndali **121** 9 50N 2 46 E
Ndareda **126** 4 12S 35 30 E
Ndélé **117** 8 25N 20 36 E
Ndendeé **124** 2 29S 10 46 E
Ndjamena **117** 12 4N 15 8 E
Ndjolé **124** 0 10S 10 45 E
Ndola **127** 13 0S 28 34 E
Ndoto Mts. **126** 2 0N 37 0 E
Ndrhamcha, Sebkra de **120** 18 30N 15 55W
Nduguti **126** 4 18S 34 41 E
NE Frt. Agency = Arun. Pradesh □ **98** 28 0N 95 0 E
Nea **71** 63 15N 11 0 E
Néa Epidhavros **69** 37 40N 23 7 E
Néa Filippiás **68** 39 12N 20 53W
Néa Kallikrátiá **68** 40 21N 23 1 E
Néa Vissi **68** 41 34N 26 33 E
Neagari **111** 36 26N 136 25 E
Neagh, Lough **38** 54 35N 6 25W
Neah Bay **160** 48 25N 124 40W
Neale L. **137** 24 15S 130 0 E
Neamarrói **127** 15 58S 36 50 E
Neamţ □ **70** 47 0N 26 20 E
Neápolis, Kozan, Greece **68** 40 20N 21 24 E
Neápolis, Kriti, Greece **69** 35 15N 25 36 E
Neápolis, Lakonia, Greece **69** 36 27N 23 8 E
Near Is. **147** 53 0N 172 0W
Neath **31** 51 39N 3 49W
Neath, R. **23** 51 46N 3 35W
Nebbou **121** 11 9N 1 51W
Nebine Cr. **139** 29 7S 146 56 E
Nebo **138** 21 42S 148 42 E
Nebolchy **81** 59 12N 32 58 E
Nebraska □ **158** 41 30N 100 0W
Nebraska City **158** 40 40N 95 52W
Necedah **158** 44 2N 90 7W
Nechako, R. **152** 53 30N 122 44W
Neches, R. **159** 31 80N 94 20W
Neckar, R. **49** 48 43N 9 15 E
Necochea **172** 38 30S 58 50W
Nectar Brook **140** 32 43S 137 57 E
Nedelišće **63** 46 23N 16 22 E
Neder Rijn, R. **46** 51 57N 6 2 E
Nederbrakel **47** 50 48N 3 46 E
Nederlandsöy I. **71** 62 20N 5 35 E
Nederweert **47** 51 17N 5 45 E
Nedha, R. **69** 37 25N 21 45 E
Nedroma **118** 35 1N 1 45W
Nedstrand **71** 59 21N 5 49 E
Neede **46** 52 8N 6 37 E
Needham Market **29** 52 9N 1 2 E
Needilup **137** 33 55S 118 45 E
Needles **161** 34 50N 114 35W
Needles, Pt. **142** 36 3S 175 25 E
Needles, The **28** 50 48N 1 19W
Ñeembucú □ **172** 27 0S 58 0W
Neemuch (Nimach) **94** 24 30N 74 50 E
Neenah **156** 44 10N 88 30W
Neepawa **153** 50 20N 99 30W
Neer **47** 51 16N 5 59 E
Neerheylissem **47** 51 5N 5 42 E
Neeroeteren **47** 50 44N 4 58 E
Neerpelt **47** 51 13N 5 26 E
Nefta **119** 33 53N 7 58 E
Neftah Sidi Boubekeur **118** 35 1N 0 4 E
Neftegorsk **83** 44 25N 39 45 E
Neftenbach **51** 47 32N 8 41 E
Neftyannye Kamni **79** 40 20N 50 55 E
Nefyn **31** 52 57N 4 29W
Negapatam = Nagappattinam **97** 10 46N 79 38 E
Negaunee **156** 46 30N 87 36W
Negba **90** 31 40N 34 41 E
Negele **123** 5 20N 39 30 E
Negeri Sembilan □ **101** 2 50N 102 10 E
Negev = Hanegev **90** 30 50N 35 0 E
Negolu **70** 45 48N 24 32 E
Negombo **97** 7 12N 79 50 E
Negotin **66** 44 16N 22 37 E
Negotino **66** 41 29N 22 9 E
Negra, La **172** 23 46S 70 18W
Negra, Peña **56** 42 11N 6 30W
Negra Pt. **103** 18 40N 120 50 E
Negrais C. **98** 16 0N 94 30 E
Negreira **56** 42 54N 8 45W
Negreşti **70** 46 50N 27 30 E
Négrine **119** 34 30N 7 30 E
Negro, C. **118** 35 40N 5 11W
Negro, R., Argent. **176** 40 0S 64 0W
Negro, R., Brazil **174** 0 25S 64 0W
Negro, R., Uruguay **173** 32 30S 55 30W
Negros, I. **103** 10 0N 123 0 E
Negru Vodǎ **70** 43 47N 28 21 E
Nehbandān **93** 31 35N 60 5 E
Neheim-Hüsten **48** 51 27N 7 58 E
Nehoiaşu **70** 45 24N 26 20 E
Neichiang **108** 29 35N 105 0 E
Neich'iu **106** 37 17N 114 31 E
Neidpath **153** 50 12N 107 20W
Neihart **160** 47 0N 110 52W
Neihsiang **106** 33 3N 111 53 E
Neilrex **141** 31 44S 149 20 E
Neilston **34** 55 47N 4 27W
Neilton **160** 47 24N 123 59W
Neira de Jusá **56** 42 53N 7 14W
Neisse, R. **48** 51 0N 15 0 E
Neiva **174** 2 56N 75 18W
Nejanilini L. **153** 59 33N 97 48W
Nejo **123** 9 30N 35 28 E
Nekemte **123** 9 4N 36 30 E
Nêkheb **122** 25 10N 33 0 E
Neksø **73** 55 4N 15 8 E
Nelas **56** 40 32N 7 52W
Nelaug **71** 58 39N 8 40 E
Nelgowrie **141** 30 54S 148 7 E
Nelia **138** 20 39S 142 12 E
Nelidovo **80** 56 13N 32 49 E
Neligh **158** 42 11N 98 2W
Nelkan **77** 57 50N 136 15 E
Nellikuppam **97** 11 46N 79 43 E
Nellore **97** 14 27N 79 59 E
Nelma **77** 47 30N 139 0 E
Nelson, Can. **152** 49 30N 117 20W
Nelson, N.Z. **143** 41 18S 173 16 E
Nelson, U.K. **32** 53 50N 2 14W
Nelson, Ariz., U.S.A. **161** 35 35N 113 24W
Nelson, Nev., U.S.A. **161** 35 46N 114 55W
Nelson □ **143** 42 11S 172 15 E
Nelson, C., Austral. **140** 38 26S 141 32 E
Nelson, C., P.N.G. **135** 9 0S 149 20 E
Nelson, Estrecho **176** 51 30S 75 0W
Nelson Forks **152** 59 30N 124 0W
Nelson House **153** 55 47N 98 51W
Nelson I. **147** 60 40N 164 40W
Nelson L. **153** 55 48N 100 7W
Nelson, R. **153** 54 33N 98 2W
Nelspruit **126** 25 29S 30 59 E
Néma **120** 16 40N 7 15W
Neman (Nemunas), R. **80** 53 30N 25 10 E
Neméa **69** 37 49N 22 40 E
Nemegos **150** 47 40N 83 15W
Nemeiben L. **153** 55 20N 105 20W
Nemira, Mt. **70** 46 17N 26 19 E
Nemiscau **150** 49 30N 111 15W
Nemours **43** 48 16N 2 40 E
Nemunas, R. **80** 55 25N 21 10 E
Nemuro **112** 43 20N 145 35 E
Nemuro-Kaikyō **112** 43 30N 145 30 E
Nemuy **77** 55 40N 135 55 E
Nenagh **39** 52 52N 8 11W
Nenana **147** 64 30N 149 0W
Nenasi **101** 3 9N 103 23 E
Nenchiang **105** 49 11N 125 13 E
Nene, R. **29** 52 38N 0 7 E
Neno **127** 15 25S 34 40 E
Nenusa, Kepulauan **103** 4 45N 127 1 E
Neodesha **159** 37 30N 95 37W
Néon Petrítsi **68** 41 16N 23 15 E
Neópolis **170** 10 18S 36 35W
Neosho **159** 36 56N 94 28W
Neosho, R. **159** 35 59N 95 10W
Nepal ■ **95** 28 0N 84 30 E
Nepalganj **95** 28 0N 81 40 E
Nephi **160** 39 43N 111 52W
Nephin Beg Ra. **38** 54 0N 9 40W
Nephin, Mt. **38** 54 1N 9 21W
Nepomuk **52** 49 29N 13 35 E
Neptune City **162** 40 13N 74 4W
Néra, R. **66** 44 52N 21 45 E
Nerac **44** 44 19N 0 20 E
Nerchinsk **77** 52 0N 116 39 E
Nerchinskiy Zavod **77** 51 10N 119 30 E
Nereju **70** 45 43N 26 43 E
Nerekhta **81** 57 26N 40 38 E
Neret L. **151** 54 45N 70 44W
Neretva, R. **66** 43 30N 17 50 E
Neretvanski **66** 43 7N 17 10 E
Neringa **80** 55 21N 21 5 E
Nerja **57** 36 43N 3 55W
Nerl, R. **81** 56 30N 40 30 E
Nerokoúrou **69** 35 29N 24 3 E
Nerpio **59** 38 11N 2 16W
Nerva **57** 37 42N 6 30W
Nes, Iceland **74** 65 53N 17 24W
Nes, Neth. **46** 53 26N 5 47 E
Nes Ziyyona **90** 31 56N 34 48W
Nesbyen **71** 60 34N 9 6 E
Nescopeck **162** 41 3N 76 12W
Nesebyr **67** 42 41N 27 46 E
Nesflaten **71** 59 38N 6 48 E
Neskaupstaður **74** 65 9N 13 42W
Nesland **71** 59 31N 7 59 E
Neslandsvatn **71** 58 57N 9 10 E
Nesle **43** 49 45N 2 53 E
Nesodden **71** 59 48N 10 40 E
Ness, dist. **36** 58 27N 6 20W
Ness, Loch **37** 57 15N 4 30W
Nesslau **51** 47 14N 9 13 E
Neston **32** 53 17N 3 3W
Nestórion Óros **68** 40 24N 21 16 E
Néstos, R. **68** 41 20N 24 35 E
Nesttun **71** 60 19N 5 21 E
Nesvizh **80** 53 14N 26 38 E
Netanya **90** 32 20N 34 51 E
Nèthe, R. **47** 51 5N 4 55 E
Netherdale **138** 21 10S 148 33 E
Netherlands ■ **47** 52 0N 5 30 E
Netherlands Guiana = Surinam **170** 4 0N 56 0W
Nethy Bridge **37** 57 15N 3 40W
Netley **28** 50 53N 1 21W
Netley Gap **28** 32 43S 139 59 E
Netley Marsh **28** 50 55N 1 32W
Neto, R. **65** 39 10N 16 58 E
Netrakong **98** 24 53N 90 47 E
Nettancourt **43** 48 51N 4 57 E
Nettilling L. **149** 66 30N 71 0W
Nettlebed **29** 51 34N 0 54W
Nettleham **33** 53 15N 0 28W
Nettuno **64** 41 29N 12 40 E
Netzahualcoyotl, Presa **165** 17 10N 93 30W
Neu-Isenburg **49** 50 3N 8 42 E
Neu Ulm **49** 48 23N 10 2 E
Neubrandenburg **48** 53 33N 13 17 E
Neubrandenburg □ **48** 53 30N 13 20 E
Neubukow **48** 54 1N 11 40 E
Neuburg **49** 48 43N 11 11 E
Neuchâtel **50** 47 0N 6 55 E
Neuchâtel □ **50** 47 0N 6 55 E
Neuchâtel, Lac de **50** 46 53N 6 50 E
Neudau **52** 47 11N 16 6 E
Neuenegg **50** 46 54N 7 18 E
Neuenhaus **48** 52 30N 6 55 E
Neuf-Brisach **43** 48 0N 7 30 E
Neufchâteau, Belg. **47** 49 50N 5 25 E
Neufchâteau, France **43** 48 21N 5 40 E
Neufchâtel **43** 49 43N 1 30 E
Neufchâtel-sur-Aisne **43** 49 26N 4 0 E
Neuhaus **48** 53 16N 10 54 E
Neuhausen **51** 47 41N 8 37 E
Neuilly-St. Front **43** 49 10N 3 15 E
Neukalen **49** 53 49N 12 48 E
Neumarkt **49** 49 16N 11 28 E
Neumünster **48** 54 4N 9 58 E
Neung-sur-Beuvron **43** 47 30N 1 50 E
Neunkirchen, Austria **52** 47 43N 16 4 E
Neunkirchen, Ger. **49** 49 23N 7 6 E
Neuquén **176** 38 0S 68 0 E
Neuquén □ **172** 38 0S 69 50W
Neuruppin **48** 52 56N 12 48 E
Neuse, R. **157** 35 5N 77 40W
Neusiedl **53** 47 57N 16 50 E
Neusiedler See **53** 47 50N 16 47 E
Neuss **48** 51 12N 6 39 E
Neussargues-Moissac **44** 45 9N 3 1 E
Neustadt, Bay., Ger. **49** 49 42N 12 10 E
Neustadt, Bay., Ger. **49** 48 48N 11 47 E
Neustadt, Bay., Ger. **49** 49 34N 10 37 E
Neustadt, Bay., Ger. **49** 50 23N 11 0 E
Neustadt, Gera, Ger. **48** 50 45N 11 43 E
Neustadt, Hessen, Ger. **48** 50 51N 9 9 E
Neustadt, Niedersachsen, Ger. **48** 52 30N 9 30 E
Neustadt, Potsdam, Ger. **48** 52 50N 12 27 E
Neustadt, Rhld-Pfz., Ger. **49** 49 21N 8 10 E
Neustadt, S.-Holst., Ger. **48** 54 6N 10 49 E
Neustrelitz **48** 53 22N 13 4 E
Neuveville, La **50** 47 4N 7 6 E
Neuvic **44** 45 23N 2 16 E
Neuville, Belg. **95** 50 11N 4 32 E
Neuville, France **43** 45 52N 4 51 E
Neuville-aux-Bois **43** 48 4N 2 3 E
Neuvy-St.-Sépulchure **43** 46 35N 1 48 E
Neuvy-sur-Barangeon **43** 47 20N 2 15 E
Neuwerk, I. **48** 53 55N 8 30 E
Neuwied **48** 50 26N 7 29 E
Neva, R. **78** 59 50N 30 30 E
Nevada **159** 37 20N 94 40W
Nevada □ **160** 39 20N 117 0W
Nevada City **163** 39 20N 121 0W
Nevada de Sta. Marta, Sa. **174** 10 55N 73 50W
Nevada, Sierra, Spain **59** 37 3N 3 15W
Nevada, Sierra, U.S.A. **160** 39 0N 120 30W
Nevado, Cerro **172** 35 30S 68 20W
Nevado de Colima, Mt. **164** 19 35N 103 45W
Nevanka **77** 56 45N 98 55 E
Nevasa **94** 19 34N 75 0 E
Nevel **80** 56 0N 29 55 E
Nevele **47** 51 3N 3 28 E
Nevern **31** 52 2N 4 49W
Nevers **43** 47 0N 3 9 E
Nevertire **141** 31 50S 147 44 E
Neville **153** 49 58N 107 39W
Nevillé-Pont-Pierre **42** 47 33N 0 33 E

Place	Page	Lat.	Long.
Nevinnomyssk	83	44 40N	42 0E
Nevis I.	167	17 0N	62 30W
Nevis, L.	36	57 0N	5 43W
Nevlunghavn	71	58 58N	9 53E
Nevoria	137	31 25S	119 25E
Nevrokop = Gotse Delchev	67	41 43N	23 46E
Nevşehir	92	38 33N	34 40E
Nevyansk	84	57 30N	60 13E
New Abbey	35	54 59N	3 38W
New Aberdour	37	57 39N	2 12W
New Adawso	121	6 50N	0 2W
New Albany, Ind., U.S.A.	156	38 20N	85 50W
New Albany, Miss., U.S.A.	159	34 30N	89 0W
New Albany, Pa., U.S.A.	162	41 35N	76 28W
New Alresford	28	51 6N	1 10W
New Amsterdam	174	6 15N	57 30W
New Angledool	139	29 10S	147 55E
New Bedford	162	41 40N	70 52W
New Berlin, N.Y., U.S.A.	162	42 38N	75 20W
New Berlin, Pa., U.S.A.	162	40 50N	76 57W
New Bern	157	35 8N	77 3W
New Birmingham	39	52 36N	7 38W
New Boston	159	33 27N	94 21W
New Braunfels	159	29 43N	98 9W
New Brighton, N.Z.	143	43 29S	172 43E
New Brighton, U.K.	32	53 27N	3 2W
New Britain	162	41 41N	72 47W
New Britain, I.	135	5 50S	150 20E
New Brunswick	162	40 30N	74 28W
New Brunswick □	151	46 50N	66 30W
New Buildings	38	54 57N	7 21W
New Bussa	121	9 53N	4 31E
New Byrd	13	80 0S	120 0W
New Caledonia, I.	130	21 0S	165 0E
New Castile = Castilla La Neuva	57	39 45N	3 20W
New Castle, Del., U.S.A.	162	39 40N	75 34W
New Castle, Ind., U.S.A.	156	39 55N	85 23W
New Castle, Pa., U.S.A.	156	41 0N	80 20W
New Chapel Cross	39	51 51N	10 12W
New City	162	41 8N	74 0W
New Cumnock	34	55 24N	4 13W
New Cuyama	163	34 57N	119 38W
New Deer	37	57 30N	2 10W
New Delhi	94	28 37N	77 13E
New Denver	152	50 0N	117 25W
New England	158	46 36N	102 47W
New England Ra.	139	30 20S	151 45E
New Forest	28	50 53N	1 40W
New Freedom	162	39 44N	76 42W
New Galloway	35	55 4N	4 10W
New Glasgow	151	45 35N	62 36W
New Gretna	162	39 35N	74 28W
New Guinea, I.	135	4 0S	136 0E
New Hampshire □	156	43 40N	71 40W
New Hampton	158	43 2N	92 20W
New Hanover	129	29 22S	30 31E
New Hanover I.	135	2 30S	150 10E
New Hartford	162	43 4N	75 18W
New Haven	162	41 20N	72 54W
New Hazelton	152	55 20N	127 30W
•New Hebrides, Is.	130	15 0S	168 0E
New Holland, U.K.	33	53 42N	0 22W
New Holland, U.S.A.	162	40 6N	76 5W
New Iberia	159	30 2N	91 54W
New Inn	39	53 5N	7 10W
New Ireland, I.	135	3 20S	151 50E
New Jersey □	162	39 50N	74 10W
New Kensington	156	40 36N	79 43W
New Kent	162	37 31N	76 59W
New Lexington	156	39 40N	82 15W
New Liskeard	150	47 31N	79 41W
New London, Conn., U.S.A.	162	41 23N	72 8W
New London, Minn., U.S.A.	158	45 17N	94 55W
New London, Wis., U.S.A.	158	44 23N	88 43W
New Luce	34	54 57N	4 50W
New Madrid	159	36 40N	89 30W
New Meadows	160	45 0N	116 10W
New Mexico □	154	34 30N	106 0W
New Milford, Conn., U.S.A.	162	41 35N	73 25W
New Milford, Pa., U.S.A.	162	41 50N	75 45W
New Mills	32	53 22N	2 0W
New Norcia	137	30 57S	116 13E
New Norfolk	138	42 46S	147 2E
New Orleans	159	30 0N	90 5W
New Oxford	162	39 52N	77 4W
New Philadelphia	156	40 29N	81 25W
New Pitsligo	37	57 35N	2 11W
New Plymouth, Bahamas	166	26 56N	77 20W
New Plymouth, N.Z.	142	39 4S	174 5E
New Point Comfort	162	37 18N	76 15W
New Providence I.	166	25 0N	77 30W
New Quay	31	52 13N	4 21W
New Radnor	31	52 15N	3 10W
New Richmond	158	45 6N	92 34W
New Roads	159	30 43N	91 30W
New Rockford	158	47 44N	99 7W
New Romney	29	50 59N	0 57E
New Ross	39	52 24N	6 58W
New Rossington	33	53 30N	1 4W
New Salem	158	46 51N	101 25W
New Siberian Is. = Novosibirskiye Os.	77	75 0N	140 0E
New Smyrna Beach	157	29 0N	80 50W
New South Wales □	139	33 0S	146 0E
New Springs	137	25 49S	120 1E
New Tamale	121	9 10N	1 10W
New Tredegar	31	51 43N	3 15W
New Ulm	158	44 15N	94 30W
New Waterford	151	46 13N	60 4W
New Westminster	152	49 10N	122 52W
New York □	156	42 40N	76 0W
New York City	162	40 45N	74 0W
New Zealand ■	143	40 0S	176 0E
Newala	127	10 58S	39 10E
Newala □	127	10 46S	39 20E
Newark, U.K.	33	53 6N	0 48W
Newark, Del., U.S.A.	162	39 42N	75 45W
Newark, N.J., U.S.A.	162	40 41N	74 12W
Newark, N.Y., U.S.A.	162	43 2N	77 10W
Newark, Ohio, U.S.A.	156	40 5N	82 30W
Newark Valley	162	42 14N	76 11W
Newberg	160	45 22N	123 0W
Newberry	156	46 20N	85 32W
Newberry Springs	163	34 50N	116 41W
Newbiggin-by-the-Sea	35	55 12N	1 31W
Newbigging	35	55 42N	3 33W
Newbliss	38	54 10N	7 8W
Newborough	31	53 10N	4 22W
Newbridge, Kildare, Ireland	39	53 11N	6 50W
Newbridge, Limerick, Ireland	38	52 33N	9 0W
Newbridge-on-Wye	31	52 13N	3 27W
Newbrook	152	54 24N	112 57W
Newburgh, Fife, U.K.	35	56 21N	3 15W
Newburgh, Grampian, U.K.	37	57 19N	2 0W
Newburgh, U.S.A.	162	41 30N	74 1W
Newburn	35	54 57N	1 45W
Newbury	28	51 24N	1 19W
Newburyport	162	42 48N	70 50W
Newby Bridge	32	54 16N	2 59W
Newbyth	37	57 35N	2 17W
Newcastle, Austral.	141	33 0S	151 40E
Newcastle, Can.	151	47 1N	65 38W
Newcastle, Ireland	39	53 5N	6 4W
Newcastle, S. Afr.	125	27 45S	29 58E
Newcastle, U.K.	38	54 13N	5 54W
Newcastle, U.S.A.	158	43 50N	104 12W
Newcastle Emlyn	31	52 2N	4 29W
Newcastle Ra.	136	15 45S	130 15E
Newcastle-under-Lyme	32	53 2N	2 15W
Newcastle-upon-Tyne	35	54 59N	1 37W
Newcastle Waters	136	17 30S	133 28E
Newcastle West	38	52 27N	9 3W
Newcastleton	35	55 10N	2 50W
Newchurch	31	52 9N	3 10W
Newdegate	137	33 6S	119 0E
Newe Etan	90	32 30N	35 32E
Newe Sha'anan	90	32 47N	34 59E
Newe Zohar	90	31 9N	35 21E
Newell	158	44 48N	103 25W
Newenham, C.	147	58 40N	162 15W
Newent	28	51 56N	2 24W
Newfield, N.J., U.S.A.	162	39 33N	75 1W
Newfield, N.Y., U.S.A.	162	42 18N	76 33W
Newfound L.	162	43 40N	71 47W
Newfoundland	151	48 30N	56 0W
Newfoundland □	151	48 28N	56 0W
Newhalem	152	48 41N	121 16W
Newhalen	147	59 40N	155 0W
Newhall	163	34 23N	118 32W
Newham	29	51 31N	0 2E
Newhaven	29	50 47N	0 4E
Newington, N. Kent, U.K.	29	51 21N	0 40E
Newington, S. Kent, U.K.	29	51 5N	1 8E
Newinn	39	52 28N	7 54W
Newkirk	159	36 52N	97 3W
Newlyn	30	50 6N	5 33W
Newlyn East	30	50 22N	5 3W
Newmachar	37	57 16N	2 11W
Newman	163	37 19N	121 1W
Newman, Mt.	137	23 20S	119 34E
Newmarket, Ireland	39	52 13N	9 0W
Newmarket, Lewis, U.K.	36	58 14N	6 24W
Newmarket, Suffolk, U.K.	29	52 15N	0 23E
Newmarket, U.S.A.	162	43 4N	70 57W
Newmarket-on-Fergus	39	52 46N	8 54W
Newmill	37	57 34N	2 58W
Newmills	38	54 56N	7 49W
Newmilns	34	55 36N	4 20W
Newnan	157	33 22N	84 48W
Newnes	139	33 9S	150 16E
Newnham	28	51 48N	2 27W
Newport, Essex, U.K.	29	51 58N	0 13E
Newport, Gwent, U.K.	31	51 35N	3 0W
Newport, I. of W., U.K.	28	50 42N	1 18W
Newport, Salop, U.K.	28	52 47N	2 22W
Newport, Ark., U.S.A.	159	35 38N	91 15W
Newport, Ky., U.S.A.	156	39 5N	84 23W
Newport, N.H., U.S.A.	162	43 23N	72 8W
Newport, Oreg., U.S.A.	160	44 41N	124 2W
Newport, R.I., U.S.A.	162	41 30N	71 19W
Newport, Tenn., U.S.A.	157	35 39N	83 12W
Newport, Wash., U.S.A.	160	48 11N	117 2W
Newport B.	38	53 52N	9 38W
Newport Beach	163	33 40N	117 58W
Newport News	162	37 2N	76 54W
Newport on Tay	35	56 27N	2 56W
Newport Pagnell	29	52 5N	0 42W
Newquay	30	50 24N	5 6W
Newry	38	54 10N	6 20W
Newry & Mourne □	38	54 10N	6 15W
Newton, Iowa, U.S.A.	158	41 40N	93 3W
Newton, Kans., U.S.A.	159	38 2N	97 30W
Newton, Mass., U.S.A.	156	42 21N	71 10W
Newton, N.C., U.S.A.	157	35 42N	81 10W
Newton, N.J., U.S.A.	162	41 3N	74 46W
Newton, Texas, U.S.A.	159	30 54N	93 42W
Newton Abbot	30	50 32N	3 37W
Newton Arlosh	32	54 53N	3 15W
Newton-Aycliffe	33	54 36N	1 33W
Newton Boyd	139	29 45S	152 16E
Newton Ferrers	30	50 19N	4 3W
Newton le Willows	32	53 28N	3 27W
Newton St. Cyres	30	50 46N	3 35W
Newton Stewart	34	54 57N	4 30W
Newtonabbey □	38	54 45N	6 0W
Newtongrange	35	55 52N	3 4W
Newtonhill	37	57 1N	20 52E
Newtonmore	37	57 4N	4 7W
Newtown, Ireland	39	52 20N	8 47W
Newtown, Scot, U.K.	35	55 34N	2 38W
Newtown, Wales, U.K.	31	52 31N	3 19W
Newtown Crommelin	38	54 59N	6 13W
Newtown Cunningham	38	55 0N	7 32W
Newtown Forbes	38	53 46N	7 50W
Newtown Gore	38	54 3N	7 41W
Newtown Hamilton	38	54 12N	6 35W
Newtownabbey	38	54 40N	5 55W
Newtownards	38	54 37N	5 40W
Newtownbutler	38	54 12N	7 22W
Newtownmount-kennedy	39	53 5N	6 7W
Newtownstewart	38	54 43N	7 22W
Nexon	48	45 41N	1 10E
Neya	81	58 21N	43 49E
Neyland	31	51 43N	4 58W
Neyrīz	93	29 15N	54 55E
Neyshābūr	93	36 10N	58 20E
Neyyattinkara	97	8 26N	77 5E
Nezhin	80	51 5N	31 55E
Nezperce	160	46 13N	116 15W
Ngabang	102	0 30N	109 55E
Ngaiphaipi	98	22 14N	93 15E
Ngambé	121	5 48N	11 29E
Ngami Depression	128	20 30S	22 46E
Ngamo	127	19 3S	27 25E
Ngandjuk	103	7 32S	111 55E
Ngao	100	18 46N	99 59E
Ngaoundéré	124	7 15N	13 35E
Ngapara	143	44 57S	170 46E
Ngara	126	2 29S	30 40E
Ngara □	126	2 29S	30 40E
Ngaruawahia	142	37 42S	175 11E
Ngatapa	142	38 32S	177 45E
Ngathainggyaung	98	17 24N	95 5E
Ngauruhoe, Mt.	142	39 13S	175 45E
Ngawi	103	7 24S	111 26E
Ngetera	121	12 40S	12 46E
Ngha Lo	101	21 33N	104 28E
Nghia Lo	100	21 33N	104 28E
Ngoma	127	13 8S	33 45E
Ngomahura	127	20 33S	30 57E
Ngomba	127	8 20S	32 53E
Ngonye Falls	128	16 35S	23 30E
Ngop	123	6 17N	30 9E
Ngorkou	120	15 40N	3 41W
Ngorongoro	126	3 11S	35 32E
Ngozi	126	2 54S	29 50E
Ngudu	126	2 58S	33 25E
N'Guigrai	117	14 20N	13 20E
Nguna, I.	100	17 26S	168 21E
Ngunga	126	3 37S	33 37E
Ngungu	143	6 15N	28 16E
Ngunguru	94	35 37S	174 30E
Nguru	121	12 56N	10 29E
Nguru Mts.	126	6 0S	37 30E
Nguyen Binh	100	22 39N	105 56E
Ngwenya	129	26 5S	31 7E
Nha Trang	101	12 16N	109 10E
Nhacoongo	129	24 18S	35 14E
Nhangutazi, Lago	129	24 0S	34 30E
Nhill	140	36 18S	141 40E
Nho Quan	100	20 18N	105 45E
Nhulunbuy	138	12 10S	136 45E
Nia-nia	126	1 30N	27 40E
Niafounké	120	16 0N	4 5W
Niagara	156	45 45N	88 0W
Niagara Falls, Can.	150	43 7N	79 5W
Niagara Falls, N. Amer.	150	43 5N	79 5W
Niah	102	3 58N	113 46E
Niamey	121	13 27N	2 6E
Nianforando	120	9 37N	10 36W
Nianfors	72	61 36N	16 46E
Niangara	126	3 50N	27 50E
Niantic	162	41 19N	72 12W
Nias, I.	102	1 0N	97 40E
Niassa □	127	13 30S	36 0E
Niassa, Lago	127	12 30S	34 30E
Nibbiano	62	44 54N	9 20E
Nibe	73	56 59N	9 38E
Nibong Tebal	101	5 10N	100 29E
Nicaragua ■	166	11 40N	85 30W
Nicaragua, Lago de	166	12 50N	85 30W
Nicastro	65	39 0N	16 18E
Nice	45	43 42N	7 14E
Niceville	157	30 30N	86 30W
Nichinan	110	31 38N	131 23E
Nicholas, Chan.	166	23 30N	80 30W
Nicholasville	156	37 54N	84 31W
Nichols	162	42 1N	76 22W
Nicholson, Austral.	136	18 2S	128 54E
Nicholson, Can.	150	47 58N	83 47W
Nicholson, U.S.A.	162	41 37N	75 47W
Nicholson, R.	138	17 31S	139 36E
Nicholson Ra.	137	27 15S	116 30E
Nicobar Is.	86	9 0N	93 0E
Nicoclí	174	8 26N	76 48W
Nicola	152	50 8N	120 40W
Nicolet	150	46 17N	72 35W
Nicolls Town	166	25 8N	78 0W
Nicosia, Cyprus	92	35 10N	33 25E
Nicosia, Italy	65	37 45N	14 22E
Nicótera	65	38 33N	15 57E
Nicoya	166	10 9N	85 27W
Nicoya, Golfo de	166	10 0N	85 0W
Nicoya, Pen. de	166	9 45N	85 40W
Nidau	50	47 7N	7 15E
Nidd, R.	33	54 1N	1 32W
Nidda	48	50 24N	9 2E
Nidda, R.	49	50 25N	9 2E
Nidderdale	33	54 5N	1 46W
Nidzica	54	53 25N	20 28E
Niebüll	48	54 47N	8 49E
Niederaula	48	50 48N	9 37E
Niederbipp	50	47 16N	7 42E
Niederbronn	43	48 57N	7 39E
Niedere Tauern	93	47 18N	14 0E
Niedermarsberg	48	51 28N	8 52E
Niederösterreich □	52	48 25N	15 40E
Niedersachsen □	48	54 45N	9 0E
Niel	47	51 7N	4 20E
Niellé	120	10 5N	5 38W
Niemba	126	5 58S	28 24E
Niemcza	54	50 42N	16 47E
Niemodlin	54	50 38N	17 38E
Niemur	140	35 17S	144 9E
Nienburg	48	52 38N	9 15E
Niench'ingt'angkula Shan	105	30 10N	90 0E
Niepołomice	54	50 3N	20 13E
Niesen	50	46 38N	7 39E
Niesky	48	51 18N	14 48E
Nieszawa	54	52 52N	18 42E
Nieuw Amsterdam	46	52 43N	6 52E
Nieuw Beijerland	46	51 49N	4 20E
Nieuw-Buinen	46	52 58N	6 56E
Nieuw-Dordrecht	46	52 45N	6 59E
Nieuw Hellevoet	46	51 51N	4 8E
Nieuw Loosdrecht	46	52 12N	5 8E
Nieuw Nickerie	175	6 0N	57 10W
Nieuw-Schoonebeek	46	52 39N	7 0E
Nieuw-Vassemeer	47	51 34N	4 12E
Nieuw-Vennep	46	52 16N	4 38E
Nieuw-Weerdinge	46	52 51N	6 59E
Nieuwe-Niedorp	46	52 44N	4 54E
Nieuwe-Pekela	46	53 5N	6 58E
Nieuwe-Schans	46	53 11N	7 12E
Nieuwe-Tonge	47	51 43N	4 10E
Nieuwendijk	46	51 46N	4 55E
Nieuwerkerken	47	50 52N	5 12E
Nieuwkoop	46	52 9N	4 48E
Nieuwleusen	46	52 34N	6 17E
Nieuwnamen	47	51 18N	4 9E
Nieuwolda	46	53 15N	6 58E
Nieuwpoort	47	51 8N	2 45E
Nieuwveen	46	52 12N	4 46E
Nieves	56	42 7N	8 26W
Nièvre □	43	47 10N	5 40E
Nigata	110	34 13N	132 39E
Nigde	92	38 0N	34 40E
Nigel	129	26 27S	28 25E
Niger □	121	10 0N	5 0E
Niger ■	121	13 30N	10 0E
Niger, R.	121	10 0N	4 40E
Nigeria ■	121	8 30N	8 0E
Nigg B.	37	57 41N	4 5W
Nightcaps	143	45 57S	168 14E
Nigrita	68	40 56N	23 29E
Nihtaur	94	29 27N	78 23E
Nii-Jima	111	34 20N	139 15E
Niigata	112	37 58N	139 0E
Niigata-ken □	112	37 15N	138 45E
Niihama	110	33 55N	133 10E
Niihau, I.	147	21 55N	160 10W
Niimi	110	34 59N	133 28E
Nijar	59	36 53N	2 15W
Nijkerk	47	52 13N	5 30E
Nijlen	47	51 10N	4 40E
Nijmegen	47	51 50N	5 52E
Nijverdal	46	52 22N	6 28E
Nike	121	6 26N	7 29E
Nikel	74	69 30N	30 5E
Nikiniki	103	9 40S	124 30E
Nikitas	68	40 17N	23 34E
Nikki	121	9 58N	3 21E
Nikkō	111	36 45N	139 35E
Nikolayev	82	46 58N	32 7E
Nikolayevsk-na-Amur	77	53 40N	140 50E
Nikolayevski	81	50 10N	45 35E
Nikolsk	81	59 30N	45 28E
Nikolski	147	53 0N	168 50W
Nikolskoye, Amur, U.S.S.R.	77	47 50N	131 5E
Nikolskoye, Kamandorskiye, U.S.S.R.	77	55 12N	166 0E
Nikopol, Bulg.	67	43 43N	24 54E
Nikopol, U.S.S.R.	82	47 35N	34 25E
Niksar	82	40 31N	37 2E
Nikshah	93	26 15N	60 10E
Nik ió	66	42 50N	18 57E
Nîl el Abyad, Bahr	123	9 30N	31 40E

• Renamed Vanuatu

Nîl el Azraq □ 123 12 30N 34 30 E
Nîl el Azraq, Bahr 123 10 30N 35 0 E
Nîl, Nahr el 122 27 30N 30 30 E
Nila 103 8 24 S 120 29 E
Niland 161 33 16N 115 30W
Nile □ 126 2 0N 31 30 E
Nile Delta 122 31 40N 31 0 E
Nile, R. = Nîl, Nahr el 122 27 30N 30 30 E
Niles 156 41 8N 80 40W
Nilgiri Hills 97 11 30N 76 30 E
Nilo Peçanha 171 13 37 S 39 6W
Nilpena 140 30 58 S 138 20 E
Nimach = Neemuch 94 24 30N 74 50 E
Nimar 96 21 49N 76 22 E
Nimba, Mt. 120 7 39N 8 30W
Nimbahera 94 24 37N 74 45 E
Nîmes 45 43 50N 4 23 E
Nimfaíon, Ákra 68 40 5N 24 20 E
Nimingarra 132 20 31 S 119 55 E
Nimmitabel 141 36 29 S 149 15 E
Nimneryskiy 77 58 0N 125 10 E
Nimule 123 3 32N 32 3 E
Nimy 47 50 28N 3 57 E
Nin 63 44 16N 15 12 E
Nindigully 139 28 21 S 148 50 E
Ninemile 152 56 0N 130 7W
Ninemilehouse 39 52 28N 7 29W
Ninety Mile Beach 130 34 45 S 173 0 E
Ninety Mile Beach, The 133 38 15 S 147 24 E
Nineveh 92 36 25N 43 10 E
Ninfield 29 50 53N 0 26 E
Ningaloo 136 22 41 S 113 41 E
Ningan 107 44 23N 129 26 E
Ningch'eng 107 41 34N 119 20 E
Ningch'iang 106 32 49N 106 13 E
Ningchin 106 37 37N 114 55 E
Ningching Shan 108 31 45N 97 15 E
Ninghai 109 29 18N 121 25 E
Ninghsiang 109 28 15N 112 30 E
Ninghsien 106 35 35N 107 58 E
Ninghua 109 26 14N 116 36 E
Ningkang 109 26 45N 113 58 E
Ningkuo 109 30 38N 118 58 E
Ninglang 108 27 19N 100 53 E
Ningling 106 34 27N 115 19 E
Ningming 108 22 12N 107 5 E
Ningnan 108 27 7N 102 42 E
Ningpo 109 29 53N 121 33 E
Ningshan 106 33 12N 108 29 E
Ningsia Hui A.R. □ 106 37 45N 106 0 E
Ningte 109 26 45N 120 0 E
Ningtsin 99 29 44N 98 28 E
Ningtu 109 26 22N 115 48 E
Ningwu 106 29 2N 112 15 E
Ningyang, Fukien, China 109 25 44N 117 8 E
Ningyang, Shantung, China 106 35 46N 116 47 E
Ningyüan 109 25 36N 111 54 E
Ninh Binh 100 20 15N 105 55 E
Ninh Giang 100 20 44N 106 24 E
Ninh Hoa 100 12 30N 109 7 E
Ninh Ma 100 12 48N 109 21 E
Ninian, oilfield 19 60 42N 1 30 E
Ninove 47 50 51N 4 2 E
Nioaque 173 21 5 S 55 50W
Niobrara 158 42 48N 97 59W
Niobrara R. 158 42 30N 103 0W
Nioki 124 2 47 S 17 40 E
Niono 120 14 15N 6 0W
Nioro 120 15 30N 9 30W
Nioro du Rip 120 13 40N 15 50W
Nioro du Sahel 120 15 30N 9 30W
Niort 44 46 19N 0 29W
Niou 121 12 42N 2 1W
Nipa 135 6 9 S 143 29 E
Nipan 138 24 45 S 150 0 E
Nipani 96 16 20N 74 25 E
Nipawin 153 53 20N 104 0W
Nipawin Prov. Park 153 54 0N 104 37W
Nipigon 150 49 0N 88 17W
Nipigon, L. 150 49 50N 88 30W
Nipin, R. 153 55 46N 109 2W
Nipishish L. 151 54 12N 60 45W
Nipissing L. 150 46 20N 80 0W
Nipomo 163 35 4N 120 29W
Niquelândia 171 14 33 S 48 23W
Nira, R. 96 18 5N 74 25 E
Nirasaki 111 35 42N 138 27 E
Nirmal 96 19 3N 78 20 E
Nirmali 95 26 20N 86 35 E
Niš 66 43 19N 21 58 E
Nisa 57 39 30N 7 41W
Nisab 91 14 25N 46 29 E
Nišava, R. 66 43 20N 22 10 E
Niscemi 65 37 8N 14 21 E
Nishi-Sonogi-Hantō 110 32 55N 129 45 E
Nishinomiya 111 34 45N 135 20 E
Nishinoomote 111 30 43N 130 59 E
Nishio 111 34 52N 137 3 E
Nishiwaki 110 34 59N 134 48 E
Nisíros, I. 69 36 35N 27 12 E
Niskibi, R. 150 56 29N 88 9W
Nisko 54 50 35N 22 7 E
Nispen 47 51 29N 4 28 E
Nisporeny 70 47 4N 28 10 E
Nissafors 73 57 25N 13 37 E
Nissan 73 56 40N 12 51 E
Nissan I. 138 4 30 S 154 10 E
Nissedal 71 59 10N 8 30 E
Nisser 71 59 7N 8 28 E
Nissum Fjord 73 56 20N 8 11 E
Nistelrode 47 51 42N 5 34 E
Nisutlin, R. 152 60 14N 132 34W
Nitchequon 151 53 10N 70 58W
Niterói 173 22 52 S 43 0W
Nith, R. 35 55 20N 3 5W
Nithsdale 35 55 14N 3 50W
Niton 28 50 35N 1 14W
Nitra 53 48 19N 18 4 E
Nitra, R. 53 48 30N 18 7 E
Nitsa, R. 84 57 29N 64 33 E
Nittedal 71 60 1N 10 57 E
Niuchieh 108 27 47N 104 16 E
Niuchuang 107 40 58N 122 38 E
Niue I. (Savage I.) 130 19 2 S 169 54W
Niulan Chiang, R. 108 27 24N 103 9 E
Niut, Mt. 102 0 55N 109 30 E
Nivelles 47 50 35N 4 20 E
Nivernais 43 47 0N 3 40 E
Nixon, Nev., U.S.A. 160 39 54N 119 22W
Nixon, Tex., U.S.A. 159 29 17N 97 45W
Nizam Sagar 96 18 10N 77 58 E
Nizamabad 96 18 45N 78 7 E
Nizamghat 98 28 20N 95 45 E
Nizhanaya Tunguska 77 64 20N 93 0 E
Nizhiye Sergi 84 56 40N 59 18 E
Nizhne Kolymsk 77 68 40N 160 55 E
Nizhne-Vartovskoye 76 60 56N 76 38 E
Nizhneangarsk 77 56 0N 109 30 E
Nizhnegorskiy 82 45 27N 34 38 E
Nizhneudinsk 77 55 0N 99 20 E
Nizhniy Lomov 81 53 34N 43 38 E
Nizhniy Novgorod = Gorkiy 81 56 20N 44 0 E
Nizhniy Pyandzh 85 37 12N 68 35 E
Nizhniy Tagil 84 57 55N 59 57 E
Nizhny Salda 84 58 8N 60 42 E
Nizké Tatry 53 48 55N 20 0 E
Nizza Monferrato 62 44 46N 8 22 E
Njakwa 127 11 1 S 33 56 E
Njinjo 127 8 34 S 38 44 E
Njombe 124 9 20 S 34 50 E
Njombe □ 127 9 20 S 34 49 E
Njombe, R. 126 7 15 S 34 30 E
Nkambe 121 6 35N 10 40 E
Nkana 127 13 0 S 28 8 E
Nkawkaw 121 6 36N 0 49W
Nkhata Bay 124 11 33 S 34 16 E
Nkhota Kota 127 12 56 S 34 15 E
Nkongsamba 121 4 55N 9 55 E
Nkunka 127 14 57 S 25 58 E
Nkwanta 120 6 10N 2 10W
Nmai Pit, R. 99 25 30N 98 0 E
Nmai, R. 99 25 30N 98 0 E
Nmaushahra 95 33 11N 74 15 E
Nnewi 121 6 0N 6 59 E
Noakhali = Maijdi 98 22 50N 90 45 E
Noatak 147 67 32N 163 10W
Noatak, R. 147 68 0N 161 0W
Nobber 38 53 49N 6 45W
Nobeoka 110 32 36N 131 41 E
Nōbi-Heiya 111 35 15N 136 45 E
Noblejas 58 39 58N 3 26W
Noblesville 156 40 1N 85 59W
Noce, R. 62 46 22N 11 0 E
Nocera Inferiore 65 40 45N 14 37 E
Nocera Terinese 65 39 2N 16 9 E
Nocera Umbra 63 43 8N 12 47 E
Nochixtlán 165 17 28N 97 14W
Noci 65 40 47N 17 7 E
Nockatunga 139 27 42 S 142 42 E
Nocona 159 33 48N 97 45W
Nocrich 70 45 55N 24 26 E
Noda, Japan 111 35 56N 139 52 E
Noda, U.S.S.R. 77 47 30N 142 5 E
Noel 159 36 36N 94 29W
Nogales, Mexico 164 31 36N 94 29W
Nogales, U.S.A. 161 31 33N 115 50W
Nōgata 110 33 48N 130 54 E
Nogent-en-Bassigny 43 48 0N 5 20 E
Nogent-le-Rotrou 42 48 20N 0 50 E
Nogent-sur-Seine 43 48 30N 3 30 E
Noggerup 137 33 32 S 116 5 E
Noginsk, Moskva, U.S.S.R. 81 55 50N 38 25 E
Noginsk, Sib., U.S.S.R. 77 64 30N 90 50 E
Nogoa, R. 138 23 33 S 148 32 E
Nogoyá 172 32 24 S 59 48W
Nógrád □ 53 48 0N 19 30 E
Nogueira de Ramuin 56 42 21N 7 43W
Noguera Pallaresa, R. 58 42 15N 1 0 E
Noguera Ribagorzana, R. 58 42 15N 0 45 E
Nohar 94 29 11N 74 49 E
Noi, R. 101 14 50N 100 15 E
Noire, Mts. 42 48 11N 3 40W
Noirétable 44 45 48N 3 46 E
Noirmoutier 42 47 0N 2 15W
Noirmoutier, Î. de 42 46 58N 2 10W
Nojane 128 23 15 S 20 14 E
Nojima-Zaki 111 34 54N 139 53 E
Nok Kundi 93 28 50N 62 45 E
Nokaneng 128 19 47 S 22 17 E
Nokhtuysk 77 60 0N 117 45 E
Nokomis 153 51 35N 105 0W
Nokomis L. 153 57 0N 103 0W
Nokou 124 14 35N 14 47 E
Nol 73 57 56N 12 5 E
Nola, C. Afr. Emp. 124 3 35N 16 10 E
Nola, Italy 65 40 54N 14 29 E
Nolay 43 46 58N 4 35 E
Nolby 72 62 17N 17 26 E
Noli, C. di 62 44 12N 8 26 E
Nolinsk 84 57 28N 49 57 E
Noma Omuramba, R. 128 19 6 S 20 30 E
Noma-Saki 110 31 25N 130 7 E
Nomad 135 6 19 S 142 13 E
Noman L. 153 62 15N 108 55W
Nombre de Dios 166 9 34N 79 28W
Nome 147 64 30N 165 30W
Nomo-Zaki 110 32 35N 129 44 E
Nonacho L. 153 61 57N 109 28W
Nonancourt 42 48 47N 1 11 E
Nonant-le-Pin 42 48 42N 0 12 E
Nonda 138 20 40 S 142 28 E
Nong Chang 100 15 23N 99 51 E
Nong Het 100 19 29N 103 59 E
Nong Khae 101 14 29N 100 53 E
Nong Khai 100 17 50N 102 46 E
Nonoava 164 27 22N 106 38W
Nonopapa 147 21 50N 160 15W
Nonthaburi 100 13 51N 100 34 E
Nontron 44 45 31N 0 40 E
Noonamah 136 12 40 S 131 4 E
Noonan 158 48 51N 102 59W
Noondoo 139 28 35 S 148 30 E
Noonkanbah 102 18 30 S 124 50 E
Noord-Bergum 46 53 14N 6 1 E
Noord Brabant □ 47 51 40N 5 0 E
Noord Holland □ 46 52 30N 4 45 E
Noordbeveland 47 51 45N 3 50 E
Noordeloos 46 51 55N 4 56 E
Noordhollandsch Kanaal 46 52 55N 4 48 E
Noordhorn 46 53 16N 6 24 E
Noordoostpolder 46 52 45N 5 45 E
Noordwijk aan Zee 46 52 14N 4 26 E
Noordwijk-Binnen 46 52 14N 4 27 E
Noordwijkerhout 46 52 16N 4 30 E
'Noordwinning', gasfield 19 53 13N 3 10 E
Noordzee Kanaal 46 52 28N 4 35 E
Noorvik 147 66 50N 161 14W
Noorwolde 46 52 54N 6 8 E
Nootka 152 49 38N 126 38W
Nootka I. 152 49 40N 126 50W
Noqui 124 5 55 S 13 30 E
Nora, Ethiopia 123 16 6N 40 4 E
Nora, Sweden 72 59 32N 15 2 E
Noranda 150 48 20N 79 0W
Norberg 72 60 4N 15 56 E
Norbottens län □ 74 66 58N 20 0 E
Nórcia 63 42 50N 13 5 E
Norco 163 33 56N 117 33W
Nord □ 43 50 15N 3 30 E
Nord-Ostee Kanal 48 54 5N 9 15 E
Nord-Süd Kanal 48 53 0N 10 32 E
Nord-Trondelag Fylke □ 74 64 20N 12 0 E
Nordagutu 71 59 25N 9 20 E
Nordaustlandet 12 79 55N 23 0 E
Nordborg 73 55 5N 9 50 E
Nordby, Fanø, Denmark 73 55 27N 8 24 E
Nordby, Samsø, Denmark 73 55 58N 10 32 E
Norddal 71 62 15N 7 14 E
Norddalsfjord kpl. 71 61 39N 5 23 E
Norddeich 48 53 37N 7 10 E
Nordegg 152 52 29N 116 5W
Nordelph 29 52 34N 0 18 E
Norden 48 53 35N 7 12 E
Nordenham 48 53 29N 8 28 E
Norderhov 71 60 7N 10 17 E
Norderney 48 53 42N 7 9 E
Norderney, I. 48 53 42N 7 15 E
Nordfjord 71 61 55N 5 30 E
Nordfriesische Inseln 48 54 40N 8 20 E
Nordhausen 48 51 29N 10 47 E
Nordhorn 48 52 27N 7 4 E
Nordjyllands Amt □ 73 57 0N 10 0 E
Nordkapp, Norway 74 71 10N 25 44 E
Nordkapp, Svalb. 12 80 31N 20 0 E
Nordkinn 16 71 3N 28 0 E
Nordland Fylke □ 74 65 40N 13 0 E
Nördlingen 49 48 50N 10 30 E
Nordrhein-Westfalen □ 48 51 45N 7 30 E
Nordstrand, I. 48 54 27N 8 50 E
Nordvik 77 73 40N 110 57 E
Nore 71 60 10N 9 0 E
Nore R. 39 52 40N 7 20W
Noreena Cr. 136 22 20 S 120 25 E
Norefjell 71 60 16N 9 29 E
Norembega 150 48 59N 80 43W
Noresund 71 60 11N 9 37 E
Norfolk, Nebr., U.S.A. 158 42 3N 97 25W
Norfolk, Va., U.S.A. 156 36 52N 76 15W
Norfolk □ 29 52 39N 1 0 E
Norfolk Broads 29 52 30N 1 15 E
Norfolk I. 130 28 58 S 168 3 E
Norfork Res. 159 36 25N 92 0W
Norg 46 53 4N 6 28 E
Norham 35 55 44N 2 9W
Norilsk 77 69 20N 88 0 E
Norley 139 27 45 S 143 48 E
Normal 158 40 30N 89 0W
Norman 159 35 12N 97 30W
Norman, R. 138 19 20 S 142 35 E
Norman Wells 147 65 17N 126 45W
Normanby 142 39 32 S 174 18 E
Normanby I. 135 10 55 S 151 5 E
Normanby, R. 138 14 23 S 144 10 E
Normandie 42 48 45N 0 10 E
Normandie, Collines de 42 48 55N 0 45W
Normandin 150 48 49N 72 31W
Normandy = Normandie 42 48 45N 0 10 E
Normanhurst, Mt. 137 25 13 S 122 30 E
Normanton, Austral. 138 17 40 S 141 10 E
Normanton, U.K. 33 53 41N 1 26W
Normanville 140 35 27 S 138 18 E
Norna, Mt. 138 20 55 S 140 42 E
Nornalup 137 35 0 S 116 48 E
Norquay 153 51 53N 102 5W
Norquinco 176 41 51 S 70 55W
Norrahammar 73 57 43N 14 7 E
Norrbottens län □ 74 66 50N 18 0 E
Norrby 74 64 55N 18 15 E
Nørre Åby 73 55 27N 9 52 E
Nørre Nebel 73 55 47N 8 17 E
Nørresundby 73 57 5N 9 52 E
Norris 160 45 40N 111 48W
Norristown 162 40 9N 75 15W
Norrköping 73 58 37N 16 11 E
Norrland □ 74 66 50N 18 0 E
Norrtälje 72 59 46N 18 42 E
Norseman 137 32 8 S 121 43 E
Norsholm 73 58 31N 15 59 E
Norsk 77 52 30N 130 0 E
Norte de Santander □ 174 8 0N 73 0W
North Adams 162 42 42N 73 6W
North America 50 40 0N 70 0W
North Andaman I. 101 13 15N 92 40 E
North Atlantic Ocean 14 30 0N 50 0W
North Ballachulish 36 56 42N 5 9W
North Battleford 153 52 50N 108 17W
North Bay 150 46 20N 79 30W
North Belcher Is. 150 56 50N 79 50W
North Bend, Can. 152 49 50N 121 35W
North Bend, U.S.A. 160 43 28N 124 7W
North Bennington 162 42 56N 73 15W
North Berwick, U.K. 35 56 4N 2 44W
North Berwick, U.S.A. 162 43 18N 70 43W
North Br., Ashburton R. 143 43 30 S 171 30 E
North Buganda □ 126 1 0N 32 0 E
North Canadian, R. 159 36 48N 103 0W
North C., Antarct. 13 71 0N 166 0 E
North C., Can. 151 47 2N 60 20W
North, Cape 151 47 2N 60 25W
North C., N.Z. 142 34 23 S 173 4 E
North C., P.N.G. 135 2 32 S 150 50 E
North C., Spitsbergen 12 80 40N 20 0 E
North Caribou L. 150 52 50N 90 40W
North Carolina □ 157 35 30N 80 0W
North Cerney 28 51 45N 1 58W
North Channel, Br. Is. 34 55 0N 5 30W
North Channel, Can. 150 46 0N 83 0W
North Chicago 156 42 19N 87 50W
North Collingham 33 53 8N 0 46W
North Dakota □ 158 47 30N 100 0W
North Dandalup 137 32 30 S 116 2 E
N. Dorset Downs 28 50 50N 2 30W
North Down □ 38 54 40N 5 45W
North Downs 29 51 17N 0 30W
North East 162 39 36N 75 56W
North Eastern □ 126 1 30N 40 0 E
North Esk, R. 37 56 44N 2 25W
North European Plain 16 55 0N 20 0 E
N. Foreland, Pt. 29 51 22N 1 28 E
North Fork 163 37 14N 119 29W
N. Frisian Is. = Nordfr'sche Inseln 48 54 50N 8 20 E
N. Harris, dist. 36 58 0N 6 55W
North Henik L. 153 61 45N 97 40W
North Hill 30 50 33N 4 26W
North Horr 126 3 20N 37 8 E
North Hykeham 33 53 10N 0 35W
North I., Kenya 126 4 5N 36 5 E
North I., N.Z. 143 38 0 S 175 0 E
North Kamloops 152 50 40N 120 25W
North Kessock 37 57 30N 4 15W
North Knife L., Can. 153 58 0N 97 0W
North Knife L., Man., Can. 153 58 5N 97 5W
North Knife, R. 153 58 53N 94 45W
North Koel, R. 95 23 50N 84 5 E
North Korea ■ 105 40 0N 127 0 E
N. Lakhimpur 99 27 15N 94 10 E
N. Las Vegas 161 36 15N 115 6W
North Mara □ 126 1 20 S 34 20 E
North Minch 36 58 5N 5 55W
North Molton 30 51 3N 3 48W
North Nahanni, R. 152 62 15N 123 20W
North Ossetian A.S.S.R. □ 83 43 30N 44 30 E
North Palisade 163 37 6N 118 32W
North Petherton 28 51 6N 3 1W
North Platte 158 41 10N 100 50W
North Platte, R. 160 42 50N 106 50W
North Pt., Austral. 108 27 23 S 153 14 E
North Pt., Can. 151 47 5N 65 0W
North Pole 12 90 0N 0 0 E
North Portal 153 49 0N 102 33W
North Powder 160 45 2N 117 59W
North Queensferry 35 56 1N 3 22W
North Riding (□) 26 54 22N 1 30W
North Roe, dist. 36 60 40N 1 22W
North Ronaldsay, I. 37 59 20N 2 30W
North Sea 19 56 0N 4 0 E
North Sentinel, I. 101 11 35N 92 15 E
North Somercotes 33 53 28N 0 9 E
North Sound 39 53 10N 9 48W
North Sound, The 37 59 18N 2 45W
North Sporades = Voríai Sporádhes 69 39 0N 24 10 E
North Stradbroke I. 133 27 35 S 153 28 E
North Sunderland 35 55 35N 1 40W
North Sydney 151 46 12N 60 21W
North Syracuse 162 43 9N 76 7W
N. Taranaki Bt. 82 38 45 S 174 20 E

North Tawton 30 50 48N 3 55W
North Thompson, R. 152 50 40N 120 20W
North Thoresby 33 53 27N 0 3W
North Tidworth 28 51 14N 1 40W
North Tolsta 36 58 21N 6 13W
N. Tonawanda 156 43 5N 78 50W
N. Truchas Pk. 161 36 0N 105 30W
North Twin I. 150 53 20N 80 0W
North Tyne, R. 35 54 59N 2 7W
North Uist I. 36 57 40N 7 15W
North Vancouver 152 49 25N 123 20W
North Vermilion 152 58 25N 116 0W
North Vernon 156 39 0N 85 35W
North Vietnam ■ 100 22 0N 105 0E
North Wabasca L. 152 56 0N 113 55W
North Walsham 29 52 49N 1 22E
North West C. 136 21 45S 114 9E
North West Highlands 36 57 35N 5 2W
North West River 151 53 30N 60 10W
North Western □ 127 13 30S 25 30E
North York Moors 33 54 25N 0 50W
North Yorkshire □ 33 54 15N 1 25W
Northallerton 33 54 20N 1 26W
Northam, Austral. 132 31 35S 116 42E
Northam, S. Afr. 137 24 55S 27 15E
Northam, U.K. 30 51 2N 4 13W
Northampton, Austral. 137 28 21S 114 33E
Northampton, U.K. 29 52 14N 0 54W
Northampton, Mass., U.S.A. 162 42 22N 72 39W
Northampton, Pa., U.S.A. 162 40 38N 75 24W
Northampton □ 29 52 16N 0 55W
Northampton Downs 138 24 35S 145 48E
Northbridge 162 42 12N 71 40W
Northcliffe 137 34 39S 116 7E
N.E. Land 12 80 0N 24 0E
N.E. Providence Chan. 166 26 0N 76 0W
Northeast Providence Channel 166 26 0N 76 0W
Northeim 42 51 42N 10 0E
Northern □, Malawi 127 11 0S 34 0E
Northern □, Uganda 126 3 5N 32 30E
Northern □, Zambia 127 10 30S 31 0E
Northern Circars 96 17 30N 82 30E
Northern Indian L. 153 57 20N 97 20W
Northern Ireland □ 38 54 45N 7 0W
Northern Light, L. 150 48 15N 90 39W
Northern Province □ 120 9 0S 11 30W
Northern Territory □ 136 16 0S 133 0E
Northfield, Minn., U.S.A. 158 44 37N 93 10W
Northfield, N.J., U.S.A. 162 39 22N 74 33W
Northfleet 29 51 26N 0 20E
Northiam 29 50 59N 0 39E
Northland □ 143 35 30S 173 30E
Northleach 28 51 49N 1 50W
Northome 158 47 53N 94 15W
Northop 31 53 13N 3 8W
Northport, Ala., U.S.A. 157 33 15N 87 35W
Northport, Mich., U.S.A. 156 45 8N 85 39W
Northport, N.Y., U.S.A. 162 40 53N 73 20W
Northport, Wash., U.S.A. 160 48 55N 117 48W
Northrepps 29 52 53N 1 20E
Northumberland □ 35 55 12N 2 0W
Northumberland, C. 140 38 5S 140 40E
Northumberland Is. 138 21 30S 149 50E
Northumberland Str. 151 46 20N 64 0W
Northville 162 43 13N 74 11W
Northway Junction 147 63 0N 141 55W
N.W. Providence Chan. 166 26 0N 78 0W
Northwest Terr. 148 65 0N 100 0W
N.W.Basin 137 25 45S 115 0E
Northwich 32 53 16N 2 30W
Northwold 29 52 33N 0 37E
Northwood, Iowa, U.S.A. 158 43 27N 93 12W
Northwood, N.D., U.S.A. 158 47 44N 97 30W
Norton, Rhod. 127 17 52S 30 40E
Norton, N. Yorks., U.K. 33 54 9N 0 48W
Norton, Suffolk, U.K. 29 52 15N 0 52E
Norton, U.S.A. 158 39 50N 100 0W
Norton B. 147 64 40N 162 0W
Norton Fitzwarren 28 51 1N 3 10W
Norton Sd. 147 64 0N 165 0W
Norton Summit 109 34 56S 138 43E
Nortorf 48 54 14N 9 47E
Norwalk, Calif., U.S.A. 163 33 54N 118 5W
Norwalk, Conn., U.S.A. 162 41 9N 73 25W
Norwalk, Ohio, U.S.A. 156 41 13N 82 38W
Norway 156 45 46N 87 57W
Norway ■ 74 67 0N 11 0E
Norway House 153 53 59N 97 50W
Norwegian Dependency 13 66 0N 15 0E
Norwegian Sea 14 66 0N 1 0E
Norwich, U.K. 29 52 38N 1 17E
Norwich, Conn., U.S.A. 162 41 33N 72 5W
Norwich, N.Y., U.S.A. 162 42 32N 75 30W
Norwood, Austral. 109 34 56S 138 39E
Norwood, U.S.A. 162 42 10N 71 10W
Noshiro 112 40 12N 140 0E
Noshiro, R. 112 40 15N 140 15E
Nosok 76 70 10N 82 20E
Nosovka 80 50 50N 31 30E
Nosratābād 93 29 55N 60 0E
Noss Hd. 37 58 29N 3 4W
Noss, I. of 36 60 8N 1 1W
Nossa Senhora da Glória 170 10 14S 37 25W
Nossa Senhora das Dores 170 10 29S 37 13W
Nossebro 73 58 12N 12 43E
Nossob 128 22 15S 17 48E
Nossob, R. 128 25 15S 20 30E
Nosy Bé, I. 125 13 25S 48 15E
Nosy Mitsio, I. 125 12 54S 48 36E
Nosy Varika 125 20 35S 48 32E
Notigi Dam 153 56 40N 99 10W
Notikewin 152 56 55N 117 50W
Notikewin, R. 152 56 59N 117 38W
Notios Evvoïkós Kólpos 69 38 20N 24 0E
Noto 65 36 52N 15 4E
Notò, G. di 65 36 50N 15 10E
Notodden 71 59 35N 9 17E
Notre Dame 151 46 18N 64 46W
Notre Dame B. 151 49 45N 55 30W
Notre Dame de Koartac 149 60 55N 69 40W
Notre Dame d'Ivugivic 149 62 20N 78 0W
Nottaway, R. 150 51 22N 78 55W
Nøtterøy 71 59 14N 10 24E
Nottingham 33 52 57N 1 10W
Nottingham □ 33 53 10N 1 0W
Nottoway, R. 156 37 0N 77 45W
Notwani, R. 128 24 14S 26 20E
Nouadhibou 116 21 0N 17 0W
Nouakchott 120 18 20N 15 50W
Nouméa 130 22 17S 166 30E
Noup Hd. 37 59 20N 3 2W
Noupoort 128 31 10S 24 57E
Nouveau Comptoir (Paint Hills) 150 53 0N 78 49W
Nouvelle Calédonie 142 21 0S 165 0E
Nouzonville 43 49 48N 4 44E
Nova-Annenskiy 81 50 32N 42 39E
Nová Bana 53 48 28N 18 39E
Nová Bystrice 52 49 2N 15 8E
Nova Chaves 124 10 50S 21 15E
Nova Cruz 170 6 28S 35 25W
Nova Era 171 19 45S 43 3W
Nova Esperança 173 23 8S 52 13W
Nova Friburgo 173 22 10S 42 30W
Nova Gaia 124 10 10S 17 35E
Nova Gradiška 66 45 17N 17 28E
Nova Granada 171 20 30S 49 20W
Nova Iguaçu 173 22 45S 43 28W
Nova Iorque 170 7 0S 44 5W
Nova Lamego 120 12 19N 14 11W
Nova Lima 173 19 59S 43 51W
Nova Lisboa = Huambo 125 12 42S 15 54E
Nova Lusitânia 127 19 50S 34 34E
Nova Mambone 129 21 0S 35 3E
Nova Mesto 63 45 47N 15 12E
Nova Paka 52 50 29N 15 30E
Nova Ponte 171 19 8S 47 41W
Nova Preixo 127 14 45S 36 22E
Nova Scotia □ 151 45 10N 63 0W
Nova Sofala 129 20 7S 34 48E
Nova Varoš 66 43 29N 19 48E
Nova Venécia 171 18 45S 40 24W
Nova Zagora 67 42 32N 25 59E
Novaci, Rumania 70 45 10N 23 42E
Novaci, Yugo. 66 41 5N 21 29E
Novaleksandrovskaya 83 45 29N 41 17E
Novalorque 171 6 48S 44 0W
Novara 62 45 27N 8 36E
Novato 163 38 6N 122 35W
Novaya Kakhovka 82 46 42N 33 27E
Novaya Ladoga 78 60 7N 32 16E
Novaya Lyalya 84 58 50N 60 35E
Novaya Sibir, O. 77 75 10N 150 0E
Novaya Zemlya 76 75 0N 56 0E
Novelda 59 38 24N 0 45W
Novellara 62 44 50N 10 43E
Noventa Vicentina 63 45 18N 11 30E
Novgorod 80 58 30N 31 25E
Novgorod Severskiy 80 52 2N 33 10E
Novgorod Volynski 80 50 38N 27 47E
Novi Bečej. 66 45 36N 20 10E
Novi Grad 63 45 19N 13 33E
Novi Knezeva 66 46 4N 20 8E
Novi Krichim 67 42 22N 24 31E
Novi Lígure 62 44 45N 8 47E
Novi-Pazar 67 43 25N 27 15E
Novi Pazar 66 43 12N 20 28E
Novi Sad 66 45 18N 19 52E
Novi Vinodolski 63 45 10N 14 48E
Novigrad 63 44 10N 15 32E
Noville 47 50 4N 5 46E
Novo Acôrdo 170 13 10S 46 48W
Nôvo Cruzeiro 171 17 29S 41 53W
Novo Freixo 127 14 49S 36 30E
Nôvo Hamburgo 173 29 37S 51 7W
Novo Horizonte 171 21 25S 49 10W
Novo Luso 103 4 3S 126 6E
Novo Redondo 124 11 10S 13 48E
Novo Selo 66 44 11N 22 47E
Novo-Sergiyevskiy 84 52 5N 53 38E
Novo-Zavidovskiy 81 56 32N 36 29E
Novoalekseyevka 84 50 8N 55 39E
Novoataysk 76 53 30N 84 0E
Novoazovsk 82 47 15N 38 4E
Novobelitsa 80 52 27N 31 2E
Novobogatinskoye 83 47 26N 51 17E
Novocherkassk 83 47 27N 40 5E
Novodevichye 81 53 37N 48 58E
Novograd Volynskiy 80 50 40N 27 35E
Novogrudok 80 53 40N 25 50E
Novokayakent 83 42 45N 42 52E
Novokazalinsk 76 45 40N 61 40E
Novokhopersk 81 51 5N 41 50E
Novokuybyshevsk 84 53 7N 49 58E
Novokuznetsk 76 54 0N 87 10E
Novomirgorod 82 48 57N 31 33E
Novomoskovsk, R.S.F.S.R., U.S.S.R. 81 54 5N 38 15E
Novomoskovsk, Ukrainian S.S.R., U.S.S.R. 81 48 33N 35 17E
Novoorsk 84 51 21N 59 2E
Novopolotsk 80 55 38N 28 37E
Novorossiysk 82 44 43N 37 52E
Novorzhev 80 57 3N 29 25E
Novoselitsa 82 48 14N 26 15E
Novoshakhtinsk 83 47 39N 39 58E
Novosibirsk 76 55 0N 83 5E
Novosibirskiye Ostrava 77 75 0N 140 0E
Novosil 81 52 58N 36 58E
Novosokolniki 80 56 33N 28 42E
Novotroitsk 84 51 10N 58 15E
Novotroitskoye 85 43 42N 73 46E
Novotulskiy 81 54 10N 37 36E
Novoukrainka 82 48 25N 31 30E
Novouzensk 81 50 32N 48 17E
Novovolynsk 80 50 45N 24 4E
Novovyatsk 84 58 24N 49 45E
Novozybkov 80 52 30N 32 0E
Novska 66 45 19N 17 0E
Novy Bug 82 47 34N 34 29E
Nový Bydzov 52 50 14N 15 29E
Novy Dwór Mazowiecki 54 52 26N 20 44E
Nový Jičin 53 49 15N 18 0E
Novyy Oskol 81 50 44N 37 55E
Novyy Port 76 67 40N 72 30E
Novyye Aneny 70 46 51N 29 13E
Now Shahr 93 36 40N 51 40E
Nowa Deba 54 50 26N 21 41E
Nowa Nowa 141 37 44S 148 3E
Nowa Skalmierzyce 54 51 43N 18 0E
Nowa Sól 54 51 48N 15 44E
Nowe 54 53 41N 18 44E
Nowe Miasteczko 54 51 42N 15 42E
Nowe Miasto 54 51 38N 20 34E
Nowe Miasto Lubawskie 54 53 27N 19 33E
Nowe Warpno 54 53 42N 14 18E
Nowen Hill 39 51 42N 9 15W
Nowendoc 141 31 32S 151 44E
Nowgong 98 26 20N 92 50E
Nowingi 140 34 33S 142 15E
Nowogard 54 53 41N 15 10E
Nowogród 54 53 14N 21 53E
Nowra 141 34 53S 150 35E
Nowthanna Mt. 137 27 0S 118 40E
Nowy Dwór 54 53 40N 23 0E
Nowy Korczyn 54 50 19N 20 48E
Nowy Sącz 54 49 40N 20 41E
Nowy Sącz □ 54 49 30N 20 30E
Nowy Staw 54 54 13N 19 2E
Nowy Targ 53 49 30N 20 2E
Nowy Tomyssl 54 52 19N 16 10E
Noxen 162 41 25N 76 4W
Noxon 160 48 0N 115 54W
Noya 56 42 48N 8 53W
Noyant 42 47 30N 0 6E
Noyers 43 47 40N 4 0E
Noyes, I. 152 55 30N 133 40W
Noyon 43 49 34N 3 0E
Nriquinha 125 16 0S 21 25E
Nsa, O. en 119 32 23N 5 20E
Nsanje 127 16 55S 35 12E
Nsawam 121 5 50N 0 24W
Nsomba 127 10 45S 29 59E
Nsopzup 98 25 51N 97 30E
Nsukka 121 7 0N 7 50E
Nuanetsi 125 21 15S 30 48E
Nuanetsi, R. 127 21 10S 31 20E
Nuatja 121 7 0N 1 10E
Nuba Mts. = Nubāh, Jibālan 123 12 0N 31 0E
Nubāh, Jibālan 123 12 0N 31 0E
Nûbîya, Es Sahrâ En 122 21 30N 33 30E
Ñuble □ 172 37 0S 72 0W
Nuboai 103 2 10S 136 30E
Nubra, R. 95 34 50N 77 25E
Nudgee 108 27 22S 153 5E
Nudgee Beach 108 27 21S 153 6E
Nûdlac 66 46 10N 20 50E
Nudo Ausangate, Mt. 174 13 45S 71 10W
Nudo de Vilcanota 174 14 30S 70 0W
Nueces, R. 159 28 18N 98 39W
Nueltin L. 153 60 30N 99 30W
Nuenen 47 51 29N 5 33E
Nueva Antioquia 174 6 5N 69 26W
Nueva Casas Grandes 164 30 25N 107 55W
Nueva Esparta □ 174 11 0N 64 0W
Nueva Gerona 166 21 53N 82 49W
Nueva Imperial 176 38 45S 72 58W
Nueva Palmira 172 33 52S 58 20W
Nueva Rosita 164 28 0N 101 20W
Nueva San Salvador 166 13 40N 89 25W
Nuéve de Julio 172 35 30S 61 0W
Nuevitas 166 21 30N 77 20W
Nuevo, Golfo 176 43 0S 64 30W
Nuevo Guerrero 165 26 34N 99 15W
Nuevo Laredo 165 27 30N 99 40W
Nuevo León □ 164 25 0N 100 0W
Nuevo Rocafuerte 174 0 55S 76 50W
Nugget Pt. 143 46 27S 169 50E
Nugrus Gebel 122 24 58N 39 34E
Nuhaka 142 39 3S 177 45E
Nuhurowa, I. 103 5 30S 132 45E
Nuits 43 47 10N 4 56E
Nuits-St.-Georges 43 47 10N 4 56E
Nukey Bluff, Mt. 132 32 32S 135 40E
Nukheila (Merga) 122 19 1N 26 21E
Nukus 76 42 20N 59 40E
Nuland 46 51 44N 5 26E
Nulato 147 64 40N 158 10W
Nules 58 39 51N 0 9W
Nullagine 136 21 53S 120 6E
Nullagine, R. 136 21 20S 120 20E
Nullarbor 137 31 28S 130 55E
Nullarbor Plain 137 30 45S 129 0E
Numalla, L. 139 28 43S 144 20E
Numan 121 9 29N 12 3E
Numansdorp 46 51 43N 4 26E
Numata 111 36 45N 139 4E
Numatinna, W. 123 6 38N 27 15E
Numazu 111 35 7N 138 51E
Numbulwar 138 14 15S 135 45E
Numfoor, I. 103 1 0S 134 50E
Numurkah 141 36 0S 145 26E
Nun, R. 105 47 30N 124 40E
Nunaksaluk, I. 151 55 49N 60 20W
Nundah 108 27 24S 152 54E
Nuneaton 28 52 32N 1 29W
Nungo 127 13 23S 37 43E
Nungwe 126 2 48S 32 2E
Nunivak I. 147 60 0N 166 0W
Nunkun, Mt. 95 33 57N 76 8E
Nunney 28 51 13N 2 20W
Nunspeet 46 52 21N 5 45E
Nuoro 64 40 20N 9 20E
Nŭousa 68 40 42N 22 9E
Nuqayy, Jabal 119 23 11N 19 30E
Nuquí 174 5 42N 77 17W
Nurata 85 40 33N 65 41E
Nuratau, Khrebet 85 40 40N 66 30E
Nure, R. 62 44 40N 9 32E
Nuremburg = Nürnberg 49 49 26N 11 5E
Nuri 164 28 2N 109 22W
Nurina 137 30 44S 126 23E
Nuriootpa 140 34 27S 139 0E
Nurlat 84 54 29N 50 45E
Nürnberg 49 49 26N 11 5E
Nurrari Lakes 137 29 1S 130 5E
Nurri 64 39 43N 9 13E
Nusa Barung 103 8 22S 113 20E
Nusa Kambangan 103 7 47S 109 0E
Nusa Tenggara □ 102 7 30S 117 0E
Nusa Tenggara Barat 102 8 50S 117 30E
Nusa Tenggara Timur 103 9 30S 122 0E
Nushki 94 29 35N 65 65E
Nŭsŭud 70 47 19N 24 29E
Nutak 149 57 28N 61 52W
Nuth 47 50 55N 5 53E
Nutwood Downs 138 15 49S 134 10E
Nuwaiba 122 28 58N 34 40E
Nuwakot 95 28 10N 83 55E
Nuwara Eliya 97 6 58N 80 55E
Nuwefontein 128 28 1S 19 6E
Nuweveldberge 128 32 10S 21 45E
Nuyts Arch. 139 32 12S 133 20E
Nuyts, C. 137 32 2S 132 21E
Nuyts, Pt. 132 35 4S 116 38E
Nuzvid 96 16 47N 80 53E
NW Tor, oilfield 19 56 42N 3 13E
Nyaake (Webo) 120 4 52N 7 37W
Nyabing 137 33 30S 118 7E
Nyack 162 41 5N 73 57W
Nyadal 72 62 48N 17 59E
Nyagyn 76 62 8N 63 36E
Nyah West 140 35 11S 143 21E
Nyahanga 126 2 20S 33 37E
Nyahua 126 5 25S 33 23E
Nyahururu 126 0 2N 36 27E
Nyahururu Falls 126 0 2N 36 27E
Nyakanazi 126 3 2S 31 10E
Nyakasu 126 3 58S 30 6E
Nyakrom 121 5 40N 0 50W
Nyâlâ 123 12 2N 24 58E
Nyamandhlovu 127 19 55S 28 16E
Nyambiti 126 2 48S 33 27E
Nyamwaga 126 1 27S 34 33E
Nyandekwa 126 3 57S 32 32E
Nyanga, L. 137 29 57S 126 10E
Nyangana 128 18 0S 20 40E
Nyanguge 126 2 30S 33 12E
Nyangwena 127 15 18S 28 45E
Nyanji 127 14 25S 31 46E
Nyankpala 121 9 21N 0 58W
Nyanza, Burundi 126 4 21S 29 36E
Nyanza, Rwanda 126 2 20S 29 42E
Nyanza □ 126 0 10S 34 15E
Nyarling, R. 152 60 41N 113 23W
Nyasa, L. = Malawi, L. 127 12 0S 34 30E
Nyaunglebin 98 17 52N 96 42E
Nyazepetrovsk 84 56 3N 59 36E
Nyazwidzi, R. 127 19 35S 32 0E
Nyborg 73 55 18N 10 47E
Nybro 73 56 44N 15 55E
Nybster 37 58 34N 3 6W
Nyda 76 66 40N 73 10E
Nyenchen Tanglha Shan 99 30 30N 95 0E
Nyeri 126 0 23S 36 56E
Nyeri □ 126 0 25S 36 55E
Nyerol 123 8 41N 32 1E
Nyhem 72 62 54N 15 37E
Nyiel 123 6 9N 31 4E
Nyika Plat. 127 10 30S 33 50E
Nyilumba 127 10 30S 40 22E
Nyinahin 120 6 43N 2 3W
Nyirbátor 53 47 49N 22 9E

Name	Page	Lat.	Long.
Nyíregyháza	**53**	48 0N	21 47 E
Nykarleby (Uusikaarlepyy)	**74**	63 32N	22 31 E
Nykobing	**73**	54 56N	11 52 E
Nykøbing, Falster, Denmark	**73**	54 56N	11 52 E
Nykøbing, Mors, Denmark	**73**	56 48N	8 51 E
Nykøbing, Sjælland, Denmark	**73**	55 55N	11 40 E
Nyköbing	**73**	56 49N	8 50 E
Nyköping	**73**	58 45N	17 0 E
Nykroppa	**72**	59 37N	14 18 E
Nykvarn	**72**	59 11N	17 25 E
Nyland	**72**	63 1N	17 45 E
Nylstroom	**129**	24 42 S	28 22 E
Nymagee	**141**	32 7 S	146 20 E
Nymburk	**52**	50 10N	15 1 E
Nymindegab	**73**	55 50N	8 12 E
Nynäshamn	**72**	58 54N	17 57 E
Nyngan	**141**	31 30 S	147 8 E
Nyon	**50**	46 23N	6 14 E
Nyons	**45**	44 22N	5 10 E
Nyora	**141**	38 20 S	145 41 E
Nyord	**73**	55 4N	12 13 E
Nysa	**54**	50 40N	17 22 E
Nysa, R.	**54**	52 4N	14 46 E
Nyssa	**160**	43 56N	117 2W
Nysted	**73**	54 40N	11 44 E
Nytva	**84**	57 56N	55 20 E
Nyūgawa	**110**	33 56N	133 5 E
Nyunzu	**126**	5 57 S	27 58 E
Nyurba	**77**	63 17N	118 20 E
Nzega	**126**	4 10 S	33 12 E
Nzega □	**126**	4 10 S	33 10 E
N'Zérékoré	**120**	7 49N	8 48W
Nzilo, Chutes de	**127**	10 18 S	25 27 E
Nzubuka	**126**	4 45 S	32 50 E
O			
O-Shima, Fukuoka, Japan	**110**	33 54N	130 25 E
O-Shima, Nagasaki, Japan	**110**	33 29N	129 33 E
O-Shima, Shizuoka, Japan	**111**	34 44N	139 24 E
Oa, Mull of	**34**	55 35N	6 20W
Oa, The, Pen.	**34**	55 36N	6 17W
Oacoma	**158**	43 50N	99 26W
Oadby	**28**	52 37N	1 7W
Oahe	**158**	44 33N	100 29W
Oahe Dam	**158**	44 28N	100 25W
Oahe Res	**158**	45 30N	100 15W
Oahu I.	**147**	21 30N	158 0W
Oak Creek	**160**	40 15N	106 59W
Oak Harb.	**160**	48 20N	122 38W
Oak Lake	**153**	49 45N	100 45W
Oak Park	**156**	41 55N	87 45W
Oak Ridge	**157**	36 1N	84 5W
Oak View	**163**	34 24N	119 18W
Oakbank, S. Australia, Austral.	**109**	34 59 S	138 51 E
Oakbank, S. Australia, Austral.	**140**	33 4 S	140 33 E
Oakdale, Calif., U.S.A.	**163**	37 49N	120 56W
Oakdale, La., U.S.A.	**159**	30 50N	92 38W
Oakengates	**28**	52 42N	2 29W
Oakes	**158**	46 14N	98 4W
Oakesdale	**160**	47 11N	117 9W
Oakey	**139**	27 25 S	151 43 E
Oakham	**29**	52 40N	0 43W
Oakhill	**156**	38 0N	81 7W
Oakhurst	**163**	37 19N	119 40W
Oakland	**163**	37 50N	122 18W
Oakland City	**156**	38 20N	87 20W
Oaklands, N.S.W., Austral.	**141**	35 34 S	146 10 E
Oaklands, S. Australia, Austral.	**109**	35 1 S	138 32 E
Oakley	**160**	42 14N	113 55W
Oakley Creek	**141**	31 37 S	149 46 E
Oakover, R.	**136**	20 43 S	120 33 E
Oakridge	**160**	43 47N	122 31W
Oakwood	**159**	31 35N	95 47W
Oamaru	**143**	45 5 S	170 59 E
Oamishirasato	**111**	35 23N	140 18 E
Oarai	**111**	36 21N	140 40 E
Oasis, Calif., U.S.A.	**163**	33 28N	116 6W
Oasis, Nev., U.S.A.	**163**	37 29N	117 55W
Oates Coast	**13**	69 0 S	160 0 E
Oatman	**161**	35 1N	114 19W
Oaxaca	**165**	17 2N	96 40W
Oaxaca □	**165**	17 0N	97 0W
Ob, R.	**76**	62 40N	66 0 E
Oba	**150**	49 4N	84 7W
Obala	**121**	4 9N	11 32 E
Obama, Eukui, Japan	**111**	35 30N	135 45 E
Obama, Nagasaki, Japan	**110**	32 43N	130 13 E
Oban, N.Z.	**143**	46 55 S	168 10 E
Oban, U.K.	**34**	56 25N	5 30W
Obatogamau L.	**150**	49 34N	74 26W
Obbia	**91**	5 25N	48 30 E
Obdam	**46**	52 41N	4 55 E
Obed	**152**	53 30N	117 10W
Obeh	**93**	34 28N	63 10 E
Ober-Aagau	**50**	47 10N	7 45 E
Obera	**173**	27 21 S	55 2W
Oberalppass	**51**	46 39N	8 35 E
Oberalpstock	**51**	46 45N	8 47 E
Oberammergau	**49**	47 35N	11 3 E
Oberdrauburg	**52**	46 44N	12 58 E
Oberengadin	**51**	46 35N	9 55 E
Oberentfelden	**50**	47 21N	8 2 E
Oberhausen	**48**	51 28N	6 50 E
Oberkirch	**49**	48 31N	8 5 E
Oberland	**50**	46 30N	7 30 E
Oberlin, Kans., U.S.A.	**158**	39 52N	100 31W
Oberlin, La., U.S.A.	**159**	30 42N	92 42W
Obernai	**43**	48 28N	7 30 E
Oberndorf	**49**	48 17N	8 35 E
Oberon	**141**	33 45 S	149 52 E
Oberösterreich □	**52**	48 10N	14 0 E
Oberpfalzer Wald	**49**	49 30N	12 25 E
Oberseebach	**51**	48 53N	7 58 E
Obersiggenthal	**51**	47 29N	8 18 E
Oberstdorf	**49**	47 25N	10 16 E
Oberwil	**50**	47 32N	7 33 E
Obi, Kepulauan	**103**	1 30 S	127 30 E
Obiaruku	**121**	5 51N	6 9 E
Óbidos, Brazil	**175**	1 50 S	55 30W
Óbidos, Port.	**57**	39 19N	9 10W
Obihiro	**112**	42 25N	143 12 E
Obilnoye	**83**	47 32N	44 30 E
Obisfelde	**48**	52 27N	10 57 E
Objat	**44**	45 16N	1 24 E
Obluchye	**77**	49 10N	130 50 E
Obninsk	**81**	55 8N	36 13 E
Obo, C. Afr. Emp.	**123**	5 20N	26 32 E
Obo, Ethiopia	**123**	3 34N	38 52 E
Oboa, Mt.	**126**	1 45N	34 45 E
Obock	**123**	12 0N	43 20 E
Oborniki	**54**	52 39N	16 59 E
Oborniki Śl.	**54**	51 17N	16 53 E
Obot	**123**	4 32N	37 13 E
Obout	**121**	3 28N	11 47 E
Oboyan	**81**	51 20N	36 28 E
Obrenovac	**66**	44 40N	20 11 E
O'Briensbridge	**39**	52 46N	8 30W
Obrovac	**63**	44 11N	15 41 E
Observatory Inlet	**152**	55 25N	129 45W
Obshchi Syrt	**16**	52 0N	53 0 E
Obskaya Guba	**76**	70 0N	73 0 E
Obuasi	**121**	6 17N	1 40W
Obubra	**121**	6 8N	8 20 E
Obyachevo	**84**	60 20N	49 37 E
Obzor	**67**	42 50N	27 52 E
Ocala	**157**	29 11N	82 5W
Ocampo	**164**	28 9N	108 8W
Ocaña	**58**	39 55N	3 30W
Ocanomowoc	**158**	43 7N	88 30W
Ocate	**159**	36 12N	104 59W
Occidental, Cordillera	**174**	5 0N	76 0W
Ocean City, Md., U.S.A.	**162**	38 20N	75 5W
Ocean City, N.J., U.S.A.	**162**	39 18N	74 34W
Ocean Falls	**152**	52 25N	127 40W
Ocean I.	**130**	0 45 S	169 50 E
Ocean Park	**160**	46 30N	124 2W
Oceanlake	**160**	45 0N	124 0W
Oceano	**163**	35 6N	120 37W
Oceanside	**163**	33 13N	117 26W
Ochagavia	**58**	42 55N	1 5W
Ochakov	**82**	46 35N	31 30 E
Ochamchire	**83**	42 46N	41 32 E
Ochamps	**47**	49 56N	5 16 E
Och'eng	**109**	30 20N	114 51 E
Ocher	**84**	57 53N	54 42 E
Ochiai	**110**	35 1N	133 45 E
Ochil Hills	**35**	56 14N	3 40W
Ochiltree	**34**	55 26N	4 23W
Ochre River	**153**	51 4N	99 47W
Ochsenfurt	**49**	49 38N	10 3 E
Ocilla	**157**	31 35N	83 12W
Ockelbo	**72**	60 54N	16 45 E
Ocmulgee, R.	**157**	32 0N	83 19W
Ocna Mureş	**70**	46 23N	23 49 E
Ocna-Sibiului	**70**	45 52N	24 2 E
Ocnele Mari	**70**	45 8N	24 18 E
Oconee, R.	**157**	32 30N	82 55W
Oconto	**156**	44 52N	87 53W
Oconto Falls	**156**	44 52N	88 10W
Ocós	**166**	14 31N	92 11W
Ocosingo	**165**	18 4N	92 15W
Ocotal	**166**	13 41N	86 41W
Ocotlán	**164**	20 21N	102 42W
Ocquier	**47**	50 24N	5 24 E
Ocreza, R.	**56**	39 50N	7 35W
Ócsa	**53**	47 17N	19 15 E
Octave	**161**	34 10N	112 43W
Octeville	**42**	49 38N	1 40W
Octyabrskoy Revolyutsii, Os.	**77**	79 30N	97 0 E
Ocumare del Tuy	**174**	10 7N	66 46W
Ocussi	**103**	9 20 S	124 30 E
Oda, Ghana	**121**	5 50N	1 5W
Oda, Ehime, Japan	**110**	33 36N	132 53 E
Oda, Shimane, Japan	**110**	35 11N	132 30 E
Ödåkra	**73**	56 9N	12 45 E
Ödåkra	**73**	56 7N	12 45 E
Odanakumadona	**128**	20 55 S	24 46 E
Ódáoahraun	**74**	65 5N	17 0W
Odate	**112**	40 16N	140 34 E
Odawara	**111**	35 20N	139 6 E
Odda	**71**	60 3N	6 35 E
Odder	**73**	55 58N	10 10 E
Oddobo	**123**	12 21N	42 6 E
Oddur	**91**	4 0N	43 35 E
Ödeborg	**73**	58 32N	11 58 E
Odei, R.	**153**	56 6N	96 54W
Odemira	**57**	37 35N	8 40W
Ödemiş	**92**	38 15N	28 0 E
Odense	**73**	55 22N	10 23 E
Odenton	**162**	39 5N	76 42W
Odenwald	**48**	49 18N	9 0 E
Oder, R.	**48**	53 0N	14 12 E
Oderzo	**63**	45 47N	12 29 E
Odessa, Del., U.S.A.	**162**	39 27N	75 40W
Odessa, Tex., U.S.A.	**159**	31 51N	102 23W
Odessa, Wash., U.S.A.	**160**	47 25N	118 35W
Odessa, U.S.S.R.	**82**	46 30N	30 45 E
Odiel, R.	**57**	37 30N	6 55W
Odienné	**120**	9 30N	7 34W
Odiham	**29**	51 16N	0 56W
Odin, gasfield	**19**	60 5N	2 10 E
Odoben	**121**	5 38N	0 56W
Odobeşti	**70**	45 43N	27 4 E
Odolanów	**54**	51 34N	17 40 E
O'Donnell	**159**	33 0N	101 48W
Odoorn	**46**	52 51N	6 51 E
Odorheiul Secuiesc	**70**	46 21N	25 21 E
Odoyevo	**81**	53 56N	36 42 E
Odra, R., Czech.	**53**	49 43N	17 47 E
Odra, R., Poland	**54**	52 40N	14 28 E
Odra, R., Spain	**56**	42 30N	4 15W
Odzaci	**66**	45 30N	19 17 E
Odzak	**66**	45 3N	18 18 E
Odzi	**125**	19 0 S	32 20 E
Oedelem	**47**	51 10N	3 21 E
Oegstgeest	**46**	52 11N	4 29 E
Oeiras, Brazil	**170**	7 0 S	42 8W
Oeiras, Port.	**57**	38 41N	9 18W
Oelrichs	**158**	43 11N	103 14W
Oelsnitz	**48**	50 24N	12 11 E
Oenpelli	**136**	12 20 S	133 4 E
Oensingen	**50**	47 17N	7 43 E
Oerhtossu, reg.	**106**	39 20N	108 30 E
Ofanto, R.	**65**	41 8N	15 50 E
Ofen Pass	**51**	46 37N	10 17 E
Offa	**121**	8 13N	4 42 E
Offaly □	**39**	53 15N	7 30W
Offenbach	**49**	50 6N	8 46 E
Offenbeek	**47**	51 17N	6 5 E
Offenburg	**126**	48 27N	7 56 E
Offerdal	**72**	63 28N	14 0 E
Offida	**63**	42 56N	13 40 E
Offranville	**42**	49 52N	1 0 E
Ofidhousa, I.	**69**	36 33N	26 8 E
Ofotfjorden	**74**	68 27N	16 40 E
Oga-Hantō	**111**	39 58N	139 59 E
Ogahalla	**150**	50 6N	85 51W
Ōgaki	**111**	35 21N	136 37 E
Ogallala	**158**	41 12N	101 40W
Ogbomosho	**121**	8 1N	3 29 E
Ogden, Iowa, U.S.A.	**158**	42 3N	94 0W
Ogden, Utah, U.S.A.	**160**	41 13N	112 1W
Ogdensburg	**156**	44 40N	75 27W
Ogeechee, R.	**157**	32 30N	81 32W
Oglio, R.	**62**	45 15N	10 15 E
Ogmore	**138**	22 37 S	149 35 E
Ogmore, R.	**31**	51 29N	3 37W
Ogmore Vale	**30**	51 35N	3 32W
Ogna	**71**	58 31N	5 48 E
Ognon, R.	**43**	47 43N	6 32 E
Ogoja	**121**	6 38N	8 39 E
Ogoki	**150**	51 35N	86 0W
Ogoki L.	**150**	50 50N	87 10W
Ogoki, R.	**150**	51 38N	85 57W
Ogoki Res.	**150**	50 45N	88 15W
Ogooué, R.	**124**	1 0 S	10 0 E
Ogori	**110**	34 6N	131 24 E
Ogosta, R.	**67**	43 35N	23 35 E
Ogowe, R. = Ogooué, R.	**124**	1 0 S	10 0 E
Ograzden	**66**	41 30N	22 50 E
Ogrein	**122**	17 55N	34 50 E
Ogulin	**63**	45 16N	15 16 E
Ogun □	**121**	7 0N	3 0 E
Oguni	**110**	33 4N	131 2 E
Oguta	**121**	5 44N	6 44 E
Ogwashi-Uku	**121**	6 15N	6 30 E
Ogwe	**121**	5 0N	7 14 E
Ohai	**143**	44 55 S	168 0 E
Ohakune	**142**	39 24 S	175 24 E
Ohara	**111**	35 15N	140 23 E
Ohau, L.	**143**	44 15 S	169 53 E
Ohaupo	**142**	37 56 S	175 20 E
Ohey	**47**	50 26N	5 8 E
O'Higgins □	**172**	34 15 S	71 1W
Ohio □	**156**	40 20N	83 0W
Ohio, R.	**156**	38 0N	86 0W
Ohiwa Harbour	**142**	37 59 S	177 10 E
Ohre, R.	**52**	50 10N	12 30 E
Ohrid	**66**	41 8N	20 52 E
Ohridsko, Jezero	**66**	41 8N	20 52 E
Ohrigstad	**129**	24 41 S	30 36 E
Öhringen	**49**	49 11N	9 31 E
Oi Ho	**108**	28 37N	98 16 E
Oignies	**47**	50 28N	3 0 E
Oil City	**156**	41 26N	79 40W
Oildale	**163**	35 25N	119 1W
Oilgate	**39**	52 25N	6 30W
Oinousa, I.	**69**	38 33N	26 14 E
Oirschot	**47**	51 30N	5 18 E
Oise □	**43**	49 28N	2 30 E
Oise, R.	**43**	49 53N	3 50 E
Oisterwijk	**47**	51 35N	5 12 E
Oita	**110**	33 14N	131 36 E
Oita-ken □	**110**	33 15N	131 30 E
Oiticica	**170**	5 3 S	41 5W
Ojai	**163**	34 28N	119 16W
Ojinaga	**164**	29 34N	104 25W
Ojocaliente	**164**	30 25N	106 30W
Ojos del Salado	**172**	27 0 S	68 40W
Oka, R.	**81**	56 20N	43 59 E
Okahandja	**128**	22 0 S	16 59 E
Okahukura	**142**	38 48N	175 14 E
Okaihau	**142**	35 19 S	173 36 E
Okakune	**142**	39 26 S	175 24 E
Okanagan L.	**152**	50 0N	119 30W
Okanogan	**160**	48 22N	119 35W
Okanogan, R.	**160**	48 40N	119 24W
Okány	**53**	46 52N	21 21 E
Okapa	**135**	6 38 S	145 39 E
Okaputa	**128**	20 5 S	17 0 E
Okara	**94**	30 50N	73 25 E
Okarito	**143**	43 15 S	170 9 E
Okato	**142**	39 12 S	173 53 E
Okaukuejo	**125**	19 10 S	16 0 E
Okavango, R. = Cubango, R.	**125**	16 15 S	18 0 E
Okavango Swamp	**128**	19 30 S	23 0 E
Okawa	**110**	33 9N	130 21 E
Okaya	**111**	36 0N	138 10 E
Okayama	**110**	34 40N	133 54 E
Okayama-ken □	**110**	35 0N	133 50 E
Okazaki	**111**	34 57N	137 10 E
Oke-Iho	**121**	8 1N	3 18 E
Okeechobee	**157**	27 16N	80 46W
Okeechobee L.	**157**	27 0N	80 50W
Okefenokee Swamp	**157**	30 50N	82 15W
Okehampton	**30**	50 44N	4 1W
Okene	**121**	7 32N	6 11 E
Oker, R.	**48**	52 7N	10 34 E
Okha	**77**	53 40N	143 0 E
Ókhi Óros	**69**	38 5N	24 25 E
Okhotsk	**77**	59 20N	143 10 E
Okhotsk, Sea of	**77**	55 0N	145 0 E
Okhotskiy Perevoz	**77**	61 52N	135 35 E
Okhotsko Kolymskoy	**77**	63 0N	157 0 E
Oki-no-Shima	**110**	32 44N	132 33 E
Oki-Shotō	**110**	36 15N	133 15 E
Okiep	**128**	29 39 S	17 53 E
Okigwi	**121**	5 52N	7 20 E
Okija	**121**	5 54N	6 55 E
Okinawa-Jima	**112**	26 32N	128 0 E
Okinawa-Shotō	**112**	27 0N	128 0 E
Okinoerabu-Jima	**112**	27 21N	128 33 E
Okitipupa	**121**	6 31N	4 50 E
Oklahoma □	**159**	35 20N	97 30W
Oklahoma City	**159**	35 25N	97 30W
Okmulgee	**159**	35 38N	96 0W
Oknitsa	**82**	48 25N	27 20 E
Okolo	**126**	2 37N	31 8 E
Okondeka	**128**	21 38 S	15 37 E
Okondja	**124**	0 35 S	13 45 E
Okonek	**54**	53 32N	16 51 E
Okrika	**121**	4 47N	7 4 E
Oksby	**73**	55 33N	8 8 E
Oktyabr	**85**	43 41N	77 12 E
Oktyabrskiy	**84**	54 28N	53 28 E
Okuchi	**110**	32 4N	130 37 E
Okulovka	**80**	58 19N	33 28 E
Okuru	**143**	43 55 S	168 55 E
Okushiri-Tō	**112**	42 15N	139 30 E
Okuta	**121**	9 14N	3 12 E
Okwa, R.	**128**	22 25 S	22 30 E
Okwoga	**121**	7 3N	7 42 E
Ola	**159**	35 2N	93 10W
Ólafsfjörður	**74**	66 4N	18 39W
Ólafsvík	**74**	64 53N	23 43W
Olancha	**163**	36 15N	118 1W
Olancha Pk.	**163**	36 15N	118 7W
Olanchito	**167**	15 30N	86 30W
Öland	**73**	56 45N	16 50 E
Olargues	**44**	43 34N	2 53 E
Olary	**140**	32 18 S	140 19 E
Olascoaga	**172**	35 15 S	60 39W
Olathe	**158**	38 50N	94 50W
Olavarría	**172**	36 55 S	60 20W
Oława	**54**	50 57N	17 20 E
Olbia	**64**	40 55N	9 30 E
Ólbia, G. di	**64**	40 55N	9 35 E
Old Bahama Chan.	**166**	22 10N	77 30W
Old Baldy Pk = San Antonio, Mt.	**163**	34 17N	117 38W
Old Castile = Castilla la Vieja	**56**	41 55N	4 0W
Old Castle	**38**	53 46N	7 10W
Old Cork	**138**	22 57 S	142 0 E
Old Dale	**163**	34 8N	115 47W
Old Deer	**37**	57 30N	2 3W
Old Dongola	**122**	18 11N	30 44 E
Old Factory	**150**	52 36N	78 43W
Old Forge, N.J., U.S.A.	**162**	43 43N	74 58W
Old Forge, N.Y., U.S.A.	**162**	43 43N	74 58W
Old Forge, Pa., U.S.A.	**162**	41 20N	75 46W
Old Fort, R.	**153**	58 36N	110 24W
Old Harbor	**147**	57 12N	153 22W
Old Kilpatrick	**34**	55 56N	4 34W
Old Leake	**33**	53 2N	0 6 E
Old Leighlin	**39**	52 46N	7 2W
Old Man of Hoy	**37**	58 53N	3 25W
Old Point Comfort	**162**	37 0N	76 20W
Old Radnor	**31**	52 14N	3 7W
Old Serenje	**127**	13 7 S	30 45 E
Old Shinyanga	**126**	3 33 S	33 27 E
Old Town	**151**	45 0N	68 50W
Old Wives L.	**153**	50 5N	106 0W
Oldbury	**28**	52 30N	2 0W
Oldeani	**126**	3 22 S	35 35 E
Oldenburg, Niedersachsen, Ger.	**48**	53 10N	8 10 E
Oldenburg, S.-Holst, Ger.	**48**	54 16N	10 53 E
Oldenzaal	**46**	52 19N	6 53 E
Oldham	**32**	53 33N	2 8W
Oldman, R.	**152**	49 57N	111 42W
Oldmeldrum	**37**	57 20N	2 19W

Olds **152** 51 50N 114 10W
Olean **156** 42 8N 78 25W
Oléggio **62** 45 36N 8 38E
Oleiros **56** 39 56N 7 56W
Olekma, R. **77** 58 0N 121 30E
Olekminsk **77** 60 40N 120 30E
Olema **163** 38 3N 122 47W
Olen **47** 51 9N 4 52E
Olenek **77** 68 20N 112 30E
Olenek, R. **77** 71 0N 123 50E
Olenino **80** 56 15N 33 20E
Oléron, I. d' **44** 45 55N 1 15W
Olesno **54** 50 51N 18 26E
Oleśnica **54** 51 13N 17 22E
Olevsk **80** 51 18N 27 39E
Olga **77** 43 50N 135 0E
Olga, L. **150** 49 47N 77 15W
Olga, Mt. **137** 25 20S 130 40E
Olgastretet **12** 78 35N 25 0E
Ølgod **73** 55 49N 8 36E
Olgrinmole **37** 58 29N 3 33W
Olhão **57** 37 3N 7 48W
Olib **63** 44 23N 14 44E
Olib, I. **63** 44 23N 14 44E
Oliena **64** 40 18N 9 22E
Oliete **58** 41 1N 0 41W
Olifants, R. **125** 24 5S 31 20E
Olifantshoek **128** 27 57S 22 42E
Ólimbos **69** 35 44N 27 11E
Ólimbos, Óros **68** 40 6N 22 23E
Olímpia **173** 20 44S 48 54W
Olimpo□ **172** 20 30S 58 45W
Olinda **170** 8 1S 34 51W
Olindiná **170** 11 22S 38 21W
Oling Hu **105** 34 52N 97 30E
Olite **58** 42 29N 1 40W
Oliva, Argent. **172** 32 0S 63 38W
Oliva, Spain **59** 38 58N 0 15W
Oliva de la Frontera **57** 38 17N 6 54W
Oliva, Punta del **56** 43 37N 5 28W
Olivares **58** 39 46N 2 20W
Oliveira, Bahia, Brazil **171** 12 23S 38 35W
Oliveira, Minas Gerais, Brazil **171** 20 50S 44 50W
Oliveira de Azemeis **56** 40 49N 8 29W
Oliveira dos Brejinhos **171** 12 19S 42 54W
Olivença **127** 11 47S 35 13E
Olivenza **57** 38 41N 7 9W
Oliver **152** 49 20N 119 30W
Oliver L. **153** 56 56N 103 22W
Olivine Ra. **143** 44 15S 168 30E
Olivone **51** 46 32N 8 57E
Olkhovka **83** 49 48N 44 32E
Olkusz **54** 50 18N 19 33E
Ollagüe **172** 21 15S 68 10W
Ollerton **33** 53 12N 1 1W
Olloy **47** 50 5N 4 36E
Olmedo **56** 41 20N 4 43W
Olmos, L. **172** 33 25S 63 19W
Olney, U.K. **29** 52 9N 0 42W
Olney, Ill., U.S.A. **156** 38 40N 88 0W
Olney, Tex., U.S.A. **159** 33 25N 98 45W
Olofström **73** 56 17N 14 32E
Oloma **121** 3 29N 11 19E
Olomane, R. **151** 50 14N 60 37W
Olomouc **53** 49 38N 17 12E
Olonets **78** 61 10N 33 0E
Olongapo **103** 14 50N 120 18E
Oloron-Ste.-Marie **44** 43 11N 0 38W
Olot **58** 42 11N 2 30E
Olovo **66** 44 8N 18 35E
Olovyannaya **77** 50 50N 115 10E
Olpe **48** 51 2N 7 50E
Olsene **47** 50 58N 3 28E
Olshanka **82** 48 16N 30 58E
Olst **46** 52 20N 6 7E
Olsztyn **54** 53 48N 20 29E
Olsztyn□ **54** 54 0N 21 0E
Olsztynek **54** 53 34N 20 19E
Olt□ **70** 44 20N 24 30E
Olt, R. **70** 43 50N 24 40E
Olten **50** 47 21N 7 53E
Oltenita **70** 44 7N 26 42E
Olton **159** 34 16N 102 7W
Oltu **92** 40 35N 41 50E
Oluanpi **109** 21 54N 120 51E
Oluego **58** 41 47N 2 0W
Olvera **57** 36 55N 5 18W
Olympia, Greece **69** 37 39N 21 39E
Olympia, U.S.A. **160** 47 0N 122 58W
Olympic Mts. **160** 47 50N 123 45W
Olympic Nat. Park **160** 47 48N 123 30W
Olympus, Mt. **160** 47 52N 123 40W
Olympus, Mt. = Olimbos, Oros **68** 40 6N 22 23E
Olyphant **162** 41 28N 75 37W
Om Hajer **123** 14 20N 36 41E
Om Koi **100** 17 48N 98 22E
Omachi **111** 36 30N 137 50E
Omae-Zaki **111** 34 36N 138 14E
Omagh **38** 54 36N 7 20W
Omagh□ **38** 54 35N 7 15W
Omaha **158** 41 15N 96 0W
Omak **160** 48 24N 119 31W
Oman■ **92** 23 0N 58 0E
Oman, G. of **93** 24 30N 58 30E
Omaruru **128** 21 26S 16 0E
Omaruru, R. **128** 21 44S 14 30E
Omate **174** 16 45S 71 0W
Ombai, Selat **103** 8 30S 124 50E
Ombersley **28** 52 17N 2 12W
Ombo **71** 59 18N 6 0E
Ombombo **128** 18 43S 13 57E
Omboué **124** 1 35S 9 15E
Ombrone, R. **62** 42 48N 11 15E
Omchi **119** 21 22N 17 53E
Omdraai **128** 20 5S 21 56E
Omdurmân **121** 15 40N 32 28E
Ome **111** 35 47N 139 15E
Omegna **62** 45 52N 8 23E
Omeonga **126** 3 40S 24 22E
Ometepe, Isla de **166** 11 32N 85 35W
Ometepec **165** 16 39N 98 23W
Omez **90** 32 22N 35 0E
Omi-Shima, Ehime, Japan **110** 34 15N 133 0E
Omi-Shima, Yamaguchi, Japan **110** 34 15N 131 9E
Omihachiman **111** 35 7N 136 3E
Omineca, R. **152** 56 3N 124 16W
Omiš **63** 43 28N 16 40E
Omisalj **63** 45 13N 14 32E
Omitara **128** 22 16S 18 2E
Ōmiya **111** 35 54N 139 38E
Omme **73** 55 56N 8 32E
Ommen **46** 52 31N 6 26E
Ömnöovi□ **106** 43 15N 104 0E
Omono, R. **112** 39 46N 140 3E
Omsk **76** 55 0N 73 38E
Omsukchan **77** 62 32N 155 48E
Omul, Mt. **70** 45 27N 25 29E
Omura **110** 33 8N 130 0E
Omura-Wan **110** 32 57N 129 52E
Omuramba, R. **125** 19 10S 19 20E
Omurtag **67** 43 8N 26 26E
Ōmuta **110** 33 0N 130 26E
Omutninsk **84** 58 45N 52 4E
On **47** 50 11N 5 18E
On-Take **110** 31 35N 130 39E
Oña **58** 42 43N 3 25W
Onaga **158** 39 32N 96 12W
Onalaska **158** 43 53N 91 14W
Onamia **158** 46 4N 93 38W
Onancock **162** 37 42N 75 49W
Onang **103** 3 2S 118 55E
Onaping L. **150** 47 3N 81 30W
Onarheim **71** 59 57N 5 35E
Oñate **58** 43 3N 2 25W
Onavas **164** 28 28N 109 30W
Onawa **158** 42 2N 96 2W
Onaway **156** 45 21N 84 11W
Oncesti **70** 43 56N 25 52E
Onchan **32** 54 11N 4 27W
Oncocua **128** 16 30S 13 40E
Onda **58** 39 55N 0 17W
Ondaejin **107** 41 34N 129 40E
Ondangua **128** 17 57S 16 4E
Ondárroa **58** 43 19N 2 25W
Ondas, R. **171** 12 8S 45 0W
Ondava, R. **53** 48 50N 21 40E
Onderdijk **46** 52 45N 5 8E
Ondo, Japan **110** 24 11N 132 32E
Ondo, Nigeria **121** 7 4N 4 47E
Ondo□ **121** 7 0N 5 0E
Ondombo **128** 21 3S 16 5E
Öndörhaan **105** 47 19N 110 39E
Öndörshil **106** 45 33N 108 5E
Ondverdarnes **74** 64 52N 24 0W
One Tree Hill **109** 34 43S 138 46E
Onega **78** 64 0N 38 10E
Onega, G. of = Onezhskaya G. **78** 64 30N 37 0E
Onega, L. = Onezhskoye Oz. **78** 62 0N 35 30E
Onega, R. **78** 63 0N 39 0E
Onehunga **142** 36 55N 174 30E
Oneida **162** 43 5N 75 40W
Oneida L. **162** 43 12N 76 0W
O'Neill **158** 42 30N 98 38W
Onekotan, Ostrov **77** 49 59N 154 0E
Onema **126** 4 35S 24 30E
Oneonta, Ala., U.S.A. **157** 33 58N 86 29W
Oneonta, N.Y., U.S.A. **162** 42 26N 75 5W
Onerahi **142** 35 45S 174 22E
Onezhskaya Guba **78** 64 30N 37 0E
Onezhskoye Ozero **78** 62 0N 35 30E
Ongarue **142** 38 42S 175 19E
Ongerup **137** 33 58S 118 28E
Ongjin **107** 37 56N 125 21E
Ongkharak **100** 14 8N 101 1E
Ongoka **126** 1 20S 26 0E
Ongole **97** 15 33N 80 2E
Ongon **106** 45 41N 113 5E
Onhaye **47** 50 15N 4 50E
Oni **83** 42 33N 43 26E
Onida **158** 44 42N 100 5W
Onilahy, R. **129** 23 30S 44 0E
Onitsha **121** 6 6N 6 42E
Onkaparinga, R. **109** 35 2S 138 47E
Onmaka **98** 22 17N 96 41E
Onny, R. **28** 52 30N 2 50W
Ono, Japan **110** 34 51N 134 56E
Ono, Japan **111** 35 59N 136 29E
Onoda **110** 33 59N 131 11E
Onomichi **110** 34 25N 133 12E
Onpyŏngni **107** 33 25N 126 55E
Ons, Islas de **56** 42 23N 8 55W
Onsala **73** 57 26N 12 0E
Onslow **136** 21 40S 115 0E
Onslow B. **157** 34 10N 77 0W
Onstwedde **46** 52 2N 7 4E
Ontake-San **111** 35 53N 137 29E
Ontaneda **56** 43 12N 3 57W
Ontario, Calif., U.S.A. **163** 34 2N 117 40W
Ontario, Oreg., U.S.A. **160** 44 1N 117 1W
Ontario□ **150** 52 0N 88 10W
Ontario, L. **150** 43 40N 78 0W
Onteniente **59** 38 50N 0 35W
Ontonagon **158** 46 52N 89 19W
Ontur **59** 38 38N 1 29W
Onyx **163** 35 41N 118 14W
Oodnadatta **139** 27 33S 135 30E
Ooglaamie **12** 72 1N 157 0W
Ookala **147** 20 1N 155 17W
Ooldea **137** 30 27S 131 50E
Ooltgensplaat **47** 51 41N 4 21E
Oona River **152** 53 57N 130 16W
Oordegem **47** 50 58N 3 54E
Oorindi **138** 20 40S 141 1E
Oost-Vlaanderen□ **47** 51 5N 3 50E
Oost-Vlieland **46** 53 18N 5 4E
Oostakker **47** 51 6N 3 46E
Oostburg **47** 51 19N 3 30E
Oostduinkerke **47** 51 7N 2 41E
Oostelijk-Flevoland **46** 52 31N 5 38E
Oostende **47** 51 15N 2 50E
Oosterbeek **46** 51 59N 5 51E
Oosterdijk **46** 52 44N 5 14E
Oosterend, Frise, Neth. **46** 53 24N 5 23E
Oosterend, Holl. Sept., Neth. **46** 53 5N 4 52E
Oosterhout, Brabank, Neth. **47** 51 39N 4 52E
Oosterhout, Gueldre, Neth. **46** 51 53N 5 50E
Oosterschelde **47** 51 33N 4 0E
Oosterwolde **46** 53 0N 6 17E
Oosterzele **47** 50 57N 3 48E
Oostkamp **47** 51 9N 3 14E
Oostmalle **47** 51 18N 4 44E
Oostrozebekke **47** 50 55N 3 21E
Oostvleteven **47** 50 56N 2 45E
Oostvoorne **46** 51 55N 4 5E
Oostzaan **46** 52 26N 4 52E
Ootacamund **97** 11 30N 76 44E
Ootha **141** 33 6S 147 29E
Ootmarsum **46** 52 24N 6 54E
Ootsa L. **152** 53 50N 126 20W
Ootsi **128** 25 2S 25 45E
Opaka **67** 43 28N 26 10E
Opala, U.S.S.R. **77** 52 15N 156 15E
Opala, Zaïre **124** 1 11S 24 45E
Opalenica **54** 52 18N 16 24E
Opalton **138** 23 15S 142 46E
Opan **67** 42 13N 25 41E
Opanake **97** 6 35N 80 40E
Opapa **142** 39 47S 176 42E
Opasatika **150** 49 30N 82 50W
Opasquia **153** 53 16N 93 34W
Opatija **63** 45 21N 14 17E
Opatów **54** 50 50N 21 27E
Opava **53** 49 57N 17 58E
Opawica, L. **150** 49 35N 75 55W
Opeinde **46** 53 8N 6 4E
Opelousas **159** 30 35N 92 0W
Opémisca L. **150** 50 0N 75 0W
Open Bay Is. **143** 43 51S 168 51E
Opglabbeek **47** 51 3N 5 35E
Opheim **160** 48 52N 106 30W
Ophir, U.K. **147** 58 56N 3 11W
Ophir, U.S.A. **147** 63 10N 156 40W
Ophthalmia Ra. **136** 23 15S 119 30E
Opi **121** 6 36N 7 28E
Opien **108** 29 15N 103 24E
Opinaca L. **150** 52 39N 76 20W
Opinaca, R. **150** 52 15N 78 2W
Opioo **47** 51 37N 5 54E
Opiskotish, L. **151** 53 10N 67 50W
Opmeer **46** 52 42N 4 57E
Opobo **121** 4 35N 7 34E
Opochka **80** 56 42N 28 45E
Opoczno **54** 51 22N 20 18E
Opole **54** 50 42N 17 58E
Opole□ **54** 50 40N 17 56E
Oporto = Porto **56** 41 8N 8 40W
Opotiki **142** 38 1S 177 19E
Opp **157** 31 19N 86 13W
Oppegård **71** 59 48N 10 48E
Oppenheim **49** 49 50N 8 22E
Opperdoes **46** 52 45N 5 4E
Oppido Mamertina **65** 38 16N 15 59E
Oppland fylke□ **71** 61 15N 9 30E
Oppstad **71** 60 17N 11 40E
Opua **142** 35 19S 174 9E
Opunake **142** 39 26S 173 52E
Opuzen **66** 43 1N 17 34E
Or Yehuda **90** 32 2N 34 50E
Ora **63** 46 20N 11 19E
Ora Banda **137** 30 20S 121 0E
Oracle **161** 32 45N 110 46W
Oradea **70** 47 2N 21 58E
Öræfajökull **74** 64 2N 16 39W
Orahovac **66** 42 24N 20 40E
Orahovica **66** 45 35N 17 52E
Orai **95** 25 58N 79 30E
Oraison **45** 43 55N 5 55E
Oran, Alg. **118** 35 37N 0 39W
Oran, Argent. **172** 23 10S 64 20W
Oran, Ireland **38** 53 40N 8 20W
Orange, Austral. **141** 33 15S 149 7E
Orange, France **45** 44 8N 4 47E
Orange, Calif., U.S.A. **163** 33 47N 117 51W
Orange, Mass., U.S.A. **162** 42 35N 72 15W
Orange, Tex., U.S.A. **159** 30 0N 93 40W
Orange, Va., U.S.A. **156** 38 17N 78 5W
Orange, C. **175** 4 20N 51 30W
Orange Cove **163** 36 38N 119 19W
Orange Free State = Oranje Vrystaat **128** 28 30S 27 0E
Orange Free State□ **128** 28 30S 27 0E
Orange Grove **159** 27 57N 97 57W
Orange, R. = Oranje, R. **128** 28 30S 18 0E
Orange Walk **165** 18 6N 88 33W
Orangeburg **157** 33 27N 80 53W
Orangerie B. **138** 10 30S 149 30E
Orangeville **150** 43 55N 80 5W
Oranienburg **48** 52 45N 13 15E
Oranje, R. **128** 28 30S 18 0E
Oranje Vrystaat□ **128** 28 30S 27 0E
Oranjemund (Orange Mouth) **128** 28 32S 16 29E
Oranmore **39** 53 16N 8 57W
Orapa **128** 21 13S 25 25E
Oras **103** 12 9N 125 22E
Orašje **66** 45 1N 18 42E
Oraşul Stalin = Braşov **70** 45 7N 25 39E
Orava, R. **53** 49 24N 19 20E
Oraviţa **66** 45 6N 21 43E
Orb, R. **44** 43 28N 3 5E
Orba, R. **62** 44 45N 8 40E
Ørbæk **73** 55 17N 10 39E
Orbe **50** 46 43N 6 32E
Orbec **42** 49 1N 0 23E
Orbetello **63** 42 26N 11 11E
Órbigo, R. **56** 42 40N 5 45W
Orbost **141** 37 40S 148 29E
Örbyhus **72** 60 15N 17 43E
Orbyhus **72** 60 13N 17 43E
Orce **59** 37 44N 2 28W
Orce, R. **59** 37 45N 2 30W
Orchies **43** 50 28N 3 14E
Orchila, Isla **167** 11 48N 66 10W
Orco, R. **62** 45 20N 7 45E
Orcutt **163** 34 52N 120 27W
Ord **136** 17 23S 128 51E
Ord, Mt. **136** 17 20S 125 34E
Ord, R. **136** 15 33S 128 35E
Ordenes **56** 43 5N 8 29W
Orderville **161** 37 18N 112 43W
Ordhead **37** 57 10N 2 31W
Ordie **37** 57 6N 2 54W
Ordos (Oerhtossu) **106** 39 0N 108 0E
Ordu **92** 40 55N 37 53E
Orduña **58** 42 58N 2 58W
Orduña, Mte. **59** 37 20N 3 30W
Ordway **158** 38 15N 103 42W
Ordzhonikidze, R.S.F.S.R., U.S.S.R. **83** 43 0N 44 35E
Ordzhonikidze, Ukraine S.S.R., U.S.S.R. **82** 47 32N 34 3E
Ordzhonikidze, Uzbek S.S.R., U.S.S.R. **85** 41 21N 69 22E
Ordzhonikidzeabad **85** 38 34N 69 1E
Ore, Sweden **72** 61 8N 15 10E
Ore, Zaïre **126** 3 17N 29 30E
Ore Mts. = Erzgebirge **49** 50 25N 13 0E
Orebic **66** 43 0N 17 11E
Örebro **72** 59 20N 15 18E
Örebro län□ **72** 59 27N 15 0E
Oregon **158** 42 1N 89 20W
Oregon□ **160** 44 0N 120 0W
Oregon City **160** 45 21N 122 35W
Öregrund **72** 60 21N 18 30E
Öregrundsgrepen **72** 60 25N 18 15E
Orekhov **82** 47 30N 35 32E
Orekhovo-Zuyevo **81** 55 50N 38 55E
Orel **81** 52 57N 36 3E
Orel, R. **82** 49 5N 35 25E
Orellana, Canal de **57** 39 2N 6 0W
Orellana la Vieja **57** 39 1N 5 32W
Orellana, Pantano de **57** 39 5N 5 10W
Orem **160** 40 27N 111 45W
Oren **69** 37 3N 27 57E
Orenburg **84** 51 45N 55 6E
Orense **56** 42 19N 7 55W
Orense□ **56** 42 15N 7 30W
Orepuki **143** 46 19S 167 46E
Orestiás **68** 41 30N 26 33E
Øresund **73** 55 45N 12 45E
Oreti, R. **143** 45 39S 168 14E
Orford **29** 52 6N 1 31E
Orford Ness **29** 52 6N 1 31E
Orgañá **58** 42 13N 1 20E
Orgaz **57** 39 39N 3 53W
Orgeyev **82** 47 9N 29 10E
Orgon **45** 43 47N 5 3E
Orhon Gol, R. **105** 50 21N 106 5E
Oria **65** 40 30N 17 38E
Orient **139** 28 7S 143 3E
Orient Bay **150** 49 20N 88 10W
Oriente **172** 38 44S 60 37W
Origny **43** 49 50N 3 30E
Origny-Ste.-Benoîte **43** 49 50N 3 30E
Orihuela **59** 38 7N 0 55W
Orihuela del Tremedal **58** 40 33N 1 39W
Oriku **68** 40 20N 19 30E
Orinoco, Delta del **167** 8 30N 61 0W
Orinoco, R. **174** 5 45N 67 40W
Orion **153** 49 28N 110 49W
Oriskany **162** 43 9N 75 20W
Orissa□ **96** 21 0N 85 0E
Oristano **64** 39 54N 8 35E
Oristano, Golfo di **64** 39 50N 8 22E
Orizaba **165** 18 50N 97 10W
Orizare **67** 42 44N 27 39E
Orizona **171** 17 3S 48 18W
Ørje **71** 59 29N 11 39E
Orjen, mt. **66** 42 35N 18 34E
Orjiva **59** 36 53N 3 24W
Orkanger **71** 63 18N 9 52E
Orkelljunga **73** 56 17N 13 17E
Örken, L. **73** 57 11N 15 0E

Örkény 53 47 9N 19 26 E
Orkla 71 63 18N 9 51 E
Orkla, R. 74 63 18N 9 51 E
Orkney 128 26 42 S 26 40 E
Orkney □ 37 59 0N 3 0W
Orkney Is. 37 59 0N 3 0W
Orland 160 39 46N 122 12W
Orlando 157 28 30N 81 25W
Orlando, C.d' 65 38 10N 14 43 E
Orléanais 43 48 0N 2 0 E
Orléans 43 47 54N 1 52 E
Orleans, I. d' 156 46 54N 70 58W
Orlice, R. 52 50 5N 16 10 E
Orlické Hory 53 50 15N 16 30 E
Orlov 53 49 17N 20 51 E
Orlov Gay 81 51 4N 48 19 E
Orlovat 66 45 14N 20 33 E
Ormara 93 25 16N 64 33 E
Ormea 62 44 9N 7 54 E
Ormesby St. Margaret 29 52 39N 1 42 E
Ormília 68 40 16N 23 33 E
Ormoc 103 11 0N 124 37 E
Ormond, N.Z. 142 38 33 S 177 56 E
Ormond, U.S.A. 157 29 13N 81 5W
Ormondville 142 40 5 S 176 19 E
Ormoz 63 46 25N 16 10 E
Ormskirk 32 53 35N 2 53W
Ornans 43 47 7N 6 10 E
Orne □ 42 48 40N 0 0 E
Orneta 54 54 8N 20 9 E
Ørnhøj 73 56 13N 8 34 E
Ornö 72 59 4N 18 24 E
Örnsköldsvik 72 63 17N 18 40 E
Oro Grande 163 34 36N 117 20W
Oro, R. 164 26 8N 105 58W
Orocué 174 4 48N 71 20W
Orodo 121 5 34N 7 4 E
Orogrande 161 32 20N 106 4W
Orol 56 43 34N 7 39W
Oromocto 151 45 54N 66 29W
Oron, Israel 90 30 55N 35 1 E
Oron, Nigeria 121 4 48N 8 14 E
Oron, Switz. 50 46 34N 6 50 E
Oron, R. 77 69 21N 95 43 E
Oronsay I. 34 56 0N 6 14W
Oronsay, Pass of 34 56 0N 6 10W
Oropesa 56 39 57N 5 10W
Oroquieta 103 8 32N 123 44 E
Orori 107 40 1N 127 27 E
Orós 170 6 15 S 38 55W
Orosei, G. di 64 40 15N 9 40 E
Orosháza 53 46 32N 20 42 E
Orotukan 77 62 16N 151 42 E
Oroville, Calif., U.S.A. 160 39 31N 121 30W
Oroville, Wash., U.S.A. 160 48 58N 119 30W
Orowia 143 46 1 S 167 50 E
Orphir 37 58 56N 3 8W
Orrefors 73 56 50N 15 45 E
Orroroo 140 32 43 S 138 38 E
Orsa 72 61 7N 14 37 E
Orsara di Puglia 65 41 17N 15 16 E
Orsasjön 72 61 7N 14 37 E
Orsha 80 54 30N 30 25 E
Orsières 50 46 2N 7 9 E
Orsk 84 51 12N 58 34 E
Ørslev 73 55 23N 11 56 E
Orsogna 63 42 13N 14 17 E
Orşova 70 44 41N 22 25 E
Ørsted 73 56 30N 10 20 E
Orta, L. d' 62 45 48N 8 21 E
Orta Nova 65 41 20N 15 40 E
Orte 63 42 28N 12 23 E
Ortegal, C. 56 43 43N 7 52W
Orthez 44 43 29N 0 48W
Ortho 47 50 8N 5 37 E
Ortigueira 56 43 40N 7 50W
Ortles, mt. 62 46 31N 10 33 E
Orto, Tokay 85 42 20N 76 1 E
Ortón, R. 174 10 50 S 67 0W
Orton Tebay 32 54 28N 2 35W
Ortona 63 42 21N 14 24 E
Orune 64 40 25N 9 20 E
Oruro 174 18 0 S 67 19W
Orust 73 58 10N 11 40 E
Orăştie 70 45 50N 23 10 E
Oruzgan 94 32 30N 66 35 E
Orvault 42 47 17N 1 38 E
Orvieto 63 42 43N 12 8 E
Orwell 162 43 35N 75 60W
Orwell, R. 29 52 2N 1 12 E
Orwigsburg 162 40 38N 76 6W
Oryakhovo 66 43 40N 23 57 E
Orzinuovi 62 45 24N 9 55 E
Orzysz 54 53 50N 21 58 E
Os 71 60 9N 5 30 E
Osa 84 57 17N 55 26 E
Osa, Pen. de 166 8 0N 84 0W
Osage, Iowa, U.S.A. 158 43 15N 92 50W
Osage, Wyo., U.S.A. 158 43 59N 104 25W
Osage City 158 38 43N 95 51W
Osage, R. 158 38 15N 92 30W
Ōsaka 111 34 30N 135 30 E
Osaka-fu □ 111 34 40N 135 30 E
Osaka-Wan 111 34 30N 135 18 E
Osan 107 37 11N 127 4 E
Osawatomie 158 38 30N 94 55W
Osborne 158 39 30N 98 45W
Osby 73 56 23N 13 59 E
Osceola, Ark., U.S.A. 159 35 40N 90 0W
Osceola, Iowa, U.S.A. 158 41 0N 93 20W
Oschatz 48 51 17N 13 8 E
Oschersleben 48 52 2N 11 13 E
Oschiri 64 40 43N 9 7 E
Osečina 66 44 23N 19 34 E
Ösel = Saaremaa 80 58 30N 22 30W
Osenovka 66 70 40N 120 50 E
Osëry 81 54 52N 38 28 E
Osh 85 40 37N 72 49 E
Oshan 108 24 11N 102 24 E
Oshawa 150 43 50N 78 45W
Oshikango 128 17 9 S 16 10 E
Oshima 110 33 11N 132 24 E
Oshkosh, Nebr., U.S.A. 156 41 27N 102 20W
Oshkosh, Wis., U.S.A. 156 44 3N 88 35W
Oshmyany 80 54 26N 25 58 E
Oshogbo 121 7 48N 4 37 E
Oshwe 124 3 25 S 19 28 E
Osica de Jos 70 44 14N 24 20 E
Osieczna 54 51 55N 16 40 E
Osijek 66 45 34N 18 41 E
Osilo 64 40 45N 8 41 E
Osimo 63 43 40N 13 30 E
Osintorf 80 54 34N 30 31 E
Osipovichi 80 53 25N 28 33 E
Oskaloosa 158 41 18N 92 40W
Oskarshamn 73 57 15N 16 27 E
Oskelaneo 150 48 5N 75 15W
Oskol, R. 81 50 20N 38 0 E
Oslo 71 59 55N 10 45 E
Oslob 103 9 31N 123 26 E
Oslofjorden 71 59 20N 10 35 E
Osmanabad 96 18 5N 76 10 E
Osmancık 82 40 45N 34 47 E
Osmand Ra. 136 17 10 S 128 45 E
Osmaniye 92 37 5N 36 10 E
Osmo 72 58 58N 17 55 E
Osmotherley 33 54 22N 1 18W
Osnabrück 48 52 16N 8 2 E
Osobláha 53 50 17N 17 44 E
Osolo 71 59 53N 10 52 E
Osona 128 22 3 S 16 59 E
Osorio 173 29 53 S 50 17W
Osorno, Chile 176 40 25 S 73 0W
Osorno, Spain 56 42 24N 4 22W
Osorno, Vol. 176 41 0N 72 30W
Osoyoos 152 49 0N 119 30W
Ospika, R. 152 56 20N 124 0W
Osprey Reef 138 13 52 S 146 36 E
Oss 46 51 46N 5 32 E
Ossa de Montiel 59 38 58N 2 45W
Ossa, Mt. 138 41 52 S 146 3 E
Ossa, Oros 68 39 47N 22 42 E
Ossabaw I. 157 31 45N 81 8W
Ossendrecht 47 51 24N 4 20 E
Ossett 33 53 40N 1 35W
Ossining 162 41 9N 73 50W
Ossipee 162 43 41N 71 9W
Osśno Lubuskie 54 52 28N 14 51 E
Ossokmanuan L. 151 53 25N 65 0W
Ossora 77 59 20N 163 13 E
Oświecim 54 50 2N 19 11 E
Ostashkov 80 57 4N 33 2 E
Oste, R. 48 53 30N 9 12 E
Ostend = Oostende 47 51 15N 2 50 E
Oster 80 50 57N 30 46 E
Osterburg 48 52 47N 11 44 E
Österby 72 60 13N 17 55 E
Österbymo 73 57 49N 15 15 E
Österdalälven 72 61 30N 13 45 E
Östergötlands Län □ 73 58 35N 15 45 E
Osterholz-Scharmbeck 48 53 14N 8 48 E
Østerild 73 57 3N 8 50 E
Østerild 73 57 2N 8 51 E
Österkorsberga 73 57 18N 15 6 E
Ostermundigen 50 46 58N 7 30 E
Østerøya 71 60 32N 5 30 E
Östersund 72 63 10N 14 38 E
Østfold fylke □ 71 59 25N 11 25 E
Ostfriesische Inseln 48 53 45N 7 15 E
Ostia Lido (Lido di Roma) 64 41 43N 12 17 E
Ostiglía 63 45 4N 11 9 E
Ostrava 53 49 51N 18 18 E
Ostrgrog 54 52 37N 16 33 E
Ostróda 54 53 42N 19 58 E
Ostrog 80 50 20N 26 30 E
Ostrogozhsk 81 50 55N 39 7 E
Ostrołeka 54 53 4N 21 38 E
Ostrołeka □ 54 53 0N 21 30 E
Ostrov, Bulg. 67 43 40N 24 9 E
Ostrov, Rumania 70 44 6N 27 24 E
Ostrov, U.S.S.R. 80 57 25N 28 20 E
Ostrów Mazowiecka 54 52 50N 21 51 E
Ostrów Wielkopolski 54 51 36N 17 44 E
Ostrowiec-Swietokrzyski 54 50 55N 21 22 E
Ostrozac 66 43 43N 17 49 E
Ostrzeszów 54 51 25N 17 52 E
Ostseebad-Kühlungsborn 48 54 10N 11 40 E
Östsinni 71 60 53N 10 3 E
Ostuni 65 40 44N 17 34 E
Osum, R. 67 43 35N 25 0 E
Osumi-Hanto 110 31 20N 130 55 E
Osumi-Kaikyō 112 30 55N 130 50 E
Osumi, R. 68 40 40N 20 10 E
Osumi-Shoto 112 30 30N 130 40 E
Osuna 57 37 14N 5 8W
Oswaldtwistle 32 53 44N 2 27W
Oswego 162 43 29N 76 30W
Oswestry 28 52 52N 3 3W
Ota, Japan 111 35 11N 136 38 E
Ota, Japan 111 36 18N 139 22 E
Ota-Gawa 110 34 21N 132 18 E
Otago □ 143 45 20 S 169 20 E
Otago Harb. 143 45 47 S 170 42 E
Otago Pen. 143 45 48 S 170 45 E
Otahuhu 142 36 56 S 174 51 E
Otake 110 34 12N 132 13 E
Otaki, Japan 111 35 17N 140 15 E
Otaki, N.Z. 142 40 45 S 175 10 E
Otane 142 39 54 S 176 39 E
Otar 85 43 32N 75 12 E
Otaru 112 43 10N 141 0 E
Otaru-Wan 112 43 25N 141 1 E
Otautau 143 46 9 S 168 1 E
Otava, R. 52 49 16N 13 32 E
Otavalo 174 0 20N 78 20W
Otavi 128 19 40 S 17 24 E
Otchinjau 128 16 30 S 13 56 E
Otelec 66 45 36N 20 50 E
Otero de Rey 56 43 6N 7 36W
Othello 160 46 53N 119 8W
Othonoí, I. 68 39 52N 19 22 E
Othris, Mt. 69 39 4N 22 42 E
Otira 143 42 49 S 171 35 E
Otira Gorge 143 42 53 S 171 33 E
Otis 158 40 12N 102 58W
Otjiwarongo 128 20 30 S 16 33 E
Otley 33 53 54N 1 41W
Otmuchow 54 50 28N 17 10 E
Otočac 63 44 53N 15 12 E
Otoineppu 112 44 44N 142 16 E
Otorohanga 142 38 12 S 175 14 E
Otoskwin, R. 150 52 13N 88 6W
Otosquen 153 53 17N 102 1W
Otoyo 110 33 43N 133 45 E
Otra 71 58 8N 8 1 E
Otranto 65 40 9N 18 28 E
Otranto, C.d' 65 40 7N 18 30 E
Otranto, Str. of 65 40 15N 18 40 E
Otrøy 71 62 43N 6 50 E
Otsuki 111 35 36N 138 57 E
Otta 71 61 46N 9 32 E
Ottapalam 97 10 46N 76 23 E
Ottawa, Can. 150 45 27N 75 42W
Ottawa, Ill., U.S.A. 156 41 20N 88 55W
Ottawa, Kans., U.S.A. 158 38 40N 95 10W
Ottawa Is. 149 59 35N 80 16W
Ottawa, R. 150 47 45N 78 35W
Ottélé 121 3 38N 11 19 E
Ottenby 73 56 15N 16 24 E
Otter L. 153 55 35N 104 39W
Otter R. 30 50 47N 3 12W
Otter Rapids, Ont., Can. 150 50 11N 81 39W
Otter Rapids, Sask., Can. 153 55 38N 104 44W
Otterburn 35 55 14N 2 12W
Otterndorf 48 53 47N 8 52 E
Otteröy, I. 71 62 45N 6 50 E
Ottersheim 52 48 21N 14 12 E
Otterup 73 55 30N 10 22 E
Ottery St. Mary 30 50 45N 3 16W
Ottignies 47 50 40N 4 33 E
Otto Beit Bridge 127 15 59 S 28 56 E
Ottosdal 128 26 46 S 25 59 E
Ottoshoop 128 25 45 S 26 58 E
Ottsjö 72 63 13N 13 2 E
Ottter Ferry 34 56 1N 5 20W
Ottumwa 158 41 0N 92 25W
Otu 121 8 14N 3 22 E
Otukpa (Al Owuho) 121 7 9N 7 41 E
Oturkpo 121 7 10N 8 15 E
Otway, Bahia 176 53 30 S 74 0W
Otway, C. 140 38 52 S 143 30 E
Otwock 54 52 5N 21 20 E
Ötz 52 47 13N 10 53 E
Otz, Fl. 52 47 13N 10 53 E
Ötz, R. 52 47 14N 10 50 E
Ötztaler Alpen 52 46 58N 11 0 E
Ou, Neua 100 22 18N 101 48 E
Ou, R. 100 20 4N 102 13 E
Ouachita Mts. 159 34 50N 94 30W
Ouachita, R. 159 33 0N 92 15W
Ouadane 116 20 50N 11 40W
Ouadda 117 8 15N 22 20 E
Ouagadougou 121 12 25N 1 30W
Ouahigouya 120 13 40N 2 25W
Ouahila 118 27 50N 5 0W
Ouahran = Oran 118 35 37N 0 39W
Oualâta 121 17 20N 6 55W
Ouallene 118 24 41N 1 11 E
Ouanda Djallé 117 8 55N 22 53 E
Ouango 124 4 19N 22 30 E
Ouargla 119 31 59N 5 25 E
Ouarkziz, Djebel 118 28 50N 8 0W
Ouarzazate 118 30 55N 6 55W
Ouatagouna 121 15 11N 0 43 E
Oubangi, R. 124 1 0N 17 50 E
Oubarakai, O. 119 27 20N 9 0 E
Ouche, R. 43 47 11N 5 10 E
Oud-Gastel 47 51 35N 4 28 E
Oud Turnhout 47 51 19N 5 0 E
Ouddorp 46 51 50N 3 57 E
Oude-Pekela 46 53 6N 7 0 E
Oude Rijn, R. 46 52 12N 4 24 E
Oudega 46 53 8N 6 0 E
Oudenaarde 47 50 50N 3 37 E
Oudenbosch 47 51 35N 4 32 E
Oudenburg 47 51 11N 3 1 E
Ouderkerk, Holl. Mérid., Neth. 46 51 56N 4 38 E
Ouderkerk, Utrecht, Neth. 46 52 18N 4 55 E
Oudeschild 46 53 2N 4 50 E
Oudewater 46 52 2N 4 52 E
Oudkarspel 46 52 43N 4 49 E
Oudon 42 47 22N 1 19W
Oudon, R. 42 47 47N 1 2W
Oudtshoorn 128 33 35 S 22 14 E
Oued Sbita 118 25 50N 5 2W
Ouellé 120 7 26N 4 1W
Ouessa 120 11 4N 2 47W
Ouessant, Île d' 42 48 28N 5 6W
Ouesso 124 1 37N 16 5 E
Ouezzane 118 34 51N 5 42W
Ouffet 47 50 26N 5 28 E
Oughter L. 38 54 2N 7 30W
Oughterard 38 53 26N 9 20W
Ougrée 47 50 36N 5 32 E
Ouidah 121 6 25N 2 0 E
Ouimet 150 48 43N 88 35W
Ouistreham 42 49 17N 0 18W
Ouj, R. 118 51 15N 29 45 E
Oujda □ 118 33 18N 1 25W
Oujeft 116 20 2N 13 0W
Oulad Naïl, Mts. des 118 34 30N 3 30 E
Ouled Djellal 119 34 28N 5 2 E
Oulmès 118 33 17N 6 0W
Oulton 29 52 29N 1 40 E
Oulton Broad 29 52 28N 1 43 E
Oulu 74 65 1N 25 29 E
Oulu □ 74 65 10N 27 20 E
Oulujärvi 74 64 25N 27 0 E
Oulujoki 74 64 45N 26 30 E
Oulun Lääni □ 74 64 36N 27 20 E
Oulx 62 45 2N 6 49 E
Oum el Bouaghi 119 35 55N 7 6 E
Oum el Ksi 118 29 4N 6 59W
Oum-er-Rbia 118 32 30N 6 30W
Oum-er-Rbia, O. 118 32 30N 6 30W
Oumè 120 5 21N 5 27W
Ounane, Dj. 119 25 4N 7 10 E
Ounasjoki 74 66 31N 25 44 E
Oundle 29 52 28N 0 28W
Ounguati 128 21 54 S 15 46 E
Ounianga Kébir 117 19 4N 20 29 E
Ounlivou 121 7 20N 1 34 E
Our, R. 47 49 55N 6 5 E
Ouray 161 38 3N 107 48W
Oureg, Oued el 118 32 34N 2 10 E
Ourém 170 1 33 S 47 6W
Ouricuri 170 7 53 S 40 5W
Ourinhos 173 23 0 S 49 54W
Ourini 117 16 7N 22 25 E
Ourique 57 37 38N 8 16W
Ouro Fino 173 22 16 S 46 25W
Ouro Prêto 173 20 20 S 43 30W
Ouro Sogui 120 15 36N 13 19W
Oursi 121 14 41N 0 27W
Ourthe, R. 47 50 29N 5 35 E
Ouse 138 42 25 S 146 42 E
Ouse, R., Sussex, U.K. 29 50 58N 0 3 E
Ouse, R., Yorks., U.K. 33 54 3N 0 7 E
Oust 44 42 52N 1 13 E
Oust, R. 42 48 8N 2 49W
Out Skerries, Is. 36 60 25N 0 50W
Outardes, R. 151 50 0N 69 4W
Outer Hebrides, Is. 36 57 30N 7 40W
Outer I. 151 51 10N 58 35W
Outes 56 42 52N 8 55W
Outjo 128 20 5 S 16 7 E
Outlook, Can. 153 51 30N 107 0W
Outlook, U.S.A. 158 48 53N 104 46W
Outreau 43 50 40N 1 36 E
Outwell 29 52 36N 0 14 E
Ouyen 140 35 1 S 142 22 E
Ouzouer-le-Marché 42 47 54N 1 32 E
Ovada 62 44 39N 8 40 E
Ovalle 172 30 33 S 71 18W
Ovamboland = Owambo 128 17 20 S 16 30 E
Ovar 56 40 51N 8 40W
Ovejas 174 9 32N 75 14W
Ovens 141 36 35 S 146 46 E
Over Flakkee, I. 47 51 45N 4 5 E
Over Wallop 28 51 9N 1 35W
Overbister 37 59 16N 2 33W
Overdinkel 46 52 14N 7 2 E
Overflakkee 46 51 44N 4 10 E
Overijse 47 50 47N 4 32 E
Overijssel 46 50 46N 4 32 E
Overijssel □ 46 52 25N 6 35 E
Overijsselsch Kanaal 46 52 31N 6 6 E
Överkalix 74 66 19N 22 50 E
Overpelt 47 51 12N 5 20 E
Overstand 29 52 55N 1 20W
Overton, Clwyd, U.K. 31 52 58N 2 56W
Overton, Hants, U.K. 28 51 14N 1 16W
Overton, U.S.A. 161 36 32N 114 31W
Övertorneå 74 66 23N 23 40 E
Overum 73 58 0N 16 20 E
Ovid, Colo., U.S.A. 158 41 0N 102 17W
Ovid, N.Y., U.S.A. 162 42 41N 76 49W
Ovidiopol 82 46 15N 30 30 E
Oviedo 56 43 25N 5 50W
Oviedo □ 56 43 20N 6 0W
Oviken 72 63 0N 14 23 E
Oviksfjällen 72 63 0N 13 49 E
Övör Hangay □ 106 45 0N 102 30 E
Ovoro 121 5 26N 7 16 E
Övre Sirdal 71 58 48N 6 43 E
Øvre Sirdal 71 58 48N 6 47 E
Ovruch 80 51 25N 28 45 E
Owaka 143 46 27 S 169 40 E
Owambo 128 17 20 S 16 30 E
Owasco L. 162 42 50N 76 31W
Owase 111 34 7N 136 5 E
Owatonna 158 44 3N 93 17W
Owego 162 42 6N 76 17W
Owel, L. 38 53 34N 7 24W
Owen 140 34 15 S 138 32 E

Owen Falls **126** 0 30N 33 5 E
Owen Mt. **143** 41 35S 152 33 E
Owen Sound **150** 44 35N 80 55W
Owen Stanley Range **135** 8 30S 147 0 E
Owendo **124** 0 17N 9 30 E
Oweniny R. **38** 54 13N 9 32W
Owenkillew R. **38** 54 44N 7 15W
Owens L. **163** 36 20N 118 0W
Owens, R. **163** 36 32N 117 59W
Owensboro **156** 37 40N 87 5W
Owensville **158** 38 20N 91 30W
Owerri **121** 5 29N 7 0 E
Owhango **142** 39 51S 175 20 E
Owl, R. **153** 57 51N 92 44W
Owo **121** 7 18N 5 30 E
Owosso **156** 43 0N 84 10W
Owston Ferry **33** 53 28N 0 47W
Owyhee **160** 42 0N 116 3W
Owyhee, R. **160** 43 10N 117 37W
Owyhee Res. **160** 43 30N 117 30W
Ox Mts. **38** 54 6N 9 0W
Oxberg **72** 61 7N 14 11 E
Oxelösund **73** 58 43N 17 15 E
Oxford, N.Z. **143** 43 18S 172 11 E
Oxford, U.K. **28** 51 45N 1 15W
Oxford, Mass., U.S.A. **162** 42 7N 71 52W
Oxford, Miss., U.S.A. **159** 34 22N 89 30W
Oxford, N.C., U.S.A. **157** 36 19N 78 36W
Oxford, N.Y., U.S.A. **162** 42 27N 75 36W
Oxford, Ohio, U.S.A. **156** 39 30N 84 40W
Oxford, Pa., U.S.A. **162** 39 47N 75 59W
Oxford □ **28** 51 45N 1 15W
Oxford L. **153** 54 51N 95 37W
Oxilithos **69** 38 35N 24 7 E
Oxley **140** 34 11S 144 6 E
Oxley Cr. **108** 27 35S 153 0 E
Oxnard **163** 34 10N 119 14W
Oya **102** 2 55N 111 55 E
Oyabe **111** 36 47N 136 56 E
Oyama **111** 36 18N 139 48 E
Oyana **110** 32 32N 130 18 E
Oyem **124** 1 42N 11 43 E
Oyen **153** 51 22N 110 28W
Øyeren **71** 59 48N 11 14 E
Öyeren **71** 59 50N 11 15 E
Oykel Bridge **37** 57 58N 4 45W
Oykell, R. **37** 57 55N 4 26W
Oymyakon **77** 63 25N 143 10 E
Oyo **121** 7 46N 3 56 E
Oyo □ **121** 8 0N 3 30 E
Oyonnax **45** 46 16N 5 40 E
Oyster B. **138** 42 15S 148 5 E
Öystese **71** 60 22N 6 9 E
Øystese **71** 60 24N 6 12 E
Oytal **85** 42 54N 73 17 E
Ozamis (Mizamis) **103** 8 15N 123 50 E
Ozark, Ala., U.S.A. **157** 31 29N 85 39W
Ozark, Ark., U.S.A. **159** 35 30N 93 50W
Ozark, Mo., U.S.A. **159** 37 0N 93 15W
Ozark Plateau **159** 37 20N 91 40W
Ozarks, L. of **158** 38 10N 93 0W
Ózd **53** 48 14N 20 15 E
Ozerhinsk **80** 53 40N 27 7 E
Ozërnyy **84** 51 8N 60 50 E
Ozieri **64** 40 35N 9 0 E
Ozimek **54** 50 41N 18 11 E
Ozona **159** 30 43N 101 11W
Ozorków **54** 51 57N 19 16 E
Ozren, Mt. **66** 43 55N 18 29 E
Ozu **110** 33 30N 132 33 E
Ozu Kumamoto **110** 32 52N 130 52 E
Ozuluama **165** 21 40N 97 50W
Ozun **70** 45 47N 25 50 E

P

Pa **120** 11 33N 3 19W
Pa-an **98** 16 45N 97 40 E
Pa Mong Dam **100** 18 0N 102 22 E
Pa Sak, R. **101** 15 30N 101 0 E
Paal **47** 51 2N 5 10 E
Paar, R. **49** 48 42N 11 27 E
Paarl **128** 33 45S 18 56 E
Paatsi, R. **74** 68 55N 29 0 E
Paauilo **147** 20 3N 155 22W
Pab Hills **94** 26 30N 66 45 E
Pabbay I. **36** 57 46N 7 12W
Pabbay, Sd. of **36** 57 45N 7 4W
Pabianice **54** 51 40N 19 20 E
Pabna **98** 24 1N 89 18 E
Pabo **126** 2 56N 32 3 E
Pacajá, R. **170** 1 56S 50 50W
Pacajus **170** 4 10S 38 38W
Pacasmayo **174** 7 20S 79 35W
Pacaudière, La **43** 46 11N 3 52 E
Paceco **64** 37 59N 12 32 E
Pachhar **94** 24 40N 77 42 E
Pachino **65** 36 43N 15 4 E
Pacho **174** 5 8N 74 10W
Pachora **96** 20 38N 75 29 E
Pachpadra **93** 25 58N 72 10 E
Pachuca **165** 20 10N 98 40W
Pachung **108** 31 58N 106 40 E
Pacific **152** 54 48N 128 28W
Pacific Grove **163** 36 38N 121 58W
Pacific Ocean **143** 10 0N 140 0W
Pacifica **163** 37 36N 122 30W
Packsaddle **140** 30 36S 141 58 E
Pacoh **152** 53 0N 132 30W
Pacov **52** 49 27N 15 0 E
Pacsa **53** 46 44N 17 2 E
Pacuí, R. **171** 16 46S 45 1W
Pacy-sur-Eure **171** 49 1N 1 23 E
Paczkow **54** 50 28N 17 0 E
Padaido, Kepulauan **103** 1 5S 138 0 E
Padalarang **103** 7 50S 107 30 E
Padang **102** 1 0S 100 20 E
Padang, I. **102** 1 0S 100 10 E
Padangpanjang **102** 0 30S 100 20 E
Padangsidimpuan **102** 1 30N 99 15 E
Padatchuang **98** 19 41N 96 35 E
Padborg **73** 54 49N 9 21 E
Paddock Wood **29** 51 13N 0 24 E
Paddockwood **153** 53 30N 105 30W
Paderborn **48** 51 42N 8 44 E
Padesul **70** 45 40N 22 22 E
Padiham **32** 53 48N 2 20W
Padina **70** 44 50N 27 8 E
Padlei **153** 62 10N 97 5W
Padloping Island **149** 67 0N 63 0W
Padma, R. **98** 23 22N 90 32 E
Padmanabhapuram **97** 8 16N 77 17 E
Pádova **63** 45 24N 11 52 E
Padra **94** 22 15N 73 7 E
Padrauna **95** 26 54N 83 59 E
Padre I. **159** 27 0N 97 20W
Padrón **56** 42 41N 8 39W
Padstow **32** 50 33N 4 57W
Padstow Bay **30** 50 35N 4 58W
Padua = Pádova **63** 45 24N 11 52 E
Paducah, Ky., U.S.A. **156** 37 0N 88 40W
Paducah, Tex., U.S.A. **159** 34 3N 100 16W
Padul **57** 37 1N 3 38W
Padula **65** 40 20N 15 40 E
Padwa **96** 18 27N 82 37 E
Paekakariki **142** 40 59S 174 58 E
Paektu-san **107** 42 0N 128 3 E
Paengaroa **142** 37 49S 176 29 E
Paengnyŏng Do **107** 37 57N 124 40 E
Paeroa **142** 37 23S 175 41 E
Paesana **62** 44 40N 7 18 E
Pag **63** 44 27N 15 5 E
Pag, I. **63** 44 50N 15 0 E
Paga **121** 11 1N 1 8W
Pagadian **103** 7 55N 123 30 E
Pagai Selatan, I. **102** 3 0S 100 15W
Pagai Utara, I. **102** 2 35S 100 0 E
Pagalu, I. **114** 1 35S 3 35 E
Pagaralam **102** 4 0S 103 17 E
Pagastikós Kólpos **68** 39 15N 23 12 E
Pagatan **102** 3 33S 115 59 E
Page **158** 47 11N 97 37W
Paglieta **63** 42 10N 14 30 E
Pagnau **123** 8 15N 34 7 E
Pagny-sur-Moselle **43** 48 59N 6 2 E
Pagosa Springs **161** 37 16N 107 4W
Pagwa River **150** 50 2N 85 14W
Pahala **147** 20 25N 156 0W
Pahang □ **101** 3 40N 102 20 E
Pahang, R. **101** 3 30N 103 9 E
Pahang, st. **101** 3 30N 103 9 E
Pahiatua **142** 40 27S 175 50 E
Pahoa **147** 19 30N 154 57W
Pahokee **157** 26 50N 80 30W
Pahrump **161** 36 15N 116 0W
Pahsien **106** 39 10N 116 20 E
Pahsientung **107** 43 11N 120 57 E
Pai **100** 19 19N 98 27 E
Paia **147** 20 54N 156 22W
Paible **36** 57 35N 7 30W
Paich'eng **105** 45 40N 122 52 E
Paich'i **109** 28 2N 111 18 E
P'aichou **109** 30 12N 113 56 E
Paicines **163** 36 44N 121 17W
Paide **80** 58 57N 25 31 E
Paignton **30** 50 26N 3 33W
Paiho, China **109** 32 49N 110 3 E
Paiho, Taiwan **109** 23 21N 120 25 E
Paihok'ou **109** 31 46N 110 13 E
Päijänne **75** 61 30N 25 30 E
Pailin **101** 12 46N 102 36 E
Pailolo Chan. **147** 21 5N 156 42W
Paimbœuf **42** 47 17N 2 0W
Paimboeuf **44** 47 17N 2 2W
Paimpol **42** 48 48N 3 4W
Painan **102** 1 15S 100 40 E
Painesville **156** 41 42N 81 18W
Painiu **109** 32 51N 112 10 E
Painscastle **31** 52 7N 3 13W
Painswick **28** 51 47N 2 11W
Paint l. **153** 55 28N 97 57W
Painted Desert **161** 36 40N 112 0W
Paintsville **156** 37 50N 82 50W
Paipa **174** 5 47N 73 7W
Paise **108** 23 55N 106 28 E
Paisha **106** 34 23N 112 32 E
Paisley, U.K. **34** 55 51N 4 27W
Paisley, U.S.A. **160** 42 43N 120 40W
Paita **174** 5 5S 81 0W
Paiva, R. **56** 40 50N 7 55W
Paiyin **105** 36 45N 104 4 E
Paiyü **99** 31 12N 98 45 E
Paiyunopo **106** 41 46N 109 58 E
Pajares **56** 39 57N 1 48W
Pak Lay **100** 18 15N 101 27 E
Pak Phanang **101** 8 21N 100 12 E
Pak Sane **100** 18 22N 103 39 E
Pak Song **100** 15 11N 106 14 E
Pak Suong **100** 19 58N 102 15 E
Pakala **97** 13 29N 79 8 E
Pakanbaru **102** 0 30N 101 15 E
Pakaraima, Sierra **174** 6 0N 60 0W
Pakemba **127** 13 3S 29 58 E
Pakenham **141** 38 6S 145 30 E
Pakhoi = Peihai **108** 21 30N 109 5 E
Pakhtakor **85** 40 2N 65 46 E
Pakistan ■ **93** 30 0N 70 0 E
Pakistan, East = Bangladesh ■ **99** 24 0N 90 0 E
Pakkading **100** 18 19N 103 59 E
Paknam = Samut Prakan **100** 13 36N 100 36 E
P'ako **105** 30 52N 81 19 E
Pakokku **98** 21 30N 95 0 E
Pakpattan **94** 30 25N 73 16 E
Pakrac **66** 45 27N 17 12 E
Paks **53** 46 38N 18 55 E
Pakse **100** 15 5N 105 52 E
Paksikori **107** 42 27N 130 31 E
Paktya □ **93** 33 0N 69 15 E
Pakwach **126** 2 28N 31 27 E
Pal **93** 33 45N 79 33 E
Pala, Chad **117** 9 25N 15 5 E
Pala, U.S.A. **163** 33 22N 117 5W
Pala, Zaïre **126** 6 45S 29 30 E
Palabek **126** 3 22N 32 33 E
Palacious **159** 28 44N 96 12W
Palafrugell **58** 41 55N 3 10 E
Palagiano **65** 40 35N 17 0 E
Palagonia **65** 37 20N 14 43 E
Palagruza **63** 42 24N 16 15 E
Palaiókastron **69** 35 12N 26 18 E
Palaiokhora **69** 35 16N 23 39 E
Pálairos **69** 38 45N 20 51 E
Palais, Le **42** 47 20N 3 10W
Palakol **96** 16 31N 81 46 E
Palam **96** 19 0N 77 0 E
Palamás **68** 39 26N 22 4 E
Palamós **58** 41 50N 3 10 E
Palampur **94** 32 10N 76 30 E
Palana, Austral. **138** 39 45S 147 55 E
Palana, U.S.S.R. **77** 59 10N 160 10 E
Palanan **103** 17 8N 122 29 E
Palandri **95** 33 42N 73 40 E
Palanpur **94** 24 10N 72 25 E
Palapye **128** 22 30S 27 7 E
Palar, R. **97** 12 27N 80 13 E
Palas **95** 35 4N 73 4 E
Palatka **157** 29 40N 81 40W
•Palau Is. **130** 7 30N 134 30 E
Palauig **103** 15 26N 119 54 E
Palauk **101** 13 10N 98 40 E
Palavas **44** 43 32N 3 56 E
Palawan, I. **102** 10 0N 119 0 E
Palayancottai **97** 8 45N 77 45 E
Palazzo San Gervásio **65** 40 53N 15 58 E
Palazzolo Acreide **65** 37 4N 14 43 E
Paldiski **80** 59 23N 24 9 E
Pale **66** 43 50N 18 38 E
Palel **98** 24 27N 94 2 E
Paleleh **103** 1 10N 121 50 E
Palembang **102** 3 0S 104 50 E
Palencia **56** 42 1N 4 34W
Palencia □ **56** 42 31N 4 33W
Palermo, Colomb. **174** 2 54N 75 26W
Palermo, Italy **64** 38 8N 13 20 E
Palermo, U.S.A. **160** 39 30N 121 37W
Palestine, Asia **90** 32 0N 35 0 E
Palestine, U.S.A. **159** 31 42N 95 35W
Palestrina **64** 41 50N 12 52 E
Paletwa **98** 21 30N 92 50 E
Palghat **97** 10 46N 76 42 E
Palgrave **29** 52 22N 1 7 E
Palgrave, Mt. **136** 23 22S 115 58 E
P'ali **105** 27 45N 89 10 E
Pali **94** 25 50N 73 20 E
Palik'un **105** 43 35N 92 51 E
Palimé **121** 6 57N 0 37 E
Palintaoch'i **107** 43 59N 119 20 E
Palinuro, C. **65** 40 1N 15 14 E
Palinyuch'i (Tapanshang) **107** 43 40N 118 20 E
Palisade **158** 40 35N 101 10W
Paliseul **47** 49 54N 5 8 E
Palitana **94** 21 32N 71 49 E
Palizada **165** 18 18N 92 8W
Palizzi **65** 37 58N 15 59 E
Palk Bay **97** 9 30N 79 30 E
Palk Strait **97** 10 0N 80 0 E
Palkonda **96** 18 36N 83 48 E
Palkonda Ra. **97** 13 50N 79 20 E
Pallasgreen **39** 52 35N 8 22W
Pallaskenry **39** 52 39N 8 53W
Pallasovka **81** 50 4N 47 0 E
Palleru, R. **96** 17 30N 79 40 E
Pallinup **137** 34 0S 117 55 E
Pallisa **126** 1 12N 33 43 E
Palliser Bay **142** 41 26S 175 5 E
Palliser, C. **142** 41 37S 175 14 E
Pallu **94** 28 59N 74 14 E
Palm Beach **157** 26 46N 80 0W
Palm Desert **163** 33 43N 116 22W
Palm Is. **138** 18 40S 146 35 E
Palm Springs **163** 33 51N 116 35W
Palma, Canary Is. **116** 28 40N 17 50W
Palma, Mozam. **127** 10 46S 40 29 E
Palma, Spain **58** 39 33N 2 39 E
Palma, Bahía de **59** 39 30N 2 39 E
Palma del Río **57** 37 43N 5 17W
Palma di Montechiaro **64** 37 12N 13 46 E
Palma, I. **116** 28 45N 17 50W
Palma, La, Panama **166** 8 15N 78 0W
Palma, La, Spain **57** 37 21N 6 38W
Palma, R. **171** 10 10N 71 50W
Palma Soriano **166** 20 15N 76 0W
Palmanova **63** 45 54N 13 18 E
Palmares **170** 8 41S 35 36W
Palmarito **174** 7 37N 70 10W
Palmarola, I. **64** 40 57N 12 50 E
Palmas **173** 26 29S 52 0W
Palmas, C. **120** 4 27N 7 46W
Palmas de Monte Alto **171** 14 16S 43 10W
Pálmas, G. di **64** 39 0N 8 30 E
Palmdale **163** 34 36N 118 7W
Palmeira **171** 25 25S 50 0W
Palmeira dos Índios **170** 9 25S 36 37W
Palmeirais **170** 12 31S 41 34W
Palmeiras, R. **171** 12 22S 47 8W
Palmeirinhas, Pta. das **124** 9 2S 12 57 E
Palmela **57** 38 32N 8 57W
Palmelo **171** 17 20S 48 27W
Palmer, Alaska, U.S.A. **147** 61 35N 149 10W
Palmer, Mass., U.S.A. **162** 42 9N 72 21W
Palmer Arch **13** 64 15S 65 0W
Palmer Lake **158** 39 10N 104 52W
Palmer Pen. **13** 73 0S 60 0W
Palmer, R., N. Terr., Austral. **138** 24 30S 133 0 E
Palmer, R., Queens., Austral. **138** 16 5S 142 43 E
Palmerston **142** 45 29S 170 43 E
Palmerston, C. **133** 21 32S 149 29 E
Palmerston North **143** 40 21S 175 39 E
Palmerton **162** 40 47N 75 36W
Palmetto **157** 27 33N 82 33W
Palmi **65** 38 21N 15 51 E
Palmira, Argent. **172** 32 59S 68 25W
Palmira, Colomb. **174** 3 32N 76 16W
Palmyra, Mo., U.S.A. **158** 39 45N 91 30W
Palmyra, N.J., U.S.A. **162** 40 0N 75 1W
Palmyra, Pa., U.S.A. **162** 40 18N 76 36W
Palmyra = Tadmor **92** 34 30N 37 55 E
Palni **97** 10 30N 77 30 E
Palni Hills **97** 10 14N 77 33 E
Palo Alto **163** 37 25N 122 8W
Palo del Colle **65** 41 4N 16 43 E
Paloe **103** 8 20S 121 43 E
Paloma, La **172** 30 35S 71 0W
Palombara Sabina **63** 42 4N 12 45 E
Palopo **103** 3 0S 120 16 E
Palos, Cabo de **59** 37 38N 0 40W
Palos Verdes **163** 33 48N 118 23W
Palos Verdes, Pt. **163** 33 43N 118 26W
Palouse **160** 46 59N 117 5W
Palparara **138** 24 47S 141 22 E
Pålsboda **73** 59 3N 15 22 E
Palu, Indon. **103** 1 0S 119 59 E
Palu, Turkey **92** 38 45N 40 0 E
Paluan **103** 13 35N 120 29 E
Palwal **94** 28 8N 77 19 E
Pama, China **108** 24 9N 107 15 E
Pama, Upp. Vol. **121** 11 19N 0 44 E
Pamanukan **103** 6 16S 107 49 E
Pamban I. **97** 9 24N 79 35 E
Pamekasan **103** 7 10S 113 29 E
Pameungpeuk **103** 7 38S 107 44 E
Pamiench'eng **107** 43 13N 124 2 E
Pamiers **44** 43 7N 1 39 E
Pamir, R. **85** 37 1N 72 41 E
Pamirs, Ra. **85** 37 40N 73 0 E
Pamlico, R. **157** 35 25N 76 40W
Pamlico Sd. **157** 35 20N 76 0W
Pampa **159** 35 35N 100 58W
Pampa de las Salinas **172** 32 1S 66 58W
Pampa, La □ **172** 36 50S 66 0W
Pampanua **103** 4 22S 120 14 E
Pamparato **62** 44 16N 7 54 E
Pampas, Argent. **172** 34 0S 64 0W
Pampas, Peru **174** 12 20S 74 50W
Pamplona, Colomb. **174** 7 23N 72 39W
Pamplona, Spain **58** 42 48N 1 38W
Pampoenpoort **128** 31 3S 22 40 E
Pamunkey, R. **162** 37 32N 76 50W
Pana **158** 39 25N 89 0W
Panaca **161** 37 51N 114 50W
Panagyurishte **67** 42 49N 24 15 E
Panaitan, I. **103** 6 35S 105 10 E
Panaji (Panjim) **97** 15 25N 73 50 E
Panamá **166** 9 0N 79 25W
Panama ■ **166** 8 48N 79 55W
Panama Canal **166** 9 10N 79 56W
Panama Canal Zone **166** 9 10N 79 56W
Panama City **157** 30 10N 85 41W
Panamá, Golfo de **166** 8 4N 79 20W
Panamint Mts. **161** 36 15N 117 20W
Panamint Springs **163** 36 20N 117 28W
Panão **174** 9 55S 75 55W
Panare **101** 6 51N 101 30 E
Panarea, I. **65** 38 38N 15 3 E
Panaro, R. **62** 44 48N 11 5 E
Panarukan **103** 7 40S 113 52 E
Panay, G. **103** 11 0N 122 30 E
Panay I. **103** 11 10N 122 30 E
Pancake Ra. **161** 38 30N 116 0W
Pančevo **66** 44 52N 20 41 E
Panciu **70** 45 54N 27 8 E
Pancorbo, Paso **58** 42 32N 3 5W
Pandan **103** 11 45N 122 10 E
Pandangpanjang **102** 0 40S 100 20 E
Pandeglang **103** 6 25S 106 0 E
Pandharpur **96** 17 41N 75 20 E
Pandhurna **96** 21 36N 78 35 E
Pandilla **58** 41 32N 3 43W
Pando **173** 34 30S 56 0W
Pando, L. = Hope L. **139** 28 24S 139 18 E
Panevėzys **80** 55 42N 24 25 E
Panfilov **76** 44 30N 80 0 E
Panfilovo **81** 50 25N 42 46 E
Pang-Long **99** 23 11N 98 45 E
Pang-Yang **99** 22 7N 98 48 E

*Renamed Belau

Panga 126 1 52N 26 18 E
Pangaion Óros 68 40 50N 24 0 E
Pangalanes, Canal des 129 22 48 S 47 50 E
Pangani 126 5 25 S 38 58 E
Pangani □ 126 5 25 S 39 0 E
Pangani, R. 126 4 40 S 37 50 E
Pangbourne 28 51 28N 1 5W
P'angchiang 106 42 50N 113 1 E
Pangfou 109 32 55N 117 25 E
Pangi 126 3 10 S 26 35 E
Pangkai 98 22 40N 97 31 E
Pangkalanberandan 102 4 1N 98 20 E
Pangkalansusu 102 4 2N 98 42 E
Pangkoh 102 3 5 S 114 8 E
Pangnirtung 149 66 0N 66 0W
Pangong Tso, L. 95 34 0N 78 20 E
Pangrango 103 6 46 S 107 1 E
Pangsau Pass 98 27 15N 96 10 E
Pangta 105 30 14N 97 24 E
Pangtara 98 20 57N 96 40 E
Panguitch 161 37 52N 112 30W
Pangutaran Group 103 6 18N 120 34 E
Panhandle 159 35 23N 101 23W
P'anhsien 108 25 46N 104 39 E
Pani Mines 94 22 29N 73 50 E
Panipat 94 29 25N 77 2 E
Panjal Range 94 32 30N 76 50 E
Panjgur 93 27 0N 64 5 E
Panjim = Panaji 93 15 25N 73 50 E
Panjinad Barrage 93 29 22N 71 15 E
Panjwai 94 31 26N 65 27 E
Pankadjene 103 4 46 S 119 34 E
Pankal Pinang 102 2 0 S 106 0 E
Pankshin 121 9 25N 9 25 E
P'anlung Chiang, R. 108 21 18N 105 25 E
Panmunjŏm 107 37 59N 126 38 E
Panna 95 24 40N 80 15 E
Panna Hills 95 24 40N 81 15 E
Pannuru 97 16 5N 80 34 E
Panorama 173 21 21 S 51 51W
Panruti 97 11 46N 79 35 E
P'anshan 107 41 12N 122 4 E
P'anshih 107 42 55N 126 3 E
Pant'anching 106 39 7N 103 52 E
Pantano 161 32 0N 110 32W
Pantar, I. 103 8 28 S 124 10 E
Pantelleria 64 36 52N 12 0 E
Pantelleria, I. 64 36 52N 12 0 E
Pantha 98 24 7N 94 17 E
Pantin Sakan 98 18 38N 97 33 E
Pantjo 103 8 42 S 118 40 E
Pantón 56 42 31N 7 37W
Pantukan 103 7 17N 125 58 E
Panuco 165 22 0N 98 25W
Panyam 121 9 27N 9 8 E
P'anyü 109 23 2N 113 20 E
Pão de AçIcar 171 9 45 S 37 26W
Paoan 109 22 32N 114 8 E
Paoch'eng 106 33 14N 106 56 E
Paochi 106 34 25N 107 11 E
Paochiatun 107 33 56N 120 12 E
Paoching 108 28 41N 109 35 E
Paok'ang 109 31 57N 111 20 E
Paokuot'u 107 42 20N 120 42 E
Páola 65 39 21N 16 2 E
Paola 158 38 36N 94 50W
Paonia 161 38 56N 107 37W
Paoshan, Shanghai, China 109 31 25N 121 29 E
Paoshan, Yunnan, China 105 25 7N 99 9 E
Paote 106 39 7N 111 13 E
Paoti 107 39 44N 117 18 E
Paoting 106 38 50N 115 30 E
Paot'ou 106 40 35N 110 3 E
Paoua 117 7 25N 16 30 E
Paoying 107 33 15N 119 20 E
Papá 53 47 22N 17 30 E
Papa Sd. 37 59 20N 2 56W
Papa, Sd. of 36 60 19N 1 40W
Papa Stour I. 36 60 20N 1 40W
Papa Stronsay I. 37 59 10N 2 37W
Papa Westray I. 37 59 20N 2 55W
Papagayo, Golfo de 166 10 4N 85 50W
Papagayo, R., Brazil 164 12 30 S 58 10W
Papagayo, R., Mexico 165 16 36N 99 43W
Papagni R. 97 14 10N 78 30 E
Papaikou 147 19 47N 155 6W
Papakura 142 37 4 S 174 59 E
Papaloapan, R. 164 18 2N 96 51W
Papantla 165 20 45N 97 21W
Papar 102 5 45N 116 0 E
Paparoa 142 36 6 S 174 16 E
Paparoa Range 143 42 5 S 171 35 E
Pápas, Akra 69 38 13N 21 6 E
Papatoetoe 142 36 59 S 174 51 E
Papenburg 48 53 7N 7 25 E
Papien Chiang, R. (Da) 108 22 56N 101 47 E
Papigochic, R. 164 29 9N 109 40W
Paposo 172 25 0 S 70 30W
Paps, The, mts. 39 52 0N 9 15W
Papua, Gulf of 135 9 0 S 144 50 E
Papua New Guinea ■ 135 8 0 S 145 0 E
PapuCa 63 44 22N 15 30 E
Papudo 172 32 29 S 71 27W
Papuk, mts. 66 45 30N 17 30 E
Papun 98 18 0N 97 30 E
Pará = Belém 170 1 20 S 48 30W
Pará □ 175 3 20 S 52 0W
Parábita 65 40 3N 18 8 E
Paracatú 171 17 10 S 46 50W
Paracatu, R. 171 16 30 S 45 4W
Paracel Is. 102 16 49N 111 2 E
Parachilna 140 31 10 S 138 21 E
Parachinar 94 34 0N 70 5 E
Paracombe 109 34 51 S 138 47 E
Paracuru 170 3 24 S 39 4W
Paradas 57 37 18N 5 29W
Paradela 56 42 44N 7 37W
Paradip 95 20 15N 86 35 E
Paradise 160 47 27N 114 54W
Paradise, R. 151 53 27N 57 19W
Paradise Valley 160 41 30N 117 28W
Parado 103 8 42 S 118 30 E
Paradyz 54 51 19N 20 2 E
Parafield 109 34 47 S 138 38 E
Parafield Airport 109 34 48 S 138 38 E
Paragould 159 36 5N 90 30W
Paragua, La 174 6 50N 63 20W
Paragua, R. 174 6 30N 63 30W
Paraguaçu Paulista 173 22 22 S 50 35W
Paraguaçu, R. 171 12 45 S 38 54W
Paraguai, R. 174 16 0 S 57 52W
Paraguaipoa 174 11 21N 71 57W
Paraguana, Pen. de 174 12 0N 70 0W
Paraguarí 172 25 36 S 57 0W
Paraguarí □ 172 26 0 S 57 10W
Paraguay ■ 172 23 0 S 57 0W
Paraguay, R. 172 27 18 S 58 38W
Paraíba = Joéo Pessoa 164 7 10 S 35 0W
Paraiba □ 170 7 0 S 36 0W
Paraíba do Sul, R. 173 21 37 S 41 3W
Paraibano 171 6 30 S 44 1W
Parainen 75 60 18N 22 18 E
Paraíso 165 19 3 S 52 59W
Paraiso 165 18 24N 93 14W
Parakhino Paddubye 80 58 46N 33 10 E
Parakou 121 9 25N 2 40 E
Parakylia 140 30 24 S 136 25 E
Paralion-Astrous 69 37 25N 22 45 E
Paramagudi 97 9 31N 78 39 E
Paramaribo 175 5 50N 55 10W
Parambu 170 6 13 S 40 43W
Paramillo, Nudo del 174 7 4N 75 55W
Paramirim 171 13 26 S 42 15W
Paramirim, R. 171 11 34 S 43 18W
Paramithiá 68 39 30N 20 35 E
Paramushir, Ostrov 77 40 24N 156 0 E
Paran, N. 90 30 14N 34 48 E
Paraná 172 32 0 S 60 30W
Paranã 171 12 30 S 47 40W
Paraná □ 173 24 30 S 51 0W
Paraná, R. 172 33 43 S 59 15W
Paranã, R. 171 22 25 S 53 1W
Paranaguá 173 25 30 S 48 30W
Paranaíba, R. 171 18 0 S 49 12W
Paranapanema, R. 173 22 40 S 53 9W
Paranapiacaba, Serra do 173 24 31 S 48 35W
Paranavaí 173 23 4 S 52 28W
Parang, Jolo, Phil. 103 5 55N 120 54 E
Parang, Mindanao, Phil. 103 7 23N 124 16 E
Parangaba 170 3 45 S 38 33W
Paraóin 66 43 54N 21 27 E
Paraparanma 143 40 57 S 175 3 E
Parapóla, I. 69 36 55N 23 27 E
Paraspóri, Ákra 69 35 55N 27 15 E
Paratinga 171 12 40 S 43 10W
Paratoo 140 32 42 S 139 22 E
Parattah 138 42 22 S 147 23 E
Paraúna 171 17 2 S 50 26W
Paray-le-Monial 45 46 27N 4 7 E
Parbati, R. 94 25 51N 76 34 E
Parbatipur 98 25 39N 88 55 E
Parbhani 96 19 8N 76 52 E
Parchim 48 53 25N 11 50 E
Parczew 54 51 9N 22 52 E
Pardee Res. 163 38 16N 120 51W
Pardes Hanna 90 32 28N 34 57 E
Pardilla 56 41 33N 3 43W
Pardo, R., Bahia, Brazil 171 15 40 S 39 0W
Pardo, R., Mato Grosso, Brazil 171 21 0 S 53 25W
Pardo, R., Minas Gerais, Brazil 171 15 48 S 44 48W
Pardo, R., São Paulo, Brazil 171 20 45 S 48 0W
Pardubice 52 50 3N 15 45 E
Pare 103 7 43 S 112 12 E
Pare □ 126 4 10 S 38 0 E
Pare Mts. 126 4 0 S 37 45 E
Pare Pare 103 4 0 S 119 45 E
Parecis, Serra dos 174 13 0 S 60 0W
Paredes de Nava 56 42 9N 4 42W
Parelhas 170 6 41 S 36 39W
Paren 77 62 45N 163 0 E
Parengarenga Harbour 142 34 31 S 173 0 E
Parent 150 47 55N 74 35W
Parent, Lac. 150 48 31N 77 1W
Parentis-en-Born 44 44 21N 1 4W
Parepare 103 4 0 S 119 40 E
Parfino 80 57 59N 31 34 E
Parfuri 129 22 28 S 31 17 E
Paria, Golfo de 174 10 20N 62 0W
Paria, Pen. de 174 10 50N 62 30W
Pariaguán 174 8 51N 64 43W
Pariaman 102 0 47 S 100 11 E
Paricutín, Cerro 164 19 28N 102 15W
Parigi 103 0 50 S 120 5 E
Parika 174 6 50N 58 20W
Parima, Serra 174 2 30N 64 0W
Parinari 174 4 35 S 74 25W
Parincea 70 46 27N 27 9 E
Parîng, mt. 70 45 20N 23 37 E
Parintins 175 2 40 S 56 50W
Pariparit Kyun 99 14 55 S 93 45 E
Paris, Can. 150 43 12N 80 25W
Paris, France 43 48 50N 2 20 E
Paris, Idaho, U.S.A. 160 42 13N 111 30W
Paris, Ky., U.S.A. 156 38 12N 84 12W
Paris, Tenn., U.S.A. 157 36 20N 88 20W
Paris, Tex., U.S.A. 159 33 40N 95 30W
Parish 162 43 24N 76 9W
Pariti 103 9 55 S 123 30 E
Park City 160 40 42N 111 35W
Park Falls 158 45 58N 90 27 E
Park Range 160 40 0N 106 30W
Park Rapids 158 46 56N 95 0W
Park River 158 48 25N 97 17W
Park Rynie 129 30 25 S 30 35 E
Park View 161 36 45N 106 37W
Parkent 85 41 18N 69 40 E
Parker, Ariz., U.S.A. 161 34 8N 114 16W
Parker, S.D., U.S.A. 158 43 25N 97 7W
Parker Dam 161 34 13N 114 5W
Parkersburg 156 39 18N 81 31W
Parkerview 153 51 21N 103 18W
Parkes, A.C.T., Austral. 133 35 18 S 149 8 E
Parkes, N.S.W., Austral. 141 33 9 S 148 11 E
Parkfield 163 35 54N 120 26W
Parkhar 85 37 30N 69 34 E
Parknasilla 39 51 49N 9 50W
Parkside 153 53 10N 106 33W
Parkston 158 43 25N 98 0W
Parksville 152 49 20N 124 21W
Parkville 162 39 23N 76 33W
Parlakimedi 96 18 45N 84 5 E
Parma, Italy 62 44 50N 10 20 E
Parma, U.S.A. 160 43 49N 116 59W
Parna, R. 62 44 27N 10 3 E
Parnaguá 170 10 10 S 44 10W
Parnaíba, Piauí, Brazil 170 3 0 S 41 40W
Parnaíba, São Paulo, Brazil 170 19 34 S 51 14W
Parnaíba, R. 170 3 35 S 43 0W
Parnamirim 170 8 5 S 39 34W
Parnarama 170 5 41 S 43 6W
Parnassós, mt. 69 38 17N 21 30 E
Parnassus 143 42 42 S 173 23 E
Párnis, mt. 69 38 14N 23 45 E
Párnon Óros 69 37 15N 22 45 E
Pärnu 80 58 12N 24 33 E
Parola 96 20 47N 75 7 E
Paroo Chan. 133 30 50 S 143 35 E
Paroo, R. 139 30 0 S 144 5 E
Paropamisus Range = Fī roz Kohi 93 34 45N 63 0 E
Páros 69 37 5N 25 9 E
Páros, I. 69 37 5N 25 12 E
Parowan 161 37 54N 112 56W
Parpaillon, mts. 45 44 30N 6 40 E
Parracombe 30 51 11N 3 55W
Parral 172 36 10 S 72 0W
Parramatta 141 33 48 S 151 1 E
Parramore I. 162 37 32N 75 39W
Parras 164 25 30N 102 20W
Parrett, R. 28 51 7N 2 58W
Parris I. 157 32 20N 80 30W
Parrsboro 151 45 30N 64 10W
Parry 153 49 47N 104 41W
Parry, C. 147 70 20N 123 38W
Parry Is. 12 77 0N 110 0W
Parry Sound 150 45 20N 80 0W
Parshall 158 47 56N 102 11W
Parsnip, R. 152 55 10N 123 2W
Parsons 159 37 20N 95 10W
Parsons Ra., Mts. 138 13 30 S 135 15 E
Partabpur 96 20 0N 80 42 E
Partanna 64 37 43N 12 51 E
Partapgarh 94 24 2N 74 40 E
Parthenay 42 46 38N 0 16W
Partille 73 57 48N 12 18 E
Partinico 64 38 3N 13 6 E
Partney 33 53 12N 0 7 E
Parton 32 54 34N 3 35W
Partry Mts. 38 53 40N 9 28W
Partur 96 19 40N 76 14 E
Paru, R. 175 0 20 S 53 30W
Parur 97 10 13N 76 14 E
Paruro 174 13 45 S 71 50W
Parvatipuram 96 18 50N 83 25 E
Parwan □ 93 35 0N 69 0 E
Påryd 73 56 34N 15 55 E
Parys 128 26 52 S 27 29 E
Parys, Mt. 31 53 23N 4 18W
Pas-de-Calais □ 43 50 30N 2 30 E
Pasadena, Calif., U.S.A. 163 34 5N 118 9W
Pasadena, Tex., U.S.A. 159 29 45N 95 14W
Pasaje 174 3 10 S 79 40W
Pasaje, R. 172 25 35 S 64 57W
Pascagoula 159 30 30N 88 30W
Pascagoula, R. 159 30 40N 88 35W
Paşcani 70 47 14N 26 45 E
Pasco 160 46 10N 119 0W
Pasco, Cerro de 174 10 45 S 76 10W
Pascoag 162 41 57N 71 42W
Pascoe, Mt. 137 27 25 S 120 40 E
Pasewalk 48 53 30N 14 0 E
Pasfield L. 153 58 24N 105 20W
Pasha, R. 80 60 20N 33 0 E
Pashiwari 95 34 40N 75 10 E
Pashiya 84 58 33N 58 26 E
Pashmakli = Smolyan 67 41 36N 24 38 E
Pasighat 98 28 4N 95 21 E
Pasir Mas 101 6 2N 102 8 E
Pasir Puteh 101 5 50N 102 24 E
Pasirian 103 8 13 S 113 8 E
Pasley, C. 137 33 52 S 123 35 E
Pasman I. 63 43 58N 15 20 E
Pasmore, R. 140 31 5 S 139 49 E
Pasni 93 25 15N 63 27 E
Paso de Indios 176 43 55 S 69 0W
Paso de los Libres 172 29 44 S 57 10W
Paso de los Toros 172 32 36 S 56 37W
Paso Robles 161 35 40N 120 45W
Paspebiac 151 48 3N 65 17W
Pasrur 94 32 16N 74 43 E
Passage East 39 52 15N 7 0W
Passage West 39 51 52N 8 20W
Passaic 162 40 50N 74 8W
Passau 49 48 34N 13 27 E
Passendale 47 50 54N 3 2 E
Passero, C. 65 36 42N 15 8 E
Passo Fundo 173 28 10 S 52 30W
Passos 171 20 45 S 46 37W
Passow 48 53 13N 14 3 E
Passwang 50 47 22N 7 41 E
Passy 43 45 55N 6 41 E
Pastaza, R. 174 2 45 S 76 50W
Pastek 54 54 3N 19 41 E
Pasto 174 1 13N 77 17W
Pasto Zootécnico do Cunene 128 16 20 S 15 20 E
Pastos Bons 170 6 36 S 44 5W
Pastrana 58 40 27N 2 53W
Pasuruan 103 7 40 S 112 53 E
Pasym 54 53 48N 20 49 E
Pásztó 53 47 52N 19 43 E
Patagonia, Argent. 176 45 0 S 69 0W
Patagonia, U.S.A. 161 31 35N 110 45W
Patan, India 93 23 54N 72 14 E
Patan, Gujarat, India 96 17 22N 73 48 E
Patan, Maharashtra, India 94 23 54N 72 14 E
Patan (Lalitapur) 99 27 40N 85 20 E
Pat'ang Szechwan 105 30 2N 98 58 E
Patani 103 0 20N 128 50 E
Pataohotzu 107 43 5N 127 33 E
Patapsco Res. 162 39 27N 76 55W
Pataudi 94 28 18N 76 48 E
Patay 43 48 2N 1 40 E
Patcham 29 50 52N 0 9W
Patchewollock 140 35 22 S 142 12 E
Patchogue 162 40 46N 73 1W
Patea 142 39 45 S 174 30 E
Pategi 121 8 50N 5 45 E
Pateley Bridge 33 54 5N 1 45W
Patensie 128 33 46 S 24 49 E
Paternò 65 37 34N 14 53 E
Paternoster, Kepulauan 102 7 5 S 118 15 E
Pateros 160 48 4N 119 58W
Paterson, Austral. 141 32 37 S 151 39 E
Paterson, U.S.A. 162 40 55N 74 10W
Paterson Inlet 143 46 56 S 168 12 E
Paterson Ra. 136 21 45 S 122 10 E
Paterswolde 46 53 9N 6 34 E
Pathankot 94 32 18N 75 45 E
Patharghata 98 22 2N 89 58 E
Pathfinder Res. 160 42 0N 107 0W
Pathiu 101 10 42N 99 19 E
Pathum Thani 100 14 1N 100 32 E
Páti 103 6 45 S 111 3 E
Patiala 94 30 23N 76 26 E
Patine Kouta 120 12 45N 13 45W
Patjitan 103 8 12 S 111 8 E
Patkai Bum 98 27 0N 95 30 E
Pátmos 69 37 21N 26 36 E
Pátmos, I. 69 37 21N 26 36 E
Patna, India 95 25 35N 85 18 E
Patna, U.K. 34 55 21N 4 30W
Patonga 126 2 45N 33 15 E
Patos 170 7 1 S 37 16W
Patos de Minas 171 18 35 S 46 32W
Patos, Lag. dos 173 31 20 S 51 0 E
Patosi 68 40 42N 19 38 E
Patquía 172 30 0 S 66 55W
Pátrai 69 38 14N 21 47 E
Pátraikos, Kólpos 69 38 17N 21 30 E
Patrick 32 54 13N 4 41W
Patrocínio 171 18 57 S 47 0W
Patta 126 2 10 S 41 0 E
Patta, I. 126 2 10 S 41 0 E
Pattada 64 40 35N 9 7 E
Pattanapuram 97 9 6N 76 33 E
Pattani 101 6 48N 101 15 E
Patten 151 45 59N 68 28W
Patterdale 32 54 33N 2 55W
Patterson, Calif., U.S.A. 163 37 30N 121 9W
Patterson, La., U.S.A. 159 29 44N 91 20W
Patterson, Mt. 163 38 29N 119 20W
Patti 94 31 17N 74 54 E
Patti Castroreale 65 38 8N 14 57 E
Pattoki 94 31 5N 73 52 E
Pattukkottai 97 10 25N 79 20 E
Patu 170 6 6 S 37 38W
Patuakhali 98 22 20N 90 25 E
Patuca, Punta 166 15 49N 84 14W
Patuca, R. 166 15 20N 84 40W
Patung 109 31 0N 110 30 E
Pâturages 47 50 25N 3 52 E
Patutahi 142 38 38 S 177 55 E
Pátzcuaro 164 19 30N 101 40W
Pau 44 43 19N 0 25W
Pau d' Arco 170 7 30 S 49 22W
Pau dos Ferros 170 6 7 S 38 10W
Pauillac 44 45 11N 0 46W
Pauini, R. 174 1 42 S 62 50W
Pauk 98 21 55N 94 30 E
Paul I. 151 56 30N 61 20W
Paulatuk 147 69 25N 124 0W
Paulhan 44 43 33N 3 28 E
Paulis = Isiro 126 2 53N 27 58 E
Paulista 170 7 57 S 34 53W

Paulistana 170 8 9 S 41 9 W
Paull 33 53 42 N 0 12 W
Paullina 158 42 55 N 95 40 W
Paulo Afonso 170 9 21 S 38 15 W
Paulo de Faria 171 20 2 S 49 24 W
Paulpietersburg 129 27 23 S 30 50 E
Paul's Valley 159 34 40 N 97 17 W
Pauma Valley 163 33 16 N 116 58 W
Paungde 98 18 29 N 95 30 E
Pauni 96 20 48 N 79 40 E
Pavelets 81 53 49 N 39 14 E
Pavia 62 45 10 N 9 10 E
Pavlikeni 67 43 14 N 25 20 E
Pavlodar 76 52 33 N 77 0 E
Pavlof Is. 147 55 30 N 161 30 W
Pavlograd 82 48 30 N 35 52 E
Pavlovo, Gorkiy, U.S.S.R. 81 55 58 N 43 5 E
Pavlovo, Yakut A.S.S.R., U.S.S.R. 77 63 5 N 115 25 E
Pavlovsk 81 50 26 N 40 5 E
Pavlovskaya 83 46 17 N 39 47 E
Pavlovskiy Posad 81 55 37 N 38 42 E
Pavullo nel Frignano 62 44 20 N 10 50 E
Pawahku 98 26 11 N 98 40 E
Pawhuska 159 36 40 N 96 25 W
Pawling 162 41 35 N 73 37 W
Pawnee 159 36 24 N 96 50 W
Pawnee City 158 40 8 N 96 10 W
Pawtucket 162 41 51 N 71 22 W
Paximádhia 69 35 0 N 24 35 E
Paxoi, I. 68 39 14 N 20 12 E
Paxton, Ill., U.S.A. 156 40 25 N 88 0 W
Paxton, Nebr., U.S.A. 158 41 12 N 101 27 W
Paya Bakri 101 2 3 N 102 44 E
Payakumbah 102 0 20 S 100 35 E
Payenhaot'e (Alashantsoch'i) 106 38 50 N 105 32 E
Payenk'ala Shan 105 34 20 N 97 0 E
Payerne 50 46 49 N 6 56 E
Payette 160 44 0 N 117 0 W
Paymogo 57 37 44 N 7 21 W
Payne L. 149 59 30 N 74 30 W
Payne, R. 149 60 0 N 70 0 W
Payneham 109 34 54 S 138 39 E
Paynes Find 137 29 15 S 117 42 E
Paynesville, Liberia 120 6 20 N 10 45 W
Paynesville, U.S.A. 158 45 21 N 94 44 W
Paysandú 172 32 19 S 58 8 W
Payson, Ariz., U.S.A. 161 34 17 N 111 15 W
Payson, Utah, U.S.A. 160 40 8 N 111 41 W
Paz, Bahía de la 164 24 15 N 110 25 W
Paz Centro, La 166 12 20 N 86 41 W
Paz, La, Entre Ríos, Argent. 172 30 50 S 59 45 W
Paz, La, San Luis, Argent. 172 33 30 S 67 20 W
Paz, La, Boliv. 174 16 20 S 68 10 W
Paz, La, Hond. 166 14 20 N 87 47 W
Paz, La, Mexico 164 24 10 N 110 20 W
Paz, La, Bahia de 164 24 20 N 110 40 W
Paz, R. 166 13 44 N 90 10 W
Pazar 92 41 10 N 40 50 E
Pazardzhik 67 42 12 N 24 20 E
Pazin 63 45 14 N 13 56 E
Pčinja, R. 66 42 0 N 21 45 E
Pe Ell 160 46 30 N 123 18 W
Peabody 162 42 31 N 70 56 W
Peace Point 152 59 7 N 112 27 W
Peace, R. 152 59 0 N 111 25 W
Peace River 152 56 15 N 117 18 W
Peace River Res. 152 55 40 N 123 40 W
Peacehaven 29 50 47 N 0 1 E
Peach Springs 161 35 36 N 113 30 W
Peak Downs 138 22 55 S 148 0 E
Peak Downs Mine 138 22 17 S 148 11 E
Peak Hill, N.S.W., Austral. 141 32 39 S 148 11 E
Peak Hill, W. A., Austral. 137 25 35 S 118 43 E
Peak Range 138 22 50 S 148 20 E
Peak, The 32 53 24 N 1 53 W
Peake 140 35 25 S 140 0 E
Peake Cr. 139 28 2 S 136 7 E
Peale Mt. 161 38 25 N 109 12 W
Pearblossom 163 34 30 N 117 55 W
Pearce 161 31 57 N 109 56 W
Pearl Banks 97 8 45 N 79 45 E
Pearl City 147 2 21 N 158 0 W
Pearl Harbor 147 21 20 N 158 0 W
Pearl, R. 159 31 50 N 90 0 W
Pearsall 159 28 55 N 99 8 W
Pearse I. 152 54 52 N 130 14 W
Peary Land 12 82 40 N 33 0 W
Pease, R. 159 34 18 N 100 15 W
Peasenhall 29 52 17 N 1 24 E
Pebane 127 17 10 S 38 8 E
Pebas 174 3 10 S 71 55 W
Pebble Beach 163 36 34 N 121 57 W
Peçanha 171 18 33 S 42 34 W
Péccioli 62 43 32 N 10 43 E
Pechea 70 45 36 N 27 49 E
Pechenezhin 82 48 30 N 24 48 E
Pechenga 78 69 30 N 31 25 E
Pechnezhskoye Vdkhr. 81 50 0 N 36 50 E
Pechora, R. 78 62 30 N 56 30 E
Pechorskaya Guba 78 68 40 N 54 0 E
Pechory 80 57 48 N 27 40 E
Pecica 66 46 10 N 21 3 E
Pečka 66 44 18 N 19 33 E
Pécora, C. 64 39 28 N 8 23 E
Pecos 159 31 25 N 103 35 W
Pecos, R. 159 31 22 N 102 30 W
Pecqueuse 47 48 39 N 2 3 E
Pécs 53 46 5 N 18 15 E
Pedasí 166 7 32 N 80 3 W
Peddapalli 96 18 40 N 79 24 E
Peddapuram 96 17 6 N 82 5 E
Peddavagu, R. 96 16 33 N 79 8 E
Pedder, L. 138 42 55 S 146 10 E
Pedernales 167 18 2 N 71 44 W
Pedirka 139 26 40 S 135 14 E
Pedjantan, I. 102 0 5 S 106 15 E
Pedra Azul 171 16 2 S 41 17 W
Pedra Grande, Recifes do 171 17 45 S 38 58 W
Pedras, Pta. de 171 7 38 S 34 47 W
Pedreiras 170 4 32 S 44 40 W
Pedrera, La 174 1 18 S 69 43 W
Pedro Afonso 170 9 0 S 48 10 W
Pedro Antonio Santos 165 18 54 N 88 15 W
Pedro Cays 166 17 5 N 77 48 W
Pedro Chico 174 1 4 N 70 25 W
Pedro de Valdivia 172 22 33 S 69 38 W
Pedro Juan Caballero 173 22 30 S 55 40 W
Pedro Muñoz 59 39 25 N 2 56 W
Pedrógão Grande 56 39 55 N 8 0 W
Peebinga 140 34 52 S 140 57 E
Peebles 35 55 40 N 3 12 W
Peebles (□) 26 55 37 N 3 4 W
Peekshill 162 41 18 N 73 57 W
Peel, Austral. 139 33 20 S 149 38 E
Peel, I. of Man 32 54 14 N 4 40 W
Peel Fell, mt. 35 55 17 N 2 35 W
Peel, R., Austral. 141 30 50 S 150 29 E
Peel, R., Can. 147 67 0 N 135 0 W
Peelwood 141 34 7 S 149 27 E
Peene, R. 48 53 53 N 13 53 E
Peera Peera Poolanna L. 139 26 30 S 138 0 E
Peers 152 53 40 N 116 0 W
Pegasus Bay 143 43 20 S 173 10 E
Peggau 52 47 12 N 15 21 E
Pego 59 38 51 N 0 8 W
Pegswood 35 55 12 N 1 38 W
Pegu 99 17 20 N 96 29 E
Pegu Yoma, mts. 98 19 0 N 96 0 E
Pegwell Bay 29 51 18 N 1 22 E
Pehčevo 66 41 41 N 22 55 E
Pehuajó 172 36 0 S 62 0 W
Pei Chiang, R. 109 23 12 N 112 45 E
Pei Wan 107 36 25 N 120 45 E
Peian 105 48 16 N 126 36 E
Peichen 107 41 38 N 121 50 E
Peichengchen 107 44 30 N 123 27 E
Peichiang 109 23 0 N 120 0 E
Peihai 108 21 30 N 109 5 E
P'eihsien, Kiangsu, China 106 34 44 N 116 55 E
P'eihsien, Kiangsu, China 107 34 20 N 117 57 E
Peiliu 109 22 45 N 110 20 E
Peine, Chile 172 23 45 S 68 8 W
Peine, Ger. 48 52 19 N 10 12 E
Peip'an Chiang, R. 108 25 0 N 106 11 E
Peip'ei 105 29 49 N 106 27 E
Peip'iao 107 41 48 N 120 44 E
Peip'ing 106 39 45 N 116 25 E
Peissenberg 49 47 48 N 11 4 E
Peitz 48 51 50 N 14 23 E
Peixe 171 12 0 S 48 40 W
Peixe, R. 171 21 31 S 51 58 W
Peize 46 53 9 N 6 30 E
Pek, R. 66 44 58 N 21 55 E
Pekalongan 103 6 53 S 109 40 E
Pekan 101 3 30 N 103 25 E
Pekin 158 40 35 N 89 40 W
Peking = Peip'ing 106 39 45 N 116 25 E
Pelabuhan Ratu, Teluk 103 7 5 S 106 30 E
Pelabuhanratu 103 7 0 S 106 32 E
Pélagos, I. 68 39 17 N 24 4 E
Pelagruza, Is. 63 42 24 N 16 15 E
Pelaihari 102 3 55 S 114 45 E
Pełczyce 54 53 3 N 15 16 E
Peleaga, mt. 70 45 22 N 22 55 E
Pelee I. 150 41 47 N 82 40 W
Pelée, Mt. 167 14 40 N 61 0 W
Pelee, Pt. 150 41 54 N 82 31 W
Pelekech, mt. 126 3 52 N 35 8 E
Peleng, I. 103 1 20 S 123 30 E
Pelham 157 31 5 N 84 6 W
Pelhrimov 52 49 24 N 15 12 E
Pelican 147 58 12 N 136 28 W
Pelican L. 153 52 28 N 100 20 W
Pelican Narrows 153 55 10 N 102 56 W
Pelican Portage 152 55 51 N 113 0 W
Pelican Rapids 153 52 45 N 100 42 W
Peligre, L. de 167 19 1 N 71 58 W
Pelkosenniemi 74 67 6 N 27 28 E
Pella 158 41 20 N 93 0 W
Pélla □ 68 40 52 N 22 0 E
Péllaro 65 38 1 N 15 40 E
Pellworm, I. 48 54 30 N 8 40 E
Pelly Bay 149 68 0 N 89 50 W
Pelly L. 148 66 0 N 102 0 W
Pelly, R. 147 62 15 N 133 30 W
Peloponnese = Pelóponnisos 69 37 10 N 22 0 E
Pelopónnisos Kai Dhitikí Iprotikí Ellas □ 69 37 10 N 22 0 E
Peloritani, Monti 65 38 2 N 15 15 E
Peloro, C. 65 38 15 N 15 40 E
Pelorus Sound 143 40 59 S 173 59 E
Pelotas 173 31 42 S 52 23 W
Pelôvo 67 43 26 N 24 17 E
Pelvoux, Massif de 45 44 52 N 6 20 E
Pelym R. 84 59 39 N 63 6 E
Pemalang 103 6 53 S 109 23 E
Pematang Siantar 102 2 57 N 99 5 E
Pemba, Mozam. 127 12 58 S 40 30 E
Pemba, Zambia 127 16 30 S 27 28 E
Pemba Channel 126 5 0 S 39 37 E
Pemba, I. 126 5 0 S 39 45 E
Pemberton, Austral. 137 34 30 S 116 0 E
Pemberton, Can. 152 50 25 N 122 50 W
Pembina 153 48 58 N 97 15 W
Pembina, R. 153 49 0 N 98 12 W
Pembine 156 45 38 N 87 59 W
Pembrey 31 51 42 N 4 17 W
Pembroke, Can. 150 45 50 N 77 7 W
Pembroke, N.Z. 143 44 33 S 169 9 E
Pembroke, U.K. 31 51 41 N 4 57 W
Pembroke, U.S.A. 157 32 5 N 81 32 W
Pembroke (□) 26 51 40 N 5 0 W
Pembroke Dock 31 51 41 N 4 57 W
Pembury 29 51 8 N 0 20 E
Pen-y-Ghent 32 54 10 N 2 15 W
Pen-y-groes, Dyfed, U.K. 31 51 48 N 4 3 W
Pen-y-groes, Gwynedd, U.K. 31 53 3 N 4 18 W
Peñíscola 58 40 22 N 0 24 E
Peña de Francia, Sierra de 56 40 32 N 6 10 W
Peña Roya, mt. 58 40 24 N 0 40 W
Peña, Sierra de la 58 42 32 N 0 45 W
Peñafiel 56 41 12 N 8 17 W
Peñafiel 56 41 35 N 4 7 W
Peñaflor 57 37 43 N 5 21 W
Peñalara, Pico 56 40 51 N 3 57 W
Penally 31 51 39 N 4 44 W
Penalva 170 3 18 S 45 10 W
Penamacôr 56 40 10 N 7 10 W
Penang = Pinang 101 5 25 N 100 15 E
Penápolis 173 21 30 S 50 0 W
Peñaranda de Bracamonte 56 40 53 N 5 13 W
Peñarroya-Pueblonuevo 57 38 19 N 5 16 W
Penarth 31 51 26 N 3 11 W
Peñas, C. de 56 43 42 N 5 52 W
Peñas de San Pedro 59 38 44 N 2 0 W
Peñas, G. de 176 47 0 S 75 0 W
Peñas, Pta. 174 11 17 N 70 28 W
Pench'i 107 41 20 N 123 48 E
Pencoed 31 51 31 N 3 30 W
Pend Oreille, L. 160 48 0 N 116 30 W
Pend Oreille, R. 160 49 4 N 117 37 W
Pendálofon 68 40 14 N 21 12 E
Pendeen 30 50 11 N 5 39 W
Pendelikón 69 38 5 N 23 53 E
Pendembu 120 9 7 N 12 14 W
Pendências 170 5 15 S 36 43 W
Pender B. 136 16 45 S 122 42 E
Pendine 31 51 44 N 4 33 W
Pendle Hill 32 53 53 N 2 18 W
Pendleton, Calif., U.S.A. 163 33 16 N 117 23 W
Pendleton, Oreg., U.S.A. 160 45 35 N 118 50 W
Pendzhikent 85 39 29 N 67 37 E
Penedo 170 10 15 S 36 36 W
Penetanguishene 150 44 50 N 79 55 W
Penfield 109 34 44 S 138 38 E
Pengalengan 103 7 9 S 107 30 E
P'engch'i 108 30 50 N 105 42 E
Penge, Kasai, Congo 126 5 30 S 24 33 E
Penge, Kivu, Congo 126 4 27 S 28 25 E
P'enghsien 108 30 59 N 103 56 E
P'enghu Liehtao 109 22 30 N 119 30 E
P'englai 107 37 49 N 120 47 E
P'engshui 108 29 19 N 108 12 E
P'engtse 109 29 53 N 116 32 E
Penguin 138 41 8 S 146 6 E
Penhalonga 127 18 52 S 32 40 E
Peniche 57 39 19 N 9 22 W
Penicuik 35 55 50 N 3 14 W
Penida, I. 102 8 45 S 115 30 E
Penistone 33 53 31 N 1 38 W
Penitentes, Serra dos 170 8 45 S 46 20 W
Penkridge 28 52 44 N 2 8 W
Penmachno 31 53 2 N 3 47 W
Penmaenmawr 31 53 16 N 3 55 W
Penmarch 42 47 49 N 4 21 W
Penmarch, Pte. de 42 47 48 N 4 22 W
Penn Yan 162 42 39 N 77 7 W
Pennabilli 63 43 50 N 12 17 E
Pennant 153 50 32 N 108 14 W
Penne 63 42 28 N 13 56 E
Penner, R. 97 14 50 N 78 20 E
Penneshaw 140 35 44 S 137 56 E
Pennines 32 54 50 N 2 20 W
Pennino, Mte. 63 43 6 N 12 54 E
Pennsburg 162 40 23 N 75 30 W
Pennsville 162 39 39 N 75 31 W
Pennsylvania □ 156 40 50 N 78 0 W
Penny 152 53 51 N 121 48 W
Peno 80 57 2 N 32 33 E
Penola 140 37 25 S 140 47 E
Penong 139 31 59 S 133 5 E
Penonomé 166 8 31 N 80 21 W
Penpont 35 55 14 N 3 49 W
Penrhyn Is. 131 9 0 S 150 30 W
Penrith, Austral. 141 33 43 S 150 38 E
Penrith, U.K. 32 54 40 N 2 45 W
Penryn 30 50 10 N 5 7 W
Pensacola 157 30 30 N 87 10 W
Pensacola Mts. 13 84 0 S 40 0 W
Pense 153 50 25 N 104 59 W
Penshurst, Austral. 140 37 49 S 142 20 W
Penshurst, U.K. 29 51 10 N 0 12 E
Pentecoste 170 3 48 S 37 17 W
Penticton 152 49 30 N 119 30 W
Pentire Pt. 30 50 35 N 4 57 W
Pentland 138 20 32 S 145 25 E
Pentland Firth 37 58 43 N 3 10 W
Pentland Hills 35 55 48 N 3 25 W
Pentland Skerries 37 58 41 N 2 53 W
Pentraeth 31 53 17 N 4 13 W
Pentre Foelas 31 53 2 N 3 41 W
Penukonda 97 14 5 N 77 38 E
Penwortham 32 53 45 N 2 44 W
Penybont 31 52 17 N 3 18 W
Penylan L. 153 61 50 N 106 20 W
Penza 81 53 15 N 45 5 E
Penzance 30 50 7 N 5 32 W
Penzberg 49 47 46 N 11 23 E
Penzhinskaya Guba 77 61 30 N 163 0 E
Penzlin 48 53 32 N 13 6 E
Peó 66 42 40 N 20 17 E
Peoria, Ariz., U.S.A. 161 33 40 N 112 15 W
Peoria, Ill., U.S.A. 158 40 40 N 89 40 W
Pepacton Res. 162 42 5 N 74 58 W
Pepingen 47 50 46 N 4 10 E
Pepinster 47 50 34 N 5 47 E
Pepmbridge 28 52 13 N 2 54 W
Pepperwood 160 40 23 N 124 0 W
Peqini 68 41 4 N 19 44 E
Pera Hd. 138 12 55 S 141 37 E
Perabumilih 102 3 27 S 104 15 E
Perakhóra 69 38 2 N 22 56 E
Peraki, R. 101 5 10 N 101 4 E
Perales de Alfambra 58 40 38 N 1 0 W
Perales del Puerto 56 40 10 N 6 40 W
Peralta 58 42 21 N 1 49 W
Pérama 69 35 20 N 24 22 E
Perast 66 42 31 N 18 47 E
Percé 151 48 31 N 64 13 W
Perche 42 48 31 N 1 1 E
Perche, Collines de la 42 42 30 N 2 5 E
Percival Lakes 136 21 25 S 125 0 E
Percy 42 48 55 N 1 11 W
Percy Is. 138 21 39 S 150 16 E
Percyville 138 19 2 S 143 45 E
Perdido, Mte. 58 42 40 N 0 50 E
Pereira 174 4 49 N 75 43 W
Pereira Barreto 171 20 38 S 51 7 W
Pereira de Eóa 128 16 48 S 15 50 E
Perekerten 140 34 55 S 143 40 E
Perenjori 137 29 26 S 116 16 E
Pereslavi-Zelesskiy 80 56 45 N 38 58 E
Pereyaslav-Khmelnitskiy 80 50 3 N 31 28 E
Perez, I. 165 22 24 N 89 42 W
Perg 52 48 15 N 14 38 E
Pergamino 172 33 52 S 60 30 W
Pergine Valsugano 63 46 4 N 11 15 E
Pérgola 63 43 35 N 12 50 E
Perham 158 46 36 N 95 36 W
Perham Down Camp 28 51 14 N 1 38 W
Perhentian, Kepulauan 101 5 54 N 102 42 E
Peri, L. 140 30 45 S 143 35 E
Periam 66 46 2 N 20 59 E
Peribonca, L. 151 50 1 N 71 10 W
Péribonca, R. 151 48 45 N 72 5 W
Perico 172 24 20 S 65 5 W
Pericos 164 25 3 N 107 42 W
Périers 42 49 11 N 1 25 W
Périgord 44 45 0 N 0 40 E
Périgueux 44 45 10 N 0 42 E
Perija, Sierra de 174 9 30 N 73 3 W
Perim, I. 91 12 39 N 43 25 E
Peristera, I. 69 39 15 N 23 58 E
Peritoró 170 4 20 S 44 18 W
Periyakulam 97 10 5 N 77 30 E
Periyar, L. 97 9 25 N 77 10 E
Periyar, R. 97 10 15 N 78 10 E
Perkam, Tg. 103 1 35 S 137 50 E
Perkasie 162 40 22 N 75 18 W
Perkovió 63 43 41 N 16 10 E
Perlas, Arch. de las 166 8 41 N 79 7 W
Perlas, Punta de 166 11 30 N 83 30 W
Perleberg 48 53 5 N 11 50 E
Perlevka 81 51 56 N 38 57 E
Perlez 66 45 11 N 20 22 E
Perlis □ 101 6 30 N 100 15 E
Perm (Molotov) 84 58 0 N 57 10 E
Përmeti 68 40 15 N 20 21 E
Pernambuco = Recife 170 8 0 S 35 0 W
Pernambuco □ 170 8 0 S 37 0 W
Pernatty Lagoon 140 31 30 S 137 12 E
Peron, C. 137 25 30 S 113 30 E
Peron Is. 136 13 9 S 130 4 E
Peron Pen. 137 26 0 S 113 10 E
Péronne 43 49 55 N 2 57 E
Péronnes 47 50 27 N 4 9 E
Perosa Argentina 62 44 57 N 7 11 E
Perouse Str., La 86 45 40 N 142 0 E
Perow 152 54 35 N 126 10 W
Perpendicular Pt. 139 31 37 S 152 52 E
Perpignan 44 42 42 N 2 53 E
Perranporth 30 50 21 N 5 9 W
Perranzabuloe 30 50 18 N 5 7 W
Perris 163 33 47 N 117 14 W
Perros-Guirec 42 48 49 N 3 28 W
Perry, Fla., U.S.A. 157 30 9 N 83 10 W
Perry, Ga., U.S.A. 157 32 25 N 83 41 W
Perry, Iowa, U.S.A. 158 41 48 N 94 5 W
Perry, Maine, U.S.A. 157 44 59 N 67 20 W
Perry, Okla., U.S.A. 159 36 20 N 97 20 W
Perry, Mt. 139 25 12 S 151 41 E
Perryton 159 36 28 N 100 48 W

Perryville, Alas., U.S.A. 147 55 54N 159 10W
Perryville, Mo., U.S.A. 159 37 42N 89 50W
Persberg 72 59 47N 14 15E
Persepolis 93 29 55N 52 50E
Pershore 28 52 7N 2 4W
Persia = Iran 93 35 0N 50 0E
Persian Gulf 93 27 0N 50 0E
Perstorp 73 56 10N 13 25E
Perth, Austral. 137 31 57S 115 52E
Perth, N.B., Can. 150 46 43N 67 42W
Perth, Ont., Can. 150 44 55N 76 15W
Perth, U.K. 35 56 24N 3 27W
Perth (□) 26 56 30N 4 0W
Perth Amboy 162 40 30N 74 25W
Perthus, Le 44 42 30N 2 53E
Pertuis 45 43 42N 5 30E
Pertuis Breton 44 46 17N 1 25W
Pertuis d'Antioche 44 46 6N 1 20W
Peru, Ill., U.S.A. 158 41 18N 89 12W
Peru, Ind., U.S.A. 156 40 42N 86 0W
Peru ■ 174 8 0S 75 0W
Perúgia 63 43 6N 12 24E
Perušić 63 44 40N 15 22E
Péruwelz 47 50 31N 3 36E
Pervomayskiy 81 53 20N 40 10E
Pervouralsk 84 56 55N 60 0E
Perwez 47 50 38N 4 48E
Pésaro 63 43 55N 12 53E
Pesca, La 165 23 46N 97 47W
Pescadores Is. (P'enghu Liehtao) 109 23 30N 119 30E
Pescara 63 42 28N 14 13E
Peschanokopskoye 83 46 14N 41 4E
Péscia 62 43 54N 10 40E
Pescina 63 42 0N 13 39E
Peseux 50 46 59N 6 53E
Peshawar 94 34 2N 71 37E
Peshawar □ 94 35 0N 72 50E
Peshkopia 68 41 41N 20 25E
Peshovka 84 59 4N 52 22E
Peshtera 67 42 2N 24 18E
Peshtigo 156 45 4N 87 46W
Peski 81 51 14N 42 12E
Peskovka 81 59 9N 52 28E
Pêso da Régua 56 41 10N 7 47W
Pesqueira 170 8 20S 36 42W
Pesquiería 164 29 23N 110 54W
Pesquiería, R. 164 25 54N 99 11W
Pessac 44 44 48N 0 37W
Pessoux 47 50 17N 5 11E
Pest □ 53 47 29N 19 5E
Pestovo 80 58 33N 35 18E
Pestravka 81 52 28N 49 57E
Péta 69 39 10N 21 2E
Petah Tiqwa 90 32 6N 34 53E
Petalídhion, Khóra 69 36 57N 21 55E
Petaling Jaya 101 3 4N 101 42E
Petaluma 163 38 13N 122 39W
Petange 47 49 33N 5 55E
Petatlán 164 17 31N 101 16W
Petauke 127 14 14S 31 12E
Petawawa 150 45 54N 77 17W
Petegem 47 50 59N 3 32E
Petén Itza, Lago 166 16 58N 89 50W
Peter 1st, I. 13 69 0S 91 0W
Peter Pond L. 153 55 55N 108 44W
Peterbell 150 48 36N 83 21W
Peterboro 162 42 55N 71 59W
Peterborough, S. Australia, Austral. 140 32 58S 138 51E
Peterborough, Victoria, Austral. 133 38 37S 142 50E
Peterborough, U.K. 29 52 35N 0 14W
Peterchurch 28 52 3N 2 57W
Peterculter 37 57 5N 2 18W
Peterhead 37 57 30N 1 49W
Peterlee 33 54 45N 1 18W
Petersburg, Alas., U.S.A. 152 56 50N 133 0W
Petersburg, Ind., U.S.A. 156 38 30N 87 15W
Petersburg, Va., U.S.A. 162 37 17N 77 26W
Petersburg, W. Va., U.S.A. 156 38 59N 79 10W
Petersfield 29 51 0N 0 56W
Peterswell 39 53 7N 8 46W
Petford 138 17 20S 144 50E
Petília Policastro 65 39 7N 16 48E
Petit Bois I. 157 30 16N 88 25W
Petit Cap 151 48 58N 63 58W
Petit Goâve 167 18 27N 72 51W
Petit-Quevilly, Le 42 49 26N 1 0E
Petitcodiac 151 45 57N 65 11W
Petite Saguenay 151 47 59N 70 1W
Petitsikapau, L. 151 54 37N 66 25W
Petlad 94 22 30N 72 45E
Peto 165 20 10N 89 0W
Petone 142 41 13S 174 53E
Petoskey 150 45 22N 84 57W
Petra, Jordan 90 30 20N 35 22E
Petra, Spain 58 39 37N 3 6E
Petra, Ostrova 12 76 15N 118 30E
Petralia 65 37 49N 14 4E
Petrel 59 38 30N 0 46W
Petrich 67 41 24N 23 13E
Petrijanec 63 46 23N 16 17E
Petrikov 80 52 11N 28 29E
Petrila 70 45 29N 23 29E
Petrinja 63 45 28N 16 18E
'Petroland', gasfield 19 53 35N 4 15E
Petrolândia 170 9 5S 38 20W
Petrolia 150 42 54N 82 9W
Petrolina 170 9 24S 40 30W
Petropavlovsk 76 55 0N 69 0E
Petropavlovsk-Kamchatskiy 77 53 16N 159 0E
Petrópolis 173 22 33S 43 9W
Petroşeni 70 45 28N 23 20E
Petrova Gora 63 45 15N 15 45E
Petrovac 66 42 13N 18 57E
Petrovaradin 66 45 16N 19 55E
Petrovsk 81 52 22N 45 19E
Petrovsk-Zabaykalskiy 77 51 26N 108 30E
Petrovskoye, R.S.F.S.R., U.S.S.R. 83 45 25N 42 58E
Petrovskoye, R.S.F.S.R., U.S.S.R. 84 53 37N 56 23E
Petrozavodsk 78 61 41N 34 20E
Petrus Steyn 129 27 38S 28 8E
Petrusburg 128 29 4S 25 26E
Pettigo 38 54 32N 7 49W
Pettitts 141 34 56S 148 10E
Petworth 29 50 59N 0 37W
Peumo 172 34 21S 71 19W
Peureulak 102 4 48N 97 45E
Pevek 77 69 15N 171 0E
Pevensey 29 50 49N 0 20E
Pevensey Levels 29 50 50N 0 20E
Peveragno 62 44 20N 7 37E
Pewsey 28 51 20N 1 46W
Pewsey, Vale of 28 51 20N 1 46W
Peyrehorade 44 43 34N 1 7W
Peyruis 45 44 1N 5 56E
Pézenas 44 43 28N 3 24E
Pezinok 53 48 17N 17 17E
Pfaffenhofen 49 48 31N 11 31E
Pfäffikon 51 47 13N 8 46E
Pfarrkirchen 49 48 25N 12 57E
Pforzheim 49 48 53N 8 43E
Pfungstadt 49 49 47N 8 36E
Phagwara 93 31 10N 75 40E
Phala 128 23 45S 26 50E
Phalodi 94 27 12N 72 24E
Phalsbourg 43 48 46N 7 15E
Phan 100 19 28N 99 43E
Phan Rang 101 11 40N 109 9E
Phan Thiet 101 11 1N 108 9E
Phanat Nikhom 100 13 27N 101 11E
Phangan, Ko 101 9 45N 100 0E
Phangnga 101 8 28N 98 30E
Phanh Bho Ho Chi Minh 101 10 58N 106 40E
Phanom Dang Raek, mts. 100 14 45N 104 0E
Phanom Sarakham 100 13 45N 101 21E
Pharenda 95 27 5N 83 17E
Phatthalung 101 7 39N 100 6E
Phayao 100 19 11N 99 55E
Phelps, N.Y., U.S.A. 162 42 57N 77 5W
Phelps, Wis., U.S.A. 158 46 2N 89 2W
Phelps L. 153 59 15N 103 15W
Phenix City 157 32 30N 85 0W
Phet Buri 100 13 1N 99 55E
Phetchabun 100 16 25N 101 8E
Phetchabun, Thiu Khao 100 16 0N 101 20E
Phetchaburi 101 13 1N 99 55E
Phi Phi, Ko 101 7 45N 98 46E
Phiafay 100 14 48N 106 0E
Phibun Mangsahan 100 15 14N 105 14E
Phichai 100 17 22N 100 10E
Phichit 100 16 26N 100 22E
Philadelphia, Miss., U.S.A. 159 32 47N 89 5W
Philadelphia, Pa., U.S.A. 162 40 0N 75 10W
Philip 158 44 4N 101 42W
Philip Smith Mts. 147 68 0N 146 0W
Philippeville 47 50 12N 4 33E
Philippi L. 138 24 20S 138 55E
Philippines ■ 103 12 0N 123 0E
Philippolis 128 30 15S 25 16E
Philippopolis = Plovdiv 67 42 8N 24 44E
Philipsburg 160 46 20N 113 21W
Philipstown 128 30 28S 24 30E
Phillip, I. 141 38 30S 145 12E
Phillips, Texas, U.S.A. 159 35 48N 101 17W
Phillips, Wis., U.S.A. 158 45 41N 90 22W
Phillips Ra. 136 16 53S 125 50E
Phillipsburg, Kans., U.S.A. 158 39 48N 99 20W
Phillipsburg, Penn., U.S.A. 162 40 43N 75 12W
Phillott 139 27 53S 145 50E
Philmont 162 42 14N 73 37W
Philomath 160 44 28N 123 21W
Phimai 100 15 13N 102 30E
Phitsanulok 100 16 50N 100 12E
Phnom Penh 101 11 33N 104 55E
Phnom Thbeng 101 13 50N 104 56E
Phoenicia 162 42 5N 74 14W
Phoenix, Ariz., U.S.A. 161 33 30N 112 10W
Phoenix, N.Y., U.S.A. 162 43 13N 76 18W
Phoenix Is. 130 3 30S 172 0W
Phoenixville 162 40 12N 75 29W
Phon 100 15 49N 102 36E
Phon Tiou 100 17 53N 104 37E
Phong, R. 100 16 23N 102 56E
Phong Saly 100 21 42N 102 9E
Phong Tho 100 22 32N 103 21E
Phongdo 99 30 14N 91 14E
Phonhong 100 18 30N 102 25E
Phonum 101 8 49N 98 48E
Photharam 100 13 41N 99 51E
Phra Chedi Sam Ong 100 15 16N 98 23E
Phra Nakhon Si Ayutthaya 100 14 25N 100 30E
Phra Thong, Ko 101 9 5N 98 17E
Phrae 100 18 7N 100 9E
Phrao 101 19 23N 99 15E
Phrom Phiram 100 17 2N 100 12E
Phu Dien 100 18 58N 105 31E
Phu Doan 101 21 40N 105 10E
Phu Loi 100 20 14N 103 14E
Phu Ly (Ha Nam) 100 20 35N 105 50E
Phu Qui 100 19 20N 105 20E
Phu Tho 100 21 24N 105 13E
Phuc Yen 100 21 16N 105 45E
Phuket 100 8 0N 98 28E
Phuket, Ko, I. 101 8 0N 98 22E
Phulbari 98 21 52N 88 8E
Phulera (Phalera) 94 26 52N 75 16E
Phun Phin 101 9 7N 99 12E
Phuoc Le (Baria) 101 10 39N 107 19E
Piabia 138 25 12S 152 45E
Piacá 170 7 42S 47 18W
Piacenza 62 45 2N 9 42E
Piaçubaçu 170 10 24S 36 25W
Piádena 62 45 8N 10 22E
Pialba 139 25 20S 152 45E
Pian, Cr. 139 30 2S 148 12E
Piancó 171 7 12S 37 57W
Pianella 63 42 24N 14 5E
Piangil 140 35 5S 143 20E
Pianoro 63 44 20N 11 20E
Pianosa, I., Puglia, Italy 63 42 12N 15 44E
Pianosa, I., Toscana, Italy 62 42 36N 10 4E
Piapot 153 49 59N 109 8W
Pias 57 38 1N 7 29W
Piaseczno 54 52 5N 21 2E
Piassabussu 171 10 24S 36 25W
Piastow 54 52 12N 20 48E
Piatá 171 13 9S 41 48W
Piatra Neamţ 70 46 56N 26 21E
Piatra Olt 70 43 51N 25 9E
Piauí □ 170 7 0S 43 0W
Piaui, R. 170 6 38S 42 42W
Piave, R. 63 45 50N 13 9E
Piazza Armerina 65 37 21N 14 20E
Pibor Post 123 6 47N 33 3E
Pibor, R. 123 7 1N 33 0E
Pica 174 20 35S 69 25W
Picard, Plaine de Picardie 43 50 0N 2 0E
Picardie 43 50 0N 2 15E
Picardy = Picardie 43 50 0N 2 15E
Picayune 159 30 40N 89 40W
Piccadilly, Austral. 109 34 59S 138 44E
Piccadilly, Zambia 127 14 0S 29 30E
Picerno 65 40 40N 15 37E
Pichiang 108 26 40N 98 53E
Pichieh 108 27 20N 105 20E
Pichilemu 172 34 22S 72 9W
Pickerel L. 150 48 40N 91 25W
Pickering 33 54 15N 0 46W
Pickering, Vale of 33 54 0N 0 45W
Pickle Lake 150 51 30N 90 12W
Pico 16 38 28N 28 18W
Pico Truncado 176 46 40S 68 10W
Picos 170 7 5S 41 28W
Picos Ancares, Sierra de 56 42 51N 6 52W
Picquigny 43 49 56N 2 10E
Picton, Austral. 141 34 12S 150 34E
Picton, Can. 150 44 1N 77 9W
Picton, N.Z. 143 41 18S 174 3E
Pictou 151 45 41N 62 42W
Picture Butte 152 49 55N 112 45W
Picuí 170 6 31S 36 21W
Picún-Leufú 176 39 30S 69 5W
Pidley 29 52 33N 0 4W
Pidurutalagala, mt. 97 7 10N 80 50E
Piedad, La 164 20 20N 102 1W
Piedecuesta 174 6 59N 73 3W
Piedicavallo 62 45 41N 7 57E
Piedmont 157 33 55N 85 39W
Piedmont = Piemonte 62 45 0N 7 30E
Piedmont Plat. 157 34 0N 81 30W
Piedmonte d'Alife 65 41 22N 14 22E
Piedra, R. 58 41 10N 1 45W
Piedrabuena 57 39 0N 4 10W
Piedrahita 56 40 28N 5 23W
Piedras Blancas Pt. 161 35 45N 121 18W
Piedras Negras 164 28 35N 100 35W
Piedras, R. de las 174 11 40S 70 50W
Piemonte 62 45 0N 7 30E
Piena 45 42 15N 8 34E
Piensk 54 51 16N 15 2E
Pier Millan 140 35 14S 142 40E
Pierce 160 46 46N 115 53W
Piería □ 68 40 13N 22 25E
Pierowall 37 59 20N 3 0W
Pierre, France 43 46 54N 5 13E
Pierre, U.S.A. 158 44 23N 100 20W
Pierrefeu 45 43 8N 6 9E
Pierrefonds 43 49 20N 3 0E
Pierrefontaine 43 47 14N 6 32E
Pierrefort 44 44 55N 2 50E
Pierrelatte 45 44 23N 4 43E
Piešťany 155 48 35N 17 50E
Piesting, R. 53 48 0N 16 19E
Pieszyce 54 50 43N 16 33E
Piet Retief 129 27 1S 30 50E
Pietarsaari 74 63 41N 22 40E
Pietermaritzburg 129 29 35S 30 25E
Pietersburg 129 23 54S 29 25E
Pietraperzia 65 37 26N 14 8E
Pietrasanta 62 43 57N 10 12E
Pietrosu 70 47 12N 25 8E
Pietrosul 70 47 35N 24 43E
Pieve di Cadore 63 46 25N 12 22E
Pieve di Teco 62 44 3N 7 54E
Pievepélago 62 44 12N 10 35E
Pigadhítsa 68 39 59N 21 23E
Pigadia 69 35 30N 27 12E
Pigeon I. 97 14 2N 74 20E
Pigeon, R. 150 48 1N 89 42W
Piggott 159 36 20N 90 10W
Pigna 62 43 57N 7 40E
Pigüé 172 37 36S 62 25W
Pihani 95 27 36N 80 15E
Pijnacker 46 52 1N 4 26E
Pikalevo 80 59 37N 34 0E
Pikes Peak 158 38 50N 105 10W
Pikesville 162 39 23N 76 44W
Piketberg 128 32 55S 18 40E
Pikeville 156 37 30N 82 30W
Pik'ochi 106 40 45N 111 17E
Pikou 106 32 45N 105 22E
Pikwitonei 153 55 35N 97 9W
Piła 54 53 10N 16 48E
Piła □ 54 53 0N 17 0E
Pila, mte. 59 38 16N 1 11W
Pilaia 68 40 32N 22 59E
Pilani 94 28 22N 75 33E
Pilão Arcado 170 10 9S 42 26W
Pilar, Brazil 170 9 36S 35 56W
Pilar, Parag. 172 26 50S 58 10W
Pilas, I. 103 6 39N 121 37E
Pilatus 51 46 59N 8 15E
Pilbara Cr. 132 21 15S 118 22E
Pilbara Mining Centre 136 21 15S 118 16E
Pilcomayo, R. 172 25 21S 57 42W
Píli 69 36 50N 27 15E
Pilibhit 95 28 40N 79 50E
Pilion, mt. 68 39 27N 23 7E
Pilis 53 47 17N 19 35E
Pilisvörösvár 53 47 38N 18 56E
Pilkhawa 94 28 43N 77 42E
Pilling 32 53 55N 2 54W
Pilltown 39 51 59N 7 49W
Pílos 69 36 55N 21 42E
Pilot Mound 153 49 15N 98 54W
Pilot Point 159 33 26N 97 0W
Pilot Rock 160 45 30N 118 58W
Pilsen = Plzen 52 49 45N 13 22E
Pilštanj 63 46 8N 15 39E
Pilton 28 51 0N 2 35W
Piltown 39 52 22N 7 18W
Pilzno 54 50 0N 21 16E
Pimba 140 31 18S 136 46E
Pimenta Bueno 174 11 35S 61 10W
Pimentel 174 6 45S 79 55W
Pimuacan, Rés. 151 49 45N 70 30W
Pina 58 41 29N 0 33W
Pinang, I. 101 5 25N 100 15E
Pinar del Río 166 22 26N 83 40W
Pinawa 149 50 9N 95 50W
Pince C. 151 46 38N 53 45W
Pinchbeck 29 52 48N 0 9W
Pincher Creek 152 49 30N 113 57W
Pinchi L. 152 54 38N 124 30W
Pinch'uan 108 25 51N 100 34E
Pinckneyville 158 38 5N 89 20W
Pîncota 66 46 20N 21 45E
Pind Dadan Khan 94 32 55N 73 47E
Pindar 137 28 30S 115 47E
Pindaré Mirim 170 3 37S 45 21W
Pindaré, R. 170 3 17S 44 47W
Pindi Gheb 94 33 14N 72 12E
Pindiga 121 9 58N 10 53E
Pindobal 170 3 16S 48 25W
Pindos Óros 68 40 0N 21 0E
Pindus Mts. = Pindos Óros 68 40 0N 21 0E
Pine 161 34 27N 111 30W
Pine Bluff 159 34 10N 92 0W
Pine, C. 151 46 37N 53 32W
Pine City 158 45 46N 93 0W
Pine Creek, N.T., Austral. 132 13 50S 131 49E
Pine Creek, Queens., Austral. 138 13 13S 142 47E
Pine Dock 153 51 38N 96 48W
Pine Falls 153 50 34N 96 11W
Pine Flat Res. 163 36 50N 119 20W
Pine Grove 162 40 33N 76 23W
Pine Hill 138 23 42S 147 0E
Pine, La 160 40 53N 80 45W
Pine Pass 152 55 25N 122 42W
Pine Point 152 60 50N 114 28W
Pine, R., Austral. 108 27 18S 153 2E
Pine, R., Can. 153 55 20N 107 38W
Pine Ridge, Austral. 141 31 10S 147 30E
Pine Ridge, U.S.A. 158 42 2N 102 35W
Pine River, Can. 153 51 45N 100 30W
Pine River, U.S.A. 158 46 40N 94 20W
Pine Valley 163 32 50N 116 32W
Pinecrest 163 38 12N 120 1W
Pinedale, Ariz., U.S.A. 161 34 23N 110 16W
Pinedale, Calif., U.S.A. 163 36 50N 119 48W
Pinega 52 64 45N 43 40E
Pinega, R. 78 64 20N 43 0E
Pinehill 138 23 38S 146 57E
Pinerolo 62 44 47N 7 21E
Pineto 63 42 36N 14 4E
Pinetop 161 34 10N 109 57W
Pinetown 129 29 48S 30 54E
Pinetree 158 43 42N 105 52W
Pineville, Ky., U.S.A. 157 36 42N 83 42W
Pineville, La., U.S.A. 159 31 22N 92 30W
Pinewood 153 48 45N 94 10W
Piney, Can. 153 49 5N 96 10W
Piney, France 43 48 22N 4 21E
Ping, R. 100 15 42N 100 9E

Pingaring 137 32 40S 118 32E
P'ingch'ang 108 31 33N 107 6E
P'ingchiang 109 28 42N 113 35E
P'ingch'uan 107 41 0N 118 36E
Pingelly 137 32 29S 116 59E
P'ingho 109 24 18N 117 2E
P'inghsiang, Kiangsi, China 109 27 39N 113 50E
P'inghsiang, Kwangsi Chuang, China 108 22 6N 106 44E
P'inghu 109 30 38N 121 0E
P'ingi, Shantung, China 107 35 30N 117 36E
P'ingi, Yünnan, China 108 25 40N 104 14E
P'ingkuo 108 23 20N 107 34E
P'ingli 108 32 26N 109 22E
P'ingliang 105 35 32N 106 50E
Pinglo, Kwangsi-Chuang, China 109 24 30N 110 45E
Pinglo, Ningsia Hui, China 106 38 58N 106 30E
P'inglu 106 37 32N 112 14E
P'ingluch'eng 106 39 46N 112 6E
P'ingnan, Fukien, China 109 26 56N 119 3E
P'ingnan, Kwangsi-Chiang, China 109 23 33N 110 23E
P'ingpa 108 26 25N 106 15E
P'ingpien 108 22 54N 103 40E
Pingrup 137 33 32S 118 29E
P'ingt'an 109 25 31N 119 47E
P'ingt'ang 108 25 50N 107 19E
P'ingting 106 37 48N 113 37E
P'ingt'ingshan 106 33 43N 113 28E
P'ingtu 107 36 47N 119 56E
P'ingtung 105 22 38N 120 30E
Pingwu 105 32 27N 104 25E
P'ingwu 108 32 25N 104 36E
P'ingyang 109 27 40N 120 33E
P'ingyangchen 107 45 11N 131 15E
P'ingyao 106 37 12N 112 10E
P'ingyin 106 36 18N 116 26E
P'ingyüan, Kwangtung, China 109 24 34N 115 54E
P'ingyüan, Ningsia Hui, China 106 37 9N 116 25E
Pinhai 107 34 0N 119 50E
Pinhal 173 22 10S 46 46W
Pinheiro 170 2 31S 45 5W
Pinhel 56 40 18N 7 0W
Pinhoe 30 50 44N 3 29W
Pinhsien, Heilung Kiang, China 107 45 44N 127 27E
Pinhsien, Shensi, China 106 35 10N 108 10E
Pini, I. 102 0 10N 98 40E
Piniós, R., Ilia, Greece 69 37 38N 21 20E
Piniós, R., Trikkala, Greece 68 39 55N 22 10E
Pinjarra 137 32 37S 115 52E
Pink, R. 153 56 50N 103 50W
Pinkafeld 53 47 22N 16 9E
Pinlebu 98 24 5N 95 22E
Pinnacles, Austral. 137 28 12S 120 26E
Pinnacles, U.S.A. 163 36 33N 121 8W
Pinnaroo 140 35 13S 140 56E
Pinon Hills 163 34 26N 117 39W
Pinos 164 22 20N 101 40W
Pinos, I. de 166 21 40N 82 40W
Pinos, Mt 163 34 49N 119 8W
Pinos Pt. 161 36 50N 121 57W
Pinos Puente 57 37 15N 3 45W
Pinotepa Nacional 165 16 25N 97 55W
Pinrang 103 3 46S 119 34E
Pinsk 80 52 10N 26 8E
Pintados 174 20 35S 69 40W
Pinto Butte Mt. 153 49 22N 107 27W
Pintumba 137 31 50S 132 18E
Pinwherry 34 55 9N 4 50W
Pinyang 108 23 17N 108 47E
Pinyug 78 60 5N 48 0E
Pinzolo 62 46 9N 10 45E
Pio XII 170 3 53S 45 17W
Pioche 161 38 0N 114 35W
Piombino 62 42 54N 10 30E
Pioner, I. 77 79 50N 92 0E
Pionki 54 51 29N 21 28E
Piorini, L. 174 3 15S 62 35W
Piotrków Trybunalski 54 51 23N 19 43E
Piotrków Trybunalski □ 54 51 30N 19 45E
Piove di Sacco 63 45 18N 12 1E
Pip 93 26 45N 60 10E
Pipar 94 26 25N 73 31E
Pipariya 96 22 45N 78 23E
Piper, oilfield 19 58 30N 0 15E
Pipéri, I. 68 39 20N 24 19E
Pipestone 158 44 0N 96 20W
Pipestone Cr. 153 53 37N 109 46W
Pipestone, R. 150 52 53N 89 23W
Pipinas 172 35 30S 57 19W
Pipiriki 142 38 28S 175 5E
Pipmuacan Res. 151 49 40N 70 25W
Pippingarra 136 20 27S 118 42E
Pipriac 42 47 49N 1 58W
Piqua 156 40 10N 84 10W
Piquet Carneiro 171 5 48S 39 25W
Piquiri, R. 173 24 3S 54 14W
Piracanjuba 171 17 18S 49 1W
Piracicaba 173 22 45S 47 30W
Piracuruca 170 3 50S 41 50W
Piræus = Piraiévs 69 37 57N 23 42E
Piraiévs 69 37 57N 23 42E
Piraiévs □ 69 37 0N 23 30E
Piráino 65 38 10N 14 52E
Pirajuí 173 21 59S 49 29W
Piran (Pirano) 63 45 31N 13 33E
Pirane 172 25 25S 59 30W
Piranhas 170 9 27S 37 46W
Pirapemas 170 3 43S 44 14W
Pirapora 171 17 20S 44 56W
Piratyin 80 50 15N 32 25E
Pirbright 29 51 17N 0 40W
Pirdop 67 42 40N 24 10E
Pires do Rio 171 17 18S 48 17W
Pirganj 98 25 51S 88 24E
Pirgos, Ilia, Greece 69 37 40N 21 27E
Pirgos, Messinia, Greece 69 36 50N 22 16E
Pirgovo 67 43 44N 25 43E
Piriac-sur-Mer 42 47 22N 2 33W
Piribebuy 172 25 26S 57 2W
Pirin Planina 67 41 40N 23 30E
Pirineos, mts. 58 42 40N 1 0E
Piripiri 170 4 15S 41 46W
Piritu 174 9 23N 69 12W
Pirmasens 49 49 12N 7 30E
Pirna 48 50 57N 13 57E
Pirojpur 98 22 35N 90 1E
Pirot 66 43 9N 22 39E
Pirsagat, R. 83 40 15N 48 45E
Pirtleville 161 31 25N 109 35W
Piru 163 34 25N 118 48W
Piryí 69 38 13N 25 59E
Pisa 62 43 43N 10 23E
Pisa Ra. 143 44 52S 169 12E
Pisagua 174 19 40S 70 15W
Pisarovina 63 45 35N 15 50E
Pisciotta 65 40 7N 15 12E
Pisco 174 13 50S 76 5W
Piscu 70 45 30N 27 43E
Písek 52 49 19N 14 10E
Pisham 108 29 37N 106 13E
P'ishan 105 37 38N 78 19E
Pishin Lora, R. 94 30 15N 66 5E
Pising 103 5 8S 121 53E
Pismo Beach 163 35 9N 120 38W
Pissos 44 44 19N 0 49W
Pisticci 65 40 24N 16 33E
Pistoia 62 43 57N 10 53E
Pistol B. 153 62 25N 92 37W
Pisuerga, R. 56 42 10N 4 15W
Pisz 54 53 38N 21 49E
Pitalito 174 1 51N 76 2W
Pitanga 171 24 46S 51 44W
Pitangui 171 19 40S 44 54E
Pitarpunga, L. 140 34 24S 143 30E
Pitcairn I. 131 25 5S 130 5W
Pite älv 74 65 44N 20 50W
Piteå 74 65 20N 21 25E
Piteşti 70 44 52N 24 54E
Pithapuram 96 17 10N 82 15E
Pithara 137 30 20S 116 35E
Pithion 68 41 24N 26 40W
Pithiviers 43 48 10N 2 13E
Pitigliano 63 42 38N 11 40E
Pitiquito 164 30 42N 112 2W
Pitlochry 37 56 43N 3 43W
Pitt I. 152 53 30N 129 50W
Pittem 47 51 1N 3 13E
Pittenweem 35 56 13N 2 43W
Pittsburg, Calif., U.S.A. 163 38 1N 121 50W
Pittsburg, Kans., U.S.A. 159 37 21N 94 43W
Pittsburg, Tex., U.S.A. 159 32 59N 94 58W
Pittsburgh 156 40 25N 79 55W
Pittsfield, Ill., U.S.A. 158 39 35N 90 46W
Pittsfield, N.H., U.S.A. 162 43 17N 71 18W
Pittston 162 41 19N 75 50W
Pittsworth 139 27 41S 151 37E
Pituri, R. 138 22 35S 138 30E
Pitzewo 107 39 28N 122 30E
Piui 171 20 28S 45 58W
Pium 170 10 27S 49 11W
Piura 174 5 5S 80 45W
Piva, R. 66 43 15N 18 50E
Pivijay 174 10 28N 74 37W
Piwniczna 54 49 27N 20 42E
Pixariá Óros 69 38 42N 23 39E
Pixley 163 35 58N 119 18W
Piyai 68 39 17N 21 25E
Piyang 109 32 50N 113 30E
Piz Bernina 49 46 23N 9 45E
Pizarro 174 4 58N 77 22W
Pizol 51 46 57N 9 23E
Pizzo 65 38 44N 16 10E
Placentia 151 47 20N 54 0W
Placentia B. 151 47 0N 54 40W
Placerville 160 38 47N 120 51W
Placetas 166 22 15N 79 44W
'Placid', gasfield 19 53 25N 4 20E
Plač kovica, mts. 66 41 45N 22 30E
Pladda, I. 34 55 25N 5 7W
Plaffein 50 46 45N 7 17E
Plain Dealing 159 32 56N 93 41W
Plainfield 162 40 37N 74 28W
Plains, Kans., U.S.A. 159 37 20N 100 35W
Plains, Mont., U.S.A. 160 47 27N 114 57W
Plains, Tex., U.S.A. 159 33 11N 102 50W
Plainview, Nebr., U.S.A. 158 42 25N 97 48W
Plainview, Tex., U.S.A. 159 34 10N 101 40W
Plainville 158 39 18N 99 19W
Plainwell 156 42 28N 85 40W
Plaisance 44 43 36N 0 3E
Pláka 68 36 45N 24 26E
Plakhino 76 67 45N 86 5E
Planá 52 49 50N 12 44E
Plana Cays 167 22 38N 73 30W
Planada 163 37 18N 120 19W
Planaltina 171 15 30S 47 45W
Plancoët 42 48 32N 2 13W
Plandište 66 45 16N 21 10E
Planeta Rica 174 8 25N 75 36W
Planina, Slovenija, Yugo. 63 45 47N 14 19E
Planina, Slovenija, Yugo. 63 46 10N 15 12E
Plankinton 158 43 45N 98 27W
Plano 159 33 0N 96 45W
Plant City 157 28 0N 82 15W
Plant, La 158 45 11N 100 40W
Plaquemine 159 30 20N 91 15W
Plasencia 56 40 3N 6 8W
Plaški 63 45 4N 15 22E
Plassen 72 61 9N 12 30E
Plast 84 54 22N 60 50E
Plaster Rock 151 46 53N 67 22W
Plata, La, Argent. 172 35 0S 57 55W
Plata, La, U.S.A. 162 38 32N 76 59W
Plata, La, Río de 172 35 0S 56 40W
Platani, R. 64 37 28N 13 23E
Plateau 13 70 55S 40 0E
Plateau □ 121 9 0N 9 0E
Plateau du Coteau du Missouri 158 47 9N 101 5W
Platí, Akra 68 40 27N 24 0E
Platinum 147 59 2N 161 50W
Plato 174 9 47N 74 47W
Platte 158 43 28N 98 50W
Platte, Piz 51 46 30N 9 35E
Platte, R. 158 41 0N 98 0W
Platteville 158 40 18N 104 47W
Plattling 49 48 46N 12 53E
Plattsburgh 156 44 41N 73 30W
Plattsmouth 158 41 0N 96 0W
Plau 48 53 27N 12 16E
Plauen 48 50 29N 12 9E
Plav 66 42 38N 19 57E
Plavnica 66 42 10N 19 20E
Plavsk 81 53 40N 37 18E
Playa Azul 164 17 59N 102 24W
Playa de Castilla 57 41 25N 0 12W
Playgreen L. 153 54 0N 98 15W
Pleasant Bay 151 46 51N 60 48W
Pleasant Hill 158 38 48N 94 14W
Pleasant Hills 141 35 28S 146 50E
Pleasant Mount 162 41 44N 75 26W
Pleasant Pt. 143 44 16S 171 9E
Pleasanton 159 29 0N 98 30W
Pleasantville 162 39 25N 74 30W
Pléaux 44 45 8N 2 13E
Pleiku (Gia Lai) 101 14 3N 108 0E
Plélan-le-Grand 42 48 0N 2 7W
Plémet 42 48 11N 2 36W
Pléneuf-Val-André 42 48 35N 2 32W
Pleniţa 70 44 14N 23 10E
Plenty, Bay of 142 37 45S 177 0E
Plenty, R. 138 23 25S 136 31E
Plentywood 158 48 45N 104 35W
Plesetsk 78 62 40N 40 10E
Plessisville 151 46 14N 71 47W
Plestin-les-Grèves 42 48 40N 3 39W
Pleszew 54 51 53N 17 47E
Pleternica 66 45 17N 17 48E
Pletipi L. 151 51 44N 70 6W
Pleven 67 43 26N 24 37E
Plevlja 66 43 21N 19 21E
Płock 54 52 32N 19 40E
Płock □ 54 52 30N 19 45E
Plöcken Passo 63 46 37N 12 57E
Plockton 36 57 20N 5 40W
Ploegsteert 47 50 44N 2 53E
Ploëmeur 42 47 44N 3 26W
Ploërmel 42 47 55N 2 26W
Ploieşti 70 44 57N 26 5E
Plomárion 69 38 58N 26 24E
Plomb du Cantal 44 45 2N 2 48E
Plombières 43 47 59N 6 27E
Plomin 63 45 8N 14 10E
Plön 48 54 8N 10 22E
Plöner See 48 53 9N 15 5E
Plonge, Lac La 153 55 8N 107 20W
Płonsk 54 52 37N 20 21E
Płoty 54 53 48N 15 18E
Plouay 42 47 55N 3 21W
Ploudalmézeau 42 48 34N 4 41W
Plougasnou 42 48 42N 3 49W
Plouha 42 48 41N 2 57W
Plouhinec 42 48 0N 4 29W
Plovdiv 67 42 8N 24 44E
Plum I. 162 41 10N 72 12W
Plumbridge 38 54 46N 7 15W
Plummer 160 47 21N 116 59W
Plumtree 127 20 27S 27 55E
Plunge 80 55 53N 21 51E
Pluvigner 42 47 46N 3 1W
Plymouth, U.K. 30 50 23N 4 9W
Plymouth, Calif., U.S.A. 163 38 29N 120 51W
Plymouth, Ind., U.S.A. 156 41 20N 86 19W
Plymouth, Mass., U.S.A. 162 41 58N 70 40W
Plymouth, N.C., U.S.A. 157 35 54N 76 55W
Plymouth, N.H., U.S.A. 162 43 44N 71 41W
Plymouth, Pa., U.S.A. 162 41 17N 76 0W
Plymouth, Wis., U.S.A. 156 43 42N 87 58W
Plymouth Sd. 30 50 20N 4 10W
Plympton 30 50 24N 4 2W
Plymstock 30 50 22N 4 6W
Plynlimon = Pumlumon Fawr 31 52 29N 3 47W
Plyussa 80 47 40N 29 0E
Plyussa, R. 80 58 40N 28 30E
Plzen 52 49 45N 13 22E
Pniewy 54 52 31N 16 16E
Pô 121 11 14N 1 5W
Po Hai 107 38 30N 119 0E
Po, R. 62 45 0N 10 45E
Poai 106 35 10N 113 4E
Pobé 121 7 0N 2 38E
Pobedino 76 49 51N 142 49E
Pobedy Pik 76 40 45N 79 58E
Pobiedziska 54 52 29N 17 19E
Pobla de Lillet, La 58 42 16N 1 59E
Pobla de Segur 58 42 15N 0 58E
Pobladura de Valle 56 42 6N 5 44W
Pocahontas, Arkansas, U.S.A. 159 37 18N 81 20W
Pocahontas, Iowa, U.S.A. 158 42 41N 94 42W
Pocatello 160 42 50N 112 25W
Pochep 80 52 58N 33 15E
Pochinki 81 54 41N 44 59E
Pochinok 80 54 28N 32 29E
Pöchlarn 52 48 12N 15 12E
Pochontas 152 53 0N 117 51W
Pochutla 165 15 50N 96 31W
Pocinhos 170 7 4S 36 3W
Pocita Casas 164 28 32N 111 6W
Pocklington 33 53 56N 0 48W
Poções 171 14 31S 40 21W
Pocomoke City 162 38 4N 75 32W
Pocomoke, R. 162 38 5N 75 34W
Poços de Caldas 173 21 50S 46 45W
Pocrane 171 19 37S 41 37W
PoC!tky 52 49 15N 15 14E
Poddebice 54 51 54N 18 58E
Poděbrady 52 50 9N 15 8E
Podensac 44 44 40N 0 22W
Podgorica = Titograd 66 42 30N 19 19E
Podkamennaya Tunguska 77 61 50N 90 26E
Podlapac 63 44 45N 15 47E
Podmokly 52 50 48N 14 10E
Podoleni 70 46 46N 26 39E
Podolínec 53 49 16N 20 31E
Podolsk 81 55 25N 37 30E
Podor 120 16 40N 14 50W
Podporozhy 78 60 55N 34 2E
Podravska Slatina 66 45 42N 17 45E
Podsreda 63 45 42N 17 41E
Podu Turcului 70 46 11N 27 25E
Podujevo 66 42 54N 21 10E
Poel, I. 48 54 0N 11 25E
Pofadder 128 29 10S 19 22E
Pogamasing 150 46 55N 81 50W
Poggiardo 65 40 3N 18 21E
Poggibonsi 63 43 27N 11 8E
Pogoanele 70 44 55N 27 0E
Pogorzela 54 51 50N 17 12E
Pogradeci 68 40 57N 20 48E
Poh 103 0 46S 122 51E
Pohang 107 36 1N 129 23E
Pohorelá 53 48 50N 20 2E
Pohorelice 53 48 59N 16 31E
Pohorje, mts. 63 46 30N 15 7E
Poiana Mare 70 43 57N 23 5E
Poiana Ruscǔi, Munţii 70 45 45N 22 25E
Pt. Augusta 140 32 30S 137 50E
Point Baker 147 56 20N 133 35W
Point Cloates 137 22 40S 113 45E
Point Edward 150 43 10N 82 30W
Point Fortin 167 10 9N 61 46W
Point Hope 147 68 20N 166 50W
Point Lay 147 69 45N 163 10W
Point Pass 140 34 5S 139 5E
Point Pedro 97 9 50N 80 15E
Point Pleasant, N.J., U.S.A. 162 40 5N 74 4W
Point Pleasant, W. Va., U.S.A. 156 38 50N 82 7W
Point Reyes Nat. Seashore 163 38 0N 122 58W
Point Rock 159 31 30N 99 56W
Pointe-à-la Hache 159 29 35N 89 55W
Pointe-à-Pitre 167 16 10N 61 30W
Pointe-Noire 124 4 48S 12 0E
Poirino 62 44 55N 7 50E
Poisonbush Ra. 136 22 30S 121 30E
Poissy 43 48 55N 2 0E
Poitiers 42 46 35N 0 20W
Poitou, Plaines du 44 46 30N 0 1W
Poix 43 49 47N 2 0E
Poix-Terron 43 49 38N 4 38E
Pojoaque 161 35 55N 106 0W
Pojuca 171 12 21S 38 20W
Pokaran 93 27 0N 71 50E
Pokataroo 139 29 30S 148 34E
Poko, Sudan 123 5 41N 31 55E
Poko, Zaïre 126 3 7N 26 52E
Pok'ot'u 105 48 46N 121 54E
Pokrovka 85 42 20N 78 0E
Pokrovsk 77 61 29N 129 6E
Pokrovsk-Uralskiy 84 60 10N 59 49E
Pol 56 43 9N 7 20W
Pola 80 57 30N 32 0E
Pola de Allande 56 43 16N 6 37W
Pola de Gordón, La 56 42 51N 5 41W
Pola de Lena 56 43 10N 5 49W
Pola de Siero 56 43 24N 5 39W
Pola de Somiedo 56 43 5N 6 15W
Polacca 161 35 52N 110 25W
Polan 93 25 30N 61 10E
Poland ■ 54 52 0N 20 0E
Polanów 54 54 7N 16 41E
Polar Bear Prov. Park 150 54 30N 83 20W
Polcura 172 37 10S 71 50W

Place	Page	Lat.	Long.
Połcyn Zdrój	**54**	53 47N	16 5 E
Polden Hills	**28**	51 7N	2 50W
Polegate	**29**	50 49N	0 15 E
Polessk	**80**	54 50N	21 8 E
Polesworth	**28**	52 37N	1 37W
Polevskoy	**84**	56 26N	60 11 E
Polewali, Sulawesi, Indon.	**103**	4 8 S	119 43 E
Polewali, Sulawesi, Indon.	**103**	3 21 S	119 31 E
Polgar	**53**	47 54N	21 6 E
Pôlgyo-ri	**107**	34 51N	127 21 E
Poli	**124**	8 34N	12 54 E
Políaigos, I.	**69**	36 45N	24 38 E
Policastro, Golfo di	**65**	39 55N	15 35 E
Police	**54**	53 33N	14 33 E
Polička	**53**	49 43N	16 15 E
Polignano a Mare	**65**	41 0N	17 12 E
Poligny	**43**	46 50N	5 42 E
Polikhnitas	**69**	39 4N	26 10 E
Polillo I.	**103**	14 56N	122 0 E
Polis	**92**	35 3N	32 30 E
Polistena	**65**	38 25N	16 4 E
Políyiros	**68**	40 23N	23 25 E
Polkowice	**54**	51 29N	16 3 E
Polla	**65**	40 31N	15 27 E
Pollachi	**97**	10 35N	77 0 E
Pollensa	**58**	39 54N	3 2 E
Pollensa, B. de	**58**	39 55N	3 5 E
Póllica	**65**	40 13N	15 3 E
Pollino, Mte.	**65**	39 54N	16 13 E
Pollock	**158**	45 58N	100 18W
Pollremon	**38**	53 40N	8 38W
Polna	**80**	58 31N	28 0 E
Polnovat	**76**	63 50N	66 5 E
Polo, Kwangtung, China	**109**	23 9N	114 17 E
Polo, S.-U., China	**105**	44 59N	81 57 E
Polo, U.S.A.	**158**	42 0N	89 38W
Pologi	**82**	47 29N	36 15 E
Polonnoye	**80**	50 6N	27 30 E
Polossu	**108**	31 12N	98 36 E
Polotsk	**80**	55 30N	28 50 E
Polperro	**30**	50 19N	4 31W
Polruan	**30**	50 17N	4 36W
Polski Trmbesh	**67**	43 20N	25 38 E
Polsko Kosovo	**67**	43 23N	25 38 E
Polson	**160**	47 45N	114 12W
Poltava	**82**	49 35N	34 35 E
Polur	**97**	12 32N	79 11 E
Polyarny	**78**	69 8N	33 20 E
Pomarance	**62**	43 18N	10 51 E
Pomarico	**65**	40 31N	16 33 E
Pomaro	**164**	18 20N	103 18W
Pombal, Brazil	**170**	6 55 S	37 50W
Pombal, Port.	**56**	39 55N	8 40W
Pômbia	**69**	35 0N	24 51 E
Pomeroy, U.K.	**38**	54 36N	6 56W
Pomeroy, Ohio, U.S.A.	**156**	39 0N	82 0W
Pomeroy, Wash., U.S.A.	**160**	46 30N	117 33W
Pomio	**135**	5 32 S	151 33 E
Pomona	**163**	34 2N	117 49W
Pomorie	**67**	42 26N	27 41 E
Pompano	**157**	26 12N	80 6W
Pompei	**65**	40 45N	14 30 E
Pompey	**43**	48 50N	6 2 E
Pompeys Pillar	**160**	46 0N	108 0W
Ponape I.	**130**	6 55N	158 10 E
Ponask, L.	**150**	54 0N	92 41W
Ponass L.	**153**	52 16N	103 58W
Ponca	**158**	42 38N	96 41W
Ponca City	**159**	36 40N	97 5W
Ponce	**147**	18 1N	66 37W
Ponchatoula	**159**	30 27N	90 25W
Poncheville, L.	**150**	50 10N	76 55W
Poncin	**45**	46 6N	5 25 E
Pond	**163**	35 43N	119 20W
Pond Inlet	**149**	72 30N	75 0W
Pondicherry	**97**	11 59N	79 50 E
Pondoland	**129**	31 10 S	29 30 E
Pondooma	**140**	33 29 S	136 59 E
Pondrôme	**47**	50 6N	5 0 E
Ponds, I. of	**151**	53 27N	55 52W
Ponferrada	**56**	42 32N	6 35W
Pongaroa	**142**	40 33 S	176 15 E
Póngo , Ponte de	**127**	19 0 S	34 0 E
Pongo, W.	**123**	8 0N	27 20 E
Poniatowa	**54**	51 11N	22 3 E
Poniec	**54**	51 48N	16 50 E
Ponnaiyar, R.	**97**	11 50N	79 45 E
Ponnani	**97**	10 45N	75 59 E
Ponnani, R.	**97**	10 45N	75 59 E
Ponneri	**97**	13 20N	80 15 E
Ponnyadaung	**99**	22 0N	94 10 E
Ponoi	**78**	67 0N	41 0 E
Ponoi, R.	**78**	67 10N	39 0 E
Ponoka	**152**	52 42N	113 40W
Ponomarevka	**84**	53 19N	54 8 E
Ponorogo	**103**	7 52 S	111 29 E
Pons, France	**44**	45 35N	0 34W
Pons, Spain	**58**	41 55N	1 12 E
Ponsul, R.	**57**	39 54N	8 45 E
Pont-à-Celles	**47**	50 30N	4 22 E
Pont-à-Mousson	**43**	45 54N	6 1 E
Pont Audemer	**42**	49 21N	0 30 E
Pont Aven	**42**	47 51N	3 47W
Pont Canavese	**62**	45 24N	7 33 E
Pont Château	**42**	47 26N	2 8W
Pont-de-Roide	**43**	47 23N	6 45 E
Pont-de-Salars	**44**	44 18N	2 44 E
Pont-de-Vaux	**43**	46 26N	4 56 E
Pont-de-Veyle	**45**	46 17N	4 53 E
Pont-l'Abbé	**42**	47 52N	4 15W
Pont Lafrance	**151**	47 40N	64 58W
Pont, Le	**50**	46 41N	6 20 E
Pont-l'Eveque	**42**	49 18N	0 11 E
Pont-St.-Esprit	**45**	44 16N	4 40 E
Pont-sur-Yonne	**43**	48 18N	3 10 E
Ponta de Pedras	**170**	1 23 S	48 52W
Ponta Grossa	**173**	25 0 S	50 10W
Ponta Pora	**173**	22 20 S	55 35W
Ponta São Sebastião	**129**	22 2 S	35 25 E
Pontacq	**44**	43 11N	0 8W
Pontailler	**43**	47 18N	5 24 E
Pontal, R.	**170**	9 8 S	40 12W
Pontalina	**171**	17 31 S	49 27W
Pontardawe	**31**	51 43N	3 51W
Pontardulais	**31**	51 42N	4 3W
Pontarlier	**43**	46 54N	6 20 E
Pontassieve	**63**	43 47N	11 25 E
Pontaubault	**42**	48 40N	1 20W
Pontaumur	**44**	45 52N	2 40 E
Pontcharra	**45**	45 26N	6 1 E
Pontchartrain, L.	**159**	30 12N	90 0W
Pontchâteau	**42**	47 25N	2 5W
Ponte Alta do Norte	**170**	10 45 S	47 34W
Ponte Alta, Serra do	**171**	19 42 S	47 40W
Ponte da Barca	**56**	41 48N	8 25W
Ponte de Sor	**57**	39 17N	7 57W
Ponte dell 'Olio	**62**	44 52N	9 39 E
Ponte di Legno	**62**	46 15N	10 30 E
Ponte do Lima	**56**	41 46N	8 35W
Ponte do Pungué	**127**	19 30 S	34 33 E
Ponte Leccia	**45**	42 28N	9 13 E
Ponte nell' Alpi	**63**	46 10N	12 18 E
Ponte Nova	**173**	20 25 S	42 54W
Ponte San Martino	**62**	45 36N	7 47 E
Ponte San Pietro	**62**	45 42N	9 35 E
Pontebba	**63**	46 30N	13 17 E
Pontecorvo	**64**	41 28N	13 40 E
Pontedera	**62**	43 40N	10 37 E
Pontefract	**33**	53 42N	1 19W
Ponteix	**153**	49 46N	107 29W
Ponteland	**35**	53 3N	1 45W
Pontelandolfo	**65**	41 17N	14 41 E
Pontemacassar Naikliu	**103**	9 30 S	123 58 E
Pontevedra	**56**	42 26N	8 40W
Pontevedra □	**56**	42 25N	8 39W
Pontevedra, R. de	**56**	42 22N	8 45W
Pontevico	**62**	45 16N	10 6 E
Ponthierville = Ubundi	**126**	0 22 S	25 30 E
Pontiac, Ill., U.S.A.	**158**	40 50N	88 40W
Pontiac, Mich., U.S.A.	**156**	42 40N	83 20W
Pontian Kechil	**101**	1 29N	103 23 E
Pontianak	**102**	0 3 S	109 15 E
Pontine Is. = Ponziane, Isole	**64**	40 55N	13 0 E
Pontine Mts. = Karadeniz D.	**92**	41 30N	35 0 E
Pontínia	**64**	41 25N	13 2 E
Pontivy	**42**	48 5N	3 0W
Pontoise	**43**	49 3N	2 5 E
Ponton, R.	**152**	58 27N	116 11W
Pontorson	**42**	48 34N	1 30W
Pontrémoli	**62**	44 22N	9 52 E
Pontresina	**51**	46 29N	9 48 E
Pontrhydfendigaid	**31**	52 17N	3 50W
Pontrieux	**28**	48 42N	3 10W
Pontrilas	**28**	51 56N	2 53W
Ponts-de Cé, Les	**42**	47 25N	0 30W
Pontypool	**31**	51 42N	3 1W
Pontypridd	**31**	51 36N	3 21W
Ponza, I.	**64**	40 55N	12 57 E
Ponziane, Isole	**64**	40 55N	13 0 E
Poochera	**139**	32 43 S	134 51 E
Poole	**28**	50 42N	2 2W
Poole Harb.	**28**	50 41N	2 0W
Poolewe	**36**	57 45N	5 38W
Pooley Bridge	**32**	54 37N	2 49W
Pooley I.	**152**	52 45N	128 15W
Poonamallee	**97**	13 3N	80 10 E
Poona = Pune	**96**	18 29N	73 57 E
Pooncarie	**140**	33 22 S	142 31 E
Poonindie	**140**	34 34 S	135 54 E
Poopelloe, L.	**140**	31 40 S	144 0 E
Poopó, Lago de	**174**	18 30 S	67 35W
Poor Knights Is.	**142**	35 29 S	174 43 E
Pooraka	**109**	34 50 S	138 38 E
Poorman	**147**	64 5N	155 48W
Popai	**108**	22 13N	109 55 E
Popak	**101**	22 15N	109 56 E
Popakai, Austral.	**170**	32 12 S	141 46 E
Popakai, Surinam	**170**	3 20N	55 30W
Popanyinning	**137**	32 40 S	117 2 E
Popayán	**174**	2 27N	76 36W
Poperinge	**47**	50 51N	2 42 E
Popigay	**77**	71 55N	110 47 E
Popilta, L.	**140**	33 10 S	141 42 E
Popio, L.	**140**	33 10 S	141 52 E
Poplar	**158**	48 3N	105 9W
Poplar Bluff	**159**	36 45N	90 22W
Poplar, R., Man., Can.	**153**	53 0N	97 19W
Poplar, R., N.W.T., Can.	**152**	61 22N	121 52W
Poplarville	**159**	30 55N	89 30W
Popocatepetl, vol.	**165**	19 10N	98 40W
Popokabaka	**124**	5 49 S	16 40 E
Pópoli	**63**	42 12N	13 50 E
Popondetta	**135**	8 48 S	148 17 E
Popovača	**63**	45 30N	16 41 E
Popovo	**67**	43 21N	26 18 E
Poppel	**47**	51 27N	5 2 E
Poprád	**53**	49 3N	20 18 E
Poprád, R.	**53**	49 15N	20 30 E
Poquoson	**162**	37 7N	76 21W
Poradaha	**98**	23 51N	89 1 E
Porali, R.	**94**	27 15N	66 24 E
Porangahau	**142**	40 17 S	176 37 E
Porangatu	**171**	13 26 S	49 10W
Porbandar	**94**	21 44N	69 43 E
Porcher I.	**152**	53 50N	130 30W
Porcos, R.	**171**	12 42 S	45 7W
Porcuna	**57**	37 52N	4 11W
Porcupine, R., Can.	**153**	59 11N	104 46W
Porcupine, R., U.S.A.	**147**	67 0N	143 0W
Pordenone	**63**	45 58N	12 40 E
Pordim	**67**	43 23N	24 51 E
Pore	**174**	5 43N	72 0W
Poreč	**63**	45 14N	13 36 E
Porecatu	**171**	22 43 S	51 24W
Poretskoye	**81**	55 9N	46 21 E
Pori	**75**	61 29N	21 48 E
Porirua	**142**	41 8 S	174 52 E
Porjus	**74**	66 57N	19 50 E
Porkhov	**80**	57 45N	29 38 E
Porkkala	**75**	59 59N	24 26 E
Porlamar	**174**	10 57N	63 51W
Porlezza	**62**	46 2N	9 8 E
Porlock	**28**	51 13N	3 36W
Porlock B.	**28**	51 14N	3 37W
Porlock Hill	**28**	51 12N	3 40W
Porma, R.	**56**	42 45N	5 21W
Pornic	**42**	47 7N	2 5W
Poronaysk	**77**	49 20N	143 0 E
Póros	**69**	37 30N	23 30 E
Póros, I.	**69**	37 30N	23 30 E
Poroshiri-Dake	**112**	42 41N	142 52 E
Poroszló	**53**	47 39N	20 40 E
Poroto Mts.	**127**	9 0 S	33 30 E
Porraburdoo	**137**	23 15 S	117 28 E
Porrentruy	**50**	47 25N	7 6 E
Porreras	**58**	39 29N	3 2 E
Porsangen	**74**	70 40N	25 40 E
Porsgrunn	**71**	59 10N	9 40 E
Port	**43**	47 43N	6 4 E
Port Adelaide	**140**	34 46 S	138 30 E
Port Alberni	**152**	49 15N	124 50W
Port Albert	**141**	38 42 S	146 42 E
Port Albert Victor	**94**	21 0N	71 30 E
Port Alexander	**147**	56 13N	134 40W
Port Alfred, Can.	**151**	48 18N	70 53W
Port Alfred, S. Afr.	**125**	33 36 S	26 55 E
Port Alice	**152**	50 25N	127 25W
Port Allegany	**156**	41 49N	78 17W
Port Allen	**159**	30 30N	91 15W
Port Alma	**138**	23 38 S	150 53 E
Port Angeles	**160**	48 7N	123 30W
Port Antonio	**166**	18 10N	76 30W
Port Aransas	**159**	27 49N	97 4W
Port Arthur, Austral.	**138**	43 7 S	147 50 E
Port Arthur, U.S.A.	**159**	30 0N	94 0W
Port Arthur = Lüshun	**107**	38 51N	121 20 E
Port Arthur = Thunder Bay	**150**	48 25N	89 10W
Port Askaig	**34**	55 51N	6 8W
Port au Port B.	**151**	48 40N	58 50W
Port-au-Prince	**167**	18 40N	72 20W
Port Augusta West	**140**	32 29 S	137 47 E
Port Austin	**150**	44 3N	82 59W
Port aux Basques	**151**	47 32N	59 8W
Port Awanui	**142**	37 50 S	178 29 E
Port Bannatyne	**34**	55 51N	5 4W
Port Bell	**126**	0 18N	32 35 E
Port Bergé Vaovao	**129**	15 33 S	47 40 E
Port Blair	**101**	11 40N	92 30 E
Port Blandford	**151**	48 30N	53 50W
Port Bolivar	**159**	29 20N	94 40W
Port Bou	**58**	42 25N	3 9 E
Port Bouet	**120**	5 16N	4 57W
Port Bradshaw	**138**	12 30 S	137 0 E
Port Broughton	**140**	33 37 S	137 56 E
Port Burwell	**150**	42 40N	80 48W
Port Campbell	**140**	35 37 S	143 1 E
Port Canning	**95**	22 17N	88 48 E
Port Carlisle	**32**	54 56N	3 12W
Port-Cartier	**151**	50 10N	66 50W
Port Chalmers	**143**	45 49 S	170 30 E
Port Charlotte	**34**	55 44N	6 22W
Port Chester	**162**	41 0N	73 41W
Port Clements	**152**	53 40N	132 10W
Port Clinton	**156**	41 30N	83 0W
Port Colborne	**150**	42 50N	79 10W
Port Coquitlam	**152**	49 20N	122 45W
Port Curtis	**138**	24 0 S	151 34 E
Port Darwin, Austral.	**136**	12 24 S	130 45 E
Port Darwin, Falk. Is.	**176**	51 50 S	59 0W
Port Davey	**138**	43 16 S	145 55 E
Port-de-Bouc	**45**	43 24N	4 59 E
Port de Paix	**167**	19 50N	72 50W
Port Deposit	**162**	39 37N	76 5W
Port Dickson	**101**	2 30N	101 49 E
Port Dinorwic	**31**	53 11N	4 12W
Port Douglas	**138**	16 30 S	145 30 E
Port Edward	**152**	54 12N	130 10W
Port Elgin	**150**	44 25N	81 25W
Port Elizabeth	**128**	33 58 S	25 40 E
Port Ellen	**34**	55 38N	6 10W
Port Erin	**32**	54 5N	4 45W
Port Erroll	**37**	57 25N	1 50W
Port Essington	**136**	11 15 S	132 10 E
Port Étienne = Nouadhibou	**116**	21 0N	17 0W
Port Ewen	**162**	41 54N	73 59W
Port Fairy	**140**	38 22 S	142 12 E
Port Fitzroy	**142**	36 8 S	175 20 E
Port Fouâd = Bûr Fuad	**122**	31 15N	32 20 E
Port Francqui	**124**	4 17 S	20 47 E
Port-Gentil	**124**	0 47 S	8 40 E
Port Gibson	**159**	31 57N	91 0W
Port Glasgow	**34**	55 57N	4 40W
Port Gregory	**137**	27 40 S	114 0 E
Port Harcourt	**121**	4 40N	7 10 E
Port Hardy	**152**	50 41N	127 30W
Port Harrison	**149**	58 25N	78 15W
Port Hawkesbury	**151**	45 36N	61 22W
Port Hedland	**136**	20 25 S	118 35 E
Port Heiden	**147**	57 0N	158 40W
Port Hood	**151**	46 0N	61 32W
Port Hope	**150**	44 0N	78 20W
Port Hueneme	**163**	34 7N	119 12W
Port Huron	**156**	43 0N	82 28W
Port Isaac	**30**	50 35N	4 50W
Port Isaac B.	**30**	50 36N	4 50W
Port Isabel	**159**	26 12N	97 9W
Port Jackson	**133**	33 50 S	151 18 E
Port Jefferson	**162**	40 58N	73 5W
Port Jervis	**162**	41 22N	74 42W
Port Joinville	**42**	46 45N	2 23W
Port Kaituma	**174**	8 3N	59 58W
Port Katon	**83**	46 27N	38 56 E
Port Kelang	**101**	3 0N	101 23 E
Port Kembla	**141**	34 29 S	150 56 E
Port La Nouvelle	**44**	43 1N	3 3 E
Port Laoise	**39**	53 2N	7 20W
Port Lavaca	**159**	28 38N	96 38W
Port Leyden	**162**	43 35N	75 21W
Port Lincoln	**140**	34 42 S	135 52 E
Port Logan	**34**	54 42N	4 57W
Port Loko	**120**	8 48N	12 46W
Port Louis	**42**	47 42N	3 22W
Port Lyautey = Kenitra	**118**	34 15N	6 40W
Port Lyttelton	**143**	43 37N	172 50 E
Port Macdonnell	**140**	38 0 S	140 39 E
Port Macquarie	**141**	31 25 S	152 54 E
Port Maitland	**151**	44 0N	66 2W
Port Maria	**166**	18 25N	76 55W
Port Mellon	**152**	49 32N	123 31W
Port Menier	**151**	49 51N	64 15W
Port Morant	**166**	17 54N	76 19W
Port Moresby	**135**	9 24 S	147 8 E
Port Mouton	**151**	43 58N	64 50W
Port Musgrave	**138**	11 55 S	141 50 E
Port Navalo	**42**	47 34N	2 54W
Port Nelson	**153**	57 3N	92 36W
Port Nicholson	**142**	41 20 S	174 52 E
Port Nolloth	**128**	29 17 S	16 52 E
Port Norris	**162**	39 15N	75 2W
Port Nouveau-Quebec (George R.)	**149**	58 30N	65 50W
Port O'Connor	**159**	28 26N	96 24W
Port of Ness	**36**	58 29N	6 13W
Port of Spain	**167**	10 40N	61 20W
Port Orchard	**160**	47 31N	122 38W
Port Oxford	**160**	42 45N	124 28W
Port Pegasus	**143**	47 12 S	167 41 E
Port Perry	**150**	44 6N	78 56W
Port Phillip B.	**139**	38 10 S	144 50 E
Port Pirie	**140**	33 10 S	137 58 E
Port Pólnocny □	**54**	54 25N	18 42 E
Port Radium = Echo Bay	**148**	66 10N	117 40W
Port Renfrew	**152**	48 30N	124 20W
Port Roper	**138**	14 45 S	134 47 E
Port Rowan	**150**	42 40N	80 30W
Port Royal	**162**	38 10N	77 12W
Port Safaga = Bûr Safâga	**122**	26 43N	33 57 E
Port Said = Bûr Sa'îd	**122**	31 16N	32 18 E
Port St. Joe	**157**	29 49N	85 20W
Port St. Johns = Umzimvubu	**129**	31 38 S	29 33 E
Port-St. Louis	**45**	43 23N	4 50 E
Port St. Louis	**129**	13 7 S	48 48 E
Port-St.-Louis-du-Rhône	**45**	43 23N	4 49 E
Port St. Mary	**32**	54 5N	4 45W
Port St. Servain	**151**	51 21N	58 0W
Port Sanilac	**150**	43 26N	82 33W
Port Saunders	**151**	50 40N	57 18W
Port Shepstone	**129**	30 44 S	30 28 E
Port Simpson	**152**	54 30N	130 20W
Port Stanley	**150**	42 40N	81 10W
Port Sudan = Bôr Sôdân	**122**	19 32N	37 9 E
Port Sunlight	**32**	53 22N	3 0W
Port Talbot	**31**	51 35N	3 48W
Port Taufiq = Bûr Taufiq	**122**	29 54N	32 32 E
Port Townsend	**160**	48 7N	122 50W
Port-Vendres	**44**	42 32N	3 8 E
Port Victoria	**140**	34 30 S	137 29 E
Port Wakefield	**140**	34 12 S	138 10 E
Port Washington	**156**	43 25N	87 52W
Port Weld	**101**	4 50N	100 38 E
Port William	**34**	54 46N	4 35W
Portachuelo	**174**	17 10 S	63 20W
Portacloy	**38**	54 20N	9 48W
Portadown (Craigavon)	**38**	54 27N	6 26W
Portaferry	**38**	54 23N	5 32W
Portage, Can.	**151**	46 40N	64 5W
Portage, U.S.A.	**158**	43 31N	89 25W
Portage la Prairie	**153**	49 58N	98 18W
Portage Mt. Dam	**152**	56 0N	122 0W
Portageville	**159**	36 25N	89 40W
Portaguiran	**36**	58 15N	6 10W
Portalegre	**57**	39 19N	7 25W
Portalegre □	**57**	39 20N	7 40W
Portales	**159**	34 12N	103 25W
Portarlington	**39**	53 10N	7 10W
Porte, La	**156**	41 40N	86 40W
Porteirinha	**171**	15 44 S	43 2W
Portel, Brazil	**170**	1 57 S	50 49W

Portel, Port. 57 38 19N 7 41W
Porter L., N.W.T., Can. 153 61 41N 108 5W
Porter L., Sask., Can. 153 56 20N 107 20W
Porterville, S. Afr. 128 33 0S 18 57E
Porterville, U.S.A. 163 36 5N 119 0W
Portet 44 43 34N 0 11W
Porteynon 31 51 33N 4 13W
Portglenone 38 54 53N 6 30W
Portgordon 37 57 40N 3 1W
Porth Neigwl 31 52 48N 4 35W
Porth Neigwl, B. 31 52 48N 4 33W
Porthcawl 31 51 28N 3 42W
Porthill 160 49 0N 116 30W
Porthleven 30 50 5N 5 19W
Porthmadog 31 52 55N 4 13W
Portile de Fier 70 44 42N 22 30E
Portimão 57 37 8N 8 32W
Portishead 28 51 29N 2 46W
Portknockle 37 57 40N 2 52W
Portland, N.S.W., Austral. 141 33 20S 150 0E
Portland, Victoria, Austral. 140 38 20S 141 35E
Portland, Conn., U.S.A. 162 41 34N 72 39W
Portland, Me., U.S.A. 151 43 40N 70 15W
Portland, Mich., U.S.A. 156 42 52N 84 58W
Portland, Oreg., U.S.A. 160 45 35N 122 40W
Portland B. 140 38 15S 141 45E
Portland Bill 28 50 31N 2 27W
Portland, C. 133 40 46S 148 0E
Portland I. 142 39 20S 177 51E
Portland, I. of 28 50 32N 2 25W
Portland, Pa. 162 40 55N 75 6W
Portland Prom. 149 58 40N 78 33W
Portlaw 39 52 18N 7 20W
Portmagee 39 51 53N 10 22W
Portmahomack 37 57 50N 3 50W
Portmarnock 38 53 25N 6 10W
Portnacroish 34 56 34N 5 24W
Portnahaven 34 55 40N 6 30W
Portneuf 151 46 43N 71 55W
Pôrto, Brazil 170 3 54S 42 42W
Pôrto, Port. 56 41 8N 8 40W
Pôrto □ 56 41 8N 8 20W
Pôrto Alegre, Mato Grosso, Brazil 170 21 40S 53 30W
Pôrto Alegre, Rio Grande do Sul, Brazil 173 30 5S 51 3W
Porto Alexandre 128 15 55S 11 55E
Porto Amboim = Gunza 124 10 50S 13 50E
Porto Amelia = Pemba 127 12 58S 40 30E
Porto Argentera 62 44 15N 7 27E
Porto Azzurro 62 42 46N 10 24E
Porto Botte 64 39 3N 8 33E
Pôrto Calvo 171 9 4S 35 24W
Porto Civitanova 63 43 19N 13 44E
Pôrto da Fôlha 170 9 55S 37 17W
Pôrto de Moz 170 1 41S 52 22W
Pôrto de Pedras 170 9 10S 35 17W
Porto Empédocle 64 37 18N 13 30E
Pôrto Esperança 174 19 37S 57 29W
Pôrto Franco 170 6 20S 47 24W
Porto Garibaldi 63 44 41N 12 14E
Porto, G. de 45 42 17N 8 34E
Pôrto Lago 68 41 1N 25 6E
Porto Mendes 173 24 30S 54 15W
Porto Murtinho 174 21 45S 57 55W
Pôrto Nacional 170 10 40S 48 30W
Porto Novo, Benin 121 6 23N 2 42E
Porto Novo, India 97 11 30N 79 38E
Porto Recanati 63 43 26N 13 40E
Porto San Giorgio 63 43 11N 13 49E
Porto San Stéfano 68 42 26N 11 6E
Porto Santo, I. 116 33 45S 16 25W
Pôrto São José 173 22 43S 53 10W
Pôrto Seguro 171 16 26S 39 5W
Porto Tolle 63 44 57N 12 20E
Porto Tórres 64 40 50N 8 23E
Pôrto União 173 26 10S 51 10W
Pôrto Válter 174 8 5S 72 40W
Porto-Vecchio 45 41 35N 9 16E
Pôrto Velho 174 8 46S 63 54W
Portobelo 166 9 35N 79 42W
Portoferráio 62 42 50N 10 20E
Portogruaro 63 45 47N 12 50E
Portola 160 39 49N 120 28W
Portomaggiore 63 44 41N 11 47E
Porton Camp 28 51 8N 1 42W
Portoscuso 64 39 12N 8 22E
Portovénere 62 44 2N 9 50E
Portoviejo 174 1 0S 80 20W
Portpatrick 34 54 50N 5 7W
Portree 36 57 25N 6 11W
Portroe 39 52 53N 8 20W
Portrush 38 55 13N 6 40W
Portsall 42 48 37N 4 45W
Portsalon 38 55 12N 7 37W
Portskerra 37 58 35N 3 55W
Portslade 29 50 50N 0 11W
Portsmouth, Domin. 167 15 34N 61 27W
Portsmouth, U.K. 28 50 48N 1 6W
Portsmouth, N.H., U.S.A. 162 43 5N 70 45W
Portsmouth, Ohio, U.S.A. 156 38 45N 83 0W
Portsmouth, R.I., U.S.A. 162 41 35N 71 44W
Portsmouth, Va., U.S.A. 156 36 50N 76 20W
Portsoy 37 57 41N 2 41W
Portstewart 38 55 12N 6 43W
Porttipahta 74 68 5N 26 30E
Portugal ■ 56 40 0N 7 0W
Portugalete 58 43 19N 3 4W
Portuguesa □ 174 9 10N 69 15W
Portuguese Guinea = Guinea Bissau 120 12 0N 15 0W
Portuguese Timor ■ = Timor 103 8 0S 126 30E
Portumna 39 53 5N 8 12W
Porvenir 176 53 10S 70 30W
Porvoo 75 60 24N 25 40E
Porzuna 57 39 9N 4 9W
Posada, R. 64 40 40N 9 35E
Posadas, Argent. 173 27 30S 56 0W
Posadas, Spain 57 37 47N 5 11W
Poschiavo 51 46 19N 10 4E
Posets, mt. 58 42 39N 0 25E
Poshan 107 36 30N 117 50E
Posídhio, Ákra 68 39 57N 23 30E
Poso 103 1 20S 120 55E
Poso Colorado 172 23 30S 58 45W
Poso, D. 103 1 20S 120 55E
Posong 107 34 46N 129 5E
Posse 171 14 4S 46 18W
Possel 124 5 5N 19 10E
Possession I. 13 72 4S 172 0E
Pössneck 48 50 42N 11 34E
Possut'eng Hu 105 42 0N 87 0E
Post 159 33 13N 101 21W
Post Falls 160 47 50N 116 59W
Postavy 80 55 4N 26 58E
Postbridge 30 50 36N 3 54W
Poste-de-la-Baleine 30 50 36N 3 54W
Poste Maurice Cortier (Bidon 5) 118 22 14N 1 2E
Postiljon, Kepulauan 103 6 30S 118 50E
Postmasburg 128 28 18S 23 5E
Postojna 63 45 46N 14 12E
Potamós 69 39 38N 19 53E
Potchefstroom 125 26 41S 27 7E
Potcoava 70 44 30N 24 39E
Poté 171 17 49S 41 49W
Poteau 159 35 5N 94 37W
Poteet 159 29 4N 98 35W
Potelu, Lacul 70 43 44N 24 20E
Potenza 65 40 40N 15 50E
Potenza Picena 63 43 22N 13 37E
Poteriteri, L. 143 46 5S 167 10E
Potes 56 43 15N 4 42W
Potgietersrus 129 24 10S 29 3E
Poti 83 42 10N 41 38E
Potiraguá 171 15 36S 39 53W
Potiskum 121 11 39N 11 2E
Potlogi 70 44 34N 25 34E
Potomac, R. 162 38 0N 76 23W
Potosí 174 19 38S 65 50W
Potosí □ 174 20 31S 67 0W
Pot'ou 106 37 57N 116 39E
Potrerillos 172 26 20S 69 30W
Potros, Cerro del 172 28 32S 69 0W
Potsdam, Ger. 48 52 23N 13 4E
Potsdam, U.S.A. 156 44 40N 74 59W
Potsdam □ 48 52 40N 12 50E
Potter 158 41 15N 103 20W
Potter Heigham 29 52 44N 1 33E
Potterne 28 51 19N 2 0W
Potters Bar 29 51 42N 0 11W
Potterspury 29 52 5N 0 52W
Pottery Hill = Abu Ballas 122 24 26N 27 36E
Pottstown 162 40 17N 75 40W
Pottsville 162 40 39N 76 12W
Pottuvil 93 6 55N 81 50E
P'otzu 109 23 30N 120 25E
Pouancé 42 47 44N 1 10W
Pouce Coupé 152 55 40N 120 10W
Poughkeepsie 162 41 40N 73 57W
Pouilly 43 47 18N 2 57E
Poulaphouca Res. 39 53 8N 6 30W
Pouldu, Le 42 47 41N 3 36W
Poulsbo 160 47 45N 122 39W
Poultney 162 43 31N 73 14W
Poulton le Fylde 32 53 51N 2 59W
Poundstock 30 50 44N 4 34W
Pouso Alegre, Mato Grosso, Brazil 175 11 55S 57 0W
Pouso Alegre, Minas Gerais, Brazil 173 22 14S 45 57W
Pouzages 44 46 40N 0 50W
Povenets 78 62 50N 34 50E
Poverty Bay 142 38 43S 178 2E
Póvoa de Lanhosa 56 41 33N 8 15W
Póvoa de Varzim 56 41 25N 8 46W
Povorino 81 51 12N 42 28E
Powassan 150 46 5N 79 25W
Poway 163 32 58N 117 2W
Powder, R. 158 46 47N 105 12W
Powell 160 44 45N 108 45W
Powell Creek 136 18 6S 133 46E
Powell River 152 49 22N 125 31W
Powers, Mich., U.S.A. 156 45 40N 87 32W
Powers, Oreg., U.S.A. 160 42 53N 124 2W
Powers Lake 158 48 37N 102 38W
Powick 28 52 9N 2 15W
Powis, Vale of 23 52 40N 3 10W
Powys □ 31 52 20N 3 20W
P'oyang 109 29 1N 116 38E
Poyang Hu 109 29 10N 116 10E
Poyarkovo 77 49 36N 128 41E
Poyntzpass 38 54 17N 6 22W
Poysdorf 53 48 40N 16 37E
Poza de la Sal 58 42 35N 3 31W
Poza Rica 165 20 33N 97 27W
Pozarevac 66 44 35N 21 18E
Pozega 66 45 21N 17 41E
Pozhva 84 59 5N 56 5E
Poznan 54 52 25N 17 0E
Pozo 163 35 20N 120 24W
Pozo Alcón 59 37 42N 2 56W
Pozo Almonte 174 20 10S 69 50W
Pozoblanco 57 38 23N 4 51W
Pozzallo 65 36 44N 15 40E
Pra, R. 121 5 30N 1 38W
Prabuty 54 53 47N 19 15E
Prača 66 43 47N 18 43E
Prachatice 52 49 1N 14 0E
Prachin Buri 100 14 0N 101 25E
Prachuap Khiri Khan 101 11 49N 99 48E
Pradelles 44 44 46N 3 52E
Pradera 174 3 25N 76 15W
Prades 44 42 38N 2 23E
Prado 171 17 20S 39 13W
Prado del Rey 57 36 48N 5 33W
Præstø 73 55 8N 12 2E
Pragersko 63 46 27N 15 42E
Prague = Praha 52 50 5N 14 22E
Praha 52 50 5N 14 22E
Prahecq 44 46 19N 0 26W
Prahita, R. 97 19 0N 79 55E
Prahova □ 70 44 50N 25 50E
Prahova, R. 70 44 50N 25 50E
Prahova, Reg. 70 44 50N 25 50E
Prahovo 66 44 18N 22 39E
Praid 70 46 32N 25 10E
Prainha, Amazonas, Brazil 174 7 10S 60 30W
Prainha, Pará, Brazil 175 1 45S 53 30W
Prairie, Queens., Austral. 138 20 50S 144 35E
Prairie, S. Australia, Austral. 109 34 51S 138 49E
Prairie City 160 45 27N 118 44W
Prairie du Chien 158 43 1N 91 9W
Prairie, R. 159 34 45N 101 15W
Praja 102 8 39S 116 27E
Prajeczno 54 51 10N 19 0E
Pramánda 68 39 32N 21 8E
Pran Buri 100 12 23N 99 55E
Prang 121 8 1N 0 56W
Prapat 102 2 41N 98 58E
Praszka 54 51 32N 18 31E
Prata, Minas Gerais, Brazil 171 19 25S 49 0W
Prata, Pará, Brazil 170 1 10S 47 35W
Prática di Mare 64 41 40N 12 26E
Prato 62 43 53N 11 5E
Prátola Peligna 63 42 7N 13 51E
Pratovécchio 63 43 44N 11 43E
Prats-de-Molló 44 42 25N 2 27E
Pratt 159 37 40N 98 45W
Pratteln 50 47 31N 7 41E
Prättigau 51 46 56N 9 44E
Prattville 157 32 30N 86 28W
Pravara, R. 96 19 30N 74 28E
Pravdinsk 81 56 29N 43 28E
Pravia 56 43 30N 6 12W
Prawle Pt. 30 50 13N 3 41W
Pré-en-Pail 42 48 28N 0 12W
Pré St. Didier 62 45 45N 7 0E
Precordillera 172 30 0S 69 1W
Predáppio 63 44 7N 11 58E
Predazzo 63 46 19N 11 37E
Predejane 66 42 51N 22 9E
Preeceville 153 51 57N 102 40W
Prees 32 52 54N 2 40W
Preesall 32 53 55N 2 58W
Préfailles 42 47 9N 2 11W
Pregonero 174 8 1N 71 46W
Pregrada 63 46 11N 15 45E
Preko 63 44 7N 15 14E
Prelate 153 50 51N 109 24W
Prelog 63 46 18N 16 32E
Premier 152 56 4N 129 56W
Premier Downs 137 30 30S 126 30E
Premont 159 27 19N 91 8W
Premuda, I. 63 44 20N 14 36E
Prenj, mt. 66 43 33N 17 53E
Prenjasi 68 41 6N 20 32E
Prentice 158 45 31N 90 19W
Prenzlau 48 53 19N 13 51E
Prepansko Jezero 68 40 45N 21 0E
Preparis I. 99 14 55N 93 45E
Preparis North Channel 101 15 12N 93 40E
Preparis South Channel 101 14 36N 93 40E
Prerov 53 49 28N 17 27E
Prescot 32 53 27N 2 49W
Prescott, Can. 150 44 45N 75 30W
Prescott, Ariz., U.S.A. 161 34 35N 112 30W
Prescott, Ark., U.S.A. 159 33 49N 93 22W
Preservation Inlet 143 46 8S 166 35E
Preševo 66 42 19N 21 39E
Presho 158 43 56N 100 4W
Preshute 28 51 24N 1 45W
Presicce 65 39 53N 18 13E
Presidencia de la Plaza 172 27 0S 60 0W
Presidencia Roque Sáenz Peña 172 26 45S 60 30W
Presidente Dutra 164 5 15S 44 30W
Presidente Epitácio 171 21 46S 52 6W
Presidente Hayes □ 172 24 0S 59 0W
Presidente Hermes 174 11 0S 61 55W
Presidente Prudente 173 22 5S 51 25W
Presidente Rogue Saena Peña 172 34 33S 58 30W
Presidio, Mexico 164 29 29N 104 23W
Presidio, U.S.A. 159 29 30N 104 20W
Preslav 67 43 10N 26 52E
Prespa, L. = Prepansko Jezero 68 40 45N 21 0E
Prespa, mt. 67 41 44N 25 0E
Presque Isle 151 46 40N 68 0W
Prestatyn 31 53 20N 3 24W
Prestea 120 5 22N 2 7W
Presteigne 31 52 17N 3 0W
Preštice 52 49 34N 13 20E
Preston, Borders, U.K. 35 55 48N 2 18W
Preston, Dorset, U.K. 28 50 38N 2 26W
Preston, Lancs., U.K. 32 53 46N 2 42W
Preston, Idaho, U.S.A. 160 42 0N 112 0W
Preston, Minn., U.S.A. 158 43 39N 92 3W
Preston, Nev., U.S.A. 160 38 59N 115 2W
Preston, C. 136 20 51S 116 12E
Prestonpans 35 55 58N 3 0W
Prestwich 32 53 32N 2 18W
Prestwick 34 55 30N 4 38W
Prêto, R., Bahia 170 11 21S 43 52W
Pretoria 129 25 44S 28 12E
Prettyboy Res. 162 39 37N 76 43W
Preuilly-sur-Claise 42 46 51N 0 56E
Préveza 69 38 57N 20 47E
Préveza □ 68 39 20N 20 40E
Prey-Veng 101 11 35N 105 29E
Priazovskoye 82 46 22N 35 28E
Pribilov Is. 12 56 0N 170 0W
Priboj 66 43 35N 19 32E
Pribram 52 49 41N 14 2E
Price 160 39 40N 110 48W
Price I. 152 52 23N 128 41W
Prichalnaya 83 48 57N 44 33E
Priego 58 40 38N 2 21W
Priego de Córdoba 57 37 27N 4 12W
Priekule 80 57 27N 21 45E
Prieska 128 29 40S 22 42E
Priest Gully Cr. 108 27 29S 153 11E
Priest L. 160 48 30N 116 55W
Priest River 160 48 11N 117 0W
Priest Valley 163 36 10N 120 39W
Priestly 152 54 8N 125 20W
Prievidza 53 48 46N 18 36E
Prijedor 63 44 58N 16 41E
Prijepolje 66 43 27N 19 40E
Prilep 66 41 21N 21 37E
Priluki 80 50 30N 32 15E
Prime Seal I. 138 40 3S 147 43E
Primeira Cruz 170 2 30S 43 26W
Primorsko 67 42 15N 27 44E
Primorsko-Akhtarsk 82 46 2N 38 10E
Primrose L. 153 54 55N 109 45W
Prince Albert 153 53 15N 105 50W
Prince Albert Nat. Park 153 54 0N 106 25W
Prince Albert Pen. 148 72 30N 116 0W
Prince Alfred C. 12 74 20N 124 40W
Prince Charles I. 149 67 47N 76 12W
Prince Edward I. □. 151 44 2N 77 20W
Prince Edward Is. 11 45 15S 39 0E
Prince Frederick 162 38 33N 76 35W
Prince George 152 53 50N 122 50W
Prince of Wales, C. 147 65 50N 168 0W
Prince of Wales I. 147 73 0N 99 0W
Prince of Wales, I. 147 53 30N 131 30W
Prince of Wales Is. 135 10 40S 142 10E
Prince Patrick I. 12 77 0N 120 0W
Prince Regent Inlet 12 73 0N 90 0W
Prince Rupert 152 54 20N 130 20W
Prince William Sd. 147 60 20N 146 30W
Princenhage 47 51 9N 4 45E
Princes Risborough 29 51 43N 0 50W
Princesa Isabel 170 7 44S 38 0W
Princess Anne 162 38 12N 75 41W
Princess Charlotte B. 138 14 25S 144 0E
Princess Mary Ranges 136 15 30S 125 30E
Princess Royal I. 152 53 0N 128 40W
Princeton, Can. 152 49 27N 120 30W
Princeton, Ill., U.S.A. 158 41 25N 89 25W
Princeton, Ind., U.S.A. 156 38 20N 87 35W
Princeton, Ky., U.S.A. 156 37 6N 87 55W
Princeton, Mo., U.S.A. 158 40 23N 93 35W
Princeton, N.J., U.S.A. 162 40 18N 74 40W
Princeton, W. Va., U.S.A. 156 37 21N 81 8W
Princetown 30 50 33N 4 0W
Principe Chan. 152 53 28N 130 0W
Principe da Beira 174 12 20S 64 30W
Principe, I. de 114 1 37N 7 27E
Prineville 160 44 17N 120 57W
Prins Albert 128 33 12S 22 2E
Prins Harald Kyst 13 70 0S 35 1E
Prinzapolca 166 13 20N 83 35W
Prior, C. 56 43 34N 8 17W
Pripet Marshes = Polesye 80 52 0N 28 10E
Pripet, R. = Pripyat, R. 80 51 30N 30 0E
Pripyat, R. 80 51 30N 30 0E
Prislop, Pasul 70 47 37N 25 15E
Pristen 81 51 15N 12 40E
Priština 66 42 40N 21 13E
Pritchard 157 30 47N 88 5W
Pritzwalk 48 53 10N 12 11E
Privas 45 44 45N 4 37E
Priverno 64 41 29N 13 10E
Privolzhsk 81 57 9N 14 9E
Privolzhskaya Vozvyshennest 81 51 0N 46 0E
Privolzhskiy 81 51 25N 46 3E
Privolzhye 81 52 52N 48 33E
Prívutnoye 83 47 12N 43 30E
Prizren 66 42 13N 20 45E
Prizzi 64 37 44N 13 24E
Prnjavor 66 44 52N 17 43E
Probolinggo 103 7 46S 113 13E
Probus 30 50 17N 4 55W
Prochowice 54 51 17N 16 20E

Procida, I. 64 40 46N 14 0 E
Proctor 162 43 40N 73 2W
Proddatur 97 14 45N 78 30 E
Proença-a-Nova 57 39 45N 7 54W
Profondeville 47 50 23N 4 52 E
Progreso 165 21 20N 89 40W
Prokhladnyy 83 43 50N 44 2 E
Prokletije 68 42 30N 19 45 E
Prokopyevsk 76 54 0N 87 3 E
Prokuplje 66 43 16N 21 36 E
Proletarskaya 83 46 42N 41 50 E
Prome = Pyè 99 18 45N 95 30 E
Prophet, R. 152 58 48N 122 40W
Propriá 170 10 13 S 36 51W
Propriano 45 41 41N 8 52 E
Proserpine 138 20 21 S 148 36 E
Prospect, Austral. 109 34 53 S 138 36 E
Prospect, U.S.A. 162 43 18N 75 9W
Prosser 160 46 11N 119 52W
Prostějov 53 49 30N 17 9 E
Proston 139 26 14 S 151 32 E
Proszowice 54 50 13N 20 16 E
Protection 159 37 16N 99 30W
Próti, I. 69 37 5N 21 32 E
Provadija 67 43 12N 27 30 E
Proven 47 50 54N 2 40 E
Provence 45 43 40N 5 46 E
Providence, Ky., U.S.A. 156 37 25N 87 46W
Providence, R.I., U.S.A. 162 41 41N 71 15W
Providence Bay 150 45 41N 82 15W
Providence C. 143 45 59 S 166 29 E
Providence Mts. 161 35 0N 115 30W
Providencia 174 0 28 S 76 28W
Providencia, I. de 166 13 25N 81 26W
Provideniya 77 64 23N 173 18 E
Province Wellesley 101 5 15N 100 20 E
Provincetown 162 42 5N 70 11W
Provins 43 48 33N 3 15 E
Provo 160 40 16N 111 37W
Provost 153 52 25N 110 20W
Prozor 66 43 50N 17 34 E
Prudentópolis 171 25 12 S 50 57W
Prudhoe 35 54 57N 1 52W
Prudhoe Bay, Austral. 138 21 30 S 149 30W
Prudhoe Bay, U.S.A. 147 70 20N 148 20W
Prudhoe I. 138 21 23 S 149 45 E
Prudhoe Land 12 78 1N 65 0W
Prud'homme 153 52 20N 105 54W
Prudnik 54 50 20N 17 38 E
Prüm 49 50 14N 6 22 E
Pruszcz 54 54 17N 19 40 E
Pruszków 54 52 9N 20 49 E
Prut, R. 70 46 3N 28 10 E
Prvič, I. 63 44 55N 14 47 E
Prvomay 67 42 8N 25 17 E
Prydz B. 13 69 0 S 74 0 E
Pryor 159 36 17N 95 20W
Przasnysz 54 53 2N 20 45 E
Przedbórz 54 51 6N 19 53 E
Przedecz 54 52 20N 18 53 E
Przemyśl 54 49 50N 22 45 E
Przemyśl □ 54 80 0N 23 0 E
Przeworsk 54 50 6N 22 32 E
Przewóz 54 51 28N 14 57 E
Przhevalsk 85 42 30N 78 20 E
Przysucha 54 51 22N 20 38 E
Psakhná 69 38 34N 23 35 E
Psarà, I. 69 38 37N 25 38 E
Psathoúra, I. 68 39 30N 24 12 E
Psel, R. 82 49 25N 33 50 E
Pserimos, I. 69 36 56N 27 12 E
Pskem, R. 85 41 38N 70 1 E
Pskemskiy Khrebet 85 42 0N 70 45 E
Pskent 85 40 54N 69 20 E
Pskov 80 57 50N 28 25 E
Psunj, mt. 66 45 25N 17 19 E
Pszczyna 54 49 59N 18 58 E
Pteleón 69 39 3N 22 57 E
Ptich, R. 80 52 30N 28 45 E
Ptolemais 68 40 30N 21 43 E
Ptuj 63 46 28N 15 50 E
Ptujska Gora 63 46 23N 15 47 E
Pua 100 19 11N 100 55 E
Puán 172 37 30 S 63 0W
P'uan 108 25 47N 104 57 E
Puan 107 35 44N 126 7 E
Pubnico 151 43 47N 65 50W
Pucallpa 174 8 25 S 74 30W
P'uchen 107 37 21N 118 1 E
P'uch'eng 109 27 45N 118 47 E
Pucheni 70 45 12N 25 17 E
P'uch'i 109 29 43N 113 53 E
Pucisce 63 43 22N 16 43 E
Puck 54 54 45N 18 23 E
Puddletown 28 50 45N 2 21W
Pudsey 33 53 47N 1 40W
Pudukkottai 97 10 28N 78 47 E
Puebla 165 19 0N 98 10W
Puebla □ 165 18 30N 98 0W
Puebla de Alcocer 57 38 59N 5 14W
Puebla de Don Fadrique 59 37 58N 2 25W
Puebla de Don Rodrigo 57 39 5N 4 37W
Puebla de Guzmán 57 37 37N 7 15W
Puebla de los Infantes, La 57 37 47N 5 24W
Puebla de Montalbán, La 56 39 52N 4 22W
Puebla de Sanabria 56 42 4N 6 38W
Puebla de Trives 56 42 20N 7 10W
Puebla del Caramiñal 56 42 37N 8 56W
Puebla, La 58 39 50N 3 0 E
Pueblo 158 38 20N 104 40W
Pueblo Bonito 161 36 4N 107 57W
Pueblo Hundido 172 26 20 S 69 30W
Pueblo Nuevo 174 8 26N 71 26W
Pueblonuevo 55 38 16N 5 16W
Puelches 172 38 5 S 66 0W
Puelén 172 37 32 S 67 38W
Puente Alto 172 33 32 S 70 35W
Puente del Arzobispo 56 39 48N 5 10W
Puente Genil 57 37 22N 4 47W
Puente la Reina 58 42 40N 1 49W
Puenteareas 56 42 10N 8 28W
Puentedeume 56 43 24N 8 10W
Puentes de García Rodríguez 56 43 27N 7 51W
Puerco, R. 161 35 10N 109 45W
Puerh 105 23 11N 100 56 E
P'uerh 108 23 5N 101 5 E
Puerhching 105 47 43N 86 53 E
Puerta, La 59 38 22N 2 45W
Puerto Aisén 176 45 10 S 73 0W
Puerto Angel 165 15 40N 96 29W
Puerto Arista 165 15 56N 93 48W
Puerto Armuelles 166 8 20N 83 10W
Puerto Ayacucho 174 5 40N 67 35W
Puerto Barrios 166 15 40N 88 40W
Puerto Bermejo 172 26 55 S 58 34W
Puerto Bermúdez 174 10 20 S 75 0W
Puerto Bolívar 174 3 10 S 79 55W
Puerto Cabello 174 10 28N 68 1W
Puerto Cabezas 166 14 0N 83 30W
Puerto Cabo Gracias a Dios 166 15 0N 83 10W
Puerto Capaz = Jebba 118 35 11N 4 43W
Puerto Carreño 174 6 12N 67 22W
Puerto Casado 172 22 19 S 57 56W
Puerto Castilla 166 16 0N 86 0W
Puerto Chicama 174 7 45 S 79 20W
Puerto Coig 176 50 54 S 69 15W
Puerto Columbia 174 10 59N 74 58W
Puerto Cortés, C. Rica 166 8 20N 82 20W
Puerto Cortés, Hond. 166 15 51N 88 0W
Puerto Cuemani 174 0 5N 73 21W
Puerto Cumarebo 174 11 29N 69 21W
Puerto de Cabras 116 28 40N 13 30W
Puerto de Morelos 165 20 49N 86 52W
Puerto de Santa María 57 36 36N 6 13W
Puerto Deseado 176 47 45 S 66 0W
Puerto Heath 174 12 25 S 68 45W
Puerto Huitoto 174 0 18N 74 3W
Puerto Juárez 165 21 11N 86 49W
Puerto La Cruz 174 10 13N 64 38W
Puerto Leguízamo 174 0 12 S 74 46W
Puerto Libertad 164 29 55N 112 41W
Puerto Limón, Meta, Colomb. 174 3 23N 73 30W
Puerto Limón, Putumayo, Colomb. 174 1 3N 76 30W
Puerto Lobos 176 42 0 S 65 3W
Puerto López 174 4 5N 72 58W
Puerto Lumbreras 59 37 34N 1 48W
Puerto Madryn 176 42 48 S 65 4W
Puerto Maldonado 174 12 30 S 69 10W
Puerto Manotí 166 21 22N 76 50W
Puerto Mazarrón 59 37 34N 1 15W
Puerto Mercedes 174 1 11N 72 53W
Puerto Montt 176 41 22 S 72 40W
Puerto Natales 176 51 45 S 72 25W
Puerto Nuevo 174 5 53N 69 56W
Puerto Ordaz 174 8 16N 62 44W
Puerto Padre 166 21 13N 76 35W
Puerto Páez 174 6 13N 67 28W
Puerto Peñasco 164 31 20N 113 33W
Puerto Pinasco 172 22 43 S 57 50W
Puerto Pirámides 176 42 35 S 64 20W
Puerto Plata 167 19 40N 70 45W
Puerto Princesa 94 9 44N 118 44 E
Puerto Quellón 176 43 7 S 73 37W
Puerto Quepos 166 9 29N 84 6W
Puerto Real 57 36 33N 6 12W
Puerto Rico 174 1 54N 75 10W
Puerto Rico ■ 147 18 15N 66 45W
Puerto Rico Trough 14 20 0N 63 0W
Puerto Sastre 172 22 25 S 57 55W
Puerto Suárez 174 18 58 S 57 52W
Puerto Tejada 174 3 14N 76 24W
Puerto Umbria 174 0 52N 76 33W
Puerto Vallarta 164 20 26N 105 15W
Puerto Villamizar 174 8 25N 72 30W
Puerto Wilches 174 7 21N 73 54W
Puertollano 57 38 43N 4 7W
Puertomarín 56 42 48N 7 37W
Pueyrredón, L. 176 47 20 S 72 0W
Puffin I., Ireland 39 51 50N 10 25W
Puffin I., U.K. 31 53 19N 4 1W
Pugachev 81 52 0N 48 55 E
Puge 126 4 45 S 33 11 E
Puget Sd. 160 47 15N 123 30W
Puget-Théniers 45 43 58N 6 53 E
Púglia 65 41 0N 16 30 E
Pugŏdong 107 42 5N 130 0 E
Pugu 126 6 55 S 39 4 E
Puha 142 38 30 S 177 50 E
P'uhsien 106 36 25N 110 4 E
Puhute Mesa 163 37 25N 116 50W
Pui 70 45 30N 23 4 E
Puieşti 70 46 25N 27 33 E
Puig Mayor, Mte. 58 39 49N 2 47 E
Puigcerdá 58 42 24N 1 50 E
Puigmal, Mt. 58 42 23N 2 7 E
Puisaye, Collines de 43 47 34N 3 28 E
Puiseaux 43 48 11N 2 30 E
Pujon-chosuji 107 40 35N 127 35 E
Puka 68 42 2N 19 53 E
Pukaki L. 143 44 4 S 170 1 E
Pukatawagan 153 55 45N 101 20W
Pukchin 107 40 12N 125 45 E
Pukchŏng 107 40 14N 128 18 E
Pukearuhe 142 38 55 S 174 31 E
Pukekohe 142 37 12 S 174 55 E
Puketeraki Ra. 143 42 58 S 172 13 E
Pukeuri 143 45 4 S 171 2 E
P'uko 108 27 27N 102 34 E
Pukoo 147 21 4N 156 48W
P'uk'ou 109 32 7N 118 43 E
Pula 64 39 0N 9 0 E
Pula (Pola) 63 44 54N 13 57 E
Pulaski, N.Y., U.S.A. 162 43 32N 76 9W
Pulaski, Tenn., U.S.A. 157 35 10N 87 0W
Pulaski, Va., U.S.A. 156 37 4N 80 49W
Pulawy 54 51 23N 21 59 E
Pulborough 29 50 58N 0 30W
Pulgaon 96 20 44N 78 21 E
Pulham Market 29 52 25N 1 15 E
Pulham St. Mary 29 52 25N 1 14 E
Pulicat, L. 97 13 40N 80 15 E
Puliyangudi 97 9 11N 77 24 E
Pullabooka 141 33 44 S 147 46 E
Pullen Cr. 108 27 33 S 152 54 E
Pullman 160 46 49N 117 10W
Pulmakong 121 11 2N 0 2 E
Pulog, Mt. 103 16 40N 120 50 E
Puloraja 102 4 55N 95 24 E
Pułtusk 54 52 43N 21 6 E
Pumlumon Fawr 31 52 29N 3 47W
Pumpsaint 31 52 3N 3 58W
Puna 174 19 45 S 65 28W
Puna de Atacama 172 25 0 S 67 0W
Puná, I. 174 2 55 S 80 5W
Punakha 98 27 42N 89 52 E
Punalur 97 9 0N 76 56 E
Punasar 94 27 6N 73 6 E
Punata 174 17 25 S 65 50W
Punch 95 33 48N 74 4 E
Pune 96 18 29N 73 57 E
Pungsan 107 40 50N 128 9 E
P'uning 109 23 19N 116 9 E
Punjab □ 94 31 0N 76 0 E
Punkatawagon 153 55 44N 101 20W
Puno 174 15 55 S 70 3W
Punt, La 51 46 35N 9 56 E
Punta Alta 176 38 53 S 62 4W
Punta Arenas 176 53 0 S 71 0W
Punta de Díaz 172 28 0 S 70 45W
Punta de Piedras 174 10 54N 64 6W
Punta del Lago Viedma 176 49 45 S 72 0W
Punta Gorda, Belize 165 16 10N 88 45W
Punta Gorda, U.S.A. 157 26 55N 82 0W
Punta Prieta 164 28 58N 114 17W
Puntabie 139 32 12 S 134 5 E
Puntarenas 166 10 0N 84 50W
Puntes de García Rodríguez 56 43 27N 7 50W
Punto Fijo 174 11 42N 70 13W
Punxsutawney 156 40 56N 79 0W
P'upei 108 22 16N 109 33 E
Puquio 174 14 45 S 74 10W
Pur, R. 76 65 30N 77 40 E
Purace, vol. 174 2 21N 76 23W
Puračió 66 44 33N 18 28 E
Purari, R. 135 7 49 S 145 0 E
Purbeck, Isle of 28 50 40N 2 5W
Purcell 159 35 0N 97 25W
Purchena Tetica 59 37 21N 2 21W
Purdy Is. 138 3 0 S 146 0 E
Purfleet 29 51 29N 0 15 E
Puri 96 19 50N 85 58 E
Purificación 174 3 51N 74 55W
Purísima, La 164 26 10N 112 4W
Purley 28 51 29N 1 4W
Purli 96 18 50N 76 35 E
Purmerend 47 52 30N 4 58 E
Purna, R. 96 19 55N 76 20 E
Purnea 95 25 45N 87 31 E
Pursat 101 12 34N 103 50 E
Puruey 174 7 35N 64 48W
Purukcahu 102 0 35 S 114 35 E
Purulia 95 23 17N 86 33 E
Purus, R. 174 5 25 S 64 0W
Purwakarta 103 6 35 S 107 29 E
Purwodadi, Jawa, Indon. 103 7 7 S 110 55 E
Purwodadi, Jawa, Indon. 103 7 51 S 110 0 E
Purworejo 103 7 43 S 110 2 E
Puryołng 107 42 0N 129 43 E
Pus, R. 96 19 50N 77 45 E
Pusad 96 19 56N 77 36 E
Pusan 107 35 5N 129 0 E
Pushchino 77 54 20N 158 10 E
Pushkin 80 59 45N 30 25 E
Pushkino 81 51 16N 47 9 E
Puskitamika L. 150 49 20N 76 30W
Püspökladány 53 47 19N 21 6 E
Pussa 129 24 30 S 33 55 E
Pustoshka 80 56 11N 29 30 E
Puszczykowo 54 52 18N 16 49 E
Putahow L. 153 59 54N 100 40W
Putao 98 27 28N 97 30 E
Putaruru 142 38 2 S 175 50 E
Putbus 48 54 19N 13 29 E
Put'ehach'i 105 48 0N 122 43 E
Puţeni 70 45 49N 27 42 E
Puthein Myit, R. 99 15 56N 94 18 E
P'ut'ien 109 25 27N 118 59 E
Putignano 65 40 50N 17 5 E
P'uting 108 26 19N 105 45 E
Putlitz 48 53 15N 12 3 E
Putna 70 47 50N 25 33 E
Putna, R. 70 45 42N 27 26 E
Putnam 162 41 55N 71 55W
Putnok 53 48 18N 20 26 E
P'ut'o 109 29 58N 122 15 E
Putorana, Gory 77 69 0N 95 0 E
Putorino 142 39 4 S 177 9 E
Putta 47 51 4N 4 38 E
Puttalam 93 8 1N 79 55 E
Puttalam Lagoon 97 8 15N 79 45 E
Putte 47 51 22N 4 24 E
Putten 46 52 16N 5 36 E
Puttgarden 48 54 28N 11 15 E
Puttur 97 12 46N 75 12 E
Putty 141 32 57 S 150 42 E
Putumayo □ 174 1 30 S 70 0W
Putumayo, R. 174 1 30 S 70 0W
Putussibau, G. 102 0 45N 113 50 E
Pututahi 142 38 39 S 177 53 E
Puurs 47 51 5N 4 17 E
Puy-de-Dôme 44 45 46N 2 57 E
Puy-de-Dôme □ 44 45 47N 3 0 E
Puy-de-Sancy 44 45 32N 2 41 E
Puy Guillaume 44 45 57N 3 28 E
Puy, Le 44 45 3N 3 52 E
Puy l'Evêque 44 44 31N 1 9 E
Puyallup 160 47 10N 122 22W
P'uyang 106 35 41N 115 0 E
Puylaurens 44 43 35N 2 0 E
Puyôo 44 43 33N 0 56W
Pwalagu 121 10 38N 0 50W
Pwani □, Tanz. 126 7 0 S 39 0 E
Pwani □, Tanz. 126 7 0 S 39 30 E
Pweto 127 8 25 S 28 51 E
Pwinbyu 98 20 23N 94 40 E
Pwllheli 31 52 54N 4 26W
Pya Ozero 78 66 8N 31 22 E
Pyana, R. 81 55 30N 45 0 E
Pyandzh 85 37 14N 69 6 E
Pyandzh, R. 85 37 6N 68 20 E
Pyapon 98 16 5N 95 50 E
Pyasina, R. 77 72 30N 90 30 E
Pyatigorsk 83 44 2N 43 0 E
Pyatikhatki 82 48 28N 33 38 E
Pyaye 98 19 12N 95 10 E
Pyè 98 18 49N 95 13 E
Pyinbauk 98 19 10N 95 12 E
Pyinmana 98 19 45N 96 20 E
Pyŏktong 107 40 37N 125 26 E
Pyŏnggang 107 38 24N 127 17 E
Pyŏngtaek 107 37 1N 127 4 E
P'yŏngyang 107 39 0N 125 45 E
Pyote 159 31 34N 103 5W
Pyramid L. 160 40 0N 119 30W
Pyramid Pk. 163 36 25N 116 37W
Pyramids 122 29 58N 31 9 E
Pyrenees 44 42 45N 0 18 E
Pyrénées-Atlantiques □ 44 43 15N 1 0W
Pyrénées-Orientales □ 44 42 35N 2 26 E
Pyrzyce 54 53 10N 14 55 E
Pyshchug 81 58 57N 45 27 E
Pyshma, R. 84 57 8N 66 18 E
Pytalovo 80 57 5N 27 55 E
Python 127 17 56 S 29 10 E
Pyttegga 71 62 13N 7 42 E
Pyu 98 18 30N 96 35 E
Pyzdry 54 52 11N 17 42 E

Q

Qaar Zeitun 122 29 10N 25 48 E
Qabalon 90 32 8N 35 17 E
Qabatiya 90 32 25N 35 16 E
Qadam 93 32 55N 66 45 E
Qadhimah 92 22 20N 39 13 E
Qadian 94 31 51N 74 19 E
Qal at Shajwa 122 25 2N 38 57 E
Qala-i-Jadid (Spin Baldak) 94 31 1N 66 25 E
Qala-i-Kirta 93 32 15N 63 0 E
Qala Nau 93 35 0N 63 5 E
Qala Punja 93 37 0N 72 40 E
Qala Yangi 94 34 20N 66 30 E
Qal'at al Akhdhar 92 28 0N 37 10 E
Qal'at Saura 122 26 10N 38 40 E
Qal'eh Shaharak 93 34 10N 64 20 E
Qalqīlya 90 32 12N 34 58 E
Qalyûb 122 30 12N 31 11 E
Qam 90 32 36N 35 43 E
Qamar, Ghubbat al 91 16 20N 52 30 E
Qamruddin Karez 94 31 45N 68 20 E
Qana 90 33 12N 35 17 E
Qâra 122 29 38N 26 30 E
Qara Qash, R. 95 35 45N 78 45 E
Qara Tagh La = Kala Shank'ou 95 35 42N 78 20 E
Qarachuk 92 37 0N 42 2 E
Qarah 92 29 55N 40 3 E
Qardud 123 10 20N 29 56 E
Qarrasa 123 14 38N 32 5 E
Qarsa 123 9 28N 41 48 E
Qaşr Bū Hadi 119 31 1N 16 45 E
Qasr-e-Qand 93 26 15N 60 45 E
Qasr Farâfra 122 27 0N 28 1 E
Qastina 90 31 44N 34 45 E
Qatar ■ 93 25 30N 51 15 E
Qattâra 122 30 12N 27 3 E
Qattara Depression = Q. Munkhafed el 122 29 30N 27 30 E
Qattâra, Munkhafed el 122 29 30N 27 30 E

Qayen 93 33 40N 59 10 E
Qazvin 92 36 15N 50 0 E
Qena 122 26 10N 32 43 E
Qena, Wadi 122 26 57N 32 50 E
Qendrevca 68 40 20N 19 48 E
Qesari 90 32 30N 34 53 E
Qeshm 93 26 55N 56 10 E
Qeshm, I. 93 26 50N 56 0 E
Qila Safed 93 29 0N 61 30 E
Qila Saifulla 94 30 45N 68 17 E
Qiryat 'Anivim 90 31 49N 35 7 E
Qiryat Bialik 90 32 50N 35 5 E
Qiryat 'Eqron 90 31 52N 34 49 E
Qiryat Hayyim 90 32 49N 35 4 E
Qiryat Shemona 90 33 13N 35 35 E
Qiryat Yam 90 32 51N 35 4 E
Qishon, R. 90 32 42N 35 7 E
Qishran 122 20 14N 40 2 E
Qizan 123 16 57N 42 34 E
Qom 93 34 40N 51 0 E
Quabbin Res. 162 42 17N 72 21W
Quabbo 123 12 2N 39 56 E
Quackenbrück 48 52 40N 7 59 E
Quadring 33 52 53N 0 9W
Quainton 29 51 51N 0 53W
Quairading 137 32 0S 117 21 E
Quakerstown 162 40 27N 75 20W
Qualeup 137 33 48S 116 48 E
Quambatook 138 35 49S 143 34 E
Quambone 141 30 57S 147 53 E
Quan Long 101 9 7N 105 8 E
Quanan 159 34 20N 99 45W
Quandialla 141 34 1S 147 47 E
Quang Nam 101 15 55N 108 15 E
Quang Ngai 101 15 13N 108 58 E
Quang Yen 100 21 3N 106 52 E
Quantock Hills, The 28 51 8N 3 10W
Quaraí 172 30 15S 56 20W
Quarré les Tombes 43 47 21N 4 0 E
Quarryville 162 39 54N 76 10W
Quartu Sant' Elena 64 39 15N 9 10 E
Quartzsite 161 33 44N 114 16W
Quatsino 152 50 30N 127 40W
Quatsino Sd. 152 50 42N 127 58W
Qubab = Mishmar Aiyalon 90 31 52N 34 57 E
Qūchān 93 37 10N 58 27 E
Que Que 127 18 58S 29 48 E
Queanbeyan 141 35 17S 149 14 E
Québec 151 46 52N 71 13W
Québec □ 151 50 0N 70 0W
Quedlinburg 48 51 47N 11 9 E
Queen Alexandra Ra. 13 85 0S 170 0 E
Queen Anne 162 38 55N 75 57W
Queen Bess Mt. 152 51 13N 124 35W
Queen Charlotte 152 53 15N 132 2W
Queen Charlotte Is. 152 53 20N 132 10W
Queen Charlotte Sd. 143 41 10S 174 15 E
Queen Charlotte Str. 152 51 0N 128 0W
Queen Elizabeth Is. 10 78 0N 95 0W
Queen Elizabeth Nat. Pk. 126 0 0S 30 0 E
Queen Mary Coast 13 70 0S 95 0 E
Queen Maud G. 148 68 15N 102 30W
Queenborough 29 51 24N 0 46 E
Queen's Chan. 136 15 0S 129 30 E
Queensbury 32 53 46N 1 50W
Queenscliff 138 38 16S 144 39 E
Queensferry 35 56 0N 3 25W
Queensland □ 138 15 0S 142 0 E
Queenstown, Austral. 138 42 4S 145 35 E
Queenstown, N.Z. 143 45 1S 168 40 E
Queenstown, S. Afr. 125 31 52S 26 52 E
Queguay Grande, R. 172 32 9S 58 9W
Queimadas 170 11 0S 39 38W
Quela 124 9 10S 16 56 E
Quelimane 127 17 53S 36 58 E
Quemado, N. Mex., U.S.A. 161 34 17N 108 28W
Quemado, Tex., U.S.A. 159 28 58N 100 35W
Quemoy, I. = Chinmen Tao, I. 109 24 25N 118 25 E
Quemú-Quemú 172 36 3S 63 36W
Quendale, B. of 36 59 53N 1 20W
Quequén 172 38 30S 58 30W
Querein 123 13 30N 34 50 E
Querétaro 164 20 40N 100 23W
Querétaro □ 164 20 30N 100 30W
Querfurt 48 51 22N 11 33 E
Quesada 59 37 51N 3 4W
Quesnel 152 53 5N 122 30W
Quesnel L. 152 52 30N 121 20W
Quesnel, R. 152 52 58N 122 29W
Quest, Pte. 151 49 52N 64 40W
Questa 161 36 45N 105 35W
Questembert 42 47 40N 2 28W
Quetico 150 48 45N 90 55W
Quetico Prov. Park 150 48 30N 91 45W
Quetta 93 30 15N 66 55 E
Quetta □ 93 30 15N 66 55 E
Quezaltenango 166 14 40N 91 30W
Quezon City 103 14 38N 121 0 E
Qui Nhon 101 13 40N 109 13 E
Quiaca, La 172 22 5S 65 35W
Quibaxi 124 8 24S 14 27 E
Quibdó 174 5 42N 76 40W
Quiberon 42 47 29N 3 9W
Quibor 174 9 56N 69 37W
Quick 152 54 36N 126 54W
Quickborn 48 53 42N 9 52 E
Quiet L. 152 61 5N 133 5W
Quiévrain 47 50 24N 3 41 E
Quiindy 172 25 58S 57 14W
Quila 164 24 23N 107 13W
Quilán, C. 176 43 15S 74 30W
Quilengues 125 14 12S 14 12 E
Quilimarí 172 32 5S 70 30W
Quilino 172 30 14S 64 29W
Quillabamba 174 12 50S 72 50W
Quillagua 172 21 40S 69 40W
Quillaicillo 172 31 17S 71 40W
Quillan 44 42 53N 2 10 E
Quillebeuf 42 49 28N 0 30 E
Quillota 172 32 54S 71 16W
Quilmes 172 34 43S 58 15W
Quilon 97 8 50N 76 38 E
Quilpie 139 26 35S 144 11 E
Quilpué 172 33 5S 71 33W
Quilty 39 52 50N 9 27W
Quilua 127 16 17S 39 54 E
Quimilí 172 27 40S 62 30W
Quimper 42 48 0N 4 9W
Quimperlé 42 47 53N 3 33W
Quin 39 52 50N 8 52W
Quinag 36 58 13N 5 5W
Quincy, Calif., U.S.A. 160 39 56N 121 0W
Quincy, Fla., U.S.A. 157 30 34N 84 34W
Quincy, Ill., U.S.A. 158 39 55N 91 20W
Quincy, Mass., U.S.A. 162 42 14N 71 0W
Quincy, Wash., U.S.A. 160 47 22N 119 56W
Quines 172 32 13S 65 48W
Quinga 127 15 49S 40 15 E
Quingey 43 47 7N 5 52 E
Quinhagak 147 59 45N 162 0W
Quintana de la Serena 57 38 45N 5 40W
Quintana Roo □ 165 19 0N 88 0W
Quintanar de la Orden 58 39 36N 3 5W
Quintanar de la Sierra 58 41 57N 2 55W
Quintanar del Rey 59 39 21N 1 56W
Quintero 172 32 45S 71 30W
Quintin 42 48 26N 2 56W
Quinto 58 41 25N 0 32W
Quinyambie 139 30 15S 141 0 E
Quipar, R. 59 37 58N 2 3W
Quirihue 172 36 15S 72 35W
Quirindi 141 31 28S 150 40 E
Quiriquire 174 9 59N 63 13W
Quiroga 56 42 28N 7 18W
Quirpon I. 151 51 32N 55 28W
Quisiro 174 10 53N 71 17W
Quissac 45 43 55N 4 0 E
Quissanga 127 12 24S 40 28 E
Quitilipi 172 26 50S 60 13W
Quitman, Ga., U.S.A. 157 30 49N 83 35W
Quitman, Miss., U.S.A. 157 32 2N 88 42W
Quitman, Tex., U.S.A. 159 32 48N 95 25W
Quito 174 0 15S 78 35W
Quixadá 170 4 55S 39 0W
Quixaxe 127 15 17S 40 4 E
Quixeramobim 170 5 12S 39 17W
Qul'ân, Jazâ'ir 122 24 22N 35 31 E
Qumran 90 31 43N 35 27 E
Quneitra 90 33 7N 35 48 E
Quoich L. 36 57 4N 5 20W
Quoile, R. 38 54 21N 5 40W
Quoin I. 136 14 54S 129 32 E
Quoin Pt., N.Z. 143 46 19S 170 11 E
Quoin Pt., S. Afr. 128 34 46S 19 37 E
Quondong 140 33 6S 140 18 E
Quorn, Austral. 140 32 25S 138 0 E
Quorn, Can. 150 49 25N 90 55W
Quorndon 28 52 45N 1 10W
Qûs 122 25 55N 32 50 E
Quseir 122 26 7N 34 16 E
Qusra 90 32 5N 35 20 E
Quthing 129 30 25S 27 36 E
Quynh Nhai 100 21 49N 103 33 E
Qytet Stalin (Kuçove) 68 40 47N 19 57 E

R

Ra, Ko 101 9 13N 98 16 E
Raa. 73 56 0N 12 45 E
Råå 73 56 0N 12 45 E
Raahana 90 32 12N 34 52 E
Raahe 74 64 40N 24 28 E
Raalte 46 52 23N 6 16 E
Raamsdonksveer 47 51 43N 4 52 E
Raasay I. 36 57 25N 6 4W
Raasay, Sd. of 36 57 30N 6 8W
Rab 63 44 45N 14 45 E
Rab, I. 63 44 45N 14 45 E
Raba 103 8 36S 118 55 E
Rába, R. 54 47 38N 17 38 E
Rabaçal, R. 56 41 41N 7 15W
Rabah 121 13 5N 5 30 E
Rabai 126 3 50S 39 31 E
Rabaraba 135 9 58S 149 49 E
Rabastens 44 43 50N 1 43 E
Rabastens, Hautes Pyrénées 44 43 25N 0 10 E
Rabat 118 34 2N 6 48W
Rabaul 135 4 24S 152 18 E
Rabbalshede 73 58 40N 11 27 E
Rabbit L. 153 47 0N 79 38W
Rabbit Lake 153 53 8N 107 46W
Rabbit, R. 152 59 41N 127 12W
Rabbitskin, R. 152 61 47N 120 42W
Rabigh 92 22 50N 39 5 E
Rabka 54 49 37N 19 59 E
Rača 66 44 14N 21 0 E
Răcale 65 39 57N 18 6 E
Racalmuto 64 37 25N 13 41 E
Racconigi 62 44 47N 7 41 E
Race, C. 151 46 40N 53 5W
Raceview 108 27 38S 152 47 E
Rach Gia 101 10 5N 105 5 E
Raciaz 54 52 46N 20 10 E
Racibórz (Ratibor) 54 50 7N 18 18 E
Racine 156 42 41N 87 51W
Rackheath 29 52 41N 1 22 E
Rackwick 37 58 52N 3 23W
Radama, Is. 129 14 0S 47 47 E
Radama, Presqu'île d' 129 14 16S 47 53 E
Radan, mt. 66 42 59N 21 29 E
Radbuza, R. 52 49 35N 13 5 E
Radcliffe, Gr. Manch., U.K. 32 53 35N 2 19W
Radcliffe, Notts., U.K. 33 52 57N 1 3W
Rade 71 59 21N 10 53 E
Radeburg 48 51 6N 13 45 E
Radeče 63 46 5N 15 14 E
Radekhov 80 50 25N 24 32 E
Radford 156 37 8N 80 32W
Radhanpur 94 23 50N 71 38 E
Radika, R. 66 41 38N 20 37 E
Radisson 153 52 30N 107 20W
Radium Hill 133 32 30S 140 42 E
Radium Hot Springs 152 50 48N 116 12W
Radkow 54 50 30N 16 24 E
Radley 28 51 42N 1 14W
Radlin 54 50 3N 18 29 E
Radna 66 46 7N 21 41 E
Radnevo 67 42 17N 25 58 E
Radnice 52 49 51N 13 35 E
Radnor (□) 26 52 20N 3 20W
Radnor Forest 31 52 17N 3 10W
Radom 54 51 23N 21 12 E
Radom □ 54 51 30N 21 0 E
Radomir 66 42 37N 23 4 E
Radomsko 54 51 5N 19 28 E
Radomyshl 80 50 30N 29 12 E
Radomysl Wielki 54 50 14N 21 15 E
Radoszyce 54 51 4N 20 15 E
Radoviš 66 41 38N 22 28 E
Radovljica 63 46 22N 14 12 E
Radöy I. 71 60 40N 4 55 E
Radstadt 52 47 24N 13 28 E
Radstock 28 51 17N 2 25W
Radstock, C. 139 33 12S 134 20 E
Raduša 66 42 7N 21 15 E
Radviliškis 80 55 49N 23 33 E
Radville 153 49 30N 104 15W
Radymno 54 49 59N 22 52 E
Radyr 31 51 32N 3 16W
Radzanów 54 52 56N 20 8 E
Radziejów 54 52 40N 18 30 E
Radzyn Chełminski 54 53 23N 18 55 E
Rae 152 62 50N 116 3W
Rae Bareli 95 26 18N 81 20 E
Rae Isthmus 149 66 40N 87 30W
Raeside, L. 137 29 20S 122 0 E
Raetihi 142 39 25S 175 17 E
Rafaela 172 31 10S 61 30W
Rafah 122 31 18N 34 14 E
Rafai 126 4 59N 23 58 E
Raffadali 64 37 23N 13 29 E
Rafhā 92 29 35N 43 35 E
Rafid 90 32 57N 35 52 E
Rafsanjān 93 30 30N 56 5 E
Raft Pt. 136 16 4S 124 26 E
Ragag 123 10 59N 24 40 E
Ragama 93 7 0N 79 50 E
Ragged Mt. 137 33 27S 123 25 E
Raglan, Austral. 138 23 42S 150 49 E
Raglan, N.Z. 142 37 55S 174 55 E
Raglan, U.K. 31 51 46N 2 51W
Ragueneau 151 49 11N 68 18W
Ragunda 72 63 6N 16 23 E
Ragusa 65 36 56N 14 42 E
Raha 103 8 20S 118 40 E
Rahad el Berdi 117 11 20N 23 40 E
Rahad, Nahr er 123 12 40N 35 30 E
Rahden 48 52 26N 8 36 E
Raheita 123 12 46N 43 4 E
Raheng = Tak 100 17 5N 99 10 E
Rahimyar Khan 94 28 30N 70 25 E
Rahotu 142 39 20S 173 49 E
Raichur 96 16 10N 77 20 E
Raiganj 95 25 37N 88 10 E
Raigarh, Madhya Pradesh, India 96 21 56N 83 25 E
Raigarh, Orissa, India 96 19 51N 82 6 E
Raiis 92 23 33N 38 43 E
Raijua 103 10 37S 121 36 E
Railton 138 41 25S 146 28 E
Rainbow 140 35 55S 142 0 E
Rainbow Lake 152 58 30N 119 23W
Rainham 29 51 22N 0 36 E
Rainier 160 46 4N 123 0W
Rainier, Mt. 160 46 50N 121 50W
Rainworth 33 53 8N 1 6W
Rainy L. 153 48 30N 92 30W
Rainy River 153 48 50N 94 30W
Raipur 96 21 17N 81 45 E
Raith 150 48 50N 90 0W
Raj Nandgaon 99 21 0N 81 0 E
Raja Empat, Kepulauan 103 0 30S 129 40 E
Raja-Jooseppi 74 68 28N 28 29 E
Raja, Ujung 102 3 40N 96 25 E
Rajahmundry 96 17 1N 81 48 E
Rajang, R. 102 2 30N 113 30 E
Rajapalaiyarm 97 9 25N 77 35 E
Rajasthan □ 94 26 45N 73 30 E
Rajasthan Canal 94 30 31N 71 0 E
Rajauri 95 33 25N 74 21 E
Rajbari 98 23 47N 89 41 E
Rajgarh, Mad. P., India 94 24 2N 76 45 E
Rajgarh, Raj., India 94 28 40N 75 25 E
Rajgród 54 53 42N 22 42 E
Rajhenburg 63 46 1N 15 29 E
Rajkot 94 22 15N 70 56 E
Rajmahal Hills 95 24 30N 87 30 E
Rajnandgaon 96 21 5N 81 5 E
Rajojooseppi 74 68 25N 28 30 E
Rajpipla 96 21 50N 73 30 E
Rajpura 94 30 32N 76 32 E
Rajshahi 98 24 22N 88 39 E
Rajshahi □ 95 25 0N 89 0 E
Rakaia 143 43 45S 172 1 E
Rakaia, R. 143 43 26S 171 47 E
Rakan, Ras 93 26 10N 51 20 E
Rakaposhi 95 36 10N 74 0 E
Rakaposhi, mt. 93 36 20N 74 30 E
Rakha 122 18 25N 41 30 E
Rakhni 94 30 4N 69 56 E
Rakitovo 67 41 59N 24 5 E
Rakkestad 71 59 25N 11 21 E
Rakoniewice 54 52 10N 16 16 E
Rakops 128 21 1S 24 28 E
Rákospalota 53 47 30N 19 5 E
Rakovica 63 44 59N 15 38 E
Rakovník 52 50 6N 13 42 E
Rakovski 67 42 21N 24 57 E
Raleigh, Can. 150 49 30N 92 5W
Raleigh, U.S.A. 150 35 46N 78 38W
Raleigh B. 157 34 50N 76 15W
Ralja 66 44 33N 20 34 E
Ralls 159 33 40N 101 20W
Ralston 162 41 30N 76 57W
Rām Allāh 90 31 55N 35 10 E
Ram Hd. 141 37 47S 149 30 E
Ram, R. 152 62 1N 123 41W
Rama, Israel 90 32 56N 35 21 E
Rama, Nic. 166 12 9N 84 15W
Ramacca 65 37 24N 14 40 E
Ramachandrapuram 96 16 50N 82 4 E
Ramadi 92 33 28N 43 15 E
Ramales de la Victoria 58 43 15N 3 28W
Ramalho, Serra do 171 13 45S 44 0W
Raman 101 6 29N 101 18 E
Ramanathapuram 97 9 25N 78 55 E
Ramanetaka, B. de 129 14 13S 47 52 E
Ramas C. 97 15 5N 73 55 E
Ramat Gan 90 32 4N 34 48 E
Ramatlhabama 128 25 37S 25 33 E
Ramban 95 33 14N 75 12 E
Rambervillers 43 48 20N 6 38 E
Rambipudji 103 8 12S 113 37 E
Rambla, La 57 37 37N 4 45W
Rambouillet 43 48 40N 1 48 E
Rambre Kyun 98 19 0N 94 0 E
Ramdurg 97 15 58N 75 22 E
Rame Head 30 50 19N 4 14W
Ramechhap 95 27 25N 86 10 E
Ramelau, Mte. 103 8 55S 126 22 E
Ramenskoye 81 55 32N 38 15 E
Ramgarh, Bihar, India 95 23 40N 85 35 E
Ramgarh, Rajasthan, India 94 27 16N 75 14 E
Ramgarh, Rajasthan, India 94 27 30N 70 36 E
Ramhormoz 92 31 15N 49 35 E
Ramla 90 31 55N 34 52 E
Ramlat Zalṭan 119 28 30N 19 30 E
Ramlu Mt. 123 13 32N 41 40 E
Ramme 73 56 30N 8 11 E
Rammun 90 31 55N 35 17 E
Ramna Stacks, Is. 36 60 40N 1 20W
Ramnad = Ramanathapuram 97 9 25N 78 55 E
Ramnagar 95 32 47N 75 18 E
Ramnäs 72 59 46N 16 12 E
Ramon 81 52 8N 39 21 E
Ramona 163 33 1N 116 56W
Ramor L. 38 53 50N 7 5W
Ramore 150 48 30N 80 25W
Ramos Arizpe 164 23 35N 100 59W
Ramos, R. 164 25 35N 105 3W
Ramoutsa 128 24 50S 25 52 E
Rampart 147 65 0N 150 15W
Rampside 32 54 6N 3 10W
Rampur, H.P., India 94 31 26N 77 43 E
Rampur, M.P., India 94 23 25N 73 53 E
Rampur, Orissa, India 96 21 48N 83 58 E
Rampur, U.P., India 94 28 50N 79 5 E
Rampura 94 24 30N 75 27 E
Rampurhat 95 24 10N 87 50 E
Ramsbottom 32 53 36N 2 20W
Ramsbury 28 51 26N 1 37W
Ramsel 47 51 2N 4 50 E
Ramsele 74 63 31N 16 27 E
Ramsey, Can. 150 47 25N 82 20W
Ramsey, Cambs., U.K. 29 52 27N 0 6W
Ramsey, Essex, U.K. 29 51 55N 1 12 E
Ramsey, I. of M., U.K. 32 54 20N 4 21W
Ramsgate 29 51 20N 1 25 E
Ramshai 98 26 44N 88 51 E
Rämshyttan 72 60 17N 15 15 E
Ramsjö 72 62 11N 15 37 E
Ramtek 96 21 20N 79 15 E
Ramu, R. 135 4 0S 144 41 E
Ramvik 72 62 49N 17 51 E
Ranaghat 95 23 15N 88 35 E
Ranahu 94 25 55N 69 45 E
Ranau 102 6 2N 116 40 E
Rancagua 172 34 10S 70 50W
Rance 47 50 9N 4 16 E
Rance, R. 42 48 34N 1 59W
Rancharia 171 22 15S 50 55W

Rancheria, R. 152 60 13N 129 7W
Ranchester 160 44 57N 107 12W
Ranchi 95 23 19N 85 27 E
Rancu 70 44 32N 24 15 E
Rand 141 35 33 S 146 32 E
Randallstown 162 39 22N 76 48W
Randalstown 38 54 45N 6 20W
Randan 44 46 2N 3 21 E
Randazzo 65 37 53N 14 56 E
Randböl 73 55 43N 9 17 E
Randers 73 56 29N 10 1 E
Randers Fjord 73 56 37N 10 20 E
Randfontein 129 26 8 S 27 45 E
Randolph, Mass., U.S.A. 162 42 10N 71 3W
Randolph, Utah, U.S.A. 160 41 43N 111 10W
Randolph, Vt., U.S.A. 162 43 55N 72 39W
Randsburg 163 35 26N 117 44W
Randsfjord 71 60 15N 10 25 E
Råne älv 74 66 26N 21 10 E
Råneå 74 65 53N 22 18 E
Ranfurly 143 45 7 S 170 6 E
Rangae 101 6 19N 101 44 E
Rangamati 98 22 38 S 92 12 E
Rangataua 142 39 26 S 175 28 E
Rangaunu B. 142 34 51 S 173 15 E
Rångedala 73 57 47N 13 9 E
Rangeley 156 44 58N 70 33W
Rangely 160 40 3N 108 53W
Ranger 159 32 30N 98 42W
Rangia 98 26 15N 91 20 E
Rangiora 143 43 19 S 172 36 E
Rangitaiki 130 38 52 S 176 23 E
Rangitaiki, R. 142 37 54 S 176 49 E
Rangitata, R. 143 43 45 S 171 15 E
Rangitikei, R. 142 40 17 S 175 15 E
Rangitoto Range 142 38 25 S 175 35 E
Rangkasbitung 103 6 22 S 106 16 E
Rangon 99 16 45N 96 20 E
Rangon, R. 99 16 28N 96 40 E
Rangoon 98 16 45N 96 20 E
Rangpur 98 25 42N 89 22 E
Rangsit 100 13 59N 100 37 E
Ranibennur 97 14 35N 75 30 E
Raniganj 95 23 40N 87 15 E
Ranipet 97 12 56N 79 23 E
Raniwara 93 24 50N 72 10 E
Ranken, R. 138 20 31 S 137 36 E
Rankin 159 31 16N 101 56W
Rankin Inlet 148 62 30N 93 0W
Rankin's Springs 141 33 49 S 146 14 E
Rannes 138 24 6 S 150 11 E
Rannoch L. 37 56 41N 4 20W
Rannoch Moor 34 56 38N 4 48W
Rannoch Sta. 37 56 40N 4 32W
Ranobe, B. de 129 23 3 S 43 33 E
Ranohira 129 22 29 S 45 24 E
Ranomafana, Tamatave, Madag. 129 18 57 S 48 50 E
Ranomafana, Tuléar, Madag. 129 24 34 S 47 0 E
Ranong 101 9 56N 98 40 E
Rantau 102 4 15N 98 5 E
Rantauprapat 102 2 15N 99 50 E
Rantemario 103 3 15 S 119 57 E
Rantis 90 32 4N 35 3 E
Rantoul 156 40 18N 88 10W
Ranum 73 56 54N 9 14 E
Ranwanlenau 128 19 37 S 22 49 E
Raon-l'Étape 43 48 24N 6 50 E
Raoui, Erg er 118 29 0N 2 0W
Rapa Iti, I. 131 27 35 S 144 20W
Rapallo 62 44 21N 9 12 E
Rapang 103 3 45 S 119 55 E
Rāpch 93 25 40N 59 15 E
Raphoe 38 54 52N 7 36W
Rapid City 158 44 0N 103 0W
Rapid, R. 152 59 15N 129 5W
Rapid River 156 45 55N 87 0W
Rapides des Joachims 150 46 13N 77 43W
Rapla 80 58 88N 24 52 E
Rapness 37 59 15N 2 51W
Raposos 171 19 57 S 43 48W
Rappahannock, R. 162 37 35N 76 17W
Rapperswil 51 47 14N 8 45 E
Raqqa 92 36 0N 38 55 E
Raquete 127 14 8 S 38 13 E
Raquette Lake 162 43 49N 74 40W
Rareagh 38 53 37N 8 37W
Rarotonga, I. 131 21 30 S 160 0W
Ras al Khaima 93 25 50N 56 5 E
Ra's Al-Unūf 119 30 25N 18 15 E
Ra's at Tannurah 92 26 40N 50 10 E
Ras Dashan, mt. 123 13 8N 37 45 E
Ras el Ma 118 34 26N 0 50W
Ras Gharib 122 28 6N 33 18 E
Ras Mallap 122 29 18N 32 50 E
Rasa, Punta 176 40 50 S 62 15W
Rasboda 72 60 8N 16 58 E
Raseiniai 80 55 25N 23 5 E
Rashad 123 11 55N 31 0 E
Rashîd 122 31 21N 30 22 E
Rashîd, Masabb 122 31 22N 30 17 E
Rasht 92 37 20N 49 40 E
Rasi Salai 100 15 20N 104 9 E
Rasipuram 97 11 30N 78 25 E
Raška 66 43 19N 20 39 E
Raso, C. 170 1 50N 50 0W
Rason, L. 137 28 45 S 124 25 E
Raşova 70 44 15N 27 55 E
Rasovo 67 43 42N 23 17 E
Rasra 95 25 50N 83 50 E
Rass el Oued 119 35 57N 5 2 E
Rasskazovo 81 52 35N 41 50 E
Rastatt 49 48 50N 8 12 E
Rastu 70 43 53N 23 16 E
Raszków 54 51 43N 17 40 E
Rat Buri 100 13 30N 99 54 E
Rat, Is. 147 51 50N 178 15 E
Rat, R. 152 56 0N 99 30W
Rat River 152 61 7N 112 36W
Rätan 72 62 27N 14 33 E
Ratangarh 94 28 5N 74 35 E
Rath 95 25 36N 79 37 E
Rath Luirc (Charleville) 39 52 21N 8 40W
Rathangan 39 53 13N 7 0W
Rathconrah 38 53 30N 7 32W
Rathcoole 39 53 17N 6 29W
Rathcormack 39 52 5N 8 19W
Rathdowney 39 52 52N 7 36W
Rathdrum, Ireland 39 52 57N 6 13W
Rathdrum, U.S.A. 160 47 50N 116 58W
Ratheclaung 98 20 29N 92 45 E
Rathen 37 57 38N 1 58W
Rathenow 48 52 38N 12 23 E
Rathfriland 38 54 12N 6 12W
Rathkeale 39 52 32N 8 57W
Rathkenny 38 53 45N 6 39W
Rathlin I. 38 55 18N 6 14W
Rathlin O'Birne I. 38 54 40N 8 50W
Rathmelton 38 55 3N 7 35W
Rathmolyon 38 53 30N 6 49W
Rathmore, Cork, Ireland 39 51 30N 9 21W
Rathmore, Kerry, Ireland 39 52 5N 9 12W
Rathmore, Kildare, Ireland 39 53 13N 6 35W
Rathmullen 38 55 6N 7 32W
Rathnure 39 52 30N 6 47W
Rathvilly 72 52 54N 6 42W
Ratlam 94 23 20N 75 0 E
Ratnagiri 96 16 57N 73 18 E
Ratnapura 97 6 40N 80 20 E
Ratoath 38 53 30N 6 27W
Raton 159 37 0N 104 30W
Rattaphum 101 7 8N 100 16 E
Ratten 52 47 28N 15 44 E
Rattray 37 56 36N 3 20W
Rattray Hd. 37 57 38N 1 50W
Rättvik 72 60 52N 15 7 E
Ratz, Mt. 152 57 23N 132 12W
Ratzeburg 48 53 41N 10 46 E
Raub 101 3 47N 101 52 E
Rauch 172 36 45 S 59 5W
Raufarhöfn 74 66 27N 15 57W
Raufoss 71 60 44N 10 37 E
Raukumara Ra. 142 38 5 S 177 55 E
Raul Soares 171 20 5 S 42 22W
Rauland 71 59 43N 8 0 E
Rauma 75 61 10N 21 30 E
Rauma, R. 71 62 34N 7 43 E
Raundal 71 60 40N 6 37 E
Raunds 29 52 20N 0 32W
Raung, Mt. 103 8 8 S 114 4 E
Raurkela 96 22 14N 84 50 E
Rava Russkaya 80 50 15N 23 42 E
Ravanusa 64 37 16N 13 58 E
Ravar 93 31 20N 56 51 E
Ravels 47 51 22N 5 0 E
Ravena 162 42 28N 73 49W
Ravenglass 32 54 21N 3 25W
Ravenna, Italy 63 44 28N 12 15 E
Ravenna, U.S.A. 158 41 3N 98 58W
Ravensburg 49 47 48N 9 38 E
Ravenshoe 138 17 37 S 145 29 E
Ravenstein 46 51 47N 5 39 E
Ravensthorpe 137 33 35 S 120 2 E
Ravenstonedale 32 54 26N 2 26W
Ravenswood, Austral. 138 20 6 S 146 54 E
Ravenswood, U.S.A. 156 38 58N 81 47W
Ravensworth 141 32 26 S 151 4 E
Raventasón 174 6 10 S 81 0W
Ravi, R. 94 31 0N 73 0 E
Ravna Gora 63 45 24N 14 50 E
Ravna Reka 66 43 59N 21 35 E
Ravnstrup 73 56 27N 9 17 E
Rawa Mazowiecka 54 51 46N 20 12 E
Rawalpindi 94 33 38N 73 8 E
Rawalpindi □ 93 33 10N 72 50 E
Rawāndūz 92 36 40N 44 30 E
Rawang 101 3 20N 101 35 E
Rawdon 150 46 3N 73 40W
Rawene 142 35 25 S 173 32 E
Rawicz 54 51 36N 16 52 E
Rawlinna 137 30 58 S 125 28 E
Rawlins 160 41 50N 107 20W
Rawlinson Range 137 24 40 S 128 30 E
Rawmarsh 33 53 27N 1 20W
Rawson 176 43 15 S 65 0W
Rawtenstall 32 53 42N 2 18W
Rawuya 121 12 10N 6 50 E
Ray, N. Mex., U.S.A. 159 35 57N 104 8W
Ray, N.D., U.S.A. 158 48 21N 103 6W
Ray, C. 151 47 33N 59 15W
Ray Mts. 147 66 0N 152 10W
Rayachoti 97 14 4N 78 50 E
Rayadrug 97 14 40N 76 50 E
Rayagada 96 19 15N 83 20 E
Raychikhinsk 77 49 46N 129 25 E
Rayevskiy 84 54 4N 54 56 E
Rayin 93 29 40N 57 22 E
Rayleigh 29 51 36N 0 38 E
Raymond, Can. 152 49 30N 112 35W
Raymond, Calif., U.S.A. 163 37 13N 119 54W
Raymond, Wash., U.S.A. 160 46 45N 123 48W
Raymond Terrace 141 32 45 S 151 44 E
Raymondville 159 26 30N 97 50W
Raymore 153 51 25N 104 31W
Rayne 159 30 16N 92 16W
Rayón 164 29 43N 110 35W
Rayong 100 12 40N 101 20 E
Rayville 159 32 30N 91 45W
Raz, Pte. du 42 48 2N 4 47W
Razana 66 44 6N 19 55 E
Razanj 66 43 40N 21 31 E
Razdelna 67 43 13N 27 41 E
Razelm, Lacul 70 44 50N 29 0 E
Razgrad 67 43 33N 26 34 E
Razlog 67 41 53N 23 28 E
Razmak 94 32 45N 69 50 E
Razole 96 16 56N 81 48 E
Razor Back Mt. 152 51 32N 125 0W
Ré, Île de 44 46 12N 1 30W
Rea, L. 39 53 10N 8 32W
Reading, U.K. 29 51 27N 0 57W
Reading, U.S.A. 162 40 20N 75 53W
Realicó 172 35 0 S 64 15W
Réalmont 44 43 48N 2 10 E
Ream 101 10 34N 103 39 E
Reata 164 26 8N 101 5W
Reay 37 58 33N 3 48W
Rebais 43 48 50N 3 10 E
Rebecca L. 137 30 0 S 122 30 E
Rebi 103 5 30 S 134 7 E
Rebiana 117 24 12N 22 10 E
Rebun-Tō 112 45 23N 141 2 E
Recanati 63 43 24N 13 32 E
Recaş 66 45 46N 21 30 E
Recess 38 53 29N 9 4W
Recherche, Arch. of the 137 34 15 S 122 50 E
Rechitsa 80 52 13N 30 15 E
Recht 47 50 20N 6 3 E
Recife 170 8 0 S 35 0W
Recklinghausen 48 51 36N 7 10 E
Reconquista 172 29 10 S 59 45W
Recreo 172 29 25 S 65 10W
Reculver 29 51 22N 1 12 E
Recz 54 53 16N 15 31 E
Red B. 38 55 4N 6 2W
Red Bank 162 40 21N 74 4W
Red Bay 151 51 44N 56 25W
Red Bluff 160 40 11N 122 11W
Red Bluff L. 159 31 59N 103 58W
Red Cliffs 140 34 19 S 142 11 E
Red Cloud 158 40 8N 98 33W
Red Creek 162 43 14N 76 45W
Red Deer 152 52 20N 113 50W
Red Deer L. 153 52 55N 101 20W
Red Deer, R. 152 50 58N 110 0W
Red Deer R. 153 52 53N 101 1W
Red Dial 32 54 48N 3 9W
Red Hook 162 41 55N 73 53W
Red Indian L. 151 48 35N 57 0W
Red L. 158 48 0N 95 0W
Red Lake 153 51 1N 94 1W
Red Lake Falls 158 47 54N 96 30W
Red Lion 162 39 54N 76 36W
Red Lodge 160 45 10N 109 10W
Red Mountain 163 35 37N 117 38W
Red Oak 158 41 0N 95 10W
Red Point Rock 137 32 13 S 127 32 E
Red, R., Can. 153 50 24N 96 48W
Red, R., Minn., U.S.A. 158 48 10N 97 0W
Red, R., Tex., U.S.A. 159 33 57N 95 30W
Red, R. = Hong, R. 100 20 17N 106 34 E
Red Rock 150 48 55N 88 15W
Red Rock, L. 158 41 30N 93 15W
Red Sea 91 25 0N 36 0 E
Red Slate Mtn. 163 37 31N 118 52W
Red Sucker L 153 54 9N 93 40W
Red Tower Pass = Turnu Rosu P. 70 45 33N 24 17 E
Red Wharf Bay 31 53 18N 4 10W
Red Wing 158 44 32N 92 35W
Reda 54 54 40N 18 19 E
Rédange 47 49 46N 5 52 E
Redbank 108 27 36 S 152 52 E
Redbridge 29 51 35N 0 7 E
Redcar 33 54 37N 1 4W
Redcliff 153 50 10N 110 50W
Redcliffe 139 27 12 S 153 0 E
Redcliffe, Mt. 137 28 30 S 121 30 E
Redcliffs 139 34 16 S 142 10 E
Reddersburg 128 29 41 S 26 10 E
Redding 160 40 30N 122 25W
Redditch 28 52 18N 1 57W
Rede, R. 35 55 8N 2 12W
Redenção 170 4 13 S 38 43W
Redesmouth 35 55 7N 2 12W
Redfield 158 45 0N 98 30W
Redhill 29 51 14N 0 10W
Redknife, R. 152 61 14N 119 22W
Redland 37 59 6N 3 4W
Redlands 163 34 0N 117 11W
Redlynch 28 50 59N 1 42W
Redmile 33 52 54N 0 48W
Redmire 32 54 19N 1 55W
Redmond, Austral. 137 34 55 S 117 40 E
Redmond, U.S.A. 160 44 19N 121 11W
Redon 42 47 40N 2 6W
Redonda, I. 167 16 58N 62 19W
Redondela 56 42 15N 8 38W
Redondo 57 38 39N 7 37W
Redondo Beach 163 33 52N 118 26W
Redrock Pt. 152 62 11N 115 2W
Redruth 30 50 14N 5 14W
Redvers 153 49 35N 101 40W
Redwater 152 53 55N 113 6W
Redwood City 163 37 30N 122 15W
Redwood Falls 158 44 30N 95 2W
Ree, L. 38 53 35N 8 0W
Reed City 156 43 52N 85 30W
Reed L. 153 54 38N 100 30W
Reed, Mt. 151 52 5N 68 5W
Reeder 158 47 7N 102 52W
Reedham 29 52 34N 1 33 E
Reedley 163 36 36N 119 27W
Reedsburg 158 43 34N 90 5W
Reedsport 160 43 45N 124 4W
Reedy Creek 140 36 58 S 140 2 E
Reef Pt. 142 35 10 S 173 5 E
Reefton, N.S.W., Austral. 141 34 15 S 147 27 E
Reefton, S. Australia, Austral. 109 34 57 S 138 55 E
Reefton, N.Z. 143 42 6 S 171 51 E
Reepham 29 52 46N 1 6 E
Reeth 32 54 23N 1 56W
Refsnes 71 61 9N 7 14 E
Reftele 73 57 11N 13 35 E
Refugio 159 28 18N 97 17W
Rega, R. 54 53 52N 15 16 E
Regalbuto 65 37 40N 14 38 E
Regar 85 38 30N 68 14 E
Regavim 90 32 32N 35 2 E
Regen 49 48 58N 13 9 E
Regeneração 170 6 15 S 42 41W
Regensburg 49 49 1N 12 7 E
Regensdorf 51 47 26N 8 28 E
Réggio di Calábria 65 38 7N 15 38 E
Réggio nell' Emilia 62 44 42N 10 38 E
Regina 153 50 30N 104 35W
Registan □ 93 30 15N 65 0 E
Registro 173 24 29 S 47 49W
Reguengos de Monsaraz 57 38 25N 7 32W
Rehar 95 23 36N 82 52 E
Rehoboth, Damaraland, Namibia 128 23 15 S 17 4 E
Rehoboth, Ovamboland, Namibia 128 17 55 S 15 5 E
Rehoboth Beach 162 38 43N 75 5W
Rehovot 90 31 54N 34 48 E
Reichenbach, Ger. 48 50 36N 12 19 E
Reichenbach, Switz. 50 46 38N 7 42 E
Reid 137 30 49 S 128 26 E
Reid River 138 19 40 S 146 48 E
Reiden 50 47 14N 7 59 E
Reidsville 157 36 21N 79 40W
Reigate 29 51 14N 0 11W
Reillo 58 39 54N 1 53W
Reims 43 49 15N 4 0 E
Reina 90 32 43N 35 18 E
Reina Adelaida, Arch. 176 52 20 S 74 0W
Reinach, Aargau, Switz. 50 47 14N 8 11 E
Reinach, Basel, Switz. 50 47 29N 7 35 E
Reinbeck 158 42 18N 92 40W
Reindeer I. 153 52 30N 98 0W
Reindeer L. 153 57 15N 102 15W
Reindeer, R. 153 55 36N 103 11W
Reine, La 150 48 50N 79 30W
Reinga, C. 142 34 25 S 172 43 E
Reinosa 56 43 2N 4 15W
Reinosa, Paso 56 42 56N 4 10W
Reira 123 15 25N 34 50 E
Reiss 37 58 29N 3 7W
Reisterstown 162 39 28N 76 50W
Reitdiep 46 53 20N 6 20 E
Reitz 129 27 48 S 28 29 E
Reivilo 128 27 36 S 24 8 E
Rejmyra 73 58 50N 15 55 E
Reka, R. 63 45 40N 14 0 E
Rekovac 66 43 51N 21 3 E
Remad, Ouedber 118 33 28N 1 20W
Remanso 170 9 41 S 42 4W
Remarkable, Mt. 140 32 48 S 138 10 E
Rembang 103 6 42 S 111 21 E
Remchi 118 35 2N 1 26W
Remedios, Colomb. 174 7 2N 74 41W
Remedios, Panama 166 8 15N 81 50W
Remeshk 93 26 55N 58 50 E
Remetea 70 46 45N 29 29 E
Remich 47 49 32N 6 22 E
Remiremont 43 48 0N 6 36 E
Remo 123 6 48N 41 20 E
Remontnoye 83 47 44N 43 37 E
Remoulins 45 43 55N 4 35 E
Remscheid 48 51 11N 7 12 E
Remsen 162 43 19N 75 11W
Rena 71 61 8N 11 20 E
Renda 123 14 30N 40 0 E
Rende 65 39 19N 16 11 E
Rendeux 47 50 14N 5 30 E
Rendina 69 39 4N 21 58 E
Rendsburg 48 54 18N 9 41 E
Rene 77 66 2N 179 25W
Renee, oilfield 19 58 4N 0 16 E
Renens 50 46 31N 6 34 E
Renfrew, Can. 150 45 30N 76 40W
Renfrew, U.K. 34 55 52N 4 24W
Renfrew (□) 26 55 50N 4 30W
Rengat 102 0 30 S 102 45 E
Rengo 172 34 24 S 70 50W
Reni 82 45 28N 28 15 E
Renigunta 97 13 38N 79 30 E
Renish Pt. 36 57 44N 6 59W
Renkum 46 51 58N 5 43 E
Renmark 140 34 11 S 140 43 E
Rennell Sd. 152 53 23N 132 35W

Renner Springs Teleg. Off. 138 18 20S 133 47E
Rennes 42 48 7N 1 41W
Rennesøy 71 59 6N 5 43E
Reno 160 39 30N 119 50W
Reno, R. 63 44 45N 11 40E
Renovo 156 41 20N 77 47W
Rens 55 54 54N 9 5E
Rensselaer, Ind., U.S.A. 156 41 0N 87 10W
Rensselaer, N.Y., U.S.A. 162 42 38N 73 41W
Rentería 58 43 19N 1 54W
Renton 160 47 30N 122 9W
Renwicktown 143 41 30S 173 51E
Réo 120 12 28N 2 35E
Réole, La 44 44 35N 0 1W
Reotipur 95 25 33N 83 45E
Repalle 97 16 2N 80 45E
Répcelak 53 47 24N 17 1E
Repton 28 52 50N 1 32W
Republic, Mich., U.S.A. 156 46 25N 87 59W
Republic, Wash., U.S.A. 160 48 38N 118 42W
Republican City 158 40 9N 99 20W
Republican, R. 158 40 0N 98 30W
Repulse B., Antarct. 13 64 30S 99 30E
Repulse B., Austral. 133 20 31S 148 45E
Repulse Bay 149 66 30N 86 30W
Requena, Peru 174 5 5S 73 52W
Requena, Spain 59 39 30N 1 4W
Resele 72 63 20N 17 5E
Resen 66 41 5N 21 0E
Reserve, Can. 153 52 28N 102 39W
Reserve, U.S.A. 161 33 50N 108 54W
Resht = Rasht 92 37 20N 49 40E
Resistencia 172 27 30S 59 0W
Reşiţa 66 45 18N 21 53E
Resko 54 53 47N 15 25E
Resolution I., Can. 149 61 30N 65 0W
Resolution I., N.Z. 143 45 40S 166 40E
Resolven 31 51 43N 3 42W
Resplandes 170 6 17S 45 13W
Resplendor 171 19 20S 41 15W
Ressano Garcia 129 25 25S 32 0E
Rest Downs 141 31 48S 146 21E
Reston, Can. 153 49 33N 101 6W
Reston, U.K. 35 55 51N 2 11W
Restrepo 174 4 15N 73 33W
Reszel 54 54 4N 21 10E
Retalhuleu 166 14 33N 91 46W
Reteag 70 47 10N 24 0E
Retem, O. el 119 33 40N 0 40E
Retenue, Lac de 127 11 0S 27 0E
Rethel 43 49 30N 4 20E
Rethem 48 52 47N 9 25E
Réthímnon 69 35 15N 24 40E
Réthímnon □ 69 35 23N 24 28E
Retie 47 51 16N 5 5E
Rétiers 42 47 55N 1 25W
Retiro 172 35 59S 71 47W
Retortillo 56 40 48N 6 21W
Rétság 53 47 58N 19 10E
Reuland 47 50 12N 6 8E
Réunion, Î. 11 22 0S 56 0E
Reus 58 41 10N 1 5E
Reusel 47 51 21N 5 9E
Reuss, R. 51 47 16N 8 24E
Reuterstadt-Stavenhagen 48 53 41N 12 54E
Reutlingen 49 48 28N 9 13E
Reutte 52 47 29N 10 42E
Reuver 47 51 17N 6 5E
Revda 84 56 48N 59 57E
Revel 44 43 28N 2 0E
Revelganj 95 25 50N 84 40E
Revelstoke 152 51 0N 118 0W
Revigny 43 48 50N 5 0E
Revilla Gigedo, Is. de 131 18 40N 112 0W
Revillagigedo I. 152 55 50N 131 20W
Revin 43 49 55N 4 39E
Revolyutsii, Pix 85 38 31N 72 21E
Revuè, R. 127 19 30S 33 35E
Rewa 95 24 33N 81 25E
Rewari 94 28 15N 76 40E
Rex 147 64 10N 149 20W
Rexburg 160 43 45N 111 50W
Rey Bouba 117 8 40N 14 15E
Rey Malabo 121 3 45N 8 50E
Reyes, Pt. 163 37 59N 123 2W
Reykjahlið 74 65 40N 16 55W
Reykjanes 74 63 48N 22 40W
Reykjavík 74 64 10N 21 57E
Reynolds 153 49 40N 95 55W
Reynolds Ra. 136 22 30S 133 0E
Reynosa 165 26 5N 98 18W
•Rezā'iyeh 92 37 40N 45 0E
•Rezā'iyeh, Daryācheh-ye 92 37 30N 45 30E
Rēzekne 80 56 30N 27 17E
Rezh 84 57 23N 61 24E
Rezina 70 47 45N 29 0E
Rezovo 67 42 0N 28 0E
Rgotina 67 44 1N 22 18E
Rhaeadr Ogwen 31 53 8N 4 0W
Rharis, O. 119 26 30N 5 4E
Rhayader 31 52 19N 3 30W
Rheden 46 52 0N 6 3E
Rheidol, R. 31 52 25N 3 57W
Rhein 153 51 25N 102 15W
Rhein, R. 48 51 42N 6 20E
Rheinbach 48 50 38N 6 54E
Rheine 48 52 17N 7 25E
Rheineck 51 47 28N 9 31E
Rheinfelden 50 47 32N 7 47E
Rheinland-Pfalz □ 49 50 50N 7 0E
Rheinsberg 48 53 6N 12 52E
Rheinwaldhorn 51 46 30N 9 3E
Rhenen 46 51 58N 5 33E
Rheydt 48 51 10N 6 24E
Rhin, R. 48 51 42N 6 20E
Rhinau 43 48 19N 7 43E
Rhine, R. = Rhein 47 51 42N 6 20E
Rhinebeck 162 41 56N 73 55W
Rhinelander 158 45 38N 89 29W
Rhino Camp 126 3 0N 31 22E
Rhisnes 47 50 31N 4 48E
Rhiw 31 52 49N 4 37W
Rho 62 45 31N 9 2E
Rhode Island □ 162 41 38N 71 37W
Rhodes = Ródhos 69 36 15N 28 10E
Rhodes' Tomb 127 20 30S 28 30E
Rhodesia = Zimbabwe ■ 127 20 0S 30 0E
Rhodope Mts. = Rhodopi Planina 67 41 40N 24 20E
Rhondda 31 51 39N 3 30W
Rhône □ 45 45 54N 4 35E
Rhône, R. 45 43 28N 4 42E
Rhos-on-Sea 31 53 18N 3 46W
Rhosllanerchrugog 31 53 3N 3 4W
Rhossilli 31 51 34N 4 18W
Rhu Coigach, C. 36 58 6N 5 27W
Rhuddlan 31 53 17N 3 28W
Rhum, I. 36 57 0N 6 20W
Rhyl 31 53 19N 3 29W
Rhymney 31 51 45N 3 17W
Rhynie 37 57 20N 2 50W
Ri-Aba 121 3 28N 8 40E
Riachão 170 7 20S 46 37W
Riachão do Jacuípe 171 11 48S 39 21W
Riacho de Santana 171 13 37S 42 57W
Rialma 171 15 18S 49 34W
Rialto 163 34 6N 117 22W
Riang 98 27 31N 92 56E
Riaño 56 42 59N 5 0W
Rians 45 43 37N 5 44E
Riansares, R. 58 40 0N 3 0W
Riasi 95 33 10N 74 50E
Riau □ 102 0 0 102 35E
Riau, Kepulauan 102 0 30N 104 20E
Riaza 58 41 18N 3 30W
Riaza, R. 58 41 16N 3 29W
Riba de Saelices 58 40 55N 2 18E
Ribadavia 56 42 17N 8 8W
Ribadeo 56 43 35N 7 5W
Ribadesella 56 43 30N 5 7W
Ribamar 170 2 33S 44 3W
Ribas 58 42 19N 2 15E
Ribat 125 29 50N 60 55E
Ribatejo □ 55 39 15N 8 30W
Ribble, R. 32 54 13N 2 20W
Ribe 73 55 19N 8 44E
Ribe Amt □ 73 55 34N 8 30E
Ribeauvillé 43 48 10N 7 20E
Ribécourt 43 49 30N 2 55E
Ribeira 56 42 36N 8 58W
Ribeira do Pombal 170 10 50S 38 32W
Ribeirão Prêto 173 21 10S 47 50W
Ribeiro Gonçalves 170 7 32S 45 14W
Ribémont 43 49 47N 3 27E
Ribera 64 37 30N 13 13E
Ribérac 44 45 15N 0 20E
Riberalta 174 11 0S 66 0W
Ribnica 63 45 45N 14 45E
Ribnitz-Dangarten 48 54 14N 12 24E
Řičany 52 50 0N 14 40E
Riccall 33 53 50N 1 4W
Riccarton 143 43 32S 172 37E
Riccia 65 41 30N 14 50E
Riccione 63 44 0N 12 39E
Rice Lake 158 45 30N 91 42W
Rich 118 32 16N 4 30W
Rich Hill 159 38 5N 94 22W
Richards B. 129 28 48S 32 6E
Richards Deep 15 25 0S 73 0W
Richards L. 153 59 10N 107 10W
Richardson Mts. 143 44 49S 168 34E
Richardson, R. 153 58 25N 111 14W
Richardton 158 46 56N 102 22W
Riche, C. 137 34 36S 118 47E
Richelieu 42 47 0N 0 20E
Richey 158 47 42N 105 5W
Richfield, Idaho, U.S.A. 160 43 2N 114 5W
Richfield, Utah, U.S.A. 161 38 50N 112 0W
Richfield Springs 162 42 51N 74 59W
Richibucto 151 46 42N 64 54W
Richland, Ga., U.S.A. 157 32 7N 84 40W
Richland, Oreg., U.S.A. 160 44 49N 117 9W
Richland, Wash., U.S.A. 160 46 15N 119 15W
Richland Center 158 43 21N 90 22W
Richlands 156 37 7N 81 49W
Richmond, N.S.W., Austral. 141 33 35S 150 42E
Richmond, Queens., Austral. 138 20 43S 143 8E
Richmond, N.Z. 143 41 4S 173 12E
Richmond, S. Afr. 125 29 51S 30 18E
Richmond, N. Yorks., U.K. 33 54 24N 1 43W
Richmond, Surrey, U.K. 29 51 28N 0 18W
Richmond, Calif., U.S.A. 163 38 0N 122 21W
Richmond, Ind., U.S.A. 156 39 50N 84 50W
Richmond, Ky., U.S.A. 156 37 40N 84 20W
Richmond, Mo., U.S.A. 158 39 15N 93 58W
Richmond, Tex., U.S.A. 159 29 32N 95 42W
Richmond, Va., U.S.A. 162 37 33N 77 27W
Richmond Gulf 150 56 20N 75 50W
Richmond, Mt. 143 41 32S 173 22E
Richmond, Ra. 139 29 0S 152 45E
Richmond Ra. 143 41 32S 173 22E
Richterswil 51 47 13N 8 43E
Richton 157 31 23N 88 58W
Richwood 156 38 17N 80 32W
Rickmansworth 29 51 38N 0 28W
Ricla 58 41 31N 1 24W
Riddarhyttan 72 59 49N 15 33E
Ridderkerk 46 51 52N 4 35E
Riddes 50 46 11N 7 14E
Ridgecrest 163 35 38N 117 40W
Ridgedale 153 53 0N 104 10W
Ridgefield 162 41 17N 73 30W
Ridgeland 157 32 30N 80 58W
Ridgelands 138 23 16S 150 17E
Ridgetown 150 42 26N 81 52W
Ridgewood 162 40 59N 74 7W
Ridgway 156 41 25N 78 43W
Riding Mt. Nat. Park 153 50 50N 100 0W
Ridley Mt. 137 33 12S 122 7E
Ridsdale 35 55 9N 2 8W
Ried 52 48 14N 13 30E
Riehen 50 47 35N 7 39E
Riel 47 51 31N 5 1E
Rienne 47 50 0N 4 53E
Rienza, R. 63 46 49N 11 47E
Riesa 48 51 19N 13 19E
Riesi 65 37 16N 14 4E
Rietfontein 128 26 44S 20 1E
Rieti 63 42 23N 12 50E
Rieupeyroux 44 44 19N 2 12E
Rievaulx 33 54 16N 1 7W
Riez 45 43 49N 6 6E
Rifle 160 39 40N 107 50W
Rifstangi 74 66 32N 16 12W
Rift Valley 126 0 20N 36 0E
Rig Rig 117 14 13N 14 25E
Riga 80 56 53N 24 8E
Riga, G. of = Rīgas Jūras Līcis 80 57 40N 23 45E
Rīgas Jūras Līcis 80 57 40N 23 45E
Rigby 160 43 41N 111 58W
Riggins 160 45 29N 116 26W
Rignac 44 44 25N 2 16E
Rigo 138 9 41S 147 31E
Rigolet 151 54 10N 58 23W
Riihimäki 75 60 45N 24 48E
Riiser-Larsen halvøya 13 68 0S 35 0E
Riishiri-Tō 112 45 11N 141 15E
Rijau 121 11 8N 5 17E
Rijeka Crnojevica 66 42 24N 19 1E
Rijeka (Fiume) 63 45 20N 14 21E
Rijen 47 51 35N 4 55E
Rijkevorsel 47 51 21N 4 46E
Rijn, R. 47 52 5N 4 50E
Rijnsberg 46 52 11N 4 27E
Rijsbergen 47 51 31N 4 41E
Rijssen 46 52 19N 6 30E
Rijswijk 46 52 4N 4 22E
Rike 123 10 50N 39 53E
Rikita 123 5 5N 28 29E
Rila 67 42 7N 23 7E
Rila Planina 66 42 10N 23 30E
Rillington 33 54 10N 0 41W
Rilly 43 49 11N 4 3E
Rima 99 28 35N 97 5E
Rima, R. 121 13 15N 5 15E
Rimavská Sobota 53 48 22N 20 2E
Rimbey 152 52 35N 114 15W
Rimbo 72 59 44N 18 21E
Rimforsa 73 58 8N 15 42E
Rimi 121 12 58N 7 43E
Rimini 63 44 3N 12 33E
Rîmna, R. 70 45 36N 27 3E
Rîmnicu Sărat 70 45 26N 27 3E
Rîmnicu Vîlcece 70 45 9N 24 21E
Rimouski 151 48 27N 68 30W
Rinca 103 8 45S 119 35E
Rincón de Romos 164 22 14N 102 18W
Rinconada 172 22 26S 66 10W
Ringarum 73 58 21N 16 26E
Ringe 73 55 13N 10 28E
Ringel Spitz 51 46 53N 9 19E
Ringford 35 54 55N 4 3W
Ringim 121 12 13N 9 10E
Ringkøbing 73 56 5N 8 15E
Ringkøbing Amt □ 73 56 15N 8 30E
Ringling 160 46 16N 110 56W
Ringmer 29 50 53N 0 5E
Ringmoen 71 60 21N 10 6E
Ringsaker 71 60 54N 10 45E
Ringsend 38 55 2N 6 45W
Ringsjön L. 73 55 55N 13 30E
Ringsted 73 55 25N 11 46E
Ringvassøy 74 69 36N 19 15E
Ringville 39 52 3N 7 37W
Ringwood 28 50 50N 1 48W
Rinia, I. 69 37 23N 25 13E
Rinjani 65 8 20S 116 30E
Rinns, The, Reg. 34 54 52N 5 3W
Rintein 48 52 11N 9 3E
Rio Arica 174 1 35S 75 30W
Rio Branco 174 9 58S 67 49W
Río Branco 173 32 40S 53 40W
Rio Brilhante 173 21 48S 54 33W
Río Chico 174 10 19N 65 59W
Rio Claro, Brazil 173 22 19S 47 35W
Rio Claro, Trin 167 10 20N 61 25W
Río Colorado 176 39 0S 64 0W
Río Cuarto 172 33 10S 64 25W
Rio das Pedras 129 23 8S 35 28E
Rio de Contas 171 13 36S 41 48W
Rio de Janeiro 173 23 0S 43 12W
Rio de Janeiro □ 173 22 50S 43 0W
Rio del Rey 121 4 42N 8 37E
Rio do Prado 171 16 35S 40 34W
Rio do Sul 173 27 95S 49 37W
Río Gallegos 176 51 35S 69 15W
Río Grande 176 53 50S 67 45W
Rio Grande 173 32 0S 52 20W
Río Grande, Mexico 164 23 50N 103 2W
Río Grande, Nic. 166 12 54N 83 33W
Rio Grande City 159 26 30N 91 55W
Río Grande del Norte, R. 154 26 0N 97 0W
Rio Grande do Norte □ 170 5 40S 36 0W
Rio Grande do Sul □ 173 30 0S 53 0W
Rio Grande, R. 161 37 47N 106 15W
Río Hato 166 8 22N 80 10W
Rio Lagartos 165 21 36N 88 10W
Rio Largo 171 9 28S 35 50W
Rio Maior 57 39 19N 8 57W
Rio Marina 62 42 48N 10 25E
Rio Mulatos 174 19 40S 66 50W
Rio Muni □ = Mbini □ 124 1 30N 10 0E
Rio Negro 173 26 0S 50 0W
Rio Oriente 166 22 17N 81 13W
Rio Pardo, Minas Gerais, Brazil 171 15 55S 42 30W
Rio Pardo, Rio Grande do Sul, Brazil 173 30 0S 52 30W
Rio Prêto, Serra do 171 13 29S 39 55W
Rio, Punta del 59 36 49N 2 24W
Rio Real 171 11 28S 37 56W
Río Segundo 172 31 40S 63 59W
Río Tercero 172 32 15S 64 8W
Rio Tinto, Brazil 170 6 48S 35 5W
Rio Tinto, Port. 56 41 11N 8 34W
Rio Verde 170 17 50S 51 0W
Río Verde 165 21 56N 99 59W
Rio Vista 163 38 11N 121 44W
Ríobamba 174 1 50S 78 45W
Ríohacha 174 11 33N 72 55W
Rioja, La, Argent. 172 29 20S 67 0W
Rioja, La, Spain 58 42 20N 2 20W
Rioja, La □ 172 29 30S 67 0W
Riom 44 45 54N 3 7E
Riom-ès-Montagnes 44 45 17N 2 39E
Rion-des-Landes 44 43 55N 0 56W
Rionegro 174 6 9N 75 22W
Rionero in Vúlture 65 40 55N 15 40E
Ríos 56 41 58N 7 16W
Riosucio, Caldas, Colomb. 174 5 30N 75 40W
Riosucio, Choco, Colomb. 174 7 27N 77 7W
Riou L. 153 59 7N 106 25W
Riparia, Dora, R. 62 45 7N 7 24E
Ripatransone 63 43 0N 13 45E
Ripley, Derby, U.K. 33 53 3N 1 24W
Ripley, N. Yorks, U.K. 33 54 3N 1 34W
Ripley, U.S.A. 159 35 43N 89 34W
Ripoll 58 42 15N 2 13E
Ripon, Calif., U.S.A. 163 37 44N 121 7W
Ripon, Wis., U.S.A. 156 43 51N 88 50W
Riposto 65 37 44N 15 12E
Risalpur 94 34 3N 71 59E
Risan 66 42 32N 18 42E
Risca 31 51 36N 3 6W
Riscle 44 43 39N 0 5W
Rishon Le Zion 90 31 58N 34 48E
Rishpon 90 32 12N 34 49E
Rishton 32 53 46N 2 26W
Riska 71 58 56N 5 52E
Risle, R. 42 48 55N 0 41E
Rîsnov 70 45 35N 25 27E
Rison 159 33 57N 92 11W
Risør 71 58 43N 9 13E
Ritchie's Archipelago 101 12 5N 94 0E
Riti 121 7 57N 9 41E
Ritzville 160 47 10N 118 21W
Riu 98 28 19N 95 3E
Riva Bella Ouistreham 42 49 17N 0 18W
Riva del Garda 62 45 53N 10 50E
Rivadavia, Buenos Aires, Argent. 172 35 29S 62 59W
Rivadavia, Mendoza, Argent. 172 33 13S 68 30W
Rivadavia, Salta, Argent. 172 24 5S 63 0W
Rivadavia, Chile 172 29 50S 70 35W
Rivarolo Canavese 62 45 20N 7 42E
Rivas 166 11 30N 85 50W
Rive-de-Gier 45 45 32N 4 37E
River Cess 120 5 30N 9 25W
Rivera 173 31 0S 55 50W
Riverchapel 39 52 38N 6 14W
Riverdale 163 36 26N 119 52W
Riverhead 162 40 53N 72 40W
Riverhurst 153 50 55N 106 50W
Riverina 136 29 45S 120 40E
Riverina, dist. 133 35 30S 145 20E
Rivers 153 50 2N 100 14W
Rivers □ 121 5 0N 6 30E
Rivers Inlet 152 51 40N 127 20W
Rivers, L. of the 153 49 49N 105 44W
Riversdal 128 34 7S 21 15E
Riverside, Calif., U.S.A. 163 34 0N 117 22W
Riverside, Wyo., U.S.A. 160 41 12N 106 57W
Riversleigh 138 19 5S 138 48E
Riverton, Austral. 140 34 10S 138 46E

*Renamed Orumiyeh

Riverton, Can. 153 51 5N 97 0W
Riverton, N.Z. 143 46 21S 168 0E
Riverton, U.S.A. 160 43 1N 108 27W
Riverview 108 27 36S 152 51E
Rives 45 45 21N 5 31E
Rivesaltes 44 42 47N 2 50E
Riviera 62 44 0N 8 30E
Rivière à Pierre 151 46 57N 72 12W
Rivière-au-Renard 151 48 59N 64 23W
Rivière Bleue 151 47 26N 69 2W
Rivière-du-Loup 151 47 50N 69 30W
Rivière Pontecôte 151 49 57N 67 1W
Rívoli 62 45 3N 7 31E
Rivoli B. 140 37 32S 140 3E
Rivungo 128 16 9S 21 51E
Riwaka 143 41 5S 172 59E
Rixensart 47 50 43N 4 32E
Riyadh = Ar Riyad 92 24 41N 46 42E
Rize 92 41 0N 40 30E
Rizzuto, C. 65 38 54N 17 5E
Rjukan 71 59 54N 8 33E
Roa, Norway 71 60 17N 10 37E
Roa, Spain 56 41 41N 3 56W
Road Town 167 18 27N 64 37W
Road Weedon 28 52 14N 1 6W
Roade 29 52 10N 0 53W
Roadhead 32 55 4N 2 44W
Roag, L. 36 58 10N 6 55W
Roan Antelope 127 13 2S 28 19E
Roanne 45 46 3N 4 4E
Roanoke, Ala., U.S.A. 157 33 9N 85 23W
Roanoke, Va., U.S.A. 156 37 19N 79 55W
Roanoke I. 157 35 55N 75 40W
Roanoke, R. 157 36 15N 77 20W
Roanoke Rapids 157 36 36N 77 42W
Roaringwater B. 39 51 30N 9 30W
Roatán 166 16 18N 86 35W
Robbins I. 138 40 42S 145 0E
Robe, R., Austral. 136 21 42S 116 15E
Robe, R., Ireland 38 53 38N 9 10W
Röbel 48 53 24N 12 37E
Robert Lee 159 31 55N 100 26W
Robert Pt. 137 32 34S 115 40E
Roberton 35 55 24N 2 53W
Roberts 160 43 44N 112 8W
Robertsganj 95 24 44N 83 12E
Robertson, Austral. 132 34 37S 150 36E
Robertson, S. Afr. 128 33 46S 19 50E
Robertson I. 13 68 0S 75 0W
Robertson Ra. 136 23 15S 121 0E
Robertsport 120 6 45N 11 26W
Robertstown, Austral. 140 33 58S 139 5E
Robertstown, Ireland 39 53 16N 6 50W
Roberval 150 48 32N 72 15W
Robeson Kanal 12 82 0N 61 30W
Robesonia 162 40 21N 76 8W
Robin Hood's B. 33 54 26N 0 31W
Robinson Crusoe I. 143 33 50S 78 30W
Robinson, R. 138 16 3S 137 16E
Robinson Ranges 137 25 40S 118 0E
Robinson River 138 16 45S 136 58E
Robinvale 140 34 40S 142 45E
Robla, La 56 42 50N 5 41W
Roblin 153 51 14N 101 21W
Roboré 174 18 10S 59 45W
Robson, Mt. 152 53 10N 119 10W
Robstown 159 27 47N 97 40W
Roca, C. da 57 38 40N 9 31W
Roca Partida, I. 164 19 1N 112 2W
Roçadas 128 16 45S 15 0E
Rocas, I. 170 4 0S 34 1W
Rocca d'Aspidé 65 40 27N 15 10E
Rocca San Casciano 63 44 3N 11 30E
Roccalbegna 63 42 47N 11 30E
Roccastrada 63 43 0N 11 10E
Rocella Iónica 65 38 20N 16 24E
Rocester 32 52 56N 1 50W
Rocha 173 34 30S 54 25W
Rochdale 32 53 36N 2 10W
Roche 30 50 24N 4 50W
Roche-Bernard, La 42 47 31N 2 19W
Roche-Canillac, La 44 45 12N 1 57E
Roche-en-Ardenne, La 47 50 11N 5 35E
Roche, La, France 45 46 4N 6 19E
Roche, La, Switz. 50 46 42N 7 7E
Roche-sur-Yon, La 42 46 40N 1 25W
Rochechouart 44 45 50N 0 49E
Rochefort, Belg. 47 50 9N 5 12E
Rochefort, France 44 45 56N 0 57W
Rochefort-en-Terre 42 47 42N 2 22W
Rochefoucauld, La 44 45 44N 0 24E
Rochelle 158 41 55N 89 5W
Rochelle, La 44 46 10N 1 9W
Rocher River 152 61 23N 112 44W
Rocherath 47 50 26N 6 18E
Rocheservière 42 46 57N 1 30W
Rochester, Austral. 140 36 22S 144 41E
Rochester, Can. 152 54 22N 113 27W
Rochester, Kent, U.K. 29 51 22N 0 30E
Rochester, Northum., U.K. 35 55 16N 2 16W
Rochester, Ind., U.S.A. 156 41 5N 86 15W
Rochester, Minn., U.S.A. 158 44 1N 92 28W
Rochester, N.H., U.S.A. 162 43 19N 70 57W
Rochester, N.Y., U.S.A. 156 43 10N 77 40W
Rochford 29 51 36N 0 42E
Rochfortbridge 38 53 25N 7 19W
Rociana 57 37 19N 6 35W
Rociu 70 44 43N 25 2E
Rock Flat 141 36 21S 149 13E
Rock Hall 162 39 8N 76 14W
Rock Hill 157 34 55N 81 2W
Rock Island 158 41 30N 90 35W
Rock Lake 158 48 50N 99 13W
Rock, R. 152 60 7N 127 7W
Rock Rapids 158 43 25N 96 10W
Rock River 160 41 49N 106 0W
Rock Sound 166 24 54N 76 12W
Rock Sprs., Ariz., U.S.A. 161 34 2N 112 11W
Rock Sprs., Mont., U.S.A. 160 46 55N 106 11W
Rock Sprs., Tex., U.S.A. 159 30 2N 100 11W
Rock Sprs., Wyo., U.S.A. 160 41 40N 109 10W
Rock Valley 158 43 10N 96 17W
Rockall I. 16 57 37N 13 42W
Rockanje 46 51 52N 4 4E
Rockcliffe 32 54 58N 3 0W
Rockcorry 38 54 7N 7 0W
Rockdale 159 30 40N 97 0W
Rockefeller Plat. 13 84 0S 130 0W
Rockford 158 42 20N 89 0W
Rockglen 153 49 11N 105 57W
Rockhampton 138 23 22S 150 32E
Rockhampton Downs 138 18 57S 135 10E
Rockhill 39 52 25N 8 44W
Rockingham, Austral. 137 32 15S 115 38E
Rockingham, U.K. 29 52 32N 0 43W
Rockingham B. 138 18 5S 146 10E
Rockingham For. 29 52 28N 0 42W
Rockland, Idaho, U.S.A. 160 42 37N 112 57W
Rockland, Me., U.S.A. 151 44 0N 69 0W
Rockland, Mich., U.S.A. 158 46 40N 89 10W
Rockmart 157 34 1N 85 2W
Rockmills 39 52 13N 8 25W
Rockport, Mass., U.S.A. 162 42 39N 70 36W
Rockport, Mo., U.S.A. 158 40 26N 95 30W
Rockport, Tex., U.S.A. 159 28 2N 97 3W
Rockville, Conn., U.S.A. 162 41 51N 72 27W
Rockville, Md., U.S.A. 162 39 7N 77 10W
Rockwall 159 32 55N 96 30W
Rockwell City 158 42 20N 94 35W
Rockwood 157 35 52N 84 40W
Rocky Ford 158 38 7N 103 45W
Rocky Gully 137 34 30S 117 0E
Rocky Lane 152 58 31N 116 22W
Rocky Mount 157 35 55N 77 48W
Rocky Mountain House 152 52 22N 114 55W
Rocky Mts. 152 55 0N 121 0W
Rocky Pt. 137 33 30S 123 57E
Rockyford 152 51 14N 113 10W
Rocroi 43 49 55N 4 30E
Rod 93 28 10N 63 5E
Roda, La, Albacete, Spain 59 39 13N 2 15W
Roda, La, Sevilla, Spain 57 37 12N 4 46W
Rødberg 71 60 17N 8 56E
Rødby 73 54 41N 11 23E
Rødby Havn 73 54 39N 11 22E
Roddickton 151 50 51N 56 8W
Rødding 73 55 23N 9 3E
Rødekro 73 55 4N 9 20E
Rodel 36 57 45N 6 57W
Roden 46 53 8N 6 26E
Rødenes 71 59 35N 11 34E
Rodenkirchen 48 53 24N 8 26E
Roderick I. 152 52 38N 128 22W
Rodez 44 44 21N 2 33E
Rodholívas 68 40 55N 24 0E
Rodhópi □ 68 41 10N 25 30E
Ródhos 69 36 15N 28 10E
Ródhos, I. 69 36 15N 28 10E
Roding R. 29 51 31N 0 7E
Rödjenäs 73 57 33N 14 50E
Rodna 70 47 25N 24 50E
Rodney, C. 142 36 17S 174 50E
Rodniki 81 57 7N 41 37E
Rodriguez, I. 11 20 0S 65 0E
Roe, R. 38 55 0N 6 56W
Roebling 162 40 7N 74 45W
Roebourne 136 20 44S 117 9E
Roebuck B. 136 18 5S 122 20E
Roebuck Plains P.O. 136 17 56S 122 28E
Roelofarendsveen 46 52 12N 4 38E
Roer, R. 47 51 12N 5 59E
Roermond 47 51 12N 6 0E
Roes Welcome Sd. 149 65 0N 87 0W
Roeselare 47 50 57N 3 7E
Rœulx 47 50 31N 4 7E
Rogachev 80 53 8N 30 5E
Rogagua, L. 174 14 0S 66 50W
Rogaland fylke □ 75 59 12N 6 20E
Rogans Seat, Mt. 32 54 25N 2 10W
Rogaóica 66 44 4N 19 40E
Rogaška Slatina 63 46 15N 15 42E
Rogate 29 51 0N 0 51W
Rogatec 63 46 15N 21 46E
Rogatin 80 29 24N 24 36E
Rogers 159 36 20N 94 0W
Rogers City 156 45 25N 83 49W
Rogerson 160 42 10N 114 40W
Rogersville 157 36 27N 83 1W
Roggan River 151 54 25N 79 32W
Roggel 47 51 16N 5 56E
Roggeveldberge 128 32 10S 20 10E
Roggiano Gravina 65 39 37N 16 9E
Rogliano, France 45 42 57N 9 30E
Rogliano, Italy 65 39 11N 16 20E
Rogoaguado, L. 174 13 0S 65 30W
Rogowo 54 52 43N 17 38E
Rogozno 54 52 45N 16 59E
Rogue, R. 160 42 30N 124 0W
Rohan 42 48 4N 2 45W
Rohnert Park 163 38 16N 122 40W
Rohrbach 43 49 3N 7 15E
Rohri 94 27 45N 68 51E
Rohri Canal 94 26 15N 68 27E
Rohtak 94 28 55N 76 43E
Roi Et 100 15 56N 103 40E
Roisel 43 49 58N 3 6E
Rojas 172 34 10S 60 45W
Rojo, C., Mexico 165 21 33N 97 20W
Rojo, C., W. Indies 147 17 56N 67 11W
Rokan, R. 102 1 30N 100 50E
Rokeby 138 13 39S 142 40E
Rokiskis 80 55 55N 25 35E
Rokitnoye 81 50 57N 35 56E
Rokycany 52 49 43N 13 35E
Rolândia 173 23 5S 52 0W
Røldal 71 59 47N 6 50E
Rolde 46 52 59N 6 39E
Rolette 158 48 42N 99 50W
Rolfstorp 73 57 11N 12 27E
Rolla, Kansas, U.S.A. 159 37 10N 101 40W
Rolla, Missouri, U.S.A. 159 38 0N 91 42W
Rolla, N. Dak., U.S.A. 158 48 50N 99 36W
Rollag 71 60 2N 9 18E
Rollands Plains 141 31 17S 152 42E
Rolle 50 46 28N 6 20E
Rolleston, Austral. 138 24 28S 148 35E
Rolleston, N.Z. 143 43 35S 172 24E
Rollingstone 138 19 2S 146 24E
Rom 123 9 54N 32 16E
Roma, Austral. 139 26 32S 148 49E
Roma, Italy 64 41 54N 12 30E
Roma, Sweden 73 57 32N 18 26E
Roman, Bulg. 67 43 8N 23 54E
Roman, Rumania 70 46 57N 26 55E
Romana, La 167 18 27N 68 57W
Romang, I. 103 7 30S 127 20E
Romania ■ 61 46 0N 25 0E
Romanija planina 66 43 50N 18 45E
Romano, Cayo 166 22 0N 77 30W
Romano di Lombardía 62 45 32N 9 45E
Romanovka = Bessarabka 82 46 21N 28 51E
Romans 62 45 3N 5 3E
Romanshorn 51 47 33N 9 22E
Romanzof, C. 147 62 0N 165 50W
Rombo □ 126 3 10S 37 30E
Rome, U.S.A. 162 41 51N 76 21W
Rome, Ga., U.S.A. 157 34 20N 85 0W
Rome, N.Y., U.S.A. 162 43 14N 75 29W
Rome = Roma 64 41 54N 12 30E
Romeleåsen 73 55 34N 13 33E
Romenây 45 46 30N 5 1E
Romeo 151 47 28N 57 4W
Romerike 71 60 7N 11 10E
Romilly 43 48 31N 3 44E
Romîni 70 44 59N 24 11E
Rommani 118 33 31N 6 40W
Romney 156 39 21N 78 45W
Romney Marsh 29 51 0N 1 0E
Romny 80 50 48N 33 28E
Rømø 73 55 10N 8 30E
Romodan 80 50 0N 33 15E
Romodanovo 81 54 26N 45 23E
Romont 50 46 42N 6 54E
Romorantin-Lanthenay 43 47 21N 1 45E
Romsdal, R. 71 62 25N 8 0E
Romsdalen 74 62 25N 7 50E
Romsey 28 51 0N 1 29W
Ron 100 17 53N 106 27E
Rona I. 36 57 33N 6 0W
Ronan 160 47 30N 114 11W
Ronas Hill 36 60 33N 1 25W
Ronay I. 36 57 30N 7 10W
Roncador Cay 166 13 40N 80 4W
Roncador, Serra do 171 12 30S 52 30W
Roncesvalles, Paso 58 43 1N 1 19W
Ronceverte 156 37 45N 80 28W
Ronciglione 63 42 18N 12 12E
Ronco, R. 63 44 26N 12 15E
Ronda 57 36 46N 5 12W
Ronda, Serranía de 57 36 44N 5 3W
Rondane 71 61 57N 9 50E
Rondón 174 6 17N 71 6W
Rondônia □ 174 11 0S 63 0W
Rong, Koh 101 10 45N 103 15E
Ronge, La, Can. 153 55 5N 105 20W
Ronge, La, Sask., Can. 153 55 6N 105 17W
Ronge, Lac La 153 55 10N 105 0W
Rongotea 142 40 19S 175 25E
Rønne 73 55 6N 14 44E
Ronne Land 13 83 0S 70 0W
Ronneby 73 56 12N 15 17E
Ronsard, C. 137 24 46S 113 10E
Ronse 47 50 45N 3 35E
Roodepoort-Maraisburg 125 26 8S 27 52E
Roodeschool 46 53 25N 6 46E
Roof Butte 161 36 29N 109 5W
Roompot 47 51 37N 3 44E
Roorkee 94 29 52N 77 59E
Roosendaal 47 51 32N 4 29E
Roosevelt, Minn., U.S.A. 158 48 51N 95 2W
Roosevelt, Utah, U.S.A. 160 40 19N 110 1W
Roosevelt I. 13 79 0S 161 0W
Roosevelt, Mt. 152 58 20N 125 20W
Roosevelt Res. 161 33 46N 111 0W
Roosky 38 53 50N 7 55W
Ropczyce 54 50 4N 21 38E
Roper, R. 138 14 43S 135 27E
Ropesville 159 33 25N 102 10W
Ropsley 33 52 53N 0 31W
Roque Pérez 172 35 25S 59 24W
Roquefort 44 44 2N 0 20W
Roquefort-sur-Souizon 44 43 58N 2 59E
Roquemaure 45 44 3N 4 48E
Roquetas 58 40 50N 0 30E
Roquevaire 45 43 20N 5 36E
Roraima □ 174 2 0N 61 30W
Roraima, Mt. 174 5 10N 60 40W
Rorketon 153 51 24N 99 35W
Røros 71 62 35N 11 23E
Rorschach 51 47 28N 9 30E
Rørvik 74 64 54N 11 15E
Rosa, U.S.A. 160 38 15N 122 16W
Rosa, Zambia 127 9 33S 31 15E
Rosa Brook 137 33 57S 115 10E
Rosa, C. 119 37 0N 8 16E
Rosa, Monte 50 45 57N 7 53E
Rosal 56 41 57N 8 51W
Rosal de la Frontera 57 37 59N 7 13W
Rosalia 160 47 26N 117 25W
Rosamund 163 34 52N 118 10W
Rosans 45 44 24N 5 29E
Rosario 172 33 0S 60 50W
Rosário, Maran., Brazil 170 3 0S 44 15W
Rosário, Rio Grande do Sul, Brazil 176 30 15S 55 0W
Rosario, Baja California, Mexico 164 30 0N 116 0W
Rosario, Durango, Mexico 164 26 30N 105 35W
Rosario, Sinaloa, Mexico 164 23 0N 106 0W
Rosario, Venez. 174 10 19N 72 19W
Rosario de la Frontera 172 25 50S 65 0W
Rosario de Lerma 172 24 59S 65 35W
Rosario del Tala 172 32 20S 59 10W
Rosário do Sul 173 30 15S 54 55W
Rosarito 164 28 38N 114 4W
Rosarno 65 38 29N 15 59E
Rosas 58 42 19N 3 10E
Rosas, G. de, 55 42 10N 3 15E
Rosburgh 143 45 33S 169 19E
Roscoe 162 41 56N 74 55W
Roscoff 42 48 44N 4 0W
Roscommon, Ireland 38 53 38N 8 11W
Roscommon, U.S.A. 156 44 27N 84 35W
Roscommon □ 38 53 40N 8 15W
Roscrea 39 52 58N 7 50W
Rose Blanche 151 47 38N 58 45W
Rose Harbour 152 52 15N 131 10W
Rose Ness 37 58 52N 2 50W
Rose Pt. 152 54 11N 131 39W
Rose, R. 138 14 16S 135 45E
Rose Valley 153 52 19N 103 49W
Roseau, Domin. 167 15 20N 61 30W
Roseau, U.S.A. 158 48 51N 95 46W
Rosebery 138 41 46S 145 33E
Rosebud, Austral. 141 38 21S 144 54E
Rosebud, U.S.A. 159 31 5N 97 0W
Roseburg 160 43 10N 123 10W
Rosedale, Austral. 138 24 38S 151 53E
Rosedale, U.S.A. 159 33 51N 91 0W
Rosedale Abbey 33 54 22N 0 51W
Rosée 47 50 14N 4 41E
Rosegreen 39 52 28N 7 51W
Rosehall 37 57 59N 4 36W
Rosehearty 37 57 42N 2 8W
Rosemarkie 37 57 35N 4 8W
Rosemary 152 50 46N 112 5W
Rosenallis 39 53 10N 7 25W
Rosenberg 159 29 30N 95 48W
Rosendaël 43 51 3N 2 24E
Rosenheim 49 47 51N 12 9E
Roseto degli Abruzzi 63 42 40N 14 2E
Rosetown 153 51 35N 108 3W
Rosetta = Rashîd 122 31 21N 30 22E
Roseville 160 38 46N 121 17W
Rosewood, N.S.W., Austral. 141 35 38S 147 52E
Rosewood, N.T., Austral. 136 16 28S 128 58E
Rosewood, Queens., Austral. 139 27 38S 152 36E
Rosh Haniqra, Kefar 90 33 5N 35 5E
Rosh Pinna 90 32 58N 35 32E
Rosh Ze'ira 90 31 14N 35 15E
Roshage C. 73 57 7N 8 35E
Rosières 43 48 36N 6 20E
Rosignano Marittimo 62 43 23N 10 28E
Rosignol 174 6 15N 57 30W
Roşiorĭ-de-Vede 70 44 9N 25 0E
Rositsa 67 43 57N 27 57E
Rositsa, R. 67 43 10N 25 30E
Roskeeragh Pt. 38 54 22N 8 40W
Roskhill 36 57 24N 6 31W
Roskilde 73 55 38N 12 3E
Roskilde Amt □ 73 55 35N 12 5E
Roskilde Fjord 73 55 50N 12 2E
Roskill, Mt. 142 36 55S 174 45E
Roslavl 80 53 57N 32 55E
Roslyn 141 34 29S 149 37E
Rosmaninhal 57 39 44N 7 5W
Røsnæs 73 55 44N 10 55E
Rosneath 34 56 1N 4 49W
Rosolini 65 36 49N 14 58E
Rosporden 42 47 57N 3 50W
Ross, Austral. 138 42 2S 147 30E
Ross, N.Z. 143 42 53S 170 49E
Ross, U.K. 28 51 55N 2 34W
Ross and Cromarty (□) 26 57 43N 4 50W

Ross Dependency 13 70 0 S 170 5W
Ross I. 13 77 30 S 168 0 E
Ross Ice Shelf 13 80 0 S 180 0W
Ross L. 160 48 50N 121 0W
Ross on Wye 28 51 55N 2 34W
Ross River, Austral. 138 19 15 S 146 51 E
Ross River, Can. 147 62 30N 131 30W
Ross Sea 13 74 0 S 178 0 E
Rossa 51 46 23N 9 8 E
Rossall Pt. 32 53 55N 3 2W
Rossan Pt. 38 54 42N 8 47W
Rossano Cálabro 65 39 36N 16 39 E
Rossburn 153 50 40N 100 49W
Rosscahill 38 53 23N 9 15W
Rosscarbery 39 51 39N 9 1W
Rosscarbery B. 39 51 32N 9 0W
Rossel I. 138 11 30 S 154 30 E
Rosses B. 38 55 2N 8 30W
Rosses Point 38 54 17N 8 34W
Rosses, The 38 55 2N 8 20W
Rossignol, L., N.S., Can. 151 44 12N 65 0W
Rossignol, L., Qué., Can. 150 52 43N 73 40W
Rossing 128 22 30 S 14 50 E
Rossland 152 49 6N 117 50W
Rosslare 39 52 17N 6 23W
Rosslau 48 51 52N 12 15 E
Rosslea 38 54 15N 7 11W
Rosso 120 16 40N 15 45W
Rossosh 83 50 15N 39 20 E
Rossport 150 48 50N 87 30W
Rossum 46 51 48N 5 20 E
Røssvatnet 74 65 45N 14 5 E
Rossville 138 15 48 S 145 15 E
Rosthern 153 52 40N 106 20W
Rostock 48 54 4N 12 9 E
Rostock □ 48 54 10N 12 30 E
Rostov, Don, U.S.S.R. 83 47 15N 39 45 E
Rostov, Moskva, U.S.S.R. 81 57 14N 39 25 E
Rostrenen 42 48 14N 3 21W
Rostrevor 38 54 7N 6 12W
Roswell 159 33 26N 104 32W
Rosyth 35 56 2N 3 26W
Rota 57 36 37N 6 20W
Rotälven 72 61 30N 14 10 E
Rotan 159 32 52N 100 30W
Rotem 47 51 3N 5 45 E
Rotenburg 48 53 6N 9 24 E
Rothbury 35 55 19N 1 55W
Rothbury Forest 35 55 19N 1 50W
Rothenburg 51 47 6N 8 16 E
Rothenburg ob der Tauber 49 49 21N 10 11 E
Rother, R. 29 50 59N 0 40W
Rotherham 33 53 26N 1 21W
Rothes 37 57 31N 3 12W
Rothesay, Can. 151 45 23N 66 0W
Rothesay, U.K. 34 55 50N 5 3W
Rothhaar G., mts. 50 51 6N 8 10 E
Rothienorman 37 57 24N 2 28W
Rothrist 50 47 18N 8 54 E
Rothwell, Northants, U.K. 29 52 25N 0 48W
Rothwell, W. Yorks., U.K. 33 53 46N 1 29W
Roti, I. 103 10 50 S 123 0 E
Rotkop 128 26 44 S 15 27 E
Roto 141 33 0 S 145 30 E
Roto Aira L. 142 39 3 S 175 55 E
Rotoehu L. 142 38 1 S 176 32 E
Rotoiti L. 142 41 51 S 172 49 E
Rotoma L. 142 38 2 S 176 35 E
Rotondella 65 40 10N 16 30 E
Rotoroa Lake 143 41 55 S 172 39 E
Rotorua 142 38 9 S 176 16 E
Rotorua, L. 142 38 5 S 176 18 E
Rotselaar 47 50 57N 4 42 E
Rottal 37 56 48N 3 1W
Rotten, R. 50 46 18N 7 36 E
Rottenburg 49 48 28N 8 56 E
Rottenmann 52 47 31N 14 22 E
Rotterdam 46 51 55N 4 30 E
Rottingdean 29 50 48N 0 3W
Rottnest I. 137 32 0 S 115 27 E
Rottumeroog 46 53 33N 6 34 E
Rottweil 49 48 9N 8 38 E
Rotuma, I. 130 12 25 S 177 5 E
Roubaix 43 50 40N 3 10 E
Roudnice 52 50 25N 14 15 E
Rouen 42 49 27N 1 4 E
Rouergue 45 44 20N 2 20 E
Rough, gasfield 19 53 50N 0 27 E
Rough Pt. 39 52 19N 10 0W
Rough Ridge 143 45 10 S 169 55 E
Rouillac 44 45 47N 0 4W
Rouleau 153 50 10N 104 56W
Round Mt. 139 30 26 S 152 16 E
Round Mountain 163 38 46N 117 3W
Roundstone 38 53 24N 9 55W
Roundup 160 46 25N 108 35W
Roundwood 39 53 4N 6 14W
Rourkela 95 22 14N 84 50 E
Rousay, I. 37 59 10N 3 2W
Rousky 38 54 44N 7 10 E
Rousse, L'Île 45 43 27N 8 57 E
Roussillon 45 45 24N 4 49 E
Rouveen 46 52 37N 6 11 E
Rouxville 128 30 11 S 26 50 E
Rouyn 150 48 20N 79 0W
Rovaniemi 74 66 29N 25 41 E
Rovato 62 45 34N 10 0 E
Rovenki 83 48 5N 39 27 E
Rovereto 62 45 53N 11 3 E
Rovigo 63 45 4N 11 48 E
Rovinari 70 46 56N 23 10 E
Rovinj 63 45 18N 13 40 E
Rovira 174 4 15N 75 20W
Rovno 80 50 40N 26 10 E
Rovnoye 81 50 52N 46 3 E
Rovuma, R. 127 11 30 S 36 10 E
Rowanburn 35 55 5N 2 54W
Rowena 139 29 48 S 148 55 E
Rowes 141 37 0 S 149 6 E
Rowley Shoals 136 17 40 S 119 20 E
Rowood 161 32 18N 112 54W
Rowrah 32 54 34N 3 26W
Roxa 120 11 15N 15 45W
Roxas 103 11 36N 122 49 E
Roxboro 157 36 24N 78 59W
Roxborough Downs 138 22 20 S 138 45 E
Roxburgh, N.Z. 143 45 33 S 169 19 E
Roxburgh, U.K. 35 55 34N 2 30W
Roxburgh (□) 26 55 30N 2 30W
Roxby 33 53 38N 0 37W
Roxen 73 58 30N 15 40 E
Roy 160 47 17N 109 0W
Roy Hill 136 22 37 S 119 58 E
Roy, Le 159 38 8N 95 35W
Roya, Peña 58 40 25N 0 40W
Royal Canal 38 53 29N 7 0W
Royal Oak 156 42 30N 83 5W
Royalla 141 35 30 S 149 9 E
Royan 44 45 37N 1 2W
Roybridge 37 56 53N 4 50W
Roye 43 47 40N 6 31 E
Røyken 71 59 45N 10 23 E
Royston 29 52 3N 0 1W
Royton 32 53 34N 2 7W
Rozaj 66 42 50N 20 15 E
Rozan 54 52 52N 21 25 E
Rozdol 80 49 30N 24 1 E
Rozier, Le 44 44 13N 3 12 E
Roznava 53 48 37N 20 35 E
Rozoy 43 48 40N 2 56 E
Rozoy-sur-Serre 43 49 40N 4 8 E
Rozwadów 54 50 37N 22 2 E
Rrësheni 68 41 47N 19 49 E
Rtanj, mt. 66 43 45N 21 50W
Rtem, Oued el 119 33 40N 5 34 E
Rtishchevo 81 52 35N 43 50 E
Rúa 56 42 24N 7 6W
Ruacaná 128 17 20 S 14 12 E
Ruahine Ra. 142 39 55 S 176 2 E
Ruamahanga, R. 142 41 24 S 175 8 E
Ruapehu 142 39 17 S 175 35 E
Ruapuke I. 143 46 46 S 168 31 E
Ruatoria 142 37 55 S 178 20 E
Ruãus, W. 119 30 14N 15 0 E
Ruawai 142 36 15 S 173 59 E
Rub 'al Khali 91 21 0N 51 0 E
Rubeho, mts. 126 6 50 S 36 25 E
Rubery 28 52 24N 1 59W
Rubezhnoye 82 49 6N 38 25 E
Rubha Ardvule C. 36 57 17N 7 32W
Rubha Hunish, C. 36 57 42N 6 20W
Rubh'an Dunain, C. 36 57 10N 6 20W
Rubiataba 171 15 8 S 49 48W
Rubicone, R. 63 44 0N 12 20 E
Rubim 171 16 23 S 40 32W
Rubinéia 171 20 13 S 51 2W
Rubino 120 6 4N 4 18W
Rubio 174 7 43N 72 22W
Rubona 126 0 29N 30 9 E
Rubtsovsk 76 51 30N 80 50 E
Ruby 147 64 40N 155 35W
Ruby L. 160 40 10N 115 28W
Ruby Mts. 160 40 30N 115 30W
Rubyvale 138 23 25 S 147 45 E
Rucava 80 56 9N 20 32 E
Ruciane-Nida 54 53 40N 21 32 E
RûcûSdia 66 44 59N 21 36 E
Rud 71 60 1N 10 1 E
Ruda 73 57 6N 16 7 E
Ruda Slaska 53 50 16N 18 50 E
Rudall 140 33 43 S 136 17 E
Rudbar 93 30 0N 62 30 E
Ruden, I. 48 54 13N 13 47 E
Rüdersdorf 48 52 28N 13 48 E
Rudewa 127 10 7 S 34 47 E
Rudgwick 29 51 7N 0 54W
Rudkøbing 73 54 56N 10 41 E
Rudna 54 51 30N 16 17 E
Rudnichnyy 84 59 38N 52 26 E
Rudnik, Bulg. 67 42 36N 27 30 E
Rudnik, Yugo. 67 44 7N 20 35 E
Rudnik, mt. 67 44 7N 20 35 E
Rudnogorsk 77 57 15N 103 42 E
Rudnya 80 54 55N 31 13 E
Rudnyy 84 52 57N 63 7 E
Rudo 66 43 41N 19 23 E
Rudolstadt 48 50 44N 11 20 E
Rudozem 67 41 29N 24 51 E
Rudston 33 54 6N 0 19W
Rûducaneni 70 46 58N 27 54 E
Rûdûuţi 70 47 50N 25 59 E
Rudyard 156 46 14N 84 35 E
Rue 43 50 15N 1 40 E
Ruelle 44 45 41N 0 14 E
Rufa'a 123 14 44N 33 32 E
Ruffec Charente 44 46 2N 0 12W
Rufi 123 5 58N 30 18 E
Rufiji □ 126 8 0 S 38 30 E
Rufiji, R. 124 7 50 S 38 15 E
Rufino 172 34 20 S 62 50W
Rufisque 120 14 40N 17 15W
Rufunsa 127 15 4 S 29 34 E
Rugby, U.K. 28 52 23N 1 16W
Rugby, U.S.A. 158 48 21N 100 0W
Rugeley 28 52 47N 1 56W
Rügen, I. 48 54 22N 13 25 E
Rugezi 126 2 6 S 33 18 E
Rugles 42 48 50N 0 40 E
Ruhāma 90 31 31N 34 43 E
Ruhea 98 26 10N 88 25 E
Ruhengeri 126 1 30 S 29 36 E
Ruhla 48 50 53N 10 21 E
Ruhland 48 51 27N 13 52 E
Ruhr, R. 48 51 25N 7 15 E
Ruhuhu, R. 127 10 15 S 34 55 E
Rui Barbosa 171 12 18 S 40 27W
Ruidosa 159 29 59N 104 39W
Ruidoso 161 33 19N 105 39W
Ruinen 46 52 46N 6 21 E
Ruinen A Kanaal 46 52 54N 7 8 E
Ruinerwold 46 52 44N 6 15 E
Ruj, mt. 66 42 52N 22 42 E
Rujen, mt. 66 42 9N 22 30 E
Ruk 94 27 50N 68 42 E
Rukwa □, Tanz. 126 7 0 S 31 30 E
Rukwa □, Tanz. 126 7 0 S 31 30 E
Rukwa L. 126 7 50 S 32 10 E
Rulhieres, C. 136 13 56 S 127 22 E
Rulles 47 49 43N 5 32 E
Rully 167 46 52N 4 44 E
Rum Jungle 136 13 0 S 130 59 E
Ruma 66 45 8N 19 50 E
Rumah 92 25 35N 47 10 E
Rumania ■ 61 46 0N 25 0 E
Rumbalara 138 25 20 S 134 29 E
Rumbek 123 6 54N 29 37 E
Rumbeke 47 50 56N 3 10 E
Rumburk 52 50 57N 14 32 E
Rumelange 47 49 27N 6 2 E
Rumford 156 44 30N 70 30W
Rumia 54 54 37N 18 25 E
Rumilly 45 45 53N 5 56 E
Rumney 31 51 32N 3 7W
Rumoi 112 43 56N 141 39W
Rumonge 126 3 59 S 29 26 E
Rumsey 152 51 51N 112 48W
Rumson 162 40 23N 74 0W
Rumula 138 16 35 S 145 20 E
Rumuruti 126 0 17N 36 32 E
Runabay Hd. 38 55 10N 6 2W
Runanga 143 42 25 S 171 15 E
Runaway, C. 142 37 32 S 178 2 E
Runcorn, Austral. 108 27 36 S 153 4 E
Runcorn, U.K. 32 53 20N 2 44W
Rungwa 126 6 55 S 33 32 E
Rungwa, R. 126 7 15 S 33 10 E
Rungwe 127 9 11 S 33 32 E
Rungwe □ 127 9 25 S 33 32 E
Runka 121 12 28N 7 20 E
Runn 72 60 30N 15 40 E
Rupa 98 27 15N 92 30 E
Rupar 94 31 2N 76 38 E
Rupat, I. 102 1 45N 101 40 E
Rupea 61 46 2N 25 13 E
Rupert House = Fort Rupert 150 51 30N 78 40W
Rupert, R. 150 51 29N 78 45W
Rupsa 98 21 44N 87 20 E
Rupununi, R. 175 3 30N 59 30W
Ruquka Gie La 99 31 35N 97 55 E
Rurrenabaque 174 14 30 S 67 32W
Rus, R. 58 39 30N 2 30W
Rusambo 127 16 30 S 32 4 E
Rusape 125 18 35 S 32 8 E
Ruschuk = Ruse 67 43 48N 25 59 E
Ruse 67 43 48N 25 59 E
Rusetu 70 44 57N 27 14 E
Rush 38 53 31N 6 7W
Rushden 29 52 17N 0 37W
Rushford 158 43 48N 91 46W
Rushville, Ill., U.S.A. 158 40 6N 90 35W
Rushville, Ind., U.S.A. 156 39 38N 85 22W
Rushville, Nebr., U.S.A. 158 42 43N 102 35W
Rushworth 141 36 32 S 145 1 E
Rusken 73 57 15N 14 20 E
Ruskington 33 53 5N 0 23W
Russas 171 4 56 S 38 2W
Russell, Can. 153 50 50N 101 20W
Russell, N.Z. 142 35 16 S 174 10 E
Russell, U.S.A. 158 38 56N 98 55W
Russell L., Man., Can. 153 56 15N 101 30W
Russell L., N.W.T., Can. 152 63 5N 115 44W
Russellkonda 96 19 57N 84 42 E
Russellville, Ala., U.S.A. 157 34 30N 87 44W
Russellville, Ark., U.S.A. 159 35 15N 93 0W
Russellville, Ky., U.S.A. 157 36 50N 86 50W
Russi 63 44 21N 12 1 E
Russian Mission 147 61 45N 161 25W
Russian S.F.S.R. □ 77 62 0N 105 0 E
Russkoye Ustie 12 71 0N 149 0 E
Rust 53 47 49N 16 42 E
Rustam 94 34 25N 72 13 E
Rustam Shahr 94 26 58N 66 6 E
Rustavi 83 40 45N 44 30 E
Rustenburg 128 25 41 S 27 14 E
Ruston 159 32 30N 92 40W
Ruswil 50 47 5N 8 8 E
Rutana 126 3 55 S 30 0 E
Rutba 92 33 4N 40 15 E
Rute 57 37 19N 4 29W
Ruteng 103 8 26 S 120 30 E
Ruth 160 39 15N 115 1W
Ruth, oilfield 19 55 33N 4 55 E
Rutherglen, Austral. 141 36 5 S 146 29 E
Rutherglen, U.K. 34 55 50N 4 11W
Ruthin 31 53 7N 3 20W
Ruthven 37 57 4N 4 2W
Ruthwell 35 55 0N 3 24W
Rüti 51 47 16N 8 51 E
Rutigliano 65 41 1N 17 0 E
Rutland 162 43 38N 73 0W
Rutland (□) 26 52 38N 0 40W
Rutland I. 101 11 25N 92 40 E
Rutland Plains 138 15 38 S 141 49 E
Rutledge L. 153 61 33N 110 47W
Rutledge, R. 153 61 4N 112 0W
Rutshuru 126 1 13 S 29 25 E
Ruurlo 46 52 5N 6 24 E
Ruvo di Púglia 65 41 7N 16 27 E
Ruvu 126 6 49 S 38 43 E
Ruvu, R. 126 7 25 S 38 15 E
Ruvuma □ 127 10 20 S 36 0 E
Ruvuma, R. 127 11 30 S 36 10 E
Ruwaidha 92 23 40N 44 40 E
Ruwandiz 92 36 40N 44 32 E
Ruwenzori Mts. 126 0 30N 29 55 E
Ruwenzori, mt. 126 0 30N 29 55 E
Ruyigi 126 3 29 S 30 15 E
Ruzayevka 81 54 10N 45 0 E
Ruzhevo Konare 67 42 23N 24 46 E
Ruzomberok 53 49 3N 19 17 E
Rwanda ■ 126 2 0 S 30 0 E
Ryaberg 73 56 47N 13 15 E
Ryakhovo 67 44 0N 26 18 E
Ryan, L. 34 55 0N 5 2W
Ryazan 81 54 50N 39 40 E
Ryazhsk 81 53 45N 40 3 E
Rybache 76 46 40N 81 20 E
Rybachi Poluostrov 78 69 43N 32 0 E
Rybachye 85 42 26N 76 12 E
Rybinsk (Shcherbakov) 81 58 5N 38 50 E
Rybinsk Vdkhr. 81 58 30N 38 0 E
Rybnik 54 50 6N 18 32 E
Rybnitsa 82 47 45N 29 0 E
Rychwał 54 52 4N 18 10 E
Ryd 73 56 27N 14 42 E
Rydal 32 54 28N 2 59W
Ryde 28 50 44N 1 9W
Rydö 73 56 58N 13 10 E
Rydsnäs 73 57 47N 15 9 E
Rydułtowy 54 50 4N 18 23 E
Rydzyna 54 51 47N 16 39 E
Rye, Denmark 73 56 5N 9 45 E
Rye, U.K. 29 50 57N 0 46 E
Rye Patch Res. 160 40 45N 118 20W
Rye, R. 33 54 12N 0 53W
Ryegate 160 46 21N 109 27W
Ryhope 35 54 52N 1 22W
Rylsk 80 51 30N 34 51 E
Rylstone 141 32 46 S 149 58 E
Rymanów 54 49 35N 21 51 E
Ryn 54 53 57N 21 34 E
Ryningsnäs 73 57 17N 15 58 E
Ryōhaku-Sanchi 111 36 0N 136 49 E
Rypin 54 53 3N 19 32 E
Ryton, Tyne & Wear, U.K. 35 54 58N 1 44W
Ryton, Warwick, U.K. 28 52 23N 1 25W
Ryūgasaki 111 35 54N 140 11 E
Ryūkyū Is. = Nansei-Shotō 112 26 0N 128 0 E
Rzepin 54 52 20N 14 49 E
Rzeszów 54 50 5N 21 58 E
Rzeszów □ 54 50 0N 22 0 E
Rzhev 80 56 20N 34 20 E

S

s'-Hertogenbosch 47 51 42N 5 17 E
Sa 100 18 34N 100 45 E
Sa. da Canastra 125 19 30 S 46 5W
Sa Dec 101 10 20N 105 46 E
Sa-Koi 98 19 54N 97 3 E
Sa'ad (Muharraga) 90 31 28N 34 33 E
Sa'ādatabād 93 30 10N 53 5 E
Saale, R. 48 51 25N 11 56 E
Saaler Bodden 48 54 20N 12 25 E
Saalfelden 70 47 26N 12 51 E
Saalfield 48 50 39N 11 21 E
Saane, R. 50 46 23N 7 18 E
Saanen 50 46 29N 7 15 E
Saar (Sarre), □ 43 49 20N 6 45 E
Saarbrücken 49 49 15N 6 58 E
Saarburg 49 49 36N 6 32 E
Saaremaa 80 58 30N 22 30 E
Saariselkä 74 68 16N 28 15 E
Saarland □ 131 49 20N 6 45 E
Saarlouis 49 49 19N 6 45 E
Saas Fee 50 46 7N 7 56 E
Saas-Grund 50 46 7N 7 57 E
Saba I. 167 17 30N 63 10W
Sabac 66 44 48N 19 42 E
Sabadell 58 41 28N 2 7 E
Sabae 111 35 57N 136 11 E
Sabagalel 102 1 36 S 98 40 E
Sabah □ 102 6 0N 117 0 E
Sabak 100 3 46N 100 58 E
Sábana de la Mar 167 19 7N 69 40W
Sábanalarga 174 10 38N 74 55W
Sabang, O. 102 5 50N 95 15 E

Sabará **171** 19 55S 43 55W
Sabarania **103** 2 5S 138 18E
Sabari, R. **96** 18 0N 81 25E
Sabastiya **90** 32 17N 35 12E
Sabaudia **64** 41 17N 13 2E
Sabderat **123** 15 26N 36 42E
Sabhah **119** 27 9N 14 29E
Sabie **129** 25 4S 30 48E
Sabinal, Mexico **164** 30 50N 107 25W
Sabinal, U.S.A. **159** 29 20N 99 27W
Sabinal, Punta del **59** 36 43N 2 44W
Sabinas **164** 27 50N 101 10W
Sabinas Hidalgo **164** 26 40N 100 10W
Sabinas, R. **164** 27 37N 100 42W
Sabine **159** 29 42N 93 54W
Sabine, R. **159** 31 30N 93 35W
Sabinópolis **171** 18 40S 43 6W
Sabinov **53** 49 6N 21 5E
Sabirabad **83** 40 0N 48 30E
Sabkhat Tawurgha **119** 31 48N 15 30E
Sablayan **103** 12 5N 120 50E
Sable **42** 47 50N 0 21W
Sable, C., Can. **151** 43 29N 65 38W
Sable, C., U.S.A. **166** 25 5N 81 0W
Sable I. **151** 44 0N 60 0W
Sablé-sur-Sarthe **42** 47 50N 0 20W
Sables-D'Olonne, Les **44** 46 30N 1 45W
Saboeiro **170** 6 32S 39 54W
Sabor, R. **56** 41 16N 7 10W
Sabou **120** 12 1N 2 28W
Sabrãtah **119** 32 47N 12 29E
Sabrina Coast **13** 67 0S 120 0E
Sabugal **56** 40 20N 7 5W
Sabzevar **93** 36 15N 57 40E
Sabzvaran **93** 28 45N 57 50E
Sac City **158** 42 26N 95 0W
Sacandaga Res. **162** 43 6N 74 16W
Sacedón **58** 40 29N 2 41W
Sachigo, L. **150** 53 50N 92 12W
Sachigo, R. **150** 55 6N 88 58W
Sachinbulako **106** 43 5N 111 47E
Sachkhere **83** 42 25N 43 28E
Sachseln **51** 46 52N 8 15E
Sacile **63** 45 58N 16 7E
Säckingen **49** 47 34N 7 56E
Saco, Me., U.S.A. **162** 43 30N 70 27W
Saco, Mont., U.S.A. **160** 48 28N 107 19W
Sacquoy Hd. **37** 59 12N 3 5W
Sacramento, Brazil **171** 19 53S 47 27W
Sacramento, U.S.A. **163** 38 39N 121 30E
Sacramento Mts. **161** 32 30N 105 30W
Sacramento, R. **163** 38 3N 121 56W
Sacratif, Cabo **59** 36 42N 3 28W
Sacriston **34** 54 49N 1 38W
Sada **56** 43 22N 8 15W
Sada-Misaki-Hantō **110** 33 22N 132 1E
Sadaba **58** 2 19N 1 12W
Sa'dani **124** 5 58S 38 35E
Sadao **101** 6 38N 100 26E
Sadasivpet **96** 17 38N 77 50E
Sadberge **33** 54 32N 1 30W
Sadd el Aali **122** 24 5N 32 54E
Saddell **34** 55 31N 5 30W
Saddle, Hd. **38** 54 0N 10 10W
Saddle, The **36** 57 10N 5 27W
Sade **121** 11 22N 10 45E
Sadiba **128** 18 53S 23 1E
Sadimi **127** 9 25S 23 32E
Sado **112** 38 0N 138 25E
Sado, R. **57** 38 10N 8 22W
Sadon, Burma **99** 25 28N 98 0E
Sadon, U.S.S.R. **83** 42 52N 43 58E
Sadri **94** 24 28N 74 30E
Saduya **98** 27 50N 95 40E
Sæby **73** 57 21N 10 30E
Saelices **58** 39 55N 2 49W
Safâga **122** 26 42N 34 0E
Safaha **122** 26 25N 39 0E
Safaniya **92** 28 5N 48 42E
Safárikovo **43** 48 25N 20 20E
Safed Koh, Mts. **94** 34 15N 64 0E
Safford **61** 32 54N 109 52W
Saffron Walden **29** 52 2N 0 15E
Safi, Jordan **90** 31 2N 35 28E
Safi, Moroc. **118** 32 18N 9 14W
Safiah **42** 31 27N 34 46E
Safonovo **80** 65 40N 47 50E
Safranbolu **82** 41 15N 32 34E
Sag Harbor **162** 40 59N 72 17W
Sag Sag **135** 5 32S 148 23E
Saga, Indon. **103** 2 40S 132 55E
Saga, Kōchi, Japan **110** 33 5N 133 6E
Saga, Saga, Japan **110** 33 15N 130 16E
Saga-ken □ **110** 33 15N 130 20E
Sagåg **71** 59 46N 5 25E
Sagaing **98** 23 30N 95 30E
Sagaing □ **98** 22 0N 95 30E
Sagala **120** 14 9N 6 38W
Sagami-Nada **111** 34 58N 139 23E
Sagami-Wan **111** 35 15N 139 25E
Sagamihara **111** 35 33N 139 25E
Saganoseki **110** 33 15N 131 53E
Sagar **93** 23 50N 78 50E
Sagara, India **97** 14 14N 75 6E
Sagara, Japan **111** 34 41N 138 12E
Sagara, L. **126** 5 20S 31 0E
Sagawa **110** 33 28N 133 11E
Sågen **72** 60 17N 14 10E
Sagil **105** 50 20N 91 40E
Saginaw **156** 43 26N 83 55W
Saginaw B. **150** 43 50N 83 40W
Sagleipie **45** 45 25N 7 0E
Saglouc (Sugluk) **149** 62 30N 74 15W
Sagone **45** 42 7N 8 42E
Sagone, G. de **45** 42 4N 8 40E
Sagori **107** 35 25N 126 49E
Sagra, La, Mt. **59** 38 0N 2 35W
Sagres **57** 37 0N 8 58W
Sagu **98** 20 13N 94 46E
Sagua la Grande **166** 22 50N 80 10W
Saguache **161** 38 10N 106 4W
Saguenay, R. **151** 48 22N 71 0W
Sagunto **58** 39 42N 0 18W
Sahaba **122** 18 57N 30 25E
Sahagún, Colomb. **174** 8 57N 75 27W
Sahagún, Spain **56** 42 18N 5 2W
Saham **90** 32 42N 35 46E
Sahara **118** 23 0N 5 0W
Saharanpur **94** 29 58N 77 33E
Saharien Atlas **118** 34 9N 3 29E
Sahasinaka **129** 21 49S 47 49E
Sahaswan **95** 28 5N 78 45E
Sahel, Canal du **120** 14 20N 6 0W
Sahibganj **95** 25 12N 87 55E
Sahiwal **94** 30 45N 73 8E
Sahl Arraba **90** 37 26N 35 12E
Sahtaneh, R. **152** 59 2N 122 28W
Sahuaripa **164** 29 30N 109 0W
Sahuarita **161** 31 58N 110 59W
Sahuayo **164** 20 4N 102 43W
Sahy **53** 48 4N 18 55E
Sai Buri **101** 6 43N 101 39E
Saibai I. **135** 9 25S 142 40E
Sa'id Bundas **117** 8 24N 24 48E
Saïda **118** 34 50N 0 11E
Sa'idabad **93** 29 30N 55 45E
Saidapet **97** 13 0N 80 15E
Saidor **135** 5 40S 146 29E
Saidu **95** 34 50N 72 15E
Säle **72** 59 8N 12 55E
Saighan **93** 35 10N 67 55E
Saignelégier **50** 47 15N 7 0E
Saignes **44** 45 20N 2 31E
Saigō **110** 36 12N 133 20E
Saigon = Phanh Bho Ho Chi Minh **101** 10 58N 106 40E
Saih-al-Malih **93** 23 37N 58 31E
Saihut **91** 15 12N 51 10E
Saijō, Ehima, Japan **110** 33 55N 133 11E
Saijō, Hiroshima, Japan **110** 34 25N 132 45E
Saikhoa Ghat **99** 27 50N 95 40E
Saiki **110** 32 58N 131 57E
Saillans **45** 44 42N 5 12E
Sailolof **103** 1 7S 130 46E
Saima **107** 40 59N 124 15E
Saimaa, L. **78** 61 15N 28 15E
St. Abbs **35** 55 54N 2 7W
St. Abb's Head **35** 55 55N 2 10W
St. Aegyd **52** 47 52N 15 33E
St. Affrique **44** 43 57N 2 53E
St. Agnes **30** 50 18N 5 13W
St. Agnes Hd. **30** 50 19N 5 14W
St. Agnes I. **30** 49 53N 6 20W
St.-Agrève **45** 45 0N 4 23E
St.-Aignan **42** 47 16N 1 22E
St. Albans, Austral. **138** 24 43S 139 56E
St. Albans, Can. **151** 47 51N 55 50W
St. Albans, U.K. **29** 51 44N 0 19W
St. Albans, Vt., U.S.A. **156** 44 49N 73 7W
St. Albans, W. Va., U.S.A. **156** 38 21N 81 50W
St. Alban's Head **28** 50 34N 2 3W
St. Albert **152** 53 37N 113 40W
St. Amand **43** 50 25N 3 6E
St.-Amand-en-Puisaye **43** 47 32N 3 5E
St.-Amand-Mont-Rond **44** 46 43N 2 30E
St.-Amarin **43** 47 54N 7 0E
St.-Amour **45** 46 26N 5 21E
St. Andrä **52** 46 46N 14 50E
St. André, C. **129** 16 11S 44 27E
St.-André-de-Cubzac **44** 44 59N 0 26W
St. André de l'Eure **42** 48 54N 1 16E
St.-André-les-Alpes **45** 43 58N 6 30E
St. Andrews, Can. **151** 47 45N 59 15W
St. Andrews, N.Z. **143** 44 33S 171 10E
St. Andrews, U.K. **35** 56 20N 2 48W
St. Ann B. **151** 46 22N 60 25W
St. Anne **42** 49 43N 2 11W
St. Anne's **32** 53 45N 3 2W
St. Ann's **35** 55 14N 3 28W
St. Ann's Bay **166** 18 26N 77 15W
St. Ann's Hd. **31** 51 41N 5 11W
St. Anthony, Can. **151** 51 22N 55 35W
St. Anthony, U.S.A. **160** 44 0N 111 49W
St.-Antonin-Noble-Val **44** 44 10N 1 45E
St. Arnaud **140** 36 32S 143 16E
St. Arnaud Ra. **143** 42 1S 172 53E
St. Arthur **151** 47 47N 67 46W
St. Asaph **31** 53 15N 3 27W
St. Astier **44** 45 8N 0 31E
St.-Aubin **50** 46 54N 6 47E
St.-Aubin-du-Cormier **42** 48 15N 1 26W
St. Augustin **129** 23 33S 43 46E
St-Augustin-Saguenay **151** 51 13N 58 38W
St. Augustine **157** 29 52N 81 20W
St. Austell **30** 50 20N 4 48W
St.-Avold **43** 49 6N 6 43E
St. Barthélemy, I. **167** 17 50N 62 50W
St. Bathans **143** 44 53S 170 0E
St. Bathan's Mt. **143** 44 45S 169 45E
St. Bees **32** 54 29N 3 36W
St. Bee's Hd. **32** 54 30N 3 38E
St.-Benoît-du-Sault **44** 46 26N 1 24E
St. Bernard, Col du Grand **50** 45 53N 7 11E
St.-Blaise **50** 47 1N 6 59E
St. Blazey **32** 50 22N 4 48W
St. Boniface **153** 49 50N 97 10W
St. Bonnet **45** 44 40N 6 5E
St. Boswells **35** 55 34N 2 39W
St.-Brévin-les-Pins **42** 47 14N 2 10W
St. Briavels **28** 51 44N 2 39W
St.-Brice-en-Coglès **42** 48 25N 1 22W
St. Bride's **151** 46 56N 54 10W
St. Bride's B. **31** 51 48N 5 15W
St.-Brieuc **42** 48 30N 2 46W
St. Budeaux **30** 50 23N 4 10W
St. Buryan **30** 50 4N 5 34W
St.-Calais **42** 47 55N 0 45E
St.-Cast **42** 48 37N 2 18W
St. Catharines **150** 43 10N 79 15W
St. Catherine's I. **157** 31 35N 81 10W
St. Catherine's Pt. **28** 50 34N 1 18W
St.-Céré **44** 44 51N 1 54E
St. Cergue **50** 46 27N 6 10E
St. Cernin **44** 45 5N 2 25E
St.-Chamond **45** 45 28N 4 31E
St. Charles, Ill., U.S.A. **156** 41 55N 88 21W
St. Charles, Mo., U.S.A. **158** 38 46N 90 30W
St.-Chély-d'Apcher **44** 44 48N 3 17E
St.-Chinian **44** 43 25N 2 56E
St. Christopher (St. Kitts) **167** 17 20N 62 40W
St.-Ciers-sur-Gironde **44** 45 17N 0 37W
St. Clair **162** 40 42N 76 12W
St. Clair, L. **150** 42 30N 82 45W
St.-Claud **44** 45 54N 0 28E
St. Claude **153** 49 40N 98 20W
St.-Claude **45** 46 22N 5 52E
St. Clears **31** 51 48N 4 30W
St.-Cloud **42** 48 51N 2 12E
St. Cloud, Fla., U.S.A. **157** 28 15N 81 15W
St. Cloud, Minn., U.S.A. **158** 45 30N 94 11W
St. Coeur de Marie **151** 48 39N 71 43W
St. Columb Major **30** 50 26N 4 56W
St. Combs **37** 57 40N 1 55W
St. Cricq, C. **137** 25 17S 113 6E
St. Croix Falls **158** 45 18N 92 22W
St. Croix, I. **147** 17 45N 64 45W
St. Croix, R. **158** 45 20N 92 50W
St. Cyprien **44** 42 37N 3 0E
St.-Cyr **45** 43 11N 5 43E
St. Cyrus **36** 56 47N 2 25W
St. David's, Can. **151** 48 12N 58 52W
St. David's, U.K. **31** 51 54N 5 16W
St. David's Head **31** 51 54N 5 16W
St.-Denis **43** 48 56N 2 22E
St.-Denis-d'Orques **42** 48 2N 0 17W
St. Dennis **30** 50 23N 4 53W
St.-Dié **43** 48 17N 6 56E
St. Dizier **43** 48 40N 5 0E
St. Dogmaels **31** 52 6N 4 42W
St. Dominick **30** 50 28N 4 15W
St. Donats **31** 51 23N 3 32W
St.-Egrève **45** 45 14N 5 41E
St. Elias, Mt. **147** 60 20N 141 59W
St. Elias Mts. **147** 59 30N 137 30W
St. Eloy **44** 46 10N 2 51E
St. Emilon **44** 44 53N 0 9W
St. Endellion **30** 50 33N 4 49W
St. Enoder **30** 50 22N 4 57W
St. Erth **30** 50 10N 5 26W
St. Étienne **45** 45 27N 4 22E
St.-Étienne-de-Tinée **45** 44 16N 6 56E
St. Eustatius I. **167** 17 20N 63 0W
St. Félicien **150** 48 40N 72 25W
St. Fergus **37** 57 33N 1 50W
St. Fillans **35** 56 25N 4 7W
St. Finian's B. **39** 51 50N 10 22W
St. Fintan's **151** 48 10N 58 50W
St.-Florent **45** 42 41N 9 18E
St.-Florent-sur-Cher **43** 46 59N 2 15E
St.-Florentin **43** 48 0N 3 45E
St.-Flour **44** 45 2N 3 6E
St.-Fons **45** 45 42N 4 52E
St. Francis **158** 39 48N 101 47W
St. Francis C. **128** 34 14S 24 49E
St. Francis, R. **159** 32 25N 90 36W
St.-Fulgent **42** 46 50N 1 10W
St. Gabriel de Brandon **150** 46 17N 73 24W
St.-Gengoux-le-National **45** 46 37N 4 40E
St.-Geniez-d'Olt **44** 44 27N 2 58E
St. George, Austral. **139** 28 1S 148 41E
St. George, Can. **151** 45 11N 66 50W
St. George, P.N.G. **135** 4 10S 152 20E
St. George, S.C., U.S.A. **157** 33 13N 80 37W
St. George, Utah, U.S.A. **161** 37 10N 113 35W
St. George, C., Can. **151** 48 30N 59 16W
St. George, C., P.N.G. **135** 4 49S 152 53E
St. George, C., U.S.A. **157** 29 36N 85 2W
St. George Hd. **139** 35 11S 150 45E
St. George Ra., Mts. **136** 18 40S 125 0E
St. George West **153** 50 33N 96 7W
St.-Georges **47** 50 37N 4 20E
St. George's **151** 48 26N 58 31W
St. Georges, Qué., Can. **151** 46 8N 70 40W
St. Georges, Quebec, Can. **150** 46 42N 72 35W
St. Georges, Fr. Gui. **175** 4 0N 52 0W
St. George's **167** 12 5N 61 43W
St. George's B. **151** 48 24N 58 53W
St. George's Channel **147** 52 0N 6 0W
St. Georges-de-Didonne **44** 45 36N 1 0W
St. Georges Head **141** 35 12S 150 42E
St.-Gérard **47** 50 21N 4 44E
St. Germain **43** 48 53N 2 5E
St.-Germain-Lembron **44** 45 27N 3 14E
St.-Germain-de-Calberte **44** 44 13N 3 48E
St.-Germain-des-Fossés **44** 46 12N 3 26E
St.-Germain-du-Plain **43** 46 42N 4 58E
St.-Germain-Laval **45** 45 50N 4 1E
St. Germans **30** 50 24N 4 19W
St. Gervais, Haute Savoie, France **45** 45 53N 6 42E
St. Gervais, Puy de Dôme, France **44** 46 4N 2 50E
St.-Gervais-les-Bains **43** 45 53N 6 41E
St.-Gildas, Pte. de **42** 47 8N 2 14W
St.-Gilles **45** 43 40N 4 26E
St. Gilles Croix-de-Vie **42** 46 41N 1 55W
St.-Gingolph **50** 46 24N 6 48E
St.-Girons **44** 42 59N 1 8E
St. Gla, L. **72** 59 35N 12 30E
St. Goar **49** 50 31N 7 43E
St. Gotthard P. = San Gottardo **51** 46 33N 8 33E
St. Govan's Hd. **31** 51 35N 4 56W
St.-Guadens **44** 43 6N 0 44E
St.-Gualtier **42** 46 39N 1 26E
St.-Guénolé **42** 47 49N 4 23W
St. Harmon **31** 52 21N 3 29W
St. Heddinge **73** 55 9N 12 26E
St. Helena **160** 38 29N 122 30W
St. Helena, I. **15** 15 55S 5 44W
St. Helenabaai **128** 32 40S 18 10E
St. Helens, Austral. **138** 41 20S 148 15E
St. Helens, I.o.W., U.K. **28** 50 42N 1 6W
St. Helens, Merseyside, U.K. **32** 53 28N 2 44W
St. Helens, U.S.A. **160** 45 55N 122 50W
St. Helier **42** 49 11N 2 6W
St. Hilaire **42** 48 35N 1 7W
St. Hippolyte **43** 47 20N 6 50E
St. Hippolyte-du-Fort **44** 43 58N 3 52E
St.-Honoré **43** 46 54N 3 50E
St.-Hubert **47** 50 2N 5 23E
St. Hyacinthe **150** 45 40N 72 58W
St. Ignace **156** 45 53N 84 43W
St. Ignace I. **150** 48 45N 88 0W
St. Ignatius **160** 47 25N 114 2W
St.-Imier **50** 47 9N 6 58E
St. Issey **30** 50 30N 4 55W
St. Ives, Cambs., U.K. **29** 52 20N 0 5W
St. Ives, Cornwall, U.K. **30** 50 13N 5 29W
St. Ives Bay **30** 50 15N 5 27W
St.-James **42** 48 31N 1 20W
St. James **158** 43 57N 94 40W
St. James C. **152** 51 55N 131 0W
St. Jean **150** 45 20N 73 50W
St.-Jean **45** 48 57N 3 1E
St. Jean Baptiste **153** 49 15N 97 20W
St. Jean, C. **124** 1 5N 9 20E
St.-Jean-de-Maurienne **45** 45 16N 6 28E
St.-Jean-de-Luz **44** 43 23N 1 39W
St.-Jean-de-Monts **42** 46 47N 2 4W
St. Jean-du-Gard **44** 47 7N 3 52E
St.-Jean-en-Royans **45** 45 1N 5 18E
St.-Jean, L. **151** 48 40N 72 0W
St. Jean-Port-Joli **151** 47 15N 70 13W
St.-Jean, R. **151** 50 17N 64 20W
St. Jérôme, Qué., Can. **150** 45 47N 74 0W
St. Jérôme, Qué., Can. **151** 48 26N 71 53W
St. John, Can. **151** 45 20N 66 8W
St. John, Kans., U.S.A. **159** 37 59N 98 45W
St. John, N.D., U.S.A. **158** 48 58N 99 40W
St. John, C. **151** 50 0N 55 32W
St. John, I. **147** 18 20N 64 45W
St. John, R. **151** 45 15N 66 4W
St. Johns **167** 17 6N 61 51W
St. John's, Can. **151** 47 35N 52 40W
St. John's, U.K. **32** 54 13N 4 38W
St. Johns, Ariz., U.S.A. **161** 34 31N 109 26W
St. Johns, Mich., U.S.A. **156** 43 0N 84 38W
St. Johns Chapel **32** 54 43N 2 10W
St. John's Pt., Ireland **38** 54 35N 8 26W
St. John's Pt., U.K. **38** 54 14N 5 40W
St. Johns, R. **157** 30 20N 81 30W
St. Johnsbury **156** 44 25N 72 1W
St. Johnston **38** 54 56N 7 29W
St. Johnsville **162** 43 0N 74 43W
St. Joseph, La., U.S.A. **159** 31 55N 91 15W
St. Joseph, Mo., U.S.A. **158** 39 40N 94 50W
St. Joseph, I. **150** 46 12N 83 58W
St. Joseph, L. **150** 51 10N 90 35W
St. Joseph, R. **156** 42 7N 86 30W
St. Joseph's **156** 42 5N 86 30W
St. Jovite **150** 46 8N 74 38W
St. Juéry **44** 43 55N 2 42E
St. Julien **45** 46 8N 6 5E
St.-Julien-Chapteuil **45** 45 2N 4 4E
St. Julien du Sault **43** 48 1N 3 17E
St.-Junien **44** 45 53N 0 55E
St. Just **30** 50 7N 5 41W
St.-Just-en-Chaussée **43** 49 30N 2 25E
St.-Just-en-Chevalet **44** 45 55N 3 50E
St.-Justin **44** 43 59N 0 14W
St. Karlsö, I. **73** 57 17N 17 58E
St. Keverne **30** 50 3N 5 5W
St. Kew **30** 50 34N 4 48W
St. Kilda **143** 45 53S 170 31E
St. Kilda, I. **23** 57 40N 8 50W
St. Kitts-Nevis ■ **167** 17 20N 62 40W
St. Laurent **153** 50 25N 97 58W
St.-Laurent-du-Pont **45** 45 23N 5 45E
St.-Laurent-en-Grandvaux **45** 46 35N 5 45E
St. Lawrence, Austral. **138** 22 16S 149 31E
St. Lawrence, Can. **151** 46 54N 55 23W

St. Lawrence, Gulf of **151** 48 25N 62 0W
St. Lawrence, I. **147** 63 0N 170 0W
St. Lawrence, R. **151** 49 30N 66 0W
St.-Léger **47** 49 37N 5 39 E
St. Leonard **151** 47 12N 67 58W
St.-Léonard-de-Noblat **44** 45 49N 1 29 E
St. Leonards **29** 50 51N 0 34 E
St. Levan **30** 50 3N 5 36W
St Lewis, R. **151** 52 26N 56 11W
St. Lin **150** 45 44N 73 46W
St.-Lô **42** 49 7N 1 5W
St. Louis, Senegal **120** 16 8N 16 27W
St. Louis, Mich., U.S.A. **156** 43 27N 84 38W
St. Louis, Mo., U.S.A. **158** 38 40N 90 12W
St. Louis R. **158** 47 15N 92 45W
St.-Loup-sur-Semouse **43** 47 53N 6 16 E
St. Lucia, C. **129** 28 32 S 32 29 E
St. Lucia Channel **167** 14 15N 61 0W
St. Lucia I. **167** 14 0N 60 50W
St. Lucia, Lake **129** 28 5 S 32 30 E
St. Lunaire-Griquet **151** 51 31N 55 28W
St. Maarten, I. **167** 18 0N 63 5W
St. Mabyn **30** 50 30N 4 45W
St. Magnus B. **36** 60 25N 1 35W
St.-Maixent-l'École **44** 46 24N 0 12W
St.-Malo **42** 48 39N 2 1W
St. Malo, G. de **42** 48 50N 2 30W
St. Mandrier **45** 43 4N 5 56 E
St. Marc **167** 19 10N 72 50W
St.-Marcellin **45** 45 9N 5 20 E
St. Marcouf, Is. **42** 49 30N 1 10W
St.-Mard **47** 49 2N 2 42 E
St. Margaret's-at-Cliffe **29** 51 10N 1 23 E
St. Margaret's Hope **37** 58 49N 2 58W
St. Maries **160** 47 17N 116 34W
St. Martin **43** 50 42N 1 38 E
St.-Martin, I. **167** 18 0N 63 0W
St. Martin L. **153** 51 40N 98 30W
St. Martin-Tende-Vésubie **45** 44 4N 7 15 E
St. Martins **151** 45 22N 65 25W
St. Martin's I. **30** 49 58N 6 16W
St. Martinsville **159** 30 10N 91 50W
St.-Martory **44** 43 9N 0 56 E
St. Mary B. **151** 46 50N 53 50W
St. Mary Bourne **28** 51 16N 1 24W
St. Mary C. **120** 13 24N 13 10 E
St. Mary Is. **97** 13 20N 74 35 E
St. Mary, Mt. **135** 8 8 S 146 54 E
St. Mary Pk. **140** 31 32 S 138 34 E
St. Marys, N.S.W., Austral. **133** 33 44 S 150 49 E
St. Marys, Tas., Austral. **138** 41 32 S 148 11 E
St. Mary's, Can. **151** 46 56N 53 34W
St. Mary's, U.K. **37** 58 53N 2 55W
St. Mary's, Ohio, U.S.A. **156** 40 33N 84 20W
St. Mary's, Pa., U.S.A. **156** 41 30N 78 33W
St Marys Bay **151** 44 25N 66 10W
St. Mary's, C. **151** 46 50N 54 12W
St. Mary's I. **30** 49 55N 6 17W
St. Mary's Pk. **133** 31 30 S 138 33 E
St. Mary's Sd. **30** 49 53N 6 19W
St. Mathews I. = Zadetkyi Kyun **101** 10 0N 48 25 E
St.-Mathieu, Pte. de **42** 48 20N 4 45W
St. Matthias Grp. **135** 1 30 S 150 0 E
St.-Maur-des-Fosses **43** 48 48N 2 30 E
St. Maurice **50** 46 13N 7 0 E
St. Maurice R. **150** 47 20N 72 50W
St. Mawes **30** 50 10N 5 1W
St.-Médard-de-Guizières **44** 45 1N 0 4W
St.-Méen-le-Grand **42** 48 11N 2 12W
St. Merryn **30** 50 31N 4 58W
St. Michael **147** 63 30N 162 30W
St. Michaels, Arizona, U.S.A. **161** 35 45N 109 5W
St. Michaels, Maryland, U.S.A. **162** 38 47N 76 14W
St. Michael's Mt. **30** 50 7N 5 30W
St. Michel **45** 45 15N 6 29 E
St. Mihiel **43** 48 54N 5 30 E
St. Minver **30** 50 34N 4 52W
St. Monans **35** 56 13N 2 46W
St.-Nazaire **42** 47 17N 2 12W
St. Neots **29** 52 14N 0 16W
St.-Nicholas-de-Port **43** 48 38N 6 18 E
St. Niklaus **50** 46 10N 7 49 E
St. Ninian's, I. **36** 59 59N 1 20W
St. Olaf **73** 55 40N 14 12 E
St.-Omer **43** 50 45N 2 15 E
St. Osyth **29** 51 47N 1 4 E
St. Ouen **43** 48 50N 2 20 E
St. Pacome **151** 47 24N 69 58W
St. Palais **44** 45 40N 1 8W
St. Pamphile **151** 46 58N 69 48W
St.-Pardoux-la-Rivière **44** 45 29N 0 45 E
St. Pascal **151** 47 32N 69 48W
St. Patrickswell **39** 52 36N 8 43W
St. Paul, Can. **152** 54 59N 111 17W
St. Paul, France **44** 43 44N 1 3W
St. Paul, Minn., U.S.A. **158** 44 54N 93 5W
St. Paul, Nebr., U.S.A. **158** 41 15N 98 30W
St. Paul-de-Fenouillet **44** 42 50N 2 28 E
St. Paul, I., Atl. Oc. **14** 0 50N 31 40W
St. Paul, I., Can. **151** 47 12N 60 9W
St. Paul, I., Ind. Oc. **11** 30 40 S 77 34 E
St. Paul's B. **151** 49 48N 57 58W
St.-Peray **45** 44 57N 4 50 E
St.-Père-en-Retz **42** 47 11N 2 2W
St. Peter **158** 44 15N 93 57W
St. Peter Port **42** 49 27N 2 31W
St. Peters, N.S., Can. **151** 45 40N 60 53W
St. Peters, P.E.I., Can. **151** 46 25N 62 35W
St. Petersburg **157** 27 45N 82 40W
St.-Philbert-de-Grand-Lieu **42** 47 2N 1 39W
St Pierre **151** 46 40N 56 0W
St.-Pierre-d'Oleron **44** 45 57N 1 19W
St.-Pierre-Église **42** 49 40N 1 24W
St.-Pierre-en-Port **42** 49 48N 0 30 E
Saint-Pierre et Miquelon □ **151** 46 55N 56 10W
St.-Pierre, L. **150** 46 12N 72 52W
St.-Pierre-le-Moûtier **43** 46 47N 3 7 E
St. Pierre-sur-Dives **42** 49 2N 0 1W
St.-Pieters Leew **47** 50 47N 4 16 E
St. Pol **43** 50 21N 2 20 E
St.-Pol-de-Léon **42** 48 41N 4 0W
St.-Pol-sur-Mer **43** 51 1N 2 20 E
St. Pons **44** 43 30N 2 45 E
St.-Pourçain-sur-Sioule **43** 46 18N 3 18 E
St.-Quay-Portrieux **42** 48 39N 2 51W
St.-Quentin **43** 49 50N 3 16 E
St. Rambert-d'Albon **45** 45 17N 1 35 E
St.-Raphaël **45** 43 25N 6 46 E
St. Regis **160** 47 20N 115 3W
St.-Rémy-de-Provence **45** 43 48N 4 50 E
St.-Renan **42** 48 26N 4 37W
St.-Saëns **42** 49 41N 1 16 E
St.-Sauveur-en-Puisaye **43** 47 37N 3 12 E
St.-Sauveur-le-Vicomte **42** 49 23N 1 32W
St. Savin **44** 46 34N 0 50 E
St.-Savinien **44** 45 53N 0 42W
St. Sebastien, C. **129** 12 26 S 48 44 E
St.-Seine-l'Abbaye **43** 47 26N 4 47 E
St. Sernin **44** 43 54N 2 35 E
St.-Servan-sur-Mer **42** 48 38N 2 0 E
St.-Sever-Calvados **42** 48 50N 1 3W
St. Simeon **151** 47 51N 69 54W
St. Stephen, Can. **151** 45 16N 67 17W
St. Stephen, U.K. **30** 50 20N 4 52W
St.-Sulpice **44** 43 46N 1 41 E
St.-Sulpice-Laurière **44** 46 3N 1 29 E
St. Teath **30** 50 34N 4 45W
St.-Thegonnec **42** 48 31N 3 57W
St. Thomas **150** 42 45N 81 10W
St. Thomas, I. **147** 18 21N 64 55W
St. Tite **150** 46 45N 72 40W
St. Tropez **45** 43 17N 6 38 E
St. Troud **47** 50 48N 5 10 E
St. Tudwal's Is. **31** 52 48N 4 28W
St. Tudy **30** 50 33N 4 45W
St.-Vaast-la-Hougue **42** 49 35N 1 17W
St. Valéry **43** 50 10N 1 38 E
St.-Valéry-en-Caux **42** 49 52N 0 43 E
St.-Vallier **45** 45 11N 4 50 E
St.-Vallier-de-Thiey **45** 43 42N 6 51 E
St.-Varent **42** 46 53N 0 13W
St. Vincent **14** 18 0N 26 1W
St. Vincent C. **125** 21 58 S 43 20 E
St. Vincent, C. = São Vincente **57** 37 0N 9 0W
St. Vincent-de-Tyrosse **44** 43 39N 1 18W
St. Vincent, G. **140** 35 0 S 138 0 E
St. Vincent, I. **167** 13 10N 61 10W
St. Vincent Passage **167** 13 30N 61 0W
St.-Vith **47** 50 17N 6 9 E
St.-Yrieux-la-Perche **44** 45 31N 1 12 E
Ste.-Adresse **42** 49 31N 0 5 E
Ste.-Agathe-des-Monts **150** 46 3N 74 17W
Ste. Anne **167** 14 26N 60 53W
Ste. Anne de Beaupré **151** 47 2N 70 58W
Ste. Anne de Portneuf **151** 48 38N 69 8W
Ste.-Anne-des-Monts **151** 49 8N 66 30W
Ste. Benoîte **43** 49 47N 3 30 E
Ste. Cecile **151** 47 56N 64 34W
Ste.-Croix **43** 46 49N 6 34W
Ste.-Enimie **44** 44 22N 3 26 E
Ste.-Foy-la-Grande **44** 44 50N 0 13 E
Ste. Genevieve **158** 37 59N 90 2W
Ste. Germaine **151** 46 24N 70 24W
Ste.-Hermine **44** 46 32N 1 4W
Ste.-Livrade-sur-Lot **44** 44 24N 0 36 E
Ste. Marguerite, R. **151** 50 9N 66 36W
Ste. Marie **167** 14 48N 61 1W
Ste.-Marie-aux-Mines **43** 48 10N 7 12 E
Ste. Marie, C. **129** 25 36 S 45 8 E
Ste. Marie de la Madeleine **151** 46 26N 71 0W
Ste. Marie, I. **129** 16 50 S 49 55 E
Ste.-Maure-de-Touraine **42** 47 7N 0 37 E
Ste.-Maxime **45** 43 19N 6 39 E
Ste.-Menehould **43** 49 5N 4 54 E
Ste.-Mère-Église **42** 49 24N 1 19W
Ste. Rose **167** 16 20N 61 45W
Ste. Rose du lac **153** 51 41N 99 30W
Ste. Teresa **172** 33 33 S 60 54W
Saintes **44** 45 45N 0 37W
Saintes, I. des **167** 15 50N 61 35W
Saintes-Maries-de-la-Mer **45** 43 26N 4 26 E
Saintes Maries, Les **45** 43 27N 4 25 E
Saintfield **38** 54 28N 5 50W
Saintonge **44** 45 40N 0 50W
Sairang **99** 23 50N 92 45 E
Sairecábur, Cerro **172** 22 43 S 67 54W
Saitama-ken □ **111** 36 25N 137 0 E
Saito **110** 32 3N 131 18 E
Sajama, Nevada **174** 18 0 S 68 55W
Sajan **66** 45 50N 20 58 E
Sajószentpéter **53** 48 12N 20 44 E
Sajum, mt. **95** 33 20N 79 0 E
Saka Ilkalat **93** 27 20N 64 7 E
Sakai **111** 34 30N 135 30 E
Sakaide **110** 34 15N 133 56 E
Sakaiminato **110** 35 38N 133 11 E
Sakaka **92** 30 0N 40 8 E
Sakami, L. **150** 53 15N 76 45W
Sâkâne, 'Erg i-n **118** 20 30N 1 30W
Sakania **127** 12 43 S 28 30 E
Sakar, I. **138** 5 30 S 148 0 E
Sakarya, R. **82** 40 5N 31 0 E
Sakata **112** 36 38N 138 19 E
Sakchu **107** 40 23N 125 2 E
Sakeny, R. **129** 20 0 S 45 25 E
Sakété **121** 6 40N 2 32 E
Sakhalin, Ostrov **77** 51 0N 143 0 E
Sakhi Gopal **96** 19 58N 85 50 E
Sakhnin **90** 32 52N 35 12 E
Saki **82** 45 16N 33 34 E
Sakiai **80** 54 59N 23 0 E
Sakmara **84** 52 0N 55 20 E
Sakmara, R. **84** 51 46N 55 1 E
Sakołow Małopolski **54** 50 10N 22 9 E
Sakon Nakhon **100** 17 10N 104 9 E
Sakrand **94** 26 10N 68 15 E
Sakri **96** 21 2N 74 40 E
Sakskøbing **73** 54 49N 11 39 E
Saku **111** 36 11N 138 31 E
Sakuma **111** 35 3N 137 56 E
Sakurai **111** 34 30N 135 51 E
Sakuru **111** 35 43N 140 14 E
Säkylä **75** 61 4N 22 20 E
Sal, R. **83** 47 25N 42 20 E
Sal'a **53** 48 10N 17 50 E
Sala **72** 59 58N 16 35 E
Sala Consilina **65** 40 23N 15 35 E
Sala-y-Gomez, I. **131** 26 28 S 105 28W
Salaberry-de-Valleyfield **150** 45 15N 74 8W
Salada, La **164** 24 30N 111 30W
Saladas **172** 28 15 S 58 40W
Saladillo **172** 35 40 S 59 55W
Salado, R., Buenos Aires, Argent. **172** 35 40 S 58 10W
Salado, R., Santa Fe, Argent. **172** 27 0 S 63 40W
Salado, R., Mexico **164** 26 52N 99 19W
Salaga **121** 8 31N 0 31W
Salala, Liberia **120** 6 42N 10 7W
Salala, Sudan **122** 21 17N 36 16 E
Salalah **91** 16 56N 53 59 E
Salama **90** 32 3N 34 48 E
Salamanca, Chile **172** 32 0 S 71 25W
Salamanca, Spain **56** 40 58N 5 39W
Salamanca, U.S.A. **156** 42 10N 78 42W
Salamanca □ **56** 40 57N 5 40W
Salamaua **138** 7 10 S 147 0 E
Salamina **174** 5 25N 75 29W
Salamis **69** 37 56N 23 30 E
Salar de Atacama **176** 23 30 S 68 25W
Salar de Uyuni **174** 20 30 S 67 45W
Salard **70** 47 12N 22 3 E
Salas **56** 43 25N 6 15W
Salas de los Infantes **58** 42 2N 3 17W
Salavat **84** 53 21N 55 55 E
Salaverry **174** 8 15 S 79 0W
Salawe **126** 3 17 S 32 56 E
Salayar, I. **103** 6 15 S 120 30 E
Salazar, R. **58** 42 45N 1 8W
Salbohed **72** 59 55N 16 22 E
Salbris **43** 47 25N 2 3 E
Salcia **70** 43 56N 24 55 E
Salcombe **30** 50 14N 3 47W
Salcombe Regis **30** 50 41N 3 11W
Saldaña **56** 42 32N 4 48W
Saldanha **128** 33 0 S 17 58 E
Saldanhabaai **128** 33 6 S 18 0 E
Saldus **80** 56 45N 22 37 E
Sale **141** 38 6 S 147 6 E
Salé **118** 34 3N 6 48W
Sale **32** 53 26N 2 19W
Saléa-koïra **121** 16 54N 0 46W
Salebabu **103** 3 45N 125 55 E
Salehabad **93** 35 40N 61 2 E
Salekhard **76** 66 30N 66 25 E
Salem, India **97** 11 40N 78 11 E
Salem, Ind., U.S.A. **156** 38 38N 86 16W
Salem, Mass., U.S.A. **162** 42 29N 70 53W
Salem, Mo., U.S.A. **159** 37 40N 91 30W
Salem, N.H., U.S.A. **162** 42 47N 71 12W
Salem, N.J., U.S.A. **162** 39 34N 75 29W
Salem, N.Y., U.S.A. **162** 43 10N 73 20W
Salem, Ohio, U.S.A. **156** 40 52N 80 50W
Salem, Oreg., U.S.A. **160** 45 0N 123 0W
Salem, Va., U.S.A. **156** 37 19N 80 8W
Salembu, Kepulauan **102** 5 35 S 114 30 E
Salemi **64** 37 49N 12 47 E
Salen, Norway **75** 64 41N 11 27 E
Salen, Highland, U.K. **36** 56 42N 5 48W
Salen, Strathclyde, U.K. **34** 56 31N 5 57W
Salernes **45** 43 34N 6 15 E
Salerno **65** 40 40N 14 44 E
Salerno, G. di **65** 40 35N 14 45 E
Salfit **90** 32 5N 35 11 E
Salford **32** 53 30N 2 17W
Salford Priors **28** 52 10N 1 52W
Salgir, R. **82** 45 30N 34 30 E
Salgótarján **53** 48 5N 19 47 E
Salgueiro **170** 8 4 S 39 6W
Salies-de-Béarn **44** 43 28N 0 56W
Salima **125** 13 47 S 34 28 E
Salin **98** 20 35N 94 40 E
Salina **158** 38 50N 97 40W
Salina Cruz **165** 16 10N 95 10W
Salina, I. **65** 38 35N 14 50 E
Salina, La **174** 10 22N 71 27W
Salinas, Brazil **171** 16 20 S 42 10W
Salinas, Chile **172** 23 31 S 69 29W
Salinas, Ecuador **174** 2 10 S 80 50W
Salinas, Mexico **164** 23 37N 106 8W
Salinas, U.S.A. **163** 36 40N 121 31W
Salinas Ambargasta **172** 29 0 S 65 30W
Salinas, B. de **166** 11 4N 85 45W
Salinas, Cabo de **59** 39 16N 3 4 E
Salinas (de Hidalgo) **164** 22 30N 101 40W
Salinas Grandes **172** 30 0 S 65 0W
Salinas, Pampa de las **172** 31 58 S 66 42W
Salinas, R., Mexico **165** 16 28N 90 31W
Salinas, R., U.S.A. **163** 36 45N 121 48W
Saline, R. **158** 39 10N 99 5W
Salines-les-Bains **43** 46 58N 5 52 E
Salinópolis **170** 0 40 S 47 20W
Salir **57** 37 14N 8 2W
Salisbury, Austral. **140** 34 46 S 138 40 E
•Salisbury, Zimb. **127** 17 50 S 31 2 E
Salisbury, U.K. **28** 51 4N 1 48W
Salisbury, Md., U.S.A. **162** 38 20N 75 38W
Salisbury, N.C., U.S.A. **157** 35 42N 80 29W
Salisbury Plain **28** 51 13N 1 50W
Salitre, R. **170** 9 29 S 40 39W
Salka **121** 10 20N 4 58 E
Salle, La **158** 41 20N 89 5W
Sallent **58** 41 49N 1 54 E
Salles-Curan **44** 44 11N 2 48 E
Salling **73** 56 40N 8 55 E
Sallisaw **159** 35 26N 94 45W
Sallom Junc. **122** 19 23N 37 6 E
Sally Gap, Mt. **39** 53 7N 6 18W
Salmerón **58** 40 33N 2 29W
Salmo **152** 49 10N 117 20W
Salmon **160** 45 12N 113 56W
Salmon Arm **152** 50 40N 119 15W
Salmon Falls **160** 42 55N 114 59W
Salmon Gums **137** 32 59 S 121 38 E
Salmon, R., Can. **152** 54 3N 122 40W
Salmon, R., U.S.A. **160** 46 0N 116 30W
Salmon Res. **151** 48 05N 56 00W
Salmon River Mts. **160** 45 0N 114 30W
Salo **75** 60 22N 23 3 E
Salò **62** 45 37N 10 32 E
Salobreña **57** 36 44N 3 35W
Salome **161** 33 51N 113 37W
Salon-de-Provence **45** 43 39N 5 6 E
Salonica = Thessaloníki **68** 40 38N 22 58 E
Salonta **70** 46 49N 21 42 E
Salop □ **28** 52 36N 2 45W
Salor, R. **57** 39 39N 7 3W
Salou, Cabo **58** 41 3N 1 10 E
Salsacate **172** 31 20 S 65 5W
Salsaker **72** 62 59N 18 20 E
Salses **44** 42 50N 2 55 E
Salsette I. **96** 19 5N 72 50 E
Salsk **83** 46 28N 41 30 E
Salso, R. **65** 37 6N 13 55 E
Salsomaggiore **62** 44 48N 9 59 E
Salt **90** 32 2N 35 43 E
Salt Creek **140** 36 8 S 139 38 E
Salt Creek Telegraph Office **139** 36 0 S 139 35 E
Salt Fork R. **159** 37 25N 98 40W
Salt Lake City **160** 40 45N 111 58W
Salt, R., Can. **152** 60 0N 112 25W
Salt, R., U.S.A. **161** 33 50N 110 25W
Salt Range **94** 32 30N 72 25 E
Salta **172** 24 47 S 65 25W
Salta □ **172** 24 48 S 65 30W
Saltash **30** 50 25N 4 13W
Saltburn by Sea **33** 54 35N 0 58W
Saltcoats **34** 55 38N 4 47W
Saltee Is. **39** 52 7N 6 37W
Saltergate **33** 54 20N 0 40W
Saltfjorden **74** 67 15N 14 20 E
Saltfleet **33** 53 25N 0 11 E
Saltfleetby **33** 53 23N 0 10 E
Salthill **39** 53 15N 9 6W
Saltholm **73** 55 38N 12 43 E
Salthólmavík **74** 65 24N 21 57W
Saltillo **164** 25 30N 100 57W
Salto, Argent. **172** 34 20 S 60 15W
Salto, Uruguay **172** 31 20 S 57 59W
Salto □ **172** 31 20 S 57 59W
Salto Augusto, falls **172** 8 30 S 58 0W
Salto da Divisa **171** 16 0 S 39 57W
Salton City **163** 33 21N 115 59W
Salton Sea **163** 33 20N 115 50W
Saltpond **121** 5 15N 1 3W
Saltsjöbaden **73** 59 15N 18 20 E
Saltspring **152** 48 54N 123 37W
Saltwood **29** 51 4N 1 5 E
Saluda **162** 37 36N 76 36W
Salula, R. **157** 34 12N 81 45W
Salûm **122** 31 31N 25 7 E
Salûm, Khâlig el **122** 31 30N 25 9 E
Salur **96** 18 27N 83 18 E
Saluzzo **62** 44 39N 7 29 E
Salvador, Brazil **171** 13 0 S 38 30W
Salvador, Can. **153** 52 10N 109 25W
Salvador ■ **164** 13 50N 89 0W
Salvador, L. **159** 29 46N 90 16W
Salvaterra **170** 0 46 S 48 31W
Salvaterra de Magos **57** 39 1N 8 47W
Sálvora, Isla **56** 42 30N 8 58W
Salwa **93** 24 45N 50 55 E
Salween, R. **98** 16 31N 97 37 E
Salza, R. **52** 47 43N 15 0 E
Salzach, R. **52** 47 15N 12 25 E
Salzburg **52** 47 48N 13 2 E
Salzgitter **48** 52 2N 10 22 E
Salzwedel **48** 52 50N 11 11 E
Sam Neua **100** 20 29N 104 0 E
Sam Ngao **100** 17 18N 99 0 E

*Renamed Harare

Sam Rayburn Res. 159 31 15N 94 20W
Sam Son 100 19 44N 105 54 E
Sam Ten 100 19 59N 104 38 E
Sama 84 60 12N 60 22 E
Sama de Langreo 56 43 18N 5 40W
Samales Group 103 6 0N 122 0 E
Samalkot 96 17 3N 82 13 E
Samâlût 122 28 20N 30 42 E
Samana 94 30 10N 76 13 E
Samana Cay 167 23 3N 73 45W
Samanco 174 9 10 S 78 30W
Samanga 127 8 20 S 39 13 E
Samangan 93 36 15N 67 40 E
Samangwa 126 4 23 S 24 10 E
Samani 112 42 7N 142 56 E
Samar, I. 103 12 0N 125 0 E
Samara, R. 84 53 10N 50 4 E
Samaria 135 10 39 S 150 41 E
Samaria = Shomron 90 32 15N 35 13 E
Samarkand 85 39 40N 67 0 E
Samarra 92 34 16N 43 55 E
Samastipur 95 25 50N 85 50 E
Samatan 44 43 29N 0 55 E
Samba, Kashmir 95 32 32N 75 10 E
Samba, Zaïre 126 4 38 S 26 22 E
Sambaíba 170 7 8 S 45 21W
Sambaina 129 19 37 S 47 8 E
Sambaise 65 38 58N 16 16 E
Sambalpur 96 21 28N 83 58 E
Sambas, S. 102 1 20N 109 20 E
Sambava 129 14 16 S 50 10 E
Sambawizi 127 18 24 S 26 13 E
Sambhal 95 28 35N 78 37 E
Sambhar 94 26 52N 75 10 E
Sambonifacio 62 45 24N 11 16 E
Sambor, Camb. 100 12 46N 106 0 E
Sambor, U.S.S.R. 80 49 30N 23 10 E
Sambre, R. 47 50 27N 4 52 E
Sambuca 64 37 39N 13 6 E
Samburu □ 126 1 10N 37 0 E
Sambusu 128 17 55 S 19 21 E
Samchŏk 107 37 30N 129 10 E
Samchonpo 107 34 54N 128 6 E
Same 126 4 2 S 37 38 E
Samedan 51 46 32N 9 52 E
Samer 43 50 38N 1 44 E
Samfya 127 11 16 S 29 31 E
Sámi 69 38 15N 20 39 E
Samna 122 25 12N 37 17 E
Samnager 71 60 23N 5 39 E
Samnaun 51 46 57N 10 22 E
Samnu 119 27 15N 14 55 E
Samo Alto 172 30 22 S 71 0W
Samoan Is. 10 14 0 S 171 0W
Samobor 63 45 47N 15 44 E
Samoëns 45 46 5N 6 45 E
Samoorombón, Bahía 172 36 5 S 57 20W
Samorogouan 120 11 21N 4 57W
Samos 56 42 44N 7 20W
Samoš 66 45 13N 20 49 E
Sámos, I. 69 37 45N 26 50 E
Samosir, P. 102 2 35N 98 50 E
Samothráki 68 40 28N 25 38 E
Samothráki, I. 68 40 25N 25 40 E
Sampa 120 8 0N 2 36W
Sampacho 172 33 20 S 64 50W
Sampang 103 7 11 S 113 13 E
Samper de Calanda 58 41 11N 04 2W
Sampford Courtenay 30 50 47N 3 58W
Sampit 102 2 20 S 113 0 E
Samra 92 25 35N 41 0 E
Samreboi 120 5 34N 7 28 E
Samrée 47 50 13N 5 39 E
Samrong, Camb. 100 14 15N 103 30 E
Samrong, Thai. 100 15 10N 100 40 E
Samsø 73 55 50N 10 35 E
Samsø Bælt 73 55 45N 10 45 E
Samsonovo 85 37 53N 65 15 E
Samsun 92 41 15N 36 15 E
Samsun Daği 69 37 45N 27 10 E
Samtredia 83 42 7N 42 24 E
Samui, Ko 101 9 30N 100 0 E
Samur, R. 83 41 30N 48 0 E
Samusole 127 10 2 S 24 0 E
Samut Prakan 100 13 32N 100 40 E
Samut Sakhon 100 13 31N 100 20 E
Samut Songkhram (Mekong) 100 13 24N 100 1 E
Samwari 94 28 5N 66 46 E
Samyo La 99 29 55N 84 46 E
San 120 13 15N 4 45W
San Adrián, C. de 56 43 21N 8 50W
San Adrián, G. de 56 43 21N 8 50W
San Agustín 174 1 53N 76 16W
San Agustin, C. 103 6 20N 126 13 E
San Agustín de Valle Fértil 172 30 35 S 67 30W
San Ambrosio, I. 131 26 35 S 79 30W
San Andreas 163 38 17N 120 39W
San Andrés, I. de 166 12 42N 81 46W
San Andres Mts. 161 33 0N 106 45W
San Andrés Tuxtla 165 18 30N 95 20W
San Angelo 159 31 30N 100 30W
San Anselmo 163 37 49N 122 34W
San Antonio, Belize 165 16 15N 89 2W
San Antonio, Chile 172 33 40 S 71 40W
San Antonio, N. Mex., U.S.A. 161 33 58N 106 57W
San Antonio, Tex., U.S.A. 159 29 30N 98 30W
San Antonio, Venez. 174 3 30N 66 44W
San Antonio Abad 59 38 59N 1 19 E
San Antonio, C., Argent. 172 36 15 S 56 40W
San Antonio, C., Cuba 166 21 50N 84 57W
San Antonio, C. de 59 38 48N 0 12 E
San Antonio de Caparo 174 7 35N 71 27W
San Antonio de los Baños 166 22 54N 82 31W
San Antonio de los Cobres 172 24 16 S 66 2W
San Antonio do Zaire 124 6 8 S 12 11 E
San Antonio, Mt. (Old Baldy Pk.) 163 34 17N 117 38W
San Antonio Oeste 176 40 40 S 65 0W
San Antonio, R. 159 28 30N 97 14W
San Ardo 163 36 1N 120 54W
San Bartolomeo in Galdo 65 41 23N 15 2 E
San Benedetto 62 45 2N 10 57 E
San Benedetto del Tronto 63 42 57N 13 52 E
San Benedicto, I. 164 19 18N 110 49W
San Benito 159 26 5N 97 32W
San Benito Mtn. 163 36 22N 120 37W
San Benito, R. 163 36 53N 121 50W
San Bernardino 163 34 7N 117 18W
San Bernardino, Paso del 51 46 28N 9 11 E
San Bernardo 172 33 40 S 70 50W
San Bernardo, I. de 174 9 45N 75 50W
San Blas 164 26 10N 108 40W
San Blas, C. 157 29 40N 85 25W
San Blas, Cord. de 166 9 15N 78 30W
San Borja 174 15 0 S 67 12W
San Buenaventura 164 27 5N 101 32W
San Buenaventura = Ventura 163 34 17N 119 18W
San Carlos, Argent. 172 33 50 S 69 0W
San Carlos, Mexico 164 29 0N 101 10W
San Carlos, Nic. 166 11 12N 84 50W
San Carlos, Phil. 103 10 29N 123 25 E
San Carlos, Uruguay 173 34 46 S 54 58W
San Carlos, U.S.A. 161 33 24N 110 27W
San Carlos, Amazonas, Venez. 174 1 55N 67 4W
San Carlos, Cojedes, Venez. 174 9 40N 68 36W
San Carlos de Bariloche 176 41 10 S 71 25W
San Carlos de la Rápita 58 40 37N 0 35 E
San Carlos del Zulia 174 9 1N 71 55W
San Carlos L. 161 33 20N 110 10W
San Carlos = Butuku-Luba 121 3 29N 8 33 E
San Cataldo 64 37 30N 13 58 E
San Celoni 58 41 42N 2 30 E
San Clemente, Chile 172 35 30 S 71 39W
San Clemente, Spain 59 39 24N 2 25W
San Clemente, U.S.A. 163 33 29N 117 45W
San Clemente I. 163 32 53N 118 30W
San Constanzo 63 43 46N 13 5 E
San Cristóbal, Argent. 172 30 20 S 61 10W
San Cristóbal, Dom. Rep. 167 18 25N 70 6W
San Cristóbal, Venez. 174 7 46N 72 14W
San Cristóbal de las Casas 165 16 50N 92 33W
San Damiano d'Asti 62 44 51N 8 4 E
San Daniel del Friuli 63 46 10N 13 0 E
San Demétrio Corone 65 39 34N 16 22 E
San Diego, Calif., U.S.A. 163 32 43N 117 10W
San Diego, Tex., U.S.A. 159 27 47N 98 15W
San Diego, C. 176 54 40 S 65 10W
San Diego de la Unión 164 21 28N 100 52W
San Donà di Piave 63 45 38N 12 34 E
San Elpídio a Mare 63 43 16N 13 41 E
San Estanislao 172 24 39 S 56 26W
San Esteban de Gormaz 58 41 34N 3 13W
San Felice sul Panaro 62 44 51N 11 9 E
San Felipe, Chile 172 32 43 S 70 50W
San Felipe, Mexico 164 31 0N 114 52W
San Felipe, Venez. 174 10 20N 68 44W
San Felipe, R. 163 33 12N 115 49W
San Feliu de Guixols 58 41 45N 3 1 E
San Feliu de Llobregat 58 41 23N 2 2 E
San Fèlix 174 8 20N 62 35W
San Felix, I. 131 26 30 S 80 0W
San Fernando, Chile 172 34 30 S 71 0W
San Fernando, Mexico 164 30 0N 115 10W
San Fernando, Luzon, Phil. 103 15 5N 120 37 E
San Fernando, Luzon, Phil. 103 16 40N 120 23 E
San Fernando, Spain 57 36 22N 6 17W
San Fernando, Trin 167 10 20N 61 30W
San Fernando, U.S.A. 163 34 15N 118 29W
San Fernando de Apure 174 7 54N 67 28W
San Fernando de Atabapo 174 4 3N 67 42W
San Fernando di Puglia 65 41 18N 16 5 E
San Fernando, R. 164 25 0N 99 0W
San Francisco, Córdoba, Argent. 172 31 30 S 62 5W
San Francisco, San Luis, Argent. 172 32 45 S 66 10W
San Francisco, U.S.A. 163 37 47N 122 30W
San Francisco de Macorís 167 19 19N 70 15W
San Francisco del Monte de Oro 172 32 36 S 66 8W
San Francisco del Oro 164 26 52N 105 50W
San Francisco Javier 59 38 40N 1 25 E
San Francisco, Paso de 172 35 40 S 70 24W
San Francisco, R. 161 33 30N 109 0W
San Francisco Solano, Pta. 174 6 18N 77 29W
San Francisville 159 30 48N 91 22W
San Fratello 65 38 1N 14 33 E
San Gabriel 174 0 36N 77 49W
San Gavino Monreale 64 39 33N 8 47 E
San German 147 18 5N 67 3W
San Gil 174 6 33N 73 8W
San Gimignano 62 43 28N 11 3 E
San Giórgio di Nogaro 63 45 50N 13 13 E
San Giórgio Iônico 65 40 27N 17 23 E
San Giovanni Bianco 62 45 52N 9 40 E
San Giovanni in Fiore 65 39 16N 16 42 E
San Giovanni in Persieceto 63 44 39N 11 12 E
San Giovanni Rotondo 65 41 41N 15 42 E
San Giovanni Valdarno 63 43 32N 11 30 E
San Giuliano Terme 62 43 45N 10 26 E
San Gorgonio Mtn. 163 34 7N 116 51W
San Gottardo, Paso del 51 46 33N 8 33 E
San Gregorio, Uruguay 173 32 37 S 55 40W
San Gregorio, U.S.A. 163 37 20N 122 23W
San Guiseppe Iato 64 37 37N 13 11 E
San Ignacio, Boliv. 174 16 20 S 60 55W
San Ignacio, Mexico 164 27 27N 112 51W
San Ignacio, Parag. 172 26 52 S 57 3W
San Ignacio, Laguna 164 26 50N 113 11W
San Ildefonso, C. 103 16 0N 122 10 E
San Isidro 172 34 29 S 58 31W
San Jacinto, Colomb. 174 9 50N 75 8W
San Jacinto, U.S.A. 163 33 47N 116 57W
San Javier, Misiones, Argent. 173 27 55 S 55 5W
San Javier, Santa Fe, Argent. 172 30 40 S 59 55W
San Javier, Boliv. 174 16 18 S 62 30W
San Javier, Chile 172 35 40 S 71 45W
San Javier, Spain 59 37 49N 0 50W
San Jerónimo, Sa. de 174 8 0N 75 50W
San Joaquin 163 36 36N 120 11W
San Joaquín 174 10 16N 67 47W
San Joaquin R. 163 38 4N 121 51W
San Joaquin Valley 163 37 0N 120 30W
San Jorge 172 31 54 S 61 50W
San Jorge, Bahía de 164 31 20N 113 20W
San Jorge, Golfo de 176 46 0 S 66 0W
San Jorge, G. de 58 40 50N 0 55W
San José, Boliv. 174 17 45 S 60 50W
San José, C. Rica 166 10 0N 84 2W
San José, Guat. 164 14 0N 90 50W
San José, Luzon, Phil. 103 15 45N 120 55 E
San José, Mindoro, Phil. 103 10 50N 122 5 E
San José, Spain 59 38 55N 1 18 E
San Jose, Calif., U.S.A. 163 37 20N 121 53W
San Jose, N. Mex., U.S.A. 159 35 26N 105 30W
San José Carpizo 165 19 26N 90 32W
San José de Feliciano 172 30 26 S 58 46W
San José de Jáchal 172 30 5 S 69 0W
San José de Mayo 172 34 27 S 56 27W
San José de Ocuné 174 4 15N 70 20W
San José del Cabo 164 23 0N 109 50W
San José del Guaviare 174 2 35N 72 38W
San José, I. 164 25 0N 110 50W
San Juan, Argent. 172 31 30 S 68 30W
San Juan, Antioquía, Colomb. 174 8 46N 76 32W
San Juan, Meta, Colomb. 174 3 26N 73 50W
San Juan, Dom. Rep. 147 18 49N 71 12W
San Juan, Coahuila, Mexico 164 29 34N 101 53W
San Juan, Jalisco, Mexico 164 21 20N 102 50W
San Juan, Querétaro, Mexico 164 20 25N 100 0W
San Juan, Phil. 103 8 35N 126 20 E
San Juan, Pto Rico 147 18 28N 66 37W
San Juan □ 172 31 9 S 69 0W
San Juan Bautista, Parag. 172 26 37 S 57 6W
San Juan Bautista, Spain 59 39 5N 1 31 E
San Juan Bautista, U.S.A. 163 36 51N 121 32W
San Juan, C. 147 18 23N 65 37W
San Juan Capistrano 163 33 29N 117 40W
San Juan de Guadalupe 164 24 38N 102 44W
San Juan de los Cayos 174 11 10N 68 25W
San Juan de los Morros 174 9 55N 67 21W
San Juan de Norte, B. de 166 11 30N 83 40W
San Juan del Norte 166 10 58N 83 40W
San Juan del Puerto 57 37 20N 6 50W
San Juan del Río 165 24 47N 104 27W
San Juan del Sur 166 11 20N 86 0W
San Juan Mts. 161 38 30N 108 30W
San Juan, Presa de 164 17 45N 95 15W
San Juan, R., Argent. 172 32 20 S 67 25W
San Juan, R., Colomb. 174 4 0N 77 20W
San Juan, R., Nic. 166 11 0N 84 30W
San Juan, R., Calif., U.S.A. 163 36 14N 121 9W
San Juan, R., Utah, U.S.A. 161 37 20N 110 20W
San Julián 176 49 15 S 68 0W
San Just, Sierra de 58 40 45N 0 41W
San Justo 172 30 55 S 60 30W
San Kamphaeng 100 18 45N 99 8 E
San Lázaro, C. 164 24 50N 112 18W
San Lázaro, Sa. de 164 23 25N 110 0W
San Leandro 163 37 40N 122 6W
San Leonardo 58 41 51N 3 5W
San Lorenzo, Argent. 172 32 45 S 60 45W
San Lorenzo, Ecuador 174 1 15N 78 50W
San Lorenzo, Parag. 172 25 20 S 57 32W
San Lorenzo, Venez. 174 9 47N 71 4W
San Lorenzo de la Parilla 58 39 51N 2 22W
San Lorenzo de Morunys 58 42 8N 1 35 E
San Lorenzo, I., Mexico 164 28 35N 112 50W
San Lorenzo, I., Peru 174 12 20 S 77 35W
San Lorenzo, Mt. 176 47 40 S 72 20W
San Lorenzo, R. 164 24 15N 107 24W
San Lucas, Boliv. 174 20 5 S 65 0W
San Lucas, Baja California S., Mexico 164 27 10N 112 14W
San Lucas, Baja California S., Mexico 164 22 53N 109 54W
San Lucas, U.S.A. 163 36 8N 121 1W
San Lucas, C. de 164 22 50N 110 0W
San Lucido 65 39 18N 16 3 E
San Luis, Argent. 172 33 20 S 66 20W
San Luis, Cuba 166 22 17N 83 46W
San Luis, Guat. 166 16 14N 89 27W
San Luis, U.S.A. 161 37 14N 105 26W
San Luis, Venez. 174 11 7N 69 42W
San Luis □ 172 34 0 S 66 0W
San Luis de la Loma 164 17 18N 100 55W
San Luis de la Paz 164 21 19N 100 32W
San Luis de Potosí 164 22 9N 100 59W
San Luis de Potosí □ 164 22 10N 101 0W
San Luis, I. 164 29 58N 114 26W
San Luis Obispo 161 35 21N 120 38W
San Luis Res. 163 37 4N 121 5W
San Luis Rio Colorado 164 32 29N 114 48W
San Luis, Sierra de 172 37 25N 66 10W
San Marco Argentano 65 39 34N 16 8 E
San Marco dei Cavoti 65 41 20N 14 50 E
San Marco in Lámis 65 41 43N 15 38 E
San Marcos, Guat. 166 14 59N 91 52W
San Marcos, U.S.A. 159 29 53N 98 0W
San Marcos, I. 164 27 13N 112 6W
San Marino 63 43 56N 12 25 E
San Marino ■ 63 43 56N 12 25 E
San Martín, Argent. 172 33 5 S 68 28W
San Martín, Colomb. 174 3 42N 73 42W
San Martín de Valdeiglesias 56 40 21N 4 24W
San Martín, L. 176 48 50 S 72 50W
San Martino de Calvi 62 45 57N 9 41 E
San Mateo, Spain 58 40 28N 0 10 E
San Mateo, U.S.A. 163 37 32N 122 19W
San Matías 174 16 25 S 58 20W
San Matías, Golfo de 176 41 30 S 64 0W
San Miguel, El Sal. 166 13 30N 88 12W
San Miguel, Panama 166 8 27N 78 55W
San Miguel, Spain 59 39 3N 1 26 E
San Miguel, U.S.A. 163 35 45N 120 42W
San Miguel, Venez. 174 9 40N 65 11W
San Miguel de Salinas 59 37 59N 0 47W
San Miguel de Tucumán 172 26 50 S 65 20W
San Miguel del Monte 172 35 23 S 58 50W
San Miguel I. 163 34 2N 120 23W
San Miguel, R., Boliv. 174 16 0 S 62 45W
San Miguel, R., Ecuador/Ecuador 174 0 25N 76 30W
San Miniato 62 43 40N 10 50 E
San Narcisco 103 15 2N 120 3 E
San Nicolás de los Arroyas 172 33 17 S 60 10W
San Nicolas I. 154 33 16N 119 30W
San Onfre 163 33 22N 117 34W
San Onofre 174 9 44N 75 32W
San Pablo, Boliv. 172 21 43 S 66 38W
San Pablo, Colomb. 174 5 27N 70 56W
San Paolo di Civitate 65 41 44N 15 16 E
San Pedro, Buenos Aires, Argent. 173 33 43 S 59 45W
San Pedro, Jujuy, Argent. 172 24 12 S 64 55W
San Pedro, Chile 172 21 58 S 68 30W
San Pedro, Colomb. 174 4 56N 71 53W
San Pedro, Dom. Rep. 167 18 30N 69 18W
San Pedro, Ivory C. 120 4 50N 6 33W
San Pedro, Mexico 164 23 55N 110 17W
San Pedro □ 172 24 0 S 57 0W
San Pedro Channel 163 33 35N 118 25W
San Pedro de Arimena 174 4 37N 71 42W
San Pedro de Atacama 172 22 55 S 68 15W
San Pedro de Jujuy 172 24 12 S 64 55W
San Pedro de las Colonias 164 25 50N 102 59W
San Pedro de Lloc 174 7 15 S 79 28W
San Pedro del Norte 166 13 4N 84 33W
San Pedro del Paraná 172 26 43 S 56 13W
San Pedro del Pinatar 59 37 50N 0 50W
San Pedro Mártir, Sierra 164 31 0N 115 30W
San Pedro Mixtepec 165 16 2N 97 0W
San Pedro Ocampo = Melchor Ocampo 164 24 52N 101 40W
San Pedro, Pta. 172 25 30 S 70 38W
San Pedro, R., Chihuahua, Mexico 164 28 20N 106 10W
San Pedro, R., Michoacan, Mexico 164 19 23N 103 51W
San Pedro, R., Nayarit, Mexico 164 21 45N 105 30W
San Pedro, R., U.S.A. 161 32 45N 110 35W
San Pedro, Sierra de 57 39 18N 6 40W
San Pedro Sula 166 15 30N 88 0W
San Pedro Tututepec 165 16 9N 97 38W
San Pedro,Pta. 172 25 30 S 70 38W
San Pietro, I. 64 39 9N 8 17 E
San Pietro Vernotico 65 40 28N 18 0 E
San Quintín, Mexico 164 30 29N 115 57W

San Quintín, Phil. **103** 16 1N 120 56 E
San, R. **54** 50 25N 22 20 E
San Rafael, Argent. **172** 34 40 S 68 30W
San Rafael, Colomb. **174** 6 2N 69 45W
San Rafael, Calif., U.S.A. **163** 38 0N 122 32W
San Rafael, N. Mex., U.S.A. **161** 35 6N 107 58W
San Rafael, Venez. **174** 10 42N 71 46W
San Rafael Mtn. **163** 34 41N 119 52W
San Ramón de la Nueva Orán **172** 23 10 S 64 20W
San Remo **62** 43 48N 7 47 E
San Román, C. **174** 12 12N 70 0W
San Roque, Argent. **172** 28 15 S 58 45W
San Roque, Spain **57** 36 17N 5 21W
San Rosendo **172** 37 10 S 72 50W
San Saba **159** 31 12N 98 45W
San Salvador **166** 13 40N 89 20W
San Salvador de Jujuy **172** 23 30 S 65 40W
San Salvador (Watlings) I. **167** 24 0N 74 40W
San Sebastián, Argent. **176** 53 10 S 68 30W
San Sebastián, Spain **58** 43 17N 1 58W
San Sebastián, Venez. **174** 9 57N 67 11W
San Serverino **63** 43 13N 13 10 E
San Severo **63** 41 41N 15 23 E
San Simeon **163** 35 39N 121 11W
San Simon **161** 32 14N 109 16W
San Stéfano di Cadore **63** 46 34N 12 33 E
San Telmo **164** 30 58N 116 6W
San Tiburcio **164** 24 8N 101 32W
San Valentin, Mte. **176** 46 30 S 73 30W
San Vicente de Alcántara **57** 39 22N 7 8W
San Vicente de la Barquera **56** 43 30N 4 29W
San Vicente del Caguán **174** 2 7N 74 46W
San Vicenzo **93** 43 9N 10 32 E
San Vito al Tagliamento **63** 45 55N 12 50 E
San Vito, C. **64** 38 11N 12 41 E
San Vito Chietino **63** 42 19N 14 27 E
San Vito dei Normanni **65** 40 40N 17 40 E
San Yanaro **174** 2 47N 69 42W
San Ygnacio **159** 27 6N 92 24W
San Ysidro **161** 32 33N 117 5W
San'a **91** 15 27N 44 12 E
Sana, R. **63** 44 40N 16 43 E
Sanaba **120** 12 25N 3 47W
Sanabria, La **56** 42 0N 6 30W
Sanâfir **122** 27 49N 34 37 E
Sanaga, R. **121** 3 35N 9 38 E
Sanak I **147** 53 30N 162 30W
Sanaloa, Presa **164** 24 50N 107 20W
Sanana **103** 2 5 S 125 50 E
Sanand **94** 22 59N 72 25 E
Sanandaj **92** 35 25N 47 7 E
Sanandita **172** 21 40 S 63 35W
Sanary **45** 43 7N 5 48 E
Sanawad **94** 22 11N 76 5 E
Sanbe-San **110** 35 6N 132 38 E
Sancergues **43** 47 10N 2 54 E
Sancerre **43** 47 20N 2 50 E
Sanch'a Ho **108** 26 55N 106 6 E
Sanch'aho **107** 44 50N 126 1 E
Sánchez **167** 19 15N 69 36W
Sanchiang **108** 25 22N 109 26 E
Sanchor **94** 24 52N 71 49 E
Sanco, Pt. **103** 8 15N 126 24 E
Sancoins **43** 46 47N 2 55 E
Sancti-Spíritus **166** 21 52N 79 33W
Sand Lake **150** 47 46N 84 31W
Sand Point **147** 55 20N 160 32W
Sand, R. **129** 22 25 S 30 5 E
Sand Springs **159** 36 12N 96 5W
Sanda **111** 34 53N 135 14 E
Sanda I. **34** 55 17N 5 35W
Sandah **122** 20 35N 39 32 E
Sandakan **102** 5 53N 118 10 E
Sandalwood **140** 34 55 S 140 9 E
Sandan **101** 12 46N 106 0 E
Sandanski **67** 41 35N 23 16 E
Sandaré **120** 14 40N 10 15W
Sanday I. **36** 57 2N 6 30W
Sanday, I. **37** 59 15N 2 30W
Sanday Sd. **37** 59 11N 2 31W
Sandbach **32** 53 9N 2 23W
Sandbank **34** 55 58N 4 57W
Sande, Möre og Romsdal, Norway **71** 62 15N 5 27 E
Sande, Sogn og Fjordane, Norway **71** 61 20N 5 47 E
Sandefjord **71** 59 10N 10 15 E
Sandeid **71** 59 33N 5 52 E
Sanders **161** 35 12N 109 25W
Sanderson **159** 30 5N 102 30W
Sanderston **140** 34 46 S 139 15 E
Sandfell **74** 63 57N 16 48W
Sandfly L. **153** 55 43N 106 6W
Sandgate, Austral. **139** 27 18 S 153 3 E
Sandgate, U.K. **29** 51 5N 1 9 E
Sandhammaren, C. **73** 55 23N 14 14 E
Sandhead **34** 54 48N 4 58W
Sandhurst **29** 51 21N 0 48W
Sandía **174** 14 10 S 69 30W
Sandikli **92** 38 30N 30 20 E
Sandiman, Mt. **137** 24 21 S 115 20 E
Sandnes **71** 58 50N 5 45 E
Sandness **37** 60 18N 1 38W
Sandoa **124** 9 48 S 23 0 E
Sandomierz **54** 50 40N 21 43 E
Sandona **174** 1 17N 77 28W
Sandover, R. **138** 21 43 S 136 32 E
Sandoway **99** 18 20N 94 30 E
Sandown **28** 50 39N 1 9W
Sandpoint **160** 48 20N 116 40W
Sandray, I. **36** 56 53N 7 30W
Sandringham **29** 52 50N 0 30 E
Sandslån **72** 63 2N 17 49 E
Sandspit **152** 53 14N 131 49W
Sandston **162** 37 31N 77 19W
Sandstone **137** 27 59 S 119 16 E
Sandusky, Mich., U.S.A. **150** 43 26N 82 50W
Sandusky, Ohio, U.S.A. **156** 41 25N 82 40W
Sandveld **128** 32 0 S 18 15 E
Sandvig, Denmark **73** 55 18N 14 48 E
Sandvig, Sweden **72** 55 32N 14 47 E
Sandvika **71** 59 54N 10 29 E
Sandviken **72** 60 38N 16 46 E
Sandwich **29** 51 16N 1 21 E
Sandwich B., Can. **151** 53 40N 57 15W
Sandwich B., S. Afr. **128** 23 25 S 14 20 E
Sandwich, C. **138** 18 14 S 146 18 E
Sandwich Group **13** 57 0 S 27 0W
Sandwip Chan. **99** 22 35N 91 35 E
Sandy **29** 53 8N 0 18W
Sandy Bight **137** 33 50 S 123 20 E
Sandy C., Queens., Austral. **139** 24 42 S 153 15 E
Sandy C., Tas., Austral. **138** 41 25 S 144 45 E
Sandy Cay **167** 23 13N 75 18W
Sandy Cr. **160** 42 20N 109 30W
Sandy L. **150** 53 2N 93 0W
Sandy Lake **150** 53 0N 93 15W
Sandy Narrows **153** 55 5N 103 4W
Sanford, Fla., U.S.A. **157** 28 45N 81 20W
Sanford, Me., U.S.A. **162** 43 28N 70 47W
Sanford, N.C., U.S.A. **157** 35 30N 79 10W
Sanford, Mt. **136** 16 58 S 130 32 E
Sanford Mt. **148** 62 30N 143 0W
Sanford, R. **137** 27 22 S 115 53 E
Sang-i-Masha **94** 33 16N 67 5 E
Sanga **127** 12 22 S 35 21 E
Sanga, R. **124** 1 0N 16 30 E
Sanga Tolon **77** 61 50N 149 40 E
Sangamner **96** 19 30N 74 15 E
Sangar, Afghan. **94** 32 56N 65 30 E
Sangar, U.S.S.R. **77** 63 55N 127 31 E
Sangar Sarcai **94** 34 27N 70 35 E
Sangasanga **102** 0 29 S 117 13 E
Sangchen La **99** 31 30N 84 40 E
Sangchih **109** 29 25N 109 30 E
Sange **126** 6 58 S 84 40 E
Sangeang, I. **103** 8 12 S 119 6 E
Sanger **163** 36 47N 119 35W
Sangerhausen **48** 51 28N 11 18 E
Sanggau **102** 0 5N 110 30 E
Sangihe, Kep. **103** 3 0N 126 0 E
Sangihe, P. **103** 3 45N 125 30 E
Sangju **107** 36 25N 128 10 E
Sangkan Ho **106** 40 24N 115 19 E
Sangkapura **102** 5 52 S 112 40 E
Sangkhla **100** 15 7N 98 28 E
Sangli **96** 16 55N 74 33 E
Sangmélina **121** 2 57N 12 1 E
Sangonera, R. **59** 37 39N 2 0W
Sangpang Bum **98** 26 30N 95 50 E
Sangre de Cristo Mts. **159** 37 0N 105 0W
Sangro, R. **63** 42 10N 14 30 E
Sangudo **152** 53 50N 114 54W
Sangüesa **58** 42 37N 1 17W
Sanguinaires, I. **45** 41 51N 8 36 E
Sanhala **120** 10 3N 6 51W
Sanho **107** 39 59N 117 4 E
Sani R. **100** 13 32N 105 57 E
Sanish **158** 48 0N 102 30W
Sanje **126** 0 49 S 31 30 E
Sankaranayinarkovil **97** 9 10N 77 35 E
Sankeshwar **96** 16 23N 74 23 E
Sankosh, R. **98** 26 24N 89 47 E
Sankt Andra **52** 46 46N 14 50 E
Sankt Antönien **51** 46 58N 9 48 E
Sankt Blasien **49** 47 47N 8 7 E
Sankt Gallen **51** 47 26N 9 22 E
Sankt Gallen □ **51** 47 25N 9 22 E
Sankt Ingbert **49** 49 16N 7 6 E
Sankt Johann **52** 47 22N 13 12 E
Sankt Margrethen **51** 47 28N 9 37 E
Sankt Moritz **51** 46 30N 9 50 E
Sankt Olof **73** 55 37N 14 8 E
Sankt Pölten **52** 48 12N 15 38 E
Sankt Valentin **52** 48 11N 14 33 E
Sankt Veit **52** 46 54N 14 22 E
Sankt Wendel **49** 49 27N 7 9 E
Sankt Wolfgang **52** 47 43N 13 27 E
Sankuru, R. **124** 4 17 S 20 25 E
Sanlúcar de Barrameda **57** 37 26N 6 18W
Sanlúcar la Mayor **57** 37 26N 6 18W
Sanluri **64** 39 35N 8 55 E
Sanmártin **70** 46 19N 25 58 E
Sanmen **109** 29 5N 121 35 E
Sanmenhsia **106** 34 46N 111 30 E
Sanming **109** 26 13N 117 35 E
Sannan **111** 35 2N 135 1 E
Sannaspos **128** 29 6 S 26 34 E
Sannicandro Gargánico **65** 41 50N 15 34 E
Sânnicolaul-Maré **66** 46 5N 20 39 E
Sannidal **71** 58 55N 9 15 E
Sannieshof **128** 26 30 S 25 47 E
Sano **111** 36 19N 139 35 E
Sanok **54** 49 35N 22 10 E
Sanokwelle **120** 7 19N 8 38W
Sanpa **108** 29 43N 99 33 E
Sanpah **139** 30 32 S 141 12 E
Sanquhar **35** 55 21N 3 56W
Sansanding Dam **120** 13 37N 6 0W
Sansanné-Mango **121** 10 20N 0 30 E
Sansepolcro **63** 43 34N 12 8 E
Sanshui **109** 23 11N 112 53 E
Sanski Most **63** 44 46N 16 40 E
Sansui **108** 26 57N 108 37 E
Sant' Ágata de Gati **65** 41 6N 14 30 E
Sant' Ágata di Militello **65** 38 2N 14 40 E
Santa Ana, Ecuador **174** 1 10 S 80 20W
Santa Ana, El Sal. **166** 14 0N 89 40W
Santa Ana, Mexico **164** 30 31N 111 8W
Santa Ana, U.S.A. **163** 33 48N 117 55W
Santa Ana, El Beni **174** 13 50 S 65 40W
Sant' Ángelo Lodigiano **62** 45 14N 9 25 E
Sant' Antioco **64** 39 2N 8 30 E
Sant' Antioco, I. **64** 39 2N 8 30 E
Sant' Arcángelo di Romagna **63** 44 4N 12 26 E
Santa Bárbara, Brazil **171** 16 0 S 59 0W
Santa Bárbara, Colomb. **174** 5 53N 75 35W
Santa Barbara **166** 14 53N 88 14W
Santa Bárbara, Mexico **164** 26 48N 105 50W
Santa Bárbara, Spain **58** 40 42N 0 29 E
Santa Barbara **163** 34 25N 119 40W
Santa Bárbara **174** 7 47N 71 10W
Santa Barbara Channel **163** 34 20N 120 0W
Santa Barbara I. **163** 33 29N 119 2W
Santa Barbara Is. **161** 33 31N 119 0W
Santa Bárbara, Mt. **59** 37 23N 2 50W
Santa Catalina **174** 10 36N 75 17W
Santa Catalina, G. of **163** 33 0N 118 0W
Santa Catalina, I., Mexico **164** 25 40N 110 50W
Santa Catalina, I., U.S.A. **163** 33 20N 118 30W
Santa Catarina □ **173** 27 25 S 48 30W
Santa Catarina, I. de **173** 27 30 S 48 40W
Santa Caterina **65** 37 37N 14 1 E
Santa Cecília **173** 26 56 S 50 27W
Santa Clara, Cuba **166** 22 20N 80 0W
Santa Clara, Calif., U.S.A. **163** 37 21N 122 0W
Santa Clara, Utah, U.S.A. **161** 37 10N 113 38W
Santa Clara de Olimar **173** 32 50 S 54 54W
Santa Clotilde **174** 2 25 S 73 45W
Santa Coloma de Farnés **58** 41 50N 2 39 E
Santa Coloma de Gramanet **58** 41 27N 2 13 E
Santa Comba **56** 43 2N 8 49W
Santa Croce Camerina **65** 36 50N 14 30 E
Santa Cruz, Argent. **176** 50 0 S 68 50W
Santa Cruz, Boliv. **174** 17 43 S 63 10W
Santa Cruz, Brazil **170** 7 57 S 36 12W
Santa Cruz, Canary Is. **116** 28 29N 16 26W
Santa Cruz, Chile **172** 34 38 S 71 27W
Santa Cruz, C. Rica **166** 10 15N 85 41W
Santa Cruz, Phil. **103** 14 20N 121 30 E
Santa Cruz, Calif., U.S.A. **163** 36 55N 122 1W
Santa Cruz, N. Mexico, U.S.A. **161** 35 59N 106 1W
Santa Cruz □ **174** 17 43 S 63 10W
Santa Cruz Cabrália **171** 16 17 S 39 2W
Santa Cruz de Barahona **167** 18 12N 71 6W
Santa Cruz de Mudela **59** 38 39N 3 28W
Santa Cruz de Tenerife □ **72** 28 10N 17 20W
Santa Cruz del Norte **166** 23 9N 81 55W
Santa Cruz del Retamar **56** 40 8N 4 14W
Santa Cruz del Sur **166** 20 50N 78 0W
Santa Cruz do Rio Pardo **173** 22 54 S 49 37W
Santa Cruz do Sul **173** 29 42 S 52 25W
Santa Cruz I. **154** 34 0N 119 45W
Santa Cruz, Is. **130** 10 30 S 166 0 E
Santa Cruz, R. **176** 50 10 S 70 0W
Santa Elena, Argent. **172** 30 58 S 59 47W
Santa Elena, Ecuador **174** 2 16 S 80 52W
Santa Elena C. **167** 10 54N 85 56W
Santa Enimie **44** 44 24N 3 26 E
Sant' Eufémia, Golfo di **65** 38 50N 16 10 E
Santa Eulalia **59** 40 34N 1 20W
Santa Fe, Argent. **172** 31 35 S 60 41W
Santa Fe, Spain **57** 37 11N 3 43W
Santa Fe, U.S.A. **161** 35 40N 106 0W
Santa Fé □ **172** 31 50 S 60 55W
Santa Filomena **170** 9 0 S 45 50W
Santa Genoveva, Mt. **164** 23 18N 109 52W
Santa Groce di Magliano **65** 41 43N 14 59 E
Santa Helena **170** 2 14 S 45 18W
Santa Helena de Goiás **171** 17 43 S 50 35W
Santa Inês **171** 13 17 S 39 48W
Santa Inés, I. **176** 54 0 S 73 0W
Santa Inés, Mt. **57** 38 32N 5 37W
Santa Isabel, Argent. **172** 36 10 S 67 0W
Santa Isabel, Brazil **171** 13 45 S 56 30W
Santa Isabel = Rey Malabo **121** 3 45N 8 50 E
Santa Isabel do Araguaia **170** 6 7 S 48 19W
Santa Isabel, Pico **121** 4 43N 8 49 E
Santa Juliana **171** 19 19 S 47 32W
Santa Lucia, Corrientes, Argent. **172** 28 58 S 59 5W
Santa Lucia, San Juan, Argent. **172** 31 30 S 68 45W
Santa Lucia, Spain **59** 37 35N 0 58W
Santa Lucia **172** 34 27 S 56 24W
Santa Lucia Range **163** 36 0N 121 20W
Santa Luzia **170** 6 53 S 36 56W
Santa Magdalena, I. **164** 24 50N 112 15W
Santa Margarita, Argent. **172** 38 18 S 61 35W
Santa Margarita, U.S.A. **163** 35 23N 120 37W
Santa Margarita, I. **164** 24 30N 112 0W
Santa Margarita, R. **163** 33 13N 117 23W
Santa Margherita **62** 44 20N 9 11 E
Santa María, Argent. **172** 26 40 S 66 0W
Santa Maria, Brazil **173** 29 40 S 53 40W
Santa Maria **65** 41 3N 14 29 E
Santa María **164** 27 40N 114 40W
Santa Maria, Spain **58** 39 39N 2 45 E
Santa Maria, Switz. **51** 46 36N 10 25 E
Santa Maria, U.S.A. **163** 34 58N 120 29W
Santa Maria, Zambia **127** 11 5 S 29 58 E
Santa Maria, Bahía de **164** 25 10N 108 40W
Santa Maria, Cabo de **57** 36 39N 7 53W
Santa Maria da Vitória **171** 13 24 S 44 12W
Santa Maria del Oro **164** 25 30N 105 20W
Santa Maria di Leuca, C. **65** 39 48N 18 20 E
Santa Maria do Suaçuí **171** 18 12 S 42 25W
Santa María la Real de Nieva **56** 41 4N 4 24W
Santa María, R. **164** 31 0N 107 14W
Santa Marta, Colomb. **174** 11 15N 74 13W
Santa Marta, Spain **57** 38 37N 6 39W
Santa Marta Grande, C. **173** 28 43 S 48 50W
Santa Marta, Ría de **56** 43 44N 7 45W
Santa Marta, Sierra Nevada de **147** 10 55N 73 50W
Santa Monica **163** 34 0N 118 30W
Santa Napa **160** 38 28N 122 45W
Santa Olalla, Huelva, Spain **57** 37 54N 6 14W
Santa Olalla, Toledo, Spain **56** 40 2N 4 25W
Sant' Onofrio **65** 38 42N 16 10 E
Santa Paula **163** 34 20N 119 2W
Santa Pola **59** 38 13N 0 35W
Santa Quitéria **170** 4 20 S 40 10W
Santa Rita, U.S.A. **161** 32 50N 108 0W
Santa Rita, Guarico, Venez. **174** 8 8N 66 16W
Santa Rita, Zulia, Venez. **174** 10 32N 71 32W
Santa Rosa, La Pampa, Argent. **172** 36 40 S 64 30W
Santa Rosa, San Luis, Argent. **172** 32 30 S 65 10W
Santa Rosa, Boliv. **174** 10 25 S 67 20W
Santa Rosa, Brazil **173** 27 52 S 54 29W
Santa Rosa, Colomb. **174** 3 32N 69 48W
Santa Rosa, Hond. **164** 14 40N 89 0W
Santa Rosa, Calif., U.S.A. **163** 38 26N 122 43W
Santa Rosa, N. Mexico, U.S.A. **159** 34 58N 104 40W
Santa Rosa, Amazonas, Venez. **174** 1 29N 66 55W
Santa Rosa, Apure, Venez. **174** 6 37N 67 57W
Santa Rosa de Cabal **174** 4 52N 75 38W
Santa Rosa de Copán **166** 14 47N 88 46W
Santa Rosa de Osos **174** 6 39N 75 28W
Santa Rosa de Río Primero **172** 31 8 S 63 20W
Santa Rosa de Viterbo **174** 5 53N 72 59W
Santa Rosa I., Calif., U.S.A. **163** 34 0N 120 6W
Santa Rosa I., Fla., U.S.A. **157** 30 23N 87 0W
Santa Rosa Mts. **160** 41 45N 117 30W
Santa Rosalía **164** 27 20N 112 30W
Santa Sofia **63** 43 57N 11 55 E
Santa Sylvina **172** 27 50 S 61 10W
Santa Tecla = Nueva San Salvador **164** 13 40N 89 25W
Santa Teresa, Argent. **172** 33 25 S 60 47W
Santa Teresa, Brazil **171** 19 55 S 40 36W
Santa Teresa, Mexico **165** 25 17N 97 51W
Santa Teresa, Venez. **174** 4 43N 61 4W
Santa Teresa di Riva **63** 37 58N 15 21 E
Santa Teresa Gallura **64** 41 14N 9 12 E
Santa Teresinha **170** 12 45 S 39 32W
Santa Vitória **171** 18 50 S 50 8W
Santa Vitória do Palmar **173** 33 32 S 53 25W
Santa Ynez **163** 34 37N 120 5W
Santa Ynez, R. **163** 34 37N 120 41W
Santa Ysabel **163** 33 7N 116 40W
Sant'ai **108** 31 5N 105 2 E
Santadi **64** 39 5N 8 42 E
Santahar **98** 24 48N 88 59 E
Santaluz **171** 11 15 S 39 22W
Santana **171** 13 2 S 44 5W
Santana, Coxilha de **173** 30 50 S 55 35W
Santana do Ipanema **170** 9 22 S 37 14W
Santana do Livramento **173** 30 55 S 55 30W
Santander, Colomb. **174** 3 1N 76 28W
Santander, Spain **56** 43 27N 3 51W
Santander □ **56** 43 25N 4 0W
Santander Jiménez **165** 24 11N 98 29W
Santañy **59** 39 20N 3 5 E
Santaquin **160** 40 0N 111 51W
Santarém, Brazil **175** 2 25 S 54 42W
Santarém, Port. **57** 39 12N 8 42W
Santarém □ **57** 39 10N 8 40W
Santaren Channel **166** 24 0N 79 30W
Santèramo in Colle **65** 40 48N 16 45 E
Santerno, R. **63** 44 10N 11 38 E
Santhia **62** 45 20N 8 10 E
Santiago, Brazil **173** 29 11 S 54 52W
Santiago, Chile **172** 33 24 S 70 50W
Santiago, Dom. Rep. **167** 19 30N 70 40W

Santiago, Panama 166 8 0N 81 0W
Santiago □ 172 33 30 S 70 50W
Santiago de Compostela 56 42 52N 8 37W
Santiago de Cuba 166 20 0N 75 49W
Santiago del Estero 172 27 50 S 64 15W
Santiago del Estero □ 172 27 50 S 64 20W
Santiago do Cacém 57 38 1N 8 42W
Santiago Ixcuintla 164 21 50N 105 11W
Santiago Papasquiaro 164 25 0N 105 20W
Santiago, Punta de 121 3 12N 8 40 E
Santiaguillo, L. de 164 24 50N 104 50W
Santillana del Mar 56 43 24N 4 6W
Santipur 95 23 17N 88 25 E
Säntis 51 47 15N 9 22 E
Santisteban del Puerto 59 38 17N 3 15W
Santo Amaro 171 12 30 S 38 50W
Santo Anastácio 173 21 58 S 51 39W
Santo André 173 23 39 S 46 29W
Santo Ângelo 173 28 15 S 54 15W
Santo Antonio 170 15 50 S 56 0W
Santo Antônio de Jesus 171 12 58 S 39 16W
Santo Antonio do Zaire 124 6 7 S 12 20 E
Santo Corazón 174 18 0 S 58 45W
Santo Domingo, Dom. Rep. 167 18 30N 70 0W
Santo Domingo, Baja Calif. N., Mexico 164 30 43N 115 56W
Santo Domingo, Baja Calif. S., Mexico 164 25 32N 112 2W
Santo Domingo, Nic. 166 12 14N 84 59W
Santo Domingo de la Calzada 58 42 26N 2 27W
Santo Isabel do Morro 171 11 34 S 50 40W
Santo Stéfano di Camastro 65 38 1N 14 22 E
Santo Stino di Livenza 63 45 45N 12 40 E
Santo Tirso 56 41 29N 8 18W
Santo Tomas 164 31 33N 116 24W
Santo Tomás 174 14 34 S 72 30W
Santo Tomé 173 28 40 S 56 5W
Santoña 56 43 29N 3 20W
Santos 173 24 0 S 46 20W
Santos Dumont 173 22 55 S 43 10W
Santos, Sierra de los 57 38 7N 5 12W
Santport 46 52 26N 4 39 E
Santu 108 25 59N 107 52 E
Sanur 90 32 22N 35 15 E
Sanvignes-les-Mines 43 46 40N 4 18 E
San'yō 110 34 2N 131 5 E
Sanyuki-Sammyaku 110 34 5N 133 0 E
Sanza Pombo 124 7 18 S 15 56 E
São Anastacio 173 22 0 S 51 40W
São Bartolomeu de Messines 57 37 15N 8 17W
São Benedito 170 4 3 S 40 53W
São Bento 170 2 42 S 44 50W
São Bento do Norte 170 5 4 S 36 2W
São Borja 173 28 45 S 56 0W
São Bras d'Alportel 57 37 8N 7 58W
São Caitano 170 8 21 S 36 6W
São Carlos 173 22 0 S 47 50W
São Cristóvão 170 11 15 S 37 15W
São Domingos, Brazil 171 13 25 S 46 10W
São Domingos, Guin.-Biss. 170 12 22N 16 8W
São Domingos do Maranhão 170 5 42 S 44 22W
São Félix, Bahia, Brazil 171 12 38 S 38 58W
São Félix, Mato Grosso, Brazil 171 11 36 S 50 39W
Sao Francisco 171 16 0 S 44 50W
São Francisco do Maranhão 170 6 15 S 42 52W
São Francisco do Sul 173 26 15 S 48 36W
São Francisco, R. 170 10 30 S 36 24W
São Gabriel 173 30 10 S 54 30W
São Gabriel da Palha 171 18 47 S 40 59W
São Gonçalo 173 22 48 S 43 5W
São Gotardo 171 19 19 S 46 3W
Sao Hill 127 8 20 S 35 18 E
São João da Boa Vista 173 22 0 S 46 52W
São João da Pesqueira 56 41 8N 7 24W
São João da Ponte 171 15 56 S 44 1W
São João del Rei 173 21 8 S 44 15W
São João do Araguaia 170 5 23 S 48 46W
São João do Paraíso 171 15 19 S 42 1W
São João do Piauí 170 8 10 S 42 15W
São João dos Patos 170 6 30 S 43 42W
São João Evangelista 171 18 32 S 42 45W
São Joaquim da Barra 171 20 35 S 47 53W
São José, B. de 170 2 38 S 44 4W
São José da Laje 170 9 1 S 36 3W
São José de Mipibu 170 6 5 S 35 15W
São José do Peixe 170 7 24 S 42 34W
São José do Rio Prêto 173 20 50 S 49 20W
São José dos Campos 173 23 7 S 45 52W
São Leopoldo 173 29 50 S 51 10W
São Lourenço, Mato Grosso, Brazil 173 16 30 S 55 5W
São Lourenço, Minas Gerais, Brazil 171 22 7 S 45 3W
São Lourenço, R. 175 16 40 S 56 0W
São Luís do Curu 170 3 40 S 39 14W
São Luís Gonzaga 173 28 25 S 55 0W
São Luís (Maranhão) 170 2 39 S 44 15W
Sao Marcelino 174 1 0N 67 12W
São Marcelino 174 1 0N 67 12W
São Marcos, B. de 170 2 0 S 44 0W
São Marcos, R. 171 18 15 S 47 37W
São Martinho 56 39 30N 9 8W
São Mateus 171 18 44 S 39 50W
São Mateus, R. 171 18 35 S 39 44W
São Miguel 16 37 33N 25 27W
São Miguel do Araguaia 171 13 19 S 50 13W
São Miguel dos Campos 170 9 47 S 36 5W
São Nicolau, R. 170 5 45 S 42 2W
São Paulo 173 23 40 S 46 50W
São Paulo □ 173 22 0 S 49 0W
São Pedro do Piaui 171 5 56 S 42 43W
São Pedro do Sul 56 40 46N 8 4W
São Rafael 170 5 47 S 36 55W
São Raimundo das Mangabeiras 170 7 1 S 45 29W
São Raimundo Nonato 170 9 1 S 42 42W
São Romão, Amazonas, Brazil 174 5 53 S 67 50W
São Romão, Minas Gerais, Brazil 171 16 22 S 45 4W
São Roque, C. de 170 5 30 S 35 10W
São Sebastião do Paraíso 173 20 54 S 46 59W
São Sebastião, I. 173 23 50 S 45 18W
São Simão 171 18 56 S 50 30W
São Teotónio 57 37 30N 8 42W
São Tomé 170 5 58 S 36 4W
São Tomé, C. de 173 22 0 S 41 10W
São Tomé, I. 114 0 10N 7 0 E
São Vicente 173 23 57 S 46 23W
São Vicente, Cabo de 57 37 0N 9 0W
Saona, I. 167 18 10N 68 40W
Saône-et-Loire □ 43 46 25N 4 50 E
Saône, R. 43 46 25N 4 50 E
Saonek 103 0 28 S 130 47 E
Saoura, O. 118 29 55N 1 50W
Sapai 68 41 2N 25 43 E
Sapão, R. 170 11 1 S 45 32W
Saparua, I. 103 3 33 S 128 40 E
Sapé 170 7 6 S 35 13W
Sapele 121 5 50N 5 40 E
Sapelo I. 157 31 28N 81 15W
Sapiéntza I. 69 36 33N 21 43 E
Sapodnyy Sayan 77 52 30N 94 0 E
Sapone 121 12 3N 1 35W
Saposoa 174 6 55 S 76 30W
Sapozhok 81 53 59N 40 51 E
Sappemeer 46 53 10N 6 48 E
Sapporo 112 43 0N 141 15 E
Sapri 65 40 5N 15 37 E
Sapudi, I. 103 7 2 S 114 17 E
Sapulpa 159 36 0N 96 40W
Sapur 95 34 18N 74 27 E
Saqota 123 12 40N 39 1 E
Saqqez 92 36 15N 46 20 E
Sar-i-Pul 93 36 10N 66 0 E
Sar Planina 66 42 10N 21 0 E
Sara 120 11 40N 3 53W
Sara Buri 100 14 30N 100 55 E
Sarab 92 38 0N 47 30 E
Sarada, R. 99 28 15N 80 30 E
Saragossa = Zaragoza 58 41 39N 0 53W
Saraguro 174 3 35 S 79 16W
Sarai 70 44 43N 28 10 E
Saraipalli 96 21 20N 82 59 E
Sarajevo 66 43 52N 18 26 E
Saraktash 84 51 47N 56 22 E
Saramati 98 25 44N 95 2 E
Saran 122 19 35N 40 30 E
Saran, G. 102 0 30 S 111 25 E
Saranac Lake 156 44 20N 74 10W
Saranda, Alb. 68 39 59N 19 55 E
Saranda, Tanz. 126 5 45 S 34 59 E
Sarandí del Yi 173 33 18 S 55 38W
Sarandí Grande 172 33 20 S 55 50W
Sarangani B. 103 6 0N 125 13 E
Sarangani Is. 103 5 25N 125 25 E
Sarangarh 96 21 30N 82 57 E
Saransk 81 54 10N 45 10 E
Sarapul 84 56 28N 53 48 E
Sarasota 157 27 10N 82 30W
Saratoga, Calif., U.S.A. 163 37 16N 122 2W
Saratoga, Wyo., U.S.A. 160 41 30N 106 56W
Saratoga Springs 162 43 5N 73 47W
Saratok 102 3 5 S 110 50 E
Saratov 81 51 30N 46 2 E
Saravane 100 15 43N 106 25 E
Sarawak □ 102 2 0N 113 0 E
Saraya 120 12 50N 11 45W
Sarbaz 93 26 38N 61 19 E
Sarbisheh 93 32 30N 59 40 E
Sârbogârd 53 46 55N 18 40 E
Sarca, R. 62 46 5N 10 45 E
Sardalas 119 25 50N 10 54 E
Sardarshahr 94 28 30N 74 29 E
Sardegna, I. 64 39 57N 9 0 E
Sardhana 94 29 9N 77 39 E
Sardinata 174 8 5N 72 48W
Sardinia = Sardegna 64 39 57N 9 0 E
Sardo 123 11 56N 41 14 E
Sarektjåkkå 74 67 27N 17 43 E
Sarengrad 66 45 14N 19 16 E
Sarèyamou 120 16 25N 3 10W
Sargasso Sea 14 27 0N 72 0W
Sargent 158 41 42N 99 24W
Sargodha 94 32 10N 72 40 E
Sargodha □ 94 31 50N 72 0 E
Sarh 117 9 5N 18 23 E
Sarhro, Jebel 118 31 6N 5 0W
Sári 93 36 30N 53 11 E
Sária, I. 69 35 54N 27 17 E
Sarichef C. 147 54 38N 164 59W
Sarida, R. 90 32 4N 35 3 E
Sarikamiş 92 40 22N 42 35 E
Sarikei 102 2 8N 111 30 E
Sarina 138 21 22 S 149 13 E
Sarine, R. 50 46 32N 7 4 E
Sariñena 58 41 47N 0 10W
Sarír Tibasti 119 22 50N 18 30 E
Sarita 159 27 14N 90 49W
Sariwon 107 38 31N 125 46 E
Sariyer 67 41 10N 29 3 E
Sark, I. 42 49 25N 2 20W
Sarkad 53 46 47N 21 17 E
Sarlat-la-Canéda 44 44 54N 1 13 E
Sarles 158 48 58N 98 57W
Sarmi 103 1 49 S 138 38 E
Särna 72 61 41N 12 58 E
Sarnano 63 43 2N 13 17 E
Sarnen 50 46 53N 8 13 E
Sarnia 150 42 58N 82 23W
Sarno 65 40 48N 14 35 E
Sarnowa 54 51 39N 16 53 E
Sarny 80 51 17N 26 40 E
Särö 73 57 31N 11 57 E
Sarolangun 102 2 30 S 102 30 E
Saronikós Kólpos 69 37 45N 23 45 E
Saros Körfezi 68 40 30N 26 15 E
Sárospatak 53 48 18N 21 33 E
Sarosul Romanesc 66 45 34N 21 43 E
Sarpsborg 71 59 16N 11 12 E
Sarracín 58 42 15N 3 45W
Sarralbe 43 48 55N 7 1 E
Sarraz, La 50 46 38N 6 30 E
Sarre, La 150 48 45N 79 15W
Sarre, R. 43 48 49N 7 0 E
Sarre-Union 43 48 55N 7 4 E
Sarrebourg 43 48 43N 7 3 E
Sarreguemines 43 49 1N 7 4 E
Sarriá 56 42 41N 7 29W
Sarrión 58 40 9N 0 49W
Sarro 120 13 40N 5 5W
Sarstedt 48 52 13N 9 50 E
Sartène 45 41 38N 9 0 E
Sarthe □ 42 47 58N 0 10 E
Sarthe, R. 42 47 33N 0 31W
Sartilly 42 48 45N 1 28W
Sartynya 76 63 30N 62 50 E
Sarum 122 21 11N 39 10 E
Sarúr 93 23 17N 58 4 E
Sárvár 53 47 15N 16 56 E
Sarveston 93 29 20N 53 10 E
Särvfjället 72 62 42N 13 30 E
Sárviz, R. 53 46 40N 18 40 E
Sary Ozek 85 44 22N 77 59 E
Sary-Tash 85 39 44N 73 15 E
Saryagach 85 41 27N 69 9 E
Sarych, Mys. 82 44 25N 33 25 E
Sarykolskiy Khrebet 85 38 30N 74 30 E
Sarykopa, Ozero 84 50 22N 64 6 E
Sarymoin, Ozero 84 51 36N 64 30 E
Saryshagan 76 46 12N 73 48 E
Sarzana 70 44 7N 9 57 E
Sarzeau 42 47 31N 2 48W
Sas van Gent 47 51 14N 3 48 E
Sasa 90 33 2N 35 23 E
Sasabeneh 91 7 59N 44 43 E
Sasaram 95 24 57N 84 5 E
Sasayama 111 35 4N 135 13 E
Sasca Montanŭ 66 44 41N 21 45 E
Sasebo 110 33 10N 129 43 E
Saser Mt. 95 34 50N 77 50 E
Saskatchewan □ 153 54 40N 106 0W
Saskatchewan, R. 153 53 12N 99 16W
Saskatoon 153 52 10N 106 38W
Sasolburg 129 26 46 S 27 49 E
Sasovo 81 54 25N 41 55 E
Sassandra 120 5 0N 6 8W
Sassandra, R. 120 5 0N 6 8W
Sássari 64 40 44N 8 33 E
Sassenheim 46 52 14N 4 31 E
Sassnitz 48 54 29N 13 39 E
Sasso Marconi 63 44 22N 11 12 E
Sassocorvaro 63 43 47N 12 30 E
Sassoferrato 63 43 26N 12 51 E
Sassuolo 62 44 31N 10 47 E
Sástago 58 41 19N 0 21W
Sastown 120 4 45N 8 27W
Sasumua Dam 126 0 54 S 36 46 E
Sasyk, Ozero 70 45 45N 30 0 E
Sasykkul 85 37 41N 73 11 E
Sata-Misaki 110 30 59N 130 40 E
Satadougou 120 12 40N 11 25W
Satanta 159 37 30N 101 0W
Satara 96 17 44N 73 58 E
Satilla, R. 157 31 15N 81 50W
Satka 84 55 3N 59 1 E
Satkania 98 22 4N 92 3 E
Satkhira 98 22 43N 89 8 E
Satmala Hills 96 20 15N 74 40 E
Satna 95 24 35N 80 50 E
Sator, mt. 63 44 11N 16 43 E
Sátoraljaújhely 53 48 25N 21 41 E
Satpura Ra. 94 21 40N 75 0 E
Satrup 48 54 39N 9 38 E
Satsuma-Hantō 110 31 25N 130 25 E
Satsuna-Shotō 112 30 0N 130 0 E
Sattahip 100 12 41N 100 54 E
Sattenpalle 96 16 25N 80 6 E
Satu Mare 70 47 46N 22 55 E
Satui 102 3 50 S 115 20 E
Satumare □ 70 47 45N 23 0 E
Satun 101 6 43N 100 2 E
Saturnina, R. 174 12 15 S 58 10W
Sauce 172 30 5 S 58 46W
Sauceda 164 25 46N 101 19W
Saucillo 164 28 1N 105 17W
Sauda 71 59 38N 6 21 E
Saúde 170 10 56 S 40 24W
Sauðarkrókur 74 65 45N 19 40W
Saudi Arabia ■ 92 26 0N 44 0 E
Sauerland 48 51 0N 8 0 E
Saugerties 162 42 4N 73 58W
Saugues 44 44 58N 3 32 E
Sauherad 71 59 25N 9 15 E
Sauid el Amia 118 25 57N 6 8W
Saujon 44 45 41N 0 55W
Sauk Center 158 45 42N 94 56W
Sauk Rapids 158 45 35N 94 10W
Saulgau 49 48 4N 9 32 E
Saulieu 43 47 17N 4 14 E
Sault 45 44 6N 5 24 E
Sault Ste. Marie, Can. 150 46 30N 84 20W
Sault Ste. Marie, U.S.A. 156 46 27N 84 22W
Saumlaki 103 7 55 S 131 20 E
Saumur 42 47 15N 0 5W
Saunders 152 52 58N 115 40W
Saunders C. 143 45 53 S 170 45 E
Saunders I. 13 57 30 S 27 30W
Saunders Point, Mt. 137 27 52 S 125 38 E
Saundersfoot 31 51 43N 4 42W
Saurbær, Borgarfjarðarsýsla, Iceland 74 64 24N 21 35W
Saurbær, Eyjafjarðarsýsla, Iceland 74 65 27N 18 13W
Sauri 121 11 50N 6 44 E
Sausalito 163 37 51N 122 29W
Sautatá 174 7 50N 77 4W
Sauveterre, B. 44 43 25N 0 57W
Sauzé-Vaussais 44 46 8N 0 8 E
Savá 166 15 32N 86 15W
Sava 65 40 28N 17 32 E
Sava, R. 63 44 40N 19 50 E
Savage 158 47 43N 104 20W
Savalou 121 7 57N 2 4 E
Savanah Downs 138 19 30 S 141 30 E
Savane 127 19 37 S 35 8 E
Savanna 158 42 5N 90 10W
Savanna la Mar 166 18 10N 78 10W
Savannah, Ga., U.S.A. 157 32 4N 81 4W
Savannah, Mo., U.S.A. 158 39 55N 94 46W
Savannah, Tenn., U.S.A. 157 35 12N 88 18W
Savannah Downs 138 19 28 S 141 47 E
Savannah, R. 157 33 0N 81 30W
Savannakhet 100 16 30N 104 49 E
Savant L. 150 50 14N 90 6W
Savant Lake 150 50 30N 90 25W
Savantvadi 97 15 55N 73 54 E
Savanur 97 14 59N 75 28 E
Savda 96 21 9N 75 56 E
Savé 121 8 2N 2 17 E
Save R. 125 21 16 S 34 0 E
Saveh 92 35 2N 50 20 E
Savelovo 81 56 51N 37 20 E
Savelugu 121 9 38N 0 54W
Savenay 42 47 20N 1 55W
Saverdun 44 43 14N 1 34 E
Saverne 43 48 39N 7 20 E
Savièse 50 46 17N 7 22 E
Savigliano 62 44 39N 7 40 E
Savigny-sur-Braye 44 47 53N 0 49 E
Saviñao 56 42 35N 7 38W
Savio, R. 63 43 58N 12 10 E
Savnik 66 42 59N 19 10 E
Savognin 51 46 36N 9 37 E
Savoie □ 45 45 26N 6 35 E
Savona 62 44 19N 8 29 E
Savonlinna 78 61 55N 28 55 E
Sävsjö 73 57 20N 14 40 E
Sävsjøström 73 57 1N 15 25 E
Sawahlunto 102 0 52 S 100 52 E
Sawai 103 3 0 S 129 5 E
Sawai Madhopur 94 26 0N 76 25 E
Sawang Daen Din 100 17 28N 103 28 E
Sawankhalok 100 17 19N 99 50 E
Sawara 111 35 55N 140 30 E
Sawatch Mts. 161 38 30N 106 30W
Sawbridgeworth 29 51 49N 0 10 E
Sawdā, Jabal as 119 28 51N 15 12 E
Sawel, Mt. 38 54 48N 7 5W
Sawfajjin, W. 119 31 46N 14 30 E
Sawi 101 10 14N 99 5 E
Sawmills 127 19 30 S 28 2 E
Sawston 29 52 7N 0 11 E
Sawtry 29 52 26N 0 17W
Sawu, I. 103 10 35 S 121 50 E
Sawu Sea 103 9 30 S 121 50 E
Saxby, R. 138 18 25 S 140 53 E
Saxilby 33 53 16N 0 40W
Saxlingham Nethergate 29 52 33N 1 16 E
Saxmundham 29 52 13N 1 29 E
Saxon 50 46 9N 7 11 E
Saxony, Lower = Niedersachsen 48 52 45N 9 0 E
Say 121 13 8N 2 22 E
Saya 121 9 30N 3 18 E
Sayabec 151 48 35N 67 41W
Sayaboury 100 19 15N 101 45 E
Sayán 174 11 0 S 77 25W
Sayan, Vostochnyy 77 54 0N 96 0 E
Sayan, Zapadnyy 77 52 30N 94 0 E
Sayasan 83 42 56N 46 15 E
Sayda 92 33 35N 35 25 E
Sayhan Ovoo 106 45 27N 103 54 E
Sayhandulaan 106 44 40N 109 1 E
Saynshand 106 44 55N 110 11 E
Sayō 110 34 59N 134 22 E
Sayre, Okla., U.S.A. 159 35 20N 99 40W
Sayre, Pa., U.S.A. 162 42 0N 76 30W
Sayula 164 19 50N 103 40W
Sayville 162 40 45N 73 7W

Sazan **68** 40 30N 19 20 E
Sazin **95** 35 35N 73 30 E
Sazlika, R. **67** 42 15N 25 50 E
Sbeïtla **119** 35 12N 9 7 E
Scaër **42** 48 2N 3 42W
Scalasaig **34** 56 4N 6 10W
Scalby **33** 54 18N 0 26W
Scalby Ness **33** 54 18N 0 25W
Scalea **65** 39 49N 15 47 E
Scalloway **36** 60 9N 1 16W
Scalpay, I., Inner Hebrides, U.K. **36** 57 18N 6 0W
Scalpay, I., Outer Hebrides, U.K. **36** 57 51N 6 40W
Scamblesby **33** 53 17N 0 5W
Scammon Bay **147** 62 0N 165 49W
Scandia **152** 50 20N 112 0W
Scandiano **62** 44 36N 10 40 E
Scandinavia **16** 64 0N 12 0 E
Scansano **63** 42 40N 11 20 E
Scapa Flow **37** 58 52N 3 6W
Scarastovore **36** 57 50N 7 2W
Scarba, I. **34** 56 10N 5 42W
Scarborough, Trin **167** 11 11N 60 42W
Scarborough, U.K. **33** 54 17N 0 24W
Scargill **143** 42 56 S 172 58 E
Scariff **39** 52 55N 8 32W
Scariff I. **39** 51 43N 10 15W
Scarinish **34** 56 30N 6 48W
Scarning **29** 52 40N 0 53W
Scarp, I. **36** 58 1N 7 8W
Scarpe, R. **43** 50 31N 3 27 E
Scarsdale **140** 37 41 S 143 39 E
Scattery I. **39** 52 37N 9 30W
Scavaig, L. **36** 57 8N 6 10W
Scebeli, Uebi **91** 2 0N 44 0 E
Scědro, I. **63** 43 6N 16 43 E
Scenic **158** 43 49N 102 32W
Schaal See **48** 53 40N 10 57 E
Schaan **51** 47 10N 9 31 E
Schaesberg **47** 50 54N 6 0 E
Schaffen **47** 51 0N 5 5 E
Schaffhausen **51** 47 42N 8 39 E
Schaffhausen □ **51** 47 42N 8 36 E
Schagen **47** 52 49N 4 48 E
Schaghticoke **162** 42 54N 73 35W
Schalkhaar **46** 52 17N 6 12 E
Schalkwijk **46** 52 0N 5 11 E
Schangnau **50** 46 50N 7 47 E
Schänis **51** 47 10N 9 3 E
Schärding **52** 48 27N 13 27 E
Scharhörn, I. **48** 53 58N 8 24 E
Scharnitz **52** 47 23N 11 15 E
Scheessel **48** 53 10N 9 33 E
Schefferville **151** 54 48N 66 50W
Scheibbs **52** 48 1N 15 9 E
Schelde, R. **47** 51 10N 4 20 E
Scheldewindeke **47** 50 56N 3 46 E
Schenectady **162** 42 50N 73 58W
Schenevus **162** 42 33N 74 50W
Scherfede **48** 51 32N 9 2 E
Scherpenheuvel **47** 50 58N 4 58 E
Scherpenisse **47** 51 33N 4 6 E
Scherpenzeel **46** 52 5N 5 30 E
Schesaplana **51** 47 5N 9 43 E
Scheveningen **46** 52 6N 4 16 E
Schichallion, Mt. **37** 56 40N 4 6W
Schiedam **46** 51 55N 4 25 E
Schiermonnikoog **46** 53 29N 6 10 E
Schiermonnikoog, I. **46** 53 30N 6 15 E
Schiers **51** 47 58N 9 41 E
Schifferstadt **49** 49 22N 8 23 E
Schifflange **47** 49 30N 6 1 E
Schijndel **47** 51 37N 5 27 E
Schiltigheim **43** 48 35N 7 45 E
Schio **63** 45 42N 11 21 E
Schipbeek **46** 52 14N 6 10 E
Schipluiden **46** 51 59N 4 19 E
Schirmeck **43** 48 29N 7 12 E
Schladming **52** 47 23N 13 41 E
Schlei, R. **48** 54 45N 9 52 E
Schleiden **48** 50 32N 6 26 E
Schleswig **48** 54 32N 9 34 E
Schleswig-Holstein □ **48** 54 10N 9 40 E
Schlieren **51** 47 28N 8 27 E
Schlüchtern **49** 50 20N 9 32 E
Schmalkalden **48** 50 43N 10 28 E
Schmölln **48** 50 54N 12 22 E
Schneeberg, Austria **52** 47 53N 15 55 E
Schneeberg, Ger. **48** 50 35N 12 39 E
Schoenberg **47** 50 17N 6 16 E
Schofield **158** 44 54N 89 39W
Schoharie **162** 42 40N 74 19W
Schoharie, R. **162** 42 56N 74 18W
Schönberg, Rostock, Ger. **48** 53 50N 10 55 E
Schönberg, Schleswig-Holstein, Ger. **48** 54 23N 10 20 E
Schönebeck **48** 52 2N 11 42 E
Schönenwerd **50** 47 23N 8 0 E
Schöningen **48** 52 8N 10 57 E
Schoondijke **47** 51 21N 3 33 E
Schoonebeek **46** 52 39N 6 52 E
Schoonebeek, oilfield **19** 52 45N 6 50 E
Schoonhoven **46** 51 57N 4 51 E
Schoonoord **46** 52 51N 6 46 E
Schoorl **46** 52 42N 4 42 E
Schors **80** 51 48N 31 56 E
Schortens **48** 53 37N 7 51 E
Schoten **47** 51 16N 4 30 E
Schouten, Kepulauan **103** 1 0 S 136 0 E
Schouter I. **138** 42 20 S 148 20 E
Schouwen, I. **47** 51 43N 3 45 E
Schramberg **49** 48 12N 8 24 E
Schrankogl **52** 47 3N 11 7 E
Schreckhorn **50** 46 36N 8 7 E
Schreiber **150** 48 45N 87 20W
Schroon Lake **162** 43 47N 73 46W
Schruns **52** 47 5N 9 56 E
Schuler **153** 50 20N 110 6W
Schuls **51** 46 48N 10 18 E
Schumacher **150** 48 30N 81 16W
Schüpfen **50** 47 2N 7 24 E
Schüpfheim **50** 46 57N 8 2 E
Schurz **163** 38 57N 118 48W
Schuyler **158** 41 30N 97 3W
Schuylerville **162** 43 6N 73 35W
Schuylkill Haven **162** 40 37N 76 11W
Schuylkill, R. **162** 39 53N 75 12W
Schwabach **49** 49 19N 11 3 E
Schwäbisch Gmünd **49** 48 49N 9 48 E
Schwäbisch Hall **49** 49 7N 9 45 E
Schwäbischer Alb **49** 48 30N 9 30 E
Schwanden **51** 47 1N 9 5 E
Schwarzach, R. **52** 50 30N 11 30 E
Schwarzenberg **48** 50 31N 12 49 E
Schwarzenburg **50** 46 49N 7 20 E
Schwarzwald **49** 48 0N 8 0 E
Schwaz **52** 47 20N 11 44 E
Schwedt **48** 53 4N 14 18 E
Schweinfurt **49** 50 3N 10 12 E
Schweizer Mittelland **50** 47 0N 7 15 E
Schweizer Reneke **128** 27 11 S 25 18 E
Schwerin **48** 53 37N 11 22 E
Schwerin □ **48** 53 35N 11 20 E
Schweriner See **48** 53 45N 11 26 E
Schwetzingen **49** 49 22N 8 35 E
Schwyz **51** 47 2N 8 39 E
Schwyz □ **51** 47 2N 8 39 E
Sciacca **64** 37 30N 13 3 E
Scicli **65** 36 48N 14 41 E
Scie, La **151** 49 57N 55 36W
Scillave **91** 6 22N 44 32 E
Scilly, Isles of **30** 49 55N 6 15W
Scinawa **54** 51 25N 16 26 E
Scioto, R. **156** 39 0N 83 0W
Scituate **162** 42 12N 70 44W
Sclayn **47** 50 29N 5 2 E
Scobey **158** 48 47N 105 30W
Scole **29** 52 22N 1 10 E
Scone **141** 32 0 S 150 52 E
Scopwick **33** 53 6N 0 24W
Scórdia **65** 37 19N 14 50 E
Score Hd. **36** 60 12N 1 5W
Scoresby Sund **12** 70 20N 23 0W
Scorno, Punta dello **64** 41 7N 8 23 E
Scotia, Calif., U.S.A. **160** 40 36N 124 4W
Scotia, N.Y., U.S.A. **162** 42 50N 73 58W
Scotia Sea **13** 56 5 S 56 0W
Scotland **158** 43 10N 97 45W
Scotland □ **51** 57 0N 4 0W
Scotland Neck **157** 36 6N 77 24W
Scott **13** 77 0 S 165 0 E
Scott, C., Antarct. **13** 71 30 S 168 0 E
Scott, C., Austral. **136** 13 30 S 129 49 E
Scott City **158** 38 30N 100 52W
Scott, I. **13** 67 0 S 179 0 E
Scott Inlet **149** 71 0N 71 0W
Scott Is. **152** 50 48N 128 40W
Scott L. **153** 59 55N 106 18W
Scott Reef **136** 14 0 S 121 50 E
Scottburgh **129** 30 15 S 30 47 E
Scottsbluff **158** 41 55N 103 35W
Scottsboro **157** 34 40N 86 0W
Scottsburg **156** 38 40N 85 46W
Scottsdale **138** 41 9 S 147 31 E
Scottsville **157** 36 48N 86 10W
Scottville, Austral. **138** 20 33 S 147 49 E
Scottville, U.S.A. **156** 43 57N 86 18W
Scourie **36** 58 20N 5 10W
Scousburgh **36** 59 58N 1 20W
Scrabby **38** 53 53N 7 32W
Scrabster **37** 58 36N 3 31W
Scram, gasfield **19** 52 55N 2 42 E
Scramoge **38** 53 46N 8 4W
Scranton **162** 41 22N 75 41W
Screebe Lodge **38** 53 23N 9 33W
Screggan **42** 53 15N 7 32W
Scremerston **35** 55 44N 1 59W
Scridain, L. **34** 56 23N 6 7W
Scunthorpe **33** 53 35N 0 38W
Scuol **51** 46 48N 10 17 E
Scusciuban **91** 10 28N 50 5 E
SE Tor, oilfield **19** 56 38N 3 27 E
Sea Isle City **162** 39 9N 74 42W
Seabra **171** 12 25 S 41 46W
Seabrook, L. **137** 30 55 S 119 40 E
Seaford, Austral. **141** 38 10 S 145 11 E
Seaford, U.K. **29** 50 46N 0 8 E
Seaford, U.S.A. **162** 38 37N 75 36W
Seaforth **150** 43 35N 81 25W
Seaforth, L. **36** 57 52N 6 36W
Seagraves **159** 32 56N 102 30W
Seaham **35** 54 51N 1 20W
Seahouses **35** 55 35N 1 39W
Seal Cove **151** 49 57N 56 22W
Seal L. **151** 54 20N 61 30W
Seal, R. **153** 58 50N 97 30W
Sealga, L. na **36** 57 50N 5 18W
Sealy **159** 29 46N 96 9W
Seamer **33** 54 14N 0 27W
Sean, gasfield **19** 53 13N 2 50 E
Searchlight **161** 35 31N 114 55W
Searcy **159** 35 15N 91 45W
Searles, L. **163** 35 47N 117 17W
Seascale **32** 54 24N 3 29W
Seaside, Calif., U.S.A. **163** 36 37N 121 50W
Seaside, Oreg., U.S.A. **160** 46 12N 121 55W
Seaside Park **162** 39 55N 74 5W
Seaspray **141** 38 25 S 147 15 E
Seaton, U.K. **30** 50 42N 3 3W
Seaton, U.K. **32** 54 40N 3 31W
Seaton Delaval **35** 55 5N 1 33W
Seattle **160** 47 41N 122 15W
Seaview Ra. **138** 18 40 S 145 45 E
Seaward Kaikouras, Mts. **143** 42 10 S 173 44 E
Sebago Lake **162** 43 50N 70 35W
Sebastián Vizcaíno, Bahía **164** 28 0N 114 30W
Sebastopol **160** 38 24N 122 49W
Sebastopol = Sevastopol **82** 44 35N 33 30 E
Sebderat **123** 15 26N 36 42 E
Sebdou **118** 34 38N 1 19W
Sebeşului, Mţii. **70** 45 56N 23 40 E
Sebewaing **156** 43 45N 83 27W
Sebezh **80** 56 14N 28 22 E
Sebi **120** 15 50N 4 12W
Sebinkarahisar **82** 40 22N 38 28 E
Sebiş **70** 46 23N 22 13 E
Sebkra Azzel Mati **118** 26 10N 0 43 E
Sebkra Mekerghene **118** 26 21N 1 30 E
Sebou, Oued **118** 34 16N 6 40W
Sebring **157** 27 36N 81 47W
Sebta = Ceuta **118** 35 52N 5 26W
Sebuku, I. **102** 3 30 S 116 25 E
Sebuku, Teluk **102** 4 0N 118 10 E
Sečanj **66** 45 25N 20 47 E
Secchia, R. **62** 44 30N 10 40 E
Sechelt **152** 49 25N 123 42W
Sechura, Desierto de **174** 6 0 S 80 30W
Seclin **43** 50 33N 3 2 E
Secondigny **42** 46 37N 0 26W
Sečovce **53** 48 42N 21 40 E
Secretary I. **143** 45 15 S 166 56 E
Secunderabad **96** 17 28N 78 30 E
Seda, R. **57** 39 6N 7 53W
Sedalia **158** 38 40N 93 18W
Sedan, Austral. **140** 34 34 S 139 19 E
Sedan, France **43** 49 43N 4 57 E
Sedan, U.S.A. **159** 37 10N 96 11W
Sedano **58** 42 43N 3 49W
Sedbergh **32** 54 20N 2 31W
Seddon **143** 41 40 S 174 7 E
Seddonville **143** 41 33 S 172 1 E
Sede Ya'aqov **90** 32 43N 35 7 E
Sederberg, Mt. **128** 32 22 S 19 7 E
Sedgefield **33** 54 40N 1 27W
Sedgewick **152** 52 48N 111 41W
Sedhiou **120** 12 50N 15 30W
Sedičany **52** 49 40N 14 25 E
Sedico **63** 46 8N 12 6 E
Sedinenie **67** 42 16N 24 33 E
Sedley **153** 50 10N 104 0W
Sedom **90** 31 5N 35 20 E
Sedova, Pik **76** 73 20N 55 10 E
Sédrata **119** 36 7N 7 31 E
Sedro Woolley **160** 48 30N 122 15W
Sedrun **51** 46 36N 8 47 E
Seduva **80** 55 45N 23 45 E
Sedziszów Małapolski **54** 50 5N 21 45 E
Seebad Ahlbeck **48** 53 56N 14 10 E
Seefeld **52** 47 19N 11 13 E
Seehausen **48** 52 52N 11 43 E
Seeheim **128** 26 32 S 17 52 E
Seekoe, R. **128** 30 30 S 24 45 E
Seeland **50** 47 0N 7 6 E
Seelaw **48** 52 32N 14 22 E
Seend **28** 51 20N 2 2W
Sées **42** 48 38N 0 10 E
Seesen **48** 51 53N 10 10 E
Sefadu **120** 8 35N 10 58W
Séfeto **120** 14 8N 9 49W
Sefrou **118** 33 52N 4 52W
Sefton **143** 43 15 S 172 41 E
Sefton Mt. **143** 43 40 S 170 5 E
Sefuri-San **110** 33 28N 130 18 E
Sefwi Bekwai **120** 6 10N 2 25W
Seg-ozero **76** 63 0N 33 10 E
Segamat **101** 2 30N 102 50 E
Segarcea **70** 44 6N 23 43 E
Segbwema **120** 8 0N 11 0W
Segeston **31** 51 41N 4 48W
Seget **103** 1 24 S 130 58 E
Seggueur, O. **118** 32 4N 2 4 E
Segid **123** 16 55N 42 0 E
Segonzac **44** 45 36N 0 14W
Segorbe **58** 39 50N 0 30W
Ségou **120** 13 30N 6 10W
Segovia **56** 40 57N 4 10W
Segovia □ **56** 40 55N 4 10W
Segré **42** 47 40N 0 52W
Segre, R. **58** 41 40N 0 43 E
Seguam **147** 52 0N 172 30W
Seguam Pass. **147** 53 0N 175 30W
Séguéla **120** 7 55N 6 40W
Segula I. **147** 52 0N 178 5W
Segundo **159** 37 12N 104 50W
Segundo, R. **172** 30 53 S 62 44W
Segura, R. **59** 38 9N 0 40W
Segura, Sierra de **59** 38 5N 2 45W
Sehithwa **125** 20 30 S 22 30 E
Sehore **94** 23 10N 77 5 E
Sehwan **94** 26 28N 67 53 E
Seica Mare **70** 46 1N 24 7 E
Seikpyu **98** 20 54N 94 48 E
Seil, I. **34** 56 17N 5 37W
Seilandsjøkelen **74** 70 25N 23 16 E
Seiling **159** 36 10N 99 5W
Seille, R. **45** 46 31N 4 57 E
Seilles **47** 50 30N 5 6 E
Sein, I. de **42** 48 2N 4 52W
Seinäjoki **74** 62 48N 22 43 E
Seine-Maritime □ **42** 49 40N 1 0 E
Seine □ **43** 49 0N 3 0 E
Seine-et-Marne □ **43** 48 45N 3 0 E
Seine, R. **42** 49 28N 0 15 E
Seine-Saint-Denis □ **43** 48 58N 2 24 E
Seini **70** 47 44N 23 21 E
Seistan **93** 30 50N 61 0 E
Seiyala **122** 22 57N 32 41 E
Sejal **174** 2 45N 68 0W
Sejerby **73** 55 54N 11 10 E
Sejerø **73** 55 54N 11 15 E
Sejerø Bugt **73** 55 53N 11 9 E
Seka **123** 8 10N 36 52 E
Sekaju **102** 2 58 S 103 58 E
Seke **126** 3 20 S 33 31 E
Sekenke **126** 4 18 S 34 11 E
Seki **111** 35 29N 136 55 E
Sekigahara **111** 35 22N 136 28 E
Sekiu **160** 48 30N 124 29W
Sekkane, Erg in **118** 20 30N 1 30W
Sekondi **120** 5 2N 1 48W
Sekondi-Takoradi **120** 5 0N 1 48W
Sekuma **128** 24 36 S 23 57 E
Sela Dingay **123** 9 58N 39 32 E
Selah **160** 46 44N 120 30W
Selama **101** 5 12N 100 42 E
Selangor □ **101** 3 20N 101 30 E
Selargius **64** 39 14N 9 14 E
Selaru, I. **103** 8 18 S 131 0 E
Selat Bangka **102** 2 30 S 105 30 E
Selawik **147** 66 55N 160 10W
Selb **49** 50 9N 12 9 E
Selborne **29** 51 5N 0 55W
Selby, U.K. **33** 53 47N 1 5W
Selby, U.S.A. **158** 45 34N 99 55W
Selbyville **162** 38 28N 75 13W
Selce **63** 43 20N 16 50 E
Selden **158** 39 24N 100 39W
Seldovia **147** 59 30N 151 45W
Sele, R. **65** 40 27N 15 0 E
Selenica **68** 40 33N 19 39 E
Selenter See **48** 54 19N 10 26 E
Selestat **43** 48 10N 7 26 E
Selet **72** 63 15N 15 45 E
Seletan, Tg. **102** 4 10 S 114 40 E
Seletin **70** 47 50N 25 12 E
Selevac **66** 44 44N 20 52 E
Selfridge **158** 46 3N 100 57W
Sélibaby **120** 15 20N 12 15W
Seliger, Oz. **80** 57 15N 33 0 E
Seligman **161** 35 17N 112 56W
Selim, C. Afr. **126** 5 31N 23 48 E
Selim, Turkey **83** 40 15N 42 58 E
Selîma, El Wâhât el **122** 21 28N 29 31 E
Selinda Spillway **128** 18 35 S 23 10 E
Selinoús **69** 37 35N 21 37 E
Selinsgrove **162** 40 48N 76 52W
Selipuk Gompa **95** 31 23N 82 49 E
Selizharovo **80** 57 1N 33 17 E
Selje **71** 62 3N 5 22 E
Seljord **71** 59 30N 8 40 E
Selkirk, Can. **153** 50 10N 97 20W
Selkirk, U.K. **35** 55 33N 2 50W
Selkirk (□) **26** 55 30N 3 0W
Selkirk I. **153** 53 20N 99 6W
Selkirk Mts. **152** 51 15N 117 40W
Selles-sur-Cher **43** 47 16N 1 33 E
Sellières **43** 46 50N 5 32 E
Sells **161** 31 57N 111 57W
Sellye **53** 45 52N 17 51 E
Selma, Ala., U.S.A. **157** 32 30N 87 0W
Selma, Calif., U.S.A. **163** 36 39N 119 39W
Selma, N.C., U.S.A. **157** 35 32N 78 15W
Selmer **157** 35 9N 88 36W
Sêlo, Óros **68** 41 10N 126 0 E
Selongey **43** 47 36N 5 10 E
Selowandoma Falls **127** 21 15 S 31 50 E
Selpele **103** 0 1 S 130 5 E
Selsey **29** 50 44N 0 47W
Selsey Bill **29** 50 44N 0 47W
Seltz **43** 48 48N 8 4 E
Selu, I. **103** 7 26 S 130 55 E
Selukwe **127** 19 40 S 30 0 E
Sélune, R. **42** 48 38N 1 22W
Selva, Argent. **172** 29 50 S 62 0W
Selva, Spain **58** 41 13N 1 8 E
Selva Beach, La **163** 36 56N 121 51W
Selva, La **58** 42 0N 2 45 E
Selvas **174** 6 30 S 67 0W
Selwyn **133** 21 30 S 140 29 E
Selwyn L. **153** 60 0N 104 30W
Selwyn Mts. **147** 63 0N 130 0W
Selwyn P.O. **138** 21 32 S 140 30 E
Selwyn Ra. **138** 21 10 S 140 0 E
Semani, R. **68** 40 45N 19 50 E
Semarang **103** 7 0 S 110 26 E
Sembabule **126** 0 4 S 31 25 E
Semeih **123** 12 43N 30 53 E
Semenov **81** 56 43N 44 30 E
Semenovka **82** 49 37N 33 2 E
Semeru, Mt. **103** 8 4 S 113 3 E
Sémi **120** 15 4N 13 41W
Semiluki **81** 51 41N 39 10 E
Seminoe Res. **160** 42 0N 107 0W
Seminole, Okla., U.S.A. **159** 35 15N 96 45W
Seminole, Tex., U.S.A. **159** 32 41N 102 38W
Semiozernoye **84** 52 22N 64 8 E
Semipalatinsk **76** 50 30N 80 10 E
Semirara Is. **103** 12 0N 121 20 E

Semisopochnoi I. **147** 52 0N 179 40W
Semitau **102** 0 29N 111 57 E
Semiyarskoye **76** 50 55N 78 30 E
Semmering Pass. **52** 47 41N 15 45 E
Semnan **93** 35 55N 53 25 E
Semnan □ **93** 36 0N 54 0 E
Semois, R. **47** 49 53N 4 44 E
Semporna **103** 4 30N 118 33 E
Semuda **102** 2 51 S 112 58 E
Semur-en-Auxois **43** 47 30N 4 20 E
Sen. R. **101** 13 45N 105 12 E
Sena Madureira **174** 9 5 S 68 45W
Senador Pompeu **170** 5 40 S 39 20W
Senai **101** 1 38N 103 38 E
Senaja **102** 6 49 S 117 2 E
Senanga **128** 16 2 S 23 14 E
Senatobia **159** 34 38N 89 57W
Sendafa **123** 9 11N 39 3 E
Sendai, Kagoshima, Japan **110** 31 50N 130 20 E
Sendai, Miyagi, Japan **112** 38 15N 141 0 E
Sendamangalam **97** 11 17N 78 17 E
Sendeling's Drift **128** 28 12 S 16 52 E
Sendenhorst **48** 51 50N 7 49 E
Sendurjana **96** 21 32N 78 24 E
Senec **53** 48 12N 17 23 E
Seneca, Oreg., U.S.A. **160** 44 10N 119 2W
Seneca, S.C., U.S.A. **157** 34 43N 82 59W
Seneca Falls **162** 42 55N 76 50W
Seneca L. **162** 42 40N 76 58W
Seneffe **47** 50 32N 4 16 E
Senegal ■ **120** 14 30N 14 30W
Senegal, R. **120** 16 30N 15 30W
Senekal **129** 28 18 S 27 36 E
Senftenberg **48** 51 30N 13 51 E
Senga Hill **127** 9 19 S 31 11 E
Senge Khambab (Indus), R. **94** 28 40N 70 10 E
Sengerema □ **126** 2 10 S 32 20 E
Sengiley **81** 53 58N 48 54 E
Sengwa, R. **127** 17 10 S 28 15 E
Senhor-do-Bonfim **170** 10 30 S 40 10W
Senica **53** 48 41N 17 25 E
Senigállia **63** 43 42N 13 12 E
Seniku **98** 25 32N 97 48 E
Senio, R. **63** 44 18N 11 47 E
Senj **63** 45 0N 14 58 E
Senja **74** 69 25N 17 20 E
Senlis **43** 49 13N 2 35 E
Senmonorom **100** 12 27N 107 12 E
Sennâr **123** 13 30N 33 35 E
Senne, R. **47** 50 42N 4 13 E
Sennen **30** 50 4N 5 42W
Senneterre **150** 48 25N 77 15W
Senno **80** 54 45N 29 58 E
Sennori **64** 40 49N 8 36 E
Senny Bridge **31** 51 57N 3 35W
Seno **100** 16 41N 105 1 E
Senonches **42** 48 34N 1 2 E
Senorbi **64** 39 33N 9 8 E
Senoze e **63** 45 43N 14 3 E
Sens **43** 48 11N 3 15 E
Senta **66** 45 55N 20 3 E
Sentein **44** 42 53N 0 58 E
Senteny **126** 5 17 S 25 42 E
Sentier, Le **51** 46 37N 6 15 E
Sentinel **161** 32 56N 113 13W
Sento Sé **170** 9 40 S 41 18W
Sentolo **103** 7 55 S 110 13 E
Senya Beraku **121** 5 28N 0 31W
Seo de Urgel **58** 42 22N 1 23 E
Seohara **95** 29 15N 78 33 E
Seoni **95** 22 5N 79 30 E
Seorinayan **96** 21 45N 82 34 E
Separation Point **151** 53 37N 57 25W
Seph, R. **33** 54 17N 1 9W
Sepik, R. **135** 3 49 S 144 30 E
Sepólno Krajenskie **54** 53 26N 17 30 E
Sepone **100** 16 45N 106 13 E
Sepopa **128** 18 49 S 22 12 E
Sepopol **54** 54 16N 21 2 E
Sepori **107** 38 57N 127 25 E
Sept Îles **151** 50 13N 66 22W
Septemvri **67** 42 13N 24 6 E
Septimus **138** 21 13 S 148 47 E
Sepúlveda **56** 41 18N 3 45W
Sequeros **56** 40 31N 6 2W
Sequim **160** 48 3N 123 9W
Sequoia Nat. Park **163** 36 30N 118 30W
Serafimovich **83** 49 30N 42 50 E
Seraing **47** 50 35N 5 32 E
Seraja **101** 2 41N 108 35 E
Seram, I. **103** 3 10 S 129 0 E
Serampore **95** 22 44N 88 30 E
Serang **103** 6 8 S 106 10 E
Serasan **101** 2 31N 109 2 E
Serasan, I. **102** 2 29N 109 4 E
Seravezza **62** 43 59N 10 13 E
Serbia = Srbija **66** 43 30N 21 0 E
Sercaia **70** 45 49N 25 9 E
Serdo **123** 11 56N 41 14 E
Serdobsk **81** 52 28N 44 10 E
Seredka **80** 58 12N 28 3 E
Seregno **62** 45 40N 9 12 E
Seremban **101** 2 43N 101 53 E
Serena, La, Chile **172** 29 55 S 71 10W
Serena, La, Spain **57** 38 45N 5 40W
Serengeti □ **126** 2 0 S 34 30 E
Serengeti Plain **126** 2 40 S 35 0 E
Serenje **125** 13 14 S 30 15 E
Sergach **81** 55 30N 45 30 E
Serge, R. **58** 42 5N 1 21 E
Sergievsk **81** 54 0N 51 10 E
Sergipe □ **170** 10 30 S 37 30W
Seria **102** 4 37N 114 30 E
Serian **102** 1 10N 110 40 E
Seriate **62** 45 42N 9 43 E
Sérifontaine **43** 49 20N 1 45 E
Sérifos, I. **69** 37 9N 24 30 E
Sérignan **44** 43 17N 3 17 E
Serik **92** 36 55N 31 10 E
Seringapatam Reef **136** 13 38 S 122 5 E
Sermaize-les-Bains **43** 48 47N 4 54 E
Sermata, I. **103** 8 15 S 128 50 E
Sérmide **63** 45 0N 11 17 E
Sernovdsk **76** 61 20N 73 28 E
Sernovodsk **84** 53 54N 51 16 E
Sero **120** 14 42N 10 59W
Serón **59** 37 20N 2 29W
Serós **58** 41 27N 0 24 E
Serov **84** 59 36N 60 35 E
Serowe **128** 22 25 S 26 43 E
Serpa **57** 37 57N 7 38 E
Serpeddi, Punta **64** 39 19N 9 28 E
Serpentara **64** 39 8N 9 38 E
Serpentine **137** 32 23 S 115 58 E
Serpentine L. **137** 28 30 S 129 10 E
Serpent's Mouth **174** 10 0N 61 30W
Serpis, R. **59** 38 45N 0 21W
Serpukhov **81** 54 55N 37 28 E
Serra **171** 20 7 S 40 18W
Serra Capriola **65** 41 47N 15 12 E
Serra do Salitre **74** 19 6 S 46 41W
Serra Talhada **170** 7 59 S 38 18W
Serradilla **56** 39 50N 6 9W
Sérrai □ **68** 41 5N 23 37 E
Serramanna **64** 39 26N 8 56 E
Serranía de Cuenca **58** 40 10N 1 50W
Serrat, C. **119** 37 14N 9 10 E
Serres **45** 44 26N 5 43 E
Serrezuela **172** 30 40 S 65 20W
Serrinha **171** 11 39 S 39 0W
Serrita **170** 7 56 S 39 19W
Serro **171** 18 37 S 43 23W
Sersale **65** 39 1N 16 44 E
Sertã **56** 39 48N 8 6W
Sertânia **170** 8 5 S 37 20W
Sertanópolis **173** 23 4 S 51 2W
Sertão **170** 10 0 S 40 20W
Sertig **51** 46 44N 9 52 E
Serua, P. **103** 6 18 S 130 1 E
Serui **103** 1 45 S 136 10 E
Serule **128** 21 57 S 27 11 E
Sérvia **68** 40 9N 21 58 E
Sesajap Lama **102** 3 32N 117 11 E
Sese Is. **126** 0 30 S 32 30 E
Sesepe **103** 1 30 S 127 59 E
Sesfontein **128** 19 7 S 13 39 E
Sesheke **128** 17 29 S 24 13 E
Sesia, R. **62** 45 35N 8 23 E
Sesimbra **57** 38 28N 9 20W
Seskanore **38** 54 31N 7 15W
Sessa Aurunca **64** 41 14N 13 55 E
Sestao **58** 43 18N 3 0W
Sesto S. Giovanni **62** 45 32N 9 14 E
Sestri Levante **62** 44 17N 9 22 E
Sestrières **62** 44 58N 6 56 E
Sestrunj, I. **63** 44 10N 15 0 E
Sestu **64** 39 18N 9 6 E
Sesvenna **51** 46 42N 10 25 E
Seta **108** 32 20N 100 41 E
Setaka **110** 33 9N 130 28 E
Setana **112** 42 26N 139 51 E
Sète **44** 43 25N 3 42 E
Sete Lagoas **171** 19 27 S 44 16W
Sétif **119** 36 9N 5 26 E
Seto **111** 35 14N 137 6 E
Seto Naikai **110** 34 20N 133 30 E
Setouchi **112** 28 8N 129 19 E
Setsan **98** 16 3N 95 23 E
Settat **118** 33 0N 7 40W
Setté Cama **124** 2 32 S 9 57 E
Séttimo Tor **62** 45 9N 7 46 E
Setting L. **153** 55 0N 98 38W
Settle **32** 54 5N 2 18W
Settlement Pt. **157** 26 40N 79 0W
Setto Calende **62** 45 44N 8 37 E
Setúbal **57** 38 30N 8 58W
Setúbal □ **57** 38 25N 8 35W
Setúbal, B. de **57** 38 40N 8 56W
Seul L. **150** 50 25N 92 30W
Seul Reservoir, Lac **150** 50 25N 92 30W
Seulimeum **102** 5 27N 95 15 E
Seuzach **51** 47 32N 8 49 E
Sevastopol **82** 44 35N 33 30 E
Sevelen **51** 47 7N 9 30 E
Seven Emu **138** 16 20 S 137 8 E
Seven Heads **39** 51 35N 8 43W
Seven Hogs, Is. **39** 52 20N 10 0W
Seven, R. **33** 54 11N 0 51W
Seven Sisters **31** 51 46N 3 43W
Seven Sisters, mt **152** 54 56N 128 10W
Sevenoaks **29** 51 16N 0 11 E
Sevenum **47** 51 25N 6 2 E
Sever, R. **57** 39 40N 7 32W
Sévérac-le-Chateau **44** 44 20N 3 5 E
Severn Beach **28** 51 34N 2 39W
Severn L. **150** 53 54N 90 48W
Severn, R., Can. **150** 56 2N 87 36W
Severn, R., U.K. **28** 51 35N 2 38W
Severn Stoke **28** 52 5N 2 13W
Severnaya Zemlya **77** 79 0N 100 0 E
Severnyye Uvaly **78** 58 0N 48 0 E
Severo-Kurilsk **77** 50 40N 156 8 E
Severodonetsk **83** 48 50N 38 30 E
Severodvinsk **78** 64 27N 39 58 E
Severomoravsky □ **53** 49 38N 17 40 E
Severouralsk **84** 60 9N 59 57 E
Sevier **161** 38 39N 112 11W
Sevier L. **160** 39 0N 113 20W
Sevier, R. **161** 39 10N 112 50W
Sevilla, Colomb. **174** 4 16N 75 57W
Sevilla, Spain **57** 37 23N 6 0W
Sevilla □ **57** 37 0N 6 0W
Seville = Sevilla **57** 37 23N 6 0W
Sevnica **63** 46 2N 15 19 E
Sevsk **80** 52 10N 34 30 E
Seward **147** 60 0N 149 40W
Seward Pen. **147** 65 0N 164 0W
Sewell **172** 34 10 S 70 45W
Sewer **103** 5 46 S 134 40 E
Sexbierum **46** 53 13N 5 29 E
Sexsmith **152** 55 21N 118 47W
Seychelles, Is. **11** 5 0 S 56 0 E
Seyðisfjörður **74** 65 16N 14 0W
Seym, R. **80** 51 45N 35 0 E
Seymchan **77** 62 40N 152 30 E
Seymour, Austral. **141** 37 0 S 145 10 E
Seymour, Conn., U.S.A. **162** 41 23N 73 5W
Seymour, Ind., U.S.A. **156** 39 0N 85 50W
Seymour, Tex., U.S.A. **159** 33 35N 99 18W
Seymour, Wis., U.S.A. **156** 44 30N 88 20W
Seyne **45** 44 21N 6 22 E
Seyne-sur-Mer, La **45** 43 7N 5 52 E
Sezana **63** 45 43N 13 41 E
Sézanne **43** 48 40N 3 40 E
Sezze **64** 41 30N 13 3 E
Sfântu Gheorghe **70** 45 52N 25 48 E
Sfax **119** 34 49N 10 48 E
Sgurr Mor **36** 57 42N 5 0W
Sgurr na Ciche **36** 57 0N 5 29W
Sgurr na Lapaich **36** 57 23N 5 5W
Sha Ch'i, R. **109** 26 35N 118 8 E
Shaartuz **85** 37 16N 68 8 E
Shaba **126** 8 0 S 25 0 E
Shaba Gamba **99** 32 8N 88 55 E
Shaballe, R. **123** 5 0N 44 0 E
Shabani **127** 20 17 S 30 2 E
Shabbear **30** 50 52N 4 12W
Shabla **67** 43 31N 28 32 E
Shabogamo L. **151** 48 40N 77 0W
Shabunda **126** 2 40 S 27 16 E
Shackleton **13** 78 30 S 36 1W
Shackleton Inlet **13** 83 0 S 160 0 E
Shaddad **122** 21 25N 40 2 E
Shadi **95** 33 24N 77 14 E
Shadrinsk **84** 56 5N 63 58 E
Shadwân **122** 27 30N 34 0 E
Shaffa **121** 10 30N 12 6 E
Shafter **163** 35 32N 119 14W
Shaftesbury **28** 51 0N 2 12W
Shag Pt. **143** 45 29 S 170 52 E
Shagamu **121** 6 51N 3 39 E
Shagram **95** 36 24N 72 20 E
Shah Bunder **94** 24 13N 67 50 E
Shahabad, And. P., India **96** 17 10N 78 11 E
Shahabad, Punjab, India **94** 30 10N 76 55 E
Shahabad, Raj., India **94** 25 15N 77 11 E
Shahabad, Uttar Pradesh, India **95** 27 36N 79 56 E
Shāhābād **93** 37 40N 56 50 E
Shahada **96** 21 33N 74 30 E
Shahapur **96** 15 50N 74 34 E
Shāhbād **92** 34 10N 46 30 E
Shahdād **93** 30 30N 57 40 E
Shahdadkot **94** 27 50N 67 55 E
Shahddpur **94** 25 55N 68 35 E
Shahganj **95** 26 3N 82 44 E
Shahgarh **93** 27 15N 69 50 E
Shahhat (Cyrene) **117** 32 40N 21 35 E
Shāhī **93** 36 30N 52 55 E
Shahjahanpur **95** 27 54N 79 57 E
Shaho **106** 36 31N 114 35 E
Shahpur, Mad. P., India **94** 22 12N 77 58 E
Shahpur, Mysore, India **97** 16 40N 76 48 E
Shahpur, Iran **92** 38 12N 44 45 E
Shahpur, Pak. **94** 28 46N 68 27 E
Shahpura **95** 23 10N 80 45 E
Shahr-e Babak **93** 30 10N 55 20 E
Shahr Kord **93** 32 15N 50 55 E
Shahraban **92** 34 0N 45 0 E
Shahreza **93** 32 0N 51 55 E
Shahrig **94** 30 15N 67 40 E
Shahriza **93** 32 0N 51 50 E
Shahrud **93** 36 30N 55 0 E
Shahrukh **93** 33 50N 60 10 E
Shahsavar **93** 36 45N 51 12 E
Shahsien **109** 26 25N 117 50 E
Shahuk'ou **106** 40 20N 112 18 E
Shaibâra **123** 25 26N 36 47 E
Shaikhabad **94** 34 0N 68 45 E
Shaim **84** 60 21N 64 10 E
Shajapur **94** 23 20N 76 15 E
Shakargarh **94** 32 17N 75 43 E
Shakawe **128** 18 28 S 21 49 E
Shakhristan **85** 39 47N 68 49 E
Shakhrisyabz **85** 39 3N 66 50 E
Shakhty **83** 47 40N 40 10 E
Shakhunya **81** 57 40N 47 0 E
Shaki **121** 8 41N 3 21 E
Shakopee **158** 44 45N 93 30W
Shaktolik **147** 64 30N 161 15W
Shala Lake **123** 7 30N 38 30 E
Shaldon **30** 50 32N 3 31W
Shalkar Karashatau, Ozero **84** 50 26N 61 12 E
Shalkar Yega Kara, Ozero **84** 50 45N 60 54 E
Sham, J. ash **93** 23 10N 57 5 E
Shama **121** 5 1N 1 42W
Shamâl Dâfû □ **123** 15 0N 25 0 E
Shamâl Kordofân □ **123** 15 0N 30 0 E
Shamar, Jabal **92** 27 40N 41 0 E
Shamattawa **153** 55 51N 92 5W
Shamattawa, R. **150** 55 1N 85 23W
Shambe **123** 7 2N 30 46 E
Shambu **123** 9 32N 37 3 E
Shamgong Dzong **98** 27 19N 90 35 E
Shamil, India **94** 29 32N 77 18 E
Shamil, Iran **93** 27 30N 56 55 E
Shamkhor **83** 40 56N 46 0 E
Shamo, L. **123** 5 45N 37 30 E
Shamokin **162** 40 47N 76 33W
Shamrock **159** 35 15N 100 15W
Shamva **125** 17 20 S 31 32 E
Shan □ **98** 21 30N 98 30 E
Shanagolden **39** 52 35N 9 6W
Shanan, R. **123** 8 0N 40 20 E
Shanch'eng **109** 31 45N 115 30 E
Shandon **163** 35 39N 120 23W
Shandon Downs **138** 17 45 S 134 50 E
Shanga **121** 9 1N 5 2 E
Shangalowe **127** 10 50 S 26 30 E
Shangani **127** 19 1 S 28 51 E
Shangani, R. **127** 18 35 S 27 45 E
Shangchih, (Chuho) **107** 45 10N 127 59 E
Shangching **106** 33 9N 110 2 E
Shangch'iu **105** 34 26N 115 40 E
Shangch'uan Shan, I. **109** 21 45N 112 45 E
Shanghai **109** 31 10N 121 25 E
Shanghang **109** 25 5N 116 30 E
Shangho **107** 37 19N 117 9 E
Shanghsien **106** 33 30N 109 58 E
Shangjao **109** 28 25N 117 57 E
Shangkao **109** 28 16N 114 50 E
Shanglin **108** 23 26N 108 36 E
Shangnan **106** 33 35N 110 49 E
Shangpanch'eng **107** 40 50N 118 0 E
Shangshui **106** 33 42N 114 34 E
Shangssu **108** 22 10N 108 0 E
Shangtsai **106** 33 15N 114 20 E
Shangtu **106** 41 31N 113 35 E
Shangyu **109** 25 59N 114 29 E
Shanhaikuan **107** 40 2N 119 48 E
Shanhot'un **107** 44 42N 127 12 E
Shanhsien **106** 34 51N 116 9 E
Shani **121** 10 14N 12 2 E
Shaniko **160** 45 0N 120 15W
Shanklin **28** 50 39N 1 9W
Shannon, Greenl. **12** 75 10N 18 30W
Shannon, N.Z. **142** 40 33 S 175 25 E
Shannon Airport **39** 52 42N 85 7W
Shannon Bridge **39** 53 17N 8 2W
Shannon I. **12** 75 0N 18 0W
Shannon, Mouth of the **39** 52 30N 9 55W
Shannon, R. **39** 53 10N 8 10W
Shansi □ **106** 37 30N 112 15 E
Shantar, Ostrov Bolshoi **77** 55 9N 137 40 E
Shant'ou **109** 23 28N 116 40 E
Shantung □ **105** 36 0N 117 30 E
Shantung Pantao **107** 37 5N 121 0 E
Shanyang **106** 33 39N 110 2 E
Shanyin **106** 39 34N 112 50 E
Shaohing **109** 30 0N 120 32 E
Shaokuan **109** 24 50N 113 35 E
Shaowu **109** 27 25N 117 30 E
Shaoyang **109** 27 10N 111 30 E
Shap **32** 54 32N 2 40W
Shap'ing **109** 22 46N 112 57 E
Shapinsay, I. **37** 59 2N 2 50W
Shapinsay Sd. **37** 59 0N 2 51W
Shaqra **92** 25 15N 45 16 E
Sharafa (Ogr) **123** 11 59N 27 7 E
Sharavati, R. **97** 14 32N 74 0 E
Sharhjui **93** 32 30N 67 22 E
Shari **92** 27 20N 43 45 E
Sharjah **93** 25 23N 55 26 E
Shark B., N. Territory, Austral. **132** 11 20 S 130 35 E
Shark B., W. Australia, Austral. **137** 25 55 S 113 32 E
Sharm el Sheikh **122** 27 53N 34 15 E
Sharon, Mass., U.S.A. **162** 42 5N 71 11W
Sharon, Pa., U.S.A. **156** 41 18N 80 30W
Sharon, Plain of = Hasharon **90** 32 12N 34 49 E
Sharon Springs **162** 42 48N 74 37W
Sharp Pt. **138** 10 58 S 142 43 E
Sharpe, L. **150** 54 10N 93 21W
Sharpe L. **153** 50 23N 95 30W
Sharpness **28** 51 43N 2 28W
Sharya **81** 58 12N 45 40 E
Shasha **123** 6 29N 35 59 E
Shashemene **123** 7 13N 38 33 E
Shashi **125** 21 15 S 27 27 E
Shashi, R. **127** 21 40 S 28 40 E
Shashih **109** 30 19N 112 14 E
Shasta, Mt. **160** 41 45N 122 0W
Shasta Res. **160** 40 50N 122 15W
Shati **109** 26 6N 114 51 E
Shatsk **81** 54 0N 41 45 E
Shattuck **159** 36 17N 99 55W
Shaumyani **83** 41 13N 44 45 E
Shaunavon **153** 49 35N 108 25W
Shaver Lake **163** 37 9N 119 18W
Shaw I. **138** 20 30 S 149 2 E
Shaw, R. **136** 20 21 S 119 17 E
Shawan **105** 44 21N 85 37 E
Shawangunk Mts. **162** 41 40N 74 25W
Shawano **156** 44 45N 88 38W
Shawbost **36** 58 20N 6 40W

Shawbury 28 52 48N 2 40W
Shawinigan 150 46 35N 72 50W
Shawnee 159 35 15N 97 0W
Shaymak 85 37 33N 74 50E
Shaziz 99 33 10N 82 43E
Shchëkino 81 54 1N 37 28E
Shcherbakov = Rybinsk 81 58 5N 38 50E
Shchigri 81 51 55N 36 58E
Shchuchinsk 76 52 56N 70 12E
Shchuchye 84 55 12N 62 46E
Shchurovo 81 55 0N 38 51E
Shebekino 81 50 28N 37 0E
Shebele, Wabi 123 2 0N 44 0E
Sheboygan 156 43 46N 87 45W
Shechem 90 32 13N 35 21E
Shech'i 106 33 3N 112 57E
Shediac 151 46 14N 64 32W
Sheefry Hills 38 53 40N 9 40W
Sheelin, Lough 38 53 48N 7 20W
Sheep Haven 38 55 12N 7 55W
Sheeps Hd. 39 51 32N 9 50W
Sheerness 29 51 26N 0 47E
Sheet Harbour 151 44 56N 62 31W
Shefar'am 90 32 48N 35 10E
Shefeiya 90 32 35N 34 58E
Sheffield, U.K. 33 53 23N 1 28W
Sheffield, Ala., U.S.A. 157 34 45N 87 42W
Sheffield, Mass., U.S.A. 162 42 6N 73 23W
Sheffield, Tex., U.S.A. 159 30 42N 101 49W
Shefford 29 52 2N 0 20W
Shegaon 96 20 48N 76 59E
Sheho 153 51 35N 103 13W
Shehojele 123 10 40N 35 27E
Shehsien, Anhwei, China 109 29 52N 118 26E
Shehsien, Hopeh, China 106 36 33N 113 40E
Shehung 108 31 0N 105 12E
Shehy Mts. 39 51 47N 9 15W
Sheikhpura 95 25 9N 85 53E
Shek Hasan 123 13 5N 35 58E
Shekar Dzong 95 28 45N 87 0E
Shekhupura 94 31 42N 73 58E
Sheki 83 41 10N 47 5E
Sheksna, R. 81 59 30N 38 30E
Shelburne, N.S., Can. 151 43 47N 65 20W
Shelburne, Ont., Can. 150 44 4N 80 15W
Shelburne B. 133 11 50S 143 0E
Shelburne Falls 162 42 36N 72 45W
Shelby, Mich., U.S.A. 156 43 34N 86 27W
Shelby, Mont., U.S.A. 160 48 30N 111 59W
Shelby, N.C., U.S.A. 157 35 18N 81 34W
Shelbyville, Ill., U.S.A. 158 39 25N 88 45W
Shelbyville, Ind., U.S.A. 156 39 30N 85 42W
Shelbyville, Tenn., U.S.A. 157 35 30N 86 25W
Sheldon 158 43 6N 95 51W
Sheldon Point 147 62 30N 165 0W
Sheldrake 151 50 20N 64 51W
Shelikef, Str. 147 58 0N 154 0W
Shelikhova, Zaliv 77 59 30N 157 0E
Shell, L. 36 58 0N 6 28W
Shell Lake 153 53 19N 107 14W
Shell Lakes 137 29 20S 127 30E
Shellbrook 153 53 13N 106 24W
Shellharbour 141 34 31S 150 51E
Shelon, R. 80 58 10N 30 30E
Shelter Bay 151 50 30N 67 20W
Shelter I 162 41 5N 72 21W
Shelton, Conn., U.S.A. 162 41 18N 73 7W
Shelton, Wash., U.S.A. 160 47 15N 123 6W
Shemakha 83 40 50N 48 28E
Shenandoah, Iowa, U.S.A. 158 40 50N 95 25W
Shenandoah, Pa., U.S.A. 162 40 49N 76 13W
Shenandoah, Va., U.S.A. 156 38 30N 78 38W
Shenandoah, R. 156 38 30N 78 38W
Shencha 105 30 56N 88 38E
Shench'ih 106 39 8N 112 10E
Shenchingtzu 107 44 48N 124 32E
Shench'iu 106 33 26N 115 2E
Shencottah 97 8 59N 77 18E
Shendam 121 9 10N 9 30E
Shendî 123 16 46N 33 33E
Shendurni 96 20 39N 75 36E
Shenfield 29 51 39N 0 21E
Shengfang 106 39 5N 116 42E
Shëngjergji 68 41 2N 20 10E
Shëngjini 68 41 50N 19 35E
Shenmëria 68 42 7N 20 13E
Shenmu 106 38 54N 110 24E
Shensi □ 106 34 50N 109 25E
Shenton, Mt. 137 27 57S 123 22E
Shenyang 107 42 50N 123 25E
Sheopur Kalan 93 25 40N 76 40E
Shepetovka 80 50 10N 27 0E
Shephelah = Hashefela 90 31 30N 34 43E
Shepparton 141 36 23S 145 26E
Sheppey, I. of 29 51 23N 0 50E
Shepshed 28 52 47N 1 18W
Shepton Mallet 28 51 11N 2 31W
Sher Khan Qala 94 29 55N 66 10E
Sher Qila 95 36 7N 74 2E
Sherada 123 7 25N 36 30E
Sherborne 28 50 56N 2 31W
Sherborne St. John 28 51 18N 1 7W
Sherbro I. 120 7 30N 12 40W
Sherbrooke 151 45 8N 81 57W
Sherburn, N. Yorks., U.K. 33 54 12N 0 32W
Sherburn, N. Yorks., U.K. 33 53 47N 1 15W
Sherburne 162 42 41N 75 30W
Shercock 38 54 0N 6 54W
Sherda 119 20 7N 16 46E
Shere 29 51 13N 0 28W
Shereik 122 18 52N 33 40E
Sherfield English 28 51 1N 1 35W
Sheridan, Ark., U.S.A. 159 34 20N 92 25W
Sheridan, Col., U.S.A. 158 39 44N 105 3W
Sheridan, Wyo., U.S.A. 160 44 50N 107 0W
Sheriff Hutton 33 54 5N 1 0W
Sheriff Muir 35 56 12N 3 53W
Sheringham 29 52 56N 1 11E
Sherkin I. 39 51 38N 9 25W
Sherkot 95 29 22N 78 35E
Sherman 159 33 40N 96 35W
Sherpur 98 24 41N 89 25E
Sherridon 153 55 8N 101 5W
Sherston 28 51 35N 2 13W
Sherwood, N.D., U.S.A. 158 48 59N 101 36W
Sherwood, Tex., U.S.A. 159 31 18N 100 45W
Sherwood For. 33 53 5N 1 5W
Shesheke 125 17 14S 24 22E
Sheslay 152 58 17N 131 45W
Sheslay, R. 152 58 48N 132 5W
Shethanei L. 153 58 48N 97 50W
Shetland □ 36 60 30N 1 30W
Shetland Is. 36 60 30N 1 30W
Shevaroy Hills 97 11 58N 78 12E
Shevchenko 83 44 25N 51 20E
Shewa □ 123 9 33N 38 10E
Sheyenne 159 47 52N 99 8W
Sheyenne, R. 158 47 40N 98 15W
Shiant Is. 36 57 54N 6 20W
Shiant, Sd. of Scot. 36 57 54N 6 30W
Shibam 91 16 0N 48 36E
Shibata 112 37 57N 139 20E
Shiberghan □ 93 35 45N 66 0E
Shibetsu 112 44 10N 142 23E
Shibîn El Kôm 122 30 31N 30 55E
Shibogama L. 150 53 35N 88 15W
Shibukawa 111 36 29N 139 0E
Shibushi 110 31 25N 131 0E
Shibushi-Wan 110 31 24N 131 8E
Shickshinny 162 41 9N 76 9W
Shido 110 34 19N 134 10E
Shiel, L. 36 56 48N 5 32W
Shield, C. 138 13 20S 136 20E
Shieldaig 36 57 31N 5 39W
Shifnal 28 52 40N 2 23W
Shiga-ken □ 111 35 20N 136 0E
Shigaib 117 15 5N 23 35E
Shigaraki 111 34 57N 136 2E
Shihch'eng 109 26 19N 116 15E
Shihchiachuangi 106 38 2N 114 30E
Shihch'ien 108 27 30N 108 14E
Shihchiu Hu 109 31 28N 118 53E
Shihchu 108 30 4N 108 10E
Shihch'üan 106 33 3N 108 17E
Shihhsing 109 24 57N 114 4E
Shihku 108 26 52N 99 56E
Shihkuaikou 106 40 42N 110 20E
Shihlung 109 23 55N 113 35E
Shihmen 109 29 36N 111 23E
Shihmenchien 109 29 33N 116 47E
Shihmien 108 29 20N 102 28E
Shihping 108 27 2N 108 7E
Shihp'ing 108 23 43N 102 30E
Shihshou 109 29 43N 112 26E
Shihtai 109 30 22N 117 57E
Shihtien 108 24 44N 99 11E
Shiht'ouhotzu 107 44 52N 128 41E
Shihtsuishan 106 39 15N 106 50E
Shihtsung 108 24 51N 103 59E
Shiiba 110 32 29N 131 4E
Shijaku 68 41 21N 19 33E
Shikarpur, India 94 28 17N 78 7E
Shikarpur, Pak. 94 27 57N 68 39E
Shikine-Jima 111 34 19N 139 13E
Shikohabad 93 27 6N 78 38E
Shikoku 110 33 30N 133 30E
Shikoku □ 110 33 30N 133 30E
Shikoku-Sanchi 110 33 30N 133 30E
Shilbottle 35 55 23N 1 42W
Shilda 84 51 49N 59 47E
Shildon 33 54 37N 1 39W
Shilka 77 52 0N 115 55E
Shilka, R. 77 57 30N 93 18E
Shillelagh 39 52 46N 6 32W
Shillingstone 28 50 54N 2 15W
Shillington 162 40 18N 75 58W
Shillong 98 25 35N 91 53E
Shiloh 90 32 4N 35 10E
Shilovo 81 54 25N 40 57E
Shima-Hantō 111 34 22N 136 45E
Shimabara 110 32 48N 130 20E
Shimada 111 34 49N 138 19E
Shimane-Hantō 110 35 30N 133 0E
Shimane-ken □ 110 35 0N 132 30E
Shimenovsk 77 52 15N 127 30E
Shimizu 111 35 0N 138 30E
Shimo-Jima 110 32 15N 130 7E
Shimo-Koshiki-Jima 110 31 40N 129 43E
Shimoda 111 34 40N 138 57E
Shimodate 111 36 20N 139 55E
Shimoga 97 13 57N 75 32E
Shimoni 126 4 38S 39 20E
Shimonita 111 36 13N 138 47E
Shimonoseki 110 33 58N 131 0E
Shimotsuma 111 36 11N 139 58E
Shimpuru Rapids 128 17 45S 19 55E
Shimsha, R. 97 13 15N 76 54E
Shimsk 80 58 15N 30 50E
Shin Dand 93 33 12N 62 8E
Shin, L. 37 58 7N 4 30W
Shin, R. 37 58 0N 4 26W
Shin-Tone-Gawa 111 35 57N 140 27E
Shingbwiyang 98 26 41N 96 13E
Shingleton 150 46 33N 86 33W
Shingu 111 33 40N 135 55E
Shinji 110 35 24N 132 54E
Shinji Ko 110 35 26N 132 57E
Shinjō 112 38 46N 140 18E
Shinkafe 121 13 8N 6 29E
Shinminato 111 36 47N 137 4E
Shinonoi 111 36 35N 138 9E
Shinrone 39 53 0N 7 58W
Shinshiro 111 34 54N 137 30E
Shinyanga 126 3 45S 33 27E
Shinyanga □ 126 3 30S 33 30E
Shio-no-Misaki 111 33 25N 135 45E
Shiogama 112 38 19N 141 1E
Shiojiri 111 36 6N 137 58E
Ship I. 159 30 16N 88 55W
Ship Shoal I. 162 37 10N 75 45W
Shipbourne 29 51 13N 0 19E
Shipdham 29 52 38N 0 53E
Shipehenski Prokhod 67 42 39N 25 28E
Shipki La 93 31 45N 78 40E
Shipley 33 53 50N 1 47W
Shippegan 151 47 45N 64 45W
Shippensburg 156 40 4N 77 32W
Shiprock 161 36 51N 108 45W
Shipston-on-Stour 28 52 4N 1 38W
Shipton-under-Wychwood 28 51 51N 1 35W
Shir Kūh 93 31 45N 53 30E
Shirabad 85 37 40N 67 1E
Shirahama 111 33 41N 135 20E
Shirakawa 111 36 17N 136 56E
Shirane-San, Gumma, Japan 111 36 48N 139 22E
Shirane-San, Yamanashi, Japan 111 35 34N 138 9E
Shiraoi 112 42 33N 141 21E
Shirati 126 1 10S 34 0E
Shiraz 93 29 42N 52 30E
Shire, R. 127 16 30S 35 0E
Shirebrook 33 53 13N 1 11W
Shiresh 85 39 58N 70 59E
Shirinab, R. 94 29 30N 66 30E
Shiringushi 81 42 54N 53 56W
Shiriya-Zaki 112 41 25N 141 30E
Shirol 96 16 47N 74 41E
Shirpur 96 21 21N 74 57E
Shirvan 93 37 30N 57 50E
Shirwa L. = Chilwa L. 127 15 15S 35 40E
Shishmanova 67 42 58N 23 12E
Shishmaref 147 66 15N 166 10W
Shivali, (Sirkall) 97 11 15N 79 41E
Shivpuri 94 25 18N 77 42E
Shivta 90 30 53N 34 40E
Shiwele Ferry 127 11 25S 28 31E
Shiyata 122 29 25N 25 7E
Shizuoka 111 35 0N 138 30E
Shizuoka-ken □ 111 35 15N 138 40E
Shklov 80 54 10N 30 15E
Shkoder = Shkodra 68 42 6N 19 20E
Shkodra 68 42 6N 19 20E
Shkodra □ 68 42 5N 19 20E
Shkumbini, R. 68 41 5N 19 50E
Shmidt, O. 77 81 0N 91 0E
Shō Gawa, R. 111 36 47N 137 4E
Shoa Ghimirra, (Wota) 123 7 4N 35 51E
Shoal, C. 137 33 52S 121 10E
Shoal Lake 153 50 30N 100 35W
Shōbara 110 34 51N 133 1E
Shōdo-Shima 110 34 30N 134 15E
Shoeburyness 29 51 31N 0 49E
Shokpar 85 43 49N 74 21E
Sholapur 96 17 43N 75 56E
Shologontsy 77 66 13N 114 14E
Shomera 90 33 4N 35 17E
Shōmrōn 90 32 15N 35 13E
Shona I. 36 56 48N 5 50W
Shongopovi 161 35 49N 110 37W
Shoranur 97 10 46N 76 19E
Shorapur 96 16 31N 76 48E
Shoreham-by-Sea 29 50 50N 0 17W
Shortland I. 135 7 0S 155 45E
Shoshone, Calif., U.S.A. 163 35 58N 116 16W
Shoshone, Idaho, U.S.A. 160 43 0N 114 27W
Shoshone L. 160 44 0N 111 0W
Shoshone Mts. 160 39 30N 117 30W
Shoshong 125 22 56S 26 31E
Shoshoni 160 43 13N 108 5W
Shostka 80 51 57N 33 32E
Shotts 35 55 49N 3 47W
Shouch'ang 109 29 22N 119 13E
Shouhsien 109 32 35N 116 48E
Shoukuang 107 36 53N 118 42E
Shouning 109 27 26N 119 27E
Shouyang 106 37 59N 113 9E
Show Low 161 34 16N 110 0W
Shpola 82 49 1N 31 30E
Shreveport 159 32 30N 93 50W
Shrewsbury 28 52 42N 2 45W
Shrewton 28 51 11N 1 55W
Shrivardhan 96 18 10N 73 3E
Shrivenham 28 51 36N 1 39W
Shropshire □ 28 52 36N 2 45W
Shrule 38 53 32N 9 7W
Shuangch'eng 107 45 25N 126 20E
Shuangchiang 108 23 33N 99 45E
Shuangfeng 109 27 26N 112 10E
Shuangfeng Tao 109 26 35N 120 8E
Shuangkou 107 34 3N 117 34E
Shuangliao 105 43 31N 123 30E
Shuangpai 108 24 50N 101 36E
Shuangshantzu 107 40 21N 119 12E
Shuangyang 107 43 32N 125 40E
Shuangyashan 105 46 37N 131 22E
Shuch'eng 109 31 27N 116 57E
Shugden Gomba 99 29 35N 96 55E
Shuguri Falls 127 8 33S 37 22E
Shuich'eng 108 26 35N 104 54E
Shuichi 109 27 28N 118 21E
Shuiyeh 106 36 8N 114 6E
Shujalpur 94 23 43N 76 40E
Shulan 107 44 27N 126 57E
Shumagin Is. 147 55 0N 159 0W
Shumerlya 81 55 30N 46 10E
Shumikha 84 55 10N 63 15E
Shunan 109 29 37N 119 0E
Shunch'ang 109 26 48N 117 47E
Shungay 83 48 30N 46 45E
Shungnak 147 66 55N 157 10W
Shunning 99 24 35N 99 50E
Shunte 109 22 48N 113 17E
Shuohsien 106 39 19N 112 25E
Shupka Kunzang 95 34 22N 78 22E
Shuqra 91 13 22N 45 34E
Shur, R. 93 28 30N 55 0E
Shurab 85 40 3N 70 33E
Shurchi 85 37 59N 67 47E
Shurkhua 98 22 15N 93 38E
Shurma 84 56 58N 50 21E
Shusf 93 31 50N 60 5E
Shūshtar 92 32 0N 48 50E
Shuswap L. 152 50 55N 119 3W
Shuweika 90 32 20N 35 1E
Shuya 81 56 50N 41 28E
Shuyak I. 147 58 35N 152 30W
Shuzenji 111 34 58N 138 56E
Shwebo 98 22 30N 95 45E
Shwegu 98 18 49N 95 26E
Shwegun 98 17 9N 97 39E
Shweli Myit 99 23 45N 96 45E
Shweli, R. 99 23 45N 96 45E
Shwenyaung 98 20 46N 96 57E
Shyok 95 34 15N 78 5E
Shyok, R. 95 34 30N 78 15E
Si Chon 101 9 0N 99 54E
Si Kiang = Hsi Chiang, R. 39 22 20N 113 20E
Si Prachan 100 14 37N 100 9E
Si Racha 101 13 10N 100 56E
Siah 92 22 0N 47 0E
Siahan Range 93 27 30N 64 40E
Siaksriinderapura 102 0 51N 102 0E
Sialkot 94 32 32N 74 30E
Sialsuk 98 23 24N 92 45E
Siam 140 32 35S 136 41E
Siam, G. of 101 11 30N 101 0E
Siam = Thailand ■ 100 16 0N 102 0E
Sian = Hsian 106 34 17N 109 0E
Siantan, P. 101 3 10N 106 15E
Siareh 93 28 5N 60 20E
Siargao, I. 103 9 52N 126 3E
Siari 95 34 55N 76 40E
Siasi 103 5 34N 120 50E
Siassi 135 5 40S 147 51E
Siátista 68 40 15N 21 33E
Siau, I. 103 2 50N 125 25E
Siauliai 80 55 56N 23 15E
Siaya □ 126 0 0N 34 20E
Siazan 83 41 3N 48 7E
Sibâi, Gebel el 122 25 45N 34 10E
Sibari 65 39 47N 16 27E
Sibay 84 52 42N 58 39E
Sibaya, L. 129 27 20S 32 45E
Sibbald 153 51 24N 110 10W
Sibenik 63 43 48N 15 54E
Siberia 77 60 0N 100 0E
Siberut, I. 102 1 30S 99 0E
Sibi 94 29 30N 67 48E
Sibil 103 4 59S 140 35E
Sibiti 124 3 38S 13 19E
Sibiu 70 45 45N 24 9E
Sibiu □ 70 45 50N 24 15E
Sible Hedingham 29 51 58N 0 37E
Sibley, Iowa, U.S.A. 158 43 21N 95 43W
Sibley, La., U.S.A. 159 32 34N 93 16W
Sibolga 102 1 50N 98 45E
Sibret 47 49 58N 5 38E
Sibsagar 98 27 0N 94 36E
Sibsey 33 53 3N 0 1E
Sibuco 103 7 20N 122 10E
Sibuguey B. 103 7 50N 122 45E
Sibuko 103 7 20N 122 10E
Sibut 117 5 52N 19 10E
Sibutu, I. 102 4 45N 119 30E
Sibutu Passage 103 4 50N 120 0E
Sibuyan, I. 103 12 25N 122 40E
Sicamous 152 50 49N 119 0W
Sicapoo 103 18 9N 121 34E
Sicasica 154 17 20S 67 45W
Siccus, R. 140 31 42S 139 25E
Sicilia, Canale di 64 37 25N 12 30E
Sicilia, I. 65 37 30N 14 30E
Sicily = Sicilia 65 37 30N 14 30E
Sicuani 174 14 10S 71 10W
Siculiana 64 37 20N 13 23E
Sid 63 45 6N 19 16E
Sidamo □ 123 5 0N 37 50E
Sidaouet 121 18 34N 8 3E
Sidaradougou 120 10 42N 4 12W
Sidbury 30 50 43N 3 12W
Siddeburen 46 53 15N 6 52E

Siddipet **96** 18 0N 79 0 E
Sidensjo **72** 63 20N 18 20 E
Sidéradougou **120** 10 42N 4 12W
Siderno Marina **65** 38 16N 16 17 E
Sidheros, Ákra **69** 35 19N 26 19 E
Sidhirókastron **68** 37 20N 21 46 E
Sidhpur **94** 23 56N 71 25 E
Sîdi Abd el Rahman **122** 30 55N 28 41 E
Sîdi Barrâni **122** 31 32N 25 58 E
Sidi-Bel-Abbès **118** 35 13N 0 10W
Sidi Bennour **118** 32 40N 9 26W
Sidi Haneish **122** 31 10N 27 35 E
Sidi Ifni **118** 29 29N 10 3W
Sidi Kacem **118** 34 11N 5 40W
Sīdī Miftāh **119** 31 8N 16 58 E
Sidi Moussa, O. **118** 33 0N 8 50W
Sidi Omar **122** 31 24N 24 57 E
Sīdī Yahya **119** 30 55N 16 30 E
Sidlaw Hills **35** 56 32N 3 10W
Sidlesham **29** 50 46N 0 46W
Sidmouth **30** 50 40N 3 13W
Sidmouth, C. **138** 13 25 S 143 36 E
Sidney, Can. **152** 48 39N 123 24W
Sidney, Mont., U.S.A. **158** 47 51N 104 7W
Sidney, N.Y., U.S.A. **162** 42 18N 75 20W
Sidney, Ohio, U.S.A. **156** 40 18N 84 6W
Sidoardjo **103** 7 30 S 112 46 E
Sidoktaya **98** 20 27N 94 15 E
Sidon, (Saida) **92** 33 38N 35 28 E
Sidra, G. of = Khalīj Surt **61** 31 40N 18 30 E
Siedlce **54** 52 10N 22 20 E
Siedlce □ **54** 52 0N 22 0 E
Siegburg **48** 50 48N 7 12 E
Siegen **48** 50 52N 8 2 E
Siem Pang **100** 14 7N 106 23 E
Siem Reap **100** 13 20N 103 52 E
Siena **63** 43 20N 11 20 E
Sieniawa **54** 50 11N 22 38 E
Sieradź **54** 51 37N 18 41 E
Sieradź □ **54** 51 30N 19 0 E
Sieraków **54** 52 39N 16 2 E
Sierck-les-Bains **43** 49 26N 6 20 E
Sierpc **54** 52 55N 19 43 E
Sierpe, Bocas de la **174** 10 0N 61 30W
Sierra Alta **58** 40 31N 1 30W
Sierra Blanca **161** 31 11N 105 17W
Sierra Blanca, mt. **161** 33 20N 105 54W
Sierra City **160** 39 34N 120 42W
Sierra Colorado **176** 40 35 S 67 50W
Sierra de Gädor **59** 36 57N 2 45W
Sierra de Yeguas **57** 37 7N 4 52W
Sierra Gorda **172** 23 0 S 69 15W
Sierra Leone ■ **120** 9 0N 12 0W
Sierra Majada **164** 27 19N 103 42W
Sierre **50** 46 17N 7 31 E
Sifnos **69** 37 0N 24 45 E
Sifton **153** 51 21N 100 8W
Sifton Pass **152** 57 52N 126 15W
Sig **118** 35 32N 0 12W
Sigaboy **103** 6 39N 126 10 E
Sigdal **71** 60 4N 9 38 E
Sigean **44** 43 2N 2 58 E
Sighetul Marmatiei **70** 47 57N 23 52 E
Sighişoara **70** 46 12N 24 50 E
Sighty Crag **35** 55 8N 2 37W
Sigli **102** 5 25N 96 0 E
Siglufjörður **74** 66 12N 18 55W
Sigma **103** 11 29N 122 40 E
Sigmaringen **49** 48 5N 9 13 E
Signakhi **83** 40 52N 45 57 E
Signau **50** 46 56N 7 45 E
Signy I. **13** 60 45 S 46 30W
Signy-l'Abbaye **43** 49 40N 4 25 E
Sigsig **174** 3 0 S 78 50W
Sigtuna **72** 59 36N 17 44 E
Sigüenza **58** 41 3N 2 40W
Siguiri **120** 11 31N 9 10W
Sigulda **80** 57 10N 24 55 E
Sigurd **161** 38 57N 112 0W
Sihanoukville = Kompong Som **101** 10 40N 103 30 E
Si'ir **90** 31 35N 35 9 E
Siirt **92** 37 57N 41 55 E
Sijarira, Ra. **127** 17 36 S 27 45 E
Sijsele **13** 51 12N 3 20 E
Sikandarabad **94** 28 30N 77 39 E
Sikandra Rao **93** 27 43N 78 24 E
Sikar **94** 27 39N 75 10 E
Sikasso **120** 11 7N 5 35W
Sikerete **128** 19 0 S 20 48 E
Sikeston **159** 36 52N 89 35W
Sikhote Alin, Khrebet **77** 46 0N 136 0 E
Sikiá. **68** 40 2N 23 56 E
Sikinos, I. **69** 36 40N 25 8 E
Sikionia **69** 38 0N 22 44 E
Sikkani Chief, R. **152** 57 47N 122 15W
Sikkim ■ **98** 27 50N 88 50 E
Siklós **53** 45 50N 18 19 E
Sikoro **120** 12 19N 7 8W
Sikqo **101** 7 34N 99 21 E
Sil, R. **56** 42 23N 7 30W
Sila, La, Mts. **65** 39 15N 16 35 E
Silacayoapán **165** 17 30N 98 9W
Silandro **62** 46 38N 10 48 E
Silat adh Dhahr **90** 32 19N 35 11 E
Silba **63** 44 24N 14 41 E
Silba, I. **63** 44 24N 14 41 E
Silchar **98** 24 49N 92 48 E
Silcox **153** 57 12N 94 10W
Silenrieux **47** 50 14N 4 27 E
Siler City **157** 35 44N 79 30W
Sileru, R. **96** 18 0N 82 0 E
Silesia = Slask **54** 51 0N 16 30 E
Silet **118** 22 44N 4 37 E
Silgarhi Doti **95** 29 15N 82 0 E
Silghat **98** 26 35N 93 0 E
Silifke **92** 36 22N 33 58 E
Siliguri **98** 26 45N 88 25 E
Siliqua **64** 39 20N 8 49 E
Silistra **67** 44 6N 27 19 E
Siljan, L. **72** 60 55N 14 45 E
Silkeborg **73** 56 10N 9 32 E
Sillajhuay, Cordillera **174** 19 40 S 68 40W
Sillé-le Guillaume **42** 48 10N 0 8W
Silloth **32** 54 53N 3 25W
Siloam Springs **159** 36 15N 94 31W
Silogui **102** 1 10 S 98 46 E
Silsbee **159** 30 20N 94 8W
Silsden **32** 53 55N 1 55W
Silute **80** 55 21N 21 33 E
Silva Porto = Bié **125** 12 22 S 16 55 E
Silvaplana **51** 46 28N 9 48 E
Silver City, Calif., U.S.A. **160** 36 19N 119 44W
Silver City, N. Mex., U.S.A. **161** 32 50N 108 18W
Silver Cr., R. **160** 43 30N 119 30W
Silver Creek **156** 42 33N 79 9W
Silver L. **163** 38 39N 120 6W
Silver Lake, Calif., U.S.A. **163** 35 21N 116 7W
Silver Lake, Oreg., U.S.A. **160** 43 9N 121 4W
Silver Springs **162** 39 2N 77 3W
Silverhojden **72** 60 2N 15 0 E
Silvermine, Mts. **39** 52 47N 8 15W
Silvermines **39** 52 48N 8 15W
Silverpeak, Ra. **163** 37 35N 117 45W
Silverstone **28** 52 5N 1 3W
Silverton, Austral. **140** 31 52 S 141 10 E
Silverton, U.K. **30** 50 49N 3 29W
Silverton, Colo., U.S.A. **161** 37 51N 107 45W
Silverton, Tex., U.S.A. **159** 34 30N 101 16W
Silves **57** 37 11N 8 26W
Silvia **174** 2 37N 76 21W
Silvies, R. **160** 43 57N 119 5W
Silvolde **46** 51 55N 6 23 E
Silvretta Gruppe **51** 46 50N 10 6 E
Silwa Bahari **122** 24 45N 32 55 E
Silwan **90** 31 59N 35 15 E
Silwani **93** 23 18N 78 27 E
Silz **52** 47 16N 10 56 E
Sim, C. **118** 31 26N 9 51W
Simanggang **102** 1 15N 111 25 E
Simão Dias **170** 10 44 S 37 49W
Simard, L. **150** 47 40N 78 40W
Simarun **93** 31 16N 51 40 E
Simba **126** 1 41 S 34 12 E
Simbach **49** 48 16N 13 3 E
Simbo **126** 4 51 S 29 41 E
Simcoe **150** 42 50N 80 20W
Simcoe, L. **150** 44 25N 79 20W
Simenga **77** 62 50N 107 55 E
Simeon **47** 50 45N 5 36 E
Simeulue, I. **102** 2 45N 95 45 E
Simferopol **82** 44 55N 34 3 E
Simi **69** 36 35N 27 50 E
Simi, I. **69** 36 35N 27 50 E
Simi Valley **163** 34 16N 118 47W
Simikot **95** 30 0N 81 50 E
Simití **174** 7 58N 73 57W
Simitli **66** 41 52N 23 7 E
Simla **94** 31 2N 77 15 E
Simleu-Silvaniei **70** 47 17N 22 50 E
Simme, R. **50** 46 38N 7 25 E
Simmern **48** 49 59N 7 32 E
Simmie **153** 49 56N 108 6W
Simmler **163** 35 21N 119 59W
Simões **170** 7 30 S 40 49W
Simojärvi **74** 66 5N 27 10 E
Simojoki **74** 65 46N 25 15 E
Simojovel **165** 17 12N 92 38W
Simonette, R. **152** 55 9N 118 15W
Simonsbath **28** 51 8N 3 45W
Simonside, Mt. **35** 55 17N 2 0W
Simonstown **128** 34 14 S 18 26 E
Simontornya **53** 46 45N 18 33 E
Simpang **101** 4 50N 100 40 E
Simpleveld **47** 50 50N 5 58 E
Simplício Mendes **170** 7 51 S 41 54W
Simplon **50** 46 12N 8 4 E
Simplon Pass **50** 46 15N 8 0 E
Simplon Tunnel **50** 46 15N 8 7 E
Simpson Des. **138** 25 0 S 137 0 E
Simpungdong **107** 41 56N 129 29 E
Simrishamn **73** 55 33N 14 22 E
Simsbury **162** 41 52N 72 48W
Simunjan **102** 1 25N 110 45 E
Sîmŭrtin **70** 46 19N 25 58 E
Simushir, Ostrov **77** 46 50N 152 30 E
Sina, R. **97** 18 25N 75 28 E
Sinaai **47** 51 9N 4 2 E
Sinabang **102** 2 30N 46 30 E
Sinai = Es Sînâ' **122** 29 0N 34 0 E
Sinai, Mt. = Musa, G. **122** 28 32N 33 59 E
Sinaia **70** 45 21N 25 38 E
Sinaloa **164** 25 50N 108 20W
Sinaloa □ **164** 25 0N 107 30W
Sinalunga **63** 43 12N 11 43 E
Sinamaica **174** 11 5N 71 51W
Sînandrei **70** 45 52N 21 13 E
Sīnāwan **119** 31 0N 10 30 E
Sinbaung we **98** 19 43N 95 10 E
Sinbo **98** 24 46N 97 3 E
Sincé **174** 9 15N 75 9W
Sincelejo **174** 9 18N 75 24W
Sinchangni, Kor., N. **107** 40 7N 128 28 E
Sinchangni, Kor., N. **107** 39 24N 126 8 E
Sinclair **160** 41 47N 107 35W
Sinclair Mills **152** 54 5N 121 40W
Sinclair's B. **37** 58 30N 3 0W
Sincorá, Serra do **171** 13 30 S 41 0W
Sind, R. **95** 34 18N 75 0 E
Sind Sagar Doab **94** 32 0N 71 30 E
Sinda **127** 17 28 S 25 51 E
Sindal **73** 57 28N 10 10 E
Sindangan **103** 8 10N 123 5 E
Sindangbarang **103** 7 27 S 107 9 E
Sindjai **103** 5 0 S 120 20 E
Sinelnikovo **82** 48 25N 35 30 E
Sines **57** 37 56N 8 51W
Sines, Cabo de **57** 37 58N 8 53W
Sineu **58** 39 39N 3 0 E
Sinewit, Mt. **135** 4 44 S 152 2 E
Sinfra **120** 6 35N 5 56W
Sing Buri **100** 14 53N 100 25 E
Singa **123** 13 10N 33 57 E
Singanallurt **97** 11 2N 77 1 E
Singaparna **103** 7 23 S 108 4 E
Singapore ■ **101** 1 17N 103 51 E
Singapore, Straits of **101** 1 15N 104 0 E
Singaraja **102** 8 15 S 115 10 E
Singen **49** 47 45N 8 50 E
Singida **126** 4 49 S 34 48 E
Singida □ **126** 6 0 S 34 30 E
Singitikós, Kólpos **68** 40 6N 24 0 E
Singkaling Hkamti **98** 26 0N 95 45 E
Singkang **103** 4 8 S 120 1 E
Singkawang **102** 1 0N 109 5 E
Singkep, I. **102** 0 30 S 104 20 E
Singleton, Austral. **141** 32 33 S 151 10 E
Singleton, U.K. **29** 50 55N 0 45W
Singleton, Mt. **137** 29 27 S 117 15 E
Singö **72** 60 12N 18 45 E
Singoli **94** 25 0N 75 16 E
Singora = Songkhla **101** 7 12N 100 36 E
Singosan **107** 38 52N 127 25 E
Sinhailian (Lienyünchiangshih) **107** 34 31N 118 15 E
Sinhung **107** 40 11N 127 34 E
Siniatsikon, Óros **68** 40 25N 21 35 E
Siniscóla **64** 40 35N 9 40 E
Sinj **63** 43 42N 16 39 E
Sinjajevina, Planina **66** 42 57N 19 22 E
Sinjil **90** 32 3N 35 15 E
Sinkat **122** 18 55N 36 49 E
Sinkiang-Uighur □ **105** 42 0N 86 0 E
Sinmark **107** 38 25N 126 14 E
Sinnai Sardinia **64** 39 18N 9 13 E
Sinnar **96** 19 48N 74 0 E
Sinni, R. **65** 40 6N 16 15 E
Sinnicolau-Maré **70** 46 5N 20 39 E
Sinnûris **122** 29 26N 30 31 E
Sinoe, L. **70** 44 35N 28 50 E
Sinoia **127** 17 20 S 30 8 E
Sinop **92** 42 1N 35 11 E
Sinop, R. **82** 42 1N 35 2 E
Sinpo **107** 40 0N 128 13 E
Sins **51** 47 12N 8 24 E
Sinskoye **77** 61 8N 126 48 E
Sint Annaland **47** 51 36N 4 6 E
Sint Annaparochie **46** 53 16N 5 40 E
Sint-Denijs **47** 50 45N 3 23 E
Sint Eustatius, I. **167** 17 30N 62 59W
Sint-Genesius-Rode **47** 50 45N 4 22 E
Sint-Gillis-Waas **47** 51 13N 4 6 E
Sint-Huibrechts-Lille **47** 51 13N 5 29 E
Sint-Katelinje-Waver **47** 51 5N 4 32 E
Sint-Kruis **47** 51 13N 3 15 E
Sint-Laureins **47** 51 14N 3 32 E
Sint Maarten, I. **167** 18 4N 63 4W
Sint-Michiels **47** 51 11N 3 15 E
Sint Nicolaasga **46** 52 55N 5 45 E
Sint Niklaas **47** 51 10N 4 9 E
Sint Oedenrode **47** 51 35N 5 29 E
Sint Pancras **46** 52 40N 4 48 E
Sint-Pauwels **47** 51 11N 3 57 E
Sint Philipsland **47** 51 37N 4 10 E
Sint Truiden **47** 50 48N 5 12 E
Sint Willebroad **47** 51 33N 4 33 E
Sîntana Ano **70** 46 20N 21 30 E
Sintang **102** 0 5N 111 35 E
Sintjohannesga **46** 52 55N 5 52 E
Sinton **159** 28 1N 97 30W
Sintra **57** 38 47N 9 25W
Sinŭiju **107** 40 5N 124 24 E
Sinuk **147** 64 42N 166 22W
Sinyang = Hsinyang **109** 32 10N 114 6 E
Sinyukha, R. **82** 48 31N 30 31 E
Siófok **53** 46 54N 18 4 E
Sióma **128** 16 25 S 23 28 E
Sion **50** 46 14N 7 20 E
Sion Mills **38** 54 47N 7 29W
Sioua, El Wâhât es **122** 29 10N 25 30 E
Sioux City **158** 42 32N 96 25W
Sioux Falls **158** 43 35N 96 40W
Sioux Lookout **150** 50 10N 91 50W
Sip Song Chaw Thai, reg. **100** 21 30N 103 30 E
Sipan **66** 42 45N 17 52 E
Sipera, I. **102** 2 18 S 99 40 E
Sipiwesk L. **153** 55 5N 97 35W
Sipul **138** 5 50 S 148 28 E
Siquia, R. **166** 12 30N 84 30W
Siquijor, I. **103** 9 12N 123 45 E
Siquirres **166** 10 6N 83 30W
Siquisique **174** 10 34N 69 42W
Sir Edward Pellew Group **138** 15 40 S 137 10 E
Sir Graham Moore Is. **136** 13 53 S 126 34 E
Sir Samuel Mt. **137** 27 45 S 120 40 E
Sir Thomas, Mt. **137** 27 10 S 129 45 E
Sira **97** 13 41N 76 49 E
Sira, R. **71** 58 43N 6 40 E
Siracusa **65** 37 4N 15 17 E
Sirajganj **95** 24 25N 89 47 E
Sirake **138** 9 1 S 141 2 E
Sirakoro **120** 12 41N 9 14W
Sirasso **120** 9 16N 6 6W
Siret **70** 47 55N 26 5 E
Siret, R. **70** 47 58N 26 5 E
Siria **66** 46 16N 21 38 E
Sirinhaém **171** 8 35 S 35 7W
Sirkall (Shivali) **97** 11 15N 79 41 E
Sirna, I. **69** 36 22N 26 42 E
Sirnach **51** 47 28N 8 59 E
Sirohi **94** 24 52N 72 53 E
Siroki Brijeg **66** 43 21N 17 36 E
Sironj **94** 24 5N 77 45 E
Siros **69** 37 28N 24 57 E
Siros, I. **69** 37 28N 24 57 E
Sirretta Pk. **163** 35 56N 118 19W
Sirsa **94** 29 33N 75 4 E
Sirsi **97** 14 40N 74 49 E
Siruela **57** 38 58N 5 3W
Sisak **63** 45 30N 16 21 E
Sisaket **100** 15 8N 104 23 E
Sisante **59** 39 25N 2 12W
Sisargas, Islas **56** 43 21N 8 50W
Sishen **128** 27 55 S 22 59 E
Sisipuk I. **153** 55 40N 102 0W
Sisipuk L. **153** 55 45N 101 50W
Sisophon **100** 13 31N 102 59 E
Sissach **50** 47 27N 7 48 E
Sisseton **158** 45 43N 97 3W
Sissonne **43** 49 34N 3 51 E
Sistan-Baluchistan □ **93** 27 0N 62 0 E
Sistema Central **56** 40 40N 5 55W
Sistema Ibérico **58** 41 0N 2 10W
Sisteron **45** 44 12N 5 57 E
Sisters **160** 44 21N 121 32W
Sitamarhi **95** 26 37N 85 30 E
Sitapur **95** 27 38N 80 45 E
Siteki **129** 26 32 S 31 58 E
Sitges **58** 41 17N 1 47 E
Sithoniá **68** 40 0N 23 45 E
Sitia **69** 35 13N 26 6 E
Sitio da Abadia **171** 14 48 S 46 16W
Sitka **147** 57 9N 134 58W
Sitona **123** 14 25N 37 23 E
Sitoti **128** 23 15 S 23 40 E
Sitra **122** 28 40N 26 53 E
Sittang Myit, R. **99** 18 20N 96 45 E
Sittang, R. **98** 17 10N 96 58 E
Sittard **47** 51 0N 5 52 E
Sittaung **98** 24 10N 94 35 E
Sittensen **48** 53 17N 9 32 E
Sittingbourne **29** 51 20N 0 43 E
Sittwe **99** 20 15N 92 45 E
Situbondo **103** 7 45 S 114 0 E
Siuch'uan **109** 26 20N 114 30 E
Siuna **166** 13 37N 84 45W
Sivaganga **97** 9 50N 78 28 E
Sivagiri **97** 9 16N 77 26 E
Sivakasi **97** 9 24N 77 47 E
Sivand **93** 30 5N 52 55 E
Sivas **92** 39 43N 36 58 E
Siverek **92** 37 50N 39 25 E
Sivrihisar **92** 39 30N 31 35 E
Sivry **47** 50 10N 4 12 E
Siwa **122** 29 11N 25 31 E
Siwalik Range **95** 28 0N 83 0 E
Siwan **95** 26 13N 84 27 E
Sixmile Cross **38** 54 34N 7 7W
Sixmilebridge **39** 52 45N 8 46W
Siyâl, Jazâ'ir **122** 22 49N 36 6 E
Siyana **94** 28 37N 78 6 E
Sizewell **29** 52 13N 1 38 E
Sjaelland **73** 55 30N 11 30 E
Sjaellands Odde **73** 56 0N 11 15 E
Själevad **72** 63 18N 18 36 E
Sjarinska Banja **66** 42 45N 21 38 E
Sjenica **66** 43 16N 20 0 E
Sjernaröy **71** 59 15N 5 50 E
Sjoa **71** 61 41N 9 40 E
Sjöbo **73** 55 37N 13 45 E
Sjöholt **71** 62 27N 6 52 E
Sjönsta **74** 67 10N 16 3 E
Sjösa **73** 58 47N 17 4 E
Skadovsk **82** 46 17N 32 52 E
Skælskör **73** 55 16N 11 18 E
Skagafjörður **74** 65 54N 19 35W
Skagastölstindane, mt. **75** 61 25N 8 10 E
Skagen **75** 68 37N 14 27 E
Skagen, pt. **73** 57 43N 10 35 E
Skagern **72** 59 0N 14 20 E
Skagerrak **73** 57 30N 9 0 E
Skagway **147** 59 30N 135 20W
Skaidi **74** 70 26N 24 30 E
Skala Podolskaya **82** 48 50N 26 15 E
Skalat **80** 49 23N 25 55 E
Skalbmierz **54** 50 20N 20 25 E
Skalderviken **73** 56 22N 12 30 E
Skalicd **53** 48 50N 17 15 E
Skallingen, Odde **73** 55 32N 8 13 E
Skalni Dol = Kamenyak **67** 43 24N 26 57 E
Skals **73** 56 34N 9 24 E
Skanderborg **73** 56 2N 9 55 E
Skaneateles **162** 42 57N 76 26W

Skaneateles L. **162** 42 51N 76 22W
Skånevik **71** 59 43N 5 53E
Skanninge **73** 58 24N 15 5E
Skanör **73** 55 24N 12 50E
Skanor **73** 55 24N 12 50E
Skantzoúra I. **69** 39 5N 24 6E
Skara **73** 58 25N 13 30E
Skaraborgs län □ **73** 58 20N 13 30E
Skarblacka **73** 58 36N 15 50E
Skardhö **71** 62 30N 8 47E
Skardu **95** 35 20N 75 35E
Skaresta **73** 58 26N 16 22E
Skarszewy **54** 54 4N 18 25E
Skarvane, Mt. **71** 63 18N 11 27E
Skarzysko Kamienna **54** 51 7N 20 52E
Skatöy **71** 50 50N 9 30E
Skattungbyn **72** 61 10N 14 56E
Skaw (Grenen) **73** 57 46N 10 34E
Skaw Taing **36** 60 23N 0 57W
Skebo **72** 59 58N 18 37E
Skebokvarn **72** 59 7N 16 45E
Skeena Mts. **152** 56 40N 128 30W
Skeena, R. **152** 54 9N 130 5W
Skeggjastadir **74** 66 3N 14 50W
Skegness **33** 53 9N 0 20E
Skeldon **174** 6 0N 57 20W
Skellefte älv **74** 65 30N 18 30E
Skellefteå **74** 64 45N 20 58E
Skelleftehamn **74** 64 41N 21 14E
Skellig Rocks **39** 51 47N 10 32W
Skellingthorpe **33** 53 14N 0 37W
Skelmersdale **32** 53 34N 2 49W
Skelmorlie **34** 55 52N 4 53W
Skelton, Cleveland., U.K. **33** 54 33N 0 59W
Skelton, Cumb., U.K. **32** 54 42N 2 50W
Skender Vakuf **66** 44 29N 17 22E
Skene **73** 57 30N 12 37E
Skerries, Rks. **38** 55 14N 6 40W
Skerries, The **31** 53 27N 4 40W
Skhirra, La = Cekhira **119** 34 20N 10 5E
Skhíza, I. **69** 36 41N 20 40E
Skhoinoúsa, I. **69** 36 53N 25 31E
Ski **71** 59 43N 10 52E
Skiathos, I. **69** 39 12N 23 30E
Skibbereen **39** 51 33N 9 16W
Skiddaw, Mt. **32** 54 39N 3 9W
Skidegate, Inlet **48** 53 20N 132 0W
Skien **71** 59 12N 9 35E
Skierniewice **54** 51 58N 20 19E
Skikda **119** 36 50N 6 58E
Skillingaryd **73** 57 27N 14 5E
Skillinge **73** 55 30N 14 16E
Skillingmark **72** 59 48N 120 1E
Skinari, Akra **69** 37 56N 20 40E
Skipness **34** 55 46N 5 20W
Skipsea **33** 53 58N 0 13W
Skipton, Austral. **140** 37 39S 143 21E
Skipton, U.K. **32** 53 57N 2 1W
Skirild **73** 55 58N 8 53E
Skirmish Pt. **138** 11 59S 134 17E
Skiropoúla, I. **69** 38 50N 24 21E
Skiros **69** 38 55N 24 34E
Skíros, I. **69** 38 55N 24 34E
Skivarp **73** 55 26N 13 34E
Skive **73** 56 33N 9 2E
Skjåk **71** 61 52N 8 22E
Skjálfandafljót **74** 65 15N 17 25W
Skjálfandi **74** 66 5N 17 30W
Skjeberg **71** 59 12N 11 12E
Skjern **73** 55 57N 8 30E
Skjönne **71** 60 16N 9 1E
Skoczów **54** 49 49N 18 45E
Skodje **71** 62 30N 6 43E
Skofja Loka **63** 46 9N 14 19E
Skoger **71** 59 42N 10 16E
Skoghall **72** 59 20N 13 30E
Skoghult **73** 56 59N 15 55E
Skokholm, I. **31** 51 42N 5 16W
Skoki **54** 52 40N 17 11E
Skole **80** 49 3N 23 30E
Skomer, I. **31** 51 44N 5 19W
Skonsberg **72** 62 25N 17 21E
Skópelos **69** 39 9N 23 47E
Skópelos, I. **69** 39 9N 23 47E
Skopin **81** 53 55N 39 32E
Skopje **66** 42 1N 21 32E
Skorcz **54** 43 47N 18 30E
Skorped **72** 63 23N 17 55E
Skotfoss **71** 59 12N 9 30E
Skoudas **80** 56 21N 21 45E
Skövde **73** 58 15N 13 59E
Skovorodino **77** 54 0N 125 0E
Skowhegan **151** 44 49N 69 40W
Skowman **153** 51 58N 99 35W
Skradin **63** 43 52N 15 53E
Skreanäs **73** 56 52N 12 35E
Skudeneshavn **71** 59 10N 5 10E
Skull **39** 51 32N 9 40W
Skultorp **73** 58 24N 13 51E
Skulyany **82** 47 19N 27 39E
Skunk, R. **158** 40 42N 91 7W
Skurup **73** 55 28N 13 30E
Skutskär **73** 60 37N 17 25E
Skvira **82** 49 44N 29 32E
Skwaner, Pegunungan **102** 1 0S 112 30E
Skwierzyna **54** 52 46N 15 30E
Skye, I. **36** 57 15N 6 10W
Skykomish **160** 47 43N 121 16W
Skyros (Skiros), L. **69** 38 52N 24 37E
Slagelse **73** 55 23N 11 19E
Slagharen **46** 52 37N 6 34E
Slaidburn **32** 53 57N 2 28W
Slaley **35** 54 55N 2 4W
Slamannon **140** 32 1S 143 41E
Slamet, G. **102** 7 16S 109 8E
Slane **38** 53 42N 6 32W
Slaney, R. **39** 52 52N 6 45W
Slangerup **73** 55 50N 12 11E
Slănic **70** 45 14N 25 58E
Slankamen **66** 45 8N 20 15E
Slano **66** 42 48N 17 53E
Slantsy **80** 59 7N 28 5E
Slany **52** 50 13N 14 6E
Slask **54** 51 25N 16 0E
Slatbaken **73** 58 28N 16 30E
Slate Is. **150** 48 40N 87 0W
Slatina **70** 44 28N 24 22E
Slatington **162** 40 45N 75 37W
Slaton **159** 33 27N 101 38W
Slave Coast **121** 6 0N 2 30E
Slave Lake **152** 55 17N 114 50W
Slave Pt. **152** 61 11N 114 56W
Slave, R. **152** 61 18N 113 39W
Slavgorod **76** 53 10N 78 50E
Slavinja **66** 43 14N 22 50E
Slavkov (Austerlitz) **53** 49 10N 16 52E
Slavnoye **80** 54 24N 29 15E
Slavonski Brod **66** 45 11N 18 0E
Slavonski Pozega **66** 45 20N 17 40E
Slavuta **80** 50 15N 27 2E
Slavyans **82** 48 55N 37 30E
Slavyansk **82** 45 15N 38 11E
Sława **54** 51 52N 16 2E
Sławno **54** 54 20N 16 41E
Sławoborze **54** 53 55N 15 42E
Slea Hd. **39** 52 7N 10 30W
Sleaford **33** 53 0N 0 22W
Sleaford B. **139** 34 55S 135 45E
Sleat, Pt. of **36** 57 1N 6 0W
Sleat, Sd. of **36** 57 5N 5 47W
Sledmere **33** 54 4N 0 35W
Sleeper, Is. **149** 56 50N 80 30W
Sleepers, The **149** 58 30N 81 0W
Sleepy Eye **158** 44 15N 94 45W
Sleidinge **47** 51 8N 3 41E
Sleights **33** 54 27N 0 40W
Sleipner, gasfield **19** 58 30N 1 48E
Sleman **103** 7 40S 110 20E
Slemmestad **71** 59 47N 10 30E
Slemon L. **152** 63 13N 116 4W
Slesin **54** 52 22N 18 14E
Sletterhage, Kap **73** 56 7N 10 31E
Slide Mt. **162** 42 0N 74 23W
Slidell **159** 30 20N 89 48W
Sliedrecht **46** 51 50N 4 45E
Slieve Anierin **38** 54 5N 7 58W
Slieve Aughty **39** 53 4N 8 30W
Slieve Bernagh **39** 52 50N 8 30W
Slieve Bloom **39** 53 4N 7 40W
Slieve Callan **39** 52 51N 9 16W
Slieve Donard **38** 54 10N 5 57W
Slieve Felim **39** 52 40N 8 20W
Slieve Gamph **38** 54 6N 9 0W
Slieve Gullion **38** 54 8N 6 26W
Slieve League **38** 54 40N 8 42W
Slieve Mish **39** 52 12N 9 50W
Slieve Miskish **39** 51 40N 10 10W
Slieve More **38** 54 1N 10 3W
Slieve Snaght **38** 54 59N 8 7W
Slieve Tooey **38** 54 46N 8 39W
Slievenamon Mt. **39** 52 25N 7 37W
Sligachan **36** 57 17N 6 10W
Sligo **38** 54 17N 8 28W
Sligo □ **38** 54 10N 8 35W
Sligo B. **38** 54 20N 8 40W
Slikkerveer **46** 51 53N 4 36E
Slioch, mt. **36** 57 40N 5 20W
Slipje **47** 51 9N 2 51E
Slite **75** 57 42N 18 48E
Sliven **67** 42 42N 26 19E
Slivnitsa **66** 42 50N 23 0E
Sljeme, mt. **63** 45 57N 15 58E
Słupsk □ **54** 54 15N 17 30E
Sloansville **162** 42 45N 74 22W
Slobodskoy **84** 58 40N 50 6E
Slobozia, Ialomiţa, Rumania **70** 44 34N 27 23E
Slobozia, Valahia, Rumania **70** 44 30N 25 14E
Slocan **152** 49 48N 117 28W
Slochteren **46** 53 12N 6 48E
Slochteren-Groningen, gasfield **19** 53 10N 6 45E
Slöinge **73** 56 51N 12 42E
Słomniki **54** 50 16N 20 4E
Slonim **80** 53 4N 25 19E
Slotermeer **46** 52 55N 5 38E
Slough **29** 51 30N 0 35W
Sloughhouse **163** 38 26N 121 12W
Slovakia □ **53** 48 30N 19 0E
Slovenia = Slovenija **63** 45 58N 14 30E
Slovenija □ **63** 45 58N 14 30E
Slovenska Bistrica **63** 46 24N 15 35E
Slovenske Krusnohorie **53** 48 45N 20 0E
Slovenské Rhudhorie **52** 48 45N 19 0E
Słubice **54** 52 22N 14 35E
Sluis **47** 51 18N 3 23E
Slunchev Bryag **67** 42 40N 27 41E
Slunj **63** 45 6N 15 33E
Słupca **54** 52 15N 17 52E
Słupsk **54** 54 30N 17 3E
Slurry **128** 25 49S 25 42E
Slyne Hd. **38** 53 25N 10 10W
Slyudyanka **77** 51 40N 103 30E
Smål-Taberg **73** 57 42N 14 5E
Smålandsfarvandet **73** 55 10N 11 20E
Smalandsstenar **73** 57 9N 13 24E
Smålandstarvandet **73** 55 10N 11 20E
Smalltree L. **153** 61 0N 105 0W
Smallwood Reservoir **151** 54 20N 63 10W
Smara **118** 26 48N 11 31W
Smarje **63** 46 15N 15 34E
Smart Syndicate Dam **128** 30 45S 23 10E
Smeaton **153** 53 30N 105 49W
Smedberg **73** 58 35N 12 0E
Smederevo **66** 44 40N 20 57E
Smedstorp **73** 55 38N 13 58E
Smela **82** 49 30N 32 0E
Smerwick Harb. **39** 52 12N 10 23W
Smethwick **28** 52 29N 1 58W
Smidovich **77** 48 36N 133 49E
Smilde **46** 52 58N 6 28E
Smiley **153** 51 38N 109 29W
Smilyan **67** 41 29N 24 46E
Smith **152** 55 10N 114 0W
Smith Arm **152** 66 15N 123 0W
Smith Center **158** 39 50N 98 50W
Smith I. **162** 38 0N 76 0W
Smith, R. **152** 59 34N 126 30W
Smith Sund **12** 78 30N 74 0W
Smithborough **38** 54 13N 7 8W
Smithburne, R. **138** 17 3S 140 57E
Smithers **152** 54 45N 127 10W
Smithfield, U.K. **32** 54 59N 2 51W
Smithfield, U.S.A. **157** 35 31N 78 16W
Smith's Falls **150** 44 55N 76 0W
Smithton, N.S.W., Austral. **139** 31 0S 152 48E
Smithton, Tas., Austral. **138** 40 53S 145 6E
Smithtown **141** 30 58S 152 56E
Smithville **159** 30 2N 97 12W
Smjörfjöll **74** 65 30N 15 42W
Smoky Bay **139** 32 22S 133 56E
Smoky Falls **150** 50 4N 82 10W
Smoky Hill, R. **158** 38 45N 98 0W
Smoky Lake **152** 54 10N 112 30W
Smola **71** 63 23N 8 3E
Smolensk **80** 54 45N 32 0E
Smolikas, Óros **68** 40 9N 20 58E
Smolnik **53** 48 43N 20 44E
Smolyan **67** 41 36N 24 38E
Smooth Rock Falls **150** 49 17N 81 37W
Smoothstone L. **153** 54 40N 106 50W
Smorgon **80** 54 28N 26 24E
Smulţi **70** 45 57N 27 44E
Smyadovo **67** 43 2N 27 1E
Smyrna **162** 39 18N 75 36W
Smyrna = İzmir **92** 38 25N 27 8E
Snaefell **30** 54 18N 4 26W
Snaefells Jökull **74** 64 45N 23 25W
Snainton **33** 54 14N 0 33W
Snaith **33** 53 42N 1 1W
Snake I. **141** 38 47S 146 33E
Snake L. **153** 55 32N 106 35W
Snake, R. **160** 46 31N 118 50W
Snake Ra., Mts. **160** 39 0N 114 30W
Snake River Plain **160** 43 13N 113 0W
Snap, The **36** 60 35N 0 50W
Snape **29** 52 11N 1 29E
Snarum **71** 60 1N 9 54E
Snasahogarha **72** 63 10N 12 20E
Snedsted **73** 56 55N 8 32E
Sneek **46** 53 2N 5 40E
Sneeker-meer **46** 53 2N 5 45E
Sneem **39** 51 50N 9 55W
Snejbjerg **73** 56 8N 8 54E
Snĕka **52** 50 41N 15 50E
Snelling **163** 37 31N 120 26W
Snettisham **29** 52 52N 0 30E
Snezhnoye **83** 48 0N 38 58E
Sneznik, mt. **63** 45 36N 14 35E
Snigirevka **82** 47 2N 32 35E
Snina **53** 49 0N 22 9E
Snizort, L. **36** 57 33N 6 28W
Snohetta **71** 62 19N 9 16E
Snohomish **160** 47 53N 122 6W
Snonuten **71** 59 31N 6 50E
Snoul **101** 12 4N 106 26E
Snow Hill **162** 38 10N 75 21W
Snow L. **153** 54 52N 100 3W
Snowbird L. **153** 60 45N 103 0W
Snowdon, Mt. **31** 53 4N 4 8W
Snowdrift **153** 62 24N 110 44W
Snowdrift, R. **153** 62 24N 110 44W
Snowflake **161** 34 30N 110 4W
Snowshoe **152** 53 43N 121 0W
Snowtown **140** 33 46S 138 14E
Snowville **160** 41 59N 112 47W
Snowy Mt. **162** 43 45N 74 26W
Snowy Mts. **141** 36 30S 148 20E
Snowy, R. **141** 37 46S 148 30E
Snug Corner **167** 22 33N 73 52W
Snyder, Okla., U.S.A. **159** 34 4N 99 0W
Snyder, Tex., U.S.A. **159** 32 45N 100 57W
Soacha **174** 4 35N 74 13W
Soahanina **129** 18 42S 44 13E
Soalala **129** 16 6S 45 20E
Soan, R. **94** 33 20N 72 40E
Soanierana-Ivongo **129** 16 55S 49 35E
Soap Lake **160** 47 29N 119 31W
Soay, I. **36** 57 9N 6 13W
Soay Sd. **36** 57 10N 6 15W
Sobat, Nahr **123** 8 32N 32 40E
Sobĕslav **52** 49 16N 14 45E
Sobhapur **94** 22 47N 78 17E
Sobinka **81** 56 0N 40 0E
Sobo-Yama **110** 32 51N 131 16E
Sobótka **54** 50 54N 16 44E
Sobrado **56** 43 2N 8 2W
Sobral **170** 3 50S 40 30W
Sobreira Formosa **57** 39 46N 7 51W
Soc Giang **100** 22 54N 106 1E
Soc Trang = Khonh Hung **101** 9 37N 105 50E
Soča, R. **63** 46 20N 13 40E
Socha **174** 6 0N 72 41W
Sochaczew **54** 52 15N 20 13E
Soch'e **105** 38 24N 37 20E
Sochi **83** 43 35N 39 40E
Société, Is. de la **131** 17 0S 151 0W
Socompa, Portezuelo de **172** 24 27S 68 18W
Socorro **174** 6 29N 73 16W
Socorro, I. **164** 18 45N 110 58W
Socotra, I. **91** 12 30N 54 0E
Socúellmos **59** 39 16N 2 47W
Soda Creek **152** 52 25N 122 10W
Soda L. **161** 35 7N 116 2W
Soda Plains **94** 35 30N 79 0E
Soda Springs **160** 42 4N 111 40W
Sodankylä **74** 67 29N 26 40E
Söderfjärden **72** 62 3N 17 25E
Söderfors **72** 60 23N 17 25E
Söderhamn **72** 61 18N 17 10E
Söderköping **72** 58 31N 16 35E
Södermanlands län □ **72** 59 10N 16 30E
Södertälje **72** 59 12N 17 50E
Sodium **128** 30 15S 15 45E
Sodo **123** 7 0N 37 57E
Södra Vi **73** 57 45N 15 45E
Sodrazica **63** 45 45N 14 39E
Sodus **162** 43 13N 77 5W
Soekmekaar **129** 23 30S 29 55E
Soest, Ger. **48** 51 34N 8 7E
Soest, Neth. **46** 52 9N 5 19E
Soestdijk **46** 52 11N 5 17E
Sofádhes **68** 39 28N 22 4E
Sofara **120** 13 59N 4 9W
Sofia = Sofiya **67** 42 45N 23 20E
Sofia, R. **129** 15 25S 48 40E
Sofievka **82** 47 58N 34 14E
Sofikón **69** 37 47N 23 3E
Sofila **67** 42 45N 23 20E
Sofiya **67** 42 45N 23 20E
Sogad **103** 10 30N 125 0E
Sogakofe **121** 6 2N 0 39E
Sogamoso **174** 5 43N 72 56W
Sögel **48** 52 50N 7 32E
Sogeri **135** 9 26S 147 35E
Sogipo **107** 33 13N 126 34E
Sogn og Fjordane fylke □ **71** 61 40N 6 0E
Sogndal **71** 58 20N 6 15E
Sogndalsfjøra **75** 61 14N 7 5E
Sognefjorden **71** 61 10N 5 50E
Sohâg **122** 26 27N 31 43E
Soham **29** 52 20N 0 20E
Sohano **135** 5 22S 154 37E
Sŏhori **107** 40 7N 128 23E
Soignies **47** 50 35N 4 5E
Soira, Mt. **123** 14 45N 39 30E
Soissons **43** 49 25N 3 19E
Soitava, R. **53** 49 30N 16 37E
Sojat **94** 25 55N 73 38E
Sok, R. **84** 53 24N 50 8E
Sokal **80** 50 31N 24 15E
Söke **69** 37 48N 27 28E
Sokhós **68** 40 48N 23 22E
Sokhta Chinar **93** 35 5N 67 35E
Sokna **71** 60 16N 9 50E
Soknedal **71** 62 57N 10 13E
Soko Banja **66** 43 40N 21 51E
Sokodé **121** 9 0N 1 11E
Sokó'ka **54** 53 25N 23 30E
Sokol **81** 59 30N 40 5E
Sokolo **120** 14 42N 6 8W
Sokolov **52** 50 12N 12 40E
Sokoł ó w Matopolski **53** 50 12N 22 7E
Sokoł ó w Podlaski **54** 52 25N 22 15E
Sokoto **121** 13 2N 5 16E
Sokoto □ **121** 12 30N 5 0E
Sokoto, R. **121** 12 30N 6 10E
Sokuluk **85** 42 52N 74 18E
Sol Iletsk **84** 51 10N 55 0E
Sola **71** 58 53N 5 36E
Sola, R. **126** 49 38N 19 8E
Solai **126** 0 2N 36 12E
Solana, La **59** 38 59N 3 14W
Solano **103** 16 25N 121 15E
Solares **56** 43 23N 3 43W
Solberga **73** 57 45N 14 43E
Solca **70** 47 40N 25 50E
Solec Kujawski **54** 53 5N 18 14E
Soledad, Colomb. **174** 10 55N 74 46W
Soledad, U.S.A. **163** 36 27N 121 16W
Soledad, Venez. **174** 8 10N 63 34W
Solemint **163** 34 25N 118 27W
Solent, The **28** 50 45N 1 25W
Solenzara **45** 41 53N 9 23E
Solesmes **43** 50 10N 3 30E
Solfonn, Mt. **71** 60 2N 6 57E
Soligalich **81** 59 5N 42 10E
Solihull **28** 52 26N 1 47W
Solikamsk **84** 59 38N 56 50E
Solila **129** 21 25S 46 37E
Soliman **119** 36 42N 10 30E
Solimões, R. **174** 2 15S 66 30W
Solingen **48** 51 10N 7 4E
Sollas **36** 57 39N 7 20W
Sollebrunn **73** 58 8N 12 32E
Sollefteå **72** 63 12N 17 20E
Sollentuna **72** 59 26N 17 56E

Soller 58 39 43N 2 45 E
Sollerön 72 60 54N 14 38 E
Solna 72 59 22N 18 1 E
Solnechnogorsk 81 56 10N 36 57 E
Sölnkletten, Mt. 71 61 55N 10 18 E
Sologne 59 47 40N 2 0 E
Solojärg 73 56 50N 10 8 E
Solok 102 0 55 S 100 40 E
Sololá 166 14 49N 91 10 E
Solomon Is. ■ 135 6 0 S 155 0 E
Solomon, N. Fork, R. 158 39 45N 99 0W
Solomon Sea 135 7 0 S 150 0 E
Solomon, S. Fork, R. 158 39 25N 99 12W
Solomon's Pools = Burak Sulayman 90 31 42N 35 7 E
Solon Springs 158 46 19N 91 47W
Solonópole 170 5 44 S 39 1W
Solor, I. 103 8 27 S 123 0 E
Solotcha 81 54 48N 39 53 E
Solothurn 50 47 13N 7 32 E
Solothurn □ 50 47 18N 7 40 E
Solotobe 85 44 37N 66 3 E
Solsona 58 42 0N 1 31 E
Solt 53 46 45N 19 1 E
Solta, I. 63 43 24N 16 15 E
Soltanabad 93 36 29N 58 5 E
Soltaniyeh 92 36 20N 48 55 E
Soltau 48 52 59N 9 50 E
Soltsy 80 58 10N 30 10 E
Solun 105 46 40N 120 40 E
Solund 71 61 5N 4 50 E
Solund I. 71 61 7N 4 50 E
Solunska Glava 66 41 44N 21 31 E
Solva 31 51 52N 5 12W
Solvang 163 34 36N 120 8W
Solvay 162 43 5N 76 17W
Solvesborg 73 56 5N 14 35 E
Sölvesborg 73 56 5N 14 35 E
Solway Firth 32 54 45N 3 38W
Solwezi 127 12 20 S 26 21 E
Somali Rep. ■ 91 7 0N 47 0 E
Somaliland 123 12 0N 43 0 E
Sombe Dzong 98 27 13N 89 8 E
Sombernon 43 47 20N 4 40 E
Sombor 66 45 46N 19 17 E
Sombrerete 164 23 40N 103 40W
Sombrero I. 167 18 30N 63 30W
Somerby 29 52 42N 0 49W
Someren 47 51 23N 5 42 E
Somers 160 48 4N 114 18W
Somerset, Austral. 138 10 45 S 142 25 E
Somerset, Can. 153 49 25N 98 39W
Somerset, Colo., U.S.A. 161 38 55N 107 30W
Somerset, Ky., U.S.A. 156 37 5N 84 40W
Somerset, Mass., U.S.A. 162 41 45N 71 10W
Somerset □ 28 51 9N 3 0W
Somerset East 128 32 42 S 25 35 E
Somerset, I. 148 73 30N 93 0W
Somerset West 128 34 8 S 18 50 E
Somersham 29 52 24N 0 0W
Somersworth 162 43 15N 70 51W
Somerton, U.K. 28 51 3N 2 45W
Somerton, U.S.A. 161 32 41N 114 47W
Somerville 162 40 34N 74 36W
Someş, R. 70 47 15N 23 45 E
Someşul Mare, R. 70 47 18N 24 30 E
Somma Lombardo 62 45 41N 8 42 E
Somma Vesuviana 65 40 52N 14 23 E
Sommariva 139 26 24 S 146 36 E
Sommatino 65 37 20N 14 0 E
Somme □ 43 50 0N 2 20 E
Somme, B. de la 42 5 22N 1 30 E
Sommelsdijk 46 51 46N 4 9 E
Sommen 73 58 12N 15 0 E
Sommen, L. 73 58 0N 15 15 E
Sommepy-Tahure 43 49 15N 4 31 E
Sömmerda 48 51 10N 11 8 E
Sommersted 73 55 19N 9 18 E
Sommesous 43 48 44N 4 12 E
Sommières 45 43 47N 4 6 E
Somogy □ 53 46 19N 17 30 E
Somogyszob 53 46 18N 17 20 E
Somoto 166 13 28N 86 37W
Sompolno 54 52 26N 18 45 E
Somport, Paso 58 42 48N 0 31W
Somport, Puerto de 58 42 48N 0 31W
Sompting 29 50 51N 0 20W
Son, Neth. 47 51 31N 5 30 E
Son, Norway 71 59 32N 10 42 E
Son, Spain 56 42 43N 8 58W
Son Hoa 100 13 2N 108 58 E
Son La 100 21 20N 103 50 E
Son Ma 100 15 3N 108 34 E
Son Tay 100 21 8N 105 30 E
Soná 166 8 0N 81 10W
Sonamarg 95 34 18N 75 21 E
Sonamukhi 95 23 18N 87 27 E
Sonamura 98 23 29N 91 15 E
Sŏnchŏn 107 39 48N 124 55 E
Soncino 62 45 24N 9 52 E
Sondags, R. 128 32 10N 24 40 E
Sóndala 62 46 20N 10 20 E
Sondar 95 33 28N 75 56 E
Sönder Hornum 73 56 32N 9 38 E
Sønder Omme 73 55 50N 8 54 E
Sønderborg 73 54 55N 9 49 E
Sonderhausen 48 51 22N 10 50 E
Sonderjyllands Amt □ 73 55 10N 9 10 E
Sondre Höland 71 59 44N 11 30 E
Sondre Land 71 60 44N 10 21 E
Söndre Stromfjord 12 66 30N 50 52W
Sóndrio 62 46 10N 9 53 E
Sone 127 17 23 S 34 55 E
Sonepat 94 29 0N 77 5 E
Sonepur 96 20 55N 83 50 E
Song 100 18 28N 100 11 E
Song Cau 100 13 20N 109 18 E
Songa, R. 71 59 57N 7 30 E
Sŏngchŏn 107 39 12N 126 15 E
Songea 127 10 40 S 35 40 E
Songea □ 127 10 30 S 36 0 E
Songeons 43 49 32N 1 50 E
Songjin 107 40 40N 129 10 E
Songjŏngni 107 35 8N 126 47 E
Songkhla 101 7 13N 100 37 E
Songnim 107 38 45N 125 39 E
Songwe, Malawi 127 9 44 S 33 58 E
Songwe, Zaïre 127 3 20 S 26 16 E
Sonkel, Ozero 85 41 50N 75 12 E
Sonkovo 81 57 50N 37 5 E
Sonmiani 94 25 25N 66 40 E
Sonning 29 51 28N 0 53W
Sonnino 64 41 25N 13 13 E
Sono, R., Goias, Brazil 170 8 58 S 48 11W
Sono, R., Minas Gerais, Brazil 171 17 2 S 45 32W
Sonobe 111 35 6N 135 28 E
Sonogno 51 46 22N 8 47 E
Sonoma 163 38 17N 122 27W
Sonora, Calif., U.S.A. 163 37 59N 120 27W
Sonora, Texas, U.S.A. 159 30 33N 100 37W
Sonora □ 164 28 0N 111 0W
Sonora P. 160 38 17N 119 35W
Sonora, R. 164 28 30N 111 33W
Sonoyta 164 31 51N 112 50W
Sŏnsan 107 36 14N 128 17 E
Sonskyn 128 30 47 S 26 28 E
Sonsonate 166 13 43N 89 44W
Sonthofen 49 47 31N 10 16 E
Soo Junction 156 46 20N 85 14W
Soochow = Suchou 109 31 15N 120 40 E
Söonder Nissum 73 56 19N 8 11 E
Sop Hao 100 20 33N 104 27 E
Sop Prap 100 17 53N 99 20 E
Sopi 103 2 40N 128 28 E
Sopo, Nahr 123 8 40N 26 30 E
Sopot, Poland 54 54 27N 18 31 E
Sopot, Yugo. 66 44 29N 20 30 E
Sopotnica 66 41 23N 21 13 E
Sopron 49 47 41N 16 37 E
Sop's Arm 151 49 46N 56 56W
Sör-Fron 71 61 35N 9 59 E
Sor, R. 57 39 7N 9 52 E
Sør-Rondane 13 72 0 S 25 0 E
Sør Trøndelag fylke □ 71 63 0N 11 0 E
Sora 64 41 45N 13 36 E
Sorada 96 19 32N 84 45 E
Sorah 94 27 13N 68 56 E
Söråker 72 62 30N 17 32 E
Sorano 63 42 40N 11 42 E
Sorata 174 15 50 S 68 50W
Sorbas 59 37 6N 2 7W
Sorbie 34 54 46N 4 26W
Sordale 37 58 33N 3 26W
Sordeval 42 48 44N 0 55W
Sorel 150 46 0N 73 10W
Sörenberg 50 46 50N 8 2 E
Soresina 62 45 17N 9 51 E
Sörfold 74 67 5N 14 20 E
Sorgues 45 44 1N 4 53 E
Soria 58 41 43N 2 32W
Soria □ 58 41 46N 2 28W
Soriano 172 33 24 S 58 19W
Soriano □ 176 33 30 S 58 0W
Sorisdale 34 56 40N 6 28W
Sorn 34 55 31N 4 18W
Sorø 73 55 26N 11 32 E
Soro 120 10 9N 9 48W
Sorocaba 173 23 31 S 47 35W
Sorochinsk 84 52 26N 53 10 E
Soroki 82 48 8N 28 12 E
Soroksár 53 47 24N 19 9 E
Soron 94 27 55N 78 45 E
Sorong 103 0 55 S 131 15 E
Sororoca 174 0 43N 61 31W
Soroti 126 1 43N 33 35 E
Soröy Sundet 74 70 25N 23 0 E
Soröya 74 70 35N 22 45 E
Soroyane 71 62 25N 5 32 E
Sorraia, R. 57 38 55N 8 35W
Sorrento, Austral. 139 38 22 S 144 47 E
Sorrento, Italy 65 40 38N 14 23 E
Sorris Sorris 128 21 0 S 14 46 E
Sorsele 74 65 31N 17 30 E
Sorso 64 40 50N 8 34 E
Sorsogon 103 13 0N 124 0 E
Sortat 37 58 32N 3 12W
Sortino 65 37 9N 15 1 E
Sos 58 42 30N 1 13W
Sŏsan 107 36 47N 126 27 E
Soscumica, L. 150 50 15N 77 27W
Sosdala 73 56 2N 13 41 E
Sosna, R. 81 52 30N 38 0 E
Sosnowiec 54 50 20N 19 10 E
Sospel 45 43 52N 7 27 E
Soštanj 63 46 23N 15 4 E
Sŏsura 107 42 16N 130 36 E
Sosva 84 59 10N 61 50 E
Sosva, R. 84 59 32N 62 20 E
Soto la Marina, R. 165 23 40N 97 40W
Soto y Amío 56 42 46N 5 53W
Sotra I. 71 60 15N 5 0 E
Sotteville 42 49 24N 1 5 E
Souanké 124 2 10N 14 10 E
Souderton 162 40 19N 75 19W
Soufi 120 15 13N 12 17W
Souflíon 68 41 12N 26 18 E
Soufrière 167 13 51N 61 4W
Soufrière, vol. 167 13 10N 61 10W
Sougne-Remouchamps 47 50 29N 5 42 E
Souillac 44 44 53N 1 29 E
Souk-Ahras 119 36 17N 7 57 E
Souk el Arba du Rharb 118 34 50N 5 59W
Souk el Khemis 119 36 36N 8 58 E
Soukhouma 100 14 38N 105 48 E
Sŏul 105 37 31N 127 6 E
Soulac-sur-Mer 44 45 30N 1 7W
Soultz 43 48 57N 7 52 E
Soumagne 47 50 37N 5 44 E
Sound, The 75 56 7N 12 30 E
Soúnion, Ákra 69 37 37N 24 1 E
Sour el Ghozlane 119 36 10N 3 45 E
Sources, Mt. aux 129 28 45 S 28 50 E
Sourdeval 42 48 43N 0 55W
Soure, Brazil 170 0 35 S 48 30W
Soure, Port. 56 40 4N 8 38W
Souris, Man., Can. 153 49 40N 100 20W
Souris, P.E.I., Can. 151 46 21N 62 15W
Souris, R. 153 49 40N 99 34W
Soúrpi 69 39 6N 22 54 E
Sous, R. 118 30 31N 9 27W
Sousa 170 6 45 S 38 10W
Sousel, Brazil 170 2 38 S 52 29W
Sousel, Port. 57 38 57N 7 40W
Souss, O. 118 30 23N 8 24W
Sousse 119 35 50N 10 38 E
Soustons 44 43 45N 1 19W
Souterraine, La 44 46 15N 1 30 E
South Africa, Rep. of, ■ 125 30 0 S 25 0 E
South Amboy 162 40 29N 74 17W
South America 168 10 0 S 60 0W
South Auckland & Bay of Plenty □ 142 38 30 S 177 0 E
South Aulatsivik I. 151 56 45N 61 30W
South Australia □ 136 32 0 S 139 0 E
South Baldy, Mt. 161 34 6N 107 27W
South Bend, Indiana, U.S.A. 156 41 38N 86 20W
South Bend, Wash., U.S.A. 160 46 44N 123 52W
South Benfleet 29 51 33N 0 34 E
South Blackwater 138 24 00 S 148 35 E
South Boston 157 36 42N 78 58W
South Br. Ashburton, R. 143 43 30 S 171 15 E
South Branch, Can. 151 47 55N 59 2W
South Branch, U.S.A. 151 44 30N 83 55W
South Brent 30 50 26N 3 50W
South Brook 151 49 26N 56 5W
South Buganda □ 126 0 15 S 31 30 E
South Cape 147 18 58N 155 24 E
South Carolina □ 157 33 45N 81 0W
South Cave 33 53 46N 0 37W
South Charleston 156 38 20N 81 40W
South China Sea 101 7 0N 107 0 E
South Dakota □ 158 45 0N 100 0W
South Dell 36 58 28N 6 20W
South Dorset Downs 28 50 40N 2 26W
South Downs 29 50 53N 0 10W
South East C. 138 43 40 S 146 50 E
South East Is. 137 34 17 S 123 30 E
South Elkington 33 53 22N 0 5W
South Esk, R. 37 56 44N 3 3W
South Foreland 29 51 7N 1 23 E
S. Fork, American, R. 163 38 45N 121 5W
South Fork, R. 160 47 54N 113 15W
South Gamboa 164 9 4N 79 40W
South Gate 163 33 57N 118 12W
South Georgia 13 54 30 S 37 0W
South Glamorgan □ 31 51 30N 3 20W
South Grafton 139 29 41 S 152 47 E
South Harris, district 36 56 51N 3 10W
South Haven 156 42 22N 86 20W
South Hayling 29 50 47N 0 56W
South Henik, L. 153 61 30N 97 30W
South Horr 126 2 12N 36 56 E
South I., Kenya 126 2 35N 36 35 E
South I., N.Z. 143 43 0 S 170 0 E
South Invercargill 143 46 26N 168 23 E
South Kirby 33 53 35N 1 25W
South Knife, R. 153 58 55N 94 37W
S. Kolok 101 6 2N 101 58 E
South Korea ■ 107 36 0N 128 0 E
S. Lembing 101 3 55N 103 3 E
South Magnetic Pole 13 66 30 S 139 30 E
South Marsh Is. 162 38 6N 76 1W
South Milwaukee 156 42 50N 87 52W
South Molton 30 51 1N 3 50W
South Nahanni, R. 152 61 3N 123 21W
South Nesting B. 36 60 18N 1 5W
South Orkney Is. 13 63 0 S 45 0W
South Pass 160 42 20N 108 58W
South Passage 137 26 07 S 113 09 E
S. Petani 101 5 37N 100 30 E
South Petherton 28 50 57N 2 49W
South Petherwin 30 50 35N 4 22W
South Pines 157 35 10N 79 25W
South Platte, R. 158 40 50N 102 45W
South Pt. 151 49 6N 62 11W
South Pole 13 90 0 S 0 0 E
South Porcupine 150 48 30N 81 12W
South Portland 162 43 38N 70 15W
South River, Can. 150 45 52N 79 29W
South River, U.S.A. 162 40 27N 74 23W
South Ronaldsay, I. 37 58 46N 2 58W
S. Sandwich Is. 15 57 0 S 27 0W
South Saskatchewan, R. 153 53 15N 105 5W
South Sd. 39 53 4N 9 28W
South Seal, R. 153 58 48N 98 8W
South Sentinel, I. 101 11 1N 92 16 E
South Shetland Is. 13 62 0 S 59 0W
South Shields 35 54 59N 1 26W
South Sioux City 158 42 30N 96 30W
South Taranaki Bight 142 39 40 S 174 5 E
South Tawton 30 50 44N 3 55W
South Thompson, R. 152 50 40N 120 20W
South Twin I. 150 53 7N 79 52W
South Tyne, R. 35 54 46N 2 25W
South Uist, I. 37 57 4N 7 21W
South Ulvön, I. 72 63 0N 18 45 E
South Walls, I. 37 58 45N 3 7W
South West Africa ■ = Namibia 128 22 0 S 18 9 E
South West C. 138 43 34 S 146 3 E
South West Cape 143 47 16 S 167 31 E
South Williamsport 162 41 14N 77 0W
South Yarmouth 162 41 35N 70 10W
South Yemen ■ 91 15 0N 48 0 E
South Yorkshire □ 33 53 30N 1 20W
Southam 28 52 16N 1 24W
Southampton, Can. 150 44 30N 81 25W
Southampton, U.K. 28 50 54N 1 23W
Southampton, U.S.A. 162 40 54N 72 22W
Southampton I. 149 64 30N 84 0W
Southampton Water 28 50 52N 1 21W
Southborough 29 51 10N 0 15 E
Southbridge, N.Z. 143 43 48 S 172 16 E
Southbridge, U.S.A. 162 42 4N 72 2W
Southeast C. 147 62 55N 169 40W
Southend, Can. 153 56 19N 103 14W
Southend, U.K. 34 55 18N 5 38W
Southend-on-Sea 29 51 32N 0 42 E
Southern □, Malawi 127 15 0 S 35 0 E
Southern □, S. Leone 120 0 8N 12 30 E
Southern □, Uganda 122 0 30 S 30 30 E
Southern □, Zambia 127 16 20 S 26 20 E
Southern Alps 143 43 41 S 170 11 E
Southern Cross 137 31 12 S 119 15 E
Southern Hills 137 32 15 S 122 40 E
Southern Indian L. 153 57 10N 98 30W
Southern Indian Lake 153 57 0N 99 0W
Southern Ocean 13 62 0 S 160 0W
Southern Uplands 35 55 30N 3 3W
Southery 29 52 32N 0 23 E
Southington 162 41 37N 72 53W
Southland □ 143 45 51 S 168 13 E
Southminster 29 51 40N 0 51 E
Southold 162 41 4N 72 26W
Southport, Austral. 139 27 58 S 153 25 E
Southport, U.K. 32 53 38N 3 1W
Southport, U.S.A. 157 33 55N 78 0W
Southwark 29 51 29N 0 5W
Southwell 33 53 4N 0 57W
Southwick 29 50 50N 0 14W
Southwold 29 52 19N 1 41 E
Soutpansberge 129 23 0 S 29 30 E
Souvigny 44 46 33N 3 10 E
Sovata 70 46 35N 25 3 E
Sovetsk, Lithuania, U.S.S.R. 80 55 6N 21 50 E
Sovetsk, R.S.F.S.R., U.S.S.R. 81 57 38N 48 53 E
Sovetskaya Gavan 77 48 50N 140 0 E
Sovicille 63 43 16N 11 12 E
Sovra 66 42 44N 17 34 E
Sowerby 33 54 13N 1 19W
Sōya-Misaki 112 45 30N 142 0 E
Soyopa 164 28 41N 109 37W
Sozh, R. 80 53 50N 31 50 E
Sozopol 67 42 23N 27 42 E
Spa 47 50 29N 5 53 E
Spain ■ 55 40 0N 5 0W
Spakenburg 46 52 15N 5 22 E
Spalding, Austral. 140 33 30 S 138 37 E
Spalding, U.K. 29 52 47N 0 9W
Spalding, U.S.A. 158 41 45N 98 27W
Spandet 73 55 15N 8 54 E
Spånga 72 59 23N 17 55 E
Spångenäs 73 57 36N 16 7 E
Spangereid 71 58 3N 7 9 E
Spaniard's Bay 151 47 38N 53 20W
Spanish 150 46 12N 82 20W
Spanish Fork 160 40 10N 111 37W
Spanish Pt. 39 52 51N 9 27W
Spanish Sahara □ = Western Sahara 116 25 0N 13 0W
Spanish Town 166 18 0N 77 20W
Sparkford 28 51 2N 2 33W
Sparrows Point 162 39 13N 76 29W
Sparta, Ga., U.S.A. 157 33 18N 82 59W
Sparta, N.J., U.S.A. 162 41 2N 74 38W
Sparta, Wis., U.S.A. 158 43 55N 91 10W
Sparta = Spárti 69 37 5N 22 25 E
Spartanburg 157 35 0N 82 0W
Spartel, C. 118 35 47N 5 56W
Spárti 69 37 5N 22 25 E
Spartivento, C., Calabria, Italy 65 37 56N 16 4 E
Spartivento, C., Sard., Italy 65 38 52N 8 50 E
Spas-Demensk 80 54 20N 34 0 E
Spas-Klepiki 81 54 34N 40 2 E
Spassk-Dalniy 77 44 40N 132 40 E
Spassk-Ryazanskiy 81 54 30N 40 25 E
Spatha Ákra. 69 35 42N 23 43 E
Spatsizi, R. 152 57 42N 128 7W
Spean Bridge 36 56 53N 4 55W
Spearfish 158 44 32N 103 52W
Spearman 159 36 15N 101 10W
Speculator 162 43 30N 74 25W
Speed 140 35 21 S 142 27 E
Speer 51 47 12N 9 8 E

Speers **153** 52 43N 107 34W
Speightstown **167** 13 15N 59 39W
Speke **32** 53 21N 2 51W
Speke Gulf, L. Victoria **126** 2 20S 32 50E
Spekholzerheide **47** 50 51N 6 2E
Spelve, L. **34** 56 22N 5 45W
Spenard **147** 61 5N 149 50W
Spencer, Idaho, U.S.A. **160** 44 18N 112 8W
Spencer, Iowa, U.S.A. **158** 43 5N 95 3W
Spencer, Nebr., U.S.A. **158** 42 52N 98 43W
Spencer, N.Y., U.S.A. **162** 42 14N 76 30W
Spencer, W. Va., U.S.A. **156** 38 47N 81 24W
Spencer B. **128** 25 30S 14 47E
Spencer Bay **148** 69 32N 93 32W
Spencer, C. **140** 35 20S 136 45E
Spencer G. **140** 34 0S 137 20E
Spences Bridge **152** 50 25N 121 20W
Spennymoor **33** 54 43N 1 35W
Spenser Mts. **143** 42 15S 172 45E
Sperkhiós, R. **69** 38 57N 22 3E
Sperrin Mts. **38** 54 50N 7 0W
Spessart **49** 50 0N 9 20E
Spetsai **69** 37 16N 23 9E
Spétsai, I. **69** 37 15N 23 10E
Spey B. **37** 57 41N 3 0W
Spey Bay **37** 57 39N 3 4W
Spey, R. **37** 57 26N 3 25W
Speyer **49** 49 19N 8 26E
Speyer, R. **41** 49 18N 7 52E
Spezia = La Spézia **62** 44 7N 9 49E
Spézia, La **62** 44 8N 9 50E
Spezzano Albanese **65** 39 41N 16 19E
Spiddal **39** 53 14N 9 19W
Spiekeroog, I. **48** 53 45N 7 42E
Spielfeld **63** 46 43N 15 38E
Spiez **50** 46 40N 7 40E
Spijk **46** 53 24N 6 50E
Spijkenisse **46** 51 51N 4 20E
Spili **69** 35 13N 24 31E
Spilimbergo **63** 46 7N 12 53E
Spillimacheen **152** 51 6N 117 0W
Spilsby **33** 53 10N 0 6E
Spin Baldak **93** 31 3N 66 16E
Spinazzola **65** 40 58N 16 5E
Spincourt **43** 49 20N 5 39E
Spind **71** 58 6N 6 53E
Spineni **70** 44 43N 24 37E
Spirit Lake **160** 47 56N 116 56W
Spirit River **152** 55 45N 118 50W
Spiritwood **153** 53 24N 107 33W
Spiš šká Nová Ves **53** 48 58N 20 34E
Spiš šké Podhradie **53** 49 0N 20 48E
Spit Pt. **136** 20 4S 118 59E
Spithead **29** 50 43N 0 56W
Spittal **52** 46 48N 13 31E
Spitzbergen (Svalbard) **12** 78 0N 17 0E
Split **63** 43 31N 16 26E
Split L. **153** 56 8N 96 15W
Splitski Kan **63** 43 31N 16 20E
Splügen **51** 46 34N 9 21E
Splügenpass **51** 46 30N 9 20E
Spoffard **159** 29 10N 100 27W
Spofforth **33** 53 57N 1 28W
Spokane **160** 47 45N 117 25W
Sponvika **71** 59 7N 11 15E
Spooner **158** 45 49N 91 51W
Sporádhes **69** 37 0N 27 0E
Sporyy Navolok, M. **76** 75 50N 68 40E
Spotswood **162** 40 23N 74 23W
Spragge **150** 46 15N 82 40W
Sprague **160** 47 25N 117 59W
Sprague River **160** 42 49N 121 31W
Spratly, I. **102** 8 20N 112 0E
Spray **160** 44 56N 119 46W
Spree, R. **48** 52 23N 13 52E
Sprimont **47** 50 30N 5 40E
Spring City, Pa., U.S.A. **162** 40 11N 75 33W
Spring City, Utah, U.S.A. **160** 39 31N 111 28W
Spring Grove **162** 39 55N 76 56W
Spring Hill **141** 33 23S 149 9E
Spring Mts. **161** 36 20N 115 43W
Spring Valley, Minn., U.S.A. **158** 43 40N 92 30W
Spring Valley, N.Y., U.S.A. **162** 41 7N 74 4W
Springbok **128** 29 42S 17 54E
Springburn **143** 43 40S 171 32E
Springdale, Can. **151** 49 30N 56 6W
Springdale, Ark., U.S.A. **159** 36 10N 94 5W
Springdale, Wash., U.S.A. **160** 48 1N 117 50W
Springe **48** 52 12N 9 35E
Springerville **161** 34 10N 109 16W
Springfield, N.Z. **143** 43 19S 171 56E
Springfield, Colo., U.S.A. **159** 37 26N 102 40W
Springfield, Ill., U.S.A. **158** 39 48N 89 40W
Springfield, Mass., U.S.A. **162** 42 8N 72 37W
Springfield, Mo., U.S.A. **159** 37 15N 93 20W
Springfield, Ohio, U.S.A. **156** 39 50N 83 48W
Springfield, Oreg., U.S.A. **160** 44 2N 123 0W
Springfield, Tenn., U.S.A. **157** 36 35N 86 55W
Springfield, Va., U.S.A. **162** 38 45N 77 13W
Springfield, Vt., U.S.A. **162** 43 20N 72 30W
Springfontein **128** 30 15S 25 40E
Springhill **151** 45 40N 64 4W
Springhouse **152** 51 56N 122 7W
Springhurst **141** 36 10S 146 31E
Springs **129** 26 13S 28 25E
Springsure **138** 24 8S 148 6E
Springvale, Queens., Austral. **138** 23 33S 140 42E
Springvale, W. Australia, Austral. **136** 17 48S 127 41E
Springvale, U.S.A. **162** 43 28N 70 48W
Springville, Calif., U.S.A. **163** 36 8N 118 49W
Springville, N.Y., U.S.A. **156** 42 31N 78 41W
Springville, Utah, U.S.A. **160** 40 14N 111 35W
Springwater **153** 51 58N 108 23W
Sproatley **33** 53 46N 0 9W
Spur **159** 33 28N 100 50W
Spurn Hd. **33** 53 34N 0 8E
Spuz **66** 42 32N 19 10E
Spuzzum **152** 49 37N 121 23W
Spydeberg **71** 59 37N 11 4E
Squam L. **162** 43 45N 71 32W
Squamish **152** 49 45N 123 10W
Square Islands **151** 52 47N 55 47W
Squillace, Golfo di **65** 38 43N 16 35E
Squinzano **65** 40 27N 18 1E
Squires, Mt. **137** 26 14S 127 46E
Sragen **103** 7 28S 110 59E
Srbac **66** 45 7N 17 30E
Srbija □ **66** 43 30N 21 0E
Srbobran **66** 45 32N 19 48E
Sre Khtum **101** 12 10N 106 52E
Sre Umbell **101** 11 8N 103 46E
Srebrnica **66** 44 10N 19 18E
Sredinyy Khrebet **77** 57 0N 160 0E
Središce **63** 46 24N 16 17E
Sredna Gora **67** 42 40N 25 0E
Sredne Tambovskoye **77** 50 55N 137 45E
Srednekolymsk **77** 67 20N 154 40E
Srednevilyuysk **77** 63 50N 123 5E
Sredni Rodopi **67** 41 40N 24 45E
Sredniy Ural, mts. **166** 59 0N 59 0E
Srem **54** 52 6N 17 2E
Srepok, R. **100** 13 33N 106 16E
Sretensk **77** 52 10N 117 40E
Sri Lanka ■ **97** 7 30N 80 50E
Sriharikota, I. **97** 13 40N 81 30E
Srikakulam **96** 18 14N 84 4E
Srinagar **95** 34 12N 74 50E
Sripur **98** 24 14N 90 30E
Srirangam **97** 10 54N 78 42E
Srirangapatnam **97** 12 26N 76 43E
Şrivilliputtur **97** 9 31N 77 40E
Šroda Wlkp. **54** 52 15N 17 19E
Srpska Crnja **66** 45 38N 20 44E
Srpska Itabej **66** 45 35N 20 44E
Ssu Chiao **109** 30 43N 122 28E
Ssuhsien **107** 33 25N 117 54E
Ssuhui **109** 23 20N 112 41E
Ssunan **108** 27 56N 108 14E
Ssup'ing **105** 43 10N 124 25E
Ssushui, Honan, China **106** 34 51N 113 12E
Ssushui, Shantung, China **107** 35 39N 117 15E
Ssutzuwangch'i **106** 41 30N 111 37E
Staaten, R. **138** 16 24S 141 17E
Stabroek **47** 51 20N 4 22E
Stack's Mts. **39** 52 20N 9 34W
Stad Delden **46** 52 16N 6 43E
Stade **48** 53 35N 9 31E
Staden **47** 50 59N 3 1E
Staðarhólskirkja **74** 65 23N 21 58W
Stadil **73** 56 12N 8 12E
Städjan **72** 61 56N 12 30E
Stadlandet **71** 62 10N 5 10E
Stadsforsen **72** 63 0N 16 45E
Stadskanaal **46** 53 4N 6 48E
Stadthagen **48** 52 20N 9 14E
Stadtlohn **48** 51 59N 6 52E
Stadtroda **48** 50 51N 11 44E
Stäfa **51** 47 14N 8 45E
Stafafell **74** 64 25N 14 52W
Staffa, I. **34** 56 26N 6 21W
Stafford, U.K. **28** 52 49N 2 9W
Stafford, Kansas, U.S.A. **159** 38 0N 98 35W
Stafford, Va., U.S.A. **162** 38 2S 77 30W
Stafford □ **28** 52 53N 2 10W
Stafford Springs **162** 41 58N 72 20W
Stagnone, I. **64** 37 50N 12 28E
Staindrop **33** 54 35N 1 49W
Staines **29** 51 26N 0 30W
Stainforth **33** 53 37N 0 59W
Stainmore For. **32** 54 29N 2 5W
Stainton **33** 53 17N 0 23W
Stainz **52** 46 53N 15 17E
Staithes **33** 54 33N 0 47W
Stakkroge **73** 55 53N 8 51E
Stala **66** 43 43N 21 28E
Stalbridge **28** 50 57N 2 22W
Stalden **50** 46 14N 7 52E
Stalham **29** 52 46N 1 31E
Stalingrad = Volgograd **83** 48 40N 44 25E
Staliniri = Tskhinvali **83** 42 14N 44 1E
Stalino = Donetsky **82** 48 0N 37 45E
Stalinogorsk = Novomoskovsk **81** 54 5N 38 15E
Stallingborough **33** 53 36N 0 11W
Stalowa Wola **54** 50 34N 22 3E
Stalybridge **32** 53 29N 1 56W
Stamford, Austral. **138** 21 15S 143 46E
Stamford, U.K. **29** 52 39N 0 29W
Stamford, Conn., U.S.A. **162** 41 5N 73 30W
Stamford, N.Y., U.S.A. **162** 42 25N 74 37W
Stamford, Tex., U.S.A. **159** 32 58N 99 50W
Stamford Bridge **33** 53 59N 0 53W
Stamfordham **35** 55 3N 1 53W
Stampersgat **47** 51 37N 4 26E
Stamps **159** 33 22N 93 30W
Stanberry **158** 40 12N 94 32W
Standerton **129** 26 55S 29 13E
Standish, U.K. **32** 53 35N 2 39W
Standish, U.S.A. **156** 43 58N 83 57W
Standon **29** 51 53N 0 2E
Stanford **160** 47 11N 110 10W
Stanford on Teme **28** 52 17N 2 26W
Stange Hedmark **71** 60 43N 11 11E
Stanger **129** 29 18S 31 21E
Stanhope, Austral. **141** 36 27S 144 59E
Stanhope, U.K. **32** 54 45N 2 0W
Stanišic **53** 45 53N 19 12E
Stanislaus, R. **163** 37 40N 121 15W
Stanislav = Ivano-Frankovsk **80** 49 0N 24 40E
Stanke Dimitrov **66** 42 27N 23 9E
Stanley, Austral. **138** 40 46S 145 19E
Stanley, N.B., Can. **151** 46 20N 66 50W
Stanley, Sask., Can. **153** 55 24N 104 22W
Stanley, Falk. Is. **176** 51 40S 58 0W
Stanley, Durham, U.K. **33** 54 53N 1 42W
Stanley, Tayside, U.K. **35** 56 29N 3 28W
Stanley, Idaho, U.S.A. **160** 44 10N 114 59W
Stanley, N.D., U.S.A. **158** 48 20N 102 23W
Stanley, Wis., U.S.A. **158** 44 57N 91 0W
Stanley Res. **97** 11 50N 77 40E
Stanleyville = Kisangani **126** 0 35N 25 15E
Stanlow **32** 53 17N 2 52W
Stann Creek **165** 17 0N 88 20W
Stannington **35** 55 7N 1 41W
Stanovoy Khrebet **77** 55 0N 130 0E
Stans **51** 46 58N 8 21E
Stansmore Ra. **136** 21 23S 128 33E
Stansted Mountfitchet **29** 51 54N 0 13E
Stanthorpe **139** 28 36S 151 59E
Stanton, Can. **147** 69 45N 128 52W
Stanton, U.S.A. **159** 32 8N 101 45W
Stantsiya Karshi **85** 38 49N 65 47E
Stanwix **32** 54 54N 2 56W
Staphorst **46** 52 39N 6 12E
Stapleford **33** 52 56N 1 16W
Staplehurst **29** 51 9N 0 35E
Stapleton **158** 41 30N 100 31W
Staporkow **54** 51 9N 20 31E
Star City **153** 52 55N 104 20W
Stara-minskaya **83** 46 33N 39 0E
Stara Moravica **66** 45 50N 19 30E
Stara Pazova **66** 45 0N 20 10E
Stara Planina **67** 43 15N 23 0E
Stara Zagora **67** 42 26N 25 39E
Starachowice-Wierzbnik **54** 51 3N 21 2E
Staraya Russa **80** 57 58N 31 10E
Starbuck I. **131** 5 37S 155 55W
Stargard **48** 53 29N 13 19E
Stargard Szczecinski **54** 53 20N 15 0E
Stari Bar **66** 42 7N 19 13E
Stari Trg. **63** 45 29N 15 7E
Staritsa **80** 56 33N 35 0E
Starke **157** 30 0N 82 10W
Starkville, Colo., U.S.A. **159** 37 10N 104 31W
Starkville, Miss., U.S.A. **157** 33 26N 88 48W
Starnberg **49** 48 0N 11 20E
Starnberger See **49** 48 0N 11 20E
Starobelsk **83** 49 27N 39 0E
Starodub **80** 52 30N 32 50E
Starogard **54** 53 55N 18 30E
Start Bay **30** 50 15N 3 35W
Start Pt., Devon, U.K. **30** 50 13N 3 38W
Start Pt., Orkney, U.K. **37** 59 17N 2 25W
Stary Sacz **54** 49 33N 20 26E
Staryy Biryuzyak **83** 44 46N 46 50E
Staryy Kheydzhan **77** 60 0N 144 50E
Staryy Krym **82** 44 48N 35 8E
Staryy Oskol **81** 51 12N 37 55E
Stassfurt **48** 51 51N 11 34E
State College **156** 40 47N 77 49W
State Is. **150** 48 40N 87 0W
Staten I. **162** 40 35N 74 10W
Staten, I. = Los Estados, I. de **176** 54 40S 64 0W
Statesboro **157** 32 26N 81 46W
Statesville **157** 35 48N 80 51W
Statfjord, oilfield **19** 61 15N 1 50E
Stathelle **71** 59 3N 9 41E
Stauffer **163** 34 45N 119 3W
Staunton, U.K. **28** 51 58N 2 19W
Staunton, Ill., U.S.A. **158** 39 0N 89 49W
Staunton, Va., U.S.A. **156** 38 7N 79 4W
Stavanger **71** 58 57N 5 40E
Staveley, Cumbria, U.K. **32** 54 24N 2 49W
Staveley, Derby, U.K. **33** 53 16N 1 20W
Stavelot **47** 50 23N 5 55E
Stavenisse **47** 51 35N 4 1E
Staveren **46** 52 53N 5 22E
Stavern **71** 59 0N 10 1E
Stavfjord **71** 61 30N 5 0E
Stavre **72** 62 51N 15 19E
Stavropol **83** 45 5N 42 0E
Stavroúpolis **68** 41 12N 24 45E
Stavsjö **73** 48 42N 16 30E
Stawell **140** 37 5S 142 47E
Stawell, R. **138** 20 38S 142 55E
Stawiszyn **54** 51 56N 18 4E
Staxigoe **37** 58 28N 3 2W
Steamboat Springs **160** 40 30N 106 58W
Stebark **54** 53 30N 20 10E
Stebleva **68** 41 18N 20 33E
Steckborn **51** 47 44N 8 59E
Steele **158** 46 56N 99 52W
Steelton **162** 40 17N 76 50W
Steelville **159** 37 57N 91 21W
Steen, R. **152** 59 35N 117 10W
Steen River **152** 59 40N 117 12W
Steenbergen **47** 51 35N 4 19E
Steenvoorde **43** 50 48N 2 33E
Steenwijk **46** 52 47N 6 7E
Steep Pt. **137** 26 08S 113 8E
Steep Rock **153** 51 30N 98 48W
Steep Rock Lake **150** 48 50N 91 38W
Stefănesti **70** 47 44N 27 15E
Stefanie L. = Chew Bahir **123** 4 40N 30 50E
Steffisburg **50** 46 47N 7 38E
Stefŭnesti **70** 47 44N 27 15E
Stege **73** 55 0N 12 18E
Steierdorf Anina **66** 45 6N 21 51E
Steiermark □ **52** 47 26N 15 0E
Steigerwald **49** 49 45N 10 30E
Stein, Neth. **47** 50 58N 5 45E
Stein, Switz. **51** 47 40N 8 50E
Stein, U.K. **36** 57 30N 6 35W
Steinbach **153** 49 32N 96 40W
Steinfort **47** 49 39N 5 55E
Steinheim **48** 51 50N 9 6E
Steinkjer **74** 63 59N 11 31E
Steinkopf **125** 29 15S 17 48E
Stekene **47** 51 12N 4 2E
Stella Land **128** 26 45S 24 50E
Stellarton **151** 45 32N 62 45W
Stellenbosch **128** 33 58S 18 50E
Stellendam **46** 51 49N 4 1E
Stelvio, Paso dello **51** 46 32N 10 27E
Stemshaug **71** 63 19N 8 44E
Stendal **48** 52 36N 11 50E
Stene **47** 51 12N 2 56E
Stenhousemuir **35** 56 2N 3 46W
Stenmagle **73** 55 49N 11 39E
Stenness, L., of **37** 59 0N 3 15W
Stensele **74** 65 3N 17 8E
Stenstorp **73** 58 17N 13 45E
Stenungsund **73** 58 6N 11 50E
Stepanakert **79** 40 0N 46 25E
Stephan **158** 48 30N 96 53W
Stephens Cr. **140** 32 15S 141 55E
Stephens I., Can. **152** 54 10N 130 45W
Stephens I., N.Z. **143** 40 40S 174 1E
Stephenville, Can. **151** 48 31N 58 30W
Stephenville, U.S.A. **159** 32 12N 98 12W
Stepnica **54** 53 38N 14 36E
Stepnoi = Elista **83** 46 25N 44 17E
Stepnoye **84** 54 4N 60 26E
Sterkstroom **128** 31 32S 26 32E
Sterlego, Mys **12** 80 30N 90 0E
Sterling, Colo., U.S.A. **158** 40 40N 103 15W
Sterling, Ill., U.S.A. **158** 41 45N 89 45W
Sterling, Kans., U.S.A. **158** 38 17N 98 13W
Sterling City **159** 31 50N 100 59W
Sterlitamak **84** 53 40N 56 0E
Sternberg **48** 53 42N 11 48E
Sternberk **53** 49 45N 17 15E
Stettin = Szczecin **54** 53 27N 14 27E
Stettiner Haff **48** 53 50N 14 25E
Stettler **152** 52 19N 112 40W
Steubenville **156** 40 21N 80 39W
Stevenage **29** 51 54N 0 11W
Stevens Port **158** 44 32N 89 34W
Stevens Village **147** 66 0N 149 10W
Stevenson L. **153** 53 55N 95 9W
Stevenson, R. **136** 46 15S 134 10E
Stevenston **34** 55 38N 4 46W
Stevns Klint **73** 55 17N 12 28E
Stewart **152** 55 56N 129 57W
Stewart, C. **138** 11 57S 134 45E
Stewart, I. **176** 54 50S 71 30W
Stewart I. **143** 46 58S 167 54E
Stewart River **147** 63 19N 139 26W
Stewarton **34** 55 40N 4 30W
Stewartstown **38** 54 35N 6 40W
Stewiacke **151** 45 9N 63 22W
Steyning **29** 50 54N 0 19W
Steynsburg **128** 31 15S 25 49E
Steyr **52** 48 3N 14 25E
Steyr, R. **52** 48 57N 14 15E
Steytlerville **128** 33 17S 24 19E
Stia **63** 43 48N 11 41E
Stiens **46** 53 16N 5 46E
Stigler **159** 35 19N 95 6W
Stigliano **65** 40 24N 16 13E
Stigsnæs **73** 55 13N 11 18E
Stigtomta **73** 58 47N 16 48E
Stikine Mts. **148** 59 30N 129 30W
Stikine, R. **147** 58 0N 131 12W
Stilfontein **128** 26 50S 26 50E
Stilís **69** 38 55N 22 37E
Stillington **33** 54 7N 1 5W
Stillwater, Minn., U.S.A. **158** 45 3N 92 47W
Stillwater, N.Y., U.S.A. **162** 42 55N 73 41W
Stillwater, Okla., U.S.A. **159** 36 5N 97 3W
Stillwater Mts. **160** 39 45N 118 6W
Stilwell **159** 35 52N 94 36W
Stimfalias, L. **69** 37 51N 22 27E
Stimson **150** 48 58N 80 30W
Stinchar, R. **34** 55 10N 4 50W
Stingray Pt. **162** 37 35N 76 15W
Stip **66** 41 42N 22 10E
Stiperstones Mt. **28** 52 36N 2 57W
Stira **69** 38 9N 24 14E

Stiring Wendel 43 49 12N 6 57 E
Stirling, Austral. 138 17 12 S 141 35 E
Stirling, Can. 152 49 30N 112 30W
Stirling, N.Z. 143 46 14 S 169 49 E
Stirling, U.K. 35 56 17N 3 57W
Stirling (□) 26 56 3N 4 10W
Stirling Ra. 137 34 0 S 118 0 E
Stjárneborg 73 57 53N 14 45 E
Stjarnsfors 72 60 2N 13 45 E
Stjördalshalsen 71 63 29N 10 51 E
Stobo 35 55 38N 3 18W
Stoborough, oilfield 19 50 38N 2 8W
Stockaryd 73 57 19N 14 36 E
Stockbridge 28 51 7N 1 30W
Stockerau 53 48 24N 16 12 E
Stockett 160 47 23N 111 7W
Stockholm 72 59 20N 18 3 E
Stockholms län □ 72 59 30N 18 20 E
Stockhorn 50 46 42N 7 33 E
Stockport 32 53 25N 2 11W
Stocksbridge 33 53 30N 1 36W
Stockton, Austral. 141 32 56 S 151 47 E
Stockton, Calif., U.S.A. 163 38 0N 121 20W
Stockton, Kans., U.S.A. 158 39 30N 99 20W
Stockton, Mo., U.S.A. 159 37 40N 93 48W
Stockton-on-Tees 33 54 34N 1 20W
Stockvik 72 62 17N 17 23 E
Stoczek Łukowski 54 51 58N 22 22 E
Stode 72 62 28N 16 35 E
Stoer 36 58 12N 5 20W
Stogovo, mts. 66 41 31N 20 38 E
Stoke, N.Z. 143 41 19N 173 14 E
Stoke, U.K. 29 51 26N 0 41 E
Stoke Ferry 29 52 34N 0 31 E
Stoke Fleming 30 50 19N 3 36W
Stoke Mandeville 29 51 46N 0 47W
Stoke Prior 28 52 18N 2 5W
Stokenham 30 50 15N 3 40W
Stokes Bay 150 45 0N 81 22W
Stokes Pt. 138 40 10 S 143 56 E
Stokes Ra. 136 15 50 S 130 50 E
Stokesley 33 54 27N 1 12W
Stokke 71 59 13N 10 17 E
Stokkem 47 51 1N 5 45 E
Stokken 71 58 31N 8 53 E
Stokkseyri 74 63 50N 20 58W
Stokksnes 74 64 14N 14 58W
Stolac 66 43 8N 17 59 E
Stolberg, Germ., E. 48 51 33N 11 0 E
Stolberg, Germ., W. 48 50 48N 6 13 E
Stolbovaya, R.S.F.S.R., U.S.S.R. 77 64 50N 153 50 E
Stolbovaya, R.S.F.S.R., U.S.S.R. 81 55 10N 37 32 E
Stolbtsy 80 53 22N 26 43 E
Stolin 80 51 53N 26 50 E
Stolnici 70 44 31N 24 48 E
Stolwijk 46 51 59N 4 47 E
Ston 66 42 51N 17 43 E
Stone, Bucks., U.K. 29 51 48N 0 52W
Stone, Stafford, U.K. 32 52 55N 2 10W
Stone Harbor 162 39 3N 74 45W
Stonecliffe 150 46 13N 77 56W
Stonehaven 37 56 58N 2 11W
Stonehenge, Austral. 138 24 22 S 143 17 E
Stonehenge, U.K. 28 51 9N 1 45W
Stonehouse, Glous., U.K. 28 51 45N 2 18W
Stonehouse, Strathclyde, U.K. 35 55 42N 4 0W
Stonewall 153 50 10N 97 19W
Stongfjord 71 61 28N 14 0 E
Stonham Aspall 29 52 11N 1 7 E
Stony L. 153 58 51N 98 40W
Stony Point 162 41 14N 73 59W
Stony Rapids 153 59 16N 105 50W
Stony River 147 61 48N 156 48W
Stony Stratford 29 52 4N 0 51W
Stony Tunguska = Tunguska, Nizhmaya 77 64 0N 95 0 E
Stopnica 54 50 27N 20 57 E
Stor Elvdal 71 61 30N 11 1 E
Stora Borge Fjell, Mt. 48 65 12N 14 0 E
Stora Gla 72 59 30N 12 30 E
Stora Karlsö 73 57 17N 17 59 E
Stora Lulevatten 74 67 10N 19 30 E
Stora Sjøfallet 74 67 29N 18 40 E
Storavan 74 65 45N 18 10 E
Stord Leirvik, I. 71 59 48N 5 27 E
Store Bælt 73 55 20N 11 0 E
Store Creek 141 32 54 S 149 6 E
Store Heddinge 73 55 18N 12 23 E
Storen 71 63 3N 10 18 E
Storfjorden 71 62 25N 6 30 E
Storm B. 138 43 10 S 147 30 E
Storm Lake 158 42 35N 95 5W
Stormberg 125 31 16 S 26 17 E
Stormsrivier 128 33 59 S 23 52 E
Stornoway 36 58 12N 6 23W
Storozhinets 82 48 14 S 25 45 E
Storr, The, mt. 36 57 30N 6 12W
Storrs 162 41 48N 72 15W
Storsjö 72 62 49N 13 5 E
Storsjöen, Hedmark, Norway 71 60 20N 11 40 E
Storsjöen, Hedmark, Norway 71 61 30N 11 14 E
Storsjön, Gavleborg, Sweden 72 60 35N 16 45 E
Storsjön, Jämtland, Sweden 72 62 50N 13 8 E
Storstroms Amt □ 73 49 50N 11 45 E
Stort, R. 29 51 50N 0 7 E
Storuman 74 65 5N 17 10 E
Storuman, L. 74 65 5N 17 10 E
Storvätteshagna, Mt. 72 62 6N 12 30 E
Storvik 72 60 35N 16 33 E
Stotfold 29 52 2N 0 13W
Stoughton 153 49 40N 103 0W
Stour, R., Dorset, U.K. 28 50 48N 2 7W
Stour, R., Heref. & Worcs., U.K. 28 52 25N 2 13W
Stour, R., Kent, U.K. 29 51 15N 0 57 E
Stour, R., Suffolk, U.K. 29 51 55N 1 5 E
Stourbridge 28 52 28N 2 8W
Stourport 28 52 21N 2 18W
Stout, L. 153 52 0N 94 40W
Stove Pipe Wells Village 163 36 35N 117 11W
Stow 35 55 41N 2 50W
Stow Bardolph 29 52 38N 0 24 E
Stow-on-the-Wold 28 51 55N 1 42W
Stowmarket 29 52 11N 1 0 E
Stowupland 29 52 12N 1 3 E
Strabane 38 54 50N 7 28W
Strabane □ 38 54 45N 7 25W
Strachan 37 57 1N 2 31W
Strachur 34 56 10N 5 5W
Stracin 66 42 13N 22 2 E
Stradbally, Kerry, Ireland 39 52 15N 10 4W
Stradbally, Laoighis, Ireland 39 53 2N 7 10W
Stradbally, Waterford, Ireland 39 52 7N 7 28W
Stradbroke 29 52 19N 1 16 E
Strade 38 53 56N 9 8W
Stradella 62 45 4N 9 20 E
Stradone 38 54 0N 7 12W
Strahan 138 42 9 S 145 20 E
Straldzha 67 42 35N 26 40 E
Stralkonice 52 49 15N 13 53 E
Stralsund 48 54 17N 13 5 E
Strand, Hedmark, Norway 71 61 18N 11 15 E
Strand, Rogaland, Norway 71 59 3N 5 56 E
Strand, S. Afr. 128 34 9 S 18 48 E
Stranda 71 62 19N 6 58 E
Strandby 73 56 47N 9 13 E
Strandebarm 71 60 17N 6 0 E
Strandhill 38 54 16N 8 34W
Strandvik 71 60 9N 5 41 E
Strangford 38 54 23N 5 34W
Strängnäs 72 59 23N 17 8 E
Stranorlar 38 54 58N 7 47W
Stranraer 34 54 54N 5 0W
Strasbourg, Can. 153 51 4N 104 55W
Strasbourg, France 43 48 35N 7 42 E
Strasburg, Ger. 48 53 30N 13 44 E
Strasburg, U.S.A. 158 46 12N 101 9W
Strassen 47 49 37N 6 4 E
Stratford, N.S.W., Austral. 141 32 7 S 151 55 E
Stratford, Vic., Austral. 141 37 59 S 147 7 E
Stratford, Can. 150 43 23N 81 0W
Stratford, N.Z. 142 39 20 S 174 19 E
Stratford, Calif., U.S.A. 163 36 10N 119 49W
Stratford, Conn., U.S.A. 162 41 13N 73 8W
Stratford, Tex., U.S.A. 159 36 20N 102 3W
Stratford-on-Avon 28 52 12N 1 42W
Stratford St. Mary 29 51 58N 0 59 E
Strath Avon 37 57 19N 3 23W
Strath Dearn 37 57 20N 4 0W
Strath Earn 35 56 20N 3 50W
Strath Glass 37 57 20N 4 40W
Strath Naver 37 58 24N 4 12W
Strath Spey 37 57 15N 3 40W
Strathalbyn 140 35 13 S 138 53 E
Strathaven 35 55 40N 4 4W
Strathbogie, Dist. 37 57 25N 2 45W
Strathclyde □ 34 56 0N 4 50W
Strathcona Prov. Park 152 49 38N 125 40W
Strathdon 37 57 12N 3 4W
Strathkanaird 36 57 58N 5 5W
Strathmore, Austral. 138 17 50 S 142 35 E
Strathmore, Can. 152 51 5N 113 25W
Strathmore, Highland, U.K. 37 58 20N 4 40W
Strathmore, Tayside, U.K. 37 56 40N 3 4W
Strathmore, U.S.A. 163 36 9N 119 4W
Strathnaver 152 53 20N 122 33W
Strathpeffer 37 57 35N 4 32W
Strathroy 150 42 58N 81 38W
Strathy 37 58 30N 4 0W
Strathy Pt. 37 58 35N 4 0W
Strathyre 34 56 14N 4 20W
Stratmiglo Scot. 35 56 16N 3 15W
Stratton, U.K. 30 50 49N 4 31W
Stratton, U.S.A. 158 39 20N 102 36W
Stratton St. Margaret 28 51 35N 1 45W
Straubing 49 48 53N 12 35 E
Straumnes 74 66 26N 23 8W
Straumsnes Åsskard 71 63 4N 8 2 E
Strausberg 48 52 40N 13 52 E
Strawberry Res. 160 40 0N 111 0W
Strawn 159 32 36N 98 30W
Strážnice 53 48 54N 17 19 E
Streaky B. 139 32 51 S 134 18 E
Streaky Bay 139 32 48 S 134 13 E
Streatley 28 51 31N 1 9W
Streator 158 41 9N 88 52W
Stredočeský □ 52 49 55N 14 30 E
Stredoslovenský □ 53 48 30N 19 15 E
Streé 47 50 17N 4 18 E
Street 28 51 7N 2 43W
Strehaia 70 44 37N 23 10 E
Strelcha 67 42 30N 24 19 E
Strelka 77 58 5N 93 10 E
Streng, R. 100 13 12N 103 37 E
Strengelvåg 74 68 58N 15 11 E
Strensall 33 54 3N 1 2W
Stretford 32 53 27N 2 19W
Stretton 32 53 21N 2 34W
Strezhevoy 76 60 42N 77 34 E
Strezhnoye 76 57 45N 84 2 E
Stribro 52 49 44N 13 0 E
Strichen 37 57 35N 2 5W
Strickland, R. 135 7 35 S 141 36 E
Strijen 46 51 45N 4 33 E
Strimón, R. 68 41 0N 23 30 E
Strimonikós Kólpos 68 40 33N 24 0 E
Striven, L. 34 55 58N 5 9W
Strofadhes, I. 69 37 15N 21 0 E
Strokestown 38 53 47N 8 6W
Strom 71 60 17N 11 44 E
Ström 72 61 52N 17 20 E
Stroma, I. of 37 58 40N 3 8W
Strombacka 72 61 58N 16 44 E
Strómboli, I. 65 38 48N 15 12 E
Stromeferry 36 57 20N 5 33W
Stromemore 36 57 22N 5 33W
Stromness 37 58 58N 3 18W
Ströms Vattudal L. 74 64 0N 15 30 E
Strömsberg 72 60 28N 17 44 E
Strömsnäsbruk 73 56 35N 13 45 E
Strömstad 72 58 55N 11 15 E
Stromsund 74 63 51N 15 35 E
Stronachlachar 34 56 15N 4 35W
Strone 34 55 59N 4 54W
Stróngoli 65 39 16N 17 2 E
Stronsay Firth 37 59 4N 2 50W
Stronsay, I. 37 59 8N 2 38W
Strontian 36 56 42N 5 32W
Strood 29 51 23N 0 30 E
Stroove 38 55 13N 6 57W
Stropkov 53 49 13N 21 39 E
Stroud 28 51 44N 2 12W
Stroud Road 141 32 18 S 151 57 E
Stroudsberg 162 40 59N 75 15W
Struer 73 56 30N 8 35 E
Struga 66 41 13N 20 44 E
Strugi Krasnye 80 58 21N 28 51 E
Struma, R. 67 41 50N 23 18 E
Strumble Hd. 31 52 3N 5 6W
Strumica 66 41 28N 22 41 E
Strumica, R. 66 41 26N 27 46 E
Strusshamn 71 60 24N 5 10 E
Struthers 150 48 41N 85 51W
Struy 37 57 25N 4 40W
Stryama 67 42 16N 24 54 E
Stryi 80 49 16N 23 48 E
Stryker 152 48 40N 114 44W
Stryków 54 51 55N 19 33 E
Strzegom 54 50 58N 16 20 E
Strzelce Krajenskie 54 52 52N 15 33 E
Strzelecki Creek 139 29 37 S 139 59 E
Strzelin 54 50 46N 17 2 E
Strzelno 54 52 35N 18 9 E
Strzyzów 54 49 52N 21 47 E
Stuart, Fla., U.S.A. 157 27 11N 80 12W
Stuart, Nebr., U.S.A. 158 42 39N 99 8W
Stuart I. 147 63 55N 164 50W
Stuart L. 152 54 30N 124 30W
Stuart Mts. 143 45 2 S 167 39 E
Stuart, R. 152 54 0N 123 35W
Stuart Range 139 29 10 S 134 56 E
Stuart's Ra. 136 29 10 S 135 0 E
Stubbekøbing 73 54 53N 12 9 E
Stuben 52 46 58N 10 31 E
Stuberhuk 48 54 23N 11 18 E
Studholme Junc. 143 44 42 S 171 9 E
Studland 28 50 39N 1 58W
Studley 28 52 16N 1 54W
Stugsund 72 61 16N 17 18 E
Stugun 72 63 10N 15 40 E
Stull, L. 153 54 24N 92 34W
Stung-Treng 100 13 31N 105 58 E
Stupart, R. 153 56 0N 93 25W
Stupino 81 54 57N 38 2 E
Sturgeon B. 153 52 0N 97 50W
Sturgeon Bay 156 44 52N 87 20W
Sturgeon Falls 150 46 25N 79 57W
Sturgeon L., Alta., Can. 152 55 6N 117 32W
Sturgeon L., Ont., Can. 150 50 0N 90 45W
Sturgis, Mich., U.S.A. 156 41 50N 85 25W
Sturgis, S.D., U.S.A. 158 44 25N 103 30W
Sturko, I. 73 56 5N 15 42 E
Sturminster Marshall 28 50 48N 2 4W
Sturminster Newton 28 50 56N 2 18W
Stúrovo 53 47 48N 18 41 E
Sturt Cr. 136 19 0 S 128 15 E
Sturt Creek 136 19 0 S 128 15 E
Sturt, R. 136 34 58 S 138 31 E
Sturton 33 53 22N 0 39W
Sturts Meadows 140 31 18 S 141 42 E
Stutterheim 128 32 33 S 27 28 E
Stuttgart, Ger. 49 48 46N 9 10 E
Stuttgart, U.S.A. 159 34 30N 91 33W
Stuyvesant 162 42 23N 73 45W
Stykkishólmur 74 65 2N 22 40W
Styr, R. 80 51 4N 25 20 E
Styria = Steiermark 52 47 26N 15 0 E
Su-no-Saki 111 34 58N 139 45 E
Suakin 122 19 0N 37 20 E
Suan 107 38 42N 126 22 E
Suaqui 164 29 12N 109 41W
Suay Rieng 101 11 9N 105 45 E
Subang 103 7 30 S 107 45 E
Subansiri, R. 98 26 48N 93 50 E
Subi 101 2 55N 108 50 E
Subi, I. 102 2 58N 108 50 E
Subiaco 63 41 56N 13 5 E
Subotica 66 46 6N 19 29 E
Success 153 50 28N 108 6W
Suceava 70 47 38N 26 16 E
Suceava □ 70 47 37N 26 18 E
Suceava, R. 70 47 38N 26 16 E
Sucha-Beskidzka 54 49 44N 19 35 E
Suchan 54 53 18N 15 18 E
Suchedniów 54 51 3N 20 49 E
Such'i 109 21 23N 110 16 E
Suchien 107 33 58N 118 17 E
Suchil 164 23 18N 103 55W
Suchitoto 166 13 56N 89 0W
Suchou 109 31 15N 120 40 E
Süchow = Hsüchou 107 34 15N 117 10 E
Suchowola 54 53 33N 23 3 E
Sucio, R. 174 6 40N 77 0W
Suck, R. 39 53 17N 8 10W
Suckling, Mt. 135 9 43 S 148 59 E
Sucre, Boliv. 174 19 0 S 65 15W
Sucre, Venez. 174 10 25N 64 5W
Sucre □, Colomb. 174 8 50N 75 40W
Sucre □, Venez. 174 10 25N 63 30W
Sůcueni 70 47 20N 22 5 E
Sucunduri, R. 174 6 20N 58 35W
SuCuraj 63 43 10N 17 8 E
Sucuriju 170 1 39N 49 57W
Sud-Ouest, Pte. du 151 49 23N 63 36W
Sud, Pte. 151 49 3N 62 14W
Suda, R. 81 59 40N 36 30 E
Sudak 82 44 51N 34 57 E
Sudan ■ 117 15 0N 30 0 E
Sudan, The 114 11 0N 9 0 E
Suday 81 59 0N 43 15 E
Sudbury, Can. 150 46 30N 81 0W
Sudbury, Derby, U.K. 33 52 53N 1 43W
Sudbury, Suffolk, U.K. 29 52 2N 0 44 E
Sûdd 123 8 20N 29 30 E
Süderbrarup 48 54 38N 9 47 E
Süderlügum 48 54 50N 8 46 E
Sudetan Mts. = Sudety 53 50 20N 16 45 E
Sudety 53 50 20N 16 45 E
Sudi 127 10 11 S 39 57 E
Sudirman, Pengunungan 103 4 30N 137 0 E
Sudiţi 70 44 35N 27 38 E
Sudogda 81 55 55N 40 50 E
Sudr 122 29 40N 32 42 E
Sudzha 80 51 14N 34 25 E
Sueca 59 39 12N 0 21W
Sueur, Le 158 44 25N 93 52W
Suez = Suweis 122 28 40N 33 0 E
Suf 90 32 19N 35 49 E
Sufaina 92 23 6N 40 44 E
Suffield 153 50 12N 111 10W
Suffolk 156 36 47N 76 33W
Suffolk □ 29 52 16N 1 0 E
Suffolk, East, □ 29 52 16N 1 10 E
Suffolk, West, □ 29 52 16N 0 45 E
Sufi-Kurgan 85 40 2N 73 30 E
Sufuk 93 23 50N 51 50 E
Suga no-Sen 110 35 25N 134 25 E
Sugag 70 45 47N 23 37 E
Sugar City 158 38 18N 103 38W
Sugarloaf Pt. 126 32 22 S 152 30 E
Sugluk = Sagloue 149 62 10N 75 40W
Sugny 47 49 49N 4 54 E
Suhaia, L. 70 43 45N 25 15 E
Suhār 93 24 20N 56 40 E
Suhbaatar 105 46 54N 113 25 E
Suhl 48 50 35N 10 40 E
Suhl □ 48 50 37N 10 43 E
Suhr 50 47 22N 8 5 E
Suhsien 106 33 40N 117 0 E
Suhum 121 6 5N 0 27W
Suian 109 29 28N 118 44 E
Suica 66 43 52N 17 11 E
Suich'ang 109 28 36N 119 16 E
Suichiang 108 28 40N 103 58 E
Suifenho 107 44 30N 131 2 E
Suihsien 109 31 41N 113 20 E
Suihua 98 46 37N 127 0 E
Suilu 108 22 20N 107 48 E
Suining, Hunan, China 108 26 21N 110 0 E
Suining, Kiangsu, China 107 33 54N 117 56 E
Suining, Szechwan, China 108 30 31N 105 34 E
Suippes 43 49 8N 4 30 E
Suir, R. 39 52 31N 7 59W
Suita 111 34 45N 135 32 E
Suiteh 106 37 35N 110 5 E
Suiyang, Heilungkiang, China 107 44 26N 130 51 E
Suiyang, Kweichow, China 108 27 57N 107 11 E
Sujangarh 94 27 42N 47 31 E
Sukabumi 103 6 56 S 106 57 E
Sukadana 102 1 10 S 110 0 E
Sukandja 102 2 28 S 110 25 E
Sukarnapura = Jajapura 103 2 28N 140 38 E
Sukarno, G. = Jaja, Puncak 103 3 57 S 137 17 E
Sukchŏn 107 39 22N 125 35 E
Sukhinichi 80 54 8N 35 10 E
Sukhona, R. 78 60 30N 45 0 E
Sukhothai 100 17 1N 99 49 E
Sukhoy Log 84 56 55N 62 1 E
Sukhumi 83 43 0N 41 0 E
Sukkur 94 27 50N 68 46 E

Sukkur Barrage 93 27 50N 68 45 E
Sukma 96 18 24N 81 37 E
Sukovo 66 43 4N 22 37 E
Sukumo 110 32 56N 132 44 E
Sukunka, R. 152 55 45N 121 15W
Sul, Canal do 170 0 10S 48 30W
Sula, Kepulauan 103 1 45S 125 0 E
Sula, R. 80 50 0N 33 0 E
Sulaco, R. 166 15 2N 87 44W
Sulaiman Range 94 30 30N 69 50 E
Sulaimanke Headworks 94 30 27N 73 55 E
Sŭlaj □ 70 47 15N 23 0 E
Sulak, R. 83 43 20N 47 20 E
Sulam Tsor 90 33 4N 35 6 E
Sulawesi □ 103 2 0S 120 0 E
Sulawesi, I. 103 2 0S 120 0 E
Sulby 32 54 18N 4 29W
Sulechów 54 52 5N 15 40 E
Sulecin 54 52 26N 15 10 E
Sulejów 54 51 26N 19 53 E
Sulejówek 54 52 13N 21 17 E
Sulgen 51 47 33N 9 7 E
Sulima 120 6 58N 11 32W
Sulina 70 45 10N 29 40 E
Sulingen 48 52 41N 8 47 E
Sülişte 70 45 45N 23 56 E
Sulița 70 47 39N 20 59 E
Sulitälma 74 67 17N 17 28 E
Sulitjelma 74 61 7N 16 8 E
Sułkowice 54 49 50N 19 49 E
Sullana 174 5 0S 80 45W
Sullivan, Ill., U.S.A. 158 39 40N 88 40W
Sullivan, Ind., U.S.A. 156 39 5N 87 26W
Sullivan, Mo., U.S.A. 158 38 10N 91 10W
Sullivan Bay 152 50 55N 126 50W
Sullom Voe 36 60 30N 1 20W
Sully-sur-Loire 43 47 45N 2 20 E
Sulmierzyce 57 51 36N 17 30 E
Sulmona 63 42 3N 13 55 E
Sulo 105 39 25N 76 6 E
Sulphur, La., U.S.A. 159 30 20N 93 22W
Sulphur, Okla., U.S.A. 159 34 35N 97 0W
Sulphur Pt. 152 60 56N 114 48W
Sulphur Springs 159 33 5N 95 30W
Sulphur Springs, Cr. 159 32 50N 102 8W
Sultan 150 47 36N 82 47W
Sultanpur 95 26 18N 82 10 E
Sulu Arch. 103 6 0N 121 0 E
Sulu Sea 103 8 0N 120 0 E
Sululta 123 9 10N 38 43 E
Sulung Shan 108 31 30N 99 30 E
Suluq 119 31 44N 20 14 E
Sulyukta 85 39 56N 69 34 E
Sulzbach-Rosenburg 49 49 30N 11 46 E
Sumalata 103 1 0N 122 37 E
Sumampa 172 29 25S 63 29W
Sumatera, I. 102 0 40N 100 20 E
Sumatera Selatan □ 102 3 30S 104 0 E
Sumatera Tengah □ 102 1 0S 100 0 E
Sumatera Utara □ 102 2 0N 99 0 E
Sumatra 160 46 45N 107 37W
Sumatra = Sumatera 102 0 40N 100 20 E
Sumba, I. 103 9 45S 119 35 E
Sumba, Selat 103 9 0S 118 40 E
Sumbawa 102 8 26S 117 30 E
Sumbawa, I. 103 8 34S 117 17 E
Sumbawanga □ 126 8 0S 31 30 E
Sumbing, mt. 103 7 19S 110 3 E
Sumburgh Hd. 36 59 52N 1 17W
Sumdo 95 35 6N 79 43 E
Sumé 170 7 39S 36 55W
Sumedang 103 6 49S 107 56 E
Sümeg 53 46 59N 17 20 E
Sumenep 103 7 3S 113 51 E
Sumgait 83 40 34N 49 10 E
Sumisu-Jima 111 31 27N 140 3 E
Sumiswald 50 47 2N 7 44 E
Summer Is. 36 58 0N 5 27W
Summer L. 160 42 50N 120 50W
Summerhill 38 53 30N 6 44W
Summerland 152 49 32N 119 41W
Summerside 151 46 24N 63 47W
Summerville, Ga., U.S.A. 157 34 30N 85 20W
Summerville, S.C., U.S.A. 157 33 2N 80 11W
Summit, Can. 150 47 50N 72 20W
Summit, U.S.A. 147 63 20N 149 20W
Summit L. 152 54 20N 122 40W
Summit Pk. 161 37 20N 106 48W
Sumner, N.Z. 143 43 35S 172 48 E
Sumner, U.S.A. 158 42 49N 92 7W
Sumner L. 143 42 42S 172 15 E
Sumoto 110 34 21N 134 54 E
Sumperk 53 49 59N 17 0 E
Sumprabum 98 26 33N 97 4 E
Sumter 157 33 55N 80 10W
Sumy 80 50 57N 34 50 E
Sun City 163 33 41N 117 11W
Suna 126 5 23S 34 48 E
Sunan 107 39 15N 125 40 E
Sunart, dist. 36 56 40N 5 40W
Sunart, L. 36 56 42N 5 43W
Sunburst 160 48 56N 111 59W
Sunbury, Austral. 141 37 35S 144 44 E
Sunbury, U.S.A. 162 40 50N 76 46W
Sunchales 172 30 58S 61 35W
Suncho Corral 172 27 55S 63 14W
Sunchŏn 107 34 52N 127 31 E
Suncook 162 43 8N 71 27W
Sund 71 60 13N 5 10 E
Sunda Ketjil, Kepulauan 102 7 30S 117 0 E
Sunda, Selat 102 6 20S 105 30 E
Sundalsöra 71 62 40N 8 36 E
Sundance 158 44 27N 104 27W
Sundarbans, The 98 22 0N 89 0 E
Sundargarh 96 22 10N 84 5 E
Sunday Str. 136 16 25S 123 18 E
Sundays, R. 128 32 10S 24 40 E
Sundby 73 56 53N 8 40 E
Sundbyberg 72 59 22N 17 58 E
Sunderland, U.K. 35 54 54N 1 22W
Sunderland, U.S.A. 162 42 27N 72 36W
Sundre 152 51 49N 114 38W
Sundridge, Can. 150 45 45N 79 25W
Sundridge, U.K. 29 51 15N 0 10 E
Sunds 73 56 13N 9 1 E
Sundsjö 72 62 59N 15 9 E
Sundsvall 72 62 23N 17 17 E
Sung Hei 101 10 20N 106 2 E
Sungaipakning 102 1 19N 102 0 E
Sungaipenuh 102 2 1S 101 20 E
Sungaitiram 102 0 45S 117 8 E
Sungari, R. = Sunghua Chiang 107 44 30N 126 20 E
Sungch'i 109 27 2N 118 19 E
Sungchiang 109 31 2N 121 14 E
Sungei Lembing 101 2 53N 103 4 E
Sungei Patani 101 5 38N 100 29 E
Sungei Siput 101 4 51N 101 6 E
Sungfou 109 31 5N 114 42 E
Sungguminasa 103 5 17S 119 30 E
Sunghsien 106 34 10N 112 10 E
Sunghua Chiang, R. 105 47 42N 132 30 E
Sungikai 123 12 20N 29 51 E
Sungk'an 108 28 33N 106 52 E
Sungming 108 25 22N 103 2 E
Sungpan 105 32 50N 103 20 E
Sungp'an 108 32 36N 103 36 E
Sungt'ao 108 28 12N 109 12 E
Sungtzu Hu 109 30 10N 111 45 E
Sungü 129 21 18S 32 28 E
Sungurlu 82 40 12N 34 21 E
Sungyang 109 28 16N 119 29 E
Sunja 63 45 21N 16 35 E
Sunk Island 33 53 38N 0 7W
Sunkar, Gora 85 44 15N 73 50 E
Sunnäsbruk 72 61 10N 7 12 E
Sunne, Jamtland, Sweden 72 63 7N 14 25 E
Sunne, Varmland, Sweden 72 59 52N 13 12 E
Sunnfjord 71 61 25N 5 18 E
Sunnhordland 71 59 50N 5 30 E
Sunninghill 29 51 25N 0 40W
Sunnmöre 71 62 15N 6 30 E
Sunnyside, Utah, U.S.A. 160 39 40N 110 24W
Sunnyside, Wash., U.S.A. 160 46 24N 120 2W
Sunnyvale 163 37 23N 122 2W
Sunray 159 36 1N 101 47W
Sunshine 141 37 48S 144 52 E
Sunson 121 9 35N 0 2W
Suntar 77 62 15N 117 30 E
Sunyani 120 7 21N 2 22W
Suō-Nada 110 33 50N 131 30 E
Suolahti 74 62 34N 25 52 E
Suonenjoki 74 62 37N 27 7 E
Supai 161 36 14N 112 44W
Supaul 95 26 10N 86 40 E
Supe 123 8 34N 35 35 E
Superior, Ariz., U.S.A. 161 33 19N 111 9W
Superior, Mont., U.S.A. 160 47 15N 114 57W
Superior, Nebr., U.S.A. 158 40 3N 98 2W
Superior, Wis., U.S.A. 158 46 45N 92 0W
Superior, L. 155 47 40N 87 0W
Supetar 63 43 25N 16 32 E
Suphan Buri 100 14 30N 100 10 E
Suprasśl 54 53 13N 23 19 E
Suq al Jumah 119 32 58N 13 12 E
Sūr, Leb. 90 33 19N 35 16 E
Sūr, Oman 93 22 34N 59 32 E
Sur, Pt. 163 36 18N 121 54W
Sura, R. 81 55 30N 46 20 E
Surab 94 28 25N 66 15 E
Surabaja = Surabaya 103 7 17S 112 45 E
Surabaya 103 7 17S 112 45 E
Surahammar 72 59 43N 16 13 E
Suraia 70 45 40N 27 25 E
Surakarta 103 7 35S 110 48 E
Surakhany 83 40 13N 50 1 E
Surandai 97 8 58N 77 26 E
Surany 53 48 6N 18 10 E
Surat, Austral. 139 27 10S 149 6 E
Surat, India 96 21 12N 72 55 E
Surat, Khalīj 119 31 40N 18 30 E
Surat Thani 101 9 6N 99 14 E
Suratgarh 94 29 18N 73 55 E
Surazh 80 53 5N 32 27 E
Surduc 70 47 15N 23 25 E
Surduc Pasul 70 45 21N 23 23 E
Surdulica 66 42 41N 22 11 E
Sûre, R. 47 49 51N 6 6 E
Surendranagar 94 22 45N 71 40 E
Surf 163 34 41N 120 36W
Surf Inlet 152 53 8N 128 50W
Surgères 44 46 7N 0 47W
Surhuisterveen 46 53 11N 6 10 E
Suri 95 23 50N 87 34 E
Surianu, mt. 70 45 33N 23 31 E
Suriapet 96 17 10N 79 40 E
Surif 90 31 40N 35 4 E
Surin 100 14 50N 103 34 E
Surin Nua, Ko 101 9 30N 97 55 E
Surinam ■ 175 4 0N 56 15W
Suriname, R. 170 4 30N 55 30W
Surkhandarya, R. 85 37 12N 67 20 E
Sûrmasu 70 46 45N 25 13 E
Sürmene 83 41 0N 40 1 E
Surovikino 83 48 32N 42 55 E
Surprise L. 152 59 40N 133 15W
Surrey □ 29 51 16N 0 30W
Surry 162 37 8N 76 50W
Sursee 50 47 11N 8 6 E
Sursk 81 53 3N 45 40W
Surt 119 31 11N 16 46 E
Surt, Al Hammādah al 119 30 0N 17 50 E
Surtsey 74 63 20N 20 30W
Surubim 170 7 50S 35 45W
Suruga-Wan 111 34 45N 138 30 E
Surup 103 6 27N 126 17 E
Surur 93 23 20N 58 10 E
Susa 62 45 8N 7 3 E
Susaa, R. 73 55 20N 11 42 E
Sušac, I. 63 42 46N 16 30 E
Susak, I. 63 44 30N 14 28 E
Susaki 110 33 22N 133 17 E
Susamyr 85 42 12N 73 58 E
Susamyrtau, Khrebet 85 42 8N 73 15 E
Susangerd 92 31 35N 48 20 E
Susanino 77 52 50N 140 14 E
Susanville 160 40 28N 120 40W
Susch 51 46 46N 10 5 E
Sušice 52 49 17N 13 30 E
Susquehanna Depot 162 41 55N 75 36W
Susquehanna, R. 156 41 50N 76 20W
Susques 172 23 35S 66 25W
Sussex, Can. 151 45 45N 65 37W
Sussex, U.S.A. 162 41 12N 74 38W
Sussex (□) 26 50 55N 0 20W
Sussex, E. □ 29 51 0N 0 0 E
Sussex, W. □ 29 51 0N 0 30W
Susten Pass 51 46 43N 8 26 E
Susteren 47 51 4N 5 51 E
Sustut, R. 152 56 20N 127 30W
Susuman 77 62 47N 148 10 E
Susuna 103 3 20S 133 25 E
Susung 109 30 9N 116 6 E
Susz 54 53 44N 19 20 E
Suțești 70 45 13N 27 27 E
Sutherland, Austral. 141 34 2S 151 4 E
Sutherland, Can. 153 52 15N 106 40W
Sutherland, S. Afr. 125 32 33S 20 40 E
Sutherland, U.S.A. 158 41 12N 101 11W
Sutherland (□) 26 58 10N 4 30W
Sutherland Falls 143 44 48S 167 46 E
Sutherland Pt. 133 28 15S 153 35 E
Sutherland Ra. 137 25 42S 125 21 E
Sutherlin 160 43 28N 123 16W
Sutivan 63 43 23N 16 30 E
Sutlej, R. 94 30 0N 73 0 E
Sutter Creek 163 38 24N 120 48W
Sutterton 33 52 54N 0 8W
Sutton, N.Z. 143 45 34S 170 8 E
Sutton, U.K. 29 51 22N 0 13W
Sutton, U.S.A. 158 40 40N 97 50W
Sutton Bridge 29 52 46N 0 12 E
Sutton Coldfield 28 52 33N 1 50W
Sutton Courtenay 28 51 39N 1 16W
Sutton-in-Ashfield 33 52 8N 1 16W
Sutton-on-Sea 33 53 18N 0 18 E
Sutton, R. 150 55 15N 83 45W
Sutton Scotney 28 51 9N 1 20W
Suttor, R. 138 20 36S 147 2 E
Sutwik I. 147 56 35N 157 10W
Suva 143 17 40S 178 8 E
Suva Gora 66 41 45N 21 3 E
Suva Planina 66 43 10N 22 5 E
Suva Reka 66 42 21N 20 50 E
Suvarov Is. 131 13 15S 163 30W
Suvo Rudište 66 43 17N 20 49 E
Suvorovo 67 43 20N 27 35 E
Suwa 111 36 2N 138 8 E
Suwa-Ko 111 36 3N 138 5 E
Suwałki 54 54 8N 22 59 E
Suwałki □ 54 54 0N 22 30 E
Suwannaphum 100 15 33N 105 47 E
Suwannee, R. 157 30 0N 83 0W
Suwanose-Jima 112 29 38N 129 38 E
Suweis, El 122 29 58N 32 31 E
Suweis, Khalîg es 122 28 40N 33 0 E
Suweis, Qanâl es 122 31 0N 32 20 E
Suwŏn 107 37 17N 127 1 E
Suykbulak 84 50 25N 62 33 E
Suzak 85 44 9N 68 27 E
Suzaka 111 36 39N 138 19 E
Sŭzava, R. 52 49 50N 15 0 E
Suzdal 81 56 29N 40 26 E
Suze, La 42 47 54N 0 2 E
Suzuka 111 34 55N 136 36 E
Suzuka-Sam 111 35 5N 136 30 E
Suzzara 62 45 0N 10 45 E
Svalbard, Arctica 12 78 0N 17 0 E
Svalbard, Iceland 74 66 12N 15 43W
Svalöv 73 55 57N 13 8 E
Svanå 72 59 46N 15 23 E
Svanvik 74 69 38N 30 3 E
Svappavaari 74 67 40N 21 03 E
Svarstad 71 59 27N 9 56 E
Svartisen 74 66 40N 14 16 E
Svartvik 72 62 19N 17 24 E
Svatovo 82 49 35N 38 5 E
Svay Chek 100 13 48N 102 58 E
Svay Rieng 101 11 5N 105 48 E
Svealand □ 75 59 55N 15 0 E
Svedala 73 55 30N 13 15 E
Sveg 72 62 2N 14 21 E
Sveio 71 59 33N 5 23 E
Svelvik 71 59 37N 10 24 E
Svendborg 73 55 4N 10 35 E
Svene 71 59 45N 9 31 E
Svenljunga 73 57 29N 13 29 E
Svensbro 73 58 15N 13 52 E
Svenstavik 72 62 45N 14 26 E
Svenstrup 73 56 58N 9 50 E
Sverdlovsk 84 56 50N 60 30 E
Sverdrup Is. 12 79 0N 97 0W
Svetac 63 43 3N 15 43 E
Sveti Ivan Zelina 63 45 57N 16 16 E
Sveti Jurij 63 46 14N 15 24 E
Sveti Lenart 63 46 36N 15 48 E
Sveti Nikola 66 41 51N 21 56 E
Sveti Trojica 63 46 37N 15 33 E
Svetlogorsk 80 52 38N 29 46 E
Svetlograd 83 45 25N 42 58 E
Svetlovodsk 80 49 2N 33 13 E
Svetlyy 84 50 48N 60 51 E
Svetozarevo 66 44 0N 21 15 E
Svidník 53 49 20N 21 37 E
Svilaja Pl. 63 43 49N 16 31 E
Svilajnac 66 44 15N 21 11 E
Svilengrad 67 41 49N 26 12 E
Svinö 73 55 6N 11 44 E
Svir, R. 78 61 2N 34 50 E
Svishov 67 43 36N 25 23 E
Svisloch 80 53 26N 24 2 E
Svitavy 53 49 47N 16 28 E
Svobodnyy 77 51 20N 128 0 E
Svoge 67 42 59N 23 23 E
Svolvær 74 68 15N 14 34 E
Svratka, R. 53 49 27N 16 12 E
Svrljig 66 43 25N 22 6 E
Swa 98 19 15N 96 17 E
Swabian Alps 49 48 30N 9 30 E
Swadlincote 28 52 47N 1 34W
Swaffham 29 52 39N 0 42 E
Swain Reefs 138 21 45S 152 20 E
Swainsboro 157 32 38N 82 22W
Swakopmund 128 22 37S 14 30 E
Swale, R. 34 54 18N 1 20W
Swallowfield 29 51 23N 0 56W
Swalmen 47 51 13N 6 2 E
Swan Hill 140 35 20S 143 33 E
Swan Hills 152 54 42N 115 24W
Swan Islands 166 17 22N 83 57W
Swan L. 153 52 30N 100 50W
Swan Pt. 136 16 22S 123 1 E
Swan, R. 132 32 3S 115 35 E
Swan Reach 140 34 35S 139 37 E
Swan River 153 52 10N 101 16W
Swanage 28 50 36N 1 59W
Swanlinbar 38 54 11N 7 42W
Swansea, Austral. 141 33 3S 151 35 E
Swansea, U.K. 31 51 37N 3 57W
Swansea Bay 31 51 34N 3 55W
Swar, R. 95 35 15N 72 24 E
Swartberg 128 30 15S 29 23 E
Swartberge 128 33 20S 22 0 E
Swarte Bank, gasfield 19 53 27N 2 10 E
Swartruggens 128 25 39S 26 42 E
Swarzedz 54 52 25N 17 4 E
Swastika 150 48 7N 80 6W
Swatow = Shant'ou 109 23 28N 116 40 E
Swatragh 38 54 55N 6 40W
Swaziland ■ 129 26 30S 31 30 E
Sweden ■ 74 67 0N 15 0 E
Swedru 121 5 32N 0 41W
Sweet Home 160 44 26N 122 38W
Sweetwater, Nev., U.S.A. 163 38 27N 119 9W
Sweetwater, Tex., U.S.A. 159 32 30N 100 28W
Sweetwater, R. 160 42 31N 107 30W
Swellendam 128 34 1S 20 26 E
Świdin 54 53 47N 15 49 E
Swidnica 54 50 50N 16 30 E
Świdnik 54 51 13N 22 39 E
Świebodzice 54 50 51N 16 20 E
Swiebodzin 54 52 15N 15 37 E
Swiecie 54 53 25N 18 30 E
Swietorkrzyskie, Góry 54 51 0N 20 30 E
Swift Current 153 50 20N 107 45W
Swiftcurrent Cr. 153 50 38N 107 44W
Swilly L. 38 55 12N 7 35W
Swilly, R. 38 54 56N 7 50W
Swindle, I. 152 52 30N 128 35W
Swindon 28 51 33N 1 47W
Swinemünde = Świnoujście 54 53 54N 14 16 E
Swineshead 33 57 57N 0 9W
Swinford 38 53 57N 8 57W
Świnoujście 54 53 54N 14 16 E
Swinton, Borders, U.K. 35 55 43N 2 14W
Swinton, Gr. Manch., U.K. 32 53 31N 2 21W
Swinton, S. Yorks., U.K. 33 53 28N 1 20W
Switzerland ■ 49 46 30N 8 0 E
Swona, I. 37 58 30N 3 3W
Swords 38 53 27N 6 15W
Syasstroy 80 60 5N 32 15 E
Sybil Pt. 39 52 12N 10 28W
Sychevka 80 55 45N 34 10 E
Syców 54 51 19N 17 40 E
Sydney, Austral. 141 33 53S 151 10 E
Sydney, Can. 151 46 7N 60 7W
Sydney, U.S.A. 158 41 12N 103 0W
Sydney Mines 151 46 18N 60 15W
Sydproven 12 60 30N 45 35W
Sydra, G. of = Surt 61 31 40N 18 30 E

Syke **48** 52 55N 8 50 E
Syktyvkar **78** 61 45N 50 40 E
Sylacauga **157** 33 10N 86 15W
Sylarna, Mt. **72** 63 2N 12 11 E
Sylhet **98** 24 54N 91 52 E
Sylt, I. **48** 54 50N 8 20 E
Sylva, R. **84** 58 0N 56 54 E
Sylvan Beach **162** 43 12N 75 44W
Sylvan Lake **152** 52 20N 114 10W
Sylvania **157** 32 45N 81 37W
Sylvester **157** 31 31N 83 50W
Sym **76** 60 20N 87 50 E
Symington **35** 55 35N 3 36W
Symón **164** 24 42N 102 35W
Symonds Yat **28** 51 50N 2 38W
Synnott Ra. **136** 16 30 S 125 20 E
Syr Darya **76** 45 0N 65 0 E
Syracuse, Kans., U.S.A. **159** 38 0N 101 40W
Syracuse, N.Y., U.S.A. **162** 43 4N 76 11W
Syrdarya **85** 40 50N 68 40 E
Syria ■ **92** 35 0N 38 0 E
Syriam **98** 16 44N 96 19 E
Syrian Des. **92** 31 30N 40 0 E
Sysert **84** 56 29N 60 49 E
Syston **28** 52 42N 1 5W
Syuldzhyukyor **77** 63 25N 113 40 E
Syutkya, mt. **67** 41 50N 24 16 E
Syzran **81** 53 12N 48 30 E
Szabolcs-Szatmár □ **53** 48 2N 21 45 E
Szamocin **54** 53 2N 17 7 E
Szamotuły **54** 52 35N 16 34 E
Szaraz, R. **53** 46 28N 20 44 E
Szazhalombatta **53** 47 20N 18 58 E
Szczara, R. **53** 53 15N 25 10 E
Szczebrzeszyn **54** 50 42N 22 59 E
Szczecin **54** 53 27N 14 27 E
Szczecin □ **54** 53 25N 14 32 E
Szczecinek **54** 53 43N 16 41 E
Szczekocimy **54** 50 38N 19 48 E
Szczrk **53** 49 42N 19 1 E
Szczuczyn **54** 53 36N 22 19 E
Szczytno **54** 53 33N 21 0 E
Szechwan □ **109** 30 15N 103 15 E
Szécsény **53** 48 7N 19 30 E
Szeged **53** 46 16N 20 10 E
Szeghalom **53** 47 1N 21 10 E
Székesfehérvár **53** 47 15N 18 25 E
Szekszárd **53** 46 22N 18 42 E
Szendrö **53** 48 24N 20 41 E
Szentendre **53** 47 39N 19 4 E
Szentes **53** 46 39N 20 21 E
Szentgotthárd **53** 46 58N 16 19 E
Szentlörinc **53** 46 3N 18 1 E
Szerencs **53** 48 10N 21 12 E
Szeshui **33** 34 50N 113 20 E
Szigetvár **53** 46 3N 17 46 E
Szlichtyogowa **54** 51 42N 16 15 E
Szob **53** 47 48N 18 53 E
Szolnok **53** 47 10N 20 15 E
Szolnok □ **53** 47 15N 20 30 E
Szombathely **53** 47 14N 16 38 E
Szprotawa **54** 51 33N 15 35 E
Sztum **54** 53 55N 19 1 E
Sztuto **54** 54 20N 19 15 E
Sztutowo **54** 54 20N 19 15 E
Szûrvas **53** 46 50N 20 38 E
Szydłowiec **54** 51 15N 20 51 E
Szypliszki **54** 54 17N 23 2 E

T

't Harde **46** 52 24N 5 54 E
't Zandt **46** 53 22N 6 46 E
Ta-erh Po, L. **106** 43 15N 116 35 E
Ta Khli Khok **100** 15 18N 100 20 E
Ta Lai **101** 11 24N 107 23 E
Taalintehdas **74** 60 2N 22 30 E
Taan **107** 45 30N 124 18 E
Taavetti **75** 60 56N 27 32 E
Taba **92** 26 55N 42 30 E
Tabacal **172** 23 15 S 64 15W
Tabaco **103** 13 22N 123 44 E
Tabagné **120** 7 59N 3 4W
Tabar Is. **135** 2 50 S 152 0 E
Tabarca, Isla de **59** 38 17N 0 30W
Tabarka **119** 36 56N 8 46 E
Tabarra **59** 38 37N 1 44 E
Tabas, Khorasan, Iran **93** 33 35N 56 55 E
Tabas, Khorasan, Iran **93** 32 48N 60 12 E
Tabasará, Serrania de **166** 8 35N 81 40W
Tabasco □ **165** 17 45N 93 30W
Tabatinga **174** 4 11 S 69 58W
Tabatinga, Serra da **170** 10 30 S 44 0W
Tabayin **98** 22 42N 95 20 E
Tabelbala, Kahal de **118** 28 47N 2 0W
Taber **152** 49 47N 112 8W
Taberg **162** 43 18N 75 37W
Tabernas **59** 37 4N 2 26W
Tabernas de Valldigna **59** 39 5N 0 13W
Tabigha **90** 32 53N 35 33 E
Tabira **170** 7 35 S 37 33W
Tablas, I. **103** 12 25N 122 2 E
Table B. **151** 53 40N 56 25W
Table Mt. **128** 34 0 S 18 22 E
Table Top, Mt. **138** 23 24 S 147 11 E
Tableland **136** 17 16 S 126 51 E
Tabletop, mt. **137** 22 32 S 123 50 E
Tábor **52** 49 25N 14 39 E
Tabor **90** 32 42N 35 24 E
Tabora **126** 5 2 S 32 57 E
Tabora □ **126** 5 0 S 33 0 E
Tabory **84** 58 31N 64 33 E
Tabou **120** 4 30N 7 20W
Tabouda **118** 34 44N 5 14W
Tabrīz **92** 38 7N 46 20 E
Tabūk **92** 28 30N 36 25 E
Täby **72** 59 29N 18 4 E
Tacámbaro **164** 19 14N 101 28W
Tacarigua, L. de **174** 11 3N 68 25W
Tach'aitan **105** 37 50N 95 18 E
T'ach'eng **105** 46 45N 82 57 E
Tach'eng **106** 38 35N 116 39 E
Tach'engtzu **107** 41 44N 118 52 E
Tach'i **109** 24 51N 121 14 E
Tachia **109** 24 25N 120 28 E
Tachiai **108** 23 44N 103 57 E
Tachibana-Wan **110** 32 45N 130 7 E
Tachikawa **111** 35 42N 139 25 E
Tach'in Ch'uan, R. **108** 31 57N 102 11 E
Tach'ing Shan, mts. **106** 40 50N 111 0 E
Tachira **174** 8 7N 72 21W
Tachira □ **174** 8 7N 72 15W
Tachov **52** 49 47N 12 39 E
Tachu **108** 30 45N 107 13 E
Tacina, R. **65** 39 5N 16 51 E
Tacloban **103** 11 15N 124 58 E
Tacna **174** 18 0 S 70 20W
Tacoma **160** 47 15N 122 30W
Tacuarembó **173** 31 45 S 56 0W
Tacumshin L. **39** 52 12N 6 28W
Tadcaster **33** 53 53N 1 16W
Tademaït, Plateau du **118** 28 30N 2 30 E
Tadent, O. **119** 22 30N 7 0 E
Tadjerdjert, O. **119** 26 0N 8 0W
Tadjerouna **118** 33 31N 2 3 E
Tadjettaret, O. **119** 22 0N 7 30W
Tadjmout, O. **118** 25 37N 3 48 E
Tadjoura **123** 11 50N 42 55 E
Tadjoura, Golfe de **123** 11 50N 43 0 E
Tadley **28** 51 21N 1 8W
Tadmor, N.Z. **143** 41 27 S 172 45 E
Tadmor, Syria **92** 34 30N 37 55 E
Tado **174** 5 16N 76 32W
Tadotsu **110** 34 16N 133 45 E
Tadoule L **153** 58 36N 98 20W
Tadoussac **151** 48 11N 69 42W
Tadzhik S.S.R. □ **85** 35 30N 70 0 E
Taechŏnni **107** 36 21N 126 36 E
Taegu **107** 35 50N 128 37 E
Taegwandong **107** 40 13N 125 12 E
Taejŏn **107** 36 20N 127 28 E
Taerhhanmaoming-anlienhoch'i **106** 41 50N 110 27 E
Taerhting **105** 37 15N 92 36 E
Taf, R. **31** 51 55N 4 36W
Tafalla **58** 42 30N 1 41W
Tafang **108** 27 10N 105 39 E
Tafar **123** 6 52N 28 15 E
Tafas **90** 32 44N 36 5 E
Tafassasset, O. **119** 23 0N 9 11 E
Tafelbaai **128** 33 35 S 18 25 E
Tafelney, C. **118** 31 3N 9 51W
Tafermaar **103** 6 47 S 134 10 E
Tafí Viejo **172** 26 43 S 65 17W
Tafiré **120** 9 4N 5 10W
Tafnidilt **118** 28 47N 10 58W
Tafraout **118** 29 50N 8 58W
Taft, Phil. **103** 11 57N 125 30 E
Taft, Ala., U.S.A. **163** 35 10N 119 28W
Taft, Tex., U.S.A. **159** 27 58N 97 23W
Taga Dzong **98** 27 5N 90 0 E
Taganrog **83** 47 12N 38 50 E
Taganrogskiy Zaliv **82** 47 0N 38 30 E
Tagant **120** 18 20N 11 0W
Tagap Ga **98** 26 56N 96 13 E
Tagbilaran **103** 9 39N 123 51 E
Tage **135** 6 19 S 143 20 E
Tággia **62** 43 52N 7 50 E
Taghmon **39** 52 19N 6 40W
Taghrīfat **119** 29 5N 17 26 E
Taghzout **118** 33 30N 4 49W
Tagish **152** 60 19N 134 16W
Tagish L. **147** 60 10N 134 20W
Tagliacozzo **63** 42 4N 13 13 E
Tagliamento, R. **63** 45 38N 13 5 E
Táglio di Po **63** 45 0N 12 12 E
Tagomago, Isla de **59** 39 2N 1 39 E
Tagua, La **174** 0 3N 74 40W
Taguatinga **171** 12 26 S 46 26W
Tagula **135** 11 22 S 153 15 E
Tagula I. **135** 11 30 S 153 30 E
Tagum (Hijo) **103** 7 33N 125 53 E
Tagus = Tajo, R. **55** 39 44N 5 50W
Tahahbala, I. **102** 0 30 S 98 30 E
Tahakopa **143** 46 30 S 169 23 E
Tahala **118** 34 0N 4 28W
Tahan, Gunong **101** 4 45N 102 25 E
Tahara **111** 34 40N 137 16 E
Tahat Mt. **119** 23 18N 5 21 E
Tāherī **93** 27 43N 52 20 E
Tahiti, I. **131** 17 37 S 149 27W
Tahoe **160** 39 12N 120 9W
Tahoe, L. **160** 39 0N 120 9W
Tahora **142** 39 2 S 174 49 E
Tahoua **121** 14 57N 5 16 E
Tahsien **108** 31 17N 107 30 E
Tahsin **108** 22 48N 107 23 E
Tahsinganling Shanmo **105** 49 0N 122 0 E
Tahsingkou **107** 43 23N 129 39 E
Tahsintien **107** 37 37N 120 50 E
Tahsüeh Shan, mts. **108** 31 15N 101 20 E
Tahta **122** 26 44N 31 32 E
Tahulandang, I. **103** 2 27N 125 23 E
Tahuna **103** 3 45N 125 30 E
Tahung Shan, mts. **109** 31 30N 112 50 E
Tai **108** 30 41N 103 29 E
Taï **120** 5 55N 7 30W
T'ai Hu **105** 31 10N 120 0 E
Tai Shan **109** 30 17N 122 10 E
T'aian **107** 36 12N 117 7 E
T'aichiang **108** 26 40N 108 19 E
T'aichou **109** 32 22N 119 45 E
T'aichou Liehtao **109** 28 30N 121 53 E
T'aichung **105** 24 9N 120 37 E
T'aichunghsien **109** 24 15N 120 35 E
Taieri, R. **143** 46 3 S 170 12 E
Taiga Madema **119** 23 46N 15 25 E
T'aihang Shan, mts. **106** 35 40N 113 20 E
Taihape **142** 39 41 S 175 48 E
T'aiho, Anhwei, China **109** 33 10N 115 36 E
T'aiho, Kiangsi, China **109** 26 50N 114 53 E
T'aihsien **109** 32 17N 120 10 E
T'aihsing **109** 32 10N 120 4 E
Taihu **109** 30 30N 116 25 E
T'aik'ang **106** 34 4N 114 52 E
Taikkyi **98** 17 20N 96 0 E
T'aiku **106** 37 23N 112 34 E
Tailem Bend **140** 35 12 S 139 29 E
Tailfingen **49** 48 15N 9 1 E
Taïma **92** 27 35N 38 45 E
Taimyr = Taymyr **77** 75 0N 100 0 E
Taimyr, Oz. **77** 74 20N 102 0 E
Tain **37** 57 49N 4 4W
T'ainan **109** 23 0N 120 10 E
T'ainanhsien **109** 23 21N 120 17 E
Tainaron, Akra **69** 36 22N 22 27 E
Tainggya **98** 17 49N 94 29 E
T'aining **109** 26 55N 117 12 E
Taintignies **47** 50 33N 3 22 E
Taiobeiras **171** 15 49 S 42 14W
T'aipei **109** 25 2N 121 30 E
T'aip'ing **109** 30 18N 118 6 E
Taiping **101** 4 51N 100 44 E
Taipu **170** 5 37 S 35 36W
T'aip'ussuchi **106** 41 55N 115 23 E
Taisha **110** 35 24N 132 40 E
T'aishan **109** 22 17N 112 43 E
Taishun **109** 27 33N 119 43 E
Taita □ **126** 4 0 S 38 30 E
Taita Hills **126** 3 25 S 38 15 E
Taitao, Pen. de **176** 46 30 S 75 0W
T'aitung **105** 22 43N 121 4 E
Taivalkoski **74** 65 33N 28 12 E
Taiwan (Formosa) ■ **109** 23 30N 121 0 E
Taiwara **93** 33 30N 64 24 E
Taïyetos Óros **69** 37 0N 22 23 E
Taiyiba, Israel **90** 32 36N 35 27 E
Taiyiba, Jordan **90** 31 55N 35 17 E
T'aiyüan **106** 37 55N 112 40 E
Ta'izz **91** 13 43N 44 7 E
Tajapuru, Furo do **170** 1 50 S 50 25W
Tajarhī **119** 24 15N 14 46 E
Tajicaringa **164** 23 15N 104 44W
Tajima **112** 35 19N 135 8 E
Tajimi **111** 35 19N 137 8 E
Tajimi Gifu **55** 35 25N 137 5 E
Tajitos **164** 30 58N 112 18W
Tajo, R. **57** 40 35N 1 52W
Tajumulco, Volcán de **165** 15 20N 91 50W
Tājūrā **119** 32 51N 13 27 E
Tak **100** 16 52N 99 8 E
Takachiho **110** 32 42N 131 18 E
Takahashi **110** 34 51N 133 39 E
Takaka **143** 40 51N 172 50 E
Takamatsu **110** 34 20N 134 5 E
Takanabe **110** 32 8N 131 30 E
Takaoka **111** 36 40N 137 0 E
Takapau **142** 40 2 S 176 21 E
Takapuna **142** 36 47 S 174 47 E
Takasago **110** 34 45N 134 48 E
Takasaki **111** 36 20N 139 0 E
Takase **110** 34 7N 133 48 E
Takatsuki **111** 34 51N 135 37 E
Takaungu **126** 3 38 S 39 52 E
Takawa **110** 33 47N 130 51 E
Takayama **111** 36 18N 137 11 E
Takayama-Bonchi **111** 36 0N 137 18 E
Takefu **111** 35 50N 136 10 E
Takehara **110** 34 21N 132 55 E
Takeley **29** 51 52N 0 16 E
Takeo, Camb. **101** 10 59N 104 47 E
Takeo, Japan **110** 33 12N 130 1 E
Tåkern **73** 58 22N 14 45 E
Takestan **92** 36 0N 49 50 E
Taketa **110** 32 58N 131 24 E
Takh **95** 33 6N 77 32 E
Takhman **101** 11 29N 104 57 E
Taki **135** 6 29 S 155 52 E
Takingeun **102** 4 45N 96 50 E
Takla L. **152** 55 15N 125 45W
Takla Landing **152** 55 30N 125 50W
Takla Makan **105** 39 0N 83 0 E
Takoradi **120** 4 58N 1 55W
Taku, China **107** 38 59N 117 41 E
Taku, Japan **110** 33 18N 130 3 E
Taku, R. **152** 58 30N 133 50W
Takuan **108** 27 44N 103 53 E
Takum **121** 7 18N 9 36 E
Takuma **110** 34 13N 133 40 E
Takushan **107** 39 55N 123 30 E
Tal-y-llyn **31** 52 40N 3 44W
Tal-y-sarn **31** 53 3N 4 12W
Tala, Uruguay **173** 34 21 S 55 46W
Tala, U.S.S.R. **77** 72 40N 113 30 E
Talach'in **106** 36 42N 104 54 E
Talagante **172** 33 40 S 70 50W
Talaint **118** 29 37N 9 45W
Talak **121** 18 0N 5 0 E
Talamanca, Cordillera de **166** 9 20N 83 20W
Talara **174** 4 30 S 81 10 E
Talas **85** 42 45N 72 0 E
Talas, R. **85** 44 0N 70 20 E
Talasea **135** 5 20 S 150 2 E
Talasskiy, Khrebet **85** 42 15N 72 0 E
Talata Mafara **121** 12 38N 6 4 E
Talaud, Kepulauan **103** 4 30N 127 10 E
Talavera de la Reina **56** 39 55N 4 46W
Talawana **136** 22 51 S 121 9 E
Talawgyi **98** 25 4N 97 19 E
Talayan **103** 6 52N 124 24 E
Talbot, C. **136** 13 48 S 126 43 E
Talbragar, R. **141** 32 5 S 149 15 E
Talca **172** 35 20 S 71 46W
Talca □ **172** 35 20 S 71 46W
Talcahuano **172** 36 40 S 73 10W
Talcher **96** 20 55N 85 3 E
Talcho **121** 14 35N 3 22 E
Taldom **81** 56 45N 37 29 E
Taldy Kurgan **76** 45 10N 78 45 E
Taleqan □ **93** 36 40N 69 30 E
Talesh, Kūhhā-Ye **92** 39 0N 48 30 E
Talfit **90** 32 5N 35 17 E
Talga, R. **136** 21 2 S 119 51 E
Talgar **85** 43 19N 77 15 E
Talgar, Pic **85** 43 5N 77 20 E
Talgarth **31** 51 59N 3 15W
Talguharai **122** 18 19N 35 56 E
Talguppa **93** 14 10N 74 45 E
Tali, Shensi, China **106** 34 48N 109 48 E
Tali, Yunnan, China **108** 25 45N 100 5 E
Tali Post **123** 5 55N 30 44 E
Taliabu, I. **103** 1 45 S 125 0 E
Taliang Shan **108** 28 0N 103 0 E
Talibong, Ko **101** 7 15N 99 23 E
Talihina **159** 34 45N 95 1W
Talikoti **96** 16 29N 76 17 E
Talimardzhan **85** 38 23N 65 37 E
Taling Ho, R. **107** 40 54N 121 38 E
Taling Sung **101** 15 5N 99 11 E
Talitsa **84** 57 0N 63 43 E
Taliwang **102** 8 50 S 116 55 E
Talkeetna **147** 62 20N 150 0W
Talkeetna Mts. **147** 62 20N 149 0W
Tall 'Asūr **90** 31 59N 35 77 E
Talla **122** 28 5N 30 43 E
Talladale **36** 57 41N 5 20W
Talladega **157** 33 28N 86 2W
Tallahassee **157** 30 25N 84 15W
Tallangatta **141** 36 15 S 147 10 E
Tallarook **141** 37 5 S 145 6 E
Tallåsen **72** 61 52N 16 2 E
Tallawang **141** 32 12 S 149 28 E
Tällberg **72** 60 51N 15 2 E
Tallebung **141** 32 42 S 146 34 E
Tallering Pk **137** 28 6 S 115 37 E
Tallinn (Reval) **80** 59 29N 24 58 E
Tallow **39** 52 6N 8 0W
Tallowbridge **39** 52 6N 8 1W
Tallulah **159** 32 25N 91 12W
Talluza **90** 32 17N 35 18 E
Talmage **153** 49 46N 103 40W
Talmest **118** 31 48N 9 21W
Talmont **44** 46 27N 1 37W
Talnoye **82** 48 57N 30 35 E
Taloda **96** 21 34N 74 19 E
Talodi **123** 10 35N 30 22 E
Talou Shan, mts. **108** 28 20N 107 10 E
Talovaya **81** 51 13N 40 38 E
Talpa de Allende **164** 20 23N 104 51W
Talsarnau **31** 52 54N 4 4W
Talsinnt **118** 32 33N 3 27W
Taltal **172** 25 23 S 70 40W
Taltson L. **153** 61 30N 110 15W
Taltson R. **152** 61 24N 112 46W
Talwood **139** 28 29 S 149 29 E
Talyawalka Cr. **140** 32 28 S 142 22 E
Talybont **31** 52 29N 3 59W
Tam Chau **101** 10 48N 105 12 E
Tam Ky **100** 15 34N 108 29 E
Tam Quan **100** 14 35N 109 3 E
Tama **158** 41 56N 92 37W
Tama Abu, Pegunungan **102** 3 10N 115 0 E
Tamala **137** 26 35 S 113 40 E
Tamalameque **174** 8 52N 73 49W
Tamale **121** 9 22N 0 50W
Taman **82** 45 14N 36 41 E
Tamana **110** 32 58N 130 32 E
Tamanar **118** 31 1N 9 46W
Tamano **110** 34 35N 133 59 E
Tamanrasset **119** 22 56N 5 30 E
Tamanrasset, O. **118** 22 0N 2 0 E
Tamanthi **98** 25 19N 95 17 E
Tamaqua **162** 40 46N 75 58W
Tamar, R. **30** 50 33N 4 15W
Tâmara **174** 5 50N 72 10W
Tamarang **141** 31 27 S 150 5 E
Tamarite de Litera **58** 41 52N 0 25 E
Tamashima **110** 34 32N 133 40 E
Tamási **53** 46 40N 18 18 E
Tamaské **121** 14 55N 5 55 E
Tamatave **129** 18 10 S 49 25 E
Tamatave □ **129** 18 0 S 49 0 E
Tamaulipas □ **165** 24 0N 99 0W
Tamaulipas, Sierra de **165** 23 30N 98 20W
Tamazula **164** 24 55N 106 58W
Tamazunchale **165** 21 16N 98 47W
Tambacounda **120** 13 55N 13 45W
Tambai **123** 16 32N 37 13 E
Tambelan, Kepulauan **102** 1 0N 107 30 E

Tambellup **137** 34 4S 117 37E
Tambo **138** 24 54S 146 14E
Tambo de Mora **174** 13 30S 76 20W
Tambohorano **129** 17 30S 43 58E
Tambora, G. **102** 8 12S 118 5E
Tamboritha, Mt. **141** 37 31S 146 51E
Tambov **81** 52 45N 41 20E
Tambre, R. **56** 42 55N 8 30W
Tambuku, G. **103** 7 8S 113 40E
Tamburâ **123** 5 40N 27 25E
Tamchaket **120** 17 25N 10 40W
Tamchok Khambab (Brahmaputra) **99** 29 25N 88 0E
Tamdybulak **85** 41 46N 64 36E
Tame **174** 6 28N 71 44W
Tame, R. **28** 52 43N 1 45W
Tamega, R. **56** 41 12N 8 5W
Tamelelt **119** 26 30N 6 14E
Tamenglong **98** 25 0N 93 35E
Tamerfors **75** 61 30N 23 50E
Tamerlanovka **85** 42 36N 69 17E
Tamerton Foliot **30** 50 25N 4 10W
Tamerza **119** 34 23N 7 58E
Tamgak, Mts. **121** 19 12N 8 35E
Tamiahua, Laguna de **165** 21 30N 97 30W
Tamil Nadu □ **97** 11 0N 77 0E
Tamines **47** 50 26N 4 36E
Taming **106** 36 20N 115 10E
Tamins **51** 46 50N 9 24E
Tamluk **95** 22 18N 87 58E
Tammisaari (Ekenäs) **75** 60 0N 23 26E
Tammun' **90** 32 18N 35 23E
Tamnaren **72** 60 10N 17 25E
Tamou **121** 12 45N 2 11E
Tampa **157** 27 57N 82 30W
Tampa B. **157** 27 40N 82 40W
Tampere **75** 61 30N 23 50E
Tampico **165** 22 20N 97 50W
Tampin **101** 2 28N 102 13E
Tamri **118** 30 49N 9 50W
Tamrida = Hadibu **91** 12 35N 54 2E
Tamsagbulag **105** 47 14N 117 21E
Tamsagout **118** 24 5N 6 35W
Tamsalu **80** 59 11N 26 8E
Tamsweg **52** 47 7N 13 49E
Tamu **99** 24 13N 94 12E
Tamuja, R. **57** 39 33N 6 8W
Tamworth, Austral. **141** 31 0S 150 58E
Tamworth, U.K. **28** 52 38N 1 41W
Tamyang **107** 35 19N 126 59E
Tan An **101** 10 32N 106 25E
Tana **74** 70 7N 28 5E
Tana Fd. **74** 70 35N 28 30E
Tana, L. **123** 13 5N 37 30E
Tana, R., Kenya **126** 0 50S 39 45E
Tana, R., Norway **48** 69 50N 26 0E
Tanabe **111** 33 44N 135 22E
Tanabi **171** 20 37S 49 37W
Tanacross **147** 63 40N 143 30W
Tanafjorden **74** 70 45N 28 25E
Tanagro, R. **65** 40 35N 15 25E
Tanahdjampea, I. **103** 7 10S 120 35E
Tanahgrogot **102** 1 55S 116 15E
Tanahmasa, I. **102** 0 5S 98 29E
Tanahmerah **103** 6 0S 140 7E
Tanami **136** 19 59S 129 43E
Tanami Des. **136** 18 50S 132 0E
Tanana **147** 65 10N 152 15W
Tanana, R. **147** 64 25N 145 30W
Tananarive **129** 18 55S 47 31E
Tananarive □ **129** 19 0S 47 0E
Tananarive = Antananarivo **125** 18 55S 47 31E
Tananger **71** 58 57N 5 37E
Tanant **118** 31 54N 6 56W
Tánaro, R. **62** 44 9N 7 50E
Tanaunella **64** 40 42N 9 45E
Tanba-Sanchi **111** 35 7N 135 48E
Tanbar **97** 25 55S 142 0E
Tancarville **42** 49 29N 0 28E
Tanchai **108** 25 58N 107 49E
T'anch'eng **107** 34 38N 118 21E
Tanda, U.P., India **95** 26 33N 82 35E
Tanda, U.P., India **95** 28 57N 78 56E
Tanda, Ivory C. **120** 7 48N 3 10W
Tandag **103** 9 4N 126 9E
Tandala **127** 9 25S 34 15E
Tândărei **70** 44 39N 27 40E
Tandil **172** 37 15S 59 6W
Tandjungpandan **102** 2 43S 107 38E
Tandlianwald **94** 31 3N 73 9E
Tando Adam **94** 25 45N 68 40E
Tandou L. **140** 32 40S 142 5E
Tandragee **38** 54 22N 6 23W
Tandsbyn **72** 63 0N 14 45W
Tandur **96** 19 11N 79 30E
Tane-ga-Shima **112** 30 35N 130 59E
Taneatua **142** 38 4S 177 1E
Tanen Range **101** 19 40N 99 0E
Tanen Tong Dan, Burma **99** 16 30N 98 30E
Tanen Tong Dan, Thai. **100** 19 43N 98 30E
Taneytown **162** 39 40N 77 10W
Tanezrouft **118** 23 9N 0 11E
Tanfeng **106** 33 45N 110 18E
Tang **38** 53 31N 7 49W
Tang, Koh **101** 10 16N 103 7E
Tang Krasang **101** 12 34N 105 3E
Tang La **99** 32 59N 92 17E
Tang Pass **99** 32 59N 92 17E
Tanga **99** 5 5S 39 2E
Tanga □ **126** 5 20S 38 0E
Tanga Is. **135** 3 20S 153 15E
Tangail **98** 24 15N 89 55E
Tanganyika, L. **126** 6 40S 30 0E
T'angch'i **109** 29 3N 119 24E
Tanger **118** 35 50N 5 49W
Tangerang **103** 6 12S 106 39E
Tangerhütte **48** 52 26N 11 50E
Tangermünde **48** 52 32N 11 57E
T'angho **109** 32 10N 112 20E
Tangier **162** 37 49N 75 59W
Tangier = Tanger **118** 35 50N 5 49W
Tangier I. **162** 37 50N 76 0W
Tangier Sd. **162** 38 3N 75 5W
Tangkak **101** 2 18N 102 34E
T'angku **107** 39 4N 117 45E
T'angkula Shanmo **98** 33 0N 92 0E
Tanglha Shan **99** 33 0N 90 0E
Tangorin P.O. **138** 21 47S 144 12E
Tangra Tso **99** 31 25N 85 30E
Tangshan **106** 34 25N 116 24E
T'angshan **107** 39 40N 118 10E
T'angt'ang **108** 26 29N 104 12E
T'angt'ou **107** 35 21N 118 32E
Tangt'u **109** 31 34N 118 29E
Tanguiéta **121** 10 40N 1 21E
Tangyang, Chekiang, China **109** 29 17N 120 14E
Tangyang, Hupeh, China **109** 30 50N 111 45E
Tangyen Ho, R. **108** 28 55N 108 36E
Tanimbar, Kepulauan **103** 7 30S 131 30E
Taning **106** 36 32N 110 47E
Taniyama **110** 31 31N 130 31E
Tanjay **103** 9 30N 123 5E
Tanjore = Thanjavur **97** 10 48N 79 12E
Tanjung **102** 2 10S 115 25E
Tanjung Malim **101** 3 42N 101 31E
Tanjungbalai **102** 2 55N 99 44E
Tanjungbatu **102** 2 23N 118 3E
Tanjungkarang **102** 5 20S 105 10E
Tanjungpinang **102** 1 5N 104 30E
Tanjungpriok **103** 6 8S 106 55E
Tanjungredeb **102** 2 9N 117 29E
Tanjungselor **102** 2 55N 117 25E
Tank **94** 32 14N 70 25E
Tankan Shan **109** 22 3N 114 16E
Tanleng **108** 30 2N 103 33E
Tanndalen **72** 62 33N 12 18E
Tannin **150** 49 40N 91 0W
Tannis B. **73** 57 40N 10 15E
Tano, R. **120** 6 0N 2 30W
Tanoumrout **119** 23 2N 5 31E
Tanout **121** 14 50N 8 55E
Tanquinho **171** 12 42S 39 43W
Tanshui **109** 25 10N 121 28E
Tanta **122** 30 45N 30 57E
Tantan **118** 28 29N 11 1W
Tantoyuca **165** 21 21N 98 10W
Tantung **107** 40 10N 124 23E
Tantura = Dor **90** 32 37N 34 55E
Tanuku **96** 16 45N 81 44E
Tanum **73** 58 42N 11 20E
Tanunda **140** 34 30S 139 0E
Tanur **97** 11 1N 75 46E
Tanus **44** 44 8N 2 19E
Tanworth **28** 52 20N 1 50W
Tanzania ■ **126** 6 40S 34 0E
Tanzawa-Sanchi **111** 35 27N 139 0E
Tanzilla, R. **152** 58 8N 130 43W
T'aoan **107** 45 20N 122 50E
Taoch'eng **108** 29 3N 100 10E
Taoerh Ho **107** 45 42N 124 5E
Taofu **108** 31 0N 101 9E
Taohsien **109** 25 37N 111 24E
T'aohua Tao **109** 29 48N 122 17E
T'aolo **106** 38 45N 106 40E
Taormina **65** 37 52N 15 16E
Taos **161** 36 28N 105 35W
Taoudenni **118** 22 40N 3 55W
Taoudrart, Adrar **118** 24 25N 2 24E
Taounate **118** 34 32N 4 41W
Taourirt, Alg. **118** 26 37N 0 8E
Taourirt, Moroc. **118** 34 20N 2 47W
Taouz **118** 31 2N 4 0W
T'aoyüan, China **109** 28 54N 111 29E
T'aoyüan, Taiwan **109** 25 0N 121 4E
Tapa **80** 59 15N 26 0E
Tapa Shan **108** 31 45N 109 30E
Tapachula **165** 14 54N 92 17W
Tapah **101** 4 12N 101 15E
Tapajós, R. **175** 4 30S 56 10W
Tapaktuan **102** 3 30N 97 10E
Tapanui **143** 45 56S 169 18E
Tapauá **174** 5 40S 64 20W
Tapauá, R. **174** 6 0S 65 40W
Tapeta **120** 6 36N 8 52W
Taphan Hin **100** 16 13N 100 16E
Tapia **56** 43 34N 6 56W
Tapieh Shan, mts. **109** 31 20N 115 30E
T'ap'ingchen **106** 33 42N 111 44E
Tapini **135** 8 19S 147 0E
Tápiószele **53** 47 45N 19 55E
Tapiraí **171** 19 52S 46 1W
Tapirapé, R. **170** 10 41S 50 38W
Tapirapecó, Serra **174** 1 10N 65 0W
Taplan **140** 34 33S 140 52E
Tapolca **53** 46 53N 17 29E
Tappahannock **162** 37 56N 76 50W
Tapsing **99** 30 22N 96 25E
Tapti, R. **96** 21 25N 75 0E
Tapu **109** 24 31N 116 41E
Tapuaenuku, Mt. **143** 41 55S 173 50E
Tapul Group, Is. **103** 5 35N 120 50E
Tapun **98** 18 22N 95 27E
Taquara **173** 29 36N 50 46W
Taquari, R. **173** 18 10S 56 0W
Taquaritinga **171** 21 24S 48 30W
Tara, Austral. **139** 27 17S 150 31E
Tara, Japan **110** 33 2N 130 11E
Tara, U.S.S.R. **76** 56 55N 74 30E
Tara, Zambia **127** 16 58S 26 45E
Tara-Dake **110** 32 58N 130 6E
Tara, R. **66** 43 10N 19 20E
Tarabagatay, Khrebet **77** 48 0N 83 0E
Tarābulus, Leb. **92** 34 31N 33 52E
Tarābulus, Libya **119** 32 49N 13 7E
Taradale **142** 39 33S 176 53E
Tarahouahout **119** 22 47N 5 59E
Tarakan **102** 3 20N 117 35E
Tarakit, Mt. **126** 2 2N 35 10E
Taralga **141** 34 26S 149 52E
Taramakau, R. **143** 42 34S 171 8E
Tarana **141** 33 31S 149 52E
Taranagar **94** 28 43N 75 9E
Taranaki □ **142** 39 5S 174 51E
Tarancón **58** 40 1N 3 1W
Taranga **94** 23 56N 72 43E
Taranga Hill **94** 24 0N 72 40E
Taransay, I. **36** 57 54N 7 0W
Taransay, Sd. of **36** 57 52N 7 0W
Táranto **65** 40 30N 17 11E
Táranto, G. di **65** 40 0N 17 15E
Tarapacá **174** 2 56S 69 46W
Tarapacá □ **172** 20 45S 69 30W
Tarare **45** 45 54N 4 26E
Tararua Range **142** 40 45S 175 25E
Tarascon, Ariège, France **44** 42 50N 1 37E
Tarascon, Bouches-du-Rhône, France **45** 43 48N 4 39E
Tarashcha **82** 49 30N 30 31E
Tarat, Bj. **119** 26 4N 9 7E
Tarauacá **174** 8 6S 70 48W
Tarauacá, R. **174** 7 30S 70 30W
Taravo, R. **45** 41 48N 8 52E
Tarawera **142** 39 2S 176 36E
Tarawera L. **142** 38 13S 176 27E
Tarawera Mt. **142** 38 14S 176 32E
Tarazat, Massif de **119** 20 2N 8 30E
Tarazona **58** 41 55N 1 43W
Tarazona de la Mancha **59** 39 16N 1 55W
Tarbat Ness **37** 57 52N 3 48W
Tarbela Dam **94** 34 0N 72 52E
Tarbert, Ireland **39** 52 34N 9 22W
Tarbert, Strathclyde, U.K. **34** 55 55N 5 25W
Tarbert, W. Isles, U.K. **36** 57 54N 6 49W
Tarbert, L. E. **36** 57 50N 6 45W
Tarbert, L. W., Strathclyde, U.K. **34** 55 58N 5 30W
Tarbert, L. W., W. Isles, U.K. **36** 57 55N 6 56W
Tarbes **44** 43 15N 0 3E
Tarbet, Highland, U.K. **36** 56 58N 5 38W
Tarbet, Strathclyde, U.K. **34** 56 13N 4 44W
Tarbolton **34** 55 30N 4 30W
Tarboro **157** 35 55N 77 3W
Tarbrax **138** 21 7S 142 26E
Tarbū **119** 26 0N 15 5E
Tarcento **63** 46 12N 13 12E
Tarcoola **139** 30 44S 134 36E
Tarcoon **139** 30 15S 146 35E
Tarcău, Munţii **70** 46 39N 26 7E
Tardets-Sorholus **44** 43 17N 0 52W
Taree **141** 31 50S 152 30E
Tarentaise **45** 45 30N 6 35E
Tarf Shaqq al Abd **122** 26 50N 36 6E
Tarfa, Wadi el **122** 28 16N 31 15E
Tarfaya **116** 27 55N 12 55W
Targon **44** 44 44N 0 16W
Targuist **118** 34 59N 4 14W
Tarhbalt **118** 30 48N 5 10W
Tarhit **118** 30 58N 2 0W
Tarhūnah **119** 32 15N 13 28E
Tari **135** 5 54S 142 59E
Tarib, Wadi **122** 18 30N 43 23E
Táriba **174** 7 49N 72 13W
Tarifa **57** 36 1N 5 36W
Tarija **172** 21 30S 64 40W
Tarija □ **172** 21 30S 63 30W
Tarim, R. **105** 41 5N 86 40E
Tarime □ **126** 1 15S 34 0E
Taringo Downs **141** 32 13S 145 33E
Taritoe, R. **103** 3 0S 138 5E
Tarka, R. **128** 32 10S 26 0E
Tarkastad **128** 32 0S 26 16E
Tarkhankut, Mys **82** 45 25N 32 30E
Tarko Sale **76** 64 55N 77 50E
Tarkwa **120** 5 20N 2 0W
Tarlac **103** 15 29N 120 35E
Tarland **37** 57 8N 2 51W
Tarleton **32** 53 41N 2 50W
Tarlsland **152** 57 03N 111 40W
Tarlton Downs **138** 22 40S 136 45E
Tarm **73** 55 56N 8 31E
Tarma **174** 11 25S 75 45W
Tarn □ **44** 43 49N 2 8E
Tarn-et-Garonne □ **44** 44 8N 1 20E
Tarn, R. **44** 44 5N 1 2E
Tärna **74** 65 45N 15 10E
Tarna, R. **53** 48 0N 20 5E
Tårnby **73** 55 37N 12 36E
Tarnobrzeg □ **54** 50 40N 22 0E
Tarnów **54** 50 3N 21 0E
Tarnów □ **54** 50 0N 21 0E
Tarnowskie Góry **54** 50 27N 18 54E
Táro, R. **62** 44 37N 9 58E
Tarong **139** 26 47S 151 51E
Taroom **139** 25 36S 149 48E
Taroudannt **118** 30 30N 8 52W
Tarp **48** 54 40N 9 25E
Tarpon Springs **157** 28 8N 82 42W
Tarporley **32** 53 10N 2 42W
Tarquinia **63** 42 15N 11 45E
Tarqumiyah **90** 31 35N 35 1E
Tarragona **58** 41 5N 1 17E
Tarragona □ **58** 41 0N 1 0E
Tarrasa **58** 41 26N 2 1E
Tárrega **58** 41 39N 1 9E
Tarrytown **162** 41 5N 73 52W
Tarshiha = Me'ona **90** 33 1N 35 15E
Tarso Emissi **119** 21 27N 18 36E
Tarso Ovrari **119** 21 27N 17 27E
Tarsus **92** 36 58N 34 55E
Tartagal **172** 22 30S 63 50W
Tartan, oilfield **19** 58 22N 0 5E
Tartas **44** 43 50N 0 49W
Tartna Point **140** 32 54S 142 24E
Tartu **80** 58 25N 26 58E
Tartus **92** 34 55N 35 55E
Tarumirim **171** 19 16S 41 59W
Tarumizu **110** 31 29N 130 42E
Tarussa **81** 54 44N 37 10E
Tarutao, Ko **101** 6 33N 99 40E
Tarutung **102** 2 0N 99 0E
Tarves **37** 57 22N 2 13W
Tarvisio **63** 46 31N 13 35E
Tarz Ulli **119** 25 46N 9 44E
Tas-Buget **85** 44 46N 65 33E
Tasahku **98** 27 33N 97 52E
Tasāwah **119** 26 0N 13 37E
Taschereau **150** 48 40N 78 40W
Taseko, R. **152** 52 4N 123 9W
Tasgaon **96** 17 2N 74 39E
Ta'shan **123** 16 31N 42 33E
Tashauz **76** 42 0N 59 20E
Tashet'ai **106** 41 0N 109 21E
Tashi Chho Dzong **98** 27 31N 89 45E
Tashihch'iao (Yingk'ou) **107** 40 38N 122 30E
T'ashihk'uerhkan **85** 37 47N 75 14E
Tashkent **85** 41 20N 69 10E
Tashkumyr **85** 41 40N 72 10E
Tashkurghan **93** 36 45N 67 40E
Tashtagol **76** 52 47N 87 53E
Tasikmalaya **103** 7 18S 108 12E
Tasjön **74** 64 15N 15 45E
Taşköpru **82** 41 30N 34 15E
Tasman Bay **143** 40 59S 173 25E
Tasman Glacier **143** 43 45S 170 20E
Tasman, Mt. **143** 43 34S 170 12E
Tasman Mts. **143** 41 3S 172 25E
Tasman Pen. **138** 43 10S 148 0E
Tasman, R. **143** 43 48S 170 8E
Tasman Sea **142** 36 0S 160 0E
Tasmania, I., □ **138** 49 0S 146 30E
Tassil Tin-Rerhoh **118** 20 5N 3 55E
Tassili n-Ajjer **119** 25 47N 8 1E
Tassili-Oua-Ahaggar **119** 20 41N 5 30E
Tasty **85** 44 47N 69 7E
Tasu Sd. **152** 52 47N 132 2W
Tata, Hung. **53** 47 37N 18 19E
Tata, Moroc. **118** 29 46N 7 50W
Tatabánya **53** 47 32N 18 25E
Tatar A.S.S.R. □ **84** 55 30N 51 30E
Tatarsk **76** 55 20N 75 50E
*Tatarskiy Proliv **77** 54 0N 141 0E
Tatebayashi **111** 36 15N 139 32E
Tateshina-Yama **111** 36 8N 138 11E
Tateyama **111** 35 0N 139 50E
Tathlina L. **152** 60 33N 117 39W
Tathra **141** 36 44S 149 59E
Tat'ien, Fukien, China **109** 25 42N 117 50E
Tat'ien, Szechwan, China **108** 26 18N 101 45E
Tatinnai L. **153** 60 55N 97 40W
Tatlayoka Lake **152** 51 35N 124 24W
Tatnam, C. **153** 57 16N 91 0W
Tato Ho, R. **108** 31 25N 100 42E
Tatra = Tatry **54** 49 20N 20 0E
Tatry **54** 49 20N 20 0E
Tatsu **108** 29 40N 105 45E
Tatsuno **110** 34 52N 134 33E
Tatta **94** 24 42N 67 55E
Tattenhall **32** 53 7N 2 47W
Tatu Ho, R. **108** 29 35N 103 47E
Tatuí **173** 23 25S 48 0W
Tatum **159** 33 16N 103 16W
Tat'ung, Anhwei, China **109** 30 48N 117 44E
Tat'ung, Shansi, China **106** 40 9N 113 19E
Tatura **141** 36 29S 145 16E
Tatvan **92** 37 28N 42 27E
Tauá **170** 6 1S 40 26W
Taubaté **173** 23 5S 45 30W
Tauberbischofsheim **49** 49 37N 9 40E
Taucha **48** 51 22N 12 31E
Tauern, mts. **52** 47 15N 12 40E
Tauern-tunnel **52** 47 0N 13 12E
Taufikia **123** 9 24N 31 37E
Taumarunui **142** 38 53S 175 15E
Taumaturgo **174** 9 0S 73 50W
Taung **128** 27 33S 24 47E
Taungdwingyi **98** 20 1N 95 40E
Taunggyi **98** 20 50N 97 0E
Taungtha **98** 20 45N 94 50E
Taungup **98** 18 51N 94 14E
Taungup Pass **98** 18 40N 94 45E
Taungup Taunggya **99** 18 20N 93 40E
Taunsa Barrage **95** 31 0N 71 0E
Taunton, U.K. **28** 51 1N 3 7W

**Renamed Sakhalinskiy Zalir*

Taunton, U.S.A. 162 41 54N 71 6W
Taunus 49 50 15N 8 20E
Taupo 142 38 41S 176 7E
Taupo, L. 142 38 46S 175 55E
Tauq 92 35 12N 44 29E
Taurage 80 55 14N 22 28E
Tauramena 174 5 1N 72 45W
Tauranga 142 37 35S 176 11E
Tauranga Harb. 142 37 30S 176 5E
Taureau, Lac 150 46 50N 73 40W
Tauri, R. 135 8 8S 146 8E
Taurianova 65 38 22N 16 1E
Taurus Mts. = Toros Dağlari 92 37 0N 35 0E
Táuste 58 41 58N 1 18W
Tauz 83 41 0N 45 40E
Tavani 153 62 10N 93 30W
Tavannes 50 47 13N 7 12E
Tavas 92 37 35N 29 8E
Tavda 84 58 7N 65 8E
Tavda, R. 84 59 30N 63 0E
Taverny 43 49 2N 2 13E
Taveta 124 3 31N 37 37E
Taviche 165 16 38N 96 32W
Tavignano, R. 45 42 7N 9 33E
Tavira 57 37 8N 7 40W
Tavistock 30 50 33N 4 9W
Tavolara, I. 64 40 55N 9 40E
Távora, R. 56 41 0N 7 30W
Tavoy 101 14 7N 98 18E
Tavoy, I. = Mali Kyun 99 13 0N 98 20E
Taw, R. 30 50 58N 3 58W
Tawang 99 27 37N 91 50E
Tawas City 156 44 16N 83 31W
Tawau 102 4 20N 117 55E
Tawngche 98 26 34N 95 38E
Tawnyinah 38 53 55N 8 45W
Tāworgha' 119 32 1N 15 2E
Taxila 94 33 42N 72 52E
Tay Bridge 35 56 28N 3 0W
Tay, Firth of 35 56 25N 3 8W
Tay, L., Austral. 137 32 55S 120 48E
Tay, L., U.K. 35 56 30N 4 10W
Tay Ninh 101 11 20N 106 5E
Tay, R. 35 56 37N 3 38W
Tay Strath 37 56 38N 3 40W
Tayabamba 174 8 15S 77 10W
Tayao 108 25 41N 101 18E
Tayaparva La 95 31 35N 83 20E
Tayeh 109 30 5N 114 57E
Taylor, Can. 152 56 13N 120 40W
Taylor, Alaska, U.S.A. 147 65 40N 164 50W
Taylor, Pa., U.S.A. 162 41 23N 75 43W
Taylor, Tex., U.S.A. 159 30 30N 97 30W
Taylor, Mt. 143 43 30S 171 20E
Taylor Mt. 161 35 16N 107 50W
Taylorville 158 39 32N 89 20W
Taymyr, Oz. 77 74 50N 102 0E
Taymyr, P-ov. 77 75 0N 100 0E
Taynuilt 34 56 25N 5 15W
Tayport 34 56 27N 2 52W
Tayr Zebna 90 33 14N 35 23E
Tayshet 77 55 58N 97 25E
Tayside □ 35 56 25N 3 30W
Taytay 103 10 45N 119 30E
Tayu 109 25 38N 114 9E
Tayülo 105 29 13N 98 13E
Tayung 109 29 8N 110 30E
Taz, R. 76 65 40N 82 0E
Taza 118 34 10N 4 0W
Taze 98 22 57N 95 24E
Tazenakht 118 30 46N 7 3W
Tazin L. 153 59 44N 108 42W
Tazin, R. 153 60 26N 110 45W
Tazoult 119 35 29N 6 11E
Tazovskiy 76 67 30N 78 30E
Tbilisi (Tiflis) 83 41 50N 44 50E
Tchad (Chad) ■ 117 12 30N 17 15E
Tchad, Lac 117 13 30N 14 30E
Tchaourou 121 8 58N 2 40E
Tchentlo L. 152 55 15N 125 0W
Tchibanga 124 2 45S 11 12E
Tchin Tabaraden 121 15 58N 5 50E
Tczew 54 54 8N 18 50E
Te Anau L. 143 45 15S 167 45E
Te Araroa 142 37 39S 178 25E
Te Aroha 142 37 32S 175 44E
Te Awamutu 142 38 1S 175 20E
Te Horo 142 40 48S 175 6E
Te Kaha 142 37 44S 177 44E
Te Karaka 142 38 26S 177 53E
Te Kauwhata 142 37 25S 175 9E
Te Kinga 143 42 35S 171 31E
Te Kopuru 142 36 2S 173 56E
Te Kuiti 142 38 20S 175 11E
Te Puke 142 37 46S 176 22E
Te Waewae B. 143 46 13S 167 33E
Tea Tree 136 22 11S 133 17E
Teacá 70 46 55N 24 30E
Teague 159 31 40N 96 20W
Tean 109 29 21N 115 42E
Teangue 36 57 7N 5 52W
Teano 65 41 15N 14 1E
Teapa 165 17 35N 92 56W
Teba 57 36 59N 4 55W
Tebay 32 54 25N 2 35W
Teberda 83 43 30N 43 54E
Tébessa 119 35 22N 8 8E
Tebicuary, R. 172 26 36S 58 16W
Tebing Tinggi 102 3 38S 102 1E
Tébourba 119 36 49N 9 51E
Téboursouk 119 36 29N 9 10E
Tebulos 83 42 36N 45 25E
Tecapa 163 35 51N 116 14W
Tecate 164 32 34N 116 38W
Techa, R. 84 56 13N 62 58E
Tech'ang 108 27 22N 102 10E
Techiang 108 28 19N 108 5E
Techiman 120 7 35N 1 58W
Tech'in 108 28 30N 98 52E
Tech'ing 109 23 8N 111 46E
Techirghiol 70 44 4N 28 32E
Techou 106 37 19N 116 19E
Tecomán 164 18 55N 103 53W
Tecoripa 164 28 37N 109 57W
Tecuci 70 45 51N 27 27E
Tecumseh 156 42 1N 83 59W
Tedavnet 38 54 19N 7 2W
Tedesa 123 5 10N 37 40E
Tedzhen 76 37 23N 60 31E
Tees B. 72 54 37N 1 10W
Tees, R. 33 54 36N 1 25W
Teesdale 32 54 37N 2 10W
Teesside 33 54 37N 1 13W
Tefé 174 3 25S 64 50W
Tegal 103 6 52S 109 8E
Tegelen 47 51 20N 6 9E
Teggiano 65 40 24N 15 32E
Teghra 95 25 30N 85 34E
Tegid, L. 31 52 53N 3 38W
Tegina 121 10 5N 6 11E
Tegucigalpa 166 14 10N 87 0W
Tehachapi 163 35 11N 118 29W
Tehachapi Mts. 163 35 0N 118 40W
Tehamiyam 122 18 26N 36 45E
Tehilla 122 17 42N 36 6E
Téhini 120 9 39N 3 32W
Tehrān 93 35 44N 51 30E
Tehrān □ 93 35 0N 49 30E
Tehsing 109 28 54N 117 34E
Tehua 109 25 30N 118 14E
Tehuacán 165 18 20N 97 30W
Tehuantepec 165 16 10N 95 19W
Tehuantepec, Golfo de 165 15 50N 95 0W
Tehuantepec, Istmo de 165 17 0N 94 30W
Tehui 107 44 32N 125 42E
Teich, Le 44 44 38N 0 59W
Teifi, R. 31 52 4N 4 14W
Teign, R. 30 50 41N 3 42W
Teignmouth 30 50 33N 3 30W
Teikovo 81 56 55N 40 30E
Teil, Le 45 44 33N 4 40E
Teilleul, Le 42 48 32N 0 53W
Teishyai 80 55 59N 22 14E
Teiuş 70 46 12N 23 40E
Teixeira 170 7 13S 37 15W
Teixeira de Sousa = Luau 124 10 40S 22 10E
Teixeira Pinto 120 12 10N 13 55E
Tejo, R. 57 39 15N 8 35W
Tejon Pass 163 34 49N 118 53W
Tejung 108 28 46N 99 19E
Tekamah 158 41 48N 96 14W
Tekapo, L. 143 43 53S 170 33E
Tekax 165 20 20N 89 30W
Tekeli 85 44 50N 79 0E
Tekeze, W. 123 13 50N 37 50E
Tekija 66 44 42N 22 26E
Tekirdağ 92 40 58N 27 30E
Tekkali 96 18 43N 84 24E
Teko 108 31 49N 98 40E
Tekoa 160 47 19N 117 4W
Tekoulât, O. 118 22 30N 2 20E
Tel Adashim 90 32 39N 35 17E
Tel Aviv-Yafo 90 32 4N 34 48E
Tel Hanan 90 32 47N 35 3E
Tel Hazor 90 33 2N 35 2E
Tel Lakhish 90 31 34N 34 51E
Tel Malhata 90 31 13N 35 2E
Tel Megiddo 90 32 35N 38 11E
Tel Mond 90 32 15N 34 56E
Tela 166 15 40N 87 28W
Télagh 118 34 51N 0 32W
Telanaipura = Jambi 102 1 38S 103 30E
Telavi 83 42 0N 45 30E
Telciu 70 47 25N 24 24E
Telefomin 135 5 10S 141 40E
Telega = Doftana 70 45 17N 25 45E
Telegraph Cr. 152 58 0N 131 10W
Telekhany 80 52 30N 25 46E
Telemark fylke □ 71 59 25N 8 30E
Telén 172 36 15S 65 31W
Teleneshty 70 47 35N 28 24E
Teleño 56 42 23N 6 22W
Teleorman □ 70 44 0N 25 0E
Teleorman, R. 70 44 15N 25 20E
Teles Pires (São Manuel), R. 174 8 40S 57 0W
Telescope Peak, Mt. 163 36 6N 117 7W
Teletaye 121 16 31N 1 30E
Telford 28 52 42N 2 31W
Telfs 52 47 19N 11 4E
Telgte 48 51 59N 7 46E
Telichie 139 31 45S 139 59E
Télimélé 120 10 54N 13 2W
Telkwa 152 54 41N 126 56W
Tell 90 32 12N 35 12E
Tell City 156 38 0N 86 44W
Teller 147 65 12N 166 24W
Tellicherry 97 11 45N 75 30E
Tellin 47 50 5N 5 13E
Telluride 161 37 58N 107 54W
Telok Anson 101 4 3N 101 0E
Teloloapán 165 18 21N 99 51W
Telom, R. 101 4 20N 101 46E
Telpos Iz. 78 63 35N 57 30E
Telsen 176 42 30S 66 50W
Teltow 48 52 24N 13 15E
Telukbetung 102 5 29S 105 17E
Telukbutun 101 4 5N 108 7E
Telukdalem 102 0 45N 97 50E
Tema 121 5 41N 0 0E
Temagami L. 150 47 0N 80 10W
Temanggung 103 7 18S 110 10E
Temapache 165 21 4N 97 38W
Temax 165 21 10N 88 50W
Tembe 126 0 30S 28 25E
Tembeling, R. 101 4 20N 102 23E
Tembleque 58 39 41N 3 30W
Temblor Ra, mts. 163 35 30N 120 0W
Tembuland □ 129 31 35S 28 0E
Teme, R. 28 52 23N 2 15W
Temecula 163 33 26N 117 6W
Temelelt 118 31 50N 7 32W
Temerloh 101 3 27N 102 25E
Temir Tau 76 53 10N 87 20E
Temirtau 76 50 5N 72 56E
Témiscaming 150 46 44N 79 5W
Temma 138 41 12S 144 42E
Temnikov 81 54 40N 43 11E
Temo, R. 64 40 20N 8 30E
Temora 141 34 30S 147 30E
Temosachic 164 28 58N 107 50W
Tempe, S. Afr. 161 29 1S 26 13E
Tempe, U.S.A. 161 33 26N 111 59W
Tempe Downs 136 24 22S 132 24E
Temperanceville 162 37 54N 75 33W
Tempestad 174 1 20S 74 56W
Tempino 102 1 55S 103 23E
Témpio Pausania 64 40 53N 9 6E
Temple 159 31 5N 97 28W
Temple B. 138 12 15S 143 3E
Temple Combe 28 51 0N 2 25W
Temple Ewell 29 51 9N 1 16W
Temple Sowerby 30 54 38N 2 33W
Templemore 39 52 48N 7 50W
Templenoe 39 51 52N 9 40W
Templeton, Austral. 138 18 30S 142 30E
Templeton, U.K. 31 51 46N 4 45W
Templeton, U.S.A. 163 35 33N 120 42W
Templeton, R. 138 21 0S 138 40E
Templeuve 47 50 39N 3 17E
Templin 48 53 8N 13 31E
Tempo 38 54 23N 7 28W
Tempoal 165 21 31N 98 23W
Temryuk 82 45 15N 37 11E
Temse 47 51 7N 4 13E
Temska, R. 66 43 17N 22 33E
Temuco 176 38 50S 72 50W
Temuka 143 44 14S 171 17E
Ten Boer 46 53 16N 6 42E
Tena 174 0 59S 77 49W
Tenabo 165 20 2N 90 12W
Tenaha 159 31 57N 94 15W
Tenali 96 16 15N 80 35E
Tenancingo 165 19 0N 99 33W
Tenango 165 19 0N 99 40W
Tenasserim 100 12 6N 99 3E
Tenasserim □ 100 14 0N 98 30E
Tenay 45 45 55N 5 30E
Tenbury 28 52 18N 2 35W
Tenby 31 51 40N 4 42W
Tenda 45 44 5N 7 34E
Tenda, Col de 45 44 9N 7 32E
Tendaho 123 11 39N 40 54E
Tende 45 44 5N 7 35E
Tendelti 123 13 1N 31 55E
Tendjedi, Adrar 119 23 41N 7 32E
Tendrara 118 33 3N 1 58W
Tendre, Mt. 50 46 35N 6 18E
Teneida 122 25 30N 29 19E
Ténéré 119 23 2N 16 0E
Tenerife, I. 116 28 20N 16 40W
Ténès 118 36 31N 1 14E
T'eng Ch'ung 99 25 9N 98 22E
Teng, R. 101 20 30N 98 10E
Tengah □ 103 2 0S 122 0E
Tengah Kepulauan 102 7 5S 118 15E
Tengchow = P'englai 107 37 49N 120 47E
Tengch'uan 108 26 0N 100 4E
Tengch'ung 108 25 2N 98 28E
Tengfeng 106 34 27N 113 2E
Tenggara □ 103 3 0S 122 0E
Tenggol, P. 101 4 48N 103 41E
T'enghsien, Honan, China 109 32 41N 112 5E
T'enghsien, Kwangsi Chuang, China 109 23 23N 110 54E
T'enghsien, Shantung, China 105 35 8N 117 9E
Tengiz, Ozero 76 50 30N 69 0E
Tengko 99 32 30N 98 0E
Tengk'o 108 32 32N 97 35E
Tengk'ou 106 40 18N 106 59E
Tenigerbad 51 46 42N 8 57E
Tenille 157 32 58N 82 50W
Tenindewa 137 28 30S 115 20E
Tenkasi 97 8 55N 77 20E
Tenke, Congo 127 11 22S 26 40E
Tenke, Zaïre 127 10 32S 26 7E
Tenkodogo 121 12 0N 0 10W
Tenna, R. 63 43 12N 13 43E
Tennant Creek 136 19 30S 134 0E
'Tenneco', oilfield 19 54 6N 4 42E
Tennessee □ 155 36 0N 86 30W
Tenneville 47 50 6N 5 32E
Tennsift, Oued 118 32 3N 9 28W
Tenom 102 5 4N 115 38E
Tenosique 165 17 30N 91 24W
Tenri 111 34 46N 135 55E
Tenryū 111 34 52N 137 55E
Tent L. 153 62 25N 107 54W
Tenterden 29 51 4N 0 42E
Tenterfield 139 29 0S 152 0E
Teófilo Otôni 171 17 50S 41 30W
Tepa 120 6 57N 2 30W
Tepalcatepec, R. 164 18 35N 101 59W
Tepao 108 23 21N 106 33E
Tepehuanes 164 25 21N 105 44W
Tepetongo 164 22 28N 103 9W
Tepic 164 21 30N 104 54W
Tepi'ng 107 37 28N 116 67E
Teploklyuchenka 85 42 30N 78 30E
Tepoca, C. 164 29 20N 112 25W
Tequila 164 20 54N 103 47W
Ter Apel 46 52 53N 7 5E
Ter, R. 58 42 0N 2 30E
Téra 121 14 0N 0 57E
Tera, R. 56 41 54N 5 44W
Téramo 63 42 40N 13 40E
Terang 140 38 15S 142 55E
Terawhiti, C. 142 41 16S 174 38E
Terborg 46 51 56N 6 22E
Tercan 92 39 50N 40 30E
Terceira 16 38 43N 27 13W
Tercero, R. 172 32 58S 61 47W
Terdal 96 16 33N 75 9E
Terebovlya 80 49 18N 25 44E
Teregova 70 45 10N 22 16E
Terek-Say 85 41 30N 71 11E
Terembone Cr. 139 30 25S 148 50E
Terengganu □ 101 4 55N 103 0E
Tereshka, R. 81 52 0N 46 36E
Teresina 170 5 2S 42 45W
Terewah L. 139 29 52S 147 35E
Terezinha 174 0 44N 69 27W
Terges, R. 57 37 49N 7 41W
Tergnier 43 49 40N 3 17E
Terhazza 118 23 45N 4 59W
Terheijden 47 51 38N 4 45E
Teriang 101 3 15N 102 26E
Terkezi 117 18 27N 21 40E
Terlizzi 65 41 8N 16 32E
Termas de Chillan 172 36 50S 71 31W
Terme 82 41 11N 37 0E
Termez 85 37 0N 67 15E
Términi Imerese 43 37 59N 13 51E
Términos, Laguna de 165 18 35N 91 30W
Termoli 63 42 0N 15 0E
Termon 38 55 3N 7 50W
Termonfeckin 38 53 47N 6 15W
Tern, oilfield 19 61 17N 0 55E
Ternate 103 0 45N 127 25E
Terneuzen 47 51 20N 3 50E
Terney 77 45 3N 136 37E
Terni 63 42 34N 12 38E
Ternitz 52 47 43N 16 2E
Ternopol 80 49 30N 25 40E
Terowie, N.S.W., Austral. 139 32 27S 147 52E
Terowie, Vic., Austral. 140 33 10S 138 50E
Terra Bella 163 35 58N 119 3W
Terra Nova B. 13 74 50S 164 40E
Terrace 152 54 30N 128 35W
Terrace Bay 150 48 47N 87 10W
Terracina 64 41 17N 13 12E
Terralba 64 39 42N 8 38E
Terranuova 63 43 38N 11 35E
Terrasini Favarotta 64 38 10N 13 4E
Terrasson 44 45 7N 1 19E
Terrebonne B. 159 29 15N 90 28W
Terrecht 118 20 10N 0 10W
Terrell 159 32 44N 96 19W
Terrenceville 151 47 40N 54 44W
Terrick Terrick 138 24 44S 145 5E
Terry 158 46 47N 105 20W
Terryglass 39 53 3N 8 14W
Terryville 162 41 41N 73 1W
Terschelling, I. 46 53 25N 5 20E
Terskey Alatau, Khrebet 85 41 50N 77 0E
Terter, R. 83 40 5N 46 15E
Teruel 58 40 22N 1 8W
Teruel □ 58 40 48N 1 0W
Tervel 67 43 45N 27 28E
Tervola 74 66 6N 24 49E
Teryaweyna L. 140 32 18S 143 22E
Tešanj 66 44 38N 17 59E
Teseney 123 15 5N 36 42E
Tesha, R. 81 55 32N 43 0E
Teshio 112 44 53N 141 44E
Teshio-Gawa, R. 112 44 53N 141 45E
Tešica 66 43 27N 21 45E
Tesiyn Gol, R. 105 50 28N 93 4E
Teslin 147 60 10N 132 43W
Teslin L. 152 60 15N 132 57W
Teslin, R. 152 61 34N 134 35W
Teslió 66 44 37N 17 54E
Teso □ = Eastern □ 126 1 50N 33 45E
Tessalit 121 20 12N 1 0E
Tessaoua 121 13 47N 7 56E
Tessenderlo 47 51 4N 5 5E
Tessier 153 51 48N 107 26W
Tessin 48 54 2N 12 28E
Tessit 121 15 13N 0 18E
Test, R. 28 51 7N 1 30W
Testa del Gargano 65 41 50N 16 10E
Teste, La 44 44 37N 1 8W
Tét 53 47 30N 17 33E
Tetachuck L. 152 53 18N 125 55W
Tetas, Pta. 172 23 31S 70 38W
Tetbury 28 51 37N 2 9W

Tete 127 16 13 S 33 33 E
Tete □ 127 15 15 S 32 40 E
Teterev, R. 80 50 30N 29 30 E
Teteringen 47 51 37N 4 49 E
Teterow 48 53 45N 12 34 E
Teteven 67 42 58N 24 17 E
Tethull, R. 152 60 35N 112 12W
Tetiyev 82 49 22N 29 38 E
Tetlin 147 63 14N 142 50W
Tetlin Junction 147 63 29N 142 55W
Tetney 33 53 30N 0 1W
Teton, R. 160 47 58N 111 0W
Tétouan 118 35 35N 5 21W
Tetovo 66 42 1N 21 2 E
Tettenhall 28 52 35N 2 7W
Tetuán = Tétouan 118 35 30N 5 25W
Tetyukhe 77 44 45N 135 40 E
Teuco, R. 172 25 30 S 60 25W
Teufen 51 47 24N 9 23 E
Teulada 64 38 59N 8 47 E
Teulon 153 50 23N 97 16W
Tevere, R. 63 42 30N 12 20 E
Teviot, R. 35 55 21N 2 51W
Teviotdale 35 55 25N 2 50W
Teviothead 35 55 19N 2 55W
Tewantin 139 26 27 S 153 3 E
Tewkesbury 28 51 59N 2 8W
Texada I. 152 49 40N 124 25W
Texarkana, Ark., U.S.A. 159 33 25N 94 0W
Texarkana, Tex., U.S.A. 159 33 25N 94 3W
Texas 139 28 49 S 151 15 E
Texas □ 159 31 40N 98 30W
Texas City 159 27 20N 95 20W
Texel, I. 46 53 5N 4 50 E
Texhoma 159 36 32N 101 47W
Texline 159 36 26N 103 0W
Texoma L. 159 34 0N 96 38W
Teyang 108 31 8N 104 24 E
Teykovo 81 56 55N 40 30 E
Teynham 29 51 19N 0 50 E
Teyr Zebna 90 33 14N 35 23 E
Teza, R. 81 56 41N 41 45 E
Tezin 94 34 24N 69 30 E
Teziutlán 165 19 50N 97 30W
Tezpur 98 26 40N 92 45 E
Tezzeron L. 152 54 43N 124 30W
Tha-anne, R. 153 60 31N 94 37W
Tha Deua, Laos 100 17 57N 102 38 E
Tha Deua, Laos 100 19 26N 101 50 E
Tha Nun 101 8 12N 98 17 E
Tha Pia 100 17 48N 100 32 E
Tha Rua 100 14 34N 100 44 E
Tha Sala 101 8 40N 99 56 E
Tha Song Yang 101 17 34N 97 55 E
Thaba Putsoa, mt. 129 29 45 S 28 0 E
Thabana Ntlenyana, Mt. 129 29 30 S 29 9 E
Thabazimbi 129 24 40 S 26 4 E
Thabeikkyin 98 22 53N 95 59 E
Thai Binh 100 20 27N 106 20 E
Thai Muang 101 8 24N 98 16 E
Thai Nguyen 100 21 35N 105 46 E
Thailand (Siam) ■ 100 16 0N 102 0 E
Thakhek 100 17 25N 104 45 E
Thakurgaon 98 26 2N 88 28 E
Thal 94 33 28N 70 33 E
Thal Desert 93 31 0N 71 30 E
Thala 119 35 35N 8 40 E
Thala La 99 28 25N 97 23 E
Thalabarivat 100 13 33N 105 57 E
Thalkirch 51 46 39N 9 17 E
Thallon 139 28 30 S 148 57 E
Thalwil 51 47 17N 8 35 E
Thame 29 51 44N 0 58W
Thame, R. 29 51 52N 0 47W
Thames 142 37 7 S 175 34 E
Thames, Firth of 142 37 0 S 175 25 E
Thames, R., Can. 150 42 20N 82 25W
Thames, R., N.Z. 142 37 32 S 175 45 E
Thames, R., U.K. 28 51 30N 0 35 E
Thames, R., U.S.A. 162 41 18N 72 9W
Thāmit, W. 119 30 51N 16 14 E
Than Uyen 100 22 0N 103 54 E
Thana 96 19 12N 72 59 E
Thanbyuzayat 98 15 58N 97 44 E
Thanesar 94 30 1N 76 52 E
Thanet, I. of 29 51 21N 1 20 E
Thang Binh 101 15 50N 108 20 E
Thangoo P.O. 136 18 10 S 122 22 E
Thangool 138 24 29 S 150 35 E
Thanh Hoa 100 19 48N 105 46 E
Thanh Hung 101 9 55N 105 43 E
Thanh Thuy 100 22 55N 104 51 E
Thanjavur (Tanjore) 97 10 48N 79 12 E
Thanlwin myit, R. 99 20 0N 98 0 E
Thann 43 47 48N 7 5 E
Thaon 43 48 15N 6 25 E
Thap Sakae 101 11 30N 99 37 E
Thap Than 100 15 27N 99 54 E
Thar (Great Indian) Desert 94 28 25N 72 0 E
Tharad 94 24 30N 71 30 E
Thargomindah 139 27 58 S 143 46 E
Tharrawaddy 98 17 38N 95 48 E
Tharrawaw 98 17 41N 95 28 E
Tharthār, Bahr ath 92 34 0N 43 0 E
Thasopoúla, I. 68 40 49N 24 45 E
Thásos 68 40 50N 24 50 E
Thásos, I. 68 40 40N 24 40 E
That Khe 100 22 16N 106 28 E
Thatcham 28 51 24N 1 17W
Thatcher, Ariz., U.S.A. 161 32 54N 109 46W
Thatcher, Colo., U.S.A. 161 37 38N 104 6W
Thaton 98 16 55N 97 22 E
Thau, Étang de 44 43 23N 3 36 E
Thaungdut 98 24 30N 94 40 E
Thaxted 29 51 57N 0 20 E
Thayer 159 36 34N 91 34W
Thayetmyo 98 19 20N 95 18 E
Thayngen 51 47 49N 8 43 E
Thazi 99 21 0N 96 5 E
The Alberga, R. 139 27 6 S 135 33 E
The Bight 167 24 19N 75 24W
The Corrong 139 36 0 S 139 30 E
The Dalles 160 45 40N 121 11W
The Diamantina 139 26 45 S 139 30 E
The English Company's Is. 138 11 50 S 136 32 E
The Entrance 141 33 21 S 151 30 E
The Four Archers 138 15 31 S 135 22 E
The Frome, R. 139 29 8 S 137 54 E
The Granites 136 20 35 S 130 21 E
The Great Divide 141 35 0 S 149 17 E
The Grenadines, Is. 167 12 30N 61 30W
The Hague (s'Gravenhage) 47 52 7N 7 14 E
The Hamilton, R. 139 26 40 S 135 19 E
The Johnston Lakes 137 32 25 S 120 30 E
The Lake 167 21 5N 73 34W
The Loup 38 54 42N 6 32W
The Macumba, R. 139 27 52 S 137 12 E
The Neales, R. 139 28 8 S 136 47 E
The Oaks 141 34 3 S 150 34 E
The Officer, R. 137 27 46 S 129 46 E
The Pas 153 53 45N 101 15W
The Range 127 19 2 S 31 2 E
The Rock 141 35 15 S 147 2 E
The Salt Lake 139 30 6 S 142 8 E
The Stevenson, R. 139 27 6 S 135 33 E
The Thumbs, Mts. 143 43 35 S 170 40 E
The Warburton, R. 139 28 4 S 137 28 E
Theale 28 51 26N 1 5W
Thebes 122 25 40N 32 35 E
Thedford 158 41 59N 100 31W
Theebine 139 25 57 S 152 34 E
Thekulthili L. 153 61 3N 110 0W
Thelma, oilfield 19 58 25N 1 18 E
Thelon, R. 153 62 35N 104 3W
Thénezay 42 46 44N 0 2W
Thenon 44 45 9N 1 4 E
Theodore 138 24 55 S 150 3 E
Thepha 101 6 52N 100 58 E
Thérain, R. 43 49 15N 2 27 E
Thermaïkos Kólpos 68 40 15N 22 45 E
Thermopílai P. 69 38 48N 22 45 E
Thermopolis 160 43 14N 108 10W
Thesprotia □ 68 39 27N 20 22 E
Thessalía □ 68 39 30N 22 0 E
Thessalon 150 46 20N 83 30W
Thessaloníki 68 40 38N 23 0 E
Thessaloníki □ 68 40 45N 23 0 E
Thessaly = Thessalía 68 39 30N 22 0 E
Thetford 29 52 25N 0 44 E
Thetford Mines 151 46 8N 71 18W
Theun, R. 100 18 19N 104 0 E
Theunissen 128 28 26 S 26 43 E
Theux 47 50 32N 5 49 E
Thevenard 139 32 9 S 133 38 E
Thiámis, R. 68 39 34N 20 18 E
Thiberville 42 49 8N 0 27 E
Thicket Portage 153 55 19N 97 42W
Thief River Falls 159 48 15N 96 10W
Thiel 120 14 55N 15 5W
Thiene 63 45 42N 11 29 E
Thierache 43 49 51N 3 45 E
Thiers 44 45 52N 3 33 E
Thies 120 14 50N 16 51W
Thiet 123 7 37N 28 49 E
Thika 126 1 1 S 37 5 E
Thika □ 126 1 1 S 37 5 E
Thille-Boubacar 120 16 31N 15 5W
Thillot, Le 43 47 53N 6 46 E
Thimphu (Tashi Chho Dzong) 98 27 31N 89 45 E
þingvallavatn 74 64 11N 21 9W
Thionville 43 49 20N 6 10 E
Thírá 69 36 23N 25 27 E
Thirasiá, I. 69 36 26N 25 21 E
Thirlmere, L. 32 54 32N 3 4W
Thirsk 33 54 15N 1 20W
Thisted 75 56 58N 8 40 E
Thistle I. 140 35 0 S 136 8 E
Thistle, oilfield 19 61 20N 1 35 E
Thitgy 98 18 15N 96 13 E
Thitpokpin 98 19 24N 96 1 E
Thiu Khao Phetchabun 101 16 20N 100 55 E
Thívai 69 38 19N 23 19 E
Thiviers 44 45 25N 0 54 E
Thizy 45 46 2N 4 18 E
þjorsa 74 63 47N 20 48W
Thlewiaza, R., Man., Can. 153 59 43N 100 5W
Thlewiaza, R., N.W.T., Can. 153 60 29N 94 40W
Thmar Puok 100 13 57N 103 4 E
Tho Vinh 100 19 16N 105 42 E
Thoa, R. 153 60 31N 109 47W
Thoen 100 17 36N 99 12 E
Thoeng 100 19 41N 100 12 E
Thoissey 45 46 12N 4 48 E
Tholdi 95 35 5N 76 6 E
Tholen 47 51 32N 4 13 E
Thomas, Okla., U.S.A. 159 35 48N 98 48W
Thomas, W. Va., U.S.A. 156 39 10N 79 30W
Thomas, L. 139 26 4 S 137 58 E
Thomas Street 38 53 27N 8 15W
Thomastown 39 52 32N 7 10W
Thomasville, Ala., U.S.A. 157 31 55N 87 42W
Thomasville, Fla., U.S.A. 157 30 50N 84 0W
Thomasville, N.C., U.S.A. 157 35 5N 80 4W
Thommen 47 50 14N 6 5 E
Thompson, Can. 153 55 45N 97 52W
Thompson, U.S.A. 162 41 52N 75 31W
Thompson Falls 160 47 37N 115 26W
Thompson Landing 153 62 56N 110 40W
Thompson, R., Can. 152 50 15N 121 24W
Thompson, R., U.S.A. 158 39 46N 93 37W
Thompsons 161 39 0N 109 50W
Thompsonville 162 42 0N 72 37W
Thomson, R. 138 25 11 S 142 53 E
Thomson's Falls = Nyahururu Falls 126 0 2N 36 27 E
Thon Buri 100 13 43N 100 29 E
Thonburi 101 13 50N 100 36 E
Thônes 45 45 54N 6 18 E
Thongwa 98 16 45N 96 33 E
Thonon-les-Bains 45 46 22N 6 29 E
Thonze 98 17 38N 95 47 E
Thorez 83 48 4N 38 34 E
þorlákshöfn 74 63 51N 21 22W
Thornaby on Tees 33 54 36N 1 19W
Thornborough 138 16 54 S 145 2 E
Thornbury, N.Z. 143 46 17 S 168 9 E
Thornbury, U.K. 28 51 36N 2 31W
Thorndon 29 52 16N 1 8 E
Thorne, U.K. 33 53 36N 0 56W
Thorne, U.S.A. 163 38 36N 118 34W
Thorne Glacier 13 87 30N 150 0 E
Thorney 29 52 37N 0 8W
Thornham 29 52 59N 0 35 E
Thornhill 35 55 15N 3 46W
Thornthwaite 32 54 36N 3 13W
Thornton-Beresfield 141 32 50 S 151 40 E
Thornton Celveleys 32 53 52N 3 1W
Thornton Dale 33 54 14N 0 41W
Thorpe 29 52 38N 1 20 E
Thorpe le Soken 29 51 50N 1 11 E
Thouarcé 43 47 17N 0 30W
Thouin, C. 136 20 20 S 118 10 E
Thousand Oakes 163 34 10N 118 50W
Thrace = Thráki 68 41 10N 25 30 E
Thráki 68 41 9N 25 30 E
Thrakikón Pélagos 68 40 30N 25 0 E
Thrapston 29 52 24N 0 32W
Three Bridges 29 51 7N 0 9W
Three Forks 160 45 5N 111 40W
Three Hills 152 51 43N 113 15W
Three Hummock I. 138 40 25 S 144 55 E
Three Kings Is. 142 34 10 S 172 10 E
Three Lakes 158 45 41N 89 10W
Three Pagodas P. 100 15 16N 98 23 E
Three Points, C. 120 4 42N 2 6W
Three Rivers, Austral. 137 25 10 S 119 5 E
Three Rivers, Calif., U.S.A. 163 36 26N 118 54W
Three Rivers, Tex., U.S.A. 159 28 30N 98 10W
Three Sisters, Mt. 160 44 10N 121 52W
Threlkeld 32 54 37N 3 2W
Threshfield 32 54 5N 2 2W
þ ó risvatn 74 64 50N 19 26W
Throssell, L. 137 27 27 S 124 16 E
Throssell Ra. 136 17 24 S 126 4 E
þ ó rshöfn 74 66 12N 15 20W
Thrumster 37 58 24N 3 8W
Thuan Moa 101 8 58N 105 30 E
Thubun Lakes 153 61 30N 112 0W
Thueyts 45 44 41N 4 9 E
Thuillies 47 50 18N 4 20 E
Thuin 47 50 20N 4 17 E
Thuir 44 42 38N 2 45 E
Thule 12 77 30N 69 0W
Thun 50 46 45N 7 38 E
Thundelarra 137 28 53 S 117 7 E
Thunder B. 156 45 0N 83 20W
Thunder Bay 150 48 20N 89 0W
Thunder River 152 52 13N 119 20W
Thundulda 137 32 15 S 126 3 E
Thunersee 50 46 43N 7 39 E
Thung Song 101 8 10N 99 40 E
Thunkar 98 27 55N 91 0 E
Thuong Tra 100 16 2N 107 42 E
Thur, R. 51 47 32N 9 10 E
Thurgau □ 51 47 34N 9 10 E
Thüringer Wald 48 50 35N 11 0 E
Thurlby 29 52 45N 0 21W
Thurles 39 52 40N 7 53W
Thurloo Downs 139 29 15 S 143 30 E
Thurmaston 28 52 40N 1 8W
Thurmont 162 39 37N 77 25W
Thurn P. 49 47 20N 12 15 E
Thursby 32 54 40N 3 3W
Thursday I. 138 10 30 S 142 3 E
Thurso, Can. 150 45 36N 75 15W
Thurso, U.K. 37 58 34N 3 31W
Thurso, R. 37 58 36N 3 30W
Thurston I. 13 72 0 S 100 0W
Thury-Harcourt 42 49 0N 0 30W
Thusis 51 46 42N 9 26 E
Thutade L. 152 57 0N 126 55W
Thuy, Le 100 17 14N 106 49 E
Thylungra 139 26 4 S 143 28 E
Thyolo 127 16 7 S 35 5 E
Thysville = Mbanza Ngungu 124 5 12 S 14 53 E
Ti-n-Amzi, O. 121 17 35N 4 20 E
Ti-n-Barraouene, O. 121 18 40N 4 5 E
Ti-n-Emensan 118 22 59N 4 45 E
Ti-n-Geloulet 118 25 58N 4 2 E
Ti-n-Medjerdam, O. 118 25 45N 1 30W
Ti-n-Tarabine, O. 119 21 37N 7 11 E
Ti-n-Zaouaténe 118 48 55 S 77 9W
Tia 141 31 10 S 151 50 E
Tiahualilo 164 26 20N 103 30W
Tianguá 170 3 44 S 40 59W
Tiankoura 120 10 47N 3 17W
Tiaret (Tagdent) 118 35 28N 1 21 E
Tiarra 141 32 46 S 145 1 E
Tiassalé 120 5 58N 4 57W
Tibagi 173 24 30 S 50 24W
Tibagi, R. 173 22 47 S 51 1W
Tibari 123 5 2N 31 48 E
Tibati 121 6 22N 12 30 E
Tiber = Tevere, R. 63 42 30N 12 20 E
Tiber Res. 160 48 20N 111 15W
Tiberias 90 32 47N 35 32 E
Tiberias, L. = Kinneret, Yam 90 32 49N 35 36 E
Tibesti 119 21 0N 17 30 E
Tibet 99 32 30N 86 0 E
Tibet □ 105 32 30N 86 0 E
Tibiri 121 13 34N 7 4 E
Tibleş, mt. 70 47 32N 24 15 E
Tibleş, Mţii 70 47 41N 24 6 E
Tibnīn 90 33 12N 35 24 E
Tibooburra 139 29 26 S 142 1 E
Tibro 73 58 28N 14 10 E
Tibugá, Golfo de 174 5 45N 77 20W
Tiburón, I. 164 29 0N 112 30W
Ticehurst 29 51 2N 0 23 E
Tichit 120 18 35N 9 20W
Ticino □ 51 46 20N 8 45 E
Ticino, R. 62 45 23N 8 47 E
Tickhill 33 53 25N 1 8W
Ticonderoga 162 43 50N 73 28W
Ticul 165 20 20N 89 50W
Tidaholm 73 58 12N 13 55 E
Tiddim 98 23 20N 93 45 E
Tideridjaouine, Adrar 118 23 0N 2 15 E
Tideswell 33 53 17N 1 46W
Tidikelt 118 26 58N 1 30 E
Tidjikdja 120 18 4N 11 35W
Tidore 103 0 40N 127 25 E
Tidra, I. 120 19 45N 16 20W
Tiébélé 121 11 6N 0 59W
Tiébissou 120 7 9N 5 18W
Tiéboro 119 21 20N 17 7 E
Tiefencastel 51 46 40N 9 33 E
Tiego 120 12 6N 2 38 E
T'iehling 107 42 17N 123 50 E
Tiel 46 51 53N 5 26 E
Tielt 47 51 0N 3 20 E
Tien Shan 85 42 0N 80 0 E
Tien Yen 100 21 20N 107 24 E
T'ienchang 107 32 41N 118 59 E
T'ienchen 106 40 30N 114 6 E
Tiench'eng 109 21 31N 111 18 E
T'ienching 107 39 10N 117 15 E
T'ienchu 108 26 55N 109 12 E
T'iench'üan 108 30 4N 102 50 E
T'ienchuangt'ai 107 40 49N 122 6 E
Tienen 47 50 48N 4 57 E
T'ienho 108 24 47N 108 42 E
T'ienhsi 108 24 26N 106 5 E
Tiénigbé 120 8 11N 5 43W
Tienkianghsien 69 30 25N 107 30 E
T'ienlin 108 24 19N 106 15 E
T'ienmen 109 30 37N 113 10 E
T'ieno 108 25 9N 106 57 E
Tienpai 109 21 30N 111 1 E
T'ienshui 105 34 35N 105 15 E
T'ient'ai 109 29 9N 121 2 E
Tientsin = T'ienching 105 39 10N 117 15 E
T'ientung 108 23 39N 107 8 E
T'ienyang 108 23 43N 106 44 E
Tierp 72 60 20N 17 30 E
Tierra Alta 174 8 11N 76 4W
Tierra Amarilla 172 27 28 S 70 18W
Tierra Colorada 165 17 10N 99 35W
Tierra de Barros 57 38 40N 6 30W
Tierra de Campos 56 42 10N 4 50W
Tierra del Fuego, I. Gr. de 176 54 0 S 69 0W
Tiétar, R. 56 39 55N 5 50W
Tieté, R. 171 20 40 S 51 35W
Tieyon 139 26 12 S 133 52 E
Tiffin 156 41 8N 83 10W
Tifi 123 6 12N 36 55 E
Tiflèt 118 33 54N 6 20W
Tiflis = Tbilisi 83 41 50N 44 50 E
Tifrah 90 31 19N 34 42 E
Tifton 157 31 28N 83 32W
Tifu 103 3 39 S 126 18 E
Tigalda I. 147 54 9N 165 0W
Tighnabruaich 34 55 55N 5 13W
Tigil 77 58 0N 158 10 E
Tignish 151 46 58N 64 2W
Tigre □ 123 13 35N 39 15 E
Tigre, R. 174 3 30 S 74 58W
Tigu 99 29 48N 91 38 E
Tiguentourine 119 28 8N 8 58 E
Tiguila 121 14 44N 1 50W
Tigveni 70 45 10N 24 31 E
Tigyaing 98 23 45N 96 10 E
Tîh, Gebel el 122 29 32N 33 26 E
Tihodaine, Dunes de 119 25 15N 7 15 E
Tîjî 119 32 0N 11 18 E
Tijiamis 103 7 16 S 108 29 E
Tijibadok 103 6 53 S 106 47 E

Tijirit, O. 120 19 30N 6 15W
Tijuana 164 32 30N 117 3W
Tikal 166 17 2N 89 35W
Tikamgarh 95 24 44N 78 57 E
Tikan 138 5 58 S 149 2 E
Tikhoretsk 83 45 56N 40 5 E
Tikhvin 80 59 35N 33 30 E
Tikkadouine, Adrar 118 24 28N 1 30 E
Tiko 121 4 4N 9 20 E
Tikrit 92 34 35N 43 37 E
Tiksi 77 71 50N 129 0 E
Tilamuta 103 0 40N 122 15 E
Tilburg 47 51 31N 5 6 E
Tilbury, Can. 150 42 17N 84 23W
Tilbury, U.K. 29 51 27N 0 24 E
Tilcara 172 23 30 S 65 23W
Tilden 158 42 3N 97 45W
Tilemsès 121 15 37N 4 44 E
Tilemsi, Vallée du 121 17 42N 0 15 E
Tilghman 162 38 42N 76 20W
Tilhar 95 28 0N 79 45 E
Tilia, O. 118 27 32N 0 55 E
Tilichiki 77 61 0N 166 5 E
Tiligul, R. 82 47 35N 30 30 E
Tililane 118 27 49N 0 6W
Tilin 98 21 41N 94 6 E
Tilissos 69 38 15N 25 0 E
Till, R. 35 55 35N 2 3W
Tillabéri 121 14 7N 1 28 E
Tillamook 160 45 29N 123 55W
Tillberga 72 59 42N 16 39 E
Tilley 152 50 28N 111 38W
Tillia 121 16 8N 4 47 E
Tillicoultry 35 56 9N 3 44W
Tillsonburg 150 42 53N 80 44W
Tilmanstone 29 51 13N 1 18 E
Tilos, I. 69 36 27N 27 27 E
Tilpa 139 30 57 S 144 24 E
Tilrhemt 118 33 9N 3 22 E
Tilsit = Sovetsk 80 55 6N 21 50 E
Tilt, R. 37 56 50N 3 50W
Tilton 162 43 25N 71 36W
Timahoe 39 52 59N 7 12W
Timanskiy Kryazh 78 65 58N 50 5 E
Timaru 143 44 23 S 171 14 E
Timashevo 84 53 22N 51 9 E
Timashevsk 83 45 35N 39 0 E
Timau 126 0 4N 37 15 E
Timbákion 69 35 4N 24 45 E
Timbaúba 170 7 31 S 35 19W
Timbédra 120 16 17N 8 16W
Timber L. 158 45 29N 101 0W
Timber Mtn. 163 37 6N 116 28W
Timbío 174 2 20N 76 40W
Timbiquí 174 2 46N 77 42W
Timboon 140 38 30 S 142 58 E
Timbuktu = Tombouctou 120 16 50N 3 0W
Timdjaouine 118 21 47N 4 30 E
Timétrine Montagnes 121 19 25N 1 0W
Timfi Óros 68 39 59N 20 45 E
Timfristós, Óros 69 38 57N 21 50 E
Timhadite 118 33 15N 5 4W
Timimoun 118 29 14N 0 16 E
Timimoun, Sebkha de 118 28 50N 0 46 E
Timiris, C. 120 19 15N 16 30W
Timiş □ 66 45 40N 21 30 E
Timiş, R. 70 45 30N 21 0 E
Timişoara 66 45 43N 21 15 E
Timmins 150 48 28N 81 25W
Timmoudi 118 29 20N 1 8W
Timok, R. 66 44 10N 22 40 E
Timoleague 39 51 40N 8 51W
Timolin 39 52 59N 6 49W
Timon 170 5 8 S 42 52W
Timor □ 103 8 0 S 126 30 E
Timor, I. 103 9 0 S 125 0 E
Timor Sea 136 10 0 S 127 0 E
Timur □ 103 9 0 S 125 0 E
Tin Alkoum 119 24 30N 10 17 E
Tin Gornai 121 16 38N 0 38W
Tin Mtn. 163 36 54N 117 28W
Tîna, Khalîg el 122 31 20N 32 42 E
Tinaca Pt. 103 5 30N 125 25 E
Tinaco 174 9 42N 68 26W
Tinafak, O. 119 27 10N 7 0W
Tinahely 39 52 48N 6 28W
Tinambacan 103 12 5N 124 32 E
Tinapagee 139 29 25 S 144 15 E
Tinaquillo 174 9 55N 68 18W
Tinaroo Falls 138 17 5 S 145 4 E
Tinca 70 46 46N 21 58 E
Tinchebray 42 48 47N 0 45W
Tindivanam 97 12 15N 79 35 E
Tindouf 118 27 50N 8 4W
Tindzhe Dzong 95 28 20N 88 8 E
Tineo 56 43 21N 6 27W
Tinerhir 118 31 29N 5 31W
Tinfouchi 118 28 58N 5 54W
T'ing Chiang, R. 109 24 24N 116 35 E
Tingan 100 19 42N 110 18 E
Tingch'u, R. 108 28 20N 99 12 E
Tingewick 28 51 59N 1 4W
Tinggi, Pulau, Is. 101 2 18N 104 7 E
Tinghai 109 30 0N 122 10 E
Tinghsi 106 35 33N 104 32 E
Tinghsiang 106 38 32N 112 59 E
Tinghsien 106 38 30N 115 0 E
Tingkawk Sakun 98 26 4N 96 44 E
Tingk'ouchen 106 39 48N 106 36 E
Tinglev 73 54 57N 9 13 E
Tingnan 109 24 47N 115 2 E
Tingo María 174 9 10 S 76 0W
Tingpien 106 37 36N 107 38 E
Tingshan 109 31 16N 119 51 E
Tingsryd 73 56 31N 15 0 E
Tingt'ao 106 35 4N 115 34 E
Tingvalla 73 58 47N 12 2 E
Tingyüan 109 32 32N 117 41 E
Tinh Bien 101 10 36N 104 57 E
Tinharé, I. de 171 13 30 S 38 58W
Tinié 121 14 17N 1 30W
Tinioulig, Sebkra 118 22 30N 6 45W
Tinjoub 118 29 45N 5 40W
Tinkurrin 137 32 59 S 117 46 E
Tinnia 172 27 0 S 62 45W
Tinnoset 71 59 45N 9 3 E
Tinnsjø 71 59 55N 8 54 E
Tinogasta 172 28 0 S 67 40W
Tinos 69 37 33N 25 8 E
Tiñoso, C. 59 37 32N 1 6W
Tinsukia 98 27 29N 95 26 E
Tintagel 30 50 40N 4 45W
Tintagel Hd. 30 50 40N 4 46W
Tintern 31 51 42N 2 41W
Tintern Abbey 39 52 14N 6 50W
Tintigny 47 49 41N 5 31 E
Tintina 172 27 2 S 62 45W
Tintinara 140 35 48 S 140 2 E
Tinto, R. 57 37 30N 5 33W
Tinui 142 40 52 S 176 5 E
Tinwald 143 43 55 S 171 43 E
Tioga 162 41 54N 77 9W
Tioman, I. 101 2 50N 104 10 E
Tioman, Pulau, Is. 101 2 50N 104 10 E
Tionaga 150 48 0N 82 0W
Tione di Trento 62 46 3N 10 44 E
Tior 123 6 26N 31 11 E
Tioulilin 118 27 1N 0 2W
Tipongpani 99 27 20N 95 55 E
Tipperary 39 52 28N 8 10W
Tipperary □ 39 52 37N 7 55W
Tipton, U.K. 28 52 32N 2 4W
Tipton, Calif., U.S.A. 163 36 3N 119 19W
Tipton, Ind., U.S.A. 156 40 17N 86 30W
Tipton, Iowa, U.S.A. 158 41 45N 91 12W
Tiptonville 159 36 22N 89 30W
Tiptree 29 51 48N 0 46 E
Tiptur 97 13 15N 76 26 E
Tira 90 32 14N 34 56 E
Tiracambu, Serra do 170 3 15 S 46 30W
Tirahart, O. 118 23 55N 2 0W
Tiran 93 32 45N 51 0 E
Tirân 122 27 56N 34 35 E
Tirana 68 41 18N 19 49 E
Tirana-Durrësi □ 68 41 35N 20 0 E
Tirano 62 46 13N 10 11 E
Tirarer, Mont 121 19 35N 1 10W
Tiraspol 82 46 55N 29 35 E
Tirat Carmel 90 32 46N 34 58 E
Tirat Tsevi 90 32 26N 35 31 E
Tirat Yehuda 90 32 1N 34 56 E
Tiratimine 118 25 56N 3 37 E
Tirdout 121 16 7N 1 5W
Tire 92 38 5N 27 50 E
Tirebolu 92 40 58N 38 45 E
Tiree, I. 34 56 31N 6 55W
Tiree, Passage of 34 56 30N 6 30W
Tîrgoviste 70 44 55N 25 27 E
Tîrgu Frumos 70 47 12N 27 2 E
Tîrgu-Jiu 70 45 5N 23 19 E
Tîrgu Mureş 70 46 31N 24 38 E
Tîrgu Neamţ 70 47 12N 26 25 E
Tîrgu Ocna 70 46 16N 26 39 E
Tîrgu Secuiesc 70 46 0N 26 10 E
Tirich Mir Mt. 93 36 15N 71 35 E
Tiriola 65 38 57N 16 32 E
Tiririca, Serra da 171 17 6 S 47 6W
Tirlyanskiy 84 54 14N 58 35 E
Tirna, R. 96 18 5N 76 30 E
Tîrnava = Botoroaga 70 44 8N 25 32 E
Tîrnava Mare, R. 70 46 15N 24 30 E
Tîrnava Mica, R. 70 46 17N 24 30 E
Tirnavos 68 39 45N 22 18 E
Tîrnova 70 45 23N 22 1 E
Tîrnăveni 70 46 19N 24 13 E
Tirodi 96 21 35N 79 35 E
Tirol □ 52 47 3N 10 43 E
Tiros 171 19 0 S 45 58W
Tirschenreuth 49 49 51N 12 20 E
Tirso, L. 64 40 8N 8 56 E
Tirso, R. 64 40 33N 9 12 E
Tirstrup 73 56 18N 10 42 E
Tirua 142 38 25 S 174 40 E
Tiruchchirappalli 97 10 45N 78 45 E
Tiruchendur 97 8 30N 78 11 E
Tiruchengodu 97 11 23N 77 56 E
Tirumangalam 97 9 49N 77 58 E
Tirunelveli (Tinnevelly) 97 8 45N 77 45 E
Tirupati 97 13 45N 79 30 E
Tiruppattur 97 12 30N 78 30 E
Tiruppur 97 11 12N 77 22 E
Tiruturaipundi 97 10 32N 79 41 E
Tiruvadaimarudur 97 11 2N 79 27 E
Tiruvallar 97 13 9N 79 57 E
Tiruvannamalai 97 12 10N 79 12 E
Tiruvarur (Negapatam) 97 10 46N 79 38 E
Tiruvatipuram 97 12 39N 79 33 E
Tiruvottiyur 97 13 10N 80 22 E
Tisa, R. 66 45 30N 20 20 E
Tisdale 153 52 50N 104 0W
Tiseirhatène, Mares de 118 22 51N 9 30W
Tishomingo 159 34 14N 96 38W
Tisjön 72 60 56N 13 0 E
Tisnaren 72 58 58N 15 56 E
Tisno 63 44 45N 15 41 E
Tišnov 53 49 21N 16 25 E
Tisovec 53 48 41N 19 56 E
Tissemsilt 118 35 35N 1 50 E
Tissit, O. 119 27 28N 9 58W
Tissø 73 55 35N 11 18 E
Tista, R. 98 25 23N 89 43 E
Tisted 73 56 58N 8 40 E
Tisza, R. 53 47 38N 20 44 E
Tiszaföldvár 53 47 0N 20 14 E
Tiszafüred 53 47 38N 20 50 E
Tiszalök 53 48 0N 21 10 E
Tiszavasvári 53 47 58N 21 18 E
Tit, Alg. 118 27 0N 1 37 E
Tit, Alg. 119 23 0N 5 10 E
Tit-Ary 77 71 50N 126 30 E
Titaguas 58 39 53N 1 6W
Titahi Bay 142 41 6 S 174 50 E
Titai Damer 123 16 43N 37 25 E
Titchfield 28 50 51N 1 13W
Titel 66 45 29N 20 18 E
Tithwal 95 34 21N 73 50 E
Titicaca, L. 174 15 30 S 69 30W
Titilagarh 96 20 15N 83 5 E
Tititira Head 98 43 38 S 169 26 E
Titiwa 121 12 14N 12 53 E
Titlis 51 46 46N 8 27 E
Titograd 66 42 30N 19 19 E
Titov Veles 66 41 46N 21 47 E
Titova Korenica 63 44 45N 15 41 E
Titovo Uzice 66 43 55N 19 50 E
Titule 126 3 15N 25 31 E
Titumate 174 8 19N 77 5W
Titusville 156 41 35N 79 39W
Tiumpan Hd. 36 58 15N 6 10W
Tivaouane 120 14 56N 16 45W
Tivat 66 42 28N 18 43 E
Tiveden 73 58 50N 14 30 E
Tiverton 30 50 54N 3 30W
Tívoli 63 41 58N 12 45 E
Tiwi 93 22 45N 59 12 E
Tiyo 123 14 41N 40 57 E
Tizga 118 32 1N 5 9W
Tizi n'Isly 118 32 28N 5 47W
Tizi Ouzou 119 36 42N 4 3 E
Tizmín 165 21 0N 88 1W
Tiznados, R. 174 8 50N 67 50W
Tiznit 118 29 48N 9 45W
Tjalang 103 4 30N 95 43 E
Tjangkuang, Tg. 102 7 0 S 105 0 E
Tjareme, G. 103 6 55 S 108 27 E
Tjeggelvas 74 66 37N 17 45 E
Tjepu 103 7 12 S 111 31 E
Tjeukemeer 46 52 53N 5 48 E
Tjiandjur 103 6 51 S 107 7 E
Tjibatu 103 7 8 S 107 59 E
Tjikadjang 103 7 25 S 107 48 E
Tjimahi 103 6 53 S 107 33 E
Tjirebon = Cirebon 103 6 45 S 108 32 E
Tjöllong 71 59 6N 10 3 E
Tjöme 71 59 8N 10 26 E
Tjonger Kanaal 46 52 52N 6 52 E
Tjörn 73 58 0N 11 35 E
Tjörnes 74 66 12N 17 9W
Tjuls 73 57 30N 18 15 E
Tjurup 102 4 26 S 102 13 E
Tkibuli 83 42 26N 43 0 E
Tkvarcheli 83 42 47N 41 52 E
Tlacolula 165 16 57N 96 29W
Tlacotalpán 165 18 37N 95 40W
Tlaquepaque 164 20 39N 103 19W
Tlaxcala 165 19 20N 98 14W
Tlaxcala □ 165 19 30N 98 20W
Tlaxiaco 165 17 10N 97 40W
Tlell 152 53 34N 131 56W
Tlemcen 118 34 52N 1 15W
Tleta di Sidi Bouguedra 118 32 16N 8 58W
Tleta Sidi Bouguedra 118 32 16N 9 59W
Tlumach 80 48 46N 25 0 E
Tłuszcz 54 52 25N 21 25 E
Tlyarata 83 42 9N 46 26 E
Tmassah 119 26 19N 15 51 E
Tmisan 119 27 23N 13 30 E
To Bong 100 12 45N 109 16 E
T'o Chiang, R. 108 28 56N 105 33 E
To-Shima 111 34 31N 139 17 E
Toad, R. 152 59 25N 124 57W
Toay 172 36 43 S 64 30W
Toba 111 34 30N 136 45 E
Toba Kakar 94 31 30N 69 0 E
Toba, L. 102 2 40N 98 50 E
Toba Tek Singh 94 30 55N 72 25 E
Tobago, I. 167 11 10N 60 30W
Tobarra 59 38 35N 1 41W
Tobelo 103 1 25N 127 56 E
Tobercurry 38 54 3N 8 43W
Tobermore 38 54 49N 6 43W
Tobermorey 138 22 12 S 138 0 E
Tobermory, Can. 150 45 12N 81 40W
Tobermory, U.K. 34 56 37N 6 4W
Tobin, L. 136 21 45 S 125 49 E
Tobin L. 153 53 35N 103 30W
Toboali 102 3 0 S 106 25 E
Tobol 84 52 40N 62 39 E
Tobol, R. 84 58 10N 68 12 E
Toboli 103 0 38 S 120 12 E
Tobolsk 84 58 0N 68 10 E
Tobruk = Tubruq 117 32 7N 23 55 E
Tobyhanna 162 41 10N 75 15W
Tocantínia 170 9 33 S 48 22W
Tocantinópolis 170 6 20 S 47 25W
Tocantins, R. 170 14 30 S 49 0W
Tocca 157 34 6N 83 17W
Toce, R. 62 46 5N 8 29 E
Tochigi 111 36 25N 139 45 E
Tochigi-ken □ 111 36 45N 139 45 E
Tocina 57 37 37N 5 44W
Toconao 172 34 35N 83 19W
Toconhão, Serra do 171 14 30 S 47 46W
Tocópero 174 11 30N 69 16W
Tocopilla 172 22 5 S 70 10W
Tocumwal 141 35 45 S 145 31 E
Tocuyo, R. 174 10 50N 69 0W
Todd, R. 138 24 52 S 135 48 E
Toddington 29 51 57N 0 31W
Todeli 103 1 38 S 124 34 E
Todenyang 126 4 35N 35 56 E
Todi 63 42 47N 12 24 E
Tödi 51 46 48N 8 55 E
Todjo 103 1 20 S 121 15 E
Todmorden 32 53 43N 2 7W
Todos os Santos, Baía de 171 12 48 S 38 38W
Todos Santos 164 23 27N 110 13W
Todos Santos, Bahia de 164 31 48N 116 42W
Todtnau 49 47 50N 7 56 E
Toe Hd., Ireland 39 51 29N 9 13W
Toe Hd., U.K. 36 57 50N 7 10W
Toecé 121 11 50N 1 16W
Toetoes B. 143 46 42 S 168 41 E
Tofield 152 53 25N 112 40W
Tofino 152 49 11N 125 55W
Töfsingdalems National Park 72 62 15N 12 44 E
Tofta 73 57 11N 12 20 E
Toftlund 73 55 11N 9 2 E
Tōgane 111 35 33N 140 22 E
Togba 120 17 26N 10 25W
Toggenburg 51 47 16N 9 9 E
Togian, Kepulauan 103 0 20 S 121 50 E
Togliatti 81 53 37N 49 18 E
Togo ■ 121 6 15N 1 35 E
Toguzak, R. 84 54 3N 62 44 E
Tōhoku □ 112 39 50N 141 45 E
Toi 111 34 54N 134 47 E
Toinya 123 6 17N 29 46 E
Toiyabe Dome 163 38 51N 117 22W
Toiyabe, Ra. 163 39 10N 117 10W
Tōjō 110 34 53N 133 16 E
Tok, R. 84 52 46N 52 22 E
Tokaanu 142 38 58 S 175 46 E
Tokachi, R. 112 42 44N 143 42 E
Tokaj 53 48 8N 21 27 E
Tokala, G. 103 1 30 S 121 40 E
Tokanui 143 46 34 S 168 56 E
Tokarahi 143 44 56 S 170 39 E
Tokat 92 40 22N 36 35 E
Tŏkchŏn 107 39 45N 126 18 E
Tokelau Is. 130 9 0 S 172 0W
Toki 111 35 18N 137 8 E
Tokmak, Kirgizia, U.S.S.R. 84 42 55N 75 45 E
Tokmak, Ukraine, U.S.S.R. 82 47 16N 35 42 E
Toko Ra. 138 23 5 S 138 20 E
Tokomaru Bay 142 38 8 S 178 22 E
Tokombere 121 11 18N 3 30 E
Tókomlós 53 46 24N 20 45 E
Tokoname 111 34 53N 136 51 E
Tokong 101 5 27N 100 23 E
Tokoroa 142 38 20 S 175 50 E
Tokorozawa 111 35 47N 139 28 E
T'ok'ot'o 106 40 15N 111 12 E
Toktogul 85 41 50N 72 50 E
Tokuii 110 34 11N 131 42 E
Tokule 123 14 54N 38 26 E
Tokunoshima 112 27 56N 128 55 E
Tokushima 110 34 4N 134 34 E
Tokushima-ken □ 110 35 50N 134 30 E
Tokuyama 110 34 0N 131 50 E
Tōkyō 111 35 45N 139 45 E
Tōkyō-to □ 111 35 40N 139 30 E
Tōkyō-Wan 111 35 25N 139 47 E
Tolaerh 105 35 8N 81 33 E
Tolaga Bay 142 38 21 S 178 20 E
Tolageak 147 70 2N 162 50W
Tolbukhin 67 43 37N 27 49 E
Toledo, Spain 56 39 50N 4 2W
Toledo, Ohio, U.S.A. 156 41 37N 83 33W
Toledo, Oreg., U.S.A. 160 44 40N 123 59W
Toledo, Wash., U.S.A. 160 42 29N 122 58W
Toledo, Montes de 57 39 33N 4 20W
Tolentino 63 43 12N 13 17 E
Tolfino 152 49 6N 125 54W
Tolga, Alg. 119 34 46N 5 22 E
Tolga, Norway 71 62 26N 11 1 E
Tolima □ 174 3 45N 75 15W
Tolima, Vol. 174 4 40N 75 19W
Tolitoli 103 1 5N 120 50 E
Tolkamer 46 51 52N 6 6 E
Tolkmicko 54 54 19N 19 31 E
Tollarp 73 55 55N 13 58 E
Tollesbury 29 51 46N 0 51 E
Tolleson 161 33 29N 112 10W
Tollhouse 163 37 1N 119 24W
Tolmachevo 80 58 56N 29 57 E
Tolmezzo 63 46 23N 13 0 E
Tolmino 63 46 11N 13 45 E
Tolna 53 46 25N 18 48 E
Tolna □ 53 46 30N 18 30 E
Tolne 73 57 28N 10 20 E
Tolo 124 2 50 S 18 40 E
Tolo, Teluk 103 2 20 S 122 10 E
Tolokiwa I. 138 5 30 S 147 30 E
Tolon 121 9 26N 1 3W
Tolosa 58 43 8N 2 5W
Tolox 57 36 41N 4 54W

Tolsta Hd. **36** 58 20N 6 10W
Toluca **165** 19 20N 99 50W
Tolun **106** 42 22N 116 30E
Tom Burke **129** 23 5S 28 4E
Tomahawk **158** 45 28N 89 40W
Tomakomai **112** 42 38N 141 36E
Tomales **163** 38 15N 122 53W
Tomales B. **163** 38 15N 123 58W
Tomar **57** 39 36N 8 25W
Tómaros Óros **68** 39 29N 20 48E
Tomaszów Lubelski **54** 50 29N 23 23E
Tomaszów Mazowiecki **54** 51 30N 19 57E
Tomatin **37** 57 20N 4 0W
Tomatlán **164** 19 56N 105 15W
Tombé **123** 5 53N 31 40E
Tombigbee, R. **157** 32 0N 88 6W
Tombodor, Serra do **171** 12 0S 41 30W
Tombouctou **120** 16 50N 3 0W
Tombstone **161** 31 40N 110 4W
Tomdoun **36** 57 4N 5 2W
Tomé **172** 36 36S 73 6W
Tomé-Açu **170** 2 25S 48 9W
Tomelilla **73** 55 33N 13 58E
Tomelloso **59** 39 10N 3 2W
Tomingley **141** 32 31S 148 16E
Tomini **103** 0 30N 120 30E
Tomini, Teluk **103** 0 10S 122 0E
Tominian **120** 13 17N 4 35W
Tomiño **56** 41 59N 8 46W
Tomintoul **37** 57 15N 3 22W
Tomioka **111** 36 15N 138 54E
Tomkinson Ranges **137** 26 11S 129 5E
Tommot **77** 58 50N 126 20E
Tomnavoulin **37** 57 19N 3 18W
Tomnop Ta Suos **101** 11 20N 104 15E
Tomo, Colomb. **174** 2 38N 67 32W
Tomo, Japan **110** 34 23N 133 23E
Tomobe **111** 36 40N 140 41E
Toms Place **163** 37 34N 118 41W
Toms River **162** 39 59N 74 12W
Tomsk **76** 56 30N 85 12E
Tomtabacken **73** 57 30N 14 30E
Tonalá **165** 16 8N 93 41W
Tonale, Passo del **62** 46 15N 10 34E
Tonalea **161** 36 17N 110 58W
Tonami **111** 36 56N 136 58E
Tonantins **174** 2 45S 67 45W
Tonasket **160** 48 45N 119 30W
Tonawanda **156** 43 0N 78 54W
Tonbridge **29** 51 12N 0 18E
Tondano **103** 1 35N 124 54E
Tondela **56** 40 31N 8 5W
Tønder **73** 54 58N 8 50E
Tondi **97** 9 45N 79 4E
Tondi Kiwindi **121** 14 28N 2 02E
Tondibi **121** 16 39N 0 14W
Tone-Gawa, R. **111** 35 44N 140 51E
Tone, R. **137** 34 23S 116 25E
Tone R. **30** 50 59N 3 15W
Tong **28** 52 39N 2 18W
Tonga Is. ■ **130** 20 0S 173 0W
Tonga Trench **143** 18 0S 175 0W
Tongaat **129** 29 33S 31 9E
Tongala **141** 36 14S 144 56E
Tongaland **129** 27 0S 32 0E
Tongareva I **143** 9 0S 158 0W
Tongariro, mt. **142** 39 7S 175 50E
Tongchŏnni **107** 39 50N 127 25E
Tongeren **47** 50 47N 5 28E
Tongio **141** 37 14S 147 44E
Tongjosŏn Man **107** 39 30N 128 0E
Tongking = Bac-Phan **101** 21 30N 105 0E
Tongking, G. of **101** 20 0N 108 0E
Tongnae **107** 35 12N 129 5E
Tongobory **129** 23 32S 44 20E
Tongoy **172** 30 25S 71 40W
Tongres = Tongeren **47** 50 47N 5 28E
Tongsa Dzong **98** 27 31N 90 31E
Tongue **37** 58 29N 4 25W
Tongue, Kyle of **37** 58 30N 4 30W
Tongue, R. **160** 48 30N 106 30W
Tongyang **107** 39 9N 126 53E
Tonj **123** 7 20N 28 44E
Tonk **94** 26 6N 75 54E
Tonkawa **159** 36 44N 67 22W
Tonkin = Bac-Phan **100** 22 0N 105 0E
Tonkin, G. of **100** 20 0N 108 0E
Tonlé Sap **100** 13 0N 104 0E
Tonnay-Charente **44** 45 56N 0 55W
Tonneins **44** 44 24N 0 20E
Tonnerre **43** 47 51N 3 59E
Tönning **48** 54 18N 8 57E
Tonopah **163** 38 4N 117 12W
Tonoshō **110** 34 29N 134 11E
Tonosí **166** 7 20N 80 20W
Tonsberg **71** 59 19N 10 25E
Tonstad **71** 58 40N 6 45E
Tonto Basin **61** 33 58N 111 15W
Tonyrefail **31** 51 35N 3 26W
Tonzang **98** 23 36N 93 42E
Tonzi **98** 24 39N 94 57E
Tooele **160** 40 30N 112 20W
Toolonda **140** 36 58S 141 5E
Toombeolo **38** 53 26N 9 52W
Toomevara **39** 52 50N 8 2W
Toompine **139** 27 15S 144 19E
Toongi **141** 32 28S 148 30E
Toonpan **138** 19 28S 146 48E
Toora **141** 38 39S 146 23E
Toora-Khem **77** 52 28N 96 9E
Toormore **39** 51 31N 9 41W
Toowoomba **139** 27 32S 151 56E
Top **93** 34 15N 68 35E
Top Ozero **78** 65 35N 32 0E
Topalu **70** 44 31N 28 3E
Topaz **163** 38 41N 119 30W
Topeka **158** 39 3N 95 40W
Topki **76** 55 25N 85 20E
Topla, R. **53** 49 0N 21 36E
Topley **152** 54 32N 126 5W
Toplica, R. **66** 43 15N 21 30E
Toplița **70** 46 55N 25 27E
Topocalma, Pta. **172** 34 10S 72 2W
Topock **161** 34 46N 114 29W
Topola **66** 44 17N 20 32E
Topol'čany **53** 48 35N 18 12E
Topoli **83** 47 59N 51 45E
Topolnitsa, R. **67** 42 21N 24 0E
Topolobampo **164** 25 40N 109 10W
Topolovgrad **67** 42 5N 26 20E
Topolvăţ Mare **66** 45 46N 21 41E
Toppenish **160** 46 27N 120 16W
Topsham **30** 50 40N 3 27W
Topusko **63** 45 18N 15 59E
Toquima, Ra. **163** 39 0N 117 0W
Tor Bay, Austral. **137** 35 5S 117 50E
Tor Bay, U.K. **23** 50 26N 3 31W
Tor Ness **37** 58 47N 3 18W
Tor, oilfield **19** 56 40N 3 35E
Torá **58** 41 49N 1 25E
Tora Kit **123** 11 2N 32 30E
Torata **174** 17 3S 70 1W
Torbat-e Heydarīyeh **93** 35 15N 59 12E
Torbat-e Jām **93** 35 8N 60 35E
Torbay, Can. **151** 47 40N 52 42W
Torbay, U.K. **30** 50 26N 3 31W
Torchin **80** 50 45N 25 0E
Tordal **71** 59 10N 8 45E
Tordesillas **56** 41 30N 5 0W
Tordoya **56** 43 6N 8 36W
Töre **74** 65 55N 22 40E
Töreboda **73** 58 41N 14 7E
Torfajökull **74** 63 54N 19 0W
Torgau **48** 51 32N 13 0E
Torgelow **48** 53 40N 13 59E
Torhout **47** 51 5N 3 7E
Tori **123** 7 53N 33 35E
Torigni-sur-Vire **42** 49 3N 0 58W
Torija **58** 40 44N 3 2W
Torin **164** 27 33N 110 5W
Toriñana, C. **56** 43 3N 9 17W
Torino **62** 45 4N 7 40E
Torit **123** 4 20N 32 55E
Torkovichi **80** 58 51N 30 30E
Tormac **66** 45 30N 21 30E
Tormentine **151** 46 6N 63 46W
Tormes, R. **56** 41 7N 6 0W
Tornado Mt. **152** 49 55N 114 40W
Tornby **73** 57 32N 9 56E
Torne älv **74** 65 50N 24 12E
Torneå = Tornio **74** 65 50N 24 12E
Torness **37** 57 18N 4 22W
Torneträsk **74** 68 24N 19 15E
Tornio **74** 65 50N 24 12E
Tornionjoki **74** 65 50N 24 12E
Tornquist **172** 38 0S 62 15W
Toro **56** 41 35N 5 24W
Torö **73** 58 48N 17 50E
Toro, Cerro del **172** 29 0S 69 50W
Toro Pk. **163** 33 34N 116 24W
Törökszentmjklés **53** 47 11N 20 27E
Toronátos Kólpos **68** 40 5N 23 30E
Toronto, Austral. **141** 33 0S 151 30E
Toronto, Can. **150** 43 39N 79 20W
Toronto, U.S.A. **156** 40 27N 80 36W
Toronto, L. **164** 27 40N 105 30W
Toropets **80** 56 30N 31 40E
Tororo **126** 0 45N 34 12E
Toros Dağlari **92** 37 0N 35 0E
Torphins **37** 57 7N 2 37W
Torpoint **30** 50 23N 4 12W
Torpshammar **72** 62 29N 16 20E
Torquay, Austral. **140** 38 20S 144 19E
Torquay, Can. **153** 49 9N 103 30W
Torquay, U.K. **30** 50 27N 3 31W
Torquemada **56** 42 2N 4 19W
Torralba de Calatrava **57** 39 1N 3 44W
Torran Rocks **34** 56 14N 6 24W
Torrance **163** 33 50N 118 19W
Torrão **57** 38 16N 8 11W
Torre Annunziata **64** 40 45N 14 26E
Tôrre de Moncorvo **56** 41 12N 7 8W
Torre del Greco **65** 40 47N 14 22E
Torre del Mar **57** 36 44N 4 6W
Torre-Pacheco **29** 37 44N 0 57W
Torre Pellice **62** 44 49N 7 13E
Torreblanca **58** 40 14N 0 12E
Torrecampo **57** 38 29N 4 41W
Torrecilla en Cameros **58** 42 15N 2 38W
Torredembarra **58** 41 9N 1 24W
Torredonjimeno **57** 37 46N 3 57W
Torrejoncillo **56** 39 54N 6 28W
Torrelaguna **58** 40 50N 3 38W
Torrelavega **56** 43 20N 4 5W
Torremaggiore **65** 41 42N 15 17E
Torremolinos **57** 36 38N 4 30W
Torrens Cr. **138** 22 23S 145 9E
Torrens Creek **138** 20 48S 145 3E
Torrens, L. **140** 31 0S 137 50E
Torrente **59** 39 27N 0 28W
Torrenueva **59** 38 38N 3 22W
Torreón **164** 25 33N 103 25W
Torreperogil **59** 38 2N 3 17W
Torres, Mexico **164** 28 46N 110 47W
Torres, Spain **56** 41 6N 5 0W
Tôrres Novas **57** 39 27N 8 33W
Torres Strait **135** 9 50S 142 20E
Torres Vedras **57** 39 5N 9 15W
Torrevieja **59** 37 59N 0 42W
Torrey **161** 38 12N 111 30W
Torridge, R. **30** 50 51N 4 10W
Torridon **36** 57 33N 5 34W
Torridon, L. **36** 57 35N 5 50W
Torrijos **56** 39 59N 4 18W
Törring **73** 55 52N 9 29E
Torrington, Conn., U.S.A. **162** 41 50N 73 9W
Torrington, Wyo., U.S.A. **158** 42 5N 104 8W
Torroboll **37** 58 0N 4 23W
Torroella de Montgri **58** 42 2N 3 8E
Torrox **57** 36 46N 3 57W
Torsås **73** 56 24N 16 0E
Torsby **72** 60 7N 13 0E
Torsjok **72** 57 5N 34 55E
Torsö **73** 58 48N 13 45E
Torthorwald **35** 55 7N 3 30W
Tortola, I. **147** 18 19N 65 0W
Tórtoles de Esgueva **56** 41 49N 4 2W
Tortona **62** 44 53N 8 54E
Tortoreto **63** 42 50N 13 55E
Tortorici **65** 38 2N 14 48E
Tortosa **58** 40 49N 0 31E
Tortosa C. **58** 40 41N 0 52E
Tortosendo **56** 40 15N 7 31W
Tortue, I. de la **167** 20 5N 72 57W
Tortuga, Isla la **167** 11 8N 67 2W
Torud **93** 35 25N 55 5E
Torugart, Pereval **85** 40 32N 75 24E
Torun **54** 53 0N 18 39E
Torup **73** 56 57N 13 5E
Torvastad **71** 59 23N 5 15E
Torver **32** 54 20N 3 7W
Tory I. **38** 55 17N 8 12W
Torysa, R. **53** 48 50N 21 15E
Torzhok **80** 57 5N 34 55E
Tosa **110** 33 24N 133 23E
Tosa-shimizu **110** 32 52N 132 58E
Tosa-Wan **110** 33 15N 133 30E
Tosa-yamada **110** 33 36N 133 38E
Toscaig **36** 57 23N 5 49W
Toscana **62** 43 30N 11 5E
Tosno **80** 59 30N 30 58E
Töss, R. **51** 47 32N 8 39E
Tossa **58** 41 43N 2 56E
Tostado **172** 29 15S 61 50W
Tostedt **48** 53 17N 9 42E
Tosu **110** 33 22N 130 31E
Toszek **54** 50 27N 18 32E
Totak **71** 59 40N 7 45E
Totana **59** 37 45N 1 30W
Toten **71** 60 37N 10 53E
Toteng **128** 20 22S 22 58E
Tôtes **42** 49 41N 1 3E
Totland **28** 50 41N 1 32W
Totley **33** 53 18N 1 32W
Totma **81** 60 0N 42 40E
Totnes **30** 50 26N 3 41W
Totonicapán **166** 14 50N 91 20W
Totskoye **84** 52 32N 52 45E
Tottenham **141** 32 14S 147 21E
Totton **28** 50 55N 1 29W
Tottori **110** 35 30N 134 15E
Tottori-ken □ **110** 35 30N 134 12E
Touamotou, Archipel des **131** 17 0S 144 0W
Touat **118** 27 30N 0 30E
Touba **120** 8 15N 7 40W
Toubkal, Djebel **118** 31 0N 8 0W
Toubouai, Îles **131** 25 0S 150 0W
Toucy **43** 47 44N 3 15E
Tougan **120** 13 11N 2 58W
Touggourt **119** 33 10N 6 0E
Tougué **120** 11 25N 11 50W
Toukmatine **119** 24 49N 7 11E
Toul **43** 48 40N 5 53E
Toulepleu **120** 6 32N 8 24W
Toulon **45** 43 10N 5 55E
Toulouse **44** 43 37N 1 27E
Toummo **119** 22 45N 14 8E
Toummo Dhoba **119** 22 30N 14 31E
Toumodi **120** 6 32N 5 4W
Tounan **109** 23 41N 120 28E
Tounassine, Hamada **118** 28 48N 5 0W
Toungoo **98** 19 0N 96 30E
Touques, R. **42** 49 22N 0 8E
Touquet, Le **43** 50 30N 1 36E
Tour-du-Pin, La **45** 45 33N 5 27E
Touraine **42** 47 20N 0 30E
Tourane = Da Nang **100** 16 4N 108 13E
Tourcoing **43** 50 42N 3 10E
Tourcoingbam **121** 13 23N 1 33W
Tournai **47** 50 35N 3 25E
Tournan-en-Brie **43** 48 44N 2 46E
Tournay **44** 43 13N 0 13E
Tournon **45** 45 4N 4 50E
Tournon-St.-Martin **42** 46 45N 0 58E
Tournus **45** 46 35N 4 54E
Tours **42** 47 22N 0 40E
Touside, Pic **119** 21 1N 16 18E
T'outaokou **107** 42 44N 129 12E
Touwsrivier **128** 33 20S 20 0E
Tovar **174** 8 20N 71 46W
Tovarkovskiy **81** 53 40N 38 5E
Tovdal **71** 58 47N 8 10E
Tovdalselva **71** 58 20N 8 16E
Towamba **141** 37 6S 149 43E
Towanda **162** 41 46N 76 30W
Towcester **29** 52 7N 0 56W
Tower **158** 47 49N 92 17W
Towerhill Cr. **138** 22 28S 144 35E
Town Yetholm **35** 55 33N 2 19W
Towner **158** 48 25N 100 26W
Townsend **160** 46 25N 111 32W
Townshend, C. **133** 22 18S 150 30E
Townshend, I. **138** 22 16S 150 31E
Townsville **138** 19 15S 146 45E
Towson **162** 39 26N 76 34W
Toyah **159** 31 20N 103 48W
Toyahvale **159** 30 58N 103 45W
Toyama **111** 36 40N 137 15E
Toyama-ken □ **111** 36 45N 137 30E
Tōyō **110** 33 26N 134 16E
Toyohashi **111** 34 45N 137 25E
Toyokawa **111** 34 48N 137 27E
Toyonaka **111** 34 50N 135 28E
Toyooka **110** 35 35N 134 55E
Toyota **111** 35 3N 137 7E
Toyoura **110** 34 6N 130 57E
Toytepa **85** 41 3N 69 20E
Tozeur **119** 33 56N 8 8E
Tra On **101** 9 58N 105 55E
Trabancos, R. **56** 41 0N 5 3E
Trabzon **92** 41 0N 39 45E
Tracadie **151** 47 30N 64 55W
Tracy, Calif., U.S.A. **163** 37 46N 121 27W
Tracy, Minn., U.S.A. **158** 44 12N 95 3W
Tradate **62** 45 43N 8 54E
Trafalgar **141** 38 14S 146 12E
Trafalgar, C. **57** 36 10N 6 2W
Traghan **119** 26 0N 14 30E
Traian **70** 45 2N 28 15E
Trail **152** 49 5N 117 40W
Trainor L. **152** 60 24N 120 17W
Traipu **171** 9 58S 37 1W
Tralee **39** 52 16N 9 42W
Tralee B. **39** 52 17N 9 55W
Tramelan **50** 47 13N 7 7E
Tramore **39** 52 10N 7 10W
Tramore B. **39** 52 9N 7 10W
Tran Ninh, Cao Nguyen **100** 19 30N 103 10E
Tranas **73** 58 3N 14 59E
Tranås **73** 55 37N 13 59E
Trancas **172** 26 20S 65 20W
Tranche-sur-Mer, La **42** 46 20N 1 27W
Trancoso **56** 40 49N 7 21W
Tranebjerg **73** 55 51N 10 36E
Tranemo **73** 57 30N 13 20E
Tranent **35** 55 57N 2 58W
Trang **101** 7 33N 99 38E
Trangahy **129** 19 7S 44 43E
Trangan, I. **103** 6 40S 134 20E
Trangie **141** 32 4S 148 0E
Trångsviken **72** 63 19N 14 0E
Trani **65** 41 17N 16 24E
Tranoroa **129** 24 42S 45 4E
Tranquebar **97** 11 1N 79 54E
Tranqueras **173** 31 8S 56 0W
Trans Nzoia □ **126** 1 0N 35 0E
Transcona **153** 49 50N 97 0W
Transilvania **70** 46 19N 25 0E
Transkei □ **129** 32 15S 28 15E
Transtrand **72** 61 6N 13 20E
Transvaal □ **128** 25 0S 29 0E
Transylvania = Transilvania **70** 46 19N 25 0E
Transylvanian Alps **70** 45 30N 25 0E
Trápani **64** 38 1N 12 30E
Trappe Peak, Mt. **160** 45 56N 114 29W
Traqowel **140** 35 50S 144 0E
Traralgon **141** 38 12S 146 34E
Traryd **73** 56 35N 13 45E
Trarza □ **120** 17 30N 15 0W
Tras os Montes e Alto-Douro □ **55** 41 25N 7 20W
Trasacco **63** 41 58N 13 30E
Trasimeno, L. **63** 43 10N 12 5E
Träslöv **73** 57 8N 12 21E
Trat **101** 12 14N 102 33E
Traun **52** 48 14N 14 15E
Traun-see **49** 47 48N 13 45E
Traunstein **49** 47 52N 12 40E
Tråvad **73** 58 15N 13 5E
Traveller's L. **140** 33 20S 142 0E
Travemünde **48** 53 58N 10 52E
Travers, Mt. **143** 42 1S 172 45E
Traverse City **156** 44 45N 85 39W
Traverse I. **13** 48 0S 28 0E
Travnik **66** 44 17N 17 39E
Trawbreaga B. **38** 55 20N 7 25W
Trawsfynydd **31** 52 54N 3 55W
Trayning **137** 31 7S 117 46E
Traynor **153** 52 20N 108 32W
Trazo **56** 43 0N 8 30W
Trbovlje **63** 46 12N 15 5E
Trebbia, R. **62** 44 52N 9 30E
Trebel, R. **48** 54 0N 12 50E
Trebinje **66** 42 44N 18 22E
Trebisacce **65** 39 52N 16 32E
Trebišnica, R. **66** 42 47N 18 8E
Trebišov **53** 48 38N 21 41E
Trebizat **66** 43 15N 17 30E
Třebon **52** 48 59N 14 48E
Trebujena **57** 36 52N 6 11W
Trecate **62** 45 29N 8 42E
Tredegar **31** 51 47N 3 16W
Trefeglwys **31** 52 31N 3 31W
Trefriw **31** 53 9N 3 50W
Tregaron **31** 52 14N 3 56W
Trégastel-Plage **42** 48 49N 3 31W
Tregnago **63** 45 31N 11 10E

Tregrasse Is. 138 17 41 S 150 43 E
Tréguier 42 48 47N 3 16W
Trégunc 42 47 51N 3 51W
Tregynon 31 52 32N 3 19W
Treharris 31 51 40N 3 17W
Treherne 153 49 38N 98 42W
Tréia 63 43 30N 13 20 E
Treig, L. 37 56 48N 4 42W
Treignac 44 45 32N 1 48 E
Treinta y Tres 173 33 10 S 54 50W
Treis 49 50 9N 7 19 E
Trekveid 128 30 35 S 19 45 E
Trelde Næs 73 55 38N 9 53 E
Trelech 31 51 56N 4 28W
Trelew 176 43 10 S 65 20W
Trélissac 44 45 11N 0 47 E
Trelleborg 73 55 20N 13 10 E
Trélon 43 50 5N 4 6 E
Tremadoc 31 52 57N 4 9W
Tremadoc, Bay 31 52 51N 4 18W
Tremblade, La 44 45 46N 1 8W
Tremelo 47 51 0N 4 42 E
Trementina 159 35 27N 105 30W
Tremiti, I. 63 42 8N 15 30 E
Tremonton 160 41 45N 112 10W
Tremp 58 42 10N 0 52 E
Trenary 156 46 12N 86 59W
Trenčin 53 48 52N 18 4 E
Trenche, R. 150 47 46N 72 53W
Trenggalek 103 8 5 S 111 44 E
Trenque Lauquen 172 36 0 S 62 45W
Trent, R. 33 53 33N 0 44W
Trentham 32 52 59N 2 12W
Trentino-Alto Adige □ 62 46 5N 11 0 E
Trento 62 46 5N 11 8 E
Trenton, Can. 150 44 10N 77 40W
Trenton, Mo., U.S.A. 158 40 5N 93 37W
Trenton, Nebr., U.S.A. 158 40 14N 101 4W
Trenton, N.J., U.S.A. 162 40 15N 74 41W
Trenton, Tenn., U.S.A. 159 35 58N 88 57W
Trepassey 151 46 43N 53 25W
Tréport, Le 42 50 3N 1 20 E
Treptow 48 53 42N 13 15 E
Trepuzzi 65 40 26N 18 4 E
Tres Arroyos 172 38 20 S 60 20W
Três Corações 173 21 30 S 45 30W
Três Lagoas 171 20 50 S 51 50W
Tres Marias, Is. 164 21 25N 106 28W
Três Marias, Represa 171 18 12 S 45 15W
Tres Montes, C. 176 47 0 S 75 35W
Tres Pinos 163 36 48N 121 19W
Três Pontas 173 21 23 S 45 29W
Tres Puentes 172 27 50 S 70 15W
Três Puntas, C. 176 47 0 S 66 0W
Tres Rios 173 22 20 S 43 30W
Tres Valles 165 18 15N 96 8W
Tresco I. 30 49 57N 6 20W
Treshnish Is. 34 56 30N 6 25W
Treska, R. 66 41 45N 21 11 E
Treskavika Planina 66 43 40N 18 20 E
Trespaderne 58 42 47N 3 24W
Tretower 31 51 53N 3 11W
Trets 45 43 27N 5 41 E
Treuchtlingen 49 48 58N 10 55 E
Treuddyn 31 53 7N 3 8W
Treuenbrietzen 48 52 6N 12 51 E
Treungen 75 59 1N 8 31 E
Treviglio 62 45 31N 9 35 E
Trevinca, Peña 56 42 15N 6 46W
Treviso 63 45 40N 12 15 E
Trevose Hd. 30 50 33N 5 3W
Trévoux 45 45 57N 4 47 E
Trgovište 66 42 20N 22 10 E
Triabunna 138 42 30 S 147 55 E
Triánda 69 36 25N 28 10 E
Triang 101 3 13N 102 27 E
Triangle 162 38 33N 77 20W
Triaucourt-en-Argonne 43 48 59N 5 2 E
Tribsees 48 54 4N 12 46 E
Tribulation, C. 138 16 5 S 145 29 E
Tribune 158 38 30N 101 45W
Tricárico 65 40 37N 16 9 E
Tricase 65 39 56N 18 20 E
Trichinopoly = Tiruchchirappalli 97 10 45N 78 45 E
Trichur 97 10 30N 76 18 E
Trida 141 33 1 S 145 1 E
Trier 49 49 45N 6 37 E
Trieste 63 45 39N 13 45 E
Trieste, G. di 63 45 37N 13 40 E
Triggiano 65 41 4N 16 58 E
Triglav 63 46 30N 13 45 E
Trigno, R. 63 41 55N 14 37 E
Trigueros 57 37 24N 6 50W
Tríkeri 69 39 6N 23 5 E
Tríkhonis, Límni 69 38 34N 21 30 E
Tríkkala 68 39 34N 21 47 E
Tríkkala □ 68 39 41N 21 30 E
Trikora, G. 103 4 11 S 138 0 E
Trilj 63 43 38N 16 42 E
Trillick 38 54 27N 7 30W
Trillo 58 40 42N 2 35W
Trim 38 53 34N 6 48W
Trimdon 33 54 43N 1 23W
Trimley 29 51 59N 1 19 E
Trincomalee 97 8 38N 81 15 E
Trindade 171 16 40 S 49 30W
Trindade, I. 15 20 20 S 29 50W
Trinidad, Boliv. 174 14 54 S 64 50W
Trinidad, Colomb. 174 5 25N 71 40W
Trinidad, Cuba 166 21 40N 80 0W
Trinidad, Uruguay 172 33 30 S 56 50W
Trinidad, U.S.A. 159 37 15N 104 30W
Trinidad & Tobago ■ 167 10 30N 61 20W
Trinidad, I., Argent. 176 39 10 S 62 0W
Trinidad, I., S. Amer. 167 10 30N 61 15W
Trinidad, R. 165 17 49N 95 9W
Trinitápoli 65 41 22N 16 5 E
Trinity, Can. 151 48 22N 53 29W
Trinity, U.S.A. 159 30 50N 95 20W
Trinity B., Austral. 133 16 30 S 146 0 E
Trinity B., Can. 151 48 20N 53 10W
Trinity Mts. 159 40 20N 118 50W
Trinity R. 159 30 30N 95 0W
Trino 62 45 10N 8 18 E
Trion 157 34 35N 85 18W
Trionto C. 65 34 38N 16 47 E
Triora 62 44 0N 7 46 E
Tripoli = Tarabulus 92 34 31N 33 52 E
Tripoli = Tarâbulus 119 32 49N 13 7 E
Trípolis 69 37 31N 22 25 E
Tripp 158 43 16N 97 58W
Tripura □ 98 24 0N 92 0 E
Trischen, I. 48 54 3N 8 32 E
Tristan da Cunha, I. 15 37 6 S 12 20W
Trivandrum 97 8 31N 77 0 E
Trivento 65 41 48N 14 31 E
Trnava 53 48 23N 17 35 E
Trobriand Is. 135 8 30 S 151 0 E
Trochu 152 51 50N 113 13W
Trodely I. 150 52 15N 79 26W
Trogir 63 43 32N 16 15 E
Troglav, mt. 63 43 56N 16 36 E
Trögstad 71 59 37N 11 16 E
Tróia 65 41 22N 15 19 E
Troilus, L. 150 50 50N 74 35W
Troina 65 37 47N 14 34 E
Trois Fourches, Cap des 118 35 26N 2 58W
Trois Pistoles 151 48 5N 69 10W
Trois-Rivières 150 46 25N 72 40W
Troisvierges 47 50 8N 6 0 E
Troitsk 84 54 10N 61 35 E
Troitskiy 84 55 29N 37 18 E
Troitsko-Pechorsk 78 62 40N 56 10 E
Trölladyngja 74 64 54N 17 15W
Trolladyngja 74 64 49N 17 29W
Trollhättan 73 58 17N 12 20 E
Trollheimen 71 62 46N 9 1 E
Tromöy 71 58 28N 8 53 E
Troms fylke □ 74 68 56N 19 0 E
Tromsø 74 69 40N 18 56 E
Trona 163 35 46N 117 23W
Tronador, Mt. 176 41 53 S 71 0W
Tröndelag, N. □ 74 65 0N 12 0 E
Tröndelag, S. □ 71 62 0N 10 0 E
Trondheim 71 63 25N 10 25 E
Trondheimsfjorden 74 63 35N 10 30 E
Trönninge 73 56 38N 12 59 E
Trönö 72 61 22N 16 54 E
Tronto, R. 63 42 50N 13 46 E
Troodos, mt. 128 34 58N 32 55 E
Troon 34 55 33N 4 40W
Tropea 65 38 40N 15 53 E
Tropic 161 37 44N 112 4W
Tropoja 68 42 23N 20 10 E
Trossachs, The 34 56 14N 4 24W
Trostan Mt. 38 55 4N 6 10W
Trostberg 49 48 2N 12 33 E
Trotternish, dist. 36 57 32N 6 15W
Troup 159 32 10N 95 3W
Troup Hd. 37 57 41N 2 18W
Trout L., N.W. Terr., Can. 152 60 40N 121 40W
Trout L., Ont., Can. 153 51 20N 93 15W
Trout Lake 150 46 10N 85 2W
Trout, R. 152 61 19N 119 51W
Trout River 151 49 29N 58 8W
Trout Run 162 41 23N 77 3W
Trouville 42 49 21N 0 5 E
Trowbridge 28 51 18N 2 12W
Troy, Turkey 92 39 55N 26 20 E
Troy, Alabama, U.S.A. 157 31 50N 85 58W
Troy, Kans., U.S.A. 158 39 47N 95 2W
Troy, Mo., U.S.A. 158 38 56N 90 59W
Troy, Montana, U.S.A. 160 48 30N 115 58W
Troy, N.Y., U.S.A. 162 42 45N 73 39W
Troy, Ohio, U.S.A. 156 40 0N 84 10W
Troy, Pa., U.S.A. 162 41 47N 76 47W
Troyan 67 42 57N 24 43 E
Troyes 43 48 19N 4 3 E
Trpanj 66 43 1N 17 15 E
Trstena 53 49 21N 19 37 E
Trstenik 66 43 36N 21 0 E
Trubchevsk 80 52 33N 33 47 E
Truc Giang 101 10 14N 106 22 E
Trucial States = Utd. Arab Emirates 93 24 0N 54 30 E
Truckee 160 39 20N 120 11W
Trujillo, Colomb. 174 4 10N 76 19W
Trujillo, Hond. 166 16 0N 86 0W
Trujillo, Peru 174 8 0 S 79 0W
Trujillo, Spain 57 39 28N 5 55W
Trujillo, U.S.A. 159 35 34N 104 44W
Trujillo, Venez. 174 9 22N 70 26W
Truk Is. 131 7 25N 151 46 E
Trull 28 50 58N 3 8W
Trumann 159 35 42N 90 32W
Trumansburg 162 42 33N 76 40W
Trumbull, Mt. 161 36 25N 113 32W
Trumpington 29 52 11N 0 6 E
Trún 66 42 51N 22 38 E
Trun, France 42 48 50N 0 2 E
Trun, Switz. 51 46 45N 8 59 E
Trundle 141 32 53 S 147 42 E
Trung-Phan, reg. 100 16 0N 108 0 E
Truro, Austral. 140 34 24 S 139 9 E
Truro, Can. 151 45 21N 63 14 E
Truro, U.K. 30 50 17N 5 2W
Trûscŭu, Muntii 70 46 14N 23 14 E
Truskmore, mt. 38 54 23N 8 20W
Truslove 137 33 20 S 121 45 E
Trustrup 73 56 20N 10 46 E
Truth or Consequences 161 33 9N 107 16W
Trutnov 52 50 37N 15 54 E
Truxton 162 42 45N 76 2W
Truyère, R. 44 44 38N 2 34 E
Trwyn Cilan 31 52 47N 4 31W
Tryavna 67 42 54N 25 25 E
Tryon 157 35 15N 82 16W
Trzciarka 54 53 3N 16 25 E
Trzciel 54 52 23N 15 50 E
Trzcinsko-Zdroj 54 52 58N 14 35 E
Trzebiez 54 53 38N 14 31 E
Trzebinia 54 50 11N 19 30 E
Trzeblatów 54 54 3N 15 18 E
Trzebnica 54 51 20N 17 1 E
Trzemeszno 54 52 33N 17 48 E
Tržič 63 46 22N 14 18 E
Tsafriya 90 31 59N 34 51 E
Tsaidam 105 37 0N 95 0 E
Tsak'o 108 31 56N 99 35 E
Tsamandás 68 39 46N 20 21 E
Tsamkong = Chanchiang 109 21 15N 110 20 E
Tsana Dzong 99 28 0N 91 55 E
Tsanga 99 30 43N 100 32 E
Ts'angchi 108 31 48N 105 57 E
Ts'angchou 106 38 10N 116 50 E
Tsangpo 99 29 40N 89 0 E
Ts'angyüan 108 23 9N 99 15 E
Ts'ao Ho, R. 107 40 32N 124 11 E
Tsaochuang 107 34 30N 117 49 E
Tsaochwang 174 35 11N 115 28 E
Ts'aohsien 106 34 50N 115 31 E
Tsaoyang 109 32 8N 112 42 E
Tsaratanana 129 16 47 S 47 39 E
Tsaratanana, Mt. de 129 14 0 S 49 0 E
Tsarevo = Michurin 67 42 9N 27 51 E
Tsaring Nor 99 34 40N 97 20 E
Tsaritsáni 68 39 53N 15 14 E
Tsau 128 20 8 S 22 29 E
Tsaukaib 128 26 37 S 15 39 E
Tsebrikovo 82 47 9N 30 10 E
Ts'ehung 108 25 2N 105 47 E
Tselinograd 76 51 10N 71 30 E
Tsengch'eng 109 23 17N 113 49 E
Ts'enkung 108 27 13N 108 45 E
Tsetserleg 105 47 36N 101 32 E
Tshabong 128 26 2 S 22 29 E
Tshane 125 24 5 S 21 54 E
Tshela 124 5 4 S 13 0 E
Tshesebe 129 20 43 S 27 32 E
Tshhinvali 83 42 14N 44 1 E
Tshibeke 126 2 40 S 28 35 E
Tshibinda 126 2 23 S 28 30 E
Tshikapa 124 6 17 S 21 0 E
Tshilenge 126 6 12 S 23 40 E
Tshinsenda 127 12 15N 28 0 E
Tshofa 124 5 8 S 25 8 E
Tshombe 129 25 18 S 45 29 E
Tshwane 128 22 24 S 22 1 E
Tsigara 128 20 22 S 25 54 E
Tsihombe 125 25 10 S 45 41 E
Tsilmamo 123 6 1N 35 10 E
Tsimlyansk 83 47 45N 42 0 E
Tsimlyanskoye Vdkhr. 83 48 0N 43 0 E
Tsinan = Chinan 106 36 32N 117 0 E
Tsineng 128 27 05 S 23 05 E
Tsinga, mt. 68 41 23N 24 44 E
Tsinghai □ 105 36 0N 96 0 E
Tsingtao = Ch'ingtao 107 36 5N 120 25 E
Tsinjomitondraka 129 15 40 S 47 8 E
Tsiroanomandidy 129 18 46 S 46 2 E
Tsivilsk 81 55 50N 47 25 E
Tsivory 129 24 4 S 46 5 E
Tskhinali 79 42 22N 43 52 E
Tso Chiang, R. 108 22 52N 108 5 E
Tso Morari, L. 95 32 50N 78 20 E
Tsochou 108 22 36N 107 36 E
Tsoch'üan 106 37 3N 113 27 E
Tsodilo Hill 128 18 49 S 21 43 E
Tsogttsetsiy 106 43 43N 105 35 E
Tsokung 108 29 55N 97 44 E
Tsona Dzong 99 28 0N 91 55 E
Tsoshui 106 33 40N 109 9 E
Tsouhsien 106 35 24N 116 58 E
Tsu 111 34 45N 136 25 E
Tsu L. 152 60 40N 111 52W
Tsuchiura 111 36 12N 140 15 E
Tsugaru-Kaikyō 112 41 35N 141 0 E
Tsukumi 110 33 4N 131 52 E
Tsukushi-Sanchi 110 33 25N 130 30 E
Tsumeb 128 19 9 S 17 44 E
Tsumis 128 23 39 S 17 29 E
Tsuna 110 34 28N 134 56 E
Ts'ungchiang 108 25 45N 108 54 E
Tsunhua 107 40 12N 117 56 E
Tsuni 108 27 43N 106 52 E
Tsuno-Shima 110 34 21N 130 52 E
Tsuru 111 35 31N 138 57 E
Tsuruga 111 35 45N 136 2 E
Tsuruga-Wan 111 35 50N 136 3 E
Tsurugi 111 36 37N 136 37 E
Tsurugi-San 110 33 51N 134 6 E
Tsurumi-Saki 110 32 56N 132 5 E
Tsuruoka 112 38 44N 139 50 E
Tsurusaki 110 33 14N 131 41 E
Tsushima 111 35 10N 136 43 E
Tsushima, I. 110 34 20N 129 20 E
Tsvetkovo 82 49 15N 31 33 E
Tu, R. 98 22 50N 97 15 E
Tua, R. 57 41 19N 7 15W
Tuai 143 38 47 S 177 15 E
Tuakau 142 37 16 S 174 59 E
Tual 103 5 30 S 132 50 E
Tuam 38 53 30N 8 50W
Tuamarina 143 41 25 S 173 59 E
Tuamgraney 39 52 54N 8 32W
Tuamotu Arch = Touamotou 131 17 0 S 144 0W
Tuan 108 23 59N 108 3 E
T'uanch'i 108 27 28N 107 7 E
T'uanfeng 109 30 38N 114 52 E
Tuao 103 17 47 S 121 30 E
Tuapse 83 44 5N 39 10 E
Tuatapere 143 46 8 S 167 41 E
Tuath, Loch 34 56 30N 6 15W
Tuba City 161 36 8N 111 12W
Tubac 161 31 45N 111 2W
Tubai Is. = Touboua, Îles 131 25 0 S 150 0W
Tuban 102 6 57 S 112 4 E
Tubarão 173 28 30 S 49 0W
Tubas 90 32 20N 35 22 E
Tubau 102 3 10N 113 40 E
Tubayq, Jabal at 122 29 30N 27 30 E
Tubbergen 46 52 24N 6 48 E
Tübingen 48 48 31N 9 4 E
Tubize 47 50 42N 4 13 E
Tubja, W. 122 25 27N 38 55 E
Tubruq, (Tobruk) 117 32 7N 23 55 E
Tubuai, Îles 131 25 0 S 150 0W
Tuc Trung 101 11 1N 107 12 E
Tucacas 174 10 48N 68 19W
Tucano 170 10 58 S 38 48W
Tuch'ang 109 29 15N 116 13 E
T'uch'ang 109 24 42N 121 25 E
Tuchodi, R. 152 58 17N 123 42W
Tuchola 54 53 33N 17 52 E
Tuchów 54 49 54N 21 1 E
T'uch'üan 107 45 22N 121 41 E
Tuckanarra 137 27 8 S 118 1 E
Tuckernuck I. 162 41 15N 70 17W
Tucson 161 32 14N 110 59W
Tucumán 172 26 50 S 65 20W
Tucumán □ 172 26 48 S 66 2W
Tucumcari 159 35 12N 103 45W
Tucupido 174 9 17N 65 47W
Tucupita 174 9 14N 62 3W
Tucuracas 174 11 45N 72 22W
Tucuruí 170 3 42 S 49 27W
Tuczno 54 53 13N 16 10 E
Tudela 58 42 4N 1 39W
Tudela de Duero 56 41 37N 4 39W
Tudor, Lac 151 55 50N 65 25W
Tudora 70 47 31N 26 45 E
Tudweiliog 31 52 54N 4 37W
Tuella, R. 56 41 50N 7 10W
Tuen 139 28 33 S 145 37 E
Tueré, R. 170 2 48 S 50 59W
Tufi 135 9 8 S 149 19 E
Tugidak I. 147 56 30N 154 40W
Tuguegarao 103 17 35N 121 42 E
Tugur 77 53 50N 136 45 E
Tugwa 128 17 27 S 18 33 E
Tukangbesi, Kepulauan 103 6 0 S 124 0 E
Tukarak I. 150 56 15N 78 45W
Tukobo 120 5 1N 2 47W
Tūkrah 119 32 30N 20 37 E
Tuku, mt. 123 9 10N 36 43 E
Tukums 80 57 2N 23 3 E
Tukuyu 127 9 17 S 33 35 E
Tukzar 93 35 55N 66 25 E
Tula, Hidalgo, Mexico 165 20 0N 99 20W
Tula, Tamaulipas, Mexico 165 23 0N 99 40W
Tula, Nigeria 121 9 51N 11 27 E
Tula, U.S.S.R. 81 54 13N 37 32 E
Tulak 93 33 55N 63 40 E
Tulancingo 165 20 5N 98 22W
Tulanssu 105 36 52N 98 24 E
Tulare 163 36 15N 119 26W
Tulare Basin 163 36 0N 119 48W
Tulare Lake 161 36 0N 119 53W
Tularosa 161 33 4N 106 1W
Tulbagh 128 33 16 S 19 6 E
Tulcán 174 0 48N 77 43W
Tulcea 70 45 13N 28 46 E
Tulcea □ 70 45 0N 29 0 E
Tulchin 82 48 41N 28 55 E
•Tuléar 129 23 21 S 43 40 E
••Tuléar □ 129 21 0 S 45 0 E
Tulemalu L. 153 62 58N 99 25W
Tulgheş 70 4 58N 25 45 E
Tuli, Indon. 103 1 24 S 122 26 E
Tuli, Zimb. 127 21 58 S 29 13 E
Tuliuchen 106 39 1N 116 54 E
Tulkarm 90 32 19N 35 10 E
Tulla, Ireland 39 52 53N 8 45W
Tulla, U.S.A. 159 34 35N 101 44W
Tulla, L. 34 56 33N 4 47W
Tullaghoge 38 54 36N 6 43W
Tullaghought 39 52 25N 7 22W
Tullahoma 157 35 23N 86 12W
Tullamore, Austral. 141 32 39 S 147 36 E
Tullamore, Ireland 39 53 17N 7 30W
Tullaroan 39 52 40N 7 27W
Tulle 44 45 16N 0 47 E
Tullibigeal 141 33 25 S 146 44 E
Tullins 45 45 18N 5 29 E
Tulln 52 48 20N 16 4 E
Tullow 39 52 48N 6 45W

*Renamed Toliara
**Renamed Toliara □

Tullus **123** 11 7N 24 40 E
Tully, Austral. **138** 17 56 S 145 55 E
Tully, Ireland **38** 53 44N 8 9W
Tully, U.S.A. **162** 42 48N 76 7W
Tully Cross **38** 53 35N 9 59W
Tůlmaciu **70** 45 38N 24 19 E
Tulmaythah **117** 32 40N 20 55 E
Tulmur **138** 22 40 S 142 20 E
Tulnici **70** 45 51N 26 38 E
Tulovo **67** 42 33N 25 32 E
Tulsa **159** 36 10N 96 0W
Tulsequah **152** 58 39N 133 35W
Tulsk **38** 53 47N 8 15W
Tulu Milki **123** 9 55N 38 14 E
Tulu Welel, Mt. **123** 8 56N 35 30 E
Tulua **174** 4 6N 76 11W
T'ulufan **105** 42 56N 89 10 E
Tulun **77** 54 40N 100 10 E
Tulungagung **103** 8 5 S 111 54 E
Tum **103** 3 28 S 130 21 E
Tuma **81** 55 10N 40 30 E
Tuma, R. **166** 13 18N 84 50W
Tumaco **174** 1 50N 78 45W
Tumatumari **174** 5 20N 58 55W
Tumba **72** 59 12N 17 48 E
Tumba, L. **124** 0 50 S 18 0 E
Tumbarumba **141** 35 44 S 148 0 E
Tumbaya **172** 23 50 S 65 20W
Tumbes **174** 3 30 S 80 20W
Tumbwa **127** 11 25 S 27 15 E
Tumby B. **140** 34 21 S 136 8 E
T'umen **107** 42 55N 129 50 E
T'umen Kiang, R. **107** 42 18N 130 41 E
Tumeremo **174** 7 18N 61 30W
Tumiritinga **171** 18 58 S 41 38W
Tumkur **97** 13 18N 77 12 E
Tumleberg **73** 58 16N 12 52 E
Tummel, L. **37** 56 43N 3 55W
Tummel, R. **37** 56 42N 4 5W
T'umot'eyuch'i **106** 40 42N 111 8 E
Tump **93** 26 7N 62 16 E
Tumpat **101** 6 11N 102 10 E
Tumsar **96** 21 26N 79 45 E
Tumu **120** 10 56N 1 56W
Tumucumaque, Serra de **175** 2 0N 55 0W
Tumut **141** 35 16 S 148 13 E
Tumutuk **84** 55 1N 53 19 E
Tumwater **160** 47 0N 122 58W
Tuna, Pta. **147** 17 59N 65 53W
Tunas de Zaza **166** 21 39N 79 34W
Tunbridge Wells **29** 51 7N 0 16 E
T'unch'i **105** 29 50N 118 26 E
Tuncurry **141** 32 9 S 152 29 E
Tunduru **127** 11 0 S 37 25 E
Tunduru □ **127** 11 5 S 37 22 E
Tundzha, R. **67** 42 0N 26 35 E
Tune **71** 59 16N 11 2 E
Tung Chiang, R. **109** 22 55N 113 35 E
Tung-Pei **77** 44 0N 126 0 E
Tunga La **99** 29 0N 94 14 E
Tunga Pass **98** 29 0N 94 14 E
Tunga, R. **97** 13 42N 75 20 E
Tungabhadra Dam **97** 15 21N 76 23 E
Tungabhadra, R. **97** 15 30N 77 0 E
Tungachen **106** 36 15N 165 12 E
Tungan **109** 26 24N 111 17 E
T'ungan **109** 24 44N 118 9 E
T'ungcheng, Anhwei, China **109** 31 3N 116 58 E
T'ungcheng, Hupeh, China **109** 29 15N 113 49 E
Tungch'i **108** 28 43N 106 42 E
T'ungchiang, Heilungkiang, China **105** 47 40N 132 30 E
T'ungchiang, Szechwan, China **108** 31 56N 107 15 E
Tungchingch'eng **107** 44 9N 129 7 E
Tungchuan **105** 35 4N 109 2 E
T'ungch'uan **106** 35 95N 109 5 E
Tungch'uan **108** 26 9N 103 7 E
Tungfanghsien, (Paso) **100** 18 50N 108 33 E
Tungfeng **107** 42 40N 125 34 E
T'unghai **108** 24 8N 102 43 E
Tunghai Tao **109** 21 2N 110 25 E
Tunghsiang **109** 28 14N 116 35 E
T'unghsien **105** 39 45N 116 43 E
T'unghsin **106** 37 9N 106 28 E
T'unghua **107** 41 45N 126 0 E
Tungi **98** 23 53N 90 24 E
T'ungjen **105** 27 43N 109 10 E
Tungkan **108** 23 22N 105 9 E
Tungkou **107** 39 52N 124 8 E
Tungku **108** 31 52N 100 14 E
T'ungku **109** 28 32N 114 23 E
Tungkuan **109** 23 0N 113 39 E
T'ungkuan **105** 34 37N 110 27 E
Tungkuang **106** 37 53N 116 32 E
Tungla **166** 13 24N 84 15W
Tunglan **108** 24 30N 107 23 E
T'ungliang **108** 29 52N 106 2 E
T'ungliao **107** 43 37N 122 16 E
Tungling **109** 31 0N 117 54 E
Tungliu **109** 30 13N 116 55 E
T'unglu **109** 29 49N 119 40 E
Tungnafellsjökull **74** 64 45N 17 55W
T'ungnan **108** 30 14N 105 48 E
Tungning **107** 44 3N 131 7 E
T'ungpai **109** 32 22N 113 24 E
Tungp'ing **106** 35 55N 116 18 E
Tungpu **99** 31 42N 98 19 E
Tungshan **109** 23 40N 117 31 E
Tungshih **109** 24 12N 120 43 E
Tungsten, Can. **152** 61 57N 128 16W
Tungsten, U.S.A. **160** 40 50N 118 10W
Tungt'ai **109** 32 50N 120 46 E
T'ungtao **108** 26 21N 109 36 E
T'ungtien **108** 26 40N 99 32 E
Tungt'ing Hu **109** 29 18N 112 45 E
Tungtzu **108** 28 8N 106 49 E
Tunguchumuch'inch'i **106** 45 33N 116 50 E
Tunguska, Nizhmaya, R. **77** 64 0N 95 0 E
Tunguska, Podkammenaya, R. **77** 61 0N 98 0 E
T'ungwei **106** 35 18N 105 10 E
T'ungyü **107** 44 48N 123 6 E
Tunhua **107** 43 20N 128 10 E
Tunhuang **105** 40 10N 94 50 E
Tuni **96** 17 22N 82 43 E
Tunia **174** 2 41N 76 31W
Tunica **159** 34 43N 90 23W
Tunis **119** 36 50N 10 11 E
Tunis, Golfe de **119** 37 0N 10 30 E
Tunisia ■ **119** 33 30N 9 10 E
Tunja **174** 5 40N 73 25W
Tunkhannock **162** 41 32N 75 56W
T'unliu **106** 36 19N 112 54 E
Tunnsjøen **74** 64 45N 13 25 E
Tuno I. **73** 55 58N 10 27 E
T'unpuli Shan **105** 35 0N 89 30 E
Tunstall **29** 52 7N 1 28 E
Tuntatuliag **147** 60 20N 162 45W
Tunungayualuk I. **151** 56 0N 61 0W
Tunuyán **172** 33 55 S 69 0W
Tunuyán, R. **172** 33 33 S 67 30W
Tuolumne **163** 37 59N 120 16W
Tuolumne, R. **163** 37 36N 121 13W
Tuoy-Khaya **77** 62 32N 111 18 E
Tupã **173** 21 57 S 50 28W
Tupaciguara **171** 18 35 S 48 42W
Tuparro, R. **174** 5 0N 68 40W
Tupelo **157** 34 15N 88 42W
Tupik **77** 54 26N 119 57 E
Tupinambaranas, I. **174** 3 0 S 58 0W
Tupirama **170** 8 58 S 48 12W
Tupiratins **170** 8 23 S 48 8W
Tupiza **172** 21 30 S 65 40W
Tupman **163** 35 18N 119 21W
Tupper **152** 55 32N 120 1W
Tupper L. **156** 44 18N 74 30W
Tupungato, Cerro **172** 33 15 S 69 50W
Tuque, La **150** 47 30N 72 50W
Túquerres **174** 1 5N 77 37W
Tur **90** 31 47N 35 14 E
Tura, India **98** 25 30N 90 16 E
Tura, U.S.S.R. **77** 64 20N 99 30 E
Tura, R. **84** 57 12N 66 56 E
Turaba, W. **122** 21 15N 41 32 E
Turagua, Serranía **174** 7 20N 64 35W
Turaiyur **97** 11 9N 78 38 E
Turakina **142** 40 3 S 175 16 E
Turakirae Hd. **142** 41 26 S 174 56 E
Tūrān **93** 35 45N 56 50 E
Turan **77** 51 38N 101 40 E
Turbenthal **51** 47 27N 8 51 E
Tureburg **72** 59 30N 17 58 E
Turégano **56** 41 9N 4 1W
Turek **54** 52 3N 18 30 E
Turen **174** 9 17N 69 6W
Turfan Depression **105** 42 45N 89 0 E
Turgay **84** 49 38N 63 30 E
Turgay, R. **84** 48 1N 62 45 E
Tŭrgovishte **67** 43 17N 26 38 E
Turgutlu **92** 38 30N 27 48 E
Turhal **82** 40 24N 36 19 E
Turia, R. **58** 39 43N 1 0W
TuriaçI **170** 1 40 S 45 28W
TuriaçI, R. **170** 3 0 S 46 0W
Turigshih **100** 18 42N 109 27 E
Turin = Torino **62** 45 3N 7 40 E
Turin Taber **152** 49 47N 112 24W
Turinsk **84** 58 3N 63 42 E
Turkana □ **126** 3 0N 35 30 E
Turkana, L. **80** 4 10N 32 10 E
Turkestan **76** 43 10N 68 10 E
Turkestanskiy, Khrebet **85** 39 35N 69 0 E
Túrkeve **53** 47 6N 20 44 E
Turkey ■ **92** 39 0N 36 0 E
Turkey Creek P.O. **136** 17 2 S 128 12 E
Turki **81** 52 0N 43 15 E
Turkmen S.S.R. □ **85** 39 0N 59 0 E
Turks Is. **167** 21 20N 71 20W
Turks Island Passage **167** 21 30N 71 20W
Turku (Åbo) **75** 60 30N 22 19 E
Turku-Pori □ **75** 60 27N 22 15 E
Turkwell, R. **126** 2 30N 35 20 E
Turlock **163** 37 30N 120 55W
Turnagain, C. **142** 40 28 S 176 38 E
Turnagain, R. **152** 59 12N 127 35W
Turnberry, Can. **153** 53 25N 101 45W
Turnberry, U.K. **34** 55 19N 4 50W
Turneffe Is. **165** 17 20N 87 50W
Turner **160** 48 52N 108 25W
Turner Pt. **138** 11 47 S 133 32 E
Turner River **136** 17 52 S 128 16 E
Turner Valley **152** 50 40N 114 17W
Turners Falls **162** 42 36N 72 34W
Turnhout **47** 51 19N 4 57 E
Tŭrnitz **52** 47 55N 15 29 E
Turnor L. **153** 56 35N 108 35W
Turnov **52** 50 34N 15 10 E
Turnovo **67** 43 5N 25 41 E
Turnovo □ **67** 43 4N 25 39 E
Turnu Mǔgurele **70** 43 46N 24 56 E
Turnu Roşu Pasul **70** 45 33N 24 17 E
Turnu-Severin **70** 44 39N 22 41 E
Turö **73** 55 2N 10 40 E
Turon **159** 37 48N 98 27W
Tuross Head **141** 36 3 S 150 8 E
Turriff **37** 57 32N 2 28W
Tursha **81** 56 50N 47 45 E
Tursi **65** 40 15N 16 27 E
Turtle Hd. I. **138** 10 50 S 142 37 E
Turtle L., Can. **153** 53 36N 108 38W
Turtle L., N.D., U.S.A. **158** 47 30N 100 55W
Turtle L., Wis., U.S.A. **158** 45 22N 92 10W
Turtleford **153** 53 23N 108 57W
Turua **142** 37 14 S 175 35 E
Turubah **92** 28 20N 43 15 E
Turukhansk **77** 65 50N 87 50 E
Turun ja Porin lääni □ **75** 60 27N 22 15 E
Turzovka **53** 49 25N 18 41 E
Tuscaloosa **157** 33 13N 87 31W
Tuscánia **63** 42 25N 11 53 E
Tuscany = Toscana **62** 43 28N 11 15 E
Tuscola, Ill., U.S.A. **156** 39 48N 88 15W
Tuscola, Tex., U.S.A. **159** 32 15N 99 48W
Tuscumbia **157** 34 42N 87 42W
Tushan **106** 25 50N 107 33 E
Tushino **81** 55 44N 37 29 E
Tuskar Rock **39** 52 12N 6 10W
Tuskegee **157** 32 24N 85 39W
Tŭšnad **70** 47 30N 22 33 E
Tustna **71** 63 10N 8 5 E
Tuszyn **54** 51 36N 19 33 E
Tutaryd **73** 56 54N 13 59 E
Tutbury **28** 52 52N 1 41W
Tutikorin **97** 8 50N 78 12 E
Tutin **66** 43 0N 20 20 E
Tutóia **170** 2 45 S 42 20W
Tutoko Mt. **143** 44 35 S 168 1 E
Tutong **102** 4 47N 114 34 E
Tutova, R. **70** 46 20N 27 30 E
Tutrakan **67** 44 2N 26 40 E
Tutshi L. **152** 59 56N 134 30W
Tuttlingen **49** 47 59N 8 50 E
Tutuaia **103** 8 25 S 127 15 E
Tutye **140** 35 12 S 141 29 E
Tuva, A.S.S.R. □ **77** 51 30N 95 0 E
Tuxford **33** 53 14N 0 52W
Tuxpan **165** 20 50N 97 30W
Tuxtla Gutiérrez **165** 16 50N 93 10W
Tuy **56** 42 3N 8 39W
Tuy An **100** 13 17N 109 16 E
Tuy Doc **101** 12 15N 107 27 E
Tuy Hoa **100** 13 5N 109 17 E
Tuy Phong **101** 11 14N 108 43 E
Tuya L. **152** 59 7N 130 35W
Tuyen Hoa **100** 17 50N 106 10 E
Tuyen Quang **100** 21 50N 105 10 E
Tuymazy **84** 54 36N 53 42 E
Tuyun **108** 26 15N 107 32 E
Tuz Gölü **92** 38 45N 33 30 E
Tuz Khurmatli **92** 34 52N 44 41 E
Tuz Khurmatu **92** 34 50N 44 45 E
Tuzkan, Ozero **85** 40 35N 67 28 E
Tuzla **66** 44 34N 18 41 E
Tuzlov, R. **83** 47 28N 39 45 E
Tvåaker **73** 57 4N 12 25 E
Tværsted **73** 57 36N 10 12 E
Tvarskog **73** 56 34N 16 0 E
Tved **73** 56 12N 10 25 E
Tvedestrand **71** 58 38N 8 58 E
Tveitsund **71** 59 2N 8 31 E
Tvelt **71** 60 30N 7 11 E
Tvyrditsa **67** 42 42N 25 53 E
Twain Harte **163** 38 2N 120 14W
Twardogóra **54** 51 23N 17 28 E
Twatt **37** 59 6N 3 15W
Tweed, R. **35** 55 42N 2 10W
Tweede Exploërmond **46** 52 55N 6 56 E
Tweedmouth **35** 55 46N 2 1W
Tweedshaws **35** 55 26N 3 29W
Tweedsmuir Prov. Park **152** 52 55N 126 20W
Twello **46** 52 14N 6 6 E
Twelve Pins **38** 53 32N 9 50W
Twentynine Palms **163** 34 10N 116 4W
Twillingate **151** 49 42N 54 45W
Twin Bridges **160** 45 33N 112 23W
Twin Falls **160** 42 30N 114 30W
Twin Valley **158** 47 18N 96 15W
Twinnge **98** 21 58N 96 23 E
Twisp **160** 48 21N 120 5W
Twistringen **48** 52 48N 8 38 E
Two Harbors **158** 47 1N 91 40W
Two Hills **152** 53 43N 111 45W
Two Mile Borris **39** 52 41N 7 43W
Two Rivers **156** 44 10N 87 31W
Two Thumbs Ra. **143** 43 45 S 170 44 E
Two Tree **138** 18 25 S 140 3 E
Twofold B. **141** 37 8 S 149 59 E
Twong **123** 5 18N 28 29 E
Twyford, Berks., U.K. **29** 51 29N 0 51W
Twyford, Hants., U.K. **28** 51 1N 1 19W
Ty **73** 56 27N 8 32 E
Tyborön **73** 56 42N 8 12 E
Tychy **54** 50 9N 18 59 E
Tyczyn **54** 49 58N 22 2 E
Tydd St. Mary **29** 52 45N 0 9 E
Tykocin **54** 53 13N 22 46 E
Tyldal **71** 62 8N 10 48 E
Tyldesley **32** 53 31N 2 29W
Tyler, Minn., U.S.A. **158** 44 18N 96 15W
Tyler, Tex., U.S.A. **159** 44 18N 96 15W
Tylldal **71** 62 7N 10 45 E
Tylösand **73** 56 33N 12 40 E
Týn nad Vltavou **52** 49 13N 14 26 E
Tynagh **39** 53 10N 8 22W
Tyndall, Mt. **143** 43 15 S 170 55 E
Tyndinskiy **77** 55 10N 124 43 E
Tyndrum **34** 56 26N 4 41W
Tyne & Wear □ **35** 54 55N 1 35W
Tyne, R., Eng., U.K. **35** 54 58N 1 28W
Tyne, R., Scot., U.K. **35** 55 58N 2 45W
Tynemouth **35** 55 1N 1 27W
Tynset **71** 62 17N 10 47 E
Tyre = Sūr **90** 33 19N 35 16 E
Tyrifjorden **71** 60 2N 10 8 E
Tyringe **73** 56 9N 13 35 E
Tyristrand **71** 60 5N 10 5 E
Tyrnyauz **83** 43 21N 42 45 E
Tyrol = Tirol **52** 46 50N 11 20 E
Tyrone □ **38** 54 40N 7 15W
Tyrone, Co. **38** 54 40N 7 15W
Tyrrell Arm **153** 62 27N 97 30W
Tyrrell, L. **140** 35 20 S 142 50 E
Tyrrell L. **153** 63 7N 105 27W
Tyrrell, R. **140** 35 26 S 142 51 E
Tyrrhenian Sea **60** 40 0N 12 30 E
Tysfjörden **74** 68 10N 16 10 E
Tysmenitsa **80** 48 58N 24 50 E
Tysnes **71** 60 1N 5 30 E
Tyssedal **71** 60 7N 6 35 E
Tystberga **73** 58 51N 17 15 E
Tyulgan **84** 52 22N 56 12 E
Tyumen **84** 57 0N 65 18 E
Tyumen-Aryk **85** 44 2N 67 1 E
Tyup **85** 42 45N 78 20 E
Tyvoll **71** 62 43N 11 21 E
Tywardreath **30** 50 21N 4 40W
Tywi, R. **31** 51 48N 4 20W
Tywyn **31** 52 36N 4 5W
Tzaneen **129** 23 47 S 30 9 E
Tzefa **90** 31 7N 35 12 E
Tzermiadhes Neapolis **69** 35 11N 25 29 E
Tzoumérka, Óros **68** 39 30N 21 26 E
Tzu Shui, R. **109** 29 2N 112 55 E
Tzuch'ang **106** 37 12N 109 44 E
Tzuch'eng **107** 36 39N 117 56 E
Tzuch'i **109** 27 42N 116 58 E
Tz'uch'i **109** 29 59N 121 14 E
Tzuchien **99** 27 43N 98 34 E
Tzuchin **109** 23 38N 115 10 E
Tzuchung **108** 29 49N 104 55 E
Tz'uhsien **106** 36 22N 114 23 E
Tzuhsing **109** 25 58N 113 24 E
Tzukuei **105** 31 0N 110 38 E
Tzukung **108** 29 20N 104 50 E
Tz'uli **109** 29 25N 111 6 E
Tzummarum **46** 53 14N 5 32 E
Tzupo **105** 36 49N 118 5 E
T'zuyang **108** 32 31N 108 32 E
Tzuyang **108** 30 7N 104 39 E
Tzuyün **108** 25 45N 106 5 E

U

U Taphao **100** 12 35N 101 0 E
Uad Erni, O. **118** 26 30N 9 30W
Uainambi **174** 1 43N 69 51W
Uanda **138** 21 37 S 144 55 E
Uarsciek **91** 2 28N 45 55 E
Uasadi-jidi, Sierra **174** 4 54N 65 18W
Uasin □ **126** 0 30N 35 20 E
Uassem **90** 32 59N 36 2 E
Uato-Udo **103** 4 3 S 126 6 E
Uatumã, R. **174** 1 30 S 59 25W
Uauá **170** 9 50 S 39 28W
Uaupés **174** 0 8 S 67 5W
Uaxactún **166** 17 25N 89 29W
Ub **66** 44 28N 20 6 E
Ubá **173** 21 0 S 43 0W
Ubaitaba **171** 14 18 S 39 20W
Ubangi, R. = Oubangi **124** 1 0N 17 50 E
Ubaté **174** 5 19N 73 49W
Ubauro **94** 28 15N 69 45 E
Ube **110** 33 56N 131 15 E
Ubeda **59** 38 3N 3 23W
Uberaba **171** 19 50 S 47 55W
Uberlândia **171** 19 0 S 48 20W
Ubiaja **121** 6 41N 6 22 E
Ubolratna Phong, L. **100** 16 45N 102 30 E
Ubombo **129** 27 31 S 32 4 E
Ubon Ratchathani **100** 15 15N 104 50 E
Ubondo **126** 0 55 S 25 42 E
Ubort, R. **80** 51 45N 28 30 E
Ubrique **57** 36 41N 5 27W
Ubundi **126** 0 22 S 25 30 E
Ucayali, R. **174** 6 0 S 75 0W
Uccle **47** 50 48N 4 22 E
Uchaly **84** 54 19N 59 27 E
Uchi Lake **153** 51 10N 92 40W
Uchiko **110** 33 33N 132 39 E
Uchiura-Wan **112** 42 25N 140 40 E
Uchte **48** 52 29N 8 52 E
Uchterek **85** 41 45N 73 12 E
Uckerath **48** 50 44N 7 22 E
Uckfield **29** 50 58N 0 6 E
Ucluelet **152** 48 57N 125 32W
Ucolta **107** 32 56 S 138 59 E
Ucuriş **70** 46 41N 21 58 E
Uda, R. **77** 54 42N 135 14 E
Udaipur **94** 24 36N 73 44 E
Udaipur Garhi **95** 27 0N 86 35 E
Udamalpet **97** 10 35N 77 15 E
Udbina **63** 44 31N 15 47 E
Uddeholm **72** 60 1N 13 38 E
Uddel **46** 52 15N 5 48 E
Uddevalla **73** 58 21N 11 55 E
Uddingston **35** 55 50N 4 3W

Name	Page	Lat.	Long.
Uddjaur	74	65 55N	17 50 E
Uden	47	51 40N	5 37 E
Udgir	96	18 25N	77 5 E
Udhampur	95	33 0N	75 5 E
Udi	121	6 23N	7 21 E
Udine	63	46 5N	13 10 E
Udine □	63	46 3N	13 13 E
Udipi	97	13 25N	74 42 E
Udmurt, A.S.S.R. □	84	57 30N	52 30 E
Udon Thani	100	17 29N	102 46 E
Udubo	121	11 52N	10 35 E
Udvoj Balken	67	42 50N	26 50 E
Udzungwa Range	127	11 15 S	35 10 E
Ueckermünde	48	53 45N	14 1 E
Ueda	111	36 24N	138 16 E
Uedineniya, Os.	12	78 0N	85 0 E
Uele, R.	124	3 50N	22 40 E
Uelen	77	66 10N	170 0W
Uelzen	48	53 0N	10 33 E
Ueno	111	34 53N	136 14 E
Uere, R.	124	3 45N	24 45 E
Uetendorf	50	46 47N	7 34 E
Ufa	84	54 45N	55 55 E
Ufa, R.	84	56 30N	58 10 E
Uffculme	30	50 45N	3 19W
Ufford	29	52 6N	1 22 E
Ugad R.	125	20 55 S	14 30 E
Ugalla, R.	126	6 0 S	32 0 E
Ugamas	128	28 0 S	19 41 E
Uganda ■	126	2 0N	32 0 E
Ugborough	30	50 22N	3 53W
Ugchelen	46	52 11N	5 56 E
Ugento	65	39 55N	18 10 E
Ugep	121	5 53N	8 2 E
Ugie	129	31 10 S	28 13 E
Ugijar	59	36 58N	3 7W
Ugine	45	45 45N	6 25 E
Ugla	122	25 40N	37 42 E
Uglich	81	57 33N	38 13 E
Ugljane	63	43 35N	16 46 E
Ugra, R.	80	54 45N	35 30 E
Ugurchin	67	43 6N	24 26 E
Uh, R.	53	48 40N	22 0 E
Uherske Hradiště	53	49 4N	17 30 E
Uhersky Brod	53	49 1N	17 40 E
Uhrichsville	156	40 23N	81 22W
Uig, Lewis, U.K.	36	58 13N	7 1W
Uig, Skye, U.K.	36	57 35N	6 20W
Uinta Mts.	160	40 45N	110 30W
Uitenhage	128	33 40 S	25 28 E
Uitgeest	46	52 32N	4 43 E
Uithoorn	46	52 14N	4 50 E
Uithuizen	46	53 24N	6 41 E
Uitkerke	47	51 18N	3 9 E
Ujda = Oujda	118	34 45N	2 0W
Ujfehértó	53	47 49N	21 41 E
Ujh, R.	95	32 40N	75 30 E
Ujhani	95	28 0N	79 6 E
Uji	111	34 53N	135 48 E
Ujjain	94	23 9N	75 43 E
Ujpest	53	47 22N	19 6 E
Ujszász	53	47 19N	20 7 E
Ujung Pandang	103	5 10 S	119 20 E
Uka	77	57 50N	162 0 E
Ukara I.	126	1 44 S	33 0 E
Ukehe	121	6 40N	7 24 E
Ukerewe □	126	2 0 S	32 30 E
Ukerewe Is.	126	2 0 S	33 0 E
Ukholovo	81	54 47N	40 30 E
Ukhrul	98	25 10N	94 25 E
Ukhta	78	63 55N	54 0 E
Ukiah	160	39 10N	123 9W
Ukki Fort	95	33 28N	76 54 E
Ukmerge	80	55 15N	24 45 E
Ukraine S.S.R. □	82	48 0N	35 0 E
Uksyanskoye	84	55 57N	63 1 E
Ukwi	128	23 29 S	20 30 E
Ulaanbaatar	105	47 55N	106 53 E
Ulaangom	105	49 58N	92 2 E
Ulak I.	147	51 24N	178 58W
Ulamambri	141	31 19 S	149 23 E
Ulamba	127	9 3 S	23 38 E
Ulan Bator = Ulaanbaatar	105	47 55N	106 53 E
Ulan Ude	77	52 0N	107 30 E
Ulanbel	85	44 50N	71 7 E
Ulanga □	127	8 40 S	36 50 E
Ulanów	54	50 30N	22 16 E
Ulaya, Morogoro, Tanz.	126	7 3 S	36 55 E
Ulaya, Shinyanga, Tanz.	126	4 25 S	33 30 E
Ulbster	37	58 21N	3 9W
Ulceby Cross	33	53 14N	0 6 E
Ulcinj	66	41 58N	19 10 E
Ulco	128	28 21 S	24 15 E
Ulefoss	71	59 17N	9 16 E
Ulëza	68	41 46N	19 57 E
Ulfborg	73	56 16N	8 20 E
Ulft	46	51 53N	6 23 E
Ulhasnagar	96	19 15N	73 10 E
Ulinda	141	31 35 S	149 30 E
Uljma	66	45 2N	21 10 E
Ulla, R.	56	42 45N	8 30W
Ulladulla	141	35 21 S	150 29 E
Ullånger	72	62 58N	18 16 E
Ullapool	36	57 54N	5 10W
Ullared	73	57 8N	12 42 E
Ulldecona	58	40 36N	0 20 E
Ullswater, L.	32	54 35N	2 52W
Ullvättern, L.	72	59 30N	14 21 E
Ulm	49	48 23N	10 0 E
Ulmarra	139	29 37 S	153 4 E
Ulmeni	70	45 4N	46 40 E
Ulricehamn	73	57 46N	13 26 E
Ulrum	46	53 22N	6 20 E
Ulsberg	71	62 45N	9 59 E
Ulsfeinvik	71	62 21N	5 53 E
Ulster □	38	54 45N	6 30W
Ulster Canal	38	54 15N	7 0W
Ulstrem	67	42 1N	26 27 E
Ultima	140	35 22 S	143 18 E
Ulubaria	95	22 31N	88 4 E
Ulugh Muztagh	99	36 40N	87 30 E
Uluguru Mts.	126	7 15 S	37 30 E
Ulva, I.	34	56 30N	6 12W
Ulvenhout	47	51 33N	4 48 E
Ulverston	32	54 13N	3 7W
Ulverstone	138	41 11 S	146 11 E
Ulvik	71	60 35N	6 54 E
Ulvo	73	56 40N	14 37 E
Ulya	77	59 10N	142 0 E
Ulyanovsk	81	54 25N	48 25 E
Ulyasutay	105	47 45N	96 49 E
Ulysses	159	37 39N	101 25W
Ulzio	62	45 2N	6 49 E
Um Qeis	90	32 40N	35 41 E
Umag	63	45 26N	13 31 E
Umala	174	17 25 S	68 5W
Uman	82	48 40N	30 12 E
Umánaé	12	70 40N	52 10W
Umánaé Fjord	10	70 40N	52 0W
Umaria	99	23 35N	80 50 E
Umarkhed	96	19 37N	77 38 E
Umarkot	93	25 15N	69 40 E
Umatilla	160	45 58N	119 17W
Umba	78	66 50N	34 20 E
Umbertide	63	43 18N	12 20 E
Umboi I.	135	5 40 S	148 0 E
Umbrella Mts.	143	45 35 S	169 5 E
Umbria □	63	42 53N	12 30 E
Ume, R.	74	64 45N	18 30 E
Umeå	74	63 45N	20 20 E
Umera	103	0 12 S	129 30 E
Umfuli, R.	127	17 50 S	29 40 E
Umgusa	127	19 29 S	27 52 E
Umi	110	33 34N	130 30 E
Umiat	147	69 25N	152 20W
Umka	66	44 40N	20 19 E
Umkomaas	129	30 13 S	30 48 E
Umm al Aranib	119	26 10N	14 54 E
Umm al Qaiwain	93	25 30N	55 35 E
Umm Arda	123	15 17N	32 31 E
Umm az Zamul	93	22 35N	55 18 E
Umm Bel	123	13 35N	28 0 E
Umm Digulgulaya	123	10 28N	24 58 E
Umm Dubban	123	15 23N	32 52 E
Umm el Fahm	90	32 31N	35 9 E
Umm Hagar	123	14 20N	36 41 E
Umm Koweika	123	13 10N	32 16 E
Umm Lajj	92	25 0N	37 23 E
Umm Merwa	122	18 4N	32 30 E
Umm Qurein	123	16 3N	28 49 E
Umm Rumah	122	25 50N	36 30 E
Umm Ruwaba	123	12 50N	31 10 E
Umm Said	93	25 0N	51 40 E
Umm Sidr	123	14 29N	25 10 E
Ummanz I.	48	54 29N	13 9 E
Umnak.	147	53 20N	168 20W
Umnak I.	147	53 0N	168 0W
Umniati, R.	127	18 0 S	29 0 E
Umpang	101	16 3N	98 54 E
Umpqua, R.	160	43 30N	123 30W
Umrer	96	20 51N	79 18 E
Umreth	94	22 41N	73 4 E
Umshandige Dam	127	20 10 S	30 40 E
Umtali	127	18 58 S	32 38 E
Umtata	129	31 36 S	28 49 E
Umuahia-Ibeku	121	5 33N	7 29 E
Umvukwe Ra..	127	16 45 S	30 45 E
Umvuma	127	19 16 S	30 30 E
Umzimvubu, R.	129	31 38 S	29 33 E
Umzingwane, R.	127	21 30 S	29 30 E
Umzinto	129	30 15 S	30 45 E
Una	94	20 46N	71 8 E
Una, Mt.	143	42 13 S	172 36 E
Una, R.	63	44 50N	16 15 E
Unac, R.	63	44 42N	16 15 E
Unadilla	162	42 20N	75 17W
Unalanaska I.	147	54 0N	164 30W
Uncastillo	58	42 21N	1 8W
Uncia	174	18 25 S	66 40W
Uncompahgce Pk., Mt.	161	38 5N	107 32W
Unden	73	58 45N	14 25 E
Underbool	140	35 10 S	141 51 E
Undersaker	72	63 19N	13 21 E
Undersvik	72	61 36N	16 20 E
Undredal	71	60 57N	7 6 E
Unecha	80	52 50N	32 37 E
Ungarie	141	33 38 S	146 56 E
Ungarra	140	34 12 S	136 2 E
Ungava B.	149	59 30N	67 30W
Ungava Pen.	50	60 0N	75 0W
Ungeny	82	47 11N	27 51 E
Unggi	105	42 16N	130 28 E
Ungwatiri	123	16 52N	36 10 E
Uni	84	56 44N	51 47 E
União	170	4 50 S	37 50W
União da Vitória	173	26 5 S	51 0W
União dos Palamares	170	9 10 S	36 2W
Uniejów	54	51 59N	18 46 E
Unije, I.	63	44 40N	14 15 E
Unimak I.	147	54 30N	164 30W
Unimak Pass.	148	53 30N	165 15W
Union, Mo., U.S.A.	158	38 25N	91 0W
Union, S.C., U.S.A.	157	34 49N	81 39W
Union City, N.J., U.S.A.	162	40 47N	74 5W
Union City, Ohio, U.S.A.	156	40 11N	84 49W
Union City, Pa., U.S.A.	156	41 53N	79 50W
Union Gap	157	46 38N	120 29W
Unión, La, Chile	176	40 10 S	73 0W
Unión, La, Colomb.	174	1 35N	77 5W
Unión, La, El Sal.	165	13 20N	87 50W
Union, La	164	17 58N	101 49W
Unión, La, Spain	59	37 38N	0 53W
Unión, La, Venez.	174	7 28N	67 53W
Union, Mt.	161	34 34N	112 21W
Union of Soviet Soc. Rep. ■	77	47 0N	100 0 E
Union Springs	157	32 9N	85 44W
Uniondale Road	128	33 39 S	23 7 E
Uniontown	156	39 54N	79 45W
Unirea	70	44 15N	27 35 E
United Arab Emirates ■	93	23 50N	54 0 E
United Arab Republic ■	113	27 5N	30 0 E
United Kingdom ■	27	55 0N	3 0W
United States of America ■	155	37 0N	96 0W
Unity	153	52 30N	109 5W
Unjha	94	23 46N	72 24 E
Unnao	95	26 35N	80 30 E
Uno, Ilha	120	11 15N	16 13W
Unshin, R.	38	54 8N	8 26W
Unst, I.	36	60 50N	0 55W
Unstrut, R.	48	51 16N	11 29 E
Unter-Engadin	51	46 48N	10 20 E
Unterägeri	51	47 8N	8 36 E
Unterkulm	50	47 18N	8 7 E
Unterseen	50	46 41N	7 50 E
Unterwalden nid dem Wald □	51	46 50N	8 25 E
Unterwalden ob dem Wald □	51	46 55N	8 15 E
Unterwaldner Alpen	51	46 55N	8 15 E
Unterwasser	51	46 32N	8 21 E
Unturán, Sierra de	174	1 35N	64 40W
Unuk, R.	152	56 5N	131 3W
Ünye	82	41 5N	37 15 E
Unzen-Dake	111	32 45N	130 17 E
Unzha	81	57 40N	44 8 E
Unzha, R.	81	58 0N	43 40 E
Uors	51	46 42N	9 12 E
Uozu	111	36 48N	137 24 E
Upa, R.	53	50 45N	16 15 E
Upal	123	6 56N	34 12 E
Upata	174	8 1N	62 24W
Upavon	28	51 17N	1 49W
Upemba, L.	127	8 30 S	26 20 E
Upernavik	12	72 49N	56 20W
Upington	128	28 25 S	21 15 E
Upleta	94	21 46N	70 16 E
Upolu Pt.	147	20 16N	155 52W
Upper Alkali Lake	160	41 47N	120 0W
Upper Arrow L.	152	50 30N	117 50W
Upper Austria = Oberösterreich	52	48 15N	14 10 E
Upper Chapel	31	52 3N	3 26W
Upper Foster L.	153	56 47N	105 20W
Upper Heyford	28	51 54N	1 16W
Upper Hutt	142	41 8 S	175 5 E
Upper Klamath L.	160	42 16N	121 55W
Upper L. Erne	38	54 14N	7 22W
Upper Lake	160	39 10N	122 55W
Upper Manilla	141	30 38 S	150 40 E
Upper Marlboro	162	38 49N	76 45W
Upper Musquodoboit	151	45 10N	62 58W
Upper Sandusky	156	40 50N	83 17W
Upper Volta ■	120	12 0N	0 30W
Upperchurch	39	52 43N	8 2W
Upphärad	73	58 9N	12 19 E
Uppingham	29	52 36N	0 43W
Uppsala	72	59 53N	17 38 E
Uppsala län □	72	60 0N	17 30 E
Upshi	95	33 48N	77 52 E
Upstart, C.	138	19 41 S	147 45 E
Upton, U.K.	32	53 14N	2 52W
Upton, U.S.A.	158	44 8N	104 35W
Upton-upon-Severn	28	52 4N	2 12W
Upwey	28	50 40N	2 29W
Ur	92	30 55N	46 25 E
Ura-Tyube	85	39 55N	69 1 E
Urabá, Golfo de	174	8 25N	76 53W
Uracará	174	2 20 S	57 50W
Urach	49	48 29N	9 25 E
Uraga-Suidō	111	35 13N	139 45 E
Urakawa	112	42 9N	142 47 E
Ural, Mt.	141	33 21 S	146 12 E
Ural Mts. = Uralskie Gory	78	60 0N	59 0 E
Ural, R.	84	49 0N	52 0W
Uralla	141	30 37 S	151 29 E
Uralsk	84	51 20N	51 20 E
Uralskie Gory	78	60 0N	59 0 E
Urambo	126	5 4 S	32 47 E
Urambo □	126	5 0 S	32 0 E
Urana	141	35 15 S	146 21 E
Urandangi	138	21 32 S	138 14 E
Uranium City	153	59 34N	108 37W
Uraricaá, R.	174	3 20N	61 56W
Uravakonda	97	14 57N	77 12 E
Urawa	111	35 50N	139 40 E
Uray	76	60 5N	65 15 E
Urbana, Ill., U.S.A.	156	40 7N	88 12W
Urbana, Ohio, U.S.A.	156	40 9N	83 44W
Urbana, La	174	7 8N	66 56W
Urbánia	63	43 40N	12 31 E
Urbano Santos	170	3 12 S	43 23W
Urbel, R.	58	42 30N	3 49W
Urbino	63	43 43N	12 38 E
Urbión, Picos de	58	42 1N	2 52W
Urcos	174	13 30 S	71 30W
Urda, Spain	57	39 25N	3 43W
Urda, U.S.S.R.	83	48 52N	47 23 E
Urdinarrain	172	32 37 S	58 52W
Urdos	44	42 51N	0 35W
Urdzhar	76	47 5N	81 38 E
Ure, R.	33	54 20N	1 25W
Uren	81	57 35N	45 55 E
Ures	164	29 30N	110 30W
Ureshino	110	33 6N	129 59 E
Urfa	92	37 12N	38 50 E
Urfahr	52	48 19N	14 17 E
Urgench	76	41 40N	60 30 E
Urgun	93	32 55N	69 12 E
Urgut	85	39 23N	67 15 E
Uri	95	34 8N	74 2 E
Uri □	51	46 43N	8 35 E
Uribante, R.	174	7 25N	71 50W
Uribe	174	3 13N	74 24W
Uribia	174	11 43N	72 16W
Urim	90	31 18N	34 32 E
Uriondo	172	21 41 S	64 41W
Urique	164	27 13N	107 55W
Urique, R.	164	26 29N	107 58W
Urirotstock	51	46 52N	8 32 E
Urk	46	52 39N	5 36 E
Urla	92	38 20N	26 55 E
Urlati	70	44 59N	26 15 E
Urlingford	39	52 43N	7 35W
Urmia, L.	92	37 30N	45 30 E
Urmia	92	37 40N	45 0 E
Urmston	32	53 28N	2 22W
Urner Alpen	51	46 45N	8 45 E
Uroševac	66	42 23N	21 10 E
Urrao	174	6 20N	76 11W
Urshult	73	56 31N	14 50 E
Urso	123	9 35N	41 33 E
Ursus	54	52 21N	20 53 E
Uruaca	171	15 30 S	49 41W
Uruaçu	171	14 30 S	49 10W
Uruapán	164	19 30N	102 0W
Urubamba	174	13 5 S	72 10W
Urubamba, R.	174	11 0 S	73 0W
Uruçuca	171	14 35 S	39 16W
Uruçuí	170	7 20 S	44 28W
Uruçuí Prêto, R.	170	7 20 S	44 38W
Uruçuí, Serra do	170	9 0 S	44 45W
Urucuia, R.	171	16 8 S	45 5W
Uruguai, R.	173	24 0 S	53 30W
Uruguaiana	172	29 50 S	57 0W
Uruguay ■	172	32 30 S	55 30W
Uruguay, R.	172	28 0 S	56 0W
Urumchi = Wulumuchi	105	43 40N	87 50 E
Urup, I.	77	43 0N	151 0 E
Urup, R.	83	44 19N	41 30 E
Urutai	171	17 28 S	48 12W
Uruyên	174	5 41N	62 25W
Uruzgan □	93	33 30N	66 0 E
Uryupinsk	81	50 45N	42 3 E
Urzhum	81	57 10N	49 56 E
Urziceni	70	44 46N	26 42 E
Usa	110	33 31N	131 21 E
Usa, R.	78	66 20N	56 0 E
Uşak	92	38 43N	29 28 E
Usakos	128	22 0 S	15 31 E
Usambara Mts.	126	4 50 S	38 20 E
Usedom	48	53 50N	13 55 E
Useko	124	5 8 S	32 24 E
Usfan	122	21 58N	39 27 E
Ush-Tobe	76	45 16N	78 0 E
Ushakova, O.	12	82 0N	80 0 E
Ushant = Ouessant, Île d'	42	48 25N	5 5W
Ushashi	126	1 59 S	33 57 E
Ushat	123	7 59N	29 28 E
Ushibuka	110	32 11N	130 1 E
Ushuaia	176	54 50 S	68 23W
Ushumun	77	52 47N	126 32 E
Usk	31	51 42N	2 53W
Usk, R.	31	51 37N	2 56W
Uskedal	71	59 56N	5 53 E
Üsküdar	92	41 0N	29 5 E
Uslar	48	51 39N	9 39 E
Usman	81	52 5N	39 48 E
Usoga □	126	0 5N	33 30 E
Usoke	126	5 7 S	32 19 E
Usolye Sibirskoye	77	52 40N	103 40 E
Usoro	121	5 33N	6 11 E
Uspallata, P. de	172	32 30 S	69 28W
Uspenskiy	76	48 50N	72 55 E
Usquert	46	53 24N	6 36 E
Ussel	44	45 32N	2 18 E
Ussuriysk	77	43 40N	131 50 E
Ust	52	50 41N	14 2 E
Ust Aldan = Batamay	77	63 30N	129 15 E
Ust Amginskoye = Khandyga	77	62 30N	134 50 E
Ust-Bolsheretsk	77	52 40N	156 30 E
Ust Buzulukskaya	81	50 8N	42 11 E
Ust Doneckij	83	47 35N	40 55 E
Ust Donetskiy	83	47 35N	40 55 E
Ust Ilga	77	55 5N	104 55 E
Ust Ilimpeya = Yukti	77	63 20N	105 0 E
Ust-Ilimsk	77	58 3N	102 39 E
Ust Ishim	76	57 45N	71 10 E
Ust Kamchatsk	77	56 10N	162 0 E
Ust Kamenogorsk	76	50 0N	82 20 E
Ust Karenga	77	54 40N	116 45 E
Ust Khayryuzova	77	57 15N	156 55 E
Ust Kut	77	56 50N	105 10 E
Ust Kuyga	77	70 1N	135 36 E

Ust Labinsk 83 45 15N 39 50 E
Ust Luga 80 59 35N 28 26 E
Ust Maya 77 60 30N 134 20 E
Ust Mil 77 59 50N 133 0 E
Ust Nera 77 64 35N 143 15 E
Ust Olenek 77 73 0N 120 10 E
Ust-Omchug 77 61 9N 149 38 E
Ust Port 76 70 0N 84 10 E
Ust Tsilma 78 65 25N 52 0 E
Ust-Tungir 77 55 25N 120 15 E
Ust Urt = Ustyurt 76 44 0N 55 0 E
Ust Usa 78 66 0N 56 30 E
Ust-Uyskoye 84 54 16N 63 54 E
Ust Vorkuta 76 67 7N 63 35 E
Ustaoset 71 60 30N 8 2 E
Ustaritz 44 43 24N 1 27W
Uste 81 59 35N 39 40 E
Uster 51 47 22N 8 43 E
Usti na Orlici 53 49 58N 16 38 E
Usti nad Labem 52 50 41N 14 3 E
Ustica, I. 64 38 42N 13 10 E
Ustka 54 54 35N 16 55 E
Ustron 54 49 45N 18 48 E
Ustrzyki Dolne 54 49 27N 22 40 E
Ustye 77 55 30N 97 30 E
Ustyurt, Plato 76 44 0N 55 0 E
Ustyuzhna 81 58 50N 36 32 E
Ušće 66 43 43N 20 39 E
Usuki 110 33 8N 131 49 E
Usulután 166 13 25N 88 28W
Usumacinta, R. 165 17 0N 91 0W
Usva 84 58 41N 57 37 E
Uta 66 45 24N 21 13 E
Utah □ 160 39 30N 111 30W
Utah, L. 160 40 10N 111 58W
Ute Cr. 159 36 5N 103 45W
Utena 80 55 27N 25 40 E
Ütersen 48 53 40N 9 40 E
Utete 124 8 0S 38 45 E
Uthai Thani 100 15 22N 100 3 E
Uthal 94 25 44N 66 40 E
Uthmaniyah 92 25 5N 49 6 E
Utiariti 174 13 0S 58 10W
Utica 162 43 5N 75 18W
Utiel 58 39 37N 1 11W
Utik L. 153 55 15N 96 0W
Utikuma L. 152 55 50N 115 30W
Utinga 171 12 6S 41 5W
Uto 110 32 41N 130 40 E
Utrecht, Neth. 46 52 3N 5 8 E
Utrecht, S. Afr. 129 27 38S 30 20 E
Utrecht □ 46 52 6N 5 7 E
Utrera 57 37 12N 5 48W
Utsjoki 74 69 51N 26 59 E
Utsunomiya 111 36 30N 139 50 E
Uttar Pradesh □ 95 27 0N 80 0 E
Uttaradit 100 17 36N 100 5 E
Uttersberg 72 59 45N 15 39 E
Uttersley 73 54 56N 11 11 E
Uttoxeter 32 52 53N 1 50W
Utva, R. 84 51 28N 52 40 E
Utze 48 52 28N 10 11 E
Uudenmaan lääni □ 75 60 25N 25 0 E
Uusikaarlepyy 74 63 32N 22 31 E
Uusikaupunki 75 60 47N 21 25 E
Uva 84 56 59N 52 13 E
Uvac, R. 66 43 35N 19 40 E
Uvalde 159 29 15N 99 48W
Uvarovo 81 51 59N 42 14 E
Uvat 76 59 5N 68 50 E
Uvelskiy 84 54 26N 61 22 E
Uvinza 126 5 5S 30 24 E
Uvira 126 3 22S 29 3 E
Uvlova, R. 52 49 34N 13 20 E
Uvs Nuur, L. 105 50 20N 92 45 E
Uwa 110 33 22N 132 31 E
Uwainhid 92 24 50N 46 0 E
Uwajima 110 33 10N 132 35 E
Uxmal 165 20 22N 89 46W
Uyeasound 36 60 42N 0 55W
Uyo 121 5 1N 7 53 E
Uyu, R. 98 24 51N 94 57 E
Uyuk 85 43 36N 71 16 E
Uyuni 172 20 35S 66 55W
Uyuni, Salar de 172 20 10S 68 0W
Uzbekistan S.S.R. □ 85 40 5N 65 0 E
Uzen, Bol. 81 50 0N 49 30 E
Uzen, Mal. 81 50 0N 48 30 E
Uzerche 44 45 25N 1 35 E
Uzès 45 44 1N 4 26 E
Uzgen 85 40 46N 73 18 E
Uzh, R. 80 51 15N 29 45 E
Uzhgorod 80 48 36N 22 18 E
Uzlovaya 81 54 0N 38 5 E
Uzun-Agach 85 43 35N 76 20 E
Uzunköprü 67 41 16N 26 43 E
Uzure 126 4 40S 34 22 E
Uzwil 51 47 26N 9 9 E

V

Vaal, R. 128 27 40S 25 30 E
Vaaldam 129 27 0S 28 14 E
Vaals 47 50 46N 6 1 E
Vaalwater 129 24 15S 28 8 E
Vaasa 74 63 16N 21 35 E
Vaasan lääni □ 74 63 2N 22 50 E
Vaassen 46 52 17N 5 58 E
Vabre 44 43 42N 2 24 E
Vác 53 47 49N 19 10 E
Vacaria 173 28 31S 50 52W
Vacaville 163 38 21N 122 0W
Vach, R. 76 60 56N 76 38 E
Vache, I.-à 167 18 2N 73 35W
Väddö 72 59 55N 18 50 E
Väderum 73 57 32N 16 11 E
Vadnagar 94 23 47N 72 40 E
Vado Ligure 62 44 16N 8 26 E
Vadodara 94 22 20N 73 10 E
Vadsø 74 70 3N 29 50 E
Vadstena 73 58 28N 14 54 E
Vaduz 51 47 8N 9 31 E
Vaerøy, Nordland Fylke, Norway 74 67 40N 12 40 E
Vaerøy, Sogn og Fjordane, Norway 71 61 17N 4 45 E
Vagney 43 48 1N 6 43 E
Vagnhärad 72 58 57N 17 33 E
Vagos 56 40 33N 8 42W
Vagsöy, I. 71 62 0N 5 0 E
Váh, R. 53 49 10N 18 20 E
Vaigach 76 70 10N 59 0 E
Vaigai, R. 97 9 47N 78 23 E
Vaiges 42 48 2N 0 30W
Vaihingen 49 48 44N 8 58 E
Vaihsel B. 13 75 0S 35 0W
Vaijapur 96 19 58N 74 45 E
Vaikam 97 9 45N 76 25 E
Vaila I. 36 60 12N 1 34W
Vailly Aisne 43 49 25N 3 30 E
Vaippar, R. 97 9 0N 78 25 E
Vaison 45 44 14N 5 4 E
Vajpur 96 21 24N 73 45 E
Vakarel 67 42 35N 23 40 E
Vakhsh, R. 85 37 6N 68 18 E
Vaksdal 71 60 29N 5 45 E
Vál 53 47 22N 18 40 E
Val d' Ajol, Le 43 47 55N 6 30 E
Val-de-Marne □ 43 48 45N 2 28 E
Val-d'Oise □ 43 49 5N 2 0 E
Val d'Or 150 48 7N 77 47W
Val Marie 153 49 15N 107 45W
Val-St.-Germain 47 48 34N 2 4 E
Valadares 56 41 5N 8 38W
Valahia 70 44 35N 25 0 E
Valais □ 50 46 12N 7 45 E
Valais, Alpes du 50 46 47N 7 30 E
Valandovo 66 41 19N 22 34 E
Valasské MeziríU5 53 49 29N 17 59 E
Valaxa, I. 69 38 50N 24 29 E
Valcheta 176 40 40S 66 20W
Valdagno 63 45 38N 11 18 E
Valdahon, Le 43 47 8N 6 20 E
Valday 80 57 58N 31 9 E
Valdayskaya Vozvyshennost 80 57 0N 33 40 E
Valdeazogues, R. 57 38 45N 4 55W
Valdemarsvik 73 58 14N 16 40 E
Valdepeñas, Ciudad Real, Spain 57 38 43N 3 25W
Valdepeñas, Jaén, Spain 57 37 33N 3 47W
Valderaduey, R. 56 42 30N 5 0W
Valderrobres 58 40 53N 0 9 E
Valdes Pen. 176 42 30S 63 45W
Valdez 147 61 14N 146 10W
Valdivia 176 39 50S 73 14W
Valdivia □ 176 40 0S 73 0W
Valdivia, La 172 34 43S 72 5W
Valdobbiádene 63 45 53N 12 0 E
Valdosta 157 30 50N 83 48W
Valdoviño 56 43 36N 8 8W
Valdres 71 60 55N 9 28 E
Vale, U.S.A. 160 44 0N 117 15W
Vale, U.S.S.R. 83 41 30N 42 58 E
Valea lui Mihai 70 47 32N 22 11 E
Valença, Brazil 171 13 20S 39 5W
Valença, Port. 56 42 1N 8 34W
Valença do Piauí 170 6 20S 41 45W
Valence 45 44 57N 4 54 E
Valence-d'Agen 44 44 8N 0 54 E
Valencia, Spain 59 39 27N 0 23W
Valencia, Venez. 174 10 11N 68 0W
Valencia □ 59 39 20N 0 40W
Valencia, Albufera de 59 39 20N 0 27W
Valencia de Alcántara 57 39 25N 7 14W
Valencia de Don Juan 56 42 17N 5 31W
Valencia des Ventoso 57 38 15N 6 29W
Valencia, G. de 59 39 30N 0 20 E
Valencia, L. de 167 10 13N 67 40W
Valenciennes 43 50 20N 3 34 E
Valensole 45 43 50N 5 59 E
Valentia Hr. 39 51 56N 10 17W
Valentia I. 39 51 54N 10 22W
Valentine, Nebr., U.S.A. 158 42 50N 100 35W
Valentine, Tex., U.S.A. 159 30 36N 104 28W
Valenton 160 48 45N 2 28 E
Valenza 62 45 2N 8 39 E
Våler 71 60 41N 11 50 E
Valera 174 9 19N 70 37W
Valguarnera Caropepe 65 37 30N 14 22 E
Valhall, oilfield 19 56 17N 3 25 E
Valier 160 48 15N 112 9W
Valinco, G. de 45 41 40N 8 52 E
Valjevo 66 44 18N 19 53 E
Valkeakoski 75 61 16N 24 2 E
Valkenburg 47 50 52N 5 50 E
Valkenswaard 47 51 21N 5 29 E
Vall de Uxó 58 40 49N 0 15W
Valla 72 59 2N 16 20 E
Valladolid, Mexico 165 20 30N 88 20W
Valladolid, Spain 56 41 38N 4 43W
Valladolid □ 56 41 38N 4 43W
Vallata 65 41 3N 15 16 E
Valldalssæter 71 59 56N 6 57 E
Valle 71 59 13N 7 33 E
Valle d'Aosta □ 62 45 45N 7 22 E
Valle de Arán 58 42 50N 0 55 E
Valle de Cabuérniga 56 43 14N 4 18W
Valle de la Pascua 174 9 13N 66 0W
Valle de Santiago 164 20 25N 101 15W
Valle de Zaragoza 164 27 28N 105 49W
Valle del Cauca □ 174 3 45N 76 30W
Valle Fértil, Sierra del 172 30 20S 68 0W
Valle Hermosa 165 25 35N 102 25 E
Valle Nacional 165 17 47N 96 19W
Vallecas 56 40 23N 3 41W
Valledupar 174 10 29N 73 15W
Vallejo 163 38 12N 122 15W
Vallenar 172 28 30S 70 50W
Valleraugue 44 44 6N 3 39 E
Vallet 42 47 10N 1 15W
Valletta 60 35 54N 14 30 E
Valley 31 53 17N 4 31W
Valley Center 163 33 13N 117 2W
Valley City 158 46 57N 98 0W
Valley Falls 160 42 33N 120 8W
Valley Okolona 159 34 0N 88 45W
Valley Springs 163 38 11N 120 50W
Valley View 162 40 39N 76 33W
Valleyfield 150 45 15N 74 8W
Valleyview 152 55 5N 117 17W
Valli di Comácchio 63 44 40N 12 15 E
Vallimanca, Arroyo 172 35 40S 59 10W
Vallo della Lucánia 65 40 14N 15 16 E
Vallon 45 44 25N 4 23 E
Vallorbe 50 46 42N 6 20 E
Valls 58 41 18N 1 15 E
Vallsta 72 61 31N 16 22 E
Valmaseda 58 43 11N 3 12W
Valmiera 80 57 37N 25 38 E
Valmont 42 49 45N 0 30 E
Valmontone 64 41 48N 12 55 E
Valmy 43 49 5N 4 45 E
Valnera, Mte. 58 43 9N 3 40W
Valognes 42 49 30N 1 28W
Valona (Vlora) 68 40 32N 19 28 E
Valongo 56 40 37N 8 27W
Valpaços 56 41 36N 7 17W
Valparaíso, Chile 172 33 2S 71 40W
Valparaíso, Mexico 164 22 50N 103 32W
Valparaiso 156 41 27N 87 2W
Valparaíso □ 172 33 2S 71 40W
Valpovo 66 45 39N 18 25 E
Valréas 45 44 24N 5 0 E
Vals 51 46 39N 10 11 E
Vals-les-Bains 45 44 42N 4 24 E
Vals, R. 128 27 28S 26 52 E
Vals, Tanjung 103 8 32S 137 32 E
Valsbaai 128 34 15S 18 40 E
Valskog 72 59 27N 15 57 E
Vålta 68 40 3N 23 25 E
Valtellina 62 46 9N 10 2 E
Valverde del Camino 57 37 35N 6 47W
Valverde del Fresno 56 40 15N 6 51W
Valyiki 80 50 10N 38 5 E
Vama 70 47 34N 25 42 E
Vambarra Ra. 136 15 13S 130 24 E
Vamdrup 50 55 26N 9 10 E
Vammala 75 61 20N 22 55 E
Vámos 69 35 24N 24 13 E
Vamsadhara, R. 96 18 22N 84 15 E
Van 92 38 30N 43 20 E
Van Alstyne 159 33 25N 96 36W
Van Bruyssel 151 47 56N 72 9W
Van Buren, Can. 151 47 10N 67 55W
Van Buren, Ark., U.S.A. 159 35 28N 94 18W
Van Buren, Me., U.S.A. 157 47 10N 68 1W
Van Buren, Mo., U.S.A. 159 37 0N 91 0W
Van Canh 100 13 37N 109 0 E
Van der Kloof Dam 128 30 04S 24 40 E
Van Diemen, C., N.T., Austral. 136 11 9S 130 24 E
Van Diemen, C., Queens., Austral. 138 16 30S 139 46 E
Van Diemen G. 136 11 45S 131 50 E
Van Gölü 92 38 30N 43 0 E
Van Horn 161 31 3N 104 55W
Van Ninn 100 12 42N 109 14 E
Van Reenen P. 129 28 22S 29 27 E
Van Tassell 158 42 40N 104 3W
Van Tivu, I. 97 8 51N 78 15 E
Van Wert 156 40 52N 84 31W
Van Yen 100 21 4N 104 42 E
Vanavara 77 60 22N 102 16 E
Vancouver, Can. 152 49 20N 123 10W
Vancouver, U.S.A. 160 45 44N 122 41W
Vancouver, C. 137 35 2S 118 11 E
Vancouver I. 152 49 50N 126 0W
Vandalia, Ill., U.S.A. 158 38 57N 89 4W
Vandalia, Mo., U.S.A. 158 39 18N 91 30W
Vandeloos Bay 97 8 0N 81 45 E
Vandenburg 163 34 35N 120 44W
Vanderbijlpark 86 26 42S 27 54 E
Vanderhoof 152 54 0N 124 0W
Vanderlin I. 138 15 44S 137 2 E
Vandyke 138 24 10S 147 51 E
Vänern 73 58 47N 13 30 E
Vänersborg 73 58 26N 12 27 E
Vang Vieng 100 18 58N 102 32 E
Vanga 126 4 35S 39 12 E
Vangaindrano 129 23 21S 47 36 E
Vanguard 153 49 55N 107 20W
Vanier 150 45 27N 75 40W
Vanimo 135 2 42S 141 21 E
Vanivilasa Sagara 97 13 45N 76 30 E
Vaniyambadi 97 12 46N 78 44 E
Vankleek Hill 150 45 32N 75 40W
Vanna 74 70 6N 19 50 E
Vannas 74 63 58N 19 48 E
Vannes 42 47 40N 2 47W
Vanoise, Massif de la 45 45 25N 6 40 E
Vanrhynsdorp 128 31 36S 18 44 E
Vanrook 138 16 57S 141 57 E
Vans, Les 45 44 25N 4 7 E
Vansbro 72 60 32N 14 15 E
Vanse 71 58 6N 6 41 E
Vansittart B. 136 14 3S 126 17 E
Vanthli 94 21 28N 70 25 E
Vanua Levu, I. 130 16 33S 178 8 E
Vanwyksvlei 128 30 18S 21 49 E
Vanylven 71 62 5N 5 33 E
Vapnyarka 82 48 32N 28 45 E
Var □ 45 43 27N 6 18 E
Vara 73 58 16N 12 55 E
Varada, R. 97 14 46N 75 15 E
Varades 42 47 25N 1 1W
Varaita, R. 62 44 35N 7 15 E
Varaldsöy 71 60 6N 5 59 E
Varallo 62 45 50N 8 13 E
Varanasi (Benares) 95 25 22N 83 8 E
Varangerfjorden 74 70 3N 29 25 E
Varazdin 63 46 20N 16 20 E
Varazze 62 44 21N 8 36 E
Varberg 73 57 17N 12 20 E
Vardar, R. 66 41 25N 22 20 E
Varde 73 55 38N 8 29 E
Varde Å 73 55 35N 8 19 E
Vardø 74 70 23N 31 5 E
Varel 48 53 23N 8 9 E
Varella, Mui 100 12 54N 109 26 E
Varena 80 54 12N 24 30 E
Värendseke 73 57 4N 15 0 E
Varennes-sur-Allier 44 49 12N 5 0 E
Vareš 66 44 12N 18 23 E
Varese 62 45 49N 8 50 E
Varese Ligure 62 44 22N 9 33 E
Vårgårda 73 58 2N 12 49 E
Vargem Bonita 171 20 20S 46 22W
Vargem Grande 170 3 33S 43 56W
Varginha 173 21 33S 45 25W
Vargön 73 58 22N 12 20 E
Varhaug 71 58 37N 5 41 E
Varillas 172 24 0S 70 10W
Varing 73 58 30N 14 0 E
Värmdö, I. 72 59 18N 18 45 E
Värmeln 72 59 35N 13 0 E
Värmlands län □ 72 59 45N 13 20 E
Varmlandssaby 72 59 7N 14 15 E
Varna, Bulg. 67 43 13N 27 56 E
Varna, U.S.S.R. 84 53 24N 60 58 E
Varna, R. 96 17 13N 73 50 E
Varnamo 73 57 10N 14 3 E
Varnsdorf 52 49 56N 14 38 E
Värö 73 51 16N 12 15 E
Varpelev 73 55 22N 12 17 E
Värsjö 73 56 23N 13 27 E
Varsseveld 46 51 56N 6 29 E
Varteig 71 59 23N 11 12 E
Varto 92 39 10N 41 28 E
Vartofta 73 58 6N 13 40 E
Vartry Res. 39 53 3N 6 12W
Varvarin 66 43 43N 21 20 E
Varzaneh 93 32 25N 52 40 E
Várzea Alegre 170 6 47S 39 17W
Várzea da Palma 171 17 36S 44 44W
Varzi 62 44 50N 9 12 E
Varzo 62 46 12N 8 15 E
Varzy 43 47 22N 3 20 E
Vas □ 53 47 10N 16 55 E
Vasa 74 63 6N 21 38 E
Vasa Barris, R. 170 11 10S 37 10W
Vásárosnamény 53 48 9N 22 19 E
Vasby 73 56 13N 12 37 E
Vascâo, R. 57 37 44N 8 15W
Vascongadas 58 42 50N 2 45W
Vaşcǎu 70 46 28N 22 30 E
Väse 72 59 23N 13 52 E
Vasht = Khāsh 93 28 20N 61 6 E
Vasii Levski 67 43 23N 25 26 E
Vasilevichi 80 52 15N 29 50 E
Vasilikón 69 38 25N 23 40 E
Vaslkov 80 50 7N 30 28 E
Vaslui 70 46 38N 27 42 E
Vaslui □ 71 46 30N 27 30 E
Väsman 72 60 9N 15 5 E
Vassa 74 63 6N 21 38 E
Vassar, Can. 153 49 10N 95 55W
Vassar, U.S.A. 156 43 23N 83 33W
Vast Silen, L. 72 59 15N 12 15 E
Västerås 73 59 37N 16 38 E
Västerbottens län □ 74 64 58N 18 0 E
Västerdalälven 72 60 50N 13 25 E
Västernorrlands län □ 72 63 30N 17 40 E
Västervik 73 57 43N 16 43 E
Västmanland □ 72 59 55N 16 30 E
Vasto 63 42 8N 14 40 E
Vasvár 53 47 3N 16 47 E
Vatan 43 47 4N 1 50 E
Vaternish Pt. 36 57 36N 6 40W
Vatersay, I. 36 56 55N 7 32W
Vathí 69 37 46N 27 1 E
Váthia 69 36 29N 22 29 E
Vatican City ■ 63 41 54N 12 27 E
Vatin 66 45 12N 21 20 E
Vatnajökull 74 64 30N 16 48W
Vatnås 71 59 58N 9 37 E
Vatne 71 62 33N 6 38 E
Vatneyri 74 65 35N 24 0W
Vatoloha, Mt. 129 17 52S 47 48 E

Vatomandry 129 19 20 S 48 59 E
Vatra-Dornei 70 47 22N 25 22 E
Vats 71 59 29N 5 45 E
Vättern, L. 73 58 25N 14 30 E
Vättis 51 46 55N 9 27 E
Vaucluse □ 45 44 3N 5 10 E
Vaucouleurs 43 48 37N 5 40 E
Vaud □ 50 46 35N 6 30 E
Vaughan 161 34 37N 105 12W
Vaughn 160 47 37N 111 36W
Vaulruz 50 46 38N 7 0 E
Vaupés □ 174 1 0N 71 0W
Vaupés, R. 174 1 0N 71 0W
Vauvert 45 43 42N 4 17 E
Vauxhall 152 50 5N 112 9W
Vavincourt 43 48 49N 5 12 E
Vavoua 120 7 23N 6 29W
Vaxholm 72 59 25N 18 20 E
Växjö 73 56 52N 14 50 E
Vaygach, Ostrov 76 70 0N 60 0 E
Vaza Barris, R. 171 10 0 S 37 30W
Veadeiros 171 14 7 S 47 31W
Veagh L. 38 55 3N 7 57W
Vechta 48 52 47N 8 18 E
Vechte, R. 46 52 34N 6 6 E
Vecilla, La 56 42 51N 5 27W
Vecsés 53 47 26N 19 19 E
Vedaraniam 97 10 25N 79 50 E
Vedbæk 73 55 50N 12 33 E
Veddige 73 57 17N 12 20 E
Vedea, R. 70 44 0N 25 20 E
Vedelgem 47 51 7N 3 10 E
Vedia 172 34 30 S 61 31W
Vedra, Isla del 59 38 52N 1 12 E
Vedrin 47 50 30N 4 52 E
Veendam 46 53 5N 6 52 E
Veenendaal 46 52 2N 5 34 E
Veenwouden 46 53 14N 6 0 E
Veerle 47 51 4N 4 59 E
Vefsna 74 65 48N 13 10 E
Vega, Norway 74 65 40N 11 55 E
Vega, U.S.A. 159 35 18N 102 26W
Vega Baja 147 18 27N 66 23W
Vega Fd. 74 65 37N 12 0 E
Vega, I. 74 65 42N 11 50 E
Vega, La 167 19 20N 70 30W
Vegadeo 56 43 27N 7 4W
Vegesack 48 53 10N 8 38 E
Vegfjorden 74 65 37N 12 0 E
Veggerby 73 56 54N 9 39 E
Veggli 71 60 3N 9 9 E
Veghel 47 51 37N 5 32 E
Vegorritis, Limni 68 40 45N 21 45 E
Vegreville 152 53 30N 112 5W
Vegusdal 71 58 32N 8 10 E
Veii 63 42 0N 12 24 E
Veinticino de Mayo 172 38 0 S 67 40W
Veitch 140 34 39 S 140 31 E
Vejen 73 55 30N 9 9 E
Vejer de la Frontera 57 36 15N 5 59W
Vejle 73 55 43N 9 30 E
Vejle Amt □ 73 55 2N 11 22 E
Vejle Fjord 73 55 40N 9 50 E
Vejlo 73 55 10N 11 45 E
Vela Luka 63 42 59N 16 44 E
Velanai I. 97 9 45N 79 45 E
Velarde 161 36 11N 106 1W
Velas, C. 166 10 21N 85 52W
Velasco 159 29 0N 95 20W
Velasco, Sierra de. 172 29 20 S 67 10W
Velay, Mts. du 44 45 0N 3 40 E
Velb 46 52 0N 5 59 E
Velddrif 128 32 42 S 18 11 E
Velden 47 51 25N 6 10 E
Veldhoven 47 51 24N 5 25 E
Veldwezelt 47 50 52N 5 38 E
Velebit Planina 63 44 50N 15 20 E
Velebitski Kanal 63 44 45N 14 55 E
Veleka, R. 67 42 4N 27 30 E
Velenje 63 46 23N 15 8 E
Velestínon 68 39 23N 22 43 E
Vélez 174 6 1N 73 41W
Velez 66 43 19N 18 2 E
Vélez Blanco 57 37 41N 2 5W
Vélez Málaga 57 36 48N 4 5W
Vélez Rubio 59 37 41N 2 5W
Velhas, R. 171 17 13 S 44 49W
Velika 66 45 27N 17 40 E
Velika Gorica 63 45 44N 16 5 E
Velika Kapela 63 45 10N 15 5 E
Velika Kladuša 63 45 11N 15 48 E
Velika Morava, R. 66 44 30N 21 9 E
Velika Plana 66 44 20N 21 1 E
Velikaya, R. 80 56 40N 28 40 E
Veliké Kapušany 53 48 34N 22 5 E
Velike Lašče 63 45 49N 14 45 E
Veliki Backa Kanal 68 45 45N 19 15 E
Veliki Jastrebac 66 43 25N 21 30 E
Veliki Ustyug 78 60 47N 46 20 E
Velikiye Luki 80 56 25N 30 32 E
Velíko Turnovo 67 43 5N 25 41 E
Velikonda Range 97 14 45N 79 10 E
Velikoye, Oz. 81 55 15N 40 0 E
Velingrad 67 42 4N 23 58 E
Velino, Mt. 63 42 10N 13 20 E
Velizh 80 55 30N 31 11 E
Velké Karlovice 53 49 20N 18 17 E
Velke Mezirici 52 49 21N 16 1 E
Velký ostrov Zitný 53 48 5N 17 20 E
Vellar, R. 97 11 30N 79 36 E
Velletri 64 41 43N 12 43 E
Velling 73 56 2N 8 20 E
Vellinge 73 55 29N 13 0 E
Vellir 74 65 55N 18 28W
Vellore 97 12 57N 79 10 E
Velsen-Noord 46 52 27N 4 40 E
Velsk 78 61 10N 42 5 E
Velten 48 52 40N 13 11 E
Veluwe Meer 46 52 24N 5 44 E
Velva 158 48 6N 100 56W
Velvendós 68 40 15N 22 6 E
Vem 73 56 21N 8 21 E
Vembanad Lake 97 9 36N 76 15 E
Veme 71 60 14N 10 7 E
Ven 73 55 55N 12 45 E
Vena 73 57 31N 16 0 E
Venado 164 22 50N 101 10W
Venado Tuerto 172 33 50 S 62 0W
Venafro 65 41 28N 14 3 E
Venarey-les-Laumes 43 47 32N 4 26 E
Venaria 62 45 12N 7 39 E
Venčane 66 44 24N 20 28 E
Vence 45 43 43N 7 6 E
Vendas Novas 57 38 39N 8 27W
Vendée 42 46 50N 1 35W
Vendée □ 44 46 40N 1 20W
Vendée, Collines de 42 46 35N 0 45W
Vendée, R. 42 46 30N 0 45W
Vendeuvre-sur-Barse 43 48 14N 4 28 E
Vendôme 42 47 47N 1 3 E
Vendrell 58 41 10N 1 30 E
Vendsyssel 73 57 22N 10 0 E
Veneta, Laguna 63 45 19N 12 13 E
Venetie 147 67 0N 146 30W
Véneto □ 63 45 30N 12 0 E
Venev 81 54 22N 38 17 E
Venézia 63 45 27N 12 20 E
Venézia, Golfo di 63 45 20N 13 0 E
Venezuela ■ 174 8 0N 65 0W
Venezuela, Golfo de 174 11 30N 71 0W
Vengurla 97 15 53N 73 45 E
Vengurla Rocks 97 15 50N 73 22 E
Venice = Venézia 63 45 27N 12 20 E
Vénissieux 45 45 43N 4 53 E
Venjansjön 72 60 58N 14 2 E
Venkatagiri 97 14 0N 79 35 E
Venkatapuram 96 18 20N 80 30 E
Venlo 47 51 22N 6 11 E
Vennesla 71 58 15N 8 0 E
Venø, Is. 73 56 33N 8 38 E
Venraij 47 51 31N 6 0 E
Venta de Cardeña 57 38 16N 4 20W
Venta de San Rafael 56 40 42N 4 12W
Venta, La 165 18 8N 94 3W
Ventana, Punta de la 164 24 4N 109 48W
Ventersburg 128 28 7 S 27 9 E
Ventimíglia 62 43 50N 7 39 E
Ventnor 28 50 35N 1 12W
Ventotene, I. 64 40 48N 13 25 E
Ventry 39 52 8N 10 21W
Ventspils 80 57 25N 21 32 E
Ventuari, R. 174 5 20N 66 0W
Ventucopa 163 34 50N 119 29W
Ventura 163 34 16N 119 18W
Ventura, La 164 24 38N 100 54W
Venturosa, La 174 6 8N 68 48W
Venus B. 141 38 40 S 145 42 E
Veoy 71 62 45N 7 30 E
Veoy Is. 71 62 45N 7 30 E
Vera, Argent. 172 29 30 S 60 20W
Vera, Spain 59 37 15N 1 15W
Veracruz 165 19 10N 96 10W
Veracruz □ 165 19 0N 96 15W
Veraval 94 20 53N 70 27 E
Verbánia 62 45 50N 8 55 E
Verbicaro 65 39 46N 15 54 E
Verbier 50 46 6N 7 13 E
Vercelli 62 45 19N 8 25 E
Verdalsøra 74 63 48N 11 30 E
Verde Grande, R. 171 16 13 S 43 49W
Verde Pequeno, R. 171 14 48 S 43 31W
Verde, R., Argent. 176 41 55 S 66 0W
Verde, R., Goiás, Brazil 171 18 1 S 50 14W
Verde, R., Goiás, Brazil 171 19 11 S 50 44W
Verde, R., Chihuahua, Mexico 164 26 59N 107 58W
Verde, R., Oaxaca, Mexico 164 15 59N 97 50W
Verde, R., Veracruz, Mexico 165 21 10N 102 50W
Verde, R., Parag. 172 23 9 S 57 37W
Verden 48 52 58N 9 18 E
Verdhikoúsa 68 39 47N 21 59 E
Verdigre 158 42 38N 98 0W
Verdon-sur-Mer, Le 44 45 33N 1 4W
Verdun 43 49 12N 5 24 E
Verdun-sur-le Doubs 43 46 54N 5 0 E
Vereeniging 129 26 38 S 27 57 E
Vérendrye, Parc Prov. de 150 47 20N 76 40W
Vereshchagino 84 58 5N 54 40 E
Verga, C. 120 10 30N 14 10W
Vergara 58 43 9N 2 28W
Vergato 62 44 18N 11 8 E
Vergemont 138 23 33 S 143 1 E
Vergemont Cr. 138 24 16 S 143 16 E
Vergt 44 45 2N 0 43 E
Verín 56 41 57N 7 27W
Veriña 56 43 32N 5 43W
Verkhnedvinsk 80 55 45N 27 58 E
Verkhneuralsk 84 53 53N 59 13 E
Verkhniy-Avzyan 84 53 32N 57 33 E
Verkhniy Baskunchak 83 48 5N 46 50 E
Verkhniy Tagil 84 57 22N 59 56 E
Verkhniy Ufaley 84 56 4N 60 14 E
Verkhniye Kigi 84 55 25N 58 37 E
Verkhnyaya Salda 84 58 2N 60 33 E
Verkhoturye 84 58 52N 60 48 E
Verkhovye 81 52 55N 37 15 E
Verkhoyansk 77 67 50N 133 50 E
Verkhoyanskiy Khrebet 77 66 0N 129 0 E
Verlo 153 50 19N 108 35W
Verma 71 62 21N 8 3 E
Vermenton 43 47 40N 3 42 E
Vermilion 153 53 20N 110 50W
Vermilion, B. 159 29 45N 91 55W
Vermilion Bay 153 49 50N 93 20W
Vermilion Chutes 152 58 22N 114 51W
Vermilion, R., Alta., Can. 153 53 22N 110 51W
Vermilion, R., Qué., Can. 150 47 38N 72 56W
Vermillion 158 42 50N 96 56W
Vermont □ 156 43 40N 72 50W
Vern, oilfield 19 55 35N 4 45 E
Vernal 160 40 28N 109 35W
Vernalis 163 37 36N 121 17W
Vernayez 50 46 8N 7 3 E
Verner 150 46 25N 80 8W
Verneuil, Bois de 50 48 59N 1 59 E
Verneuil-sur-Avre 42 48 45N 0 55 E
Vernier 50 46 13N 6 5 E
Vernon, Can. 152 50 20N 119 15W
Vernon, France 42 49 5N 1 30 E
Vernon, U.S.A. 159 34 0N 99 15W
Vero Beach 157 27 39N 80 23W
Véroia 68 40 34N 22 18 E
Verolanuova 62 45 20N 10 5 E
Véroli 64 41 43N 13 24 E
Verona 62 45 27N 11 0 E
Veropol 77 66 0N 168 0 E
Verrieres, Les 50 46 55N 6 28 E
Versailles 43 48 48N 2 8 E
Versoix 50 46 17N 6 10 E
Vert, C. 120 14 45N 17 30W
Vertou 42 47 10N 1 28W
Vertus 43 48 54N 4 0 E
Verulam 129 29 38 S 31 2 E
Verviers 47 50 37N 5 52 E
Vervins 43 49 50N 3 53 E
Verwood, Can. 153 49 30N 105 40W
Verwood, U.K. 28 50 53N 1 53W
Veryan 30 50 13N 4 56W
Veryan Bay 30 50 12N 4 51W
Verzej 63 46 34N 16 13 E
Vesdre, R. 47 50 36N 6 0 E
Veseli nad Luznicí 52 49 12N 14 15 E
Veselie 67 42 18N 27 38 E
Veselovskoye Vdkhr. 83 47 0N 41 0 E
Veselyy Res. 83 47 0N 41 0 E
Veshenskaya 83 49 35N 41 44 E
Vesle, R. 43 49 17N 3 50 E
Veslyana, R. 84 60 20N 54 0 E
Vesoul 43 60 40N 6 11 E
Vessigebro 73 56 58N 12 40 E
Vest-Agder fylke □ 71 58 30N 7 15 E
Vest Fjorden 71 68 0N 15 0 E
Vesta 166 9 43N 83 3W
Vestby 71 59 37N 10 45 E
Vester Hassing 73 57 4N 10 8 E
Vesterålen 74 68 45N 14 30 E
Vestersche Veld 46 52 52N 6 9 E
Vestfjorden 74 67 55N 14 0 E
Vestfold fylke □ 71 59 15N 10 0 E
Vestmannaeyjar 74 63 27N 20 15W
Vestmarka 71 59 56N 11 59 E
Vestnes 71 62 39N 7 5 E
Vestone 62 45 43N 10 25 E
Vestsjaellands Amt □ 73 55 30N 11 20 E
Vestspitsbergen 12 78 40N 17 0 E
Vestvågøy 74 68 18N 13 50 E
Vesuvio 65 40 50N 14 22 E
Vesuvius, Mt. = Vesuvio 65 40 50N 14 22 E
Veszprém 53 47 8N 17 57 E
Veszprém □ 53 47 5N 17 55 E
Vésztö 53 46 55N 21 16 E
Vetapalam 97 15 47N 80 18 E
Vetlanda 73 57 24N 15 3 E
Vetluga 81 57 53N 45 45 E
Vetluzhskiy 81 57 17N 45 12 E
Vetovo 67 43 42N 26 16 E
Vetralia 63 42 20N 12 2 E
Vetren 67 42 15N 24 3 E
Vettore, Mte. 63 44 38N 7 5 E
Veurne 47 51 5N 2 40 E
Vevey 50 46 28N 6 51 E
Vévi 68 40 47N 21 38 E
Veys 92 31 30N 49 0 E
Vézelise 43 48 30N 6 5 E
Vezhen, mt. 67 42 50N 24 20 E
Vi Thanh 101 9 42N 105 26 E
Viacha 174 16 30 S 68 5W
Viadana 62 44 55N 10 30 E
Viana, Brazil 170 3 0 S 44 40W
Viana, Port. 55 38 20N 8 0W
Viana, Spain 58 42 31N 2 22W
Viana do Castelo 56 41 42N 8 50W
Vianden 47 49 56N 6 12 E
Vianen 46 51 59N 5 5 E
Vianna do Castelo □ 56 41 50N 8 30W
Vianópolis 171 16 40 S 48 35W
Viar, R. 56 37 45N 5 54W
Viaréggio 62 43 52N 10 13 E
Vibank 153 50 20N 103 56W
Vibey, R. 56 42 21N 7 15 E
Vibo Valéntia 65 38 40N 16 5 E
Viborg 73 56 27N 9 23 E
Viborg Amt □ 73 56 30N 9 20 E
Vic-en-Bigorre 44 43 24N 0 3 E
Vic-Fezensac 44 43 45N 0 18 E
Vic Fézensac 44 43 47N 0 19 E
Vic-sur-Cère 44 44 59N 2 38 E
Vic-sur-Seille 43 48 45N 6 33 E
Vicarstown 39 53 5N 7 7W
Vicenza 63 45 32N 11 31 E
Vich 58 41 58N 2 19 E
Vichada □ 174 5 0N 69 30W
Vichuga 81 57 25N 41 55 E
Vichy 44 46 9N 3 26 E
Vickerstown 32 54 8N 3 17W
Vicksburg, Mich., U.S.A. 156 42 10N 85 30W
Vicksburg, Miss., U.S.A. 159 32 22N 90 56W
Vico, L. di 63 42 20N 12 10 E
Viçosa, Min. Ger., Brazil 170 20 45 S 42 53W
Viçosa, Pernambuco, Brazil 170 9 28 S 36 14W
Viçosa do Ceará 170 3 34 S 41 5W
Vicosoprano 51 46 22N 9 38 E
Victor 158 38 43N 105 7W
Victor Emanuel Ra. 135 5 20 S 142 15 E
Victor Harbour 139 35 30 S 138 37 E
Victoria, Argent. 172 32 40 S 60 10W
Victoria, Austral. 138 21 16 S 149 3 E
*Victoria, Camer. 121 4 1N 9 10 E
Victoria, Can. 152 48 30N 123 25W
Victoria, Chile 176 38 13 S 72 20W
Victoria, Guin. 120 10 50N 14 32W
Victoria, H. K. 109 22 25N 114 15 E
Victoria, Malay. 102 5 20N 115 20 E
Victoria, Tex., U.S.A. 159 28 50N 97 0W
Victoria, Va., U.S.A. 158 38 52N 99 8W
Victoria □, Austral. 131 37 0 S 144 0 E
Victoria □, Zimb. 127 21 0 S 31 30 E
Victoria Beach 153 50 40N 96 35W
Victoria de las Tunas 166 20 58N 76 59W
Victoria Falls 127 17 58 S 25 45 E
Victoria, Grand L. 150 47 31N 77 30W
Victoria Harbour 150 44 45N 79 45W
Victoria I. 148 71 0N 111 0W
Victoria, L., N.S.W., Austral. 140 33 57 S 141 15 E
Victoria, L., Vic., Austral. 139 38 2 S 147 34 E
Victoria, L., E. Afr. 126 1 0 S 33 0 E
Victoria, La 174 10 14N 67 20W
Victoria Ld. 13 75 0 S 160 0 E
Victoria, Mt., Burma 98 21 15N 93 55 E
Victoria, Mt., P.N.G. 135 8 55 S 147 32 E
Victoria Nile R. 126 2 25N 31 50 E
Victoria, R. 136 15 10 S 129 40 E
Victoria R. Downs 136 16 25 S 131 0 E
Victoria Ra. 143 42 12 S 172 7 E
Victoria Res. 151 48 20N 57 27W
Victoria Taungdeik 99 21 15N 93 55 E
Victoria West 128 31 25 S 23 4 E
Victoriaville 151 46 4N 71 56W
Victorica 172 36 20 S 65 30W
Victorino 174 2 48N 67 50W
Victorville 163 34 32N 117 18W
Vicuña 172 30 0 S 70 50W
Vicuña Mackenna 172 33 53 S 64 25W
Vidalia 157 32 13N 82 25W
Vidauban 45 43 25N 6 27 E
Videlv, R. 71 58 50N 8 32 E
Vidigueira 57 38 12N 7 48W
Vidin 66 43 59N 22 28 E
Vidio, Cabo 56 43 35N 6 14W
Vidisha (Bhilsa) 94 23 28N 77 53 E
Vidöstern 73 57 5N 14 0 E
Vidra 70 45 56N 26 55 E
Viduša, mts. 66 42 55N 18 21 E
Vidzy 80 54 40N 26 37 E
Viedma 176 40 50 S 63 0W
Viedma, L. 176 49 30 S 72 30W
Vieira 56 41 38N 8 8W
Viejo Canal de Bahama 166 22 10N 77 30W
Viella 58 42 43N 0 44 E
Vielsalm 47 50 17N 5 54 E
Vien Pou Kha 101 20 45N 101 5 E
Vienenburg 48 51 57N 10 35 E
Vieng Pou Kha 100 20 41N 101 4 E
Vienna, Illinois, U.S.A. 159 37 29N 88 54W
Vienna, Va., U.S.A. 162 38 54N 77 16W
Vienna = Wien 53 48 12N 16 22 E
Vienne 45 45 31N 4 53 E
Vienne □ 44 45 53N 0 42 E
Vienne, R. 42 47 5N 0 30 E
Vientiane 100 17 58N 102 36 E
Vieques, I. 147 18 8N 65 25W
Vierlingsbeek 47 51 36N 6 1 E
Viersen 48 51 15N 6 23 E
Vierwaldstättersee 51 47 0N 8 30 E
Vierzon 43 47 13N 2 5 E
Vieux-Boucau-les-Bains 44 43 48N 1 23W
Vif 45 45 5N 5 41 E
Vigan 103 17 35N 120 28 E
Vigan, Le 44 44 0N 3 36 E
Vigevano 62 45 18N 8 50 E
Vigia 170 0 50 S 48 5W
Vigía Chico 165 19 46N 87 35W
Vignacourt 43 50 1N 2 15 E
Vignemale, Pic du 44 42 47N 0 10W
Vigneulles 43 48 59N 5 40 E
Vignola 62 44 29N 11 0 E
Vigo 56 42 12N 8 41W
Vigo, Ría de 56 42 15N 8 45W
Vihiers 42 47 10N 0 30W
Vijayadurg 96 16 30N 73 25 E

*Renamed Limbe

Vijayawada (Bezwada) 96 16 31N 80 39 E
Vijfhuizen 46 52 22N 4 41 E
Vikedal 71 59 30N 5 55 E
Viken, L. 73 58 40N 10 2 E
Vikersund 71 59 58N 10 2 E
Viking 152 53 7N 111 50W
Viking, gasfield 19 53 30N 2 20 E
Vikna 74 64 52N 10 57 E
Vikramasingapuram 97 8 40N 76 47 E
Viksjö 72 62 45N 17 26 E
Vikulovo 76 56 50N 70 40 E
Vila Alferes Chamusca 129 24 27 S 33 0 E
Vila Arriaga 125 14 35 S 13 30 E
Vila Bittencourt 174 1 20 S 69 20W
Vila Cabral = Lichinga 127 13 13 S 35 11 E
Vila Caldas Xavier 127 14 28 S 33 0 E
Vila Coutinho 127 14 37 S 34 19 E
Vila da Maganja 127 17 18 S 37 30 E
Vila da Ponte 125 14 35 S 16 40 E
Vila de Aljustrel 125 13 30 S 19 45 E
Vila de João Belo = Xai-Xai 129 25 6 S 33 31 E
Vila de Liquica 103 8 40 S 125 20 E
Vila de Manica 125 18 58 S 32 59 E
Vila de Rei 57 39 41N 8 9W
Vila de Sena = Sena 127 17 25 S 35 0 E
Vila do Bispo 57 37 5N 8 53W
Vila do Conde 56 41 21N 8 45W
Vila Fontes 125 17 51 S 35 24 E
Vila Fontes Velha 127 17 51 S 35 24 E
Vila Franca de Xira 57 38 57N 8 59W
Vila Gamito 127 14 12 S 33 0 E
Vila General Machado 125 11 58 S 17 22 E
Vila Gomes da Costa 129 24 20 S 33 37 E
Vila Henrique de Carvalho = Lunda 124 9 40 S 20 12 E
Vila Junqueiro 127 15 25 S 36 58 E
Vila Luisa 129 25 45 S 32 35 E
Vila Luso = Moxico 125 11 53 S 19 55 E
Vila Machado 127 19 15 S 34 14 E
Vila Marechal Carmona = Uige 124 7 30 S 14 40 E
Vila Mariano Machado 125 13 3 S 14 35 E
Vila Moatize 127 16 11 S 33 40 E
Vila Mouzinho 127 14 48 S 34 25 E
Vila Murtinho 174 10 20 S 65 20W
Vila Nova de Fozcôa 56 41 5N 7 9W
Vila Nova de Ourém 57 39 40N 8 35W
Vila Nova do Seles 125 11 35 S 14 22 E
Vila Novo de Gaia 56 41 4N 8 40W
Vila Paiva Couceiro 125 14 37 S 14 40 E
Vila Paiva de Andrada 127 18 37 S 34 2 E
Vila Pery = Chimoio 127 19 4 S 33 30 E
Vila Pouca de Aguiar 56 41 30N 7 38W
Vila Real 56 41 17N 7 48W
Vila Real de Santo Antonio 57 37 10N 7 28W
Vila Robert Williams 125 12 46 S 15 30 E
Vila Salazar, Angola 124 9 12 S 14 48 E
Vila Salazar, Indon. 103 5 25 S 123 50 E
Vila Teixeira da Silva 125 12 10 S 15 50 E
Vila Vasco da Gama 127 14 54 S 32 14 E
Vila Velha 173 20 20 S 40 17W
Vila Verissimo Sarmento 124 8 15 S 20 50 E
Vila Viçosa 57 38 45N 7 27W
Vilaboa 56 42 21N 8 39W
Vilaine, R. 42 47 35N 2 10W
Vilanculos 129 22 1 S 35 17 E
Vilar Formosa 56 40 38N 6 45W
Vilareal □ 56 41 36N 7 35W
Vileyka 80 54 30N 27 0 E
Vilhelmina 74 64 35N 16 39 E
Vilhena 174 12 30 S 60 0W
Viliga 77 60 2N 156 56 E
Viliya, R. 80 54 57N 24 35 E
Viljandi 80 58 28N 25 30 E
Villa Abecia 172 21 0 S 68 18W
Villa Ahumada 164 30 30N 106 40W
Villa Ana 172 28 28 S 59 40W
Villa Ángela 172 27 34 S 60 45W
Villa Bella 174 10 25 S 65 30W
Villa Bens (Tarfaya) 116 27 55N 12 55W
Villa Cañas 172 34 0 S 61 35W
Villa Cisneros = Dakhla 116 23 50N 15 53W
Villa Colón 172 31 38 S 68 20W
Villa Constitución 172 33 15 S 60 20W
Villa de Cura 174 10 2N 67 29W
Villa de María 172 30 0 S 63 43W
Villa de Rosario 172 24 30 S 57 35W
Villa Dolores 172 31 58 S 65 15W
Villa Franca 172 26 14 S 58 20W
Villa Frontera 164 26 56N 101 27W
Villa Guillermina 172 28 15 S 59 29W
Villa Hayes 172 25 0 S 57 20W
Villa Iris 172 38 12 S 63 12W
Villa Julia Molina 167 19 5N 69 45W
Villa Madero 164 24 28N 104 10W
Villa María 172 32 20 S 63 10W
Villa Mazán 172 28 40 S 66 30W
Villa Mentes 172 21 10 S 63 30W
Villa Minozzo 62 44 21N 10 30 E
Villa Montes 172 21 10 S 63 30W
Villa Ocampo, Argent. 172 28 30 S 59 20W
Villa Ocampo, Mexico 164 26 29N 105 30W
Villa Ojo de Agua 172 29 30 S 63 44W
Villa San Agustín 172 30 35 S 67 30W
Villa San Giovanni 65 38 13N 15 38 E
Villa San José 172 32 12 S 58 15W
Villa San Martín 172 28 9 S 64 9W
Villa Santina 63 46 25N 12 55 E
Villa Unión 164 23 12N 106 14W
Villablino 56 42 57N 6 19W
Villabruzzi 91 3 3N 45 18 E
Villacampo, Pantano de 56 41 31N 6 0W
Villacañas 58 39 38N 3 20W
Villacarlos 58 39 53N 4 17 E
Villacarriedo 58 43 14N 3 48W
Villacarrillo 59 38 7N 3 3W
Villacastín 56 40 46N 4 25W
Villach 52 46 37N 13 51 E
Villaciaro 64 39 27N 8 45 E
Villada 56 42 15N 4 59W
Villadiego 56 42 31N 4 1W
Villadossóla 62 46 4N 8 16 E
Villafeliche 58 41 10N 1 30W
Villafranca 58 42 17N 1 46W
Villafranca de los Barros 57 38 35N 6 18W
Villafranca de los Caballeros 59 39 26N 3 21W
Villafranca del Bierzo 56 42 38N 6 50W
Villafranca del Cid 58 40 26N 0 16W
Villafranca del Panadés 58 41 21N 1 40 E
Villafranca di Verona 62 45 20N 10 51 E
Villagarcía de Arosa 56 42 34N 8 46W
Villagrán 165 24 29N 99 29W
Villaguay 172 32 0 S 58 45W
Villaharta 57 38 9N 4 54W
Villahermosa, Mexico 165 17 45N 92 50W
Villahermosa, Spain 59 38 46N 2 52W
Villaines-la-Juhel 42 48 21N 0 20W
Villajoyosa 59 38 30N 0 12W
Villalba 56 40 36N 3 59W
Villalba de Guardo 56 42 42N 4 49W
Villalón de Campos 56 42 5N 5 4W
Villalpando 56 41 51N 5 25W
Villaluenga 56 40 2N 3 54W
Villamañán 56 42 19N 5 35W
Villamartín 56 36 52N 5 38W
Villamayor 58 41 42N 0 43W
Villamblard 44 45 2N 0 32 E
Villanova Monteleone 64 40 30N 8 28 E
Villanueva, Colomb. 174 10 37N 72 59W
Villanueva, U.S.A. 161 35 16N 105 31W
Villanueva de Castellón 59 39 5N 0 31W
Villanueva de Córdoba 57 38 20N 4 38W
Villanueva de la Fuente 59 38 42N 2 42W
Villanueva de la Serena 57 38 59N 5 50W
Villanueva de la Sierra 56 40 12N 6 24W
Villanueva de los Castillejos 57 37 30N 7 15W
Villanueva del Arzobispo 59 38 10N 3 0W
Villanueva del Duque 57 38 20N 4 38W
Villanueva del Fresno 57 38 23N 7 10W
Villanueva y Geltrú 58 41 13N 1 40 E
Villaodrid 56 43 20N 7 11W
Villaputzu 64 39 28N 9 33 E
Villar del Arzobispo 58 39 44N 0 50W
Villar del Rey 57 39 7N 6 50W
Villarcayo 58 42 56N 3 34W
Villard 45 45 4N 5 33 E
Villard-Bonnot 45 45 14N 5 53 E
Villard-de-Lans 45 45 3N 5 33 E
Villarino de los Aires 56 41 18N 6 23W
Villarosa 65 37 36N 14 9 E
Villarramiel 56 42 2N 4 55W
Villarreal 58 39 55N 0 3W
Villarrica, Chile 176 39 15 S 72 30W
Villarrica, Parag. 172 25 40 S 56 30W
Villarrobledo 59 39 18N 2 36W
Villarroya de la Sierra 58 41 27N 1 46W
Villarrubia de los Ojos 59 39 14N 3 36W
Villars 45 46 0N 5 2 E
Villarta de San Juan 59 39 15N 3 25W
Villasayas 58 41 24N 2 39W
Villaseca de los Gamitos 56 41 2N 6 7W
Villastar 58 40 17N 1 9W
Villatobas 58 39 54N 3 20W
Villavicencio, Argent. 172 32 28 S 69 0W
Villavicencio, Colomb. 174 4 9N 73 37W
Villaviciosa 56 43 32N 5 27W
Villazón 172 22 0 S 65 35W
Ville de Paris □ 43 48 50N 2 20 E
Ville Marie 150 47 20N 79 30W
Ville Platte 159 30 45N 92 17W
Villedieu 42 48 50N 1 12W
Villefort 44 44 28N 3 56 E
Villefranche 43 47 19N 146 0 E
Villefranche-de-Lauragais 44 43 25N 1 44 E
Villefranche-de-Rouergue 44 44 21N 2 2 E
Villefranche-du-Périgord 44 44 38N 1 5 E
Villefranche-sur-Saône 45 45 59N 4 43 E
Villel 58 40 14N 1 12W
Villemaur 43 48 14N 3 40 E
Villemur-sur-Tarn 44 43 51N 1 31 E
Villena 59 38 39N 0 52W
Villenauxe 43 48 36N 3 30 E
Villenave 44 44 46N 0 33W
Villeneuve, France 43 48 42N 2 25 E
Villeneuve, Italy 62 45 40N 7 10 E
Villeneuve, Switz. 50 46 24N 6 56 E
Villeneuve-l'Archevèque 43 48 14N 3 32 E
Villeneuve-lès-Avignon 45 43 57N 4 49 E
Villeneuve-sur-Allier 44 46 40N 3 13 E
Villeneuve-sur-Lot 44 44 24N 0 42 E
Villeréal 44 44 38N 0 45 E
Villers Bocage 42 49 3N 0 40W
Villers Bretonneux 43 49 50N 2 30 E
Villers-Cotterets 43 49 15N 3 4 E
Villers-Farlay 47 47 0N 5 45 E
Villers-le-Bouillet 47 50 34N 5 15 E
Villers-le-Gambon 47 50 11N 4 37 E
Villers-sur-Mer 42 49 21N 0 2W
Villersexel 43 47 33N 6 26 E
Villerslev 73 56 49N 8 29 E
Villerupt 43 49 28N 5 55 E
Villerville 42 49 26N 0 5 E
Villiers 129 27 2 S 28 36 E
Villingen = Schwenningen 49 48 3N 8 29 E
Villisca 158 40 55N 94 59W
Villupuram 97 11 59N 79 31 E
Vilna 152 54 7N 111 55W
Vilnius 80 54 38N 25 25 E
Vils 52 47 33N 10 37 E
Vilsbiburg 49 48 27N 12 23 E
Vilslev 73 55 24N 8 42 E
Vilusi 66 42 44N 18 34 E
Vilvoorde 47 50 56N 4 26 E
Vilyuy, R. 77 63 58N 125 0 E
Vilyuysk 77 63 40N 121 20 E
Vimercate 62 45 38N 9 25 E
Vimiosa 56 41 35N 6 13W
Vimmerby 73 57 40N 15 55 E
Vimo 72 60 50N 14 20 E
Vimoutiers 42 48 57N 0 10 E
Vimperk 52 49 3N 13 46 E
Viña del Mar 172 33 0 S 71 30W
Vinaroz 58 40 30N 0 27 E
Vincennes 156 38 42N 87 29W
Vincent 163 34 33N 118 11W
Vinchina 172 28 45 S 68 15W
Vindel älv 74 64 20N 19 20 E
Vindeln 74 64 12N 19 43 E
Vinderup 73 56 29N 8 45 E
Vindhya Ra. 94 22 50N 77 0 E
Vinegar Hill 39 52 30N 6 28W
Vineland 162 39 30N 75 0W
Vinga 66 46 0N 21 14 E
Vingnes 71 61 7N 10 26 E
Vinh 100 18 45N 105 38 E
Vinh Linh 100 17 4N 107 2 E
Vinh Loi 101 9 20N 104 45 E
Vinh Long 101 10 16N 105 57 E
Vinh Yen 100 21 21N 105 35 E
Vinhais 56 41 50N 7 0W
Vinica 63 45 28N 15 16 E
Vinita 159 36 40N 95 12W
Vinkeveen 46 52 13N 4 56 E
Vinkovci 66 45 19N 18 48 E
Vinnitsa 82 49 15N 28 30 E
Vinstra 71 61 37N 9 44 E
Vinton, Iowa, U.S.A. 158 42 8N 92 1W
Vinton, La., U.S.A. 159 30 13N 93 35W
Vintu de Jos 70 46 0N 23 30 E
Viöl 48 54 32N 9 12 E
Violet Town 141 36 38 S 145 42 E
Vipava 63 45 51N 13 38 E
Vipiteno 63 46 55N 11 25 E
Viqueque 103 8 42 S 126 30 E
Vir 85 37 45N 72 5 E
Vir, I. 63 44 17N 15 3 E
Virac 103 13 30N 124 20 E
Virachei 100 13 59N 106 49 E
Virago Sd. 152 54 0N 132 42W
Virajpet 97 12 15N 75 50 E
Viramgam 94 23 5N 72 0 E
Virarajendrapet (Virajpet) 97 12 10N 75 50 E
Viravanallur 97 8 40N 79 30 E
Virden 153 49 50N 100 56W
Vire 42 48 50N 0 53W
Virgem da Lapa 171 16 49 S 42 21W
Vírgenes, C. 176 52 19 S 68 21W
Virgin Gorda, I. 147 18 45N 64 26W
Virgin Is. 147 18 40N 64 30W
Virgin, R., Can. 153 57 2N 108 17W
Virgin, R., U.S.A. 161 36 50N 114 10W
Virginia, Ireland 38 53 50N 7 5W
Virginia, S. Afr. 128 28 8 S 26 55 E
Virginia, U.S.A. 158 47 30N 92 32W
Virginia □ 156 37 45N 78 0W
Virginia Beach 156 36 54N 75 58W
Virginia City, Mont., U.S.A. 160 45 25N 111 58W
Virginia City, Nev., U.S.A. 160 39 19N 119 39W
Virginia Falls 152 61 38N 125 42W
Virginiatown 150 48 9N 79 36W
Virgins, C. 176 52 10 S 68 30W
Virieu-le-Grand 45 45 51N 5 39 E
Virje 66 46 4N 16 59 E
Viroqua 158 43 33N 90 57W
Virovitica 66 45 51N 17 21 E
Virpaza, R. 66 42 14N 19 6 E
Virserum 73 57 20N 15 35 E
Virton 47 49 35N 5 32 E
Virtsu 80 58 32N 23 33 E
Virudhunagar 97 9 30N 78 0 E
Vis 63 43 0N 16 10 E
Vis, I. 63 43 0N 16 10 E
Vis Kanal 63 43 4N 16 5 E
Visalia 163 36 25N 119 18W
Visayan Sea 103 11 30N 123 30 E
Visby 73 57 37N 18 18 E
Viscount Melville Sd. 12 74 10N 108 0W
Visé 47 50 44N 5 41 E
Višegrad 66 43 47N 19 17 E
Viseu, Brazil 170 1 10 S 46 20W
Viseu, Port. 56 40 40N 7 55W
Vişeu 70 47 45N 24 25 E
Viseu □ 56 40 40N 7 55W
Vishakhapatnam 96 17 45N 83 20 E
Vishera, R. 84 59 55N 56 25 E
Vishnupur 95 23 8N 87 20 E
Visikoi I. 13 56 30 S 26 40 E
Visingsö 73 58 2N 14 20 E
Viskafors 73 57 37N 12 50 E
Vislanda 73 56 46N 14 30 E
Vislinskil Zaliv (Zalew Wislany) 54 54 20N 19 50 E
Visnagar 94 23 45N 72 32 E
Višnja Gora 63 45 58N 14 45 E
Viso del Marqués 59 38 32N 3 34W
Viso, Mte. 62 44 38N 7 5 E
Visoko 66 43 58N 18 10 E
Visp 50 46 17N 7 52 E
Vispa, R. 50 46 9N 7 48 E
Visselhovde 48 52 59N 9 36 E
Vissoie 50 46 13N 7 36 E
Vista 163 33 12N 117 14W
Vistonis, Limni 68 41 0N 25 7 E
Vistula, R. = Wisła, R. 54 53 38N 18 47 E
Vit, R. 67 43 30N 24 30 E
Vitanje 63 46 40N 15 18 E
Vitebsk 80 55 10N 30 15 E
Viterbo 63 42 25N 12 8 E
Viti Levu, I. 143 17 30 S 177 30 E
Vitiaz Str. 135 5 40 S 147 10 E
Vitigudino 56 41 1N 6 35W
Vitim 77 59 45N 112 25 E
Vitim, R. 77 58 40N 112 50 E
Vitina 69 37 40N 22 10 E
Vitina 66 43 17N 17 29 E
Vitória 171 20 20 S 40 22W
Vitoria 58 42 50N 2 41W
Vitória da Conquista 171 14 51 S 40 51W
Vitória de São Antão 170 8 10 S 37 20W
Vitorino Friere 170 4 4 S 45 10W
Vitré 42 48 8N 1 12W
Vitry-le-François 43 48 43N 4 33 E
Vitsi, Mt. 68 40 40N 21 25 E
Vittangi 74 67 41N 21 40 E
Vitteaux 43 47 24N 4 30 E
Vittel 43 48 12N 5 57 E
Vittória 65 36 58N 14 30 E
Vittório Véneto 63 45 59N 12 18 E
Vitu Is. 135 4 50 S 149 25 E
Vivegnis 47 50 42N 5 39 E
Viver 58 39 55N 0 36W
Vivero 56 43 39N 7 38W
Viviers 45 44 30N 4 40 E
Vivonne, Austral. 140 35 59 S 137 9 E
Vivonne, France 44 46 36N 0 15 E
Vivonne B. 140 35 59 S 137 9 E
Vivsta 72 62 30N 17 18 E
Vizcaíno, Desierto de 164 27 40N 113 50W
Vizcaíno, Sierra 164 27 30N 114 0W
Vizcaya □ 58 43 15N 2 45W
Vizianagaram 96 18 6N 83 10 E
Vizille 45 45 5N 5 46 E
Vizinada 63 45 20N 13 46 E
Viziru 70 45 0N 27 43 E
Vizovice 53 49 12N 17 56 E
Vizzini 65 37 9N 14 43 E
Vlaardingen 46 51 55N 4 21 E
Vladicin Han 66 42 42N 22 1 E
Vladimir 81 56 0N 40 30 E
Vladimir Volynskiy 80 50 50N 24 18 E
Vladimirci 66 44 36N 19 45 E
Vladimirovac 66 45 1N 20 53 E
Vladimirovka, U.S.S.R. 83 44 37N 44 41 E
Vladimirovka, U.S.S.R. 83 48 27N 46 5 E
Vladimirovo 67 43 32N 23 22 E
Vladislavovka 82 45 15N 35 15 E
Vladivostok 82 43 10N 131 53 E
Vlamertinge 47 50 51N 2 49 E
Vlaming Head 137 21 48 S 114 5 E
Vlasenica 66 44 11N 18 59 E
Vlasim 52 49 40N 14 53 E
Vlasinsko Jezero 66 42 44N 22 37 E
Vlašić, mt. 66 44 19N 17 37 E
Vlasotinci 66 42 59N 22 7 E
Vleuten 46 52 6N 5 1 E
Vlieland, I. 46 53 30N 4 55 E
Vliestroom 46 53 19N 5 8 E
Vlijmen 47 51 42N 5 14 E
Vlissingen 47 51 26N 3 34 E
Vlora 68 40 32N 19 28 E
Vlora □ 68 40 12N 20 0 E
Vltava, R. 52 49 35N 14 10 E
Vlădeasa, mt. 70 46 47N 22 50 E
Vo Dat 101 11 9N 107 31 E
Vobarno 62 45 38N 10 30 E
Vočin 66 45 37N 17 33 E
Vodice 63 43 47N 15 47 E
Vodnany 52 49 9N 14 11 E
Vodnjan 63 44 59N 13 52 E
Voe 36 60 21N 1 15W
Voga 121 6 23N 1 30 E
Vogelkop = Doberai, Jazirah 103 1 25 S 133 0 E
Vogelsberg 48 50 37N 9 30 E
Voghera 62 44 59N 9 1 E
Vohémar 129 13 25 S 50 0 E
Vohipeno 129 22 22 S 47 51 E
Voi 126 3 25 S 38 32 E
Void 43 48 40N 5 36 E
Voil, L. 34 56 20N 4 25W
Voineşti, Iaşi, Rumania 70 47 5N 27 27 E
Voineşti, Ploeşti, Rumania 70 45 5N 25 14 E
Voiotía □ 69 38 20N 23 0 E
Voiron 45 45 22N 5 35 E
Voiseys B. 151 56 15N 61 50W
Voitsberg 52 47 3N 15 9 E

Voiviis Limni, L. 68 39 30N 22 45 E
Vojens 73 55 16N 9 18 E
Vojmsjön 74 64 55N 16 40 E
Vojnió 63 45 19N 15 43 E
Vojvodina, Auton. Pokragina 66 45 20N 20 0 E
Vokhma 81 59 0N 46 45 E
Vokhma, R. 81 59 0N 46 44 E
Vokhtoga 81 58 46N 41 8 E
Volary 52 48 54N 13 52 E
Volborg 158 45 50N 105 44W
Volchansk 81 50 17N 36 58 E
Volchya, R. 82 48 0N 37 0 E
Volda 71 62 9N 6 5 E
Volendam 46 52 30N 5 4 E
Volga 81 57 58N 38 16 E
Volga Hts. = Privolzhskaya V.S. 79 51 0N 46 0 E
Volga, R. 83 52 20N 48 0 E
Volgodonsk 83 47 33N 42 5 E
Volgograd 83 48 40N 44 25 E
Volgogradskoye Vdkhr. 81 50 0N 45 20 E
Volgorechensk 81 57 28N 41 14 E
Volissós 69 38 29N 25 54 E
Volkerak 47 51 39N 4 18 E
Völkermarkt 52 46 39N 14 39 E
Volkhov 80 59 55N 32 15 E
Volkhov, R. 80 59 30N 32 0 E
Völklingen 49 49 15N 6 50 E
Volkovysk 80 53 9N 24 30 E
Volksrust 129 27 24 S 29 53 E
Vollenhove 46 52 40N 5 58 E
Volnovakha 82 47 35N 37 30 E
Volo 140 31 37 S 143 0 E
Volochayevka 77 48 40N 134 30 E
Volodary 81 56 12N 43 15 E
Vologda 81 59 25N 40 0 E
Volokolamsk 81 56 5N 36 0 E
Volokonovka 81 50 33N 37 58 E
Volontirovka 82 46 28N 29 28 E
Vólos 68 39 24N 22 59 E
Volosovo 80 59 27N 29 32 E
Volozhin 80 54 3N 26 30 E
Volsk 81 52 5N 47 28 E
Volstrup 73 57 19N 10 27 E
Volta, L. 121 7 30N 0 15 E
Volta, R. 121 8 0N 0 10W
Volta Redonda 173 22 31 S 44 5W
Voltaire, C. 136 14 16 S 125 35 E
Volterra 62 43 24N 10 50 E
Voltri 62 44 25N 8 43 E
Volturara Áppula 65 41 30N 15 2 E
Volturno, R. 65 41 18N 14 20 E
Volubilis 118 34 2N 5 33W
Vólvi, L. 68 40 40N 23 34 E
Volzhsk 81 55 57N 48 23 E
Volzhskiy 83 48 56N 44 46 E
Vondrozo 129 22 49 S 47 20 E
Vónitsa 69 38 53N 20 58 E
Voorburg 46 52 5N 4 24 E
Voorne Putten 46 51 52N 4 10 E
Voorst 46 52 10N 6 8 E
Voorthuizen 46 52 11N 5 36 E
Vopnafjörður 74 65 45N 14 40W
Vorarlberg □ 52 47 20N 10 0 E
Vóras Óros 68 40 57N 21 45 E
Vorbasse 73 55 39N 9 6 E
Vorden 46 52 6N 6 19 E
Vorderrheim, R. 51 46 49N 9 25 E
Vordingborg 73 55 0N 11 54 E
Voreppe 45 45 18N 5 39 E
Voriai Sporádhes 69 39 15N 23 30 E
Vórios Evvoïkós Kólpos 69 38 45N 23 15 E
Vorkuta 78 67 48N 64 20 E
Vorma 71 60 9N 11 27 E
Vorona, R. 81 52 0N 42 20 E
Voronezh, R.S.S.R., U.S.S.R. 81 51 40N 39 10 E
Voronezh, Ukraine, U.S.S.R. 80 51 47N 33 28 E
Voronezh, R. 81 52 30N 39 30 E
Vorontsovo-Aleksandrovskoïe = Zelenokumsk. 83 44 30N 44 1 E
Voroshilovgrad 83 48 38N 39 15 E
Voroshilovsk = Kommunarsk 83 48 3N 38 40 E
Vorovskoye 77 54 30N 155 50 E
Vorselaar 47 51 12N 4 46 E
Vorskla, R. 82 49 30N 34 31 E
Vorukh 85 39 52N 70 35 E
Vorupør 73 56 58N 8 22 E
Vosges 43 48 20N 7 10 E
Vosges □ 43 48 12N 6 20 E
Voskopoja 68 40 40N 20 33 E
Voskresensk 81 55 27N 38 31 E
Voskresenskoye 81 56 51N 45 30 E
Voss 71 60 38N 6 26 E
Vosselaar 47 51 19N 4 52 E
Vostok I. 131 10 5 S 152 23W
Vostotnyy Sayan 77 54 0N 96 0 E
Votice 52 49 38N 14 39 E
Votkinsk 84 57 0N 53 55 E
Votkinskoye Vdkhr. 78 57 30N 55 0 E
Vouga, R. 56 40 46N 8 10W
Voulte-sur-Rhône, La 45 44 48N 4 46 E
Vouvry 50 46 21N 6 21 E
Voúxa, Ákra 69 35 37N 20 32 E
Vouzela 56 40 43N 8 7W
Vouziers 43 49 22N 4 40 E
Voves 43 48 15N 1 38 E
Voxna 72 61 20N 15 30 E
Voy 37 59 1N 3 16W
Vozhe Oz. 78 60 45N 39 0 E
Vozhgaly 81 58 24N 50 1 E
Voznesensk 82 47 35N 31 15 E
Voznesenye 78 61 0N 35 45 E
Vráble 53 48 15N 18 16 E
Vrácevšnica 66 44 2N 20 34 E
Vrådal 71 59 20N 8 25 E
Vradiyevka 82 49 56N 30 38 E
Vraka 68 42 8N 19 28 E
Vrakhnéika 69 38 10N 21 40 E
Vrancea □ 70 45 50N 26 45 E
Vrancei, Munţii 70 46 0N 26 30 E
Vrangelja, Ostrov 77 71 0N 180 0 E
Vrangtjarn 72 62 14N 16 37 E
Vranica, mt. 66 43 59N 18 0 E
Vranje 66 42 34N 21 54 E
Vranjska Banja 66 42 34N 22 1 E
Vranov 53 48 53N 21 40 E
Vransko 63 46 17N 14 58 E
Vratsa 67 43 13N 23 30 E
Vratsa □ 67 43 30N 23 30 E
Vrbas 66 45 0N 17 27 E
Vrbas, R. 66 44 30N 17 10 E
Vrbnik 63 45 4N 14 32 E
Vrboviec 63 45 53N 16 28 E
Vrbovsko 63 45 24N 15 5 E
Vrchlabí 52 49 38N 15 37 E
Vrede 129 27 24 S 29 6 E
Vredefort 128 27 0 S 26 58 E
Vredenburg 128 32 51 S 18 0 E
Vredendal 128 31 41 S 18 35 E
Vreeswijk 46 52 1N 5 6 E
Vrena 73 58 54N 16 41 E
Vrgorac 66 43 12N 17 20 E
Vrhnika 63 45 58N 14 15 E
Vriddhachalam 97 11 30N 79 10 E
Vridi 120 5 15N 4 3W
Vridi Canal 120 5 15N 4 3W
Vries 46 53 5N 6 35 E
Vriezenveen 46 52 25N 6 38 E
Vrindaban 94 27 37N 77 40 E
Vrnograč 63 43 12N 17 20 E
Vrondádhes 69 38 25N 26 7 E
Vroomshoop 46 52 27N 6 34 E
Vrpolje 66 43 42N 16 1 E
Vršac 66 45 8N 21 18 E
Vršački Kanal 66 45 15N 21 0 E
Vrsheto 67 43 15N 23 23 E
Vryburg 128 26 55 S 24 45 E
Vryheid 129 27 54 S 30 47 E
Vsetín 53 49 20N 18 0 E
Vu Liet 100 18 43N 105 23 E
Vŭcha, R. 67 41 53N 24 26 E
Vučitrn 66 42 49N 20 59 E
Vught 47 51 38N 5 20 E
Vuka, R. 66 45 28N 18 30 E
Vukovar 66 45 21N 18 59 E
Vulcan, Can. 152 50 25N 113 15W
Vulcan, Rumania 70 45 23N 23 17 E
Vulcan, U.S.A. 156 45 46N 87 51W
Vŭlcani 66 46 0N 20 26 E
Vulcano, I. 65 38 25N 14 58 E
Vulchedrŭma 67 43 42N 23 16 E
Vulci 63 42 23N 11 37 E
Vŭleni 70 44 15N 24 45 E
Vulkaneshty 82 45 35N 28 30 E
Vunduzi, R. 127 18 0 S 33 45 E
Vung Tau 101 10 21N 107 4 E
Vûrbitsa 67 42 59N 26 40 E
Vutcani 70 46 26N 27 59 E
Vuyyuru 96 16 28N 80 50 E
Vvedenka 84 54 0N 63 53 E
Vyara 96 21 8N 73 28 E
Vyasniki 81 56 10N 42 10 E
Vyatka, R. 84 56 30N 51 0 E
Vyatskiye Polyany 84 56 5N 51 0 E
Vyazemskiy 77 47 32N 134 45 E
Vyazma 80 55 10N 34 15 E
Vyborg 78 60 43N 28 47 E
Vychegda R. 78 61 50N 52 30 E
Vychodné Beskydy 53 49 30N 22 0 E
Východočeský □ 52 50 20N 15 45 E
Východoslovenský □ 53 48 50N 21 0 E
Vyg-ozero 78 63 30N 34 0 E
Vyja, R. 81 41 53N 24 26 E
Vypin, I. 97 10 10N 76 15 E
Vyrnwy, L. 31 52 48N 3 30W
Vyrnwy, R. 31 52 43N 3 15W
Vyshniy Volochek 80 57 30N 34 30 E
Vyškov 53 49 17N 17 0 E
Vysoké Mýto 53 49 58N 16 23 E
Vysoké Tatry 53 49 30N 20 0 E
Vysokovsk 81 56 22N 36 30 E
Vysotsk 80 51 43N 36 32 E
Vyssi Brod 92 48 36N 14 20 E
Vytegra 52 61 15N 36 40 E

W

Wa 121 10 7N 2 25W
Waal, R. 46 51 59N 4 8 E
Waalwijk 47 51 42N 5 4 E
Waarschoot 47 51 10N 3 36 E
Waasmunster 47 51 6N 4 5 E
Wabag 135 5 32 S 143 53 E
Wabakimi L. 150 50 38N 89 45W
Wabana 151 47 40N 53 0W
Wabasca 152 55 57N 113 45W
Wabash 156 40 48N 85 46W
Wabash, R. 156 39 10N 87 30W
Wabawng 98 25 18N 97 46 E
Wabeno 156 45 25N 88 40W
Wabi Gestro, R. 123 6 0N 41 35 E
Wabi, R. 123 7 35N 40 5 E
Wabi Shaballe, R. 123 8 0N 40 45 E
Wabigoon, L. 153 49 44N 92 34W
Wabowden 153 54 55N 98 38W
Wabrzezno 54 53 16N 18 57 E
Wabuk Pt. 150 55 20N 85 5W
Wabush City 151 52 55N 66 52W
Wabuska 160 39 16N 119 13W
W.A.C. Bennett Dam 152 56 2N 122 6W
Wachapreague 162 37 36N 75 41W
Wachtebeke 47 51 11N 3 52 E
Waco 159 31 33N 97 5W
Waconichi, L. 150 50 8N 74 0W
Wad ar Rimsa 92 26 5N 41 30 E
Wad Ban Naqa 123 16 32N 33 9 E
Wad Banda 123 13 10N 27 50 E
Wad el Haddad 123 13 50N 33 30 E
Wad en Nau 123 14 10N 33 34 E
Wad Hamid 123 16 20N 32 45 E
Wâd Medanî 123 14 28N 33 30 E
Wad Thana 94 27 22N 66 23 E
Wadayama 110 35 19N 134 52 E
Waddān 119 29 9N 16 45 E
Waddān, Jabal 119 29 0N 16 15 E
Waddeneilanden 46 53 25N 5 10 E
Waddenzee 46 53 6N 5 10 E
Wadderin Hill 137 32 0 S 118 25 E
Waddesdon 29 51 50N 0 54W
Waddingham 33 53 28N 0 31W
Waddington 33 53 10N 0 31W
Waddington, Mt. 152 51 23N 125 15W
Waddinxveen 46 52 2N 4 40 E
Waddy Pt. 139 24 58 S 153 21 E
Wadebridge 30 50 31N 4 51W
Wadena, Can. 153 51 57N 103 38W
Wadena, U.S.A. 158 46 25N 95 2W
Wädenswil 51 47 14N 8 30 E
Wadesboro 157 35 2N 80 2W
Wadhams 152 51 30N 127 30W
Wadhurst 29 51 3N 0 21 E
Wadi 121 13 5N 11 40 E
Wādī ash Shāfī' 119 27 30N 15 0 E
Wādī Banī Walīd 119 31 49N 14 0 E
Wadi Gemâl 122 24 35N 35 10 E
Wadi Halfa 122 21 53N 31 19 E
Wadi Masila 91 16 30N 49 0 E
Wadi Sabha 92 23 50N 48 30 E
Wadlew 54 51 31N 19 23 E
Wadowice 54 49 52N 19 30 E
Wadsworth 160 39 44N 119 22W
Waegwan 107 35 59N 128 23 E
Waenfawr 31 53 7N 4 10W
Wafou Hu 109 32 19N 116 56 E
Wafra 92 28 33N 48 3 E
Wagenberg 47 51 40N 4 46 E
Wageningen 46 51 58N 5 40 E
Wager B. 149 65 26N 88 40W
Wager Bay 149 65 56N 90 49W
Wagga Wagga 141 35 7 S 147 24 E
Waghete 103 4 10 S 135 50 E
Wagin, Austral. 137 33 17 S 117 25 E
Wagin, Nigeria 137 12 42N 7 10 E
Wagon Mound 159 36 10N 105 0W
Wagoner 159 36 0N 95 20W
Wagrowiec 54 52 48N 17 19 E
Wah 94 33 45N 72 40 E
Wahai 103 2 48 S 129 35 E
Wahiawa 147 21 30N 158 2W
Wahnai 94 32 40N 65 50 E
Wahoo 158 41 15N 96 35W
Wahpeton 158 46 20N 96 35W
Wahratta 140 31 58 S 141 50 E
Wai 96 17 56N 73 57 E
Wai, Koh 101 9 55N 102 55 E
Waiai, R. 143 45 36 S 167 45 E
Waianae 147 21 25N 158 8W
Waiau 143 42 39 S 173 5 E
Waiau, R. 143 42 47 S 173 22 E
Waiawe Ganga 97 6 15N 81 0 E
Waibeem 103 0 30 S 132 50 E
Waiblingen 49 48 49N 9 20 E
Waidhofen, Niederösterreich, Austria 52 48 49N 15 17 E
Waidhofen, Niederösterreich, Austria 52 47 57N 14 46 E
Waigeo, I. 103 0 20 S 130 40 E
Waihao Downs 143 44 48 S 170 55 E
Waihao, R. 143 44 52 S 171 11 E
Waiheke Islands 142 36 48 S 175 6 E
Waihi 142 37 23 S 175 52 E
Waihola 143 46 1 S 170 8 E
Waihola L. 143 45 59 S 170 8 E
Waihou, R. 143 37 15 S 175 40 E
Waika 126 2 22 S 25 42 E
Waikabubak 103 9 45 S 119 25 E
Waikaka 143 45 55 S 169 1 E
Waikaoti 131 45 36 S 170 41 E
Waikare, L. 142 37 26 S 175 13 E
Waikaremoana 142 38 42 S 177 12 E
Waikaremoana L. 142 38 49 S 177 9 E
Waikari 143 42 58 S 172 41 E
Waikato, R. 142 37 23 S 174 43 E
Waikawa Harbour 143 46 39 S 169 9 E
Waikerie 140 34 9 S 140 0 E
Waikiekie 142 35 57 S 174 16 E
Waikokopu 142 39 3 S 177 52 E
Waikokopu Harb. 142 39 4 S 177 53 E
Waikouaiti 143 45 36 S 170 41 E
Wailuku 147 20 53N 156 26W
Waimakariri, R. 143 42 23 S 172 42 E
Waimangaroa 143 41 43 S 171 46 E
Waimanola 147 21 19N 157 43W
Waimarie 143 41 35 S 171 58 E
Waimarino 143 40 40 S 175 20 E
Waimate 143 44 53 S 171 3 E
Waimea 147 21 57N 159 39W
Waimea Plain 143 45 55 S 168 35 E
Waimes 47 50 25N 6 7 E
Wainfleet All Saints 33 53 7N 0 16 E
Wainganga, R. 96 21 0N 79 45 E
Waingapu 103 9 35 S 120 11 E
Waingmaw 98 25 21N 97 26 E
Wainiha 147 22 9N 159 34W
Wainuiomata 142 41 17 S 174 56 E
Wainwright, Can. 153 52 50N 110 50W
Wainwright, U.S.A. 147 70 39N 160 10W
Waiotapu 142 38 21 S 176 25 E
Waiouru 142 39 28 S 175 41 E
Waipahi 143 46 6 S 169 15 E
Waipahu 147 21 23N 158 1W
Waipapa Pt. 143 46 40 S 168 51 E
Waipara 143 43 3 S 172 46 E
Waipawa 142 39 56 S 176 38 E
Waipiro 142 38 2 S 176 22 E
Waipori 131 45 50 S 169 52 E
Waipu 142 35 59 S 174 29 E
Waipukurau 142 40 1 S 176 33 E
Wairakei 142 38 37 S 176 6 E
Wairarapa I. 142 41 14 S 175 15 E
Wairau, R. 143 41 32 S 174 7 E
Wairio 143 45 59 S 168 3 E
Wairoa 142 39 3 S 177 25 E
Wairoa, R. 142 36 5 S 173 59 E
Waitaki Plains 143 44 22 S 170 0 E
Waitaki, R. 143 44 23 S 169 55 E
Waitara 142 38 59 S 174 15 E
Waitchie 140 35 22 S 143 8 E
Waitoa 142 37 37 S 175 35 E
Waitotara 142 39 49 S 174 44 E
Waitsburg 160 46 15N 118 10W
Waiuku 142 37 15 S 174 45 E
Wajir 126 1 42N 40 20 E
Wajir □ 126 1 42N 40 20 E
Wakaia 143 45 44 S 168 51 E
Wakasa 110 35 20N 134 24 E
Wakasa-Wan 111 34 45N 135 30 E
Wakatipu, L. 143 45 5 S 168 33 E
Wakaw 153 52 39N 105 44W
Wakayama 111 34 15N 135 15 E
Wakayama-ken □ 111 33 50N 135 30 E
Wake 110 34 48N 134 8 E
Wake Forest 157 35 58N 78 30W
Wake I. 130 19 18N 166 36 E
Wakefield, N.Z. 143 41 24 S 173 5 E
Wakefield, U.K. 33 53 41N 1 31W
Wakefield, Mass., U.S.A. 162 42 30N 71 3W
Wakefield, Mich., U.S.A. 158 46 28N 89 53W
Wakema 98 16 40N 95 18 E
Wakhan □ 93 37 0N 73 0 E
Wakkanai 112 45 28N 141 35 E
Wakkerstroom 129 27 24 S 30 10 E
Wako 150 49 50N 91 22W
Wakool 140 35 28 S 144 23 E
Wakool, R. 140 35 5 S 143 33 E
Wakre 103 0 30 S 131 5 E
Waku 135 6 5 S 149 9 E
Wakuach L. 151 55 34N 67 32W
Walachia □ 70 44 40N 25 0 E
Walamba 127 13 30 S 28 42 E
Walberswick 29 52 18N 1 39 E
Walbrzych 54 50 45N 16 18 E
Walbury Hill 28 51 22N 1 28W
Walcha 141 30 55 S 151 31 E
Walcha Road 141 30 55 S 151 24 E
Walcheren, I. 46 51 30N 3 35 E
Walcott 160 41 50N 106 55W
Walcz 54 53 17N 16 27 E
Wald 51 47 17N 8 56 E
Waldbröl 48 50 52N 7 36 E
Waldeck 48 51 12N 9 4 E
Walden, Colo., U.S.A. 160 40 47N 106 20W
Walden, N.Y., U.S.A. 162 41 32N 74 13W
Waldenburg 50 47 23N 7 45 E
Waldorf 162 38 37N 76 54W
Waldport 160 44 30N 124 2W
Waldron, Can. 153 50 53N 102 35W
Waldron, U.K. 29 50 56N 0 13 E
Waldron, U.S.A. 159 34 52N 94 4W
Waldshut 49 47 37N 8 12 E
Waldya 123 11 50N 39 34 E
Walebing 137 30 40 S 116 15 E
Walembele 120 10 30N 1 14W
Walensee 51 47 7N 9 13 E
Walenstadt 51 47 8N 9 19 E
Wales 147 65 38N 168 10W
Walewale 121 10 21N 0 50W
Walgett 133 30 0 S 148 5 E
Walhalla, Austral. 141 37 56 S 146 29 E
Walhalla, U.S.A. 153 48 55N 97 55W
Waliso 123 8 33N 38 1 E
Walkaway 137 28 59 S 114 48 E
Walker 158 47 4N 94 35W
Walker L., Man., Can. 153 54 42N 96 57W
Walker L., Qué., Can. 151 50 20N 67 11W
Walker L., U.S.A. 163 38 56N 118 46W
Walkerston 138 21 11 S 149 8 E
Wall 158 44 0N 102 14W
Walla Walla, Austral. 141 35 45 S 146 54 E
Walla Walla, U.S.A. 160 46 3N 118 25W

Place	Page	Lat.	Long.
Wallabadah	138	17 57 S	142 15 E
Wallace, Idaho, U.S.A.	160	47 30N	116 0W
Wallace, N.C., U.S.A.	157	34 50N	77 59W
Wallace, Nebr., U.S.A.	158	40 51N	101 12W
Wallaceburg	150	42 40N	82 23W
Wallacetown	143	46 21 S	168 19 E
Wallachia = Valahia	70	44 35N	25 0 E
Wallal	139	26 32 S	146 7 E
Wallal Downs	136	19 47 S	120 40 E
Wallambin, L.	137	30 57 S	117 35 E
Wallaroo	140	33 56 S	137 39 E
Wallasey	32	53 26N	3 2W
Walldurn	49	49 34N	9 23 E
Wallerawang	141	33 25 S	150 4 E
Wallhallow	138	17 50 S	135 50 E
Wallingford	162	43 27N	72 50W
Wallis Arch.	142	13 20 S	176 20 E
Wallisellen	51	47 25N	8 36 E
Wallowa	160	45 40N	117 35W
Wallowa, Mts.	160	45 20N	117 30W
Walls	36	60 14N	1 32W
Wallsend, Austral.	141	32 55 S	151 40 E
Wallsend, U.K.	35	54 59N	1 30W
Wallula	160	46 3N	118 59W
Wallumbilla	139	26 33 S	149 9 E
Walmer, S. Afr.	128	33 57 S	25 35 E
Walmer, U.K.	29	51 12N	1 23 E
Walmsley, L.	153	63 25N	108 36W
Walney, Isle of	32	54 5N	3 15W
Walnut Ridge	159	36 7N	90 58W
Walpeup	140	35 10 S	142 2 E
Walpole	29	52 44N	0 13 E
Walsall	28	52 36N	1 59W
Walsenburg	159	37 42N	104 45W
Walsh, Austral.	138	16 40 S	144 0 E
Walsh, U.S.A.	159	37 28N	102 15W
Walsh, R.	138	16 31 S	143 42 E
Walshoutem	47	50 43N	5 4 E
Walsoken	29	52 41N	0 12 E
Walsrode	48	52 51N	9 37 E
Waltair	96	17 44N	83 23 E
Walterboro	157	32 53N	80 40W
Walters	159	34 25N	98 20W
Waltershausen	48	50 53N	10 33 E
Waltham, Can.	150	45 57N	76 57W
Waltham, U.K.	29	53 32N	0 6W
Waltham, U.S.A.	34	42 22N	71 12W
Waltham Abbey	29	51 40N	0 1 E
Waltham Forest	29	51 37N	0 2 E
Waltham on the Wolds	29	52 49N	0 48W
Waltman	160	43 8N	107 15W
Walton	162	42 12N	75 9W
Walton-le-Dale	32	53 45N	2 41W
Walton-on-the-Naze	29	51 52N	1 17 E
Walu	98	23 54N	96 57 E
Walvis Ridge	15	30 0 S	3 0 E
Walvisbaai	128	23 0 S	14 28 E
Walwa	141	35 59 S	147 44 E
Wamaza	126	4 12 S	27 2 E
Wamba, Kenya	126	0 58N	37 19 E
Wamba, Nigeria	126	8 58N	8 34 E
Wamba, Zaïre	121	2 10N	27 57 E
Wamego	158	39 14N	96 22W
Wamena	103	3 58 S	138 50 E
Wampo	99	31 30N	86 38 E
Wamsasi	103	3 27 S	126 7 E
Wan Hat	98	20 14N	97 53 E
Wan Kinghao	98	21 34N	98 17 E
Wan Lai-Kam	98	21 21N	98 22 E
Wan Tup	98	21 13N	98 42 E
Wana	94	32 20N	69 32 E
Wanaaring	139	29 38 S	144 0 E
Wanaka L.	143	44 33 S	169 7 E
Wanan	109	26 25N	114 50 E
Wanapiri	103	4 30 S	135 50 E
Wanapitei	150	46 30N	80 45W
Wanapitei L.	150	46 45N	80 40W
Wanaque	162	41 3N	74 17W
Wanbi	140	34 46 S	140 17 E
Wanborough	28	51 33N	1 40W
Wanch'eng	108	22 51N	107 25 E
Wanch'üan	106	35 26N	110 50 E
Wanch'uan	106	40 50N	114 56 E
Wandanian	141	35 6 S	150 30 E
Wanderer	127	19 36 S	30 1 E
Wandiwash	97	12 30N	79 30 E
Wandoan	139	26 5 S	149 55 E
Wandre	47	50 40N	5 39 E
Wandsworth	29	51 28N	0 15W
Wanfercée-Baulet	47	50 28N	4 35 E
Wanfuchuang	107	40 10N	122 34 E
Wang Kai (Ghâbat el Arab)	123	9 3N	29 23 E
Wang Noi	100	14 13N	100 44 E
Wang, R.	100	17 8N	99 2 E
Wang Saphung	100	17 18N	101 46 E
Wang Thong	100	16 50N	100 26 E
Wanga	126	2 58N	29 12 E
Wangal	103	6 8 S	134 9 E
Wanganella	141	35 6 S	144 49 E
Wanganui	142	39 35 S	175 3 E
Wanganui, R., N.I., N.Z.	142	39 25 S	175 4 E
Wanganui, R., S.I., N.Z.	143	43 3 S	170 26 E
Wangaratta	141	36 21 S	146 19 E
Wangchiang	109	30 7N	116 41 E
Wangch'ing	107	43 14N	129 38 E
Wangdu Phodrang	98	27 28N	89 54 E
Wangerooge I.	48	53 47N	7 52 E
Wangi	126	1 58 S	40 58 E
Wangiwangi, I.	103	5 22 S	123 37 E
Wangmo	108	25 14N	105 59 E
Wangts'ang	108	32 12N	106 21 E
Wangtu	106	38 42N	115 4 E
Wanhsien, Hopeh, China	106	38 49N	115 7 E
Wanhsien, Kansu, China	105	36 45N	107 24 E
Wankaner	94	22 42N	71 0 E
Wanki Nat. Park	128	19 0 S	26 30 E
Wankie	127	18 18 S	26 30 E
Wankie □	127	18 18 S	26 30 E
Wanless	153	54 11N	101 21W
Wanna Lakes	137	28 30 S	128 27 E
Wannien	109	28 40N	116 55 E
Wanon Niwar	100	17 38N	103 46 E
Wanshengch'ang	108	28 58N	106 55 E
Wanssum	47	51 32N	6 5 E
Wanstead	143	40 8 S	176 30 E
Wantage	28	51 35N	1 25W
Wantsai	109	28 5N	114 22 E
Wanyin	98	20 23N	97 15 E
Wanyüan	108	32 4N	108 5 E
Wanzarīk	119	27 3N	13 30 E
Wanze	47	50 32N	5 13 E
Wapakoneta	156	40 35N	84 10W
Wapato	160	46 30N	120 25W
Wapawekka L.	153	54 55N	104 40W
Wapikopa L.	150	42 50N	88 10W
Wapiti, R.	150	55 5N	118 18W
Wappingers Fs.	162	41 35N	73 56W
Wapsipinican, R.	158	41 44N	90 19W
Warabi	111	35 49N	139 41 E
Warandab	91	7 20N	44 2 E
Warangal	96	17 58N	79 45 E
Waratah	138	41 30 S	145 30 E
Waratah B.	139	38 54 S	146 5 E
Warboys	29	52 25N	0 5W
Warburg	48	51 29N	9 10 E
Warburton	141	37 47 S	145 42 E
Warburton, R.	143	27 30 S	138 30 E
Warburton Ra.	137	25 55 S	126 28 E
Ward, Ireland	38	53 25N	6 19W
Ward, N.Z.	143	41 49 S	174 11 E
Ward Cove	152	55 25N	132 10W
Ward Hunt, C.	135	8 2 S	148 10 E
Ward Hunt Str.	135	9 30 S	150 0 E
Ward Mtn.	163	37 12N	118 54W
Ward, R.	139	26 32 S	146 6 E
Warden	129	27 50 S	29 0 E
Wardha	96	20 45N	78 39 E
Wardha, R.	93	19 57N	79 11 E
Wardington	28	52 8N	1 17W
Wardle	32	53 7N	2 35W
Wardlow	152	50 56N	111 31W
Wardoan	133	25 59 S	149 59 E
Wards River	141	32 11 S	151 56 E
Ward's Stone, mt.	32	54 2N	2 39W
Ware, Can.	152	57 26N	125 41W
Ware, U.K.	29	51 48N	0 2W
Ware, U.S.A.	162	42 16N	72 15W
Waregem	47	50 53N	3 27 E
Wareham, U.K.	28	50 41N	2 8W
Wareham, U.S.A.	162	41 45N	70 44W
Wareham, oilfield	19	50 40N	2 8W
Waremme	47	50 43N	5 15 E
Waren	48	53 30N	12 41 E
Warendorf	48	51 57N	8 0 E
Warialda	139	29 29 S	150 33 E
Wariap	103	1 30 S	134 5 E
Warin Chamrap	100	15 12N	104 53 E
Wark	35	55 5N	2 14W
Warkopi	103	1 12 S	134 9 E
Warkworth, N.Z.	142	36 24 S	174 41 E
Warkworth, U.K.	35	55 22N	1 38W
Warley	28	52 30N	2 0W
Warm Springs, Mont., U.S.A.	160	46 11N	112 56W
Warm Springs, Nev., U.S.A.	161	38 16N	116 32W
Warman	153	52 19N	106 30W
Warmbad, Namibia	128	19 14 S	13 51 E
Warmbad, Namibia	128	28 25 S	18 42 E
Warmbad, S. Afr.	129	24 51 S	28 19 E
Warmenhuizen	46	52 43N	4 44 E
Warmeriville	43	49 20N	4 13 E
Warminster	28	51 12N	2 11W
Warmond	46	52 12N	4 30 E
Warnambool Downs	138	22 48 S	142 52 E
Warnemünde	48	54 9N	12 5 E
Warner	152	49 17N	112 12W
Warner Range, Mts.	160	41 30 S	120 20W
Warner Robins	157	32 41N	83 36W
Warneton	47	50 45N	2 57 E
Warnow, R.	48	54 0N	12 9 E
Warnsveld	46	52 8N	6 14 E
Waroona	137	32 50 S	115 58 E
Warora	96	20 14N	79 1 E
Warracknabeal	140	36 9 S	142 26 E
Warragul	141	38 10 S	145 58 E
Warrawaqine	136	20 51 S	120 42 E
Warrayelu	123	10 40N	39 28 E
Warrego, R.	139	30 24 S	145 21 E
Warrego Ra.	138	25 15 S	146 0 E
Warren, Austral.	141	31 42 S	147 51 E
Warren, Ark., U.S.A.	159	33 35N	92 3W
Warren, Pa., U.S.A.	156	41 52N	79 10W
Warren, R.I., U.S.A.	156	41 43N	71 19W
Warrenpoint	38	54 7N	6 15W
Warrens Landing	153	53 40N	98 0W
Warrensburg	158	38 45N	93 45W
Warrenton, S. Afr.	128	28 9 S	24 47 E
Warrenton, U.S.A.	160	46 11N	123 59W
Warrenville	139	25 48 S	147 22 E
Warri	121	5 30N	5 41 E
Warrie	136	22 12 S	119 40 E
Warrina	136	28 12 S	135 50 E
Warrington, N.Z.	143	45 43 S	170 35 E
Warrington, U.K.	32	53 25N	2 38W
Warrington, U.S.A.	157	30 22N	87 16W
Warrnambool	140	38 25 S	142 30 E
Warroad	158	49 0N	95 20W
Warsaw	156	41 14N	85 50W
Warsaw = Warszawa	54	52 13N	21 0 E
Warsop	33	53 13N	1 9W
Warstein	48	51 26N	8 20 E
Warszawa	54	52 13N	21 0 E
Warszawa □	54	52 30N	17 0 E
Warta	54	51 43N	18 38 E
Warta, R.	54	52 40N	16 10 E
Waru	103	3 30 S	130 36 E
Warud	96	21 30N	78 16 E
Warwick, Austral.	139	28 10 S	152 1 E
Warwick, U.K.	28	52 17N	1 36W
Warwick, N.Y., U.S.A.	162	41 16N	74 22W
Warwick, R.I., U.S.A.	162	41 43N	71 25W
Warwick □	28	52 20N	1 30W
Wasa	152	49 45N	115 50W
Wasatch, Mt., Ra.	160	40 30N	111 15W
Wasbank	129	28 15 S	30 9 E
Wasbister	37	59 11N	3 2W
Wasco, Calif., U.S.A.	163	35 37N	119 16W
Wasco, Oreg., U.S.A.	160	45 45N	120 46W
Waseca	158	44 3N	93 31W
Wasekamio L.	153	56 45N	108 45W
Wash, The	33	52 58N	0 20W
Washburn, N.D., U.S.A.	158	47 23N	101 0W
Washburn, Wis., U.S.A.	158	46 38N	90 55W
Washford	28	51 9N	3 22W
Washington, U.K.	35	54 55N	1 30W
Washington, D.C., U.S.A.	162	38 52N	77 0W
Washington, Ga., U.S.A.	157	33 45N	82 45W
Washington, Ind., U.S.A.	156	38 40N	87 8W
Washington, Iowa, U.S.A.	158	41 20N	91 45W
Washington, Miss., U.S.A.	158	38 35N	91 20W
Washington, N.C., U.S.A.	157	35 35N	77 1W
Washington, N.J., U.S.A.	162	40 45N	74 59W
Washington, Ohio, U.S.A.	156	39 34N	83 26W
Washington, Pa., U.S.A.	156	40 10N	80 20W
Washington, Utah, U.S.A.	161	37 10N	113 30W
Washington □	160	47 45N	120 30W
Washington Court House	156	39 34N	83 26W
*Washington I., Pac. Oc.	131	4 43N	160 25W
Washington I., U.S.A.	156	45 24N	86 54W
Washington Mt.	156	44 15N	71 18W
Washir	93	32 15N	63 50 E
Wasian	103	1 47 S	133 19 E
Wasilków	54	53 12N	23 13 E
Wasior	103	2 43 S	134 30 E
Waskaiowaka, L.	153	56 33N	96 23W
Waskesiu Lake	153	53 55N	106 5W
Wasm	122	18 2N	41 32 E
Waspik	47	51 41N	4 57 E
Wassen	51	46 42N	8 36 E
Wassenaar	46	52 8N	4 24 E
Wasserburg	49	48 4N	12 15 E
Wassy	43	48 30N	4 58 E
Wast Water, L.	32	54 26N	3 18W
Waswanipi	150	49 40N	75 59W
Waswanipi, L.	150	49 35N	76 40W
Watangpone	103	4 29 S	120 25 E
Wataroa	143	43 18 S	170 24 E
Wataroa, R.	143	43 7 S	170 16 E
Watawaha, P.	103	6 30 S	122 20 E
Watchet	28	51 10N	3 20W
Water Park Pt.	138	22 56 S	150 47 E
Water Valley	159	34 9N	89 38W
Waterberg, Namibia	128	20 30 S	17 18 E
Waterberg, S. Afr.	129	24 14 S	28 0 E
Waterberg, mt.	128	20 26 S	17 13 E
Waterbury	162	41 32N	73 0W
Waterbury L.	153	58 10N	104 22W
Waterford, Ireland	39	52 16N	7 8W
Waterford, S. Afr.	128	33 6 S	25 0 E
Waterford, U.S.A.	163	37 38N	120 46W
Waterford □	39	51 10N	7 40W
Waterford Harb.	39	52 10N	6 58W
Watergate Bay	30	50 26N	5 4W
Watergrasshill	39	52 1N	8 20W
Waterhen L., Man., Can.	153	52 10N	99 40W
Waterhen L., Sask., Can.	153	54 28N	108 25W
Wateringen	46	52 2N	4 16 E
Waterloo, Belg.	47	50 43N	4 25 E
Waterloo, Can.	150	43 30N	80 32W
Waterloo, S. Leone	120	8 26N	13 8W
Waterloo, U.K.	32	53 29N	3 2W
Waterloo, Ill., U.S.A.	158	38 22N	90 6W
Waterloo, Iowa, U.S.A.	158	42 27N	92 20W
Waterloo, N.Y., U.S.A.	162	42 54N	76 53W
Watermeal-Boitsford	47	50 48N	4 25 E
Watermeet	158	46 15N	89 12W
Waternish	36	57 32N	6 35W
Waterton Lakes Nat. Park	152	49 5N	114 15W
Watertown, Conn., U.S.A.	162	41 36N	73 7W
Watertown, N.Y., U.S.A.	162	43 58N	75 57W
Watertown, S.D., U.S.A.	158	44 57N	97 5W
Watertown, Wis., U.S.A.	158	43 15N	88 45W
Waterval-Boven	129	25 40 S	30 18 E
Waterville, Ireland	39	51 49N	10 10W
Waterville, Me., U.S.A.	151	44 35N	69 40W
Waterville, N.Y., U.S.A.	162	42 56N	75 23W
Waterville, Wash., U.S.A.	160	47 45N	120 1W
Watervliet, Belg.	47	51 17N	3 38 E
Watervliet, U.S.A.	162	42 46N	73 43W
Wates	103	7 53 S	110 6 E
Watford	29	51 38N	0 23W
Watford City	158	47 50N	103 23W
Wath	33	53 29N	1 20W
Wathaman, R.	153	57 16N	102 59W
Watheroo	137	30 15 S	116 0W
Watien	109	32 45N	112 30 E
Wat'ing	106	35 25N	106 46 E
Watkins Glen	162	42 25N	76 55W
Watlings I.	167	24 0N	74 35W
Watlington, Norfolk, U.K.	29	52 40N	0 24 E
Watlington, Oxford, U.K.	29	51 38N	1 0W
Watonga	159	35 51N	98 24W
Watou	47	50 51N	2 38 E
Watraba	139	31 58 S	133 13 E
Watrous, Can.	153	51 40N	105 25W
Watrous, U.S.A.	159	35 50N	104 55W
Watsa	126	3 4N	29 30 E
Watseka	156	40 45N	87 45W
Watson, Austral.	137	30 29 S	131 31 E
Watson, Can.	153	52 10N	104 30W
Watson Lake	147	60 6N	128 49W
Watsontown	162	41 5N	76 52W
Watsonville	163	36 55N	121 49W
Watten	37	21 1 S	144 3 E
Wattenwil	50	46 46N	7 30 E
Wattiwarriganna Cr.	139	28 57 S	136 10 E
Watton	29	52 35N	0 50 E
Wattwil	51	47 18N	9 6 E
Watubela, Kepulauan	103	4 28 S	131 54 E
Wau	135	7 21 S	146 47 E
Waubach	47	50 55N	6 3 E
Waubay	158	45 42N	97 17W
Waubra	140	37 21 S	143 39 E
Wauchope	141	31 28 S	152 45 E
Wauchula	157	27 35N	81 50W
Waugh	153	49 40N	95 20W
Waukegan	156	42 22N	87 54W
Waukesha	156	43 0N	88 15W
Waukon	158	43 14N	91 33W
Wauneta	158	40 27N	101 25W
Waupaca	158	44 22N	89 8W
Waupun	158	43 38N	88 44W
Waurika	159	34 12N	98 0W
Wausau	158	44 57N	89 40W
Wautoma	158	44 3N	89 20W
Wauwatosa	156	43 6N	87 59W
Wave Hill	136	17 32N	131 0 E
Waveney, R.	29	52 24N	1 20 E
Waver R.	32	54 50N	3 15W
Waverley	142	39 46 S	174 37 E
Waverly, Iowa, U.S.A.	158	42 40N	92 30W
Waverly, N.Y., U.S.A.	162	42 0N	76 33W
Wavre	47	50 43N	4 38 E
Wavreille	47	50 7N	5 15 E
Wâw	123	7 45N	28 1 E
Waw an Namus	119	24 24N	18 11 E
Wawa, Can.	150	47 59N	84 47W
Wawa, Nigeria	121	9 54N	4 27 E
Wawa, Sudan	122	20 30N	30 22 E
Wawanesa	153	49 36N	99 40W
Wawoi, R.	135	7 48 S	143 16 E
Wawona	163	37 32N	119 39W
Waxahachie	159	32 22N	96 53W
Waxweiler	49	50 6N	6 22 E
Way, L.	137	26 45 S	120 16 E
Wayabula Rau	103	2 29N	128 17 E
Wayatinah	138	42 19 S	146 27 E
Waycross	157	31 12N	82 25W
Wayi	123	5 8N	30 10 E
Wayne, Nebr., U.S.A.	158	42 16N	97 0W
Wayne, W. Va., U.S.A.	156	38 15N	82 27W
Waynesboro, Miss., U.S.A.	157	31 40N	88 39W
Waynesboro, Pa., U.S.A.	156	39 46N	77 32W
Waynesboro, Va., U.S.A.	156	38 4N	78 57W
Waynesburg	156	39 54N	80 12W
Waynesville	157	35 31N	83 0W
Waynoka	159	36 38N	98 53W
Waza	94	33 22N	69 22 E
Wâzin	119	31 58N	10 51 E
Wazirabad, Afghan.	93	36 44N	66 47 E
Wazirabad, Pak.	94	32 30N	74 8 E
We	102	6 3N	95 56 E
Weald, The	29	51 7N	0 9 E
Wear, R.	35	54 55N	1 22W
Weardale	32	54 44N	2 5W
Wearhead	32	54 45N	2 14W
Weatherford, Okla., U.S.A.	159	35 30N	98 45W
Weatherford, Tex., U.S.A.	159	32 45N	97 48W
Weaver, R.	32	53 17N	2 35W
Weaverham	32	53 15N	2 30W

*Renamed Teraina

Webb City 159 37 9N 94 30W
Weber 142 40 24S 176 20E
Webera, Bale, Ethiopia 123 6 29N 40 33E
Webera, Shewa, Ethiopia 123 9 40N 39 0E
Webster, Mass., U.S.A. 162 42 4N 71 54W
Webster, S.D., U.S.A. 158 45 24N 97 33W
Webster, Wis., U.S.A. 158 45 53N 92 25W
Webster City 158 42 30N 93 50W
Webster Green 158 38 38N 90 20W
Webster Springs 156 38 30N 80 25W
Wecliniec 54 51 18N 15 10E
Weda 103 0 30N 127 50E
Weda, Teluk 103 0 30N 127 50E
Weddell I. 176 51 50S 61 0W
Weddell Sea 13 72 30S 40 0W
Wedderburn 140 36 20S 143 33E
Wedge I. 132 30 50S 115 11E
Wedgeport 151 43 44N 65 59W
Wedmore 28 51 14N 2 50W
Wednesbury 28 52 33N 2 1W
Wednesfield 28 52 36N 2 3W
Wedza 127 18 40S 31 33E
Wee Elwah 141 32 2S 145 14E
Wee Waa 139 30 11S 149 26E
Weed 160 41 29N 122 22W
Weedsport 162 43 3N 76 35W
Weemelah 139 29 2S 149 7E
Weenen 129 28 48S 30 7E
Weener 48 53 10N 7 23E
Weert 47 51 15N 5 43E
Weesen 51 47 7N 9 4E
Weesp 46 52 18N 5 2E
Weggis 51 47 2N 8 26E
Wegierska-Gorka 54 49 36N 19 7E
Wegorzewo 54 54 13N 21 43E
Wegroów 54 52 24N 22 0E
Wehl 46 51 58N 6 13E
Wei Ho, R., Honan, China 106 34 58N 113 32E
Wei Ho, R., Shensi, China 106 34 38N 110 20E
Wei-si 99 27 18N 99 18E
Weich'ang 107 41 56N 117 34E
Weichou Tao 108 21 3N 109 2E
Weich'uan 106 34 19N 114 0E
Weida 48 50 47N 12 3E
Weiden 49 49 40N 12 10E
Weifang 107 36 47N 119 10E
Weihai 107 37 30N 122 10E
Weihsi 108 27 18N 99 18E
Weihsin 108 27 48N 105 5E
Weilburg 48 50 28N 8 17E
Weilheim 49 47 50N 11 9E
Weimar 48 51 0N 11 20E
Weinan 106 34 30N 109 35E
Weinfelden 51 47 34N 9 6E
Weingarten 49 47 49N 9 39E
Weinheim 49 49 33N 8 40E
Weining 108 26 50N 104 19E
Weipa 138 12 24S 141 50E
Weir, R., Austral. 139 28 20S 149 50E
Weir, R., Càn. 153 56 54N 93 21W
Weir River 153 56 49N 94 6W
Weisen 51 46 42N 9 43E
Weiser 160 44 10N 117 0W
Weishan, Shantung, China 107 34 49N 47 6E
Weishan, Yunnan, China 108 25 16N 100 21E
Weissenburg 49 49 2N 10 58E
Weissenfels 48 51 11N 11 58E
Weisshorn 50 46 7N 7 43E
Weissmies 50 46 8N 8 1E
Weisstannen 51 46 59N 9 22E
Weisswasser 48 51 30N 14 36E
Weiswampach 47 50 8N 6 5E
Wéitra 52 48 41N 14 54E
Weiyüan 106 35 6N 104 14E
Weiyuan 106 35 10N 104 20E
Weiz 52 47 13N 15 39E
Wejherowo 54 54 35N 18 12E
Wekusko 153 54 45N 99 45W
Wekusko L. 153 54 40N 99 50W
Welbourn Hill 139 27 21S 134 6E
Welby 153 50 33N 101 29W
Welch 156 37 29N 81 36W
Welcome 138 15 20S 144 40E
Weldon 35 55 16N 1 46W
Welega □ 123 9 25N 34 20E
Welford, Berks., U.K. 28 51 28N 1 24W
Welford, Northampton, U.K. 28 52 26N 1 5W
Welkenraedt 47 50 39N 5 58E
Welkite 123 8 15N 37 42E
Welkom 128 28 0S 26 50E
Welland 150 43 0N 79 10W
Welland, R. 29 52 43N 0 10W
Wellen 47 50 50N 5 21E
Wellesley Is. 138 17 20S 139 30E
Wellin 47 50 5N 5 6E
Wellingborough 29 52 18N 0 41W
Wellington, Austral. 141 32 35S 148 59E
Wellington, Can. 150 43 57N 77 20W
Wellington, N.Z. 142 41 19S 174 46E
Wellington, S. Afr. 128 33 38S 18 57E
Wellington, U.K. 28 50 58N 3 13W
Wellington, Col., U.S.A. 158 40 43N 105 0W
Wellington, Kans., U.S.A. 159 37 15N 97 25W
Wellington, Nev., U.S.A. 163 38 47N 119 28W
Wellington, Okla., U.S.A. 159 34 55N 100 13W
Wellington □ 143 40 8S 175 36E
Wellington Bridge 39 52 15N 6 45W
Wellington, I. 176 49 30S 75 0W
Wellington, L. 141 38 6S 147 20E
Wellington, Mt. 142 36 55S 174 52E
Wellington (Telford) 28 52 42N 2 31W
Wello, L. 137 26 43S 123 10E
Wellow 28 51 20N 2 22W
Wells, Norfolk, U.K. 29 52 57N 0 51E
Wells, Somerset, U.K. 28 51 12N 2 39W
Wells, Me., U.S.A. 162 43 18N 70 35W
Wells, Minn., U.S.A. 158 43 44N 93 45W
Wells, Nev., U.S.A. 160 41 8N 115 0W
Wells, N.Y., U.S.A. 162 43 24N 74 17W
Wells Gray Prov. Park 152 52 30N 120 15W
Wells L. 137 26 44S 123 15E
Wellsboro 156 41 46N 77 20W
Wellsford 142 36 16S 174 32E
Wellsville, Mo., U.S.A. 158 39 4N 91 30W
Wellsville, N.Y., U.S.A. 156 42 9N 77 53W
Wellsville, Ohio, U.S.A. 156 40 36N 80 40W
Wellsville, Utah, U.S.A. 160 41 35N 111 59W
Wellton 161 32 46N 114 6W
Welmel, W. 123 6 0N 40 20E
Welney 29 52 31N 0 15E
Welo □ 123 11 50N 39 48E
Wels 52 48 9N 14 1E
Welshpool 31 52 40N 3 9W
Welton 33 53 19N 0 29W
Welwel 91 7 5N 45 25E
Welwitschia 128 20 16S 14 59E
Welwyn 153 50 20N 101 30W
Welwyn Garden City 29 51 49N 0 11W
Wem 28 52 52N 2 45W
Wembere, R. 126 4 45S 34 0E
Wembury 30 50 19N 4 6W
Wemmel 47 50 55N 4 18E
Wemyss Bay 34 55 52N 4 54W
Wenatchee 160 47 30N 120 17W
Wench'ang 100 19 38N 110 42E
Wencheng 109 27 48N 120 5E
Wenchi 120 7 46N 2 8W
Wenchiang 108 30 43N 103 56E
Wenchou 109 28 1N 120 39E
Wench'uan 108 31 28N 103 35E
Wendell 160 42 50N 114 51W
Wendesi 103 2 30S 134 10E
Wendo 123 6 40N 38 27E
Wendover, U.K. 29 51 46N 0 45W
Wendover, U.S.A. 160 40 49N 114 1W
Wenduine 47 51 18N 3 5E
Wengan 108 27 0N 107 32E
Wengch'eng 109 24 22N 113 50E
Wenge 126 0 3N 24 0E
Wengen 50 46 37N 7 55E
Wengniut'ech'i 107 42 59N 118 48E
Wengpu 108 32 55N 98 30E
Wengyüan 109 24 21N 114 7E
Wenhsi 106 35 23N 111 8E
Wenhsiang 106 34 36N 110 34E
Wenhsien, Honan, China 106 34 56N 113 4E
Wenhsien, Kansu, China 106 58 0N 104 39E
Wenling 109 28 22N 121 18E
Wenlock 138 13 5S 142 58E
Wenlock Edge 23 52 30N 2 43W
Wenlock, R. 133 12 2S 141 55E
Wenshan 108 23 22N 104 13E
Wenshang 106 35 37N 116 33E
Wenshui, Kweichow, China 108 28 27N 106 31E
Wenshui, Shansi, China 106 37 25N 112 1E
Wensleydale 32 54 18N 2 0W
Wensu 105 41 15N 80 14E
Wenteng 107 37 10N 122 0E
Wentworth 140 34 2S 141 54E
Wentworth, Mt. 138 24 12S 147 1E
Wenut 103 3 11S 133 19E
Weobley 28 52 9N 2 52W
Weott 160 40 19N 123 56W
Wepener 128 29 42S 27 3E
Werbomont 47 50 23N 5 41E
Werda 128 25 24S 23 15E
Werdau 48 50 45N 12 20E
Werder, Ethiopia 91 6 58N 45 1E
Werder, Ger. 48 52 23N 12 56E
Werdohl 48 51 15N 7 47E
Weri 103 3 10S 132 30E
Werkendam 46 51 50N 4 53E
Werne 48 51 38N 7 38E
Wernigerode 48 51 49N 0 45E
Werribee 140 37 54S 144 40E
Werrimull 140 34 25S 141 38E
Werrington 30 50 31N 4 22W
Werris Creek 141 31 18S 150 38E
Wersar 103 1 30S 131 55E
Wertheim 49 49 44N 9 32E
Wervershoof 46 52 44N 5 10E
Wervik 47 50 47N 3 3E
Wesel 48 51 39N 6 34E
Weser, R. 48 53 33N 8 30E
Wesiri 103 7 30S 126 30E
Wesleyville 151 49 8N 53 36W
Wessel, C. 138 10 59S 136 46E
Wessel Is. 138 11 10S 136 45E
Wesselburen 48 54 11N 8 53E
Wessem 47 51 11N 5 49E
Wessington 158 44 30N 98 40W
Wessington Springs 158 44 10N 98 35W
West 159 31 50N 97 5W
West Auckland 33 54 38N 1 42W
West B. 151 45 53N 82 8W
West, B. 159 29 5N 89 27W
West Baines, R. 136 15 36S 129 58E
West Bend 156 43 25N 88 10W
West Bengal □ 95 25 0N 90 0E
West Branch 156 44 16N 84 13W
West Bridgford 33 52 56N 1 8W
West Bromwich 28 52 32N 2 1W
West Burra, I. 36 60 5N 1 21W
West Calder 35 55 51N 3 34W
West Canada Cr. 162 43 1N 74 58W
West Cape Howe 137 35 8S 117 36E
West Chester 162 39 58N 75 36W
West Coker 28 50 55N 2 40W
West Columbia 159 29 10N 95 38W
West Covina 163 34 4N 117 54W
West Derry 162 42 55N 71 19W
West Des Moines 158 41 30N 93 45W
West End 166 26 41N 78 58W
West Falkland Island 176 51 30S 60 0W
West Fen 33 53 5N 0 5W
West Frankfort 158 37 56N 89 0W
West Glamorgan □ 31 51 40N 3 55W
West Grinstead 29 50 58N 0 19W
West Haddon 28 52 21N 1 5W
West Harbour 131 45 51S 170 33E
West Hartford 162 41 45N 72 45W
West Haven 162 41 18N 72 57W
West Hazleton 162 40 58N 76 0W
West Helena 159 34 30N 90 40W
West Hurley 162 41 59N 74 7W
West Indies 158 15 0N 70 0W
West Kilbride 34 55 41N 4 50W
West Kirby 32 53 22N 3 11W
West Lavington 28 51 16N 1 59W
West Linton 35 55 45N 3 24W
West Looe 30 50 21N 4 29W
West Lulworth 28 50 37N 2 14W
West Lunga, R. 127 12 35S 24 45E
West Magpie R. 151 51 2N 64 42W
West Malling 29 51 16N 0 25E
West Memphis 159 35 5N 90 3W
West Meon 28 51 2N 1 3W
West Mersea 29 51 46N 0 55E
West Midlands □ 28 52 30N 1 55W
West Milton 162 41 1N 76 50W
West Monroe 159 32 32N 92 7W
West Nicholson 127 21 2S 29 20E
West Pakistan = Pakistan 93 27 0N 67 0W
West Palm Beach 157 26 44N 80 3W
West Paris 101 44 18N 70 30W
West Parley 28 50 46N 1 52W
West Plains 159 36 45N 91 50W
West Pt. 140 35 1S 135 56E
West Point, Can. 151 49 55N 64 30W
West Point, Jamaica 166 18 14N 78 30W
West Point, Ga., U.S.A. 157 32 54N 85 10W
West Point, Miss., U.S.A. 157 33 36N 88 38W
West Point, Nebr., U.S.A. 158 41 50N 96 43W
West Point, Va., U.S.A. 162 37 35N 76 47W
West Pokot □ 126 1 30N 35 40E
West, R. 162 42 52N 72 33W
West Rasen 33 53 23N 0 23W
West Reading 162 40 20N 75 57W
West Riding (□) 26 53 50N 1 30W
West Road R. 152 53 18N 122 53W
West Rutland 162 43 36N 73 3W
West Schelde = Westerschelde 47 51 23N 3 50E
West Sole, gasfield 19 53 40N 1 15E
West Spitsbergen 12 78 40N 17 0E
West Sussex □ 29 50 55N 0 30W
West-Terschelling 46 53 22N 5 13E
West Virginia □ 156 39 0N 18 0W
West-Vlaanderen □ 47 51 0N 3 0E
West Walker, R. 163 38 54N 119 9W
West Wittering 29 50 44N 0 53W
West Wyalong 141 33 56S 147 10E
West Yellowstone 160 44 47N 111 4W
West York 162 39 57N 76 46W
West Yorkshire □ 33 53 45N 1 40W
Westall 139 32 55S 134 4E
Westbank 152 49 50N 119 25W
Westbourne 29 50 53N 0 55W
Westbrook, Maine, U.S.A. 162 43 40N 70 22W
Westbrook, Tex., U.S.A. 159 32 25N 101 0W
Westbury, Austral. 138 41 30S 146 51E
Westbury, Salop, U.K. 28 52 40N 2 57W
Westbury, Wilts., U.K. 28 51 16N 2 11W
Westbury-on-Severn 28 51 49N 2 24W
Westby 158 48 52N 104 3W
Westend 163 35 42N 117 24W
Wester Ross, dist. 36 57 37N 5 0W
Westerbork 46 52 51N 6 37E
Westerham 29 51 16N 0 5E
Westerland 48 54 51N 8 20E
Western □, Kenya 126 0 30N 34 30E
Western □, Uganda 126 1 45N 31 30E
Western □, Zambia 127 13 15N 27 30E
Western Australia □ 137 25 0S 118 0E
Western Bay 151 46 50N 52 30W
Western Germany ■ 48 50 0N 8 0E
Western Ghats 97 15 30N 74 30E
Western Is. □ 36 57 40N 7 0W
Western River 140 35 42S 136 56E
Western Samoa ■ 130 14 0S 172 0W
Westernport 156 30 30N 79 5W
Westerschelde, R. 47 51 25N 4 0E
Westerstede 48 51 15N 7 55E
Westervoort 46 51 58N 5 59E
Westerwald, mts. 48 50 39N 8 0E
Westfield, U.K. 29 50 53N 0 30E
Westfield, U.S.A. 162 42 9N 72 49W
Westgat 47 51 39N 3 44E
Westhope 158 48 55N 101 0W
Westhoughton 32 53 34N 2 30W
Westkapelle, Belg. 47 51 19N 3 19E
Westkapelle, Neth. 47 51 31N 3 28E
Westland □ 143 43 33S 169 59E
Westland Bight 143 42 55S 170 5E
Westlock 152 54 9N 113 55W
Westmalle 47 51 18N 4 42E
Westmeath □ 38 53 30N 7 30W
Westmine 137 29 2S 116 8E
Westminster 162 39 34S 77 1W
Westmorland 161 33 2N 115 42W
Westmorland (□) 26 54 28N 2 40W
Weston, Malay. 102 5 10N 115 35E
Weston, U.K. 28 52 51N 2 2W
Weston, Oreg., U.S.A. 160 45 50N 118 30W
Weston, W. Va., U.S.A. 156 39 3N 80 29W
Weston I. 150 52 33N 79 36W
Weston-super-Mare 28 51 20N 2 59W
Westport, Ireland 38 53 44N 9 31W
Westport, N.Z. 143 41 46S 171 37E
Westport, U.S.A. 160 46 48N 124 4W
Westport B. 38 53 48N 9 38W
Westray 153 53 36N 101 24W
Westray Firth 37 59 15N 3 0W
Westray, I. 37 59 18N 3 0W
Westree 150 47 26N 81 34W
Westruther 35 55 45N 2 34W
Westview 152 49 50N 124 31W
Westville, Ill., U.S.A. 156 40 3N 87 36W
Westville, Okla., U.S.A. 159 36 0N 94 33W
Westward Ho 30 51 2N 4 16W
Westwood 160 40 26N 121 0W
Wetar, I. 103 7 30S 126 30E
Wetaskiwin 152 52 55N 113 24W
Wetherby 33 53 56N 1 23W
Wethersfield 162 41 43N 72 40W
Wetlet 98 21 13N 95 53E
Wettingen 51 47 28N 8 20E
Wetwang 33 54 2N 0 35W
Wetzikon 51 47 19N 8 48E
Wetzlar 48 50 33N 8 30E
Wevelgem 47 50 49N 3 12E
Wewak 135 3 38S 143 41E
Wewaka 159 35 10N 96 35W
Wexford 39 52 20N 6 28W
Wexford □ 39 52 20N 6 25W
Wexford Harb. 39 52 20N 6 25W
Wey, R. 29 51 19N 0 29W
Weybourne 29 52 57N 1 9E
Weybridge 29 51 22N 0 28W
Weyburn 153 49 40N 103 50W
Weyburn L. 152 63 0N 117 59W
Weyer 52 47 51N 14 40E
Weymouth, Can. 151 44 30N 66 1W
Weymouth, U.K. 28 50 36N 2 28W
Weymouth, U.S.A. 162 42 13N 70 53W
Weymouth, C. 133 12 37S 143 27E
Wezep 46 52 28N 6 0E
Whakamaru 142 38 23S 175 63E
Whakatane 142 37 57S 177 1E
Whale Cove 148 62 11N 92 36W
Whale Firth 36 60 40N 1 10W
Whale, R. 151 58 15N 67 40W
Whales 13 78 0S 165 0W
Whaley Bridge 32 53 20N 2 0W
Whalley 32 53 49N 2 25W
Whalsay, I. 36 60 22N 1 0W
Whalton 35 55 7N 1 46W
Whangamomona 142 39 8S 174 44E
Whangarei 142 35 43S 174 21E
Whangarei Harbour 142 35 45S 174 28E
Whangaroa 142 35 4S 173 46E
Whangumata 142 37 12S 175 53E
Whaplode 29 52 42N 0 3W
Wharanui 143 41 55S 174 6E
Wharfe, R. 33 53 55N 1 30W
Wharfedale 31 54 7N 2 4W
Wharton, N.J., U.S.A. 162 40 53N 74 36W
Wharton, Tex., U.S.A. 159 29 20N 96 6W
Whauphill 34 54 48N 4 31W
Whayjonta 139 29 40S 142 35E
Wheatland 158 42 4N 105 58W
Wheatley Hill 33 54 45N 1 23W
Wheaton, Md., U.S.A. 162 39 3N 77 3W
Wheaton, Minn., U.S.A. 158 45 50N 96 29W
Wheeler, Oreg., U.S.A. 160 45 45N 123 57W
Wheeler, Tex., U.S.A. 159 35 29N 100 15W
Wheeler Peak, Mt. 160 38 57N 114 15W
Wheeler, R. 153 57 34N 104 15W
Wheeler Ridge 163 35 0N 118 57W
Wheeling 156 40 2N 80 41W
Whichham 32 54 14N 3 22W
Whidbey I. 152 48 15N 122 40W
Whidbey Is. 136 34 30S 135 3E
Whiddy, I. 39 51 41N 9 30W
Whimple 30 50 46N 3 21W
Whipsnade 29 51 51N 0 32W
Whiskey Gap 152 49 0N 113 3W
Whiskey Jack L. 153 58 23N 101 55W
Whissendine 29 52 43N 0 46W
Whistleduck Cr. 138 20 15S 135 18E
Whistler 157 30 50N 88 10W
Whiston 32 53 25N 2 45W
Whitburn 35 55 52N 3 41W
Whitby 33 54 29N 0 37W

Whitchurch, U.K. 31 51 32N 3 15W
Whitchurch, Devon, U.K. 30 50 31N 4 7W
Whitchurch, Hants., U.K. 28 51 14N 1 20W
Whitchurch, Here., U.K. 28 51 51N 2 41W
Whitchurch, Salop, U.K. 32 52 58N 2 42W
Whitcombe, Mt. 131 43 12S 171 0E
Whitcombe, P. 131 43 12S 171 0E
White B. 151 50 0N 56 35W
White Bear Res. 151 48 10N 57 05W
White Bird 160 45 46N 116 21W
White Bridge 35 57 11N 4 32W
White Butte 156 46 23N 103 25W
White City 158 38 50N 96 45W
White Cliffs, Austral. 140 30 50S 143 10E
White Cliffs, N.Z. 143 43 26S 171 55E
White Deer 159 35 30N 101 8W
White Esk, R. 35 55 14N 3 11W
White Hall 158 39 25N 90 27W
White Haven 162 41 3N 75 47W
White Horse Hill 28 51 35N 1 35W
White I. 142 37 30S 177 13E
White L., Austral. 136 24 43S 121 44E
White L., U.S.A. 159 29 45N 92 30W
White Mts. 163 37 30N 118 15W
White Nile = Nîl el Abyad, Bahr 123 9 30N 31 40E
White Nile Dam 123 15 24N 32 30E
White Otter L. 150 49 5N 91 55W
White Pass 147 59 40N 135 3W
White Plains, Liberia 120 6 28N 10 40W
White Plains, U.S.A. 162 41 2N 73 44W
White, R., Ark., U.S.A. 159 36 28N 93 55W
White, R., Colo., U.S.A. 160 40 8N 108 52W
White, R., Ind., U.S.A. 156 39 25N 86 30W
White, R., S.D., U.S.A. 158 43 10N 102 52W
White River, Can. 150 48 35N 85 20W
White River, S. Afr. 129 25 20S 31 00E
White River, U.S.A. 158 43 48N 100 5W
White River Junc. 162 43 38N 72 20W
White Russia = Byelorussia, SSR 80 53 30N 27 0E
White Sea = Beloye More 78 66 30N 38 0E
White Sulphur Springs, Mont., U.S.A. 160 46 35N 111 0W
White Sulphur Springs, W. Va., U.S.A. 160 37 50N 80 16W
White Volta, R., (Volta Blanche) 121 10 0N 1 0W
White Well 137 31 25S 131 3E
Whiteadder Water, R. 35 55 47N 2 20W
Whitecourt 152 54 10N 115 45W
Whiteface 159 33 35N 102 40W
Whitefish 160 48 25N 114 22W
Whitefish L. 153 62 41N 106 48W
Whitefish Pt. 156 46 45N 85 0W
Whitegate, Clare, Ireland 39 52 58N 8 24W
Whitegate, Cork, Ireland 39 51 49N 8 15W
Whitegull, L. 151 55 27N 64 17W
Whitehall, Ireland 39 52 42N 7 2W
Whitehall, U.K. 37 59 9N 2 36W
Whitehall, Mich., U.S.A. 156 43 21N 86 20W
Whitehall, Mont., U.S.A. 160 45 52N 112 4W
Whitehall, N.Y., U.S.A. 162 43 32N 73 28W
Whitehall, Wis., U.S.A. 158 44 20N 91 19W
Whitehaven 32 54 33N 3 35W
Whitehead 38 54 45N 5 42W
Whitehorse 147 60 43N 135 3W
Whitehorse, Vale of 28 51 37N 1 30W
Whitekirk 35 56 2N 2 36W
Whiteman Ra. 135 5 55S 150 0E
Whitemark 138 40 7S 148 3E
Whitemouth 153 49 57N 95 58W
Whiten Hd. 37 58 34N 4 35W
Whitesail, L. 152 53 35N 127 45W
Whitesand B. 30 50 18N 4 20W
Whitesboro, N.Y., U.S.A. 162 43 8N 75 20W
Whitesboro, Tex., U.S.A. 159 33 40N 96 58W
Whiteshell Prov. Park 153 50 0N 95 40W
Whitetail 158 48 54N 105 15W
Whiteville 157 34 20N 78 40W
Whitewater 156 42 50N 88 45W
Whitewater Baldy, Mt. 161 33 20N 108 44W
Whitewater L. 150 50 50N 89 10W
Whitewood, Austral. 138 21 28S 143 30E
Whitewood, Can. 153 50 20N 102 20W
Whitfield 141 36 42S 146 24E
Whithorn 162 54 55N 4 25W
Whitianga 142 36 47S 175 41E
Whitland 31 51 49N 4 38W
Whitley Bay 35 55 4N 1 28W
Whitman 162 42 4N 70 55W
Whitmire 157 34 33N 81 40W
Whitney 150 45 31N 78 14W
Whitney, Mt. 163 36 35N 118 14W
Whitney Pt. 162 42 19N 75 59W
Whitstable 29 51 21N 1 2E
Whitsunday I. 138 20 15S 149 4E
Whittier 147 60 46N 148 48W
Whittington, Derby, U.K. 33 53 17N 1 26W
Whittington, Salop, U.K. 28 52 53N 3 0W
Whittle, C. 151 50 11N 60 8W
Whittlesea 141 37 27S 145 9E
Whittlesey 29 52 34N 0 8W
Whittlesford 29 52 6N 0 9E
Whitton 33 53 42N 0 39W
Whitwell, Derby, U.K. 33 53 16N 1 11W
Whitwell, Isle of Wight, U.K. 28 50 35N 1 19W
Whitwell, U.S.A. 157 35 15N 85 30W
Whitwick 28 52 45N 1 23W
Whitworth 32 53 40N 2 11W
Whixley 33 54 2N 1 19W
Wholdaia L. 153 60 43N 104 20W
Whyalla 140 33 2S 137 30E
Whyjonta 139 29 41S 142 28E
Whyte Yarcowie 107 33 13S 138 54E
Wiarton 150 44 50N 81 10W
Wiawso 120 6 10N 2 25W
Wiay I. 36 57 24N 7 12W
Wiazow 54 50 50N 17 10E
Wibaux 158 47 0N 104 13W
Wichian Buri 100 15 39N 101 7E
Wichita 159 37 40N 97 29W
Wichita Falls 159 33 57N 98 30W
Wick, Scot., U.K. 37 58 26N 3 5W
Wick, Wales, U.K. 31 51 24N 3 32W
Wick R. 37 58 28N 3 14W
Wickenburg 161 33 58N 112 45W
Wickepin 137 32 50S 117 30E
Wickett 159 31 37N 102 58W
Wickford 29 51 37N 0 31E
Wickham 28 50 54N 1 11W
Wickham, C. 138 39 35S 143 57E
Wickham Market 29 52 9N 1 21E
Wicklow 39 53 0N 6 2W
Wicklow □ 39 52 59N 6 25W
Wicklow Gap 39 53 3N 6 23W
Wicklow Hd. 39 52 59N 6 3W
Wicklow Mts. 39 53 0N 6 30W
Wickwar 28 51 35N 2 23W
Widawa 54 51 27N 18 51E
Widdrington 35 55 15N 1 35W
Wide B. 138 4 52S 152 0E
Wide Firth 37 59 2N 3 0W
Widecombe 30 50 34N 3 48W
Widemouth 30 50 45N 4 34W
Widgiemooltha 137 31 30S 121 34E
Widnes 32 53 22N 2 44W
Wiek 48 54 37N 13 17E
Wielbark 54 53 24N 20 55E
Wielén 54 52 53N 16 9E
Wieliczka 54 50 0N 20 5E
Wielun 54 51 15N 18 40E
Wien 53 48 12N 16 22E
Wiener Neustadt 53 47 49N 16 16E
Wieprz, R., Koszalin, Poland 54 54 26N 16 35E
Wieprz, R., Lublin, Poland 54 51 15N 22 50E
Wierden 46 52 22N 6 35E
Wiers 47 50 30N 3 32E
Wieruszów 54 51 19N 18 9E
Wiesbaden 49 50 7N 8 17E
Wiesental 49 49 15N 8 30E
Wigan 32 53 33N 2 38W
Wiggins, Colo., U.S.A. 158 40 16N 104 3W
Wiggins, Miss., U.S.A. 159 30 53N 89 9W
Wight, I. of 28 50 40N 1 20W
Wigmore 28 52 19N 2 51W
Wigston 28 52 35N 1 6W
Wigton 32 54 50N 3 9W
Wigtown 34 54 52N 4 27W
Wigtown (□) 26 54 53N 4 45W
Wigtown B. 34 54 46N 4 15W
Wihéries 47 50 23N 3 45E
Wijangala 139 33 57S 148 59E
Wijchen 46 51 48N 5 44E
Wijhe 46 52 23N 6 8E
Wijk bij Duurstede 46 51 59N 5 21E
Wil 51 47 28N 9 3E
Wilamowice 53 49 55N 19 9E
Wilangee 140 31 28S 141 20E
Wilber 158 40 34N 96 59W
Wilburton 159 34 55N 95 15W
Wilcannia 140 31 30S 143 26E
Wildbad 49 48 44N 8 32E
Wildervank 46 53 5N 6 52E
Wildeshausen 48 52 54N 8 25E
Wildhorn 50 46 22N 7 21E
Wildon 52 46 52N 15 31E
Wildrose, Calif., U.S.A. 163 36 14N 117 11W
Wildrose, N. Dak., U.S.A. 158 48 36N 103 17W
Wildspitze 52 46 53N 10 53E
Wildstrubel 50 46 24N 7 32E
Wildwood 162 38 59N 74 46W
Wilgaroon 141 30 52S 145 42E
Wilhelm II Coast 13 67 0S 90 0E
Wilhelm Mt. 135 5 50S 145 1E
Wilhelm-Pieck-Stadt Guben 48 51 59N 14 48E
Wilhelmina Kanaal 47 51 36N 5 6E
Wilhelmina, Mt. 175 3 50N 56 30W
Wilhelmsburg, Austria 52 48 6N 15 36E
Wilhelmsburg, Ger. 48 53 28N 10 1E
Wilhelmshaven 48 53 30N 8 9E
Wilhelmstal 128 21 58S 16 21E
Wilkes-Barre 162 41 15N 75 52W
Wilkes Land 13 69 0S 120 0E
Wilkesboro 157 36 10N 81 9W
Wilkie 153 52 27N 108 42W
Wilkinson Lakes 137 29 40S 132 39E
Willamina 160 45 9N 123 32W
Willamulka 140 33 55S 137 52E
Willandra Billabong Creek 140 33 22S 145 52E
Willapa, B. 160 46 44N 124 0W
Willard, N. Mex., U.S.A. 161 34 35N 106 1W
Willard, N.Y., U.S.A. 162 42 40N 76 50W
Willard, Utah, U.S.A. 160 41 28N 112 1W
Willaumez Pen. 138 5 3S 150 3E
Willaura 140 37 31S 142 45E
Willberforce, C. 138 11 54S 136 35E
Willbriggie 141 34 28S 146 2E
Willcox 161 32 13N 109 53W
Willebroek 47 51 4N 4 22E
Willemstad 167 12 5N 69 0W
Willenhall 28 52 36N 2 3W
Willeroo 136 15 14S 131 37E
Willesborough 29 51 8N 0 55E
Willet 162 42 28N 75 55W
William Cr. 139 28 58S 136 22E
William, Mt. 140 37 17S 142 35E
William, R. 153 59 8N 109 19W
Williambury 137 23 45S 115 12E
Williams, Austral. 137 33 2S 116 52E
Williams, U.S.A. 161 35 16N 112 11W
Williams Lake 152 52 2N 122 10W
Williamsburg, Ky., U.S.A. 157 36 45N 84 10W
Williamsburg, Va., U.S.A. 162 37 17N 76 44W
Williamsburg, Va., U.S.A. 162 37 16N 79 43W
Williamson 156 37 46N 82 17W
Williamsport 162 41 18N 77 1W
Williamston 157 35 50N 77 5W
Williamstown, Austral. 141 37 51S 144 52E
Williamstown, Ireland 38 53 41N 8 34W
Williamstown, Mass., U.S.A. 162 42 43N 73 12W
Williamstown, N.Y., U.S.A. 162 43 25N 75 53W
Williamstown, N.Y., U.S.A. 162 43 25N 75 54W
Williamsville 159 37 0N 90 33W
Willimantic 162 41 45N 72 12W
Willingdon 29 50 47N 0 17E
Willis Group 138 16 18S 150 0E
Willisau 50 47 7N 8 0E
Williston, S. Afr. 128 31 20S 20 53E
Williston, Fla, U.S.A. 157 29 25N 82 28W
Williston, N.D., U.S.A. 158 48 10N 103 35W
Williston L. 152 56 0N 124 0W
Williton 28 51 9N 3 20W
Willits 160 39 28N 123 17W
Willmar 158 45 5N 95 0W
Willoughby 33 53 14N 0 12E
Willow Bunch 153 49 20N 105 35W
Willow L. 152 62 10N 119 8W
Willow Lake 158 44 40N 97 40W
Willow River 152 54 6N 122 28W
Willow Springs 159 37 0N 92 0W
Willow Tree 141 31 40S 150 45E
Willow Wall 107 41 30N 120 40E
Willowlake, R. 152 62 42N 123 8W
Willowmore 128 33 15S 23 30E
Willows, Austral. 138 23 45S 147 25E
Willows, U.S.A. 160 39 30N 122 10W
Wills Cr. 138 22 43S 140 2E
Wills, L. 136 21 25S 128 51E
Wills Pt. 159 32 42N 95 57W
Willunga 140 35 15S 138 30E
Wilmete 156 42 6N 87 44W
Wilmington, Austral. 140 32 39S 138 7E
Wilmington, U.K. 30 50 46N 3 8W
Wilmington, Del., U.S.A. 162 39 45N 75 32W
Wilmington, Ill., U.S.A. 156 41 19N 88 10W
Wilmington, N.C., U.S.A. 157 34 14N 77 54W
Wilmington, Ohio, U.S.A. 156 39 29N 83 46W
Wilmington, Vt., U.S.A. 162 42 52N 72 52W
Wilmslow 32 53 19N 2 14W
Wilnecote 28 52 36N 1 40W
Wilpena Cr. 140 31 25S 139 29E
Wilrijk 47 51 9N 4 22E
Wilsall 160 45 59N 110 4W
Wilson, U.S.A. 162 40 41N 75 15W
Wilson, N.C., U.S.A. 157 35 44N 77 54W
Wilson Bluff 137 31 41S 129 0E
Wilson Inlet 137 35 0S 117 20E
Wilson, Mt. 161 37 55N 105 3W
Wilson, R., Queens., Austral. 139 27 38S 141 24E
Wilson, R., W. Australia, Austral. 136 16 48S 128 16E
Wilson's Promontory 141 38 55S 146 25E
Wilster 48 53 55N 9 23E
Wilton, U.K. 28 51 5N 1 52W
Wilton, U.S.A. 158 47 12N 100 53W
Wilton, R. 138 14 45S 134 33E
Wiltshire □ 28 51 20N 2 0W
Wiltz 47 49 57N 5 55E
Wiluna 137 26 36S 120 14E
Wimblington 29 52 31N 0 5E
Wimborne Minster 28 50 48N 2 0W
Wimereux 43 50 45N 1 37E
Wimmera 133 36 30S 142 0E
Wimmera, R. 140 36 8S 141 56E
Winam G. 126 0 20S 34 15E
Winburg 128 28 30S 27 2E
Wincanton 28 51 3N 2 24W
Winchelsea, Austral. 140 38 10S 144 1E
Winchelsea, U.K. 29 50 55N 0 43E
Winchendon 162 42 40N 72 3W
Winchester, N.Z. 143 44 11S 171 17E
Winchester, U.K. 28 51 4N 1 19W
Winchester, Conn., U.S.A. 162 41 53N 73 9W
Winchester, Conn., U.S.A. 162 41 55N 73 8W
Winchester, Idaho, U.S.A. 160 46 11N 116 32W
Winchester, Ind., U.S.A. 156 40 10N 84 56W
Winchester, Ky., U.S.A. 156 38 0N 84 8W
Winchester, Mass., U.S.A. 162 42 28N 71 10W
Winchester, N.H., U.S.A. 162 42 47N 72 22W
Winchester, Tenn., U.S.A. 157 35 11N 86 8W
Winchester, Va., U.S.A. 156 39 14N 78 8W
Wind, R. 160 43 30N 109 30W
Wind River Range, Mts. 160 43 0N 109 30W
Windber 156 40 14N 78 50W
Winder 157 34 0N 83 40W
Windera 139 26 17S 151 51E
Windermere 32 54 24N 2 56W
Windermere, L. 32 54 20N 2 57W
Windfall 152 54 12N 116 13W
Windflower L. 152 62 52N 118 30W
Windhoek 128 22 35S 17 4E
Windischgarsten 52 47 42N 14 21E
Windmill Pt. 162 37 35N 76 17W
Windom 158 43 48N 95 3W
Windorah 138 25 24S 142 36E
Window Rock 161 35 47N 109 4W
Windrush, R. 28 51 48N 1 35W
Windsor, Austral. 141 33 37S 150 50E
Windsor, Newf., Can. 151 48 57N 55 40W
Windsor, N.S., Can. 151 44 59N 64 5W
Windsor, Ont., Can. 150 42 18N 83 82W
Windsor, N.Z. 143 44 59S 170 49E
Windsor, U.K. 29 51 28N 0 36W
Windsor, Col., U.S.A. 158 40 33N 104 55W
Windsor, Conn., U.S.A. 162 41 50N 72 40W
Windsor, Miss., U.S.A. 158 38 32N 93 31W
Windsor, N.Y., U.S.A. 162 42 5N 75 37W
Windsor, Vt., U.S.A. 162 43 30N 72 25W
Windsorton 128 28 16S 24 44E
Windward Is. 167 13 0N 63 0W
Windward Passage 167 20 0N 74 0W
Windy L. 153 60 20N 100 2W
Windygap 39 52 28N 7 24W
Windygates 35 56 12N 3 1W
Winefred L. 153 55 30N 110 30W
Winejok 123 9 1N 27 30E
Winfield 159 37 15N 97 0W
Wing 29 51 54N 0 41W
Wingate Mts. 136 14 25S 130 40E
Wingen 141 31 54S 150 54E
Wingene 47 51 3N 3 17E
Wingham, Austral. 141 31 48S 152 22E
Wingham, Can. 150 43 55N 81 20W
Wingham, U.K. 29 51 16N 1 12E
Winifred 160 47 30N 109 28W
Winisk 150 55 20N 85 15W
Winisk L. 150 52 55N 87 22W
Winisk, R. 150 55 17N 85 5W
Wink 159 31 49N 103 9W
Winkleigh 30 50 49N 3 57W
Winkler 153 49 15N 97 56W
Winklern 52 46 52N 12 52E
Winneba 121 5 25N 0 36W
Winnebago 158 43 43N 94 8W
Winnebago L. 156 44 0N 88 20W
Winnecke Cr. 136 18 35S 131 34E
Winnemucca 160 41 0N 117 45W
Winnemucca, L. 160 40 25N 19 21W
Winner 158 43 23N 99 52W
Winnetka 156 42 8N 87 46W
Winnett 160 47 2N 108 28W
Winnfield 159 31 57N 92 38W
Winnibigoshish L. 158 47 25N 94 12W
Winning Pool 136 23 9S 114 30E
Winnipeg 153 49 50N 97 9W
Winnipeg Beach 153 50 30N 96 58W
Winnipeg, L. 153 52 0N 97 0W
Winnipeg, R. 153 50 38N 96 19W
Winnipegosis 153 51 39N 99 55W
Winnipegosis L. 153 52 30N 100 0W
Winnipesaukee, L. 162 43 38N 71 21W
Winnisquam L. 162 43 33N 71 30W
Winnsboro, Lou, U.S.A. 159 32 10N 91 41W
Winnsboro, S.C., U.S.A. 157 34 23N 81 5W
Winnsboro, Tex., U.S.A. 158 32 56N 95 15W
Winokapau, L. 151 53 15N 62 50W
Winona, Miss., U.S.A. 159 33 30N 89 42W
Winona, Wis., U.S.A. 158 44 2N 91 45W
Winooski 156 44 31N 73 11W
Winschoten 46 53 9N 7 3E
Winsen 48 53 21N 10 11E
Winsford 32 53 12N 2 31W
Winslow, U.K. 29 51 57N 0 52W
Winslow, U.S.A. 161 35 2N 110 41W
Winstead 162 41 55N 73 5W
Winster 33 53 9N 1 42W
Winston-Salem 157 36 7N 80 15W
Winsum 46 53 20N 6 32E
Winter Garden 157 28 33N 81 35W
Winter Haven 157 28 0N 81 42W
Winter Park 157 28 34N 81 19W
Winterberg 48 51 12N 8 30E

Winterborne Abbas **28** 50 43N 2 30W
Winters **159** 31 58N 99 58W
Winterset **158** 41 18N 94 0W
Winterswijk **46** 51 58N 6 43 E
Winterthur **51** 47 30N 8 44 E
Winterton, Humberside, U.K. **33** 53 39N 0 37W
Winterton, Norfolk, U.K. **29** 52 43N 1 43 E
Winthrop, Minn., U.S.A. **158** 44 31N 94 25W
Winthrop, Wash., U.S.A. **160** 48 27N 120 6W
Winton, Austral. **138** 22 24 S 143 3 E
Winton, N.Z. **143** 46 8 S 168 20 E
Winton, U.S.A. **157** 36 25N 76 58W
Wirksworth **33** 53 5N 1 34W
Wirral **23** 53 25N 3 0W
Wirraminna **140** 31 12 S 136 13 E
Wirrulla **139** 32 24 S 134 31 E
Wisbech **29** 52 39N 0 10 E
Wisborough Green **29** 51 2N 0 30W
Wisconsin □ **158** 44 30N 90 0W
Wisconsin Dells **158** 43 38N 89 45W
Wisconsin, R. **158** 45 25N 89 45W
Wisconsin Rapids **158** 44 25N 89 50W
Wisdom **147** 45 36N 113 1W
Wiserman **147** 67 25N 150 15W
Wishaw **35** 55 46N 3 55W
Wishek **158** 46 20N 99 35W
Wiske, R. **33** 54 26N 1 27W
Wisła **53** 49 38N 18 53 E
Wisła, R. **54** 53 38N 18 47 E
Wisłok, R. **53** 50 7N 22 25 E
Wisłoka, R. **53** 49 50N 21 28 E
Wismar **48** 53 53N 11 23 E
Wismar B. **48** 54 0N 11 15 E
Wisner **158** 42 0N 96 46W
Wissant **43** 50 52N 1 40 E
Wissembourg **43** 48 57N 7 57 E
Wissenkerke **47** 51 35N 3 45 E
Wistoka, R. **54** 49 50N 21 28 E
Witbank **129** 25 51 S 29 14 E
Witchita **159** 37 40N 97 22W
Witchyburn **37** 57 37N 2 37W
Witdraai **128** 26 58 S 20 48 E
Witham **29** 51 48N 0 39 E
Witham, R. **33** 53 3N 0 8W
Withern **33** 53 19N 0 9 E
Withernsea **33** 53 43N 0 2W
Witkowo **54** 52 26N 17 45 E
Witley **29** 51 9N 0 39W
Witmarsum **46** 53 6N 5 28 E
Witney **28** 51 47N 1 29W
Witnossob, R. **128** 23 0 S 18 40 E
Wittdün **48** 54 38N 8 23 E
Witten **48** 51 26N 7 19 E
Wittenberg **48** 51 51N 12 39 E
Wittenberge **48** 53 0N 11 44 E
Wittenburg **48** 53 30N 11 4 E
Wittenoom, W. Australia, Austral. **132** 22 15 S 118 20 E
Wittenoom, W. Australia, Austral. **136** 18 34 S 128 51 E
Wittersham **29** 51 1N 0 42 E
Wittingen **48** 52 43N 10 43 E
Wittlich **49** 50 0N 6 54 E
Wittmund **48** 53 39N 7 35 E
Wittow **48** 54 37N 13 21 E
Wittstock **48** 53 10N 12 30 E
Witzenhausen **48** 51 20N 9 50 E
Wiveliscombe **28** 51 2N 3 20W
Wivenhoe **29** 51 51N 0 59 E
Wiyeb, W. **123** 7 15N 40 15 E
Wladyslawowo **54** 52 6N 18 28 E
Wlen **160** 51 0N 15 39 E
Wlingi **103** 8 5 S 112 25 E
Włocławek **54** 52 40N 19 3 E
Włodawa **54** 51 33N 23 31 E
Włoszczowa **54** 50 50N 19 55 E
Woburn, U.K. **29** 51 59N 0 37W
Woburn, U.S.A. **162** 42 31N 71 7W
Woburn Sands **29** 51 1N 0 38W
Wodonga **141** 36 5 S 146 50 E
Wodzisław Sl. **54** 50 1N 18 26 E
Woerden **46** 52 5N 4 54 E
Woerht'ukou **106** 42 35N 112 19 E
Woerth **43** 48 57N 7 45 E
Woevre **43** 49 15N 5 45 E
Wognum **46** 52 40N 5 1 E
Wohlen **51** 47 21N 8 17 E
Wokam, I. **103** 5 45 S 134 28 E
Wokha **98** 26 6N 94 16 E
Woking, Can. **152** 55 35N 118 50W
Woking, U.K. **29** 51 18N 0 33W
Wokingham **29** 51 25N 0 50W
Wolbrom **54** 50 24N 19 45 E
Woldegk **48** 53 27N 13 35 E
Wolf Creek **160** 47 1N 112 2W
Wolf L. **152** 60 24N 133 42W
Wolf Point **158** 48 6N 105 40W
Wolf, R. **152** 60 17N 132 33W
Wolf Rock **30** 49 56N 5 50W
Wolfe I. **150** 44 7N 76 20W
Wolfeboro **162** 43 35N 71 12W
Wolfenbüttel **48** 52 10N 10 33 E
Wolfenden **152** 52 0N 119 25W
Wolfheze **46** 52 0N 5 48 E
Wolfram **138** 17 6 S 145 0 E
Wolf's Castle **31** 51 53N 4 57W
Wolfsberg **52** 46 50N 14 52 E
Wolfsburg **48** 52 27N 10 49 E
Wolgast **48** 54 3N 13 46 E
Wolhusen **50** 47 4N 8 4 E
Wolin **54** 53 40N 14 37 E
Wollaston, Islas **176** 55 40 S 67 30W
Wollaston L. **153** 58 7N 103 10W
Wollaston Pen. **148** 69 30N 115 0W
Wollogorang **138** 17 13 S 137 57 E
Wollongong **141** 34 25 S 150 54 E
Wolmaransstad **128** 27 12 S 26 13 E
Wolmirstedt **48** 52 15N 11 35 E
Wołomin **54** 52 19N 21 15 E
Wołow **54** 51 20N 16 38 E
Wolseley, Austral. **140** 36 23 S 140 54 E
Wolseley, Can. **153** 50 25N 103 15W
Wolseley, S. Afr. **128** 33 26 S 19 7 E
Wolsingham **32** 54 44N 1 52W
Wolstenholme Sound **12** 74 30N 75 0W
Wolsztyn **54** 52 8N 16 5 E
Wolvega **46** 52 52N 6 0 E
Wolverhampton **28** 52 35N 2 6W
Wolverton **29** 52 3N 0 48W
Wolviston **33** 54 39N 1 25W
Wombera **123** 10 45N 35 49 E
Wombwell **33** 53 31N 1 23W
Wommels **46** 53 6N 5 36 E
Wonarah P.O. **138** 19 55 S 136 20 E
Wonboyn **141** 37 15 S 149 55 E
Wonck **47** 50 46N 5 38 E
Wondai **139** 26 20 S 151 49 E
Wondelgem **47** 51 5N 3 44 E
Wonder Gorge **127** 14 40 S 29 0 E
Wongalarroo L. **140** 31 32 S 144 0 E
Wongan **137** 30 51 S 116 37 E
Wongan Hills **137** 30 53 S 116 42 E
Wongawal **137** 25 5 S 121 55 E
Wonosari **103** 7 38 S 110 36 E
Wŏnsan **107** 39 11N 127 27 E
Wonston **28** 51 9N 1 18W
Wonthaggi **141** 38 37 S 145 37 E
Wonyulgunna Hill, Mt. **137** 24 52 S 119 44 E
Woocalla **140** 31 42 S 137 12 E
Wood Buffalo Nat. Park **152** 56 28N 113 41W
Wood Green **138** 22 26 S 134 12 E
Wood Is. **136** 16 24 S 123 19 E
Wood L. **153** 55 17N 103 17W
Wood Lake **158** 42 38N 100 14W
Wood Mt. **153** 49 14N 106 30W
Woodah I. **138** 13 27 S 136 10 E
Woodanilling **137** 33 31 S 117 24 E
Woodbine **162** 39 14N 74 49W
Woodbourne **162** 41 46N 74 35W
Woodbridge **29** 52 6N 1 19 E
Woodburn **139** 29 6 S 153 23 E
Woodbury, U.K. **30** 50 40N 3 24W
Woodbury, U.S.A. **162** 39 50N 75 9W
Woodchopper **147** 65 25N 143 30W
Wooden Bridge **39** 52 50N 6 13W
Woodend **140** 37 20N 144 33 E
Woodford **39** 53 3N 8 23W
Woodfords **163** 38 47N 119 50W
Woodhall Spa. **33** 53 10N 0 12W
Woodham Ferrers **29** 51 40N 0 37 E
Woodlake **163** 36 25N 119 6W
Woodland **160** 38 40N 121 50W
Woodlands **137** 24 46 S 118 8 E
Woodlark I. **135** 9 10 S 152 50 E
Woodley **29** 51 26N 0 54W
Woodpecker **152** 53 30N 122 40W
Woodplumpton **32** 53 47N 2 46W
Woodridge **153** 49 20N 96 9W
Woodroffe, Mt. **137** 26 20 S 131 45 E
Woodruff, Ariz., U.S.A. **161** 34 51N 110 1W
Woodruff, Utah, U.S.A. **160** 41 30N 111 4W
Woods, L., Austral. **138** 17 50 S 133 30 E
Woods, L., Can. **151** 54 30N 65 13W
Woods, Lake of the **153** 49 30N 94 30W
Woodside, S. Australia, Austral. **140** 34 58 S 138 52 E
Woodside, Victoria, Austral. **141** 38 31 S 146 52 E
Woodstock, N.S.W., Austral. **141** 33 45 S 148 53 E
Woodstock, Queens., Austral. **138** 19 35 S 146 50 E
Woodstock, W.A., Austral. **136** 21 41 S 118 57 E
Woodstock, N.B., Can. **151** 46 11N 67 37W
Woodstock, Ont., Can. **150** 43 10N 80 45W
Woodstock, U.K. **28** 51 51N 1 20W
Woodstock, Ill., U.S.A. **158** 42 17N 88 30W
Woodstock, Vt., U.S.A. **162** 43 37N 72 31W
Woodstown **162** 39 39N 75 20W
Woodville, N.Z. **142** 40 20 S 175 53 E
Woodville, U.S.A. **159** 30 45N 94 25W
Woodward **159** 36 24N 99 28W
Woodward, Mt. **137** 26 0 S 131 0 E
Woody **163** 35 42N 118 50W
Wookey **28** 51 13N 2 41W
Wookey Hole **28** 51 13N 2 41W
Wool **28** 50 41N 2 13W
Woolacombe **30** 51 10N 4 12W
Woolamai, C. **141** 38 30 S 145 23 E
Wooler **35** 55 33N 2 0W
Woolgangie **137** 31 12 S 120 35 E
Woolyeenyer, Mt. **137** 32 16 S 121 47 E
Woombye **139** 26 40 S 152 55 E
Woomera **140** 31 11 S 136 47 E
Woonona **141** 34 21 S 150 54 E
Woonsocket **162** 42 0N 71 30W
Woonsockett **158** 44 5N 98 15W
Wooramel **137** 25 45 S 114 40 E
Wooramel, R. **137** 25 30 S 114 30 E
Wooroloo **137** 31 48 S 116 18 E
Wooroorooka **139** 29 0 S 145 41 E
Wooster **156** 40 38N 81 55W
Wootton Bassett **28** 51 32N 1 55W
Wootton Wawen **28** 52 16N 1 47W
Worb **50** 46 56N 7 33 E
Worcester, S. Afr. **125** 33 39 S 19 27 E
Worcester, U.K. **28** 52 12N 2 12W
Worcester, Mass., U.S.A. **162** 42 14N 71 49W
Worcester, N.Y., U.S.A. **162** 42 35N 74 45W
Worcestershire (□) **26** 52 13N 2 10W
Worfield **28** 52 34N 2 22W
Wörgl **52** 47 29N 12 3 E
Worikambo **121** 10 43N 0 11W
Workington **32** 54 39N 3 34W
Worksop **33** 53 19N 1 9W
Workum **46** 52 59N 5 26 E
Worland **160** 44 0N 107 59W
Wormerveer **46** 52 30N 4 46 E
Wormhoudt **43** 50 52N 2 28 E
Wormit **35** 56 26N 2 59W
Worms **49** 49 37N 8 21 E
Worms Head **29** 51 33N 4 19W
Worplesdon **29** 51 16N 0 36W
Worsley **137** 33 15 S 116 2 E
Wortham, U.K. **29** 52 22N 1 3 E
Wortham, U.S.A. **159** 31 48N 96 27W
Wörther See **52** 46 37N 14 19 E
Worthing **29** 50 49N 0 21W
Worthington **158** 43 35N 95 30W
Wosi **103** 0 15 S 128 0 E
Wota (Shoa Ghimirra) **123** 7 4N 35 51 E
Wotton-under-Edge **28** 51 37N 2 20W
Woubrugge **46** 52 10N 4 39 E
Woudenberg **46** 52 5N 5 25 E
Woudsend **46** 52 56N 5 38 E
Wour **119** 21 14N 16 0 E
Wouw **47** 51 31N 4 23 E
Wowoni, I. **103** 4 5 S 123 5 E
Woy Woy **141** 33 30 S 151 19 E
Wragby **33** 53 17N 0 18W
Wrangell **147** 56 30N 132 25W
Wrangell, I. **152** 56 20N 132 10W
Wrangell Mts. **147** 61 40N 143 30W
Wrangle **33** 53 3N 0 9 E
Wrath, C. **36** 58 38N 5 0W
Wray **158** 40 8N 102 18W
Wreck I. **162** 37 12N 75 48W
Wrekin, The, Mt. **28** 52 41N 2 35W
Wrens **157** 33 13N 82 23W
Wrentham **29** 52 24N 1 39 E
Wrexham **31** 53 5N 3 0W
Wriezen **48** 52 43N 14 9 E
Wright, Can. **152** 51 52N 121 40W
Wright, Phil. **103** 11 42N 125 2 E
Wright, Mt. **151** 52 40N 67 25W
Wrightlington **28** 51 18N 2 16W
Wrightson, Mt. **161** 31 49N 110 56W
Wrightsville **162** 40 2N 76 32W
Wrightwood **163** 34 21N 117 38W
Wrigley **148** 63 16N 123 27W
Writtle **29** 51 44N 0 27 E
Wrocław **54** 51 5N 17 5 E
Wrocław □ **54** 51 0N 17 0 E
Wronki **54** 52 41N 16 21 E
Wrotham **29** 51 18N 0 20 E
Wroughton **28** 51 31N 1 47W
Wroxham **29** 52 42N 1 23 E
Września **54** 52 21N 17 36 E
Wschowa **54** 51 48N 16 20 E
Wu Chiang, R. **108** 29 42N 107 20 E
Wu Shui, R. **109** 27 7N 109 57 E
Wuan **106** 36 45N 114 2 E
Wubin **137** 30 6 S 116 37 E
Wuch'ang, Heilungkiang, China **107** 44 55N 127 10 E
Wuch'ang, Hupeh, China **109** 30 30N 114 15 E
Wuch'eng **108** 30 48N 98 46 E
Wuch'i **108** 31 28N 109 36 E
Wuchiang **109** 31 10N 120 37 E
Wuchih Shan, mts. **100** 18 45N 109 45 E
Wuch'ing **107** 39 25N 117 7 E
Wuchou **105** 23 33N 111 18 E
Wuch'uan, Inner Mong., China **106** 41 8N 111 24 E
Wuch'uan, Kwangsi-Chuang, China **109** 21 29N 110 49 E
Wuch'uan, Kweichow, China **108** 28 30N 107 58 E
Wuchung **106** 38 4N 106 12 E
Wufeng **109** 30 12N 110 36 E
Wuhan **109** 30 35N 114 15 E
Wuho **107** 33 9N 117 53 E
Wuhsi **105** 31 30N 120 20 E
Wuhsiang **106** 36 50N 112 52 E
Wuhsing **109** 30 49N 120 5 E
Wuhsüan **108** 23 36N 109 39 E
Wuhu **105** 31 18N 118 20 E
Wuhu (Wou-tou) **109** 31 21N 118 30 E
Wui, Anhwei, China **109** 28 53N 119 48 E
Wui, Hopeh, China **106** 37 49N 115 54 E
Wui Shan, mts. **105** 27 30N 117 30 E
Wukang **109** 26 50N 110 15 E
Wukari **121** 7 57N 9 42 E
Wulachieh **107** 44 5N 126 27 E
Wulanhaot'e **105** 46 5N 122 5 E
Wulanpulang **106** 41 8N 110 56 E
Wulehe **121** 3 42N 0 0 E
Wuliang Shan, mts. **108** 24 0N 100 55 E
Wuliaru, I. **103** 7 10 S 131 0 E
Wulien **107** 35 45N 119 12 E
Wuluk'omushih Ling **105** 36 25N 87 25 E
Wulumuchi **105** 43 40N 87 50 E
Wulunku Ho, R. **105** 46 58N 87 28 E
Wum **121** 6 40N 10 2 E
Wuming **108** 23 11N 108 12 E
Wuneba **123** 4 49N 30 22 E
Wuning **109** 29 16N 115 0 E
Wunnummin L. **150** 52 55N 89 10W
Wunsiedel **49** 50 2N 12 0 E
Wunstorf **48** 52 26N 9 29 E
Wuntho, Burma **98** 21 44N 96 2 E
Wuntho, Burma **99** 23 55N 95 45 E
Wupao **106** 37 35N 110 45 E
Wup'ing **109** 25 9N 116 5 E
Wuppertal, Ger. **48** 51 15N 7 8 E
Wuppertal, S. Afr. **128** 32 13 S 19 12 E
Wurarga **137** 28 25 S 116 15 E
Würenlingen **51** 47 32N 8 16 E
Wurung **138** 19 13 S 140 38 E
Würzburg **49** 49 46N 9 55 E
Wurzen **48** 51 21N 12 45 E
Wushan, Kansu, China **106** 34 42N 104 58 E
Wushan, Szechwan, China **108** 31 3N 109 57 E
Wushench'i **106** 38 57N 109 15 E
Wustrow **48** 54 4N 11 33 E
Wusu **105** 44 27N 84 37 E
Wutai **106** 38 44N 113 18 E
Wuti **107** 37 46N 117 39 E
Wuting **108** 25 33N 102 26 E
Wuting = Huimin **107** 37 32N 117 33 E
Wuting Ho, R. **106** 37 8N 110 25 E
Wut'ungch'iao **108** 29 24N 104 0 E
Wutunghaolan **107** 42 49N 120 11 E
Wuustwezel **47** 51 23N 4 36 E
Wuwei, Anhwei, China **109** 31 22N 117 55 E
Wuwei, Kansu, China **105** 37 55N 102 48 E
Wuyang **106** 33 25N 113 36 E
Wuyo **121** 10 23N 11 50 E
Wuyüan, Inner Mong., China **106** 41 6N 108 16 E
Wuyüan, Kiangsi, China **109** 29 17N 117 54 E
Wuyün **105** 49 17N 129 40 E
Wyaaba Cr. **138** 16 27 S 141 35 E
Wyalkatchem **137** 31 8 S 117 22 E
Wyalong **139** 33 54 S 147 16 E
Wyalusing **162** 41 40N 76 16W
Wyandotte **156** 42 14N 83 13W
Wyandra **139** 27 12 S 145 56 E
Wyangala Res. **141** 33 54 S 149 0 E
Wyara, L. **139** 28 42 S 144 14 E
Wych Farm, oilfield **19** 50 38N 2 2W
Wycheproof **140** 36 0N 143 17 E
Wye **29** 51 11N 0 56 E
Wye, R. **28** 52 0N 2 36W
Wyemandoo, Mt. **137** 28 28 S 118 29 E
Wyk **48** 54 41N 8 33 E
Wylfa Hd. **31** 53 25N 4 28W
Wylye, R. **28** 51 8N 1 53W
Wymondham, Leicester, U.K. **29** 52 45N 0 42W
Wymondham, Norfolk, U.K. **29** 52 34N 1 7 E
Wymore **158** 40 10N 97 8W
Wynberg **128** 34 2 S 18 28 E
Wynbring **139** 30 33 S 133 32 E
Wyndham, Austral. **136** 15 33 S 128 3 E
Wyndham, N.Z. **143** 46 20 S 168 51 E
Wynne **159** 35 15N 90 50W
Wynnstay **31** 52 36N 3 33W
Wynnum **139** 27 27 S 153 9 E
Wynyard **153** 51 45N 104 10W
Wyola, L. **137** 29 8 S 130 17 E
Wyoming □ **154** 42 48N 109 0W
Wyong **141** 33 14 S 151 24 E
Wyre Forest **28** 52 24N 2 24W
Wyre, I. **37** 59 7N 2 58W
Wyre, R. **37** 53 52N 2 57W
Wyrzysk **54** 53 10N 17 17 E
Wysoka **54** 53 13N 17 2 E
Wyszków **54** 52 36N 21 25 E
Wyszogród **54** 52 23N 20 9 E
Wytheville **156** 37 0N 81 3W

X

Xai-Xai **129** 25 6 S 33 31 E
Xambioá **170** 6 25 S 48 40W
Xanten **48** 51 40N 6 27 E
Xanthi **68** 41 10N 24 58 E
Xanthi □ **68** 41 10N 24 58 E
Xapuri **174** 10 35 S 68 35W
Xau **128** 21 15 S 24 44 E
Xavantina **173** 21 15 S 52 48W
Xenia **156** 39 42N 83 57W
Xieng Khouang **100** 19 17N 103 25 E
Xilókastron **69** 38 4N 22 43 E
Xinavane **129** 25 2 S 32 47 E
Xingu, R. **175** 2 25 S 52 35W
Xiniás, L. **69** 39 2N 22 12 E
Xique-Xique **170** 10 50 S 42 40W
Xuan Loc **101** 10 56N 107 14 E
Xuyen Moc **101** 10 34N 107 25 E

Y

Ya'Bud **90** 32 27N 35 10 E
Yaamba **138** 23 8 S 150 22 E
Yaan **108** 30 0N 102 59 E
Yaapeet **140** 35 45 S 142 3 E

CIB

Yabassi 121 4 30N 9 57 E
Yabba North 141 36 13 S 145 42 E
Yabelo 123 4 57N 38 8 E
Yablanitsa 67 43 2N 24 5 E
Yablonovyy Khrebet 77 53 0N 114 0 E
Yabrīn 92 23 7N 48 52 E
Yach'i 108 27 35N 106 40 E
Yachiang 108 30 4N 101 7 E
Yacuiba 172 22 0 S 63 25W
Yadgir 96 16 45N 77 5 E
Yadkin, R. 157 36 15N 81 0W
Yadrin 81 55 57N 46 6 E
Yaeyama-Shotō 112 24 25N 124 0 E
Yagaba 121 10 14N 1 20W
Yagoua 124 10 20N 14 58 E
Yagur 90 32 45N 35 4 E
Yaha 101 6 29N 101 8 E
Yahk 152 49 6N 116 10W
Yahuma 124 1 0N 22 5 E
Yaihsien 100 18 14N 109 29 E
Yaizu 111 34 52N 138 20 E
Yajua 121 11 27N 12 49 E
Yakage 110 34 37N 133 35 E
Yakataga 147 60 5N 142 32W
Yakiang 99 30 4N 101 15 E
Yakima 160 46 42N 120 30W
Yakima, R. 160 47 0N 120 30W
Yako 120 12 59N 2 15W
Yakoruda 67 42 1N 23 29 E
Yakshur Bodya 84 57 11N 53 7 E
Yaku-Jima 112 30 20N 130 30 E
Yakut A.S.S.R. □ 77 62 0N 130 0 E
Yakutat 147 59 50N 139 44W
Yakutsk 77 62 5N 129 40 E
Yala 101 6 33N 101 18 E
Yalabusha, R. 159 33 53N 89 50W
Yalbalgo 137 25 10 S 114 45 E
Yalboroo 138 20 50 S 148 40 E
Yalgoo 137 28 16 S 116 39 E
Yalikavak 69 37 6N 27 18 E
Yalinga 117 6 20N 23 10 E
Yalkubul, Punta 165 21 32N 88 37W
Y'allaq, G. 122 30 21N 33 31 E
Yalleroi 138 24 3 S 145 42 E
Yallourn 141 38 10 S 146 18 E
Yalpukh, Oz. 70 45 30N 28 41 E
Yalta 82 44 30N 34 10 E
Yalu Chiang, R. 107 39 45N 124 20 E
Yalung Chiang, R. 105 26 35N 101 45 E
Yalutorovsk 76 56 30N 65 40 E
Yam Kinneret 90 32 49N 35 36 E
Yamada 110 33 43N 130 49 E
Yamaga 110 33 1N 130 41 E
Yamagata 112 38 15N 140 15 E
Yamagata-ken □ 112 38 30N 140 0 E
Yamagawa 110 31 12N 130 39 E
Yamaguchi 110 34 10N 131 32 E
Yamaguchi-ken □ 110 34 20N 131 40 E
Yamal, Poluostrov 76 71 0N 70 0 E
Yamana 92 24 5N 47 30 E
Yamanaka 111 36 15N 136 22 E
Yamanashi-ken □ 111 35 40N 138 40 E
Yamankhalinka 83 47 43N 49 21 E
Yamantau 78 54 20N 57 40 E
Yamantau, Gora 84 54 15N 58 6 E
Yamato 111 35 27N 139 25 E
Yamatotakada 111 34 31N 135 45 E
Yamazaki 110 35 0N 134 32 E
Yamba, N.S.W., Austral. 139 29 26 S 153 23 E
Yamba, S. Australia, Austral. 140 34 10 S 140 52 E
Yambah 138 23 10 S 133 50 E
Yâmbiô 123 4 35N 28 16 E
Yambol 67 42 30N 26 36 E
Yamdena 103 7 45 S 131 20 E
Yame 110 33 13N 130 35 E
Yamethin 98 20 29N 96 18 E
Yamil 121 12 53N 8 4 E
Yamma-Yamma L. 139 26 16 S 141 20 E
Yampa, R. 160 40 37N 108 0W
Yampi Sd. 136 16 8 S 123 38 E
Yampol 82 48 15N 28 15 E
Yamrat 121 10 11N 9 55 E
Yamrukohal, Mt. 67 42 44N 24 52 E
Yamun 90 32 29N 35 14 E
Yamuna (Jumna), R. 94 27 0N 78 30 E
Yan 121 10 5N 12 11 E
Yan Oya 97 9 0N 81 10 E
Yana, R. 77 69 0N 134 0 E
Yanac 140 36 8 S 141 25 E
Yanagawa 110 33 10N 130 24 E
Yanahara 110 34 58N 134 2 E
Yanam 96 16 47N 82 15 E
Yanaul 84 56 25N 55 0 E
Yanbu 'al Bahr 92 24 0N 38 5 E
Yancannia 139 30 12 S 142 35 E
Yanchep 137 31 30 S 115 45 E
Yanco 141 34 38 S 146 27 E
Yanco Cr. 141 35 14 S 145 35 E
Yandabome 138 7 1 S 145 46 E
Yandal 137 27 35 S 121 10 E
Yandanooka 137 29 18 S 115 29 E
Yandaran 138 24 43 S 152 6 E
Yandil 137 26 20 S 119 50 E
Yandoon 98 17 0N 95 40 E
Yanfolila 120 11 11N 8 9W
Yangambi 126 0 47N 24 20 E
Yangch'angtzukou 106 41 31N 109 1 E
Yangch'eng 106 35 32N 112 26 E
Yangchiang 109 21 55N 111 55 E
Yangchiaoch'iao 109 29 45N 112 45 E
Yangchiapa 106 42 6N 113 46 E
Yangchou 109 32 24N 119 26 E
Yangchoyung Hu 105 29 0N 90 40 E
Yangch'ü = T'aiyüan 106 37 55N 112 40 E
Yangch'üan 106 37 54N 113 36 E
Yangch'un 109 22 10N 111 47 E
Yanghsien 106 33 20N 107 30 E
Yanghsin 109 29 53N 115 10 E
Yangi-Yer 76 40 17N 68 48 E
Yangibazar 85 41 40N 70 53 E
Yangikishlak 85 40 25N 67 10 E
Yangiyul 85 41 0N 69 3 E
Yangku 106 36 8N 115 48 E
Yangliuch'ing 107 39 11N 117 9 E
Yangp'i 108 25 40N 100 0 E
Yangp'ing 109 31 13N 111 33 E
Yangp'ingkuan 106 33 2N 105 56 E
Yangshan 109 24 28N 112 38 E
Yangshuo 109 24 45N 110 24 E
Yangtze (Ch'ang Chiang) 109 1 48N 121 53 E
Yangyang 107 38 4N 128 38 E
Yangyüan 106 40 5N 114 12 E
Yanhee Res. 101 17 30N 98 45 E
Yanko Cr. 139 35 17 S 145 15 E
Yankton 158 42 55N 97 25W
Yanna 139 26 58 S 146 0 E
Yanonge 126 0 35N 24 38 E
Yantabulla 139 29 21 S 145 0 E
Yantra, R. 67 43 35N 25 37 E
Yany Kurgan 85 43 55N 67 15 E
Yao, Chad 117 12 56N 17 33 E
Yao, Japan 111 34 32N 135 36 E
Yao Yai, Ko 101 8 0N 98 35 E
Yaoan 108 25 32N 101 12 E
Yaoundé 121 3 50N 11 35 E
Yaowan 107 34 10N 118 3 E
Yap Is. 103 9 30N 138 10 E
Yapen 103 1 50 S 136 0 E
Yapen, Selat 103 1 20 S 136 10 E
Yapo, R. 174 0 30 S 77 0W
Yappar, R. 138 18 22 S 141 16 E
Yaqui, R. 164 28 28N 109 30W
Yar 84 58 14N 52 5 E
Yar-Sale 76 66 50N 70 50 E
Yaracuy □ 174 10 20N 68 45W
Yaraka 138 24 53 S 144 3 E
Yaransk 81 57 13N 47 56 E
Yaratishky 80 54 3N 25 52 E
Yarcombe 30 50 51N 3 6W
Yarda 117 18 35N 19 0 E
Yardea P.O. 139 32 23 S 135 32 E
Yare, R. 29 52 36N 1 28 E
Yarensk 78 61 10N 49 8 E
Yarfa 122 24 40N 38 35 E
Yarí, R. 174 1 0N 73 40W
Yaringa North 137 25 53 S 114 30 E
Yaringa South 137 26 3 S 114 28 E
Yarkand = Soch'e 105 38 24N 77 20 E
Yarkhun, R. 95 36 30N 72 45 E
Yarm 33 54 31N 1 21W
Yarmouth, Can. 151 43 53N 65 45W
Yarmouth, U.K. 28 50 42N 1 29W
Yaroslavl 81 57 35N 39 55 E
Yarra Yarra Lakes 137 29 40 S 115 45 E
Yarraden 138 14 28 S 143 15 E
Yarraloola 136 21 33 S 115 52 E
Yarram 141 38 29 S 146 40 E
Yarraman 139 26 50 S 152 0 E
Yarraman Cr. 139 26 46 S 152 1 E
Yarranvale 139 26 50 S 145 20 E
Yarras 141 31 25 S 152 20 E
Yarrawonga 141 36 0 S 146 0 E
Yarrow 35 55 32N 3 0W
Yarrowee, R. 140 38 18 S 144 30 E
Yarto 140 35 28 S 142 16 E
Yartsevo 77 60 20N 90 0 E
Yarumal 174 6 58N 75 24W
Yaselda, R. 80 52 26N 25 30 E
Yashi 121 12 23N 7 54 E
Yashiro-Jima 110 33 55N 132 15 E
Yasin 95 36 24N 73 15 E
Yasinovataya 82 48 7N 37 57 E
Yasinski, L. 150 53 16N 77 35W
Yasnogorsk 81 54 32N 37 38 E
Yasothon 100 15 50N 104 10 E
Yass 141 34 49 S 148 54 E
Yasugi 110 35 26N 133 15 E
Yas'ur 90 32 54N 35 10 E
Yatagan 69 37 20N 28 10 E
Yate 28 51 32N 2 26W
Yates Center 159 37 53N 95 45W
Yates Pt. 143 44 29 S 167 49 E
Yathkyed L. 153 62 40N 98 0W
Yathong 141 32 37 S 145 33 E
Yatsuo 111 36 34N 137 8 E
Yatsushiro 110 32 30N 130 40 E
Yatsushiro-Kai 110 32 30N 130 25 E
Yatta 90 31 27N 35 6 E
Yatta Plat. 126 2 0 S 38 0 E
Yattah 90 31 27N 35 6 E
Yatton 28 51 23N 2 50W
Yauyos 174 12 10 S 75 50W
Yaval 96 21 10N 75 42 E
Yavan 85 38 19N 69 2 E
Yavari R. 174 4 50 S 72 0W
Yavorov 80 49 55N 23 20 E
Yawatahama 110 33 27N 132 24 E
Yawri B. 120 8 22N 13 0W
Yaxley 29 52 31N 0 14W
Yazagyo 98 23 30N 94 6 E
Yazd (Yezd) 93 31 55N 54 27 E
Yazdan 93 33 30N 60 50 E
Yazoo City 159 32 48N 90 28W
Yazoo, R. 159 32 35N 90 50W
Ybbs 52 48 12N 15 4 E
Yding Skovhøj 75 55 59N 9 46 E
Yea 141 37 14 S 145 26 E
Yealering 137 32 36 S 117 36 E
Yealmpton 30 50 21N 4 0W
Yearinan 141 31 10 S 149 11 E
Yebbi-Souma 119 21 7N 17 54 E
Yebbigué 119 22 30N 17 30 E
Yebel Jarris Tighzert, O. 118 28 10N 9 37W
Yebyu 99 14 15N 98 13 E
Yechŏn 107 36 39N 128 27 E
Yecla 59 38 35N 1 5W
Yécora 164 28 20N 108 58W
Yedashe 98 17 24N 95 50 E
Yeddou 118 28 5N 9 2W
Yeeda River 136 17 31 S 123 38 E
Yeelanna 139 34 9 S 135 45 E
Yefremov 81 53 15N 38 3 E
Yegorlyk, R. 83 46 15N 41 30 E
Yegorlykskaya 83 46 5N 40 35 E
Yegoryevsk 81 55 27N 38 55 E
Yegros 172 26 20 S 56 25W
Yehchih 108 27 39N 99 0 E
Yehsien 106 33 37N 113 20 E
Yehud 90 32 3N 34 53 E
Yehuda, Midbar 90 31 35N 34 57 E
Yei 123 4 3N 30 40 E
Yei, Nahr 123 5 50N 30 20 E
Yelan 81 50 55N 43 43 E
Yelan Kolenovski 81 51 16N 40 45 E
Yelandur 97 12 6N 77 0 E
Yelanskoye 77 61 25N 128 0 E
Yelarbon 139 28 33 S 150 49 E
Yelatma 81 55 0N 41 52 E
Yelets 81 52 40N 38 30 E
Yelimané 120 15 9N 22 49 E
Yell, I. 36 60 35N 1 5W
Yell Sd. 36 60 33N 1 15W
Yellamanchilli (Elamanchili) 96 17 26N 82 50 E
Yellow Sea 105 35 0N 123 0 E
Yellowdine 137 31 17 S 119 40 E
Yellowhead P. 152 52 53N 118 25W
Yellowknife 152 62 27N 114 21W
Yellowknife, R. 152 62 31N 114 19W
Yellowstone L. 160 44 30N 110 20W
Yellowstone National Park 160 44 35N 110 0W
Yellowstone, R. 158 46 35N 105 45W
Yelnya 80 54 35N 33 15 E
Yelsk 80 51 50N 29 3 E
Yelvertoft 138 20 13 S 138 53 E
Yelwa 122 10 49N 8 41 E
Yemanzhelinsk 84 54 58N 61 18 E
Yemen ■ 91 15 0N 44 0 E
Yemen, South ■ 91 15 0N 48 0 E
Yen Bai 100 21 42N 104 52 E
Yenakiyevo 82 48 15N 38 5 E
Yenan 106 36 42N 109 25 E
Yenangyaung 98 20 30N 95 0 E
Yenanma 98 19 46N 96 48 E
Yenchang 106 36 44N 110 2 E
Yench'eng, Honan, China 106 33 37N 114 0 E
Yench'eng, Kiangsu, China 107 33 24N 120 10 E
Yench'i 105 42 4N 86 34 E
Yenchi 107 42 53N 129 31 E
Yench'ih 106 37 47N 107 24 E
Yenchihsien 107 42 46N 129 24 E
Yenchin 108 28 4N 104 14 E
Yench'ing 106 40 28N 115 58 E
Yenching 108 29 7N 98 33 E
Yenchou 105 35 40N 116 50 E
Yench'uan 106 36 52N 110 11 E
Yenda 141 34 13 S 146 14 E
Yendéré 120 10 12N 4 59W
Yendi 121 9 29N 0 1W
Yenfeng 108 25 52N 101 5 E
Yenho 108 28 35N 108 28 E
Yenhsing 108 25 22N 101 44 E
Yenisaia 68 41 1N 24 57 E
Yenisey, R. 76 68 0N 86 30 E
Yeniseysk 77 58 39N 92 4 E
Yeniseyskiy Zaliv 76 72 20N 81 0 E
Yenne 45 45 43N 5 44 E
Yenotyevka 83 47 15N 47 0 E
Yenpien 108 26 54N 101 34 E
Yenshan, Hopeh, China 107 38 3N 117 12 E
Yenshan, Yunnan, China 108 23 40N 104 22 E
Yenshou 107 45 27N 128 19 E
Yent'ai 107 37 35N 121 25 E
Yent'ing 108 31 19N 105 20 E
Yenyüan 108 27 25N 101 33 E
Yenyuka 77 58 20N 121 30 E
Yeo, L. 137 28 0 S 124 30 E
Yeo, R. 28 51 1N 2 46W
Yeola 96 20 0N 74 30 E
Yeotmal 96 20 20N 78 15 E
Yeoval 141 32 41 S 148 39 E
Yeovil 28 50 57N 2 38W
Yepes 56 39 55N 3 39W
Yeppoon 138 23 5 S 150 47 E
Yeráki 69 37 0N 22 42 E
Yerbogachen 77 61 16N 108 0 E
Yerevan 83 40 10N 44 20 E
Yerilla 137 29 24 S 121 47 E
Yerington 163 38 59N 119 10W
Yerla, R. 96 17 35N 74 30 E
Yermakovo 77 52 35N 126 20 E
Yermo 163 34 58N 116 50W
Yermolayevo 78 52 58N 56 12 E
Yerofey Pavlovich 77 54 0N 122 0 E
Yerseke 47 51 29N 4 3 E
Yershov 81 51 15N 48 27 E
Yerūshalayim 90 31 47N 35 10 E
Yerville 42 49 40N 0 53 E
Yes Tor, Mt. 30 50 41N 3 59W
Yesagyo 98 21 38N 95 14 E
Yesan 107 36 41N 126 51 E
Yeşilirmak 82 41 0N 36 40 E
Yeso 159 34 29N 104 87W
Yessentuki 83 44 0N 42 45 E
Yeste 59 38 22N 2 19W
Yeu, I. d' 42 46 42N 2 20W
Yevlakh 83 40 39N 47 7 E
Yevpatoriya 82 45 15N 33 20 E
Yevstratovskiy 81 50 11N 39 2 E
Yeya, R. 83 46 40N 39 0 E
Yeysk Staro 82 46 40N 38 12 E
Yhati 172 25 45 S 56 35W
Yhú 173 25 0 S 56 0W
Yi, R. 172 33 7 S 57 8W
Yialí, I. 69 36 41N 27 11 E
Yiáltra 69 38 51N 22 59 E
Yiànisádhes, I. 69 35 20N 26 10 E
Yiannitsa 68 40 46N 22 24 E
Yibal 91 22 10N 56 8 E
Yidhá 68 40 35N 22 53 E
Yinchiang 108 27 58N 108 20 E
Yinch'uan 105 38 30N 106 20 E
Yindarlgooda, L. 137 30 40 S 121 52 E
Ying Ho, R. 109 32 30N 116 32 E
Yingch'eng 109 30 55N 113 33 E
Yingchiang 108 24 48N 98 5 E
Yinghsien 106 39 36N 113 12 E
Yingk'ou 107 40 38N 122 30 E
Yingp'an, Chiang, G. 108 21 20N 109 30 E
Yingp'anshan 108 27 56N 105 34 E
Yingshan, Hupeh, China 109 31 37N 113 46 E
Yingshan, Hupeh, China 109 30 50N 115 45 E
Yingshan, Szechwan, China 108 31 6N 106 35 E
Yingshang 109 32 36N 116 16 E
Yingtan 105 28 12N 117 0 E
Yingte 109 24 10N 113 24 E
Yinkanie 140 34 22 S 140 17 E
Yinmabin 99 22 10N 94 55 E
Yinnietharra 137 24 39 S 116 12 E
Yioúra, I. 68 39 23N 24 10 E
Yipang 101 22 15N 101 26 E
Yirga Alem 124 6 34N 38 29 E
Yíthion 69 36 46N 22 34 E
Yizre'el 90 32 34N 35 19 E
Ylitornio 74 66 19N 23 39 E
Ylivieska 74 64 4N 24 28 E
Yngaren 73 58 50N 16 35 E
Ynykchanskiy 77 60 15N 137 43 E
Yoakum 159 29 20N 97 10W
Yobuko 110 33 32N 129 54 E
Yog Pt. 103 13 55N 124 20 E
Yogyakarta 103 7 49 S 110 22 E
Yoho Nat. Park 152 51 25N 116 30W
Yojoa, L. de 166 14 53N 88 0W
Yŏju 107 37 20N 127 35 E
Yokadouma 124 3 35N 14 50 E
Yŏkaichi 111 35 6N 136 12 E
Yŏkaichiba 111 35 42N 140 33 E
Yokkaichi 111 35 0N 136 30 E
Yoko 121 5 50N 12 20 E
Yokohama 111 35 27N 139 39 E
Yokosuka 111 35 20N 139 40 E
Yokote 112 39 20N 140 30 E
Yola 121 9 10N 12 29 E
Yolaina, Cordillera de 166 11 30N 84 0W
Yom Mae Nam 101 15 15N 100 20 E
Yonago 110 35 25N 133 19 E
Yŏnan 107 37 55N 126 11 E
Yonezawa 112 37 57N 140 4 E
Yong Peng 101 2 0N 103 3 E
Yong Sata 101 7 8N 99 41 E
Yongampo 107 39 56N 124 23 E
Yŏngchon 107 35 58N 128 56 E
Yŏngdŏk 107 36 24N 129 22 E
Yŏngdŭngpo 107 37 31N 126 54 E
Yŏnghŭng 107 39 31N 127 18 E
Yŏngju 107 36 50N 128 40 E
Yŏngwŏl 107 37 11N 128 28 E
Yonibana 120 8 30N 12 19W
Yonker 153 52 40N 109 40W
Yonkers 162 40 57N 73 51W
Yonne □ 43 47 50N 3 40 E
Yonne, R. 43 48 23N 2 58 E
Yonov 121 7 33N 8 42 E
Yoqueam 90 32 40N 35 6 E
York, Austral. 137 31 52 S 116 47 E
York, U.K. 33 53 58N 1 7W
York, Ala., U.S.A. 157 32 30N 88 18W
York, Nebr., U.S.A. 158 40 55N 97 35W
York, Pa., U.S.A. 162 39 57N 76 43W
York, C. 138 10 42 S 142 31 E
York Factory 153 57 0N 92 18W
York Haven 162 40 7N 76 46W
York, Kap 12 75 55N 66 25W
York, R. 162 37 15N 76 23W
York Sd. 136 14 50 S 125 5 E
York, Vale of 23 54 15N 1 25W
Yorke Pen. 140 34 50 S 137 40 E
Yorkshire Wolds 33 54 0N 0 30W
Yorkton 153 51 11N 102 28W
Yorktown, Tex., U.S.A. 159 29 0N 97 29W

Yorktown, Va., U.S.A. 162 37 14N 76 30W
Yornup 137 34 2S 116 10E
Yoro 166 15 9N 87 7W
Yosemite National Park 163 38 0N 119 30W
Yosemite Village 163 37 45N 119 35W
Yoshii 110 33 16N 129 46E
Yoshimatsu 110 32 0N 130 47E
Yoshkar Ola 81 56 49N 47 10E
Yŏsu 107 34 47N 127 45E
Youanmi 137 28 37S 118 49E
Youbou 152 48 53N 124 13W
Youghal 39 51 58N 7 51W
Youghal B. 39 51 55N 7 50W
Youkounkoun 120 12 35N 13 11W
Young, Austral. 141 34 19S 148 18E
Young, Can. 153 51 47N 105 45W
Young, Uruguay 172 32 44S 57 36W
Young, U.S.A. 161 34 9N 110 56W
Young Ra. 143 44 10S 169 30E
Younghusband, L. 140 30 50S 136 5E
Younghusband Pen. 140 36 0S 139 25E
Youngstown, Can. 153 51 35N 111 10W
Youngstown, U.S.A. 156 41 7N 80 41W
Youssoufia 118 32 16N 8 31W
Yoweragabbie 137 28 14S 117 39E
Yowrie 141 36 17S 149 46E
Yoxall 28 52 45N 1 49W
Yoxford 29 52 16N 1 30E
Yozgat 92 39 51N 34 47E
Ypané, R. 172 23 29S 57 19W
Yport 42 49 45N 0 15E
Ypres 47 50 50N 2 52E
Ypsilanti 156 42 18N 83 40W
Yreka 160 41 44N 122 40W
Ysabel Chan. 135 2 0S 150 0E
Ysbyty Ystwyth 31 52 20N 3 50W
Ysleta 161 31 45N 106 24W
Yssingeaux 45 45 9N 4 8E
Ystad 73 55 26N 13 50E
Ystalyfera 31 51 46N 3 48W
Ystradgynlais 31 51 47N 3 45W
Ystwyth, R. 31 52 24N 4 2W
Ythan, R. 37 57 26N 2 12W
Ytre Adal 71 60 15N 10 14E
Ytterhogdal 72 62 12N 14 56E
Ytyk-Kel 77 62 20N 133 28E
Yü Chiang, R., China 105 22 50N 108 6E
Yü Chiang, R., China 108 22 50N 108 6E
Yu Shui, R. 108 28 37N 110 23E
Yüan Chiang, R. 109 29 0N 111 50E
Yüan Chiang, R (Hong.) 108 29 12N 111 43E
Yüanan 109 31 3N 111 34E
Yüanchiang, Hünan, China 109 28 50N 112 23E
Yüanchiang, Yunnan, China 108 23 40N 102 0E
Yüanch'ü 106 35 18N 111 41E
Yüanli 109 24 27N 120 39E
Yüanlin 109 23 45N 120 30E
Yuanling 109 28 30N 110 5E
Yüanmou 108 25 42N 101 32E
Yuanyang 108 23 10N 102 58E
Yüanyang 108 35 3N 113 57E
Yuat, R. 135 4 10S 143 52E
Yuba City 160 39 12N 121 37W
Yübari 112 43 4N 141 59E
Yübetsu 112 43 13N 144 5E
Yucatán □ 165 21 30N 86 30W
Yucatán Basin 14 20 0N 84 0W
Yucatán Channel 166 22 0N 86 30W
Yucca 161 34 56N 114 6W
Yucca Valley 163 34 8N 116 30W
Yücha 108 26 55N 101 24E
Yucheng 106 36 55N 116 40E
Yüch'i 108 24 25N 102 35E
Yuch'i 109 26 10N 118 11E
Yüchiang 109 28 24N 116 53E
Yüch'ien 109 30 12N 119 24E
Yüch'ing 108 27 13N 107 54E
Yudino 76 55 10N 67 55E
Yüehhsi, Anhwei, China 109 30 54N 116 22E
Yüehhsi, Szechwan, China 108 28 36N 102 35E
Yüehyang 109 29 20N 113 7E
Yuendumu 136 22 16S 131 49E
Yufu-Dake 110 33 17N 131 33E
Yugoslavia ■ 66 44 0N 20 0E
Yühsien 106 34 10N 113 30E
Yuhsien, Hunan, China 109 27 2N 113 20E
Yuhsien, Shansi, China 106 38 5N 113 24E
Yühuan Tao, I. 109 28 5N 121 15E
Yukan 109 28 43N 116 35E
Yukhnov 80 54 44N 35 15E
Yüki 111 36 18N 139 53E
Yukon □ 147 63 0N 135 0W
Yukon, R. 147 65 30N 150 0W
Yukti 77 63 20N 105 0E
Yukuhashi 110 33 44N 130 59E
Yule, R. 136 20 24S 118 12E
Yuli 122 9 44N 10 12E
Yülin 100 18 10N 109 31E
Yulin, Guangdong, China 109 22 36N 110 7E
Yulin, Shensi, China 105 38 15N 109 30E
Yuma, Ariz., U.S.A. 161 32 45N 114 37W
Yuma, Colo., U.S.A. 158 40 10N 102 43W
Yuma, B. de 167 18 20N 68 35W
Yumali 140 35 32S 139 45E
Yumbe 126 3 28N 31 15E
Yumbi 126 1 12S 26 15E
Yumbo 174 3 35N 76 28W
Yümenhsien 105 40 17N 97 12E
Yün Ho 107 33 16N 118 45E
Yun Ho 109 35 0N 117 0E
Yuna 137 28 20S 115 0E
Yünan 109 23 14N 111 31E
Yunaska I. 147 52 40N 170 40W
Yünch'eng, Shansi, China 106 35 1N 110 59E
Yünch'eng, Shantung, China 106 35 35N 115 56E
Yunfou 109 22 56N 112 2E
Yungan 109 25 50N 117 25E
Yungas 174 17 0S 66 0W
Yungay 172 37 10S 72 5W
Yungch'eng 106 33 56N 116 22E
Yungchi 106 34 52N 110 26E
Yungch'ing 106 39 19N 116 29E
Yungch'uan 108 20 22N 105 52E
Yungch'un 109 25 19N 118 17E
Yungfeng 109 27 20N 115 27E
Yungfu 109 24 59N 109 59E
Yungho 106 36 44N 110 39E
Yunghsin 109 16 55N 114 18E
Yunghsing 109 26 8N 113 6E
Yunghsiu 109 29 8N 115 42E
Yungjen 108 26 4N 101 42E
Yungk'ang, Chekiang, China 109 28 53N 120 2E
Yungk'ang, Kwangsi Chuang Aut. Region, China 108 22 48N 107 51E
Yungnien 106 36 49N 114 33E
Yungning, Kwangsi Chuang A. R., China 108 22 45N 108 29E
Yungning, Ningsia Hui A. R., China 106 38 18N 106 18E
Yungning, Yunnan, China 108 27 50N 100 40E
Yungningchai 106 36 35N 108 51E
Yungp'ing 108 25 25N 99 36E
Yungshan 108 28 11N 103 35E
Yungsheng 108 26 42N 100 45E
Yungshun, Hunan, China 108 29 3N 109 50E
Yungshun, Kwangsi Chuang, China 108 22 48N 108 55E
Yungt'ai 109 25 52N 118 55E
Yungteng 106 36 44N 103 24E
Yungting 109 24 49N 116 46E
Yunho = Lishui 109 28 6N 119 34E
Yünhsi 109 33 0N 110 22E
Yünhsiao 109 24 1N 117 15E
Yünhsien, Hupeh, China 105 32 50N 110 53E
Yünhsien, Yunnan, China 108 24 25N 100 6E
Yünlin 109 23 42N 120 31E
Yunling Shan, mts. 108 28 30N 98 50E
Yunlung 99 25 50N 99 25E
Yünmeng 109 31 1N 113 39E
Yunnan □ 108 25 0N 102 30E
Yunndaga 137 29 45S 121 0E
Yunomae 110 32 12N 130 59E
Yunotso 110 35 5N 132 21E
Yunquera de Henares 58 40 47N 3 11W
Yunta 140 32 34S 139 36E
Yünyang 108 30 55N 108 56E
Yüp'ing 108 27 14N 108 54E
Yupyongdong 107 41 49N 128 53E
Yur 77 59 52N 137 49E
Yurga 76 55 42N 84 51E
Yuria 84 59 22N 54 10E
Yuribei 76 71 20N 76 30E
Yurimaguas 174 5 55S 76 0W
Yurya 81 59 1N 49 13E
Yuryev Polskiy 81 56 30N 59 47E
Yuryevets 81 57 25N 43 2E
Yuryuzan 84 54 27N 58 28E
Yuscarán 166 13 58N 86 51W
Yusha, Jebel 90 32 4N 35 41E
Yüshan 109 28 40N 118 15E
Yüshanchen 108 29 31N 108 25E
Yushe 106 37 4N 112 58E
Yüshu 105 33 1N 96 44E
Yushu 107 44 46N 126 34E
Yüt'ai 106 35 2N 116 40E
Yüt'ien 107 39 53N 117 45E
Yütu 109 26 0N 115 24E
Yütz'u 106 37 42N 112 44E
Yüwang 106 37 9N 106 28E
Yüyang 108 28 44N 108 46E
Yüyang 109 30 12N 119 56E
Yüyao 109 30 3N 121 9E
Yüyao 109 30 0N 121 20E
Yuyu 105 40 20N 112 30E
Yuyü 106 40 10N 112 25E
Yüyuan 109 28 9N 121 11E
Yuzha 81 56 40N 42 10E
Yuzhno-Sakhalinsk 77 47 5N 142 5E
Yuzhno-Surkhanskoye Vodokhranilishehe 85 37 53N 67 42E
Yuzhno-Uralsk 84 54 26N 61 15E
Yuzhnyy Ural, mts. 84 53 0N 58 0E
Yvelines □ 43 48 40N 1 45E
Yverdon 50 46 47N 6 39E
Yvetot 42 49 37N 0 44E
Yvonand 50 46 48N 6 44E

Z

Za, O. 118 34 5N 2 30W
Zaalayskiy Khrebet 85 39 20N 73 0E
Zaamslag 47 51 19N 3 55E
Zaan, R. 46 52 25N 4 52E
Zaandam 47 52 26N 4 49E
Zab, Monts du 119 34 55N 5 0E
Zabalj, Yugo. 66 45 21N 20 5E
Zabalj, Yugo. 66 45 23N 20 5E
Zabari 66 44 22N 21 15E
Zabarjad 122 23 40N 36 12E
Zabaykalskiy 77 49 40N 117 10E
Zabkowice Slaskie 54 50 22N 19 17E
Zabljak 66 42 19N 19 10E
Zabludow 54 53 0N 23 19E
Zabno 54 50 9N 20 53E
Zābol 93 31 0N 61 25E
Zābolī 93 27 10N 61 35E
Zabré 121 11 12N 0 36W
Zabrze 54 50 24N 18 50E
Zacapa 166 14 59N 89 31W
Zacapu 164 19 50N 101 43W
Zacatecas 164 22 49N 102 34W
Zacatecas □ 164 23 30N 103 0W
Zacatecolua 166 13 29N 88 51W
Zacaultipán 165 20 39N 98 36W
Zacoalco 164 20 10N 103 40W
Zadar 63 44 8N 15 8E
Zadawa 121 11 33N 10 19E
Zadetkyi Kyun 101 10 0N 98 25E
Zadonsk 81 52 25N 38 56E
Zafed 90 32 58N 35 29E
Zafora, I. 69 36 5N 26 24E
Zafra 57 38 26N 6 30W
Zagan 54 51 39N 15 22E
Zagazig 122 30 40N 31 12E
Zaghouan 119 36 23N 10 10E
Zaglivérion 68 40 36N 23 15E
Zaglou 118 27 17N 0 3W
Zagnanado 121 7 18N 2 28E
Zagorá 68 39 27N 23 6E
Zagora 118 30 14N 5 51W
Zagórów 54 52 10N 17 54E
Zagorsk 81 56 20N 38 10E
Zagórz 54 49 30N 22 14E
Zagreb 63 45 50N 16 0E
Zāgros, Kudha-ye 93 33 45N 47 0E
Zagubica 66 44 15N 21 47E
Zaguinaso 120 10 1N 6 14W
Zāhedān 93 29 30N 60 50E
Zahirabad 96 17 43N 77 37E
Zahlah 92 33 52N 35 50E
Zahna 48 51 54N 12 47E
Zahrez Chergui 118 35 0N 3 30E
Zahrez Rharbi 118 34 50N 2 55E
Zailiyskiy Alatau, Khrebet 85 43 5N 77 0E
Zainsk 84 55 18N 52 4E
Zaïr 118 29 47N 5 51W
Zaïre, R. 124 1 30N 28 0E
Zaïre, Rep. of ■ 124 3 0S 23 0E
Zaječar 66 43 53N 22 18E
Zakamensk 77 50 23N 103 17E
Zakariya 90 31 43N 34 57E
Zakataly 83 41 38N 46 35E
Zakavkazye 83 42 0N 44 0E
Zakhu 92 37 10N 42 50E
Zákinthos 69 37 47N 20 54E
Zåkinthos, I. 69 37 45N 27 45E
Zakopane 54 49 18N 19 57E
Zala □ 53 46 42N 16 50E
Zala, R. 53 46 53N 17 6E
Zalaegerszeg 53 46 53N 16 47E
Zalakomár 53 46 33N 17 10E
Zalalövö 53 46 51N 16 35E
Zalamea de la Serena 57 38 40N 5 38W
Zalamea la Real 57 37 41N 6 38W
Zalau 121 10 30N 8 58E
Zalazna 84 58 39N 52 31E
Zalec 63 46 16N 15 10E
Zaleshchiki 82 48 45N 25 45E
Zalewo 54 53 55N 19 41E
Zalingei 117 13 5N 23 10E
Zalţan, Jabal 119 28 46N 19 45E
Zaltbommel 46 51 48N 5 15E
Zalŭ 121 47 12N 23 5E
Zambeke 126 2 8N 25 17E
Zambèze, R. 127 18 46S 36 16E
Zambezi, R. 127 18 46S 36 16E
Zambezia □ 127 16 15S 37 30E
Zambia ■ 125 15 0S 28 0E
Zamboanga 103 6 59N 122 3E
Zambrano 174 9 45N 74 49W
Zametchino 81 53 30N 42 30E
Zamora, Mexico 164 20 0N 102 21W
Zamora, Spain 56 41 30N 5 45W
Zamora □ 56 41 30N 5 46W
Zamość 54 50 50N 23 22E
Zamuro, Sierra del 174 4 0N 62 30W
Zamzam, W. 119 31 0N 14 30E
Zan 121 9 26N 0 17W
Zanaga 124 2 48S 13 48E
Záncara, R. 58 39 20N 3 0W
Zandvoort 46 52 22N 4 32E
Zanesville 156 39 56N 82 2W
Zangue, R. 127 18 5S 35 10E
Zanjan 92 36 40N 48 35E
Zannone, I. 64 40 38N 13 2E
Zante = Zákinthos 69 37 47N 20 54E
Zanthus 137 31 2S 123 34E
Zanzibar 126 6 12S 39 12E
Zanzibar I. 126 6 12S 39 12E
Zanzūr 119 32 55N 13 1E
Zaouatalaz 119 24 57N 8 16E
*Zaouiet El Kahla 119 27 10N 6 40E
Zaouiet Reggane 118 26 32N 0 3E
Zapadna Morava, R. 66 43 50N 20 15E
Zapadnaya Dvina 80 56 15N 32 3E
Západné Beskydy 54 49 30N 19 0E
Západočesky □ 52 49 35N 13 0E
Západoslovenský □ 53 48 30N 17 30E
Zapala 176 39 0S 70 5W
Zapaleri, Cerro 172 22 49S 67 11W
Zapata 159 26 56N 92 17W
Zapatón, R. 57 39 0N 6 49W
Zaporozhye 82 47 50N 35 10E
Zapponeta 65 41 27N 15 57E
Zara 92 39 58N 37 43E
Zaragoza, Colomb. 174 7 30N 74 52W
Zaragoza, Coahuila, Mexico 164 28 30N 101 0W
Zaragoza, Nuevo León, Mexico 165 24 0N 99 36W
Zaragoza, Spain 58 41 39N 0 53W
Zaragoza □ 58 41 35N 1 0W
Zarand 93 30 46N 56 34E
Zarasai 80 55 40N 26 12E
Zarate 172 34 7S 59 0W
Zaraysk 81 54 48N 38 53E
Zaraza 174 9 21N 65 19W
Zarembo I. 152 56 20N 132 50W
Zari 73 13 8N 12 37E
Zaria 121 11 0N 7 40E
Zarisberge 128 24 30S 16 15E
Zarki 54 50 38N 19 21E
Zarnów 54 51 16N 20 9E
Zarnuqa 90 31 53N 34 47E
Zarów 54 50 56N 16 29E
Zarqa, R. 90 32 10N 35 37E
Zaruma 174 3 40S 79 30W
Zary 54 51 37N 15 10E
Zarza de Alange 57 38 49N 6 13W
Zarza de Granadilla 56 40 14N 6 3W
Zarza, La 57 37 42N 6 51W
Zarzaîtine 119 28 32N 9 5E
Zarzal 174 4 24N 76 4W
Zarzis 119 33 31N 11 2E
Zas 56 43 4N 8 53W
Zashiversk 77 67 25N 142 40E
Zaskar Mountains 95 33 15N 77 30E
Zaskar, R. 95 33 55N 77 2E
Zastron 128 30 18S 27 7E
Zatec 52 50 20N 13 32E
Zator 54 49 59N 19 28E
Zavala 66 42 50N 17 59E
Zavareh 93 33 35N 52 28E
Zaventem 47 50 53N 4 28E
Zavetnoye 83 47 13N 43 50E
Zavidovići 66 44 27N 18 13E
Zavitinsk 77 50 10N 129 20E
Zavodoski, I. 13 56 0S 27 45W
Zavolzhye 81 56 37N 43 18E
Zawadzkie 54 50 37N 18 28E
Zawidów 54 51 1N 15 1E
Zawiercie 54 50 30N 19 13E
Zâwyet Shammâs 122 31 30N 26 37E
Zâwyet Um el Rakham 122 31 18N 27 1E
Zâwyet Ungeila 122 31 23N 26 42E
Zayandeh, R. 93 32 35N 32 0E
Zayarsk 77 56 20N 102 55E
Zaysan 76 47 28N 84 52E
Zaysan, Oz. 76 48 0N 83 0E
Zāzamt, W. 119 30 29N 14 30E
Zazir, O. 119 22 0N 5 40E
Zázrivá 53 49 16N 19 7E
Zbarazh 80 49 43N 25 44E
Zbaszyn 54 52 14N 15 56E
Zbaszynek 54 52 16N 15 51E
Zblewo 54 53 56N 18 19E
Zdandijk 46 52 82N 4 49E
Zdolbunov 80 50 30N 26 15E
Zdrelo 66 44 16N 21 28E
Zdunska Wola 54 51 37N 18 59E
Zduny 54 51 39N 17 21E
Zeballos 152 49 59N 126 50W
Zebediela 129 24 20S 29 17E
Zedelgem 47 51 8N 3 8E
Zeebrugge 47 51 19N 3 12E
Zeehan 138 41 52S 145 25E
Zeeland 47 51 41N 5 40E
Zeeland □ 47 51 30N 3 50E
Ze'elim 90 31 13N 34 32E
Zeelst 47 51 25N 5 25E
Zeerust 128 25 31S 26 4E
Zefat 90 32 58N 35 29E
Zegdou 118 29 51N 4 53W
Zege 123 11 43N 37 18E
Zegelsem 47 50 49N 3 43E
Zegoua 120 10 32N 5 35W
Zehdenick 48 52 59N 13 20E
Zeil, Mt. 136 23 24S 132 23E
Zeila 91 11 15N 43 30E
Zeist 46 52 5N 5 15E
Zeita 90 32 23N 35 2E
Zeitz 48 51 3N 12 9E
Zele 47 51 4N 4 2E
Zelendolsk 81 55 55N 48 30E
Zelengora, mts. 66 43 22N 18 30E
Zelenika 66 42 27N 18 37E
Zelenogradsk 80 54 53N 20 29E
Zelenokumsk 83 44 30N 44 1E
Zelenovski 83 48 6N 50 45E
Zelhem 47 52 0N 6 21E
Zell 49 47 42N 7 50E

Renamed Bordj Omar Driss

Zell am See **52** 47 19N 12 47 E
Zella Mehlis **48** 50 40N 10 41 E
Zelouane **86** 35 1N 2 58W
Zelzate **47** 51 13N 3 47 E
Zémio **126** 5 2N 25 5 E
Zemmora **118** 35 44N 0 51 E
Zemora, I. **119** 37 5N 10 56 E
Zemoul, W. **118** 29 15N 7 30W
Zemst **47** 50 59N 4 28 E
Zemun **66** 44 51N 20 25 E
Zenica **66** 44 10N 17 57 E
Zenina **118** 34 30N 2 37 E
Zentsûji **110** 34 14N 133 47 E
Zepce **66** 44 28N 18 2 E
Zeravshan **85** 39 10N 68 39 E
Zeravshan, R. **85** 39 32N 63 45 E
Zeravshanskiy, Khrebet **85** 39 20N 69 0 E
Zerbst **48** 51 59N 12 8 E
Zerhamra **118** 29 58N 2 30W
Zerków **54** 52 4N 17 32 E
Zermatt **50** 46 2N 7 46 E
Zernez **51** 46 42N 10 7 E
Zernograd **83** 46 52N 40 11 E
Zeroud, O. **119** 35 30N 9 30 E
Zerqani **68** 41 30N 20 20 E
Zestafoni **83** 42 6N 43 0 E
Zetel **48** 53 33N 7 57 E
Zetland (□) **26** 60 30N 0 15W
Zetten **46** 51 56N 5 44 E
Zeulenroda **48** 50 39N 12 0 E
Zeven **48** 53 17N 9 19 E
Zevenaar **46** 51 56N 6 5 E
Zevenbergen **47** 51 38N 4 37 E
Zévio **62** 45 23N 11 10 E
Zeya **77** 54 2N 127 20 E
Zeya, R. **77** 53 30N 127 0 E
Zeyse **123** 5 44N 37 23W
Zeytin **92** 37 53N 36 53 E
Zêzere, R. **56** 40 0N 7 55W
Zgierz **54** 51 45N 19 27 E
Zgorzelec **54** 51 10N 15 0 E
Zhabinka **80** 52 13N 24 2 E
Zhailma **84** 51 30N 61 50 E
Zhalanash **85** 43 3N 78 38 E
Zhamensk **80** 54 37N 21 17 E
Zhanadarya **85** 44 45N 64 40 E
Zhanatas **76** 43 11N 81 18 E
Zharkol **84** 49 57N 64 5 E
Zharkovskiy **80** 55 56N 32 19 E
Zhashkov **82** 49 15N 30 5 E
Zhdanov **82** 47 5N 37 31 E
Zheleznogorsk-Ilimskiy **77** 56 34N 104 8 E
Zherdevka **81** 51 56N 41 21 E
Zhetykol, Ozero **84** 51 2N 60 54 E
Zhigansk **77** 66 35N 124 10 E
Zhigulevsk **81** 53 28N 49 45 E
Zhirhovsk **81** 50 57N 44 49 E
Zhitomir **80** 50 20N 28 40 E
Zhizdra **80** 53 45N 34 40 E
Zhlobin **80** 52 55N 30 0 E
Zhmerinka **82** 49 2N 28 10 E
Zhodino **80** 54 5N 28 17 E
Zhovtnevoye **82** 47 54N 32 2 E
Zhuantobe **85** 43 43N 78 18 E
Zhukovka **80** 53 35N 33 50 E
Zhupanovo **77** 51 59N 15 9 E
Ziarat **94** 30 25N 67 30 E
Zichem **47** 51 2N 4 59 E
Ziebice **54** 50 37N 17 2 E
Ziel, Mt. **136** 23 20 S 132 30 E
Zielona Góra **54** 51 57N 15 31 E
Zielona Góra □ **54** 51 57N 15 30 E
Zierikzee **47** 51 40N 3 55 E
Ziesar **48** 52 16N 12 19 E
Zifta **122** 30 43N 31 14 E
Zigazinskiy **84** 53 50N 57 20 E
Zigey **117** 14 50N 15 50 E
Ziguinchor **120** 12 25N 16 20W
Zihuatanejo **164** 17 38N 101 33W
Zikhron Ya'Aqov **90** 32 34N 34 56 E
Zile **92** 40 15N 36 0 E
Zilfi **92** 26 12N 44 52 E
Zilina **53** 49 12N 18 42 E
Zillah **119** 28 40N 17 41 E
Zillertaler Alpen **52** 47 6N 11 45 E
Zima **77** 54 0N 102 5 E
Zimane, Adrar in **118** 22 10N 4 30 E
Zimapán **165** 20 40N 99 20W
Zimba **127** 17 20 S 26 25 E
Zimbabwe ■ **127** 20 16 S 31 0 E
Zimovniki **83** 47 10N 42 25 E
Zinal **50** 46 8N 7 38 E
Zinder **121** 13 48N 9 0 E
Zinga **127** 9 16 S 38 41 E
Zingem **47** 50 54N 3 40 E
Zingst **48** 54 24N 12 45 E
Zini, Yebel **118** 28 0N 11 0W
Ziniaré **121** 12 44N 1 10W
Zinjibar **91** 13 5N 46 0 E
Zinkgruvan **73** 58 50N 15 6 E
Zinnowitz **48** 54 5N 13 54 E
Zion Nat. Park **161** 37 25N 112 50W
Zipaquirá **174** 5 0N 74 0W
Zippori **90** 32 64N 35 16 E
Zirc **53** 47 17N 17 42 E
Ziri **63** 47 17N 11 14 E
Zirje, I. **63** 43 39N 15 42 E
Zirl **52** 47 17N 11 14 E
Zisterdorf **53** 48 33N 16 45 E
Zitácuaro **164** 19 20N 100 30W
Zitava, R. **53** 48 14N 18 21 E
Zitiste **66** 45 30N 2 32 E
Zitsa **68** 39 47N 20 40 E
Zittau **48** 50 54N 14 47 E
Zitundo **129** 26 48 S 32 47 E
Zivinice **66** 44 27N 18 36 E
Ziway, L. **123** 8 0N 38 50 E
Ziz, Oued **118** 31 40N 4 15W
Zizip **92** 37 5N 37 50 E
Zlarin **63** 43 42N 15 49 E
Zlatar **63** 46 5N 16 3 E
Zlataritsa **67** 43 2N 24 55 E
Zlatibor **66** 43 45N 19 43 E
Zlatista **67** 42 41N 24 7 E
Zlatna **70** 46 8N 23 11 E
Zlatograd **67** 41 22N 25 7 E
Zlatoust **78** 55 10N 59 40 E
Zletovo **66** 41 59N 22 17 E
Zlitan **119** 32 25N 14 35 E
Złocieniec **54** 53 30N 16 1 E
Złoczew **54** 51 24N 18 35 E
Zlot **66** 44 1N 22 0 E
Złotoryja **54** 51 8N 15 55 E
Złotów **54** 53 22N 17 2 E
Złoty Stok **54** 50 27N 16 53 E
Zmeinogorsk **76** 51 10N 82 13 E
Zmigród **54** 51 28N 16 53 E
Zmiyev **82** 49 45N 36 27 E
Znamenka **82** 48 45N 32 30 E
Znin **54** 52 51N 17 44 E
Znojmo **52** 48 50N 16 2 E
Zoar **128** 33 30 S 21 26 E
Zobia **126** 3 0N 25 50 E
Zoetermeer **46** 52 3N 4 30 E
Zofingen **50** 47 17N 7 56 E
Zogno **62** 45 49N 9 41 E
Zolder **47** 51 1N 5 19 E
Zollikofen **50** 47 0N 7 28 E
Zollikon **51** 47 21N 8 34 E
Zolochev **80** 49 45N 24 58 E
Zolotonosha **82** 49 45N 32 5 E
Zomba **127** 15 30 S 35 19 E
Zombi **126** 3 35N 29 10 E
Zomergem **47** 51 7N 3 33 E
Zongo **124** 4 12N 18 0 E
Zonguldak **82** 41 28N 31 50 E
Zonhoven **47** 50 59N 5 23 E
Zorgo **121** 12 22N 0 35W
Zorita **57** 39 17N 5 39W
Zorleni **70** 46 14N 27 44 E
Zornitsa **67** 42 23N 26 58 E
Zorritos **174** 3 50 S 80 40W
Zory **54** 50 3N 18 44 E
Zorzor **120** 7 46N 9 28W
Zossen **48** 52 13N 13 28 E
Zottegam **47** 50 52N 3 48 E
Zouar **119** 20 30N 16 32 E
Zouérabe **116** 22 35N 12 30W
Zousfana, O. **118** 31 51N 1 30W
Zoutkamp **46** 53 20N 6 18 E
Zqorzelec **54** 51 9N 15 0 E
Zrenjanin **66** 45 22N 20 23 E
Zuarungu **121** 10 49N 0 52W
Zuba **121** 9 11N 7 12 E
Zubair, Jazâir **123** 15 0N 42 10 E
Zubia **57** 37 8N 3 33W
Zubtsov **80** 56 10N 34 34 E
Zueitina **119** 30 58N 20 7 E
Zuénoula **120** 7 34N 6 3W
Zuera **58** 41 51N 0 49W
Zug **51** 47 10N 8 31 E
Zug □ **51** 47 9N 8 35 E
Zugar **123** 14 0N 42 40 E
Zugdidi **83** 42 30N 41 48 E
Zugersee **51** 47 7N 8 35 E
Zugspitze **49** 47 25N 10 59 E
Zuid-Holland □ **46** 52 0N 4 35 E
Zuid-horn **46** 53 15N 6 23 E
Zuidbeveland **47** 51 30N 3 50 E
Zuidbroek **46** 53 10N 6 52 E
Zuidelijk-Flevoland **46** 52 22N 5 22 E
Zuidlaarder meer **46** 53 8N 6 42 E
Zuidland **46** 51 49N 4 15 E
Zuidlaren **46** 53 6N 6 42 E
Zuidwolde **46** 52 40N 6 26 E
Zújar **59** 37 34N 2 50W
Zújar, Pantano del **57** 38 55N 5 35W
Zújar, R. **59** 38 30N 5 30 E
Zula **123** 15 17N 39 40 E
Zulia □ **174** 10 0N 72 10W
Zülpich **48** 50 41N 6 38 E
Zululand **129** 43 19N 2 15W
Zumaya **58** 43 19N 2 15W
Zumbo **127** 15 35 S 30 26 E
Zummo **121** 9 51N 12 59 E
Zumpango **165** 19 48N 99 6W
Zundert **47** 51 28N 4 39 E
Zungeru **121** 9 48N 6 8 E
Zuni **161** 35 7N 108 57W
Zupania **66** 45 4N 18 43 E
Zur **66** 42 13N 20 34 E
Zura **84** 57 36N 53 24 E
Zürandului **70** 46 14N 22 7 E
Zürich **51** 47 22N 8 32 E
Zürich □ **51** 47 26N 8 40 E
Zürichsee **51** 47 18N 8 40 E
Zuromin **54** 53 4N 19 57 E
Zuru **121** 11 27N 5 4 E
Zurzach **51** 47 35N 8 18 E
Zut, I. **63** 43 52N 15 17 E
Zutendaal **47** 50 56N 5 35 E
Zutphen **46** 52 9N 6 12 E
Zuwárrah **119** 32 58N 12 1 E
Zuyevka **84** 58 27N 51 10 E
Zuzemberk **63** 45 52N 14 56 E
Zvenigorodka **82** 49 4N 30 56 E
Zverinogolovskoye **84** 55 0N 62 30 E
Zvezdets **67** 42 6N 27 26 E
Zvolen **53** 48 33N 19 10 E
Zvonce **66** 42 57N 22 34 E
Zvornik **66** 44 26N 19 7 E
Zwaag **46** 52 40N 5 4 E
Zwanenburg **46** 52 23N 4 45 E
Zwarte Meer **46** 52 38N 5 57 E
Zwarte Waler **46** 52 39N 6 1 E
Zwartemeer **46** 52 43N 7 2 E
Zwartsluis **46** 52 39N 6 4 E
Zwedru (Tchien) **120** 5 59N 8 15W
Zweibrücken **49** 49 15N 7 20 E
Zwenkau **48** 51 13N 12 19 E
Zwetti **52** 48 35N 15 9 E
Zwickau **48** 50 43N 12 30 E
Zwijnaarde **47** 51 0N 3 43 E
Zwijndrecht, Belg. **47** 51 13N 4 20 E
Zwijndrecht, Neth. **46** 51 50N 4 39 E
Zwolle **46** 52 31N 6 6 E
Zymoelz, R. **152** 54 33N 128 31W
Zyrardów **54** 52 3N 20 35 E
Zywiec **54** 44 42N 19 12 E

Recent Place-Name Changes

The following place-name changes have recently occurred in Angola, Iran, Madagascar, Mozambique, Vietnam and Zimbabwe. The new names are given on the maps but the former names are in the index.

Angola

Former Name	*New name*
Ambrizete	Nzeto
Artur de Paiva	Capelongo
Bié	Kuito
Cassinga	Kassinga
Dundo	Luachimo
General Machado	Camacupa
João de Almeida	Chibia
Macedo do Cavaleiros	Andulo
Mariano Machado	Ganda
Moçâmedes	Namibe
Nova Redondo	Ngunza
Ongiva	Ngiva
Paiva Couceiro	Gambos
Robert Williams	Caála
Roçadas	Xangongo
San António do Zaïre	Soyo
Teixeira da Silva	Bailundo
Vila Ariaga	Bibala
Vila Marechal Carmona	Uíge

Iran

Former name	*New name*
Bandar-e Pahlavi	Bandar-e Anzalī
Bandar-e Shah	Bandar-e Torkeman
Bandar-e Shahpur	Bandar-e Khomeynī
Dehkhvareqan	Āzar Shahr
Dezh Shahpur	Marīvan
Kermanshah	Qahremānshahr
Khorramshahr	Khorramshahr (Khūnīnshahr)
Naft Shah	Naftshahr
Reza'iyeh	Orūmīyeh
Reza'iyeh, Daryacheh-ye	Orūmīyeh, Daryācheh-ye
Sar Eskand Khan	Āzarān
Shāhābād	Eslāmābād-e Gharb
Shāhī	Qā'emshahr
Shahpur	Salmās
Shahreza	Qomsheh
Shāhrud	Emāmrūd
Shahsavar	Tunekābon
Soltaniyeh	Sa'īdīyeh

Madagascar

Former name	*New name*
Ambre, C. de	Bobaomby, Tanjon' i
Ambre, Mt. d'	Ambohitra
Brickaville	Vohibinany
Chesterfield I.	Vestale, Toraka
Diégo Suarez	Antsirañana
Fénérive	Fenoarivo Atsinanana
Fort-Dauphin	Faradofay
Majunga	Mahajanga
Midongy du Sud	Midongy Atsimo
Ste. Marie, C.	Vohimena, T.' i
Ste. Marie, I.	Boraha, Nosy
Tamatave	Toamasina
Tuléar	Toliara

Mozambique

Former name	*New name*
Augusto Cardosa	Metangula
Entre Rios	Malema
Malvérnia	Chicualacuala
Mau-é-ele	Marão
Olivença	Lupilichi
Vila Alferes Chamusca	Guijá
Vila Caldas Xavier	Muende
Vila Coutinho	Ulonguè
Vila Fontes	Caia
Vila de Junqueiro	Gurué
Vila Luísa	Marracuene
Vila Paiva de Andrada	Gorongoza

Vietnam

Former name	*New name*
An Loc	Hon Quan
An Tuc	An Khe
Chau Phu	Chau Doc
Dien Bien Phu	Dien Bien
Hau Bon	Cheo Reo
Khanh Hung	Soc Trang
Kien Hung	Go Quao
Phuoc Le	Ba Ria
Quan Long	Ca Mau
Truc Giang	Ben Tre

Zimbabwe

Former name	*New name*
Balla Balla	Mbalabala
Belingwe	Mberengwa
Chipinga	Chipinge
Dett	Dete
Enkeldoorn	Chivhu
Essexvale	Esigodini
Fort Victoria	Masvingo
Gwelo	Gweru
Hartley	Chegutu
Gatooma	Kadoma
Inyazura	Nyazura
Marandellas	Marondera
Mashaba	Mashava
Melsetter	Chimanimani
Mrewa	Murewa
Mtoko	Mutoko
Nuanetsi	Mwenezi
Que Que	Kwekwe
Salisbury	Harare
Selukwe	Shurugwi
Shabani	Zvishavane
Sinoia	Chinhoyi
Somabula	Somabhula
Tjolotjo	Tsholotsho
Umvuma	Mvuma
Umtali	Mutare
Wankie	Hwange

Chinese Place-Names

The following list gives the Pin Yin nameform and the modified Wade-Giles nameform for the principal places in China. Pin Yin is officially approved by the Chinese and is gaining in use throughout the world. Wade-Giles is the transcription selected for the maps and index in this atlas and is still extensively used in the West.

Pin Yin	*Wade-Giles*
Anhui	Anhwei
Anqing	Anch'ing
Baoding	Paoting
Baoji	Paochi
Baotou	Paot'ou
Bei'an	Peian
Beihai	Peihai
Beijing	Peip'ing
Bengbu	Pangfou
Benxi	Pench'i
Boshan	Poshan
Cangzhou	Ts'angchou
Changchi	Ch'angchih
Changchun	Ch'angch'un
Changde	Changt'e
Changsha	Ch'angsha
Changshu	Ch'angshu
Changzhou	Ch'angchou
Chengde	Ch'engte
Chengdu	Ch'engtu
Chongqing	Ch'ungch'ing
Da Hinggan Ling	Tahsinganling Shanmo
Datong	Tat'ung
Dezhou	Techou
Dongchuan	Tungch'uan
Duyun	Tuyün
Fujian	Fukien
Fuxin	Fouhsinshin
Fuzhou	Fuchou
Gansu	Kansu
Ganzhou	Kanchou
Gejiu	Kochiu
Guangdong	Kwangtung
Guangxi Zhuangzu Zizhiqu	Kwangsi-Chuang
Guangzhou	Kuangchou
Guilin	Kueilin
Guiyang	Kueiyang
Guizhou	Kweichow
Hangzhou	Hangchou
Harbin	Haerhpin
Hebei	Hopei
Hebi	Haopi
Hechuan	Hoch'uan
Hefei	Hofei
Hegang	Haokang
Heilong Jiang	Heilungkiang
Henan	Honan
Hohhot	Huhohaot'e
Huaide	Huaite
Huangshi	Huangshih
Hubei	Hupei
Jiamusi	Chiamussu
Ji'an	Chian
Jiangmen	Chiangmen
Jiangsu	Kiangsu
Jiangxi	Kiangsi
Jiaxing	Chiahsing
Jilin	Chilin
Jinan	Chinan
Jingdezhen	Chingtechen
Jinhua	Chinhua
Jining	Chining
Jinxi	Chinhsi
Jinxian	Chinhsien
Jinzhou	Chinchou
Jiujiang	Chiuchiang
Jixi	Chihsi
Junggur Pendi	Dzungaria
Kashi	Kashgar
Lanzhou	Lanchou
Lianyungan	Lienyünchiangshih
Liuzhou	Liuchou
Lüda	Lüta
Luoshan	Loshan
Luoyang	Loyang
Luzhou	Luchou
Manzhouli	Manchouli
Meixian	Meihsien
Mudanjiang	Mutanchiang
Nanchong	Nanch'ung
Nanjing	Nanching
Nantong	Nant'ung
Nanzhang	Nanch'ang
Neijiang	Neichiang
Ningbo	Ningpo
Ningxia Huizu Zizhiqu	Ningsia Hui
Pingdingshan	P'ingt'ingshan
Pingxiang	P'inghsiang
Qaidam Pendi	Tsaidam
Qingdao	Ch'ingtao
Qinghai	Tsinghai
Qingjiang	Ch'ingchiang
Qinhuangdao	Ch'inhuangtao
Qiqihar	Ch'ich'ihaerh
Quanzhou	Ch'üanchou
Rugao	Jukao
Sanmenxia	Sanmenhsia
Shaanxi	Shensi
Shandong	Shantung
Shangqiu	Shangch'iu
Shangrao	Shangjao
Shanxi	Shansi
Shaoguan	Shaokuan
Shaoxing	Shaohsing
Shijiazhuang	Shihchiachuangi
Shizuishan	Shihtsuishan
Shunde	Shunte
Sichuan	Szechwan
Siping	Ssup'ing
Suxian	Suhsien
Suzhou	Suchou
Taizhou	T'aichou
Tandong	T'antung
Tanggula Shan	T'angkula Shanmo
Tian Shan	Tien Shan
Tianjin	T'ienching
Tianshui	Tienshui
Tongchuan	Tungchwan
Tonghua	T'unghua
Tongling	Tungling
Ürümqi	Wulumuchi
Wanxian	Wanhsien
Wenzhou	Wenchou
Wutongqiao	Wut'ungchi'ao
Wuxi	Wuhsi
Wuzhou	Wuchou
Xiaguan	Hsiakuan
Xiamen	Hsiamen
Xi'an	Hsian
Xiangfan	Hsiangfan
Xiangtan	Hsiangt'an
Xianyang	Hsienyang
Xiao Hinggan Ling	Hsiaohsinganling Shanmo
Xingtai	Hsingt'ai
Xining	Hsinging
Xinjiang Uygur Zizhiqu	Singkiang-Uigur
Xinjin	Hsinchin
Xinxiang	Hsinhsiang
Xuanhua	Hsüanhua
Xuchang	Hsüch'ang
Xuzhou	Hsüchou
Yangquan	Yangch'üan
Yangzhou	Yangchou
Yanji	Yenchi
Yanjin	Yench'eng
Yantai	Yent'ai
Yibin	Ipin
Yichang	Ich'ang
Yingchuan	Yinch'uan
Yining	Ining
Yiyang	Iyang
Yuci	Yutz'ü
Zaozhuang	Tsaochuang
Zhangjiakou	Changchiak'ou
Zhangjiang	Chanchiang
Zhangzhou	Changchou
Zhao'an	Ch'aoan
Zhejiang	Chekiang
Zhengzhou	Chengchou
Zhenjiang	Chenchiang
Zhuhai	Chuhai
Zhuzhou	Chuchou
Zigong	Tzukung
Zunyi	Tsuni

Geographical Terms

This is a list of some of the geographical words from foreign languages which are found in the place names on the maps and in the index. Each is followed by the language and the English meaning.

Afr. afrikaans
Alb. albanian
Amh. amharic
Ar. arabic
Ber. berber
Bulg. bulgarian
Bur. burmese
Chin. chinese
Cz. czechoslovakian
Dan. danish
Dut. dutch
Fin. finnish
Flem. flemish
Fr. french
Gae. gaelic
Ger. german
Gr. greek
Heb. hebrew
Hin. hindi
I.-C. indo-chinese
Ice. icelandic
It. italian
Jap. japanese
Kor. korean
Lapp. lappish
Lith. lithuanian
Mal. malay
Mong. mongolian
Nor. norwegian
Pash. pashto
Pers. persian
Pol. polish
Port. portuguese
Rum. rumanian
Russ. russian
Ser.-Cr. serbo-croat
Siam. siamese
Sin. sinhalese
Som. somali
Span. spanish
Swed. swedish
Tib. tibetan
Turk. turkish

A. (Ain) *Ar.* spring
–á *Ice.* river
a *Dan., Nor., Swed.* stream
–abad *Pers., Russ.* town
Abyad *Ar.* white
Ad. (Adrar) *Ar., Ber.* mountain
Ada, Adasi *Tur.* island
Addis *Amh.* new
Adrar *Ar., Ber.* mountain
Ain *Ar.* spring
Ākra *Gr.* cape
Akrotíri *Gr.* cape
Alb *Ger.* mountains
Albufera *Span.* lagoon
–ålen *Nor.* islands
Alpen *Ger.* mountain pastures
Alpes *Fr.* mountains
Alpi *It.* mountains
Alto *Port.* high
–älv, –älven *Swed.* stream, river
Amt *Dan.* first-order administrative division
Appennino *It.* mountain range
Arch. (Archipiélago) *Span.* archipelago
Arcipélago *It.* archipelago
Arq. (Arquipélago) *Port.* archipelago
Arr. (Arroyo) *Span.* stream
–Ås, –åsen *Nor., Swed.* hill
Autonomna Oblast *Ser.-Cr.* autonomous region
Ayios *Gr.* island
Ayn *Ar.* well, waterhole

B(a). (Baía) *Port.* bay
B. (Baie) *Fr.* bay
B. (Bahía) *Span.* bay
B. (Ben) *Gae.* mountain
B. (Bir) *Ar.* well
B. (Bucht) *Ger.* bay
B. (Bugt.) *Dan.* bay
Baai, –baai *Afr.* bay
Bāb *Ar.* gate
Bäck, –bäcken *Swed.* stream
Back, backen, *Swed.* hill
Bad, –baden *Ger.* spa
Bādiya, -t *Ar.* desert
Baek *Dan.* stream
Baelt *Dan.* strait
Bahía *Span.* bay
Bahr *Ar.* sea, river
Bahra *Ar.* lake
Baía *Port.* bay
Baie *Fr.* bay
Bajo, –a, *Span.* lower
Bakke *Nor.* hill
Bala *Pers.* upper
Baltă *Rum.* marsh, lake
Banc *Fr.* bank
Bander *Ar., Mal.* port
Bandar *Pers.* bay
Banja *Ser. Cr.* spa. resort
Barat *Mal.* western
Barr. (Barrage) *Fr.* dam
Barracão *Port.* dam, waterfall
Bassin *Fr.* bay
Bayt *Heb.* house, village
Bazar *Hin.* market, bazaar
Be'er *Heb.* well
Beit *Heb.* village
Belo-, Belyy, Belaya, Beloye, *Russ.* white
Ben *Gae.* mountain
Bender *Somal.* harbour
Berg,(e) –berg(e) *Afr.* mountain(s)
Berg, –berg *Ger.* mountain
–berg, –et *Nor., Swed.* hill, mountain, rock
Bet *Heb.* house, village
Bir, Bîr *Ar.* well
Birket *Ar.* lake, bay, marsh
Bj. (Bordj) *Ar.* port
–bjerg *Dan.* hill, point
Boca *Span.* river mouth
Bodden *Ger.* bay, inlet
Bogaz, Boğaz, –ı *Tur.* strait
Boka *Ser.-Cr.* gulf, inlet
Bol. (Bolshoi) *Russ.* great, large
Bordj *Ar.* fort
–borg *Dan., Nor., Swed.* castle, fort
–botn *Nor.* valley floor
bouche(s) *Fr.* mouth
Br. (Burnu) *Tur.* cape
Braţul *Rum.* distributary stream
–breen *Nor.* glacier
–bruck *Ger.* bridge
–brunn *Swed.* well, spring
Bucht *Ger.* bay
Bugt, –bugt *Dan.* bay
Buheirat *Ar.* lake
Bukit *Mal.* hill
Bukten *Swed.* bay
–bulag *Mong.* spring
Bûr *Ar.* port
Burg. *Ar.* fort
Burg, –burg *Ger.* castle
Burnu *Tur.* cape
Burun *Tur.* cape
Butt *Gae.* promontory
–by *Dan., Nor., Swed.* town
–byen *Nor., Swed.* town

C. (Cabo) *Port., Span.* headland, cape
C. (Cap) *Fr.* cape
C. (Capo) *It.* cape
Cabeza *Span.* peak, hill
Camp *Port., Span.* land, field
Campo *Span.* plain
Campos *Span.* upland
Can. (Canal) *Fr., Span.* canal
Canale *It.* canal
Canalul *Ser.-Cr.* canal
Cao Nguyên *Thai.* plateau, tableland
Cap *Fr.* cape
Capo *It.* cape
Cataracta *Sp.* cataract
Cauce *Span.* intermittent stream
Causse *Fr.* upland (limestone)
Cayi *Tur.* river
Cayo(s) *Span.* rock(s), islet(s)
Cerro *Span.* hill, peak
Ch. (Chaîne(s)) *Fr.* mountain range(s)
Ch. (Chott) *Ar.* salt lake
Chaco *Span.* jungle
Chaîne(s) *Fr.* mountain range(s)
Chap. (Chapada) *Port.* hills, upland
Chapa *Span.* hills, upland
Chapada *Port.* hills, upland
Chaung *Bur.* stream, river
Chen *Chin.* market town
Ch'eng *Chin.* town
Chiang *Chin.* river
Ch'ih *Chin.* pool
Ch'ŏn *Kor.* river
–chŏsuji *Kor.* reservoir
Chott *Ar.* salt lake, swamp
Chou *Chin.* district
Chu *Tib.* river
Chung *Chin.* middle
Chute *Fr.* waterfall
Co. (Cerro) *Span.* hill, peak
Coch. (Cochilla) *Port.* hills
Col *Fr., It.* Pass
Colline(s) *Fr.* hill(s)
Conca *It.* plain, basin
Cord. (Cordillera) *Span.* mountain chain
Costa *It., Span.* coast
Côte *Fr.* coast, slope, hill
Cuchillas *Spain* hills
Cu-Lao *I.-C.* island

D. (Dolok) *Mal.* mountain
Dāgh *Pers.* mountain
Dağ(ı) *Tur.* mountain(s)
Dağları *Tur.* mountain range
Dake *Jap.* mountain
–dal *Nor.* valley
–dal, –e *Dan., Nor.* valley
–dal, –en *Swed.* valley, stream
Dalay *Mong.* sea, large lake
–dalir *Ice.* valley
–dalur *Ice.* valley
–damm, –en *Swed.* lake
Danau *Mal.* lake
Dao *I.-C.* island
Dar *Ar.* region
Darya *Russ.* river
Daryācheh *Pers.* marshy lake, lake
Dasht *Pers.* desert, steppe
Daung *Bur.* mountain, hill
Dayr *Ar.* depression, hill
Debre *Amh.* hill
Deli *Ser.-Cr.* mountain(s)
Denizi *Tur.* sea
Dépt. (Département) *Fr.* first-order administrative division
Desierto *Span.* desert
Dhar *Ar.* region, mountain chain
Dj. (Djebel) *Ar.* mountain
Dō *Jap., Kor.* island
Dong *Kor.* village, town
Dong *Thai.* jungle region
–dorf *Ger.* village
–dorp *Afr.* village
–drif *Afr.* ford
–dybet *Dan.* marine channel
Dzong *Tib.* town, settlement

Eil.-eiland(en) *Afr., Dut.* island(s)
–elv *Nor.* river
–'emeq *Heb.* plain, valley
'erg *Ar.* desert with dunes
Estrecho *Span.* strait
Estuario *Span.* estuary
Étang *Fr.* lagoon
–ey(jar) *Ice.* island(s)

F. (Fiume) *It.* river
F. Folyó *Hung.* river
Fd. (Fjord) *Nor.* Inlet of sea
–feld *Ger.* field
–fell *Ice.* mountain, hill
–feng *Chin.* mountain
Fiume *It.* river
Fj. (–fjell) *Nor.* mountain
–fjall *Ice.* mountain(s), hill(s)
–fjäll(et) *Swed.* hill(s), mountain(s), ridge
–fjällen *Swed.* mountains
–fjard(en) *Swed.* fjord, bay, lake
Fjeld *Dan.* mountain
–fjell *Nor.* mountain, rock
–fjord(en) *Nor.* inlet of sea
–fjorden *Dan.* bay, marine channel
–fjörður *Ice.* fjord
Fl. (Fleuve) *Fr.* river
Fl. (Fluss) *Ger.* river
–flói *Ice.* bay, marshy country
Fluss *Ger.* river
foce, –i *It.* mouth(s)
Folyó *Hung.* river
–fontein *Afr.* fountain, spring
–fors, –en, *Swed.* rapids, waterfall
Foss *Ice., Nor.* waterfall
–furt *Ger.* ford
Fylke *Nor.* first-order administrative division

G. (Gebel) *Ar.* mountain
G. (Gebirge) *Ger.* hills, mountains
G. (Golfe) *Fr.* gulf
G. (Golfo) *It.* gulf
G. (Gora) *Bulg., Russ., Ser-Cr.* mountain
G. (Gunong) *Mal.* mountain
–gang *Kor.* river
Ganga *Hin., Sin.* river
–gat *Dan.* sound
–gau *Ger.* district
Gave *Fr.* stream
–gawa *Jap.* river
Geb. (Gebirge) *Ger.* hills, mountains
Gebel *Ar.* mountain
Geziret *Ar.* island
Ghat *Hin.* range of hills
Ghiol *Rum.* lake
Ghubbat *Ar.* bay, inlet
Gji *Alb.* bay
Gjol *Alb.* lagoon, lake
Gl. (Glava) *Ser.-Cr.* mountain, peak
Glen. *Gae.* valley
Gletscher *Ger.* glacier
Gobi *Mong.* desert
Gol *Mong.* river
Golfe *Fr.* gulf
Golfo *It., Span.* gulf
Gomba *Tib.* settlement
Gora *Bulg., Russ., Ser.-Cr.* mountain(s)
Góry *Pol., Russ.* mountain
Gölü *Tur.* lake
–gorod *Russ.* small town
Grad *Bulg., Russ., Ser-Cr.* town, city
Grada *Russ.* mountain range
Guba *Russ.* bay
–Guntō *Jap.* island group
Gunong *Mal.* mountain
Gură *Rum.* passage

H. Hadabat *Ar.* plateau
–hafen *Ger.* harbour, port
Haff *Ger.* bay
Hai *Chin.* sea
Haihsia *Chin.* strait
–hale *Dan.* spit, peninsula
Hals *Dan., Nor.* peninsula, isthmus
Halvø *Dan.* peninsula
Halvøya *Nor.* peninsula
Hāmad, Hamada, Hammādah *Ar.* stony desert, plain
–hamn *Swed., Nor.* harbour, anchorage
Hāmūn *Ar.* plain
Hāmūn *Pers.* low-lying marshy area
–Hantō *Jap.* peninsula
Harju *Fin.* hill
Hassi *Ar.* well
–haug *Nor.* hill
Hav *Swed.* gulf
Havet *Nor.* sea
–havn *Dan., Nor.* harbour
Hegyseg *Hung.* forest
Heide *Ger.* heath
Hi. (hassi) *Ar.* well
Ho *Chin.* river
–hø *Nor.* peak
Hochland *Afr.* highland
Hoek, –hoek *Afr., Dut.* cape
Höfn *Ice.* harbour, port
–hög, –en, –högar, –högarna *Swed.* hill(s), peak, mountain
Höhe *Ger.* hills
Holm *Dan.* island
–holm, –holme, –holzen, *Swed.* island
Hon *I.-C.* island
Hora *Cz.* mountain
–horn *Nor.* peak
Hory *Cz.* mountain range, forest
–hoved *Dan.* point, headland, peninsula
Hraun *Ice.* lava
–hsi *Chin.* mountain, stream
–hsiang *Chin.* village
–hsien *Chin.* district
Hu *Chin.* lake
Huk *Dan., Ger.* point
Huken *Nor.* head

I. (Île) *Fr.* island
I. (Ilha) *Port.* island
I. (Insel) *Ger.* island
I. (Isla) *Span.* island
I. (Isola) *It.* island
Idehan *Ar., Ber.* sandy plain
Île(s) *Fr.* island(s)
Ilha *Port.* island
Insel(n) *Ger.* island(s)
Irmak *Tur.* river
Is. (Inseln) *Ger.* islands
Is. (Islas) *Span.* islands
Is. (Isola) *It.* island
Isola, –e *It.* island(s)
Istmo *Span.* isthmus

J. (Jabal) *Ar.* mountain
J. (Jazīra) *Ar.* island
J. (Jebel) *Ar.* mountain
J. (Jezioro) *Pol.* lake
Jabal *Ar.* mountain, range
–jaur *Swed.* lake
–järvi *Fin.* lake, bay, pond
Jasovir *Bulg.* reservoir
Jazā'ir *Ar.* islands
Jazīra *Ar.* island
Jazireh *Pers.* island
Jebel *Ar.* mountain
Jezero *Ser.-Cr.* lake
Jezioro *Pol.* lake
–Jima *Jap.* island
Jøkelen *Nor.* glacier
–joki *Fin.* stream
–jökull *Ice.* glacier
Jūras Līcis *Lat.* bay, gulf

K. (Kap) *Dan.* cape
K (Khalig) *Ar.* gulf
K. (Kiang) *Chin.* river
K. (Kuala) *Mal.* confluence, estuary
Kaap *Afr.* cape
Kai *Jap.* sea
Kaikyō *Jap.* strait
Kamennyy *Russ.* stony
Kampong *Mal.* village
Kan. (Kanal) *Ser.-Cr.* channel, canal
Kanaal *Dut., Flem.* canal
Kanal *Dan.* channel, gulf
Kanal *Ger., Swed.* canal, stream
kanal *Ser.-Cr.* channel, canal
Kang *Kor.* river, bay
Kangri *Tib.* mountain glacier
Kap *Dan., Ger.* cape
Kapp *Nor.* cape
Kas *I.-C.* island
–kaupstaður *Ice.* market town
–kaupunki *Fin.* town
Kavīr *Pers.* salt desert
Kébir *Ar.* great
Kéfar *Heb.* village, hamlet
–ken *Jap.* first-order administrative division
Kep *Alb.* cape
Kepulauan *Mal.* archipelago
Ketjil *Mal.* lesser, little
Khalīg, Khalij *Ar.* gulf
khamba, –īdg *Tib.* source, spring
Khawr *Ar.* wadi
Khirbat *Ar.* ruins
Kho Khot *Thai.* isthmus
Khōr *Pers.* creek, estuary
Khrebet *Russ.* mountain range
Kiang *Chin.* river
–klint *Dan.* cliff
–Klintar *Swed.* hills
Kloof *Afr.* gorge
Knude *Dan.* point
Ko *Jap.* lake
Ko *Thai.* island
Kohi *Pash.* mountains
Kol *Russ.* lake
Kolymskoye *Russ.* mountain range
Kólpos *Gr., Tur.* gulf, bay
Kompong *Mal.* landing place
–kop *Afr.* hill

–köping *Swed.* market town
Körfezi *Tur.* gulf
Kosa *Russ.* spit
–koski *Fin.* cataract, rapids
–kraal *Afr.* native village
Krasnyy *Russ.* red
Kryash *Russ.* ridge, hills
Kuala *Mal.* confluence, estuary
kuan *Chin.* pass
Kuh –hha *Pers.* mountains
Kul *Russ.* lake
Kulle *Swed.* hill, shoal
Kum *Russ.* sandy desert
Kumpu *Fin.* hill
Kurgan *Russ.* mound
Kwe *Bur.* bay, gulf
Kyst *Dan.* coast
Kyun, –zu, –umya *Bur.* island(s)

L. (Lac) *Fr.* lake
L. (Lacul) *Rum.* lake
L. (Lago) *It., Span.* lake, lagoon
L. (Lagoa) *Port.* lagoon
L. (Límni) *Gr.* lake
L. (Loch) *Gae.* (lake, inlet)
L. (Lough) *Gae.* (lake, inlet)
La *Tib.* pass
La (Lagoa) *Port.* lagoon
–laagte *Afr.* watercourse
Läani *Fin.* first-order administrative division
Län *Swed.* first-order administrative division
Lac *Fr.* lake
Lacul *Rum.* lake, lagoon
Lago *It., Span.* lake, lagoon
Lagoa *Port.* lagoon
Laguna *It., Span.* lagoon, intermittent lake
Lagune *Fr.* lake
Lahti *Fin.* bay, gulf, cove
Lakhti *Russ.* bay, gulf
Lampi *Fin.* lake
Land *Ger.* first-order administrative division
–land *Dan.* region
–land *Afr., Nor.* land, province
Lido *It.* beach, shore
Liehtao *Chin.* islands
Lilla *Swed.* small
Límni *Gr.* lake
Ling *Chin.* mountain range, ice
Linna *Fin.* historical fort
Llano *Span.* prairie, plain
Loch *Gae.* (lake)
Lough *Gae.* (lake)
Lum *Alb.* river
Lund *Dan.* forest
–lund, –en *Swed.* wood(s)

M. (Maj, Mai) *Alb.* mountain, peak
M. (Mont) *Fr.* mountain peak
M. (Mys) *Russ.* cape
Madīna(h) *Ar.* town, city
Madiq *Ar.* strait
Maj *Alb.* peak
Mäki *Fin.* hill, hillside
Mal *Alb.* mountain
Mal *Russ.* little, small
Mal/a, –i, –o *Ser.-Cr.* small, little
Man *Kor.* bay
Mar *Span.* lagoon, sea
Mare *Rum.* great
Marisma *Span.* marsh
–mark *Dan., Nor.* land
Marsâ *Ar.* anchorage, bay, inlet
Masabb *Ar.* river mouth
Massif *Fr.* upland, plateau
Mato *Port.* forest
Mazar *Pers.* shrine, tomb
Meer *Afr., Dut., Ger.* lake sea

Mi., Mti. (Monti) *It.* mountains
Miao *Chin.* temple, shrine
Midbar *Heb.* wilderness
Mif. (Massif) *Fr.* upland, plateau
Misaki *Jap.* cape, point
–mo *Nor., Swed.* heath, island
–mon *Swed.* heath
Mong *Bur.* town
Mont *Fr.* hill, mountain
Montagna *It.* mountain
Montagne *Fr.* hill, mountain
Montaña *Span.* mountain
Monte *It., Port., Span.* mountain
Monti *It.* mountains
More *Russ.* sea
Mörön *Hung.* river
Mt. (Mont) *Fr.* mountain
Mt. (Monti) *It.* mountain
Mt. (Montaña) *Span.* mountain range
Mte. (Monte) *It., Port., Span.* mountain
Mţi. (Munţi) *Rum.* mountain
Mts. (Monts) *Fr.* mountains
Muang *Mal.* town
Mui *Ar., I.-C.* cape
Mull *Gae.* (promontory)
Mund, –mund *Afr.* mouth
Munkhafed *Ar.* depression
Munte *Rum.* mount
Munţ(i) *Rum.* mountain(s)
Muong *Mal.* village
Myit *Bur.* river
Myitwanya *Bur.* mouths of river
–mýri *Ice.* bog
Mys *Russ.* cape

N. (Nahal) *Heb.* river
Naes *Dan.* point, cape
Nafūd *Ar.* sandy desert
Nahal *Heb.* river
Nahr *Ar.* river, stream
Najd *Ar.* plateau, pass
Nakhon *Thai.* town
Nam *I.-C.* river
–nam *Kor.* south
–näs *Swed.* cape
–nes *Ice., Nor.* cape
Ness, –ness *Gae.* promontory, cape
Nez *Fr.* cape
–niemi *Fin.* cape, point, peninsula, island
Nizhne, –iy *Russ.* lower
Nizmennost *Russ.* plain, lowland
Nísos, Nísoi *Gr.* island(s)
Nor *Chin.* lake
Nor *Tib.* peak
Nos *Bulg., Russ.* cape, point
Nudo *Span.* mountain
Nuruu *Mong.* mountain range
Nuur *Mong.* lake

O. (Ostrov) *Russ.* island
O (Ouâdi, Oued) *Ar.* wadi
–ö *Swed.* island, peninsula, point
–öar, (–na) *Swed.* islands
Oblast *Russ.* administrative division
Öbor *Mong.* inner
Occidental *Fr., Span.* western
Odde *Dan., Nor.* point, peninsula, cape
Oji *Alb.* bay
Ojo *Span.* spring
Oki *Jap.* bay
–ön *Swed.* island peninsula
Ondör *Mong.* high, tall

–ör *Swed.* island, peninsula, point
Oraşul *Rum.* city
Ord *Gae.* point
Óri *Gr.* mountains
Oriental *Span.* eastern
Órmos *Gr.* bay
Óros *Gr.* mountain
Ort *Ger.* point, cape
Ostrov(a) *Russ.* island(s)
Otok(–i) *Ser.-Cr.* island(s)
Ouadi, –edi *Ar.* dry watercourse, wadi
Ouzan *Pers.* river
Ova (–si) *Tur.* plains, lowlands
–øy, (–a) *Nor.* island(s)
Oya *Hin.* point
Oya *Sin.* river
Oz. (Ozero, a) *Russ.* lake(s)

P. (Passo) *It.* pass
P. (Pasul) *Rum.* pass
P. (Pico) *Span.* peak
P. (Prokhod) *Bulg.* pass
–pää *Fin.* hill(s), mountain
Pahta *Lapp.* hill
Pampa, –s *Span.* plain(s) salt flat(s)
Pan. (Pantano) *Span.* Reservoir
Pantao *Chin.* peninsula
Parbat *Urdu* mountain
Pas *Fr.* gap
Paso *Span.* pass, marine channel
Pass *Ger.* pass
Passo *It.* pass
Pasul *Rum.* pass
Patam *Hin.* small village
Patna, –patnam *Hin.* small village
Pegunungan *Mal.* mountain, range
Pei, –pei *Chin.* north
Pélagos *Gr.* sea
Pen. (Península) *Span.* peninsula
Peña *Span.* rock, peak
Península *Span.* peninsula
Per. (Pereval) *Russ.* pass
Pertuis *Fr.* channel
Peski *Russ.* desert, sands
Phanom *I.-C., Thai.* mountain
Phnom *I.-C.* mountain
Phu *I.-C.* mountain
Pic *Fr.* peak
Pico(s) *Span.* peak(s)
Pik *Russ.* peak
Piz., pizzo *It.* peak
Pl. (Planina) *Ser.-Cr.* mountain, range
Plage *Fr.* beach
Plaine *Fr.* plain
Planalto *Span.* plateau
Planina *Bulg., Ser.-Cr.* mountain, range
Plat. (Plateau) *Fr.* level upland
Plato *Russ.* plateau
Playa *Span.* beach
P-ov. (Poluostrov) *Russ.* peninsula
Pointe *Fr.* point, cape
Pojezierze *Pol.* lakes plateau
Polder *Dut.* reclaimed farmland
–pólis *Gr.* city, town
Poluostrov *Russ.* peninsula
Półwysep *Pol.* peninsula
Pont *Fr.* bridge
Ponta *Port.* point, cape
Ponte *It.* bridge
Poort *Afr.* passage, gate
–poort *Dut.* port
Porta *Port.* pass
Porţil, –e *Rum.* gate
Portillo *Span.* pass
Porto *It.* port
Porto *Port., Span.* port

Pot. (Potámi, Potamós) *Gr.* river
Poulo *I.-C.* island
Pr. (Průsmyk) *Cz.* pass
Pradesh *Hin.* state
Presa *Span.* reservoir
Presqu'île *Fr.* peninsula
Prokhod *Bulg.* pass
Proliv *Russ.* strait
Prusmyk *Cz.* pass
Pso. (Passo) *It.* pass
Pta. (Ponta) *Port.* point, cape
Pta. (Punta) *It., Span.* point, cape, peak
Pte. (Pointe) *Fr.* point cape
Puerto *Span.* port, pass
Puig *Cat.* peak
Pulau *Mal.* island
Puna *Span.* desert plateau
Punta *It., Span.* point, peak
Puy *Fr.* hill

Qal'at *Ar.* fort
Qanal *Ar.* canal
Qasr *Ar.* fort
Qiryat *Heb.* town
Qolleh *Pers.* mountain

Ramla *Ar.* sand
Rann *Hin.* swampy region
Rao *I.-C.* river
Ras *Amh.* cape, headland
Rās *Ar.* cape, headland
Recife(s) *Port.* reef(s)
Reka *Bulg., Cz., Russ.* river
Repede *Rum.* rapids
Represa *Port.* dam
Reshteh *Pers.* mountain range
–Rettō *Jap.* group of islands
Ría *Span.* estuary, bay
Ribeirão *Port.* river
Rijeka *Ser.-Cr.* river
Rio *Port.* river
Río *Span.* river
Riv. (Riviera) *It.* coastal plain, coast, river
Rivier *Afr.* river
Riviera *It.* coast
Rivière *Fr.* river
Roche *Fr.* rock
Rog *Russ.* horn
–rück *Ger.* ridge
Rūd *Pers.* stream, river
Rudohorie *Cz.* ore mountains
Rzeka *Pol.* river

S. (Sungei) *Mal.* river
Sa. (Serra) *It., Port.* range of hills
Sa. (Sierra) *Span.* range of hills
–saari *Fin.* island
Sadd *Ar.* dam
Sagar, –ara *Hin., Urdu* lake
Saharā *Ar.* desert
Sahrâ *Ar.* desert
Sa'id *Ar.* highland
Sakar *Fin.* mountain
–Saki *Jap.* point
Sal. (Salar) *Span.* salt pan
Salina(s) *Span.* salt flat(s)
–salmi *Fin.* strait, sound, lake, channel
Saltsjöbad *Swed.* resort
Sammyaku *Jap.* mountain, range
Samut *Thai.* gulf
–San *Jap.* hill, mountain
Sap. (Sapadno) *Russ.* west
Sasso *It.* mountain
Se, Sé *I.-C.* river
Sebkha, –kra *Ar.* salt flats
See *Ger.* lake
–see *Ger.* sea
–şehir *Turk.* town
Selat *Mal.* strait
–selkä *Fin.* bay, lake, sound, ridge, hills

Selva *Span.* forest, wood
Seno *Span.* bay, sound
Serír *Ar.* desert of small stones
Serra *It., Port.* range of hills
Serranía *Span.* mountains
Sev. (Severo) *Russ.* north
–shahr *Pers.* city, town
Shan *Chin.* hills, mountains, pass
Shan-mo *Chin.* mountain range
Shatt *Ar.* river
–Shima *Jap.* island
Shimāli *Ar.* northern
–Shotō *Jap.* group of islands
Shuik'u *Chin.* reservoir
Sierra *Span.* hill, range
Sjö, sjön *Swed.* lake, bay, sea
Sjøen *Dan.* sea
Skär *Swed.* island, rock, cape
Skog *Nor.* forest
–skog, –skogen *Swed.* wood(s)
–skov *Dan.* forest
Slieve *Gae.* range of hills
–sø *Dan., Nor.* lake
Sør *Nor.* south, southern
Solonchak *Russ.* salt lake, marsh
Souk *Ar.* market
Spitze *Ger.* peak, mountain
–spruit *Afr.* stream
–stad *Afr., Nor., Swed.* town
–stadt *Ger.* town
Staður *Ice.* town
Stausee *Ger.* reservoir
Stenón *Gr.* strait, pass
Step *Russ.* plain
Str. (Stretto) *It.* strait
–strand *Dan., Nor.* beach
–strede *Nor.* straits
Strelka *Russ.* spit
–strete *Nor.* straits
Stretto *It.* strait
Stroedet *Dan.* strait
–ström, –strömmen *Swed.* stream(s)
–stroom *Afr.* large river
Suidō *Jap.* strait, channel
Sûn *Bur.* cape
Sund *Dan.* sound
–sund, –sundet *Swed.* sound, estuary, inlet
–sund(et) *Nor.* sound
Sungai, –ei *Mal.* river
Sungei *Mal.* river
Sur *Span.* south, southern
Sveti *Bulg.* pass
Syd *Dan., Swed.* south

Tai –tai *Chin.* tower
Tal *Mong.* plain, steppe
–tal *Ger.* valley
Tall *Ar.* hills, hummocks
Tandjung *Mal.* cape, headland
Tao *Chin.* island
Tassili *Ar.* rocky plateau
Tau *Russ.* mountain, range
Taung *Bur.* mountain, south
Taunggya *Bur.* pass
Tělok *I.-C., Mal.* bay bight
Teluk *Mal.* bay, gulf
Tg. (Tandjung) *Mal.* cape, headland
–thal *Ger.* valley
Thok *Tib.* town
Tierra *Span.* land, country
–tind *Nor.* peak
Tjärn, –en, –et *Swed.* lake
Tong *Nor.* village, town
Tong *Bur., Thai.* mountain range
Tonle *I.-C.* large river, lake
–träsk *Swed.* bog, swamp
Tsangpo *Tib.* large river
Tso *Tib.* lake

Tsu *Jap.* entrance, bay
Tulur *Ar.* hill
T'un *Chin.* village
Tung *Chin.* east
Tunnel *Fr.* tunnel
Tunturi *Fin.* hill(s), mountain(s), ridge

Uad *Ar.* dry watercourse, wadi
Udjung *Mal.* cape
Udd, udde, udden *Swed.* point, peninsula
Uebi *Somal.* river
Us *Mong.* water
Ust *Russ.* river mouth
Uul *Mong., Russ.* mountain, range

V. (Volcán) *Span.* volcano
–vaara *Fin.* hill, mountain, ridge, peak
–våg *Nor.* bay
Val *Fr., It.* valley
Valea *Rum.* valley
–vall, –vallen *Swed.* mountain
Valle *Span.* valley
Vallée *Fr.* valley
Valli *It.* lake, lagoon
Väst *Swed.* west
–vatn *Ice., Nor.* lake
Vatten *Swed.* lake
Vdkhr. (Vodokhranilishche) *Russ.* reservoir
–ved, –veden *Swed.* range, hills
Veld, –veld *Afr.* field
Velik/a, –e, –i, –o *Ser.Cr.* large
–vesi *Fin.* water, lake, bay sound, strait
Vest *Dan., Nor.* west
Vf. (Vîrful) *Rum.* peak, mountain
–vidda *Nor.* plateau
Vig *Dan.* bay, inlet, cove, lagoon, lake, bight
–vik, –vika, –viken *Nor., Swed.* bay, cove, gulf, inlet, lake
Vila *Port.* small town
Villa *Span.* town
Ville *Fr.* town
Vinh *I.-C.* bay
Vîrful *Rum.* peak, mountain
–vlei *Afr.* pond, pool
Vodokhranilishche *Russ.* reservoir
Vol. (Volcán) *Span.* volcano, mountain
Vorota *Russ.* gate
Vostochnyy *Russ.* eastern
Vozyshennost *Russ.* heights, uplands
Vrata *Bulg.* gate, pass
Vrchovina *Cz.* mountainous country
Vrchy *Cz.* mountain range
Vung *I.-C.* gulf
–vuori *Fin.* mountain, hill

W. (Wādī) *Ar.* dry watercourse
Wâhât *Ar.* oasis
Wald *Ger.* wood, forest
Wan *Chin., Jap.* bay
Webi *Amh.* river
Woestyn *Afr.* desert

Yam *Heb.* sea
Yang *Chin.* ocean
Yazovir *Bulg.* reservoir
Yoma *Bur.* mountain range
–yüan *Chin.* spring

–**Z**aki *Jap.* peninsula
Zalew *Pol.* lagoon, swamp
Zaliv *Russ.* bay
Zan *Jap.* mountain
Zatoka *Pol.* bay
Zee *Dut.* sea
Zemlya *Russ.* land, island(s)